INTRODUCTORY

THE CONCISE STANDARD DICTIONARY is abridged from the Funk & Wagnalls New Standard Dictionary of the English Language, and contains about 35,000 words and phrases. The basis of selection has been the inclusion of all words that are sure to be used by the average person in his speaking and writing, with the addition of such words and phrases as will occur in the books, papers, and magazines which are most likely to be read; in short, the choice has been for the most part of words at once the simplest and the most common. Only such words as should be written with capital initial letters are capitalized in the vocabulary.

I. The Vocabulary.

The pronunciations are those of the New Standard Dictionary as finally determined with the aid of the Advisory Committee of twenty-five leading Philologists and Educators. The pronunciation of words is indicated by phonetic respelling in the characters of the Revised Scientific Alphabet, which is designated as Key 1, and also by means of a system of diacritic marks such as is much used in text-books and the older dictionaries, this older system being called Key 2. The Revised Scientific Alphabet is believed to be at once the simplest and most exact alphabet yet devised for use in books of general reference. An explanation of the values of the symbols and of the principles of the alphabet will be found on the concluding introductory pages.

II. Pronunciation.

In definitions the aim has been to secure the utmost brevity and simplicity consistent with accuracy. So far as practicable, the method of beginning each definition with a definitive statement, as in the New Standard Dictionary, has been here employed. This has been done, even at the cost of somewhat enlarging the volume, with the belief that the reading public will especially appreciate this feature of fulness of definition. Where definition by synonym has been necessary for the sake of brevity, the endeavor has been to define by a word which is itself more fully defined, or by one so simple and familiar that its meaning can not be for a moment in doubt. Tables of *coins, measures*, and *weights* are given under these words, and the tables of the *metric system* under *metric*.

III. Definitions.

The most important prefixes and suffixes are fully treated in the main vocabulary. Many of these, especially of suffixes, form derivatives which are self-explaining when the meaning of the principal word and that of the affix are known. Hence such a word is often indicated by simply giving the suffix after the word to which it is to be adjoined, or by entering the derivative in full under the principal word, to give spelling and accent, with assurance that the meaning will be readily understood.

The illustrations, 780 in number (17 of these filling each a page and containing several individual illustrations), selected as aids to definition, convey the meaning of terms through the eye to the mind, as mere words can not do. Thus no words can express the contrasted terms *endogen* and *exogen*, so clearly and readily as it is given by a good picture; and for totally new products, as the *aeroplane*, or for very complex subjects, as *architecture*, illustrations are indispensable.

IV. The Illustrations.

In the Appendix will be found a set of simple Rules for Spelling; a treatment of common faults in diction, with rules and examples helpful in the avoidance of such faults; an extensive pronouncing list of Proper Names, ancient and modern, personal, geographical, literary, etc.; Foreign Words and Phrases, with their translations; a list of Symbolic Flowers and Gems, with the significance of each explained; and, finally, an explanatory list of common Abbreviations.

V. The Appendix.

It is believed that the book will find favor among the many persons who desire a small, inexpensive, and handy dictionary which will give them in a moment the most necessary information as to the spelling, pronunciation, and meaning of the words and phrases in common use.

J. C. F.

SPECIAL EXPLANATORY NOTES

Comparison of Adjectives; Plurals of Nouns.

☞ Where the COMPARATIVE AND SUPERLATIVE DEGREES OF ADJECTIVES and the PLURALS OF NOUNS are not given, they are formed regularly, according to the simplest rules of grammar.

The pronunciation of plurals of nouns is indicated either by respelling or by the sign (z) inserted after the plural form. EXAMPLE: **du′ty,** diů′tĭ, *n.* [DU′TIES^z, *p′.*] The sign (z) is used to indicate that the pronunciation of the plural is obtained by adding "z" to the pronunciation of the vocabulary word. Thus, DU′TIES is pronounced diů′tĭz.

Verbs and Their Participles, Etc.

☞ Where the TENSE AND PARTICIPIAL FORMS OF A VERB are not given, add -*ed* to the vocabulary word for the imperfect tense and the past participle, and -*ing* for the present particiⱼⱼe, except in compound verbs.

The pronunciation of the participles of verbs is indicated as follows:

The sign (t) added after a verb, or after Roman I., as I**ᵗ.** (when sever9l p rts of speech are grouped under one vocabulary entry), indicates that the pronunciation of the past participle or imperfect of this verb is obtained by adding "t" to the pronunciation of the vocabulary word. EXAMPLE: **look**ᵗ, lŭk, *v.* By adding "t" to the pronunciation of **look,** the pronunciation of **looked,** *pp.*, is obtained, thus: lŭk + t = lŭkt; so **blotch,** blŏch. I**ᵗ.** *vt.,* indicates that the past participle or imp9rfect, **blotched,** is pronounced blŏcht.

The sign (d) added after a verb, or after Roman I., as I**ᵈ.** (when several parts of speech are grouped under one vocabulary entry), indicates that the pronunciation of the past participle or imperfect of this verb is obtained by adding "ed" to the pronunciation of the vocabulary word. EXAMPLES: **amend**ᵈ, ə-mend′. By adding "ed" to the pronunciation of **amend,** the pronunciation of **amended,** *tmp.* and *pp.*, is obtained, thus: ə-mend′ + ed = ə-mend′ed; so **amount,** ə-mount′. I**ᵈ.** *vt.,* indicates that the past participle or imperfect is pronounced ə-mount′ed.

The pronunciation of the past participle and imperfect of the verbs is indicated, where no sign is given, by adding "d" to the pronunciation of the vocabulary word. EXAMPLES: **love,** lŭv; **loved,** lŭvd; **cable,** kā′bl; **cabled,** kā′bld.

Homonyms: Words spelled in the same way, but having different meanings, are distinguished by superior numbers ^{1}, ^{2} or ^{3}.

Compound Words.

COMPOUND WORDS are defined under their ârst element, except when grouped under the second element.

The participles and imperfects of verbs (if not given with the entry), as **disabuse,** ⱼill be found under the final element of each compound, as under **abuse.**

(iv)

Suffixes in Definitions.

DERIVATIVES formed by means of familiar suffixes, when entered without definition, will be understood to have the meaning of the principal word, plus the meaning of the suffix (prefixes and suffixes are entered and defined in their vocabulary places). EXAMPLE: Under the verb **embalm** will be found the noun of agency **embalmer,** readily understood to mean "one who embalms."

SUFFIXES, as -**ly, -ness,** following the treatment of any vocabulary word denote that the suffix is to be added directly to the bold-face word that immediately precedes it, to form the corresponding adverb, or other derivative. EXAMPLE: Under **harm** will be found **harmful,** *a.,* * * * -**ly,** *adv.,* -**ness,** *n.,* indicating that the adverb is **harmfully** and the verbal noun **harmfulness;** also, **harmless,** *a.,* * * * -**ly,** *adv.,* -**ness,** *n.,* indicating that the adverb is in this latter case **harmlessly,** and the noun **harmlessness.**

Hyphens and Accents.

THE SINGLE HYPHEN (-) connects parts of a worⱼ that are arbitrarilᵛ separated, as at the end of a line, or in the division of words into syllables, the syllables which it connects being closely joined in ordinary writing or printing. The single hyphen is omitted when the primary or secondary accent is used, as in vocabulary words: **as-tron′o-my** for *astronomy;* **in″di-vid′u-al** for *individual.*

THE DOUBLE HYPHEN (⸗) connects only the parts of a compound word, and indicates that the parts so joined are to be connected by a hyphen in ordinary writing or printing; as, **half-mast** (written ordinarily *half-mast*).

THE SINGLE ACCENT (′) indicates the primary or chief accent; as, **a′ble.**

THE DOUBLE ACCENT (″) indicates the secondary accent; as, **as-so″ci-a′tion; mul″ti-pli-ca′tion.**

Abbreviations and Arbitrary Signs.

[Colloq.] Colloquial.	† = *obsolete.*
[Dial.] Dialectic.	‖ = *archaic.*
[Prov.] Provincial.	§ = *rare.*
[Poet.] Poetical.	‡ = *variant.*

For other abbreviations, see the list of Abbreviations in the Appendix.

Reformed Spellings.

The reformed spellings recommended by the American Philological Association and the Philological Society of England are marked with a small superior ᵖ; those recommended by the Simplified Spelling Board are marked with superior ˢ. The reformed spellings are given sometimes in fully respelled form, sometimes by putting a parenthesis mark before (and, if necessary, after) a letter in the vocabulary spelling which in the reformed spelling is omitted. Thus, **ca′pa-bl**(eᵖ, **fys′ic**ᵖ (*physic*) are spellings recommended by the two philological societies; **fo′no-grafˢ, con-serv**(e′ˢ, **con-serv**(e)dˢ, spellings recommended by the Simplified Spelling Board—the *e* being dropped from the last two.

METHOD OF COMPOUNDING WORDS

General Principles

1. When used in regular grammatical relation and construction, all words should be separate except they are applied jointly in some arbitrary way.

2. The unification of sense is generally indicated by the normal association of words, and therefore compounding is necessary.

3. No expression in the language can be changed from two or more words combined as one or hyphenated without conveying a change of sense.

Under these principles no adjective should be hyphenated with a noun, and no noun used with adjectival force with another noun. So we have *spinal column*, *brick house*, *brown horse*, *brother officer*, etc.

Arbitrary use requires joining, as when we use *bluestocking* to indicate a learned or a literary woman, *bluebird* when we refer to the thrush like bird commonly designated by that name, or *browntail* when we refer to the moth that we recognize as a common pest, or to its lava that strips trees of their leaves.

Under the second principle, compounding is required (1) when two adjectives, a noun and an adjective, or any two or more parts of speech are used in abnormal association to express one attribution, as, *dark=brown* hair, *well=known* man, *free=trade* doctrines, *silk=and=cotton* fabric; (2) when a verb, an adverb, or any part of speech is used in a manner contrary to the rules of grammar, as in to *halter=break* a horse, to go *down=town*, *after=ages*, *broad=mindedly*, a *cross=action*.

The first principle keeps a regular adverb separate from the adjective it modifies, even when the two express one attribution; as "*highly colored* wings," "*recently published* book."

The second principle makes two nouns used together as one name become one word, if the first is not really attributive. Thus, while *brick* is attributive in *brick house* (a house made of bricks), it is *not* attributive in *brick=yard* (a yard where bricks are made). *Brick* in the first instance has the same qualifying sense that *bricken* would have if that were used, and so is an adjective, properly standing alone; but in the second instance it has no other sense than the naming of what is made in the yard, and no quality or attribute of the yard is noted, except in the name as a whole.

Rules for the Selection of Forms

From these principles we deduct the fact that if one term having elements of a certain kind is properly a compound word, so is every other exactly similar term.

Every name that shows ellipsis or inversion is a compound noun. For example, a box for a hat is a *hat=box*, a brush for the hair is a *hair=brush*, a stove for cooking is a *cooking=stove* or a *cook=stove*; likewise, *collar=box*, *paper=box*, *pill=box*, *shoe=box*, etc.

Some nouns that are unquestionably compounds in their nature have never been compounded, so we frequently find the words *association*, *asylum*, *company*, *corporation* used in conjunction with others without hyphenization, as, *racing association*, *lunatic asylum*, *railroad company*, *corporation council*.

Seeming Exceptions

I. In certain nouns used in combination the first is actually an adjective having the sense of

(1) "Made of," as in *apple pie*, *bean soup*, *feather bed*, *silk dress*, *stone wall*;

(2) "Having the character, quality, or shape of," as, *man servant*, *bull calf*, *barrel cart*, *mesh structure*;

(3) "Relating to, suitable for, pertaining to, or representing," as, *city officer*, *parlor clock*, *district attorney*, *government employee*, *church furniture*;

(4) "Characterized by," as in *diamond ring*, *cylinder press*, *cupola furnace*;

(5) "Situated in, having a character naturally implied from situation or connection," as, *country gentleman*, *mountain stream*, *ocean steamer*, etc.

But in certain instances names of this kind, where they denote specification, should be compounded, as, *mountain=dew* (illicit whisky), *field=mouse*, *house=fly*, *sea=gull*, *proof=reader*.

(6) "Advocating, or acting in support of," as, *prohibition candidate*, *war propagandist*, *disarmament supporter*;

(7) "Residing, existing, originating in, or coming from some place," as *New York boy*, *Bermuda onion*, *British politics*, *Bath brick*, *New York schools*, *Florida oranges*;

(8) "Originated or made by or named for," as, *Crookes tube*, *Williams College*.

II. 1. When nouns are placed in apposition, the first one is used as an adjective in effect, but there are certain constructions in which either word may be used alone for the thing named, as, *monarch oak*, *knight templar*, *knight companion*.

2. Phrases used in the possessive as specific names are compound words and should be hyphenated, as in *rabbit's=foot*, *hare's=tail*, *ass's=foot*, *lamb's=tongue*. There are, however, in the language certain terms, originally possessive in form, long established in continuous form, such as, *coltsfoot*, *sheepshead*.

3. Certain terms, originally phrases, are now established as fixed forms, such as, *daylight*, *hillside*, *loophole*, and *sunbeam*. Others, designating certain classes, are used in combination, such as, *coachman*, *footman*, *oarsman*, *statecraft*, *witchcraft*, *handicraft*, *shipmaster*, *schoolmaster*, *seaweed*, all of which have solid form in this work.

4. Certain monosyllabic words when used with *fish* take continuous form, that is, are not hyphenated. Of these, there are: *bluefish*, *catfish*, *dogfish*, *goldfish*, etc. Polysyllabic names are, in general, hyphenated.

5. There are some words that designate a characteristic or an adjunct, as, a *blue*-coated man who is called a *bluecoat* (policeman, sailor, etc.). A seaman who serves as a lookout is the *lookout*. The plant that looks like a golden rod is called the *goldenrod*. The fruit that bears a black berry is called the *blackberry*, etc.

Throughout this dictionary the double hyphen (=) is used to indicate words that should be hyphenated. The single hyphen (-) is merely a mark of syllabication.

KEYS TO PRONUNCIATION

As in the NEW STANDARD DICTIONARY two pronunciation keys are used here. The first (Key 1) is the Revised Scientific Alphabet; the second (Key 2), using many diacritical marks, is such as is in use in text-books and in earlier dictionaries.

The following table gives the values of the symbols in the two Keys based on the phonic values of the symbols of Key 1. For example, u in "burn," indicated in Key 1 by ū, is the equivalent of û in Key 2, in which the symbol ê is also used for the same sound when it occurs in "fern." The latter symbol and ī and y̆ are classed with ū, as in Key 2 four symbols are used for the same sound—û, ê, ī, y̆. Other symbols are classed in the same manner.

KEY	KEY	
1	2	ILLUSTRATIVE WORDS
a	ă	as in *artistic*, *cartoon*.
ā	ä	as in *art*, *cart*, *alms*, *father*.
a	ă	as in *add*, *fat*, *man*, *lap*, *baffle*.
ā	â, ê	as in *air*, *fare*, *pear*, *heir*, *there*.
ā	à	as in *ask*, *chant*, *dance*, *fast*.
e	ĕ	as in *get*, *bell*, *says*, *leopard*, *said*, *dead*, *bury*, *added*.
ē	ā, ę	as in *prey*, *wait*, *fame*, *great*, *neighbor*.
i	ĭ, y̆	as in *hit*, *tin*, *miss*, *cyst*, *physic*.
ī	ē, ĭ, ȳ	as in *police*, *mete*, *greet*, *sea*.
o	o	as in *obey*, *window*, *photo*.
ō	ō	as in *go*, *note*, *glory*, *blow*, *soul*, *goat*, *door*, *beau*.
o	ŏ, ą	as in *not*, *odd*, *what*, *was*.
ō	ô, ą	as in *or*, *north*, *all*, *haul*, *walk*.
u	ụ, ọ, ōō	as in *full*, *push*, *could*, *stood*.
ū	ụ, ọ, ōō	as in *rule*, *true*, *food*, *who*, *lose*.
u	ŭ, ŏ	as in *but*, *under*, *son*, *other*.
ū	û, ê, ĭ, ȳ	as in *burn*, *cur*, *earn*, *whirl*, *myrrh*.
ai	ī, ȳ	as in *aisle*, *pine*, *sign*, *light*, *type*, *height*.
au	ou, ow	as in *sauerkraut*, *out*, *now*.
iu	ū	as in *duration*, *futility*.
iū	ū	as in *feud*, *tube*, *pupil*, *beauty*.
oi	ŏi, ŏy	as in *oil*, *coin*, *boy*, *oyster*, *loyal*.
k	k, ç	as in *kin*, *cat*, *back*, *ache*, *pique*, *quit*.
g	g̃	as in *go*, *dog*, *egg*, *ghost*, *guard*.

KEY	KEY	
1	2	ILLUSTRATIVE WORDS
ŋ	n̦, ng	as in *sing*, *long*, *ringing*, *link*.
th	th	as in *thin*, *bath*, *faith*, *ether*, *Luther*.
th	th	as in *this*, *with*, *breathe*, *rather*, *either*.
s	s, ç	as in *so*, *house*, *this*, *missing*, *cent*, *scene*, *psychology*.
z	z, ş	as in *zest*, *lazy*, *buzz*, *was*, *houses*.
ch	ch	as in *chin*, *rich*, *church*, *watch*.
j	j, ġ	as in *jet*, *gin*, *gist*, *judge*, *pigeon*.
sh	sh, çh	as in *ship*, *dish*, *issue*, *nation*, *ocean*, *function*, *machine*.
ʒ	zh	as in *azure*, *seizure*, *leisure*, *vision*.
ə	a,e,o,u	as in *about*, *final*, *sofa*, *over*, *separate*, *mystery*, *guttural*, *martyrdom* (always unstressed).
ɪ	a,e,i,y	as in *habit*, *senate*, *surfeit*, *biscuit*, *min'ute*, *menace*, *average*, *privilege*, *valley*, *Sunday*, *cities*, *renew* (always unstressed).
H	H	as in *loch* (Scotch), *ach*, *mich* (German).
ü	ü	as in *Lübeck* (German), *Du-mas* (French).
ṅ	ṅ	as in *bon* (French).

Of the consonant and semi-vowel symbols b, d, f, h, l, m, n, p, r, t, v, w, y, and z, these, as initials, have the familiar and unmistakable sounds heard in *be*, *do*, *fee*, *he*, *let*, *met*, *net*, *pet*, *red*, *ten*, *vow*, *wet*, *yet*, and *zest*; as finals, l, m, n, and r have the sounds heard in *able*, *prism*, *fasten* and *flour*.

The foreign sounds (H, ü, ṅ), not represented in English, are described below

H is made with the tongue almost in position for k (as in *lock*). The difference is that for H the tongue does not wholly close the passage, so that the breath rushes out with great friction, making a sound like a very rough h. If the vowel preceding H is made in the front of the mouth (as German *i, e, ü, ä*) the H is also forward, and is then made by forcing the breath out while the tongue is held firmly in the initial position for English y.

ü represents a sound made by pronouncing ī (the vowel-sound of *see*) with the lips at the same time fully pursed or rounded as for whistling. It may be noted, also, that the foreign sound represented in this dictionary by the symbol **ū** (as French *danseuse*, daṅ"sœz′) is not exactly the vowel heard in the English *burn*, *earn*, etc., but is approximately that vowel sounded while the lips are fully pursed or rounded.

ṅ is a symbol indicating that the n itself is silent, but has imparted a nasal quality to the preceding vowel.

The Concise Standard Dictionary

A, a, 1 ē; 2 ā (*unaccented*, 1 ə; 2 a), *indef. article or adjective.* [AES, A's, or As, 1 ēz: 2 āş, *pl.*] One; any; each: before a vowel, *an.*

a-, *prefix.* **1.** On, awry, out, off, from, to: as *a* mere intensive; as, *a*down, *a*thirst. **2.** Not, in-, un-: in words derived from the Greek; as, *a*chromatic. **an-:**. [abs-:.]

ab-, *prefix.* Off; from; away; as, *ab*solve.

ab′a-ca, 1 ab′ə-kə; 2 ăb′a-ca, *n.* A plant of the banana family, native to the Philippine Islands, or its inner fiber, used for cloth, paper, cordage, etc.: commonly known as *Manila hemp.*

a-back′, 1 ə-bak′; 2 a-băk′, *adv.* So as to be pressed backward, as sails; backward.

ab′a-cus, 1 ab′ə-kus; 2 ăb′a-cŭs, *n.* [-ES, 1 -ez, 2 -ĕş, or -CI, 1 -sai, 2 -çī, *pl.*] **1.** A reckoning-table with sliding balls. **2.** A slab forming the top of a capital.

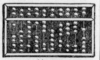

Abacus.

a-baft′, 1 ə-baft′; 2 a-băft′. *Naut.* **I.** *adv.* Toward the stern; back. **II.** *prep.* Further aft than.

ab″a-lo′ne, 1 ab″ə-lō′ni; 2 ăb″a-lō′ne, *n.* A shell-fish having a perforated ear-shaped shell.

a-ban′don, 1 ə-ban′dən; 2 a-băn′don, *vt.* To forsake or renounce utterly; give up wholly; quit.— **a-ban′don(e)d³,** *pa.* Given over; profligate.—**a-ban′don-ment,** *n.* The act of abandoning, or the state of being abandoned; a giving up; yielding (of oneself).

a-base′, 1 ə-bēs′; 2 a-bās′, *vt.* [A-BASED′t, A-BAS′ING.] To make low or lowly; lower, as in rank; humble.— **a-base′ment,** *n.*

a-bash′, 1 ə-bash′; 2 a-băsh′, *vt.* [A-BASHED′t or A-BASHT′; A-BASH′ING.] To make ashamed; confuse; embarrass.

a-bate′, 1 ə-bēt′; 2 a-bāt′, *v.* [A-BAT′ED⁴, A-BAT′ING.] **I.** *t.* To lessen; reduce; do away with. **II.** *i.* To grow less; decrease.— **a-bate′ment,** *n.* The act of abating, or the amount abated.

ab′a-tis, } 1 ab′ə-tis; 2 ăb′a-tĭs, *n.* *Mil.* **ab′at-tis,** { An obstruction of felled trees.

a′′bat′′toir′, 1 ɑ″bɑ″twär′; 2 ä″bä″twär′, *n.* A slaughter-house.

ab′ba, 1 ab′ə; 2 ăb′a, *n.* Father.— **ab′ba-cy,** *n.* The dignity or office of an abbot.

ab′bess, 1 ab′es; 2 ăb′ĕs, *n.* The lady superior of a nunnery.

ab′bey, 1 ab′i; 2 ăb′y, *n.* [AB′BEYS², *pl.*] A monastery or nunnery governed by an abbot or abbess; a chapel of such an institution; the residence of an abbot or abbess.

ab′bot, 1 ab′ət; 2 ăb′ot, *n.* *Eccl.* The superior of a monastery.— **ab′bot-ship,** *n.*

ab-bre′vi-ate, 1 a-brī′vi-ēt; 2 ă-brē′vi-āt, *vt.* [-AT′ED⁴; -AT′ING.] To cut short; contract; reduce; condense.— **ab-bre′vi-a′tion,** *n.* A shortening; an abridgment.

ab′di-cate, 1 ab′di-kēt; 2 ăb′di-eāt, *vt. & vi.* [-CAT′ED⁴; -CAT′ING.] To give up voluntarily; renounce office, etc.— **ab″di-ca′tion,** *n.*

ab-do′men, 1 ab-dō′men *or* ab′do-men; 2 ăb-dō′mĕn *or* ăb′do-mĕn, *n.* The visceral cavity; belly.— **ab-dom′i-nal,** *a.*

ab-duct′d, 1 ab-dukt′; 2 ăb-dŭct′, *vt.* To carry away wrongfully; kidnap; draw aside.— **ab-duc′tion,** *n.*— **ab-duc′tor,** *n.*

a-bed′, 1 ə-bed′; 2 a-bĕd′, *adv.* In bed; on a bed; to bed.

ab″er-ra′tion, 1 ab″ər-ē′shən; 2 ăb″er-ā′shŏn, *n.* Deviation from a natural course or condition; wandering; insanity.

a-bet′, 1 ə-bet′; 2 a-bĕt′, *vt.* [A-BET′TED⁴; A-BET′TING.] To encourage (wrong-doing or a wrong-doer), as by approval or aid; incite; instigate; as, to *abet* a person *in* a crime.— **a-bet′ter** *or* **-tor,** *n.*

a-bey′ance, 1 ə-bē′əns; 2 a-bẹ′anç, *n.* Suspense; inaction.

1: ärtistic, ärt; făt, fâre; fạst; get; prȩy; hit, police; obey, gō; not, ôr; fⱳll, rûle; bụt, bûrn.
2: ärt, āpe, făt, fâre, fạst, whạt, ạll; mē, gĕt, prȩy, fẽrn; hĭt, īce; ĭ=ĕ; ĩ=ē; gō, nŏt, ôr, wŏn,
1: ə = final; ı = habit; aïsle; au = out; oïl; īū = feud; chin; go; ŋ = sing; thin, this.
2: wǫlf, dǫ; bŏŏk, bŏŏt; full, rụle, cûre, bŭt, bûrn; ŏïl, bŏy; ḡo, ḡem; ıŋk; thin, this.

ab-hor′, 1 ab-hôr′; 2 ăb-hôr′, *vt.* [AB-HORRED′, AB-HORD′ˢ; AB-HOR′RING.] To view with horror; detest.— **ab-hor′rence,** *n.* —**ab-hor′rent,** *a.*

a-bide′, 1 ə-baid′; 2 a-bīd′, *v.* [A-BODE′; A-BID′ING.] **I.** *t.* To await expectantly or defiantly; endure. **II.** *i.* To remain; dwell.—**a-bid′ing. I.** *pa.* Enduring; permanent. **II.** *n.* Continuance; abode.

a-bil′i-ty, 1 ə-bil′i-ti; 2 a-bĭl′i-ty, *n.* [-TIES²,* *pl.*] The state of being able; power; talent; faculty.

ab′ject, 1 ab′jekt; 2 ăb′jĕct, *a.* Sunk to a low state; mean; despicable; servile. **-ly,** *adv.*—**ab′ject-ness,** *n.* **ab-jec′tion‡.**

ab-jure′, 1 ab-jūr′; 2 ăb-jur′, *vt.* [AB-JURED′; AB-JUR′ING.] To renounce under oath: recant.— **ab′ju-ra′tion,** *n.*

ab′la-tiv(eˢ, 1 ab′la-tiv; 2 ăb′la-tĭv, *n.* A case of Latin nouns, denoting *from, with, in, by,* etc.

a-blaze′, 1 ə-blēz′; 2 a-blāz′, *a. & adv.* On fire; in a blaze.

a′ble, 1 ē′bl; 2 ā′bl, *a.* [A′BLER; A′BLEST.] Having adequate power; competent; capable.— **a′bly,** *adv.* In an able manner.

-a-ble(eⁱ, *suffix.* Given to; tending to; like to; fit to; worthy of; capable of; able to; as, change*able,* honor*able,* think*able.*

ab-lu′tion, 1 ab-lū′[*or* -liū′]shən; 2 ăb-lṳ′- [*or* -lĭ′]shon, *n.* The act of washing; a cleansing; bath.

ab″ne-ga′tion, 1 ab″nɪ-gē′shən; 2 ăb″ne-gā′shon, *n.* The act of renouncing; renunciation.

ab-nor′mal, 1 ab-nôr′məl; 2 ăb-nôr′mal, *a.* That does not conform to rule; unnatural. **-ly,** *adv.*— **ab″nor-mal′i-ty,** *n.* [-TIES², *pl.*] Irregularity; something abnormal.

a-board′, 1 ə-bōrd′; 2 a-bôrd′. **I.** *adv.* On board; alongside. **II.** *prep.* On board or alongside of.

a-bode′, 1 ə-bōd′; 2 a-bōd′. **I.** *v. Imp.* of ABIDE. **II.** *n.* Dwelling-place; home.

a-bol′ishⁱd, 1 ə-bɒl′ish; 2 a-bŏl′ish, *vt.* To do away with; put an end to; annul; destroy. **-a-bl(eⁱ,** *a.* **-er,** *n.*— **ab″o-li′tion,** 1 ab″o-lish′an; 2 ăb″o-lish′on, *n.* The act of abolishing; extinction.— **ab″o-li′tion-istⁱ,** *n.* [U. S.] One who favors abolition; as, formerly, of negro slavery.

a-bom′i-nate, 1 ə-bɒm′ɪ-nēt; 2 a-bŏm′i-nāt, *vt.* [-NAT″EDᵈ;-NAT″ING.] To regard with horror; abhor; hate.— **a-bom′i-na-bl(eⁱ,** *a.* Very hateful; detestable; horrible. — **a-bom′i-na - bly,** *adv.*— **a - bom″i - na′-tion,** *n.* Something detested or abhorred; loathing.

ab″o-rig′i-nal, 1 ab″o-rij′i-nəl; 2 ăb″o-rĭg′i-nal. **I.** *a.* Native to the soil; in-

digenous; primitive. **II.** *n.* An original inhabitant.— **ab″o-rig′i-nes,** 1 ab″o-rij′- ɪ-nīz; 2 ăb″o-rĭg′i-nēz, *n. pl.* The original inhabitants of a country.

a-bor′tion, 1 ə-bôr′shan; 2 a-bôr′shon, *n.* An untimely birth; failure.— **a-bor′tiv(eˢ,** *a.* Brought forth prematurely; imperfect; unsuccessful. **-ly,** *adv.* **-ness,** *n.*

a-bound′ᵈ, 1 ə-baund′; 2 a-bound′, *vi.* To be or have in abundance.

a-bout′, 1 ə-baut′; 2 a-bout′. **I.** *adv.* On every side; around; almost; ready; to and fro. **II.** *prep.* On the outside or on every side of; all around; over; beside; somewhere near; in connection with; engaged in.

a-bove′, 1 ə-buv′; 2 a-bŏv′. **I.** *adv.* Ver-
a-buv′ᴾ, ʃ tically up; overhead; on the upper side. **II.** *prep.* Vertically over; upon; in excess of; superior to; beyond; free from. — **a-bove′board″,** *n. & adv.* Open; openly.

ab-rade′, 1 ab-rēd′; 2 ăb-rād′, *vt.* [AB-RAD′EDᵈ; AB-RAD′ING.] To rub or wear away.— **ab-ra′sion,** 1 ab-rē′ʒən; 2 ăb-rā′-zhon, *n.* The act or result of abrading.

a-breast′, 1 ə-brest′; 2 a-brĕst′, *adv.* Side
a-brest′ˢ, ʃ by side.

a-bridge′, 1 ə-brij′; 2 a-brĭdg′, *vt.* [A-BRIDGED′; A-BRIDG′ING.] **1.** To make shorter; condense; cut short. **2.** To deprive of.— **a-bridg′ment,** 1 ə-brij′ment *or* -ment; 2 a-brĭdg′ment *n.* The act of abridging; the state of being abridged; an epitome or abstract. **a-bridge′ment‡.**

a-broad′, 1 ə-brōd′; 2 a-brôd′, *adv.* Beyond the bounds of one's home or country; out-of-doors; away; at large.

ab′ro-gate, 1 ab′ro-gēt; 2 ăb′ro-gāt, *vt.* [-GAT″EDᵈ; -GAT″ING.] To do away with; annul; abolish; repeal.— **ab″ro-ga′tion,** *n.* Authoritative repeal.

ab-rupt′, 1 ab-rupt′; 2 ăb-rŭpt′, *a.* Not expected; sudden; broken off; disconnected; steep. **-ly,** *adv.* **-ness,** *n.*

ab′scess, 1 ab′ses; 2 ăb′sĕs, *n.* A collection of pus in a tissue of the body; a tumor; boil.

ab-scond′ᵈ, 1 ab-skɒnd′; 2 ăb-scŏnd′, *vi.* To depart suddenly and secretly; hide oneself.

ab′sence, 1 ab′sens; 2 ăb′sĕnç, *n.* The state, fact, or time of being absent; lack; want.   [keep (oneself) away.

ab-sent′ᵈ, 1 ab-sent′; 2 ăb-sĕnt′, *vt.* To

ab′sent, 1 ab′sent; 2 ăb′sĕnt, *a.* Not present; lacking; missing; absent-minded. **-ly,** *adv.*— **ab″sen-tee′,** 1 ab″sen-tī′; 2 ăb″sĕn-tē′, *n.* One who is absent; a non-resident.— **ab″-sent·mind′ed,** *a.* Abstracted; forgetful; oblivious.

ab'sinth,) 1 ab'sinth; 2 ăb'sĭnth, *n.* A
ab'sinthe,) bitter, aromatic liqueur flavored with wormwood.

ab'so-lute, 1 ab'so-liūt; 2 ăb'so-lūt, *a.* **1.**
Not limited; unrestricted; independent.
2. Without restraint in the exercise of
power or will; arbitrary; unconditional.
3. Complete; perfect. **4.** Not adulterated; pure. **5.** Positive; entire; total.
-ly, *adv.* **-ness,** *n.*— **ab-so-lu″tism,** *n.*
Arbitrary government; absoluteness.

ab-solv(e'ʳˢ, 1 ab-sŏlv'; 2 ăb-sŏlv', *vt.* [AB-
SOLV(E)D'ˢ; AB-SOLV'ING.] To set free; forgive; pardon; acquit.— **ab″so-lu'tion,** 1
ab'so-liū'shan; 2 ăb'so-lū'shon, *n.* An ab-
solving, or a being absolved; forgiveness.

ab-sorb', 1 ab-sŏrb'; 2 ăb-sŏrb', *vt.* To
drink in or suck up; engross completely;
swallow up.— **ab-sorb'ent,** 1 ab-sŏrb'ent; 2
ăb-sŏrb'ĕnt. **I.** *a.* Absorbing, or tending to
absorb. **II.** *n.* Something that absorbs.—
ab-sorp'tion, 1 ab-sŏrp'shan; 2 ăb-sŏrp'-
shon, *n.* The act of absorbing; the condition
of being absorbed.— **ab-sorp'tive(ˢ,** *a.*

ab-stain', 1 ab-stēn'; 2 ăb-stān', *vi.* To keep
back; refrain: with *from.*— **ab-stain'er,** *n.*

aᵇ-ste'mi-ous, 1 ab-stī'mi-us; 2 ăb-stē'mi-
ŭs, *a.* Sparing in food and drink; temperate. **-ly,** *adv.* **-ness,** *n.*

ab-sten'tion, 1 ab-sten'shan; 2 ăb-stĕn'-
shon, *n.* A refraining or abstaining.—
ab-sten'tious, *a.* Self-restraining. **-ly,** *adv.*

ab-sterge', 1 ab-stŭrj'; 2 ăb-stŭrg', *vt.* To
wipe away; wipe; cleanse.— **ab-ster'gent.**
I. *a.* Cleansing. **ab-ster'sive(ˢ.** **II.** *n.* A
cleansing application or remedy.— **ab-ster'-
sion,** *n.* The act of cleansing or purging.

ab'sti-nence, 1 ab'stɪ-nens; 2 ăb'sti-nĕnç,
n. The act or practise of abstaining; self-
denial.— **ab'sti-nent,** *a.* Abstemious. **-ly,**
adv.

ab-stract'ᵈ, 1 ab-strakt'; 2 ăb-străct', *vt.*
1. To take away; separate; divert;
remove; purloin. **2.** To make an abstract of; abridge.

ab'stract, 1 ab'strakt; 2 ăb'străct, *a.* Existing in thought only; not concrete;
theoretical; imaginary; abstruse.

ab'stract, *n.* A brief statement of facts
that are set forth in full elsewhere; summary; compendium. **-ly,** *adv.* **-ness,** *n.*—
ab-stract'ed, *a.* **1.** Absent-minded. **2.**
Separated from everything else; apart; abstruse; abstract. **-ly,** *adv.*— **ab-strac'tion,**
n. **1.** An abstracting. **2.** An abstract idea;
something unreal. **3.** Removal; theft. **4.**
Absence of mind.

ab-struse', 1 ab-strūs'; 2 ăb-strŭs', *a.* Hard
to be understood; difficult. **-ly,** *adv.*
-ness, *n.*

ab-surd', 1 ab-sŭrd'; 2 ăb-sûrd', *a.* Not
consistent with reason or common sense;
irrational; preposterous.— **ab-surd'i-ty,** *n.*
[-TIESᶻ, *pl.*] **1.** The quality of being absurd.
ab-surd'ness‡. **2.** Something absurd.—
ab-surd'ly, *adv.* In an absurd manner.

a-bun'dant, 1 a-bŭn'dant; 2 a-bŭn'dant,
a. Affording a large quantity, number,
or measure, or a surplus; plentiful; ample.
-ly, *adv.*— **a-bun'dance,** *n.* Plenty.

a-buse',) 1 a-biūz'; 2 a-būs', *vt.* [A-BUSED';
a-buze'ʳᵖ,) A-BUS'ING.] To use improperly;
wrong; hurt; revile; vio-
late.

a-buse', 1 a-biūs'; 2 a-
būs', *n.* Improper use; ill
treatment; misuse; vi-
cious conduct; insulting
speech.— **a-bu'sive(eˢ,** *a.*
Of the nature of or marked
by abuse.— **a-bu'siv(e-lyˢ,**
adv.— **a-bu'siv(e-nessˢ,** *n.*

a-but', 1 a-but'; 2 a-bŭt',
vt. & vi. [A-BUT'TEDᵈ;
A-BUT'TING.] To touch
upon; border; with *on,*
upon, or *against.*— **a-but'ment,** *n.* The act
of abutting; a supporting structure, as at the
end of a bridge or wall.

Abutment (A)

a-byss', 1 a-bis'; 2 a-bўs', *n.* A bottomless
gulf; vast depth.— **a-bysm',** 1 a-bizm'; 2
a-bўsm', *n.* An abyss.— **a-bys'mal,** *a.*
Pertaining to an abyss; unfathomable.

ac-, *prefix.* Form of AD- before *c* and *q.*

-ac, *suffix.* Having, pertaining to, affected
by, as in demon*iac*, man*iac.*

A-ca'cia, 1 a-ke'sha; 2 a-cā'sha, *n.* A genus
of thorny flowering trees
or shrubs.

ac″a-dem'ic, 1
ak'a-dĕm'ik; 2
ăe″a-dĕm'ie. **I.**
a. **1.** Pertain-
ing to an acad-
emy; scholar-
ly; literary. **2.**
Theoretical;
not practical.

Acacia.

3. [A-] Belonging to the school or philosophy of Plato. **-i-cal‡.** **II.** *n.* **1.** A college student. **2.** A member of a learned
society. **3.** [A-] A Platonist. **4.** *pl.* [A-]
The teachings of Plato.— **ac″a-dem'i-cal-
ly,** *adv.*— **ac″a-dem'i-cals,** *n. pl.* Special
dress worn at an institution of learning.

a-cad'e-my, 1 a-kad'i-mi; 2 a-căd'e-my, *n.*
[-MIESᶻ, *pl.*] **1.** A school intermediate between a common school and a college. **2.**
A learned society. **3.** [A-] The school of
Plato in Athens; the Platonic philosophy.
— **a-cad″e-mi'cian,** 1 a-kad'ı-mish'an; 2
a-căd'e-mish'an, *n.* A member of an academy.

a-can'thus, 1 ə-kan'thus; 2 a-căn'thŭs, *n.*
1. A perennial flowering plant. **2.** An ornament like its leaf.

a ca-pel'la, 1 ɑ ka-pel'la; 2 ä cä-pĕl'lä. *Mus.* In church style, *i.e.*, without instrumental accompaniment.

Acanthus.

ac-cede', 1 ak-sēd'; 2 ăe-cĕd'. *vi.* [AC-CED'ED; AC-CED'ING.] **1.** To agree; assent. **2.** To succeed, as to a throne.

ac-ce''le - ran'do, 1 ɑ-chē''lē-rän'do; 2 ä-chē''le - rän'do, *adv.*
*Mus.*With gradual quickening of the time.

ac-cel'er-ate, 1 ak-sel'er-ēt; 2 ăe-çĕl'er-āt, *vt. & vi.* [-AT'ED⁴; -AT'ING.] To quicken; hasten.— ac-cel'er-a-tive(eˢ, *a.* Tending to accelerate.— ac-cel'er-a-to-ry‡.— ac-cel'er-a'tion, *n.*

ac-cent'd, 1 ak-sent';2 ăe-çĕnt', *vt.* To speak, write, or print with an accent; emphasize.

ac'cent, 1 ak'sent; 2 ăe'çĕnt, *n.* A stress of voice on a syllable of a word, or a mark used to indicate such stress known as primary (′) and secondary (″).— ac-cen'tu-al, 1 ak-sen'chu-al *or* -tiu-al; 2 ăe-çĕn'chu̧-al *or* -tū-al, *a.* Pertaining to accent.— ac-cen'tu-ate, *vt.* [-AT'ED⁴; -AT'ING.] To give accent to; emphasize.— ac-cen''tu-a'tion, *n.*

ac-cept'd, 1 ak-sept';2ăe-çĕpt',*vt.* **1.** To take when offered; agree to; receive; believe. **2.** To agree to pay, as a draft. **3.** To acknowledge (as valid or as received).— ac-cept'a-bl(eᴾ, *a.* Worthy of being accepted; pleasing; welcome.— ac-cept''a-bil'-i-ty‡.— ac-cept'a-bly, *adv.*— ac-cep'tance, *n.* The act of accepting; state of being accepted or acceptable; acceptation; an accepted bill or the like.— ac''cep-ta'tion, *n.* **1.** The accepted meaning of a word. **2.** The state of being accepted or acceptable.— ac-cept'er *or* ac-cep'tor, *n.* One who accepts, as a check, draft, or the like: *acceptor* preferred in legal use.

ac'cess, 1 ak'ses; 2 ăe'çĕs, *n.* The act or opportunity of approaching; admission; approach; increase; attack, as of disease.— ac-ces''si-bil'i-ty, *n.*— ac-ces'si-bl(eᴾ, *a.* Easy of access; approachable; attainable.— ac-ces'si-bly, *adv.*

ac-ces'sa-ry, *a. & n.* Same as ACCESSORY.

ac-ces'sion, 1 ak-sesh'ən; 2 ăe-çĕsh'ŏn, *n.* Attainment; assent; agreement; person or thing added.

ac-ces'so-ry, 1 ak-ses'a-rı; 2 ăe-çĕs'o-ry. **I.** *a.* Aiding subordinately; contributory.

II. *n.* [-RIES²*, pl.*] **1.** An aid; adjunct; accomplice. **2.** A supplemental attachment.

ac'ci-dent, 1 ak'si-dent; 2 ăe'çi-dĕnt, *n.* Something that happens unexpectedly; a casualty; mishap.— ac''ci-den'tal, *a.* Happening by chance; casual; non-essential; incidental.— ac''ci-den'tal-ly, *adv.*

ac-claim', 1 a-klēm'; 2 ä-clām'. **I.** *vt & vi.* To shout applause; applaud; proclaim. **II.** *n.* A shout, as of applause.— ac''cla-ma'tion, 1 ak''lə-mē'shən; 2 ăc'la-mä'shon, *n.* A shout, as of applause; a unanimous oral vote of approval.

ac-cli'mate, 1 a-klai'mēt; 2 ä-clī'māt, *vt.* [-MAT-ED‡; -MAT-ING.] To habituate to a foreign climate. ac-cli'ma-tize *or* -tise‡.— ac''cli-ma'tion, *n.* ac-cli''ma-ta'tion‡.— ac-cli''ma-ti-za'tion *or* -sa'tion, *n.*

ac-cliv'i-ty, 1 a-kliv'i-tı; 2 ä-clīv'i-ty, *n.* [TIES², *pl.*] An upward slope.

ac-com'mo-date, 1 a-kəm'o-dēt; 2 ä-kŏm'o-dāt, *vt.* [-DAT'ED⁴; -DAT'ING.] **1.** To do a favor to; oblige; help. **2.** To provide for; lodge. **3.** To adapt; conform; compromise.— ac-com'mo-dat''ing, *pa.* Obliging.— ac-com''mo-da'tion, *n.* **1.** Adjustment; compromise. **2.** A convenience; entertainment; loan. **3.** An accommodating disposition; obligingness.

ac-com'pa-ny, 1 a-kum'pə-nı; 2 ä-kŏm'pa-ny, *vt. & vi.* [-NIED'; -NY-ING.] To go with; attend; escort; play an accompaniment.— ac-com'pa-ni-ment, *n.* **1.** Anything that accompanies. **2.** *Mus.* A subordinate part, voice, or instrument.— ac-com'pa-nist, *n.*

ac-com'plice, 1 a-kəm'plis; 2 ä-kŏm'plĭç, *n.* An associate in wrong or crime.

ac-com'plish†, 1 a-kəm'plish; 2 ä-kŏm'plĭsh, *vt.* To bring to pass; perform; effect.— ac-com'plished†, *pa.* **1.** Proficient; polite; polished. **2.** Completed.— ac-com'plish-ment, *n.* **1.** An accomplishing; completion. **2.** An elegant acquirement.

ac-cord'd, 1 a-kōrd'; 2 ä-côrd', *v.* **I.** *t.* **1.** To grant; allow. **2.** To bring to agreement. **II.** *i.* To agree; harmonize.

ac-cord', *n.* **1.** Harmony; agreement. **2.** Spontaneous impulse; choice.— ac-cord'ance, *n.* Agreement; accord.— ac-cord'ant, *a.* Harmonious. -ly, *adv.*

ac-cord'ing, 1 a-kōrd'ıŋ; 2 ä-côrd'ing, *pa.* Agreeing; harmonizing.— according to, in conformity to; as stated by.— ac-cord'ing-ly, *adv.* Suitably; consequently.

Bellows-accordion.

ac-cor'di-on, 1 a-kôr'di-ən; 2 ä-côr'di-on, *n.* A portable musical wind-instrument.

ac-cost′d, 1 a-kŏst′; 2 ă-cŏst′, *vt.* To speak first to; address.

ac″couche″ment, 1 a″kūsh′măn′; 2 ä″euçh′-măn′, *n.* Delivery in childbed; confinement.

ac-count′d, 1 a-kaunt′; 2 ă-count′, *v.* **I.** *t.* To consider; estimate; count; compute. **II.** *i.* **1.** To answer (*to* a person *for* a thing). **2.** To explain: followed by *for.*

ac-count′, *n.* **1.** A reckoning; computation; record; statement; description; notice. **2.** An explanation. **3.** Importance; consideration.— **ac-count″a-bil′i-ty,** *n.* · The state of being accountable. **ac-count′a- bl(e-ness′‡.— ac-count′a-bl(e²,** *a.* Liable to be called to account; responsible.— **ac-count′a-bly,** *adv.—* **ac-count′ant,** *n.* One who keeps accounts.

ac-cou′ter, 1 a-kū′tẽr; 2 ă-cụ′ter, *vt.*
ac-cou′tre, 1 [-TER(E)D⁸ or -TRED; -TER-ING or -TRING.] To furnish with dress or trappings; equip.— **ac-cou′ter-ment, ac-cou′-tre-ment,** *n.* Equipment; dress; trappings.

ac-cred′it d, 1 a-kred′it; 2 ă-erĕd′it, *vt.* To give credit to; furnish with credentials.

ac-cre′tion, 1 a-krī′shạn; 2 ă-erē′shon, *n.* Growth; increase.

ac-crue′, 1 a-krū′; 2 ă-erụ′, *vi.* [AC-CRUED′; AC-CRU′ING.] To arise as an addition; be added; accumulate.

ac-cum′bent, 1 a-kum′bent; 2 ă-eŭm′bĕnt, *a.* **1.** *Bot.* Lying against something.

ac-cu′mu-late, 1 a-kiū′miu-lēt; 2 ă-eū′mū-lāt, *v.* [-LAT′ED d; -LAT′ING.] **I.** *t.* To heap or pile up; amass; collect. **II.** *i.* To increase, as profits, etc.— **ac-cu″mu-la′-tion,** *n.* An amassing; increase; mass.— **ac-cu′mu-la-tiv(e⁸,** *a.* Tending to accumulate; accumulating.— **ac-cu′mu-la′tor,** *a.*

ac′cu-ra-cy, 1 ak′yu-ra-sı; 2 ăe′yụ-ra-çy, *n.* The quality of being accurate; correctness.

ac′cu-rate, 1 ak′yu-rıt; 2 ăe′yụ-rat, *a.* Conforming exactly to fact; precise; exact; correct. **-ly,** *adv.* **-ness,** *n.*

ac-curs′ed, 1 a-kūrs′ed or a-kūrst′; 2 ă-eûrs′ĕd or a-eûrst′,*a.* Cursed; detestable.

ac-cu′sa-tiv(e⁸, 1 a-kiū′zạ-tiv; 2 ă-eū′sa-tĭv. *Gram.* **I.** *a.* Objective. **II.** *n.* The case of the direct object; objective case.

ac-cuse′, 1 a-kiūz′; 2 ă-eūs′, *vt. & vi.* [AC-CUSED′; AC-CUS′ING.] To charge with fault or error; censure; make accusation.— **ac″cu-sa′tion,** *n.* An accusing; a charge.— **ac-cu′sa-to-ry,** *a.* Pertaining to an accusation. **— ac-cus′er,** *n.* One who accuses.

ac-cus′tom, 1 a-kus′tạm; 2 ă-eŭs′tom, *vt.* To make familiar by use; habituate.— **ac-cus′tom(e)d⁸,** *a.* Habitual; usual.

ace, 1 ēs; 2 āç, *n.* A single spot on a card or die; a unit; particle. **2.** A military airman who has destroyed five enemies.

-a′ceous, *suffix.* Of the nature of; pertaining to; like; as, cret*aceous*, of or like chalk, chalky.

a-cer′bi-ty, 1 a-sûr′bı-tı; 2 a-çẽr′bi-ty, *n.* [-TIES², *pl.*] Sourness, as of temper, etc.; harshness. [acetic acid.

ac′e-tate, 1 as′ı-tēt; 2 ăç′e-tāt, *n.* A salt of

a-cet′ic, 1 a-set′ık or a-sī′tık; 2 a-çẽt′ie or a-çē′tie, *a.* Pertaining to or like vinegar; sour.— **acetic acid,** acid found in vinegar.— **a-cet′i-fy,** *vt. & vi.* [-FIED; -FY′ING.] To make acid.

a-cet′y-lene, 1 a-set′ı-līn; 2 a-çĕt′y-lēn, *n.* A brilliant illuminating gas produced by the action of water on certain compounds of quicklime.

ache,) 1 ēk; 2 āe. **I.** *vi.* [ACHED†, AKED⁸;
akes,) ACH′ING, AK′ING⁸.] · To suffer dull, continued pain. **II.** *n.* A dull, continued pain.

a-chiev(e′⁸, 1 a-chīv′; 2 a-chēv′, *vt. & vi.* [A-CHIEV(E)D′⁸; A-CHIEV′ING.] To accomplish, as by an exploit; perform; finish; win; attain an object.

a-chieve′ment, 1 a-chĭv′ment or -mạnt; 2 a-chēv′ment, *n.* A noteworthy and successful action.

ach″ro-mat′ic, 1 ak″ro-mat′ık; 2 ăe″ro-măt′ie, *a.* Free from color; transmitting pure white light, as a lens.

ac′id, 1 as′ıd; 2 ăç′id. **I.** *a.* Sharp to the taste, as vinegar; sour; of or like an acid. **II.** *n.* **1.** Any sour substance. **2.** *Chem.* A compound of hydrogen capable of uniting with a base to form a salt.— **a-cid′i-fy,** 1 a-sıd′ı-faı; 2 a-çĭd′ı-fŷ, *vt. & vi.* To make or become acid.— **a-cid′i-ty,** 1 -ı-tı; 2 -i-ty, *n.* The quality of being acid; strength of an acid. **ac′id-ness‡.— a-cid′u-late,** *vt.* To acidify.— **a-cid′u-lous,** *a.* Slightly acid.

-a′cious, *suffix.* Abounding in; characterized by; given to; as, ver*acious*, truthful.

ac-knowl′edge, 1 ak-nŏl′ej; 2 ăe-nŏl′ĕdg, *vt.* [-EDGED; -EDG-ING.] To own as obligatory, genuine, or valid; confess; avow; certify.— **ac-knowl′edg-ment,** *n.* Avowal; confession; recognition.

ac′me, 1 ak′mı; 2 ăe′me, *n.* The highest point or summit; perfection; climax.

ac′o-lyte, 1 ak′o-lait; 2 ăe′o-lŷt, *n.* An attendant in religious service; altar-boy.

ac′o-nite, 1 ak′o-nait; 2 ăe′o-nīt, *n.* *Med.* A poisonous plant; monk′s-hood or wolf′s-bane.

a′corn, 1 ē′kŏrn or ē′kạrn; 2 ā′eôrn or ā′corn, *n.* The fruit of the oak, a nut, fixed in a natural woody cup.

Acorn.

a-cous′tic, 1 a-kūs′[or -kạus′]tık; 2 a-eụs′-

1: ə = final; ı = habit; aısle; au = out; oıl; iū = feud; chin; go; ŋ = sing; chin, this.
2: wǫlf, dǫ; bŏŏk, bōōt; fụll, rụle, cūre, bŭt, bûrn; ŏıl, bŏy; gǫ, gem; ıŋk; thin, this.

[or -cous′]tie, a. Pertaining to the act or sense of hearing; adapted for conveying sound. — **a-cous′tics,** n. The science of sound; the sound-producing qualities.

ac-quaint′d, 1 a-kwĕnt′; 2 ă-kwänt′, vt. To cause to know; inform: followed by with. — **ac-quaint′ed,** pa. Personally knowing or known.

ac-quain′tance, 1 a-kwēn′təns; 2 ă-kwän′tans, n. **1.** Knowledge. **2.** A person or persons known.

ac″qui-esce′, 1 ak″wi-es′; 2 ăe″wi-ĕs′, vt. [-ESCED′t; -ESC′ING.] To tacitly consent; accept; assent. — **ac″qui-es′cence,** n. Passive consent. — **ac″qui-es′cent,** a.

ac-quire′, 1 a-kwair′; 2 ă-kwīr′, vt. [AC-QUIRED′; AC-QUIR′ING.] To obtain; get as one's own; receive; gain. — **ac-quire′ment,** n. The act of acquiring; an acquired power; attainment. — **ac″qui-si′tion,** 1 ak″wi-zish′ən; 2 ăe″wi-ṣish′on, n. **1.** The act of acquiring. **2.** Anything acquired; acquirement; possession. — **ac-quis′i-tiv**(e⁵, 1 a-kwiz′i-tiv; 2 ă-kwiṣ′i-tiv, a. Able or inclined to acquire. -ly, adv. -ness, n.

ac-quit′, 1 a-kwit′; 2 ă-kwĭt′, vt. [AC-QUIT′TEDᵈ or AC-QUIT′; AC-QUIT′TING.] **1.** To declare innocent; exculpate; exonerate. **2.** To relieve, as of an obligation; absolve. **3.** To deport (oneself). **4.** To repay; requite. — **ac-quit′tal,** n. The act of acquitting, or the state of being acquitted. — **ac-quit′tance,** n. Release or discharge, as from indebtedness; a receipt; an acquittal.

a′cre, 1 ē′kər; 2 ā′eer, n. A measure of land, 43,560 square feet; a field.

ac′rid, 1 ak′rıd; 2 ăe′rid, a. Of a cutting, burning taste; pungent; bitter. — **a-crid′i-ty,** n. **ac′rid-ness**⁂. — **ac′rid-ly,** adv.

ac″ri-mo′ni-ous, 1 ak″rı-mō′nı-us; 2 ăe″ri-mō′ni-ŭs, a. Bitter; sarcastic; sharp. -ly, adv. -ness, n.

ac′ri-mo-ny, 1 ak′rı-mo-nı; 2 ăe′ri-mo-ny, n. [-NIES², pl.] Bitterness of speech or temper; harshness.

ac′ro-bat, 1 ak′ro-bat; 2 ăe′ro-băt, n. One who practises certain athletic exercises, as vaulting, tumbling, etc.; a rope-dancer. — **ac″ro-bat′ic,** a.

a-crop′o-lis, 1 a-krop′o-lis; 2 a-erŏp′o-līs, n. The citadel of an ancient Greek city.

a-cross′, 1 a-krŏs′; 2 a-erŏs′, adv. & prep. From side to side; over; beyond; crosswise.

a-cros′tic, 1 a-krŏs′tık; 2 a-erŏs′tıe, n. Pros. A rime in which the initial letters of each line form a word or phrase.

actᵈ, 1 akt; 2 ăet, n. & v. **I.** t. To perform; do; play; feign. **II.** i. To perform an act; behave; do; perform on the stage.

— **act′ing.** **I.** pa. Operating; officiating; doing (service) in place of another. **II.** n. Action; performance.

act, n. **1.** The exertion of power; something done; a deed. **2.** A section of a play or drama. **3.** A law.

ac′tin-ism, 1 ak′tın-izm; 2 ăe′tin-iṣm, n. Chemical power or effect of the sun's rays. — **ac-tin′ic,** a.

ac′tion, 1 ak′shən; 2 ăe′shon, n. **1.** The process or mode of acting; operation; activity. **2.** The thing done; deed; a battle; lawsuit. — **ac′tion-a-bl**(e⁵, a. Affording ground for prosecution, as a libel.

ac′tiv(e⁵, 1 ak′tıv; 2 ăe′tiv, a. **1.** Abounding in action; lively; brisk; busy. **2.** Gram. Expressing action, as a verb. -ly, adv. -ness, n.

ac-tiv′i-ty, 1 ak-tiv′ı-tı; 2 ăe-tĭv′i-ty, n. [-TIES², pl.] The quality of being active; action.

ac′tor, 1 ak′tər; 2 ăe′tŏr, n. One who acts; a stage-player. — **ac′tress,** n. fem.

ac′tu-al, 1 ak′chu-[or -tiu-]al; 2 ăe′chu-[or -tū-]al. **I.** a. Existing in fact; real. **II.** n. Something real. — **ac″tu-al′i-ty,** n. [-TIES², pl.] The quality of being actual; reality. **ac′tu-al-ness**⁂. — **ac′tu-al-ly,** adv. In reality; truly.

ac′tu-a-ry, 1 ak′chu-[or -tiu-]ē-rı; 2 ăe′chu-[or -tū-]ā-ry, n. [-RIES², pl.] A statistician; accountant.

ac′tu-ate, 1 ak′chu-[or -tiu-]ēt; 2 ăe′chu-[or -tū-]āt, v. [-AT′EDᵈ; -AT′ING.] **I.** t. To incite to action; influence; impel. **II.** i. To act.

a-cu′men, 1 a-kiū′men; 2 a-cū′mĕn, n. Quickness of insight; keenness of intellect.

a-cute′, 1 a-kiūt′; 2 a-eūt′, a. **1.** Keenly discerning or sensitive. **2.** Intense; violent. **3.** Sharp at the end; sharp-pointed. -ly, adv. -ness, n. — **acute angle,** an angle less than a right angle.

a-cy, suffix. Forming nouns denoting quality, condition, office, etc.; as, delicacy.

ad-, prefix. To; as, adhere.

ad′age, 1 ad′ıj; 2 ăd′ag, n. An old saying; maxim.

a-da′gio, 1 a-dä′jo; 2 ä-dä′go, a. & adv. Mus. Slow.

a″da-gis′si-mo, 1 ä″da-jis′si-mo; 2 ä″dä-ğis′si-mo, a. & adv. Mus. As slow as possible.

ad′a-mant, 1 ad′ə-mant; 2 ăd′a-mănt, n. A very hard mineral; formerly, the diamond. — **ad″a-man′tin**(e⁵, a. Unyielding.

a-dapt′d, 1 ə-dapt′; 2 a-dăpt′, vt. To make suitable; adjust; fit; conform; remodel. — **a-dapt′a-bil′i-ty,** n. **a-dapt′a-bl**(e-ness⁂‡. — **a-dapt′a-bl**(e⁵, a. Capable of being adapted. — **ad″ap-ta′tion,** n. An adapting; that which is adapted.

add⁴,⎱ 1 ad; 2 ăd, v. **I.** t. To join or unite, so
ad⁰,⎰ as to increase; find the sum of. **II.** i.
To make or be an addition; perform addition.— **add'a-bl(e⁰,** a. That can be added.
— **added line** (Mus.), a short line above or
below the staff.

ad-den'dum, 1 a-den'dum; 2 ă-dĕn'dŭm,
n. [-DA, pl.] Something added, or to be
added.

ad'der, 1 ad'ər; 2 ăd'ẽr, n. A poisonous
serpent; the common European viper.

ad-dict'⁴, 1 a-dikt'; 2 ă-dĭct'. **I.**
vt. To apply (oneself) persistently; give (oneself) up: followed by to. **II.** n. One addicted to some habit.— **ad-dic'tion,** n. Habitual inclination;
bent. **ad-dict'ed-ness‡.**

ad-di'tion, 1 a-dish'ən; 2
ă-dĭsh'on, n. The act of adding, or that which is added; Adder. ¹/₁₀
an increase; accession.— **ad-di'tion-al,** a. Being in addition. **-ly,** adv.

ad'dle,⎱ 1 ad'l; 2 ăd'l. **I.** vt. & vi. [AD-
ad'l⁰,⎰ DLED, AD'L,D⁰; AD'DLING.] To
spoil or become spoiled, as eggs; muddle.
II. a. Spoiled, as eggs; rotten; worthless.
— **ad'dled‡.**

ad-dress', 1 a-dres'; 2 ă-drĕs', vt. [AD-
DRESSED'† or AD-DREST'; AD-DRESS'ING.] **1.** To
speak to; accost. **2.** To direct, as a letter.
3. To devote (oneself); apply. **4.** To woo.

ad-dress', n. **1.** A discourse; greeting; petition. **2.** A person's name, residence, etc.
3. Manner; bearing. **4.** pl. Courteous
attentions; wooing. **5.** Adroitness; tact.

ad-duce', 1 a-diūs'; 2 ă-dūç', vt. [AD-
DUCED'†; AD-DUC'ING.] To bring forward;
cite; allege.— **ad-duce'a-bl(e⁰,** **ad-du'ci-
bl(e⁰,** a. [dular tumor.

ad'e-noid, 1 ad'ı-noid; 2 ăd'e-nöid, n. A glandular tumor.

a-dept', 1 a-dept'; 2 a-dĕpt'. **I.** a. Highly
skilful; proficient. **II.** n. An expert.

ad'e-quate, 1 ad'ı-kwıt or -kwĕt; 2 ăd'e-
kwat, a. Fully sufficient.— **ad'e-qua-cy,** 1
ad'ı-kwə-sı; 2 ăd'e-kwa-cy, n. The state
or fact of being adequate. **ad'e-quate-
ness‡.— ad'e-quate-ly,** adv.

ad-here', 1 ad-hīr'; 2 ăd-hēr', vi. [AD-
HERED'; AD-HER'ING.] To stick fast; be
attached; cling: with to.— **ad-her'ence,** n.
Adhesion. **ad-her'en-cy‡.— ad-her'ent.**
I. a. Clinging or sticking fast. **II.** n. One
who is attached, as to a cause or leader.

ad-he'sion, 1 ad-hī'zən; 2 ăd-hē'zhon, n.
The act of adhering; fidelity; adherence;
assent.— **ad-he'siv(e⁰,** 1 ad-hī'sıv; 2 ăd-hē'-
sıv. **I.** a. Adhering; clinging; sticky. **II.**
n. Something that causes adhesion. **-ly,**
adv. **-ness,** n.

a-dieu', 1 ə-diū'; 2 a-dū', n. & interj. [A-
DIEUS' or A-DIEUX', 1 ə-diūz'; 2 a-dūz', pl.]
Farewell.

ad'i-pose, 1 ad'ı-pōs; 2 ăd'ı-pōs, a. & n. Fat.

ad-ja'cent, 1 a-jē'sent; 2 ă-jā'çĕnt, a.
Near; adjoining; contiguous.

ad'jec-tiv(e⁰, 1 aj'ek-tiv; 2 ăj'ĕc-tĭv. **I.** a.
Pertaining to or like an adjective. **ad'jec-
tiv-al‡. II.** n. A word used to qualify a
noun.— **ad'jec-tiv(e-ly⁰,** adv. **ad'jec-tiv"-
al-ly‡.**

ad-join', 1 a-join'; 2 ă-jŏin', vt. & vi. To join;
append; be close together; be in contact.
— **ad-join'ing,** pa. Lying next; near by;
contiguous.

ad-journ', 1 a-jūrn'; 2 ă-jûrn', vt. & vi. To
close (a meeting or session); postpone (a
matter).— **ad-journ'ment,** n. The act of
adjourning; postponement.

ad-judge, 1 a-juj'; 2 ă-jŭdg', vt. & vi.
[AD-JUDGED'; AD-JUDG'ING.] To pass sentence; award; decree; condemn.

ad-ju'di-cate, 1 a-jū'dı-kēt; 2 ă-jŭ'dı-cāt,
vt. & vi. [-CAT"ED⁴: -CAT'ING.] To determine judicially; adjudge.— **ad-ju"di-ca'-
tion,** n. A judicial decision.— **ad-ju'di-ca-
tor,** n.

ad'junct, 1 aj'uŋkt; 2 ăj'ŭnçt. **I.** a.
Joined subordinately; auxiliary. **II.** n.
An auxiliary.— **ad-junc'tion,** n. The act of
joining; also, the thing joined.— **ad-junc'-
tiv(e⁰,** a. Forming an adjunct. **-ly,** adv.

ad-jure', 1 a-jūr'; 2 ă-jur', vt. [AD-JURED';
AD-JUR'ING.] To charge solemnly; appeal
to; invoke.— **ad"ju-ra'tion,** n.

ad-just'⁴, 1 a-just'; 2 ă-jŭst', vt. To cause
to fit; arrange; regulate; settle.— **ad-just'a-
bl(e⁰,** a. Capable of being adjusted.— **adjust'er,** n. **ad-jus'tor‡.— ad-just'ment,**
n. Regulation; arrangement; settlement.

ad'ju-tant, 1 ad'ju-tənt; 2 ăd'ju-tant. **I.** a.
Assistant; auxiliary. **II.** n. **1.** Mil. A
staff-officer who assists the commander.
2. A carrion-eating East-Indian stork.
— **ad'ju-tan-cy,** n. The office or rank of
an adjutant. **ad'ju-tant-shlp‡.**

ad-mea'sure, 1 ad-mez'ur; 2 ăd-mĕzh'ur,
ad-me'sure⁵, ⎰ vt. [-SURED: -SUR-ING.] To
apportion.— **ad-mea'sure-ment,** n. **1.** An
admeasuring. **2.** Measure; size; dimensions.

ad-min'is-ter, 1 ad-min'ıs-tər; 2 ăd-mĭn'ıs-
ter, v. **I.** t. **1.** To take or have the
charge of; manage; settle, as an estate.
2. To apply; inflict; cause to take. **II.** i.
1. To contribute; minister: with to. **2.**
Law. To act as administrator.— **ad-min"ıs-
tra'tion,** n. An administering.— **ad-min'ıs-
tra"tiv(e⁰,** a. Pertaining to administration;
executive.— **ad-min"ıs-tra"tor,** n. One who

1: ə = final; ı = habıt; aisle; au = out; oil; iū = feud; chin; go; ŋ = sing; thin, this.
2: wolf, dọ; bōōk, bōōt; fụll, rụle, cūre, bŭt, bûrn; ŏil, bŏy; g̣o, g̣em; iŋk; thin, this.

administers.— **ad-min″ls-tra′trix,** *n. fem.*
[-TRI′CES, 1 -trə-trai′sĭz; 2 -tra-trĭ′çĕs, *pl.*]

ad′mi-ra-bl(e², 1 ad′mi-rə-bl; 2 ăd′mi-ra-bl, *a.* Worthy of admiration; excellent.— **ad′mi-ra-bly,** *adv.*

ad′mi-ral, 1 ad′mi-rəl; 2 ăd′mi-ral, *n.* A naval officer of the highest rank; the commander-in-chief of a fleet.— **ad′mi-ral-ship,** *n.* The office or rank of an admiral. — **ad′mi-ral-ty,** *n.* A court of maritime affairs; the office of an admiral.

ad″mi-ra′tion, 1 ad″mi-rē′shən; 2 ăd″mi-rā′shon, *n.* 1. Wonder combined with approbation; gratified contemplation. 2. That which is admired.

ad-mire′, 1 ad-mair′; 2 ăd-mīr′, *vt.* [AD-MIRED′; AD-MIR′ING.] To regard with wondering pleasure.— **ad-mir′er,** *n.* One who admires; a lover.

ad-mis′si-bl(e², 1 ad-mĭs′i-bl; 2 ăd-mĭs′i-bl, *a.* Such as may be admitted; allowable. — **ad-mis″si-bil′i-ty,** *n.* — **ad-mis′si-bly,** *adv.*

ad-mis′sion, 1 ad-mĭsh′ən; 2 ăd-mĭsh′on, *n.* Right or privilege of entrance; an admitting; concession.

ad-mit′, 1 ad-mĭt′; 2 ăd-mĭt′, *v.* [AD-MIT′TED⁴; AD-MIT′TING.] **I.** *t.* To allow to enter; receive; permit; concede. **II.** *i.* 1. To give scope, warrant, or permission: with *of.* 2. To give entrance: often with *to.*— **ad-mit′tance,** *n.* An admitting or being admitted; entrance; admission.

ad-mix′ture, 1 ad-miks′chur *or* -tiur; 2 ăd-mĭks′chur *or* -tūr, *n.* Mixture.— **ad-mix′,** *vt.*

ad-mon′ish, 1 ad-mon′ish; 2 ăd-mŏn′ish, *vt.* To advise of a fault; caution; exhort; instruct solemnly; warn.— **ad″mo-ni′tion,** 1 ad″mo-nĭsh′ən; 2 ăd″mo-nĭsh′on, *n.* The act of admonishing; gentle reproof.— **ad-mon′i-to-ry,** *a.* Giving admonition.

a-do′, 1 ə-dū′; 2 a-do̱′, *n.* Unnecessary activity; fuss; trouble.   [brick.

a-do′be, 1 ə-dō′bi; 2 a-do̱′be, *n.* Sun-dried

ad″o-les′cent, 1 ad″o-les′ent; 2 ăd″o-lĕs′ĕnt. **I.** *a.* Approaching maturity; pertaining to youth. **II.** *n.* A youth.— **ad″o-les′cence,** *n.* The period of youth.

a-dopt′ᵈ, 1 ə-dopt′; 2 a-dŏpt′, *vt.* To accept as one's own.— **a-dop′tion,** *n.* The act of adopting, or the state of being adopted.— **a-dop′tiv(e³,** *a.* Pertaining or tending to adoption.

a-dore′, 1 ə-dōr′; 2 a-dōr′, *vt. & vi.* [A-DORED′; A-DOR′ING.] To regard with reverence; love intensely; worship.— **a-dor′a-bl(e³,** *a.* Worthy of adoration or devoted affection. — **a-dor′a-bly,** *adv.*— **ad″o-ra′tion,** *n.* The act of adoring; worship or devotion.— **a-dor′er,** *n.* One who adores; a lover.

a-dorn′, 1 ə-dōrn′; 2 a-dōrn′, *vt.* To make

beautiful; ornament.— **a-dorn′ing. I.** *pa.* Ornamental. **II.** *n.* Adornment.— **a-dorn′ment,** *n.* The act of adorning, or that which adorns; ornament.

ad-re′nal-in, 1 ad-rĭ′nəl-in; 2 ăd-rē′nal-ĭn, *n.* The most powerful chemical astringent known.

a-drift′, 1 ə-drift′; 2 a-drĭft′, *adv.* Drifting.

a-droit′, 1 ə-droit′; 2 a-drŏit′, *a.* Skilful; dexterous.

ad″u-la′tion, 1 ad″yu-lē′shən; 2 ăd″yu-lā′shon, *n.* Servile flattery; fulsome compliment.— **ad′u-la-to-ry,** *a.* Obsequiously flattering.

a-dult′, 1 ə-dult′; 2 a-dŭlt′. **I.** *a.* Full-grown. **II.** *n.* One who has attained maturity

a-dul′ter-ate, 1 a-dul′tər-ēt; 2 a-dŭl′ter-āt. **I.** *vt.* [-AT′ED⁴; -AT′ING.] To make impure by admixture; corrupt. **II.** *a.* Adulterated.— **a-dul″ter-a′tion,** *n.*— **a-dul′ter-a″tor,** *n.*— **a-dul′ter-y,** *n.* [-IES², *pl.*] Violation of the marriage vow; unchastity. — **a-dul′ter-er, a-dul′ter-ess,** *n.* A man or woman guilty of adultery.— **a-dul′ter-ous,** *a.*

ad-vance′, 1 ad-vɑns′; 2 ăd-vȧnç′. **I.** *vt. & vi.* [AD-VANCED′ᵗ; AD-VANC′ING.] 1. To move, bring, or go forward; accelerate; increase; progress. 2. To pay beforehand. 3. To elevate; promote. **II.** *a.* Being an advance. **III.** *n.* 1. An advancing; progress; improvement; prepayment; proposal. 2. The front; lead; start; van. — **ad-vanced′,** *pa.* Being at the front; mature; far extended; progressive; highly developed.— **ad-vance′ment,** *n.* An advancing; furtherance; promotion.

ad-van′tage, 1 ad-vɑn′tij; 2 ăd-vȧn′tag. **I.** *vt. & vi.* [-TAGED⁴; -TAG-ING.] To give or gain advantage; favor; profit. **II.** *n.* Anything favorable to success; superiority; profit; utility.— **ad″van-ta′geous,** 1 ad″van-tē′jus; 2 ăd″van-tā′gŭs, *a.* Affording advantage; profitable; favorable. **-ly,** *adv.* **-ness,** *n.*

ad′vent, 1 ad′vent; 2 ăd′vĕnt, *n.* 1. A coming. 2. [A-] (1) The coming of Christ. (2) The four weeks before Christmas.

ad″ven-ti′tious, 1 ad″ven-tish′us; 2 ăd″vĕn-tĭsh′ŭs, *a.* Not inherent; extrinsic; accidental. **-ly,** *adv.*

ad-ven′ture, 1 ad-ven′chur *or* -tiur; 2 ăd-vĕn′chur *or* -tūr. **I.** *vt. & vi.* [-TURED; -TUR-ING.] To venture. **II.** *n.* A hazardous experience; daring feat; venture; speculation.— **ad-ven′tur-er,** *n.*— **ad-ven′tur-ess,** *n.* A seeker of adventures, or of fortune by questionable means.— **ad-ven′tur-ous,** *a.* 1. Disposed to seek adventures; venturesome. 2. Hazardous. **-ly,** *adv.* **-ness,** *n.*

ad'verb, 1 ad'vûrb; 2 ăd'věrb, *n. Gram.* Any word used to modify verbs, adjectives, or other adverbs.— **ad-ver'bi-al,** *a.* **-ly,** *adv.*

ad'ver-sa-ry, 1 ad'věr-sē-rı; 2 ăd'ver-sā-ry, *n.* [-RIES²*, pl.*] An opponent; antagonist; enemy.

ad'verse, 1 ad'vûrs; 2 ăd'věrs, *a.* Opposing or opposed; antagonistic. **-ly,** *adv.* **-ness,** *n.*— **ad-ver'si-ty,** *n.* [-TIES², *pl.*] Hardship or affliction; misfortune; poverty.

ad-vert', 1 ad-vûrt'; 2 ăd-věrt', *vi.* To turn the mind; refer incidentally.— **ad-ver'tence,** *n.* Attention; notice.

ad'ver-tise or **-tize,** 1 ad'věr-taiz; 2 ăd'ver-tīz, *vt. & vi.* [-TISED; -TIS'ING.] To make known by public notice. — **ad-ver'tise-ment,** 1 ad-vûr'tız-měnt *or* ad'věr-taiz'ment; 2 ăd-věr'tĭş-měnt *or* ăd'-ver-tīş'měnt. *n.* A printed public notice, as in a newspaper. **ad-ver'tiz-ment**ᴾ‡.— **ad'-ver-tis'er** or **-tiz'er,** *n.* One who advertises.

ad-vice', 1 ad-vais'; 2 ăd-vīç', *n.* **1.** Encouragement or dissuasion; counsel. **2.** Information; notification: frequently in the plural, *advices.* **3.** Deliberation; forethought.

ad-vise', 1 ad-vaiz'; 2 ăd-vīz', *v.* [AD-
ad-vize'ᴾ, VISED'; AD-VIS'ING.] **I.** *t.* **1.** To give advice to; counsel; warn; recommend. **2.** To apprize (of); notify; inform. **II.** *i.* To take or give counsel; consult.— **ad-vis'a-bil'i-ty,** *n.* **ad-vis'a-ble-ness**‡. — **ad-vis'a-ble**ᴾ, *a.* Proper to be advised; expedient.— **ad-vis'a-bly,** *adv.*— **ad-vis'ed-ly,** *adv.* With forethought or advice; not hastily.— **ad-vis'er,** *n.* One who advises.— **ad-vi'so-ry,** *a.* Having power to advise; advising.

ad'vo-cate, 1 ad'vo-kēt; 2 ăd'vo-eāt. **I.** *vt.* [-CAT'ED^d; -CAT'ING.] To speak in favor of; plead for. **II.** *n.* An intercessor; counselor.— **ad'vo-ca-cy,** *n.* Act of advocating.

adz, 1 adz; 2 ădz. *n.* A hand cutting-
adze, tool with blade at right angles to its handle.

æ-. For words so beginning, see E-.

Æ-ge'an, 1 ī-jī'ən; 2 ē-gē'an, *a.* Pertaining to a sea between Greece and Asia Minor, part of the Mediterranean; the Greek Archipelago.

a'er-ate, 1 ē'ər-ēt; 2 ā'er-āt, *vt.* [-AT'-
ED^d; -AT'ING.] To supply or charge with air or gas.

a-e'ri-al, 1 ē-ī'rı-əl; 2 ā-ē'ri-al, **I.** *a.* Of or like the air; high in air; growing in air; airy; spiritual. **II.** *n.* A radio antenna.

a'er-ie, 1 ē'er-ı; 2 ā'er-i, *n.* The nest or brood of a predatory bird, as the eagle on a crag. **a'er-y**‡.

a'er-i-form, 1 ē'ər-ı-fôrm; 2 ā'er-i-fôrm, *a.*

Like air; gaseous; unsubstantial; intangible.

a'er-o, 1 ē'ər-o; 2 ā'er-o, *abbr.* [Colloq.] An aeroplane or other aerial vehicle.— **a'er-o-boat",** *n.* A flying boat; hydroaeroplane.— **a'er-o-bus",** *n.* An aeroplane or airship that carries passengers.

a'er-o-drome, 1 ē'ər-o-drōm; 2 ā'er-o-drōm, *n.* A mechanism for gliding on the air; place for storing flying-machines.

a'er-o-gram, 1 ē'ər-o-gram; 2 ā'er-o-grăm, *n.* A wireless message.   [meteorite.

a'er-o-lite, 1 ē'ər-o-lait; 2 ā'er-o-līt, *n.* A

a'er-o-naut, 1 ē'ər-o-nôt; 2 ā'er-o-nạt, *n.* A balloonist; aviator.

a"er-o-nau'tic, 1 ē'ər-o-nō'tık; 2 ā"er-o-nạ'tie, *a.* Pertaining to aeronauts.

a"er-o-nau'tics, 1 ē'ər-o-nō'tıks; 2 ā"er-o-nạ'tiçs,*n.* The science of navigating the air.

a'er-o-plane, 1 ē'ər-o-plēn; 2 ā'er-o-plān, *n.* A kite-like machine for flying: a "heavier-than-air" machine, having one plane (*monoplane*) or two planes (*biplane*), and sustained by the gliding motion imparted by its own propeller.

a'er-o-stat, 1 ē'ər-o-stat; 2 ā'er-o-stăt, *n.* **1.** A balloon or flying-machine. **2.** [Rare.] An aeronaut or aviator.— **a"er-o-stat'ic,** *a.* **-i-cal**‡.— **a"er-o-stat'ics,** *n. pl.* **1.** The scientific study of air and gases at rest. **2.** Aerostatics.— **a"er-o-sta'tion,** *n.* The art or practise of raising and supporting bodies in the air, as balloons or flying-machines.

æs-thet'ic, etc. See ESTHETIC, etc.

a-far', 1 ə-fär';2 a-fär', *adv.* At or to a distance.

af'fa-bleᴾ, 1 af'ə-bl; 2 ăf'a-bl, *a.* Easy and courteous in manner.— **af"fa-bil'i-ty,** *n.* The quality of being affable; easy courtesy.— **af'fa-bl(e-ness**ᴾ‡.— **af'fa-bly,** *adv.*

af-fair', 1 a-fâr'; 2 ă-fâr', *n.* Anything done or to be done; business; matter; thing.

af-fect'ᴵ^d, 1 a-fekt'; 2 ă-fĕet', *vt.* To act upon: influence; move emotionally. — **af-fect'ed**ᴵ, *pa.* Acted upon; influenced; moved emotionally.— **af-fect'ing,** *pa.* Moving; pathetic.— **af-fect'ing-ly,** *adv.*

af-fect'²^d, *vt.* **1.** To be fond of; love; haunt; frequent. **2.** To pretend; counterfeit.— **af"fec-ta'tion,** 1 af"ek-tē'shən: 2 ăf"ee-tā'-shon, *n.* Pretense; display.— **af-fect'ed**², *pa.* Showing affectation; inclined; frequented; unnatural. **-ly,** *adv.* **-ness,** *n.*

af-fec'tion¹, 1 a-fek'shən; 2 ă-fĕe'shon, *n.* The act of influencing, or state of being influenced; state of mind or body; disease.

af-fec'tion², *n.* **1.** Strong and tender attachment; love. **2.** Any natural feeling. — **af-fec'tion-ate,** *a.* Having or expressing love; loving; fond. **-ly,** *adv.*

af'fer-ent, 1 af'ər-ent; 2 ăf'er-ĕnt, *a.* Con-

1: **ə** = final; **ı** = habıt; **aı**sle = out; **oıl**; **ıū** = feud; **ch**in; go; **ŋ** = sing; **th**in, this.
2: **wo**lf, **do**; b**oo**k, b**oo**t; f**u**ll, r**u**le, c**u**re, b**u**t, b**u**rn; **oi**l, b**o**y; **go**, **ge**m; **ink**; **th**in, thus.

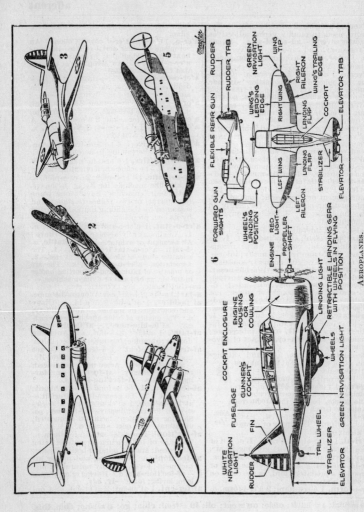

AEROPLANES.

1. Douglas Transport (1934), a notably successful modern design. 2. Curtis "Hawk" (1940). 3. Curtis Pursuit Plane (1940). 4. Boeing Bomber (1940). 5. Boeing "Atlantic Clipper" (1940), designed to carry 72 passengers. 6. A two-place Seversky,

ducting inward or toward the center: opposed to *efferent*.

af-fi′ance, 1 a-fai′əns; 2 ă-fī′anç. **I.** *vt.* [-ANCED^t; -ANC-ING.] To betroth; pledge. **II.** *n.* A betrothal; pledge of faith; confidence. [who makes an affidavit.

af-fi′ant, 1 a-fai′ənt; 2 ă-fī′ant, *n.* One

af′fi-da-vit, 1 af′ı-dē′vıt; 2 ăf′ĭ-dā′vit, *n.* A voluntary sworn declaration in writing.

af-fil′i-ate, 1 a-fil′ı-ēt; 2 ă-fĭl′ĭ-āt, *v.* [-AT′ED^d; -AT′ING.] **I.** *t.* To associate with; adopt; ally. **II.** *i.* To be intimate; sympathize; consort.— **af-fil′i-a′tion,** *n.*

af-fin′i-ty, 1 a-fin′ı-tı; 2 ă-fĭn′ĭ-ty, *n.* [-TIES^z, *pl.*] Natural inclination; chemical attraction.

af-firm′, 1 a-fūrm′; 2 ă-fĭrm′, *vt.* & *vi.* To state positively; maintain; assert; aver; make affirmation.— **af-firm′ance,** *n.* **1.** Affirmation. **2.** *Law.* Ratification.— **af′′fir-ma′tion,** *n.* A solemn declaration; statement.— **af-firm′a-tiv(e^s.** **I.** *a.* Taking the "yes" side; asserting something as fact. **II.** *n.* That which affirms or asserts; assent. **-ly,** *adv.*

af-fix′^t, 1 a-fiks′; 2 ă-fĭks′, *vt.* To attach; fasten; append.— **af′fix,** 1 af′ıks; 2 ăf′iks, *n.* That which is attached or added; a prefix or suffix.

af-flict′^d, 1 a-flikt′; 2 ă-flĭet′, *vt.* To oppress; trouble; grieve; distress.— **af-flic′tion,** *n.* Distress of body or mind, or its cause; grief; calamity.— **af-flic′tiv(e^s,** *a.* Causing distress; grievous. **-ly,** *adv.*

af′flu-ent, 1 af′lu-ent; 2 ăf′lụ-ĕnt. **I.** *a.* Abounding, as in wealth; rich; also, flowing freely; fluent. **II.** *n.* A tributary stream.— **af′flu-ence,** *n.* A profuse or abundant supply; wealth.

af-ford′^d, 1 a-fōrd′; 2 ă-fôrd′, *vt.* **1.** To be able to meet, as expense; bear; stand. **2.** To produce; yield.

af-for′est, 1 a-fər′est; 2 ă-fŏr′ĕst, *vt.* To convert into a forest; declare subject to forest laws. [brawl; fight; fray.

af-fray′, 1 a-frē′; 2 ă-frā′, *n.* A public

af-fright′‖, 1 a-froit′; 2 ă-frīt′. **I^d.** *vt.* To frighten. **II.** *n.* Fright.

af-front′, 1 a-frunt′; 2 ă-frŏnt′. **I^d.** *vt.* To insult openly. **II.** *n.* An open insult.

af-fu′sion, 1 a-fiū′ʒən; 2 ă-fū′zhon, *n.* Pouring.

a-field′, 1 ə-fīld′; 2 a-fēld′, *adv.* In, to, or on the field. [burning.

a-fire′, 1 ə-fair′; 2 a-fīr′, *adv.* & *a.* On fire;

a-flame′, 1 ə-flēm′; 2 a-flăm′, *adv.* & *a.* Flaming; glowing; in a flame.

a-float′, 1 ə-flōt′; 2 a-flŏt′, *adv.* & *a.* Floating; circulating; adrift; unfixed. [ing.

a-flow′, 1 ə-flō′; 2 a-flō′, *adv.* & *a.* Flow-

a-foot′, 1 ə-fut′; 2 a-fŏŏt′, *adv.* On foot; able to walk; on the move; astir.

a-fore′, 1 ə-fōr′; 2 a-fōr′, *adv.*, *prep.*, & *conj.* Before.— **a-fore′said′,** *a.* Said or mentioned before.— **a-fore′time′,** *adv.* At a previous time; formerly.

a-fore′thought′, 1 ə-fōr′thŏt′; 2 a-fōr′thôt′, *a.* Intended; premeditated.— **malice afore-thought,** a preconceived intent to kill.

a-foul′, 1 ə-faul′; 2 a-foul′, *adv.* & *a.* In entanglement or collision.

a-fraid′, 1 ə-frēd′; 2 a-frād′, *a.* Filled with fear; fearful. [more; again.

a-fresh′, 1 ə-fresh′; 2 a-frĕsh′, *adv.* Once

Af′ri-ca, 1 af′rı-kə; 2 ăf′ri-ca, *n.* A continent; area, 11,513.579 square miles.— **Af′ri-can,** *a.* & *n.*

aft, 1 uft; 2 ăft. *Naut.* **I.** *a.* Of or near the stern. **II.** *adv.* At, toward, or near the stern.

af′ter, 1 af′tər; 2 ăf′ter. **I.** *a.* **1.** *Naut.* Farther aft. **2.** Following in time. **II.** *adv.* **1.** At a later time. **2.** In the rear; behind. **III.** *prep.* **1.** In succession to, subsequently to; because of; notwithstanding. **2.** Behind, back of, or below in rank; inferior to; in pursuit of; in search of. **3.** In relation to; about; for; in imitation of; in obedience to; according to. **4.** For the sake of; by the name of.— **af′ter-crop′,** *n.* A second crop in a season.— **af′ter-math′,** *n.* The second mowing of the season.— **af′ter-most,** *a.* *superl.* **1.** *Naut.* Aftmost. **2**†. Last or latest.— **af′ter-noon′,** *n.* That part of the day between noon and sunset; figuratively. the closing part.— **af′ter-piece′,** *n.* **1.** A farce or the like after a play. **2.** A sequel.— **af′ter-ward.** *adv.* In time following; subsequently. **af′ter-wards**†. [Nearest the ster.ı.

aft′most, 1 aft′mōst; 2 ăft′mōst, *a. Naut.*

a-gain′, 1 ə-gen′; 2 a-gĕn′, *adv.* At a second or another time; once more; anew; afresh; back; in reply; repeatedly; further; moreover; on the other hand.

a-gainst′, 1 ə-genst′; 2 a-gĕnst′, *prep.* **1.** Into contact or collision with; in movement toward; opposite or contrary to; in contact with; also, opposite to; in contrast with. **2.** In preparation for; in readiness for. **3.** In exchange for. **4.** To the debit of; as a charge upon.

ag′ate, 1 ag′ıt; 2 ăg′at, *n.* **1.** A variegated waxy quartz; a gem. **2.** A child's playing marble. **3.** *Print.* The size of type in which this line is set.

A-ga′ve, 1 ə-gē′vı; 2 a-gā′ve, *n.* A genus of plants, embracing the century-plant.

age, 1 ēj; 2 ăg. **I.** *vt.* & *vi.* [AGED; AG′ING.] To make, grow, or seem to grow old. **II.** *n.* **1.** Period of life or existence; length

---

1: ə = final; ı = habit; aisle; au = out; oil; iū = feud; chin; go; ŋ = sing; thin, this.
2: wolf, do; book, boot; full, rule, cūre, bŭt, bŭrn; oil, boy; go, gem; ink; thin, this.

of life already passed. **2.** The decline of life; the state of being old. **3.** Legal majority; maturity. **4.** An era: generation: century.— **a'ged,** 1 ē'jed; 2 ā'gĕd, *pa.* **1.** Advanced in years; of or like old age; old. **2.** Of or at the age of.

-age, *suffix.* Used to fo m nouns: (1) Collective, as bagg*age*, leaf*age;* (2) Of condition, connection, office, etc., as, dray*age*, pilgrim*age*.

a-gen'dum, 1 ə-jen'dum, 2 ā-gĕn'dŭm, *n.* [-DA, *pl.*] A list of business matters to be attended to.

a'gent, 1 ē'jent; 2 ā'gĕnt, *n.* **1.** One who acts; actor; doer. **2.** One who or that which acts for another; a deputy.— **a'gen-cy,** *n.* [-CIES², *pl.*] **1.** Active power or operation; activity; instrumentality. **2.** The relation, business, or place of business, of an agent.

ag-glom'er-ate, 1 a-glom'er-ēt; 2 ă-glŏm'er-āt. **I.** *vt. & vi.* [-AT"ED^d; -AT"-ING.] To gather, form, or grow into a ball or mass. **II.** *a.* Gathered into a mass or heap; clustered. **III.** *n.* A heap or mass of things thrown together. — **ag-glom"er-a'tion,** *n.* A confused mass.

ag-glu'ti-nate, 1 a-glū'ti-nēt; 2 ă-glŭ'ti-nāt. **I.** *vt.* [-NAT"ED^d; -NAT"ING.] **1.** To unite, as by glue. **2.** To convert into glue. **II.** *a.* Adhering.— **ag-glu'ti-nant. I.** *a.* Tending to cause adhesion. **ag-glu-ti-na-tive**(es¹. **II.** *n.* A substance or remedy that causes adhesion.— **ag-glu"ti-na'tion,** *n.*

ag'gran-dize or -dise, 1 ag'ran-daiz; 2 ăg'ran-dīz, *vt. & vi.* [-DIZED; -DIZ'ING.] To increase; exalt.— **ag'gran-dize"ment,** *n.* An aggrandizing; increase; exaltation.

ag'gra-vate, 1 ag'ra-vēt; 2 ăg'ra-vāt, *vt.* [-VAT"ED^d; -VAT'ING.] To make worse; increase; intensify.— **ag"gra-va'tion,** *n.* A making heavier or worse; an enhancement.

ag'gre-gate, 1 ag'ri-gēt; 2 ăg're-gāt. **I.** *vt. & vi.* [-GAT"ED^d; -GAT'ING.] To bring or come together, as into a mass, sum, or body; collect; mass; amount to. **II.** *a.* Collected into a sum, mass, or total; collective. **III.** *n.* The entire number, sum, or quantity; amount; total.— **ag"gre-ga'tion,** *n.* A collection or mass; aggregate.

ag-gres'sion, 1 a-gresh'ən; 2 ă-grĕsh'on, *n.* An unprovoked attack.— **ag-gres'sive**(es, *a.* Disposed to attack or to vigorous activity. **-ly,** *adv.* **-ness,** *n.*— **ag-gres'sor,** *n.* One who begins a quarrel.

ag-griev'e(eᴵᴾ, 1 a-grīv'; 2 ă-grēv', *vt.* [AG-GRIEV(E)D'ˢ; AG-GRIEV'ING.] To cause sorrow to; injure; oppress.

a-ghast', 1 ə-gast'; 2 ă-gȧst', *a.* Struck **a-gast'ˢ,** dumb with horror.

ag'il(es, 1 aj'il; 2 ăg'il, *a.* Active; nimble. — **a-gil'i-ty,** *n.* Quickness and readiness in movement; nimbleness.

ag'i-tate, 1 aj'i-tēt; 2 ăg'i-tāt, *vt. & vi.* [-TAT"ED^d; -TAT"ING.] To excite; disturb; shake; discuss.— **ag"i-ta'tion,** *n.* Violent motion or emotion; open, active discussion. — **ag'i-ta"tor,** *n.*

a"gi-ta'to, 1 ä"ji-tā'to; 2 ä'gī-tä'to, *a. Mus.* Stirred; restless; agitated.

a-glow', 1 ə-glō'; 2 ă-glō', *adv. & a.* In a glow; glowing.

ag-nos'ti-cism, 1 ag-nŏs'ti-sizm, ag-nŏs'-**ag-nos'tics,** tiks; 2 ăg-nŏs'ti-çĭşm, ăg-nŏs'tics, *n.* The doctrine that all being, including God and the human soul, is unknown or unknowable.— **ag-nos'tic. I.** *a.* Professing agnosticism. **II.** *n.* A believer in agnosticism.

a-go', 1 ə-gō'; 2 ă-gō', *pa. & adv.* Gone by; in the past; since.

a-gog', 1 ə-gog'; 2 ă-gŏg', *adv. & a.* Excited with interest or expectation.

ag'o-nize, 1 ag'o-naiz; 2 ăg'o-nīz, *vt. & vi.* **ag'o-nise,** [-NIZED; -NIZ'ING.] To torture; be in agony; writhe; strive.

ag'o-ny, 1 ag'o-ni; 2 ăg'o-ny, *n.* [-NIES², *pl.*] Intense suffering; anguish; struggle.

a-gra'ri-an, 1 ə-grē'ri-an; 2 ă-grā'ri-an. **I.** *a.* Pertaining to land or its distribution; pertaining to agrarianism. **II.** *n.* An advocate of agrarianism.— **a-gra'ri-an-ism,** *n.* The theory or practise of or the demand for an equal or general distribution of lands.

a-gree', 1 ə-grī'; 2 ă-grē', *vi.* [A-GREED'; A-GREE'ING.] To be of one mind; concur; consent; promise; correspond; match.

a-gree-a-bl(eᴾ, 1 ə-grī'ə-bl; 2 ă-grē'a-bl, *a.* Agreeing; pleasurable; suitable; correspondent; willing.— **a-gree"a-bil'i-ty,** *n.* **a-gree'a-bl**(e-ness²‡.— **a-gree'a-bly,** *adv.*

a-gree'ment, 1 ə-grī'ment *or* -mənt; 2 ă-grē'ment, *n.* Mutual assent; conformity; concord; a contract.

ag'ri-cul'ture, 1 ag'ri-kul'ᴄhur *or* -tiur; 2 ăg'ri-cŭl'ᴄhur *or* -tûr, *n.* The cultivation of the soil; tillage; farming.— **ag"ri-cul'tur-al,** *a.* Of, pertaining to, or engaged in agriculture.— **ag"ri-cul'tur-ist,** *n.* A farmer.

a-ground', 1 ə-graund'; 2 ă-ground', *adv. & a.* On the shore or bottom, as a vessel; stranded.

a'gue, 1 ē'giū; 2 ā'gū, *n.* Chills and fever; also, a chill.— **a'gu-ish,** *a.*

a-head', 1 ə-hed'; 2 ă-hĕd', *adv.* At the **a-hed'ˢ,** head; in advance; forward.

a-hoy', 1 ə-hoi'; 2 ă-hōy', *interj. Naut.* Ho there! as, ship *ahoy!*

aid, 1 ēd; 2 ād. **I.** *vt. & vi.* To help; succor; assist. **II.** *n.* Cooperation: assistance; a helper; assistant.

aide'=de=camp', 1 ēd"=de=kamp' *or* äd'=de=kän'; 2 ād'=de=cămp' *or* äd'=de=cän',

1: ȧrtistic, ȧrt; fat, fāre; fȧst; get, prᴇy; hit, police; obey, gō; not, ŏr; full, rūle; but, būrn.

2: ärt, āpe, făt, fâre, fȧst, whąt, ąll; mē, gĕt, prᴇy, fērn; hĭt, īce; ĭ=ē; ĭ=ĕ̃; gō, nŏt, ôr, wŏn,

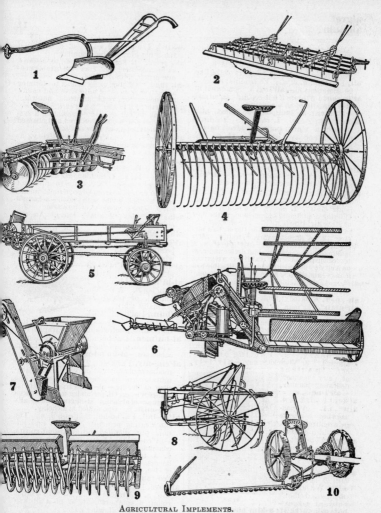

AGRICULTURAL IMPLEMENTS.

1. Walking-plow.　2. Tooth-harrow.　3. Disk-harrow.　4. Hay-rake.　5. Manure-spreader.　6. owing- and Binding-machine (rear view).　7. Feed-grinder.　8. Riding-cultivator.　9. Disk-harrow th seeder attachment.　10. Mowing-machine.

['AIDES'=DE=CAMP", *pl.*] *Mil.* An officer who assists a general: called also *aid.*

ai'gret, 1 ē'gret; 2 ā'grĕt, *n.* **1.** A heron, the egret. **2.** A tuft of feathers or the like.

ail, 1 ēl; 2 āl, *vt.* & *vi.* To trouble; make or be somewhat ill.— **ail'ing,** *a.* Somewhat ill.

ai'le-ron, 1 ē'li-ron; 2 ā'le-rŏn, *n.* An adjustable wing=tip of an air=plane.

— **ail'ment,** *n.* Indisposition; illness. **ail‡.**

aim, 1 ēm; 2 ām. **I.** *vt.* & *vi.* To direct toward a mark; point or level; have a purpose; endeavor earnestly. **II.** *n.* The act of aiming; line of direction of anything aimed; object or point aimed at: purpose.

— **aim'less,** *a.* Wanting in aim or purpose.

air, 1 ār; 2 âr, *vt.* To expose to the air; purify; ventilate; make public.— **air'ing,** *n.* Exposure to or exercise in the air.

air¹, *n.* The gaseous substance surrounding the earth; the atmosphere; wind; breeze.
— **air'=flow".** **I.** *n.* The flow of air. **II.** *a.* Offering a minimum of resistance to the flow of air.— **air'=line",** *n.* **1.** The shortest distance between two points on the earth's surface. **2.** A direct railroad route. — **air'=plane",** *n.* An aeroplane.— **air'=port",** *n.* A landing=place or loading= and delivering=center for air=planes.— **air'=raid",** *n.* An attack on a city by armed air=planes or dirigible balloons.— **air'=ship",** *n.* A dirigible balloon.

air², *n.* **1.** Characteristic appearance; mien; manner. **2.** Affectation: in the plural.

air¹, *n.* **1.** A melody; tune. **2.** The soprano.

air'man", 1 ār'man"; 2 âr'măn", *n.* One who operates a balloon or flying=machine.

air'way", *n.* **1.** Any passageway for air. **2.** A route of travel selected for aircraft.

air'y, *a.* **1.** Of or pertaining to the air; breezy; delicate; ethereal; buoyant; visionary. **2.** Putting on airs; affected. **3.** Vivacious; gay.— **air'i=ly,** *adv.* In a light or airy manner; delicately; jauntily. — **air'i=ness,** *n.*

aisle, 1 ail; 2 īl, *n.*

alle⁵, ¦ 1. A passage between seats in a church. **2.** A wing of a church.

a-jar', 1 ə-jär'; 2 a-jär', *a.* & *adv.* Partly open, as a door.

a-kim'bo, 1 ə-kim'-bo; 2 a-kĭm'bo, *adv.* With hands on hips and elbows outward. **a-kem'-bo‡; a-kem'bow‡; a-kim'bow‡.**

Aisle.

a-kin', 1 ə-kin'; 2 a-kĭn', *a.* & *adv.* Of the same kin; related; similar.

al-, *prefix.* **1.** Form of Latin *ad-,* to, before *l,* as in *al*location. **2.** The: the Arabic definite article, as in *Al*koran.

-al, *suffix.* Of, like, or pertaining to: forming adjectives from other adjectives and nouns, and nouns from verbs; as, deni*al,* music*al.*

à la carte', 1 ɑ lɑ kärt'; 2 ä lä cärt'. [F.] According to bill of fare; designating a system where each dish is ordered and charged separately: opposed to *table d'hôte.*

a-lac'ri-ty, 1 ə-lak'rĭ-tĭ; 2 a-lăc'ri-ty, *n.* Willingness and promptitude; readiness; facility.

a-larm', 1 ə-lärm'; 2 a-lärm'. **I.** *vt.* To strike with sudden fear; give alarm to; arouse. **II.** *n.* **1.** Sudden fear arousing to defense or escape. **2.** A sound to apprize of danger or arouse from sleep; a mechanism, as of a clock, giving such signal.— **a-larm'-ist,** *n.* One disposed to excite alarm.

a-las', 1 ə-las'; 2 a-lás', *interj.* An exclamation of sorrow.

[ment.

alb, 1 alb; 2 ălb, *n.* A priest's linen vestment.

al'ba-tross, 1 al'ba-tros; 2 ăl'ba-trŏs, *n.* [-TROSS-ES, *pl.*] A large, long= winged sea=bird.

al"be'it, 1 ōl'bī'it; 2 al'bē'it, *conj.* Altho.

al-bi'no, 1 al-bai'no; 2 ăl-bī'no, *n.* A person, animal, or plant abnormally white.

al'bum, 1 al'bum; 2 ăl'bŭm, *n.* A blank book for holding photographs, autographs, etc.

Albatross. ¹/₅₁

al-bu'men, 1 al-biū'men; 2 ăl-bū'mĕn, *n.* The white of an egg or a similar viscous substance.— **al-bu'mi-nous,** *a.*

al'che-my, 1 al'ki-mi; 2 ăl'ee-my, *n.* The medieval chemistry that sought the transmutation of base metals into gold, the elixir of life, etc.— **al-chem'ic,** 1 al-kem'ik; 2 al-cĕm'ie, *a.* Of, pertaining to, or produced by means of alchemy. **al-chem'i-cal‡.— al'che-mist,** *n.* One skilled in alchemy.

al'co-hol, 1 al'ko-hol; 2 ăl'co-hŏl, *n.* The intoxicating principle of wines and liquors; pure distilled spirits; ardent spirits.
— **al"co-hol'ic. I.** *a.* Pertaining to, like, containing, or preserved in alcohol. **II.** *n.* **1.** A toper; drunkard. **2.** *pl.* Alcoholic liquors.— **al'co-hol-ism,** *n.*— **al'co-hol-ize** or **-ise,** *vt.*

[as KORAN.

Al"co-ran', 1 al'ko-rän'; 2 al'co-rän', *n.* Same

al'cove, 1 al'kŏv or al-kōv'; 2 ăl'eŏv or ăl-eōv', *n.* A recess connected with a larger room; a compartment, as of a library. See illus. on following page.

al′der, 1 ŏl′dər; 2 al̤′der, *n.* A small tree of the oak family.

al′der-man, 1 ŏl′dər-mən; 2 al̤′der-man, *n.* [-MEN, *pl.*] A city magistrate.

ale, 1 ēl; 2 āl, *n.* A fermented malt liquor.

a-lem′bic, 1 ə-lĕm′bĭk; 2 a-lĕm′bic, *n.* An old-style distilling apparatus; anything that tests or purifies.

a-lert′, 1 ə-lûrt′; 2 a-lērt′, *a.* Keenly watchful; on the lookout; ready for sudden action; also, lively; nimble. **-ly,** *adv.* **-ness,** *n.*

Alcove.

al-fal′fa, 1 al-fal′fə; 2 ăl-fäl′fa, *n.* A forage-plant with leaflets and clover-like flower heads.

al fi′ne, 1 ɑl fĭ′nē; 2 äl fĭ′nẹ. *Mus.* To the end.

al′ge-bra, 1 al′jı-brə; 2 ăl′ğe-bra, *n.* Mathematical calculation by letters and symbols; a treatise on this branch.— **al″ge-bra′ic,** *a.* Pertaining to algebra. **al″ge-bra′i-cal‡.** — **al″ge-bra′i-cal-ly,** *adv.*

a′li-as, 1 ē′lı-əs; 2 ā′li-as. **I.** *a.* Another. **II.** *n.* An assumed name. **III.** *adv.* Otherwise; otherwise called.

al′i-bi, 1 al′ı-baı; 2 ăl′i-bī, *n.* *Law.* A plea of being elsewhere when a crime was committed.

a′lien, 1 ēl′yen; 2 āl′yĕn. **I.** *a.* Of another country; foreign. **II.** *n.* An unnaturalized foreigner; a stranger.— **a″lien-a-bi**(ı⁰ᵉ, *a.* That may be alienated.— **a′lien-age,** *n.* The state or quality of being an alien.— **a′lien-ate,** *vt.* [-AT′EDᵈ; -AT′ING.] **1.** To make alien: estrange. **2.** To transfer: sell.— **a″lien-a′tion,** *n.* Estrangement; sale; mental derangement.— **a′lien-ism,** *n.* **1.** *Rhet.* The use of foreign words or idioms.— **a′lien-ist,** *n.* One who studies or treats insanity.

a-light′, 1 ə-laıt′; 2 a-līt′. **I.** *vi.* [A-LIGHT′EDᵈ; A-LIGHT′ING.] To descend and come to rest; dismount; settle; rest: with *on* or *upon.* **II.** *a. & adv.* Lighted; on fire.

a-lign′, etc. Same as ALINE, etc.

a-like′, 1 ə-laık′; 2 a-līk′. **I.** *a.* Similar; like one another. **II.** *adv.* In like manner.

al′i-ment, 1 al′ı-ment *or* -mənt; 2 ăl′i-ment, *n.* Food; nutriment; sustenance. — **al″i-men′tal,** *a.* Nutritious.— **al″i-men′-ta-ry,** *a.* Supplying nourishment; connected with nutrition.— **al″i-men-ta′tion,** *n.* The supplying or partaking of food.

al′i-mo-ny, 1 al′ı-mō-nı; 2 ăl′i-mō-ny, *n.* *Law.* Separate maintenance to a wife.

a-line′, 1 ə-laın′; 2 a-līn′, *v.* [A-LINED′; A-LIN′ING.] **I.** *t.* To arrange in line, as in military tactics. **II.** *i.* To fall into line.— **a-line′ment,** *n.* Position in line; formation in line; a straight line.

al′i-quant, 1 al′ı-kwənt; 2 ăl′i-kwant, *a.* Contained in another number, but with remainder.

al′i-quot, 1 al′ı-kwŏt; 2 ăl′i-kwŏt, *a.* Contained in another number without remainder. [tive; vigorous; active.

a-live′, 1 ə-laıv′; 2 a-līv′, *a.* Living; sensi-

al′ka-hest, 1 al′kə-hest; 2 ăl′ka-hĕst, *n.* *Alchemy.* An imaginary infallible solvent.

al′ka-li, 1 al′kə-laı *or* -lı; 2 ăl′ka-lī *or* -li, *n.* [-LISᶻ *or* -LIESᶻ, *pl.*] A caustic substance neutralizing acids.— **al″ka-lin**(eˢ, 1 al′kə-laın *or* -lın; 2 ăl′ka-līn *or* -lin, *a.* Of, containing, or like an alkali.

al′ka-loid, 1 al′kə-lɔıd; 2 ăl′ka-lŏid. **I.** *a.* Of or like an alkali. **II.** *n.* A nitrogenous organic substance (generally vegetable) of poisonous properties.

Al″ko-ran′, etc. Same as KORAN, etc.

all, 1 ŏl; 2 al̤. **I.** *a.* The whole of. **II.** *n.* The whole; each and every person or thing. **III.** *adv.* Wholly; entirely; quite.

al′la bre′ve, 1 äl′lä brē′vē; 2 äl′lä brẹ′vẹ. *Mus.* In quick (common) time.

Al′lah, 1 al′ə; 2 äl′a, *n.* The one supreme being; God.

al-lay′, 1 a-lē′; 2 a-lā′, *vt.* [AL-LAYED′, AL-LAYDʳˢ; AL-LAY′ING.] To calm; reduce; relieve; soothe; pacify.

al-lege′, 1 a-lej′; 2 a-lĕğ′, *vt.* [AL-LEGED′; AL-LEG′ING.] To assert without proving; state; plead.— **al″le-ga′tion,** 1 al′ı-gē′shən; 2 äl′e-ğä′shon, *n.* The act of alleging, or that which is alleged.

al-le′giance, 1 ə-lī′jəns; 2 a-lē′ğanç, *n.* Fidelity or duty to a government, a superior, or a principle.

al″le-gor′ic, 1 al′ı-gor′ık, -ı-kəl; 2 äl′e-. [1 al′ı-gor′ı-cal, a. Pertaining **al″le-gor′i-cal,** į gŏr′ie, -i-cal, *a.* Pertaining to or containing allegory; figurative.— **al″le-gor′i-cal-ly,** *adv.*

al″le-go′ry, 1 al′ı-gō′rı; 2 äl′e-gō′ry, *n.* [-RIESᶻ, *pl.*] A symbolic representation; a parable.

al″le-gret′to, 1 ɑl′lē-gret′to; 2 äl′lē-grĕt′to, *a. & adv.* *Mus.* Moderately fast; slower than allegro.

al-le′gro, 1 ɑl-lē′gro; 2 äl-lē′gro. *Mus.* **I.** *a. & adv.* Quick; lively. **II.** *n.* Music in quick time.

al″le-lu′ia, *n. & interj.* See HALLELUJAH.

al'ler-gy, 1 ăl'ur-jı; 2 ăl'ĕr-ġy, n. A condition of susceptibility to substances harmless to most individuals.—**al-ler'ġic,** a.

al-le'vi-ate, 1 ə-lī''vı-ēt; 2 a-lē'vi-āt, vt. [-AT''ED^d; -AT''ING.] To make lighter or easier to bear; relieve; mitigate.—**al-le''vi-a'tion,** n. An alleviating, or that which alleviates.

al'ley, 1 ăl'ı; 2 ăl'y, n. A narrow passageway; a space or building for bowling.

al-li'ance, 1 a-laı'ans; 2 ă-lī'anç, n. A formal union, as between states; intimate relationship.

al'li-ga''tor, 1 ăl'ı-gē''tər; 2 ăl'i-ġā''tor, n. A large American crocodilian reptile.

al-lit''er-a'tion, 1 a-lit''ər-ē''shən; 2 ă-lĭt''er-ā'shon, n. The use of a number of words with the same initial letter; as, a *tale* of *terror*.— **al-lit'er-a-tiv(e^s,** a.

al'lo-cate, 1 ăl'o-kēt; 2 ăl'o-eāt, vt. To set apart; apportion; place.—**al''lo-ca'tion,** n. Apportionment; allowance.

al''lo-cu'tion, 1 ăl''o-kiū'shən; 2 ăl'lo-eū'-shon, n. A formal address, as by the Pope to the clergy.

al''lo-path'ic, 1 ăl''o-pặth'ık; 2 ăl''o-pă̄th'ic, a. Pertaining to the system of medical treatment opposed to the homeopathic: a popular term not recognized by physicians as a class.— **al-lop'a-thist,** n. An advocate or practitioner of the allopathic system. **al''lo-path;**— **al-lop'a-thy,** n. The so-called allopathic system of medicine.

al-lot', 1 a-lɒt'; 2 ă-lŏt', vt. [AL-LOT'TED^d; AL-LOT'TING.] To assign by lot; distribute; appoint; assign.— **al-lot'ment,** n. The act of allotting, or that which is allotted.

al-low', 1 a-lau'; 2 ă-low', v. I. t. 1. To put no obstacle in the way of; permit; tolerate; approve. 2. To grant; allot; give; admit; acknowledge. 3. To make allowance for; deduct. II. i. To make allowance, concession, or abatement.— **al-low'a-bl(e^r,** a. That may be allowed; permissible; admissible.— **al-low'a-bly,** adv.— **al-low'ance.** I^t. vt. To put on an allowance; limit in amount. II. n. 1. That which is allowed: a limited amount, as of income or food. 2. Concession; a difference allowed. 3. Acknowledgment.

al-loy', 1 a-loı'; 2 ă-loy'. I. vt. & vi. To mix with or form into an alloy; temper; debase. II. n. 1. A mixture of two or more metals, or the baser metal in such mixture. 2. Anything that reduces purity or excellence.

all'spice', 1 ɒl'spaıs''; 2 al'spĭç'', n. The dried berry of a West-Indian tree, the pimento.

al-lude', 1 a-liūd'; 2 ă-lūd', vi. [AL-LUD'ED^d; AL-LUD'ING.] To refer (to something) without express mention; make indirect reference.

al-lure', 1 a-liūr'; 2 ă-lūr', vt. & vi. [AL-LURED'; AL-LUR'ING.] To attract; entice; tempt.— **al-lure'ment,** n. 1. The act, quality, or power of alluring; enticement; fascination; attraction. 2. A charm; lure.

al-lu'sion, 1 a-liū'ʒən; 2 ă-lū'zhon, n. An alluding; indirect reference; suggestion.

al-lu'siv(e^s, 1 a-liū'sıv; 2 ă-lū'sĭv, a. Suggestive; figurative.

al-lu'vi-al, 1 a-liū'vı-əl; 2 ă-lū'vi-al, a. Pertaining to or composed of earth deposited by water.

al-lu'vi-um, 1 a-liū'vı-um; 2 ă-lū'vi-ŭm, n. [-VI-A or -VI-UMS^z, pl.] Earth deposited by water.

al-ly', 1 a-laı'; 2 ă-lȳ'. I. vt. & vi. [AL-LIED'; AL-LY'ING.] To unite by relationship, treaty, or marriage. II. n. [AL-LIES'^z, pl.] A state or ruler leagued with another by treaty; an associate; a kinsman.

al'ma-nac, 1 ɒl'mə-nak; 2 al'ma-năc, n. A book giving the days of the week and month through the year, with various data; a yearly calendar.

al-might'y, 1 ɒl-maıt'ı; 2 al-mīt'y. I. a. Able to do all things. II. n. [A-] God; the Supreme Being.

al'mond, 1 ä'mənd or al'mənd; 2 ä'mond or ăl'mond, n. The almond-tree, a native of Barbary or Morocco; also, the stone of its nutlike fruit.

al'mon-er, 1 ăl'mon-ər or ăm'-nər; 2 ăl'mon-er or ăm'ner, n. An official dispenser of alms; formerly, a household chaplain. — **al'mon-ry,** n. [-RIES^z, pl.] The residence of an almoner; place where alms are dispensed.

Almond.

a, flowering branch; b, c, fruit; d, stone.

al'most, 1 ɒl'-mōst; 2 al'mōst, adv. Approximately; very nearly.

alms, 1 ämz; 2 äms, n. sing. & pl. A gift or gifts for the poor; charitable offerings; charity.— **alms'house',** n. A home for the destitute; poorhouse.

al'oe, 1 al'o; 2 ăl'o, n. A plant with thick, fleshy leaves. — **American aloe,** the cen-

1: ȧrtistic, ärt; fat, fāre; fạst; get, prēy; hĭt, police; obey, gō; nɒt, ȯr; fṳll, rūle; bᴜt, bᴜrn.

2: ärt, āpe, făt, fâre, fȧst, whạt, ạll; mē, gĕt, prĕy, fērn; hĭt, īce; ī=ē; ĭ=ē; gō, nŏt, ȯr, wŏn,

tury-plant.— **al'oes,** *n. sing. & pl.* A bitter cathartic from certain species of aloe.

a-loft', 1 ə-lôft'; 2 a-lôft', *adv.* In or to a high or higher place; on high; high up.

-alogy, *suffix.* See -LOGY.

a-lone', 1 ə-lōn'; 2 a-lōn', *a. & adv.* Without company; solitary; unique; only.

a-long', 1 ə-lŏṅ'; 2 a-lŏṅg'. **I.** *adv.* **1.** Lengthwise; onward. **2.** In company (with). **II.** *prep.* On the line of; by the side of; throughout.— **a-long'side".** **I.** *adv.* Close to or along the side. **II.** *prep.* Side by side with.

a-loof', 1 ə-lūf'; 2 a-lōōf', *adv.* At a distance apart.   [or audibly.

a-loud', 1 ə-laud'; 2 a-loud', *adv.* Loudly

alp, 1 ălp; 2 ălp, *n.* A lofty mountain.— **al'pen-horn',** 1 al'pen-hôrn'; 2 ăl'pĕn-hôrn', *n.* A long curved horn used by cowherds on the Alps.— **al'pen-stock',** 1 al'pen-stŏk"; 2 ăl'pĕn-stŏk", *n.* A mountaineers' long iron-pointed staff.— **Al'pine,** 1 al'pin or -pain; 2 ăl'pin or -pĭn, *a.* Pertaining to the Alps, a mountainous region of Europe.

al-pac'a, 1 al-pak'ə; 2 ăl-păc'a, *n.* A sheep-like ruminant of South America, having long, silky wool; a thin cloth made of or in imitation of its wool.

al'pha, 1 al'fə; 2 ăl'fa, *n.* The first letter in the Greek alphabet, equal to the English A, a; hence, the beginning or the first of anything.

Alpaca. 1/70

al'pha-bet, 1 al'fə-bet; 2 **al'fa-bet**, *n.* The letters that form the elements of written language, in order as fixed by usage; the simplest elements or rudiments of anything.— **al''pha-bet'ic,** *a.* **1.** Pertaining to, having, or expressed by an alphabet. **2.** Alphabetical.— **al''pha-bet'i-cal,** *a.* **1.** Arranged in the order of the alphabet. **2.** Alphabetic.— **al''pha-bet'i-cal-ly,** *adv.*

al-read'y, 1 ôl-red'i; 2 al-rĕd'y, *adv.* Before or by this time or the time mentioned; even now.

al'so, 1 ôl'so; 2 al'so, *adv. & conj.* Besides; too; likewise.

al'ta, 1 ôl'ta; 2 ăl'tä, *a. & n. Mus.* High: feminine of ALTO.

al'tar, 1 ôl'tər; 2 al'tar, *n.* **1.** A raised place for burning sacrifices or incense. **2.** The communion-table; a place of prayer.

al'ter, 1 ôl'tər; 2 al'ter, *v.* **I.** *t.* To change; vary; modify; transform. **II.** *i.* To become different.— **al'ter-a-bl(e²,** *a.* Capable of alteration.— **al''ter-a-bly,** *adv.*— **al''ter-a'tion,** *n.* The act or result of altering; modification; change.— **al''ter-a-tiv(e²,**

I. *a.* Tending to change gradually the bodily condition to a normal state. **II.** *n.* An alterative medicine. **al'ter-ant;**

al'ter-cate, 1 al'[*or* ôl']tər-kĕt; 2 ăl'[*or* al']-ter-cāt, *vi.* [-CAT"ED^d; -CAT"ING.] To dispute; wrangle.— **al''ter-ca'tion,** *n.* Angry controversy; disputing.

al'ter-nate, 1 al'[*or* ôl']tər-nēt; 2 ăl'[*or* al']-ter-nāt, *vt. & vi.* [-NAT"ED^d; -NAT"ING.] To change, perform, or occur by turns.— **alternating current** (*Elec.*), a current that changes from the positive to the negative direction and back rapidly; a vibrating or pulsating current.— **al''ter-na'tion,** *n.* Occurrence in turn; permutation.

al-ter'nate, 1 al-[*or* ôl-]tûr'nit; 2 ăl-[*or* al-]-tẽr'nat. **I.** *a.* **1.** Existing, occurring, or following by turns; reciprocal. **2.** Every other (of a series); pertaining to such a series. **II.** *n.* [U. S.] A substitute or second.— **al-ter'nate-ly,** *adv.* In alternate order; by turns.

al-ter'na-tiv(e², 1 al-[*or* ôl-]tûr'nə-tiv; 2 ăl-[*or* al-]tẽr'na-tiv. **I.** *a.* Affording a choice between two things. **II.** *n.* Something instead of something else; a choice of two (or more) things.— **al-ter'na-tiv(e-ly²,** *adv.* In an alternative manner.

al'ter-na"tor, 1 al'[*or* ôl']tər-nē"tər; 2 ăl'[*or* al']ter-nā"tŏr, *n.* **1.** One who or that which alternates. **2.** A dynamo giving an alternating current.

al-tho', 1 ôl-thō'; 2 al-thō', *conj.*
al-though', Admitting or granting that; even tho; notwithstanding.

al'ti-tude, 1 al'ti-tiūd; 2 ăl'ti-tūd, *n.* Vertical elevation; height.

al'to, 1 al'to *or* ôl'to; 2 ăl'to *or* äl'to. *Mus.* **I.** *a.* Sounding or ranging between tenor and treble. **II.** *n.* The lowest female voice.

al''to-geth'er, 1 ôl'tə-geth'ər; 2 al'to-gĕth'er, *adv.* Completely; wholly; permanently.

al'tru-ism, 1 al'tru-izm; 2 ăl'tru-ĭsm, *n.* Disinterested benevolence.— **al'tru-ist,** *n.* One who holds to altruism.— **al''tru-is'tic,** *a.*

al'um, 1 al'um; 2 ăl'ŭm, *n.* An astringent mineral salt.

a-lu'mi-na, 1 ə-liū'mi-nə; 2 a-lū'mi-na, *n. Chem.* Aluminum oxid; pure clay.

a-lu'mi-nous, 1 ə-liū'mi-nus; 2 a-lū'mi-nŭs, *a.* Pertaining to or containing alum or alumina.

a-lu'mi-num, 1 ə-liū'mi-num; 2 a-lū'mi-nŭm, *n.* A light silvery metallic element, which does not tarnish.— **al''u-min'i-um;**

a-lum'na, 1 ə-lum'nə; 2 a-lŭm'na, *n.* [-NÆ, 1 -nī; 2 -nē, *pl.*] A woman graduate, as of a college.

a-lum'nus, 1 ə-lum'nus; 2 a-lŭm'nŭs, *n.*

[-NI, 1 -nai; 2 -nĭ, pl.] A male graduate, as of a college.

al'ways, 1 ôl'wiz; 2 al'waȥ, adv. **1.** Perpetually; ceaselessly. **2.** Regularly; invariably. **al'wayȥ** [Poet.].

A-lys'sum, 1 ə-lis'um; 2 a-lȳs'ŭm, n. Bot. **1.** A large genus of plants of the mustard family, bearing racemes of white or yellow flowers. **2.** [a-] Any plant of this genus, a sweet alyssum.

am, 1 am; 2 ăm, 1st per. sing. pres. ind. of BE.

a-main', 1 ə-mēn'; 2 a-mān', adv. Vehemently; exceedingly; without delay.

a-mal'gam, 1 ə-mal'gəm; 2 a-măl'găm, n. An alloy of mercury; a combination.

a-mal'ga-mate, 1 ə-mal'gə-mēt; 2 a-măl'ga-māt, vt. & vi. [-MAT'ED⁴; -MAT'-ING.] To unite in an alloy with mercury; combine; mix.— **a-mal''ga-ma'tion,** n. The forming of an amalgam; mingling; mixture.

a-man''u-en'sis, 1 ə-man'yu-en'sis; 2 a-măn'yu-ĕn'sis, n. [-SES, 1 -sīz; 2 -sēȥ, pl.] One who copies manuscript or takes dictation.

am'a-ranth, 1 am'ə-ranth; 2 ăm'a-rănth, n. A plant with flowers that do not fade when gathered; also, an imaginary neverfading flower.— **am''a-ran'thin(e⁵,** a. Unfading; immortal; of purplish hue.

a-mass', 1 ə-mas'; 2 a-măs', vt. To heap up; accumulate.— **a-mass'ment,** n.

am''a-teur', 1 am'ə-tūr'; 2 ăm'a-tûr', I. a. Pertaining to, like, or done by an amateur. II. n. One who practises an art or a sport merely for the love of it.

am'a-tive, 1 am'ə-tiv; 2 ăm'a-tĭv, a. Pertaining to sexual love; amorous.— **am'a-tiv(e-ness⁵,** n.— **am'a-to-ry,** a. Characterized by, expressing, or given to sexual love.

a-maze', 1 ə-mēz'; 2 a-māz', vt. [A-MAZED'; A-MAZ'ING.] To confound or bewilder; astonish greatly.— **a-maz'ed-ly,** adv.— **a-maze'ment,** n. Wonder; surprise; astonishment.— **a-maz'ing,** pa. Causing amazement; wonderful.— **-ly,** adv.

Am'a-zon, 1 am'ə-zən; 2 ăm'a-zŏn, n. **1.** One of a mythical race of female warriors. **2.** [A- or a-] Any female warrior; a virago.— **Am''a-zo'ni-an,** a. Pertaining to the Amazons or to the Amazon river in South America; the largest in the world; length, 4,000 miles; has 12 tributaries, each 1,000 miles long; warlike; masculine.

am-bas'sa-dor, 1 am-bas'ə-der; 2 ăm-băs'a-dŏr, n. A diplomatic envoy of highest rank; minister plenipotentiary; any official messenger. **em-bas'sa-dorȷ.**— **am-bas'sa-dress,** n. **1.** A female ambassador. **2.** The wife of an ambassador.

am'ber, 1 am'bər; 2 ăm'ber. I. a. Pertaining to or like amber. II. n. A yellowish fossilized vegetable resin, hard, brittle, and translucent.

am'ber-gris, 1 am'bər-grĭs; 2 ăm'ber-grĭs, n. A waxy substance from the sperm-whale, used in perfumery.

am''bi-dex'ter, 1 am'bi-deks'tər; 2 ăm'bi-dĕks'ter. I. a. Using both hands equally well. **am''bi-dex'trousȷ.** II. n. **1.** One who uses both hands equally well. **2.** A double-dealer; hypocrite.— **am''bi-dex-ter'i-ty,** n.

am'bi-ent, 1 am'bi-ent; 2 ăm'bi-ĕnt, a. Encompassing.

am-big'u-ous, 1 am-big'yu-us; 2 ăm-bĭg'-yu-ŭs, a. Having a double meaning; equivocal. **-ly,** adv. **-ness,** n.— **am''bi-gu'i-ty,** n. [-TIES², pl.] The quality of being ambiguous; an ambiguous expression.

am-bi'tion, 1 am-bish'ən; 2 ăm-bĭsh'on, n. **1.** Inordinate desire of power or distinction. **2.** Worthy eagerness to achieve something great and good. **3.** An object of ambitious effort.— **am-bi'tious,** a. **1.** Characterized by ambition; aspiring. **2.** Pretentious; showy. **-ly,** adv. **-ness,** n.

am'bl(e⁵, 1 am'bl; 2 ăm'bl. I. vi. [AM'-BL(E)D⁶; AM'BLING.] To move with an easy pace or swaying motion. II. n. An easy gait, as of a horse, in which both legs on one side move at once.— **am'bler,** n.

am''bly-o'pi-a, 1 am'bli-ō'pi-ə; 2 ăm''bly-ō'-pi-a, n. Pathol. Dimness of vision, without discoverable change in the eye. **am'bly-o-pyȷ.**—**am''bly-op'ic,** a.

am-bro'si-a, 1 am-brō'ȝi-ə; 2 ăm-brō'zhi-a, n. The fabled food of the gods; delicious food.— **am-bro'sial,** a. Pertaining to or like ambrosia; fragrant; delicious; also, belonging to or worthy of the gods; heavenly. —**am-bro'slanȷ.**

am'bu-lance, 1 am'biu-lans; 2 ăm'bū-lançȥ, n. A covered wagon for conveying the sick and wounded.— **am''bu-la'tion,** walking about.— **am''bu-la'tiv(e⁵,** a.— **am'bu-la'tor,** n.— **am'bu-la-to-ry,** I. a. Walking; shifting. II. n. [-RIES², pl.] A place for walking.

am''bus-cade', 1 am''bus-kēd'; 2 ăm'bŭs-cād', v. & n. Ambush.

am'bush, 1 am'bush; 2 ăm'bush. Iᵗ. vt. **1.** To hide, as troops, for attack by surprise. **2.** To attack from an ambush; waylay. II. n. The lying concealed to attack by surprise; the hiding-place, or the persons hidden.

a-me'ba, 1 ə-mī'ba; 2 a-mē'ba, n. A microscopic organism, consisting of a jelly-like mass, able to move by throwing out

finger-like extensions of its substance.

a-mœ'ba‡.— a-me'bold. I. *a.* Like an ameba. **II.** *n* An organism resembling an ameba.**— a-mœ'boid‡.**

a-meer', 1 ə-mīr'; 2 a-mēr', *n.* A Mohammedan prince or governor; especially, the sovereign of Afghanistan.

a-me'lio-rate, 1 ə-mīl'yo-rēt; 2 a-mēl'yo-rāt, *vt. & vi.* [-RAT'ED‡; -RAT'ING.] To make or grow better; improve; relieve. **— a-me''lio-ra'tion,** *n.* An ameliorating; improvement.**— a-me'lio-ra-tiv(e⁵, *a.

a''men', 1 ē''men'; 2 ä''mĕn' *or* (*Mus.*) 1 ä''men'; 2 ä''mĕn',*interj.* So it is,or so be it.

a-me'na-bl(e⁵, 1 ə-mī'nə-bl; 2 a-mē'na-bl, *a.* Accountable; subject; submissive; tractable.**— a-me'na-bly,** *adv.*

a-mend'd, 1 ə-mend'; 2 a-mĕnd', *vt. & vi.* To change for the better; correct; improve.**— a-mend'a-to-ry,** *a.* Tending to amend.**— a-mend'ment,** *n.* Change or a changing for the better; improvement; modification.**— a-mends',** *n. pl.* Reparation, satisfaction, or compensation.

a-men'i-ty, 1 ə-men'i-tı; 2 a-mĕn'i-ty, *n.* [-TIES², *pl.*] Agreeableness; pleasantness.

am'ent, 1 am'ent; 2 ăm'ĕnt, *n.* A catkin.

a-merce', 1 ə-mūrs'; 2 a-mērç', *vt.* [A-MERCED't; A-MERC'ING.] To mulct; fine. **-ment,** *n.*

A-mer'i-ca, 1 ə-mer'i-kə; 2 a-mĕr'i-ca, *n.* **1.** Either of two continents forming the western hemisphere: (1) **North A.,** area, 8,037,- 714 sq. m. (2) **South A.,** area, 6,800,000 sq. m. **2.** A national anthem of the United States, written by Dr. Samuel F. Smith to the air of "God Save the King."

A-mer'i-can, 1 ə-mer'i-kən; 2 a-mĕr'i-can. **I.** *a.* Pertaining to America, or to the United States. **II.** *n.* **1.** A citizen of the United States. **2.** An inhabitant of America.**— A-mer'i-can-ism,** *n.* **1.** A word, phrase, custom, etc., peculiar to the people of the United States. **2.** American citizenship; devotion to America.**— A-mer'i-can-ize or -ise,** *vt.*

am'e-thyst, 1 am'i-ŧhist; 2 ăm'e-thỹst, *n.* Quartz of a clear purple or violet color; also, the color.**— am''e-thys'tin(e⁵, *a.

a'mi-a-bl(e⁵, 1 ē'mi-ə-bl; 2 ā'mi-a-bl, *a.* Pleasing in disposition; kind-hearted; friendly.**— a''mi-a-bil'i-ty,** *n.* Sweetness of disposition; lovableness. **a'mi-a-bl(e-ness²‡.— a'mi-a-bly.adv.**

am'i-ca-bl(e⁵, 1 am'i-kə-bl; 2 ăm'i-ca-bl, *a.*

Friendly; peaceable.**— am''i-ca-bil'i-ty, am'i-ca-bl(e-ness²,** *n.* The quality of being amicable.**— am'i-ca-bly,** *adv.*

am'ice, 1 am'ıs; 2 ăm'íç, *n. Eccl.* A vestment, as an embroidered collar and hood of fine white linen.

a-mid', 1 ə-mid'; 2 a-mĭd', *prep.* In the midst of; among. **a-midst'‡.**

a-mid'ships, 1 ə-mid'ships; 2 a-mĭd'shĭps, *adv.* Half-way between stem and stern.

a-miss', 1 ə-mis'; 2 a-mĭs'. **I.** *a.* Out of order; unsuitable; wrong; improper. **II.** *adv.* Improperly; erroneously.

am'i-ty, 1 am'i-tı; 2 ăm'i-ty, *n.* Peaceful relations; mutual good will; friendship.

am'me-ter, 1 am'i-tər; 2 ăm'e-ter, *n.* An instrument showing by direct reading the number of amperes of current passing through a circuit. **am'pere-me''ter‡.**

am-mo'ni-a, 1 a-mō'nı-ə; 2 a-mō'ni-a, *n.* A pungent gas; also, a solution of this gas in water, called **spirits of hartshorn, aqua ammonia,** etc.**— am''mo-ni'a-cal,** 1 am''o-nai'ə-kəl; 2 ăm'o-nī'a-cal, *a.* **am-mo'ni-a‡.**

am''mu-ni'tion, 1 am''yu-nish'ən; 2 ăm'- yu-nĭsh'on, *n.* Powder, shot, etc., for firearms; resources for conflict.

am'nes-ty, 1 am'nes-tı; 2 ăm'nĕs-ty, *n.* [-TIES², *pl.*] A general act of pardon of offenses against a government.

a-mœ'ba, etc. See AMEBA, etc.

a-mong', 1 ə-muŋ'; 2 a-muŋst';
a-mongst', mŏng', a-mŏngst', *prep.* In or into the midst of; mingled with; in the country or time of.

am'o-rous, 1 am'o-rus; 2 ăm'o-rŭs, *a.* Pertaining to sexual love, or influenced by it; ardent in affection; enamored. **-ly, -ness,** *n.*

a-mor'phous, 1 ə-mōr'fus; 2 a-môr'fŭs, *a.*
a-mor'fous², Formless; uncrystallized. **-ly,** *adv.* **-ness,** *n.*

a-mount', 1 ə-mount'; 2 a-mount'. I‡d. *vi.* To reach in the aggregate; be equivalent: with *to.* **II.** *n.* A sum total; aggregate result.

am-pere', 1 am-pīr'; 2 ăm-pēr', *n. Elec.* The practical unit of electric-current strength, such as would be given with an electromotive force of one volt through a wire having a resistance of one ohm (see OHM; VOLT).**— am-per'age,** *n.* The strength of a current in amperes.**— am'pere-me''ter,** *n.* See AMMETER.

am-phib'i-ous, 1 am-fib'i-us; 2 ăm-fĭb'i-**am-fib'i-ous²,** ŭs, *a.* Living both on land and in water, as a frog. **-ly,** *adv.* **-ness,** *n.* **— am-phib'i-an,** *n.* An amphibious animal.

1: ə = final; ɪ = habit; aisle; au = out; oil; iū = feud; chin; go; ŋ = sing; thin, this.
2: wǫlf, dǫ; bōōk, bōōt; full, rụle, cūre, bŭt, bûrn; ôil, bǫy; ḡo, ḡem; iŋk; thin, this.

am″phi-the′a-ter,⎫ 1 am″fi-thī′ə-tər; 2
am″phi-the′a-tre,⎬ ăm″fi-thē′ə-ter, *n.* An
am″fi-the′a-ter,⎭ oval edifice having rows of seats which slope upward from an enclosed arena.

am′pl(e**r**, 1 am′pl; 2 ăm″pl, *a.* Spacious; large; complete; abundant.— **am′pl**(e**-ness**ᴿ, *n.*— **am′pli-fi″er,** *n.* One who o· that which increases or intensifies; as, a radio *amplifier*.— **am′pli-fy,** *vt.* & *vi.* [-FIED; -FY″ING.] To enlarge; expand; expatiate.— **am″pli-fi-ca′-tion,** *n.*— **am′pli-tude,** *n.* Largeness; scope; fulness.— **am′ply,** *adv.* Largely; liberally; sufficiently.

am′pu-tate, 1 am′piu-tēt; 2 ăm″pu-tāt, *vt.* [-TAT″ED⁴; -TAT″ING.] To cut off, as a limb.— **am″pu-ta′tion,** *n.*

am′u-let, 1 am′yu-let; 2 ăm″yu-lĕt, *n.* A small object worn as a charm against evil.

a-muse′, 1 ə-miūz′; 2 a-mūs′, *vt.* [A-MUSED′; A-MUS′ING.] **1.** To occupy pleasingly; divert; entertain. **2.** To excite to mirth.— **a-muse′ment,** *n.* Diversion; recreation; an entertainment.— **a-mus′ing-ly,** *adv.*

an, 1 an; 2 ăn, *indef. art.* or *adjective.* One, or any: used for the article *a* before words beginning with a vowel sound.

-an, *suffix* (often with euphonic -*i*-). Pertaining to: used in nouns or adjectives denoting country, origin, race, etc.; as, Itali*an*, amphib*ian.*

an′a-, *prefix.* Up; back; again; anew: sometimes = *re*-; as, *ana*baptism, rebaptism.

-ana, *suffix* (often with euphonic -*i*-). Pertaining to: connected with (a certain notable subject, person, place, etc.); as, Johnson*iana*, etc.

a-nach′ro-nism, 1 ə-nak′ro-nizm; 2 a-năĕ′ro-nĭşm, *n.* A confusion of dates; something out of time.— **a-nach″ro-nis′tic,** *a.*

an″a-con′da, 1 an″ə-kon′də; 2 ăn′a-kŏn″da, *n.* A large trop· cal serpent that crushes its prey; a boa or python.

a-næ′mi-a, an″æs-the′si-a. See ANEMIA, etc.

an′a-gram, 1 an′ə-gram; 2 ăn′a-grăm, *n.* A word or phrase formed from another by transposing letters. — **an″ a-gram-mat′ic, -i-cal, a.**

a-nal′o-gy, 1 ə-nal′o-ji; 2 a-năl′o-ğv, *n.* [-GIES², *pl.*] Resemblance of relations; similarity without identity.— **an″a-log′i-cal,** *a.* Figurative. **an″a-log′ic‡.**— **an″a-log′i-cal-ly,** *adv.*— **a-nal′o-gous,** *a.* Resembling in certain respects.— **an′a-log,** 1 an′ə-log; 2 ăn′a-lŏğ, *n.* Anything analogous to something else. **an′a-logue‡.**

a-nal′y-sis, 1 ə-nal′y-sis; 2 a-năl′y-sĭs, *n.* [-SES², *pl.*] The resolution of a compound into its elements; also, a logical synopsis. — **an″a-lyt′ic,** *a.* Pertaining to or proceeding by analysis. **an″a-lyt′i-cal‡.**— **an″a-lyt′i-cal-ly,** *adv.*

an′a-lyze,⎫ 1 an′ə-laiz; 2 ăn′a-lўz, *vt.*
an′a-lyse,⎬ [-LYZED, -LYSED; -LYZ″ING, -LYS″ING.] To make an analysis of; examine minutely or critically.— **an′a-lyst,** *n.* One who analyzes; an expert in analysis.

an′ar-chy, 1 an′ar-ki; 2 ăn′ar-ey, *n.* Absence or disregard of government; lawlessness.— **an-ar′chic,** *a.* Without or opposed to government; lawless. **an-ar′chi-cal‡.**— **an′-arch-ism,** *n.* Opposition to all government. — **an′arch-ist,** *n.* An opponent of all government.— **an″arch-is′tic,** *a.*

a-nath′e-ma, 1 ə-nath′i-mə; 2 a-năth′e-ma, *n.* [-MAS or AN″A-THEM′A-TA, *pl.*] A formal ecclesiastical curse; also, a person or thing anathematized.— **a-nath′e-ma-tize** or **-tise,** *vt.* & *vi.* To pronounce an anathema against; utter anathemas.

a-nat′o-my, 1 ə-nat′o-mi; 2 a-năt′o-my, *n.* [-MIES², *pl.*] **1.** The science of the structure of organisms, as of the human body. **2.** Dissection; a corpse or skeleton; an emaciated person.— **an″a-tom′i-cal,** *a.* Pertaining to anatomy.— **an″a-tom′ic‡.**— **an″a-tom′i-cal-ly,** *adv.*— **a-nat′o-mist,** *n.* One skilled in anatomy.— **an-at′o-mize,** *vt.* [-MIZED; -MIZ″-ING.] To dissect; analyze. **-mise‡.**

-ance, *suffix.* Forming from adjectives in -*ant*, and also directly from verbs, nouns denoting action, quality, or state; as, abun-d*ance*, forbear*ance.*

an′ces-tor, 1 an′ses-tər or -tər; 2 ăn′ĉes-tor, *n.* A forefather.— **an-ces′tral,** *a.* Of, pertaining to, or inherited from an ancestor.— **an′-ces-tress,** *n.* A female ancestor.— **an′ces-try,** *n.* [-TRIES², *pl.*] **1.** One's ancestors collectively. **2.** Descent; noble or worthy lineage.

an′chor,⎫ 1 aŋ′kər; 2 ăŋ′eor. **I.** *vt.* & *vi.*
an′ker,⎬ To secure by an anchor; come to anchor; lie at anchor; fix; fasten. **II.** *n.* An implement for holding a vessel to the bottom by means of a connecting cable.

Anchor.
f, f, flukes.

an′chor-age,⎫ 1 aŋ′-
an′ker-age⁊,⎬ kər-ij;
2 aŋ′eor-ag, *n.* **1.** A place for anchoring. **2.** A coming to or lying at anchor.

an′cho-ret, 1 aŋ′ko-ret; 2 ăn′cho-rĕt, *n.* A recluse; hermit. **an′cho-rite‡.**

an-cho′vy, 1 an-chō′vi; 2 ăn-chō′vy, *n.* [-VIES², *pl.*] A very small, herring=like fish.

an′cient, 1 ēn′shent; 2 ān′chĕnt, *a.* Belonging to remote antiquity; of great age; very old.— **an′cient-ly,** *adv.*   [times.

an′cient⁊, *n.* One who lived in ancient **an′cient²‖,** *n.* A flag= or a standard=bearer.

1: ȧrtistic, ȧrt; fat, fāre; fȧst; get, prēy; hĭt, police; obey, gō; nŏt, ôr; fŭll, rūle; bŭt, bûrn.
2: ärt, āpe, făt, fâre, fȧst, whạt, ạll; mē, gĕt, prey, fêrn; hĭt, īce; ĭ=ē; ĭ=ĕ; gō, nŏt, ôr. wŏn.

an'cil·la·ry, 1 an'si-lĕ-rı; 2 ăn'çĭ-lā-ry, *a.* Secondary; subsidiary.

and, 1 and; 2 ănd, *conj.* A particle denoting addition: used as a connective.

an·dan'te, 1 ɑn-dän'tĕ *or* an-dan'tı; 2 än-dän'tę *or* än-dän'tĕ, *a. & adv. Mus.* Rather slow, between adagio and allegretto.

an''dan·ti'no, 1 ɑn''dɑn-tī'no; 2 än''dän-tī'no, *a. & adv. Mus.* Slower than andante.

and'i'ron, 1 and'ī'ərn; 2 ănd'ī'ern, *n.* A metallic support for wood in an open fireplace.

Andirons.

-ane, *suffix.* Same as -AN: where, howe·er, both forms exist, it is with a difference in meaning, as in hum*an*, hum*ane*.

an'ec·dote, 1 an'ek-dōt; 2 ăn'ĕc-dōt, *n.* A short story. — **an''ec·dot'ic,** *a.* Pertaining to anecdotes. **an ec·do''talǂ.**

a·ne'mi·a, 1 ə-nī'mı-ə; 2 a·nae'mi·a, } a-nē'mi-a, *n.* Deficiency of blood; bloodlessness. — **a·ne'mic or a·nae'mic,** *a.*

an''e·mom'e·ter, 1 an''ı-mem'ı-tər; 2 ăn''e-mŏm'e-ter. An instrument for measuring the force or velocity of wind.— **an''e·mo·met'ric,** *a.* **-ri·calǂ.**

a·nem'o·ne, 1 ə-nem'o-nı; 2 a·něm'o-ne, *n.* A plant of the crowfoot family; a windflower.

Anemone. *a,* fruit.

an'e·roid, 1 an'ı-roid; 2 ăn'e-rŏid, **I.** *a.* Not employing a fluid. **II.** *n.* An aneroid barometer or battery.— **aneroid barometer,** an instrument showing atmospheric pressure by the movements of the elastic top of a metallic box from which the air has been exhausted.

an''es·the'si·a, 1 an·es-thī'- } sı-ə *or* -zı-s; **an''æs·the'si·a,** 2 ăn'es-thē'si-ə *or* -zhï-a, *n.* Insensibility to pain. **an''es·the'sist.**— **an''es·thet'ic or an''æs·thet'ic,** 1 an'es-thet'ık; 2 ăn'es-thĕt'ïe. **I.** *a.* Pertaining to or producing insensibility. **II.** *n.* Anything that produces anesthesia, as ether.

an'eu·rism, } 1 an'yu-rizm; 2 ăn'yu-rĭʂm, **an'eu·rysm,** } *n.* A tumor formed by dilatation of the coats of an artery.

a·new', 1 ə-niū'; 2 a-nū', *adv.* Once more; again.

an'gel, 1 ēn'jel; 2 ăn'ǧĕl **I.** *a.* Angelic. **II.** *n.* **1.** A spiritual being, especially one of celestial purity. **2.** A former English gold coin.— **an·gel'ic,** 1 an-jel'ık; 2 än-ǧĕl'ic, *a.* Of or like angels; celestial; pure; beautiful; saintly. **an·gel'i·calǂ.**— **an·gel'i·cal·ly,** *adv.*

an''ge·lus, 1 an'jı-lus; 2 än'ge-lŭs, *n. R. C. Ch.* A prayer commemorating the Annunciation; also, a bell rung at morning, noon, and night, calling the faithful to recite it: commemorated in a famous painting by Millet, called *The Angelus.*

an'ger, 1 aŋ'gər; 2 ăŋ'ger. **I.** *vt.* To provoke; irritate. **II.** *n.* Sudden and strong displeasure; wrath; ire.

an·gi'na, 1 an'jı-nə *or* an-jaï'nə; 2 än'ǧi-na *or* än-ǧï'na, *n.* An inflammatory disease of the throat.— **an·gi'na pec'to·ris,** neuralgia of the heart.

an'gl(e*r*, 1 aŋ'gl; 2 ăŋ'ǧl, *vt. & vi.* [AN'GL(E)D*F*; AN'GLING.] To fish with rod, hook, and line: with *for.*— **an'gler,** *n.*— **an'gling,** *n.* Fishing with rod, hook, and line.

Angles.

an'gle[1], *n.* The figure, concept, or relation of two straight lines emanating from one point; a corner; point; inclination. See illus.

an'gle[2], *n.* A fish=hook; fishing=tackle; a fishing with hook and line.

An'gli·can, 1 aŋ'glı-kən; 2 ăŋ'gli·can. **I.** *a.* **1.** Pertaining to the Church of England or the churches derived from it, or the High=Church party. **2.** Pertaining to England; English. **II.** *n.* A member of the Church of England or of the High=Church party.— **An'gli·can·ism,** *n.* **1.** The spirit and practise of the Church of England, or of the High=Church party. **2.** Attachment to the Church of England, or to England and its institutions.

An'gli·ce, 1 aŋ'glı-sı; 2 ăŋ'ǧli·çe, *adv.* In English; according to the usage of the English language.

An'gli·cize, } 1 aŋ'glı-saiz; 2 ăŋ'ǧli·çīz, *vt.* **An'gli·cise,** } & *vi.* To give an English form, style, or idiom to, make or become like the English.— **An'gli·cism,** *n.*

Anglo-. The combining form for *English, England.*— **An''glo·ma'ni·a,** *n.* Fondness for England and things English.— **An''glo·pho'bi·a,** *n.* Hatred of England or things English.— **An''glo·Sax'on,** *n.* **1.** One of the Anglo=Saxons or their race or language. **2.** *pl.* The mixed tribes, chiefly of Angles and Saxons, who conquered Britain in the 5th and immediately following centuries: often applied to the entire English race, with its various branches.— **An''glo·Sax'on,** *a.*

1: ə = final; ı = habit; aisle; au = out; ɵıl; ıū = feud; ᴄhin; go; ŋ = sing; thin, this.

2: wolf, do; book, boot; full, rule, cure, bŭt, bûrn; ɵil, bŏy; ǧo, ǧem; ıŋk; thin, this.

an′gry, 1 aŋ′grı; 2 ăŋ′gry, *a.* [AN′GRI-ER; AN′GRI-EST.] Moved with anger; indignant; inflamed.— **an′gri-ly,** *adv.*— **an′gri-ness,** *n.*

an′guish, 1 aŋ′gwısh; 2 ăŋ′gwish, *n.* Excruciating pain; agony; torture.

an′gu-lar, 1 aŋ′giu-lər; 2 ăŋ′gū-lar, *a.* Having or pertaining to an angle or angles; sharp-cornered; pointed.— **an′gu-lar′i-ty,** *n.* [-TIES², *pl.*] The state or condition of being angular. **an′gu-lar-ness‡.**— **an′gu-lar-ly,** *adv.*

an′il, 1 an′ıl; 2 ăn′il, *n.* A West-Indian indigo-plant; the dye indigo.

an′ile, 1 an′ıl *or* -ail; 2 ăn′il *or* -ïl, *a.* Like an old woman; feeble-minded.— **a-nil′i-ty,** *n.*

an′i-lin, } 1 an′ı-lin; 2 ăn′ı-lĭn, *n.* A
an′i-line, } colorless oily compound, the base of many coal-tar dyes.

an″i-mad-vert′d, 1 an″ı-mad-vŭrt′; 2 ăn″ı-măd-vĕrt′, *vi.* To criticize or censure: followed by *upon.*— **an″i-mad-ver′sion,** *n.* Criticism or censure.

an″i-mal, 1 an′ı-məl; 2 ăn′ı-mal. **I.** *a.* Pertaining to an animal or animals. **II.** *n.* **1.** A sentient living organism other than a plant. **2.** A sentient creature other than a human being; a brute.— **an′i-mal-ism,** *n.* The state of being a mere animal.

an″i-mal′cu-la, *n.* Plural of ANIMALCULUM.

an″i-mal′cule, 1 an″ı-mal′kiūl; 2 ăn″ı-măl′eūl, *n.* [-CULES², *pl.*] A microscopic animal.— **an″i-mal′cu-lum‡.**— **an″i-mal′cu-lar,** *a.* Pertaining to or like animalcules.

an′i-mate, 1 an′ı-mēt; 2 ăn′ı-māt. **I.** *vt.* [-MAT′ED^d; -MAT′ING.] To make alive; arouse; enliven; inspire. **II.** *a.* Possessing animal life; living; lively. **an′i-mat″ed‡.**— **an′i-ma′tion,** *n.* The act of imparting or the state of possessing life; liveliness; vivacity.

a″ni-ma′to, 1 ɑ″nī-mā′to; 2 ä″nī-mä′to, *adv. Mus.* With animation.

an′i-mism, 1 an′ı-mizm; 2 ăn′ı-mĭşm, *n.* **1.** Belief in spiritual existence, as the soul of man or the world-soul of Greek philosophy. **2.** A widely prevalent form of polytheism, which attributes a soul to the lower animals, to inanimate objects, and to natural phenomena, as winds, storms, etc.— **an′i-mist,** *n.* A believer in animism.— **an′i-mis′tic,** *a.*

an″i-mos′i-ty, 1 an″ı-mɒs′ı-tı; 2 ăn″ı-mŏs′ı-ty, *n.* [-TIES², *pl.*] Active enmity; hatred; ill will.

an′i-mus, 1 an′ı-mus; 2 ăn′ı-mŭs, *n.* The animating thought; spirit; intention; temper.

an′is(e², 1 an′ıs; 2 ăn′ıs, *n.* A small North-African plant.— **an′i-seed″,** *n.* The fragrant, warm-tasting seed of the anise-plant.

an′kl(e², 1 aŋ′kl; 2 ăŋ′kl, *n.* The joint connecting the foot and the leg.— **an′klet,** *n.* A band for the ankle.

an′nals, 1 an′əlz; 2 ăn′alş, *n. pl.* A record of events in the order of time.— **an′nal-ist,** *n.* A writer of annals.

an-neal′, 1 a-nīl′; 2 ă-nēl′, *vt.* To render soft and tough by heating and then slowly cooling.

an-nex′t, 1 a-neks′; 2 ă-nĕks′, *vt.* To add or affix; join; unite; attach.— **an-nex′,n.** An addition; appendix; addendum.— **an″nex-a′tion,** *n.* The act of annexing; an addition.

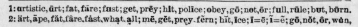

Anise.
a, root; *b,* top.

an-ni′hi-late, 1 a-naı′hi-lēt; 2 ă-nī′hi-lāt, *vt.* [-LAT′ED^d; -LAT′ING.] To reduce to nothing; destroy.— **an-ni″hi-la′tion,** *n.* An annihilating; destruction.

an″ni-ver′sa-ry, 1 an″ı-vŭr′sə-rı; 2 ăn″i-vēr′sa-ry. **I.** *a.* Recurring annually. **II.** *n.* [-RIES², *pl.*] A day on which some special event is annually celebrated, as a birthday.

an′no Dom′i-ni, 1 an′o dɒm′ı-naı *or* -nī; 2 ăn′o dŏm′ī-nī *or* -nī. In the year of our Lord, *i. e.,* of the Christian era: abbreviated *A. D.*

an′no-tate, 1 an′o-tēt; 2 ăn′o-tāt, *vt. & vi.* [-TAT′ED^d; -TAT′ING.] To make critical notes (on or upon).— **an″no-ta′tion,n.** The act of annotating; a note.— **an″no-ta′tor,** *n.* A commentator.

an-nounce′, 1 a-nɑuns′; 2 ă-nounç′, *vt.* [AN-NOUNCED′t; AN-NOUNC′ING.] To give intelligence of; proclaim; declare.— **an-nounce′ment,** *n.* The act of announcing; publication; declaration.

an-noy′, 1 a-nɒi′; 2 ă-nŏy′, *vt.* To trouble; worry; bother; irritate.— **an-noy′ance,** *n.* The act of annoying or that which annoys; the state of being annoyed.— **an-noy′ing-ly,** *adv.*

an′nu-al, 1 an′yu-al; 2 ăn′yu-al. **I.** *a.* Returning every year; pertaining to the year; lasting only one year. **II.** *n.* **1.** A book or pamphlet issued once a year. **2.** A plant living but for a single year.— **an′nu-al-ly,** *adv.* Year by year; yearly.

an-nu′i-ty, 1 a-niū′ı-tı; 2 ă-nū′ı-ty, *n.* [-TIES², *pl.*] An annual allowance or income.

an-nul', 1 a-nul'; 2 ă-nŭl', vt. [AN-NULLED', AN-NULD^s; AN-NUL'LING.] To render or declare void; nullify; at·olish.— **an-nul'ment**, n.

an'nu-lar, 1 an'yu-lər; 2 ăn'yu-lar, a. Of or like a ring; ring-shaped; marked with rings.

an'nu-late, 1 an'yu-lēt; 2 ăn'yu-lāt, a. Having rings; ringed. **an'nu-lat"ed±**.

an-nun'ci-ate, } 1 a-nun'shi[or -si-]-ēt; 2
an-nun'ti-ate, } ă-nŭn'shi[or -çi-]-āt, vt. [-AT"ED^d; -AT"ING.] To make known; announce.— **an-nun"ci-a'tion**, n. 1. The act of announcing; a proclamation. 2. [A-] The festival (March 25) commemorating the announcement by the angel to the Virgin (Luke i, 28-38).— **an-nun'ci-a"tor**, n. That which announces; an instrument showing a number or name when a bell is rung.

an'ode, 1 an'ōd; 2 ăn'ōd, n. The positive voltaic pole: opposed to cathode.

an'o-dyne, 1 an'o-dain; 2 ăn'o-dyn. I. a. Allaying pain; soothing. II. n. Anything that relieves pain, calms, or soothes: an opiate. [oil upon; consecrate.

a-noint'^d, 1 a-neint'; 2 a-nŏint', vt. To put

a-nom'a-lous, 1 ə-nem'ə-lus; 2 a-nŏm'a-lŭs, a. Deviating from rule; irregular; abnormal.—**a-nom'a-lous-ly**, adv.—**a-nom'a-ly**, 1 ə-nem'ə-li; 2 a-nŏm'a-ly, n. [-LIES², pl.] Irregularity; anything abnormal.

a-non'¹, 1 ə-nen'; 2 a-nŏn', adv. 1. Soon; presently. 2. At another time; again.

a-non'². A common abbreviation of anonymous.

a-non'y-mous, 1 ə-nən'ı-mus; 2 a-nŏn'y-mŭs, a. Bearing no name; not known by name. **-ly**, adv. **-ness**, n.

an-oth'er, 1 an-uth'ər; 2 ăn-ŏth'er, a. & pron. Not the same; distinct; different; one more.

An'schluss, 1 an'shlus; 2 ăn'shlŭs, n. [G.] Political union; specif., that between Germany and Austria.

an'swer, 1 an'sər; 2 ăn'ser, v. I. t. 1. To speak or act in response to; acknowledge; reply; especially, to reply favorably; retaliate; controvert; solve, as a riddle. 2. To be sufficient for; correspond to; atone for; expiate. II. i. 1. To reply or respond; correspond; be sufficient. 2. To be responsible; atone.

an'swer, n. A reply or response; refutation; retaliation; solution.—**an'swer-a-bl(e⁴**, 1 -ə-bl; 2 -a-bȷl, a. Responsible; corresponding; adequate; suitable. [emmet.

ant, 1 ant; 2 ănt, n. A small insect; an **ant-**, prefix. Against. See ANTI-.

-ant, suffix. 1. In the act or process of doing; as, militant, litigant, etc. 2. One who does; as, servant, one who serves.

an-tag'o-nize, } 1 an-tag'o-naiz; 2 ăn-tăg'-**an-tag'o-nise**, } o-nīz, vt. & vi. [-NIZED, -NISED; -NIZ"ING, -NIS"ING.] To oppose; contend with; counteract; neutralize; check; act in antagonism.— **an-tag'o-nism**, 1 -nizm; 2 -nȷsm, n. Opposition; hostility.— **an-tag'o-nist**, n. An adversary; opponent.— **an-tag"o-nis'tic**, a. Opposed; hostile. **-i-cal-ly**, adv.

ant-arc'tic, 1 ant-ārk'tik; 2 ănt-äre'tie, a. Pertaining to or designating the south pole or the regions near it.— **antarctic circle**, an imaginary circle of the earth parallel to the equator, and distant from the south pole 23° 28'.— **Antarctic ocean**, the ocean within the antarctic circle.

an'te-, prefix. Before, in time, order, or position; as, antechristian, etc. Compare ANTI-.

ant'eat"er, 1 ant'ēt"ər; 2 ănt'-ēt"er, n. A mammal that feeds on ants.

Ant-eater. ⅛

an"te-ce'dent, 1 an"ti-sī'dent; 2 ăn"te-çē'dĕnt. I. a. Going before; preceding. II. n. 1. One who or that which goes before. 2. The noun to which a relative pronoun refers. 3. pl. The previous history of a person or thing. **-ly**, adv.— **an"te-ce'dence**, n. The fact or state of being antecedent.

an"te-cham'ber, 1 an"ti-chĕm"bər; 2 ăn"te-chām"ber, n. A room serving as an entranceway to another apartment.

an"te-date', 1 an"ti-dēt; 2 ăn"te-dāt, vt. [-DAT"ED^d; -DAT"ING.] To date back; precede in time.

an"te-di-lu'vi-an, 1 an"ti-di-liū'vi-ən; 2 ăn"te-di-lū'vi-an. I. a. Earlier than the flood; antiquated; primitive. II. n. One that lived before the flood; an old or old-fashioned person.

Antelope. ⅟₂₅

an"te-lope', 1 an"ti-lōp; 2 ăn"te-lōp, n. A deer-like animal, intermediate between cattle and goats, as the gazel, ibex.

an"te-me-rid'i-an, 1 an"ti-mı-rid'i-ən; 2 ăn"te-me-rid'i-an, a. Before noon.

ante meridiem, [L.] Before noon: abbreviated a. m. or A. M.

an"te-mun'dane, 1 an"ti-mun'dēn; 2 ăn"te-mŭn'dān, a. Preceding the world's creation. [a. Preceding birth.

an"te-na'tal, 1 an"ti-nē'təl; 2 ăn"te-nā'tal, **an-ten'na**, 1 an-ten'ə; 2 ăn-tĕn'a, 1

[-NÆ, 1 -ĭ; 2 -ē, *pl.*] **1.** One of the feelers of an insect. **2.** A wire for receiving or sending electric waves in radio.

an-te′ri-or, 1 an-tī′rĭ-ẽr; 2 ăn-tē′ri-or, *a.* **1.** Antecedent; prior; earlier. **2.** Farther front; situated at the front.

an′te-room″, 1 an′tɪ-rūm″; 2 ăn′te-rōōm″, *n.* Waiting-room; antechamber.

an′them, 1 an′them; 2 ăn′thĕm, *n.* A joyous or triumphal song or hymn.

an′ther, 1 an′thẽr; 2 ăn′ther, *n.* *Bot.* The pollen-bearing part of a stamen.

an-thol′o-gy, 1 an-thŏl′o-jɪ; 2 ăn-thŏl′o-gy, *n.* [-GIES², *pl.*] A collection of choice literary extracts.

an′thra-cite, 1 an′thrɑ-saɪt; 2 ăn′thra-çīt, *n.* Mineral coal of nearly pure carbon; hard coal.

an′thro-poid, 1 an′thro-pɔɪd; 2 ăn′thro-pŏĭd. **I.** *a.* Somewhat like a human being in form; manlike. **II.** *n.* An anthropoid ape.

an″thro-pol′o-gy, 1 an″thro-pŏl′o-jɪ; 2 ăn″thro-pŏl′o-gy, *n.* [-GIES², *pl.*] The science of man.— **an″thro-po-log′i-cal,** *a.* Pertaining to anthropology or to man. **an″thro-po-log′ic‡.— an″thro-pol′o-gist,** *n.* A student of anthropology.

an′ti-, *prefix.* Against; opposed to; opposite to; corresponding to; in return for; instead of; as, *anti*christian, *anti*aircraft (said of guns).

an′tic, 1 an′tɪk; 2 ăn′tĭc. **I.** *a.* Odd; fantastic; ludicrous. **II.** *n.* A prank; caper; clown; buffoon.

An′ti-christ, 1 an′tɪ-kraɪst; 2 ăn′ti-crīst, *n.* An enemy of Christ; a false Christ.— **an″ti-chris′tian,** *a.* & *n.*

an-tic′i-pate, 1 an-tis′ɪ-pēt; 2 ăn-tiç′i-pāt, *vt.* & *vi.* [-PAT″ED‡; -PAT″ING.] **1.** To look forward to; foresee; expect; cherish expectation. **2.** To act sooner than; forestall; prevent; fulfil beforehand; foretaste.— **an-tic″i-pa′tion,** *n.* The act of anticipating; prevision; foretaste; expectation.— **an-tic′i-pa-to-ry,** *a.* Marked by anticipation.

an″ti-cli′max, 1 an″tɪ-klaɪ′maks; 2 ăn″ti-clī′măks, *n.* A sudden descent or fall: the opposite of *climax*.

an′ti-dote, 1 an′tɪ-dōt; 2 ăn′ti-dōt, *n.* Anything having power to counteract the effects of poison or of any evil.— **an′ti-do″tal,** *a.* Of, like, or pertaining to an antidote or antidotes.

an′ti-mo-ny, 1 an′tɪ-mo-nɪ; 2 ăn′ti-mo-ny, *n.* A silver-white, hard, crystalline, metallic element.— **an″ti-mo′ni-al,** 1 an″tɪ-mō′nɪ-al; 2 ăn″ti-mō′ni-al, *a.* Of or containing antimony.

an-tip′a-thy, 1 an-tɪp′ɑ-thɪ; 2 ăn-tĭp′a-thy, *n.* [-THIES², *pl.*] An instinctive aversion,

or that which excites it.— **an″ti-pa-thet′ic,** *a.* Having antipathy; naturally repugnant.

an-tip′o-des, 1 an-tɪp′o-dīz; 2 ăn-tĭp′o-dēs, *n.* *sing.* & *pl.* A place or people on the opposite side of the earth; the opposite extreme.— **an-tip′o-dal,** 1 an-tip′o-dəl; 2 ăn-tĭp′o-dal, *a.* Pertaining to the antipodes; diametrically opposed.— **an′ti-pode,** 1 an′tɪ-pōd; 2 ăn′ti-pŏd, *n.* **1.** An exact opposite. **2.** One of the antipodes.

an′ti-qua-ry, 1 an′tɪ-kwē-rɪ; 2 ăn′ti-kwā-ry, *n.* [-RIES², *pl.*] One who collects, examines, or deals in ancient objects, as coins, etc.— **an″ti-qua′ri-an. I.** *a.* Pertaining to antiquity or antiquities. **II.** *n.* An antiquary. **-ism,** *n.*

an′ti-quate, 1 an′tɪ-kwēt; 2 ăn′ti-kwāt, *vt.* [-QUAT″ED‡; -QUAT″ING.] To make old or obsolete.— **an′ti-quat″ed,** *pa.* Out of date; old-fashioned; obsolete; ancient; superannuated.

an-tique′, 1 an-tīk′; 2 ăn-tīk′. **I.** *a.* Ancient in fact or in style. **II.** *n.* The style of ancient art, or some specimen of it; antiquity.

an-tiq′ui-ty, 1 an-tik′wɪ-tɪ; 2 ăn-tĭk′wi-ty, *n.* [-TIES², *pl.*] The state or quality of being ancient; ancient times; an ancient object.

an″ti-sep′tic, 1 an″tɪ-sep′tɪk; 2 ăn″ti-sĕp′tie. **I.** *a.* Preventing putrefaction, etc. **-i-cal‡. II.** *n.* Anything having antiseptic qualities.— **an″ti-sep′sis,** *n.* The exclusion, as from wounds, of germs that cause infection, blood-poisoning, etc., or the system of surgery by which this is done.

an-tith′e-sis, 1 an-tĭth′ɪ-sĭs; 2 ăn-tĭth′e-sĭs, *n.* [-SES, 1 -sīz; 2 -sēs, *pl.*] **1.** Opposition of words or ideas. **2.** The contrary; a contrast.— **an″ti-thet′i-cal,** 1 an″tɪ-thet′ɪ-kal; 2 ăn″ti-thĕt′i-cal, *a.* Directly opposed; contrasted.— **an″ti-thet′ic‡. -i-cal-ly,** *adv.*

an″ti-tox′in, 1 an″tɪ-tɒks′ɪn; 2 ăn″ti-tŏks′ĭn, *n.* A substance formed in the body which neutralizes the poisonous products of microbes.

an′ti-type, 1 an′tɪ-taɪp; 2 ăn′ti-tȳp, *n.* That which a type prefigures.— **an″ti-typ′i-cal,** *a.*

ant′ler, 1 ant′lẽr; 2 ănt′ler, *n.* A deciduous bony outgrowth or horn on the head of a deer.

an′to-nym, 1 an′to-nim; 2 ăn′to-nȳm, *n.* A word directly opposed to another in meaning.

Anvil.

an′vil, 1 an′vɪl; 2 ăn′vil, *n.* A heavy block of iron or steel on which metal may be forged.

anx′ious, 1 aŋk′shus; 2 ăŋk′shŭs, *a.*

Mentally troubled or perplexed; also, eager; solicitous. **2.** Worrying; distressing.— **anx-i′e-ty,** 1 aŋ-zaī′i-tɪ; 2 aŋ-zī′e-ty, *n.* [-TIES², *pl.*] Misgiving; solicitude; eagerness.— **anx′ious-ly,** *adv.*— **anx′ious-ness,** *n.* Anxiety.'

an′y, 1 en′ɪ; 2 ĕn′y. **I.** *a.* **1.** One; a; an; some. **2.** Some of a number, class, or total. **II.** *pron.* One or more out of a number. **III.** *adv.* Somewhat; in the least; at all. — **an′y-bod″y,** 1 en′ɪ-bod″ɪ; 2 ĕn′y-bŏd″y, *pron.* Any person whatever.— **an′y-how″,** 1 en′ɪ-hou″; 2 ĕn′y-how″, *adv.* In any way whatever; by any means; however; notwithstanding.— **an′y-thing,** 1 en′ɪ-thɪŋ; 2 ĕn′y-thĭng, *pron.* A thing of any sort; something or other.— **an′y-way,** 1 en′ɪ-wē; 2 ĕn′y-wā, *adv.* **1.** No matter what happens; in any event. **2.** At all events; anyhow. **3.** In any manner; to any degree or extent. — **an′y-where,** 1 en′ɪ-hwâr; 2 ĕn′y-hwêr, *adv.* In or at any place whatever.— **an′y-wise,** 1 en′ɪ-waɪz; 2 ĕn′y-wĭş, *adv.* In any manner; to any degree.

An′zac, 1 an′zak; 2 ăn′zăe². **I.** *a.* Pertaining to the Australian and New Zealand Army Corps in the World War (1914–18). **II.** *n.* A member of this army corps: a word formed from the initial letters of the name.

a-or′ta, 1 ē-ôr′tə; 2 ā-ôr′ta, *n.* [-TÆ, 1 -tī; 2 -tē, *pl.*] The great artery springing from the heart. [fast.

a-pace′, 1 ə-pēs′; 2 a-pāç′, *adv.* Rapidly;

a-part′, 1 ə-pärt′; 2 a-pärt′, *adv.* Separately; aside; by itself; asunder.

a-part′ment, 1 ə-pärt′ment *or* -mənt; 2 a-pärt′ment, *n.* A room or suite of rooms.

ap′a-thy, 1 ap′ə-thɪ; 2 ăp′a-thy, *n.* [-THIES², *pl.*] Lack of feeling; insensibility; indifference.— **ap″a-thet′ic,** 1 ap″ə-thet′ɪk; 2 ăp″a-thĕt′ĭc, *a.* Without feeling; unconcerned; impassive. **-i-cal‡.**— **ap″a-thet′i-cal-ly,** *adv.*

ape, 1 ēp; 2 āp. **I.** *vt.* [APED‡; AP′ING.] To imitate absurdly; mimic. **II.** *n.* An Old World man-like monkey; also, any monkey; a mimic.

a-pe′ri-ent, 1 ə-pī′rɪ-ent; 2 a-pē′rĭ-ĕnt. **I.** *a.* Laxative. **II.** *n.* A gently purgative remedy.

ap′er-ture, 1 ap′ər-chur *or* -tiur; 2 ăp′ér-chur *or* -tūr, *n.* An opening; orifice; hole; cleft.

a′pex, 1 ē′peks; 2 ā′pĕks, *n.* [A′PEX-ES *or* AP′I-CES, 1 ē′peks-ez *or* ap′ɪ-sīz; 2 ā′pĕks-ĕş *or* ăp′ĭ-çēş, *pl.*] The highest point; tip; top.

a-pha′si-a, 1 ə-fē′ʒɪ-ə; 2 a-fā′zhi-a, *n.* Loss of the power of speech, or of coherent speech.

a-phe′li-on, 1 ə-fī′lɪ-ɒn; 2 a-fē′lĭ-ŏn, *n.* [-LI-A, 1 -lɪ-ə; 2 -li-a, *pl.*] The point in an orbit, as of a planet, farthest from the sun.

a′phis, 1 ē′fɪs; 2 ā′fĭs, *n.* [APH′I-DES, 1 af′ɪ-dīz; 2 ăf′ĭ-dēş, *pl.*] A plant-louse. **aph′id‡.**

aph′o-rism, 1 af′o-rizm; 2 ăf′o-rĭşm, *n.* A proverb; maxim.— **aph″o-ris′tic,** *a.* **-ti-cal‡.**

Aph″ro-di′te, *n.* See VENUS.

a′pi-a-ry, 1 ē′pɪ-ē-rɪ; 2 ā′pi-a-ry, *n.* [-RIES², *pl.*] A place where bees are kept; also, a set of hives, bees, and appliances.— **a′pi-cul″ture,** *n.* Bee-keeping.

a-piece′, 1 ə-pīs′; 2 a-pēç′, *adv.* For each person or thing; to each one; each.

A′pis, 1 ē′pɪs; 2 ā′pĭs, *n. Myth.* The sacred bull of ancient Egypt.

ap′ish, 1 ēp′ɪsh; 2 āp′ĭsh, *a.* Like an ape; servilely imitative; foolish; tricky.— **ap′ish-ly,** *adv.*— **ap′ish-ness,** *n.*

a″plomb′, 1 a″plôn′; 2 ä″plôn′, *n.* **1.** Assurance; self-confidence; self-possession. **2.** Upright posture; erectness.

a-poc′a-lypse, 1 ə-pok′ə-lips; 2 a-pŏc′a-lýps, *n.* **1.** A revelation. **2.** [A-] Revelations, the last book of the Bible.— **a-poc″a-lyp′tic,** *a.* **a-poc″a-lyp′ti-cal‡.**

a-poc′o-pe, 1 ə-pok′o-pɪ; 2 a-pŏc′o-pe, *n.* A cutting off of the last letter or syllable of a word.

A-poc′ry-pha, } 1 ə-pok′rɪ-fə; 2 a-pŏc′ry-**A-poc′ry-fa″,** } fa, *n. sing.* & *pl.* Books of disputed authority, included by some in the Old Testament Scriptures.— **A-poc′ry-phal,** *a.* **1.** Pertaining to the Apocrypha. **2.** [a-] Of doubtful authenticity; spurious.

ap′o-gee, 1 ap′o-jī; 2 ăp′o-gē, *n.* That point of the moon's orbit farthest from the earth.

A-pol′lo, 1 ə-pol′o; 2 a-pŏl′o, *n. Myth.* Son of Zeus (Jupiter) and Leto (Latona); god of the sun, divination, medicine, music, poetry, etc.

a-pol′o-gize, -gise, 1 ə-pol′o-jaɪz; 2 a-pŏl′o-gīz, *vi.* [-GIZED; -GIZ′ING.] To offer an apology or excuse.— **a-pol″o-get′ic,** 1 ə-pol″o-jet′ɪk; 2 a-pŏl″o-gĕt′ĭc. **I.** *a.* Of the nature of an apology.— **a-pol″o-get′i-cal‡. II.** *n.* An apology or defense.— **a-pol′o-gist,** *n.* One who argues in defense of any person or cause; a defender. [fable.

ap′o-logue, 1 ap′o-lɒg; 2 ăp′o-lŏg, *n.* A

a-pol′o-gy, 1 ə-pol′o-jɪ; 2 a-pŏl′o-gy, *n.* [-GIES², *pl.*] **1.** An acknowledgment of error; excuse. **2.** A justification or defense: the original meaning. **3.** A poor substitute.

ap′o-phthegm, *n.* See APOTHEM.

ap′o-plex-y, 1 ap′o-pleks-ɪ; 2 ăp′o-plĕks-y, *n.* Sudden loss of sensation and motion; a stroke of paralysis.— **ap″o-plec′tic,** 1 ap″o-plek′tɪk; 2 ăp″o-plĕc′tĭc, *a.* Pertaining to, affected with, or tending toward apoplexy. **-ti-cal‡.**

1: ə = final; ɪ = habit; aɪsle; au = out; oil; iū = feud; chin; go; ŋ = sing; thin, this.
2: wolf, dǫ; bŏŏk, bōōt; fŭll, rṳle, cūre, bŭt, bûrn; ŏil, bŏy; go, ġem; iŋk; thin, this.

a-port′, 1 ə-pōrt′; 2 a-pōrt′, *adv.* On or toward the port side, or the left as one faces the bow.

a-pos′ta-sy, 1 ə-pos′tə-si; 2 a-pŏs′tɑ-sy, *n.* [-SIES², *pl.*] Desertion of one's faith or principles.— **a-pos′tate,** 1 ə-pos′tēt; 2 a-pŏs′tāt. I. *a.* Guilty of apostasy; false. II. *n.* One who apostatizes.— **a-pos′ta-tize,** *vi.* [-TIZED; -TIZ′ING.] To forsake one's faith or principles.

a-pos′tl(e², 1 ə-pos′l; 2 a-pŏs′l, *n.* 1. One of the twelve chosen by Christ to proclaim his gospel (*Matt.* x, 2–4). 2. Any zealous advocate of a cause.— **a-pos′tl(e-ship²,** *n.* **a-pos′to-late‡.**— **ap″os-tol′ic,** ap′əs-tol′ik, -i-kəl; 2 ăp′ŏs-tŏl′ic, -i-cal, *a.*

a-pos′tro-phe¹, 1 ə-pos′tro-fı; 2 a-pŏs′tro-fe, *n.* A symbol (′) above the line, to mark omission, or possessive, etc.

a-pos′tro-phe², *n.* An address to an absent person, an attribute, etc.— **a-pos′tro-phize,** *vt. & vi.* To address by or in a rhetorical apostrophe; utter an apostrophe.

a-poth′e-ca-ry, 1 ə-pŏθ′ı-kē-rı; 2 a-pŏth′e-cā-ry, *n.* [-RIES², *pl.*] One who sells and compounds drugs; a druggist.

ap′o-them, 1 ap′o-ᵺem; 2 ăp′o-thĕm, *n.* A terse, practical saying; a sententious maxim. **ap′o-thegm‡.**

ap″o-the′o-sis, 1 ap′o-ᵺı′o-sis; 2 ăp′o-the′o-sis, *n.* [-SES, *pl.*] Exaltation to divine honors; deification.

ap-pal′, 1 ə-pōl′; 2 ă-pạl′, *vt.* [AP-PALL′**ap-pall′,**] PALL(E)D′S; AP-PAL′LING.] To fill with horror; terrify; shock.— **ap-pal′ling,** *pa.* Causing or fitted to cause dismay or terror; frightful. **-ly,** *adv.*

ap″pa-ra′tus, 1 ap′ə-rē′tus *or* -rā′tus; 2 ăp′ɑ-rā′tŭs *or* -rā′tus, *n.* [-TUS *or* (rarely) -TUS-ES, *pl.*] A complex machine, or a set of tools, etc.

ap-par′el, 1 ə-par′el; 2 ă-păr′ĕl. I. *vt.* [-ELED *or* -ELLED; -EL-ING *or* -EL-LING.] To clothe. II. *n.* Raiment; clothing.

ap-par′ent, 1 ə-pâr′ent; 2 ă-pâr′ĕnt, *a.* 1. Evident; obvious; visible. 2. Seeming; not necessarily real or true.— **ap-par′ent-ly,** *adv.*

ap″pa-ri′tion, 1 ap′ə-rish′ən; 2 ăp′ɑ-rĭsh′on, *n.* A specter; fantom.

ap-peal′, 1 ə-pīl′; 2 ă-pēl′. I. *vt. & vi.* 1. To beseech; entreat; awaken response or sympathy: followed by *to.* 2. To take (a cause) to a higher court. II. *n.* 1. An earnest request; entreaty. 2. A resort to a higher authority, for sanction or aid.— **ap-peal′a-bl(e²,** *a.*— **ap-peal′ing,** *pa.* Making, containing, or conveying an appeal; imploring. **-ly,** *adv.*

ap-pear′, 1 ə-pīr′; 2 ă-pēr′, *vi.* 1. To come into view; become visible. 2. To seem, or seem likely.

ap-pear′ance, 1 ə-pīr′əns; 2 ă-pēr′anç, *n.* An appearing; that which appears; aspect; semblance; indication; advent; publication.

ap-pease′, 1 ə-pīz′; 2 ă-pēg′, *vt.* [AP-PEASED′; AP-PEAS′ING.] To soothe; pacify; calm; still; allay.— **ap-peas′a-bl(e²,** *a.*— **ap-peas′a-bly,** *adv.*

ap-pel′lant, 1 ə-pel′ənt; 2 ă-pĕl′ant, *n.* One who appeals.— **ap-pel′late,** 1 ə-pel′et; 2 ă-pĕl′āt, *a.* Pertaining to or having jurisdiction of appeals.

ap″pel-la′tion, 1 ap′ē-lē′shən; 2 ăp′ĕ-lā′shon, *n.* A name or title; the act of calling or naming.— **ap-pel′la-tiv(e²,** 1 a-pel′a-tiv; 2 ă-pĕl′ɑ-tiv. I. *a.* Serving to designate or name, as common nouns. II. *n.* A title; appellation; a common noun. **-ly,** *adv.* **-ness,** *n.*

ap-pend′d, 1 ə-pend′; 2 ă-pĕnd′, *vt.* To add or attach (something subordinate).— **ap-pen′dage,** 1 ə-pen′dij; 2 ă-pen′dag, *n.* [AP-PEN′DAGES, *pl.*] A subordinate addition or adjunct.

ap-pen′di-ces, *n.* A plural of APPENDIX.

ap-pen″di-ci′tis, 1 ə-pen″dı-sai′tıs *or* -sī′tıs; 2 ă-pĕn″di-çī′tis *or* -çī′tis, *n.* Inflammation of the vermiform appendix.

ap-pen′dix, 1 ə-pen′dıks; 2 ă-pĕn′diks, *n.* [-DIX-ES *or* -DI-CES, 1 -sīz; 2-çēs, *pl.*] 1. An addition or supplement, as at the end of a book. 2. A small intestinal organ called the *vermiform appendix.*

ap″per-tain′, 1 ap′ər-tēn′; 2 ăp′ĕr-tān′, *vi.* To belong; relate: with *to.*

ap′pe-tence, 1 ap′ı-tens, -ten-sı; 2 ăp′e-**ap′pe-ten-cy,** tenç, -tĕn-çy, *n.* [-TEN-CES², -TEN-CIES², *pl.*] Strong craving; appetite; propensity; affinity.

ap′pe-tite, 1 ap′ı-tait; 2 ăp′e-tīt, *n.* A physical craving, as for food; a mental craving; longing.— **ap′pe-tize,** *vt.* [-TIZED; -TIZ′ING.] To give an appetite.— **ap′pe-tiz″er,** *n.* Anything that excites appetite or gives relish.— **ap′pe-tiz″ing,** *pa.* Giving relish; tempting.

ap-plaud′d, 1 ə-plōd′; 2 ă-plạd′, *vt. & vi.* To express approval, as by clapping the hands; commend; praise.— **ap-plause′,** 1 ə-plōz′; 2 ă-plạs′, *n.* The act of applauding; acclamation; approval.— **ap-plaus′iv(e²,** *a.* Expressing applause.— **ap-plaus′iv(e-ly²,** *adv.*

ap′pl(e², 1 ap′l; 2 ăp′l, *n.* The fruit of a **ap′l²,** tree of the rose family, or the tree that bears it.— **apple of the eye,** the pupil of the eye; something precious.

1: ȧrtistic, ȧrt; fat, fāre; fȧst; get, prēy; hit, police; obey, gō; net, ȯr; full, rūle; but, būrn.
2: ärt, āpe, făt, fâre, fȧst, whạt, ạll; mē, gĕt, prey, fern; hĭt, īce; ĭ=ĕ; ī=ĕ; gō, nŏt, ôr, wọn,

ap·pli´ance, 1 a-plai´əns: 2 ă-plī´anç, *n.*
The act of applying; a device; tool; instrument.

ap″pli·ca´tion, 1 ap″li-kē´shən; 2 ăp″li-eā´-
shon, *n.* **1.** The act of applying; appropriation. **2.** That which is applied; a
remedy. **3.** A request. **4.** Close and
continuous attention.— **ap″pli·ca·bil´i·ty,**
n. [-TIES², *pl.*] Suitability; fitness. **ap´pli-
ca·ble(e·ness²†.—** ap´pli-ka-bl(e²,1 ap´li-kə-
bl; 2 ăp´li-ca-bl, *a.* That may be applied;
suitable for application; relevant; fitting.—
ap´pli·ca·bly, *adv.—* **ap″pli·cant,** *n.* One
who applies; a candidate.

ap″pli·qué´, 1 a″pli-kē´; 2 ä″pli-kē´. **I.** *a.*
Applied; laid on. **II.** *n.* Any ornament
cut out and applied to another surface in
cloth, wood, or metal; also, the article so
ornamented.

ap·ply´, 1 a-plai´; 2 ă-plī´, *v.* [AP-PLIED´,
AP-PLY´ING.] **I.** *t.* **1.** To put or place
(to); devote; attach; refer; test. **2.** To
give wholly (to); devote (oneself), as to
study. **II.** *i.* **1.** To make request; ask;
petition. **2.** To have reference.

ap·pog´gia·tu´ra, 1 ap-pej´a-tū´ra; 2 ap-
põg″ä-tū´rä, *n.* A musical embellishment
consisting of a single note introduced as a
suspension before any note of a melody.

ap·point´, 1 a-point´; 2 ă-põint´, *vt. & vi.*
1. To name designate; assign; command;
prescribe. **2.** To fit out; equip; furnish.
— **ap·point´ed,** *a.* Designated; equipped.
— **ap·point·ee´,** *n.* One who is appointed.
— **ap·point´er,** *n.* One who appoints.— **ap·
point´ment,** *n.* An appointing or being appointed; position; service; station; office; an
agreement, as for meeting at a given time;
an engagement; stipulation; equipment.

ap·por´tion, 1 a-pōr´shən; 2 ă-pôr´shon, *vt.*
To divide proportionally; allot. **-ment,** *n.*

ap´po·site(e², 1 ap´o-zit; 2 ăp´o-sĭt, *a.* Well
adapted; appropriate; apt. **-ly,** *adv.* **-ness,** *n.*

ap″po·si´tion, 1 ap″o-zish´ən; 2 ăp″o-
sĭsh´on, *n.* **1.** *Gram.* The relation between nouns in the same subject or predicate and in the same case. **2.** A placing or
being in immediate connection; application.

ap·praise´, 1 a-prēz´; 2 ă-prāş´, *vt.* [AP-
PRAISED´; AP-PRAIS´ING.] To put a value
on officially; value.— **ap·prais´al,** *n.* An appraising; official valuation. **ap·praise´-
ment†.— ap·prais´er,** *n.*

ap·pre´ci·a·ble(e², 1 a-prī´shi-a-bl; 2 ă-prē´-
shi-a-bl, *a.* That may be appreciated, per-

ceptible.— **ap·pre´ci·a·bly,** *adv.—* **ap·pre″-
ci·a´tion,** 1 a-prī´shi-ē´shən; 2 ă-prē´shi-ā´-
shon, *n.* An appreciating; true estimation;
recognition; increase in value.— **ap·pre´ci·a-
tiv(e²,** *a.* Having or manifesting appreciation.

ap″pre·hend´, 1 ap″ri-hend´; 2 ăp″re-
hĕnd´, *v.* **I.** *t.* **1.** To grasp mentally;
perceive. **2.** To have an impression of.
3. To expect with anxious foreboding. **4.**
To arrest; seize. **II.** *i.* **1.** To suppose;
surmise; conjecture. **2.** To look forward
with foreboding. **3.** To perceive.—
ap″pre·hen´si·ble(e², *a.* Capable of being
apprehended.— **ap″pre·hen´sion,** *n.* **1.**
Anxious foreboding. **2.** Idea; opinion; perception. **3.** Legal arrest.— **ap″pre·hen´-
siv(e²,** *a.* **1.** Anticipative of evil; anxious;
fearful. **2.** Quick to apprehend; sensitive;
conscious. **-ly,** *adv.* **-ness,** *n.*

ap·pren´tice, 1 a-pren´tis; 2 ă-prĕn´tiç. **I.**
vt. [-TICED†, -TIST³] **-TIC-
ING.**] To bind as an apprentice. **II.** *n.*
One who is bound to serve another in
order to learn a trade; a learner; beginner.— **ap·pren´tice·ship,** *n.*

ap·prise´, } 1 a-praiz´; 2 ă-prīş´, *vt.* [AP-
ap·prize´, } PRIZED´, AP-PRISED´; AP-PRIZ´-
ING, AP-PRIS´ING.] To notify; advise; inform.

ap·proach´, 1 a-prōch´; 2 ă-prōch´. **I.** *vt.
& vi.* To come or cause to come near or
nearer (to); make advances (to). **II.** *n.*
1. The act of approaching; a coming
nearer; access. **2.** Nearness; approximation. **3.** Opportunity, means, or way of
approaching. **4.** *pl.* Advances, as to
friendship, etc. **5.** *pl. Mil.* Works, as
trenches, etc., by which besiegers approach a fortified place.— **ap·proach´a·
ble(e²,** *a.* **-ness,** *n.*

ap″pro·ba´tion, 1 ap″ro-bē´shən; 2 ăp″ro-
bā´shon, *n.* The act of approving; approval; commendation.

ap·pro´pri·ate, 1 a-prō´pri-ēt; 2 ă-prō´-
pri-āt. **I.** *vt.* [-AT´ED³, -AT´ING.] **1.** To
set apart for a particular use; assign.
2. To take for one's own use; make use
of. **II.** *a.* Suitable for the person, circumstance, place, etc. **-ly,** *adv.* **-ness,** *n.*—
ap·pro″pri·a´tion, *n.* An appropriating or
something appropriated.

ap·prove´, 1 a-prūv´; 2 ă-prǫv´, *v.* [AP-
PROVED´; AP-PROV´ING.] **I.** *t.* **1.** To regard as worthy; commend; sanction. **2.**
To show (oneself) worthy. **3†.** To prove
by trial; test. **II.** *i.* To think with favor;
often with *of.—* **ap·prov´a·ble(e²,** *a.* Worthy
of approval.— **ap·prov´al,** *n.* Approbation;
sanction; commendation.— **ap·prov´ing·ly,**
adv. In an approving manner.

1: ə = final; ı = habit; aisle; ɑu = out; oil; iū = feud; chin; go; ŋ = sing; thin, this.
2: wǫlf, dǫ; bꝏk, bꝏt; fl̥l, rl̥e, cūre, bŭt, bûrn; ȯil, bȯy; g̣o, g̣em; iŋk; thin, this.

ap-prox'i-mate, 1 a-proks'i-mēt; 2 ă-prŏks'-i-māt, *v.* [-MAT'ED^d; -MAT'ING.] **I.** *vt.* & *vi.* To approach or cause to approach closely without exact coincidence. **II.** *i.* 1 a-proks'i-mit; 2 ă-prŏks'i-mat, *a.* Nearly but not exactly accurate or complete; near. — **ap-prox'i-mate-ly,** *adv.* Nearly; about. — **ap-prox''i-ma'tion,** *n.* The act of approximating; an approximate result.— **ap-prox'i-ma-tiv(e**^s, *a.* Obtained by or involving approximation; approximate. — **-ly,** *adv.*

ap-pur'te-nance, 1 a-pūr'te-nəns; 2 ă-pûr'te-nanç, *n.* An accessory or adjunct.— **ap-pur'te-nant,** 1 a-pūr'te-nənt; 2 ă-pûr'te-nant, *a.* Appertaining; accessory.

a'pri-cot, 1 ē'pri-ket; 2 ā'pri-cŏt, *n.* A plum-like fruit, or the tree that yields it.

A'pril, 1 ē'pril; 2 ā'pril, *n.* The fourth month.

a'pron, 1 ē'prən; 2 ā'pron, *n.* A covering for the front of a person's clothes; a covering on the front of a carriage.

Apricot.

ap'ro-pos', 1 ap'ro-pō'; 2 ăp'ro-pō'. *a.* Pertinent; opportune. **II.** *adv.* 1. Pertinently; appropriately. 2. By the way.— **apropos of,** with reference to; as suggested by; in respect.

apse, 1 aps; 2 ăps, *n.* 1. A recess or termination, as of a church, properly semicircular, with a semidome. 2. The eastern or altar end of a church.

apt, 1 apt; 2 ăpt, *a.* 1. Tending; liable; likely. 2. Quick to learn; skilful. 3. Pertinent; apposite; pat. — **apt'ly,** *adv.*— **apt'ness,** *n.* Aptitude.

ap'ter-yx, 1 ap'tər-iks; 2 ăp'ter-ўks, *n.* A New Zealand bird with small and undeveloped wings.

apt'i-tude, 1 apt'i-tiūd; 2 ăpt'i-tūd, *n.* 1. Adaptation; bent; tendency; fitness. 2. Quickness of understanding; readiness; aptness.

a'qua, 1 ē'kwə; 2 ā'kwa, *n.* Water.— **a'qua for'tis,** nitric acid.— **a. vitæ,** distilled spirits.

a-qua'ri-um, 1 a-kwē'ri-um; 2 a-kwā'ri-ŭm, *n.* [-RI-UMS or -RI-A, *pl.*] A tank or building for aquatic animals or plants.

a-quat'ic, 1 a-kwat'ik; 2 a-kwăt'ic. **I.** *a.* Pertaining to, living in, or adapted to the water. **II.** *n.* An aquatic animal or plant.

aq'ue-duct, 1 ak'wi-dukt; 2 ăk'we-dŭct, *n.* A pipe or channel for supplying water from a distance.

a'que-ous, 1 ē'kwi-us; 2 ā'kwe-ŭs, *a.* Pertaining to or containing water; watery.

aq'ui-lin(e^s, 1 ak'wi-lin; 2 ăk'wi-lĭn, *a.* Of or like an eagle or an eagle's beak; curving; hooked.

-ar, *suffix.* Pertaining to; like; as, regul*ar*, singul*ar*; also, the person or thing pertaining to; as, schol*ar*.

Ar'ab, 1 ar'əb; 2 ăr'ab, *n.* 1. An Arabian, or an Arabian horse. 2. [a-] A homeless street wanderer.— **ar''a-besque,** 1 ar'ə-besk'; 2 ăr''a-běsk', *n. Art.* Fanciful grouping of animal- and plant-forms, or flat ornamentation employing the interlaced lines of Arabian architecture.— **ar''a-besque,** *a.*— **A-ra'bi-an,** 1 ə-rē'bi-ən; 2 a-rā'bi-an. **I.** *a.* Of or pertaining to Arabia or its inhabitants. **II.** *n.* A native or naturalized inhabitant of Arabia.— **Ar'a-bic,** 1 ar'ə-bik; 2 ăr'a-bie. **I.** *a.* Arabian. **II.** *n.* The language of the Arabians.— **Arabic figures,** the numerals 1, 2, 3, 4, 5, 6, 7, 8, 9, 0.

ar'a-bl(e^s, 1 ar'ə-bl; 2 ăr'a-bl, *a.* Capable of being plowed or cultivated.

ar'bi-ter, 1 ar'bi-tər; 2 ăr'bi-ter, *n.* An arbitrator or umpire; a final judge.— **ar-bit'ra-ment,** 1 ar-bit'ra-ment or -mənt; 2 ar-bit'ra-ment, *n.* Decision by an arbiter.

ar'bi-tra-ry, 1 ar'bi-trē-ri; 2 ăr'bi-trā-ry, *a.* Fixed, made, or done capriciously; absolute; despotic.— **ar'bi-tra-ri-ly,** *adv.*

ar'bi-trate, 1 ar'bi-trēt; 2 ăr'bi-trāt, *vt.* & *vi.* [-TRAT'ED^d; -TRAT'ING.] To decide as arbitrator; settle by arbitration.— **ar''bi-tra'tion,** *n.* The settling of a controversy by an arbitrator or arbitrators.— **ar'bi-tra''tor,** *n.* A person chosen by agreement of parties to decide a dispute between them; an arbiter.

ar'bor¹, 1 ar'bər; 2 ăr'bor, *n.* 1. A spindle or axle. 2. *Bot.* A tree.— **ar-bo're-al,** *a.* Pertaining to a tree or trees; living or situated among trees.— **ar''bo-res'cent,** *a.* Treelike; branching.— **ar''bor-i-cul'ture,** *n.* The cultivation of trees or shrubs.— **ar''bor-i-cul'tur-al,** *a.*— **ar''bor-i-cul'tur-ist,** *n.*

ar'bor², *n.* A vine-clad bower; a shaded walk or nook. [The Mayflower.]

ar-bu'tus, 1 ar-biū'tus; 2 ăr-bū'tŭs, *n.*

arc, 1 ark; 2 ăre, *n.* Part of the circumference of a circle; a bow; an arch.

ar-cade', 1 ar-kēd'; 2 ăr-cād', *n.* A vaulted passageway or roofed street; a range of arches.

Ar-ca'di-an, 1 ar-kē'di-ən; 2 ăr-cā'di-an, *a.* Pertaining to Arcadia; rural; pastoral.

ar-ca'num, 1 ar-kē'num; 2 ăr-cā'nŭm, *n.* [AR-CA'NA, *pl.*] An inner secret or mystery.

arch^t, 1 ārch; 2 ărch, *vt.* & *vi.* To form into an arch; form an arch; curve; span with an arch or arches.

arch, *a.* Innocently cunning; roguish; playfully sly; coy. 2. Chief.— **arch'ly,** *adv.*— **arch'ness,** *n.*

arch, *n.* **1.** A bow-like curve, structure, or object. **2.** *Arch.* A curved structure supported at the sides or ends only, and formed of distinct pieces fitted together to span an opening.

arch-, 1 ärch-; 2 ärch-, *prefix.* Chief or principal; very great; extreme. In words beginning with the prefix *arch-*, the syllable *arch-* is pronounced *arc-*, 1 ärk-, 2 ärc-, before a vowel; as, *arch-* an'gel, 1 ark'ĕn'jel, 2 ärc'än'gĕl; before a consonant the pronunciation is *arch-*, 1 ärch-, 2 ärch-; as, *arch'*bish'op, 1 ärch'bish'ap, 2 ärch'bish'op; *arch'*duch'ess, 1 ärch'duch'es, 2 ärch'dŭch'ĕs. [This rule does not apply to the prefix *archi-*. See ARCHI-.]

Round Arch.

ar"chæ-ol'o-gy, etc. See ARCHEOLOGY, etc.

ar-cha'ic, 1 är-kē'ik; 2 är-cā'ie, *a.* Belonging to a former period; going out of use; antiquated. **-i-cal‡.— ar'cha-ism,** *n.* Anything archaic, as an archaic word, idiom, style, etc.

arch"an'gel, 1 ark"ēn'jel; 2 äre"än'gĕl, *n.* An angel of highest rank.

arch"bish'op, 1 ärch"bish'ap; 2 ärch"-bish'op, *n.* The chief bishop of a province.— **arch"bish'op-ric,** *n.* The office and jurisdiction of an archbishop.

arch"dea'con, 1 ärch"dī'kn; 2 ärch"dē'en, *n.* A high official in a diocese.— **arch"dea'-con-ate, arch"dea'con-ry,** *n.* [-RIES‡, *pl.*] The office or jurisdiction of an archdeacon.

ar"che-ol'o-gy, ⎱ 1 är"kɪ-el'o-jɪ; 2 är"ee-
ar"chæ-ol'o-gy, ⎰ ŏl'o-ġy, *n.* [-GIES‡, *pl.*] The science or study of history from relics and remains of antiquity.— **ar"che-o-log'-ic, ar"che-o-log'i-cal,** 1 är"kɪ-o-loj'ik, -ɪ-kal; 2 är"ee-o-lŏġ'ie, -ieal, *a.* Pertaining to archeology.— **ar"che-ol'o-gist,** *n.* One skilled in archeology.

arch'er, 1 ärch'er; 2 ärch'er, *n.* One who uses the bow and arrow.— **arch'er-y,** 1 ärch'er-ɪ; 2 ärch'er-y, *n.* [-IES‡, *pl.*] **1.** The art of shooting with the bow. **2.** Archers collectively.

ar'che-type, 1 är'kɪ-taip; 2 är"ee-tȳp, *n.* A primitive or standard pattern; a model.— **ar'che-ty"pal,** *a.*— **ar'che-typ'-ic** or **-i-cal,** *a.* [itive. See ARCH-.

ar'chi-, 1 är'kɪ-; 2 är'ei-, *prefix.* Chief; primar"chi-pel'a-go,** 1 är"kɪ-pel'a-go; 2 är'ei-pĕl'a-ḡo, *n.* [-GOES^z or -GOS^z, *pl.*] A

sea studded with islands, or the islands collectively.— **ar"chi-pe-lag'ic,** *a.*

ar'chi-tect, 1 är'kɪ-tekt; 2 är'ei-tĕct, *n.* One who plans buildings, etc., and directs their construction.— **ar'chi-tec"ture,** 1 är'-kɪ-tek'chur or -tiur; 2 är'ei-tĕe'chur or -tûr, *n.* **1.** The science and art of designing and constructing buildings. **2.** A style of building. **3.** Buildings, etc., collectively.— **ar"chi-tec'tur-al,** *a.*

ar'chive, 1 är'kaiv; 2 är'eīv, *n.* **1.** A depository for public documents: used mostly in the plural. **2.** A public document or record. [arched passage.

arch'way", 1 ärch'wē"; 2 ärch'wā", *n.* An

arc'tic, 1 ärk'tik; 2 äre'tie. **I.** *a.* Pertaining to the north pole; far northern; cold; frigid. **II.** *n.* **1.** The arctic circle or regions. **2.** [U. S.] A warm, waterproof overshoe.

Arctic ocean, 1 ärk'tik; 2 äre'tie. A body of water, largely frozen, surrounding the north pole; open to the Atlantic through Baffin bay, and to the Pacific through Bering strait.

-ard, *suffix.* Used to form from adjectives personal nouns denoting the possession in a high degree of the quality denoted by the adjective; as, drunk*ard*: sometimes changed to *-art*, as in bragg*art*.

ar'dent, 1 är'dent; 2 är'dĕnt, *a.* Vehement; passionate; intense; also, hot, burning. **-ly,** *adv.* **-ness,** *n.*— **ar'den-cy,** *n.* Intensity; warmth; eagerness.

ar'dor, 1 är'dor or -dȯr; 2 är'dor, *n.* Warmth; intensity; eagerness; vehemence; zeal. **ar'dour‡.**

ar'du-ous, 1 är'jŭ[or -diū-]us; 2 är'jŭ[or -diū-]ŭs, *a.* **1.** Laborious; difficult. **2.** Steep and lofty. **-ly,** *adv.* **-ness,** *n.*

are, 1 är; 2 är, *1st, 2d,* & *3d per. pl. pres. ind.* of BE, *v.*; also *2d per. pl.* (used as a sing.) *pres. ind.*

are, ⎱ 1 är; 2 är, *n.* A land-measure = 119.38-
ar^z, ⎰ square yards. See METRIC SYSTEM.

a're-a, 1 ē'rɪ-a; 2 ā're-a, *n.* **1.** An open space; a tract. **2.** Extent of surface. **3.** A small sunken basement-court.

a-re'na, 1 a-rī'na; 2 a-rē'na, *n.* The space for contestants in a Roman amphitheater; sphere of action or contest.

A'res, *n.* See MARS.

ar'gent, 1 är'jent; 2 är'ġĕnt, *a.* Like or made of silver; white; silvery.— **ar"gen-tif'-er-ous,** *a.* Silver-bearing.

ar"gil-la'ceous, 1 är"jɪ-lē'shus; 2 är"ġi-lā'shŭs, *a.* Containing, consisting of, or like clay; clayey.

ar'gon, 1 är'gon; 2 är'ġŏn, *n.* A gaseous constituent of the atmosphere, discovered in 1894.

ar'go-naut, 1 är'go-nȯt; 2 är'ġo-nạt, *n.* **1.** One of the legendary seekers for the golden fleece; hence, a gold-seeker. **2.** A

1: ə = final; ɪ = habit; aisle; au = *out*; oil; iū = *feud*; ċhin; go; ŋ = *sing*; ċhin, this.
2: wolf, dọ; bŏŏk, bōōt; fụll, rụle, cūre, bŭt, bûrn; ŏil, bọ̈y; ḡo, ġem; iŋk; thin, this.

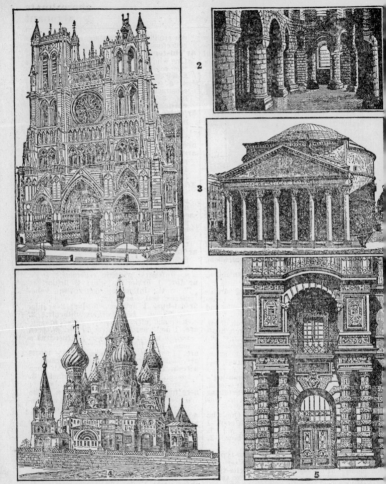

ARCHITECTURE.—I.

1. Gothic (Amiens Cathedral, France). 2. Norman (Chapel of St. John in the Tower of London, England). 3. Roman (Pantheon, Rome). 4. Russo-Byzantine (Church of St. Basil, Moscow). 5. Renaissance (Doorway of the Palace of Fontainebleau, France).

Architecture.—II.

1. Modern American (Metropolitan Tower, New York). 2. Byzantine (St. Mark's, Venice). 3. Egyptian (Temple of Karnak, Egypt). 4. Greek (Parthenon, Athens). 5. Chinese (Pagoda, Shanghai). 6. Colonial (Jumel Mansion, New York). 7. Moorish (La Giralda, Seville). 8. French (Château of Theil, France). 9. Moslem (Taj Mahal, India).

cuttlefish with papery shell. Called also *paper-nautilus.*

ar'go-sy, 1 är'go-sɪ; 2 är'go-sy, *n.* [-SIES², *pl.*] A large, richly laden ship.

ar'gue, 1 är'gi̇u; 2 är'gu, *vt. & vi.* [AR'-GUED; AR'GU-ING.] To reason; debate; discuss; influence by argument; prove; show; imply.

ar'gu-ment, 1 är'gi̇u-ment *or* -mᴇnt; 2 är'gu-ment, *n.* 1. A reason or course of reasoning; demonstration; debate; discussion. 2. The plot or gist of a work: a summary.— **ar"gu-men-ta'tion,** *n.* Debate; argument.— **ar"gu-men'ta-tiv(e⁸,** *a.* Pertaining to, consisting of, or marked by argument; given to argumentation. **-ly,** *adv.* **-ness,** *n.*

Ar'gus, 1 är'gᴜs; 2 är'gŭs, *n.* 1. *Myth.* A monster with 100 eyes; killed by Mercury; Juno set his eyes in the tail of the peacock. 2. A sharp-eyed, watchful person. 3. An East-Indian pheasant.

a'ri-a, 1 ä'ri-ɑ; 2 ä'ri-ä, *n. Mus.* An air or song; especially, an elaborate solo.

-a'ri-an, *suffix.* Used in forming adjectives and adjectival nouns denoting occupation, age, sect, etc.; as, predestin*arian.*

ar'id, 1 ar'ɪd; 2 är'id, *a.* Parched; dry; barren.— **a-rid'i-ty,** *n.* [-TIES², *pl.*] The state or quality of being arid. **ar'id-ness‡.**

a-right', 1 ə-rait'; 2 a-rīt', *a. & adv.* Rightly.

a-rise', ⎱1 ə-raɪz'; 2 a-rīz', *vi.* [A-ROSE', **a-rize'ᴾ,** ⎰A-ROZE'ᴾ; A-RIS'EN, A-RIZ'Nᴾ; A-RIS'ING.] To spring forth; appear; issue; originate; rise; ascend.

a-ris'ta, 1 ə-ris'tɑ; 2 a-ris'ta, *n.* [-TÆ, *pl.*] An awn.

ar"is-toc'ra-cy, 1 ar"ɪs-tɒk'rɑ-sɪ; 2 är"ɪs-tŏc'ra-çy, *n.* [-CIES², *pl.*] A hereditary nobility, or government by such a nobility.— **a-ris'to-crat,** 1 ə-ris'to-krat; 2 a-ris'to-crät, *n.* A member of an aristocracy; a proud and exclusive person.— **ar"is-to-crat'ic,** *a.* Pertaining to aristocracy; haughty; exclusive. **-i-cal‡.**

a-rith'me-tic, 1 ə-rith'mɪ-tik; 2 a-rĭth'me-tĭe, *n.* The science of numbers, or a treatise upon it.— **ar"ith-met'i-cal,** *a.* **-ly,** *adv.*— **a-rith"me-ti'cian,** 1 ə-rith"me-tish'ᴀn; 2 a-rith"me-tish'an, *n.* One skilled in arithmetic.

-a'ri-um, *suffix.* Forming nouns denoting a place for or connection with; as, aqu*arium,* honor*arium.*

ark, 1 ärk; 2 ärk, *n.* 1. *Script.* (1) The ship of Noah (*Gen.* vi, 14–22). (2) The chest containing the tables of the law (*Ex.* xxv, 10, etc.). (3) The papyrus cradle of Moses (*Ex.* ii, 3). 2. Any sacred repository. 3. A flat-bottomed freight-boat.

arm, 1 ärm; 2 ärm, *vt. & vi.* To provide with arms or armor; equip; fortify; have or take arms.

arm¹, *n.* The upper limb of the human body; an arm-like part or branch.

arm², *n.* 1. A weapon. 2. A branch of the military service.

ar-ma'da, 1 ɑr-mē'dɑ; 2 är-mä'dä, *n.* A fleet of war-vessels, as the so-called *Invincible Armada,* defeated off the coast of England in 1588.

ar"ma-dil'lo, 1 är"-mɑ-dil'o; 2 är"ma-dil'o, *n.* An American mammal with armor-like covering.

ar'ma-ment, 1 är'-mɑ-ment *or* -mᴇnt; 2 är'ma-ment, *n.* A land or naval force; the guns and munitions of a fort or vessel.

Armadillo. 1/20

ar'ma-ture, 1 är'mɑ-chur *or* -tiur; 2 är'ma-chur *or* -tūr, *n.* A piece of soft iron or wire-wound metal joining or rotating near the poles of a magnet.

arm'ful, 1 ärm'ful; 2 ärm'ful, *n.* That which is held, or can be held, in the arm or arms.

ar'mi-stice, ⎱1 är'mɪ-stis; 2 är'mi-stĭç, *n.* **ar'mi-stis⁸,** ⎰*Mil.* A suspension of hostilities; a truce.

arm'let, 1 ärm'let; 2 ärm'lĕt, *n.* A little arm; a band or armor for the arm.

ar'mor, 1 är'mᴇr; 2 är'mor, *n.* A defensive covering, as of mail for a warrior, or of metallic plates for a war-vessel, a diver's suit, etc.— **ar'mor-er,** *n.* A maker, repairer, or custodian of arms or armor.— **ar-mo'ri-al,** 1 är-mō'ri-ᴀl; 2 är-mō'ri-al, *a.* Pertaining to heraldry or heraldic arms.— **ar'mo-ry,** 1 är'mo-rɪ; 2 är'mo-ry, *n.* [-RIES², *pl.*] A place for the storing of arms, the assembling of troops, etc.

ar'mour, etc. Same as ARMOR, etc.

arms, 1 ärmz; 2 ärmz, *n. pl.* 1. Weapons of offense, collectively. 2. The military service. 3. Armorial bearings.

ar'my, 1 är'mɪ; 2 är'my, *n.* [AR'MIES², *pl.*] A large organized body of men armed for military service on land.

ar'ni-ca, 1 är'nɪ-kɑ; 2 är'ni-ea, *n.* A plant of the aster family, or a tincture prepared from it.

a-ro'ma, 1 ə-rō'mɑ; 2 a-rō'ma, *n.* [-MAS² *or* -MA-TA, 1 -mɑ-tɑ; 2 -ma-ta, *pl.*] Fragrance, as from plants; agreeable odor.— **ar"o-mat'ic. I.** *a.* Fragrant; spicy. **II.** *n.* An aromatic substance.

a-rose′, 1 ə-rōz′; 2 a-rōṣ′, *imp.* of ARISE, *v.*

a-round′, 1 ə-raund′; 2 a-round′. **I.** *adv.*
1. So as to encompass; in various directions; in the opposite direction; about.
2. From place to place; here and there.
II. *prep.* On all or various sides of; about.

a-rouse′, 1 ə-rauz′; 2 a-rouṣ, *vt.* [A-ROUSED′; A-ROUS′ING.] To awaken; excite; animate; rouse.— **a-rous′al,** *n.* An arousing; awakening.

ar-peg′gi-o, 1 ɑr-pej′o; 2 är-pĕg′o, *n.* The sounding of the notes of a chord in succession instead of together, as in playing the harp.

ar-raign′, 1 a-rēn′; 2 ä-rān′, *vt.* To accuse formally before a court; accuse.— **ar-raign′ment,** *n.* The act of arraigning; accusation.

ar-range′, 1 a-rēnj′; 2 ä-rāng′, *vt.* & *vi.* [AR-RANGED′; AR-RANG′ING.] To put in order; agree upon, as a plan; adjust; adapt; prepare; settle.— **ar-range′ment,** *n.* An arranging, or that which is arranged; disposition; order; preparation; plan; settlement; adjustment.

ar′rant, 1 ar′ənt; 2 är′ant, *a.* Notoriously bad; unmitigated.

ar′ras, 1 ar′əs; 2 är′as, *n.* Tapestry.

ar-ray′, 1 a-rē′; 2 ä-rā′. **I.** *vt.* **1.** To marshal; set in order. **2.** To clothe; dress. **II.** *n.* **1.** Regular or proper order; arrangement, as for battle; a military force. **2.** Clothing; dress.

ar-rear′, 1 a-rīr′; 2 ä-rēr′, *n.* A part, as of a debt, overdue and unpaid: commonly in the plural.— **ar-rear′age,** *n.* Arrears.

ar-rest′, 1 a-rest′; 2 ä-rĕst′. **I**ᵈ. *vt.* **1.** To stop suddenly; check; fix. **2.** To take into custody. **II.** *n.* An arresting; a stop, check, or stay; seizure by legal authority.

ar-rive′, 1 a-raiv′; 2 ä-rīv′, *vi.* [AR-RIVED′; AR-RIV′ING.] To come to a destination, conclusion, or result; come: followed by *at.*— **ar-ri′val,** 1 a-rai′vəl; 2 ä-rī′val, *n.* An arriving, or that which arrives.

ar′ro-gant, 1 ar′o-gənt; 2 är′o-ḡant, *a.* Having or showing excessive pride; supercilious; overbearing; haughty.— **ar′ro-gance,** 1 ar′o-gəns; 2 är′o-ḡanç, *n.* The being arrogant; haughtiness.— **ar′ro-gant-ly,** *adv.*

ar′ro-gate, 1 ar′o-gēt; 2 är′o-ḡāt, *vt.* [-GAT′EDᵈ; -GAT′ING.] To take, demand, or claim unreasonably; assume; usurp.— **ar′ro-ga′tion,** 1 ar′o-gē′shən; 2 är′o-ḡā′shon, *n.* The act of arrogating; unwarrantable assumption.

ar′row, 1 ar′o; 2 är′o, *n.* A slender shaft with pointed head, to be shot from a bow. See illus. in next column.— **ar′row-y,** 1 ar′o-ı; 2 är′o-y, *a.* Like an arrow; swift; sharp; direct.

ar′row-root″, 1 ar′o-rūt″; 2 är′o-rōōt″, *n.* A nutritious starch from a tropical American plant; also, the plant.

ar′se-nal, 1 är′sı-nəl; 2 är′se-nal, *n.* A repository for or manufactory of arms and munitions of war.

ar′se-nic, 1 är′sı-nik; 2 är′se-nĭe, *n.* A chemical element; also, a poisonous compound of this element.

Indian Arrow-heads.

ar′son, 1 är′sən; 2 är′son, *n.* The malicious burning of a dwelling or other structure.

art, 1 ärt; 2 ärt, *2d per. sing. pres. ind.* of BE, *v.*

art, *n.* **1.** Skill in some practical work; dexterity; facility; a system of rules; as, the industrial or mechanical *arts.* **2.** The embodiment of beautiful thought in artistic forms; also, the works thus produced, collectively; as, the esthetic or fine *arts;* also, artistic skill. **3.** Craft; cunning. **4.** An organized body of trained craftsmen; a gild.

Ar′te-mis, *n.* See DIANA.

ar′ter-y, 1 är′tər-ı; 2 är′ter-y, *n.* [-IESᶻ, *pl.*] One of the vessels which convey blood away from the heart; any great channel.— **ar-te′ri-al,** 1 ɑr-tī′rı-əl; 2 är-tē′ri-al, *a.*

Ar-te′sian, 1 ɑr-tī′ʒən; 2 är-tē′zhan, *a.* Of or pertaining to Artois, France.— **Artesian well,** a well bored down to a depth whence water is forced out at the surface.

art′ful, 1 ärt′ful; 2 ärt′ful, *a.* **1.** Crafty; cunning. **2.** Artificial. **3.** Skilful; ingenious.— **art′ful-ly,** *adv.*— **art′ful-ness,** *n.*

ar′ti-choke, 1 är′tı-chōk; 2 är′ti-chōk, *n.* A thistle-like garden plant or its edible head.

ar′ti-cl(eᵖ, 1 är′tı-kl; 2 är′ti-el. **I.** *vt.* [-CLED; -CLING.] To bind by or set forth in articles. **II.** *n.* **1.** A particular thing; item; proposition. **2.** An essay; paper. **3.** One of a class of limiting adjectives, as *a, an,* and *the.*

ar-tic′u-lar, 1 ɑr-tik′yu-lər; 2 är-tĭe′yu-lar, *a.* Pertaining to an articulation or joint.

ar-tic′u-late, 1 ɑr-tik′yu-lēt; 2 är-tĭe′yu-lāt. **I.** *vt.* & *vi.* [-LAT′EDᵈ; -LAT′ING.] **1.** To pronounce; enunciate; utter articulate sounds. **2.** To joint together. **II.** *a.* **1.** Having distinct syllables; distinctly uttered. **2.** Jointed; segmented. **III.** *n.* An invertebrate animal with segmented body, as an insect. **-ly,** *adv.* **-ness,** *n.*—

1: ə = final; ı = habıt; ɑisle; ɑu = out; oıl; ıū = feud; ℭhin; go; ŋ = sing; ℭhin, this.
2: wǫlf, dǫ; bŏŏk, bōōt; fu̇ll, rų̈le, cūre, bŭt, bûrn; oĭl, bŏy; ḡo, ġem; iŋk; thin, this.

ar-tic″u-la′tion, *n.* **1.** The utterance of articulate sounds; enunciation; an articulate sound. **2.** A jointing together; joint.

ar′ti-fice, } 1 är′tu-fis; 2 är′ti-fĭç, *n.* Trick-
ar′ti-fiss, } ery; stratagem; maneuver.

ar-tif′i-cer, 1 är-tif′ı-sər; 2 är-tif′ı-çer, *n.* A skilful handicraftsman; also, an inventor; a contriver.

ar″ti-fi′cial, 1 är″tı-fish′əl; 2 är″ti-fĭsh′al, *a.* Produced by art; not natural; affected. **-ly,** *adv.*

ar-til′ler-y, 1 ar-til′ər-ı; 2 är-tĭl′er-y, *n.* **1.** Cannon, or the troops operating it. **2.** Implements of ancient warfare.

art′ist, 1 ärt′ist; 2 ärt′ĭst, *n.* One who is skilled in the fine arts; one who works artistically.— **ar-tis′tic, ar-tis′ti-cal,** *a.* Of or pertaining to art or artists; conformable to the principles of art; tasteful; elegant; beautiful.— **ar-tis′ti-cal-ly,** *adv.*

ar′ti-zan, } 1 är′tı-zən; 2 är′ti-zan, *n.* A
ar′ti-san, } trained workman; superior mechanic.

art′less, 1 ärt′les; 2 ärt′lĕs, *a.* Without art or craft; unaffected; ingenuous; simple; sincere. **-ly,** *adv.* **-ness,** *n.*

-a-ry, *suffix.* Denoting in nouns, persons, things, or places; as, not*ary*, libr*ary*: also used to form adjectives; as, prim*ary*.

Ar′yan, 1 är′yan; 2 är′yan. **I.** *a.* Indo-European or Indo-Germanic; of or belonging to the Aryans. **II.** *n.* **1.** One of a primitive people who are believed to have spread from the highlands of Central Asia into Europe and India, and to be the parent stock alike of the Hindus, Greeks, Latins, Celts, Anglo-Saxons, etc. **2.** The language of this people.

as, 1 az; 2 ăz, *adv. & conj.* Like; for instance; in the character of; when; because; since.

as″a-fet′i-da, 1 as″ə-fet′ı-də; 2 ăs″ə-fĕt′i-da, *n.* A fetid drug.

as-bes′tos, 1 as-bes′tos; 2 ăs-bĕs′tos, *n.* A fibrous fire-proof mineral.

as-cend′d, 1 a-send′; 2 ă-çĕnd′, *vt. & vi.* To go or move up; slope upward; mount; climb; rise.

as-cen′den-cy, } 1 a-sen′den-sı, -dən-sı; 2
as-cen′dan-cy, } ă-çĕn′dĕn-çy, -dan-çy, *n.* Paramount influence; domination; sway.

as-cen′dent, } 1 a-sen′dent, -dənt; 2 ă-
as-cen′dant, } çĕn′dĕnt, -dant. **I.** *a.* Ascending; rising; superior; dominant. **II.** *n.* Preeminence; domination.

as-cen′sion, 1 a-sen′shən; 2 ă-çĕn′shon, *n.* **1.** The act of ascending. **2.** [A-] Christ's ascent from earth; Ascension day (the 40th day after Easter).

as-cent′, 1 a-sent′; 2 ă-çĕnt′, *n.* The act of ascending; a rising, soaring, or climb-

ing; promotion; a way of ascending; an acclivity.

as″cer-tain′, 1 as″ər-tēn′; 2 ăs′er-tān′, *vt.* To make certain; find out; determine.— **as″cer-tain′a-bl(e)²,** *a.*

as-cet′ic, 1 a-set′ik; 2 ă-çĕt′ĭc. **I.** *a.* Practising extreme abstinence; severely self-denying. **II.** *n.* One austerely self-denying; a hermit.— **as-cet′i-cal-ly,** *adv.*— **as-cet′i-cism,** *n.* Ascetic belief and conduct.

a-scribe′, 1 a-skraib′; 2 ă-scrīb′, *vt.* [A-SCRIBED′; A-SCRIB′ING.] To refer, as to a cause or source; attribute.— **as-crib′a-bl(e)²,** *a.*— **a-scrip′tion,** 1 a-skrip′shən; 2 ă-scrip′shon, *n.* The act of ascribing, or that which is ascribed.

a-sep′tic, 1 a-sep′tık; 2 ă-sĕp′tic, *a.* Free from disease-germs or tendency to putrefaction.

a-sex′u-al, 1 ē-[or ɑ-]seks′yu-al; 2 ā-[or ă-]sĕks′yu-al, *a.* Of neither sex.

ash¹, 1 ash; 2 ăsh, *n.* [ASH′ES², *pl.*] A tree of the olive family, or its light, tough, elastic wood. — **ash′en¹,** *a.* Pertaining to or made of the ash.

Ash.
1. Tree. 2. Leaflet.

ash², *n.* **1.** The residue of a substance that has been burnt: usually in the plural. **2.** *pl.* Remains, as of the dead.— **ash′en²,** *a.* Of, pertaining to, or like ashes; pale. **ash′y‡.**

a-shamed′, 1 a-shēmd′; 2 a-shāmd′, *a.* **1.** Feeling shame; abashed. **2.** Deterred by shame or modesty; reluctant.

ash′en, ash′es (*pl.*), **ash′y.** See ASH¹ or ASH².

a-shore′, 1 a-shōr′; 2 a-shōr′, *adv.* To or on shore.

A′sia, 1 ē′shə; 2 ā′sha, *n.* The largest continent in the world, in the eastern hemisphere; area, 17,057,666 sq. m.

A″si-at′ic, 1 ē″shi-at′ik; 2 ā′shi-ăt′ic. **I.** *a.* Of or pertaining to Asia. **II.** *n.* A native or inhabitant of Asia.

a-side′, 1 a-said′; 2 a-sīd′. **I.** *n.* Something said or done aside. **II.** *adv.* On or to one side; away; apart; out of consideration; out of hearing.

as′i-nine, 1 as′ı-nin *or* -nain; 2 ăs′i-nin *or* -nīn, *a.* Pertaining to or like an ass; stupid; silly.— **as″i-nin′i-ty,** 1 as′ı-nin′ı-tı; 2 ăs′i-nin′i-ty, *n.*

ask‡, 1 ask; 2 ásk, *vt. & vi.* **1.** To request; solicit; demand; claim. **2.** To question; inquire. **3.** To invite.

a-skance', 1 ə-skŭns', 2 a-skănç', *adv.* With a side or indirect glance; disdainfully; distrustfully. **a-skant'‡.**

a-skew', 1 ə-skiū'; 2 a-skū', *a. & adv.* Obliquely; awry.

a-slant', 1 ə-slant'; 2 a-slănt'. **I.** *a. & adv.* Slanting; oblique; slantingly; obliquely. **II.** *prep.* Across slantingly; athwart.

a-sleep, 1 ə-slīp'; 2 a-slēp', *a. & adv.* In or into a state of sleep; dormant; dead; benumbed.

a-slope, 1 ə-slōp'; 2 a-slōp', *a. & adv.* In a sloping position. [viper.

asp, 1 asp; 2 ásp, *n.* A venomous serpent;

as-par'a-gus, 1 as-par'ə-gŭs; 2 ăs-păr'a-gŭs, *n.* A plant of the lily family, or its edible shoots.

as'pect, 1 as'pekt; 2 ăs'pĕct, *n.* Appearance; mien; look; view; exposure; outlook.

asp'en, 1 asp'n; 2 ăsp'n. **I.** *a.* Of or pertaining to the aspen; shaking; tremulous. **II.** *n.* A poplar with tremulous leaves.

as-per'i-ty, 1 as-per'ı-tı; 2 ăs-pĕr'i-ty, *n.* [-TIES²*, pl.*] Roughness; harshness; hardship.

as-perse', 1 as-pūrs'; 2 ăs-pērs', *vt.* [AS-PERSED'ᵗ, AS-PERST'ˢ; AS-PERS'- a, branch; b, ament. ING.] **1.** To censure harshly and falsely; slander. **2.** To besprinkle.— **as-per'sion,** 1 as-pūr'sʜən; 2 ăs-pĕr'sʜon, *n.* **1.** A slanderous report or charɡe. **2.** Sprinkling.

Aspen.

as'phalt, 1 as'falt; 2 ăs'fălt, *n.* Mineral
as'falt⁽ᴾ⁾, pitch; hard bitumen, or a pavement made of it. **as-phal'tum‡.— as-phal'tic,** *a.*

as-phyx'i-a, 1 as-fiks'ı-ə; 2 ăs-fy̆ks'i-a, *n.*
as-fyx'i-aᴾ, Suffocation.— **as-phyx'i-ate,** 1 as-fiks'ı-ēt; 2 ăs-fy̆ks'i-āt, *vt.* [-ATᴬED⁽ᵈ⁾; -AT'ING.] To suffocate.— **as-phyx''i-a'tion,** *n.* Suffocation; asphyxia.

as-pir'ant, 1 as-pair'ənt; 2 ăs-pīr'ant. **I.** *a.* Aspiring. **II.** *n.* One who aspires; a candidate.

as'pi-rate, 1 as'pı-rēt; 2 ăs'pi-răt. **I.** *vt.* [-RATᴬEDᵈ; -RAT'ING.] **1.** To utter with a breathing or as if preceded by the letter *h.* **2.** To draw out by suction. **II.** *a.* Uttered with a strong *h* sound. **as'pi-rat''ed‡.**

as'pi-rate, *n.* The letter *h,* or its sound.

as''pi-ra'tion, 1 as''pı-rē'sʜən; 2 ăs''pi-rā'sʜon, *n.* The act of aspiring or of aspirating; exalted desire; a breath; inspiration; suction.

as-pire', 1 as-pair'; 2 ăs-pīr', *vi.* [AS-

PIRED'; AS-PIR'ING.] To desire something high and good; reach upward; ascend.— **as-pir'ing,** *pa.* Upreaching; nobly ambitious. **-ly,** *adv.*

as'pi-rin, 1 as'pı-rin; 2 ăs'pi-rin, *n.* A white powder used as a remedy for rheumatism.

a-squint, 1 ə-skwint'; 2 a-skwint', *a. & adv.* Askance; squinting; squintingly.

ass, 1 as; 2 ăs, *n.* [ASS'ES², *pl.*] A long-eared equine quadruped; a stupid person.

as''sa-fet'i-da, *n.* Same as ASAFETIDA.

as'sa-gai, 1 as'ə-gai; 2 ăs'a-gī, *n.* A light spear.

as-sail', 1 a-sēl'; 2 ă-sāl', *vt.* To attack violently; assault; upbraid.— **as-sail'a-bl(eᴾ,** *a.*— **as-sail'ant. I.** *a.* Attacking; hostile. **II.** *n.* One who assails.

as-sas'sin, 1 a-sas'ın'; 2 ă-săs'in, *n.* One who assassinates.— **as-sas'si-nate,** *v.* [-NATᴬEDᵈ; -NAT'ING.] **I.** *t.* To kill by secret or treacherous assault. **II.** *i.* To commit treacherous murder.— **as-sas''si-na'tion,** *n.* The act of assassinating; secret or treacherous murder.

as-sault', 1 a-sôlt'; 2 ă-sȧlt'. **Iᵈ.** *vt.* To attack with violence; assail. **II.** *n.* Any attack; charge of troops.

as-say', 1 a-sē'; 2 ă-sā'. **I.** *vt. & vi.* To subject to an assay; essay; prove; test; show by test a certain value. **II.** *n.* The testing of an alloy or ore for valuable metal.— **as-say'er,** *n.*

as'se-gai, *n.* Same as ASSAGAI.

as-sem'blage, 1 a-sem'blıj; 2 ă-sĕm'blăg, *n.* An assembling; gathering; collection; assembly.

as-sem'bl(eᴾ, 1 a-sem'bl; 2 ă-sĕm'bl, *vt. & vi.* [-BL(E)Dᴾ; -BLING.] To collect; join together; come together; meet; congregate.

as-sem'bly, 1 a-sem'blı; 2 ă-sĕm'bly, *n.* [-BLIES², *pl.*] An assembling; persons assembled; military signal for assembling.

as-sent', 1 a-sent'; 2 ă-sĕnt'. **Iᵈ.** *vi.* To express agreement; concur; acquiesce. **II.** *n.* Concurrence; agreement; consent; sanction.

as-sertᵈ, 1 a-sūrt'; 2 ă-sērt', *vt.* To state positively; affirm without proof; maintain as a right or claim.— **as-ser'tion,** *n.* The act of asserting; a positive declaration without attempt at proof.

as-sessᵗ, 1 a-sɛs'; 2 ă-sĕs', *vt.* To tax; estimate or value for taxation.— **as-sess'a-bl(eᴾ,** *a.*— **as-sess'a-bly,** *adv.*— **as-sess'ment,** *n.* An assessing, or the amount assessed.— **as-sess'or,** *n.* [assets.

as'set, 1 as'et; 2 ăs'ĕt, *n.* An item in one's

as'sets, 1 as'ets; 2 ăs'ĕts, *n. pl.* Available property, as for payment of debts, legacies, etc.

as-sev'er-ate, 1 a-sev'ər-ēt; 2 ă-sĕv'er-ăt

vt. [-AT"ED^d; -AT"ING.] To affirm emphatically or solemnly.— **as-sev"er-a'tion,** 1 a-sev'ər-ē'shan; 2 ā-sĕv'er-ā'shon, *n.* An emphatic or solemn declaration.

as-sid'u-ous, 1 a-sid'yu-us; 2 ă-sĭd'yu-ŭs, *a.* Devoted or constant; unremitting; diligent. **-ly,** *adv.* **-ness,** *n.*— **as"si-du'i-ty,** 1 as"i-dū'i-ti; 2 ăs"i-dū'i-ty, *n.* [-TIES², *pl.*] Close application; diligence.

as-sign', 1 a-sain'; 2 ă-sīn'. **I.** *vt. & vi.* **1.** To set apart; designate; appoint; allot; attribute. **2.** To make over, as property, to an assignee; make an assignment. **II.** *n.* A person to whom property, rights, or powers are transferred by another.— **as-sign'a-bl**(e³, *a.* That may be assigned or specified.— **as"sig - na'tion,** 1 as"ig-nē'shən; 2 as"ĭg-nā'shon, *n.* **1.** An assigning; assignment. **2.** An appointment for meeting: usually in a bad sense.— **as"sign-ee',** 1 as"i-nī'; 2 ăs"i-nē', *n.* One to whom property has been assigned in trust; an agent or trustee.— **as-sign'ment,** *n.* **1.** An assigning. **2.** The transfer of a property, or the writing of transfer.— **as"sign-or',** *n.* One who assigns. **as-sign'er**‡.

as-sim'i-late, 1 a-sim'i-lēt; 2 ă-sĭm'i-lāt, *vt. & vi.* [-LAT"ED^d; -LAT"ING.] **1.** To take up and incorporate, as food. **2.** To make or become like; liken; compare; become alike.— **as-sim'i-la-bl**(e³, *a.* That may be assimilated.— **as-sim"i-la'tion,** *n.* An assimilating or being assimilated; transformation. — **as-sim'i-la-tiv**(e³, *a.* Capable of or tending to assimilation.

as-sist'^d, 1 a-sist'; 2 ă-sĭst', *vt. & vi.* **1.** To give succor or support to; aid; help; relieve. **2.** To attend as a helper; act as assistant.— **as-sist'ance,** *n.* Help; aid; support; relief.— **as-sis'tant.** **I.** *a.* Affording aid; assisting subordinately. **II.** *n.* One who or that which assists; a deputy.

as-size', 1 a-saiz'; 2 ă-sīz', *n.* [AS-SIZ'ES², *pl.*] A court or its session, or time and place of sitting: used chiefly in the plural.

as-so'ci-ate, 1 a-sō'shi-ēt; 2 ă-sō'shi-āt. **I.** *vt. & vi.* [-AT"ED^d; -AT"ING.] To bring together; combine; connect in thought; have fellowship; unite; join. **II.** *a.* Joined together; united; allied. **III.** *n.* **1.** A companion; colleague. **2.** A concomitant.

as-so"ci-a'tion, 1 a-sō"si-ē'shən; 2 ă-sō"-çi-ā'shon, *n.* **1.** The act of associating; fellowship; combination; society; corporation. **2.** Connection of ideas.

as-sort'^d, 1 a-sōrt'; 2 ă-sôrt', *vt. & vi.* To distribute into classes; classify; associate; consort.— **as-sort'ment,** *n.* **1.** The act or process of assorting. **2.** A collection of various things.

as-suage', 1 a-swēj'; 2 ă-swăg', *vt.* [AS-SUAGED'; AS-SUAG'ING.] To make less violent; alleviate; soothe; allay; abate; calm. **-ment,** *n.* — **as-sua'siv**(e³, *a.* Tending to assuage; soothing.

as-sume', 1 a-siūm'; 2 ă-sūm', *vt. & vi.* [AS-SUMED'; AS-SUM'ING.] **1.** To take upon oneself; adopt. **2.** To take for granted; suppose. **3.** To affect; pretend. — **as-sum'ing,** *pa.* Presumptuous; arrogant.

as-sump'tion, 1 a-sump'shən; 2 ă-sŭmp'-shon, *n.* **1.** An assuming; a supposition. **2.** Arrogance.

as-sur'ance, 1 a-shūr'əns; 2 ă-shụr'anç, *n.* **1.** The act of assuring; a promise. **2.** Full confidence; conviction. **3.** Self-confidence; boldness; effrontery. **4.** Insurance.

as-sure', 1 a-shūr'; 2 ă-shụr', *vt.* [AS-SURED'; AS-SUR'ING.] **1.** To offer assurances to. **2.** To give confidence to; convince. **3.** To insure.— **as-sur'ed-ly,** *adv.* Without doubt; certainly. — **as-sur'ed-ness,** *n.*

as'ter, 1 as'tər; 2 ăs'ter, *n.* A plant having alternate leaves, and flowers with white, purple, or blue rays and yellow disk.

as'ter-isk, 1 as'tər-isk; 2 ăs'ter-ĭsk, *n.* A star (*) used in writing and printing, for references, etc.

a-stern', 1 a-stûrn'; 2 a-stĕrn', *adv.* *Naut.* Behind; backward.

as'ter-oid, 1 as'tər-oid; 2 ăs'ter-ŏid, *n.* One of the very small China planets between Mars and Jupiter. Aster. — **as"ter-oid'al,** *a.*

asth'ma, 1 az'ma; 2 ăṣ'ma, *n.* Chronic difficulty of breathing.— **asth-mat'ic,** 1 az-mat'ik; 2 ăṣ-măt'ie. **I.** *a.* Of, pertaining to, or affected with asthma or shortness of breath. **-i-cal**‡. **II.** *n.* A person subject to asthma.— **asth-mat'i-cal-ly,** *adv.*

a-stig'ma-tism, 1 a-stig'mə-tizm; 2 a-stĭg'ma-tĭṣm, *n.* A defect of vision due to faulty curvature of the cornea.

a-stir', 1 a-stûr'; 2 a-stîr', *adv. & a.* In action; stirring.

a-ston'ish^d, 1 a-ston'ish; 2 a-stŏn'ish, *vt.* To affect with wonder and surprise; amaze; confound. — **a - ston'ish - ing,** *pa.* Causing astonishment. **-ly,** *adv.*— **a-ston'ish-ment,** *n.* The state of being astonished; surprise; amazement.

a-stound'^d, 1 a-staund'; 2 a-stound', *vt. & vi.* To overwhelm with wonder; confound; stupefy.   [starry.

as'tral, 1 as'trəl; 2 ăs'tral, *a.* Starlike;

a-stray', 1 a-strē'; 2 a-strā', *a. & adv.* Wandering; out of the way; evil.

a-stride', 1 a-straid'; 2 a-strīd', *adv. &*

prep. With one leg on each side of, or with the legs far apart; bestriding.

as-trin′gent, 1 as-trin′jent; 2 ăs-trĭn′gĕnt. **I.** *a.* Binding; constipative; styptic. **II.** *n.* An astringent substance, as alum, etc. — **as-trin′gen-cy,** *n.*—**as-trin′gent-ly,** *adv.*

as-trol′o-gy, 1 as-trol′o-ji; 2 ăs-trŏl′o-gy, *n.* Ancient divination by the stars.— **as-trol′o-ger,** 1 as-trol′o-jər; 2 ăs-trŏl′o-gẽr, *n.* One practising astrology.— **as″tro-log′ic,** 1 as″tro-loj′ık; 2 ăs″tro-lŏg′ĭe , *a.* **-i-cal‡.**

as-tron′o-my, 1 as-tron′o-mı; 2 ăs-trŏn′o-my, *n.* The science of the heavenly bodies.— **as-tron′o-mer,** *n.* A skilled observer of the stars.— **as″tro-nom′ic,** 1 as″tro-nom′ık; 2 ăs″tro-nŏm′ĭe, *a.* Of or pertaining to astronomy. **as″tro-nom′i-cal‡.** — **as″tro-nom′i-cal-ly,** *adv.*

as-tute′, 1 as-tūt′; 2 ăs-tūt′, *a.* Keen in discernment; acute; sagacious; cunning. **-ly,** *adv.* **-ness,** *n.* [Apart; in or into pieces.]

a-sun′der, 1 ə-sun′dər; 2 a-sŭn′der, *adv.*

a-sy′lum, 1 ə-sai′lum; 2 a-sȳ′lŭm, *n.* An institution for the care of invalids; a refuge; retreat.

at, 1 at; 2 ăt, *prep.* **1.** On; upon; close to; by; near; in; within. **2.** To; toward; after; by way of; through. **3.** On the point of; during. **4.** On the happening of; in response to; because of. **5.** Up to; to the extent of; corresponding to. **6.** In; connected with; dependent on; in a state or condition of.

at′a-vism, 1 at′ə-vizm; 2 ăt′a-vĭşm, *n.* Reversion to an ancestral type or trait.

ate, 1 ēt; 2 ăt, *imp.* of EAT, *v.*

-ate, *suffix.* **1.** Forming adjectives; as, desolate. **2.** Forming verbs; as, assassinate. **3.** Forming nouns denoting office, etc.; as, magistrate; also, in chemistry, various salts formed from acids whose names end in -*ic*; as, nitrate.

a tem′po, 1 ä tem′po; 2 ä těm′po. See TEMPO.

a′the-ism, 1 ē′thĭ-izm; 2 ā′thē-ĭşm, *n.* The denial of or disbelief in the existence of God.— **a′the-ist,** *n.* One who holds or advocates atheism.— **a″the-is′tic,** *a.* Characterized by atheism. **a″the-is′ti-cal‡.**— **a″the-is′ti-cal-ly,** *adv.*

A-the′na, 1 a-fhī′nə; 2 a-thē′na, *n.* The Greek goddess of wisdom, corresponding to the Roman Minerva. **A-the′nē‡** [Gr.].

ath″e-ne′um, 1 afh′ı-nī′um; 2 ăth′e- **ath″e-næ′um,** ⎰ nē′ŭm, *n.* A literary club or academy; a reading-room or the like.

A-the′ni-an, 1 a-fhī′nı-ən; 2 a-thē′ni-an, *a.* Of, pertaining to, or characteristic of Athens, the most famous city of ancient Greece and capital of modern Greece.

a-thirst′, 1 ə-thûrst′; 2 a-thĭrst′, *a.* Thirsting; thirsty.

ath′lete, 1 afh′lēt; 2 ăth′lĕt, *n.* One skilled in feats of physical strength and agility.— **ath-let′ic,** 1 afh-let′ık; 2 ăth-lĕt′ĭc, *a.* Pertaining to feats of physical strength and agility; of or like an athlete; strong; vigorous; muscular.— **ath-let′i-cal,** *a.* **-ly,** *adv.*— **ath-let′ics,** *n.* Athletic exercises collectively; a system of athletic training.

a-thwart′, 1 ə-thwôrt′; 2 a-thwart′, *adv.* & *prep.* Across; transversely; in opposition to; perversely.

-at′ic, *suffix.* Of; of the kind of: used in adjectives of Latin or Greek origin; as, *erratic, grammatic.*

-a′tion, *suffix.* A form used in nouns of action of Latin origin and, by analogy, in nouns of non-Latin origin; as, *creation, flirtation.*

At-lan′tic o′cean, 1 at-lan′tık; 2 ăt-lăn′tĭe. Vast waters between America and Europe and Africa; 10,000 miles long; 3,000 miles wide; average depth, about 13,000 feet; area, 30,000,000 sq. m.

at′las, 1 at′las; 2 ăt′las, *n.* **1.** A volume of maps or the like. **2.** A size of paper, 26 by 33 (34) inches. **3.** [A-] *Myth.* Son of Iapetus and Clymene; leader of Titans in war against Jupiter; condemned, when defeated, to bear the heavens on his shoulders.

at′mos-phere, ⎱ 1 at′mas-fīr; 2 ăt′mos-fēr, **at′mos-fere,** ⎰ *n.* The mass of gases, chiefly air, surrounding the earth or any heavenly body; any surrounding element or influence; environment.— **at″mos-pher′ic,** 1 at′mas-fer′ık; 2 ăt′mos-fēr′ĭe, *a.* Pertaining to the atmosphere. **at″mos-pher′i-cal‡.**

a-toll′, 1 ə-tŏl′; 2 a-tŏl′, *n.* A ring-like coral island.

at′om, 1 at′-əm; 2 ăt′-om, *n.* One of the parts of which all matter is supposed to

Atoll.

be formed; any exceedingly small particle or thing; an iota.— **a-tom′ic, -i-cal,** *a.* Of or pertaining to an atom or atoms; minute; infinitesimal; elemental.— **at′om-ize,** 1 at′-əm-aiz; 2 ăt′om-iz, *vt.* [-IZED; -IZ′ING.] To reduce to atoms; pulverize. **at′om-ise‡.**— **at′om-iz″er,** 1 at′əm-aiz′ər; 2 ăt′om-iz′ẽr, *n.* An apparatus for transforming a liquid to spray. **at′om-is″er‡.**

at′om-y¹, 1 at′əm-ı; 2 ăt′o-my, *n.* [-IES²**,** *pl.*] An atom; pigmy.

at′o-my², 1 at′o-mı; 2 ăt′o-my, *n.* [-MIES², *pl.*] A skeleton; an emaciated person.

a-tone′, 1 a-tōn′; 2 ä-tōn′, *vt.* & *vi.* [A-TONED²; A-TON′ING.] To make expiation for; make amends; propitiate; appease; reconcile.— **a-tone′ment,** 1 a-tōn′ment *or*

-mənt; 2 ă-tōn′ment, *n.* Satisfaction, reparation, or expiation made for wrong or harm; the sacrificial work of Christ.

a-top′, 1 ə-top′; 2 ă-tŏp′, *adv. & prep.* On the top; up above.

ator, *suffix.* An agent; doer; actor; one who or that which; as, arbitr*ator*.

-atory, *suffix.* Of or pertaining to; producing or produced by; of the nature of; expressing; as, exclam*atory*.

a′tri-um, 1 ē′tri-um; 2 ā′tri-ŭm, *n.* A stately and spacious entrance-hall, as of a Roman dwelling.

a-tro′cious, 1 ə-trō′shus; 2 a-trō′shŭs, *a.* Outrageously wicked, vile, or cruel; heinous; horrible.— **a-tro′cious-ly,** *adv.*— **a-troc′i-ty,** 1 ə-tros′i-tī; 2 a-trŏc′i-ty, *n.* [-TIES², *pl.*] **1.** The being atrocious. **a-tro′cious-ness‡. 2.** An atrocious deed; shocking cruelty or wickedness.

at′ro-phy, 1 at′ro-fī; 2 ăt′ro-fy **I.** *vt. &*
at′ro-fyʳ, *vi.* [-PHIED; -PHY-ING.] To cause to waste away; wither. **II.** *n.* [-PHIES², *pl.*] A wasting or withering of the body or any of its parts; a stoppage of growth.

at-tach′ᵗ, 1 a-tach′; 2 ă-tăch′, *vt. & vi.* To fasten; join; connect; attribute; assign; unite; win; seize by legal process.

at″ta″ché′, 1 ā″tā″shē′; 2 ā″tă″che′, *n.* One attached to a company or suite, as of an ambassador.

at-tach′ment, 1 a-tach′ment *or* -mənt; 2 ă-tăch′ment, *n.* An attaching, or a being attached; adherence; affection; also, a bond; band; tie; appendage; adjunct; legal seizure.

at-tack′, 1 a-tak′; 2 ă-tăk′. **I**ᵗ. *vt. & vi.* **1.** To begin battle or conflict with; assail; assault; make an onset; criticize; censure. **2.** To start vigorously on (a task). **3.** To set upon vigorously, as acid upon metal. **II.** *n.* The act of attacking; an onset; an attacking force; a seizure, as by disease.

at-tain′, 1 a-tēn′; 2 ă-tān′, *v.* **I.** *t.* To arrive at (a desired object); acquire; achieve; reach. **II.** *i.* To arrive or reach with effort: with *to.*— **at-tain″a-bil′i-ty, at-tain′a-bl(e-ness**ʳ, *n.*— **at-tain′a-bl(e**ʳ, *a.* That can be attained; practicable.— **at-tain′ment,** *n.* The act of attaining; an acquisition; achievement.

at-tain′der, 1 a-tēn′der; 2 ă-tān′der, *n. Eng. Law.* A sentence of confiscation and outlawry against a person, as for treason: forbidden by the Constitution of the United States.

at-taint′, 1 a-tēnt′; 2 ă-tānt′. **I**ᵈ. *vt.* To disgrace; condemn; seize upon. **II.** *n.*

1. Imputation; stigma; attainder. **2.** A touch; hit.

at′tar, 1 at′ər; 2 ăt′ar, *n.* The fragrant essential oil extracted from rose-petals.

at-tem′per, 1 a-tem′pər; 2 ă-tĕm′per, *vt.* To modify by mixture; soften; moderate; temper.

at-tempt′, 1 a-tempt′; 2 ă-tĕmpt′. **I**ᵈ. *vt.* To make an effort to do or to conquer; endeavor; try; essay. **II.** *n.* A trial; endeavor; essay; attack.

at-tend′ᵈ, 1 a-tend′; 2 ă-tĕnd′, *v.* **I.** *t.* To wait upon; minister to; be present at; follow; accompany. **II.** *i.* **1.** To give attention; listen; give attendance: with *to.* **2.** To be present: with *at, on,* or *upon.* **3.** To follow as a result: with *on* or *upon.*— **at-ten′dance,** *n.* An attending; those who attend; an audience; a retinue.— **at-ten′dant,** 1 a-ten′dənt; 2 ă-tĕn′dant. **I.** *a.* Following; consequent; waiting upon. **II.** *n.* One who attends; a servant; companion; suitor.

at-ten′tion, 1 a-ten′shən; 2 ă-tĕn′shon, *n.* **1.** The act, fact, or power of attending. **2.** An act of courtesy; consideration; care. **3.** *Mil.* The soldierly posture of readiness.

at-ten′tive, 1 a-ten′tiv; 2 ă-tĕn′tiv, *a.*
at-ten′tivˢ, Giving attention; observant; thoughtful; polite. **-ly,** *adv.* **-ness,** *n.*

at-ten′u-ate, 1 a-ten′yu-ēt; 2 ă-tĕn′yu-āt, *vt. & vi.* [-AT″ED̃ᵈ; -AT″ING.] To make or become thin; draw out, as a wire; emaciate; weaken; enfeeble.— **at-ten″u-a′tion,** *n.*

at-test′, 1 a-test′; 2 ă-tĕst′. **I**ᵈ. *vt. & vi.* To certify; confirm; vouch for. **II.** *n.* One who or that which attests; testimony; attestation.— **at″tes-ta′tion,** 1 at″es-tē′shən; 2 ăt″ĕs-tā′shon, *n.* The act of attesting; evidence; testimony.

At′tic, 1 at′ik; 2 ăt′ic, *a.* Of or pertaining to Attica or Athens in Greece; classic; witty.— **Attic salt,** refined classical wit.— **At′ti-cism,** *n.* An Attic idiom; pure Greek; elegance of diction. [ret.

at′tic, *n.* A half-story next the roof; a garret.

at-tire′, 1 a-tair′; 2 ă-tīr′. **I.** *vt.* [AT-TIRED′; AT-TIR′ING.] To dress; array; adorn. **II.** *n.* Dress or clothing; apparel; garments; costume; adornment.

at′ti-tude, 1 at′i-tiūd; 2 ăt′i-tŭd, *n.* **1.** Position of the body, as suggesting some thought, feeling, or action. **2.** State of mind, behavior, or conduct.— **at″ti-tu′di-nal,** *a.*— **at″ti-tu′di-nize,** *vi.* [-NIZED; -NIZ″ING.] To strike attitudes; pose for effect. **-nise‡.**

at-tor′ney, 1 a-tŭr′ni; 2 ă-tŭr′ny, *n.* [-NEYS², *pl.*] One empowered to act for another; a lawyer.

at-tract′d, 1 a-trakt′; 2 ă-trăct′, *v.* **I.** *t.*
To draw; charm; allure; entice; win. **II.**
i. To exert attractive influence or power.
— **at-trac′tion,** *n.* The act or process of
attracting; attractive power; anything pleasing or alluring.— **at-trac′tiv**(e[s], *a.* Having
the power or quality of attracting; drawing;
pleasing; winning. **-ly,** *adv.* **-ness,** *n.*

at-trib′ute, 1 a-trib′yut; 2 ă-trib′yut, *vt.*
[-UT-ED[d]; -UT-ING.] To ascribe (something) as due and belonging; assign; refer;
with *to.*— **at-trib′u-ta-bl**(e[r], *a.*— **at″tri-
bu′tion,** 1 at′rı-biū′shan; 2 ăt′rı-bū′shon, *n.*
The act of attributing; an attribute.— **at-
trib′u-tiv**(e[s]. **I.** *a.* Of or pertaining to an
attribute; expressing or assigning an attribute.
II. *n.* *Gram.* An attributive word, as an
adjective.— **at-trib′u-tiv**(e-ly[s], *adv.*

at′tri-bute, 1 at′rı-biūt; 2 ăt′rı-būt, *n.* **1.**
That which is attributed; a characteristic.
2. A distinctive mark or symbol.

at-tri′tion, 1 a-trĭsh′an; 2 ă-trĭsh′on, *n.* A
rubbing or grinding down.

at-tune′, 1 a-tiūn′; 2 ă-tūn′, *vt.* [AT-
TUNED′; AT-TUN′ING.] To tune; harmonize; adjust.

au′burn, 1 ŏ′barn; 2 ạ′burn. **I.** *a.* Reddish-brown; as, *auburn* hair. **II**[l]. *n.* A
reddish-brown color.

auc′tion, 1 ŏk′shạn; 2 ạc′shon. **I.** *vt.*
To sell by or at auction. **II.** *n.* A public sale of property to the highest bidder.
— **auc″tion-eer′,** 1 ŏk″shạn-ır′; 2 ạc′shon-ēr′.
I. *vt.* To sell by or at auction. **II.** *n.* One who
sells by or at auction.

au-da′cious, 1 o-dē′shŭs; 2 ạ-dā′shŭs, *a.*
Defiant of law or decorum; bold; shame-
less; insolent. **-ly,** *adv.* **-ness,** *n.*— **au-dac′-
i-ty,** 1 o-das′ı-tı; 2 ạ-dăç′ı-tı, *n.* [-TIES[z],
pl.] The being audacious; impudence; boldness; daring; recklessness.

au′di-bl(e[r], 1 ŏ′dı-bl; 2 ạ′dı-bl, *a.* Perceptible by the ear; loud enough to be
heard.— **au″di-bil′i-ty,** *n.* The state or fact
of being audible. **au′di-ble-ness**‡.— **au′di-
bly,** *adv.*

au′di-ence, 1 ŏ′dı-ens; 2 ạ′dı-ĕnç, *n.* An assembly of hearers; a hearing; conference.

au′di-phone, 1 ŏ′dı-fōn; 2 ạ′dı-fōn, *n.* An
instrument for enabling the deaf to hear:
(1) A device for directing sound through
the teeth, etc., to the auditory nerve; (2)
an electrical device, resembling the receiver of a telephone instrument, which
in churches, halls, etc., may be connected
to a common telephone circuit, of which
the transmitter is placed near the mouth
of the speaker, while the receiver communicates the sound directly to the ear
of the hearer.

au′dit, 1 ŏ′dıt; 2 ạ′dıt. **I**[d]. *vt.* To examine, adjust, and certify, as accounts. **II.**
n. An official examination of accounts;
a settlement; balance-sheet.

au′di-tor, *n.* **1.** One who audits accounts.
2. One who listens; a hearer.

au″di-to′ri-um, 1 ŏ′dı-tō′rı-um; 2 ạ′dı-
tō′rı-ŭm, *n.* [-RI-UMS[z] or -RI-A, *pl.*] An
audience-room, or a large building for
public meetings.

au′di-to-ry, 1 ŏ′dı-to-rı; 2 ạ′dı-to-ry. **I.** *a.*
Of or pertaining to hearing, to sense of
hearing, or to an audience-room. **II.** *n.*
[-RIES[z], *pl.*] An assembly of hearers; an
audience; auditorium.   [boring.

au′ger, 1 ŏ′gạr; 2 ạ′gẹr, *n.* A large tool for

aught, 1 ŏt; 2 ạt, *n.* Anything; any part or item.

aug-ment′d, 1 og-ment′; 2
ăg-mĕnt′, *vt. & vi.* To increase; enlarge; intensify.
— **aug″men-ta′tion,** *n.* The
act of augmenting; enlargement; increase; addition.—
aug-men′ta-tiv(e[s], *a.*
Having the quality or power
of augmenting.

aug′ment, 1 ŏg′ment; 2
ăg′mĕnt, *n.* **1.** In certain
languages, as the Greek,
a vowel or syllable prefixed
to a verb, or a lengthening
of the initial vowel, to mark
past time. **2‖.** Increase; enlargement.

au′gur, 1 ŏ′gạr; 2 ạ′gẹr, *n.* **I.** *vt. & vi.* To
prognosticate; divine; predict; betoken;
portend. **II.** *n.* A soothsayer; prophet.
— **au′gu-ral,** *a.* Of or pertaining to an au-
gur or an augury.— **au′gu-ry,** *n.* [-RIES[z], *pl.*]
The foretelling by signs or omens; divination;
prediction; portent or omen.

au-gust′, 1 o-gust′; 2 ạ-gŭst′, *a.* **1.** Majestic; imposing. **2.** Of high rank; venerable; eminent.

Au′gust, 1 ŏ′gust; 2 ạ′gŭst, *n.* The eighth
month of the year, containing 31 days.

auk, 1 ŏk; 2 ạk, *n.* A diving bird of
northern seas.

aunt, 1 ant; 2 ånt, *n.* A
father's or mother's sister or
uncle's wife.

au′ral, 1 ŏ′ral; 2 ạ′ral, *a.* Pertaining to the ear.

au′re-ole, 1 ŏ′rı-ōl; 2 ạ′re-ōl, *n.*
A halo or radiance, as the radiance around the sun, called the
corona, or in art around the head or the
entire figure of Christ or of a saint: known
also as the *aureola.*

Augers.
1. Twisted. 2.
Post-hole. 3. Ship.

Auk. ¹⁄₈

au'ri·cl(e**r**, 1 ō'rɪ-kl; 2 a̯'ri-cl, *n.* **1.** A chamber of the heart. **2.** The external ear; an ear-shaped part; an ear-trumpet. **– au·ric'u·lar,** 1 e-rɪk'yu-lẽr; 2 a̯-rĭc'yu-lar, *a.* **1.** Of or pertaining to the ear or the hearing; audible; confidential. **2.** Ear-shaped. **3.** Of or pertaining to an auricle.

au·rif'er·ous, 1 e-rɪf'er-ŭs; 2 a̯-rĭf'er-ŭs, *a.* Gold-bearing.   [diseases of the ear.

au'rist, 1 ō'rɪst; 2 a̯'rist, *n.* One who treats

au·ro'ra, 1 e-rō'rə; 2 a̯-rō'ra, *n.* **1.** A brilliant nocturnal radiance of the sky, in northern latitudes called **aurora borealis** or **northern lights,** in southern latitudes called **aurora australis** or **southern lights. 2.** The glow of early morning; dawn. **3.** [A-] The Roman goddess of dawn. **– au·ro'ral,** *a.* Pertaining to or like the dawn; dawning; roseate.

aus'pice, } 1 ôs'pɪs; 2 a̯s'piç, *n.* Favoring
aus'pisᵉ, } influence or guidance; patronage: commonly in the plural, *auspices.* **– aus·pi'cious,** 1 ôs-pɪsh'ŭs; 2 a̯s-pĭsh'ŭs, *a.* Of good omen; propitious; fortunate; happy. **-ly,** *adv.* **-ness,** *n.*

aus·tere', 1 ôs-tīr'; 2 a̯s-tēr', *a.* **1.** Severe; stern; strict; abstemious. **2.** Sour and astringent. **3.** Severely simple. **-ly,** *adv.* **-ness,** *n.* **– aus·ter'i·ty,** 1 ôs-ter'ɪ-tɪ; 2 a̯s-tẽr'i-ty, *n.* [-TIES**z**,] *pl.* Gravity or rigor; severe self-restraint; severity.   [torrid.

aus'tral, 1 ôs'trəl; 2 a̯s'tral, *a.* Southern.

Aus·tra'li·a, 1 ôs-trē'lɪ-ə; 2 a̯s-trā'li-a, *n.* British island continent in the Indian and Pacific oceans; 2,974,581 sq. m.

au·then'tic, 1 e-ꜩhen'tɪk; 2 a̯-then'tie, *a.* Authorized; trustworthy; genuine. **au·then'ti·cal**‡. **– au·then'ti·cal·ly,** *adv.* **au·then'ti·cate,** 1 e-ꜩhen'tɪ-kēt; 2 a̯-then'tĭ-cāt, *vt.* [-CAT**ᵉᴇᴅ**; -CAT**ᴵᴺɢ**.] To make or show to be authentic. **– au·then'ti·ca'tion,** *n.* An authenticating; attestation; confirmation. **– au''then·tic'i·ty,** 1 ō''ꜩhen-tɪs'ɪ-tɪ; 2 a̯''then-tiç'i-ty, *n.* The state of being authentic, authoritative, or genuine.

au'thor, 1 ō'ꜩhẽr; 2 a̯'thor, *n.* An originator; creator; the original writer, as of a book; also, one who makes a profession of writing. **– au'thor·ess,** *n.fem.:* now little used. **– au'thor·ship,** *n.* **1.** The state, quality, or function of an author. **2.** Origination or source.

au·thor'i·ty, 1 e-ꜩhor'ɪ-tɪ; 2 a̯-thŏr'i-ty, *n.* [-TIES**z**,] *pl.* **1.** The right to command; power; control. **2.** A ruler or rulers; that which commands confidence. **– au·thor'i·ta''tive**(e**s**, 1 -tē''tɪv; 2 -ta''tiv, *a.* Having authority; positive; commanding. **-ly,** *adv.*

au'thor·ize, 1 ō'ꜩhẽr-aɪz; 2 a̯'thor-īz, *vt.* [-IZED; -IZ''ING.] To confer authority upon; empower; commission; justify; sanc-

tion. **– au''thor·i·za'tion,** 1 ō''ꜩhẽr-ɪ-zē'shẽn; 2 a̯'thor-i-zā'shon, *n.* The act of authorizing; legal sanction.

au'to, 1 ō'to; 2 a̯'to, *n.* [Colloq.] An automobile: a common abbreviation.

au'to-, 1 ō'to-; 2 a̯'to-. From the Greek *autos,* self: a combining form, signifying action of, from within, by, or upon self.

au''to·bi·og'ra·phy, 1 ō''to-baɪ-og'rə-fɪ; 2 a̯''to-bī-ŏg'ra-fy, *n.* [-PHIES**z**, *pl.*] The story of one's life written by oneself. **– au''to·bi·og'ra·pher,** *n.* **– au''to·bi''o·graph'i·cal,** *a.* **au''to·bi''o·graph'ic**‡.

au'to·boat, au'to·bus, au'to·car, au'to·cy''cle, *n.* A boat, an omnibus, a car, or bicycle propelled by motor power within itself.

au'to·crat, 1 ō'to-krat; 2 a̯'to-erăt, *n.* A supreme and irresponsible ruler. **– au·toc'ra·cy,** 1 e-tŏk'rə-sɪ; 2 a̯-tŏc'ra-çy, *n.* [-CIES**z**, *pl.*] The rule of an autocrat; absolute government. **– au''to·crat'ic,** 1 ō''to-krat'ɪk; 2 a̯''to-erăt'ie, *a.* Irresponsible; despotic.

au'to·dyne, 1 ō'to-daɪn; 2 a̯'to-dȳn, *a. Radio.* Designating the manner of producing oscillations in a radiodetector to obtain beats.

au'to·graph, } 1 ō'to-graf; 2 a̯'to-gráf. **I.**
au'to·grafᶠ, } *a.* Written by one's own hand, as a note. **II.** *n.* Writing done with one's own hand; one's own signature. **– au''to·graph'ic,** 1 -graf'ɪk; 2 -gräf'ie, *a.* Of the nature of an autograph. **-i·cal**‡.

au''to·gy'ro, 1 ō''to-jaɪ'ro; 2 a̯''to-gȳ'ro, *n.* An aeroplane having horizontal rotary blades which act only as a means of lift and support.

au''to·hyp·no'sis, *n.* Self-hypnotism.

au'to·mat, 1 ō'to-mat; 2 a̯'to-măt, *n.* [U. S.] A restaurant where the service is automatic.

au''to·mat'ic, 1 ō''to-mat'ɪk; 2 a̯''to-măt'ie, *a.* Self-moving; acting mechanically; done without volition. **– au''to·mat'i·cal**‡.

au·tom'a·ton, 1 e-tom'ə-ten; 2 a̯-tŏm'a̯-tŏn, *n.* [-TONS or -TA, 1 -tə; 2 -ta, *pl.*] A machine that imitates actions of living beings.

au''to·mo·bile', 1 ō''to-mo-bīl'; 2 a̯''to-mo-bĭl', *n.* A self-propelling motor-driven vehicle; motor-car.

au''to·mo'bil·ist, *n.* One who owns, drives, or rides in an automobile.

au·ton'o·my, 1 e-ton'o-mɪ; 2 a̯-tŏn'o-my, *n.* [-MIES**z**, *pl.*] Self-government; practical independence with nominal subordination; self-determination, as of the will.

au'top·sy, 1 ō'top-sɪ; 2 a̯'tŏp-sy, *n.* [-SIES**z**, *pl.*] Examination of a human body after death.

au'tumn, 1 ō'tum; 2 a̯'tŭm, *n.* The third **au'tum**ᶠ, } season of the year: often called *fall.* **– au·tum'nal,** *a.* Of or like autumn; ripening; declining.

aux·il'ia·ry, 1 ogz-ɪl'ya-rɪ; 2 a̯gz-ĭl'ya-ry. **I.** *a.* Giving aid; subsidiary; accessory.

II. *n.* [-RIES^z, *pl.*] **1.** One who or that which aids, as one verb in the conjugation of another. **2.** *pl.* Allied troops. **aux·il'i·art.**

a·vail', 1 ə·vēl'; 2 a·vāl', *v.* **I.** *t.* **1.** To help; aid; profit. **2.** To take; secure. **II.** *i.* To be of advantage; suffice.

a·vail', *n.* **1.** Utility for a purpose; profit; benefit. **2.** *pl.* Proceeds.— **a·vail'a·bil'i·ty,** *n.* Fitness to serve a given purpose. **a·vail'a·bl(e·ness^zt.**— **a·vail'a·bl(e^r,** 1 ə·vēl'ə·bl; 2 a·vāl'a·bl, *a.* Capable of being used advantageously; usable; profitable; valid; at one's disposal.— **a·vail'a·bly,** *adv.*

av'a·lanch(e^r, 1 av'ə·lanċh; 2 ăv'a·lånch, *n.* The fall of a mass of snow or ice down a mountain-slope; also, the mass so falling.

av'a·rice, 1 av'ə·ris; 2 ăv'a·rĭç, *n.* Passion for riches; covetousness; cupidity.— **av"a·ri'cious,** 1 av'ə·rish'ŭs; 2 ăv'a·rish'ŭs, *a.* Greedy of gain; grasping; miserly. **-ly,** *adv.* **-ness,** *n.*

av'a·ris^s, } for riches; covetousness; cupidity.

a·vast', 1 ə·vast'; 2 a·vàst', *interj. Naut.* Stop! hold!

a·vaunt', 1 ə·vänt'; 2 a·vänt', *interj.* Begone! away!

A've, 1 ē'vi; 2 ä'vē, *n.* A prayer to the Virgin, beginning *Ave Maria* (Hail Mary).

a·venge', 1 ə·venj'; 2 a·vĕnġ', *v.* [A·VENGED'; A·VENG'ING.] **I.** *t.* To take vengeance for (an act) or in behalf of (a person). **II.** *i.* To take vengeance; exact satisfaction.— **a·veng'er,** *n.* One that avenges.

av'e·nue, 1 av'i·niu; 2 ăv'e·nū, *n.* A [broad road.

a·ver', 1 ə·vūr'; 2 a·vẽr', *vt.* [A·VERRED', A·VERD'^s; A·VER'ING.] To declare confidently; affirm; — **a·ver'ment,** *n.* Positive affirmation.

av'er·age, 1 av'ər·ıj; 2 ăv'ẽr·aġ. **I.** *vt.* [-AGED; -AG·ING.] To fix, or be the average of; apportion on the average; take as an average. **II.** *a.* Obtained by calculating the mean of several; medium; ordinary. **III.** *n.* **1.** The quotient of any sum divided by the number of its terms; the mean amount, quantity, or the like. **2.** The ordinary degree or amount; general type.

a·verse', 1 ə·vūrs'; 2 a·vẽrs', *a.* Opposed; unfavorable; reluctant: with *to.* **-ly,** *adv.* **-ness,** *n.*— **a·ver'sion,** 1 ə·vūr'shən; 2 a·vẽr'shon, *n.* **1.** Mental opposition; antipathy. **2.** That to which one is averse.

a·vert', 1 ə·vūrt'; 2 a·vẽrt', *vt.* **1.** To turn away or aside. **2.** To prevent; ward off.

a'vi·a·ry, 1 ē'vi·ĕ·ri; 2 ā'vi·å·ry, *n.* [-RIES^z, *pl.*] An enclosure for live birds.

a'vi·a"tor, 1 ē'vi·ē"tər or -tẽr; 2 ā'vi·ā"tor,

n. An operator of an aeroplane.— **a'vi·at"rice,** *n. fem.*— **a'vi·a'tion,** *n.* The art of flying.

a·vid'i·ty, 1 ə·vid'i·ti; 2 a·vĭd'i·ty, *n.* Eager appetite; greediness; chemical affinity.

av"o·ca'tion, 1 av"o·kē'shən; 2 ăv"o·cā'-shon, *n.* A transient occupation; diversion; business.

a·void'^d, 1 ə·void'; 2 a·vŏid', *vt.* To keep away from; shun; evade.— **a·void'a·bl(e^r,** *a.* — **a·void'a·bly,** *adv.*— **a·void'ance,** *n.* The act of avoiding or shunning.

av"oir·du·pois', 1 av"ər·du·pɔiz'; 2 ăv"or-du·pŏis', *n.* The ordinary system of weights of the United States and Great Britain. See WEIGHT.

a·vouch'^t, 1 ə·vauċh'; 2 a·vouch', *vt.* To affirm positively; proclaim; vouch for; acknowledge.

a·vow', 1 ə·vau'; 2 a·vow', *vt.* To declare openly; own or confess frankly; acknowledge.— **a·vow'al,** *n.* Open declaration; acknowledgment.— **a·vow'ed·ly,** *adv.* Confessedly; openly.

a·wait'^d, 1 ə·wēt'; 2 a·wāt', *vt.* **1.** To wait for; expect. **2.** To be ready or in store for.

a·wak(e', 1 ə·wēk'; 2 a·wāk', *v.* [A·WOKE, 1 ə·wōk'; 2 a·wōk', or A·WAKED; A·WAK'ING.] **I.** *t.* To rouse, as from sleep; excite; arouse; wake; waken. **II.** *i.* To cease to sleep; become awake or alert.

a·wake', 1 ə·wēk'; 2 a·wāk', *a.* Not asleep; vigilant.

a·wak'en, 1 ə·wēk'n; 2 a·wāk'n, *vt.* To awake.— **a·wak'en·ing,** 1 ə·wēk'n·ıŋ; 2 a·wāk'n·ing. **I.** *pa.* Stirring; exciting. **II.** *n.* The act of waking; an arousing; revival.

a·ward'^d, 1 ə·wōrd'; 2 a·wǎrd'. **I.** *vt.* To adjudge; apportion; assign; allow. **II.** *n.* A decision, as by a judge, umpire, or arbitrator, or that which is awarded.

a·ware', 1 ə·wâr'; 2 a·wâr', *a.* Knowing; conscious; cognizant.

a·way', 1 ə·wē'; 2 a·wā', *adv.* At or to a distance; off; absent; aside; on and on continuously.

aw(e^r, 1 ō; 2 a. **I.** *vt.* [AW(E)D^s; AW'ING or AWE'ING.] To impress with reverential fear. **II.** *n.* Reverential fear; dread mingled with veneration.— **aw'ful,** 1 ō'ful; 2 a'ful, *a.* **1.** Inspiring awe; majestic and terrible. **2.** Filled with awe.— **aw'ful·ly,** *adv.*— **aw'ful·ness,** *n.*— **awe'struck,** *pa.* Impressed with awe.

a·while', 1 ə·hwil'; 2 a·hwîl', *adv.* For a time. [the wing; flying.

a·wing', 1 ə·wiŋ'; 2 a·wíng', *adv. & a.* On

awk'ward, 1 ōk'wərd; 2 ak'wård, *a.* **1.** Ungraceful; unskilful; bungling. **2.** Em-

barrassing or perplexing; also, difficult or dangerous. **-ly,** *adv.* **-ness,** *n.*

awl, 1 ôl; 2 ạl, *n.* A pointed steel instrument for making small holes.

awn, 1 ôn; 2 ạn, *n.* A bristle of the beard of a grass, as of wheat or rye.

awn'ing, 1 ôn'ɪŋ; 2 ạn'ɪŋ, *n.* A roof=like shelter from sun or rain.

a-woke', 1 ə-wōk'; 2 a-wōk', *imp. & pp.* of AWAKE, *v.*

a-wry', 1 ə-rɑɪ'; 2 a-rī', *adv. & a.* Toward one side; crooked; oblique-ly; perversely.

ax, 1 aks; 2 ăks, *n.* An edge=tool
axe, for chopping, hewing, or the like.

Awns.

ax'i-al, 1 aks'i-əl; 2 ăks'i-al, *a.* Of, pertaining to, or constituting an axis.

ax'il, 1 aks'ɪl; 2 ăks'il, *n.* **1.** The angle which a leaf, branch, etc., makes with the stem at the junction. **2.** The axilla.

ax-il'la, 1 aks-ɪl'ə; 2 ăks-ɪl'a, *n.* The armpit.

ax'i-om, 1 aks'i-əm; 2 ăks'i-om, *n.* A self=evident or necessary truth.— **ax''i-o-mat'ic,** 1 aks''i-o-mat'ɪk; 2 ăks''i-o-măt'ic, *a.* Of the nature of an axiom; self=evident. **-i-cal‡. -i-cal-ly,** *adv.*

ax'is, 1 aks'ɪs; 2 ăks'is, *n.* [-ES, 1 -ɪz; 2 -ĕş, *pl.*] A line on which something rotates, or any central line or pivotal point.

ax'le, 1 aks'l; 2 ăks'l, *n.* A shaft or
ax'l‡, spindle on which a wheel turns.

ay, 1 ē; 2 ā, *adv.* Ever; always. **aye‡.**=
for **ay** or **aye,** forever; eternally.

aye, 1 ɑɪ; 2 ɪ. **I.** *n.* An expression of assent; affirmative vote. **II.** *adv.* Yes; yea. **ay‡.**

a-za'le-a, 1 ə-zē'lɪ-ə; 2 a-zā'le-a, *n.* A flowering shrub of the heath family.

az'o-, 1 az'o-; 2 ăz'o-. *Chem.* A combining form indicating the presence of nitrogen; as, *azo*-benzene: often used separately; as, the *azo* compounds.

a-zo'ic, 1 ə-zō'ɪk; 2 a-zō'ic. **I.** *a.* Without life; without organic remains, as fossils. **II.** *n. Geol.* The azoic age.

az'ote, 1 az ōt; 2 ăz'ōt, *n. Chem.* Nitrogen: old name.

Azalea.

Az'ra-el, 1 az'rɪ-el; 2 ăz'ra-ĕl, *n.* The angel of death: so called by Mohammedans.

az'ure, 1 az'ur; 2 ăzh'ur. **I.** *a.* Like the blue of the sky; sky=blue; cloudless; spotless. **II.** *n.* **1.** A clear sky=blue color or pigment. **2.** The clear sky; the blue vault of heaven.

az'ym, 1 az'ɪm; 2 ăz'ym, *n.* The
az'yme, Jewish paschal loaf; unleavened bread.

B

B, b, 1 bɪ; 2 bē, *n.* [BEES, B's, or *Bs,* 1 bɪz; 2 bēş, *pl.*] The second letter in the English alphabet.

baa, 1 bä; 2 bä. **I.** *vi.* To bleat as a sheep. **II.** *n.* The bleat of a sheep.

bab'ble, 1 bab'l; 2 băb'l. **I.** *vt. & vi.*
bab'l‡, [BAB'BLED, BAB'LD‡; BAB'BLING.] To utter unintelligibly; utter inarticulate sounds; tell thoughtlessly; murmur, as a stream; prattle. **II.** *n.* The rippling sound of a stream; prattle; gossip.— **bab'bler,** *n.*

babe, 1 bēb; 2 bāb, *n.* An infant; baby.

Ba'bel, 1 bē'bel; 2 bā'bĕl, *n.* **1.** The tower described in Gen. xi, 9; also, Babylon. **2.** [b- or B-] Confusion of many voices or languages; tumult.

bab-oon', 1 bab-ūn'; 2 băb-ōōn', *n.* A ferocious Old World monkey. See illus. in preceding column.

ba'by, 1 bē'bɪ; 2 bā'by. **I.** *vt.* [BA'BIED; BA'BY-ING.] To treat as a baby; play with. **II.** *n.* [BA'BIES‡, *pl.*] A child in arms; an infant.— **ba'by-hood,** *n.* The period of infancy; the condition of being a baby. — **ba'by-ish,** *a.* Like a baby; infantile.

Bab'y-lon, 1 bab'ɪ-lən; 2 băb'y-lon, *n.* **1.** An ancient splendid city, the capital of Babylonia; now in ruins. **2.** Any great city regarded as a seat of luxury and vice.

bac'cha-nal, 1 bak'ə-nal; 2 băc'a-nal, *n.* A votary of Bacchus; a drunken reveler. **bac'chant‡; bac'chante‡,** 1 bak'ant, 2 băc'ant *(fem.).*— **bac''cha-na'li-a,** 1 bak''a-nē'lɪ-ə; 2 bac'a-nā'li-a, *n. pl.* **1.** [B-] *Rom. Antiq.* A festival of Bacchus. **2.** Drunken revelries; orgies.— **bac''cha-na'li-an. I.** *a.* Of or like bacchanalia. **II.** *n.* A bacchanal.

Baboon. 1/48

1: **a**rtistic, **ā**rt; f**ă**t; f**ā**re; f**a**st; get; pr**ē**y; hit; pol**i**ce; **o**bey, g**ō**; n**o**t, **ǒ**r; full, r**ū**le; b**u**t, b**ū**rn.

2: ärt, āpe, fặt, fāre, fàst, whạt, ạll; mē gĕt, prey, fẽrn; hĭt, īce; ĭ=ē; ī=ē; gō, nŏt, ôr, wǒn,

Bac'chus, 1 bak'ŭs; 2 băc'ŭs, *n.* *Gr. & Rom. Myth.* God of wine and of the drama. **Di"o-ny'sos‡** [Gr.].

bach'e-lor, 1 bach'l-lẽr; 2 băch'e-lŏr, *n.* **1.** An unmarried man. **2.** One who has taken his first university degree.

ba-cil'lus, 1 bə-sil'us; 2 bă-çĭl'ŭs, *n.* [BA-CIL'LI, 1 -ai; 2 -ī, *pl.*] A microscopic organism; microbe.

backᵗ, 1 bak; 2 băk, *v.* **I.** *t.* **1.** To force backward. **2.** To stand; uphold; sustain; support. **3.** To mount; ride. **4.** To address or indorse. **II.** *i.* To move rearward.— **back'er,** *n.* A supporter.

back, *a.* **1.** In the rear; behind. **2.** Remote or retired. **3.** In arrears; overdue; not paid: as, *back* pay.

back, *n.* That side of the trunk nearest the spine, in man the hinder, in quadrupeds the upper part; the reverse or rear part of anything.

back, *adv.* To or toward the rear; behind; backward; in return; again.— **back'bite",** *vt.* To revile or traduce behind one's back.— **back'bit"er,** *n.* A secret slanderer. — **back'bit"ing,** *a. & n.*— **back'bone",** *n.* The spine or vertebral column; firmness; resolution.— **back'ground",** *n.* The part of a picture which is represented as behind the principal objects; a subordinate position; obscurity.— **back'hand"ed,** *a.* **1.** Delivered with the hand turned backward; equivocal; ironical. **2.** Sloping to the left, as writing.— **back'side",** *n.* The rear or hinder side.— **back'slide",** *vi.* To relapse; apostatize.— **back'slid'er,** *n.*— **back'woods",** *n.* Wild, sparsely settled districts.— **back'woods"-man,** *n.* [-MEN, *pl.*]

back'gam"mon, 1 bak'gam"ən; 2 băk'găm"on, *n.* A game played by two persons on a special board, the moves being determined by dice-throws.

back'ward, 1 bak'wẽrd; 2 băk'ward, *a.* **1.** Turned to the back or rear; reversed. **2.** Retiring; bashful. **3.** Slow; dull. **4.** Late; behindhand.— **back'ward,** *adv.* **back'-wards‡.**— **back'ward-ly,** *adv.*— **back'ward-ness,** *n.*

ba'con, 1 bē'kən; 2 bā'eon, *n.* The salted and dried or smoked flesh of the hog.

bac-te'ri-um, 1 bak-tī'ri-um; 2 băe-te'ri-ŭm, *n.* A microscopic organism; microbe. — **bac-te'ri-al,** *a.*— **bac-te'ri-cide,** *n.* An agent that destroys bacteria.— **bac-te'ri-cid"al,** *a.*— **bac-te"ri-ol'o-gy,** *n.* The department of science that treats of bacteria.

bad, 1 bad; 2 băd, **I.** *a.* [WORSE; WORST.] Opposite to *good*; vicious; wicked; deficient; incorrect; worthless; unfortunate; disagreeable. **II.** *n.* **1.** That which is

bad; those who are bad. **2.** A bad state or condition. **-ly,** *adv.* **-ness,** *n.*

bad(e)**,** 1 bad; 2 băd, *imp.* of BID, *v.*

badge, 1 baj; 2 bădg, *n.* A token or decoration. [or persecute; bait.

badg'er, 1 baj'ẽr; 2 bădg'er, *vt.* To worry

badg'er, *n.* A small, burrowing, nocturnal, and carnivorous mammal.

ba"di-nage', 1 ba"di-naʒ'; 2 bä"di-näzh', *n.* Playful raillery; banter.

American Badger. ¹⁄₂₄

baf'fle, 1 baf'l; **baf'l**ᶠ, 2 băf'l, *vt.* [BAF'FLED; BAF'LD**ᴾ**; BAF'FLING.] To defeat foil, or frustrate; circumvent.

bag, 1 bag; 2 băg. **I.** *vt. & vi.* [BAGGED, BAGD**ˢ**; BAG'GING.] **1.** To put into a bag; capture or kill, as game. **2.** To fill out like a bag; swell; bulge; sag. **II.** *n.* **1.** A sack or pouch; the udder of a cow. **2.** What a bag will hold; game bagged. — **bag'gy,** *a.* Like a bag; loose; bulging.

bag"a-tel(leᶠ**,** 1 bag"a-tel'; 2 băg"a-těl', *n.* **1.** A trifle. **2.** *Games.* A modification of billiards.

bag'gage, 1 bag'ij; 2 băg'ăg, *n.* **1.** [U. S.] The trunks, packages, etc., of a traveler; luggage. **2.** An army's movable equipment.

bag'ging, 1 bag'iŋ; 2 băg'ing, *n.* **1.** The putting into bags. **2.** Material for making bags.

bag'pipe, 1 bag'paip; 2 băg'pĭp, *n.* A Scotch musical wind-instrument. See illus. on page 374.— **bag'pip"er,** *n.*

bail, 1 bēl; 2 băl, *vt.* To admit to bail; set free on bail; also, to become surety for. — **bail-ee',** *n.* One who receives personal property in trust.— **bail'or,** *n.* One who delivers personal property in trust; one who gives bail for another. **bail'er‡.**— **bail'a-bl(e**ᶠ**,** *a.* Admitting of bail.

bail², *vt.* To provide with a bail or handle.

bail³, *vt. & vi.* **1.** To dip out, as water. **2.** To clear of water by dipping it out.

bail⁴, *n.* *Law.* **1.** One who becomes surety for another. **2.** The security given or agreed upon. **3.** Release, or privilege of release, on security for future appearance.

bail⁵, *n.* The handle of a pail.

bail⁶, *n.* **1.** A division in a stable. **2.** *Cricket.* One of the crosspieces of the wicket. [magistrate.

bai'lif(fᶠ**,** 1 bē'lif; 2 bā'lĭf, *n.* A local

bai'li-wick, 1 bē'li-wik; 2 bā'li-wĭk, *n.* The office, jurisdiction, or district of a bailiff.

bairn, 1 bärn; 2 bârn, *n.* [Scot.] A child.

baitd, 1 bēt; 2 bãt, *v.* **I.** *t.* **1.** To put a bait on or in. **2.** To feed while resting. **3.** To torment, as by setting dogs upon; harass; worry. **II.** *i.* To stop for rest and refreshment.

bait, *n.* **1.** Anything used to allure a fish or other animal. **2.** A luncheon.

baize, 1 bēz; 2 bãz, *n.* A napped woolen
baizᴿ, } fabric used as for table=covers.

bake, 1 bēk; 2 bāk, *vt. & vi.* [BAKED; BAK′EN‖; BAK′ING.] To cook or become cooked by dry and continued heat; vitrify by heat, as bricks; do the work of baking. — **bak′er,** *n.* One who bakes and sells bread, cake, etc.— **bak′er-y,** *n.* [-IES², *pl.*] A place for baking bread, cake. etc.— **bak′ing,** *n.* The act of baking; the quantity baked.

bal′ance, 1 bal′ɑns; 2 băl′ɑnç. **I.** *vt. & vi.* [BAL′ANCED; BAL′-ANC-ING.] **1.** To put into or be in equilib-rium; poise. **2.** To adjust or be ad-justed, as an account. **3.** To offset. **4.** To weigh; deliberate; ponder; hesitate. **II.** *n.* **1.** A pair of scales or other instrument for weighing. **2.** The act of balancing. **3.** The being in equilibrium; equipoise. **4.** Equality of debit and credit; also, the difference or excess on either side; re-mainder: surplus. **5.** The balance=wheel of a watch.

A Balance.

bal′co-ny, 1 bal′ko-nɪ; 2 băl′co-ny, *n.* [-NIES², *pl.*] A projected balustrade platform before a window; a tier of seats in a theater.

bald, 1 bēld; 2 bạld, *a.* Des-titute of hair or other natural covering; bare; unadorned. **-ly,** *adv.* **-ness,** *n.*

bal′der-dash, 1 bȯl′dɐr-dash; 2 bạl′der-dăsh, *n.* An empty and pretentious flow of words.

bale, 1 bēl; 2 bāl, *vt.* [BALED; BAL′ING.] To make into a bale.

A Balcony.

bale¹, *n.* A pack of goods prepared for transportation.

bale²‖, *n.* Calamity; ruin; sorrow; wo.— **bale′-ful,** *a.* Hurtful; malign; malignant; perni-cious.— **bale′ful-ly,** *adv.*

balkt, } 1 bȯk; 2 bạk, *v.* **I.** *t.* To disap-
baulk, } point; thwart; frustrate. **II.** *i.*

To stop and refuse to proceed.— **balk′y,** *a.* Disposed to balk.

balk, } *n.* **1.** An obstruction; hindrance;
baulk, } disappointment; defeat. **2.** A failure; miss; blunder. **3.** A stop; feint.

ball, 1 bȯl; 2 bạl, *vt. & vi.* To form into a ball or balls.— **ball bearing,** a bearing, as of an axle, that turns upon small steel balls: used also adjectively.

ball¹, *n.* Any round or spherical body; a game played with a ball. [ing.

ball², *n.* An evening assembly for danc-

bal′lad, 1 bal′ɑd; 2 băl′ad, *n.* Any popular narrative poem.

bal′last, 1 bal′ɑst; 2 băl′ast. **I**d. *vt.* To supply with ballast; steady. **II.** *n.* Any heavy substance in the hold of a vessel to steady it; solid filling for a railroad= bed.

bal′let, 1 bal′e; 2 băl′e, *n.* A dance by women on the stage; also, the dancers collectively.

bal-loon′, 1 ba-kūn′; 2 bă-lōōn′, *n.* A bag inflated with a light gas so that it rises and floats in the air.— **bal-loon′ist,** *n.* One who navigates a balloon; an aeronaut.

bal′lot, 1 bal′ɐt; 2 băl′ot. **I**d. *vi.* To vote by ballot. **II.** *n.* **1.** A written or printed ticket or a little ball for voting. **2.** The voting secretly by balls or tick-ets; number of votes so cast.

balm, 1 bäm; 2 bäm. **I.** *vt.* To anoint, as with balm. **II.** *n.* **1.** A soothing appli-cation. **2.** An aromatic resin; balsam; also, a tree or shrub that yields balm. — **balm′y,** *a.* **1.** Fragrant; aromatic. **2.** Healing; soothing; mild.

bal′sam, 1 bȯl′sɑm; 2 bạl′sam, *n.* **1.** An aromatic, oily prep-aration used for healing; balm. **2.** An aromatic resin, or the tree that yields it; also, a flowering plant.

bal′us-ter, 1 bal′us-tɐr; 2 băl′ŭs-ter, *n.* One of a set of small pillars that support a hand=rail and form with the hand= rail a balustrade.— **bal″us-trade′,** 1 bal′-us-trēd′; 2 băl′ŭs-trād′, *n.* A hand=rail supported by balus-ters.

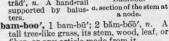

Bamboo.
a, section of the stem at a node.

bam-boo′, 1 bam-bū′; 2 băm-bōō′, *n.* A tall tree=like grass, its stem, wood, leaf, or fiber, or any article made from it.

ban, 1 ban; 2 băn. **I.** *vt. & vi.* [BANNED; BAND⁸; BAN′NING.] To place under a ban; issue a ban. **II.** *n.* **1.** A proclamation; a sentence of outlawry; oath. **2.** *pl.* A statement of intention to marry.

ba′nal, 1 ba′nal; 2 bä′nal, *a.* [F.] Meaningless from overuse; commonplace; trivial.—**ba-nal′i-ty,** *n.*

ba-nan′a, 1 ba-nan′a *or* ba-nä′na; 2 ba-năn′a *or* ba-nä′na, *n.* The fruit of a large herbaceous tropical plant; also, the plant.

band, 1 band; 2 bănd. **I**ᵈ. *vt.* **1.** To bind; unite. **2.** To stripe. **II.** *n.* **1.** A bond; a flat flexible strip used for binding. **2.** A company, as of musicians. **ban-dan′a‡.**

band′age, 1 band′ij; 2 bănd′ag. **I.** *vt.* [-AGED; -AG-ING.] To put a bandage on. **II.** *n.* A strip, as of soft cloth, used in dressing wounds, etc.; any band.

ban-dan′na, 1 ban-dan′a; 2 băn-dăn′a, *n.* A large, bright-colored handkerchief with spots or figures. **ban-dan′a‡.**

band′box″, 1 band′boks″; 2 bănd′bŏks″, *n.* A light round box for carrying hats.

ban′dit, 1 ban′dit; 2 băn′dit, *n.* [BAN′DITS or BAN-DIT′TI, *pl.*] A highwayman; brigand.

ban′dy, 1 ban′di; 2 băn′dy, *vt.* [BAN′DIED; BAN′DY-ING.] To exchange, as words, blows, etc.; knock or pass to and fro.

ban′dy, *a.* Crooked outward at the knees.— **ban′dy-legged″,** 1 -legd″; 2 -lĕgd′, *a.* Bow-legged.

ban′dy, *n.* [BAN′DIES², *pl.*] **1.** Hockey. **2.** A hockey-stick.

bane, 1 bēn; 2 băn. Anything noxious; a scourge; disease: poison.—**bane′ful,** *a.* Noxious; poisonous; deadly. **-ly,** *adv.*

bang¹, 1 baŋ; 2 băng, *vt. & vi.* To strike with a heavy sound; knock; beat.

bang², *vt.* To cut straight across, as the front hair. [whack, or explosion.]

bang¹, *n.* A sudden or noisy blow, thump,

bang², *n.* Front hair cut straight across.

bang, *adv.* With a violent blow or loud and sudden noise; abruptly.

ban′ian, } 1 ban′yan; 2 băn′yan, *n.* An
ban′yan, } East-Indian tree, which sends down from its branches roots that develop into accessory trunks; Indian fig.

ban′ish‡, 1 ban′ish; 2 băn′ish, *vt.* To expel from one's country; drive away; exile.— **ban′ish-ment,** *n.* Exile; expulsion.

ban′is-ter, 1 ban′is-tər; 2 băn′is-ter, *n.* **1.** A baluster. **2.** *pl.* A balustrade: a corruption.

ban′jo, 1 ban′jo; 2 băn′jo, *n.* A musical instrument of the guitar class. See illus. in next column.

bank¹‡, 1 baŋk; 2 băŋk. **I.** *vt. & vi.* To make into a bank; shelter under a bank; form banks. **II.** *n.* **1.** A long acclivity; a rising ground. **2.** The land at the edge of a watercourse. **3.** A shallow; shoal. — **bank′ing‡,** *n.* The forming of a ridge or mound; an embankment.

A Banjo.

bank²‡. **I.** *vt. & vi.* To deposit in a bank; do business as or with a bank or banker. **II.** *n.* An institution for lending, borrowing, issuing, or caring for money.— **bank′a-ble(e″,** *a.* Receivable by a bank.— **bank′er,** *n.* One engaged in banking.— **bank′ing‡,** *n.* The business of a bank or banker. — **bank′-note″,** *n.* **1.** A promissory note issued by a bank. **2.** A note payable at a bank.

bank′rupt, 1 baŋk′rupt; 2 băŋk′rŭpt. **I**ᵈ. *vt.* To make bankrupt. **II.** *a.* Unable to pay one's debts; insolvent. **III.** *n.* A person unable to pay his debts. — **bank′rupt-cy,** *n.* [-CIES²; *pl.*] The state of being bankrupt; failure; insolvency.

ban′ner, 1 ban′ər; 2 băn′er, *n.* A cloth bearing a device, suspended from a pole by a cross-bar; any flag or standard.

ban′nis-ter, *n.* Same as BANISTER.

ban′quet, 1 baŋ′kwet; 2 băn′kwĕt. **I**ᵈ. *vt. & vi.* To feast richly. **II.** *n.* A sumptuous feast.

bans, banns, 1 banz; 2 bănz, *n. pl.* of BAN.

ban′tam, 1 ban′təm; 2 băn′tam, *n.* A breed of small domestic fowl.

ban′ter, 1 ban′tər; 2 băn′ter. **I.** *vt.* To make sport of; joke. **II.** *n.* Good-humored ridicule.

bant′ling, 1 bant′liŋ; 2 bănt′lĭng, *n.* A young child; infant; youth.

ban′yan, *n.* Same as BANIAN.

ban″za-i′, 1 ban′za-i′ ;2 băn′zä-ī′, *interj.* [Jap.] Ten thousand years: the equivalent of "long live the Emperor !"

bap-tise′, *vt. & vi.* Same as BAPTIZE.

bap′tism, 1 bap′tizm; 2 băp′tĭzm, *n.* The act of baptizing; the sacramental use of water in acknowledgment of consecration to Christ.— **bap-tis′mal,** *a.* Pertaining to baptism.

Bap′tist, 1 bap′tist; 2 băp′tist, *n.* One holding that the only valid baptism is the immersion of a believer; originally, one who baptizes.

bap′tis-ter-y, } 1 bap′tis-tər-ı, -trı; 2 băp′-
bap′tis-try, } tis-ter-y, -try, *n.* [-TER-IES², -TRIES².] *pl.*] A reservoir or place in a church, for baptizing, as by immersion.

---

bap·tize′, 1 bap-taiz′; 2 băp-tīz′, *vt.* & *vi.*
[-TIZED′; -TIZ′ING.] To administer baptism to; administer baptism; christen; name; consecrate; dedicate. **bap·tise′**‡.

bar, 1 bär; 2 bär. **I.** *vt.* [BARRED, BARD⁸; BAR′RING.] **1.** To close; obstruct; prohibit; except. **2.** To mark with bars. **II.** *n.* **1.** A long, solid strip, as of wood or iron; rail; barrier; obstruction; a bank, as of sand in a harbor. **2.** An enclosed place in a court=room; a court of justice; the legal profession. **3.** A counter where liquors are sold. **4.** A stripe. **5.** *Mus.* The vertical line that divides a staff. [a bar[d]; make cutting.

barb, 1 bärb; 2 bärb, *vt.* To provide with barb[1], *n.* A backward=projecting point, as on a fish=hook, etc.

barb[2], *n.* A horse of the breed brought by the Moors from Barbary into Spain.

bar′ba·rous, 1 bär′ba-rus; 2 bär′ba-rŭs, *a.* Pertaining to or like a barbarian; uncultivated; rude; cruel; brutal; savage. **-ly,** *adv.* **-ness,** *n.*— **bar·ba′ri·an,** 1 bar-bē′rɪ-ən; 2 bär-bā′rɪ-an. **I.** *a.* Uncivilized; cruel; barbarous. **II.** *n.* An uncivilized, coarse, or rude person; anciently, a foreigner. — **bar·bar′ic,** 1 bɑr-bar′ɪk; 2 bär-bär′ɪc, *a.* Rudely splendid, striking, or picturesque.— **bar′ba·rism,** 1 bär′ba-rizm; 2 bär′ba-rĭṣm, *n.* **1.** The condition of a people between savagery and civilization; rudeness. **2.** A foreign or disapproved word or idiom.— **bar·bar′i·ty,** 1 bar-bar′ɪ-tɪ; 2 bär-bär′ɪ-ty, *n.* [-TIES², *pl.*] Brutal or barbarous conduct; a barbarous deed.

bar′be·cue, 1 bär′bɪ-kiū; 2 bär′be-eū. **bar·ba·cue,** ⸗ **I.** *vt.* [-CUED; -CU′ING.] To roast whole. **II.** *n.* An animal roasted whole as an ox.

bar′ber, 1 bär′bər; 2 bär′ber, *n.* One who cuts the hair, shaves the beard, etc.

bard, 1 bärd; 2 bärd, *n.* A Celtic minstrel; any poet.

bare[1], 1 bâr; 2 bâr, *vt.* [BARED, BAR′ING.] To lay bare; strip; reveal; expose.

bare[2]‡, *imp.* of BEAR, *v.*

bare, *a.* **1.** Uncovered; naked; empty; unsheathed. **2.** Scanty; simple; mere. **3.** Manifest; undisguised.— **bare′faced″,** *a.* Undisguised; impudent; audacious.— **bare′foot″,** *a.* & *adv.* With the feet bare.— **bare′ly,** *adv.* Only just; scarcely; boldly; plainly. — **bare′ness,** *n.*

bar′gain, 1 bär′gɪn; 2 bär′gĭn. **I.** *vt.* & *vi.* To trade; negotiate; stipulate. **II.** *n.* A mutual agreement, or that which is agreed upon; an advantageous transaction; an article low in price.

barge, 1 bärj; 2 bärǵ, *n.* A flat=bottomed freight=boat; a large boat for excursions.

bar′i·tone, *n.* Same as BARYTONE. [as a dog.

bark[1]‡, 1 bärk; 2 bärk, *vi.* To utter a bark,

bark[2]‡, *vt.* **1.** To scrape bark off; girdle. **2.** To abrade the skin of.

bark[1], *n.* A short, abrupt, explosive sound, as of a dog. [plant.

bark[2], *n.* The covering of a tree or other

bark[3], *n.* A three=masted vessel, square=rigged except for the mizzenmast, which is fore=and=aft rigged; in poetical use, any vessel. **barque**‡. [[U. S.] A bartender.

bar′keep″er, 1 bär′kīp″ər; 2 bär′kēp″er, *n.*

bar′ley, 1 bär′lɪ; 2 bär′ly, *n.* A hardy, bearded grain.

barm, 1 bärm; 2 bärm, *n.* The froth rising on fermented malt liquors; brewers' yeast.

barn, 1 bärn; 2 bärn, *n.* A storehouse for hay, etc.

bar′na·cle(e², 1 bär′na-kl; 2 bär′na-el, *n.* A shell=fish that clings to rocks, ships, etc.

ba·rom′e·ter, 1 ba-rŏm′ɪ-tər; 2 ba-rŏm′e-ter, *n.* An instrument for indicating atmospheric pressure: used for foretelling the weather, etc.— **bar″o·met′ric, -met′ri·cal,** *a.*— **bar″o·met′ri·cal·ly,** *adv.*— **ba·rom′e·try,** *n.* Scientific calculation of the tension and pressure of the air.

bar′on, 1 bär′an; 2 bär′on, *n.* A member of the lowest order of nobility in several European countries. — **bar′on·ess,** *n. fem.* — **ba·ro′ni·al,** *a.*— **bar′on·y,** *n.* [-IES², *pl.*] The rank, dignity, or domain of a baron.

bar′on·et, 1 bar′an-et; 2 bär′on-ĕt, *n.* An English title, below that of baron; also, the bearer of the title.— **bar′on·et·cy,** *n.* [-CIES², *pl.*] The rank of a baronet. **-ship**‡.

ba·rouche′, 1 ba-rūsh′; 2 ba-ruçh′, *n.* A four=wheeled carriage with folding top.

bar′rack, 1 bar′ək; 2 bär′ak, *n.* A building for the lodgment of soldiers; a roof for sheltering hay, etc.

bar′rage, 1 bär′ɪj; 2 bär′aǵ (*Fr.* 1 bȧ′rȧʒ), *n.* **1.** A barrier, as in a watercourse, to raise its depth. **2.** *Mil.* Concentrated fire on an enemy's line to prevent reenforcement.

bar′rel, 1 bar′el; 2 băr′ĕl. **I.** *vt.* [BAR′RELED or BAR′RELLED, BAR′RELD⁸; BAR′REL-ING or BAR′REL·LING.] To put or pack in a barrel. **II.** *n.* **1.** A round vessel, made with staves and hoops, about 31 inches high. **2.** As much as a barrel will hold. **3.** Something like a barrel, as the tube of a fire=arm, the body of an animal, etc.

Hay=barrack.

bar′ren, 1 bar′en; 2 băr′ĕn. **I.** *a.* Sterile; unproductive; dull. **II.** *n.* A tract of barren land. **-ly,** *adv.* **-ness,** *n.*

bar′ri-cade′, 1 bar′ï-kēd′; 2 băr′ï-kād′. **I.** *vt.* [-CAD′ED⁴; -CAD′ING.] To defend with a barricade. **II.** *n.* A defensive barrier closing a passage. **bar′ri-ca′dọ.**

bar′ri-er, 1 bar′ï-ər; 2 băr′ï-er, *n.* Something that obstructs progress; a boundary; obstruction.

bar′ris-ter, 1 bar′ıs-tər; 2 băr′is-ter, *n. Eng. Law.* An advocate; lawyer; attorney.

bar′room″, 1 băr′rūm″; 2 băr′rōōm″, *n.* A room where liquors and refreshments are served. [vehicle propelled by hand.

bar′row¹, 1 bar′o; 2 băr′o, *n.* A small

bar′row², *n.* A burial-mound; cairn; heap.

bar′tend″er, 1 băr′tend″ər; 2 băr′tĕnd″er, *n.* One who serves liquors, etc., at a bar.

bar′ter, 1 băr′tər; 2 băr′ter. **I.** *vt. & vi.* To exchange; trade by exchange of commodities. **II.** *n.* Exchanging of commodities, or a commodity given in exchange.

bar′y-tone, 1 bar′ı-tōn; 2 băr′y-tōn. **I.** *a. Mus.* Having a register higher than bass and lower than tenor. **II.** *n. Mus.* A barytone male voice, or a person having such a voice.

ba′sal, 1 bē′sal; 2 bā′sal, *a.* Pertaining to, of, or at the base; fundamental.

ba-salt′, 1 ba-sölt′; 2 ba-sạlt′, *n.* A dark-colored igneous rock, often of columnar structure.— **ba-salt′ïc,** *a.*

base, 1 bēs; 2 bās, *vt.* [BASED; BAS′ING.] To place upon a base or basis; establish.

base, *a.* **1.** Low; ignoble; abject. **2.** *Mus.* Bass. **-ly,** *adv.* **-ness,** *n.*— **base′-born″,** *a.* Born out of wedlock; also, of low birth; plebeian.

base, *n.* **1.** The lowest part; foundation. **2.** *Mus.* Bass. **3.** *Chem.* A compound capable of forming a salt with an acid. **4.** *Mil.* A basis of operations or of supplies. **5.** *Gram.* The form of a word used in making derivatives, as by adding suffixes. — **base′less,** *a.* Without foundation; unfounded; groundless.— **base′ment,** *n.* The ground floor of a building, beneath the principal story.

base′ball″, 1 bēs′bôl″; 2 bās′bạl″, *n.* A game played with bat and ball about four bases.

ba-shaw′, 1 ba-shô′; 2 ba-shô′, *n.* See PASHA.

bash′ful, 1 bash′ful; 2 băsh′fụl, *a.* Shrinking from notice; shy; timid. **-ly,** *adv.* **-ness,** *n.* [to, or like a base.

ba′sic, 1 bē′sık; 2 bā′sïe, *a.* Of, pertaining

bas′i-lisk, 1 bas′ı-lisk; 2 băs′i-lĭsk, *n.* **1.** A fabled deadly serpent. **2.** A crested lizard.

ba′sin, 1 bē′sn; 2 bā′sn, *n.* A shallow vessel, with sloping sides; any similar cavity; a pond; dock; hollow.

ba′sis, 1 bē′sıs; 2 bā′sis, *n.* [BA′SES, bē′sīz; 2 bā′sĕs, *pl.*] A support; foundation; chief ingredient. [as in warmth.

bask⁴, 1 busk; 2 bȧsk, *vi.* To luxuriate.

bas′ket, 1 bas′ket; 2 bás′kĕt, *n.* **1.** A vessel of interwoven twigs, splints, or strips. **2.** What a basket will hold. **bas′ket-ful†.— bas′ket-ball,** *n.* A game in which opposing teams of five players endeavor to score against one another by tossing a ball into basket-like goals.

bas″-re-lief′, 1 bä″-rı-lïf′; 2 bä″-re-lëf′, *n.* Sculpture in which the figure projects but slï₂tly from the background. **bass″-re-lief′†.** [or compass.

bass, 1 bēs; 2 bās, *a. Mus.* Low in tone

bass¹, 1 bas; 2 bás, *n.* A food-fish.

bass², 1 bēs; 2 bās, *n. Mus.* The lowest tones of the male voice or of an instrument.

bass³, 1 bus; 2 bás, *n.* Same as BASSWOOD.

bas-soon′, 1 ba-sūn′; 2 bă-sōōn′, *n.* A wooden reed-instrument with curved mouthpiece.

bas″so-ri-lie′vo, 1 bä″so-rï-lyē′vo; 2 bä″so-rï-lyē′vo, *n.* Same as BAS-RELIEF.

bass vi′ol, 1 bēs vai′al; 2 bás vi′ol. A large stringed instrument of the violin type.

bass′wood″, 1 bas′wud″; 2 bás′wŏŏd″, *n.* The American linden- or whitewood-tree. **bass†.**

bast, 1 bust; 2 bȧst, *n.* The fibrous inner bark of trees; also, cordage, etc., made from it.

bas′tard, 1 bas′tərd; 2 băs′tard. **I.** *a.* Illegitimate; spurious. **II.** *n.* An illegitimate child.— **bas′tard-y,** *n.* Illegitimacy.

baste¹, 1 bast; 2 bȧst, *vt.* [BAST′ED⁴; BAST′ING.] To sew loosely together.

baste²ᵈ, *vt.* To cover with gravy or the like while cooking.

bas″ti-na′do, 1 bas″tı-nē′do; 2 băs″ti-nā′do. **I.** *vt.* To beat on the soles of the feet; flog. **bas″ti-nade′†.** **II.** *n.* A beating on the soles of the feet.

bas′tion, 1 bas′chan; 2 băs′chon, *n.* A projecting part of a fortification.

bat, 1 bat; 2 băt, *vt. & vi.* [BAT′TED⁴; BAT′TING.] To strike with or as with a bat.

bat¹, *n.* A stick for striking the ball in baseball, cricket, etc.

bat², *n.* A nocturnal mammal with limbs connected by a membrane to form wings.

batch, ⟩1 bach; 2 băch, **bach²,** ⟩*n.* The dough for one baking or the bread, etc., baked; quantity made or done at one time.

Bat.¹/₆

1: ə = final; ı = habıt; aısle; au = out; oıl; ıū = feud; chin; go; ŋ = sing; thin, this.
2: wọlf, dọ; bŏŏk, bŏŏt; fụll, rụle, cūre, bŭt, bûrn; ōil, bŏy; ḡo, ḡem; iŋk; thin, this.

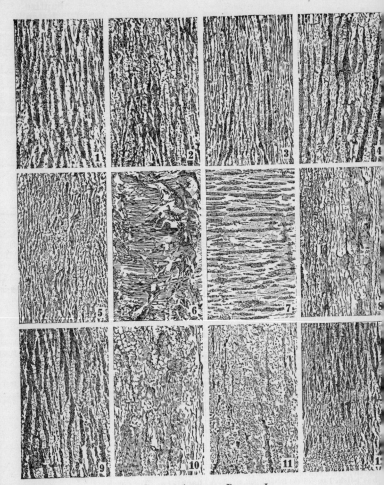

COMMON AMERICAN BARKS.—I.

1. Basswood. 2. White elm. 3. White cedar. 4. White oak. 5. Box-elder. 6. Yell
birch. 7. Sweet cherry. 8. Red maple. 9. Black walnut. 10. Horse-chestnut. 11. Red p
12. White ash.

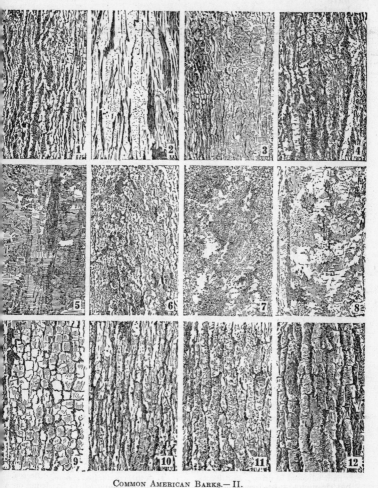

COMMON AMERICAN BARKS.— II.

1. Brittle willow.   2. Shagbark hickory.   3. Honey-locust.   4. Chestnut.   5. Blue beech.   6.
hite spruce.   7. Great laurel.   8. Wich-hazel.   9. Persimmon.   10. Fragrant crab.   11. Hemlock.
. Sassafras.

bate, 1 bēt; 2 băt, *vt.* [BAT′ED^d; BAT′ING.] **1.** To lessen; moderate; abate. **2.** To deduct.

ba-teau′, 1 bȧ-tō′; 2 bä-tō′, *n.* [BA-TEAUX′, 1 -tōz′; 2 -tōz′, *pl.*] A flat=bottomed boat; a pontoon for a bridge.

bath, 1 bȧth; 2 bȧth, *n.* A bathing; a building, room, or receptacle for bathing.

bathe, 1 bēth; 2 bāth, *v.* [BATHED; BATH′-ING.] **I.** *t.* To wash or immerse; wet; lave. **II.** *i.* To take a bath.—**bath′er,** *n.*

ba′thos, 1 bē′thos; 2 bā′thŏs, *n.* A ridiculous descent from the lofty to the commonplace in discourse.

bath′y-sphere, 1 băth′i-sfīr; 2 băth′y-sfēr, *n.* A diving=chamber for deep=sea observation.

bat′on, 1 bat′ən; 2 băt′on, *n.* A short staff or rod.

bat-tal′ion, 1 ba-tal′yən; 2 bă-tăl′yon, *n.* Two or more companies of infantry; a body of troops.

bat′ten¹, 1 bat′n; 2 băt′n, *vt. & vi.* To make or grow fat; gratify a craving, as for cruelty.

bat′ten², *vt.* To put battens on.

bat′ten, *n.* A narrow strip of wood; a cleat.

bat′ter, 1 bat′ər; 2 băt′ėr, *vt. & vi.* To strike repeatedly; beat; dent; mar; deface.

bat′ter¹, *n.* A thick liquid mixture beaten up for use in cookery.

bat′ter², *n.* A heavy blow; also, repeated blows, or the condition resulting from them.

bat′ter³, *n.* One who uses the bat, as in baseball. **bats′man**‡.

bat′ter-ing-ram″, 1 bat′ər-iŋ-ram″; 2 băt′ėr-ing-răm″, *n.* A long beam, with heavy head, anciently used to beat down gates and walls.

bat′ter-y, 1 bat′ər-i; 2 băt′ėr-y, *n.* [-IES^z, *pl.*] **1.** *Mil.* (1) An earthwork enclosing cannon. (2) A company of artillerymen or their guns and other equipment. **2.** *Elec.* A group of cells, dynamos, etc. **3.** *Law.* The unlawful use of force by one person upon another.

Battering=ram.

bat′ting, 1 bat′iŋ; 2 băt′ing, *n.* Cotton or wool prepared in sheets; also, the act of batting in any sense of the verb.

bat′tle, 1 bat′l; 2 băt′l. **I.** *vi.* [BAT′TL(E)D^p; **bat′tl^p,** BAT′TLING.] To fight; struggle; strive. **II.** *n.* **1.** A combat between hostile armies or fleets; a fight; conflict; contest. **2**‖. Arms, or an armed force.

bat′tle-dore, 1 bat′l-dōr; 2 băt′l-dōr, *n.* A light bat used to drive a shuttlecock.

bat′tle-ment, 1 bat′l-ment *or* -mənt; 2 băt′l-ment, *n.* An indented parapet.

bau′ble(e^p, 1 bɔ′bl; 2 bạ′bl, *n.* A worthless, showy trinket; toy; wand of a court jester. **baw′ble**‡.

baulk, *v. & n.* Same as BALK.

bawl, 1 bɔl; 2 bạl, *vt. & vi.* To cry or wail loudly.

bay, 1 bē; 2 bā, *vt. & vi.* To bark at; drive; bark hoarsely.

bay, *a.* Red=brown: said of horses.

bay¹, *n.* **1.** A body of water partly enclosed by land; an arm of the sea. **2.** Any recess. **3.** A coarse mahogany. **bay′=wood″**‡.

bay², *n.* **1.** The laurel=tree. **bay′=tree″**‡. **2.** A laurel=wreath; poetic renown.

bay³, *n.* A bay horse.

bay⁴, *n.* **1.** A deep bark, as of dogs in hunting. **2.** The situation of a hunted creature compelled to turn on its pursuers.

bay⁵, *n.* **1.** A large space in a barn for hay. **2.** A division between piers or columns.

bay′ber″ry, 1 bē′ber″i; 2 bā′ber″y, *n.* One of various trees, as the wax=myrtle, etc.

bay′o-net, 1 bē′o-net; 2 bā′o-nĕt. **I**^d. *vt.* To stab or charge with a bayonet. **II.** *n.* A dagger=weapon attachable to a rifle.

bay′ou, 1 bai′ū; 2 bī′ụ, *n.* A sluggish inlet or outlet of a lake or bay.

bay win′dow, *Arch.* A projecting window=structure of angular plan.

ba-zoo′ka, 1 ba-zū′ka; 2 ba-zōō′ka, *n.* **1.** A trombone=type wind=instrument. **2.** A long, tubular weapon from which explosive rockets are fired.

ba-zaar′, 1 ba-zär′; 2 ba-zär′, *n.* **1.** An Oriental market=place or range of shops. **2.** A fancy fair for charity. **ba-zar′,**

be, 1 bī; 2 bē, *vi.* To exist; happen.

be-, *prefix.* By; near; on; about. *Be-* forms numerous compounds which are readily understood by combining the meaning of the prefix with that of the second element; as, *be*numb, *be*times.

beach, 1 bīch; 2 bēch. **I**^t. *vt.* To run or haul up on a beach. **II.** *n.* The sloping shore of a body of water; a wave=washed margin.

bea′con, 1 bī′kən; 2 bē′con. **I.** *vt. & vi.* To light up; shine; guide by a light. **II.** *n.* A prominent object, set up as a guide or warning to mariners; a signal=fire or =light.

bead, 1 bīd; 2 bēd. **I**^d. *vt. & vi.* To decorate with or as with beads; collect in beads; bubble; foam; sparkle. **II.** *n.* **1.** A little perforated sphere, or the like, intended to be strung on a thread. **2.** *pl.* A rosary; hence, prayers.

Beacon.

1: ȧrtistic, ärt; fat, fâre; fast; get, prēy; hit, police; obey, gō; net, ȯr; full, rūle; but, būrn.

2: ärt, āpe, făt, fâre, fȧst, whạt, ạll; mē, gĕt, prey, fērn; hĭt, īce; ï=ē; ï=ĕ; gō, nŏt, ȯr, wȯn,

3. A bubble or bubbles of gas on a liquid; froth; a knob used as the front sight of a gun. **4.** A small convex molding.—**bead′y,** a.

bea′dl(eᴿ, 1 bī′dl; 2 bē′dl, n. [Eng.] A petty parish or university official; a crier or messenger of a court.

bea′gl(eᴿ, 1 bī′gl; 2 bē′gl, n. **1.** A small hunting-hound. **2.** A constable.

beak, 1 bīk; 2 bēk, n. The projecting jaws of a bird; bill; also, the prow of a ship.

beak′er, 1 bīk′ər; 2 bēk′er, n. A large goblet.

beam, 1 bīm; 2 bēm, v. **I.** t. **1.** To send out as rays of light. **2.** To furnish with beams. **3.** To burnish. **II.** i. To shine; be radiant.—**beam′ing,** pa. Radiant; bright; cheerful.

beam, n. **1.** A long horizontal piece of wood, stone, or metal in the frame of a building. **2.** The bar of a balance. **3.** A ray of light, or a group of rays.—**beam′y,** 1 bīm′ɪ; 2 bēm′y, a. **1.** Radiant; joyous; gladsome. **2.** Like a beam; massive.

bean, 1 bīn; 2 bēn, n. The oval edible seed of certain plants; a plant that bears beans.

bear¹, 1 bār; 2 bâr, vt. & vi. [BORE or BARE‖; BORNE or BORN; BEAR′ING.] **1.** To support at rest; sustain. **2.** To support in motion; carry. **3.** To show; display; exhibit. **4.** To suffer; endure; hold; maintain. **5.** To produce; give birth to; yield fruit. **6.** To conduct (oneself); behave.—**bear′a-bl(e**ᴿ, a. Capable of being borne.—**bear′a-bly,** adv.—**bear′er,** n. One who or that which bears or has in possession.—**bear′ing,** n. **1.** The act of sustaining, producing, etc. **2.** Deportment; manner. **3.** Relation; meaning. **4.** A part (of a machine) that rests on something, or on which something rests. **5.** A heraldic device.

bear², vt. [U. S.] Finance. To depress the price of (stocks, etc.).

bear, n. **1.** A large carnivorous animal, with massive body and short tail. **2.** A speculator who seeks to depress prices. **3.** One of two constellations: the Great Bear or Little Bear. See URSA MAJOR, etc.—**bear′ish,** a. Like a bear; rough; surly.

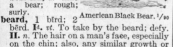

American Black Bear. ¹/₉₀

beard, 1 bīrd; 2 bērd. **I**ᵈ. vt. To take by the beard; defy. **II.** n. The hair on a man's face, especially on the chin; also, any similar growth or appendage; an awn, as of grass; the barb of an arrow, etc.—**beard′ed,** a. Having a beard.—**beard′less,** a. Without a beard; young; inexperienced.

beast, 1 bīst; 2 bēst, n. **1.** One of the inferior animals; a quadruped. **2.** A rude or filthy person.—**beast′ly,** a.

beat, 1 bīt; 2 bēt, v. [BEAT; BEAT′EN or BEAT; BEAT′ING.] **I.** t. **1.** To strike repeatedly. **2.** To excel; overcome; vanquish. **3.** To range over in hunting. **II.** i. **1.** To strike repeated blows; throb; pulsate. **2.** Naut. To work up against the wind by tacking. **3.** To conquer; win.

beat, 1 bīt; 2 bēt, n. **1.** A stroke or blow; a pulsation. **2.** A space regularly traversed, as by a sentry or a policeman.

be-at′i-fy, 1 bɪ-at′ɪ-faɪ; 2 be-ăt′i-fî, vt. [-FIED; -FY′ING.] To make supremely happy; enroll among the saints.—**be″a-tif′ic,** 1 bī″ə-tif′ɪk; 2 bē″a-tif′ie, a. Imparting or expressing supreme happiness; blissful.—**be-at′i-fi-ca′tion,** 1 bɪ-at″ɪ-fɪ-kē′shən; 2 be-ăt″i-fi-câ′shon, n. The act of blessing, or the state of being blessed.

be-at′i-tude, 1 bɪ-at′ɪ-tiūd; 2 be-ăt′i-tūd, n. Supreme blessedness; a declaration of blessedness, as in Matt. v, 3-11.

beau, 1 bō; 2 bô, n. [BEAUS or BEAUX, 1 bōz; 2 bôṣ, pl.] **1.** A ladies' man; a dandy. **2.** [Colloq.] An escort or lover.

beau′-i-de′al, 1 bō″-ɑi-dī′al; 2 bô″-î-dē′al, n. The highest conceivable type of excellence.

beau′te-ous, 1 biū′tɪ-us; 2 bū′te-ŭs, a.
beu′te-ousᴿ, ⎱ Full of beauty; beautiful. **-ly,** adv. **-ness,** n.

beau′ti-ful, 1 biū′tɪ-ful; 2 bū′ti-ful, a.
beu′ti-fulᴿ, ⎱ Possessing conspicuous beauty; fair. **-ly,** adv.—**beau′ti-fy,** 1 biū′tɪ-faɪ; 2 bū′ti-fî, vt. & vi. [-FIED; -FY′ING.] To make or grow beautiful; adorn.

beau′ty, 1 biū′tɪ; 2 bū′ty, n. [BEAU′TIES ᶻ,
beu′tyᴿ, ⎱ pl.] **1.** That which charms the eye; harmonious perfection of form. **2.** A person or thing that is beautiful.

beaux, 1 bōz; 2 bôz, n. Plural of BEAU.

bea′ver¹, 1 bī′vər; 2 bē′ver, n. **1.** An aquatic rodent noted for skill in damming streams, and valued for its fur. **2.** The fur of the beaver, or a hat made of it; a high silk hat.

Beaver. ¹/₆₀

bea′ver², n. A movable piece of medieval armor covering the lower part of the face.

be-calm′, 1 bɪ-kām′; 2 be-căm′, vt. To

make calm; still; delay (a ship, etc.), by a calm. [BECOME, *v.*

be-came', 1 bɪ-kām'; 2 be-cām', *imp.* of **be-cause'**, 1 bɪ-kôz'; 2 be-caṣ'. **I.** *adv.* By reason (of). **II.** *conj.* For the reason that since.

beck¹, 1 bek; 2 bĕk, *vt. & vi.* To beckon.

beck¹, *n.* A nod or other sign of wish or command. [which it runs.

beck², *n.* A small brook, or the valley in

beck'on, 1 bek'n; 2 bĕk'n, *v.* **I.** *t.* To summon by gesture. **II.** *i.* To signal, as with the hand.

be-come', 1 bɪ-kum'; 2 be-cŏm', *v.* [BE-**be-cum**ᵖ, ʃ CAME'; BE-COME'; BE-COM'ING.] **I.** *t.* **1.** To accord with; befit. **2.** To set off; grace. **II.** *i.* **1.** To come to a state or condition; begin; come to pass. **2.** To be fit or suitable.

be-com'ing, 1 bɪ-kum'ɪŋ; 2 be-cŏm'ing, **be-cum'ing**ᵖ, ʃ *pa.* Appropriate; suitable; pleasing. **-ly,** *adv.*

Becque"rel' rays, 1 bek"rel'; 2 bĕc"rĕl'. Invisible rays emitted by uranium and polonium.

bed, 1 bed; 2 bĕd. **I.** *vt. & vi.* [BED'DEDᵈ; BED'DING.] To put to bed; plant in a bed; sleep. **II.** *n.* **1.** Something for sleeping in or on; a couch. **2.** A place for plants; a layer; stratum; foundation or support. **—bed'cham"ber,** *n.* A sleeping-room.

be-dab'ble, 1 bɪ-dab'l; 2 be-dăb'l, *vt.* **be-dab'l**ᵖ, ʃ [-BLED, -BLDᵖ; -BLING.] To sprinkle; splash; dabble.

be-daub', 1 bɪ-dôb'; 2 be-dạb', *vt.* To smear; soil; abuse; bedizen; flatter.

bed'ding, 1 bed'ing; 2 bĕd'ing, *n.* Furnishings for a bedstead; materials for a bed; a foundation.

be-deck'ᵗ, 1 bɪ-dek'; 2 be-dĕk', *vt.* To deck; adorn. [ten with or as with dew.

be-dew', 1 bɪ-diū'; 2 be-dū', *vt.* To moisten.

be-dim', 1 bɪ-dim'; 2 be-dĭm', *vt.* [BE-DIMMED', BE-DIMDᵈ'ˢ; BE-DIM'MING.] To make dim; obscure.

be-diz'en, 1 bɪ-diz'n; 2 be-dĭz'n, *vt.* To dress out; adorn with tawdry splendor. **be-diz'zen**‡.

bed'lam, 1 bed'ləm; 2 bĕd'lam, *n.* An excited crowd; an uproar; an insane asylum. **—bed'lam-ite,** *n.* A lunatic.

Bed'ou-in, 1 bed'u-ɪn; 2 bĕd'u-in, *n.* A nomadic Arab; nomad; vagabond. **Bed'u-in**‡.

be-drag'gle, 1 bɪ-drag'l; 2 be-drăg'l, *vt. &* **be-drag'l**ᵖ, ʃ *vi.* [-GLED, -GLDᵖ; -GLING.] To wet or soil, as by dragging.

bed'rid"den, 1 bed'rid"n; 2 bĕd'rĭd"n, *a.* **bed'rid"n**ᵖ, ʃ Confined to bed by sickness or weakness. **bed'rid"**‡.

bed'room", 1 bed'rūm'; 2 bĕd'rōōm', *n.* A bedchamber.

bed'stead, ʃ 1 bed'sted; 2 bĕd'stĕd, *n.* A **bed'sted**ˢ, ʃ framework for supporting a mattress, bedding, etc.

bee, 1 bī; 2 bē, *n.* **1.** A social honey-gathering insect. **2.** A gathering of neighbors or friends for work or amusement.**—bee'hive"**, *n.* A hive for bees; a place filled with busy workers.—

bee-line, *n.* The shortest course from one place to another.

beech, 1 bīch; 2 bēch, *n.* A forest tree of the oak family, with hard wood. **beech'en**, *a.* Pertaining to the beech-tree or its wood. **beech'nut"**, *n.* The — Leaves and Fruit of the English Beech. edible triangular nut, the fruit of the beech. **beech'mast"**‡.

beef, 1 bīf; 2 bēf, *n.* **1.** The flesh of a slaughtered adult bovine animal. **2.** [BEEVES, *pl.*] Any adult bovine animal. **—bully-beef,** *n.* Canned or pickled beef. **beef'steak"**, 1 bīf'stēk'; 2 bēf'stāk', *n.* A slice of beef for broiling.

been, 1 bin *or* bīn; 2 bin *or* bēn, *pp.* of BE, *v.*

beer, 1 bīr; 2 bēr, *n.* An alcoholic fermented liquor.

bees'wax", 1 bīz'waks"; 2 bēṣ'wăks", *n.* The wax of which honey-bees make their comb

beet, 1 bīt; 2 bēt, *n.* The fleshy edible root of a biennial herb; also, the plant.

bee'tleᵖ¹, 1 bī'tl; 2 bē'tl, *vi.* [BEE'TL(E)Dᵖ; BEE'TLING.] To jut out; overhang.

bee'tle², *vt.* To beat or stamp with or as with a beetle, mallet, etc.

bee'tle³, *a.* Overhanging; prominent; as, a *beetle*brow. **bee'tling**‡.**—bee'tle-browed"**,*a.*

bee'tle¹, *n.* Any coleopterous insect.

bee'tle², *n.* A heavy wooden mallet.

beeves, 1 bīvz; 2 bēvṣ, *n.* Plural of BEEF.

be-fall', 1 bɪ-fôl'; 2 be-fạl', *v.* [BE-FELL', BE-FEL'ᵖ; BE-FEL'; BE-FĕL'; BE-FALL'EN, BE-FAL'Nᵖ; BE-FALL'ING.] **I.** *t.* To occur or happen to. **II.** *i.* To happen.

be-fell', 1 bɪ-fel'; 2 be-fĕl', *imp.* of BEFALL, *v.*

be-fit', 1 bɪ-fit'; 2 be-fĭt', *vt.* [BE-FIT'TEDᵈ; BE-FIT'TING.] To be suitable for; be worthy of.**—be-fit'ting**, *pa.* Becoming; suitable.

be-fog', 1 bɪ-fog'; 2 be-fŏg', *vt.* [BE-FOGGED', BE-FOGDᵈ'ˢ; BE-FOG'GING.] To envelop in fog; confuse.

be-fore', 1 bı-fōr'; 2 be-fōr'. **I.** *adv.* In front; ahead; earlier. **II.** *prep.* **1.** In front of; ahead of; anterior to; in advance of; in preference to. **2.** Face to face with; in the presence of. **III.** *conj.* Rather than; sooner than.

be-fore'hand", 1 bı-fōr'hand"; 2 be-fōr'hănd". **I.** *a.* Being in easy circumstances; forehanded. **II.** *adv.* In advance; before the time.

be-friend'd, 1 bı-frend'; 2 be-frĕnd', *vt.*
be-frend'r, To be a friend to; stand by; help in time of need.

beg, 1 beg; 2 bĕg, *vt.* & *vi.* [BEGGED, BEGD⁵; BEG'GING.] To ask pleadingly; entreat; supplicate; beseech; ask alms.— **to beg the question**, to take for granted the matter in dispute.

be-gan', 1 bı-gan'; 2 be-găn', *imp.* of BEGIN, *v.*

be-gat', 1 bı-gat'; 2 be-găt', *imp.* of BEGET, *v.*

be-get', 1 bı-get'; 2 be-gĕt', *vt.* [BE-GOT', 1 bı-got',2 be-gŏt',or BE-GAT',1 bı-gat',2 be-găt'; BE-GOT' or BE-GOT'TEN, BE-GOT'N⁵; BE-GET'TING.] To generate; produce.

beg'gar, 1 beg'ər; 2 bĕg'ar. **I.** *vt.* To reduce to want; impoverish. **II.** *n.* One who requests alms; a destitute person.— **beg'gar-li-ness,** *n.*— **beg'gar-ly,** *a.* Miserably poor; mean; wretched.— **beg'gar-ly,** *adv.*— **beg'-gar-y,** *n.* **1.** Extreme poverty. **2.** Beggars as a class. **3.** The act or habit of begging.

be-gin', 1 bı-gin'; 2 be-gĭn', *v.* [BE-GAN' or BE-GUN'; BE-GUN'; BE-GIN'NING.] **I.** *t.* To take the first step in; give origin to; start; commence. **II.** *i.* **1.** To take the first step; start. **2.** To come into existence; originate.— **be-gin'ner,** *n.* **1.** A founder; originator. **2.** A novice; tyro.— **be-gin'ning,** *n.* The starting-point; origin; first part; source.

be-gone', 1 bı-gŏn'; 2 be-gŏn', *interj.* De-
be-gonᴾ, part! away!

be-got', 1 bı-got'; 2 be-gŏt', *imp.* of BEGET, *v.*

be-got'ten, *pp.* of BEGET, *v.*

be-grudge', 1 bı-gruj'; 2 be-grŭdg', *vt.* [BE-GRUDGED'; BE-GRUDG'ING.] To envy; grudge.

be-guile', 1 bı-gail'; 2 be-gīl', *vt.* [BE-GUILED'; BE-GUIL'ING.] To deceive; amuse.

be-gun', 1 bı-gun'; 2 be-gŭn', *imp.* & *pp.* of BEGIN, *v.*

be-half', 1 bı-haf'; 2 be-hȧf', *n.* The interest or defense (of any one); preceded by *in, on,* or *upon.*

be-have', 1 bı-hēv'; 2 be-hāv', *vt.* & *vi.* [BE-HAVED'; BE-HAV'ING.] To conduct (oneself); act; act properly or suitably.— **be-ha'vior,** *n.* Manner or mode of action; demeanor; deportment. **be-ha'viour‡.**

be-head'd, 1 bı-hed'; 2 be-hĕd', *vt.* To
be-hed'⁵, take the head from; decapitate.

be-held', 1 bı-held'; 2 be-hĕld', *imp.* & *pp.* of BEHOLD, *v.*

be-hest', 1 bı-hest'; 2 be-hĕst', *n.* An authoritative request; command.

be-hind', 1 bı-haind'; 2 be-hīnd'. **I.** *adv.* In, toward, or at the rear; backward; in reserve; behindhand. **II.** *prep.* At the back of; on the other side of; inferior to. — **be-hind'hand",** *a.* & *adv.* Behind time; late; behind; backward; in arrears.

be-hold', 1 bı-hōld', 2 be-hōld', *vt.* & *vi.* [BE-HELD', 1 bı-held', 2 be-hĕld'; BE-HOLD'ING.] To look at or upon; look; view; see.— **be-hold'en,** *a.* Indebted.— **be-hold'er,** *n.* An eye-witness; spectator.

be-hoof', 1 bı-hūf'; 2 be-hōōf', *n.* Advantage; use.— **be-hoove',** 1 bı-hūv'; 2 be-hōōv', *vt.* [BE-HOOVED'; BE-HOOV'ING.] To be becoming to; needful, or right for.

be'ing, 1 bī'ıŋ; 2 bē'ĭng. **I.** *ppr.* of BE, *v.* Existing; continuing to be. **II.** *n.* Anything that exists; existence. [beat; thrash.

be-la'bor, 1 bı-lē'bər; 2 be-lā'bŏr, *vt.* To

be-late', 1 bı-lēt'; 2 be-lāt', *vt.* [BE-LAT-ED⁴; BE-LAT'ING.] To cause to be late.

be-lay', 1 bı-lē'; 2 be-lā', *vt.* To make fast by winding, as a rope.— **be-lay'ing-pin",** *n.* A pin on which rope is wound.

belch'ᵗ, 1 belch'; 2 bĕlch, *vt.* & *vi.* To eject noisily, as gas from the stomach; cast forth, as ashes from a volcano; vomit; eject; come forth forcibly, as flame from a furnace.— **belch,** *n.* A belching; eructation.

bel'dam, 1 bel'dam, -dĕm; 2 bĕl'dăm,
bel'dame, -dām, *n.* An evil hag.

be-lea'guer, 1 bı-lī'gər;
be-lea'gerᴾ, 2 be-lē'-ger, *vt.* To besiege.

bel'fry, 1 bel'frı; 2 bĕl'-fry, *n.* [BEL'FRIES²,*pl.*] A tower, or that part of a tower in which a bell is hung.

Belfry.

bel'ga, 1 bel'jā'; 2 bĕl'-gä', *n.* A unit of Belgian currency. See COIN.

be-lie', 1 bı-lai'; 2 be-lī', *vt.* [BE-LIED'; BE-LY'-ING.] To give the lie to; contradict; disappoint.

be-lief', 1 bı-līf'; 2 be-lēf', *n.* **1.** Acceptance of something as true; trust; conviction; assurance. **2.** That which is believed; opinion; creed.

be-lieve', 1 bı-līv'; 2 be-lēv', *vt.* & *vi.* [BE-
be-lievᴾ, LIEV(E)D'⁵; BE-LIEV'ING.] To accept as true; be convinced of; credit; accept the word of; trust; think; suppose.

1: ə = final; ı = habit; aisle; au = out; oil; iū = feud; chin; go; ŋ = sing; thin, this.
2: wolf, dǫ; bŏŏk, bōōt; full, rule, cūre, bŭt, bûrn; oil, bǒy; go, ġem; ink; thin, this.

— **be-liev'er,** *n.* One who believes; an adherent of a religious faith. [probably.

be-like', 1 bı-laik'; 2 be-līk', *adv.* Perhaps;

be-lit'tle, | **be-lit'l**P, 1 bı-lit'l; 2 be-lĭt'l, *vt.* [-TL(E)DP; -TLING.] To treat slightingly; disparage; depreciate.

bell, | **bel**P, 1 bel; 2 bĕl, *vt.* & *vi.* To put a bell on; shape like a bell; make a bell=like sound.

bell, *n.* A hollow metallic instrument for giving forth a sound when struck.

"Czar Kolokol," the Great Bell of Moscow.

bel"la-don'na, 1 bel"ə-don'ə; 2 bĕl"a-dŏn'a, *n.* A poisonous herb; deadly nightshade; also, a medicinal preparation made from it.

belle, 1 bel; 2 bĕl, *n.* A beautiful and attractive woman.

belles"=let'tres, 1 bel"=let'r; 2 bĕl"=lĕt'r, *n. pl.* Polite literature.

bel'li-cose, 1 bel'ı-kōs; 2 bĕl'i-cōs, *a.* Pugnacious; warlike.

bel-lig'er-ent, 1 be-lij'ər-ent; 2 bĕ-lĭg'er-ĕnt. **I.** *a.* **1.** Warlike; bellicose. **2.** Engaged in or pertaining to warfare. **II.** *n.* A nation engaged in legitimate warfare.

bell'man, 1 bel'mən; 2 bĕl'man, *n.* [-MEN, *pl.*] A town crier.

bel'low, 1 bel'o; 2 bĕl'o. **I.** *vt.* & *vi.* To proclaim vociferously; roar; shout. **II.** *n.* A loud hollow cry or roar.

bel'lows, 1 bel'oz; 2 bĕl'os, *n. sing.* & *pl.* An instrument for forcing air upon a fire, for blowing organs, etc.

bel'ly, 1 bel'ı; 2 bĕl'y. **I.** *vt.* & *vi.* [BEL'LIED; BEL'LY-ING.] To fill, as a sail. **II.** *n.* [BEL'LIESz, *pl.*] The abdomen, or something resembling it; as, the *belly* of a sail.

be-long', 1 bı-lēŋ'; 2 be-lông', *vi.* To be a possession or part; be an attribute; be suitable; appertain: followed by *to*.— **be-long'ing,** *n.* Something that belongs to a person or thing: usually in the plural.

be-lov'ed, | **be-luv'ed**P, 1 bı-luv'ed *or* bı-luvd'; 2 be-lòv'ĕd *or* be-lòvd'. **I.** *a.* Greatly loved; very dear. **II.** *n.* One greatly loved.

be-low', 1 bı-lō'; 2 be-lō'. **I.** *adv.* In or to a lower place; farther down; on earth; in Hades or in hell. **II.** *prep.* Beneath; under; lower than; inferior to.

belt, 1 belt; 2 bĕlt. **I**d. *vt.* To gird with a belt; mark with belts; drive by a belt, as a machine. **II.** *n.* A band worn around the waist; a band for transmitting power in machinery; any broad encircling band; a zone; strip; strait. [lament.

be-moan', 1 bı-mōn'; 2 be-mōn', *vt.* To

bench, 1 bench; 2 bĕnch, *n.* **1.** A long wooden seat. **2.** A stout table, as for carpenters' work. **3.** The judges' seat in court; the judge or the judges.

bend, 1 bend; 2 bĕnd, *v.* [BENT or BEND'EDd; BEND'ING.] **I.** *t.* **1.** To curve; crook; deflect; direct; apply. **2.** To subdue. **3.** *Naut.* To make fast; tie. **II.** *i.* **1.** To become curved or deflected. **2.** To yield; submit; devote oneself. **3.** To overhang. [loop or knot.

bend, *n.* A curve or crook; a bending; a

be-neath', 1 bı-nīth'; 2 be-nēth'. **I.** *adv.* At a lower point; below. **II.** *prep.* Under; lower than; below the surface of; under the power of: unworthy of.

ben'e-dick, 1 ben'ı-dik; 2 bĕn'e-dĭk, *n.* A newly married man. **ben'e-dict**‡.

ben"e-dic'tion, 1 ben"ı-dik'shən; 2 bĕn"e-dĭc'shon, *n.* The act of blessing, as at the close of worship; blessing; favor.

ben"e-fac'tion, 1 ben"ı-fak'shən; 2 bĕn"e-fac'shon, *n.* A kindly or generous act; a gift; beneficence.— **ben"e-fac'tor,** *n.* A friendly helper; a patron.— **ben"e-fac'tress,** *n. fem.*

ben'e-fice, | **ben'e-fis**s, 1 ben'ı-fis; 2 bĕn'e-fıç, *n.* An ecclesiastical living.— **ben'e-ficed, -fist**s, *a.* Holding a benefice.

be-nef'i-cent, 1 bı-nef'ı-sent; 2 be-nĕf'i-çĕnt, *a.* Doing good; charitable; kind. **-ly,** *adv.*— **be-nef'i-cence,** *n.*— **ben"e-fi'cial,** 1 ben"ı-fish'əl; 2 bĕn"e-fĭsh'al, *a.* Conferring benefits; helpful. **-ly,** *adv.*

ben"e-fi'ci-a-ry, 1 ben"ı-fish'ı-ē-rı *or* -ə-ri; 2 bĕn"e-fĭsh'i-ā-ry *or* -a-ry. **I.** *a.* Pertaining to benefits or benevolence. **II.** *n.* [-RIESz, *pl.*] A recipient of charity, benefit, or profit; the holder of a benefice.

ben'e-fitd, 1 ben'ı-fit; 2 bĕn'e-fĭt. **I.** *vt.* & *vi.* To be helpful or useful to; profit; improve. **II.** *n.* **1.** Profit; advantage. **2.** A favor bestowed; privilege.

be-nev'o-lence, 1 bı-nev'o-lens; 2 be-nĕv'o-lĕnç, *n.* Desire for the good of others; charitableness; charity; humanity. — **be-nev'o-lent,** *a.* Characterized by benevolence; kindly; charitable. **-ly,** *adv.*

be-night'ed, 1 bı-nait'ed; 2 be-nīt'ĕd, *pa.* Overtaken by night; ignorant; depraved.

be-nign', 1 bı-nain'; 2 be-nīn', *a.* Gracious; generous; genial; propitious; mild. **-ly,** *adv.*

1: ɑrtistic, ɑrt; fat, fāre; fɑst; get, prēy; hit, polīce; obey, gō; net, ēr; full, rūle; but, būrn.
2: ärt, āpe, făt, fâre, fȧst, what, all; mē, gĕt, prey, fẽrn; hĭt, īce; ï=ē; ĩ=ẽ; gō, nŏt, ôr, wòn,

be-nig′nant, 1 bɪ-nĭg′nənt; 2 be-nĭg′nant, *a.*
1. Kindly; benign; gentle; gracious. **2.**
Helpful; salutary. **-ly,** *adv.*—**be-nig′ni-ty,**
n. [-TIES², *pl.*] **1.** Kindliness; beneficence.
3. Healthfulness; salubrity.

ben′i-son, 1 benʹi-sən; 2 bĕnʹi-son, *n.* A
benediction; blessing.

bent, 1 bent; 2 bĕnt, *imp. & pp.* of BEND, *v.*

bent¹, *n.* **1.** Tendency; disposition. **2.**
The limit of endurance or capacity.

bent², *n.* A stiff wiry grass.

be-numb′, ⎱ 1 bɪ-num′; 2 be-nŭm′, *v.t.*
be-nrm′ᵇ, ⎰ To make numb; stupefy.—
be-numbed′, *pa.*

ben′zene, 1 ben′zīn; 2 bĕn′zēn, *n.* A
colorless, inflammable liquid obtained
chiefly from coal-tar.

ben′zin, ⎱ 1 ben′zin, -zin *or* -zīn; 2 bĕn′zin
ben′zine, ⎰ -zīn *or* -zĭn, *n.* A colorless inflammable, and explosive liquid obtained
from petroleum, used to cleanse clothing,
etc.   [der used in preserving food.

ben′zo-ate of so′da. *Chem.* A white pow-
ben′zo-in, 1 ben′zo-in *or* -zoin; 2 bĕn′zo-ĭn
or -zŏin, *n.* **1.** A fragrant medicinal
Oriental gum resin. **2.** A shrub of North
America and eastern Asia, the spice-bush.
3. A product prepared artificially, as from
oil of bitter almonds.— **ben-zo′ïc,** *a.*

be-queath′, 1 bɪ-kwēth′; 2 be-kwĕth′, *vt.*
To give by will; transmit by inheritance.
—**be-quest′,** 1 bɪ-kwest′; 2 be-kwĕst′, *n.* The
act of bequeathing; a legacy.

be-rate′, 1 bɪ-rēt′; 2 be-rāt′, *vt.* [BE-
RAT′EDᵈ; BE-RAT′ING.] To chide harshly;
scold; rail at.

be-reave′, ⎱ 1 bɪ-rīv′; 2 be-rēv′, *vt.* [BE-
REAVED′ᴾ, ⎰ REAVED′, BE-REAVD′ᵛˢ, *or* BE-
REFT′, 1 bɪ-reft′, 2 be-rĕft′; BE-REAV′ING.]
To deprive, as of something valuable or beloved; despoil; rob.— **be-reave′ment,** *n.* The
act of bereaving, or the state of being be-
reaved; an afflictive loss.

berg, 1 bûrg; 2 bĕrg, *n.* An iceberg.

Ber-mu′da lil′y. The Easter lily. See LILY.

ber′ry, 1 berʹɪ; 2 bĕrʹy, *n.* [BER′RIESᶻ, *pl.*]
1. A small succulent fruit. **2.** A coffee-
bean or the like.

berth, 1 bûrth; 2 bĕrth, *n.* **1.** A bunk or
bed in a vessel, sleeping-car, etc. **2.** A place
in which a vessel can lie. **3.** A place
of employment, as on a vessel. **birth‡.**

Ber″til″lon′ sys′tem, 1 ber″tɪ″yŏn′; 2 bĕr″-
tĭ″yŏn′ *or* (*Fr.*) bār″tĭ″yoñ′. A system of
human measurements for identification.

ber′yl, 1 berʹɪl; 2 bĕr′yl, *n.* A precious
stone, commonly green in color.

be-seech′, 1 bɪ-sīch′; 2 be-sēch′, *vt.* [BE-
SOUGHT′, 1 bɪ-sôt′; 2 be-sôt′; BE-SEECH′-

ING.] To ask with supplicating earnest-
ness; implore; beg; entreat.

be-seem′, 1 bɪ-sīm′; 2 be-sēm′, *v. I. t.* To be
becoming to; befit. **II.** *i.* To seem.— **be-
seem′ing,** *pa.*—**be-seem′ing-ly,** *adv.*

be-set′, 1 bɪ-set′; 2 be-sĕt′, *vt.* [BE-SET′;
BE-SET′TING.] To attack; harass; embarrass; waylay.—**be-set′ting,** *pa.* Constantly
assailing.

be-side′, 1 bɪ-said′; 2 be-sīd′. **I.** *adv.*
Close by; at hand. **II.** *prep.* At or by
the side of; near; in comparison with; in
addition to; apart from; except.

be-sides′, 1 bɪ-saidz′; 2 be-sīdz′. **I.** *adv.*
1. In addition; also. **2.** Aside from. **II.**
prep. In addition to; other than; except.

be-siege′, 1 bɪ-sīj′; 2 be-sēj′, *vt.* [BE-
SIEGED′; BE-SIEG′ING.] To lay siege to;
beset or harass.—**be-sieg′er,** *n.*

be-smear′, 1 bɪ-smīr′; 2 be-smēr′, *vt.* To
smear over; sully.

be-smirch′ᵗ, 1 bɪ-smûrch′; 2 be-smĭrch′, *vt.*
To soil; stain; defile.

be′som, 1 bi′zəm; 2 bē′som, *n.* A broom;
something that sweeps away or destroys.

be-sot′, 1 bɪ-sot′; 2 be-sŏt′, *vt.* [BE-SOT′-
TEDᵈ; BE-SOT′TING.] To intoxicate; in-
fatuate.   [BESEECH, *v.*

be-sought′, 1 bɪ-sôt′; 2 be-sôt′, *imp. & pp.* of

be-speak′, 1 bɪ-spīk′; 2 be-spēk′, *vt.* [BE-
SPOKE′; BE-SPOKE′ *or* BE-SPOK′EN; BE-
SPEAK′ING.] **1.** To ask for in advance.
2. To give token of; indicate.

Bes′se-mer, 1 besʹɪ-mər; 2 bĕsʹe-mer, *n.*
Steel prepared by forcing air through the
molten metal.

best, 1 best; 2 bĕst. **I.** *a.* [*Superl.* of
GOOD.] Most excellent. **II.** *n.* The
most excellent; the highest degree; the
utmost. **III.** *adv.* [*Superl.* of WELL.] In
the most excellent manner; with the most
favorable result; to the utmost degree.

be-sted′, ⎱ 1 bɪ-sted′; 2 be-stĕd′, *pa.* Sit-
be-stead′, ⎰ uated; circumstanced; beset.

bes′tial, 1 bes′chəl; 2 bĕs′chal. *a.* Beastly;
animal; brutish; sensual.— **bes″ti-al′i-ty,**
1 bes″chi-alʹɪ-tɪ; 2 bĕs″chi-ăl′ɪ-ty, *n.* Character or conduct befitting beasts. **-ly,** *adv.*

be-stir′, 1 bɪ-stûr′; 2 be-stîr′, *vt.* [BE-
STIRRED′, BE-STIRD′ᵛˢ; BE-STIR′RING.]
To move vigorously; arouse.

be-stow′, 1 bɪ-stō′; 2 be-stō′, *vt.* **1.** To
confer as a gift: with *on* or *upon.* **2.** To
use; apply.— **be-stow′a-ble(eᵖ,** *a.*— **be-
stow′al,** *n.* The act of bestowing; gift.

be-strew′, 1 bɪ-strū′; 2 be-strū′, *vt.* [BE-
STREWED′ *or* BE-STREWN′; BE-STREW′ING.]
To sprinkle; scatter about.

be-stride′, 1 bɪ-straid′; 2 be-strīd′, *vt.* [BE-

1: ə = final; ɪ = habɪt; aɪsle; au = *out*; oɪl; ɪū = *feud*; ℭhin; go; ŋ = sɪng; thɪn, **this.**
2: wolf, do; bōok, bōot; full, rṳle, cūre, bŭt, bûrn; oɪl, bŏy; ḡo, ġem; iŋk; thin, this.

STRODE', 1 bi-strōd', 2 be-strŏd', or BE-3TRID', 1 bi-strĭd', 2 be-strĭd'; BE-STRID'-DEN or BE-STRID'; BE-STRID'ING.] To stand over or sit upon astride; step over at a stride.

be-strow', 1 bi-strō'; 2 be-strō', vt. [BE-STROWED' BE-STROWED' or BE-STROWN^P; BE-STROW'ING.] Same as BESTREW.

bet, 1 bet; 2 bĕt, v. [BET or BET'TED^d; BET'TING.] I. t. To stake or pledge on an uncertain issue. II. i. To wager money, etc., upon some uncertain matter.

bet, n. The act of betting; wager; stake.

be-take', 1 bi-tēk'; 2 be-tāk', vt. [BE-TOOK', 1 bi-tuk', 2 be-tŏŏk'; BE-TAK'EN; BE-TAK'ING.] To resort (to); take (one-self), remove, or go (to).

be-think', 1 bi-thĭnk'; 2 be-thĭnk', vt. & vi. [BE-THOUGHT, 1 bi-thŏt', 2 be-thôt'; BE-THINK'ING.] To remind (oneself); take thought; deliberate.

be-tide', 1 bi-taid'; 2 be-tīd', vt. & vi. [BE-TID'ED^d; BE-TID'ING.] To happen to; betoken.

be-times', 1 bi-taimz'; 2 be-tīmz', adv. In good season or time; soon.

be-to'ken, 1 bi-tō'kn; 2 be-tō'kn, vt. To be a sign of; give promise of.

be-took', imp. & pp. of BETAKE, v.

be-tray', 1 bi-trē'; 2 be-trā', vt. 1. To deliver up or disclose treacherously; lead astray; seduce. 2. To reveal uninten-tionally; show signs of.— be-tray'al, n.— be-tray'er, n.

be-troth'^t, 1 bi-trŏth' or bi-trōth'; 2 be-trŏth' or be-trōth', vt. To engage to marry; promise in marriage.— be-troth'al, n. Engagement to marry. be-troth'ment; [prove; surpass; excel.

bet'ter, 1 bet'ər; 2 bĕt'er, vt. & vi. To im-bet'ter, a. [Compar. of GOOD.] Superior; preferable; surpassing; improved in health: convalescent. [2. A superior.

bet'ter¹, n. 1. Advantage; superiority.

bet'ter², n. One who makes bets. -tor¦.

bet'ter, adv. [Compar. of WELL.] In a su-perior manner; more excellently; more correctly; in a higher degree.

bet'ter-ment, 1 bet'ər-ment or -mənt; 2 bĕt'er-ment, n. Improvement; addition to value of real estate.

be-tween', 1 bi-twīn'; 2 be-twēn'. I. adv. In the interval; at intervals. II. prep. In the space which separates; intermedi-ate in relation to; with relation to both of; common to. [prep. Between.

be-twixt', 1 bi-twikst'; 2 be-twĭkst', prep. & bev'el, 1 bev'el; 2 bĕv'ĕl. I. vt. & vi. [BEV'-ELED or BEV'ELLED, BEV'ELD^s; BEV'EL-

ING or BEV'EL-LING.] To give a sloping edge to; have a sloping edge. II. a. Oblique; slanting; beveled. III. n. A sloping edge, or an in-strument for measur-ing it, called a bevel-square.

Bevel-square.

bev'er-age, 1 bev'ər-ij; 2 bĕv'er-aġ, n. Drink; liquor for drinking.

bev'y, 1 bev'i; 2 bĕv'y, n. [BEV'IES², pl.] A flock of birds; a group of women.

be-wail', 1 bi-wēl'; 2 be-wāl', vt. & vi. To mourn for; lament.

be-ware', 1 bi-wār'; 2 be-wâr', vt. & vi. To look out for, be wary of; be cautious or wary; look out: often with of.

be-wil'der, 1 bi-wil'dər; 2 be-wĭl'der, vt. To confuse; perplex; daze.— be-wil'der-ment, n.

be-witch', 1 bi-wich'; 2 be-wĭch', vt. To be-wich'^P, 1 gain magical power over; charm; fascinate.— be-witch'ing, pa. Charming; captivating.— be-witch'ing-ly, adv.— be-witch'ment, n. The act or power of bewitching, or the state of being bewitched.

bey, 1 bē; 2 be, n. The governor of a Turkish town or district; also, some other Turkish official of high rank.

be-yond', 1 bi-yond'; 2 be-yŏnd'. I. n. That which is on the other side or farther on; the future life. II. adv. On the other side of something intervening; yonder; far off. III. prep. Farther or later than; out of reach of; superior to; more than.

bi-, 1 bai-; 2 bī-, prefix. Twice; doubly; two; as, biannual, biweekly. bin-¦¦; bis-¦.

bi-an'nu-al, 1 bai-an'yu-əl; 2 bī-ăn'yu̇-al, a. Occurring twice a year; semiannual. -ly, adv.

bi'as, 1 bai'əs; 2 bī'as. I. vt. [BI'ASED^t or BI'ASSED^t, BI'AST^s; BI'AS-ING or BI'AS-SING.] To cause to incline; influence un-duly; prejudice. II. a. Running diago-nally across the texture; cut slantingly, as cloth. III. n. [BI'AS-ES^Z or BI'AS-SES, pl.] 1. A line, cut, or seam running obliquely across the threads of a fabric. 2. A mental leaning or prejudice.

bib, 1 bib; 2 bĭb. I. vt. & vi. [BIBBED, BIBD^s; BIB'BING.] To tipple. II. n. A cloth worn under the chin by children at meals.— bib'ber, 1 bib'ər; 2 bĭb'er, n. A tippler.

Bi'ble, 1 bai'bl; 2 bī'bl, n. The Sacred Scriptures of the Old and New Testa-ments.— Bib'li-cal, 1 bib'li-kal; 2 bĭb'li-cal, a. Pertaining to or in harmony with the Bible.

bib″li·og′ra·pher, 1 bĭb″lĭ-ŏg′rə-fər; 2 **bib″li·og′ra·fers,** b̄ĭb″li-ŏḡ′ra-fer, *n.* One skilled in bibliography. — **bib″li·o·graph′ic,** *a.* **bib″li·o·graph′i·cal‡.—bib″li·og′ra·phy,** *n.* [-PHIES^z, *pl.*] **1.** The description and history of books. **2.** A list of the works of an author, or of the literature bearing on a subject.

bib″li·o·ma′ni·a, 1 bĭb″lĭ-o-mē″nĭ-ə; 2 b̄ĭb″lĭ-o-mā′ni-a, *n.* Book-madness; the passion for collecting books.—**bib″li·o·ma′ni·ac,** *a.* & *n.*—**bib″li·o·ma·ni′a·cal,** *a.* **-ly,** *adv.*

bib″li·o·phile, 1 bĭb″lĭ-o-fail *or* -fil; 2 b̄ĭb″li-o-fil *or* -fīl, *n.* One who loves books.

bib″li·o·pole, 1 bĭb″lĭ-o-pōl; 2 bĭb″li·o-pōl, *n.* A dealer in rare books.

bib″li·o·the′ca, 1 bĭb″lĭ-o-thī′ka; 2 bĭb″li-o-thē′ca, *n.* A library, or a collection of books.

bib′u·lous, 1 bĭb′yu-lŭs; 2 b̄ĭb′yu-lŭs, *a.* Given to drink; absorbing moisture readily.

bi′ceps, 1 bai′seps; 2 bī′çĕps, *n.* The large muscle of the upper arm.

bick′er, 1 bĭk′ər; 2 b̄ĭk′er, *vi.* To dispute; wrangle; chatter; flow noisily, as a brook; splutter, as a flame.

bi′cy·cle, 1 bai′sĭ-kl; 2 bī′çy-el. **I.** *vi.* [-CLED; -CLING.] To ride a bicycle. **II.** *n.* A vehicle with two wheels set tandem, and propelled by the rider's feet.—**bi′cy·clist,** *n.* One who rides on a bicycle; a wheelman. **bi′cy·cler‡; cy′clist‡** (1 sai′klist; 2 çī′elist).

bid, 1 bĭd; 2 b̄ĭd. **I.** *vt.* & *vi.* [BADE, BAD, *or* BID; BID′DEN *or* BID; BID′DING.] To offer; command; order. **II.** *n.* An offer to pay or accept a price.—**bid′der,** *n.*—**bid′ding,** *n.* A command; invitation; offer.

bide, 1 baid; 2 b̄ĭd, *vt.* & *vi.* [BID′ED^d *or* BODE; BID′ING.] To wait for; await; dwell; stay; abide; endure.

bi·en′ni·al, 1 bai-en′ĭ-əl; 2 bī-ĕn′i-al. **I.** *a.* Occurring every two years; lasting two years. **II.** *n.* A plant that lives two years.

bier, 1 bīr; 2 b̄ēr, *n.* A framework for carrying the dead; a coffin; hearse; the grave.

bi·fo′cal, 1 bai-fō′kəl; 2 bī-fō′eal, *a.* Having two foci, as a pair of eye-glasses that can be used for reading or distance view at pleasure of the wearer.

bi·fo′li·ate, 1 bai-fō′lĭ-ēt; 2 bī-fō′li-āt, *a. Bot.* Having two leaves.

bi·fur′cate^d, 1 bai-fûr′kĕt *or* bai′fur-kĕt; 2 bī-fûr′eāt *or* bī′fŭr-eāt, *v.* To fork; divide into two branches or stems.—**bi·fur′cate,** *a.* Forked. **bi·fur′cat·ed‡.— bi″fur·ca′tion,** *n.*

big, 1 big; 2 b̄ĭg, *a.* [BIG′GER; BIG′GEST.] Large; great; bulky; haughty; pompous. —**big′ness,** *n.*

big′a·my, 1 big′ə-mı; 2 b̄ĭg′a-my, *n.* The crime of having two wives or husbands at once.—**bi·gam′ic,** *a.* **big′a·mous‡.—big′a·mist,** *n.* One guilty of bigamy.

bight, 1 bait; 2 b̄ĭt, *n.* **1.** A small bay. **2.** *Naut.* A loop or turn in a rope.

big′ot, 1 big′ət; 2 b̄ĭg′ot, *n.* An illiberal adherent of a creed, party, or opinion. —**big′ot·ed,** *a.* Stubbornly attached to a creed, party, system, or opinion.—**big′ot·ry,** *n.* [-RIES^z, *pl.*] Obstinate and intolerant attachment to a cause or creed.

bi′jou′, 1 bĭ″ẕū′; 2 bī″zhụ′, *n.* [BI′JOUX′,] 1 bĭ″ẕūz′; 2 bī″zhụz′, *pl.*] A jewel; a trinket. —**bi″jou′te·rie′,** 1 bĭ″zhū″te-rī′; 2 bī″zhụ″te-rē′, *n.* Jewelry. **bi·jou′try‡.**

bi·lat′er·al, 1 bai-lat′ər-əl; 2 bī-lăt′er-al, *a.* Pertaining to two sides; two-sided.

bile, 1 bail; 2 b̄ĭl, *n.* **1.** A bitter greenish fluid secreted by the liver. **2.** Anger; peevishness.

bilge, 1 bilj; 2 b̄ĭlḡ. **I.** *vt.* & *vi.* [BILGED; BILG′ING.] *Naut.* To stave or be stove in; make or be leaky. **II.** *n.* **1.** The flat part of a ship's bottom. **2.** The bulge of a barrel.—**bilge′wa″ter,** *n.* Foul water that collects in the bilge of a ship.

bil′i·a·ry, 1 bĭl′ĭ-ē-rı; 2 b̄ĭl′i-ā-ry, *a.* Pertaining to or conveying bile.

bi·lin′gual, 1 bai-lĭŋ′gwəl; 2 bī-lĭŋ′gwal, *a.* Recorded or expressed in two languages; speaking two languages.—**bi·lin′guist,** *n.* One who speaks two languages.

bil′ious, 1 bĭl′yus; 2 b̄ĭl′yŭs, *a.* **1.** Suffering from liver-complaint; ill-natured. **2.** Of, pertaining to, containing, or consisting of bile.—**bil′ious·ness,** *n.*

bi·lit′er·al, 1 bai-lĭt′ər-əl; 2 bī-lĭt′er-al, *a.* Composed of two letters.

bill¹, 1 bil; 2 b̄ĭl, *vt.* **1.** To enter in a bill; **bill²,** charge; advertise by bills or placards. **bill²,** *vi.* To join bills, as doves; caress.

bill¹, *n.* **1.** A statement of an account. **2.** [U. S.] A bank- or government-note. **3.** A list of items. **4.** The draft of a proposed law. **5.** A public notice.

bill², *n.* A beak, as of a bird.

bill³, *n.* A hook-shaped instrument or weapon; a halberd.

bil′let^d, 1 bĭl′et; 2 b̄ĭl′ĕt, *vt.* & *vi.* To lodge, as soldiers, in a private house.

Bill of the
time of
Henry
VII.

bil′let², 1 bĭl′et; 2 b̄ĭl′ĕt, *n.* A note; requisition; a soldiers' lodging; quarters.

bil′let², *n.* A short thick stick of wood.

---

bil″let:doux′, 1 bil′ı:dū′; 2 bĭl″i:dū′, *n.* [BIL′-LETS:DOUX′, *pl.*] A lover's note.

bill:fold, *n.* A folding case, as of leather, for bills, or bank:notes, into which they are placed flat, then folded.

bil′liards, 1 bil′yɑrdz; 2 bĭl′yårds, *n.* A game played with ivory balls on a cloth:covered table.

bil′lings:gate, 1 bil′ıŋz:gēt; 2 bĭl′ĭngs:gāt, *n.* Vulgar and abusive language: named from Billingsgate fish:market, London.

bil′lion, 1 bil′yɐn; 2 bĭl′yon, *n.* **1.** [U. S. & Fr.] A thousand millions (1,000,000,-000). **2.** [Eng.] A million millions (1,000,-000,000,000). [typical Australian.

Bill′jim″, 1 bil′jim″; 2 bĭl′jĭm″, *n.* The

bil′low, 1 bil′o; 2 bĭl′o. **I.** *vt. & vi.* To roll in billows; surge; swell. **II.** *n.* A great wave, as of the sea, or of sound, etc.; in the plural, the sea.— **bil′low:y,** *a.*

bil′ly, 1 bil′ı; 2 bĭl′y, *n.* [BIL′LIES², *pl.*] A short bludgeon; a policeman's club.

bi″me:tal′lic, 1 bai′mı:tal′ık; 2 bī″me:tăl′ic, *a.* Consisting of or relating to two metals.— **bi:met′al:ism,** 1 bai:met′al:izm; 2 bī:mĕt′al:ĭsm, *n.* The concurrent use of both gold and silver as money at a fixed relative value.— **bi:met′al:ist,** *n.*

bi:month′ly, 1 bai:munth′lı; 2 bī:mŏnth′-ly, *a. & adv.* Once in two months.

bin, 1 bin; 2 bĭn, *n.* A receptacle, as for coal.

bi′na:ry, 1 bai′nɐ:rı; 2 bī′na:ry. **I.** *a.* Pertaining to or made up of two; double. **II.** *n.* [-RIES², *pl.*] A couple; duality.

bind, 1 baind; 2 bīnd, *vt. & vi.* [BOUND, 1 baund; 2 bound; BOUND or BOUND′EN; BIND′ING.] **1.** To tie together; make fast by tying; fasten; constrain; have moral or legal force; be obligatory. **2.** To put a bandage or a binding on; secure between covers, as the sheets of a book.— **bind′er,** *n.* One who or that which binds.— **bind′er:y,** 1 baind′ɐr:ı; 2 bīnd′er:y, *n.* [-IES², *pl.*]. A place where books are bound. — **bind′ing.** **I.** *pa.* Obligatory. **II.** *n.* The act of fastening or joining; anything that binds, as the cover of a book.

bin′na:cle, 1 bin′ɐ:kl; 2 bĭn′a:cl, *n.* A case for a ship's compass.
bin′na:cl², *f*

bin:oc′u:lar, 1 bin:ok′yu:lɐr; 2 bĭn:ŏc′yu:lar. **I.** *a.* **1.** Having two eyes. **2.** Pertaining to the use of both eyes at once. **II.** *n.* A glass, as a telescope or microscope, adapted to vision by both eyes at once.

bi″o:gen′e:sis, 1 bai″o:jen′ı:sis; 2 bī″o:gĕn′-e:sĭs, *n. Biol.* The doctrine that life is generated only from antecedent life.

bi:og′e:ny, 1 bai:oj′ı:nı; 2 bī:ŏg′e:ny, *n. Biol.* The evolution of living things.

bi′o:graph, 1 bai′o:grɑf; 2 bī′o:gråf, *n.* See KINETOGRAPH.

bi:og′ra:phy, 1 bai:og′rɐ:fı; 2 bī:ŏg′ra:fy, *n.* **bi:og′ra:fy²,** [-PHIES², *pl.*] A written account of a person's life.— **bi:og′ra:pher,** 1 bai:og′rɐ:fɐr; 2 bī:ŏg′ra:fer, *n.* One who writes a biography.— **bi″o:graph′ic, bi″o:graph′i:cal,** 1 bai″o:graf′ık, -ı:kɐl; 2 bī″o:gråf′ic, -i:cal, *a.* Pertaining to or consisting of biography.

bi:ol′o:gy, 1 bai:ol′o:jı; 2 bī:ŏl′o:gy, *n.* The science of life or living organisms. — **bi″o:log′ic,** 1 bai″o:loj′ık; 2 bī″o:lŏg′ic, *a.* **bi″o:log′i:cal‡.— bi:ol′o:gist,** *n.* A student of or expert in biology.

bi′o:plasm, 1 bai′o:plazm; 2 bī′o:plăsm, *n.* Formative living matter. Compare PRO-TOPLASM.

bi′o:scope, 1 bai′o:skōp; 2 bī′o:scōp, *n.* A machine for showing moving pictures.

bi:par′tite, 1 bai:pɑr′tait; 2 bī:pär′tīt, *a.* Consisting of two corresponding parts.

bi′ped, 1 bai′ped; 2 bī′pĕd. **I.** *a.* Having two feet. **II.** *n.* An animal having two feet.— **bip′e:dal,** *a.* Of or pertaining to a biped.

bi′plane, 1 bai′plēn; 2 bī′plān, *n.* An aero-plane having two plane surfaces.

birch, 1 bûrch; 2 bîrch, *n.* **1.** A tree of the oak family with outer bark separable in thin lay-ers. **2.** The wood of the birch; a birch rod; a canoe made of birch bark.— **birch′en,** *a.* Pertaining to or made of birch.

Birch:bark Canoe.

bird, 1 bûrd; 2 bîrd, *n.* A feathered, egg:laying vertebrate animal, having the fore limbs modified as wings.— **bird′-lime″,** *n.* A sticky substance smeared on twigs to catch small birds.— **bird′s′:eye″,** *a.* **1.** Marked as if with birds' eyes. **2.** Seen from above, as if by a flying bird.

birth, 1 bûrth; 2 bîrth, *n.* **1.** The coming into life or being born; nativity; ori-gin. **2.** Ancestry or descent; lineage. **3.** Issue; offspring; the giving birth to off-spring.— **birth′day″,** *n.* The day of one's birth, or its anniversary: used also adjectively. — **birth′right″,** *n.* **1.** A right or privilege to which one is born. **2.** Primogeniture.

bis, 1 bis; 2 bĭs, *adv. Mus.* Twice; repeat.

bis′cuit, 1 bis′kıt; 2 bĭs′eit, *n.* **1.** A small soft cake; also, a cracker. **2.** Bisque.

bi:sect′d, 1 bai:sekt′; 2 bī:sĕct′, *vt.* To divide into two equal parts.— **bi:sec′tion,** *n.*

BIRDS.

1. Blue jay. ¹/₆ 2. Cardinal. ¹/₆ 3. Scarlet tanager. ¹/₆ 4. Purple martin. ¹/₇ 5. Swallow. ¹/₉
American robin. ¹/₆ 7. Catbird. ¹/₅ 8. Baltimore oriole. ¹/₇ 9. Bluebird. ¹/₅ 10. Humming-
d. ¹/₆ 11. Red-winged blackbird. ¹/₆ 12. Crow. ¹/₉ 13. Sparrow. ¹/₆ 14. Meadow-lark. ¹/₉
Downy woodpecker. ¹/₉ 16. Wren. ¹/₃ 17. Thrush. ¹/₃ 18. Barn-owl. ¹/₃

bish′op, 1 bĭsh′əp; 2 bĭsh′op, *n.* **1.** An overseer in the church, having charge of a diocese. **2.** A piece in chess.—**bish′op-ric,** *n.* The office or province of a bishop; a diocese.

bi′son, 1 bai′sən; 2 bī′son, *n.* A bovine ruminant akin to the ox; [N. Am.] a buffalo.

bis-sex′tile, } 1 bi-seks′tĭl; 2 bi-sĕks′til. **I.**
bis-sex′til⁵, } *a.* Pertaining to a leap-year. **II.** *n.* A leap-year.

bit¹, 1 bit; 2 bĭt, *vt.* [BIT′TED⁴; BIT′TING.] To put a bit in the mouth of; train to or control by the bit; curb; restrain.

bit², *imp. & pp.* of BITE, *v.*

bit¹, *n.* **1.** A wood-boring tool adapted to be used with a stock or brace. **2.** The metallic mouthpiece of a bridle.

bit², *n.* A small piece, portion, or fragment; a little.

Bits and Bit-stock or Brace.

bitch, 1 bĭch; 2 bĭch, *n.* The female of the dog or other canine animal.

bite, 1 bait; 2 bĭt. **I.** *vt. & vi.* [BIT, 1 bit, 2 bĭt; BIT′TEN or BIT; BIT′N²; BIT′ING.] To seize, cut, grind, or tear with the teeth; cause to grip; take hold of; act upon; smart; sting; corrode. **II.** *n.* The act of biting, or the hurt inflicted by biting; a morsel of food. —**bit′er,** *n.* One who or that which bites.

bit′ter, 1 bit′ər; 2 bĭt′ẽr. **I.** *a.* **1.** Having a peculiar acrid taste, as of quinin. **2.** Painful; keen; poignant; stinging; sharp; severe. **3.** Resentful; harsh; hateful. **II.** *n.* **1.** That which is bitter; bitterness. **2.** *pl.* An infusion of bitter ingredients, often with spirits. **-ly,** *adv.* **-ness,** *n.*

bit′tern, 1 bit′ərn; 2 bĭt′ẽrn, *n.* A small heron.

bi-tu′men, 1 bi-tiū′men; 2 bi-tū′mĕn, *n.* A native mineral containing naphtha or asphalt; mineral pitch.—**bi-tu′mi-nous,** *a.*

bi′valve, } 1 bai′valv; 2 bī′-
bi′valv⁵, } vălv. **I.** *a.* Having two valves, as a mollusk. **bi′valv(e)d⁵ᵗ;** **bi-val′vous‡;** **bi-val′vu-lar‡.** **II.** *n.* A headless mollusk having a shell of two valves, as the oyster.

Bittern. **¹/17**

biv′ou-ac, 1 bĭv′u-ak; 2 bĭv′u-ăc. **I.** *vi.* [BIV′OU-ACKED⁴; BIV′OU-ACK-ING.] To

encamp for the night without tents. **II.** *n.* A temporary encampment without shelter.

bi-week′ly, 1 bai-wĭk′lĭ; 2 bi-wēk′ly. **I.** *a.* Occurring or appearing once in two weeks. **II.** *n.* A biweekly publication. [odd.

bi-zarre′, 1 bi-zär′; 2 bi-zär′, *a.* Grotesque;

blab, 1 blab; 2 blăb, *vt. & vi.* [BLABBED, BLABD⁵; BLAB′BING.] To talk or tell indiscreetly; tattler.

black, 1 blak; 2 blăk. **I¹.** *vt. & vi.* To make or become black; blacken. **II.** *a.* Reflecting little or no light; dark; swarthy; gloomy; dismal; forbidding; sad; evil; malignant; deadly. **III.** *n.* **1.** The absence of color, or the darkest of all colors; sable. **2.** Anything black. **3.** A negro.

black′ball″, 1 blak′bôl″; 2 blăk′bal″. **I.** *vt.* To vote against; ostracize. **II.** *n.* A vote rejecting application for membership.

black′ber″ry, 1 blak′ber″ĭ; 2 blăk′bẽr″y, *n.* [-BER″RIES²; *pl.*] The black edible fruit of certain shrubs, or a plant producing it.

black′bird″, 1 blak′bŭrd″; 2 blăk′bĭrd″, *n.* A European thrush, black with yellow bill; one of various black American birds.

black′board″, 1 blak′bôrd″; 2 blăk′bôrd″, *n.* A blackened surface, for marking upon with chalk.

black′en, 1 blak′n; 2 blăk′n, *vt. & vi.* To make or become black; darken; defame.

black′guard, } 1 blag′ard; 2 blăg′ärd. **I⁴.**
black′gard⁵, } *vt.* To revile. **II.** *a.* Scurrilous; low; vile. **III.** *n.* A low, rude, vicious fellow.

black′ing, 1 blak′ɪŋ; 2 blăk′ing, *n.* A preparation used to give blackness or luster, or both.

black′leg″, 1 blak′leg″; 2 blăk′lĕg″, *n.* A professional swindler or gambler; sharper.

black′mail″, 1 blak′mēl″; 2 blăk′māl″. **I.** *vt.* To levy blackmail upon. **II.** *n.* Extortion by threats of accusation.

black′out″, *n.* A state of darkness of an otherwise lighted area; especially as a military measure.—**black′-out″,** *v.*

black′smith″, 1 blak′smith″; 2 blăk′-smith″, *n.* One who works in or welds iron.

black′thorn″, 1 blak′thôrn″; 2 blăk′thôrn″, *n.* A thorny shrub of the rose family; a cane made of its wood.

blad′der, 1 blad′ər; 2 blăd′ẽr, *n.* A sac for retention of urine; an air-vessel.

blade, 1 blēd; 2 blād, *n.* **1.** The flat, cutting part of a knife, sword, etc., or something resembling it, as the leaf of grasses. **2.** A rakish young man.

blame, 1 blēm; 2 blām. **I.** *vt.* [BLAMED;

BLAM'ING.] To find fault with; censure.
II. *n.* **1.** The act of faultfinding; censure; also, fault; culpability. — **blam'a-bl**(e², *a.* Deserving censure; wrong; faulty. **blame'ful**‡; **blame'wor''thy**‡.— **blam'a-bly**, *adv.*— **blame'ful-ly**, *adv.*— **blame'ful-ness**, *n.*— **blame'less**, *a.* Innocent; guiltless. **-ly**, *adv.* **-ness**, *n.*

blanch‡, 1 blanch; 2 blånch, *vt. & vi.* To whiten; bleach; pale.

blanc''-mange, 1 blä''-mäng'; 2 blä''-mänzh', *n.* A whitish jelly-like preparation for desserts.

bland, 1 bland; 2 blånd, *a.* Affable in manner; gentle; mild; balmy; genial. **-ly**, *adv.* **-ness**, *n.*

blan'dish‡, 1 blan'dish; 2 blån'dish, *vt.* To wheedle; caress; coax; please.— **blan'-dish-ment**, *n.*

blank, 1 blaŋk; 2 blåŋk. **I.** *a.* **1.** Free from writing or print; white; empty; void; unsigned. **2.** Without rime; as, *blank* verse. **3.** Disconcerted; confused. **4.** Utter; downright. **II.** *n.* **1.** A blank paper, or one with blank spaces. **2.** A vacant space. **3.** A lottery-ticket which draws no prize; a disappointing result.

blan'ket, 1 blaŋ'ket; 2 blåŋ'kĕt. **I**ᵈ. *vt.* To cover, as with a blanket. **II.** *n.* A heavy woolen or other covering, as of a bed.

blare, 1 blãr; 2 blâr. **I.** *vt. & vi.* [BLARED; BLAR'ING.] To sound loudly, as a trumpet. **II.** *n.* A loud brazen sound.

blar'ney, 1 blär'nı; 2 blär'ny. **I.** *vt. & vi.* To flatter; cajole. **II.** *n.* Wheedling; flattery: in allusion to the Blarney stone in Blarney Castle, near Cork, Ireland, said to give to those who kiss it a cajoling tongue.

bla''sé', 1 blä''zē'; 2 blä''se', *a.* Sated with pleasure; wearied by dissipation.

blas-pheme', 1 blas-fēm'; 2 blås-fēm', *v.* **blas-feme''r**, ʃ[BLAS-PHEMED'; BLAS-PHEM'-ING.] **I.** *t.* To speak irreverently of God or sacred things. **II.** *i.* To speak blasphemy; use profane language; swear.— **blas-phem'er**, *n.*— **blas'phe-mous**, *a.* Impious; irreverent; profane. **-ly**, *adv.*— **blas'phe-my**, **-fe-mıʸ**, 1 blas'fı-mı; 2 blås'fe-my, *n.* [-MIES², *pl.*] Evil or profane speaking of God or sacred things.

blast, 1 blast; 2 blåst. **I**ᵈ. *vt. & vi.* To rend in pieces by explosion; wither, as by a wind; blight; shrivel; destroy; ruin; curse. **II.** *n.* **1.** A strong wind; strong artificial current as of air, steam, etc. **2.** The discharge of an explosive; a loud, sudden sound. **3.** A blight, or blighting influence.

bla'tant, 1 blē'tənt; 2 blä'tant, *a.* Noisy; blustering.

blaze¹, 1 blēz; 2 blāz. **I.** *vt. & vi.* [BLAZED; BLAZ'ING.] To cause to burn with a bright flame; shine; flame; gleam. **II.** *n.* A vivid glowing flame; brightness; effulgence; ardor.

blaze². **I.** *vt.* To publish abroad; proclaim **II**‡. *n.* A proclamation or report.

blaze³. **I.** *vt.* To mark (a tree) by chipping or peeling; hence, to mark out (a path) in this way. **II.** *n.* **1.** A white spot on the face of an animal, as a horse. **2.** A mark chipped on a tree, to indicate a path; a path so indicated.

bla'zon, 1 blē'zn; 2 blā'zn. **I.** *vt.* To proclaim; publish; inscribe; decorate; emblazon. **II.** *n.* A coat of arms; show; proclamation.— **bla'zon-ry**, *n.* The art of depicting heraldic devices; coat of arms; decoration; show.

-bl(e², *suffix.* Used in forming adjectives from verbs: usually preceded by a vowel (see *-able, -ible*). [whiten; blanch.

bleach‡, 1 blĭch; 2 blēch, *vt. & vi.* To

bleak, 1 blĭk; 2 blēk, *a.* **1.** Exposed to wind; bare; barren; dreary. **2.** Cold; cutting. **-ly**, *adv.* **-ness**, *n.*

blear, 1 blĭr; 2 blēr. **I.** *vt.* To dim; obscure; blur. **II.** *a.* Dimmed; dull; bleared.

bleat, 1 blĭt; 2 blēt. **I**ᵈ. *vi.* To cry as a sheep. **II.** *n.* The cry of the sheep or goat.

bleed, 1 blĭd; 2 blēd, *vt. & vi.* [BLED; BLEED'ING.] To lose or cause to lose blood, sap, or other fluid; shed; exude; grieve; sympathize; suffer or die, as in battle.

blem'ish, 1 blem'ısh; 2 blĕm'ish. **I**‡. *vt.* To mar; disfigure. **II.** *n.* A disfiguring defect; reproach; dishonor.

blench‡, 1 blench; 2 blĕnch, *vi.* To shrink back; quail.

blend, 1 blend; 2 blĕnd, *vt. & vi.* [BLEND'ED; BLEND'EDᵈ or BLENT; BLEND'ING.] To mix; combine.

bless, 1 bles; 2 blĕs, *vt.* [BLESSED‡ or BLEST; BLESS'ING.] **1.** To bring or wish happiness or good fortune to; prosper; felicitate. **2.** To invoke God's favor upon. **3.** To consecrate. **4.** To praise; glorify.

bless'ed, 1 bles'ed, blest; 2 blĕs'ĕd, blĕst, **blest**, ʃ *a.* **1.** Heavenly. **2.** Worthy of blessing. **3.** Joyful; happy; favored.— **bless'ed-ly**, *adv.*— **bless'ed-ness**, *n.*

bless'ing, 1 bles'ıŋ; 2 blĕs'ing, *n.* **1.** That which makes happy or prosperous; a divine favor. **2.** A benediction. **3.** Grateful adoration; worship.

blew, 1 blū; 2 blṳ, *imp.* of BLOW, *v.*

blight, 1 blait; 2 blīt. **I**d. *vt. & vi.* To cause to decay; blast; wither. **II.** *n.* A diseased state of plants; anything that withers hopes or prospects.

Bligh′ty, 1 blai′ti; 2 blī′ty, *n.* England; corruption of *Bilayati*, Europe.

blind, 1 blaind; 2 blīnd. **I**d. *vt.* To make blind; screen; hide; eclipse. **II.** *a.* Destitute of sight; ignorant; inconsiderate; acting at random; illegible; unintelligible; hidden; obscure.— **blind′ly,** *adv.* Without sight or without foresight; at random; recklessly.— **blind′ness,** *n.*

blind, *n.* Something that obscures or shades; a shutter: a subterfuge; ruse. — **blind′er,** *n.* One who or that which blinds; a flap on the side of a horse's head-stall.

Venetian Blind.

blind′fold, 1 blaind′fōld; 2 blīnd′-fōld, *vt.* To cover the eyes; hoodwink; mislead.— **blind′fold,** *a.*

blink, 1 bliŋk; 2 blīŋk. **I**t. *vt. & vi.* **1.** To peer at; evade seeing; pass by; wink; get a hasty glimpse. **2.** To twinkle; glimmer. **II.** *n.* **1.** A glance or glimpse. **2.** A shimmer or glimmer.—**blink′er,** *n.* **1.** A horse's blinder. **2.** One who or that which blinks. **blink′ard**‡.

bliss, 1 blis; 2 blĭs, *n.* Superlative happiness.—**bliss′ful,** *a.* -**ly,** *adv.* -**ness,** *n.*

blis′ter, 1 blis′tər; 2 blĭs′ter. **I.** *vt. & vi.* To produce a blister or blisters upon; hurt, as by a blister; gall. **II.** *n.* A thin vesicle on the skin.—**blis′ter-y,** *a.*

blithe, 1 blaith *or* blaith; 2 blīth *or* blīth, *a.* Joyous; gay; merry; sprightly. **blithe′-** some‡.—**blithe′ly,** *adv.*

Blitz′krieg, 1 blits′krēg; 2 blĭts′krēg, *n.* [G.] Lightning war; sudden overwhelming attack with powerful force.

bliz′zard, 1 bliz′ard; 2 blĭz′ard, *n.* A high cold wind with blinding snow.

bloat, 1 blōt; 2 blōt. **I**d. *vt. & vi.* To puff up; swell. **II.** *n.* One who is bloated; a drunkard.

bloat′er, 1 blōt′ər; 2 blōt′er, *n.* A selected smoked herring.

block, 1 blek; 2 blŏk. **I**t. *vt.* To stop; impede; obstruct: often with *up.* **II.** *n.* **1.** A solid piece, as of wood, metal, or stone; an obstruction. **2.** A section; a row, as of houses. **3.** A pulley, or set of pulleys, in a frame.— **block′he(a)d′′s,** *n.* A stupid person.— **block′house′,** *n.* A fort of logs.

Block (3).

block-ade′, 1 blek-ēd′; 2 blŏk-ād′. **I**d. *vt.* To close to traffic by military or naval force; obstruct; block up. **II.** *n.* The closing of a seaport, etc., by hostile forces.

blond, 1 blend; 2 blŏnd. **I.** *a.* **1.** Having a fair skin with light eyes and hair. **2.** Flaxen or golden, as hair. **II.** *n.* A blond person: in the feminine, **blonde.**

blood, 1 blud; 2 blŏd, *n.* **1.** The fluid that circulates in the heart, arteries, and veins. **2.** Kinship by descent; lineage; nobility. **3.** Passion; bloodshed.— **blood′-heat,** *n.* The normal temperature of the human body, about 98½° Fahr.— **b.-horse,** *n.* A horse of a fine breed, especially of the English-Arab cross.— **blood′hound′′,** *n.* A keen-scented hound for tracing fugitives.— **blood′less,** *a.* **1.** Having no blood; pale; lifeless; cold-hearted. **2.** Free from bloodshed. **-ly,** *adv.* **-ness,** *n.*— **blood′shed′′,** *n.* The shedding of blood; slaughter; carnage.— **blood′shot′′,** *a.* Streaked with blood; inflamed.— **blood′thirst′′y,** *a.* Eager to shed blood; murderous; cruel.— **blood′y,** 1 blud′i; 2 blŏd′y, *a.* [BLOOD′I-ER; BLOOD′I-EST.] Stained with, containing, or mixed with blood; sanguinary; bloodthirsty. — **blood′i-ly,** *adv.* **blood′i-ness,** *n.*

blood′ed, 1 blud′ed; 2 blŏd′ĕd, *pa.* **1.** Of pure blood or breed; as, a *blooded* horse (better *blood-horse*). **2.** Having blood of a certain kind; metaphorically, of a certain temperament or character; as, cold-*blooded.* [with blood; bloody.]

blood′ied, 1 blud′id; 2 blŏd′id, *a.* Stained

bloom, 1 blūm; 2 blōōm, *vi.* To blossom; grow luxuriantly; glow with health and beauty.— **bloom′ing,** *pa.*

bloom1, *n.* The blooming or being in flower; fulness and freshness; a flower or flowers collectively; the downy covering of certain fruits.

bloom2, *n.* *Metal.* A mass of malleable iron from which the slag has been beaten.

bloom′er, 1 blūm′ər; 2 blōōm′er, *n.* A trouser-like dress for women: commonly in the plural.

blos′som, 1 bles′əm; 2 blŏs′om. **I.** *vt. & vi.* To bloom. **II.** *n.* A flower; bloom.

blot, 1 blet; 2 blŏt. **I.** *vt. & vi.* [LOT′TED‡; BLOT′TING.] **1.** To spot; stain; disgrace; sully. **2.** To obliterate, as writing; obscure; darken: often with *out.* **3.** To dry with blotting-paper. **II.** *n.* A spot or stain; reproach; blemish.— **blot′ter,** *n.* **1.** A sheet, pad, or book of blotting-paper. **2.** The first record-book, as in a police-station. — **blot′ting-pa′′per,** *n.* Unsized paper for absorbing any excess of ink.

blotch, 1 blech; 2 blŏch. **I**t. *vt.* To mark with blotches. **II.** *n.* **1.**

1: urtistic, **ûr**t; f**a**t, f**ä**re; f**a**st; g**e**t, pr**ey**; h**i**t, pol**i**ce; **o**bey, g**ō**; n**o**t, **ô**r; f**u**ll, r**u**le; b**u**t, b**û**rn.

2: ärt, **ä**pe, f**ä**t, f**ä**re, f**a**st, wh**a**t, **a**ll; m**ē**, g**ĕ**t, pr**ey**, f**ê**rn; h**ĭ**t, **ī**ce; **ĩ**=ē; **ĩ**=ē; g**ō**, n**ŏ**t, **ô**r, w**ŏ**n,

A blot. **2.** An inflamed eruption on the skin. [garment, as of a workman.
blouse, 1 blauz; 2 blous, *n.* A loose upper
blow¹, 1 blō; 2 blō, *v.* [BLEW, 1 blū, 2 blu; BLOWN; BLOW'ING.] **I.** *t.* **1.** To move or affect by a current of air; inflate, as molten glass; sound, as a trumpet. **2.** To put out of breath. **3.** To lay eggs in, as flies in meat. **II.** *i.* **1.** To emit a current, as of air; move in or be carried by the wind. **2.** To sound by being blown. **3.** To pant; be winded.
blow², *vi.* To bloom.
blow¹, *n.* A sudden or violent stroke; thump; shock; calamity.
blow², *n.* **1.** The act of blowing; a blast. **2.** The egg of a fly; a flyblow.
blow³, *n.* The state of flowering; a mass of blossoms.
blow'er, 1 blō'er; 2 blō'er, *n.* One who or that which blows; a device for increasing a draft.
blow'pipe, 1 blō'paip; 2 blō'pīp, *n.* A tube by which air or gas is blown through a flame for the purpose of heating or melting something.
blowz'y, 1 blauz'ɪ; 2 blowz'y, *a.* Having a red or flushed face; slatternly or unkempt.
blub'ber, 1 blʌb'er; 2 blŭb'er, *vi.* To sob noisily. [skin of a whale, or the like.
blub'ber, *n.* The layer of fat beneath the
blu'cher, 1 blū'cher *or* -kər; 2 blū'cher: *or* -cer, *n.* A half-boot or high shoe: named from the Prussian Field-marshal von Blücher, whose arrival gave Wellington the victory at Waterloo. [short club.
bludg'eon, 1 blʌj'ən; 2 blŭdg'on, *n.* A
blue, 1 blū; 2 blu. **I.** *vt.* [BLUED; BLU'-ING.] To make blue. **II.** *a.* [BLU'ER; BLU'EST.] Having the color of the clear sky. **III.** *n.* The color of the clear sky; azure; also, a dye or pigment of this color.— **blue'bell",** *n.* A plant with blue, bell-shaped flowers.— **b l u e ' b i r d",** *n.* A small American bird, of a prevailing blue above.— **blue'bot"tle,** *n.* **1.** A fleshy-fly of a dark-blue color. **2.** A garden flower with tubular florets, mostly blue.— **blue'-stock"ing,** *n.* A learned or literary w o m a n.— **blu'ish,** *a.*— **the blues,** low spirits; melancholy.
bluff¹, {1 bluf; 2 blŭf, *vt.*
bluf², { & *vi.* To over-awe by bold assumption; boast in order to mislead and daunt.
bluff, *a.* **1.** Blunt, frank, and hearty. **2.**

Bluebird. ⅕

Steep and bold, as a cliff. **-ly,** *adv.* **-ness,** *n.*
bluff¹, *n.* Boldness assumed in order to overawe or deceive.
bluff², *n.* A bold, steep headland.
blun'der, 1 blun'der; 2 blŭn'der. **I.** *vt.* & *vi.* To err egregiously; act stupidly. **II.** *n.* A stupid mistake.— **blun'der-er,** *n.*
blun'der-buss, 1 blun'der-bus; 2 blŭn'der-bŭs, *n.* A short gun with large bore and flaring mouth.
blunt, 1 blunt; 2 blŭnt. **I.** *vt.* & *vi.* To make or become blunt; dull. **II.** *a.* **1.** Having a thick end or edge; not sharp; dull. **2.** Abrupt in manner; plain-spoken; brusk.— **blunt'ly,** *adv.*— **blunt'ness,** *n.*
blur, 1 blūr; 2 blûr. **I.** *vt.* & *vi.* [BLURRED, BLURᵇᵉᵈˢ; BLUR'RING.] **1.** To make or become obscure; dull; soil; blemish. **2.** To become indistinct or smeared. **II.** *n.* A smeared or indistinct marking; a blemish.
blurb, 1 blurb; 2 blûrb, *n.* A publishers' statement concerning a book or its author.
blurt, 1 blurt; 2 blûrt, *vt.* To utter abruptly; burst out with: often with *out*.
blush, 1 blush; 2 blŭsh. **I.** *vt.* & *vi.* To make or become red; flush; redden. **II.** *n.* **1.** A reddening, as of the face; a red or rosy tint; flush. **2.** A glance; glimpse.
blus'ter, 1 blus'ter; 2 blŭs'ter. **I.** *vi.* To blow in gusts; fume with anger; threaten; swagger. **II.** *n.* Boisterous talk; a fitful and noisy wind; blast.— **blus'ter-er,** *n.* — **blus'ter-ing,** *pa.* Windy; disagreeable; noisy; swaggering. **blus'ter-ous‡; blus'-ter-y‡; blus'trous‡; blus'try‡.**
bo'a, 1 bō'ə; 2 bō'a, *n.* **1.** Any large non-poisonous serpent that crushes its prey. **2.** A long fur or feather neck-piece.
boar, 1 bēr; 2 bôr, *n.* A male hog.
board, 1 bōrd; 2 bôrd. **I**ᵈ. *vt.* & *vi.* **1.** To enclose with boards. **2.** To furnish or be supplied with meals for pay. **3.** To come alongside or go on board of (a ship, etc.). **II.** *n.* **1.** A thin and broad flat piece of wood. **2.** A table, or the food served; meals furnished for pay. **3.** An official body. **4.** *pl.* The stage of a theater. **5.** Pasteboard; a book-cover. **6.** The deck of a vessel; as, on *board.*
board'er, 1 bōrd'er; 2 bôrd'er, *n.* **1.** One who receives meals for pay. **2.** One detailed to board an enemy's ship.
boast, 1 bōst; 2 bōst. **I**ᵈ. *vt.* & *vi.* To proclaim ostentatiously; vaunt; exult; glory. **II.** *n.* **1.** A boastful speech. **2.** A source of pride.— **boast'er,** *n.*— **boast'ful,** *a.* Inclined to boast. **-ly,** *adv.* **-ness,** *n.*
boat, 1 bōt; 2 bōt. **I**ᵈ. *vt.* & *vi.* To carry or place in a boat; go in a boat; row;

1: ə = final; ɪ = habit; aɪsle; au = out; oil; iū = feud; ᴄhin; go; ŋ = sing; ᴛhin, this.
2: wolf, do; book, boot; full, rule, cūre, bŭt, bûrn; oil, boy; go, gem; iŋk; thin, this.

sail; navigate. **II.** *n.* A water-craft; especially, a small vessel for oars or sails.

Whale-boat.

boat'swain, 1 bŏt'swĕn *or* (*Naut.*) bō'sn; 2 bŏt'swān *or* (*Naut.*) bō'sn, *n.* A ship's petty officer in charge of rigging, etc.

bob, 1 bŏb; 2 bŏb. **I.** *vt. & vi.* [BOBBED, BOBD²; BOB'BING.] **1.** To move with a jerky motion. **2.** To angle with a bob. **3.** To cut short; as, to *bob* a woman's hair. **II.** *n.* **1.** A cork or float on a fishing-line. **2.** A small pendent object, as a pendulum. **3.** A jerky movement. **4.** A woman's head of hair cut short.— **bob'-sled",** *n.* Either of two short sleds, connected tandem by a top plank, or the vehicle so formed.— **bob'tail".** **I.** *a.* Short-tailed; docked; deficient. **bob'tail(e)d"²‡.** **II.** *n.* **1.** A short or docked tail, or an animal marked by it. **2.** The rabble; refuse.

bob'bin, 1 bŏb'in; 2 bŏb'in, *n.* A spool to hold thread.

bob'o-link", 1 bŏb'o-lingk; 2 bŏb'o-lingk, *n.* A small American singing bird. **reed'-bird"‡; rice'-bird"‡.**

bob'-white", 1 bŏb'-hwait"; 2 bŏb'-hwīt", *n.* The North-American quail; also, its cry.

Boche, 1 bŏsh; 2 bŏch, *n.* [Fr. slang.] A blockhead.

bode, 1 bōd; 2 bōd, *vt. & vi.* [BOD'ED²; BOD'ING.] To have a token or presentiment of; presage good or ill.

Bobolink. 1/7

bod'ice, 1 bŏd'is; 2 bŏd'iç, *n.* The close-fitting waist of a woman's dress.

bod'iss, 1 bed'i-les; 2 bŏd'i-lĕs, *a.* Having no body; corporeal.

bod'i-ly, 1 bed'i-li; 2 bŏd'i-ly. **I.** *a.* Pertaining to the body; corporeal. **II.** *adv.* In the body; in person; wholly; completely.

bod'kin, 1 bed'kin; 2 bŏd'kin, *n.* A needle-like perforator.

bod'y, 1 bed'i; 2 bŏd'y, *n.* [BOD'IED, 1 bed'id, 2 bŏd'id; BOD'Y-ING.] To embody; represent. **II.** *n.* [BOD'IES², *pl.*] **1.** The entire physical part of a man or other animal; also, the trunk, exclusive of the limbs; the principal part of anything. **2.** A person. **3.** A solid. **4.** A collection of persons or things, as one whole.

Boer, 1 būr; 2 bur, *n.* A Dutch colonist, or person of Dutch descent in South Africa.

bog, 1 bŏg; 2 bŏg. **I.** *vt. & vi.* [BOGGED, BOGD²; BOG'GING.] To sink or stick in a bog. **II.** *n.* Wet and spongy ground; marsh; morass.— **bog'gy,** *a.* Swampy; miry.

bog'gle, ⎱ 1 bŏg'l; 2 bŏg'l, *vt. & vi.* [BOG'-
bog'l‡, ⎰ GLED, BOG'LD²; BOG'GLING.] To bungle; hesitate; quibble.

bog'le, 1 bŏg'i; 2 bō'gi, *n.* Same as BOGY.

bo'gus, 1 bō'gus; 2 bō'gŭs, *a.* Counterfeit, as money; hence, fraudulent.

bo'gy, ⎱ 1 bō'gi; 2 bō'gy, *n.* [BO'GIES²;
bo'gey, ⎰ BO'GEYS², *pl.*] A goblin; bugbear.

Bo-he'mi-an, 1 bo-hī'mi-an; 2 bo-hē'mi-an, *n.* **1.** One of the people of Bohemia, now part of Czecho-Slovakia, or their language. **2.** A Gipsy. **3.** [B- or b-] A person, as an author, artist, or actor, of unconventional and irregular life.— **Bo-he'mi-an,** *a.*— **Bo-he'mi-an-ism,** *n.*

boil, 1 bŏil; 2 bŏil, *vt. & vi.* To bring or come to the boiling-point; cook, affect, or produce by boiling; bubble up; be agitated.— **boil'er,** *n.* A vessel in which a liquid is boiled or steam generated.

boil¹, *n.* A painful tumor in the skin.

boil², *n.* **1.** The act or state of boiling. **2.** An immersion in boiling water.

bois'ter-ous, 1 bois'ter-us; 2 bŏis'ter-ŭs, *a.* Vociferous and rude; tempestuous. **-ly,** *adv.* **-ness,** *n.*

bold, 1 bōld; 2 bōld, *a.* **1.** Possessing, showing, or requiring courage; fearless; audacious; impudent. **2.** Striking; vigorous; prominent. **-ly,** *adv.* **-ness,** *n.*

bole¹, 1 bōl; 2 bōl, *n.* The trunk of a tree.

bole², *n.* A fine, compact, soft clay.

bo-le'ro, 1 bo-lē'ro; 2 bo-lĕ'ro, *n.* **1.** A Spanish dance in 3/4 time, commonly with castanets; the music for it. **2.** A blouse worn by ladies.

boll, 1 bōl; 2 bōl. **I.** *vi.* To form pods. **II.** *n.* **1.** A round pod, as of flax. **2.** A knob.

Bol"she-vi'ki, 1 bel"she-vi'kī *or* -vī-kī'; 2 bŏl"-she-vī'kī *or* -vī-kī', *n. pl.* [Rus.] A dominating revolutionary political party in Russia.— **Bol'she-vism,** *n.*— **Bol'she-vist,** *n.*

bol'ster, 1 bōl'ster; 2 bōl'ster. **I.** *vt.* To prop up; aid; abet. **II.** *n.* A long under-pillow for a bed.

bolt¹ᵈ, 1 bōlt; 2 bōlt, *v.* **I.** *t.* **1.** To fasten with a bolt. **2.** [U. S.] To refuse to support, as a candidate. **3.** To swallow hurriedly. **4.** To expel; blurt out. **II.** *i.* **1.** To run away, as a horse. **2.** [U. S.] To repudiate a party measure or candi-

1: **ur**tistic, **ûrt**; fat, fāre; fast; get, prēy; hit, police; obey, gō; net, ĕr; full, rūle; but, būrn.

2: ärt, āpe, fät, fâre, fåst, what, all; mē, gĕt, prey, fêrn; hit, īce; i=ĕ; ĩ=ẽ; gō, nŏt, ôr, won.

date.— **bolt′er**[1], *n.* One who or that which bolts in any sense.

bolt[2]**d**, *vt.* To sift; examine as by sifting. — **bolt′er**[2], *n.* Same as BOLT[2], *n.*

bolt[1], *n.* **1.** A sliding bar for fastening a door, etc.; any pin or rod used for fastening. **2.** An arrow; a long shot for a cannon; anything coming suddenly. **3.** [U. S.] Desertion of a party, candidate, or policy. **4.** A sudden start, or runaway. **5.** A roll, as of cloth.

bolt[2], *n.* A rotating frame for sifting flour.

bolt, *adv.* Like an arrow; swiftly; straight. — **bolt upright**, erect.

bo′lus, 1 bō′lus; 2 bō′lŭs, *n.* A large pill.

bomb, 1 bem; 2 bŏm, *n.* A hollow iron
bom[2], ∫ shell filled with explosive material to be shot from a cannon; also, any similar receptacle containing an explosive. **bomb′shell**.

bom-bard[′d], 1 bem-bärd′; 2 bŏm-bärd′, *vt.* To attack with or as with cannon-balls or shells.— **bom″bar-dier′**, *n.* The crew-man of a bombing plane who determines range and releases bombs.— **bom-bard′ment**, *n.*

bom′bast, 1 bem′bast; 2 bŏm′băst, *n.* Pompous language; rant.— **bom-bas′tic**, *a.*

bo′na fi′de, 1 bō′na fai′di; 2 bŏn′ä fī′de. In good faith; without deceit.

bo-nan′za, 1 bo-nan′zo; 2 bo-năn′za, *n.* [U. S.] A rich mine or vein of ore; profitable speculation.

bon′bon, 1 ben′ben *or* (F.) bėṅ″bŏṅ′; 2 bŏn′bŏn *or* (F.) bôṅ″bôṅ, *n.* A sugarplum; confection.

bond[d], 1 bend; 2 bŏnd, *vt.* To put under bond; mortgage; bind.

bond, *a.* Subject to servitude; enslaved. — **bond′maid**″, *n.* A female slave.— **bond′man**, *n.* [-MEN, *pl.*] A male slave or serf. **bonds′man**.— **bond′wo″man**, *n. fem.*

bond, *n.* **1.** That which binds; a band; obligation. **2.** *pl.* Fetters; captivity. **3.** An interest-bearing debt-certificate.— **Liberty bond**, a war interest-bearing debt-certificate, issued by the United States Government, 1917–19.

bond′age, 1 bend′ij; 2 bŏnd′aġ, *n.* Compulsory restraint; slavery; imprisonment; captivity.

bond′ed, 1 bend′ed; 2 bŏnd′ĕd, *pa.* **1.** Mortgaged, as property; secured by bonds, as a debt. **2.** Held in bond for payment of duties.

bonds′man, 1 bendz′mən; 2 bŏndz′man, *n.* [-MEN, *pl.*] **1.** *Law.* One who is bound as security for another; a surety. **2.** A bondman.

bone, 1 bōn; 2 bŏn, *vt.* [BONED; BON′ING.] **1.** To remove the bones from. **2.** To

stiffen with whalebone. **3.** To fertilize with bone-dust.

bone, *n.* **1.** The skeleton of a vertebrate animal, or any portion of it. **2.** *pl.* The mortal remains. **3.** Something made of bone or the like.— **bone′dust″**, *n.* Pulverized bone: used as a fertilizer.— **bone′less**, *a.*

bon′fire″, 1 ben′fair″; 2 bŏn′fīr″, *n.* A large fire, as of brush, in the open air.

bon″naz′, 1 bo″naz′; 2 bo′năz′, *n.* An embroidering-machine; embroidery made by it.

bonne, 1 ben; 2 bŏn, *n.* A French nurse-maid.

bon′net, 1 ben′et; 2 bŏn′ĕt, *n.* A covering for the head, especially for women.

bon′ny, 1 ben′i; 2 bŏn′y, *a.* [BON′NI-ER;
BON′NI-EST.∫ Having homelike beauty; sweet and fair; merry; cheery.

bo′nus, 1 bō′nus; 2 bō′nŭs, *n.* A premium or extra allowance; a gift for service.

bon′y, 1 bōn′i; 2 bŏn′y, *a.* **1.** Of or like bone. **2.** Having prominent bones; thin; gaunt. [*pl.*] A dull fellow; dunce.

boo′by, 1 bū′bi; 2 bōō′by, *n.* [BOO′BIES[2].]
boo′dle, 1 bū′dl; 2 bōō′dl, *n.* [Slang, U. S.] **1.** Bribe-money or corruption funds. **2.** A lot or pack; crowd.— **bood′ler**, *n.*

book, 1 buk; 2 bŏŏk. I[t]. *vt. & vi.* To enter in a book; engage beforehand. II. *n.* **1.** A number of sheets of paper bound or stitched together; a printed and bound volume. **2.** A treatise, or one of its subdivisions.— **book′bind″er**, *n.* One whose trade is the binding of books.— **book′ish**, *a.* Fond of books: pedantic; unpractical.— **book′keep″er**, *n.* One who keeps accounts; an accountant.— **book′keep″ing**, *n.* The art or practise of recording business transactions systematically.— **book′sell″ing**, *n.*— **book′worm**″, *n.* **1.** A close student. **2.** The larva of an insect destructive to books.

boom[1], 1 būm; 2 bōōm. I. *vt. & vi.* To sound with a deep, resonant tone; rush onward impetuously. II. *n.* A deep, reverberating sound, as of a cannon.

boom[2]. I. *vt.* To control or confine by means of a boom.
II. *n.* **1.** A spar holding the foot of a fore-and-aft sail. **2.** A chain of logs to confine floating logs, etc.

boom[3]. I. *vt. & vi.* To push forward; advance with a rush; gain rapidly. II. *n.* A torrent; sudden activity or prosperity.

Sloop, showing boom and bowsprit.
b, boom; *bs.* bowsprit.

boom′e-rang, 1 būm′i-raŋ; 2 bōōm′e-răŋg,

n. A curved Australian missile some forms of which will return to the thrower.

boon, 1 bŭn; 2 bōōn, *a.* Genial; jovial; prosperous; bounteous.

boon, *n.* A good gift; favor; blessing.

boor, 1 bŭr; 2 bōōr, *n.* **1.** A coarse rustic; a rude fellow. **2.** A Dutch peasant. **3.** [B-] Same as BOER.— **boor'ish,** *a.* Rude; clownish.

boose, *v. & n.* Same as BOOZE.

boost, 1 bŭst; 2 bōōst. **I**[d]. *vt.* To push or lift up. **II.** *n.* A lift; help.

boot[1], 1 bŭt; 2 bōōt. **I**[d]. *vt. & vi.* To put boots on; kick. **II.** *n.* **1.** A leather covering for the foot, or foot and leg. **2.** A carriage receptacle, for carrying parcels, etc. — **boot'black",** *n.* One who cleans shoes.— **boot'jack",** *n.* A device for removing boots.

boot[2]. **I**[d]. *vi.* To profit; avail. **II.** *n.* **1.** Something over and above given in barter. **2.** Advantage; resource: help.— **boot'less,** *a.* Profitless; useless: unavailing. **-ly,** *adv.* **-ness,** *n.*—**to boot,** in addition. See BOOT[1], *n.,* 1.

booth, 1 bŭth *or* bŭth; 2 bōōth *or* bōōth, *n.* A stall, as at a fair; a temporary shelter.

boot'leg", *vt. & vi.* To sell (liquor) against the law; engage in the illicit sale of liquor.— **boot'leg"ger,** *n.*

boo'ty, 1 bū'tɪ; 2 bōō'tɪ, *n.* [BOO'TIES[z], *pl.*] The spoil of war; plunder; gain.

booze, 1 bŭz; 2 bōōz. **I**[d]. *vi.* To drink to excess; **II.** *n.* Strong drink; a carouse.

bo'rax, 1 bō'raks; 2 bō'răks, *n.* A white crystalline compound used as an antiseptic and as a flux.— **bo-rac'ic,** *a.*

bor'der, 1 bȇr'dər; 2 bôr'dȇr. **I.** *vt. & vi.* **1.** To put a border on. **2.** To lie on the border; adjoin; approach; resemble: often with *on or upon.* **II.** *n.* A margin or edge; brink; verge; frontier.

bore[1], 1 bōr; 2 bôr, *vt. & vi.* [BORED; BOR'-ING.] To make a hole in; pierce; perforate; tire; weary; annoy.— **bor'er,** *n.* One who or that which bores; especially, an insect or mollusk that bores in wood.

bore[2], *imp.* of BEAR, *v.*

bore, *n.* **1.** A hole made by boring; the interior diameter, as of a firearm. **2.** A tiresome person; an annoyance.

bo're-al, 1 bō'rɪ-əl; 2 bō're-al, *a.* Pertaining to the north or the north wind; northern. [north wind.]

Bo're-as, 1 bō'rɪ-əs; 2 bō're-as, *n.* The [north wind.]

born, } Forms of *pp.* of BEAR[1], *v.:* the form
borne, } *born* being restricted to the sense *given birth to, brought forth,* and *borne* used as *pp.* in all other senses.

born, 1 bȇrn; 2 bôrn, *pa.* **1.** Brought forth, as offspring. **2.** Natural; ingrained.

bor'ough, } 1 bur'o; 2 bŭr'o, *n.* **1.** [U.S.]
bor'o[s], } An incorporated village; sec-

tion of a city. **2.** [Eng.] A municipal corporation or a privileged town.

bor'row, 1 bȇr'o; 2 bŏr'o, *vt. & vi.* To obtain on promise of return; copy; adopt; pretend; feign. [words; nonsense.]

bosh, 1 bŏsh; 2 bŏsh, *n.* [Colloq.] Empty

bo'som, 1 bu'zəm; 2 bo'sŏm, *n.* The breast, or the part of a garment covering the breast; the affections.

boss[1], 1 bɔs; 2 bôs. **I**[t]. *vt.* To work in relief; emboss. **II.** *n.* A circular prominence; a knob; stud.— **boss'y,** *a.*

boss[2], 1 bɔs; 2 bôs. [Colloq., U.S.] **I**[t]. *vt. & vi.* To master; manage; dominate. **II.** *n.* **1.** A superintendent or employer; manager; foreman. **2.** A dictator of a political party.

bot, 1 bŏt; 2 bŏt, *n.* A bot=fly, or its larva— **bot'=fly",** *n.* A fly, the larvæ of which are parasitic, as in horses.

bot'a-ny, 1 bŏt'ɑ-nɪ; 2 bŏt'a-ny, *n.* [-NIES[z], *pl.*] The science that treats of plants.— **bo-tan'i-cal,** 1 bo-tan'ɪ-kəl; 2 bo-tăn'ɪ-cal, *a.* **bo-tan'ic.—** **bo-tan'i-cal-ly,** *adv.*— **bot'a-nist,** *n.* One versed in botany.— **bot'a-nize,** 1 bŏt'ɑ-naɪz; 2 bŏt'a-nɪz, *vt. & vi.* [-NIZED; -NIZ'ING.] To make botanical studies; explore as a botanist. **bot'a-nise†.**

botch, 1 bŏch; 2 bŏch. **I**[t]. *vt. & vi.* To **boch**[r], } do in a bungling way; mar; spoil; disfigure; bungle. **II.** *n.* A bungled piece of work; a bungling workman.— **botch'y,** *a.*

both, 1 bōth; 2 bōth. **I.** *a.* The two together; the one and the other alike. **II.** *pron.* The two, including the one and the other; the pair. **III.** *adv. & conj.* Equally; alike; as well.

both'er, 1 bŏth'ȇr; 2 bŏth'ȇr. **I.** *vt. & vi.* To trouble; annoy. **II.** *n.* A source of annoyance; perplexity; vexation.— **both"er-a'tion,** *n.* Annoyance; vexation.

bott, *n.* Same as BOT.

bot'tle, } 1 bŏt'l; 2 bŏt'l, *vt.* [BOT'TLED;
bot'l[r], } BOT'LD[r]; BOT'TLING.] To put into a bottle or bottles; shut in.

bot'tle[1], *n.* **1.** A narrow-mouthed vessel for liquids. **2.** What a bottle will hold. **bot'tle-ful†.**

bot'tle[2]†, *n.* A bundle or truss of hay.

bot'tom, 1 bŏt'əm; 2 bŏt'om. **I.** *vt. & vi.* To base or found (upon); fathom; rest; touch bottom. **II.** *a.* Lowest; fundamental; basal. **III.** *n.* **1.** The lowest part of anything; base; support; root; dregs. **2.** The ground beneath or low land near a body of water. **3.** The part of a vessel below the water=line; hence, a vessel. **4.** Endurance; stamina; grit.— **bot'tom-less,** *a.* Having no bottom; unfathomable; baseless; visionary.

1: ᴀrtistic, ȃrt; fat, fare; fast; get, prēy; hĭt, police; obey, gō; nŏt, ȏr; fŭll, rŭle; bŭt, bŭrn;

2: ärt, āpe, făt, fâre, fȧst, whạt, ạll; mē, gĕt, prey, fȇrn; hĭt, īce; ĭ=ĕ; ĩ=ĕ; gō, nŏt, ôr, wŏn,

bou"doir', 1 bū"dwär'; 2 bụ"dwär', *n.* A lady's private sitting-room.

bough, 1 bau; 2 bou. *n.* A limb of a tree.

bought, 1 bôt; 2 bôt, *imp. & pp.* of BUY, *v.*

bouil'lon, 1 būl'yǒn; 2 bụl'yǒn, *n.* Clear beef soup.

boul'der, 1 bōl'dẽr; 2 bōl'der, *n.* A large detached angular or rounded stone. **bowl'der‡.**

bou'le-vard, 1 bū'lẹ-värd; 2 bụ'le-värd. *n.* A broad avenue, usually planted with trees.

bounce, 1 bauns; 2 bounç. **I.** *vt. & vi.* [BOUNCED‡; BOUNC'ING.] To cause to bound; move with a bound. **II.** *n.* A bounding or elastic motion; spring; leap; bound; rebound.— **bounc'er**, *n.* Something that bounces; a big, strong person or thing; an audacious lie.— **bounc'ing**, *pa.* Strong; large; exaggerated; boastful; untruthful.

bound¹, 1 baund; 2 bound. **I**d. *vi.* To leap lightly; spring; rebound. **II.** *n.* A light elastic spring; a rebound.

bound². **I**d. *vt.* To set bounds to; form the boundary of; adjoin; name the boundaries of. **II.** *n.* **1.** That which circumscribes; a boundary. **2.** *pl.* The district included within a boundary or limits. — **bound'less**, *a.* Having no limit; vast; infinite. **-ly**, *adv.*

bound, *imp. & pp.* of BIND, *v.*

bound, *pa.* **1.** Made fast; tied; confined; compelled. **2.** Having a cover or binding.

bound, *a.* Having one's course directed; destined; with *for* or *to.*

bound'a-ry, 1 baund'ạ-rɪ; 2 bound'a-ry, *n.* [-RIES²‚ *pl.*] A limiting line or mark; limit. [Obligatory; necessary; obliged.

bound'en, 1 baund'en; 2 bound'ĕn, *a.*

boun'te-ous, 1 baun'tɪ-us; 2 boun'te-ŭs, *a.* Generous; beneficent; plentiful. **-ly**, *adv.* **-ness₂** *n.*

boun'ti-ful, 1 baun'tɪ-fyl; 2 boun'ti-fụl, *a.* Bounteous; generous; abundant. **-ly**, *adv.* **-ness₂** *n.*

boun'ty, 1 baun'tɪ; 2 boun'ty, *n.* [-TIES²‚ *pl.*] Liberality; munificence; generous gifts; an allowance from a government.

bou"quet', 1 bū"kẽ'; 2 bụ"ke', *n.* **1.** A bunch of flowers; a nosegay. **2.** Aroma.

bourn, ⎰1 bōrn; 2 bōrn. **1.** A limit;
bourne, ⎱ bound; goal; end. **2.** A burn.

bourse, 1 būrs; 2 bụrs, *n.* **1.** *Finance.* An exchange or money market, especially the Paris stock exchange. **2.** *Anat.* A sac-like structure.

bout, 1 baut; 2 bout, *n.* **1.** A single turn; a set-to; a revel. **2.** A bend or turn, as of a rope; bight. [slow; stupid.

bo'vine, 1 bō'vɪn; 2 bō'vin, *a.* Ox-like;

bow¹, 1 bau; 2 bow, *v.* [BOWED, BOWD³; baud, 2 bowd; BOW'ING, 1 bau'ɪŋ, 2 bow'-ing.] **I.** *t.* To bend or cause to bend forward, as in reverence; subdue; humiliate; oppress. **II.** *i.* To bend; assent; worship; submit; yield.

bow², 1 bō; 2 bō, *vt.* [BOWED, BOWD³; 1 bōd, 2 bōd; BOW'ING, 1 bō'ɪŋ, 2 bō'ing.] To curve like a bow; bend.

bow¹, 1 bō; 2 bō, *n.* A bending of body or head forward and downward, as in salutation.

bow², 1 bō; 2 bō, *n.* **1.** A bend or curve, or something bent or curved, as a loop of rib-

Bow and Arrows

bon, rim of spectacles, etc. **2.** An elastic weapon, bent by a cord, for shooting arrows. **3.** A rod bearing parallel hairs, used with a violin.— **bow'-knot"**, *n.* A knot made to be readily untied.— **bow window**, a curved projecting window built up from the ground-level.

bow³, 1 bau; 2 bow, *n.* The forward part of a vessel; prow.

bow'el, 1 bau'el; 2 bow'ĕl, *n.* An intestine; in the plural, the intestinal regions; formerly, pity; compassion; heart.

bow'er, 1 bau'ẽr; 2 bow'er, *n.* A shady recess; private apartment; arbor; boudoir.

bow'ie-knife", 1 bō'ɪ-naif"; 2 bō'i-nīf", *n.* [U. S.] A strong hunting-knife.

bowl, 1 bōl; 2 bōl, *v.* **I.** *t.* To roll; trundle along; hit with anything rolled; knock down; prostrate. **II.** *i.* To roll a bowl; deliver a cricket-ball or the like; move smoothly, as on wheels.— **bowl'er**, *n.* **1.** One who plays at bowls. **2.** *Cricket.* The player who delivers the ball.

bowl¹, *n.* A concave vessel, larger than a cup; a large goblet. [pins.

bowl², *n.* A large wooden ball for ten-

bow'sprit, 1 bō'sprit; 2 bō'sprĭt, *n.* A spar projecting forward from the bow of a vessel. See illus. under BOOM.

box¹t, 1 bɒks; 2 bŏks, *vt.* To put into or furnish with a box: often with *up.*

box²t, *v.* **I.** *t.* To cuff or buffet. **II.** *i.* To spar, as with boxing-gloves.— **box'ing**, *n.* Sparring; pugilism.

box¹, *n.* **1.** A case, as of wood or metal; a coachman's raised seat. **2.** The quantity that a box will hold.

box², *n.* A slap or cuff.

box³, *n.* A small tree or shrub of the spurge family; also, its wood, called *boxwood.*

box'er¹, *n.* One who packs things in boxes.

box'er², *n.* One who spars or boxes; a pugilist.

Box'er³, *n.* A member of a Chinese secret society, active in 1900, which aimed to rid China of foreigners by massacre, etc.

boy, 1 boi; 2 boy, *n.* A male child; lad; youth.— **boy'hood**, *n.* The state or period of being a boy; boys collectively.— **boy'ish**, *a.* Of, pertaining to, or like boys or boyhood.

boy'cott, 1 boi'kŏt; 2 bŏy'eŏt. **I**ᵈ. *vt.* To exclude from all dealings or intercourse; ostracize. **II**. *n.* Refusal of all dealings with a person or persons.

brace, 1 brēs; 2 brāç. **I**. *vt.* [BRACED^t; BRAC'ING.] To strengthen; prop; bind. **II**. *n.* **1.** A support to hold something firmly in place. **2.** A crank-like handle, as for a bit. See illus. at BIT. **3.** A clasp; a curved line (⌒) for uniting words, etc. **4.** A pair; couple; two.

brace'let, 1 brēs'let; 2 brāç'lĕt, *n.* An ornamental band encircling the wrist or arm.

brack'et, 1 brak'et; 2 brăk'ĕt. **I**ᵈ. *vt.* To put in brackets; join; couple. **II**. *n.* **1.** A piece projecting from a wall, as a support, a gas-fixture, etc. **2.** In printing or writing: (1) One of two enclosing marks [ ]. (2) A brace.

brack'ish, 1 brak'ish; 2 brăk'ish, *a.* Salty; salt.

bract, 1 brakt; 2 brăet, *n.* A modified leaf in a flower-cluster.   [der nail.

brad, 1 brad; 2 brăd. *n.* A small and slender.

brag, 1 brag; 2 brăg. **I**. *vt. & vi.* [BRAGGED, BRAGD³; BRAG'GING.] To boast; vaunt oneself. **II**. *n.* Boastfulness; boast; a boaster.— **brag'gart**, 1 brag'ərt; 2 brăg'ärt, *n.* A vain boaster.

Bráh'má, 1 brä'ma; 2 brä'ma, *n.* Hindu divinity; first of the triad, Bráhmá, Vishnu, and Siva.

braid, 1 brēd; 2 brād. **I**ᵈ. *vt.* To weave together; plait; put braid on. **II**. *n.* A narrow flat strip for binding or ornamenting fabrics; anything braided or plaited.

brain, 1 brēn; 2 brān, *n.* That part of the central nervous system that is within the skull; hence, mind; intellect: often in the plural.— **brain'less**, *a.* Without brain; senseless; stupid.

Brain Trust. [U.S.] A phrase coined in 1933 to designate a group of educators in political science and economy who advised the Chief Executive.

brake¹, 1 brēk; 2 brāk, *v.* [BRAKED; BRAK'ING.] **I**. *t.* To apply a brake to; reduce the speed of; bruise, as flax. **II**. *i.* To act as brakeman.

brake² [Archaic or Poet.], *imp.* of BREAK, *v.*

brake¹, *n.* **1.** A device for retarding motion, as of a wheel. **2.** A harrow. **3.** An implement for separating the fiber of flax, hemp, etc.— **brake'man, brakes'man**, *n.* [-MEN, *pl.*] One who tends a brake or brakes.

brake², *n.* A variety of fern; bracken.

brake³, *n.* A thicket.

bram'ble, 1 bram'bl; 2 brăm'bl, *n.* The
bram'bl', European blackberry; hence, any prickly shrub.

bran, 1 bran; 2 brăn, *n.* The coarse outer coat of wheat, rye, and other cereals.

branch, 1 branch; 2 brănch. **I**ᵗ. *vt. & vi.* To divide into or adorn with branches; put forth branches. **II**. *a.* Diverging from or merging in a trunk, stock, or main part. **III**. *n.* A secondary stem, as of a tree; an offshoot; side issue; division; department; tributary.

brand, 1 brand; 2 brănd. **I**ᵈ. *vt.* To mark with a brand; stigmatize; imprint indelibly. **II**. *n.* **1.** A firebrand; a mark burnt with a hot iron; trade-mark; stigma. **2.** Quality; kind. **3.** A branding-iron. **4.** A sword.

bran'dish, 1 bran'dish; 2 brăn'dish, *vt.* To wave triumphantly or defiantly.

brand'-new', 1 brand'-niū'; 2 brănd'-nū', *a.* Quite new; fresh and bright.

bran'dy, 1 bran'di; 2 brăn'dy, *n.* [BRAN'-DIES², *pl.*] An alcoholic liquor distilled from wine.

bra'sier, *n.* Same as BRAZIER.

brass, 1 bras; 2 brás, *n.* An alloy of copper and zinc.— **bras'sy**, *a.* Covered with, made of, or like brass.   [tuously.

brat, 1 brat; 2 brăt, *n.* A child: contemp-

bra-va'do, 1 bra-vē'[*or* -vä']do; 2 brava'[*or* -vä']do, *n.* [-DOS² *or* -DOES², *pl.*] Arrogant defiance; affectation of bravery.

brave, 1 brēv; 2 brāv. **I**. *vt.* [BRAVED; BRAV'ING.] To meet with courage; defy; dare; challenge. **II**. *a.* [BRAV'ER; BRAV'-EST.] **1.** Having or showing courage; intrepid; courageous. **2**‖. Elegant; showy; splendid. **III**. *n.* A man of courage; a soldier; a North-American Indian warrior; a bravo.— **ly**, *adv.*— **bra'ver-y**, 1 brē'ver-ı; 2 brā'ver-y, *n.* [-IES², *pl.*] **1.** Valor; gallantry; heroism. **2.** Elegance of attire; show; splendor.

bra'vo, 1 brē'vo *or* brä'vo; 2 brä'vo *or* brä'vo. **I**. *n.* [BRA'VOS² *or* BRA'VOES², *pl.*] **1.** A daring villain; hired assassin; bandit. **2.** A shout of applause. **I**. 1 brä'vo; 2 brä'vo, *interj.* Good! well done!

---

brawl, 1 brôl; 2 brạl. **I.** *vt. & vi.* To utter noisily; wrangle; flow noisily, as water. **II.** *n.* A noisy quarrel or wrangle; a row; a roaring of a stream.

brawn, 1 brôn; 2 brạn, *n.* **1.** Flesh; firm muscle; strength. **2.** The flesh of the boar.— **brawn′y,** 1 brôn′i; 2 brạn′y, *a.* Muscular; strong. [or mix, as in mortar.

bray[1], 1 brē; 2 brā, *vt.* To bruise, pound, [cry of an ass.

bray[2], *vt. & vi.* To utter loudly and harshly; give forth a bray.

bray, *n.* Any loud, harsh sound, as the

braze[1], 1 brēz; 2 brāz, *vt.* [BRAZED; BRAZ′ING.] To make of or like brass; ornament with brass.

braze[2], *vt.* To join by hard solder.

bra′zen, 1 brē′zn; 2 brā′zn, *a.* Made of or like brass; impudent; shameless. **-ly,** *adv.* **-ness,** *n.* [who works in brass.

bra′zier[1], 1 brē′ʒər; 2 brā′zher, *n.* One

bra′zier[2], *n.* A pan for holding live coals.

breach, 1 brīch; 2 brēch. **I**[t]. *vt.* To make a breach in; break through. **II.** *n.* The act of breaking; a gap or break; a quarrel.

bread, 1 bred; 2 brĕd, *n.* An article of
breds, food made of flour or meal; provisions; subsistence.

— **bread′fruit″,** *n.* The fruit of a tree of the South Sea Islands: when roasted, resembling bread; also, the tree.— **bread′stuff″,** *n.* Material for bread; grain, meal, or flour.

breadth, 1 bredth;
bredths, 2 brĕdth, *n.* Measure or distance from side to side; width; liberality; a piece of a fabric of uniform width.

break, 1 brēk; 2 brāk, *v.* [BROKE, 1 brōk, 2 brōk, *or* BRAKE (poet.); BRO′KEN, 1 brō′kn, 2 brō′kn, *or* BROKE; BREAK′ING.]
I. *t.* **1.** To separate into parts or fragments, as by a blow; rupture; shatter. **2.** To fail to keep; violate; transgress. **3.** To make bankrupt. **4.** To degrade, as a military or naval officer; cashier. **5.** To disclose cautiously, as ill tidings. **6.** To reduce to discipline; tame. **II.** *i.* **1.** To become fractured, as by a blow; part; burst. **2.** To change suddenly; dawn, as the day; begin. **3.** To fail; become bankrupt.— **break′a-ble**(e[r]), *a.*— **break′age,** *n.* **1.** A breaking, or being broken. **2.** Articles broken.— **break′down″,** *n.* The act of

Breadfruit. 1/11

breaking down; a collapse.— **break′er,** *n.* One who or that which breaks; a wave that breaks on a beach, etc.— **break′neck″. I.** *a.* Likely to break the neck; dangerous. **II.** *n.* A steep and dangerous place.— **break′wa″ter,** *n.* A mole or wall for protecting a harbor from the force of waves.

break, 1 brēk; 2 brāk, *n.* **1.** A breach; interruption. **2.** A starting or opening out; as, the *break* of day.

break′fast, 1 brek′fəst; 2 brĕk′fast. **I**[d].
brek′fasts, *vt. & vi.* To give a breakfast to; eat breakfast. **II.** *n.* The first meal of the day.

breast, 1 brest; 2 brĕst. **I**[d]. *vt.* To en-
brests, counter; buffet; stem. **II.** *n.* **1.** The front of the chest. **2.** One of the mammary glands; the bosom. **3.** The seat of the affections: mind; heart.— **breast′plate″,** *n.* Defensive plate armor for the breast.— **breast′work″,** *n* *Fort* A low temporary defensive work; a parapet.

breath, 1 breth; 2 brĕth, *n.* **1.** Air re-
breths, spired; respiration; life. **2.** A breathing-time; pause; instant.— **breath′less,** *a.* **1.** Out of breath; taking away the breath; intense; eager. **2.** Without breath; dead. **-ly,** *adv.* **-ness,** *n.*

breathe, 1 brīth; 2 brēth, *v.* [BREATHED, BREATHD[s]; BREATH′ING.] **I.** *t.* **1.** To inhale and exhale, as air; respire; emit; utter; manifest. **2.** To exercise; overtire. **3.** To rest, as for breath. **II.** *i.* **1.** To inhale and exhale air; respire; be alive. **2.** To pause for breath. **3.** To exhale.

bred, *imp. & pp.* of BREED, *v.*

breech, 1 brīch; 2 brēch, *n.* The posterior and lower part of the body; the rear end of a gun.

breech′es, 1 brich′ez; 2 brĭch′ĕş, *n. pl.* A garment for men, covering the waist, hips, and thighs.

breech′ing, 1 brich′ɪŋ; 2 brĭch′ĭng, *n.* A hold=back strap passing behind a horse's haunches.

breed, 1 brīd; 2 brēd, *v.* [BRED; BREED′ING.] **I.** *t.* **1.** To produce, as offspring; beget; hatch; raise; originate; cause. **2.** To bring up; train. **II.** *i.* **1.** To produce young. **2.** To be born; develop; originate.— **breed′ing,** 1 brid′ɪŋ; 2 brēd′ĭng, *n.* **1.** The production of offspring. **2.** Nurture; training; manners.

breed, *n.* The progeny of one stock; a race or strain; a sort or kind.

breeze, 1 brīz; 2 brēz, *n.* A light wind.—
breez[r], breez′y, 1 brīz′ɪ; 2 brēz′y, *a.* Airy; windy; animated.

breth′ren, 1 breth′ren; 2 brĕth′rĕn, *n. pl.* Brothers.

bre-vet′, 1 bri-vet′; 2 bre-vĕt′. **I.** *vt.* [BRE-VET′TED^d; BRE-VET′TING.] To promote by brevet. **II.** *a.* Held or conferred by brevet; holding rank by brevet; brevetted. **III.** *n.* *Mil.* A commission giving an officer an honorary rank above his pay. [*pl.*] A prayer-book.

bre′vi-a-ry, 1 brī′vi-ĕ-ri; 2 brē′vi-ā-ry, *n.* [-RIES^z.]

brev′i-ty, 1 brev′i-tı; 2 brĕv′i-ty, *n.* [-TIES^z, *pl.*] Shortness; conciseness.

brew, 1 brū; 2 brụ. **I.** *vt. & vi.* To make by fermentation, as beer; concoct; plot; contrive; be preparing. **II.** *n.* That which is brewed; the product of brewing. — **brew′er,** 1 brū′ər; 2 brụ′er, *n.* — **brew′er-y,** 1 brū′ər-ı; 2 brụ′er-y, *n.* [-IES^z, *pl.*] An establishment for brewing.

bribe, 1 braib; 2 brīb. **I.** *vt. & vi.* [BRIBED; BRIB′ING.] To give a bribe; give or offer bribes. **II.** *n.* Any gift used corruptly to influence public or official action; anything that seduces or allures; an allurement.— **brib′er,** *n.* One who gives or offers a bribe.— **brib′er-y,** *n.* [-IES^z, *pl.*] The giving, offering, or accepting of a bribe.

bric′-a-brac′, 1 brik′=a=brak″; 2 brĭc′=a=brăc″, *n.* Objects of curiosity; rarities; antiques.

brick, 1 brik; 2 brĭk. **I^t.** *vt.* To cover or line with bricks. **II.** *n.* A molded block of clay, usually burned; bricks collectively.— **brick′bat″,** *n.* A piece of a brick. — **brick′=kiln″,** 1 brik′=kĭl″; 2 brĭk′=kĭl″, *n.* A structure in which bricks are burned.— **brick′lay″er,** *n.* One who builds with bricks.

bri′dal, 1 brai′dəl; 2 brī′dal. **I.** *a.* Pertaining to a bride or wedding. **II.** *n.* A wedding.

bride, 1 braid; 2 brīd, *n.* A newly married woman; woman about to be married.

bride′groom″, 1 braid′grūm″; 2 brĭd′grōōm″, *n.* A man newly married or about to be married.

brides′maid″, 1 braidz′mēd″; 2 brĭdʒ′mād″, *n.* An unmarried woman who attends a bride at her wedding.

bridge, 1 brij; 2 brĭdʒ. **I.** *vt.* [BRIDGED; BRIDG′ING.] To span, as with a bridge; get over; pass. **II.** *n.* A structure erected to afford passage across a waterway, gorge, or the like; a raised support.

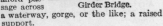

Girder Bridge.

bridge whist. A variety of the game of whist.

bri′dle, 1 brai′dl; 2 brī′dl, *v.* [BRI′DLED; BRI′DLING.] **I.** *t.* To put a bridle on; check; curb; control. **II.** *i.* To raise the head and draw in the chin, as through resentment, etc.

bri′dle, *n.* The head-harness of a horse, including bit and reins; any check; curb.

brief, 1 brīf; 2 brēf. **I^t.** *vt.* To epitomize; abridge. **II.** *a.* Short in time or space; quickly passing; concise; limited. **III.** *n.* Any short statement, as of a law-case; an epitome. — **brief′ly,** *adv.*

bri′er, 1 brai′ər; 2 brī′er, *n.* A prickly bush or shrub. **bri′ar‡.— bri′er-y,** *a.*

brig, 1 brig; 2 brĭg, *n.* A two-masted square-rigged vessel.

bri-gade′, 1 bri-gēd′; 2 bri-gād′. *Mil.* **I.** *vt.* [BRI-GAD′ED^d; BRI-GAD′ING.] To form into a brigade. **II.** *n.* A force of two or more regiments.

brig″a-dier′, 1 brig″ə-dīr′; 2 brĭg″a-dēr′, *n.* A general who commands a brigade. **brigadier=general‡.**

brig′and, 1 brig′ənd; 2 brĭg′and, *n.* A robber; a bandit.— **brig′and-age,** *n.* Robbery; brigands collectively.

brig′an-tine, 1 brig′an-tin; 2 brĭg′an-tĭn, *n.* A vessel like a brig, except for having a fore-and-aft mainsail: once much used by pirates.

bright, 1 brait; 2 brīt, *a.* Full of light; shining; brilliant; quick-witted; cheery; illustrious. **-ly,** *adv.* **-ness,** *n* — **bright′en,** 1 brait′n; 2 brīt′n, *vt. & vi.* To make or become bright or brighter; illuminate; cheer.

bril′liance, } 1 bril′yəns, -yən-sı; 2 brĭl′-
bril′lian-cy, } yanç, -yan-çy, *n.* Brightness; luster.

bril′liant, 1 bril′yənt; 2 brĭl′yant. **I.** *a.* Glowing with light; gleaming; splendid; accomplished; illustrious. **II.** *n.* A diamond of the finest cut. **-ly,** *adv.* **-ness,** *n.*

brim, 1 brim; 2 brĭm. **I.** *vt. & vi.* [BRIMMED; BRIMD^s; BRIM′MING.] To fill or be filled to the brim. **II.** *n.* The rim, as of a cup; margin; edge; border. — **brim′ful′,** *a.* Full to the brim. **brim′full″‡.**

brim′stone, 1 brim′stōn″; 2 brĭm′stŏn″, *n.* Sulfur.

brin′dled, 1 brin′dld; 2 brĭn′dld, *a.* Irregularly streaked with color. **brin′ded‡.— brin′dle‡,** 1 brin′dl; 2 brĭn′dl. **I.** *a.* Brindled. **II.** *n.* A brindled color, or a brindled animal.

brine, 1 brain; 2 brīn, *n.* Salt water; the sea; tears.— **brin′y,** *a.*

bring, 1 brin; 2 brĭng, *vt.* [BROUGHT, 1 brɔt; 2 brôt; BRING′ING.] **1.** To convey or conduct to or toward the speaker; cause to

come; fetch. **2.** To influence; persuade; produce; render; fetch as a price.

brink, 1 brĭŋk; 2 brĭŋk, *n.* The verge, as of a precipice; margin; bank; shore.

bri′o, 1 brī′o; 2 brī′o, *adv. Mus.* With animation; spiritedly. **con brio‡.**

brisk, 1 brisk; 2 brisk, *a.* Quick; sprightly; lively. **-ly,** *adv.* **-ness,** *n.*

bris′ket, 1 bris′ket; 2 bris′kĕt, *n.* The breast of an animal.

bris′tle, 1 bris′l; 2 bris′l. **I.** *vt. & vi.* [BRIS′TLED, BRIS′TLD²; BRIS′TLING.] **1.** To erect, or stand erect, as bristles; make bristly; excite; irritate; agitate. **2.** To be thickly beset, as with bristles. **II.** *n.* A coarse, stiff hair, as of swine.— **bris′tly,** 1 bris′li; 2 bris′li, *a.* Having or resembling bristles.— **bris′tli-ness,** *n.*

Brit′ish, 1 brit′ish; 2 brit′ish. **I.** *a.* Pertaining to Great Britain, the United Kingdom, or the British Empire. **Bri-tan′nic‡. II.** *n.* **1.** *pl.* The people of Great Britain or of the British Empire. **2.** The language of the ancient Britons.

Brit′on, 1 brit′ən; 2 brit′on, *n.* **1.** One of the ancient Celtic people of Great Britain. **2.** A native or citizen of Great Britain.

brit′tle, 1 brit′l; 2 brit′l, *a.* Liable to **brit′l²,** break; fragile.— **brit′tle-ness,** *n.*

broach, 1 brōch; 2 brōch. **I‡.** *vt.* **1.** To mention or introduce (a matter); make public. **2.** To tap, as a cask. **II.** *n.* **1.** A boring-tool; reamer. **2.** A brooch.

broad, 1 brɵd; 2 brôd, *a.* **1.** Extended in width; wide; vast. **2.** Comprehensive; catholic; liberal; tolerant. **3.** Strong, rude, or coarse, as speech. **-ly,** *adv.* **-ness,** *n.*
— **broad′cast″. I.** *vt.* To scatter widely; send by radio or wireless. **II.** *a. & adv.* Scattered abroad, as seed. **III.** *n.* A casting or scattering of seed, etc., over the ground.—
broad′cloth″, *n.* A fine quality of woven fabric.—**broad′side″. I.** *n.* **1.** All the guns on one side of a man-of-war, or their simultaneous discharge; any sweeping attack. **2.** A vessel's side above the water-line. **3.** A large sheet of paper, printed on one side. **II.** *adv.* With the broadside turned, presented, or exposed.— **broad′sword″,** *n.* A sword with a broad cutting blade and obtuse point.

broad′en, 1 brɵd′n; 2 brôd′n, *vt. & vi.* To make or become broad or broader.

bro-cade′, 1 bro-kēd′; 2 bro-cād′, *n.* A silken fabric woven with raised figures.

bro″chure′, 1 bro″shūr′; 2 bro″çhūr′, *n.* A pamphlet; slight sketch.

bro′gan, 1 brō′gan; 2 brō′găn, *n.* A coarse, heavy shoe.

brogue, 1 brōg; 2 brōg, *n.* A manner of pronouncing English peculiar to some of the Irish.

broil, 1 brɵil; 2 brɵil, *vt. & vi.* To cook by direct heat, as over coals.

broil¹, *n.* A turmoil; noisy quarrel; brawl.

broil², *n.* Something broiled; a broiling heat.

broke, *imp.* **bro′ken,** *pp.,* of BREAK, *v.*

bro′ker, 1 brō′kər; 2 brō′ker, *n.* One who buys and sells for another on commission.
— **bro′ker-age,** *n.* The business or commission of a broker.

bron′chi-al, 1 brɵŋ′kɪ-əl; 2 brɵŋ′ei-al, *a.* Of or pertaining to the chief air-passages of the lungs, called the *bronchial tubes.*—
bron-chi′tis, 1 brɵŋ-kai′tis or -kī′tis; 2 brɵŋ-ei′tis or -ei′tis, *n.* Inflammation of the bronchial tubes.

bron′co, 1 brɵŋ′ko; 2 brɵŋ′eo, *n.* [U. S.] A native American horse; mustang. **bron′cho‡.**

bronze, 1 brenz; 2 brŏnz. **I.** *vt.*
bronz², [BRONZ(E)D³; BRONZ′ING.] To harden or color like bronze; brown; tan. **II.** *n.* A reddish-brown alloy of copper and tin, or a statue made of it; a bronze-like pigment.—**bron′zy,** *a.* [*n.* A breastpin.

brooch, 1 brōch or rūch; 2 brōch or brōōch.

brood, 1 brūd; 2 brōōd. **I.** *vt. & vi.* To cover, as a bird its young; incubate; cherish; nurse; meditate. **II.** *a.* All the young birds of a single hatching; offspring; progeny.

brook¹, 1 bruk; 2 brŏŏk, *vt.* To put up with; endure. [*let.*

brook, *n.* A small natural stream; a rivu-
room, 1 brūm; 2 brōōm, *n.* **1.** A brush for sweeping. **2.** A shrub of the bean family, with stiff green branches.— **broom′-corn″,** *n.* A cane-like grass, of which brooms are made.— **broom′stick″,** *n.* The handle of a broom.

broth, 1 brɵth; 2 brôth, *n.* The liquor in which meat has been boiled; a thin or strained soup.

broth′er, 1 bruth′ər; 2 brŏth′er, *n.* [BROTH′ERS or BRETH′REN, 1 breth′ren; 2 brĕth′ren, *pl.*] A son of the same parents or parent; a close companion or associate.
— **broth′er-hood,** *n.* Fraternal relationship; a society or fraternity.— **broth′er-in-law″,** *n.* A brother of a husband or of a wife; the husband of a sister or of a wife's sister.
— **broth′er-ly,** *a.* Pertaining to or like a brother; fraternal.

brough′am, 1 brū′am; 2 brṳ′am, *n.* A close four-wheeled vehicle.

brought, 1 brɵt; 2 brôt, *imp. & pp.* of BRING, *v.*

brow, 1 brau; 2 brow, *n.* The forehead; eyebrow; Brougham. countenance; upper edge of a cliff or the like.

1: ə = fin*al*; **ɪ** = hab*it*; **aɪsle**; **au** = *out*; **ɵil**; **iū** = f*eu*d; **ch**in; **g**o; **ŋ** = si*ng*; **th**in, **this**.
2: wolf, do̧; bŏŏk, bōōt; fṳll, rṳle, cūre, bŭt, bûrn; ɵil, bŏy; g̑o, g̑em; iŋk; thin, this.

brow'beat", 1 brau'bīt"; 2 brow'bĕt", *vt.* [BROW'BEAT"; BROW'BEAT"EN; BROW'BEAT"ING.] To intimidate; cow; bully.

brown, 1 braun; 2 brown. **I.** *vt. & vi.* To make or become brown; bronze; tan. **II.** *a.* Of a color made up of red, yellow, and black. **III.** *n.* A dusky color, as of faded leaves, or a pigment or dye producing it; a thing or part that is brown. **— brown'ish,** *a.* Of a color inclining to brown.— **brown study,** absent-mindedness; deep reverie.

brown'ie, 1 braun'i; 2 brown'i, *n.* A homely good-natured sprite.

bru'in, 1 brū'in; 2 brụ'in, *n.* A bear.

bruise, 1 brūz; 2 brụs. **I.** *vt. & vi.* [BRUISED; BRUIS'ING.] To batter; dent; inflict a bruise or bruises; contuse; crush. **II.** *n.* A surface injury caused by violent contact; contusion. — **bruis'er,** *n.* A pugilist.

bruit, 1 brūt; 2 brụt. **I**d. *vt. & vi.* To noise abroad; report; proclaim. **II.** *n.* A rumor noised abroad; a din; clamor.

bru-nette', 1 bru-net'; 2 brụ-nĕt', *n.* A woman or girl of dark complexion, eyes, and hair.   [shock or stress; hardest part.

brunt, 1 brunt; 2 brụnt, *n.* The main

brush, 1 brush; 2 brụsh. **I**t. *vt. & vi.* To use a brush on; sweep; touch or move lightly. **II.** *n.* **1.** An implement, as of bristles, for cleansing, smoothing, etc. **2.** The act of brushing. **3.** A thicket; wooded country; brushwood. **4.** A bushy object, as the tail of the fox. **5.** A smart skirmish; a dashing ride; chase. — **brush'wood",** *n.* A low thicket; underwood; cut bushes or branches.

brusk, } 1 brusk, brụsk; 2 brŭsk, brụsk,
brusque, } *a.* Rude or curt; blunt; offhand. **-ly,** *adv.* **-ness,** *n.*

brute, 1 brūt; 2 brụt. **I.** *a.* Animal; unintelligent; material, unconscious; brutal. **II.** *n.* Any animal other than man; a brutal person.— **bru'tal,** *a.* Characteristic of or like a brute; sensual; cruel; unfeeling; rude.— **bru-tal'i-ty,** *n.* [-TIES², *pl.*] The being brutal; a brutal action.— **bru'tal-ize,** *vt.* [-IZED; -IZ'ING.] To make brutal.— **bru'tal-ly,** *adv.*— **bru'tish,** *a.* Of or like a brute; stupid; irrational; sensual.— **brut'ish-ly,** *adv.*— **brut'ish-ness,** *n.*

bub'ble, } 1 bub'l; 2 bŭb'l. **I.** *vi.* [BUB'-
bub'le, } BLED, BUB'LD²; BUB'BLING.] To form bubbles; rise in bubbles; make an intermittent liquid sound. **II.** *n.* **1.** A vesicle of liquid, filled with air or other gas. **2.** Anything unsubstantial; a delusion; cheat; fraud.

buc"ca-neer', } 1 buk"a-nīr'; 2 bŭc"a-nēr',
buc"a-nier', } *n.* A pirate or freebooter.

Bu-ceph'a-lus, 1 biu-sef'a-lus; 2 bū-çĕf'a-lŭs, *n.* The war-horse of Alexander the Great.

buckt, 1 buk, 2 bŭk, *vt. & vi.* To spring viciously from the ground, as a horse or mule; throw (a rider) by vicious plunges.

buck¹, *n.* **1.** The male of various animals, as of deer. **2.** A dashing fellow.

buck², *n.* The act of bucking.

buck'board", 1 buk'bōrd"; 2 bŭk'bōrd", *n.* [U. S.] A light, four-wheeled vehicle with elastic board instead of body and springs.

buck'et, 1 buk'et; 2 bŭk'ĕt, *n.* A vessel, with a bail, for dipping or carrying liquids; a compartment on a water-wheel, or the like.

buck'eye", 1 buk'ai"; 2 bŭk'-I", *n.* The horse-chestnut of the United States.

Bucket.

buck'le¹, 1 buk'l; 2 bŭk'l. *v.*
buck'le, {[BUCK'L(E)D²; BUCK'LING.] **I.** *t.* To fasten with or as with a buckle. **II.** *i.* To apply oneself vigorously: with *to* or *down to*.

buck'le², 1 buk'l; 2 bŭk'l, *vt. & vi.* To bend, warp, curl, or crumple.

buck'ler¹, *n.* A metal frame with movable tongue, for fastening straps, etc.

buck'ler², *n.* distortion.

buck'ler, 1 -lər; 2 -ler, *n.* A small round shield.

buck'ram, 1 buk'ram; 2 bŭk'ram. **I.** *a.* Of or like buckram; stiff; precise. **II.** *n.* A coarse fabric, for stiffening garments.

buck'shot", 1 buk'shet"; 2 bŭk'shŏt", *n.* Large shot, used in hunting, as for deer.

buck'skin", 1 buk'skin"; 2 bŭk'skin". **I.** *a.* Made of or colored like buckskin. **II.** *n.* The skin of a buck; a soft, strong, grayish-yellow leather.

buck'wheat", 1 buk'hwīt"; 2 bŭk'hwēt", *n.* A plant, or its triangular seeds, from which a flour is made.

bu-col'ic, 1 biu-kol'ik; 2 bū-cŏl'ic. **I.** *a.* Of or like shepherds or herdsmen; pastoral; rustic. **II.** *n.* A pastoral poem.

bud, 1 bud; 2 bŭd. **I.** *vt. & vi.* [BUD'DED²; BUD'DING.] **1.** To graft by inserting a bud into the slit bark. **2.** To put forth, as buds; begin to grow. **II.** *n.* **1.** An undeveloped stem, branch, or flower. **2.** The act or stage of budding.

Bud'dha, 1 bud'a; 2 bud'a, **Gotama Sa-kya-sinha** (d. about 480 B. C.). The founder of Buddhism. — **Bud'dhism,** *n.* A religious cult, widely prevalent in Asia.

bud'dy, 1 bud'i; 2 bŭd'y, *n.* [-DIES², *pl.*] A son or daughter; hence, a companion; chum.

budge, 1 buj; 2 bŭdj, *vt. & vi.* [BUDGED; BUDG'ING.] To move a little; give way; go.

1: ärtistic, ärt; fat, fāre; fast; get, prēy; hit, police; obey, gō; not, ẽr; full, rūle; but, bŭrn.
2: ärt, āpe, fät, fâre, fàst, whạt, ạll; mē, gĕt, prey, fẽrn; hit, īce; ī=ĕ; ĩ=ĕ; gō, nŏt, ôr, wǒo,

budg′et, 1 buj′et; 2 bŭdg′ĕt, *n.* Formerly, a small sack, or its contents; a collection of news; financial estimate.

buff, 1 buf; 2 bŭf.
bufᴿ, I. *a.* Made of buff = leather; brownish = yellow. II. *n.* 1. A thick, soft, flexible leather. **buff′=leath″=erʇ.** 2. A light brownish = yellow. 3. A coat made of buff=leather.

buf′fa-lo, 1 buf′a-lo; 2 bŭf′a-lo, *n.* [-LOESᶻ *or* -LOSᶻ *pl.*] 1. A large Old World ox. 2. The North=American bison.

Buffalo. ¹⁄₄₅

buf′fer, 1 buf′er; 2 bŭf′er, *n.* A device for lessening the shock of concussion.

buf′fetᵈ, 1 buf′et; 2 bŭf′ĕt, *vt. & vi.* To strike; beat; struggle against; contend.

buf′fet¹, 1 buf′et *or* bu-fē′ *or* bu-fā′, *n.* 1. A sideboard. 2. A public lunch=room. [cuff; assault.

buf′fet², 1 buf′et; 2 bŭf′ĕt, *n.* A blow;

buf-foon′, 1 bu-fūn′; 2 bŭ-fōōn′, *n.* A professional clown; low jester.— **buf-foon′er-y,** *n.* [-IESᶻ *pl.*] Low drollery.

bug, 1 bug; 2 bŭg, *n.* Any one of various insects or small crustaceans.

bug′bear″, 1 bug′bār″; 2 bŭg′bâr″, *n.* An imaginary object of terror; a specter. **bug′-a-boo**ʇ.

bug′gy, 1 bug′i; 2 bŭg′y, *n.* [BUG′GIESᶻ *pl.*] A light four=wheeled vehicle with or without a hood.

bu′gle, 1 biū′gl; 2 bū′gl, *n.* A wind=instrument resembling a horn or trumpet; a huntsman's horn. **bu′gle=horn″**ʇ. — **bu′gler,** 1 biū′glẹr; 2 bū′glẹr, *n.* One who plays on the bugle.

Bugle.

buhl, 1 būl; 2 bul, *n.* Metal or tortoise= shell inlaid in furniture; also, cabinet= work so decorated.

build, 1 bild; 2 bĭld, *v.* [BUILT *or* BUILD′EDᵈ; BUILD′ING.] I. *t.* To frame, construct, or erect as a house; fabricate; establish; found; strengthen: often with *up.* II. *i.* 1. To follow the business of building; construct. 2. To rely; depend: with *on* or *upon.*— **build,** *n.* The manner or style in which anything is built; form; figure. — **build′er,** *n.*— **build′ing,** *n.* That which is built; an edifice; the art of building.

bulb, 1 bulb; 2 bŭlb, *n.* 1. *Bot.* A cluster of thickened leaves, growing usually un-

derground. 2. A bulbous protuberance. — **bulb′ous,** *a.* 1. Having or growing from bulbs. 2. Of, pertaining to, or like a bulb.

bulge, 1 bulj; 2 bŭlg. I. *vt. & vi.* [BULGED; BULG′-ING.] To swell out; press out of shape. II. *n.* The most convex part, as of a cask; a swelling.

bulk, 1 bulk; 2 bŭlk, *n.* Magnitude; mass; size; a large body; the greater part.— **bulk′y,** *a.* [BULK′I-ER; BULK′I-EST.] Huge; large; unwieldy.— **bulk′i-ness,***n.*

bulk′age, 1 bulk′ij; 2 bŭlk′ag, *n.* The non=assimilable accessory of food elements, such as vegetable fiber, that stimulates intestinal activity.

Bulb of Lily.
a, flower; *b,* bulb.

bulk′head″, 1 bulk′hed″; 2 bŭlk′hĕd″, *n.*
bulk′hed″ˢ, A partition, as in a ship.

bull¹, 1 bul; 2 bul, *n.* 1. The male of
bullᴾ, domestic cattle or of some other animals. 2. A dealer who seeks or expects higher prices.

bull², *n.* An official document of the Pope.

bull³, *n.* A ridiculous contradiction in terms; a blundering statement.

bull′dog″, 1 bul′dôg″; 2 bul′dôg″, *n.* A squat and muscular dog.

bull′doze′, 1 bul′dōz′; 2 bul′dōz′, *vt.* [BULL′-DOZED′; BULL′DOZ′ING.] [Slang, U. S.] To intimidate; bully.

bul′let, 1 bul′et; 2 bul′ĕt, *n.* A small projectile for a firearm.— **dumdum bullet,** an expanding or man=stopping bullet.

bul′le-tin, 1 bul′i-tin; 2 bul′e-tĭn, *n.* A brief official summary or publication.

bull′finch″, 1 bul′finch″; 2 bul′fĭnch″, *n.* A singing bird having a short stout bill.

bull′frog″, 1 bul′frôg″; 2 bul′frŏg, *n.* A large North=American frog.

bul′lion, 1 bul′yan; 2 bul′yon, *n.* Gold or silver uncoined or in mass. [ox.

bul′lock, 1 bul′ak; 2 bul′ok, *n.* A young

bull's′=eye″, 1 bulz′=ai″; 2 buls′=ī″, *n.* The center of a target; a circular window; a thick lens of glass, or a lantern fitted with one; a small perforated wooden block.

bul′ly, 1 bul′i; 2 bul′y. I. *vt. & vi.* [BUL′-LIED; BUL′LY-ING.] To browbeat; terrorize; coerce; quarrel; bluster. II. *n.* [BUL′LIESᶻ *pl.*] A quarrelsome, swaggering, cowardly fellow.

---

bul′rush″, 1 bul′rush″; 2 bȕl′rŭsh″, *n.* A tall rush.

bul′wark, 1 bul′wərk; 2 bȕl′wark, *n.* A rampart; defense; raised side of a ship.

bum′ble-bee″, 1 bum′bl-bī″; 2 bŭm′bl-bē″, *n.* A large hairy social bee. **hum′ble-bee″‡.**

bum′boat, 1 bum′bōt; 2 bŭm′bōt, *n.* A clumsy boat for peddling provisions to ships in port, etc.

bump, 1 bump; 2 bŭmp. **I**[t]. *vt.* To thump; knock; jolt. **II.** *n.* **1.** A violent impact or collision; a heavy blow. **2.** A protuberance like that caused by a blow.

Bumblebee. ²/₃

bump′er[1], 1 bump′ər; 2 bŭmp′er, *n.* **1.** Something that bumps or causes a bump. **2.** A buffer.

bump′er[2], *n.* A glass filled to the brim.

bump′kin, 1 bump′kin; 2 bŭmp′kin, *n.* An awkward rustic; a clown; lout.

bun, 1 bun; 2 bŭn, *n.* A small sweet cake.

bunch, 1 bunch; 2 bŭnch. **I**[t]. *vt. & vi.* To make into or form a bunch; collect; gather; group. **II.** *n.* **1.** A compact collection; group; cluster. **2.** A hump; protuberance.— **bunch′y,** *a.* Being, growing in, or having bunches; like a bunch.

bun′dle, 1 bun′dl; 2 bŭn′dl. **I.** *vt. &*
bun′dl[P], *j vi.* [BUN′DLED, BUN′DLD[P]; BUN′-DLING.] **1.** To make into a bundle: often with *up.* **2.** To dismiss or quit summarily: often with *off* or *out.* **II.** *n.* A package; group; collection.

bung, 1 bung; 2 bŭng, *n.* A stopper for the large hole of a cask; also, the hole itself. **bung′-hole″‡.**

bun′ga-low, 1 bung′gə-lō; 2 bŭng′gȧ-lō, *n.* A country house, of one story.

bun′gle, 1 bung′gl; 2 bŭn′gl. **I.** *vt. &*
bun′gl[P], *j vi.* [BUN′GLED, BUN′GLD[P]; BUN′-GLING.] To make or do badly; botch. **II.** *n.* An awkward imperfect job; botch.— **bun′gler,** *n.*— **bun′gling,** *pa.* Awkward; clumsy; unskilful.

bun′ion, 1 bun′yən; 2 bŭn′yon, *n.* A painful swelling of the basal joint of the great toe.

bunk, 1 bunk; 2 bŭnk. **I**[t]. *vi.* To sleep in a bunk; go to bed. **II.** *n.* A shelf or recess, etc., used for a bed.

bun′ker, 1 bung′kər; 2 bŭn′ker, *n.* A large receptacle, as a coal-bin on a ship.

bun′ting[1], 1 bun′tiŋ; 2 bŭn′ting, *n.* A light, woolen stuff used for flags; hence, flags, etc.

bun′ting[2], *n.* A finchlike bird.

bun′yon, *n.* Same as BUNION.

buoy, 1 boi; 2 bŏy. **I.** *vt.* To keep afloat; support; mark with buoys. **II.** *n.* A float moored, as on a rock or shoal, for a guide to navigators.— **buoy′an-cy,** 1 boi′an-si; 2 bŏy′an-cy, *n.* **1.** Power or tendency to keep afloat. **2.** Elasticity of spirits; cheerfulness.— **buoy′ant,** 1 boi′ant; 2 bŏy′ant, *a.* Having the power to float; vivacious; cheerful; hopeful. **-ly,** *adv.*

Buntings. ¹/₈

1. The Snow-bunti g. 2. The Corn-bunting.

bur, *{* 1 bur; 2 bûr, *n.* **1.** A prick-
burr, *{ n.* ly flower-head, or the like. **2.** The burdock. **3.** A protuberance; lump. **4.** An unwelcome adherent. **5.** A burrstone. See BURR.

bur′bot, 1 bur′bət; 2 bûr′bot, *n.* A fish with barbels on the nose and chin.

bur′den, 1 bur′dn; 2 bûr′dn, *vt.* To load or overload.

bur′den[1], *n.* **1.** Something heavy to bear; a load. **2.** The carrying capacity of a vessel.— **bur′den-some,** *a.* Hard or heavy to bear; oppressive.

bur′den[2], *n.* The refrain of a song.

bur′dock, 1 bur′dok; 2 bûr′dŏk, *n.* A coarse weed with a globular bur.

bu′reau, 1 biū′ro; 2 bū′ro, *n.* [BU′REAUS or BU′REAUX, 1 biū′rōz; 2 bū′rōɔ, *pl.*] **1.** [U. S.] A chest of drawers for clothing, etc. **2.** A public department; a staff of literary workers, or the place where the work is done. **3.** A writing-desk. [village.

burg, 1 bûrg; 2 bûrg, *n.* A borough;

bur′gess, 1 bûr′jes; 2 bûr′gĕs, *n.* A free-man, citizen, or officer of a borough or burg.

burgh, 1 bûrg; 2 bûrg, *n.* An incorporated town or village; borough; originally, a castle.— **burgh′er,** *n.* An inhabitant or citizen of a burgh.

bur′glar, 1 bûr′glər; 2 bûr′glar, *n.* One who commits a burglary.— **bur-gla′ri-ous,** *a.*— **bur′gla-ry,** *n.* [-RIES[Z], *pl.*] The break-ing and entering of a building with intent to rob.

bur′go-mas″ter, 1 bûr′go-mas″tər; 2 bûr′-go-más″ter, *n.* A Dutch magistrate; mayor.

bur′i-al, 1 ber′i-al; 2 bĕr′i-al, *n.* The burying of a dead body; sepulture.

bu'rin, 1 biū'rin; 2 bū'rin, *n.* An engravers' tool; graver.

bur'lap, 1 bŭr'lap; 2 bûr'lăp, *n.* A coarse stuff for wrapping.

bur-lesque', 1 bŭr-lĕsk'; 2 bûr-lĕsk'. **I.** *vt. & vi.* [BUR-LESQUED't; BUR-LESQU'ING.] To represent ludicrously; caricature. **II.** *a.* Marked by ludicrous incongruity. **III.** *n.* Ludicrous representation; caricature.

bur'ly, 1 bŭr'li; 2 bûr'ly, *a.* [BUR'LI-ER; BUR'LI-EST.] Large of body; bulky; stout; lusty.— **bur'li-ness,** *n.*

burn, 1 bŭrn; 2 bûrn, *v.* [BURNED or BURNT, BURND⁸; BURN'ING.] **I.** *t.* To affect or destroy by or as by fire; consume; scorch. **II.** *i.* To be on fire; appear or feel hot; be eager or excited; glow.

burn¹, *n.* An effect or injury from burning; a burnt place.

burn², *n.* [Scot.] A brook or rivulet.
bournt; bourne‡.

burn'er, 1 bŭrn'ėr; 2 bûrn'er, *n.* One who or that which burns; the part of a lamp, or the like, that carries the flame.

bur'nisht, 1 bŭr'nĭsh; 2 bûr'nish, *vt. & vi.* To polish by friction; make or become bright. [BURN, *v.*]

burnt, 1 bŭrnt; 2 bûrnt, *imp. & pp.* of **burr,** 1 bŭr; 2 bûr, *n.* **1.** A roughness or **bur⁸,** } rough edge, or a tool that produces it. **2.** A burrstone or a millstone made of it. See BUR.— **burr'stone",** *n.* A hard, compact rock, from which millstones are made.

bur'ro, 1 bur'o; 2 bŭr'o, *n.* [Sp. or Southwestern U. S.] A small donkey, used as a pack-animal.

bur'row, 1 bur'o; 2 bŭr'o. **I.** *vt. & vi.* To dig into or through; perforate; make or live in a burrow. **II.** *n.* **1.** A hole made in and under the ground, as by a rabbit. **2.** A mound or barrow.

burst, 1 bŭrst; 2 bûrst, *v.* [BURST; BURST'-ING.] **I.** *t.* To rend, break, or disrupt suddenly or violently. **II.** *i.* To suffer rupture from an internal force. **2.** To exhibit some sudden and violent activity; break forth; break away. **3.** To be filled or stirred to overflowing or breaking, as with passion.

burst, *n.* **1.** A sudden or violent explosion or breaking forth; sudden rending or disruption. **2.** A sudden effort; spurt; rush; as a *burst* of speed.

bur'then, 1 bŭr'thn; 2 bûr'thn, *v. & n.* Same as BURDEN.

bur'y, 1 ber'i; 2 bĕr'y, *vt.* [BUR'IED, 1 ber'id, 2 bĕr'id; BUR'Y-ING.] To put in or under the ground; inter; hide; cover up; engross deeply; absorb.— **bur'y-ing-ground",** *n.* A cemetery.

bus, 1 bus; 2 bŭs, *n.* [Colloq.] An omnibus. **buss‡.**

bush, 1 bush; 2 bush, *n.* **1.** A thickly branching shrub. **2.** A forest with undergrowth. **3.** A bough.— **bush'y,** *a.* Covered with bushes; shaggy.— **bush'i-ly,** *adv.* — **bush'i-ness,** *n.*

bush'el, 1 bush'el; 2 bush'ĕl, *n.* A measure of capacity; four pecks, or a vessel that holds it.

bush'ing, 1 bush'ĭŋ; 2 bush'ing, *n.* A metallic lining for a hole, as in the hub of a wheel. [industriously.]

bus'i-ly, 1 biz'i-li; 2 bĭs'i-ly, *adv.* Actively;

bus'i-ness, 1 biz'i-nes; 2 bĭs'i-nĕs, *n.* **1.** An occupation; trade; profession; calling. **2.** A matter or affair; interest; concern; duty.

bus'kin, 1 bus'kin; 2 bŭs'kin, *n.* A laced half=boot, worn by Athenian tragic actors; hence, tragedy. [Dial.] Kiss.

buss¹, 1 bus; 2 bŭs, *v. & n.* [Archaic or **buss²,** *n.* A fishing=smack.

buss³, *n.* Same as BUS.

bust, 1 bust; 2 bŭst, *n.* The human chest or breast; a piece of statuary representing the human head, shoulders, and breast.

bus'tard, 1 bus'tərd; 2 bŭs'tard, *n.* A large Old World game=bird.

bus'tle, } 1 bus'l; 2 bŭs'l. **I.** *vt. & vi.* [BUS'-**bus'tlᴾ,** } TL(E)D̄ᴾ; BUS'TLING.] To hurry; hustle; make a stir or fuss. **II.** *n.* Excited activity; noisy stir; fuss.

bus'y, 1 biz'i; 2 bĭs'y. **I.** *vt. & vi.* [BUS'-IED, 1 biz'id, 2 bĭs'id; BUS'Y-ING.] To make or be busy; occupy oneself. **II.** *a.* [BUS'I-ER; BUS'I-EST.] **1.** Intensely active; habitually occupied; industrious; diligent. **2.** Officiously active; prying. — **bus'y-bod"y,** 1 biz'i-bod'i; 2 bĭs'y-bŏd"y, *n.* [-BOD"IES᷄, *pl.*] A meddlesome person.

bu"ta-di'ene, 1 biū"ta-dai'īn; 2 bū"ta-di'ēn, *n.* A chemical used in synthetic rubber production.

but, 1 but; 2 bŭt. **I.** *adv.* Not otherwise than; no more than; only. **II.** *prep.* Leaving out; except; barring. **III.** *conj.* Except; yet; nevertheless; however.

butch'er, 1 buch'ėr; 2 buch'er. **I.** *vt.* To slaughter (animals) for market; kill (men) barbarously. **II.** *n.* **1.** One who slaughters animals or deals in meats. **2.** A bloody or cruel murderer.— **butch'er-ly,** *a.* Of or pertaining to a butcher.— **butch'er-y,** 1 buch'ər-i; 2 buch'er-y, *n.* [-IES᷄, *pl.*] Wanton or wholesale slaughter; an abattoir.

1: ə = final; ɪ = habit; aisle; au = out; oil; iū = feud; chin; go; ŋ = sing; thin, this.
2: wolf, dọ; bŏŏk, bŏŏt; full, rụle, cūre, bŭt, bûrn; oil, bŏy; g̣o, g̣em; iŋk; thin, this.

but′ler, 1 but′lẽr; 2 bŭt′ler, *n.* A man servant in charge of the dining-room, wine, etc.

buttᵗᵈ, 1 but; 2 bŭt, *vt. & vi.* **1.** To strike with or as with the head or horns. **2.** To project; jut; abut. **but**ᶠ‡.

butt², *v.* **I.** *t.* To cut off the butt smoothly, as of a log. **II.** *i.* To cut through the butt of a log.

butt¹, ⎱ *n.* **1.** The larger or thicker end of
butᶠ, ⎰ anything. **2.** A hinge. **3.** A target.

butt², *n.* A stroke or push with or as with the head.

butt³, *n.* A large cask; a measure of wine, 126 U. S. gallons; a pipe.

butte, 1 biūt; 2 būt, *n.* A conspicuous hill or natural turret.

but′ter, 1 but′ẽr; 2 bŭt′er. **I.** *vt.* To put butter upon. **II.** *n.* The fat of milk, separated by churning.— **but′ter-milk″,** *n.* The liquid left after churning.— **but′ter-scotch″,** *n.* Taffy containing butter.

but′ter², *n.* A person or animal that butts.

but′ter-cup″, 1 but′ẽr-kup″; 2 bŭt′er-cŭp″, *n.* A plant with yellow cup-shaped flowers; also, the flower.

but′ter-fly″, 1 but′ẽr-flai″; 2 bŭt′er-flī″, *n.* [-FLIES″², *pl.*] **1.** An insect with brightly colored wings. **2.** A gay idler or trifler.

but′ter-in, ⎱ 1 bŭt′ẽr-in,
but′ter-ine, ⎰ -in *or* -īn; 2 bŭt′er-ĭn, -ĭn *or* -īn, *n.* Artificial butter.

but′ter-nut″, 1 but′ẽr-nut″; 2 bŭt′er-nŭt″, *n.* The North-American white walnut, or its fruit.

but′ter-y, 1 but′ẽr-ɪ; 2 bŭt′er-y. **I.** *a.* Containing, like, or smeared with butter. **II.** *n.* [-IES², *pl.*] A pantry; a wine-room or wine-cellar.

but′tock, 1 but′ak; 2 bŭt′ok, *n.* **1.** The hinder part of a ship's hull. **2.** *pl.* The rump.

but′ton, 1 but′n; 2 bŭt′n. **I.** *vt. & vi.* To fasten with or as with a button or buttons; admit of being buttoned. **II.** *n.* A small knob or disk, as of bone, for fastening a garment by passing through a buttonhole; a pivoted fastener for a door, window, etc.; a knob or protuber-

ance.— **but′ton-hole″,** 1 but′n-hōl″; 2 bŭt′n-hōl″, *n.* A slit to receive and hold a button.

but′ton-wood″, 1 but′n-wud″; 2 bŭt′n-wŏŏd″, *n.* The American plane-tree. syc′a-more‡.

but′tress, 1 but′res; 2 bŭt′rĕs. **I**ᵗ. *vt.* To support with a buttress; sustain; uphold. **II.** *n.* A structure built against a wall to strengthen it; a support. See illus. in preceding column.

Buzzard. ¹⁄₁₅

bux′om, ⎱ 1 buks′-
bux′umᶠ, ⎰ əm; 2 bŭks′om, *a.* Plump, healthy, and comely; brisk and cheerful.

buy, 1 bai; 2 bī, *vt. & vi.* [BOUGHT, 1 bōt, 2 bôt; BUY′ING.] To obtain for a price; purchase; be a price for; make a purchase or purchases.— **buy′er,** *n.*

buzz, ⎱ 1 buz; 2 bŭz. **I.** *vt. & vi.* To whis-
buzᶠ, ⎰ per; gossip; hum, as a bee; murmur. **II.** *n.* A low murmur, as of bees, of talk, or of distant sounds; rumor; gossip.

buz′zard, 1 buz′ẽrd; 2 bŭz′ard, *n.* **1.** A large hawk. **2.** An American vulture. tur′key-buz″zard‡.

by, 1 bai; 2 bī, *adv.* **1.** At hand; near. **2.** Beyond; past. **3.** Aside; apart off; up.— **by and by.** **1.** After a time; at some future time. **2.** The hereafter. **3**‖. At once; immediately.— **by′-pro′duct,** *n.* Something produced incidentally; as, leather is a *by-product* of the beef-industry.— **by′way″,** *n.* A side or secluded lane, road, or way: opposed to *highway.* **by-path‡; by-road‡.**

by, *prep.* **1.** Beside; past; over (a course). **2.** Through the agency or help of; with. **3.** In accordance with; according to. **4.** To the extent of; multiplied into.— **by the bye** or **by, by the way,** incidentally; in passing.

by′gon(**e**ᶠᴿ, ⎱ 1 bai′gon″; 2 bī′gŏn″, *a. & n.* Gone by; former; past; something past.

by′-law″, 1 bai′-lɔ̄″; 2 bī′-la″, *n.* A subordinate rule or law. **bye′-law″‡.**

by′stand″er, 1 bai′stand″ẽr; 2 bī′ständ″er, *n.* One who stands by; a looker-on.

by′word″, 1 bai′wũrd″; 2 bī′wûrd″, *n.* An object of derision; nickname; a trite saying; proverb.

Buttresses.

1: **a**rtistic, **ā**rt; f**a**t, f**ā**re; f**a**st; get, prēy; hit, pol**ī**ce; obey, gō; n**o**t, **o**r; full, rūle; b**u**t, bũrn.
2: **ä**rt, **ā**pe, f**ă**t, f**â**re, f**å**st, wh**ạ**t, **ạ**ll; mē, gĕt, prẹy, fẽrn; hĭt, īce; ī=ĕ; ĩ=ẽ; gō, nŏt, ôr, wọn,

C

C, c, 1 sī; 2 çē, *n.* [CEES, C's, or *C*s, 1 sīz; 2 çēs, *pl.*] The third letter in the English alphabet.

cab, 1 kab; 2 căb, *n.* A one=horse public carriage; the covered part of a locomotive.

ca-bal', 1 ka-bal'; 2 ca-băl'. **I.** *vt.* To plot. **II.** *n.* A number of persons secretly united for some private purpose; intrigue.

cab'a-ret, 1 ka″ba′rē′; 2 că″bä′rę, *n.* A vaude-ville entertainment in a restaurant.

cab'bage, 1 kab'ıj; 2 căb'aġ, *n.* The close-leaved head of any one of certain plants; also, the plant.

cab'in, 1 kab'ın; 2 căb'ın. **I.** *vt. & vi.* To shut up or dwell in a cabin; hamper; confine; limit. **II.** *n.* **1.** A small, rude house; hut. **2.** A small room on a vessel.

cab'i-net, 1 kab'ı-net; 2 căb'ı-nĕt, *n.* **1.** A state council, or its meeting=place; a room for specimens, etc.; a study or closet. **2.** A piece of furniture having shelves and drawers.— **cab'i-net-mak″er,** *n.* One who makes household furniture.

ca'ble, 1 kē'bl; 2 eā'bl. **I.** *vt. & vi.* [CA-BLED; CA'BLING.] **1.** To fasten, as by a cable. **2.** To send a message by sub-marine telegraph. **II.** *n.* **1.** A heavy rope or chain. **2.** A cable's=length, 100 fathoms. **3.** An insulated telegraph=wire or =wires, as for a submarine telegraph.

ca-boose', 1 ka-būs'; 2 ca-boōs', *n.* **1.** A car for a freight=train crew. **2.** The cook's galley on a ship.

cab'ri-o-let', 1 kab'rı-o-lē'; 2 căb'rı-o-le', *n.* A one=horse covered carriage; a cab.

ca-ca'o, 1 ka-kē'o or ka-kā'o; 2 ca-eā'o or ca-eā'o. Chocolate=nuts, or the tree producing them.

cache, kash; 2 eaçh. **I.** *vt.* To place in a cache; hide. **II.** *n.* A place for hiding something, as in the ground.

cach″in-na'tion, 1 kak'ı-nē'shan; 2 eae'ı-nā'shon, *n.* Loud laughter.

cack'le, } 1 kak'l; 2 eăk'l. **I.** *vi.* [CACK-
cack'lP, } L(E)Dᴾ; CACK'LING.] To make a cackle; chatter. **II.** *n.* The shrill, broken cry made by a hen after laying an egg; idle talk; chattering; chuckling.

cac'tus, 1 kak'tus; 2 eăe'tŭs, *n.* [CAC'TI, 1 -taī, 2 -tī, or CAC'TUS-ES, *pl.*] A green, fleshy, spiny plant. See illus. in following column.

cad, 1 kad; 2 eăd, *n.* **1.** A low fellow. **2.** [Eng.] The conductor of an omnibus.

ca-dav'er-ous, 1 ka-dav'er-us; 2 ca-dăv'er-ūs, *a.* Like a corpse; pale; ghastly.

cad'die, 1 kad'ı; 2 eăd'ı, *n.* An errand-boy, as one carrying clubs for golf=players.

cad'dy.

cad'dy, 1 kad'ı; 2 eăd'y, *n.* [CAD'DIESᶻ, *pl.*] A receptacle for tea.

Cactus.

ca'dence, 1 kē'dens; 2 eā'dĕnç, *n.* Rhyth-mical movement, as in music.

ca-den'za, 1 ka-den'dza; 2 eā-dĕn'dzä, *n. Mus.* An ornamental passage introduced into a musical piece or song.

ca-det', 1 ka-det'; 2 ca-dĕt', *n.* **1.** A pupil in a military or naval school. **2.** A younger son or brother serving in the army without a commission.

ca″fé', 1 ka″fē'; 2 eä″fę', *n.* A coffee-house; restaurant; coffee.

caf″e-te'ri-a, 1 kaf′ı-tē′rı-a; 2 eăf'e-tę'ri-a, *n.* [Colloq., U. S.] A restaurant in which the patrons wait upon themselves.

cage, 1 kēj; 2 eāġ. **I.** *vt.* [CAGED; CAG'ING.] To shut up in a cage; confine; imprison. **II.** *n.* A structure, with openwork of wire or bars, as for confining birds or beasts. [heap of stones.

cairn, 1 kārn; 2 eârn, *n.* A monumental

cais'son, 1 kē'san; 2 eā'son, *n.* **1.** An ammunition=chest or =wagon. **2.** A large water=tight box within which work is done under water.

cai'tiff, } 1 kē'tıf; 2 eā'tif. **I.** *a.* Vile;
cai'tifᴾ, } cowardly; base. **II.** *n.* A base, wicked wretch.

ca-jole', 1 ka-jōl'; 2 ca-jōl', *vt. & vi.* [CA-JOLED; CA-JOL'ING.] To impose on by flattery; dupe.— **ca-jol'er-y,** *n.* [-IESᶻ, *pl.*]

cake, 1 kēk; 2 eāk. **I.** *vt. & vi.* [CAKEDᵗ; CAK'ING.] To form into a hardened mass. **II.** *n.* A sweetened and baked article of food; any small, thin mass, as of dough, etc., baked or fried.

cal'a-bash, 1 kal'a-bash; 2 eăl'a-băsh, *n.* A gourd or a vessel made from it.

ca-lam'i-ty, 1 ka-lam'ı-tı; 2 ca-lăm'ı-ty, *n.* [-TIESᶻ, *pl.*] A misfortune or disaster; adversity.— **ca-lam'i-tous,** *a.* -iy, *adv.* -ness,*n.*

cal'a-mus, 1 kal'a-mus; 2 eăl'a-mŭs, *n.*

1: ə = final; ı = habıt; aısle; au = out; oıl; ıū = feud; ¢hin; go; ŋ = sıng; ŧhin, **this.**
2: wǫlf, dǫ; boŏk, boōt; fˬull, rˬule, cūre, bŭt, bûrn; oıl, bŏy; ġo, ġem; ıŋk; thin, **this.**

[-MI, 1 -mɑi; 2 -mī, pl.] **1.** A kind of flag. **sweet′=flag″‡. 2.** A climbing rattan; reed; quill; pen; flute.

ca-lash′, 1 kə-lash′; 2 cắ-lăsh′, n. A low light carriage with folding top; a folding carriage=top.

Calash.

cal-ca′re-ous, 1 kal-kē′rɪ-ŭs; 2 cắl-cā′-re-ŭs, a. Of, containing, or like lime or limestone.

cal′ci-mine, 1 kal′sɪ-mɑin; 2 cắl′çi-mīn. **I.** vt. [-MINED; -MIN′ING.] To apply calcimine to. **II.** n. A white or tinted wash for ceilings, walls of rooms, etc.

cal′cine, 1 kal′sɪn; 2 cắl′çin, vt. & vi. [CAL′-CINED; CAL′CIN-ING.] To make or become friable by heat.— **cal″ci-na′tion,** n.

cal′cu-late, 1 kal′kiu-lēt; 2 cắl′cū-lāt, vt. & vi. [-LAT″ED^d; -LAT′ING.] To compute mathematically; figure up or out; reckon; estimate; plan.— **cal′cu-la-bl(e)²,** a. That may be calculated or counted upon.— **cal″-cu-la′tion,** n. The act or art of computing; computation; reckoning.— **cal′cu-la″tor,** n. One who calculates; a calculating=machine; a set of tables for calculations.

cal′cu-lus, 1 kal′kiu-lŭs; 2 cắl′cū-lŭs, n. [-LI, 1 -lɑi; 2 -lī, pl.] **1.** A stone=like concretion, as in the bladder. **2.** A method of calculating by algebraic symbols.— **cal′-cu-lous,** a. Stony; gritty.

cal′dron, 1 kôl′drən; 2 cạl′dron, n. A large kettle.

cal′en-dar, 1 kal′en-dər; 2 cắl′ĕn-dar, n. **1.** A systematic arrangement of days, months, and years. **2.** An almanac.

cal′en-der, 1 kal′en-dər; 2 cắl′ĕn-der. **I.** vt. To press between rollers. **II.** n. A machine for giving to cloth, paper, etc., a gloss by pressing between rollers.

calf¹, 1 kaf; 2 cäf, n. [CALVES, 1 kavz; 2 cävz, pl.] The young of the cow, its skin, or leather made from it, called calfskin.

calf², n. [CALVES, pl.] The hinder part of the human leg below the knee.

cal′i-ber, } 1 kal′ɪ-bər; 2 cắl′i-ber, n. The
cal′i-bre, } size of bore, as of a gun=barrel; individual capacity or power.

cal′i-co, 1 kal′ɪ-kō; 2 cắl′i-cō, n. [-COES or -COS, 1 -kōz; 2 -cōs, pl.] **1.** [U. S.] Cotton printed in colors. **2.** [Eng.] White cotton cloth.

ca′lif, } 1 kē′lɪf or kal′ɪf; 2 cā′lif or cắl′if,
ca′liph, } n. The spiritual and civil head of a Mohammedan state.— **cal′i-fate, cal′i-**

phate, 1 kal′ɪ-fēt; 2 cắl′i-fāt, n. The office, dignity, or reign of a calif.

ca-lig′ra-phy, }
ca-lig′ra-fy², } n. Same as CALLIGRAPHY.

cal′i-per, 1 kal′ɪ-pər; 2 cắl′i-per, n. An instrument like a pair of compasses, for measuring diameters: usually in the plural.

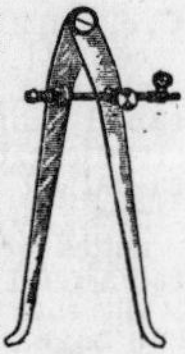

Calipers.

cal″is-then′ics, n. Same as CALLISTHENICS.

ca′lix, n. Same as CALYX.

calk¹ᵗ, } 1 kôk; 2 cạk, vt. To
caulk¹ᵗ, } make tight, as a boat's seams, by plugging with soft material.— **calk′ing,** n.

calk²ᵗ, vt. **1.** To furnish with calks, as a horseshoe. **2.** To wound with a calk.

calk, n. A spur on a horse's shoe, to prevent slipping.

call, 1 kôl; 2 cạl, v. **I.** t. To name; summon; invite; invoke; utter aloud. **II.** i. To cry out; appeal; signal; make a brief visit: often with on or upon.— **call′er,** n.

call, n. **1.** A shout or cry; summons; invitation; divine vocation; claim; right; obligation. **2.** A brief visit.

cal′la, 1 kal′ə; 2 cắl′a, n. Bot. A South African plant, with a large milk=white blossom. **cal″la=lil′y‡.**

cal-lig′ra-phy, } 1 ka-lig′rə-fɪ; 2 cắ-lĭg′ra-
cal-lig′ra-fy², } fy, n. Beautiful penmanship.— **cal″li-graph′ic,** a.

call′ing, 1 kôl′ɪŋ; 2 cạl′ing, n. **1.** A summons. **2.** Habitual occupation; vocation; business.

Cal-li′o-pe, 1 ka-lɑi′o-pɪ; 2 cắ-lī′o-pe, n. **1.** Myth. Muse of epic poetry; ordinarily represented with a tablet and stylus. **2.** [c-] A series of steam=whistles played by means of a keyboard.

cal′li-per, n. Same as CALIPER.

cal″lis-then′ics, 1 kal′ɪs-�′ɪks; 2 cắl′-is-thĕn′ics, n. pl. Light gymnastics.— **cal″lis-then′ic,** a.

cal′lous, 1 kal′ŭs; 2 cắl′ŭs, a. Like thickened and hardened skin; insensible; unfeeling. **-ly,** adv. **-ness,** n.— **cal-los′i-ty,** 1 ka-lŏs′ɪ-tɪ; 2 cắl-lŏs′i-ty, n. [-TIES, 1 -tɪz; 2 -tĭs, pl.] A thickened, hardened portion of the skin; hardness; insensibility.

cal′low, 1 kal′o; 2 cắl′o, a. Unfledged; inexperienced; youthful.

calm, 1 kām; 2 cäm, v. **I.** t. To still; soothe; tranquilize. **II.** i. To become quiet. [Id; serene. **-ly,** adv. **-ness,** n.

calm, a. Free from agitation; quiet; placid.

calm, n. Tranquillity; stillness; serenity.

cal′o-mel, 1 kal′o-mel; 2 cắl′o-mĕl, n. Med. A compound of chlorin and mercury.

1: artistic, ärt; fat, fāre; fạst; get, prēy; hit, polīce; obey, gō; nǒt, ôr; fŭll, rūle; bŭt, bûrn.

2: ärt, āpe, fặt, fâre, fạ̈st, whạt, ạll; mē, gĕt, prey, fẽrn; hĭt, īce; ī=ē; ĭ=ĕ; gō, nǒt, ôr, wǒn,

ca·lor'ic, 1 kə-lor'ık; 2 ca-lŏr'ic, n. Heat; formerly, a supposed principle of heat.

cal'o·ry, 1 kal'o-rı; 2 căl'o-ry, n. [-RIES, 1 -rız; 2 -rıs, pl.] The generally accepted unit of heat, being the amount of heat necessary to raise the temperature of one kilogram of water one degree centigrade; a heat-unit **cal'o·rie‡.**

cal'u·met, 1 kal'yu-met; 2 căl'yu-mĕt, n. The Indian pipe of peace.

cal'um·ny, 1 kal'ŭm-nı; 2 căl'ŭm-ny, n. [-NIES, 1 -nız; 2 -nıs, pl.] A false accusation; defamation; slander.— **ca·lum'ni·ate,** 1 kə-lum'nı-ēt; 2 ca-lūm'nı-āt, vt. & vi. [-AT'ED‡, -AT'ING.] To accuse falsely; defame. — **ca·lum'ni·a'tion,** n.— **ca·lum'ni·a"tor,** n.— **ca·lum'ni·ous,** 1 kə-lum'nı-us; 2 ca-lūm'nı-ŭs, a. Slanderous; defamatory. **ca·lum'ni·a·to·ry‡.**

calve, 1 kɑv; 2 cäv, vt. & vi. [CALVED, CALVD‡; CALV'ING.] To bring forth (a calf).

ca'lyx, 1 kē'lıks; 2 cā'lyks, n. [CAL'Y·CES or CA'LYX·ES, 1 kal'ı-sīz or kē'lıks-ez; 2 căl'y-çĕs or cā'lyks-ĕs, pl.] **1.** The outermost series of leaves of a flower. **2.** A cup-shaped part or organ.

Cam.

cam, 1 kam; 2 căm, n. Mech. A non-circular rotating piece, to give motion to and fro.

The cam revolves with the shaft, s, and gives a reciprocal motion

cam'bric, 1 kēm'brık; 2 căm'-brie, n. A fine white linen or a coarse glazed cotton fabric.

to the fly-rod, r.

came, 1 kēm; 2 căm, imp. of COME, v.

cam'el, 1 kam'el; 2 căm'ĕl, n. A large Asiatic or African ruminant, having a humped back, and able to subsist long without water.

ca·mel'li·a, 1 kə-mel'-ı-ə; 2 ca-mĕl'i-a, n. A tropical Eastern tree or shrub with white or rose flowers.

Camels. 1/175

ca·mel'o·pard, 1 kə-mel'o-pārd; 2 ca-mĕl'-o-pärd, n. The giraffe.

cam'e·o, 1 kam'ı-o; 2 căm'e-o, n. A striated stone or shell, carved in relief.

cam'er·a, 1 kam'er-ə; 2 căm'er-a, n. [-AS or -Æ, 1 -əz or -ī; 2 -aş or -ē, pl.] **1.** A box within which the image of an exterior object is received through a lens or lenses. **2.** A chamber.— **cam'er·al,** a.

cam'o·mile, 1 kam'o-moil; 2 căm'o-mīl, n. A strong-scented herb of the aster family.

cam"ou"flage', 1 kă"mū"fläჳ'; 2 că"mų"fläzb', n. [Fr.] Disguise, as by masking.

camp, 1 kamp; 2 cămp. **I¹.** vt. & vi. To encamp; lodge temporarily. **II.** n. A group of tents, or the place so occupied; a tent, cabin, etc.; the army; military life.

cam·paign', 1 kam-pēn'; 2 căm-pān', n.
cam·pain's, The time an army keeps the field; a political or other contest.— **cam·paign'er,** n.

cam'phor, 1 kam'fər; 2 căm'for, n. A
cam'fors, fragrant Asiatic gum-like compound.— **cam'phor·ate,** vt. [-AT'ED‡; -AT'ING.] To treat with camphor. **-ic,** a.

can¹, 1 kan; 2 căn, v. def. [COULD, 1 kud; 2 cud.] To be able (to do something).

can², vt. [CANNED, CANDS; CAN'NING.] To put up in cans. [liquids.

can, n. A vessel for holding or preserving

Can'a·da, 1 kan'a-də; 2 căn'a-da, **Dominion of.** A federation of colonies and provinces (3,457,484 sq. m.; pop. 10,376,786) of British North America (except Newfoundland and Labrador).—**Ca·na'di·an,** a. & n.

ca·nal', 1 kə-nal'; 2 ca-năl', n. An artificial waterway; a channel, or duct.

ca·nard', 1 kə-nārd'; 2 ca-närd', n. A fabricated sensational story.

ca·na'ry, 1 kə-nē'rı; 2 ca-nā'ry, n. [-RIES, 1 -rız; 2 -rıs, pl.] **1.** A finch, originally of the Canary Islands. **2.** A bright yellow color. **3.** Wine from the Canary Islands.

can'cel, 1 kan'sel; 2 căn'çĕl, vt. [CAN'-CELED or CAN'CELLED, CANCELD‡; CAN'-CEL·ING or CAN'CEL·LING.] To mark out or off; annul; revoke.— **can"cel·a'tion,** n.

can'cer, 1 kan'sər; 2 căn'çer, n. **1.** A malignant and commonly fatal tumor; any inveterate and spreading evil. **2.** [C-] The Crab, a zodiacal constellation or sign. See TROPIC.— **can'cer·ous,** a.

can"de·la'brum, 1 kan"dı-lē'brum; 2 căn"de-lä'brŭm, n. [-BRA, pl.] A branched candlestick or lamp-stand.

can'did, 1 kan'dıd; 2 căn'-did, a. Sincere; ingenuous; frank; fair. **-ly,** adv. **-ness,** n.

can'di·date, 1 kan'dı-dēt; 2 căn'dı-dāt, n. A nominee or aspirant for any position. — **can'di·da·cy,** 1 kan'dı-dē-sı; 2 căn'dı-dā-çy, n. [-CIES, 1 -sız; 2 -çıs, pl.] The state or position of being a candidate. **can'di·date"ship‡;** **can'di·da·ture‡.**

Candelabrum.

can'dle, 1 kan'dl; 2 căn'dl, n. A cylin-
can'dl², der, as of tallow or wax, containing a wick, for lighting; a light.— **can'dle·stick",** n. A support for a candle or candles.

---

can'dor, 1 kan'dər; 2 căn'dor, *n.* Sincerity; frankness; impartiality; fairness. **can'dour‡.**

can'dy, 1 kan'di; 2 căn'dy. **I.** *vt. & vi.* [CAN'DIED; CAN'DY-ING.] To cover with or become like hardened sugar. **II.** *n.* [CAN'-DIES²*, pl.*] A sweetmeat of sugar or molasses or both.

cane, 1 kēn; 2 cān. **I.** *vt.* [CANED; CAN'-ING.] **1.** To beat with a cane. **2.** To bottom or back with cane, as a chair. **II.** *n.* **1.** A walking-stick. **2.** A slender flexible woody stem or plant, as a rattan or the sugar-cane. — **cane'-brake″,** *n.* Land overgrown with canes.

ca-nine', 1 kə-nīn'; 2 ca-nīn', *a.* Of, pertaining to, or like a dog.

can'is-ter, 1 kan'is-tər; 2 căn'is-ter, *n.* **1.** A metal case, as for tea, etc. **2.** A metallic cylinder filled with bullets to be fired from a cannon.

can'ker, 1 kaŋ'kər; 2 căŋ'ker. **I.** *vt. & vi.* To infect with canker; eat like a canker; corrode; fester. **II.** *n.* An ulcerous sore; a group of small ulcers in the mouth; a disease of fruit-trees; any secret or spreading evil. — **can'ker-worm″,** *n.* An insect destructive to fruit-trees.

can'ni-bal, 1 kan'i-bəl; 2 căn'i-bal, *n.* A human being that eats human flesh. — **can'-ni-bal-ism,** *n.* — **can″ni-bal-is'tic,** *a.*

can'non, 1 kan'ən; 2 căn'on, *n.* [CAN'-NONS or CAN'NON, *pl.*] A great gun for heavy shot. — **can″non-ade′,** 1 kan'an-ēd'; 2 căn'on-ād'. **I.** *vt. & vi* [-AD'ED^d; -AD'ING.] To attack with cannon-shot; fire cannon repeatedly. **II.** *n.* A continued attack with or discharge of cannon. — **can″non-eer′,** *n.* A soldier who serves as a gunner. **can″non-ier'‡.**

can'not, 1 kan'ət; 2 căn'ot. Can not. See CAN¹, *v.*

can'ny, 1 kan'i; 2 căn'y, *a.* [Scot.] **1.** Careful in planning for action; shrewd; thrifty. **2.** Pleasing; comely; worthy. **can'nie,**

ca-noe', 1 kə-nū'; 2 ca-nọ', *n.* A light boat, as of bark, propelled by paddles. **ca-noe'ist,** *n.*

can'on¹, 1 kan'ən; 2 căn'on, *n.* **1.** A rule or law; standard. **2.** The books of the Bible that are recognized by the Church as inspired.

can'on², *n.* A dignitary of the Church of England.

ca-ñon', *n.* See CANYON.

ca-non'i-cal, 1 kə-nɔn'i-kəl; 2 ca-nŏn'i-kăl,
ca-non'ic, 2 ca-nŏn'i-cal, ca-nŏn'ic, *a.* Belonging to the canon of Scripture; lawful; accepted or approved. — **ca-non'i-cal-ly,** *adv.* — **ca-non'i-cals,** 1 kə-nɔn'i-kəlz; 2 ca-nŏn'i-cals, *n. pl.* Official robes of the clergy. — **can″on-ic'i-ty,** 1 kan″ən-is'i-ti; 2 căn″on-ĭç'i-ty, *n.* The quality of being canonical.

can'on-ize, 1 kan'ən-aiz; 2 căn'on-īz, *vt.* [-IZED; -IZ'ING.] To enroll among the saints. — **can″on-i-za'tion,** *n.*

can'o-py, 1 kan'o-pi; 2 căn'o-py. **I.** *vt.* [-PIED; -PY-ING.] To cover with or as with a canopy. **II.** *n.* [-PIES, 1 -piz; 2-pis, *pl.*] A suspended covering, as over a throne, shrine, bed, etc.

cant¹, 1 kant; 2 cănt. **I^d.** *vt. & vi.* To slant; tip up; tilt. **II.** *n.* An inclination or tipping; a slant.

cant². **I^d.** *vt. & vi.* To talk with affected religiousness; speak in a hypocritical way. **II.** *n.* **1.** Formal, ostentatious religious talk. **2.** Any technical or professional phraseology. [contraction.

can't, 1 kant; 2 cănt. Can not: a colloquial

can-ta'bi-le, 1 kan-tä'bi-lē; 2 can-tä'bi-le, *adv. Mus.* Gracefully, in a style characterized by melodious swing.

can'ta-loup, 1 kan'a-lūp; 2 căn'ta-lụp, *n.* A variety of muskmelon.

can-ta'ta, 1 kan-tä'ta; 2 căn-tä'tä, *n. Mus.* A choral composition in the style of oratorio.

can-teen', 1 kan-tīn'; 2 căn-tēn', *n. Mil.* **1.** A soldiers' drinking-flask. **2.** A sutlers' refreshment and liquor-shop.

can'ter, 1 kan'tər; 2 căn'ter. **I.** *vt. & vi.* To ride or move at a canter. **II.** *n.* A moderate, easy gallop.

can'ti-cle, 1 kan'ti-kl; 2 căn'ti-cl, *n.*
can'ti-cl², 2 non-metrical hymn, to be chanted. — **Can'ti-cles,** *n. pl. Bib.* The Song of Solomon.

can'ti-lev″er, 1 kan'ti-lev″ər; 2 căn'ti-lĕv″er, *n.* A heavy bracket supporting a balcony, or reaching out from a pier, and joining with another to form a bridge.

can'to¹, 1 kan'to; 2 căn'to, *n.* A division of a poem.

can'to², *n. Mus.* The part to which the melody is assigned; the air; formerly, the tenor; in modern use, the soprano.

can'ton, 1 kan'tən; 2 căn'ton. **I.** *vt. & vi.* **1.** To divide into cantons. **2.** To assign to or enter into quarters. **II.** *n.* **1.** A district, as of the Swiss confederation. **2.** The part of a flag next the staff. — **can'ton-ment,** 1 kan'ton-mənt; 2 căn'ton-ment, *n.* A place for lodging troops, as in a town; a military station.

---

can′vas, 1 kan′vəs; 2 eăn′vas, *n.* A heavy, strong cloth for sails, paintings, etc.

can′vass¹, 1 kan′vəs; 2 eăn′vas, *v.* **I.** *t.* To solicit personally, as votes; examine; scrutinize; sift. **II.** *i.* To go about soliciting votes, orders, etc. **-er,** *n.*

can′vass, *n.* **1.** The going about to solicit orders, interest, or votes. **2.** A detailed examination; inquiry; scrutiny.

can′yon, 1 kan′yon *or* (*Sp.*) kɑ-nyŏn′; 2 ca-ñon′, } eăn′yon *or* (*Sp.*) eä-nyŏn′. *n.* A deep gorge or ravine. [India-rubber.

caout′chouc, 1 kū′chuk; 2 eu′chue, *n.*

cap, 1 kap; 2 eăp. **I.** *vt. & vi.* [CAPPED, CAPT⁶; CAP′PING.] **1.** To put a cap on; cover; crown; excel. **2.** To doff the cap, as in salutation. **II.** *n.* A covering without a brim; to be worn upon the head; a covering at the top or end of anything.

ca′pa-ble, } 1 kē′pə-bl; 2 eā′pa-bl, *a.* Able **ca′pa-bl²,** } to do or to receive; efficient; qualified; competent.—**ca″pa-bil′i-ty,** 1 kē′-pə-bil′ɪ-tɪ; 2 eā′pa-bil′i-ty, *n.* [-TIES, 1 -tɪz; 2 -tĭs, *pl.*] The state or quality of being capable. **ca′pa-ble-ness‡.—ca′pa-bly,** *adv.*

ca-pa′cious, 1 kɑ-pē′shus; 2 ea-pā′shŭs, *a.* Able to contain much; spacious; roomy. **-ly,** *adv.* **-ness,** *n.*

ca-pac′i-ty, 1 kɑ-pas′ɪ-tɪ; 2 ea-păç′i-ty, *n.* [-TIES, 1 -tɪz; 2 -tĭs, *pl.*] Ability to receive, contain, understand, etc.; cubic extent; ability; talent; character or office; also, legal qualification.— **ca-pac′i-tate,** 1 kɑ-pas′-ɪ-tēt; 2 ea-păç′i-tăt, *vt.* [-TAT′ED⁴; -TAT′-ING.] To make capable; qualify.

cap″·a·pie′, 1 kap′·ə·pī′; 2 eăp′·ə·pē′, *adv.* From head to foot. **cap″·a·pe′‡.**

ca-par′i-son, 1 kɑ-par′ɪ-sən; 2 ea-pär′i-son. **I.** *vt.* To put housings on; clothe richly. **II.** *n.* Showy trappings (for a horse); sumptuous apparel.

cape¹, 1 kēp; 2 eăp, *n.* A point of land extending into the sea or a lake.

cape², *n.* A short cloak.

ca′per, 1 kē′pər; 2 eā′per, *vi.* To leap playfully; frisk.

ca′per¹, *n.* Leaping or frisking; prank.

ca′per², *n. pl.* The flower-buds of a Mediterranean shrub, used as a condiment.

cap′il-la-ry, 1 kap′ɪ-lē-rɪ; 2 eăp′il-lā-ry. **I.** *a.* Of, pertaining to, or like hair; slender; having a hair-like bore, as a tube. **II.** *n.* [-RIES², *pl.*] A minute vessel, as those connecting the arteries and veins; any tube with a fine bore.

cap′i-tal, 1 kap′ɪ-təl; 2 eăp′i-tal, *a.* **1.** Chief; principal; admirable. **2.** Of or pertaining to the death-penalty; punishable with death.— **cap′i-tal-ly,** *adv.* **1.** Excellently. **2.** So as to deserve death.

cap′i-tal¹, *n.* **1.** A chief city; the seat of government. **2.** A large letter used at the beginning of a sentence, of a proper name, etc. **capital letter‡.**

cap′i-tal², *n.* Wealth employed in or available for production; resources; advantages.— **cap′i-tal-ist,** *n.* An owner of capital.

cap′i-tal³, *n.* The upper member of a column or pillar.

cap′i-tal-ize¹, 1 kap′ɪ-təl-aiz; 2 eăp′i-tal-īz, *vt.* [-IZED; -IZ′ING.] To begin with a capital letter.

cap′i-tal-ize², *vt.* [-IZED; -IZ′ING.] To convert into capital or cash.

Egyptian Capital.

cap″i-ta′tion, 1 kap′ɪ-tē′shən; 2 eăp′i-tā′shon, *n.* An individual assessment or tax.

Cap′i-tol, 1 kap′ɪ-təl; 2 eăp′i-tŏl, *n.* **1.** [U. S.] The official building of Congress; a State-house. **2.** The temple of Jupiter Maximus in ancient Rome, or the hill on which it stood.

ca-pit′u-late, 1 kɑ-pit′yu-lēt; 2 ea-pĭt′yu-lāt, *vt. & vi.* [-LAT′ED⁴; -LAT′ING.] To surrender on conditions; make terms.— **ca-pit″u-la′tion,** *n.* A conditional surrender; a treaty.

ca′pon, 1 kē′pən; 2 eā′pon, *n.* A cock gelded to improve the flesh for the table.

ca-price′, 1 kɑ-prīs′; 2 ea-prīç′, *n.* A sudden unreasonable change; a whim; freak; capricious disposition.— **ca-pri′cious,** 1 kɑ-prish′us; 2 ea-prish′ŭs, *a.* Fickle; whimsical. **-ly,** *adv.* **-ness,** *n.*

Cap′ri-corn, 1 kap′rɪ-kērn; 2 eăp′ri-eôrn, *n.* A constellation or sign of the zodiac. See TROPIC.

cap′si-cum, 1 kap′sɪ-kum; 2 eăp′si-eŭm, *n.* The plant producing red pepper, or its fruit.

cap-size′, 1 kap-saiz′; 2 eăp-sīz′, *vt. & vi.* [CAP-SIZED′; CAP-SIZ′ING.] To upset; overturn.

cap′stan, 1 kap′stən; 2 eăp′stan, *n.* An upright windlass for hoisting anchors, etc.

cap′sule, 1 kap′siūl; 2 eăp′sūl, *n.* A seed-vessel, as of a pink or a lily; a small case, shell, cap, or seal.

cap′tain, 1 kap′tɪn; 2 eăp′tin, *n.* The commander of a vessel, or of a company of soldiers; a chief; leader.— **cap′tain-cy,** *n.* [-CIES, 1 -sɪz; 2 -çĭs, *pl.*] The position, rank, or term of office of a captain. **cap′tain-ship‡.**

Capstan.

cap′tion, 1 kap′shən; 2 căp′shon, *n.* A title, introduction, or heading.

cap′tious, 1 kap′shus; 2 căp′shŭs, *a.* **1.** Faultfinding; overcritical. **2.** Perplexing; sophistical. **-ly,** *adv.* **-ness,** *n.*

cap′ti-vate, 1 kap′tɪ-vēt; 2 căp′tɪ-vāt, *vt.* [-VAT′EDᵈ; -VAT′ING.] To charm; win; fascinate.

cap′tive, } 1 kap′tɪv; 2 căp′tĭv. **I.** *a.*
cap′tivˢ, } Taken prisoner; held in confinement or bondage. **II.** *n.* One captured and held in restraint; a prisoner. — **cap-tiv′i-ty,** *n.* Imprisonment; bondage; thraldom. — **cap′tor,** *n.* One who takes or holds captive.

cap′ture, 1 kap′chur *or* -tiur; 2 căp′chur *or* -tūr. **I.** *vt.* [CAP′TURED; CAP′TUR-ING.] To take captive or possession of; win. **II.** *n.* The act of capturing; that which is captured.

car, 1 kär; 2 cär, *n.* A wheeled vehicle; railway-carriage; basket of a balloon.

ca″ra-ba′o, 1 kä″rä-bä′o; 2 cä″rä-bä′o, *n.* [P. I.] A water-buffalo.

car′a-bine, *n.* Same as CARBINE.

ca-ra′fe, 1 kə-räf′; 2 ca-räf′, *n.* A glass water-bottle.

car′a-mel, 1 kar′ə-mel; 2 căr′a-mĕl, *n.* **1.** A confection of sugar, butter, etc. **2.** Burnt sugar.

car′at, 1 kar′ət; 2 căr′at, *n.* **1.** A twenty-fourth part of the fineness of gold. **2.** A unit of weight for gems, about 3.2 grains.

car′a-van, 1 kar′ə-van; 2 căr′a-văn, *n.* An Oriental armed company of traders, etc.; a traveling menagerie. — **car″a-van′sa-ry,** 1 -sə-rɪ; 2-sa-ry, *n.* [-RIES, -rɪz; 2-rɪs, *pl.*] An Oriental hostelry or inn. — **car″a-van′se-raï.**

car′a-way, 1 kar′ə-wē; 2 căr′a-wā, *n.* A European herb or its spicy fruit, the so-called seeds.

car′bine, 1 kär′baɪn; 2 cär′bĭn, *n.* A horseman's rifle. — **car″bi-neer′,** 1 kär′bɪ-nīr′; 2 cär′bi-nēr′, *n.* A soldier armed with a carbine.

car-bol′ic, 1 kɑr-bŏl′ɪk; 2 cär-bŏl′ic, *a.* Of or pertaining to coal-tar oil. — **carbolic acid,** a caustic poison, used as an antiseptic and disinfectant.

car′bon, 1 kär′bən; 2 cär′bon, *n.* A non-metallic chemical element; pure charcoal. — **car″bon-a′ceous,** 1 kär′bən-ē′shus; 2 cär′bon-ā′shŭs, *a.* Of, pertaining to, or yielding carbon. — **car′bon-ate.** **I.** *vt.* [-AT′EDᵈ; -AT′ING.] To charge with carbonic acid. **II.** *n.* A salt of carbonic acid. — **car-bon′ic,** 1 kär-bən′ik; 2 cär-bŏn′ic, *a.* Of, pertaining to, or obtained from carbon. — **carbonic acid,** a heavy, colorless, incombustible gas. — **car″bon-if′er-ous,** *a.* Containing or yielding car-

bon or coal. — **car′bon-ize,** 1 kär′bən-aɪz; 2 cär′bon-īz, *vt.* [-IZED; -IZ′ING.] To reduce to carbon; coat or charge with carbon. — **carbonized cloth,** cloth charred in vacuo: used for high resistance. — **car″bon-pa″per,** *n.* Tissue paper so prepared with carbon or other material that it will reproduce on paper underneath a copy of anything impressed on it, as by pencil or typewriter.

car′boy, 1 kär′bɔɪ; 2 cär′bŏy, *n.* A large glass bottle enclosed in a box or in wickerwork, for corrosive acids, etc.

car′bun-cle, } 1 kär′bun-kl; 2 cär′bŭn-el,
car′bun-clᵉ, } *n.* **1.** A malignant boil. **2.** A gem of brilliant fire and deep red color.

car′bu-ret″er, 1 kär′biu-ret″ər; 2 cär′bū-rĕt″er, *n.* **1.** A device to charge air or gas with volatile substances for illuminating purposes. **2.** A device to carry a current of air through or over a liquid fuel, so that the air may take up the vapor to form an explosive mixture for operating the motor, as of an aeroplane, automobile, etc. **car′bu-ret″or or -terᵗ.**

car′cass, } 1 kär′kəs; 2 cär′eas, *n.* **1.** The
car′case, } dead body of an animal. **2.** The frame, as of a house or ship.

cardᵈ, 1 kärd; 2 cärd, *vt.* To comb, dress, or cleanse with a card. See CARD², *n.*

card¹, *n.* **1.** A piece of cardboard bearing a name, etc., or symbols for use in play. **2.** Cardboard. — **card′board″,** *n.* A thin pasteboard of fine quality and finish.

card², *n.* A wire-toothed brush, as for carding wool.

car′di-ac, 1 kär′dɪ-ak; 2 cär′di-ăe, *a.* Pertaining to, situated near, or affecting the heart.

car′di-nal, 1 kär′dɪ-nəl; 2 cär′di-nal, *a.* **1.** Of prime importance; chief. **2.** Of a rich red color; vermilion.

car′di-nal, 1 kär′dɪ-nəl; 2 cär′di-nal, *n.* **1.** One of the princes of the Roman Catholic Church. **2.** The American red-bird, a red crested finch. **cardi-nal-bird″‡.** **3.** A bright and rich red color. — **car′di-nal-ate,** *n.* The rank, dignity, or term of office of a cardinal. **car′di-nal-ship‡.**

care, 1 kār; 2 cär. **I.** *vi.* [CARED; CAR′ING.] To be interested or concerned; be inclined or disposed; desire. **II.** *n.* **1.** Anxiety or concern; solicitude. **2.** Charge or oversight. **3.** Regard or attention; heed. **4.** Any object of solicitude. — **care′ful,** *a.* Exercising, marked by, or done with care; attentive; prudent; circumspect. **-ly,** *adv.* **-ness,** *n.* — **care′less,**

Cardinal.
1/12

---

a. Free from care; neglectful; heedless; light-hearted; negligent; easy. **-ly,** *adv.* **-ness,** *n.*

ca-reen', 1 ke-rīr'; 2 ca-rēn', *vt. & vi.* To tip or incline to one side, as a vessel.

ca-reer', 1 ke-rīr'; 2 ca-rēr'. **I.** *vi.* To rush; sweep on. **II.** *n.* A free and swift course, run, or charge; a life or period of notable achievement.

care'ful, care'less, etc. See under CARE.

ca-ress', 1 ke-res'; 2 ca-rĕs'. **I**ᵗ. *vt.* To touch endearingly; fondle; embrace; pet. **II.** *n.* A gentle, affectionate movement.

ca'ret, 1 kē'ret; 2 cā'rĕt, *n.* A sign (∧) denoting an omission.

car'go, 1 kär'go; 2 cär'gọ, *n.* Goods and merchandise taken on board of a vessel; lading; load.

car'i-bou, 1 kar'ı-bū; 2 cär'ı-bụ, *n.* The North-American reindeer.

car'i-ca-ture, 1 kar'ı-ke-chur *or* -tiūr; 2 cär'ı-ca-chụr *or* -tūr. **I.** *vt.* [-TURED; -TUR'ING.] To represent so as to make ridiculous; burlesque. **II.** *n.* A picture or description marked by ridiculous exaggeration; burlesque.— **car'i-ca-tur-ist,** *n.* A maker of caricatures.

Caribou Antlers.

ca'ri-es, 1 kē'rı-īz; 2 cā'rı-ĕş, *n.* Decay of a bone or of a tooth.— **ca'ri-ous,** *a.* Affected with caries; decayed.

car'i-ole, 1 kar'ı-ōl; 2 cär'ı-ōl, *n.* A small carriage.

Car"ma'gnole', 1 kär"mɑ'nyōl'; 2 cär'mä-nyōl', *n.* A wild dance and song of the French revolutionists of 1789.

car'man, 1 kär'men; 2 cär'man, *n.* [CAR'MEN, *pl.*] One who drives a car or cart.

car'mine, 1 kär'mĭn; 2 cär'min, *n.* A rich purplish-red color, prepared from cochineal; rouge.

car'nage, 1 kär'nĭj; 2 cär'nag, *n.* Extensive and bloody slaughter; massacre; also, the bodies of the slain.

car'nal, 1 kär'nel; 2 cär'nal, *a.* Pertaining to the fleshly nature or to bodily appetites; sensual; formerly, worldly; not spiritual.— **car-nal'i-ty,** *n.* The quality of being carnal; sensuality.— **car'nal-ize,** *vt.* To make carnal.— **car'nal-ly,** *adv.*

car-na'tion, 1 kar-nē'shon; 2 cär-nā'shon, *n.* **1.** Flesh-color. **2.** A pink of southern Europe.

car-ne'lian, 1 kar-nīl'yen; 2 cär-nēl'yan, *n.* A red chalcedony, often cut as a gem.

car'ni-val, 1 kär'nı-val; 2 cär'nı-val, *n.* A period of gaiety, just before Lent; a revel.

car-niv'o-rous, 1 kar-nĭv'o-rus; 2 cär-nĭv'o-rŭs, *a.* Eating or living on flesh.

car'ol, 1 kar'el; 2 cär'ol. **I.** *vt. & vi.* [CAR'OL(E)Dˢ *or* CAR'OLLED; CAR'OL-ING *or* CAR'OL-LING.] To sing as a bird; warble. **II.** *n.* A song of joy, as of a bird; a joyous hymn; a Christmas ballad

car'om, 1 kar'em; 2 cär'om. **I.** *vi.* To make a glancing movement. **II.** *n.* The impact of a ball against two others in succession.

ca-rot'id, 1 ke-rot'id; 2 ca-rŏt'id, *n.* One of the great arteries of the neck. **carotid artery†.**

ca-rou'sal, 1 ke-rau'zel; 2 ca-rou'gal, *n.* A jovial feast or banquet; boisterous revelry.

ca-rouse', 1 ke-rauz'; 2 ca-rouş'. **I.** *vi* [CA-ROUSED'; CA-ROUS'ING.] To drink deeply and boisterously. **II.** *n.* A carousal.

car'ou-sel, 1 kar'u-zel; 2 cär'ụ-şĕl, *n.* **1.** A merry-go-round. **2.** A tournament.

carp†, 1 kärp; 2 cärp, *vi.* To find fault unreasonably; cavil.

carp, *n.* [CARP, formerly CARPS, *pl.*] A fresh-water food-fish.

car'pen-ter, 1 kär'pen-ter; 2 cär'pĕn-ter, *n.* A builder or repairer of wooden structures.— **car'pen-try,** *n.* The art, trade, or work of a carpenter.

car'pet, 1 kär'pet; 2 cär'pĕt. **I**ᵈ. *vt.* To cover with or as with a carpet. **II.** *n.* A heavy ornamental floor-covering.— **car'pet-bag",** *n.* A hand-bag, especially one made of carpeting.— **car'pet-ing,** *n.* Material for carpets; carpets collectively.

car'riage, 1 kar'ıj; 2 cär'ag, *n.* **1.** A wheeled vehicle for carrying persons; that which carries something, as in a machine; transportation; the cost of carrying. **2.** Deportment; bearing. **3**†. Something carried.

car'ri-er, 1 kar'ı-er; 2 cär'ı-er, *n.* One who or that which carries.

car'ri-on, 1 kar'ı-en; 2 cär'ı-on, *n.* Dead and putrefying flesh; a carcass.

car'rot, 1 kar'et; 2 cär'ot, *n.* A reddish-yellow edible root, or the plant producing it.— **car'rot-y,** *a.*

car'ry, 1 kar'ı; 2 cär'y, *v.* [CAR'RIED; CAR'-RY-ING.] **I.** *t.* **1.** To take, as in the hand or arms, from one place to another; transport; transfer; convey. **2.** To hold; contain; include; involve; imply. **3.** To influence; win; capture. **4.** To bear up; sustain. **5.** To demean or conduct; behave. **II.** *i.* To have influence, propelling power, or the like.

cart, 1 kärt; 2 cärt. I^d. *vt. & vi.* To carry in or as in a cart; drive a cart. **II.** *n.* A two=wheeled vehicle, heavy for loads, or light, with springs, for pleasure.— **cart′age, n.** The act or cost of carting.— **cart′er, n.** One who drives a cart; a teamster.

carte[1], 1 kärt; 2 cärt, *n.* A card or paper; a bill of fare.— **carte blanche,** 1 kärt blänsh, 2 cärt blänçh, an order signed in blank; unconditional permission or authority.

carte[2], *n.* A position in fencing.

car′tel, 1 kär′tel *or* kar-tel′; 2 cär′tĕl *or* cär-tĕl′, *n.* **1.** A written agreement for exchange of prisoners. **2.** A challenge.

car′ti-lage, 1 kär′tĭ-lĭj; 2 cär′ti-laġ, *n.* Gristle.— **car′ti-lag′i-nous,** 1 kär′tĭ-laj′ĭ-nŭs; 2 cär′ti-lăġ′i-nŭs, *a.* Gristly; having a gristly skeleton, as sharks.

car-toon′, 1 kar-tūn′; 2 cär-tōon′, *n.* **1.** A large sketch, as for a fresco. **2.** A caricature.— **car-toon′ist, n.**

car′tridge, 1 kär′trĭj; 2 cär′tridġ, *n.* A charge for a firearm or for blasting, enclosed in a case.— **blank cartridge,** a cartridge containing powder only.

carve, 1 kärv; 2 cärv, *vt. & vi.* [CARV(E)D⁸; **carv**^s, CARV′ING.] **1.** To make or decorate by cutting or chiseling; sculpture. **2.** To cut up, as cooked meat.— **carv′er, n.— carv′ing, n.** [small waterfall.

cas-cade′, 1 kas-kēd′; 2 căs-cād′, *n.* A

case, 1 kēs; 2 cās, *vt.* [CASED; CAS′ING.] To cover with a case; incase.

case[1], *n.* **1.** The state of things; condition; situation; instance; event; contingency; in law, a cause of action; a suit. **2.** *Gram.* The relation of a noun, pronoun, or adjective to other words.

case[2], 1 kēs; 2 cās, *n.* A covering in which something may be kept; quantity or number so contained; a set; a tray for holding type.

case′=hard′en, 1 kēs′=härd′n; 2 cās′=härd′n, *vt.* To harden the surface of (iron); make callous or insensible.

ca′se-in, 1 kē′si-in; 2 cā′se-ĭn, *n.* A constituent of milk, the chief ingredient in cheese.

case′mate, 1 kēs′mēt; 2 cās′māt, *n.* A chamber, as in a fort, with openings for guns.

case′ment, 1 kēs′ment *or* -mənt; 2 cās′ment, *n.* A hinged window=sash; window.

cash[t], 1 kash; 2 căsh, *vt.* To convert into cash.

cash[1], *n.* Current money in hand.

cash[2], *n.* [CASH, *pl.*] A former coin of China, worth one=fifth of a cent.

cash-ier′, 1 kash-ir′; 2 căsh-ēr′, *vt.* To dismiss in disgrace, as a military officer.

cash-ier′, *n.* A cash=keeper or paymaster.

cash′mere, 1 kash′mir; 2 căsh′mēr, *n.* A fine, soft fabric from Kashmir in India.

ca-si′no, 1 kə-sī′no; 2 ca-sī′no, *n.* **1.** A room or building for public resort and diversion. **2.** A game of cards.

cask, 1 kask; 2 căsk, *n.* A barrel=shaped wooden vessel, or the quantity it will hold.

cas′ket, 1 kas′ket; 2 căs′kĕt, *n.* **1.** A jewel=case. **2.** [U.S.] A burial=case.

casque, 1 kask; 2 căsk, *n.* A helmet.

cas-sa′va, 1 ka-sä′və; 2 că-sä′va, *n.* **1.** A tropical American shrub or herb. **2.** Tapioca.

cas′sia, 1 kash′ə *or* -i-ə; 2 căsh′a *or* -i-a, *n.* A coarse variety of cinnamon; also, the tree yielding it.

cas′si-mere, 1 kas′i-mir; 2 căs′i-mèr, *n.* A woolen cloth for men's wear.

cas-si′no, *n.* Same as CASINO.

cas′sock, 1 kas′ək; 2 căs′ok, *n.* A long close=fitting garment for a clergyman.

cas′so-wa-ry, 1 kas′o-wē-ri; 2 căs′o-wä-ry *n.* [-RIES, 2 -riz.]
A large, fleet, ostrich=like bird of Australia.

Helmeted Cassowary. ¹/₆₀

cast, 1 kast; 2 cäst, *vt. & vi.* [CAST; CAST′ING.] **1.** To throw with force; fling; hurl. **2.** To throw off, out, or over; emit; shed; deposit; give; impute. **3.** To shape in a mold; found; stereotype. **4.** To compute; calculate. **5.** *Theat.* To assign, as an actor of a part.

cast, *n.* **1.** A throw; anything thrown. **2.** An object shaped in a mold. **3.** An impression, as in wax. **4.** A characteristic formation; stamp; shade. **5.** A squint. **6.** *Theat.* The distribution of parts to performers. **7.** The performers as a body.

cas′ta-net, 1 kas′ta-net; 2 căs′ta-nĕt, *n.* A pair of small clappers, used as an accompaniment to song or dance.

cast′a-way, 1 kast′ə-wē; 2 cäst′a-wā, *n.* One who is wrecked or abandoned; an outcast.

caste, 1 kast; 2 cäst, *n.* A hereditary social class, as in Hindustan.

cas′tel-lat″ed, 1 kas′te-lēt″ed; 2 căs′tĕ-lăt″ĕd, *pa.* Having battlements; fortified.

cast′er, 1 kast′ər, -ər *or* -ŏr; 2 cäst′er, *n.* **1.** One who or that

which casts. **2.** A cruet, or a stand for cruets. **3.** A small roller for furniture.

cas′ti-gate, 1 kas′tɪ-gāt; 2 ĕăs′tĭ-gāt, *vt.* [-GAT″ED^d; -GAT″ING.] To whip; chastise; correct. — **cas″ti-ga′tion,** 1 kas″tɪ-gē′shən; 2 ĕăs″tĭ-gā′shon, *n.* A whipping; severe rebuke or criticism.

cast′ing, 1 kas′tɪŋ; 2 eăst′ing, *n.* The act of casting, or any metal object cast in a mold.

cas′tle, 1 kas′l; 2 eăs′l, *n.* **1.** A fortress. **2.** *Chess.* A castle-shaped piece; a rook.

cas′tlᴾ, a fortified residence. **2.** *Chess.* A castle-shaped piece; a rook.

cas′tor¹, 1 kus′tər *or* -tər; 2 eăs′tor, *n.* **1.** A beaver, or its fur; a hat. **2.** A heavy fabric for overcoats, etc.

cas′tor², *n.* Same as CASTER.

cas′tor-oil″, 1 kas′tər-[*or* -tər-]oil″; 2 eăs′-tor-öil″, *n.* A thick vegetable oil: used as a cathartic.

cas′trate, 1 kas′trēt; 2 eăs′trāt, *vt.* To remove the sexual germ-bearing glands from (the male); emasculate.

cas′u-al, 1 kaʒ′u-əl; 2 eăzh′u-al, **I.** *a.* Occurring by chance; accidental; unusual. **II.** *n.* A casual laborer or pauper. — **cas′u-al-ly,** *adv.* — **cas′u-al-ty,** 1 kaʒ′u-əl-tɪ; 2 eăzh′u-al-ty, *n.* [-TIES, 1 -tɪz; 2 -tĭs, *pl.*] **1.** A fatal or serious accident. **2.** A chance occurrence.

cas′u-ist-ry, 1 kaʒ′u-ɪst-rɪ; 2 eăzh′u-ĭst-ry, *n.* [-RIES, 1 -rɪz; 2 -rĭs, *pl.*] **1.** The determination of duty in doubtful cases. **2.** Sophistical reasoning. — **cas′u-ist,** *n.* An expert in casuistry; a sophist. — **cas″u-is′tic,** *a.* **cas″u-is′ti-cal‡.**

cat, 1 kat; 2 eăt, *n.* **1.** A domestic animal, kept to kill mice and rats. **2.** One of various fishes. **3.** A purchase for hoisting an anchor. **4.** A cat-o′-nine-tails.

cat′a-clysm, 1 kat′ə-klizm; 2 eăt′a-elȳsm, *n.* An overwhelming flood or convulsion.

cat′a-comb, 1 kat′ə-kōm; 2 eăt′a-eōm, *n.* An underground gallery for coffined dead.

cat′a-lep-sy, 1 kat′ə-lep-sɪ; 2 eăt′a-lĕp-sy, *n.* Sudden loss of consciousness, with muscular rigidity. — **cat″a-lep′tic,** *a.* & *n.*

cat′a-lo, 1 kat′ə-lo; 2 eăt′a-lo, *n.* A hybrid between the North-American buffalo and the domestic cow.

cat′a-log, 1 kat′ə-ləg; 2 eăt′a-lŏg. **I.** *vt.* [-LOGED, -LOGUED; -LOG″ING, LOGU″ING.] To list. **II.** *n.* An alphabetical list of names, persons, or things.

cat′a-logue, [-LOGED, -LOGUED; -LOG″ING, LOGU″ING.] To list. **II.** *n.* An alphabetical list of names, persons, or things.

ca-tal′pa, 1 kə-tal′pə; 2 ea-tăl′pa, *n.* A tree of North America and the Orient, with ovate leaves and bell-shaped flowers.

cat″a-ma-ran′, 1 kat″ə-ma-ran′; 2 eăt″a-ma-răn′, *n.* A long raft with outrigger.

cat′a-mount, 1 kat′ə-maunt; 2 eăt′a-mount, *n.* A wildcat, cougar, or lynx.

cat′a-plasm, 1 kat′ə-plazm; 2 eăt′a-plăsm, *n.* A poultice.

cat′a-pult, 1 kat′ə-pult; 2 eăt′a-pŭlt, *n.* An ancient military engine for throwing stones, etc.

cat′a-ract, 1 kat′ə-rakt; 2 eăt′a-răet, *n.* **1.** A great waterfall. **2.** Opacity of a lens of the eye.

ca-tarrh′, 1 kə-tūr′; 2 ea-tär′, *n.* Excessive secretion from a mucous membrane, as of the throat and head. — **ca-tarrh′al,** *a.*

ca-tas′tro-phe, 1 kə-tas′tro-fɪ; 2 ca-tas′tro-fe, *n.* **1.** A final event; fatal conclusion; sudden misfortune. **2.** *Geol.* A sudden, violent change.

ca-tas′tro-feᴾ, tăs′tro-fe, *n.*

cat′bird″, 1 kat′bŭrd″; 2 eăt′bĭrd″, *n.* A small slate-colored North-American thrush with cat-like cry.

catch, 1 kaćh; 2 cach, *v.* **cach^ᴾ,** Catbird. ¹/₁₄ [CAUGHT, 1 kȯt, 2 eạt; CATCH′ING.] **I.** *t.* **1.** To take; seize; capture; ensnare; surprise. **2.** To grasp; apprehend; engage; captivate. **II.** *i.* **1.** To seize or attempt to seize something: with *at*. **2.** *Baseball.* To act as catcher. **3.** To become entangled or fastened. **4.** To be contagious. — **catch′er,** *n.* — **catch′ing,** *pa.* Infectious; contagious; captivating. — **catch′pen″ny.** **I.** *a.* Cheap, poor, and showy. **II.** *n.* [-NIES^z, *pl.*] An inferior article, made merely to sell.

catch, *n.* **1.** The act of catching. **2.** That which catches; a fastening. **3.** Something caught or gained. **4.** A trick. **5.** An impediment; a break. **6.** *Mus.* A round; a scrap of song.

catch′up, 1 kaćh′up; 2 eăch′ŭp, *n.* A spiced condiment for meats.

cat′e-chism, 1 kat′ɪ-kizm; 2 eăt′e-eĭsm, *n.* A book of religious instruction by question and answer. — **cat″e-chet′ic, -i-cal,** 1 kat′ɪ-ket′ɪk, -ɪ-kəl; 2 eăt″e-eĕt′ĭe, -ĭ-eal, *a.* Of or pertaining to a catechism or to instruction by question and answer.

cat′e-chize, -chise, 1 kat′ɪ-kaiz; 2 eăt′e-eīz, *vt.* [-CHIZED, -CHISED; -CHIZ″ING, -CHIS″ING.] To interrogate; instruct as by catechism. — **cat′e-chist,** *n.* One who catechizes. — **cat′e-chiz″er or -chis″er‡.**

cat′e-chu, 1 kat′ɪ-ćhu; 2 eăt′e-chụ, *n.* An astringent extract from various Oriental plants.

cat″e-chu′men, 1 kat″ɪ-kiū′men; 2 eăt″e-

1: ə = final; ɪ = habĭt; aisle; au = out; oil; iū = feud; ćhin; go; ŋ = sing; thin, this.

2: wolf, do; bŏŏk, bŏŏt; full, rụle, cūre, bŭt, bûrn; ö̤l, bŏy; ḡo, ḡem; iŋk; thin, this.

REPRESENTATIVE TYPES OF CATS. ⅓

1. Manx. 2. Silver tabby. 3. Angora. 4. Short-haired brown tabby. 5. Smoke Persian.
6. Siamese. 7. Short-haired blue. 8. Short-haired tortoise-shell. 9. Shaded silver.

cŭ′mĕn, *n*. One under catechetic instruction; a new convert.

cat′e-go-ry, 1 kat′ı̆-go-rı; 2 căt′e-g̅o-ry, *n*. [-RIES*z*, *pl.*] A class or order.— **cat″e-gor′i-cal,** 1 kat′ı̆-gŏr′i-kəl; 2 căt″e-gŏr′i-cal, *a*. Unqualified; absolute, positive. **-ly,** *adv.*

ca′ter, 1 kē′tər; 2 cā′ter, *vi*. To furnish food or entertainment.— **ca′ter-er,** *n*. One who furnishes food, etc.. for entertainments.

cat′er-pil″lar, 1 kat′ər-pil″ər ; 2 căt′er-pil″ar, *n*. The larva of a butterfly, moth, or the like.

cat′er-waul, 1 kat′ər-wōl; 2 căt′er-wa̤l, *vi*. To utter a discordant cry like a cat.

cat′fish″, 1 kat′fish″, 2 căt′fĭsh″, *n*. Any one of various fishes.

cat′gut″, 1 kat′gut″; 2 căt′g̅ŭt″, *n*. A very tough cord, made from the intestines of animals, for stringing musical instruments, etc.

ca-thar′tic, 1 kə-thär′tı̆k; 2 ca-thär″tie. **I.** *a.* purgative; purifying. **II.** *n*. A purgative medicine.

ca-the′dral, 1 kə-thī′drəl; 2 ca-thē′dral, *n*. The chief church of a diocese; the church containing the official throne or chair of the bishop.

cath′ode, 1 kăth′ōd; 2 căth′ōd, *n*. The negative pole of a galvanic battery; opposed to *anode*.

Cath′o-lic, 1 kăth′o-lik; 2 căth′o-lie. **I.** *a.* **1.** Pertaining to the whole Christian church. **2.** Specif.: Of or pertaining (1) to the Church of Rome, (2) to the Church of England, or (3) to the Greek Church. **3.** [c-] Large = minded; liberal; universal. **II.** *n*. A member of the Roman Catholic Church.— **Ca-thol′i-cism,** 1 kə-thŏl′i-sizm; 2 ca-thŏl′i-çĭsm, *n*. The tenets of the Roman Catholic Church.— **cath″-o-lic′i-ty,** 1 kăth″o-lis′i-tı̆; 2 căth″o-lĭç′i-ty, *n*. Comprehensiveness; liberality; universality.

cat′kin, 1 kat′kı̆n; 2 căt′kĭn, *n*. A scaly spike of flowers, as in the willow; an ament.

cat′mint″, 1 kat′mı̆nt″; 2 căt′mĭnt″, *n*. An aromatic herb of which cats are fond. **cat′nip″**‡.

cat″o′-nine′-tails, 1 kat″o=nain′=tēlz; 2 căt″o=nīn′=tāls, *n*. A whip with nine lashes: formerly used for flogging in the army and navy.

cats′paw″, 1 kats′pō″; 2 căts′pạ″, *n*. **1.** A person used as a tool or dupe: in allusion to the fable of the monkey's using the cat's paw to draw chestnuts from the fire. **2.** *Naut.* A light wind barely ruffling the water. **cat's′=paw″**‡.

cat′sup, 1 *n*. Same as CATCHUP.

cat′tle, 1 kat′l; 2 căt′l, *n, pl*. **1.** Domesticated bovine animals; formerly any live stock kept for use or profit, as horses, camels, sheep, etc. **2.** Human beings: said contemptuously. **cat′lP**‡,

Cau-ca′sian, 1 kŏ-kash′ən *or* -kē′shən; 2 ca-căsh′an *or* -cā′shan, *n*. A member of the white division of the human species: also used adjectively.

cau′cus. 1 kō′kus; 2 ca̤′cŭs, *n*. [U. S.] A private or preliminary meeting of members of a political party to select candidates or to concert measures.

cau′dal, 1 kŏ′dəl; 2 ca̤′dal, *a*. Of, pertaining to, or near the tail.— **cau′date,** *a*. Having a tail.

cau′dle, 1 kŏ′dl; 2 ca̤′dl, *n*. A warm drink of wine, eggs, etc. **cau′dlP**‡,

caught, 1 kŏt; 2 ca̤t, *imp. & pp.* of CATCH, *v*.

caul, 1 kōl; 2 ca̤l, *n*. A membrane, as a fold of the peritoneum.

caul′dron, 1 kōl′drən; 2 ca̤l′dron, *n*. Same as CALDRON.

cau′li-flow″er, 1 kō′lı̆-flau″ər; 2 ca̤′li-flow″er, *n*. A variety of cabbage.

caulk, caulk′er, etc. Same as CALK, etc.

cause, 1 kŏz; 2 ca̤s. **I.** *vt*. [CAUSED; CAUS′-ING.] To produce; effect; compel. **II.** *n*. **1.** That which produces any thing or event. **2.** A reason; purpose; aim. **3.** A great enterprise. **4.** A lawsuit.— **caus′al,** *a*. Pertaining to, constituting, or expressing a cause.— **cau-sal′i-ty,** *n*. [-TIES*z*, *pl.*] **1.** The relation of cause and effect. **2.** Causal action or agency.— **cau-sa′tion,** *n*. The principle of causality; causative power, action, or agency.— **caus′a-tive**(e*s*, *a*. Effective as a cause; expressing cause; causal.— **cause′less,** *a*. **1.** Having no just cause; groundless. **2.** Uncaused. **-ly,** *adv*. **-ness,** *n*.

cause′way, 1 kōz′wē; 2 ca̤s′wā, *n*. A raised road, as over marshy ground.

caus′tic, 1 kŏs′tı̆k; 2 ca̤s′tic. **I.** *a.* Corroding; corrosive; sarcastic. **II.** *n*. A caustic substance.— **caus-tic′i-ty,** 1 kŏs-tis′i-tı̆; 2 ca̤s-tĭç′i-ty, *n*. **caus′tic-ness**‡.

cau′ter-ize *or* **-ise,** 1 kō′tər-aiz; 2 ca̤′ter-īz, *vt*. [-IZED; -IZ′ING.] To sear with a caustic or a hot iron.— **cau″ter-i-za′**[or **-sa′**]**tion,** *n*.

cau′ter-y, 1 kō′tər-ı̆; 2 ca̤′ter-y, *n*. [-IES*z*, *pl.*] The act of cauterizing; a cauterizing agent.

cau′tion, 1 kō′shən; 2 ca̤′shon. **I.** *vt*. To warn. **II.** *n.* **1.** Care to avoid injury or misfortune; prudence; wariness. **2.** A warning.— **cau′tion-a-ry,** 1 kō′shən-ē-rı̆; 2 ca̤′shon-ā-ry, *a*. Warning.— **cau′tious,** 1 kō′shus; 2 ca̤′shŭs, *a*. Exercising caution; wary; prudent. **-ly,** *adv*. **-ness,** *n*.

1: ə = final; ı = habit; aisle; au = out; oil; iū = feud; chin; go; ŋ = sing; thin, this.
2: wo̤lf, dǫ; bo̅o̅k, bo̅o̅t; full, rule, cūre, bŭt, bûrn; o̤il, bo̤y; g̅o, g̅em; iŋk; thin, this.

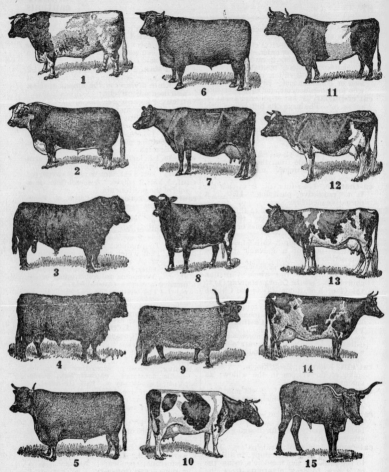

REPRESENTATIVE TYPES OF CATTLE.

1. Shorthorn bull. 2. Hereford bull. 3. Aberdeen-Angus bull. 4. Galloway bull. 5. Devon bull.
6. Sussex steer. 7. Red Polled cow. 8. Polled Durham cow. 9. West Highland cow. 10. Holstein-
Friesian cow. 11. Dutch Belted bull. 12. Jersey cow. 13. Guernsey cow. 14. Ayrshire cow. 15.
Texas Longhorn steer.

cav″al-cade′, 1 kav″əl-kēd′; 2 eăv″al-eād′, *n.* A company of riders; a parade.

cav″a-lier′, 1 kav″ə-līr′; 2 eăv″a-lēr′. **I.** *a.* Free and easy; offhand; haughty. **II.** *n.* **1.** [-C-] A royalist opponent of the English Puritans. **2.** A horseman; knight; lover; escort.— **cav″a-lier′ly,** *adv.*

cav′al-ry, 1 kav′əl-rɪ; 2 eăv′al-ry, *n.* Mounted troops.

ca″va-ti′na, 1 kä″va-tī′na; 2 eä″vä-tī′nä, *n.* *Mus.* A short and simple aria; a song without a second part.

cave, 1 kēv; 2 eäv. **I.** *vt.* & *vi.* [CAVED; CAV′ING.] To hollow out; cause to fall in; give way. **II.** *n.* A natural cavity in earth or rock.

cav′ern, 1 kav′ern; 2 eăv′ern, *n.* A large cave; a den; cavity.— **cav′ern-ous,** 1 kav′ərn-us; 2 eăv′ern-ŭs, *a.* Of or like a cavern or caverns; hollow; hollow-sounding.— **cav′ern-ous-ly,** *adv.*

cav″i-ar′, 1 kav″ɪ-är′; 2 eăv″i-är′, *n.* The salted roe of the sturgeon.

cav′il, 1 kav′il; 2 eăv′il. **I.** *vi.* [CAV′IL(E)D⁸ or CAV′ILLED; CAV′IL-ING or CAV′IL-LING.] To raise frivolous objections. **II.** *n.* A captious objection; caviling.— **cav′il-er, cav′il-ler,** *n.*

cav′i-ty, 1 kav′ɪ-tɪ; 2 eăv′i-ty, *n.* [-TIES²; *pl.*] A hollow or sunken space; hole.

caw, 1 kɔ; 2 eą. **I.** *vi.* To cry like a crow. **II.** *n.* The cry of the crow.

Cay-enne′, 1 kē-en′ *or* kai-en′; 2 eā-ĕn′ or **Cay-en′,** *or* eī-ĕn′, *n.* Red pepper.

cay′man, 1 kē′mən; 2 eā′man, *n.* An American alligator.

cay-use′, 1 kai-yūs′; 2 eỹ-yus′, *n.* [Northwestern U. S.] An Indian pony; a bronco.

cease, 1 sīs; 2 çēs, *vt.* & *vi.* [CEASED⁴, CEAST⁸; CEAS′ING.] To leave off; end; stop; desist.— **cease′less,** *a.* Continuing without pause or stop. -**ly,** *adv.* -**ness,** *n.*

ce′dar, 1 sī′dər; 2 çē′dar, *n.* A large evergreen tree of the pine family.

cede, 1 sīd; 2 çēd, *vt.* [CED′ED⁴; CED′ING.] To surrender title to; transfer; give up: said especially of territory.

ceil, 1 sīl; 2 çēl, *vt.* To furnish with a [ceiling.

ceil′ing, 1 sīl′ɪŋ; 2 çēl′ing, *n.* The overhead covering of a room.

cel′e-brate, 1 sel′ɪ-brēt; 2 çĕl′e-brāt, *vt.* [-BRAT″ED⁴; -BRAT′ING.] To commemorate joyfully; keep; observe; make famous, as by song or poem.— **cel′e-brant,** *n.* One who celebrates, as mass.— **cel′e-brat″ed,** *pa.* **1.** Famous. **2.** Performed with customary rites. — **cel′e-bra′tion,** *n.* The act of celebrating; a festal observance.— **ce-leb′ri-ty,** 1 sɪ-leb′-**

rɪ-tɪ; 2 çe-lĕb′ri-ty, *n.* [-TIES²; *pl.*] Fame; distinction; a celebrated person.

ce-ler′i-ty, 1 sɪ-ler′ɪ-tɪ; 2 çe-lĕr′i-ty, *n.* Quickness; speed.

cel′er-y, 1 sel′ər-ɪ; 2 çĕl′er-y, *n.* A biennial herb, whose blanched stems are used as a salad.

ce-les′tial, 1 sɪ-les′ehəl; 2 çe-lĕs′chal. **I.** *a.* **1.** Of or pertaining to the sky or heaven; heavenly. **2.** [-C-] Chinese. **II.** *n.* **1.** A heavenly being. **2.** [-C-] A Chinese. — **ce-les′tial-ly,** *adv.*

cel′i-ba-cy, 1 sel′ɪ-bə-sɪ; 2 çĕl′i-ba-çy, *n.* The state of being unmarried.— **cel′i-bate,** *n.* An unmarried person.

cell, } 1 sel; 2 çĕl, *n.* **1.** A small chamber, **celⁱ,** } space, cavity, or vesicle. **2.** *Elec.* A single element of a voltaic battery.

cel′lar, 1 sel′ər; 2 çĕl′ar, *n.* An underground room.— **cel′lar-age,** *n.* A cellar or cellars; storage in a cellar, or the charge for it.

cel′lo, 1 chel′lo; 2 chĕl′lo, *n.* *Mus.* A violoncello.

cel′lu-lar, 1 sel′yu-lər; 2 çĕl′yu-lar, *a.* Of, pertaining to, or like a cell or cells.

cel′lu-loid, 1 sel′yu-leid; 2 çĕl′yu-löid, *n.* A hard elastic compound, prepared from guncotton.

Celt¹, 1 selt; 2 çĕlt, *n.* One of the family that includes the Irish, Welsh, Bretons, etc.— **Celt′ic,** *a.* & *n.*

celt², *n.* A prehistoric implement or weapon of stone or bronze.

ce-ment′, 1 sɪ-ment′; 2 çe-mĕnt′. **I**ᵈ. *vt.* & *vi.* To cover with or join by cement; unite; cohere. **II.** *n.* A substance for joining objects by adhesion; a mortar-like substance for producing a hard, smooth, or water-proof surface.

cem″en-ta′tion, 1 sem″en-tē′shən; 2 çĕm″-ĕn-tā′shon, *n.* **1.** The act of cementing. **2.** A process of modifying a metal by heat.

cem′e-ter-y, 1 sem′ɪ-ter-ɪ; 2 çĕm′e-tĕr-y, *n.* [-IES²; *pl.*] A place for the burial of the dead.

cen′o-bite, 1 sen′o-bait; 2 çĕn′o-bĭt, *n.* A monk.— **cen″o-bit′ic, cen″o-bit′i-cal,** *a.*

cen′o-taph, 1 sen′o-taf; 2 çĕn′o-táf, *n.* **cen′o-tafᵖ,** } An empty tomb.

cen′ser, 1 sen′sər; 2 çĕn′ser, *n.* A vessel for burning incense.

cen′sor, 1 sen′sər *or* -ser; 2 çen′sor, *n.* **1.** An official examiner empowered to prohibit publication of manuscripts; one who censures; a critic. **2.** An ancient Roman magistrate.— **cen-so′ri-ous,** *a.* Given to censure; faultfinding. -**ly,** *adv.* -**ness,** *n.*— **cen′sor-ship,** *n.* The office, term, or powers of a censor or critic.

1: ə = final; ɪ = habɪt; aɪsle; au = out; oɪl; iū = feud; chin; go; ŋ = sing; ℂhin, this.
2: wolf, dǫ; book, boot; fŭll, rŭle, cūre, bŭt, bûrn; ŏil, bŏy; ḡo, ḡem; iŋk; thin, this.

cen'sure, 1 sen'shur; 2 çĕn'shur. **I.** *vt.* [CEN'SURED; CEN'SUR-ING.] To blame; condemn; reprimand. **II.** *n.* The act of censuring; disapproval; blame; reprimand.— **cen'sur-a-ble**(er, *a.* Deserving censure; blameworthy.

cen'sus, 1 sen'sus; 2 çĕn'sus, *n.* An official numbering of the people of a country.

cent, 1 sent; 2 çĕnt, *n.* The one-hundredth part of a dollar.— **per cent.,** see PER.

cen'tal, 1 sen'tal; 2 çĕn'tal. **I.** *a.* Of or pertaining to a hundred. **II.** *n.* An English hundredweight, 112 pounds.

cen'tare, 1 sen'tār *or* (F.) sañ'tär'; 2 çĕn'tär *or* (F.) çäñ'tär', *n.* See METRIC SYSTEM.

cen'taur, 1 sen'tōr; 2 çĕn'tạr, *n.* A fabled monster, half man and half horse.

cen'te-na'ry, 1 sen'tɪ-nē"rɪ; 2 çĕn'te-nā"ry. **I.** *a.* Of or pertaining to a hundred or a century. **II.** *n.* [-RIES², *pl.*] **1.** A hundredth anniversary. **2.** A period of a hundred years. —**cen"te-na'ri-an,** *n.* One a hundred years old.

cen-ten'ni-al, 1 sen-ten'ɪ-al; 2 çĕn-tĕn'i-al. **I.** *a.* Happening once in a century. **II.** *n.* A hundredth anniversary.

cen'ter, } 1 sen'tar; 2 çĕn'ter. **I.** *vt. & vi.*
cen'tre, } [CEN'TERED, CEN'TRED, CEN'-TERD⁸; CEN'TERING, CEN'TRING.] To place in or on a center; draw to a center; determine the center of; be or converge in the center. **II.** *n.* The middle point of anything, especially of a circle.— **cen'ter-**[or **-tre-**]**bit**⁰, *n.* A bit with a cutting edge that revolves about a central point.

cen-tes'i-mal, 1 sen-tes'ɪ-mal; 2 çĕn-tĕs'i-mal, *a.* One-hundredth.

cen'ti-grade, 1 sen'tɪ-grēd; 2 çĕn'tɪ-grād, *a.* Graduated to a scale of 100°. On the centigrade thermometer the freezing-point of water is zero and its boiling-point 100°; its symbol is C.; as, 100° C. Compare FAHRENHEIT.

cen'ti-gram *or* **-gramme,** 1 sen'tɪ-gram; 2 çĕn'tɪ-gräm, **cen'ti-li"ter** *or* **-li"tre,** 1 sen'-tɪ-lī"tər; 2 çĕn'tɪ-lī"ter, **cen'ti-me"ter** *or* **-me"tre,** 1 sen'tɪ-mī"tər; 2 çĕn'tɪ-mē"ter. See METRIC SYSTEM.

cen'time', 1 sañ'tīm'; 2 çäñ'tīm', *n.* The smallest unit in the French monetary system, ¹/₁₀₀ of a franc or ¹/₅ of a cent.

cen'ti-ped, } 1 sen'tɪ-ped, -pīd; 2 çĕn'tɪ-
cen'ti-pede, } pĕd, -pēd, *n.* A many-legged insect.

cen'tral, 1 sen'tral; 2 çĕn'tral, *a.* Of or pertaining to or acting from the center; chief. **-ly,** *adv.* — **cen"tral-i-za'tion** *or* **-sa'tion,** *n.* The concentration of control in a central authority.— **cen'tral-ize** *or* **-ise,**

1 sen'tral-aiz; 2 çĕn'tral-īz, *vt. & vi.* [-IZED; -IZ"ING.] To make central; concentrate.

cen'tre, 1 Same as CENTER.

cen'tric, 1 sen'trik; 2 çĕn'trie, *a.* Central; related to a nerve-center. **cen'tri-cal‡.**

cen-trif'u-gal, 1 sen-trif'yu-gal; 2 çĕn-trif'yu̯-gal, *a.* Tending away from a center. **-ly,** *adv.*

cen-trip'e-tal, 1 sen-trip'ɪ-tal; 2 çĕn-trĭp'e-tal, *a.* Tending toward a center. **-ly,** *adv.*

cen'tu-ple, } 1 sen'tiu-pl; 2 çĕn'tū-pl, *a.*
cen'tu-plȳ, } Increased a hundredfold.

cen-tu'ri-on, 1 sen-tiū'rɪ-ạn; 2 çĕn-tū'ri-on, *n.* A Roman captain, originally of a hundred men.

cen'tu-ry, 1 sen'chu-[or -tiu-]rɪ; 2 çĕn'chu̯-[or -tū-]ry, *n.* [-RIES², *pl.*] **1.** A period of 100 years. **2.** A hundred things of the same kind.— **c e n't u-r y-plant",** *n.* The American aloe, formerly supposed to flower once in a century.

ce-phal'ic, } 1 sɪ-fal'ik; 2
ce-fal'icᵖ, } çe-fǎl'ie, *a.* Of, pertaining to, on, in, or near the head.

ce-ra'ceous, 1 sɪ-rē"shus; 2 çe-rā"shus, *a.* Of or like wax.

ce-ram'ic, 1 sɪ-ram'ik; 2 çe-răm'ie, *a.* Relating to pottery.

Century-plant.

ce'rate, 1 sī'rēt; 2 çē'rāt, *n.* An ointment of oil or lard, with wax, etc.

ce'rat-ed, 1 sī'rēt-ed; 2 çē'rāt-ĕd, *a.* Covered with wax.

ce're-al, 1 sī'rɪ-al; 2 çē're-al. **I.** *a.* Pertaining to edible grain. **II.** *n.* Any edible grain, or a grain-yielding plant.

cer'e-bel'lum, 1 ser'ɪ-bel'um; 2 çĕr'e-bĕl'ŭm, *n.* [-BEL'LA, *pl.*] The little or hinder brain.

cer'e-brum, 1 ser'ɪ-brum; 2 çĕr'e-brŭm, *n.* [-BRA, *pl.*] The front and upper part of the brain.— **cer'e-bral,** *a.* Of, pertaining to, or like the brain; mental.— **cer"e-bra'tion,** *n.* Brain-action.

cere'ment, 1 sīr'ment *or* -mant; 2 çēr'ment, *n.* A garment or wrapping for the dead.

cer'e-mo-ny, 1 ser'ɪ-mo-nɪ; 2 çĕr'e-mo-ny, *n.* [-NIES², *pl.*] A formal act, rite, or observance; formal civility.— **cer"e-mo'ni-al. I.** *a.* Of or pertaining to ceremony; ritual; formal. **II.** *n.* A system of rules of ceremony; ritual; etiquette. **-ly,** *adv.*— **cer"e-mo'ni-ous,** *a.* Observant of or conducted with ceremony; formal. **-ly,** *adv.* **-ness,** *n.*

Ce'res, 1 sī'rīz; 2 çē'rēs, *n.* Roman goddess of corn and harvests; sister of Jupiter and mother of Proserpine. **De-me'ter‡** [Gr.].

1: ạrtistic, ärt; fat, fāre; fạst; get, prẹy; hit, police; obey, gō; nøt, ör; fưll, rūle; but, būrn.
2: ärt, āpe, făt, fâre, fȧst, whạt, ạll; mē, gĕt, prẹy, fērn; hĭt, īce; Ī=ē; ĭ=ĕ; gō, nŏt, ôr, wŏn,

cer'tain, 1 sŭr'tın; 2 çẽr'tin, *a.* **1.** Sure, as matter of fact, expectation, purpose, or the like. **2.** Having a settled belief; assured; confident; positive. **3.** Indefinite; one; some.— **cer'tain-ly,** 1 sŭr'tın-lı; 2 çẽr'tin-ly, *adv.*— **cer'tain-ty,** 1 sŭr'tın-tı; 2 çẽr'tin-ty, *n.* [-TIES², *pl.*] Confidence; precision; accuracy; a known truth.

cer-tif'i-cate, 1 sᴀr-tif'ı-kıt; 2 çer-tif'i-cat, *n.* A written declaration or testimonial. — **cer"ti-fi-ca'tion,** *n.* The act of certifying.

cer'ti-fy, 1 sŭr'tı-fαı; 2 çẽr'ti-fī, *vt. & vi.* [-FIED²; -FY"ING.] To give certain knowledge of; inform or state positively, as in writing; attest.

cer'ti-tude, 1 sŭr'tı-tiūd; 2 çẽr'ti-tūd, *n.* Perfect confidence; assured fact; sureness.

ce-ru'le-an, 1 sı-rū'lı-ᴀn; 2 çe-ru'le-an, *a.* Sky-blue.

cer'vi-cal, 1 sŭr'vı-kᴀl; 2 çẽr'vi-cal, *a.* Of, pertaining to, or near the neck.

ces-sa'tion, 1 se-sē'shᴀn; 2 çĕ-sā'shon, *n.* A stop; pause.

ces'sion, 1 sesh'ᴀn; 2 çĕsh'on, *n.* The act of ceding; surrender.

cess'pool", 1 ses'pūl"; 2 çĕs'pōōl", *n.* A pit for drainage, as from sinks. **cess'pit"**‡.

ce-ta'cean, 1 sı-tē'shᴀn; 2 çe-tā'shan, *n.* An aquatic mammal of fish-like form, as a whale or porpoise.

chafe, 1 chēf; 2 chāf, *vt. & vi.* [CHAFED†; CHAF'ING.] To injure or make sore by rubbing; gall; irritate; annoy; fret; fume; warm by rubbing.

chaff¹,) 1 chaf; 2 chäf, *n.* The husks of **chaf²,**) grain.

chaff², *n.* Good-natured raillery; banter. — **chaff,** *vt. & vi.* To poke fun (at); banter.

chaf'fer, 1 chaf'ᴀr; 2 chäf'er. **I.** *vi.* To dispute about price; bargain; haggle; chatter. **II.** *n.* A disputatious bargaining. [European song-bird.]

chaf'finch, 1 chaf'ınch; 2 chäf'ınch, *n.*

chaf'ing-dish", 1 chēf'ın-dish"; 2 chāf'ıng-dish", *n.* A vessel for holding live coals, a lamp, or hot water, for heating or cooking.

cha-grin', 1 sha-grın' *or* -grīn'; 2 çha-grın' *or* -grīn'. **I.** *vt.* To humiliate; mortify. **II.** *n.* Disappointment and wounded pride; mortification.

chain, 1 chēn; 2 chān. **I.** *vt.* To fasten, as with a chain. **II.** *n.* A string of interlinked rings or links; a series; range, as of mountains; a surveyors' measuring-line of 100 links.

chair, 1 chār; 2 châr, *n.* **1.** A movable seat with four legs and a back; a seat of office, as of a moderator; a chairman. **2.**

Railroad. An iron block for holding rails in place. **3‖.** A sedan.

chair'man, 1 chār'mᴀn; 2 châr'man, *n.* [-MEN, *pl.*] One who presides over an assembly.

chaise, 1 shēz; 2 chāş, *n.* **1.** A two-wheeled, one-horse vehicle for two persons. **2.** A light four-wheeled carriage.

French Chaise of 1760.

chal-ced'o-ny, 1 kal-sed'o-nı *or* kal'sı-do-nı; 2 cᴀl-çĕd'o-ny *or* cᴀl'çe-do-ny, *n.* A waxy, translucent quartz. **cal-ced'o-ny‡.**

cha'let', 1 sha'lē' *or* shal'ı; 2 chä'lẹ' *or* chäl'e, *n.* A Swiss cottage.

chal'ice,) 1 chal'ıs; 2 chăl'iç, *n.* A cup used **chal'is²,**) in the Lord's Supper.

chalk, 1 chôk; 2 chąk. **I†.** *vt.* To mark with chalk. **II.** *n.* A soft, white limestone, or a piece of it, used for marking. — **chalk'y,** *a.* Of, containing, or like chalk.

chal'lenge, 1 chal'enj; 2 chăl'ĕng. **I.** *vt. & vi.* [-LENGED; -LENG-ING.] To dare; invite; defy; claim; question; call out to a duel; dispute; object to. **II.** *n.* A call or defiance; summons to a duel; objection, as to a voter.— **chal'leng-er,** *n.*

chal'lis, 1 shal'ı; 2 chăl'i, *n.* A light, all-wool fabric.

cha-lyb'e-ate, 1 kᴀ-lib'ı-ēt; 2 ca-lÿb'e-āt, *a.* Impregnated with iron.

cham'ber, 1 chēm'bᴀr; 2 chām'ber, *n.* A room, especially a bedroom; any enclosed space, as at the breech of a gun. **cham'ber-lain,** 1 chēm'bᴀr-lın; 2 chām'ber-lın, *n.* A palace official; a steward or treasurer.— **cham'ber-maid",** *n.* A woman having care of bedchambers.

cha-me'le-on, 1 kᴀ-mī'lı-ᴀn; 2 ea-mē'le-on, *n.* A lizard that has the power of changing color.

cham'fer, 1 cham'fᴀr; 2 chăm'fer. **I** *vt.* To bevel. **II.** *n.* A bevel.

cham'ois, 1 sham'ı; 2 chăm'ei; 2 chăm'i *or* chăm'ŏi, *n.* **1.** A mountain antelope. **2.** A soft leather.

cham'o-mile, *n.* Same as CAMOMILE.

champ†, 1 champ; 2 chămp, *vt. & vi.* To bite impatiently, as a horse the bit.

cham-pagne', 1 sham-pēn'; 2 chăm-pān', *n.* An effervescent wine, typically amber-colored; originally, any wine produced in the former province of Champagne, France.

cham-paign', 1 sham-pēn'; 2 chăm-pān', *n.* Flat and open ground.

cham'pi-on, 1 cham'pı-ᴀn; 2 chăm'pi-on.

I. *vt.* To contend for; advocate. **II.** *n.*
1. One who defends a person, principle, etc. **2.** The victor in an open contest. **— cham'pi-on-ship,** *n.*

chance, 1 cháns; 2 chánç. **I.** *vi.* [CHANCED[t]; CHANC'ING.] **1.** To happen. **2.** To come unexpectedly (*on* or *upon*). **II.** *a.* Occurring by chance; casual. **III.** *n.* Fortune; luck; accident; opportunity; contingency; possibility; probability.

chan'cel, 1 chan'sel; 2 chăn'çĕl, *n.* The space about the altar in a church, for the clergy.

chan'cel-lor, ⎱ 1 chan'se-lẽr *or* lẽr; 2 chăn'-
chan'cel-or, ⎰ çĕ-lor, *n.* A high officer of state or of a university.**—chan'cel-lor-ship,**
chan'cel-or-ship, *n.*

chan'cer-y, 1 chan'sẽr-1; 2 chăn'çer-y, *n.* A court of equity.

chan"de-lier', 1 shan"de-lîr'; 2 chăn"de-lēr', *n.* A branched support for lights suspended from a ceiling.

chan'dler, 1 chan'dlẽr; 2 chăn'dler, *n.* A trader; dealer, especially in candles. **— chan'dler-y,** *n.* [-IES[z], *pl.*] A chandler's shop or goods; place for keeping candles.

Chandelier.

change, 1 chēnj; 2 chāng. **I.** *vt. & vi.* [CHANGED; CHANG'ING.] **1.** To make or become different; convert; alter; vary. **2.** To exchange; interchange. **II.** *n.* **1.** The act or fact of changing; alteration; substitution; a substitute. **2.** Small money. **3.** An exchange. **— change"a-bil'-i-ty,** *n.* **change'a-bl(e-ness?‡.— change'a-bl(e?,** 1 chēnj'a-bl; 2 chāng'a-bl, *a.* Capable of change; likely to change; inconstant.— **change'a-bly,** *adv.*— **change'ful,** 1 chēnj'-ful; 2 chāng'ful, *a.* Full of or given to change.— **change'less,** *a.* Free from change; immutable.

change'ling, 1 chēnj'lin; 2 chāng'lǐng, *n.* **1.** An ill-favored child supposed to have been substituted for a beautiful one stolen away. **2.** A fickle person.

chan'nel, 1 chan'el; 2 chăn'ĕl. **I.** *vt.* [CHAN'NELED *or* CHAN'NELLED, CHAN'-NELD[s]; CHAN'NEL-ING *or* CHAN'NEL-LING.] To cut or wear channels in. **II.** *n.* The bed of a stream; deep part of a river; a wide strait; any groove or passage.

chant, 1 chant; 2 chânt. **I.** *vt. & vi.* To recite musically; sing. **II.** *n.* A musical recitation, as of Scripture; a song; melody. **— chant'er,** *n.* **chan'tor‡.— chan'tress,** *n. fem.*

chan'ti-cleer, 1 chan'tı-klîr; 2 chăn'ti-elēr, *n.* A cock.

cha'os, 1 kē'os; 2 cā'ŏs, *n.* A condition of utter disorder, as the unformed primal state of the universe.**— cha-ot'ic,** 1 kē-ot'ık; 2 cā-ŏt'ie, *a.* Of or like chaos; unformed; disordered.

chap, 1 chap; 2 chăp, *vt. & vi.* [CHAPPED[t] *or* CHAPT; CHAP'PING.] To crack and roughen, as the skin.

chap[1], *n.* A crack, as in the skin.

chap[2], *n.* [Colloq.] A fellow; lad.

chap[3], 1 chop; 2 chăp, *n.* A jaw; in the plural, the mouth and cheeks.

chap"ar-ral', 1 chap"a-ral'; 2 chăp"a-răl', *n.* A tangle of dwarf oak, low thorny shrubs, etc.

chap'el, 1 chap'el; 2 chăp'ĕl, *n.* **1.** A place of worship. **2.** A chapel service.

chap'er-on, 1 shap'ẽr-ōn; 2 chăp'er-ōn. **I.** *vt.* To attend as chaperon. **II.** *n.* A woman who acts as attendant or protector of a young unmarried woman in public.

chap'fall"en, ⎱ 1 chop'fôl"n; 2 chăp'fal"n,
chop'fall"en, ⎰ *a.* Dejected; crestfallen.

chap'lain, 1 chap'lın; 2 chăp'lin, *n.* A minister or clergyman assigned to special duties, as holding the religious services of a legislature, a regiment, or on board ship. **— chap'lain-cy,** *n.* [-CIES[z], *pl.*] The office of a chaplain. **chap'lain-ship‡.**

chap'let, 1 chap'let; 2 chăp'lĕt, *n.* A wreath or garland; necklace; rosary.

chap'man, 1 chap'man; 2 chăp'man, *n.* [CHAP'MEN, *pl.*] A pedler.

chap'ter, 1 chap'tẽr; 2 chăp'ter, *n.* **1.** A division of a book. **2.** The clergy of a cathedral. **3.** A branch of a society.

char, 1 chär; 2 chär, *vt. & vi.* [CHARRED; CHAR'RING.] To scorch; burn to charcoal.

char'ac-ter, 1 kar'ak-tẽr; 2 eăr'ae-ter. **I.** *vt.* To impress, engrave, or depict; characterize. **II.** *n.* **1.** Mental or moral quality, or qualities, good or bad; also, moral excellence. **2.** Reputation. **3.** An assumed part; also, the person holding it. **4.** A figure; mark; sign; letter.**— char"ac-ter-is'-tic. I.** *a.* That characterizes; distinguishing; specific. **II.** *n.* A distinctive feature; peculiarity.**— char"ac-ter-is'ti-cal-ly,** *adv.*

char'ac-ter-ize *or* **-ise,** 1 kar'ak-tẽr-aiz; 2 eăr'ae-ter-īz, *vt.* [-IZED; -IZ'ING.] To describe; designate; distinguish.**— char"ac-ter-1-za'tion** *or* **-sa'tion,** *n.*

cha-rade', 1 sha-rēd' *or* -rād'; 2 cha-rād' *or* -rād', *n.* An acted riddle.

char'coal, 1 chär'kōl; 2 chär'eōl", *n.* A black, porous substance, made by charring wood; nearly pure carbon.

charge, 1 chärj; 2 chärg. **I.** *vt. & vi.*

[CHARGED; CHARG'ING.] **1.** To lay or impose something upon; instruct; enjoin. **2.** To set as a price; demand; set down something against; debit; accuse. **3.** To make an onset upon; attack. **II.** *n.* **1.** A load, as for a firearm. **2.** Care and custody, or the object cared for. **3.** A price; entry of indebtedness; tax; expense; cost. **4.** An admonitory address; instruction; command. **5.** An accusation. **6.** An impetuous onset; also, the signal for it.— **charge'a=bl**(e², *a.* Capable of being charged.— **charg'er,** *n.* **1.** A war=horse. **2‖.** A large dish.

char'i-ly, 1 ĉhār'ı-lı; 2 chār'i-ly, *adv.* In a chary manner.— **char'i-ness,** *n.* The quality of being chary.

char'i-ot, 1 ĉhar'ı-ət; 2 chăr'i-ot, *n.* Anciently, a two=wheeled vehicle, as for war; now, an ornate four=wheeled carriage.— **char'i-ot-eer',** 1 ĉhar'ı-ət-ır'; 2 chăr'i-ot-ēr', *n.* The driver of a chariot.

char'i-ty, 1 ĉhar'ı-tı; 2 chăr'i-ty, *n.* [-TIES², *pl.*] **1.** Liberality; almsgiving; alms. **2.** Benevolence; Christian love; leniency; readiness to forgive.— **char'i-ta-bl**(e², *a.* Generous; considerate; lenient; indulgent. **-ness,** *n.* **-ta-bly,** *adv.*

char'la-tan, 1 ŝhār'la-tən; 2 chār'la-tan, *n.* A pretender; quack; impostor; swindler. — **char'la-tan-ry,** *n.* **char'la-tan-ism‡.**

charm, 1 ĉhārm; 2 chärm. **I.** *vt.* & *vi.* To captivate; fascinate; delight; be fascinating. **II.** *n.* **1.** The power of alluring or delighting; winsomeness; fascination; beauty. **2.** A magical spell; amulet. — **charm'er,** *n.*— **charm'ing,** *pa.* Having power to charm. **-ly,** *adv.* **-ness,** *n.*

char'nel, 1 ĉhār'nel; 2 chär'nĕl. **I.** *a.* Sepulchral. **II.** *n.* A sepulcher. **char'nel- house"‡.**

Cha'ron, 1 kē'rən; 2 ēa'ron, *n. Myth.* Son of Erebus and Nox who ferried spirits across the river Styx.

chart, 1 ĉhārt; 2 chärt. **I**d. *vt.* To lay out on a chart. **II.** *n.* A map, as of the sea with its coast, etc.

char'ter, 1 ĉhār'tər; 2 chär'ter. **I.** *vt.* To hire by charter; establish by charter. **II.** *n.* An act of incorporation; document granting special rights or privileges; lease of a vessel, a railroad=train, etc.

char'y, 1 ĉhār'ı or ĉhē'rı; 2 chär'y or chā'ry, *a.* Cautious; wary.

Cha-ryb'dis, 1 ka-rīb'dıs; 2 ea-rўb'dis, *n. Myth.* A ravenous woman, whom Jupiter transformed into a treacherous whirlpool on the Sicilian coast. See SCYLLA.

chase¹, 1 ĉhēs; 2 chās, *vt.* & *vi.* [CHASED²; CHAS'ING.] **1.** To follow with intent to catch; pursue; hunt. **2.** To drive away.

chase²ᵗ, *vt.* To ornament by embossing.

chase¹, *n.* **1.** Earnest pursuit. **2.** That which is pursued. **3.** Hunting; hunters collectively; the hunt. **4.** [Eng.] A private game=preserve.

chase², *n.* A frame into which type is fastened, as for printing. [hollow; deep gorge.

chasm, 1 kazm; 2 căsm, *n.* A yawning

chas"sé', 1 ŝha'sē'; 2 chä'se'. **I.** *vi.* To perform a chassé. **II.** *n.* In dancing, a movement across, or to right and to left.

chas-seur', 1 ŝha-sör'; 2 chä-sūr', *n.* [F.] A light=armed horse= or foot=soldier.

chas'sis, 1 ĉhas'ıs or (F.) ŝha'sī'; 2 chăs'is or (F.) chä'sī', *n.* The frame of a motor=car.

chaste, 1 ĉhēst; 2 chāst, *a.* **1.** Sexually pure; modest; virtuous. **2.** Pure in style. **-ly,** *adv.* **-ness,** *n.*

chast'en, 1 ĉhēs'n; 2 chās'n, *vt.* **1.** To discipline by pain or trial; moderate; soften; purify. **2‖.** To chastise.

chas-tise', 1 ĉhas-taiz'; 2 chăs-tīẓ', *vt.* [CHAS-TISED'; CHAS-TIS'ING.] **1.** To correct with the rod. **2.** To punish, as an enemy. **chas-tize'sᵗ.— chas'tise-ment,** 1 ĉhas'tız-ment or -mənt; 2 chăs'tiẓ-ment, *n.* Punishment; correction.

chas'ti-ty, 1 ĉhas'tı-tı; 2 chăs'ti-ty, *n.* The state or quality of being chaste; purity.

chat, 1 ĉhat; 2 chăt. **I.** *vi.* [CHAT'TEDᵈ; CHAT'TING.] To converse in an easy manner. **II.** *n.* Easy and familiar speech.

châ"teau', 1 ŝha"tō'; 2 chä"tō', *n.* [CHA'- TEAUX', 1 -tōz'; 2 -tōz', *pl.*] A castle; country mansion.

French Château.

chat'e-laine, 1 ŝhat'ı-lēn; 2 chăt'e-lān, *n.* **1.** A chain or chains hanging from a woman's belt for holding small articles. **2.** The mistress of a château.

chat'tel, 1 ĉhat'el; 2 chăt'ĕl, *n. Law.* An article of personal property; a movable.

chat'ter, 1 ĉhat'ər; 2 chăt'er. **I.** *vt.* & *vi.* **1.** To click (the teeth) rapidly together. **2.** To talk fast and trivially; jabber, as a monkey. **II.** *n.* Idle prattle; jabbering; rattling of the teeth.— **chat'ter-box".** *n.* A voluble talker.— **chat'ty,** 1 ĉhat'ı; 2 chăt'y, *a.* Given to chat; loquacious.

chauf'feur, 1 ŝhō'fər or (F.) shō"fûr'; 2 chō'fer or (F.) çhō"fûr', *n.* A driver of an automobile.

cheap, 1 chip; 2 chĕp, a. Low in price; poor; mean. — **cheap′en,** 1 chip′n; 2 chĕp′n, vt. & vi. **1.** To make or become cheap. **2∥.** To beat down the price of; bargain. — **cheap′ly,** adv. — **cheap′ness,** n.

cheat, 1 chīt; 2 chēt. **I**d. vt. & vi. To deceive; defraud; delude; beguile. **II.** n. **1.** A fraud; imposture. **2.** A swindler. **3.** A weed; chess. — **cheat′er,** n.

check, 1 chek; 2 chĕk. **I**t. vt. & vi. **1.** To restrain sharply; stop; curb. **2.** To mark or provide with a check. **3.** To put in check, as in chess. **II.** n. **1.** A checking, or something that checks. **2.** A written order for money; a tag; a mark for verification. **3.** A checkered pattern. **4.** In chess, a menace to the king.

check′er, 1 chek′ər; 2 chĕk′er. **I.** vt. To mark with squares; diversify. **II.** n. **1.** A piece in the game of checkers. **2.** A square in a checkered surface. **3.** pl. A game played on a checker-board; draughts. — **check′er-board″,** n. A board divided into 64 squares.

check′mate, 1 chek′mēt″; 2 chĕk′māt″. **I**d. vt. Chess. To put (a king) in a check from which no escape is possible; defeat by a skilful maneuver. **II.** n. The act or position of checkmating.

cheek, 1 chīk; 2 chēk, n. Either side of the face below the eye; an analogous part of any object. [peep, as a young bird.

cheep, 1 chip; 2 chēp, v. & n. Chirp or

cheer, 1 chīr; 2 chēr. **I.** vt. & vi. To make or become cheerful; applaud with cheers; utter cheers. **II.** n. **1.** A shout of applause. **2.** Cheerfulness. **3.** Provisions for a feast. — **cheer′ful,** a. In good spirits; joyous; lively; willing. — **cheer′ful·ly,** adv. — **cheer′ful·ness,** n. — **cheer′less,** a. Destitute of cheer; gloomy. **-ly,** adv. **-ness,** n.

cheer′y, 1 chīr′ĭ; 2 chēr′y, a. Cheerful; cheering. — **cheer′i·ly,** adv. — **cheer′i·ness,** n.

cheese, 1 chīz; 2 chēs, n. The pressed curd of milk. — **chees′y,** a. [**chee′tat.**

chee′tah, 1 chī′tȧ; 2 chē′ta, n. See CHETAH.

chef, 1 shef; 2 chĕf, n. A male head cook.

chem′i·cal, 1 kem′ĭ-kȧl; 2 ĕm′i-cal. **I.** a. Of or pertaining to chemistry. **chem′le‡.** [Poet.]. **II.** n. A chemical substance. — **chem′i·cal·ly,** adv.

che·mise′, 1 she·mīz′; 2 çhe·mīş′, n. A woman's garment worn next to the skin.

chem′ist, 1 kem′ist; 2 ĕm′ist, n. One versed in chemistry; a dealer in chemicals; an apothecary.

chem′is·try, 1 kem′is-trĭ; 2 ĕm′is-try, n. That science which treats of matter considered as composed of atoms and of their relations and affinities.

che·nille′, 1 shĭ-nīl′; 2 çhe-nīl′, n. A soft tufted or fluffy cord of cotton, wool, silk or worsted.

cheque, 1 chek; 2 chĕk, n. Same as CHECK, 2.

cheq′uer, etc. Same as CHECKER, etc.

cher′ish†, 1 cher′ish; 2 chĕr′ish, vt. To care for kindly; entertain fondly; foster.

che·root′, 1 shĭ·rut′; 2 çhe·rōōt′, n. A tapering cigar cut off at both ends.

cher′ry, 1 cher′ĭ; 2 chĕr′y. **I.** a. **1.** Like a cherry; red. **2.** Made of cherry-wood. **II.** n. [CHER′RIES², pl.] A small red, reddish yellow, or black stone-fruit; also, the tree that bears it, or its wood.

cher′ub, 1 cher′ub; 2 chĕr′ub, n. **1.** [CHER′UBS², pl.] A beautiful winged child, as in painting or sculpture. **2.** [CHER′U-BĬM, pl.] An angelic being. — **che·ru′bic, che·ru′bi·cal,** a.

Chess-board.

cher′up, 1 cher′up; 2 chĕr′ŭp, v. & n. Chirrup; chirp.

chess, 1 ches; 2 chĕs, n. A game played by two persons on a checkered board, with 16 pieces on each side.

Pieces as arranged at opening of game: a, rook; b, knight; c, bishop; d, queen; e, king; f, bishop; g, knight; h, rook; i, i,— i, i, pawns.

chest, 1 chest; 2 chĕst, n. **1.** A large box, as for packing. **2.** The part of the body enclosed by the ribs; the thorax. — **chest of drawers,** a box-like frame containing drawers. **bu′reau‡** [U. S.]. — **c·tone,** n. A tone of the voice produced in the chest.

chest′nut, 1 ches′nut; 2 chĕs′nŭt. **I.** a. Made of or colored like chestnut. **II.** n. An edible nut; also, the tree that bears it, or its wood; a reddish-brown color. [**ches′nut.**

che′tah, 1 chī′tȧ; 2 chē′ta, n. The hunting-leopard of southwestern Asia and northern Africa.

chev′a·lier′, 1 shev′ȧ-līr′; 2 çhev′a-lēr′, n. A knight; cavalier.

chev′ron, 1 shev′rȧn; 2 chĕv′ron, n. Mil.

Chestnut

1. Leaf of the American chestnut. 2. Leaves of European chestnut; a, a bur; b, a nut.

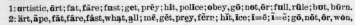

1: ȧrtistic, ärt; fȧt, fāre; fȧst; get, prēy; hit, police; obey, gō; net, ôr; full, rūle; but, bûrn.
2: ärt, āpe, fȧt, fâre, fȧst, whạt, ạll; mē, gĕt, prey, fẽrr; hit, īce; ĭ=ĕ; ī̄=ĕ; gō, nŏt, ôr, wŏn,

A V=shaped bar or bars on the sleeve of a non=commissioned officer's coat.

chew, 1 chū; 2 chu. **I.** *vt. & vi.* To cut or grind with the teeth; work the jaws and teeth; ruminate. **II.** *n.* The act of chewing, or something chewed.

chi-cane', 1 shi-kēn'; 2 chi-cān', *n.* Mean, petty trickery, with fair pretense. **chi-can'-er-y‡.**

chick, 1 chik; 2 chĭk, *n.* A young chicken.

chick'en, 1 chik'en; 2 chĭk'ĕn, *n.* The young of the common fowl; a fowl, or its flesh. — **chick'en=heart"ed,** *a.* Faint=hearted; cowardly.

chic'o-ry, 1 chik'o-ri; 2 chĭc'o-pǎn. A perennial herb used in adulterating coffee. **chic'co-ry‡.**

chide, 1 chaid; 2 chīd, *vt. & vi.* [CHID, 1 chid, 2 chĭd (CHODE, 16th cent.); CHID'DEN, 1 chid'n, 2 chĭd'n, or CHID, CHID'N²; CHID'ING.] **1.** To rebuke; scold. **2.** To beat with murmuring sound, as waves; bay, as hounds.

chief, 1 chīf; 2 chēf. **I.** *a.* Highest; greatest; of great importance. **II.** *n.* A ruler, leader, or head; principal part.— **chief'ly,** *adv.*

chief'tain, 1 chīf'tin; 2 chēf'tin, *n.* The head of a Highland clan; chief; leader. — **chief'tain-cy,** *n.* The rank or territory of a chieftain. **chief'tain-ship‡.**

chif"fo-nier', 1 shif"o-nīr'; 2 chĭf"o-nēr', *n.* **1.** An ornamental cabinet or a high, narrow bureau. **2.** A ragpicker.

chil'blain, 1 chil'blēn; 2 chĭl'blān, *n.* Inflammation of hands or feet from exposure to cold.

child, 1 chaild; 2 chīld, *n.* [CHIL'DREN, 1 chil'dren; 2 chĭl'drĕn, *pl.*] A human being in early youth; a son or daughter. — **child'hood,** *n.* The state or time of being a child. — **child'ish,** *a.* Like a child; puerile; petty. **-ly,** *adv.* **-ness,** *n.*— **child'less,** *a.* Having no children. **-ly,** *adv.* **-ness,** *n.*— **child'like",** *a.* Like a child; artless; confiding; docile. **-ness,** *n.*

chil'i-ad, 1 kil'i-ad; 2 eĭl'ĭ-ăd, *n.* A thousand; specifically, a thousand years; the millennium.

chill, 1 chil; 2 chĭl. **I.** *vt. & vi.* To reduce or come to a low temperature; make or become chilly; discourage. **II.** *a.* Somewhat cold; chilly. **III.** *n.* Coldness; a sensation of cold; a check to ardor, joy, etc.— **chill'i-ness,** *n.*— **chill'y,** *a.* Producing or feeling a chill.

chi-mæ'ra, *n.* Same as CHIMERA.

chimb, *n.* See CHIME².

chime¹, 1 chaim; 2 chīm. **I.** *vt. & vi.* [CHIMED; CHIM'ING.] To ring musically; harmonize; agree. **II.** *n.* A set of

bells tuned to a scale; harmony; agreement.

chime², *n.* The rim formed by the projecting staves around the edge of a barrel, cask, or tub, or one of the stave=ends so projecting.

chi-me'ra, 1 ki-[*or* kai-]mī'ra; 2 ei-[*or* eī-]mē'ra, *n.* A mythical fire=breathing monster; a groundless fancy.— **chi-mer'i-cal,** 1 ki-[*or* kai-]mer'i-kǝl; 2 ei-[*or* eī-]mĕr'ĭ-cal, *a.* Like a chimera; impracticable; visionary.— **chi-mer'i-cal-ly,** *adv.*

chim'ney, 1 chim'ni; 2 chĭm'ny, *n.* A flue for the smoke or gases from a fire.

chim-pan'zee, 1 chim-pan'zī; 2 chĭm-păn'zē, *n.* A West=African ape, about 5 feet in height.

chin, 1 chin; 2 chĭn, *n.* The central and front part of the lower jaw.

chi'na, 1 chai'na; 2 chī'na, *n.* **1.** [C-] A country of Asia. **2.** Porcelain. **chi'na-ware"‡.**— **Chi'na-man,** *n.* One of the Chinese.

chinch, 1 chinch; 2 chĭnch, *n.* **1.** A bug destructive to grain. **2.** The bedbug.

chin-chil'la, 1 chin-chil'a; 2 chĭn-chĭl'a, *n.* A squirrel=like rodent of the Andes, with soft, pearly=gray fur, or a woolen imitation of it. [back-bone]

chine, 1 chain; 2 chīn, *n.* The back-bone

Chi-nese', 1 chai-nīs' *or* -nīz'; 2 chī-nēs' *or* -nēg'. **I.** *a.* Of or pertaining to China. **II.** *n. sing. or pl.* A native of China; the race or the language of China.

chink, 1 chink; 2 chĭnk. **I¹.** *vt. & vi.* To open in chinks; make a chink; crack; ring. **II.** *n.* A narrow crack; crevice; metallic sound, as of money.

chints, 1 chints; 2 chĭnts, *n.* A cotton fabric printed in colors. **chintz‡.**

chip, 1 chip; 2 chĭp. **I.** *vt. & vi.* [CHIPPED†, CHIPT⁸; CHIP'PING.] To break off a chip from; break open; scale off. **II.** *n.* **1.** A small piece cut or broken off. **2.** A small disk or counter used in games.

chip'munk, 1 chip'-munk; 2 chĭp'-munk, *n.* A North=American squirrel=like rodent.

Chipmunk. ¹⁄₇

chi-rog'ra-phy, 1 kai-rog'ra-fi; 2 eī-rŏg'- **chi-rog'ra-fy²,** ra-fy, *n.* Style or character of handwriting.— **chi-rog'ra-pher,** *n.* — **chi"ro-graph'i-cal,** *a.*

chi-rop'o-dist, 1 kai-rep'o-dist; 2 eī-rŏp'o-

dist, *n.* One who specializes in the treatment of ailments of the hands and feet.

chi′ro-prac′tic, 1 kaɪ′ro-prak′tɪk; 2 eɪ′ro-prăc′tie, *n.* A method of treating disease by manipulating the spinal column.—**chi′ro-prac′tor,** *n.*

chirp, 1 chŭrp; 2 chĭrp. I^t. *vt. & vi.* To utter with a chirp; give a chirp. II. *n.* A short, shrill sound, as of a cricket.

chir′rup, 1 chir′up; 2 chĭr′ŭp. I^t. *vt. & vi.* To chirp. II. *n.* A chirp; a cheery sound.

chis′el, 1 chiz′el; 2 chĭş′ĕl. I. *vt.* [CHIS′-ELED or CHIS′ELD; CHIS′-EL-ING or CHIS′EL-LING.] To cut; carve. II. *n.* A cutting=tool with a beveled edge.

Chisel.

chiv′al-ry, 1 shiv′əl-rɪ; 2 chĭv′al-ry, *n.* **1.** The knightly system of feudal times; lofty courtesy; bravery; magnanimity. **2.** A body of knights.— **chiv′al-ric,** *a.* Pertaining to chivalry.— **chiv′al-rous,** *a.* Knightly; gallant; courteous; brave; chivalric. **-ly,** *adv.* **-ness,** *n.*

chlo′ral, 1 klō′rəl; 2 elō′ral, *n.* A sedative prepared from chlorin and alcohol. **chlo′ral hy′drate‡.**

chlo′rin, ⎱1 klō′rɪn, -rɪn *or* -rīn; 2 elō′rĭn;
chlo′rine, ⎰ -rɪn *or* -rīn, *n. Chem.* A greenish=yellow, poisonous gas, useful for bleaching and disinfecting.

chlo′ro-form, 1 klō′ro-fêrm; 2 elō′ro-fôrm. I. *vt.* To administer chloroform to. II. *n.* A colorless liquid compound, used to produce insensibility to pain.

chlo′ro-phyl, ⎱1 klō′ro-fil; 2 elō′ro-fȳl,
chlo′ro-phyll, ⎰ *n.* The green coloring=matter of plants.

chock, 1 chok; 2 chŏk. I^t. *vt. & vi.* To fit in tightly. II. *n.* A block or wedge.

chock′=full″, 1 chok′=ful″; 2 chŏk′=fụl″, *a.* Completely full; full to crowding.

choc′o-late, 1 chok′o-lɪt; 2 chŏk′o-lat, *n.* A preparation of cacao=nuts, or a beverage made from it.

choice, 1 cheis; 2 chŏiç. I. *a.* [CHOIC′ER; CHOIC′EST.] **1.** Select; excellent. **2.** Fastidious; dainty. II. *n.* **1.** The act or privilege of choosing; preference; variety to choose from. **2.** One who or that which is chosen.— **choice′ly,** *adv.*— **choice′ness,** *n.*

choir, 1 kwair; 2 chwīr, *n.* A body of trained singers, or that part of a church occupied by them; chancel.

choke, 1 chōk; 2 chōk. I. *vt. & vi.* [CHOKED^t; CHOK′ING.] To arrest the breathing or; suffocate; clog; stop; obstruct. II. *n.* The act of choking.

— **choke′=damp″,** *n.* A poisonous gas in mines.— **chok′y.**

choke′=full″, *a.* Same as CHOCK=FULL.

chol′er, ⎱1 kol′ər; 2 eŏl′ĕr, *n.* Hastiness of
col′er^p, ⎰ temper.— **chol′er-ic,** 1 kol′ər-ɪk; 2 eŏl′er-ic, *a.* Irascible.

chol′er-a, ⎱1 kol′ər-ə; 2 eŏl′er-a, *n.* An
col′er-a^p, ⎰ acute, infectious disease caused by bacilli. **A″si-at′ic chol′er-a‡.**— **cholera infantum,** an acute summer disease of infants.— **c. morbus,** an acute and prostrating disease, not epidemic.

choose, 1 chûz; 2 chŏŏş, *vt. & vi.* [CHOSE, 1 chōz, 2 chōş, CHOZE^p; CHO′SEN, 1 chō′zn, 2 chō′şn, CHO′ZEN^p; CHOOS′ING.] To take by preference; select.— **choos′er,** *n.*

chop, 1 chop; 2 chŏp. I. *vt. & vi.* [CHOPPED^t; CHOP′PING.] **1.** To cut by strokes; make cutting strokes; hew; mince. **2.** To chop. **3.** To veer, as wind. II. *n.* **1.** A cut of meat containing a rib. **2.** A cleft or fissure. **3.** An act of chopping, or a tool for chopping. **4.** A jaw.

chop′fal″len, *a.* Same as CHAPFALLEN.

chop′per, *n.* One who or that which chops.

chop′=sticks, ⎱1 chop′=
stiks″; 2 chŏp′=stiks″, *n. pl.* Slender rods, used in China, to convey food to the mouth.

chop″su′ey, 1 chop′=sū′ɪ; 2 chŏp′=su̯′y, *n.* A dish of chicken or pork and vegetables.

Chop=sticks.

cho′ral, 1 kō′rəl; 2 eō′ral, *a.* Pertaining to a chorus or a choir.— **cho′ral-ly,** *adv.*

chord, 1 kêrd; 2 eôrd. I^d. *vt. & vi.* To furnish with chords; bring into or be in harmony; accord. II. *n.* **1.** A harmonious combination of tones. **2.** A string of a musical instrument; hence, sensibility or emotion. **3.** A straight line connecting the extremities of an arc. **4.** A truss; cord; tendon.

chore, 1 chōr; 2 chōr, *n.* [U. S. & Prov. Eng.] A small job: commonly in the plural.

chor′is-ter, 1 kər′ɪs-tər; 2 eŏr′is-ter, *n.* **1.** A member of a choir. **2.** [U. S.] A musical director.

cho′rus, 1 kō′rus; 2 eō′rŭs, *n.* A song or refrain for several voices; a body of singers.

chose, 1 chōz; 2 chōş, *imp.* of CHOOSE, *v.*

Chough. 1/16

cho′sen, ⎱1 chō′zn; 2 chō′şn, *pp.* of CHOOSE, *v.*
cho′zen^p, ⎰

chough, ⎱1 chuf; 2 chŭf, *n.* A crow=like
chuf^p, ⎰ bird.

chow'=chow", 1 chau'=chau"; 2 chow'=chow", *n.* A mixture, as of pickles; medley.

chow'der, 1 chau'dər; 2 chow'der, *n.* A stew of clams or fish.

chrism, 1 krizm; 2 erĭsm, *n.* A consecrated ointment; an anointing.— **chris'mal**, *a.*

Christ, 1 kraist; 2 erĭst, *n.* The Anointed; the Messiah.

chris'ten, 1 kris'n; 2 erĭs'n, *vt.* To name in or as in baptism; baptize.— **Chris'ten-dom**, 1 kris'n-dəm; 2 eris'n-dom, *n.* Christian lands, or Christians collectively; the Christian world.

Chris'tian, 1 kris'chən; 2 erĭs'chan. **I.** *a.* Relating to Christ or his doctrine or his followers. **II.** *n.* A disciple of Christ, or one of a Christian nation. [See CHRIST.]— **Chris"ti-an'I-ty**, 1 kris'chi-an'ĭ-tɪ; 2 eris'-chi-ăn'ĭ-ty, *n.* The Christian religion.— **Christian Science**, a system of moral and religious instruction, founded by Mary Baker G. Eddy (1866), and combined with a method of treating diseases mentally.

Christ'mas, 1 kris'məs; 2 erĭs'mas, *n.* The 25th of December, celebrated as the anniversary of the birth of Christ.

chro-mat'ic, 1 kro-mat'ik; 2 ero-măt'ic, *a.* **1.** Pertaining to color. **2.** *Mus.* Proceeding by semitones. **chro-mat'I-cal‡.— chro-mat'ics**, *n.* **1.** The science of colors. **2.** *pl.* Chromatic tones or intervals.

chro'mo, 1 krō'mo; 2 erō'mo, *n.* A print in colors. **chro"mo-lith'o-graph‡.**

chron'ic, } 1 krɒn'ik; 2 erŏn'ic, *a.* Con-
cron'ics, } tinuing for a long period; inveterate, as disease.

chron'I-cle, } 1 krɒn'i-kl; 2 erŏn'i-el. **I.** *vt.*
chron'I-cl‡, } [-CL(E)D‡; -CLING.] To record. **II.** *n.* A register of events in the order of time.— **chron'I-cler,** *n.*

chro-nol'o-gy, 1 kro-nɒl'o-jɪ; 2 ero-nŏl'o-ġy, *n.* [-GIES²; *pl.*] The science that treats of time, or the order of events.— **chro-nol'o-ger,** *n.* One who studies or is versed in chronology. **chro-nol'o-gist‡.— chron"o-log'I-cal,** *a.* **chron"o-log'Ic‡.— chron"o-log'I-cal-ly,** *adv.*

chro-nom'e-ter, 1 kro-nɒm'ĭ-tər; 2 ero-nŏm'e-ter, *n.* A portable timekeeper of high precision.

chrys'a-lis, 1 kris'ə-lis; 2 erỹs'a-lĭs, *n.* [-LIS-ES, 1 -lis-ez, 2 -lĭs-ĕs, or -AL'I-DES, 1 al'-dĭz, 2 -ăl'i-dĕs, *pl.*] The pupa of an insect, enclosed in a shell from which the perfect insect emerges.— **chrys'a-lid,** *a. & n.*

chrys-an'the-mum, 1 kris-an'thi-mum; 2 erỹs-ăn'the-mŭm, *n.* A plant of the aster family, with large heads of showy flowers.

chrys'o-lite, 1 kris'o-lait; 2 erỹs'o-lĭt, *n.* An olive=green mineral: used as a gem.

chub'by, 1 chub'ı; 2 chŭb'y, *a.* Plump; rounded. [as under the chin.

chuckit, 1 chuk; 2 chŭk, *vt.* To pat or tap, **chuck²t**, *vi.* To cluck, like a fowl.

chuck¹, *n.* A playful pat or toss.

chuck², *n.* A clamp; chock.

chuck³, *n.* A cluck. [Chock=full.

chuck'=full", 1 chuk'=ful"; 2 chŭk'=ful", *a.*

chuck'le, } 1 chuk'l; 2 chŭk'l. **I.** *vi.*
chuck'l‡p, } [CHUCK'L(E)D‡; CHUCK'LING.] To laugh to oneself. **II.** *n.* A low, suppressed, or broken laugh.

chum, 1 chum; 2 chŭm, *n.* A roommate; intimate companion.

chunk, 1 chunk; 2 chŭŋk, *n.* A short, stout thing, person, or animal.— **chunk'y,** *a.* [U. S.] Short and thick=set.

church, 1 church; 2 chûrch, *n.* **1. A.** building for Christian worship. **2.** A distinct body of Christians; also, all Christian believers collectively. **3.** The clergy. — **church'ly,** *a.*— **church'man,** *n.* [-MEN, *pl.*] **1.** An adherent or member of a church. **2**‖. A clergyman; ecclesiastic. — **church'war"den,** *n.* An officer of an Anglican church having the care of church property and of the poor. — **church'yard",** *n.* A yard or graveyard adjoining a church; a cemetery.

churl, 1 chûrl; 2 chûrl, *n.* **1.** A low=bred, surly fellow; a sordid person. **2.** A peasant.— **churl'Ish,** *a.* Of or like a churl; rude; sordid. **-ly,** *adv.* **-ness,** *n.*

churn, 1 chûrn; 2 chûrn. **I.** *vt. & vi.* To agitate, as cream in a churn. **II.** *n.* A vessel in which milk or cream is agitated to separate the butter.— **churn'ing,** *n.*

chute, 1 shūt; 2 chụt, *n.* An inclined trough or channel; a rapid. **shute‡.**

chyle, 1 kail; 2 ɛïl, *n.* A nutritive fluid formed during digestion.

chyme, 1 kaim; 2 eïm, *n.* Food reduced to liquid form in the process of digestion.

cic'a-trice, } 1 sik'ə-tris; 2 çĭe'a-trĭç, *n.*
cic'a-triss, } *scar.* **cic'a-trix‡.— cic'a-trize** or **-trise**, 1 sik'ə-traiz; 2 çĭe'a-trĭz, *vt.* [-TRIZED; -TRIZ'ING.] To form a scar.— **cic"-a-tri-za'tion** or **-sa'tion,** *n.*

ci''ce-ro'ne, 1 chĭ"chē-rō'nē or sis'i-rō'nı; 2 chĭ"che-rō'ne or çïç"e-rō'ne, *n.* [-NI, -NES, 1 -nĭ, -nēs; 2 -nĭ, -ngs, *pl.*] A local guide.

ci'der, 1 sai'dər; 2 çï'der, *n.* The expressed juice of apples. [Former.

ci''=de-vant', 1 sı"də-vän'; 2 çï'=de-vän', *a.*

ci-gar', 1 sı-gär'; 2 çi-ġär', *n.* A small roll of tobacco=leaves for smoking.— **cig"a-ret',** 1 sig"ə-ret'; 2 çiġ"a-rĕt', *n.* A small roll of fine-ly cut tobacco in thin paper. **cig"a-rette'‡.**

cim'e-ter, *n.* Same as SIMITAR.

Cim-me'ri-an, 1 si-mĭ'rı-ən; 2 çĭ-mē'ri-an, *a.* Densely dark; shrouded in gloom.

---

cinch, 1 sinch; 2 çĭnch, *n.* [Western U. S.] A broad saddle=girth, knotted into place.

cin-cho'na, 1 sin-kō'na; 2 çĭn-cō'na, *n.* Peruvian bark: the source of quinin; the tree that yields this bark.

cinc'ture, 1 sink'chur *or* -tiur; 2 çĭ̄ŋe'chur *or* -tŭr, *n.* A belt or girdle.

cin'der, 1 sin'dər; 2 çĭn'der, *n.* A burnt= out coal; a scale from forged iron; slag.

cin"e-mat'o-graph, *n.* A kinetograph.

cin'na-mon, 1 sin'ə-mən; 2 çĭn'a-mon, *n.* The aromatic inner bark of a tropical laurel.

cinque'foil, 1 sink'feil; 2 çĭnk'foil, *n.* **1.** *Arch.* A five=cusped ornament or window. **2.** *Bot.* A plant with five=lobed leaves.

ci'pher, } 1 sai'fər; 2 çī'fer.
ci'fers, } *vt. & vi.* **1.** To calculate arithmetically. **2.** To write in secret char= acters. **II.** *n.* **1.** The character 0; zero. **2.** A method of secret writing; anything so written. **3.** A monogram. **cy'phers.**

Cinnamon.
1. Flowering branch. **2.** Cin= namon=bark, pre= pared for market.

Cir-ce'an, 1 sər-sī'an; 2 çĭr-çē'an, *a.* Be= witching and degrading, like the enchant= ress Circe, who transformed men into swine.

cir'cle, } 1 sur'kl; 2 çĭr'el, *vt. & vi.* [CIR'-
cir'clⁱ, } CL(E)Dᴾ; CIR'CLING.] To encircle; move in a circle.

cir'cle, *n.* **1.** *Geom.* A plane figure bounded by a curved line called the circumference, everywhere equally distant from a point within called the center; also, the circum= ference. **2.** Anything circular; a ring. **3.** An association; set; coterie; class.— **cir'clet,** *n.* A small ring.

cir'cuit, 1 sur'kit; 2 çĭr'eit, *n.* **1.** A passing or traveling round; distance around; dis= trict traveled over. **2.** The entire course of an electric current.— **cir'cuit-break"er,** *n.* An electro=mechanical protective device which automatically opens an electric cir= cuit when the current flowing therein be= comes excessive.— **cir-cu'i-tous,** 1 sər-kiū'-ı-tus; 2 çĭr-eū'i-tŭs, *a.* Of or like a circuit; indirect; roundabout.— **cir-cu'i-tous-ly,** *adv.*— **cir-cu'i-tous-ness,** *n.*

cir'cu-lar, 1 sur'kiu-lar; 2 çĭr'eū-lar. **I.** *a.* Forming, bounded by, or moving in a circle; round; circulating. **II.** *n.* A let= ter, or the like for general circulation.— **cir"cu-lar'i-ty,** *n.* [-TIESᶻ, *pl.*]

cir'cu-late, 1 sur'kiu-lēt; 2 çĭr'eū-lāt, *v.* [-LATᴱᴰᵈ; -LAT'ING.] **I.** *t.* To spread

abroad; disseminate. **II.** *i.* To move in a complete circuit, as the blood through the body; become diffused, as a report.— **cir'cu-la'tion,** *n.* Transmission; dissemina= tion; extent or amount of distribution; a cur= rent medium of exchange.— **cir'cu-la'tor,** *n.* — **cir'cu-la-to-ry,** 1 sur'kiu-lə-to-rı; 2 çĭr'-eū-la-to-ry, *a.* Of or pertaining to circula= tion; circulating.

cir'cum-, 1 sur'kum-; 2 çĭr'eŭm-, *prefix.* About; around; on all sides; surrounding; as, *circum*flex, *circum*locution.

cir"cum-am'bi-ent, 1 sur"kum-am'bi-ent; 2 çĭr'eŭm-ăm'bi-ĕnt, *a.* Extending around; encompassing.

cir"cum-cise, } 1 sur"kum-saiz; 2 çĭr'-
cir"cum-cizeᴾ, } eŭm-çĭs, *vt.* [-CISED; -CIS'-ING.] To perform circumcision upon.— **cir"cum-ci'sion,** 1 sur"kum-siʒ'an; 2 çĭr'-eŭm-çĭʒh'on, *n.* The initiatory rite of Juda= ism; spiritual purification; the Jewish people.

cir-cum'fer-ence, 1 sər-kum'fer-ens; 2 çĭr-eŭm'fer-ĕnç, *n.* The boundary=line of a circle; distance around; circuit.— **cir"cum-fer-en'tial,** *a.*

cir'cum-flex, 1 sur'kum-fleks; 2 çĭr'eŭm-flĕks, *n.* A mark (⌃ ‿ ꙴ) used over a letter to indicate the combination of a rising with a falling tone.

cir"cum-ja'cent, 1 sur'kum-jē'sent; 2 çĭr'eŭm-jā'çĕnt, *a.* Surrounding.

cir"cum-lo-cu'tion, 1 sur'kum-lo-kiū'-shan; 2 çĭr'eŭm-lo-eū'shon, *n.* Indirect or roundabout expression.

cir"cum-nav'i-gate, 1 sur"kum-nav'i-gēt; 2 çĭr'eŭm-năv'i-gāt, *vt.* [-GAT"EDᵈ; -GAT'-ING.] To sail around.— **cir"cum-nav'i-ga'tion,** *n.*— **cir"cum-nav'i-ga-tor,** *n.*

cir"cum-po'lar, 1 sur'kum-pō'lar; 2 çĭr'eŭm-pō'lar, *a.* Near, surrounding, or revolving about a pole.

cir"cum-scribe', 1 sur"kum-skraib'; 2 çĭr'eŭm-serĭb', *vt.* [-SCRIBED'; -SCRIB'-ING.] To draw around; limit; define.— **cir"cum-scrip'tion,** *n.*

cir'cum-spect, 1 sur'kum-spekt; 2 çĭr'-eŭm-spĕet, *a.* Watchful, as against dan= ger or error; cautious; well=considered. — **cir"eum-spec'tion, cir'cum-spect"ly,** *adv.*

cir'cum-stance, 1 sur'kum-stans; 2 çĭr'-eŭm-stăng, *n.* **1.** Something incidental; an incident. **2.** *pl.* Environment; situ= ation, income, etc.— **cir"cum-stan'tial,** *a.* **1.** Consisting of details; minute; particular. **2.** Pertaining to or dependent on circumstances. **-ly,** *adv.*— **cir"cum-stan'ti-ate,** *vt.* [-AT"EDᵈ; -AT'ING.] To set forth or prove by circum= stances.

cir"cum-vent'd, 1 sur"kum-vent'; 2 çĭr'-

1: artistic, ärt; fat, fāre; fast; get, prēy; hit, police; obey, gō; not, ör; full, rūle; but, būrn.
2: ärt, āpe, fät, fâre, fâst, whąt, ạll; mē, gĕt, prey, fērn; hĭt, īce; ī=ē; ĭ=ē̆: gō, nŏt, ör, wŏn.

eŭm-vĕnt′, *vt.* To get around; get the better of, as by craft.— **cir″cum-ven′tion,** *n.*

cir′cus, 1 sŭr′kus; 2 çir′çŭs, *n.* A show of feats of horsemanship, etc.; also, the enclosure where it is given.

cir′rus, 1 sir′us; 2 çir′ŭs, *n.* [CIR′RI, 1 sir′ai; 2 çir′ī, *pl.*] A tufted form of cloud.

cis′tern, 1 sis′tərn; 2 çis′tern, *n.* A reservoir for holding water.

cit′a-del, 1 sit′a-del; 2 çit′a-dĕl, *n.* A fortress commanding a city.

cite, 1 sait; 2 çit, *vt.* [CIT′ED^d; CIT′ING.] **1.** To quote or name; refer to. **2.** *Law.* To summon before a tribunal.— **ci-ta′tion,** 1 sai-tⁱ′shan; 2 çi-tä′shon, *n.* **1.** The act of citing, or a passage cited. **2.** *Law.* A judicial summons.

cit′i-zen, 1 sitⁱ-zn; 2 çit′i-zn, *n.* **1.** One owing allegiance to, and entitled to protection from, a government. **2.** A resident of a city or town. **3.** A private person; one who is not a public officer nor a soldier.— **cit′i-zen-ship,** *n.* The status of a citizen, with its rights and privileges.

cit′range, 1 sit′rinj, 2 çit′rang, *n.* A citrus fruit produced by crossing the common sweet orange with the trifoliate orange.

cit′ric, 1 sit′rik; 2 çit′rie, *a.* Derived from fruits of the genus *Citrus*, which includes the orange, lemon, lime, etc.

cit′ron, 1 sit′rən; 2 çit′ron, *n.* A fruit like a lemon, but larger and less acid; also, the tree (citron=tree) yielding it.

cit′y, 1 sitⁱ; 2 çit′y, *n.* [CIT′IES^z, *pl.*] A place inhabited by a large, permanent, organized community.

Citron.

civ′et, 1 siv′et; 2 çiv′ĕt, *n.* An animal secretion of musk=like odor; the animal secreting it, often called *civet=cat*.

civ′ic, 1 siv′ik; 2 çiv′ic, *a.* Of or pertaining to a city, a citizen, or citizenship.

civ′il, 1 siv′il; 2 çiv′il, *a.* **1.** Formally polite. **2.** Of or pertaining to a citizen. **3.** Occurring between citizens of the same country, as a war.— **civil service,** the departments of the public service that are neither military nor naval.— **ci-vil′ian,** 1 si-vil′yan; 2 çi-vil′yan, *n.* One occupied with civil life; one not a soldier.— **ci-vil′i-ty,** 1 si-vil′i-tɪ; 2 çi-vil′i-ty, *n.* [-TIES^z, *pl.*] Formal politeness; also, a civil act or speech.— **civ′il-ly,** *adv.*

civ′i-lize or **-lise,** 1 siv′i-laiz; 2 çiv′i-līz, *vt.* [-LIZED; -LIZ″ING.] To bring into a condition of organization, enlightenment, and progress; reclaim from savagery.— **civ″i-li-za′tion** or **-sa′tion,** 1 siv″i-li-zē′shan; 2 çiv′i-li-zä′shon, *n.* The act of civilizing, or the state of being civilized.

clack, 1 klak; 2 elăk. **I^t.** *vt. & vi.* To clap; rattle; chatter. **II.** *n.* A clapping sound, or something producing it; chatter.

clad, 1 klad; 2 elăd, *imp. & pp.* OF CLOTHE, *v.*

claim, 1 klēm; 2 elăm. **I.** *vt. & vi.* To lay claim to; make a claim; maintain. **II.** *n.* **1.** The demand of something as a right; assertion of a right; a right or title. **2.** The asserting, as of a fact. **3.** Anything claimed, as a settler's tract.— **claim′ant,** *n.* One who makes a claim.

clair-voy′ance, 1 klār-vei′əns; 2 elăr-vöy′anç, *n.* Assumed preternatural knowledge, as in a trance.— **clair-voy′ant,** *a. & n.*

clam, 1 klam; 2 elăm, *n.* An edible bivalve mollusk; one of various shell-fishes.

clam′ber, 1 klam′bər; 2 elăm′ber, *vi.* To climb with difficulty.

clam′my, 1 klamⁱ; 2 elăm′y, *a.* Damp and cold; soft and sticky.— **clam′mi-ly,** *adv.* — **clam′mi-ness,** *n.*

clam′or, 1 klam′ər; 2 elăm′or. **I.** *vi.* To cry out; vociferate. **II.** *n.* A loud repeated outcry; vociferation; noisy confusion of voices. **clam′our‡.**— **clam′or-ous,** *a.* Making or made with clamor. **clam′our-ous‡.** -**ly,** *adv.* -**ness,** *n.*

clamp, 1 klamp; 2 elămp. **I^t.** *vt.* To join as by a clamp. **II.** *n.* A device for holding or binding together two or more parts.

clan, 1 klan; 2 elăn, *n.* A tribe, as of Scottish Highlanders; set; clique.— **clan′nish,** *a.* Like a clan; clinging together. -**ly,** *adv.* -**ness,** *n.*— **clan′ship,** *n.* Union under a chief.

Clamps.
1. Screw = clamp.
2. Dentists'. 3. Jewelers'.

clan-des′tine, } 1 klan-des′tin; 2 elăn-dĕs′-
clan-des′tin′, } tin, *a.* Kept secret; concealed. -**ly,** *adv.* Secretly.

clang, 1 klaŋ; 2 elăng. **I.** *vt. & vi.* To send forth as a clang. **II.** *n.* A ringing sound, as of metal struck.

clan′gor, 1 klăŋ′gər; 2 elăn′gor, *n.* Repeated clanging; clamor. **clan′gour‡.**— **clan′gor-ous,** *a.*

clank, 1 klaŋk; 2 elăŋk. **I^t.** *vt. & vi.* To send forth as a clank. **II.** *n.* An abrupt, short, harsh metallic sound.

clap, 1 klap; 2 elăp. **I.** *vt. & vi.* [CLAPPED^t or CLAPT; CLAP′PING.] To strike together with a sharp sound, as the palms of the hands; applaud by clapping; place

quickly or suddenly. **II.** *n.* The act or sound of clapping.— **clap'per,** *n.* One who or that which claps.— **clap'trap",** *n.* A cheap artifice designed to evoke applause.

clap'board, 1 klap'bord; 2 elăp'bord, *n.* An overlapping board in the sheathing of a house; a weather-board.

claque, 1 klak; 2 elăk, *n.* Hired applauders in a theater. [table-wine.

clar'et, 1 klar'et; 2 elăr'ĕt, *n.* A red

clar'i-fy, 1 klar'ĭ-fɑi; 2 elăr'i-fĭ, *vt.* [-FIED, 1 -faid, 2 -fĭd; -FY"ING.] To make clear or transparent; free from impurities.— **clar"i-fi-ca'tion,** *n.*— **clar'i-fi"er,** *n.*

clar'i-net, 1 klar'ĭ-net; 2 elăr'i-nĕt, *n.* Mus. A wooden wind-instrument with keys. **clar'i-o-net‡.**

clar'i-on, 1 klar'ĭ-ən; 2 elăr'i-on, *n.* A small trumpet, or its sound.

clash, 1 klash; 2 elăsh. **I‡.** *vt. & vi.* To strike together with a clash; collide; conflict; interfere. **II.** *n.* A confused resounding metallic noise; collision; conflict.

clasp, 1 klɑsp; 2 elăsp. **I‡.** *vt.* To take hold of; fasten. **II.** *n.* 1. An overlapping fastening, as of a book. **2.** A firm grasp or embrace.

class, 1 klɑs; 2 elăs. **I‡.** *vt.* To group in classes; assign to a class. **II.** *n.* A body of persons or things somewhat alike; a number of students having the same teacher or studies.

clas'sic, 1 klas'ĭk; 2 elăs'ĭc. **I.** *a.* Of the first rank in literature or art; pertaining to Greek or Latin authors. **clas'si-cal‡.** **II.** *n.* A standard work of literature or art, as of Greek or Roman genius; the author of such a work.— **clas"si-cal'i-ty,** *n.* The quality of being classical. **clas'si-cal-ness‡.**— **clas'si-cal-ly,** *adv.*

clas'si-fy, 1 klas'ĭ-fɑi; 2 elăs'i-fĭ, *vt.* [-FIED, -FY"ING.] To arrange in a class or classes.— **clas"si-fi-ca'tion,** 1 klas'ĭ-fi-kĕ'shən; 2 elăs'ĭ-fi-eă'shon, *n.* A classifying, or a system of things classified.

clat'ter, 1 klat'ər; 2 elăt'er. **I.** *vt. & vi.* To rattle; make a clatter. **II.** *n.* A rattling noise; noisy talk; chatter.— **clat'ter-er,** *n.*

clause, 1 klɔz; 2 elɑs, *n.* **1.** A distinct part of a composition, as a paragraph, division, or article. **2.** *Gram.* A subordinate sentence. [Cloistral.

claus'tral, 1 klɔs'trəl; 2 elɑs'tral, *a.*

clave‖, 1 klĕv; 2 elăv, *imp.* of CLEAVE[1] or CLEAVE[2], *v.*

clav'i-cl(e[p], 1 klav'ĭ-kl; 2 elăv'i-cl, *n.* The collar-bone.— **cla-vic'u-lar,** *a.*

claw, 1 klɔ; 2 elɑ. **I.** *vt. & vi.* To tear or scratch as with claws; use the claws or nails. **II.** *n.* A sharp, curved, horny nail; a claw-like part; a stroke or movement as with claws.

clay, 1 klĕ; 2 elă, *n.* A common plastic earth; the human body.— **clay'ey,** 1 klĕ'i; 2 elă'y, *a.*

clay'more, 1 klĕ'mōr; 2 elă'mōr, *n.* The two-handed broadsword of the Scottish Highlanders.

-cle, *suffix.* A diminutive; as, icicle, particle.

clean, 1 klĭn; 2 elēn. **I.** *vt.* To make clean; cleanse. **II.** *a.* Free from dirt, impurity, or defilement; unblemished; pure; complete. **III.** *adv.* In a clean manner; unqualifiedly; wholly.— **clean'er,** *n.*— **clean'ness,** *n.*

clean'ly, } 1 klen'li; 2 elĕn'ly, *a.* Neat; **clen'ly**[s], } tidy; pure.— **clean'li-ly,** *adv.*— **clean'li-ness,** *n.* [clean manner.

clean'ly, 1 klĭn'li; 2 elēn'ly, *adv.* In a

cleanse, } 1 klenz; 2 elĕns, *vt.* [CLEANSED;] **clense**[s], } CLEANS'ING.] To free from dirt or defilement; clean; purge.

clear, 1 klĭr; 2 elēr. **I.** *vt. & vi.* To make or become clear; brighten; clarify; clean; free; acquit. **2.** To gain over and above expenses. **II.** *a.* **1.** Free from anything that dims or darkens; unclouded; unobstructed; distinct; intelligible. **2.** Free from responsibility, defect, guilt, or blemish. **3.** Without deduction; net. **4.** Undisturbed; serene. **5.** Plain; evident. **III.** *n.* Unbroken or unobstructed distance or space. **IV.** *adv.* Wholly; completely; quite; clearly; plainly.— **clear'ly,** *adv.*— **clear'ness,** *n.*

clear'ance, 1 klĭr'əns; 2 elēr'anç, *n.* **1.** A clearing. **2.** A certificate permitting a vessel to sail.

clear'ing, 1 klĭr'ɪŋ; 2 elēr'ing, *n.* A making or becoming clear; that which is clear; a tract of cleared land.— **clear'ing-house",** *n.* An office where bankers exchange drafts and checks and adjust balances.

cleat, 1 klĭt; 2 elēt. **I**d. *vt.* To furnish with a cleat or cleats. **II.** *n.* A cross-strip, as of wood or iron.

cleave[1], } 1 klĭv; 2 elēv, *vt. & vi.* [CLEFT, **cleav**[p], } CLOVE, or CLAVE, 1 kleft, klōv, klĕv; 2 elĕft, elōv, elăv; CLEFT, CLO'VEN, 1 klō'vn, 2 elō'vn, or CLEAV(E)D[p]; CLEAV'ING.] To cut through; sunder; split. — **cleav'a-bl**(e[p], 1 klĭv'ə-bl; 2 elēv'a-bl, *a.* Capable of being cleft.— **cleav'age,** 1 klĭv'ij; 2 elĕv'ag̶, *n.* A splitting or tendency to split; a split; cleft; division.— **cleav'er,** *n.* One who or that which cleaves; a butchers' chopper.

cleave[2], } *vi.* [CLEAV(E)D[s]; CLEAV(E)D[s] or **cleav**[s], } CLAVE; CLEAV'ING.] To stick fast; cling; adhere.

1: **a**rtistic, **ā**rt; fat, fāre; fast; get, prẽy; hĭt, police; obey, gō; nŏt,ŏr; full, rūle; bŭt, bŭrn.

2: ärt, āpe, făt,fâre,fȧst,whạt,ạll; mē, gĕt, prẹy, fẽrn; hĭt, īce; ĭ=ē; ĭ=ė; gō,nŏt,ŏr, wŏn.

clef, 1 klef; 2 elĕf, *n. Mus.* A character placed upon the staff to determine the pitch.

Clefs.
1. Treble or G clef. 2. Bass or F clef.

cleft, 1 kleft; 2 elĕft, *imp. & pp.* of CLEAVE[1], *v.*

cleft, *pa.* Divided partially or completely.

cleft, *n.* An opening made by cleaving; fissure; crevice; rift.

clem'a·tis, 1 klĕm'a-tĭs; 2 elĕm'a-tĭs, *n.* A perennial flowering plant of the crow-foot family.

clem'en·cy, 1 klem'en-sı; 2 elĕm'ĕn-çy, *n.* Mildness toward offenders; leniency; mercy.— **clem'ent,** *a.* Lenient; mild; pleasant. **-ly,** *adv.*

clench, 1 klench; 2 elĕnch. **I**[t]. *vt.* To grasp firmly; close tightly, as the fist or the teeth; clinch. **II.** *n.* A clenching; firm grip; clinch.— **clench'er,** *n.* One who or that which clenches; a clenching-tool; an unanswerable argument. **clinch'er†.** [etc.

clep'to·ma'ni·a, etc. See KLEPTOMANIA.

cler'gy, 1 klŭr'jı; 2 elĕr'ġy, *n.* [CLER'-GIES[2], *pl.*] The body of men ordained to the Christian ministry.— **cler'gy·man,** *n.* [-MEN, *pl.*] A Christian minister.

cler'ic, 1 kler'ık; 2 elĕr'ıe. **I.** *a.* Clerical. **II.** *n. Ang. Ch.* A clerk in holy orders.

cler'i·cal, 1 kler'i-kəl; 2 elĕr'i-eal, *a.* **1.** Of or belonging to the clergy. **2.** Of or pertaining to a clerk or clerks or of penmanship.— **clerical error,** an error of inadvertence in a writing.

clerk, 1 klŭrk (*Eng.* klärk); 2 elĕrk (*Eng.* elärk), *n.* **1.** One who keeps records or accounts; a secretary; [U. S.] a salesman. **2.** *Ang. Ch.* One who leads in the responses.— **clerk'ship,** *n.*

clev'er, 1 klev'ər; 2 elĕv'er, *a.* Ready and adroit; capable; talented. **-ly,** *adv.* **-ness,** *n.*

clew, 1 klū; 2 elų. **I.** *vt.* **1.** To move or fasten by or as by a clew. **2.** To coil or roll up into a bunch. **II.** *n.* **1.** A thread that guides through a maze; something that leads to the solution of a mystery. **2.** A loop at the corner of a sail. **3.** A ball of yarn. **clue†.**

click, 1 klik; 2 elĭk. **I**[t]. *vt. & vi.* To make or cause to make a click. **II.** *n.* A short dull sound, as from a light blow.

cli'ent, 1 klai'ent; 2 elĭ'ĕnt, *n.* One for whom an attorney acts.

cli'en·tele', 1 klai'en-tĭl' *or* -tel'; 2 elĭ'ĕn-tēl' *or* -tēl', *n.* A body of clients or adherents.

cliff, 1 klif; 2 elĭf, *n.* A high, steep rock; precipice.
clif[p], } a precipice.

cli'mate, 1 klai'mıt; 2 elĭ'mat, *n.* **1.** The temperature and atmospheric conditions of a locality. **2.** A region; clime.— **cli·mat'ic,** *a.*

cli'max, 1 klai'maks; 2 elĭ'măks, *n. Rhet.* A progressive increase in force to a culmination; the culmination; acme.

climb, 1 klaim; 2 elĭm. **I.** *vt. & vi.* [CLIMBED *or* CLOMB (poetical), 1 klŏm, 2 elŏm: CLIMB'ING.] To ascend as by means of the hands and feet; mount or rise by gradual ascent. **II.** *n.* The act or process of climbing.— **climb'er,** *n.*

clime, 1 klaim; 2 elĭm, *n.* [Poet.] A region; climate.

clinch, 1 klinch; 2 elĭnch. **I**[t]. *vt. & vi.* **1.** To fasten, as a driven nail, by bending down the point; confirm, as a bargain or an argument. **2.** To grapple; clench. **II.** *n.* A clinching, or that which clinches or is clinched; a decisive argument.— **clinch'er,** *n.*

cling, 1 klıŋ; 2 elĭŋg, *vi.* [CLUNG, 1 klųŋ, 2 elųŋg; CLING'ING.] To hold firmly, as by grasping; adhere; stick.

clin'ic, 1 klin'ık; 2 elĭn'ie, *n.* Medical instruction at the bedside of patients. **cli·nique'†,** 1 kli-nīk'; 2 eli-nīk'.— **clin'i·cal,** *a.* Of or pertaining to a sick-bed or a clinic.

clink, 1 kliŋk; 2 elĭŋk. **I**[t]. *vt. & vi.* To make a clink; strike smartly. **II.** *n.* A slight ringing sound, as of glass.— **clink'er,** *n.* A thing that clinks, as a mass left by coal in burning.

Cli'o, 1 klai'o; 2 elĭ'o, *n. Gr. Myth.* Muse of epic poetry and history. **Klei-ō'†** [Gr.]

clip, 1 klip; 2 elĭp, *vt.* [CLIPPED[t] *or* CLIPT; CLIP'PING.] To trim with shears; snip a part from, as a coin.

clip[1], *n.* The act of clipping, or that which is clipped off.

clip[2], *n.* A clasp for holding letters, etc.

clip'per, 1 klip'ər; 2 elĭp'er, *n.* **1.** A swift sailing vessel. **2.** An implement for clipping hair.

clip'ping, 1 klip'ıŋ; 2 elĭp'ing, *n.* A cutting; a slip cut, as from a newspaper.

clique, 1 klĭk; 2 elĭk, *n.* An exclusive set.

cloak, 1 klōk; 2 elōk. **I**[t]. *vt. & vi.* To cover with or put on a cloak; disguise; conceal. **II.** *n.* A loose outer garment; a cover; disguise.

clock, 1 klŏk; 2 elŏk, *n.* A machine for measuring and indicating time.— **clock'-work",** 1 klek'wŭrk"; 2 elŏk'wûrk", *n.* Machinery, as of a clock.

clod, 1 kled; 2 elŏd. **I.** *vt. & vi.* [CLOD'-DED[d]; CLOD'DING.] **1.** To throw clods (at). **2.** To turn into clods. **II.** *n.* A lump of clay; the soil; anything earthy

---

1: ə = *final;* ı = *habit;* ɑisle; ɑu = *out;* oil; ıū = *feud;* ᴄhin; go; ŋ = *sing;* ᴛhin, this.
2: wọlf, dọ; bōōk, bōōt; fụll, rụle, cūre, bŭt, bûrn; ọil, bŏy; ġo, ġem; iŋk; thin, this.

and gross.— **clod'hop"per,** *n.* A plowman; rustic; lout.

clog, 1 klŏg; 2 elŏg, *v.* [CLOGGED, CLOGD⁸; CLOG'GING.] **I.** *t.* To put a clog on; hinder; obstruct. **II.** *i.* **1.** To become choked up; be hindered. **2.** To adhere in a mass.

clog, *n.* **1.** Anything that impedes motion, as a block attached to an animal's foot; an encumbrance; hindrance. **2.** A wooden-soled shoe.

clois'ter, 1 klois'tẽr; 2 elŏis'ter. **I.** *vt.* **1.** To seclude, as in a cloister. **2.** To provide with cloisters. **II.** *n.* A covered walk, as for monks; a monastery; convent.— **clois'tral,** *a.* Of or pertaining to a cloister; secluded; solitary.

close, 1 klōz; 2 elŏs, *v.* [CLOSED; CLOS'-
cloze², } ING.] **I.** *t.* To shut; stop; end; terminate; conclude. **II.** *i.* **1.** To come together; shut; end; terminate. **2.** To join; coalesce; agree; also, to join battle; grapple.

close, 1 klōs; 2 elŏs, *a.* **1.** Shut; shut in; confined; secluded; secret; secretive. **2.** Near, or near together; dense; compact. **3.** Trusty; intimate; as, *close* friends. **4.** Watchful; strict; as, *close* attention. **5.** Nearly even or equal; as, a *close* contest. **6.** Avaricious; stingy. **-ly,** *adv.* **-ness,** *n.*

close¹, 1 klōz; 2 elŏs, *n.* **1.** The end; conclusion. **2.** A grapple. **3.** A junction; meeting.

close², 1 klōs; 2 elŏs, *n.* **1.** An enclosed place. **2.** A narrow lane or passage.

close, *adv.* Closely.

clos'et, } 1 klŏz'et; 2 elŏs'ĕt. **I**ᵈ. *vt.* To
cloz'et², } shut up; conceal; admit to a private interview. **II.** *n.* A small chamber or the like.

clo'sure, } 1 klō'zur; 2 elŏ'zhur, *n.* A
clo'zureᴾ, } closing or enclosure; that which closes or encloses; a close, as of debate; conclusion. **clō"ture'‡.**

clot, 1 klŏt; 2 elŏt. **I.** *vt. & vi.* [CLOT'TED**d**; CLOT'TING.] To form into or fill with clots; coagulate. **II.** *n.* A coagulated mass.

cloth, 1 klŏth; 2 elŏth, *n.* A woven fabric.

clothe, 1 klōth; 2 elŏth, *vt.* [CLOTHED or CLAD, 1 klad, 2 elăd; CLOTH'ING.] To cover or provide with clothes; dress.

clothes, 1 klōthz; 2 elŏths, *n. pl.* Garments; raiment; clothing; covering.

cloth'ler, 1 klōth'yẽr; 2 elŏth'yer, *n.* One who makes or sells cloths or clothing.

cloth'ing, 1 klōth'ĭŋ; 2 elŏth'ing, *n.* Dress; garments; raiment; covering.

clo"ture'¹, 1 klō'tūr; 2 elŏ'tūr, *n.* A closing of debates.

cloud, 1 klaud; 2 eloud. **I**ᵈ. *vt. & vi.* To cover or be covered with clouds; make or become dark; darken; obscure. **II.** *n.* A mass of visible vapor floating in the air; something that obscures, darkens, or threatens; a defect; blemish.— **cloud'less,** *a.* Unclouded; clear.— **cloud'y,** *a.* Of, like, or covered with a cloud or clouds; darkened; gloomy; obscure; vague; confused.— **cloud'i-ly,** *adv.*— **cloud'i-ness,** *n.*

clout, 1 klaut; 2 elout. **I.** *vt.* To beat; cuff. **II.** *n.* **1.** A piece, as of cloth; patch; rag. **2.** The center of a target. **3.** An iron plate; a short, stout nail.

clove, 1 klōv; 2 elŏv, *imp.* of CLEAVE¹, *v.*

clove, *n.* A dried flower-bud of a tropical tree (the *clove= tree*): used as a spice.

clo'ven, 1 klō'vn; 2 elŏ'vn, *pa.* Parted: pp. of CLEAVE¹, *v.*— **clo'ven=foot"ed,** *a.* **1.** Having the foot cleft or divided. **2.** Satanic.— **c.=hoofed,** *a.*

Common Clove.

clo'ver, 1 klō'vẽr; 2 elŏ'ver, *n.* A three-leaved plant of the bean family.

clown, 1 klaun; 2 elown, *n.* **1.** A professional buffoon; jester. **2.** A rude fellow; boor. **3.** A countryman.— **clown'ish,** *a.* Rude; ill-bred. **-ly,** *adv.* **-ness,** *n.*

cloy, 1 klŏi; 2 elŏy, *vt.* To satiate, as with sweetness; surfeit.

club¹, 1 klub; 2 elŭb. **I.** *vt.* [CLUBBED, CLUBD⁸; CLUB'BING.] To beat with a club; use like a club. **II.** *n.* **1.** A stout stick; cudgel. **2.** A black three-lobed spot on a playing-card; a card so marked. — **clubbed,** *a.* Shaped or used like a club. — **club'foot",** *n.* Congenital distortion of the foot.— **club'=foot"ed,** *a.*

club². **I.** *vt. & vi.* To contribute to a common purpose; combine; join; form a club. **II.** *n.* An organization of persons, as for social intercourse; a club-house or club-room.

cluck, 1 kluk; 2 elŭk. **I**ᵗ. *vt. & vi.* To call with or utter a cluck. **II.** *n.* A sound made, or like that made, by a brooding hen in calling her chicks.

clue, 1 klū; 2 elu. **I.** *vt.* Same as CLEW, *vt.* **II.** *n.* Figuratively, anything that guides through a perplexity; a suggestion; hint; as, a *clue* to a theft. For mechanical uses see CLEW, *n.* [tuft; lump.— **clump'y,** *a.*

clump, 1 klump; 2 elŭmp, *n.* A thick cluster;

clum'sy, 1 klum'zi; 2 elŭm'sy, *a.* [CLUM'-SI-ER; CLUM'SI-EST.] Unhandy; ungrace-

ful; awkward; unwieldy; ungainly.— **clum'-
si-ly,** *adv.*— **clum'si-ness,** *n.*

clung, 1 kluŋ; 2 elŭng, *imp. & pp.* of CLING, *v.*

clus'ter, 1 klŭs'ter; 2 elŭs'ter. **I.** *vt. & vi.*
To grow or gather in a cluster or clusters.
II. *n.* A group or bunch, as of grapes;
an assembly; aggregation.

clutch, 1 kluch; 2 elŭch, *v.* **I**ᵗ. *t.* To
cluchᴾ, ∫ seize eagerly; grasp firmly. **II.**
i. To snatch; catch; with *at.*

clutch¹, *n.* **1.** A powerful grasp; tight
grip; an attempt at seizure. **2.** A talon,
claw, paw, or hand. **3.** A device for
transmitting power, as by friction.

clutch², *n.* A sitting of eggs; a brood.

clut'ter¹, 1 klut'ər; 2 elŭt'er. **I.** *vt.* To
disorder; litter. **II.** *n.* A disordered
state; confused heap; litter.

clut'ter², **I.** *vi.* To clatter; make a
noise. **II.** *n.* A clattering noise.

co-¹, *prefix.* With; together. See COM-. *Co-*
is often joined to purely English words; as,
*co*mate, *co*partner, *co*respondent (distinguished from *correspondent*).

co-², *prefix.* Of the complement; as, *co*sine.

coach, 1 kōch; 2 eōch. **I**ᵗ. *vt. & vi.* **1.** To
tutor or train; study with a tutor or
trainer. **2.** To carry or be carried in a
coach. **II.** *n.* **1.** A large close carriage.
2. A tutor; trainer.— **coach'man,** *n.* [-MEN,
pl.] One who drives a coach. **coach'eeʇ.**

co''ad-ju'tor, 1 kō''ə-jū'tər *or* -ter; 2 eō''-
a-jū'tor, *n.* A coworker or colleague.
— **co''ad-ju'tress, co''ad-ju'trix,** *n. fem.*

co-æ'**val,** *a.* Same as COEVAL.

co-ag'u-late, 1 ko-ag'yu-lēt; 2 eo-ăg'yu-
lāt, *vt. & vi.* [-LATᵉᵈᵈ; -LAT''ING.] To
change into a curd=like mass; curdle.— **co-
ag''u-la'tion,** *n.*— **co-ag'u-u-len,** *a.* A coag-
ulating powder used in surgery.

coal, 1 kōl; 2 eōl. **I.** *vt. & vi.* To supply
with coal. **II.** *n.* A combustible substance derived from ancient vegetation,
found in beds or veins in the earth; a
piece of partly burned wood.— **coal'y,** *a.*

co''a-lesce', 1 kō''ə-les'; 2 eō'a-lĕs', *vi.*
[-LESCEDᵗ; -LESC'ING.] To grow or come
together into one; fuse; blend.— **co''a-les'-
cence,** *n.*— **co''a-les'cent,** *a.*

co''a-li'tion, 1 kō''ə-lish'ən; 2 eō''a-lĭsh'on,
n. An alliance of persons, parties, or states.

coam'ing, *n.* The raised margin or curb
of a hatchway, well, etc. **comb'ingʇ.**

coarse, 1 kōrs; 2 eōrs, *a.* [COARS'ER;
COARS'EST.] Composed of large or rough
parts or particles; inferior; rude; low;
vulgar; indelicate. **-ly,** *adv.* **-ness,** *n.*

coast, 1 kōst; 2 eōst. **I.** *vt. & vi.* **1.** To
sail or travel along (a shore or border).
2. [U. S.] To ride down a slope by force

of gravity, as on a sled. **II.** *n.* **1.** The
land next to the sea; the seashore; formerly, a boundary; region. **2.** [U. S.] A
coasting, as on a sled.— **coast'er,** *n.*

coat, 1 kōt; 2 eōt. **I**ᵈ. *vt.* To cover as
with a coat. **II.** *n.* An upper and
outer garment with sleeves; any outer
covering, as of fur, paint, etc.— **coat'ing,** *n.*
1. A covering layer; coat. **2.** Cloth for coats.

coax,ᵗ 1 kōks; 2 eōks, *vt. & vi.* To persuade;
wheedle; win; soothe.— **coax'er,** *n.*

cob, 1 kɒb; 2 eŏb, *n.* **1.** A roundish mass.
2. [U. S.] The spike of an ear of maize.
3. A strong, thick=set, short=legged horse.

co'balt, 1 kō'bȯlt; 2 eō'bạlt, *n.* A tough
steel=gray metallic element that forms
blue pigments.

cob'ble,) 1 kɒb'l; 2 eŏb'l, *v.* [COB'BLED, COB'-
cob'lᴾ, ∫ LDᴾ; COB'BLING.] **I.** *t.* To repair,
as boots; make clumsily. **II.** *i.* To work
as a cobbler.— **cob'bler,** *n.* One who patches
boots and shoes.

cob'ble-stone'', 1 kɒb'l-stōn''; 2 eŏb'l-stōn'',
n. A rounded water=worn stone, as for
paving.

co'bra, 1 kō'brə; 2 eō'bra, *n.* A very
venomous snake of India that can dilate
its neck into a broad hood. **co'bra
de=ca-pel'loʇ.**

cob'web'', 1 kɒb'web''; 2 eŏb'wĕb''. **I.** *vt.*
[COB'WEBBED; COB'WEB'BING.] To cover
as with cobwebs. **II.** *n.* The network
or fine thread spun by a spider.

co'ca, 1 kō'kə; 2 eō'ea, *n.* The dried leaves of
a South=American shrub, used as a tonic.

co'ca-in,) 1 kō'kə-in, -in *or* -ĭn; 2 eō'ea-ken';
co'ca-ine, ∫ 2 eō'ea-ĭn, -ĭn *or* -ĭn, *or* eo-kĕn',
n. A white, bitter substance obtained
from coca; used as an anesthetic.

coch'i-neal, 1 kɒch'i-nīl; 2 eŏch'i-nēl, *n.*
A scarlet dyestuff consisting of certain
tropical insects killed and dried by heat.

cock, 1 kɒk; 2 eŏk. **I**ᵗ. *vt.* **1.** To raise
the cock of (a gun or pistol),
in readiness for firing. **2.** To
turn up, as the head or hat;
prick up, as the ears. **II.**
n. **1.** A male of the domestic
fowl; any male bird. **2.** A
faucet. **3.** The hammer of
a firearm, or its position when Self=closing
raised. **4.** A tip or upward turn, as of the Cock.
head or of a hat=brim. **5.** A small conical
pile, as of hay.

cock-ade', 1 kɒk-ēd'; 2 eŏk-ād', *n.* A ro-
sette, or the like, worn on the hat.

cock''a-too', 1 kɒk''ə-tū'; 2 eŏk''a-tōō', *n.*
A crested parrot.

cock'a-trice, 1 kɒk'ə-tris *or* -trȧis; 2 eŏk'a-

-trĭç *or* -trĭç, *n.* A fabulous serpent, said to kill by its breath or glance.

cock′boat″, 1 kĕk′bōt″; 2 ĕŏk′bŏt″, *n.* A small rowboat.

cock′crow″, 1 kĕk′krō″; 2 ĕŏk′erō″, *n.* The early morning. **cock′crow″ing‡.**

cock′er-el, 1 kĕk′ẽr-el; 2 ĕŏk′er-ĕl, *n.* A young cock.

cock′l(e², 1 kĕk′l; 2 ĕŏk′l, *n.* **1.** A weed that grows among grain. **2.** An edible European bivalve.

cock′loft″, 1 kĕk′lôft″; 2 ĕŏk′lôft″, *n.* A loft under the roof. [doner.

cock′ney, 1 kĕk′ny; 2 ĕŏk′ny, *n.* A Lon-

cock′pit″, 1 kĕk′pit″; 2 ĕŏk′pit″, *n.* **1.** A pit for cock-fighting. **2.** An apartment for the wounded in a war-ship. **3.** In small yachts, the space inside the coaming, lower than the deck. **4.** The operator's seating-place in an air-plane.

cock′roach″, 1 kĕk′rōch″; 2 ĕŏk′rōch″, *n.* An insect with a flat oval body infesting houses and ships.

cocks′comb″, 1 kĕks′kōm″; 2 ĕŏks′eōm″, *n.* **1.** A plant with red flowers. **2.** A coxcomb. **3.** A scarlet ridge on a jester's cap; also, the cap.

cock′swain, *n.* Same as COXSWAIN.

cock′tail″, 1 kĕk′tēl″; 2 ĕŏk′tāl″, *n.* [U. S.] A drink of spirits mixed with sugar and flavoring.

co′co, 1 kō′ko; 2 eō′eo, *n.* The palm-
co′coa¹, ∫ tree that produces coconuts.
co′co▪palm″‡.

co′coa², *n.* The powdered seed-kernels of the cacao; also, a beverage made from it.

co′co-nut″, 1 kō′ko-nut″; 2 eō′eo-nŭt″,
co′coa-nut″, ∫ *n.* The large, white-meated fruit of a tree called the *coco▪palm.*

co-coon′, 1 ko-kūn′; 2 eo-eōōn′, *n.* The envelop in which larvæ, as of silkworms, are enclosed in the chrysalis state.— **co-coon′-er-y,** *n.* A place for rearing silkworms.

cod, 1 ked; 2 eŏd, *n.* A food-fish of temperate northern seas. **cod′fish″‡.**

co′da, 1 kō′dä; 2 eō′dä, *n. Mus.* An independent concluding passage; finale.

cod′dle, 1 ked′l; 2 eŏd′l, *vt.* [COD′DLED,
cod′l, ∫ COD′DLD²; COD′DLING.] To treat as a baby or an invalid; pamper.

code, 1 kōd; 2 eōd, *n.* A system of laws, signals, or rules.

codg′er, 1 kej′ẽr; 2 eŏdg′er, *n.* A testy or eccentric old man; fellow.

cod′i-cil, 1 ked′i-sil; 2 eŏd′i-çĭl, *n.* A supplement to a will.

cod′i-fy, 1 ked′i-fai *or* kō′di-fai; 2 eŏd′i-fī *or* eō′di-fī, *vt.* [-FIED; -FY′ING.] To systematize, as laws.— **cod″i-fi-ca′tion,** *n.*

co-ed″u-ca′tion, 1 ko-ej′u-[*or* -ed″yu-]kē′-shən; 2 eo-ĕj′u-[*or* -ĕd″yu-]eā″shon, *n.* The education of both sexes, or of whites and negroes, together.

co″ef-fi′cient, 1 kō″e-fĭsh′ent; 2 eō″ĕ-fĭsh′-ĕnt. **I.** *a.* Jointly efficient. **II.** *n.* **1.** A cooperating agent. **2.** A number or letter put before an algebraic expression showing how many times it is to be taken.

cœ′no-bite, *n.* Same as CENOBITE.

co-e′qual, 1 kō-ī′kwəl; 2 eo-ē′kwal. **I.** *a.* Equal and conjoined. **II.** *n.* The equal of another or others.

co-erce′, 1 ko-ūrs′; 2 eo-ẽrç′, *vt.* [co-ERCED′ᵗ, CO-ERST⁸; CO-ERC′ING.] To constrain by force or fear; compel; restrain or repress.— **co-er′cion,** *n.* Compulsion.— **co-er′civ**(e⁸, *a.* Coercing or tending to coerce.

co-e′val, 1 ko-ī′vəl; 2 eo-ē′val, *a.* Of or belonging to the same age or period.

co″ex-ist′d, 1 kō″egz-ist″; 2 eō″ĕgz-ist′, *vi.* To exist together.— **co″ex-is′tence,** or **-tens⁸,** *n.*— **co″ex-is′tent,** *a.* Existing together; coexisting.

co″ex-tend′d, 1 kō″eks-tend″; 2 eō″ĕks-tĕnd″, *vt. & vi.* To make or be coextensive.— **co″-ex-ten′siv**(e⁸, *a.* Having the same limits or extent.

cof′fee, 1 kêf′ɪ; 2 eôf′e, *n.* The seeds of a tropical tree; also, a beverage made from them, or the tree producing them.

cof′fer, 1 kêf′ẽr; 2 eôf′er, *n.* **1.** A chest; strong box; safe. **2.** *pl.* A treasury; financial resources.— **cof′fer-dam″,** *n.* A frame built in the water and pumped dry, to protect workmen.

cof′fin, 1 kêf′in; 2 eôf′in. **I.** *vt.* To put into or as into a coffin. **II.** *n.* **1.** The case in which a corpse is buried. **2.** The lower part of a horse's hoof.

cog, 1 keg; 2 eŏg, *n.* A tooth projecting from the surface of a wheel.— **cog′wheel″,** *n.* A wheel with cogs.

co′gent, 1 kō′jent; 2 eō′gĕnt, *a.* Compelling belief; forcible; convincing.— **-ly,** *adv.*— **co′gen-cy,** *n.* Convincing power.

cog′i-tate, 1 koj′i-tēt; 2 eŏg′i-tāt. *vt. & vi.* [-TAT″ED⁴; -TAT″ING.] To meditate; reflect; think.— **cog″i-ta′tion,** *n.* Consideration; reflection; thought.

co′gnac, 1 kō′nyak; 2 eō′nyäe, *n.* French brandy: named from the town of Cognac, France. **co′gniac‡.**

cog′nate, 1 keg′nēt; 2 eŏg′nāt, *a.* Allied by blood; kindred; akin.— **cog-na′tion,** *n.*

cog-ni′tion, 1 keg-nish′ən; 2 eŏg-nĭsh′on, *n.* The act, power, or faculty of knowing; knowledge.— **cog′ni-tiv**(e⁸, *a.* Pertaining to cognition; knowing.

cog′nize or **-nise,** 1 keg′naiz; 2 eŏg′nīz, *vt.*

[-NIZED; -NIZ-ING.] To know, perceive, or recognize.— **cog′ni-za-bl(e**^{P}, 1 kɒg′nɪ-za-bl; 2 cŏg′nɪ-za-bl, *a.* Capable of being known or of being judicially tried or examined.— **cog′ni-zance,** 1 kɒg′nɪ-zəns; 2 cŏg′nɪ-zanç, *n.* **1.** Apprehension; knowledge; judicial notice or jurisdiction. **2.** A badge or mark.— **cog′nizant,** *a.* Taking notice; aware. **cog′ni-sant‡.**

cog-no′men, 1 kɒg-nō′men; 2 cŏg-nō′mĕn, *n.* [-NO′MENS or -NOM′I-NA, 1 -nom′ɪ-nə; 2 -nŏm′ɪ-na, *pl.*] A surname; colloquially, any name.

co-hab′it^d, 1 ko-hab′ɪt; 2 eo-hăb′ɪt, *vi.* To dwell together as husband and wife.— **co-hab′i-ta′tion,** *n.*

co-heir′, 1 kō-âr′; 2 cō-êr′, *n.* An heir with another or others.— **co-heir′ess,** *n. fem.*

co-here′, 1 ko-hɪr′; 2 eo-hēr′, *vi.* [co-HERED′; CO-HER′ING.] To stick or hold firmly together.— **co-her′ence,** *n.* Conjunction; consistency; agreement. **co-her′en-cy‡.**— **co-her′ent,** *a.* Cleaving together; consistent; adapted; accordant; intelligible.— **co-her′ent-ly,** *adv.*— **co-her′er,** *n.* A small glass tube for holding particles of nickel

and silver used in wireless telegraphy.— **co-he′sion,** 1 ko-hī′ʒən; 2 co-hē′zhon, *n.* The act or state of cohering; attraction between atoms.— **co-he′siv(e**^{8}, *a.* Belonging to, exerting, or having the property of cohesion. **-ly,** *adv.* **-ness,** *n.*

co′hort, 1 kō′hŏrt; 2 cō′hôrt, *n.* An armed company; originally, the tenth of a Roman legion, 500 to 600 men. [dress.

coif‖, 1 kɒɪf; 2 cŏɪf, *n.* A close-fitting head-**coif′fure,** 1 kɒɪf′yur or (*F.*) kwa′für′; 2 cŏɪf′-yur or (*F.*) ewä′für′, *n.* An arrangement or dressing of the hair; a head-dress.

coign, 1 kɒɪn; 2 eŏɪn, *n.* A projecting angle or stone; a corner. **coigne‡.— coign of vantage,** an advantageous position.

coil, 1 kɒɪl; 2 cŏɪl, *vt. & vi.* To wind spirally.— **coil**^{1}, *n.* A ring or spiral; perplexity.— **coil‖**^{2}, *n.* Confusion or tumult; turmoil.

coin, 1 kɒɪn; 2 cŏɪn. **I.** *vt. & vi.* To make into coins; stamp or mint; originate; counterfeit. **II.** *n.* A piece of metallic money; such money collectively.— **coin′age,** *n.* Coining or fabricating coins, or the system of coins of a country; the cost of coining money.

VALUES OF FOREIGN COINS BASED ON THE REPORT OF THE TREASURY DEPARTMENT OF THE UNITED STATES.

Entries of merchandise into the United States liquidated upon the values proclaimed below are subject to reliquidation upon the order of the Secretary of the Treasury whenever satisfactory evidence is produced to show that the values in the United States currency of the foreign money specified are, at the date of certification of the invoices, for such merchandise at least five *per centum* or more from the values measured by the buying rate at New York determined by the Federal Reserve Bank of New York.

COUNTRY.	MONETARY UNIT.	LEGAL STANDARD	NORMAL VALUES.*		REMARKS.*
			U.S. MONEY.	ENG. MONEY.	
Argentine Rep. ...	peso	g	$1.6335	£0 3s 11.58d	Currency: Paper normally convertible at 44% of face value.
Austria..........	schilling	g	.2382	... ... 6.93	
Belgium..........	belga	g	.1695	... ... 4.94	Based on decree of March 31, 1935; 1 belga = 5 Belgian paper francs.
Bolivia..........	boliviano	g	.6180	... 1 6.00	13⅓ bolivianos = £1.0.0.
Brazil..........	milreis	g	.2025	... 2 5.89	Currency: Government paper; ratio of 8 paper to 1 gold milreis for collection of taxes and duties decreed Nov. 22, 1933.
British Colonies in Australasia and Africa..........	pound sterling	g	8.2397	1	
Bulgaria..........	lev (*pl.* leva)	g	.0112	... ... 0.35	
Canada..........	dollar	g	1.6931	... 4 1.31	
Chile..........	peso	g	.2060	... ... 6.02	
China..........	yuan, prior to March, 1933	s¹	.4870	... 1 2.20	The yuan (sometimes known as yuan dollar) of 100 fen (cents) is the monetary unit minted by the Central Government of the Republic.
	yuan, established March 3, 1933		.4786	... 1 1.95	

* Exchange rates fluctuate. ¹ Stated values are estimated market values in gold, of silver content of units.

1: ə = final; ɪ = habit; aɪsle; au = out; ɒɪl; ɪū = feud; ɟhin; go; ŋ = sing; ƒhin, this.
2: wọlf, dọ; bōōk, bŏŏt; fụll, rụle, cūre, bŭt, bûrn; ŏɪl, bŏy: ḡo, ġem; iŋk; thin, this.

VALUES OF FOREIGN COINS, ETC.—*Continued.*

COUNTRY.	MONETARY UNIT.	LEGAL STANDARD	NORMAL VALUES.*			REMARKS.*
			U. S. MONEY.	ENG. MONEY.		
Colombia........	peso	g	$1.6479	... 4	......	Currency: Govt. paper and silver.
Costa Rica......	colon	g	.7879	... 1	10.95	Law establishing conversion office fixes ratio 4 colons (nongold) = $1.
Cuba...........	peso	g	1.0000	... 2	5.12	By law of May 25, 1934.
Czechoslovakia...	koruna	g	.0418	......	1.22	Effective Feb. 17, 1934.
Denmark........	krone	g	.4537	... 1	1.22	
Dominican Rep. .	dollar	g	1.6931	... 4	1.31	U. S. money is principal circulating medium.
Ecuador........	sucre	g	.3386	......	9.83	
Egypt...........	pound (100 piasters)	g	8.3692	1 ...	3.78	
Estonia.........	kroon	g	.4537	... 1	1.22	
Finland.........	markka	g	.0426	......	1.24	
France..........	franc	g	.0663	......	1.93	
Germany........	reichsmark	g	.4033	......	11.74	
Great Britain....	pound sterling	g	8.2397	1 ...	......	Obligation to sell gold at legal monetary par suspended, effective Sept. 21, 1931.
Greece..........	drachma	g	.0220	......	0.64	
Guatemala......	quetzal	g	1.6931	... 4	1.31	
Haiti...........	gourde	g	.2000	......	5.82	Currency: National bank notes redeemable on demand in American dollars.
Honduras.......	lempira	g	.8466	... 2	0.66	Lempira circulates as equivalent of half of U. S. dollar.
Hungary........	pengö	g	.2961	......	8.62	
India (British)...	rupee	g	.6180	... 1	6.00	
Italy...........	lira	g	.0891	......	2.59	
Japan..........	yen	g	.8440	... 2	0.58	
Latvia.........	lat	g	.3267	......	9.51	
Liberia.........	dollar	g	1.6931	... 4	1.31	British money only is used.
Lithuania.......	litas	g	.1693	......	4.93	
Mexico.........	peso	g	.8440	... 2	0.58	By law of July 25, 1931, gold has no legal tender status but it may be held as monetary reserve for use in foreign exchange operations.
Netherlands.....	guilder (florin)	g	.6806	... 1	7.82	
Newfoundland...	dollar	g	1.6931	... 4	1.31	
Nicaragua.......	cordoba	g	1.6933	... 4	1.32	
Norway.........	krone	g	.4537	... 1	1.22	
Panama........	balboa	g	1.6933	... 4	1.32	
Paraguay........	peso (Argentine)	g	1.6335	... 3	11.58	Depreciated Paraguayan paper currency is used.
Persia..........	rial	g	.0824	......	2.40	Rial currency effective March 21, 1932, with 1 rial equivalent to 1 kran of old system.
Peru...........	sol	g	.4740	... 1	1.80	
Philippine Isls....	peso	g	.5000	... 1	2.58	By act approved March 16, 1935.
Poland.........	zloty	g	.1899	......	5.53	
Portugal........	escudo	g	.0748	......	2.18	
Roumania.......	leu (*pl.* lei)	g	.0101	......	0.29	
Salvador........	colon	g	.8466	... 2	0.66	
Siam...........	baht (tical)	g	.7491	... 1	9.82	
Spain..........	peseta	g	.3267	......	9.51	Valuation is for gold peseta; currency is notes of Bank of Spain.
StraitsSettlements	dollar	g	.9613	... 2	4.00	
Sweden.........	krona	g	.4537	... 1	1.22	
Switzerland.....	franc	g	.3267	......	9.51	
Turkey.........	piaster	g	.0744	......	2.16	(100 piasters = to the Turkish £.)
Uruguay........	peso	g	1.7511	... 4	3.00	Currency: inconvertible paper.
U.S.S.R........	chervonetz	g	8.7123	1 1	1.78	
Venezuela......	bolivar	g	.3267	......	9.51	
Yugoslavia......	dinar	g	.0298	......	0.86	

* Exchange rates fluctuate. *Abbreviations:* $ = dollar; £ = pound; *s* = shilling; *d* = penny; U. S. = United States; Eng. = England; g = gold; s = silver; abt. = about; approx. = approximately; ex. = exchange rate.

co″in-cide′, 1 kō″in-said′; 2 cō″in-çīd′, vi. [-CID′ED^d; -CID′ING.] To agree exactly; concur.— **co-in′ci-dence,** n. Agreement; correspondence.— **co-in′ci-dent,** a.

coke, 1 kōk; 2 cōk, n. Coal from which the volatile portion has been expelled by heating.

col′an-der, 1 kul′ən-dər; 2 cŏl′an-der, n. A perforated vessel for straining liquids, etc.

cold, 1 kōld; 2 cōld, a. 1. Of a low temperature; frigid; chilled; chilly. 2. Lacking ardor or sympathy; stolid; not cordial; discouraging. **-ly,** adv. **-ness,** n.— **cold′ chis′el,** n. A steel chisel for cutting cold metal.

cold, n. 1. A low temperature, or the sensation caused by it. 2. A disorder caused by exposure to cold.

Col″e-op′ter-a, 1 kŏl″ī-ŏp′tər-ə; 2 cŏl″e-ŏp′ter-a, n. pl. An order of insects having horny wing-cases; beetles.— **col′e-op′ter,** n. A beetle.— **col′e-op′ter-ous,** a.

col′ic, 1 kŏl′ik; 2 cŏl′ic, n. Acute pain in the bowels.— **col′ick-y,** 1 kŏl′ik-ı; 2 cŏl′ik-y, a.

col-lab′o-rate, 1 kə-lab′o-rēt; 2 cŏl-lăb′o-rāt, vi. [-RAT′ED^d; -RAT′ING.] To cooperate with another or others, as in scientific or literary work.— **col-lab″o-ra′tion,** n.— **col-lab′o-ra′tor,** n. **col-lab′o-ra″teur‡.**

col-lapse′, 1 kə-laps′; 2 cō-lăps′. I. vi. & **col-laps′^r,** 2 [vi. [-LAPSED′^t, -LAPST^s; -LAPS′ING.] To cause to shrink; fall in; fall together; fail utterly; be prostrated; succumb. II. n. A falling or sinking together; prostration; failure; ruin.

col′lar, 1 kŏl′ər; 2 cŏl′ar. I. vt. To grasp by or provide with a collar. II. n. A band for the neck; a ring or band on or about anything.— **col′lar-bone″,** n. The bone connecting the shoulder-blade and breast-bone; the clavicle.

col-late′, 1 kə-lēt′; 2 cō-lāt′, vt. [COL-LAT′-ED^d; COL-LAT′ING.] To compare critically; examine.— **col-la′tion,** n. 1. A collating; comparison. 2. A light repast.

col-lat′er-al, 1 kə-lat′ər-əl; 2 cō-lăt′er-al, I. a. 1. Attendant; incidental; confirmatory. 2. Parallel; bordering; descended from the same ancestor in a different line. II. n. Security subject to forfeiture in case of default. **-ly,** adv.

col′league, 1 kŏl′īg; 2 cŏl′ēg, n. An associate in office. **col′leags^s,**)

col-lect′^d, 1 kə-lekt′; 2 cō-lĕct′, vt. & vi. To bring or come together; gather; assemble; accumulate.— **col-lect′a-ble^r** or **col-lect′i-ble^r,** a. [condensed prayer.

col′lect, 1 kŏl′ekt; 2 cŏl′ĕct, n. A short

col-lect′ed, pa. 1. Assembled; gathered. 2. Composed; self-possessed.

col-lec′tion, 1 kə-lek′shən; 2 cō-lĕc′shon, n. A collecting; persons or things collected; an accumulation.

col-lec′tive,) 1 kə-lek′tiv; 2 cō-lĕc′tiv, a. **col-lec′tiv^s,**) Relating to an aggregate or group; tending to collect; bringing together.— **col-lec′tiv(e-ly^s,** adv. Unitedly; at once.

col-lec′tor, 1 kə-lek′tər or -tōr; 2 cō-lĕc′tor, n. One who collects, as duties, taxes, or debts.— **col-lec′tor-ate, col-lec′tor-ship,** n. The office or jurisdiction of a collector.

col′lege, 1 kŏl′ij; 2 cŏl′eg, n. 1. A school of higher learning. 2. A body of associates or colleagues. [A college student.

col-le′gi-an, 1 kə-lī′ji-ən; 2 cō-lē′gi-an, n.

col-le′gi-ate, 1 kə-lī′ji-ēt; 2 cō-lē′gi-āt. I. a. Pertaining to a college. II. n. A collegian.

col-lide′, 1 kə-laid′; 2 cō-līd′, vi. [COL-LID′ED^d; COL-LID′ING.] To meet and strike violently; clash. [dog. **col′ley‡.**

col′lie, 1 kŏl′ī; 2 cŏl′i, n. A Scotch sheep-

col′lier, 1 kŏl′yər; 2 cŏl′yer, n. A coal-miner; a vessel employed in coal-carrying, or one of her crew.— **col′lier-y,** n. [-IES^z, pl.] A coal-mine; the coal-trade.

col-li′sion, 1 kə-liz′ən; 2 cō-lĭzh′on, n. The act of colliding; clashing; antagonism.

col′lo-cate, 1 kŏl′o-kēt; 2 cŏl′o-cāt, vt. [-CAT′ED^d; -CAT′ING.] To arrange together; station.— **col″lo-ca′tion,** n.

col-lo′di-on, 1 kə-lō′di-ən; 2 cō-lō′di-on, n. A solution of guncotton in ether and alcohol that forms an adhesive film.

col′loid, 1 kŏl′oid; 2 cŏl′oid. I. a. Jelly-like. II. n. A jelly-like substance.— **col-lol′dal,** a.

col-lo′qui-al, 1 kə-lō′kwi-əl; 2 cō-lō′kwi-al, a. Pertaining to conversation; used in conversation, but not in literary or oratorical style. **-ly,** adv.— **col-lo′qui-al-ism,** n. A form of speech used only or chiefly in conversation; a colloquial expression.

col′lo-quy, 1 kŏl′o-kwı; 2 cŏl′o-kwy, n. [-QUIES^z, pl.] An informal conference; conversation.

col-lude′, 1 kə-liūd′; 2 cō-lūd′, vi. [-LUD′-ED^d; -LUD′ING.] To cooperate secretly; conspire; connive.— **col-lu′sion,** n. Fraudulent cooperation.— **col-lu′siv(es,** a. Fraudulently concerted. **-ly,** adv. **-ness,** n.

co-logne′, 1 kō-lōn′; 2 cō-lōn′, n. A perfume made of alcohol mingled with aromatic oils: named from the city of Cologne, Germany.

co′lon‡, 1 kō′lən; 2 cō′lon, n. A punctua-

tion-mark (:) indicating a pause greater than a semicolon, but less than a period.

co'lon², n. The large intestine.

colo'nel, 1 kûr'nel; 2 eûr'nĕl, n. The highest officer of a regiment.— **colo'nel-cy,** n. **colo'nel-ship‡.**

col''on-nade', 1 kŏl'o-nēd'; 2 eŏl'o-nād', n. A range of columns connected by an entablature.

col'o-ny, 1 kŏl'o-nɪ; 2 eŏl'o-ny, n. [-NIES², pl.] A body of emigrants in a remote region under the control of the parent country; the region so occupied; any association of individuals, as a swarm of bees.— **co-lo'ni-al**, 1 ko-lō'nɪ-al; 2 eo-lō'nɪ-al, a.— **col'o-nist**, 1 kŏl'o-nɪst; 2 eŏl'o-nĭst, n. A member or inhabitant of a colony; a settler.— **col'o-nize**, 1 kŏl'o-naɪz; 2 eŏl'o-nɪz, vt. & vi. [-NIZED‡; -NIZ'ING.] To emigrate to and settle in a region; establish, unite in, or settle in a colony or colonies. **colo-nise‡.— col''o-ni-za'tion or -sa'tion**, n.

col'or, ⎰ 1 kul'ər; 2 eŏl'or, v. **I.** t. **1.**
col'our, ⎰ give a color to; dye; tint; stain. **2.** To modify; misrepresent. **II.** i. To change color; blush.— **col'or-a-ble**, a.— **col''or-a'tion**, n.— **col'ored**, pa. Having color; of a dark-skinned race; embellished or exaggerated.— **col'or-er**, n.— **col'or-ist**, n. One skilled in the use of color.

col'or, n. **1.** Any one of the hues of the rainbow, or a blending of those hues; loosely, any hue including black and white. **2.** A paint or pigment. **3.** An appearance; pretense; disguise. **4.** pl. An ensign, flag, or badge.— **col'or-less**, a. Without color; impartial; negative; dull.

col'or-a-ture, 1 kul'ər-a-chur or -tiur; 2 eŏl-or-a-chur or -tūr, n. [-TU'RA, pl.] **1.** The effect of giving color to vocal music, by means of runs, trills, or other florid decorations. **2.** A singer who produces such effect. [It.]

co-los'sus, 1 ko-los'us; 2 eo-los'ŭs, n. [-Sɪ, 1 -aɪ; 2 -ɪ, or -SUS-ES, pl.] A gigantic statue, as of Apollo at ancient Rhodes.— **co-los'sal**, a. Enormous; huge; gigantic. **-ly**, adv.

col'our, col''our-a-bl(eᴿ, etc. Color, etc.: the usual spelling in England.

col'por-teur, 1 kŏl'pōr-tər; 2 eŏl'pôr-tər, n. A traveling distributor of Bibles, religious books, etc. **col'por-ter‡.— col'por-tage**, n. A colporteur's work.

colt, 1 kōlt; 2 eōlt, n. A young horse.— **colt'ish**, a. Like a colt; frisky; wanton.

col'ter, 1 kōl'tər; 2 eōl'ter, n. A blade on the beam of a plow, to cut the sod. **coul'ter‡.**

Co-lum'bi-a, 1 ko-lum'bɪ-a; 2 eo-lŭm'bi-a, n. The personification of the United States.

col'um-bine, 1 kŏl'um-baɪn; 2 eŏl'ŭm-bīn, n. A herbaceous plant with flowers of five petals. See illus. in next column.

col'umn, 1 kŏl'um; 2 eŏl'ŭm, n. **1.** A pillar; a prop or support. **2.** A vertical series of lines, words, figures, or the like. **3.** A long array of troops with narrow front; a fleet in single file. — **co-lum'nar**, a.

Columbine.
a, the fruit.

com-, con-, prefix. Together: with: often used with intensive force; as, complex, compress. Co-, col-, and cor- are variant forms.

co'ma¹, 1 kō'ma; 2 eō'ma, n. A state of unconsciousness, with slow, heavy breathing; stupor.— **co'ma-tose**, 1 kō'mə-tōs; 2 eō'ma-tōs, a. Relating to or affected with coma; abnormally sleepy. **co'ma-tous‡.**

co'ma², n. [co'MÆ, 1 -mī; 2 -mē, pl.] **1.** The glowing, hazy mass around the nucleus of a comet. **2.** A tuft of silky hairs.

comb, 1 kōm; 2 eōm, v. **I.** t. To dress with a comb. **II.** i. To curl over and break into foam, as waves.— **comb'er**, n. One who or that which combs; a combing wave.— **comb'ing**, n. **1.** The act of using a comb. **2.** That which is combed away, as hair, etc. **3.** A coaming.

comb, n. **1.** A thin piece of horn, or the like, with teeth: for dressing the hair or holding it in place. **2.** The fleshy crest on the head of a fowl. **3.** The crest of a hill or wave. **4.** Honeycomb.

com'bat, 1 kŏm'bat or kum'bat; 2 eŏm'bat or eŏm'băt. **I.** d. vt. & vi. To fight or contend with; oppose; resist; do battle; contend. **II.** n A battle or fight; struggle; contest.— **com'bat-ant. I.** a. Contending in fight; combative. **II.** n. One engaged in combat.— **com'bat-iv(eᴺ**, a. Disposed to combat; contentious; pugnacious. **-ly**, adv. **-ness**, n.

com-bine', 1 kəm-baɪn'; 2 eŏm-bīn', vt. & vi. [-BINED'; -BIN'ING.] To bring or come into a close union; blend; unite.— **com''bi-na'tion**, n. A joining together; union; alliance; compound.— **com-bin'er**, n.

com-bus'ti-bl(eᴿ, 1 kəm-bus'tɪ-bl; 2 eŏm-bŭs'ti-bl. **I.** a. Capable of burning; inflammable. **II.** n. Any substance that will readily burn.— **com-bus'ti-bl(e- nessᴿ**, n. The quality of being combustible. **com-bus''ti-bil'i-ty‡.**

com-bus'tion, 1 kəm-bus'chən; 2 eŏm-bŭs'chon, n. The act or process of burning.

come, ⎰ 1 kum; 2 eŏm, vi. [CAME, 1 kēm,
cumᴿ, ⎰ eām; COME, COM'ING.] To move to

or toward the speaker; draw nigh; arrive; happen.— **com′er**, *n.*

com′e-dy, 1 kŏm′ĭ-dĭ; 2 cŏm′e-dy, *n.* [-DIES², *pl.*] An amusing drama; anything comical.— **co-me′di-an**, 1 ko-mĭ′dĭ-ən; 2 co-mē′di-an, *n.* A comic actor.— **co-mē′di-enne′**, 1 ko-mē′dĭ-en′; 2 co-mē′di-ĕn′, *n. fem.*

come′ly, 1 kŭm′lĭ; 2 cóm′ly, *a.* [COME′-cum′ly**ᵖ**, LI-ER; COME′LI-EST.] **1.** Pleasing in person; handsome. **2.** Suitable; becoming.— **come′li-ly**, *adv.* **come′ly‡.— come′li-ness**, *n.*

com′et, 1 kŏm′et; 2 cŏm′ĕt, *n.* A heavenly body, consisting of a coma surrounding a star-like nucleus, with a nebulous train.— **com′et-a-ry**, *a.* **com′et-ic‡.**

com′fit, 1 kŭm′fĭt; 2 cóm′fit, *n.* A dry sweetmeat, confection. **com′fi-ture‡.**

Comet.

com′fort, 1 kŭm′fərt; 2 cóm′fort. **I** *d.* **cum′fort**ᵖ, *vt.* To encourage; console; solace. **II.** *n.* Freedom or relief from pain or trouble; ease; satisfaction; also, anything that contributes to such a state.— **com′fort-a-ble**, *a.* Having or imparting comfort.— **com′fort-a-ble-ness**, *n.*— **com′fort-a-bly**, *adv.*— **com′fort-er**, *n.* **1.** One who comforts; a consoler; [C-], the Holy Spirit. **2.** A long woolen scarf.— **com′fort-less**, *a.* Destitute of comfort.

com′ic, 1 kŏm′ĭk; 2 cŏm′ĭc, *a.* **1.** Pertaining to or like comedy. **2.** Comical.

com′i-cal, 1 kŏm′ĭ-kəl; 2 cŏm′ĭ-cal, *a.* **1.** Droll; ludicrous; diverting. **2.** Comic. **-ly**, *adv.*

com′i-ty, 1 kŏm′ĭ-tĭ; 2 cŏm′i-ty, *n.* Kindly consideration; friendliness; courtesy.

com′ma, 1 kŏm′ə; 2 cŏm′a, *n.* A punctuation=mark (,) denoting the slightest separation.

com-mand′ᵈ, 1 ko-mand′; 2 cŏ-mänd′, *v.* **I.** *t.* **1.** To order with authority; require; enjoin. **2.** To have under control; be master of; overlook, as from a height; cover; guard; be able to obtain. **3.** To claim irresistibly. **II.** *i.* To be in authority; rule.— **com′man-dant′**, 1 kŏm′-an-dant′; 2 cŏm′än-dänt′. *n.* An officer in command, as of a military post.— **com-mand′er**, 1 ko-mand′ər; 2 cŏ-mänd′er, *n.* One in command; a military or a naval officer.— **com-mand′ing**, *pa.* Fitted to command; authoritative; dignified.— **com-mand′ment**, *n.* An edict; order; law.

com-mand′, *n.* **1.** The right to command; act of commanding; control; mastery; authority. **2.** An order; commandment. **3.** The force or district commanded.

com″man-deer′, 1 kŏm″ən-dīr′; 2 cŏm″an-dēr′, *vt.* [S. Afr.] To force into military service.

com-man′do, 1 ko-man′do; 2 cŏ-män′do, *n.* [-DOS or -DOES, 1 -doz; 2 -dōs, *pl.*] A military raiding unit; also, a member of such unit.

com-mem′o-rate, 1 ko-mem′o-rēt; 2 cŏ-mĕm′o-rāt, *vt.* [-RAT′ED**d**; -RAT′ING.] To celebrate the memory of; keep in remembrance.— **com-mem″o-ra′tion**, *n.*— **com-mem′o-ra-tiv**(es, *a.*

com-mence′, 1 ko-mens′; 2 cŏ-mĕnç′, *v.* [-MENCED**t**; -MENC′ING.] **I.** *t.* To begin; give origin to; initiate. **II.** *i.* To make a beginning; originate; start; begin to be.— **com-mence′ment**, *n.* **1.** A beginning; origin. **2.** A celebration at the close of a college course, when degrees are conferred.

com-mend′ᵈ, 1 ko-mend′; 2 cŏ-mĕnd′, *vt.* **1.** To express a favorable opinion of; approve; recommend. **2.** To commit with confidence; entrust.— **com-mend′a-bl**(e**ᵖ**, *a.* Laudable; creditable.— **com-mend′a-bl**(e-ness**ᵖ**, *n.*—**com-mend′a-bly**, *adv.*— **com″men-da′tion**, *n.* **1.** The act of commending; approbation. **2.** Something that commends.— **com-mend′a-to-ry**, *a.* Expressing commendation; commending.

com-men′su-ra-bl(e**ᵖ**, 1 ko-men′shu-ra-bl; 2 cŏ-mĕn′shu-ra-bl, *a.* Measurable by a common unit; proportionate.— **com-men″su-ra-bil′i-ty**, *n.*— **com-men′su-ra-bl**(e-ness**ᵖt**.— **com-men′su-ra-bly**, *adv.*

com-men′su-rate, 1 ko-men′shu-rēt; 2 cŏ-mĕn′shu-rāt, *a.* **1.** Commensurable. **2.** In proper proportion. **-ly**, *adv.* **-ness**, *n.*

com′ment, 1 kem′ent; 2 cŏm′ĕnt. **I** *d.* *vi.* To make comments; followed by *on* or *upon*. **II.** *n.* A note in explanation or criticism.— **com′men-ta-ry**, *n.* [-RIES², *pl.*] A body of comments; exposition.— **com′men-ta″tor**, *n.* A writer of commentaries; an annotator.

com-merce′, 1 ko-mûrs′; 2 cŏ-mẽrs′, *vi.* [COM-MERCED′t; COM-MERC′ING.] To commune.

com′merce, 1 kŏm′ərs; 2 cŏm′erç, *n.* Exchange of goods or productions, as between states or nations; extended trade; intercourse.— **com-mer′cial**, *a.* Pertaining to trade or commerce.— **com-mer′cial-ly**, *adv.*

com-min′gle, 1 ko-miŋ′gl; 2 cŏ-mĭŋ′gl, **cum-min′gl**ᵖ, *vt. & vi.* [-GL(E)D**ᵖ**; -GLING.] To mix together; mingle.

com′mi-nute, 1 kŏm′ĭ-niūt; 2 cŏm′i-nut, *vt.* [-NUT′ED**d**; -NUT′ING.] To reduce to minute particles; crush; pulverize.— **com″mi-nu′tion**, *n.*

com-mis′er-ate, 1 ko-miz′ər-ēt; 2 cŏ-mĭṣ′er-āt, *vt.* [-AT′ED**d**; -AT′ING.] To feel pity for.— **com-mis″er-a′tion**, *n.*

com′·mis·sa·ry, 1 kŏm′ĭ-sē-rĭ; 2 cŏm′-ĭ-să-ry, *n.* [-RIES^z, *pl.*] **1.** A commissioner. **2.** *Mil.* An officer in charge of subsistence, etc. — **com′mis·sa′rĭ·at,** 1 kŏm′ĭ-sē′rĭ-at; 2 cŏm′ĭ-sä′rĭ-ăt, *n.* An army department supplying food and other necessaries; also, military supplies.

com·mis′sion, 1 kẹ-mĭsh′ən; 2 cŏ-mĭsh′on. **I.** *vt.* To give a commission to; appoint; empower; delegate. **II.** *n.* **1.** The act of committing; a trust; charge. **2.** A document conferring rank or authority, or the rank or authority conferred. **3.** A body of persons acting under public authority. **4.** Agency, or the compensation of an agent. — **to put in** or **into commission,** to put in direct command of a designated officer, as a ship of war, for active service.

com·mis′sion·er, 1 kẹ-mĭsh′ən·ər; 2 cŏ-mĭsh′on·er, *n.* An official specially commissioned.

com·mit′, 1 kẹ-mĭt′; 2 cŏ-mĭt′, *vt.* [COM-MIT′TED^d; COM·MIT′TING.] **1.** To do; perpetrate. **2.** To consign; entrust; refer. **3.** To devote; pledge; compromise or bind (oneself). **4.** To memorize, as a speech. — **com·mit′ment,** *n.* The act of committing, or the state of being committed, as to prison. **com·mit′tal‡.**

com·mit′tee, 1 kẹ-mĭt′ĭ; 2 cŏ-mĭt′e, *n.* A person or persons appointed to act upon some matter.

com·mo′di·ous, 1 kẹ-mō′dĭ-us; 2 cŏ-mō′-dĭ-ŭs, *a.* Affording ample accommodation; suitable; convenient; spacious. **-ly,** *adv.* **-ness,** *n.*

com·mod′i·ty, 1 kẹ-mŏd′ĭ-tĭ; 2 cŏ-mŏd′-ĭ-ty, *n.* [-TIES^z, *pl.*] A movable article of value.

com′mo·dore, 1 kŏm′ọ-dōr; 2 cŏm′ọ-dōr, *n.* The commander of a squadron.

com′mon, 1 kŏm′ən; 2 cŏm′on. **I.** *a.* **1.** Frequent or usual; customary; regular. **2.** Pertaining to two or more persons or things; joint; general. **3.** Commonplace; coarse; vulgar; low. **II.** *n.* Land owned by a town; land open to the use of the public. — **com′mon·al·ty,** *n.* [-TIES^z, *pl.*] The common people; the lower classes. — **common chord,** a chord consisting of a fundamental tone with its third and fifth. — **com′mon·er,** 1 kŏm′ən·ər; 2 cŏm′on·er, *n.* [Gt. Brit.] One of the common people; any subject not a peer. — **com′mon·ly,** *adv.* — **com′mon·ness,** *n.* — **com′mon·place′. I.** *a.* Not remarkable or interesting; ordinary; trite. **II.** *n.* **1.** A trite remark; familiar truth. **2.** A memorandum. — **com′mons,** *n. pl.* **1.** The common people; commonalty. **2.** [C-] [Gt. Brit.] The legislators of the lower house of Parliament; the House of Commons. **3.** A company eating at a common table, or the meals so furnished. — **com′mon·weal′,** *n.* The general welfare. — **com′mon·wealth″,** *n.* **1.** The people of a state; the state. **2.** A republic.

com·mo′tion, 1 kẹ-mō′shạn; 2 cŏ-mō′-shon, *n.* A violent agitation; excitement; tumult.

com·mune′, 1 kẹ-miūn′; 2 cŏ-mūn′, *vi.* [COM·MUNED′; COM·MUN′ING.] **1.** To hold communion; interchange thoughts or feelings. **2.** To partake of the eucharist.

com′mune, 1 kŏm′yūn; 2 cŏm′yụn, *n.* **1.** The smallest political division of France. **2.** A self-governing community. — **com′mu·nal,** 1 kŏm′yu·nạl; 2 cŏm′yu·nal, *a.* Of or pertaining to a commune; public.

com·mu′ni·cate, 1 kẹ-miū′nĭ-kēt; 2 cŏ-mū′nĭ-cāt, *v.* [-CAT″ED^d; -CAT″ING.] **I.** *t.* To impart; make known. **II.** *i.* **1.** To make or hold a communication. To partake of the Lord's Supper; commune. — **com·mu′ni·ca·ble,** *a.* — **com·mu′ni·cant,** *n.* One who partakes of the Lord's Supper. — **com·mu′ni·ca′tion,** *n.* **1.** The act of communicating, or something communicated; a message. **2.** Means of communicating, as a highway. — **com·mu′ni·ca·tive,** *a.* Ready to communicate; frank. **-ly,** *adv.* **-ness,** *n.* — **com·mu′ni·ca″tor,** *n.*

com·mu′nion, 1 kẹ-miū′nyạn; 2 cŏ-mū′-nyon, *n.* **1.** The act of communing; sympathetic intercourse. **2.** The Lord's Supper, or the act of partaking of it. **3.** Religious fellowship; a denomination of Christians.

com′mu′ni·qué′, 1 kẹ-mū′nĭ·kē′; 2 cŏ-mū′-nĭ·ke′, *n.* [F.] An official announcement.

com′mu·nism, 1 kŏm′yu·nizm; 2 cŏm′-yu·nĭsm, *n.* Common ownership of property with state control of labor, religion, social relations, etc. — **com′mu·nist,** *n.* One who advocates communism. — **com″mu·nis′tic,** *a.*

com·mu′ni·ty, 1 kẹ-miū′nĭ-tĭ; 2 cŏ-mū′ni-ty, *n.* [-TIES^z, *pl.*] **1.** A body politic; people of any place; the public. **2.** Participation; identity; likeness.

com·mute′, 1 kẹ-miūt′; 2 cŏ-mūt′, *v.* [COM·MUT′ED^d; COM·MUT′ING.] **I.** *t.* To reduce to something less. **II.** *i.* To pay at a reduced rate. — **com″mu·ta′tion,** *n.* A substitution, reduction of penalty. — **com′mu·ta″tor,** *n.* *Elec.* A device to change the direction or vary the strength of an electric current in a dynamo, motor, etc. — **com·mut′er,** *n.* One who travels steadily at a reduced rate.

com·pact′^d, 1 kẹm-pakt′; 2 cŏm-păct′, *v.* To pack closely; compress; unite closely; compose; make a compact; conspire.

com-pact', *a.* Closely united; solid; dense; brief; terse. **-ly**, *adv.* **-ness**, *n.*

com'pact, 1 kŏm'păkt; 2 cŏm'păct. *n.* A covenant or contract.

com-pan'ion, 1 kŏm-pan'yŏn; 2 cŏm-păn'yon, *n.* One who or that which accompanies; a comrade; associate.— **com-pan'ion-a-bl(e**[P], *a.* Sociable; agreeable. — **com-pan'ion-ship**, *n.* Association; company.

com-pan'ion-way", 1 kŏm-pan'yŏn-wē"; 2 cŏm-păn'yon-wā", *n.* *Naut.* A staircase leading from a deck to a cabin.

com'pa-ny, 1 kum'pa-nı; 2 cŏm'pa-ny, *n.* [-NIES[z], *pl.*] **1.** The society of another or others; fellowship; association. **2.** A gathering of persons for social purposes; an assemblage; a corporation. **3.** *Mil.* A body of men commanded by a captain.

com-pare', 1 kŏm-pâr'; 2 cŏm-pâr', *v.* [-PARED'; -PAR'ING.] **I.** *t.* **1.** To examine as to similarity or dissimilarity. **2.** To liken. **II.** *i.* To be like or equal. — **com'pa-ra-bl(e**[P], 1 kŏm'pa-ra-bl; 2 cŏm'-pa-ra-bl, *a.* Worthy to be compared; similar. — **com'pa-ra-bly**, *adv.*— **com-par'a-tiv(e**[S], *a.* **1.** Pertaining to comparison. **2.** Estimated by comparison; relative. **-ly**, *adv.*

com-par'i-son, 1 kŏm-păr'ı-sŏn; 2 cŏm-păr'ı-son, *n.* A comparing; an estimate of likeness or unlikeness; a simile; example; resemblance.

com-part'ment, 1 kŏm-pärt'ment *or* -mɛnt; 2 cŏm-pärt'ment, *n.* A separate section, as of a ship.

com'pass, 1 kum'pɐs; **cum'pass**[P], 2 cŏm'pɐs. **I**[t]. *vt.* To attain; plan for; comprehend; surround; encompass. **II.** *n.* **1.** Extent within limits; scope; circuit; a boundary; bounds; due limits. **2.** *Mus.* The range of a voice or instrument. **3.** An instrument for determining directions by the pointing of a magnetic needle northward, as in the *mariners' compass.*

com'pass-es, 1 kum'pɐs-ez; 2 cŏm'pas-ĕs, *n. pl.* A jointed instrument for describing circles, etc.

1. Ordinary Compasses. 2. Proportional Compasses for reducing and enlarging in proportion. 3. Bow-spring Pencil-compasses.

com-pas'sion, 1 kŏm-pash'ɐn; 2 cŏm-păsh'on, *n.* Pity for suffering, with desire to relieve.— **com-pas'sion-ate. I.** *vt.*

[-AT"ED[d]; -AT"ING.] To have compassion for; commiserate. **II.** *a.* Feeling compassion; merciful; sympathetic. **-ly**, *adv.* **-ness**, *n.*

com-pat'i-ble, 1 kŏm-pat'ı-bl; 2 cŏm-**com-pat'i-bl**[P], păt'ı-bl, *a.* Capable of existing together; congenial. — **com-pat'l-bll'i-ty**, *n.* The state of being compatible; congeniality; consistency. **com-pat'i-bl(e-ness**[F]t.— **com-pat'i-bly**, *adv.*

com-pa'tri-ot, 1 kŏm-pē'trı-ŏt; 2 cŏm-pā'-tri-ot, *n.* A fellow countryman.

com-peer', 1 kŏm-pīr'; 2 cŏm-pēr', *n.* One of equal rank; a comrade; associate.

com-pel', 1 kŏm-pel'; 2 cŏm-pĕl', *v.* [COM-PELLED'; COM-PEL'LING.] **I.** *t.* To urge irresistibly; constrain; coerce; force; obtain by force. **II.** *i.* To use compulsion.

com'pend, 1 kŏm'pend; 2 cŏm'pĕnd, *n.* An abridgment; digest; compendium.

com-pen'di-ous, 1 kŏm-pen'dı-us; 2 cŏm-pĕn'di-ŭs, *a.* Briefly stated; concise. **-ly**, *adv.* **-ness**, *n.*

com-pen'di-um, 1 kŏm-pen'dı-um; 2 cŏm-pĕn'di-ŭm, *n.* [-DI-UMS[z] or -DI-A, *pl.*] A brief comprehensive summary; an abridgment.

com'pen-sate, 1 kŏm'pen-sēt; 2 cŏm'pĕn-săt, *v.* [-SAT"ED[d]; -SAT"ING.] **I.** *t.* **1.** To make payment to or for; requite; repay. **2.** To make amends for; counterbalance. **II.** *i.* To make amends.— **com"pen-sa'tion**, *n.* Payment; amends.

com-pete', 1 kŏm-pīt'; 2 cŏm-pēt', *vi.* [-PET"ED[d]; -PET"ING.] To strive for the same object; rival; vie.— **com"pe-ti'tion**, 1 kŏm"pı-tish'ɐn; 2 cŏm"pe-tish'on, *n.* Contention for the same object; rivalry.— **com-pet'i-tiv(e**[S], *a.* Pertaining to or characterized by competition. — **com-pet'i-tor**, *n.* One who competes.

com'pe-tence, 1 kŏm'pı-tens, -ten-sı; 2 **com'pe-ten-cy**, cŏm'pe-tĕnç, -tĕn-çy, *n.* **1.** The state of being competent; ability; qualification. **2.** Sufficient means; sufficiency.

com'pe-tent, 1 kŏm'pı-tent; 2 cŏm'pe-tĕnt, *a.* Having sufficient ability, authority, or qualifications; fulfilling all requirements; sufficient; adequate; able; qualified. **-ly**, *adv.*

com-pile', 1 kŏm-paıl'; 2 cŏm-pīl', *vt.* [-PILED'; -PIL'ING.] To compose, as a book, by borrowing or transcribing; put together extracts.— **com"pi-la'tion**, 1 kŏm"-pı-lē'shɐn; 2 cŏm"pi-lā'shon, *n.* The act of compiling a book or collection of extracts.— **com-pil'er**, *n.*

com-pla'cence, 1 kŏm-plē'sens, -sen-sı; **com-pla'cen-cy**, 2 cŏm-plā'çĕnç, -çĕn-çy, *n.* Satisfaction; self-approval; serenity.

1: ə = final; ı = habit; aisle; au = out; oil; iū = feud; chin; go; ŋ = sing; chin, this.
2: wǫlf, dǫ; bōōk, bōōt; fụll, rụle, cūre, bŭt, bûrn; ŏll, bŏy; go, ġem; iŋk; thin, this.

com-pla′cent, 1 kəm-plē′sent; 2 eŏm-plä′-çĕnt, *a.* Feeling or showing gratification. **-ly,** *adv.*

com-plain′, 1 kəm-plēn′; 2 eŏm-plān′, *vi.* To make a statement of grievance; find fault; murmur.— **com-plain′ant,** *n.* One who complains.

com-plaint′, 1 kəm-plēnt′; 2 eŏm-plānt′, *n.* **1.** A statement of grievance or injury. **2.** A grievance. **3.** A physical ailment; disease.

com′plai-sant″, 1 kŏm′plē-zant″; 2 eŏm′-plä-ġänt″, *a.* Showing a desire to please; courteous.— **com′plai-sance″,** 1 kŏm′plē-zans″; 2 eŏm′plä-ġänç″, *n.* The desire or endeavor to please: politeness.

com′ple-ment, 1 kŏm′pli-ment *or* -mənt; 2 eŏm′ple-měn. **I**d. *vt.* To add or form a complement to; supplement. **II.** *n.* Full number; completeness; that which completes; an accessory.— **com″ple-men′tal,** *a.* Completing; additional; accessory. **com″-ple-men′ta-ry‡.**

com-plete′, 1 kəm-plīt′; 2 eŏm-plēt′. **I.** *vt.* [-PLET′ED**d**; -PLET′ING.] To make complete; accomplish; finish; fulfil. **II.** *a.* Lacking nothing; entire; perfect; full; finished.— **com-plete′ly,** *adv.*— **com-plete′-ness,** *n.*— **com-ple′tion,** 1 kəm-plī′shən; 2 eŏm-plē′shon, *n.* The act of completing, or the state of being completed: finish; fulfilment.— **com-ple′tive,** *a.* Completing or tending to complete.

com′plex, 1 kŏm′pleks; 2 eŏm′plĕks, *a.* Consisting of various parts; complicated; intricate.— **com-plex′i-ty,** *n.* [-TIES**z**, *pl.*] The state of being complex; something complex.

com-plex′ion, 1 kəm-plek′shən; 2 eŏm′plĕk′shon, *n.* **1.** The color of the skin, especially of the face. **2.** Aspect; character; quality.

com-pli′ance, 1 kəm-plai′əns; 2 eŏm-plī′-anç, *n.* **1.** The act of complying. **2.** Complaisance.

com-pli′ant, 1 kəm-plai′ənt; 2 eŏm-plī′ant, *a.* Complying; yielding.— **com-pli′ant-ly,** *adv.*

com′pli-cate, 1 kŏm′pli-kēt; 2 eŏm′pli-eät. **I.** *vt.* & *vi.* [-CAT′ED**d**; -CAT′ING.] To make or become complex, difficult, or perplexing: mix; confuse; entangle. **II.** *a.* Complicated; complex.— **com″pli-ca′tion,** *n.* **1.** The act of complicating, or the state of being complicated; complexity. **2.** Anything that complicates.

com-plic′i-ty, 1 kəm-plis′i-tɪ; 2 eŏm-plĭç′i-ty, *n.* [-TIES**z**, *pl.*] The act or state of being an accomplice; participation, as in wrong-doing.

com′pli-ment, 1 kŏm′pli-ment *or* -mənt;

2 eŏm′pli-ment. **I**d. *vt.* & *vi.* To pay a compliment to; use or exchange compliments. **II.** *n.* **1.** An expression of admiration, congratulation, or the like. **2.** A formal greeting: usually in the plural. — **com″pli-men′ta-ry,** *a.* Expressing or expressive of compliment.

com-ply′, 1 kəm-plai′; 2 eŏm-plī′, *vi.* [-PLIED′; -PLY′ING.] To conform; consent; obey.

com-po′nent, 1 kəm-pō′nent; 2 eŏm-pō′-něnt. **I.** *a.* Forming a part. **II.** *n.* A constituent element or part; ingredient.

com-port′d, 1 kəm-pōrt′; 2 eŏm-pôrt′, *v.* **I.** *t.* To conduct (oneself). **II.** *i.* To be compatible; agree.

com-pose′, 1 kəm-pōz′; 2 eŏm-pōġ′, *v.* [-POSED′; -POS′ING.] **I.** *t.* **1.** To make up of parts; construct; form; constitute. **2.** To tranquilize; calm; reconcile; arrange; settle. **II.** *i.* To engage in composition.— **com-posed′,** *pa.* Free from agitation; calm.— **com-pos′er,** *n.*

com-pos′it(es, 1 kəm-pez′it *or* kəm′po-zit; 2 eŏm-pŏġ′it *or* eŏm′po-ġĭt, *a.* Made up of distinct parts; combined or compounded.

com″po-si′tion, 1 kŏm″po-zish′ən; 2 eŏm″-po-ġĭsh′on, *n.* **1.** The act of composing, or that which is composed, as a literary, artistic, or musical production; a combination. **2.** Typesetting. **3.** An agreement or settlement; compromise.— **com-pos′i-tor,** 1 kəm-pez′i-tər *or* -tər; 2 eŏm-pŏġ′i-tor, *n.* A typesetter.

com′post, 1 kŏm′pōst; 2 eŏm′pōst, *n.* A fertilizing mixture; manure.

com-po′sure, 1 kəm-pō′ʒur; 2 eŏm-pō′-zhur, *n.* Tranquillity; calmness; serenity.

com-pound′d, 1 kəm-paund′; 2 eŏm-pound′, *v.* **I.** *t.* **1.** To mix, or make by mixture; combine. **2.** To settle at a reduction, as a debt; conceal, as a crime, for a consideration. **II.** *i.* To come to terms; settle.

com′pound, 1 kŏm′paund; 2 eŏm′pound, *a.* Composed of ingredients or parts; composite.

com′pound¹, *n.* A compound substance.

com′pound², *n.* The walled or fenced enclosure of a European residence or factory in the Orient.

com″pre-hend′d, 1 kŏm″pri-hend′; 2 eŏm″-pre-hěnd′, *vt.* **1.** To grasp mentally; understand fully. **2.** To include; comprise; encompass. — **com″pre-hen″si-bil′i-ty,** *n.* The state of being comprehensible. **com″-pre-hen′si-ble-ness‡.**— **com″pre-hen′-si-bl**(e**r**, *a.* Capable of being comprehended;

conceivable.— **com″pre·hen′si·bly,** *adv.*— **com″pre·hen′sion,** *n.* **1.** The act or power of comprehending; understanding. **2.** Inclusion; comprehensiveness.— **com″pre·hen′siv**(es, *a.* Large in scope; inclusive; broad. **-ly,** *adv.* **-ness,** *n.*

com·press′t, 1 kəm-pres′; 2 cŏm-prĕs′, *vt.* To press together; condense; concentrate. — **com·press′i·bil′i·ty,** *n.* **com·press′i·bl**(e·ness‡t.— **com·press′i·bl**(er, *a.* Capable of being compressed.— **com·pres′sion,** *n.* The act of compressing, or the state of being compressed.

com′press, 1 kŏm′pres; 2 cŏm′prĕs, *n.* A device for compressing.

com·prise′, 1 kəm-praiz′; 2 cŏm-prīg′, *vt.* [-PRISED′; -PRIS′ING.] To include; consist of; embrace. **com·prize′**‡.

com′pro·mise, 1 kŏm′pro-maiz; 2 cŏm′-pro-mīs. **I.** *vt. & vi.* [-MISED′; -MIS″ING.] **1.** To adjust or make a settlement by concessions. **2.** To expose to risk or suspicion. **II.** *n.* **1.** A settlement by mutual concession. **2.** The habit or spirit of concession. [Controller.

comp·trol′ler, 1 kən-trōl′ər; 2 cŏn-trōl′er, *n.*

com·pul′sion, 1 kəm-pul′shən; 2 cŏm-pŭl′shon, *n.* The act of compelling, or the state of being compelled; coercion. — **com·pul′siv**(es, *a.* Compelling, or tending to compel; compulsory. **-ly,** *adv.* **-ness,** *n.*—**com·pul′so·ry,** *a.* Compelling; coercive; enforced; forced. — **com·pul′so·ri·ly,** *adv.*— **com·pul′so·ri·ness,** *n.*

com·punc′tion, 1 kəm-puŋk′shən; 2 cŏm-pŭŋc′shon, *n.* Self-reproach; slight regret.

com·pute′, 1 kəm-piūt′; 2 cŏm-pūt′, *vt. & vi.* [-PUT′ED⁴; -PUT′ING.] To estimate numerically; calculate; reckon.— **com·put″a·bil″i·ty,** *n.* — **com·put′a·bl**(er, *a.* — **com″pu·ta′tion,** *n.* The act of computing; amount computed.— **com·put′er,** *n.*

com′rade, 1 kŏm′rad; 2 cŏm′rắd, *n.* An intimate companion or associate, as in arms.— **com′rade·ship,** *n.* **com′rade·ry**‡.

con, 1 kən; 2 cŏn, *vt.* [CONNED, COND⁵; CON′NING.] To study with care; peruse; learn.

con, *n. & adv.* The contrary; against.

con·cat′e·nate, 1 kən-kat′i-nēt; 2 cŏn-că̆t′e-nāt, *vt.* [-NAT″ED⁴; -NAT″ING.] To link together; connect in a series.— **con·cat″e·na′tion,** *n.* A chain-like series.

con′cave, 1 kən′kēv; 2 cŏn′cāv. **I.** *a.* Hollow and rounded, as the interior of a sphere or circle. **II.** *n.* A concave surface; vault, as of heaven.— **con·cav′i·ty,** *n.* [-TIESᶻ, *pl.*] The state of being concave; a concave surface; hollow.

con·ceal′, 1 kən-sēl′; 2 cŏn-çēl′, *vt.* To hide; secrete.— **con·ceal′ment,** *n.* **1.** The act of

concealing, or state of being concealed. **2.** A hiding-place.

con·cede′, 1 kən-sīd′; 2 cŏn-çēd′, *vt.* [-CED′ED⁴; -CED′ING.] To yield; acknowledge; admit.

con·ceit′, 1 kən-sīt′; 2 cŏn-çēt′, *n.* **1.** Overweening self-esteem. **2.** A fancy; clever thought or expression. **3.** Apprehension; understanding.— **con·ceit′ed,** *pa.* Having an excessive opinion of oneself; vain. **-ly,** *adv.*

con·ceiv(er, 1 kən-sīv′; 2 cŏn-çēv′, *vt. & vi.* [-CEIV(E)D′s; -CEIV′ING.] **1.** To form an idea of; think; imagine. **2.** To become pregnant; engender; originate.— **con·ceiv′a·bl**(er, *a.*— **con·ceiv′a·bly,** *adv.*

con′cen·trate, 1 kən′sen-trēt *or* kən-sen′trĕt; 2 cŏn′çĕn-trāt *or* cŏn-çĕn′trăt, *vt. & vi.* [-TRAT′ED⁴; -TRAT′ING.] To draw to a common center; condense; intensify.— **con″cen·tra′tion,** *n.* The act of concentrating, or that which is concentrated; condensation.

con·cen′tric, 1 kən-sen′trik; 2 cŏn-çĕn′tric, *a.* Having a common center. **con·cen′tri·cal**‡.

con′cept, 1 kən′sept; 2 cŏn′çĕpt, *n.* An abstract general notion; idea.

con·cep′tion, 1 kən-sep′shən; 2 cŏn-çĕp′shon, *n.* The act or faculty of conceiving or that which is conceived; an idea; notion

con·cern′, 1 kən-sūrn′; 2 cŏn-çẽrn′. **I.** *vt.* To relate or belong to; interest; affect; trouble. **II.** *n.* **1.** That which concerns one; affair; business; anxiety. **2.** Solicitude; interest.

con·cern′ing, 1 kən-sūrn′iŋ; 2 cŏn-çẽrn′-ing, *prep.* In relation to; about.

con·cert′d, 1 kən-sūrt′; 2 cŏn-çẽrt′, *vt.* To arrange in concert; contrive.

con′cert, 1 kən′sart; 2 cŏn′çert, *n.* **1.** A musical entertainment. **2.** Harmony; agreement.

con·cer′to, 1 kən-chér′to; 2 cŏn-chĕr′to, *n.* *Mus.* A musical composition in several parts, written with an orchestral accompaniment.

con·ces′sion, 1 kən-sesh′ən; 2 cŏn-çĕsh′on, *n.* The act of conceding, or that which is conceded.

conch, 1 kəŋk; 2 cŏŋe, *n.* A large marine shell.— **con·chol′dal,** 1 kəŋ-kŏl′dəl; 2 cŏŋ-cŏl′dal, *a.* Shell-shaped. **con′chold**‡.— **con·chol′o·gist,** 1 kəŋ-kŏl′o-jist; 2 cŏŋ-cŏl′o-gist, *n.* One versed in conchology.— **con·chol′o·gy,** *n.* The study of shells.

con·cil′i·ate, 1 kən-sil′i-ēt; 2 cŏn-çĭl′i-āt, *vt.* [-AT″ED⁴; -AT″ING.] To pacify; soothe; gain; win.— **con·cil′i·a′tion,** *n.*— **con·cil′i·a·to·ry,** *a.* Tending to conciliate.

1: ə = final; ɪ = habit; aisle; au = out; oil; iū = feud; chin; go; ŋ = sing; thin, this.
2: wọlf, dọ; bŏŏk, bōŏt; fųll, rųle, cūre, bŭt, bûrn; ŏil, bŏy; ḡo, ḡem; iŋk; thin, this.

con-cise', 1 kən-sais'; 2 cŏn-çīs', a. Expressing much in brief form; compact; terse. **-ly**, adv. **-ness**, n.

con'clave, 1 kon'klēv; 2 cŏn'clāv, n. A secret council.

con-clude', 1 kən-klūd'; 2 cŏn-clụd'. vt. & vi. [c_n-clud'ed^d; con-clud'ing.] **1.** To determine; decide; also, to infer; deduce. **2.** To terminate; finish; settle; end.

con-clu'sion, 1 ken-klū'ʒən; 2 cŏn-clụ'-zhon, n. The act of concluding; termination; end; inference; decision.

con-clu'siv(e^s, 1 ken-klū'sɪv; 2 cŏn-clụ'sɪv, a. Decisive; final. **-ly**, adv. **-ness**, n.

con-coct'^d, 1 ken-kokt'; 2 cŏn-cŏct', vt. To prepare by mixing ingredients; contrive; plan.— **con-coc'tion**, n. The act of concocting, or the thing concocted; contrivance; mixture.

con-com'i-tant, 1 ken-kom'ı-tənt; 2 cŏm'i-tant. **I.** a. Existing or occurring together; attendant. **II.** n. An attendant circumstance.— **con-com'i-tant-ly**, adv.

con'cord, 1 koŋ'kŏrd; 2 cŏŋ'côrd, n. Unity; agreement; harmony.

con-cor'dance, 1 kən-kōr'dəns; 2 cŏn-côr'danç, n. An index of words or topics, as of the Bible.

con-cor'dant, 1 ken-kōr'dənt; 2 cŏn-côr'dant, a. Existing in concord; consonant. **-ly**, adv.

con'course, 1 koŋ'[or ken']kōrs; 2 coŋ'-[or cŏn']çôrs, n. **1.** An assembling; assembly; throng. **2.** A place of assembly.

con-crete', 1 ken-krīt'; 2 cŏn-erēt', vt. & vi. [con-cret'ed^d; con-cret'ing.] To form into a hardened mass; coalesce; congeal; supply with concrete.

con'crete, 1 ken'krīt; 2 cŏn'erēt, a. **1.** Joined in or constituting a mass. **2.** Actually existing; real; individual; particular. **3.** Made of concrete. **-ly**, adv. **-ness**, n.— **con-cre'tion**, n. The act of concreting; a hardened mass.

con'crete, n. **1.** A hardened mass, as of gravel and hydraulic cement. **2.** A concrete object.

con'cu-bine, 1 koŋ'kiu-bain; 2 cŏŋ'eū-bīn, n. A woman who cohabits with a man without marriage; a mistress.— **con-cu'bi-nage**, n.

con-cu'pis-cence, 1 ken-kiū'pɪs-ens; 2 cŏn-eū'pis-ênç, n. **1.** Undue or illicit sexual desire; lust. **2.** Any inordinate desire.— **con-cu'pis-cent**, a. Sensual.

con-cur', 1 ken-kūr'; 2 cŏn-eûr', vi. [con-curred', con-curd^s; con-cur'ring.] To come or happen together; agree; coincide; cooperate; unite.— **con-cur'rence**, 1 ken-kur'ens; 2 cŏn-eûr'ĕnç, n. Combination;

agreement; coincidence; approval; assent.— **con-cur'rent**, a. Occurring or acting together; coordinate; concomitant. **-ly**, adv.

con-cus'sion, 1 ken-kush'ən; 2 cŏn-eūsh'on, n. A violent shaking; shock; jar.

con-demn', 1 ken-dem'; 2 cŏn-dĕm', vt. **con-demn'**^s, } **1.** To speak against; declare guilty; censure; blame; sentence. **2.** To officially reject as unfit for use; also, to appropriate for public use; declare forfeited.— **con''dem-na'tion**, n. The act of condemning, or the state of being condemned. — **con-dem'na-to-ry**, a. Containing or expressing condemnation.

con-dense', 1 ken-dens'; 2 cŏn-dĕns', vt. & vi. [-densed'^t, -denst'^s; -dens'ing.] To make or become dense; compress; consolidate; abridge.— **con-den'sa-[or -ı-]bl**(e^r, a.— **con''den-sa'tion**, 1 kon''den-sē'shən; 2 cŏn''dĕn-sā'shon, n. The act of making dense or denser, or the state of being condensed; a product of condensing.— **con-dens'er**, 1 ken-dens'ər; 2 cŏn-dĕns'er, n.

con''de-scend'^d, 1 kon''dı-send'; 2 cŏn''de-sĕnd', vi. To be gracious, affable, or social, as with an inferior; deign.— **con''de-scend'ing**, pa. Showing condescension; gracious; patronizing. **-ly**, adv.— **con''de-scen'sion**, n. Graciousness or courtesy to inferiors.

con-dign', 1 ken-dain'; 2 cŏn-dīn', a. Well deserved; merited; deservedly severe. **-ly**, adv. **-ness**, n.

con'di-ment, 1 kon'dı-ment or -mənt; 2 cŏn'di-ment, n. A relish, spice, etc.

con-di'tion, 1 ken-dish'ən; 2 cŏn-dish'on. **I.** vt. To limit by conditions; be prerequisite to; require. **II.** n. **1.** The state of existence or of health; state of highest health. **2.** A modifying circumstance; a prerequisite. **3.** A grade or rank; high social position.— **con-di'tion-al**, a. Expressing or imposing conditions; not absolute.— **con-di'tion-al-ly**, adv.

con-di'tioned, 1 ken-dish'ənd; 2 cŏn-dish'ond, pa. **1.** Limited by conditions. **2.** Circumstanced; placed.

con-dole', 1 ken-dōl'; 2 cŏn-dōl', vi. [-doled'; dol'ing.] To express sympathy with another.— **con-do'lence**, n.

con-done', 1 ken-dōn'; 2 cŏn-dōn', vt. [-doned'; don'ing.] To treat as forgiven; forgive.— **con''do-na'tion**, n. Forgiveness.

con'dor, 1 ken'dor; 2 cŏn'dôr, n. A large vulture of the high Andes.

con-duce', 1 ken-diūs'; 2 cŏn-dūç', vt. [-duced'^t; duc'ing.] To help or tend toward a result; contribute.— **con-du'cɪv**(e^s, 1 ken-diū'sɪv; 2 cŏn-dū'çɪv, a. Contributing to a result; leading; helping. **-ly**, adv. **-ness**, n.

con·duct'd, 1 kən-dŭkt'; 2 cŏn-dŭet', *v.*
I. *t.* **1.** To guide; escort. **2.** To manage; carry on; also, to behave (oneself).
3. To transmit, as electricity. **II.** *i.* **1.**
To be a conductor. **2.** To direct; lead;
behave; act.— **con·duc'tion,** 1 kən-dŭk'shən;
2 cŏn-dŭe'shon, *n.* Transmission or conveyance, as of heat, etc.— **con"duc·tiv'i·ty,** *n.*
Power to conduct, as heat or electricity.—
con·duc'tor, *n.* **1.** A guide; leader; manager. **2.** A body having conducting power.
con'duct, 1 kon'dŭkt; 2 cŏn'dŭet, *n.* **1.**
Behavior. **2.** Escort; convoy; direction;
control; skilful management.
con'duit, 1 kon'dit *or* dwit; 2 cŏn'dit *or*
dwĭt, *n.* A means of conducting, as a tube
or pipe.
cone, 1 kōn; 2 cŏn, *n.* A solid figure that
tapers uniformly from a circular base to
a point; a scaly fruit, as of the pine, having such a shape.
con·fab'u·late, 1
kən-făb'yu-lēt; 2
cŏn-făb'yu-lāt, *vi.*
[-LAT'ED²; -LAT'-
ING.] To chat;
gossip; converse.
— **con·fab"u·la'-
tion,** *n.* Familiar
conversation; chat.

Cone of Pine-tree.

con·fec'tion, 1 kən-fek'shən; 2 cŏn-fĕe'-
shon, *n.* A sweetmeat; conserve. **con'-
fect‡.— con·fec'tion·er,** *n.* One who
makes or deals in confectionery.— **con·fec'-
tion·er·y,** *n.* [-IES², *pl.*] Candies, sweetmeats, etc., or a shop where they are sold.
con·fed'er·a·cy, 1 kən-fed'ər-ə-sı; 2 cŏn-
fĕd'er-a-çy, *n.* [-CIES², *pl.*] A number
of states or persons allied; a league; confederation.
con·fed'er·ate, 1 kən-fed'er-ēt; 2 cŏn-
fĕd'er-āt. **I.** *vt. & vi.* [-AT'ED^d; -AT'ING.]
To form or join in a confederacy. **II.** *a.*
Associated in a confederacy. **III.** *n.* An
ally; associate; accomplice.— **con·fed"er·a'-
tion,** *n.* **1.** The act of confederating. **2.**
A confederacy.
con·fer', 1 kən-fūr'; 2 cŏn-fēr', *v.* [-FERRED',
-FERD'²; -FER'RING.] **I.** *t.* To grant as a
benefit; bestow. **II.** *i.* To hold a conference; consult.— **con"fer·ee',** *n.* **1.** [U.S.]
A person taking part in a conference. **2.**
One upon whom something is conferred.
con'fer·ence, 1 kon'fər-ens; 2 cŏn'fer-ĕnç,
n. **1.** A meeting for counsel; an official
council. **2.** Conversation; discourse.
con·fess', 1 kən-fes'; 2 cŏn-fĕs', *v.* [CON-
FESSED'ᵗ, sometimes CON-FEST'; CON-
FESS'ING.] **I.** *t.* **1.** To acknowledge; own;
admit, as a fault or error. **2.** To avow.
3. To disclose; reveal. **II.** *i.* To make

acknowledgment.— **con·fess'ed·ly,** *adv.* By
confession; indisputably.— **con·fes'sion,** 1
kən-fesh'ən; 2 cŏn-fĕsh'on, *n.* The act of
confessing; avowal; acknowledgment; a creed.
— **con·fes'sion·al. I.** *a.* Pertaining to a confession. **II.** *n.* *R. C. Ch.* A priest's cabinet
for hearing confessions.— **con·fes'sor,** 1 kon-
fes'ər; 2 cŏn-fĕs'or, *n.* **1.** One who confesses
the Christian faith, as under persecution. **2.**
R. C. Ch. A priest who hears confessions; a
spiritual adviser.
con"fi·dant', 1 kon'fı-dant'; 2 cŏn'fĭ-dänt', *n.*
A person to whom secrets are entrusted.
— **con"fi·dante',** 1 kon'fı-dant'; 2 cŏn'fĭ-
dänt', *n. fem.*
con·fide', 1 kən-faid'; 2 cŏn-fīd', *v.* [CON-
FID'ED^d; CON-FID'ING.] **I.** *t.* To reveal in
trust or confidence; entrust (to). **II.** *i.*
To repose confidence (in).
con'fi·dence, 1 kon'fı-dens; 2 cŏn'fĭ-dĕnç,
n. **1.** Trust; reliance; belief in a person
or thing. **2.** Assurance; self-reliance. **3.**
Private communication; a secret.— **con'fi·-
dent,** 1 kon'fı-dent; 2 cŏn'fĭ-dĕnt, *a.* Having confidence; assured; self-reliant. **-ly,**
adv.— **con"fi·den'tial,** 1 kon"fı-den'shəl; 2
cŏn"fĭ-dĕn'shal, *a.* **1.** Having private relations with another; trusted; intimate. **2.**
Given in confidence; secret. **3.** Disposed to
confide.— **con"fi·den'tial·ly,** *adv.*
con·fig"u·ra'tion, 1 kon-fig"yur-ē'shən; 2
cŏn-fĭg"yur-ā'shon, *n.* Structural arrangement; figure; shape.
con·fine', 1 kən-faın'; 2 cŏn-fīn', *vt.* [CON-
FINED'; CON-FIN'ING.] To shut up; imprison; limit; restrict.— **con'fine,** 1 kon'fain;
2 cŏn'fīn, *n.* A boundary; limit; frontier.—
con·fine'less, *a.* Unbounded; boundless.—
con·fine'ment, *n.* The state of being confined; restraint; imprisonment.
con·firm', 1 kən-fūrm'; 2 cŏn-fĭrm', *vt.* **1.**
To verify; make certain; strengthen. **2.**
Law. To ratify; sanction. **3.** *Eccl.* To
receive into the church.— **con"fir·ma'tion,**
n. **1.** The act of confirming; that which
confirms; corroboration; proof. **2.** The rite
of full induction into certain churches.— **con·-
firm'a·to·ry,** 1 kən-fūrm'ə-to-ri; 2 cŏn-fĭrm'-
a-to-ry, *a.* Helping to confirm or establish.
con·firm'a·tiv(e²ᵗ.
con·fis'cate, 1 kən'fıs-kēt *or* kən-fis'kēt; 2
cŏn'fıs-cāt *or* cŏn-fis'cāt, *vt.* [-CAT'ED^d;
-CAT'ING.] *Law.* To appropriate as forfeited to the public use or treasury.— **con·fis'-
ca·ble**(e²ᵗ, *a.* Liable to confiscation. **con"fis-
cat'a·bl**(e²ᵗ.— **con"fis·cate,** *a.* Confiscated
or forfeited.— **con"fis·ca'tion,**n. Forfeiture
or appropriation to public use.
con"fla·gra'tion, 1 kən'flə-grē'shən; 2
cŏn"fla-grā'shon, *n.* A great or extensive
fire.
con·flict'd, 1 kən-flikt'; 2 cŏn-flĭet', *vi.*

To come into collision; be in mutual opposition; contend.　[contest; strife.
con'flict, 1 kən'flikt; 2 cŏn'flĭct, *n.* A
con'flu-ent, 1 kŏn'flu-ent; 2 cŏn'flu-ĕnt.
I. *a.* Flowing together; blended. **II.** *n.*
A branch of a river.— **con'flu-ence**, *n.* A
junction of streams; union.

con-form', 1 kən-fôrm'; 2 cŏn-fôrm', *v.* **1.**
t. To make like in form; with *to.* **II.** *i.*
To act in accord; correspond; comply.
— **con-form'a-ble**(ᵉᵖ, *a.* Being in conformity; correspondent; compliant; obedient.—
con-form'a-bly, *adv.*— **con''for-ma'tion**,
n. General structure, form, or outline.—
con-form'i-ty, *n.* Correspondence; agreement; acquiescence.

con-found'ᵈ, 1 kən-found'; 2 cŏn-found',
vt. **1.** To strike with confusion; amaze;
perplex; overwhelm; abash. **2.** To confuse with something else; mix.

con''fra-ter'ni-ty, 1 kŏn''frä-tûr'nĭ-tĭ; 2
cŏn''fra-tēr'nĭ-ty, *n.* [-TIESᶻ, *pl.*] An
association; brotherhood.

con-front'ᵈ,) 1 kən-frunt'; 2 cŏn-frŏnt',
con-frunt'ᵖ,) *vt.* To stand face to face
with; face defiantly; put face to face.

con-fuse', 1 kən-fiūz'; 2 cŏn-fūs', *vt.* [CON-
FUSED'; CON-FUS'ING.] **1.** To perplex; bewilder; disconcert. **2.** To mix in disorder; derange.— **con-fus'ed-ly**, *adv.*—
con-fu'sion, 1 kən-fiū'ʒən; 2 cŏn-fū'zhon, *n.*
The act of confusing, or the state of being
confused; perplexity; distraction; embarrassment; shame.

con-fute', 1 kən-fiūt'; 2 cŏn-fūt', *vt.* [CON-
FUT'EDᵈ; CON-FUT'ING.] **1.** To prove
false; refute. **2.** To prove (a person) to be
in error.— **con'fu-ta'tion**, *n.* The act of
confuting; disproof.

con''gé', 1 kŏn'ʒē'; 2 cŏn'zhē', *n.* **1.** Leave-
taking; parting. **2.** Dismissal. **con''gee'**‡.

con-geal', 1 kən-jīl'; 2 cŏn-gēl', *v.* & *vi.*
To change from a fluid to a solid condition; coagulate; harden; freeze.— **con''ge-
la'tion**, *n.* A congealing; clot; concretion.

con'ge-ner, 1 kən'jĭ-nər; 2 cŏn'ge-nẽr. *n.*
A member of the same genus or kind with
another.

con-ge'nial, 1 kən-jīn'yəl; 2 cŏn-ḡẽn'yal, *a.*
Having similar character or tastes: sympathetic; agreeable.— **con-ge''ni-al'i-ty**, *n.*
—**con-ge'nial-ly**, *adv.*

con-gen'i-tal, 1 kən-jen'ĭ-təl; 2 cŏn-ḡẽn'ĭ-
tal, *a.* Born with one; existing from
birth.— **con-gen'i-tal-ly**, *adv.*

con-gest'ᵈ, 1 kən-jest'; 2 cŏn-ḡĕst', *vi.* To
become overcrowded.— **con-ges'tion**, 1 kən-
jes'chən; 2 cŏn-ḡĕs'chon, *n.* An excessive
accumulation; crowding; thickening.— **con-
ges'tiv**(eˢ, *a.* Pertaining to, characterized
by, or indicative of congestion.

con-glom'er-ate, 1 kən-glŏm'ər-ēt; 2 cŏn-
glŏm'er-āt. **I.** *vt.* & *vi.* [-AT"EDᵈ;
-AT'ING.] To gather into a cohering mass.
II. 1 kən-glŏm'ər-ĭt; 2 cŏn-glŏm'er-at, *a.*
Massed or clustered; heterogeneous. **III.**
n. A heterogeneous collection; a rock
composed of pebbles loosely cemented together.— **con-glom''er-a'tion**, *n.* **1.** A
conglomerated mass. **2.** The act of conglomerating.

con-grat'u-late, 1 kən-grach'u-[or -grat'-
yu-]lēt; 2 cŏn-grăch'u-[or -grăt'yu-]lāt, *vt.*
[-LAT"EDᵈ; -LAT'ING.] To express sympathetic pleasure in the joy or good fortune of (another).— **con-grat''u-la'tion**, *n.*
The act of congratulating; a congratulatory expression.— **con-grat'u-la-to-ry**, *a.*
Expressing congratulation.

con'gre-gate, 1 kŏn'grĭ-gēt; 2 cŏn'ḡrē-gāt,
vt. & *vi.* [-GAT"EDᵈ; -GAT'ING.] To bring
or come together into a crowd; assemble.

con''gre-ga'tion, 1 kŏn'grĭ-gē'shən; 2
cŏn''ḡrē-gā'shon, *n.* **1.** The act of congregating. **2.** An assemblage, as for worship; a religious body.

con''gre-ga'tion-al, 1 kŏn'grĭ-gē'shən-əl;
2 cŏn''ḡrē-gā'shon-al, *a.* **1.** Pertaining to
a congregation. **2.** [-C-] Pertaining to
Congregationalism or to the Congregationalists.— **con''gre-ga'tion-al-ism**, *n.*
The church polity that makes the authority
of the local congregation supreme within its
own domain, or [-C-] the religious denomination founded on that polity.— **Con''gre-ga'-
tion-al-ist**, *n.* A member of the Congregational denomination.

con'gress, 1 kŏn'gres; 2 cŏn'grĕs, *n.* **1.**
An assembly; conference; meeting; intercourse. **2.** [-C-] The national legislative
body of the United States.— **con-gres'sion-
al**, *a.* Pertaining to a congress, especially
[-C-] the United States Congress.— **Con'-
gress-man**, *n.* [-MEN, *pl.*] A member of
the United States Congress.— **Con'gress-
wo"man**. A woman elected to Congress.

con'gru-ent, 1 kŏn'gru-ent; 2 cŏn'gru-ĕnt,
a. Having mutual agreement, as figures
or propositions; correspondent. **-ly**, *adv.*—
con'gru-ence, *n.* **con'gru-en-cy**‡.

con'gru-ous, 1 kŏn'gru-us; 2 cŏn'gru-ŭs,
a. Harmoniously related or combined;
appropriate; consistent. **-ly**, *adv.*— **con-
gru'i-ty**, 1 kən-gru'ĭ-tĭ; 2 cŏn-grū'ĭ-ty, *n.*
[-TIESᶻ, *pl.*] Harmoniousness; appropriateness.
con'gru-ous-ness‡.

con'ic, 1 kŏn'ĭk; 2 cŏn'ĭc, *a.* Cone-shaped.
con'i-cal‡.　　　　[*a.* Cone-bearing.

co-nif'er-ous, 1 ko-nĭf'ər-us; 2 co-nĭf'er-ŭs,

con-jec'ture, 1 kən-jek'chur *or* -tiur; 2
cŏn-jĕc'chur *or* -tūr. **I.** *vt.* & *vi.* [-TURED;
-TUR-ING.] To surmise; guess. **II.** *n.*

An indecisive opinion; a guess; surmise. — **con-jec'tur-al,** *a.* Of the nature of or dependent on conjecture.

con-join', 1 kən-join'; 2 eŏn-join', *vt. & vi.* To join together; associate; unite. — **con-joint',** *a.* Associated; conjoined.

con'ju-gal, 1 kŏn'ju-gəl; 2 eŏn'ju-găl, *a.* Pertaining to marriage; matrimonial. **-ly,** *adv.*

con'ju-gate, 1 kŏn'ju-gēt; 2 eŏn'ju-găt. **I,** *vt.* [-GAT°ED⁴; -GAT'ING.] To give the modes, tenses, etc., of (a verb). **II,** *a.* Joined in pairs; coupled; paired.— **con'-ju-ga'tion,** *n.* 1. Conjunction; union. 2. *Gram.* The inflection of a verb.

con-junc'tion, 1 kən-juŋk'shən; 2 eŏn-jŭŋe'shon, *n.* 1. A joining; combination; league. 2. A part of speech that connects words, clauses, and sentences. 3. The nearest apparent approach of two heavenly bodies to each other.— **con-junc'tiv(e⁵,** *a.* Joining or joined together.— **con-junc'ture,** 1 kən-juŋk'chur or -tiur; 2 eŏn-jŭŋe'chur or -tūr, *n.* 1. A combination of circumstances; juncture; crisis. 2. The act of joining; union.

con''ju-ra'tion, 1 kŏn''ju-rē'shən; 2 eŏn'-ju-rä'shon, *n.* 1. A solemn invocation. 2. An incantation; spell.

con'jure, 1 kun'jər; 2 eŏn'jur, *vt. & vi.* [CON'JURED; CON'JUR-ING.] To effect or control by magic art; practise magic.— **con'jur-er,** *n.* A juggler.

con-jure'², 1 kən-jūr'; 2 eŏn-jur', *v.* [CON-JURED; CON-JUR'ING.] **I.** *t.* To appeal to solemnly, as in the name of God; adjure. **II.** *i.* To bind oneself by oath with others.

con-nate', 1 kə-nēt'; 2 eŏ-nāt', *a.* Born in and with one; innate; congenital.

con-nect'⁴, 1 kə-nekt'; 2 eŏ-nĕet', *vt. & vi.* To join, unite, or combine; associate or be associated.— **con-nect'ed-ly,** *adv.* Jointly; coherently.— **con-nec'tion,** 1 kə-nek'-shən; 2 eŏ-nĕe'shon, *n.* 1. The act of connecting; union; direct transfer, as by rail. 2. Family relationship; a relative. 3. A company; denomination.— **con-nec'tiv(e⁵,** *a.* Capable of connecting; causing or involving connection. **-ly,** *adv.*— **con-nec'tor,** *n.*

con-nex'ion, etc. Same as CONNECTION, etc.

con'ning-tow"er, 1 kŏn'ıŋ-tau"ər; 2 eŏn'ıŋe-tow"er, *n.* The low shot-proof pilot-house of a war-vessel.

con-nive', 1 kə-naiv'; 2 eŏ-nīv', *vi.* [-NIVED'; -NIV'ING.] 1. To encourage wrong by silence: followed by *at.* 2. To be in collusion: followed by *with.*— **con-ni'vance,** *n.*

con''nois-seur', 1 kŏn''ı-sūr'; 2 eŏn'ı-sûr', *n.* A competent critical judge of art.

con'no-tate, 1 kŏn'o-tēt; 2 eŏn'o-tăt, *vt. & vi.* [-TAT°ED⁴; -TAT'ING.] To indicate indirectly or by implication: opposed to *denote.* **con-note'‡.— con''no-ta'tion,** *n.*— **con-no'ta-tiv(e⁵,** *a.*

con-nu'bi-al, 1 kə-niū'bɪ-əl; 2 eŏ-nū'bi-al, *a.* Pertaining to matrimony; matrimonial; conjugal.

con'quer, 1 kŏŋ'kər; 2 eŏŋ'ker, *v.* **I.** *t.* 1. To overcome; subdue; vanquish. 2. To obtain as in war, or by any conflict. **II.** *i.* To be victorious.— **con'quer-a-bl(e⁵,** *a.*— **con'quer-or,** *n.*

con'quest, 1 kŏŋ'kwest; 2 eŏŋ'kwĕst, *n.* The act of conquering; the thing conquered.

con''san-guin'e-ous, 1 kŏn''san-gwın'ı-us; 2 eŏn'săn-gwīn'e-ŭs, *a.* Descended from the same parent or ancestor.— **con''san-guin'i-ty,** *n.* Blood-relationship.

con'science, 1 kŏn'shens; 2 eŏn'shĕŋe, *n.* The faculty which distinguishes between right and wrong; moral sense.— **con''sci-en'-tious,** 1 kŏn''si-en'shus; 2 eŏn'si-ĕn'shŭs, *a.* Governed or dictated by conscience. **-ly,** *adv.* **-ness,** *n.*

con'scion-a-bl(e⁵, 1 kŏn'shən-a-bl; 2 eŏn'-shon-a-bl, *a.* Conformable to conscience; right; just.— **con'scion-a-bly,** *adv.*

con'scious, 1 kŏn'shus; 2 eŏn'shŭs, *a.* 1. Knowing one's own existence and mental operations. 2. Unduly self-conscious. 3. Cognizant; aware. 4. Present to the mind. — **con'scious-ly,** *adv.*— **con'scious-ness,** *n.* The state of being conscious; sensation; knowledge; the power of self-knowledge.

con-script'⁴, 1 kən-skript'; 2 eŏn-serîpt', *vt.* To force into military service; draft.

con'script, 1 kŏn'skript; 2 eŏn'serîpt. **I.** *a.* Registered; enrolled. **II.** *n.* One who is compulsorily enrolled for military service.— **con-scrip'tion,** *n.* A compulsory enrolment of men for military service; draft.

con'se-crate, 1 kŏn'sı-krēt; 2 eŏn'se-erăt, *vt.* [-CRAT°ED⁴; -CRAT'ING.] To appropriate to sacred uses; devote; dedicate; hallow.— **con''se-cra'tion,** *n.* Devotion to a sacred purpose.

con-sec'u-tiv(e⁵, 1 kən-sek'yu-tiv; 2 eŏn-sĕe'yu-tîv, *a.* 1. Following in order without a break; successive. 2. Consequent.— **con-sec''u-tiv(e-ly⁵,** *adv.*— **con-sec'u-tiv(e-ness⁵,** *n.*

con-sen'sus, 1 kən-sen'sus; 2 eŏn-sĕn'sŭs, *n.* A general agreement.

con-sent', 1 kən-sent'; 2 eŏn-sĕnt'. **I⁴.** *vi.* To yield voluntarily; accede; acquiesce. **II.** *n.* 1. A voluntary yielding; compliance. 2. Agreement; concord.

con''sen-ta'ne-ous, 1 kŏn''sen-tē'nı-us; 2

cŏn′sĕn-tā′ne-ŭs, *a.* Mutually consenting; acquiescent.

con-sen′tient, 1 kən-sen′shent; 2 cŏn-sĕn′shĕnt, *a.* Mutually agreeing.

con′se-quence, 1 kon′sı̆-kwens; 2 cŏn′se-kwĕns, *n.* **1.** That which naturally follows. **2.** Distinction; importance.

con′se-quent, 1 kon′sı̆-kwent; 2 cŏn′se-kwĕnt, *a.* Following as a result or conclusion; logical.— **con′se-quent-ly,** *adv.* As a consequence; therefore.

con″se-quen′tial, 1 kon″sı̆-kwen′shəl; 2 cŏn″se-kwĕn′shal, *a.* **1.** Having or showing importance; self-important. **2.** Consequent. **-ly,** *adv.*

con-serve′(e′s, 1 kən-sûrv′; 2 cŏn-sĕrv′, *vt.* [-SERV(E)D′s; -SERV′ING.] To keep from loss, decay, or injury; preserve.— **con″serva′tion,** *n.* The act of conserving.— **conserv′a-tism,** *n.* Disposition to be conservative.— **con-ser′va-tiv(es.** I. *a.* **1.** Adhering to the existing order of things; opposed to change or progress. **2.** Conserving. II. *n.* A conservative person.— **con′ser-va′tor,** 1 kon′sər-vē′tər *or* -ter; 2 cŏn′ser-vā′tor, *n.* A protector; guardian.— **con-ser′va-to-ry.** I. *a.* Adapted to preserve. II. *n.* [-RIESᶻ, *pl.*] **1.** A glazed apartment for tender plants. **2.** A school of art or science.

con′serve, 1 kon′sûrv; 2 cŏn′sĕrv, *n.* Fruit preserved in sugar.

con-sid′er, 1 kən-sid′ər; 2 cŏn-sĭd′er, *v.* I. *t.* **1.** To reflect upon; ponder. **2.** To think to be; estimate; believe. **3.** To think well of; treat well. **4.** To make allowance for. II. *i.* To think closely; cogitate.— **con-sid′er-a-bl(eʳ,** *a.* Of noteworthy size, quantity, or importance; large; ample.— **con-sid′er-a-bly,** *adv.* To a considerable extent.— **con-sid′er-ate,** 1 kon-sid′ər-it; 2 cŏn-sĭd′er-at, *a.* Exhibiting consideration; thoughtful; kind; prudent. **-ly,** *adv.* **-ness,** *n.*

con-sid″er-a′tion, 1 kən-sid″ər-ē′shən; 2 cŏn-sĭd″er-ā′shon, *n.* **1.** The act of considering. **2.** Thoughtful and kindly feeling or treatment. **3.** A circumstance to be considered. **4.** Something given or paid; remuneration. **5.** Importance; consequence.

con-sid′er-ing, 1 kən-sid′ər-ıŋ; 2 cŏn-sĭd′er-ing, *prep.* In view of; taking all things into account.

con-sign′, 1 kən-sain′; 2 cŏn-sīn′, *vt.* To deliver; entrust; commit.— **con″sign-ee′,** 1 kon″sain-ī′; 2 cŏn″sĭn-ē′, *n.* One to whom property is consigned.— **con-sign′ment,** 1 kən-sain′ment *or* -mənt; 2 cŏn-sīn′ment, *n.* The consigning of property to a person, or property consigned.— **con″sign-or′,** 1 kon″sı̆-nôr′ *or* kon-sain′ər *or* -ər; 2 cŏn′sı̆-nôr′ *or* cŏn-sĭn′or, *n.* One who consigns or makes a consignment. **con-sign′er‡.**

con-sist′d, 1 kən-sist′; 2 cŏn-sĭst′, *vi.* **1.** To be made up: followed by *of.* **2.** To have as its substance or nature; be: followed by *in.* **3.** To harmonize: followed by *with.* **4.** To stand together; subsist.

con-sis′tent, 1 kən-sis′tent; 2 cŏn-sĭs′tĕnt, *a.* **1.** Agreeing with itself; not self-contradictory. **2.** Congruous; compatible. **3.** Firmly united; solid. **-ly,** *adv.*— **con-sis′tence, con-sis′ten-cy,** *n.* [-CESᶻ or -CIESᶻ, *pl.*] **1.** Harmony between things, acts, or statements. **2.** Degree of firmness or density.

con-sis′to-ry, 1 ken-sis′to-rı; 2 cŏn-sĭs′to-ry, *n.* [-RIESᶻ, *pl.*] An ecclesiastical court.— **con′sis-to′ri-al,** *a.*

con-sole′, 1 kən-sōl′; 2 cŏn-sōl′. *vt.* [-SOLED′; -SOL′ING.] To comfort; solace; cheer.— **con-sol′a-bl(eʳ,** *a.* That may be consoled.— **con″so-la′tion,** *n.* The act of consoling, or the state of being consoled; something that comforts or consoles.— **con-sol′a-to-ry,** 1 kon-sŏl′ə-to-rı; 2 cŏn-sŏl′a-to-ry, *a.* Tending to console.

con′sole, 1 kon′sōl; 2 cŏn′sōl, *n.* A bracket; a corbel.

con-sol′i-date, 1 kən-sŏl′ı-dēt; 2 cŏn-sŏl′ı-dāt, *v.* [-DAT″EDd; -DAT″ING.] I. *t.* To make solid or firm; unite. II. *i.* To become united, solid, or firm.— **con-sol″i-da′tion,** *n.*

con-sols′, 1 kən-solz′; 2 cŏn-sŏlz′, *n. pl.* A contraction for "consolidated annuities," a British governmental security.

con″som-mé′, 1 kŏn″so-mē′; 2 cŏn″so-mę́, *n.* Clear meat soup.

con′so-nant, 1 kon′so-nant; 2 cŏn′so-nant. I. *a.* **1.** Being in harmony; consistent. **2.** Consonantal. II. *n.* An alphabetic sound not easily uttered without a vowel; a letter representing such a sound. **-ly,** *adv.*— **con′so-nance,** *n.* Agreement; accord; concord. **con′so-nan-cy‡.**

con-sort′d, 1 kən-sôrt′; 2 cŏn-sôrt′, *vt. & vi.* To join; associate.

con′sort, 1 kon′sôrt; 2 cŏn′sôrt, *n.* A companion; a husband or wife; a ship that accompanies another; company.

con-spec′tus, 1 kon-spek′tus; 2 cŏn-spĕc′tŭs, *n.* A general view; summary.

con-spic′u-ous, 1 kon-spik′yu-us; 2 cŏn-spĭc′yu-ŭs, *a.* Clearly visible; prominent; obvious; striking. **-ly,** *adv.* **-ness,** *n.*

con-spire′, 1 kən-spair′; 2 cŏn-spīr′, *vt. & vi.* [CON-SPIRED′; CON-SPIR′ING.] **1.** To plot; form a conspiracy. **2.** To concur.— **con-spir′a-cy,** 1 kən-spir′ə-sı; 2 cŏn-spĭr′a-çy, *n.* [-CIESᶻ, *pl.*] A secret combination, especially for an evil purpose; plot.— **con-spir′a-tor,** *n.* One who engages in a conspiracy.— **con-spir′er,** *n.*

con′sta-bl(eᵖ, 1 kun′stə-bl; 2 eŏn-stā-bl, *n.*
1. A police officer. **2.** Anciently, a high
military officer.—**con′sta-ble-ship,** *n.*— **con-
stab′u-la-ry,** 1 kən-stab′yu-lē-rī; 2 eŏn-stăb′-
yu-lā-ry. **I.** *a.* Pertaining to or consisting
of constables. **II.** *n.* [-RIES²*, pl.*] Constables
collectively; a military police force.

con′stan-cy, 1 kŏn′stan-sı; 2 eŏn′stan-çy,
n. Steadiness; faithfulness; stability.

con′stant, 1 kŏn′stənt; 2 eŏn′stant, *a.*
Steady; persevering; faithful; invariable.

con″stel-la′tion, 1 kŏn″ste-lē′shən; 2 eŏn″-
stĕ-lā′shon, *n.* A cluster
of stars.

con″ster-na′tion, 1 kŏn″stər-
nē′shən; 2 eŏn″ster-nā′-
shon, *n.* Sudden over-
whelming fear.

con′sti-pate, 1 kŏn′stı-pēt;
2 eŏn′stı-pāt, *vt.* [-PAT″ED**d**;
-PAT″ING.] To fill and stop (the bowels).
— **con″sti-pa′tion,** *n.*

con-stit′u-ent, 1 kən-stit′yu-ent; 2 eŏn-
stĭt′yu-ĕnt. **I.** *a.* Being a constituent;
composing. **II.** *n.* **1.** One represented;
a voter; a client. **2.** A necessary part.
— **con-stit′u-en-cy,** 1 kən-stit′yu-en-sı; 2
eŏn-stĭt′yu-ĕn-çy, *n.* [-CIES², *pl.*] A body
of constituents.

con′sti-tute, 1 kŏn′stı-tiūt; 2 eŏn′stı-tūt,
vt. [-TUT″ED**d**; -TUT″ING.] **1.** To make
up; frame; compose. **2.** To establish;
enact; appoint.— **con′sti-tu″tiv(e**ˢ, *a.* Helping or having power to constitute.

con″sti-tu′tion, 1 kŏn″stı-tiū′shən; 2 eŏn″-
stı-tū′shon, *n.* **1.** The act of constituting.
2. A system of related parts; composition;
bodily frame or temperament; the organic
law, as of a State.— **con″sti-tu′tion-al,** *a.*
Pertaining to, consistent with, or controlled
by a constitution; lawful.— **con″sti-tu″tion-
al′i-ty,** *n.* Accordance with a constitution;
lawfulness. — **con″sti-tu′tion-al-ly,** *adv.*

con-strain′, 1 kən-strēn′; 2 eŏn-strān′, *vt.*
To compel; urge; oblige; compress.— **con-
strain(e)d′s,** *pa.* Compulsory; repressed.
— **con-strain′ed-ly,** *adv.*— **con-straint′,**
1 kən-strēnt′; 2 eŏn-strānt′, *a.* Compulsion; repression; embarrassment.

con-strict′d, 1 kən-strikt′; 2 eŏn-strĭct′, *vt.*
To compress; bind; cramp.— **con-stric′tion,**
n. A constricting; or a constricted part.—
con-stric′tiv(eˢ, *a.* Tending to constrict.
— **con-stric′tor,** *n.* That which constricts;
a serpent, as a boa, that crushes its prey.

con-struct′d, 1 kən-strukt′; 2 eŏn-strŭet′,
vt. To put together; build; arrange; make.
— **con-struct′er, con-struc′tor,** *n.*— **con-
struc′tion,** *n.* **1.** The act of constructing; a
structure. **2.** Style of building; grammatical arrangement and relation of words. **3.**

The act of construing; interpretation; meaning.— **con-struc′tiv(e**ˢ, *a.* **1.** Involving or
tending to construction; positive; affirmative.
2. Depending on inference rather than explicit statement or established fact. **-ly,** *adv*
— **con-struc′tiv(e-ness**ˢ, *n.* The faculty of
construction; mechanical ability.

con′strue, 1 kŏn′strū *or* kən-strū′; 2 eŏn′-
strụ *or* eŏn-strụ′, *vt.* & *vi.* [CON′STRUED;
CON′STRU″ING.] To translate; interpret;
explain.

con′sul, 1 kŏn′sul; 2 eŏn′sŭl, *n.* **1.** An
officer representing his country in a
foreign port or city. **2.** A chief magistrate of ancient Rome, or of the French
republic (1799–1804).— **con′su-lar,** 1 kŏn′-
slu-lar; 2 eŏn′sū-lar, *a.* Pertaining to a consul.
— **con′su-late,** *n.* **1.** The office or term of
office of a consul. **con′sul-ship‡.** **2.** The
official place of business of a consul.

con-sult′d, 1 kən-sult′; 2 eŏn-sŭlt′, *v.* **I.** *t.*
To ask the advice of; regard; consider.
II. *i.* To ask advice; take counsel: followed by *with*.— **con″sul-ta′tion,** *n.* The
act of consulting; a conference.

con-sume′, 1 kən-siūm′; 2 eŏn-sūm′, *vt.* &
vi. [CON-SUMED′; CON-SUM′ING.] To destroy or disappear gradually, as by burning; waste; spend.— **con-sum′er,** *n.*

con′sum-mate, 1 kŏn′su-mēt; 2 eŏn′sŭ-
māt, *vt.* [-MAT″ED**d**; -MAT″ING.] To bring
to completion.— **con-sum′mate,** 1 kən-
sum′it; 2 eŏn-sŭm′at, *a.* Of the highest degree; perfect; complete. **-ly,** *adv.*— **con″-
sum-ma′tion,** *n.* Completion; perfection.

con-sump′tion, 1 kən-sump′shan; 2 eŏn-
sŭmp′shon, *n.* **1.** The act or process of
consuming. **2.** *Med.* A wasting disease;
phthisis.— **con-sump′tiv(e**ˢ. **I.** *a.* Tending
to, causing, or affected with consumption.
II. *n.* A person affected by phthisis. **-ly,**
adv. **-ness,** *n.*

con′tact, 1 kŏn′takt; 2 eŏn′tăet, *n.* The
coming together of two bodies.

con-ta′gion, 1 kən-tē′jən; 2 eŏn-tā′gon,
n. The communication of disease, as
by contact; pestilence; plague.

con-ta′gious, 1 kən-tē′jus; 2 eŏn-tā′gŭs, *a.*
Transmissible, as a disease; catching;
spreading; pestilential. **-ly,** *adv.* **-ness,** *n.*

con-tain′, 1 kən-tēn′; 2 eŏn-tān′, *vt.* **1.**
To have room for; hold; enclose. **2.** To
restrain.

con-tam′i-nate, 1 kən-tam′i-nēt; 2 eŏn-
tăm′i-nāt, *vt.* [-NAT″ED**d**; -NAT″ING.] To
make impure by contact or admixture;
taint; defile; pollute.— **con-tam″i-na′tion,**
n. A contaminating; taint.

con-temn′, } 1 kən-tem′; 2 eŏn-tĕm′, *vt.*
con-tems, } To despise; scorn.— **c o n-
tem′ner,** *n.*

con'tem-plate, 1 kən'tem-plēt or kən-tem'-plēt; 2 cŏn'tĕm-plāt or cŏn-tĕm'plāt, vt. & vi. [-PLAT'ED⁴; -PLAT'ING.] To look at attentively; consider; meditate; muse. — **con'tem-pla'tion,** n. The act of contemplating; meditation.— **con-tem'pla-tiv(e⁵,** a. Given or pertaining to contemplation.

con-tem'po-ra'ne-ous, 1 kən-tem"po-rē'-ni-us; 2 cŏn-tĕm"po-rā'ne-ŭs, a. Living or occurring at the same time. -ly, adv. -ness, n.

con-tem'po-ra-ry, 1 kən-tem'po-rē-ri; 2 cŏn-tĕm'po-rā-ry. I. a. Contemporaneous. II. n. [-RIES².] A person living at the same time with another or with others.

con-tempt', 1 kən-tempt'; 2 cŏn-tĕmpt', n. The act of despising; disdain; scorn; disregard; disgrace; shame.— **con-tempt'l-bil'-i-ty,** n. **con-tempt'l-bl(e-ness⁵‡.**— **con-tempt'l-bl(e⁵,** a. Deserving of contempt; despicable; vile.— **con-temp't'l-bly,** adv.— **con-temp'tu-ous,** 1 kən-temp'chu-[or -tiu-]us; 2 cŏn-tĕmp'chu-[or -tū-]ŭs, a. Showing, feeling, or expressing contempt; disdainful. -ly, adv. -ness, n.

con-tend'd, 1 kən-tend'; 2 cŏn-tĕnd', v. I. t. To maintain in argument. II. i. To struggle; strive; debate; dispute.

con-tent'd, 1 kən-tent'; 2 cŏn-tĕnt', vt. To satisfy.— **con-tent'ed,** pa. Satisfied with things as they are; resigned; willing. -ly, adv. -ness, n.

con-tent', a. Contented; satisfied.

con-tent'¹, n. Rest of mind; satisfaction; contentment.

con'tent², 1 kən'tent; 2 cŏn'tĕnt, n. All that a thing contains: usually in the plural.

con-ten'tion, 1 kən-ten'shən; 2 cŏn-tĕn'-shon, n. The act of contending; strife; conflict; dispute; a matter in controversy.

con-ten'tious, 1 kən-ten'shus; 2 cŏn-tĕn'shŭs, a. Given to contention; quarrelsome. -ly, adv. -ness, n.

con-tent'ment, 1 kən-tent'ment or -mənt; 2 cŏn-tĕnt'ment, ×. The state of being contented.

con-ter'mi-nous, 1 kən-tûr'mi-nus; 2 cŏn-tĕr'mi-nŭs, a. Having a common boundary-line; coextensive. **con-ter'mi-nal‡.**

con-test'd, 1 kən-test'; 2 cŏn-tĕst', v. I. t. To dispute; strive to win. II. i. To contend strenuously.

con'test, 1 kən'test; 2 cŏn'tĕst, n. A struggle; conflict.— **con-tes'tant,** n. One who contests.

con'text, 1 kən'tekst; 2 cŏn'tĕkst, n. The portions associated with a passage quoted; connection.— **con-tex'tu-al,** a. -ly, adv.

con-tex'ture, 1 kən-teks'chur or -tiur; 2

eŏn-tĕks'chụr or -tūr, n. Texture.— **con-tex'tur-al,** a.

con-tig'u-ous, 1 kən-tig'yu-us; 2 eŏn-tĭg'-yụ-ŭs, a. Touching at the edge; adjacent. -ly, adv. -ness, n.— **con'ti-gu'l-ty,** 1 kən'ti-gū'i-ti; 2 eŏn'ti-gū'i-ty, n. Nearness; contact; continuity.

con'ti-nent, 1 kən'ti-nent; 2 eŏn'ti-nĕnt, a. self-restrained; abstinent; chaste. -ly, adv. — **con'ti-nence, -nen-cy,** n. Self-restraint; chastity.

con'ti-nent, n. One of the great bodies of land on the globe.— **con'ti-nen'tal,** a.

con-tin'gent, 1 kən-tin'jent; 2 eŏn-tĭn'gĕnt. I. a. Likely but not certain to occur: probable. II. n. 1. A contingency. 2. A quota, as of troops. -ly, adv.— **con-tin'gen-cy,** 1 kən-tin'jen-si; 2 eŏn-tĭn'gĕn-çy, n. [-CIES², pl.] A contingent event. **con-tin'gence‡.**

con-tin'u-al, 1 kən-tin'yu-al; 2 eŏn-tĭn'-yụ-al, a. 1. Constantly renewed; often repeated. 2. Continuous. -ly, adv.

con-tin'ue, 1 kən-tin'yu; 2 eŏn-tĭn'yụ, v. [-UED; -U-ING.] I. t. To extend or prolong. II. i. To be durable; last; endure; abide; keep on; persist.— **con-tin'u-ance,** n. The state of continuing; duration; succession; survival.— **con-tin'u-a'tion,** n. The act of continuing; an addition.

con-tin'u-ous, 1 kən-tin'yu-us; 2 eŏn-tĭn'yụ-ŭs, a. Connected without a break; unbroken; uninterrupted. -ly, adv. -ness, n.— **con'ti-nu'l-ty,** 1 kən'ti-niū'i-ti; 2 eŏn'-ti-nū'i-ty, n. The state or quality of being continuous.

con-tort'd, 1 kən-tört'; 2 eŏn-tôrt', vt. To twist violently; wrench out of shape.— **con-tor'tion,** 1 kən-tör'shan; 2 eŏn-tôr'shon, n. The act of contorting; writhing, as of the limbs.— **con-tor'tiv(e⁵,** a.

con-tour', 1 kən-tūr' or kən'tūr; 2 eŏn-tụr' or eŏn'tụr, n. Outline.

con'tra-, prefix. Against; opposite; contrary; as, contradict, contraindicate.

con'tra-band, 1 kən'tra-band; 2 eŏn'tra-bănd. I. a. Prohibited, as by military law; forbidden. II. n. Contraband goods or trade.

con-tract'd, 1 kən-trakt'; 2 eŏn-trăet', v. I. t. 1. To draw together; narrow; limit; shorten; condense. 2. To take; become affected with, as a disease. 3. To arrange by contract. II. i. 1. To shrink. 2. To make a contract.— **con-tract'ed,** pa. Narrow; mean; scanty. -ly, adv. -ness, n. — **con-tract'l-bl(e⁵,** a. Capable of contraction. **con-trac'til(e⁵‡; con-trac'tiv(e⁵‡.**

con'tract, 1 kən'trakt; 2 eŏn'trăet, n. A formal agreement, or the writing containing it.

con-trac′tion, 1 kən-trak′shən: 2 cŏn-trăe′shon, *n.* **1.** The act of contracting, or the state of being contracted. **2.** That which is contracted.

con-trac′tor, 1 kən-trak′tər *or* -tẽr; 2 cŏn-trăe′tor, *n.* A party to a contract; one who works, builds, etc., under contract; a muscle that serves to contract.

con″tra-dict′d, 1 kən″trə-dikt′; 2 cŏn″-tra-dïct′, *v.* **I.** *t.* To deny; oppose by denial; be inconsistent with. **II.** *i.* To utter a contradiction.— **con″tra-dic′tion,** *n.* The act of contradicting; inconsistency; direct negation.— **con″tra-dic′to-ry. I.** *a.* Characterized by opposition; inconsistent; diametrically opposed. **II.** *n.* [-RIES²*, pl.*] A proposition that is the absolute denial of another.— **con″tra-dic′to-ri-ly,** *adv.*— **con″-tra-dic′to-ri-ness,** *n.*

con″tra-dis-tinct′, 1 kən″trə-dis-tiŋkt′; 2 cŏn″tra-dis-tïŋkt′, *a.* Distinct as having or indicating points of contrast.— **con″tra-dis-tinc′tion,** *n.* Distinction by contrary qualities or by contrast.— **con″tra-dis-tin′guish,** *vt.*

con″tra-in′di-cate, 1 kən″trə-in′dı-kēt; 2 cŏn″tra-ïn′di-cāt, *vt.* [-CAT′ED⁴; -CAT″ING.] *Med.* To indicate the contrary of.— **con″tra-in′di-cant,** *n.*— **con″tra-in′di-ca′tion,** *n.*

con-tral′to, 1 kən-tral′to *or* -träl′to; 2 cŏn-trăl′to *or* -träl′to, *n.* **1.** In singing, the part between soprano and tenor. **2.** A contralto singer.

con′tra-ry, 1 kən″trē-rı; 2 cŏn″trā-ry. **I.** *a.* Opposite; opposing; captious; perverse. **II.** *n.* [-RIES², *pl.*] One of two contrary things; the opposite.— **con″tra-ri′e-ty,** 1 kən″tra-rai′ı-tı; 2 cŏn″tra-rī′e-ty, *n.* [-TIES², *pl.*] **1.** The quality or state of being contrary. **2.** Something contrary; an inconsistency; a contrary.— **con′tra-ri-ly,** *adv.*— **con′tra-ri-ness,** *n.*— **con′tra-ri-wise,** *adv.* On the contrary; on the other hand; conversely.

con-trast′d, 1 kən-trast′; 2 kən-trast′, *v.* **I.** *t.* To compare in order to show unlikeness. **II.** *i.* To stand in opposition; show unlikeness.

con′trast, 1 kən′trast; 2 cŏn′trăst, *n.* Partial unlikeness between things compared; also, the things thus opposed.

con″tra-vene′, 1 kən″trə-vīn′; 2 cŏn″tra-vēn′, *vt.* [-VENED′; -VEN″ING.] To prevent or obstruct.— **con″tra-ven′tion,** *n.*

con″tre-temps′, 1 kŏn″trə-tän̈; 2 cŏn″tre-tän̈′, *n.* An awkward incident.

con-trib′ute, 1 kən-trib′yūt; 2 cŏn-trïb′-yụt, *v.* [-UT-ED⁴; -UT-ING.] **I.** *t.* To supply as part of a common stock; give in aid of some object. **II.** *i.* To share in effecting a result.— **con″tri-bu′tion,** *n.* The act of contributing; a gift; subscription.

— **con-trib′u-tor,** *n.* One who contributes.
— **con-trib′u-to-ry,** *a.* Contributing. **con-trib′u-tiv**(e)‡.

con′trite, 1 kən′trait; 2 cŏn′trït, *a.* Broken in spirit under a sense of sin; penitent. **-ly,** *adv.*— **con-tri′tion,** 1 kən-trish′ən; 2 cŏn-trïsh′on, *n.* Sincere sorrow for sin; repentance. **con′trite-ness‡.**

con-trive′, 1 kən-traiv′; 2 cŏn-trïv′, *vt. & vi.* [CON-TRIVED′; CON-TRIV″ING.] To plan ingeniously; invent; scheme; plot. — **con-tri′vance,** *n.* **1.** The act of contriving. **2.** An artifice; stratagem; device; invention. — **con-triv′er,** *n.*

con-trol′, 1 kən-trōl′; 2 cŏn-trōl′. **I.** *vt. & vi.* [CON-TROLLED′; CON-TROLD′ˢ; CON-TROL′LING.] To direct; govern; influence; regulate; manage. **II.** *n.* The act of controlling; influence; regulation; government; command.— **con-trol′ler,** *n.* One who controls; an officer to examine and verify accounts.

con′tro-ver″sy, 1 kən′tro-vũr″sı; 2 cŏn′-tro-vēr″sy, *n.* [-SIES², *pl.*] Debate; disputation; dispute.— **con″tro-ver′sial,** 1 kən″tro-vũr′shəl; 2 cŏn″tro-vẽr′shal, *a.* Pertaining to controversy; contentious.— **con″tro-ver′sial-ist,** *n.* A disputant.— **con′tro-ver′sial-ly,** *adv.*

con″tro-vert′d, 1 kən″tro-vũrt′; 2 cŏn″tro-vērt, *vt.* To argue against; oppose.

con′tu-ma-cy, 1 kən′tiu-mə-sı; 2 cŏn′tū-ma-çy, *n.* [-CIES², *pl.*] Insolent obstinacy.— **con″tu-ma′cious,** 1 kən″tiu-mē′-shus; 2 cŏn″tū-mā′shüs, *a.* Rebellious; refractory. **-ly,** *adv.* **-ness,** *n.*

con″tu-me-ly, 1 kən′tiu-mī-lı; 2 cŏn′tū-mē-ly, *n.* [-LIES², *pl.*] Scornful insolence.— **con″tu-me′li-ous,** 1 kən″tiu-mī′lı-us; 2 cŏn″tū-mē′li-ŭs, *a.* Scornfully offensive or insolent. **-ly,** *adv.*

con-tuse′, 1 kən-tiūz′; 2 cŏn-tūs′, *vt.* [CON-TUSED′; CON-TUS′ING.] To bruise by a blow.— **con-tu′sion,** 1 kən-tiū′zən; 2 cŏn-tū′zhon, *n.* The act of bruising; a bruise.

co-nun′drum, 1 ko-nun′drum; 2 co-nŭn′-drŭm, *n.* A riddle; perplexity.

con″va-lesce′, 1 kən″va-les′; 2 cŏn″va-lĕs′, *vi.* [-LESCED′ᵗ; -LESC″ING.] To recover after a sickness.— **con″va-les′cence,** *n.* Gradual recovery from illness.— **con″va-les′cent. I.** *a.* Recovering health after sickness. **II.** *n.* One who is convalescing.

con-vene′, 1 kən-vīn′; 2 cŏn-vēn′, *v.* [CON-VENED′; CON-VEN′ING.] **I.** *t.* To call together; convoke. **II.** *i.* To come together; assemble.

con-ve′nient, 1 kən-vī′nyent; 2 cŏn-vēn′-yĕnt, *a.* Suitable; handy; commodious; favorable; timely.— **con-ve′nience,** 1 kən-vīn′yens; 2 cŏn-vēn′yĕnç, *n.* Serviceableness;

suitableness; fitness; something convenient.
con-ve'nien-cy‡.— con-ve'nient-ly, *adv.*

con'vent, 1 kŏn'vent; 2 cŏn'vĕnt, *n.* A
body of monks or nuns, or the house
occupied by them.

con-ven'ti-cl(er, 1 kən-ven'ti-kl; 2 cŏn-
vĕn'ti-el, *n.* A religious meeting, as of
Scottish Covenanters.

con-ven'tion, 1 kən-ven'shən; 2 cŏn-vĕn'-
shon, *n.* A meeting: assembly; compact;
general consent.— **con-ven'tion-al,** *a.* Established by convention or custom; agreed;
customary: formal. **-ly,** *adv.*— **con-ven'-
tion-al-ism,** *n.* Regard for conventionality.
— **con-ven''tion-al'i-ty,** *n.* [-TIESᶻ, *pl.*] The
state of being conventional; a formality.

con-ven'tu-al, 1 kən-ven'chu-[or -tiu-]əl;
2 cŏn-vĕn'chu-[or -tū-]al, *a.* Belonging
to a convent.

con-verge', 1 kən-vūrj'; 2 cŏn-vĕrg', *vt.* &
vi. [CON-VERGED'; CON-VERG'ING.] To
draw toward one point; come together by
gradual approach.— **con-ver'gence,** *n.*—
con-ver'gent, *a.* Tending to one point.

con'ver-sant, 1 kɒn'ver-sənt; 2 cŏn'ver-
sant, *a.* Knowing fully; versed; engaged;
concerned: followed by *with* or *about.*

con''ver-sa'tion, 1 kɒn''var-sē'shən; 2 cŏn''-
ver-sā'shon, *n.* 1. Familiar talk; association; intercourse. 2∥. Deportment.— **con''-
ver-sa'tion-al,** *a.* Pertaining to conversation. **-ly,** *adv.*

con-verse', 1 kən-vūrs'; 2 cŏn-vĕrs', *vi.*
[-VERSED'ᵗ, -VERST'ˢ; -VERS'ING.] 1. To
speak together informally and alternately.
2∥. To associate; commune.— **con-vers'a-
bl(eᵖ,** *a.* Disposed to converse; ready in
conversation; sociable.— **con-vers'er,** *n.*
One who converses.

con'verse, 1 kɒn'vūrs; 2 cŏn'vĕrs, *a.* Trans-
posed; reversed.— **con'verse-ly,** *adv.*

con'verse¹, *n.* Conversation; intercourse;
communion. [proposition.]

con'verse², *n.* The reverse; an inverted

con-ver'sion, 1 kən-vūr'shən; 2 cŏn-vĕr'-
shon, *n.* The act of converting, or state
of being converted.

con-vert'ᵈ, 1 kən-vūrt'; 2 cŏn-vĕrt', *vt.* To
change; transform.— **con-vert'er,** *n.* One
who or that which converts; especially, a vessel in which iron is converted into steel.
**con-vert'or‡.— con-vert''i-bil'i-ty, con-
vert'i-bl(e-nessᵖ,** *n.*— **con-vert'i-bl(eᵖ,** *a.*
1. Capable of conversion. 2. Equivalent in
meaning; interchangeable.— **con-vert'i-bly,**
adv.

con'vert, 1 kən'vūrt; 2 cŏn'vĕrt, *n.* A
person who has been converted.

con'vex, 1 kɒn'veks; 2 cŏn'vĕks. I. *a.*
Curving outward like a segment of a
globe or of a circle; bulging out. II. *n.*

A convex surface or body; convexity.
— **con-vex'i-ty,** *n.* 1. The state of being con-
vex. 2. A convex surface. **con-vex'ed-
ness‡; con'vex-ness‡.**

con-vey', 1 kən-vē'; 2 cŏn-vẹ', *vt.* 1. To
transport from one place to another;
carry; transmit; communicate. 2. *Law.*
To transfer, as the title to real estate.
— **con-vey'ance,** 1 kən-vē'əns; 2 cŏn-vẹ'anç,
n. The act of conveying; a vehicle; a deed
transferring title.— **con-vey'anc-er,** *n.* One
whose business is conveyancing.— **con-vey'-
anc-ing,** *n.* The business of preparing conveyances, including the investigation of titles.

con-vict'ᵈ, 1 kən-vikt'; 2 cŏn-viet', *vt.* To
prove guilty; condemn.

con'vict, 1 kɒn'vikt; 2 cŏn'viet, *n.* One
found guilty of crime; a criminal.

con-vic'tion, 1 kən-vik'shən; 2 cŏn-vie'-
shon, *n.* The state of being convinced or
convicted; act of convicting; that which
one firmly believes.

con-vince', 1 kən-vins'; 2 cŏn-vĭnç', *vt.*
[CON-VINCED'ᵈ; CON-VINC'ING.] To compel belief by argument or evidence.

con-viv'i-al, 1 kən-viv'i-əl; 2 cŏn-vĭv'i-al,
a. Pertaining to a feast; festive; jovial.
-ly, *adv.*— **con-viv''i-al'i-ty,** *n.* [-TIESᶻ, *pl.*]
Festive merriment or joviality.

con-voke', 1 kən-vōk'; 2 cŏn-vōk', *vt.*
[CON-VOKED'ᵗ; CON-VOK'ING.] To call together; summon.— **con''vo-ca'tion,** *n.* 1.
The act of convoking. 2. [C-] An ecclesiastical congress or council.

con-volve', 1 kən-vŏlv'; 2 cŏn-vŏlv', *vt.*
con-volv'ˢ, & *vi.* [CON-VOLVED', CON-
VOLVD'ˢ; CON-VOLV'ING.] To roll together;
twist; turn.— **con'vo-lute,** 1 kɒn'vo-lūt;
2 cŏn'vo-lūt, *a.* Rolled one part on another
or inward from one side. **con'vo-lut''ed‡.—
con''vo-lu'tion,** 1 kɒn''vo-liū'shən; 2 cŏn''-
vo-lū'shon, *n.* The act of convolving; a turn;
fold; especially, one of the folds of the brain.

con-vol'vu-lus, 1 kən-vŏl'viu-lus; 2 cŏn-
vŏl'vū-lŭs, *n.* A twining herb with large
showy trumpet-shaped flowers.

con-voy', 1 kən-voi'; 2 cŏn-vǒy', *vt.* To
act as convoy to; escort and protect.

con'voy, 1 kɒn'voi; 2 cŏn'vǒy, *n.* The act
of convoying; that which convoys or is
convoyed.

con-vulse', 1 kən-vuls'; 2 cŏn-vŭls', *vt.*
[-VULSED'ᵗ, -VULST'ˢ; -VULS'ING.] To throw
into convulsions; agitate violently.— **con-
vul'sion,** 1 kən-vul'shən; 2 cŏn-vŭl'shon, *n.*
A violent and abnormal muscular contraction of the body; spasm; fit; any violent
commotion.— **con-vuls'iv(eˢ,** *a.* Producing,
resulting from, or characterized by convulsions. **-ly,** *adv.*

1: ȧrtistic, ärt; fat, fāre; fast; get, prẹy; hit, police; obey, gō; net, ôr; full, rūle; but, būrn.
2: ärt, āpe, făt, fâre, fȧst, whąt, ạll; mē, gĕt, prey, fėrn; hĭt, īce; ī=ē; ĭ=ĕ; gō, nŏt, ôr, wŏn,

co'ny, 1 kō'nı; 2 cō'nỵ, n. [CO'NIES², pl.] A rabbit. **co'ney‡**.

coo, 1 kū; 2 cōō. **I.** vt. & vi. To utter as the note of a dove; make love in low, murmuring tones. **II.** n. A murmuring note, as of a dove.

cook, 1 kuk; 2 cōŏk. **I**t. vt. & vi. To prepare for food by heat; do the work of a cook. **II.** n. One who prepares food for eating.— **cook'er**, n.— **cook'er- y**, n. [-IES², pl.] The art or practise of cooking.

cook'y, 1 kuk'ı; 2 cōŏk'ỵ, n. [-IES², pl.] A small, sweet cake. **cook'ey‡**; **cook'ie‡**.

cool, 1 kūl; 2 cōōl. **I.** vt. & vi. To make or become cool or cooler. **II.** a. Moderate in temperature, feeling, or temperament; self-controlled; self-possessed; apathetic; chilling; slighting. **III.** n. A moderate temperature approaching cold.— **cool'er**, n. That which cools, as a vessel to cool liquids. — **cool'ly**, adv.— **cool'ness**, n.

coo'lie, 1 kū'lı; 2 cōō'li, n. An Oriental laborer. **coo'ly‡**.

coon, kūn; 2 cōōn, n. The raccoon.

coop, 1 kūp; 2 cōōp. **I.** vt. To confine, as in a coop. **II.** n. An enclosure for small animals, as fowls.

coo'per, 1 kū'pər; 2 cōō'per, n. One who makes casks, barrels. etc.— **coo'per-age**, n. The work of a cooper, or the cost of it.

co-op'er-ate, 1 ko-ŏp'er-ēt; 2 co-ŏp'er-ăt, vi. [-AT'ED̶d; -AT'ING.] To work together for a common object: followed by with.— **co-op'er-a'tion**, n. Joint action; profit-sharing.— **co-op'er-a-tiv(e‡**, a. Operating together, by industrial cooperation, as for providing supplies.— **co-op'er-a''tor**, n.

co-or'di-nate, 1 ko-ōr'dı-nēt; 2 co-ŏr'dı-năt. **I.** vt. & vi. [-NAT'ED̶d; -NAT'ING.] To put or be in the same rank, class, or order. **II.** 1 ko-ōr'dı-nıt; 2 co-ŏr'dı-nat, a. Of the same order or rank; existing together in similar relation. **III.** 1 ko-ōr'dı-nıt; 2 co-ŏr'dı-nat, n. One of a number of coordinate persons or things. **-ly,** adv.— **co-or'di-na'tion**, n. The act of coordinating, or the state of being coordinate. [bird.

coot, 1 kūt; 2 cōōt, n. A rail-like aquatic

coo'tie, 1 kū'tı; 2 cōō'tı, n. [Soldiers' Slang.] A body-louse.

co'pal, 1 kō'pəl; 2 cō'pal, n. A hard transparent resin used for varnishes.

American Coot. ¹/₁₈

co-part'ner, 1 ko-pärt'nər; 2 co-pärt'ner, n. A sharer; partner.— **co-part'ner-ship**, n.

cope, 1 kōp; 2 cōp, vt. [COPED̶t; COP'ING.] To contend on equal terms: followed by with.

cope, n. **1.** Anything that arches overhead; a coping. **2.** A long mantle, as of a priest.

Co-per'ni-can, 1 ko-pūr'nı-kən; 2 co-pĕr'ni-can, a. Pertaining to the astronomer Copernicus, or to his theory that makes the sun the center of the solar system.

cop'i-er, 1 kŏp'ı-ər; 2 cŏp'i-er, n. A copyist: imitator. [or top course of a wall.

cop'ing, 1 kōp'ın; 2 cōp'ing, n. The cap

co'pi-ous, 1 kō'pı-us; 2 cō'pi-ŭs, a. Abundant; ample. **-ly,** adv. **-ness,** n.

cop'per, 1 kŏp'ər; 2 cŏp'er. **I.** vt. To cover with copper. **II.** n. A reddish ductile metal.— **cop'per-head''**, n. **1.** A venomous North-American snake. **2.** [Colloq.] U. S. Hist. A Northern sympathizer with the Southern secessionists: in the Civil War (1861-1865).— **cop'per-plate''**, n. An engraved plate of copper, or an engraving printed from it.— **cop'per-y**, a. Like copper.

cop'per-as, 1 kŏp'ər-as; 2 cŏp'er-as, n. A green sulfate of iron. **green vit'ri-ol‡**.

cop'pice, 1 kŏp'ıs; 2 cŏp'iç, n. A low **cop'piss**,) growing thicket. **copse‡**.

cop'u-la, 1 kŏp'yu-la; 2 cŏp'yu-la, n. A word uniting the subject and predicate of a sentence, as the present indicative of the verb to be.

cop'u-late, 1 kŏp'yu-lēt; 2 cŏp'yu-lăt, vt. & vi. [-LAT'ED̶d; -LAT'ING.] To couple; unite.— **cop'u-la'tion**, n. A coupling or union.— **cop'u-la-tiv(e‡**, a.

cop'y, 1 kŏp'ı; 2 cŏp'ỵ. **I.** vt. & vi. [COP'-IED, 1 kŏp'ıd, 2 cŏp'ıd; COP'Y-ING.] To reproduce; imitate. **II.** n. [COP'IES², pl.] **1.** A reproduction; imitation; duplicate; one of an edition or issue. **2.** A pattern for imitation, as manuscript to be set up in type.— **cop'y-ist**, n. One whose business it is to copy; also, an imitator.— **cop'y-right''**. **I**d. vt. To secure copyright for, as a book. **II.** n. The right of authors, composers, playwrights, and artists to publish and sell their works for a limited time.

co-quet', 1 ko-ket'; 2 co-kĕt', vt. & vi. [CO-QUET'TED̶d; CO-QUET'TING.] To deceive with affected fondness; trifle in love — **co'quet-ry**, 1 kō'ket-rı; 2 cō'kĕt-rỵ, n. [-RIES², pl.] Trifling in love.— **co-quette'**, 1 ko-ket'; 2 co-kĕt', n. A woman addicted to coquetry; a flirt.— **co-quet'tish**, a. **-ly,** adv. **-ness,** n.

cor'al, 1 ker'əl; 2 cŏr'al. **I.** a. Of or like coral. **II.** n. A calcareous secretion of various marine zoophytes, often forming reefs or islands. See cut on next page.— **cor'al-lin(e‡**, 1 ker'ə-lin; 2 cŏr'a-lin, a. Of, pertaining to, producing, or like coral. — **cor'al-leid,** a.

cor'bel, 1 kör'bel; 2 cŏr'bĕl, n. Arch. **1.** A

projecting bracket. **2.** The basket-shaped portion of a Corinthian capital. **cor'bil‡.**

cord, 1 kŏrd; 2 côrd. **Id.** *vt.* **1.** To bind with cord; furnish with cords. **2.** To pile (fire-wood) by the cord. **II.** *n.* **1.** A string of several strands. **2.** A measure for wood (128 cubic feet).—**cord'age,** 1 kŏrd'ij; 2 côrd'ag, *n.* Ropes and cords collectively.

cor'date, 1 kŏr'dĕt; 2 côr'dāt, *a. Bot.* Heart-shaped, as a leaf.

Red Coral.

cor'dial, 1 kŏr'jal *or* kŏrd'yal; 2 côr'jal *or* côrd'yal. **I.** *a.* Proceeding from the heart; kindly; hearty; encouraging; cheering. **II.** *n.* **1.** Something that invigorates. **2.** A sweet and aromatic alcoholic liquor.—**cor-dial'i-ty,** *n.* [-TIES², *pl.*] The quality of being cordial. **cor'dial-ness‡.** **cor'dial-ly,** *adv.*

cor'don, 1 kŏr'dən; 2 côr'don, *n.* **1.** An extended line, as of men, ships, forts, etc. **2.** An ornamental lace, ribbon, or the like.

cor'du-roy, 1 kŏr'du-rei *or* kŏr"du-rei'; 2 côr'du-rŏy *or* côr"du-rŏy', *n.* A thick and durable cotton stuff, corded or ribbed. — **corduroy road,** a road made of transverse logs laid side by side.

core, 1 kōr; 2 côr, *n.* The heart, as of an apple, containing the seeds; center; heart; pith.

co"re-spon'dent, 1 kō"rĭ-spon'dent; 2 cō"re-spŏn'dĕnt, *n.* A joint respondent, as in a suit for divorce.

co"ri-an'der, 1 kō"rĭ-an'dər; 2 cō"rĭ-ăn'der, *n.* A plant of the parsley family, bearing aromatic seeds.

Co-rin'thi-an, 1 ko-rin'thĭ-ən; 2 co-rĭn'thĭ-an, *a.* Pertaining to Corinth, in ancient Greece, or to an order of architecture marked by slender fluted columns with ornate capitals.

cork, 1 kŏrk; 2 côrk. **I‡.** *vt.* To stop with a cork, as a bottle. **II.** *n.* **1.** The light, porous bark of a tree (the *cork=oak*). **2.** Anything made of cork, as a stopper for a bottle.—**cork'screw",** *n.* A spirally shaped instrument for drawing corks from bottles.—**cork'y,** *a.*

Greek Corinthian Capital and Base.

cor'mo-rant, 1 kŏr'mo-rant; 2 côr'mo-rant, *n.* A large voracious aquatic bird; a glutton or avaricious person.

corn, 1 kŏrn; 2 côrn. *vt.* To preserve in salt or in brine.

corn¹, *n.* The edible seeds of cereal plants: in England, wheat, barley, rye, and oats collectively: in America, maize, or Indian corn. [ticle, common on the feet.

corn², *n.* A horny thickening of the cu-

cor'ne-a, 1 kŏr'nĭ-ə; 2 côr'ne-a, *n.* The front part of the outer coat of the eyeball.

corned, 1 kŏrnd; 2 côrnd, *a.* Preserved

cornd⁸, ∫ by laying down in brine; as, *corned* beef.

cor'nel, 1 kŏr'nel; 2 côr'nel, *n.* A tree with hard, compact wood, as the dogwood.

cor-ne'lian, *n.* Same as CARNELIAN.

cor'ner, 1 kŏr'nər; 2 côr'ner. **I.** *vt.* To drive into a corner; make a corner in; secure a monopoly of. **II.** *n.* **1.** An angle; recess; nook. **2.** A position of embarrassment or difficulty; the securing of a monopoly in the market with control of price.—**cor'ner-stone",** *n.* A stone uniting two walls at the corner of a building, at or near the foundation.

cor'net¹, 1 kŏr'net; 2 côr'nĕt, *n.* A small wind-instrument of the tru pet class.

cor-net'², 1 kŏr-net'; 2 côr-nĕt', *n. Mil.* [Eng.] Formerly, a cavalry officer; a flag or standard.—**cor'net-cy,** *n.* The rank or commission of a cornet.

cor'nice, ∫ 1 kŏr'nis; 2 côr'nĭs, *n.* A

cor'nis⁸, ∫ molding round the top of a building or wall of a room.

cor"nu-co'pi-a, 1 kŏr"niu-kō'pĭ-ə; 2 côr"nū-cō'pĭ-a, *n.* [-AS^Z *or* -Æ, 1 -Ī; 2 -ē, *pl.*] The horn of plenty, symbolizing prosperity.

co-rol'la, 1 ko-rŏl'ə; 2 co-rŏl'a, *n. Bot.* The inner circle or set of leaves of a flower.

cor'ol-la-ry, 1 kŏr'ə-lē-rĭ; 2 cor'o-lā-ry, *n.* [-RIES², *pl.*] A consequence; obvious deduction.

co-ro'na, 1 ko-rō'nə; 2 co-rō'na, *n.* [-NAS⁸ *or* -NÆ, 1 -nī; 2 -nē, *pl.*] A crown or garland: a luminous circle; halo.—**cor'o-nal,** 1 kŏr'o-nəl; 2 côr'o-nal. **I.** *a.* Of or pertaining to a corona or halo, or to the crown of the head. **II.** *n.* A crown or garland. **cor'o-na-ry‡.**—**cor"o-na'tion,** 1 kŏr"o-ne'shən; 2 côr"o-nā'shon, *n.* The act or ceremony of crowning a monarch.

cor'o-ner, 1 kŏr'o-nər; 2 côr'o-ner, *n.* An officer who inquires into the cause of sudden or violent death of persons.

cor'o-net, 1 kŏr'o-net; 2 côr'o-nĕt, *n.* An inferior crown, denoting noble rank less than sovereign.

1: artistic, ärt; fat, fāre; fast; get, prey; hit, police; obey, gō; not, ôr; full, rūle; but, būrn.
2: ärt, āpe, fät, fâre, fàst, what, all; mē, gĕt, prey, fėrn; hı̆t, īce; ı̆=ē; ı̆=ĕ; gō, nŏt, ôr, wŏn,

cor'po-ral, 1 kẽr'po-rəl; 2 côr'po-ral, *a.* Belonging or relating to the body as opposed to the mind. **-ly,** *adv.*

cor'po-ral, *n. Mil.* The lowest non-commissioned officer in a company.

cor'po-rate, 1 kẽr'po-rɪt; 2 côr'po-rat, *a.* Incorporated, or belonging to a corporation. **cor'po-ra-tiv(e‡.—cor'po-rate-ly,** *adv.* **1.** As a corporate body. **2.** In the body; bodily.—**cor'po-ra'tion,** 1 kẽr"po-re'shən; 2 côr"po-rā'shon, *n.* A body of persons legally associated for the transaction of business.

cor-po're-al, 1 ker-pō'rɪ-əl; 2 côr-pō're-al, *a.* Having a body; material; physical. —**cor'po-re'i-ty,** 1 kẽr"po-rī'ɪ-tɪ; 2 côr"po-rē'i-ty, *n.* Corporeal existence. **cor-po're-al'i-ty‡; cor-po're-al-ness‡.—cor-po're-al-ly,** *adv.*

corps, 1 kōr; 2 côr, *n.* A number of persons acting together, as a section of an army.

corpse, 1 kôrps; 2 côrps, *n.* A dead body, as of a human being.

cor'pu-lent, 1 kẽr'pɪu-lent; 2 côr'pu-lĕnt, *a.* Excessively fat.—**cor'pu-lence,** *n.* **cor'pu-len-cy‡.—cor'pu-lent-ly,** *adv.*

cor'pus-cle, 1 kẽr'pʉs-l; 2 côr'pŭs-l, *n.* A minute particle or body; cell; atom. **cor'pus-cule‡.—cor-pus'cu-lar,** *a.* Of or pertaining to corpuscles; molecular.

cor-ral', 1 ke-rɑl'; 2 cô-rӓl'. **I.** *vt.* [COR-RALLED, COR-RALD'S; COR-RAL'ING.] To pen up. **II.** *n.* An enclosed space or pen for live stock.

cor-rect', 1 ke-rekt'; 2 cô-rĕct'. **I.** *vt.* To make right; rectify; remedy; set right; punish. **II.** *a.* Free from fault or mistake; true, right, or proper; accurate. —**cor-rect'a-bl(e‡.—cor-rect'i-bl(e*, *a.* **cor-rec'tion,** 1 ke-rek'shən; 2 cô-rĕc'shon, *n.* The act of correcting; rectification; amendment; improvement; punishment. **cor-rec'tion-al,** *a.* Tending to or intended for correction.—**cor-rec'tiv(e‡,** *a.* Adapted to correct.—**cor-rect'ly,** *adv.*—**cor-rect'-ness,** *n.*—**cor-rec'tor,** *n.*

cor"re-spond'‡, 1 kẽr'ɪ-spond'; 2 côr"e-spônd', *vi.* **1.** To be adequate, equal, or like. **2.** To communicate by letter.

cor"re-spon'dence, 1 kẽr'ɪ-spon'dens; 2 côr"e-spôn'dĕnç, *n.* **1.** Mutual adaptation; agreement. **2.** Communication by letters; also, the letters themselves.—**cor"re-spon'dent. I.** *a.* Agreeing; adapted: with *to.* **II.** *n.* One who communicates with another by mail or telegraph.

cor"re-spond'ing, 1 kẽr'ɪ-spond'ɪŋ; 2 côr"e-spônd'ing, *pa.* **1.** Correspondent; similar: with *to.* **2.** Carrying on a correspondence: followed by *with.* **-ly,** *adv.*

cor'ri-dor, 1 kẽr'ɪ-dẽr; 2 côr'i-dôr, *n.* A wide gallery or passage in a building.

cor'ri-gi-bl(e‡, 1 kẽr'ɪ-jɪ-bl; 2 côr'i-gi-bl, *a.* Capable of being corrected.

cor-rob'o-rate, 1 ke-rob'o-rēt; 2 cô-rŏb'o-rāt, *vt.* [-RAT"ED⁴; -RAT"ING.] To strengthen, as conviction or proof; confirm. —**cor-rob''o-ra'tion,** *n.* The act of corroborating; confirmation.—**cor-rob''o-ra-tiv(e‡,** *a.* Tending to confirm; verifying. **cor-rob'o-ra-to-ry‡.**

cor-rode', 1 ke-rōd'; 2 cô-rōd', *vt. & vi.* [-ROD"ED⁴; -ROD'ING.] To eat away gradually; be eaten away; rust.—**cor-ro'sion,** 1 ke-rō'ʒən; 2 cô-rō'zhon, *n.* Gradual decay. —**cor-ro'siv(e‡,** 1 ke-rō'sɪv; 2 cô-rō'siv. **I.** *a.* Having the power of corroding. **II.** *n.* That which corrodes; a corroding agent. **-ly,** *adv.* **-ness,** *n.*

cor'ru-gate, 1 kẽr'u-gēt; 2 côr'u-gāt, *vt. & vi.* [-GAT"ED⁴; -GAT"ING.] To contract into ridges and furrows; wrinkle. **II.** *a.* Wrinkled. **cor'ru-gat"ed‡.—cor'-ru-ga'tion,** *n.* The act of corrugating; a wrinkle.

cor-rupt', 1 ke-rupt'; 2 cô-rŭpt'. **I⁴.** *vt. & vi.* To subject to decay; spoil; putrefy; vitiate; deprave; pollute; pervert, as by bribery. **II.** *a.* **1.** Decomposing; tainted; putrid. **2.** Given to bribery; dishonest; depraved.—**cor-rupt'er, cor-rup'tor,** *n.*—**cor-rupt'i-bil'i-ty,** *n.* The quality of being corruptible.—**cor-rupt'i-bl(e‡,** *a.* That may be corrupted.—**cor-rupt'i-bl(e-ness*, *n.*—**cor-rupt'i-bly,** *adv.*—**cor-rup'tiv(e‡,** *a.* Of a corrupting character.—**cor-rupt'ly,** *adv.*—**cor-rupt'ness,** *n.*

cor-rup'tion, 1 ke-rup'shən; 2 cô-rŭp'shon, *n.* The act of corrupting; rottenness; decay; dishonesty; bribery.

cor'sage, 1 kẽr'sɪj; 2 côr'saᵹ, *n.* The bodice or waist of a woman's dress.

cor'sair, 1 kẽr'sãr; 2 côr'sâr, *n.* A pirate, or his vessel.

corse, 1 kōrs; 2 côrs, *n.* **1.** A ribbon. **2.** A corpse.

corse'let, 1 kōrs'let; 2 côrs'lĕt, *n.* The complete armor of a soldier; also, a breastplate.

cor'set, 1 kẽr'set. 2 côr'sĕt, *n.* A close-fitting laced bodice, worn as a support, usually by women.

cor-tège', 1 ker-tāᵹ'; 2 côr-tȇzh', *n.* A train of attendants.

cor'ti-cal, 1 kẽr'tɪ-kəl; 2 côr'ti-cal, *a.* Of, pertaining to, or like bark; external.

co-run'dum, 1 ko-run'dəm; 2 co-rŭn'dŭm, *n.* An extremely hard mineral, an oxid of aluminum, of which the inferior varieties are used for polishing and the

---

finely colored as gems. Emery is the granular variety.

cor′us-cate, 1 kŏr′us-kāt; 2 eŏr′ŭs-cāt, *vi.* [-CAT′ED‡; -CAT′ING.] To sparkle.— **cor″us-ca′tion**, *n.* A burst of sparks.

cor-vette′, 1 kŏr-vet′; 2 eŏr-vĕt′, *n.* A wooden war-vessel. **cor′vet‡.**

cor′vine, 1 kŏr′vin; 2 eŏr′vin, *a.* Of or pertaining to a crow; crow-like.

co′sey, *a.* Same as COZY. **cosy‡.**

cos-met′ic, 1 kez-met′ik; 2 eŏs-mĕt′ie. **I.** *a.* Pertaining to the art of beautifying the complexion. **cos-met′i-cal‡. II.** *n.* A compound applied to the skin to improve its appearance.

cos″mo-pol′i-tan, 1 kez″mo-pel′i-tən; 2 eŏs″mo-pŏl′i-tan. **I.** *a.* Common to all the world; at home in all parts of the world; widely distributed. **II.** *n.* A citizen of the world. **cos-mop′o-lite‡.**

cos′mos, 1 kez′mos; 2 eŏs′mŏs, *n.* The universe as a system; any complete system.

Cos′sack, 1 kŏs′ak; 2 eŏs′ăk, *n.* One of a race inhabiting S. E. Russia, supplying irregular cavalrymen to the Russian army.

cos′set, 1 kŏs′et; 2 eŏs′ĕt. **I‡.** *vt.* To fondle; pet. **II.** *n.* A pet lamb; any pet.

cost, 1 kŏst; 2 eŏst. **I.** *vt.* [COST; COST′ING.] To require as a price; cause the loss of, as of life. **II.** *n.* The price paid for anything; outlay; expense; charge.

cos′tal, 1 kŏs′təl; 2 eŏs′tal, *a.* Of, pertaining to, on, or near a rib.

cos′tive, 1 kŏs′tiv; 2 eŏs′tiv, *a.* Constipated. **-ly,** *adv.* **-ness,** *n.*

cost′ly, 1 kŏst′li; 2 eŏst′ly, *a.* Of great cost; expensive.— **cost′li-ness,** *n.*

cos′tume, 1 kŏs′tiūm; 2 eŏs′tūm, *n.* Dress, especially of a country, period, class, etc.

cot, 1 kŏt; 2 eŏt, *n.* **1.** A cottage. **2.** A light, portable bedstead. **3.** A cover, as of kid, for an injured finger. [NEOUS, etc.

co-tem″po-ra′ne-ous, etc. See CONTEMPORA-

co″te-rie′, 1 kō″ta-rī′; 2 eō″te-rē′, *n.* A set of persons who meet habitually; a clique.

co-ter′mi-nous, *a.* Same as CONTERMINOUS.

co-til′lion, 1 ko-til′yən; 2 eo-til′yon, *n.* A square dance; also, the music for it.

cot′tage, 1 kŏt′ij; 2 eŏt′aġ, *n.* **1.** A humble dwelling; small house; hut. **2.** [U. S.] A country residence.— **cot′tag-er,** *n.* The occupant of a cottage.— **cot′ter,** *n.* A cottager; farm tenant. **cot′tar‡. cot′ti-er‡.**

cot′ton, 1 kŏt′n; 2 eŏt′n, *n.* **1.** The soft, fibrous material appendant to the seeds of a plant (the *cotton-plant*); also, the plant itself. See illus. in next column. **2.** Cotton cloth or thread.— **cot′ton-ġin″,** *n.* A machine used to separate the seeds from the fiber of cotton.

cot″y-le′don, 1 kŏt″-i-lī′dən; 2 eŏt″y-lē′don, *n.* A seed-leaf, or first leaf of an embryo.— **cot″y-led′o-nous,** 1 kŏt′i-led′o-nus; 2 eŏt″y-lĕd′o-nŭs,** *a.* Of, pertaining to, or like cotyledons. **cot″y-led′o-nal‡.**

couch‡, 1 kauch; 2 eouch. *v.* **I.** *t.* **1.** To lay down; lower, as a spear, for attack. **2.** To express in a form of words. **3.** *Surg.* To remove, as a cataract. **II.** *i.* To lie down; rest; crouch.

couch, *n.* A bed or other support for sleeping or reclining.

Cotton-plant.
a, the boll ready for picking.

cou′gar, 1 kū′gar, 2 eụ′ġar, *n.* The puma.

cough‡, 1 kŏf; 2 eŏf, *v.* **I.** *t.* To expel by **cof‡‡,** a cough: with *up.* **II.** *i.* To expel air from the lungs with a sudden, harsh sound.

cough, *n.* A sudden, harsh expulsion of breath; a disease productive of coughing.

could, 1 kud; 2 eụd, *imp. of* CAN‡, *v.*

cou-lomb′, 1 kū-lem″; 2 eụ-lŏm″, *n.* The practical unit of quantity in measuring electricity; the amount conveyed by one ampere in one second: named from *Coulomb*, a French physicist (1736-1806).

coul′ter, *n.* Same as COLTER.

coun′cil, 1 kaun′sil; 2 eoun′eil, *n.* An assembly for consultation.— **coun′cil-man, coun′cil-or,** *n.* A member of a council.

coun′sel, 1 kaun′sel; 2 eoun′sĕl. **I.** *vt. & vi.* [-SELED or -SELLED, -SELD³; -SEL-ING or -SEL-LING.] To consult; admonish; advise; deliberate. **II.** *n.* **1.** Mutual consultation; opinion; advice; purpose; prudence. **2.** An advocate.— **coun′sel-or,** 1 kaun′sel-ər *or* -er; 2 eoun′sĕl-or, *n.* One who gives counsel; a lawyer; advocate. **coun′sel-lor‡.**

count‡, 1 kaunt; 2 eount. *v.* **I.** *t.* **1.** To number; compute. **2.** To consider to be; judge. **3.** To ascribe: with *to.* **II.** *i.* **1.** To number. **2.** To be important. **3.** To rely: with *on* or *upon.*

count‡, 1 kaunt; 2 eount, *n.* The act of counting; number; estimation; a separate charge, as in an indictment. [Europe.

count², *n.* A nobleman of continental

coun′te-nance, 1 kaun′ti-nans; 2 eoun′te-nanç. **I.** *vt.* [-NANCED‡; -NANC-ING.] To approve; encourage; abet. **II.** *n.* The face; expression; aspect; approval; support.

coun'ter, 1 kaun'tər; 2 ĕoun'ter, *a.* Contrary; opposing.

count'er¹, 1 kaunt'ər; 2 ĕount'er, *n.* One who counts; a counting-machine; a piece of wood, ivory, etc., used in counting.

coun'ter², *n.* A table on which to count money or expose goods for sale.

coun'ter³, *n.* **1.** An opposite; a parry; return blow. **2.** The portion of a shoe that surrounds the heel.

coun'ter, *adv.* Contrary; reversely.

counter-, *prefix.* Contrary; opposite; as, *counteract, counterpart.*

coun"ter-act'ᵈ, 1 kaun"tər-akt'; 2 ĕoun"ter-ăĕt', *vt.* To oppose; check; frustrate; hinder.— **coun"ter-ac'tion,** *n.*

coun"ter-bal'ance, 1 kaun"tər-bal'əns; 2 ĕoun"ter-băl'anç. **I.** *vt.* [-ANCEDᵗ; -ANC-ING.] To oppose with an equal force; offset. **II.** *n.* Any power equally opposing another; a counterpoise.

coun'ter-feit, 1 kaun'tər-fit; 2 ĕoun'ter-**coun'ter-fitˢ,** fit. ᵗᵈ. *vt.* To make fraudulently, as money; imitate deceitfully; feign; pretend. **II.** *a.* Fraudulently imitated; spurious. **III.** *n.* Something spurious, as a counterfeit coin; also, any imitation, as a portrait or copy.— **coun'ter-feit-er,** *n.* One who counterfeits money; a pretender.

coun"ter-mand', 1 kaun"tər-mand'; 2 ĕoun"ter-mănd'. ᴵᵈ. *vt.* To revoke, as an order; contradict; oppose. **II.** *n.* An order contrary to or revoking one previously issued.

coun"ter-march', 1 kaun"tər-mārch'; 2 ĕoun"ter-märch'. **Iᵗ.** *vt.* & *vi.* To march back. **II.** *n.* A return march; change of front or of conduct, etc.

coun"ter-pane", 1 kaun'tər-pēn'; 2 ĕoun'ter-pān'. *n.* A coverlet or quilt.

coun"ter-part", 1 kaun'tər-pärt'; 2 ĕoun'ter-pärt'. *n.* **1.** A facsimile; duplicate. **2.** Something corresponding reversely, as the right hand to the left; a complement; opposite.

coun"ter-poise", 1 kaun'tər-pɔiz'; 2 ĕoun"ter-pŏiẓ'. **I.** *vt.* [-POISED'; -POIS-ING.] To offset with an equal weight; counterbalance; frustrate. **II.** *n.* A counterbalancing weight, effort, power, etc.; equilibrium.

coun'ter-sign", 1 kaun'tər-sain"; 2 ĕoun'ter-sīn". **I.** *vt.* To authenticate by an additional signature. **II.** *n.* A secret password; watchword.

count'ess, 1 kaunt'es; 2 ĕount'ĕs, *n.* The wife of a count, or, in Great Britain, of an earl.

count'ing-house", *n.* An office for accounts. **count'ing-room"**‡.

count'less, 1 kaunt'les; 2 ĕount'lĕs, *a.* That can not be counted.

coun'tri-fy, 1 kun'tri-fai; 2 ĕŭn'tri-fȳ, *vt.* [-FIED; -FY'ING.] To make rural or rustic.

coun'try, 1 kun'tri; 2 ĕŭn'try. **I.** *a.* Of or pertaining to the country; **cun'tryᴾ,** rural; rustic; simple; unpolished. **II.** *n.* [COUN'TRIESᶻ, *pl.*] **1.** A region or nation; district; tract of land; native land. **2.** With the definite article, a rural region.— **coun'try-dance",** *n.* A dance in which the partners are ranged in opposite lines.— **coun'try-man,** *n.* [-MEN, *pl.*] One living in the country or in the same country; a rustic; a fellow citizen.— **coun'try-seat",** *n.* A dwelling or mansion in the country.— **coun'try-wo"man,** *n.*

coun'ty, 1 kaun'ti; 2 ĕoun'ty, *n.* [COUN'-TIESᶻ, *pl.*] A civil division, as of a state; also its inhabitants.

coup, 1 kū; 2 ĕụ, *n.* A sudden telling blow; a master-stroke; stratagem.— **coup de grâce,** 1 kū de grås; 2 ĕụ de gräç, the finishing or mortal stroke; mercy, a stroke of mercy.— **c. d'é'tat',** 1 kū dē'tä'; 2 ĕụ dĕ'-tä', a sudden stroke of policy or statesmanship, often accompanied by violence.

cou"pé', 1 kū"pē'; 2 ĕụ"pẹ', *n.* A low closed carriage, or a closed motor-car with seats for two to four persons.

coup'le, 1 kup'l; 2 ĕụp'l. **I.** *vt.* & *vi.* **cup'lᴾ,** [COUP'LED, CUP'LDᴾ; COUP'LING.] To join; place together in a pair; connect; unite. **II.** *n.* Two of a kind; a pair.

coup'let, 1 kup'let; 2 ĕụp'lĕt, *n.* Two **cup'letᴾ,** successive lines of verse riming together.

cou'pon, 1 kū'pɔn; 2 ĕụ'pŏn, *n.* A detachable portion of a bond, ticket, etc.

cour'age, 1 kur'ij; 2 ĕụr'aǵ, *n.* Intrepid-**cur'age,** ity, calmness, and firmness in face of danger; bravery.— **cou-ra'geous,** 1 ku-rē'jus; 2 ĕụ-rā'ǵụs, *a.* Having or showing courage; brave; intrepid. **-ly,** *adv.*

cou'ri-er, 1 kū'ri-ər; 2 ĕụ'ri-er, *n.* A messenger; also, a traveling attendant.

course, 1 kōrs; 2 ĕōrs. **I.** *vt.* & *vi.* [COURSEDᵗ; COURS'ING.] To run, or cause to run; hunt; chase. **II.** *n.* The act of moving onward; path; direction; series or sequence, as of events; career; line of conduct; portion of a meal served at once; a row or layer.— **cours'er,** *n.* A fleet and spirited horse.

court, 1 kōrt; 2 ĕōrt. ᴵᵈ. *vt.* & *vi.* To woo; seek; solicit. **II.** *a.* Of or pertaining to court. **III.** *n.* **1.** A judicial tribunal, or the judge or judges. **2.** The residence, or

the council and retinue, of a sovereign. **3.** A courtyard or a blind alley. **4.** Obsequious attention.— **court'li·ness,** n.— **court'ly,** a. Of or befitting a court; elegant in manners.— **court martial** [COURTS MARTIAL, pl.], a court to try offenses against military or naval law.— **court'·plas"ter,** n. A thin, fine adhesive plaster.— **court'ship,** n. The act or period of wooing.— **court'·yard",** n. An enclosed yard adjoining or within a building.

cour'te·ous, } 1 kŭr'tɪ·us; 2 cûr'te·ŭs, a.
cur'te·uss, } Showing courtesy; polite. **-ly, adv. -ness,** n.

cour'te·san, n. Same as COURTEZAN.

courte'sy, } 1 kŭrt'sɪ; 2 cûrt'sy, vi. [-SIED;
cur'te·sys, } -SY-ING.] To make a courtesy.

courte'sy¹, n. [-SIES², pl.] An old-time gesture of civility or respect, somewhat resembling a bow, made by women; a curtsy.

cour'te·sy², } 1 kŭr'tɪ·sɪ; 2 cûr'te·sy, n.
[-SIES², pl.] Genuine politeness; courtliness; a courteous favor or act. **cur'te·sy‡.**

cour'te·zan, } 1 kŭr'tɪ·zən; 2 cûr'te·zan, n. A prostitute.

court'ier, 1 kōrt'yer; 2 eōrt'yer, n. A member of the court circle.

cous'in, 1 kuz'n; 2 cŭg'n, n. The child of an uncle or aunt, or a descendant of one so related. [recess.

cove, 1 kōv; 2 eōv, n. A small bay or

cov'e·nant, } 1 kuv'ɪ·nənt; 2 eóv'e·nant.
cuv'e·nantᴿ, } I. vt. & vi. To promise; pledge oneself. II. n. An agreement; compact.— **cov'e·nant·er,** n. One who enters into a covenant. **cov'e·nant·or‡.**

cov'er, } 1 kuv'er; 2 eóv'er. I. vt. & vi.
cuv'erᴿ, } 1. To overspread; overlay; enwrap; hide; screen; command, as with a weapon. **2.** To suffice or compensate for. **3.** To accomplish; pass over, as a distance. II. n. **1.** That which covers; a veil or disguise; a shelter, as a thicket; defense; protection. **2.** Table furniture for one person.— **cov'er·ing,** n. Anything that covers.— **cov'er·let,** n. A bedquilt. **cov'er·lid‡.**

cov'ert, } 1 kuv'ert; 2 eóv'ert. I. a. Concealed; secret; sheltered. II. n.
cuv'ertᴿ, } A hiding-place, as a thicket. **-ly, adv.**

cov'er·ture, 1 kuv'er-chur or -tiur; 2 eóv'er-chur or -tūr, n. Marriage; legal state of a married woman.

cov'et, } 1 kuv'et; 2 eóv'ĕt, vt. & vi. To de-
cuv'etᴿ, } sire wrongfully or eagerly; crave.
— **cov'et·ous,** a. Inordinately eager to acquire and possess; avaricious. **-ly, adv. -ness,** n.

cov'ey, cuv'eyᴿ, 1 kuv'ɪ; 2 eóv'y, n. A flock, as of quails. [timidate.

cow, 1 kau; 2 eow, vt. To overawe; in-

cow, n. The female of domestic cattle and of some other animals which yield milk.

cow'ard, 1 kau'erd; 2 eow'ard, n. One lacking in courage; a craven; poltroon. — **cow'ard,** a. Cowardly.— **cow'ard·ice,** 1 kau'ard·is; 2 eow'ard-iç, n. Unworthy timidity.— **cow'ard·li·ness,** n.— **cow'ard·ly.** I. a. Like or befitting a coward; fearful; timorous; pusillanimous. II. adv. In a cowardly manner.

cow'er, 1 kau'er; 2 eow'er, vi. To crouch tremblingly; quail.

cow'herd", 1 kau'hŭrd"; 2 eow'hĕrd", n. A herdsman.

cow'hide", 1 kau'haid"; 2 eow'hīd". I. vt. [COW'HID"EDᵈ; COW'HID"ING.] To whip as with a cowhide. II. n. The hide of a cow, or a whip made from it.

cowl, 1 kaul; 2 eowl, n. **1.** A monk's hood. **2.** A hood-like covering.

co·work'er, 1 kō–wûrk'er; 2 eo–wûrk'er, n. A fellow worker.

cow'slip", 1 kau'slip"; 2 eow'slĭp", n. A wild flower of the primrose family.

cox'comb", 1 keks–kōm"; 2 eŏks'eŏm", n. **1.** A pretentious fop. **2.** Same as COCKS-COMB.

cox'swain, 1 kek'swĕn or (naut.) kek'sn; 2 eŏk'swān or (naut.) eŏk'sn, n. One who steers or has charge of a rowboat.

Cowslip.

coy, 1 kei; 2 eóy, a. Shrinking from notice; shy; coquettish. **-ly, adv. -ness,** n.

co·yo'te, 1 ko–yō'tɪ or kai'ōt; 2 eo–yō'te or ei'ōt, n. The prairie-wolf of the western United States.

coz'en, } 1 kuz'n; 2 eŏz'n, vt. & vi. To
cuz'enᴿ, } cheat.

co'zy, 1 kō'zɪ; 2 eō'zy, a. [CO'ZI-ER; CO'ZI-EST.] Snugly comfortable; contented; sociable. **cosy‡.— co'zi-ly, co'si-ly,** adv.

craal, n. Same as KRAAL.

crab¹, 1 krab; 2 erāb, n. **1.** A 10-footed crustacean having the abdomen or tail folded under the body. **2.** [C-] A constellation, Cancer.

crab², n. **1.** A kind of small, sour apple. **2.** A tree bearing this fruit. **crab'·ap"ple‡.**

crab'bed, 1 krab'ed; 2 erāb'ĕd, a. Sour-tempered; harsh; sour; cramped and irregular. **-ly, adv. -ness,** n.

crack, 1 krak; 2 erāk. I². vt. & vi. To burst; split; break open; snap; tell with spirit. II. n. A partial breakage; a fissure; a sharp sound; a sounding blow. — **crack'er,** 1 krak'er; 2 erāk'er, n. A

person or thing that cracks; a firecracker; a brittle biscuit. — **crack⁼up.** Same as CRASH¹, 2.

crack'l(e², 1 krak'l; 2 erăk'l. **I.** *vt. & vi.* [CRACK'L(E)D⁹; CRACK'LING.] To crack slightly and repeatedly. **II.** *n.* A succession of light, cracking sounds; a small crack; a network of fine cracks, as on china.— **crack'ling,** 1 krak'lŋ; 2 erăk' ing, *n.* **1.** A crackling sound. **2.** The crisp browned skin of roasted pork.

cra'dle, 1 krē'dl; 2 erā'dl. **I.** *vt. & vi.* [CRA'DLED; CRA'DLING.] **1.** To put into or rock in a cradle; soothe; nurse; nurture. **2.** To reap or wash with a cradle, as wheat or ore. **II.** *n.* **1.** A rocking or swinging bed for an infant; birthplace; origin. **2.** A scythe with fingers that catch the grain when cut. **3.** A frame for sustaining a vessel. **4.** A box on rockers for washing ore.

craft, 1 kraft; 2 erăft, *n.* **1.** Cunning or skill; trickery. **2.** A trade, or those employed in it. **3.** A vessel; also, collectively, vessels.— **craft'i‑ly,** *adv.*— **craft'i‑ness,** *n.*— **crafts'man,** *n.* [-MEN, *pl.*] A skilled mechanic.— **craft'y,** 1 kraft'ı; 2 erăft'y, *a.* Skilful in deceiving; cunning.

crag, 1 krag; 2 erăg. *n.* A rough, steep rock.— **crag'ged,** *a.* Having numerous crags.

cram, 1 kram; 2 erăm, *vt. & vi.* [CRAMMED, CRAMD⁸; CRAM'MING.] To press together; eat greedily; stuff; crowd; overfill.

cramp¹, 1 kramp; 2 erămp. **Iᵗ.** *vt.* To fasten with a cramp. **II.** *n.* A bent iron for binding two pieces firmly together.

cramp², 1ᵗ. *vt.* To affect with cramps. **II.** *n.* An involuntary, sudden, painful, muscular contraction.

cran'ber'ry, 1 kran'ber'ı; 2 erăn'bĕr'y, *n.* [-RIES², *pl.*] The bright⁼scarlet acid berry of a marshy plant, or the plant itself.

crane¹, 1 krēn; 2 erān, *n.* A large long‑legged heron⁼like bird.— **crane¹,** *vt.* To stretch out (the neck) as a crane does.

crane², *n.* A hoisting⁼machine: a support for kettles in a fireplace.— **crane²,** *vt.* To raise by or as by a crane.

cra'ni‑um, 1 krē'nı‑um; 2 erā'ni‑ŭm, *n.* [CRA'NI‑A, *pl.*] The skull.— **cra'ni‑al,** *a.*

crank, 1 kraŋk; 2 erăŋk, *a.* Unsteady; easily capsized; shaky; lively.

crank, *n.* **1.** A bent arm attached to an axis, or a bent portion of an axle, for con‑

Cranes.

verting rotary into reciprocating motion, or vice versa. **2.** [Colloq., U.S.] An unbalanced person; a monomaniac.— **crank'y,** *a.* Crooked; unsteady; rickety; mentally unbalanced.

cran'ny, 1 kran'ı; 2 erăn'y, *n.* [CRAN'NIES², *pl.*] A narrow opening; fissure. [like fabric.

crape, 1 krēp; 2 erāp, *n.* A gauze⁼

craps, 1 kraps; 2 erăps, *n. pl.* [Slang.] A gambling game played with two dice. Crank.

crash¹, 1 krash; 2 erăsh, *vt. & vi.* **1.** To break with a sharp, sudden noise. **2.** To bring to the ground in such a way as to cause damage or breakage; as, to crash an air⁼plane.

crash¹, *n.* **1.** A loud noise of sudden breakage; destruction; ruin. **2.** An air⁼plane wreck. [toweling.

crash², *n.* A coarse linen fabric, as for

crate, 1 krēt; 2 erāt. **I.** *vt.* [CRAT'ED⁹; CRAT'ING.] To put in a crate. **II.** *n.* A large hamper or framework for transporting various articles.

cra'ter, 1 krē'tər; 2 erā'ter, *n.* The bowl‑shaped outlet of a volcano. [neck⁼cloth.

cra‑vat', 1 kra‑vat'; 2 era‑văt', *n.* A

crave, 1 krēv; 2 erāv, *v.* [CRAVED; CRAV'ING.] **I.** *t.* To beg for; long for. **II.** *i.* To desire or entreat humbly: with *for.*

cra'ven, 1 krē'vn; 2 erā'vn. **I.** *a.* Cowardly. **II.** *n.* A base coward. **‑ly,** *adv.*

cra'ven‑ette', 1 krē'vn‑et'; 2 erā'vn‑ĕt', *n.* A water‑proofed woolen cloth used for outer garments. [or crop, of a bird.

craw, 1 krô; 2 era, *n.* The first stomach,

craw'fish, 1 krô'fish''; 2 erạ'fĭsh'', *n.* A small fresh‑water lobster‑like crustacean.

crawl, 1 krôl; 2 erạl, *vi.* To move as a worm; move slowly; creep.— **crawl'ing‑ly,** *adv.* [crawfish.

cray'fish, 1 krē'fish''; 2 erā'fĭsh'', *n.* A

cray'on, 1 krē'ən; 2 erā'on, *n.* A pencil, as of charcoal or prepared chalk, for drawing; a drawing made with crayons.

craze, 1 krēz; 2 erāz. **I.** *vt. & vi.* [CRAZED⁹; CRAZ'ING.] **1.** To make or become insane. **2.** To crackle, as pottery. **II.** *n.* **1.** Mental disorder; freak of fashion; a caprice. **2.** A flaw in the glaze of pottery. — **crazed,** *a.* **1.** Insane. **2.** Cracked, as glaze.— **craz'i‑ly,** *adv.*— **craz'i‑ness,** *n.*— **craz'y,** *a.* [CRAZ'I‑ER; CRAZ'I‑EST.] **1.** Insane. **2.** Dilapidated; rickety.

creak, 1 krīk; 2 erēk. **Iᵗ.** *vt. & vi.* To make, or cause to make, a creak. **II.** *n.* A sharp, squeaking sound, as from friction.— **creak'y,** *a.* Apt to creak; creaking.

cream, 1 krīm; 2 erēm. **I.** *vt. & vi.* To

skim cream from or supply cream to; be covered with cream. **II.** *n.* A gathering of fatty globules on the surface of milk; the choicest or best part of anything. — **cream′er-y,** *n.* [-IES^z, *pl.*] A place for cream; a butter-making establishment.— **cream′y,** *a.* Like or containing cream.

crease, 1 krēs; 2 erēs, *vt.* [CREASED†, CREAST^s; CREAS′ING.] To make a crease or wrinkle in. [or the like.

crease[1], *n.* The mark of a wrinkle, fold, crease[2], *n.* Same as CREESE.

cre′a-sote, *n.* Same as CREOSOTE.

cre-ate′, 1 krī-ēt′; 2 erē-āt′, *vt.* [CRE-AT′ED^d, CRE-AT′ING.] To bring into existence; make out of nothing; originate; produce; occasion; appoint.— **cre-a′tion,** 1 krī-ē′shon; 2 erē-ā′shon, *n.* The act of creating; that which is created; the universe.— **cre-a′tiv**(e^s, *a.* Having the power to create; productive.— **cre-a′tor,** *n.* One who creates; [C-]. God as the maker of the universe.— **crea′ture,** 1 krī′chur *or* -tiur; 2 erē′chur *or* -tūr, *n.* A living being; a dependent; tool.

crèche, 1 krāsh; 2 erēçh, *n.* **1.** A public day-nursery. **2.** A foundling-asylum.

cre′dence, 1 krī′dens; 2 erē′dĕnç, *n.* Belief.

cre-den′tial, 1 krī-den′shal; 2 erē-dĕn′shal, *n.* That which certifies one's authority or claim to confidence.

cred′i-bl(e^r, 1 kred′ı-bl; 2 erĕd′i-bl, *a.* Capable of being believed; worthy of acceptance.— **cred′i-bil′i-ty,** *n.* The state or quality of being credible; trustworthiness. **cred′i-bl**(e-ness^r‡.— **cred′i-bly,** *adv.*

cred′it, 1 kred′ıt; 2 erĕd′it. **I**^{d}. *vt.* To give credit to or for; believe. **II.** *n.* **1.** Belief; trust; character; repute; honor. **2.** Time allowed for payment; amount in one's favor, or the record of it.— **cred″it-a-bil′i-ty,** *n.* **cred′it-a-bl**(e-ness^r‡.— **cred′it-a-bl**(e^r, *a.* Deserving credit; praiseworthy; meritorious.— **cred′it-a-bly,** *adv.*— **cred′i-tor,** *n.* One to whom another owes money.

cred′u-lous, 1 kred′yu-lus; 2 erĕd′yu-lŭs, *a.* Apt or disposed to believe on slight evidence. **-ly,** *adv.*— **cre-du′li-ty,** 1 krı-diū′lı-tı; 2 erē-dū′li-tу, *n.* Readiness to believe on inadequate evidence. **cred′u-lous-ness‡.**

creed, 1 krīd; 2 erēd, *n.* A formal summary of religious belief; doctrine.

creek, 1 krīk; 2 erēk, *n.* A small inlet or stream.

creel, 1 krīl; 2 erēl, *n.* A fishing-basket.

creep, 1 krīp; 2 erēp, *vi.* [CREPT, 1 krept, 2 erĕpt; CREEP′ING.] **1.** To move as a serpent; crawl; move slowly or stealthily. **2.** To show servility; cringe.— **creep′er,** *n.* One who or that which creeps; a creeping or climbing plant.

creese, 1 krīs; 2 erēs, *n.* A Malayan dagger with a waved blade.

cre-mate′, 1 krī-mēt′; 2 erē-māt′, *vt.* [-MAT′ED^d; -MAT′ING.] To burn up; reduce to ashes.— **cre-ma′tion,** *n.*— **cre′ma-to-ry,** *n.* [-RIES^z, *pl.*] A place for cremating the dead.

cre′nate, 1 krī′nēt; 2 erē′nāt, *a.* Scalloped or toothed, as a leaf. **cre′nat-ed‡.**

cre′ole, 1 krī′ōl; 2 erē′ōl, *n.* A native of Spanish America, or of the West Indies, of European parentage.

cre′o-sote, 1 krī′o-sōt; 2 erē′o-sōt, *n.* An oily liquid of smoky odor distilled from wood.

crep′i-tate, 1 krep′ı-tēt; 2 erĕp′i-tāt, *vi.* [-TAT′ED^d; -TAT′ING.] To make a succession of light crackling sounds; crackle. — **crep′i-tant,** *a.*— **crep′i-ta′tion,** *n.*

crept, 1 krept; 2 erĕpt, *imp.* of CREEP, *v.*

cres-cen′do, 1 kre-shen′do *or* kre-sen′do; 2 erē-shĕn′do *or* erĕ-sĕn′do, *a. Mus.* Slowly increasing in loudness or power: indicated by the sign < or abbreviated *cresc.*

cres′cent, 1 kres′ent; 2 erĕs′ĕnt. **I.** *a.* **1.** Increasing, as the new moon. **2.** Crescent-shaped. **II.** *n.* The moon in its first quarter, or something so shaped, as the device on the Turkish standard.

cress, 1 kres; 2 erēs, *n.* A plant of the mustard family, with pungent taste.

cres′set, 1 kres′et; 2 erĕs′ĕt, *n.* A frame to hold a torch; a burning light.

Cresset.

crest, 1 krest; 2 erĕst, *n.* **1.** A comb or tuft on the head of a fowl; a plume, tuft, or the like, on a helmet; the ridge of a wave or of a mountain; the top of anything; head. **2.** A coat of arms. — **crest′ed,** *a.* Bearing a crest.— **crest′-fall″en,** *a.* Dispirited; dejected.

cre-ta′ceous, 1 krı-tē′shus; 2 ere-tā′shŭs, *a.* Chalky.

Crest (a Dragon) upon a 16th-century Helmet.

cre-tonne′, 1 krı-ton′; 2 ere-tŏn′, *n.* An unglazed cotton fabric printed on one side.

cre-vasse′, 1 krı-vas′; 2 ere-vås′, *n.* A deep fissure, as in a glacier.

crev′ice, 1 krev′ıs; 2 erĕv′iç, *n.* A small crev′is^s, fissure or crack.

crew‖, 1 krū; 2 erų, *imp.* of CROW, *v.*

crew, *n.* The company of seamen belonging to a vessel; any company of workmen; a crowd; gang.

---

crew'el, 1 krū'el; 2 crŭ'el, *n.* A soft worsted yarn, used in fancy-work.

crib, 1 krib; 2 erĭb, *n.* **1.** A rack, manger, or stall for cattle. **2.** A child's bedstead, with side railings. **3.** A box or bin for grain. **4.** A wooden frame, as to retain a bank of earth.— **crib'bing**, *n.* The biting of the crib, as by a horse. [of cards.

crib'bage, 1 krib'ıj; 2 crĭb'ag, *n.* A game

crick, 1 krik; 2 erĭk, *n.* A spasmodic affection of the muscles, as of the neck; a cramp.

crick'et¹, 1 krik'et; 2 erĭk'ĕt, *n.* A leaping insect, the male of which makes a chirping sound.

crick'et², *n.* An outdoor game played with bats, a ball, and wickets.

crick'et³, *n.* A small footstool.

crick'et-er, 1 krik'et-ər; 2 erĭk'ĕt-er, *n.* A cricket-player.

cried, 1 kraid; 2 crid, *imp.* of CRY, *v.*

cri'er, 1 krai'ər; 2 crī'er, *n.* One who publicly cries sales, losses, etc.

crime, 1 kraim; 2 erīm, *n.* An act punishable by law; sin; any grave offense.— **crim'i-nal**, 1 krim'ı-nəl; 2 erim'i-nal. **I.** *a.* Relating to or guilty of crime. **II.** *n.* One who has committed a crime.— **crim"i-nal'i-ty**, *n.*— **crim'i-nal-ly**, *adv.*— **crim'i-nate**, 1 krim'ı-nēt; 2 erim'i-nāt, *vt.* [-NAT"ED⁴; -NAT"ING.] To accuse of or implicate in crime.— **crim"i-na'tion**, *n.* The act of criminating.

crim"i-nol'o-gy, 1 krim"ı-nəl'o-jı; 2 erim"-i-nŏl'o-gy, *n.* The scientific study of crime and criminals.

crimp, 1 krimp; 2 erĭmp. **I**t. *vt.* To bend into folds; corrugate; flute. **II.** *a.* Brittle and crisp; stiff; friable. **III.** *n.* Anything crimped, as a lock of hair.— **crim'-pl(e**ᴾ, 1 krim'pl; 2 erĭm'pl. **I.** *vt. & vt.* [CRIM'PL(E)D²; CRIM'PLING.] To wrinkle. **II.** *n.* A wrinkle.— **crimp'y**, *a.* Wavy; frizzled.

crim'son, 1 krim'zn; 2 erĭm'sn. **I.** *vt. & vi.* To make or become crimson; redden; blush. **II.** *a.* Deep-red; deep-dyed. **III.** *n.* A red color having a tinge of blue; deep-red.

cringe, 1 krinj; 2 erĭng. **I.** *vt.* [CRINGED; CRING'ING.] To crouch; fawn. **II.** *n.* A servile crouching.

crin'kl(eᴾ, 1 kriŋ'kl; 2 erĭŋ'kl. **I.** *vt. & vi.* [CRIN'KL(E)D²; CRIN'KLING.] To fold; wrinkle. **II.** *n.* A wrinkle; ripple; twist.— **crin'kly**, *a.* Wrinkled; crimpy.

crip'ple,) 1 krip'l;) 2 erĭp'l. **I.** *vt.* [CRIP'- **crip'l**ᴾ,) PLED, CRIP'LD²; CRIP'PLING.] To lame; disable. **II.** *n.* One lacking the natural use of a limb or limbs.

cri'sis, 1 krai'sis; 2 erī'sis, *n.* [CRI'SES,

1-sīz; 2-sēg, *pl.*] A turning-point; a critical moment.

crisp, 1 krisp; 2 erĭsp. **I**t. *vt. & vi.* To crinkle; curl; make or become crisp. **II.** *a.* **1.** Somewhat firm and brittle. **2.** Crinkled; crisped.

cri-te'ri-on, 1 krai-tī'rı-ən; 2 erī-tē'ri-on, *n.* [-RI-A, *pl.*] A standard; test.

crit'ic, 1 krit'ık; 2 erĭt'ic, *n.* **1.** One who judges anything by some standard. **2.** A faultfinder; caviler.— **crit'i-cal**, *a.* **1.** Of or pertaining to a critic or criticism; judicious; fastidious; thorough; exact; faultfinding. **2.** Of or preliminary to a crisis; perilous. **-ly**, *cdv.*— **crit'i-cism**, 1 krit'ı-sizm; 2 erĭt'i-çism, *n.* The act or art of criticizing; a critical judgment.— **crit'i-cize** or **-cise**, 1 krit'ı-saiz; 2 erĭt'i-çiz, *vt. & vi.* [-CIZED, -CISED; -CIZ'ING, -CIS'ING.] **1.** To examine critically. **2.** To judge severely; censure.— **cri-tique'**, 1 krı-tīk; 2 eri-tĭk', *n.* A criticism; critical review.

croak, 1 krōk; 2 erōk. **I**t. *vi.* To make a croak; talk dolefully; forbode evil. **II.** *n.* A hoarse, guttural sound, as of a frog or raven; a doleful or foreboding speech. — **croak'er**, *n.*

cro-chet', 1 krō-shē'; 2 erō-çhe'. **I.** *vt. & vi.* [CRO-CHETED', 1 krō-shēd', 2 erō-çhed'; CRO-CHET'ING, 1 krō-shē'ıŋ, 2 erō-çhe'ing.] To form or knit, as crochet. **II.** *n.* Fancy-work produced by looping thread with a hooked needle.

crock¹, 1 krok; 2 erōk. **I**t. *vt.* To stain or dye. **II.** *n.* The coloring-matter that rubs off from a dyed stuff, as c oth.

crock², *n.* An earthen pot or jar.

crock'er-y, 1 krek'ər-ı; 2 erōk'er-y, *n.* Earthenware.

croc'o-dile, 1 krek'o-dail; 2 erōe'o-dil, *n.* A large carnivorous amphibious reptile. — **croc"o-dil'-i-an**, *a. & n.* Like a crocodile.— **croc"o-dil'e-an.**

Skull of the Common Crocodile.

cro'cus, 1 krō'kus; 2 erō'eŭs, *n.* A plant of the iris family, with long grass-like leaves and large flowers. [farm.

croft, 1 krŏft; 2 erōft, *n.* A small field or

crone, 1 krōn; 2 erōn, *n.* A withered old woman.

cro'ny, 1 krō'nı; 2 erō'ny, *n.* [CRO'NIES⁸, *pl.*] A familiar friend.

crook, 1 kruk; 2 erōōk. **I**t. *vt. & vi.* To bend; make or grow crooked. **II.** *n.* **1.** A bend or curve; something crooked, as a staff with a hooked end. **2.** A criminal; sharper.— **crook'ed**, 1 kruk'ed; 2

erŏŏk'ĕd, *a.* Not straight; having angles or curves; dishonest. **-ly,** *adv.* **-ness,** *n.*

croon, 1 krūn; 2 erŏŏn, *vt. & vi.* To sing or hum in a low, monotonous manner.

crop, 1 krŏp; 2 erŏp, *vt.* [CROPPED⁴ or CROPT⁵; CROP′PING.] To cut off closely; mow; reap; eat down.

crop, *n.* **1.** Produce; harvest. **2.** The first stomach of a bird; a craw.

cro-quet', 1 kro-kē'; 2 ero-kę', *n.* A lawn-game played with balls and mallets.

cro-quette', 1 kro-ket'; 2 ero-kĕt', *n.* A cake of minced food, fried brown.

cro'sier, cros'let, *n.* See CROZIER, CROSSLET.

cross, 1 krôs; 2 erôs. **I⁴.** *vt. & vi.* **I.** To place or move across; traverse; intersect; cancel (cross *off* or *out*); obstruct; contradict; irritate. **2.** To make the sign of the cross upon. **3.** To mix with a different variety. **II.** *a.* Ill-tempered; peevish. **III.** *n.* **1.** An ancient instrument of torture and death, consisting of two crossed timbers, on which the condemned were fastened. **2.** [C-] The crucifixion of Christ; the Atonement. **3.** Something endured for Christ's sake; trial; tribulation. **4.** A mark resembling a cross. **5.** A mixing of breeds; an animal of mixed breed.—**cross'ly,** *adv.* Peevishly.—**cross'ness,** *n.*—**cross'bow'',** *n.* A bow, fixed transversely upon a stock.—**c.=bred,** *a.* Hybrid; mongrel.—**c.=breed,** *n.* A hybrid.—**c.=breeding,** *n.*—**c.=cut,** *n.* A cut across; a short cut.—**c.=examine,** *vt. Law.* To cross-question.—**c.=examination,** *n.*—**c.=examiner,** *n.*—**c.=eyed,** *a.* Having a squint; squinting.—**c.=purpose,** *n.* A conflicting aim.—**c.=question,** *vt.* To question minutely, as in order to elicit facts from a reluctant witness.

cross'ing, 1 krôs'ıŋ; 2 erôs'ing, *n.* Intersection, as of roads; act or place of crossing.

cross'=road'', 1 krôs'=rōd''; 2 erôs'=rōd'', *n.* A road that crosses another. **cross'=way''‡.**—**cross'roads'',** *n.* A place where roads cross: often marked by a settlement.

cross'wise, 1 krôs'waiz; 2 erôs'wįs, *adv.* **1.** Across: sometimes with *to.* **2.** In the form of a cross.

crotch, 1 krŏch; 2 erŏch, *n.* A point of division of branches; fork.

crotch'et, 1 krŏch'et; 2 erŏch'ĕt, *n.* **1.** A whim; eccentricity. **2.** *Mus.* A quarter note. **3.** A small hook.—**crotch'et-i-ness,** *n.*—**crotch'et-y,** *a.* Whimsical; eccentric.

crouch, 1 krauch; 2 erouch, *vi.* To stoop low, as in fear or in readiness to spring; cringe.

croup¹, 1 krūp; 2 erųp, *n.* A membranous

disease of the throat.—**croup'ous,** *a.* Of, like, or affected by croup. **croup'y‡.**

croup², 1 krūp; 2 erųp, *n.* The rump of a horse. **croupe‡.**

crow, 1 krō; 2 erō, *vi.* [CROWED, CROWD⁵; 1 krŏd, 2 erŏd; CROW′ING.] **1.** To utter the cry of a cock; exult; boast. **2.** To utter sounds of infantile delight.

crow, *n.* **1.** A bird with glossy black plumage. **2.** The cry of a cock, or any like sound.—**crow'bar'',** 1 krō'bär''; 2 erō'-bär'', *n.* A straight iron or steel bar: used as a lever.—**crow'foot'',** *n.* A plant, the buttercup.—**crows'=foot'',** *n.* **1.** One of the wrinkles diverging from the outer corner of the eye. **2.** One of various mechanical devices so named from their shape.

crowd, 1 kraud; 2 erowd. **I⁴.** *vt. & vi.* To fill to overflowing; pack; throng; push forward; urge. **II.** *n.* A numerous collection; multitude; throng.

crown, 1 kraun; 2 erown. **I.** *vt.* **1.** To put a crown on; invest with royal dignity; honor; reward. **2.** To form the top part of; cap; complete. **II.** *n.* **1.** A circlet or covering for the head, as a mark of sovereign power; any wreath or garland for the head. **2.** A sovereign ruler; sovereignty. **3.** A reward; prize. **4.** The top, as of the head; summit; perfect state; acme. **5.** An English coin, worth 5 shillings.

Crown.

cro'zier, 1 krō'ʒər; 2 erō'zher, *n.* A bishop's official staff surmounted by a crook or a cross. **cro'sier.**

cru'cial, 1 krū'shəl; 2 erų'shal, *a.* **1.** Decisive; searching; severe. **2.** Having the form of a cross.

cru'ci-bl(e⁰, 1 krū'sı-bl; 2 erų'çį-bl, *n.* A vessel, as of clay, for melting metals, etc.; a test; purifying agency.

cru'ci-fix, 1 krū'sı-fiks; 2 erų'çį-fïks, *n.* A cross bearing an effigy of Christ crucified.

cru'ci-fix'ion, 1 krū'sı-fik'shan; 2 erų'çį-fïk'shon, *n.* The act of crucifying; death upon the cross; specifically [C-], the death of Christ on Calvary.

cru'ci-form, 1 krū'sı-fêrm; 2 erų'ei-fôrm, *a.* Cross=shaped.

cru'ci-fy, 1 krū'sı-fai; 2 erų'çį-fī, *vt.* [-FIED; -FY′ING.] To put to death by fastening to a cross.

crude, 1 krūd; 2 erųd, *a.* Not mature; raw; unripe; superficial; unfinished. **-ly,** *adv.*—**cru'di-ty,** 1 krū'dı-tı; 2 erų'dį-ty, *n.* [-TIES²,* pl.*] **1.** The state of being crude. **2.** That which is crude. **crude'ness‡.**

cru'el, 1 krū'el; 2 erų'ĕl, *a.* Disposed to

inflict suffering; pitiless; unreasonably severe; harsh; distressing. **-ly,** adv.— **cru′el-ty,** 1 krū′el-tı; 2 erụ′ĕl-ty, n. [-TIES² pl.] A cruel disposition or act; inhumanity.

cru′et, 1 krū′et; 2 erụ′ĕt, n. A small glass bottle, as for vinegar or oil; a caster.

cruise, 1 krūz; 2 erụṣ. **I.** vt. & vi. [CRUISED; CRUIS′ING.] To sail over or through; sail to and fro. **II.** n. A voyage at sea; a sailing to and fro.— **cruis′er,** n. A person or ship that cruises; a war-vessel inferior to a battle-ship.

crul′ler, 1 krul′ər; 2 erŭl′er, n. A ring-shaped cake of dough, fried brown in boiling lard.

crum, } 1krum; 2 erŭm. **I.** vt. [CRUMMED,
crumb, } CRUMBED, CRUMB⁸; CRUM′MING, CRUMB′ING.] To break into small pieces; crumble. **II.** n. **1.** A small bit, as of bread; a morsel. **2.** The soft inner part of a loaf.

crum′ble, } 1 krum′bl; 2 erŭm′bl, vt. & vi.
crum′bl′, } [CRUM′BL(E)D⁸; CRUM′BLING.] To break into small pieces; cause to fall to pieces; disintegrate; decay.— **crum′bly,** a. Apt to crumble; friable.

crum′pet, 1 krum′pet; 2 erŭm′pĕt, n. A sort of muffin.

crum′ple, } 1 krum′pl; 2 erŭm′pl, vt. &
crum′pl′, } vi. [CRUM′PL(E)D⁸; CRUM′PLING.] To press into wrinkles; become wrinkled; rumple.

crunch, 1 krunch; 2 erŭnch, **I.** vt. & vi. To crush with the teeth; chew audibly; crush or grind noisily. **II.** n. The act of crunching.

crup′per, 1 krup′ər; 2 erŭp′er, n. **1.** The looped strap that goes under a horse's tail. **2.** The rump of a horse.

cru-sade′, 1 krū-sēd′; 2 erụ-sād′. **I**d. vi. To go on or engage in a crusade. **II.** n. A medieval gathering of the Christians of Europe for the conquest of the Holy Sepulcher; any vigorous concerted movement.— **cru-sad′er,** n.

cruse, 1 krūs; 2 erụs, n. A small bottle, flask, or jug; cruet. **cruize‡.**

crush, 1 krush; 2 erŭsh. **I**t. vt. & vi. To press out of shape; break or be broken by pressure; conquer. **II.** n. **1.** A violent colliding; breaking by violent pressure. **2.** A crowd; jam.— **crush′er,** n.

crust, 1 krust; 2 erŭst. **I**d. vt. & vi. To cover with or acquire a crust. **II.** n. A hard, thin coating; the outer part of bread; a bit of bread.

crus-ta′cean, 1 krus-tē′shan; 2 erŭs-tā′shan. **I.** a. Of or pertaining to the Crustacea. **II.** n. One of the Crustacea, animals having crust-like shells, including lobsters, crabs, sow-bugs, etc.— **crus-ta′ceous,** a. **1.** Having a crust-like shell. **2.** Crustacean.

crust′y, 1 krust′ı; 2 erŭst′y, a. Crust-like; curt; surly.— **crust′1-ly,** adv.— **crust′1-ness,** n.

crutch, } 1 kruch; 2 erŭch, n. A staff with
crutch⁸, } a crosspiece fitting under the armpit, as for support in walking; any mechanical device of similar shape.

cry, 1 krai; 2 erī, n. [CRIED; CRY′ING.] **I.** t. To utter loudly; shout out; proclaim. **II.** i. **1.** To call loudly; shout. **2.** To utter lamentations; weep.

cry, 1 krai; 2 erȳ, n. [CRIES², pl.] **1.** A loud call; shout; yell. **2.** The act of weeping. **3.** Advertisement by outcry; proclamation; public demand.

crypt, 1 kript; 2 erȳpt, n. A recess or vault, as under a church.

cryp′to-gam, 1 krip′to-gam; 2 erȳp′to-găm, n. Bot. A plant that has no true flowers, but propagates by spores.— **cryp″to-gam′ic,** a.

cryp′to-gram, 1 krip′to-gram; 2 erȳp′to-grăm, n. A writing in cipher.

cryp-tog′ra-phy, 1 krip-tog′ra-fı; 2 erȳp⸗ tŏg′ra-fy, n. The art of cipher-writing.

crys′tal, 1 kris′təl; 2 erȳs′tal. **I.** a. Of or like crystal; clear; limpid. **II.** n. **1.** The solid mathematical form assumed by many minerals. **2.** Transparent quartz; flint glass; a watch-glass.— **crys′tal-line,** 1 kris′təl-in; 2 erȳs′tal-in, a. Of, pertaining to, or like crystals or crystal; transparent; pure.— **crys″tal-log′ra-phy,** n. The science of crystals.

crys′tal-lize or **-lise,** 1 kris′təl-aiz; 2 erȳs′-tal-īz, vt. & vi. [-LIZED; -LIZ″ING.] To form crystals; bring or come to definite and permanent form.— **crys″tal-li-za′tion,** n.

cub, 1 kub; 2 eŭb, n. The young of the bear, fox, wolf, etc.; a whelp.

cube, 1 kiūb; 2 eūb, n. **1.** A solid bounded by six equal squares and having all its angles right angles. **2.** The third power of a quantity; the product of three equal factors.— **cu′bic,** 1 kiū′bık; 2 eū′bĭc, a. Of, equal to, or like a cube. **cu′bi-cal‡.— cu′-bi-cal-ly,** adv. **— cu′bi-cal-ness,** n.

cu′bit, 1 kiū′-bit;2 eū′bit, n. An ancient measure of length: about 20 inches.

American Yellow-billed Cuckoo and Nest. 1/14

cuck′oo, 1 kuk′ū; 2 eụk′ŏŏ, n. A bird, many species of which deposit their eggs

to be hatched in the nests of other birds.

cu'cum·ber, 1 kiū'kum-bər; 2 eū'eŭm-ber, *n.* The oblong fruit of a creeping plant of the gourd family; also, the plant.

cud, 1 kud; 2 eŭd, *n.* Food chewed over again, as by ruminants.

cud'dle, 1 kud'l; 2 eŭd'l, *vt. & vi.* [CUD'-DLED, CUD'DLING.] To protect and caress within a close embrace; lie close together.

cud'dy, 1 kud'i; 2 eŭd'y, *n.* [CUD'DIESᶻ, *pl.*] *Naut.* A small cabin; a cook's galley.

cudg'el, 1 kuj'el; 2 eŭdg'ĕl. **I.** *vt.* To beat, as with a cudgel. **II.** *n.* A short thick stick; a club.

cue, 1 kiū; 2 eū, *n.* **1.** A tail; a long braid of hair. **2.** The words serving as a signal for an actor; a hint; suggestion. **3.** A straight tapering rod, used in billiards, etc.

cufft, } 1 kuf; 2 eŭf, *v.* **I.** *t.* To strike, as **cufᴿ,** } with the open hand; buffet. **II.** *i.* To scuffle; box.

cuff¹, *n.* A blow, as with the open hand.

cuff², *n.* A band about the wrist; the lower part of a sleeve.

cui·rass', 1 kwĭ-ras'; 2 ewĭ-răs', *n.* A breastplate. — **cui'ras·sier',** 1 kwĭ'rə-sīr'; 2 ewĭ'ra-sēr', *n.* A mounted soldier wearing a cuirass.

cui·sine', 1 kwĭ-zīn'; 2 ewĭ-sĭn', *n.* The kitchen; cooking department; style or quality of cooking.

cui''=de·sac', 1 kü''də-sak'; 2 eü''de-săc', *n.* [CULS''=DE·SAC', 1 kü''=; 2 eü''=, *pl.*] A passage open only at one end; blind alley; trap.

-cule, *suffix.* A diminutive; as, animal*cule.*

cu'li·na·ry, 1 kiū'lɪ-nē-rɪ; 2 eū'lĭ-nă-ry, *a.* Of or pertaining to cooking or the kitchen.

cull, 1 kul; 2 eŭl. **I.** *vt.* [CULLED, CULDˢ; CULL'ING.] To pick or sort out. **II.** *n.* Something sorted out; something rejected. — **cull'er,** *n.*

cul'len·der, *n.* Same as COLANDER.

culm, 1 kulm; 2 eŭlm, *n.* The jointed stem of a grass.

cul'mi·nate, 1 kul'mɪ-nēt; 2 eŭl'mĭ-nāt, *vi.* [-NAT''EDᵈ; -NAT''ING.] To attain the highest point or degree. — **cul'mi·na'tion,** *n.* The highest point, condition, or degree.

cul'pa·ble, } 1 kul'pə-bl; 2 eŭl'pa-bl, *a.* **cul'pa·blᴿ,** } Deserving of blame. — **cul'pa·bil'i·ty, cul'pa·bl(e=nessᴿ,** *n.* — **cul'pa·bly,** *adv.*

cul'prit, 1 kul'prit; 2 eŭl'prĭt, *n.* A guilty person; criminal; offender.

cult, 1 kult; 2 eŭlt, *n.* A system of religious observances; also, a fad.

cul'ti·vate, 1 kul'tɪ-vēt; 2 eŭl'tĭ-vāt, *vt.* [-VAT''EDᵈ; -VAT''ING.] **1.** To till, as land; raise, as a plant, by tillage. **2.** To develop by study or training; devote oneself to; foster. — **cul'ti·va'tion,** *n.* The act of cultivating; improvement; culture. — **cul'ti·va''tor,** *n.* One who cultivates; a machine for cultivating.

cul'ture, 1 kul'chur *or* -tiur; 2 eŭl'chur *or* -tūr, *n.* **1.** Cultivation: training; improvement: refinement of mind, morals, or taste; enlightenment. **2.** The development of micro=organisms, or the organisms so developed. — **cul'tur·al,** *a.* Of or pertaining to culture. — **cul'tured,** *pa.* Educated; refined.

cul'tus, 1 kul'tus; 2 eŭl'tŭs, *n.* A cult.

cul'vert, 1 kul'vərt; 2 eŭl'vert, *n.* An artificial covered channel for water, as under a road.

cum'ber, 1 kum'bər; 2 eŭm'ber, *vt.* To burden; hamper; weigh down; oppress. — **cum'ber·some,** 1 kum'bər-səm; 2 eŭm'ber-som, *a.* Moving or working heavily; unwieldy; burdensome. **-ly,** *adv.* **-ness,** *n.*

cum'brous, 1 kum'brus; 2 eŭm'brŭs, *a.* Cumbersome. **-ly,** *adv.* **-ness,** *n.*

cum'in, 1 kum'ɪn; 2 eŭm'ĭn, *n.* A plant of the parsley family, or its seeds. **cum'mint.**

cu'mu·late, 1 kiū'miu-lēt; 2 eū'mū-lāt, *vt.* [-LAT''EDᵈ; -LAT''ING.] To collect into a heap; accumulate. — **cu'mu·la'tion,** *n.* The process of massing or heaping together; a heap. — **cu'mu·la·tiv(eˢ,** *a.* Increasing by addition or repetition.

cu'ne·i·form, 1 kiū'nī-ɪ-fôrm; 2 eū'nē-ɪ-fôrm, *a.* Wedge-shaped, as the characters in ancient Assyrian inscriptions. **cu'ne·ate‡.**

Cuneiform Inscription.

cun'ner, 1 kun'ər; 2 eŭn'er, *n.* A small brownish=blue food= fish common on the Atlantic coast of the United States.

cun'ning, 1 kun'ɪŋ; 2 eŭn'ing. **I.** *a.* Crafty or shrewd; artful; guileful. **II.** *n.* A crafty disposition; craft; guile; artifice.

cup, 1 kup; 2 eŭp. **I.** *vt. & vi.* [CUPPEDᵈ, CUPᵀˢ; CUP'PING.] **1.** To draw blood under an exhausted cup. **2.** To shape like or place in a cup. **II.** *n.* A small drinking=vessel; its contents; one's lot. — **cup'ful,** *n.* As much as a cup will hold.

cup'board, 1 kub'ərd; 2 eŭb'ord, *n.* A closet with shelves, as for tableware.

Cu′pid, 1 kiū′pıd; 2 cū′pĭd, *n.* *Myth.* The Roman god of love.

cu-pid′i-ty, 1 kiu-pid′ı-tı; 2 cū-pĭd′ĭ-ty, *n.* An inordinate desire, as for gain; avarice.

cu′po-la, 1 kiū′po-lə; 2 cū′po-la, *n.* A dome; a small structure above a roof; a turret on an armored ship.

cur, 1 kŭr; 2 cŭr, *n.* A worthless dog; a mean or malicious person.— **cur′rish,** *a.*

cur′a-ble, } 1 kiūr′ə-bl; 2 cūr′a-bl, *a.*
cur′a-bl², } Susceptible of being cured.— **cur″a-bil′i-ty,** *n.* **cur′a-bl(e-ness²‡.—** **cur′a-bly,** *adv.*

cu′ra-cy, 1 kiū′rə-sı; 2 cū′ra-çy, *n.* [-CIES², *pl.*] The position, duties, or term of office of a curate.

cu′rate, 1 kiū′rıt; 2 cū′rat, *n.* A rector's or a vicar's assistant.— **cu′rate-ship,** *n.* A curacy.

cur′a-tive, } 1 kiūr′ə-tiv; 2 cūr′a-tĭv. **I.** *a.*
cur′a-tiv², } Possessing power or tendency to cure; relating to the cure of diseases. **II.** *n.* A remedy.— **cur′a-tiv(e-ly²,** *adv.*

cu-ra′tor, 1 kiu-rē′tər *or* -tər; 2 cū-rā′tor, *n.* A superintendent; guardian.

curb, 1 kŭrb; 2 cûrb. **I.** *vt.* To subject, control, as with reins and curb. **II.** *n.* **1.** A chain or strap to add power to a bit; also, a bit so arranged; restraint; control. **2.** A curbstone. **3.** The framework around the top of a well.

curb′stone, 1 kŭrb′stōn; 2 cûrb′stōn″, *n.* A stone forming the outer edge of a sidewalk.

curd, 1 kŭrd; 2 cûrd, *n.* The coagulated portion of milk of which cheese is made. — **cur′dle,** *vt.* & *vt.* [CUR′DLED; CUR′DLING.] To change to curd; coagulate.

cure, 1 kiūr; 2 cūr. **I.** *vt.* & *vi.* [CURED; CUR′ING.] **1.** To restore to health; cause recovery. **2.** To eradicate, as disease; heal. **3.** To preserve, as fish, by salting and drying. **II.** *n.* **1.** A restoration to health. **2.** That which restores health. **3.** Spiritual care; a curacy; as, the *cure* of souls.

cur′few, 1 kŭr′fiu; 2 cûr′fū, *n.* An ancient law for the putting out of fires and lights at the tolling of a bell; also, the bell, or the act or hour of ringing.

cu″ri-os′i-ty, 1 kiū″rı-os′ı-tı; 2 cū″rĭ-ŏs′i-ty, *n.* [-TIES², *pl.*] **1.** Habitual anxiety for knowledge; inquisitiveness. **2.** A rare and interesting object.

cu′ri-ous, 1 kiū′rı-us; 2 cū′rĭ-ŭs, *a.* **1.** Eager for information; inquisitive. **2.** Adapted to excite interest; novel; odd; strange; mysterious; ingenious. **-ly,** *adv.* **-ness,** *n.*

curl, 1 kŭrl; 2 cûrl. **I.** *vt.* & *vi.* To curl into ringlets or curves; adorn with curls; take spiral shape. **II.** *n.* Anything coiled or spiral, as a ringlet.— **curl′y,** *a.*— **curl′i-ness,** *n.*

cur′lew, 1 kŭr′liu; 2 cûr′lū, *n.* A shorebird with long bill and legs.

curl′ing, 1 kŭrl′ıŋ; 2 cûrl′ĭng, *n.* 1. [Scot.] A game played by sliding large circular stones, called *curling-stones,* on the ice. **2.** The act of forming curls. — **curl′ing-i′ron,** *n.* An implement of metal, used when heated for curling the hair. **curl′ing-tongs″‡.**

Curlew. ¹/₂₅

cur-mudg′eon, 1 kər-muj′ən; 2 cûr-mŭdg′on, *n.* A miserly or churlish person.

cur′rant, 1 kŭr′ənt; 2 cûr′ant, *n.* A small round, acid berry, or the bush producing it; also, a small seedless raisin.

cur′rent, 1 kŭr′ent; 2 cûr′ĕnt. **I.** *a.* **1.** Circulating freely; generally accepted. **2.** In actual progress; present. **II.** *n.* A movement as of a stream; a fluid thus flowing; any connected onward movement; course. **-ly,** *adv.* **-ness,** *n.*— **cur′ren-cy,** 1 kŭr′en-sı; 2 cûr′ĕn-çy, *n.* [-CIES², *pl.*] **1.** The current medium of exchange; coin or bank-notes. **2.** The state of being current.

cur-ric′u-lum, 1 ku-rik′yu-lum; 2 cû-rĭc′yu-lŭm, *n.* A prescribed course of study, as in a college. [curries leather.

cur′ri-er, 1 kŭr′ı-ər; 2 cûr′i-er, *n.* One who

cur′ry, 1 kŭr′ı; 2 cûr′y, *vt.* [CUR′RIED, 1 -rid, 2 -rid; CUR′RY-ING.] **1.** To clean or groom, as a horse. **2.** To dress for use, as leather.

cur′ry, *n.* [CUR′RIES², *pl.*] A pungent sauce, or a dish served with it.

curse, 1 kŭrs; 2 cûrs, *v.* [CURSED† *or* CURST; CURS′ING.] **I.** *t.* **1.** To invoke evil upon; anathematize; excommunicate. **2.** To cause great evils to. **II.** *i.* To utter imprecations; swear; blaspheme. — **curs′ed,** 1 kŭrs′ed; 2 cûrs′ĕd, *a.* Under or deserving a curse; execrable; detestable. — **curs′ed-ly,** *adv.*

curse, *n.* An imprecation of evil; profane oath. **2.** Calamity invoked; a source of evil.

cur′sive, } 1 kŭr′sıv; 2 cûr′siv. **I.** *a.* Run-
cur′siv², } ning or flowing, as writing with letters joined. **II.** *n.* A letter or character used in cursive writing.

cur′so-ry, 1 kŭr′so-rı; 2 cûr′so-ry, *a.*

Rapid and superficial; hasty.— **cur'so·ri·ly,** *adv.*— **cur'so·ri·ness,** *n.*

curt, 1 kŭrt; 2 eûrt, *a.* Concise and abrupt; short; sharp; brusk. **-ly,** *adv.* **-ness,** *n.*

cur·tail', 1 kər-tāl'; 2 eur-tăl', *vt.* To cut short; abbreviate; reduce. **-ment,** *n.*

cur'tain, 1 kûr'tın; 2 eûr'tın. **I.** *vt.* To supply with curtains; separate, as by a curtain. **II.** *n.* **1.** An adjustable hanging covering, as of a window. **2.** Something that conceals or separates. **3.** Part of a rampart that connects two bastions or towers.— **curtain of fire** (*Mil.*), shell-fire designed to prevent the advance of reenforcements.

curt'sy, 1 kûrt'sı; 2 eûrt'sy. **I.** *vi.* To make a courtesy. **II.** *n.* An old-time gesture of deference. See COURTESY. **curt'sey‡.**

curve, 1 kûrv; 2 eûrv. **I.** *vt. & vi.* **curvᴮ,** ⎰[CURV(E)Dᴮ; CURV'ING.] To form a curve; move in a curve; bend. **II.** *a.* Having a different direction at every point. **III.** *n.* A line continuously bent, as the arc of a circle; a bending, or something bent.

cur'va·ture, 1 kûr'və-chur *or* -tıur; 2 eûr'va-chur *or* -tūr, *n.* The act of bending, or the state of being curved; amount or rate of bending.

cur'vet, 1 kûr'vet; 2 eûr'vĕt. **Iᵈ.** *vt. & vi.* To prance or cause to prance. **II.** *n.* A light, low leap of a horse.

cur''vi·lin'e·ar, 1 kûr''vi-lin'ı-ər; 2 eûr''vi-lín'e-ar, *a.* Formed by curved lines. **cur''vi·lin'e·al‡.**

cush'ion, 1 kush'ən; 2 eush'on. **I.** *vt.* To place on or provide with a cushion. **II.** *n.* A flexible casing filled with soft material, as feathers; any device to deaden jar.

cusp, 1 kusp; 2 eusp, *n.* One of the points of the crescent moon; a prominence; point.— **cus'pi·date,** 1 kus'pı-dēt; 2 eûs'pı-dāt, *a.* Having a cusp or cusps. **cus'pi·dal‡; cus'pi·dat''ed‡.**

cus'pi·dor, 1 kus'pı-dôr; 2 eûs'pi-dôr, *n.* A spittoon. **cus'pi·dore‡.**

cus'tard, 1 kus'tərd; 2 eûs'tard, *n.* A mixture of milk, eggs, sugar, etc., boiled or baked.

cus'to·dy, 1 kus'to-dı; 2 eûs'to-dy, *n.* A keeping; guardianship; restraint; imprisonment.— **cus·to'di·an,** 1 kus-tō'dı-ən; 2 eûs-tō'di-an, *n.* One having the custody of a person or thing; a guardian.

cus'tom, 1 kus'tam; 2 eûs'tom, *n.* **1.** Habitual practise; common or recognized usage. **2.** Business support; patronage. **3.** A tariff or duty.— **cus'tom·a·ry,** 1 kus'təm-ē-rı; 2 eûs'tom-ā-ry, *a.* Conforming to

or established by custom.— **cus'tom·a·ri·ly,** *adv.* In the customary manner; ordinarily. — **cus'tom·er,** *n.* A purchaser.— **cus'tom·house",** *n.* The place where duties are collected.

cut, 1 kut; 2 eŭt, *vt. & vi.* [CUT; CUT'TING.] **1.** To divide, trim, or shape, as with a knife; make a cut; sever; clip; hew; wound. **2.** To hurt; pain; grieve. **3.** To reduce. **4.** To pass without recognition.— **cut'ter,** 1 kut'ər; 2 eŭt'er, *n.* One who cuts; a cutting-tool or -machine; a small, swift vessel; a small sleigh.— **cut'throat",** *n.* A bloodthirsty ruffian.— **cut'wa''ter,** *n.* *Naut.* The forward part of the prow of a vessel.— **cut'worm",** *n.* A larval moth that cuts off young plants.

cut, *pa.* Formed or affected by cutting; wounded; severed.

cut, *n.* **1.** An incision; a gash; slit. **2.** A cutting motion or action. **3.** A short way, as across a corner. **4.** Fashion; form; style. **5.** *Print.* An engraved block, or a picture printed from it.

cu·ta'ne·ous, 1 kiu-tē'nı-us; 2 eū-tā'ne-ŭs, *a.* Consisting of, pertaining to, or like skin.

cute, 1 kiut; 2 eŭt, *a.* [CUT'ER; CUT'EST.] **1.** Clever; sharp. **2.** [Colloq., U. S.] Bright and winsome, as a child.

cu'ti·cle, ⎰1 kū'tı-kl; 2 eū'ti-el, *n.* The **cu'ti·clᴾ,** ⎰ outer layer of skin; epidermis; any superficial covering.— **cu·tic'u·lar,** *a.*

cut'las, 1 kut'ləs; 2 eŭt'las, *n.* A short, heavy sword-like weapon. **cut'lass‡.**

cut'ler, 1 kut'lər; 2 eŭt'lər, *n.* One who makes or deals in cutlery.— **cut'ler·y,** *n.* Cutting-instruments collectively.

British Cutlas of the 10th Century.

cut'let, 1 kut'let; 2 eŭt'lĕt, *n.* A thin piece of veal or mutton for broiling or frying.

cut'tle, ⎰1 kut'l; 2 eŭt'l, *n.* **1.** A cuttlefish. **cut'lᴾ,** ⎰ **2.** Cuttlebone. — **cut'tle·bone",** *n.* The internal calcareous plate of a cuttlefish.— **cut'tle·fish",** *n.* A marine mollusk, with 8 or 10 arms and an internal shell or bone, having the power of ejecting an inky fluid to conceal itself.

Cuttlefish. ¹/₂₁
a, the cuttlebone.

-cy, *suffix.* Denoting condition, quality, office, rank, etc.; as, aristocra*cy*, captain*cy*, magistra*cy.*

cy'cle, 1 sai'k‖; 2 çȳ'el, *n.* **1.** A recurring period of time; a round of years or of ages; a vast period. **2.** A turn or circle; loop. **3.** A bicycle, tricycle, etc. **4.** *Elec.* A full period of an alternating current.—**cye'lic,** 1 sik'lık; 2 çȳc'lic, *a.*—**cy'cling,** *n.* The riding of the bicycle.—**cy'clist,** *n.* One who rides a bicycle or the like. **cy'clert.**

cy'cloid, 1 sai'kloid; 2 çȳ'elöïd, *n.* *Geom.* The curve described by a point in the plane of a circle that rolls along a straight line.—**cy-cloï'dal,** *a.*

cy-clom'e-ter, 1 sai-klem'ı-tər; 2 çȳ-elöm'e-ter, *n.* An instrument for recording the rotations of a wheel, as of a bicycle.

cy'clone, 1 sai'klōn; 2 çȳ'elōn, *n.* A violent and destructive wind-storm; tornado.—**cy-clon'ic,** *a.*

Cy"clo-pe'an, 1 sai"klo-pi'ən; 2 çȳ'elo-pē'an, *a.* Of or pertaining to the Cyclopes, a race of mythical giants, or their work; gigantic; colossal.

cy"clo-pe'di-a, 1 sai"klo-pi'dı-ə; 2 çȳ'elo-pē'di-a, *n.* A work giving a summary of some branch of knowledge; in broader use, an encyclopedia.—**cy"clo-pe'**[or **-pæ'**]**die,** *a.* [swan.

cyg'net, 1 sig'net; 2 çȳg'nĕt, *n.* A young

cyl'in-der, 1 sil'ın-dər; 2 çȳl'in-der, *n.* A circular body of uniform diameter, the extremities of which are equal parallel circles.—**cy-lin'dric,** *a.* **cy-lin'dri-cal‡.**—**cy-lin'dri-cal-ly,** *adv.*

cym'bal, 1 sim'bəl; 2 çȳm'bal, *n.* One of a pair of plate-like metallic musical instruments played by being clashed together.

cyn'ic, 1 sin'ık; 2 çȳn'ie, *n.* **1.** [C-] One of a sect of Greek philosophers who taught contempt for pleasure, intellectual or sensual. **2.** A sneering, captious person; a misanthrope; pessimist.—**cyn'i-cal,** *a.* Of or like a cynic: misanthropic: morose; sarcastic.—**cyn'i-cal-ly,** *adv.*—**cyn'i-cism,** 1 sin'ı-sizm; 2 çȳn'i-çism, *n.* The state or quality of being cynical; contempt for the virtuous or generous sentiments of others.

Turkish
Cymbals.

cy'no-sure, 1 sai'no-shūr; 2 çȳ'no-shur, *n.* An object of general interest or attention.

cy'press, 1 sai'pres; 2 çȳ'près, *n.* An evergreen tree yielding durable timber; also, a kindred plant, funeral cypress, with pendulous branches like a weeping willow.

cyst, 1 sist; 2 çȳst, *n.* A membranous sac or vesicle in living organisms.

czar, 1 zär; 2 zär, *n.* An emperor: especially [C-], the emperor of Russia, when an empire. **tsar‡; tzar‡.**—**Czar'e-vitch,** 1 zär'ı-vıch; 2 zär'e-vich, *n.* The eldest son of a Czar of Russia. **Tsar'e-vitch‡.**—**Cza-ri'na,** 1 za-ri'na; 2 zä-rī'na, *n.* An empress of Russia, when an empire. **Tsa-ri'na‡.**

Czech'o-Slo'vak, 1 chek'o-slō'vak; 2 chĕc'o-slō'vak, *a.* Of or pertaining to the Czechs (peoples of Bohemia) and the Slovaks (peoples of Moravia, Silesia, etc.), or to their country, **Czech"o-Slo-va'ki-a,** in S. E. Europe.

D

D, d, 1 dī; 2 dē, *n.* [DEES, D's, or Ds, 1 dīz; 2 dēs, *pl.*] The fourth letter in the English alphabet; as a Roman numeral, 500.

dab, 1 dab; 2 dăb, *vt. & vi.* [DABBED; DAB'BING.] To strike softly: pat.—**dab'ber,** *n.*

dab[1], *n.* **1.** A gentle blow; pat. **2.** A small lump of soft substance, as butter.

dab[2], *n.* A skilful person; adept. **dab'ster‡.**

dab'ble, ⎰1 dab'l; 2 dăb'l, *v.* [DAB'BLED,
dab'l[?], ⎱ DAB'LD[?]; DAB'BLING.] **I.** *t.* To dip lightly; splash; sprinkle. **II.** *i.* To play, as with the hands, in a fluid; splash gently; engage slightly.—**dab'bler,** *n.*

da ca'po, 1 dɑ kä'po; 2 dä cä'po. *Mus.* From the beginning; a direction to repeat: abbreviated *D. C.* [fish.

dace, 1 dēs; 2 dāc, *n.* A small fresh-water

dac'tyl, 1 dak'tıl; 2 dăc'tyl, *n.* A foot consisting of a long syllable followed by two short ones (— ‿ ‿).—**dac-tyl'ic,** *a.*

dad, 1 dad; 2 dăd, *n.* A father: used by children. **dad'dy‡.**—**dad'dy-long'-legs",** *n.* A spider-like insect with small body and very long legs.

da'do, 1 dē'do; 2 dā'do, *n.* A flat, often decorated surface at the base of a wall; one of the faces of a pedestal.

daf'fo-dil, 1 daf'o-dil; 2 dăf'o-dil, *n.* A plant with solitary yellow flowers. **daf'fa-dil"ly‡; daf'fo-dil"ly‡.**

daft, 1 daft; 2 dăft, *a.* Silly; imbecile; insane.

dag'ger, 1 dag'ər; 2 dăg'er, *n.* **1.** A short, edged, and pointed weapon, for stabbing, etc. **2.** A reference-mark (†).

da-guerre'o-type, 1 da-ger'o-taip; 2 da-gĕr'o-tȳp. *n.* A former photographic process, in which silver-coated metallic plates were used; a picture so made.

dah'lia, 1 dēl'ya *or* dăl'ya; 2 dăl'ya *or* däl'ya, *n.* A flowering plant of the aster family. See illus. on next page.

1: ə = final; ı = habit; aisle; au = out; oil; ıū = feud; chin; go; ŋ = sing; thin, this.
2: wolf, do; book, boot; full, rule, cure, but, burn; oil, boy; g̣o. g̣em; iŋk; thin, this.

Da'il Eire'ann, 1 dē'il ār'ən; 2 dạ'il ār'an. The Assembly of the Irish Free State; originally the Sinn Fein Party.

dai'ly, 1 dē'lı; 2 dā'ly. **I.** *a.* Occurring every day; diurnal. **II.** *n.* [DAI'LIES², *pl.*] A daily paper. **III.** *adv.* Day after day; on every day.

dain'ty, 1 dēn'tı; 2 dān'ty. **I.** *a.* [DAIN'TI-ER; DAIN'TI-EST.] Delicate; delicious; fastidious; refined; decorous. **II.** *n.* [-TIES², *pl.*] Something delicious; a delicacy.— **dain'ti-ly,** *adv.*— **dain'ti-ness,** *n.*

dai'ry, 1 dē'rı; 2 dā'ry, *n.* [DAI'RIES², *pl.*] A place for keeping milk, making butter and cheese, and where milk products are sold.

da'is, 1 dē'ıs; 2 dā'ıs, *n.* A raised platform, as at the upper end of a room.

dai'sy, 1 dē'zı; 2 dā'gy, *n.* [DAI'SIES², *pl.*] A flower having a yellow disk with white or rose-colored rays.

Dahlia.

dale, 1 dēl; 2 dāl, *n.* A small valley.

dal'ly, 1 dal'ı; 2 dăl'y, *vi.* [DAL'LIED, 1 dal'id, 2 dăl'id; DAL'LY-ING.] To trifle; loiter; delay; play amorously.— **dal'li-ance,** *n.* The act of dallying; fondling; social chat.

dam, 1 dam; 2 dăm, *vt.* [DAMMED, DAMD⁸; DAM'MING.] To stop by a dam; restrain.

dam¹, *n.* A barrier to check the flow of a stream.

dam², *n.* A female parent of the lower animals.

dam'age, 1 dam'ıj; 2 dăm'ag̃. **I.** *vt. & vi.* [DAM'AGED; DAM'AG-ING.] To harm; impair or become impaired. **II.** *n.* 1. Injury; harm. 2. *pl.* Money recoverable for a wrong or an injury.

dam'ask, 1 dam'ask; 2 dăm'ask. **I.** *a.* Of or like damask. **II.** *n.* A fine silk or linen fabric woven in elaborate patterns.

dame, 1 dēm; 2 dām, *n.* A lady; married woman; matron.

damn, 1 dam; 2 dăm, *v.* **I.** *t.* 1. To condemn; doom to perdition. 2. To curse profanely. **II.** *i.* To swear.— **dam'na-bl(e)ᴾ,** *a.* Meriting or causing damnation; detestable; outrageous.— **dam'na-bly,** *adv.*— **dam-na'tion,** *n.* Condemnation to punishment after death; perdition.— **dam'na-to-ry,** *a.* Tending to convict or condemn; consigning to damnation.

damp, 1 damp; 2 dămp. **I**ᵗ. *vt. & vi.* To make moist; dampen; discourage; check. **II.** *a.* Somewhat wet; moist. 2. Clammy; cold. **III.** *n.* Moisture; dampness; fog; mist; poisonous gas in mines.— **damp'en,** 1 damp'n; 2 dămp'n, *vt. & vi.* To make damp; moisten; check; chill or depress.— **damp'en-er,** *n.*— **damp'er,** *n.* One who

or that which damps or checks; a device to check the draft, as of a stove.— **damp'ly,** *adv.* — **damp'ness,** *n.*

dam'sel, 1 dam'zel; 2 dăm'ŝĕl, *n.* A young girl; maiden. **dam'o-sel‡.**

dam'son, 1 dam'zən; 2 dăm'ŝon, *n.* A small purple plum; also, the tree producing it.

dance, 1 dans; 2 dáns̃. **I.** *vt. & vi.* [DANCED†; DANC'ING.] 1. To move or cause to move rhythmically to music. 2. To dandle; leap, quiver, flit, or skip lightly. **II.** *n.* 1. A series of rhythmic concerted movements timed to music. 2. A dancing-party; tune to dance by.— **danc'er,** *n.*

dan'de-li'on, 1 dan'dı-loi"ən; 2 dăn'de-li"on, *n.* A milky herb with a large yellow flower.

dan'dle,)1 dan'dl; 2 dăn'dl, *vt.* [DAN'-
dan'dlᴾ,) DL(E)Dᴾ; DAN'DLING.] To dance, as an infant on the lap; tondle; caress.

dan'druff, 1 dan'druf; 2 dăn'drŭf, *n.* A fine scurf on the head. **dan'driff‡.**

dan'dy, 1 dan'dı; 2 dăn'dy. **I.** *a.* Like a dandy. **II.** *n.* [DAN'DIES², *pl.*] A man fastidious in dress and affected in manner; a fop.

dan'ger, 1 dēn'jər; 2 dăn'ger, *n.* Exposure to chance of injury or loss; peril; risk. — **dan'ger-ous,** 1 dēn'jər-us; 2 dăn'ger-ŭs, *a.* Hazardous; perilous; unsafe. **-ly,** *adv.* **-ness,** *n.*

dan'gle,)1 daŋ'gl; 2 dăŋ'gl, *vt. & vi.* [DAN'-
dan'glᴾ,) GL(E)Dᴾ; DAN'GLING.] To hang or swing loosely; be an attendant: with *before, about,* or *after.*— **dan'gler,** *n.*

dank, 1 daŋk; 2 dăŋk, *a.* Damp and cold; moist. [professional female dancer; ballet-girl.

dan"seuse', 1 dɒn"sūz'; 2 dăn"sŭs', *n.* A

Daph'ne, 1 daf'nı; 2 dăf'ne, *n. Myth.* Daughter of river-god Peneus; changed into a laurel while fleeing from Apollo.

dap'per, 1 dap'ər; 2 dăp'er, *a.* Trim and pretty; neat; also, little and active.

dap'ple,)1 dap'l; 2 dăp'l. **I.** *vt.* [DAP'-
dap'lᴾ,) PLED, DAP'LDᴾ; DAP'PLING.] To make spotted. **II.** *a.* Spotted; variegated **dap'pled‡; dap'ldᴾ‡. III.** *n.* A spot or dot, as on the skin of a horse; an animal marked with spots.

dare, 1 dâr; 2 dâr, *v.* [DURST, 1 dŭrst, 2 dûrst, OR DARED; DAR'ING.] **I.** *t.* 1. To be bold enough (to do or attempt). 2. To challenge; defy. **II.** *i.* To have courage; venture.— **dar'ing,** 1 dâr'iŋ; 2 dâr'ing. **I.** *pa.* Bold; brave; venturesome; also, audacious; presuming. **II.** *n.* Heroic courage; bravery. **-ly,** *adv.*

dark, 1 dārk; 2 därk. **I.** *a.* Lacking light; of a deep shade; obscure; gloomy; atrocious. **II.** *n.* Lack of light; a place without light; a shadow. **-ly,** *adv.* **-ness,** *n.*

1: ȧrtistic, ärt; fat, fāre; fạst; get, prey; hit, police; obey, gō; net, ȯr; full, rūle; but, būrn.

2: ärt, āpe, făt, fâre, fȧst, whạt, ạll; mē, gĕt, prey, fẽrn; hĭt, īce; ĭ=ĕ; ĭ=ẽ; gō, nŏt, ȏr, wọn,

—**dark'en,** 1 därk'n; 2 därk'n, *vt. & vi.* To make or grow dark or darker.—**dark'ling.**
I. *a.* Dim; gloomy. **II.** *adv.* In the dark; blindly.—**dark'some,** *a.* [Poet.] Dark.

dar'ling, 1 där'lıŋ; 2 där'ling. **I.** *a.* Tenderly loved; very dear. **II.** *n.* One beloved; a pet.

darn, 1 därn; 2 därn. **I.** *vt.* To mend by filling in yarn or thread with a needle.
II. *n.* A place mended by darning.

dar'nel, 1 där'nel; 2 där'nĕl, *n.* A noxious weed.

dart, 1 därt; 2 därt. **I**d. *vt. & vi.* To shoot out, as a dart; shoot darts; move swiftly. **II.** *n.* A pointed missile weapon, as a javelin; a sudden, swift motion.

dasht, 1 dash; 2 dăsh, *v.* **I.** *t.* **1.** To throw suddenly and violently; hurl; shatter; splash. **2.** To sketch hastily: with *off.* **3.** To discourage; abash. **II.** *i.* To rush impetuously.

dash, *n.* **1.** A sudden onset; rush; impetuosity; spirit; display. **2.** A check; collision. **3.** A slight admixture. **4.** A line (——), as a mark of punctuation, etc.

da"sheen', 1 dɑ"shĭn'; 2 dä"shĕn', *n.* A tuberous-rooted plant used as a food in the tropics: recently introduced into the southern United States.

dash'ing, 1 dash'ıŋ; 2 dăsh'ing, *pa.* Spirited; bold; impetuous; showy or gay.

das'tard, 1 das'tərd; 2 dăs'tard. **I.** *a.* Base and cowardly. **das'tard-ly**‡. **II.** *n.* A base coward; poltroon.

da'ta, 1 dē'tɑ; 2 dā'ta, *n. pl.* Things assumed, known, or conceded; premises; given facts.

date, 1 dēt; 2 dāt, *v.* [DAT'ED^d; DAT'ING.]
I. *t.* To mark with a date; assign a date to. **II.** *i.* To bear date: with *from.*

date¹, *n.* The time of some event; a point of time.—
date'less, *a.* Without date; not assignable to any date; of indefinite duration.

date², *n.* A sweet Oriental stone-fruit, or the tree bearing it.

da'tive, 1 dē'tıv; } *a.* Denoting
da'tivs, } *a. & n.* in various languages the case of the indirect object, represented in English by *to* or *for.*

Date.

a, a date-tree, bearing f r u i t; *b,* growth of ripening fruit (dates); *c,* a single date.

da'tum, 1 dē'tŭm; 2 dā'tŭm, *n.* [DA'TA, *pl.*] A fact given or assumed; a premise: used chiefly in the plural; as, the *data* are sufficient.

daub, 1 dɔb; 2 dạb. **I.** *vt. & vi.* To smear with something sticky; plaster; paint

badly. **II.** *n.* A sticky application; a smear; a poor, coarse painting.— **daub'er,**n.

daugh'ter, 1 dȯ'tɑr; 2 dạ'tẽr, *n.* A female child or descendant.— **daugh'ter-in-law",** *n.* The wife of one's son.— **daugh'ter-ly,** *a.* Like a daughter.

dauntd, 1 dänt; 2 dȧnt, *vt.* To intimidate; cow; tame.— **daunt'less,** *a.* Fearless; intrepid. -**ly,** *adv.* -**ness,** *n.*

dau'phin, 1 dȯ'fın; 2 dạ'fĭn, *n.* The eldest
dau'finr, } son of the king of France. —
dau'phine, *n.* The wife of a dauphin.

dav'it, 1 dav'ıt; 2 dȧv'ĭt, *n.* A small crane on a ship's side, as for hoisting or lowering boats.

daw, 1 dȯ; 2 dạ, *n.* A jackdaw.

daw'dle, 1 dȯ'dl; 2 dạ'dl, *vt. & vi.* [DAW-DL(E)D^p; DAW'DLING.] To loiter; trifle.—
daw'dler, *n.*

dawn, 1 dȯn; 2 dạn. **I.** *vi.* To begin to grow light. **II.** *n.* The first appearance of light in the morning; daybreak; a beginning.

day, 1 dē; 2 dā, *n.* **1.** The period of daylight. **2.** The twenty-four hours from midnight to midnight. **3.** A period; an age; a battle, or its result.— **day'-book",** *n.* The book in which transactions are recorded as they take place.— **day'break",** *n.* Dawn.— **day=dream",** *n.* A reverie.— **day'light",** *n.* The light of day.— **day'-spring",** *n.* [Poet.] The early dawn.— **day = star,** *n.* The star of morning or dawn; an emblem of hope.— **day'time",** *n.* The time between sunrise and sunset.

daze, 1 dēz; 2 dāz. **I.** *vt.* [DAZED; DAZ'-ING.] To stupefy; bewilder. **II.** *n.* Stupefaction; bewilderment.

daz'zle, 1 daz'l; 2 dăz'l, *vt. & vi.* [DAZ-
daz'le, } ZLED, DAZ'LD^p; DAZ'ZLING.] To blind for a moment by excess of light; to blindingly bright; fascinate; bewilder.

de-, *prefix.* From; down; out: used with privative, intensive, or completive force; as, *de*-face, *de*grade, *de*prave, *de*rail. In some words it is equivalent to DIS-.

dea'con, 1 dī'kn; 2 dē'en, *n.* A subordinate church officer.— **dea'con-ess,** *n. fem.*
— **dea'con-ry, dea'con-ship,** *n.* The office, or term of office, of a deacon or deaconess.

dead, 1 ded; 2 dĕd. **I.** *a.* **1.** Lifeless;
deds, } insensible; numb; motionless; inanimate; dull. **2.** Complete; utter; absolute. **3.** Unproductive; useless. **II.** *n.* **1.** The most lifeless period, as of night. **2.** Dead persons collectively.—
dead'en, 1 ded'n; 2 dĕd'n, *vt.* To diminish in force; dull; retard.— **dead'lioness,** *n.*— **dead'ly,** 1 ded'lı; 2 dĕd'lı. **I.** *a.* **1.** Liable or certain to cause death; fatal. **2.** Aiming to kill; mortal; implacable. **3.** Like

death; deathly. **II.** *adv.* In a deadly manner.— **dead'ness,** *n.*

deaf, 1 def; 2 dĕf, *a.* Incapable or hard of

defs, hearing; unwilling to hear or comply. — **deaf'en,** 1 def'n; 2 dĕf'n, *vt.* To make deaf; stun, as with noise.— **deaf'ly,** *adv.*— **deaf'-mute'',** *n.* A deaf-and-dumb person. — **deaf'ness,** *n.*

deal, 1 dīl; 2 dēl, *v.* [DEALT, DELTs; 1 delt, 2 dĕlt; DEAL'ING.] **I.** *t.* To distribute; apportion; inflict. **II.** *i.* **1.** To do business; trade. **2.** To behave.— **deal'er,** *n.* One who deals in any sense; a trader.— **deal'ing,** *n.* A transaction; business.

deal¹, *n.* **1.** A quantity or degree. **2.** A distribution of cards; a single round. **3.** A secret bargain.

deal², *n.* A board or plank, or the wood, as pine, of which it is made.

dean, 1 dīn; 2 dēn, *n.* The chief officer of a cathedral; an executive officer of a college.— **dean'er-y,** *n.* [-IESz, *pl.*] The office, residence, or jurisdiction of a dean.— **dean'ship,** *n.* The office, rank, or title of a dean.

dear, 1 dīr; 2 dēr. **I.** *a.* Beloved; precious; costly. **II.** *n.* One greatly beloved; a darling. **III.** *adv.* Dearly. **IV.** *interj.* An exclamation of regret, surprize, etc. **-ly,** *adv.* **-ness,** *n.*

dearth, 1 dûrth; 2 dērth, *n.* Scarcity; famine.

death, 1 defh; 2 dĕth, *n.* Cessation of life; extinction; destruction.— **death'less,** *a.* Undying; unending; perpetual. — **death'li-ness,** *n.*— **death'ly. I.** *a.* **1.** Having the semblance or suggestion of death. **death'-like².** **2.** Deadly. **II.** *adv.* Like death.

de-bar', 1 dı-bār'; 2 de-bär', *vt.* To bar or shut out; preclude; hinder; commonly with *from*.

de-bark't, 1 dı-bärk'; 2 de-bärk', *vt. & vi.* To set or go ashore.— **de'bar-ka'tion,** *n.*

de-base', 1 dı-bēs'; 2 de-bās', *vt.* [DE-BASED't; DE-BAS'ING.] To lower in character or quality; depreciate; degrade. **-ment,** *n.*— **de-bas'er,** *n.*— **de-bas'ing-ly,** *adv.*

de-bate', 1 dı-bēt'; 2 de-bāt'. **I.** *vt. & vi.* [DE-BAT'EDd; DE-BAT'ING.] To discuss; argue; consider; reflect. **II.** *n.* The discussing of any question; argumentation; dispute.— **de-bat'a-bl(e²,** *a.*— **de-bat'er,** *n.*

de-bauch', 1 dı-bôch'; 2 de-bạch'. **I**t. *vt. & vi.* To make or become corrupt in morals; lead astray; seduce; pervert. **II.** *n.* An act or process of debauchery; a carouse.— **deb''au-chee',** 1 dĕb''o-shī'; 2 dĕb'o-çhē', *n.* A drunkard or libertine.— **de-bauch'er-y,** *n.* [-IESz, *pl.*] Licentiousness; drunkenness.

de-ben'ture, 1 dı-bĕn'chur *or* -tiur; 2 de-

bĕn'chur *or* -tūr, *n.* A bond, certificate, or the like.

de-bil'i-tate, 1 dı-bĭl'ı-tēt; 2 de-bĭl'i-tāt, *vt.* [-TAT'EDd; -TAT'ING.] To weaken.— **de-bil'i-ty,** *n.* Abnormal weakness; languor.

deb'it, 1 deb'ıt; 2 dĕb'ıt. **I**d. *vt.* To enter on the debtor side of an account; charge, as with debt. **II.** *n.* The debtor side of an account; a record of debt; something owed.

deb''o-nair', 1 deb''o-nār'; 2 dĕb''o-nâr', *a.* Gentle or courteous; affable; complaisant. — **deb''o-nair'ly,** *adv.*

de-bouch't, 1 dı-būsh'; 2 de-bụch', *vi.* To emerge or issue, as a river.— **dé''bou''-chure',** 1 dĕ''bū'shūr'; 2 de'bụ'çhūr', *n.* The opening out of a valley, stream, or the like.

dé''bris', 1 dĕ''brī' *or* de''brı, deb''rī'; 2 de''-

deb''ris', brī' *or* de'brı, dĕb''rī', *n.* Accumulated fragments; rubbish.

debt, 1 det; 2 dĕt, *n.* That which one owes; an obligation; indebtedness; trespass.— **debt'or,** *n.* One who is in debt.

dé''but', 1 dĕ''bū'; 2 de'bū', *n.* A first appearance, as in society; first attempt. — **dé''bu'tant',** 1 dĕ''bū'tän'; 2 de'bū'tän', *n.* One who makes a début.— **dé''bu'-tante',** 1 dĕ''bū'tänt'; 2 de'bū'tänt', *n. fem.*

dec'ade, 1 dek'ĕd; 2 dĕc'ād *n.* A period of ten years; a set of ten. **dec'adt.**

de-ca'dence, 1 dı-kē'dens; 2 de-cā'dĕnç, *n.* Deterioration; decline; decay. **de-ca'den-cyt.**— **de-ca'dent,** *a.* Falling into ruin: decaying; declining.

dec'a-gon, 1 dek'ạ-gon; 2 dĕc'a-gŏn, *n.* A figure with ten sides and ten angles.

dec'a-gram, dec'a-li''ter *or* **-tre, dec'a-me''ter** *or* **-tre.** See METRIC SYSTEM.

dec''a-he'dron, 1 dek''ạ-hī'dron; 2 dĕc'a-hē'dron, *n.* A solid bounded by ten plane faces.

dec'a-log, dek'ạ-log; 2 dĕc'a-lŏg, *n.*

dec'a-logue, The ten commandments; the moral law.

de-camp't, 1 dı-kamp'; 2 de-cămp', *vi.* To break camp; run away.— **de-camp'ment,** *n.*

de-cant'd, 1 dı-kant'; 2 de-cănt', *vt.* To pour off gently.— **de''can-ta'tion,** *n.*— **de-cant'er,** *n.* An ornamental bottle for wine, water, etc.

de-cap'i-tate, 1 dı-kap'ı-tēt; 2 de-căp'i-tāt, *vt.* [-TAT'EDd; -TAT'ING.] To behead.— **de-cap''i-ta'tion,** *n.*

de-cay', 1 dı-kē'; 2 de-cā'. **I.** *vt. & vi.* To affect or be affected by decay; impair; deteriorate; decline. **II.** *n.* A gradual decline; decomposition; corruption; rottenness.

de-cease', 1 dı-sīs'; 2 de-çēs'. **I.** *vi.* [DE-CEASED't; DE-CEAS'ING.] To die. **II.** *n.* Death.— **de-ceas't,** *pa.* Dead.

1: **a**rtistic, **ä**rt; f**a**t, f**ā**re; f**a**st; get, pr**ey**; h**i**t, pol**i**ce; **o**bey, g**ō**; n**o**t, **ô**r; f**u**ll, r**u**le; b**u**t, b**û**rn.

2: **ä**rt, **ā**pe, f**ä**t, f**â**re, f**à**st, wh**a**t, **ạ**il; m**ē**, gĕt, prey, f**ê**rn; h**ı**t, **Ī**ce; **ī**=ē; **ĭ**=ē; g**ō**, n**ŏ**t, **ôr**, w**ŏ**n,

de-ceit′, 1 dĭ-sīt′; 2 de-çēt′, *n.* The act of deceiving; deception; fraud.— **de-ceit′ful,** *a.* False; tricky; fraudulent. **-ly,** *adv.* **-ness,** *n.*

de-ceive′, ⎱ 1 dĭ-sīv′; 2 de-çēv′, *vt.* [DE-
de-ceiv′ᴿᴰ, ⎰ CEIV(E)D′ˢ; DE-CEIV′ING.] To mislead, as by falsehood; impose upon; delude.— **de-ceiv′a-bl(e)ᴾ,** *a.* Capable of being deceived.— **de-ceiv′er,** *n.* One who deceives.

De-cem′ber, 1 dĭ-sem′bər; 2 de-çĕm′ber, *n.* Twelfth month of the year, having 31 days.

de′cen-cy, 1 dī′sen-sı; 2 dē′çĕn-çy, *n.* [-CIESᶻ, *pl.*] Propriety; modesty; that which is decent.

de-cen′ni-al, 1 dı-sen′ı-əl; 2 de-çĕn′i-al, *a.* Continuing for ten years; occurring every ten years.

de′cent, 1 dī′sent; 2 dē′çĕnt, *a.* **1.** Proper; decorous; respectable; modest; chaste. **2.** Sufficient; passable; moderate. **-ly,** *adv.* **-ness,** *n.*

de-cep′tion, 1 dı-sep′shən; 2 de-çĕp′shon, *n.* The act of deceiving; deceit; a delusion.

de-cep′tive, ⎱ 1 dı-sep′tıv; 2 de-çĕp′tĭv, *a.*
de-cep′tivˢ, ⎰ Having power or tendency to deceive. **-ly,** *adv.*

dec′i-gram or -gramme, 1 des′ı-gram; 2 dĕç′i-gräm, **dec′i-li′′ter or -tre, dec′i-me′′ter or -tre, dec′i-stère′.** See METRIC SYSTEM.

de-cide′, 1 dı-said′; 2 de-çīd′, *vt. & vi.* [DE-CID′EDᵈ; DE-CID′ING.] To determine authoritatively; conclude; adjudge; arbitrate; resolve.— **de-cid′ed,** *pa.* **1.** Unquestionable; unmistakable. **2.** Determined; resolute; emphatic.— **de-cid′ed-ly,** *adv.*

de-cid′u-ous, 1 dı-sid′yu-us; 2 de-çĭd′yu-ŭs, *a.* **1.** A falling off at maturity, as leaves, etc. **2.** Shedding leaves annually, as a tree, etc.— **de-cid′u-ous-ly,** *adv.*— **de-cid′u-ous-ness,** *n.*

dec′i-mal, 1 des′ı-məl; 2 dĕç′i-mal. **I.** *a.* Pertaining to or founded on the number 10; proceeding by tens or tenths. **II.** *n.* A decimal fraction, or one of its digits.— **decimal fraction,** a fraction whose denominator (usually unexpressed) is 10 or a power of 10.— **d. point,** a dot or period used before a decimal fraction.— **dec′i-mal-ly,** *adv.*— **dec′i-mate,** 1 des′ı-mēt; 2 dĕç′i-māt, *vt.* [-MAT′-EDᵈ; -MAT′ING.] To kill one out of every ten of; destroy numbers of.— **dec′i-ma′tion,** *n.*— **dec′i-ma′′tor,** *n.*

de-ci′pher, 1 dı-sai′far; 2 de-çī′fer, *vt.* To
de-ci′ferˢ, ⎰ make out, as secret or difficult writing.— **de-ci′pher-a-bl(e)ᴾ,** *a.*— **de-ci′pher-er,** *n.*

de-ci′sion, 1 dı-siʒ′ən; 2 de-çĭʒh′on, *n.* **1.** The act of deciding; a fixed intention; settlement; judgment of a court. **2.** firmness; determination.

de-ci′sive, ⎱ 1 dı-sai′sıv; 2 de-çī′sĭv, *a.*
de-ci′sivˢ, ⎰ Putting an end to debate or question; conclusive; positive; decided. **-ly,** *adv.* **-ness,** *n.*

deckᵗ, 1 dek; 2 dĕk, *vt.* **1.** To dress elegantly; adorn; decorate. **2.** To put a deck on.

deck, *n.* **1.** *Naut.* A platform or floor across a vessel; the space between two such platforms. **2.** A car-roof. **3.** A pack of playing-cards.

de-claim′, 1 dı-klēm′; 2 de-elām′, *vt. & vi.* To deliver oratorically; recite.— **de-claim′er,** *n.*— **dec′′la-ma′tion,** *n.* The act of declaiming; empty oratory; something recited or to be recited from memory.— **de-clam′a-to-ry,** 1 dı-klam′ə-to-rı; 2 de-elăm′a-to-ry, *a.* Using, characterized by, or pertaining to declamation.

de-clare′, 1 dı-klār′; 2 de-elār′, *vt. & vi.* [DE-CLARED′; DE-CLAR′ING.] To reveal; explain; assert positively; announce formally.— **dec′′la-ra′tion,** 1 dek′la-rē′shan; 2 dĕe′la-rä′shon, *n.* A formal, positive, or explicit statement.— **de-clar′a-to-ry,** 1 dı-klar′ə-to-rı; 2 de-elăr′a-to-ry, *a.* Making a declaration; affirmative. **de-clar′a-tivᶜ(eˢ‡.**

de-clen′sion, 1 dı-klen′shan; 2 de-elĕn′shon, *n.* **1.** *Gram.* The inflection, as of nouns by cases. **2.** The act of declining. **3.** A slope; incline; decline; deterioration.

de-cline′, 1 dı-klaın′; 2 de-elīn′. **I.** *vt. & vi.* [DE-CLINED′; DE-CLIN′ING.] **1.** To refuse; reject. **2.** To bend down; depress; decay; diminish. **3.** To inflect, as a noun. **II.** *n.* The act or result of declining; deterioration; decay.— **de-clin′a-bl(e)ᴾ,** 1 dı-klaın′ə-bl; 2 de-elīn′a-bl, *a.* Capable of being declined.— **dec′′li-na′tion,** 1 dek′lı-nē′shan; 2 dĕe′li-nā′shon, *n.* **1.** The act of declining; descent; slope; deterioration; decay. **2.** Refusal; non-acceptance. **3.** *Astron.* The angular distance of a heavenly body from the celestial equator.

de-cliv′i-ty, 1 dı-kliv′ı-tı; 2 de-elĭv′i-ty, *n.* [-TIESᶻ, *pl.*] A downward slope, as of a hill or mountain.— **de-cliv′i-tous,** *a.* Sloping.

de-coc′tion, 1 dı-kok′shən; 2 de-eŏe′shon, *n.* The act of boiling; an extract made by boiling.— **de-coct′d,** *vt.* To make a decoction of; cook.

de′′co-here′, 1 dī′′ko-hīr′; 2 dē′eo-hēr′, *vt.* To cause to cease cohering.

de′′col′′le-té′, 1 dē′′kŏl′ə-tē′; 2 dĕ′eŏl′ē- te′, *pa.* **1.** Cut low in the neck, as a dress. **2.** Having the neck and shoulders bare.

de-col′or, ⎱ 1 dī′-kul′ər; 2 de-eŏl′or, *vt.* To
de-col′orᴾ, ⎰ bleach. **de-col′or-ize or-iseᶻ‡; de-col′or-izeᴿ‡.— de-col′′or-a′tion,** *n.* A bleaching or a bleached condition.

de′′com-pose′, 1 dī′′kəm-pōz′; 2 dē′eŏm-

pōs′, _vt._ & _vi._ [-POSED′; -POS′ING.] To separate into constituent parts; decay; putrefy.— **de-com″po-si′tion,** _n._ The act, process, or result of decomposing; dissolution.

dec′o-rate, 1 dek′o-rēt; 2 dĕe′o-rāt, _vt._ [-RAT″ED^d; -RAT′ING.] To adorn; ornament.

dec″o-ra′tion, 1 dek″o-rē′shᴀn; 2 dĕe′o-rā′shon, _n._ The act or art of decorating; ornamentation: an ornament: a badge of honor. **Decoration Day.** [U. S.] May 30; set apart in memory of those who fell in the Civil War.— **dec′o-ra′tive,** _a._ Ornamental. —**dec′o-ra″tor,** _n._

de-co′rous, 1 dɪ-kō′rᴜs _or_ dek′o-rᴜs; 2 de-cō′rᴜs _or_ dĕe′o-rᴜs, _a._ Proper; becoming; suitable. **-ly,** _adv._ **-ness,** _n._

de-co′rum, 1 dɪ-kō′rᴜm; 2 de-cō′rᴜm, _n._ Propriety, as in manner, conduct, etc.

de-coy′, 1 dɪ-kɔi′; 2 de-cŏy′. **I.** _vt._ To entice, as into a snare: draw on so as to entrap. **II.** _n._ One who or that which decoys; a lure.

de-crease′, 1 dɪ-krēs′; 2 de-crēs′. **I.** _vt._ & _vi._ [DE-CREASED′ᵗ; DE-CREAS′ING.] To diminish gradually; reduce. **II.** _n._ The act, process, or state of decreasing; the amount or degree of loss; diminution.

de-cree′, 1 dɪ-krī′; 2 de-crē′. **I.** _vt._ & _vi._ [DE-CREED′; DE-CREE′ING.] To order, ordain, or appoint by law or by edict; issue a decree. **II.** _n._ A law; edict.

dec′re-ment, 1 dek′rɪ-ment _or_ -mᴀnt; 2 dĕe′re-ment, _n._ A decreasing; loss by decrease; waste.

de-crep′it, 1 dɪ-krep′ɪt; 2 de-erĕp′ɪt, _a._ Enfeebled, as by old age; broken down. **de-crep′idt.— de-crep′i-tude,** _n._ Enfeeblement, as through old age.

de″cre-scen′do, 1 dē″kre-shen′do; 2 dĕ′erĕ-shĕn′do, _n._ _Mus._ Gradual decrease in tone. See DIMINUENDO.

de-cry′, 1 dɪ-kraɪ′; 2 de-erȳ′, _vt._ [DE-CRIED′; DE-CRY′ING.] To disparage; traduce.— **de-cri′al,** _n._ The act of decrying.

ded′i-cate, 1 ded′ɪ-kēt; 2 dĕd′i-eāt. **I.** _vt._ [-CAT″ED^d; -CAT′ING.] **1.** To consecrate; devote. **2.** To preface with a dedication. **II.** _a._ Dedicated; devoted.— **ded″i-ca′tion,** _n._ **1.** The act of dedicating. **2.** An inscription, as to a friend, prefixed to a book.— **ded′i-ca-to-ry,** _a._

de-duce′, 1 dɪ-diūs′; 2 de-dūe′, _vt._ [DE-DUCED′ᵗ; DE-DUC′ING.] **1.** To infer; conclude. **2.** To trace, as derivation.— **de-duc′i-bl(e^r,** _a._ Capable of being deduced.

de-duct′ᵈ, 1 dɪ-dᴜkt′; 2 de-dŭet′, _vt._ To subtract; take away.— **de-duc′tion,** 1 dɪ-dᴜk′shᴀn; 2 de-dŭe′shon, _n._ The act of deducting or of deducting; an inference; con-

clusion, subtraction; abatement.— **de-duc′-tiv(es,** _a._ Proceeding by deduction; inferential; deducible. **-ly,** _adv._

deed, 1 dīd; 2 dēd. **I**^d. _vt._ To convey by deed. **II.** _n._ **1.** Anything done; an act; achievement. **2.** Fact; truth; reality. **3.** A document conveying property.

deem, 1 dīm; 2 dēm, _vt._ & _vi._ To decide, judge; consider; regard; believe.

deep, 1 dīp; 2 dēp. **I.** _a._ **1.** Extending far downward, backward, or inward; profound; extreme; heartfelt. **2.** Sagacious; penetrating; also, scheming; designing. **3.** Low in tone; dark in hue. **II.** _n._ That which has great depth; an abyss; the sea. **III.** _adv._ Deeply. **-ly,** _adv._ **-ness,** _n._— **deep′en,** 1 dīp′n; 2 dēp′n, _vt._ & _vt._ To make or become deep or deeper.

deer, 1 dīr; 2 dēr, _n._ [DEER, _pl._] A fleet ruminant, as the moose, elk, and reindeer.

de-face′, 1 dɪ-fēs′; 2 de-fāc′, _vt._ [DE-FACED′ᵗ; DE-FAC′ING.] To mar; disfigure. — **de-face′ment,** _n._ The act of defacing, or state of being defaced.

de fac′to, 1 dɪ fak′to; 2 dē fāe′to. Actually existing, as a government.

def″al-ca′tion, 1 def″al-kē′shᴀn; 2 dĕf′ăl-eā′shon, _n._ A fraudulent appropriation of funds; embezzlement; also, a deficit.

de-fame′, 1 dɪ-fēm′; 2 de-fām′, _vt._ & _vi._ [DE-FAMED′; DE-FAM′ING.] To calumniate; slander.— **def″a-ma′tion,** 1 def″a-mē′shan; 2 dĕf′a-mā′shon, _n._ The act of defaming; aspersion; calumny.— **de-fam′a-to-ry,** _a._ Slanderous.

de-fault′ᵈ, 1 dɪ-fôlt′; 2 de-fạlt′, _v._ **I.** _t._ To make default in; neglect; declare in default. **II.** _i._ To make a default.— **de-fault′er,** _n._ One who defaults; an embezzler.

de-fault′, _n._ **1.** A failure in an obligation or duty; failure to appear or plead in a suit. **2.** Want or deficiency; lack.

de-fea′sance, 1 dɪ-fī′zᴀns; 2 de-fē′sạnç, _n._ Annulment.— **de-fea′si-bl(e^r,** 1 dɪ-fī′zɪ-bl; 2 de-fē′sɪ-bl, _a._ Capable of being annulled.

de-feat′, 1 dɪ-fīt′; 2 de-fēt′. **I**^d. _vt._ To overcome; vanquish; frustrate. **II.** _n._ An overthrow; frustration; an annulment.

de-fect′, 1 dɪ-fekt′; 2 de-fĕet′, _n._ Lack of something essential; imperfection; blemish; failing; fault.— **de-fec′tion,** 1 dɪ-fek′shᴀn; 2 de-fĕe′shon, _n._ Abandonment of allegiance; desertion.— **de-fec′tiv(es,** _a._ Incomplete; imperfect; faulty. **-ly,** _adv._ **-ness,** _n._

de-fence′, -less, etc. Same as DEFENSE, etc.

de-fend′ᵈ, 1 dɪ-fend′; 2 de-fĕnd′, _vt._ & _vi._ To protect; maintain; justify; vindicate; make defense.— **de-fend′a-bl(e^r,** _a._— **de-fen′dant,** _n._ One against whom a legal ac-

tion is brought; also, a defender.— **de-fend'-er,** *n.* One who defends; a champion.

de-fense', } 1 dɪ-fens'; 2 de-fĕns', *n.* The
de-fence', } act of defending; anything that defends; a plea in justification; excuse; apology.— **de-fense'less, de-fence'less,** *a.* Unprotected.— **de-fen"si-bil'i-ty, de-fen'si-bl(e-ness²,** *n.*— **de-fen'si-bl(e²,** *a.* Capable of being defended.— **de-fen'siv(e⁵. I.** *a.* Intended or suitable for defense; done in defense; making defense. **II.** *n.* An attitude or condition of defense. **-ly,** *adv.*

de-fer'¹, 1 dɪ-fûr'; 2 de-fẽr', *v.* [DE-FERRED', DE-FERD'ˢ; DE-FER'RING.] **I.** *t.* To put off; postpone. **II.** *i.* To delay; wait.

de-fer'², *v.* [DE-FERRED'; DE-FER'RING.] **I.** *t.* To submit or refer (something) respectfully: with *to* before the indirect object. **II.** *i.* To yield respectfully; submit: with *to.*— **def'er-ence,** 1 def'ẽr-ens; 2 dĕf'ẽr-ĕnç, *n.* Respectful yielding; respect; regard.— **def"er-en'tial,** *a.* Respectful. **-ly,** *adv.*

de-fi'ant, 1 dɪ-fai'ǎnt; 2 de-fi'ant, *a.* Characterized by defiance.— **de-fi'ance,** *n.* The act of defying; a challenge; bold opposition.

de-fi'cient, 1 dɪ-fish'ent; 2 de-fĭsh'ĕnt, *a.* Lacking; incomplete; imperfect; defective. **-ly,** *adv.*— **de-fi'cien-cy,** 1 dɪ-fish'en-sɪ; 2 de-fĭsh'ĕn-çy, *n.* [-CIES², *pl.*] Lack; insufficiency; defect.

def'i-cit, 1 def'ɪ-sit; 2 dĕf'ĭ-çĭt, *n.* A deficiency, or falling short in amount; shortage.

de-file'¹, 1 dɪ-fail'; 2 de-fĭl', *vt.* [DE-FILED'; DE-FIL'ING.] To pollute; debauch; violate.— **de-file'ment,** *n.* The act of defiling, or state of being defiled; uncleanness; pollution.— **de-fil'er,** *n.*

de-file'², *vi.* To march by files; file off.

de-file', *n.* **1.** A long narrow pass; gorge. **2.** *Mil.* A marching in file.

de-fine', 1 dɪ-fain'; 2 de-fīn', *v.* [DE-FINED'; DE-FIN'ING.] **1.** To state the meaning of; explain. **2.** To bring out the outlines of; determine exactly.— **de-fin'a-bl(e²,** *a.* Capable of being defined.— **de-fin'er,** *n.*

def'i-nite, } 1 def'ɪ-nit; 2 dĕf'ĭ-nĭt, *a.* Hav-
def'i-nit⁵, } ing precise limits; determined; clear; precise. **-ly,** *adv.* **-ness,** *n.*— **de-fin'i-tiv(e⁵. I.** *a.* Sharply defining or limiting; explicit; positive. **II.** *n.* A word that defines or limits. **-ly,** *adv.* **-ness,** *n.*

def"i-ni'tion, 1 def"ɪ-nish'ǎn; 2 dĕf'ĭ-nĭsh'on, *n.* **1.** An explanation of a word or thing that distinguishes it from all other things. **2.** The act of defining. **3.** The state of being definite; definitiveness; the power of a lens to give a distinct image.

de-flect'ᵈ, 1 dɪ-flekt'; 2 de-flĕet', *vt. & vi.* To swerve or cause to swerve; bend or turn from a course.— **de-flec'tion,** *n.* A turning aside; deviation.

de-flow'er, 1 dɪ-flau'ǝr; 2 dē-flow'er, *vt.* To deprive of flowers or bloom; despoil; ravish.

de-form', 1 dɪ-fôrm'; 2 de-fôrm', *vt.* To render misshapen; distort; disfigure.— **def"or-ma'tion,** *n.*— **de-formed',** *pa.*— **de-for'mi-ty,** 1 dɪ-fôr'mɪ-tɪ; 2 de-fôr'mi-ty, *n.* [-TIES², *pl.*] A deformed state; a misshapen part; disfigurement; unsightliness.

de-fraud'ᵈ, 1 dɪ-frɔd'; 2 de-frạd', *vt.* To deprive of something by fraud; cheat; swindle.— **de-fraud'er,** *n.*

de-fray', 1 dɪ-frē'; 2 de-frā', *vt.* To make payment for; bear the expense of; pay.— **de-fray'al,** *n.* The act of defraying. **de-fray'ment‡.**— **de-fray'er,** *n.*

deft, 1 deft; 2 dĕft, *a.* Neat and skilful; handy; apt; clever. **-ly,** *adv.* **-ness,** *n.*

de-funct', 1 dɪ-fuŋkt'; 2 de-fŭɳct'. **I.** *a.* Dead; deceased; extinct. **II.** *n.* A dead person; the dead.

de-fy', 1 dɪ-fai'; 2 de-fȳ', *vt.* [DE-FIED', 1 -faid', 2 -fid'; DE-FY'ING.] To challenge or dare; act in despite of; resist boldly.

de-gauss', 1 dɪ-gaus'; 2 de-ġous, *vt.* To protect a ship from magnetic mines.

de-gen'er-ate, 1 dɪ-jen'ẽr-ēt; 2 de-ġĕn'er-ăt. **I.** *vi.* [-AT"EDᵈ; -AT"ING.] To become worse; decline; deteriorate. **II.** 1 dɪ-jen'ǝr-ɪt; 2 de-ġĕn'er-at, *a.* Deteriorated; degraded. **III.** *n.* A deteriorated or degraded individual. **-ly,** *adv.* **-ness,** *n.*— **de-gen'er-a-cy,** 1 dɪ-jen'ǝr-ạ-sɪ; 2 de-ġĕn'er-a-çy, *n.* The state of being degenerate; the act or process of degenerating.— **de-gen"er-a'tion,** *n.* The act, state, or process of degenerating; degeneracy.

deg"lu-ti'tion, 1 deg"lu-tish'ǎn; 2 dĕġ'lу-tĭsh'on, *n.* The act, process, or power of swallowing.

de-grade', 1 dɪ-grēd'; 2 de-ġrād', *v.* [DE-GRAD'EDᵈ; DE-GRAD'ING.] **I.** *t.* To reduce in rank; debase in character or quality; make mean or contemptible. **II.** *i.* To decline in character, reputation, or standing; degenerate.— **deg"ra-da'tion,** *n.* The act of degrading, or the state of being degraded.— **de-grad'ing-ly,** *adv.*

de-gree', 1 dɪ-grī'; 2 de-ġrē', *n.* **1.** One of a series of steps; grade; rank; station; amount; intensity. **2.** One of the three forms in which an adjective or an adverb is compared; as, the positive, comparative, and superlative *degrees.* **3.** An honorary title.

1: ǝ = final; ɪ = habĭt; aisle; ɑu = out; oil; iū = feud; ᴄhin; go; ŋ = sing; thin, this.
2: wolf, dǫ; bŏŏk, bŏŏt; full, rұle, cūre, bŭt, bûrn; ŏil, bŏy; ġo, ġem; iɳk; thin, this.

de-his′cence, 1 dɪ-his′ens; 2 de-hĭs′ĕnç, *n.* A gape; opening.— **de-his′cent,** *a.*

de′i-fy, 1 dī′ɪ-fai; 2 dē′i-fī, *vt.* [-FIED, 1 -faid, 2 -fīd; -FY′ING.] To regard or worship as a god; adore.— **de′i-fi-ca′tion,** *n.*

deign, 1 dēn; 2 dēn, *vt.* To stoop to compliance; condescend; vouchsafe.

de′ism, 1 dī′izm; 2 dē′ism, *n.* The belief of the existence of God, with disbelief of Christianity.— **de′ist,** *n.* A believer in deism. — **de-is′tic,** *a.* **de-is′ti-cal**‡.

de′i-ty, 1 dī′ɪ-tɪ; 2 dē′i-ty, *n.* [-TIES‡, *pl.*] **1.** A divine person; god. **2.** [D-] The one true God. **3.** Godhead; divinity.

de-ject′ᵈ, 1 dɪ-jekt′; 2 de-jĕct′, *vt.* To depress the spirits of; discourage.— **de-ject′-ed,** *pa.* Depressed; disheartened. **-ly,** *adv.* **-ness,** *n.*— **de-jec′tion,** *n.* Depression; melancholy.

dek′a-gram, etc. Same as DECAGRAM, etc.

de-lay′, 1 dɪ-lē′; 2 de-lā′, *v.* **I.** *t.* To put off; postpone; detain; retard; hinder. **II.** *i.* To act slowly; procrastinate.

de-lay′, *n.* A putting off; postponement; procrastination; hindrance. [delete.

de′le, 1 dī′lī; 2 dē′lē, *vt.* Print. To take out;

de-lec′ta-ble, 1 dɪ-lek′ta-bl; 2 de-lĕc′ta-**de-lec′ta-bl**ᴾ, bl, *a.* Delightful; charming. **-ness,** *n.*— **de-lec′ta-bly,** *adv.*— **de′lec-ta′tion,** *n.* Delight.

del′e-gate, 1 del′ɪ-gēt; 2 dĕl′e-gāt. **I.** *vt.* [-GAT′′ED**d**; -GAT′ING.] **1.** To send as a representative; depute. **2.** To commit; entrust. **II.** *a.* Sent as a deputy. **III.** *n.* A representative; deputy.— **del′′e-ga′-tion,** *n.* The act of delegating; a delegate; delegates collectively.

de-lete′, 1 dɪ-līt′; 2 de-lēt′, *vt.* [DE-LET′-ED**d**; DE-LET′ING.] To blot out; erase; cancel; dele.— **de-le′tion,** *n.* Erasure.

del′′e-te′ri-ous, 1 del′ɪ-tī′rɪ-us; 2 dĕl′e-tē′ri-ŭs, *a.* Hurtful; injurious; pernicious. **-ness,** *n.*

delft, 1 delft, delf; 2 dĕlft, dĕlf, *n.* A colored **delf,** glazed earthenware made first at Delft, in Holland.

de-lib′er-ate, 1 dɪ-lib′ər-ēt; 2 de-lĭb′er-āt. **I.** *vt.* & *vi.* [-AT′′ED**d**; -AT′ING.] To weigh in the mind; consider; ponder; hesitate. **II.** 1 dɪ-lib′ər-ɪt; 2 de-lĭb′er-at, *a.* Acting with deliberation; slow; cautious; leisurely; intentional. **-ly,** *adv.* **-ness,** *n.*— **de-lib′′er-a′tion,** *n.* The act of deliberating; slowness in action; forethought; intention. — **de-lib′er-a-tive**(es, *a.* Pertaining to, characterized by, or existing for deliberation.

del′i-cate, 1 del′ɪ-kɪt; 2 dĕl′i-eat, *a.* **1.** Fine and light; daintily pleasing; finely wrought; tender; frail; fragile. **2.** Refined: pure; chaste; dainty; sensitive. **-ly,** *adv.* **-ness,** *n.*— **del′i-ca-cy,** 1 del′ɪ-

kə-sɪ; 2 dĕl′i-ca-çy, *n.* [-CIES‡, *pl.*] **1.** Fineness; daintiness; sensitiveness; fragility. **2.** A luxury; dainty. **3.** Refinement; fastidiousness; nicety.

del′′i-ca-tes′sen, 1 del′ɪ-kə-tes′en; 2 dĕl′i-ca-tĕs′ĕn, *n. pl.* Table delicacies.

de-li′cious, 1 dɪ-lish′us; 2 de-lĭsh′ŭs, *a.* Extremely pleasant or grateful. **-ly,** *adv.* **-ness,** *n.*

de-light′ᵈ, 1 dɪ-lait′; 2 de-līt′, *v.* **I.** *t.* To **de-lite′**ᴾ, please or gratify highly; charm. **II.** *i.* To rejoice: followed by *in* or an infinitive.

de-light′, *n.* Joyful satisfaction, or that which affords it.— **de-light′ful,** *a.* Affording delight; gratifying; charming. **de-light′-some**‡. **-ly,** *adv.* **-ness,** *n.*

de-lin′e-ate, 1 dɪ-lin′ɪ-ēt; 2 de-lĭn′e-āt, *vt.* [-AT′′ED**d** -AT′ING.] To draw in outline; portray; depict; describe.— **de-lin′′e-a′tion,** *n.* The act or art of delineating; a portrait; sketch.— **de-lin′e-a′tor,** *n.*

de-lin′quent, 1 dɪ-liŋ′kwent; 2 de-lĭn′kwĕnt. **I.** *a.* **1.** Neglectful of duty; faulty. **2.** Due and unpaid, as taxes. **II.** *n.* One who fails in duty or who commits a fault.— **de-lin′quen-cy,** *n.* [-CIES‡, *pl.*] The fact of being delinquent; neglect; fault.

del′′i-quesce′, 1 del′ɪ-kwes′; 2 dĕl′i-kwĕs′, *vi.* [-QUESCED′t; -QUESC′ING.] To become liquid by absorption of moisture from the air.— **del′′i-ques′cence,** *n.*— **del′′i-ques′-cent,** *a.*

de-lir′i-ous, 1 dɪ-lir′ɪ-us; 2 de-lĭr′i-ŭs, *a.* Suffering from delirium. **-ly,** *adv.* **-ness,** *n.*

de-lir′i-um, 1 dɪ-lir′ɪ-um; 2 de-lĭr′i-ŭm, *n.* **1.** Mental aberration, as in fever; wandering of the mind. **2.** Intense excitement; rapture.

de-liv′er, 1 dɪ-liv′ər; 2 de-lĭv′er, *vt.* **1.** To set free; rescue; save. **2.** To give; give up; communicate. **3.** To utter; speak formally.— **de-liv′er-ance,** *n.* The act of delivering; rescue; release; expression of opinion.— **de-liv′er-er,** *n.* One who delivers. — **de-liv′er-y,** *n.* [-IES‡, *pl.*] **1.** The act of delivering; release; transference; surrender. **2.** Mode of utterance, as in public speaking.

dell, 1 del; 2 dĕl, *n.* A small secluded **del**ᴾ, valley.

del′ta, 1 del′tə; 2 dĕl′ta, *n.* The fourth letter in the Greek alphabet (Δ, δ); a triangle, as of land; the mouth of a river.

de-lude′, 1 dɪ-liūd′; 2 de-lūd′, *vt.* [DE-LUD′-ED**d**; DE-LUD′ING.] To mislead; beguile; deceive.— **de-lud′er,** *n.*

del′uge, 1 del′yuj; 2 dĕl′yŭg. **I.** *vt.* [DEL′-UGED; DEL′UG-ING.] To overwhelm with water; inundate. **II.** *n.* A flood; inundation.

1: ärtistic, ärt; fat, fãre; fäst; get, prēy; hit, police; obey, gō; nŏt, ôr; full, rūle; but, bûrn.
2: ärt, āpe, fät, fãre, fàst, whạt, ạll; mē, gĕt, prey, fẽrn; hĭt, īce; ĩ=ē; ĩ=ē; gō, nŏt, ôr, wŏn,

de-lu'sion, 1 dɪ-liū'ʒən; 2 de-lū'zhon, *n.* The act of deluding; belief of what does not exist; deception.— **de-lu'siv**(e⁵, *a.* Tending to delude; misleading; deceptive. **-ly,** *adv.* **-ness,** *n.*

delve, 1 delv; 2 dĕlv, *vt. & vi.* [DELV(E)D⁸; **delv⁸,** DELV'ING.] To make laborious research; dig; fathom.

dem'a-gog, 1 dem'ə-gɔg; 2 dĕm'a-gŏg,
dem'a-gogue, *n.* An artful and unprincipled politician.

de-main', 1 *n.* Same as DEMESNE.

de-mand', 1 dɪ-mand'; 2 de-mănd'. **I**ᵈ. *vt. & vi.* To claim as due; insist upon; need; require; make claim. **II.** *n.* The act of demanding, or that which is demanded; requirement; claim; need.

de''mar-ca'tion, 1 dī''mɑr-kē'shən; 2 dē''mär-cā'shon, *n.* The fixing of boundaries; limitation; limit fixed. **de''mar-ka'tion‡.**

dé''marche', 1 dê''märsh'; 2 dę''märçh', *n.* [F.] **1.** Change in plan. **2.** Manner of procedure.

de-mean', 1 dɪ-mīn'; 2 de-mēn', *vt.* To behave; conduct: used reflexively.— **de-mean'or,** *n.* Behavior; bearing; deportment. **de-mean'our‡.**

de-ment'ed, 1 dɪ-ment'ed; 2 de-mĕnt'ĕd, *pa.* Deprived of reason; insane; imbecile. — **de-men'ti-a,** 1 dɪ-men'shɪ-ə; 2 de-mĕn'shi-a, *n.* Imbecility or insanity.

de-mer'it, 1 dī-mer'ɪt; 2 dē-mĕr'it, *n.* Ill desert; misconduct, or a mark denoting it.

de-mesne', *n.* 1 dɪ-mēn' *or* de-mēn'; 2 de-mẹn' *or* de-mēn', *n.* A manor-house and adjoining lands; domain.

demi-, *prefix.* Half; as, *demi*god, *demi*circle.

dem'i-god, 1 dem'ɪ-gɔd; 2 dĕm'i-gŏd, *n.* The fabled offspring of a god and a mortal; a godlike man.

dem'i-john, 1 dem'ɪ-jɔn; 2 dĕm'i-jŏn, *n.* A glass jug enclosed in wickerwork.

de-mise', 1 dɪ-maɪz'; 2 de-mīz'. **I.** *vt. & vi.* [DE-MISED'; DE-MIS'ING.] To bequeath; pass by bequest; give; convey; lease. **II.** *n.* Death, as of a sovereign; a transfer of property. [up; resign.

de-mit'¹, 1 dɪ-mit'; 2 de-mĭt', *vt.* To give **de-mit',** *n.* A letter of dismissal.

de-moc'ra-cy, 1 dɪ-mok'rə-sɪ; 2 de-mŏc'ra-çy, *n.* [-CIES⁷, *pl.*] **1.** Government directly by the people; the mass of the people. **2.** [D-] *U. S. Polit.* The policy of the Democratic party; Democrats collectively.— **dem'o-crat,** *n.* **1.** One who favors a democracy. **2.** [D-] [U. S.] A member of the Democratic party.— **dem''o-crat'ic,** *a.* Of or pertaining to a democracy or to democrats, or in United States politics [D-] to the party so designated. **dem''o-crat'i-cal‡. -cal-ly,** *adv.*

de-mol'ishᵗ, 1 dɪ-mɒl'ɪsh; 2 de-mŏl'ish, *vt.* To tear or throw down; destroy; ruin. — **dem''o-li'tion,** 1 dem''o-lish'ən; 2 dĕm'-o-lish'on, *n.* The act of demolishing; destruction.

de'mon, 1 dī'mən; 2 dē'mon, *n.* **1.** An evil spirit; devil. **2.** *Gr. Myth.* A guardian spirit. **dæ'mon‡; dai'mon‡.**

de-mon'e-tize *or* **-tise,** 1 dɪ-mun'ɪ-taɪz; 2 de-mŏn'e-tīz, *vt.* [-TIZED; -TIZ'ING.] To divest of the character of standard money. — **de-mon''e-ti-za'tion** or **-sa'tion,** *n.*

de-mo'ni-ac, 1 dɪ-mō'nɪ-ak; 2 de-mō'ni-ăc. **I.** *a.* Of or like a demon: devilish. **de''mo-ni'a-cal‡,** 1 dī''mo-naɪ'ə-kəl; 2 dē''mo-nī'a-cal. **de-mon'ic‡. II.** *n.* One possessed of a demon; a lunatic.

dem'on-strate, 1 dem'ən-strēt *or* dɪ-mŏn'-strēt; 2 dĕm'on-strāt *or* de-mŏn'strāt, *vt.* [-STRAT'EDᵈ; -STRAT'ING.] To prove with mathematical certainty; point out; make clear.— **de- mon'stra-bl**(e⁵, *a.* Capable of positive proof.— **de-mon'stra-bl**(e-ness⁷, *n.*— **de-mon'stra-bly,** *adv.*

dem''on-stra'tion, 1 dem''ən-strē'shən; 2 dĕm''on-strā'shon, *n.* **1.** A process of reasoning that leads to an absolutely certain conclusion, as in mathematics. **2.** A pointing out; manifestation; exhibition. — **de-mon'stra-tiv**(e⁵, 1 dɪ-men'strə-tiv; 2 de-mŏn'stra-tiv, *a.* **1.** Convincing; conclusive. **2.** Inclined to emotional manifestation. **-ly,** *adv.* **-ness,** *n.*— **dem'on-stra''tor,** *n.*

de-mor'al-ize *or* **-ise,** 1 dɪ-mor'əl-aɪz; 2 de-mŏr'al-īz, *vt.* [-IZED; -IZ'ING.] **1.** To corrupt or deprave. **2.** To disorganize and dishearten, as troops.— **de-mor''al-i-za'tion** *or* **-sa'tion,** *n.*

de-mote', 1 dɪ-mōt'; 2 de-mōt', *vt.* [DE-MOT'-EDᵈ; DE-MOT'ING.] [Local, U.S.] To reduce to a lower class or grade: applied to school-children, and opposed to promote.— **de-mo'tion,** *n.*

de-mul'cent, 1 dɪ-mul'sent; 2 de-mŭl'çent. *Med.* **I.** *a.* Soothing. **II.** *n.* A soothing application.

de-mur', 1 dɪ-mūr'; 2 de-mûr'. **I.** *vi.* [-MURRED',-MURD'⁸:-MUR'RING.] To object; hesitate. **II.** *n.* Hesitation; objection.

de-mure', 1 dɪ-miūr'; 2 de-mūr', *a.* Sedate; modest; also, prim; coy. **-ly,** *adv.* **-ness,** *n.*

de-mur'rage, 1 dɪ-mūr'ɪj; 2 de-mûr'ag, *n.* **1.** The detention of a vessel or car beyond the specified time. **2.** The compensation demanded or allowed for such delay.

de-mur'rer, 1 dɪ-mūr'ər; 2 de-mûr'er, *n.* **1.** One who demurs. **2.** *Law.* A denial of cause of action.

den, 1 den; 2 dĕn, *n.* A cavern occupied by animals; a lair; a low haunt.

1: ə = final; ɪ = habit; aisle; au = out; oil; iū = feud; ɔhin; go; ŋ = sing; ɔhin, this.
2: wolf, dǫ; bōōk, bōōt; full, rųle, cūre, bŭt, bûrn; ŏil, bŏy; g̣o, g̣em; iŋk; thin, this.

de-na′tion-al-ize or **-ise,** 1 dĭ-năsh′ən-əl-aiz; 2 dē-năsh′on-al-īz, *vt.* [-IZED; -IZ″-ING.] To deprive of nationality; change the nationality of.— **de-na″tion-al-i-za′tion** or **-sa′tion,** *n.*

de-nat′u-ral-ize or **-ise,** 1 dĭ-năch′u-[or -nat′yu-]rəl-aiz; 2 dē-năch′u-[or -năt′yu-]ral-īz, *vt.* [-IZED; -IZ″ING.] **1.** To render unnatural. **2.** To denationalize. **3.** To denature.

de-na′ture, 1 dĭ-nē′chur or -tiur; 2 dē-nā′chur or -tūr, *vt.* [-TURED; -TUR-ING.] To change the natural qualities of; adulterate; specifically, of alcohol, to render unpalatable for drinking by disagreeable admixture, and thus free from internal-revenue tax, for use in industry and the arts. **de-na′tur-ize‡.— de-na″tur-a′tion,** *n.*

den′droid, 1 děn′droid; 2 děn′drŏid, *a.* Treelike. **den′droi-dal‡.**

de-ni′al, 1 dĭ-nai′əl; 2 de-nī′al, *n.* The act of denying; contradiction; disavowal; refusal. [citizen; inhabitant.

den′i-zen, 1 děn′i-zn; 2 děn′i-zn, *n.* A

de-nom′i-nate, 1 dĭ-nŏm′i-nēt; 2 de-nŏm′i-nāt, *vt.* [-NAT″ED; -NAT″ING.] To name; call.— **de-nom′i-na-tive**(es, *a.* That gives or constitutes a name; appellative.— **de-nom′i-na″tor,** *n.* **1.** One who or that which names. **2.** That term of a fraction denoting the number of parts into which the unit is divided.

de-nom′i-na′tion, 1 dĭ-nŏm″i-nē′shən; 2 de-nŏm″i-nā′shon, *n.* **1.** The act of naming; a name; appellation. **2.** A distinct body of Christians; a sect.— **de-nom″i-na′tion-al,** *a.*

de-note′, 1 dĭ-nōt′; 2 de-nōt′, *vt.* [DE-NOT′ED^d; DE-NOT′ING.] To represent; signify; indicate.

dé-noue′ment, 1 dē-nū′māṅ; 2 de̱-nu̱′mäṅ-n.* The catastrophe, as of a play; issue; outcome. **dé-nou′ment‡.**

de-nounce′, 1 dĭ-nauns′; 2 de-nounç′, *vt.* [DE-NOUNCED′^t; DE-NOUNC′ING.] To censure vehemently; stigmatize; arraign; accuse; announce threateningly, as vengeance; menace.— **de-nounce′ment,** *n.*

dense, 1 dens; 2 děns, *a.* [DENS′ER; DENS′-EST.] **1.** Compact in structure; thick; solid; close. **2.** Obtuse; stupid; dull. **-ly,** *adv.*— **den′si-ty,** 1 den′si-tɪ; 2 děn′si-ty, *n.* **dense′ness‡.**

dent, 1 dent; 2 děnt. **I**^d. *vt.* To make a dent in; indent. **II.** *n.* A small depression, as from a blow; indentation.

den′tal, 1 den′təl; 2 děn′tal, *a.* Of or pertaining to the teeth or dentistry.— **den′tate,** 1 den′tēt; 2 děn′tāt, *a.* Having teeth or tooth-like processes. **-ly,** *adv.*— **den′ti-frice,** 1 den′ti-fris; 2 děn′ti-friç, *n.* A preparation for clean-

ing the teeth.— **den′tist,** *n.* One who operates on the teeth.— **den′tist-ry,** *n.* Dental surgery.— **den-ti′tion,** 1 den-tish′ən; 2 děn-tish′on, *n.* **1.** The process or period of cutting the teeth. **2.** *Zool.* The system of teeth peculiar to an animal.

de-nude′, 1 dĭ-niūd′; 2 de-nūd′, *vt.* [DE-NUD′ED^d; DE-NUD′ING.] To strip naked.

de-nun′ci-a′tion, 1 dĭ-nŭn′si-ē′shən; 2 de-nŭn′çi-ā′shon, *n.* The act of denouncing; arraignment; accusation.— **de-nun′ci-a-to-ry,** *a.* **de-nun′ci-a-tiv**(es‡.

de-ny′, 1 dĭ-nai′; 2 de-nī′, *vt. & vi.* [DE-NIED′, 1 -naid′, 2 -nīd′; DE-NY′ING.] To declare to be untrue; disown; refute; forbid; answer in the negative.

de-o′dor-ize or **-ise,** 1 dĭ-ō′dər-aiz; 2 dē-ō′dor-īz, *vt.* [-IZED^d; -IZ″ING.] To destroy the odor of, as by disinfectants.— **de-o″dor-i-za′tion** or **-sa′tion,** *n.*— **de-o′dor-iz″er** or **-is″er,** *n.*

de-ox′i-dize or **-dise,** 1 dĭ-ŏks′i-daiz; 2 dē-ŏks′i-dīz, *vt.* [-DIZED^d; -DIZ″ING.] To deprive of oxygen.— **de-ox′i-date‡.— de-ox″i-di-za′tion** or **-sa′tion,** *n.*

de-part′, ^d 1 dĭ-pärt′; 2 de-pärt′, *vi.* To go away; withdraw; deviate; die.— **de-part′ment,** *n.* A division for a distinct purpose.— **de″part-men′tal,** *a.*— **de-par′ture,** 1 dĭ-pär′chur or -tiur; 2 de-pär′chur or -tūr, *n.* The act of departing; deviation; death.

de-pend′, ^d 1 dĭ-pend′; 2 de-pěnd′, *vi.* **1.** To trust; rely; be dependent. **2.** To hang down.

de-pen′dent, 1 dĭ-pen′dent; 2 de-pěn′děnt. **I.** *a.* **1.** Depending upon something exterior; subordinate; contingent; needy. **2.** Hanging down; pendent. **II.** *n.* **1.** One who depends on another; a retainer. **2.** A consequence; corollary. **de-pen′dant‡.— de-pen′dence,** *n.* The act of depending, or the state of being dependent; reliance; trust; subordination; something relied upon. **de-pen′dance.— de-pen′den-cy,** *n.* [-CIES^z, *pl.*] That which is dependent; a subject or tributary state; dependence.— **de-pen′dent-ly,** *adv.*

de-pict′, ^d 1 dĭ-pikt′; 2 de-pīct′, *vt.* To picture; describe; represent vividly.

de-plane′, 1 dĭ-plēn′; 2 de-plān′, *vt. & vi.* To descend from (an air-plane) on arrival; also, remove from (an air-plane), as goods.

de-plete′, 1 dĭ-plīt′; 2 de-plīt′, *vt.* [-PLET′-ED^d; -PLET′ING.] To lessen or exhaust, as the quantity of blood in the veins.— **de-ple′tion,** *n.*

de-plore′, 1 dĭ-plōr′; 2 de-plŏr′, *vt.* [-PLORED′; -PLOR′ING.] To regret; lament.— **de-plor-a-ble**(es, *a.*— **de-plor′a-bly,** *adv.*— **de-plor′ing-ly,** *adv.*

de-ploy′, 1 dĭ-plŏi′; 2 de-plŏy′, *vt. & vi.*

Mil. To spread out in line of battle, as troops.

de-po′nent, 1 di-pō′nent; 2 de-pō′něnt. **I.** *a.* Laying down; passive in form, but active in meaning, as certain Latin verbs. **II.** *n.* **1.** *Gram.* A deponent verb. **2.** *Law.* One who deposes; a witness who gives written testimony.

de-pop′u-late, 1 dī-pŏp′yu-lēt; 2 dē-pŏp′yu-lāt, *vt.* [-LAT″ED⁴; -LAT″ING.] To deprive of inhabitants; unpeople.— **de-pop′-u-la′tion,** *n.*

de-port′, 1 di-pōrt′; 2 de-pôrt′, *vt.* **1.** To carry away; banish. **2.** To behave or conduct (oneself).— **de″por·ta′tion,** *n.* Transportation; exile.

de-port′ment, 1 di-pōrt′ment *or* -mənt; 2 de-pôrt′ment, *n.* Conduct or behavior; demeanor; bearing.

de-pose′, 1 di-pōz′; 2 de-pōs′, *vt. & vi.* [DE-POSED′; DE-POS′ING.] **1.** To deprive of rank or office; remove; degrade. **2.** To state on oath; testify.

de-pos′it, 1 di-pŏz′it; 2 de-pŏs′it. **I**ᵈ. *vt. & vi.* To place, as for safe-keeping; lay down; let fall, as sediment; form or make a deposit. **II.** *n.* The act of depositing; sediment; money or property deposited.

de-pos′i-ta-ry, 1 di-pŏz′i-tĕ-ri; 2 de-pŏs′i-tā-ry, *n.* [-RIES²; *pl.*] **1.** A person entrusted with anything; a trustee. **2.** A depository.

dep″o-si′tion, 1 dep″o-zish′ən; 2 dĕp″o-sish′on, *n.* **1.** The act of depositing; a deposit. **2.** *Law.* Written testimony under oath. **3.** Removal from office.

de-pos′i-tor, 1 di-pŏz′i-tər *or* -tor; 2 de-pŏs′i-tor, *n.* One who makes a deposit.

de-pos′i-to-ry, 1 di-pŏz′i-to-ri; 2 de-pŏs′i-to-ry, *n.* [-RIES²; *pl.*] A place where anything is deposited.

de′pot, 1 dī′po *or* dep′o; 2 dē′po *or* dep′o, *n.* **1.** A storehouse. **2.** [U. S.] A railroad station.

de-prave′, 1 di-prēv′; 2 de-prāv′, *vt.* [DE-PRAVED′; DE-PRAV′ING.] To render bad or worse; corrupt; vitiate.— **dep″ra-va′tion,** 1 dep″ra-vē′shan; 2 dĕp″ra-vā′shon, *n.* The act of depraving, or the state of being depraved.— **de-prav′i-ty,** 1 di-prav′i-ti; 2 de-prăv′i-ty, *n.* The state of being depraved; a depraved condition; wickedness.

dep′re-cate, 1 dep′ri-kēt; 2 dĕp′re-cāt, *vt.* [-CAT″ED⁴; -CAT″ING.] To plead against; pray for deliverance from.— **dep′re-cat″ing-ly,** *adv.*— **dep′re-ca′tion,** *n.*— **dep′re-ca-to-ry,** *a.* Tending to deprecate; protesting; deprecating. **dep′re-ca-tiv(e‡.**

de-pre′ci-ate, 1 di-prī′shi-ēt; 2 de-prē′shi-āt, *vt. & vi.* [-AT″ED⁴; -AT″ING.] **1.** To

lessen in value; lower the price of; fall in price. **2.** To underrate; disparage. — **de-pre″ci-a′tion,** *n.* The act of depreciating, or the state of being depreciated.— **de-pre′ci-a-tiv(e‡,** *a.* Tending to depreciate. **de-pre′ci-a-to-ry‡.**

dep′re-date, 1 dep′ri-dēt; 2 dĕp′re-dāt, *vt. & vi.* [-DAT″ED⁴; -DAT″ING.] To prey upon; despoil; pillage; plunder.— **dep′re-da′tion,** *n.* A plundering; robbery.— **dep′re-da″tor,** *n.* A robber.— **dep′re-da″to-ry,** *a.*

de-press′, 1 di-pres′; 2 de-prěs′, *vt.* **1.** To press down; lower. **2.** To dispirit; sadden. **3.** To humble.— **de-pres′sion,** *n.* The act of depressing, or the state of being depressed; low spirits or vitality; dejection; melancholy. **2.** That which is depressed; a low or hollow place.— **de-pres′siv(e‡,** *a.*— **de-pres′sor,** *n.*

de-prive′, 1 di-praiv′; 2 de-prīv′, *vt.* [DE-PRIVED′; DE-PRIV′ING.] **1.** To take away from; dispossess; divest: with *of* before the object taken away. **2.** To keep from acquiring or enjoying something; debar.— **dep″ri-va′tion,** 1 dep″ri-vē′shan; 2 dĕp″ri-vā′shon, *n.* The act of depriving, or the state of being deprived.

depth, 1 depth; 2 dĕpth, *n.* **1.** The state or degree of being deep; distance downward, inward, or backward; profundity; extremity. **2.** A deep place; the innermost part.— **depth-bomb,** *n.* An explosive bomb dropped from a vessel's stern to sink a submarine.

de-pute′, 1 di-piūt′; 2 de-pūt′, *vt.* [DE-PUT″ED⁴; DE-PUT′ING.] To appoint as an agent; delegate; send with authority.— **dep″u-ta′tion,** 1 dep″yu-tē′shan; 2 dĕp″yu-tā′shon, *n.* **1.** A deputy, or deputies collectively; a delegation. **2.** The act of deputing, or the state of being deputed.— **dep′u-ty,** 1 dep′yu-ti; 2 dĕp′yu-ty, *n.* [-TIES²; *pl.*] A person delegated to act for another or others; representative.

de-rail′, 1 di-rēl′; 2 dē-rāl′, *vt.* To run off from the rails, as a car or train. **-ment,** *n.*

de-range′, 1 di-rēnj′; 2 de-rānġ′, *vt.* [DE-RANGED′; DE-RANG′ING.] To disarrange; disorder; craze.— **de-ranged′,** *pa.* Insane. — **de-range′ment,** *n.* The act of deranging, or state of being deranged; insanity.

der′e-lict, 1 der′i-likt; 2 dĕr′e-lict. **I.** *a.* **1.** Neglectful of obligation; unfaithful. **2.** Deserted; abandoned. **II.** *n.* That which is abandoned; a deserted wreck at sea.— **der″e-lic′tion,** 1 der″i-lik′shan; 2 dĕr″e-lic′shon, *n.* Neglect or wilful omission.

de-ride′, 1 di-raid′; 2 de-rīd′, *vt.* [DE-RID″ED⁴; DE-RID′ING.] To treat with scornful mirth; ridicule.— **de-rid′er,** *n.*— **de-rid′ing-ly,** *adv.*— **de-ri′sion,** 1 di-riȝ′ən; 2 de-

rizh'on, *n.* Ridicule; mockery; an object of ridicule or scorn.— **de-ri'siv**(e³, 1 dɪ-raɪ'sɪv; 2 de-rī'sɪv, *a.* Marked by derision; mocking. **de-ri'so-ry‡.— de-ri'siv(e-ly³,** *adv.* **— de-ri'siv(e-ness³,** *n.*

de-rive', 1 dɪ-raɪv'; 2 de-rīv', *vt.* [DE-RIVED'; DE-RIV'ING.] To draw, as from a source; deduce, as a conclusion; trace the derivation of.— **de-riv'a-bl**(e², 1 dɪ-raɪv'-ə-bl; 2 de-rīv'a-bl, *a.* Capable of being derived.— **der''i-va'tion,** 1 der'i-vē'shən; 2 dẽr'i-vā'shon, *n.* The act of deriving, or the condition of being derived.— **de-riv'a-tiv**(e³, 1 dɪ-riv'a-tiv; 2 de-riv'a-tiv. **I.** *a.* Of or pertaining to derivation; derived. **II.** *n.* That which is derived; a word derived from another.

der'o-gate, 1 der'o-gēt; 2 dẽr'o-gāt, *vi.* [-GAT'ED⁴; -GAT'ING.] To take away something; detract: used with *from.*— **der''o-ga'tion,** *n.* The act of derogating; detraction; disparagement.— **de-rog'a-to-ri-ly,** *adv.*— **de-rog'a-to-ri-ness,**— **de-rog'a-to-ry,** *a.* Lessening in good repute; disparaging. **de-rog'a-tiv**(e³.

der'rick, 1 der'ɪk; 2 dẽr'ik, *n.* An apparatus, as a mast with a hinged boom, for hoisting and swinging weights into place.

der'rin-ger, 1 der'in-jər; 2 dẽr'in-ger, *n.* A short pistol of large bore.

der'vish, 1 dūr'vɪsh; 2 dẽr'vish, *n.* A Mohammedan mendicant friar; a Moslem fanatic of upper Egypt. **der'viset.**

des-cant'ᵈ, 1 des-kant'; 2 dẽs-eänt', *vi.* To discourse at length; hold forth: with *on* or *upon.*

des'cant, 1 des'kant; 2 dẽs'eänt, *n.* The act of descanting; a discourse; a varied melody or song.

de-scend'ᵈ, 1 dɪ-send'; 2 de-sẽnd', *vt.* & *vi.* **1.** To go down or downward; fall. **2.** To be handed down; be sprung or derived: with *from,* formerly *of.*— **de-scen'dant,** *n.* One who is descended lineally from another. **de-scen'dent‡.— de-scen'dent,** *a.* Descending. **de-scen'dant‡.— de-scent',** *n.* **1.** The act of descending; decline; fall. **2.** A declivity; slope. **3.** Lineage; birth. **4.** Descendants; issue. **5.** An invasion.

de-scribe', 1 dɪ-skraɪb'; 2 de-serīb', *v.* [DE-SCRIBED'; DE-SCRIB'ING.] **I.** *t.* To give the characteristics of; represent; delineate. **II.** *t.* To make a description.— **de-scrip'tion,** 1 dɪ-skrɪp'shən; 2 de-serip'shon, *n.* **1.** The act of describing; a portrayal or explanation. **2.** A sort; kind.— **de-scrip'tiv**(e³, *a.* Marked by description; serving to describe. **-ly,** *adv.* **-ness,** *n.*

de-scry', 1 dɪ-skraɪ'; 2 de-serȳ', *v.* [DE-SCRIED', 1-skraid', 2-serīd'; DE-SCRY'ING.] To discover with the eye; discern; detect.

des'e-crate, 1 des'i-krēt; 2 dẽs'e-crät, *vt.* [-CRAT'ED⁴; -CRAT'ING.] To divert from a sacred to a common use; profane.— **des''e-cra'tion,** *n.* Profanation.

de-sert'ᵈ, 1 de-zūrt'; 2 de-sẽrt', *v.* **I.** *t.* To leave unwarrantably; forsake; abandon. **II.** *i.* To forsake a post or service without leave.— **de-sert'er,** *n.* One who deserts; an absconding soldier or sailor.— **de-ser'tion,** 1 de-zūr'shən; 2 de-sẽr'shon, *n.* The act of deserting.

des'ert, 1 dez'ərt; 2 dẽs'ert, *a.* Of or like a desert; barren; waste.

des'ert¹, *n.* *Geog.* A region destitute of vegetation, rainless, and commonly uninhabitable.

de-sert'², 1 dɪ-zūrt'; 2 de-sẽrt', *n.* The state of deserving, or that which is deserved; merit or demerit.

de-serve', 1 dɪ-zūrv'; 2 de-sẽrv', *v.* [DE-SERVED'; ſSERV(E)D'³; DE-SERV'ING.] **I.** *t.* To be entitled to or worthy of, by either merit or demerit. **II.** *i.* To be worthy or deserving.— **de-serv'ed-ly,** *adv.* According to desert; justly.— **de-serv'ing,** 1 *pa.* Worthy; meritorious. **II.** *n.* The act of deserving. **-ly,** *adv.*

des''ha-bille', *n.* Same as DISHABILLE.

des'ic-cate, 1 des'i-kēt; 2 dẽs'i-eät, *v.* [-CAT'ED⁴; -CAT'ING.] **I.** *t.* To dry thoroughly, as for preserving. **II.** *i.* To become dry.— **des''ic-ca'tion,** *n.*— **des'ic-ca-tiv**(e³ *a.* & *n.*

de-sid'er-ate, 1 de-sid'ər-ēt; 2 de-sīd'er-āt, *vt.* [-AT'ED⁴; -AT'ING.] To feel desire for; be in want of; miss.

de-sid''er-a'tum, 1 de-sid'ər-ē'tum; 2 de-sīd'er-ā'tûm, *n.* [-A'TA, *pl.*] Something not possessed, but needed or desired.

de-sign', 1 dɪ-zaɪn'; 2 de-sīn', *v.* **I.** *t.* **1.** To plan; invent. **2.** To plan for a purpose; purpose; intend. **3.** To draw; sketch in outline. **II.** *i.* To form designs; contrive.— **de-sign'a-bl**(e², *a.*— **de-sign'ed-ly,** *adv.* By design; purposely; intentionally.— **de-sign'er,** *n.* One who forms designs; a contriver; schemer.— **de-sign'ing,** *pa.* Artful; scheming.

de-sign', *n.* **1.** A pattern; preliminary sketch, the art of designing. **2.** The adaptation of means to an end; plan; contrivance; also, the object or end sought; purpose; intention.

des'ig-nate, 1 des'ig-nēt; 2 dẽs'ig-nāt, *vt.* [-NAT'ED⁴; -NAT'ING.] To point out; name; appoint.— **des''ig-na'tion,** *n.* The act of designating; a distinctive name or title.— **des'ig-na-tiv**(e³, *a.*— **des'ig-na'tor,** *n.*

de-sire', 1 dɪ-zaɪr'; 2 de-sīr', *v.* **I.** *vt.* [DE-SIRED'; DE-SIR'ING.] To wish for; covet;

crave; request. **II.** *n.* **1.** An earnest wishing for something; longing; craving; appetite; passion. **2.** A request; wish; prayer. **3.** An object desired.— **de-sir′a-bil′i-ty, de-sir′a-bl(e-ness²,** *n.*— **de-sir′a-bl(e²,** *a.* Worthy to be desired; worth having.— **de-sir′a-bly,** *adv.*— **de-sir′ous,** *a.* Having desire; wishing; craving.— **de-sir′-ous-ly,** *adv.*

de-sist′ᵈ, 1 dɪ-zist′; 2 de-sĭst′, *vi.* To cease from action; forbear; stop: often followed by *from*.

desk, 1 desk; 2 dĕsk, *n.* **1.** A table for writing or study. **2.** A stand for public reading; pulpit.

des′o-late. I. 1 des′o-lĕt; 2 dĕs′o-lāt, *vt.* [-LAT′-EDᵈ; -LAT′ING.] To lay waste; make desolate. **II.** 1 des′o-lĭt; 2 dĕs′o-lat, *a.*

Desk Used by Washington.

1. Laid waste, as a country; deserted; abandoned. **2.** Without friends; forlorn; afflicted; lonely.— **des′o-late-ly,** *adv.*— **des′o-late-ness,** *n.*— **des′o-la′tion,** *n.* **1.** The state of being desolate; loneliness; dreariness; affliction. **2.** A desolate region; a waste. **3.** The act of making desolate; devastation.

de-spair′, 1 dɪ-spār′; 2 de-spâr′. **I.** *vi.* To abandon hope; be or become hopeless: often with *of*. **II.** *n.* **1.** Utter hopelessness. **2.** That which causes despair or which is despaired of.— **de-spair′ing-ly,** *adv.*

des-patch′, *v.* & *n.* Same as DISPATCH.

des″per-a′do, 1 des″pər-ē′do *or* -ā′do; 2 dĕs″pĕr-ā′dᴼ *or* -ä′do, *n.* [-DOES² or -DOS², *pl.*] A ruffian.

des′per-ate, 1 des′pər-ɪt; 2 dĕs′per-at, *a.* **1.** Without care for danger; reckless, as from despair. **2.** Resorted to in extremity; hazardous: furious. **3.** Regarded as hopeless; despaired of.— **des′per-ate-ly,** *adv.*— **des′per-ate-ness,** *n.*— **des′per-a′tion,** *n.* The state of being desperate; recklessness; blind fury.

des′pi-ca-ble, 1 des′pɪ-ka-bl; 2 dĕs′pi-ca-**des′pi-ca-bl²,** } bl, *a.* Deserving to be despised; contemptible; mean; vile.— **des′-pi-ca-bil′i-ty,** *n.* The quality of being despicable.— **des′pi-ca-bl(e-ness²‡.— des′pi-ca-bly,** *adv.*

de-spise′, 1 dɪ-spaiz′; 2 de-spīz′, *vt.* [DE-SPISED′; DE-SPIS′ING.] To regard as contemptible; disdain; scorn.

de-spite′, 1 dɪ-spait′; 2 de-spīt′. **I.** *n.* Extreme aversion; spite; disdain with defiance. **II.** *prep.* In spite of; notwithstanding.— **de-spite′ful,** *a.* Full of spite; malignant.— **de-spite′ful-ly,** *adv.*— **de-spite′ful-ness,** *n.*

de-spoil′, 1 dɪ-spoil′; 2 de-spŏil′, *vt.* To deprive of something, as by force; plunder: with *of*.— **de-spoil′er,** *n.*— **de-spo″li-a′tion,** *n.*

de-spond′ᵈ, 1 dɪ-spond′; 2 de-spŏnd′, *vi.* To lose courage or hope; be depressed.

de-spon′dent, 1 dɪ-spon′dent; 2 de-spŏn′dĕnt, *a.* Dejected; disheartened.— **-ly,** *adv.*— **de-spon′den-cy,** *n.* Dejection. **de-spon′-dence‡.**

des′pot, 1 des′pɒt; 2 dĕs′pot, *n.* An absolute monarch; autocrat; tyrant.— **des-pot′ic,** *a.* Of or like a despot or despotism; tyrannical.— **des-pot′i-cal-ly,** *adv.*

des′pot-ism, 1 des′pɒt-izm; 2 dĕs′pot-ĭṣm, *n.* Absolute power; autocracy; tyranny.

des-sert′, 1 de-zûrt′; 2 dĕ-ṣêrt′, *n.* A service of sweetmeats, etc., at the close of a repast.

des″ti-na′tion, 1 des″tɪ-nē′shən; 2 dĕs″ti-nā′shon, *n.* A point to which a journey is directed; end; goal; appointment.

des′tine, } 1 des′tɪn; 2 dĕs′tin, *vt.* [DES′-**des′tin²,** } TINED, DES′TIND²; DES′TIN-ING.] To design for or appoint to a distinct purpose; foreordain.

des′ti-ny, 1 des′tɪ-nɪ; 2 dĕs′ti-ny, *n.* [-NIES², *pl.*] That to which any person or thing is destined; fortune; doom; fate.

des′ti-tute, 1 des′tɪ-tiūt; 2 dĕs′ti-tūt, *a.* **1.** Not possessing; entirely lacking: with *of*. **2.** Being in want; extremely poor.— **des″ti-tu′tion,** *n.*

de-stroy′, 1 dɪ-strɔi′; 2 de-strŏy′, *vt.* To break down; demolish; put an end to; ruin; kill.— **de-stroy′er,** *n.*

de-struc′tion, 1 dɪ-struk′shən; 2 de-strŭc′shon, *n.* **1.** The act of destroying, or state of being destroyed; demolition; ruin. **2.** That which destroys.— **de-struc′ti-bl(e²,** *a.* Liable to destruction.— **de-struc′tiv(e²,** *a.* Tending to destroy; pernicious; ruinous.— **de-struc′tiv(e-ly²,** *adv.*— **de-struc′tiv(e-ness²,** *n.*

des′ue-tude, 1 des′wɪ-tiūd; 2 dĕs′we-tūd, *n.* Disuse.

des′ul-to-ry, 1 des′ul-to-rɪ; 2 dĕs′ŭl-to-ry, *a.* Changing abruptly and irregularly from one thing to another; fitful; changeable.

de-tach′ᵗ, 1 dɪ-tach′; 2 de-tăch′, *vt.* To disconnect; sever; separate.— **de-tach′ment,** *n.* A detaching; something detached, as a body of troops for special service.

de-tail′, 1 dɪ-tēl′; 2 de-tāl′. **I.** *vt.* **1.** To report minutely. **2.** To select for special service. **II.** *n.* **1.** A particular or item; accessory. **2.** A minute narrative. **3.** *Mil.* A small detachment for some subordinate service.

de-tain′, 1 dɪ-tēn′; 2 de-tān′, *vt.* To stop; withhold; keep back.— **de-tain′er,** *n.*

de-tect′d, 1 dɪ-tekt′; 2 de-tĕct′, *vt.* To discover, as something hidden; find out; determine; disclose.— **de-tec′tion,** *n.* The act of detecting; discovery.— **de-tec′tiv(es.** **I.** *a.* Skilled in or employed for detection; belonging to detectives. **II.** *n.* One employed to ferret out crime and capture criminals.

de-ten′tion, 1 dɪ-ten′shən; 2 de-tĕn′shon, *n.* The act of detaining, or the state of being detained; restraint; confinement.

de-ter′, 1 dɪ-tūr′; 2 de-tēr′, *vt.* [DE-TERRED′, DE-TER′D′S; DE-TER′RING.] To prevent or restrain, as by fear.

de-ter′gent, 1 dɪ-tūr′jent; 2 de-tēr′gĕnt. **I.** *a.* Cleansing. **II.** *n.* A cleansing medicine.— **de-ter′gen-cy,** *n.*

de-te′ri-o-rate, 1 dɪ-tī′rɪ-o-rēt; 2 de-tē′ri-o-rāt, *vt. & vi.* [-RAT″ED′d; -RAT″ING.] To make or grow worse; impair; degenerate. — **de-te″ri-o-ra′tion,** *n.*

de-ter′mi-nate, 1 dɪ-tūr′mɪ-nɪt; 2 de-tēr′mi-nat, *a.* Definite; fixed.

de-ter″mi-na′tion, 1 dɪ-tūr″mi-nē′shən; 2 de-tēr′mi-nā′shon, *n.* **1.** The act of determining; a firm resolve; firmness; resolution. **2.** Authoritative settlement.

de-ter′mine, 1 dɪ-tūr′mɪn; 2 de-tēr′min, **de-ter′mins**, *v.* [-MIN(E)D′S; -MIN′ING.] **I.** *t.* **1.** To resolve; decide; fix; settle; decree. **2.** To terminate; end. **II.** *i.* **1.** To decide; resolve: with *on.* **2.** To come to an end.— **de-ter′mi-na-bl(e′r,** *a.*— **de-ter′mi-na-tiv(es,** *a.* **-ly,** *adv.* **-ness,** *n.*— **de-ter′mined,** *pa.* Resolute; settled; determinate. **-ly,** *adv.*

de-test′d, 1 dɪ-test′; 2 de-tĕst′, *vt.* To dislike intensely; hate; abhor.— **de-test′a-bl(e′r,** *a.* Hateful; abominable.— **de-test′a-bly,** *adv.*— **de′′tes-ta′tion,** *n.* Extreme dislike; hatred; abhorence.

de-throne′, 1 dī-thrōn′; 2 dē-thrŏn′, *vt.* [DE-THRONED′; DE-THRON′ING.] To deprive of royal authority; depose.

det′o-nate, 1 det′o-nēt; 2 dĕt′o-nāt, *vt. & vi.* [-NAT″ED′d; -NAT″ING.] To explode with a sudden loud report.— **det′′o-na′tion,** *n.* A report or explosion.

de′′tour′, 1 de-tūr′; 2 de-tur′, *n.* A roundabout way.

de-tract′d, 1 dɪ-trakt′; 2 de-trăct′, *v.* **I.** *t.* To take away so as to lessen value or estimation. **II.** *i.* To lessen reputation or credit: commonly with *from.*— **de-trac′tion,**

n. The act of detracting; slander; defamation.— **de-trac′tor, de-tract′er,** *n.* A defamer.— **de-trac′tor-y,** *a.*

det′ri-ment, 1 det′rɪ-ment *or* -mənt; 2 dĕt′ri-ment, *n.* Something that impairs or injures; damage; loss.— **det′′ri-men′tal,** *a.* Injurious.

de trop′, 1 də trō′; 2 de trō′. Too much; out of place; not wanted.

deuce¹, 1 diūs; 2 dūͅc, *n.** Two: a card, or side of a die, having two spots.

deuce², *n.* The devil.

dev′as-tate, 1 dev′əs-tēt; 2 dĕv′as-tāt, *vt.* [-TAT″ED′d; -TAT″ING.] To lay waste, as by war, fire, flood, etc.; destroy; ravage. — **dev′′as-ta′tion,** *n.*

de-vel′op, 1 dɪ-vel′əp; 2 de-vĕl′op, *v.* **I.** *t.* To uncover or unfold; perfect by degrees; increase. **II.** *i.* To advance by degrees; come to light or completion gradually; disclose itself. **de-vel′ope‡.**— **de-vel′-op-ment,** *n.* Gradual evolution or completion.

de′vi-ate, 1 dī′vɪ-ēt; 2 dē′vi-āt, *vi.* [-AT″ED′d; -AT″ING.] To turn aside; wander; diverge; differ.— **de′′vi-a′tion,** *n.* The act of deviating, or its result; variation; error.

de-vice′, 1 dɪ-vais′; 2 de-viç′, *n.* A contrivance; design; plan; scheme; heraldic emblem or motto.

dev′il, 1 dev′l; 2 dĕv′l, *vt.* To cook by broiling or frying with the use of pungent spices.

dev′il, *n.* An evil spirit; demon; Satan. — **dev′il-ish,** *a.* Having the qualities of the devil; diabolical; malicious. **-ly,** *adv.* **-ness,** *n.*— **dev′il-try,** *n.* Wanton and malicious mischief, or the spirit inciting to it.

de′vi-ous, 1 dī′vɪ-us; 2 dē′vi-ŭs, *a.* Winding about; rambling. **-ly,** *adv.* **-ness,** *n.*

de-vise′, 1 dɪ-vaiz′; 2 de-vīz′. **I.** *t.* & *vi.* **de-vize′F**, [DE-VISED′; DE-VIS′ING.] **1.** To invent; contrive; plan. **2.** *Law.* To transmit by will. **II.** *n. Law.* A bequest of real estate; also, the will or clause conveying it.— **dev′l-see′,** *n.* The person to whom a devise is made.— **de-vis′er,** *n.* One who contrives.— **de-vi′sor,** *n.* One who gives by will.

de-void′, 1 dɪ-void′; 2 de-vŏid′, *a.* Destitute: with *of.*

de-voir′, 1 dɪ-vwār′; 2 de-vwär′, *n.* Service or duty; respectful attention: often in the plural.

de-volve′, 1 dɪ-vǫlv′; 2 de-vǫlv′, *v.* [DE-VOLVED′; DE-VOLV″ING.] **I.** *t.* To deliver over; transmit. **II.** *i.* To pass to a successor or substitute: sometimes followed by *to,* oftener by *on* or *upon.*

de-vote′, 1 dɪ-vōt′; 2 de-vōt′, *vt.* [DE-VOT″ED′d; DE-VOT″ING.] **1.** To set apart; dedicate; consecrate. **2.** To doom.— **de-**

vot′ed, 1 dɪ-vōt′ed; 2 de-vŏt′ĕd, *pa.* **1.** Feeling or showing devotion; ardent; devout. **2.** Consecrated; also, doomed. **-ly,** *adv.* **-ness,** *n.*— dev″o-tee′, 1 dev′o-tī′; 2 dĕv′o-tē′, *n.* One zealously devoted, as to religion; a zealot.

de-vo′tion, 1 dɪ-vō′shən; 2 de-vō′shon, *n.* **1.** The act of devoting, or the state of being devoted; devoutness; zeal. **2.** An act of worship; prayer: usually in the plural.— de-vo′tion-al, *a.* Of or pertaining to devotion; devout.

de-vour′, 1 dɪ-vaur′; 2 de-vour′, *vt.* To eat up greedily; consume; destroy. **-er,** *n.*

de-vout′, 1 dɪ-vaut′; 2 de-vout′, *a.* **1.** Earnestly religious; pious; reverent. **2.** Warmly devoted; heartfelt; sincere. **-ly,** *adv.* **-ness,** *n.*

dew, 1 dɪū; 2 dū. **I.** *vt.* To wet with or as with dew; bedew. **II.** *n.* Moisture condensed from the atmosphere in small drops upon the upper surface of plants, etc.— dew′-claw″, *n.* A rudimentary toe or hoof in dogs or cattle.— dew′drop″, *n.* A drop of dew.— dew′lap″, *n.* The pendulous skin under the throat of cattle.— dew′y, 1 dɪū-ı; 2 dū′y, *a.* Moist, as with dew; of, like, or yielding dew.

dex′ter, 1 deks′tər; 2 dĕks′ter, *a.* **1.** Right-hand; right. **2.** Favorable; propitious.— dex-ter′i - ty, 1 deks-ter′ı-tɪ; 2 dĕks-tĕr′ï-ty, *n.* Readiness with the hands; expertness; adroitness; skill.— dex′ter-ous, dex′tral, dex′trous, *a.* Characterized by dexterity; skilful; expert; clever; artful. **-ly,** *adv.* **-ness,** *n.* [doubly.

di-¹, *prefix.* Two; twofold; double; twice.

di-², *prefix.* Form of DIS- before b, d, g, j, l, m, n, r, v: used to indicate separation.

di-³, *prefix.* Form of DIA- before a vowel.

dia-, *prefix.* Through; thoroughly.

di″a-bol′ic, ⎱ 1 dai″ə-bŏl′ık, -ı-kəl; 2 dī″-
di″a-bol′i-cal, ⎰ a-bŏl′ïc, -ï-cal, *a.* Of, pertaining to, or like the devil. **-cal-ly,** *adv.* **-cal-ness,** *n.*

di-ab′o-lo, 1 dɪ-ab′o-lō; 2 dĭ-ăb′o-lō, *n.* A game in which a reel-like top is kept spinning continuously by means of a string attached to two sticks.

di-ac′o-nal, 1 dɪ-ak′o-nəl; 2 dĭ-ăc′o-nal, *a.* Of or pertaining to a deacon.— di-ac′o-nate, *n.* The office of a deacon.

di″a-crit′ic, 1 dai″ə-krit′ık; 2 dī″a-crĭt′ĭc. **I.** *a.* Marking a distinctive; distinctive. **II.** *n.* A diacritic mark attached to a letter.

di″ac-tin′ic, 1 dai″ak-tin′ık; 2 dī″ăc-tĭn′ĭc, *a.* Capable of transmitting actinic rays. See ACTINIC.

di-a-dem, 1 dai′ə-dem; 2 dī′a-dĕm, *n.* A crown; sovereignty. See illus. in next column.

di-ær′e-sis, etc. Same as DIERESIS, etc.

di″ag-nose′, 1 dai′ag-nōs′; 2 dī″ăg-nōs′, *vt.* [-NOSED′; -NOS′ING.] *Med.* To make a diagnosis of, as a disease.— di″ag-no′sis, 1 dai′ag-nō′sıs; 2 dī″ăg-nō′sĭs, *n.* The determination of the nature of a disease.

Head with Diadem.

di-ag′o-nal, 1 dai-ag′o-nəl; 2 dĭ-ăg′o-nal. **I.** *a.* Crossing obliquely; oblique. **II.** *n.* A straight line or plane passing from one angle, as of a square, to any other angle not adjacent.— di-ag′o-nal-ly, *adv.*

di′a-gram, 1 dai′ə-gram; 2 dī′a-grăm, *n.* A mechanical plan or outline; a map.— di″a-gram-mat′ic, *a.*

di′al, 1 dai′əl; 2 dī′al, *n.* **1.** A device for indicating time by a shadow thrown upon a marked plate; as, a sun-*dial*. **2.** Any graduated circular plate or face, as of a watch or clock, a mariners' compass, etc.

di′a-lect, 1 dai′ə-lekt; 2 dī′a-lĕct, *n.* A provincial mode of speaking a language, as differing from the accepted literary standard; idiom.

Vertical Sun-dial.

di″a-lec′tic, 1 dai″ə-lek′tık; 2 dī″a-lĕc′tĭe, *a.* **1.** Pertaining to a dialect. di″a-lec′tal‡. **2.** Pertaining to dialectics; argumentative. di″a-lec′ti-cal‡.— di″a-lec′ti-cal-ly, *adv.*

di″a-lec′tic, *n.* **1.** Logic in general: often in the plural, *dialectics*. **2.** A specific mode of argument. **3.** Argumentative ability.— di″a-lec-ti′cian, *n.* A logician.

di′a-log, ⎱ 1 dai′ə-log; 2 dī′a-lŏg, *n.* A
di′a-logue, ⎰ formal conversation between two or more speakers.

di-am′e-ter, 1 dai-am′i-tər; 2 dĭ-ăm′e-ter, *n.* A line through the center, as of a circle or sphere, terminated at the boundary thereof; the length of such a line.— di″a-met′ri-cal, *a.* **1.** Of or pertaining to a diameter. di-am′e-tral‡. **2.** Of or pertaining to the ends of a diameter; directly opposite, and as far removed as possible; irreconcilable. di″-a-met′ric‡.— di″a - met′ri-cal-ly, *adv.* **1.** In the manner of a diameter. **2.** Irreconcilably.

Forms of Cut Diamonds.

di′a-mond, 1 dai′ə-mənd; 2 dī′a-mond, *n.* **1.** A gem of great refractive power,

consisting essentially of crystallized carbon. **2.** A figure bounded by four equal straight lines, and having two of the angles acute and two obtuse; a rhomb or lozenge. **3.** A very small size of type: 4² or 4¹/₂°point.

Di-an′a, 1 dai-an′ə; 2 dī-ǎn′a, *n. Myth.* Roman goddess of the chase and the moon. **Ar′te-mis‡** [Gr.].

di″a-pa′son, 1 dai′ə-pē′sən *or* zən; 2 dī″a-pā′son *or* ṣon, *n.* **1.** *Mus.* A principal stop in a pipe=organ, characterized by fulness and richness of tone. **2.** Comprehensive or fundamental harmony; accord.

di′a-per, 1 dai′ə-pər; 2 dī′a-per, *n.* A fine figured silken or linen cloth.

di-aph′a-nous, } 1 dai-af′a-nʋs; 2 dī-ǎf′a-**di-af′a-nous″,** } nʋs, *a.* Transparent.

di′a-phragm, } 1 dai′ə-fram; 2 dī′a-frăm, **di′a-fram⁸,** } *n.* **1.** *Anat.* An important muscle used in respiration, situated between the thoracic and abdominal cavities. **2.** Any dividing membrane or partition. **mid′riff‡.— di″a-phrag-mat′ic,** *a.*

di″ar-rhe′a, 1 dai″ə-rī′ə; 2 dī″a-rē′a, *n.* Looseness of the bowels. **di″ar-rhœ′a‡.**

di′a-ry, 1 dai′ə-rɪ; 2 dī′a-ry, *n.* [-RIES³, *pl.*] A record of daily events.

di″a-ton′ic, 1 dai″ə-tɒn′ɪk; 2 dī″a-tŏn′ic, *a. Mus.* Designating the regular tones of a key (or scale).

di′a-tribe, 1 dai′ə-traib; 2 dī′a-trīb, *n.* An abusive discourse; invective.

dib′ble, } 1 dib′l; 2 dib′l, *n.* A pointed **dib′l⁸,** } tool for planting seeds, setting slips, etc.

dice, 1 dais; 2 dīç, *n. pl.* [DIE, 1 dai; 2 dī, *sing.*] **1.** Cubes, usually of bone or ivory, marked on each side with black spots, from one to six. **2.** A game played with dice.

dick′er, 1 dik′ər; 2 dīk′er, *vt. & vi.* [U. S.] To make a petty trade; barter; bargain. **— dick′er,** *n.*

dic′tate, 1 dik′tēt; 2 dīc′tāt. **I.** *vt. & vi.* [DIC′TAT-ED⁴; DIC′TAT-ING.] **1.** To declare with authority; command. **2.** To communicate orally, as an amanuensis. **II.** *n.* An authoritative suggestion; a rule; maxim; order.**— dic-ta′tion,** *n.* The act of dictating; that which is dictated; arbitrary control.

dic-ta′tor, 1 dik-tē′tər *or* -tər; 2 dīc-tā′tor, *n.* **1.** One possessing absolute power. **2.** One who dictates.**— dic″ta-to′ri-al,** *a.* Overbearing; imperious; absolute. **-ly,** *adv.* **-ness,** *n.***— dic-ta′tor-ship,** *n.* The office, or term of office, of a dictator.

dic′tion, 1 dik′shən; 2 dīc′shon, *n.* The choice and arrangement of words and modes of expression.

dic′tion-a-ry, 1 dik′shən-ē-rɪ; 2 dīc′shon-ā-ry, *n.* [-RIES³, *pl.*] A book containing the words of a language, arranged alphabetically and defined; a lexicon; book of definitions.

dic′tum, 1 dik′tum; 2 dīc′tŭm, *n.* [DIC′TA, *pl.*] An authoritative or positive utterance.

did, 1 did; 2 did, *imp.* of DO, *v.*

di-dac′tic, 1 dai-dak′tik; 2 dī-dăc′tic, *a.* Pertaining to teaching; instructive; preceptive; expository. **di-dac′ti-cal‡.— di-dac′ti-cal-ly,** *adv.* [DO, *v.*

didst, 1 didst; 2 didst, *2d per. sing. imp.* of

die, 1 dai; 2 dī, *vi.* [DIED; DY′ING.] To suffer death; decease; expire.

die, *n.* [DICE, 1 dais, 2 dīç, *pl.*, in def. 1; DIES, 1 daiz, 2 dīṣ, *pl.*, in def. 2.] **1.** A small figured cube (see DICE); a cast, as in dice=playing; stake. **2.** A hard metal device for stamping or cutting out some object, as a coin.

di-er′e-sis, } 1 dai-er′ɪ-sis; 2 dī-ĕr′e-sĭs, *n.* **di-ær′e-sis,** } [-SES³, *pl.*] Two dots (¨) placed over a vowel, denoting that it is to be pronounced separately from the vowel just before it: used in the text of this dictionary only in foreign words.

di′et⁴, 1 dai′et; 2 dī′ĕt, *vt. & vi.* To regulate the food and drink of; take food and drink by rule; eat sparingly.

di′et¹, *n.* A regulated course of eating and drinking; the daily fare; victuals.**— di′et-a-ry,** dai′et-ə-rɪ; 2 dī′ĕt-ā-ry. **I.** *a.* Of or pertaining to diet. **II.** *n.* [-RIES³, *pl.*] A system of diet.**— di″e-tet′ic, di″e-tet′i-cal,** 1 dai′ı-tet′ık, -ı-kəl; 2 dī′e-tĕt′ic, -ı-cal, *a.* Relating to diet. **dietitian,** *n.* An expert in diet.

di′et², *n.* A legislative body; council.

dif′fer, 1 dif′ər; 2 dīf′er, *vi.* **1.** To be unlike; be different: commonly followed by *from.* **2.** To disagree; dissent: followed by *from* or *with.*

dif′fer-ence, 1 dif′ər-ens; 2 dīf′er-ĕnç, *n.* **1.** The state or quality of being unlike; that in which two things are unlike; unlikeness; distinction; discrimination. **2.** A disagreement; controversy; quarrel.

dif′fer-ent, 1 dif′ər-ent; 2 dīf′er-ĕnt, *a.* Not the same; distinct; other; unlike. **— dif′fer-ent-ly,** *adv.*

dif″fer-en′tial, 1 dif″ər-en′shəl; 2 dĭf″er-ĕn′shal. **I.** *a.* Denoting or making a difference; distinctive. **II.** *n. Math.* An infinitesimal difference between two values of a quantity.**— dif″fer-en′tial-ly,** *adv.*

dif″fer-en′ti-ate, 1 dif″ər-en′shı-ēt; 2 dīf″-

1: artistic, ūrt; făt, fāre; făst; get, prĕy; hĭt, police; obey, gō; nŏt, ŏr; fŭll, rūle; bŭt, bûrn.
2: ärt, ăpe, făt, fâre, făst, whạt, ạll; mē, gĕt, prĕy, fêrn; hĭt, īce; ĩ=ē; ĭ=ĕ; gō, nŏt, ôr, wŏn,

er-ĕn'shi-āt, v. [-AT'ED^d; -AT'ING.] **I.** t. To constitute or note a difference between. **II.** i. To become different or distinct.— **dif''fer-en-ti-a'tion,** n.

dif'fi-cult, 1 dif'ĭ-kult; 2 dif'ĭ-cŭlt, a. **1.** Hard to do or be done; arduous; perplexing. **2.** Hard to influence or satisfy; intractable; exacting.— **dif'fi-cul-ty,** 1 dif'ĭ-kul-tɪ; 2 dif'ĭ-cŭl-ty, n. [-TIES^z, pl.] The state or quality of being difficult; an obstacle; hindrance; objection; trouble; distress.

dif'fi-dent, 1 dif'ĭ-dent; 2 dif'ĭ-dĕnt, a. Self-distrustful; timid; shy; modest.— **dif'fi-dent-ly,** adv.— **dif'fi-dence,** n. Self-distrust; shyness; modesty. **dif'fi-dent-ness‡.**

dif-fuse', 1 dĭ-fiūz'; 2 dĭ-fūs', vt. & vi. [DIF-FUSED'; DIF-FUS'ING.] To spread abroad; circulate; permeate.— **dif-fus'i-bil'i-ty,** 1 dĭ-fūs'ɪ-ble-ness‡.— **dif-fus'i-ble,** a. Spreading rapidly and energetically.— **dif-fu'sion,** 1 dĭ-fiū'ʒən; 2 dĭ-fū'-zhon, n. The act or process of diffusing; a scattering; dissemination; circulation.— **dif-fu'siv(e^s),** 1 dĭ-fiū'sɪv; 2 dĭ-fū'sĭv, a. Diffusing or tending to diffuse; spreading abroad. **-ly,** adv. **-ness,** n.

dif-fuse', 1 dĭ-fiūs'; 2 dĭ-fūs', a. Redundant; prolix; verbose; extended.— **dif-fuse'-ly,** adv.— **dif-fuse'ness,** n.

dig, 1 dig; 2 dĭg, v. [DUG, 1 dug, 2 dŭg or DIGGED, DIGD^s; DIG'GING.] **I.** t. **1.** To break up, or throw up or out, as earth with a spade; excavate. **2.** To push or force in, as a spade into the ground. **II.** i. To work, as with a spade; toil; plod.— **to dig in** (Mil.), to entrench (oneself). —**dig'ger,** n.

di-gest'^d, 1 dɪ-jest'; 2 di-gĕst', vt. & vi. **1.** To change in the stomach, as food; take into the physical or mental organism; assimilate. **2.** To analyze and classify; form into a digest. **3.** To tolerate; endure. — **di-gest'er,** n.— **di-gest''i-bil'i-ty,** n. The quality of being digestible. **di-gest'i-bl(e-ness^z‡.— di-gest'i-bl(e^s,** a. Capable of being digested.— **di-ges'tiv(e^s,** a. Pertaining or conducing to digestion.

di'gest, 1 dai'jest; 2 dī'gĕst, n. A systematic arrangement; summary; compilation.

di-ges'tion, 1 dɪ-jes'ʧən; 2 di-gĕs'chon, n. **1.** The process of changing food in the stomach, so that it can be taken up by the blood and furnish nutriment to the body. **2.** The power to digest; the digestive functions. **3.** Mental assimilation.

dig'it, 1 dij'ɪt; 2 dĭg'ĭt, n. **1.** A finger or toe. **2.** An Arabic numeral. **3.** An ancient measure of length: about two-thirds of an inch.

dig'ni-fy, 1 dig'nɪ-fai; 2 dĭg'ni-fȳ, vt. [-FIED; -FY'ING.] To impart dignity to; invest with dignities; honor; promote; exalt. — **dig'ni-fied,** 1 dig'nɪ-faid; 2 dĭg'ni-fīd, pa. Characterized by dignity; stately; honored.

dig'ni-ta-ry, 1 dig'nɪ-tē-rɪ; 2 dĭg'ni-tā-ry, n. [-RIES^z, pl.] One who holds high official position.

dig'ni-ty, 1 dig'nɪ-tɪ; 2 dĭg'ni-ty, n. [-TIES^z, pl.] **1.** Grave or stately bearing. **2.** High rank or position; distinction; excellence; worth. **3.** A dignitary.

di'graph, 1 dai'graf; 2 dī'grăf, n. A union of two characters with a single sound, as oa in boat or ch in church.

di-gress't, 1 dɪ-gres'; 2 di-grĕs', vi. To turn aside; deviate; wander.— **di-gres'sion,** n. The act of digressing; a turning aside, as from a subject; deviation; wandering.

dike, 1 daik; 2 dīk. **I.** n. [DIKED^t; DIK'ING.] To furnish with a dike; drain by ditching. **II.** n. An embankment to protect low land from inundation.

di-lap'i-date, 1 dɪ-lap'ɪ-dēt; 2 di-lăp'i-dāt, vt. & vi. [-DAT'ED^d; -DAT'ING.] To fall or cause to fall into partial ruin; impair by neglect or misuse.— **di-lap''i-da'tion,** n.

di-late', 1 dɪ-lēt'; 2 di-lāt', vt. & vi. [DI-LAT'ED^d; DI-LAT'ING.] To swell or puff out; distend; expand; expatiate.— **di-la'tion,** 1 dɪ-lē'shon; 2 di-lā'shon, n. Expansion.

dil'a-to-ry, 1 dil'ə-to-rɪ; 2 dĭl'a-to-ry, a. Given to or tending to cause delay; tardy; slow.— **dil'a-to-ri-ly,** adv.— **dil'a-to-ri-ness,** n.

di-lem'ma, 1 dɪ-lem'ə; 2 di-lĕm'a, n. A necessary choice between equally undesirable alternatives; a perplexive predicament.

dil''et-tan'te, 1 dil''e-tan'tɪ; 2 dĭl''ĕ-tăn'te, n. [-TI, pl.] A dabbler in art; a superficial amateur. **dil''et-tant'‡.— dil''et-tan'te-ism,** n.— **dil''et-tan'te-ism‡.**

dil'i-gence¹, 1 dil'ɪ-jens; 2 dĭl'i-gĕnç, n. Assiduous application; industry; care.

dil'i-gence², 1 dil'ɪ-jens or (F.) dī"lī'-zãns'; 2 dĭl'i-gĕnç or (F.) dī"lī'zhäṅç', n. A French stage-coach.

dil'i-gent, 1 dil'-i-jent; 2 dĭl'i-gĕnt, a. Industrious; painstaking; laborious. **-ly,** adv.

Diligence.

dill, 1 dil; 2 dĭl, n. An old-world annual plant of the parsley family, with yellow flowers and aromatic seeds.

di-lute', 1 dɪ-liūt'; 2 di-lūt', vt. & vi. [DI-

lut′ed^d; di-lut′ing.] To weaken; thin,
as by adding water to a liquid preparation.— **di-lu′tion,** 1 dɪ-liū′shən; 2 dɪ-lū′-
shon, *n.* The act of diluting, or the state of
being diluted; something diluted.

di-lu′vi-al, 1 dɪ-liū′vɪ-əl; 2 di-lū′vi-al, *a.*
Of, pertaining to, or produced by a flood.

dim, 1 dim; 2 dĭm. **I.** *vt. & vi.* [DIMMED,
DIMD^s; DIM′MING.] To render or grow dim;
tarnish; fade. **II.** *a.* [DIM′MER; DIM′-
MEST.] **1.** Obscure; indistinct; shadowy;
misty. **2.** Not seeing clearly; purblind;
obtuse.— **dim′ly,** *adv.*— **dim′ness,** *n.*

dime, 1 daim; 2 dĭm, *n.* [U. S.] A silver
coin worth ten cents.

di-men′sion, 1 dɪ-men′shən; 2 di-měn′-
shon, *n.* Extent, as length, breadth, or
thickness.

di-min′ish^t, 1 dɪ-min′ish; 2 di-mĭn′ish, *vt.
& vi.* To make or grow smaller or less;
decrease.— **dim″i-nu′tion,** 1 dim′ɪ-niū′shən;
2 dĭm′i-nū′shon, *n.* The act of diminishing, or
the condition of being diminished; reduction.

di-min″u-en′do, 1 dɪ-min″yu-en′do; 2 di-
mĭn′yu-ĕn′do, *a. & adv. Mus.* Gradually
diminishing in volume of sound: abbreviated *dim., dimin.,* or expressed by the sign >:
used in English as *a., n.,* or *adv.*

di-min′u-tive, } 1 dɪ-min′yu-tiv; 2 di-
di-min′u-tiv^s, } mĭn′yu-tĭv. **I.** *a.* Small;
little. **II.** *n.* A derivative word expres-
sive of diminished size; as, duck*ling.* **-ly,**
adv. **-ness,** *n.*

dim′i-ty, 1 dim′ɪ-tɪ; 2 dĭm′i-ty, *n.* [-TIES^z,
pl.] A variety of cotton cloth.

dim′ple, } 1 dim′pl; 2 dĭm′pl. **I.** *vt. & vi.*
dim′pl^z, } [DIM′PL(E)D^p; DIM′PLING.] To
mark with dimples; form dimples. **II.**
n. A slight depression on the cheek or
chin, or on any smooth surface.

din, 1 din; 2 dĭn. **I.** *vt. & vi.* [DINNED,
DIND^s; DIN′NING.] To assail with confusing noise; urge with clamor; make a din.
II. *n.* A loud continuous noise or clam-
or; a rattling or clattering sound.

dine, 1 dain; 2 dĭn, *v.* [DINED; DIN′ING.]
I. *t.* To give a dinner to. **II.** *i.* To
take dinner. [boat. **din′gy†.**

din′gey, 1 din′gɪ; 2 dĭn′gy, *n.* A small
din′gle, } 1 din′gl; 2 dĭn′gl, *n.* A narrow
din′gl^z, } valley.

din′gy, 1 din′jɪ; 2 dĭn′gy, *a.* Of a dusky
color, as if soiled; dull; tarnished.— **din′gi-ly,**
adv.— **din′gi-ness,** *n.*

din′ner, 1 din′ər; 2 dĭn′ĕr, *n.* The principal meal of the day; a banquet.

dint, 1 dint; 2 dĭnt. **I.** *vt.* To make a
dent or dint in. **II.** *n.* **1.** A dent. **2.**
Active agency; efficacy; as, by *dint* of
hard work.

di′o-cese, 1 dai′o-sīs; 2 dī′o-cēs, *n.* The
territory or the churches under a bishop's
jurisdiction.— **di-oc′e-san.** **I.** *a.* Of or pertaining to a diocese. **II.** *n.* A bishop.

di″o-ra′ma, 1 dai″o-rā′ma; 2 dī′o-rä′ma, *n.*
A painting, as of a battle, arranged for
exhibition.

dip, 1 dip; 2 dĭp, *v.* [DIPPED^t or DIPT; DIP′-
PING.] **I.** *t.* **1.** To put into or under a
fluid and withdraw again; lower and then
raise, as a flag. **2.** To lift up and out,
as liquor with a ladle. **II.** *i.* **1.** To
plunge partly or momentarily; engage
slightly: with *in* or *into.* **2.** To incline
downward, as a compass-needle; lie at
an angle with the horizon, as strata.

dip, *n.* **1.** The act of dipping; a plunge;
bath; dipping up; depression. **2.** Inclination, as of strata, etc. **3.** A candle made
by dipping.

diph-the′ri-a, 1 dif-thī′rɪ-ə; 2 dĭf-thē′ri-a,
n. An infectious disease with tendency
to form a false membrane in the throat.—
diph″the-rit′ic, *a.* **diph-ther′ic‡, -i-cal†.**

diph′thong, 1 dif′thɒŋ; 2 dĭf′thŏng, *n.*
The union of two vowels in one sound.
— **diph-thon′gal,** *a.*

Dip-lod′o-cus, 1 dip-led′o-kus; 2 dĭp-lŏd′o-
eŭs, *n.* A genus of enormous fossil reptiles
found in the United States.

di-plo′ma, 1 dɪ-plo′ma; 2 di-plō′ma, *n.* An
official honorary certificate, as of graduation.

di-plo′ma-cy, 1 dɪ-plo′mə-sɪ; 2 di-plō′ma-
cy, *n.* [-CIES^z, *pl.*] **1.** The art, science,
or practise of conducting negotiations
between nations. **2.** Tact; shrewdness;
skill.— **dip′lo-mat,** 1 dip′lo-mat; 2 dĭp′lo-
mắt, *n.* One employed or skilled in diplomacy.— **dip″lo-mat′ic,** *a.* **1.** Of or pertaining to diplomacy. **2.** Marked by tact
in negotiation; dexterous; adroit. **dip″lo-
mat′i-cal‡.**— **dip″lo-mat′i-cal-ly,** *adv.*—
di-plo′ma-tist, *n.* **1.** One employed in or
skilled in diplomacy. **2.** One remarkable
for tact and shrewd man-
agement.

dip′per, 1 dip′ər; 2
dĭp′er, *n.* One who or
that which dips; a ves-
sel with long handle for
dipping. **2.** A small diving bird. **3.** [D-] [U. S.]
The group of seven
bright stars in the con-
stellation Ursa Major.

American Dipper.

dip″so-ma′ni-a, 1 dip″-
so-mē′nɪ-ə; 2 dĭp″so-
mā′ni-a, *n.* An uncontrollable craving for
alcoholic drink.— **dip″so-ma′ni-ac,** *n.*

dire, 1 dair; 2 dīr, *a.* [DIR′ER; DIR′EST.] Extremely calamitous; dreadful; terrible. **-ly,** *adv.* **-ness,** *n.*

di-rect′d, 1 dı-rekt′; 2 dı-rĕct′, *v.* **I.** *t.* **1.** To point; aim; point out a way to (a person). **2.** To regulate; control; govern. **3.** To address, as a letter. **II.** *i.* To act as a guide, conductor, or leader.

di-rect′, *a.* Straight; straightforward; shortest; nearest; plain; immediate.— **di-rect′ly,** *adv.* **1.** In a direct line or manner. **2.** Immediately; at once; as soon as possible. — **di-rect′ness,** *n.* Straightness; straightforwardness.— **di-rec′tor,** *n.* One who or that which directs.

di-rec′tion, 1 dı-rek′shən; 2 dı-rĕe′shon, *n.* **1.** The position of one point in relation to another; relative position; tendency; aim. **2.** Superintendence; command; order. **3.** The name and residence of a person; address.

di-rec′to-ry, 1 dı-rek′to-rı; 2 dı-rĕe′to-ry, *n.* [-RIES², *pl.*] A classified list of names and addresses, as of the people of a city.

dire′ful, 1 dair′ful; 2 dīr′ful, *a.* Most dire; dreadful; terrible. **-ly,** *adv.* **-ness,** *n.*

dirge, 1 dûrj; 2 dûrj, *n.* A funeral hymn.

dir′i-gi-bl(eᴾ, 1 dir′ı-ji-bl; 2 dîr′ı-gı-bl, **I.** *a.* That may be directed; as, a *dirigible* balloon. **II.** *n.* A dirigible balloon. [poniard.

dirk, 1 dûrk; 2 dirk, *n.* A dagger or **dirt,** 1 dûrt; 2 dîrt, *n.* **1.** Any foul or filthy substance; refuse. **2.** [Colloq., U. S.] Loose earth; garden-loam.— **dirt′y,** 1 dûrt′ı; 2 dîrt′y. **I.** *vt.* [DIRT′IED; DIRT′Y-ING.] To soil; sully; tarnish. **II.** *a.* [DIRT′I-ER; DIRT′I-EST.] Unclean; foul; filthy.— **dirt′i-ly,** *adv.* **-dirt′i-ness,** *n.*

dis-, *prefix.* Apart; asunder. In numerous words having this prefix, *dis-* has simply a negative force, causing the word to express the contrary of what is implied by the second element.

dis-a′bl(eᴾ, 1 dis-ē′bl; 2 dis-ā′bl, *vt.* To render incapable of effective action; cripple; impair.— **dis″a-bil′i-ty,** [-TIES², *pl.*] Lack of ability; inability.

dis″a-buse, } 1 dis″ə-biūz′; 2 dis″a-būs′, **dis″a-buze′ᴾ,** } *vt.* To rid of a false notion; undeceive.

dis″ad-van′tage, 1 dis″ad-van′tıj; 2 dis″-ăd-văn′tăg. **I.** *vt.* To injure; prejudice; hinder. **II.** *n.* **1.** That which hinders; a drawback; injury. **2.** A state of inferiority; preceded by *at*; as, the army was *at* a *disadvantage.*— **dis-ad″van-ta′geous,** *a.* Attended with disadvantage; detrimental; inconvenient. **-ly,** *adv.* **-ness,** *n.*

dis″af-fect′d, 1 dis″a-fekt′; 2 dis″-ă-fĕct′, *vt.* To alienate.— **dis″af-fect′ed,** *pa.* Alienated; estranged; unfriendly.— **dis″af-fec′tion,** *n.* Discontent; estrangement.

dis″a-gree′, 1 dis″ə-grī′; 2 dis″a-grē′, *vi.* **1.** To differ; fail to agree; contend; quarrel. **2.** To be unfavorable in effect, as food; be injurious: followed by *with.*— **dis″-a-gree′a-bl(eᴾ,** 1 dis″ə-grī′ə-bl; 2 dis″a-grē′-a-bl, *a.* Repugnant; displeasing; unpleasant. — **dis″a-gree′ment,** *n.* Failure to agree; dissimilarity; variance; incongruity; altercation; quarrel.

dis″al-low′, 1 dis″a-lau′; 2 dis″ă-low′, *vt.* & *vi.* To refuse to allow or permit; disapprove.— **dis″al-low′ance,** *n.*

dis″ap-pear′, 1 dis″a-pīr′; 2 dis″ă-pēr′, *vi.* To pass from view; vanish.— **dis″ap-pear′-ance,** *n.*

dis″ap-point′d, 1 dis″a-point′; 2 dis″ă-point′, *vt.* **1.** To defeat the expectation, hope, or desire of (a person). **2.** To frustrate (a hope or plan).— **dis″ap-point′-ment,** *n.* The state, condition, or sense of being disappointed; failure; frustration.

dis-ap″pro-ba′tion, 1 dis-ap″ro-bē′shən; 2 dis-ăp″ro-bā′shon, *n.* Disapproval; unfavorable judgment.

dis″ap-prove′, 1 dis″a-prūv′; 2 dis″ă-prǫv′, *v.* **I.** *t.* To regard with disfavor; condemn: often with *of.* **2.** To refuse; reject. **II.** *i.* To feel or express disapproval.— **dis″ap-prov′al,** *n.* The act of disapproving; disapprobation.— **dis″ap-prov′-ing-ly,** *adv.*

dis-arm′, 1 dis-ärm′; 2 dis-ärm′, *v.* **I.** *t.* To deprive of weapons; quell; allay. **II.** *i.* To lay aside arms.— **dis-arm′a-ment,** *n.*

dis″ar-range′, 1 dis″a-rēnj′; 2 dis″ă-rāng′, *vt.* To disturb; derange. **-ment,** *n.*

dis-as′ter, 1 diz-as′tər; 2 dis̠-ăs′ter, *n.* Crushing misfortune; a calamity.— **dis-as′-trous,** 1 diz-as′trus; 2 dis̠-ăs′trŭs, *a.* Full of disaster: calamitous; gloomy; dismal. **-ly,** *adv.* **-ness,** *n.*

dis″a-vow′, 1 dis″a-vau′; 2 dis″a-vow′, *vt.* To deny; disclaim; disown.— **dis″a-vow′-al,** *n.* A disowning; denial.

dis-band′d, 1 dis-band′; 2 dis-bănd′, *vt.* & *vi.* To break up, as an army; discharge from united service, as soldiers; dismiss; discharge.— **dis-band′ment,** *n.* A disbanding.

dis-bar′, 1 dis-bär′; 2 dis-bär′, *vt.* *Law.* To deprive of the right to appear in court as an attorney.

dis″be-lief′, 1 dis″bı-līf′; 2 dis″be-lēf′, *n.* A conviction that a statement is untrue; want of belief.

dis″be-lieve′, } 1 dis″bı-līv′; 2 dis″be-lēv′, **dis″be-liev′ᴾ,** } *vt.* & *vi.* To refuse to be-

lieve; withhold belief; deem false.— **dis″be-liev′er,** n.

dis-bur′den, 1 dis-bûr′dn; 2 dĭs-bûr′dn, vt. & vi.   To unload; get rid of; unburden.

dis-burse′, 1 dis-bûrs′; 2 dĭs-bûrs′, vt. [DIS-BURSED′t, DIS-BURST′s; DIS-BURS′ING.] To pay out, as money.— **dis-burse′ment,** n. Expenditure.

disc, n.   Same as DISK.— **dis′cal,** 1 dĭs′kəl; 2 dĭs′cal, a.   Of, pertaining to, or like a disk.

dis-card′d, 1 dis-kärd′; 2 dĭs-cärd′, vt. & vi. To reject; dismiss.

dis-cern′, 1 di-zûrn′; 2 di-sẽrn′, vt. & vi. To see distinctly; perceive; distinguish; discriminate.— **dis-cern′i-bl(e′r,** a.   Capable of being discerned; perceivable.— **dis-cern′ment,** n.   The act or power of discerning; keenness; insight.

dis-charge′, 1 dis-chärj′; 2 dĭs-chärg′, v. [DIS-CHARGED′; DIS-CHARG′ING.] I. t.   To send forth; emit; unload, as a ship or cargo; fire, as a gun; dismiss, as an employee; set free, as a prisoner; pay, as a debt; perform, as a duty. II. i.   To deliver a charge; unload a cargo or burden; send forth contents; shoot; fire; pour.

dis-charge′, n.   1. The act of discharging; an unloading; dismissal; release. 2. That which discharges, as a certificate. 3. That which is discharged, or thrown out or off, as from a wound.

dis-ci′pl(e′r, 1 di-sai′pl; 2 di-çī′pl. I. vt. [DIS-CI′PLED; DIS-CI′PLING.] To convert. II. n.   A pupil; learner; follower.— **dis-ci′-ple-ship,** n.

dis′ci-pline, ⎰ 1 dĭs′i-plin; 2 dĭs′i-plĭn. 1.
dis′ci-plins, ⎰ vt. [DIS′CI-PLIN(E)Ds; DIS′-CI-PLIN-ING.] 1. To train to obedience or effectiveness; drill; educate. 2. To punish. II. n.   1. Systematic training, as of a soldier; subjection; progressive molding of character and conduct. 2. Punishment; correction; chastisement. 3. A system of rules, as of a church.— **dis′ci-pli-na′ri-an,** 1 dĭs′i-pli-nē′ri-an; 2 dĭs′i-plĭ-nā′ri-an. I. a.   Of or pertaining to discipline. II. n.   One who disciplines; one strict in discipline.— **dis′ci-pli-na-ry,** 1 dĭs′i-plĭ-nē-rï; 2 dĭs′i-plĭ-nā-ry, a.   Of or relating to discipline; employed in discipline.

dis-claim′, 1 dis-klēm′; 2 dĭs-clām′, vt.   To disavow; disown; reject; deny.— **dis-claim′-er,** n.   One who or that which disclaims.

dis-close′, ⎰ 1 dis-klōz′; 2 dĭs-clōz′, vt. & vi.
dis-cloze′r, ⎰ [DIS-CLOSED′; DIS-CLOS′ING.] To lay bare; uncover; make known; reveal; tell.— **dis-clo′sure or -zure′,** 1 dis-klō′ʒur; 2 dĭs-clō′zhur, n.   1. The act or process of disclosing. 2. Anything disclosed.

dis-col′or, ⎰ 1 dis-kul′ər; 2 dĭs-cŏl′or, vt.
dis-cul′or′, ⎰ To give an unnatural color to; stain.— **dis-col″or-a′tion,** n.

dis-com′fit, ⎰ 1 dis-kum′fit; 2 dĭs-cŏm′fit,
dis-cum′fit′, ⎰ vt.   To defeat utterly; frustrate; rout; vanquish.— **dis-com′fi-ture,** n. Defeat.

dis-com′fort, ⎰ 1 dis-kum′fərt; 2 dĭs-
dis-cum′fort′, ⎰ cŏm′fort, n.   The state of being uncomfortable, or that which causes it; disturbance; disquietude.

dis″com-mode′, 1 dĭs″kə-mōd′; 2 dĭs″cŏm-mōd′, vt.   [-MOD′EDd; -MOD′ING.] To cause inconvenience to; trouble; annoy.

dis″com-pose′, 1 dĭs″kem-pōz′; 2 dĭs″cŏm-pōʒ′, vt.   [-POSED′; -POS′ING.] To disarrange; derange; agitate; disturb.— **dis″com-po′sure,** n.   Agitation; disorder.

dis″con-cert′d, 1 dĭs″kon-sûrt′; 2 dĭs″cŏn-çẽrt′, vt.   1. To confuse, as by surprise; discompose.   2. To disarrange, as a plan; frustrate.

dis″con-nect′d, 1 dĭs″kə-nekt′; 2 dĭs″cŏn-nĕct′, vt.   To dissolve the connection of; separate.— **dis″con-nec′tion,** n.

dis-con′so-late, 1 dis-kon′so-lĭt; 2 dĭs-cŏn′so-lat, a.   Sorrowful; inconsolable; gloomy; cheerless; sad.

dis″con-tent′, 1 dĭs″kon-tent′; 2 dĭs″cŏn-tĕnt′. Id. vt.   To dissatisfy. II. n. Lack of content; dissatisfaction; uneasiness.   **dis″con-tent′ment‡.**

dis″con-tent′ed, a.   Ill at ease; dissatisfied.   **-ly,** adv.   **-ness,** n.

dis″con-tin′ue, 1 dĭs″kon-tin′yu; 2 dĭs″cŏn-tĭn′yu, vt. & vi.   [-TIN′UED; -TIN′U-ING.] To break off; bring to an end; cease; stop; intermit; separate; be disunited.— **dis″con-tin′u-ance,** 1 dĭs″kon-tĭn′yu-əns; 2 dĭs″cŏn-tĭn′yu-anç, n.   The act of discontinuing; interruption; intermission.   — **dis″con-tin″u-a′tion,** n.— **dis″con-tin′-u-ous,** a.   Not continuous; interrupted; broken.

dis′cord, 1 dĭs′kord; 2 dĭs′cŏrd, n.   1. Variance; strife; contention.   2. A combination of inharmonious sounds; lack of harmony.— **dis-cor′dance,** n.   A discordant state or quality; discord.   **dis-cor′dan-cy‡.** — **dis-cor′dant,** a.   Contradictory; harsh; dissonant.   **-ly,** adv.

dis-count′d, 1 dis-kaunt′; 2 dĭs′count′, vt. & vi.   1. To deduct; make an allowance; take with exception or doubt, as a statement; discredit.   2. To buy or cash, as notes, for less than face value; cash with deduction of interest yet to accrue.   3. To draw on in advance, as income or prospects; anticipate.

dis′count, 1 dĭs′kaunt; 2 dĭs′count, n.   1.

1: artistic, ûrt; fat, fāre; fast; get, prēy; hit, police; obey, gō; net, ēr; full, rûle; but, bûrn.
2: ärt, āpe, fặt, fâre, fâst, whạt, ạll; mē, gĕt, prey, fẽrn; hit, īce; i̅=ĕ; ĩ=ĕ; gō, nŏt, ôr, wŏn,

An amount deducted; interest deducted in advance for cashing notes, etc. **2.** The act of discounting. **3.** The rate of discount.

dis-coun′te-nance†, 1 dis-koun′tɪ-nəns; 2 dĭs-coun′te-nạnç, *vt.* To disapprove; discourage.

dis-cour′age,) 1 dis-kur′ɪj; 2 dĭs-eŭr′ag,
dis-cur′age†, ∫ *vt.* [-AGED′; -AG-ING.] To damp the courage of; dispirit; dishearten; oppose; obstruct.— **dis-cour′age-ment,** *n.* The act of discouraging, or the state of being discouraged; also, that which discourages; dejection. **-ly,** *adv.* **-ness,** *n.*

dis-course′, 1 dis-kōrs′; 2 dĭs-cōrs′. **I.** *vt.* & *vi.* [DIS-COURSED′†, DIS-COURST′ᴮ; DIS-COURS′ING.] To talk; speak; converse; make an address. **II.** *n.* Connected communication of thought; conversation; a formal address.

dis-cour′te-sy, 1 dis-kûr′tɪ-sɪ; 2 dĭs-
dis-cur′te-syᴮ, ∫ eŭr′te-sy, *n.* [-SIESᶻ, *pl.*] Rude behavior; impoliteness.— **dis-cour′te-ous,** 1 dis-kûr′tɪ-us; 2 dĭs-eŭr′te-ŭs, *a.* Impolite; rude. **-ly,** *adv.* **-ness,** *n.*

dis-cov′er,) 1 dis-kuv′ər; 2 dĭs-cŏv′er, *vt.*
dis-cuv′er†, ∫ To find out; disclose; reveal; expose.— **dis-cov′er-a-ble,** *a.*— **dis-cov′er-er,** *n.*— **dis-cov′er-y,** 1 dis-kuv′ar-ɪ; 2 dĭs-eŏv′er-y, *n.* [-IESᶻ, *pl.*] The act of discovering; disclosure; something discovered.

dis-cred′it†, 1 dis-kred′it; 2 dĭs-erĕd′it. **Iᵈ.** *vt.* To disbelieve; injure the credit of; destroy faith in. **II.** *n.* **1.** The act of discrediting. **2.** Lack of credit; impaired reputation; dishonor.— **dis-cred′it-a-ble†ᵖ,** *a.* Hurtful to credit or reputation; disreputable.

dis-creet′, 1 dis-krīt′; 2 dĭs-erēt′, *a.* Wise in avoiding errors; judicious; prudent. **-ly,** *adv.* **-ness,** *n.*

dis-crep′ant, 1 dis-krep′ənt *or* dis′krɪ-pant; 2 dĭs-erĕp′ant *or* dis′ere-pănt, *a.* Different; opposite; contrary.— **dis-crep′an-cy,** 1 dis-krep′an-sɪ; 2 dĭs-erĕp′an-cy, *n.* [-CIESᶻ, *pl.*] A disagreement or difference. **dis-crep′ance†.**

dis-crete′, 1 dis-krīt′; 2 dĭs-erēt′, *a.* **1.** Distinct or separate. **2.** Made up of distinct parts. **-ly,** *adv.* **-ness,** *n.*

dis-cre′tion, 1 dis-kresh′an; 2 dĭs-erĕsh′on, *n.* **1.** Cautious and correct judgment; prudence; sagacity. **2.** Freedom of judgment and action.— **dis-cre′tion-a-ry,** *a.* Left to discretion; uncontrolled except by discretion. **dis-cre′tion-al†.**

dis-crim′i-nate, 1 dis-krim′ɪ-nēt; 2 dĭs-erĭm′i-nāt. **I.** *vt.* & *vi.* [-NAT″EDᵈ; -NAT″ING.] To note the differences between; note as different; distinguish; make a distinction. **II.** *a.* Noting differences; discriminating; discriminated. **-ly,** *adv.* **-ness,** *n.*— **dis-crim′i-nat″ing,** *pa.* Having power on serving to distinguish; differential. **-ly,** *adv.*— **dis-crim′i-na′tion,** *n.* The act or power of discriminating; distinction.— **dis-crim′i-na-tiv(eᴮ,** *a.* Discriminating; distinctive. **dis-crim′i-na-to-ry†.**

dis-crown′, 1 dis-kraun′; 2 dĭs-erown′, *vt.* To remove a crown from; dethrone.

dis-cur′sive,) 1 dis-kûr′sɪv; 2 dĭs-eŭr′siv,
dis-cur′sivᴮ, ∫ *a.* Passing from subject to subject; wandering. **-ly,** *adv.* **-ness,** *n.*

dis′cus, 1 dis′kus; 2 dĭs′eŭs, *n.* A heavy disk thrown in athletic contests; quoit.

dis-cuss′†, 1 dis-kus′; 2 dĭs-eŭs′, *vt.* To argue for and against; debate.— **dis-cus′sion,** 1 dis-kush′ən; 2 dĭs-eŭsh′on, *n.* The act of discussing; examination; debate.

dis-dain′, 1 dis-dēn′; 2 dĭs-dān′. **I.** *vt.* To regard with proud indifference; despise. **II.** *n.* Proud contempt.— **dis-dain′ful,** *a.* Scornful. **-ly,** *adv.* **-ness,** *n.*

dis-ease′, 1 diz-īz′; 2 dĭz-ēṣ′. **I.** *vt.* [DIS-EASED′; DIS-EAS′ING.] To cause disease in; disorder. **II.** *n.* Disturbed action in the living organism; sickness; illness.

dis″em-bark′†, 1 dis″em-bārk′; 2 dĭs″ĕm-bärk′, *vt.* & *vi.* To put or go ashore; land; unload.— **dis-em″bar-ka′tion** or **-ca′tion,** *n.*

dis″em-bar′rass†, 1 dis″em-bar′as; 2 dĭs″ĕm-băr′as, *vt.* To free from embarrassment. **-ment,** *n.*

dis″em-bod′y, 1 dis″em-bed′ɪ; 2 dĭs″ĕm-bŏd′y, *vt.* **1.** To free from the body. **2.** To disband, as troops.

dis″em-bow′el, 1 dis″em-bau′el; 2 dĭs″ĕm-bow′el, *vt.* To take or let out the bowels of.

dis″en-chant′ᵈ, 1 dis″en-chant′; 2 dĭs″ĕn-chänt′, *vt.* To free from enchantment. **-ment,** *n.*

dis″en-cum′ber, 1 dis″en-kum′bər; 2 dĭs″-ĕn-eŭm′ber, *vt.* To free from encumbrance.

dis″en-gage′, 1 dis″en-gēj′; 2 dĭs″ĕn-ḡāḡ′, *vt.* & *vi.* To set or be free from engagement; become detached; withdraw. **-ment,** *n.*

dis″en-tan′gle,) 1 dis″en-taŋ′gl; 2 dĭs″ĕn-
dis″en-tan′glᴾ, ∫ tăŋ′ḡl, *vt.* To relieve of entanglement; unravel.

dis″en-thrall′, -thral′, 1 dis″en-thrēl′; 2 dĭs″ĕn-thral′, *vt.* To release from thraldom; set free. **-ment,** *n.*

dis″en-trance′, 1 dis″en-trans′; 2 dĭs″ĕn-trănç′, *vt.* To arouse from a trance; free from illusion.

dis″es-tab′lish†, 1 dis″es-tab′lish; 2 dĭs″ĕs-tăb′lish, *vt.* To deprive of established character; withdraw state patronage from, as a church. **-ment,** *n.*

dis-fa'vor, 1 dis-fē'vər; 2 dĭs-fā'vor. **I.** *vt.* To withdraw or withhold favor from; discountenance. **II.** *n.* Disapproval; dislike.

dis-fig'ure, 1 dis-fig'yur; 2 dĭs-fĭg'yur, *vt.* To impair or injure the beauty of; render unsightly; deform.— **dis-fig'ure-ment,** *n.* **1.** That which disfigures. **2.** The act of disfiguring, or the state of being disfigured. **dis-fig"u-ra'tion‡.**

dis-fran'chise, 1 dis-fran'chiz *or* -chaiz; 2 dĭs-frăn'chĭs *or* -chīs, *vt.* [-CHISED; -CHIS-ING.] To deprive of a citizen's privileges, as of the ballot. **-ment,** *n.*

dis-gorge', 1 dis-gōrj'; 2 dĭs-gôrg', *vt. & vi.* To eject; vomit; restore; make restitution.

dis-grace', 1 dis-grēs'; 2 dĭs-grāç'. **I‡.** *vt.* To bring reproach upon; dismiss with ignominy. **II.** *n.* Reproach; infamy; ignominy.— **dis-grace'ful,** *a.* Characterized by or causing disgrace; shameful. **-ly,** *adv.* **-ness,** *n.*

dis-guise', ⎱1 dis-gaiz'; 2 dĭs-gīg'. **I.** *vt.*
dis-guize'ᴾ, ⎰[DIS-GUISED'; DIS-GUIS'ING.] To change in appearance, as by a mask; hide; alter. **II.** *n.* The act of disguising or the state of being disguised; something that disguises; concealment.

dis-gust', 1 dis-gust'; 2 dĭs-gŭst'. **Iᵈ.** *vt.* To cause to loathe or hate. **II.** *n.* Strong aversion; loathing; abhorrence.— **dis-gust'ing,** *pa.* Odious; revolting.— **dis-gust'ing-ly,** *adv.*

dishᵗ, 1 dish; 2 dĭsh, *v.* **I.** *t.* **1.** To place in a dish or dishes; serve, as food. **2.** To make concave, as a wheel. **II.** *i.* To be or become concave.

dish, *n.* **1.** A concave vessel for serving food at meals. **2.** The food served in a dish. **3.** Concavity.— **dish'ful,** *n.*

dis"ha-bille', 1 dis"ə-bĭl' *or* -bĭl'; 2 dĭs"-a-bĭl' *or* -bĭl,,*n.* Undress, or negligent attire.

dis-heart'en, ⎱1 dis-härt'n; 2 dĭs-härt'n,
dis-hart'enˢ, ⎰ *vt.* To discourage.

di-shev'el, 1 di-shev'el; 2 dĭ-shĕv'ĕl,*vt. & vi.* [-ELED *or* -ELLED, -ELDˢ; EL-ING *or* -EL-LING.] To disorder (the hair); disarrange (the dress).

dis-hon'est, 1 dis-ɵn'est; 2 dĭs-ŏn'ĕst, *a.* Lacking in honesty; fraudulent; false. **-ly,** *adv.*— **dis-hon'es-ty,** *n.* Falsity; insincerity; violation of trust; fraud.

dis-hon'or, 1 dis-ɵn'ər; 2 dĭs-ŏn'or. **I.** *vt.* **1.** To disgrace; insult; seduce. **2.** *Com.* To decline or fail to pay, as a note. **II.** *n.* **1.** Lack of honor; degradation; insult; reproach; strain. **2.** Refusal or failure to pay a note, etc., when due.— **dis-hon'or-a-bl(eᴾ,** *a.* Characterized by or bringing dishonor; discreditable; ignoble. **-ness,** *n.*— **dis-hon'or-a-bly,** *adv.*

dis"in-cline', 1 dis"in-klain'; 2 dĭs"in-elīn',

vt. To make unwilling; indispose.— **dis-in"cli-na'tion,** *n.* Aversion; unwillingness.

dis"in-fect'ᵈ, 1 dis"in-fekt'; 2 dĭs"in-fĕct', *vt.* To purify from infection.— **dis"in-fec'-tant. I.** *a.* Disinfecting. **II.** *n.* A substance used to disinfect.— **dis"in-fec'tion,** *n.*

dis"in-gen'u-ous, 1 dis"in-jen'yu-us; 2 dĭs"in-gĕn'yu-ŭs, *a.* Not sincere; deceitful. **-ly,** *adv.* **-ness,** *n.*

dis"in-her'itᵈ, 1 dis"in-her'it; 2 dĭs"in-hĕr'it, *vt.* To deprive of an inheritance.— **dis"-in-her'i-tance,** *n.*

dis-in'te-grateᵈ, 1 dis-in'ti-grēt; 2 dĭs-in'te-grāt, *vt. & vi.* To break or fall in pieces; crumble.— **dis-in"te-gra'tion,** *n.*

dis"in-ter', 1 dis"in-tūr'; 2 dĭs"in-tẽr', *vt.* To dig up, as from a grave; exhume. **-ment,** *n.*

dis-in'ter-est-ed, 1 dis-in'ter-est-ed; 2 dĭs-in'ter-ĕst-ĕd, *a.* Unselfish; impartial. **-ly,** *adv.* **-ness,** *n.*

dis-join', 1 dis-join'; 2 dĭs-jŏin', *vt. & vi.* To sever or be severed; separate; sunder; part.

dis-joint'ᵈ, 1 dis-joint'; 2 dĭs-jŏint', *vt.* To divide at the joints; dislocate; disconnect. — **dis-joint'ed,** *pa.* Dislocated; disconnected; incoherent. **-ly,** *adv.* **-ness,** *n.*

dis-junc'tive, ⎱1 dis-juŋk'tiv; 2 dĭs-jŭge'-
dis-junc'tivˢ, ⎰ *tiv.* **I.** *a.* Helping or serving to disjoin. **II.** *n.* That which disjoins, as one of certain conjunctions. **-ly,** *adv.*

disk, ⎱1 disk; 2 dĭsk, *n.* Any plane or sur-
disc, ⎰ face that is flat and round.

dis-like', 1 dis-laik'; 2 dĭs-līk'. **Iᵗ.** *vt.* To regard with aversion. **II.** *n.* Distaste; repugnance; aversion.

dis'lo-cate, 1 dis'lo-kēt; 2 dĭs'lo-eāt, *vt.* [-CAT"EDᵈ; -CAT"ING.] To put out of joint or out of order; displace.— **dis"lo-ca'tion,** *n.*

dis-lodge', 1 dis-lej'; 2 dĭs-lŏdg', *vt.* To drive out; eject; displace.— **dis-lodg'ment,** *n.*

dis-loy'al, 1 dis-lei'əl; 2 dĭs-lŏy'al, *a.* False to one's allegiance; faithless. **-ly,** *adv.* **-ty,** *n.*

dis'mal, 1 diz'məl; 2 dĭs'mal, *a.* Cheerless; doleful; gloomy. **-ly,** *adv.* **-ness,** *n.*

dis-man'tle, 1 dis-man'tl; 2 dĭs-măn'tl,
dis-man'tlᴾ, ⎰ *vt.* [-TL(E)Dᴾ; -TLING.] To strip of fittings, furniture, defenses, etc.

dis-mast'ᵈ, *vt.* To remove the masts of.

dis-may', 1 dis-mē'; 2 dĭs-mā'. **I.** *vt.* To fill with fear; appal; affright. **II.** *n.* Overwhelming fright; consternation; terror.

dis-mem'ber, 1 dis-mem'bər; 2 dĭs-mĕm'-ber, *vt.* To separate limb from limb. **-ment,** *n.*

dis-miss'ᵗ, 1 dis-mis'; 2 dĭs-mĭs', *vt.* To put out of office; discharge; set aside; send away; reject.— **dis-mis'sal,** *n.* A dismissing; discharge. **dis-mis'sion‡.**

dis-mount'ᵈ, 1 dis-maunt'; 2 dĭs-mount', *v.* **I.** *t.* To remove from a horse, as a

soldier, or from a mounting, as a cannon. **II.** *i.* To get off or alight, as from a horse; come down; descend.

dis″o-bey′, 1 dis″o-bē′; 2 dĭs′o-bẹ̄′, *vt.* & *vi.* To refuse to obey; be disobedient.— **dis″o-be′di-ence,** *n.*— **dis″o-be′di-ent,** 1 dis″o-bī′di-ent; 2 dĭs′o-bẹ̄′dĭ-ĕnt, *a.* Neglecting or refusing to obey; refractory. **-ly,** *adv.*

dis″.-blige′, 1 dis″o-blaij′; 2 dĭs″o-blīǧ′, *vt.* To neglect or refuse to oblige.— **dis″o-blig′-ing,** *pa.* Not disposed to oblige; unaccommodating. **-ly,** *adv.*

dis-or′der, 1 dis-ôr′dẹr; 2 dĭs-ôr′der. **I.** *vt.* To throw out of order; disarrange; derange. **II.** *n.* **1.** Disarrangement; disorderliness; disease. **2.** A disturbance of the peace.— **dis-or′der-ly,** 1 dis-ôr′dẹr-lĭ; 2 dĭs-ôr′der-lỵ, *a.* & *adv.* Being in disorder; lawless; disreputable.— **dis-or′der-li-ness,** *n.*

dis-or′gan-ize, 1 dis-ôr′gan-aiz; 2 dĭs-ôr′gȧn-īz, *vt.* To deprive of organization; break up.— **dis-or″gan-i-za′tion,** *n.*

dis-own′, 1 dis-ōn′; 2 dĭs-ōn′, *vt.* To refuse to acknowledge or to admit; deny; reject.

dis-par′age, 1 dis-par′ĭj; 2 dĭs-păr′aǧ, *vt.* [-AGED; -AG-ING.] To speak of slightingly; undervalue.— **dis-par′age-ment,** *n.* The act of depreciating or undervaluing; detraction.

dis-par′i-ty, 1 dis-par′ĭ-tĭ; 2 dĭs-păr′ĭ-tỵ, *n.* [-TIES[z], *pl.*] The state of being dissimilar; inequality.

dis-pas′sion-ate, 1 dis-pash′ạn-ēt; 2 dĭs-păsh′on-ȧt, *a.* Free from passion; without prejudice. **-ly,** *adv.*

dis-patch′,} 1 dis-pach′; 2 dĭs-păch′. **I**[t].
dis-pach′[r],} *vt.* To send off swiftly; do promptly; execute; accomplish; kill outright. **II.** *n.* **1.** The act of dispatching. **2.** A message sent with haste, as by telegraph. **3.** Promptness; expedition; speed.

dis-pel′, 1 dis-pel′; 2 dĭs-pĕl′, *vt.* [DIS-PELLED′, DIS-PELD′[s]; DIS-PEL′LING.] To scatter; disperse; dissipate.

dis-pense′, 1 dis-pens′; 2 dĭs-pĕns′, *v.* [DIS-PENSED′[t], DIS-PENST′[s]; DIS-PENS′ING.] **I.** *t.* **1.** To deal out in portions; administer, as laws. **2.** To relieve or excuse, as from obligation. **II.** *i.* To grant dispensation. **— to dispense with,** to do without; relinquish; forego.— **dis-pen′sa-bl(e[r],** *a.* Capable of being dispensed or dispensed with. — **dis-pen′sa-ry,** 1 dis-pen′sa-rĭ; 2 dis-pĕn′sa-ry, *n.* [-RIES[z], *pl.*] A place where medicines are kept and compounded, especially where they are given freely to the poor.— **dis″pen-sa′tion,** 1 dis″pen-sē′shạn; 2 dĭs″pĕn-sā′shon, *n.* **1.** The act of dispensing. **2.** Exemption as from an ecclesiastical rule. **3.** A special divine revelation or dealing.— **dis-pen′sa-to-ry,** 1 dis-pen′sa-to-rĭ; 2 dĭs-pĕn′sa-to-ry. **I.** *a.* Of or pertaining to dispensing or dis-

pensation. **II.** *n.* [-RIES[z], *pl.*] A book in which medicinal substances are described; pharmacopeia.

dis-perse′, 1 dis-pʉrs′; 2 dĭs-pērs′, *vt.* & *vi.* [DIS-PERSED′[t], DIS-PERST′[s]; DIS-PERS′ING.] To scatter.— **dis-per′sion,** 1 dis-pʉr′shạn; 2 dis-pēr′shon, *n.* The act of dispersing, or the state of being dispersed; something dispersed. [depress; dishearten.

dis-pir′it[d], 1 dis-pir′it; 2 dĭs-pir′it, *vt.* To

dis-place′[t], 1 dis-plēs′; 2 dĭs-plāç′, *vt.* To put out of place; take the place of. **-ment,** *n.*

dis-play′, 1 dis-plē′; 2 dĭs-plā′. **I.** *vt.* & *vi.* To make manifest or conspicuous; parade; open; unfold; expose; make a display. **II.** *n.* The act of spreading out, unfolding, or bringing to the view or to the mind; ostentatious show.

dis-please′, 1 dis-plīz′; 2 dĭs-plēş′, *vt.* & *vi.* To vex; annoy; offend; give offense.— **dis-pleas′ing,** *pa.* Offensive. **-ly,** *adv.*— **dis-plea′sure,** 1 dis-pleʒ′ur; 2 dĭs-plĕʒh′ur, *n.* **1.** The state of being displeased; dissatisfaction; vexation; indignant disapproval. **2.** An annoyance; offense.

dis-port′, 1 dis-pōrt′; 2 dĭs-pôrt′. **I**[d]. *vt.* & *vi.* To divert; play; sport **II.** *n.* Diversion; sport.

dis-pose′, 1 dis-pōz′; 2 dĭs pōŝ′, *vt.* & *vi.* [DIS-POSED′; DIS-POS′ING.] **1.** To arrange; settle; order; regulate. **2.** To incline; render favorable.— **to dispose of,** to part with; get rid of; sell.— **dis-po′sal,** *n.* The act of disposing; arrangement; distribution; sale; control; outlay.— **dis-pos′er,** *n.* One who disposes or orders.

dis″po-si′tion, 1 dis″po-zish′ạn; 2 dĭs″po-ŝish′on, *n.* **1.** The act of disposing; disposal; settlement. **2.** Natural temper; temperament; spirit; propensity; inclination.

dis″pos-sess′[t], 1 dis″po-zes′; 2 dĭs″po-ĝĕs′, *vt.* To eject; oust.— **dis″pos-ses′sion,** *n.*

dis-praise′, 1 dis-prēz′; 2 dĭs-prāŝ′, *n.* Blame; censure.

dis-proof′, 1 dis-prūf′; 2 dĭs-prōōf′, *n.* Refutation; confutation.

dis″pro-por′tion, 1 dis″pro-pōr′shạn; 2 dĭs″pro-pōr′shon. **I.** *vt.* To make unsymmetrical. **II.** *n.* Want of due proportion or relation.— **dis″pro-por′tion-ate,** *a.* Out of proportion; disproportioned. **dis″pro-por′tion-al**[t]. **-ly,** *adv.*

dis-prove′, 1 dis-prūv′; 2 dĭs-prọv′, *vt.* To prove to be false; confute; refute.— **dis-prov′al,** *n.* Disproof.

dis-pute′, 1 dis-pūt′; 2 dĭs-pūt′, *v.* [DIS-PUT′ED[d]; DIS-PUT′ING.] **I.** *t.* To question; challenge; discuss; contest. **II.** *i.* To debate; quarrel.— **dis′pu-ta-bl(e[r],** *a.* That may be disputed; controvertible; doubtful.—

1: ạ = final; ɪ = habɪt; aisle; au = out; oil; iū = feud; chin; go; ŋ = sing; thin, this.
2: wolf, dọ; bōōk, bōōt; full, rule, cūre, bŭt, bûrn; ôil, bŏy; ĝo, ĝem; iŋk; thin, this.

dis'pu-tant. I. *a.* Engaged in controversy; disputing. **II.** *n.* One who disputes. — **dis″pu-ta'tion,** *n.* The act of disputing; controversy; discussion; argumentation. — **dis″pu-ta'tious,** 1 dis″piu-tē'shus; 2 dis″pū-tā'shŭs, *a.* Tending or pertaining to disputation.— **dis-put'er,** *n.*

dis-pute', *n.* A controversial discussion; a contest; altercation; wrangle; quarrel.

dis-qual'i-fy, 1 dis-kwŏl'ı-faı; 2 dĭs-kwặl'ĭ-fȳ, *vt.* To deprive of qualifications; incapacitate; debar.— **dis-qual″i-fi-ca'tion,** *n.*

dis-qui'et, 1 dis-kwaı'et; 2 dĭs-kwī'ĕt. **I**d. *vt.* To make uneasy; harass; disturb. **II.** *n.* Restlessness; uneasiness. **dis-qui'e-tude‡.**

dis″qui-si'tion, 1 dis″kwı-zish'ən; 2 dĭs″kwı-sĭsh'on, *n.* A systematic treatise or discourse.

dis″re-gard', 1 dis″rı-gärd'; 2 dĭs″re-gärd'. **I**d. *vt.* To slight; overlook. **II.** *n.* Want of regard; neglect.

dis-rel'ish, 1 dis-rel'ish; 2 dĭs-rĕl'ĭsh. **I.** *vt.* **1.** To dislike. **2.** To make unpalatable or offensive. **II.** *n.* **1.** A feeling of slight repugnance; distaste; dislike. **2.** The quality of being displeasing or distasteful.

dis″re-pute', 1 dis″rı-piūt'; 2 dĭs″re-pūt', *n.* Lack or loss of reputation; ill repute. — **dis″rep'u-ta-ble**(er, 1 dis-rep'yu-ta-bl; 2 dĭs-rĕp'yu-ta-bl, *a.* Being in or causing ill repute; disgraceful.— **dis-rep'u-ta-bly,** *adv.*

dis″re-spect', 1 dis″rı-spekt'; 2 dĭs″re-spĕkt', *n.* Lack of respect; discourtesy. — **dis″re-spect'ful,** *a.* Wanting in respect; discourteous.— **dis″re-spect'ful-ly,** *adv.*

dis-robe', 1 dis-rōb'; 2 dĭs-rōb', *vt. & vi.* To unclothe; undress.

dis-rupt'd, 1 dis-rupt'; 2 dĭs-rŭpt', *vt.* To burst asunder.— **dis-rup'tion,** 1 dis-rup'shən; 2 dĭs-rŭp'shon, *n.* The act of bursting asunder; the state of being disrupted.

dis″sat'is-fy, 1 dis-sat'ıs-faı; 2 dĭs-săt'ĭs-fȳ, *vt.* To disappoint; displease.— **dis-sat″is-fac'tion,** *n.* A dissatisfied state or feeling; discontent.

dis-sect'd, 1 dis-sekt'; 2 dĭs-sĕkt', *vt.* To cut apart and analyze; anatomize.— **dis-sec'tion,** 1 di-sek'shən; 2 dĭ-sĕe'shon, *n.* The act of dissecting; a dissected object; critical analysis.— **dis-sec'tor,** *n.*

dis″sem'ble, } 1 di-sem'bl; 2 dĭ-sĕm'bl, *vt.*
dis-sem'blr, } & *vi.* [-BLED, -BLDr; -BLING.] To hide by false pretense; pretend; feign; dissimulate.— **dis-sem'bler,** *n.*

dis-sem'i-nate, 1 dis-sem'ı-nēt; 2 dĭs-sĕm'ĭ-nặt, *vt.* [-NATed, -NAT'ING.] To sow broadcast; diffuse; promulgate.— **dis-sem″i-na'tion,** *n.*

dis-sen'sion, 1 dis-sen'shən; 2 dĭ-sĕn'shon, *n.* Bitter disagreement; discord; strife.

dis-sent', 1 dı-sent'; 2 dĭ-sĕnt'. **I**d. *vi.* To disagree. **II.** *n.* The act or state of dissenting; disagreement; non-conformity.— **dis-sent'er,** *n.* One who dissents, as from an established church; a non-conformist.

dis″ser-ta'tion, 1 dis″ər-tē'shən; 2 dĭs″er-tā'shon, *n.* An argumentative treatise or discourse; disquisition.

dis-sev'er, 1 di-sev'ər; 2 dĭ-sĕv'er, *vt. & vi.* To sever; disjoin; separate; part. **dis-sev'er-ance,** *n.* Separation.

dis'si-dent, 1 dis'ı-dent; 2 dĭs'ĭ-dĕnt. **I.** *a.* Dissenting; differing. **II.** *n.* A dissenter.— **dis'si-dence,** *n.* Disagreement; dissent.

dis-sim'i-lar, 1 dis-sim'ı-lər; 2 dĭs-sĭm'ĭ-lar. *a.* Unlike; different. **-ly,** *adv.*— **dis″sim″i-lar'i-ty,** *n.* Unlikeness; difference. **dis‴si-mil'i-tude‡.**

dis-sim'u-lated, 1 dis-sim'yu-lēt; 2 dĭs-sĭm'yu-lặt, *vt. & vi.* To dissemble.— **dis-sim″u-la'tion,** *n.* False pretense.

dis'si-pate, 1 dis'ı-pēt; 2 dĭs'ĭ-pặt, *v.* [-PATedd; -PAT'ING.] **I.** *t.* To disperse; dispel; waste; squander. **II.** *i.* **1.** To scatter; vanish. **2.** To be wasteful or dissolute.— **dis'si-pat″ed,** *pa.* Pursuing pleasure to excess; dissolute.— **dis″si-pa'tion,** *n.* The act of dissipating; excess; indulgence in vicious pleasures.

dis-so'ci-ate, 1 di-sō'shı-ēt; 2 dĭ-sō'shĭ-ặt, *vt.* [-ATedd, -AT'ING.] To disconnect; separate.— **dis-so″ci-a'tion,** *n.*

dis'so-lu-ble, } 1 dis'o-liū-bl *or* di-sŏl'yu-
dis'so-lu-blr, } bl; 2 dĭs'o-lū-bl *or* dĭ-sŏl'-yu-bl, *a.* Separable into parts; that may be dissolved or decomposed.

dis'so-lute, 1 dis'o-liūt; 2 dĭs'o-lūt, *a.* Abandoned; profligate.— **dis'so-lute-ly,** *adv.* — **dis'so-lute-ness,** *n.*

dis″so-lu'tion, 1 dis″o-liū'shən; 2 dĭs″o-lū'shon, *n.* The act of dissolving; separation; disintegration; decomposition; death.

dis-solve', 1 di-zolv'; 2 dĭ-zŏlv', *vt. & vi.*

dis-solv'es, } [dis-solv(e)d'/s; dis-solv'ing.] To melt; break up; abrogate; relax; destroy.— **dis-solv'a-bl**(er, *a.*— **dis-sol'vent,** *a. & n.*

dis'so-nant, 1 dis'o-nant; 2 dĭs'o-nant, *a.* Harsh; inharmonious.— **dis'so-nance,** *n.* Discord; disagreement.

dis-suade', 1 di-swēd'; 2 dĭ-swād', *vt. & vi.* [dis-suadedd; dis-suad'ing.] To persuade against (an act): with *from.*— **dis-sua'sion,** *n.* 1. The act of dissuading. **2.** A dissuasive.— **dis-sua'sive**(es. **I.** *a.* Tending or intended to dissuade; dissuading. **II.** *n.* A dissuading argument or consideration. **dis-sua'sive-ly,** *adv.*

dis-syl′la-ble, 1 di-sil′ə-bl; 2 dĭ-sўl′a-bl, **dis-syl′la-blᴾ,** n. A word of two syllables. — **dis″syl-lab′ic,** a.

dis′taff, 1 dis′tạf; 2 dĭs′tȧf, n. [DIS′-DIS′TAVES or (rarely) DIS′TAVES, pl.] **dis′tafᴾ,** TAFFS A rotating vertical staff that holds the bunch of flax or wool in hand=spinning.

dis-tain′, 1 dis-tēn′; 2 dĭs-tān′, vt. To stain; sully.

dis′tance, 1 dis′təns; 2 dĭs′tănç. **I.** vt. [DIS′TANCEᵗ; DIS′TANC-ING.] To leave hopelessly behind in a race; outstrip. **II.** n. **1.** Length of separation in space. **2.** Remoteness; a remote point. **3.** Reserve; deference; coldness; haughtiness.

dis′tant, 1 dis′tənt; 2 dĭs′tȧnt, a. **1.** Separated in space or time; remote; indistinct. **2.** Reserved; formal. **-ly,** adv.

dis-taste′, 1 dis-tēst′; 2 dĭs-tāst′, n. Aversion; disrelish; dislike. — **dis-taste′ful,** a. Offensive; displeasing. **-ly,** adv. **-ness,** n.

dis-tem′per, 1 dis-tem′pər; 2 dĭs-tĕm′per, vt. **1.** To affect with disease. **2.** To anger; ruffle.

dis-tem′per¹, n. **1.** A malady, as of brutes. **2.** Ill humor; disturbance.

dis-tem′per², n. Water=color, as for scene=painting, or the painting so executed.

dis-tend′ᵈ, 1 dis-tend′; 2 dĭs-tĕnd′, vt. & vi. To expand; swell; inflate. — **dis-ten″-si-bil′i-ty,**n.— **dis-ten′si-bl(eᴾ,** a. Capable of being distended. — **dis-ten′tion,** n. The act of distending, or the state of being distended. **dis-ten′sion‡.**

dis′tich, 1 dis′tɪk; 2 dĭs′tie, n. Pros. A couplet.

dis-til′, 1 dis-til′; 2 dĭs-tĭl′, vt. & vi. **1.** **dis-till′,** To vaporize and condense; also, to make extracts by such process. **2.** To give forth or exude in drops; shed; emit. — **dis″til-la′tion,** n. The act or product of distilling. — **dis-til′ler,** n. One who distils; a condenser used in distilling. — **dis-til′ler-y,**n. [-IESᶻ, pl.] An establishment for distilling, especially for distilling alcoholic liquors.

dis-tinct′, 1 dis-tiŋkt′; 2 dĭs-tĭŋt′, a. Clear; plain; disjoined; separate. **-ly,** adv. **-ness,** n.— **dis-tinc′tion,** 1 dis-tiŋk′shən; 2 dis-tĭŋe′shon, n. **1.** A distinguishing mark or quality; a mark of honor; eminence. **2.** The act of distinguishing; discrimination.— **dis-tinc′tiv(eˢ,** a. Characteristic; distinguishing. **-ly,** adv. **-ness,** n.

dis-tin′guish, 1 dis-tiŋ′gwɪsh; 2 dĭs-tĭŋ′-gwĭsh, v. **I.** t. **1.** To note as different; discriminate. **2.** To make eminent. **II.** i. To discriminate; followed by between. — **dis-tin′guish-a-bl(eᴾ,** a.— **dis-tin′-guished,** pa. Conspicuous; eminent.

dis-tort′ᵈ, 1 dis-tôrt′; 2 dĭs-tôrt′, vt. To twist into an unnatural form; misinterpret; pervert. — **dis-tor′tion,** n. The act of distorting; a deformity; perversion.

dis-tract′ᵈ, 1 dis-trakt′; 2 dĭs-trăct′, vt. To divert or turn aside; bewilder; craze. — **dis-tract′ed,** pa. Bewildered or harassed; crazed.— **dis-trac′tion,** n. **1.** A diversion of the mind; confusion; interruption. **2.** Agitation; frenzy.— **dis-tract′ing,** a.

dis-train′, 1 dis-trēn′; 2 dĭs-trān′, v. **I.** t. To seize for debt. **II.** i. To make a levy on personal property for debt.— **dis-train′er** or **-or,** n.— **dis-traint′,** n. The seizure of personal property for debt.

dis-trait′, 1 dis-trē′; 2 dĭs-trā′, a. Absent-minded. [Distracted.

dis-traught′, 1 dis-trôt′; 2 dĭs-trȧt′, a.

dis-tress′, 1 dis-tres′; 2 dĭs-trĕs′. **I**ᵗ. vt. **1.** To cause to suffer; afflict; grieve; agitate. **2.** Law. To distrain. **II.** n. **1.** Acute or extreme suffering; pain; trouble. **2.**Law. Distraint.— **dis-tress′ful,** a. **-ly,** adv.

dis-trib′ute, 1 dis-trib′yut; 2 dĭs-trĭb′yut, vt. & vi. [-UT-EDᵈ; -UT-ING.] To divide among a number; apportion; share; classify.— **dis″tri-bu′tion,** 1 dis″tri-biū′shən; 2 dĭs″trĭ-bū′shon, n. Apportionment; arrangement; disposition.— **dis-trib′u-tiv(eˢ,** 1 dis-trib′yu-tiv; 2 dĭs-trĭb′yu-tĭv, a. Serving or tending to distribute; pertaining to distribution; applying to individuals. **-ly,** adv.

dis′trict, 1 dis′trikt; 2 dĭs′trict. **I.** vt. To divide into districts. **II.** n. A portion of territory specially set off; a region; tract.

dis-trust′, 1 dis-trust′; 2 dĭs-trŭst′. **I**ᵈ. vt. To doubt; suspect. **II.** n. Doubt. suspicion.— **dis-trust′ful,** a. **-ly,** adv. **-ness,** n.

dis-turb′, 1 dis-tûrb′; 2 dĭs-tûrb′, vt. **1.** To rouse from rest; disquiet; agitate; trouble. **2.** To disarrange.— **dis-tur′bance,** n. The act of disturbing; a public tumult; mental confusion.— **dis-turb′er,** n.

dis″u-nite′ᵈ, 1 dis″yu-nait′; 2 dĭs″yu-nīt′, vt. & vi. To separate; alienate or become alienated; estrange.— **dis-u′nion,** 1 dis-yūn′yən; 2 dĭs-yųn′yon, n. The state of being disunited; severance; rupture.

dis-use′, 1 dis-yūz′; 2 dĭs-yųg′, vt. To **dis-uze′ᴾ,** discontinue.

dis-use′, 1 dis-yūs′; 2 dĭs-yųs′, n. The act of disusing; abandonment. **dis-u′sage‡.**

ditch, 1 dich; 2 dĭch. **I**ᵗ. vt. & vi. To dig a ditch or ditches in; drain by ditching; run into a ditch; make ditches. **II.** n. A narrow trench in the ground, as for drainage.— **ditch′er,** n.

dit′to, 1 dit′o; 2 dĭt′o. **I.** n. The same thing repeated; the aforesaid. **II.** adv. As before; likewise.

dit′ty, 1 dit′i; 2 dĭt′y, *n.* [DIT′TIES², *pl.*] A short simple air; song.

di-ur′nal, 1 dai-ûr′nal; 2 dī-ûr′nal, *a.* **1.** Daily. **2.** Pertaining to the daytime. — **di-ur′nal-ly,** *adv.*

di-van′, 1 di-van′; 2 di-văn′, *n.* **1.** An Oriental council or council=chamber. **2.** A couch.

dive, 1 daiv; 2 dīv. **I.** *vi.* [DIVED or (Colloq.) DOVE, 1 dōv, 2 dōv; DIV′ING.] To make a dive; plunge or rush in. **II.** *n.* **1.** A plunge head foremost into or as into water. **2.** A disreputable resort.— **div′er,** *n.* — **div′ing=bell″,** *n.* A hollow, water=tight vessel in which men may work under water.

di-verge′, 1 di-vûrj′; 2 di-vẽrg′, *vi.* [DI-VERGED′; DI-VERG′ING.] To deviate; differ.— **di-ver′gence,** *n.* **di-ver′gen-cy‡.**— **di-ver′gent,** *a.* Differing; deviating. **di-verg′ing‡.** [various.]

di′vers, 1 dai′vɚz; 2 dī′vɚs, *a.* Several;

di-verse′, 1 di-vûrs′; 2 di-vẽrs′, *a.* Differing; distinct. **-ly,** *adv.*— **di-ver″si-fi-ca′tion,** *n.* Variation; variety.— **di-ver′si-fy,** *vt.* [-FIED′; -FY′ING.] To make diverse; variegate.

di-ver′sion, 1 di-vûr′shən; 2 di-vẽr′shon, *n.* The act of diverting, or that which diverts; recreation.

di-ver′si-ty, 1 di-vûr′si-ti; 2 di-vẽr′si-ty, *n.* [-TIES², *pl.*] The state of being diverse; unlikeness.

di-vert′ᵈ, 1 di-vûrt′; 2 di-vẽrt′, *vt.* **1.** To turn aside; deflect. **2.** To amuse; entertain.

di-vest′ᵈ, 1 di-vest′; 2 di-vĕst′, *vt.* To strip; dispossess; deprive.

di-vide′, 1 di-vaid′; 2 di-vīd′, *vt. & vi.* [DI-VID′EDᵈ; DI-VID′ING.] To separate into parts; sunder; part; diverge; differ; portion out; apportion.— **di-vid′ed-ly,** *adv.*— **di-vid′er,** 2 di-vaid′ɚr; 2 di-vīd′ɚr, *n.* **1.** One who or that which divides. **2.** *pl.* Compasses.

di-vide′, *n.* A watershed.

div′i-dend, 1 div′i-dend; 2 dĭv′i-dĕnd, *n.* **1.** *Math.* A quantity divided, or to be divided, into equal parts. **2.** *Com.* A distribution of profit on shares or the like.

di-vine′, 1 di-vain′; 2 di-vīn′. **I.** *vt. & vi.* [DI-VINED′; DI-VIN′ING.] To find out or foretell by assumed supernatural aid; prognosticate; surmise; guess. **II.** *a.* **1.** Pertaining to, proceeding from, or of the nature of God or of a god; sacred; excellent; godlike. **2.** Pertaining to divinity or theology. **III.** *n.* A theologian; clergyman. **-ly,** *adv.*— **div″i-na′tion,** *n.* **1.** The act or art of divining. **2.** An instinctive presentiment.— **di-vin′er,** *n.*— **di-vin′i-ty,** *n.* [-TIES², *pl.*] **1.** The quality or character of being divine. **2.** A being (real or imaginary) re-

garded as possessing divine attributes; especially [D-] The Deity; God. **3.** Theology.

di-vi′sion, 1 di-vig′ən; 2 di-vĭzh′on, *n.* **1.** The act of dividing. **2.** A part; section. **3.** Separation; disagreement. **4.** That which divides.— **di-vis″i-bil′i-ty,** *n.* **di-vis′i-bl(e-ness²‡.**— **di-vis′i-bl(e²,** 1 di-viz′-i-bl; 2 di-vĭz′i-bl, *a.* Capable of being divided.— **di-vis′i-bly,** *adv.*— **di-vi′siv(e²,** 1 di-vai′siv; 2 di-vī′siv, *a.* Causing or expressing division.— **di-vi′sor,** 1 di-vai′zɚr or -zɚr; 2 di-vī′sɚr, *n.* *Math.* That by which a number or quantity is divided.

di-vorce′, 1 di-vōrs′; 2 di-vôrc′. **I.** *vt.* [DI-VORCED′‡; DI-VORC′ING.] To separate legally, as husband and wife; sunder; put away. **II.** *n.* Legal dissolution of a marriage contract; severance; separation. — **di-vorce′a-bl(e²,** *a.* **di-vorc′i-bl(e²‡.**— **di-vor-cée′,** 1 di-vor-sē′; 2 di-vor′cē′, *n.* A divorced woman.

di-vulge′, 1 di-vulj′; 2 di-vŭlg′, *vt.* [DI-VULGED′; DI-VULG′ING.] To tell, as a secret; disclose.

diz′zy, 1 diz′i; 2 dĭz′y. **I.** *vt.* [DIZ′ZIED; DIZ′ZY-ING.] To make giddy; confuse. **II.** *a.* [DIZ′ZI-ER; DIZ′ZI-EST.] Having a feeling of whirling and confusion, with a tendency to fall; giddy; causing giddiness. — **diz′zi-ly,** *adv.*— **diz′zi-ness,** *n.*

do, 1 dū; 2 dọ, *v.* [DID, 1 dĭd, 2 dĭd; DO′ING; DONE, 1 dun, 2 dŏn.] **I.** *t.* To bring to accomplishment; perform; execute; effect; transact; finish. **II.** *i.* **1.** To act; work. **2.** To conduct oneself; fare, as in health. **3.** To answer the purpose; suffice.— **do′er,** *n.*

doatᵈ, *vt.* Same as DOTE.

doc′ile, } 1 dos′il or dō′sil; 2 dŏc′il or dō′çil,
doc′il², } *a.* Easy to train or manage; tractable.— **do-cil′i-ty,** *n.*

dockᵗ, 1 dɒk; 2 dŏk, *vt.* To shorten; cut off, as the tail of a horse.

dock²ᵗ, *vt.* To lay up in or as in dock.— **dock′age,** *n.* The act of docking; provision for or charge for docking a vessel.

dock¹, *n.* Any one of various plants of the buckwheat family.

dock², *n.* **1.** An artificial basin for vessels; also, a wharf. **2.** An enclosed space for prisoners in a court=room.

dock³, *n.* The stump of a tail.

dock′et, 1 dɒk′et; 2 dŏk′ĕt. **I**ᵈ. *vt.* To place on a docket; record. **II.** *n.* A summary; calendar of cases to be called in court; any calendar of business.

dock′yard″, 1 dɒk′yärd′; 2 dŏk′yärd″, *n.* A shipyard provided with docks.

doc′tor, 1 dɒk′tɚr or -tɚr; 2 dŏc′tor, *n.* **1.** A physician. **2.** A person who has re-

ceived the highest degree in a faculty, as of divinity law, etc.— **doc′tor-ate,** *n.*

doc′trine,) 1 dek′trɪn; 2 doe′trɪn, *n.* **1.**
doc′trin,) That which is truth, especially in religion; a tenet, or body of tenets. **2**‖. Instruction.— **doc″tri-nal,** *a.* Pertaining to doctrine; instructive.

doc′u-ment, 1 dok′yu-ment *or* -ment; 2 dŏc′yu-ment, *n.* A written or printed paper conveying information or evidence. — **doc″u-men′ta-ry,** *a.* Of, pertaining to, or based upon documents. **doc″u-men′tal‡.**

do-dec′a-gon, 1 do-dek′ɑ-gɔn; 2 do-dĕc′ɑ-gŏn, *n.* A figure with twelve sides and twelve angles.— **do-dec″a-he′dron,** *n.* A solid bounded by twelve plane faces.

dodge, 1 dej; 2 dŏj, *v.* [DODGED; DODG′-ING.] **I.** *t.* To avoid by a sudden turn. **II.** *i.* To move quickly to one side; shift; evade; skulk.— **dodg′er,** 1 dej′ər; 2 dŏdg′er, *n.*

dodge, *n.* An evasion; trick.

doe, 1 dō; 2 dō, *n.* The female of the deer, antelope, hare, rabbit, or kangaroo.

does, 1 duz; 2 dŏs, *3d per. sing. ind. pres.* of DO, *v.*

doe′skin″, 1 dō′skin″; 2 dō′skĭn″, *n.* **1.** The skin of a doe. **2.** A fine woolen cloth.

doff‡,) 1 def; 2 dŏf, *v.* **I.** *t.* To take off, as **doff**ᴾ,) a hat or cloak. **II.** *i.* To take off the hat in salutation.

dog, 1 deg; 2 dŏg. **I.** *vt.* [DOGGED, DOGᴅˢ; DOG′GING.] To follow closely; hound; hunt. **II.** *n.* **1.** A carnivorous mammal, commonly domesticated, and remarkable for its intelligence and its attachment to man. **2.** A catch or detent; implement.— **dog′-cart″,** *n.* A two-wheeled one-horse vehicle, having two seats set back to back, and with an enclosed space for dogs beneath the seats.— **dog-days,** *n. pl.* The hot, sultry season in July and August, when the dog-star (Sirius) rises with the sun.— **dog-ear,** *v.* To bend over a corner of a leaf in a book so as to resemble a dog's ear. **dog′s-ear‡.** — **dog-star,** *n.* The star Sirius, the most brilliant star in the heavens.— **dog′wood″,** *n.* A flowering tree of the United States and Canada, or its wood.

doge, 1 dōj; 2 dōg, *n.* Formerly, the elective chief magistrate, holding princely rank in Venice or Genoa.

Dogwood.

dog′ged, 1 deg′ed; 2 dŏg′ĕd, *a.* Silently or sullenly persistent; stubborn. **-ly,** *adv.* **-ness,** *n.*

dog′ger-el, 1 deg′ər-el; 2 dŏg′er-ĕl, *n.* Trivial, ill-made verse: used also adjectivally.

dog′gish, 1 deg′ɪsh; 2 dŏg′ish, *a.* Like a dog; snappish.

dog′ma, 1 deg′mə; 2 dŏg′ma, *n.* [DOG′MASᶻ *or* DOG′MA-TA, *pl.*] A doctrine, as of a creed resting on authority; a dictum.— **dog-mat′ic,** *a.* **1.** Marked by positive and authoritative assertion. **2.** Like or pertaining to dogma. **dog-mat′i-cal‡.**— **dog-mat′i-cal-ly,** *adv.*— **dog′ma-tism,** 1 deg′ma-tizm; 2 dŏg′ma-tism, *n.* Positive or arrogant assertion, as of belief, without proof.— **dog′ma-tist,** *n.*— **dog′ma-tize** *or* **-tise,** *vi.* [-TIZED; -TIZ′ING.] To express oneself dogmatically.

doi′ly, 1 dei′lɪ; 2 dŏi′ly, *n.* [DOI′LIESᶻ, *pl.*] A small table napkin. **doy′ley‡.**

do′ings, 1 dū′ɪŋz; 2 dō′ings, *n. pl.* Proceedings; acts; course of conduct.

doit, 1 deit; 2 dŏit, *n.* Formerly, a small copper coin of the Netherlands; a trifle.

dole, 1 dōl; 2 dōl, *vt.* [DOLED; DOL′ING.] To deal out in small quantities.

dole, *n.* That which is doled out; a gratuity.

dole′ful, 1 dōl′ful; 2 dōl′ful, *a.* Melancholy; mournful. **-ly,** *adv.* **-ness,** *n.*

doll,) 1 del; 2 dŏl, *n.* A toy representing **doll**ᴾ,) a person.

dol′lar, 1 del′ər; 2 dŏl′ar, *n.* The monetary unit of the United States and Canada, equal to 100 cents, or normally about 4*s.* 1¹⁄₂*d.* English money; also, a similar coin of various other countries.

dol′o-rous, 1 del′o-rus; 2 dŏl′o-rŭs, *a.* Sad; pathetic. **-ly,** *adv.*

dol′phin,) 1 del′fɪn; 2 dŏl′fin, *n.* **1.** A **dol′fin**ᴾ,) cetacean of the Mediterranean and Atlantic. **2.** A large fish, noted for the changes in its color when dying.

dolt, 1 dōlt; 2 dōlt, *n.* A stupid person; dunce. **-ish,** *a.* **-ish-ly,** *adv.* **-ish-ness,** *n.*

do-main′, 1 do-mēn′; 2 do-mān′, *n.* **1.** A territory; province; estate. **2.** A department, as of knowledge; range. **3.** Dominion; rule.

dome, 1 dōm; 2 dōm, *n.* **1.** The vaulted roof of a rotunda; a cupola. **2.** [Poet.] A majestic building.

do-mes′tic, 1 do-mes′tɪk; 2 do-mĕs′tic. **I.** *a.* **1.** Belonging to or fond of the house or household. **2.** Domesticated; tame. **3.** Of or pertaining to one's own country; home-made. **II.** *n.* A family servant. — **do-mes′ti-cal-ly,** *adv.*— **do-mes′ti-cate,** 1 do-mes′tɪ-kēt; 2 do-mĕs′tĭ-cāt, *vt.* [-CAT′ED‡; -CAT′ING.] To train for domestic use;

REPRESENTATIVE TYPES OF DOGS.

1. Scotch terrier. 1/24   2. Dachshund. 1/24   3. Poodle. 1/28   4. Pug. 1/18   5. Smooth fox-terrier. 1/26
6. Pomeranian. 1/13   7. Irish water-spaniel. 1/45   8. American foxhound. 1/41   9. Collie. 1/28   10. Airedale. 1/42   11. Boston terrier. 1/21   12. Bulldog. 1/24   13. Bloodhound. 1/12   14. Bull-terrier. 1/26   15. Greyhound. 1/29   16. Dalmatian. 1/30   17. Great Dane. 1/40   18. Setter. 1/45   19. Mastiff. 1/
20. Pointer. 1/33

make domestic; tame.— **do-mes″ti-ca′tion,**
n.— **do″mes-tic′i-ty,** 1 dō″mes-tis′i-ti; 2 dō″-
mĕs-tic′i-ty, *n.* [-TIES^z, *pl.*] The state of
being domestic

dom′i-cil, } 1 dŏm′i-sil; 2 dŏm′i-çĭl. **I.** *vt.*
dom′i-cile, } [-CILED, -CILD^s; -CIL-ING.] To
provide with a domicil. **dom″i-cil′i-ate‡.**
II. *n.* A home, house, or dwelling.— **dom″i-
cil′i-a-ry,** 1 dŏm′i-sil′i-a-ri; 2 dŏm′i-çĭl′i-a-
ry, *a.* Pertaining to a private residence.

dom′i-nate, 1 dŏm′i-nēt; 2 dŏm′i-nāt, *v.*
[-NAT′ED^d; -NAT′ING.] **I.** *t.* To control;
govern; rule. **II.** *i.* To prevail; pre-
dominate.— **dom′i-nance,** *n.* Control; ascendency. **dom′i-nan-cy‡.**— **dom′i-nant,**
1 dŏm′i-nant; 2 dŏm′i-nant. **I.** *a.* Ruling;
governing; predominant. **II.** *n.* *Mus.* The
fifth tone of a diatonic scale.— **dom″i-na′-
tion,** *n.* Control; dominion. [son.

do′mi-ne, 1 dō′mi-ni; 2 dō′mi-ne, *n.* A par-
dom″i-neer′, 1 dŏm′i-nīr′, 2 dŏm′i-nēr′, *v.*
I. *t.* To dominate. **II.** *i.* To rule arrogantly or insolently: commonly followed by *over.*— **dom″i-neer′ing,** *pa.* Overbearing.— **dom″i-neer′ing-ly,** *adv.*

do-min′i-cal, 1 do-mĭn′i-kal; 2 do-mĭn′i-cal,
a. Relating to Christ or to the Lord's day.

dom′i-nie, 1 dŏm′i-ni; 2 dŏm′i-ni, *n.* A
schoolmaster.

do-min′ion, 1 do-min′yən; 2 do-mĭn′yon,
n. **1.** Sovereign authority; rule; sway.
2. A realm.

dom′i-no, 1 dŏm′i-no; 2 dŏm′i-no, *n.*
[-NOES, 1 -nōz; 2 -nōş, *pl.*] **1.** A robe and
hood, as worn at masquerades; also, the
wearer. **2.** *pl.* A game played with
flat pieces marked like dice, each piece
being also called a *domino.*

don, 1 dən; 2 dŏn, *vt.* [DONNED, DOND^s;
DON′NING.] To put on, as a garment.

don, *n.* **1.** Signor; sir. **2.** A gentleman.

do′nate, 1 dō′nēt; 2 dō′nāt, *vt.* [DO′NAT-
ED^d; DO′NAT-ING.] To bestow as a gift;
contribute.— **do-na′tion,** *n.* The act of
donating; a gift.— **don′a-tive** (e^s, 1 dən′ə-tiv;
2 dŏn′a-tiv. **I.** *a.* Belonging by deed of
gift. **II.** *n.* A donation; gift.

done, 1 dun; 2 dŏn, *pp.* of DO, *v.*

don′key, 1 dŏŋ′ki or duŋ′ki; 2 dŏŋ′ky or
dŭŋ′ky, *n.* An ass.

do′nor, 1 dō′ner; 2 dō′nŏr, *n.* A giver.

doom, 1 dūm; 2 dōōm. **I.** *vt.* To consign
to death or ruin; condemn. **II.** *n.* The
act of dooming, or the state of being
doomed; sad or evil destiny; condemnation; sentence.— **dooms′day″,** 1 dūmz′dē″;
2 dōōmṣ′dā″, *n.* The day of final judgment.

door, 1 dēr; 2 dôr, *n.* An entrance, as to
a house, or the hinged or sliding cover
that closes it; passageway; access.

Dor′ic, 1 dər′ik; 2 dôr′ic. **I.** *a.* **1.** Relating to or characteristic of the district
of Doris, in ancient Greece. **Do′ri-an‡.** **2.**
Of or pertaining to Doric architecture, a style
marked by strength and simplicity. **II.** *n.*
The Doric dialect.

dor′mant, 1 dôr′mənt; 2 dôr′mant, *a.*
Being in a state of sleep; torpid; inactive; unused.— **dor′man-cy,** *n.* Torpidity;
lethargy.

dor′mer, 1 dôr′mər; 2 dôr′mer, *n.* A
vertical window rising from a sloping roof.
dor′mer-win″dow‡.

dor′mi-to-ry, 1 dər′mi-to-ri; 2 dôr′mi-
to-ry, *n.* [-RIES^z, *pl.*] A students' lodg-
ing-house; any large room in which many
persons sleep.

dor′mouse″, 1 dōr′-
maus″; 2 dôr′mous″,
n. [DOR′MICE″, 1 dōr′-
mais″; 2 dôr′mīç″, *pl.*]
A small squirrel=like
rodent.

dor′sal, 1 dōr′sal; 2
dôr′sal, *a.* **1.** Of, pertaining to, on, or near
the **D**ACK. **2.** Per-
taining to the under
surface, as of a leaf.

Dormouse. ¹/₄

do′ry, 1 dō′ri; 2 dō′ry, *n.* [DO′RIES^z, *pl.*]
1. A sharp flat=bottomed rowboat, much
used by fishermen.
2. One of various
fishes.

dose, 1 dōs; 2 dōs.
I. *vt. & vi.* [DOSED^t;
DOS′ING.] To give
or take in doses;
take doses repeatedly. **II.** *n.* The quantity
of medicine to be taken at one time.

Fisherman's Dory.

dost, 1 dust; 2 dŏst, *2d per. sing. pres. ind.* of
DO, *v.*

dot, 1 det; 2 dŏt. **I.** *vt. & vi.* [DOT′TED^d;
DOT′TING.] To mark with a dot or dots;
make dots. **II.** *n.* A minute mark;
speck; spot.

do′tage, 1 dō′tij; 2 dō′taḡ, *n.* Feebleness
of mind, due to old age; senility.— **do′tard,**
1 dō′tard; 2 dō′tard, *n.* One who is in his
dotage.

dote, 1 dōt; 2 dōt, *vi.* [DOT′ED^d; DOT′ING.]
1. To lavish fondness: with *on* or *upon.*
2. To be in one's dotage. **doat‡.**— **dot′ing-
ly,** *adv.* [DO, *v.*

doth, 1 duth; 2 dŏth, *3d per. sing. pres. ind.* of

doub′le, } 1 dŭb′l; 2 dŭb′l, *v.* [DOUB′LED,
dub′l′, } DUB′LD^p; DOUB′LING, DUB′LING^p.]
I. *t.* **1.** To make or be twice as many or
twice as great. **2.** To fold together: with
up, over, etc. **3.** To repeat. **4.** To pass,

march, or sail round. **II.** *i.* **1.** To become twice as great or many. **2.** To turn and go back on the same track.

doub'le, *a.* **1.** Being in pairs; coupled. **2.** Twice as large, much, strong, heavy, or many. **3.** Twofold; hence, ambiguous or deceitful.— **double=deal'ing. I.** *a.* Treacherous; deceitful. **II.** *n.* Treachery; duplicity.

doub'le, *n.* **1.** Something that is twice as much. **2.** A fold or plait. **3.** A person or thing that closely resembles another. **4.** A backward turn, as of a hunted fox; a trick.

doub'let, | 1 dub'let; 2 dŭb'lĕt, *n.* **1.** One
dub'letᴾ, | of a pair of like things; loosely, a pair or couple. **2.** A close=fitting outer body=garment (15th to 17th centuries).

doub-loon', | 1 dub-lūn'; 2 dŭb-loͤon', *n.* A
dub-loon'ᴾ, | former Spanish gold coin worth about $8.

doubtᵈ, | 1 daut; 2 dout, *v.* **I.** *t.* To hold
doutˢ, | as uncertain; distrust. **II.** *i.* To be in doubt.— **doubt'er,** *n.* One who doubts.

doubt, *n.* **1.** Lack of certain knowledge; uncertainty; indecision. **2.** A question; perplexity; problem.— **doubt'ful, dout'ful**ˢ, *a.* **1.** Subject to doubt; uncertain; contingent. **2.** Indistinct; vague. **3.** Questionable; dubious. **-ly,** *adv.* **-ness,** *n.*— **doubt'less, dout'less**ˢ, *adv.* Without doubt; unquestionably. **-ly**‡. [present; bribe; tip.

dou"ceur', | 1 dū̇'sŏr'; 2 du'çûr', *n.* A small

douche, 1 dūsh; 2 duçh, *n.* A jet of water or vapor, or the instrument for administering it.

dough, 1 dō; 2 dō, *n.* Moistened flour or meal, for cooking into bread, cake, etc.; any soft, pasty mass.— **dough'nut,** *n.* A small cake of dough fried in lard.— **dough'y,** *a.*

dough'ty, 1 dau'tı; 2 dou'ty, *a.* Brave; valiant.— **dough'ti-ly,** *adv.*— **dough'ti-ness,** *n.*

douse, 1 daus; 2 dous, *vt.* [DOUSED‡;
DOUS'ING.] To plunge into a liquid; duck; drench.

dove, | 1 duv; 2 dŏv,
duvᴾ, | *n.* A pigeon.—
dove'=cot", **d.=cote,**
n. A house for tame pigeons. **d.=house**‡.

dove'tail", | 1 duv'tāl';
duv'tail"ᴾ, | 2 dŭv'tāl'.
I. *vt.* To join by interlocking. **II.** *n.* A
manner of joining boards, timbers, etc., by interlocking wedge=shaped tenons and spaces; the joint so made. See illus. in next column.

Dove. 1/12

dow'a-ger, 1 dau'ə-jər; 2 dow'a-ger, *n.* [Eng.] A widow holding dower.

dow'dy, | 1 dau'dı; 2 dow'dy. **I.** *a.* [DOW-
DI-ER; DOW'DI-EST.] Ill=dressed, ill=fitting, and in bad taste; shabby. **dow'dy-ish**‡. **II.** *n.* A slatternly woman.

dow'el, 1 dau'el; 2 dow'ĕl, *n.* A pin or peg fitted into two adjacent pieces to fasten them together.

Dovetailed Joint.

dow'er, 1 dau'ər; 2 dow'er.
I. *vt.* To provide with a dower; endow. **II.** *n.* A
widow's life=portion (usually a third) of her husband's lands and tenements; the sum of one's natural gifts; endowment.

a. open; *b*, closed.

down¹, 1 daun; 2 down, *n.* Fine soft plumage, hair, or fibers.

down², *n.* [Eng.] A flat=topped treeless hill; undulating tract of upland.

down, *adv.* From a higher to or toward a lower place or position; downward to or on the ground; below the horizon.— **down'cast,** 1 daun'kast'; 2 down'cåst', *a.* Directed downward; dejected; depressed.— **down'fall",** *n.* A falling or flowing downward; a fall; disgrace.— **down'fall"en,** *a.* Fallen; ruined.— **down'heart"ed,** *a.* Dejected; discouraged.— **down'=hill".** **I.** *a.* Descending; sloping. **II.** *a.* With a downward direction.— **down'right". I.** *a.* **1.** Straight to the point; plain; outspoken; utter. **2.** Directed downward. **II.** *adv.* **1.** Directly downward. **2.** Without doubt or qualification. **3.** In the extreme; utterly.— **down'trod"den,** *a.* Oppressed.— **down'ward,** 1 daun'ward; 2 down'ward. **I.** *a.* Descending; tending from a higher to a lower level. **II.** *adv.* **1.** From a higher to a lower position. **2.** From that which is more remote, as in place or time. **3.** Toward the extremities. **down'wards**‡.

down, 1 daun; 2 down, *prep.* In a descending direction along, upon, or within.

down'y, 1 daun'ı; 2 down'y, *a.* Of, pertaining to, like, or covered with down; soft; restful.

dow'ry, 1 dau'rı; 2 dow'ry, *a.* [DOW-
RIES², *pl.*] The property a wife brings to her husband in marriage; an endowment or gift.

dox-ol'o-gy, 1 dŏks-el'o-jı; 2 dŏks-ŏl'o-gy,*n.* [-GIES², *pl.*] An exultant hymn of praise.

doze, 1 dōz; 2 dōz. **I.** *vi.* [DOZED; DOZ'-
ING.] To sleep lightly; drowse. **II.** *n.* A light sleep; a drowse.— **doz'y,** *a.* Drowsy; soporific.

doz'en, | 1 duz'n; 2 dŏz'n, *n.* Twelve
duz'enᴾ, | things of a kind, collectively.

drab¹, 1 drab; 2 drăb, *n.* A yellowish≈gray color.

drab², *n.* A slattern; lewd woman.

drab′ble, }1 drab′l; 2 drăb′l, *vt.* [DRAB′-
drab′lᵖ, } BLED, DRAB′LDᵖ; DRAB′BLING.]
To draggle.

drachm, 1 dram; 2 drăm, *n.* Same as DRAM.

draft, }1 draft; 2 dråft. **I.** *vt.* **1.** To
draught, } outline; sketch; delineate. **2.**
To conscript. **II.** *n.* **1.** A current of
air. **2.** The act of drinking; a drink.
3. The depth to which a vessel sinks in
the water. **4.** The act of drawing; a
haul; pull; drag. **5.** A plan; sketch.
6. A money≈order; bill of exchange. **7.**
A military or naval conscription. **8.** An
exhausting demand.

drafts′man, }1 drafts′mən; 2 dråfts′-
draughts′man, } man, *n.* [-MEN, *pl.*] One
who draws or prepares plans, designs, etc.

drag, 1 drag; 2 drăg, *v.* [DRAGGED; DRAGDᵖ;
DRAG′GING.] **I.** *t.* **1.** To pull along by
main force; haul. **2.** To search by drag-
ging, as for a dead body; search carefully.
II. *i.* **1.** To move slowly or heavily. **2.**
To dredge.

drag, *n.* **1.** The act of dragging, or that
which drags or is dragged; a clog;
impediment;
brake. **2.** A
long, high, four≈
wheeled carriage.
— drag′net″, *n.*
A net to be drawn
along the bottom
of the water.

Drag and Four.

drag′gle, }1 drag′l; 2 drăg′l, *vt. & vi.*
drag′lᵖ, } [DRAG′GLED, DRAG′LDᵖ; DRAG′-
GLING.] To drag or trail on the ground
so as to wet or soil; drabble; befoul.

drag′o≈man, 1 drag′o≈mən; 2 drăg′o-man,
n. [-MANSᶻ, improperly -MEN, *pl.*] An interpreter or agent for travelers in the East.

drag′on, 1 drag′ən; 2 drăg′on, *n.* A
fabulous, serpent≈like, winged monster.
— drag′on≈fly″, *n.* An insect with slender
body, four large wings, and enormous eyes.
Called also *darning≈needle* and *devil's darning-
needle*.

dra≈goon′, 1 drə≈gūn′; 2 dra-gōōn′. **I.** *vt.*
To harass; coerce; browbeat. **II.** *n.* In
the British army, a cavalryman.

drain, 1 drēn; 2 drān, *v.* **I.** *t.* **1.** To draw
off, as a fluid; draw a fluid from. **2.** To
exhaust. **II.** *i.* To flow off or leak away
gradually; become exhausted.

drain, *n.* **1.** The act of draining; continuous strain, leak, or outflow. **2.** A pipe
or trench for draining.

drain′age, 1 drēn′ɪj; 2 drān′ag, *n.* The act
or means of draining; that which is
drained off; a system of drains.

drake, 1 drēk; 2 drāk, *n.* A male duck.

dram, 1 dram; 2 drăm, *n.* **1.** In apothecaries' weight, 60 grains; in avoirdupois
weight, 27.34 grains. **drachm‡. 2.** A
drink of spirits.

dra′ma, 1 drā′mə; 2 drä′ma, *n.* A composition for the stage; a play; the theater;
— dra≈mat′ic, *a.* Of or like the drama;
theatrical. **dra≈mat′i≈cal‡. — dra≈mat′i-
cal≈ly,** *adv.* **— dra′ma≈tist,** *n.* A dramatic
author. **— dra′ma≈tize** or **-tise,** *vt.* [-TIZED;
-TIZ′ING.] To set forth in dramatic form;
relate or represent dramatically.

drank, 1 draŋk; 2 drăŋk, *imp.* of DRINK, *v.*

drape, 1 drēp; 2 drăp, *vt. & vi.* [DRAPED‡;
DRAP′ING.] To cover, as with hanging
cloth; arrange, as drapery. **— drap′er,** *n.* A
dealer in cloths. **— drap′er≈y,** *n.* [-IESᶻ, *pl.*]
1. Loosely hanging attire; also, curtains,
tapestry, etc. **2.** The business of a draper.
3. Cloth in general.

dras′tic, 1 dras′tɪk; 2 drăs′tic. **I.** *a.* Acting vigorously; effective. **II.** *n.* A strong
purgative.

draught, *vt. & n.* See DRAFT.

draughts, 1 drafts; 2 dråfts, *n. pl.* Checkers.**— draughts′man,** *n.* A piece used in the
game of checkers; a draftsman.

draw, 1 drɔ; 2 drą, *v.* [DREW; DRAWN;
DRAWN; DRAW′ING.] **I.** *t.* **1.** To pull;
haul; lead; attract. **2.** To pull out; extract; call forth; obtain. **3.** To draft:
commonly with *up.* **4.** To sketch; portray. **5.** To require the depth of (so
much water), as a vessel. **II.** *i.* **1.** To
have attractive influence; be attractive.
2. To have a free draft, as a stove or
chimney. **3.** To move as if drawn; as, to
draw away. **4.** To obtain money, etc.,
on application. **5.** To delineate, as with
a pencil; practise drawing. **6.** To un-
sheathe a sword.**— draw′back″,** *n.* **1.**
A disadvantage. **2.** A rebate. **— draw′-
bridge″,** *n.* A bridge of which the whole or
a part may be drawn up or aside. **— draw≈ee′,**
1 drɔ-ī′; 2 drą-ē′, *n.* The one upon whom an
order for money is drawn. **— draw′er,** *n.* **1.**
One who draws; formerly, a waiter. **2.** A
sliding receptacle, as in a bureau, table, etc.
— draw′ers, *n. pl.* A trouser≈like under-
garment. **— draw′ing,** *n.* **1.** The act of one
who draws. **2.** A picture, sketch, or design;
also, the art of representing objects by lines;
delineation.

draw, *n.* **1.** An act of drawing. **2.** A tie,
as in a game. **3.** The movable section
of a drawbridge.

draw′ing≈room″, 1 drɔ′ɪŋ≈rūm″; 2 dra′ing-

room', *n.* A room for the reception of company; also, the company assembled.

drawl, 1 drôl; 2 drạl. **I.** *vt. & vi.* To speak slowly and lazily. **II.** *n.* Spiritless utterance.

dray, 1 drē; 2 drā, *n.* A strong, heavy, low vehicle.

Two-wheeled Dray.

dray'age, 1 drē'ij; 2 drā'ag, *n.* **1.** The act of conveying in a dray. **2.** The charge for draying.

dread, } 1 dred; 2 dred. **I**^d. *vt.* To an-
dread^s, } ticipate fearfully. **II.** *a.* **1.** Causing great fear; terrible. **2.** Exciting awe or reverence. **III.** *n.* **1.** Shrinking horror; terrifying anticipation. **2.** Fear with respect; awe. **3**‖. That which causes awe or fear.—**dread'ful**, *a.* Inspiring dread; terrible; awful.—**dread'ful-ly**, *adv.*—**dread'ful-ness**, *n.*

dream, 1 drīm; 2 drēm. **I.** *vt. & vi.* [DREAMED or DREAMT, 1 dremt, 2 drĕmt, DREMT^s; DREAM'ING.] To have a vision of while sleeping; have a dream or dreams; fancy; hope; imagine; meditate. **II.** *n.* A train of thoughts or images passing through the mind in sleep; also, a visionary idea or anticipation.—**dream'er**, *n.* One who dreams; a visionary.—**dream'-ful**, *a.*—**dream'I-ly**, *adv.*—In a dreamy manner.—**dream'I-ness**, *n.*—**dream'less**, *a.* **dream'y**, 1 drīm'ī; 2 drēm'ÿ, *a.* Of, pertaining to, or given to dreams.

drear, 1 drīr; 2 drēr, *a.* [Poet.] Dreary.

drear'y, 1 drīr'ī; 2 drēr'ÿ, *a.* [DREAR'I-ER; DREAR'I-EST.] Forlorn; lonely; gloomy.—**drear'I-ly**, *adv.*—**drear'I-ness**, *n.*

dredge^1, 1 drej; 2 drĕdg. **I.** *vt. & vi.* [DREDGED, DREDGD^s; DREDG'ING.] To clean out by a dredge; remove by a dredge; use a dredge. **II.** *n.* An appliance for bringing up mud, silt, etc., from under water.

dredge^2. **I.** *vt.* To sprinkle flour or the like upon. **II.** *n.* A box with perforated lid, for dredging meat. **dredg'ing-box**^‡.

dredg'er^1, 1 drej'er; 2 drĕdg'er, *n.* One who dredges; a boat or machine for dredging.

dredg'er^2, *n.* In cookery, a dredging-box.

dregs, 1 dregz; 2 drĕgs, *n. pl.* Sediment; lees; refuse.—**dreg'gi-ness**, *n.*—**dreg'gish**, *a.*—**dreg'gy**, *a.* Containing dregs; foul.

drench^t, 1 drench; 2 drĕnch, *vt.* To wet thoroughly; soak; give a potion to.

drench, *n.* A large draft of fluid; a liquid medicine.

dress, 1 dres; 2 drĕs. **I.** *vt. & vi.* [DRESSED^t or DREST; DRESS'ING.] To clothe; array; adorn; arrange; adjust; cleanse and bind up, as a wound; prepare. **II.** *n.* **1.** Clothes collectively; elegant attire. **2.** A gown of a woman or child.—**dress'er**^1, *n.* One who or that which dresses.—**dress'er**^2, *n.* A kitchen table with shelves; a cupboard; sideboard.—**dress'ing**, *n.* The act of dressing, or that with which anything, as a wound, is dressed.—**dress'mak"er**, *n.* One who makes dresses for women or children.—**dress'mak"ing**, *n.*—**dress'y**, *a.* [Colloq.] Fond of dress; showy; elegant.

drew, 1 drū; 2 drų, *imp.* of DRAW, *v.*

drib'ble, } 1 drib'l; 2 drĭb'l. **I.** *vt. & vi.* **drib'lr**, } [DRIB'BLED, DRIB'LD^p; DRIB'-BLING.] To drip; give out by piecemeal. **II.** *n.* Liquid falling in drops.—**drib'let**, *n.* A scanty portion. **drib'blet**‡.

dried, 1 draid; 2 drīd, *imp. & pp.* of DRY, *v.*

dri'er, 1 drai'er; 2 drī'er, *n.* One who or that which dries. **dry'er**‡.

dri'er, **dri'est**, *compar. & superl.* of DRY, *a.*

drift^d, 1 drift; 2 drĭft, *vt. & vi.* To carry or be carried along, as on a current; accumulate by force of wind, as snow.

drift, *n.* **1.** Something driven onward or piled up by a current. **2.** A course; tendency. **3.** A driving; an urgent force.

drill, } 1 dril; 2 drĭl, *vt. & vi.* **1.** To bore, **drill**^r, } as with a drill. **2.** To train, as soldiers. **3.** To plant in drills.

drill, *n.* **1.** A boring-tool for metal. **2.** A machine for planting seeds in rows; a row so planted. **3.** Military training.

drill'ing, 1 dril'ĭŋ; 2 drĭl'ĭng, *n.* A firm twilled fabric of linen or cotton.

dri'ly, *adv.* Same as DRYLY.

drink, 1 drink; 2 drĭŋk, *vt. & vi.* [*imp.* DRANK, 1 drank; 2 drạ̈ŋk (formerly DRUNK, 1 drụŋk, 2 drŭŋk); *pp.* DRUNK (formerly DRUNK'EN); DRINK'ING.] To swallow, as a liquid; absorb; receive eagerly.—**drink'a-bl(e**^r. **I.** *a.* Capable of use as a drink. **II.** *n.* A beverage.—**drink'er**, *n.*

drink, *n.* Any liquid that is or may be swallowed; a beverage; a draft.

drip, 1 drip; 2 drĭp. **I.** *vt. & vi.* To fall, or let fall, in drops. **II.** *n.* A falling, or letting fall, in drops.—**drip'ping**, *n.* That which falls in drops; the fat from roasting meat.

drive, 1 draiv; 2 drīv, *v.* [DROVE, 1 drōv, 2 drōv; DRIV'EN, 1 driv'n, 2 drĭv'n; DRIV'ING.] **I.** *t.* **1.** To urge forward forcibly; impel; prosecute urgently, as a business. **2.** To convey in a carriage. **II.** *i.* **1.** To be impelled forcibly onward; press forward furiously; aim a blow; direct one's action. **2.** To ride in a carriage, or direct the animal or animals by which it is

1: artistic, ärt; fat, fāre; fạst; get, prēy; hĭt, police; obey, gō; net, ȯr; full, rūle; but, bûrn.

2: ärt, āpe, făt, fâre, fȧst, whạt, ạll; mē, gĕt, prey, fêrn; hĭt, īce; ī=ē; ĭ=ē; gō, nŏt, ȯr, wọn,

drawn.— **driv′er**, *n.* One who or that which drives; a coachman; driving-wheel.— **driv′-ing-wheel″**, *n.* A wheel imparting motion to other wheels.

drive, *n.* **1.** The act of driving. **2.** A road for driving. **drive′way″**‡. **3.** A trip in a carriage. **4.** Urgent pressure, as of business. **5.** An advance of troops in mass against an enemy.

driv′el, 1 driv′l; 2 driv′l. **I.** *vi.* [DRIV′ELED or DRIV′ELLED, DRIV′ELD⁸; DRIV′EL-ING or DRIV′EL-LING.] To let spittle flow from the mouth; be weak or silly. **II.** *n.* **1.** An involuntary flow of saliva from the mouth. **2.** Senseless, empty talk.— **driv′el-er**, *n.* **driv′el-ler**‡.

driv′en, 1 driv′n; 2 driv′n, *pp.* of DRIVE, *v.*

driz′zle, } 1 driz′l; 2 driz′l. **I.** *vt. & vi.*
driz′l′, } [DRIZ′ZLED, DRIZ′LD⁸; DRIZ′-ZLING.] To shed or fall in fine drops. **II.** *n.* A light rain.— **driz′zly**, *a.*

droll, 1 drōl; 2 drōl, *a.* Odd; comical; funny.— **droll′er-y**, *n.* [-IES⁸, *pl.*] Waggish-ness; facetiousness; humor; oddity.— **droll′-ing-ly**, *adv.*

drom′e-da-ry, 1 drum′ı-dē-rı; 2 drŭm′e-dä-ry, *n.* [-RIES⁸, *pl.*] A fleet, ele-gant, one-humped riding-camel.

drone¹, 1 drōn; 2 drōn. **I.** *vt. & vi.* [DRONED; DRON′-ING.] To hum. **II.** *n.* **1.** A dull, monotonous hum-ming. **2.** One of the three long tubes of the bag-pipe, each of which produces a fixed note operating as a sustained bass, or its sound; a bass of one note running through a piece.

Dromedary. ¹/₁₂₆

drone². **I.** *vt.* To idle. **II.** *n.* A male bee, that gathers no honey; an idler.

droop, 1 drūp; 2 drōop. **I**‡. *vt. & vi.* To allow to hang listlessly; bend downward; sink as from weakness; despond; decline. **II.** *n.* A sinking or hanging down.

drop, 1 drɒp; 2 drŏp. **I.** *vt. & vi.* [DROPPED‡ or DROPT; DROP′PING.] **1.** To fall, or let fall, in drops. **2.** To fall, or let fall, in any way; give up; dismiss; subside; sink. **II.** *n.* **1.** A globule of liquid; anything hanging down; a pendant. **2.** A fall; descent.

drop′sy, 1 drɒp′sı; 2 drŏp′sy, *n.* An ab-normal accumulation of liquid in some part of the body.— **drop′si-cal**, *a.* Of, like, or affected with dropsy.

drosh′ky, } 1 drɒsh′kı, drɒs′kı; 2 drŏsh′ky,
dros′ky, } drɒs′ky, *n.* A light open Rus-sian carriage; also, a cab.

dross, 1 drɒs; 2 drôs, *n.* Impurity in melt-ed metal; slag; cinders; refuse.

drought, } 1 draut, drauᵗh; 2 drout,
drouth, } drouth, *n.* Long-continued dry weather; want of rain; dearth; thirst. — **drought′y, drouth′y**, 1 draut′ı, drauᵗh′ı; 2 drout′y, drouth′y, *a.* Marked by or suf-fering from drought or thirst; thirsty.— **drought′i-ness, drouth′i-ness**, *n.*

drove, *imp.* of DRIVE, *v.*

drove, 1 drōv; 2 drōv, *n.* A number of animals driven or herded for driving. — **dro′ver**, *n.* One who drives animals to market.

drown, 1 draun; 2 drown, *v.* **I.** *t.* To kill by immersion, as in water; deluge; overwhelm. **II.** *i.* To die by suffocation in liquid.

drowse, 1 drauz; 2 drows. **I.** *vt. & vi.* [DROWSED; DROWS′ING.] To doze; be list-less. **II.** *n.* A doze.— **drow′sy**, *a.* [DROW′SI-ER; DROW′SI-EST.] Heavy with sleepiness; dull.— **drow′si-ly**, *adv.*— **drow′si-ness**, *n.*

drub, 1 drub; 2 drŭb. **I.** *vt. & vi.* [DRUBBED; DRUBD⁸; DRUB′BING.] To beat; thrash. **II.** *n.* A blow; thump.— **drub′bing**, *n.* A thrashing.

drudge, 1 druj; 2 drŭdg. **I.** *vi.* [DRUDGED; DRUDG′ING.] To toil without spirit; work hard at mean or slavish tasks. **II.** *n.* One who toils at menial tasks.— **drudg′er-y**, *n.* [-IES⁸, *pl.*] Dull, wearisome, or menial work.

drug, 1 drug; 2 drŭg. **I.** *vt. & vi.* [DRUGGED; DRUGD⁸; DRUG′GING.] To mix drugs with, or administer drugs to; stupefy; also, to take drugs. **II.** *n.* **1.** Any substance used medicinally. **2.** An unsalable com-modity.— **drug′gist**, *n.* A dealer in drugs; an apothecary.

drug′get, 1 drug′et; 2 drŭg′ĕt, *n.* A coarse woolen fabric for rugs and the like.

dru′id, 1 drū′ıd; 2 drų′id, *n.* A priest of ancient Gaul and Britain.— **dru-id′i-cal**, *a.* Of or pertaining to the druids. **dru-id′ic**‡.

drum, 1 drum; 2 drŭm. **I.** *vt. & vi.* [DRUMMED, DRUMD⁸; DRUM′MING.] To play on a drum; beat a drum. **II.** *n.* **1.** A hollow cylinder, the ends of which are cov-ered with skin, to be beaten with drum-sticks. **2.** A cylindrical organ, as the tym-panum, or middle ear.— **drum′mer**, *n.* **1.** One who drums. **2.** [U. S.] A traveling salesman.— **drum′stick″**, *n.* A stick for beating a drum. [formerly *imp.*

drunk, 1 drunk; 2 drŭnk, *pp.* of DRINK, *v.*

1: ə = final; ı = habit; aisle; au = out; oil; Iŭ = feud; chin; go; ŋ = sing; thin, this.
2: wolf, dg; book, boot; full, rule, cūre, bŭt, bûrn; oil, bŏy; g̃o, g̃em; iŋk; thin, this.

drunk, *a.* Inebriated; intoxicated.—
drunk'ard, *n.* One who habitually drinks to
intoxication; a sot.—**drunk'en,** *a.* Given to
or characterized by drunkenness; drunk;
tipsy. **-ly,** *adv.* **-ness,** *n.*

dry, 1 draɪ; 2 drī. **I.** *vt. & vi.* [DRIED; DRY-
ING.] To make or become dry; evapo-
rate; wither: often followed by *up.* **II.** *a.*
[DRI'ER; DRI'EST.] **1.** Lacking moisture;
not fresh; not green. **2.** Thirsty. **3.**
Lacking interest; lifeless; dull. **4.** Slyly
jocose or satirical. **5.** [U. S.] Favoring prohibition.—**dry'ly,** *adv.* **drɪ'ly‡.**—**dry-ness,** *n.*

dry'ad, 1 draɪ'ad; 2 drī'ăd, *n. Gr. Myth.*
A wood-nymph.

dry'er, dry'est, *n.* Same as DRIER, DRIEST.

dry'ing, 1 draɪ'ɪŋ; 2 drī'ĭng, *ppr. & verbal n.*
of DRY, *v.*

du'al, 1 diū'əl; 2 dū'ăl, *a.* Denoting or
relating to two; twofold.—**du'al-is'tic,** *a.*—
du-al'i-ty, *n.* The state or being two or of
being composed of two.

dub, 1 dʌb; 2 dŭb, *vt.* [DUBBED, DUBBᵈ;
DUB'BING.] To confer knighthood upon;
name; entitle.

du'bi-ous, 1 diū'bɪ-ʊs; 2 dū'bĭ-ŭs, *a.*
Doubting; doubtful; problematic; questionable; ambiguous. **-ly,** *adv.* **-ness,** *n.*

du'cal, 1 diū'kəl; 2 dū'cal, *a.* Of or pertaining to a duke or a duchy.

duc'at, 1 dʌk'ət; 2 dŭc'ăt, *n.* One of
several European coins, ranging in value
from about 83 cents to $2.25.

duch'ess, 1 dʌch'es; 2 dŭch'ĕs, *n.* The
wife or widow of a duke.

duch'y, 1 dʌch'ɪ; 2 dŭch'y, *n.* [DUCH'IESᶻ,
pl.] The territory or dominion of a duke.

duckᵗ, 1 dʌk; 2 dŭk, *vt. & vi.* To plunge
suddenly under water; dive; bob; dodge;
cringe.—**duck'ing,** *n.* A sudden immersion.

duck¹, *n.* A web-footed, short-legged water-fowl.—**duck'ling,** *n.* A young duck.

duck², *n.* A strong linen or cotton fabric.

duct, 1 dʌkt; 2 dŭct, *n.* A tube for conveying fluid.

duc'tile, 1 dʌk'tɪl; 2 dŭc'til, *a.* Capable
duc'tilᵉ, of being drawn out, as into wire;
easily led; tractable; pliant.—**duc-til'i-ty,**
n. The state or degree of being ductile.
duc'til(e-nessᵗ‡.

dud, 1 dʌd; 2 dŭd, *n.* [Colloq.] **1.** An article of clothing; personal belongings:
commonly in the plural, *duds.* **2.** A shell
that fails to explode.

dude, 1 diūd; 2 dūd, *n.* One excessively
fastidious in dress, manners, speech, or
the like; an exquisite.   [displeasure.

dudg'eon, 1 dʌj'ən; 2 dŭdg'on, *n.* Sullen

due, 1 diū; 2 dū. **I.** *a.* **1.** Owing and
demandable; owed; proper; appropriate;

fairly to be ascribed. **2.** Scheduled to
arrive, as a train. **II.** *n.* A debt, or
obligation. **III.** *adv.* Directly; exactly;
as, *due* east.

du'el, 1 diū'el; 2 dū'ĕl, *n.* A prearranged
combat between two persons.—**du'el-ing,**
n. The fighting of duels. **du'el-ling‡.**—
du'el-ist, *n.* **du'el-list‡.**

du-en'na, 1 diū-en'ə; 2 dū-ĕn'a, *n.* An
elderly woman who watches over a young
woman.

du-et', 1 diū-et'; 2 dū-ĕt', *n.* A composition
for two voices, performers, or instruments.

dug, 1 dʌg; 2 dŭg, *imp. & pp.* of DIG, *v.*—
dug'out", *n.* An underground shelter, as
from bombs or shells.

dug, *n.* A teat or udder.

duke, 1 diūk; 2 dūk, *n.* **1.** A nobleman of
the highest rank. **2.** A reigning prince
inferior to a king.—**duke'dom,** *n.* **1.** A
duchy. **2.** The dignity or title of a duke.

dul'cet, 1 dʌl'set; 2 dŭl'çĕt, *a.* Sweet;
harmonious.

dul'ci-mer, 1 dʌl'sɪ-mər; 2 dŭl'çi-mer, *n.*
1. A stringed instrument played with
two shaped hammers. **2.** An ancient
wind-instrument.

dul-cin'e-a, 1 dʌl-sin'ɪ-ə; 2 dŭl-çĭn'e-a, *n.* A
sweetheart: from *Dulcinea* del Toboso, the
lady-love of the hero in Cervantes's novel
Don Quixote.

dull, 1 dʌl; 2 dŭl. **I.** *vt. & vi.* To make or
dulᶫ, become dull. **II.** *a.* Not sharp,
keen, bright, or acute; blunt; sluggish;
wearisome; sad; dismal; obscure; dim.—
dull'ard, 1 dʌl'ərd; 2 dŭl'ard, *n.* A dull or
stupid person; a dolt.—**dul'ly,** *adv.*—**dull'-
ness,** *n.* **dull'ness‡.**

du'ly, 1 diū'lɪ; 2 dū'ly, *adv.* In accordance
with what is due; fitly; regularly.

dumb, 1 dʌm; 2 dŭm, *a.* Lacking the
dumbᵇ, power of speech; mute; silent.
—**dumb'-bell",** A gymnastic implement consisting of a
handle with a ball at
each end.—**dumb'ly,**
adv.—**dumb' ness,** *n.*
—**d.-walter,** *n.* **1.** A
movable framework for
carrying things from
one room or floor to   Dumb-bells
another. **2.** [Eng.] An adjustable stand for
holding dishes.

dum'my, 1 dʌm'ɪ; 2 dŭm'y. **I.** *a.* Sham;
counterfeit. **II.** *n.* [DUM'MIESᶻ, *pl.*] A silent
person or actor; something made to represent
something else; a steam-motor car.

dump, 1 dʌmp; 2 dŭmp. **Iᵗ.** *vt. & vi.* To
unload or remove in mass. **II.** *n.* [U. S.]
A dumping-ground; also, that which is
dumped.

1: artistic, ärt; fat, fāre; fʌst; get, prēy; hit, polīce; ɒᴅᴇy, gō; not, ôr; full, rūle; but, būrn.
2: ärt, āpe, făt, fâre, fȧst, whȧt, ạll; mē, gĕt, prey, fẽrn; hit, īce; ī=ĕ; ĭ=ē; gō, nŏt, ôr, wŏn,

dump'ling, 1 dump'liŋ; 2 dŭmp'ling, *n.* A dessert, as of fruit enclosed in pastry and boiled or baked.

dumps, 1 dumps; 2 dŭmps, *n. pl.* A gloomy state of mind; melancholy.— **dump'ish,** *a.* Dull and inactive; low=spirited.

dump'y, 1 dump'i; 2 dŭmp'y, *a.* Short and thick; stocky.

dun, 1 dun; 2 dŭn, *vt. & vi.* [DUNNED, DUND⁸; DUN'NING.] To press for payment; make a din; clamor.

dun, *a.* Of a dull, dark=brown color.

dun, *n.* One who duns; a demand for payment.

dunce, 1 duns; 2 dŭnç, *n.* A stupid or ignorant person.

dune, 1 diūn; 2 dūn, *n.* A hill of loose sand; a down.

dung, 1 duŋ; 2 dŭng, *n.* Animal excrement.

dun'geon, 1 dun'jən; 2 dŭn'gon, *n.* A dark underground cell; any prison.

dung'hill', 1 duŋ'hil'; 2 dŭng'hĭl'. **I.** *a.* From or of the dunghill; ignoble. **II.** *n.* A heap of manure.

du'o, 1 diū'o; 2 dū'o, *n. Mus.* A duet.

du''o-dec'i-mal, 1 diū''o-des'i-məl; 2 dū''-o-dĕç'i-mal, *a.* Denoting a system of reckoning by twelves.

du''o-dec'i-mal, *n.* **1.** One of the numbers used in duodecimal reckoning. **2.** A method of using the duodecimal system.

du''o-dec'i-mo, 1 diū''o-des'i-mō; 2 dū''o-dĕç'i-mō, *n.* **1.** A book=page of about 4¹⁄₂ by 7¹⁄₂ inches; a book having such pages: often written *12mo.* **2.** *Mus.* An interval of a twelfth.

dupe, 1 diūp; 2 dūp. **I.** *vt.* [DUPED†; DUP'-ING.] To impose upon. **II.** *n.* One mis-led through credulity.

du'plex, 1 diū'pleks; 2 dū'plĕks, *a.* Having two parts; twofold; also, working in two ways or directions.

du'pli-cate, 1 diū'pli-kēt; 2 dū'pli-cāt, *a.* **I.** *vt. & vi.* [-CAT''ED⁴; -CAT''ING.] To make a duplicate of; reproduce; copy; repeat. **II.** 1 diū'pli-kit; 2 dū'pli-eat, *a.* **1.** Made or done exactly like an original. **2.** Growing in pairs; double, **III.** *n.* Originally one of two, now one of any number of objects exactly alike; an exact copy; a reproduction.— **du''pli-ca'tion,** *n.* The act of duplicating, or the state of being duplicated.

du-plic'i-ty, 1 diu-plis'i-ti; 2 dū-plĭç'i-ty, *n.* [-TIES⁶, *pl.*] Tricky deceitfulness; double=dealing.

du'ra-ble, 1 diū'ra-bl; 2 dū'ra-bl, *a.* Able to continue long unchanged;

lasting.— **du''ra-bil'i-ty,** *n.* **du'ra-ble(e-ness‡)ʳ.— dur'a-bly,** *adv.*

dur'ance, 1 diūr'əns; 2 dūr'anç, *n.* Personal restraint; imprisonment.

du-ra'tion, 1 diu-rē'shən; 2 dū-rā'shon, *n.* The period during which anything lasts; time.

du'ress, 1 diū'res *or* diu-res'; 2 dū'rĕs *or* dū-rĕs', *n.* Constraint; compulsion; imprisonment. **du-resse'‡.**

dur'ing, 1 diūr'iŋ; 2 dūr'ing, *prep.* In or within the time of.

durst, 1 dūrst; 2 dŭrst, *imp.* of DARE, *v.*

dusk, 1 dusk; 2 dŭsk, *n.* **1.** A state between darkness and light; twilight. **2.** Swarthiness; shadowiness.— **dusk'i-ly,** *adv.*— **dusk'i-ness,** *n.* Moderate darkness.— **dusk'y,** *a.* [DUSK'I-ER; DUSK'I-EST.] Somewhat dark; dim; obscure; swarthy. **dusk‡** [Poetic].

dust, 1 dust; 2 dŭst. **I**ᵈ. *vt.* To free from dust; sprinkle with dust; reduce to dust. **II.** *n.* **1.** Any substance, as earth, reduced to powder. **2.** A dead body; remains; the grave. **3.** [Eng.] Ashes and household sweepings.— **dust'y,** *a.* [DUST'I-ER; DUST'I-EST.] **1.** Covered with or as with dust. **2.** Of the color of dust.

Dutch, 1 duch; 2 dŭch, *n.* **1.** The people of Holland, or their language. **2.** Loosely, the German race or language.— **Dutch'man,** 1 duch'mən; 2 dŭch'man, *n.* [DUTCH'MEN, *pl.*] A Hollander.

du'ty, 1 diū'ti; 2 dū'ty, *n.* [DU'TIES², *pl.*] **1.** That which is due; moral obligation. **2.** An impost, as upon imports. **3‖.** A formal expression of respect.— **du'te-ous,** *a.* Rendering due respect and obedience; dutiful. **-ly,** *adv.* **-ness,** *n.*— **du'ti-a-ble(eᴿ,** *a. Law.* Subject to impost.— **du'ti-ful,** *a.* Performing the duties of one's position; submissive; respectful. **-ly,** *adv.* **-ness,** *n.*

dwarf, 1 dwôrf; 2 dwᴀrf. **I**ᵗ. *vt.* **1.** To stunt. **2.** To cause to look small by comparison. **II.** *a.* Smaller than others of its kind; diminutive. **III.** *n.* A person, animal, or plant that is unnaturally small.— **dwarf'ish,** *a.* **-ness,** *n.*

dwell, 1 dwel; 2 dwĕl, *vi.* [DWELT or **dwelᵗ,** DWELLED, DWELD⁸; DWELL'ING.] **1.** To have a fixed abode; reside. **2.** To linger; pause; expatiate: with *on* or *upon.*— **dwell'er,** *n.* Inhabitant.— **dwell'ing,** *n.* A residence; family abode.

dwin'dle, 1 dwin'dl; 2 dwĭn'dl, *vi.* [DWIN'-**dwin'dlᵖ,** DL(E)Dᴾ; DWIN'DLING.] To waste; diminish; become less; decline.

dye, 1 dai; 2 dȳ. **I.** *vt. & vi.* [DYED; DYE'-ING.] To color; stain; tinge; take a color.

II. *n.* A fluid coloring=matter; a color produced by or as by dyeing; hue.— **dye′= house″,** *n.* A building where dyeing is done. — **dye′ing,** *n.* The act, process, or trade of fixing colors in cloth or the like.— **dy′er,** *n.* One who dyes.— **dye′stuff″,** *n.* Any material used for dyeing.

dy′ing, 1 dai′iŋ; 2 dȳ′ing, *ppr.* of DIE & *pa.* Expiring; failing; mortal; perishable; pertaining to death or the time of approaching death.

dyke, *n.* Same as DIKE.

dy-nam′ic,) 1 dai-nam′ik, -ı-kəl; 2 di-
dy-nam′i-cal,) năm′ie, -i-cal, *a.* 1. Pertaining to mechanical force or its effects. 2. Producing action; efficient; causal. — **dy-nam′i-cal-ly,** *adv.*— **dy-nam′ics,** *n.* The branch of science that treats of the laws of force.

dy′na-mite, 1 dai′nə-mait; 2 dȳ′na-mīt, *n.* An explosive composed of an absorbent saturated with nitroglycerin.

dy′na-mo, 1 dai′nə-mo; 2 dȳ′na-mo, *n.*

Elec. A machine for producing electricity by mechanical action.— **dy′na-mo=e-lec′-tric, -tri-cal,** *a.* Pertaining to the conversion of mechanical into electrical energy, or the reverse.

dy″na-mom′e-ter, 1 dai″nə-mom′ı-tər; 2 dȳ″na-mŏm′e-tĕr, *n.* An instrument for measuring force exerted or power expended in doing work.— **dy″na-mo-met′-ric, -ri-cal,** *a.*

dy′nas-ty, 1 dai′nas-tı; 2 dȳ-nas-ty, *n.* [-TIES², *pl.*] A succession of sovereigns in one family.— **dy-nas′tic, -ti-cal,** *a.*

dys′en-ter-y, 1 dis′en-ter-ı; 2 dȳs′ĕn-tĕr-y, *n.* Inflammation of the large intestine; diarrhea.— **dys″en-ter′ic,** *a.* Pertaining to or suffering from dysentery. **dys″en-ter′-i-cal‡.**

dys-pep′si-a, 1 dis-pep′sı-ə; 2 dȳs-pĕp′si-a, *n.* Difficult and painful digestion, generally chronic.— **dys-pep′tic. I.** *a.* Relating to, of the nature of, or suffering from dyspepsia; tending to produce dyspepsia. **dys-pep′ti-cal‡. II.** *n.* A dyspeptic person.

E

E, e, 1 ī; 2 ē, *n.* [EES, E's, or Es, 1 īz; 2 ēs, *pl.*] The fifth letter in the English alphabet.

e-, *prefix.* Out of; out; from: a shortened form of EX- used before consonants.

each, 1 ĭch; 2 ēch. **I.** *a.* Being one of two or more; every. **II.** *pron.* Every one individually; each one.

ea′ger, 1 ī′gər; 2 ē′ger, *a.* Impatiently anxious for something; intent; vehement. **-ly,** *adv.* **-ness,** *n.*

ea′gle,) 1 ī′gl; 2 ē′gl, *n.*
ea′gl³,) 1. A very large diurnal bird of prey. 2. A gold coin of the United States, value $10. 3. A Roman standard bearing the image of an eagle.— **ea′glet,** *n.* A young eagle.

Head and Talon of an Eagle.

ear¹, 1 īr; 2 ēr, *n.* 1. The organ or sense of hearing; attention; heed. 2. Any projecting piece, handle, etc.— **ear′drum″,** *n.* A thin membrane stretched across a passage of the ear.— **ear′less,** *a.* Destitute or deprived of ears.— **ear′mark″,** *n.* A mark of identification, as on an animal's ear.— **ear′-ring″,** *n.* A pendant worn at the ear.— **ear′-wig″,** *n.* An insect with horny wing=covers and a caudal forceps.

ear², *n.* A head, as of wheat; spike of maize.

earl,) 1 ürl; 2 ĕrl, *n.* A member of the
erlᴾ,) British nobility next above a viscount.— **earl′dom,** *n.* The dignity, prerogative, or territory of an earl.

ear′ly,) 1 ür′lı; 2 ĕr′ly. **I.** *a.* [EAR′LI-ER;
er′lyᴾ,) EAR′LI-EST.] Occurring among the first in a series or sooner than is usual; soon to occur. **II.** *adv.* At or near the beginning of a period of time.— **ear′li-ness,** *n.*

earn,) 1 ürn; 2 ĕrn, *vt.* To gain as a
ernᴾ,) recompense for labor; merit.— **earn′ing,** *n.* That which is earned; compensation; wages, commonly in the plural.

ear′nest,) 1 ür′nest; 2 ĕr′nĕst, *a.* 1.
er′nest²,) Zealous; fervent. 2. Serious; important. **-ly,** *adv.* **-ness,** *n.*

ear′nest¹, *n.* Seriousness; reality.

ear′nest², *n.* Money paid in advance to bind a bargain; an assurance of something to come.

earth,) 1 ürth; 2 ĕrth, *n.* The globe on
erthᴾ,) which we dwell; the world; ground; land; soil.— **earth′en,** 1 ür′th'n; 2 ĕrth'n, *a.* Made of earth or of burnt clay.— **earth′en-ware″,** *n.* Pottery.— **earth′i-ness,** *n.* The quality of being earthy or like earth.— **earth′li-ness,** *n.* The quality of being earthly; earthiness; worldliness.— **earth′ly,** 1 ür′thlı; 2 ĕrth′ly, *a.* Pertaining

to the earth or to the present world; material; worldly.— **earth′quake″,** *n.* A vibration of a portion of the earth's crust.— **earth′worm″,** *n.* A burrowing terrestrial worm.— **earth′y,** *a.* **1.** Of or pertaining to earth or soil; made of earth. **2.** Like earth. **3.** Unrefined; coarse.

ease, 1 ĭz; 2 ēs. **I.** *vt.* [EASED; EAS′ING.] To give ease; relieve; lighten. **II.** *n.* **1.** Freedom from disturbance; tranquillity; comfort. **2.** Freedom from strain or constraint; facility; naturalness.

ea′sel, 1 ĭ′zl; 2 ē′sl, *n.* A folding frame for supporting a picture.

ease′ment, 1 ĭz′ment *or* -mənt; 2 ēs′ment, *n.* **1.** *Law.* A right distinct from ownership of the soil, as to running water or free air. **2.** That which gives ease or relief. [manner.

eas′i-ly, 1 ĭz′ĭ-lĭ; 2 ēs′i-ly, *adv.* In an easy

eas′i-ness, 1 ĭz′ĭ-nes; 2 ēs′i-nĕs, *n.* The state of being easy or at ease.

east, 1 ĭst; 2 ēst. **I.** *a.* Being at the east; coming from the east. **II.** *n.* **1.** That point of the compass at which the sun rises at the equinox. **2.** Any region to the eastward; [E-] the Orient. **III.** *adv.* In an easterly direction.— **east′er-ly,** *a.* **1.** Situated, moving or directed, toward the east; eastward. **2.** Coming from the east.— **east′er-ly, east′ern-ly,** *adv.* Toward the east.— **east′ern,** *a.* **1.** [E-] Of, pertaining to, or being in the East; Oriental. **2.** Moving to or from the east; easterly.— **east′ward. I.** *a.* Running in an easterly direction. **II.** *adv.* Toward the east.

East″-In′di-an, 1 ĭst″-ĭn′dĭ-an; 2 ēst″-ĭn′di-an. **I.** *a.* Of or pertaining to the East Indies, a vague general name formerly much used for India, Indo=China, and Malay Archipelago. **II.** *n.* A native or resident of the East Indies.

East′er, 1 ĭst′ẽr; 2 ēst′er, *n.* A Christian festival commemorating the resurrection of Christ.

eas′y, 1 ĭz′ĭ; 2 ēs′y, *a.* [EAS′I-ER; EAS′I-EST.] **1.** Marked by ease; free from difficulty, discomfort, or affectation; comfortable; natural; unconstrained. **2.** Yielding; indulgent. **3.** Gentle.

eat, 1 ĭt; 2 ēt, *v.* [ATE *or* EAT, 1 et, 2 ĕt; EAT′E(N)ᴾ, 1 ĭt′n, 2 ēt′n (sometimes EAT, 1 et, 2 ĕt); EAT′ING.] **I.** *t.* **1.** To chew and swallow, as food. **2.** To consume or corrode. **II.** *i.* **1.** To take sustenance; feed. **2.** To gnaw; penetrate; corrode. — **eat′a-ble**(eᴾ, 1 ĭt′ə-bl; 2 ēt′a-bl. **I.** *a.* Fit to be eaten; edible. **II.** *n.* Something edible.— **eat′er,** *n.*

eaves, 1 ĭvz; 2 ēvs, *n. pl.* The projecting edge of a roof.— **eaves′drop″t,** 1 ĭvz′drŏp″; 2 ēvs′drŏp″, *vt. & vi.* To overhear; listen clan-

destinely.— **eaves′ drop″per,** *n.*— **eaves′-drop″ping,** *n.*

ebb, 1 eb; 2 ĕb. **I.** *vi.* To recede, as the tide; decline; fail. **II.** *n.* **1.** The reflux of tide=water to the ocean. **ebb′=tide″‡. 2.** Decrease; decline.

eb′on, 1 eb′ən; 2 ĕb′on. **I.** *a.* Of ebony; very black. **II.** *n.* Ebony.— **eb′on-ite,** *n.* Black vulcanite, or hard rubber.— **eb′on-ize** *or* -**ise,** *vt.* To polish in imitation of ebony.

eb′o-ny, 1 eb′o-nĭ; 2 ĕb′o-ny, *n.* [-NIESᶻ, *pl.*] A hard, heavy wood, usually black.

eb″ul-li′tion, 1 eb″ʋ-lĭsh′ən; 2 ĕb′ŭ-lĭsh′on, *n.* The bubbling of a liquid; boiling; violent agitation.

ec-, *prefix.* From; out of: used before many words beginning with a consonant; as, *ec*centric.

ec-cen′tric, 1 ek-sen′trĭk; 2 ĕc-çĕn′tric. **I.** *a.* **1.** Peculiar; erratic. **2.** Not in the center; not having the same center; not circular. **II.** *n.* **1.** *Mech.* A disk mounted out of center on a driving=shaft so as to have the effect of a crank motion. **2.** One who or that which is eccentric. **ec-cen′tri-cal.**— **ec-cen′tri-cal-ly,** *adv.*— **ec″cen-tric′i-ty,** 1 ek′sen-tris′ĭ-tĭ; 2 ĕc-çĕn-tric′i-ty, *n.* [-TIESᶻ, *pl.*] The state, quality, or degree of being eccentric; oddity; singularity: an eccentric, odd, or capricious act.

ec-cle′si-as′tic, 1 e-klī′zĭ-as′tĭk; 2 ĕ-clē′-şi-ăs′tic. **I.** *a.* Ecclesiastical. **II.** *n.* A clergyman or church official.— **ec-cle″si-as′ti-cal,** *a.* Of or pertaining to the church. **-ly,** *adv.*

ec-dem′ic, 1 ek-dem′ĭk; 2 ĕc-dĕm′ic, *a.* Arising in a distant locality, as a disease.

ech′o, 1 ek′ō; 2 ec′ō. **I.** *vt. & vi.* To return as an echo; reproduce; imitate. **II.** *n.* [ECH′OESᶻ, *pl.*] A sound given back by an opposing surface and returned to its source; a close reproduction or imitation.

é″clair′, 1 ē″klâr′; 2 ē″clär′, *n.* A small cake with sweet filling and icing, as of chocolate.

é″clat′, 1 ē″klä′; 2 ē″clä′, *n.* Brilliancy; celebrity.

ec-lec′tic, 1 ek-lek′tĭk; 2 ĕc-lĕc′tic. **I.** *a.* Selecting, or made by selection; broad; liberal. **II.** *n.* One who practises selection from all systems, as in medicine.— **ec-lec′ti-cism,** 1 ek-lek′tĭ-sizm; 2 ĕc-lĕc′ti-çĭsm, *n.* An eclectic method or system.

e-clipse′, } 1 1-klips′; 2 e-clĭps′. **I.** *vt.* [E-**e-clips′ᴾ,** } CLIPSED′ᵗ, E-CLIPST′ˢ; E-CLIPS′-ING.] To darken or hide by intervention; cast into the shade; surpass; obscure. **II.** *n.* The obscuration of a heavenly body by the intervention of another; any hiding, obscuring, or overshadowing. See illus. on next page.

---

e-clip'tic, 1 ɪ-klĭp'tĭk; 2 e-clĭp'tie, *n.* **1.** That plane, passing through the center of the sun, which contains the orbit of the earth. **2.** The apparent path of the sun around the celestial sphere.

Eclipses of tne Sun and Moon.

s, the sun; *m*[1], the moon passing between the sun and the earth (*e*), and causing an eclipse of the former, total in the depth of the shadow; *m*[2], the moon in position to be totally eclipsed by the earth.

ec'log, } 1 ek'lŏg; 2 ĕc'lŏg, *n.* A short
ec'logue, } pastoral poem.

e-con'o-my, 1 ɪ-kẽn'o-mɪ; 2 e-cŏn'o-my, *n.* [-MIES[z], *pl.*] **1.** Disposition to save; frugality; cheapness. **2.** Practical, systematic management of affairs.— **ec"o-nom'ic,** 1 ek'o-[*or* ɪ'ko-]nem'ɪk; 2 ĕc'o-[*or* ē'co-]nŏm'ie, *a.* Relating to economics; economical.— **ec"o-nom'i-cal,** 1 ek'o-nem'ɪ-kəl; 2 ĕc'o-nŏm'i-cal, *a.* Careful; frugal; prudent. **-ly,** *adv.*— **ec"o-nom'ics,** 1 ek'o-nŏm'ɪks; 2 ĕc'-o-nŏm'ies, *n.* The science of the production and distribution of wealth; political economy.— **e-con'o-mist,** *n.*— **e-con'o-mize** *or* **-mise,** *vt. & vi.* [-MIZED; -MIZ'ING.] To use economically; be frugal or economical.

ec'sta-sy, 1 ek'stə-sɪ; 2 ĕc'sta-sy, *n.* [-SIES[z], *pl.*] Rapturous excitement or exaltation; rapture.— **ec-stat'ic,** *a.* Enraptured. **ec-stat'i-cal‡.— ec-stat'i-cal-ly,** *adv.*

ec"u-men'i-cal, 1 ek"yu-men'ɪ-kəl; 2 ĕc'yu-mĕn'i-cal, *a.* Of or pertaining to the habitable world or to the entire Christian church; universal. **ec"u-men'ic‡.**

ec'ze-ma, 1 ek'ze-mə; 2 ĕc'ze-ma, *n.* An inflammatory skin-disease.

-ed, *suffix.* Termination (1) of the past tense, and (2) of the past participle of regular verbs and of adjectives formed on the model of such participles; as, hot-head*ed*.

ed'dy, 1 ed'ɪ; 2 ĕd'y. **I.** *vt. & vi.* [ED'DIED; ED'DY-ING.] To move in or as in an eddy. **II.** *n.* [ED'DIES[z], *pl.*] A circling current, as of water; a turning aside; diversion.

e'del-weiss, 1 ē'del-vaɪs; 2 ē'dĕl-vīs, *n.* A small Alpine plant and flower of the aster family, growing up to the snow-line.

e-den'tate, 1 ɪ-den'tēt; 2 ĕ-dĕn'tāt. **I.** *a.* Toothless. **II.** *n.* A toothless animal. **— e-den'tat-ed,** *a.*

edge, 1 ej; 2 ĕdg. **I.** *vt. & vi.* [EDGED; EDG'ING.] **1.** To sharpen; incite. **2.** To move sidewise; sidle. **II.** *n.* **1.** The thin, sharp cutting part of a blade; sharpness. **2.** A border; margin.— **edge'wise,** *a. & adv.* Having the edge directed forward;

in the direction of the edge. **edge'ways‡.** **— edg'ing,** *n.* Anything serving as or attached to an edge; a border.

ed'i-ble, } 1 ed'ɪ-bl; 2 ĕd'i-bl. **I.** *a.* Eat-
ed'i-bl², } able. **II.** *n.* Something suitable for food.— **ed"i-bil'i-ty,** *n.*— **ed'i-bl(e-ness[r],** *n.*

e'dict, 1 ī'dikt; 2 ē'dĭet, *n.* A proclamation of command; ordinance; decree.

ed'i-fice, } 1 ed'ɪ-fis; 2 ĕd'i-fĭç, *n.* A large
ed'i-fiss, } building.

ed'i-fy, 1 ed'ɪ-faɪ; 2 ĕd'i-fī, *vt. & vi.* [-FIED; -FY'ING.] To build up, as in religion; improve.— **ed"i-fi-ca'tion,** *n.* The act of edifying; instruction; enlightenment.— **ed'i-fi²er,** *n.*— **ed'i-fy"ing,** *pa.*

ed'it, 1 ed'ɪt; 2 ĕd'it, *vt.* To prepare for publication; compile; arrange.— **e-di'tion,** 1 ɪ-dĭsh'ən; 2 e-dĭsh'on, *n.* Number of copies of a book, paper, etc., issued at one time.— **ed'i-tor,** 1 ed'ɪ-tər; 2 ĕd'i-tor, *n.* One who edits; one having charge of a publication.— **ed"i-to'ri-al. I.** *a.* Of or pertaining to an editor. **II.** *n.* An editorial article. **-ly,** *adv.*— **ed'i-tor-ship,** *n.*

ed'u-cate, 1 ej'u-kēt *or* ed'yu-kēt; 2 ĕg'u-eāt *or* ĕd'yu-eāt, *vt.* [-CAT'ED[d]; -CAT'-ING.] To develop the natural powers; teach; train; instruct.— **ed"u-ca'tion,** 1 ej"u-[*or* ed'yu-]kē'shən; 2 ĕg'u-[*or* ĕd'yu-]-eā'shon, *n.* The systematic development and cultivation of the natural powers; instruction and training.— **ed"u-ca'tion-al,** *a.* Of or pertaining to education.— **ed'u-ca-tiv(e²,** *a.*— **ed'u-ca"tor,** *n.* A teacher.

e-duce', 1 ɪ-diūs'; 2 e-dūç', *vt.* [E-DUCED't; E-DUC'ING.] To call forth; draw out.

-ee¹, *suffix.* Denoting the recipient of something; as, employ*ee*, grant*ee*, pay*ee*.

-ee², *suffix.* Diminutive; as, boot*ee*.

eel, 1 īl; 2 ēl, *n.* A fish of snake-like form.

e'en, *adv.* Same as EVEN: a contraction.

-eer, *suffix.* **1.** Denoting agency; as, engin*eer*. Same as -ER. **2.** Denoting residence; as, mountain*eer*. [traction.

e'er, 1 âr; 2 êr, *adv.* Same as EVER: a contraction.

ee'ry, 1 ī'rɪ; 2 ē'ry, *a.* [Scot.] Causing or affected by fear or awe; weird.

ef-face', 1 e-fēs'; 2 ĕ-fāç', *vt.* [EF-FACED't; EF-FAC'ING.] To obliterate, as written characters; wipe out; cancel. **-ment,** *n.*

ef-fect', 1 e-fekt'; 2 ĕ-fĕct'. **I**[d]. *vt.* To cause; produce; achieve; accomplish. **II.** *n.* **1.** A result; product; consequence. **2.** The substance of a statement; gist. **3.** Active operation; execution. **4.** Fact or reality; following *in.* **5.** *pl.* Movable goods.— **ef-fec'tiv(e²,** *a.* Producing effect; efficient. **-ly,** *adv.* **-ness,** *n.*— **ef-fec'tu-al,** 1 e-fek'chu-al *or* -tiu-əl; 2 ĕ-fĕc'chu-al *or* -tū-al, *a.* Producing or capable of

producing an effect; adequate and operative; effective. **-ly,** *adv.* **-ness,** *n.*— **ef-fec'tu-ate,** *vt.* [-AT″ED^d; -AT″ING.] To render effectual; effect; accomplish.

ef-fem'i-nate, 1 e-fem'ɪ-nēt; 2 ĕ-fĕm'ɪ-nāt. **I.** *vt.* & *vi.* [-NAT″ED^d; -NAT″ING.] To make or become womanish; weaken. **II.** *a.* Womanish; unmanly. **-ly,** *adv.* **-ness,** *n.*— **ef-fem'i-na-cy,** 1 e-fem'ɪ-na-sɪ; 2 ĕ-fĕm'ɪ-na-cy, *n.* Womanishness; unmanly weakness.

ef″fer-vesce', 1 ef″ɑr-ves'; 2 ĕf″er-vĕs', *vi.* [-VESCED′^t; -VESC′ING.] To bubble, as in boiling; gush.— **ef″fer-ves'cence,** *n.* The bubbling of a liquid from escaping gas; irrepressible excitement or emotion.— **ef″fer-ves'cent,** *a.* Effervescing.

ef-fete', 1 e-fīt'; 2 ĕ-fēt', *a.* Worn out; exhausted; barren.

ef-fi-ca'cious, 1 ef″ɪ-kē'shŭs; 2 ĕf″ɪ-cā'shŭs, *a.* Having efficacy; effective; effectual. **-ly,** *adv.* **-ness,** *n.*— **ef'fi-ca-cy,** *n.* Power to produce effect; effective energy.

ef-fi'cient, 1 e-fish'ent; 2 ĕ-fĭsh'ĕnt, *a.* **1.** Acting effectively; competent. **2.** Productive of effects; causative.— **ef-fi'cien-cy,** *n.* The character of being efficient; effectiveness.— **ef-fi'cient-ly,** *adv.*

ef'fi-gy, 1 ef'ɪ-jɪ; 2 ĕf'ɪ-gy, *n.* [-GIES^z, *pl.*] A picture or a stuffed figure representing a person.

ef'fort, 1 ef'ɑrt; 2 ĕf'ort, *n.* A voluntary exertion of power; strenuous endeavor; attempt; achievement.

ef-front'er-y, 1 e-frunt'ɑr-ɪ; 2 ĕ-frŏnt'er-y, *n.* Insolent assurance; audacity; impudence.

ef-ful'gence, 1 e-ful'jens; 2 ĕ-fŭl'gĕnc, *n.* A shining forth brilliantly; brightness; splendor.— **ef-ful'gent,** *a.* **-ly,** *adv.*

ef-fuse', ⎱ 1 e-fiūz'; 2 ĕ-fūs', *v.* [EF-FUSED′; **ef-fuze^r,** ⎰ EF-FUS′ING.] **I.** *t.* To pour forth; shed. **II.** *i.* To emanate.

ef-fu'sion, 1 e-fiū'ʒen; 2 ĕ-fū'zhon, *n.* A pouring forth, or that which is poured forth; a literary production; show of feeling.

ef-fu'sive, ⎱ 1 e-fiū'sɪv; 2 ĕ-fū'sĭv, *a.* Overflowing; demonstrative; gushing. **-ly,** *adv.* **-ness,** *n.* [eft‡.

eft, 1 eft; 2 ĕft, *n.* A newt; a small lizard.

egg, ⎱ 1 eg; 2 ĕg, *vt.* To instigate or incite; **egg^s,** ⎰ *urge:* commonly followed by *on.*

egg, *n.* A body containing the germ and food=yolk, as of birds, enclosed in a membranous or shelly covering.

e'gis, 1 ī'jɪs; 2 ē'gɪs, *n.* [Classic form Æ-GIS.] A shield or defensive armor, as the mantle of Minerva, bearing the Gorgon's head; any protecting influence or power.

eg'lan-tine, 1 eg'lan-tɪn; 2 ĕg'lan-tɪn, *n.* A plant of the genus *Rosa*; the sweetbrier.

eg'o-ism, 1 eg'o-[*or* ī'go-]izm; 2 ĕg'o-[*or* ē'go-]ĭsm, *n.* Self=development and self-satisfaction as the supreme end of existence; refined selfishness: opposed to *altru-ism.*— **eg'o-ist,** *n.*

eg'o-tism, 1 eg'o-[*or* ī'go-]tɪzm; 2 ĕg'o-[*or* ē'go-]tĭsm, *n.* The habit of thinking and talking much of oneself; self-conceit.

eg'o-tist, 1 eg'o-[*or* ī'go-]tist; 2 ĕg'o-[*or* ē'go-]tĭst, *n.* One characterized by egotism.— **eg″o-tis'tic,** *a.* **eg″o-tis'ti-cal‡.**

e-gre'gious, 1 e-grī'jus; 2 e-grē'gŭs, *a.* Surpassing; excessive. **-ly,** *adv.* **-ness,** *n.*

e'gress, 1 ī'gres; 2 ē'grĕs, *n.* A going out; place of exit. **e-gres'sion‡.**

e'gret, 1 ī'gret *or* eg'ret; 2 ē'grĕt *or* ĕg'rĕt, *n.* A white heron, or a plume or tuft of its feathers.

Great White Egret. ¹⁄₃₃

E-gyp'tian, 1 ɪ-jip'-shan; 2 e-gyp'shan. **I.** *a.* Of or pertaining to Egypt. **II.** *n.* **1.** A native of Egypt. **2.** The language of Egypt.

ei'der, 1 ai'dɑr; 2 ī'der, *n.* A large sea-duck of northern regions. **ei'der-duck″‡.**— **ei'der-down″,** *n.* The soft down of the eider.

eight, 1 ēt; 2 ĕt. **I.** *a.* Consisting of one more than seven. **II.** *n.* Eight units. — **eighth,** 1 ētth; 2 ĕtth. **I.** *a.* **1.** Next in order after the seventh. **2.** Being one of eight equal parts. **II.** *n.* One of eight equal parts.— **eighth'ly,** *adv.*

eight-een', 1 ēt-īn'; 2 ĕt-ēn'. **I.** *a.* Consisting of eight more than ten. **II.** *n.* The sum of ten and eight.— **eight-eenth',** 1 ēt-īnth'; 2 ĕt-ēnth'. **I.** *a.* Eighth in order after the tenth. **II.** *n.* One of eighteen equal parts.

eight'y, 1 ēt'ɪ; 2 ĕt'y. **I.** *a.* Consisting of ten more than seventy. **II.** *n.* Eight times ten.— **eight'i-eth.** **I.** *a.* **1.** Tenth in order after the seventieth. **2.** Being one of eighty equal parts. **II.** *n.* One of eighty equal parts. **-ly,** *adv.*

ei'ther, 1 ī'thɑr *or* ai'thɑr; 2 ē'ther *or* ī'ther. **I.** *a.* **1.** One or the other of two. **2.** Each of two. **II.** *pron.* One of two; one or the other. **III.** *conj.* In one of two or more cases.

e-jac'u-late, 1 ɪ-jak'yu-lēt; 2 e-jăc'yu-lāt, *vt.* & *vi.* [-LAT″ED^d; -LAT″ING.] To utter suddenly; exclaim.— **e-jac″u-la'tion,** 1 ɪ-jak″yu-lē'shan; 2 e-jăc″yu-lā'shon, *n.* Exclamation.— **e-jac'u-la-to-ry,** *a.*

e-ject'd, 1 ı-jekt'; 2 e-jĕet', *vt.* To throw out by sudden force; expel; dispossess. — **e-jee'tion,** *n.* The act of ejecting; expulsion; something ejected. — **e-ject'ment,** *n.* A casting out; eviction. — **e-jec'tor,** *n.*

eke, 1 īk; 2 ēk, *vt.* [EKED⁵; EK'ING.] To piece out: followed by *out.*

ekell, *adv. & conj.* Likewise; also.

e-lab'o-rate, 1 ı-lab'o-rēt; 2 e-lăb'o-rāt. **I.** *vt.* [-RAT'ED⁴; -RAT'ING.] To produce by thorough and careful work. **II.** 1-lab'o-rit; 2 e-lăb'o-rat, *a.* Developed with thoroughness or exactness. **-ly,** *adv.* **-ness,** *n.* — **e-lab'o-ra'tion,** *n.* The act of elaborating; that which is elaborated.

e-lapse', } 1 ı-laps'; 2 e-lăps', *vi.* [E-LAPSED'; **e-laps'e,** } E-LAPST'⁵; E-LAPS'ING.] To glide by; pass, as time.

e-las'tic, 1 ı-las'tık; 2 e-lăs'tie. **I.** *a.* Spontaneously returning to its original shape; springy; accommodating; buoyant. **II.** *n.* A band of elastic material. — **e-las'ti-cal-ly,** *adv.* — **e'las-tie'i-ty,** 1 ı'las-tis'ı-tı; 2 ē'lăs-tĭe'ĭ-tι, *n.* The property or quality of being elastic.

e-late', 1 ı-lēt'; 2 e-lāt'. **I.** *vt.* [E-LAT'ED⁴; E-LAT'ING.] To raise the spirits of; excite. **II.** *a.* Exalted or triumphant; exultant. — **e-la'tion,** *n.* A jubilant state of mind; exaltation.

el'bow, 1 el'bo; 2 ĕl'bo. **I.** *vt. & vi.* To push with the elbows; jostle. **II.** *n.* The joint at the bend of the arm, or anything resembling it.

eld, 1 eld; 2 ĕld, *n.* [Archaic & Poet.] Old times; antiquity; old age.

eld'er, 1 eld'er; 2 ĕld'er, *a., compar.* of OLD. Having lived longer; senior; older. — **eld'er-ly,** *a.* Somewhat old. — **eld'est,** *a., superl.* of OLD. First-born; oldest.

eld'er¹, *n.* An older or aged person ; patriarch; church officer or minister.

el'der², 1 el'dər; 2 ĕl'der, *n.* A shrub with white flowers and purple-black or red berries. — **el'der-ber"ry,** *n.* [-RIES², *pl.*] The fruit of the common elder.

Red-berried Elder.
a, the flower, enlarged.

El Do-ra'do, } 1 el'do-rä'dō; 2 ĕl'do-rä'dō, **El"do-ra'do,** } *n.* **1.** A region rich in gold;

a golden opportunity. **2.** An imaginary land, rich in gold and precious stones, supposed by the Spaniards and by Raleigh to have existed between the Amazon and Orinoco rivers, South America.

e-lect', 1 ı-lekt'; 2 e-lĕet'. **I.** *vt.* To choose by vote; select; appoint to salvation. **II.** *a.* **1.** Elected, as to office. **2.** Chosen of God for salvation; of saintly character. **III.** *n.* A person or persons elected, favored, or preferred.

e-lec'tion, 1 ı-lek'shan; 2 e-lĕe'shon, *n.* The act of electing; a vote; choice.— **e-lec'tion-eer',** 1 ı-lek"shan-ır'; 2 e-lĕe"shon-ēr', *vi.* To canvass for votes.

e-lec'tive, } 1 ı-lek'tıv; 2 e-lĕe'tiv, *a.* **1.** **e-lec'tive⁵,** } Of or pertaining to election. **2.** Exercising or subject to choice; optional. — **e-lec'tive-ly,** *adv.*

e-lec'tor, 1 ı-lek'ter; 2 e-lĕe'tor, *n.* **1.** One who elects or votes. **2.** Formerly, one of the great princes of Germany. — **e-lec'to-ral,** *a.* Pertaining to electors or elections. — **e-lec'to-rate,** *n.* **1.** The body of electors or voters, collectively. **2.** Formerly, the rank or territory of an elector in the old German empire.

e-lec-tric'i-ty, 1 ı-lek-tris'ı-tı; 2 e-lĕe-trĭe'ĭ-tι, *n.* An imponderable and invisible agent manifested in lightning, magnetism, heat, motion, etc.— **e-lec'tric,** 1 ı-lek'trık; 2 e-lĕe'trie, *a.* **1.** Relating to, produced, or operated by electricity. **2.** Spirited; magnetic; thrilling. **e-lec'tric-al,** *a.* — **electric fish,** a fish capable of giving an electric shock, as an *electric* eel.— **e. motor,** see ELECTROMOTOR, under ELECTRO-.— **e-lec'tri-cal-ly,** *adv.* — **e-lec-tri'cian,** 1 ı-lek-trish'an; 2 e-lĕe-trish'an, *n.* **1.** One versed in electricity. **2.** An inventor or manager of electrical apparatus.— **e-lec'tri-cute,** *vt.* To kill by electricity.— **e-lec'tri-cu'tion,** *n.*

e-lec'tri-fy, 1 ı-lek'trı-faı; 2 e-lĕe'tri-fī, *vt. & vi.* [-FIED; -FY'ING.] To act upon or charge or become charged with electricity; arouse; startle; thrill.— **e-lec"tri-fi-ca'tion,** *n.* The process of electrifying, or the state of being electrified.

e-lec'tro-, 1 ı-lek'tro-; 2 e-lĕe'tro-. A combining form representing *electric* in composition.— **e-lec"tro-chem'is-try,** *n.* The branch of chemistry that treats of electricity as active in effecting chemical change.— **e-lec"tro-chem'i-cal,** *a.* — **e-lec"tro-chem'i-cal-ly,** *adv.* — **e-lec"tro-chem'ist,** *n.* — **e-lec"tro-cul'ture,** *n.* Hort. Cultivation of plants by the aid of an electric current or by electric light.— **e-lec'tro-cute,** etc., see ELECTRICUTE, etc.— **e-lec"tro-de-pos'it,** **I.** *d.* *vt.* To deposit chemically, or

metal from a solution, by means of an electric current. **II.** *n.* That which is so deposited.— **e-lec″tro-dep″o-sī′tion,** *n.* The process of electrodepositing.— **e-lec″tro-dy-nam′ic,** *a.* Relating to forces of attraction and repulsion, produced by electric currents. — **e-lec″tro-ki-net′ic,** *a.* Pertaining to or caused by electricity in motion.— **e-lec-trol′y-sis,** *n.* Decomposition by passage ,f an electric current.— **e-lec″tro-lyt′ic,** *a.* **e-lec″-tro-lyt′i-cal‡.**— **e-lec″tro-mag′net,** *n.* A core, as of soft iron, made magnetic by the passage of an electric current through a surrounding coil of wire, and losing its magnetism when the current ceases.— **e-lec″tro-mag-net′ic,** *a.* Pertaining to an electromagnet, or to the relations between electricity and magnetism.— **e-lec″tro-mag′net-ism,** *n.*— **e-lec-trom′e-ter,** *n.* An instrument for measuring electricity.— **e-lec″tro-mo′tor,** *n.* A motor moved by an electric current: the reverse of a *dynamo.*— **e-lec-trop′a-thy,** *n.* See ELECTROTHERAPEUTICS.— **e-lec″tro-path′ic,** *a.*— **e-lec″tro-plate,** *vt.* To coat with metal by means of electricity.— **e-lec″-tro-scope,** *n.* An instrument for detecting the presence of electricity.— **e-lec″tro-stat′-ics,** *n.* The branch of science treating of electricity at rest, or of frictional electricity. — **e-lec″tro-stat′ic, -i-cal,** *a.*— **e-lec″tro-tech′nics,** *n.* The branch of science that treats of the applications of electricity in the industrial arts.— **e-lec″tro-tech′nic, -ni-cal,** *a.*— **e-lec″tro-te-leg′ra-phy,** *n.* Telegraphy by electricity.— **e-lec″tro-tel″e-graph′ic,** *a.* — **e-lec″tro-ther″a-peu′tics,** *n.* Healing by electricity, or the laws, etc., of such treatment. **e-lec″tro-ther″a-py‡.**— **e-lec″tro-ther″a-peu′tic, -ti-cal,** *a.*— **e-lec′tro-type. I.** *vt.* To copy by electrodeposition. **II.** *n.* A copy, as of a page of type, made by securing a deposit of metal over the surface from a solution by means of electricity; the mold thus obtained is filled with molten metal forming a cast which exactly reproduces the original. See STEREOTYPE. [Electrotyped matter is commonly said to be *cast.* See CAST, *v.,* 3.]— **e-lec′tro-typ″er,** *n.* **e-lec′tro-typ″ist‡.**— **e-lec′tro-typ″ing,** *n.* **e-lec′tro-typ″y‡.**

e-lec′trode, 1 =lek′trōd; 2 e-lĕc′trŏd, *n.* Either of the two poles of a battery or dynamo.

e-lec″tro-lier′, 1 =lek″tro-lir′; 2 e-lĕe″tro-lēr′, *n.* A fixture for holding electric lamps.

e-lec′tron. 1 =lek′tren; 2 e-lĕc′trŏn, *n.* The electric charge of an atom: believed to exist as a separate entity.

el″e-e-mos′y-na-ry, 1 el′i-=-mŏs′i-nē-ri; 2 ĕl′e-e-mŏs′y-nā-ry. **I.** *a.* Of, pertaining to, or dependent on alms; charitable. **II.** *n.* [-RIES^z, *pl.*] A recipient of charity.

el′e-gant, 1 el′i-gent; 2 ĕl′e-gănt, *a.* Graceful; symmetrical; refined. **-ly,** *adv.*— **el′e-**

gance, *n.* The state or quality of being elegant. **el′e-gan-cy‡** [-CIES^z, *pl.*].

el′e-gy, 1 el′i-ji; 2 ĕl′e-ǵy, *n.* [-GIES^z, *pl.*] A funeral song; a plaintive meditative poem. — **e-le′gi-ac,** 1 =-lī′ji-ak *or* el′i-jɑi′ak; 2 e-lē′-ǵi-ăc *or* ĕl′e-ǵi′ăc, *a.* Pertaining to elegies; sad; plaintive. **el″e-gi′a-cal‡.**

el′e-ment, 1 el′i-ment *or* -ment; 2 ĕl′e-ment, *n.* **1.** A component; constituent; ingredient. **2.** *pl.* Rudiments. **3.** *pl.* The bread and wine of the Lord's Supper. **4.** *pl.* Natural agencies, as of earth, air, fire, and water. **5.** The natural sphere or environment. **6.** *Chem.* A form of matter which can not be decomposed by any known means.— **el″e-men′tal,** *a.* Relating to an element; pertaining to the great forces of nature; rudimentary.— **el″e-men′tal-ly,** *adv.*— **el″e-men′ta-ry,** *a.* Of, pertaining to, or being an element or elements, in any sense.

el′e-phant, 1 el′i-fent; 2 ĕl′e-fant, *n.* A large quadruped with tusks and a flexible proboscis.— **el″e-phan′tine,** 1 el′i-fan′tin; 2 ĕl″e-făn′tin, *a.* Of or pertaining to an elephant; enormous; unwieldy.

Asiatic Elephant. 1/100

el′e-vate, 1 el′-i-vēt; 2 ĕl′e-vāt, *vt.* [-VAT″ED^d; -VAT″ING.] To raise; promote; exalt; cheer; inspire.— **el″e-va′tion,** *n.* The act of elevating; exaltation; an elevated place; front view of a building.— **el′e-va″tor,** *n.* One who or that which elevates; a hoisting mechanism for grain, freight, or passengers; also, a warehouse for grain.

e-lev′en, 1 =-lev′n; 2 e-lĕv′n. **I.** *a.* Consisting of one more than ten. **II.** *n.* The sum of ten and one.— **e-lev′enth,** *a.* & *n.* **1.** Next in order after the tenth. **2.** One of eleven equal parts.

elf, 1 elf; 2 ĕlf, *n.* [ELVES, 1 elvz; 2 ĕlvs, *pl.*] A dwarfish, mischievous sprite; a dwarf. — **elf′in,** *a.* Relating or belonging to elves. — **elf′ish,** *a.* Elfin; mischievous.

e-lic′it‡, 1 =-lis′it; 2 e-lĭç′it, *vt.* To draw out.

e-lide′, 1 =-laid′; 2 e-līd′, *vt.* [E-LID′ED^d; E-LID′ING.] To strike out or omit, as a part of a word.

el′i-gi-ble, 1 el′i-ji-bl; 2 ĕl′i-ǵi-bl, *a.* **el″i-gi-bil^F‡,** pable of being chosen; worthy of acceptance.— **el″i-gi-bil′i-ty,** *n.* **el″i-gi-bl{e-ness^F‡.**

e·lim'i·nate, 1 ɪ-lĭm'ɪ-nēt; 2 e-lĭm'ĭ-nät, *vt.* [-NAT″ED^d; -NAT″ING.] To cast out from; a system of algebraic equations; remove; get rid of.— **e·lim″i·na'tion,** *n.*

e·li'sion, 1 ɪ-lĭʒ'ən; 2 e-lĭzh'on, *n.* The act of eliding.

e·lix'ir, 1 ɪ-lĭks'ər; 2 e-lĭks'ir, *n.* An alcoholic medicinal preparation; a cordial.

elk, 1 elk; 2 ĕlk, *n.* A large deer of northern forests, with palmated antlers.

ell, } 1 el; 2 ĕl, *n.* A measure of length **el**^s, } now rarely used: in England, 45 inches.

el·lipse', } 1 e·lips'; 2 ĕ·lĭps', *n.* An oval. **el·lips″,** }

el·lip'sis, 1 e·lĭp'sɪs; 2 ĕ·lĭp'sis, *n.* [-SES, 1 -sīz; 2 -sēs, *pl.*] The omission of a word or words.

el·lip'tic, } 1 e·lĭp'tɪk, -tɪ-kəl; 2 ĕ·lĭp'tic; **el·lip'ti·cal,** } -ti·cal, *a.* **1.** Of, pertaining to, or like an ellipse. **2.** Characterized by ellipsis; shortened.

elm, 1 elm; 2 ĕlm, *n.* A shade-tree with a broad, spreading, or overarching top.

el″o·cu'tion, 1 el″o·kiū'shən; 2 ĕl″o·kū'shon, *n.* The art of correct utterance in public speaking or reading; manner of utterance.— **el″o·cu'tion·a·ry,** *a.* — **el″o·cu'tion·ist,** *n.* One who is skilled in or teaches elocution.

White Elm.
a, flowers; *b*, leaves and fruit.

e·lon'gate, 1 ɪ-lŏŋ'gēt; 2 e·lŏŋ'gät, *vt.* & *vi.* [-GAT″ED^d; -GAT″ING.] To lengthen.— **e″lon·ga'tion,** *n.* A lengthening; extension.

e·lope', 1 ɪ-lōp'; 2 e·lōp', *vi.* [E·LOPED'; E·LOP'ING.] To run away from home with a lover.— **e·lope'ment,** *n.*

el'o·quent, 1 el'o·kwent; 2 ĕl'o·kwĕnt, *a.* Possessed of or manifesting eloquence; persuasive; convincing; expressive of emotion. **-ly,** *adv.*— **el'o·quence,** 1 el'o·kwens; 2 ĕl'o·kwĕnç, *n.* Lofty, impassioned, and convincing utterance; the quality of being eloquent.

else, 1 els; 2 ĕls, *adv.* Other; besides: instead; otherwise.— **else'where″,** *adv.* Somewhere else.

e·lu'ci·date, 1 ɪ-liū'sɪ-dēt; 2 e·lū'çi·dät, *vt.*

[-DAT″ED^d; -DAT″ING.] To throw light upon; clear up.— **e·lu″ci·da'tion,** *n.*

e·lude', 1 ɪ-liūd'; 2 e·lūd', *vt.* [E·LUD'ED^d; E·LUD'ING.] To avoid adroitly; evade; baffle.— **e·lu'sion,** 1 ɪ-liū'ʒən; 2 e·lū'zhon, *n.* The act of eluding or escaping.— **e·lu'sive,** 1 ɪ-liū'sɪv; 2 e·lū'siv, *a.* Tending to slip away or escape. **-ly,** *adv.* **-ness,** *n.* **e·lu'so·ry**‡.

elves, *n.* Plural of ELF.— **elv'ish,** *a.*

E·lys'i·an, 1 ɪ-lĭz'ɪ-ən; 2 e·lÿʒ'i·an, *a.* Belonging to Elysium; happy; heavenly.

E·lys'i·um, 1 ɪ-lĭz'ɪ-um; 2 e·lÿʒ'i·ŭm, *n. Gr. Myth.* The abode of the blessed dead.

e·ma'ci·ate, 1 ɪ-mē'shɪ-ēt; 2 e·mā'çhi·ät, *vt.* [-AT″ED^d; -AT″ING.] To reduce in flesh; make lean or thin.— **e·ma″ci·a'tion,** *n.*

em'a·nate, 1 em'ə-nēt; 2 ĕm'a·nät, *vi.* [-NAT″ED^d; -NAT″ING.] To flow forth, as from a source.— **em″a·na'tion,** 1 em″ə-nē'shən; 2 ĕm″a·nä'shon, *n.* The act of emanating; an effluence or outflowing, as of the Divine Essence.

e·man'ci·pate, 1 ɪ-man'sɪ-pēt; 2 e·măn'çi·pät, *vt.* [-PAT″ED^d; -PAT″ING.] To set free, as from slavery.— **e·man″ci·pa'tion,** *n.* — **e·man'ci·pa″tor,** *n.*

e·mas'cu·late, **I.** *vt.* [-LAT″ED^d; -LAT″ING.] 1 ɪ-mas'kiu-lēt; 2 e·măs'cū-lät. **1.** To deprive of masculine strength; weaken; impair. **2.** To castrate; geld. **II.** *a.* Emasculated.— **e·mas″cu·la'tion,** *n.*

em·balm', 1 em·bäm'; 2 ĕm·bäm', *vt.* To preserve from decay, as a dead body, by antiseptics.— **em·balm'er,** *n.*

em·bank', 1 em·baŋk'; 2 ĕm·băŋk', *vt.* To confine or protect by a bank.— **em·bank'ment,** *n.* A protecting or supporting bank.

em″bar·ca'tion, *n.* Same as EMBARKATION.

em·bar'go, 1 em·bär'go; 2 ĕm·bär'go, *n.* A prohibition of ships from leaving port; an impediment; a check.

em·bark', 1 em·bärk'; 2 ĕm·bärk', *vt.* & *vi.* To put or go on board a vessel; venture; engage; invest.— **em″bar·ka'tion,** *n.*

em·bar'rass, 1 em·bar'as; 2 ĕm·băr'as, *vt.* To confuse; abash; perplex; hamper; encumber.— **em·bar'rass·ment,** *n.* **1.** Discomposure; entanglement; difficulty. **2.** An impediment; hindrance. [etc.

em·bas'sa·dor, etc. Same as AMBASSADOR.

em'bas·sy, 1 em'ba·sɪ; 2 ĕm'ba·si, *n.* [-SIES^z, *pl.*] **1.** An ambassador and his suite. **2.** An ambassador's office, mission, or official residence.

em·bat'tled, } 1 em·bat'ld; 2 ĕm·băt'ld, *pa.* **em·bat'tld**^r, } Drawn up in battle array; having battlements.— **em·bat'tle,** *vt.*

em·bed', 1 em·bed'; 2 ĕm·bĕd', *vt.* [EM·BED'DED^d; EM·BED'DING.] To lay as in a bed. **im·bed'**‡.

1: **a**rtistic, **ä**rt; fat, fāre; fast; get, prēy; hĭt, polīce; obey, gō; net, ŏr; full, rūle; but, bŭrn.
2: **ä**rt, **ā**pe, făt, fâre, fȧst, whạt, ạll; mē, gĕt, prey, fèrn; hĭt, īce; ī=ē; ĭ=ĕ; gō, nŏt, ôr, wŏn,

em·bel'lish[t], 1 em-bel'ısh; 2 ĕm-bĕl'ish, *vt.* To ornament; decorate.— **em·bel'lish - er,** *n.*— **em·bel'lish-ment,** *n.*

em'ber, 1 em'bər; 2 ĕm'ber, *n.* A live coal.

em·bez'zle, } 1 em-bez'l; 2 ĕm-bĕz'l, *vt.* **em·bez'l**[e], } [-zl(e)d⁴; -zling.] To appropriate fraudulently.— **em·bez'zle·ment,** *n.*— **em·bez'zler,** *n.*

em·bit'ter, 1 em-bit'ər; 2 ĕm-bĭt'er, *vt.* To render bitter, unhappy, or resentful. **im·bit'ter**[t].

em·bla'zon, 1 em-blē'zn; 2 ĕm-blā'zn, *vt.* To adorn with armorial ensigns; display; celebrate.— **em·bla'zon-ry,** *n.*

em'blem, 1 em'blem; 2 ĕm'blĕm, *n.* A figurative representation; symbol.— **em''blem·at'ic,** *a.* **em''blem·at'i-cal**[t].

em·bod'y, 1 em-bod'ı; 2 ĕm-bŏd'y, *vt. & vi.* [em-bod'ied; em-bod'y-ing.] **1.** To put into bodily form; express, as in words. **2.** To unite in one whole; incorporate; coalesce.— **em·bod'i-ment,** *n.* The act of embodying, or that which embodies, as a description or picture. [To make bold.

em·bold'en, 1 em-bōld'n; 2 em-bōld'n, *vt.*

em·bo'som, 1 em-bu'zəm; 2 ĕm-bo'som, *vt.* To place in the bosom; envelop; shelter; cherish.

em·boss'[t], 1 em-bos'; 2 ĕm-bŏs', *vt.* To ornament with raised work; cause to stand out.— **em·boss'er, em·boss'ment,** *n.*

em·bow'er, 1 em-bau'ər; 2 ĕm-bow'er, *vt. & vi.* To place or rest in or as in a bower.

em·brace', 1 em-brēs'; 2 ĕm-brāç'. **I.** *vt. & vi.* [em-braced'[t]; em-brac'ing.] To infold in the arms; clasp; hug; accept willingly; comprehend; include. **II.** *n.* The act of embracing; a clasping in the arms; a hug.

em·bra'sure, 1 em-brē'ʒur; 2 ĕm-brā'zhur, *n.* An opening in a wall, as for a cannon.

em''bro·ca'tion, 1 em''bro-kē'shən; 2 ĕm''bro-cā'shon, *n.* A liniment, or its application.— **em'bro·cate,** *vt.*

em·broi'der, 1 em-brei'dər; 2 ĕm-brŏi'der, *v.* **I.** *t.* To ornament with needlework; execute in needlework. **II.** *i.* To make embroidery.— **em·broi'der-er,** *n.*— **em·broi'der-y,** *n.,* [-ies²; *pl.*] Ornamental needlework, or the art of producing it; ornamentation.

em·broil', 1 em-breil'; 2 ĕm-brŏil', *vt. & vi.* To involve, or become involved, in dissension or strife.— **em·broil'ment,** *n.*

em'bry-o, 1 em'brı-o; 2 ĕm'bry-o. **I.** *a.* Rudimentary. **II.** *n.* The germ or rudimentary form of anything, as of an animal or plant.— **em''bry·on'ic,** *a.*

e·meer', 1 ı-mīr'; 2 e-mēr',*n.* An emir.

e·mend'[d], 1 ı-mend'; 2 e-mĕnd', *vt.* To

correct, as a result of criticism.— **e''men·da'-tion,** 1 ı''men-dā'shən; 2 ē''mĕn-dā'shon, *n.* A correction or alteration.

em'er·ald, 1 em'ar-ald; 2 ĕm'er-ald, *n.* A bright-green variety of beryl; a rich and vivid green hue.

e·merge', 1 ı-mūrj'; 2 e-mērg', *vi.* [e-merged'; e-merg'ing.] To rise, as from a fluid; come forth; come into view.— **e·mer'gence,** *n.* **1.** The process or result of emerging. **e·mer'sion**[t]. **2.** That which emerges; an outgrowth.

e·mer'gen-cy, 1 ı-mūr'jen-sı; 2 e-mēr'gĕn-çy, *n.* [-cies²; *pl.*] A sudden condition calling for immediate action.— **e·mer'gent,** *a.*— **e·mer'gent-ly,** *adv.*

e·mer'i-tus, 1 ı-mer'ı-tus; 2 e-mēr'i-tŭs, *a. & n.* Denoting one retired from active service, but retained in an honorary position.

em'er-y, 1 em'ar-ı; 2 ĕm'er-y, *n.* A very hard black mineral: used in powder for polishing, etc.

e·met'ic, 1 ı-met'ık; 2 e-mĕt'ic. **I.** *a.* Tending to produce vomiting. **II.** *n.* A medicine used to produce vomiting.

em'i-grate, 1 em'ı-grēt; 2 ĕm'i-grāt, *vi.* [-grat'ed⁴; -grat'ing.] To go from one country to settle in another.— **em'i-grant. I.** *a.* Emigrating. **II.** *n.* One who emigrates.— **em''i-gra'tion,** *n.*

em'i·nence, 1 em'ı-nens; 2 ĕm'i-nĕnç, *n.* A lofty place; hill; rank; distinction.— **em'i-nen-cy**[t].— **em'i-nent,** *a.* High in station or esteem; distinguished. **-ly,** *adv.*

e·mir', 1 ē-mīr'; 2 e-mīr', *n.* A Mohammedan prince; a high Turkish official.

em'is·sa·ry, 1 em'ı-sē-rı; 2 ĕm'i-sā-ry, *n.* [-ries²; *pl.*] A secret agent; spy.

e·mit', 1 ı-mit; 2 e-mīt, *vt.* [e-mit'ted⁴; e-mit'ting.] To send or give out; issue.— **e·mis'sion,** 1 ı-mish'ən; 2 e-mish'on, *n.* The act of emitting, or that which is emitted.

em'met, 1 em'et; 2 ĕm'ĕt, *n.* An ant.

e·mol'li-ent, 1 ı-mel'ı-ent; 2 e-mŏl'i-ĕnt. **I.** *a.* Softening; soothing. **II.** *n.* A softening or soothing application.

e·mol'u-ment, 1 ı-mel'yu-ment *or* -ment; 2 e-mŏl'yu-ment, *n.* Remuneration; gain; profit.

e·mo'tion, 1 ı-mō'shən; 2 e-mō'shon, *n.* Excitement of mind; feeling; sensibility; sentiment.— **e·mo'tion-al,** *a.* **1.** Of, pertaining to, or expressive of emotion. **2.** Capable of emotion.— **e·mo'tiv(e**[t], *a.* Marked by or tending to excite emotion.

em·pale', } 1 em-pēl'; 2 ĕm-pāl',*vt.* [em-**im·pale'**, } paled'⁴; em-pal'ing.] **1.** To put to death by fixing upon a pale or sharp stake. **2.** To fence in.— **em·[or im-]-**

pale'ment, *n.* The act of empaling, in either sense of the verb.

em″pen′nage, 1 añ″pen″näz′; 2 äñ″pĕn″näzh′, *n.* The rear steering parts of an aeroplane.

em′per-or, 1 em′pər-ər *or* er; 2 ĕm′pei-or, *n.* **1.** The sovereign of an empire. **2.** One of various butterflies and moths.

em′pha-sis, ‖
em′fa-sis², ‖
1 em′fa-sis; 2 ĕm′fa-sĭs, *n.* [-SES, 1-sĭz, 2 -sēg, *pl.*] A stress laid upon some word or words in speaking or reading. — **em′pha-size, em′fa-saiz;** 2 ĕm′fa-sĭz, *vt.* [-SIZED; -SIZ″ING.] To articulate with special force; make distinct.

Emper-or-moth. ¹/₈

em-phat′ic, ‖ 1 em-fat′ĭk; 2 ĕm-făt′ie, *a.*
em-fat′ic², ‖ Speaking or spoken with emphasis; forcible; positive; earnest. **em-phat′i-cal:**. — **em-phat′i-cal-ly,** *adv.*

em′pire, 1 em′pair; 2 ĕm′pīr, *n.* A country governed by an emperor; a powerful nation; wide and supreme dominion.

em-pir′ic, 1 em-pir′ĭk; 2 ĕm-pĭr′ie. **I.** *a.* Experimental rather than scientific. **II.** *n.* One whose methods are empirical; a quack. — **em-pir′i-cal:**. — **em-pir′i-cal-ly,** *adv.* — **em-pir′i-cism,** 1 em-pir′i-sizm; 2 ĕm-pir′i-çigm, *n.* **1.** Quackery; unscientific experimenting. **2.** *Philos.* The doctrine that all knowledge is derived from experience.

em-ploy′, 1 em-ploi′; 2 ĕm-plŏy′. **I.** *vt.* To have in service; furnish work for; use; apply. **II.** *n.* The state of being employed; service. — **em″ploy-ee′,** 1 em′ploi-ī′; 2 ĕm′plŏy-ē′, *n.* One who is employed by another. **em″ploy-é′:;** 1 em′ploi-ē′; 2 ĕm′plŏy-ḡ′. — **em-ploy′er,** *n.* One who employs. — **em-ploy′ment,** *n.* The act of employing; service; work.

em-po′ri-um, 1 em-pō′ri-um; 2 ĕm-pō′ri-ŭm, *n.* [-RI-UMSᶻ *or* -RI-A, *pl.*] An important trading-place; a mart; a bazaar or large department-store.

em-pow′er, 1 em-pau′ər; 2 ĕm-pow′er, *vt.* To authorize.

em′press, 1 em′pres; 2 ĕm′prĕs, *n.* A woman who rules an empire; the wife or widow of an emperor.

emp′ty, 1 emp′ti; 2 ĕmp′ty. **I.** *a. vt. & vi.* [EMP′TIED; EMP′TY-ING.] To make or become empty; pour out; remove, as contents. **II.** *a.* [EMP′TI-ER; EMP′TI-EST.] Having nothing within; without contents or substance; vacant; hollow; unmeaning. — **emp′ti-ness,** *n.*

em″py-re′an, 1 em″pi-rī′ən; 2 ĕm″py-rē′an, *n.* The highest heaven; upper sky. — **em-**

pyr′e-al, 1 em-pir′i-əl; 2 ĕm-pȳr′e-al, *a. & n.* Celestial.

e′mu, 1 ī′miu; 2 ē′mū, *n.* A large Australian ostrich-like bird.

em′u-late, 1 em′yu-lĕt; 2 ĕm′yu-lāt, *vt.* [-LAT″EDᵈ; -LAT″ING.] To strive to equal or surpass; vie with. — **em″u-la′tion,** *n.* Effort or ambition to equal or excel another. — **em′u-la-tive,** *a.* Inclined to emulation. — **em′u-lous,** *a.* Eager to equal or excel another; competitive. — **ly,** *adv.* — **em′u-lous-ness,** *n.*

Emu. ¹/₉₀

e-mul′sion, 1 i-mul′shan; 2 e-mŭl′shon, *n.* A liquid mixture in which a fatty substance is suspended in minute globules; any milky liquid. — **e-mul′siv(e³,** *a.* Of the nature of an emulsion; softening; oily.

en¹-, *prefix.* In; into; as, *en*shrine; *en*throne. [words.

en-², *prefix.* In: used chiefly in scientific **-en,** *suffix.* Used (1) to form verbs; as, fatt*en*; (2) to form past participles in strong verbs; as, fall*en*; (3) to form plural of verbs; (4) to form feminine of nouns; (5) to form plural of nouns; as, ox*en*; (6) to form adjectives denoting material; as, wool*en*; (7) as a form of -AN.

en-a′ble, ‖ 1 en-ē′bᵊl; 2 ĕn-ā′bl, *vt.* [EN-
en-a′blᵖ, ‖ A′BL(E)Dᴾ; EN-A′BLING.] To make able; empower.

en-act′ᵈ, 1 en-akt′; 2 ĕn-ăct′, *vt.* **1.** To make into a law. **2.** To carry out in action; perform. — **en-act′ment,** *n.* A law; statute; the act of enacting.

en-am′el, 1 en-am′el; 2 ĕn-ăm′ĕl. **I.** *vt.* [-ELED *or* -ELLED, -ELDˢ; -EL-ING *or* -EL-LING.] To cover with enamel; decorate in enamel. **II.** *n.* A hard and glossy coating, as of the teeth. — **en-am′el-er or -ler,** *n.*

en-am′or, ‖ 1 en-am′ər *or* -ōr; 2 ĕn-ăm′or,
en-am′our, ‖ *vt.* To inspire with love.

en-cage′, 1 en-kēj′; 2 ĕn-eāg′, *vt.* To shut up in a cage.

en-camp′ᵗ, 1 en-kamp′; 2 ĕn-eămp′, *vt. & vi.* To settle and lodge in a camp; form a camp. — **en-camp′ment,** *n.* The act of pitching a camp; a camp; persons encamped.

en-caus′tic, 1 en-kɒs′tɪk; 2 ĕn-eas′tie, *a.* Having colors fixed as by heat, as tiles.

en-chain′, 1 en-chēn′; 2 ĕn-chān′, *vt.* To bind with or as with a chain; confine. — **en-chain′ment,** *n.*

en-chant′ᵈ, 1 en-chant′; 2 ĕn-chànt′, *vt.* To bewitch; fascinate; delight. — **en-chant′er,** *n.* One who enchants; a magician. — **en-chant′-**

ing-ly, *adv.*— en-chant′ment, *n.* The act of enchanting, or the state of being enchanted; illusive charm.— en-chant′ress, *n.* 1. A sorceress. 2. A bewitching woman.

en-cir′cle, ⎱ 1 en-sŭr′kl; 2 ĕn-çĭr′el, *vt.*
en-cir′cl′, ⎰ [-CL(E)D^p; -CLING.] To surround; environ.

en-close′, 1 en-klōz′; 2 ĕn-clōs′, *vt.* [EN-CLOSED′; EN-CLOS′ING.] 1. To insert, as in an envelop. 2. To fence in, as land. 3. To surround. in-close′‡.— en-clo′sure, 1 en-klō′zhur; 2 ĕn-clō′zhur, *n.* The act of enclosing; that which encloses or is enclosed. in-clo′sure‡.

en-co′mi-um, 1 en-kō′mi-um; 2 ĕn-cō′mi-ŭm, *n.* [-UMS^z or -A, *pl.*] A formal expression of praise; a eulogy.— en-co′mi-ast, 1 en-kō′mi-ast; 2 ĕn-cō′mi-ăst, *n.* A eulogist.

en-com′pass, ⎱ 1 en-kum′pas; 2 ĕn-eŏm′-
en-cum′pas′, ⎰ pas, *vt.* To encircle; surround; shut in. -ment, *n.*

en′′core, 1 añ″kōr′; 2 än′eōr′, I. *vt.* & *vi.* [EN-CORED′; EN-COR′ING.] To call for a repetition, as of a performance. II. *n.* The call for a repetition, as of a performance; also, the repetition itself. III. *adv.* Again; once more.

en-coun′ter, 1 en-kaun′ter; 2 ĕn-koun′ter. I. *vt.* & *vi.* To come upon; meet face to face or in conflict. II. *n.* A sudden or hostile meeting; conflict; battle.

en-cour′age, 1 en-kur′ij; 2 ĕn-eŭr′aġ, *vt.* [-AGED; -AG-ING.] To inspire with courage or hope; incite; promote; countenance.— en-cour′age-ment, *n.* The act of encouraging, or that which encourages.

en-croach′^t, 1 en-krōch′; 2 ĕn-erŏch′, *vi.* To trench on another's limits or rights; intrude; make inroads.— en-croach′er, *n.*— en-croach′ing-ly, *adv.*— en-croach′ment, *n.*

en-cum′ber, 1 en-kum′ber; 2 ĕn-eŭm′ber, *vt.* To obstruct; hinder; burden.— en-cum′brance, *n.* That which encumbers; a burdensome addition.

en-cy′clo-pe′di-a, ⎱ 1 en-sai″klo-pī′di-ə; 2
en-cy′clo-pæ′di-a, ⎰ ĕn-çȳ″elo-pē′di-a, *n.* A work containing information on all subjects, or exhaustive of one subject.— en-cy′clo-pe′dic or -pæ′dic, *a.* Of or like an encyclopedia; erudite; comprehensive.

en-cyst′, 1 en-sist′; 2 ĕn-çȳst′, *vt.* & *vi.* [-CYST′ED; -CYST′ING.] To envelop in or become enclosed in a sac or cyst, as a bullet in the human body.

end^d, 1 end; 2 ĕnd, *v.* I. *t.* To put an end to; come to the end of; finish; terminate; kill. II. *i.* To come to an end; conclude; result.— end′ing, 1 end′iŋ; 2 ĕnd′iŋ, *n.* Termination; end; conclusion.

end, *n.* 1. The terminal point or part of an object; conclusion; object; purpose; result. 2. The close of life.— end′less, *a.* Having no end. -ly, *adv.* -ness, *n.*— end′-wise, *adv.* With the end foremost or uppermost; on end. end′ways‡.

en-dan′ger, 1 en-dēn′jər; 2 ĕn-dān′ġer, *vt.* To put in danger.

en-dear′, 1 en-dīr′; 2 ĕn-dēr′, *vt.* To make dear.— en-dear′ment, *n.* The act of endearing; an expression of love; a caress.

en-deav′or, ⎱ 1 en-dev′ər; 2 ĕn-dĕv′or. I.
en-dev′or^z, ⎰ *vt.* & *vi.* To make an effort to do; undertake; try. II. *n.* An attempt or effort to do or attain something; earnest exertion for an end.— en-deav′or-er, *n.*

en-dem′ic, 1 en-dem′ik; 2 ĕn-dĕm′ie, *a.* Peculiar to or prevailing in a locality.

en′dive, 1 en′dīv; 2 ĕn′dȳv, *n.* A plant or its blanched leaves; used as a salad.

en′do-gen, 1 en′do-jen; 2 ĕn′do-ġĕn, *n.* A plant that increases by growth from within.— en-dog′e-nous, 1 en-dej′i-nus; 2 ĕn-dŏġ′e-nŭs, *a.* Of or pertaining to an endogen; growing from within, as a palm.

en-dorse′^t, etc. See INDORSE, etc.

en-dow′, 1 en-dau′; 2 ĕn-dow′, *vt.* 1. To provide with a permanent fund or income. 2. To furnish or equip, as with natural gifts.— en-dow′ment, *n.* The act of endowing; a fund; gift; talent.

en-due′, 1 en-diū′; 2 ĕn-dū′, *vt.* [EN-DUED′; EN-DU′ING.] 1. To invest, as with spiritual grace. 2. To put on; assume; clothe; invest.

en-dure′, 1 en-diūr′; 2 ĕn-dūr′, *v.* [EN-DURED′; EN-DUR′ING.] I. *t.* To bear, as pain, without giving way; withstand; suffer patiently; tolerate. II. *i.* 1. To have duration; continue. 2. To be firm in trial.— en-dur′a-ble, *a.* That may be endured; bearable.— en-dur′a-bl(e-ness^z, *n.*— en-dur′a-bly, *adv.*— en-dur′ance, *n.* The power to endure; fortitude; durability; duration.

Leaf and Divided Stem of an Endogen, showing characteristic structure.

En-dym′i-on, 1 en-dim′i-en; 2 ĕn-dȳm′i-ŏn, *n.* *Gr. Myth.* Beautiful youth, forever asleep; beloved by Diana.

en′e·ma, 1 en′i-mə; 2 ĕn′e-ma, *n.* [-MAS² or E-NEM′A-TA, *pl.*] *Med.* An injection.

en′e·my, 1 en′i-mɪ; 2 ĕn′e-my, *n.* [-MIES², *pl.*] **1.** One who cherishes resentment or malice; an adversary; foe. **2.** One of a hostile army or nation; also, such nation or army collectively.

en′er·gize, 1 en′ər-jɑɪz; 2 ĕn′er-gĭz, *vt. & vi.* [-GIZED; -GIZ′ING.] To impel or act with energy. **en′er·gise‡.**

en′er·gy, 1 en′ər-jɪ; 2 ĕn′er-gy, *n.* [-GIES², *pl.*] Power to move or change, or to accomplish a result; vigor; force.— **en″er·get′ic,** 1 en″ər-jet′ɪk; 2 ĕn″er-gĕt′ic, *a.* Full of energy; forceful; strenuous. **en″er·get′i·cal‡.** — **en″er·get′i·cal·ly,** *adv.*

en′er·vate, 1 en′ər-vēt *or* ɪ-nûr′vēt; 2 ĕn′er-vāt *or* e-nẽr′vāt. **I.** *vt.* [EN′ER-VAT′-ED⁴ *or* E-NER′VAT-ED⁴; EN′ER-VAT′ING *or* E-NER′VAT-ING.] To deprive of energy or vigor; weaken. **II.** *a.* Rendered feeble or effeminate; weakened.— **en″er·va′tion,** *n.* The act of enervating, or the state of being enervated; debility.

en·fee′ble, 1 en-fī′bl; 2 ĕn-fē′bl, *vt.*
en·fee′biⁱ, } [-BL(E)D⁴; -BLING.] To render feeble.— **en·fee′ble·ment,** *n.*

en″fi·lade′, 1 en″fi-lēd′; 2 ĕn″fi-lād′, *vt.* [-LAD′ED⁴; -LAD′ING.] To rake lengthwise, as with shot.

en·fold′, etc. Same as INFOLD, etc.

en·force′ᵗ, 1 en-fōrs′; 2 ĕn-fôrç′, *vt.* **1.** To execute, as laws. **2.** To exact or obtain by force. **3.** To urge forcibly; impress.— **en·force′ment,** *n.* The act of enforcing, or the state of being enforced.

en·fran′chise, 1 en-fran′chɪz *or* en-fran′chaɪz; 2 ĕn-frăn′chĭg *or* ĕn-frăn′chiz, *vt.* [-CHISED; -CHIS-ING.] **1.** To endow with a franchise, as the right to vote. **2.** To set free, as from bondage. **-ment,** *n.*

en·gage′, 1 en-gēj′; 2 ĕn-gāg′, *v.* [EN-GAGED′; EN-GAG′ING.] **I.** *t.* **1.** To bind by promise. **2.** To attract. **3.** To occupy. **4.** To join in conflict with. **II.** *i.* **1.** To bind oneself by promise. **2.** To busy oneself. **3.** To begin or maintain a conflict.— **en·gaged′,** *pa.* **1.** Affianced. **2.** Occupied or busy.— **en·gage′ment,** *n.* The act of engaging; a betrothal; an obligation; a battle.— **en·gag′ing,** *pa.* Interesting; winning.— **en·gag′ing·ly,** *adv.*

en·gen′der, 1 en-jen′dər; 2 ĕn-gĕn′der, *v.* **I.** *t.* To bring into existence; produce. **II.** *i.* To come into being.

en′gine, } 1 en′jɪn; 2 ĕn′gin, *n.* A machine
en′ginˢ, } by which power, as of steam, is applied to the doing of work; any powerful mechanism or instrumentality.— **en′gine·driv″er,** *n.* [Eng.] A locomotive-engineer.

en″gi·neer′, 1 en″jɪ-nīr′; 2 ĕn″gi-nēr′. **I.** *vt.* **1.** To execute by contrivance. **2.** To plan and superintend the construction of. **II.** *n.* **1.** One versed in or practising engineering. **2.** One who runs an engine.— **en″gi·neer′ing,** *n.* The art of making, building, or using engines, or of designing and constructing public works, as roads, railroads, etc.

En′glish, 1 ɪŋ′glɪsh; 2 ĭŋ′glĭsh. **I.** *a.* Of or pertaining to England, its people, or its language. **II.** *n.* **1.** *pl.* The English race collectively. **2.** The language of England and of the English-speaking peoples.— **En′glish·man, En′glish·wo″man,** *n.* [-MEN, *pl.*] A man or woman of English race or belonging to the English people.

en·grain′, 1 en-grēn′; 2 ĕn-grān′, *vt.* Same as INGRAIN.

en·grave′, 1 en-grēv′; 2 ĕn-grāv′, *vt.* [EN-GRAVED′; EN-GRAV′ING.] To cut or carve, as a design on metal; carve figures or inscriptions upon; impress deeply.— **en·grav′er,** *n.* One who engraves.— **en·grav′ing,** *n.* The act or art of cutting designs on a plate; an engraved design, plate, or print.

en·gross′ᵗ, 1 en-grōs′; 2 ĕn-grōs′, *vt.* **1.** To write in a bold, round hand; make a formal copy of. **2.** To occupy completely; absorb.— **en·gross′ment,** *n.*

en·gulf′ᵗ, 1 en-gulf′; 2 ĕn-gŭlf′, *vt.* To swallow up in or as in a gulf. **In·gulf′‡.**

en·hance′, 1 en-hans′; 2 ĕn-hȧnç′, *vt. & vi.* [EN-HANCED′ᵗ; EN-HANC′ING.] To heighten; increase.— **en·hance′ment,** *n.* An enhancing circumstance; increase; advance.

e·nig′ma, 1 ɪ-nig′ma; 2 ē-nĭg′ma, *n.* A riddle; puzzle.— **e″nig·mat′ic, -i·cal,** *a.* Ambiguous; puzzling.— **e″nig·mat′i·cal·ly,** *adv.*

en·join′, 1 en-jɔɪn′; 2 ĕn-jōin′, *vt.* To command; charge; prohibit.

en·joy′, 1 en-jɔɪ′; 2 ĕn-jŏy′, *vt. & vi.* **1.** To experience joy or pleasure in; receive pleasure. **2.** To have the use or benefit of.— **en·joy′a·ble(e)ᵖ,** *a.* Giving, or capable of giving, enjoyment.— **en·joy′ment,** 1 en-jɔɪ′ment *or* -mant; 2 ĕn-jŏy′ment, *n.* The act or state of enjoying; pleasure; a source of enjoyment, joy, or satisfaction.

en·kin′dle, } 1 en-kin′dl; 2 ĕn-kĭn′dl, *vt.* To
en·kin′dlⁱ, } set on fire; kindle.

en·large′, 1 en-lārj′; 2 ĕn-lärg′, *v.* [EN-LARGED′; EN-LARG′ING.] **I.** *t.* **1.** To make larger; increase; expand. **2.** To set at liberty. **II.** *i.* **1.** To become large or larger. **2.** To expatiate.— **en·large′ment,** *n.*

en·light′en, 1 en-laɪt′n; 2 ĕn-līt′n, *vt.* To bestow mental or spiritual light upon; impart knowledge to.— **en·light′en·ment,** *n.* Moral and intellectual advancement.

1: ȧrtistic, ärt; fat, fȧre; fast; get, prēy; hit, police; obey, gō; net, ôr; full, rūle; but, būrn.
2: ärt, āpe, făt, fâre, fȧst, whạt, ạll; mē, gĕt, prey, fẽrn; hĭt, īce; ĭ=ĕ; ĭ=ē; gō, nŏt, ôr, wŏn,

en-list′ᵈ, 1 en-list′; 2 ĕn-lĭst′, *v.* **I.** *t.* To enroll for service, as in the army; gain the interest and assistance of. **II.** *i.* To engage. as in the military or naval service. — **en-list′ment,** *n.*

en-li′ven, 1 en-laī′vn; 2 ĕn-lī′vn, *vt.* To make lively or cheerful; stimulate.

en′mi-ty, 1 en′mi-tı; 2 ĕn′mi-ty, *n.* [-TIESᶻ, *pl.*] The spirit of an enemy; hostility.

en-no′ble, 1 e-nō′bl; 2 ĕ-nō′bl, *vt.* [-BLED; -BLING.] To make noble; confer a title of nobility upon.— **en-no′ble-ment,** *n.*

en″nui′, 1 ȧn″nwî′; 2 ȧn″nwî′, *n.* Listless weariness resulting from satiety.

e-nor′mous, 1 ı-nôr′mus; 2 e-nôr′mŭs, *a.* **1.** Extraordinary in size, amount, or degree. **2.** Wicked above measure; atrocious. **-ly** *adv.* **-ness,** *n.*— **e-nor′mi-ty,** *n.* [-TIESᶻ, *pl.*] Extreme wickedness; a flagrant offense.

e-nough′, 1 ı-nuf′; 2 e-nŭf′. **I.** *a.* Adequate; sufficient. **II.** *n.* An ample supply; a sufficiency. **III.** *adv.* Sufficiently. **IV.** *interj.* It is enough; stop. **e-nuf′,**

en-plane′, 1 en-plēn′; 2 ĕn-plān′, *vt. & vi.* To go or put aboard (an air-plane), as passengers or goods.

en-quire′, etc. Same as INQUIRE, etc.

en-rage′, 1 en-rēj′; 2 ĕn-rāj′, *vt.* [EN-RAGED′; EN-RAG′ING.] To throw into a rage; exasperate.

en-rap′ture, 1 en-rap′chur *or* -tiur; 2 ĕn-răp′chur *or* -tūr, *vt.* [-TURED; -TUR-ING.] To fill with rapture; delight exceedingly.

en-rich′ᵗ, 1 en-rich′; 2 ĕn-rich′, *vt.* To make rich; render fertile; improve; adorn. — **en-rich′ment,** *n.*

en-roll′, 1 en-rōl′; 2 ĕn-rōl′, *vt.* To register; enlist; record.— **en-rol′ment,** *n.* **1.** The act of enrolling. **2.** A record. **en-rol′,**

en route, 1 ȧn rūt; 2 ȧn rṳt. On the road.

en-sconce′, 1 en-skens′; 2 ĕn-scŏnç′, *vt.* [EN-SCONCED′ᵗ; EN-SCONC′ING.] To settle snugly.

en″sem′ble, 1 ȧn″sȧn′bl; 2 ȧn″sän′bl, *n.* The parts of a thing taken or viewed together as a whole; the general effect.

en-shrine′, 1 en-shrain′; 2 ĕn-shrīn′, *vt.* To place in or as in a shrine; cherish devoutly; be a shrine for.

en-shroud′ᵈ, 1 en-shraud′; 2 ĕn-shroud′, *vt.* To cover with a shroud; enwrap; conceal.

en′si-form, 1 en′sı-fôrm; 2 ĕn′si-fôrm, *a.* Sword-shaped, as certain leaves.

en′sign, 1 en′sain; 2 ĕn′sīn, *n.* **1.** A flag or banner; standard; badge; symbol. **2.** A military or naval officer.

en′si-lage, 1 en′sı-lıj; 2 ĕn′si-laǧ, *n.* The process of preserving green fodder in air-tight pits; fodder thus preserved. **sī′lage‡.**

en-slave′, 1 en-slēv′; 2 ĕn-slāv′, *vt.* To make a slave of; bring into bondage.— **slave′ment,** *n.* Bondage.

en-snare′, 1 en-snâr′; 2 ĕn-snâr′, *vt.* [EN-SNARED′; EN-SNAR′ING.] To entrap; inveigle; seduce.

en-sue′, 1 en-siū′; 2 ĕn-sū′, *vt. & vi.* [EN-SUED′; EN-SU′ING.] To follow; result.

en-sure′, *v.* Same as INSURE.

en-tab′la-ture, 1 en-tab′lạ-chur *or* -tiur; 2 ĕn-tăb′la-chur *or* -tūr, *n.* *Arch.* The structure that rests horizontally upon the columns and sustains the roof.

en-tail′, 1 en-tēl′; 2 ĕn-tāl′. **I.** *vt.* To devolve upon a successor; bring upon another as a consequence or legacy; limit by entail. **II.** *n.* **1.** An inalienable inheritance. **2.** An estate limited to a particular class of heirs. **3.** The act of entailing, or the state of being entailed.— **en-tail′ment,** *n.*

en-tan′gle, 1 en-taŋ′gl; 2 ĕn-tăŋ′gl, *vt.* **en-tan′glᵖ,** ∫ To catch as in a snare; hamper; perplex; tangle; snarl. **-ment,** *n.*

en′ter, 1 en′tạr; 2 ĕn′tẽr, *v.* **I.** *t.* **1.** To come or go into; pass through; penetrate; join, as a society. **2.** To enroll; record; file. **II.** *i.* To come or go inward.

en′ter-prise, 1 en′tạr-praiz; 2 ĕn′tẽr-prīṣ, *n.* **1.** An undertaking; bold or difficult attempt. **2.** Boldness, energy, and invention in practical affairs. **en′ter-prizet.** — **en′ter-pris′ing,** *pa.* Energetic and progressive.

en″ter-tain′, 1 en″tạr-tēn′; 2 ĕn″tẽr-tān′, *v.* **I.** *t.* **1.** To receive and care for, as a guest; amuse; divert. **2.** To take into consideration; hold, as an opinion. **II.** *i.* To receive and care for guests.— **en″ter-tain′er,** *n.*— **en″ter-tain′ing,** *a.* **-ly,** *adv.*— **en″ter-tain′ment,** *n.* The act of entertaining; amusement.

en-thrall′, 1 en-thrōl′; 2 ĕn-thrạl′, *vt.* To enslave.

en-throne′, 1 en-thrōn′; 2 ĕn-thrōn′, *vt.* [EN-THRONED′; EN-THRON′ING.] To put upon a throne; invest with sovereign power.— **en-throne′ment,** *n.*

en-thu′si-asm, 1 en-thiū′zı-azm; 2 ĕn-thū′si-ăṣm, *n.* **1.** Earnest and fervent feeling; ardent zeal. **2‖.** Irrational religious ecstasy.— **en-thu′si-ast,** *n.* One moved by enthusiasm; an ardent adherent.— **en-thu″si-as′tic,** *a.* Given to enthusiasm; ardent; zealous.— **en-thu″si-as′ti-cal-ly,** *adv.*

en-tice′, 1 en-tais′; 2 ĕn-tīç′, *vt.* [EN-TICED′ᵗ; EN-TIC′ING.] To draw, or attempt to draw (especially into evil); allure; seduce. **-ment,** *n.*— **en-tic′er,** *n.*

1: ə = final; ı = habit; aisle; au = out; oil; lū = feud; chin; go; ŋ = sing; thin, this.
2: wolf, do; book, boot; full, rule, cūre, bŭt, bûrn; oil, boy; go, gem; iŋk; thin, this.

en-tire′, 1 en-tair′; 2 ĕn-tīr′. **I.** *a.* Complete; undivided; unqualified; whole. **II.** *n.* The whole.— **en-tire′ly,** *adv.*— **en-tire′-ness,** *n.* The state of being entire.— **en-tire′ty,** 1 en-tair′tı; 2 ĕn-tīr′tẏ, *n.* **1.** Entireness. **2.** That which is entire; whole.

en-ti′tle, 1 en-tai′tl; 2 ĕn-tī′tl, *vt.* [-TLED; -TLING.] To give a right or title to; authorize to receive; name; style.

en′ti-ty, 1 en′tı-tı; 2 ĕn′tĭ-tẏ, *n.* [-TIESᶻ, *pl.*] Anything that exists; a real thing or substance.

en-tomb′, 1 en-tūm′; 2 ĕn-tọm′, *vt.* To place in a tomb; bury.— **en-tomb′ment,** *n.*

en″to-mol′o-gy, 1 en″to-mol′o-jı; 2 ĕn″-to-mŏl′o-ġẏ, *n.* The branch of zoology that treats of insects.— **en″to-mo-log′i-cal,** *a.* **en″to-mo-log′icǂ.**— **en″to-mol′o-gist,** *n.* A student of entomology.

en′tr′acte, 1 añ′trăkt; 2 äñ′trăct, *n.* The time between two acts of a play or opera, or a musical interlude then performed.

en′trails, 1 en′trĕlz; 2 ĕn′trâlṣ, *n. pl.* The internal parts, especially the intestines, of an animal.

en-trance′, 1 en-trans′; 2 ĕn-trȧnç′, *vt.* [EN-TRANCED′ᵗ, EN-TRANC′ING.] **1.** To transport; enrapture. **2.** To throw into a trance.— **en-trance′ment,** *n.*

en′trance, 1 en′trans; 2 ĕn′tranç, *n.* **1.** The act, right, or power of entering. **2.** A place or passage for entering.

en-trap′ᵗ, 1 en-trap′; 2 ĕn-trăp′, *vt.* To catch in or as in a trap; ensnare.

en-treat′ᵈ, 1 en-trīt′; 2 ĕn-trēt′, *vt.* To solicit earnestly; supplicate.— **en-treat′y,** *n.* [-IESᶻ, *pl.*] An earnest request; supplication.

en″trée′, 1 añ′trē′; 2 äñ′trē′, *n.* **1.** The act or privilege of entering; admission. **2.** A dish between courses.

en-trench′ᵗ, 1 en-trench′; 2 ĕn-trĕnch′, *v.* **I.** *t.* **1.** To protect, as by a trench. **2.** To make a trench or trenches in. **II.** *i.* To encroach; trespass. **in-trench′‡.**— **en-trench′ment,** *n.* The act of entrenching; a breastwork; defense; protection. **in-trench′mentǂ.**

en-trust′ᵈ, 1 en-trust′; 2 ĕn-trŭst′, *vt.* **1.** To give in trust. **2.** To place in charge. **in-trust′‡.**

en′try, 1 en′trı; 2 ĕn′trẏ, *n.* [EN′TRIESᶻ, *pl.*] **1.** The act of entering; entrance; enrolment. **2.** A place of entrance; a small hallway.

en-twine′, 1 en-twain′; 2 ĕn-twīn′, *vt. & vi.* To twine round; twine or twist together.

en-twist′ᵈ, 1 en-twist′; 2 ĕn-twĭst′, *vt.* To twist; intertwist.

e-nu′mer-ate, 1 ı-niū′mər-ĕt; 2 e-nū′mer-āt, *vt.* [-AT″EDᵈ; -AT″ING.] To name one by one; count.— **e-nu″mer-a′tion,** *n.* A counting; number; list.

e-nun′ci-ate, 1 ı-nun′sı-ĕt; 2 e-nŭn′çĭ-āt, *vt. & vi.* [-AT″EDᵈ; -AT″ING.] To articulate; utter; speak.— **e-nun″ci-a′tion,** *n.* 1 ı-nun″sı-ē′shən; 2 e-nŭn″çĭ-ā′shon, *n.* The utterance, or mode of utterance, of vocal sounds; definite statement.— **e-nun′ci-a-tiv**(eˢ, *a.* **e-nun′ci-a-to-ry‡.**

en-vel′op′, ⎱1 en-vel′əp; 2 ĕn-vĕl′op,
en-vel′ope‡, ⎰ *vt.* To surround as a wrapper; enclose.— **en-vel′op-ment,** *n.*

en′vel-ope, ⎱1 en′vel′op or en′vı′op;
en′vel-ope, ⎰ lŏp; 2 ĕn-vĕl′op, ĕn-vĕl′ŏp or ĕn′ve-lŏp, *n.* A wrapper of paper with gummed edges, as for enclosing a letter; any enclosing covering.

en-ven′om, 1 en-ven′əm; 2 ĕn-vĕn′om, *vt.* To poison; render vindictive.

en′vi-ous, 1 en′vı-us; 2 ĕn′vĭ-ŭs, *a.* Cherishing envy; characterized by envy. **-ly,** *adv.* **-ness,** *n.*— **en′vi-a-bl**(eᴾ, *a.* To be envied; desirable.— **en′vi-a-bly,** *adv.*

en-vi′ron, 1 en-vai′rən; 2 ĕn-vī′ron, *vt.* To enclose; surround.— **en-vi′ron-ment,** *n.* The act of environing; whatever environs; one's surroundings collectively.— **en-vi′rons,** 1 en-vai′rənz; 2 ĕn-vī′ronṣ, *n. pl.* The surrounding region; outskirts; suburbs.

en′voy, 1 en′vei; 2 ĕn′vŏy, *n.* A diplomatic agent below an ambassador; a messenger.

en′vy, 1 en′vı; 2 ĕn′vẏ. **I.** *vt. & vi.* [EN′-VIED, 1 en′vıd, 2 ĕn′vıd; EN′VY-ING.] To regard with envy; feel envy; covet; grudge. **2.** To admire and covet without ill will. **II.** *n.* [EN′VIESᶻ, *pl.*] **1.** Bitterness or hatred in view of what another enjoys; envious desire. **2.** A worthy longing for a good possessed by another, without ill will toward the possessor. **3.** An object of envy.

E-o′li-an, ⎱1 ī-ō′lı-ən; 2 e-ō′lĭ-an, *a.* **1.**
Æ-o′li-an, ⎰ Pertaining to Æolus, the god of the winds. **2.** [e-] Pertaining to the winds; produced, moved, or borne by the wind; aerial.— **e o l i a n harp,** e. **lyre,** a stringed instrument that gives forth musical sounds when exposed to a current of air.

Eolian Harp.

a, pegs; *b b, b b,* bridges; *c,* chords; *d d, d,* roses.

e′on, ⎱1 ī′ən; 2 ē′ŏn, *n.* An incalculable
æ′on, ⎰ period of time; an age; eternity.

ep′au-let, 1 ep′o-let; 2 ĕp′ạ-lĕt, *n.* A fringed shoulder-ornament of commis-

stoned officers: now rarely worn. **ep′au-
lette‡.**

e-phem′er-al, ⎫ 1 1-fem′ər-əl; 2 e-fĕm′er-al,
e-fem′er-al‡, ⎭ *a.* Living one day only, as
May=flies; hence, transitory.

eph′od, 1 ef′od; 2 ĕf′ŏd, *n.* A Jewish priestly
vestment.

ep′ic, 1 ep′ık; 2 ĕp′ĭe. **I.** *a.* Of, pertaining
to, or like an epic; heroic. **II.** *n.* A poem
celebrating in stately verse the achievements of heroes; a heroic poem.

ep′i-cure, 1 ep′ı-kiur; 2 ĕp′ĭ-eūr, *n.* One
given to dainty indulgence in the pleasures of the table.— **Ep″i-cu-re′an,** 1 ep′ı-
kiu-rī′ən; 2 ĕp′ĭ-eū-rē′an. **I.** *a.* **1.** Pertaining to the Greek philosopher Epicurus
or to his doctrine that pleasure is the chief
good. **2.** [e-] Of, pertaining to, or like an
epicure. **II.** *n.* **1.** A follower of Epicurus.
2. [e-] A pleasure=seeker; an epicure.

ep″i-dem′ic, 1 ep′ı-dem′ık; 2 ĕp′ĭ-dĕm′ie.
I. *a.* *Med.* Affecting many in a community at once. **II.** *n.* Wide=spread disease, excitement, influence, etc.

ep″i-der′mis, 1 ep′ı-dŭr′mıs; 2 ĕp′ĭ-dẽr′-
mis, *n.* The cuticle, or outer skin.

ep″i-glot′tis, 1 en ı-glŏt′ıs; 2 ĕp′ĭ-glŏt′is, *n.*
[-TI-DES‡, 1 -ı-dīz; 2 -ĭ-dēṣ, *pl.*] The leaf-
shaped lid that covers the larynx during
the act of swallowing.

ep′i-gram, 1 ep′ı-grȧm; 2 ĕp′ĭ-grăm, *n.* A
pithy saying or brief poem.— **ep″i-gram-
mat′ic, ep″i-gram-mat′i-cal,** *a.* Pertaining to or marked by epigram; witty; anti-
thetical.— **ep″i-gram-mat′i-cal-ly,** *adv.*

ep′i-lep-sy, 1 ep′ı-lep-sı; 2 ĕp′ĭ-lĕp-sy, *n.*
A chronic nervous disease characterized
by convulsions or fits.— **ep″i-lep′tic. I.** *a.*
Pertaining to or affected with epilepsy. **II.**
n. One affected with epilepsy.

ep′i-log, ⎫ 1 ep′ı-lŏg; 2 ĕp′ĭ-lŏg, *n.* The
ep′i-logue, ⎭ conclusion, as of a discourse,
poem, or play; a concluding speech.

e-piph′a-ny, 1 1-pif′ə-nı; 2 e-pĭf′a-ny, *n.*
1. [E-] A festival (Jan. 6) in commemo-
ration of the visit of the Magi to Bethle-
hem. **2.** Any bodily manifestation, as of
a deity.

e-pis′co-pal, 1 1-pıs′ko-pəl; 2 e-pĭs′eo-pal,
a. Of or pertaining to bishops; governed
by bishops.— **e-pis′co-pa-cy,** 1 1-pıs′ko-pa-
sı; 2 e-pis′eo-pa-cy, *n.* **1.** Government by
bishops. **2.** A bishop's office. **3.** The body
of bishops.— **E-pis′co-pa′lian,** 1 1-pıs′ko-
pēl′yən; 2 e-pis′eo-pāl′yan. **I.** *a.* **1.** Pertaining to the Protestant Episcopal Church.
2. [e-] Episcopal. **II.** *n.* **1.** A member of
the Protestant Episcopal Church. **2.** [e-]
An advocate of episcopacy.— **e-pis′co-pate,**
1 1-pıs′ko-pēt; 2 e-pis′eo-pāt, *n.* The office
of a bishop; a bishopric; the body of bishops.

ep′i-sode, 1 ep′ı-sōd; 2 ĕp′ĭ-sŏd, *n.* An
incidental story; incident.

e-pis′tle, 1 1-pis′l; 2 e-pĭs′l, *n.* A letter.
— **e-pis′to-la-ry,** 1 1-pıs′to-lē-rı; 2 e-pis′to-
lā-ry, *a.* Belonging or suitable to correspondence by letter.

ep′i-taph, ⎫ 1 ep′ı-tạf; 2 ĕp′ĭ-tȧf, *n.* An in-
ep′i-taf‡, ⎭ scription, as on a tomb, in
memory of the dead.

ep′i-thet, 1 ep′ı-thet; 2 ĕp′ĭ-thĕt, *n.* A
descriptive phrase or word, good or bad,
added to a noun.

e-pit′o-me, 1 1-pit′o-mı; 2 e-pĭt′o-me, *n.*
A summary.— **e-pit′o-mize** or **-mise,** *vt. &
vi.* [-MIZED; -MIZ′ING.] To make an epitome.

ep″i-zo-ot′ic, 1 ep′ı-zō-ŏt′ık; 2 ĕp′ĭ-zō-ŏt′-
ie, *n.* An epidemic disease of animals.
ep″i-zo′o-ty‡.

ep′och, 1 ep′ȧk; 2 ĕp′oe, *n.* An important
point or memorable period of history; era.

e′qua-ble, ⎫ 1 ī′kwə-bl; 2 ē′kwa-bl, *a.* Uni-
e″qua-bl‡, ⎭ form; regular; even; steady.
— **e″qua-bil′i-ty,** 1 ī′kwə-bil′ı-tı; 2 ē′kwa-
bil′i-ty, *n.* Evenness, as of temper or action.
e′qua-bl(e=ness‡.— e′qua-bly, *adv.*

e′qual, 1 ī′kwal; 2 ē′kwal. **I.** *vt.* [E′-
QUALED or E′QUALLED, E′QUALD‡; E′QUAL-
ING or E′QUAL-LING.] To be or become
equal to; make equal; equalize. **II.** *a.* **1.**
Exactly corresponding in magnitude or
value; neither greater nor less. **2.** Equable. **3.** Adequate. **4.** Equitable; just. **III.**
n. A person or thing equal to another;
one of the same rank. **-ly,** *adv.* **-ness,** *n.*—
e-qual′i-ty, 1 1-kwel′ı-tı; 2 e-kwạl′i-ty, *n.*
[-TIES‡, *pl.*] The state of being equal; exact
agreement; uniformity.— **e″qual-i-za′tion** or
-sa′tion, *n.* The act of equalizing.— **e′qual-
ize** or **-ise,** *vt.* [-IZED; -IZ′ING.] To make
equal.

e″qua-nim′i-ty, 1 ī″kwa-nim′ı-tı; 2 ē″-
kwa-nĭm′i-ty, *n.* Evenness of mind or
temper; composure; calmness.

e-qua′tion, 1 1-kwē′shən; 2 e-kwā′shon, *n.*
A proposition expressing the equality of
two quantities.— **e-quate′,** 1 1-kwēt′; 2 e-
kwāt′, *vt.* [E-QUAT′ED‡; E-QUAT′ING.] To
make equal; represent as equivalent; put
into the form of an equation.

e-qua′tor, 1 1-kwē′tɘr or -tɘr; 2 e-kwā′tor,
n. A great circle of a globe, as the earth,
midway between the poles.— **e″qua-to′ri-
al,** 1 ī″kwa-tō′ri-al; 2 ē″kwa-tō′ri-al, *a.*

eq′uer-ry, 1 ek′wɘr-ı; 2 ĕk′wer-y, *n.*
[-RIES‡, *pl.*] An officer having charge of
the horses of a royal household who also attends the sovereign.

e-ques′tri-an, 1 1-kwes′trı-ən; 2 e-kwĕs′-
tri-an. **I.** *a.* Pertaining to horses or
horsemanship. **II.** *n.* One skilled in
horsemanship; a horseman.

1: ə = final; ı = habıt; ɑisle; ɑu = out; oıl; iū = feud; ℂhin; go; ŋ = sing; ℂhin, this.
2: wọlf, dọ; boͦok, boͦot; fμll, rμle, cūre, bŭt, bûrn; ŏil, bŏy; g̣o, g̣em; iŋk; thin, this.

e'qui-, 1 ī'kwı-; 2 ē'kwı-. A combining form signifying equal; as, *equi*distant.

e"qui-an'gu-lar, 1 ī'kwı-aŋ'giu-lẽr; 2 ē"-kwı-ăŋ'gū-lar, *a.* Having equal angles.

e"qui-dis'tant, 1 ī'kwı-dis'tənt; 2 ē"kwı-dĭs'tant, *a.* Situated at equal distances from a point or from each other.

e"qui-lat'er-al, 1 ī'kwı-lat'ẽr-əl; 2 ē"kwı-lăt'er-ăl, *a.* Having all the sides equal.

e"qui-li'bra-tor, 1 ī'kwı-lai'brē-tẽr; 2 ē"-kwı-lĭ'bra-tor, *n.* A device for establishing or restoring equilibrium, as in an aeroplane or dirigible balloon.

e"qui-lib'ri-um, 1 ī"kwı-lib'rı-um; 2 ē"kwı-lĭb'rĭ-ŭm, *n.* Even poise or balance.

e'quine, 1 ī'kwain *or* ī'kwın; 2 ē'kwīn *or* ē'kwin, *a.* Of, pertaining to, or like a horse.

e"qui-nox, 1 ī'kwı-nɔks; 2 ē'kwı-nŏks, *n.* One of two points at which the sun crosses the equator, when the days and nights are equal; also, the time of this crossing (about Mar. 21 and Sept. 22).— e"qui-noc'tial, 1 ī'kwı-nɔk'shal; 2 ē"kwı-nŏc'shal. **I.** *a.* Occurring at or pertaining to the equinox. **II.** *n.* **1.** A severe storm occurring at or near the equinox. **2.** The equator.

e-quip', 1 ı-kwip'; 2 e-kwĭp', *vt.* [E-QUIPPED[t], E-QUIPT[s]; E-QUIP'PING.] To furnish; fit out; dress; array.— e-quip'ment, *n.* The act of equipping, or the state of being equipped; a complete outfit.

eq'ui-page, 1 ek'wı-pij; 2 ĕk'wı-paġ, *n.* **1.** Equipment. **2.** A carriage, with its horses, attendants, etc.; retinue.

e"qui-poise, 1 ī'kwı-pɔiz; 2 ē'kwı-pŏiġ, *n.* **1.** Equality, as of weight and power; equilibrium. **2.** A counterpoise.

eq'ui-ty, 1 ek'wı-tı; 2 ĕk'wı-ty, *n.* [-TIES[z], *pl.*] Fairness; impartiality; equal justice. — eq'ui-ta-ble[e²], *a.* Impartial; just; fair. -ness, *n.*— eq'ui-ta-bly, *adv.*

e-quiv'a-lent, 1 ı-kwiv'ə-lent; 2 e-kwĭv'a-lĕnt. **I.** *a.* Equal in value, area, force, meaning, or the like. **II.** *n.* That which is equivalent.— e-quiv'a-lence, *n.* e-quiv'-a-len-cy‡.

e-quiv'o-cal, 1 ı-kwiv'o-kəl; 2 e-kwĭv'o-eal, *a.* Having a doubtful meaning; ambiguous; questionable. -ly, *adv.* -ness, *n.*— e-quiv'o-cate, 1 ı-kwiv'o-kēt; 2 e-kwĭv'o-eăt, *vi.* [-CAT"ED[d]; -CAT'ING.] To use ambiguous language with intent to deceive.— e-quiv"o-ca'tion, *n.* The act of equivocating.— e-quiv'o-ca"tor, *n.*— eq'ui-voke, eq'ui-voque, 1 ek'wı-vōk; 2 ĕk'wı-vōk, *n.* An equivocal term; a play upon words.

-er, *suffix.* Used (1) to form nouns of agency; as, mak*er*, knock*er*, pension*er*, etc.; (2) to form the comparative degree; as, larg*er*, long*er*; (3) to form frequentative and diminutive verbs; as, flutt*er* (from FLOAT).

e'ra, 1 ī'rə; 2 ē'ra, *n.* A period dating from a fixed epoch; as, the Christian *era*.

e-rad'i-cate, 1 ı-rad'ı-kēt; 2 e-răd'ĭ-eăt, *vt.* [-CAT"ED[d]; -CAT'ING.] To root out; extirpate.— e-rad"i-ca'tion, *n.*

e-rase', 1 ı-rēs'; 2 e-rās', *vt.* [E-RASED[t]; E-RAS'ING.] To obliterate, as by scraping out; efface.— e-ras'er, 1 ı-rēs'ẽr; 2 e-rās'er, *n.*— e-ra'sure, 1 ı-rē'ʒur; 2 e-rā'ʒhur, *n.* The act of erasing; anything erased.

ere, 1 ãr; 2 êr, *prep. & conj.* Sooner than; before; rather than.— ere"long', *adv.* Ere long; before long.

e-rect', 1 ı-rekt'; 2 e-rĕct'. **I**[d]. *vt.* To set upright; build; establish; exalt. **II.** *a.* Upright; vertical. -ly, *adv.* -ness, *n.*

e-rec'tion, 1 ı-rek'shən; 2 e-rĕe'shon, *n.* The act of erecting, or the state of being erected; a building or structure.

er'e-mite, 1 er'ı-mait; 2 ĕr'e-mīt, *n.* A hermit.

er'go-graph, 1 ūr'go-graf; 2 ĕr'go-gráf, *n.* An instrument used as an index of mental excitement, fatigue, etc.

er'mine, 1 ū̃r'mın; 2 ĕr'min, *n.* **1.** A weasel-like carnivore, especially in its winter dress of white, with black tail-tip. **2.** Its fur, used in Europe for the facings of official robes, as of judges; hence, the judicial office, or its ideal purity.
er'mins,

e-ro'sion, 1 ı-rō'ʒən; 2 e-rō'zhon, *n.* The wearing away of rocks, as by water.

Ermine. 1/8

e-rot'ic, 1 ı-rɔt'ık; 2 e-rŏt'ie, *a.* Amorous; amatory.

err, 1 ūr; 2 êr, *vi.* [ERRED, ERD[s]; ERR'ING.] To wander from the truth or right; mistake; sin.

er'rand, 1 er'ənd; 2 ĕr'and, *n.* A message or commission; also, the going to carry or accomplish it.

er'rant, 1 er'ənt; 2 ĕr'ant, *a.* Wandering; erratic.

er-ra'ta, *n.* Plural of ERRATUM.

er-rat'ic, 1 e-rat'ık; 2 e-răt'ie, *a.* Deviating from the wise, natural, or usual course; irregular; eccentric; wandering; straying. er-rat'i-eal.

er-ra'tum, 1 e-rē'tum; 2 ĕ-rā'tŭm, *n.* [-TA, *pl.*] An error, as in writing or printing.

er-ro'ne-ous, 1 e-rō'nı-us; 2 ĕ-rō'ne-ŭs, *a.* Marked by error; mistaken. -ly, *adv.* -ness, *n.*

er'ror, 1 er'ẽr; 2 ĕr'or, *n.* A mistake; fault; transgression.

erst, 1 ūrst; 2 ĕrst, *adv.* **1.** Formerly;

long ago; once. **2.** In the beginning.— **erst′while″,** *adv.*

e″ruc·ta′tion, 1 ĭ″rŭk-tē′shən; 2 ē″rŭc-tā′shon, *n.* The throwing off of gas from the stomach; belching.— **e-ruct′, e-ruc′tate,** *vt.*

er′u·dite, 1 er′u-dait; 2 ĕr′u-dīt, *a.* Learned; scholarly. **-ly,** *adv.* **-ness,** *n.*— **er″u·di′tion,** 1 er′u-dish′ən; 2 ĕr′u-dish′on, *n.* Complete and various scholarship.

e-rupt′d, 1 1-rupt′; 2 e-rŭpt′, *vt.* & *vi.* To burst or cause to burst forth.— **e-rup′tion, n. 1.** A bursting out, as of a volcano. **2.** That which bursts forth, as lava from a volcano. **3.** A breaking out, as in a rash.

e-rup′tive, 1 1-rup′tiv; 2 e-rŭp′tiv, *a.* Per- **e-rup′tivᵉ,** } taining or tending to eruption.

-ery, *suffix.* Denoting a business, place of business, etc.; as, confectionery.

er″y·sip′e·las, 1 er′1-sip′1-ləs; 2 ĕr″y-sĭp′e-las, *n.* An inflammatory disease of the skin.

es″ca′drille, 1 es″kä′drĭl′; ĕs″eä′drĭl′, *n.* [Fr.] A squadron of military aeroplanes.

es″ca·lade′, 1 es″kə-lēd′; 2 ĕs″ea-lād′. **I.** *vt.* [-LADᴇᴅᵈ; -LAD′ING.] To scale, as a wall. **II.** *n.* Passing of ramparts, etc., by scaling.

es″ca·la″tor, 1 es″kə-lē″tər *or* -ter; 2 ĕs″ea-lā″tor, *n.* A moving stairway.

es-cal′lop, *v.* & *n.* Same as SCALLOP.

es′ca·pade, 1 es′kə-pēd; 2 ĕs′ea-pād, *n.* A mischievous prank.

es-cape′, 1 es-kēp′; 2 ĕs-cāp′, *v.* [ES-CAPEDᵗ; ES-CAP′ING.] **I.** *t.* To flee and get away from. **II.** *i.* To succeed in getting away from something; also, to elude notice.

es-cape′, *n.* **1.** A successful flight; deliverance from some evil. **2.** Issue, as of a fluid; leakage.

es-cape′ment, 1 es-kēp′ment *or* -mənt; 2 ĕs-cāp′ment, *n.* **1.** A device used in timepieces for securing a uniform movement. **2.** The act of escaping.

es-chew′, 1 es-chū′; 2 ĕs-chu′, *vt.* To shun, as something unworthy.

es-cort′d, 1 es-kôrt′; 2 ĕs-eôrt′, *vt.* To accompany and guard; conduct; convoy.

Anchor Escapement of a Watch.

a. anchor; *l*, lever or fork; *lp,* impulse-pallet; *lp,* locking pallet; *r,* roller operating the balance - wheel; *s,* escape-wheel.

es′cort, 1 es′kôrt; 2 ĕs′eôrt, *n.* A guard accompanying a person or property in transit; an attendant; safe-guard; protection.

es″cri·toire′, 1 es″kri-twär′; 2 ĕs″eri-twär′, *n.* A secretary; writing-desk.

es′cu·lent, 1 es′kiu-lent; 2 ĕs′eū-lĕnt, *a.* Suitable for food; edible.

es-cutch′eon, 1 es-kuch′ən; 2 ĕs-eŭch′on, *n.* A heraldic shield.

Es′ki·mo, 1 es′ki-mō; 2 ĕs′ki-mō, *n.* [-MOS, *pl.*] One of the American natives of northern North America: also used adjectively. **Es′ki·mau‡; Es′qui·mau‡** [-MAUX, *pl.*].

e·soph′a·gus, 1 1-sof′ə-gus; 2 e-sŏf′a-gŭs, **œ·soph′a·gus,** } *n.* The tube through which food passes from the mouth to the stomach; the gullet.

es″o·ter′ic, 1 es″o-ter′ik; 2 ĕs″o-tĕr′ie, *a.* Confined to a select circle; confidential.— **es″o·ter′i·cal·ly,** *adv.*

es·pal′ler, 1 es-pal′yər; 2 ĕs-păl′yer, *n.* A trellis on which to train small fruits.

es·pe′cial, 1 es-pesh′əl; 2 ĕs-pĕsh′al, *a.* Exceptional; noteworthy; special.— **es·pe′cial·ly,** *adv.* Preeminently; particularly.

es·pi′al, 1 es-pai′ə; 2 ĕs-pī′al, *n.* The action of a spy; a watching in secret.

es′pi·o·nage, 1 es′pi-o-nij; 2 ĕs′pi-o-nag, *n.* The practise of spying, as to secure military information; offensive surveillance.

es″pla·nade′, 1 es″plə-nēd′; 2 ĕs″pla-nād′, *n.* A level open space, as before a fortress, for promenading.

es·pouse′, 1 es-pauz′; 2 ĕs-pous′, *vt.* [ES-POUSED′; ES-POUS′ING.] **1.** To marry; engage or bestow in marriage. **2.** To become an advocate of, as a cause or claim.— **es·pou′sal,** 1 es-pauz′əl; 2 ĕs-pou′sal. **I.** *a.* Of or pertaining to a betrothal or a marriage. **II.** *n.* The act of espousing; marriage.

es·py′, 1 es-pai′; 2 ĕs-pī′, *v.* [ES-PIED′; ES-PY′ING.] **I.** *t.* To get sight of; discover; observe. **II.** *i.* To keep close watch.

Es′qui·mau, 1 es′ki-mō; 2 ĕs′ki-mō, *n.* Same as ESKIMO.

es·quire′, 1 es-kwair′; 2 ĕs-kwīr′, *n.* **1.** A title of office or courtesy. **2.** [Eng.] A landed proprietor; squire. **3‖.** A knight's attendant. [tempt.

es·say′, 1 e-sē′; 2 ĕ-sā′, *vt.* To try; attempt.

es′say, 1 es′ē; 2 ĕs′ā, *n.* **1.** A composition on some special subject. **2.** An endeavor; attempt; effort.— **es′say·ist,** 1 es′ē-ist; 2 ĕs′ā-ist, *n.* **1.** A writer of essays. **2.** One who makes an attempt.

es′sence, 1 es′ens; 2 ĕs′ĕnç, *n.* **1.** The intrinsic nature of anything. **2.** Being or existence; a spiritual being. **3.** A solution, as of an essential oil in alcohol. **4.** Perfume; scent.— **es·sen′tial,** 1 e-sen′shal; 2 ĕ-sĕn′shal. **I.** *a.* Pertaining to the essence of anything; real; requisite; necessary. **II.** *n.* That which is essential or characteristic; a necessary element.— **es·sen′tial·ly,** *adv.*

es·tab′lish‡, 1 es-tab′lish; 2 ĕs-tăb′lish, *vt.*

To fix firmly; prove; verify; ratify; sanction. **-er,** *n.*— **es-tab'lish-ment,** *n.* The act of establishing; that which is established; a residence or place of business; an organization.

es''ta'mi'net', 1 es''tä'mĭ'nĕ'; 2 ĕs'tä'mĭ'ng' *n.* [Fr.] A drinking-place; wine-shop.

es-tate', 1 es-tēt'; 2 ĕs-tāt', *n.* **1.** One's entire property; a tract of land; property left after death. **2.** Condition; rank; dignity; means. **3.** A class or order in a state.

es-teem', 1 es-tīm'; 2 ĕs-tēm'. **I.** *vt.* **1.** To prize. **2.** To hold in estimation; value; estimate. **II.** *n.* Favorable opinion, as that based on moral worth.

es-thet'ic, 1 es-thĕt'ık; 2 ĕs-thĕt'ie, *a.* Pertaining to or loving the beautiful; artistic.— **es-thet'ics,** 1 es-thĕt'ıks; 2 ĕs-thĕt'ics, *n.* The science of beauty and taste; knowledge of the fine arts.

es'ti-ma-ble, 1 es'tı-mə-bl; 2 ĕs'tı-ma-es'ti-ma-bl**,** bl, *a.* **1.** Deserving of esteem. **2.** Capable of being estimated.— **es'ti-ma-bly,** *adv.*

es'ti-mate, 1 es'tı-mēt; 2 ĕs'tı-māt. **I.** *vt.* [-MAT'ED⁴; -MAT'ING.] To form a general opinion thereon; compute; rate. **II.** 1 es'tı-mēt; 2 ĕs'tı-māt, *n.* A valuation based on opinion.— **es-ti-ma'tion,** 1 es'tı-mē'shən; 2 ĕs'tı-mā'shon, *n.* **1.** The act of estimating; an estimate. **2.** Esteem; regard.

es-trange', 1 es-trēnj'; 2 ĕs-trānj', *vt.* [ES-TRANGED'; ES-TRANG'ING.] To make strange or distant; alienate. **-ment,** *n.*

es-tray', 1 es-trē'; 2 ĕs-trā', *n.* *Law.* A stray or unclaimed domestic beast.

es'tu-a-ry, 1 es'chu-[*or* -tiu-]ē-rı; 2 ĕs'chu-[*or* -tū-]ā-ry, *n.* [-RIES²; *pl.*] A wide lower part of a tidal river.

-et. A diminutive suffix.

é''ta''gère', 1 ē'tɑ'ȝär'; 2 ę'tä'zhĕr', *n.* An ornamental stand with shelves; a whatnot.

etchᵗ, etch; 2 ĕch, *vt.* & *vi.* To engrave **ech**ʳ, by means of a corrosive fluid.— **etch'ing,** 1 ech'ıŋ; 2 ĕch'ing, *n.* **1.** A process of engraving by means of the biting of an acid. **2.** An impression from an etched plate.

e-ter'nal, 1 ı-tūr'nəl; 2 e-tẽr'nal, *a.* Having neither beginning nor end; everlasting; timeless; pertaining to eternity.— **e-ter'nal-ly,** *adv.* Forever.

e-ter'ni-ty, 1 ı-tūr'nı-tı; 2 e-tẽr'nı-ty, *n.* [-TIES²; *pl.*] **1.** Infinite duration; endless time; immortality. **2.** That which is eternal or immortal.

e'ther, 1 ī'thər; 2 ē'ther, *n.* **1.** A colorless volatile liquid, used as an anesthetic. **2.**

A supposed medium filling all space, and transmitting the vibrations of light, heat, and electricity. **3.** The upper air.

e-the're-al, 1 ı-thī'rı-əl; 2 e-thē're-al, *a.* Having the nature of ether or air; light; airy; subtile; aerial.— **e-the're-al-ize** or **-ise,** *vt.* & *vi.* To make or become ethereal; spiritualize.— **e'ther-ize** or **-ise,** *vt.* To subject to the influence of ether.

eth'i-cal, 1 eth'ı-kəl; 2 ĕth'ı-cal, *a.* Pertaining or relating to ethics or morals.— **eth'i-cal-ly,** *adv.*

eth'ics, 1 eth'ıks; 2 ĕth'ies, *n.* The science of human duty; moral science; the principles of right action; also, a treatise on the science.

E''thi-o'pi-an, 1 ī''thı-ō'pı-an; 2 ē''thi-ō'pi-an. **I.** *a.* Pertaining to Ethiopia; African; negro. **II.** *n.* **1.** A negro. **2.** A native of Ethiopia, an ancient region south of Egypt, including modern Nubia, Abyssinia, etc. **Æ''thi-opt; Æ''thi-o'pi-an; E''thi-opt.**

et'i-quette'', 1 et'ı-ket''; 2 ĕt'i-kĕt', *n.* The usages of polite society.

é''tude', 1 ē'tüd'; 2 ę'tüd', *n.* A study; an exercise; a musical composition for practise.

et''y-mol'o-gy, 1 et'ı-mol'o-ȷı; 2 ĕt'y-mŏl'o-ġy, *n.* [-GIES²; *pl.*] **1.** That branch of philology which treats of the derivation of words; derivation, as of a word. **2.** The branch of grammar that treats of the parts of speech.— **et''y-mo-log'i-cal,** *a.* **et''y-mo-log'ic;** — **et''y-mo-log'i-cal-ly,** *adv.*— **et''y-mol'o-gist,** *n.* A student of etymology.

eu''ca-lyp'tus, 1 yū'kə-lip'tus; 2 yu''ca-lyp'tŭs, *n.* An evergreen tree of the myrtle family which grows, in Australia, to a height of 400 or 500 feet.

eu'cha-rist, 1 yū'kə-ıist; 2 yu'ca-rıst, *n.* **1.** The Lord's Supper; the holy sacrament; the communion of the body and blood of Christ. **2.** Hence, the bread and wine in the communion.— **eu''cha-ris'tic,** *a.* **eu''cha-rıs'tic-al‡.**

eu'chre, 1 yū'kər; 2 yu'ẽer. **I.** *vt.* [EU'-CHRED; EU'CHRING.] In the game of euchre, to check (an opponent); outwit; defeat. **II.** *n.* **1.** A game of cards played by from two to six persons. **2.** The act of euchring or of being euchred.

eu'lo-gy, 1 yū'lō-ȷı; 2 yu'lo-ġy, *n.* [-GIES², *pl.*] A discourse in praise of a person. **eu-lo'gi-un‡.**— **eu'lo-gist,** *n.* The author of a eulogy; one who speaks in high praise. — **eu''lo-gis'tic,** *a.* Laudatory. **eu''lo-gis'ti-cal‡.**— **eu''lo-gis'ti-cal-ly,** *adv.*— **eu'lo-gize,** *vt.* [-GIZED; -GIZ'ING.] To speak or write a eulogy upon. **eu'lo-gise‡.**

eu′nuch, 1 yū′nŭk; 2 yụ′nŭk, *n.* An Oriental palace official; a chamberlain.

eu′phe-mism, 1 yū′fĭ-mĭzm; 2 yụ′fe-mĭṣm, *n.* A mild expression for something disagreeable.— **eu″phe-mis′tic,** *a.*

eu′pho-ny, 1 yū′fō-nĭ; 2 yụ′fo-n␣, *n.* **1.** Agreeableness of sound. **2.** Well-sounding combination of words.— **eu-phon′ic,** 1 yu-fŏn′ik; 2 yu-fŏn′ie, *a.* Pertaining to euphony; euphonious.— **eu-pho′ni-ous,** 1 yu-fō′nĭ-us; 2 yu-fō′ni-ŭs, *a.* Characterized by euphony; well-sounding, as a word.

eu-re′ka, 1 yu-rī′kạ; 2 yụ-re′ka, *interj.* I have found (it): a cry of exultation over a discovery, said to have been uttered by Archimedes, on discovering how to find the amount of alloy in the crown of Hiero, tyrant of Syracuse.

Eu′rope, 1 yū′rŏp; 2 yụ′rop, *n.* A continent on the N. W. of the eastern hemisphere; 3,844,000 sq. m.

Eu″ro-pe′an, 1 yū″ro-pī′ạn; 2 yụ″ro-pē′an. **I.** *a.* Relating to or derived from Europe. **II.** *n.* One of a European race.

e-vac′u-ate, 1 ı̆-vak′yu-ēt; 2 e-văc′yu-āt, *v.* [-AT″ED^d; -AT″ING.] **I.** *t.* **1.** To withdraw from, as a fortress; vacate; make empty. **2.** To eject or discharge, as from the bowels. **II.** *i.* To pass or flow out.— **e-vac″u-a′tion,** 1 ı̆-vak″yu-ē′shạn; 2 e-văc″yu-ā′shon, *n.* The act of evacuating or that which is evacuated.

e-vade′, 1 ı̆-vēd′; 2 e-vād′, *vt.* [E-VAD″ED^d; E-VAD′ING.] To avoid by artifice; elude.

ev″a-nes′cent, 1 ev″a-nes′ent; 2 ĕv′a-nĕs′ent, *a.* Passing away, or liable to pass away, gradually; fading; fleeting.— **ev″a-nes′cence,** *n.*

e-van′gel, 1 ı̆-van′jel; 2 e-văn′ğĕl, *n.* Good news; a gospel.— **ev″an-gel′i-cal. I.** *a.* Pertaining to the gospel or to its fundamental doctrines; spiritually minded. **II.** *n.* One who holds evangelical doctrines. **ev″an-gel′ic‡.— ev″an-gel′i-cal-ly,** *adv.* **e-van′gel-ism,** *n.* Zeal in spreading the gospel.— **e-van′gel-ist,** *n.* **1.** A traveling revivalist. **2.** One of the four writers of the Gospels.

e-vap′o-rate, 1 ı̆-vap′o-rēt; 2 e-văp′o-rāt, *vt. & vi.* [-RAT″ED^d; -RAT′ING.] To turn into vapor, as by heat; dry; pass off like vapor.— **e-vap″o-ra′tion,** *n.* The act or process of evaporating.— **e-vap′o-ra″tor,** *n.* An apparatus for drying fruits, etc.

e-va′sion, 1 ı̆-vē′zhạn; 2 e-vā′zhon, *n.* The act, means, or result of evading; equivocation; subterfuge.— **e-va′sive(e⁵,** *a.* Tending or seeking to evade; marked by evasion. **-ly,** *adv.* **-ness,** *n.*

eve, 1 īv; 2 ēv, *n.* **1.** The evening before a festival; evening or time immediately pre-

ceding any event. **2.** [Poet.] Evening.

e′ven, 1 ī′vn; 2 ē′vn. **I.** *vt. & vi.* To make or become even or level; balance. **II.** *a.* **1.** Free from inequalities; level; uniform; equal. **2.** Divisible by 2 without remainder. **III.** *n.* [Archaic or Poet.] Evening; eve. **IV.** *adv.* To a like degree; at the very time; fully; quite; so far as; evenly. **-ly,** *adv.* **-ness,** *n.*— **e′ven-tide″,** *n.* Evening.

eve′ning, 1 īv′nı̆ŋ; 2 ēv′ning, *n.* The closing part of the day.

e-vent′, 1 ı̆-vent′; 2 e-věnt′, *n.* **1.** Anything that happens. **2.** The result of any action. **3.** A contingent occurrence. **4.** One incident in a series, as of games.— **e-vent′ful,** *a.* Attended or characterized by important events; momentous.

e-ven′tu-al, 1 ı̆-ven′chu-al *or* -tiu-al; 2 e-věn′chu-al *or* -tū-al, *a.* Pertaining to or being a result; ultimate; final.— **e-ven′tu-al-ly,** *adv.* Ultimately; finally.— **e-ven′tu-ate,** *vi.* [-AT″ED^d; -AT′ING.] To result; turn out; happen.

ev′er, 1 ev′er; 2 ĕv′er, *adv.* **1.** At any time; in any case; in any degree; at all. **2.** Under all circumstances; always; perpetually.— **ev′er-green″,** **I.** *a.* Green throughout the year. **II.** *n.* A tree or plant always green.— **ev′er-last′ing. I.** *a.* Lasting forever; eternal. **-ly,** *adv.* **-ness,** *n.* **II.** *n.* **1.** Past or future endless duration; eternity. **2.** [E-] The one who is eternal; God.— **ev′er-more″,** *adv.* During all time; always.

ev′er-glade, 1 ev′er-glēd″; 2 ĕv′er-glād″, *n.* A grass-covered tract of swamp land.

eve′ry, 1 ev′rı̆ *or* ev′er-ı̆; 2 ĕv′ry *or* ĕv′er-y. **I.** *a.* Each, as of a number; all taken one by one. **II.** *pron.* Every one; each.— **eve′ry-bod″y,** *n.* Every person; people in general.— **eve′ry-day″,** *a.* Suitable for every day; ordinary; usual.— **eve′ry-thing,** *n.* Each one of a number of things; all that exists; something supremely important.— **eve′ry-where″,** *adv.* At or in every place.

e-vict′d, 1 ı̆-vikt′; 2 e-vĭet′, *vt.* To dispossess by legal process; oust; expel.— **e-vic′tion,** *n.* The act of evicting; forcible ejectment.

ev′i-dence, 1 ev′ı̆-dens; 2 ĕv′i-dĕnç, *n.* Fact on which a judgment is based; proof.— **ev′i-dent,** *a.* Plain; manifest; obvious. **-ly,** *adv.*— **ev″i-den′tial,** *a.* Of the nature of evidence; indicative. **-ly,** *adv.*

e′vil, 1 ī′vl; 2 ē′vl. **I.** *a.* Morally bad; wicked; injurious; calamitous; sorrowful. **II.** *n.* Wicked conduct; moral depravity; affliction; calamity. **III.** *adv.* In an evil manner.

e-vince′, 1 ı̆-vins′; 2 e-vĭnç′, *vt.* [E-VINCED′t; E-VINC′ING.] To show plainly; prove.

1: ə = *final*; ı = *habit*; aisle; au = *out*; oil; iū = *feud*; chin; go; ŋ = *sing*; thin, this.
2: wolf, do; book, boot; full, rule, cure, but, burn; oil, boy; go, gem; ink; thin, this.

e·vis′cer·ate, 1 ɪ-vɪs′ər-ēt; 2 e-vĭs′er-āt, *vt.* [-AT″ᴇᴘᵈ; -AT′ING.] To disembowel.— **e·vis′′- cer·a′tion,** *n.*

e·voke′, 1 ɪ-vōk′; 2 e-vōk′, *vt.* [E-VOKED′ᵗ; E-VOK′ING.] To call forth or out.

ev″o·lu′tion, 1 ev″o-liū′shən; 2 ĕv″o-lū′- shon, *n.* The act of evolving; development.

e·volve′, } 1 ɪ-volv′; 2 e-vŏlv′, *vt. & vi.*
e·volv′ᵉ, } [E-VOLVED′, E-VOLVD′ᵈ; E-VOLV′- ING.] To unfold; develop.

ewe, 1 yū; 2 yu, *n.* A female sheep.

ew′er, 1 yū′ər; 2 yu′er, *n.* A wide-mouthed water-pitcher.

ex-, *prefix.* Out; out of; off; beyond: used also with privative and intensive force. Prefixed to a word denoting office, it indicates one who formerly occupied the position; as, *ex-*President.

ex·act′, 1 egz-akt′; 2 ĕgz-ăkt′. Iᵈ. *vt.* To compel the payment of; extort; demand. **II.** *a.* Perfectly conformed to a standard; precise; accurate; methodical.— **ex·act′- ing,** *pa.* Making unreasonable demands; taxing.— **ex·ac′tion,** 1 egz-ak′shan; 2 ĕgz-ăe′shon, *n.*— **ex·act′ly,** *adv.*— **ex·act′ness,** *n.* **ex·act′i·tude‡.**

ex·ag′ger·ate, 1 egz-aj′ər-ēt; 2 ĕgz-ăg′er-āt, *vt. & vi.* [-AT″ᴇᴘᵈ; -AT′ING.] To represent extravagantly; make statements beyond fact.— **ex·ag″ger·a′tion,** *n.* The act of exaggerating; overstatement; hyperbole.

ex·alt′ᵈ, 1 egz-ôlt′; 2 ĕgz-ạlt′, *v.* **I.** *t.* To raise; magnify; glorify; elate. **II.** *i.* To produce exaltation; promote.— **ex″al·ta′- tion,** *n.* Elevation; promotion; elation.

ex·am′ine, } 1 egz-am′in; 2 ĕgz-ăm′in, *vt.*
ex·am′inᵉ, } [-IN(E)ᴅˢ, -IN-ING.] To investigate critically; scrutinize; test; question.— **ex·am″i·na′tion,** *n.*

ex·am′ple, } 1 egz-am′pl; 2 ĕgz-ăm′pl, *n.* **1.**
ex·am′plᵉ, } A copy; sample; illustration; precedent; warning. **2.** A problem to be solved.

ex·as′per·ate, 1 egz-as′pər-ēt; 2 ĕgz-ăs′- per-āt, *vt.* [-AT″ᴇᴘᵈ; -AT′ING.] To anger; enrage; intensify; inflame.— **ex·as″per·a′- tion,** *n.* Extreme anger; rage; intensity.

ex′ca·vate, 1 eks′ca-vēt; 2 ĕks′ea-vāt, *vt.* [-VAT″ᴇᴘᵈ; -VAT′ING.] To dig into; make by digging out; remove or uncover by digging.— **ex″ca·va′tion,** *n.* A digging out; a cavity; hollow.— **ex′ca·va″tor,** *n.*

ex·ceed′ᵈ, } 1 eks-sīd′; 2 ĕk-çēd′, *vt.* To go
ex·ceed′ˢ, } beyond; surpass.— **ex·ceed′ing,** *pa.* Greater than usual; surpassing.— **ex·ceed′ing·ly,** *adv.* Extremely; remarkably.

ex·cel′, 1 eks-sel′; 2 ĕk-çĕl′, *vt. & vi.* [EX-CELLED′, EX-CELD′ˢ; EX-CEL′LING.] To be superior to; be more excellent than; be or do more or better; surpass.— **ex′cel·lence,** *n.*

Possession of eminently good qualities; a superior trait.— **ex′cel·len·cy,** *n.* [-CIESᶻ, *pl.*] **1.** An honorary title. **2.** Excellence.— **ex′- cel·lent,** *a.* Having good qualities in a high degree. **-ly,** *adv.*

ex·cel′si·or, 1 ek-sel′sɪ-ɵr; 2 ĕk-çĕl′si-ŏr. **I.** *a.* Still higher; ever upward. **II.** *n.* A packing-material composed of long, fine wood-shavings.

ex·cept′, 1 ek-sept′; 2 ĕk-çĕpt′. Iᵈ. *vt. & vi.* To leave out; omit; object; take exception (to). **II.** *prep.* With the exception of. **III.** *conj.* If not that; unless.— **ex·cept′ing,** *prep. & conj.* Except.

ex·cep′tion, 1 ek-sep′shan; 2 ĕk-çĕp′shon, *n.* The act of excepting, or that which is excepted; exclusion.— **ex·cep′tion·a·bl(eᵖ,** *a.* Open to exception or objection.— **ex·cep′- tion·al,** *a.* Unusual or uncommon; superior.

ex·cerpt′, 1 ek-sûrpt′; 2 ĕk-çẽrpt′, *n.* An extract, as from a book.

ex·cess′, 1 ek-ses′; 2 ĕk-çĕs′, *n.* **1.** That which passes the due limit. **2.** Inordinate gratification. **3.** The amount by which one thing is greater than another; overplus.— **ex·ces′siv(eˢ,** *a.* Exceeding the proper amount or degree; immoderate; extreme. **-ly,** *adv.* **-ness,** *n.*

ex·change′, 1 eks-chēnj′; 2 ĕks-chāng′, *v.* [EX-CHANGED′; EX-CHANG′ING.] **I.** *t.* To part with in return for something else; barter; interchange. **II.** *i.* To be given or received in exchange; make an exchange.

ex·change′, *n.* **1.** The act of exchanging or that which is exchanged; barter; trade. **2.** Change. **3.** Any transfer of value, as by credits, drafts, etc., or the rate at which it is effected. **4.** A place where merchants effect exchanges. **5.** A central telephone-office.— **ex·change″a·bil′i·ty,** *n.*— **ex·change′a·bl(eᵖ,** 1 eks-chēnj′a-bl; 2 ĕks-chāng′a-bl, *a.* That may be exchanged.

ex·cheq′uer, 1 eks-chek′ər; 2 ĕks-chĕk′er, *n.* **1.** The treasury of a state; finances; pecuniary resources. **2.** [E-] [Eng.] A court of revenue.

ex·cise′¹, 1 ek-saiz′; 2 ĕk-çīẓ′, *vt.* [EX-CISED′; EX-CIS′ING.] To cut out or off.— **ex·ci′sion,** *n.* The removal of a part; extirpation.

ex·cise′², *vt.* To tax.— **ex·cis′a·ble,** *a.*

ex·cise′, *n.* A charge levied upon commodities, especially upon liquors.

ex·cite′, 1 ek-sait′; 2 ĕk-çīt′, *vt.* [EX-CIT′ᴇᴘᵈ; EX-CIT′ING.] To agitate; stimulate; bring about, as by stimulating.— **ex·cit″- a·bil′i·ty,** *n.*— **ex·cit′a·bl(eᵖ,** *a.* Easily excited.— **ex·cit′ant,** 1 ek-soi′tənt; 2 ĕk-çī′tant. **I.** *a.* Adapted to excite or stimulate. **II.** *n.* A

stimulant.— **ex-cite'ment,** n. 1. The act of exciting, or that which excites. 2. The state of being excited. **ex″ci-ta'tion‡.— ex-cit'er,** n.

ex-claim', 1 eks-klēm'; 2 ĕks-elām', vt. & vi. To cry out abruptly or with passion. — **ex″cla-ma'tion,** n. Sudden outcry; an emphatic expression; an interjection.— **ex-clam'a-to-ry,** a. 1. Of the nature of exclamation. 2. Given to the use of exclamation.

ex-clude', 1 eks-klūd'; 2 ĕks-clud', vt. [EX-CLUD′ED‡; EX-CLUD′ING.] To shut out; debar; reject; eject.— **ex-clu'sion,** 1 eks-klū'ʒen; 2 ĕks-clu'zhon, n. The act of excluding, or the state of being excluded; that which is excluded.— **ex-clu'sive,** 1 eks-klū'siv; 2 ĕks-clu'siv, a. Excluding or tending to exclude as from social relations. **-ly,** adv. **-ness,** n.

ex-cog'i-tate, 1 eks-kej'i-tēt; 2 ĕks-cŏg'i-tāt, vt. [-TAT′ED‡; -TAT′ING.] To think out carefully; devise.— **ex-cog″i-ta'tion,** n.

ex″com-mu'ni-cate, 1 eks″ke-miū'ni-kēt; 2 ĕks-cŏ-mū'ni-eāt, vt. [-CAT′ED‡; -CAT′-ING.] To cut off from church-membership and communion; exclude; expel. — **ex″com-mu″ni-ca'tion,** n. The act of excommunicating, or the state of having been excommunicated.

ex-co′ri-ate, 1 eks-kō'ri-et; 2 ĕks-eō'ri-āt, vt. [-AT′ED‡; -AT′ING.] To strip off the skin or covering of; abrade; gall.— **ex-co″ri-a'tion,** n.

ex'cre-ment, 1 eks'kri-ment; 2 ĕks'cre-mĕnt, n. Refuse matter discharged from an animal body; feces; dung.

ex-cres'cence, 1 eks-kres'ens; 2 ĕks-erĕs'ĕnç, n. An unnatural outgrowth.

ex-crete', 1 eks-krīt'; 2 ĕks-erēt', vt. [EX-CRET′ED‡; EX-CRET′ING.] To throw off, as waste matter.— **ex-cre'tion,** n. The act of excreting; matter excreted.

ex-cru'ci-ate, 1 eks-krū'shi-et; 2 ĕks-eru'çhi-āt, vt. [-AT′ED‡; -AT′ING.] To inflict extreme pain upon; torture.— **ex-cru″ci-a'tion,** n.

ex-cul'pate, 1 eks-kul'pēt; 2 ĕks-eŭl'pāt, vt. [-PAT′ED‡; -PAT′ING.] To exonerate; excuse.— **ex″cul-pa'tion,** n.— **ex-cul'pa-to-ry,** a.

ex-cur'sion, 1 eks-kūr'shan; 2 ĕks-eûr'shon, n. 1. A short journey; trip for pleasure. 2. A body of excursionists. 3. A digression.— **ex-cur'siv(e‡,** a. Wandering; desultory; digressive. **-ly,** adv.

ex-cuse', 1 eks-kiūz'; 2 ĕks-eūş', vt. [EX-CUSED′; EX-CUS′ING.] 1. To exculpate; vindicate; justify. 2. To overlook; pardon. 3. To release from a service, demand, or claim.— **ex-cus'a-ble,** a. Admitting of excuse or pardon; justifiable.— **ex-cus'a-bly,** adv.

ex-cuse', 1 eks-kiūs'; 2 ĕks-eūs', n. 1. A

plea in extenuation of an offense, neglect, or failure; apology. 2. The act of excusing. 3. A reason for excusing.

ex'e-crate, 1 eks'i-krēt; 2 ĕks'e-erāt, vt. [-CRAT′ED‡; -CRAT′ING.] To curse; detest. — **ex'e-cra-bl(e‡,** a. Worthy of execration; abominable.— **ex'e - cra - bly,** adv.— **ex″e-cra'tion,** n. 1. The act of execrating; imprecation. 2. An accursed thing.

ex'e-cute, 1 eks'i-kiūt; 2 ĕks'e-eūt, v. [-CUT′ED‡; -CUT′ING.] I. t. 1. To effect; accomplish. 2. To put to death according to legal sentence. II. i. To accomplish something.— **ex-ec'u-tor,** 1 egz-ek'yu-ter; 2 ĕgz-ĕe'yu-tôr, n. One appointed to execute a will.— **ex-ec'u-to-ry,** a. Pertaining to execution; executive; administrative. — **ex-ec'u-trix,** n. A woman who serves as an executor.

ex″e-cu'tion, 1 eks′i-kiū'shan; 2 ĕks'e-eū'shon, n. The act of executing; performance; enforcement; signing, as of a deed; capital punishment; a judicial writ. — **ex″e-cu'tion-er,** n. One who executes a death sentence.

ex-ec'u-tive, 1 egz-ek'yu-tiv; 2 ĕgz-ĕe'-
ex-ec'u-tivs, 1 yu-tiv. I. a. Having the power or capacity of executing; administrative. II. n. A person or body that executes the law.

ex″e-ge'sis, 1 eks'i-jī'sis; 2 ĕks'e-ġē'sis, n. [-SES, 1 -sīz; 2 -sĕs, pl.] Explanation or interpretation, as of the Bible.— **ex″e-get'ic,** 1 eks'i-jet'ik; 2 ĕks'e-ġĕt'ie, a. Pertaining to exegesis; expository; explanatory. **ex″e-get'i-cal‡.**

ex-em'plar, 1 egz-em'plər; 2 ĕgz-ĕm'plar, n. A model; pattern; example; specimen. — **ex'em-pla-ry,** 1 egz'em-plĕ-ri; 2 ĕgz'ĕm-plā-ry, a. Serving as a model or a warning.

ex-em'pli-fy, 1 egz-em'phi-fai; 2 ĕgz-ĕm'-pli-fī, vt. [-FIED, 1 -faid, 2 -fīd; -FY′ING.] To explain by example; illustrate.— **ex-em″pli-fi-ca'tion,** n. The act of exemplifying; an example.

ex-empt', 1 egz-empt'; 2 ĕgz-ĕmpt'. I d. vt. To free or excuse, as from some obligation. II. a. Free; clear; excused. III. n. One who is exempt.— **ex-emp'tion,** 1 egz-emp'shan; 2 ĕgz-ĕmp'shon, n. Freedom; immunity.

ex'er-cise, 1 eks'er-saiz; 2 ĕks'er-çīş, v. [-CISED; -CIS′ING.] I. t. 1. To exert; train by practise. 2. To make anxious. II. i. To take exercise.

ex'er-cise, n. Activity; practise; training.

ex-ert'd, 1 egz-ūrt'; 2 ĕgz-ērt', vt. To put forth, or put in action, as force or faculty. — **ex-er'tion,** 1 egz-ūr'shan; 2 ĕgz-ēr'shon, n. Vigorous action; a strong effort.

1: ə = final; ɪ = habit; aisle; au = out; oil; iū = feud; chin; go; ŋ = sing; thin, this.
2: wolf, do; book, boot; full, rule, cure, but, burn; oil, boy; go, gem; ink; thin, this.

ex′e-unt, 1 eks′ı-unt; 2 ĕks′e-ŭnt. Plural of EXIT, he goes out; a stage direction.— **ex′e-unt om′nes,** all go off or out.

ex-hale′, 1 eks-hēl′; 2 ĕks′e-hāl′, *vt.* & *vi.* [EX-HALED′; EX-HAL′ING.] To breathe forth; send out, as vapor or perfume; emit; evaporate.— **ex″ha-la′tion,** *n.* A breathing out; anything exhaled; a vapor; fume.

ex-haust′d, 1 egz-ōst′; 2 ĕgz-ȧst′, **I.** *vt.* **1.** To draw off entirely; empty; drain. **2.** To reduce; weaken. **3.** To examine or discuss to the uttermost. **II.** *n.* That which is exhausted or drawn off.— **ex-haust′i-bl**(er̷, *a.*— **ex-haus′tion,** 1 egz-ōs′chȧn; 2 ĕgz- s′chon, *n.* The act of exhausting, or the state of being exhausted; weakness; fatigue.— **ex-haus′tiv**(es̷, *a.* Exhausting; tending to exhaust. **-ly,** *adv.*— **ex-haust′less,** *a.* Inexhaustible.

ex-hib′it, 1 egz-ib′it; 2 ĕgz-ĭb′ıt, **I**d. *vt.* & *vi.* To present to view; show; display. **II.** *n.* Any object or objects exhibited; a document or object marked for use as evidence.— **ex″hi-bi′tion,** 1 eks′ı-bish′ȧn; 2 ĕks′ı-bish′on, *n.* **1.** The act of exhibiting; display. **2.** Anything exhibited; a show.— **ex-hib′it-or,** *n.* One who exhibits. **ex-hib′it-er‡.**

ex-hil′a-rate, 1 egz-il′ȧ-rēt; 2 ĕgz-ĭl′a-rāt, *vt.* [-RAT″ED**d**; -RAT′ING.] To enliven; cheer; stimulate.— **ex-hil′a-rant. I.** *a.* Causing exhilaration. **II.** *n.* Something that exhilarates.— **ex-hil″a-ra′tion,** *n.*

ex-hort′d, 1 egz-ōrt′; 2 ĕgz-ôrt′, *v.* **I.** *t.* To urge earnestly to well-doing; advise; admonish. **II.** *i.* To deliver or practise exhortation.— **ex″hor-ta′tion,** *n.* The act of exhorting; earnest advice; admonition.— **hort′er,** 1 egz-ōrt′ȧr; 2 ĕgz-ôrt′er, *n.*

ex-hume′, 1 eks-hiūm′; 2 ĕks-hūm′, *vt.* [EX-HUMED′; EX-HUM′ING.] To dig up; disinter.— **ex″hu-ma′tion,** *n.*

ex′i-gen-cy, 1 eks′ı-jen-sı; 2 ĕks′ı-gĕn-cy, [-CIES²; *pl.*] The state of being urgent; a pressing necessity.— **ex′i-gence‡.**— **ex′i-gent,** *a.* Demanding immediate aid or action; urgent; pressing.

ex′ile, 1 eks′ail; 2 ĕks′īl. **I.** *vt.* [EX′ILED; EX′IL-ING.] To banish. **II.** *n.* **1.** Banishment; expatriation. **2.** One driven or wandering away from country or home.

ex-ist′d, 1 egz-ist′; 2 ĕgz-ĭst′, *vi.* To be, or continue to be; live.— **ex-is′tence,** *n.* Being; life; anything that exists; an entity.— **ex-is′tent,** *a.* Having being or existence.

ex′it, 1 eks′it; 2 ĕks′ĭt, *n.* A way out; egress; departure.

ex′o-dus, 1 eks′o-dus; 2 ĕks′o-dŭs, *n.* **1.** A departure, as of a multitude, from any place. **2.** [E-] The departure of the Israelites from Egypt. **3.** [E-] The second book of the Old Testament.

ex′o-gen, 1 eks′o-jen; 2 ĕks′o-gĕn, *n. Bot.* A plant which increases in size by successive additions or rings on the outside of the wood, next the bark.— **ex-og′e-nous,** 1 eks-oj′ı-nus; 2 ĕks-ŏg′e-nŭs, *a.* **1.** Pertaining to or like an exogen. **2.** Originating or growing from without.

Exogen.

1. Vertical section of an exogenous stem. 2. Cross-section. (Letters apply to both figures.) *s*, pith; *m*, medullary sheath; *h*, heart-wood, representing the rings of growth of three successive years (1, 2, 3); *s*, sapwood; *c*, cambium layer; *b*, bark.

ex-on′er-ate, 1 egz-on′ȧr-ēt; 2 ĕgz-ŏn′er-āt, *vt.* [-AT″ED**d**; -AT′ING.] **1.** To vindicate from accusation. **2.** To free, as from a responsibility.— **ex-on″er-a′tion,** *n.*

ex-or′bi-tance, 1 egz-ōr′bı-tȧns; 2 ĕgz-ôr′bi-tanc, *n.* Excessiveness; extravagance. — **ex-or′bi-tant,** *a.* Excessive, as a price or charge; extravagant. **-ly,** *adv.*

ex′or-cise, 1 eks′er-saiz; 2 ĕks′ôr-çīs, *v.* [-CISED; -CIS′ING.] **I.** *t.* To cast out (an evil spirit). **II.** *i.* To use or practise exorcisms.— **ex′or-cism,** 1 eks′er-sizm; 2 ĕks′ôr-çism, *n.* The act of exorcising evil spirits.— **ex′or-cist,** *n.*

ex-or′di-um, 1 egz-ōr′dı-um; 2 ĕgz-ôr′di-ŭm, *n.* [-UMS² or -A, *pl.*] An introduction of a discourse; prelude.

ex″o-ter′ic, 1 eks″o-ter′ik; 2 ĕks′o-tĕr′ie, *a.* Belonging to the outside world; opposed to *esoteric.* **ex″o-ter′i-cal‡.**

ex-ot′ic, 1 eks-ot′ik; 2 ĕks-ŏt′ie. **I.** *a.* Of foreign origin. **II.** *n.* Something not native, as a plant.

ex-pand′d, 1 eks-pand′; 2 ĕks-pănd′, *vt.* & *vi.* To enlarge; swell; spread out. — **ex-panse′,** 1 eks-pans′; 2 ĕks-pâns′, *n.* That which lies spread out; a vast continuous area.— **ex-pan″si-bil′i-ty,** *n.*— **ex-pan′si-bl**(er̷, *a.*— **ex-pan′si-bly,** *adv.*— **ex-pan′sion,** *n.* The act of expanding; increase; enlargement.— **ex-pan′siv**(es̷, *a.* Capable of enlarging; causing or marked by expansion; broad. **-ly,** *adv.* **-ness,** *n.*

ex-pa′ti-ate, 1 eks-pē′shı-ēt; 2 ĕks-pā′shi-āt, *vi.* [-AT″ED**d**; -AT′ING.] To give full and diffuse statement; discuss at length. — **ex-pa″ti-a′tion,** *n.*

ex·pa′tri·ate, 1 eks-pē′trı-ēt; 2 ĕks-pā′-tri-āt, *vt.* [-AT″ED^d; -AT″ING.] To banish. **— ex·pa″tri·a′tion,** *n.*

ex·pect′^d, 1 eks-pekt′; 2 ĕks-pĕet′, *vt.* To look forward to as probable; anticipate; look for; rely upon; require.**— ex·pec′tan·cy,** 1 eks-pek′tan-sı; 2 ĕks-pĕe′tan-çy, *n.* The act or state of expecting; expectation. **ex·pec′tance‡.— ex·pec′tant,** 1 eks-pek′-tǝnt; 2 ĕks-pĕe′tant. **I.** *a.* Looking forward in expectation. **II.** *n.* One who is anticipating confidently.**— ex″pec·ta′tion,** *n.* **1.** The act of looking confidently for something future; expectancy. **2.** Something expected; a hopeful prospect, as of wealth: often plural.

ex·pec′to·rate, 1 eks-pek′to-rēt; 2 ĕks-pĕe′to-rāt, *vt. & vi.* [-RAT″ED^d; -RAT″ING.] To cough up and spit forth; spit.**— ex·pec′to·rant. I.** *a.* Relating to expectoration. **II.** *n.* A medicine to promote expectoration.**— ex·pec″to·ra′tion,** *n.* The act of expectorating; matter expectorated.

ex·pe′di·ent, 1 eks-pī′dı-ent; 2 ĕks-pē′di-ĕnt. **I.** *a.* Suitable under the circumstances; advantageous; advisable. **II.** *n.* That which promotes an end; resource.**— ex·pe′di·en·cy,** *n.* The quality of being expedient; the principle of utility or self-interest. **ex·pe′di·ence‡.— ex·pe′di·ent·ly,** *adv.*

ex′pe·dite, 1 eks′pı-dait; 2 ĕks′pe-dīt, *vt.* [-DIT″ED^d; -DIT″ING.] To hasten; quicken; dispatch.**— ex″pe·di′tion,** 1 eks′pı-dish′ən; 2 ĕks′pe-dish′on, *n.* **1.** A journey, as of many persons; also, the body of persons journeying. **2.** The quality of being expeditious; speed; dispatch.**— ex″pe·di′tion·a·ry,** 1 eks′pı-dish′ən-ĕ-rı; 2 ĕks′pe-dish′on-ā-ry, *a.* Constituting an expedition; as, an American *expeditionary* force of troops.**— ex″pe·di′tious,** *a.* Accomplished with energy and dispatch; quick; speedy. **-ly,** *adv.* **-ness,** *n.*

ex·pel′, 1 eks-pel′; 2 ĕks-pĕl′, *vt.* [EX-PELLED′, EX-PELD′^s; EX-PEL′LING.] To drive out forcibly.

ex·pend′^d, 1 eks-pend′; 2 ĕks-pĕnd′, *vt. & vi.* To pay out; disburse.**— ex·pen′di·ture,** 1 eks-pen′dı-chur or -tiūr; 2 ĕks-pĕn′dı-chur or -tūr, *n.* The act of expending; outlay.

ex·pense′, 1 eks-pens′; 2 ĕks-pĕns′, *n.* The spending, as of money: money spent; outlay; cost.**— ex·pen′sive(e^s,** *a.* Involving great expense; costly. **-ly,** *adv.* **-ness,** *n.*

ex·pe′ri·ence, 1 eks-pī′rı-ens; 2 ĕks-pē′ri-ĕnç. **I.** *vt.* [-ENCED^t; -ENC-ING.] To undergo personally; feel. **II.** *n.* **1.** Knowledge derived from one's own action, perception, or endurance. **2.** Something undergone, enjoyed, etc.**— ex·pe′ri·enced,** 1 eks-pī′rı-enst; 2 ĕks-pē′ri-ĕnçt, *pa.* Taught by experience; practised; skilled.**— ex·pe″ri·en′tial,** *a.*

ex·per′i·ment, 1 eks-per′ı-ment *or* -mənt; 2 ĕks-pĕr′i-ment. **I^d.** *vi.* To make experiments; make a test or trial. **II.** *n.* An action designed as a test; a trial; essay; attempt.**— ex·per″i·men′tal,** *a.* Pertaining to or known by experiment or experience. **-ly,** *adv.*

ex·pert′, 1 eks-pūrt′; 2 ĕks-pĕrt′, *a.* Skilful through practise; dexterous; marked by skill.

ex′pert, 1 eks′pūrt; 2 ĕks′pĕrt, *n.* One who has special skill or knowledge; a specialist. **-ly,** *adv.* **-ness,** *n.*

ex′pi·ate, 1 eks′pı-ēt; 2 ĕks′pi-āt, *vt.* [-AT″ED^d; -AT″ING.] To atone for, as by suffering or restitution.**— ex′pi·a·bl(e^s,** *a.***— ex″pi·a′tion,** *n.* The act or means of expiating; atonement.**— ex′pi·a·to·ry,** *a.* Having the character of or offered in expiation.

ex·pire′, 1 eks-pair′; 2 ĕks-pīr′, *v.* [EX-PIRED′; EX-PIR′ING.] **I.** *t.* To breathe out; emit from the lungs. **II.** *i.* **1.** To send forth breath; die; perish. **2.** To terminate.**— ex″pi·ra′tion,** 1 eks′pı-rē′shən; 2 ĕks′pi-rā′shon, *n.* **1.** The natural termination of anything, as of a lease. **2.** A breathing out; death.

ex·plain′, 1 eks-plēn′; 2 ĕks-plān′, *vt. & vi.* To make plain or clear; interpret; elucidate.**— ex″pla·na′tion,** 1 eks′pla-nē′shan; 2 ĕks′pla-nā′shon, *n.* **1.** The act or means of explaining. **2.** Meaning; significance; sense.**— ex·plan′a·to·ry,** 1 eks-plan′a-to-rı; 2 ĕks-plăn′a-to-ry, *a.* Serving or tending to explain.

ex′ple·tive, } 1 eks′plı-tiv; 2 ĕks′ple-tĭv. **I.** **ex′ple·tiv^s,** } *a.* Added for emphasis; redundant. **II.** *n.* **1.** An interjection, often profane. **2.** A word or phrase serving merely to fill out.

ex′pli·cate, 1 eks′plı-kēt; 2 ĕks′pli-eāt, *vt. & vi.* [-CAT″ED; -CAT″ING.] To clear from obscurity or perplexity; explain clearly.**— ex′pli·cate,** *a.***— ex′pli·ca′tion,** *n.***— ex′pli·ca·tiv(e^s,** *a.* **ex′pli·ca·to·ry‡.**

ex·plic′it, 1 eks-plis′ıt; 2 ĕks-plĭç′it, *a.* Plainly expressed, or that plainly expresses. **-ly,** *adv.* **-ness,** *n.*

ex·plode′, 1 eks-plōd′; 2 ĕks-plŏd′, *vt. & vi.* [EX-PLOD′ED^d; EX-PLOD′ING.] **1.** To burst; drive out violently; flash up noisily, as gunpowder. **2.** To disprove utterly.

ex·ploit′, 1 eks-pleit′; 2 ĕks-ploit′. **I^d.** *vt.* To utilize selfishly, as workingmen. **II.** *n.* A heroic deed or act.**— ex″ploi·ta′tion,** *n.*

ex·plore′, 1 eks-plōr′; 2 ĕks-plŏr′, *vt. & vi.* [EX-PLORED′; EX-PLOR′ING.] To travel over, as new lands; scrutinize; make thorough search.**— ex″plo·ra′tion,** *n.* The act of exploring.**— ex·plor′er,** *n.*

ex-plo'sion, 1 eks-plō'zən; 2 ĕks-plō'zhon, *n.* The act of exploding; a sudden and violent outbreak.— **ex-plo'siv**(e^s. **I.** *a.* Pertaining to explosion; liable to explode. **II.** *n.* An explosive substance.

ex-po'nent, 1 eks-pō'nent; 2 ĕks-pō'nĕnt, *n.* **1.** One who or that which explains or expounds. **2.** *Alg.* A symbol indicating a power.

ex-port'^d, 1 eks-pōrt'; 2 ĕks-pôrt', *vt.* To carry or send away, as from one country to another.— **ex"por-ta'tion,** *n.* **1.** The act or practise of exporting. **2.** An exported commodity.— **ex-port'er,** *n.*

ex'port, 1 eks'pōrt; 2 ĕks'pôrt, *n.* The act of exporting, or that which is exported; merchandise sent from one country to another.

ex-pose', 1 eks-pōz'; 2 ĕks-pōs', *vt.* [EX-POSED'; EX-POS'ING.] **1.** To lay open; display; disclose. **2.** To place in a perilous situation; abandon to probable destruction.

ex"po-sé', 1 eks"po-zē'; 2 ĕks"po-sē', *n.* An undesirable or embarrassing disclosure or exposure.

ex"po-si'tion, 1 eks"po-zish'ən; 2 ĕks"po-sĭsh'on, *n.* **1.** A public exhibition. **2.** An explanation; commentary.— **ex-pos'i-tor,** *n.* One who expounds.— **ex-pos'i-to-ry,** *a.* Pertaining to exposition.

ex-pos'tu-late, 1 eks-pos'chu-[or -tiu-]lēt; 2 ĕks-pŏs'chu-[or -tū-]lāt, *vi.* [-LAT'ED^d; -LAT'ING.] To plead with a person against some action.— **ex-pos"tu-la'tion,** *n.*

ex-po'sure, 1 eks-pō'zur; 2 ĕks-pō'zhur, *n.* **1.** The act of exposing; an exposed state or situation. **2.** Outlook or aspect.

ex-pound'^d, 1 eks-paund'; 2 ĕks-pound', *vt.* To explain; interpret.— **ex-pound'er,** *n.*

ex-press', 1 eks-pres'; 2 ĕks-prĕs'. **I.** *vt.* **1.** To set forth; declare. **2.** To press out. **3.** To send by express. **II.** *a.* **1.** Set forth distinctly; explicit; plain; direct. **2.** Done or carried by express or with speed. **3.** Exactly like; very. **III.** *n.* **1.** A system of rapid transportation. **2.** A message; dispatch; also, a messenger bearing dispatches; a currier.— **ex-press'age,** 1 eks-pres'ɪj; 2 ĕks-prĕs'aġ, *n.* **1.** Amount charged for carrying by express. **2.** Things carried by express.— **ex-press'i-ble,** *a.*— **ex-press'ly,** *adv.*

ex-pres'sion, 1 eks-presh'ən; 2 ĕks-prĕsh'on, *n.* **1.** The act or mode of uttering or representing. **2.** That which is uttered. **3.** Aspect; look; looks. **4.** A pressing out. **-less,** *a.*— **ex-press'iv**(e^s, *a.* Conveying expression; full of meaning. **-ly,** *adv.* **-ness,** *n.*

ex-pul'sion, 1 eks-pul'shən; 2 ĕks-pŭl'shon, *n.* Forcible ejection.— **ex-pul'siv**(e^s, *a.* Tending to expel.

ex-punge', 1 eks-punj'; 2 ĕks-pŭng', *vt.* [EX-PUNGED'; EX-PUNG'ING.] To blot out; obliterate; efface; destroy.

ex'pur-gate, 1 eks'pur-gēt or eks-pūr'gēt; 2 ĕks'pûr-gāt or ĕks-pûr'gāt, *vt.* [-GAT'-ED^d; -GAT'ING.] To clear, as a book, of whatever is objectionable.— **ex"pur-ga'tion,** *n.*

ex'qui-site, 1 eks'kwɪ-zit; 2 ĕks'kwi-sĭt; **ex'qui-sit**^s, } **I.** *a.* **1.** Delicate; refined. delicately beautiful. **2.** Sensitive; fastidious. **3.** Intense. **II.** *n.* A dainty person; a fop; dandy. **-ly,** *adv.* **-ness,** *n.*

ex'tant, 1 eks'tant or eks-tant'; 2 ĕks'tant or ĕks-tănt', *a.* Still existing; living.

ex-tem'po-re, 1 eks-tem'po-rɪ; 2 ĕks-tĕm'po-re. **I.** *a.* Extemporaneous. **II.** *adv.* Without special preparation.— **ex-tem"po-ra'ne-ous,** 1 eks-tem"po-rē'nɪ-us; 2 ĕks-tĕm"po-rā'ne-ŭs, *a.* Done or made with little or no preparation; offhand; speaking or spoken without notes. **ex-tem'po-ra-ry‡. -ly,** *adv.*— **ex-tem'po-rize,** *vt.* & *vi.* [-RIZED'; -RIZ'ING.] To speak or compose offhand. **ex-tem'po-riseǂ.**— **ex-tem'po-riz"er** or **-ris"er,** *n.*

ex-tend'^d, 1 eks-tend'; 2 ĕks-tĕnd', *v.* **I.** *t.* **1.** To make larger; enlarge; prolong. **2.** To reach or stretch out. **II.** *i.* To reach; stretch.— **ex-ten'si-bil'i-ty,** *n.*— **ex-ten'si-bl**(e^r, *a.* That may be extended. **ex-ten'sil**(e^s‡.— **ex-ten'sion,** *n.* **1.** The act of extending; extent. **2.** An annex; addition. **3.** The property of occupying space. — **ex-ten'siv**(e^s, *a.* Extended widely in space, time, or scope. **-ly,** *adv.* **-ness,** *n.*

ex-tent', 1 eks-tent'; 2 ĕks-tĕnt', *n.* Amount or degree of extension; size; compass; reach.

ex-ten'u-ate, 1 eks-ten'yu-ēt; 2 ĕks-tĕn'yu-āt, *vt.* [-AT'ED^d; -AT'ING.] To palliate; make thin or thinner.— **ex-ten"u-a'tion,** *n.* Palliation.

ex-te'ri-or, 1 eks-tī'rɪ-ər or -ǝr; 2 ĕks-tē'ri-or. **I.** *a.* External; outside. **II.** *n.* The outside.

ex-ter'mi-nate, 1 eks-tūr'mɪ-nēt; 2 ĕks-tēr'mi-nāt, *vt.* [-NAT'ED^d; -NAT'ING.] To destroy; annihilate.— **ex-ter"mi-na'tion,** *n.* Annihilation; extirpation.— **ex-ter'mi-na"tor,** *n.*

ex-ter'nal, 1 eks-tūr'nǝl; 2 ĕks-tēr'nal. **I.** *a.* Outside; superficial. **II.** *n.* An exterior part; an outward form or symbol, as of religion.— **ex-ter'nal-ly,** *adv.*

ex-tinct', 1 eks-tiŋkt'; 2 ĕks-tĭŋet', *a.* Extinguished; disused; inactive; non‑existent.

1: ŭrtistic, **ärt; fat, fāre; fȧst; get, prey; hit, police; obey, gō; net, ôr; full, rūle; but, būrn.**
2: ärt, āpe, fȧt, fâre, fȧst, wha**t,** ǎ**ll; mē, gĕt, prey, fērn; hĭt, īce; ī=ē; ĩ=ē; gō, nŏt, ôr, won,**

— **ex-tinc'tion,** *n.* **1.** An extinguishing. **ex-tin'guish-ment‡.** **2.** Destruction; annihilation.

ex-tin'guish⁴, 1 eks-tiŋ'gwish; 2 ĕks-tiŋ'gwish, *vt.* To put out; quench; destroy.— **ex-tin'guish-a-bl**(e², *a.* — **ex-tin'guish-er,** *n.*

ex'tir-pate, 1 eks'tẽr-pēt; 2 ĕks'tir-pāt, *vt.* [-PAT ED⁴; -PAT'ING.] To root out or up; eradicate.— **ex'tir-pa'tion,** *n.* The act of extirpating; total removal.

ex-tol', 1 eks-tōl' *or* -tel'; 2 ĕks-tōl' *or* -tŏl', *vt.* [EX-TOLLED, EX-TOLD'S; EX-TOL'LING.] To praise in the highest terms; magnify.

ex-tort'⁴, 1 eks-tõrt'; 2 ĕks-tôrt', *v.* **I.** *t.* To obtain by compulsion; wring; wrest; also, to exact illegally. **II.** *i.* To practise extortion.— **ex-tor'tion,** *n.* Forcible or unjust exaction; something extorted.— **ex-tor'tion-a-ry,** *a.* — **ex-tor'tion-ate,** *a.* Characterized by extortion; oppressive.— **ex-tor'tion-er,** *n.*

ex'tra, 1 eks'trə; 2 ĕks'tra. **I.** *a.* More than usual; additional. **II.** *n.* Something beyond what is usual or required.

ex'tra-, *prefix.* Outside; beyond; besides; as, *extra*ordinary.

ex'tract'⁴, 1 eks-trakt'; 2 ĕks-trăct', *vt.* To draw or pull out; obtain; select; quote.— **ex-trac'tion,** *n.* **1.** The act of extracting. **2.** That which is extracted. **3.** Lineage.— **ex-trac'tor,** *n.*

ex'tract, 1 eks'trakt; 2 ĕks'trăct, *n.* **1.** Something extracted, as by distillation. **2.** A selection, as from a book.

ex'tra-dite, 1 eks'trə-dait; 2 ĕks'tra-dīt, *vt.* [-DIT'ED⁴; -DIT'ING.] To deliver up, as to another state or nation.— **ex''tra-dit'a-ble,** *a.* Liable to or warranting extradition.

ex''tra-di'tion, 1 eks''trə-dish'ən; 2 ĕks''tra-dīsh'on, *n.* The surrender of an accused person to the justice of another government.

ex-tra'ne-ous, 1 eks-trē'nɪ-ʊs; 2 ĕks-trā'ne-ŭs, *a.* Not intrinsic or essential; foreign. **-ly,** *adv.*

ex-traor'di-na-ry, 1 eks-trõr'dɪ-nē-rɪ *or* eks''trə-ôr'dɪ-nē-rɪ; 2 ĕks-trôr'dɪ-nā-ry *or* ĕks''tra-ôr'dɪ-nā-ry, *a.* Being beyond the ordinary; remarkable; special.— **ex-traor'di-na-ri-ly,** *adv.*

ex-trav'a-gant, 1 eks-trav'ə-gənt; 2 ĕks-trăv'a-gănt, *a.* Extreme; immoderate; fantastic; lavish in expenditure. **-ly,** *adv.* **-ness,** *n.* — **ex-trav'a-gance,** 1 eks-trav'ə-ganҫe; 2 ĕks-trăv'a-gănҫ, *n.* Lavish expendi-

ture; prodigality; irregularity; wildness. **ex-trav'a-gan-cy‡.**

ex-treme', 1 eks-trīm'; 2 ĕks-trēm'. **I.** *a.* Farthest; outermost; utmost; severe; excessive. **II.** *n.* The highest or utmost degree; farthest point or limit; extremity; first or last term of a proportion or series.— **ex-trem'lst,** *n.* — **ex-trem'i-ty,** *n.* [-TIES²*, pl.*] **1.** The farthest point; end; edge. **2.** The highest degree. **3.** Extreme distress or need. **4.** *pl.* Extreme measures. **5.** A hand, foot, etc.

ex'tri-cate, 1 eks'trɪ-kēt; 2 ĕks'trɪ-eāt, *vt.* [-CAT'ED⁴; -CAT'ING.] To liberate from entanglement.— **ex'tri-ca-bl**(e², *a.* — **ex''tri-ca'tion,** *n.*

ex-trin'sic, 1 eks-trɪn'sɪk; 2 ĕks-trĭn'sɪk, *a.* Non-essential; foreign.— **ex-trin'si-cal-ly,** *adv.*

ex-u'ber-ant, 1 eks-yū'bər-ənt; 2 ĕks-yy'ber-ant, *a.* Marked by plentifulness; producing copiously.— **ex-u'ber-ance,** *n.* — **ex-u'ber-an-cy‡.**

ex-ude', 1 eks-yūd; 2 ĕks-yyd', *vt. & vi.* [EX-UD'ED⁴; EX-UD'ING.] To discharge; trickle forth, as through pores.— **ex''u-da'tion,** *n.*

ex-ult'⁴, 1 egz-ult'; 2 ĕgz-ŭlt', *vi.* To rejoice in or as in triumph; take a lively delight.— **ex-ul'tant,** *a.* **1.** Rejoicing triumphantly. **2.** Denoting great joy.— **ex''ul-ta'tion,** *n.* The act or state of exulting; triumphant joy.— **ex-ult'ing-ly,** *adv.*

eye, 1 ai; 2 ī. **I.** *vt.* [EYED, EY'ING ey², *or* EYE'ING.] To look at fixedly; scrutinize. **II.** *n.* **1.** The organ of vision; sight. **2.** Anything that resembles the organ of sight, as in shape, place, or office; as, the *eye* of a needle.— **eye'-ball'',** *n.* The globe or ball of the eye. — **eye'brow'',** *n.* The arch over the eye, or its hairy covering.— **eye'lash'',** *n.* One of the stiff curved hairs growing from the edge of the eyelids.— **eye'less,** *a.* Lacking eyes; deprived of sight.— **eye'let,** *n.* A small hole or opening; a metal ring for protecting a hole in canvas, paper, etc.— **eye'lid'',** *n.* One of the fleshy curtains that can be closed over the eyes.— **eye'ser''vant,** *n.* One who does his duty only when watched.— **eye-ser-vice,** *n.* — **eye'sight'',** *n.* **1.** The power or sense of sight. **2.** Extent of vision; view.— **eye'sore'',** *n.* Anything that offends the eye.— **eye'tooth,** *n.* One of the upper canine teeth.— **eye-witness,** *n.* One who sees a thing with his own eyes or attests what he has seen.

ey'ry, *n.* An aerie. **ey'rie‡.**

F

F, f, 1 ef; 2 ĕf, *n.* [EFS, F's, or *F*s, 1 efs; 2 ĕfs, *pl.*] A letter: the sixth in the English alphabet.

fa'ble, 1 fē'bl; 2 fā'bl, *n.* A fictitious story embodying a moral, as where animals are the speakers; any fiction; legend; myth.

fab'ric, 1 fab'rik; 2 făb'rie, *n.* **1.** A woven, felted, or knitted material, as cloth, etc. **2.** A system; structure; edifice; workmanship; texture.— **fab'ri-cate,** *vt.* [-CAT⁻ ED⁴; -CAT'ING.] To form; make; build; forge.— **fab''ri-ca'tion,** *n.* The act of fabricating; structure; fabric; invention; falsehood.— **fab'ri-ca'tor,** *n.*

fab'u-lous, 1 fab'yu-lus; 2 făb'yu̇-lŭs, *a.* Belonging to fable; fictitious; mythical; false. **-ly,** *adv.* **-ness,** *n.*— **fab'u-list,** *n.* A composer of fables; one who falsifies or fabricates. [chief face of a building.

fa''çade', 1 fa̤''sād'; 2 fä̱''çäd',*n.* The front or

face, 1 fēs; 2 fāç. **I.** *vt. & vi.* [FACED⁻; FAC'ING.] **1.** To meet in front; confront; oppose. **2.** To cover; smooth the surface of. **II.** *n.* **1.** The front part of the head; the countenance. **2.** The surface; front; aspect; look; show; direct statement. **3.** Personal presence; sight. **4.** Effrontery; assurance. **5.** A grotesque expression.

fac'et, 1 fas'et; 2 făç'ĕt, *n.* A small face or surface, as on a diamond.

fa'ce-tious, 1 fa̤-si'shus; 2 fa-çē'shŭs, *a.* Witty; jocose; funny; humorous. **-ly,** *adv.* **-ness,** *n.*

fa'cial, 1 fē'shal; 2 fā'shal, *a.* Of, near, or affecting the face.

fac'ile, 1 fas'il; 2 făç'il, *a.* **1.** Easy; **fac'ilᴱ,** pliant; yielding; affable. **2.** Dexterous; skilful.

fa-cil'i-ty, 1 fa̤-sil'i-ti; 2 fa-çil'i-ty, *n.* [-TIES², *pl.*] **1.** Ease in doing; dexterity. **2.** Any aid or convenience: commonly in the plural.— **fa-cil'i-tate,** *vt.* [-TAT'ED⁴;-TAT'- ING.] To make easier or more convenient.

fac'ing, 1 fēs'iŋ; 2 fāç'iŋg, *n.* A covering or edging in front; outer coating.

fac-sim'i-le, 1 fak-sim'i-li; 2 făe-sĭm'i-lē, *n.* An exact copy or reproduction.

fact, 1 fakt; 2 făet, *n.* Anything that is, is done, or happens; an act; deed; truth; reality.

fac'tion, 1 fak'shan; 2 făe'shon, *n.* **1.** A party within a party; a cabal. **2.** Violent opposition, as to a government; dissension.— **fac'tious,** *a.* Given to or promoting faction; turbulent; partizan. **-ly,** *adv.* **-ness,** *n.*

fac-ti'tious, 1 fak-tish'us; 2 făe-tĭsh'ŭs, *a.* Artificial; conventional.

fac'tor, 1 fak'tər *or* -tẽr; 2 făe'tor, *n.* **1.** A commission merchant; agent. **2.** One of two or more quantities that, when multiplied together, produce a given quantity.

fac'to-ry, 1 fak'to-ri; 2 făe'to-ry, *n.* [-RIES², *pl.*] **1.** A manufactory. **2.** A business establishment in charge of factors in a foreign country.

fac-to'tum, 1 fak-tō'tum; 2 făe-tō'tŭm, *n.* A man of all work.

fac'ul-ty, 1 fak'ul-ti; 2 făe'ŭl-ty,*n.* [-TIES², *pl.*] **1.** Any special power of mind or body. **2.** The members of a profession, or the instructors in a school or college, collectively. [hobby.

fad, 1 fad; 2 făd, *n.* A passing fashion;

fade, 1 fēd; 2 făd, *vt. & vi.* [FAD'ED⁴; FAD'- ING.] To make or become pale, dull, or dim; disappear gradually.— **fade'less,** *a.* Unfading.

fæ'ces, *n. pl.* Same as FECES.

fag, 1 fag; 2 făg. **I.** *vt. & vi.* [FAGGED; FAGD²; FAG'GING.] To work as a fag; fatigue; tire out. **II.** *n* **1.** One who does menial service for another: a drudge.- **2.** [Soldiers' Slang.] A cigarette.- **fag'ᵉend'',** *n.* The frayed end, as of a rope; a remnant.

fag'ot, 1 fag'at; 2 făg'ot, *n.* A bundle of sticks, as used for fuel. **fag'got‡.**

Fah'ren-heit, 1 fä'ren-hait; 2 fä'rĕn-hīt, *a.* Designating that thermometer-scale in which the freezing-point of water is 32° and the boiling-point 212°: named from *Fahrenheit,* German physicist (1686-1736).

fa-ience', 1 fa-yäns'; 2 fä-yäṇç', *n.* A kind of majolica, usually highly decorated.

fail, 1 fēl; 2 fāl, *v.* **I.** *t.* To be wanting to; disappoint. **II.** *i.* To prove inadequate; waste away; decline; dwindle; be unsuccessful or insolvent.— **fail'ing,** *n.* A minor fault; foible; infirmity; failure.

fail'ure, 1 fēl'yur; 2 fāl'yu̇r, *n.* **1.** The act of failing, or the state of having failed; cessation; neglect; bankruptcy. **2.** That which fails; anything unsuccessful.

fain, 1 fēn; 2 fān. **I.** *a.* **1.** Reluctantly willing; content. **2.** Glad; rejoiced. **II.** *adv.* Gladly.

faint, 1 fēnt; 2 fānt. **I**d. *vi.* To swoon; become spiritless; despond; grow weak; fade; vanish. **II.** *a.* **1.** Despondent; timid; weak. **2.** Indistinct; feeble; dim. **III.** *n.* A swoon. **-ly,** *adv.* **-ness,** *n.*

fair, 1 fār; 2 fâr, *a.* **1.** Free from cloud or blemish; sunshiny; clear. **2.** Impartial; just; according to rule. **3.** Having light color or complexion. **4.** Pleasing; beautiful; flattering; plausible. **5.** Tolerable; passable. **6.** In the direction of a ship's course. **-ly,** *adv.* **-ness,** *n.*

fair, *n.* An exhibit of wares or products; a stated market.

fair, *adv.* In a fair manner; fairly.

fair′y, 1 fār′ı; 2 fâr′y, *n.* [-IESᶻ, *pl.*] An imaginary being of small size and supernatural power.—**fair′y-land″,** *n.* The fancied abode of the fairies.

faith, 1 fēth; 2 fāth, *n.* A firm belief; trust; a religious creed; honor; fidelity.—**faith′ful,** *a.* Trustworthy; accurate; truthful; firm in faith.—**faith′ful-ly,** *adv.*—**faith′ful-ness,** *n.*—**faith′less,** *a.* Unfaithful; untrustworthy; unbelieving. **-ly,** *adv.* **-ness,** *n.* [ascetic.

fa-kir′, 1 fə-kīr′; 2 fa-kīr′, *n.* An Oriental

fal′chion, 1 fōl′chən; 2 fạl′chon, *n.* A broad-bladed sword.

fal′con, 1 fō′kn *or* fal′kən; 2 fạ′en *or* fâl′con, *n.* A diurnal bird of prey; hawk.—**fal′con-er,** 1 fō′kn-ər; 2 fạ′en-er, *n.* One who breeds, trains, or hunts with falcons for sport.—**fal′con-ry,** 1 fō′kn-rı; 2 fạ′en-ry, *n.* The training or using of falcons for sport.

fall, 1 fōl; 2 fạl, *vi.* [FELL, 1 fel, 2 fĕl; FALL′EN; FALL′ING.] **1.** To descend by the force of gravity; drop; sink; decline; decrease; droop; die. **2.** To sin; err; apostatize. **3.** To pass or be transferred as by chance, inheritance, etc.; happen; come to pass.—**fall′en,** *a.* Overthrown; disgraced; ruined; dead.

Great-footed Falcon, or Duckhawk. ¹/₂₀

fall, *n.* **1.** The act of falling. **2.** A waterfall. **3.** Autumn. **4.** The rope of a tackle.

fal′la-cy, 1 fal′ə-sı; 2 fãl′a-çy, *n.* [-CIESᶻ, *pl.*] Delusion; error; false reasoning.—**fal-la′cious,** 1 fa-lē′shus; 2 fã-lā′shŭs, *a.* Deceitful; deceptive. **-ly,** *adv.* **-ness,** *n.*

fal′li-ble, } 1 fal′ı-bl; 2 fãl′ı-bl, *a.* Liable **fal′li-blᴾ,** } to error; misleading.—**fal′li-bil′i-ty,** *n.* **fal′li-bl(e-nessᴾ˟.—fal′li-bly,** *adv.*

fal′low, 1 fal′o; 2 fãl′o. **I.** *vt. & vi.* To make, keep, or become fallow. **II.** *a.* **1.** Left unseeded after being plowed; uncultivated; neglected. **2.** Pale-yellow or pale-red. **III.** *n.* Land left fallow; also, cleared woodland.—**fal′low deer,** a European deer, about 3 feet high.

false, 1 fōls; 2 fạls. **I.** *a.* Contrary to truth or fact; counterfeit; artificial; incorrect; not real; unfaithful; treacherous. **II.** *adv.* Falsely.—**false′hood,** *n.* Falseness; untruthfulness; a lie; counterfeit.—**false′ly,** *adv.*—**false′ness,** *n.* The quality or state of being false.—**fal″si-fi-ca′tion,** 1 fōl″sı-fı-kē′-shən; 2 fạl″sı-fı-câ′shon, *n.* The act or process of falsifying; a false statement.—**fal′si-fi″er,** *n.*—**fal′si-fy,** 1 fōl′sı-foı; 2 fạl′sı-fÿ, *vt. & vi.* [-FIED; -FY′ING.] To misrepresent; disprove; counterfeit; tamper with or pervert; lie.—**fal′si-ty,** 1 fōl′sı-tı; fạl′sı-ty, *n.* [-TIESᶻ, *pl.*] The quality of being false; a false statement, thing, or appearance.

fal-set′to, 1 fōl-set′o; 2 fạl-sĕt′o, *n.* The artificial tones of the voice, higher than the natural voice.

fal′ter, 1 fōl′tər; 2 fạl′ter, *vt. & vi.* To speak brokenly; act with weakness; waver; totter.—**fal′ter-ing-ly,** *adv.*

fame, 1 fēm; 2 fām, *n.* Public reputation; renown; rumor.—**famed,** *a.*

fa-mil′iar, 1 fə-mil′yər; 2 fa-mîl′yar. **I.** *a.* **1.** Well acquainted; thoroughly versed. **2.** Intimate; informal; forward; free. **3.** Well known; common; unaffected. **II.** *n.* **1.** A familiar friend. **2.** An attendant demon. **3.** A servant of the Inquisition. **-ly,** *adv.*—**fa-mil″i-ar′i-ty,** *n.* [-TIESᶻ, *pl.*] The state of being familiar; intimacy; unceremoniousness; freedom.—**fa-mil′iar-ize,** *vt.* [-IZED; -IZ′ING.] To make familiar; accustom

fam′i-ly, 1 fam′ı-lı; 2 fãm′i-ly. **I.** *a.* Of, belonging to, or suitable for a family. **II.** *n.* [-LIESᶻ, *pl.*] **1.** A group of persons, consisting of parents and their children; a household; house; line; clan; tribe; race. **2.** Distinguished or ancient lineage; descent. **3.** A class or group of like or related things.

fam′ine, } 1 fam′ın; 2 fãm′in, *n.* A wide-**fam′inˢ,** } spread scarcity of food; dearth.

fam′isht, 1 fam′ish; 2 fãm′ish, *vt. & vi.* To perish or cause to perish from hunger or thirst; starve.

fa′mous, 1 fē′mus; 2 fā′mŭs, *a.* Having fame; celebrated; renowned. **-ly,** *adv.*

fan, 1 fan; 2 fãn. **I.** *vt.* [FANNED, FANDˢ; FAN′NING.] To excite, as fire, by a fan; winnow, as grain. **II.** *n.* A light, flat implement or other device for agitating the air.

fa-nat'ic, 1 fə-nat'ık; 2 fă-năt'ĭe. *n.* One intemperate in zeal; a religious zealot. —**fa-nat'l-cal,** *a.* **fa-nat'ĭc‡.**—**fa-nat'ĭ-cal-ly,** *adv.*—**fa-nat'ĭ-cism,** *n.* The spirit or conduct of a fanatic; unreasonable zeal.

fan'cl-er, 1 fan'sı-ər; 2 făn'çĭ-er, *n.* **1.** A breeder and seller of birds and animals; an amateur. **2.** A dreamer.

fan'ci-ful, 1 fan'sı-ful; 2 făn'çĭ-ful, *a.* Proceeding from or produced by fancy; ideal; odd; unreal; visionary; whimsical. **-ly,** *adv.* **-ness,** *n.*

fan'cy, 1 fan'sı; 2 făn'çy. **I.** *vt.* & *vi.* [FAN'CIED; FAN'CY-ING.] To suppose; conceive in the fancy; have a notion of; form a fancy; imagine; take a liking to. **II.** *a.* Pertaining to or proceeding from fancy. **III.** *n.* [FAN'CIES‡, *pl.*] **1.** The power or act of forming mental images at random; imagination in its lower form. **2.** A visionary notion; vagary. **3.** A liking; that which one likes; a pet pursuit; hobby; fad.

fan-dan'go, 1 fan-dan'go; 2 făn-dăn'go, *n.* A Spanish dance.

fane, 1 fēn; 2 făn, *n.* A sanctuary; temple.

fang, 1 faŋ; 2 făng, *n.* A long tooth or tusk, as of a serpent; the root of a tooth. —**fanged,** *a.*

fan'ta-sĭ'a, 1 fan"ta-zi'ə *or* fan-tä'zı-ə; 2 făn"tă-ḡĭ'ä *or* făn-tä'ḡĭ-a, *n. Mus.* A fanciful composition of irregular form.

fan'tasm, 1 fan'tazm; 2 făn'tặṣm, *n.* **phan'tasm,** } An imaginary appearance; a fantom; fancy.

fan-tas'mal, 1 fan-taz'məl; 2 făn-tăḡ'-məl, *a.* Relating to or of the nature of a fantasm; unsubstantial; apparitional; imaginary; illusive. **fan-tas'mic‡; fan-tas'mĭ-cal‡.**—**fan-tas'mal-ly, fan-tas'mĭ-cal-ly,** *adv.*

fan-tas'tic, 1 fan-tas'tık; 2 făn-tăs'tĭe, *a.* **1.** Odd; grotesque; capricious; whimsical. **2.** Fanciful; illusory. **fan-tas'tĭ-cal‡.**—**fan-tas'tĭ-cal-ly,** *adv.*

fan'ta-sy, } 1 fan'tə-sı; 2 făn'ta-sy, *n.* **phan'ta-sy,** } [-SIES‡, *pl.*] Fancy; a fantastic notion, device, or design.

fan'tom, } 1 fan'təm; 2 făn'tom, *n.* **phan'tom,** } Something that exists only in appearance; an apparition; ghost; specter; a vision; an illusion; mirage: often used adjectively: as, a *fantom* ship.—**fan-tom'ic,** *a.* Denoting that which is in the nature of a fantom. **fan"tom-at'ĭc‡; fan-tom'ĭ-cal‡.**—**fan-tom'ĭ-cal-ly,** *adv.*

far, 1 fär; 2 fär. **I.** *a.* [FAR'THER *or* FUR'-THER; FAR'THEST *or* FUR'THEST.] Remote; distant; reaching a long way. **II.** *adv.* **1.** At a distance. **2.** To a great distance or degree; by very much. **3.** From afar.

far'ad, 1 far'ad; 2 făr'ăd, *n.* The unit of electromagnetic capacity: named from the English physicist *Faraday* (1791–1867).

farce, 1 färs; 2 färç, *n.* A short, grotesque comedy; something ridiculous; an absurd failure.—**far'cl-cal,** 1 fär'sı-kəl; 2 fär'çĭ-cal. *a.* Burlesque; absurd.

fare, 1 fär; 2 fär. **I.** *vi.* [FARED; FAR'ING.] To be in any state; get on; happen; turn out; be provided as regards food and drink. **II.** *n.* **1.** Passage-money. **2.** A passenger. **3.** Food and drink; diet; eatables.

fare'well', } 1 fär'wel'; 2 fär'wĕl'. **I.** *a.* **fare'wel'ʳ,** } Parting; closing. **II.** *n.* A parting salutation; a good-by; adieu; parting. **III.** *interj.* May you fare well: used only at parting.

fa-ri'na, 1 fə-ri'nə *or* -raı'nə; 2 fa-rī'na *or* -rī'na, *n.* A meal or flour made from Indian corn or other cereals.—**far'ĭ-na'ceous,** 1 far'ı-nē'shus; 2 făr'ĭ-nä'shŭs, *a.* **1.** Consisting or made of meal or flour. **2.** Containing or yielding starch.

farm, 1 fûrm; 2 färm, *v.* **I.** *t.* To cultivate as a farm. **2.** To contract for at a fixed percentage, as taxes, etc. **II.** *i.* To carry on farming.—**farm'er,** *n.* One who farms; an agriculturist.—**farm'ĭng,** *n.* The management of or labor on a farm; agriculture.

farm, 1 fûrm; 2 färm, *n.* A landed property devoted to agriculture. [game of cards.

far'o, 1 fär'o *or* fē'ro; 2 fär'o *or* fä'ro, *n.* A far'rı-er, 1 far'ı-ər; 2 făr'ĭ-er, *n.* One who shoes horses; a veterinarian.—**far'rĭ-er-y,** *n.* The business or shop of a farrier.

far'row, 1 far'o; 2 făr'o. **I.** *vt.* & *vi.* To give birth to; bring forth young: said of swine. **II.** *n.* A little pig, or a litter of pigs.

far'row, *a.* Not producing young during a given year, as a cow. [of FAR.

far'ther, far'thest, *a.* & *adv.*, *compar.* & *superl.*

far'thing, 1 fär'thıŋ; 2 fär'thing, *n.* One-fourth of an English penny.

fas'cl-nate, 1 fas'ı-nēt; 2 făs'ĭ-nāt, *vt.* & *vi.* [-NAT'ED‡; -NAT'ING.] To bewitch; enchant; captivate.—**fas"cĭ-na'tion,** *n.* The act of fascinating; enchantment; charm.

Fa-scis'ti, 1 fa-shĭs'ti; 2 fä-çhĭs'tĭ, *n. pl.* [It.] Members of a society formed to oppose Bolshevism in Italy.—**Fa'scism,** *n.* The doctrine of the Fascisti.

fash'ion, 1 fash'ən; 2 făsh'on. **I.** *rt.* To frame; mold; make; fit. **II.** *n.* **1.** The prevailing mode, as in dress. **2.** Manner; method; way. **3.** The make or shape of a thing; appearance; form.—**fash'ion-a-bl(eʳ,** *a.* Conforming to the fashion; approved by polite usage.—**fash'ion-a-bly,** *adv.*

fast[d], 1 fast; 2 fȧst, *vi.* To abstain from food.— **fast′ing**, *n.* Abstinence from food.

fast[1], *a.* Firm; secure; lasting; stedfast. — **fast**[1], *adv.* Firmly; securely; soundly.

fast[2], *a.* **1.** Swift; speedy. **2.** Ahead of the standard, as a timepiece. **3.** Dissipated; dissolute.— **fast**[2], *adv.* Rapidly; swiftly.

fast, *n.* Abstinence from food, or a period prescribed for it.— **fast′-day″,** *n.* A day set apart for religious fasting.

fast′en, 1 fas′n; 2 fȧs′n, *v.* **I.** *t.* To make fast; secure; attach; fix; bind. **II.** *i.* To take fast hold; cleave; cling.— **fast′en-er,** *n.* One who or that which fastens.— **fast′en-ing,** *n.* **1.** The act of making fast. **2.** That which fastens, as a bolt.

fas-tid′i-ous, 1 fas-tid′i-us; 2 făs-tĭd′ĭ-ŭs, *a.* Hard to please; overnice; squeamish. **-ly,** *adv.* **-ness,** *n.*

fast′ness, 1 fast′nes; 2 fȧst′nĕs, *n.* **1.** A fortress; stronghold. **2.** The state of being fast.

fat, 1 fat; 2 făt. **I.** *vt.* & *vi.* [FAT′TED[d]; FAT′TING.] To fatten. **II.** *a.* [FAT′TER; FAT′TEST.] **1.** Having much fat; corpulent; plump. **2.** Prosperous; thriving; lucrative. **III.** *n.* **1.** A white greasy compound found in animal or vegetable tissues. **2.** The richest part of anything. — **fat′ly,** *adv.*— **fat′ness,** *n.*

fa′tal, 1 fē′tal; 2 fā′tal, *a.* **1.** Bringing or connected with death or ruin; destructive; deadly; ominous. **2.** Fateful.— **fa′-tal-ism,** *n.* The doctrine that every event is predetermined and inevitable.— **fa′tal-ist,** *n.* A believer in fatalism.— **fa-tal′-i-ty,** 1 fa-tal′i-tı; 2 fa-tăl′ĭ-ty, *n.* [-TIES[z], *pl.*] **1.** A state of being fated; destiny. **2.** A fatal event; death.— **fa′tal-ly,** *adv.* Ruinously; mortally.

fate, 1 fēt; 2 fāt, *n.* **1.** Predetermined and inevitable necessity; destiny; fortune; lot; doom; death. **2.** *pl.* [F-] *Gr.* & *Rom. Myth.* The three goddesses supposed to control all destinies.— **fat′ed,** *pa.* Appointed by fate; destined; doomed.— **fate′ful,** *a.* **1.** Determined by fate; deciding destiny. **2.** Fatal.

fa′ther, 1 fā′thₑr; 2 fä′ther. **I.** *vt.* **1.** To adopt. **2.** To charge the responsibility for: with *on* or *upon.* **II.** *n.* **1.** The male parent of a child. **2.** Any male ancestor; forefather; patriarch. **3.** A venerable man; priest; clergyman; ancient church writer; author; founder. **4.** [F-] The Deity; God; the first person in the Trinity.— **fa′ther-hood,** *n.* The state or relation of a father.— **fa′ther-in-law″,** *n.* The father of one's spouse.— **fa′ther-land″,** *n.* The land of one's birth.— **fa′ther-less,** *a.* Not having a living father.— **fa′ther-li-**

ness, *n.*— **fa′ther-ly,** *a.* Of or pertaining to a father; paternal.

fath′om, 1 fath′ₑm; 2 fằth′om. **I.** *vt.* To find the depth of; sound; comprehend. **II.** *n.* [FATH′OMS or FATH′OM, *pl.*] A measure of length, 6 feet.— **fath′om-less,** *a.* Unfathomable.— **fath′om-a-bl(e[r], *a.*

fa-tigue′, 1 fa-tīg′; 2 fa-tĭg′. **I.** *vt.* [FA-TIGUED′; FA-TIGU′ING.] To weary; tire out. **II.** *n.* Exhaustion of strength by toil; weariness; also, labor.

fat′ling, 1 fat′lıŋ; 2 făt′ling. **I.** *a.* Fat; plump. **II.** *n.* A young animal fattened for slaughter.

fat′ten, 1 fat′n; 2 făt′n, *vt.* & *vi.* To make or become fat, plump, or productive; grow rich. — **fat′ten-er,** *n.*

fat′ty, 1 fat′ı; 2 făt′y, *a.* Fat; unctuous.

fat′u-ous, 1 fat′yu-us; 2 făt′yu-ŭs, *a.* Stubbornly foolish; idiotic; inane.— **fa-tu′i-ty,** 1 fa-tiū′i-tı; 2 fa-tū′ĭ-ty, *n.* Obstinate or conceited folly; imbecility.

fau′cet, 1 fɔ′set; 2 fa′çĕt, *n.* A spout with a valve, for drawing liquids through a pipe.

faugh, 1 fɔ; 2 fạ, *interj.* An exclamation of disgust.

fault, 1 fɔlt; 2 falt, *n.* **1.** An offense; failing; neglect. **2.** A defect; blemish; break in strata.— **fault′less,** *a.* Without fault. **-ly,** *adv.* **-ness,** *n.*— **fault′y,** *a.* Having faults; erroneous.— **fault′i-ly,** *adv.*— **fault′i-ness,** *n.*

faun, 1 fɔn; 2 fạn, *n.* *Rom. Myth.* A deity of the woods and herbs, half-human, with pointed ears and goats' feet.

fau′na, 1 fɔ′na; 2 fạ′na, *n.* [FAU′NÆ, 1 fɔ′nī, 2 fạ′nē, or FAU′NAS, 1 fɔ′naz, 2 fạ′nạs, *pl.*] The animals living within a given area or a stated period.

fa′vor, 1 fē′vₑr; 2 fā′vor. **I.** *vt.* **1.** To treat with favor; befriend; promote. **2.** [Colloq.] To look like. **II.** *n.* **1.** Kind feeling; a kind and helpful act; a token; a letter. **2**‖. Aspect; looks; beauty.— **fa′-vor-a-bl(e[r], *a.* Convenient; advantageous; friendly.— **fa′vor-a-bly,** *adv.*— **fa′vor-er,** *n.*

fa′vor-ite, 1 fē′vₑr-ıt; 2 fā′vor-it. **I.** *a.* **fa′vor-it**[8], } Favored; preferred. **II.** *n.* A person or thing particularly liked or favored.— **fa′vor-it-ism,** *n.* A favoring unfairly; partiality.

fawn, 1 fɔn; 2 fạn, *vi.* To show cringing fondness, as a dog.

fawn, *n.* A young deer; a light yellowish-brown color.

fay, 1 fē; 2 fā, *n.* A fairy.

F clef. *Mus.* The bass clef: an indication that F below the middle C is on the fourth line of the staff.

fe′al-ty, 1 fī′al-tı; 2 fē′al-ty, *n.* Fidelity, as of a vassal to his lord; loyalty.

1: ə = final; ı = habit; aisle; au = *out*; oil; iū = *feud*; ₡hin; go; ŋ = sing; ₡hin, this.
2: wolf, dǫ; bōōk, bōōt; fu̧ll, ru̧le, cūre, bu̧t, bûrn; oil, bǫy; ḡo, ḡem; iŋk; thin, this.

fear, 1 fĭr; 2 fēr. **I.** *vt. & vi.* To be apprehensive or afraid of; be fearful or afraid; venerate; revere. **II.** *n.* **1.** An emotion excited by threatening or apprehended evil; alarm; dread; terror. **2.** A cause of fear. **3.** Reverence; awe.— **fear'ful,** *a.* **1.** Afraid; apprehensive; timid. **2.** Inspiring fear; terrible. **-ly,** *adv.* **-ness,** *n.*— **fear'less,** *a.* Being without fear. **-ly,** *adv.* **-ness,** *n.*— **fear'some,** *a.* Fearful.

fea'si·ble, } 1 fĭ'zĭ-bl; 2 fē'sĭ-bl, *a.* That
fea'si·bl[P]**,** } may be done; practicable. — **fea''si·bil'i·ty,** *n.* Capability of being effected or accomplished; practicability.— **fea'si·bl(e-ness**[P]**,** *n.*— **fea'si·bly,** *adv.*

feast, 1 fĭst; 2 fēst. **I**[d]**.** *vt. & vi.* To give or enjoy a feast; delight. **II.** *n.* A sumptuous repast; great enjoyment; a festival.

feat, 1 fĭt; 2 fēt. *n.* A notable act or performance, as one showing skill, endurance, or daring.

feath'er, } 1 feth'er; 2 feth'er. **I.** *vt. & vi.*
feth'er[s]**,** } **1.** To cover or be covered with feathers. **2.** To turn the blade of (an oar) nearly horizontal in recovering. **II.** *n.* **1.** One of the fluffy growths that form the plumage of a bird. **2.** In rowing, the act of feathering.— **feath'ered,** *a.*— **feath'er-y,** *a.* Covered with or resembling feathers; light, soft, or fluffy.

fea'ture, 1 fĭ'chur *or* -tiur; 2 fē'chur *or* -tūr, *n.* **1.** Any part of the human face. **2.** *pl.* The face. **3.** A salient point.

feb'rile, } 1 feb'rıl *or* fī'brıl; 2 feb'rıl *or* fē'-
feb'ril[s]**,** } bril, *a.* Pertaining to fever.

Feb'ru·a·ry, 1 feb'ru-ē-rı; 2 feb'ru-ā-ry, *n.* The second month of the year, having twenty=eight or, in leap=years, twenty= nine days.

fe'ces, 1 fĭ'sēz; 2 fē'çēs, *n. pl.* Animal excrement. **fæ'cest,**— **fe'cal,** 1 fī'kal; 2 fē'cal, *a.*

fec'und, 1 fek'und *or* fī'kund; 2 fē̆'ŭnd *or* fē'cŭnd, *a.* Fruitful; prolific.— **fec'un·date,** *vt.* [-DATᴇD[d]; -DAT'ING.] To make fruitful; impregnate.— **fe·cun'di·ty,** *n.* Productiveness; fruitfulness.

fed, 1 fed; 2 fĕd, *imp. of* FEED, *v.*

fed'er·al, 1 fed'ər-əl; 2 fĕd'er-al, *a.* **1.** Pertaining to a union of states under one general government. **2.** Pertaining to a treaty, league, or covenant.— **fed'er·ate. I.** *vt. & vi.* To unite in a federation. **II.** *a.* Leagued; confederate; federal.— **fed''er·a'tion,** 1 fed'ər-ē'shan; 2 fĕd'ēr-ā'shon, *n.* The act of uniting under a federal government; a federated body; league.

fee, 1 fĭ; 2 fē, *vt.* [FEED; FEE'ING.] To pay a fee to; tip; hire; bribe.

fee[1]**,** *n.* **1.** A payment, as for professional service. **2.** A charge for some privilege.

fee[2]**,** *n.* **1.** *Law.* An estate of inheritance. **2.** *Feudal Law.* A fief. **3.** Ownership; property.— **fee simple,** an estate of inheritance free from condition.

fee'ble, } 1 fī'bl; 2 fē'bl, *a.* Lacking strength
fee'bl[P]**,** } or vigor; weak.— **fee'ble-ness,** *n.* — **fee'bly,** *adv.*

feed, 1 fĭd; 2 fēd. **I.** *vt. & vi.* [FED, 1 fed, 2 fĕd; FEED'ING.] To give food to; use for food; take food; eat; nourish; supply. **II.** *n.* Food, as of animals.

feel, 1 fĭl; 2 fēl, *v.* [FELT, 1 felt, 2 fĕlt; FEEL'ING.] **I.** *t.* **1.** To perceive, as by the touch. **2.** To be conscious of; be moved by. **II.** *i.* **1.** To have a (specified) feeling; as, to *feel* cold. **2.** To give a sensation to the touch; as, to *feel* rough. **3.** To be full of feeling.— **feel'er,** *n.* **1.** One who or that which feels. **2.** An antenna; tentacle. **3.** An indirect approach; a venture.— **feel'ing. I.** *pa.* Possessed of warm sensibilities; sympathetic; fervent; impassioned. **II.** *n.* Touch; sensation; sentiment; emotion; sensibility. **-ly,** *adv.*

feet, 1 fĭt; 2 fēt, *n.* Plural of FOOT.

feign, } 1 fēn; 2 fēn, *v.* **I.** *t.* **1.** To simulate;
fein[P]**,** } pretend. **2.** To invent or imagine. **II.** *t.* To dissimulate.— **feign'ed·ly,** *adv.*

feint, 1 fēnt; 2 fēnt. **I**[d]**.** *vi.* To make a feint. **II.** *n.* An appearance assumed to mislead; a deceptive movement; pretended attack.

feld'spar, } 1 feld'spär; 2 fĕld'spär, *n.* A
feld'spath[s]**,** } mineral consisting chiefly of aluminum and silica. **feld'spath"t.**

fe·lic'i·tate, } 1 fēn; 2 fe-lĭç'ĭ-tāt, *vt.*
fe·lic'i·tāt[P]**,** } [-TATᴇD[d]; -TAT'ING.] To wish joy or happiness to.— **fe·lic''i·ta'tion,** *n.*

fe·lic'i·ty, 1 fı-lis'ĭ-tı; 2 fe-lĭç'ĭ-ty, *n.* [-TIES[z], *pl.*] **1.** Happiness; content; bliss. **2.** Happy faculty; a clever expression; appropriateness.— **fe·lic'i·tous,** *a.* Marked by or producing felicity; happy; appropriate. **-ly,** *adv.*

fe'line, 1 fī'lıne; 2 fē'līn, *a.* Of or pertaining to cats; cat-like; sly.

fell, 1 fel; 2 fĕl, *vt.* **1.** To cause to fall; cut down. **2.** To finish with a fell (compare FELL[1], *n.*): said of seams.— **fell'er,** *n.*

fell, *imp. of* FALL, *v.*

fell, *a.* Fierce; cruel; inhuman; hideous.

fell[1]**,** *n.* A seam finished with a flat, smooth strip.

fell[2]**,** *n.* **1.** Hair. **2**‖**.** A hide or pelt.

fel'lah, 1 fel'a; 2 fĕl'ä, *n.* [FEL'LAHS[z] *or* FEL'-LAH-EEN'', *pl.*] A peasant; laborer, as in Egypt.

fel'loe, 1 fel'o; 2 fĕl'o, *n.* Same as FELLY.

fel'low, 1 fel'o; 2 fĕl'o. **I.** *a.* Joined; associated; associate. **II.** *n.* **1.** A person;

companion; counterpart; equal. **2.** An inferior or worthless person. **3.** The holder of a fellowship. **4.** A member of a society.— **fel'low-feel'ing,** 1 fel'o-fil'iŋ; 2 fĕl'o-fēl'ing, n. Sympathy.— **fel'low-ship,** 1 fel'o-ship; 2 fĕl'o-ship, n. **1.** The state of being a comrade or companion; friendly intercourse; communion. **2.** A band; company. **3.** A privileged position, as of a graduate in a college.

fel'ly, } 1 fel'i, fel'o; 2 fĕl'y, fĕl'o, n. [FEL'-
fel'loe, } LIES², FEL'LOES², pl.] A segment of the rim of a wooden wheel.

fel'on, 1 fel'ən; 2 fĕl'on. **I.** a. **1.** Obtained by felony. **2.** Wicked; criminal; treacherous. **II.** n. **1.** One who has committed a felony. **2.** Inflammation of the periosteum, as on a finger.

fel'o-ny, 1 fel'o-ny; 2 fĕl'o-ny, n. [-NIES², pl.] A grave or capital crime.— **fe-lo'ni-ous,** 1 fi-lō'ni-us; 2 fe-lō'ni-ŭs, a. Showing criminal purpose. **-ly,** adv. [FELDSPAR.

fel'spar", 1 fel'spär"; 2 fĕl'spär", n. Same as **felt,** 1 felt; 2 fĕlt, n. A fabric of matted wool, fur, or hair.

felt, imp. of FEEL, v.

fe-luc'ca, 1 fi-luk'ə; 2 fe-lŭc'a, n. A small, swift, Mediterranean coasting-vessel, propelled by lateen sails and by oars.

fe'male, 1 fī'mēl; 2 fē'māl. **I.** a. Of or pertaining to the sex that brings forth young or produces ova; feminine. **II.** n. A person or animal of the female sex.

fem'i-nine, } 1 fem'i-nin; 2 fĕm'i-nĭn, a.
fem'i-nin⁸, } Belonging to or characteristic of womankind; womanly.— **fem"i-nin'i-ty,** n. **fem'i-nine-ness‡.**

fem'o-ral, 1 fem'o-ral; 2 fĕm'o-ral, a. Pertaining to the thigh.

fen, 1 fen; 2 fĕn, n. A marsh; bog.

fence, } 1 fens; 2 fĕnç, v. [FENCED‡; FENC'-
fense⁵, } ING.] **I.** t. To enclose with a fence; secure; protect. **II.** i. **1.** To practise with a foil or sword; strive skilfully, as in debate. **2.** To provide a fence or defense.— **fenc'er,** n.— **fenc'ing,** n. **1.** The art of attacking and defending, as with a foil or sword. **2.** Material for fences; fences collectively.

fence, n. **1.** A structure, as of rails, for enclosing land; a defense; shield; bulwark. **2.** The use of weapons, as in fencing; repartee.

fend⁴, 1 fend; 2 fĕnd, v. **I.** t. To ward off; defend; guard. **II.** i. To fence; parry.— **fend'er,** 1 fend'ər; 2 fĕnd'ĕr, n. One who or that which defends or wards off; any protecting device, as a guard before an open fire.

Fe'ni-an, 1 fī'ni-ən; 2 fē'ni-an, n. One of

an Irish society seeking independence for Ireland.— **Fe'ni-an-ism,** n.

fen'nel, 1 fen'el; 2 fĕn'el, n. A tall aromatic European herb with yellow flowers.

fer-ment'ᵈ, 1 far-ment'; 2 fer-mĕnt', v. **I.** t. To produce fermentation in; agitate. **II.** i. To undergo fermentation; be in agitation.— **fer-ment"a-bil'i-ty,** n.— **fer-ment'a-bl**(eᵖ or **-i-bl**(eᵖ, a.

fer'ment, 1 fûr'ment; 2 fĕr'mĕnt, n. **1.** A substance productive of fermentation. **2.** Excitement or agitation.— **fer"men-ta'-tion,** n. **1.** A chemical decomposition of an organic compound, as of sugar in the production of alcohol. **2.** Commotion; excitement.— **fer-men'ta-tiv**(e⁵, a. Causing, or capable of causing, fermentation; fermenting.

fern, 1 fûrn; 2 fĕrn, n. A flowerless plant with feathery leaves.— **fern'y,** a. Abounding in or resembling ferns.

fe-ro'cious, 1 fur-ō'shus; 2 fe-rō'shŭs, a. Fierce; savage; rapacious. **-ly,** adv. **-ness,** n.— **fe-roc'i-ty,** 1 fi-ros'i-ti; 2 fe-rŏç'i-ty, n. [-TIES², pl.] The state or quality of being ferocious; fierce cruelty.

-ferous, suffix. Producing, containing, yielding; as, carboniferous.

fer'ret, 1 fer'et; 2 fĕr'ĕt. **I**ᵈ. vt. **1.** To find by keen search: with out. **2.** To hunt with ferrets. **II.** n. A weasel-like carnivore, usually white with red eyes: used to hunt rabbits, rats, etc.

Ferns.

fer'ri-age, 1 fer'i-ij; 2 fĕr'i-ag, n. The act of ferrying; conveyance by ferry; toll charged for ferrying.

fer-ru'gi-nous, 1 fe-rū'ji-nus; 2 fĕ-rụ'gi-nŭs, a. Of or like iron.

fer'rule, 1 fer'il or -ul; 2 fĕr'il or -ul, n. A metal ring or cap, as on the end of a cane.

fer'ry, 1 fer'i; 2 fĕr'y. **I.** vt. & vi. [FER'-RIED; FER'RY-ING.] To convey or go over water on a boat. **II.** n. [FER'RIES², pl.] A system of ferriage; boat for crossing a river or the like; place of crossing by boat.— **fer'ry-boat",** n.— **fer'ry-man,** n.

fer'tile, } 1 fûr'til; 2 fĕr'til, a. Producing,
fer'til⁸, } or capable of producing, abundantly; fruitful; plentiful.— **fer'til**(e-ly⁵, adv.— **fer-til'i-ty,** n. **fer'til**(e-ness⁵‡.

fer'til-ize or **-ise,** 1 fûr'til-aiz; 2 fĕr'til-īş, vt. [-IZED; -IZ'ING.] To render fertile or fruitful; enrich.

---

fer'ule, 1 fer'ul; 2 fĕr'ŭl, *n.* A flat stick for punishing children.

fer'vent, 1 fŭr'vent; 2 fẽr'vĕnt, *a.* **1.** Ardent in feeling; fervid. **2.** Burning; hot. **-ly,** *adv.* **-ness,** *n.*— **fer'ven-cy,** *n.* Fervor; zeal.

fer'vid, 1 fŭr'vid; 2 fẽr'vid, *a.* **1.** Burning with zeal; eager; vehement. **2.** Hot; fiery. **-ly,** *adv.*— **fer-vid'i-ty, fer'vid-ness,** *n.*

fer'vor, 1 fŭr'var; 2 fẽr'vor, *n.* **1.** Intensity of feeling; ardor; zeal. **2.** Heat; warmth.

fes'tal, 1 fes'tal; 2 fĕs'tal, *a.* Pertaining to a festival or a feast; festive. **-ly,** *adv.*

fes'ter, 1 fes'tar; 2 fĕs'ter. **I.** *vt. & vi.* To ulcerate; corrupt. **II.** *n.* The act of festering; an ulcerous sore.

fes'ti-val, 1 fes'ti-val; 2 fĕs'ti-val. **I.** *a.* Festive. **II.** *n.* A period of feasting or celebration.

fes'tive, ⎱ 1 fes'tiv; 2 fĕs'tiv, *a.* Pertaining
fes'tiv⁵, ⎰ or suited to a feast; gay. See FEAST.— **fes'tive-ly,** *adv.*— **fes-tiv'i-ty,** *n.* [-TIES²,* pl.*] A festive celebration; gaiety; merrymaking.

fes-toon', 1 fes-tūn'; 2 fĕs-tōon'. **I.** *vt.* To decorate with or make into festoons. **II.** *n.* A decorative band hanging in a curve between two points.

fe'tal, 1 fī'tal; 2 fē'tal, *a.* Of or pertaining to a fetus. **fœ'tal‡.**

fetch, ⎱ 1 fech; 2 fĕch. **Iᵗ.** *vt.* **1.** To go
fech⁰, ⎰ after and bring; bring; convey; accomplish; reach. **2.** To bring as a price. **II.** *n.* **1.** An act of fetching. **2.** A stratagem.

fête, 1 fēt; 2 fẹt, *n.* A festival; holiday.

fe'tich, fe'tich-ism, etc. Same as FETISH, etc.

fet'id, 1 fet'id; 2 fĕt'id, *a.* Emitting an offensive odor. **-ness,** *n.*

fet'ish, ⎱ 1 fī'tish *or* fet'ish; 2 fē'tish *or* fĕt'-
fet'ich, ⎰ ish, *n.* An object worshiped among savages as the incarnation of a spirit.— **fe'tish-ism,** *n.*

fet'lock, 1 fet'lok; 2 fĕt'lŏk, *n.* The tuft of hair above a horse's hoof; also, the projection and the joint at this place.

fet'ter, 1 fet'ar; 2 fĕt'ter. **I.** *vt.* To fasten fetters upon; shackle. **II.** *n.* A shackle for the feet; any bond. [spring.

fe'tus, 1 fes'tus; 2 fē'tŭs, *n.* Unborn offspring.

feud¹, 1 fiūd; 2 fūd, *n.* Vindictive hostility between families or clans, commonly hereditary.

feud², *n.* Land held of a superior on condition of rendering service.— **feu'dal,** 1 fiū'-dal; 2 fū'dal, *a.* Pertaining to the relation of lord and vassal.— **feu'dal-ism,** *n.* The medieval European system of land-tenure on condition of military service. **feudal system‡.**— **feu'da-to-ry.** **1.** *a.* Holding or held

by feudal tenure. **II.** *n.* [-RIES²,* pl.*] A vassal or the lands held by him.— **feu'dal-ly,** *adv.*

fe'ver, 1 fī'ver; 2 fē'ver. **I.** *vt.* To affect with fever. **II.** *n.* **1.** A disorder marked by high temperature, quickened pulse, etc. **2.** Extreme excitement.— **fe'ver-ish,** *a.* Affected with fever; hot; impatient.

few, 1 fiū; 2 fū, *a.* Small or limited in number; not many.— **few'ness,** *n.*

fez, 1 fez; 2 fẽz, *n.* A brimless Turkish felt cap, usually red, with a black tassel: named from Fez, a city in Morocco.

fi"an"cé', 1 fī"an̈'sē'; 2 fī'än̈'çẹ', *n.* [FI"-AN"CÉE',* fem.*] An affianced or betrothed person. [ating failure.

fi-as'co, 1 fi-as'ko; 2 fi-äs'co, *n.* A humili-

fi'at, 1 fai'at; 2 fī'ăt, *n.* An authoritative command.

fib, 1 fib; 2 fĭb. **I.** *vi.* [FIBBED, FIBD⁵; FIB'BING.] To tell a fib. **II.** *n.* A petty falsehood.

fi'ber, ⎱ 1 fai'bar; 2 fī'ber, *n.* **1.** A fine
fi'bre, ⎰ thread; a substance composed of threads or filaments. **2.** The essence of anything; strength; nerve.— **fi'brin,** 1 fai'-brin; 2 fī'brin, *n.* A white threadlike substance found in coagulated blood and in cereals.— **fi'brous,** *a.* Composed of or having the character of fibers.

fick'le, ⎱ 1 fik'l; 2 fĭk'l, *a.* Inconstant;
fick'l⁵, ⎰ changeful; capricious. **-ness,** *n.*

fic'tile, 1 fik'til; 2 fĭc'til, *a.* Pertaining to pottery; plastic.

fic'tion, 1 fik'shan; 2 fic'shon, *n.* A representation of that which is not true; a fabrication; fictitious narrative; novel.— **fic-ti'-tious,** 1 fik-tish'us; 2 fic-tish'ŭs, *a.* Imaginary; counterfeit; false.

fid'dle, ⎱ 1 fid'l; 2 fĭd'l. **I.** *vt. & vi.* [FID'-
fid'l⁵, ⎰ DLED, FID'LD⁵; FID'DLING.] To play on a fiddle; trifle or toy with. **II.** *n.* A violin.— **fid'dler,** *n.*

fi-del'i-ty, 1 fi-del'i-ti; 2 fi-dĕl'i-ty, *n.* **1.** Faithfulness; loyalty. **2.** Truthfulness; accuracy.

fidg'et, 1 fij'et; 2 fĭdg'ĕt. **I.** *vt. & vi.* To make fidgety; worry; move restlessly. **II.** *n.* Nervous restlessness.— **fidg'et-y,** *a.* Nervous; uneasy; restless.

fie, 1 fai; 2 fī, *interj.* An expression of impatience or disapproval.

fief, 1 fīf; 2 fẽf, *n.* A landed estate held under feudal tenure.

field, 1 fild; 2 fẽld,* n.* **1.** A large piece of land enclosed. **2.** A region; open expanse; the open country. **3.** A sphere of action; battle-ground; battle.— **field'-day",** *n.* A day devoted to open-air exercise, as of troops; day of excitement; gala-day.— **field'-glass,** *n.* A small, portable terrestrial tele-

scope, monocular or binocular.— **f. =gun,** *n.* A cannon mounted on wheels for rapid movement in the field.— **f. =marshal,** *n. Mil.* A European general officer of the highest rank.— **f. =officer,** *n. Mil.* An officer above a captain and below a general; a major, lieutenant=colonel, or colonel.— **f. =piece,** *n.* Same as FIELD=GUN.— **f. =sports,** *n. pl.* Outdoor sports, as hunting, shooting, and racing.

fiend, 1 fīnd; 2 fênd, *n.* **1.** A devil; demon. **2.** A devotee, as of opium.— **fiend′ish,** *a.* **-ly,** *adv.* **-ness,** *n.*

fierce, 1 fīrs; 2 fêrç, *a.* Savage; ferocious; furious; passionate. **-ly,** *adv.* **-ness,** *n.*

fier′y, 1 fair′i; 2 fīr′y, *a.* [FIER′I-ER; FIER′I-EST.] Of, pertaining to, or like fire; burning; hot; passionate; spirited.— **fier′i-ly,** *adv.*— **fier′i-ness,** *n.*

fife, 1 faif; 2 fīf, *n.* **1.** A small shrill=toned flute=like martial wind=instrument.— **fif′er,** *n.*

fif-teen′, 1 fif-tīn′; 2 fif-tēn′. **I.** *a.* Consisting of five more than ten. **II.** *n.* The sum of ten and five, or the symbols (15 or XV) representing this number.— **fif-teenth′. I.** *a.* **1.** Fifth in order after the tenth. **2.** Being one of fifteen equal parts of a thing. **II.** *n.* One of fifteen equal parts of anything.

fifth, 1 fifth; 2 fĩfth. **I.** *a.* **1.** Next in order after the fourth. **2.** Being one of five equal parts of a thing. **II.** *n.* One of five equal parts of anything.— **fifth′ly,** *adv.*

fif′ty, 1 fif′ti; 2 fĩf′ty. **I.** *a.* Consisting of ten more than forty or five times ten. **II.** *n.* [FIF′TIES², *pl.*] **1.** The sum of ten and forty; five times ten. **2.** The symbols representing this number.— **fif′ti-eth. I.** *a.* **1.** Tenth in order after the fortieth. **2.** Being one of fifty equal parts of a thing. **II.** *n.* One of fifty equal parts.

fig, 1 fig; 2 fĩg, *n.* The sweet fruit of a tree, grown in warm climates; also, the tree.

fight, 1 fait; 2 fīt, *v.* [FOUGHT, 1 fôt, 2 fôt; FIGHT′ING.] **I.** *t.* To contend with; carry on (a contest); direct in battle. **II.** *i.* To contend or strive; give battle.

fight, *n.* Strife; battle; conflict; combat. — **fight′er,** *n.*— **fight′ing. I.** *a.* Qualified, equipped, or ready to fight; pertaining to or used for conflict. **II.** *n.* Strife; battle; conflict.

fig′ment, 1 fig′ment *or* -mənt; 2 fĩg′ment, *n.* Something imagined or feigned; a fiction.

fig′ure, 1 fig′yur; 2 fĩg′yur, *v.* [FIG′URED; FIG′UR-ING.] **I.** *t.* **1.** To form an image of; depict; imagine. **2.** To mark with figures. **3.** To compute; calculate. **4.** To symbolize; prefigure. **II.** *i.* **1.** To make a figure; be conspicuous. **2.** To compute; cipher.— **fig′ur-a-tiv(es,** *a.* **1.** Metaphorical; symbolic; ornate; florid. **2.** Pertaining to form or figure. **-ly,** *adv.* **-ness,** *n.*

fig′ure, *n.* **1.** Shape; appearance. **2.** A drawing or other representation; figurative language; a metaphor; a type. **3.** An active or conspicuous person; distinction. **4.** A numeral; hence, amount; price. **5.** One of the regular movements of a dance in which a certain set of steps is completed.— **fig′ured,** *a.*

fil′a-gree, *n.* Same as FILIGREE.

fil′a-ment, 1 fil′ə-ment *or* -mənt; 2 fĩl′a-ment, *n.* A fine thread or fiber.— **fil′a-men′tous,** *a.* Threadlike.

fil′bert, 1 fil′bərt; 2 fĩl′bert, *n.* The nut of the hazel.

filch[b], 1 filċh; 2 fĩlċh, *vt.* To steal in small amounts; pilfer.— **filch′er,** *n.*

file[1], 1 fail; 2 fīl. **I.** *vt.* [FILED; FIL′ING.] To cut or sharpen with a file. **II.** *n.* A hard steel abrading instrument.

file[2]. **I.** *vt. & vi.* **1.** To put on file, as papers. **2.** To march in file, as soldiers. **II.** *n.* **1.** Any device to keep papers in order for reference. **2.** A collection of papers arranged for reference. **3.** *Mil.* A row of men standing or marching one behind another. **4.** A roll; list.

fil′ial, 1 fil′yəl; 2 fĩl′yal, *a.* Of, pertaining to, or befitting a son or daughter; due to parents.— **fil′ial-ly,** *adv.*

fil′i-bus″ter, 1 fil′i-bus″tər; 2 fĩl′i-būs″ter. **I.** *vi.* **1.** To act like a filibuster. **2.** To delay action on a law in an effort to defeat it. **II.** *n.* One who engages in plundering.

fil′i-gree, 1 fil′i-grī; 2 fĩl′i-grē, *n.* Delicate ornamental work; anything fanciful but unserviceable.

fil′ing, 1 fail′iŋ; 2 fīl′ing, *n.* **1.** The act of using a file. **2.** A particle removed by a file.

Fil″i-pi′no, 1 fil″i-pī′no; 2 fĩl′i-pī′no, *n.* [-NA, *fem.*] A native of the Philippine Islands.

fill, 1 fil; 2 fĩl. **I.** *vt. & vi.* **1.** To make or become full. **2.** To occupy; pervade. **3.** To satisfy; glut. **II.** *n.* That which fills; a supply.— **fill′er,** *n.*

fil′let, 1 fil′et; 2 fĩl′ĕt, *n.* **1.** A narrow band, as for binding the hair. **2.** A strip of lean meat.

fil′lip, 1 fil′ip; 2 fĩl′ip. **I**[t]. *vt.* To strike by or as by a fillip. **II.** *n.* A snap or blow with the end of a finger; hence, incitement.

fil′ly, 1 fil′i; 2 fĩl′y, *n.* [FIL′LIES², *pl.*] **1.** A young mare. **2.** A bold, frisky girl.

film, 1 film; 2 fĩlm, *n.* A thin coating, layer, or membrane.— **film,** *vt. & vi.*— **film′i-ness,** *n.*— **film′y,** *a.* Like a film; gauzy.

fil′ter, 1 fil′tər; 2 fĩl′ter. **I.** *vt. & vi.* To pass through a filter; separate by a filter.

II. *n.* A strainer for clearing or purifying liquids.— **fil'trate**, 1 fīl'trēt; 2 fīl'trāt. **I.** *vt.* [FIL'TRAT-ED⁺; FIL'TRAT-ING.] To filter. **II.** *n.* The liquid separated by filtration.— **fil-tra'tion**, *n.* The act or process of filtering.

filth, 1 filth; 2 filth, *n.* Anything that soils or defiles; defilement; nastiness; dirt.— **filth'y**, *a.* [FILTH'I-ER; FILTH'I-EST.] Of the nature of or containing filth; foul; obscene.— **filth'i-ly**, *adv.*— **filth'i-ness**, *n.*

fin, 1 fin; 2 fin, *n.* A membranous extension from the body of a fish or other aquatic animal.— **fin'less**, *a.* Without fins.

fin'a-bl(e², 1 faɪn'ə-bl; 2 fīn'a-bl, *a.* Liable to or involving a fine.

fi'nal, 1 faɪ'nəl; 2 fī'nal, *a.* **1.** Pertaining to the end; ultimate; last; conclusive. **2.** Relating to the end aimed at; as, a *final* cause.— **fi-nal'i-ty**, *n.* [-TIES², *pl.*] The state of being final; a final or decisive act, offer, etc.— **fi'nal-ly**, *adv.*

fi-na'le, 1 fi-nä'lē; 2 fi-nä'le, *n.* The last act, part, scene, or movement; end.

fi-nance', 1 fi-nans'; 2 fi-nănç', *n.* The science of monetary affairs; pecuniary resources; funds; revenue.— **fi-nan'cial**, 1 fi-nan'shəl; 2 fi-năn'shal, *a.* Of or pertaining to finance; monetary.— **fi-nan'cial-ly**, *adv.*— **fin'an-cier'**, 1 fin'ən-sīr'; 2 fin'an-çēr', *n.* One skilled in or occupied with financial affairs.

finch, 1 finch; 2 finch, *n.* A small seed-eating bird, as a sparrow, goldfinch, or canary.

find, 1 faɪnd; 2 fīnd, *vt.* & *vi.* [FOUND, 1 faʊnd, 2 found; FIND'ING.] **1.** To discover accidentally or by search or study; learn by experience; perceive; ascertain. **2.** *Law.* To decide judicially. **3.** To furnish; provide; support.— **find'er**, **find'ing**, *n.*

Finch. 1/6

fine¹, 1 faɪn; 2 fīn, *vt.* [FINED; FIN'ING.] To punish by fine; mulct.

fine², *vt.* & *vi.* To make or become fine, pure, thin, or slender: with *down*.— **fin'er**, *n.* A refiner.

fine, *a.* [FIN'ER; FIN'EST.] **1.** Excellent; elegant. **2.** Light or delicate; thin; keen; refined; sensitive; nice; pure. **3.** Showy.— **-ly**, *adv.* **-ness**, *n.*— **fin'er-y**, *n.* [-IES², *pl.*] Showy decoration.

fine, *n.* A penalty in money.

fi'ne, 1 fī'nē; 2 fī'ne, *n. Mus.* The end; finis.

fi-nesse', 1 fi-nes'; 2 fi-něs', **I.** *vi.* [FI-NESSED'⁺; FI-NESS'ING.] To use artifice. **II.** *n.* Subtle contrivance; artifice; artfulness; skill.

fin'ger, 1 fiŋ'gər; 2 fiŋ'ğer. **I.** *vt.* & *vi.* To toy or tamper with. **II.** *n.* One of the digits of the hand, excluding or including the thumb.— **fin'ger-board"**, *n.* A keyboard.

fin'i-cal, 1 fin'ɪ-kəl; 2 fin'i-cal, *a.* Over-nice or fastidious in dress, etc. **-ly**, *adv.*

fi'nis, 1 faɪ'nɪs; 2 fī'nis, *n.* The end.

fin'ish, 1 fin'ish; 2 fin'ish. **I⁺.** *vt.* & *vi.* To end; perfect finally or in detail; complete; cease. **II.** *n.* Conclusion; completion; perfection in detail; polish. **-er**, *n.*

fi'nite, 1 faɪ'naɪt; 2 fī'nīt. **I.** *a.* Having bounds or limits; opposed to *infinite*; limited; bounded. **II.** *n.* That which is finite. **-ly**, *adv.*— **fi'nite-ness**, *n.* The state or quality of being finite. [fishlike.]

fin'ny, 1 fin'ɪ; 2 fin'y, *a.* Having fins;

fiord, 1 fyôrd; 2 fyôrd, *n.* A long and narrow arm of the sea, with high rocky banks.

fir, 1 fûr; 2 fir, *n.* An evergreen tree of the pine family. **fir'-tree"**‡.

fire, 1 faɪr; 2 fīr, *v.* [FIRED; FIR'ING.] **I.** *t.* **1.** To set on fire; kindle; bake, as pottery; discharge, as a firearm; impel, as from a gun; hurl. **2.** To inflame; excite. **II.** *i.* **1.** To take fire; be kindled, inflamed, or excited. **2.** To discharge firearms.

Fir-tree and Cone.

fire, *n.* **1.** The evolution of heat and light by burning; flame; flash; fuel as burning. **2.** The discharge of firearms. **3.** Intensity; ardor; passion; vivacity. **4.** Affliction; trial.— **fire'arm"**, *n.* A weapon from which a missile is hurled, as by gunpowder.— **fire'brand"**, *n.* A burning piece of wood.— **fire'clay**, *n.* A fire-resisting clay.— **f.-clay**, *n.* Clay containing nothing fusible.— **f.-company**, *n.* A company of men employed to extinguish fires.— **f.-damp**, *n.* An explosive gas generated in coal-mines.— **f.-engine**, *n.* An engine for pumping water through hose to extinguish fires.— **f.-escape**, *n.* A ladder or other device furnishing a means of escape from a burning building.— **fire'fly"**, *n.* A winged, luminous insect.— **fire'man**, *n.* [FIRE'MEN, *pl.*] **1.** One who aids in extinguishing fires. **2.** A

1: ärtistic, ärt; fat, fāre; fạst; get, prēy; hit, police; obey, gō; nŏt, ôr; fụll, rūle; but, bûrn.

2: ärt, āpe, făt, fâre, fȧst, whạt, ạll; mē, gĕt, prey, fẽrn; hĭt, īce; ī=ē; ĭ=ē; gō, nŏt, ôr, wŏn,

fire-tender, as on a locomotive; a stoker.—
f.-proof, *a.* Proof against fire; incombustible.— **fire'side"**, *n.* The hearth or space about the fireplace; hence, home.— **f.-trench**, *n.* A first-line trench on a line of fire.— **f.-wood**, *n.* Wood used, or fit to use, as fuel.— **fire'work"**, *n.* **1.** A combustible or expossive to be fired for display. **2.** *pl.* A pyrotechnic display.— **liquid f.**, see under LIQUID.

fir'kin, 1 fŭr'kin, *n.* **1.** A wooden vessel for lard, etc. **2.** [Eng.] A measure, one-fourth of a barrel.

firm, 1 fŭrm; 2 fĭrm. **I.** *a.* Compact; unyielding; solid; stable; stedfast; determined; vigorous; resolute. **II.** *n.* A partnership; business house. **-ly**, *adv.* **-ness**, *n.*

fir'ma-ment, 1 fŭr'ma-ment *or* -ment; 2 fĭr'ma-ment, *n.* The expanse of heaven; sky.— **fir"ma-men'tal**, *a.*

first, 1 fŭrst; 2 fŏrst. **I.** *a.* Before all others; earliest; nearest; leading; chief; best. **II.** *n.* That which is first. **III.** *adv.* In the first place; earlier; rather; sooner.— **first'-class"**, *a.* Belonging to the first class; of the highest rank or best quality. **f.-rate†.— first'ling**, *n.* The one first born, as of a flock.— **first'ly**, *adv.* Same as FIRST, *adv.* [of the sea.

firth, 1 fŭrth; 2 fĭrth, *n.* [Scot.] An arm

fis'cal, 1 fis'kəl; 2 fĭs'cal. **I.** *a.* Pertaining to the treasury or finances of a government; financial. **II.** *n.* A financial secretary.— **fisc**, *n.* The treasury, as of a state.

fish†, 1 fĭsh; 2 fĭsh, *v.* **I.** *t.* **1.** To catch, or try to catch, fish in a (stream or the like). **2.** To catch, as fish, in or under water; search for and bring to light: often with *up or out*. **II.** *i.* To catch, or try to catch, fish; be employed in catching fish.— **fish'er**, *n.* One who fishes; a fisherman.— **fish'er-man**, *n.* [-MEN, *pl.*] One who catches fish; a fisher.— **fish'er-y**, *n.* [-IES², *pl.*] **1.** The operation or business of catching fish; fishing industry. **2.** A place for fishing.— **fish'ing**, *n.* The act or operation of catching fish.

fish, 1 fĭsh; 2 fĭsh, *n.* [FISH *or* FISH'ES², *pl.*] **1.** A vertebrate animal with permanent gills, adapted to live under water. **2.** Loosely, any animal habitually living in the water. See illus. on next page.— **fish'-hook"**, *n.* A hook for catching fish on a line.— **fish'mon"ger**, 1 fĭsh'muŋ"ger; 2 fĭsh'mŏŋ"ger, *n.* A dealer in fish.— **fish'y**, *a.* **1.** Of, pertaining to, or like fish. **2.** Abounding in fish.— **fish'i-ness**, *n.*

fis'sile, 1 fĭs'il; 2 fĭs'il, *a.* Readily split or │ separated into layers.— **fis'sion**, *n.* A splitting or separating.

fis'sure, 1 fĭsh'ur; 2 fĭsh'ur. **I.** *vt. & vi.* [FIS'SURED; FIS'SUR-ING.] To crack; split.

II. *n.* A narrow opening; cleft; crevice.

fist, 1 fist; 2 fĭst, *n.* The clenched hand.— **fist'l-cuff"**, *n.* A cuff with the fist; in the plural, a fight with fists.

fis'tu-la, 1 fĭs'chu-la *or* -tiu-la; 2 fĭs'chu-la *or* -tū-la, *n.* A long narrow canal caused by diseased action.— **fis'tu-lar**, *a.*

fit, 1 fit; 2 fĭt, *v.* [FIT'TED d; FIT'TING.] **I.** *t.* **1.** To render suitable; adapt; prepare; equip: commonly with *out or up.* **2.** To be of the proper size and shape for. **3.** To be suitable for; befit. **II.** *i.* **1.** To be of the proper size, shape, etc.; be suitable, proper, or becoming. **2.** To receive suitable equipment.— **fit'ter**, *n.*

fit, *a.* [FIT'TER; FIT'TEST.] Adapted to a purpose; adequate; competent; suitable; appropriate.— **fit'ly**, *adv.* In a fit manner; properly.— **fit'ness**, *n.*

fit¹, *n.* A convulsion; spasm; mood; caprice.— **fit'ful**, *a.* Occurring in fits; spasmodic. **-ly**, *adv.* **-ness**, *n.* [tion.

fit², *n.* Adjustment; suitability; adaptation.

fit'ting, 1 fĭt'ɪŋ; 2 fĭt'ing. **I.** *pa.* Fit or suitable; proper; appropriate. **II.** *n.* **1.** The act of adjusting. **2.** *pl.* Fixtures.— **fit'ting-ly**, *adv.* **fit'ting-ness**, *n.*

five, 1 faiv; 2 fĭv. **I.** *a.* Consisting of one more than four. **II.** *n.* **1.** The sum of four and one. **2.** A symbol denoting this number, as 5 or V.— **five'fold"**. **I.** *a.* Five times as much or as great. **II.** *adv.* In a fivefold manner or degree.

fix†, 1 fĭks; 2 fĭks, *v.* **I.** *t.* **1.** To fasten or secure firmly; make firm; establish; settle; determine; solidify. **2.** To direct steadily and intently, as the gaze. **3.** To arrange; put in order; adjust. **II.** *i.* To settle permanently; become firm or solid; crystallize; solidify.— **fix-a'tion**, 1 fĭks-ē'shən; 2 fĭks-ā'shon, *n.* The act of fixing, or the state of being fixed; stability.— **fixed**, 1 fĭkst; 2 fĭkst, *pa.* **1.** Established; fastened; settled; stable; lasting. **2.** Keeping nearly the same relative position; as, *fixed* stars.— **fix'ed-ly**, 1 fĭks'ed-lɪ; 2 fĭks'ĕd-ly, *adv.*— **fix'ed-ness**, 1 fĭks'ed-nes; 2 fĭks'ĕd-nĕs, *n.*— **fix'l-ty**, *n.* The state of being fixed; permanence; fixedness; stability.— **fix'ture**, 1 fĭks'chur *or* -tiur; 2 fĭks'chur *or* -tūr, *n.* Anything fixed firmly in its place; as, gas-*fixtures.*

fjord, *n.* Same as FIORD.

flab'by, 1 flab'ɪ; 2 flăb'y, *a.* [FLAB'BI-ER; FLAB'BI-EST.] Lacking muscle; flaccid; languid; feeble.— **flab'bi-ly**, *adv.*— **flab'bi-ness**, *n.*

flac'cid, 1 flak'sɪd; 2 flăc'çid, *a.* Lacking firmness or elasticity; flabby. **-ly**, *adv.*— **flac-cid'l-ty**, **flac'cid-ness**, *n.*

flag¹, 1 flag; 2 flăg, *vt.* [FLAGGED; FLAGD²; FLAG'GING.] To signal by a flag.

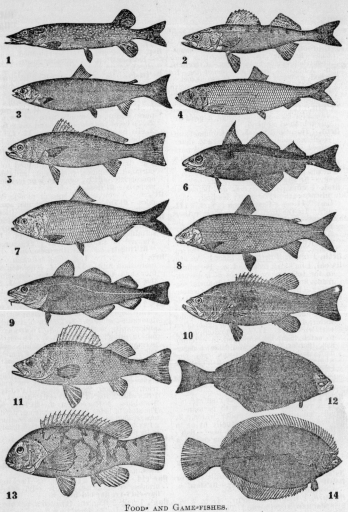

FOOD= AND GAME=FISHES.

1. Pike. $1/22$ 2. Pike=perch. $1/21$ 3. Atlantic salmon. $1/23$ 4. Herring. $1/7$ 5. Weak=
fish. $1/14$ 6. Haddock. $1/11$ 7. American shad. $1/7$ 8. Whitefish. $1/9$ 9. Cod. $1/21$ 10.
Large=mouthed black bass. $1/9$ 11. Yellow perch. $1/7$ 12. Halibut. $1/29$ 13. Tautog or
blackfish. $1/8$ 14. Winter flounder. $1/9$

flag², *vt.* To pave with flagstones.

flag³, *vi.* To grow languid; become tired; droop; drag.

flag¹, *n.* A piece of cloth commonly bearing a device and attached to a staff or halyard: used as a standard, symbol, or signal.— **black flag,** the emblem of piracy and of no quarter.— **Flag Day** [U. S.], June 14.— **flag″man,** *n.* One who carries a flag, as for signaling trains on a railway.— **flag″ of″fi·cer,** *n.* **1.** Formerly, the captain of a flag-ship. **2.** An admiral, vice-admiral, or rear-admiral.— **f. of truce,** a white flag displayed to denote that a conference or truce is desired.— **f. ship,** *n.* The ship carrying a flag-officer and displaying his flag.— **flag″staff″,** *n.* A pole on which a flag is hung.

flag², *n.* A flagstone.

flag³, *n.* A plant having sword-shaped leaves and growing in moist places.

flag′el·late, 1 flaj′e·lēt; 2 flăġ′ĕ·lāt, *vt.* [-LAT″ED⁴; -LAT″ING.] To beat with a rod; whip; scourge.— **flag″el·la′tion,** *n.*

flag′eo·let″, 1 flaj′o·let″; 2 flăġ′o·lĕt″, *n.* A musical instrument resembling the flute.

fla·gi′tious, 1 fla·jish′us; 2 fla·ġish′ŭs, *a.* Flagrantly wicked; atrocious; heinous. **-ly,** *adv.* **-ness,** *n.*

flag′on, 1 flag′an; 2 flăġ′on, *n.* A vessel with a handle and a narrow mouth, used to serve liquors.

fla′grant, 1 flē′grant; 2 flā′ġrant, *a.* Openly scandalous; notorious; heinous. **-ly,** *adv.* — **fla′gran·cy,** *n.*

flag′stone″, 1 flag′stōn″; 2 flăġ′stōn″, *n.* A broad, flat stone suitable for foot-pavements.

flail, 1 flēl; 2 flāl, *n.* An implement for separating grain from chaff by beating.

flake, 1 flēk; 2 flāk. **I.** *vt. & vi.* [FLAKED⁴; FLAK′ING.] To peel off in flakes; fleck. **II.** *n.* A small flat fragment; scale; fleck.— **flak′y,** 1 flēk′ı; 2 flāk′y, *a.* Resembling or consisting of flakes; separable into flakes.— **flak′i·ness,** *n.*

flam′beau, 1 flam′bō; 2 flăm′bō, *n.* [FLAM′-BEAUX or -BEAUS, 1 flam′bōz; 2 flăm′-bōz, *pl.*] A flaring torch.

flame, 1 flēm; 2 flām. **I.** *vi.* [FLAMED; FLAM′ING.] **1.** To blaze; shine like a flame; flash. **2.** To burst forth, as in violence of passion. **II.** *n.* **1.** A stream of vapor or gas made luminous by heat; a blaze. **2.** Excitement, as from rage, strife, or passion; an ardent affection; passionate love. **-less,** *a.*

fla·min′go, 1 fla·miŋ′go; 2 fla·miṅ′ġo, *n.* A long-necked, small-bodied bird of a red color, having very long legs, webbed feet, and a bent bill. See illus. in next col.

flange, 1 flanj; 2 flăṅġ, *n.* A projecting rim or edge, as on a car-wheel.

flank, 1 flaŋk; 2 flăṅk.
I. *vt. & vi.* **1.** To border. **2.** *Mil.* To turn, guard, or threaten the flank (of). **II.** *a.* Pertaining to the flank or side. **III.** *n.* **1.** The part of an animal's side between the ribs and the hip. **2.** The side of anything, as of an army.

American Flamingo.¹⁄₄₀

flan′nel, 1 flan′l; 2 flăn′l, *n.* A loosely woven woolen stuff with soft, nap-like surface.

flap, 1 flap; 2 flăp. **I.** *vt. & vi.* [FLAPPED⁴, FLAPT⁸; FLAP′PING.] **1.** To strike, or strike at, as with a wing. **2.** To move to and fro rapidly, as wings; swing or wave; droop. **II.** *n.* **1.** A broad, limber, and loosely hanging part or attachment. **2.** The act of flapping; a light blow.— **flap′per,** *n.* One who or that which flaps; also, a young girl.

flare, 1 flār; 2 flâr. **I.** *vt. & vi.* [FLARED; FLAR′ING.] **1.** To burn fiercely and fitfully. **2.** To display ostentatiously; make a show. **3.** To spread outward like a funnel. **II.** *n.* **1.** A bright but unsteady light; show; ostentation. **2.** A spreading outward, as of the sides of a funnel.

flash, 1 flash; 2 flăsh. **I⁴.** *vt. & vi.* To send or burst forth, as a sudden brilliant light. **II.** *a.* Relating to or connected with thieves or thieves' talk; cheap and tawdry; loud. **III.** *n.* **1.** A sudden and transient blaze; gleam; outburst, as of wit, anger, etc. **2.** A moment; instant.— **flash-light″,** *n.* **1.** A light shown only at intervals. **2.** A brief and brilliant light for taking photographs.— **flash′y,** *a.* Pretentious; showy; tawdry.— **flash′i·ly,** *adv.* — **flash′i·ness,** *n.* [the like.

flask, 1 flask; 2 flăsk, *n.* A small bottle or flat.

flat, 1 flat; 2 flăt, *vt. & vi.* [FLAT′TED⁴; FLAT′TING.] To lower; flatten.

flat, *a.* [FLAT′TER; FLAT′TEST.] **1.** Level; prostrate. **2.** Positive; absolute. **3.** Monotonous; dull. **4.** *Mus.* Below pitch. — **flat′-i″ron,** *n.* An iron with a smooth, polished under-surface for smoothing cloth.— **flat′ly,** *adv.* — **flat′ness,** *n.* — **flat′ten,** 1 flat′n; 2 flăt′n, *vt. & vi.* To make or become flat.— **flat′wise,** 1 flat′waiz; 2 flăt′wis, *adv.* With the flat side downward or next to another object. **flat′ways″‡.**

flat[1], *n.* **1.** A level; low land washed by the tide; shoal. **2.** Anything that is flat; the flat side of a thing. **3.** *Mus.* A tone a half step lower than a tone from which it is named, represented by the character ♭. [ment.

flat[2], *n.* A set of rooms on one floor; apart-

flat, *adv.* In a level position; so as to be flat; flatly.

flat′ter, 1 flat′ẽr; 2 flăt′er, *v.* **I.** *t.* **1.** To praise unduly or insincerely; fawn on; cajole. **2.** To encourage with visionary hopes; delude. **II.** *i.* To use fulsome or undue praise.—**flat′ter-er**, *n.* One who flatters.—**flat′ter-y**, *n.* [-IES[2], *pl.*] Undue or insincere praise; adulation.

flat′u-lent, 1 flat′yu-lent; 2 flăt′yu-lĕnt, *a.* **1.** Affected with gas in the stomach and bowels, as a person. **2.** Tending, as food or medicine, to produce such a condition. **3.** Puffy; vain; conceited. **-ly,** *adv.*— **flat′u-lence,** *n.*

flaunt, 1 flänt *or* flŏnt; 2 flänt *or* flant. **I**[d]. *vt. & vi.* To display ostentatiously; parade. **II.** *n.* **1.** The act of flaunting. **2.** A boast; vaunt.

fla′vor, 1 flē′vẽr; 2 flā′vor. **I.** *vt.* To impart flavor to. **II.** *n.* The taste of a thing, especially if pleasant: often used figuratively. **fla′vour**‡.

flaw, 1 flô; 2 flạ, *vt.* To make flaws in; mar; crack.

flaw[1], *n.* An inherent defect; weak spot; crack; fissure.—**flaw′less**, *a.* Having no flaw.—**flaw′y**, *a.*

flaw[2], *n.* A sudden puff of wind; a transient wind-storm.

flax, 1 flaks; 2 flăks, *n.* **1.** The soft fiber obtained from the bark of the flax =plant. **2.** An annual plant having a mucilaginous seed, called *flaxseed* or *linseed*, and a fibrous inner bark. —**flax′en**, *a.* Of, pertaining to, or made of flax; like flax; of a light golden color.

flay, 1 flē; 2 flā, *vt.* To strip off the skin from; skin.

flea, 1 flī; 2 flē, *n.* A parasitic wingless insect, having limbs adapted for leaping and a head armed with blood-sucking organs.

fleck, 1 flek; 2 flĕk. **I.** *vt.* To spot; dapple. **II.** *n.* A dot or streak; dapple.—**fleck′less**, *a.* Spotless; stainless.

Flax.

flec′tion, 1 flek′shạn; 2 flĕc′shon, *n.* The act of bending; a curved or bent part. **flex′ion**‡.

fled, 1 fled; 2 flĕd, *imp. & pp.* of FLEE, *v.*

fledge, 1 flej; 2 flĕdg, *vi.* [FLEDGED. FLEDGD[8]; FLEDG′ING.] To acquire feathers enough for flight.—**fledg′ling. I.** *a.* Just fledged; hence, little known, as a young poet. **II.** *n.* A young bird just fledged. **fledge′ling‡.**

flee, 1 flī; 2 flē, *v.* [FLED, 1 fled, 2 flĕd; FLEE′ING.] **I.** *t.* To run away from; shun; avoid. **II.** *i.* To seek safety in flight; run away.

fleece, 1 flīs; 2 flēç. **I.** *vt.* [FLEECED[t]; FLEEC′ING.] **1.** To shear off the fleece from; swindle. **2.** To cover as with a fleece. **II.** *n.* The woolly covering of a sheep.—**fleec′er**, *n.*—**fleec′y**, *a.* [FLEEC′I-ER; FLEEC′I-EST.] Pertaining to, like, or covered with a fleece.

fleer, 1 flīr; 2 flēr. **I.** *vt. & vi.* To jeer at; deride. **II.** *n.* Derision; a leer.

fleet[d], 1 flīt; 2 flēt, *vi.* To fly or pass swiftly.—**fleet′ing**, *pa.* Passing quickly; transitory.

fleet, *a.* Moving, or capable of moving, swiftly; rapid; nimble; swift. **-ly,** *adv.* **-ness,** *n.* [as ships of war.

fleet, *n.* A number of vessels in company,

Flem′ish, 1 flem′ish; 2 flĕm′ish. **I.** *a.* Of or pertaining to Flanders, its people, literature, or language. **II.** *n.* The Flemish people collectively, or the language of Flanders.

flense, 1 flens; 2 flĕns, *vt.* To strip the blubber or the skin from, as a whale or a seal.

flesh, 1 flesh; 2 flĕsh. **I**[t]. *vt.* To glut with flesh; satiate; also, to tempt with a taste of flesh, as a dog; embolden with success; flush. **II.** *n.* The softer tissues of an animal body; the soft part of fruits and vegetables; the body as opposed to the soul; the carnal or sinful nature; the human race.—**flesh′i-ness**, *n.* Plumpness; corpulence.—**flesh′li-ness**, *n.* Carnality.— **flesh′ly**, *a.* Pertaining to the body; corporeal; carnal; worldly; human.—**flesh′y**, *a.* [FLESH′I-ER; FLESH′I-EST.] **1.** Having much flesh; corpulent; succulent, as a plant. **2.** Pertaining to flesh or to the carnal nature; composed of flesh.

fleur″-de-lis′, 1 flûr″-də-līs′; 2 flûr″-de-lis′, *n.* [FLEURS″ DE-LIS′, *pl.*] A heraldic device, the bearing of the former royal family of France. **fleur″-de-lys′**‡.

Fleur-de-lis.

flew, 1 flū; 2 flu, *imp.* of FLY, *v.*

flex, 1 fleks; 2 flĕks. **I**[t]. *vt.* To bend; subject to flexure. **II.** *n.* A bend; flexure.—**flex″i-**

1: **a**rtistic, **ä**rt; fat, fāre; fast; get, prey; hit, police; **o**bey, gō; n**o**t, **o**r; full, rūle; but, bûrn.
2: ärt, āpe, făt, fâre, făst, whạt, ạll; mē, gĕt, prey, fẽrn; hĭt, īce; ĭ=ē; ĩ=ē; gō, nŏt, ôr, wŏn.

bil'i-ty, *n.* **flex'i-bl(e-ness**ᴾ‡.— **flex'i-bl(e**ᴾ, *a.* Bending readily; pliable; pliant; plastic; tractable; yielding. **flex'il(e**ˢ‡.— **flex'i-bly,** *adv.*

flex'ion. Same as FLECTION.

flex'ure, 1 flek'shur *or* fleks'yur; 2 flĕk'shụr *or* flĕks'yụr, *n.* A bending; bent part; turn; curve; fold.

flick, 1 flik; 2 flĭk. **I**ᵗ. *vt.* To give a flip to. **II.** *n.* A quick, light stroke, as with a whip.

flick'er, 1 flik'ər; 2 flĭk'er, *vi.* To be unsteady or wavering, as a flame.

flick'er¹, *n.* A waving or fluctuating light; a flickering or fluttering motion.

flick'er², *n.* The golden-winged woodpecker of eastern North America.

fli'er, / **fly'er,** 1 flai'ər; 2 flī'er, *n.* That which flies; a flying bird; a fugitive.

flight, 1 flait; 2 flīt, *n.* **1.** The act, process, or power of flying or of fleeing; swift movement; the distance traveled, as by a projectile. **2.** A flock or swarm of flying creatures. **3.** A lofty and sustained effort. **4.** An ascent or series, as of stairs.

flight'y, 1 flait'ı; 2 flīt'y, *a.* [FLIGHT'I-ER; FLIGHT'I-EST.] Capricious; giddy; delirious.— **flight'i-ly,** *adv.*— **flight'i-ness,** *n.*

flim'sy, 1 flim'zı; 2 flĭm'sy, *a.* [FLIM'SI-ER; FLIM'SI-EST.] Thin and weak; ineffective. — **flim'si-ly,** *adv.*— **flim'si-ness,** *n.*

flinchᵗ, 1 flinch; 2 flĭnch, *vi.* To shrink back, as from pain or danger; waver; wince.

fling, 1 fliŋ; 2 flĭng, *v.* [FLUNG, 1 fluŋ, 2 flŭng; FLING'ING.] **I.** *t.* **1.** To cast with force; throw; hurl; sling; emit freely. **2.** To throw to the ground; overpower. **II.** *i.* To throw a missile; cast aspersions; flout; start and rush with impatience; dash; flounce.

fling, *n.* **1.** The act of casting out, down, or away; a sneering insinuation; aspersion. **2.** A kick, flounce, or leap; a lively Scotch dance. **3.** Free range for indulgence; dash; swagger.

flint, 1 flint; 2 flĭnt, *n.* A hard, dull-colored variety of quartz; a piece of such stone, shaped for some purpose.— **flint'-lock",** *n.* A gun-lock that fires the charge by a spark produced by the striking of flint on steel. — **flint'lock",** *n.* A firearm, as a musket, with a flint-lock.— **flint'i-ness,** *n.*— **flint'y,** *a.* [FLINT'I-ER; FLINT'I-EST.] Made of, containing, or resembling flint; hard; cruel; obdurate.

flip, 1 flip; 2 flĭp, *vt.* [FLIPPEDᵗ, FLIPTˢ; FLIP'PING.] To snap or flick; toss or strike lightly and quickly.

flip¹, *n.* A quick movement of the hand or finger; sudden toss; snap; flick.

flip², *n.* A hot drink of ale, spiced and sugared.

flip'pant, 1 flip-ənt; 2 flĭp'ant, *a.* Light, pert, and trifling.— **flip'pan-cy,** *n.* **flip'pant-ness**‡.— **flip'pant-ly,** *adv.*

flip'per, 1 flip'ər; 2 flĭp'er, *n.* A limb used to swim with, as in seals, turtles, etc.

flirtᵈ, 1 flūrt; 2 flĩrt, *v.* **I.** *t.* To fling; jerk. **II.** *i.* **1.** To make love for mere amusement; coquet. **2.** To flounce; act flippantly.— **flir-ta'tion,** *n.* insincere love-making. **flirt'ing**‡.

flirt, *n.* **1.** One who flirts; a coquet; trifler. **2.** The act of flirting; a toss; fling.

flit, 1 flit; 2 flĭt, *vi.* [FLIT'TEDᵈ; FLIT'TING.] To fly rapidly and lightly; dart; skim. — **flit'ting,** *n.*

flitch, 1 flich; 2 flĭch, *n.* A side (of a hog) [salted and cured.

fliv'ver, 1 fliv'ər; 2 flĭv'er, *n.* [Slang.] A motor-car of cheap grade,

floatᵈ, 1 flōt; 2 flōt, *v.* **I.** *t.* **1.** To keep up on or in a fluid. **2.** To put in circulation; find a market for. **II.** *i.* To be supported or carried along by a liquid or gas; move lightly and freely.— **float'age,** *n.* See FLOTAGE.— **float'er,** *n.*

float, *n.* An object that floats or buoys up [something.

floc'cu-lent, 1 flok'yu-lent; 2 flŏc'yụ-lĕnt, *a.* Woolly; downy.— **floc'cu-lence,** *n.*

flock, 1 flok; 2 flŏk. **I**ᵗ. *vi.* To assemble; congregate. **II.** *n.* **1.** A company or herd of animals, as sheep or birds. **2.** A congregation, church, or parish.

floe, 1 flō; 2 flō, *n.* A mass of floating polar [ice.

flog, 1 flog; 2 flŏg, *vt.* [FLOGGED, FLOGDˢ; FLOG'GING.] To chastise with a rod; whip. — **flog'ger,** *n.*— **flog'ging,** *n.*

floodᵈ, 1 flud; 2 flŏd, *v.* **I.** *t.* To inundate; deluge; supply to excess. **II.** *i.* To rise to or be at the flood; overflow.

flood, *n.* **1.** A freshet; inundation; deluge. **2.** The tide at its height; high tide. **3.** A copious flow, as of sunlight; abundant or excessive supply.— **flood'-gate",** *n.* A gate for regulating the flow of water; any removable restraint for an outpouring, as of contention or vice.

floor, 1 flōr; 2 flōr. **I.** *vt.* **1.** To provide with a floor. **2.** To throw to the floor; overthrow; vanquish. **II.** *n.* **1.** The bottom surface in a room or building; also, a story. **2.** Space appropriated to members; the right to speak.— **floor'ing,** *n.* **1.** Material for a floor. **2.** Floors collectively; a floor.

flop, 1 flop; 2 flŏp, *v.* & *n.* Same as FLAP.

flo'ra, 1 flō'rə; 2 flō'ra, *n.* **1.** The aggregate of plants of a country. **2.** [F-] *Rom. Myth.* The goddess of flowers.— **flo'ral,** *a.* Of, like, or pertaining to flowers.

flo-res'cence, 1 flo-res'ens; 2 flo-rĕs'ĕnç, *n.* *Bot.* **1.** The state of being in blossom. **2.** Inflorescence.— **flo-res'cent,** *a.* Expanding into flowers.

flo'ri-cul-ture, 1 flō'rī-kul-chur *or* -tiur; 2 flō'rī-eŭl-chur *or* -tūr, *n.* The cultivation of flowers or ornamental plants.

flor'id, 1 flor'ĭd; 2 flŏr'ĭd, *a.* **1.** Having a bright color; of a lively red. **2.** Excessively ornate; flowery.— **flor'id'l-ty,** *n.* **flor'id-ness‡.**

flo-rif'er-ous, 1 flo-rif'ẽr-ŭs; 2 flo-rĭf'ẽr-ŭs, *a.* Bearing flowers.

flor'in, 1 flor'ĭn; 2 flŏr'ĭn, *n.* A European silver coin; also, a gold coin of Tuscany.

flo'rist, 1 flō'rĭst; 2 flō'rĭst, *n.* A grower of or dealer in flowers.

floss, 1 flos; 2 flŏs, *n.* **1.** Floss-silk. **2.** The silk of some plants, as Indian corn.— **floss'-silk",** *n.* A soft, downy embroidery-silk.— **floss'y,** *a.* [FLOSS'I-ER; FLOSS'I-EST.] Of, pertaining to, or like floss; light; downy.

flo'tage, 1 flō'tĭj; 2 flō'tag, *n.* Things that float, collectively, or capacity to float.

flo-ta'tion, 1 flo-tē'shən; 2 flo-tā'shon, *n.* **1.** The act or state of floating. **2.** The science of bodies that float.

flo-til'la, 1 flo-til'ə; 2 flo-til'a, *n.* A fleet of small vessels; a small fleet.

flot'sam, 1 flŏt'səm; 2 flŏt'sam, *n.* *Law.* Goods found floating at sea.

flounce¹, 1 flauns; 2 flounç. **I.** *vt.* [FLOUNCED‡; FLOUNC'ING.] To furnish with flounces. **II.** *n.* A gathered or plaited strip on a skirt.

flounce², **I.** *vi.* To fling oneself about petulantly. **II.** *n.* The act of flouncing; a fling.

floun'der, 1 flaun'dər; 2 floun'der, *vi.* To stumble or struggle awkwardly or helplessly.

floun'der¹, *n.* A fish with broad flat body.

floun'der², *n.* A stumbling motion.

flour, 1 flaur; 2 flour, *vt. & vi.* **1.** To pulverize. **2.** To sprinkle flour upon.

flour, *n.* **1.** The ground and bolted substance of wheat; also, of some other cereal. **2.** Any finely powdered substance.

flour'ish‡, ⎱ 1 flur'ĭsh; 2 flŭr'ĭsh, *v.* **I.** *t.* To **flur'ish**ᴿ, ⎰ **1.** To swing about; brandish; flaunt. **2.** To embellish with flourishes. **II.** *i.* **1.** To thrive; prosper; live. **2.** To swing or wave about. **3.** To use flourishes.— **flour'ish-ing,** *pa.* Thriving; prosperous.

flour'ish, *n.* **1.** An ornamental mark in writing; something for display. **2.** The act of brandishing or waving.

flout, 1 flaut; 2 flout. **I**ᵈ. *vt. & vi.* To scoff at; jeer. **II.** *n.* A gibe; scoff.

flow, 1 flō; 2 flō, *v.* **I.** *t.* To overflow; flood. **II.** *i.* **1.** To move, as a stream; glide; issue; result. **2.** To rise, as the tide; abound.

flow, *n.* The act of flowing; a stream or current; incoming of the tide; a copious outpouring.

flow'er, 1 flau'ər; 2 flow'er, *v.* **I.** *t.* To decorate with flowers. **II.** *i.* To bloom; blossom.

flow'er, *n.* **1.** The blossom of a plant; bloom. **2.** A flowering plant. See illus. on next page. **3.** The best of anything. **4.** An ornament; figure of speech. **5.** *pl.* A very light powder.— **flow'er-i-ness,** *n.*— **flow'er-y,** *a.* Abounding with flowers; flowered; florid; figurative; poetic.

flown, 1 flōn; 2 flōn, *pp.* of FLY, *v.*

fluc'tu-ate, 1 fluk'chu-ēt *or* -tiu-ēt; 2 flŭe'chu-āt *or* -tū-āt, *vt. & vi.* [-AT'ED⁴; -AT'ING.] To move like waves; undulate; waver; oscillate.— **fluc"tu-a'tion,** *n.* Frequent irregular change; varying movement or action.

flue, 1 flū; 2 flu, *n.* A channel or passage for smoke, air, or gas from a fire; a chimney.

flu'ent, 1 flū'ent; 2 flu'ĕnt, *a.* **1.** Ready in speaking or writing; voluble. **2.** Copious; flowing; smooth, as style.— **flu'en-cy,** *n.* The quality of being fluent; readiness and ease of speech or expression. **flu'ent-ness‡.**— **flu'ent-ly,** *adv.*

fluff, 1 fluf; 2 flŭf, *n.* Nap, down, or the like.— **fluff'i-ness,** *n.*— **fluff'y,** *a.* Downy.

flu'id, 1 flū'ĭd; 2 flu'ĭd. **I.** *a.* Capable of flowing; liquid or gaseous. **II.** *n.* A liquid or gas.— **flu-id'i-ty,** *n.* The state or quality of being fluid. **flu'id-ness‡.**

fluke, 1 flūk; 2 fluk, *n.* The part of an anchor that holds to the ground; a lobe of a whale's tail; a barb on a harpoon.

flume, 1 flūm; 2 flum, *n.* A narrow passage through which water flows, as for a mill.

flum'mer-y, 1 flum'ẽr-ĭ; 2 flŭm'ẽr-y, *n.* **1.** Anything insipid; humbug. **2.** A dish of pasty food.

flung, 1 fluŋ; 2 flŭng, *imp. & pp.* of FLING, *v.*

flunk'y, ⎱ 1 fluŋk'ĭ; 2 flŭŋk'y, *n.* [FLUNK'-**flunk'ey,** ⎰ IES²; *pl.*] **1.** An obsequious fellow; toady. **2.** [Colloq.] A servant in livery.

flu'or, 1 flū'ər; 2 flu'ŏr, *n.* A cleavable, brittle mineral substance, a compound of calcium and fluorin, phosphorescent when heated. **flu'or-lte‡; flu'or-spar"‡.**

flu"o-res'cence, 1 flū"o-res'ens; 2 flu"o-rĕs'ĕnç, *n.* The property, possessed by some transparent bodies, of giving off,

1: artistic, ärt; fat, fāre; fast; get, prēy; hit, police; obey, gō; net, ôr; full, rūle; but, bûrn.

2: ärt, āpe, fät, fâre, fåst, what, all; mē, gĕt, prey, fẽrn; hĭt, īce; ī=ĕ; ĩ=ē; gō, nŏt, ôr, wŏn,

FLOWERS.

1. Cultivated rose. 2. Wild rose. 3. Carnation. 4. Honeysuckle 5. Violet. 6. White water-lily. 7. Jonquil. 8. Chrysanthemums. 9. Daisy. 10. Hyacinth. 11. Ketmia. 12. Sweet pea. 13. Poppy. 14. Magnolia. 15. Narcissus. 16. Iris. 17. Calla-lily. 18. Easter lily. 19. Morning-glory. 20. Tiger-lily. 21. Crocus. 22. Tulip. 23. Orchid. 24. Pansies. 25. Lilacs. 26. Butter-cup.

when illuminated, light different in color from their own and from that of the light thrown upon them.— **flu″o-res′cent,** *a.*

flu′o-rin, } 1 flū′o-rin, -rin *or* -rīn; 2 flṳ′o-
flu′o-rine, } rĭn, -rĭn *or* -rĭn, *n.* A pale-greenish, gaseous, chemical element.

flu′or-o-scope, 1 flū′ẽr-o-skōp; 2 flṳ′ẽr-o-seōp, *n.* A device for observing the shadows of objects cast by Roentgen rays through a fluorescent screen.

flur′ry, 1 flur′ĭ; 2 flŭr′y. **I.** *vt.* [FLUR′-RIED; FLUR′RY-ING.] To bewilder; agitate; fluster. **II.** *n.* [FLUR′RIES², *pl.*] A sudden commotion; flutter; hurry; a light gust of wind.

[redden; blush.
flush[it], 1 flush; 2 flŭsh, *vt. & vi.* To
flush²[t], *vt. & vi.* To deluge with water; wash out. [start up, as birds.
flush³[t], *vt. & vi.* To drive from cover;
flush⁴[t], *vt.* To encourage and excite; elate: chiefly in the past participle. [with *up.*
flush⁵[t], *vt.* To make flush or even: often
flush¹, *a.* Level; even.
flush², *a.* Full; well supplied with money.
flush³, *a.* Full of life; vigorous.
flush¹, *n.* **1.** A heightened color; blush. **2.** Sudden elation. **3.** A blossoming out; bloom.
flush², *n.* The act of flushing a bird; a bird or birds startled from cover.
flush³, *n.* A hand of cards all of one suit.
flush⁴, *n.* A sudden gush or rush of water.
flush⁵, *n.* Abundance.

flus′ter, 1 flus′tẽr; 2 flŭs′ter. **I.** *vt.* To confuse; flurry. **II.** *n.* Confusion of mind; flurry.

flute, 1 flūt; 2 flṳt, *vt. & vi.* [FLUT′ED[d]; FLUT′ING.] **1.** To corrugate; crimp. **2.** To play on a flute; make a flute-like sound.— **flut′ed,** *pa.* **1.** Channeled; crimped. **2.** Having the tone of a flute.— **flut′ing,** *n.* **1.** A groove or channel; fluted work. **2.** A crimp, as in a woman's ruffle.

flute, *n.* **1.** A small tubular wind-instrument with holes along the sides. **2.** A groove, as in a column; a corrugation; crimping.

flut′ter, 1 flut′ẽr; 2 flŭt′er, *v.* **I.** *t.* To shake; agitate; vibrate. **II.** *i.* To make the wings vibrate rapidly; move fitfully; be agitated. [tion.
flut′ter, *n.* The act of fluttering; agita-
flu′vi-al, 1 flū′vĭ-əl; 2 flṳ′vi-al, *a.* Of, pertaining to, or formed by a river. **flu′vi-a-tile‡.**

flux, 1 fluks; 2 flŭks. **I**[t]. *vt.* To melt; purge; treat with a flux. **II.** *n.* **1.** A flowing or melting. **2.** *Med.* Diarrhea. **3.** A substance that promotes the fusing

of minerals and metals.— **bloody flux,** dysentery.

flux′ion, 1 fluk′[sh]ən; 2 flŭk′shon, *n.* **1.** The act of flowing or melting; that which flows or melts. **2.** *Math.* The rate of variation of a changing quantity.— **flux′-ion-al,** *a.* **flux′ion-a-ry‡.**

fly, 1 flai; 2 flī, *v.* [FLEW, 1 flū; 2 flṳ; FLOWN, 1 flōn, 2 flōn; FLY′ING.] **I.** *t.* **1.** To cause to take flight. **2.** To flee from; shun. **II.** *i.* **1.** To move in the air, as by wings. **2.** To move quickly; hasten; dart; flee. **3.** To float in air or water; wave. **4.** To be violently impelled; explode; burst.—

Flying-fish. ¹⁄₂₄

fly′ing-boat, *n.* A hydroaeroplane.— **fly″ing-fish″,** *n.* A fish with large pectoral fins that buoy it up as it moves through the air.— **flying squirrel. 1.** A squirrel of parts of Europe and America, having on each side a fold of skin joining the fore and hind legs, and forming, when they are extended, a parachute by which the animal can make long gliding leaps. **2.** A marsupial of Australia similarly provided, known also as the *flying phalanger.*

fly¹, *n.* [FLIES², *pl.*] **1.** One of various small two-winged insects. **2.** [FLYS², *pl.*] A light carriage.— **fly′blow″. I.** *vt. & vi.* [FLY′BLOWN″, 1 flai′blōn″, 2 flī′blōn″; FLY′-BLOW″ING.] To taint with flyblows. **II.** *n.* The egg or young larva of a fly.— **fly′-speck″. I**[t]. *vt.* To mark with fly-specks. **II.** *n.* The dot made by the excrement of a fly; hence, any slight speck.

fly², *n.* **1.** One of various rapidly moving objects or devices; as, the *fly* of a printing-press. **2.** A flap. **3.** The act of flying.— **fly′leaf″,** *n.* A blank leaf at the beginning or end of a book.— **fly-wheel,** *n.* A heavy wheel whose weight resists sudden speed-changes, thus securing uniform motion.

fly′er, *n.* Same as FLIER.

foal, 1 fōl; 2 fōl. **I.** *vt. & vi.* To give birth to, as a foal; produce a foal. **II.** *n.* The young of an equine animal; a colt or filly.

foam, 1 fōm; 2 fōm. **I.** *vt. & vi.* To gather, produce, or emit foam; make or become foamy; froth. **II.** *n.* A collection of minute bubbles forming a frothy mass.— **foam′y,** *a.* Covered with foam; foam-like.

fob, 1 fob; 2 fŏb, *n.* A watch-pocket in the waistband of trousers, or a chain or ribbon hanging from it.

fo′cal, 1 fō′kəl; 2 fō′eal, *a.* Of, pertaining

to, situated at, or constituting a focus.—
fo'cal-ize or **-ise,** vt. To bring to a focus.

fo'cus, 1 fō'kŭs; 2 fō'cŭs. **I.** vt. [FO′-
CUSED† or FO′CUSSED†, FO′CUST⁵; FO′CUS-
ING or FO′CUS-SING.] To adjust or bring
to a focus; concentrate. **II.** n. [FO′CUS-ES²
or FO′CI, 1 -sai; 2 -sī, pl.] **1.** A point of
meeting of rays of light; any point of concentration. **2.** Geom. One of two points,
as in an ellipse, the sum or difference of
whose distances to any point of the curve
is always the same.

fod'der, 1 fɒd′ər; 2 fŏd′er, n. Coarse feed,
for horses, cattle, etc., as the stalks and
leaves of Indian corn.

foe, 1 fō; 2 fō, n. An enemy; adversary.
— **foe'man,** 1 fō′mən; 2 fō′man, n. [FOE′-
MEN, pl.] An active or open enemy.

fœ'tal, fœ'tid, a. Same as FETAL, FETID.

fœ'tus, n. Same as FETUS.

fog, 1 fɒg; 2 fŏg, n. **1.** Condensed watery
vapor suspended in the air near the earth;
mist. **2.** Bewilderment; perplexity; obscurity.— **fog'gi-ly,** adv.— **fog'gi-ness,** n.—
fog'gy, 1 fɒg′ɪ; 2 fŏg′y, a. Full of or covered
with fog; obscure; confused.

fo'gy, 1 fō′gɪ; 2 fō′gy, n. [FO′GIES², pl.]
A person of old-fashioned notions.— **fo'gy-
ism,** n.

foi'ble,) 1 fɔi′bl; 2 fŏi′bl, n. A personal
foi'bl²,) weakness; slight fault of character.

foil, 1 fɔil; 2 fŏil, vt. To render ineffectual;
frustrate; balk.

foil¹, n. **1.** Metal in
very thin sheets, as
on the back of a mir-
ror. **2.** Anything
that sets off some-
thing else by con-
trast. **3.** A leaf-like
division in architec-
tural ornamenta-
tion.

foil², n. A sword-like
implement, with a
button on its end,
used in fencing.

foist^d, 1 fɔist; 2 fŏist,
vt. To thrust in
slyly; palm off.

fold^d, 1 fōld; 2 fōld, v. **I.** t. **1.** To lay or
bend over upon itself; lap. **2.** To em-
brace; envelop. **II.** i. To shut in folds.

fold²^d, vt. To shut up in a fold, as sheep.

fold¹, n. **1.** One part doubled over another; a plait; ply. **2.** An embrace.

fold², n. **1.** A pen, as for sheep. **2.** A
flock of sheep; a church.

fold'er, 1 fōld′ər; 2 fōld′er, n. One who or
that which folds.

Foils.

Foliated tracery in
a window of Grace
Church Chantry, New
York.

fo'li-age, 1 fō′lɪ-ɪj; 2 fō′li-aġ, n. Any
growth of leaves; leaves collectively.

fo'li-ate, 1 fō′lɪ-ēt; 2 fō′li-ăt. **I.** vt.
[-AT′ED^d; -AT′ING.] To beat into a leaf;
coat with foil, as a mirror. **II.** a. Having leaves; leafy; leaf-shaped; beaten into
a leaf.— **fo'li-a'tion,** n. **1.** The leafing out
of plants. **2.** The act of foliating.

fo'li-o, 1 fō′lɪ-ō; 2 fō′li-ō, n. A sheet of
paper folded once; a book of the largest
size.

folk, 1 fōk; 2 fōk, n. **1.** People collectively.
2. pl. [Colloq.,U.S.] Those of one's family;
relatives. **3.** A nation or race.

fol'li-cle, 1 fɒl′ɪ-kl; 2 fŏl′i-cl, n. A minute
cavity; a dry seed-vessel; a cocoon.— **fol-
lic'u-lar,** a.

fol'low, 1 fɒl′o; 2 fŏl′o,v. **I.** t. **1.** To go or
come after; accompany; attend; pursue;
engage in; obey. **2.** To result from. **II.**
i. **1.** To go or move after something;
pursue. **2.** To be a natural consequence.
— **fol'low-er,** n. One who or that which
follows; an adherent, imitator, or attendant.
— **fol'low-ing.** **1.** pa. Next in order; succeeding. **II.** n. A body of adherents or
attendants.

fol'ly, 1 fɒl′ɪ; 2 fŏl′y, n. [FOL′LIES², pl.]
The state of being foolish; foolish conduct,
or its result.

fo-ment'^d, 1 fo-ment′; 2 fo-mĕnt′, vt. **1.**
To apply warm or medicated lotions to.
2. To stir up to heat or violence; instigate.— **fo″men-ta'tion,** n. The act of fomenting, in any sense; any lotion or medicinal substance used in fomenting.

fond, 1 fɒnd; 2 fŏnd, a. **1.** Loving;
affectionate; sometimes, foolishly affectionate. **2.** Foolishly prized; trivial; silly.
-ly, adv. **-ness,** n.

fon'dle,) 1 fɒn′dl; 2 fŏn′dl, vt. & vi.
fon'dl²,) [FON′DL(E)D^d; FON′DLING.] To
handle lovingly; caress.

font¹, 1 fɒnt; 2 fŏnt, n. **1.** A receptacle
for the water used in baptizing. **2.** A
fountain.

font², n. Print. A full assortment of type
of a particular kind.

food, 1 fūd; 2 fōod, n. Nourishment;
nutriment; aliment.

fool, 1 fūl; 2 fōol. **I.** vt. & vi. To make a
fool of; impose upon; deceive; play the
fool. **II.** n. **1.** A person lacking sense;
a simpleton. **2.** An idiot; imbecile. **3.**
A court jester.— **fool'er-y,** n. [-IES², pl.]
Foolish conduct; anything foolish.— **fool'-
har'dy,** a. Bold without judgment; reckless; rash.— **fool'har'di-ly,** adv.— **fool'-
har'di-ness,** n.— **fool'ish,** a. Of or like a
fool; weak-minded; marked by folly. **-ly,**

---

adv. **-ness,** *n.*— **fools'cap",** *n.* A size of writing-paper about 13 by 8 inches.

footᵈ, 1 fut; 2 fŏŏt, *v.* **I.** *t.* **1.** To tread; set the foot on; travel. **2.** To add, as a column of figures. **II.** *i.* To go afoot: walk.

foot, *n.* [FEET, 1 fīt; 2 fēt, *pl.*] **1.** The part below the ankle in man, or the corresponding part in other animals. **2.** Anything in any way like an animal's foot; the lowest part of a thing; the last of a series. **3.** A measure: twelve inches. **4.** Unmounted troops; infantry. **5.** *Pros.* A division of a verse.— **foot'ball",** *n.* A large inflated ball to be kicked in play; also, the game in which it is used.— **foot'fall",** *n.* The sound of a footstep.— **foot'hold",** *n.* A place where the foot may rest; secure footing; established position.— **foot'ing,** *n.* **1.** A place to stand or walk on; hence, secure position. **2.** The adding or the sum of a column of figures.— **foot'lights",** *n. pl.* Lights in a row near the front of the stage, as in a theater.— **foot'man,** *n.* [-MEN, *pl.*] **1.** A man servant who attends a carriage, etc. **2**‖. A foot-soldier.— **foot'pad",** *n.* A highwayman or robber on foot.— **foot'print",** *n.* An impression of a foot. **foot'-mark"**‡.— **foot'-sol"dier,** *n.* A soldier who marches and fights on foot; an infantryman.— **foot'-step",** *n.* A step; footfall; footprint.— **foot'stool",** *n.* A low stool for the feet.

fop, 1 fŏp; 2 fŏp, *n.* A man affectedly fastidious in dress or deportment; a dandy.— **fop'per-y,** *n.* [-IESᶻ, *pl.*] The conduct or practises of a fop.

for, 1 fôr; 2 fôr. **I.** *prep.* Because of; on account of; with a view to; in behalf of; in place of; in honor of; by the name of. **II.** *conj.* Seeing that; since; because.

for'age, 1 fẽr'ij; 2 fŏr'ag. **I.** *vt. & vi.* [FOR'AGED; FOR'AG-ING.] To overrun in search of forage; collect food for men and stock by roving search. **II.** *n.* **1.** Any food suitable for horses or cattle. **2.** The act of foraging.— **for'ag-er,** *n.*

for"as-much", 1 fŏr"az-muᶜh'; 2 fŏr"ăs-much'. *conj.* Seeing or considering that: used with *as.*

for'ay, 1 fŏr'ē; 2 fŏr'ā. **I.** *vt. & vi.* To ravage; pillage; raid. **II.** *n.* A marauding expedition; raid.

for-bade', } 1 fẽr-bad'; 2 fŏr-băd', *imp.* of
for-bad'ᵖ, } FORBID, *v.*

for-bear', 1 fẽr-bâr'; 2 fŏr-bâr', *v.* [FOR-BORE, 1 fẽr-bōr'; 2 fŏr-bōr'; FOR-BORNE', 1 fẽr-bōrn', 2 fŏr-bōrn'; FOR-BEAR'ING.] **I.** *t.* To refrain or abstain from. **II.** *i.* **1.** To refrain from some action. **2.** To be patient. **-ing,** *a.*— **for-bear'ance,** *n.* The act of forbearing; patience; mildness.— **for-bear'ing-ly,** *adv.*

for-bid', 1 fẽr-bid'; 2 fŏr-bĭd', *vt.* [FOR-BADE', 1 fẽr-bad', 2 fŏr-băd'; FOR-BID'DEN, 1 fẽr-bid'n, 2 fŏr-bĭd'n, or FOR-BID'; FOR-BID'DING.] To command against: prohibit; oppose effectually; prevent.— **for-bid'ding,** *pa.* Such as to repel; repellent; repulsive. [*pp.* of FORBEAR, *v.*

for-bore', *imp.* of FORBEAR, *v.*— **for-borne',** *pp.* of FORBEAR, *v.*

force, 1 fōrs; 2 fŏrç. **I.** *vt.* [FORCED**ᵗ**; FORC'ING.] **1.** To compel. **2.** To stimulate artificially. **II.** *n.* **1.** Any operating energy; constraint; compulsion; coercion; cogency; efficacy; import. **2.** An organized body, as of troops; an army.— **force'-ful,** *a.*— **force'ful-ly,** *adv.*— **force'-pump",** *n.* A pump that forces fluid out or up by means of compressed air.

A Side-suc-tion Force-pump.

for'ceps, 1 fŏr'seps; 2 fŏr'çĕps, *n.* Pincers for grasping or removing small objects or foreign bodies.

for'ci-ble, } 1 fŏr'sı-bl; 2 fŏr'çi-bl, *a.* **1.**
for'ci-blᵖ, } Accomplished by force. **2.** Energetic; cogent.— **for'ci-bl(e-ness**ᵖ, *n.*— **for'ci-bly,** *adv.*

ford, 1 fōrd; 2 fôrd. **I**ᵈ. *vt.* To wade across. **II.** *n.* A place where a stream may be waded across.— **ford'a-bl(e**ᵖ, *a.*

fore, 1 fōr; 2 fôr. **I.** *a.* Preceding in place or time; forward; antecedent; prior. **II.** *n.* The foremost part; the leading place. **III.** *adv.* **1.** *Naut.* At or toward the bow. **2.** Before; forward; in front. **IV.** *prep.* Before.— **fore'-and-aft",** *a.* Lying or going in the direction of a ship's length.

fore-, *prefix.* Before; as, *fore*arm.

fore-arm', 1 fōr-ärm'; 2 fŏr-ärm', *vt.* To arm beforehand.

fore'arm", 1 fōr'ärm"; 2 fŏr'ärm", *n.* The part of the arm that is between the elbow and the wrist.

fore-bode', 1 fōr-bōd'; 2 fŏr-bōd', *v.* [-BOD'-ED**ᵈ**; -BOD'ING.] **I.** *t.* **1.** To be an omen of; presage. **2.** To have a premonition of. **II.** *i.* To foretell; prognosticate.— **fore-bod'ing,** *n.* The apprehension of coming misfortune.

fore-cast'ᵈ, 1 fōr-kȧst'; 2 fŏr-cȧst', *vt.* To calculate or plan beforehand; predict.

fore'cast", 1 fōr'kȧst"; 2 fŏr'cȧst", *n.* An antecedent calculation or contrivance.

fore'cas"tle, 1 fōr'kȧs"l *or* (*Naut.*) fōk'sl; 2 fŏr'cȧs"l *or* (*Naut.*) fōc'sl, *n.* The forward part of a ship; compartment for common sailors.

fore-close', 1 fōr-klōz'; 2 fŏr-clōṣ', *vt.* [FORE-CLOSED'; FORE-CLOS'ING.] To bar by judicial proceedings the right to redeem,

---

1: **u**rtistic, **är**t; **f**at, **f**āre; **f**ȧst; get, pr**ē**y; h**ĭ**t, pol**i**ce; ob**e**y, g**ō**; n**o**t, **ŏ**r; f**u**ll, r**ū**le; b**u**t, b**ûr**n.
2: **ä**rt, **ā**pe, f**ă**t, f**â**re, f**ȧ**st, wh**ạ**t, ạll; mē, gĕt, prẹy, fẽrn; hĭt, īce; **ī**=ē; **ĭ**=ē; gō, nŏt, ôr, wọn,

as mortgaged property; shut out; exclude.— **fore-clo'sure,** 1 fōr-klō'ʒur; 2 fōr-clō'zhur, *n.* The act of foreclosing.

fore'fa"ther, 1 fōr'fā"thər; 2 fōr'fä"ther, *n.* An ancestor.

fore-fend', 1 fōr-fend'; 2 fōr-fĕnd', *vt.* Same as FORFEND.

fore'fin"ger, 1 fōr'fiŋ"gər; 2 fōr'fĭŋ"ger, *n.* The finger next to the thumb.

fore'foot", 1 fōr'fut"; 2 fōr'fŏŏt", *n.* A fore foot.

fore'front", 1 fōr'frunt"; 2 fōr'frŏnt", *n.* The foremost part or position.

fore-go'[1], 1 fōr-gō'; 2 fōr-gō', *vt.* [FORE-WENT'; FORE-GONE'; FORE-GO'ING.] To give up; relinquish.

fore-go'[2], *vt. & vi.* To go in advance of; go before.— **fore-go'ing,** *pa.* Occurring previously; antecedent.— **fore'gon**(eᵖ, *pa.* Determined already.

fore'ground", 1 fōr'graund"; 2 fōr'ground", *n.* That part of a landscape nearest the spectator.

fore'hand"ed, 1 fōr'hand"ed; 2 fōr'hănd"-ĕd, *a.* **1.** Done in good time. **2.** [U. S.] Having money saved; thrifty.

fore'head,) 1 fŏr'ed; 2 fŏr'ĕd, *n.* The
fore'heds,) upper part of the face, between the eyes and the hair.

for'eign,) 1 fŏr'in; 2 fŏr'in, *a.* Of or from
for'ens,) another country; alien; not belonging where found; not pertinent; irrelevant.— **for'eign-er, for'en-ers,** 1 fŏr'-in-ər; 2 fŏr'ĭn-ẽr, *n.* A citizen of a foreign country; an alien.

fore-know', 1 fōr-nō'; 2 fōr-nō', *vt.* [FORE-KNEW'; -KNOWN'; -KNOW'ING.] To know beforehand.— **fore-knowl'edge,** 1 fōr-nol'ij; 2 fōr-nōl'edĝ, *n.* Knowledge before the event.

fore'land, 1 fōr'land; 2 fōr'lănd, *n.* A projecting point of land.

fore'lock, 1 fōr'lek"; 2 fōr'lŏk", *n.* A lock of hair growing over the forehead, as of a horse.

fore'man, 1 fōr'mən; 2 fōr'man, *n.* [FORE-MEN, *pl.*] The head man overseeing a body of workmen.

fore'mast", 1 fōr'mɑst"; 2 fōr'mȧst", *n.* The foremost mast of a vessel.

fore'most, 1 fōr'mōst; 2 fōr'mōst, *a.* First in place, time, rank, or order; chief.

fore'noon", 1 fōr'nūn"; 2 fōr'nŏŏn", *n.* The period of daylight preceding midday; the morning.

fo-ren'sic, 1 fo-ren'sık; 2 fo-rĕn'sie, *a.* Pertaining to courts or justice or to public disputation.

fore"or-dain', 1 fōr"ər-dēn'; 2 fōr"ŏr-dān', *vt.* To ordain beforehand; predestinate.

— **fore-or"di-na'tion,** *n.* Predestination; predetermination.

fore-run', 1 fōr-run'; 2 fōr-rŭn', *vt.* To run before; precede; announce.— **fore-run'-ner,** *n.* A herald.

fore'sail",) fōr'sēl" *or* (*Naut.*) fō'sl; 2 fōr'sāl.
or (*Naut.*) fō'sl, *n.* A sail on a foremast'

fore-see', 1 fōr-sī'; 2 fōr-sē', *v.* [FORE-SAW'; FORE-SEEN'; FORE-SEE'ING.] **I.** *t.* To see beforehand; anticipate. **II.** *i.* To have foresight.

fore-shad'ow, 1 fōr-shad'o; 2 fōr-shăd'o. **I.** *vt.* To suggest beforehand. **II.** *n.* The dim representation of something to come

fore-short'en, 1 fōr-shŏrt'n; 2 fōr-shŏrt'n, *vt.* To shorten parts of in drawing, so as to give the effect of distance.

fore'sight", 1 fōr'sait"; 2 fōr'sīt", *n.* The act or power of foreseeing; forethought.

for'est, 1 fŏr'est; 2 fŏr'est, *n.* A tract of land overgrown with trees.— **for'est-er, n.** One who has charge of a forest.— **for'est-ry,** *n.* The art of developing or managing forests.

fore-stall', 1 fōr-stŏl'; 2 fōr-stạl', *vt.* **1.** To hinder; anticipate; prevent. **2.** To control in one's own favor; as, to *forestall* the market.

fore'taste", 1 fōr'tēst"; 2 fōr'tāst", *n.* A taste or brief experience beforehand.

fore-tell', 1 fōr-tel'; 2 fōr-tĕl', *vt. & vi.* [FORE-TOLD'; FORE-TELL'ING.] To predict.

fore'thought", 1 fōr'thŏt"; 2 fōr'thôt", *n.* Consideration beforehand; prudent care for the future.

fore"to'ken, *vt.* Same as FORESHADOW.

fore'top", 1 fōr'tɒp"; 2 fōr'tŏp", *n.* **1.** The forelock. **2.** A platform at the head of a foremast.

for-ev'er, 1 fɒr-ev'ər; 2 fŏr-ĕv'ẽr, *adv.* Eternally; endlessly; incessantly.

fore-warn', 1 fōr-wŏrn'; 2 fōr-wạrn', *vt.* To warn beforehand; instruct in advance. — **fore-warn'ing,** *n.*

for'feit,) 1 fōr'fit; 2 fōr'fit. **I**d. *vt.* To
for'fits,) lose through some fault, neglect, or error. **II.** *a.* Forfeited. **III.** *n.* **1.** A thing lost by default. **2.** *pl.* Any game in which some playful penalty is imposed.— **for'feit-a-ble,** *a.*— **for'fei-ture,** 1 fōr'fi-chur *or* -tiur; 2 fōr'fi-chur *or* -tūr, *n.* The act of forfeiting, or that which is forfeited.

for-fend'[|ᵈ, 1 fər-fend'; 2 fōr-fĕnd', *vt.* To ward off; prevent. [GIVE, *v.*

for-gave', 1 fɒr-gēv'; 2 fŏr-gāv', *imp.* of FOR-

forge', 1 fōrj *or* fōrj; 2 fôrg *or* fôrg, *v.* [FORGED; FORG'ING.] **I.** *t.* **1.** To shape (heated metal), as with a hammer; shape; frame. **2.** *Law.* To make or alter with

intent to defraud.— **II.** *i.* To be guilty of forgery.— **forg′er,** *n.*— **forger-y,** 1 fōr′jər-ɪ *or* fôr′jər-ɪ; 2 fôr′ger-y *or* fôr′ger-y, *n.* [-ɪESᶻ, *pl.*] **1.** The act of forging. **2.** A forged paper or document.

forge², *v.* **I.** *t.* To impel forward.— **II.** *i.* To go slowly or with difficulty.

forge, *n.* **1.** An open fireplace or hearth with forced draft, as for blacksmithing. **2.** A place where metal is forged.

for-get′, 1 fər-get′; 2 fŏr-gĕt′, *vt.* & *vi.* [FOR-GOT′, 1 fər-got′, 2 fŏr-gŏt′; FOR-GOT′TEN, 1 fər-got′n, 2 fŏr-gŏt′n; FOR-GET′TING.] **1.** To lose from the memory. **2.** To lose interest in; neglect.— **for-get′ful,** *a.* Forgetting easily; neglectful. **-ly,** *adv.* **-ness,** *n.*— **for-get′me-not′′,** *n.* A perennial herb, with small sky-blue flowers.

for-give′, 1 fər-giv′; 2 fŏr-gĭv′, *v.* [FOR-giv′ᴾ, 1 GAVE′, 1 fər-gĕv′, 2 fŏr-gāv′; FOR-GIV′EN; FOR-GIV′ING.] **I.** *t.* To pardon; excuse; remit, as a debt. **II.** *i.* To show forgiveness.— **for-give′(e′nessᴾ,** *n.* **1.** The act of forgiving; pardon. **2.** A disposition to forgive. **for-giv′ing-ness‡.**— **for-giv′ing,** *pa.* Disposed to forgive. **-ly,** *adv.*

for-got′, *imp.* & *pp.* of FORGET, *v.*— **for-got′ten,** *pp.* of FORGET, *v.*

fork, 1 fŏrk; 2 fôrk. **I.** *vt.* & *vi.* To lift, toss, or dig with a fork; diverge; divide. **II.** *n.* A device consisting of a handle and tines or prongs; also, anything of like shape or use.— **forked,** 1 fŏrkt *or* fôrk′ed; 2 fôrkt *or* fôrk′ĕd, *a.* Having a fork, or shaped like a fork; diverging into two branches.

for-lorn′, 1 fər-lŏrn′; 2 fŏr-lôrn′, *a.* Left in distress; miserable; lonely; dreary. **-ly,** *adv.* **-ness,** *n.*— **forlorn hope,** a military detachment detailed for a desperate enterprise; also, such an enterprise.

form, 1 fŏrm; 2 fôrm, *v.* **I.** *t.* To make; construct; conceive; compose. **II.** *i.* To assume a specific form.— **form′er,** *n.*

form, *n.* **1.** The shape of a body; figure; contour; appearance; style; kind. **2.** Ritual; ceremony. **3.** A mold; model; formula; type in a chase ready for the press. **4.** A long bench without a back.

form′al, 1 fŏrm′al; 2 fôrm′al, *a.* **1.** According with established forms; ceremonial; ceremonious. **2.** Pertaining to form as opposed to substance; outward; external.— **form′al-ism,** *n.* Scrupulous observance of forms.— **form′al-ist,** *n.*— **for-mal′i-ty,** *n.* [-TIESᶻ, *pl.*] The state or character of being formal; a formal observance; empty ceremony.— **form′al-ly,** *adv.*

for-mal′de-hyde, 1 fər-mal′də-hold; 2 fŏr-măl′de-hȳd, *n.* A colorless gas obtained from methyl alcohol: a powerful antiseptic and disinfectant.

for-ma′tion, 1 fər-mē′shən; 2 fŏr-mā′shon, *n.* The act of forming; construction; arrangement; development.— **form′a-tiv(es,** 1 fōrm′ə-tiv; 2 fôrm′a-tiv. **I.** *a.* **1.** Serving or aiding to form. **2.** Pertaining to formation. **II.** *n.* An element added to a word; an affix.

for′mer, 1 fŏr′mər; 2 fôr′mer, *a.* Earlier; previous; preceding; ancient.— **for′mer-ly,** *adv.* Some time ago; once.

for′mic, 1 fŏr′mɪk; 2 fôr′mie, *a.* Pertaining to or derived from ants.— **formic acid,** a colorless liquid compound, found in ants, stinging nettles, etc., and also produced artificially.

for′mi-da-ble, 1 fŏr′mɪ-də-bl; 2 fôr′mi-da-bl‡, } da-bl, *a.* Exciting fear; dangerous to encounter; difficult to accomplish.— **for′mi-da-bly,** *adv.*

for′mu-la, 1 fŏr′miu-lə; 2 fôr′mū-la, *n.* [-LASᶻ *or* -LÆ, *pl.*] A fixed rule; exact statement.— **for′mu-la-ry,** 1 fŏr′miu-lē-rɪ; 2 fôr′mū-lā-ry, *a.* Stated in or as in a formula; formal. **II.** *n.* [-RIESᶻ, *pl.*] A collection of forms or formulas; a ritual.— **for′mu-late,** *vt.* [-LAT′EDᵈ; -LAT′ING.] To express in or as a formula.— **for′′mu-la′tion,** *n.*

for′ni-ca′tion, 1 fŏr′nɪ-kē′shən; 2 fôr′ni-cā′shon, *n.* Illicit sexual intercourse.— **for′ni-ca′′tor,** *n.*— **for′ni-ca′′tress,** *n. fem.*

for-sake′, 1 fər-sēk′; 2 fŏr-sāk′, *vt.* [FOR-SOOK′, 1 fər-sūk′, 2 fŏr-sook′; FOR-SAK′EN *or* FOR-SOOK′; FOR-SAK′ING.] To leave; abandon; reject.

for-sooth′, 1 fər-sūth′; 2 fŏr-sooth′, *adv.* In truth; certainly: chiefly ironical.

for-swear′, 1 fər-swār′; 2 fŏr-swâr′, *vt.* & *vi.* [-SWORE′; -SWORN′; -SWEAR′ING.] To renounce upon oath; repudiate; perjure (oneself).

A Round Fort.
Castle William, on Governors Island, New York Bay.

fort, 1 fōrt; 2 fôrt, *n.* A defensive work; a fortification; fortress.

forte, 1 fōrt; 2 fôrt, *n.* That which one does most readily or excellently.

for′te, 1 fōr′tē; 2 fôr′te, *a.*, *n.*, & *adv.* *Mus.* Loud; a passage to be loudly performed.

forth, 1 fōrth; 2 fôrth, *adv.* Forward; outward; away; out; abroad.— **forth′com′′ing,** *a.* Ready or about to appear.— **forth′with′,** *adv.* Without delay; immediately; directly.

for′ti-eth, 1 fŏr′tɪ-efh; 2 fôr′ti-ĕth. **I.** *a.* **1.** Tenth in order after the thirtieth. **2.**

1: **a**rtistic, **ä**rt; fat, f**ā**re; f**a**st; get, pr**ē**y; h**ɪ**t, pol**i**ce; obey, g**ō**; n**o**t, **ŏ**r; f**u**ll, r**ū**le; b**u**t, b**ū**rn.
2: **ä**rt, **ā**pe, f**ă**t, f**â**re, f**a**st, wh**a**t, **a**ll; m**ē**, g**ĕ**t, pr**e**y, f**ẽ**rn; h**ɪ**t, **ī**ce; ī=ē; ĭ=ĕ; g**ō**, n**ŏ**t, **ô**r, w**o**n,

Being one of forty equal parts. **II.** *n.* One of forty equal parts.— **for″ti-eth-ly,** *adv.*

for″ti-fi-ca′tion, 1 fôr″tɪ-fɪ-kē′shan; 2 fôr″ti-fi-cā′shon, *n.* **1.** The act, art, or science of fortifying. **2.** A military defensive work; a fort.

for′ti-fy, 1 fôr′tɪ-faɪ; 2 fôr′ti-fȳ, *vt. & vi.* [-FIED; -FY′ING.] To provide with or raise defensive works; give strength, security, or power to.— **for′ti-fi″a-bl(eᴿ,** *a.*

for-tis′si-mo, 1 fẽr-tɪs′ɪ-mō; 2 fôr-tɪs′ɪ-mō, *a. & adv. Mus.* Very loud.

for′ti-tude, 1 fôr′tɪ-tiūd; 2 fôr′ti-tūd, *n.* Strength of mind to endure suffering or peril.

fort′night″, 1 fôrt′naɪt″ or fôrt′nɪt; 2 fôrt′-nɪt″ or fôrt′nɪt, *n.* A period of two weeks. **-ly,** *a. & adv.*

for′tress, 1 fôr′tres; 2 fôr′trĕs, *n.* A large permanent fort; a stronghold; castle.

for-tu′i-tous, 1 fer-tiū′ɪ-tus; 2 fôr-tū′i-tŭs, *a.* Occurring by chance; casual; accidental. **-ly,** *adv.* **-ness,** *n.*

for-tu′i-ty, 1 fer-tiū′ɪ-tɪ; 2 fôr-tū′i-ty, *n.* Chance occurrence.

for′tu-nate, 1 fôr′chu-[or -tiu-]nɪt; 2 fôr′-chu[or -tū-]nat, *a.* **1.** Happening by a favorable chance; lucky. **2.** Favored with good fortune.— **for′tu-nate-ly,** *adv.*

for′tune, 1 fôr′chun or -tiun; 2 fôr′chun or -tūn, *n.* Chance; especially, favorable chance; lot; luck; success; a large estate; wealth.

for′ty, 1 fôr′tɪ; 2 fôr′ty. **I.** *a.* Consisting of ten more than thirty. **II.** *n.* The sum of ten and thirty.

fo′rum, 1 fō′rum; 2 fō′rŭm, *n.* [FO′RUMSᶻ or FO′RA, *pl.*] A place of public assembly, as in ancient Rome; an assembly; tribunal; court.

for′ward, 1 fôr′werd; 2 fôr′ward. **Iᵈ.** *vt.* To send forward; help onward; further; transmit. **II.** *a.* **1.** Located at or near the front. **2.** Advanced; advancing. **3.** Eager; prompt; officious; impertinent. **III.** *adv.* Toward the front; onward; ahead. **for′wards:. -ly,** *adv.* **-ness,** *n.*

fos′sil, 1 fos′ɪl; 2 fŏs′il. **I.** *a.* Petrified; outworn; antiquated. **II.** *n.* **1.** A body, as the petrified form of a plant or an animal, preserved in earth or rock. **2.** A person or thing out of date.— **fos″sil-if′er-ous,** *a.* Containing fossils.— **fos′sil-ize,** *vt. & vi.* [-IZED; -IZ′ING.] To convert into a fossil: petrify; make or become antiquated. **fos′sil-ize‡.**

fos′ter, 1 fes′ter; 2 fŏs′ter, *vt.* To nourish; rear; aid; encourage.— **fos′ter=broth″er, f.= child, f.=father, f.=mother, f.=parent, f.= sister, f.=son,** one considered as holding the

relationship indicated, in consequence of nursing and rearing, tho not related by blood.

fought, 1 fôt; 2 fôt, *imp. & pp.* of FIGHT, *v.*

fought′en, *pp.* of FIGHT, *v.* Obsolete except in the phrase *a foughten field.*

foul, 1 faul; 2 foul. **I.** *vt. & vi.* To collide (with); make or become foul or dirty; commit a breach of rule. **II.** *a.* **1.** Offensive; loathsome; filthy. **2.** Obstructing, entangling, or injuring; unfair. **III.** *n.* An act of fouling; a collision; breach of rule. **IV.** *adv.* Foully.— **foul′ly,** *adv.* In a foul manner.— **foul′ness,** *n.*

found, 1 faund; 2 found, *imp. & pp.* of FIND, *v.*

found¹ᵈ, *v.* **I.** *t.* To lay the foundation of; originate; establish. **II.** *i.* To form and base one's belief or opinion: followed by *on* or *upon.*— **foun-da′tion,** *n.* **1.** The act of founding; base; basis. **2.** An endowment; endowed institution.— **found′erᴵ,** *n.* One who founds or endows.— **found′ress,** *n. fem.*

found²ᵈ, *vt.* To cast, as iron, by melting and pouring.— **found′er²,** *n.* One who makes castings.— **found′ing,** *n.* The business of making articles of cast iron, brass, etc.

foun′der, 1 faun′dẽr; 2 foun′der, *vt. & vi.* **1.** To fill with water and sink, as a vessel. **2.** To fail; be ruined. **3.** To make or go lame, as a horse, through inflammation in the feet.— **foun′der³,** *n.* Inflammation of the tissue in the foot of a horse.

found′ling, 1 faund′lɪŋ; 2 found′ling, *n.* A deserted infant of unknown parentage.

foun′dry, 1 faun′drɪ; 2 foun′dry, *n.* [FOUN′DRIESᶻ, *pl.*] A place where articles are cast from metal. **foun′der-y‡.**

fount, 1 faunt; 2 fount, *n.* **1.** A fountain. **2.** A font.

foun′tain, 1 faun′tɪn; 2 foun′tan, *n.* **1.** A spring, jet, or spray of water; also, any structure enclosing it. **2.** A cause; origin; source.— **foun′tain-head″,** *n.* The source, as of a stream.

four, 1 fōr; 2 fôr. **I.** *a.* Consisting of one more than three. **II.** *n.* The sum of three and one.— **four′fold″,** *a. & adv.* Quadruple; in quadrupled measure.— **four′score″,** *a. & n.* Eighty.— **four-teen′,** 1 fôr-tīn′; 2 fôr-tēn′. **I.** *a.* Consisting of four more than ten. **II.** *n.* The sum of ten and four.— **four-teenth′,** *a. & n.*— **fourth,** 1 fôrth; 2 fôrth. **I.** *a.* Next in order after the third. **II.** *n.* One of four equal parts. **-ly,** *adv.*

fowl, 1 faul; 2 fowl, *n.* **1.** The common domestic cock or hen. **2.** *pl.* Poultry in general. **3.** Birds collectively; as, wild *fowl.* See illus. on next page.— **fowl′er,** *n.* One who catches or kills birds for sport or food.— **fowl′ing=piece″,** *n.* A light smooth-bore shotgun for bird=shooting.

REPRESENTATIVE TYPES OF FOWLS.

1. Houdans. 2. White-faced Black Spanish 3. Barred Plymouth Rocks. 4. Silver-laced Wyan-dottes. 5. Japanese Bantams. 6. Sebright Bantams. 7. Silver-gray Dorkings. 8. Buff Cochins. 9. Partridge-cochins. 10. Light Brahmas. 11. Indian Games. 12. Silver-spangled Hamburgs. 13. White Leghorns.

fox, 1 foks; 2 fŏks, *n.* **1.** A burrowing canine mammal, noted for its cunning. **2.** A sly, crafty person.— **fox′y,** 1 foks′i; 2 fŏks′y, *a.* [FOX′I-ER; FOX′I-EST.] Of or like a fox; crafty in character; reddish-brown in color.— **fox′i-ness,** *n.*

foy″er′, 1 fwä″yē′ *or* foi′ər; 2 fwä″yē′ *or* foy′er, *n.* A public room near the auditorium and lobby, as in a theater, etc.

fra′cas, 1 frē′kəs; 2 frā′cas, *n.* A noisy fight or quarrel; uproar.

frac′tion, 1 frak′shən; 2 frăc′shon, *n.* **1.** A fragment; portion. **2.** The sum of a number of equal parts of a unit, as ½, ⅔, 0.35.— **frac′tion-al,** *a.* **-ly,** *adv.*

frac′tious, 1 frak′shus; 2 frăc′shŭs, *a.* Ill-tempered; unruly; peevish. **-ly,** *adv.* **-ness,** *n.*

frac′ture, 1 frak′chur *or* -tiūr; 2 frăc′chŭr *or* -tūr. **I.** *vt.* & *vi.* [FRAC′TURED; FRAC′TUR-ING.] To break. **II.** *n.* The act of breaking; a break.

frag′ile, ⎱ 1 fraj′il; 2 frăg′il, *a.* Easily
frag′il⁸, ⎰ broken; frail; delicate.— **fra-gil′i-ty,** *n.* Fragile quality.

frag′ment, 1 frag′ment *or* mənt; 2 frăg′ment, *n.* A part broken off; a small detached portion.— **frag′men-ta-ry,** *a.* Composed of fragments; broken.

fra′grant, 1 frē′grənt; 2 frā′grant, *a.* Having an agreeable smell.— **fra′grance,** *n.* The state or quality of being fragrant. **fra′gran-cy‡.— fra′grant-ly,** *adv.*

frail, 1 frēl; 2 frāl, *a.* Delicately constituted; easily broken or destroyed; easily tempted; liable to be led astray. **-ly,** *adv.*— **frail′ty,** *n.* [FRAIL′TIES², *pl.*] The state of being frail; a moral infirmity. **frail′ness‡.**

frame, 1 frēm; 2 frām. **I.** *vt.* [FRAMED; FRAM′ING.] To put together; contrive; arrange; shape; surround with a frame. **II.** *n.* **1.** Something composed of parts united in a system; arrangement; constitution; framework; case. **2.** A mental state or condition.— **frame′work″,** *n.* A skeleton structure as a support or enclosure; plan; outline.

franc, 1 frank; 2 frănc, *n.* A French silver coin, of the value of about 19½ cents.

fran′chise, 1 fran′chiz *or* fran′chaiz; 2 frăn′chiş *or* frăn′chĭş, *n.* A political right, privilege, or exemption; suffrage; citizenship.

fran′gi-ble, ⎱ 1 fran′ji-bl; 2 frăn′gi-bl,
fran′gi-bl², ⎰ *a.* Easily broken; fragile.— **fran″gi-bil′i-ty,** *n.*

frank⁴, 1 frank; 2 frănk, *vt.* To send free of charge, as a letter.

frank, *a.* **1.** Candid and open; ingenuous. **2.** Free; privileged; exempt. **-ly,** *adv.* **-ness,** *n.*

frank¹, *n.* The right to send mail-matter free, the package so sent, or the signature that authenticates it.

Frank², *n.* **1.** A member of one of the Germanic tribes settled on the Rhine early in the Christian era. **2.** In the Orient, any European.— **Frank′ish,** *a.*

frank′furt-er, 1 frank′fərt-ər; 2 frănk′-furt-er, *n.* A highly seasoned sausage of mixed meats.

frank′in-cense, 1 frank′in-sens; 2 frănk′-in-cĕns, *n.* An aromatic gum: used as an incense.

fran′tic, 1 fran′tik; 2 frăn′tic, *a.* Wildly excited; frenzied.— **fran′ti-cal-ly,** *adv.*

fra-ter′nal, 1 frə-tūr′nal; 2 fra-tẽr′nal, *a.* Brotherly. **-ly,** *adv.*— **fra-ter′ni-ty,** *n.* [-TIES² *pl.*] Brotherhood; brotherly affection; a fraternal association.— **frat′er-nize** *or* **-nise,** 1 frat′ər-naiz; 2 frăt′er-nĭz, *vt.* & *vi.* To bring into or hold fellowship.— **frat″er-ni-za′[or -sa′]tion,** *n.*

frat′ri-cide, 1 frat′ri-said; 2 frăt′ri-çĭd, *n.* **1.** One who kills his brother. **2.** The killing of a brother by a brother.— **frat″ri-ci′dal,** *a.*

fraud, 1 frēd; 2 frạd, *n.* Deceitful dealing; craft; trickery; a cheat; a spurious thing.— **fraud′u-lent,** *a.* Practising or characterized by fraud.— **fraud′u-lent-ly,** *adv.* [full.

fraught, 1 frēt; 2 frạt, *pa.* [Poet.] Freighted;

fray, 1 frē; 2 frā, *v.* **I.** *t.* To wear; fret. **II.** *i.* To ravel at the edge.

fray¹, *n.* A fretted spot in a cloth, cord, etc.

fray² n. An affray; fracas; combat.

fraz″′le, ⎱ 1 fraz′l; 2 frăz′l. **I.** *vt.* & *vt.* To
fraz′l⁸ ⎰ fray or tatter; become frayed. **II.** *n.* Frayed ends; state of being frayed; worn out.

freak, 1 frik; 2 frēk, *n.* **1.** A sudden causeless change of mind; a whim. **2.** A monstrosity.— **freak′ish,** *a.* **-ly,** *adv.* **-ness,** *n.*

freck′le, ⎱ 1 frek′l; 2 frĕk′l. **I.** *vt.* & *vi.*
freck′l⁸, ⎰ [FRECK′L(E)D⁸; FRECK′LING.] To mark or be marked with freckles. **II.** *n.* A small, colored spot on the skin.— **freck′ly,** *adv.*

free, 1 frī; 2 frē. **I.** *vt.* [FREED; FREE′ING.] To set free; release; relieve. **II.** *a.* [FRE′-ER; FRE′EST.] **1.** Not restrained; uncontrolled; independent. **2.** Exempt: followed by *from.* **3.** Ingenuous; frank; easy; careless; familiar. **4.** Gratuitous. **5.** Liberal; generous. **III.** *adv.* Freely; gratuitously; willingly. **-ly,** *adv.* **-ness,** *n.*— **free′boot″er,** *n.* A robber.

freed′man, 1 frīd′man; 2 frēd′man, *n.* An emancipated slave.

free′dom, 1 frī′dəm; 2 frē′dom, *n.* **1.** The state of being free; liberty. **2.** Facility; ease; ingenuousness; also, undue familiarity.

free'-hand"ed, a. 1. Having the hands free. 2. Open-handed; generous.— **free'hold"**, n. 1. An estate in fee simple.— **free'hold"er**, n. The owner of a freehold estate.— **free'man**, n. A man who is free; one not a slave; a citizen.— **Free'ma"son**, n. A member of a widely extended secret fraternity.— **Free'ma"son-ry**, n. The institutions and principles of Freemasons; hence, community of feeling and interest.— **free'stone"**, n. 1. An easily wrought sandstone. 2. A peach easily freed from its pit.— **free'think"er**, n. One who claims the right to think for himself, unbiased by any authority, as of the Christian Scriptures.— **free trade**, commerce unrestricted by tariff or customs.— **free'-will"**, a. Made, done, or given of one's own free will.

freeze, 1 frīz; 2 frēz, vt. & vi. [FRO'ZEN, freez^P, 1 frō'zn, 2 frō'zn, or FROZE, 1 frōz, 2 frōz; FREEZ'ING.] To harden with cold; congeal, kill or be killed by cold.— **freez'er**, 1 frīz'ar; 2 frēz'er, n. One who or that which freezes.

freight, 1 frēt: 2 frēt. I^d. vt. To load; transport. II. n. Goods transported, or the price of transportation; that with which anything is laden.— **freight'age**, n.— **freight'er**, n.

French, 1 french; 2 frĕnch. I. a. Pertaining to France. II. n. The language or people of France.— **French'man**, n. [-MEN, pl.] One of the French people.

fren'zy, 1 fren'zı; 2 frĕn'zy. I. vt. [FREN'-ZIED; FREN'ZY-ING.] To make frantic. II. n. [FREN'ZIES^z, pl.] Violent agitation; fury; madness; delirium.— **fren'zi-cal**, a.

fre-quent'^d, 1 frı-kwent'; 2 fre-kwĕnt', vt. To visit often.

fre'quent, 1 frī'kwent; 2 frē'kwĕnt, a. Occurring or appearing often.— **fre'quen-cy**, n. The property of being frequent.— **fre-quen'ta-tiv**(es, a. & n. Gram. Applying to a verb that denotes repeated action.— **fre-quent'er**, n.— **fre'quent-ly**, adv. Often; repeatedly.— **fre'quent-ness**, n.

fres'co, 1 fres'ko; 2 frĕs'co. I. vt. To paint in fresco. II. n. [FRES'COES^z or FRES'COS^z, pl.] The art of painting on plaster, as on a wall or ceiling; a picture or design so painted.

fresh, 1 fresh; 2 frĕsh, a. 1. Newly prepared or produced; unfaded; untainted; recent; new. 2. Vigorous; strong; brisk. 3. Unsalted. **-ly**, adv. **-ness**, n.— **fresh'en**, 1 fresh'n; 2 frĕsh'n, vt. & vi. To make or become fresh.

fresh'et, 1 fresh'et; 2 frĕsh'ĕt, n. A sudden flood in a stream; an inundation.

fresh'man, 1 fresh'man; 2 frĕsh'man, n.

[FRESH'MEN, pl.] A college student in his first year.

fret^1, 1 fret; 2 frĕt, v. [FRET'TED^d; FRET'-TING.] I. t. To wear or eat away; irritate; worry; vex; agitate. II. i. 1. To be worn away. 2. To complain; be agitated.

fret^2d, vt. To ornament as with fretwork.

fret^1, n. The act of fretting; irritation; agitation.

fret^2, n. Ornament in relief. **fret'work"**‡.

fret^3, n. A bar on a musical instrument, as a guitar, against which the strings may be stopped.

fret'ful, 1 fret'ful; 2 frĕt'fụl, a. Inclined to fret; peevish; worrying; agitated. **-ly**, adv. **-ness**, n.

fri'a-ble, 1 frai'a-bl; 2 frī'a-bl, a. Easily **fri'a-blr**, crumbled.— **fri"a-bil'i-ty**, n. **fri'-a-ble-ness**‡.

fri'ar, 1 frai'ar; 2 frī'ar, n. A mendicant monk.— **fri'ar-y**, n. A monastery.

fric"as-see', 1 frik"a-sī'; 2 frĭc"a-sē'. I. vt. To make into a fricassee. II. n. A dish of meat cut small, stewed or fried, and served with gravy.

fric'tion, 1 frik'shan; 2 frĭc'shon, n. The rubbing together of two bodies, or the hindrance to motion so produced; attrition.— **fric'tion-al**, a.

Fri'day, 1 frai'dı; 2 frī'dy, n. The sixth day of the week.— **Good Friday**, the Friday before Easter.

fried, 1 fraid; 2 frīd, imp. & pp. of FRY, q. v.

friend, 1 frend; 2 frĕnd, n. 1. One who **friend**^P, cherishes kind regard for another; an adherent; ally. 2. [F-] One of the Society of Friends; a Quaker.— **friend'less**, a. Having no friends; forlorn.— **friend'-less-ness**, n.— **friend'li-ness**, n.— **friend'-ly**, a. Pertaining to or like a friend; propitious; favorable.— **friend'ship**, n. Mutual regard; the state or fact of being friends or being friendly.

frieze^1, 1 frīz; 2 frēz, n. Arch. The **friez**^P, middle division of an entablature.

frieze^2, n. A coarse, shaggy woolen cloth. — **friezed**, a.

frig'ate, 1 frig'it; 2 frĭg'at, n. An old-style war-vessel of moderate size.

fright, 1 frait; 2 frīt. I^d. vt. [Poet.] To frighten. II. n. Sudden fear.— **fright'en**, 1 frait'n; 2 frīt'n, vt. To alarm suddenly; scare.— **fright'ful**, a. Apt to induce terror; shocking. **-ly**, adv. **-ness**, n.

frig'id, 1 frij'id; 2 frĭg'id, a. Of low temperature; cold; formal and forbidding. **-ly**, adv. **-ness**, n.— **fri-gid'i-ty**, 1 fri-jid'-ı-tı; 2 fri-gĭd'i-ty, n. Coldness; formality.

frill, 1 fril; 2 frĭl. I. vt. & vi. To make **frill**^P, into a frill; put frills on: be frilled.

II. *n.* An ornamental band; a flounce; ruffle.

fringe, 1 frinj; 2 frĭng. **I.** *vt.* [FRINGED, FRING'ING.] To border with a fringe. **II.** *n.* A border, as of pendent cords; an edging.— **fring'y,** *a.*

frip'per-y, 1 frĭp'er-ı; 2 frĭp'er-y. **I.** *a.* Worthless. **II.** *n.* [-IES², *pl.*] Worthless things; trumpery; cast=off clothes.

fri''seur', 1 frī''zŭr'; 2 frī''sur', *n. masc.* A hair=dresser.— **fri''seuse',** 1 frī''zŭz'; 2 frī''süs', *n. fem.*

frisk, 1 frisk; 2 frĭsk. **I³.** *vi.* To leap about playfully; frolic. **II.** *n.* A playful skipping about.— **frisk'I-ly,** *adv.*— **frisk'I-ness,** *n.*— **frisk'y,** *a.* Lively or playful.

frith, 1 frith; 2 frĭth, *n.* Same as FIRTH.

frit'ter, 1 frit'er; 2 frĭt'er. **I.** *vt.* To waste little by little: with *away.* **II.** *n.* **1.** A small fried cake. **2.** A shred.

friv'o-lous, 1 friv'o-lus; 2 frĭv'o-lŭs, *a.* Trivial; trifling; silly. **-ly,** *adv.* **-ness,** *n.*— **fri-vol'i-ty,** 1 fri-vol'i-tı; 2 fri-vŏl'i-ty, *n.* [-TIES², *pl.*] The quality of being frivolous; something frivolous.

frizz, 1 friz; 2 frĭz. **I.** *vt.* [FRIZZED, friz²ᵖ; FRIZD³; FRIZZ'ING.] To crimp. **II.** *n.* That which is frizzed, as hair. **friz'zlet.**— **frizz'ly,** *a.* Crinkled; crisped.

fro, 1 frō; 2 frō, *adv.* Away from; back.

frock, 1 frek; 2 frŏk, *n.* Any loose outer garment, as a woman's or child's gown; dress.

frog¹, 1 freg; 2 frŏg, *n.* A small, tailless, amphibious, web=footed animal.

frog², *n.* **1.** The triangular prominence in the sole of a horse's foot. **2.** A joint of rails of a railway=track.

Development of the Frog.
a, eggs; *b, b,* aquatic young (tadpoles) in various stages of growth; *c,* adult.

frog³, *n.* **1.** An ornamental fastening of a garment. **2.** The loop of a scabbard. **3.** A sailor's coat or frock.

frol'ic, 1 frol'ik; 2 frŏl'ic. **I.** *vi.* [FROL'ICKEDᵗ, FROL'ICTˢ; FROL'ICK-ING.] To play mirthful pranks; sport. **II.** *a.* Merry; sportive. **III.** *n.* A playful act; merriment; sport.— **frol'ic-some,** *a.* Full of frolic; playful.— **frol'ic-some-ness,** *n.*

from, 1 frem; 2 frŏm, *prep.* **1.** Out of; starting at; beginning with; after. **2.** In a relation of contrast with; as *from* grave to gay. **3.** Having as a cause or origin; by means of; due to.

frond, 1 frond; 2 frŏnd, *n.* A leaf=like expansion, as of ferns.

frontᵈ, 1 frunt; 2 frŏnt, *v.* **I.** *t.* To
fruntᵖ, face toward; confront. **II.** *i.* To have the front in a certain direction: with *on* or *upon.*

front, *a.* Situated at the front; frontal.

front, *n.* **1.** The foremost part of anything; the forehead; brow; face. **2.** Position in advance. **3.** Boldness; effrontery.— **front'age,** *n.* Linear extent of front.— **fron'tal,** 1 fren'tal; 2 frŏn'tal. **I.** *a.* Pertaining to the front or to the forehead. **II.** *n.* A front part; frontal bone.

fron-tier', 1 fren-tir' or fren'tir; 2 frŏn-tēr' or frŏn'tēr, *n.* The border of a country; the confines of civilization.

fron'tis-piece, 1 fren'tis-pis''; 2 frŏn'tis-pēç'', *n.* An illustration in the front of a book.

front'let, 1 frunt'let; 2 frŏnt'let, *n.* A band worn on the forehead.

frostᵈ, 1 frest; 2 frŏst, *v.* **I.** *t.* To cover with or injure by frost; apply frosting to. **II.** *i.* To freeze; assume the appearance of frost.

frost, *n.* Minute crystals of ice formed directly from vapor in the air.— **frost'I-ly,** *adv.*— **frost'I-ness,** *n.*— **frost'ing,** *n.* A surface imitating frost, as a sugared covering of cake.— **frost'y,** *a.* [FROST'I-ER; FROST'I-EST.] Attended with frost; chilly; forbidding.

froth, 1 freth; 2 frŏth. **Iᵗ.** *vt. & vi.* To cause to foam; foam. **II.** *n.* A mass of bubbles, as from fermentation; any light, unsubstantial matter.— **froth'y,** *a.* Of, like, or full of froth; empty; pretentious.

fro'ward, 1 frō'werd; 2 frō'ward, *a.* Disobedient; perverse. **-ly,** *adv.* **-ness,** *n.*

frown, 1 fraun; 2 frown, *v.* **I.** *t.* To rebuke indignantly: commonly with *down.* **II.** *i.* To knit the brow, as in displeasure; scowl; threaten; lower.— **frown'ing,** *pa.* **-ly,** *adv.*

frown, *n.* A wrinkling of the brow, as in anger.

frow'zy, 1 frau'zı; 2 frow'zy, *a.* [FROW'ZI-ER; FROW'ZI-EST.] Unkempt; slovenly.

froze, 1 frōz; 2 frŏz, *imp.*; **fro'zen,** *pp.* of FREEZE, *v.*

fro'zen, 1 frō'zn; 2 frō'zn, *pa.* Solidified, benumbed, or killed by cold; overspread with ice.

fruc'ti-fy, 1 fruk'ti-fai; 2 frŭe'ti-fy, *v.* [-FIED; -FY'ING.] **I.** *t.* To render fruitful. **II.** *i.* To yield fruit.— **fruc''ti-fi-ca'tion,** *n.*

fru′gal, 1 frū′gəl; 2 fru̇′gal, *a.* Economical; saving; sparing; meager. **-ly,** *adv.*— **fru-gal′i-ty,** *n.* [-TIES^z, *pl.*] Strict economy; thrift.

fru-gif′er-ous§, 1 fru-jif′ər-us; 2 fru-gif′er-ŭs, *a.* Fruit=bearing; fruitful.

fru-giv′o-rous, 1 fru-jiv′o-rus; 2 fru-gĭv′o-rŭs, *a.* Fruit=eating.

fruit, 1 frūt; 2 fru̇t. **I**^d. *vt. & vi.* To produce as fruit; bear fruit. **II.** *n.* **1.** The matured seed=vessel of a flowering plant; edible product of a plant. **2.** Offspring; product; result.— **fruit′age,** 1 frūt′ij; 2 fru̇t′ag, *n.* Fruit collectively; result; effect.— **fruit′er-er,** *n.* A dealer in fruits.— **fruit′ful,** *a.* Prolific; productive. **-ly,** *adv.* **-ness,** *n.*— **fruit′less,** *a.* Yielding no fruit; barren; useless; vain. **-ly,** *adv.* **-ness,** *n.*

fru-i′tion, 1 frū-ish′ən; 2 fru̇-ish′on, *n.* The bearing of fruit; realization; fulfilment.

frus′trate, 1 frus′trēt; 2 frŭs′trāt, *vt.* [FRUS′TRAT-ED^d; FRUS′TRAT-ING.] To cause to fail; baffle; foil.— **frus-tra′tion,** *n.* Failure; defeat.

frus′tum, 1 frus′tum; 2 frŭs′tŭm, *n.* [-TUMS^z or -TA, *pl.*] That which is left of a solid after cutting off the top parallel to the base; a fragment.

Frustum of a Pyramid.

fry¹, 1 frai; 2 frȳ, *vt. & vi.* [FRIED; FRY′ING.] **1.** To cook in hot oil, lard, or butter. **2.** To vex; worry.

fry¹, *n.* [FRIES^z, *pl.*] A dish of anything fried.

fry², *n. sing. & pl.* **1.** Very young fish. **2.** A multitude of petty persons or things.

fuch′sia, 1 fiū′shə; 2 fū′sha, *n.* A plant with drooping, four=petaled flowers.

fud′dle, 1 fud′l; 2 fŭd′l, *vt. & vi.* [FUD′-DLED; FUD′DLING.] To intoxicate or be intoxicated.

fudge, 1 fuj; 2 fŭḍg, *n.* A humbug; nonsense: commonly used as an interjection.

fu′el, 1 fiū′el; 2 fū′ĕl, *n.* Material, as wood or coal, used to feed a fire.

fu′gi-tive, 1 fiū′ji-tiv; 2 fū′gi-tĭv. **I.** *a.* Fleeing; escaping or escaped; evanescent; momentary. **II.** *n.* One who or that which flees; a runaway; deserter; anything evanescent. **-ly,** *adv.* **-ness,** *n.*

fugue, 1 fiūg; 2 fūg, *n. Mus.* A composition in which a theme introduced by one part is repeated and imitated by the others in succession.

-ful, *suffix.* **1.** Full of; abounding in; containing; as, art*ful;* beauti*ful.* **2.** The quantity or number that will fill; as, a cup*ful;* a spoon*ful.*

ful′crum, 1 ful′krum; 2 fŭl′erŭm, *n.* [FUL′CRUMS^z or FUL′CRA, *pl.*] The support on which a lever rests.

ful-fil′, 1 ful-fil′; 2 fu̇l-fil′, *vt.* [FUL-FIL-LING.] To bring to pass; accomplish; perform fully; meet; come up to.— **ful-fil′-ment, ful-fill′ment,** *n.*

full¹, 1 ful; 2 fu̇l, *vt. & vi.* To make or become full; show fulness.

full², *v.* **I.** *t.* To make (cloth) thicker, as in a fulling=mill. **II.** *i.* To thicken by shrinking, as cloth.

full, *a.* Containing all that the space will hold; filled; ample; complete.— **full′y,** *adv.* **ful′ness,** *n.* **full′ness‡.**

full, *n.* The highest state, point, or degree; the state of being full; fulness. [quite.

full, *adv.* Without abatement; fully;

full′er, 1 ful′ər; 2 fu̇l′er, *n.* One who fulls and cleanses cloth.— **fullers′ earth,** a clay used in fulling cloth.— **full′er-y,** *n.* A place where cloth is fulled.

ful′mi-nate, 1 ful′mi-nēt; 2 fŭl′mi-nāt, *v.* [-NAT′ED^d; -NAT′ING.] **I.** *t.* To explode; utter as a threat. **II.** *i.* To thunder; censure or threaten stormily.— **ful′mi-na′tion,** *n.* The act of fulminating, or that which is fulminated.— **ful′mi-na-to″ry,** *a.* Uttering fulminations.

ful′mi-nate, *n.* A substance that explodes under percussion.

ful′some, 1 ful′sam; 2 fu̇l′som, *a.* Offensive from excess of praise; **ful′sum²,** coarse; indelicate. **-ly,** *adv.* **-ness,** *n.*

fum′ble, 1 fum′bl; 2 fŭm′bl, *vt. & vi.* **fum′bl²,** To feel about clumsily. [FUM′BL(E)D^d; FUM′BLING.]

fume, 1 fiūm; 2 fūm. **I.** *vi.* [FUMED; FUM′ING.] To emit smoke, gas, or vapor; rage; rave. **II.** *n.* **1.** Vapor, especially as narcotic or choking. **2.** Furious anger.

fu′mi-gate, 1 fiū′mi-gēt; 2 fū′mi-gāt, *vt.* [-GAT″ED^d; -GAT′ING.] To subject to smoke or fumes; disinfect.— **fu″mi-ga′tion,** *n.*

fun, 1 fun; 2 fŭn, *n.* That which excites merriment; frolic; drollery; joke.

func′tion, 1 funk′shan; 2 fŭnɡ′shon, *n.* **1.** The appropriate business, duty, or office of any person or thing. **2.** A public ceremony or entertainment. **3.** *Math.* A dependent quantity.— **func′tion-al,** *a.*— **func′tion-al-ly,** *adv.*— **func′tion-a-ry,** 1 funk′shan-ē-ri; 2 fŭnɡ′shon-ă-ry, *n.* [-RIES^z, *pl.*] A public official.

fund, 1 fund; 2 fŭnd. **I**^d. *vt.* To convert (various debts) into a single fund secured by stocks or bonds. **II.** *n.* **1.** A sum of money or stock of convertible wealth; a

reserve; ample stock. **2.** Money lent to a government; a funded debt: used in the plural.

fun″da-men′tal, 1 fun″də-men′təl; 2 fŭn′da-měn′tal. **I.** *a.* Relating to or constituting a foundation; indispensable; basal. **II.** *n.* A foundation; a necessary truth; an essential. **-ly,** *adv.*

fu′ner-al, 1 fiū′nər-əl; 2 fū′ner-al. **I.** *a.* Pertaining to a funeral. **fu′ner-a-ry‡. II.** *n.* The ceremonies or persons attending the burial of the dead.

fu-ne′re-al, 1 fiū-nī′ri-əl; 2 fū-nē′re-al, *a.* Pertaining to or suitable for a funeral; mournful.

fun′gus, 1 fuŋ′gus; 2 fŭŋ′gŭs, *n.* [FUN′GI, 1 fun′jai, 2 fŭn′gī, or FUN′GUS-ES^z, *pl.*] One of a group of plants, including mushrooms, toadstools, etc.; also, a soft, spongy growth on an animal body.—**fun′gous,** 1 fuŋ′gus; 2 fŭŋ′gŭs, *a.*

fun′nel, 1 fun′el; 2 fŭn′ĕl, *n.* **1.** A wide-mouthed conical vessel for filling close vessels with liquids; tunnel. **2.** A smoke-pipe.

fun′ny, 1 fun′i; 2 fŭn′y, *a.* [FUN′NI-ER; FUN′NI-EST.] Affording fun; comical; ludicrous.

fur, 1 fūr; 2 fûr. **I.** *vt.* [FURRED, FURD^s; FUR′RING.] To cover, line, or trim with fur. **II.** *n.* **1.** The soft, fine coat covering the skin of many mammals. **2.** *pl.* or *collect. sing.* Skins of fur-bearing animals; also, apparel made of them. **3.** Any fuzzy covering.—**fur′ring,** *n.*

fur′be-low, 1 fūr′bi-lō; 2 fûr′be-lō, *n.* A plaited flounce or other ornament.

fur′bish‡, 1 fūr′bish; 2 fûr′bish, *vt.* To rub bright; burnish; renovate.

fur′cate, 1 fūr′kēt; 2 fûr′cāt, *a.* Forked. **fur′cat-ed‡.**

Fu′ries, The. *Class. Myth.* The avenging goddesses, Alecto, Tisiphone, Megæra.

fu′ri-ous, 1 fiū′ri-us; 2 fū′ri-ŭs, *a.* Full of fury; raging; frantic; tempestuous. **-ly,** *adv.* **-ness,** *n.*

furl, 1 fūrl; 2 fûrl, *vt.* To roll up and secure, as a sail to a spar.

fur′long, 1 fūr′lɔŋ; 2 fûr′lông, *n.* A measure: one-eighth of a mile.

fur′lough, 1 fūr′lō; 2 fûr′lō. **I.** *vt.* To grant a furlough to. **II.** *n.* Leave of absence, as of a soldier.

fur′nace, 1 fūr′nis; 2 fûr′naç, *n.* A structure enclosing a fire-chamber, as for smelting or heating.

fur′nish, 1 fūr′nish; 2 fûr′nish, *vt.* To fit out, as with furniture; supply; yield.—**fur′nish-ing,** *n.* **1.** *pl.* Fixtures or fittings. **2.** The act of supplying with furniture.

fur′ni-ture, 1 fūr′ni-chur *or* -tiur; 2 fûr′ni-

chur *or* -tūr, *n.* Outfit, as of chairs, tables, etc.; the trappings of a horse.

fu′ror, 1 fiū′ror, -rōr; 2 fū′rŏr, -rōr, *n.* **fu′rore,** Overmastering passion for anything; rage; mania. [dealer in furs.

fur′ri-er, 1 fūr′i-ər; 2 fûr′i-er, *n.* A

fur′row, 1 fur′o; 2 fûr′o. **I.** *vt. & vi.* To cut furrows in, as land; plow. **II.** *n.* A trench made by a plow; groove; wrinkle.

fur′ry, 1 fūr′i; 2 fûr′y, *a.* Of or like fur; fur-covered.

fur′ther, 1 fūr′ther; 2 fûr′ther. **I.** *vt.* To help forward; promote. **II.** *a. compar.* [*Positive* wanting: used as *compar.* of FAR.] More distant or advanced; fuller; additional. **III.** *adv.* More remotely; farther; in addition; besides.—**fur′ther-ance,** *n.* **1.** The act of furthering advancement. **2.** That which furthers.—**fur′ther-more,** *adv.* Besides; moreover.—**fur′ther-most,** *a.* Furthest or most remote.—**fur′thest. I.** *a. superl.* [*Positive* wanting: used as *superl.* of FAR.] Most distant, remote, or advanced. **II.** *adv.* At or to the greatest distance.

fur′tive, 1 fūr′tiv; 2 fûr′tiv, *a.* Stealthy **fur′tiv^s,** or sly; stolen; secret; elusive. **-ly,** *adv.* **-ness,** *n.*

fu′ry, 1 fiū′ri; 2 fū′ry, *n.* [FU′RIES^z, *pl.*] **1.** Ungovernable rage; any vehement passion or excitement; frenzy. **2.** A turbulent woman; termagant.

furze, 1 fūrz; 2 fûrz, *n.* A spiny shrub **furz^p,** having many branches and yellow flowers.—**furz′y,** *a.*

fuse, 1 fiūz; 2 fūs. **I.** **fuze^p,** *vt. & vi.* [FUSED, FUS′ING.] To melt; blend by melting. **II.** *n.* A tube, cord, or the like, to convey fire to an explosive.—**fu″si-bil′i-ty,** *n.*—**fu′si-ble,** *a.* Capable of being fused.

fu-see′^1, 1 fiu-zī′; 2 fū-sē′, *n.* **1.** A match not extinguishable by wind. **2.** A fuse. **3†.** A flint-lock musket.

fu-see′^2, *n.* A spirally grooved cone to equalize motion in a watch

Furze.
a, a single flower.

fu′se-lage, 1 fiū′si-lij; 2 fū′se-lag, *n.* The body of an air-plane.

fu′sel-oil″, 1 fiū′zel-ɔil″; 2 fū′gĕl-ôil″, *n.* A bitter, poisonous, oily compound, often present in unrectified or ill-rectified spirits.

fu″sil-lade′, 1 fiū″zi-lēd′; 2 fū′ġi-lād′, *n.* A simultaneous discharge of firearms.

fu'sion, 1 fiū'ʒən; 2 fū'zhon, *n.* The act or process of fusing; blending; coalition.

fuss, 1 fus; 2 fŭs. **I**. *vt. & vi.* To trouble about trifles; fret; worry. **II.** *n.* Disturbance about trifles; trouble; ado.— **fuss'y,** *a.* Inclined to fuss; fidgety; fretful. — **fuss'i-ly,** *adv.*— **fuss'i-ness,** *n.*

fus'tian, 1 fus'chən; 2 fŭs'chan. **I.** *a.* Made of fustian; pompous; bombastic. **II.** *n.* **1.** A coarse twilled stuff. **2.** Verbiage; bombast.

fust'y, 1 fust'ĭ; 2 fŭst'y, *a.* [FUST'I-ER; FUST'I-EST.] Musty; moldy.— **fust'i-ness,** *n.*

fu'tile, 1 fiū'tĭl; 2 fū'til, *a.* Useless; **fu'til⁸,** vain.— **fu-til'i-ty,** *n.* [-TIES², *pl.*] The quality of being futile; anything futile.

fut'tock, 1 fut'ək; 2 fŭt'ok, *n.* A crooked timber in the built-up rib or frame of a wooden vessel.

fu'ture, 1 fiū'chur *or* -tiur; 2 fū'chur *or* -tūr. **I.** *a.* That will be hereafter; pertaining to time to come. **II.** *n.* The time yet to come; that which is to be; prospect; outlook.— **fu-tu'ri-ty,** 1 fiu-tiū'rĭ-tĭ; 2 fū-tū'rĭ-ty, *n.* [-TIES², *pl.*] **1.** The future. **2.** The state of being future.

fuzz, 1 fuz; 2 fŭz, *n.* Down, or downy **fuzᵖ,** fiber, as on cloth or on some fruits.— **fuzz'i-ly,** *adv.*— **fuzz'i-ness,** *n.*— **fuzz'y,** *a.*

fy, 1 fai; 2 fī, *interj.* Same as FIE.

-fy, *suffix.* Make; as, beauti*fy*.

G

G, g, gee, 1 jī; 2 gē, *n.* [GEES, G's, or Gs, 1 jīz; 2 gēs, *pl.*] The seventh letter in the English alphabet.

gab''ar-dine', 1 gab''ar-dīn'; 2 găb''ar-dĭn', *n.* 1. A long cloak. 2. A waterproof coat or cloth suited for making one.

gab'ble, 1 gab'l; 2 găb'l. **I.** *vt. & vi.* **gab'lᵖ,** [GAB'BLED; GAB'LDᵖ; GAB'BLING.] To chatter; talk inarticulately. **II.** *n.* Noisy and incoherent talk; cackling.

ga'bi-on, 1 gē'bi-ən; 2 gā'bi-on, *n.* A wicker basket to be filled with sand.

ga'ble, 1 gē'bl; 2 gā'bl, *n.* The triangular end of a wall, above the eaves; end wall of a building.

gad, 1 gad; 2 găd, *vi.* [GAD'DEDᵈ; GAD'-DING.] To roam abroad; ramble; stray.— **gad'der,** *n.*

gad, 1 gad; 2 găd, *n.* A goad or the like.

gad'fly'', 1 gad'flai''; 2 găd'flȳ'', *n.* [-FLIES²; *pl.*] A large fly that torments cattle. **horse'-fly''**‡.

gad'get, 1 gad'jet; 2 găd'gĕt, *n.* [Slang, U.S.] Some thing of which the name can not be recalled.

Gael, 1 gēl; 2 gāl, *n.* A Scottish highlander. — **Gael'ic,** 1 gēl'ĭk; 2 gāl'ic. **I.** *a.* Belonging to the Scottish Highlanders. **II.** *n.* The Celtic language.

gaff, 1 gaf; 2 găf, *n.* **1.** A sharp iron **gafᵖ,** hook at the end of a pole, for landing large fish. **2.** A spar for extending a sail. **3.** A game-cock's steel spur.

gag, 1 gag; 2 găg. **I.** *vt. & vi.* [GAGGED, GAGDˢ; GAG'GING.] To silence by force; nauseate or be nauseated. **II.** *n.* **1.** Any appliance for preventing utterance; any re-

straint upon speech. **2.** Something nauseating. **3.** An actor's interpolation in a play.

gage¹, 1 gēj; 2 găg. **I.** *vt.* [GAGED or **gauge,** GAUGED; GAG'ING or GAUG'ING.] To measure; estimate. **II.** *n.* An instrument for measuring capacity or dimensions; a standard.— **gag'er, gaug'er,** *n.* One who gages; an officer of the revenue service.

gage², 1 gēj. **I.** *vt.* [GAGED; GAG'ING.] To give as a pledge; pawn; wager. **II.** *n.* Something given or thrown down as security, as for a combat; a pledge; a challenge.

gai'e-ty, 1 gē'i-tĭ; 2 gā'e-ty, *n.* [-TIES²; **gay'e-ty,** *pl.*] The state of being gay; merriment; merrymaking; festivity; fun.

gai'ly, 1 gē'lĭ; 2 gā'ly, *adv.* In a gay man- **gay'ly,** ner; joyously; merrily; showily.

gain, 1 gēn; 2 găn, *v.* **I.** *t.* **1.** To get; win; arrive at; reach. **2.** To win over; propitiate. **II.** *i.* To make progress; improve; advance; obtain the advantage: often followed by *on* or *upon*.

gain, *n.* An advantage; acquisition; profit; increase.— **gain'ful,** 1 gēn'ful; 2 găn'ful, *a.* Profitable; lucrative.

gain''say', 1 gēn'sē'; 2 găn'sā', *vt.* [-SAID'; -SAY'ING.] To contradict; controvert.— **gain''say'er,** *n.*

gait, 1 gēt; 2 găt, *n.* The manner of walking or stepping; carriage; walk; way.

gai'ter, 1 gē'tar; 2 gā'ter, *n.* A covering for the lower leg or ankle; a high shoe.

ga'la, 1 gē'lə; 2 gā'la, *n.* A festivity; show. — **ga'la-day'',** *n.* A holiday; festival.

Gal'ax-y, 1 gal'əks-ĭ; 2 găl'aks-y, *n.* **1.** A starry band in the heavens, called the *Milky Way.* **2.** [g-] [-IES², *pl.*] A brilliant group, as of persons.

gale, 1 gāl; 2 găl, *n.* A wind=storm; a strong wind.　[mon ore of lead.

ga·le′na, 1 gə-lī′nə; 2 gà-lē′na, *n.* A com-

gall, 1 gôl; 2 găl, *vt.* To render sore by friction; abrade; fret.

gall¹, *n.* An excrescence on plants, due to insects or to a fungus.— **gall″=in″sect,** *n.* An insect that produces galls on plants.— **gall′nut″,** *n.* The gall of a species of oak.

gall², *n.* An abrasion or excoriation.

gall³, *n.* The bile; hence, bitter feeling; malignity.

gal′lant¹, 1 gal′ənt; 2 găl′ant. **I.** *a.* Intrepid; brave; chivalrous. **II.** *n.* A dashing fellow; an intrepid youth. **-ly¹,** *adv.*

gal·lant′², 1 gə-lant′; 2 gà-lănt′. **I.** *a.* Polite and attentive to women; courteous. **II.** *n.* A man who pays court to women. **-ly²,** *adv.* **-ness,** *n.*

gal′lant·ry, 1 gal′ənt-rɪ; 2 găl′ant-ry, *n.* [-RIES², *pl.*] **1.** Courage; chivalrousness. **2.** Politeness to women.

gal′le·on, 1 gal′ē-ən; 2 găl′e-ŏn, *n.* A large Spanish ship.

gal′ler·y, 1 gal′ər-ɪ; 2 găl′er-y, *n.* [-IES², *pl.*] **1.** An elevated floor, commonly furnished with seats, along the side of an audience=room; or the people seated there. **2.** A corridor; a place for the display of statues, paintings, etc.

gal′ley, 1 gal′ɪ; 2 găl′y, *n.* **1.** A seagoing vessel propelled by oars; barge. **2.** The cooking=place on board ship. **3.** *Print.* A long tray for holding composed type. — **gal′ley=slave″,** *n.* A convict sentenced to labor at the oar of a galley.

Gal′lic¹, 1 gal′ɪk; 2 găl′ic, *a.* Of or pertaining to ancient Gaul or modern France. — **Gal′li·cism,** 1 gal′ɪ-sizm; 2 găl′i-çism, *n.* A French idiom used in another language.

gal′lic², *a.* Derived from gallnuts.

gal′li·na′ceous, 1 gal′ɪ-nē′shus; 2 găl′i-nā′shŭs, *a.* Pertaining to the common hen, turkeys, partridges, etc.

gal′li·pot, 1 gal′ɪ-pət; 2 găl′i-pŏt, *n.* A small jar for ointments.

gal′lon, 1 gal′ən; 2 găl′on, *n.* **1.** A liquid measure. (1) U. S. standard, 231 cubic inches. (2) Brit. imperial, 277.274 cubic inches. **2.** A dry measure; ⅛ of a bushel.

gal·loon′, 1 gə-lūn′; 2 gà-lōōn′, *n.* A worsted lace; narrow trimming.

gal′lop, 1 gal′əp; 2 găl′op. **I.** *vi. & vi.* To move at a gallop. **II.** *n.* **1.** Motion, as of a horse, by a succession of leaps. **2.** The act of riding at a gallop.

gal′lows, 1 gal′oz; 2 găl′ōş, *n.* [GAL′LOWS² or GAL′LOWS=ES², *pl.*] A framework for hanging criminals.

gal′op, 1 gal′əp *or* ga″lō′; 2 găl′op *or* gä″lō′, *n.* A lively dance, or the music for it.

ga·losh′, 1 gə-losh′; 2 gà-lŏsh′, *n.* A wooden or other overshoe.

gal′o·yak, 1 gal′ō-yak; 2 găl′ō-yăk, *n.* A hybrid between an Asiatic yak and a Galloway cow; a portmanteau=word.

gal·van′ic, 1 gal-van′ɪk; 2 găl-văn′ic, *a.* Pertaining to galvanism.— **gal′va·nism,** 1 gal′və-nɪzm; 2 găl′va-nĭşm, *n.* Current electricity arising from chemical action: a term no longer in scientific use: named from the Italian physicist Galvani (1737-1798).— **gal′va·nize** *or* **-nise,** *vt.* [-NIZED; -NIZ′ING.] To treat with a continuous electric current; excite (a corpse) to muscular action by electricity; rouse to a false show of life and energy.— **galvanized iron,** iron coated with tin or zinc.

gal′va·nom′e·ter, 1 gal″və-nom′ɪ-tər; 2 găl″va-nŏm′e-ter, *n.* *Elec.* An apparatus for measuring current=strength or potential difference.

gam′ble, 1 gam′bl; 2 găm′bl, *v.* [GAM′-**gam′bl,** BL(E)D²; GAM′BLING.] **I.** *t.* To squander by gaming. **II.** *i.* To game; risk or wager moments of value upon a chance.

gam′ble, *n.* A gambling venture.

gam·boge′, 1 gam-bōj′ *or* gam-būj′; 2 găm-bōg′ *or* găm-bug′, *n.* A brownish Oriental gum resin.

gam′bol, 1 gam′bəl; 2 găm′bol. **I.** *vi.* [-BOLED *or* -BOLLED, -BOLD³; -BOL·ING *or* -BOL·LING.] To skip sportively about. **II.** *n.* A skipping about in sport.

gam′brel, 1 gam′brel; 2 găm′brĕl, *n.* **1.** The hock of an animal, as a horse. **2.** A curved stick used to support a carcass while dressing it. **3.** A gambrel roof.— **gambrel roof,** a roof having its slope broken by an outward obtuse angle. Called also a *double=pitched roof; curb roof.*

game, 1 gēm; 2 găm. **I.** *vi.* [GAMED; GAM′-ING.] To play a game for a stake. **II.** *a.* **1.** Of or pertaining to game. **2.** Ready to fight; unflinching. **III.** *n.* **1.** A contest for recreation or amusement; a jest; joke; sport. **2.** A scheme; plot. **3.** Wild animals collectively, or their flesh; any object of pursuit.— **game′=cock″,** *n.* The male of one of several hardy and pugnacious breeds of fowls (game=fowl), bred and trained for fighting.— **game′some,** *a.*

Gambrel Roof.

Playful; sportive; gay; merry.— **game'ster,** *n.* A gambler.

gam'in, 1 gam'in *or* (*F.*) gȧ″mȧn'; 2 găm'in *or* (*F.*) gä″măn', *n.* A street arab.

gam'mon¹, 1 gam'ən; 2 găm'on, *n.* **1.** [Colloq.] A hoax. **2.** In backgammon, a sweeping defeat.

gam'mon², *n.* A cured ham.

gam'ut, 1 gam'ut; 2 găm'ŭt, *n.* The diatonic scale of musical notes. [goose.

gan'der, 1 gan'dẽr; 2 găn'der, *n.* A male

gang, 1 gang; 2 găng, *n.* A group; squad.

gan'gli·on, 1 gaŋ'glı·ən; 2 găŋ'gli·on, *n.* [GAN'GLI·ONSᶻ *or* GAN'GLI·A, *pl.*] **1.** *Anat.* (1) A collection of nerve·cells. (2) A gland·like organ. **2.** A tumor proceeding from a tendon.

gan'grene, 1 gaŋ'grīn; 2 găŋ'grēn. I. *vt.* & *vi.* [GAN'GRENED; GAN'GREN·ING.] To affect or be affected by gangrene. II. *n.* The death of a part; mortification.— **gan'gre·nous,** *a.* [passageway.

gang'way″, 1 gaŋ'wē″; 2 găng'wā″, *n.* A

gan'net, 1 gan'et; 2 găn'ĕt, *n.* A bird related to the pelicans.

gant'let¹, 1 gant'let; 2 gänt'lĕt, *n.* A
gaunt'let, punishment wherein the victim ran between two rows of men who struck him with clubs as he passed.

gant'let², *n.* Same as GAUNTLET.

gaol, gaol'er, etc. Same as JAIL, etc.

gap, 1 gap; 2 găp. I. *vt.* [GAPPEDᵗ, GAPTˢ; GAP'PING.] To notch; make a breach in. II. *n.* A passage or aperture; breach; ravine.

gape, 1 gāp; 2 găp. I. *vi.* [GAPEDᵗ; GAP'ING.] To open the mouth wide; yawn; open wide, as a chasm. II. *n.* The act of gaping; a chasm; fissure. [snout.

gar, 1 gär; 2 gär, *n.* A fish with spear·like

ga″rage′, 1 gȧ″räʒ′ *or* (*Anglicized*) gar'ij; 2 gä″räzh′ *or* găr'ȧg. [F.] I. *vt.* [GA″RAGED′; GA″RAG′ING.] To store and care for (motor·vehicles). II. *n.* A building in which motor·vehicles are cared for. [form.

garb, 1 gärb; 2 gärb, *n.* Dress; outward

gar'bage, 1 gär'bɪj; 2 gär'bag, *n.* Refuse.

gar'ble, 1 gär'bl; 2 gär'bl, *vt.* [GAR'BL(E)D⸳;
gar'bl², GAR'BLING.] To change injuriously; mutilate; pervert.

gar'den, 1 gär'dn; 2 gär'dn. I. *vt.* & *vi.* To cultivate; till a garden. II. *n.* A place for the cultivation of flowers, vegetables, or small plants.— **gar'den·er,** 1 gär'dn·ẽr; 2 gär'dn·er, *n.* One who tends gardens.— **gar'den·ing,** *n.* The caring for a garden.

gar'gle, 1 gär'gl; 2 gär'gl. I. *vt.* [GAR'-
gar'gl², GL(E)D⸳; GAR'GLING.] (1) To rinse (the throat) with a liquid agitated by air from the windpipe. (2) To use as a gargle. II. *n.* A liquid for gargling.

gar'goyle, 1 gär'goil; 2 gär'gŏyl, *n.* A projecting stone spout, grotesquely carved.

gar'ish, 1 gār'ɪsh; 2 găr'ish, *a.* Marked by a dazzling glare; gaudy. **-ly,** *adv.* **-ness,** *n.*

Gargoyle.

gar'land, 1 gär'lənd; 2 gär'land, *n.* A wreath as a token of victory or honor.

gar'lic, 1 gär'lɪk; 2 gär'lie, *n.* A bulbous plant of the same genus as the onion.— **gar'lick·y,** *a.*

gar'ment, 1 gär'ment *or* -mənt; 2 gär'ment, *n.* An article of clothing.

gar'ner, 1 gär'nẽr; 2 gär'ner. I. *vt.* To store, as grain; gather. II. *n.* A granary; gathering; store.

gar'net, 1 gär'nĕt; 2 gär'nĕt, *n.* A vitreous transparent stone, used as a gem; deep·red color.

gar'nish, 1 gär'nɪsh; 2 gär'nish. Iᵗ. *vt.* **1.** To decorate; furnish. **2.** *Law.* To warn one to answer to an action. II. *n.* An ornament, as around a dish at table.— **gar'nish·ment,** *n.* The act of garnishing.— **gar'ni·ture,** 1 gär'nı·chur *or* -tiūr; 2 gär'ni·chur *or* -tūr, *n.* Anything used to garnish; embellishment.

gar'ret, 1 gar'et; 2 găr'ĕt, *n.* A story or room directly under a sloping roof.

gar'ri·son, 1 gar'ı·sən; 2 găr'i·son. I. *vt.* **1.** To supply with soldiers. **2.** To put (soldiers) into a fortification. II. *n.* The military force defending a fort, town, or the like.

gar·rote′, 1 gȧ·rōt′; 2 gä·rōt′. I. *vt.* [GAR·ROT′EDᵈ; GAR·ROT′ING.] To execute with a garrote; throttle, as in order to rob. II. *n.* A Spanish instrument for capital punishment by strangling; strangulation.— **gar·rot'er,** 1 gȧ·rōt'ẽr; 2 gä·rōt'er, *n.*

gar'ru·lous, 1 gar'u·lus; 2 găr'ṵ·lŭs, *a.* Given to tedious talking; loquacious. **-ly,** *adv.*— **gar·ru'li·ty,** 1 gȧ·rū'lı·tɪ; 2 gä·ru'li·ty, *n.* Idle and empty loquacity. **gar·ru·lous·ness⸳**

gar'ter, 1 gär'tẽr; 2 gär'ter. I. *vt.* To put a garter upon; fasten with a garter. II. *n.* **1.** A band to hold a stocking in place. **2.** The badge of the highest order of knighthood in Great Britain, called the Order of the Garter; the order itself.

gas, 1 gas; 2 găs, *n.* [GAS'ES͎, *pl.*] **1.** An aeriform elastic fluid; such a fluid used for lighting or heating. **2.** A single jet or flame supplied by gas. **3.** [Colloq., U. S.] Gasoline. **gas'‖jet"‡; gas"light"‡;— gas'‖hel"met,** *n.* A protective covering for the head and face to prevent poisoning by noxious gas.—**gas‖mask‡.— gas'‖me"ter,** *n.* An apparatus for measuring the consumption of gas.

gas"con-ade', 1 gas"kən-ēd'; 2 găs'con-ād'. **I.** *vi.* [-AD'ED^d; -AD'ING.] To brag; bluster. **II.** *n.* Boastful or blustering talk.

gas'e-ous, 1 gas'i-us; 2 găs'e-ŭs, *a.* Of or like gas; aeriform; unsubstantial.

gash, 1 gash; 2 găsh. **I.** *vt.* To make a long, deep cut in. **II.** *n.* A long, deep incision; a flesh wound.

gas'o-line, ⎱ 1 gas'o-lin *or* -līn; 2 găs'o-lĭn *or*
gas'o-lin͎, ⎰ -lĭn, *n.* A colorless, volatile, inflammable liquid distilled from petroleum.

ʒas-om'e-ter, 1 gas-om'i-tər; 2 găs-ŏm'e-ter, *n.* A tank for storing or an apparatus for measuring gas.

gasp, 1 gasp; 2 găsp. **I.** *vt. & vi.* To utter or emit brokenly; breathe convulsively. **II.** *n.* An act of gasping.

gas'tric, 1 gas'trik; 2 găs'tric, *a.* Of, pertaining to, or near the stomach.

gas-tron'o-my, 1 gas-tren'o-mɪ; 2 găs-trŏn'o-my, *n.* The art of preparing and serving appetizing food.—**gas-tron'o-mer,** *n.* An epicure.—**gas"tro-nom'ic,** *a.*

gate, 1 gēt; 2 gāt, *n.* **1.** A passageway, as in a fence; a portal; also, a movable frame that serves to close it. **2.** Any means of access, power; supremacy.—**gate'way",** *n.* An opening that is or may be closed by a gate; an entrance; approach.

Gate of a Walled City.

gath'er, 1 gath'- ər; 2 găth'er. *v.* **I.** *t.* **1.** To bring together; assemble; collect. **2.** To deduce; infer. **3.** To draw into folds. **II.** *i.* **1.** To congregate. **2.** To increase; accumulate. **3.** To come to a head; concentrate.—**gath'er-ing,** *n.* The act of gathering; an assemblage; **a collection; an abscess.**

gath'er, *n.* A plait or fold in cloth.

gaud, 1 gôd; 2 ḡad, *n.* An article of vulgar finery.—**gaud'i-ly,** *adv.*—**gaud'i-ness,** *n.*—**gaud'y,** 1 gâd'ɪ; 2 ḡad'y, *a.* [GAUD'I-ER; GAUD'I-EST.] Obtrusively brilliant in color; garish; flashy.

gauge, gaug'er, etc. Same as GAGE, etc.

Gaul, 1 gôl; 2 ḡal, *n.* **1.** A native of Gaul, an ancient region comprising what is now northern Italy, France, Belgium, etc. **2.** A Frenchman.

gaunt, 1 gänt *or* gônt; 2 gänt *or* ḡant, *a.* Emaciated; lank; lean; meager.—**-ly,** *adv.* **-ness,** *n.*

gaunt'let, 1 gônt'let *or* gänt'let; 2 gänt'lĕt *or* ḡant'lĕt, *n.* A knight's leather glove covered with metal plates; a glove with long wristlet; also, the wristlet.

gaunt'let², *n.* Same as GANTLET.

gauze, ⎱ 1 gôz; 2 ḡaz, *n.* A light open-
gauz², ⎰ woven fabric.—**gauz'y,** *a.* Thin and diaphanous like gauze.

gave, *imp.* of GIVE, *v.*

gav'el, 1 gav'el; 2 găv'ĕl, *n.* A masons' mallet; mallet used by a presiding officer.

ga'vi-al, 1 gē'vi-əl; 2 ḡā'vi-al, *n.* The great Indian crocodile, having long, slender jaws.

gav'ot, 1 gav'ət *or* gə-vot'; 2 ḡăv'ot *or* ḡa-vŏt', *n.* A dignified, vivacious French dance, resembling the minuet; also, a dance‖tune in common time, and in two periods, each repeated. **ga-vot'ta‡; ga-votte'‡.**

gawk, 1 gôk; 2 ḡak. **I.** *vi.* To stare or behave awkwardly. **II.** *n.* An awkward, stupid fellow.—**gawk'i-ly,** *adv.*—**gawk'i-ness,** *n.*—**gawk'y. I.** *a.* Awkward and dull; clownish. **II.** *n.* A gawk.

gay, 1 gē; 2 ḡā, *a.* **1.** Merry; sportive. **2.** Brilliant; showy. **3.** Wanton.—**gai'ly** *or* **gay'ly,** *adv.*—**gay'ness,** *n.*

gay'e-ty, *n.* Same as GAIETY.

gaze, 1 gēz; 2 ḡāz. **I.** *vi.* [GAZED; GAZ'ING.] To look steadily; followed by *at, on,* or *upon.* **II.** *n.* A continued or intense look.

ga-zel', ⎱ 1 ḡa-zel'; 2 ḡa-zĕl',
ga-zelle', ⎰ *n.* A small, delicately formed antelope with large, gentle eyes.

ga-zette', ⎱ 1 ḡa-zet';
ga-zet'‡, ⎰ 2 ḡa-zĕt'. **I.** *vt.* [GA-ZET'TED^d; GA-ZET'TING.] To report officially; hence, to appoint. **II.** *n.* A newspaper, or printed account of current events; any official announcement.

Gazel. ¹/₄₃

— gaz″et-teer′, 1 gaz′e-tīr′; 2 găz″ĕ-tēr′, n. **1.** A dictionary of geographical names. **2.** A writer for a gazette.

G clef. Treble clef, indicating that the second line of the staff has the pitch of the first G above the middle C.

gear, 1 gīr; 2 gēr, v. **I.** t. To equip; make ready; put into gear. **II.** i. To come into or be in gear.

gear, n. **1.** Any set of appliances, as of cog-wheels, serving to transmit motion; a cog-wheel. **2.** Equipment, as dress, tools, etc. **3.** Same as GEARING, n., 1.—**gear′ing,** n. **1.** Mech. Gear in general; working parts collectively. **2.** Naut. Ropes and tackle.

gee, 1 jī; 2 gē, vt. & vi. To turn to the right or from the driver: said of or to draft-animals.

geese, 1 gīs; 2 gēs, n. Plural of GOOSE.

gel′a-tin, 1 jel′a-tin; 2 gĕl′a-tĭn, n. } **gel′a-tine,** } Hard, transparent, tasteless substance obtained from animal tissue, as skin or horns.—**ge-lat′i-nous,** a. Of the nature of gelatin; like jelly.

geld, 1 geld; 2 gĕld, vt. [GELD′ED⁴ or GELT; GELD′ING.] To castrate, as a horse.—**geld′ing,** n. A castrated horse.

gem, 1 jem; 2 gĕm. **I.** vt. [GEMMED, GEMD⁸; GEM′MING.] To adorn with gems. **II.** n. A precious stone.

gem′i-na′tion, 1 jem′i-nē′shan; 2 gĕm″i-nā′shon, n. A doubling or duplicating.

gem′mate, 1 jem′ēt; 2 gĕm′āt, a. Bearing buds; reproducing by buds.—**gem-mif′er-ous‡; gem-mip′a-rous‡.—gem-ma′tion,** n. Budding, as of plants.

gen″darme′, 1 zən̈′därm′; 2 zhän-därm′, n. [GEN′DARMES′, GENS D′ARMES, pl.] Originally, in France, a man-at-arms; now, an armed policeman.—**gen″dar′me-rie′,** n. Gendarmes collectively.—**gen-dar′mer-y‡.**

gen′der, 1 jen′dər; 2 gĕn′der. **I.** vt. To beget. **II.** n. A property of certain words whereby they indicate sex.

gene, 1 jīn; 2 gēn, n. The unit of inheritance, transmitted from parents to offspring through germ-cells.

gen″e-al′o-gy, 1 jen′i-al′o-ji; 2 gĕn″e-ăl′o-gy, n. [-GIES², pl.] **1.** A record of descent from an ancestry. **2.** Descent in a direct line; pedigree.—**gen″e-a-log′i-cal,** a. **gen″e-a-log′ic‡.—gen″e-a-log′i-cal-ly,** adv.—**gen″e-al′o-gist,** n. [GENUS.

gen′er-a, 1 jen′i-rə; 2 gĕn′e-ra, n. Plural of

gen′er-al, 1 jen′ər-al; 2 gĕn′er-al. **I.** a. **1.** Pertaining to a genus; relating to all of a class. **2.** Large; sweeping; indefinite. **3.** Common; customary; wide-spread. **4.** Viewed as a whole. **II.** n. **1.** Mil. An officer who commands any body of troops not less than a brigade. **2.** A general principle, statement, or notion; totality.—**gen″er-al′i-ty,** n. [-TIES², pl.] **1.** The main part. **2.** A general statement. **3.** The state of being general or generalized.—**gen″er-al-i-za′tion,** n. The act of generalizing; a general inference; an induction.—**gen′er-al-ize,** v. [-IZED; -IZ′ING.] **I.** t. To treat as general; infer (a general law) from particulars. **II.** i. To form objects into classes; form general ideas or inferences.—**gen′er-al-ise‡.—gen′er-al-ly,** adv. **1.** Ordinarily. **2.** Without going into particulars. **3.** Collectively.—**gen′er-al-ship,** n. A general's office, rank, or skill; tactics or strategy; leadership.

gen″er-al-is′si-mo, 1 jen″ər-al-is′i-mō; 2 gĕn″er-al-ĭs′i-mō, n. A supreme military commander.

gen′er-ate, 1 jen′ər-ēt; 2 gĕn′er-āt, vt. [-AT′ED⁴; -AT′ING.] To produce; create; beget.—**gen″er-a′tion,** n. **1.** The act of generating; reproduction; origination. **2.** A step in descent; the individuals existing at one time, or their average lifetime. **3.** Race; progeny.—**gen′er-a-tive,** a. Of or pertaining to generation.—**gen′er-a″tor,** n. One who or that which generates; a machine for the production of gas or electricity.

ge-ner′ic, 1 ji-ner′ik; 2 ge-nĕr′ĭc, a. Pertaining to a genus or class: opposed to specific.—**i-cal,** a. **-i-cal-ly,** adv.

gen′er-ous, 1 jen′ər-ūs; 2 gĕn′er-ŭs, a. **1.** Giving liberally; magnanimous. **2.** Cheering or stimulating, as wine.—**ly,** adv.—**ness,** n.—**gen″er-os′i-ty,** n. [-TIES², pl.] Liberality; a generous act.

gen′e-sis, 1 jen′i-sis; 2 gĕn′e-sĭs, n. [-SES, 1 -sīz; 2 -sĕs, pl.] **1.** The act of originating; creation; origin. **2.** [G-] The first book of the Bible.

ge′ni-al, 1 jī′ni-al; 2 gē′ni-al, a. Kindly; cordial; pleasant; cheering.—**ge″ni-al′i-ty,** n.—**ge′ni-al-ly,** adv.—**ge′ni-al-ness,** n.

gen′i-tal, 1 jen′i-tal; 2 gĕn′i-tal, a. Pertaining to generation.

gen′i-tive, 1 jen′i-tiv; 2 gĕn′i-tĭv. **I.** a. **gen′i-tiv‡,** } Gram. Indicating source, possession, or the like. **II.** n. In Latin, Greek, etc., the genitive case.

gen′ius, 1 jīn′yus; 2 gĕn′yŭs, n. [GE′NI-I or (def. 3) GEN′IUS-ES², pl.] **1.** Exalted intellectual power and creative ability. **2.** Remarkable special aptitude. **3.** A person of remarkable intellect and creative power. **4.** The essential principle of anything; a representative type.

ge′ni-us², 1 jī′ni-us; 2 gē′ni-ŭs, n. [-NI-I, 1 -aī or -ī; 2 -I or -ī, pl.] A beneficent guardian spirit.

gen're, 1 zͦän're; 2 zhän're, *n.* A style of art illustrative of common life.

gen·teel', 1 jen-tēl'; 2 gĕn-tēl', *a.* Well=bred or refined; elegant; fashionable. **-ly,** *adv.* **-ness,** *n.*

gen'tian, 1 jen'shan; 2 gĕn'shan, *n.* A flowering plant of various species, as the *fringed gentian* of America, with blue, delicately fringed flowers.

gen'tile, 1 jen'tail; 2 gĕn'tīl, *n.* **1.** [G-] *Script.* One not a Jew. **2.** *Gram.* A word denoting race or country.

gen·til'i·ty, 1 jen-til'i·ti; 2 gĕn-tĭl'i·ty, *n.* [-TIES², *pl.*] **1.** The quality of being genteel; exclusiveness. **2.** Dignity of birth.

gen'tle, } 1 jen'tl; 2 gĕn'tl, *a.* **1.** Mild; **gen'tl²,** } kindly; soft or low; peaceful; docile; easy. **2.** Of honorable family; noble. **-ness,** *n.* — **gen'tly,** *adv.* — **gen'tle-folk²,** *n. pl.* People of good family: now more commonly *gentlefolks.* — **gen'tle- man,** *n.* [-MEN, *pl.*] **1.** A well=bred and honorable man. **2.** A man of gentle extraction. — **gen'tle-man-li-ness,** *n.* — **gen'tle-man-ly,** *a.* Pertaining to or befitting a gentleman; courteous; gracious. — **gen'tle-wo²man,** *n.* [-WO²MEN, 1-wim²en; 2-wĭm²ĕn, *pl.*] A woman of good birth and breeding; a lady.

gen'try, 1 jen'tri; 2 gĕn'try, *n.* **1.** People of good position or birth. **2.** Any specified class of people.

gen"u·flec'tion or **-flex'ion,** 1 jen"yu-flek'shan; 2 gĕn"yu-flĕk'shon, *n.* A bending of the knee, as in worship.

gen'u·ine, } 1 jen'yu-in; 2 gĕn'yu-ĭn, *a.* **1.** **gen'u·in²,** } Of the original or true stock; of the authorship claimed; not spurious, adulterated, or counterfeit. **2.** Not affected or hypocritical; frank; sincere. **-ly,** *adv.* **-ness,** *n.*

ge'nus, 1 jī'nus; 2 gē'nŭs, *n.* [GEN'ER·A, 1 jen'i·ra; 2 gĕn'e·ra, *pl.*] A group or class embracing subordinate classes or species.

ge·og'ra·phy, } 1 ji-ŏg'ra·fi; 2 ge-ŏg'ra·fy, **ge·og'ra·fy²,** } *n.* [-PHIES², *pl.*] The science that describes the surface of the earth, with its peoples and products. — **ge·og'ra·pher,** *n.* — **ge"o·graph'i·cal,** *a.* Of or pertaining to geography. **ge"o·graph'ic,** *a.*

ge·ol'o·gy, 1 ji-ŏl'o·ji; 2 ge-ŏl'o·gy, *n.* The science that treats of the structure of the earth. — **ge"o·log'ic,** 1 jī'o-lŏj'ik; 2 gē"o-lŏg'ic, *a.* Of, pertaining to, or derived from geology. **ge"o·log'i·cal.** — **ge·ol'o·gist,** *n.* One versed in geology.

ge·om'e·try, 1 ji-ŏm'i·tri; 2 ge-ŏm'e·try, *n.* [-TRIES², *pl.*] The science of space and its relations. — **ge·om'e·ter,** *n.* One skilled in geometry; a mathematician. **ge-**

om"e·tri'cian‡. — **ge"o·met'ric, ge"o·met'ri·cal,** 1 jī'o-met'rik, -ri·kal; 2 gē"o-mĕt'ric, -ri·cal, *a.* — **ge"o·met'ri·cal·ly,** *adv.*

ge·ra'ni·um, 1 ji-rē'ni·um; 2 ge-rā'ni·ŭm, *n. Bot.* A flowering plant of many species, common in cultivation.

ger'fal'con, 1 jur'fô"kn or -fal"kan; 2 gẽr'fa²en or -fäl"eon, *n.* A large falcon with feathered shanks.

germ, 1 jurm; 2 gẽrm, *n.* The earliest stage of an organism; bud; embryo; primary source. — **ger'mi·nal,** *a.*

Geranium.

Ger'man¹, 1 jur'man; 2 gẽr'man. **I.** *a.* Pertaining to Germany, its people, or its language. **II.** *n.* **1.** A native or citizen of Germany. **2.** The language of Germany. **3.** [g-] [U. S.] The cotillion. — **German'ic. I.** *a.* German. **II.** *n.* The German language.

ger'man², *a.* **1.** Having the same parents or grandparents: used after the noun; as, cousins *german.* **2.** Germane.

ger·mane', 1 jar-mēn'; 2 gẽr-mān', *a.* **1.** Appropriate; pertinent. **2.** Akin; german.

ger'mi·cide, 1 jur'mi·said; 2 gẽr'mi·çīd, *n.* Something used to destroy germs, as of disease. — **ger'mi·ci'dal,** *a.*

ger'mi·nate, 1 jur'mi·nēt; 2 gẽr'mi·nāt, *vi.* [-NAT'ED²; -NAT'ING.] To begin to grow or develop. — **ger'mi·na'tion,** *n.*

ger'ry·man'der, 1 ger'i·man'dər; 2 gĕr'y·măn'dẽr. **I.** *vt.* To reconstruct abnormally the voting districts, as of a state, to favor a political party. **II.** *n.* Such a reconstruction: named from Governor Elbridge *Gerry,* of Massachusetts, + *-mander* in SALAMANDER (because one of the districts formed while Gerry was governor was thought to resemble a salamander). — **jer"ry·man'der‡** [incorrect form].

ger'und, 1 jer'und; 2 gĕr'ŭnd, *n.* **1.** *L. Gram.* A verbal noun governing the same case as its verb. **2.** *Eng. Gram.* In the usage of some grammarians the verbal noun=form in *-ing.* [*n.* Pregnancy.

ges·ta'tion, 1 jes-tē'shan; 2 ges-tā'shon, **ges·tic'u·late,** 1 jes-tik'yu·lēt; 2 gĕs-tĭc'yu·lāt, *vi.* [-LAT'ED²; -LAT'ING.] To make gestures. — **ges·tic"u·la'tion,** *n.*

ges'ture, 1 jes'chur or -tiur; 2 gĕs'chur or -tūr, *n.* An expressive motion, as of the hand in speaking. See illus. on next page.

get, 1 get; 2 gĕt, *v.* [GOT, 1 got, 2 gŏt (GATT); GOT or GOT'TEN, 1 got'n, 2 gŏt'n,

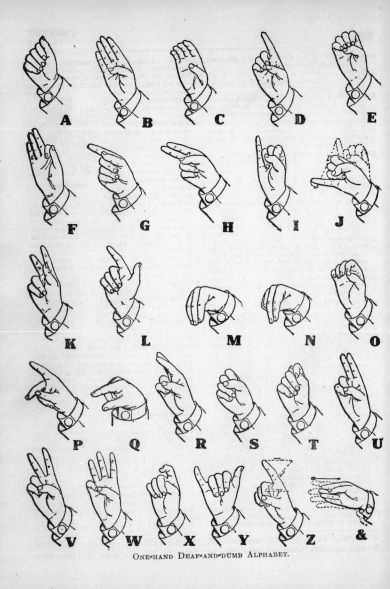

ONE-HAND DEAF-AND-DUMB ALPHABET.

GET′TING.] **I.** *t.* **1.** To gain; procure; acquire; receive; obtain. **2.** To learn. **3.** To beget; bring about; cause to be. **4.** To prevail on; persuade. **II.** *i.* To acquire wealth.

gew′gaw, 1 giū′gô; 2 gū′gạ, *n.* A flashy, useless ornament; bauble.

gey′ser, 1 gaī′zạr; 2 gȳ′ser, *n.* A hot spring from which water or mud is ejected.

ghast′ly,) 1 gast′li; 2 gȧst′ly, *a.* Death-
gast′ly²,) like; terrifying or shocking.— **ghast′li-ness,** *n.*

gher′kin, 1 gŭr′kin; 2 ġẽr′kin, *n.* Any small cucumber, used for pickling. **ger′kin‡.**

Ghet′to, 1 get′o; 2 ġet′o, *n.* [GHETTI or GHET′TOS, *pl.*] The Jews' quarter, as of a city.

ghost,) 1 gōst; 2 ġōst, *n.* A disembodied
gost⁸,) spirit; the soul; a shadow; semblance. **-like,** *a.*—**ghost′ly,** *a.* **1.** Pertaining to the soul; spiritual. **2.** Spectral. **—ghost′li-ness,** *n.*

ghoul, 1 gūl; 2 ġul, *n.* A demon supposed to prey on corpses.

gi′ant, 1 jaī′ạnt; 2 ġī′ant. **I.** *a.* Gigantic. **II.** *n.* **1.** *Myth.* A being of human form, but of enormous size. **2.** Any huge person or thing.—**gi′ant-ess,** *n. fem.*

glaour, 1 jaur; 2 ġour, *n.* An infidel: used by Mohammedans.

gib′ber, 1 gĭb′ạr; 2 ġĭb′er, *vi.* To jabber. —**gib′ber-ish. I.** *a.* Without meaning. **II.** *n.* Incoherent gabble.

gib′bet, 1 jĭb′et; 2 ġĭb′ĕt. **I.** *vt.* [-BET-ED^d; -BET-ING.] To hang; execrate. **II.** *n.* An upright timber with a crosspiece at its upper end, used as a gallows.

gib′bon, 1 gĭb′ạn; 2 ġĭb′on, *n.* A slender ape of southern Asia.

gib′bous,) 1 gĭb′ŭs; 2
gĭb′us,) *a.* **1.** Irregularly rounded, as the moon between half and full. **2.** Humpbacked.

gibe, 1 jaīb; 2 ġīb. **I.** *vt. & vi.* [GIBED; GIB′-ING.] To mock. **II.** *n.* A jeer; taunt.

Gibbon. 1/24

gib′let, 1 jĭb′let; 2 ġĭb′lĕt, *n.* **1.** Internal edible parts of a fowl, as the gizzard, etc. **2.** *pl.* Rags; tatters.

gid′dy, 1 gĭd′ĭ; 2 ġĭd′y, *a.* [GID′DI-ER; GID′DI-EST.] **1.** Dizzy; tending to cause dizziness. **2.** Thoughtless; imprudent.— **gid′di-ly,** *adv.*—**gid′di-ness,** *n.*

gift, 1 gĭft; 2 ġĭft, *n.* **1.** The act of giving; that given; a present. **2.** A natural endowment; talent.—**gift′ed,** *pa.* Talented.

gig¹, 1 gĭg; 2 ġĭg, *n.* **1.** A two-wheeled, one-horse vehicle. **2.** A ship's boat.

gig², *n.* A pronged fish-spear; a set of hooks for catching fish by dragging.

gi-gan′tic, 1 jai-gan′tik; 2 ġĭ-găn′tic, *a.* Like a giant; colossal; mighty.— **gi-gan′ti-cal-ly,** *adv.*

gig-gle,) 1 gĭg′l; 2 ġĭg′l. **I.** *vi.* [GIG′-
gig′l²,) GLED, GIG′LD²; GIG′GLING.] To laugh with an effort at suppression; titter. **II.** *n.* A convulsive laugh; titter.— **gig′gler,** *n.*

gi″go-′lette″, 1 jĭ″gō′lĕt; 2 ġĭ″gō′lĕt, *n.* [Fr.] A dance-hall employee who dances with patrons of the establishment.

gi″go-′lo″, 1 -lō′; 2 -lō′, *n.* **1.** [Fr.] A male companion of a gigolette. **2.** [U.S.] A hired escort for unattended women, as at entertainments.

gild, 1 gĭld; 2 ġĭld, *vt.* [GILD′ED^d or GILT; GILD′ING.] To coat with gold; make lustrous; illuminate.—**gild′ing,** *n.* **1.** The art of overlaying thinly with gold. **2.** An overlay of gold; gilt.

gild,) *n.* [*Gild* is the older form.] An
guild,) association of workers for mutual protection or cooperation.

gill¹, 1 gĭl; 2 ġĭl, *n.* An organ of fishes for breathing the air contained in water.

gill², 1 jĭl; 2 ġĭl, *n.* A liquid measure of one-eighth of a quart.

gil′ly-flow″er,) 1 jĭl′ĭ-flau″ạr; 2 ġĭl′y-flow″-
gil′li-flow″er,) er, *n.* A flowering plant.

gilt, 1 gĭlt; 2 ġĭlt. **I.** *a.* Gilded; yellow like gold. **II.** *n.* A thin overlay of gold.

gim′bal, 1 jĭm′bạl; 2 ġĭm′bal, *n.* A device for holding an object, as a ship's compass level.

gim′crack″, 1 jĭm′krak″; 2 ġĭm′erăk″, *n.* Something cheap; bauble. [boring-tool.

gim′let, 1 gĭm′let; 2 ġĭm′lĕt, *n.* A small

gimp, 1 gĭmp; 2 ġĭmp, *n.* A narrow, flat trimming: used for dresses, furniture, etc.

gin, 1 jĭn; 2 ġĭn, *vt.* [GINNED, GIND⁸; GIN′-NING.] **1.** To catch in a trap. **2.** To remove the seeds from (cotton).

gin¹, *n.* One of various machines or traps.

gin², *n.* An aromatic distilled liquor.

gin′ger, 1 jĭn′jạr; 2 ġĭn′ger, *n.* The pungent, spicy root of a tropical plant; also, the plant.—**gin′ger-bread″,** *n.* A light, sweet cake flavored with ginger.

gin′ger-ly, 1 jĭn′jạr-lĭ; 2 ġĭn′ger-ly, *a.* Cautious or fastidious: also, adverbially.

ging′ham, 1 gĭŋ′ạm; 2 ġĭŋ′am, *n.* A cotton dress-goods, in checks or stripes.

gin′seng, 1 jĭn′seŋ; 2 ġĭn′sĕŋg, *n.* A Chinese herb having an aromatic root.

gip′po, 1 jĭp′o; 2 ġĭp′o, *n.* [Soldiers' Slang.] **1.** Soup. **2.** Bacon.

Gip′sy, 1 jĭp′sĭ; 2 ġĭp′sy, *n.* [GIP′SIES²; *pl.*] A member of a wandering race, now

found in every part of the world; also, the language of that race.

gi-raffe′, 1 ji-raf′; 2 gi-răf′, *n.* An African ruminant having a very long neck.

gird¹, 1 gŭrd; 2 gĭrd, *vt.* [GIRD′ED^d or GIRT; GIRD′ING.] **1.** To bind around, as with a belt; encircle.

gird², *vt. & vi.* To attack with sarcasm; gibe; jeer.

gird′er, 1 gŭrd′-ər; 2 gĭrd′er, *n.* A principal horizontal beam.

Giraffe. ¹⁄₁₀₀

gir′dle, } 1 gŭr′dl; 2 gĭr′dl. **I.** *vt.* [GIR′-
gir′dl², } DL(E)D^d; GIR′DLING.] **1.** To fasten a girdle around; gird; encompass. **2.** To make an encircling cut through the bark of (a branch or tree). **II.** *n.* A belt; something encircling like a belt.

girl, 1 gŭrl; 2 gĭrl, *n.* A female infant or child, or a young unmarried woman.— **girl′hood,** *n.* The state or time of being a girl.— **girl′ish,** *a.* Like or pertaining to a girl. **-ly,** *adv.* **-ness,** *n.*

girt, 1 gŭrt; 2 gĭrt, *imp.* of GIRD, *v.*

girth, 1 gŭrth; 2 gĭrth, *n.* **1.** A band for fastening a pack or saddle to a horse's back. **2.** Anything that girds or binds. **3.** The circumference of an object.

gist, 1 jist; 2 gĭst, *n.* The main point; substance.

give, } 1 giv; 2 gĭv, *v.* [GAVE, 1 gēv, 2 găv;
giv², } GIV′EN, GIV′N^p; GIV′ING.] **I.** *t.* **1.** To bestow gratuitously. **2.** To transfer as or for a price; hand over; deliver; administer; inflict; declare; pronounce. **3.** To concede; surrender: often with *up.* **4.** To yield as a product or result. **5.** To supply; impart. **II.** *i.* **1.** To convey gratuitously something valuable. **2.** To yield as through pressure; recede.— **giv′en,** *pa.* **1.** Habitually inclined. **2.** Specified.— **giv′er,**^{n.}

giz′zard, 1 giz′ərd; 2 gĭz′ard, *n.* The second stomach of birds, in which the food is ground.

gla′cial, 1 glē′shəl; 2 glā′shal, *a.* Pertaining to glaciers; icy.

gla′cier, 1 glē′shər *or* glas′ı-ər; 2 glā′sher *or* glăç′i-ẽr, *n.* A slowly moving field or stream of ice, as on the slope of a mountain.

gla′cis, 1 glē′sıs; 2 glā′çis, *n.* A defensive slope in front of a fortification.

glad, 1 glad; 2 glăd, *a.* [GLAD′DER; GLAD′-DEST.] Joyful; pleased; gratified.— **glad′ly,** *adv.* [GLAD′LI-ER; GLAD′LI-EST.]— **glad′ness,** *n.*— **glad′some,** *a.* Causing or having a feeling of joy. **-ly,** *adv.* **-ness,** *n.*

glad′den, 1 glad′n; 2 glăd′n, *vt. & vi.* To make, be, or become glad.

glade, 1 glēd; 2 glād, *n.* A clearing or open space in a wood.

glad′i-a″tor, 1 glad′ı-ē″tər *or* -tər; 2 glăd′i-ā″tor, *n. Rom. Antiq.* A man who fought with deadly weapons, especially in the amphitheater, for popular amusement.— **glad″i-a-to′ri-al,** *a.*

gla-di′o-lus, 1 glə-dai′o-lus; 2 glä-di′o-lŭs, *n.* A plant with a fleshy bulb and sword-shaped leaves.

glair, 1 glār; 2 glâr, *n.* The white of egg; viscous matter.— **glair′y,** *a.*

glam′our, 1 glam′ər; 2 glăm′or, *n.* A
glam′er, } delusive fascination; enchantment.

glance, 1 glans; 2 glàns, *v.* [GLANCED^t; GLANC′ING.] **I.** *t.* To dart suddenly; direct momentarily. **II.** *i.* **1.** To look hurriedly or indirectly. **2.** To bound off after striking obliquely. **3.** To hint; make allusion. **4.** To flash; gleam.— **glanc′ing-ly,** *adv.*

glance, *n.* A quick look; sudden thought; momentary gleam; oblique rebound.

gland, 1 gland; 2 glănd, *n.* A secreting organ in plants or animals.— **glan′du-lar,** *a.*

glan′ders, 1 glan′dərz; 2 glăn′derṣ, *n. Vet. Med.* A contagious disease affecting the air-passages of the horse.

glare, 1 glār; 2 glâr, *vi.* [GLARED; GLAR′-ING.] To shine with fierce intensity; gaze fiercely.— **glar′ing,** *pa.* Excessively brilliant; evident; notorious; staring fiercely. **-ly,** *adv.* **-ness,** *n.* [ing look.

glare¹, *n.* **1.** A dazzling light. **2.** A piercing look. **glare²,** *n.* [U. S.] A glassy, smooth surface.

glass, 1 glas; 2 gläs. **I**ᵗ. *vt.* **1.** To reflect as in a mirror. **2.** To glaze. **II.** *n.* **1.** A transparent, brittle compound of silica with metallic oxids. **2.** Any article made wholly or partly of glass, as a mirror or a drinking-vessel; in the plural, spectacles or eye-glasses. **3.** The contents of a drinking-glass.— **glass′ful,** *n.* As much as can be contained in a drinking-glass.— **glass′y,** *a.* Composed of or like glass; having a hard, fixed look.— **glass′i-ly,** *adv.*— **glass′i-ness,** *n.*

glaze, 1 glēz; 2 glāz, *v.* [GLAZED; GLAZ′ING.] **I.** *t.* **1.** To furnish with glass. **2.** To

give a glassy appearance or coating to.
II. *i.* To become glassy.— **gla′zier,** 1 glē′-
ʒər; 2 glā′zher, *n.* **1.** One who fits panes
of glass. **2.** One who applies glaze to
pottery.— **glaz′ing,** *n.* **1.** A glaze. **2.** The
act or art of applying glaze. **3.** Window-
panes; glasswork. [used to produce it.

glaze, *n.* A glossy coating, or a substance

gleam, 1 glēm; 2 glēm. **I.** *vi.* To shine
out suddenly; glow. **II.** *n.* A glimmer;
flash.

glean, 1 glēn; 2 glēn, *vt.* & *vi.* To gather
(leavings) after reaping; gather item by
item.— **glean′er,** *n.*— **glean′ing,** *t.*

glebe, 1 glēb; 2 glēb, *n.* **1.** [Gt. Brit.] Land
of a parish church. **2**§. Turf; soil.

glee, 1 glī; 2 glē, *n.* **1.** Mirth; gaiety;
merriment. **2.** A song for three or more
voices.— **glee′ful,** *a.* Full of glee; merry.

glen, 1 glen; 2 glĕn, *n.* A small, secluded
valley.

glib, 1 glib; 2 glĭb, *a.* Fluent and plausible.
— **glib′ly,** *adv.*— **glib′ness,** *n.*

glide, 1 glaid; 2 glīd, *vi.* [GLID′ED^d or
GLID; GLID′ING.] To flow rapidly and
smoothly.— **glid′ing-ly,** *adv.*

glid′er, 1 glaid′ər; 2 glīd′er, *n.* One who or
that which glides; especially, a device for
gliding on the air.

glim′mer, 1 glim′ər; 2 glĭm′er. **I.** *vi.* To
gleam fitfully; flicker. **II.** *n.* A faint, unsteady light; a gleam.— **glim′mer-ing,** *pa.*
& *n.*

glimpse, 1 glimps; 2 glĭmps, *n.* **1.** A
glimpse^s, momentary view or look. **2.** A
swift, passing appearance; temporary
gleam.

glis′ten, 1 glis′n; 2 glĭs′n. **I.** *vi.* To
sparkle; shine; gleam. **II.** *n.* A gleam.

glit′ter, 1 glit′ər; 2 glĭt′er. **I.** *vi.* To
shine as a hard, polished surface; sparkle;
gleam. **II.** *n.* Sparkle; brilliancy.— **glit′-
ter-ing-ly,** *adv.* [twilight.

gloam′ing, 1 glōm′ıŋ; 2 glōm′ing, *n.* The
gloat^d, 1 glōt; 2 glōt, *vi.* To gaze steadily
with cruel or malign satisfaction.

globe, 1 glōb; 2 glōb, *n.* **1.** A perfectly
round body; ball; sphere. **2.** The earth.
— **glo′bose,** *a.* Nearly globular.— **glob′u-
lar,** 1 glɑb′yu-lər; 2 glŏb′yu-lar, *a.* Spherical.— **glob′ule,** 1 glɑb′yul; 2 glŏb′yul, *n.* A
small globe or spherical particle.— **glob′u-
lous,** *a.*

gloom, 1 glūm; 2 glōōm, *n.* Darkness;
obscurity; hence, melancholy; misfortune.
— **gloom′y,** *a.* [GLOOM′I-ER; GLOOM′I-EST.]
Full of gloom; dark; dismal; melancholy.—
gloom′i-ly, *adv.*— **gloom′i-ness,** *n.*

glo′ri-fy, 1 glō′rı-fɑi; 2 glō′ri-fȳ, *vt.* [-FIED;
-FY′ING.] **1.** To ascribe glory to; adore.

2. To honor; make glorious.— **glo″ri-fi-ca′-
tion,** *n.*

glo′ri-ous, 1 glō′rı-us; 2 glō′ri-ŭs, *a.* Full
of glory; illustrious; grand; noble. **-ly,** *adv.*
-ness, *n.*

glo′ry, 1 glō′rı; 2 glō′ry. **I.** *vi.* [GLO′-
RIED; GLO′RY-ING.] To exult: commonly
followed by *in.* **II.** *n.* [GLO′RIES^z, *pl.*]
1. Distinguished honor; praise; adoration.
2. Grandeur; radiance.

gloss[1], 1 glɛs; 2 glŏs. **I**^t. *vt.* **1.** To polish.
2. To excuse: usually with *over.* **II.** *n.*
Polish; deceptive show.

gloss[2]. **I**^t. *vt.* & *vi.* To annotate; write
marginal explanations. **II.** *n.* **1.** An explanatory note. **2.** A plausible excuse.

glos′sa-ry, 1 glɑs′ə-rı; 2 glŏs′a-ry, *n.*
[-RIES^z, *pl.*] A lexicon of the obsolete, obscure, or foreign words of a work.

gloss′y, *a.* [GLOSS′I-ER; GLOSS′I-EST.]
Smooth and shining.— **gloss′i-ly,** *adv.*—
gloss′i-ness, *n.*

glot′tis, 1 glɑt′ıs; 2 glŏt′is, *n.* [-TI-DES,
1 -ı-dīz; 2 -i-dĕs, *pl.*] The mouth of the
windpipe.

glove, 1 gluv; 2 glŭv, *n.* A covering for the
hand, with separate sheath for each finger.
— **glov′er,** *n.* A maker of or a dealer in
gloves.

glow, 1 glō; 2 glō. **I.** *vi.* **1.** To radiate
light and heat, especially without a flame.
2. To be ardent or excited. **3.** To flush.
II. *n.* Fervid heat; strong emotion; ardor; flush; ruddiness.— **glow′worm″,** *n.* A
phosphorescent beetle.

glow′er, 1 glɑu′ər; 2 glow′er, *vi.* To
frown; scowl.

gloze, 1 glōz; 2 glōz, *vt.* & *vi.* [GLOZED;
GLOZ′ING.] **1.** To palliate. **2**‖. To flatter.

glu′cose, 1 glū′kōs; 2 glū′cōs, *n.* A sugar
less sweet than cane-sugar, found largely
in nature, and made artificially by treating with sulfuric acid any substance containing starch.

glue, 1 glū; 2 glū. **I.** *vt.* & *vi.* [GLUED;
GLU′ING.] To stick; adhere. **II.** *n.* An
adhesive preparation derived from animal
substances, as hoofs. [silent; morose.

glum, 1 glum; 2 glŭm, *a.* Moody and

glume, 1 glūm; 2 glūm, *n.* A chaff-like
scale of the inflorescence of grasses.

glut, 1 glut; 2 glŭt. **I.** *vt.* & *vi.* [GLUT′-
TED^d; GLUT′TING.] To gorge. **II.** *n.* An
excessive supply; plethora.

glu′ten, 1 glū′ten; 2 glū′tĕn, *n.* The
tough albuminous part of wheat-flour.—
glu′ti-nous, *a.* Resembling glue; sticky.

glut′ton, 1 glut′n; 2 glŭt′n, *n.* One who
gluts himself with food and drink.— **glut′-**

1: ə = final; ı = habit; ɑisle; ɑu = out; oil; iū = feud; ℂhin; go; ŋ = sing; ℞hin, this.
2: wǫlf, dǫ; bōōk, bōōt; fṳll, rṳle, cṳre, bŭt, bûrn; oil, bǒy; ℊo, ℊem; iŋk; thin, this.

ton-ish, *a.*—**glut′ton-ous**, *a.*—**glut′ton-ous-ly**, *adv.*—**glut′ton-y**, *n.* Excess in eating.

glyc′er-in, } 1 glis′ər-in, -in *or* -īn; 2
glyc′er-ine, } glȳç′er-īn, -ĭn *or* -īn, *n.* A thick, oily, sweet liquid formed in the decomposition of fats.

gnarl, 1 närl; 2 närl, *n.* A tough knot.—**gnarl(e)d**, 1 närld; 2 närld, *a.* Knotty; distorted. **gnarl′y**‡.

gnash‡, 1 nash; 2 năsh, *vt.* & *vi.* To grind (the teeth) together, as in rage. [fly.

gnat, 1 nat; 2 năt, *n.* A small two-winged

gnaw, 1 nê; 2 na̤, *vt.* & *vi.* **1.** To eat little by little. **2.** To corrode.

gneiss, 1 nais; 2 nīs, *n.* A granitic rock. —**gneiss′ic**, **gneiss′oid**, *a.*

gnome, 1 nōm; 2 nōm, *n.* A fabled dwarfed goblin; a humming-bird; small owl.

gno′mon, 1 nō′mən; 2 nō′mŏn, *n.* The upright piece that casts the shadow on a sun-dial.

gnu, 1 nū; 2 nų, *n.* A South-African

White-tailed Gnu.
1/38

antelope having a buffalo-like head and a horse-like tail.

go, 1 gō; 2 gō, *vi.* [WENT, 1 went, 2 wĕnt; GONE, 1 gon, 2 gŏn; GO′ING.] **1.** To move from one place to another; depart; proceed; reach; tend; be about to do; intend; suit; fit. **2.** To pass away; be expended; die.

goad, 1 gōd; 2 gōd. **I**‡. *vt.* To drive; stimulate; incite. **II.** *n.* A point set in the end of a stick for urging oxen; spur; incitement.

goal, 1 gōl; 2 gōl, *n.* A point aimed at; limit; winning-point of a game.

goat, 1 gōt; 2 gōt, *n.* A hollow-horned ruminant of nearly the size of the sheep. —**goat′herd**″, *n.* One who tends goats.

goa-tee′, 1 gō-tī′; 2 gō-tē′, *n.* A pointed beard on the chin. [preventive service.

gob, *n.* [Colloq.] A sailor: originally, one in the

gob′ble¹, } 1 geb′l; 2 gŏb′l, *vt.* [GOB′BLED,
gob′l′r, } GOB′LD ; GOB′BLING.] To eat greedily.—**gob′bler**¹, *n.* A glutton.

gob′ble². **I.** *vt.* & *vi.* To utter a gobble. **II.** *n.* The sound made by the turkey-cock.—**gob′bler**², *n.* [Colloq.] A turkey-cock.

gob′let, 1 gob′let; 2 gŏb′lĕt, *n.* A drinking-vessel with stem and standard.

gob′lin, 1 gob′lin; 2 gŏb′lin, *n.* A frightful creature fabled to haunt groves and grottoes.

god, 1 god; 2 gŏd, *n.* **1.** [G-] The one Supreme Being; the Deity. **2.** An object of worship; divinity; an idol.—**god′child**″, **god′daugh**″**ter**, **god′fa**″**ther**, **god′moth**″**er**, **god′son**″, one viewed as holding a religious relationship like the natural one indicated, in consequence of sponsorship at baptism.—**god′dess**, *n.* A female divinity. —**God′head**, *n.* Deity.—**god′less**, *a.* Ungodly; wicked. **-ly**, *adv.* **-ness**, *n.*—**god′like**, *a.* Divine; of supreme excellence or beauty.—**god′li-ness**, *n.* The character of being godly.—**god′ly**, *a.* Filled with reverence and love for God; pious.—**god′send**″, *n.* An unexpected stroke of good fortune.—**God′speed**″, *n.* A wish that God will speed or prosper one.

gog′gle, } 1 geg′l; 2 gŏg′l, *n.* **1.** A rolling
gog′l′r, } of the eyes. **2.** *pl.* Tubular spectacles to protect against dust or strong light.

goi′ter, } 1 goi′tər; 2 gŏi′ter, *n.* A morbid
goi′tre, } swelling of the neck.

gold, 1 gōld; 2 gōld, *n.* A precious metal of a yellow color, very heavy, ductile, and malleable; money made of this metal; hence, wealth. —**gold′-beat**″**er**, 1 gōld′-bēt″ər; 2 gōld′-bēt″ər, *n.* One who makes gold-leaf.—**g.-beating**, *n.*—**g.-dust**, *n.* Gold in fine particles.—**gold′-finch**″, *n.* A finch with brilliant markings of black and yellow.—**gold′fish**″, *n.* A small carp of golden color.—**g. lace**, a lace wrought with gold or gilt thread.—**g.-leaf**, *n.* The finest leaf made from beaten gold.—**gold′smith**″, *n.* A worker in gold.—**g.-foil**, *n.* Thin sheets of gold, thicker than gold-leaf.

American Goldfinch.
1/5

gold′en, 1 gōld′n; 2 gōld′n, *a.* Made of or like gold; precious; prosperous.—**gold′en-rod**″, 1 gōld′n-rod″; 2 gōld′n-rŏd″, *n.* A plant of the aster family with bright-yellow flowers.

golf, 1 golf; 2 gŏlf, *n.* A Scottish game

1: ȧrtistic, ärt; fat, fāre; fạst; get, prēy; hīt, police; obey, gō; not, ŏr; full, rūle; bụt, būrn.

2: ärt, āpe, făt, fâre, fȧst, whạt, ạll; mē, gĕt, prey, fẽrn; hĭt, īce; ī=ē; ĭ=ĕ; gō, nŏt, ôr, wọn,

played with a small, resilient ball and clubs having wooden or metal heads.

gon'do-la, 1 gɛn'do-la; 2 gŏn'do-la, *n.* A long, narrow, flat=bottomed Venetian boat.— **gon"do-lier',** 1 gɛn'do-lîr'; 2 gŏn'-do-lêr', *n.* The rower of a gondola.

gone, *pp.* of GO, *v.*

gong, 1 gɛŋ; 2 gŏng, *n.* A metal instrument like a shallow dish, sounded by beating; a bell of similar shape.

good, 1 gud; 2 gōōd. **I.** *a.* [BET'TER; BEST.] **1.** Having excellent, useful, or admirable qualities; excellent; worthy; righteous; virtuous; religious. **2.** Adequate; competent; serviceable; ample. **3.** Valid; genuine. **II.** *n.* **1.** That which is good; advantage; benefit; righteousness; virtue; welfare. **2.** *pl.* Personal property; chattels.— **good'ly,** *a.* [-LI-ER; -LI-EST.] Pleasing; attractive; excellent; ample.— **good'li-ness,** *n.* Comeliness; beauty. — **good'man**‖, *n.* [-MEN, *pl.*] Master; Mr.; husband; head of a family.— **good'ness,** *n.* The state or quality of being good.— **good'-wife'**‖, 1 gud'wɑif'; 2 gōōd'wîf', *n.* [-WIVES², *pl.*] Madam; Mrs.: the correlative of *good-man.*— **good"will',** *n.* The established popularity of a business.

good"=by'‖, ⎱1 gud"=bɑi'; 2 gōōd'=bî', *a.,*
good"=bye', ⎰ *n.,* & *interj.* Farewell; adieu.

good'y, 1 gud'ı; 2 gōōd'y. **I.** *a.* Mawkishly good; weakly pious. **good'y=good'y**‡. **II.** *n.* [GOOD'IES², *pl.*] **1.** A poor old woman. **2.** A sweetmeat.

goose, 1 gūs; 2 gōōs, *n.* [GEESE, 1 gīs; 2 gês, *pl.*] **1.** A web=footed bird, larger than a duck and smaller than a swan. **2.** A tailors' smoothing=iron. **3.** A silly creature; ninny. — **goose'ber"ry,** 1 gūz'-ber'ı; 2 gōōs'bĕr"y, *n.* [-RIES², *pl.*] The tart fruit of a spiny shrub; also, the shrub.— **goose'=flesh"**, *n.* Skin roughened like that of a plucked goose as the result of cold, fear, etc.

Tailors' Goose.

go'pher, 1 gō'fər; 2 gō'fer, *n.* A burrowing American rodent.

gore¹, 1 gōr; 2 gôr, *vt.* [GORED; GOR'ING.] To make a gore of; supply with a gore.

gore², *vt.* [GORED; GOR'ING.] To pierce, as with a horn; stab.

gore¹, *n.* A wedge=shaped piece, as of cloth in a garment.

gore², *n.* Blood after effusion, especially clotted blood.— **gor'y,** *a.* Stained with or resembling gore.

gorge, 1 gɔrj; 2 gôrg, *vt.* & *vi.* [GORGED; GORG'ING.] To eat greedily; glut.

gorge, *n.* **1.** The throat. **2.** A ravine.

gor'geous, 1 gōr'jus; 2 gôr'gŭs, *a.* Resplendent; magnificent; sumptuous. **-ly,** *adv.* **-ness,** *n.*

gor'gon, 1 gōr'gɛn; 2 gôr'gon, *n. Gr. Myth.* **1.** [G-] A frightful female monster inhabiting the edge of the Western ocean. **2.** [G-] The head of the Gorgon Medusa, set in the egis of Athena, after the monster had been slain by Perseus. **3.** Any hideously ugly being or object.

Gorilla. ¹⁄₅₅

go-ril'la, 1 go-ril'ə; 2 go-rîl'a, *n.* A manlike African ape about five and a half feet in height, with a massive body and limbs.

gor'mand, ⎱1 gōr'mɛnd, gûr'mɛnd; 2
gour'mand, ⎰gôr'mand, gŭr'mand, *n.* **1.** A glutton. **2.** An epicure.— **gor'mand-ize,** *vt.* & *vi.* [-IZED; -IZ'ING.] To eat voraciously. **gor'mand-ise**‡.— **gor'mand-iz"er** or **-is"-er,** *n.*

gorse, 1 gōrs; 2 gôrs, *n.* Furze.

gor'y, 1 gōr'ı; 2 gôr'y, *a.* **1.** Stained with gore. **2.** Resembling gore.

gos'hawk", 1 gɛs'hɔk"; 2 gŏs'hạk", *n.* A short=winged hawk. [goose.

gos'ling, 1 gɛz'lıŋ; 2 gŏs'ling, *n.* A young

gos'pel, 1 gɛs'pɛl; 2 gŏs'pĕl, *n.* **1.** Good news, especially the tidings of salvation through Jesus Christ. **2.** [G-] One of the four memoirs of Christ in the New Testament.

gos'sa-mer, 1 gɛs'a-mər; 2 gŏs'a-mer. **I.** *a.* Thin and light; flimsy. **II.** *n.* **1.** An exceedingly fine web of spider's silk that may float in the air. **2.** A fine gauze; a thin water=proof outer garment.

gos'sip, 1 gɛs'ıp; 2 gŏs'ip. **I.** *vi.* [GOS'-SIPED†, GOS'SIPT²; GOS'SIP-ING.] To chat; tattle. **II.** *n.* **1.** Familiar or idle talk; mischievous tattle; rumor. **2.** One who gossips. **3.** Originally, a sponsor in baptism.— **gos'sip-y,** *a.*

got, *imp.* & *pp.* of GET, *v.*— **got'ten,** 1 gɛt'n; 2 gŏt'n, *pp.* of GET, *v.*

Goth, 1 gɛth; 2 gŏth, *n.* One of the German invaders of the Roman empire in the 3d and 4th centuries.— **Goth'ic. I.** *a.* **1.** Pertaining to the Goths; rude; barbaric. **2.** Pertaining to the Pointed style of architecture. **II.** *n.* **1.** The language of the

Goths. **2.** *Arch.* The Pointed style. **3.** *Print.* A style of type.

This Line is in Gothic Type.

gouge, 1 gauj; 2 g̯oug̯. **I.** *vt.* [GOUGED; GOUG′ING.] To scoop out, as with a gouge; cheat. **II.** *n.* A chisel with a curved cutting edge, or a cut made by it.

gourd, 1 gōrd; 2 g̯ōrd, *n.* A melon-like fruit with a hard rind; also, the plant that bears it, or a vessel made of its shell.

gour′mand, etc. See GORMAND. [cure.

gour″met′, 1 gūr′mĕ′; 2 g̯ur′me̯′, *n.* An epi-

gout, 1 gaut; 2 g̯out, *n.* A disease manifested by painful inflammation of a joint, as of the great toe.— **gout′i-ness,** *n.*— **gout′y,** *a.*

goût, 1 gū; 2 g̯u, *n.* Taste; relish.

gov′ern, 1 guv′ərn; 2 g̯ŏv′ern, *v.* **I.** *t.*
guv′ern^r, *f* To control; regulate; direct. **II.** *i.* To exercise authority; administer laws.— **gov′ern-ess,** *n.* A woman who trains and instructs children in their home.

gov′ern-ment, 1 guv′ərn-ment *or* -mənt;
guv′ern-ment^r, *f* 2 g̯ŏv′ern-ment, *n.* The act of governing; control, direction, or restraint; the controlling power in a state; the administration; territory governed.— **gov″ern-men′tal,** *a.*

gov′er-nor, 1 guv′ər-nər *or* -nər; 2 g̯ŏv′-
guv′er-nor^r, *f* er-nor, *n.* One who governs; chief executive of a state; a regulator, as of the speed of machinery.

Governor.

gown, 1 gaun; 2 g̯own. **I.** *vt. & vi.* To dress in a gown. **II.** *n.* A woman's dress; any long, loose robe.— **gowned,** *a.*

grab, 1 grab; 2 g̯răb. **I.** *vt. & vi.* [GRABBED, GRABD^S; GRAB′-BING.] To grasp rudely; clutch; seize suddenly or dishonestly. **II.** *n.* An act of grabbing; a clutch; snatch.

grace, 1 grēs; 2 g̯rāç. **I.** *vt.* [GRACED^t; GRAC′ING.] To adorn; honor; gratify. **II.** *n.* **1.** Beauty of form, motion, or speech. **2.** Any attractive quality. **3.** Clemency; divine favor or influence. **4.** A brief prayer before or after a meal.— **grace′ful,** *a.* Marked by grace; elegant; easy; becoming. **-ly,** *adv.* **-ness,** *n.*— **grace′less,** *a.* Lacking grace; immoral; vicious.— **grace-note,** *n. Mus.* An ornament or embellishment, such as the turn, trill, etc.

gra′cious, 1 grē′shus; 2 g̯rā′shŭs, *a.* Courteous; kind; affable; manifesting divine grace. **-ly,** *adv.* **-ness,** *n.*

gra-da′tion, 1 grē-dē′shən; 2 g̯rā-dā′shon, *n.* Advance by steps.

grade, 1 grēd; 2 g̯rād. **I.** *vt.* [GRAD′ED^d; GRAD′ING.] **1.** To classify by grades. **2.** To bring to a grade. **3.** To improve by cross-breeding. **II.** *n.* **1.** A degree, step, or rank in any series. **2.** An incline, or the degree of inclination. **3.** A cross-bred animal.

gra′di-ent, 1 grē′di-ent; 2 g̯rā′di-ĕnt. **I.** *a.* Advancing by steps or by a grade. **II.** *n.* **1.** *Civ. Eng.* A grade. **2.** *Meteor.* Rate of increase or decrease, as of barometric pressure.

grad′u-al, 1 graj′u-əl *or* grad′yu-əl; 2 g̯răj′u-al *or* g̯răd′yu-al, *a.* **1.** Proceeding by steps; moving slowly and regularly; slow. **2.** Divided into degrees; graduated. **-ly,** *adv.* **-ness,** *n.*

grad′u-ate, 1 graj′u-ēt *or* grad′yu-ēt; 2 g̯răj′u-āt *or* g̯răd′yu-āt. **I.** *vt. & vi.* [-AT″ED^d; -AT′ING.] **1.** To admit to or take an academic degree at the end of a course. **2.** To divide into grades or intervals; change by degrees. **II.** *a.* Having been graduated from an institution of learning. **III.** *n.* One who has been graduated by an institution of learning.— **grad″u-a′tion,** *n.* The act of graduating. — **grad′u-a″tor,** *n.*

graft^id, 1 graft; 2 g̯räft. **I.** *vt. & vi.* [GRAFT′ED^d; GRAFT′ING.] To insert, as a graft; insert a graft into. **II^1.** *n.* A shoot inserted into a tree or plant so as to unite with it.— **graft′er^1,** *n.*

graft², **I.** *vt.* **1.** To toil. **2.** To obtain something, as money, by dishonest means. **II².** *n.* **1.** Manual labor. **2.** Anything obtained by grafting, as money secured dishonestly. — **graft′er²,** *n.*

grail, 1 grēl; 2 g̯rāl, *n.* A broad bowl or chalice; in medieval legend the cup used by Chr.st at the Last Supper; the **Ho′y Grail.**

grain, 1 grēn; 2 g̯răn. **I.** *vt. & vi.* **1.** To granulate. **2.** To paint or stain in imitation of the grain of wood. **II.** *n.* **1.** Any very small hard mass; a seed; kernel; minute particle. **2.** Cereals, collectively. **3.** A weight, the $1/7000$ part of a pound avoirdupois. **4.** Texture; direction of fibers, as of wood. **5.** Innate quality or character.

gram, 1 gram; 2 g̯răm, *n.* In the
gramme, *f* metric system, a weight: 15.43 troy grains. See METRIC SYSTEM.

gram″i-niv′o-rous, 1 gram″i-niv′o-rus; 2 g̯răm″i-nĭv′o-rŭs, *a.* Feeding upon grass, or the like.

gram'mar, 1 gram'ẽr; 2 grăm'ar, *n.* The science treating the correct use of language; a treatise on this subject; any elementary treatise.— **gram-ma'ri-an,** 1 gra-mẽ'rɪ-ən; 2 grā-mā'rɪ-an, *n.* One skilled in grammar.— **gram-mat'i-cal,** *a.* According to grammar. **gram-mat'ic‡.— gram-mat'i-cal-ly,** *adv.*

gram'pus, 1 gram'pus; 2 grăm'pŭs, *n.* A large dolphin=like cetacean.

gran'a-ry, 1 gran'a-rɪ; 2 grăn'a-ry, *n.* [-RIES*z*, *pl.*] A storehouse for grain.

grand, 1 grand; 2 grănd, *a.* Of imposing character or aspect; magnificent; stately; noble; chief.— **grand'ly,** *adv.*— **grand'ness,** *n.*— **gran'dam, gran'dame,** *n.* A grandmother; an old woman.— **grand'child",** *n.* The child of one's son or daughter.— **grand'daugh"ter,** *n. fem.* **grand'fa"ther,** *n.* The father of one's father or mother. **grand'pa"‡;** **grand'pa-pa"‡.— grand'moth"er,** *n.* The mother of one's father or mother. **grand'ma"‡;** **grand'ma-ma"‡.— grand'par"ent,** *n.* The parent of one's parent.— **grand'sire",** *n.* A grandfather; any male ancestor.— **grand'son",** *n.* The son of one's child. [Spanish noble.

gran-dee', 1 gran-dī'; 2 grăn-dē', *n.* A **gran'deur,** 1 gran'jur *or* -dɪur; 2 grăn'jur *or* -dūr, *n.* The quality of being grand; sublimity; magnificence.

gran-dil'o-quent, 1 gran-dɪl'o-kwent; 2 grăn-dĭl'o-kwĕnt, *a.* Pompous or bombastic in style.— **gran-dil'o-quence,** *n.*— **gran-dil'o-quent-ly,** *adv.*

gran"di-o'so, 1 grăn"dɪ-ō'so; 2 grän'dĭ-ō'so, *a. & adv. Mus.* In a grand or imposing manner.

grange, 1 grēnj; 2 grānj, *n.* A farm, with its dwelling=house.— **grang'er,** *n.*

gran'ite, 1 gran'ɪt; 2 grăn'ɪt, *n.* A rock **gran'its,** composed of quartz, feldspar, and mica, of great strength, and taking a high polish.— **gran'ite-ware",** *n.*— **gra-nit'ic,** *a.* Of or like granite.

gra-niv'o-rous, 1 gra-nɪv'o-rŭs; 2 gra-nĭv'o-rŭs, *a.* Living on grain or seeds.

grant, 1 grant; 2 grănt. **I**d. *vt.* **1.** To bestow; confer. **2.** To admit as true; concede. **II.** *n.* **1.** The act of granting. **2.** The thing granted. **3.** An admission; concession.— **grant-ee',** 1 grant-ī'; 2 grănt-ē', *n.* The person to whom property or rights are granted.— **grant'or** *or* **-er,** *n.* One who grants.

gran'u-lar, 1 gran'yu-lẽr; 2 grăn'yu-lar, *a.* Composed of, like, or containing grains or granules. **gran'u-lous‡.— gran'u-lar-ly,** *adv.*— **gran'u-la-ry,** *a.*

gran'u-late, 1 gran'yu-lēt; 2 grăn'yu-lāt, *vt. & vi.* [-LAT"ED*d*; -LAT"ING.] To form

into grains; become granular.— **gran"u-la'tion,** *n.* The forming into grains or granules; a granulated surface.

gran'ule, 1 gran'yul; 2 grăn'yul, *n.* A small grain; particle; corpuscle.— **gran'u-lous,** *a.*

grape, 1 grēp; 2 grāp, *n.* **1.** The round edible fruit growing in clusters on a vine called the grape=vine; also, the vine. **2.** *Mil.* Grape=shot.— **grap'er-y,** 1 grēp'er-ɪ; 2 grāp'er-y, *n.* A building or enclosure for the growing of grapes.— **grape'shot",** *n.* A cluster of cast=iron shot, to be discharged from a cannon.— **g.=vine,** *n.* The vine that bears grapes.

-graph. A suffix denoting that which writes or that which is written; as, phono*graph.* See -GRAPHY.

graph'ic, 1 graf'ɪk, -ɪ-kəl; 2 grăf'ic, **graph'i-cal,** -ɪ-cal, *a.* Pertaining to or recorded in writing; describing with pictorial effect. **-ly,** *adv.*

graph'ite, 1 graf'ait; 2 grăf'ɪt, *n. Mineral.* A variety of carbon; used in the making of lead=pencils, etc.

graph'o-phone, 1 graf'o-fōn; 2 grăf'o-fōn, *n.* An instrument for recording and reproducing sounds through the medium of a disk, cylinder, or tape. See PHONOGRAPH.

-graphy, *suffix.* Description; writing: used in such words as geo*graphy*, bio*graphy*, naming a descriptive science.

grap'nel, 1 grap'nel; 2 grăp'nĕl, *n.* **1.** A device for grappling. **grap'pling-i"ron‡.** **2.** A boat's anchor with many flukes.

grap'ple, 1 grap'l; 2 grăp'l. **I.** *vt. & vi.* [GRAP'PLED; GRAP'PLING.] To seize; clinch; contend. **II.** *n.* **1.** A close hold

Grapnel.

or grip, as in wrestling. **2.** A grapnel.

grasp, 1 grasp; 2 grȧsp. **I**t. *vt.* To seize with the hand; embrace firmly; comprehend. **II.** *n.* **1.** A grip of the hand. **2.** Ability to seize and hold; possession; comprehension.— **grasp'ing,** *pa.* Greedy of gain; avaricious.

grass, 1 gras; 2 grȧs, *n.* **1.** The green plants on which cattle feed. **2.** *Bot.* Any plant with hollow, jointed stems and sheathing leaves.— **grass'hop"per,** *n.* An insect having powerful thighs adapted for leaping.— **grass'i-ness,** *n.*— **grass'y,** *a.* Abounding in, covered with, or resembling grass.

grate,1 grēt; 2 grāt, *vt. & vi.* [GRAT'ED*d*; GRAT'ING.] **1.** To rub together with a

harsh sound; rasp; irritate. **2.** To wear away in minute particles by rubbing. — **grat'er,** *n.* One who or that which grates; a utensil for grating substances.— **grat'ing,** *pa.* Harsh; rasping; irritating.

grate², *vt.* To fit with a grate or with bars.

grate, *n.* A framework of bars, as to close an opening, or to hold fuel in burning. **grat'ing².**

grate'ful, 1 grēt'ful; 2 grāt'ful, *a.* Having or expressing a due sense of benefits received; thankful. **-ly,** *adv.* **-ness,** *n.*

grat'i-fy, 1 grat'i-fai; 2 grăt'i-fī, *vt.* [-FIED; -FY'ING.] **1.** To please; satisfy. **2‖.** To recompense; reward.— **grat″i-fi-ca'tion,** 1 grat'i-fi-kē'shən; 2 grăt″i-fi-cā'shon, *n.* The act of gratifying; state of being gratified; that which gratifies.

gra'tis, 1 grē'tis; 2 grā'tis, *adv.* Without recompense; freely.

grat'i-tude, 1 grat'i-tiūd; 2 grăt'i-tūd, *n.* The state of being grateful; thankfulness.

gra-tu'i-tous, 1 grə-tiū'i-tus; 2 gra-tū'i-tŭs, *a.* Given without recompense, as a benefit, or without provocation, as an insult. **-ly,** *adv.* **-ness,** *n.*— **gra-tu'i-ty,** *n.* [-TIES², *pl.*] Something given gratuitously; a present; donation.

grat'u-late‖, 1 grach'u-[or grat'yu-]lēt; 2 grăch'u-[or grăt'yu-]lāt, *vt.* To congratulate.— **grat″u-la'tion,** *n.*— **grat'u-la-to-ry,** *a.*

grave, 1 grēv; 2 grāv, *vt.* [GRAVED; GRAVED or GRAV'EN, 1 grēv'n, 2 grāv'n; GRAV'ING.] To engrave.

grave, *a.* Important; serious; sober. **-ly,** *adv.* **-ness,** *n.*

grave, *n.* An excavation in the earth for the burial of a dead body; the abode of the dead.— **grave'stone″,** *n.* A memorial stone at a grave.— **grave'yard″,** *n.* A burial-ground; cemetery.

grav'el, 1 grav'el; 2 grăv'ĕl. **I.** *vt.* [GRAV'-ELED or GRAV'ELLED, GRAV'ELD³; GRAV'EL-ING or GRAV'EL-LING.] To cover or fill with gravel. **II.** *n.* **1.** A mixture of sand and pebbles. **2.** *Pathol.* Granular concretions formed in the kidneys.— **grav'el-ly,** *a.*

grav'er, 1 grēv'ər; 2 grāv'er, *n.* An engraver; a burin or chisel.

grav'i-tate, 1 grav'i-tēt; 2 grăv'i-tāt, *vi.* [-TAT″ED⁴; -TAT'ING.] To tend by or as by force of gravity.

grav″i-ta'tion, 1 grav″i-tē'shən; 2 grăv″i-tā'shon, *n.* The force with which all bodies attract each other.

grav'i-ty, 1 grav'i-ti; 2 grăv'i-ty, *n.* [-TIES², *pl.*] **1.** Gravitation; weight. **2.** The quality of being grave; importance; sedateness.

gra'vy, 1 grē'vi; 2 grā'vy, *n.* [GRA'VIES², *pl.*] The juice of cooked meat, or a sauce made from it.

gray, 1 grē; 2 grā. **I.** *a.* **1.** Of mingled
grey, white and black. **2.** Having gray hair; hoary; aged. **II.** *n.* A gray color; a gray animal.

gray'hound″, *n.* Same as GREYHOUND.

graze¹, 1 grēz; 2 grāz, *vt. & vi.* [GRAZED; GRAZ'ING.] To feed upon herbage; pasture.— **gra'zier,** 1 grē'зer; 2 grā'zher, *n.* One who pastures or deals in cattle.

graze², *vt. & vi.* [GRAZED; GRAZ'ING.] To touch lightly in passing; rub; abrade.

grease, 1 grīs or grīz; 2 grēs or grēs. **I.** *vt.* [GREASED, 1 grīst or grīzd, 2 grēst or grēsd; GREAS'ING.] To smear with grease. **II.** 1 grīs; 2 grēs, *n.* Animal fat; any fatty substance.— **greas'i-ly,** *adv.*— **greas'i-ness,** *n.*— **greas'y,** 1 grīs'i; 2 grēs'y, *a.* [GREAS'I-ER; GREAS'I-EST.] Smeared with, containing, or like grease; oily.

great, 1 grēt; 2 grāt, *a.* **1.** Of large size, quantity, number, or duration; big; vast; numerous; prolonged. **2.** Important; mighty; eminent; distinguished; magnanimous; grand. **3.** More remote by one generation; as, *great*-grandfather, etc. — **great'coat″,** *n.* A heavy overcoat. — **great'ly,** *adv.*— **great'ness,** *n.*

greaves, 1 grīvz; 2 grēvs, *n. pl.* Armor to protect the legs from knee to ankle.

grebe, 1 grīb; 2 grēb, *n.* A 4-toed diving bird without tail-feathers.

Gre'cian, 1 grī'shan; 2 grē'shan. **I.** *a.* Greek. **II.** *n.* **1.** A Greek. **2.** A Greek scholar.

Gre'cism, 1 grī'sizm; 2 grē'çĭsm, *n.* A Greek idiom.

greed, 1 grīd; 2 grēd, *n.* Eager and selfish desire; greediness; avarice. — **greed'i-ly,** *adv.*— **greed'i-ness,** *n.*— **greed'y,** 1 grīd'i; 2 grēd'y, *a.* [GREED'I-ER; GREED'I-EST.] Excessively eager for food or drink; selfish; avaricious.

Greek, 1 grīk; 2 grēk. **I.** *a.* Pertaining to Greece or the Greeks; Grecian. **II.** *n.* One of the people of Greece; the Greek language.

Grebe. ¹/₁₄

green, 1 grīn; 2 grēn. **I.** *a.* **1.** Of the ordinary color of growing plants. **2.** Unripe; immature. **3.** New; fresh; flourishing. **II.** *n.* **1.** A green color or object. **2.** A plot of grass-land. **-ly,** *adv.* **-ness,** *n.*— **green'back″,** *n.* A legaltender note of the United States.— **green'gro'cer,** *n.* A retailer of fresh vegetables.—

green'house", *n.* A building covered with glass, for tender plants.— **green'ish**, *a.* Somewhat green.— **green'room"**, 1 grēn'rūm"; 2 grēn'rōŏm", *n.* The common waiting-room for performers in a theater.— **green'sward"**, *n.* Green turf.

greetd, 1 grīt; 2 grēt, *vt. & vi.* To salute; accost.— **greet'ing**, *n.* Salutation; welcome.

gre-ga'ri-ous, 1 gri-gē'ri-us; 2 gre-gā'ri-ŭs, *a.* Associating in flocks or companies. **-ly,** *adv.* **-ness,** *n.*

Gre-go'ri-an, 1 gri-gō'ri-ən; 2 gre-gō'ri-an. **I.** *a.* Pertaining to one named Gregory, especially to either of two popes, Gregory I. or XIII.— **Gregorian chant,** the prescribed musical ritual of the Roman Catholic Church, ascribed to Pope Gregory (6th century).

gre-nade', 1 gri-nēd'; 2 gre-nād', *n.* An explosive shell, to be thrown by hand.— **gren"a-dier',** 1 gren"ə-dir'; 2 grĕn"a-dēr', *n.* A foot-soldier belonging to a special regiment; originally, a soldier who threw grenades.

grew, *imp.* of GROW, *v.*

grew'some, *a.* Same as GRUESOME.

grey, etc. Same as GRAY, etc.

grey'hound", 1 grē'hɑund"; 2 grē'hound", *n.* A tall, slender hunting-dog, noted for keen sight and swiftness.

grid'dle, }
grid'lP, } 1 grid'l; 2 grid'l, *n.* A shallow pan, for baking thin cakes; a cover for a hole in a cooking-stove.

Greyhound. ⅟₃₆

grid'i'ron, 1 grid'ɑi"ərn; 2 grĭd'ī"ern, *n.* A grated utensil for broiling.

gride, 1 grɑid; 2 grīd. **I.** *vt. & vi.* [GRIDED; GRID'ING.] To make a harsh, grating sound; grate. **II.** *n.* The sound so made.

grief, 1 grīf; 2 grēf, *n.* **1.** Sorrow; regret; lamentation. **2.** Affliction; grievance.

grieve, }
griev'eP, } 1 grīv; 2 grēv, *v.* [GRIEV(E)Dᵈ; GRIEV'ING.] **I.** *t.* To oppress with grief; afflict. **II.** *i.* To sorrow.— **griev'ance,** *n.* A cause of annoyance; wrong done.— **griev'ous,** *a.* Causing grief or injury; harmful; distressing; severe.— **griev'ous-ly,** *adv.*— **griev'ous-ness,** *n.*

grif'fin, 1 grif'in; 2 grĭf'in, *n.* A fabulous creature, half lion, half eagle.

grill, }
grillP, } 1 gril; 2 grĭl, *vt. & vi.* To broil. — **grill'-room",** *n.* An eating-room where grilling is done.

grim, 1 grim; 2 grĭm, *a.* Stern and forbidding; harsh; formidable. **-ly,** *adv.* **-ness,** *n.*

gri-mace', 1 gri-mēs'; 2 gri-māç'. **I.** *vi.* To make grimaces. **II.** *n.* A distortion of the features, as in contempt or pretense.

gri-mal'kin, 1 gri-mal'[or -məl']kin; 2 gri-măl'[or -mal'kin], *n.* An old cat.

grime, 1 grɑim; 2 grīm. **I.** *vt.* [GRIMED; GRIM'ING.] To soil; begrime. **II.** *n.* That which soils; dirt ground in.— **grim'y,** *a.*

grin, 1 grin; 2 grĭn. **I.** *vt. & vi.* [GRINNED; GRINNᵈ; GRIN'NING.] To make by grinning; show the teeth, as in suppressed laughter. **II.** *n.* The act of grinning; a broad smile.

grind, 1 grɑind; 2 grīnd, *v.* [GROUND, 1 grɑund, 2 ground; GRIND'ING.] **I.** *t.* To wear down or pulverize by friction; sharpen; chafe; oppress; harass. **II.** *i.* **1.** To be chafed, polished, or sharpened by rubbing. **2.** To toil mechanically.— **grind'er,** *n.* One who or that which grinds; a molar tooth.— **grind'stone",** *n.* A flat circular stone turning on an axis, for sharpening tools.

grip, 1 grip; 2 grĭp. **I.** *vt.* [GRIPPEDᵗ, GRIPTᵖ; GRIP'PING.] To gripe; grasp. **II.** *n.* **1.** The act of grasping firmly; a firm grasp. **2.** A handle; gripping mechanism.

gripe, 1 grɑip; 2 grīp. **I.** *vt. & vi.* [GRIPEDᵗ; GRIP'ING.] **1.** To grasp. **2.** To give pain to (the bowels); distress; suffer; be extortionate. **II.** *n.* **1.** A firm hold; grip; oppressive control. **2.** *pl.* Intermittent pains in the bowels.

grippe, }
grip, } 1 grip; 2 grĭp, *n.* Severe influenza or epidemic catarrh.

gris'ly, 1 griz'li; 2 grĭȥ'ly, *a.* Savage-looking; fearful.

grist, 1 grist; 2 grĭst, *n.* **1.** A portion of grain to be ground. **2.** A supply.— **grist'-mill",** *n.* A mill for grinding grain.

gris'tle, 1 gris'l; 2 grĭs'l, *n.* Tough, elastic animal tissue; cartilage.— **gris'tly,** 1 gris'li; 2 gris'ly, *a.*

grit¹, 1 grit; 2 grĭt, *n.* **1.** Rough, hard particles; sand or gravel. **2.** Firmness of character; courage.— **grit'ti-ness,** *n.*— **grit'ty,** 1 grit'i; 2 grĭt'y, *a.*

grit², *n.* **1.** Coarse meal. **2.** *pl.* Grain hulled or granulated.

griz'zle, }
griz'lP, } 1 griz'l; 2 grĭz'l, *n.* A mixture of white and black; gray.— **griz'zled,** *a.* Gray.— **griz'zly,** *a.* Grayish; somewhat gray.— **grizzly bear,** a large, ferocious, grizzly-

Grizzly Bear. ⅟₇₅

gray or brownish bear of W. North America.

groan, 1 grōn; 2 grŏn. **I.** *vi.* To utter a groan. **II.** *n.* A low, murmuring sound, as of distress.— **groan'ing,** *n.*

groat, 1 grōt; 2 grŏt, *n.* A former English silver coin: fourpence; a trifle.

groats, 1 grōts; 2 grŏts, *n. pl.* Hulled and crushed oats or wheat.

gro'cer, 1 grō'sər; 2 grō'çer, *n.* One who deals in groceries.— **gro"ce-te'ri-a,** 1 grō"sə-tē'ri-ə; 2 grō"çe-te'ri-a, *n.* [U. S.] A grocery where patrons wait on themselves and pay on leaving: a trade=mark name.— **gro'-cer-y,** 1 grō'sər-ĭ; 2 grō'çer-y, *n.* [-IES², *pl.*] **1.** [U. S.] A grocer's store or shop. **2.** *pl.* Household supplies for the table.

grog, 1 grog; 2 grŏg, *n.* A mixture of spirits and water.— **grog'gy,** *a.*— **grog's shop",** *n.* A liquor=saloon.

groin, 1 groin; 2 grŏin, *n.* **1.** *Anat.* The crease where the thigh joins the abdomen. **2.** *Arch.* The line of intersection of two arches.

groom, 1 grūm; 2 grōōm. **I.** *vt.* To take care of, as a horse. **II.** *n.* **1.** A person who cares for horses in the stable; hostler. **2.** A bridegroom. **3**‖. A menial; servitor.

groove, 1 grūv; 2 grōōv. **I.** *vt.* [GROOV(E)D⁸;
groovᵛ, GROOV'ING.] To form a groove in; shape like a groove. **II.** *n.* **1.** A furrow or long hollow, as cut by a tool. **2.** A fixed routine.

grope, 1 grōp; 2 grŏp, *vt. & vi.* [GROPED*ᵗ;* GROP'ING.] To feel one's way; search uncertainly.— **grop'ing-ly,** *adv.*

gros'beak", 1 grōs'bēk"; 2 grŏs'bĕk", *n.* One of various birds with large, stout beak, as the cardinal redbird of North America.

gross, 1 grōs; 2 grŏs. **I.** *a.* **1.** Large and coarse; glaring, as a fault. **2.** Entire. **3.** Indelicate; obscene. **4.** Dull; stupid. **II.** *n.* [GROSS, *pl.*] **1.** Twelve dozen, as a unit. **2.** The greater part; mass; entire amount. **-ly,** *adv.* **-ness,** *n.*

grot, 1 grot; 2 grŏt, *n.* [Poet.] A grotto.

gro-tesque', 1 gro-tesk'; 2 gro-tĕsk', *a.* Ludicrously odd or extravagant; fantastic. **-ly,** *adv.* **-ness,** *n.* [esque cave.

grot'to, 1 grot'o; 2 grŏt'o, *n.* A small picturesque cave.

grouch, 1 grauch; 2 grouch, *vt. & vi.* [U. S.] To grumble; be discontented.— **grouch'er,** *n.* One who grumbles.

groundᵈ, 1 graund; 2 ground, *v.* **I.** *t.* **1.** To found; establish; train in first principles. **2.** To fix in the ground; run aground. **II.** *i.* To run aground; fall to the ground.

ground, *imp. & pp.* of GRIND, *v.*

ground, *n.* **1.** The surface of the earth; land. **2.** A base; starting=point; reason. **3.** *pl.* Dregs.— **ground'=hog",** *n.* The woodchuck.— **ground'less,** *a.* Without foundation, reason, or cause. **-ly,** *adv.* **-ness,** *n.*— **ground'ling,** *n.* **1.** Any animal that lives on the ground. **2.** An underling or base person.— **ground'nut",** *n.* A peanut. — **ground'=plan",** *n.* The plan of the ground floor of a building.— **g.=rent,** *n.* The rent of grounds leased for building.— **ground'work",** *n.* A fundamental part; basis.

group, 1 grūp; 2 grup. **I**ᵗ. *vt. & vi.* To form into a group or groups. **II.** *n.* A small collection or company; cluster.

grouse, 1 grauz; 2 grous, *vi.* To grumble.— **grou'ser,** *n.* A grumbler.

grouse, 1 graus; 2 grous, *n. sing. & pl.* A small game=bird with mottled plumage.

grove, 1 grōv; 2 grŏv, *n.* A small wood.

grov'el, 1 grev'l; 2 grŏv'l, *vi.* [-ELED or -ELLED, -ELD⁸; -EL-ING or -EL-LING.] To creep on the earth; delight in what is low; be abject or mean.— **grov'el-er, -el-ler,** *n.*

Grouse. ¹⁄₁₅

grow, 1 grō; 2 grŏ, *v.* [GREW, 1 grū, 2 grụ; GROWN; GROW'ING.] **I.** *t.* To raise, as a crop. **II.** *i.* **1.** To increase in bulk, as a living organism; develop. **2.** To pass to a certain state; as, to *grow* cold. **-er,** *n.*

growl, 1 graul; 2 growl. **I.** *vt. & vi.* To utter in a surly tone; utter a growl; grumble. **II.** *n.* The guttural sound made by an angry animal; grumbling. — **growl'er,** *n.*

grown, 1 grōn; 2 grŏn, *pp.* of GROW, *v.*

growth, 1 grōth; 2 grŏth, *n.* **1.** Gradual increase, as of a living organism; augmentation; progress; promotion. **2.** Anything grown; product; effect.

grub, 1 grub; 2 grŭb, *vt. & vi.* [GRUBBED, GRUBD⁸; GRUB'BING.] To dig up or out; dig; drudge.— **grub'ber,** *n.*

grub, *n.* The larva of an insect.

grudge, 1 gruj; 2 grŭdg. **I.** *vt.* [GRUDGED, GRUDGD⁸; GRUDG'ING.] To begrudge; give reluctantly. **II.** *n.* **1.** Ill will cherished, as for remembered wrong. **2.** Reluctance.— **grudg'ing-ly,** *adv.* In a grudging manner; with reluctance or ill will.

gru'el, 1 grū'el; 2 grụ'el, *n.* A semiliquid food made by boiling meal in water or milk.

grue'some, grew'some, 1 grū'sam; 2 grụ'som, *a.* Inspiring horror and repulsion; repulsive; horrible.

gruff, 1 gruf; 2 grŭf, *a.* Rough or morose; surly. **-ly,** *adt.* **-ness,** *n.* [surly.

grum, 1 grum; 2 grŭm, *a.* Morose;

grum′ble, 1 grum′bl; 2 grŭm′bl. **I.** *vt.* **& vi.** [GRUM′BL(E)D⁴; GRUM′-BLING.] To murmur; growl; mutter; complain. **II.** *n.* The act of grumbling; a complaint; murmur.— **grum′bler,** *n.*— **grum′bling,** *pa.* & *n.*

Grun′dy, 1 grun′dı; 2 grŭn′dy, **Mrs.** A character in Morton's comedy *Speed the Plough:* used to typify society in general, regarded as a censor of morals.

grunt, 1 grunt; 2 grŭnt. **I.** *vt.* & *vi.* To utter as a grunt; emit a grunt; murmur; complain. **II.** *n.* A short, guttural sound, as of a hog.— **grunt′er,** *n.* One that grunts; a hog.

gua′no, 1 gwä′no; 2 gwä′no, *n.* The excrement of sea-birds: used as a fertilizer.

guar′an-tee′, ⎰1 gar′ən-tī′; 2 găr′an-tē′.
gar″an-tee′ᴾ, ⎱ **I.** *vt.* [-TEED′; -TEE′ING.] To warrant; secure against loss or damage. **II.** *n.* A guaranty.

guar′an-tor′, 1 gar′ən-tôr′; 2 găr′an-tôr′, *n.* One who or that which guarantees or warrants.

guar′an-ty, ⎰1 gar′ən-tı; 2 găr′an-ty, *n.*
gar′an-tyᴾ, ⎱ [-TIES², *pl.*] An undertaking by one person to be answerable for an obligation of another; the **act** of making sure, or that which assures.

guard, ⎰1 gärd; 2 gärd. **I**ᵈ. *vt.* & *vi.* To
gardˢ, ⎱ protect; defend; watch over; be on one's guard. **II.** *n.* **1.** One who or that which protects or defends. **2.** Watchful oversight; an attitude or condition of defense. **3.** One having charge, as of a train, or of baggage.— **guard′ed,** 1 gärd′ed; 2 gärd′ed, *pa.* Exhibiting caution; circumspect. **-ly,** *adv.* **-ness,** *n.*— **guard′i-an,** 1 gärd′ı-an; 2 gärd′i-an, *n.* **1.** A person who legally has the care of another, as of a minor. **2.** A guard; warden.— **guard′i-an-ship,** *n.*

gua′va, 1 gwä′vₐ; 2 gwä′va, *n.* A tropical American tree or its fruit, from which guava jelly is made.

gu″ber-na-to′ri-al, 1 giū″bər-nₐ-tō′rı-əl; 2 gū″ber-na-tō′ri-al, *a.* [U. S.] Of or pertaining to a governor.

gudg′eon¹, 1 guj′ən; 2 gŭdg′on, *n.* **1.** An Old World fish, very easily caught. **2.** A simpleton. [shaft; a pin.

gudg′eon², *n. Mech.* The bearing of a

guer′don, 1 gūr′dən; 2 gēr′don, *n.* Reward; recompense.

guer-ril′la, 1 ge-ril′ₐ; 2 gĕ-rîl′a, *n.* One of an irregular band of soldiers.

guess, ⎰1 ges; 2 ḡes. **I**ᵗ. *vt.* & *vi.* To con-
gessᴾ, ⎱ jecture; surmise; find out by con-

jecture; divine. **II.** *n.* A tentative opinion; a supposition; surmise; conjecture.

guest, ⎰1 gest; 2 ḡest, *n.* A visitor; boarder.
gestᴾ, ⎱

guf-faw′, 1 gu-fô′; 2 gŭ-fạ′, *n.* A shout of boisterous laughter.

guide, 1 gaid; 2 ḡīd. **I.** *vt.* [GUID′ED⁴; GUID′ING.] To conduct in a path; lead; manage; train. **II.** *n.* **1.** One who leads another in any path. **2.** Something serving to guide; a guide-book.— **gui′dance,** 1 gaı′dəns; 2 ḡī′danç, *n.* The act of guiding; a leading; direction.— **guide′-board″, g.-post,** *n.* A board or post to direct travelers.— **guide′-book,** *n.* A book for travelers and tourists, telling of places, sights, routes, etc.

guil′don, 1 gaı′dən; 2 ḡī′don, *n.* A forked guide-flag carried by a cavalry company or a mounted battery; also, the officer who carries it.

guild, etc. Same as GILD, etc.

guile, 1 gail; 2 ḡīl, *n.* Deceit; stratagem.— **guile′ful,** *a.* Full of deceit or guile.— **guile′less,** *a.* Free from guile; artless.

guill′lo-tine′, 1 gil″o-tīn′; 2 ḡll″o-tîn′, *vt.* [-TINED′; -TIN′ING.] To behead with the guillotine.

guil′lo-tine″, *n.* An instrument for beheading criminals by the fall of a weighted knife: used by the French.

guilt, 1 gilt; 2 ḡīlt, *n.* **1.** Desert of condemnation or punishment. **2.** Wickedness.— **guilt′i-ly,** *adv.*— **guilt′i-ness,** *n.*— **guilt′less,** *a.* Free from guilt; innocent. **-ly,** *adv.*— **guilt′y,** 1 gilt′ı; 2 ḡīlt′y, *a.* [GUILT′I-ER; GUILT′I-EST.] Having incurred guilt; involving guilt; deserving punishment.

guin′ea, 1 gin′ı; 2 ḡin′e, *n.* A former English gold coin, value 21 shillings or $5.

guin′ea-fowl″, *n.* A speckled African fowl, commonly domesticated. **guin′ea-hen″‡.**— **guin′ea-pig″,** *n.* A small South-American rodent.

guise, ⎰1 gaiz; 2 ḡīẓ, *n.* The external appearance; seeming; manner; be-
guizeᴾ, ⎱ havior.

gui-tar′, 1 gı-tär′; 2 ḡi-tär′, *n.* A musical instrument, having usually six strings played with the fingers.

gulch, 1 gulch; 2 gŭlch, *n.* A ravine.

gulf, 1 gulf; 2 gŭlf, *n.* **1.** A partly enclosed tract of water smaller than a sea. **2.** An abyss; chasm.

gull, 1 gul; 2 gŭl, *vt.* To impose upon; outwit.

gull¹, *n.* A long-winged water-fowl. See illus. on next page.

gull², *n.* **1.** A credulous person; dupe. **2.** A deceit.

gul′let, 1 gul′et; 2 gŭl′ĕt, *n.* The esophagus.

gul′li-ble, ¦ 1 gul′i-bl; 2 gŭl′i-bl, *a.* Capable of being gulled; simple; credulous.— **gul″li-bil′i-ty,** *n.*
gul′li-bl²,

gul′ly, 1 gul′i; 2 gŭl′y, *n.* [GUL′LIES^z, *pl.*] A channel cut by running water; a narrow ravine.

gulp, 1 gulp; 2 gŭlp. **I**^t. *vt.* To swallow eagerly and in large drafts. **II.** *n.* A huge swallow.

Great Black-backed Gull. 1/30

gum, 1 gum; 2 gŭm, *vt. & vi.* [GUMMED, GUMD^s; GUM′MING.] To smear, stiffen, or stick with gum; become stiff and sticky.

gum¹, *n.* **1.** The hardened sap of certain trees or shrubs. **2.** India-rubber.— **gum′mi-ness,** *n.*— **gum′my,** *a.* [GUM′MI-ER; GUM′MI-EST.] Like or covered with gum; viscous; sticky.— **gum′=tree″,** *n.* A gum-producing tree of the United States and Australia.

gum², *n.* The fleshy tissue that invests the necks of the teeth.— **gum′=boil″,** *n.* A small boil formed on the gum.

gum′bo, 1 gum′bo; 2 gŭm′bo, *n.* [Southern U. S.] **1.** The okra-plant or its pods; also a soup flavored with okra. **2.** *Geol.* A stratified portion of the Mississippi valley. **3.** The Creole patois in Louisiana.

gump, 1 gump; 2 gŭmp. *n.* [Colloq.] A simpleton.

gun, 1 gun; 2 gŭn. **I.** *vi.* [GUNNED, GUND^s; GUN′NING.] [U. S.] To shoot with a gun. **II.** *n.* A metal tube for firing projectiles by the force of gunpowder or other explosive.— **gun′=bar″rel,** *n.* The tube of a gun.— **gun′boat″,** *n.* Formerly, a small vessel having one gun; now, a man-of-war next in size below a cruiser.— **gun′cot″ton,** *n.* A compound prepared by treating cotton with nitric and sulfuric acids.— **gun′ner,** *n.* One who uses or operates a gun.— **gun′ner-y,** *n.*— **gun′ning,** *n.* The sport of hunting game with a gun.— **gun′pow″der,** *n.* An explosive mixture of niter, charcoal, and sulfur.— **gun′shot″,** *n.* **I.** *a.* Made by the shot of a gun. **II.** *n.* The range or reach of a gun.— **gun′smith″,** *n.* One who makes or repairs firearms.— **gun=stock,** *n.* The wooden part of a gun holding the lock and the barrel.

gun′ny, 1 gun′i; 2 gŭn′y, *n.* [GUN′NIES^z, *pl.*] Coarse sacking of jute or hemp.

gun′wale, 1 gun′əl *or* gun′wĕl; 2 gŭn′el *or* gŭn′wāl, *n. Naut.* The upper edge of a vessel's side.

gur′gle, ¦ 1 gūr′gl; 2 gûr′gl. **I.** *vi.* [GUR′GLED; GUR′GLING.] To flow with a murmuring sound. **II.** *n.* A gurgling flow or sound.
gur′gl², ¦ GL(E)D^F;

gush, 1 gush; 2 gŭsh. **I**^t. *vt & vi.* [GUSHED′^t, GUSHT′^s; GUSH′ING.] To pour forth or flow out freely; make an extravagant display of affection or sentiment. **II.** *n.* A sudden outpouring of fluid; an extravagant display of sentiment.— **gush′ing,** *pa.*— **gush′ing-ly,** *adv.*

gus′set, 1 gus′et; 2 gŭs′ĕt, *n.* A triangular piece of cloth fitted into a garment.

gust¹, 1 gust; 2 gŭst, *n.* A violent blast of wind; sudden outburst of feeling.— **gust′i-ness,** *n.*— **gust′y,** *a.*

gust², *n.* Taste: relish.— **gus′ta-to-ry,** *a.* Pertaining to the sense of taste.

gus′to, 1 gus′to; 2 gŭs′to, *n.* Keen enjoyment; relish.

gut, 1 gut; 2 gŭt. **I.** *vt.* [GUT′TED^d; GUT′TING.] To disembowel; despoil; plunder. **II.** *n.* The alimentary canal; an intestine: not in best usage.

gut′ta-per′cha, 1 gut′ə=pûr′chə; 2 gŭt′a=pẽr′cha, *n.* A horny substance, softening with heat, obtained from a Malayan evergreen tree.

gut′ter. 1 gut′ər; 2 gŭt′er. **I.** *vt. & vi.* To form a channel in; become channeled. **II.** *n.* A channel to carry off rain-water, as along the eaves of a house or at the side of a road; a trench; trough.

gut′tur-al, 1 gut′ur-al; 2 gŭt′ŭr-al. **I.** *a.* Pertaining to or formed in the throat. **II.** *n.* A sound produced in the throat. **-ly,** *adv.* **-ness,** *n.*

guy¹, 1 gai; 2 gī, *n.* A stay-rope, as for steadying a mast.

guy². **I.** *vt.* To ridicule; quiz. **II.** *n.* A person of grotesque appearance.

guz′zle, ¦ 1 guz′l; 2 gŭz′l, *vt. & vi.* [GUZ′ZLED, GUZ′LD^F; GUZ′ZLING.] To drink immoderately.— **guz′zler,** *n.*
guz′zl²,

gym-na′si-um, 1 jim-nē′zi-um *or* -3um; 2 gўm-nā′si-ŭm *or* -zhŭm, *n.* [-A *or* -UMS, *pl.*] **1.** A place for gymnastic exercises. **2.** A Latin or classical school, as in Germany. — **gym′nast,** *n.* An athlete.— **gym-nas′tic.** **I.** *a.* Relating to gymnastics. **II.** *n.* Disciplinary exercise: a feat of bodily skill: generally in the plural.

gyp′sum, 1 jip′sum; 2 gўp′sŭm, *n.* Sulfate of lime: when calcined, called *plaster of Paris.*

Gyp′sy, etc. See GIPSY.

gy′ral, 1 jai′ral; 2 gī′ral, *a.* **1.** Having a circular or whirling motion. **2.** *Anat.*

1: **a**rtistic, **ä**rt; f**a**t, f**a**re; f**a**st; get, prēy; h**ĭ**t, pol**i**ce; o**b**ey, gō; n**o**t, **ŏ**r; full, rūle; b**u**t, b**û**rn.

2: ärt, āpe, făt, fâre, fȧst, whạt, ạll; mē, gĕt, prey, fẽrn; hĭt, īce; ĩ=ē; ĩ=ë; gō, nŏt, ôr, wȯn,

Of or pertaining to the convolutions of the brain.

gy′rate, 1 jai′rēt; 2 gî′rāt, *vi.* [GY′RAT-ED^d; GY′RAT-ING.] To rotate or revolve; move in a spiral, as a cyclone.— **gy-ra′tion**, 1 jai-rē′shən; 2 gî-rā′shon, *n.* A whirling or rotating.— **gy′ra-to-ry**, 1 jai′rə-to-ri; 2 gî′ra-to-ry, *a.* Having a circular motion.

gy′ro-scope, 1 jai′ro-skōp; 2 gî′ro-seōp, *n.* A heavy rotating wheel that may be made to revolve as if independent of gravitation.— **gy″ro-scop′ic**, *a.* Pertaining to or like the gyroscope or its motion.

Gyroscope.

gyve, 1 jaiv; 2 gîv, *n.* A fetter.

H

H, h, 1 ēch; 2 äch, *n.* [AITCHES, H's, or Hs, 1 ēch′ez; 2 äch′ĕs, *pl.*] The eighth letter in the English alphabet.

ha, 1 hä; 2 hä, *interj.* An exclamation of surprise, joy, grief, laughter, etc.

ha′be-as cor′pus, 1 hē′bi-əs kōr′pus; 2 hä′be-as cŏr′pŭs. *Law.* A writ requiring a person in custody to be brought before a court.

hab′er-dash″er, 1 hab′ər-dash″ər; 2 hăb′er-dăsh″er, *n.* A dealer in gentlemen's furnishings, etc.

ha-bil′i-ment, 1 hə-bil′i-ment *or* -mənt; 2 ha-bĭl′i-ment, *n.* A garment: in the plural, dress; garb.

hab′it, 1 hab′it; 2 hăb′it, *n.* **1.** An acquired tendency toward the repetition of an act or thought; habitual course of action or conduct. **2.** Habitual condition; temperament. **3.** An outer garment; costume; a woman's dress for horseback-riding.

hab′it-a-ble, 1 hab′it-ə-bl; 2 hăb′it-a-bl,
hab′it-a-bl″, 1 } *a.* Fit to be inhabited.

hab′i-tat, 1 hab′i-tat; 2 hăb′i-tăt, *n.* The region where a plant or animal usually lives or is found.

hab″i-ta′tion, 1 hab″i-tē′shən; 2 hăb″i-tā′shon, *n.* **1.** A place of abode. **2.** The act or state of inhabiting.

ha-bit′u-al, 1 hə-bich′u-[*or* -bit′yu-]əl; 2 ha-bĭch′u-[*or* -bĭt′yu-]al, *a.* Pertaining to or resulting from habit; usual; ordinary; inveterate.— **ha-bit′u-al-ly,** *adv.*

ha-bit′u-ate, 1 hə-bich′u-[*or* -bit′yu-]ēt; 2 ha-bĭch′u-[*or* -bĭt′yu-]āt, *vt.* [-AT′ED^d; -AT′ING.] To make familiar by use; accustom.— **ha-bit″u-a′tion,** *n.*

hab′i-tude, 1 hab′i-tiūd; 2 hăb′i-tūd, *n.* Habitual method; customary association.

ha-bit″u-é′, 1 hə-bich′u-ē′ *or* (*Fr.*) ȧ″bī′tü′ē′; 2 ha-bĭch′u-e̦′, *or* (*Fr.*) ä″bī″tü′e̦′, *n.* A habitual frequenter, as of a social resort.

hack, 1 hak; 2 hăk, *vt. & vi.* **1.** To cut at random; chop; notch. **2.** To emit a short, dry cough.

hack¹, *n.* A gash made by or as by a sharp instrument.

hack², *n.* **1.** A horse kept for hire. **2.** [U. S.] A hackney-coach. **3.** A drudge.

hack′le, 1 hak′l; 2 hăk′l. **I.** *vt.* [HACK′-
hack′lⁱ, } L(E)D^F; HACK′LING.] To hatchel; tear. **II.** *n.* **1.** A hatchel. **2.** Unspun fiber, as raw silk. **3.** A feather from the neck or back of a cock.

hack′ney, 1 hak′ni; 2 hăk′ny. **I.** *vt.* To use up; make stale by repetition. **II.** *a.* Let out for hire; common. **III.** *n.* **1.** One of a valued breed of horses. **2.** A horse kept for hire. **3.** A hackney-coach. — **hack′ney-coach″,** *n.* A coach plying for hire.

had, 1 had; 2 hăd, *tmp.* of HAVE, *q.v.*

had′dock, 1 had′ək; 2 hăd′ok, *n.* A foodfish of the North Atlantic.

Ha′des, 1 hē′dīz; 2 hä′dēs, *n.* The condition and abode of the dead. [knife.

haft, 1 haft; 2 häft, *n.* The handle of a

hag, 1 hag; 2 hăg, *n.* A forbidding or malicious old woman.— **hag′gish,** *a.* Like a hag.

hag′gard, 1 hag′ərd; 2 hăg′ard, *a.* Worn and gaunt in appearance.

hag′gle, 1 hag′l; 2 hăg′l, *v.* [HAG′GLED;
hag′lⁱ, } HAG′LD^F; HAG′GLING.] **I.** *t.* To hack; mangle. **II.** *i.* To chaffer; bargain; cavil.

hail¹, 1 hēl; 2 hāl. **I.** *vt. & vi.* To pour out like hail; pour. down hail. **II.** *n.* Frozen rain or congealed vapor, falling in pellets.— **hail′stone″,** *n.* A pellet of hail.

hail². **I.** *vt. & vi.* To salute; call to; give a loud call. **II.** *n.* A call to attract attention; greeting. **III.** *interj.* An exclamation of greeting.— **hail′-fel″low,** 1 hēl′-fel′o; 2 hāl′-fĕl′o, *n.* A close companion.

hair, 1 hār; 2 hâr, *n.* A filament growing from the skin of an animal; such filaments collectively; any similar outgrowth. — **hair′breadth″,** *n.* A hair's breadth; an extremely small distance: used adjectively.—

hair′cloth″, *n.* A fabric having a warp of either cotton or linen with a horsehair filling. — **hair′₂dress″er,** *n.* A barber.— **h.₂dressing,** *n.*—**hair′less,** *a.* Destitute of hair.— **hair′lip″,** *n.* Same as HARELIP.— **hair′pin″,** *n.* A pin for supporting the hair or headdress.— **h.₂splitter,** *n.*—**h.₂splitting,** *a. & n.* Denoting the making of very fine or trivial distinctions.— **h.₂spring,** *n.* The fine spring of the balance-wheel, as in a watch.— **h.₂trigger,** *n.* A secondary trigger that instantaneously releases the main trigger of a firearm.— **hair′y,** *a.* Covered with, consisting of, or like hair.— **hair′i-ness,** *n.*

hal′berd, 1 hal′bərd; 2 hăl′berd, *n.* A weapon in the form of a battle-ax and pike combined, at the end of a long staff.— **hal″ber-dier′,** *n.* A soldier armed with a halberd.

hal′cy-on, 1 hal′sı-ən; 2 hăl′çy-on. **I.** *a.* Calm; peaceful. **II.** *n.* A kingfisher.

hale, 1 hēl; 2 hāl, *vt.* [HALED; HAL′-ING.] To drag by force; haul; lug.

hale, *a.* Of sound and vigorous health; robust.

half, 1 haf; 2 hàf. **I.** *a.* Having half of a standard value; partial. **II.** *n.* [HALVES², *pl.*] One of the two equal parts into which a thing is or may be divided. **III.** *adv.* To the extent of a half; partially.— **half′breed″,** *a. & n.* Half of one blood and half of another; one of such extraction. **h.₂blood†.**— **h.₂brother,** *n.* A brother related through only one parent.— **h.₂caste,** *a. & n.* Of mixed European and other blood; one of such extraction.— **h.₂hearted,** *a.* Wanting in affection, interest, or sincerity. **-ly,** *adv.* **-ness,** *n.*—**h.₂mast,** *n.* The position of a flag when half-way up the staff.— **h.₂moon,** *n.* The moon when half its disk is lit.— **half′pen″ny,** 1 hāf′[or hē′]pen′ı or hap′ən-ı; 2 hāf′[or hā′]pen″y or hāp′e-ny, *n.* [HALF′-PENCE′ or HALF′PEN″NIES², *pl.*] A British coin worth half of a penny.— **h.₂sister,** *n.* A sister by one parent.— **h. step** (*Mus.*), a semitone.— **h.₂witted,** *a.* Feeble-minded; idiotic.

hal′i-but, 1 hol′ı-but; 2 hăl′i-bŭt, *n.* A large flat fish of northern seas.

hal″i-to′sis, 1 hal″ı-tō′sıs; 2 hăl″i-tō′sis, *n.* A badly smelling breath.

hall, 1 hōl; 2 hal, *n.* A large building or room; entry; passageway.

hal″le-lu′iah, 1 hal′ı-lū′yə; 2 hăl″e-lu″ya, *n. & interj.* Praise ye the Lord. **hal″le-lu′jah‡.**

hal-loo′, 1 ha-lū′; 2 hă-lōō′, *interj.* An exclamation used in accosting or calling the attention: used also as verb and noun. **hal-lo′‡.**

hal′low, 1 hal′o; 2 hăl′o, *vt.* To devote to sacred use.

Hal′low-e′en′, 1 hal′o-īn′; 2 hăl′o-ēn′, *n.* The evening of Oct. 31, as the vigil of All Saints' day.

hal-lu″ci-na′tion, 1 ha-liū″sı-nē′shən; 2 hă-lū″çi-nā′shon, *n.* An apparent perception without external cause: delusion.

ha′lo, 1 hē′lo; 2 hā′lo, *n.* A luminous circle, as around the moon.

halt¹, 1 hōlt; 2 halt. **I⁴.** *vt. & vi.* To limp; falter; hesitate. **II.** *a.* Limping; lame. **III₂.** *n.* The act of limping; lameness.

halt². **I⁴.** *vt. & vi.* To stop. **II.** *n.* A complete stop, as of marching troops.

hal′ter, 1 hōl′tər; 2 hal′ter, *n.* A strap or rope by which to hold a horse; a hangman's rope.

halve, 1 hav; 2 hȧv, *vt.* [HALV(E)D⁸; HALV′-halv₂, } ING.] To divide into halves.

halves, 1 havz; 2 hȧvs, *n.* Plural of HALF.

hal′yard, 1 hal′yərd; 2 hăl′yard, *n. Naut.* A rope for hoisting a sail, a yard, or a flag.

ham, 1 ham; 2 hăm, *n.* The thigh of an animal, as of a hog, prepared for food.

hame, 1 hēm; 2 hām, *n.* One of two curved bars fitted to the collar, that hold the traces of a draft-harness. [village.

ham′let, 1 ham′let; 2 hăm′lĕt, *n.* A little

ham′mer, 1 ham′ər; 2 hăm′er. **I.** *vt. & vi.* To pound; drive; work out laboriously; toil. **II.** *n.* An implement for driving nails, beating, pounding, etc.

ham′mock, 1 ham′ək; 2 hăm′ok, *n.* A couch of canvas or netting, swung by the ends.

Hammers. 1. Claw. 2. Machinist's. 3. Riveting. 4. Bricklayers'. 5. Upholsterers'.

ham′per¹, 1 ham′pər; 2 hăm′per. **I.** *vt.* To hinder. **II.** *n.* 1. Rigging, etc., on a ship. **2.** A fetter.

ham′per². **I.** *vt.* To put into hampers. **II.** *n.* A large packing-basket.

ham′string″, 1 ham′strıŋ; 2 hăm′strĭng″. **I.** *vt.* To cut the hamstring of; cripple. **II.** *n.* A tendon of the human thigh, or of the hind leg of a quadruped.

hand, 1 hand; 2 hănd. **I⁴.** *vt.* To give, pass, deliver, lead, etc., with or as with the hand. **II.** *n.* 1. The extremity of the arm below the wrist, or something like or acting like it. **2.** Dexterity; touch; performance. **3.** An operative. **4.** Handwriting; signature. **5.** A measure: four inches. **6.** Possession; control. **7.** Side;

---

direction.— **hand's bar"row**, *n.* **1.** A litter. **2.** A wheelbarrow.— **hand'bill"**, *n.* A small advertising sheet.— **hand'book"**, *n.* A small guide-book.— **hand'breadth"**, *n.* The breadth of the hand; a palm.— **hand'cuff"**, *n.* I*t. vt.* To put handcuffs upon. **II.** *n.* One of two iron bands for the wrists, connected by a chain.— **hand'ful**, *n.* As much as a hand can hold.— **hand'maid"**, *n.* A female servant, **hand'maid"en.**— **hand-organ**, *n.* A musical instrument operated by a crank.— **h.-saw**, *n.* A saw made to be used with one hand.— **hand'spike"**, *n.* A bar used as a lever.— **hand'writ"ing**, *n.* The form of writing peculiar to a given person; penmanship; written matter.

hand'i-cap, 1 hand'i-kap; 2 hănd'i-căp. **I.** *vt.* [-CAPPED[t], -CAPT[s]; -CAP"PING.] To impose a handicap on; hinder; retard. **II.** *n.* The weighting of the better horses, or the allowance of time or distance in favor of a weaker rival; also, a race so conducted.

hand'i-craft", 1 hand'i-kraft"; 2 hănd'i-cráft", *n.* Skill with the hands; a mechanical trade.

hand'i-ly, *adv.*, **hand'i-ness**, *n.* See HANDY.

hand'i-work", 1 hand'i-wûrk"; 2 hănd'i-wûrk", *n.* Work done by the hands.

hand'ker-chief, 1 haŋ'kėr-chif; 2 hăn'ker-chif, *n.* A kerchief for wiping the face or nose.

han'dle, 1 han'dl; 2 hăn'dl. **I.** *vt.* [HAN'-han'dlP, } DL(E)DP; HAN'DLING.] To touch; feel; treat; deal in; train. **II.** *n.* That part of an object intended to be grasped with the hand.

hand'some, } 1 han'sǝm; 2 hăn'som, *a.*
hand'sum, } Fine-looking; liberal; magnanimous.— **hand'some-ly**, *adv.* Becomingly; liberally; generously.— **ness**, *n.*

hand'y, 1 hand'i; 2 hănd'y, *a.* [HAND'I-ER; HAND'I-EST.] **1.** Ready at hand; near by; convenient. **2.** Skilful with the hands. — **hand'i-ly**, *adv.*— **hand'i-ness**, *n.*

hang, 1 haŋ; 2 hăng, *v.* [HUNG, 1 huŋ, 2 hŭng, or HANGED, HANGD[s]; HANG'ING.] **I.** *t.* **1.** To support by attachment to something above; suspend; also, to suspend something on. **2.** To execute on the gallows (with *pp. hanged*). **II.** *i.* **1.** To droop, swing, wave, or flutter from any support. **2.** To suffer death by the gallows. **3.** To depend; wait; cling; hover; rest.— **hang'dog"**, *a. & n.* Mean; sneaking; abject; a sneak.— **hang'er**, 1 haŋ'ėr; 2 hăng'er, *n.* That which hangs, or on which something is hung; a short cut-and-thrust sword.— **hang'ing**, *n.* **1.** The act of suspending; execution on the gallows. **2.** *pl.* Drapery for a room, as tapestry.— **hang'-**

man, *n.* [-MEN, *pl.*] A public executioner. — **hang'nail"**, *n.* Skin partially torn loose near a finger-nail.

han'gar", 1 han'gär" or (*F.*) häŋ"gär'; 2 hän-gar" or (*F.*) hän"gär', *n.* [F.] A shelter or shed, as for the housing of aeroplanes.

hank, 1 haŋk; 2 hăŋk, *n.* A bundle of two or more skeins of yarn; also, a single skein.

han'ker, 1 haŋ'kėr; 2 hăŋ'ker, *vi.* To have an incessant desire; hunger; crave. — **han'ker-ing**, *n.*

han'som, 1 han'sǝm; 2 hăn'som, *n.* A low, two-wheeled, one-horse cab, with driver's seat perched back of the top: f o r m e r l y   m u c h used.

hap, 1 hap; 2 hăp. **I.** *vi.* [HAPPED[t], HAP[s]; HAP"PING.] To happen; chance. **II.** *n.* **1.** A casual occurrence; happening; chance. **2.** Luck; good fortune.— **hap'haz"ard**, *a. & n.* Accidental: chance; hazard.— **hap'less**, *a.* Having no luck or hap; unfortunate; unhappy.— **hap'ly**, *adv.* By chance; perhaps.

Hansom.

hap'pen, 1 hap'n; 2 hăp'n, *vi.* To occur or exist by chance; befall; come to pass.

hap'py, 1 hap'i; 2 hăp'y, *a.* [HAP'PI-ER; HAP'PI-EST.] Enjoying, giving, or expressing pleasure; joyous; blessed; opportune; felicitous; fortunate.— **hap'pi-ly**, *adv.*— **hap'pi-ness**, *n.* The state or quality of being happy; enjoyment; good fortune; felicitousness.

ha'ra-ki'ri, 1 hä'rᴇ-kī'rī; 2 hä'rä-kī'rĭ, *n.* A Japanese method of suicide by ripping open the bowels. Erroneously spelled *hari-kari*.

ha-rangue', } 1 hᴇ-raŋ'; 2 hȧ-răng'. **I.** *vt.*
ha-rang's, } & *vi.* [HA-RANGUED[s]; HA-RANGU'ING.] To utter a harangue to; deliver a harangue. **II.** *n.* An oration; a vehement speech.— **ha-rangu'er**, *n.*

har'ass[t], 1 har'ᴇs; 2 hăr'as, *vt.* To vex; tease; worry. [*n.* A forerunner.

har'bin-ger, 1 här'bin-jėr; 2 här'bin-ger, **har'bor**, 1 här'bėr; 2 här'bor. **I.** *vt. & vi.* To shelter; entertain; find shelter. **II.** *n.* A port or haven; place of refuge and rest.

har'bour, *n.* Harbor: usual spelling in England.

hard, 1 härd; 2 härd. **I.** *a.* **1.** Solid; firm. **2.** Difficult; rigorous; severe. **3.** Unfeeling; unsparing. **4.** Thoroughgoing and energetic. **5.** Coarse; poor; scanty; offensive. **6.** Containing mineral salts: said of water. **II.** *adv.* In a hard manner. — **ness**, *n.*— **hard'-heart"ed**, *a.* Lacking pity or sympathy; unfeeling; obdurate.

1: ǝ = final; ı = habit; aïsle; au = *out*; oïl; iū = feud; chin; go; ŋ = *sing*; thin, **this.**
2: wǫlf. dǫ; book, boot; fŭll, rᵫle, cᵫre, bŭt, bûrn; öïl, böy; ğo, ğem; iŋk; thin, **this.**

hard′en, 1 härd′n; 2 härd′n, *vt. & vi.* To make or become hard or harder.— **hard′ened,** *a.*

har′di-hood, 1 här′dı-hud; 2 här′dı-hŏŏd, *n.* Sturdy courage; presumption.

har′di-ly, 1 här′dı-lı; 2 här′dı-ly, *adv.* With hardihood.

har′di-ness, 1 här′dı-nes; 2 här′dı-nĕs, *n.* **1.** The state of being hardy. **2.** Intrepidity.

hard′ly, 1 härd′lı; 2 härd′ly, *adv.* **1.** With difficulty. **2.** Scarcely; not quite. **3.** Improbably.

hard′-pan″, 1 härd′-pan″; 2 härd′-păn″, *n.* A layer of firm earth under soft soil.

hard′ship, 1 härd′ship; 2 härd′shı̆p, *n.* Something hard to endure, as exposure.

hard′tack″, 1 härd′tak″; 2 härd′tăk″, *n.* Large, unsalted, hard-baked biscuit, as for army use.

hard′ware″, 1 härd′wâr″; 2 härd′wâr″, *n.* Manufactured articles of metal.

har′dy, 1 här′dı; 2 här′dy, *a.* [HAR′DI-ER; HAR′DI-EST.] Inured to hardship; robust; bold; audacious.

hare, 1 hâr; 2 hâr, *n.* A swift, timid, long-eared rodent with cleft upper lip.— **hare′bell″,** *n.* A perennial herb with blue bell-shaped flowers.— **hare′brained″,** *a.* Foolish; flighty; giddy.— **hare′lip″,** *n.* A cleft upper lip, like a hare's.

ha′rem, 1 hē′rem; 2 hā′rĕm, *n.* The women's apartments in a Mohammedan household; also, the women occupying them. [meat and vegetables.

har′i-cot, 1 har′ı-kō; 2 här′ı-cō, *n.* A stew of

ha′ri-ka′ri, *n.* See HARA-KIRI.

hark′, 1 härk; 2 härk, *vi.* To harken; listen.

hark′en, 1 härk′n; 2 härk′n, *vt. & vi.*
heark′en, } To hear by listening; listen.

har′le-quin, 1 här′lı-kwin; 2 här′le-kwin, *n.* A buffoon. [tute.

har′lot, 1 här′lǝt; 2 här′lot, *n.* A prosti-

harm, 1 härm; 2 härm. **I.** *vt.* To injure; hurt. **II.** *n.* That which inflicts injury or loss; injury; hurt; wrong.— **harm′ful,** *a.* Having power to injure; noxious. **-ly,** *adv.* **-ness,** *n.*— **harm′less,** *a.* Not harmful. **2.** Without hurt, loss, or liability. **-ly,** *adv.* **-ness,** *n.*

har-mon′ic, 1 har-mǝn′ık; 2 här-mŏn′ie. **I.** *a.* Producing or relating to harmony. **-i-cal‡.** **II.** *n.* **1.** An attendant or secondary tone. **2.** A note on a stringed instrument, produced by lightly stopping a string.— **har-mon′i-cal-ly,** *adv.*

har′mo-ny, 1 här′mo-nı; 2 här′mo-ny, *n.* [-NIES^z, *pl.*] **1.** Agreement of musical sounds. **2.** Accord, as in feeling or action; symmetry; unanimity; unity.— **har′mo′ni-ous,** 1 här-mō′nı-us; 2 här-mō′nı-ŭs, *a.* Possessing harmony; concordant; musical; peaceable; symmetrical. **-ly,** *adv.* **-ness,** *n.*— **har′mo-nize** or **-nise,** *vt. & vi.* [-NIZED; -NIZ′ING.] To make or become harmonious.

har′ness, 1 här′nes; 2 här′nĕs. **I.** *vt.* To equip with harness or with armor. **II.** *n.* **1.** The equipment of a horse or other draft-animal; tackle. **2.** Equipment for any work; active service. **3.** Defensive armor.

harp, 1 härp; 2 härp. **I.** *vi.* **1.** To revert to something incessantly; dwell unduly; with *on* or *upon.* **2.** To play on the harp. **II.** *n.* A stringed musical instrument played with the fingers.— **harp′er,** 1 härp′ǝr; 2 härp′er, *n.* One who plays the harp. **harp′ist‡.**

har-poon′, 1 har-pūn′; 2 här-pōōn′. **I.** *vt.* To strike with a harpoon. **II.** *n.* A barbed missile weapon, carrying a long cord for striking whales or the like.

harp′si-chord, 1 härp′sı-kŏrd; 2 härp′sı-eôrd, *n.* An old-fashioned musical instrument, resembling the pianoforte.

Harp.

har′py, 1 här′pı; 2 här′py, *n.* [HAR′PIES^z, *pl.*] **1.** A plunderer; extortioner. **2.** *Myth.* A rapacious and filthy winged monster. **3.** A large American eagle

har′que-bus, 1 här′kwı-bus; 2 här′kwe-bŭs, *n.* An ancient hand-firearm.

har′ri-dan, 1 har′ı-dǝn; 2 här′ı-dan, *n.* A vixenish old woman; hag.

har′ri-er¹, 1 har′ı-ǝr; 2 här′i-er, *n.* One who or that which harries; a buzzard-like bird destructive to poultry.

har′ri-er², *n.* A small dog used in hunting hares.

har′row, 1 har′o; 2 hăr′o. **I.** *vt.* **1.** To work with a harrow, as land. **2.** To pain; grieve; torment. **II.** *n.* A frame set with teeth, for leveling plowed ground.— **har′row-ing-ly,** *adv.*

har′ry, 1 har′ı; 2 hăr′y, *vt. & vi.* [HAR′RIED, 1 -ıd, 2 -id; HAR′RY-ING.] To pillage; strip; harass.

harsh, 1 härsh; 2 härsh, *a.* Grating or rough; irritating; severe. **-ly,** *adv.* **-ness,** *n.*

hars′let, *n.* Same as HASLET.

hart, 1 härt; 2 härt, *n.* The male of the red deer.— **harts'horn",** *n.* A preparation of ammonia, used as smelling-salts.

har'vest, 1 här'vest; 2 här'vĕst. **I**d. *vt.* To gather, as a crop; reap. **II.** *n.* A ripened crop, as of grain; the time of gathering; product; return.— **har'vest-er,** *n.* A harvest-worker; a machine that harvests grain.— **har'vest=home",** *n.* The season of gathering the harvest; an old English festival then observed, or the song then sung.

har'vey, } 1 här'vι, hür'vi-aiz; 2 här'vy,
har'vey-ize, } här'vy-iz, *vt.* **1.** To harden, as steel plate, by a process invented by H. A. *Harvey,* 1824–1893. **2.** To cover or protect such plates. [HAVE, *v.*

has, 1 haz; 2 hăs, *3d per. sing. pres. ind.* of HAVE, *v.*

hash, 1 hash; 2 hăsh. **I**t. *vt.* To chop into small pieces. **II.** *n.* A dish of hashed and cooked meat.

hash'ish, 1 hash'ish; 2 hăsh'ĭsh, *n.* An intoxicating preparation of Indian hemp. **hash'eesh**‡.

has'let, 1 has'let; 2 hăs'lĕt, *n.* The heart, liver, lungs, etc., of an animal, used as food.

hasp, 1 hasp; 2 hăsp. **I**t. *vt.* To fasten, as with a hasp. **II.** *n.* A fastening passing over a staple and secured as by a padlock. [cushion for a footstool.

has'sock, 1 has'ǝk; 2 hăs'ok, *n.* A thick

hast, 1 hast; 2 hăst, *2d per. sing. pres. ind.* of HAVE, *v.*

haste, 1 hēst; 2 hāst. **I.** *vt. & vi.* [HAST'-ED]d, HAST'ING.] To hasten. **II.** *n.* Quickness; speed; dispatch; hurry.— **hast'-en,** *vt. & vi.* To make haste; dispatch; be quick.— **hast'y,** *a.* [HAST'I-ER; HAST'I-EST.] Acting or done with haste; rash; impetuous; irascible.— **hast'i-ly,** *adv.*— **hast'i-ness,** *n.*

hat, 1 hat; 2 hăt, *n.* A covering for the head.

hatch1t, } 1 hach; 2 hăch, *vt. & vi.* To
hachp, } bring or come forth from the egg, as young birds; to contrive or plot.

hatch2t, *vt.* To mark with parallel or crossed lines.

hatch1, *n.* The act of hatching, or the brood hatched. [roof; also, its cover.

hatch2, *n.* An opening in a deck, floor, or

hatch'el, 1 hach'el; 2 hăch'ĕl. **I.** *vt.* [HATCH'ELED or HATCH'ELLED; HATCH'EL-ING or HATCH'EL-LING.] To comb, as flax or hemp. **II.** *n.* An implement for combing flax, etc.

hatch'et, 1 hach'et; 2 hăch'ĕt, *n.* A small short-handled ax, for use with one hand. [A hatch.

hatch'way", 1 hach'wē"; 2 hăch'wā", *n.*

hate, 1 hēt; 2 hāt. **I.** *vt. & vi.* [HAT'ED]d, HAT'ING.] To regard with hatred; detest;

cherish hatred. **II.** *n.* Intense aversion; animosity; malignity.— **hate'ful,** *a.* Exciting strong aversion; odious; feeling or manifesting hatred. **-ly,** *adv.* **-ness,** *n.*

hath‖, 1 hath; 2 hăth, *3d per. sing. pres. ind.* of HAVE, *v.* [aversion; enmity.

ha'tred, 1 hē'tred; 2 hā'trĕd, *n.* Bitter

hat'ter, 1 hat'ǝr; 2 hăt'er, *n.* One who makes or deals in hats.

haugh'ty, 1 hē'tι; 2 hạ'ty, *a.* [HAUGH'TI-ER; HAUGH'TI-EST.] Proud and disdainful.— **haugh'ti-ly,** *adv.*— **haugh'ti-ness,** *n.*

haul, 1 hōl; 2 hạl. **I.** *vt. & vi.* To draw or drag with force; transport by pulling. **II.** *n.* A pulling with force; something hauled in, as a draft of fishes.

haunch, 1 hänch or hōnch; 2 hänch or hạnch, *n.* **1.** The fleshy part of the hip. **2.** The part of an arch on either side of its crown.

hauntd, 1 hänt or hōnt; 2 hänt or hạnt, *vt. & vi.* To resort much to; frequent; visit persistently. [frequently

haunt, *n.* A place to which one resorts

haut'boy, 1 hō'bɔι; 2 hō'bȯy, *n.* A wooden wind-instrument.

have, } 1 hav; 2 hăv, *vt.* [HAD; HAV'ING.
havp, } *Pres. ind. sing.,* I
HAVE, thou HAST, he
HAS.] **1.** To hold; own;
possess. **2.** To feel;
realize; enjoy. **3.** To
cause to be; procure.
4. To be compelled to.
5. To bring forth; bear.

have'lock, 1 hav'lek; 2 hăv'lok, *n.* A white cover, with cape, for a military cap, as a protection from the sun: named from *Havelock,* British general. [refuge.

Havelock.

ha'ven, 1 hē'vn; 2 hā'vn, *n.* A harbor;

hav'er-sack, 1 hav'ǝr-sak; 2 hăv'er-săk, *n.* A bag, slung from the shoulder, as for a soldier's rations.

hav'oc, 1 hav'ǝk; 2 hăv'oc, *n.* General carnage or destruction. [left in driving.

haw, 1 hē; 2 hạ, *vt. & vi.* To turn to the

haw, *n.* The fruit of the hawthorn.

Ha-wai'ian, 1 ha-wɔι'yan; 2 hä-wī'yan. **I.** *a.* Of or pertaining to the island of Hawaii, or to the group of associated islands. **II.** *n.* **1.** One of the Hawaiian people. **2.** The Hawaiian language.

hawk1t, 1 hēk; 2 hạk, *vt.* To cry for sale in the streets; peddle.— **hawk'er**1, *n.* A pedler.

hawk2t, *vt. & vi.* To cough up or clear the throat forcibly.

hawk[st], *vt.* To hunt with hawks.— **hawk′er**[2], *n.* One who hunts with hawks; a falconer

hawk, *n.* A oird of prey, as a falcon.

haw′ser, 1 hê′zər; 2 hạ′ṣer, *n. Naut.* A large rope, 5 to 10 inches in circumference.

haw′thorn, 1 hê′thôrn; 2 hạ′thôrn, *n.* A thorny shrub of the rose family.

hay, 1 hē; 2 hā, *n.* Grass cut and dried.— **hay′cock″,** *n.* A dome-shaped pile of hay in the field.— **hay′mow″,** *n.* A mass of hay stored in a barn.— **hay′stack″,** *n.* A conical pile of hay stacked in the open air.

Hawk prepared for Falconry. 1/25

haz′ard, 1 haz′ərd; 2 hăz′ard, **I**[d]. *vt.* To put to hazard; imperil; risk. **II.** *n.* **1.** Exposure to the chance of loss or harm; risk; peril. **2.** A chance. **3.** That which is hazarded.— **haz′ard-ous,** *a.* Exposed to or involving danger of risk of loss. **-ly,** *adv.* **-ness,** *n.*

haze, 1 hēz; 2 hāz, *vt.* [HAZED; HAZ′ING.] To subject to ill treatment, as a student.

haze, *n.* Very fine suspended particles in the air; dimness, as of perception or knowledge.— **haz′i-ly,** *adv.*— **haz′i-ness,** *n.*— **haz′y,** 1 hēz′ĭ; 2 hāz′y, *a.* Obscured with haze; dim; confused; obscure.

ha′zel, 1 hē′zl; 2 hā′zl. **I.** *a.* Made of hazel=wood; dark=brown. **II.** *n.* A small tree of the oak family, yielding a small edible nut, the *hazelnut.*

he, 1 hī; 2 hē, *pron.* The male previously mentioned.

head[d], 1 hed; 2 hĕd, *v.* **I.** *t.* **1.** To be at the head of; lead. **2.** To be or get ahead of; intercept. **II.** *i.* To move in a given direction; come to a head; originate.

head, *a.* **1.** Being the head or at the head; chief. **2.** Bearing upon or against the head; as, a *head* wind.

head, *n.* **1.** The part of the body containing the brain; also, something analogous to it; top; front; prow; ear of grain; title or division, as of a discourse. **2.** A chief, leader, or commander. **3.** A unit; as, a hundred *head* of sheep: used both as a singular and plural. **4.** Headway; freedom.— **head′ache″,** *n.* A pain in the head.— **head′=dress″,** *n.* A covering for the head.— **head′ing,** *n.* Something located at the head, as a title.— **head′land″,** *n.* A cliff projecting into the sea.— **head′less,** *a.* Without a head.— **head′long″** or **hed′long″**[s], *n. a.* & *adv.* Head foremost; impetuous;

rash; rashly; recklessly; precipitately.— **head′quar″ters,** *n. sing.* & *pl. Mil.* The location of a commanding officer in camp, garrison, etc.— **head′ship,** *n.* The office of a chief; authority.— **heads′man,** *n.* [-MEN, *pl.*] A public executioner.— **h.=stall,** *n.* The part of a bridle that fits over the horse's head.— **head′stone″,** *n.* A stone set at the head of a grave, bearing the inscription.— **head′strong″,** *a.* Stubborn; obstinate; determined.— **head′way″,** *n.* Forward motion; momentum; progress; interval between consecutive trains.— **head′wind″,** *n.* A wind blowing directly against a vessel's course. — **head′y,** *a.* [HEAD′I-ER; HEAD′I-EST.] **1.** Headstrong. **2.** Tending to affect the head, as liquor.— **head′i-ness,** *n.*

heal, 1 hīl; 2 hēl, *v.* **I.** *t.* To restore to health; reconcile, as differences; remedy. **II.** *i.* To become sound and well.— **heal′er,** *n.*— **heal′ing,** *a.* & *n.*

health, 1 helth; 2 hĕlth, *n.* **1.** Soundness of any living organism; also, physical condition, good or ill. **2.** A toast wishing health; salubrious. **2.** Being in health: properly *healthy.* **-ly,** *adv.* **-ness,** *n.*— **health′i-ly,** *adv.*— **health′i-ness,** *n.*— **health′y,** 1 helth′ĭ; 2 hĕlth′y[s], *a.* [HEALTH′I-ER; HEALTH′I-EST.] **1.** Having health; sound; well. **2.** Conducing to health: properly *healthful.*

heap, 1 hīp; 2 hēp. **I**[t]. *vt.* To form into a heap; fill heaping full; amass. **II.** *n.* A pile; mass.

hear, 1 hīr; 2 hēr, *v.* [HEARD, 1 hûrd, 2 hĕrd; HEAR′ING.] **I.** *t.* **1.** To apprehend by the ear; listen to. **2.** To regard; favor; grant. **II.** *i.* To perceive sound; be told; receive word.— **hear′er,** *n.*— **hear′ing,** *n.* The capacity to hear; opportunity to be heard; audience.— **hear′say″,** *n.* Common talk; report; rumor. [HARKEN.

heark′en, 1 härk′n; 2 bärk′n, *v.* Same as **hear.**

hearse, 1 hûrs; 2 hêrs, *n.* A vehicle for carrying the dead to the grave.

heart, 1 härt; 2 härt, *n.* **1.** The muscular organ that propels the blood. **2.** The emotional nature; tenderness; sympathy. **3.** Courage. **4.** Vital part; center; core.— **heart′ache″,** *n.* Mental anguish; grief.— **heart′=bro″ken,** *a.* Overwhelmingly grieved.— **heart′burn″,** *n* A burning sensation in the esophagus, due to acidity of the stomach.— **heart′felt″,** *a.* Deeply felt; most sincere.— **heart′less,** *a.* Without heart; pitiless. **-ly,** *adv.* **-ness,** *n.*— **heart′rend″ing,** *a.* Extremely distressing; dreadful.— **hearts′ease″,** 1 härts′īz″; 2 härts′ẽṣ″, *n.* The pansy or violet.— **heart′sick,** *a.* Deeply disappointed. **-ness,** *n.*

hearth, 1 härth; 2 härth, *n.* The floor
harth⁸, of a fireplace; fireside; home.
    hearth′stone″‡.

heart′y, 1 härt′ĭ; 2 härt′y, *a.* [HEART′I-ER;
hart′y⁸, HEART′I-EST.] Cordial; heartfelt;
vigorous; eager.

heat, 1 hĭt; 2 hēt. I^d. *vt. & vi.* To make
or become hot; excite. II. *n.* 1. A
form of energy manifested by burning
substances; the state of being hot; intensity; vehemence. 2. A single course
of a race.— **heat′er,** *n.*— **heat′-unit″,** *n.* A
unit of quantity of heat; a calory.

heath, 1 hĭth; 2 hēth, *n.* A low hardy
evergreen shrub; open land overgrown
with heath.

hea′then, 1 hĭ′thn; 2 hē′thn. I. *a.* Gen-
tile; pagan; irreligious. II. *n.* [HEA′-
THENS or, collectively, HEA′THEN, *pl.*] One
of a non-Christian people; a pagan; idol-
ater.— **hea′then-dom,** *n.* Heathenism;
heathen or heathen lands collectively.—
hea′then-ish, *a.*— **hea′then-ism,** *n.* The
state of being a heathen.

heath′er, 1 heth′ẽr; 2 hĕth′er, *n.* Heath.
heth′er⁸, — **heath′er-y,** *a.*

heave, 1 hĭv; 2 hēv, *v.* [HEAVED
heav^P, or HOVE, HEAVD⁸; HEAV′-
ING.] I. *t.* To raise with effort;
throw with difficulty. II. *i.* To
rise or swell up; pant; strain.

heave, *n.* A heaving; throw;
swell, as of waves.

heav′en, 1 hĕv′n; 2 hĕv′n, *n.* 1.
hev′en⁸, The abode of the righteous dead; supreme happiness;
the sky. 2. [H-] God; Providence. — **heav′-**
en-ly, *a.* Of or
like heaven; ce-
lestial. — **heav′-**
en-li-ness, *n.—*

heav′en-ward,
a. & adv. Tend-
ing toward heaven.

Common Heather.

heav′y, 1 hev′ĭ; 2 hĕv′y, *a.* [HEAV′I-ER;
hev′y⁸, HEAV′I-EST.] Having great weight;
ponderous; hard to lift, bear, or suffer;
dejected; sluggish.—**heav′i-ly,** *adv.* **-ness,** *n.*

heavy water. Popular name for hydrogen
isotope of mass 2 (H₂H₂O).

heb-dom′a-dal, 1 heb-dŏm′a-dal; 2 hĕb-
dŏm′a-dal, *a.* Weekly.

He-bra′ic, 1 hĭ-brā′ĭk; 2 he-brā′ie, *a.* Relating to or characteristic of the Hebrews.
He′brew, 1 hĭ′brū; 2 hē′bru. I. *a.* Hebraic. II. *n.* A Jew; the Jewish language.

hec′a-tomb, 1 hek′a-tūm; 2 hĕc′a-tom, *n.*
A sacrifice, orig., of a hundred bulls.

hec′tare. See METRIC SYSTEM, under METRIC.

hec′tic, 1 hek′tĭk; 2 hĕc′tie. I. *a.* 1.
Constitutional. 2. Consumptive. II. *n.*
A fever connected with some organic dis-
ease, as consumption.— **hec′ti-cal-ly,** *adv.*

hec′to-gram, hec′to-li″ter, etc. See METRIC
SYSTEM, under METRIC.

hec′to-graph, 1 hek′to-graf; 2 hĕc′to-grāf,
n. A gelatin pad for producing multiple
copies of a writing or drawing.

hec′tor, 1 hek′tẽr or -tẽr; 2 hĕc′tor. I. *vt. &*
vi. To domineer over; bully; be domineering. II. *n.* A quarrelsome fellow; bully:
from Hector, a Trojan hero.

hedge, 1 hej; 2 hĕdg, *v.* [HEDGED; HEDG′-
ING.] I. *t.* To enclose with a hedge;
limit; defend. II. *i.* To make one bet to
offset another; provide a means of escape.

hedge, 1 hej; 2 hĕdg, *n.* A fence formed
by bushes set
close together.
— **hedge′hog″,**
n. A small insec-
tivorous mam-
mal armed with
stout s p i n e s;
porcupine.

European Hedgehog. 1/9

heed, 1 hĭd; 2
hēd. I^d. *vt. &*
vi. To notice;
attend to; pay
attention. II. *n.* Careful attention or
consideration.— **heed′ful,** *a.* Attentive. **-ly,**
adv. **-ness,** *n.*— **heed′less,** *a.* Careless.
-ly, *adv.* **-ness,** *n.*

heel¹, 1 hĭl; 2 hēl, *vt.* To add a heel to.

heel², *vt. & vi.* To tip or lean to one side;
cant, as a ship.

heel, *n.* The hinder part of the foot or of a
shoe, or something like it in position; lower end of a rafter; last part of a thing.

heg′i-ra, 1 hej′ĭ-ra or hĭ-jaī′ra; 2 hĕg′i-ra
or he-gī′ra, *n.* A flight; especially [H-],
the flight of Mohammed from Mekka, A.
D. 622.

heif′er, 1 hef′ẽr; 2 hĕf′er, *n.* A young
hef′er⁸, cow.

height, 1 hait; 2 hĭt, *n.* 1. Distance
hight, above a base; altitude. 2. An
eminence. 3. The acme; extreme degree.— **height′en, hight′en,** 1 hait′n; 2
hĭt′n, *v.* I. *t.* To intensify; elevate; exalt.
II. *t.* To be elevated or intensified.

hei′nous, 1 hē′nŭs; 2 he̩′nŭs, *a.* Wicked
in the extreme; atrocious. **-ly,** *adv.* **-ness,** *n.*

heir, 1 ãr; 2 êr, *n.* An inheritor of property
or of qualities, etc.— **heir apparent,** the person recognized as next in succession to a
throne.— **heir′ess,** *n. fem.*— **heir′loom″,** 1
ãr′lūm″; 2 êr′lōom″, *n.* Any movable chat-

tel, quality, etc., that descends by inheritance.

hej'i·ra, n. Same as HEGIRA.

hek'to·gram, etc. Same as HECTOGRAM. See METRIC SYSTEM, under METRIC.

held, 1 held; 2 hĕld, *imp.* of HOLD, v.

he·li'a·cal, 1 hı-lai'ə-kəl; 2 he-lĭ'a·cal, a. Pertaining to the sun.

hel'i·cal, 1 hel'ı-kəl; 2 hĕl'i-cal, a. Pertaining to or shaped like a helix.

hel''i·cop'ter, 1 hel'ı-kəp'tər; 2 hĕl'i·cŏpter", n. In aeronautics, a machine in which power to rise is produced by propellers.

he''li·o·cen'tric, 1 hī''lı-o-sen'trık; 2 hē''li-o-çĕn'tric, a. Having reference to the sun as a center.

he'li·o·graph, 1 hī'lı-o-graf; 2 hē'li-o-grȧf, n. **1.** An instrument for taking photographs of the sun. **2.** A photograph taken by sunlight. **3.** An apparatus for signaling by flashes of light.— **he''li·o·graph'ic**, a.

he'li·o·trope, 1 hī'lı-o-trōp; 2 hē'li-o-trōp, n. A shrub or herb, with small purplish or white flowers.

he'li·o·type, 1 hī'lı-o-taip; 2 hē'li-o-tȳp, n. A photoengraving from which impressions can be taken by a printing-press; a picture so made.

he'li·um, 1 hī'lı-ʊm; 2 hē'li-ŭm, n. A chemical element first inferred from lines in the spectrum to exist in the sun, now found on the earth.

he'lix, 1 hī'lıks; 2 hē'liks, n. [HE'LIX·ES or HEL'I·CES, 1 -ez or hel'ı-sīz; 2 -çĕs or hĕl'i-çēş, pl.] A spiral, as a screw-thread.

hell, 1 hel; 2 hĕl, n. The abode of evil spirits; place of punishment, torment, or evil-doing; Hades.— **hell'ish**, 1 hel'ısh; 2 hĕl'ish, a. Of or like hell; diabolical. **-ly**, adv. **-ness**, n.

hel'le·bore, 1 hel'ı-bōr; 2 hĕl'e-bōr, n. A perennial herb of cathartic or poisonous properties.

Hel·len'ic, 1 he-len'ık; 2 hĕ-lĕn'ic, a. Grecian.

helm[1], 1 helm; 2 hĕlm, n. The steering-apparatus of a vessel; tiller.— **helms'man**, n. [-MEN, pl.] *Naut.* A steersman.

helm[2], n. A helmet.

hel'met, 1 hel'met; 2 hĕl'mĕt, n. A defensive covering for the head.

Hel'ot, 1 hel'ət or hī'lət; 2 hĕl'ŏt or hē'lot, n. One of the Spartan bondmen; any slave.

help[t], 1 help; 2 hĕlp, v. **I.** t. **1.** To aid; assist; relieve. **2.** To remedy. **3.** To wait upon, as at table. **4.** To refrain from. **II.** i. To lend assistance; be useful; portion out food at table.— **help'er**, n.— **help'ful**, a. Affording aid; beneficial. **-ly**,

adv. **-ness**, n.— **help'less**, a. **1.** Unable to help oneself; feeble. **2.** Beyond remedy. **-ly**, adv. **-ness**, n.— **help'mate''**, n. A helper; coworker.— **help'meet''**, n. One who is fitted to help; a partner; companion; wife.

help, n. **1.** Assistance; aid; remedy; relief; rescue. **2.** A helper.

hel'ter·skel'ter, 1 hel'tər-skel'tər; 2 hĕl'ter-skĕl'ter. **I.** a. & adv. Hurried and confused; with haste and confusion. **II.** n. Disorderly hurry.

helve, 1 helv; 2 hĕlv, n. The handle, as helve[s], of an ax or hatchet.

hem[1], 1 hem; 2 hĕm, vt. [HEMMED, HEMD[s]; HEM'MING.] To border; edge; shut in; restrict.

hem[2], vt. & vi. [HEMMED, HEMD[s]; HEM'MING.] To throw off by coughing; cough; stammer.

hem[1], n. A folded edge of cloth sewed down on the inner side.

hem[2], n. & *interj.* A sound made, as in clearing the throat; ahem.

hem'i-, *prefix.* Half; as, *hemi*sphere.

hem'i·sphere, 1 hem'ı-sfīr; 2 hĕm'i-sfēr, n. A half-sphere.— **hem''i·spher'ic**, **hem''i·spher'i·cal**, a.

hem'i·stich, 1 hem'ı-stik; 2 hĕm'i-stĭc, n. A half of a poetic line.

hem'lock, 1 hem'lok; 2 hĕm'lŏk, n. **1.** An evergreen of the pine family. **2.** A poisonous herb of the parsley family.

hem'or·rhage, 1 hem'ə-rıj; 2 hĕm'o-rag, n. Discharge of blood from a ruptured blood-vessel. **hæm'or·rhage**[1].— **hem''or·rhag'ic**, a.— **hem'[or hæm']·or·rhoids**, n. pl. Piles.— **hem''or·rhoid·al**, a.

hemp, 1 hemp; 2 hĕmp, n. A tall annual herb of the nettle family; also, the tough fiber obtained from its bark.— **hemp'en**, 1 hemp'n; 2 hĕmp'n, a. Made of hemp; as, *hempen* rope.

Hemlock.

hem'stitch''[t], 1 hem'stich''; 2 hĕm'stĭch''. **I.** vt. To embroider with a hem. **II.** n. The ornamental finishing of the inner edge of a hem, made by pulling out several threads adjoining it and drawing together in groups the cross-threads by successive stitches.

hen, 1 hen; 2 hĕn, n. **1.** A female fowl or bird. **2.** pl. Domestic fowl, without regard to sex.— **hen'bane''**, n. A poisonous herb of the nightshade family.

hence, 1 hens; 2 hĕnç, adv. Away from hense[r], this place; hereafter; consequently;

1: ȧrtistic, ûrt; fat, fāre; fȧst; get, prēy; hĭt, polĭce; obey, gō; nŏt, ȯr; fu̇ll, rūle; bu̇t, bûrn.

2: ärt, āpe, făt, fâre, fȧst, wha̧t, a̧ll; mē, gĕt, prey, fẽrn; hĭt, īce; ī=ē; ĭ=ȩ̄; gō, nŏt, ôr, wŏn,

therefore.— **hence″forth′**, *adv.* From this time on. **hence″for′ward‡.**

hench′man, 1 hench′mən; 2 hĕnch′man, *n.* [-MEN, *pl.*] A subordinate; male servant.

hen′ner-y, 1 hen′ər-ı; 2 hĕn′er-y, *n.* [-IES^z, *pl.*] A place where hens are kept.

hen′peck″^t, 1 hen′pek″; 2 hĕn′pĕk″, *vt.* To domineer over, as a wife who controls her husband.

hen′ry, 1 hen′rı; 2 hĕn′ry, *n.* *Elec.* The unit of inductance: named from Joseph *Henry*, American physicist (1797–1878).

he-pat′ic, 1 hı-pat′ık; 2 he-păt′ie, *a.* Pertaining to the liver.

hep′ta-gon, 1 hep′tə-gən; 2 hĕp′ta-gŏn, *n.* A figure having seven sides and seven angles.— **hep-tag′o-nal,** *a.*

hep′tar-chy, 1 hep′tār-kı; 2 hĕp′tär-cy, *n.* [-CHIES^z, *pl.*] **1.** A group of seven kingdoms. **2.** Government by seven persons.

her, 1 hūr; 2 hẽr, *pron.* Objective or possessive case of SHE: used in the form *hers* in the predicate when the noun is not expressed.

her′ald, 1 her′əld, 2 hĕr′ald. **I^d.** *vt.* To announce publicly; usher in; proclaim. **II.** *n.* An official bearer of messages, as from a sovereign; any bearer of news; a forerunner.— **he-ral′dic,** 1 hı-ral′dık; 2 he-răl′dic, *a.* Relating to heralds or heraldry.— **her′ald-ry,** 1 her′əld-rı; 2 hĕr′ald-ry, *n.* The science that treats of blazoning or describing coats of arms and the like.— **her′ald-ship,** *n.* The office or rank of a herald.

herb, 1 hūrb; 2 hẽrb, *n.* A plant that dies completely, or down to the ground, after flowering; herbage.— **her-ba′ceous,** 1 hər-bē′shʊs; 2 her-bā′shŭs, *a.* Pertaining to or like herbs.— **herb′age,** 1 hūrb′ıj *or* ūrb′ıj; 2 hẽrb′aġ *or* ẽrb′aġ, *n.* Herbs collectively; hence, pasturage.— **herb′al,** 1 hūrb′əl *or* ūrb′əl; 2 hẽrb′al *or* ẽrb′al, *a.* Pertaining to herbs.— **herb′al-ist,** *n.* One skilled in the study of plants; also, a dealer in herbs.— **her-ba′ri-um,** 1 hər-bē′rı-ʊm; 2 her-bā′ri-ŭm, *n.* [-RI-UMS^z or -RI-A, *pl.*] A collection of dried plants scientifically arranged.— **her-bif′er-ous,** *a.* Producing herbs or vegetation.— **her-biv′o-rous,** *a.* Feeding on herbage.— **herb′y,** *a.*

her-cu-le′an, 1 hər-kiū-lī′ən; 2 her-eū-lē′an, *a.* [H- or h-] Like or pertaining to Hercules, the mighty ancient demigod; laborious; mighty.

Her′cu-les, 1 hūr′kiu-līz; 2 hẽr′eū-lēs, *n.* *Class. Myth.* Son of Zeus by Alcmene; a national hero of Greece; incarnation of strength; founder of Olympic games.

herd^d, 1 hūrd; 2 hẽrd. **I.** *vt.* & *vi.* To bring together; congregate; flock together. **II.** *n.* **1.** A number of animals feeding together. **2.** A crowd; rabble. **3.** A herdsman.— **herds′man″,** *n.* One who owns or tends a herd. **herd′er‡.**

here, 1 hīr; 2 hēr, *adv.* In, at, or to this place, time, or stage of proceedings; in the present life.— **here′a-bout″,** *adv.* About this place; in this vicinity. **here′a-bouts″‡.** — **here-af′ter.** **I.** *n.* A future state. **II.** *adv.* At a future time; from this time forth; after this life.— **here-at′,** *adv.* At or by reason of this.— **here-by′,** *adv.* By means or virtue of this.— **here-in′,** *adv.* In this; in this place, circumstance, etc.— **here-of′,** *adv.* **1.** Of this; about this. **2.** From this; because of this.— **here-on′,** *adv.* On this; hereupon.— **here-to′,** *adv.* To this time, place, or end.— **here″to-fore′.** **I.** *n.* Past time. **II.** *adv.* Previously; hitherto.— **here″up-on′,** *adv.* Upon or because of this. — **here-with′,** *adv.* Along with this.

he-red′i-ta-ry, 1 hı-red′ı-tē-rı; 2 he-rĕd′i-tā-ry, *a.* Descending by inheritance.— **he-red′i-ta-ri-ly,** *adv.*

he-red′i-ty, 1 hı-red′ı-tı; 2 he-rĕd′i-ty, *n.* Transmission of qualities, diseases, etc., from parent to offspring.

her′e-sy, 1 her′ı-sı; 2 hĕr′e-sy, *n.* [-SIES^z, *pl.*] A belief at variance with that of a church, school, or party.— **her′e-si-arch,** 1 her′ı-sı-ārk; 2 hĕr′e-si-äre, *n.* The chief exponent of a heresy.— **her′e-tic,** 1 her′ı-tik; 2 hĕr′e-tie, *n.* One who holds a heresy.— **he-ret′i-cal,** *a.* At variance with accepted beliefs. **-ly,** *adv.*

her′i-ta-ble, } 1 her′ı-tə-bl; 2 hĕr′i-ta-bl,
her′i-ta-bl^p, } *a.* **1.** That can be inherited. **2.** Capable of inheriting.

her′i-tage, 1 her′ı-tıj; 2 hĕr′i-taġ, *n.* That which is inherited, as an estate, quality, or condition.

her-met′ic, 1 hər-met′ık; 2 her-mĕt′ie, *a.* Made air-tight, as by fusion. **her-met′i-cal‡.**— **her-met′i-cal-ly,** *adv.*

her′mit, 1 hūr′mıt; 2 hẽr′mit, *n.* One who lives alone; an anchorite.— **her′mit-age,** 1 hūr′mıt-ıj; 2 hẽr′mit-aġ, *n.* The retreat of a hermit.

her′ni-a, 1 hūr′nı-ə; 2 hẽr′ni-a, *n.* Protrusion, as of an intestine; rupture.

he′ro, 1 hī′ro; 2 hē′ro, *n.* **1.** A man eminent for courage; anciently, a demigod. **2.** The chief male figure of a poem, play, or novel.— **he-ro′ic,** 1 hı-rō′ık; 2 he-rō′ie. **I.** *a.* **1.** Relating to or like a hero; brave; venturesome. **2.** *Art.* Larger than life. **II.** *n.* A heroic verse; in the plural, extravagances of language. **he-ro′i-cal‡.**— **her′o-in(e^s,** 1 her′o-in; 2 hĕr′o-ĭn, *n. fem.*— **her′o-ism,** 1 her′o-izm; 2 hĕr′o-ĭsm, *n.* Heroic character or action.

her'on, 1 her'ən; 2 hĕr'on, *n.* A long-necked long-legged wading bird.

her'ring, 1 her'ĭŋ; 2 hĕr'ĭng, *n.* A small food-fish.

hers, 1 hŭrz; 2 hers, *poss. pron.* See HER.

her-self', 1 hər-self'; 2 her-sĕlf', *pron.* A reflexive or emphatic form of the third-personal pronoun, feminine.

hes'i-tate, 1 hez'ĭ-tēt; 2 hĕş'ĭ-tāt, *vi.* [-TAT'ED^d; -TAT'ING.] To be in doubt; be slow in deciding; deliberate; falter.— **hes'i-tan-cy, hes'i-ta'tion,** *n.* The act or manner of one who hesitates; vacillation.— **hes'i-tant,** *a.* Hesitating; faltering; lingering; vacillating.— **hes'i-tat'ing-ly,** *adv.*

Hes'per, 1 hes'pər; 2 hĕs'per, *n.* The evening star; vesper. **Hes'per-us‡.— Hes-pe'ri-an,** 1 hes-pî'rĭ-ən; 2 hĕs-pē'rĭ-an, *a.* [Poet.] In or of the west; western.

het'er-o-dox, 1 het'ər-o-deks; 2 hĕt'er-o-dŏks, *a.* At variance with a commonly accepted belief.— **het'er-o-dox"y,** *n.* [-IES^z, *pl.*] The character of being heterodox; a heterodox doctrine.

het'er-o-dyne, 1 het'ər-o-dɑin; 2 hĕt'er-o-dyn, *a.* *Radio.* Describing the manner in which different oscillations are produced in a receiving set.

het'er-o-ge-ous, 1 het"ər-o-jĭ'nĭ-us; 2 hĕt'er-o-gē'ne-ŭs, *a.* Consisting of dissimilar elements. **-ly,** *adv.* **-ness,** *n.*

hew, 1 hiū; 2 hū, *vt. & vi.* [HEWED; HEWN or HEW'ING.] To cut with blows, as of an ax; chop; work out.— **hewer,** *n.*

hex'a-gon, 1 heks'ə-gɒn; 2 hĕks'a-gŏn, *n.* *Geom.* A figure with six sides and six angles.— **hex-ag'o-nal,** *a.* **-ly,** *adv.*— **hex"a-he'dral,** *a.*— **hex"a-he'dron,** *n.* [-DRONS^z or -DRA, *pl.*] A solid bounded by six plane faces.

hex-am'e-ter, 1 heks-am'ĭ-tər; 2 hĕks-ăm'e-ter. **I.** *a.* Pros. Having six feet in a verse. **II.** *n.* Pros. A verse of six feet.

hey, 1 hē; 2 he, *interj.* An exclamation of surprise, pleasure, inquiry, incitement, etc. **hey'day",** 1 hē'dē"; 2 hē'dā". **I.** *n.* The time of greatest vitality and vigor. **II.** *interj.* An exclamation of surprise, joy, etc.

hi-a'tus, 1 hai-ē'tus; 2 hĭ-ā'tŭs, *n.* [-TUS or -TUS-ES, 1 -tus-ez; 2 -tŭs-ĕş, *pl.*] A gap; break; interruption; the meeting of two separate vowels without an intervening consonant.

hi-ber'nal, 1 hai-bŭr'nəl; 2 hĭ-bẽr'nal, *a.* Wintry.— **hi'ber-nate,** 1 hai'ber-nēt; 2 hī'ber-nāt, *vi.* [-NAT'ED^d; -NAT'ING.] To pass the winter, especially in a torpid state.— **hi"ber-na'tion,** *n.*

Hi-ber'ni-an, 1 hai-bŭr'nĭ-ən; 2 hī-bẽr'nĭ-an. **I.** *a.* Irish. **II.** *n.* A native of Ireland.— **Hi-ber'ni-an-ism,** *n.* An Irish idiom.— **Hi-ber'ni-cism‡.**

hic'cup, } 1 hik'up; 2 hĭc'ŭp. **I**^t. *vi. &* **hic'cough,** } *vt.* To have the hiccups; **hic'cof*,** } utter a hiccup; utter with hiccups. **II.** *n.* A short, catching sound due to spasmodic contraction of the diaphragm and windpipe.

hick'o-ry, 1 hik'o-rĭ; 2 hĭk'o-rĭ, *n.* [-RIES^z, *pl.*] An American tree of the walnut family, yielding an edible nut; also, its hard, tough, heavy wood. [*vt.*

hid, hid'den. See HIDE¹.

hi-dal'go, 1 hi-dal'go; 2 hĭ-dăl'go, *n.* A Spanish nobleman.

Shagbark Hickory.
a, hickory-nut, with half the shuck resecrete; disguise. moved.

hide¹, 1 haid; 2 hīd, *vt. & vi.* [HID; HID'DEN or HID; HID'ING.] To put or keep out of sight; half

hide², *vt.* [HID'ED^d; HID'ING.] To whip with a rawhide; cover as with hide.

hide, *n.* The skin of a large animal, as an ox.— **hide'bound",** *a.* Having the skin tight-drawn; narrow-minded.

hid'e-ous, 1 hid'ĭ-us; 2 hĭd'e-ŭs, *a.* Shocking; ghastly. **-ly,** *adv.* **-ness,** *n.*

hid'ing¹, 1 haid'ĭŋ; 2 hī'ding, *n.* Concealment.

hid'ing², *n.* [Colloq.] A flogging.

hie, 1 hai; 2 hī, *vt. & vi.* [HIED; HY'ING.] To hasten; hurry.

hi'er-arch, 1 hai'ər-ɑrk; 2 hī'er-ärc, *n.* An ecclesiastical chief ruler.— **hi"er-ar'chic,** *a.* Of, pertaining to, or like a hierarchy. **hi"er-ar'chal;— hi"er-ar'chi-cal‡.— hi"er-ar'chy,** *n.* A body of organized ecclesiastical rulers; clerical or priestly government.

hi'er-o-glyph, 1 hai'ər-o-glif; 2 hī'er-o-glȳf, *n.* **1.** Picture-writing, as of the ancient Egyptians. **2.** A character or word supposed to convey a hidden meaning. **hi"er-o-glyph'ic,** *n.*— **hi"er-o-glyph'ic,** *a.* Pertaining to hieroglyphs. **hi"er-o-glyph'i-cal‡.— hi"er-o-glyph'i-cal-ly,** *adv*

hig'gle, 1 hig'l; 2 hĭg'l, *vi.* [HIG'GLED; HIG'GLING.] To dispute about trifles.— **hig'gler,** *n.*

high, 1 hai; 2 hī. **I.** *a.* Greatly elevated; lofty; chief; exalted; intense. **II.** *adv.* In a high manner; to a great altitude; also, at a high rate; luxuriously.— **high'-born',** *a.* Of noble extraction.— **h.-bred,** *a.* **1.** Having a fine pedigree. **2.** Characterized by fine manners.— **h.-flown,** *a.* Pretentious; extravagant.— **h.-handed,** *a.* Carried on in an overbearing manner.— **high'-ly,** *adv.*— **h.-minded,** *a.* Magnanimous— **high'ness,** *n.*— **h.-pressure,** *a.* Having or

1: ɑrtistic, ûrt; fat, fāre; fast; get, prȇy; hĭt, police; obey, gō; nǝt, ôr; fŭll, rūle; bŭt, būrn.

2: ärt, āpe, făt, fâre, fȧst, whạt, ạll; mē, gĕt, prȇy, fẽrn; hĭt, īce; ĭ=ĕ; ĩ=ẽ; gō, nŏt, ôr, wǫn,

using a high steam=pressure.— **h. priest**, a chief priest.— **high′road″**, n. **1.** A main road. **2.** A common or easy method.— **high school**, a school ranking between grammar=school and college; secondary school.— **h.=spirited**, a. Full of spirit; not brooking restraint. **h.=strung‡**.

high′land, 1 hai′lənd; 2 hī′land, n. **1.** An elevation of land. **2.** [H-]. pl. A mountainous region: commonly with the definite article.— **high′land-er**, n.

hight, hight′en, etc. Same as HEIGHT, etc.

high′way′, 1 hai′wē″; 2 hī′wā″, n. A public road.— **high′way″man**, n. A robber on the highway.

hi-la′ri-ous, 1 hai-lē′rɪ-ʊs; 2 hī-lā′rĭ-ŭs, a. Boisterously merry.— **hi-lar′i-ty**, n. Boisterous mirth.

hill, 1 hil; 2 hĭl, n. **1.** A conspicuous
hilᴵ, natural elevation. **2.** A small heap of earth.— **hill′ock,** n. A small hill.— **hill′y,** a. Full of hills; also, large and swelling.

hilt, 1 hilt; 2 hĭlt, n. The handle and guard of a sword or dagger.

him, 1 him; 2 hĭm, pron. The objective case of HE.

him-self′, 1 him-self″; 2 hĭm-sĕlf′, pron. [THEM-SELVES′, pl.] **1.** The intensive form of HE. **2.** One's individuality.

hind, 1 haind; 2 hĭnd, a. [HIND′MOST or HIND′ER-MOST, superl.] Belonging to the rear.

hind¹, n. A female deer.

hind‖², n. A farm=laborer.

hin′der, 1 hin′dər; 2 hĭn′der, vt. & vi. To keep from or delay in action; be or act as a check.— **hin′der-ance,** n. Same as HINDRANCE.

hind′er, 1 haind′ər; 2 hĭnd′er, a. Pertaining to or constituting the rear.— **hind′most,** a. In the extreme rear. **hind′er-most‡**.

Hin′doo, -ism, etc. Same as HINDU, etc.

hin′drance, 1 hin′drəns; 2 hĭn′drạnç, n. The act of hindering; an obstacle.

Hin′du, 1 hin′dū; 2 hĭn′du, n. A member of the native race of India; also, the language of this race.— **Hin′du-sta′ni,** 1 hin′dū-stä′nɪ; 2 hĭn′dụ-stä′nĭ, n. The official and ordinary language of India.

hinge, 1 hinj; 2 hĭnj, n. I. vt. & vi. [HINGED; HING′ING.] To furnish with a hinge; turn, as on a hinge; depend; hang. II. n. A device allowing one part to turn upon another‡

hin′ny, 1 hin′ɪ; 2 hĭn′y, n. The offspring of a stallion and a she ass.

hint, 1 hint; 2 hĭnt. I. vt. & vi. To suggest indirectly; make a suggestion. II. n. A covert or indirect allusion; suggestion.

hip, 1 hip; 2 hĭp, n. The hip=joint; haunch.

hip′po-drome, 1 hip′o-drōm; 2 hĭp′o-drōm, n. An ancient race=course or modern circus.

hip″po-pot′a-mus, 1 hip′o-pɒt′ə-mʊs; 2 hĭp′o-pŏt′ạ-mŭs. n. [-ES, or -MI, 1 ez or -mai; 2 -ĕ§ or mī, pl.] A large amphibious short=legged thick=skinned mammal; river=horse.

Hippopotamus. ¹⁄₆₀₀

hir′cine, 1 hūr′sin, 2 hĭr′çin, a. Pertaining to or like a goat.

hire, 1 hair; 2 hīr. I. vt. [HIRED; HIR′ING.] To engage for pay. II. n. Compensation for labor, services, etc.— **hire′ling.** I. a. Serving for hire; venal. II. n. One who serves for or only for hire.

hir-sute′, 1 hūr-siūt′; 2 hĭr-sūt′, a. Hairy.

his, 1 hiz; 2 hĭ§, pron. Possessive case of HE.

hiss, 1 his; 2 hĭs. Iᵗ. vt. & vi. To utter with or as a hiss; utter a hiss. II. n. The prolonged sound of s, especially as an expression of contempt; also, any similar sound.— **hiss′ing,** n. The act of uttering a hiss.
[hark!

hist, 1 hist; 2 hĭst, interj. Be silent! hush!

his′to-ry, 1 his′to-rɪ; 2 hĭs′to-ry, n. [-RIES², pl.] A systematic record of past events; past events in general.— **his-to′ri-an,** n. One who compiles a history; a chronicler.— **his-tor′ic,** a. **1.** Mentioned or celebrated in history; notable. **2.** Historical.— **his-tor′i-cal,** a. **1.** Relating to history or to the past. **2.** Historic. **-ly,** adv.

his″tri-on′ic, 1 his″trɪ-ɒn′ɪk; 2 hĭs″trĭ-ŏn′ĭc, a. Pertaining to the stage; theatrical.

hit, 1 hit; 2 hĭt, v. [HIT; HIT′TING.] I. t. To strike; get or catch cleverly. II. i. To strike together; clash; also, to attain one's aim; happen; conform; suit.

hit, n. A stroke; blow; a repartee; stroke of luck.

hitch‖, 1 hich; 2 hĭch, v. I. t. To fasten
hichᴾ, or tie. II. i. To move by jerks; become entangled.

hitch, n. **1.** A stop; obstruction. **2.** The act of fastening, as by a rope. **3.** A noose=like knot.

hith′er, 1 hith′ər; 2 hĭth′er. I. a. Near to or toward the speaker. II. adv. In this direction.— **hith″er-to′,** adv. Till now.— **hith′er-ward,** adv. Hither.

1: ə = final; ɪ = habit; aɪsle; aʊ = out; oɪl; iū = feud; ƈhin; go; ŋ = sing; ƈhin, this.
2: wǫlf, dǫ; bŏŏk, bōōt; fůll, rūle, cūre, bŭt, bûrn; ŏll, bŏy; g̣o, g̣em; iŋk; thin, this.

hive, 1 haiv; 2 hīv. **I.** *vt.* & *vi.* [HIVED; HIV'ING.] To cause to enter a hive; store, as honey; enter or dwell in a hive. **II.** *n.* A structure in which bees may dwell; also, a colony of bees; a busy place.

hives, 1 haivz; 2 hīvz, *n.* A mild fever with eruptions of the skin; also, croup.

ho, 1 hō; 2 hō, *interj.* A call to excite attention. [*hoar* frost.

hoar, 1 hōr; 2 hōr, *a.* Hoary; white; as,

hoard, 1 hōrd; 2 hōrd. **I**ᵈ. *vt.* & *vi.* To gather and store away; accumulate. **II.** *n.* That which has been accumulated and stored away; a stock or store.

hoar'hound", 1 hōr'haund"; 2 hōr'hound", *n.* A bitter perennial herb of the mint family: used as a remedy for colds.

hoarse, 1 hōrs; 2 hōrs, *a.* [HOARS'ER; HOARS'EST.] Harsh in sound; having the voice harsh or rough. **-ly,** *adv.* **-ness,** *n.*

hoar'y, 1 hōr'ı; 2 hōr'y, *a.* [HOAR'I-ER; HOAR'I-EST.] White, as from age; ancient.— **hoar'i-ness,** *n.*

hoax, 1 hōks; 2 hōks. **I**ᵗ. *vt.* To play a trick upon. **II.** *n.* A deception practised for sport.— **hoax'er,** *n.*

hob, 1 hob; 2 hŏb, *n.* A projection; hub.

hob'ble, ⎱ 1 hob'l; 2 hŏb'l. **I.** *vt.* & *vi.*
hob'lᶠ, ⎰ [HOB'BLED, HOB'LDᶠ; HOB'BLING.] To hamper; hopple; walk with a hitch. **II.** *n.* **1.** A limping gait. **2.** A fetter for the legs.— **hob'ble-de-hoy",** *n.* An awkward stripling.— **hob'ble-skirt",** *n.* A very narrow, close-fitting skirt permitting the wearer to take only short steps.

hob'by, 1 hob'ı; 2 hŏb'y, *n.* [HOB'BIESᶻ, *pl.*] An object of extravagant interest; pet idea.— **hob'by-horse",** *n.* A wooden horse; rocking-horse.

hob-gob'lin, 1 hob-gob'lın; 2 hŏb-gŏb'lin, *n.* A mischievous imp; frightful apparition.

hob'nail", 1 hob'nēl"; 2 hŏb'nāl", *n.* A nail for the soles of heavy shoes.— **hob'nailed",** *pa.* Bearing hob-nails, as heavy shoes.

hob'nob", 1 hob'nob"; 2 hŏb'nŏb", *vi.* [HOB'-NOBBED, HOB'NOBD'ᵇ; HOB'NOB"BING.] To drink together; be familiar.

hock¹, 1 hek; 2 hŏk, *n.* The joint of the hind leg in quadrupeds; back part of knee-joint in man.

hock², *n.* Any white Rhine wine.

hock'ey, 1 hek'ı; 2 hŏk'y, *n.* A game in which a ball is driven with a hooked bat; also, a hooked bat.

ho'cus-po'cus, 1 hō'kus-pō'kus; 2 hō'cŭs-pō'cŭs, *n.* A conjurer's trick; a deception: coined in imitation of Latin.

hod, 1 hod; 2 hŏd, *n.* A receptacle for carrying bricks and mortar; also, a coal-scuttle.

hodge'podge", 1 hoj'poj"; 2 hŏdg'pŏdg", *n.* A hotchpotch.

hoe, 1 hō; 2 hō. **I.** *vt.* & *vi.* [HOED; HOE'-ING.] To work with a hoe. **II.** *n.* A flat-bladed implement for digging.

Hoe.

hog, 1 hog; 2 hŏg, *n.* **1.** An omnivorous mammal; a swine: bred and raised for its meat, which is called *pork.* **2.** A filthy, gluttonous person.— **hog'gish,** *a.* Like a hog; gluttonous.

hogs'head, 1 hogz'hed; 2 hŏgs'hĕd, *n.* **1.** A large cask. **2.** A liquid measure, ordinarily 63 gallons.

hoi'den, 1 hei'dn; 2 hŏi'dn, *n.* A romping or bold girl. **hoy'den‡.— hoi'den-ish,** *a.*

hoist, 1 heist; 2 hŏist. **I**ᵈ. *vt.* To raise to a higher position. **II.** *n.* A hoisting-machine; lift; the act of hoisting.

hold, 1 hōld; 2 hōld, *v.* [HELD; HELD or HOLD'EN; HOLD'ING.] **I.** *t.* **1.** To retain so as to prevent movement or escape; grasp; keep; restrict; restrain; withhold. **2.** To maintain; sustain; adhere to. **3.** To contain; have room for. **II.** *i.* **1.** To stick; adhere. **2.** To remain firm or unbroken. **3.** To continue; proceed. **4.** To have possession. **5.** To stop; forbear.— **hold'er,** *n.*— **hold'ing,** *n.* A possession.

hold¹, *n.* The act of holding; a seizure; restraint; a place to grasp; refuge.

hold², *n.* The storage part of a ship.

hold³, *n.* A sign ⌢ over a note in music indicating that it should be prolonged.

hole, 1 hōl; 2 hōl, *n.* A cavity; hollow; den.

hol'i-day, 1 hol'ı-dē; 2 hŏl'i-dā, *n.* A day of rest or of diversion.

ho'li-ness, 1 hō'lı-nes; 2 hō'li-nĕs, *n.* The state of being holy.

hol'land, 1 hol'and; 2 hŏl'and, *n.* **1.** Unbleached linen. **2.** *pl.* Ardent spirits; gin.

hol'lo, 1 hel'o or hо-lō'; 2 hŏl'o or hō-lō', *n.* & *interj.* Same as HALLOO. **hol'la‡; hol'loa‡; hul-lo'‡.**

hol'low, 1 hel'o; 2 hŏl'o. **I.** *vt.* & *vi.* To make or become hollow. **II.** *a.* **1.** Having a cavity, as a tube, jar, or the like. **2.** Empty; vacant; sounding like the reverberation from an empty vessel or cavity; deep; murmuring. **III.** *n.* A depression or opening; an enclosed cavity. **-ness,** *n.*

hol'ly, 1 hel'ı; 2 hŏl'y, *n.* [-LIESᶻ, *pl.*] A tree or shrub with white flowers and red berries. See illus. on next page.

hol′ly-hock″, 1 hŏl′i-hŏk″; 2 hŏl′y-hŏk″, n. A tall biennial herb of the mallow family, with large flowers.

holm¹, 1 hōlm or hōm; 2 hōlm or hōm, n. Low land by a stream; an island in a river.

holm², n. **1.** An oak: the holm=oak. **2.** The holly.

hol′o-caust, 1 hel′o-kŏst; 2 hŏl′o-câst, n. **1.** A whole burnt offering. **2.** Wholesale destruction by fire and sword.

hol′ster, 1 hōl′stər; 2 hōl′ster, n. A horseman's pistol-case.

American Holly.

ho′ly, 1 hō′li; 2 hō′ly, a. [HŌ′LI-ER; HŌ′LI-EST.] Morally excellent; of highest spiritual purity; consecrated; hallowed.

hom′age, 1 hem′ij; 2 hŏm′ag, n. Reverential regard or worship; a vassal's act of fealty.

home, 1 hōm; 2 hōm. **I.** a. **1.** Pertaining to home or country. **2.** Going home; effective. **II.** n. **1.** A place of abode; family residence; resting-place; habitat. **2.** In games, a goal. **III.** adv. **1.** To or at home. **2.** To the place or point intended.— **hom′ing,** a. Readily finding its way home, as a carrier=pigeon.— **home′less,** a. Having no home.— **home′like″,** a. Like home; reminding of home.— **home′liness,** n.— **home′ly,** a. [HOME′LI-ER; HOME′LI-EST.] **1.** Having a familiar, every=day character; simple; domestic. **2.** [U. S.] Having plain features. **3.** Suffering because of absence from home.— **home′sick″,** a. **1.** Of domestic manufacture. **2.** Plain and homely in character. **II.** n. Fabric woven at home.— **home′stead,** n. A permanent family abode.— **home′ward,** adv. Toward home.

ho″me-op′a-thy, 1 hō″mi-ŏp′a-thι; 2 hō″me-ŏp′a-thy, n. A system of medicine founded on the principle that "like cures like," and prescribing minute doses of medicines that would produce in a healthy person symptoms like those of the disease to be cured.— **ho″me-o-path′ic,** a.— **ho″me-op′a-thist,** n. One who advocates or practises homeopathy. **ho′me-o-path‡.**

hom′i-cide, 1 hem′i-sɑid; 2 hŏm′i-çīd, n. The killing of a human being; one who has killed another.— **hom′i-ci′dal,** a.

hom′i-ly, 1 hem′i-lɪ; 2 hŏm′i-ly, n. [-LIES², pl.] A didactic discourse; sermon.—

hom″i-let′ic, a. Pertaining to the composition and delivery of sermons.

hom′i-ny, 1 hem′i-nɪ; 2 hŏm′i-ny. [U. S.] Maize, hulled and broken.

ho″mœ-op′a-thy, etc. Same as HOMEOPATHY, etc.

ho″mo-ge′ne-ous, 1 hō″mo-jī′nι-ŭs; 2 hō″mo-ġē′ne-ŭs, a. Made up of similar parts; uniform in texture or composition. **-ly,** adv. **-ness,** n.— **ho″mo-ge-ne′i-ty,** n. Identity or similarity of kind or structure.

ho-mol′o-gous, 1 ho-mel′o-gŭs; 2 ho-mŏl′o-ġŭs, a. Having a similar structure, proportion, value, or position.— **hom′o-log,** n.

hom′o-nym, 1 hem′o-nim; 2 hŏm′o-nўm, n. A word similar in sound to, but different in meaning from, another: fair and fare.— **ho-mon′y-mous,** a.— **ho-mon′y-my,** n.

hone, 1 hōn; 2 hōn. **I.** vt. [HONED; HON′ING.] To sharpen, as on a hone. **II.** n. A block of fine stone, as for sharpening razors.

hon′est, 1 ɒn′est; 2 ŏn′ĕst, a. Fair and candid in dealings; frank; open; just; upright; also, chaste.— **hon′est-ly,** adv.— **hon′es-ty,** n. The quality of being honest.

hon′ey, 1 hun′ι; 2 hŏn′y, n. A sweet **hun′eyᴾ,** sirup from the nectaries of flowers, deposited by bees.— **hon′ey-bee″,** n. A bee that collects honey; the common hive-bee.— **hon′ey-comb″. I.** vt. To fill with small holes or passages. **II.** n. **1.** A structure of waxen cells, made by bees to contain honey, eggs, etc. **2.** Anything full of small holes or cells.— **hon′ey-combed″,** pa. Full of cells or perforations.— **honeydew melon,** a smooth, yellow=skinned cultivated variety of winter melon with whitish=green pulp. See MELON.— **hon′eyed,** a. **1.** Covered with or full of honey. **2.** Sweet; cajoling.— **hon′ey-moon″,** n. The first month after marriage.— **hon′ey-suck″le,** n. Any one of various ornamental erect or climbing flowering shrubs.

hon′or, 1 ɒn′ər; 2 ŏn′or. **I.** vt. **1.** To regard with honor; bestow marks of honor upon; add dignity to. **2.** To pay, as a draft. **II.** n. **1.** Consideration due or paid, as to worth; respectful regard, or its outward tokens; a cause of esteem. **2.** Nobility of character; nice sense of what is right, noble, or becoming.— **hon′or-a-bl(eᴾ,** a. Worthy of honor; conferring honor; conforming to a code of honor.— **hon′or-a-bly,** adv. In an honorable manner.— **hon′or-a-ry,** 1 ɒn′ər-ē-rι; 2 ŏn′or-ā-ry, a. Conferring honor; being a token of honor.

hon″o-ra′ri-um, 1 hen″o-rē′rɪ-ŭm; 2 hŏn″o-rā′ri-ŭm, n. [-RI-A, pl.] A reward for services, which is not viewed as pay.

hon'our, hon'our-a-bl(eᴿ**, etc.** Honor, etc.

-hood, *suffix.* Condition; state; as, child*hood.*

hood, 1 hud; 2 hŏŏd. **Iᵈ.** *vt.* To cover with a hood; hide. **II.** *n.* A covering for the head and back of the neck.— **hood'- wink**ᵗ, *vt.* To deceive; blindfold.

hood'lum, 1 hūd'lum; 2 hŏŏd'lŭm, *n.* [Colloq., **U. S.**] A street ruffian; rowdy.

hoo'doo, 1 hū'dū; 2 hŏŏ'dōŏ, *n.* A person or thing that causes bad luck; an evil spell. See VOODOO.

hoof, 1 hūf; 2 hŏŏf, *n.* [HOOFS, *pl.*] The horny casing of the foot of the horse, ox, deer, etc.

hookᵗ, 1 huk; 2 hŏŏk, *vt. & vi.* **1.** To fasten with a hook; entrap. **2.** To attack with the horns, as a cow.— **hooked,** *pa.* **1.** Curved like a hook. **2.** Supplied with a hook. **3.** Fastened by a hook.— **to hook up.** *Radio.* To connect so as to form a complete electric circuit, as by assembling sets for transmission or reception of radio programs.

hook, *n.* Something bent so as to hold another object, as a fish-hook.

hoo'ka, 1 hū'ka; 2 hŏŏ'ka, *n.* An Oriental pipe, in which smoke draws through water.

hook-up, *n. Radio.* A complete assemblage of electric apparatus for the transmission or reception of radio programs.

hoop², **Iᵗ.** *vt.* **1.** To surround with hoops, as a cask. **2.** To encircle. **II.** *n.* A circular band, as on a barrel.

Hoo'sier, 1 hū'zẽr; 2 hŏŏ'zhẽr, *n.* A nickname for a native or resident of Indiana.

hoot, 1 hūt; 2 hŏŏt. **Iᵈ.** *vt. & vi.* To utter contemptuous cries; jeer; mock; cry as an owl. **II.** *n.* **1.** A cry uttered in derision. **2.** The cry of an owl.

Hoo'ver-ize, *vt.* [Colloq.] To restrict oneself to a fixed allowance of food, as meat, etc.: from H. C. HOOVER, U. S. Food Administrator, 1917–18.— **Hoo''ver-i-za'tion,** *n.*

hop, 1 hŏp; 2 hŏp, *v.* [HOPPEDᵗ or HOPTᵗ; HOP'PING.] **I.** *t.* To leap over. **II.** *i.* To move by short leaps, especially on one leg.

hop¹, *n.* The act of hopping; a dance.

hop², *n.* **1.** A perennial climbing herb with opposite lobed leaves and scaly fruit. **2.** *pl.* The fruit of this plant.

hope, 1 hōp; 2 hŏp. **I.** *vt. & vi.* [HOPEDᵗ; HOP'ING.] To desire with expectation of obtaining; cherish desire mingled with expectation. **II.** *n.* **1.** Desire accompanied by expectation. **2.** The cause of hopeful expectation.— **hope'ful. I.** *a.* Full of hope; promising. **II.** *n.* [Colloq.] A son or daughter. **-ly,** *adv.* **-ness,** *n.*— **hope'-less,** *a.* Without hope; despairing. **-ly,** *adv.* **-ness,** *n.*

hop'per, 1 hŏp'ẽr; 2 hŏp'ẽr, *n.* A funnel for sending grain to the millstones in a mill.

hop'ple, 1 hŏp'l; 2 hŏp'l. **I.** *vt.* [HOP'-

PLED; HOP'PLING.] To hamper; hobble. **II.** *n.* A fetter, as for the legs of a horse.

horde, 1 hōrd; 2 hôrd, *n.* A gathered and motley multitude of human beings.

ho-ri'zon, 1 ho-rai'zən; 2 ho-rī'zŏn, *n.* The line where the earth or sea seems to meet the sky.— **hor''i-zon'tal,** *a.* Parallel to the horizon; level. **-ly,** *adv.*

horn, 1 hẽrn; 2 hôrn, *n.* **1.** A bone-like projecting growth on the head of an animal, as an ox or deer. **2.** Something made of horn, or likened to an animal's horn, as a trumpet.— **horned,** *a.* Having a horn or horns.— **horn'pipe'',** *n.* **1.** A lively English country-dance. **2.** A former musical instrument.— **horn'y,** *a.*

hor'net, 1 hẽr'net; 2 hôr'nĕt, *n.* A large social wasp.

ho-rol'o-gy, 1 ho-rŏl'o-ji; 2 ho-rŏl'o-ġy. *n.* [-GIES², *pl.*] The science of time-measurement or of timepieces.

hor'o-scope, 1 hŏr'o-skŏp; 2 hŏr'o-scŏp, *n. Astrol.* The position of the planets at a person's birth.

hor'ri-ble, } 1 hŏr'ı-bl; 2 hŏr'i-bl, *a.* Ex-
hor'ri-bl², } citing abhorrence; terrible.—
hor'ri-bly, *adv.*— **hor-rif'ic,** *a.* Causing horror.— **hor'ri-fy,** *vt.* [-FIED; -FY'ING.] To affect or fill with horror.

hor'rid, 1 hŏr'ıd; 2 hŏr'id, *a.* Fitted to inspire horror; dreadful; outrageous. **-ly,** *adv.* **-ness,** *n.*

hor'ror, 1 hŏr'ẽr; 2 hŏr'or, *n.* **1.** Extreme fear or abhorrence; dread; repugnance. **2.** Some great calamity.

horse, 1 hẽrs; 2 hôrs. **I.** *vt.* [HORSEDᵗ, HORSTˢ; HORS'ING.] To mount or carry, as on a horse; furnish horses for. **II.** *n.* **1.** A solid-hoofed quadruped having a mane and tail of long coarse hair, and relatively small ears and head. **2.** The male of the horse. **3.** Mounted troops; cavalry. — **horse'back''. I.** *n.* **1.** A horse's back. **2.** An object shaped like a horse's back. **II.** *adv.* On a horse's back.— **horse'-chest''nut,** *n.* An Old World tree, with a large chestnut-like fruit.— **horse'man,** *n.* One who rides a horse.— **horse'man-ship,** *n.* Equestrian skill.— **horse'power,** *n.* **1.** A standard theoretical unit of the rate of work, equal to 33,000 pounds lifted one foot in one minute. **2.** A treadmill worked by a horse.— **horse'- rad''ish,** *n.* A common garden herb of the mustard family, cultivated for its pungent root.— **horse'shoe'',** *n.* A U-shaped metal shoe for a horse.— **horse'whip''. Iᵗ.** *vt.* To chastise with a horsewhip. **II.** *n.* A whip for managing horses.

hor'ta-tive, } 1 hôr'ta-tiv; 2 hôr'ta-tiv, *a.*
hor'ta-tiv³, } Of the nature of exhortation. — **hor'ta-to-ry,** *a.* Giving exhortation.

REPRESENTATIVE TYPES OF HORSES.

1. Pacing stallion. 2. Orloff stallion. 3. Belgian stallion. 4. Percheron stallion. 5. Arab stallion. 6. Hackney stallion. 7. Cleveland Bay stallion. 8. Shetland pony. 9. Trotting stallion. 10. German Coach stallion. 11. Clydesdale stallion. 12. French Coach stallion.

hor'ti-cul"ture, 1 hõr'tĭ-kul"ĉhur or -tiŭr; 2 hŏr'tĭ-cŭl"chur or -tūr, n. The cultivation of a garden, especially as a science.— **hor"ti-cul'tur-al,** a. — **hor"ti-cul'tur-ist,** n. One devoted to or skilled in horticulture.

ho-san'na, 1 ho-zan'ə; 2 ho-săn'a, interj. An exclamation of praise to God.

hose, 1 hōz; 2 hŏs, n. [HOSE, formerly HO'SEN, 1 hō'zn, 2 hō'ʂn, pl.] **1.** A stocking: mostly used as a plural. **2.** A flexible tube for conveying fluids.— **ho'sier,** 1 hō'ʒər; 2 hō'zher, n. One who deals in hose, etc.— **ho'sier-y,** n. Hosiers' wares; stockings; hose.

hos'pice, 1 hes'pɪs; 2 hŏs'pĭç, n. A place of entertainment or shelter; especially a convent in an Alpine pass.

hos'pi-ta-ble, 1 hes'pɪ-tə-bl; 2 hŏs'pi-ta-**hos'pi-ta-bl̶ᴾ,** ʃ bl, a. Disposed to entertain with generous kindness.— **hos'pi-ta-bly,** adv.

hos'pi-tal, 1 hes'pi-təl; 2 hŏs'pi-tal, n. An institution for the care and treatment of the sick or wounded.

hos"pi-tal'i-ty, 1 hes"pi-tal'ɪ-tɪ; 2 hŏs"pĭ-tăl'i-ty, n. [-TIES², pl.] The act of being hospitable. [army.

host¹, 1 hōst; 2 hŏst, n. A multitude; an **host²,** n. One who entertains guests.

host³, n. In some churches, The consecrated wafer used at the Lord's Supper.

hos'tage, 1 hes'tɪj; 2 hŏs'tağ, n. A person held as a pledge, as in war, for the performance of some stipulation.

hos"teau', 1 ōs"tō'; 2 ŏs"tō', n. [Colloq.] A château used as a hospital: a telescope word.

hos'tel-ry, 1 hes'tel-rɪ; 2 hŏs'tĕl-ry, n. An inn. **hos'tel‡; hos'tler-y‡.** [host.

host'ess, 1 hōst'es; 2 hŏst'ĕs, n. A female **hos'tile,** ʔ 1 hes'tɪl; 2 hŏs'til, a. **1.** Hav-**hos'til²,** ʃ ing a spirit of enmity. **2.** Pertaining to an enemy.— **hos-til'i-ty,** n. [-TIES², pl.] **1.** Enmity. **2.** pl. Warlike measures. [man; groom.

hos'tler, 1 hes'lər; 2 hŏs'ler, n. A stable-**hot¹,** 1 het; 2 hŏt, a. [HOT'TER; HOT'TEST.] Being heated; very warm; pungent; acrid; fiery.— **hot'bed",** n. A bed of rich earth, covered with glass, for tender plants.— **hot-head'ed,** a. Having an impulsive temperament.— **hot'house",** n. A house, as of glass, heated artificially.— **hot'ly,** adv.— **hot'ness,** n.

hotch'potch", 1 heĉh'pech"; 2 hŏch'pŏch"-n. A confused mess; jumble. **hodge'-podge"‡.**

ho-tel', 1 ho-tel'; 2 ho-tĕl', n. A house for the entertainment of travelers; an inn; also, an official residence.

hough, n. Same as HOCK.

hound, 1 haund; 2 hound. **Iᵈ.** vt. To hunt with hounds; trail; persecute; set on, as a hound. **II.** n. **1.** A hunting-dog. **2.** A dastardly fellow.

hour, 1 aur; 2 our, n. **1.** Sixty minutes. **2.** A set time.— **hour'glass",** n. A glass vessel used for measuring time by the running of sand.— **hour'ly. I.** a. Happening every hour. **II.** adv. At intervals of an hour.

hou'ri, 1 hū'rɪ or hau'rɪ; 2 hu'ri or hou'ri, n. [HOU'RIS² or HOU'RIES², pl.] One of the beautiful maidens who, according to the Mohammedan faith, are to be the companions of the faithful in Paradise.

house, ʔ 1 hauz; 2 hous, vt. & vi. [HOUSED, **houz²,** ʃ HOUZDᴾ; HOUS'ING, HOUZ'INGᴾ.] To place under cover; take shelter or lodgings.

house, 1 haus; 2 hous, n. [HOUS'ES, 1 hauz'ez; 2 hous'ĕʂ, pl.] **1.** A place of abode. **2.** A household. **3.** A tribe; stock; line. **4.** One of the divisions of a legislative body; a convention; audience. **5.** A mercantile establishment; a corporation.— **house'break"er,** n. A burglar. — **house'break"ing,** n.— **house'hold". I.** a. Domestic. **II.** n. A number of persons dwelling under the same roof.— **house'hold"er,** n. The head of a family.— **house'keep"er,** n. A woman who oversees work in a house.— **house'keep"ing,** n. The management of a household.— **house'maid",** n. A girl employed in housework.— **house'ware",** n. Kitchen equipment and labor-saving devices in a home.— **house'warm"ing,** n. A festivity on entering a new home.— **house'wife",** 1 haus'waif"; 2 hous'wif", n. The mistress of a household. **-ly,** adv.— **house'wife'ry,** n. Housekeeping. [Shelter.

hous'ing¹, 1 hauz'ɪŋ; 2 hous'ing, n.

hous'ing², n. The trappings of a horse.

hove, imp. of HEAVE, v. [dwelling.

hov'el, 1 hov'el; 2 hŏv'ĕl, n. A wretched **hov'er,** 1 huv'ər; 2 hŏv'er, v. **I.** t. To cover with the wings. **II.** i. **1.** To pause with fluttering wings. **2.** To linger about.

how, 1 hau; 2 how, adv. **1.** In what manner. **2.** To what degree. **3.** In what state. **4.** At what price. **5.** To what name. **6.** By what name. **7.** For what reason; why.— **how-be'it,** adv. & conj. Be it as it may.— **how-ev'er. I.** adv. In whatever manner; by whatever means. **II.** conj. Notwithstanding; yet.— **how"so-ev'er,** adv. Nevertheless.

how'dah, 1 hau'da; 2 how'da, n. A railed or canopied seat on the back of an elephant.

how'it-zer, 1 hau'it-sər; 2 how'it-ser, n. A short light cannon.

howl, 1 haul; 2 howl. **I.** vt. & vi. **1.** To utter a loud wail; clamor; roar. **II.** n. **1.** The cry of a wolf or of a dog in distress.

1: ɑrtistic, ärt; fat, fāre; fȧst; gět, prēy; hǐt, pŏlíce; ŏbey, gō; nět, ôr; fůll, rūle; bŭt, bûrn.
2: ärt, āpe, făt, fâre, fȧst, whạt, ạll: mē, gět, prẹy, fêrn; hĭt, īce; ĭ=ĕ; ĩ=ẽ; gō, nŏt, ôr, wŏn.

2. Any resonant mournful cry or sound. — **howl'ing,** *pa.*

hoy, 1 hoi; 2 hŏy, *interj.* Ho; halloo.

hoy'den, *n.* Same as HOIDEN.

hub, 1 hub; 2 hŭb, *n.* **1.** The central part of a wheel. **2.** Anything central. [roar.

hub'bub, 1 hub'ub; 2 hŭb'ŭb, *n.* Uproar.

huck'le-ber″ry, 1 huk'l-ber″i; 2 hŭk'l-ber″y, *n.* [-RIES², *pl.*] The edible black or dark-blue berry of a species of heath.

hur'tle-ber″ry‡.

huck'ster, 1 huk'stər; 2 hŭk'ster. **I.** *vi.* To bargain in a small way. **II.** *n.* One who retails small wares; a hawker.

hud'dle, 1 hud'l; 2 hŭd'l. **I.** *vt. & vi.* [HUD'DLED; HUD'DLING.] To collect confusedly; put in place hurriedly; gather in a huddle. **II.** *n.* A confused crowd or collection. [quality of color; tint.

hue¹, 1 hiū; 2 hū, *n.* The particular

hue², *n.* A vociferous cry; shouting.

huff, } 1 huf; 2 hŭf. **I**ᵗ. *vt. & vi.* To puff

hufᶠ, } up; swell; bully; anger. **II.** *n.* Offense suddenly taken.— **huff'ish,** *a.* Petulant; irascible. **huff'y‡.**

hug, 1 hug; 2 hŭg, *v.* [HUGGED, HUGD²; HUG'GING.] **I.** *t.* To clasp tightly within the arms; embrace; cherish. **II.** *i.* To cuddle.— **hug,** *n.* A close embrace.

huge, ¶1 hiūj; 2 hūg, *a.* Having great bulk; vast. **-ly,** *adv.* **-ness,** *n.*

Hu'gue-not, 1 hiū'gi-net; 2 hū'ḡe-nŏt, *n.* A French Protestant of the 16th and 17th centuries.

hulk, 1 hulk; 2 hŭlk, *n.* The body of an old ship; any unwieldy object.

hulk'ing, 1 hulk'iŋ; 2 hŭlk'ing, *a.* [Colloq.] Bulky; clumsy. **hulk'y‡.**

hull¹, 1 hul; 2 hŭl. **I.** *vt.* To free from the hull. **II¹.** *n.* The outer covering, as of a nut; husk.

hull². **I.** *vt.* To strike or pierce the hull of. **II².** *n.* The body of a vessel.

hul-lo', 1 hu-lō'; 2 hŭ-lō', *v., n., & interj.* Same as HALLOO.

hum, 1 hum; 2 hŭm. **I.** *vt. & vi.* [HUMMED, HUMD²; HUM'MING.] To sing in a low tone; make a droning sound. **II.** *n.* A low inarticulate sound (as of *h'm*).

hu'man, 1 hiū'mən; 2 hū'man, *a.* Pertaining to man; suitable for man.— **hu'man-ize,** *vt. & vi.* [-IZED; -IZ'ING.] To render humane or human. **hu'man-ise‡.— hu-man″i-ta'ri-an,** *n.* A philanthropist. **— hu-man'i-ty,** 1 hiu-man'i-ti; 2 hū-măn'i-ty, *n.* [-TIES², *pl.*] **1.** Mankind collectively. **2.** Human nature. **3.** The state of being humane; a humane act. **4.** *pl.* Classical learning.— **hu'man-kind″,** *n.* The human race.— **hu'man-ly,** *adv.*

hu-mane', 1 hiu-mēn'; 2 hū-mān', *a.* **1.** Having or showing kindness; compassionate. **2.** Tending to refine; polite; elegant.— **nu-mane'ly,** *adv.*

hum'ble, } 1 hum'bl; 2 hŭm'bl. **I.** *vt.*

hum'blᶠ, } [HUM'BL(E)Dᴾ; HUM'BLING.] To make humble; humiliate; lower. **II.** *a.* [HUM'BLER; HUM'BLEST.] Having or manifesting a lowly opinion of oneself; meek; unpretending; lowly.— **hum'bly,** *adv.*

hum'ble-bee″, 1 hum'bl-bī″; 2 hŭm'bl-bē″, *n.* A bumblebee.

hum'bug, 1 hum'bug; 2 hŭm'bŭg. **I.** *vt. & vi.* [HUM'BUGGED, HUM'BUGD²; HUM'BUG-GING.] To impose upon; deceive. **II.** *n.* An impostor or imposture; a sham.

hum'drum″, 1 hum'drum″; 2 hŭm'drŭm″, *a.* Tedious; monotonous.

hu'mid, 1 hiū'mid; 2 hū'mid, *a.* Moist; damp.— **hu-mid'i-ty,** *n.* Moisture; dampness; water-vapor in the atmosphere.

hu-mil'i-ate, 1 hiu-mil'i-ēt; 2 hū-mĭl'i-āt, *vt.* [-AT'ED²; -AT'ING.] To lower the pride of; bring down; humble.— **hu-mil″i-a'tion,** *n.*— **hu-mil'i-ty,** 1 hiu-mil'i-ti; 2 hū-mĭl'i-ty, *n.* [-TIES², *pl.*] The quality of being humble. [bird, related to the swift.

hum'ming-bird″, *n.* A small American

hum'mock, 1 hum'ək; 2 hŭm'ok, *n.* A small elevation.

hu'mor, 1 hiū'mər *or* yū'mər; 2 hū'mor *or* yū'mor. **I.** *vt.* To yield to the humor or caprices of; adapt oneself to. **II.** *n.* **1.** Disposition; characteristic mood; whim. **2.** A facetious turn of thought. **3.** An animal fluid. **4.** A cutaneous eruption.— **hu'mor-ist,** *n.* One who displays humor.— **hu'mor-ous,** *a.* **1.** That excites merriment; amusing. **2.** Whimsical. **-ly,** *adv.* **-ness,** *n.*— **hu'mor-some,** *a.* **1.** Full of whims. **2.** Characterized by wit; droll. **-ly,** *adv.* **-ness,** *n.*

hump, 1 hump; 2 hŭmp, *n.* A protuberance, as that formed by a curved spine.— **hump'back″,** *n.* **1.** A crooked back. **2.** A hunchback.— **hump'backed″,** *a.*

Hun, 1 hun; 2 hŭn, *n.* **1.** A barbarian of an Asiatic race that invaded Europe; hence, a ruthless soldier. **2.** A Vandal.

hunch, 1 hunch; 2 hŭnch. **I**ᵗ. *vt.* To jostle; also, to crook, as the back. **II.** *n.* **1.** A hump; lump. **2.** A sudden shove.— **hunch'back″,** *n.* A person with a hump on the back.— **hunch'backed″,** *a.*

hun'dred, 1 hun'dred; 2 hŭn'drĕd, *a. & n.* Ten times ten; also, the symbol representing it, C or 100.— **hun'dredth. I.** *a.* Tenth in order after the ninetieth. **II.** *n.* The last in a series of 100.— **hun'dred-weight″,** *n.* A weight commonly reckoned

---

1: ə = final; ɪ = habit; aisle; au = out; oil; iū = feud; ɑ́hin; go; ŋ = sing; ᵺhin, this.

2: wolf, dǫ; bŏŏk, bōōt; fu̇ll, ru̇le, cūre, bŭt, bûrn; ȯil, bŏy; ḡo, ġem; iŋk; thin, this.

in the United States, and sometimes in England, at 100 lbs. avoirdupois, but commonly in England at 112 lbs.

hung, 1 hŭng; 2 hŭng, *imp. & pp.* of HANG, *v.*

Hun-ga′ri-an, 1 huŋ-gē′ri-ən; 2 hŭŋ-gā′ri-an.
I. *a.* Of or pertaining to Hungary. **II.** *n.*
A native, or the language, of Hungary.

hun′ger, 1 huŋ′ger; 2 hŭŋ′ger. **I.** *vi.*
To crave food; have eager desire. **II.** *n.*
Craving for food; any strong desire.
— **hun′ger-strike**, *n.* Persistent abstention from food in order to obtain a certain end, as by a prisoner to secure release.—
hun′gry, 1 huŋ′gri; 2 hŭŋ′gry, *a.* [HUN′-
GRI-ER; HUN′GRI-EST.] Having or manifesting hunger.— **hun′gri-ly**, *adv.*

hunt, 1 hunt; 2 hŭnt. **I**^d. *vt. & vi.* To
pursue; chase; search. **II.** *n.* **1.** The
act of hunting game; chase. **2.** A search.
— **hunt′er**, *n.* **1.** A huntsman. **2.** A horse
used in hunting.— **hunts′man**, *n.* One who
practises hunting; the attendant who has
charge of the pack of hounds in a hunt.

hur′dle, 1 hûr′dl; 2 hûr′dl, *n.* A movable framework used for making
hur′dlr, } able framework used for making
fences, or to be leaped over in racing.

hurl, 1 hûrl; 2 hûrl, *vt. & vi.* To throw
with violence; utter with vehemence.

hur-rah′, } 1 hu-rā′; 2 hu-rä′. **I.** *vt. & vi.*
hur-ra′, } To receive with cheers; utter
cheers. **II.** *n.* A shout of triumph. **III.**
interj. An exclamation expressing triumph.

hur′ri-cane, 1 hur′i-kēn; 2 hûr′i-cān, *n.*
Originally, a cyclone; now, any gale of
unusual violence.

hur′ry, 1 hur′i; 2 hûr′y. **I.** *vt. & vi.*
[HUR′RIED, 1 -id, 2 -id; HUR′RY-ING.] To
hasten; act rapidly. **II.** *n.* [HUR′RIES^z,
pl.] The act of hurrying; haste.— **hur′ry-
ing-ly**, *adv.*

hurt, 1 hûrt; 2 hûrt. **I.** *vt. & vi.* [HURT;
HURT′ING.] To pain; injure; harm. **II.**
n. Injury, as a bruise; hence, damage.
— **hurt′ful**, *a.* Causing hurt.

hur′tle, 1 hûr′tl; 2 hûr′tl, *vt. & vi.* [HUR′-
TLED; HUR′TLING.] To move violently;
hurl; rush confusedly and noisily.

hur′tle-ber′ry, *n.* Same as HUCKLEBERRY.

hus′band, 1 huz′band; 2 hŭz′band. **I**^d.
vt. To manage economically; save. **II.**
n. A married man.— **hus′band-man**, *n.*
A farmer.— **hus′band-ry**, *n.* **1.** Agriculture. **2.** Economical management.

hush, 1 hush; 2 hŭsh. **I**^t. *vt. & vi.* To
silence; be still. **II.** *n.* Profound silence;
quiet. **III.** *interj.* Be still.

husk, 1 husk; 2 hŭsk. **I**^t. *vt.* To remove
the husk of. **II.** *n.* An outer covering; rind;
something worthless.— **husk′ing**, *n.*

husk′y^1, 1 husk′i; 2 hŭsk′y.,*a.* [HUSK′I-ER;
HUSK′I-EST.] Abounding in husks; husk-like.

husk′y^2, *a.* [HUSK′I-ER; HUSK′I-EST.]
Hoarse: said of the voice.— **husk′i-ly**, *adv.*—
husk′i-ness, *n.* [horse trooper.

hus-sar′, 1 hu-zär′; 2 hŭ-gär′, *n.* A light

hus′sy, 1 huz′i; 2 hŭg′y, *n.* [HUS′SIES^z, *pl.*]
A pert or forward girl.

hust′ing, 1 hust′in; 2 hŭst′ing, *n.* **1.** A
meeting for conference. **2.** *pl.* [Gt. Brit.]
A platform for electioneering speeches.

hus′tle, } 1 hus′l; 2 hŭs′l, *vt. & vi.* [HUS′-
hus′tlr, } TL(E)D^p; HUS′TLING.] **1.** To
shuffle together in confusion; jostle;
shuffle along. **2.** [Colloq., U. S.] To
show energy and perseverance. [ing.

hut, 1 hut; 2 hŭt, *n.* A small rude dwelling.

hutch, } 1 huch; 2 hŭch, *n.* A small room;
huch^r, } chest; coop. [Hurrah.

huz-za′, 1 hu-zä′; 2 hŭ-zä′, *v., n., & interj.*

hy′a-cinth, 1 hai′ə-sinth; 2 hī′a-çinth, *n.*
A bulbous plant with spike-like cluster of
flowers.— **hy″a-cin′thin**(e^s, *a.* Pertaining
to or like the hyacinth; lovely; beautiful.

hy-æ′na, *n.* See HYENA.

hy′brid, 1 hai′brid; 2 hī′brid. **I.** *a.* Of
mixed parentage; mongrel. **II.** *n.* A
hybrid animal or plant; a mongrel.—
hy′brid-ism, *n.*— **hy′brid′i-ty**, *n.*

hy′dra, 1 hai′drə; 2 hī′dra, *n.* [HY′DRAS^z
or HY′DRÆ, 1 hai′drī; 2 hī′drē, *pl.*] **1.**
[H-] *Gr. Myth.* The many-headed water-
serpent slain by Hercules. **2.** Any evil
of many forms. **3.** A fresh-water polyp.

hy′drant, 1 hai′drənt; 2 hī′drant, *n.* A
valved discharge-pipe on a water-main.

hy-drau′lic, 1 hai-drô′lik; 2 hī-dra′lic, *a.*
Pertaining to hydraulics.— **hy-drau′li-cal-
ly**, *adv.*— **hy-drau′lics**, *n.* The science of
liquids, as water, in motion.

hy″dro-a′er-o-plane, 1 hai″dro-ē′ər-o-plēn; 2
hī″dro-ā′er-o-plān, *n.* An aeroplane fitted to
alight on, rise from, or travel over water.

hy′dro-gen, 1 hai′dro-jen; 2 hī′dro-gĕn, *n.*
A colorless, odorless, tasteless, gaseous
element, the lightest substance known.

hy-drog′ra-phy, } 1 hai-drog′rə-fi; 2 hī-
hy-drog′ra-fy^r, } drog′ra-fy, *n.* The science of charting navigable waters, coasts,
rivers, etc.— **hy″dro-graph′ic**, *a.* Relating
to hydrography.

hy-drom′e-ter, 1 hai-drom′i-tər; 2 hī-
drŏm′e-ter, *n.* An instrument for determining specific gravity.— **hy″dro-met′ric**, *a.*—
hy″dro-met′ri-cal, *a.*— **hy-drom′e-try**, *n.*

hy-drop′a-thy, 1 hai-drop′ə-thi; 2 hī-
drŏp′a-thy, *n.* The treatment of diseases
by the use of water.— **hy″dro-path′ic**, *a.*
— **hy-drop′a-thist**, *n.* **hy-drop′a-tht**:

hy″dro-pho′bi-a, } 1 hai″dro-fō′bi-ə; 2 hī′-
hy″dro-fo′bi-a, } dro-fō′bi-a, *n.* A disease due to the bite of a rabid animal.

hy′dro-plane, 1 hai′dro-plēn; 2 hī′dro-plān, *n.* A flat-bottomed boat propelled as by a motor-engine.

hy″dro-stat′ics, 1 hai″dro-stat′iks; 2 hī″dro-stăt-ies, *n.* The science of the pressure and equilibrium of fluids, as water.— **hy″dro-stat′ic,** *a.* Pertaining to hydrostatics. **hy″dro-stat′l-cal‡.**

hy′drous, 1 hai′drŭs; 2 hī′drŭs, *a.* Watery; containing water or hydrogen.

hy-e′na, 1 hai-i′nə; 2 hī-ē′na, *n.* A cowardly carnivorous mammal having the fore-legs longer than the hind.

hy′gi-ene, 1 hai′ji-īn; 2 hī′gi-ēn, *n.* The scientific study of the preservation of health.— **hy″gi-en′ic,** *a.* Pertaining to hygiene.

Striped Hyena. ⅟₄₅

hy-grom′e-ter, 1 hai-grŏm′i-tər; 2 hī-grŏm′e-ter, *n.* An instrument for ascertaining the humidity, as of the air.

Hy′men, 1 hai′men; 2 hī′mĕn, *n.* **1.** *Gr. Myth.* The god of marriage. **2.** [h-] The wedded state.— **hy″me-ne′al.** *I. a.* Pertaining to marriage. *II. n.* A wedding-song.

hymn, 1 him; 2 hym. *I. vt. & vi.* [HYMNED, 1 himd, 2 hymd; HYMN′ING, 1 him′iŋ *or* him′niŋ, 2 hym′niŋ *or* hym′ning.] To sing hymns to; express in hymns; sing praises. *II. n.* A song expressive of praise.— **hym′nal,** *n.* A book of hymns.

hy′per-, 1 hai′pər-; 2 hī′per-, *prefix.* Over; above: above measure; as, *hyper*critical.

hy-per′bo-la, 1 hai-pūr′bo-la; 2 hī-pēr′bo-la, *n. Geom.* The figure formed when two cones, placed vertex to vertex, are cut by a plane that passes through them both.

A Hyperbola.
P, P, any points of the curve; *F, G,* foci; *C,* center; *AB,* transverse axis; *ED,* conjugate axis. The dotted curves are the branches of the conjugate hyperbola.

hy-per′bo-le, 1 hai-pūr′bo-lī; 2 hī-pēr′bo-lē, *n.* Poetic or rhetorical exaggeration.— **hy″per-bol′ic,** *a.* Relating to hyperbole. **hy″per-bol′i-cal,** *a.* exaggerating.

hy″per-bo′re-an, 1 hai″pər-bō′ri-ən; 2 hī″per-bō′re-an. *I. a.* Occupying the extreme north; very cold. *II. n.* [H-] *Gr. Myth.* One of a people supposed to dwell beyond the north wind.

hy″per-crit′ic, 1 hai″pər-krit′ik; 2 hī″per-crit′ic, *n.* A very severe critic.— **hy″per-crit′i-cal,** *a.* Given to strained or captious criticism.— **hy″per-crit′i-cism,** *n.* Unduly severe, minute, or captious criticism.

hy-per′tro-phy, 1 hai-pūr′tro-fi; 2 hī-pēr′tro-fy, *n.* Undue or excessive growth.

hy′phen, 1 hai′fen; 2 hī′fĕn, *n.* A mark

hy′fenᴾ, ⎰(- *or* ⹀) used to connect the elements of words.— **hy′phen-ate,** *vt.* [-AT′EDᵈ; -AT′ING.] To insert a hyphen between the parts of.— **hy″phen-a′tion,** *n.*

hyp′no-tism, 1 hip′no-tizm; 2 hyp′no-tism, *n.* An artificial somnambulism in which the mind becomes passive.— **hyp-not′ic,** *a.* **1.** Pertaining to or tending to produce hypnotism. **2.** Tending to produce sleep.— **hyp′no-tize,** *vt.* [-TIZED; -TIZ′ING.] To produce hypnotic sleep in.

hy′po-, hyp-, 1 hai′po-, hip-; 2 hī′po-, hyp-, *prefix.* Under; beneath; less than: opposed to *hyper-;* as, *hypo*dermic.

hyp″o-chon′dri-a, 1 hip″o-[*or* hip″o-]kŏn′dri-ə; 2 hyp″o-[*or* hī″po-]ĕŏn′dri-a, *n.* A morbid melancholy and anxiety of mind.— **hyp″o-chon′dri-ac.** *I. a.* Subject to imaginary ailments. *II. n.* A person who suffers from hypochondria.

hyp′o-crite, 1 hip′o-krit; 2 hyp′o-crĭt, *n.*

hyp′o-criteˢ, ⎰One who acts a false part or makes false professions.— **hy-poc′ri-sy,** 1 hi-pŏk′ri-si; 2 hy-pŏc′ri-sy, *n.* [-SIESᶻ, *pl.*] The feigning to be what one is not.— **hyp″o-crit′i-cal,** *a.* Pertaining to a hypocrite or hypocrisy. **-ly,** *adv.*

hy″po-der′mic, 1 hai″po-[*or* hip″o-]dŭr′mik; 2 hī″po-[*or* hyp″o-]dēr′mie, *a.* Introduced or found under the skin.

hy-pot′e-nuse, 1 hai-pot′i-niūs; 2 hī-pŏt′e-nūs, *n.* The side of a right-angled triangle opposite the right angle.

hy-poth′e-cate, 1 hai-pŏth′i-kēt; 2 hī-pŏth′e-cāt, *vt.* [-CAT′EDᵈ; -CAT′ING.] To give (personal property) in pledge as security for debt.— **hy-poth″e-ca′tion,** *n.*

hy-poth′e-nuse, *n.* Same as HYPOTENUSE.

hy-poth′e-sis, 1 hai-pŏth′i-sis; 2 hī-pŏth′e-sĭs, *n.* [-SES, 1 -sīz; 2 -sĕs, *pl.*] A supposition assumed as a basis of reasoning or experiment; a guess or conjecture.— **hy″po-thet′ic, hy″po-thet′i-cal,** *a.* Having the nature of or based on hypothesis; conjectural.— **hy″po-thet′i-cal-ly,** *adv.*

hys′sop, 1 his′əp; 2 hys′op, *n.* A bushy medicinal herb of the mint family.

hys-te′ri-a, 1 his-tī′ri-ə; 2 hys-tē′ri-a, *n.* A nervous affection occurring typically in paroxysms of laughing and crying alternately. **hys-ter′ics‡.— hys-ter′i-cal,** *a.* Pertaining to or like hysterics; fitfully emotional. **-ly,** *adv.*

I

I, i, 1 ai; 2 ī, *n.* [IES, I's, *I*s, 1 aiz; 2 īṣ, *pl.*] The ninth letter in the English alphabet; as a Roman numeral, one.

I, *pron.* The nominative case singular of the personal pronoun of the first person.

I-am'bus, 1 ai-am'bus; 2 ĭ-ăm'bŭs, *n.* [-BI, 1 -bai; 2 -bī, *pl.*] A foot consisting of a short followed by a long syllable. —**I-am'bĭc,** *a.*

-ian, *suffix.* See -AN.

I'bex, 1 ai'beks; 2 ī-bĕks, *n.* One of various wild goats, especially the Alpine.

I'bis, 1 ai'bis; 2 ī'bis, *n.* A wading bird, with cylindrical bill bent downward.

Ibex. 1/36

-ible, A suffix of adjectives: the equivalent of -ABLE; as, ed*ible*, from the Latin *ede-re,* = *eat-able.*

-ic, *suffix.* Used as an adjective termination with general sense of "of," "pertaining to," or "like," as in artist*ic.* **-ical‡.**

ice, 1 ais; 2 īç. **I.** *vt. & vi.* [ICED⁺; IC'ING.] **1.** To freeze or chill. **2.** To frost, as cake. **II.** *n.* **1.** Congealed or frozen water. **2.** Ice-cream, frosting, or icing.—**ice'berg",** *n.* A thick mass of ice found floating in the sea.—**ice'-boat",** *n.* A framework with skate-like runners and sails for sailing over ice.—**ice'-cream,** *n.* Cream, milk, or custard sweetened, flavored, and frozen.—**ice-house,** *n.* A building for storing ice.—**ic'ing,** 1 ais'iŋ; 2 īç'ing, *n.* A frosting, as for cake.

-ice, *suffix.* Same as -ISE.

ich-neu'mon, 1 ik-njū'mən; 2 ĭe-nū'mon, *n.* A carnivore, of somewhat weasellike aspect.

ich"thy-ol'o-gy, 1 ik"fhi-ɵl'o-ji; 2 ĭe"thy-ŏl'o-ġy, *n.* The branch of zoology that treats of fishes.—**ich"thy-o-log'I-cal,** *a.*—**ich"thy-ol'o-gist,** *n.*

i'ci-cle, } 1 ai'si-kl; 2 ī'çi-cl, *n.* A pendent **i'ci-cl²,** } mass of ice formed by the freezing of dripping water.

ic'i-ly, ic'i-ness, etc. See ICY.

i-con'o-clast, 1 ai-kɵn'o-klast; 2 ĭ-cŏn'o-

clăst, *n.* A breaker of images, or assailant of traditional beliefs.

ic'y, 1 ais'i; 2 īç'y, *a.* [IC'I-ER; IC'I-EST.] Pertaining to ice; frigid; chilling.—**ic'I-ly,** *adv.*—**ic'I-ness,** *n.*

i-de'a, 1 ai'dī'ə; 2 ĭ-dē'a, *n.* A mental image; conception; notion; plan; supposition; impression.—**i-de'al.** **I.** *a.* Pertaining to ideas; existing only in idea; reaching the highest conception. **II.** *n.* **1.** A model; type; highest conceivable state. **2.** Something imaginary. **-ly,** *adv.*—**i-de'al-ism,** *n.* **1.** The doctrine that ideas are the only objects immediately known. **2.** The quest of ideal perfection.—**i"de-al'I-ty,** *n.* [-TIES², *pl.*] **1.** The condition or character of being ideal. **2.** The power or tendency to form ideals.—**i-de'al-ize, i-de'al-ise,** *vt. & vi.* [-IZED²; -IZ"ING.] To render ideal; form ideals. —**i-de'al-ist,** *n.*—**i-de"al-is'tic,** *a.*—**i-de"al-i-za'tion** *or* **-sa'tion,** *n.*

i-den'ti-cal, 1 ai-den'ti-kəl; 2 ĭ-dĕn'ti-cal, *a.* **1.** Absolutely the same. **2.** Uniform. **-ly,** *adv.* **-ness,** *n.*

i-den'ti-fy, 1 ai-den'ti-fai; 2 ĭ-dĕn'ti-fȳ, *vt.* [-FIED²; -FY"ING.] **1.** To assert or prove to be the same. **2.** To unite (*with*).—**i-den"ti-fi-ca'tion,** *n.*

i-den'ti-ty, 1 ai-den'ti-ti; 2 ĭ-dĕn'ti-ty, *n.* [-TIES², *pl.*] **1.** The state of being identical. **2.** Distinctive personal character.

ides, 1 aidz; 2 īdṣ, *n. pl. Rom. Antiq.* The 15th of March, May, July, and October, and the 13th of the other months.

id'i-o-cy, 1 id'i-o-si; 2 ĭd'i-o-çy, *n.* The condition of being an idiot.

id'i-om, 1 id'i-əm; 2 ĭd'i-om, *n.* **1.** A use of words peculiar to any language. **2.** A peculiar speech or dialect.—**id"i-om-at'ic,** *a.* Marked by the distinctive idiom of a language. **id"i-om-at'i-cal‡.**

id"i-o-syn'cra-sy, 1 id"i-o-sin'krə-si; 2 ĭd'i-o-sȳn'cra-sy, *n.* [-SIES², *pl.*] A constitutional peculiarity.

id'i-ot, 1 id'i-ət; 2 ĭd'i-ot, *n.* One devoid of common sense; an imbecile.—**id"i-ot'Ic,** *a.* Like an idiot.—**id"i-ot'I-cal-ly,** *adv.*

i'dle, 1 ai'dl; 2 ī'dl. **I.** *vt. & vi.* [I'DLED; I'DLING.] To spend in idleness; waste time idly. **II.** *a.* [I'DLER; I'DLEST.] **1.** Not occupied. **2.** Averse to labor; lazy. **3.** Vain; useless. **-ness,** *n.*—**i'dler,** *n.* One who idles.—**i'dly,** *adv.*

i'dol, 1 ai'dəl; 2 ī'dol, *n.* **1.** The image of a heathen god. **2.** Any object of passionate devotion.—**i-dol'a-ter,** *n.* An adorer of

images.— **i-dol'a-tress,** *n. fem.*— **i-dol'a-trous,** *a.* **1.** Pertaining to idolatry. **2.** Extravagant in admiration.— **i-dol'a-try,** *n.* [-TRIES², *pl.*] **1.** The worship of idols. **2.** Idolatrous admiration.— **i'dol-ize,** *vt.* [-IZED; -IZ'ING.] To regard with admiration; worship idolatrously. **i'dol-ise‡.** [**i'dyll‡.**]

i'dyl, 1 ai'dil; 2 i'dýl, *n.* A short poem. **-ler,** *suffix.* See -EER, -ER.

if, 1 if; 2 ĭf, *conj.* **1.** On the supposition that; allowing that. **2.** Altho; because. **3.** Whenever. **4.** Whether.

ig'ne-ous, 1 ig'nɪ-ŭs; 2 ĭg'ne-ŭs, *a.* Pertaining to or formed by means of fire.

ig'nis fat'u-us, 1 ig'nis fat'yu-ŭs; 2 ĭg'nĭs făt'yu-ŭs. [IG'NES FAT'U-I, 1 ig'nīz fat'yu-ai; 2 ĭg'nēg făt'yu-ī, *pl.*] A phosphorescent light seen over marshy places at night; lit., "fools' fire": a Latin phrase.

ig-nite', 1 ig-naɪt'; 2 ĭg-nīt', *v.* [IG-NIT'ED^d; IG-NIT'ING.] **I.** *t.* To kindle; make luminous. **II.** *i.* To take fire; glow with heat.— **ig-ni'tion,** 1 ig-nish'ən; 2 ĭg-nĭsh'on, *n.* The act of igniting.

ig-no'ble, 1 ig-no'bl; *a.* **1.** **ig-no'bl²,** Unworthy, or degraded in character. **2.** Low-born. **3.** Of inferior kind.— **ig-no'bly,** *adv.*

ig'no-min-y, 1 ig'no-min-ɪ; 2 ĭg'no-mĭn-y, *n.* [-IES², *pl.*] Public disgrace, or that which causes it.— **ig''no-min'i-ous,** *a.* Entailing ignominy; disgraceful. **-ly,** *adv.* **-ness,** *n.*

ig''no-ra'mus, 1 ig''no-rē'mus; 2 ĭg''no-rā'mŭs, *n.* An ignorant pretender to knowledge.

ig'no-rance, 1 ig'no-rəns; 2 ĭg'no-ranç, *n.* The state of being ignorant; lack of knowledge.— **ig'no-rant,** *a.* **1.** Destitute of education or knowledge. **2.** Unacquainted. — **ig'no-rant-ly,** *adv.*

ig-nore', 1 ig-nōr'; 2 ĭg-nōr', *vt.* [IG-NORED'; IG-NOR'ING.] To pass without notice.

i-gua'na, 1 i-gwɑ'nə; 2 ĭ-gwä'na, *n.* A large lizard of tropical America.

il-¹, il-², *prefixes.* Forms of IN-¹, IN-², before *l.*

ilk¹, 1 ilk; 2 ĭlk, *a. & n.* [Scot. or Archaic.] Same.— **of that ilk,** of an estate of the same name.

the Common Iguana. 1/60

ilk², *a.* [Scot. or Archaic.] Each; every. **ilk'a‡.**

ill, 1 il; 2 ĭl. **I.** *a.* **1.** Disordered **il²,** physically; sick. **2.** Baneful; harmful; inferior. **II.** *n.* Anything bad; injury; harm; misfortune. **III.** *adv.* **1.** Not well; badly; poorly. **2.** With difficul-

ty; hardly.— **ill'=bred'',** *a.* Badly taught reared, or trained.— **ill=breeding,** *a.*— **ill fame,** immoral repute.— **ill=favored,** *a.* Repulsive; ugly.— **ill nature,** peevishness; surliness; sullenness.— **ill=natured,** *a.* Indicating surliness; cross.— **ill=starred,** *a.* Unfortunate or disastrous.— **ill temper,** irritability; moroseness.— **ill=tempered,** *a.*— **ill will,** enmity; malevolence.

il-le'gal, 1 i-li'gal; 2 ĭ-lē'gal, *a.* Contrary to the law. **-ly,** *adv.*— **il''le-gal'i-ty,** *n.* **il-le'gal-ness‡.**

il-leg'i-ble, 1 i-lej'i-bl; 2 ĭ-lĕg'i-bl, *a.* Not **il-leg'i-bl²,** legible; obscure.— **il-leg''i-bil'i-ty,** *n.* **il-leg'i-bl(e-ness²‡.**— **il-leg'i-bly,** *adv.*

il''le-git'i-mate, 1 il''ɪ-jit'ɪ-mɪt; 2 ĭl''e-gĭt'i-mat, *a.* Contrary to law; born out of wedlock; illogical. **-ly,** *adv.*— **il''le-git'i-ma-cy,** *n.*

il-lib'er-al, 1 i-lib'ər-al; 2 ĭ-lĭb'er-al, *a.* Not liberal; parsimonious; narrow-minded.— **il-lib''er-al'i-ty,** *n.*— **il-lib'er-al-ly,** *adv.* **-ly,** *adv.*

il-lic'it, 1 i-lis'it; 2 ĭ-lĭç'it, *a.* Unlawful.

il-lim'it-a-ble, 1 i-lim'it-a-bl; 2 ĭ-lĭm'it-**il-lim'it-a-bl²,** a-bl, *a.* That can not be limited.— **il-lim'it-a-bly,** *adv.*

il-lit'er-ate, 1 i-lit'ər-ɪt; 2 ĭ-lĭt'er-at, *a.* Uneducated; uncultured.— **il-lit'er-a-cy,** *n.*

ill'ness, 1 il'nes; 2 ĭl'nĕs, *n.* The state of being ill; an ailment; sickness.

il-log'i-cal, 1 i-loj'i-kəl; 2 ĭ-lŏg'i-kal, *a.* Contrary to the rules of logic or to sound reasoning.

il-lu'mi-nate, 1 i-liū'mɪ-nēt; 2 ĭ-lū'mi-nāt, *v.* [-NAT'ED^d; -NAT'ING.] **I.** *t.* To light up; enlighten; decorate. **II.** *i.* To make a display of lights. **il-lume'‡** [Poet.].— **il-lu''mi-na'tion,** *n.* A lighting up; enlightenment; embellishment.

il-lu'mine, 1 i-liū'mɪn; 2 ĭ-lū'min, *vt.* **il-lu'min²,** [-MINED, MIND²; -MIN-ING.] To make bright; enlighten.

il-lu'sion, 1 i-liū'ʒən; 2 ĭ-lū'zhon, *n.* Any misleading appearance; a false show.— **il-lu'siv(e²,** 1 i-liū'siv; 2 ĭ-lū'sĭv, *a.* Misleading; deceptive. **il-lu'so-ry‡.**— **il-lu'siv(e-ly²,** *adv.*— **il-lu'siv(e-ness²,** *n.*— **il-lu'so-ri-ness,** *n.*

il-lus'trate, 1 i-lus'trēt; 2 ĭ-lŭs'trāt, *vt.* [-TRAT-ED^d; -TRAT-ING.] **1.** To explain by means of figures, examples, etc. **2.** To adorn with pictures, borders, etc.— **il''lus-tra'tion,** *n.* That which illustrates; an example or a picture. **2.** The act or art of illustrating.— **il-lus'tra-tiv(e²,** *a.* **-ly,** *adv.*— **il'lus-tra''tor** or **il'lus-trat''er,** *n.*

il-lus'tri-ous, 1 i-lus'trɪ-ŭs; 2 ĭ-lŭs'tri-ŭs, *a.* **1.** Greatly distinguished.— Conferring luster. **-ly,** *adv.*

1: ə = final; ɪ = habit; aisle; au = out; oil; iū = feud; chin; go; ŋ = sing; chin, this.
2: wolf, dǫ; bōōk, bōōt; full, rule, cūre, bŭt, bûrn; oil, bǒy; ḡo, ǥem; iŋk; thin, this.

im-, 1 ĭm-; 2 ĭm, *prefix.* Euphonic variant of IN- before *b*, *m*, and *p*. (1) In; into; on. (2) Not.

im'age, 1 ĭm'ĭj; 2 ĭm'aĝ. **I.** *vt.* [IM'-AGED; IM'AG-ING.] To form an image of; portray; resemble. **II.** *n.* A visible representation; a statue, picture, idol, etc.; an idea; a figure of speech.— **im'age-ry,** 1 ĭm'ĭj-rĭ; 2 ĭm'aĝ-ry, *n.* [-RIES², *pl.*] The act of forming images; images collectively.

im-ag'ine, 1 ĭm-ăj'ĭn; 2 ĭm-ăĝ'in, *v.*
im-ag'ine, [-IN(E)D²; -IN-ING.] **I.** *t.* To form an image or conception of; conjecture; devise; fancy; suppose. **II.** *i.* To exercise the imagination.— **im-ag'I-na-ble,** *a.* That can be imagined.— **imag'I-na-bly,** *adv.*— **im-ag'I-na-ry,** *a.* Existing only in imagination; unreal.— **im-ag'I-na'tion,** *n.* **1.** The picturing power or act of the mind. **2.** That which is imagined; a fantasm; notion.— **im-ag'I-na-tiv(e²,** *a.* **1.** Creative or constructive. **2.** Characterized by imagination.— **-ly,** *adv.*

i-ma'go, 1 ĭ-mē'go; 2 i-mä'ĝo, *n.* An adult, sexually matured insect; the typical form.

im-bank', etc. Same as EMBANK, etc.

im'be-cile, 1 ĭm'bĭ-sĭl; 2 ĭm'be-çĭl. **I.** *a.* Feeble-minded. **II.** *n.* A person of feeble mind.— **im'be-cil'I-ty,** *n.* [-TIES², *pl.*] Imbecile condition or opinion.

im-bed', *vt.* Same as EMBED.

im-bibe', 1 ĭm-bīb'; 2 ĭm-bīb', *vt.* [IM-BIBED'; IM-BIB'ING.] To drink in; absorb.

im-bit'ter, *v.* Same as EMBITTER.

im-bod'y, im-bo'som, *v.* Same as EMBODY, EMBOSOM.

im'bri-cate, 1 ĭm'brĭ-kēt; 2 ĭm'brĭ-eāt, *a.* Overlapping; having overlapping scales.— **im'bri-cat''ed‡.— im'bri-ca'tion,** *n.*

im-bro'glio, 1 ĭm-brō'lyo; 2 ĭm-brō'lyo, *n.* A troublesome complication; intricate plot.

im-brue', 1 ĭm-brū'; 2 ĭm-brụ', *vt.* [IM-BRUED'; IM-BRU'ING.] To wet or moisten; drench. [To brutalize.

im-brute', 1 ĭm-brūt'; 2 ĭm-brụt', *vt. & vi.*

im-bue', 1 ĭm-bū'; 2 ĭm-bū', *vt.* [IM-BUED'; IM-BU'ING.] To absorb or pervade; tinge; dye.

im'i-tate, 1 ĭm'ĭ-tēt; 2 ĭm'ĭ-tāt, *vt.* [-TAT'-ED⁴; -TAT'ING.] To pattern after; copy; make in imitation.— **im'I-ta-bl(e²,** *a.* That may be imitated.— **im'I-ta'tion,** *n.* **1.** The act of imitating. **2.** Something copied.— **im'-ĭ-ta-tiv(e²,** *a.* **-ly,** *adv.*— **im'I-ta''tor,** *n.*

im-mac'u-late, 1 ĭ-mak'yu-lĭt; 2 ĭ-măe-yu-lat, *a.* Without spot or blemish.— **-ly,** *adv.* **-ness,** *n.*

im'ma-nent, 1 ĭm'a-nent; 2 ĭm'a-něnt, *a.* Indwelling; inherent.— **im'ma-nence, im'-**

ma-nen-cy, *n.* The quality of being immanent.

im''ma-te'ri-al, 1 ĭm''mə-tī'rĭ-əl; 2 ĭm'ma-tē'ri-al, *a.* **1.** Not material; incorporeal. **2.** Unimportant.— **im''ma-te'ri-al'I-ty,** *n.*— **im''ma-te'ri-al-ly,** *adv.*

im''ma-ture', 1 ĭm''mə-tiūr'; 2 ĭm''ma-tūr', *a.* Not mature; undeveloped.— **-ly,** *adv.*— **im''ma-tur'I-ty,** *n.*

im-mea'sur-a-ble, 1 ĭm-mĕzh'ur-ə-bl; 2 ĭm-mĕzh'ur-a-bl, *a.* Indefinitely extensive; measureless.— **-ness,** *n.*— **im-mea'sur-a-bly,** *adv.*

im-me'di-ate, 1 ĭ-mī'dĭ-ĭt; 2 ĭ-mē'di-at, *a.* **1.** Without delay; instant. **2.** Close. **3.** Acting without anything intervening; direct.— **-ly,** *adv.* **-ness,** *n.*

im''me-mo'ri-al, 1 ĭm''mĭ-mō'rĭ-al; 2 ĭm'-me-mō'ri-al, *a.* Reaching back beyond memory.— **-ly,** *adv.*

im-mense', 1 ĭ-mens'; 2 ĭ-mĕns', *a.* Very great; vast; huge.— **-ly,** *adv.* **-ness,** *n.*— **im-men'si-ty,** *n.* [-TIES², *pl.*]

im-merse', 1 ĭ-mūrs'; 2 ĭ-mĕrs', *vt.* [IM-MERSED'ᵗ, IM-MERST'ˢ; IM-MERS'ING.] To dip entirely, as under water; involve deeply; baptize by immersion.— **im-mer'-sion,** *n.* The act of immersing, or the state of being immersed.

im''me-thod'i-cal, 1 ĭm''mĭ-fhŏd'ĭ-kəl; 2 ĭm''me-thŏd'i-eal, *a.* Lacking method; unsystematic.— **-ly,** *adv.* **-ness,** *n.*

im'mi-grate, 1 ĭm'ĭ-grēt; 2 ĭm'i-ĝrāt, *vi.* [-GRAT'ED⁴; -GRAT'ING.] To come into a country; migrate into; opposed to EMI-GRATE.— **im'mi-grant,** *n.* One who immigrates; opposed to EMIGRANT.— **im''mi-gra'tion,** *n.*

im'mi-nent, 1 ĭm'ĭ-nent; 2 ĭm'i-něnt, *a.* Dangerous and close at hand; impending; threatening.— **im'mi-nence,** *n.*— **im'mi-nent-ly,** *adv.*

im-mo'bile, 1 ĭm-mō'bĭl; 2 ĭm-mō'bil, *a.* Unmovable.— **im''mo-bil'I-ty,** *n.* Fixedness.

im-mod'er-ate, 1 ĭm-mŏd'ər-ĭt; 2 ĭm-mŏd'er-at, *a.* Not moderate; excessive; unreasonable.— **-ly,** *adv.* **-ness,** *n.*

im-mod'est, 1 ĭm-mŏd'est; 2 ĭm-mŏd'ĕst, *a.* **1.** Wanting in modesty. **2.** Impudent.— **-ly,** *adv.*— **im-mod'es-ty,** *n.*

im'mo-late, 1 ĭm'o-lēt; 2 ĭm'o-lāt, *vt.* [-LAT'ED⁴; -LAT'ING.] To kill or offer, as in sacrifice.— **im''mo-la'tion,** *n.*

im-mor'al, 1 ĭm-mŏr'al; 2 ĭm-mŏr'al, *a.* Violating the moral law; licentious; wicked.— **-ly,** *adv.*— **im''mo-ral'I-ty,** *n.* [-TIES², *pl.*] **1.** Depravity. **2.** An immoral act.

im-mor'tal, 1 ĭm-mŏr'təl; 2 ĭm-mŏr'tal, *a.* Having endless existence; deathless; imperishable.— **-ly,** *adv.*— **im''mor-tal'I-ty,** *n.*

Exemption from death or oblivion; eternal life.— **im-mor'tal-ize,** vt. [-IZED; -IZ'ING.] To render immortal; invest with unfading honor.

im-mov'a-bl(e[r], 1 im-mūv'ə-bl; 2 ĭm-mǫv'-a-bl, *a.* That can not be moved; unchangeable; apathetic. — **im-mov"a-bil'i-ty,** *n.* **im-mov'a-ble-ness**‡.— **im-mov'a-bly,** *adv.*

im-mu'ni-ty, 1 i-miū'nɪ-tɪ; 2 ĭ-mū'nɪ-ty, *n.* [-TIES², *pl.*] Freedom; exemption; security. — **im-mune'.** **I.** *a.* Exempt, as from disease. **II.** *n.* One who is exempt.— **im-mun'-ize,** 1 -aɪz; 2 -ɪz, *vt.* [-IZED; -IZ-ING.] To make immune.

im-mure', 1 -miūr'; 2 ĭ-mūr', *vt.* [IM-MURED'; IM-MUR'ING.] To shut up within walls.

im-mu'ta-ble, 1 i-miū'tə-bl; 2 ĭ-mū'ta-**im-mu'ta-bl**[p], ∫ bl, *a.* Not mutable; unchangeable.— **im-mu"ta-bil'i-ty,** *n.* **im-mu'ta-bl(e-ness**‡.— **im-mu'ta-bly,** *adv.*

imp, 1 imp; 2 ĭmp, *n.* **1.** An imaginary evil spirit of inferior rank. **2.** [Colloq.] A mischievous person.

im'pact, 1 im'pakt; 2 ĭm'păct, *n.* The act of striking; collision.

im-pair', 1 im-pâr'; 2 ĭm-pâr', *vt.* To diminish in quantity or value.— **im-pair'-ment,** *n.*

im-pale', -ment, etc. Same as EMPALE, etc.

im-pal'pa-ble, 1 im-pal'pə-bl; 2 ĭm-păl'-**im-pal'pa-bl**[p], ∫ pa-bl, *a.* That can not be felt; ground to utmost fineness.— **im-pal'-pa-bly,** *adv.*

im-pan'el, 1 im-pan'el; 2 ĭm-păn'ĕl, *vt.* To enroll, as for jury duty.

im-part'[d], 1 im-pârt'; 2 ĭm-pärt', *vt. & vi.* To share; make known; bestow; give.

im-par'tial, 1 im-pâr'shal; 2 ĭm-pär'shal, *a.* Not partial; unbiased. **-ly,** *adv.*— **im-par"ti-al'i-ty**‡, *n.*

im-pass'a-ble, 1 im-pas'ə-bl; 2 ĭm-păs'-**im-pass'a-bl**[p], ∫ a-bl, *a.* Not passable.— **im-pass"a-bil'i-ty, im-pass'a-bl(e-ness**‡, *n.*— **im-pass'a-bly,** *adv.*

im-pas'si-ble, 1 im-pas'ɪ-bl; 2 ĭm-păs'ɪ-bl, **im-pas'si-bl**[p], ∫ *a.* Incapable of feeling or suffering; apathetic.

im-pas'sion(e)d[s], 1 im-pash'ənd; 2 ĭm-pǎsh'ond, *a.* Fervent; stirring.

im-pas'sive, 1 im-pas'ɪv; 2 ĭm-pǎs'ɪv, *a.* **im-pas'siv**[s], ∫ Unaffected by suffering; not having or not showing emotion; impassible; apathetic. **-ly,** *adv.* **-ness,** *n.*

im-pa'tient, 1 im-pē'shent; 2 ĭm-pā'shĕnt, *a.* Not patient; intolerant of opposition or delay; passionate; irritable.— **im-pa'-tience,** *n.* Lack of patience; hastiness; irritability.— **im-pa'tient-ly,** *adv.*

im-peach'[t], 1 im-pīch'; 2 ĭm-pēch', *vt.* **1.** To discredit. **2.** To accuse; charge with crime or wrong.— **im-peach'ment,** *n.* **1.** A discrediting. **2.** The act of impeaching, as of a high civil officer.

im-pec'ca-ble, 1 im-pek'ə-bl; 2 ĭm-pĕe'-**im-pec'ca-bl**[p], ∫ a-bl, *a.* Not capable of sin or error.— **im-pec"ca-bil'i-ty,** *n.*

im"pe-cu'ni-ous, 1 im'pɪ-kiū'nɪ-us; 2 ĭm'-pe-eū'nɪ-ŭs, *a.* Having no money; habitually poor. **-ly,** *adv.*— **im"pe-cu"ni-os'-i-ty,** *n.* Want of money; poverty.

im-pede'[d], 1 im-pīd'; 2 ĭm-pēd', *vt.* [IM-PED'ED; IM-PED'ING.] To be an obstacle to; hinder; obstruct.— **im-ped'i-ment,** *n.* A hindrance; obstruction.

im-pel', 1 im-pel'; 2 ĭm-pĕl', *vt.* [IM-PELLED', IM-PELD'[s]; IM-PEL'LING.] To drive or urge forward.

im-pend'[d], 1 im-pend'; 2 ĭm-pĕnd', *vi.* To be imminent; threaten.— **im-pen'dence,** *n.* **im-pen'den-cy**‡.

im-pen'e-tra-ble, 1 im-pen'ɪ-trə-bl; 2 ĭm-**im-pen'e-tra-bl**[p], ∫ pĕn'e-tra-bl, *a.* Not penetrable; possessing impenetrability.— **im-pen"e-tra-bil'i-ty,** *n.* The quality of being impenetrable; that attribute of matter which prevents two bodies from occupying the same space at the same time.— **im-pen'-e-tra-bly,** *adv.*

im-pen'i-tent, 1 im-pen'ɪ-tent; 2 ĭm-pĕn'ɪ-tĕnt, *a.* Not penitent; hardened; obdurate. **-ly,** *adv.*— **im-pen'i-tence,** *n.* **im-pen'i-ten-cy**‡.

im-per'a-tive, 1 im-per'ə-tɪv; 2 ĭm-pĕr'a-**im-per'a-tiv**[s], ∫ tɪv, **I.** *a.* Commanding; authoritative; peremptory; obligatory. **II.** *n.* **1.** That which is imperative. **2.** *Gram.* That mode of the verb which expresses command. **-ly,** *adv.* **-ness,** *n.*

im"per-cep'ti-bl(e[r], 1 im'pər-sep'tɪ-bl; 2 ĭm'per-çĕp'tɪ-bl, *a.* That can not be perceived; inappreciable. **-ness,** *n.*— **im"per-cep"ti-bil'i-ty,** *n.*— **im"per-cep'ti-bly,** *adv.*

im-per'fect, 1 im-pûr'fekt; 2 ĭm-pẽr'fĕct. **I.** *a.* **1.** Not perfect; incomplete; defective. **2.** *Gram.* Indicating past action. **II.** *n.* The imperfect tense. **-ly,** *adv.* **-ness,** *n.*— **im"per-fec'tion,** *n.* **1.** Lack of perfection. **2.** A defect.

im-pe'ri-al, 1 im-pī'rɪ-əl; 2 ĭm-pē'rɪ-al. **I.** *a.* **1.** Pertaining to an empire, an emperor, or an empress. **2.** Commanding; superior. **II.** *n.* A tuft of hair just under the lower lip.— **im-pe'ri-al-ism,** *n.* Imperial state; the system of imperial government.— **im-pe'ri-al-ist,** *n.*— **im-pe'ri-al-ly,** *adv.* [endanger.

im-per'il, 1 im-per'ɪl; 2 ĭm-pĕr'ɪl, *vt.* To

im-pe'ri-ous, 1 im-pī'rɪ-us; 2 ĭm-pē'rɪ-ŭs,

1: ə = final; ɪ = habit; aɪsle; aʊ = out; oɪl; iū = feud; ᴄhin; go; ŋ = sing; ᴛhin, this.
2: wolf, dǫ; bꝋok, bꝋot; fṳll, rṳle, cūre, bŭt, bûrn; ȯil. bȯy; ḡo, ḡem; iŋk; thin, this.

a. Domineering; urgent; imperative. **-ly,**
adv. **-ness,** *n.*

im-per'ish-a-ble, ⎱ 1 im-pẽr'ĭsh-a-bl; 2 ĭm-
im-per'ish-a-blᴇ, ⎰ pẽr'ĭsh-a-bl, *a.* Not
perishable; indestructible.— **im-per''ish-a-
bĭl'ĭ-ty,** *n.*— **im-per'ish-a-bly,** *adv.*

im-per'me-a-ble, ⎱ 1 im-pẽr'mĭ-a-bl; 2 ĭm-
im-per'me-a-blᴇ, ⎰ pẽr'me-a-bl, *a.* Not
permeable; impervious.— **im-per''me-a-
bĭl'ĭ-ty, im-per'me-a-bl**(e-ness)ᴾ, *n.*— **im-
per'me-a-bly,** *adv.*

im-per'son-al, 1 im-pẽr'sən-al; 2 ĭm-pẽr'-
son-al, *a.* **1.** Not having personality.
2. Not relating to a particular person or
thing. **-ly,** *adv.*— **im-per''son-al'ĭ-ty,** *n.*

im-per'son-ate, 1 im-pẽr'sən-ēt; 2 ĭm-
pẽr'son-āt, *vt.* [-ᴀᴛ''ᴇᴅᵈ; -ᴀᴛ'ɪɴɢ.] **1.** To
personify. **2.** To personate.— **im-per''son-
a'tion,** *n.*

im-per'ti-nent, 1 im-pẽr'tɪ-nent; 2 ĭm-
pẽr'ti-nĕnt, *a.* **1.** Offending propriety;
impudent. **2.** Irrelevant. **-ly,** *adv.*— **im-
per'ti-nence,** *n.*

im''per-turb'a-bl(eᴾ, 1 im''pẽr-tûrb'a-bl; 2
ĭm''per-tûrb'a-bl, *a.* Incapable of being
agitated.— **im''per-turb''a-bĭl'ĭ-ty,** *n.*

im-per'vi-ous, 1 im-pẽr'vɪ-us; 2 ĭm-pẽr'-
vi-ŭs, *a.* Permitting no passage. **-ly,**
adv. **-ness,** *n.*

im-pet'u-ous, 1 im-pet'yᵼ-[*or* -pech'u-]us;
2 ĭm-pĕt'yu-[*or* -pĕch'u-]ŭs, *a.* Full of
energy and dash; vehement; eager; headlong.— **im-pet''u-os'ĭ-ty,** *n.*— **im-pet'u-ous-
ness,** *n.*— **im-pet'u-ous-ly,** *adv.*

im'pe-tus, 1 im'pɪ-tus; 2 ĭm'pe-tŭs, *n.* The
energy with which anything moves or is
driven.

im-pi'e-ty, 1 im-paɪ'ɪ-tɪ; 2 ĭm-pī'e-ty, *n.* **1.**
Ungodliness; wickedness. **2.** An impi-
ous act.

im-pinge', 1 im-pinj'; 2 ĭm-pĭnġ', *vi.*
[ɪᴍ-ᴘɪɴɢᴇᴅ'; ɪᴍ-ᴘɪɴɢ'ɪɴɢ.] To come into
physical contact with an object.— **im-
pinge'ment,** *n.*

im'pi-ous, 1 im'pɪ-us; 2 ĭm'pi-ŭs, *a.* Ungodly; wicked; irreverent; blasphemous.
— im'pi-ous-ly, *adv.*— **im'pi-ous-ness,** *n.*

im-pla'ca-bl(eᴾ, 1 im-plē'ka-bl; 2 ĭm-plä'-
ca-bl, *a.* That can not be placated; inex-
orable; relentless.— **im-pla''ca-bĭl'ĭ-ty, im-
pla'ca-bl**(e-ness)ᴾ, *n.*— **im-pla'ca-bly,** *adv.*

im-plant'ᵈ, 1 im-plant'; 2 ĭm-plänt', *vt.*
To inculcate.— **im''plan-ta'tion,** *n.*

im-plead'ᵈ, 1 im-plīd'; 2 ĭm-plēd', *vt. & vi.*
To bring a suit at law; sue.— **im-plead'er,** *n.*

im'ple-ment, 1 im'plɪ-ment *or* -mənt; 2
ĭm'ple-ment, *n.* A thing used in work; a
utensil; tool.

im'pli-cate, 1 im'plɪ-kēt; 2 ĭm'pli-eāt, *vt.*
[-ᴄᴀᴛ''ᴇᴅᵈ; -ᴄᴀᴛ'ɪɴɢ.] To involve; in-

fold; entangle.— **im''pli-ca'tion,** *n.* **1.** The
act of implying; deduction; something implied. **2.** An entanglement.

im-plic'it, 1 im-plis'ɪt; 2 ĭm-plĭç'it, *a.* **1.**
Implied. **2.** Unquestioning. **-ly,** *adv.* **-ness,** *n.*

im-plore', 1 im-plōr'; 2 ĭm-plōr', *vt. & vi.*
[ɪᴍ-ᴘʟᴏʀᴇᴅ'; ɪᴍ-ᴘʟᴏʀ'ɪɴɢ.] To call for urgently or piteously; entreat; supplicate.
— im-plor'ing-ly, *adv.*

im-ply', 1 im-plaɪ'; 2 ĭm-plȳ', *vt.* [ɪᴍ-
ᴘʟɪᴇᴅ'; ɪᴍ-ᴘʟʏ'ɪɴɢ.] To involve or intimate (a meaning not expressed); signify; import.

im-pol'i-cy, 1 im-pol'ɪ-sɪ; 2 ĭm-pŏl'i-çy, *n.*
Inexpediency.

im''po-lite', 1 im''po-laɪt'; 2 ĭm''po-līt', *a.*
Lacking in politeness; rude. **-ly,** *adv.*
-ness, *n.*

im-pol'i-tic, 1 im-pol'ɪ-tik; 2 ĭm-pŏl'i-tĭc,
a. **1.** Pursuing unwise measures. **2.** In-
expedient; imprudent.

im-pon'der-a-ble, ⎱ 1 im-pon'dər-a-bl; 2
im-pon'der-a-blᴘ, ⎰ ĭm-pŏn'der-a-bl, *a.*
Without weight.— **im-pon''der-a-bĭl'ĭ-ty,** *n.*

im-port'ᵈ, 1 im-pōrt'; 2 ĭm-pōrt', *v.* **I.** *t.*
1. To bring in from abroad. **2.** To mean;
signify. **3.** To affect seriously; be important to. **II.** *i.* To be of importance.—
im-port'a-bl(eᴾ, *n.*— **im''por-ta'tion,** *n.*—
im-port'er, *n.* One who imports.

im'port, 1 im'pōrt; 2 ĭm'pōrt, *n.* **1.**
Meaning. **2.** That which is imported.
3. Importance.

im-por'tant, 1 im-pōr'tənt; 2 ĭm-pōr'tant,
a. Of great import, consequence, or
value. **-ly,** *adv.*— **im-por'tance,** *n.* The
quality of being important.

im''por-tune', 1 im''por-tiūn'; 2 ĭm''pŏr-
tūn', *vt. & vi.* [-ᴛᴜɴᴇᴅ'; -ᴛᴜɴ'ɪɴɢ.] To
urge incessantly.— **im-por'tu-nate,** *a.* Urgent; insistent; pertinacious. **-ly,** *adv.*—
im''por-tu'ni-ty, *n.* [-ᴛɪᴇꜱ², *pl.*]

im-pose', 1 im-pōz'; 2 ĭm-pōġ', *v.* [ɪᴍ-
ᴘᴏꜱᴇᴅ'; ɪᴍ-ᴘᴏꜱ'ɪɴɢ.] **I.** *t.* To levy or
exact; lay or inflict, as a burden or
trouble; palm off; followed by *in* or *upon*.
II. *i.* To place a burden or inflict a deception (upon); take unfair advantage.
— im-pos'a-bl(eᴾ, *a.*— **im-pos'ing,** *pa.* Impressive.— **im-pos'ing-ly,** *adv.*

im''po-si'tion, 1 im''po-zish'ən; 2 ĭm''po-
ġĭsh'on, *n.* The act of imposing; an
imposture; a tax or burden.

im-pos'si-ble, ⎱ 1 im-pos'ɪ-bl; 2 ĭm-pŏs'i-
im-pos'si-blᴘ, ⎰ bl, *a.* Not possible; impracticable; hopelessly objectionable.— **im-
pos''si-bĭl'ĭ-ty,** *n.*— **im-pos'si-bly,** *adv.*

im'post, 1 im'pōst; 2 ĭm'pōst, *n.* That
which is imposed as a customs duty.

im-pos'tor, 1 im-pos'tər *or* -tor; 2 ĭm-

pŏs'tor, *n.* A pretender; deceiver.— **Im-pos'ture,** *n.* Deception by false pretenses.

im'po-tent, 1 im′po-tent: 2 ĭm′po-tĕnt, *a.* Powerless. **-ly,** *adv.* — **im'po-tence,** *n.* Powerlessness. **im'po-ten-cy‡.**

im-pound′d, 1 im-paund'; 2 ĭm-pound', *vt.* To shut up, as in a pound.

im-pov'er-ish⁴, 1 im-pŏv′ẽr-ĭsh; 2 ĭm-pŏv′ẽr-ĭsh, *vt.* To make poor; deteriorate. — **im-pov'er-ish-ment,** *n.*

im-prac'ti-ca-ble, } 1 im-prak′tĭ-kə-bl; 2 ĭm- **im-prac'ti-ca-bl⁵,** } ĭm-prăc′tĭ-ca-bl, *a.* That can not reasonably or profitably be done; not feasible; intractable. — **im-prac″-ti-ca-bil'i-ty, im-prac′ti-ca-bl(e-ness)**⁵, *n.* — **im-prac'ti-ca-bly,** *adv.* [cal.

im-prac'ti-cal⁵, *a.* Not practical; unpractical.

im′pre-cate, 1 im′prĭ-kēt; 2 ĭm′pre-cāt, *vt.* [-CAT′ED⁴; -CAT′ING.] To invoke or call down, as a judgment. — **im″pre-ca'tion,** *n.*

im-preg'na-ble, } 1 im-preg′nə-bl; 2 ĭm- **im-preg'na-bl⁵,** } prĕg′na-bl, *a.* Proof against attack; unconquerable. — **im-preg″-na-bil'i-ty,** *n.*— **im-preg'na-bly,** *adv.*

im-preg'nate, 1 im-preg′nēt; 2 ĭm-prĕg′nāt, *vt.* [-NAT′ED⁴; -NAT′ING.] **1.** To make pregnant. **2.** To saturate; imbue. — **im″preg-na'tion,** *n.*

im″pre-sa'ri-o, 1 im″prĭ-sē′rĭ-ŏ; 2 ĭm″pre-sä′rĭ-ō, *n.* One who manages, conducts, or is responsible for an opera company or public musical performance.

im-press', 1 im-pres′; 2 ĭm-prĕs′. **I⁴.** *vt.* To form or fix by pressure; mark by pressure; indent. **II.** 1 im′pres; 2 ĭm′prĕs, *n.* A mark or indentation produced by pressure; effect; stamp.

im-press′²ᵗ, *vt.* To force into public service; seize for public use; conscript. — **im-press'ment,** *n.* The act of impressing, as soldiers or sailors, into the public service, or of seizing property for public use.

im-press'i-ble, } 1 im-pres′ĭ-bl; 2 ĭm-prĕs′- **im-press'i-bl⁵,** } ĭ-bl, *a.* Capable of being impressed. — **im-press″i-bil'i-ty,** *n.* — **im-press'i-bly,** *adv.*

im-pres'sion, 1 im-prĕsh′ən; 2 ĭm-prĕsh′on, *n.* **1.** The act of impressing; mark, print, etc., made by pressure; imprint; effect. **2.** A slight remembrance. — **im-pres'sion-a-bl**(e⁵, *a.* Susceptible of impression. — **im-press'iv(e**⁵, *a.* Producing an impression. **-ly,** *adv.* **-ness,** *n.*

im-print', 1 im-print′; 2 ĭm-prĭnt. **I⁴.** *vt.* To print by stamping or pressure; impress on the heart or mind. **II.** 1 im′-print; 2 ĭm′prĭnt, *n.* **1.** Something imprinted; an impression. **2.** A publisher's or printer's name, etc., printed in a book or the like.

im-pris'on, 1 im-priz′n; 2 ĭm-prĭẑ′n, *vt.* To put into prison; confine.— **im-pris'on-ment,** *n.*

im-prob'a-ble, } 1 im-prɒb′ə-bl; 2 ĭm- **im-prob'a-bl⁵,** } prŏb′a-bl, *a.* Not likely to be true or to happen.— **im-prob″a-bil'i-ty,** *n.*— **im-prob'a-bly,** *adv.*

im-promp'tu, 1 im-prɒmp′tiū; 2 ĭm-prŏmp′tū. **I.** *a.* & *adv.* Extempore; offhand. **II.** *n.* An offhand speech or performance.

im-prop'er, 1 im-prɒp′ẽr; 2 ĭm-prŏp′ẽr, *a.* Not proper; unsuitable.— **im-prop'er-ly,** *adv.*— **im″pro-pri'e-ty,** *n.* The state of being improper; anything that is improper.

im-prove', 1 im-prūv′; 2 ĭm-prŏv′, *v.* **I.** *t.* **1.** To make better. **2.** To use to good purpose. **II.** *i.* To make progress. — **im-prove'ment,** *n.* **1.** The act of improving; something that improves, as a change in a machine. **2.** The practical application, as of a sermon.

im-prov'i-dent, 1 im-prɒv′ĭ-dent; 2 ĭm-prŏv′ĭ-dĕnt, *a.* Lacking foresight or thrift; reckless; wasteful. **-ly,** *adv.*— **im-prov'i-dence,** *n.*

im″pro-vise', 1 im″prɒ-vaiz′; 2 ĭm″prɒ-vīz′, *vt.* & *vi.* [-VISED′; -VIS′ING.] To compose, sing, play, etc., offhand.— **im-prov″i-sa'tion,** *n.*

im-pru'dent, 1 im-prū′dent; 2 ĭm-prū′dĕnt, *a.* Not prudent; lacking discretion. **-ly,** *adv.*— **im-pru'dence,** *n.*

im'pu-dent, 1 im′piu-dent; 2 ĭm′pū-dĕnt, *a.* **1.** Offensively bold. **2.** Immodest; shameless.— **im'pu-dence,** *n.* Effrontery; shamelessness.— **im'pu-dent-ly,** *adv.*

im-pugn', 1 im-piūn′; 2 ĭm-pūn′, *vt.* To call in question; gainsay.

im'pulse, 1 im′puls; 2 ĭm′pŭls, *n.* **1.** An impetus. **2.** A sudden or transient feeling; impelling force.— **im-pul'sion,** *n.*— **im-pul'siv(e**⁵, *a.* **1.** Actuated by impulse. **2.** Having the power of impelling.

im-pu'ni-ty, 1 im-piū′ni-tĭ; 2 ĭm-pū′ni-ty. *n.* [-TIES²ᵍ, *pl.*] Freedom from punishment or injury.

im-pure', 1 im-piūr′; 2 ĭm-pūr′, *a.* **1.** Containing some foreign substance; adulterated. **2.** Unchaste. **3.** Unhallowed. **-ly,** *adv.* **-ness,** *n.*— **im-pu'ri-ty,** *n.*

im-pute', 1 im-piūt′; 2 ĭm-pūt′, *vt.* [IM-PUT′ED⁴; IM-PUT′ING.] To set to the account of a person; charge.— **im″pu-ta'tion,** *n.* The act of imputing; a censure or reproach.

in, 1 in; 2 ĭn. **I.** *n.* A nook or corner; one who or that which is in, as in office. **II.** *adv.* **1.** Enclosed in a place or state. **2.** Into a place or state. **3.** Close by.

---

4. Within. III. *prep.* Denoting the object; surrounded by; among; toward; by means of.

in-¹, *prefix.* In; into; on; as, *in*flame.

in-², *prefix.* Not; without; un-.

The following is a list of unimportant or self-defining words with this prefix. I all cases, *in-* as here used has the meaning of "want or lack of," "freedom from," "not," simply reversing the meaning of the main portion of the word (as *in*decorum, la k of decorum; *in*devout, not devout).

in″a-bil′i-ty
in″ac-ces″si-bil′i-ty
in″ac-ces″si-bl(e, -ness)ᴾ
in-ac′cu-ra-cy
in-ac′cu-rate, -ly
in-ad′e-qua-cy
in-ad′e-quate, -ly
in″ad-mis″si-bl(eᴾ,-bly
in-an′i-mate
in-ap′pli-ca-bl(eᴾ,-bly
in″ap-pre′ci-a-bl(e, -bly
in″ap-pro′pri-ate, -ly, -ness
in-apt′, -ly, -ness
in-apt′i-tude
in-ar-tic′u-late, -ly, -ness
in-at-ten′tion
in-at-ten′tiv(eˢ, -ly, -ness
in-au′di-bl(eᴾ, -bly
in″aus-pi′cious, -ly, -ness
in-ca′pa-bil′i-ty
in-ca′pa-bl(eᴾ, -bly
in-cau′tious, -ly, -ness
in″ci-vil′i-ty (cp. UN-CIVIL)
in″com-bus′ti-bl(eᴾ, -ness
in″com-men′su-ra-bl(eᴾ
in″com-men′su-rate
in-com-mu′ni-ca-bl(eᴾ
in″com-mu′ni-ca-tiv(eˢ
in″com-pat″i-bil′i-ty
in″com-pat′i-bl(eᴾ, -bly
in-com′pe-tence, -ten-cy
in-com′pe-tent, -ly
in-com-plete′, -ly, -ness
in-com″pre-hen″si-bl(eᴾ, -ness, -bly
in″com-pre-hen″si-bl(eᴾ
in-con-ceiv′a-bl(eᴾ, -ness, -bly
in″con-clu′siv(eˢ, -ly

in″con-sid′er-a-bl(eᴾ, -ness, -bly
in″con-sid′er-ate, -ly, -ness
in″con-sis′ten-cy
in″con-sis′tent, -ly
in-con-sol′a-bl(eᴾ, -ness, -bly
in″con-spic′u-ous, -ly
in-con′stan-cy
in-con′stant, -ly
in-con-test′a-bl(eᴾ, -bly
in-con″tro-vert′i-bil′i-ty
in-con″tro-vert′i-bl(eᴾ, -ness, -bly
in″con-ve′nience
in″con-ve′nient, -ly
in″cor-po′re-al, -ly
in″cor-rect′, -ly, -ness
in″cor-rupt″i-bil′i-ty
in″cor-rupt′i-bl(eᴾ, -ness, -bly
in″cor-rup′tion
in-cred″i-bil′i-ty
in-cred′i-bl(eᴾ, -ness, -bly
in-cur′a-bl(eᴾ, -ness, -bly
in-de′cen-cy
in-de′cent, -ly
in″de-clin′a-bl(eᴾ, -bly
in″de-co′rous, -ly, -bly
in″de-co′rum
in″de-fen″si-bl(eᴾ, -ness, -bly
in-def′i-ca-cy
in-del′i-cate, -ly
in″de-mon′stra-bl(eᴾ, -bly
in″de-scrib′a-bl(eᴾ, -bly
in″de-struc′ti-bl(eᴾ, -bly
in-dis-creet′, -ly
in-dis-cre′tion
in″dis-pen′sa-bl(eᴾ, -ness
in-dis-tinct′, -ly, -ness

in″di-vis″i-bl(eᴾ, -ness
in″di-vis′i-bly
in″ef-face′a-bl(eᴾ, -ness
in″ef-face′a-bly
in″ef-fect′iv(eˢ, -ly, -ness
in″ef-fec′tu-al, -ly
in-ef′fi-ca′cious, -ly, -ness
in-ef′fi-ca-cy
in-ef-fi′cien-cy
in″ef-fi′cient, -ly
in-el′e-gance
in-el′e-gant, -ly
in-el′i-gi-bil′i-ty
in-el′i-gi-bl(eᴾ
in-e′qual′i-ty
in″e-rad′i-ca-bl(eᴾ, -bly
in″ex-cus′a-bl(eᴾ, -bly
in″ex-haust′i-bl(eᴾ
in″ex-pe′di-ence, -en-cy
in″ex-pe′di-ent
in″ex-pen′siv(eˢ, -ly, -ness
in″ex-pe′ri-ence, in″-ex-pe′ri-enced
in-ex′pli-ca-bl(eᴾ, -bly
in″ex-plic′it, -ly, -ness
in″ex-press″i-bl(eᴾ, -bly
in″ex-press′iv(eˢ, -ly, -ness
in″ex-tin′guish-a-bl(eᴾ, -ness, -bly
in-fer′til(eˢ, -til′i-ty
in-fre′quence, -quen-cy
in-fre′quent, -ly
in-fus″i-bl(eᴾ

in″har-mo′ni-ous, -ly, -ness
in-hu′man, -ly
in″hu-man′i-ty
in-im′i-ta-bl(eᴾ, -bly
in″ju-di′cious
in″nu-tri′tion
in-nu-tri′tious
in″ob-ser′vance, -vant
in-o′dor-ous
in″of-fen′siv(eˢ, -ly, -ness
in-op′er-a-tiv(eˢ
in-op″por-tune′, -ly,
in-se-cure′, -ly, -ness
in-sep″a-ra-bil′i-ty
in-sep′a-ra-bl(eᴾ, -bly
in-sep′a-ra-bly
in″sin-cere′, -ly
in″sin-cer′i-ty
in-sol″u-bil′i-ty
in-sol′u-bl(eᴾ, -ness
in″sub-or′di-nate, -ly
in″sub-or′di-na′tion
in-suf-fi′cience, -cien-cy
in″suf-fi′cient, -ly
in″sup-port′a-bl(eᴾ, -ness
in″sup-port′a-bly
in″sur-mount′a-bl(eᴾ
in-tan′gi-bl(eᴾ, -ness, -bly
in-tan″gi-bil′i-ty, -bly
in-tan′gi-bly
in-va′ri-a-bl(eᴾ, -bly
in-vul′ner-a-bl(eᴾ, -bly
in-vul′ner-a-bl(e-ness)ᴾ

in″ac′tion, 1 in-ak′shən; 2 ĭn-ăe′shon, *n.* The state of being inactive. **in″ac-tiv′i-ty‡. — in-ac′tiv(eˢ,** *a.* Not active; indolent; inert. **-ly,** *adv.*

in″ad-ver′tent, 1 in″ad-vûr′tent; 2 ĭn″ăd-vẽr′tĕnt, *a.* Inconsiderate; thoughtless; heedless. — **in″ad-ver′tence,** *n.* **in″ad-ver′ten-cy‡. — in″ad-ver′tent-ly,** *adv.*

in-a′lien-a-ble, ┐ 1 in-ēl′yen-ə-bl; 2 ĭn-āl′
in-a′lien-a-blᴾ, ┘ yĕn-a-bl, *a.* Not transferable; that can not be rightfully taken away. — **in-a′lien-a-bly,** *adv.*

in-ane′, 1 in-ēn′; 2 ĭn-ān′, *a.* Empty; silly. — **in-an′i-ty,** 1 in-an′i-tı; 2 ĭn-ăn′i-ty, *n.* [-TIES², *pl.*] The condition of being inane or empty; inanition; lack of sense.

in″a-ni′tion, 1 in″ə-nish′ən; 2 ĭn″a-nĭsh′on, *n.* Exhaustion from want of nourishment.

in″as-much′, 1 in″az-muᴜ′ch′; 2 ″ăş-muᴜch′,

adv. Considering the fact; seeing that; in so far.

in-au'gu-rate, 1 in-ô'giu-rēt; 2 ĭn-a'gūrāt, *vt.* [-RAT^dED^d; -RAT'ING.] To introduce into office; begin; originate.— **in-au'-gu-ral,** 1 in-ô'giu-rəl; 2 ĭn-a'gū-ral. **I.** *a.* Pertaining to an inauguration. **II.** *n.* An inaugural address.— **in-au'gu-ra'tion,** *n.* The ceremony of inaugurating.— **in-au'gu-ra"tor,** *n.*— **in-au'gu-ra-to-ry,** *a.*

in'born", 1 in'bôrn"; 2 ĭn'bôrn", *a.* Implanted by nature; innate.

in'bred", 1 in'bred"; 2 ĭn'brĕd", *a.* **1.** Bred within; innate. **2.** Bred from closely related parents.— **in-breed'ing,** *n.*

in'ca, 1 iŋ'kə; 2 ĭŋ'ca, *n.* [I- *or* i-] A member or chief of the ancient native Peruvian race.

in-cal'cu-la-ble, 1 in-kal'kiu-lə-bl; 2 ĭn-căl'eū-la-bl, *a.* That can not be calculated or estimated; beyond calculation.— **in - cal" cu - la - bil'i - ty,** *n.* **in-cal'cu-la-bl(e-ness⁺‡.— in-cal'cu-la-bly,** *adv.*

in"can-des'cent, 1 in"kan-des'ent; 2 ĭn"căn-dĕs'ənt, *a.* Made luminous by heat. — **in"can-des'cence,** *n.* **in"can-des'cen-cy,** *n.*

in"can-ta'tion, 1 in"kan-tē'shən; 2 ĭn"căn-tā'shon, *n.* The utterance of supposedly magical words; a charm; spell.

in-ca-pa-bl(e⁺, in-ca'tious. For these and many similar words, see list under IN-².

in"ca-pac'i-tated, 1 in"kə-pas'i-tēt: 2 ĭn"ca-păç'i-tāt, *vt.* To make incapable; disqualify.— **in"ca-pac'i-ty,** *n.* [-TIES², *pl.*] **1.** Lack of capacity; incapability. **2.** Want of competency.

in-car'cer-ate, 1 in-kär'sər-ēt; 2 ĭn-eär'çer-āt, *vt.* [-AT"ED^d; -AT'ING.] To imprison.— **in-car"cer-a'tion,** *n.*

in-car'na-din(e⁺, 1 in-kär'na-din; 2 ĭn-eär'na-dĭn, *vt.* [-DIN(E)D^d; -DIN-ING.] To dye red; redden.

in-car'nate, 1 in-kär'nēt; 2 ĭn-eär'nāt. **I.** *vt.* [-NA-TED^d; -NAT'ING.] To embody; invest with bodily form. **II.** *a.* Invested with flesh or bodily form.— **in"car-na'tion,** *n.* The act of becoming incarnate; the assumption of human nature by Jesus Christ.

in-case'⁺, 1 in-kēs', en-kēs'; 2 ĭn-eās', en-eās'⁺ ĕn-eās', *vt.* To enclose in a case; enclose; surround. **-ment,** *n.*

in-cen'di-a-ry, 1 in-sen'di-ē-ri; 2 ĭn-çĕn'di-ā-ri. **I.** *a.* Pertaining to incendiarism; purposely kindled; inflammatory; seditious. **II.** *n.* [-RIES², *pl.*] One who maliciously sets a building on fire.— **in-cen'di-a-rism,** *n.* An incendiary act.

in-cense'⁺, 1 in-sens'; 2 ĭn-çĕns', *vt.* [IN-CENSED'⁺, IN-CENST'⁸; IN-CENS'ING.] To inflame or incite to anger.

in'cense², 1 in'sens; 2 ĭn'çĕns, *vt. & vi.* [IN-CENSED^t; IN'CENS-ING.] To perfume with incense; burn incense.

in'cense, *n.* An aromatic substance that exhales perfume in burning.

in-cen'tive, 1 in-sen'tiv; 2 ĭn-çĕn'tĭv. **I.** *a.* Encouraging or impelling. **II.** *n.* An incitement.

in-cep'tion, 1 in-sep'shən; 2 ĭn-çĕp'shon, *n.* A beginning.— **in-cep'tiv(e⁸,** *a.* Noting the beginning.

in-cer'ti-tude, 1 in-sûr'ti-tiūd; 2 ĭn-çĕr'ti-tūd, *n.* Uncertainty; obscurity.

in-ces'sant, 1 in-ses'ent; 2 ĭn-çĕs'ant, *a.* Continued or repeated without cessation. — **in-ces'sant-ly,** *adv.*

inch, 1 inch; 2 ĭnch, *n.* A measure, the twelfth part of a foot. [cipient.

in'cho-ate, 1 in'ko-ēt; 2 ĭn'eo-āt, *a.* Incipient.

in'ci-dence, 1 in'si-dens; 2 ĭn'çi-dĕnç, *n.* A falling, or the direction of fall.

in'ci-dent, 1 in'si-dent; 2 ĭn'çi-dĕnt. **I.** *a.* Falling upon; likely to befall or happen; incidental. **II.** *n.* A subordinate event or act; a happening of little importance. — **in"ci-den'tal. I.** *a.* **1.** Occurring in the course of something else; contingent. **2.** Happening without regularity or design; casual; occasional. **II.** *n.* Something incidental. **-ly,** *adv.*

in-cin'er-ate, 1 in-sin'ər-ēt; 2 ĭn-çĭn'er-āt, *vt.* [-AT"ED^d; -AT'ING.] To burn to ashes. — **in-cin"er-a'tion,** *n.* Cremation.

in-cip'i-ent, 1 in-sip'i-ent; 2 ĭn-çĭp'i-ĕnt, *a.* Belonging to the first stages; beginning. — **in-cip'i-ence,** *n.* Inception. **in-cip'i-en-cy‡.**

in-cise', 1 in-saiz'; 2 ĭn-çīẓ', *vt.* [IN-CISED'⁺, IN-CIS'ING.] To cut into; carve in intaglio; engrave.— **in-ci'sion,** 1 in-siʒ'ən; 2 ĭn-çizh'on, *n.* The act of incising; also, a cut; gash. — **in-ci'siv(e⁸,** 1 in-sai'siv; 2 ĭn-çī'sĭv, *a.* **1.** Having the power of incising; cutting; acute. **2.** Pertaining to an incisor.— **in-ci'so-ry‡. in-ci'sor. I.** *a.* Adapted for cutting. **II.** *n.* A front or cutting tooth.

in-cite', 1 in-sait'; 2 ĭn-çīt', *vt.* [IN-CIT"ED^d; IN-CIT'ING.] To impel to a particular action; instigate.— **in-ci'tant,** **I.** *a.* Inciting; instigating. **II.** *n.* An incitement.— **in"ci-ta'tion,** *n.* An incentive; incitement. — **in-cit'a-tiv(e⁸,** *n.*— **in-cite'ment,** *n.* **1.** The act of inciting. **2.** That which incites; an impelling motive.— **in-cit'ing-ly,** *adv.*

in-clem'ent, 1 in-klem'ent; 2 ĭn-elĕm'ĕnt, *a.* Not clement; severe; rigorous, as weather; stormy.— **in-clem'en-cy,** *n.* Severity, as of weather: harshness.

in"cli-na'tion, 1 in"kli-nē'shən; 2 ĭn"eli-

na'shon, *n.* **1.** A deviation from a vertical or horizontal direction; a bend; slope; angle. **2.** A mental bent; predilection.

in-cline', 1 in-klain'; 2 in-clīn', *vt.* & *vi.* [IN-CLINED'; IN-CLIN'ING.] **1.** To bend, stoop, lean, or slope. **2.** To make or be disposed (to). **3.** To bend the head or body; bow.— **in-clin-a-ble(er**, *a.*— **inclined plane,** a plane forming any angle but a right angle with a horizontal plane. [slope.

in-cline', *n.* A gradient;

in-close', etc. Same as ENCLOSE, etc.

ab, base: *bc,* height; *ac,* inclined plane.

Inclined Plane.

in-clude', 1 in-klūd'; 2 in-elụd', *vt.* [IN-CLUD-ED^d; IN-CLUD'ING.] To comprise; enclose; contain.— **in-clu'sion,** *n.* The act of including; that which is included.— **in-clu'siv(es**, *a.* Including the things mentioned; embracing; comprising. **-ly,** *adv.* **-ness,** *n.*

in-cog'ni-to, 1 in-kŏg'ni-to; 2 ĭn-cŏğ'ni-to. **I.** *a.* & *adv.* Unknown; under an assumed name. **II.** *n.* The taking of a fictitious name; the name assumed.

in"co-her'ent, 1 in"ko-hir'ent; 2 ĭn"co-hēr'ĕnt, *a.* Not coherent; incongruous; unconnected; confused. **-ly,** *adv.*— **in"co-her'ence, in"co-her'en-cy,** *n.* Want of cohesion or connection; something incoherent.

in'come, 1 in'kum; 2 ĭn'eŏm, *n.* The amount of money coming in; revenue.

in"com-mode', 1 in"ko-mōd'; 2 ĭn"eŏ-mōd', *vt.* To inconvenience; disturb.— **in"com-mo'di-ous,** *a.* Not commodious or convenient. **-ly,** *adv.* **-ness,** *n.*

in-com'pa-ra-ble,) 1 in-kem'pa-ra-bl; 2
in-com'pa-ra-bl², ∫ ĭn-eŏm'pa-ra-bl, *a.* Not admitting of comparison; peerless. **-ness,** *n.*— **in-com'pa-ra-bly,** *adv.*

in-con'gru-ous, 1 in-kŏŋ'gru-us; 2 ĭn-eŏŋ'ğru-ŭs, *a.* **1.** Not congruous. **2.** Composed of inharmonious elements. **-ly,** *adv.*— **in"con-gru'i-ty,** *n.*

in-con'se-quent, 1 in-kŏn'si-kwent; 2 ĭn-eŏn'se-kwĕnt, *a.* **1.** Contrary to reasonable inference; illogical. **2.** Not in regular sequence.— **in-con'se-quence,** *n.*

in-con'ti-nent, 1 in-kŏn'ti-nent; 2 ĭn-eŏn'ti-nĕnt, *a.* Not continent; unchaste. — **in-con'ti-nence,** *n.* Lack of continence; unchastity.— **in-con'ti-nen-cy,** *n.*— **in-con'ti-nent-ly,** *adv.* **1.** Without due restraint. **2.** Immediately.

in-cor'po-rate, 1 in-kŏr'po-rēt; 2 ĭn-eŏr'po-rāt, *v.* [RAT"ED^d; -RAT'ING.] **I.** *t. i.* **1.** To combine together to form a whole. **2.** To embody. **3.** To form into a legal corporation. **II.** *i.* To become incorporated.

in-cor'po-rate,1 in-kŏr'po-rit; 2 ĭn-eŏr'po-rat, *a.* **1.** Not consisting of matter. **2.** Not formed into a corporation.

in-cor'po-rate², *a.* Incorporated.— **in-cor"po-ra'tion,** *n.* **1.** The act of incorporating. **2.** A corporation. **3.** The combining of elements.

in"cor-po're-al, 1 in"ker-pō'ri-el; 2 ĭn"-eŏr-pō're-al, *a.* Not consisting of matter; immaterial; intangible.

in-cor'ri-gi-ble,) 1 in-ker'ri-ji-bl; 2
in-cor'ri-gi-bl², ∫ eŏr'ri-gi-bl, *a.* That can not be corrected; depraved beyond reform. **-ness,** *n.*— **in-cor'ri-gi-bly,** *adv.*— **in-cor"ri-gi-bil'i-ty,** *n.*

in-crease', 1 in-krīs'; 2 ĭn-erēs'. **I.** *vt.* & *vi.* [IN-CREASED', IN-CREAST'^s; IN-CREAS'ING.] To make or become greater; enlarge; augment; grow; multiply. **II.** 1 in'krīs; 2 ĭn'erēs, *n.* A growing larger or greater; augmentation; increment; produce.— **in-creas'ing-ly,** *adv.*

in-cred'u-lous, 1 in-krej'u-lus; 2 ĭn-erĕj'u-lụs, *a.* **1.** Refusing belief; skeptical. **2.** Characterized by doubt. **-ly,** *adv.* — **in"cre-du'li-ty,** *n.* Indisposition to believe. **in-cred'u-lous-ness‡.**

in'cre-ment, 1 in'kri-ment *or* -mənt; 2 ĭn'ere-ment, *n.* The act of increasing; enlargement; amount of increase.

in-crim'i-nate, 1 in-krim'i-nēt; 2 ĭn-erĭm'i-nāt, *vt.* [-NAT"ED^d; -NAT'ING.] To charge with a crime or fault; criminate.

in-crust'^d, 1 in-krust'; 2 ĭn-erŭst', *vt.* To cover with a crust.— **in"crus-ta'tion,** *n.* The act of incrusting, or the object incrusted; a crust.

in'cu-bate, 1 in'kiu-bēt; 2 ĭn'eū-bāt, *vt.* & *vi.* [-BAT"ED^d; -BAT'ING.] **1.** To sit upon in order to hatch; sit, as on eggs; to hatch by sitting. **2.** To study; plan.— **in"cu-ba'tion,** *n.* The act of incubating; a planning or producing.— **in'cu-ba"tor,** *n.* That which incubates; an apparatus for hatching artificially.

in'cu-bus, 1 in'kiu-bus; 2 ĭn'eū-bŭs, *n.* [-BUS-ES^z *or* -BI, 1 -bai; 2 -bī, *pl.*] Anything oppressive or discouraging; nightmare.

in'cul-cate, 1 in-kul'kēt; 2 ĭn-eŭl'eāt, *vt.* [-CAT"ED^d; -CAT'ING.] To impress upon the mind; teach.— **in"cul-ca'tion,** *n.*

in-cul'pate, 1 in-kul'pēt; 2 ĭn-eŭl'pāt, *vt.* [-PAT"ED^d; -PAT'ING.] To charge with wrong-doing; implicate.— **in"cul-pa'tion,** *n.* — **in-cul'pa-to-ry,** *a.*

in-cum'bent, 1 in-kum'bent; 2 ĭn-eŭm'bĕnt. **I.** *a.* **1.** Required; obligatory. **2.** Resting upon something. **II.** *n.* One who holds an office.— **in-cum'ben-cy,** *n.*

[-CIES^z, pl.] The state or period of holding an office.   [CUMBER, etc.

in-cum′ber, in-cum′brance, etc. See EN-

in-cur′, 1 in-kûr′; 2 ĭn-cûr′, vt. [IN-CURRED′, IN-CURD′^s; IN-CUR′RING.] To bring upon oneself, as an injury.— **in-cur′-sion,** 1 in-kûr′shän; 2 ĭn-cûr′shon, n. A hostile entrance into a territory; raid.— **in-cur′siv(e^s,** a. Disposed to make incursions.

in-curve′, 1 in-kûrv′; 2 ĭn-cûrv′, vt. & vi. To curve, or cause to curve, inward.— **in-cur′vate,** 1 in-kûr′vĕt; 2 ĭn-cûr′văt. **I.** vt. [-VAT-ED^d; -VAT-ING.] To curve; bend. **II.** a. Curved.— **in″cur-va′tion,** n.

in-debt′ed, 1 in-det′ed; 2 ĭn-dĕt′ĕd, pa. **1.** Having contracted a debt. **2.** Owing gratitude; obliged.— **in-debt′ed-ness,** n.

in″de-ci′sion, 1 in″dĭ-siz′on; 2 ĭn″de-çĭzh′on, n. Want of settled purpose or prompt resolution; irresoluteness.— **in″de-ci′sive,** a. **1.** Not definitely deciding; leaving the result unsettled; as, an indecisive battle. **2.** Not able to come to a decision; irresolute.   [in truth.

in-deed′, 1 in-dïd′; 2 ĭn-dēd′, adv. In fact;

in″de-fat′i-ga-ble,) 1 in″dĭ-fat′ĭ-ga-bl; 2
in″de-fat′i-ga-bl^e,) ĭn″de-făt′ĭ-ga-bl, a. Not exhausted by labor; unflagging.— **in″de-fat′i-ga-bly,** adv.

in″de-fea′si-ble,) 1 in″dĭ-fï′zi-bl; 2 ĭn″de-
in″de-fea′si-bl^e,) fē′ȿi-bl, a. That can not be defeated, set aside, or made void.— **in″de-fea′si-bil′i-ty,** n.— **in″de-fea′si-bly,** adv.

in″de-fin′a-ble,) 1 in″dĭ-fain′a-bl; 2 ĭn″-
in″de-fin′a-bl^e,) de-fïn′a-bl, a. That can not be defined or described; evanescent; subtle.— **in″de-fin′a-bly,** adv.

in-def′i-nit(e^s, 1 in-def′i-nit; 2 ĭn-dĕf′i-nĭt, a. Not definite, determinate, or precise. **-ly,** adv. **-ness,** n.

in-del′i-ble,) 1 in-del′ĭ-bl; 2 ĭn-dĕl′ĭ-bl, a.
in-del′i-bl^e,) That can not be blotted out; ineffaceable.— **in-del′i-bil′i-ty,** n. **in-del′-i-bl(e-ness^s‡.— in-del′i-bly,** adv.

in-dem′ni-fy, 1 in-dem′nĭ-fai; 2 ĭn-dĕm′-ni-fī, vt. [-FIED′; -FY′ING.] To compensate for loss or injury.— **in-dem″ni-fi-ca′-tion,** n.— **in-dem′ni-ty,** n.   [-TIES^z, pl.] That which is given as compensation for a loss.

in-dent′^d, 1 in-dent′; 2 ĭn-dĕnt′, vt. **1.** To make dents in. **2.** To indenture. **3.** To set in from the margin, as a line of type.— **in″den-ta′tion,** n. **1.** The act of indenting. **2.** A cut or notch.— **in-den′-tion,** n. A dent. **2.** The indenting of a line in print.— **in-den′ture.** **I.** vt. [-TURED; -TUR-ING.] To bind by contract, as an apprentice. **II.** n. **1.** Law. A contract under seal; the contract binding an apprentice. **2.** The act of indenting.

in″de-pen′dent, 1 in″dĭ-pen′dent; 2 ĭn″-de-pĕn′dĕnt, a. **1.** Not subordinate to nor dependent; free. **2.** Affording independence. **3.** Self-reliant. **4.** Separate.— **in″de-pen′dence,** n. **1.** Freedom from dependence. **2.** A competency. **3.** A spirit of self-reliance.— **in″de-pen′den-cy‡.— in″-de-pen′dent-ly,** adv.

in″de-ter′mi-na-bl(e^r, 1 in″dĭ-tûr′mi-na-bl; 2 ĭn″de-tẽr′mi-na-bl, a. That can not be determined, ascertained, or rendered definite.— **in″de-ter′mi-na-bly,** adv.

in″de-ter′mi-nate, 1 in″dĭ-tûr′mi-nit; 2 ĭn″de-tẽr′mi-nat. a. Not determinate; not precise; not exactly limited in time, as a penal sentence; indefinite. **-ly,** adv. **-ness,** n.— **in″de-ter″mi-na′tion,** n.

in′dex, 1 in′deks; 2 ĭn′dĕks. **I**^t. vt. To provide with an index; enter in an index. **II.** n. [IN′DEX-ES or IN′DI-CES, pl.] **1.** An indicator, pointer, etc. **2.** An alphabetic list of matter, as in a book.

in′di-a-rub′ber, 1 in′dĭ-a-rub′ar; 2 ĭn′di-a-rub′er, n. A soft and elastic substance derived from the sap of various tropical plants.

In′di-an, 1 in′dĭ-an; 2 ĭn′di-an. **I.** a. **1.** Pertaining to India. **2.** Pertaining to the American native races. **II.** n. **1.** A native of India. **2.** An aboriginal American.— **Indian corn,** maize.— **I. meal,** meal made from maize.— **I. ocean,** one of the five great oceans; between Africa, Asia, Australia, and 40th parallel of south latitude; estimated area, 17,320,500 square miles.

in′di-cate, 1 in′dĭ-kĕt; 2 ĭn′di-cāt, vt. [-CAT′ED^d; -CAT′ING.] **1.** To give a suggestion of. **2.** To point out; show; represent.— **in′di-cant.** **I.** a. Indicating. **II.** n. An indicator.— **in″di-ca′tion,** n. A manifestation; token.— **in-dic′a-tiv(e^s.** **I.** a. Giving intimation. **II.** n. Gram. The indicative mode, which asserts or questions directly. **-ly,** adv.— **in′di-ca″tor,** n. That which indicates, as a pointer.

in′di-ces, 1 in′dĭ-siz; 2 ĭn′di-çĕs, n. A plural of INDEX.

in-dict′^d, 1 in-dait′; 2 ĭn-dīt′, vt. To prefer an indictment against.— **in-dict′a-bl(e^r,** a.— **in-dict′ment,** n. The act of indicting; a formal charge of crime.

in-dif′fer-ent, 1 in-dif′ar-ent; 2 ĭn-dĭf′er-ĕnt, a. **1.** Having no interest; apathetic. **2.** Only passably good. **3.** Unimportant; unprejudiced. **-ly,** adv.— **in-dif′fer-ence,** n. The state of being indifferent; apathy; insensibility.

in-dig′e-nous, 1 in-dij′i-nus; 2 ĭn-dĭg′e-nŭs, a. Originating in; native; hence, inherent.

in′di-gent, 1 in′di-jent; 2 ĭn′di-gĕnt, a.

Destitute; needy; poor.— **in′di-gence**, *n.*
Poverty.

in″di-ges′tion, 1 in″di-jes′chən; 2 ĭn″di-gĕs′chon, *n.* Defective digestion; dyspepsia.— **in″di-gest′i-bl**(e)[r], *a.* Not digestible, or difficult to digest.

in-dig′nant, 1 in-dig′nənt; 2 ĭn-dĭg′nant, *a.* Having or showing just anger and scorn. **-ly,** *adv.*— **in″dig-na′tion,** *n.* Just resentment.

in-dig′ni-ty, 1 in-dig′ni-tɪ; 2 ĭn-dĭg′ni-ty, *n.* [-TIES[z], *pl.*] An act tending to degrade or mortify; insult; affront.

in′di-go, 1 in′di-go; 2 ĭn′di-go, *n.* A blue coloring-substance obtained from the indigo-plant; a deep violet-blue.

in″di-rect′, 1 in″di-rekt′; 2 ĭn″di-rĕct′, *a.* Not direct; roundabout; inferential; equivocal. **-ly,** *adv.* **-ness,** *n.*— **in″di-rec′tion,** *n.*

in″dis-crim′i-nate, 1 in″dis-krim′i-nɪt; 2 ĭn″dis-crĭm′i-nat, *a.* Making no discrimination; general; sweeping. **2.** Confused. **-ly,** *adv.* **-ness,** *n.*

in″dis-pose′, 1 in″dis-pōz′; 2 ĭn″dĭs-pōs′, *vt.* To disincline; render unfit; make ill.— **in″dis-posed′,** *pa.* **1.** Ill; unwell. **2.** Disinclined. — **in-dis″po-si′tion,** *n.* **1.** Slight illness. **2.** The state of being mentally disinclined.

in-dis′pu-ta-ble, ⎱ 1 in-dis′piu-tə-bl; 2 ĭn-
in-dis′pu-ta-bl[r], ⎰ dĭs′pū-ta-bl, *a.* Incapable of being disputed; unquestionable. **in-dis′pu-ta-bly,** *adv.*

in-dis′so-lu-ble, ⎱ 1 in-dis′o-liu-bl; 2 ĭn-
in-dis′so-lu-bl[r], ⎰ dĭs′o-lū-bl, *a.* That can not be dissolved; perpetually binding. **in-dis′so-lu-ble-ness,** *n.*— **in-dis′so-lu-bly,** *adv.*

in-dite′, 1 in-dait′; 2 ĭn-dīt′, *vt.* & *vi.* [IN-DIT′ED[d]; IN-DIT′ING.] To put into words or writing; dictate; compose. **-ment,** *n.*— **in-dit′er,** *n.*

in″di-vid′u-al, 1 in″di-vij′u-[or -vid′yu-]əl; 2 ĭn″di-vĭj′u-[or -vĭd′yu-]al. **I.** *a.* Pertaining to one thing; single. **II.** *n.* A single person, animal, or thing.— **in″di-vid″u-al′i-ty,** *n.* **1.** The state of being individual. **2.** Personality.— **in″di-vid′u-al-ly,** *adv.*

In′do-. From Greek *Indos*, Indian: a combining form, denoting connection with India and the East Indies; as, *Indo*-China, *Indo*-European; *Indo*-Germanic.

in-doc′tri-nate, 1 in-dok′tri-nēt; 2 ĭn-dŏc′tri-nāt, *vt.* [-NAT″ED[d]; -NAT″ING.] To instruct in doctrines.

in′do-lence, 1 in′do-lens; 2 ĭn′do-lĕnç, *n.* Habitual idleness; laziness.— **in′do-lent,** *a.* Averse to exertion.— **in′do-lent-ly,** *adv.*

in-dom′i-ta-ble, ⎱ 1 in-dom′i-tə-bl; 2 ĭn-
in-dom′i-ta-bl[r], ⎰ dŏm′i-ta-bl, *a.* Not to be subdued.— **in-dom′i-ta-bly,** *adv.*

in′door″, 1 in′dōr′; 2 ĭn′dôr′, *a.* Being or done within doors.— **in′doors″,** *adv.* Within a building.

in-dorse′, 1 in-dōrs′; 2 ĭn-dôrs′, *vt.* [IN-DORSED′[t], IN-DORST′[s]; IN-DORS′ING.] To write, as one's name, on the back of; sanction. **en-dorse′**‡.— **in″dor-see′,** *n.* One to whom anything is indorsed.— **in-dorse′-ment,** *n.* The writing of one's name on the back of a note, check, etc.; ratification; approval. **en-dorse′ment**‡.— **in-dors′er,** *n.* One who indorses.

in-du′bi-ta-ble, ⎱ 1 in-diū′bi-tə-bl; 2 ĭn-
in-du′bi-ta-bl[r], ⎰ dū′bi-ta-bl, *a.* Not open to doubt; unquestionable; certain. **-ness,** *n.*— **in-du′bi-ta-bly,** *adv.*

in-duce′, 1 in-diūs′; 2 ĭn-dūç′, *vt.* [IN-DUCED′[t]; IN-DUC′ING.] **1.** To influence to an act; prevail on. **2.** To lead to or produce.— **in-duce′ment,** *n.* The act of inducing; an incentive; motive.— **in-duc′er,** *n.*

in-duc′tion, 1 in-duk′shən; 2 ĭn-dŭc′shon, *n.* **1.** The process of inferring general conclusions from particular cases; inference; conclusion. **2.** Electrification by nearness without contact.— **in-duct′,** *vt.* **1.** To put in possession; introduce; install. **2.** To obtain by induction.— **in-duc′tance,** *n.* The capacity for magnetic induction.— **in-duc′tive**(e)[s], *a.* Pertaining to induction; proceeding or produced by induction.— **in-duc′tive-ly,** *adv.*— **in-duc′tor,** *n.*

in-due′[1], 1 in-diū′; 2 ĭn-dū′, *vt.* [IN-DUED′; IN-DU′ING.] To endow.

in-due′[2], *vt.* To put on, as a garment.

in-dulge′, 1 in-dulj′; 2 ĭn-dŭlj′, *vt.* [IN-DULGED′; IN-DULG′ING.] To gratify, as a desire; leave unrestrained, as a person. — **in-dul′gence,** *n.* **1.** The act of indulging; excess. **2.** That with which a person is indulged. **3.** *R. C. Ch.* Remission of temporal punishment.— **in-dul′gent,** *a.* Prone to indulge; easy; lenient.

in′du-rate, 1 in′diu-rēt; 2 ĭn′dū-rāt, *vt.* & *vi.* [-RAT″ED[d]; -RAT′ING.] To make or become hard or tough; harden.— **in′du-rate,** *a.* Hard or hardened; indurated.— **in″du-ra′tion,** *n.*

in-dus′tri-al, 1 in-dus′tri-əl; 2 ĭn-dŭs′tri-al,*a.* Pertaining to industry or manufactures. **-ly,** *adv.*

in′dus-try, 1 in′dus-trɪ; 2 ĭn′dŭs-try, *n.* [-TRIES[z], *pl.*] **1.** Earnest or constant application to work. **2.** Useful labor; any branch of productive work.— **in-dus′tri-ous,** *a.* Habitually occupied with or given to work; diligent; laborious. **-ly,** *adv.*

ir-e′bri-ate, 1 in-ī′bri-ēt; 2 ĭn-ē′bri-āt. **I.** *vt.* [-AT″ED[d]; -AT′ING.] To intoxicate. **II.** *a.* Inebriated. **III.** *n.* A habitual drunkard.— **in-e″bri-a′tion,** **in″e-bri′e-ty,** *n.*

n. Drunkenness; habitual intoxication.— **in-e'bri-ant,** *a. & n.* Intoxicant.

in-ef'fa-ble, } 1 in-ef'a-b.; 2 ĭn-ĕf'a-bl, *a.*
in-ef'fa-bl², } Too lofty or sacred for utterance; unspeakable.— **in-ef'fa-bly,** *adv.*

in-ept', 1 in-ept'; 2 ĭn-ĕpt', *a.* **1.** Not fit or suitable; unapt. **2.** Unreasonable; absurd.

in-eq'ui-ta-ble, 1 in-ek'wi-ta-bl; 2 ĭn-ĕk'wi-ta-bl, *a.* Not according to equity; unfair; unjust.— **in-eq'ui-ta-bly,** *adv.*

in-er'rant, 1 in-er'ənt; 2 ĭn-ĕr'ant, *a.* Unerring.— **in-er'ran-cy,** *n.* Freedom from all error.

in-ert', 1 in-ûrt'; 2 ĭn-ẽrt', *a.* Having no power to move; possessing inertia; sluggish. **-ly,** *adv.* **-ness,** *n.*— **in-er'ti-a,** 1 in-ûr'shi-ə; 2 ĭn-ẽr'shi-a, *n.* **1.** The state of being inert. **2.** That property of matter by virtue of which it continues at rest or in motion unless acted on by some force outside of itself.

in-es'ti-ma-ble, } 1 in-es'ti-ma-bl; 2 ĭn-
in-es'ti-ma-bl², } ĕs'ti-ma-bl, *a.* Above price; very valuable.

in-ev'i-ta-ble, } 1 in-ev'i-tə-bl; 2 ĭn-ĕv'i-
in-ev'i-ta-bl², } ta-bl, *a.* That can not be prevented; unavoidable. **-ness,** *n.*— **in-ev'i-ta-bly,** *adv.*

in-ex'o-ra-ble, } 1 in-eks'o-rə-bl; 2 ĭn-ĕks'-
in-ex'o-ra-bl², } o-ra-bl, *a.* Not to be moved by entreaty; unyielding.— **in-ex'o-ra-bly,** *adv.*

in-ex'tri-ca-ble, } 1 in-eks'tri-kə-bl; 2 ĭn-
in-ex'tri-ca-bl², } ĕks'tri-ea-bl, *a.* Involved or entangled beyond extrication. **-ness,** *n.*— **in-ex'tri-ca-bly,** *adv.*

in-fal'li-ble, } 1 in-fal'i-bl; 2 ĭn-făl'i-bl, *a.*
in-fal'li-bl², } Incapable of error or failure; inerrant; certain.— **in-fal'li-bil'i-ty,** *n.* The state of being infallible.— **in-fal'li-bly,** *adv.*

in fa-mous, 1 in'fə-mŭs; 2 ĭn'fa-mŭs, *a.* Of evil repute; notorious; detestable. **-ly,** *adv.*— **in'fa-my,** 1 in'fə-mi; 2 ĭn'fa-my, *n.* [-MIES², *pl.*] Notorious evil repute; disgrace; dishonor; something infamous or abominable.

in'fant, 1 in'fənt; 2 ĭn'fant. **I.** *a.* Pertaining to infancy; infantile. **II.** *n.* **1.** A babe. **2.** *Law.* A minor.— **in'fan-cy,** *n.* The state of being an infant; babyhood; beginning.— **in-fan'ti-cide,** *n.* Child murder, or one who commits it.— **in-fan'ti-ci'dal,** *a.*— **in'fan-til[e²,** *a.* Pertaining to infants. **in'fan-tine².**

in'fan-try, 1 in'fan-tri; 2 ĭn'fan-try, *n.* Foot-soldiery equipped with small arms.

in-fat'u-ate, 1 in-fach'u-[or -fat'yu-]ēt; 2 ĭn-făch'u-[or -făt'yu-]āt, *vt.* [-AT'ED⁴; -AT'ING.] To inspire with unreasoning passion; deprive of judgment.— **in-fat''u-a'-tion,** *n.*

in-fect', 1 in-fekt'; 2 ĭn-fĕet', *vt.* To taint

with disease; corrupt; contaminate.— **in-fec'tion,** *n.* Communication of disease, as by contact.— **in-fec'tious,** *a.* Liable to infect; contagious. **-ly,** *adv.* **-ness,** *n.*

in''fe-lic'i-ty, 1 in''fi-lis'i-ti; 2 ĭn''fe-lĭç'i-ty, *n.* Inappropriateness; unsuitableness; unhappiness; something infelicitous.— **in''fe-lic'i-tous,** 1 in''fi-lĭs'i-tus; 2 ĭn''fe-lĭç'i-tŭs, *a.* Not felicitous or happy. **-ly,** *adv.* **-ness,** *n.*

in-fer', 1 in-fûr'; 2 ĭn-fẽr', *vt. & vi.* [IN-FERRED', IN-FERD'⁸; IN-FER'RING.] To draw as a conclusion from evidence; draw inferences; give evidence of; conclude. — **in-fer'a-bl[e², in-fer'ri-bl[e², — in''fer-ence,** *n.* The act of inferring a deduction or conclusion from evidence.— **in''fer-en'tial,** *a.* Deducible by inference. **-ly,** *adv.*

in-fe'ri-or, 1 in-fî'ri-ər; 2 ĭn-fē'ri-or. **I.** *a.* Lower, as in position, rank, quality, or worth. **II.** *n.* One who is inferior; a subordinate.— **in-fe''ri-or'i-ty,** *n.* The state of being inferior; low condition, quality, or station.

in-fer'nal, 1 in-fûr'nəl; 2 ĭn-fẽr'nal, *a.* Belonging to hell; diabolical. **-ly,** *adv.*

in-fer'no, 1 in-fûr'no; 2 ĭn-fẽr'no, *n.* The infernal regions; hell.

in-fest'd, 1 in-fest'; 2 ĭn-fĕst', *vt.* To fill or overrun annoyingly or harmfully.

in-fi-del, 1 in'fi-del; 2 ĭn'fi-dĕl. **I.** *a.* Unbelieving; rejecting the Christian religion; faithless; recreant. **II.** *n.* A disbeliever in God or in the Bible; any unbeliever.— **in''fi-del'i-ty,** *n.* [-TIES², *pl.*] **1.** Unbelief in religion. **2.** Want of fidelity; unfaithfulness.

in-fil'trate, 1 in-fil'trēt; 2 ĭn-fĭl'trāt, *vt. & vi.* [-TRAT-ED⁴; -TRAT-ING.] To filter in or into; percolate.— **in''fil-tra'tion,** *n.*

in'fi-nite, } 1 in'fi-nɪt; 2 ĭn'fi-nĭt. **I.** *a.*
in'fi-nit⁸, } Immeasureable and unbounded; limitless; perfect; countless. **II.** *a.* That which is infinite; [I-] the Deity. **-ly,** *adv.* **-ness,** *n.*— **in-fin''i-tes'i-mal,** *a.* Infinitely small. **II.** *n.* An infinitesimal quantity. **-ly,** *adv.*— **in-fin'i-tive(e⁸.** **I.** *a.* Without limitation of person or number. **II.** *n. Gram.* The infinitive mode; as, *to love.*— **in-fin'i-ty,** *n.* [-TIES², *pl.*] Boundlessness; infinitely distant space; completeness; perfection. **in-fin'i-tude².**

in-firm', 1 in-fûrm'; 2 ĭn-fĩrm', *a.* **1.** Feeble, as from age. **2.** Lacking soundness, stability, or firmness. **-ly,** *adv.* **-ness,** *n.*— **in-fir'ma-ry,** *n.* [-RIES², *pl.*] A small hospital.— **in-fir'mi-ty,** *n.* [-TIES², *pl.*] Weakness or illness; a feible; flaw.

in-fix'ᵗ, 1 in-fiks'; 2 ĭn-fĭks', *vt.* To fix in, as by piercing; implant firmly.

in-flame', 1 in-flēm'; 2 ĭn-flām', *vt. & vi.* [IN-FLAMED'; IN-FLAM'ING.] To kindle;

burn; rouse; excite; affect or be affected by inflammation.— **in-flam″ma-bil′i-ty**, *n*. **in-flam′ma-ble-ness*‡‡**.— **in-flam′ma-ble**(eᴿ, *a*. Readily inflamed; easily excited.— **in-flam′ma-bly**, *adv*.— **in″flam-ma′tion**, *n*. The act of inflaming; a diseased condition attended with heat, redness, swelling, and pain.— **in-flam′ma-to-ry**, *a*. Tending to inflame; pertaining to inflammation.

in-flate′, 1 in-flēt′; 2 ĭn-flāt′, *vt. & vi*. [IN-FLAT′EDᵈ; IN-FLAT′ING.] To puff up, as with air; swell; elate; expand.— **in-flat′ing-ly**, *adv*.— **in-fla′tion**, *n*. **1**. The act of inflating; figuratively, bombast. **2**. Overissue, as of currency.

in-flect′ᵈ, 1 in-flekt′; 2 ĭn-flĕct′, *vt. & vi*. **1**. *Gram*. To be subject to inflection; give the inflections of. **2**. To deflect; swerve; bend.— **in-flec′tion**, **in-flex′ion**, *n*. **1**. An inflecting; modulation of voice. **2**. *Gram*. Changes in words to express case, gender, person, tense, etc.— **in-flec′tion-al, in-flex′ion-al**, *a*.

in-flex′i-ble(eᴿ, 1 in-fleks′ɪ-bl; 2ĭn-flĕks′ĭ-bl, *a*. Not to be bent; not to be swayed or turned from a purpose; rigid; unalterable.— **in-flex′i-bil′i-ty**, *n*. **in-flex′i-ble-ness**‡.— **in-flex′i-bly**, *adv*.

in-flict′ᵈ, 1 in-flikt′; 2 ĭn-flĭct′, *vt*. To lay on; impose.— **in-flic′tion**, *n*. A punishment; imposition.

in″flo-res′cence, 1 in″flo-res′ens; 2 ĭn″flo-rĕs′ĕnç, *n*. **1**. *Bot*. A flower-cluster. **2**. The arrangement of flowers on the stem. **3**. The act of flowering; flowers collectively.

in′flu-ence, 1 in′flu-ens; 2 ĭn′flụ-ĕnç, *vt*. [-ENCEDᵗ; -ENC-ING.] To act upon, as by mental power or unseen agency; affect; move. **II**. *n*. The gradual or unseen operation of some cause; ability to sway the will of another.— **in″flu-en′tial**, *a*. **-ly**, *adv*.

in″flu-en′za, 1 in″flu-en′zo; 2 ĭn″flụ-ĕn′za, *n*. An epidemic catarrhal disease.

in′flux, 1 in′fluks; 2 ĭn′flŭks, *n*. A flowing in; instilling. [close; embrace.

in-fold′ᵈ, 1 in-fōld′; 2 ĭn-fōld′, *vt*. To en-

in-form′, 1 in-fērm′; 2 ĭn-fôrm′, *v*. **I**. *t*. **1**. To impart knowledge to; tell. **2**. To give form or animation to. **II**. *i*. To communicate facts; make accusation.— **in-form′ant**, *n*. One who gives information.— **in-for-ma′tion**, *n*. Knowledge communicated by others.— **in-form′er**, *n*. One who informs against others; a telltale.

in-for′mal, 1 in-fôr′məl; 2 ĭn-fôr′mal, *a*. Not in usual form; without ceremony. **-ly**, *adv*.— **in″for-mal′i-ty**, *n*. [-TIESᶻ, *pl*.] Absence of regular form.

in-frac′tion, 1 in-frak′shən; 2 ĭn-frăc′shon, *n*. **1**. The act of breaking or infringing. **2**. A fracture.

in-fre′quent, **in-fus′i-bl**(eᴿ. For these and many similar words, see list under IN³.

in-fringe′, 1 in-frinj′; 2 ĭn-frĭng′, *v*. [IN-FRINGED′; IN-FRING′ING.] **I**. *t*. To encroach upon. **II**. *i*. To transgress; trespass.— **in-fringe′ment**, *n*.

in-fu′ri-ate, 1 in-fiū′rɪ-ēt; 2 ĭn-fū′ri-āt. **I**. *vt*. [-AT′EDᵈ, -AT′ING.] To make furious. **II**. *a*. Infuriated; enraged; mad.

in-fuse′, 1 in-fiūz′; 2 ĭn-fūz′, *vt*. [IN-**in-fuze′ᴿ**, ∫ FUSED′; IN-FUS′ING.] **1**. To instil; inculcate. **2**. To steep; pour in.— **in-fu′sion**, *n*. The act of infusing; a steeping or a medicinal preparation so obtained.

In″fu-so′ri-a, 1 in″fiu-sō′rɪ-a; 2 ĭn″fū-sō′ri-a, *n*. *pl*. Animalcules found in infusions of decaying substances.

in-ge′nious, 1 in-jīn′yus; 2 ĭn-gēn′yŭs, *a*. Inventive; dexterous; skilful. **-ly**, *adv*. **-ness**, *n*.— **in″ge-nu′i-ty**, *n*. Contrivance; dexterity; skill.

in-gen′u-ous, 1 in-jen′yu-us; 2 ĭn-gĕn′yu-ŭs, *a*. **1**. Free from disguise or dissimulation. **2**. High-minded; sincere. **-ly**, *adv*. **-ness**, *n*.

in′gle, 1 in′gl; 2 ĭn′gl, *n*. A fire-or fire-place.— **in′gle-side″**, *n*. Fireside.

in-glo′ri-ous, 1 in-glō′rɪ-us; 2 ĭn-glö′ri-ŭs, *a*. Marked by failure or disgrace; without glory. **-ly**, *adv*.

in′got, 1 in′got; 2 ĭn′gŏt, *n*. A mass of cast metal.

in-graft′ᵈ, 1 in-graft′; 2 ĭn-grȧft′, *vt*. To graft; incorporate vitally.

in-grain′, 1 in-grēn′; 2 ĭn-grān′, *vt*. To dye before weaving; dye with lasting color; fix deeply.

in′grain, 1 in′grēn; 2 ĭn′grān, *a*. Dyed before weaving; thoroughly inwrought.

in′grain, *n*. A carpet made of worsted or cotton warps and wool or other filling.

in′grate, 1 in′grēt; 2 ĭn′grāt. **I**. *a*. Ungrateful. **II**. *n*. One who is ungrateful.

in-gra′ti-ate, 1 in-grē′shɪ-ēt; 2 ĭn-grā′shi-āt, *vt*. [-AT′EDᵈ; -AT′ING.] To win for oneself.

in-grat′i-tude, 1 in-grat′ɪ-tiūd; 2 ĭn-grăt′i-tūd, *n*. Lack of gratitude.

in-gre′di-ent, 1 in-grī′dɪ-ent; 2 ĭn-grē′di-ĕnt, *n*. One element of a mixture.

in′gress, 1 in′gres; 2 ĭn′grĕs, *n*. Entrance; place of entrance.

in-gulf′ᵗ, 1 in-gulf′; 2 ĭn-gŭlf′, *vt*. To engulf.— **in-gulf′ment**, *n*.

in-hab′it‡ᵈ, 1 in-hab′it; 2 ĭn-hăb′it, *vt*. To live or dwell in; occupy.— **in-hab′it-a-bl**(eᴿ, *a*. Habitable.— **in-hab′i-tant**, *n*. A resident.

in-hale′, 1 in-hēl′; 2 ĭn-hāl′, *vt*. [IN-

HALED′; IN-HAL′ING.] To draw in, as a breath; breathe in.— **in″ha-la′tion,** *n.* **1.** The act of inhaling. **2.** That which is inhaled.— **in-hal′er,** *n.*

in-here′, 1 in-hīr′; 2 ĭn-hēr′, *vi.* [IN-HERED′; IN-HER′ING.] To be a permanent or essential part; belong.— **in-her′ence,** *n.* **in-her′en-cy‡.— in-her′ent,** *a.* Permanently united; innate; essential: intrinsic.

in-her′it⁴, 1 in-her′ĭt; 2 ĭn-hĕr′ĭt, *vt. & vi.* To receive by descent; be endowed with; receive property by inheritance.— **in-her′it-a-bl(e**ᴾ, *a.*— **in-her′it-ance,** *n.* The act of inheriting; something inherited.— **in-her′i-tor,** *n.*— **in-her′it-rix,** *n. fem.*

in-hib′it⁴, 1 in-hib′ĭt; 2 ĭn-hĭb′ĭt, *vt.* To hold back; prohibit.— **in″hi-bi′tion,** 1 in″-hi-bish′ən; 2 ĭn″hi-bĭsh′on, *n.*— **in-hib′i-to-ry,** *a.* **in-hib′i-tive‡.**

in-hos′pi-ta-ble, 1 in-hɒs′pi-tə-bl; 2 ĭn-hos′pi-ta-bl″, *a.* Not hospitable; barren; wild; cheerless.— **in-hos′-pi-ta-ble-ness,** *n.* **in-hos″pi-tal′i-ty‡.**

in-hume′, 1 in-hiūm′; 2 ĭn-hūm′, *vt.* [IN-HUMED′; IN-HUM′ING.] To place in the earth; bury. **in-hu′mate‡.— in″hu-ma′tion,** *n.*

in-im′i-cal, 1 in-im′ĭ-kəl; 2 ĭn-ĭm′i-eal, *a.* Antagonistic; unfriendly; hostile.

in-iq′ui-ty, 1 in-ik′wi-ti; 2 ĭn-ĭk′wi-ty, *n.* [-TIES²ᶻ, *pl.*] Wickedness; wrong; sin.— **in-iq′ui-tous,** *a.* **-ly,** *adv.*

in-i′tial, 1 in-ish′əl; 2 ĭn-ĭsh′al. **I.** *a.* Standing at the beginning or head; first. **II.** *n.* The first letter of a word.

in-i′ti-ate, 1 in-ish′i-ēt; 2 ĭn-ĭsh′i-āt. **I.** *vt.* [-AT″ED⁴; -AT″ING.] **1.** To instruct in rudiments; introduce, as into a society. **2.** To begin. **II.** *a.* Newly admitted. **III.** *n.* One who has been initiated.— **in-i″ti-a′tion,** 1 in-ish′i-ē′shan; 2 ĭn-ĭsh″i-ā′shon, *n.* **1.** The act of initiating. **2.** Ceremonious admission, as into a society.

in-i′ti-a-tiv(eᴾ, 1 in-ish′i-ə-tiv; 2 ĭn-ĭsh′i-a-tĭv. **I.** *a.* Pertaining to initiation; serving to initiate. **II.** *n.* **1.** A first move. **2.** The power of initiating; power to originate; originality. **3.** A political system by which the people may demand by vote the passage of any desired legislation: usually accompanied by the *referendum*. See REFERENDUM.— **in-i′ti-a-to-ry,** 1 in-ish′i-ə-to-ri; 2 ĭn-ĭsh′i-a-to-ry, *a.* Initiative.

in-ject′⁴, 1 in-jekt′; 2 ĭn-jĕet′, *vt.* **1.** To introduce forcibly, as a fluid. **2.** To interject.— **in-jec′tion,** *n.* The act of injecting, or that which is injected.— **in-jec′tor,** *n.*

in-join′, *v.* Same as ENJOIN.

in-junc′tion, 1 in-juŋk′shən; 2 ĭn-jŭŋe′-shon, *n.* **1.** The act of enjoining; admonition. **2.** A judicial order prohibiting something.

in′jure, 1 in′jur; 2 ĭn′jụr, *vt.* [IN′JURED; IN′JUR-ING.] To inflict harm or injury upon.— **in-ju′ri-ous,** *a.* Hurtful; detrimental.— **in′ju-ry,** *n.* [-RIES²ᶻ, *pl.*] Any wrong, damage, or mischief.

in-jus′tice, 1 in-jus′tĭs; 2 ĭn-jŭs′tĭç, *n.* **in-jus′tis**ˢ, The violation of justice; an unjust act; a wrong.

ink, 1 iŋk; 2 ĭŋk. **I**ᵗ. *vt.* To cover or stain with ink. **II.** *n.* A colored liquid used in writing, printing, etc.— **ink′stand**ⁿ, *n.* A vessel to hold ink for writing.— **ink′y,** *a.*

ink′ling, 1 iŋk′liŋ; 2 ĭŋk′.ing, *n.* A hint.

in-laid′, *pp.* of INLAY, *v.*

in′land, 1 in′lənd; 2 ĭn′land. **I.** *a.* **1.** Remote from the sea. **2.** Not foreign. **II.** *adv.* Toward the interior of a land.

in-lay′, 1 in-lē′; 2 ĭn-lā′. **I.** *vt.* [IN-LAID′; IN-LAY′ING.] To insert, as shell, ivory, or the like in cabinetwork. **II.** 1 in′lē′; 2 ĭn′lā′, *n.* That which is inlaid.

in′let′, 1 in′let′; 2 ĭn′lĕt′, *n.* **1.** A small bay or creek. **2.** An entrance.

in′ly, 1 in′li; 2 ĭn′ly, *adv.* In the inner parts; inwardly. [occupant.

in′mate, 1 in′mēt; 2 ĭn′māt, *n.* An **in′most,** 1 in′mōst; 2 ĭn′mōst, *a.* Farthest within; deepest.

inn, 1 in; 2 ĭn, *n.* A public house; tavern; [hotel.— **inn′keep′er,** *n.* The keeper of an inn. **inn′hold″er‡.**

in′nate, 1 in′nēt *or* in-nēt′; 2 ĭn′nāt *or* ĭn-nāt′, *a.* Inborn; natural. **-ly,** *adv.* **-ness,** *n.*

in′ner, 1 in′ər; 2 ĭn′er, *a.* Interior; internal; inward; recondite; hidden.— **in′ner-most**ⁿ, *a.* Inmost.

in′ning, 1 in′iŋ; 2 ĭn′ing, *n.* In baseball cricket, etc., a turn at the bat; the time that a party is in power.

in′no-cent, 1 in′o-sent; 2 ĭn′o-çĕnt. **I.** *a.* **1.** Free from guilt; pure; blameless. **2.** Harmless. **3.** Guileless; artless. **II.** *n.* **1.** One unstained by sin. **2.** An imbecile. **-ly,** *adv.*— **in′no-cence,** *n.* The state of being innocent. **in′no-cen-cy‡.**

in-noc′u-ous, 1 in-nek′yu-us; 2 ĭn-nŏe′yu-ŭs, *a.* Having no harmful qualities; harmless.

in′no-vate, 1 in′o-vēt; 2 ĭn′o-vāt, *vi.* [-VAT″ED⁴; -VAT′ING.] To make innovations; introduce new things.— **in″no-va′tion,** *n.* The changing of something established; a novelty.— **in′no-va″tor,** *n.*

in″nu-en′do, 1 in″yu-en′do; 2 ĭn″yu-ĕn′do, *n.* [-DOS²ᶻ, -DOES²ᶻ, *pl.*] An indirect aspersion; insinuation.

in-nu′mer-a-ble, ⎰ 1 in-niū′mər-ə-bl; 2 ĭn-
in-nu-mer-a-bl′, ⎱ nŭ′mer-a-bl, *a.* Countless. **-ness,** *n.* **in-nu′mer-a-bly,** *adv.*

in-oc′u-late, 1 in-ǒk′yu-lēt; 2 ĭn-ŏe′yu-lāt,
vt. [-LAT′ED⁴; -LAT′ING.] **1.** To infect
through the skin. **2.** To insert a bud in,
as a tree; bud.— **in-oc″u-la′tion,** *n.*

in-or′di-nate, 1 in-ôr′dɪ-nɪt; 2 ĭn-ôr′dĭ-
nat, *a.* Unreasonable; excessive. **-ly,** *adv.*
-ness, *n.*

in″or-gan′ic, 1 in″ər-gan′ik; 2 ĭn″ôr-găn′ie,
a. Not having organic structure; not
the result of living processes.

in′quest, 1 in′kwest; 2 ĭn′kwĕst, *n.* A
judicial inquiry, as concerning a sudden
death.

in-qui′e-tude, 1 in-kwai′ɪ-tiūd; 2 ĭn-
kwī′e-tūd, *n.* A state of restlessness;
disquietude.

in-quire′, 1 in-kwair′; 2 ĭn-kwīr′, *v.* [IN-
QUIRED′; IN-QUIR′ING.] **I.** *t.* To ask information about. **II.** *i.* To seek information by asking questions; investigate.
— **in-quir′er,** *n.*— **in-qui′ry,** 1 in-kwair′ɪ;
2 ĭn-kwīr′y, *n.* [-IES⁴, *pl.*] The act of in-
quiring; investigation; a query; interrogation.— **in″qui-si′tion,** 1 in″kwɪ-zish′ən; 2
ĭn″kwĭ-sĭsh′on, *n.* **1.** [I-] A tribunal for examination and punishment of heretics. **2.**
Judicial investigation; searching inquiry.—
in″qui-si′tion-al, *a.*— **in-quis′i-tiv**(e⁴, *a.*
Given to questioning or to investigation;
curious.— **in-quis′i-tor,** *n.* One who makes
inquisition.— **in-quis″i-to′ri-al,** *a.* Of, pertaining to, or like an inquisitor or inquisition.

in′road, 1 in′rōd; 2 ĭn′rōd, *n.* A hostile
entrance into a country; raid; encroachment.

in-sane′, 1 in-sēn′; 2 ĭn-sān′, *a.* **1.** Not
sane; crazy; irrational. **2.** Pertaining to
insanity or the insane.— **in-san′i-ty,** *n.*
Mental disorder; derangement; lunacy.

in-sa′ti-a-ble, ⎰ 1 in-sē′shɪ-ə-bl; 2 ĭn-sā′shi-
in-sa′ti-a-bl′, ⎱ a-bl, *a.* That can not be
satiated; unappeasable. **in-sa′ti-ate¹.**

in-scribe′, 1 in-skraib′; 2 in-scrib′, *vt.*
[IN-SCRIBED′; IN-SCRIB′ING.] **1.** To carve,
as characters (upon); write; enroll. **2.**
To dedicate (a book).— **in-scrip′tion,** *n.* **1.**
The act of inscribing, or that which is in-
scribed. **2.** Entry in a roll or the like.

in-scru′ta-ble, ⎰ 1 in-skrū′ta-bl; 2 ĭn-
in-scru′ta-bl′, ⎱ scrü′ta-bl, *a.* That can
not be searched into; undiscoverable.

in′sect, 1 in′sekt; 2 ĭn′sĕct, *n.* **1.** A small
six-legged animal, having the body di-
vided into segments, as a bee, fly, wasp,
or the like. **2.** Loosely, any small invertebrate; bug.— **in″sec-tiv′o-rous,** *a.* Feeding or subsisting upon insects.

in-sen′sate, 1 in-sen′sēt; 2 ĭn-sĕn′sāt, *a.*
Lacking sense or sensibility; foolish; mad.

in-sen′si-ble, ⎰ 1 in-sen′si-bl; 2 ĭn-sĕn′si-bl,
in-sen′si-bl′, ⎱ *a.* **1.** That can not be
perceived by the senses. **2.** Destitute of
sensation or perception.— **in-sen″si-bil′i-ty,**
n.— **in-sen′si-bly,** *adv.*

in-sert′ᵈ, 1 in-sŭrt′; 2 ĭn-sĕrt′, *vt.* To
put or place in among other things.—
in-ser′tion, *n.* The act of inserting; something inserted.

in′side, 1 in′said″; 2 ĭn′sīd″. **I.** *a.* Interior; internal. **II.** *n.* **1.** The side or
part that is within. **2.** Contents. **III.**
adv. In or into the interior; within. **IV.**
prep. In or into the interior of.

in-sid′i-ous, 1 in-sid′ɪ-us; 2 ĭn-sĭd′i-ŭs, *a.*
Doing or contriving secret harm; treacherous.   [lectual discernment.

in′sight″, 1 in′sait″; 2 ĭn′sīt″, *n.* Intel-

in-sig′ni-a, 1 in-sig′ni-ə; 2 ĭn-sĭg′ni-a, *n. pl.*
Badges, etc., as marks of office or distinction.

in″sig-nif′i-cant, 1 in″sig-nif′ɪ-kənt; 2 ĭn″-
sĭg-nif′i-cant, *a.* Not significant; unimportant; trivial.— **in″sig-nif′i-cance,** *n.*

in-sin′u-ate, 1 in-sin′yu-ēt; 2 ĭn-sĭn′yu-āt,
v. [-AT′ED⁴; -AT′ING.] **I.** *t.* **1.** To suggest indirectly; intimate. **2.** To worm
(oneself) in. **II.** *i.* **1.** To hint. **2.** To
work oneself into favor, etc.— **in-sin″u-a′-**
tion, *n.* Insidious suggestion or implication;
something insinuated.— **in-sin′u-a-tiv**(e⁴, *a.*

in-sip′id, 1 in-sip′ɪd; 2 ĭn-sĭp′id, *a.* Without flavor; unsavory; uninteresting. **-ly,**
adv.— **in″si-pid′i-ty,** *n.* **in-sip′id-ness‡.**

in-sist′ᵈ, 1 in-sist′; 2 ĭn-sĭst′, *vi.* To assert
or demand persistently.

in-snare′, etc. Same as ENSNARE, etc.

in′sole″, 1 in′sōl″; 2 ĭn′sōl″, *n.* An inner
sole of a boot or shoe, fixed or removable.

in′so-lent, 1 in′so-lent; 2 ĭn′so-lĕnt, *a.*
Presumptuously or defiantly offensive;
impudent; grossly disrespectful. **-ly,** *adv.*—
in′so-lence, *n.*

in-sol′vent, 1 in-sol′vent; 2 ĭn-sŏl′vĕnt
I. *a.* Bankrupt; inadequate for the payment of debts. **II.** *n.* A bankrupt.—
in-sol′ven-cy, *n.* [-CIES⁴, *pl.*] Bankruptcy.

in-som′ni-a, 1 in-som′ni-ə; 2 ĭn″so-mni′a,
n. Chronic inability to sleep.

in″so-much′, 1 in″so-mŭch′; 2 ĭn″so-mŭch′,
adv. In such wise; to such a degree.

in-spect′ᵈ, 1 in-spekt′; 2 ĭn-spĕct′, *vt.* To
examine carefully and critically.— **in-spec′-**
tion, *n.* Critical investigation; official examination.— **in-spec′tor,** *n.* **1.** A super-
visor; overseer. **2.** An officer of police.—
in-spec′tor-ate, in-spec′tor-ship, *n.* The
office or district of an inspector.

---

in-spire′, 1 ĭn-spair′; 2 ĭn-spīr′, *v.* [IN-SPIRED′; IN-SPIR′ING.] **I.** *t.* **1.** To breathe into the lungs. **2.** To animate as by spiritual influence; instil, as thoughts or emotions. **II.** *i.* To inhale air; draw in the breath.— **in″spi-ra′tion,** *n.* **1.** Inhalation. **2.** The inbreathing or imparting of an idea, emotion, etc.; lofty thought; controlling divine influence.— **in-spir′er,** *n.*

in-spir′itd, 1 ĭn-spir′ĭt; 2 ĭn-spĭr′it, *vt.* To fill with spirit; animate.

in-spis′sate, 1 ĭn-spĭs′ēt; 2 ĭn-spĭs′āt. **I.** *vt.* [-SAT-EDd; -SAT-ING.] To thicken by boiling. **II.** *a.* Thickened.— **in″spis-sa′tion,** *n.*

in″sta-bil′i-ty, 1 ĭn″stə-bĭl′ĭ-tɪ; 2 ĭn″stə-bĭl′i-tɪ. [-TIESz, *pl.*] Unstable condition; changeableness; inconstancy.

in-stall′, 1 ĭn-stôl′; 2 ĭn-stạl′, *vt.* **1.** To invest formally with office. **2.** To establish.— **in″stal-la′tion,** *n.* Ceremonial introduction; institution.— **in-stal′ment, in-stall′ment,** *n.* **1.** A partial payment; stipulated portion. **2.** The act of installing.

in′stance, 1 ĭn′stəns; 2 ĭn′stạnç. **I.** *vt.* [IN′STANCEDt; IN′STANC-ING.] To refer to as an illustration. **II.** *n.* **1.** A single case as an example. **2.** Solicitation; suggestion.

in′stant, 1 ĭn′stənt; 2 ĭn′stạnt. **I.** *a.* **1.** Immediately impending. **2.** Now passing; current. **II.** *n.* **1.** A brief point of time. **2.** A moment.— **in″stan-ta′ne-ous,** *a.* Acting instantly. **-ly,** *adv.* **-ness,** *n.*— **in-stan′ter,** *adv.* Without an instant of delay.— **in′stant-ly,** *adv.* On the instant; immediately.

in-state′, 1 ĭn-stēt′; 2 ĭn-stāt′, *vt.* [IN-STAT′EDd; IN-STAT′ING.] To place in an office or rank.

in-stau′rate, 1 ĭn-stô′rēt; 2 ĭn-stạ′rāt, *vt.* To renew; renovate; restore.— **in″stau-ra′-tion,** *n.*

in-stead′, 1 ĭn-sted′; 2 ĭn-stĕd′, *adv.* In

in-sted′s, } place (of).

in′step, 1 ĭn′step; 2 ĭn′stĕp, *n.* The arched upper part of the human foot.

in′sti-gate, 1 ĭn′stɪ-gēt; 2 ĭn′stɪ-gāt, *vt.* [-GAT′EDd; -GAT′ING.] To stimulate to a bad action.— **in″sti-ga′tion,** *n.*— **in′sti-ga″tor,** *n.*

in-stil′, 1 ĭn-stil′; 2 ĭn-stĭl′, *vt.* [IN-STILLED′, IN-STILD′s; IN-STIL′LING.] **1.** To inculcate gradually. **2.** To pour in by drops. **in-still′**t.— **in-stil′la-tion,** *n.* **in-still′ment**.

in-stinct′, 1 ĭn-stiŋkt′; 2 ĭn-stĭŋet′, *a.* Animated from within.

in′stinct, 1 ĭn′stiŋkt; 2 ĭn′stĭŋet, *n.* A natural impulse acting automatically; animal sagacity.— **in-stinc′tiv(es,** *a.* Spontaneous. **-ly,** *adv.*

in′sti-tute, 1 ĭn′stɪ-tiūt; 2 ĭn′sti-tūt. **I.** *vt.*

[-TUT′EDd; -TUT′ING.] To establish; set in operation; originate. **II.** *n.* **1.** An institution, as of learning. **2.** *pl.* Fundamental principles.— **in″sti-tu′tion,** 1 ĭn″stɪ-tiū′-shən; 2 ĭn″sti-tū′shon, *n.* **1.** That which is instituted; an established order. **2.** A corporate body, or the building occupied by it. **3.** The act of instituting.— **in″sti-tu″tor,** *n.*

in-struct′d, 1 ĭn-strukt′; 2 ĭn-strŭct′, *vt.* **1.** To impart knowledge to; educate. **2.** To give orders or directions to.— **in-struc′tion,** 1 ĭn-struk′shən; 2 ĭn-strŭe′shon, *n.* **1.** The act of instructing; teaching. **2.** Imparted knowledge. **3.** A direction or order.— **in-struc′tiv(es,** *a.* Fitted to instruct; conveying knowledge. **-ly,** *adv.*— **in-struc′tor,** *n.* A teacher.— **in-struct′er**t.— **in-struc′tress,** *n. fem.*

in′stru-ment, 1 ĭn′stru-ment *or* -mənt; 2 ĭn′stru-ment, *n.* **1.** A tool; a mechanism for scientific or musical purposes. **2.** A legal writing.— **in″stru-men′tal,** *a.* **1.** Helpful. **2.** Fitted for or played upon musical instruments.— **in″stru-men-tal′i-ty,** *n.* [-TIESz, *pl.*]

in″stru-men-ta′tion, 1 ĭn″stru-men-tē′shən; 2 ĭn″stru-mĕn-tā′shon, *n.* **1.** *Mus.* The adapting or arranging of musical compositions for performance by instruments. **2.** The use of instruments of any kind, the work done with them, or the instruments used; agency; means.

in-suf′fer-a-ble, } 1 ĭn-sŭf′ɛr-ə-bl; 2 ĭn-suf′fer-a-bl**p**, } sŭf′ɛr-a-bl, *a.* Not to be endured; intolerable.— **in-suf′fer-a-bly,** *adv.*

in′su-lar, 1 ĭn′siu-lər; 2 ĭn′sĭŭ-lar, *a.* Pertaining to an island; isolated; narrow; contracted.— **in′su-lar-ism,** *n.*— **in″su-lar′i-ty,** *n.* Narrowness or illiberality.— **in′su-late,** *vt.* [-LAT′EDd; -LAT′ING.] To separate, as by non-conductors of electricity; isolate. — **in″su-la′tion,** *n.* The act or means of insulating; isolation.— **in′su-la″tor,** *n.* One who or that which insulates.

in′su-lin, 1 ĭn′sʉ-lin; 2 ĭn′sŭ-lin, *n.* A chemical product used in treating diabetes.

in-sult′, 1 ĭn-sŭlt′; 2 ĭn-sŭlt′. **I**d. *vt.* To treat with indignity; affront. **II.** 1 ĭn′-sult; 2 ĭn′sŭlt, *n.* Something offensive said or done; an affront.

in-su″per-a-ble, } 1 ĭn-siū′pər-ə-bl; 2 ĭn-su″per-a-bl**p**, } sŭ′per-a-bl, *a.* Not to be overcome; insurmountable.— **in-su″per-a-bil′i-ty,** *n.*

in-sure′, 1 ĭn-shūr′; 2 ĭn-shụr′, *v.* [IN-SURED′; IN-SUR′ING.] **I.** *t.* To make sure; guarantee. **II.** *i.* To effect insurance.— **in-sur′ance,** *n.* An act or system of guaranteeing a stipulated payment in case of loss, accident, or death; any guaranty.

in-sur′gent, 1 ĭn-sûr′jent; 2 ĭn-sûr′gĕnt. **I.** *a.* Uprising against an existing gov-

ernment; rebellious. **II.** *n.* One who joins in an insurrection.

in″sur-rec′tion, 1 in″sŭ-rek′shən; 2 ĭn″-sŭ-rĕc′shon, *n.* An organized resistance to established government.— **in″sur-rec′tion-a-ry,** *a.* **in″sur-rec′tion-al;.**

in-tact′, 1 in-takt′; 2 ĭn-tăct′, *a.* Left complete or unimpaired.— **in-tact′ness,** *n.*

in-ta′glio, 1 in-tä′lyo; 2 ĭn-tä′lyo, *n.* [-GLII *or* -GLIOS², 1 -lyī *or* -lyoz; 2 -lyī *or* -lyog, *pl.*] Incised or countersunk work; a gem or a die so cut.

in′te-ger, 1 in′tı-jər; 2 ĭn′te-ger, *n.* A whole number; whole.— **in′te-gral,** *a.* **-ly,** *adv.*— **in′te-grate,** *v.* [-GRAT″EDᵈ; -GRAT″-ING.] **I.** *t.* To make into a whole; give the sum total of. **II. i.** To become whole.

in-teg′ri-ty, 1 in-teg′rı-tı; 2 ĭn-tĕg′ri-ty, *n.* **1.** Uprightness of character; probity. **2.** Completeness; soundness.

in-teg′u-ment, 1 in-teg′yu-ment *or* -mənt; 2 ĭn-tĕg′yu-ment, *n.* A natural outer covering, as of skin.

in′tel-lect, 1 in′te-lekt; 2 ĭn′tĕ-lĕct, *n.* The faculty of perception or thought; mind.— **in″tel-lec′tu-al,** *a.* Pertaining to or marked by intellect; mental; highly intelligent. **in″-tel-lec′tiv(e³;.—in″tel-lec″tu-al′i-ty,** *n.*

in-tel′li-gent, 1 in-tel′ı-jent; 2 ĭn-tĕl′ı-gĕnt, *a.* Marked by intelligence; discerning; rational; sensible. **-ly,** *adv.*— **in-tel′li-gence,** *n.* **1.** Mental power; understanding. **2.** News.— **in-tel′li-genc-er,** *n.*— **in-tel′li-gi-bl(e³,** *a.* Capable of being understood.— **in-tel′li-gi-bly,** *adv.*

in-tem′per-ate, 1 in-tem′pər-ıt; 2 ĭn-tĕm′per-at, *a.* Immoderate; excessive, especially in the use of alcoholic drinks. **-ly,** *adv.* **-ness,** *n.*— **in-tem′per-ance,** *n.* Lack of temperance; excess.

in-tend′ᵈ, 1 in-tend′; 2 ĭn-tĕnd′, *vt. & vi.* To purpose; design; have an intention; mean.— **in-ten′dant,** *n.* A superintendent; provincial administrator.

in-tense′, 1 in-tens′; 2 ĭn-tĕns′, *a.* Strained; strenuous; extreme. **-ly,** *adv.* **-ness,** *n.*— **in-ten′si-fy,** *vt. & vi.* To make or become intense; increase in intensity.— **in-ten′sion,** *n.* The act of straining; intensity.— **in-ten′si-ty,** *n.* The state of being intense; amount or degree of force or energy.— **in-ten′siv(e³,** *a.* Serving to intensify; thorough. **-ly,** *adv.* **-ness,** *n.*

in-tent′, 1 in-tent′; 2 ĭn-tĕnt′. **I.** *a.* Eager; earnest. **II.** *n.* Intention; meaning; aim; purpose. **-ly,** *adv.* **-ness,** *n.*— **in-ten′tion,** *n.* A purpose.— **in-ten′tion-al,** *a.* Designed. **-ly,** *adv.*

in-ter′, 1 in-tūr′; 2 ĭn-tēr′, *vt.* [IN-TERRED; IN-TERD′⁸; IN-TER′RING.] To place in a grave or tomb; bury.

in″ter-, *prefix.* Between; together; among; as, *inter*change.

in-ter′ca-late, 1 in-tūr′kə-lēt; 2 ĭn-tēr′ca-lāt, *vt.* [-LAT″Edᵈ; -LAT′ING.] To insert, as a day into the calendar.— **in-ter′ca-la-ry,** *a.*— **in-ter″ca-la′tion,** *n.*

in″ter-cede′, 1 in″tər-sīd′; 2 ĭn″tər-çēd′, *vi.* [-CED′Edᵈ; -CED′ING.] To mediate between persons; make intercession; plead.— **in″ter-ces′sion,** *n.* Entreaty in behalf of another or others.— **in″ter-ces′sor,** *n.* One who intercedes; a mediator.

in″ter-cept′ᵈ, 1 in″tər-sept′; 2 ĭn″tər-çĕpt′, *vt.* To interrupt the course of; stop in transmission.— **in″ter-cep′tion,** *n.*— **in″ter-cept′er** *or* **-or,** *n.*

in″ter-change′, 1 in″tər-chēnj′; 2 ĭn″tər-chāng′, *vt. & vi.* To put each of two things in the place of the other; alternate.— **in″ter-change′** 1 in″tər-chēnj′; 2 in″ter-chăn:′, *n.* **1.** Mutual exchange. **2.** Alternation.— **in″ter-change′a-bl(e³,** *a.* Capable of being interchanged.

in″ter-cos′tal, 1 in″tər-kəs′tal; 2 ĭn″tər-cŏs′tal. **I.** *a.* Occurring between the ribs, as a muscle; pertaining to parts between the ribs. **II.** *n.* An intercostal muscle.

in″ter-course, 1 in″tər-kōrs; 2 ĭn″tər-côrs, *n.* Communication; commerce.

in″ter-dict′, 1 in″tər-dikt′; 2 ĭn″tər-dīct′. **I**ᵈ. *vt.* To prohibit. **II.** 1 in″tər-dikt; 2 ĭn″ter-dīct, *n.* A prohibitive order; ban.— **in″ter-dic′tion,** *n.* Official prohibition.— **in″ter-dic′tiv(e³, in″ter-dic′to-ry,** *a.*

in′ter-est, 1 in″tər-est; 2 ĭn″tər-ĕst. **I**ᵈ. *vt.* To awaken the interest of; engage in. **II.** *n.* **1.** Attention with concern or desire to know. **2.** Profit; benefit. **3.** Payment for the use of money. **4.** Influence.— **in″ter-est-ed,** *pa.* Having an interest; engaged; enlisted; biased. **-ly,** *adv.*— **in″ter-est-ing,** *pa.* Awakening interest; attractive; engaging.

in″ter-fere′, 1 in″tər-fīr′; 2 ĭn″tər-fēr′, *vi.* [-FERED′; -FER′ING.] To take part in the concerns of others; interpose; intervene; also, to conflict; clash.— **in″ter-fer′ence,** *n.*

in′ter-im, 1 in′tər-ım; 2 ĭn′tər-ĭm, *n.* An intermediate season; intervening time; interval.

in-te′ri-or, 1 in-tī′rı-ər; 2 ĭn-tē′ri-or. **I.** *a.* Internal; inland. **II.** *n.* The inside; inland region of a country.

in″ter-ject′ᵈ, 1 in″tər-jekt′; 2 ĭn″tər-jĕct′, *vt. & vi.* To throw between other things.— **in″ter-jec′tion,** *n.* The act of interjecting; a word of exclamation.

in″ter-lace′ᵗ, 1 in″tər-lās′; 2 ĭn″tər-lāç′, *vt. & vi.* To weave or twine together; entwine. See illus. on next page.

in″ter-lard′d, 1 in″tər-lärd′; 2 ĭn″ter-lärd′, *vt.* To diversify; make frequent interpolations in.

in″ter-leav(e′ʳᴾ, 1 in″tər-lēv′; 2 ĭn″ter-lĕv′, *vt.* [-LEAVED′; -LEAV′ING.] To supply with additional leaves, especially blank leaves, inserted among the others, as a book.

Interlaced Arcade.

in″ter-line′, 1 in″tər-lain′; 2 ĭn″ter-līn′, *vt.* [-LINED′; -LIN′ING.] To write or print between the lines of; insert between the lines.— **in″ter-lin′e-ar,** *a.* Situated between lines; having matter inserted between the lines.— **in″ter-lin′e-al**†.— **in″ter-lin″e-a′tion,** *n.*

in″ter-lock′, 1 in″tər-lək′; 2 ĭn″ter-lŏk′, *vt.* To link into each other; clasp together.

in″ter-lo-cu′tion, 1 in″tər-lō-kiū′shən; 2 ĭn″ter-lo-eū′shon, *n.* Interchange of speech; conference; dialog.— **in″ter-loc′u-tor,** *n.* One who takes part in a conversation.

in′ter-lop″er, 1 in″tər-lōp″ər; 2 ĭn″ter-lōp″er, *n.* An intruder.

in′ter-lude, 1 in″tər-liūd; 2 ĭn″ter-lūd, *n.* An incidental action coming between others; an entertainment between acts, music between stanzas, etc.

in″ter-mar′riage, 1 in″tər-mar′ij; 2 ĭn″ter-mär′aǧ, *n.* Marriage between persons of different families or races, or between blood-kindred.— **in″ter-mar′ry,** *vt.*

in″ter-med′dle, } 1 in″tər-med′l; 2 ĭn″ter-med′l, *vi.* To interfere
in″ter-med′lᴾ, } 2 ĭn″ter-med′l, *vi.* To interfere unduly in the affairs of others.— **in″ter-med′dler,** *n.*

in″ter-me′di-a-ry, 1 in″tər-mī′di-ĕ-ri; 2 ĭn″ter-mē′di-ā-ry. I. *a.* Situated, acting, or occurring between. II. *n.* An intermediate agent or medium.

in″ter-me′di-ate, 1 in″tər-mī′di-ıt; 2 ĭn″ter-mē′di-at, *a.* Being in a middle place or degree; lying between.

in-ter′ment, 1 in-tûr′ment *or* -mənt; 2 ĭn-tēr′ment, *n.* The act of interring; burial.

in-ter′mi-na-ble, } 1 in-tûr′mi-na-bl; 2 ĭn-tēr′mi-na-bl, *a.* Endless in fact or seeming.— **in-ter′mi-na-bly,** *adv.*
in-ter′mi-na-blᴾ, }

in″ter-min′gle, 1 in″tər-miŋ′gl; 2 ĭn″ter-mĭŋ′ǧl, *vt. & vi.* To mingle together; mix.

in″ter-mit′, 1 in″tər-mit′; 2 ĭn″ter-mĭt′, *vt. & vi.* [-MIT′TEDd; -MIT′TING.] To cease temporarily; interrupt; suspend.— **in″ter-mis′sion,** 1 in″tər-mish′ən; 2 ĭn″ter-mĭsh′on, *n.* Temporary cessation; a recess; interval.

— **in″ter-mis′siv**(eˢ, *a.* — **in″ter-mit′tent,** *a.* Ceasing at intervals.

in″ter-mix′t, 1 in″tər-miks′; 2 ĭn″ter-mĭks′, *vt. & vi.* To mingle with; become mixed.
— **in″ter-mix′ture,** *n.*

in-tern′, 1 in-tûrn′; 2 ĭn-tērn′, *n.* An inmate; especially a resident hospital surgeon or physician.

in-ter′nal, 1 in-tûr′nəl; 2 ĭn-tēr′nal, *a.* Situated in the inside; interior; based on essential qualities; pertaining to the mind. -ly, *adv.*

in″ter-na′tion-al, 1 in″tər-nash′ən-əl; 2 ĭn″ter-năsh′on-al, *a.* Pertaining to two or more nations; affecting nations generally.

in″ter-ne′cine, 1 in″tər-nī′sın; 2 ĭn″ter-nē′çin, *a.* Involving mutual slaughter; sanguinary.

in-ter′po-late, 1 in-tûr′po-lēt; 2 ĭn-tēr′po-lāt, *vt.* [-LAT′EDd; -LAT′ING.] **1.** To insert, as new or unauthorized matter, in a writing. **2.** To interpose.— **in-ter″po-la′tion,** *n.*— **in-ter′po-la″tor** *or* -ter, *n.*

in″ter-pose′, 1 in″tər-pōz′; 2 ĭn″ter-pōṣ′, *vt. & vi.* [-POSED′; -POS′ING.] To place or come between; mediate; intervene; interrupt.

in″ter-po-si′tion, 1 in″tər-po-zish′ən; 2 ĭn″ter-po-zĭsh′on, *n.* **1** The act of interposing. **2.** That which is interposed.

in-ter′pretd, 1 in-tûr′pret; 2 ĭn-tēr′prĕt, *vt. & vi.* To give the meaning of; translate; explain; act as an interpreter.— **in-ter″pre-ta′tion,** *n.* **1.** The act of interpreting. **2.** The sense given by an interpreter.— **in-ter′pret-er,** *n.* One who interprets or translates.

in″ter-reg′num, 1 in″tər-reg′num; 2 ĭn″ter-rĕg′nŭm, *n.* An interval during which a throne is vacant; any period of abeyance or derangement.

in-ter′ro-gate, 1 in″tər′o-gēt; 2 ĭn-tēr′o-gāt, *vt. & vi.* [-GAT′EDd; -GAT′ING.] To question; make inquiry.— **in-ter″ro-ga′tion,** *n.* **1.** A questioning; query. **2.** An interrogation-point (?).— **in″ter-rog′a-tiv**(eˢ. I. *a.* Denoting inquiry; questioning. II. *n.* Gram. A word used to ask a question, as *who?* -ly, *adv.*— **in-ter′ro-ga″tor,** *n.* One who interrogates.— **in″ter-rog′a-to-ry.** I. *a.* Pertaining to a question. II. *n.* A question.

in″ter-rupt′d, 1 in″tə-rupt′; 2 ĭn″te-rŭpt′, *vt.* To break in upon; stop while in progress; check; hinder.— **in″ter-rup′tion,** *n.* The act of interrupting; hindrance; stop; check; break.— **in″ter-rup′tiv**(eˢ, *a.*

in″ter-sect′d, 1 in″tər-sekt′; 2 ĭn″ter-sĕct′, *vt. & vi.* To pass across; cut through or

into.— **in″ter-sec′tion,** *n.* **1.** The act of intersecting. **2.** A place of crossing or cutting.

in″ter-sperse′, 1 in″tər-spûrs′; 2 ĭn″tər-spĕrs′, *vt.* [-spersed′ᵗ, -spers′ᵗ⁸; -spers″-ing.] To scatter among other things.— **in″ter-sper′sion,** *n.*

in″ter-state′, 1 in″tər-stĕt′; 2 ĭn″tər-stāt′, *a.* Pertaining to different states or their citizens or mutual relations.

in″ter-stel′lar, 1 in″tər-stel′ər; 2 ĭn″tər-stĕl′ar, *a.* Relating to or situated in the regions of space between the stars.

in′ter-stice, 1 in′tər-stĭs *or* in-tûr′stĭs; 2 **in′ter-stis⁸,** in′ter-stĭç *or* ĭn-tĕr′stĭç, *n.* A slight opening; crack; crevice; interval.— **in″ter-sti′tial,** *a.*

in′ter-val, 1 in′tər-val; 2 ĭn′ter-val, *n.* **1.** A space between objects; distance between points; degree of difference; intervening time. **2.** *Mus. & Acoustics.* Difference of pitch between two tones.

in″ter-vene′, 1 in″tər-vīn′; 2 ĭn″ter-vēn′, *vi.* [-vened′; -ven′ing.] To come or be between things; interfere; interpose; interrupt.— **in″ter-ven′tion,** *n.*

in′ter-view, 1 in′tər-viū; 2 ĭn′ter-vū. **I.** *vt.* To visit and question, as to obtain opinions. **II.** *n.* A meeting of two persons; colloquy; conference sought for publication.

in″ter-weave′, 1 in″tər-wīv′; 2 ĭn″ter-wēv′, *vt. & vi.* [-wove′; -wo′ven, -wo′vn.] To weave in; become intermingled.

in-tes′tate, 1 in-tes′tĕt; 2 ĭn-tĕs′tāt. **I.** *a.* **1.** Not having made a valid will. **2.** Not legally bequeathed. **II.** *n.* A person who dies intestate.— **in-tes′ta-cy,** *n.*

in-tes′tine, 1 in-tes′tĭn; 2 ĭn-tĕs′tĭn. **I.** **in-tes′tin⁸,** *a.* Internal; domestic; interior. **II.** *n.* The alimentary canal; bowel: usually in the plural.— **in-tes′ti-nal,** *a.* **1.** Pertaining to the intestines. **2.** Intestine. [THRALL, etc.

in-thrall′, in-throne′, etc. Same as EN-

in′ti-mate, 1 in′ti-mĕt; 2 in′ti-māt. **I.** *vt.* [-mat″ed^d; -mat″ing.] To make known indirectly; hint. **II.** 1 in′ti-mit; 2 ĭn′ti-mat, *a.* Close; confidential, as friends. **III.** *n.* A confidential friend. **-ly,** *adv.* — **in′ti-ma-cy,** *n.* [-cies^z, *pl.*] Close or confidential friendship.— **in″ti-ma′tion,** *n.* A hint.

in-tim′i-date, 1 in-tim′i-dĕt; 2 ĭn-tĭm′i-dāt, *vt.* [-dat″ed^d; -dat″ing.] To frighten; influence by fear; put in fear.— **in-tim″i-da′tion,** *n.* The use of violence or threats to influence the conduct of another.

in′to, 1 in′tu; 2 ĭn′tọ, *prep.* To and in; to the inside of.

in-tol′er-ant, 1 in-tol′ər-ənt; 2 ĭn-tŏl′ər-ant, *a.* **1.** Unwilling to tolerate contrary beliefs; bigoted. **2.** Unable to endure; as, *intolerant* of contradiction. **-ly,** *adv.*— **in-tol′er-a-bl(e)ʳ,** *a.* That can not be borne; insufferable. **-ness,** *n.*— **in-tol′er-a-bly,** *adv.*— **in-tol′er-ance,** *n.* Refusal to tolerate opposing beliefs; bigotry.

in-tomb′, -ment. Same as ENTOMB, etc.

in-tone′, 1 in-tōn′; 2 ĭn-tōn′, *vt. & vi.* [IN-TONED′; IN-TON′ING.] To recite in or to utter a musical monotone. **in′to-nate‡,**— **in″to-na′tion,** *n.* The act of intoning; modulation of the voice.

in to′to, 1 in tō′to; 2 ĭn tō′to. Altogether; entirely; literally, in all: a Latin phrase.

in-tox′i-cant, 1 in-toks′i-kənt; 2 ĭn-tŏks′i-cant, *n.* Anything that intoxicates, as alcohol; anything that unduly exhilarates.

in-tox′i-cate, 1 in-toks′i-kĕt; 2 ĭn-tŏks′i-cāt, *v.* [-cat″ed^d; -cat″ing.] **I.** *t.* To make drunk; inebriate; elate; excite. **II.** *i.* To possess intoxicating properties.— **in-tox″i-ca′tion,** *n.* Drunkenness; intense excitement.

in′tra-, *prefix.* Within; as, *intra*cerebral.

in-trac′ta-bl(e)ʳ, 1 in-trak′tə-bl; 2 ĭn-trăc′ta-bl, *a.* Not tractable; refractory; unruly, as an animal; difficult to treat or work, as a metal. **-ness,** *n.*— **in-trac″ta-bil′i-ty,** *n.*— **in-trac′ta-bly,** *adv.*

in-tran′si-tive, 1 in-tran′si-tiv; 2 ĭn-trăn′si-tiv⁸, *a.* *Gram.* Not taking or requiring an object, as certain verbs. **II.** *n.* An intransitive verb. **-ly,** *adv.*

in-trench′ᵗ, etc. Same as ENTRENCH, etc.

in-trep′id, 1 in-trep′id; 2 ĭn-trĕp′id, *a.* Unshaken in the presence of danger; dauntless.— **in″tre-pid′i-ty,** *n.* Undaunted courage.— **in-trep′id-ly,** *adv.*

in′tri-cate, 1 in′tri-kit; 2 ĭn′tri-eat, *a.* Entangled; complicated; involved. **-ly,** *adv.* **-ness,** *n.*— **in′tri-ca-cy,** *n.*

in-trigue′, 1 in-trīg′; 2 ĭn-trĭg′. **I.** *vt. & vi.* [IN-TRIGUED′; IN-TRIGU′ING.] To plot or scheme. **II.** *n.* A secret scheme; plot. **2.** A clandestine love-affair.

in-trin′sic, 1 in-trin′sik; 2 ĭn-trĭn′sie, *a.* Pertaining to the very nature of a thing or person; inherent.— **in-trin′si-cal-ly,** *adv.*

in′tro-, *prefix.* In; into; within; as, *introduce.*

in″tro-duce′, 1 in″tro-diūs′; 2 ĭn″tro-dūs′, *vt.* [-duced′ᵗ; -duc′ing.] **1.** To make acquainted. **2.** To insert. **3.** To bring into use; usher in.— **in″tro-du′cer,** *n.*— **in″tro-duc′tion,** *n.* The act of introducing. **2.** Something that introduces; a prefatory statement; elementary treatise.— **in″tro-duc′tiv(e)⁸,** *a.*— **in″tro-duc′to-ry,** *a.* Prefatory; preliminary.

in″tro-spec′tion, 1 in″tro-spek′shən; 2 ĭn″-tro-spĕc′shon, *n.* The act of looking within; self-examination.— **in″tro-spec′tiv(e^s,** *a.*
in″tro-vert′d, 1 in″tro-vūrt′; 2 ĭn″tro-vẽrt′, *vt.* To turn within.— **in″tro-ver′sion,** *n.*
in-trude′, 1 in-trūd′; 2 ĭn-trud′, *vt.* & *vi.* [IN-TRUD′ED^d; IN-TRUD′ING.] To force in, or come in, without warrant or invitation. — **in-trud′er,** *n.*— **in-tru′sion,** *n.* The act of intruding.— **in-tru′siv(e^s,** *a.* Coming without warrant; prone to intrude.
in-trust′d, *vt.* Same as ENTRUST.
in″tu-i′tion, 1 in″tiu-ish′ən; 2 ĭn″tū-ĭsh′-on, *n.* Immediate perception of truth; something felt to be true without conscious reasoning.— **in-tu′i-tiv(e^s,** *a.* Perceived or perceiving by intuition. **-ly,** *adv.* **-ness,** *n.* [etc.
in-twine′, in-twist′, etc. Same as ENTWINE,
in′un-date, 1 in′un-dēt *or* in-un′dēt; 2 ĭn′-ŭn-dāt *or* ĭn-ŭn′dāt, *vt.* [-DAT″ED^d; -DAT″-ING.] To overflow; flood; fill to overflowing.— **in″un-da′tion,** *n.* A flood; superabundance.
in-ure′, 1 in-yūr′; 2 ĭn-yur′, *v.* [IN-URED′; IN-UR′ING.] **I.** *t.* To harden or toughen by use. **II.** *i.* To take or have effect; be applied.
in-urn′, 1 in-ūrn′; 2 ĭn-ûrn′, *vt.* To put into an urn, as the ashes of the dead.
in″u-til′i-ty, 1 in″yu-til′ı-tı; 2 ĭn″yu-tĭl′i-ty, *n.* The quality of being useless or profitless.
in-vade′, 1 in-vēd′; 2 ĭn-vād′, *vt.* [IN-VAD′ED^d; IN-VAD′ING.] To enter with a hostile armed force; encroach upon.
in-val′id¹, 1 in-val′ıd; 2 ĭn-văl′id, *a.* Having no force, weight, or cogency; null.— **in-val′i-date^d,** *vt.* To weaken or destroy the validity of.— **in-val″i-da′tion,** *n.*— **in″-va-lid′i-ty,** *n.*
in′va-lid², 1 in′və-lid; 2 ĭn′va-lĭd. **I.** *a.* Enfeebled; sickly. **II.** *n.* A sickly or disabled person.— **in′va-lid-ism,** *n.* The condition of being an invalid.
in-val′u-a-ble, / **in-val′u-a-bl^p,** 1 in-val′yu-ə-bl; 2 ĭn-văl′yu-a-bl, *a.* Valuable above estimation; exceedingly precious.
in-va′ri-a-bl(e^p, in-vul′ner-a-bl(e^p. For these and similar words, see list under IN-².
in-va′sion, 1 in-vē′ʒən; 2 ĭn-vā′zhon, *n.* The act of invading; hostile attack; encroachment.— **in-va′siv(e^s,** *a.* Encroaching; aggressive. **-ly,** *adv.* **-ness,** *n.*
in-vec′tive, / **in-vec′tiv^s,** 1 in-vek′tıv; 2 ĭn-vĕc′tiv, *n.* Railing accusation; vituperation. [vehement censure or invective.
in-veigh′, 1 in-vē′; 2 ĭn-ve′, *vi.* To utter
in-vei′gle, 1 in-vī′gl; 2 ĭn-vē′gl, *vt.* [-GLED; -GLING.] To lead astray; beguile; wheedle.
in-vent′d, 1 in-vent′; 2 ĭn-vĕnt′, *vt.* To contrive by ingenuity; originate; discover. — **in-ven′tion,** *n.* **1.** The act or process of inventing. **2.** That which is invented; a device; contrivance. **3.** Skill or ingenuity in contriving.— **in-ven′tiv(e^s,** *a.* Able to invent; quick at contrivance.— **in-ven′tor,** *n.*
in′ven-to″ry, 1 in′ven-tō″rı; 2 ĭn′vĕn-tō″ry, *n.* [-RIES^z, *pl.*] An itemized list, especially of items with values, as of property.
in-vert′d, 1 in-vūrt′; 2 ĭn-vẽrt′, *vt.* To turn inside out or upside down; reverse. — **in-verse′,** *a.* Opposite in order or effect; inverted; reciprocal. **-ly,** *adv.*— **in-ver′sion,** *n.* The act of inverting; a reversal of the natural order of things.— **in-vert′i-bl(e^p,** *a.*
in-ver′te-brate, 1 in-vūr′tı-brıt; 2 ĭn-vẽr′-te-brat. **I.** *a.* Destitute of a backbone. **II.** *n.* An invertebrate animal.
in-vest′d, 1 in-vest′; 2 ĭn-vĕst′, *v.* **I.** *t.* **1.** To lay out (money) in purchase for permanent holding. **2.** To clothe; dress. **3.** To endow, as with office. **4.** To beleaguer. **II.** *i.* To make an investment. — **in-ves′ti-ture,** *n.* **1.** A formal investing, as with robes of office. **2.** That which invests or clothes.— **in-vest′ment,** *n.* The act of investing; money invested; property invested in; a blockade; siege; investiture.— **in-ves′tor,** *n.*
in-ves′ti-gate, 1 in-ves′tı-gēt; 2 ĭn-vĕs′ti-gāt, *vt.* [-GAT″ED^d; -GAT″ING.] To inquire into systematically.— **in-ves″ti-ga′-tion,** *n.*— **in-ves′ti-ga″tor,** *n.*
in-vet′er-ate, 1 in-vet′ər-ıt; 2 ĭn-vĕt′er-at, *a.* Established by long continuance; deep-rooted; confirmed.— **in-vet′er-a-cy,** *n*
in-vid′i-ous, 1 in-vid′ı-us; 2 ĭn-vĭd′i-ŭs, *a* Unjustly discriminating; provoking envy.
in-vig′or-ate, 1 in-vig′ər-ēt; 2 ĭn-vĭg′or-āt, *vt.* [-AT″ED^d; -AT″ING.] To give vigor to; animate.— **in-vig″or-a′tion,** *n.*
in-vin′ci-ble, / **in-vin′ci-bl^p,** 1 in-vin′sı-bl; 2 ĭn-vĭn′çi-bl, *a.* Unconquerable. — **in-vin″ci-bil′i-ty,** *n*
in-vi′o-late, 1 in-vai′o-lıt; 2 ĭn-vī′o-lat, *a.* Not violated; unprofaned; inviolable.— **in-vi″o-la-bil′i-ty,** *n.*— **in-vi′o-la-bl(e^p,** *a.* That must not or can not be violated. **-bly,** *adv.*
in-vis′i-ble, / **in-vis′i-bl^p,** 1 in-viz′ı-bl; 2 ĭn-vĭs′i-bl, *a.* Not visible; not in sight; concealed. **-bly,** *adv.*— **in-vis″i-bil′i-ty,** *n.*
in-vite′, 1 in-vait′; 2 ĭn-vīt′, *v.* [IN-VIT′ED^d; IN-VIT′ING.] **I.** *t.* To ask; solicit; allure; entice. **II.** *i.* To give invitation; allure. — **in″vi-ta′tion,** *n.* **1.** The act of inviting. **2.** The means of inviting.— **in-vit′ing,** *pa.* Alluring; captivating.
in″vo-ca′tion, 1 in″vo-kē′shən; 2 ĭn″vo-cā′shon, *n.* The act of invoking; prayer at the opening of a service.

in′voice, 1 in′vois ; 2 ĭn′vŏiç. **I.** *vt.* [IN′VOICED⁴; IN′VOIC·ING.] To make an invoice of. **II.** *n.* A list of goods sent, as to a purchaser; goods so listed.

in-voke′, 1 in-vōk′; 2 ĭn-vōk′, *vt.* [IN·VOKED′ᵗ; IN·VOK′ING.] To call upon or call for, as in prayer.

in-vol′un-ta-ry, 1 in-vŏl′un-tē-rɪ; 2 ĭn-vŏl′ŭn-tā-ry, *a.* Contrary to or independent of one's will.— **in-vol′un-ta-ri-ly,** *adv.*

in″vo-lu′tion, 1 in″vo-liū′shən; 2 ĭn″vo-lū′shon, *n.* The act of involving, or that which is involved; in mathematics, the raising of a quantity to a higher power.

in-volve′, 1 in-volv′; 2 ĭn-vŏlv′, *vt.* [IN·VOLV′ᵈ⁸, VOLV(E)D′ᵈ⁸; IN·VOLV′ING.] **1.** To entangle; embroil; complicate. **2.** To include; imply. **3.** *Math.* To multiply (a quantity) by itself any number of times; raise to a power.— **in-volve′ment,** *n.*

in′ward, 1 in′wərd; 2 ĭn′ward. **I.** *a.* Situated within; inner. **II.** *n.* The inside; in the plural, the viscera. **III.** *adv.* Toward the inside or interior. **In′wards**‡. -ly, *adv.* -ness, *n.*

in-weave′, ⟩ 1 in-wīv′; 2 ĭn-wēv′, *vt.* [-WOVE′-
in-weav′ᴾ, ⟩ -WO′VEN.] To weave into; weave together.

in-wrought′, 1 in-rêt′; 2 ĭn-rôt′, *pa.* Worked into, as a fabric, so as to form a part of it.

ĭ′o-did, ⟩ 1 ai′o-did, -did *or* -daid; 2 ĭ′o-dĭd,
ĭ′o-dide, ⟩ -dĭd *or* -dĭd, *n.* A compound of iodin.

ĭ′o-din, ⟩ 1 ai′o-din, -din, -dain, *or* -dīn; 2
ĭ′o-dine, ⟩ ĭ′o-dĭn, -dĭn, -dīn, *or* -dīn, *n.* *Chem.* A bluish-black crystalline element; used medicinally.

ĭ-o′ta, 1 ai-ō′ta; 2 ĭ-ō′ta, *n.* A Greek letter (ɪ, ι), corresponding to English I, i; an insignificant item; least particle: from the smallness of the Greek letter.

ip′e-cac, 1 ip′i-kak; 2 ĭp′e-căk, *n.* A South-American plant, used as an emetic. **ip″e-cac″u-an′ha**‡.

ir-, *prefix.* Form of IN-¹ or IN-² before *r*.
In the following list *ir-* has the meaning of "not," "lack of," etc., simply reversing the meaning of the word to which it is prefixed (as *ir*reclaimable, not reclaimable; *ir-*religion, lack of religion).

ir-ra′tion-al [-bly	ir″re-fut′a-bl(eᴾ, -bly
ir″re-claim′a-bl(eᴾ,	ir-reg′u-lar
ir-rec′on-cil′a-bl(eᴾ,	ir-reg″u-lar′i-ty
-ness, -bly	ir-rel′e-van-cy
ir″re-cov′er-a-bl(eᴾ,	ir-rel′e-vant
-ness, -bly	ir-re-lig′ion
ir″re-deem′a-bl(eᴾ,	ir-re-lig′ious, -ly, -ness
-ness, -bly	ir″re-me′di-a-bl(eᴾ, -bly
ir″re-duc′i-bl(eᴾ, -bly	ir″re-mov′a-bl(eᴾ, -bly

ir″re-pres′si-bl(eᴾ	ir″re-spon′si-bl(eᴾ
ir″re-proach′a-bl(eᴾ	ir″re-triev′a-bl(eᴾ
ir″re-sis′ti-bl(eᴾ, -ness	ir-rev′er-ence
ir″re-sis′ti-bly	ir-rev′er-ent, -ly

i-ras′ci-ble, ⟩ 1 ai-ras′i-bl; 2 ĭ-răs′i-bl, *a.*
i-ras′ci-blᴾ, ⟩ Prone to or caused by anger; hot-tempered; choleric.— **i-ras′ci-bly,** *adv.*

i-rate′, 1 ai-rēt′; 2 ĭ-rāt′, *a.* Moved to anger; wrathful.

ire, 1 air; 2 ĭr, *n.* Strong resentment; wrath; anger.— **ire′ful,** *a.*

ir″i-des′cent, 1 ir′i-des′ent; 2 ĭr′i-dĕs′ĕnt, *a.* Exhibiting changing rainbow-colors.— **ir″i-des′cence,** *n.*

i-rid′i-um, 1 ai-rid′i-um; 2 ĭ-rĭd′i-ŭm, *n.* A silver-white, metallic element.

i′ris, 1 ai′ris; 2 ī′rĭs, *n.* [I′RIS·ES *or* IR′I-DES, 1 -ez *or* ir′i-dīz; 2 -ēs *or* ĭr′i-dēṣ, *pl.*] **1.** The colored circle around the pupil of the eye. **2.** The rainbow. **3.** A flowering plant with sword-shaped leaves. **4.** [I-] *Myth.* The rainbow personified as the messenger of Juno (Hera) and the gods.

I′rish, 1 ai′rish; 2 ī′rish. **I.** *a.* Pertaining to Ireland or its people. **II.** *n. pl.* The people of Ireland or their language.

irkᵗ, 1 ûrk; 2 ĭrk, *vt.* To vex or fatigue.— **irk′some,** *a.* Troublesome; tiresome; tedious.

i′ron, 1 ai′ərn; 2 ī′ĕrn. **I.** *vt.* **1.** To smooth with an iron. **2.** To fetter. **3.** To fit with iron. **II.** *a.* Made of or like iron; hard; rude; unyielding; heavy. **III.** *n.* **1.** A hard, tough, malleable metal. **2.** Something made of iron, as a tool or implement; in the plural, fetters.— **i′ron-bound″,** *a.* Bound with iron; rugged and forbidding, as a coast; unchangeable and inescapable, as a contract.— **i′ron-clad″,** *n.* A war-vessel sheathed with armor.— **i′ron-mas″ter,** *n.* A manufacturer of iron.— **i′ron-mon″ger,** *n.* A dealer in iron articles or hardware.— **i′ron-mon″ger-y,** *n.*

i′ro-ny, 1 ai′ro-nɪ; 2 ī′ro-ny, *n.* Language intended to mean the opposite of what is said; covert sarcasm.— **i-ron′i-cal,** *a.* Pertaining to irony; covertly sarcastic.— **i-ron′ic**‡.

ir-ra′di-ate, 1 i-rē′di-ēt; 2 ĭ-rā′di-āt, *vt. & vi.* [-AT′ED⁴; -AT′ING.] To illuminate; shine.

ir-ref′ra-ga-ble, ⟩ 1 i-ref′ra-ga-bl; 2 ĭ-rĕf′-
ir-ref′ra-ga-blᴾ, ⟩ ra-ga-bl, *a.* That can not be refuted or disproved.

ir-rep′a-ra-ble, ⟩ 1 i-rep′a-ra-bl; 2 ĭ-rĕp′-
ir-rep′a-ra-blᴾ, ⟩ a-ra-bl, *a.* That can not be repaired, rectified, or amended.

ir-res′o-lute, 1 i-rez′o-liūt; 2 ĭ-rĕz′o-lūt, *a.* Not resolute or resolved; wavering; hesitating. -ly, *adv.*— **ir-res″o-lu′tion,** *n.*

ir″re-spec′tive, ⟩ 1 ir″re-spek′tɪv; 2 ĭr″e-
ir″re-spec′tivᵖ, ⟩ spĕc′tiv, *a.* Lacking re-

spect or relation; taking no account; regardless. **-ly,** *adv.*

ir-rev′o-ca-ble, ⟩ 1 i-rev′o-ka-bl; 2 ĭ-rĕv′o-
ir-rev′o-ca-blᵖ, ⟩ ca-bl, *a.* Incapable of being revoked or repealed; unalterable.

ir′ri-gate, 1 ir′i-gēt; 2 ĭr′ĭ-gāt, *vt.* [-GAT″-ED; -GAT″ING.] To water, as land, artificially; wet; soak; bedew.— **ir″ri-ga′tion,** *n.* Artificial watering of land.

ir′ri-tate, 1 ir′i-tēt; 2 ĭr′ĭ-tāt, *vt.* [-TAT″-EDᵈ; -TAT″ING.] To anger; provoke; inflame.— **ir″ri-ta-bil′i-ty,** *n.*— **ir′ri-ta-bl(eᵖ,** 1 ir′i-ta-bl; 2 ĭr′ĭ-ta-bl, *a.* Impatient; easily angered or excited.— **ir′ri-ta-bly,** *adv.*— **ir′-ri-tant. I.** *a.* Causing irritation. **II.** *n.* Something that causes irritation or excitement.— **ir″ri-ta′tion,** *n.*— **ir′ri-ta″tiv(eˢ,** *a.* **ir′ri-ta″to-ryϟ.**

ir-rup′tion, 1 i-rup′shan; 2 ĭ-rŭp′shon, *n.* A breaking or rushing in; violent incursion.— **ir-rup′tiv(eˢ,** *a.* **-ly,** *adv.*

is, 1 iz; 2 ĭş, *3d per. sing. pres. ind.* of BE, *v.*

-ise, *suffix.* **1.** Used to denote "condition, quality of being"; as, franch*ise.* **-iceϟ; -izeϟ. 2.** Same as -ISH². **3.** Used to form verbs: same as -IZE, 1.

-ish¹, *suffix.* Somewhat; of the nature of: used also to form adjectives of place or country; as, child*ish,* yellow*ish,* Pol*ish.*

-ish², *suffix.* To make; give.

i′sin-glass, 1 ai′zin-glas; 2 ī′şĭn-glȧs, *n.* **1.** A preparation of gelatin. **2.** Mica.

Is′lam, 1 is′lor iz′lam; 2 ĭs′lor ĭş′lam, *n.* The Mohammedan religion or body of believers.— **Is′lam-ism,** *n.*— **Is″lam-it′ic,** *a.*

is′land, ⟩ 1 ai′land; 2 ī′land, *n.* A piece
i′landˢ, ⟩ of land surrounded by water.— **is′land-er,** *n.* An inhabitant of an island.

isle, ⟩ 1 ail; 2 īl, *n.* An island: chiefly
ileˢ, ⟩ poetical.

is′let, ⟩ 1 ai′let; 2 ī′lĕt, *n.* A little island;
i′letˢ, ⟩ something like a small island.

-ism, *suffix.* Used to denote condition, act, idiom, or doctrine; as, bapt*ism,* critic*ism,* organ*ism.*

ism, 1 izm; 2 ĭşm, *n.* A doctrine or system.

is′o-late, 1 is′o-[or ai′so-]lēt; 2 ĭs′o-[or ī′so-]lāt, *vt.* [-LAT″EDᵈ; -LAT″ING.] To detach; insulate: place by itself.— **is″o-la′tion,** *n.*

i″so-met′ric, 1 ai″so-met′rik; 2 ī″so-mĕt′-rie, *a.* Of equal measure.

i-sos′ce-les, 1 ai-sos′i-līz; 2 ī-sŏs′e-lēş, *a.* *Geom.* Having two sides equal, as a triangle.

i′so-therm, 1 ai′so-thūrm; 2 ī′so-thĕrm, *n.* A line passing through points on the earth's surface that have the same temperature.— **i″so-ther′mal,** *a.*

Is′ra-el-ite, 1 iz′ri-el-ait; 2 ĭş′ra-ĕl-īt, *n.* A descendant of Israel (or Jacob); a He-

brew; Jew.— **Is′ra-el-it″ish,** *a.* Jewish. **Is″-ra-el-it′leϟ.**

is′sue, 1 ish′u; 2 ĭsh′ụ. **I.** *vt.* & *vi.* [IS′SUED; IS′SU-ING.] To send forth; give or flow out; proceed; result. **II.** *n.* **1.** The act of issuing. **2.** That which is issued; an edition; progeny; a matter of discussion; profits; final outcome.

-ist, *suffix.* Used to denote an agent; as, organ*ist.*

isth′mus, 1 is′mus or ist′mus; 2 ĭs′mŭs or ĭst′mŭs, *n.* A narrow body of land connecting two larger bodies.

it, 1 it; 2 ĭt, *pron.* [THEY, 1 thē; 2 thę, *pl.*] The personal pronoun of the third person, singular number, and neuter gender: that one.

I-tal′ian, 1 i-tal′yan; 2 ĭ-tăl′yan. **I.** *a.* Pertaining to Italy its people, or language. **II.** *n.* The people or language of Italy.

I-tal′ic, 1 i-tal′ik; 2 ĭ-tăl′ie. **I.** *a.* **1.** Relating to the races or languages of Italy. **2.** [i- or I-] Printed in italic. **II.** *n.* [i- or I-] A style of type in which the letters slope, as *these.*— **i-tal′i-cize,** 1 i-tal′i-saiz; 2 ĭ-tăl′i-çiz, *vt.* [-CIZED; -CIZ″ING.] [i- or I-] To put in italics; emphasize. **i-tal′i-ciseϟ.**

itch, ⟩ 1 ich; 2 ĭch. **Iᵗ.** *vi.* **1.** To feel an irri-
ichᵖ, ⟩ tation of the skin with inclination to scratch the part. **2.** To have a teasing inclination to do a thing. **II.** *n.* **1.** A contagious skin-disease; an itching. **2.** A teasing desire.— **itch′y,** *a.*

i′tem, 1 ai′tem; 2 ī′tĕm. **I.** *n.* A separate article or entry in an account, etc. **II.** *adv.* Likewise.— **i′tem-ize,** *vt.* [-IZED; IZ″-ING.] To set down by items.

it′er-ate, 1 it′er-ēt; 2 ĭt′er-āt, *vt.* [-AT″EDᵈ; -AT″ING.] To utter or do again; repeat.— **it″er-a′tion,** *n.*

i-tin′er-ant, 1 ai-tin′er-ant; 2 ĭ-tĭn′er-ant. **I.** *a.* Going from place to place. **II.** *n.* One, as a preacher, who travels from place to place.— **i-tin′er-a-cy,** **i-tin′-er-an-cy,** *n.* A passing from place to place in circuit.— **i-tin′er-a-ry. I.** *a.* Pertaining to or done on a journey; itinerant. **II.** *n.* [-RIESᶻ, *pl.*] A detailed account of a journey; guide-book.— **i-tin′er-ate,** *vt.* To journey from place to place in circuit.

-itis, *suffix.* Used to denote inflammation; as, tonsil*itis.*

its, 1 its; 2 ĭts, *pron.* Possessive case of IT.

—**it-self′**, 1 it-self′; 2 ĭt-sĕlf′, *pron.* Its self: emphatic or reflexive.

—**iv(e⁵**, *suffix.* Doing; serving to do; tending to do or be; as, construct*ive*, expans*ive*, recept*ive*.

i′vo-ry, 1 ai′vo-rɪ; 2 ĭ′vo-ry. **I.** *a.* Made of or resembling ivory. **II.** *n.* [-RIES², *pl.*] The hard, white, elastic substance of the tusks of certain animals, as the elephant.

i′vy, 1 ɑi′vɪ; 2 ĭ′vy, *n.* A European evergreen climbing shrub, or one of various other climbing plants.—**i′vied**, *a.* Overgrown with ivy. See illus. on preceding page.

—**ize, -ise**, *suffix.* **1.** Used to form verbs denoting to make; give; practise; as, liberal*ize*, tyrann*ize*. **2.** Used to form nouns: same as -ISE, 1.

iz′zard, 1 ĭz′ərd; 2 ĭz′ard, *n.* The letter Z: an old name.

J

J, j, 1 jē; 2 jā, *n.* [JAYS, J's, or *J*s, 1 jēz; 2 jās, *pl.*] The tenth letter in the English alphabet.

jab′ber, 1 jab′ər; 2 jăb′er. **I.** *vt. & vi.* To chatter. **II.** *n.* Rapid or unintelligible talk; chatter.

ja′bot′, 1 ʒɑ″bŏ′; 2 zhä″bŏ′, *n.* A lace frill worn on the bosom. [F.]

jack, 1 jak; 2 jăk, *n.* **1.** [J-] A nickname for *John, James,* or *Jacob.* **2.** A handy tool.—**jack′a-napes″**, *n.* An impertinent fellow; an upstart.—**jack′ass″**, *n.* **1.** The male ass; a donkey. **2.** A fool; blockhead. —**jack′=boots″**, *n. pl.* Heavy top-boots reaching above the knee.—**jack′daw″**, *n.* A small European glossy-black, crow-like bird, often tamed.—**jack′=knife**, *n.* A large clasp-knife for the pocket.—**jack′-o′-lantern**, *n.* **1.** A will-o′-the-wisp; ignis fatuus. **2.** [U. S.] A lantern made of the hollow shell of a pumpkin or squash slashed to represent a face.

jack′al, 1 jak′ôl; 2 jăk′al, *n.* A dog-like carnivorous mammal, smaller than the wolf.

jack′et, 1 jak′et; 2 jăk′ĕt. **I**d. *vt.* To clothe or enclose in a jacket. **II.** *n.* A short coat.

jade, 1 jēd; 2 jād, *vt. & vi.* [JAD′EDd; JAD′ING.] To weary, or become weary, by hard service. [less person; hussy.

jade¹, *n.* An old worn-out horse; a worthless person.

jade², *n.* A hard, tough, greenish silicate used for making ornaments, etc.

jag, 1 jag; 2 jăg, *vt.* [JAG′GEDd; JAG′GING.] To notch.

jag′, *n.* A projecting point; notch; tooth.— **jag′ged**, *a.* Having jags or notches.

jag², *n.* **1.** [Local.] A load for one horse. **2.** [Slang.] Enough liquor to intoxicate; intoxication.

Jaguar. ⅟₅₅

jag′uar, 1 jag′wor *or* jə-gwɑr′; 2 jăg′wär *or* ja-gwär′, *n.* A large leopard-like mammal of wooded regions from Texas to Patagonia.

jail, 1 jēl; 2 jāl. **I.** *vt.* To imprison. **II.** *n.* A prison. **gaol†.**—**jail′bird″**, *n.* A convict —**jail′er**, *n.* The officer in charge of a jail

jal′ap, 1 jal′əp; 2 jăl′ap, *n.* The dried root of a Mexican plant useful as a purgative: named from *Jalapa,* a town in Mexico.

jam, 1 jam; 2 jăm, *v.* [JAMMED²; JAMD⁵; JAM′MING.] **I.** *t.* To press into a tight place; crush; crowd. **II.** *i.* To become immovable from being crowded.

jam¹, *n.* A number of people or objects crowded together.

jam², *n.* A conserve of fruit. [way, etc.

jamb, 1 jam; 2 jăm, *n.* A side of a door-

jan′gle, 1 jan′gl; 2 jăn′gl. **I.** *vt. & vi.* [JAN′GLED; JAN′GLING.] To make harsh, broken sounds; wrangle; bicker. **II.** *n.* Discordant sound; wrangling.

jan′i-tor, 1 jan′i-tər *or* -ter; 2 jăn′i-tor, *n.* One who has the care of a building.—**jan′i-tress**, *n. fem.*

jan′i-za-ry, 1 jan′i-zē-rɪ; 2 jăn′i-zā-ry, *n.* [-RIES², *pl.*] One of the former bodyguard of the Turkish sultan. **jan′is-sa-ry†.**

Jan′u-a-ry, 1 jan′yu-ĕ-rɪ; 2 jăn′yu̇-ā-ry, *n.* The first month of the year.

ja-pan′, 1 jə-pan′; 2 ja-păn′. **I.** *vt.* [JA-PANNED′, JA-PAND″⁵; JA-PAN′NING.] To lacquer with japan. **II.** *n.* **1.** Lacquered Japanese work. **2.** A hard black varnish.

Jap″a-nese′, 1 jap″ə-nīs′ *or* -nīz′; 2 jăp″-a-nēs′ *or* -nĕs′. **I.** *a.* Belonging to Japan or its people. **II.** *n.* A native of Japan or the language of Japan.

jar, 1 jɑr; 2 jär, *v.* [JARRED, JARD⁵; JAR′RING.] **I.** *t.* To cause to tremble or shake; agitate. **II.** *i.* **1.** To rattle. **2.** To clash; conflict. **3.** To shake or tremble.

jar′, *n.* **1.** A shaking, as from a sudden shock. **2.** A discordant sound; discord; strife.

jar², *n.* A deep, wide=mouthed vessel of earthenware or glass.

jar″di″niѐre′, 1 zär″dĭ″nyär′; 2 zhär″dĭ″nyĕr′, *n.* An ornamental pot or stand, as of porcelain, for flowers or plants.

jar′gon, 1 jär′gŏn; 2 jär′gon, *n.* Confused speech.

jas′mine, } 1 jas′mĭn; 2 jăs′min, *n.* An
jas′min⁵, } ornamental plant with fragrant, generally white, flowers.

jas′per, } 1 jas′pẽr, -aĭt; 2 jăs′per, -ĭt, *n.*
jas′per-ite, } An opaque, colored quartz.

jaun′dice, } 1 jän′dĭs or jǒn′dĭs, 2 jän′dĭç
jaun′dis⁵, } or jạn′dĭç, *n.* A disease characterized by yellowness of the skin.

jaunt, 1 jänt or jŏnt; 2 jänt or jạnt. **I**d. *vi.* To ramble about. **II.** *n.* A short journey; a pleasure=trip.

jaunt′y, 1 jänt′ɪ or jŏnt′ɪ; 2 jänt′y or jạnt′y, *a.* [JAUNT′I-ER; JAUNT′I-EST.] Careless; sprightly.—**jaunt′i-ly**, *adv.*—**jaunt′i-ness,**n.

jave′lin, 1 jav′lĭn; 2 jăv′lin, *n.* A short, light spear, for throwing.

jaw, 1 jɓ; 2 jạ, *n.* **1.** One of the bones of the mouth in which the teeth are set; also such bone with its attachments. **2.** Anything like or suggesting such an organ, as one of the gripping parts of a vise: often used figuratively; as, the *jaws* of death. [of brilliant coloring

jay, 1 jē; 2 jā, *n.* A small crow=like bird

jazz, 1 jaz; 2 jăz, *n.* Syncopated music played in discordant tones.—**jazz′band, n.**

jeal′ous, } 1 jel′ʊs; 2 jĕl′ŭs,
jel′ous⁵, } *a.* **1.** Apprehensive of being displaced by a rival. **2.** Anxiously watchful. **-ly,** *adv.* **-ness,** *n.*—**jeal′ous-y,** *n.* [-IES², *pl.*]

jean, 1 jēn or jĭn; 2 jän or jĕn, *n.* A twilled cotton cloth.

jeep, 1 jīp; 2 jēp, *n.* A small, military motor=vehicle with four=wheel drive.

jeer, 1 jɪr; 2 jēr. **I.** *vt. & vi.* To scoff at; mock. **II.** *n.* A derisive word or speech.

American Blue Jay. ¹/₁₅

Je-ho′vah, 1 jɪ-hō′vɑ; 2 je-hō′va, *n.* Lord; specifically, the covenant God of the Hebrew people.

je-june′, 1 jɪ-jūn′; 2 je-jụn′, *a.* Lifeless; dry; dull. **-ly,** *adv.* **-ness,** *n.*

jel′ly, 1 jel′ɪ; 2 jĕl′y. **I.** *vi.* [JEL′LIED; JEL′LY-ING.] To turn to jelly. **II.** *n.* [JEL′LIES², *pl.*] Any semisolid glutinous mass, as fruit=juice boiled with sugar.

jen′ny, 1 jen′ɪ; 2 jĕn′y, *n.* [JEN′NIES², *pl.*] **1.** A spinning=machine. **2.** A female ass.

jeop′ardd, } 1 jep′ẽrd; 2 jĕp′ard, *vt.* To
jep′ardr, } expose to loss or injury; imperil. **jeop′ard-ize**†.—**jeop′ard-y,** *n.* Exposure to danger; peril.

jerk¹, 1 jũrk; 2 jẽrk. **I**t. *vt. & vi.* To give a jerk to; move with jerks. **II**¹. *n.* A short, sharp pull, twitch, or fling.—**jerk′y,** *a.*

jerk². **I**t. *vt.* To cure (meat) by cutting into strips and drying. **II**². *n.* Meat, as beef, so cured. **jerked beef**‡; **jerked meat**‡.

jer′kin, 1 jũr′kɪn; 2 jẽr′kin, *n.* A jacket.

Jer′sey, 1 jũr′zɪ; 2 jẽr′sy, *n.* **1.** One of a breed of cattle from the island of Jersey. **2.** [j-] A seamless, knit upper garment from the island of Jersey.

jes′sa-mine, } 1 jes′ɑ-mɪn; 2 jĕs′a-mǐn, *n.*
jes′sa-min⁵, } The jasmine.

jest, 1 jest; 2 jĕst. **I**d. *vt. & vi.* To joke. **II.** *n.* A joke; raillery.—**jest′er,** *n.*

Jes′u-it, 1 jez′yu-ɪt or jez′u-ɪt; 2 jĕş′yu-it or jĕzh′u-it, *n.* **1.** R. C. Ch. A member of the Society of Jesus. **2.** A subtle reasoner.— **Jes″u-it′ic,** *a.* **Jes″u-it′i-cal**‡.

Je′sus, 1 jī′zus; 2 jē′şŭs, *n.* Personal name of the Messiah— the Christ.

jet, 1 jet; 2 jĕt, *vt. & vi.* [JET′TED**d**; JET′TING.] To shoot out in a jet or jets.

jet¹. *n.* **1.** That which spurts out. **2.** A spout or nozle.

jet², *n.* **1.** A rich black mineral coal, used for ornaments. **2.** The color of jet; deep black. **jet=black**‡.

jet′sam, 1 jet′sɑm; 2 jĕt′sam, *n.* The non-floating part of a cargo cast into the sea to lighten a vessel in danger: opposed to *flotsam*.

jet′ti-son, 1 jet′ɪ-sɑn; 2 jĕt′i-son. **I.** *vt.* To throw overboard, as goods, to lighten an endangered vessel. **II.** *n.* The throwing overboard of cargo, or goods so sacrificed; jetsam. [jet; black as jet.

jet′ty, 1 jet′ɪ; 2 jĕt′y, *a.* Like or made of

jet′ty, *n.* [JET′TIES², *pl.*] A pier.

Jew, 1 jū; 2 jụ, *n.* **1.** A Hebrew; an Israelite. — **Jew′ess,** *n.* A female Jew.— **Jew′ish,** *a.* Of or pertaining to a Jew or Jews; Hebrew.

jew′el, 1 jū′el; 2 jụ′ĕl. **I.** *vt.* [JEW′ELED or JEW′ELLED; JEW′EL-ING or JEW′EL-LING.] To adorn with jewels. **II.** *n.* A precious stone; gem; anything precious.— **jew′el-er,** *n.* A dealer in or maker of jewelry. **jew′el-ler**‡.—**jew′el-ry,** *n.* **1.** Jewels collectively. **2.** The trade of a jeweler.

jew's′=harp″, 1 jūz′=härp″; 2 jụş′=härp″, *n.* A small musical instrument with a metal frame and a bent metallic tongue.

jib, 1 jib; 2 jĭb, *n.* A triangular sail extending from the foretopmast=head to the jib=boom or the bowsprit.—**jib′=boom″,**

1: ɑ = final; ɪ = habit; aisle; ɑu = out; oil; ĭu = feud; chin; go; ŋ = sing; thin, this.
2: wolf, dǫ; bꝋꝋk, bꝋꝋt; fựll, rựle, cūre, bŭt, bũrn; ŏil, bŏy; ĝo, gem; iŋk; thin, this.

n. A spar forming part of the bowsprit.

jibe, 1 jaib; 2 jīb, *vt. & vi. Naut.* [JIBED; JIB´ING.] To shift, as a sail; tack.

jig, 1 jig; 2 jĭg, *n.* A light, rapid dance.

jilt, 1 jilt; 2 jĭlt. I. *vt. & vi.* To discard, as a lover. II. *n.* One who discards a lover.

jim´my, 1 jim´i; 2 jĭm´y, *n.* A burglar's crowbar, sometimes made in sections.

jin´gle, ⎱ 1 jiŋ´gl; 2 jĭŋ´gl. [JIN´GL(E)D³;
jin´gl², ⎰ JIN´GLING.] I. *vt. & vi.* To make a slight, tinkling sound. II. *n.* 1. A tinkling sound. 2. Any pleasing succession of rhythmical sounds.

Jin´go, 1 jiŋ´go; 2 jĭŋ´go, *n. Polit.* One in favor of an aggressive foreign policy.

jin-rik´i-sha, 1 jin-rik´i-shə; 2 jĭn-rĭk´i-sha, *n.* A small, two-wheeled Japanese carriage.
jin-rik´shaᵗ.

jit´ney, 1 jit´ni; 2 jĭt´ny, *n.* [U.S.] 1. A small coin; nickel. 2. A motor-vehicle carrying passengers for a small fare.

Jinrikisha.

job, 1 jɵb; 2 jŏb. I. *vt. & vi.* [JOBBED, JOBDˢ; JOB´BING.] To buy, sell, work, etc., by the job. II. *n.* 1. A piece of work done as a whole. 2. A corrupt money-making scheme. **job´ber,** *n.* 1. A middleman. 2. An intriguer. One who works by the job.—**job´ber-y,** *n.*

jock´ey, 1 jɵk´i; 2 jŏk´y. I. *vt. & vi.* [JOCK´EYED; JOCK´EY-ING.] To play the jockey with; be tricky; cheat. II. *n.* 1. One employed to ride horses, as at races. 2. A cheat. 3. A horse-dealer.

jo-cose´, 1 jo-kōs´; 2 jo-cōs´, *a.* Of the nature of a joke; jocular. **-ly,** *adv.* **-ness,** *n.*—**joc´u-lar,** *a.* 1. Being in a joking mood; making jokes. 2. Jocose. **-ly,** *adv.*—**joc´u-lar´i-ty,** *n.*—**joc´und,** 1 jɵk´und; 2 jŏc´und, *a.* Jovial; sportive.—**jo-cun´di-ty,** *n.*

jodh-pur´, 1 jŏd-pūr´; 2 jŏd-pᵤr´, *n.* A type of riding-breeches noted for its close fit down to the heel and fitted with a cuff; first used by British Army officers who obtained goods from Jodhpur, India, after which it was named.

jog, 1 jɵg; 2 jŏg. I. *vt. & vi.* [JOGGED, JOGDˢ; JOG´GING.] To move with a jog; nudge. II. *n.* 1. A slight push. 2. A slow, jolting motion.—**jog´ger,** *n.*

jog´gle, ⎱ 1 jɵg´l; 2 jŏg´l. I. *vt. & vi.*
jog´l², ⎰ [JOG´GLED, JOG´LDᵖ; JOG´GLING.] To shake slightly; jog. II. *n.* A jolt.

John Bull. The typical Englishman: a nickname. Hence, the English people.

join, 1 jɵin; 2 join, *vt. & vi.* 1. To put together; unite; connect; combine. 2. To engage in (battle, etc.) together.—**join´er-y,** *n.*

jointᵈ, 1 jɵint; 2 jŏint, *vt. & vi.* To form with or unite by joints.

joint, *a.* Combined; shared; joined. **-ly,** *adv.*

joint, *n.* 1. A junction, as of two movable bones; place of union; hinge. 2. A piece of meat, as for roasting.

joist, 1 jɵist; 2 jŏist, *n.* A horizontal timber in a floor or ceiling.

joke, 1 jōk; 2 jōk. I. *vt. & vi.* [JOKEDᵗ; JOK´ING.] To make sport of; attack playfully; utter witticisms; banter; jest. II. *n.* 1. A jest. 2. A subject for merriment.

jol´ly, 1 jɵl´i; 2 jŏl´y, *a.* [JOL´LI-ER; JOL´LI-EST.] 1. Full of life and mirth; jovial. 2. Expressing mirth; exciting gaiety.—**jol´li-fi-ca´tion,** *n.* [Colloq.] A merrymaking.—**jol´li-ty,** *n.*—**jol´li-ly,** *adv.*—**jol´li-ness, jol´li-tyᵗ,** *n.*

jol´ly-boat´, 1 jɵl´i-bōt´; 2 jŏl´y-bōt´, *n.* A small boat belonging to a ship.

jolt, 1 jōlt; 2 jōlt. Iᵈ. *vt. & vi.* To shake with a jarring movement. II. *n.* A sudden, jarring shock.

jon´quil, 1 jɵn´kwil; 2 jŏn´kwil, *n.* A bulbous plant related to the daffodil.

joss, 1 jes; 2 jŏs, *n.* A Chinese god or idol.—**joss´-house,** *n.* A Chinese temple or shrine for idols.—**j.-stick,** *n.* A slender stick of perfumed wood-powder and paste burnt as incense, etc.

jos´tle, ⎱ 1 jes´l; 2 jŏs´l, *vt.*
jos´tl², ⎰ & *vi.* [JOS´TL(E)Dᵖ; JOS´TLING.] To push or crowd against.—**jos´tl(e²,** *n.* A bumping against.

Jonquil.

jot, 1 jɵt; 2 jŏt. I. *vt.* [JOT´TEDᵈ; JOT´TING.] To note down or sketch offhand. II. *n.* The least bit; an iota.—**jot´ting,** *n.* A short note; memorandum.

joule, 1 jaul; 2 joul, *n.* The practical unit of electrical energy, equivalent to the work done by keeping up for one second a current of one ampere against a resistance of one ohm: named from the English physicist J. P. *Joule* (1818–1889).

jour´nal, 1 jûr´nal; 2 jûr´nal, *n.* 1. A daily record; diary. 2. A newspaper. 3. That part of a shaft which rotates in a bearing.—**jour´nal-ism,** *n.* The occupation of a journalist.—**jour´nal-ist,** *n.* One who manages, edits, or writes for a journal or newspaper.

jour´ney, ⎱ 1 jûr´ni; 2 jûr´ny. I. *vi.* To
jur´ney², ⎰ travel. II. *n.* Passage from

1: ärtistic, ärt; fat, fāre; fast; get, prey; hit, police; obey, gō; net, ôr; full, rūle; but, būrn.
2: ärt, āpe, fắt, fâre, fȧst, whạt, ạll; mē, gĕt, prey, fêrn; hĭt, īce; ī=ĕ; ĭ=ẽ; gō, nŏt, ôr, wŏn,

one place to another.— **jour'ney-man,** n. [-MEN, pl.] A skilled mechanic.

joust, 1 just; 2 jŭst, v. & n. Same as JUST.

jo'vi-al, 1 jō'vi-əl; 2 jō'vi-al, a. Mirthful; merry; jolly.— **jo''vi-al'i-ty.** n.

jowl, 1 jōl or jaul; 2 jōl or jowl, n. The cheek or jaw.

joy, 1 joi; 2 jŏy, n. **1.** A lively emotion of happiness; gladness. **2.** Something that gives delight.— **joy'ful,** a. **1.** Full of joy. **2.** Manifesting joy. **-ly,** adv. **-ness,** n.— **joy'less,** a. Destitute of joy. **-ly,** adv. **-ness,** n.— **joy'ous,** a. Joyful. **-ly,** adv. **-ness,** n.

ju'bi-lant, 1 jū'bɪ-lənt; 2 jų'bi-lant, a. Manifesting great joy; exultingly glad; triumphant.— **ju''bi-la'tion,** n. Rejoicing; exultation.— **ju'bi-lee,** n. **1.** The fiftieth anniversary of an event. **2.** Any season of rejoicing.

Ju-da'ic, 1 ju-dē'ɪk; 2 jų-dā'ic, a. Pertaining to the Jews. **Ju-da'i-cal‡.**— **Ju'da-ism,** n. The Jewish system of religion or government; Jewish beliefs or practises.

judge, 1 juj; 2 jŭdg, v. [JUDGED; JUDG'ING.] **I.** t. **1.** To come to a conclusion regarding. **2.** To decide upon evidence; try judicially. **II.** i. **1.** To form a judgment; sit in judgment; express judgment. **2.** To consider.

judge, n. **1.** An officer authorized to administer justice in a court. **2.** One who decides upon the merits of things, as in contests; a connoisseur.— **judg'ment,** n. **1.** The act or faculty of judging; power to judge wisely or well. **2.** The decision reached. **3.** The sentence of a court. **4.** A disaster or affliction regarded as a punishment for sin. **judge'ment‡.**— **judge'ship,** n.

ju'di-ca-ture, 1 jū'dɪ-kə-chur or -tiur; 2 jų'di-ea-chur or -tūr, n. **1.** The power of administering justice. **2.** The jurisdiction of a court. **3.** A court of justice.— **ju'di-ca''tiv(es,** a. Competent to judge.— **ju'di-ca-to-ry,** a. Pertaining to the administration of justice.

ju-di'cial, 1 ju-dish'əl; 2 jų-dĭsh'al, a. **1.** Pertaining to a court or to the administration of justice. **2.** Discriminating; impartial. **-ly,** adv.— **ju-di'ci-a-ry.** **I.** a. Pertaining to courts of justice. **II.** n. **1.** That department of government which administers the law. **2.** The judges collectively.

ju-di'cious, 1 ju-dish'us; 2 jų-dĭsh'ŭs, a. Manifesting forethought and sense; prudent; wise. **-ly,** adv. **-ness,** n.

jug, 1 jug; 2 jŭg, n. **1.** [U. S.] A narrow-necked stout bulging vessel for liquids,

designed to be closed with a cork. **2.** A pitcher.

jug'gle, 1 jug'l; 2 jŭg'l. **I.** **jug'l⁵,** vt. & vi. [JUG'GLED, JUG'LD⁵; JUG'GLING.] To deceive by trick; practise sleight of hand. **II.** n. A trick; deception.— **jug'gler,** n. One who practises sleight of hand.— **jug'gler-y,** n.

French Earthenware Jug.

ju'gu-lar, 1 jū'giu-lər; 2 jų'gū-lar. **I.** a. Pertaining to the throat or to the jugular vein. **II.** n. One of the large veins of the neck.

juice, 1 jūs; 2 jųç, n. The fluid part of vegetable or animal matter.— **juic'y,** a. [JUIC'I-ER; JUIC'I-EST.] Abounding with juice.— **juic'i-ly,** adv.— **juic'i-ness,** n.

ju'jut''su, 1 jū'-jut'sū; 2 jų'-jut'sų, n. [Jap.] Wrestling or throwing an opponent by sleight. **jiu''-jut'sut.**

ju'lep, 1 jū'lep; 2 jų'lĕp, n. A drink composed of sweetened liquor and mint.

ju'li-enne', 1 gū'li-en'; 2 zhū'li-ĕn', n. A clear meat soup into which vegetables have been chopped or shredded: named from Julien, a French caterer of Boston.

Ju-ly', 1 ju-lai'; 2 jų-lŷ', n. The seventh month of the year.

jum'ble, 1 jum'bl; 2 jŭm'bl. **I.** vt. & vi. **jum'bl⁵,** [JUM'BL(E)D⁵; JUM'BLING.] To mix confusedly. **II.** n. **1.** A confused mixture. **2.** A thin sweet cake.

jump, 1 jump; 2 jŭmp, v. **I.** t. **1.** To leap over. **2.** To cause to leap. **II.** i. To impel oneself through the air; leap; spring.

[spring.

jump, n. The act of jumping; a leap;

junc'tion, 1 jŭnk'shən; 2 jŭnc'shon, n. **1.** The act of joining, or condition of being joined. **2.** A place of union or meeting.— **junc'ture,** n. **1.** A junction; joint. **2.** An occasion when circumstances meet.

June, 1 jūn; 2 jųn, n. The sixth month of the year.

jun'gle, 1 jun'gl; 2 jŭn'gl, n. A dense thicket; a forest choked with undergrowth.— **jun'gly,** a.

jun'ior, 1 jūn'yər; 2 jųn'yor. **I.** a. Younger in years or lower in rank. **II.** n. The younger of two; a younger person.— **jun-ior'i-ty,** n.— **jun'ior-ship,** n.

ju'ni-per, 1 jū'nɪ-pər; 2 jų'ni-per, n. An evergreen shrub with dark-blue berries

junk, 1 junk; 2 jŭnk, n. **1.** Naut. (1) Old cordage. (2) Salt meat. **2.** Cast-off material.

junk[2], *n.* A large Chinese sailing-vessel.
jun'ket, 1 jŭn'ket; 2 jŭn'kĕt. **I**[d]. *vt. & vi.* To feast in company; revel. **II.** *n.* A feast; picnic.
Ju'no, 1 jū'no; 2 ju'no, *n. Rom. Myth.* Wife of Jupiter; queen of heaven. **He'ra**‡ [Gr.].
jun'ta, 1 jun'ta; 2 jŭn'ta, *n.* A Spanish or South-American legislative assembly or council. [cabal.
jun'to, 1 jun'to; 2 jŭn'to, *n.* A faction; a
Ju'pi-ter, 1 jū'pi-tər; 2 jụ'pi-tẽr, *n. Rom. Myth.* Chief of the gods; king of heaven. **Zeus**‡ [Gr.].
ju-rid'i-cal, 1 ju-rid'i-kal; 2 jụ-rĭd'i-cal, *a.* **1.** Relating to law. **2.** Assumed by law to exist. **ju-rid'ic**‡.
ju'ris-dic'tion, 1 jū'ris-dik'shən; 2 jū'ris-dic'shon, *n.* The right or limit of exercising authority.
ju'ris-pru'dence, 1 jū'ris-prū'dens; 2 jụ'ris-prụ'dĕnc, *n.* **1.** The science of law. **2.** A system of laws.
ju'rist, 1 jū'rist; 2 jụ'rĭst, *n.* One versed in law.
ju'ror, 1 jū'rər *or* -rɛr; 2 jụ'ror, *n.* A member of a jury.
ju'ry, 1 jū'ri; 2 jụ'ry, *n.* [JU'RIES[z], *pl.*] A body of persons sworn to give a true verdict upon the evidence in a trial; any committee of award.
ju'ry-mast", *n. Naut.* A temporary mast.

just, 1 just; 2 jŭst. **I**[d]. *vi.* To engage
joust, in a tilt or tournament. **II.** *n.* A tilting-match between mounted knights.
just. I. *a.* Righteous; honest; equitable. **II.** *adv.* **1.** Exactly; precisely. **2.** But now; this moment. **3.** Barely; only.
jus'tice, 1 jus'tis; 2 jŭs'tiç, *n.* **1.** Conformity to the principles of right;
jus'tiss, honesty; impartiality. **2.** A judge.—**jus'ti-ci-a-ry,** 1 jus-tish'i-ē-ri; 2 jŭs-tish'i-ā-ry. **I.** *a.* Pertaining to law or the administration of justice. **II.** *n.* [-RIES[z], *pl.*] A judge.
jus'ti-fy, 1 jus'ti-fai; 2 jŭs'ti-fī, *vt.* [-FIED'; -FY"ING.] **1.** To show to be just; vindicate. **2.** To declare blameless; exonerate. **3.** To adjust.—**jus"ti-fi"a-ble,** *a.* Capable of being justified. **-ness,** *n.*—**jus'ti-fi"a-bly,** *adv.*—**jus"ti-fi-ca'tion,** *n.* The state of being justified.
jut, 1 jut; 2 jŭt. **I.** *vi.* [JUT'TED[d]; JUT'TING.] To project. **II.** *n.* A projection.
jute, 1 jūt; 2 jụt, *n.* An annual Asiatic herb of the linden family, or its fiber: used for bags.
ju've-nile, 1 jū'vi-nil; 2 ju've-nĭl. **I.** *a.*
ju've-nils, Characteristic of or adapted to youth; youthful; young. **II.** *n.* A young person.—**ju"ve-nil'i-ty,** *n.* Youthfulness.
jux"ta-po-si'tion, 1 juks"ta-po-zish'ən; 2 jŭks"ta-po-gĭsh'on, *n.* A placing close together; contiguity.

K

K, k, 1 kē; 2 kā, *n.* [KAYS, K's, *or* Ks, 1 kēz; 2 kāg, *pl.*] The eleventh letter in the English alphabet.
kai'ak, 1 kai'ak; 2 kī'ăk, *n.* A hunting
kay'ak, canoe of arctic America, made of sealskin stretched over a frame.
kail, *n.* Same as KALE.
Kai'ser, 1 kai'zər; 2 kī'ser, *n.* Cæsar: the title of the German emperors from 1871 to 1918. [cabbage.

Kaiak.

kale, 1 kēl; 2 kāl, *n.* A variety of headless
ka-lei'do-scope, 1 ka-lai'do-skōp; 2 ka-lī'do-scŏp, *n.* An instrument which, by means of mirrors, presents objects viewed through it in symmetrical patterns.—**ka-lei"do-scop'ic,** *a.* [CIMINE.
kal'so-mine, *v. & n.* Incorrect form of CAL-
kan"ga-roo', 1 kaŋ'ga-rū'; 2 kăŋ"ga-rōō',

n. A marsupial quadruped of Australia, having strong hind limbs and moving by leaps. [A Chinese millet.
ka"o'li-ang, 1 kā"ō'li-aŋ; 2 kā"ō'li-ăng, *n.*
ka'o-lin, 1 kē'o-lin; 2 kā'o-lĭn, *n.* A variety of white clay: a chief ingredient of porcelain.
kat'sup, *n.* Same as CATCHUP.
ka'ty-did", 1 kē'ti-did"; 2 kā'ty-dĭd", *n.* An insect named from its cry. [əs KAIAK.
kay'ack, kay'ak, *n.* Same
kedge, 1 kej; 2 kĕdg, *n.* A light anchor.
keel, 1 kīl; 2 kēl. **I.** *vt. & vi.* **1.** To put a keel on. **2.** To turn up the keel; as, to *keel over.* **II.** *n.* The lowest lengthwise member of the framework of a vessel, projecting along the bottom from stem to stern.

Broad-winged Katydid. ¹/₂

keel'son, 1 kel'san; 2 kĕl'son, *n.* A beam running lengthwise above the keel, to stiffen a vessel.

keen, 1 kīn; 2 kēn, *a.* Very sharp and cutting; acute; shrewd. **-ly,** *adv.* **-ness,** *n.*

keep, 1 kīp; 2 kēp, *v.* [KEPT; KEEP'ING.] **I.** *t.* **1.** To have; hold; retain. **2.** To protect; guard; defend. **3.** To support; maintain. **4.** To be faithful to, as a pledge or command. **II.** *i.* To remain; stay; continue sound, sweet, fresh, or the like; endure.— **keep'er,** *n.*— **keep'ing,** *n.* **1.** Custody, charge, or possession. **2.** Right proportion; suitableness. **3.** Maintenance; support.— **keep'sake",** *n.* Anything kept for the sake of the giver; a memento.

keep, 1 kīp; 2 kēp, *n.* **1.** Means of subsistence; livelihood. **2.** A castle; fortress.

keg, 1 keg; 2 kĕg, *n.* A small strong barrel. [seaweed.

kelp, 1 kelp; 2 kĕlp, *n.* Large coarse

Kelt'ic, *a.* Same as CELTIC.

ken, 1 ken; 2 kĕn. **I.** *vi.* [KENNED or KENT, KEND²; KEN'NING.] To know; descry; see. **II** *n.* Reach of sight or knowledge.

ken'nel¹, 1 ken'el; 2 kĕn'ĕl, *n.* **1.** A house for a dog or for a pack of hounds; also, the pack. **2.** A lair; den.

ken'nel², *n.* The gutter of a street; channel; puddle.

kept, 1 kept; 2 kĕpt, *imp. & pp.* of KEEP, *v.*

ke-ram'ic, ke-ram'ics. Same as CERAMIC, etc.

ker'chief, 1 kûr'chif; 2 kẽr'chif, *n.* A square, as of linen or silk, used as a covering for the head or neck, or as a handkerchief.

ker'nel, 1 kûr'nel; 2 kẽr'nĕl, *n.* A grain or seed; edible part of a nut; gist.

ker'o-sene, 1 ker'o-sīn; 2 kẽr'o-sēn, *n.* Illuminating-oil distilled from crude petroleum.

ker'sey, 1 kûr'zı; 2 kẽr'sy, *n.* A smooth, light-weight beaver cloth: named from Kersey, England.

ketch'up, *n.* Same as CATCHUP.

ket'tle, 1 ket'l; 2 kĕt'l, *n.* A metallic vessel for stewing or boiling.
ket'l², — **ket'tle-drum",** *n.* A musical instrument, consisting of a brass hemispherical shell, with a parchment head: formerly used by mounted troops, now chiefly in orchestras.— **ket'tle-drum,** *n.* A ladies' informal afternoon party: so named from parties in India, where drumheads served for tables.

key¹, 1 kī; 2 kē, *n.* **1.** An instrument for moving the bolt in a lock. **2.** Anything that discloses or opens something; a lever to be pressed by the finger in a musical instrument or a typewriter. **3.** A key-note; quality, intensity, or pitch of tone in speaking.— **key'board",** *n.* A range of keys, as in a piano or typewriter.— **key'hole",** *n.* A hole for a key, as in a door or lock.— **key'=note",** *n.* **1.** *Mus.* The tonic of a key, from which it is named. **2.** A ruling principle or sentiment.— **key'stone',** *n.* The uppermost and completing stone of an arch.— **key'=word",** *n.* A word used as a guide to the pronunciation of other words.

key², *n.* A low island, as of coral.

key³, *n.* A quay; wharf.

kha'ki, 1 kä'ki; 2 kä'ki. [Anglo-Ind.] **I.** *a.* Of the color of dust or ashes; made of khaki. **II.** *n.* A light drab or brownish cotton cloth used as for military uniforms.

kha'lif, *n.* Same as CALIF.

khan¹, 1 kän; 2 kän, *n.* An East·rn title of respect, as for a sovereign or gentleman.

khan², *n.* An Oriental inn.

khe-dive', 1 ke-dīv'; 2 kĕ-dīv', *n.* Formerly, the viceroy of Egypt.

kick, 1 kik; 2 kĭk. **I⁴.** *vt. & vi.* **1.** To strike with the foot; recoil, as a firearm. **2.** [Colloq.] To object; complain. **II.** *n.* **1.** A blow with the foot. **2.** The recoil of a firearm.

kid, 1 kid; 2 kĭd, *n.* A young goat, or leather made from its skin.

kid'nap, 1 kid'nap; 2 kĭd'năp, *vt.* [-NAPED† or -NAPPED†, -NAPT²; -NAP-ING or -NAP-PING.] To carry off (a person) from home or country.— **kid'nap-er, -per,** *n.*

kid'ney, 1 kid'nı; 2 kĭd'ny, *n.* A glandular organ that secretes urine.

kil-am'pere, 1 kil'am-pīr; 2 kĭl'ăm-pēr, *n.* *Elec.* One thousand amperes.

kill, 1 kil; 2 kĭl, *vt.* To deprive of life,
kil², vigor, efficiency, or usefulness, etc.; deaden.

kiln, 1 kil; 2 kĭl, *n.* An oven or furnace for baking, burning, or drying industrial products.

kil'o-, etc. See METRIC SYSTEM, under METRIC.

kil'o-cy"cle, *n. Elec.* One thousand cycles.

kil'o-gram, kil'o-li"ter, kil'o-me"ter, kil'o-stere". See METRIC SYSTEM, under METRIC.

kil'o-joule", 1 kil'o-jūl" or -jaul"; 2 kĭl'o-jul" or -joul".*n. Elec.* One thousand joules.—
kil'o-watt", *n. Elec.* One thousand watts.

kilt, 1 kilt; 2 kĭlt, *n.* A short skirt, as of the Scottish Highlanders.— **kilt'ed,** *a.*— **kilt'ing,** *n.*

kin, 1 kin; 2 kĭn, *n.* Relation; consanguinity; relatives collectively. [*kin.*

-kin, *suffix.* Diminutive: as, lamb*kin*, mani-

kind, 1 kaind; 2 kĭnd, *a.* Gentle, tender; humane; kindly.— **kind'=heart"ed,** *a.* Having a kind spirit or disposition.— **kind'ness,** *n.*

kind, *n.* Sort; a class; species.

kin'der-gar"ten, 1 kin'dẽr-gär"tn; 2 kĭn'-der-gär"tn, *n.* A play-school for little

children.— **kin′der-gart″ner**, *n.* A kinder-garten=teacher.

kin′dle, } 1 kin′dl; 2 kĭn′dl, *v.* [KIN′-
kin′dl², } DL(E)D^P; KIN′DLING.] **I.** *t.* To set fire to; excite; inflame; illuminate. **II.** *i.* To take fire; become excited. — **kin′dler,** *n.*

kind′ly, 1 kaind′li; 2 kīnd′ly. **I.** *a.* [KIND′-LI-ER; KIND′LI-EST.] **1.** Having or manifesting kindness. **2.** Favorable; beneficial. **II.** *adv.* In a kind manner or spirit; congenially.— **kind′li-ness,** *n.*

kin′dred, 1 kin′dred; 2 kĭn′drĕd. **I.** *a.* Of a like nature or character; related; congenial; akin. **II.** *n.* Relationship; relatives collectively.

kine,‖ 1 kain; 2 kīn, *n.* Plural of cow.

kin′e-o-graph, 1 kin′ı-o-grȧf; 2 kĭn′e-o-grȧf, *n.* A motion-picture, as that shown by the kinetoscope.

ki-net′o-graph, 1 kı-net′o-grȧf; 2 ki-nĕt′o-grȧf, *n.* An apparatus for taking pictures of persons or things in motion for use in a moving-picture machine.

ki-net′o-scope, 1 kı-net′o-skōp; 2 ki-nĕt′o-scōp, *n.* A device by which the pictures taken by the kinetograph may be reproduced in rapid succession to the eye, as upon a screen.— **ki-net″o-scop′ic,** *a.*

king, 1 kiŋ; 2 kĭng, *n.* The sovereign male ruler of a kingdom; a leader; chief; head. — **king′=bolt″,** *n.* A vertical central bolt attaching the body of a vehicle to the fore axle.— **king′dom,** *n.* **1.** The realm ruled by a king or queen. **2.** *Nat. Hist.* A primary division of natural objects; as, the animal *kingdom.*— **king′fish″er,** *n.* A bird having a straight, deeply cleft bill, and in the habit of diving for fish.— **king′ly,** 1 kiŋ′li; 2 kĭng′ly, *a.* [KING′-LI-ER; KING′LI-EST.] Pertaining to or worthy of a king; regal. **king′like‡.**— **king′li-ness,** *n.*

kink, 1 kiŋk; 2 kĭŋk. **I**^t. *vt. & vi.* To form kinks; twist; tangle. **II.** *n.* An abrupt bend, twist, loop, or tangle, as in a rope.— **kink′y,** *a.*

kins′folk″, 1 kinz′fōk″; 2 kĭng′fōk″, *n. pl.* Relatives collectively; kindred; kin.— **kin′ship,** *n.* Relationship; consanguinity.— **kins′man,** *n.* [KINS′MEN, *pl.*] A blood relation; relative. — **kins′wo″man,** *n. fem.*

Belted King-fisher. 1/9

ki-osk′, 1 kı-ɔsk′; 2 ki-ŏsk′, *n.* *Arch.* An ornamental pavilion, common in the Orient, and imitated elsewhere.

kip, 1 kip; 2 kĭp, *n.* Untanned calfskin. — **kip′per,** *n.*

kirk, 1 kɔrk; 2 kĭrk, *n.* [Scot.] Church.

kis′met, 1 kis′met; 2 kĭs′mĕt, *n.* Appointed lot; fate.

kiss‡, 1 kis; 2 kĭs, *v.* **I.** *t.* To touch with the lips in salutation. **II.** *i.* To salute mutually with the lips; touch gently; meet.

kiss, *n.* An affectionate salutation by contact of the lips; a gentle touch.

kit¹, 1 kit; 2 kĭt, *n.* A tub, pail, or box for packing; an outfit, as of tools.

kit², *n.* **1.** A small violin. **2.** A guitar.

kitch′en, } 1 kich′en; 2 kĭch′ĕn, *n.* A
kich′en², } room for cooking food.— **kitch′-en=gar″den,** *n.* A vegetable=garden.— **kitch′en-ette″,** *n.* A small kitchen.

kite, 1 kait; 2 kīt, *n.* **1.** A hawk=like bird having long pointed wings and a forked tail. **2.** A slender frame covered with light fabric, to be flown in the air.

kith, 1 kith; 2 kĭth, *n.* One's friends: in the phrase **kith and kin.**

kit′ten, 1 kit′n; 2 kĭt′n, *n.* A young cat.

klep′to-ma′ni-a, 1 klep″to-mē′nı-a; 2 klĕp′-to-mā′ni-a, *n.* An insane propensity to steal.— **klep″to-ma′ni-ac.** **II.** *a.* Of or pertaining to kleptomania. **II.** *n.* A person affected with kleptomania.

knack, 1 nak; 2 năk, *n.* The trick of doing a thing cleverly and well; cleverness; adroitness.

knap′sack″, 1 nap′sak″; 2 năp′săk″, *n.* A case strapped across the shoulders, for carrying light luggage, etc.

knarled, knarl′y, *a.* Same as GNARLED, etc.

knave, 1 nēv; 2 nāv, *n.* **1.** A dishonest person; rogue. **2.** A playing-card.— **knav′-er-y,** *n.* [-IES^Z, *pl.*] Deceitfulness in dealing; roguery.— **knav′ish,** *a.* **-ly,** *adv.* **-ness,** *n.*

knead, 1 nīd; 2 nēd, *vt.* To mix and work, as dough.

knee, 1 nī; 2 nē, *n.* The joint between the thigh and the leg in man; a like joint in other animals, as the horse or cow. — **knee′cap″,** *n.* The round movable bone covering the knee in front. **knee′pan″‡.**

kneel, 1 nīl; 2 nēl, *vi.* [KNELT, 1 nelt, 2 nĕlt, or KNEELED, KNEELD^s; KNEEL′ING.] To rest, as on the knees.

knell, } 1 nel; 2 nĕl. **I.** *vt. & vi.* [Poet.]
knel², } To sound as a knell; give a sad or warning sound. **II.** *n.* The tolling of a bell to announce a death.

knelt, *imp. & pp.* of KNEEL, *v.*

knew, *imp.* of KNOW, *v.*

knick′er-bock″ers, 1 nik′ẽr-bok″ẽrz; 2 nĭk′er-bŏk″ers, *n. pl.* Knee-breeches gathered at the knee. [A trinket; trifle.

knick′knack″, 1 nik′nak″; 2 nĭk′năk″, *n.*

knife, 1 naif; 2 nīf, *n.* [KNIVES, 1 naivz; 2

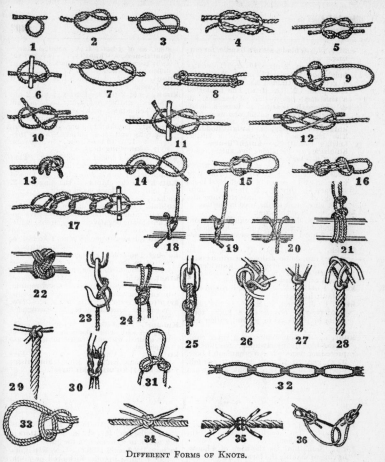

DIFFERENT FORMS OF KNOTS.

1. Bight or simple loop. 2. Simple, single, or overhand knot. 3. Figure-of-eight or German knot. 4. Granny-knot. 5. Square knot or reef-knot. 6. Boat-knot. 7. Double knot. 8. Sheepshank knot, for shortening a rope. 9. Bowline-knot. 10. Sheet-bend, becket-bend, or single bend. Called also *weavers' knot*, because used in weaving for joining threads. 11. Sheet-bend with toggle. 12. Single carrick-bend. 13. Stevedore-knot. 14. Stevedore-knot before drawing tight. 15. Single bow-knot. 16. Double Flemish loop. 17. Chain-knot with toggle. 18. Half-hitch. 19. Timberhitch. 20. Two half-hitches. Called also *builders' knot*. 21. Rolling-hitch. 22. Turk's-head. 23. Blackwall knot. 24. Fisherman's bend. 25. Round turn and half-hitch. 26, 27. Wall-knot begun and finished, the strands being knotted together to prevent their untwisting. 28, 29. Crowned wall-knot begun and finished. 30. Cat's-paw. 31. Harness-hitch. 32. Hawser-bend. 33. Bowline on a bight. 34, 35. Shroud-knot, begun and finished. 36. Two bowline-knots.

nīvẓ, *pl.*] A blade, set in a handle, for cutting.

knight, 1 naɪt; 2 nĭt. **I**^d. *vt.* To confer knighthood upon. **II.** *n.* **1.** Anciently, a gentleman trained to arms; hence, a champion. **2.** [Gt. Brit.] The holder of a title next below that of baronet. **3.** A chessman bearing a horse's head. — **knight errant,** a knight who went forth to redress wrongs or seek adventures. — **knight′er″rant-ry,** *n.* — **knight′hood,** *n.* The character or dignity of a knight; knights collectively. — **knight′li-ness,** *n.* — **knight′ly,** *a.* Pertaining to a knight; chivalrous: also used adverbially.

knit, 1 nit; 2 nĭt, *vt. & vi.* [KNIT OR KNIT′-TED^d; KNIT′TING.] **1.** To form (a fabric or garment) by a series of interlocked loops of yarn or thread. **2.** Hence, to unite closely; grow together. — **knit′ting-nee″dle,** *n.* A long, blunt needle, used in knitting.

knives, *n.* Plural of KNIFE.

knob, 1 neb; 2 nŏb, *n.* A round projection; a rounded handle, as of a door. — **knobbed,** 1 nebd; 2 nŏbd, *a.* — **knob′bi-ness,** *n.* — **knob′by,** *a.*

knock, 1 nek; 2 nŏk. **I**^t. *vt. & vi.* To strike; rap, as on a door, for admittance. **II.** *n.* A stroke; blow; rap. — **knock′er,** *n.* — **knock′-kneed″,** *a.* Having the legs bent inward at the knees; shaky; weak.

knoll, 1 nōl; 2 nōl, *n.* A small round hill; mound; hilltop.

knot, 1 net; 2 nŏt, *vt. & vi.* [KNOT′TED^d; KNOT′TING.] To tie in a knot; form knots or joints, as in plants; gather in a knot.

knot, *n.* **1.** A fastening of a rope, cord, or the like, by intertwining. See illus. on preceding page. **2.** An ornamental bow. **3.** A gnarled portion of a tree-trunk, where a branch has grown out; a joint in a

stem, as of grass. **4.** A nautical mile.— **knot′ti-ness,** *n.*— **knot′ty,** *a.* [KNOT′TI-ER; KNOT′TI-EST.] Marked by knots; like a knot; difficult; intricate.

knout, 1 naut; 2 nout, *n.* A whip used in Russia.

know, 1 nō; 2 nō, *v.* [KNEW, 1 niū, 2 nū; KNOWN; KNOW′ING.] **I.** *t.* To be certain of or acquainted with; recognize; understand. **II.** *i.* To have or get knowledge.

know′ing, 1 nō′iŋ, *pa.* Shrewd; done consciously or on purpose. — **know′ing-ly,** *adv.* **1.** With knowledge. **2.** Shrewdly; slyly. — **know′ing-ness,** *n.*

knowl′edge, 1 nol′ej; 2 nŏl′ĕdg, *n.* That which is known; information; learning.

knuck′le,) 1 nuk′l; 2 nŭk′l, *n.* **1.** One of **knuck′l^e,**) the joints of the fingers. **2.** A joint of the knee, as of a calf.

ko′balt, *n.* Same as COBALT.

ko′dak, 1 kō′dak; 2 kō′dăk, *n.* A portable photographic camera for successive instantaneous negatives: a registered trademark name.

Ko-ran′, 1 ko-rān′ *or* kō′rən; 2 ko-rän′ *or* kō′ran, *n.* The Mohammedan scripture.

ko′sher, 1 kō′shər; 2 kō′sher, *a.* [Heb.] Permitted by the requirements of the law, as food; ceremonially clean; pure.

kraal, 1 krāl; 2 kräl, *n.* [Afr.] A village, or group of native huts; also, a sheepfold, or enclosure for cattle.

kryp′ton, 1 krip′tən; 2 krўp′ton, *n.* *Chem.* A gaseous constituent of the atmosphere, isolated in 1898.

Kul-tur′, 1 kul-tūr′; 2 kul-tųr′, *n.* [G.] Progress and achievement in all phases of life secured without regard to the means employed.

ku′miss, 1 kū′mis; 2 kų′mĭs, *n.* Fermented milk, used as a drink. **kou′miss**‡ **kou′mys**‡; **ku′mys**‡; **ku′myss**‡.

L

L¹, l, 1 el; 2 ĕl, *n.* [ELS, L's, or Ls, 1 elz; 2 ĕlẓ, *pl.*] The twelfth letter in the English alphabet.

L², *n.* Something, as the wing of a house, having or making the form of an L; an ell.

la, 1 la; 2 lä, *n.* *Mus.* The sixth tone of the scale.

la′bel, 1 lē′bel; 2 lā′bĕl. **I.** *vt.* [LA′BELED OR LA′BELLED, LA′BELD^s; LA′BEL-ING OR LA′BEL-LING.] To mark; designate. **II.** *n.* A marked slip, as of paper, affixed to something to show what or whose it is.

la′bi-al, 1 lē′bi-al; 2 lā′bi-al. **I.** *a.* Pertaining to the lips. **II**†. *n.* One of the letters *p, b, m, f, v,* or *w,* formed by the lips. -**ly,** *adv.*

la′bor, 1 lē′bər; 2 lā′bor. **I.** *vt. & vi.* To toil or cause to toil; work; roll or pitch, as a ship at sea. **II.** *n.* **1.** Physical or mental exertion for some end; toil; work. **2.** The laboring class collectively. — **la′bored,** *a.* — **la′bor-er,** *n.* One who lives by manual labor. — **la-bo′ri-ous,** 1 lə-bō′rɪ-us; 2 la-bō′-ri-ŭs, *a.* Requiring much labor; toilsome; industrious. -**ly,** *adv.* -**ness,** *n.*

lab′o-ra-to″ry, 1 lab′o-rə-tō″rĭ; 2 lăb′o-ra-tō″ry, *n.* [-RIES², *pl.*] A place for conducting scientific experiments, etc.

lab′y-rinth, 1 lab′ĭ-rĭnth; 2 lăb′y-rĭnth, *n.* A confusing network of paths or passages; maze. **lab″y-rin′thi-an‡; lab″y-rin′-thin**(e‡**.—lab″y-rin′thic,** *a.* Complicated.

lac¹, 1 lak; 2 lăç, *n.* A resinous substance exuded from an East-Indian scale-insect; also, other similar substances: used for making varnishes, lacquer, shellac, etc.

lac², *n.* [Anglo-Ind.] Same as LAKH.

lace, 1 lēs; 2 lāç. **I.** *vt.* & *vi.* [LACED‡; LAC′ING.] To trim with lace; interlace. **II.** *n.* **1.** A delicate network of threads of linen, silk, cotton, etc.; also, any ornamental cord or braid. **2.** A shoe-string; any string.— **lac′ing,** *n.* **1.** The act of fastening with laces; the use of laced stays or corsets. **2.** A lace for fastening.

lac′er-ate, 1 las′ər-ēt; 2 lăç′er-āt, *vt.* [-AT″ED^d; -AT″ING.] To tear raggedly; rend; harrow.— **lac″er-a′tion,** *n.*

lach′ry-mal, -mose, etc. See LACRIMAL, etc.

lack, 1 lak; 2 lăk. **I‡.** *vt.* & *vi.* To be destitute of; be deficient; fail. **II.** *n.* Absence or deficiency of something; want; failure.

lack″a-dai′si-cal, 1 lak″ə-dē′zi-kəl; 2 lăk″-a-dā′si-cal, *a.* Affectedly pensive or sentimental.

lack′er, *v.* & *n.* Same as LACQUER.

lack′ey, 1 lak′ĭ; 2 lăk′y. **I.** *vt.* & *vi.* To wait on; attend. **II.** *n.* A male servant; a footman; menial.

la-con′ic, 1 lə-kon′ĭk; 2 la-cŏn′ic, *a.* Using few words; short and forceful; concise. **la-con′i-cal‡.— la-con′i-cal-ly,** *adv.*

lac′quer, 1 lak′ər; 2 lăk′er. **I.** *vt.* To coat with lacquer. **II.** *n.* **1.** A varnish of shellac dissolved in alcohol. **2.** Lacquered woodwork.

lac′ri-mal, 1 lak′ri-məl; 2 lăç′ri-mal, *a.* Pertaining to tears.— **lac′ri-mose,** 1 -mōs; 2 -mōs, *a.* Tearful.

la-crosse′, 1 lə-krôs′; 2 la-crôs′, *n.* A game of ball, played with a racket-like implement (called a *crosse*) between and past two goal-posts.

lac-ta′tion, 1 lak-tē′shən; 2 lăc-tā′shon, *n.* The act or period of suckling.— **lac′te-al,** *a.* Pertaining to or like milk.

lac′tic, 1 lak′tĭk; 2 lăç′tie, *a.* Chem. Of or pertaining to milk.— **lac-tom′e-ter,** 1 lak-tom′e-tər; 2 lăc-tŏm′e-ter, *n.* An instrument for determining the density of milk, particularly a hydrometer; a galactometer.

lad, 1 lad; 2 lăd, *n.* A boy or youth; companion; fellow.

lad′der, 1 lad′ər; 2 lăd′er, *n.* A device of wood,

rope, etc., for climbing or descending.

lade, 1 lēd; 2 lād, *vt.* [LAD′ED^d; LAD′ED^d or LAD′EN; LAD′ING.] **1.** To load; oppress. **2.** To ladle.— **lad′en,** *pa.* Burdened; overtaxed; oppressed.— **lad′ing,** 1 lēd′ɪŋ; 2 lād′-ing, *n.* The act of loading; a load or cargo; freight.

la′dle, 1 lē′dl; 2 lā′dl. **I.** *vt.* [LA′DLED^d; LA′DLING.] To dip up and pour with a ladle. **II.** *n.* A vessel, with a long handle, for serving liquids.

la′dy, 1 lē′dĭ; 2 lā′dy, *n.* [LA′DIES², *pl.*] A gentlewoman; the mistress of a household.— **la′dy-bird″,** *n.* A small beetle, spotted with red, yellow, or black. **la′dy-bug″‡.—la′dy-like″,** *a.* Like or suitable to a lady; gentle; delicate.—**l-′love,** *n.* A sweetheart.— **la′dy-ship,** *n.* The rank or condition of a lady.

lag, 1 lag; 2 lăg, *vi.* [LAGGED, LAG^s; LAG′GING.] To move slowly; stay or fall behind; loiter.

Ladybird. ³/₁

la′ger, 1 lä′gər; 2 lä′ger, *n.* Beer containing few hops, formerly kept long before use. **la′ger-beer″‡.**

lag′gard, 1 lag′ərd; 2 lăg′ard. **I.** *a.* Slow; tardy. **II.** *n.* A loiterer.

la-goon′, 1 lə-gūn′; 2 la-gōōn, *n.* A body of shallow water; pool; lake. **la-gune′‡.**

la′ic, 1 lē′ɪk; 2 lā′ic. **I.** *a.* Same as LAY, *a.* **la′i-cal‡. II.** *n.* A layman.

laid, 1 lēd; 2 lād, *pp.* of LAY, *v.*

lain, 1 lēn; 2 lān, *pp.* of LIE, *v.*

lair, 1 lār; 2 lâr, *n.* The couch or den of a wild animal.

laird, 1 lärd; 2 lârd,[*n.* [Scot.] A lord; land-owner. [pä″sē′, *n.* [F.] A pass.

lais″sez″-pas″ser′, 1 lē″sē″-pa′sē′; 2 lā″sē″-**la′i-ty,** 1 lē′ĭ-tɪ; 2 lā′i-ty, *n.* The people as distinguished from the clergy. [water

lake¹, 1 lēk; 2 lāk, *n.* An inland body of

lake², *n.* A deep-red pigment.

lakh, 1 lak; 2 lăk, *n.* [Anglo-Ind.] The sum of 100,000; especially 100,000 rupees.

la′ma¹, 1 lä′mə; 2 lä′ma, *n.* A priest of the religious system of Tibet.

lamb,)1 lam; 2 lăm, *n.* A young sheep; **lams,**) also, its flesh; a gentle or innocent person.— **lamb′kin,** *n.* A little lamb.

lam′bent, 1 lam′bent; 2 lăm′bĕnt, *a.* Playing, with a soft movement; flickering.

lam′bre-quin, 1 lam′brɪ-kin; 2 lăm′bre-kin, *n.* Drapery, hanging over a window or door.

lame, 1 lēm; 2 lām. **I.** *vt.* [LAMED; LAM′-ING.] To cripple or disable. **II.** *a.* [LAM′ER; LAM′EST.] Crippled or disabled in a leg; halt. **-ness,** *n.*

la-ment′, 1 lə-ment′; 2 la-mĕnt′. **I^d.** *vt.* & *vi.* To sorrow for; mourn; bewail.

II. *n.* The expression of grief; lamentation.— **lam'en-ta-bl**(e², *a.* To be lamented; mournful; sad; unfortunate.— **lam'en-ta-bly,** *adv.*— **lam'en-ta'tion,** *n.* The act of lamenting; a wailing cry.

lam'i-na, 1 lam'i-nə; 2 lăm'i-na, *n.* [-NÆ, 1 -nī; 2 -nē, *pl.*] A thin scale or sheet. — **lam'i-nate,** *a.*— **lam'i-nat'ed,** *a.* Consisting of thin layers.

lamp, 1 lamp; 2 lămp, *n.* A vessel in which oil is burnt through a wick.— **lamp'black",** *n.* Fine carbon deposited from smoke.

lam-poon', 1 lam-pūn'; 2 lăm-pōōn'. **I.** *vt.* To abuse or satirize. **II.** *n.* A personal satire in writing.

lam'prey, 1 lam'prı; 2 lăm'pry, *n.* An eel-like parasitical fish.

lance, 1 luns; 2 lȧnç. **I.** *vt.* [LANCED†; LANC'ING.] To pierce with a lance or a lancet. **II.** *n.* A spear; a bearer of a lance.

lan'cet, 1 lun'set; 2 lȧn'çĕt, *n.* **1.** A surgeons' instrument with one or more small, keen blades. **2.** An acutely pointed window.

land, 1 land; 2 lănd. **I**d. *vt.* & *vi.* To bring to the land; debark; go or come ashore. **II.** *n.* The solid surface of the earth; a continent; ground or soil; real estate.— **land'ed,** 1 land'ed; 2 lănd'ĕd, *a.* Having an estate in land.— **land'hold"er,** *n.* A landowner.— **land'ing,** *n.* The act or place of putting ashore; a platform dividing a flight of stairs.— **land'la'dy,** *n.* [-DIES²; *pl.*] A woman who keeps a boarding-house, or lets her property.— **land'locked",** *a.* Surrounded and protected by land.— **land'lord",** *n.* A man who keeps an inn or hotel, or owns and lets real estate.— **land'mark",** *n.* A boundary-mark; an object on land serving as a guide to seamen.— **land'own"er,** *n.*— **land'slide",** *n.* The slipping down of a mass of land; the land that has slipped down. **land'slip"**‡.— **lands'man,** *n.* One who lives on the land; opposed to *seaman*.— **land'ward,** *adv.* Toward the land.

lan'dau, 1 lan'dō; 2 lȧn'dȧ, *n.* A two-seated, four-wheeled carriage with a removable top.— **lan'dau-let',** *n.* A type of motor-car with movable top.

1. A Landau with Lowered Top. 2. A Landau Closed.

land'scape, 1 land'skēp; 2 lănd'scāp, *n.* A stretch of country as seen from a single point, or a picture representing it.

lane, 1 lēn; 2 lān, *n.* A narrow way or street.

lan'guage, 1 laŋ'gwıj; 2 lăŋ'gwaġ, *n.* **1.** The expression of ideas by words; speech. **2.** The words in use among any people; a tongue.

lan'guid, 1 laŋ'gwid; 2 lăŋ'gwid, *a.* Listless; feeble; weak. **-ly,** *adv.* **-ness,** *n.*

lan'guish†, 1 laŋ'gwish; 2 lăŋ'gwish, *vi.* **1.** To become weak; pine; fail; fade. **2.** To manifest tender emotion. **-ment,** *n.*

lan'guor, 1 laŋ'gər *or* -gwər; 2 lăŋ'gor *or* ġwor, *n.* Lassitude; depression; weakness.— **lan'guor-ous,** *a.*

lank, 1 laŋk; 2 lăŋk, *a.* Long and thin. **-ly,** *adv.* **-ness,** *n.*

lan'tern, 1 lan'tərn; 2 lăn'tern, *n.* **1.** A transparent case, for enclosing a light. **2.** A tower, as on a roof, to give light.

lan'yard, 1 lan'yərd; 2 lăn'yard, *n.* A small rope or a cord, as for use on shipboard.

lap¹, 1 lap; 2 lăp, *v.* [LAPPED†, LAPT³; LAP'PING.] **I.** *t.* To lay over, as a fold; infold; involve. **II.** *i.* To lie partly over something else.

lap², *vt.* & *vi.* [LAPPED†; LAP'PING.] To lick up; take up liquid with the tongue.

lap¹, *n.* That part of a substance which extends over another.

lap², *n.* The upper part of the thighs or knees of a person in a sitting posture; the clothing that covers this part.— **lap'-dog",** *n.* A small dog fondled in the lap.

la-pel', 1 lə-pel'; 2 la-pĕl', *n.* The part of the front of a coat which is folded back. **la-pelled',** *a.*

lap'i-da-ry, 1 lap'i-dē-rı; 2 lăp'i-dā-ry. **I.** *a.* Pertaining to stones or the art of working in precious stones. **II.** *n.* [-RIES²; *pl.*] One who cuts, engraves, and sets precious stones.

la'pis laz'u-li, 1 lē'pıs laz'yu-laı; 2 lā'pıs lăz'yu-lī. A rich blue mixture of minerals, largely used by the ancients for decoration.

lap'pet, 1 lap'et; 2 lăp'ĕt, *n.* A small lap or flap.

lapse, 1 laps; 2 lăps. **I.** *vi.* [LAPSED†, LAPST³; LAPS'ING.] To pass gradually; glide; slip; to pass out of possession, as a title to property; become void. **II.** *n.* A slipping or passing away; failure; error.

Lapwing. 1/16

lap'wing", 1 lap'wıŋ"; 2 lăp'wĭŋ", *n.* A plover-like bird.

lar'board″, 1 lär'börd′; 2 lär'bôrd′, *a.* & *n.* *Naut.* Same as PORT³.

lar'ce-ny, 1 lär'si-ni; 2 lär'çe-ny, *n.* [-NIES², *pl.*] The unlawful taking of another's property; theft. [pine family.

larch, 1 lärch; 2 lärch, *n.* A tree of the

lard, 1 lärd; 2 lärd. **I**ᵈ. *vt.* To stuff or smear with lard; interlard. **II.** *n.* The clarified fat of the hog.—**lar'der,** 1 lär'dər; 2 lär'der, *n.* A pantry; the provisions of a household.

large, 1 lärj; 2 lärg, *a.* [LARG′ER; LARG′EST.] Great as regards size, quantity, etc.; big; broad. **-ly,** *adv.* **-ness,** *n.* [gratuity; bounty.

lar'gess, 1 lär'jes; 2 lär'gĕs, *n.* A gift;

lar'go, 1 lär'go; 2 lär'go, *a.* & *adv.* *Mus.* **I.** *a.* Slow. **II.** *n.* A slow movement.

lar'i-at, 1 lar'i-at; 2 lăr'ĭ-ăt, *n.* A rope of horsehair for tethering animals; a lasso. [bird.

larkⁱ, 1 lärk; 2 lärk, *n.* A small singing

lark², *n.* [Colloq.] A hilarious time; frolic.

lark'spur, 1 lärk'spər; 2 lärk'spur, *n.* A showy herb, with flowers in clusters.

lar'va, 1 lär'və; 2 lär'va, *n.* A caterpillar or grub; insect-life after leaving the egg. —**lar'val,** *a.*

lar'ynx, 1 lar'iŋks; 2 lăr'yŋks, *n.* [LA-RYN′GES, 1 lə-rin'jīz; 2 la-rĭn'gēs, *pl.*] The upper part of the windpipe.— **la-ryn'ge-al,** 1 lə-rin'ji-əl; 2 la-rȳn'gē-al *a.* Pertaining to the larynx.— **lar″yn-gi'tis,** 1 lar'in-jai'tis *or* -jī'tis; 2 lär″yn-gī'tis *or* -gī'tis, *n.* Inflammation of the larynx.

las-civ'i-ous, 1 la-siv'i-us; 2 lȧ-çĭv'ĭ-us, *a.* Wanton; lewd; unchaste. **-ly,** *adv.* **-ness,** *n.*

lashᵗ, 1 lash; 2 lăsh, *vt.* & *vi.* To whip; tie with a lashing; satirize.

lash, *n.* **1.** A thong on a whip-handle; a whip; stroke with a whip. **2.** A stroke of sarcasm. **3.** An eyelash.

lass, 1 las; 2 lăs, *n.* A girl.

las'si-tude, 1 las'i-tiūd; 2 lăs'ĭ-tūd *n.* Disinclination to exertion; languor; debility.

las'so, 1 las'o; 2 lăs'o. **I.** *vt.* To capture with a lasso. **II.** *n.* A long line, as of hide, with a noose, for catching horses, etc.

lastᵈ, 1 last; 2 låst, *vi.* To remain in existence; endure.— **last'ing.** **I.** *pa.* That continues; durable; permanent. **-ly,** *adv.* **II.** *n.* A durable cloth.

last, *a.* Being at the end; latest; hindmost.

lastⁱ, *n.* A wooden form on which to make a boot or shoe.

last², *n.* The end; conclusion.

last, *adv.* After all others; finally. **-ly**‡.

latch, } 1 lach; 2 lăch. **I**ᵗ. *vt.* To fasten,
lachᴾ, } as with a latch. **II.** *n.* A catch for fastening a door or the like.

latch'et, 1 lach'et; 2 lăch'ĕt, *n.* A string that fastens a shoe or sandal.

late, 1 lēt; 2 lāt. **I.** *a.* [LAT′ER or LATT′TER; LAT′EST or LAST.] Coming after time; tardy; recent; deceased. **II.** *adv.* After or beyond the usual time; recently.— **late'ly,** *adv.* Not long ago.— **lat'er,** *adv.* At a subsequent time; hereafter.

la-teen', 1 la-tīn; 2 lȧ-tēn′, *a.* Designating a short mast, long yard and a triangular sail.

la'tent, 1 lē'tent; 2 lā'tĕnt, *a.* Not apparent; dormant. **-ly,** *adv.*

lat'er-al, 1 lat'ər-əl; 2 lăt'er-al, *a.* Pertaining to, proceeding from, or directed toward the side.— **lat'er-al-ly,** *adv.*

la'tex, 1 lē'teks; 2 lā'tĕks, *n.* The viscid, milky juice secreted by the india-rubber tree.

lath, 1 luth; 2 .ăth. **I.** *vt.* To fit with laths. **II.** *n.* A thin strip of wood or metal, as to support plastering.

lathe, 1 lēth; 2 lāth, *n.* A machine for shaping articles by turning.

lath'er, 1 lath'ər; 2 lăth'er, *n.* **I.** *vt.* & *vi.* To spread over with or form lather. **II.** *n.* Froth from soapsuds.

Lat'in, 1 lat'in; 2 lăt'ĭn. **I.** *a.* Pertaining to ancient Rome, its language or people, or to nations derived from the ancient Romans. **II.** *n.* The language of ancient Rome.— **Lat'in-ism,** *n.* A Latin idiom.— **Lat'in-ist,** *n.* One versed in Latin.— **Lat'in-ize,** *vt.*

lat'i-tude, 1 lat'i-tiūd; 2 lăt'ĭ-tūd, *n.* Distance northward or southward from the equator; range; scope.— **lat″i-tu'di-nal,** *a.*

lat'ter, 1 lat'er; 2 lăt'er, *a.* Of more recent date; modern; second of two things. **-ly,** *adv.*

lat'tice, } 1 lat'is; 2 lăt'ĭç. **I.** *vt.* [LAT′-
lat'tisᵖ, } TICED⁵, LAT′-TIST⁵; LAT′TIC-ING.] To furnish with a lattice. **II.** *n.* Openwork of crossed bars; a screen.

laud, 1 lôd; 2 lạd. **I**ᵈ. *vt.* To praise; extol. **II.** *n.* Praise; a song of praise.— **laud'er,** *n.*— **laud'a-ble**(ᵖ, *a.* Praiseworthy. **-ness,** *n.*— **laud'a-bly,** *adv.*— **lau-da'tion,** *n.* Eulogy.— **laud'a-to-ry.** **I.** *a.* Eulogizing. **laud'a-tiv**(eᵗ. **II.** *n.* [-RIES‡, *pl.*] A panegyric; eulogy.

lau'da-num, 1 lô'də-num; 2 lạ'da-nŭm, *n.* Tincture of opium.

Lattice Window.

laughᵗ, } 1 laf; 2 läf, *v.* **I.** *t.* To ridicule;
lafᴾ, } deride. **II.** *i.* **1.** To give vent

to laughter; be glad. **2.** To scoff; jeer: followed by *at*.—**laugh′a-bl**(e^r, *a.* Provoking laughter.—**laugh′ing-ly**, *adv.*

laugh, *n.* An act of laughter; merriment; ridicule.—**laugh′ing-stock″**, *n.* A butt for ridicule.

laugh′ter, } 1 laf′ter; 2 lȧf′ter, *n.* Quick
laf′ter, } convulsive breathing, with vocal sounds and facial expressions indicative of mirth.

launch, 1 lånch *or* lŏnch; 2 länch *or* lȧnch. **I**^t. *vt. & vi.* To slide into the water, as a boat; start; set out; throw, as a dart. **II.** *n.* The act of launching; a large open boat generally propelled by steam, electricity, or naphtha.

laun′der, 1 lȧn′dər; 2 län′der, *vt.* To wash and iron, as clothes.—**laun′der-er**, *n.*—**laun′dress**, 1 lȧn′dres; 2 län′dres, *n.* A washerwoman.—
laun′dry, 1 lȧn′drı; 2 län′dry, *n.* [LAUN′-DRIES^z, *pl.*] A place for washing and ironing clothes. **laun′dry-man,** *n.*

lau′re-ate, 1 lō′rı-ıt ; 2 lạ̈′re-at. **I.** *a.* Crowned with laurel. **II.** *n.* [Eng.] The poet invested with the title of laureate by the crown.

Mountain=laurel.

lau′rel, 1 lō′rel; 2 lạ̈′rĕl, *n.* An evergreen shrub with fragrant leaves.

la′va, 1 lä′və; 2 lä′va, *n.* Melted rock, as from a volcanic crater.

lav′a-to″ry, 1 lav′ə-tō″rı; 2 lăv′a-tō″ry, *n.* [-RIES^z, *pl.*] A place for washing.

lave, 1 lēv; 2 lāv, *vt. & vi.* [LAVED; LAV′ING.] To wash; bathe.—**la′ver**, 1 lē′vər; 2 lā′ver, *n.* A large basin to wash in.

lav′en-der, 1 lav′en-dər; 2 lăv′ĕn-der, *n.* **1.** An aromatic shrub. **2.** A pale lilac color.

lav′ish, 1 lav′ish; 2 lăv′ish. **I**^t. *vt.* To give out profusely; squander. **II.** *a.* Profuse; prodigal; superabundant. **-ly,** *adv.* **-ment,** *n.* **-ness,** *n.*

law, 1 lē; 2 lą, *n.* **1.** An authoritative rule of action; legislative enactment; commandment; statute. **2.** Legal science; jurisprudence.—**law′ful,** *a.* Permitted by law; right; just. **-ly,** *adv.* **-ness,** *n.*—**law′less,** *a.* Unrestrained by law; irregular; outlawed. **-ly,** *adv.* **-ness,** *n.*

lawn¹, 1 lēn; 2 lạn, *n.* A grassy space near a dwelling.—**lawn′-ten″nis,** *n.* See TENNIS.

lawn², *n.* Fine thin linen cambric.

law′suit″, 1 lē′siút″; 2 lạ′sūt″, *n.* An action in a court of law.

law′yer, 1 lō′yər; 2 lạ′yer, *n.* One who is versed in law or who practises law.

lax, 1 laks; 2 lăks, *a.* Lacking firmness; slack; flabby; negligent. **-ly,** *adv.* **-ness,** *n.*—**lax-a′tion,** *n.*—**lax′a-tiv**(e^s. **I.** *a. Med.* Gently purgative. **II.** *n.* A purgative.—**lax′i-ty,** *n.* **lax′ness**‡.

lay, 1 lē; 2 lā, *v.* [LAID; LAY′ING.] **I.** *t.* **1.** To place; deposit; impose; attribute or ascribe; impute; present. **2.** To make ready, as a table for a meal. **3.** To drop (an egg), as a fowl. **II.** *i.* To drop eggs, as fowls.—**lay′-fīg″ure,** *n.* A model, often jointed, made to put in a certain attitude, to support drapery for an artist's use; a mere puppet.

lay, 1 lē; 2 lā, *imp.* of LIE¹, *v.*

lay, *a.* Pertaining to the laity.—**la′ic,** *a.*

lay¹, *n.* The manner in which something lies or is placed; a line of work; a layer; a bet.

lay², *n.* A song; ballad.

lay′er, 1 lē′ər; 2 lā′er, *n.* **1.** A single horizontal thickness, as of strata. **2.** A shoot laid in the ground to take root and form a new plant.

lay′man, 1 lē′mən; 2 lā′man, *n.* [LAY′-MEN, *pl.*] One of the laity.

la′zar, 1 lē′zər; 2 lā′zar, *n.* One afflicted with a loathsome disease; a leper.—**laz″a-ret′to,** 1 laz″ə-ret′o; 2 lăz′a-rĕt′o, *n.* A pest=house or pest=ship; a hospital.

la′zy, 1 lē′zı; 2 lā′zy, *a.* [LA′ZI-ER; LA′ZI-EST.] Indisposed to exertion; slothful; slow.—**la′zi-ly,** *adv.*—**la′zi-ness,** *n.*

lea, 1 lī; 2 lē, *n.* A grassy field or plain.

leach, 1 līch; 2 lēch. **I**^t. *vt. & vi.* To wash, as wood=ashes; drain away. **II.** *n.* Wood=ashes, washed for the alkali contained in them.

lead¹, 1 līd; 2 lēd, *v.* [LED; LEAD′ING.] **I.** *t.* To guide by going before; precede; conduct; induce. **II.** *i.* To act as guide; extend or reach.—**lead′er,** *n.* One who leads; a guide; commander.—**lead′er-ship,** *n.*

lead², 1 led; 2 lĕd, *vt. & vi.* [LEAD′ED^d; LEAD′ING.] To cover, fasten, fit, or fill up with lead; supply with leads, as type.

lead¹, 1 līd; 2 lēd, *n.* Position in advance; priority; guidance; command.

lead², } 1 led; 2 lĕd, *n.* **1.** A soft, heavy,
leds, } bluish=gray metal; some leaden object, as a thin slip to separate lines of type, a sinker, etc. **2.** Graphite. **black lead**‡.—**lead′=pen″cil,** *n.* A pencil made of graphite (black lead) encased in wood, paper, or the like for drawing or writing.

lead′en, } 1 led′n; 2 lĕd′n, *a.* Made of or
led′en=, } like lead; heavy; dull; oppressive.

leaf, 1 līf; 2 lēf, *n.* [LEAVES, 1 līvz; 2 lēvs,

pl.] One of the breathing-organs of a plant, growing from the stem, and commonly broad, flat, thin, and green. See illus. on next page; also, something resembling this, as a fold of a book, a movable part of a table, or a valve of a door. **— leaf'age,** *n.* Leaves collectively; foliage. — **leaf'less,** *a.* Having no leafage. **— leaf'let,** *n.* A little leaf; also, a tract. **— leaf'y,** *a.* [LEAF'I-ER; LEAF'I-EST.] Abounding in leaves.

league, 1 lēg; 2 lĕg, *vt. & vi.* [LEAGUED, 1 lēagd⁸; LEAGU'ING.] To join in a league; combine.

league¹, *n.* An alliance.

league², *n.* A varying measure of distance. The marine league equals 3 geographic miles.

leak, 1 līk; 2 lēk. **I²,** *vt. & vi.* To pass or allow to pass in or out undesignedly, as a liquid. **II.** *n.* 1. An opening letting a fluid in or out undesignedly. 2. Leakage. **— leak'age,** *n.* The act of leaking; the quantity that leaks; an allowance for loss by leaking. **— leak'y,** *a.* [LEAK'I-ER; LEAK'I-EST.] Having a leak or leaks. **— leak'i-ness,** *n.*

leal, 1 līl; 2 lēl, *a.* [Poet., Prov. Eng., & Scot.] Loyal; true-hearted; faithful.

lean, 1 līn; 2 lēn, *vt. & vi.* [LEANED, 1 līnd, 2 lēnd, or LEANT, 1 lĕnt, 2 lĕnt, LEAND⁸; LEAN'ING.] To bend from an erect position; depend: with *on* or *upon.*

lean. I. *a.* Wanting flesh; not fat; thin; slender. **II.** *n.* Lean meat.

leap, 1 līp; 2 lēp. **I.** *vt. & vi.* [LEAPED or LEAPT, 1 lĭpt, 2 lēpt, or LEPT, 1 lĕpt, 2 lĕpt; LEAP'ING.] To spring over or off the ground; jump; bound. **II.** *n.* The act of leaping; a jump; bound. **— leap'-year",** *n.* Every fourth year, in which February has 29 days.

learn, 1 lûrn; 2 lērn, *vt. & vi.* [LEARNED, 1 lûrnd, 2 lērnd, or LEARNT, 1 lûrnt, 2 lērnt; LEARN'ING.] To gain knowledge of or skill in; acquire knowledge or skill. **— learn'ed,** 1 lûrn'ĕd; 2 lērn'ĕd, *pa.* Possessed of learning; erudite. **-ly,** *adv.* **-ness,** *n.* **— learn'er,** *n.* **— learn'ing,** *n.* Knowledge; eminent scholarship.

lease, 1 līs; 2 lēs. **I.** *vt.* [LEASED⁴, LEAST⁸; LEAS'ING.] To grant or obtain the temporary possession of, as lands; rent; let. **II.** *n.* The letting of land, etc., for rent, or the contract for such letting. **— lease'-hold",** 1 līs'hōld"; 2 lēs'hōld", *n.* A tenure held by a lease.

leash, 1 līsh; 2 lēsh. **I²,** *vt.* To bind or hold by a leash. **II.** A thong for holding a hunting-dog, etc.; three of the same kind, as greyhounds; three in general.

least, 1 līst; 2 lēst. **I.** *a. superl.* Smallest in size, value, etc. **II.** *adv. superl.* In the lowest or smallest degree.

leath'er, 1 lĕth'ẽr; 2 lĕth'er, *n.* The skin **leth'er⁸,** of an animal tanned or dressed for use. **— leath'ern,** *a.* Made of leather. **— leath'er-y,** *a.* Resembling leather; tough.

leave¹, 1 līv; 2 lēv, *v.* [LEFT; LEAV'ING.] **leav²,** **I.** *t.* To withdraw from; quit; abandon; refer; bequeath. **II.** *i.* To go away; depart; discontinue.

leave², *vt.* To grant leave to; permit.

leave³, *vt.* [LEAVED, LEAVD⁸; LEAV'ING.] To put forth leaves.

leave, *n.* Permission to go or to be absent; a departure; parting.

leav'en, 1 lev'n; 2 lĕv'n. **I.** *vt.* To make **lev'en⁸,** light by fermentation. **II.** *n.* A fermenting substance; ferment; influence causing change.

leaves, 1 līvz; 2 lēvs, *n.* Plural of LEAF.

leav'ing, 1 līv'ıŋ; 2 lēv'ĭng, *n.* **1.** The act of departure. **2.** *pl.* Things left; scraps; refuse; offal.

lech'er, 1 lĕch'ẽr; 2 lĕch'er, *n.* A libertine; sensualist. **— lech'er-ous,** *a.* Lewd. **-ly,** *adv.* **— lech'er-y,** *n.* Vicious sensuality; lewdness.

lec'tern, 1 lek'tẽrn; 2 lĕc'tern, *n.* A reading-desk in a church.

lec'ture, 1 lek'chur or -tiur; 2 lĕc'chur or -tūr. **I.** *vt. & vi.* [LEC'TURED; LEC'TUR-ING.] To deliver lectures to; reprimand; deliver a formal discourse. **II.** *n.* A discourse; formal reproof. **— lec'tur-er,** *n.*

led, *imp. & pp.* of LEAD, *v.*

ledge, 1 lej; 2 lĕdg, *n.* A projecting shelf, as of rock, etc.

ledg'er, 1 lej'ẽr; 2 lĕdg'er, *n.* The chief book of accounts among merchants.

lee, 1 lī; 2 lē. **I.** *a. Naut.* Pertaining to the side sheltered from the wind. **II.** *n.* The direction opposite that from which the wind comes; the side sheltered, or that gives shelter, from wind. **— lee shore,** the shore on the lee side of a ship. **— lee tide,** a tide running with the wind.

leech¹, 1 līch; 2 lēch, *vt.* To bleed with leeches; treat with medicine; heal.

leech¹, *n.* An aquatic worm used for drawing blood; bloodsucker.

leech², *n.* The edge of a square sail.

leek, 1 līk; 2 lēk, *n.* An onion-like herb.

leer, 1 līr; 2 lēr. **I.** *vt. & vi.* To look with a leer; allure. **II.** *n.* A sly, oblique, malicious, or amorous glance. **— leer'ing-ly,** *adv.*

lees, 1 līz; 2 lēs, *n. pl.* Sediment; dregs.

lee'ward, 1 lī'wẽrd or (*Naut.*) lū'ẽrd; 2 lē'-ward or (*Naut.*) lŭ'ard. **I.** *a. & n.* Lee. **II.** *adv.* Toward the lee.

1: ǝ = final; ı = habit; aisle; au = out; oil; iu = feud; chin; go; ŋ = sing; thin, this.
2: wolf, dǫ; book, boot; full, rule, cūre, but, burn; oil, boy; go, gem; ink; thin, this.

COMMON AMERICAN LEAVES.

1. Sand-bar willow. 2. Canoe-birch. 3. Honey-locust. 4. Sugar-maple. 5. Black ash.
6. Shingle-oak. 7. Lombardy poplar. 8. White elm. 9. Chestnut.

lee′way″, 1 lī′wē″; 2 lē′wā″, n. The drift of a vessel to leeward.

left, 1 left; 2 lĕft, imp. & pp. of LEAVE, v.

left. I. a. Opposite to right. II. n. The left side.

left′-hand″, 1 left′-hand″; 2 lĕft′-hănd″, a. Situated on the left side.— left′-hand″ed, a. More efficient with the left hand than right.

leg, 1 leg; 2 lĕg, n. A supporting limb of an animal or something analogous to it; as, the leg of a stocking; the leg of a table; a support.   [A bequest.

leg′a-cy, 1 leg′a-sı; 2 lĕg′ga-cy, n. [-CIES², pl.|

le′gal, 1 lī′gal; 2 lē′gal, a. Pertaining to or according to law; lawful.— le-gal′i-ty, 1 li-gal′ı-tı; 2 le-găl′i-ty, n. [-TIES², pl.] The condition of being legal; conformity to law. — le′gal-ize, vt. [-IZED; -IZ′ING.] To give the authority of law to. le′gal-ise‡.— le′gal-ly, adv. According to law; lawfully.

leg′ate, 1 leg′ıt; 2 lĕg′at, n. An ambassador; envoy.   [recipient of a legacy.

leg″a-tee′, 1 leg″a-tī′; 2 lĕg″a-tē′, n. The

le-ga′tion, 1 lı-gē′shan; 2 le-gā′shon, n. 1. The act of delegating.   2. An embassy.

le-ga′to, 1 le-gä′to; 2 le-gä′to, adv. Mus. In a smooth, connected manner.

leg′end, 1 lej′end; 2 lĕg′ĕnd, n. A traditionary narrative; fable; myth; also, a motto or inscription, as under a picture. — leg-en-da-ry, a. Pertaining to legends; traditional; fabulous.

leg″er-de-main″, 1 lej″ɛr-dı-mēn″; 2 lĕg″ɛr-de-mān′, n. Sleight of hand.

leg′ging, 1 leg′ıŋ; 2 lĕg′ing, n. A covering for the leg. leg′gint.

leg′i-ble, 1 lej′i-bl; 2 lĕg′i-bl, a. Readable, as writing.— leg″i-bil′i-ty, n. leg′i-ble-ness‡.— leg′i-bly, adv.
leg′i-bl‡,

le′gion, 1 lī′jan; 2 lē′gon, n. 1. A body of Roman soldiers, of 4,500 to 6,000 men; a military force; multitude. 2. An organization of veterans, as the American Legion.

leg′is-late, 1 lej′ıs-.ēt; 2 lĕg′is-lāt, vt. & vi. [-LAT″ED^d; -LAT″ING.] To bring about by legislation; make or enact laws.— leg′is-la′-tion, n. Enactment of laws.— leg′is-la″-tiv(e‡), 1 lej′ıs-lā″tıv; 2 lĕg′is-lā-tiv. a. Pertaining to legislation or to a legislature.— leg′is-la″tor, n. A lawgiver; member of a legislature.

leg′is-la″ture, 1 lej′ıs-lē″chur or -tiur; 2 lĕg′is-lā″chur or -tūr, n. A body of men empowered to make laws for a state.

le-git′i-mate, 1 lı-jit′ı-mēt; 2 le-gĭt′i-māt. I. vt. [-MAT″ED^d; -MAT″ING.] To make legitimate. II. 1. lı-jit′ı-mıt; 2 le-gĭt′i-mat, a. Lawful; born in wedlock; genuine. -ly, adv. — le-git′i-ma-cy, 1 lı-jit′ı-mə-sı; 2 le-gĭt′i-ma-cy, n. The

quality of being legitimate.— le-git″i-ma′-tion, n. The act of making legitimate.

leg′ume, 1 leg′yum or ıı-giūm′; 2 lĕg′yum or le-gūm′, n. A 2-valved seed-vessel or pod, as of a bean or pea.— le-gu′mi-nous, 1 lı-giū′mı-nus; 2 le-gū′mi-nus, a. Pertaining to the bean family. le-gu′mi-nose‡.

lei′sure, 1 lī′zur; 2 lē′zhur. I. a. Spare; unoccupied. II. n. Freedom from work; spare time; opportunity.— lei′sure-ly. I. a. Done at leisure; deliberate; slow. II. adv. At leisure; deliberately.— lei′sure-li-ness, n.

lem′on, 1 lem′an; 2 lĕm′on, n. An orange-like fruit, with very acid juice; also, the tree that bears it.— lem″on-ade′, n. A drink of lemon-juice and water with sugar.

lem″pi″ra′, 1 lem″pī′rä′; 2 lĕm″pī′rä′, n. The Honduran monetary unit. See COIN.

le′mur, 1 lī′mur; 2 lē′mŭr, n. A small nocturnal mammal related to the monkeys.

Lemur. 1/32

lend, 1 lend; 2 lĕnd, vt. & vi. [LENT, 1 lent, 2 lĕnt; LEND′ING.] To grant the temporary use of; furnish; afford.— lend′er, n.

length, 1 leŋth; 2 lĕngth, n. 1. Extension from end to end; reach; extent. 2. Gram. & Pros. Quantity, as of a vowel.— length′i-ly, adv.— length′i-ness, n.— length′wise, -woiz; 2 -wīs, a. & adv. In a longitudinal direction.— length′y, 1 leŋth′ı; 2lĕngth′y, a. [LENGTH′I-ER; -I-EST.] Having length; unduly long.

length′en, 1 leŋth′n; 2 lĕngth′n, vt. & vi. To make or grow longer; extend; protract.

le′nient, 1 lī′nı-ent; 2 lē′ni-ĕnt, a. Not severe; merciful; mild.— le′ni-en-cy, n. Mildness. le′ni-ence‡.— len′i-tiv(e‡, 1 len′i-tiv; 2 lĕn′i-tiv, a. Having the power of soothing. — len′i-ty, 1 len′i-tı; 2 lĕn′i-ty, n. The state or quality of being lenient; forbearance.

lens, 1 lenz; 2 lĕns, n. A curved piece of glass by which rays of light may be made to converge or to diverge.

Lens.

Lent, n. A fast of forty days immediately preceding Easter.— lent′en, 1 lent′en or lent′n; 2 lĕnt′en or lĕnt′n, a. [l- or L-] Pertaining to Lent; plain; spare; meager.

len-tic′u-lar, 1 len-tik′yu-lɛr; 2 lĕn-tiç′yu-lar, a. Resembling a double-convex lens; shaped like a lentil. -ly, adv. len′til-form‡.

len′til, 1 len′tıl; 2 lĕn′til, n. A leguminous plant or one of its pods or seeds.

len′to. len″ta-men′te, 1 len′to, lent′a-men′tē; 2 lĕn′to, lĕn″tä-mĕn′tç, a. & adv. Mus. Slow; slowly: a direction to the players.

le′o-nine, 1 lī′o-nin; 2 lē′o-nĭn, _a._ Pertaining to or like a lion; fierce; powerful.

leop′ard,
lep′ard², } 1 lep′ərd; 2 lĕp′ard, _n._ A spotted cat-like mammal, of Asia and Africa; also, the American jaguar.

lep′er, 1 lep′ər; 2 lĕp′er, _n._ One afflicted with leprosy.— **lep′ro-sy,** 1 lep′ro-sɪ; 2 lĕp′ro-sy, _n._ A chronic skin-disease with ulcerous spots and scaling off of dead tissue.— **lep′rous,** _a. Pathol._ Affected with leprosy; unclean.

lese″-maj′es-ty, 1 līz″-maj′es-tɪ; 2 lēs″-măj′ĕs-ty, _n._ A crime against or insult to the sovereign power; treason. **leze″-maj′es-ty‡.**

le′sion, 1 lī′ʒən; 2 lē′zhon, _n._ A hurt; loss; injury.

less, 1 les; 2 lĕs. **I.** _a._ [LEAST, 1 līst; 2 lēst, _superl._] Smaller; inferior. **II.** _adv._ In inferior or smaller degree; not so much. **-less,** _suffix._ A termination expressing deprivation or destitution, often equivalent to "without"; as, harm_less_.

les-see′, 1 les-ī′; 2 lĕs-ē′, _n._ One holding property by lease.

less′en, 1 les′n; 2 lĕs′n, _vt. & vi._ To make less; diminish; lower; shrink.

less′er, 1 les′ər; 2 lĕs′er, _a._ Less; smaller; inferior.

les′son, 1 les′n; 2 lĕs′n, _n._ An exercise to be learned by a pupil; instruction; reproof; portion of Scripture.

les′sor, 1 les′ər or -ɔr; 2 lĕs′or, _n._ One who grants a lease.   [not; for fear that.

lest, 1 lest; 2 lĕst, _conj._ In order that . . .

let¹, 1 let; 2 lĕt, _vt. & vi._ [LET; LET′TING.] **1.** To permit; give leave to. **2.** To hire; rent; be leased or hired.

let²‖, _vt._ [LET or LET′TED⁴; LET′TING.] To hinder or impede; obstruct; oppose.

let, _n._ That which hinders; an obstacle.

-let, _suffix._ A termination forming diminutives from French and English nouns: as, _gimlet, tablet._   [mortal; deadly; fatal.

le′thal, 1 lī′thəl; 2 lē′thal, _a._ Causing death;

leth′ar-gy, 1 leth′ar-jɪ; 2 lĕth′ar-gy, _n._ [-GIES², _pl._] A state of prolonged sleep; stupor; apathy.— **le-thar′gic,** _a._ Drowsy; stupefying.

Le′the, 1 lī′thī; 2 lē′thē, _n. Class. Myth._ The stream of oblivion in the world of the dead, causing all who drank of it to forget the past.— **Le-the′an,** 1 lɪ-thī′an; 2 le-thē′an, _a._ Causing forgetfulness or oblivion.

let′ter, 1 let′ər; 2 lĕt′er. **I.** _vt._ To mark with letters. **II.** _n._ **1.** A character used to represent a sound; a written or printed communication; literal meaning. **2.** _pl._ Literary culture; learning.— **let′tering,** _n._   [herb used as a salad.

let′tuce, 1 let′ɪs; 2 lĕt′ĭç, _n._ A kitchen

leu′co-cyte, 1 liū′ko-sait; 2 lū′co-çȳt, _n._ One of the minute colorless masses of protoplasm found in blood and lymph (white blood-corpuscles), etc.: destructive to bacteria.

Le-vant′, 1 lɪ-vant′; 2 le-vănt′, _n._ The eastern Mediterranean and its coasts.— **Le-vant′ine,** _a._

lev-ee′¹, 1 lev-ī′; 2 lĕv-ē′, _n._ [U. S.] An embankment beside a stream, to prevent overflow; wharf.

lev-ee′², _n._ A morning reception; also, a general reception at any hour.

lev′el, 1 lev′el; 2 lĕv′ĕl. **I.** _vt. & vi._ [LEV′-ELED or LEV′ELLED, LEV′ELD⁸; LEV′EL-ING, or LEV′EL-LING.] To make level; aim; point. **II.** _a._ Having a flat, even surface; horizontal. **III.** _n._ A horizontal line; surface, plane, or position; an instrument for ascertaining a horizontal line. **IV.** _adv._ In a level line; direct; straight; steadily. **-ness,** _n._— **lev′el-er, lev′el-ler,** _n._— **lev′el-ing, lev′el-ling,** _n._

lev′er, 1 lev′ər or lī′vər; 2 lĕv′er or lē′ver, _n._ A bar, turning on a fulcrum, to apply power.— **lev′er-age,** _n._ The mechanical advantage gained by use of a lever.

lev′er-et, 1 lev′ər-et; 2 lĕv′er-ĕt, _n._ A young hare.

le-vi′a-than, 1 lɪ-vai′ə-thən; 2 le-vī′a-than, _n._ A large unknown animal mentioned in the Bible.   [frivolity; flippancy.

lev′i-ty, 1 lev′ɪ-tɪ; 2 lĕv′ĭ-ty, _n._ Lightness;

lev′y, 1 lev′ɪ; 2 lĕv′y, _vt._ [LEV′IED; LEV′Y-ING.] To exact by compulsion; assess.

lev′y, _n._ [LEV′IES², _pl._] **1.** The act of levying or collecting compulsorily. **2.** That which is levied, as money or troops.

lewd, 1 liūd; 2 lūd, _a._ Lustful; licentious. **-ly,** _adv._ **-ness,** _n._

lex″i-cog′ra-phy,
lex″i-cog′ra-fy², } 1 leks″ɪ-kɒg′rə-fɪ; 2 lĕks″ĭ-cŏg′ra-fy, _n._ The art of compiling dictionaries.— **lex″i-cog′ra-pher,** _n._— **lex″i-co-graph′ic,** _a._

lex′i-con, 1 leks′ɪ-kən; 2 lĕks′ĭ-cŏn, _n._ A dictionary, as of Latin, Greek, or Hebrew.

li′a-bl(e², 1 lai′ə-bl; 2 lī′a-bl, _a._ Responsible; answerable; exposed.— **li″a-bil′i-ty,** _n._ The state of being liable; exposure to danger, accident, or injury.

li′al′son, 1 lī″ē′zōn; 2 lī′ā′zŏn′, _n._ An illicit love-affair; intrigue. **II.** _a._ Linking or joining.   [falsehood.

li′ar, 1 lai′ər; 2 lī′ar, _n._ One who utters a

li-ba′tion, 1 lai-bē′shən; 2 lī-bā′shon, _n._ Liquid poured out, as in honor of a deity.

li′bel, 1 lai′bel; 2 lī′bĕl. **I.** _vt._ [LI′BELED or LI′BELLED, LI′BELD⁸; LI′BEL-ING or LI′BEL-LING.] To defame; bring suit against (a ship or cargo). **II.** _n._ **1.** Anything tending to defame character or reputation; slander. **2.** A plaintiff's written

statement, as in a court of admiralty. — **li'bel-ous, li'bel-lous,** *a.*

lib'er-al, 1 lĭb'er-al; 2 lĭb'er-al. **I.** *a.* Free and generous; bountiful; not bigoted; broad. **II.** *n.* A member of a liberal party. **-ism,** *n.* — **lib″er-al'i-ty,** 1 lĭb″er-al'-ı-tı; 2 lĭb″er-ăl'ĭ-ty, *n.* — **lib′er-al-ly,** *adv.*

lib'er-ate, 1 lĭb'er-ēt; 2 lĭb'er-āt, *vt.* [-AT″ED⁴; -AT″ING.] To set free; release from bondage. — **lib″er-a'tion,** *n.* — **lib′er-a″tor,** *n.*

lib'er-tin(e⁵, 1 lĭb'er-tin; 2 lĭb'er-tĭn. **I.** *a.* Dissolute; licentious. **II.** *n.* A licentious man; seducer. — **lib′er-tin-ism,** *n.* Licentiousness.

lib'er-ty, 1 lĭb'er-tı; 2 lĭb'er-ty, *n.* [-TIES²; *pl.*] **1.** The state of being free from the control of others; freedom; also, undue freedom; license. **2.** Franchise; privilege. [*a.* Lewd.

li-bid'i-nous, 1 lı-bĭd'ı-nŭs; 2 lĭ-bĭd'ĭ-nŭs,

li'bra-ry, 1 laı'brē-rı; 2 lī'brā-ry, *n.* [-RIES²; *pl.*] A collection of books, pamphlets, etc.; also, the place containing it. — **li-bra'ri-an,** 1 laı-brē'rı-an; 2 lĭ-brā'rĭ-an, *n.* One who has charge of a library. **-ship,** *n.*

li-bret'to, 1 lı-bret'to; 2 lĭ-brĕt'to, *n.* A book containing the text, as of an opera; the words of the text. — **li-bret'tist,** *n.* The writer of a libretto.

lice, 1 laıs; 2 līç, *n.* Plural of LOUSE.

li'cense, 1 laı'sens; 2 lī'sens, **I.** *vt.* [LI′-CENSED⁴; LI′CENST⁵; LI′CENS-ING.] To authorize; permit. **II.** *n.* Authority granted to do or omit an act; also, unrestrained or unwarrantable liberty of action. — **li-cen'tious,** 1 laı-sen'shŭs; 2 lĭ-çĕn'shŭs, *a.* Exceeding the limits of propriety; wanton; lewd; dissolute. **-ly,** *adv.* **-ness,** *n.*

li-cen'ti-ate, 1 laı-sen'shı-ēt; 2 lĭ-çĕn'shĭ-āt, *n.* A person licensed to exercise a profession.

li'chen, 1 laı'ken; 2 lī'çĕn, *n.* *Bot.* A flowerless plant growing flat upon a surface, as of a rock.

lick⁵, 1 lık; 2 lĭk, *vt. & vi.* To lap; make a lapping movement, as a flame.

lic'o-rice, 1 lık'o-rıs; 2 lĭk'o-rĭç, *n.* An **lic'o-ris⁵,** } annual herb or a confection made from its root. [lid.

lid, 1 lıd; 2 lĭd, *n.* A movable cover; eye-

lie¹, 1 laı; 2 lī, *vi.* [LAY, 1 lē, 2 lā; LAIN, 1 lēn, 2 lān; LY′ING.] To rest or lay oneself down at full length; sleep; lodge; abide.

lie², *vi.* [LIED; LY′ING.] To utter falsehood; give a deceitful impression.

lie, *n.* An untruth; falsehood.

lief, 1 līf; 2 lēf, *adv.* Willingly; freely.

liege, 1 līj; 2 lēg. **I.** *a.* Bound by feudal

tenure; sovereign. **II.** *n.* A vassal; a citizen; also, a liege lord.

li'en, 1 lī'en *or* līn; 2 lī'ĕn *or* lēn, *n.* A legal claim on property.

lieu, 1 liū; 2 lū, *n.* Place; stead: in the phrase, *in lieu of.*

lieu-ten'ant, 1 liu-ten'ant; 2 lū-tĕn'ant, *n.* **1.** An officer empowered to act in place of a superior; deputy. **2.** A commissioned officer next below a captain in the army or a commander in the navy.

lieve, 1 līv; 2 lēv, *adv.* Same as LIEF.

life, 1 laıf; 2 līf, *n.* [LIVES, 1 laıvz; 2 līvz, *pl.*] **1.** The state of being alive; vital principle; vitality. **2.** Animate existence. **3.** Human affairs. **4.** Subsistence. **5.** A biography. — **life′boat″,** *n.* A boat made specially buoyant, for life-saving in case of shipwreck. — **life′less,** *a.* Destitute of life; dead; dull; insensible. — **life′like″,** *a.* Resembling that which is living. — **life′long″,** *a.* Lasting or continuing through life. — **life′-time″,** *n.* The whole period of a life.

lift⁴, 1 lıft; 2 lĭft, *v.* **I.** *t.* To raise; elevate; exalt. **II.** *i.* To rise, or appear to rise, as mist.

lift, *n.* **1.** The act of lifting; that which is raised or hoisted. **2.** That which lifts or assists in lifting; an elevator, a hook for raising a window-sash, etc.

lig'a-ment, 1 lıg'a-ment *or* -mant; 2 lĭg′a-ment, *n.* A fibrous band which binds related structures, as bones, together; a bond of union.

lig'a-ture, 1 lıg'a-chur *or* -tiur; 2 lĭg′a-chŭr *or* -tūr, *n.* Anything that serves for tying or connecting.

light¹, 1 laıt; 2 līt, *vt. & vi.* [LIGHT′ED⁴ or LIT; LIGHT′ING.] To set fire to or take fire; inflame; kindle; illuminate.

light², *vi.* [LIGHT′ED⁴ or LIT; LIGHT′-ING.] **1.** To alight, as a bird. **2.** To happen or stumble, as by chance; followed by *on* or *upon*. [pale in color.

light¹, *a.* Full of light; bright; faint or

light², *a.* **1.** Having little weight. **2.** Trifling; trivial. **3.** Easy in movement; cheerful; frivolous; gay.

light, *n.* That which renders objects visible; anything that gives light, as a candle, window, etc.; aspect; perception.

light, *adv.* Lightly; cheaply.

light′en¹, 1 laıt'n; 2 līt'n, *vt. & vi.* To make or become light or lighter; illuminate; enlighten; emit, as a flash of lightning.

light′en², *vt. & vi.* To relieve of weight or distress; gladden; become less weighty.

light′er¹, 1 laıt'er; 2 līt'er, *n.* A barge-like vessel used in loading ships.

---

light′er², *n.* One who or that which lights or illuminates.

light′house″, 1 lait′haus″; 2 līt′hous″, *n.* A tower bearing lamps, erected to guide seamen by night.

1. Lighthouse. 2. Flash-light Lantern, showing arrangement of Prisms and Revolving-gear.

light′ly, *adv.* With little weight or pressure; easily; with levity.

light′ness, 1 lait′nes; 2 līt′nĕs, *n.* The quality of being light, in any sense.

light′ning, 1 lait′nıŋ; 2 līt′ning, *n.* Light caused by the discharge of electricity from a cloud.   [slaughtered animal.

lights, 1 laits; 2 līts, *n. pl.* Lungs, as of a

light′-ship″, 1 lait′ship″; 2 līt′shĭp″, *n* A vessel anchored at a station, and bearing lights, to serve the purpose of a lighthouse.

light′some, 1 lait′sam; 2 līt′sŏm, *a.* Of a light or cheerful mood or character; lively; gay; playful. **-ly**, *adv.* **-ness**, *n.*

lig′ne-ous, 1 lĭg′nı-us; 2 lĭg′ne-ŭs, *a.* Having the appearance of wood; woody.

lig′nite, 1 lĭg′nait; 2 lĭg′nīt, *n.* A fuel intermediate between peat and coal.

lig′num-vi′tæ, 1 lĭg′num=vai′tī; 2 lĭg′nŭm=vī′tē, *n.* A tropical American tree, with hard, heavy wood.

like, 1 laik; 2 līk. **I.** *vt.* [LIKED‡; LIK′ING.] To please, or be pleased with; enjoy; choose. **II.** *a.* Resembling; similar; equal, or virtually equivalent. **III.** *n.* A like person or thing; counterpart; liking; inclination.— **IV.** *adv.* In the manner of; similarly to. **like′li-hood**, *n.* The character of being likely; a probability. **like-li-ness‡.— like′ly. I.** *a.* [LIKE′LI-ER; LIKE′LI-EST.] Apparently true or real; probable; promising. **II.** *adv.* Probably.— **like′ness**, *n.* Resemblance; portrait; guise.— **like′wise**, *adv. & conj.* In like manner; moreover.— **lik′ing**, *n.* Inclination; kindly feeling; preference.

lik′en, 1 laik′n; 2 līk′en, *vt.* To represent as similar; compare.

li′lac, 1 lai′lak; 2 lī′lac, *n.* A shrub having fragrant purplish flowers.

lil′y, 1 lĭl′ı; 2 lĭl′y, *n.* A bulbous plant having elegant, often pure-white, flowers. **— Easter lily**, the trumpet-like white lily, so called from the time of blooming and decorative use at Easter. **Bermuda l.‡**

Lil′li-put, 1 lĭl′ı-put; 2 lĭl′ĭ-pŭt, *n.* A fictitious island described by Swift in his *Gulliver's Travels*, where the men were six inches in height, and trees, houses, and all other objects in proportion.— **Lil″li-pu′tian. I.** *a.* Pertaining to Lilliput; tiny; diminutive. **II.** *n.* An inhabitant of Lilliput; a pigmy; dwarf. **Lil″i-pu′tian‡.**

limb¹, 1 lim; 2 lĭm, *n.* One of the jointed **lims**, parts of an animal, as a leg or arm; also, a branch of a tree.

limb², *n.* An edge, or part, as of a disk or surface.

lim′ber, 1 lĭm′bər; 2 lĭm′ber, *vt.* To make limber or pliant; fasten a limber to (a cannon.   [**lim′ber-ness**, *n.*

lim′ber, *a.* Easily bent; pliant; limp.—

lim′ber, *n.* The fore part of a gun-carriage.

lim′bo, 1 lĭm′bo; 2 lĭm′bo, *n.* **1.** *R. C. Theol.* A border region between hell and heaven. **2.** A place, real or imaginary, for worthless or foolish things.

lime, 1 laim; 2 līm, *vt.* [LIMED; LIM′ING.] To catch with birdlime; ensnare.

lime¹, *n.* A white earth-like substance produced by burning limestone, etc., used in building.— **lime′-kiln″**, *n.* A kiln for burning lime.— **lime′stone″**, *n.* A rock composed of calcium carbonate.— **lime′-water**, *n.* A saturated solution of lime in water, used medicinally.

lime², *n.* A small tree of the orange family, or its lemon-like fruit; also, a linden. **lime′-tree″‡.— lime′-juice″**, *n.* The acid juice of the lime, used medicinally.

lim′er-ick, 1 lĭm′ər-ık; 2 lĭm′er-ĭc, *n.* A form of nonsense verse in five lines.

lim′it, 1 lĭm′ıt; 2 lĭm′ĭt. **I.** *d. vt.* To bound; confine; restrict. **II.** *n.* That which limits, or is limited, or has bounds; a check; district; period.— **lim″i-ta′tion**, 1 lĭm″ı-tē′shan; 2 lĭm″ĭ-ta′shon, *n.* The act of limiting; restriction.— **lim′it-ed**, *pa.* Confined to certain limits; circumscribed.— **lim′-it-less**, *a.*

limn, 1 lĭm; 2 lĭm, *vt.* To draw or paint, as a picture; delineate.— **lim′ner**, *n.*

li″mou′sine″, 1 lī″mū′zīn′; 2 lī″mụ′sĭn″, *n.* A motor-car with a coupé-like body.

limp, 1 lĭmp; 2 lĭmp, *vi.* To walk lamely.

limp, *a.* Limber; flimsy.

limp, *n.* The step of a lame person; a halt.

lim′pet, 1 lĭm′pet; 2 lĭm′pĕt, *n.* A small shell-fish, found clinging to rocks.

lim′pid, 1 lĭm′pid; 2 lĭm′pĭd, *a.* Transparent; lucid; clear.— **lim-pid′i-ty**, *n.* **lim′-pid-ness‡.**

linch′pin″, 1 linch′pin″; 2 lĭnch′pĭn″, *n.* A pin formerly used to keep a wheel on the axle.

lin′den, 1 lin′den; 2 lĭn′dĕn, *n.* A tree with heart-shaped leaves and cream-colored flowers. See illus. in next col.

line¹, 1 lain; 2 līn, *v.* [LINED; LIN′ING.]

I. *t.* To make lines upon; read out, line by line. **II.** *i.* To form or be in line.

line², *vt.* [LINED; LIN'-ING.] To cover the inside of.

line, *n.* **1.** A string or cord; mark; outline; lineament; boundary; limit; course; route; series of conveyances; a train of thought. **2.** Kinship; descent; family. **3.** A row, as of articles or words. **4.** A stock of goods or a business. **5.** *Math.* That which has length without breadth or thickness. **6.** The equator. **7.** A measure of length, one-twelfth inch.— **the line,** the equator.

American Linden.

a, the leaf; *b,* a bract bearing flowers; *c, a* bract in fruit.

lin'e-age, 1 lĭn'ĭ-ĭj; 2 lĭn'e-aġ, *n.* Genealogy; pedigree; descent.

lin'e-al, 1 lĭn'ĭ-al; 2 lĭn'e-al, *a.* **1.** Hereditary. **2.** Made with lines. **-ly,** *adv.*

lin'e-a-ment, 1 lĭn'ĭ-ə-ment *or* -mənt; 2 lĭn'e-a-ment, *n.* A feature.

lin'e-ar, 1 lĭn'ĭ-ər; 2 lĭn'e-är, *a.* Pertaining to or composed of lines.

lin'en, 1 lĭn'en; 2 lĭn'ĕn, *n.* A fabric woven from flax; articles made of linen.

lin'ger, 1 lĭŋ'gər; 2 lĭŋ'ġer, *vt. & vi.* To protract; drag; be long about going or coming; lag.— **lin'ger-ing,** *pa.* Protracted; slow.

lin"ge-rie', 1 lăn"ʒə-rī'; 2 lăn'zhe-rē', *n.* Fine white linen or cotton articles of dress collectively.

lin'gual, 1 lĭŋ'gwal; 2 lĭŋ'ġwal. **I.** *a.* Pertaining to the tongue. **II.** *n.* A letter pronounced chiefly with the tongue, as *d, s, z, dh,* etc.

lin'guist, 1 lĭŋ'gwist; 2 lĭŋ'ġwĭst, *n.* An adept in languages.— **lin-guis'tic,** *a.* Pertaining to language.

lin'i-ment, 1 lĭn'ĭ-ment *or* -mənt; 2 lĭn'i-ment, *n. Med.* A liquid medicine for external use.

lin'ing, 1 laĭn'ĭŋ; 2 lĭn'ing, *n.* A covering of the inner surface of a thing.

link¹, 1 lĭŋk; 2 lĭŋk, *vt. & vi.* To connect by links; unite.

link¹, *n.* A loop of a chain; a part of a series; connecting-bar of a machine.

link², *n.* A torch.

links, 1 lĭŋks; 2 lĭŋks, *n. pl.* Grounds laid out for the game of golf.

lin'net, 1 lĭn'et; 2 lĭn'ĕt, *n.* A small singing bird.

li-no'le-um, 1 lĭ-nō'lĭ-um; 2 li-nō'le-ŭm, *n.*

Hardened linseed-oil, mixed with ground cork and pressed upon canvas, for covering floors.

li'no-type, 1 laĭno-[*or* lĭn'o-]taĭp; 2 lī'no-[*or* lĭn'o-]tīp, *n.* A line of type cast in one piece, or a machine for so casting material for printing

lin'seed", 1 lĭn'sĭd"; 2 lĭn'sēd", *n.* Flaxseed.— **lin'seed-oil",** *n.* An oil expressed from flaxseed.

lin"sey-wool'sey, 1 lĭn"zĭ-wul'zĭ; 2 lĭn'sy-wool'sy. **I.** *a.* Made of linen and wool mixed. **II.** *n.* A cloth of this mixture.

lint, 1 lint; 2 lĭnt, *n.* Raveled linen; also, downy feathers.

lin'tel, 1 lin'tel; 2 lĭn'tĕl, *n.* A horizontal beam over a door or window.

li'on, 1 laĭ'ən; 2 lī'on, *n.* A large yellowish-brown carnivorous mammal, of the cat family, of Africa and Asia; figuratively, a celebrity.— **li'on-ess,** *n.* A she lion.— **li'on-ize** *or* **-ise,** *vt.* To treat or regard as a prominent or notable person; distinguish with social attention.

lip, 1 lĭp; 2 lĭp, *n.* The border of the mouth; the mouth; speech; the edge of anything.— **lip'stick",** *n.* A small roll of colored cosmetic used to enchance the color of the lips.— **lipped,** 1 lĭpt; 2 lĭpt, *a.* Having lips.

liq'ue-fy, 1 lĭk'wĭ-faĭ; 2 lĭk'we-fȳ, *vt. & vi.* [-FIED; -FY'ING.] To make or become liquid; melt.— **liq'ue-fac'tion,** *n.* The act of melting; state of being melted.

li-queur', 1 lĭ-kūr'; 2 lĭ-kûr', *n.* Alcoholic liquor sweetened and flavored with aromatic substances.

liq'uid, 1 lĭk'wĭd; 2 lĭk'wid. **I.** *a.* Flowing; not solid; watery; soft or soft in sound. **II.** *n.* **1.** A flowing or fluid substance. **2.** One of the letters *l, m, n, r.* **-ly,** *adv.* **-ness,** *n.*— **liquid fire,** flaming petroleum ejected by high pressure.— **liq'ui-date,** 1 lĭk'wĭ-dēt; 2 lĭk'wi-dāt, *vt.* [-DAT'ED; DAT'ING.] To settle; adjust; make more liquid, as a sound.— **liq"ui-da'tion,** *n.*— **li-quid'i-ty,** 1 lĭ-kwĭd'ĭ-tĭ; 2 li-kwĭd'i-ty, *n.* The state of being liquid.

liq'uor, 1 lĭk'ər; 2 lĭk'or, *n.* Any alcoholic liquid; liquid in general.

lisp, 1 lĭsp; 2 lĭsp. **I.** *vi. & vt.* To speak with a lisp; pronounce *s* and *z* as *th;* speak imperfectly. **II.** *n.* **1.** The act or habit of lisping. **2.** A childish or timid utterance.

list¹ᵈ, 1 list; 2 lĭst, *vt. & vi.* To enroll; enlist.

list², *vt.* To cover with list. See LIST².

list³, *vt. & vi.* To careen, as a ship.

list⁴, *vt. & vi.* [Poet.] To listen.

list⁵ᵈ, *vt.* To enclose, as a field, for combat.

list⁶, *n.* A roll or catalog.

list², *n.* The selvage of cloth; any outer edge; boundary.

list³, *n. Naut.* A careening.

list⁴, *n.* A barrier of a justing=field; in the plural, the field itself.

lis'ten, 1 lis'n; 2 lĭs'n, *vi.* To attend for the sake of hearing; harken.— **lis'ten-er,** *n.* **lis'ten-ing=post",** *n.* *Mil.* A post for detecting the movements or mining operations of an enemy.

list'less, 1 list'les; 2 lĭst'lĕs, *a.* Inattentive; heedless; languid. **-ly,** *adv.* **-ness,** *n.*

lit, *imp. & pp.* of LIGHT, *v.*

lit'a-ny, 1 lit'a-nɪ; 2 lĭt'a-ny, *n.* [-NIES², *pl.*] A supplicatory or responsive prayer.

li'ter, 1 li'tər; 2 lī'tẽr, *n.* A measure of capacity. See METRIC SYSTEM.

lit'er-al, 1 lit'ər-al; 2 lĭt'ẽr-al, *a.* Word for word; not figurative; exact.— **lit'er-al-ly,** *adv.* — **lit'er-al-ness,** *n.*

lit'er-a-ry, 1 lit'ər-ē-rɪ; 2 lĭt'ẽr-ā-ry, *a.* Pertaining to, practised in, or devoted to literature.

lit'er-ate, 1 lit'ər-ɪt; 2 lĭt'ẽr-at. **I.** *a.* Having a knowledge of letters. **II.** *n.* One versed in letters.

lit"e-ra'ti, 1 lit"ɪ-rē'tai; 2 lĭt"e-rā'tĭ, *n. pl.* [-TUS, 1 -tus; 2 -tŭs, *sing.*] Men of letters; scholars.

lit'er-a-ture, 1 lit'ər-a-chur *or* -tiūr; 2 lĭt'ẽr-a-chur *or* -tūr, *n.* Written or printed works of superior merit; learning.

lith'arge, 1 lith'ärj; 2 lĭth'ärg, *n.* A substance made by heating lead in a current of air: used in glass=making, etc.

lithe, 1 laith; 2 lĭth, *a.* Bending easily or gracefully; supple. **-ly,** *adv.* **-ness,** *n.*— **lithe'some,** *a.* Somewhat lithe. **lis'som‡.** — **lith'some-ness,** *n.*

lith'i-a, 1 lith'ɪ-ə; 2 lĭth'ĭ-a, *n.* A white compound of lithium, soluble in water.

lith'i-um, 1 lith'ɪ-um; 2 lĭth'ĭ-ŭm, *n.* A soft metallic element, the lightest solid element.

lith'o-graph, } 1 lith'o-graf; 2 lĭth'o-gräf.
lith'o-graph᷎, } *I. & II. vt.* To produce by lithography. **II.** *n.* A lithographic print.— **li-thog'ra-pher,** *n.*— **lith"o-graph'ic,** 1 lĭth"o-graf'ik; 2 lĭth"o-gräf'ĭc, *a.* Pertaining to or produced by lithography.— **li-thog'ra-phy,** 1 lĭth-og'ra-fɪ; 2 li-thŏg'ra-fy, *n.* The art of printing from stone.

lit'i-gant, 1 lit'ɪ-gənt; 2 lĭt'i-gant. **I.** *a.* Disposed to or engaged in litigation. **II.** *n.* A party to a lawsuit.

lit'i-gate, 1 lit'ɪ-gēt; 2 lĭt'i-gāt, *vt. & vi.* [-GAT"ED᷎; -GAT'ING.] To engage in litigation.— **lit"i-ga'tion,** 1 lĭt"ɪ-gē'shan; 2 lĭt"i-gā'shon, *n.* The carrying on of a suit at law; a lawsuit.— **li-tig'ious,** 1 lɪ-tĭj'us; 2 li-tĭg'ŭs, *a.* Inclined to litigation.

li'tre, *n.* Same as LITER.

lit'ter, 1 lit'ər; 2 lĭt'ẽr. **I.** *vt. & vi.* **1.** To bring forth, as a litter of young. **2.** To scatter straw, etc., for bedding; disorder; confuse. **II.** *n.* **1.** A number of young animals at a birth. **2.** Straw, hay, etc., as bedding for animals. **3.** A state of disorder. **4.** A stretcher.

lit'tle, 1 lit'l; 2 lĭt'l. **I.** *a.* [LESS; LEAST; also (dial. or colloq.), LITT'LER; LIT'TLEST.] Below the ordinary size or amount; small; short; brief; petty. **II.** *n.* A small quantity, space, time, etc. **III.** *adv.* [LESS; LEAST.] In a small degree; slightly.— **lit'tle-ness,** *n.*

lit'to-ral, 1 lit'o-rəl; 2 lĭt'o-ral, *a.* Pertaining to the shore.

lit'ur-gy, 1 lit'ur-jɪ; 2 lĭt'ẽr-gy, *n.* [-GIES², *pl.*] Prescribed forms for public worship; a ritual.

live, 1 liv; 2 lĭv, *v.* [LIVED; LIV'ING.] **I.** *t.* To spend; pass, as time or life. **II.** *i.* To be living; pass life; enjoy life; abide; subsist; survive.— **live,** 1 laiv; 2 lïv, *a.* Alive; quick; alert.— **live'li-hood,** 1 laiv'lɪ-hud; 2 līv'lĭ-hŏŏd, *n.* Means of subsistence; living. — **live'long",** 1 liv'lon"; 2 lĭv'lŏng", *a.* That lives long; whole; entire.— **live"oak",** 1 laiv"ōk"; 2 līv"ōk", *n.* A durable tree of the oak family.

lived, 1 laivd; 2 lïvd, *a.* Having a life; used only as the final element of a compound word; as, long=*lived.*

live'ly, 1 laiv'lɪ; 2 lïv'ly, *a.* [LIVE'LI-ER; LIVE'LI-EST.] Full of life or animation; brisk; vivacious; active.— **live'li-ness,** *n.*

liv'er¹, 1 liv'ər; 2 lĭv'ẽr, *n.* One who lives; a dweller.

liv'er², *n.* An internal organ which secretes bile, and effects changes in the blood.

liv'er-y, 1 liv'ər-ɪ; 2 lĭv'ẽr-y, *n.* [-IES², *pl.*] **1.** A uniform worn as by servants. **2.** The keeping of horses and vehicles for hire. **3.** A stated allowance of food.— **liv'er-y=man,** *n.* A livery=stable keeper. — **liv'er-y=sta"ble,** *n.* A stable where horses and vehicles are kept for hire.— **liv'er-ied,** *a.* Wearing a livery, as servants.

liv'id, 1 liv'id; 2 lĭv'ĭd, *a.* Black=blue, as bruised flesh; lead=colored; ashy= pale, as the lips. **-ness,** *n.*

liv'ing, 1 liv'ɪŋ; 2 lïv'ĭng,

North=American Lizard. 1/4

n. Livelihood; benefice; those who live.

liz'ard, 1 liz'ərd; 2 lĭz'ärd, *n.* One of vari-

ous reptiles, with four legs, a scaly body, and long tail.

lla'ma, 1 lä′mə; 2 lä′ma, *n.* A South-American camel-like ruminant with woolly coat.

lo, 1 lō; 2 lō, *interj.* Behold! observe!

load^d, 1 lōd; 2 lōd, *vt. & vi.* **1.** To lay a burden on; lade; weigh down; supply abundantly. **2.** To charge, as a firearm.

load, *n.* **1.** That which is to be carried; a burden; cargo. **2.** A charge, as for a gun.

load'star″, load'stone″, *n.* Same as LODE-STAR, LODESTONE.

loaf^t, 1 lōf; 2 lōf, *vt. & vi.* To pass (the time) lazily; lounge; loiter.—**loaf'er,** 1 lōf′ər; 2 lōf′er, *n.* An idler; vagrant.

loaf, *n.* [LOAVES, 1 lōvz; 2 lōvz, *pl.*] A shaped mass, as of bread or cake.

loam, 1 lōm; 2 lōm, *n.* Sand and clay, containing organic matter.—**loam'y,** *a.*

loan, 1 lōn; 2 lōn. **I.** *vt. & vi.* [U. S.] To lend. **II.** *n.* Something lent; act of lending.

loath, 1 lōth; 2 lōth, *a.* Strongly disinclined; reluctant.

loathe, 1 lōth; 2 lōth, *vt. & vi.* [LOATHED; LOATH'ING.] To regard with hatred and disgust; abhor; detest.—**loath'ful,** *a.* Abhorring.—**loath'ing,** *n.* Extreme dislike; aversion.—**loath'ly,** *adv.*—**loath'ness,** *n.*—**loath'some,** *a.* Exciting aversion or disgust.

loaves, 1 lōvz; 2 lōvz, *n.* Plural of LOAF.

lob'by, 1 leb′i; 2 lob′y. **I.** *vt. & vi.* [LOB'-BIED; LOB'BY-ING.] [U.S.] To try to secure (legislation) by corrupt influence. **II.** *n.* [LOB'BIES^z, *pl.*] An anteroom, as of a legislative hall; men engaged in lobbying.—**lob'by-ist,** *n.*

lobe, 1 lōb; 2 lōb, *n.* A protuberance, as of the ear or of a leaf.—**lo'bu-lar,** *a.*

lob'ster, 1 leb′stər; 2 lŏb′ster, *n.* A large marine crustacean used as food.

lo'cal, 1 lō′kəl; 2 lō′cal. **I.** *a.* Pertaining to place or to a locality. **II.** *n.* An accommodation train.—**lo-cal'i-ty,** 1 lo-kal′i-ti; 2 lo-căl′i-ty, *n.* [-TIES^z, *pl.*] A definite region in any part of space; geographical position.—**lo'cal-ize,** 1 lō′kəl-aiz; 2 lō′cal-iz, *vt.* [-IZED; -IZ'ING.] To determine the exact place of.—**lo″cal-i-za'tion,** *n.*—**lo'cal-ly,** *adv.*

lo'cate, 1 lō′kēt; 2 lō′eāt, *vt.* [LO'CAT″ED^d; LO'CAT″ING.] To place in a particular spot; localize.—**lo-ca'tion,** 1 lo-kē′shən; 2 lo-eā′shon, *n.* A locating; exact position; place.

loch, 1 lɒн; 2 lŏн, *n.* [Scot.] A lake, bay, or inlet.

lock^t, 1 lɒk; 2 lŏk, *v.* **I.** *t.* To make fast; shut in or out securely. **II.** *i.* To be securely closed; be held fast.—**lock'jaw″,** 1 lɒk′jō″; 2 lŏk′jg″, *n.* A disease characterized by spasmodic contraction of the muscles of the lower jaw; tetanus.—**lock'out″,** 1 lɒk′-aut″; 2 lŏk′out″, *n.* The closing of a factory by employers to coerce employees.—**lock'-smith″,** *n.* A maker or repairer of locks.—**lock'up″,** *n.* A place for the detention of persons under arrest.

lock¹, *n.* **1.** A device to fasten doors, drawers, etc., by means of a key. **2.** A spring mechanism for discharging a firearm. **3.** An enclosure in a canal, with floodgates, to control the water-level.—**lock'age,** *n.* The material for canal-locks or the difference in their level; the toll charged for passing through canal-locks.

lock², *n.* A tuft, as of hair.

lock'er, 1 lɒk′ər; 2 lŏk′er, *n.* A closet or box fastened with a lock.

lock'et, 1 lɒk′et; 2 lŏk′ĕt, *n.* A small case, suspended to a necklace or chain, often holding a portrait.

lo″co-mo'tion, 1 lō″ko-mō′shən; 2 lō″eo-mō′shon, *n.* The act or power of moving from place to place.

lo″co-mo'tive(s, 1 lō″ko-mō′tiv; 2 lō″eo-mō′tiv. **I.** *a.* Pertaining to locomotion; moving from place to place. **II.** *n.* A self-propelling steam- or electric-engine, as on a railway.

lo'cust¹, 1 lō′kust; 2 lō′eŭst, *n.* **1.** A migratory, grasshopper-like insect. **2.** [U. S.] A cicada, as the seventeen-year locust.

lo'cust², *n.* A North-American tree, with rough bark and white flowers. Adult Seventeen-year Locust. ½

lode, 1 lōd; 2 lōd, *n.* **1.** A metal-bearing vein. **2.** A reach of water, as in a canal.

lode'star″, *n.* A guiding star; the pole-star.

lode'stone″, *n.* Magnetic iron ore.

lodge, 1 lej; 2 lŏdg, *v.* [LODGED; LODG'ING.] **I.** *t.* **1.** To furnish with or have lodging. **2.** To implant; infix, as an arrow. **3.** To beat down, or be beaten down, as grain. **II.** *n.* A small house; a cabin; a local subdivision, as of a society.—**lodg'er,** *n.*—**lodg'ing,** *n.* A temporary abode.—**lodg'-ment,** 1 lej′ment *or* -ment; 2 lŏdg′ment, *n.* The act of lodging; state of being lodged; a foothold.

loft, 1 lɒft; 2 lŏft, *n.* A low story under a roof; an elevated gallery in a large room; any floor in a building adapted for manufacture or business.

loft'y, 1 lɒft′i; 2 lŏft′y, *a.* [LOFT'I-ER; LOFT'I-EST.] Elevated; high; exalted; stately.—**loft'i-ly,** *adv.*—**loft'i-ness,** *n.*

log¹, 1 lŏg; 2 lôg. **I.** *vt.* [LOGGED, LOGD⁸; LOG′GING.] To cut, as logs. **II.** *n.* A bulky piece of timber.— **log cabin, log house, log hut**, a small, rough house of logs.

log², *n.* A weighted board for showing the speed of a vessel, by drawing a line in trailing behind; record of the daily progress and affairs of a vessel.— **log′book″**, *n.* The book in which the official record of a voyage is entered.

log′ger-head″, 1 lŏg′ẽr-hed″; 2 lŏg′er-hĕd″, *n.* A blockhead; dunce; a large marine turtle.

log′ic, 1 lŏj′ĭk; 2 lŏg′ie, *n.* The science of correct and accurate reasoning.— **log′i-cal**, *a.* Relating to or of the nature of logic. **-ly**, *adv.*— **lo-gi′cian**, 1 lo-jish′ạn; 2 lo-gĭsh′an, *n.* One versed in logic.

Ship's Log in Use.

log′wood″, 1 lŏg′wud″; 2 lôg′wŏŏd″, *n.* A Central-American tree or its wood: used in dyeing. [mineral*ogy*.

-logy, *suffix.* Used to denote a science; as,

loin, 1 lein; 2 lŏin, *n.* The part of the body between the lower rib and the hip-bone.

loi′ter, 1 lei′tẽr; 2 lŏi′ter, *vi.* To linger idly; lag.

loll, 1 lŏl; 2 lŏl. *vt. & vi.* To hang out, as the tongue; lean idly or at ease; lounge.

lone, 1 lōn; 2 lōn, *a.* Standing by itself; solitary; single; **unmarried.— lone′li-ness**, *n.* — **lone′ly**, 1 lōn′lĭ; 2 lōn′ly, *a.* [LONE′LI-ER; LONE′LI-EST.] Deserted by human beings; given to solitude; secluded; lonesome.— **lone′some**, 1 lōn′sạm; 2 lōn′som, *a.* Sad because of loneliness; secluded. **-ly**, *adv.* **-ness**, *n.*

long, 1 lŏŋ; 2 lông, *vi.* To have an eager craving or desire.

long, *a.* Having length; lasting; extended, as in space or time.— **long′-lived″**, 1 lŏŋ′-laivd″; 2 lông′-lĭvd″, *a.* Having a long life.— **l.-suffering**, *a.* Enduring injuries for a long time; patient.

long, *adv.* To, at, or through a great extent or period. [*n.* Length of life.

lon-gev′i-ty, 1 lŏn-jev′ĭ-tĭ; 2 lŏn-gĕv′ĭ-ty, *n.*

long′ing, 1 lŏŋ′ĭŋ; 2 lông′ing, *n.* An eager craving.— **long′ing-ly**, *adv.*

lon′gi-tude, 1 lŏn′jĭ-tiūd; 2 lŏn′gĭ-tūd, *n.* Distance east or west on the earth's surface; length.— **lon″gi-tu′di-nal**, *a.* Pertaining to longitude or length; running lengthwise. **-ly**, *adv.*

look¹, 1 luk; 2 lŏŏk, *v.* **I.** *t.* To influence or express by the looks. **II.** *i.* **1.** To fix the eyes; direct the sight: followed by *at, on,* or *upon.* **2.** To apply the mind; consider; expect: followed by *for.* **3.** To seem; appear. **4.** To depend: followed by *to.*— **look′ing-glass″**, 1 luk′ĭŋ-glas″; 2 lŏŏk′ing-glås″, *n.* A mirror.— **look′out″**, 1 luk′aut″; 2 lŏŏk′out″, *n.* The act of watching; a place for observation; person set to watch. [aspect; appearance.

look, *n.* A glance of the eye; expression;

loom, 1 lūm; 2 lōōm, *vi.* To rise gradually into prominence, as through a mist.

loom, *n.* A machine for weaving.

loon¹, 1 lūn; 2 lōōn, *n.* A stupid person.

loon², 1 lūn; 2 lōōn, *n.* A diving water-bird.

loop, 1 lūp; 2 lōōp. **I.** *vt. & vi.* To fasten by a loop; form into or make loops. **II.** *n.* A doubling, as of a string, to form an eye; noose; curve.— **loop′hole″**, *n.* A narrow opening for small arms; a means of escape, or place of observation.

Loon. 1/30

loose, 1 lūs; 2 lōōs. **I.** *vt.* [LOOSED⁸, LOOS⁸; LOOS′ING.] To free; release; unbind; disengage. **II.** *a.* [LOOS′ER; LOOS′EST.] **1.** Not fastened, confined, or compact. **2.** Lax; slack; dissolute. **3.** Indefinite; vague. **-ly**, *adv.* **-ness**, *n.*— **loos′en**, 1 lūs′n; 2 lōōs′n, *vt. & vi.* To make or become less tight, firm, or compact.

loot, 1 lūt; 2 lōōt. **I**d. *vt. & vi.* To plunder; sack; pillage. **II.** *n.* Booty; plunder.

lop¹, 1 lŏp; 2 lŏp, *vt.* [LOPPED⁸, LOPT⁸; LOP′PING.] To cut off, as the top of anything.

lop², *vt. & vi.* To droop, as the ears of some dogs.— **lop′-eared″**, *a.*— **lop′sld″ed**, *a.* Inclined to one side; full of idiosyncrasies.

lope, 1 lōp; 2 lōp, *n.* An easy gallop with a long stride.— **lope**, *vt. & vi.* [LOPED⁸; LOP′ING.]

lo-qua′cious, 1 lo-kwē′shus; 2 lo-kwā′shŭs, *a.* Talkative; chattering. **-ly**, *adv.* **-ness**, *n.* — **lo-quac′i-ty**, 1 lo-kwas′ĭ-tĭ; 2 lo-kwăç′ĭ-ty, *n.* Talkativeness; loquaciousness.

lord, 1 lôrd; 2 lôrd. **I**d. *vi.* To rule; domineer. **II.** *n.* **1.** One having power and authority; a ruler. **2.** [L-] The Deity; Christ. **3.** A title of nobility or office.— **lord′ly**, *a.* Pertaining to or like a lord; imperious; arrogant.— **lord′li-ness**, *n.*

1: ȧrtistic, ȧrt; fat, fāre; fạst; get, prēy; hĭt, po͡lice; o͡bey, gō; nŏt, ôr; fu͡ll, ru͡le; bu͡t, bûrn.

2: ärt, āpe, făt, fâre, fȧst, whạt, ạll; mē, gĕt, prēy, fērn; hĭt, īce; ĭ = ē; ī = ē; gō, nŏt, ôr, wŏn,

— **lord'ship,** n. The state, title, or jurisdiction of a lord; sovereignty; supremacy.

lore, 1 lōr; 2 lŏr, n. Learning; erudition.

lor"gnette', 1 lŏr"nyet'; 2 lŏr'nyĕt', n. A pair of eye-glasses carried on a long, ornamental handle; also, an opera-glass of similar construction. [lost.

lorn, 1 lōrn; 2 lŏrn, a. Forlorn; lonely;

lor'ry, 1 ler'ĭ; 2 lŏr'y, n. 1. A four-wheeled platform wagon. 2. A motor-car for heavy roads.

lose, 1 lūz; 2 lọs, vt. & vi. [LOST; LOS'ING.] To part with unintentionally; forfeit; mislay; be deprived of; miss; squander; waste. — **los'er,** n.

loss, 1 lȯs; 2 lŏs, n. The act or state of losing; that which is lost; damage; failure; waste.

lost, pp. of LOSE, v.

lost, 1 lȯst; 2 lŏst, pa. 1. Not to be found or recovered; not gained, used, or enjoyed; missed; wasted. 2. Ruined; also, bewildered; perplexed.

lot, 1 lȯt; 2 lŏt. I. vt. & vi. [LOT'TED^d; LOT'TING.] To divide or draw by lot; allot; apportion. II. n. 1. Something to be taken by chance as a means of decision; chance; fortune; share. 2. A parcel of land.

loth, 1 lōth; 2 lŏth, a. Loath. [cated wash.

lo'tion, 1 lō'shạn; 2 lō'shon, n. A medi-

lot'ter-y, 1 lȯt'ẽr-ĭ; 2 lŏt'er-y, n. [-IES², pl.] A distribution of prizes by chance.

loud, 1 laud; 2 loud, a. Making a great noise; clamorous; turbulent; vulgarly showy. — **loud'ly,** adv. **loud‡.** — **loud'ness,** n.

lounge, 1 launj; 2 loung. I. vi. [LOUNGED; LOUNG'ING.] To recline lazily; loll; idle; loaf; loiter. II. n. The act of lounging; a lounging-place; couch; sofa. — **loung'er,** n.

louse, 1 laus; 2 lous, n. [LICE, 1 lais; 2 lĭç, pl.] A small parasitic insect. — **lous'y,** 1 lauz'ĭ; 2 lous'y, a. Infested with lice. [ish, a.

lout, n. An awkward fellow; clown. — **lout'-**

lov'a-ble,) 1 luv'ạ-bl; 2 lŏv'a-bl, a.
luv'a-ble,) Worthy of love; amiable.

love,) 1 luv; 2 lŏv, v. [LOVED, LUVD²; LOV'-
luv²,) ING.] I. t. To regard with affection; delight in. II. i. To feel tender or passionate affection. — **lov'ing-ly,** adv. — **lov'-ing-ness,** n.

love, 1 luv; 2 lŏv, n. 1. Devoted affection; tender feeling; fondness; courtship. 2. One who is beloved. — **love'-lorn",** a. Forsaken by or pining for a lover. — **love'ly,** a. [LOVE'LI-ER; LOVE'LI-EST.] Charming; attractive; amiable. — **love'li-ness,** n. — **lov'er,** n. One who loves; one who is in love.

low, 1 luv; 2 lō. I. vi. To give a loud call, as cattle; bellow. II. n. The bellow of cattle.

low. I. a. Of little height; deep; depressed; cheap; moderate; inferior; vulgar; base; weak; despondent. II. adv. In a low way or position; cheaply; humbly; softly. — **-ness** n. — **low'land.** I. a. Pertaining to a low or level country. II. n. pl. Lands that lie low; level land. — **low'ly.** I. a. [LOW'LI-ER; LOW'LI-EST.] Lying low; humble; modest; submissive. II. adv. In a lowly manner. — **low'li-ness,** n. A lowly state or condition.

low'er¹, 1 lō'ẽr; 2 lō'er, vt. & vi. To bring down; make or become lower; humble; sink. — **low'er-most",** a. superl. Lowest.

low'er², 1 lau'ẽr; 2 low'er. I. vi. To look angry; scowl. II. n. A scowl; a gloomy aspect. — **low'er-ing-ly,** adv.

loy'al, 1 lei'ạl; 2 lŏy'al, a. Bearing true allegiance, as to a government or to friends. — **loy'al-ist,** n. One who is loyal, especially to a sovereign; a royalist. — **loy'al-ly,** adv. — **loy'al-ty,** n. Devoted allegiance to a government or friend.

loz'enge, 1 loz'enj; 2 lŏz'ĕng, n. 1. A rhombus with all sides equal. 2. A small sweetened tablet.

lub'ber, 1 lub'ẽr; 2 lŭb'er, n. An awkward fellow; landsman on shipboard. — **lub'ber-ly,** a. & adv.

lu'bri-cate, 1 liū'brĭ-kēt; 2 lū'brĭ-eāt, vt. [-CAT"ED^d; -CAT"ING.] To supply with oil or the like, to lessen friction. — **lu'bri-cant,** n. Something that lubricates, as oil or graphite. — **lu'bri-ca"tor,** n.

lu'cid, 1 liū'sĭd; 2 lī'çĭd, a. Easily understood; sane; clear; shining; translucent. — **lu-cid'i-ty,** n. Clearness. — **lu'cid-ness‡.** — **lu'cid-ly,** adv.

Lu'ci-fer, 1 liū'sĭ-fẽr; 2 lū'çĭ-fer, n. 1. The morning star. 2. Satan, the prince of darkness. 3. [l-] A friction-match. — **lu'ci-fer-match"‡.**

luck, 1 luk; 2 lŭk, n. Chance; fortune; lot. — **luck'less,** a. Having no luck. — **luck'-less-ly,** adv. — **luck'less-ness,** n. — **luck'i-ly,** adv. — **luck'i-ness,** n. — **luck'y,** 1 luk'ĭ; 2 lŭk'y, a. [LUCK'I-ER; LUCK'I-EST.] Favored by fortune; successful; auspicious.

lu'cra-tive,) 1 liū'krạ-tĭv; 2 lū'era-tĭv, a.
lu'cra-tiv⁵,) Highly profitable. **-ly,** adv.

lu'cre, 1 liū'kẽr; 2 lū'cer, n. Money; gain.

lu'cu-brate, 1 liū'kiu-brēt; 2 lū'eū-brāt, vt. & vi. [-BRAT"ED^d; -BRAT"ING.] To elaborate or perfect as by night study; study or write laboriously. — **lu"cu-bra'tion,** 1 liū"-kiu-brē'shạn; 2 lū"eū-brā'shon, n. Close study; literary composition.

lu'di-crous, 1 liū'dĭ-krus; 2 lū'dĭ-erŭs, a. Laughable; droll; ridiculous. **-ly,** adv. **-ness,** n.

---

luff, ⎱1 lŭf; 2 lŭf. **I**ᵗ. *vt. & vi.* To steer
lufᴾ, ⎰closer to the wind. **II.** *n.* The act
of sailing close to the wind; the rounded
part of a vessel's bow.

lug, 1 lŭg; 2 lŭg, *v.* [LUGGED, LUGDˢ; LUG'-
GING.] To pull or move heavily; drag.

lug'gage, 1 lŭg'ıj; 2 lŭg'ag, *n.* Anything
burdensome or heavy; baggage.

lu-gu'bri-ous, 1 liu-giū'brı-us; 2 lū-gū'-
bri-ŭs, *a.* Doleful; solemn; sad.

luke'warm", 1 liūk'wörm"; 2 lūk'warm", *a.*
Moderately warm; indifferent. **-ly,** *adv.*
-ness, *n.*

lull, ⎱1 lŭl; 2 lŭl. **I.** *vt. & vi.* To soothe
lufᴾ, ⎰to rest; calm; quiet; abate. **II.** *n.*
An abatement, as of noise; calm.

lull'a-by, 1 lŭl'ə-bai; 2 lŭl'a-bȳ, *n.* [-BIESᶻ,
pl.] A cradle≈song.

lum'bar, 1 lŭm'bər; 2 lŭm'bar, *a.* Pertaining to the loins. **—lum-ba'go,** 1 lŭm-
bē'go; 2 lŭm-bā'go, *n.* Rheumatic pain in
the back or loins.

lum'ber¹, 1 lŭm'bər; 2 lŭm'ber, *vt.* To fill
with or deal in lumber; encumber; heap
in disorder.

lum'ber², *vi.* To move heavily; rumble.

lum'ber, *n.* Timber sawed into merchant-
able form, especially boards; also, rubbish.

lu'mi-na-ry, 1 liū'mı-nē-rı; 2 lū'mi-nā-ry,
n. [-RIESᶻ, *pl.*] Any body that gives
light.—**lu"mi-nos'i-ty,** *n.* The quality of
being luminous. **lu'mi-nous-ness‡.—lu"-
mi-nous,** 1 liū'mı-nus; 2 lū'mi-nŭs, *a.* Giving light; shining; bright; lucid. **-ly,** *adv.*

lump, 1 lŭmp; 2 lŭmp. **I**ᵗ. *vt.* To throw
into a lump; take in the gross. **II.** *n.*
A shapeless mass of matter; swelling.
—lump'ish, *a.* Like a lump; stupid. **-ly,**
adv. **-ness,** *n.*—**lump'y,** *a.* [LUMP'I-ER;
LUMP'I-EST.] Full of lumps; gross.

lu'na-cy, 1 liū'nə-sı; 2 lū'na-çy, *n.* [-CIESᶻ,
pl.] Mental unsoundness; insanity.

lu'nar, 1 liū'nər; 2 lū'nar, *a.* Pertaining
to the moon.→**lu'na-tic,** 1 liū'nə-tık; 2 lū'-
na-tic. **I.** *a.* Affected with lunacy; crazy;
insane. **II.** *n.* An insane person.— **lu-na'-
tion,** *n.* A revolution of the moon.

lu'nate, 1 liū'nēt; 2 lū'nāt, *a.* Crescent≈
shaped; having crescent≈shaped markings.
lu'nat-ed‡.

lunch, 1 lŭnch; 2 lŭnch. **I**ᵗ. *vi.* To take
lunch. **II.** *n.* A light meal, as between
breakfast and dinner. **lunch'eon‡.**

lung, 1 lŭŋ; 2 lŭŋ, *n.* An organ of
respiration in air≈breathing creatures.

lunge, 1 lŭnj; 2 lŭnġ. **I.** *vi.* [LUNGED;
LUNG'ING.] To thrust. **II.** *n.* A long,
sudden thrust.

lu'pin(e³, 1 liū'pın; 2 lū'pin, *a.* Of or like a
wolf; wolfish.

---

lurchᵗ, 1 lūrċh; 2 lûrch. **I.** *vi.* To roll to
one side, as a ship at sea; sway. **II.** *n.*
A swaying or rolling.

lure, 1 liūr; 2 lūr. **I.** *vt. & vi.* [LURED;
LUR'ING.] To entice, as a bird; attract;
allure; tempt‡ **II.** *n.* A snare; decoy;
bait; enticement.

lu'rid, 1 liū'rıd; 2 lū'rid, *a.* Giving a
ghastly or dull≈red light; dismal.

lurkᵗ, 1 lūrk; 2 lûrk, *vi.* To lie in wait, as
for attack; hide.

lus'cious, 1 lŭsh'us; 2 lŭsh'ŭs, *a.* Rich,
sweet, and delicious; excessively sweet.
-ly, *adv.* **-ness,** *n.* [luxuriant.

lush, 1 lŭsh; 2 lŭsh, *a.* Rich and juicy;

lust, 1 lŭst; 2 lŭst. **I**ᵈ. *vi.* To have
passionate desire. **II.** *n.* Vehement or
inordinate desire.

lus'ter, ⎱1 lus'tər; 2 lŭs'ter, *n.* **1.**
lus'tre, ⎰Brilliancy; gloss; brightness. **2.**
A chandelier with glass pendants.—**lus'ter-
less,** *a.*—**lus'trous,** 1 lus'trus; 2 lŭs'trŭs,
a. Shining.

lus'tring, 1 lus'trıŋ; 2 lŭs'tring, *n.* A
plain glossy silk. **lute'string‡.**

lust'y, 1 lust'ı; 2 lŭst'y, *a.* [LUST'I-ER;
LUST'I-EST.] Full of vigor and health;
robust.—**lust'i-ly,** *adv.*—**lust'i-ness,** *n.*

lu'sus na-tu'ræ, 1 liū'sus na-tiū'rī; 2 lū'-
sŭs na-tū'rē. An abnormal natural production; a freak of nature; monstrosity: a
Latin phrase. [instrument.

lute, 1 liūt; 2 lūt, *n.* A guitar≈like musical

Lu'ther-an, 1 liū'ther-ən; 2 lū'ther-an. **I.**
a. Pertaining to the Protestant reformer
Martin Luther (1483–1546) or to his
doctrines. **II.** *n.* A follower of Luther.

lux-u'ri-ant, 1 lug-ʒū'[*or* luks-yū']rı-ənt;
2 lŭg-zhu'[*or* lŭks-yu']ri-ant, *a.* Superabundant in growth; profuse. **-ly,** *adv.*—
lux-u'ri-ance, *n.* **lux-u'ri-an-cy‡.**

lux-u'ri-ate, 1 lug-ʒū'[*or* luks-yū']rı-ēt; 2
lŭg-zhu'[*or* lŭks-yu']ri-āt, *vi.* [-AT"EDᵈ;
-AT'ING.] To grow profusely; live sump-
tuously; glory or revel.

lux-u'ri-ous, 1 lug-ʒū'[*or* luks-yū']rı-us; 2
lŭg-zhu'[*or* lŭks-yu']ri-ŭs, *a.* Pertaining
to luxury. **-ly,** *adv.* **-ness,** *n.*

lux'u-ry, 1 luk'shu-rı; 2 lŭk'shu-ry, *n.*
[-RIESᶻ, *pl.*] A free indulgence in the
pleasures of the senses; abundance of outward delights; anything giving great pleasure; delicacy.

ly-ce'um, 1 lai-sī'um; 2 lȳ-çē'ŭm, *n.*
[-UMSᶻ *or* -A, *pl.*] [U. S.] An association
for instruction, as by lectures, books, etc.;
a classical school.

lye, 1 lai; 2 lȳ, *n.* An alkaline solution, as
from leached ashes.

---

ly′ing¹, 1 laiʹiŋ; 2 lȳ′ing, *pa.* Being in a horizontal position; prostrate.

ly′ing², *pa.* Mendacious; false.— **ly′ing,** *n.* The fact or habit of speaking falsehoods; untruthfulness; mendacity.

lyd′dite, 1 lid′ait; 2 lȳd′ĭt, *n.* An exceedingly powerful explosive.

lymph, 1 limf; 2 lȳmf, *n.* A transparent,
lymfⁿ, colorless fluid, as from coagulated blood; virus.— **lym·phat′ic,** 1 lim-fat′ik; 2 lȳm-făt′ic. **I.** *a.* Pertaining to, containing, or conveying lymph; absorbent. **II.** *n.* An absorbent vessel.

lyncht, 1 linch; 2 lȳnch, *vt.* To punish by lynch-law: from Charles *Lynch*, of Virginia, who took summary measures against malcontents during the Revolutionary war.— **lynch′·law″,** *n.* Summary punishment by a mob without trial by law.

lynx, 1 liŋks; 2 lȳnks, *n.* A keen-sighted feline mammal.— **lynx′·eyed″,** *a.* Having acute sight.

Lynx. 1/30

lyre, 1 lair; 2 lȳr, *n.* An ancient harp-like stringed instrument.

lyr′ic, 1 lir′ik; 2 lȳr′ic, *a.* Belonging to a lyre; adapted for singing to a lyre. **lyr′i·cal‡.**

lyr′ic, *n.* A lyric poem, song, or verse.

M

M, m, 1 em; 2 ĕm, *n.* [EMS, M's, or *M*s, 1 emz; 2 ĕmṣ, *pl.*] The thirteenth letter in the English alphabet.

ma, 1 mā; 2 mä, *n.* Mama; mother.

ma′am, 1 mäm; 2 mäm, *n.* [Colloq.] Madam.

mac·ad′am·ize or **-ise,** 1 mak-ad′əm-aiz; 2 mac-ăd′am-īz, *vt.* [-IZED; -IZ″ING.] To pave with small broken stone: named from the Scottish engineer *Macadam* (1756–1836).— **mac·ad′am,** 1 mak-ad′əm; 2 mac-ăd′am, *n.* Broken stone; macadamized roadway.— **mac·ad′am·i·za″[or-sa′]tion,** *n.*— **mac·ad′am·iz″er** or **-is″er,** *n.*

mac″a·ro′ni, 1 mak″ə-rō′ni; 2 măc″a-rō′ni, *n.* An Italian paste of flour made into slender tubes. [cal American parrot.

ma·caw′, 1 mə-kɔ′; 2 ma-ca̤′, *n.* A tropi-

Mac″ca·be′an, 1 mak″ə-bī′ən; 2 măc″a-bē′an, *a.* Of or pertaining to a family of Jewish patriots of the 2d cent. B. C. **Mac″ca·bæ′an‡.**

mace¹, 1 mēs; 2 mās, *n.* A club-shaped staff of office; an officer who carries it.

mace², *n.* A spice made from the covering of the nutmeg-seed.

Mac″e·do′ni·an, 1 mas″ɪ-dō′nɪ-ən; 2 măc″e-dō′ni-an. **I.** *a.* Of or pertaining to Macedonia, a country north of Greece. **II.** *n.* A native or inhabitant of Macedonia.

mac′er·ate, 1 mas′ər-ēt; 2 măc′er-āt, *vt.* [-AT″EDᵈ; -AT″ING.] To reduce to a soft mass by soaking.

ma·che′te, 1 mə-chē′tē; 2 mä-chĕ′te, *n.* A heavy knife or cutlas used by the natives of tropical America. [Sp.]

Mach″i·a·vel′li·an, 1 mak″ɪ-ə-vel′ɪ-ən; 2 măc″i-a-vĕl′i-an. **I.** *a.* Of or pertaining to Niccolo Machiavelli (1469–1527), an unscrupulous Florentine statesman and writer. **II.** *n.* A follower of Machiavelli. **Mach″i·a·vel′li·an‡.**— **Mach″i·a·vel′lism,** *n.*

mach″i·na′tion, 1 mak″ɪ-nē′shən; 2 măc″i-nā′shon, *n.* A secret or hostile plan; plot.

ma·chine′, 1 mə-shīn′; 2 ma-chīn′, *n.* **1.** A mechanical arrangement for utilizing power; engine. **2.** [U. S.] An organization, as to control political patronage.— **ma·chin′er·y,** 1 mə-shīn′ər-ɪ; 2 ma-chīn′er-y, *n.* The parts of a machine; machines collectively.— **ma·chin′ist,** 1 mə-shīn′ist; 2 ma-chīn′ist, *n.* One who makes or repairs machines.

mack·er·el, 1 mak′ər-el; 2 măk′er-ĕl, *n.* A food-fish found in the North Atlantic.

mack′in·tosh, 1 mak′in-tosh; 2 măk′in-tŏsh, *n.*

Mackerel. 1/12

A water-proof overgarment: named from *Mackintosh,* the inventor.

ma′cron, 1 mē′krən; 2 mā′cron, *n.* A straight line placed over a vowel to show that it is long, as ā.

mad, 1 mad; 2 măd, *a.* [MAD′DER; MAD′DEST.] **1.** Insane; crazy; distracted; rash; eager; passionate; infatuated; angry. **2.** Having hydrophobia, as a dog.— **mad′house″,** *n.* A lunatic asylum.— **mad′ly,** *adv.*— **mad′man,** *n.* A lunatic; maniac.— **mad′ness,** *n.* Insanity.

mad′am, 1 mad′əm; 2 măd′am, *n.* My lady; mistress.

ma′dame, 1 mä′dăm; 2 mä′dăm, *n.* [MES-DAMES, 1 mē′dăm′; 2 me̤′däm′, *pl.*] Madam: the original French form.

mad′cap″, 1 mad′kap″; 2 măd′căp″. **I.** *a.* Wild; rattle-brained. **II.** *n.* One who acts wildly or rashly.

mad'den, 1 mad'n; 2 măd'n. *vt.* & *vi.* To drive or become mad; enrage.

mad'der, 1 mad'ər; 2 măd'er. *n.* A perennial herb or a red dye made from it.

made, 1 mēd; 2 mād, *pp.* of MAKE, *v.*

Ma-dei'ra, 1 mə-dī'rə; 2 ma-dē'ra. A rich red or white wine made in Madeira, a Portuguese island off the northwest coast of Africa.

ma"de-moi-selle', 1 ma"də-mwa-zel' *or* mad'i-mo-zel'; 2 mä"de-mwä-sĕl' *or* mäd'e-mo-sĕl'. *n.* Miss: the French appellation for unmarried women.

Ma-don'na, 1 mə-don'ə; 2 ma-dŏn'a, *n.* The Virgin Mary; a painting or statue of the Virgin.

mad'ri-gal, 1 mad'ri-gəl; 2 măd'ri-găl, *n.* A shepherd's song.

mael'strom, 1 mēl'strəm; 2 māl'strom, *n.* **1.** A whirlpool or current off the coast of Norway, formerly credited with resistless destructive power. **2.** Any overpowering ruinous influence.

mag"a-zine', 1 mag"ə-zīn'; 2 măg"a-zīn', *n.* A house, room, or receptacle in which anything is stored; chamber of a repeating rifle; a periodical.

mag'got, 1 mag'ət; 2 măg'ot, *n.* The larva of a fly; a grub. whim.—**mag'got-y,** *a.*

Ma'gi, 1 mē'jai; 2 mā'gĭ, *n. pl.* The Medo-Persian priestly caste.—**Ma'gi-an,** *a.* & *n.*—**Ma'gi-an-ism,** *n.*

mag'ic, 1 maj'ik; 2 măg'ic. **I.** *a.* Of the nature of magic; having magical power; magical. **II.** *n.* **1.** Any supposed supernatural art; necromancy. **2.** Sleight of hand.—**mag'i-cal,** *a.* Pertaining to or produced by or as by magic. **-ly,** *adv.*—**ma-gi'cian,** 1 mə-jish'ən; 2 ma-gish'an, *n.* An expert in magic arts; a sorcerer; wizard.

mag"is-te'ri-al, 1 maj"is-tī'ri-əl; 2 măg"-is-tē'ri-al, *a.* Pertaining to a magistrate; authoritative; judicial. **-ly,** *adv.* **-ness,** *n.*

mag'is-trate, 1 maj'is-trēt; 2 măg'is-trāt, *n.* A judicial officer.—**mag'is-tra-cy,** 1 maj'is-trə-si; 2 măg'is-tra-çy, *n.* [-CIES², *pl.*] The office of a magistrate; magistrates collectively.

Mag'na Car'ta, 1 mag'nə kār'tə; 2 măg'-na Cär'ta. [L.] The Great Charter of English liberties, delivered, not signed, June 19, 1215, by King John, at Runnymede.

mag-nan'i-mous, 1 mag-nan'i-mus; 2 măg-năn'i-mŭs, *a.* Elevated in soul; scorning what is base; unselfish. **-ly,** *adv.*—**mag"na-nim'i-ty,** *n.* [person of rank.

mag'nate, 1 mag'nēt; 2 măg'nāt, *n.* A

mag-ne'si-a, 1 mag-nī'shə; 2 măg-nē'-shi-a, *n.* A white, earthy powder, used in medicine.—**mag-ne'si-um,** 1 mag-nī'-shi-um; 2 măg-nē'shi-ŭm, *n.* A light, silver-white metallic element.

mag'net, 1 mag'net; 2 măg'nĕt, *n.* A

body capable of attracting to itself iron and steel.—**mag-net'ic,** 1 mag-net'ik; 2 măg-nĕt'ic, *a.* Pertaining to a magnet; possessing magnetism. **mag-net'i-cal**;—**mag-net'i-cal-ly,** *adv.*—**mag'net-ism,** 1 mag'net-izm; 2 măg'nĕt-ĭsm, *n.* **1.** Magnetic force. **2.** Personal attractiveness.—**mag'net-iz"**[or **-is"**]a-bl(e)", *a.*—**mag'net-ize,** 1 mag'net-aiz; 2 măg'nĕt-īz. *vt.* & *vi.* [-IZED; -IZ"ING.] To make magnetic; develop or acquire magnetic properties; attract. **mag'net-ise**;

mag-neto-electric machine, a machine in which the rotation of a coil of wire between the poles of a permanent magnet induces a current of electricity in the coil: widely used as a means of igniting the explosive mixtures used in internal-combustion engines, as in automobiles.—**mag-ne'to**; **mag-ne'to-ma-chine'**;—**mag-ne'to-ay'na-mo**;

mag-nif'i-cent, 1 mag-nif'i-sent; 2 măg-nif'i-çĕnt, *a.* Grand; majestic; splendid. **mag-nif'ic**;—**-ly,** *adv.*—**mag-nif'i-cence,** *n.*

mag'ni-fy, 1 mag'ni-fai; 2 măg'ni-fŷ, *vt.* [-FIED; -FY"ING.] To increase the apparent size of, as by a microscope; extol; glorify; enlarge.—**mag'ni-**fi"a-bl(e)", 1 mag'ni-fai"ə-bl; 2 măg'ni-fĭ"a-bl, *a.* That can be magnified.—**mag'ni-fi"er,** *n.*

mag-nil'o-quent, 1 mag-nil'o-kwent; 2 măg-nil'o-kwĕnt, *a.* Using or characterized by a pompous and bombastic style.—**mag-nil'o-quence,** *n.*—**mag-nil'o-quent-ly,** *adv.*

mag'ni-tude, 1 mag'ni-tiūd; 2 măg'ni-tūd, *n.* Size; vastness; grandeur; importance.

mag-no'li-a, 1 mag-nō'li-ə; 2 măg-nō'li-a, *n.* A flowering tree or shrub, with evergreen leaves.

mag'pie, 1 mag'pai; 2 măg'pī, *n.* A crow-like bird with black-and-white plumage capable of being taught to speak.

ma-hog'a-ny, 1 mə-hog'ə-ni; 2 ma-hŏg'a-ny, *n.* [-NIES², *pl.*] A large tropical American tree, with hard, reddish wood.

Ma-hom'ed-an, Ma-hom'et-an, etc. Same as MOHAMMEDAN, etc.

ma-hout', 1 ma-haut'; 2 ma-haut', *n.* The keeper and driver of an elephant.

Mah-rat'ta, 1 ma-rāt'ə; 2 mä-rät'a, *n.* A Hindu people in S. W. and cent. India.

maid, 1 mēd; 2 mād, *n.* An unmarried woman; virgin; female servant.

maid'en, 1 mēd'n; 2 mād'n. **I.** *a.* Pertaining to or suitable for a maiden; initiatory; unused; untried. **II.** *n.* A maid; virgin.—**maid'en-hair",** *n.* A very delicate and graceful fern.—**maid'en-hood",** *n.* The state of being a maiden or virgin.—**maid'en-ly,** *a.* Befitting a maiden; gentle; modest.

mail¹, 1 mēl; 2 māl, *vt.* [U.S.] To post, as letters, newspapers, etc.

mail², *vt.* To put a coat of mail on.

mail¹, _n._ The governmental system of letter-conveyance; the letters conveyed; a mail-car, ₌wagon, or ₌bag.

mail², _n._ Armor as of chains, rings, or scales.

maim, 1 mēm; 2 mām. **I.** _vt._ To deprive of any part of the body; mutilate; disable. **II.** _n._ A crippling; mutilation; maiming.

main, 1 mēn; 2 mān, _a._ First; chief; principal; concentrated; undivided.— **main'land**, 1 mēn'land; 2 mān'land, _n._ A principal body of land; a continent.— **main'ly**, _adv._ For the most part.— **main'mast"**, _n._ The principal mast of a vessel.— **main'sail"**, 1 mēn'sēl" _or_ (_Naut._) mēn'sl; 2 mān'sāl" _or_ (_Naut._) mān'sl, _n._ A sail on the mainmast. — **main'spring"**, _n._ The principal spring of a watch; chief cause or motive.— **main'-stay"**, _n._ 1. _Naut._ A rope to support the mainmast. 2. A chief support or dependence.— **main'top"**, _n. Naut._ A platform at the head of the mainmast, and the rigging attached to it.

main, _n._ 1. The ocean. 2. A chief conduit-pipe or conductor. 3. Violent effort; strength.

main-tain', 1 mēn-tēn'; 2 mān-tān', _v._ **I.** _t._ To hold; keep; support; uphold; vindicate; make good. **II.** _i._ To assert; affirm.— **main'te-nance**, 1 mēn'tɪ-nəns; 2 mān'te-nɑnç, _n._ The act of maintaining; means of support.— **main-tain'a-ble**, _a._

maize², 1 māz; 2 māz, _n._ A tall grass
maizᴾ, ∫ cultivated for food and fodder; its grain; Indian corn.

maj'es-ty, 1 maj'es-tı; 2 măj'ĕs-ty, _n._ [-TIESᶻ, _pl._] 1. Exalted dignity; stateliness; grandeur. 2. [M-] A title given to reigning monarchs.— **ma-jes'tic**, 1 mə-jes'tık; 2 ma-jĕs'tık, _a._ Stately; royal; august. — **ma-jes'ti-cal-ly**, _adv._

ma-jol'i-ca, 1 mə-jŏl'ı-kə, mɑ-yō'lı-kɑ; 2
ma-io'li-ca, ∫ ma-jŏl'ı-ea, mā-yō'lī-eä, _n._ Earthenware coated with a white enamel.

ma'jor, 1 mē'jər; 2 mā'jor, _a._ **I.** _a._ 1. Greater, as in number; principal. 2. _Mus._ Normal; as, the _major_ key. **II.** _n. Mil._ An officer next above a captain. — **ma"jor-do'mo**, _n._ The steward of a royal household.— **ma'jor-gen'er-al**, _n._

ma-jor'i-ty, 1 mə-jŏr'ı-tı; 2 ma-jŏr'ı-ty, _n._ [-TIESᶻ, _pl._] 1. The greater part; excess. 2. Legal age. 3. _Mil._ Rank of a major.

make, 1 mēk; 2 māk, _v._ [MADE; MAK'ING.] **I.** _t._ 1. To bring into being; produce; create; accomplish. 2. To force; induce; procure; gain. 3. _Naut._ To arrive at. 4. To reckon. **II.** _i._ To proceed or tend; contribute.— **make"-be-lieve"**, _a. & n._ Denoting a mere pretense or sham.— **mak'er,** _n._

— **make'shift"**, _a. & n._ Denoting a temporary contrivance for an emergency.

make, _n._ Structure; shape; product.

mal-, _prefix._ Bad; ill; evil; wrong; defective; imperfect; as, _mal_treat: signifying also simple negation.

mal'a-chite, 1 mal'ə-kait; 2 măl'a-eīt, _n._ A native carbonate of copper, of a green color.

mal"ad-min"is-tra'tion, 1 mal"ad-min"-ıs-trē'shan; 2 măl"ăd-mĭn"ĭs-trā'shon, _n._ Bad management, as of public affairs.

mal"a-droit', 1 mal"ə-drɔit'; 2 măl"a-drŏit', _a._ Clumsy; blundering.

mal'a-dy, 1 mal'ə-dı; 2 măl'a-dy, _n._ [-DIESᶻ, _pl._] A disease; sickness; illness.

mal'aise', 1 mal'ēz'; 2 măl'āş', _n._ Uneasiness; indisposition.

mal'a-pert, 1 mal'ə-pūrt; 2 măl'a-pĕrt, _a._ Impudent; saucy. **-ly,** _adv._ **-ness,** _n._

mal-ap"ro-pos', 1 mal-ap"ro-pō'; 2 măl-ăp"ro-pō', _a._ Out of place; inept.

ma-la'ri-a, 1 mə-lē'rı-ə; 2 ma-lā'rī-a, _n._ Any foul air or exhalation, or a disease attributed to it; chills and fever.— **ma-la'ri-al,** _a._— **ma-la'ri-ous,** _a._

Ma-lay', 1 mə-lē' _or_ mē'lē; 2 ma-lā' _or_ mā'lā, _n._ 1. One of the dominant race in Malakka and the Eastern Archipelago. 2. The language of this people.— **Ma-lay'an,** _a._

mal'con-tent, 1 mal'kən-tent; 2 măl'eon-tĕnt. **I.** _a._ Discontented. **II.** _n._ A dissatisfied person.

male, 1 mēl; 2 māl. **I.** _a._ Pertaining to the sex that begets young; masculine. **II.** _n._ A male person, animal, or plant.

mal"e-dic'tion, 1 mal"ı-dik'shen; 2 măl"e-dĭe'shon, _n._ An invocation of evil; imprecation; curse.

mal"e-fac'tor, 1 mal"ı-fak'tər _or_ -tər; 2 măl"e-făe'tor, _n._ A criminal.

ma-lev'o-lent, 1 mə-lev'o-lent; 2 ma-lĕv'o-lĕnt, _a._ Wishing evil; ill-disposed. **-ly,** _adv._ — **ma-lev'o-lence,** _n._

mal-fea'sance, 1 mal-fī'zəns; 2 măl-fē'şanç, _n._ Evil or unlawful actions; wrongdoing.

mal"for-ma'tion, 1 mal"fər-mē'shən; 2 măl"for-mā'shon, _n._ A faulty formation.

mal'ice, 1 mal'ıs; 2 măl'ıç, _n._ A disposi-
mal'isˢ, ∫ tion to injure; evil intent; spite; ill will.— **ma-li'cious,** _a._ Harboring malice; due to malice; spiteful; malevolent. **-ly,** _adv._ **-ness,** _n._

ma-lign', 1 mə-lain'; 2 ma-līn'. **I.** _vt._ To slander. **II.** _a._ Malicious; pernicious. **-er,** _n._ **-ly,** _adv._— **ma-lig'nant,** 1 mə-lig'nant; 2 ma-lĭg'nant. **I.** _a._ Extremely malevolent; virulent; deadly. **II.**

n. One who has evil intentions. **-ly,** *adv.*—
ma-lig'nan-cy, *n.* The state or quality of
being malign.— **ma-lig'ni-ty,** *n.* Violent
animosity; destructiveness; virulence.

ma-lin'ger, 1 mə-liŋ'gər; 2 ma-liŋ'ger, *vt.* To
feign sickness.— **ma-lin'ger-er,** *n.*— **ma-
lin'ger-ing,** *n.* [curse.

mal'i-son, 1 mal'ı-sən; 2 măl'ĭ-son, *n.* A

mall, 1 mêl; 2 mal, *vt.* Same as MAUL.

mall¹, *n.* A maul; war-hammer.

mall², 1 mal *or* mel; 2 măl *or* mĕl, *n.* A
level shaded walk.

mal'lard, 1 mal'ərd; 2 măl'ard, *n.* The
common wild
duck; formerly,
its drake.

Mallard. ¹⁄₂₆

mal'le - a - ble, ⎫
mal'le - a - bl², ⎬
1 mal'ı-ə-bl; 2
măl'e-a-bl, *a.*
Capable of be-
ing hammered or rolled out without
breaking; pliant. **-ness,** *n.*— **mal'le-a-
bil'i-ty,** *n.* [hammer.

mal'let, 1 mal'et; 2 măl'ĕt, *n.* A wooden

mal'low, ⎫ 1 mal'o,-oz; 2 măl'o,-ōş, *n.* A
mal'lows, ⎬ prostrate weed, with roundish
leaves and disk-like fruit.

mal-prac'tise, 1 mal-prak'tıs; 2 măl-
prăc'tis, *n.* Improper treatment, as in
medical practise.

malt, 1 mêlt; 2 malt, *n.* Grain artificially
germinated by moisture and heat.

Mal-tese', 1 mêl-tīz' *or* -tīz'; 2 mal-tēs' *or* -tēs'.
I. *a.* Of or pertaining to Malta, a British
island in the Mediterranean. **II.** *n.* 1. An
inhabitant of Malta; the people or language
of Malta. 2. A Maltese cat or terrier.

Mal-thu'sian, 1 mal-thiū'zən *or* -sı-ən; 2 măl-
thū'zhan *or* -sī'an. **I.** *a.* Of or pertaining to
Malthus (1766–1824), an English economist
who taught that the natural tendency of population is to increase so as to outrun the
means of subsistence. **II.** *n.* A follower or
adherent of Malthus.

mal-treat'd, 1 mal-trīt'; 2 măl-trĕt', *vt.*
To use ill; abuse.— **mal-treat'ment,** *n.*

ma-ma', ⎫ 1 mə-mä' *or* mä'mə; 2 ma-mä'
mam-ma', ⎬ *or* mä'ma, *n.* Mother.

mam'mal, 1 mam'əl; 2 măm'al, *n.* A
vertebrate animal whose female suckles
its young.— **Mam-ma'li-a,** 1 ma-mē'lı-ə; 2
mă-mā'lı-a, *n. pl. Zool.* Mammals collectively.— **mam-ma'li-an,** *n.*

Mam'mon, 1 mam'ən; 2 măm'on, *n.* The
Syrian god of riches; worldliness; avarice.

mam'moth, 1 mam'əth; 2 măm'oth, *n.* **I.**
a. Huge; colossal. **II.** *n.* A large ex-
tinct elephant.

man, 1 man; 2 măn. **I.** *vt.* [MANNED,
MANDˢ; MAN'NING.] To supply with men;

strengthen; make courageous. **II.** *n.*
[MEN, *pl.*] 1. A human being; the human
race; any person. 2. An adult human
male. 3. A piece, as in chess.

man'a-cle, ⎫ 1 man'ə-kl; 2 măn'a-cl. **I.**
man'a-cl², ⎬ *vt.* [-CL(E)Dᴰ; -CLING.] To
put manacles on. **II.** *n.* A handcuff.

man'age, 1 man'ıj; 2 măn'aġ, *v.* [MAN'-
AGED; MAN'AG-ING.] **I.** *t.* To control;
conduct; guide; contrive. **II.** *i.* To
conduct business or affairs.— **man'age-a-
bl(e²,** *a.* Capable of being managed; tractable; docile.— **man'age-ment,** *n.* 1. The
act of managing. 2. Managers or directors
collectively.— **man'ag-er,** *n.*

man'da-rin, 1 man'də-rın *or* man''də-
rın'; 2 măn'da-rın *or* măn''da-rīn', *n.* A
Chinese official.

man'date, 1 man'dēt; 2 măn'dāt, *n.* A
command; order; charge.— **man'da-to-ry,**
a. Expressive of positive command.

man'di-ble, 1 man'dı-bl; 2 măn'dı-bl, *n.*
The lower jaw-bone; either portion of the
beak of a bird, or of the jaws of an insect.
— **man-dib'u-lar,** *a.*

man'do-lin, ⎫ 1 man'do-lin; 2 măn'do-lĭn,
man'do-line, ⎬
n. A stringed
musical instru-
ment with an almond-
shaped body.

man'drake, 1 man'drēk; 2
măn'drāk, *n.* A com-
mon woodland plant; the
May-apple.

Mandolin.

man'drel, 1 man'drel; 2 măn'drĕl, *n.* A
shaft; spindle.

mane, 1 mēn; 2 măn, *n.* The long hair on
the neck of some animals.

ma-nège', 1 mə-nēġ'; 2 mä-nezh', *n.* [F.] 1.
The art of training or riding horses. 2. A
school of horsemanship.

ma-neu'ver, ⎫ 1 mə-nū'vər; 2 ma-nụ'ver.
ma-nœu'vre, ⎬ **I.** *vt. & vi.* [-VERED,
-VERDˢ, -VRED; -VER-ING, -VRING.] 1. To
put through or perform evolutions. 2.
To intrigue. **II.** *n.* 1. A movement, as
of troops. 2. Any dexterous or artful
proceeding.

man'ful, 1 man'ful; 2 măn'ful, *a.* Manly;
sturdy; brave. **-ly,** *adv.* **-ness,** *n.*

man''ga-nese', 1 maŋ'gə-nīs'; 2 măŋ''ga-
nēs', *n.* A hard, brittle metal.

mange, 1 mēnj; 2 mănġ, *n.* An itch-like
skin-disease, as of dogs.

man'ger, 1 man'jər; 2 mān'ġer, *n.* A
feeding-box, as for horses.

man''gl(e², 1 maŋ'gl; 2 măŋ'ġl, *vt.* [MAN'-
GLED; MAN'GLING.] To mutilate; lacerate.

man'gle², *vt.* To smooth with a mangle.

man'gle, *n.* A machine for smoothing fabrics by pressing between rollers.— **man'gler**, *n.*

man'go, 1 maŋ'go; 2 măŋ'go, *n.* **1.** An edible tropical fruit or the tree producing it. **2.** A pickled green muskmelon.

man'grove, 1 maŋ'grōv; 2 măŋ'grŏv, *n.* A tropical tree of low coasts.

man'gy, 1 mēn'jı; 2 măn'ġy, *a.* [MAN'-GI-ER; MAN'GI-EST.] Affected with the mange; squalid.— **man'gi-ness**, *n.*

man'hood, 1 man'hud; 2 măn'hŏŏd, *n.* **1.** Manly qualities collectively. **2.** The state of being a man.

ma'ni-a, 1 mē'nı-ə; 2 mā'ni-a, *n.* **1.** Mental unsoundness; raving insanity. **2.** A desire; craze.— **ma'ni-ac**. **I.** *a.* Maniacal. **II.** *n.* A person wildly insane; a madman.— **ma-nī'a-cal**, *a.* Insane; raving; mad. **-ly**, *adv.*

man'i-cure, 1 man'ı-kiūr; 2 măn'i-eūr, *n.* The care and treatment of the hands and finger-nails, or a person who makes this a business.— **man'i-cure**, *vt. & vi.*

man'i-fest, 1 man'ı-fest; 2 măn'i-fĕst. **I**ᵈ. *vt.* To make plain; reveal. **II.** *a.* Plainly apparent; evident; plain; clear. **III.** *n.* An invoice of a cargo; way-bill. **-ly**, *adv.*— **man'i-fes-ta'tion**, *n.* The act of manifesting; a revelation.

man'i-fes'to, 1 man'ı-fes'to; 2 măn'i-fĕs'to, *n.* [-TOES², *pl.*] A public official proclamation.

man'i-fold, 1 man'ı-fōld; 2 măn'i-fŏld, *a.* Of great variety; numerous. **-ly**, *adv.*

man'i-kin, 1 man'ı-kin; 2 măn'i-kĭn, *n.* **1.** A model of the human body. **2.** A dwarf.

ma-nil'a,) 1 mə-nil'ə; 2 ma-nĭl'a, *n.* **1.**
ma-nil'la,) A cheroot made in Manila, in the Philippine Islands. **2.** The fiber of a tall perennial herb; Manila hemp. See ABACA.— **Manila paper**, an inexpensive wrapping- and writing-paper originally made of Manila hemp.

ma-nip'u-late, 1 mə-nip'yu-lēt; 2 ma-nĭp'yu-lāt, *vt. & vi.* [-LAT'ED⁴; -LAT'ING.] To operate on with the hands; manage. — **ma-nip"u-la'tion**, *n.*— **ma-nip'u-la"tor**, *n.*

man"kind', 1 man"kaind'; 2 măn"kĭnd', *n.* **1.** The whole human species. **2.** Men as distinguished from women.

man'like", 1 man'laik"; 2 măn'lĭk", *a.* Like a man.

man'ly, 1 man'lı; 2 măn'ly, *a.* [MAN'LI-ER; MAN'LI-EST.] Like a true man; strong; frank and intrepid.— **man'li-ness**, *n.*

man'na, 1 man'ə; 2 măn'a, *n.* **1.** Divine-

ly given food of the Israelites in the wilderness; spiritual nourishment. **2.** A sweetish substance from the stems of a species of ash.

man'ner, 1 man'ər; 2 măn'er, *n.* **1.** The way of doing anything; habit; method. **2.** Appearance; bearing; mien. **3.** *pl.* Behavior; politeness.— **man'ner-ism**, *n.* A set manner; peculiarity.— **man'ner-ist**, *n.*— **man'ner-ly**. **I.** *a.* Well-behaved; polite. **II.** *adv.* Politely.—**man'ner-li-ness**, *n.*

ma-nœu'ver, -vre. Same as MANEUVER.

man'-of-war', *n.* [MEN'-OF-WAR', *pl.*] An armed government vessel.

man'or, 1 man'ər *or* -ēr; 2 măn'or, *n.* A nobleman's landed estate.— **ma-no'ri-al**, *a.* Pertaining to a manor.

manse, 1 mans; 2 măns, *n.* A parsonage; landholder's residence.

man'sion, 1 man'shən; 2 măn'shon, *n.* A large or handsome dwelling.

man'slaugh"ter, 1 man'slô"tər; 2 măn'slạ"ter, *n.* The killing of man by man, especially when without malice.

man'tel, 1 man'tl; 2 măn'tl, *n.* The facing about a fireplace, including the shelf above it; the shelf. **man'tel-piece"**‡.— **man'tel-shelf"**, *n.*

man-til'la, 1 man-til'ə; 2 măn-tĭl'a, *n.* A woman's light cape or head-covering, as of lace.

man'tis, 1 man'tıs; 2 măn'tis, *n.* [MAN'-TIS-ES *or* MAN'TES, 1 -ız, -tēz; 2 -ĕs, -tēg, *pl.*] An insect which assumes a position as of prayer when waiting for its insect prey.

Mantis.

man'tle,) 1 man'tl; 2 mån'tl;
man'tlᴾ,) măn'tl, *v.* [MAN'TL(E)Dᴾ; MAN'-TLING.] **I.** *t.* To conceal. **II.** *i.* To overspread; become covered.

man'tle,) *n.* A loose sleeveless cloak;
man'tlᴾ,) that which clothes, covers, or conceals.

man'tu-a-mak"er, *n.* A dressmaker.

man'u-al, 1 man'yu-əl; 2 măn'yu-al. **I.** *a.* Done, made, or used by the hand. **-ly**, *adv.* **II.** *n.* **1.** A compact volume; handbook. **2.** A keyboard, as of an organ. **3.** Training in the handling of a weapon.

man"u-fac'to-ry, 1 man"yu-fak'to-rı; 2 măn"yu-făc'to-ry, *n.* [-RIES², *pl.*] A place where anything is manufactured.

man"u-fac'ture, 1 man"yu-fak'chur *or* -tiur; 2 măn"yu-făc'chụr *or* -tūr. **I.** *vt. &*
vi. [-TURED; -TUR'ING.] To make, as

by hand or machinery.— **II.** *n.* The making of goods by industrial art; manufactured articles collectively.— **man″u-fac′-tur-er,** *n.*

man″u-mit′, 1 man′yu-mit′; 2 măn′yu-mĭt′, *vt.* [-MIT′TED⁴; -MIT′TING.] To emancipate; liberate.— **man″u-mis′sion,** *n.*

ma-nure′, 1 mə-niūr′; 2 ma-nūr′. **I.** *vt.* [MA-NURED′; MA-NUR′ING.] To fertilize. **II.** *n.* Any fertilizer, as dung, for the soil.— **ma-nur′er,** *n.*

man′u-script, 1 man′yu-skript; 2 măn′yu-skrĭpt. **I.** *a.* Written by hand. **II.** *n.* Matter written by hand: abbreviated MS.

Manx, 1 maŋks; 2 măŋks, *a.* Of or pertaining to the Isle of Man, its people, or their language.— **Manx′man,** *n.*— **Manx′-wo″man,** *n.*

man′y, 1 men′ı; 2 měn′y. **I.** *a.* [MORE; MOST.] Constituting a large number; numerous. **II.** *n.* Any large number; the masses; crowd; multitude.

Ma′o-rı, 1 mā′o-rı *or (colloq.)* mou′rı; 2 mä′o-rı *or (colloq.)* mou′ri, *n.* A Polynesian native of New Zealand.

map, 1 map; 2 măp. **I.** *vt.* [MAPPED⁴, MAPT⁴; MAP′PING.] To make a map of; plan in detail. **II.** *n.* A representation of any region, as of the earth's surface; a chart.

ma′ple, 1 mē′pl; 2 mā′pl, *n.* A deciduous tree of the north temperate zone.

mar, 1 mär; 2 mär. **I.** *vt.* [MARRED, MARD⁴; MAR′-RING.] To harm; impair; spoil. **II.** *n.* A blemish; injury.

Leaf of Red Maple.

Mar′a-thon, 1 mar′ə-thon; 2 mär′a-thŏn, *n.* A race of 26 miles 188 yards in imitation of one run originally during the Olympic games at Athens, Greece, April, 1896: from the feat of a Greek runner, who ran from Marathon to Athens to announce the victory of the Athenian arms.

ma-raud′d, 1 ma-rêd′; 2 ma-rad′, *vt. & vi.* To pillage; plunder; rob.— **ma-raud′er,** *n.* A plunderer; robber.

mar′ble,) 1 mär′bl; 2 mär′bl. **I.** *vt.*
mar′bl²,) [MAR′BL(E)D⁴; MAR′BLING.] To color in imitation of marble. **II.** *a.* Made of or like marble; unfeeling; white; cold. **III.** *n.* A fine limestone, valuable for building or sculpture; a small ball, as of this stone, used in a child's game; a piece of sculpture.— **mar′bly,** *a.*

march⁴, 1 märch; 2 märch, *vt. & vi.* To move or cause to move with measured steps, as a soldier.

march¹, *n.* Movement together, as of soldiers; the distance marched; prog-

ress; music suitable for marching troops.

March², *n.* The third month of the year, having 31 days.

march³, *n.* A boundary; frontier.

mar′chion-ess, 1 mär′shən-es; 2 mär′çhon-ĕs, *n.* The wife or widow of a marquis.

mar-co′ni-gram, 1 mar-kō′nı-gram; 2 mär-cō′ni-grăm, *n.* A wireless message: from *Marconi* (1874–1937), inventor of wireless telegraphy. [horse.

mare, 1 mâr; 2 mâr, *n.* The female of the

mar′e-o-graph, 1 mar′ı-o-graf; 2 mär′e-o-gräf, *n.* An instrument for recording tidal changes in the level of the sea.

mar′gin, 1 mär′jın; 2 mär′gin, *n.* A border; brink; edge.— **mar′gi-nal,** *a.* **-ly,** *adv.*

mar′gue-rite, 1 mär′gə-rīt; 2 mär′ge-rĭt, *n.* A daisy.

mar′i-gold, 1 mar′ı-gōld; 2 măr′ı-gōld, *n.* A plant with golden-yellow flowers.

ma-rine′, 1 mə-rīn′; 2 ma-rīn′. **I.** *a.* Pertaining to the sea; oceanic. **II.** *n.* **1.** A soldier serving on a war-vessel. **2.** Shipping. [sailor.

mar′i-ner, 1 mar′ı-nər; 2 măr′i-ner, *n.* A

mar′i-tal, 1 mar′ı-təl; 2 măr′i-tal, *a.* Pertaining to a husband or to marriage.

mar′i-time, 1 mar′ı-tim; 2 măr′i-tĭm, *a.* Situated on or near the sea; marine.

mar′jo-ram, 1 mär′jo-ram; 2 mär′jo-ram, *n.* A perennial culinary herb.

mark⁴, 1 märk; 2 märk, *v.* **I.** *t.* **1.** To make a mark or marks on; produce by marking; designate. **2.** To heed; regard. **II.** *i.* To pay special attention.— **mark′er,** *n.*

mark, *n.* **1.** A visible trace or sign; a character; badge; characteristic. **2.** A target; aim. **3.** Distinction; eminence. **4.** A German coin worth, normally, about 24 cents. See COIN.

mar′ket⁴, 1 mär′ket; 2 mär′kĕt, *vt. & vi.* To take or send to market; deal in a market.

mar′ket, *n.* A place where articles are exposed for sale; traffic; sale.— **mar′ket-a-bl(e⁴,** *a.* Salable; in demand.

marks′man, 1 märks′mən; 2 märks′man, *n.* [MARKS′MEN, *pl.*] One who shoots at a mark, especially if skilful.— **marks′man-ship,** *n.*

marl, 1 märl; 2 märl, *n.* An earthy deposit containing lime, clay, and sand.

mar′lin(e⁴, 1 mär′lin; 2 mär′lin, *n.* A small rope of two strands.— **mar′line-spike″,** *n.* A pointed iron pin used as in splicing ropes.

mar′ma-lade, 1 mär′mə-lēd; 2 mär′ma-lād, *n.* A preserve of bitter or acid fruits with sugar.

mar′mo-set, 1 mär′mo-zet; 2 mär′mo-sĕt, *n.* A small South-American monkey; a squirrel-monkey.

mar′mot, 1 mär′mǝt; 2 mär′mot, _n._ A stout, short=tailed, burrowing rodent.

ma-roon′, 1 mǝ-rūn′; 2 ma-rōōn′, _vt._ To put ashore and abandon, as on a desolate coast.

ma-roon′, _a._ Having the color maroon.

ma-roon′¹, _n._ A dull=red color.

ma-roon′², _n._ A negro living wild in the mountains of some West India islands.

mar′plot″, 1 mär′plot″; 2 mär′plŏt″, _n._ One who, by meddling, spoils a plan.

marque, 1 märk; 2 märk, _n._ A license to capture the vessels of an enemy: in the phrase **letter of marque.**

mar-quee′, 1 mɑr-kī′; 2 mär-kē′, _n._ A large field=tent.

mar′quis, 1 mär′kwɪs; 2 mär′kwis, _n._ A nobleman next in rank below a duke. — **mar′quis-ate,** _n._ The rank of a marquis.

mar′riage, 1 mar′ij; 2 mär′ag, _n._ **1.** The act of marrying, or the state of being married; a wedding. **2.** Figuratively, any close union.— **mar′riage-a-bl**(eʳ,1mar′-ij-ǝ-bl; 2 mär′ag-a-bl, _a._ Fitted by age, etc., for marriage.

mar′row, 1 mar′o; 2 măr′o, _n._ A soft tissue found in the central cavities of bones; essence; pith.— **mar′row=bone″,** _n._ A bone containing marrow; humorously, in the plural, the knees.— **mar′row-fat,** _n._ A large kind of pea.— **mar′row-y,** _a._

mar′ry, 1 mar′ɪ; 2 măr′y, _vt._ [-RIED; -RY-ING.] To unite in wedlock; espouse; wed.

Mars, 1 märz; 2 märs, _n._ **1.** The fourth planet from the sun. **2.** _Rom. Myth._ The god of war. **A′res** [Gr.].

Mar″seil-lais′, } 1 mär″sǝ-lēz′; 2 **Mar″seil′laise′,** _fem._,} mär″se-lās. _1. a._ Of or pertaining to Marseilles, a French seaport. **II.** _n._ **1.** A native or inhabitant of Marseilles. **2.** _fem._ The Marseillaise hymn, the national hymn of the French republic.

marsh, 1 märsh; 2 märsh, _n._ A tract of low wet land; swamp.— **marsh′y,** _a._— **marsh′i-ness,** _n._

mar′shal, 1 mär′shǝl; 2 mär′shal. **I.** _vt. & vi._ [MAR′SHALED or -SHALLED, -SHALDˢ; MAR′SHAL-ING or -SHAL-LING.] To array; assemble. **II.** _n._ A civic officer, as for regulating ceremonies, etc.; a military commander.

mar-su′pi-al, 1 mɑr-siū′pɪ-ǝl; 2 mär-sū′pi-al. **I.** _a._ Having a pouch for carrying the young. **II.** _n._ A marsupial mammal, as an opossum.

mart, 1 märt; 2 märt, _n._ A place of public traffic; market.

mar′ten, 1 mär′ten; 2 mär′tĕn, _n._ A weasel=like, fur=yielding animal.

mar′tial, 1 mär′shǝl; 2 mär′shal, _a._ Pertaining to or connected with war.

mar′tin, 1 mär′tɪn; 2 mär′tin, _n._ A bird of the swallow variety.

mar″ti-net′, 1 mär″tɪ-net′; 2 mär″ti-nĕt′, _n._ A strict disciplinarian.

mar′tin-gale, 1 mär′tɪn-gēl; 2 mär′tin-gāl, _n._ **1.** A forked strap for holding down a horse's head. **2.** _Naut._ A stay of a jib=boom, or a vertical spar under the bowsprit. **mar′tin-gal**‡.

mar′tyr, 1 mär′tǝr; 2 mär′tyr. **I.** _vt._ To put to death because of one's faith; persecute. **II.** _n._ One who suffers death for his faith or for any cherished object.— **mar′tyr-dom,** _n._ The condition or fate of a martyr.— **mar″tyr-ol′o-gy,** _n._ [-GIESᶻ, _pl._] A historical record of martyrs.— **mar″tyr-ol′o-gist,** _n._

mar′vel, 1 mär′vel; 2 mär′vĕl. **I.** _vt. & vi._ [-VELED or -VELLED, -VELDˢ; -VEL-ING or -VEL-LING.] To wonder. **II.** _n._ That which excites wonder; a prodigy.— **mar′vel-ous,** _a._ Wonderful; amazing. **-ly,** _adv._ **-ness,** _n._

mas′cot, 1 mas′kǝt; 2 măs′cot, _n._ [Colloq.] Some person, animal, or thing regarded as a cause of good luck.

mas′cu-line, } 1 mas′kiu-lɪn; 2 măs′eū-lĭn, **mas′cu-linˢ,** } _a._ Distinctively manly or manlike; male. **-ly,** _adv._— **mas″cu-lin′i-ty,** _n._ **más′cu-line-ness‡.**

mashᵗ, 1 maʃ; 2 măsh, _vt._ To reduce to a soft state, as by bruising.— **mash′er,** _n._— **mash′y,** _a._

mash, _n._ A mass of something beaten or soaked into a soft state.

maskᵗ, 1 mɑsk; 2 mȧsk, _vt. & vi._ To conceal as with a mask; put on or wear a mask.— **mask′er,** _n._

mask, _n._ **1.** A cover for the face; disguise; protection. **2.** A subterfuge. **3.** A play by masked actors; masquerade.

ma′son, 1 mē′sn; 2 mā′sn, _n._ **1.** A builder in brick or stone. **2.** [M-] Freemason.— **ma-son′ic,** 1 mǝ-son′ɪk; 2 ma-sŏn′ic, _a._— **ma′son-ry,** 1 mē′sn-rɪ; 2 mā′sn-ry, _n._ [-RIESᶻ, _pl._] **1.** The art of building with brick or stone. **2.** [M-] Freemasonry.

masque, _v. & n._ Same as MASK.

mas″quer-ade′, 1 mas″ker-ēd′; 2 más″ker-ād′. **I.** _vi._ [-AD′EDᵈ; -AD′ING.] To wear a disguise. **II.** _n._ **1.** A social party of persons masked. **2.** A disguise. **3.** A play by masked actors.— **mas″quer-ad′er,** _n._

massᵗ, 1 mas; 2 más, _vt. & vi._ To form into a mass.

mass¹, _n._ An assemblage; principal part; quantity of matter in a body.

mass², *n.* The celebration of the eucharist in the Roman Catholic Church.

mas'sa-cre, 1 mas'ə-kər; 2 măs'a-cer. **I.** *vt.* [-CRED; -CRING.] To butcher; slaughter. **II.** *n.* Indiscriminate butchery.

mas-sage', 1 ma-sāʒ'; 2 mä-säzh', *n.* Remedial treatment by manipulation, as by rubbing or kneading the body or any part of it.—**mas'seur**, *n.* One who massages.—**mas-sag'list‡.**—**mas'seuse'**, *n. fem.*

mas'sive, } 1 mas'ıv; 2 măs'iv, *a.* Con-
mas'sivᵉ, } stituting a large mass; ponderous. **-ly**, *adv.* **-ness**, *n.*

mast¹, 1 mast; 2 mȧst, *n.* An upright spar to sustain the yards, sails, etc., of a vessel.

mast², *n.* Nuts, acorns, etc., as food for animals.

mas'ter, 1 mas'tər; 2 màs'ter. **I.** *vt.* To overpower; subdue; rule; know; understand thoroughly. **II.** *a.* Controlling; chief. **III.** *n.* **1.** A commander; teacher; employer; owner. **2.** An adept, as in an art or profession.— **mas'ter-ful**, *a.* Commanding; arbitrary; showing mastery.— **mas'ter-key"**, *n.* A key that will unlock a number of locks.—**mas'ter-ly**, *a.* Like or befitting a master.— **mas'ter-piece"**, *n.* An admirable production.— **mas'ter-y**, *n.* Dominion; superiority; victory.

mas'tic, 1 mas'tık; 2 màs'tie, *n.* **1.** A small Mediterranean evergreen tree, or a resin obtained from it. **2.** A cement.

mas'ti-cate, 1 mas'tı-kēt; 2 màs'ti-eāt, *vt.* [-CAT"EDᵈ; -CAT"ING.] To chew.— **mas"ti-ca'tion**, *n.* [watch•dog.

mas'tiff, 1 mas'tıf; 2 màs'tif, *n.* A large

mas'to-don, 1 mas'to-dən; 2 màs'to-dŏn, *n.* An extinct elephant of great size.

mat, 1 mat; 2 măt. **I.** *vt. & vi.* [MAT"TEDᵈ; MAT"TING.] To knot into a mat; be tangled. **II.** *n.* **1.** A flat article as of straw, etc., for wiping the feet. **2.** A border for a picture.

match†, } 1 mach; 2 măch, *v.* **I.** *t.* **1.** To
mach², } set beside or against one another, as mates or competitors. **2.** To suit; to marry. **II.** *i.* To be alike; tally; agree.— **match'er**, *n.*—**match'less**, 1 mach'les; 2 măch'lĕs, *a.* Unequaled; peerless.

match¹, *n.* **1.** An equal; mate. **2.** A contest. **3.** A marriage.

match², *n.* A splinter of soft wood tipped with something that ignites by friction; also, a fuse; slow• (or quick•) match.

mate¹, 1 mēt; 2 māt, *vt. & vi.* [MAT"EDᵈ; MAT"ING.] To join, or be joined, as mates.

mate², *vt.* [MAT"EDᵈ; MAT"ING.] In chess, to checkmate.

mate¹, *n.* **1.** A companion; husband; wife; match. **2.** An officer of a merchant ship ranking below a captain. [mate.

mate², 1 mēt; 2 māt, *n.* In chess, a check-

ma-te'ri-al, 1 mə-tĭ'rı-al; 2 ma-tē'ri-al, *a.* **1.** Pertaining to matter; physical; corporeal; sensual. **2.** Essential; important. **-ly**, *adv.*— **ma-te"ri-al'i-ty**, *n.* **ma-te'ri-al-ness‡.**

ma-te'ri-al, *n.* That of which anything is or may be made.— **ma-te'ri-al-ism**, *n.* The denial of the existence of soul or spirit; devotion to material interests.— **ma-te'ri-al-ist**, *n.*— **ma-te"ri-al-is'tic**, *a.*

ma-ter'nal, 1 mə-tûr'nəl; 2 ma-tẽr'nal, *a.* Motherly. **-ly**, *adv.*— **ma-ter'ni-ty**, 1 ma-tûr'ni-tı; 2 ma-tẽr'ni-ty, *n.* [-TIES², *pl.*] The state or relation of a mother.

math"e-mat'i-cal, 1 math"ı-mat'ı-kəl; 2 măth"e-măt'i-cal, *a.* Pertaining to mathematics; rigidly exact. **-ly**, *adv.*— **math"e-ma-ti'cian**, *n.* One versed in mathematics.

math"e-mat'ics, 1 math"ı-mat'ıks; 2 măth"e-măt'ies, *n.* The science of number and quantity.

mat'in, 1 mat'ın; 2 măt'in. **I.** *a.* Of or belonging to the morning. **II.** *n. pl.* Morning service.— **mat"i-née'**, 1 mat'ı-nē'; 2 măt'i-nē', *n.* An entertainment in the daytime. [ral of MATRIX.

mat'ri-ces, 1 mat'rı-sīz; 2 măt'ri-çēs, *n.* Plu-

mat'ri-cide, 1 mat'rı-said; 2 măt'ri-çïd, *n.* The murder of one's mother: one who kills his mother.— **mat"ri-ci'dal**, *a.*

ma-tric'u-late, 1 mə-trik'yu-lēt; 2 ma-trïe'yu-lāt. **I.** *vt & vi.* [-LAT"EDᵈ; -LAT"-ING.] To enroll or be enrolled as a student in a college. **II.** *n.* One who is so enrolled.— **ma-tric"u-la'tion**, *n.*

mat'ri-mo-ny, 1 mat'rı-mo-nı; 2 măt'ri-mo-ny, *n.* Marriage.— **mat"ri-mo'ni-al**, *a.*— **mat"ri-mo'ni-al-ly**, *adv.*

ma'trix, 1 mē'trıks; 2 mā'triks, *n.* [MAT'-RI-CES, 1 mat'rı-sīz; 2 măt'ri-çēs, *pl.*] A mold; the womb.

ma'tron, 1 mē'trən; 2 mā'tron, *n.* A married woman; mother; housekeeper.— **ma'tron-age**, *n.*— **ma'tron-al**, *a.* Pertaining to a matron.— **ma'tron-ly**, *a.* Of or like a matron.— **ma'tron-hood**, *n.*

mat'ter, 1 mat'ər; 2 măt'er. **I.** *vi.* To be of concern or importance; signify. **II.** *n.* **1.** The substance of anything; material; essence; importance. **2.** That which has extension, inertia, weight, etc. **3.** A subject, as for discussion. **4.** A condition of affairs; case; trouble. **5.** Pus.— **mat'ter-less**, *a.*— **mat'ter-of-fact"**, *a.*

mat'ting, 1 mat'ıŋ; 2 măt'ing, *n.* A coarsely woven floor•covering.

---

mat'tock, 1 mat'ək; 2 măt'ok, *n.* A pick-ax-like tool having blades instead of points.

Mattock.

mat'tress, 1 mat'res; 2 măt'-rĕs, *n.* A tick stuffed with hair, straw, etc., used as a bed.

mat'u-rate, 1 mat'yu-rēt; 2 măt'yu-rāt, *vt. & vi.* [-RAT°ED°d; -RAT'ING.] To suppurate; form pus.— **mat″u-ra'tion,** *n.*— **mat″u-ra'tiv**(e⁸, *a. & n.*

ma-ture', 1 ma-tiūr'; 2 ma-tūr', *v.* [MA-TURED'; MA-TUR'ING.] **I.** *t.* To cause to ripen; bring to maturity. **II.** *i.* To become ripe; develop; become due.— **ma-tu'ri-ty,** 1 ma-tiū'ri-ti; 2 ma-tū'ri-ty, *n.* The state or condition of being mature; full development.

ma-ture', *a.* **1.** Fully developed; ripe. **2.** *Com.* Due and payable **-ly,** *adv.* **-ness,** *n.*

maud'lin, 1 mêd'lin; 2 mạd'lin, *a.* Foolishly affectionate, as from drink.

maul, 1 môl; 2 mạl. **I.** *vt.* To pound; beat; abuse. **II.** *n.* A heavy mallet.

Mau'ser ri'fle, 1 mau'zər; 2 mou'ser. A magazine rifle carrying five cartridges in the stock and sighted to over two thousand yards: named from Paul *Mauser,* the inventor.

mau″so-le'um, 1 mô'so-lī'um; 2 mạ'so-lē'ụm, *n.* A large stately tomb.

mauve, 1 mōv; 2 mōv, *n.* A delicate purple color or dyestuff.

maw, 1 mô; 2 mạ, *n.* **1.** The craw of a bird. **2.** The stomach. **3.** The air-bladder of a fish.

mawk'ish, 1 mêk'ish; 2 mạk'ish, *a.* Disgusting; insipid. **-ly,** *adv.* **-ness,** *n.*

max'il-la-ry, 1 maks'i-lē-ri; 2 măks'i-lă-ry, *a.* Pertaining to the jaw. **max'il-larǂ.**

max'im, 1 maks'im; 2 măks'im, *n.* A brief, practical saying; motto.

max'i-mum, 1 maks'i-mum; 2 măks'i-mŭm. **I.** *a.* The greatest possible; as, a *maximum* speed. **II.** *n.* [-MA, *pl.*] The greatest quantity, amount, or degree.

may, 1 mē; 2 mā, *v.* [MIGHT, *imp.*] **1.** To have permission or ability. **2.** To be possible. [The first day of May.

May, *n.* The fifth month.— **May'day″,** *n.*

may'or, 1 mē'ər *or* -ər; 2 mā'or, *n.* The chief magistrate of a city, borough, or municipality.— **may'or-al-ty,** *n.*

maze, 1 mēz; 2 māz, *n.* A labyrinth; perplexity.— **ma'zy,** *a.* Of the nature of a maze; interwoven; intricate; perplexing.— **ma'zi-ly,** *adv.*— **ma'zi-ness,** *n.* [of *I.*

me, 1 mī; 2 mē, *pron.* The objective case

mead¹, 1 mēd; 2 mēd, *n.* A liquor of fermented honey and water.

mead², *n.* [Poet.] A meadow.

mead'ow, 1 med'o; 2 mĕd'o, *n.* A hay-field.
med'ow⁸,

mea'ger, 1 mī'gər; 2 mē'ger, *a.* Thin; emaciated; scanty. **-ly,** *adv.* **-ness,** *n.*
mea'gre, [grain.

meal¹, 1 mēl; 2 mēl, *n.* Coarsely ground

meal², *n.* The portion of food taken at one time; a repast.

meal'y, 1 mīl'i; 2 mēl'y, *a.* Like meal; farinaceous.— **meal'i-ness,** *n.*— **meal'y⁸ mouthed″,** *a.*

mean, 1 mīn; 2 mēn, *v.* [MEANT, 1 ment, 2 mĕnt; MEAN'ING.] **I.** *t.* To aim at; purpose; signify. **II.** *i.* To be minded.

mean¹, *a.* **1.** Low; lowly; inferior; poor. **2.** Ignoble; base; petty; contemptible. **-ly,** *adv.* **-ness,** *n.*

mean², *a.* Intermediate; medium; average.

mean, *n.* **1.** The middle state or quantity between two extremes; hence, moderation; medium. **2.** *pl.* Instrumentality (often with singular construction; as, this is a *means*); also, property; wealth.

me-an'der, 1 mi-an'dər; 2 me-ăn'der. **I.** *vi.* To flow circuitously. **II.** *n.* A winding course. **-ing,** *a. & n.*

mean'ing, 1 mīn'iŋ; 2 mēn'ing, *n.* The intention; aim; acceptation; import.

mean'ing, *pa.* Significant; suggestive. **-ly,** *adv.*

meant, 1 ment; 2 mĕnt, *imp. & pp.* of MEAN, *v.*

mean'time″, 1 mīn'taim″, -hwail″; 2 mēn'tīm″, -hwīl″. **I.** *n.* Intervening time or occasion. **II.** *adv.* In the intervening time.
mean'while″,

mea'sles, 1 mī'zlz; 2 mē'slz, *n.* An infectious eruptive disease.
mea'sls⁸,

mea'sure, 1 meʒ'ur *or* -yiur; 2 mĕzh'ụr, *v.* [MEA'SURED; MEA'SUR-ING.] **I.** *t.* To take the dimensions of something; show on measurement, a (specified) extent. **-less,** *a.*— **mea'sur-a-bl**(e⁸, *a.*— **mea'sur-a-bly,** *adv.*— **mea'sured,** *pa.* Uniform; rhythmical.— **mea'sure-ment,** *n.* The act or result of measuring.
me'sure⁸,

mea'sure, *n.* **1.** The extent of anything. **2.** A standard, instrument, or vessel of measurement. **3.** A quantity measured. **4.** Moderation. **5.** A specific act or course of action; a legislative bill. **6.** Division of time, as in music; meter, as in verse. **7.** *pl. Geol.* Related strata.

Long or Linear Measure
(used in measuring lengths and distances).

12 inches (in.).	= 1 foot (ft.).
3 feet	= 1 yard (yd.).
5½ yds. *or* 16½ ft.	= 1 rod (rd.) or pole (p.).
40 rods	= 1 furlong (fur.).
8 furlongs	= 1 mile (mi.).
320 rds. *or* 5,280 ft.	= 1 mile.
3 miles	= 1 league.

NOTE.— A perch (p.) = 1 rod.

1: ə = final; ɪ = habit; aɪsle; aʊ = out; oɪl; ɪū = feud; ᴄhin; go; ŋ = sing; ᴛhin, this.
2: wọlf, dọ; bŏŏk, bōōt; fụll, rụle, cūre, bŭt, bûrn; ŏil, bŏy; ḡo, ḡem; iŋk; thin, this.

Square Measure
(used in measuring the area of surfaces).

144 square inches = 1 square foot (sq. ft.).
9 square feet = 1 square yard (sq. yd.).
30¼ sq. yds. or ⎱ = 1 square rod (sq. rd.).
272¼ sq. ft. ⎰
40 sq. rods or ⎱ = 1 rood.
10,890 sq. ft. ⎰
4 roods or ⎱
160 sq. rods or ⎰ = 1 acre (a.).
43,560 sq. ft.
640 acres = 1 square mile (sq. mi.).
NOTE.— A perch (p.) is a square rod.

Cubic Measure
(used in measuring things which have three dimensions, length, breadth, and thickness).

1728 cubic inches ⎱ = 1 cubic foot (cu. ft.).
(cu. in.) ⎰
27 cubic feet = 1 cubic yard (cu. yd.).
24³/₄ cubic feet = 1 perch (p.).

Wood Measure
(used in measuring wood and other merchandise).

16 cubic feet = 1 cord foot.
8 cord feet or 128 cubic feet = 1 cord (cd.).
NOTE.— A cord of wood, as generally piled, is 8 ft. long, 4 ft. wide, and 4 ft. high.

Liquid Measure
(used in measuring liquids).

4 gills (gi.) = 1 pint (pt.).
2 pints = 1 quart (qt.).
4 quarts = 1 gallon (gal.).
NOTE.— In the United States, a gallon contains 231 cu. in.; 31 gallons are considered a barrel (bbl.), and 63 gallons a hogshead (hhd.); but barrels and hogsheads are made of various sizes.

Apothecaries' Fluid Measure
(used in compounding medicines).

60 minims (♏) = 1 fluid dram (f ℨ).
8 fluid drams = 1 fluid ounce (f ℥).
16 fluid ounces = 1 pint (O.).
8 pints = 1 gallon (C.).

Dry Measure
(used in measuring dry articles).

2 pints (pt.) = 1 quart (qt.).
8 quarts = 1 peck (pk.).
4 pecks = 1 bushel (bu.).
NOTE.— In the United States, a bushel contains 2150.42 cu. in.; in Great Britain, 2218.2. See BUSHEL in the vocabulary.

Time Measure

60 seconds (sec.) = 1 minute (min.).
60 minutes = 1 hour (hr.).
24 hours = 1 day (da.).
7 days = 1 week (wk.).
365 days ⎱
12 months ⎰ = 1 common year (yr.).
366 days = 1 leap year.
100 years = 1 century.
NOTE.— One month is commonly reckoned as 30 days.

Mariners' Measure

6 feet = 1 fathom.
100 fathoms = 1 cable lgth. (or cable).
10 cable lgths. = 1 mile.
5,280 feet = 1 statute mile.
6,085 feet = 1 nautical mile.

Measure of Angles or Arcs

60 seconds (″) = 1 minute (′).
60 minutes = 1 degree (°).
90 degrees = { 1 right angle or quadrant (∟).
360 degrees = 1 circle.

meat, 1 mĭt; 2 mēt, n. **1.** The flesh of animals used as food. **2.** Victuals; nourishment. **3.** The essence, gist, or pith of a subject.

me-chan'ic, 1 mĭ-kăn'ĭk; 2 me-eăn'ie. **I.** a. Pertaining to mechanics; materialistic; atomistic. **II.** n. One exercising a mechanical employment.— **me-chan'i-cal,** a. Pertaining to mechanics; produced by or as by a machine; automatic. **-ly,** adv. **-ness,** n.— **mech″a-ni'cian,** 1 mek″ə-nĭsh'ən; 2 mĕe′a-nish′an, n. A maker of mechanism.— **me-chan'ics,** n. The science of the action of forces on material bodies.— **mech'a-nism,** n. Machinery; a machine.— **mech'a-nist,** n.

med'al, 1 med′əl; 2 mĕd′al, n. A small disk of metal, bearing a device; given as a mark of honor, a prize, or the like.— **me-dal'lion,** n. A large medal; also, a circular or oval picture.

med'dle, ⎱ 1 med′l; 2 mĕd′l, vi. [MED′-
med'l₂, ⎰ DLED, MED′LD²; MED′DLING.] To interfere in the concerns of others impertinently.— **med'dler,** n.— **med'dle-some,** a.— **med'dle-some-ly,** adv. **-ness,** n

me″di-æ'val. Same as MEDIEVAL.

me'di-an, 1 mĭ'dĭ-ən; 2 mē'di-an, a. Pertaining to the middle; situated in the middle plane. **me'di-aḷ.**

me'di-ate, 1 mĭ'dĭ-ēt; 2 mē'di-āt. **I.** vt. & vi. [-AT′ED⁴; -AT″ING.] **1.** To interpose, as for reconciliation. **2.** To be intermediate. **II.** a. Intervening; intermediate. **-ly,** adv.— **me″di-a'tion,** n. Intercession; interposition.— **me'di-a″tor,** n. One who mediates; an intercessor.— **me'di-a-to'ri-al,** a. **-ly,** adv.

med'i-cine, ⎱ 1 med′ɪ-sin or med′sɪn; 2 mĕd′-
med'i-cin₂, ⎰ i-çĭn or mĕd′çin, n. **1.** A substance that tends to cure disease. **2.** The healing art.— **med'i-cal,** 1 med′ɪ-kəl; 2 mĕd′-i-eal, a. Pertaining to medicine; curative; remedial. **-ly,** adv.— **med'i-ca-ment,** n. A medicine.— **med'i-cate,** vt. [-CAT′ED⁴; -CAT″ING.] **1.** To treat medicinally. **2.** To impregnate with medicine.— **med″i-ca'tion,** n.— **med′i-ca″tiv(es,** a. Medical treatment.— **me-dic'i-nal,** 1 mē-dĭs′ɪ-nəl; 2 me-dĭç′i-nal, a. Curative. **-ly,** adv.

me″di-e′val, 1 mĭ″dĭ-ī′vəl; 2 mē″dĭ-ē′val, *a.* Belonging to the middle ages. **me″di-æ′val‡.**

me′di-o″cre, 1 mĭ′dĭ-ō″kēr; 2 mē′dĭ-ō″cēr, *a.* Of medium quality; ordinary; commonplace.— **me″di-oc′ri-ty,** *n.* [-TIES², *pl.*] Commonplace ability or condition.

med′i-tate, 1 med′ĭ-tēt; 2 mĕd′ĭ-tāt, *vt.* & *vi.* [-TAT′ED⁴; -TAT′ING.] To plan; think; contemplate.— **med′i-ta′tion,** *n.* The act of meditating; reflection.— **med′i-ta″tiv(e⁵,** *a.* **-ly,** *adv.*

Med″i-ter-ra′ne-an, 1 med″ĭ-te-rē′nu-ən; 2 mĕd″ĭ-tĕ-rā′ne-an, *n.* An inland sea between Europe and Africa; length, 2,100 miles; about 250 to 700 miles wide; 976,781 square miles.

me′di-um, 1 mĭ′dĭ-um; 2 mē′dĭ-ŭm. **I.** *a.* Intermediate; middle; mediocre. **II.** *n.* [ME′DI-UMS² *or* ME′DI-A, *pl.*] Anything that acts intermediately; a substance in which something may exist or move. 2. One believed to be controlled by a disembodied spirit.

med′lar, 1 med′lər; 2 mĕd′lar, *n.* A small European tree, or its fruit.

med′ley, 1 med′lĭ; 2 mĕd′lȳ, *n.* A mixture; jumble.

me-dul′la, 1 mi-dul′ə; 2 me-dŭl′a, *n.* [-LÆ, 1 -lī; 2 -lē, *pl.*] Marrow; pith; the spinal cord.— **med′ul-la-ry,** *a.* **me-dul′lar‡.**

meed, 1 mīd; 2 mēd, *n.* A well-won reward; recompense.

meek, 1 mīk; 2 mēk, *a.* Gentle; submissive; humble; lowly. **-ly,** *adv.* **-ness,** *n.*

meer′schaum, 1 mĭr′shŏm or -shəm; 2 mēr′shaum or -shum, *n.* A soft, light mineral, or a pipe made of it.

Leaves, Flower, and Fruit (*a*) of the Common Medlar.

meet, 1 mīt; 2 mēt, *v.* [MET; MEET′ING.] **I.** *t.* To come to by mutual advance from opposite directions; encounter; pay; satisfy; harmonize with; refute. **II.** *i.* To come together; assemble. **[-ness,** *n.*

meet, *a.* Suitable; adapted; fit. **-ly,** *adv.*

meet, *n.* A meeting, or place of meeting, as of huntsmen.— **meet′ing,** *n.* A coming together; an assembly; encounter.

meg′a-cy″cle, 1 *n.* *Elec.* One million cycles.

meg′a-phone, *n.* An appliance for projecting the voice a long distance.

me′grim, 1 mĭ′grĭm; 2 mē′grĭm, *n.* **1.** A headache on one side of the head. **2.** *pl.* Dulness; depression.

Mek′kan, 1 mek′ən; 2 mĕk′an, *a.* Of or pertaining to Mekka, in Arabia, the sacred city of Mohammedanism.

mel′an-chol-y, } 1 mel′ən-kŏl-ĭ; 2 mĕl′an- **mel′an-col-y²,** } cŏl-y. **I.** *a.* Morbidly gloomy; dejected; sad. **II.** *n.* Low spirits; despondency.— **mel″an-chol′ic,** *a.* Of melancholy temperament or character.

Mel″e-a′ger, 1 mel′ī-ē′jər or me-lī′ə-jər; 2 mĕl′e-ā′ger or mē-lē′a-ger,n. *Gr. Myth.* Hero of Argonautic expedition; Calydonian hunt.

mê″lée′ ( ) 1 mē′lē′; 2 mē″le′, *n.* A general hand-to-hand fight; an affray.

me′lio-rate, 1 mĭl′yo-rēt; 2 mēl′yo-rāt, *vt.* & *vi.* [-RAT′ED⁴; -RAT′ING.] To make better; ameliorate.— **me″lio-ra′tion,** *n.*

mel-lif′lu-ent, *a.* See MELLIFLUOUS.— **mel-lif′lu-ence,** *n.* **-mel-lif′lu-ent-ly,** *adv.*

mel-lif′lu-ous, 1 me-lif′lu-us; 2 mĕl-lĭf′lu-ŭs, *a.* Flowing smoothly; dulcet; euphonious. **mel-lif′lu-ent‡.**

mel′low, 1 mel′o; 2 mĕl′o. **I.** *vt.* & *vi.* To make or become mellow. **II.** *a.* Soft by reason of ripeness; rich in quality. **-ness,** *n.*

me-lo′di-ous, 1 mi-lō′dĭ-us; 2 me-lō′di-ŭs, *a.* Agreeable to the ear; producing melody; tuneful. **-ly,** *adv.* **-ness,** *n.*

mel′o-dra″ma, 1 mel′o-drä″mə; 2 mĕl′o-drä″ma, *n.* A sensational drama.— **mel″o-dra-mat′ic,** *a.*

mel′o-dy, 1 mel′o-dĭ; 2 mĕl′o-dy, *n.* [-DIES², *pl.*] An agreeable succession of sounds; a tune; music.— **mel′o-dist,** *n.*

mel′on, 1 mel′ən; 2 mĕl′on, *n.* A trailing plant of the gourd family, or its fruit.

melt, 1 melt; 2 mĕlt, *vt.* & *vi.* [MELT′ED⁴ *or* MOLT′EN; MELT′ING.] **1.** To change from a solid to a liquid state; dissolve. **2.** To soften the feelings of; move to sympathy.

mem′ber, 1 mem′bər; 2 mĕm′ber, *n.* A limb; organ; part; one of an organization. — **mem′ber-ship,** *n.* The state of being a member; members collectively.

mem′brane, 1 mem′brĕn; 2 mĕm′brān, *n.* A thin sheet of animal tissue.— **mem″bra-na′ceous, mem″bra-nous,** *a.*

me-men′to, 1 mi-men′to; 2 me-mĕn′to, *n.* Something to awaken memory; a souvenir.

mem′oir, 1 mem′wor or -wur; 2 mĕm′wôr or -wär, *n.* A record or memorial; narrative of a person's life.

mem″o-ran′dum, 1 mem″o-ran′dum; 2 mĕm″o-răn′dŭm, *n.* [-DA *or* -DUMS², *pl.*] A note of something to be remembered.

me-mo′ri-al, 1 mi-mō′rĭ-əl; 2 me-mō′ri-al. **I.** *a.* Commemorating something, as the memory of the dead. **II.** *n.* **1.** Something designed to keep in remem-

brance a person, event, etc. **2.** A presentation of facts; memoir.— **Memorial day.** [U. S.] May 30, set for decorating the graves of the dead in war.— **me-mo'ri-al-ist,** *n.* One who writes or presents a memorial.— **me-mo'ri-al-ize** or **-ise,** *vt.* To present a memorial to.

mem'o-ry, 1 mem'o-rɪ; 2 měm'o-ry, *n.* [-RIES², *pl.*] The mental power of recalling the past; remembrance; recollection. — **mem'o-ra-ble,** *a.* Worthy to be remembered.— **mem'o-ra-bly,** *adv.*— **mem'o-rize,** *vt.* [-RIZED; -RIZ'ING.] To commit to memory. **mem'o-rise‡.**

men, *n.* Plural of MAN.

men'ace, 1 men'ɪs; 2 měn'aç. **I.** *vt. & vi.* [MEN'ACED‡; MEN'AC-ING.] To threaten. **II.** *n.* A threatening; threat.

me-nag'er-ie, 1 mɪ-naj'[or -naʒ']ər-ɪ; 2 me-năg'[or -năzh']er-e, *n.* A collection of wild animals kept for exhibition.

mend⁴, 1 mend; 2 měnd, *vt.* To repair; patch up; change for the better.

men-da'cious, 1 men-dē'shʊs; 2 měn-dā'shŭs, *a.* Addicted to lying; falsifying; deceitful.— **men-dac'i-ty,** *n.* Lying; falsity.

men'di-cant, 1 men'dɪ-kənt; 2 měn'di-cant. **I.** *a.* Reduced to beggary; begging. **II.** *n.* A beggar.— **men'di-can-cy, men-dic'i-ty,** *n.*

me'ni-al, 1 mī'nɪ-əl; 2 mē'ni-al. **I.** *a.* Pertaining to servants; servile. **II.** *n.* A servant.

men"in-gi'tis, 1 men"ɪn-jɑi'tɪs; 2 měn"ĭn-gī'tĭs, *n.* Inflammation of the membranes, as of the brain.

men'su-ra-ble, 1 men'shu-ra-bl; 2 měn'shu-ra-bl,*a.* Measurable.—**men'su-ra-bil'i-ty,** *n.*

men'su-ral, 1 men'shu-ral; 2 měn'shu-ral, *a.* Of or pertaining to measure.

men"su-ra'tion, 1 men"shu-rē'shən; 2 měn"shu-rā'shon, *n.* The act, art, or process of measuring.

-ment, *suffix.* Used to form from verbs nouns denoting result, condition, action, or agency; as, achievement.

men'tal, 1 men'təl; 2 měn'tal, *a.* Pertaining to the mind or due to it. **-ly,** *adv.*

men'tion, 1 men'shən; 2 měn'shon. **I.** *vt.* To refer to or name without description. **II.** *n.* The act of mentioning; brief reference. **men'tion-a-ble,** *a.* [An adviser.

men'tor, 1 men'tər or -tor; 2 měn'tor, *n.*

men-u', 1 men'yu'; 2 měn'yu, *n.* A bill of fare; also the dishes included in it.

mer'can-tile, 1 mûr'kan-til or -tail; 2 **mer'can-til‡,** ⎰ mẽr'can-tĭl or -tĭl, *a.* Pertaining to merchants; commercial.

mer'ce-na-ry, 1 mûr'sɪ-nē-rɪ; 2 mẽr'çe-nā'ry. **I.** *a.* Influenced by desire for gain; serving for pay or profit. **II.** *n.* [-RIES², *pl.*] A hired soldier in foreign service.

mer'chant, 1 mûr'ɕhənt; 2 mẽr'chant, *n.* A person who buys and sells commodities as a business.— **mer'chan-dise,** *n.* Commodities traded in by merchants.— **mer'chant-a-bl[e²,** *a.* That can be bought or sold.— **mer'chant-man,** *n. Naut.* A trading-vessel. [*adv.* See MERCY.

mer'ci-ful,*a.* **-ly,***adv.*— **mer'ci-less,** *a.* **-ly,**

mer'cu-ry, 1 mûr'kiu-rɪ; 2 mẽr'çŭ-ry, *n.* **1.** A silver-white metal, liquid at ordinary temperatures; quicksilver. **2.** [M-] The planet of our system nearest the sun. **3.** *Rom. Myth.* [M-] God of commerce; patron of travelers and thieves; messenger of the gods. **Her'mes‡** [Gr.].— **mer-cu'ri-al,** *a.* **1.** Pertaining to the god Mercury; lively; volatile. **2.** Of or relating to quicksilver.

mer'cy, 1 mûr'sɪ; 2 mẽr'çy, *n.* [MER'CIES², *pl.*] Mild treatment of an offender; compassion; clemency; charity.— **mer'ci-ful,** *a.* Full of mercy; compassionate.— **mer'ci-less,** *a.* Having or showing no mercy.

mere, 1 mīr; 2 mēr, *a.* Only; nothing but. — **mere'ly,** *adv.* Only; solely.

mere, *n.* A pond; pool; boundary-line.

mer"e-tri'cious, 1 mer'ɪ-trɪsh'ʊs; 2 mẽr'e-trĭsh'ŭs, *a.* Deceitfully or artificially attractive; vulgar and tawdry; wanton. **-ly,** *adv.* **-ness,** *n.*

merge, 1 mûrj; 2 mẽrg, *vt. & vi.* [MERGED; MERG'ING.] To sink the identity of; be absorbed into something else.— **merg'er,** *n.* Something that absorbs other things; a combination.

me-rid'i-an, 1 mɪ-rid'ɪ-ən; 2 me-rĭd'i-an. **I.** *a.* Pertaining to the meridian; highest; brightest; noonday. **II.** *n.* **1.** Noonday; hence, the highest or culminating point of anything. **2.** The vertical plane, at any place, that contains the earth's axis; also the great circle in which this intersects the surface of the earth or the celestial sphere; a north-and-south line.

me-ri'no, 1 mɪ-rī'no; 2 me-rī'no. **I.** *a.* Of or pertaining to merinos or their wool. **II.** *n.* **1.** A Spanish breed of fine-wooled sheep. **2.** A fabric of or like merino wool.

American Merino.
1/40

mer'it, 1 mer'ɪt; 2 mẽr'-it. **I**d. *vt.* To deserve. **II.** *n.* The state or fact of deserving; desert; worth; excellence.— **mer'i-to'ri-ous,** *a.* Deserving reward or praise. **-ly,** *adv.* **-ness,** *n.*

mer'maid, 1 mûr'mēd; 2 mẽr'mād, *n.* A

fabled marine creature, half woman, half fish.— **mer'man**, *n.* A fabled marine creature, half man, half fish.

mer'ry, 1 mer'ɪ; 2 mĕr'y, *a.* [MER'RI-ER; MER'RI-EST.] Full of fun; jovial; mirthful. — **mer'ry-an"drew**, *n.* A clown or buffoon.— **m.-go-round**, *n.* A revolving ring of hobby-horses or of boat-like vehicles on which people ride for amusement.— **mer'ri-ly**, *adv.*— **mer'ri-ment**, *n.*

mes"dames', 1 mē'dăm'; 2 mẹ'däm', *n.* Plural of MADAME.

mesh, 1 mesh; 2 mĕsh. I⁵. *vt. & vi.* To net; entangle; engage, as gear-teeth. II. *n.* 1. One of the open spaces of a network. 2. Anything that entangles; a trap.— **mesh'y**, *a.*

mes'mer-ism, 1 mez'mər-izm; 2 mĕs'mer-ĭsm, *n.* 1. The production of a trance-like condition by control of will; hypnotism. 2. Personal magnetism: named from Franz Mesmer (1733–1815), the originator. — **mes-mer'ic, -i-cal**, *a.*— **mes-mer'i-cal-ly**, *adv.*— **mes'mer-ize, -ise**, *vt.* [-IZED; -IZ'-ING.] To control by mesmerism; hypnotize; fascinate.— **mes'mer-iz"er** or **-is"er**, *n.* **mes'mer-ist‡.**

mess⁵, 1 mes; 2 mĕs, *vt. & vi.* To provide for at a mess; belong to a mess.

mess¹, *n.* 1. A meal. 2. A number of persons who eat together, as on board ship.

mess², *n.* [Colloq.] A state of disorder; confusion.

mes'sage, 1 mes'ɪj; 2 mĕs'aġ, *n.* Word sent; a communication sent in any way.

mes'sen-ger, 1 mes'en-jer; 2 mĕs'ĕn-ġer, *n.* One sent with a message; a forerunner; herald.

Mes-si'ah, 1 me-saɪ'ə; 2 mĕ-sī'a, *n.* The Anointed One; the Christ.— **Mes-si'ah-ship**, *n.*— **Mes"si-an'ic**, *a.*

mes'sieurs, 1 mes'yɚz; 2 mĕs'yẽrs, *n. pl.* Sirs; gentlemen: the plural of MONSIEUR: French plural of MONSIEUR.

met, *imp. & pp.* of MEET, *v.*

met'-, met'a-, met'ä-, meth'-; 2 mĕt'-, **met'a-**, mĕt'a-, mĕth'-, *prefix.* Used (1) in **meth'-**, words of Greek origin to mean "between, with, after, over, reversely"; (2) (*Chem.*) to denote resemblance. etc.

me-tab'o-lism, 1 mɪ-tab'o-lizm; 2 mẹ-tăb'o-lĭṣm, *n.* The process by which, on the one hand, food is built up into living material, and, on the other, living matter is broken up and decomposed.

met'al, 1 met'əl; 2 mĕt al, *n.* An elementary substance, usually hard, heavy, and malleable, as iron, gold, tin, etc.— **me-tal'lic**, *a.* Being, containing, or pertaining to a metal.— **met"al - lif'er - ous**, *a.* Yielding

metal.— **met'al-lur"gy**, *n.* The art of extracting metals from ores.— **met'al-lur'gic**, *a.*

met"a-mor'pho-sis, 1 met'ə-môr'fo-sis; **met"a-mor'fo-sis^P**, 2 mĕt'a-môr'fo-sĭs, *n.* [-SES, 1 -sīz; 2 -sĕs, *pl.*] Transformation, as of a caterpillar into a butterfly; chemical decomposition.— **met"a-mor'phose**, *vt.* [-PHOSED; -PHOS-ING.] To change the form of; transmute.

met'a-phor, 1 met'a-fɚ; 2 mĕt'a-for, *n.* A figure of speech in which one object is spoken of as if it were another.— **met"a-phor'i-cal**, *a.* Relating to or abounding in metaphor; figurative. **-ly**, *adv.* **met"a-phor'ic‡.**

met"a-phys'ics, 1 met'ə-fiz'ɪks; 2 mĕt'a-**met"a-fys'ics^P**, fỹs'ics, *n.* Philosophy; mental science; psychology.— **met"a-phys'i-cal**, *a.* **-ly**, *adv.*— **met"a-phy-si'cian**, *n.* One skilled in metaphysics.

mete, 1 mīt; 2 mēt. I. *vt.* [MET'ED⁴; MET'ING.] To allot by measure; apportion. II. *n.* A boundary-line; limit; measure.

me'te-or, 1 mī'tɪ-ɚ; 2 mē'te-ŏr, *n.* A luminous mass of matter from space, visiting the earth: a shooting-star. **me'te-or-old‡.**— **me"te-or'ic**, *a.* Relating to meteors; transiently brilliant.— **me'te-or-ite**, *n.* A fallen meteor; a mass that has fallen upon the earth from space. **me'te-or-o-lite‡.** — **me"te-or-ol'o-gy**, *n.* 1. The phenomena of the atmosphere, especially as relating to weather. 2. The character of the weather and of atmospheric changes.— **me"te-or-o'log'ic, me"te-or"o-log'i-cal**, *a.*— **me"te-or-ol'o-gist**, *n.* A specialist in meteorology.

me'ter, 1 mī'tɚ; 2 mē'ter, *n.* 1. Rhythmical arrangement of syllables, as **me'tre**, in poetry. 2. An instrument for measuring fluids, gases, etc. 3. The fundamental unit of length in the metric system: 39.37 inches. See METRIC SYSTEM.— **me'ter-age**, *n.*

me-thinks', 1 mɪ-thɪŋks'; 2 me-thĭŋks', *v. impers.* [ME-THOUGHT'.] It seems to me.

meth'od, 1 meth'əd; 2 mĕth'od, *n.* A way or order of doing; orderly arrangement or procedure.— **me-thod'ic, me-thod'i-cal**, *a.* Orderly; systematic. **-ly**, *adv.*— **meth'od-ize**, *v.* [-IZED; -IZ'ING.] I. *t.* To subject to method; regulate. II. *t.* To act methodically. **meth'od-ise‡.**

Meth'od-ist, 1 meth'əd-ist; 2 mĕth'od-ĭst, *n.* A member of the religious denomination originated by John Wesley.— **meth'od-ism**, *n.* 1. The state of being methodical. 2. [M-] The doctrines, polity, and worship of the Methodists.— **meth"od-is'tic, meth"od-is'ti-cal**, *a.*

1: ə = final; ɪ = habit; aɪsle; au = out; oïl; iū = feud; chin; go; ŋ = sing; thin, this.
2: wǫlf, dǫ; book, boot; fůll, růle, cūre, bŭt, bûrn; ǒil, bǒy; ġo, ġem; iŋk; thin, this.

me-thought′, 1 mɪ-fhŏt′; 2 me-thôt′, *imp.* of METHINKS, *v.*

me′tre, *n.* Same as METER.

met′ric, 1 met′rɪk; 2 mĕt′rɪc, *a.* **1.** Pertaining to measure or meter. **2.** Pertaining to the meter as a unit of measurement or to the metric system.— **met′ri-cal,** 1 met′rɪ-kəl; 2 mĕt′rɪ-cal, *a* **1.** Relating to meter; rhythmical. **2.** Pertaining to measure or the meter.— **met′ri-cal-ly,** *adv.*

THE METRIC SYSTEM.

This is a system of weights and measures depending upon the *meter*, in which the original factors are derived from the meter. The system includes measures of length, of which the *meter* is the unit; measures of surface, of which the *are* is the unit; measures of capacity, of which the *liter* is the unit; and weights, of which the *gram* is the unit. Ascending in value from each unit the measure is multiplied by ten, and bears a Greek prefix indicating its value, as *decameter*, which is 10 meters; *hectometer*, which is 100 meters; *kilometer*, which is 1000 meters; and *myriameter*, which is 10,000 meters. Similarly descending in value the terms bear Latin prefixes indicating their relation to the unit, as *decimeter*, which is 1/10 of a meter; *centimeter*, which is 1/100 of a meter; and *millimeter*, which is 1/1000 of a meter. The following tables show the various units with corresponding factors in other systems. The metric system has been legalized by the United States and Great Britain, and is in actual use in every civilized nation.

MEASURES OF LENGTH.

Metric Denomination and Value.		Equivalent in Common Use.
myr′i-a-me″ter.	10,000 m	6.214 miles
kil′o-me″ter....	1,000 m	0.62137 m i l e (3,280 feet, 10 inches)
hec′to-me″ter..	100 m	328 feet, 1 inch
dec′a-me″ter ..	10 m	393.7 inches
me″ter........	1 m	39.37 inches
dec′i-me″ter..	1/10 m	3.937 inches
cen′ti-me″ter...	1/100 m	0.3937 inch
mil′li-me″ter ..	1/1000 m	0.0394 inch

NOTE.— In the United States the value of the meter is legalized at 39.37 inches, while in Great Britain and France its exact value is given as 39.37079 inches.

FACTORS FOR CONVERSION: One inch = 0.0254 meter; one foot = 0.3048 meter; one mile = 1609.35 meters.

ABBREVIATIONS*: cm = centimeter, dm = decimeter, km = kilometer, m = meter, mm = millimeter.

MEASURES OF SURFACE.

Metric Denomination and Value.		Equivalent in Common Use.
hec′tare.....	10,000 m²	2,471 acres
are..........	100 m²	119.6 square yards
cen′tare......	1 m²	1,550 square inches

FACTORS FOR CONVERSION: One square inch = 0.0006452 square meter; one square yard = 0.836 square meter; one acre = 4,047 square meters.

ABBREVIATIONS*: a = are, ha = hectare, m² = square meter.

MEASURES OF CAPACITY.

Metric Denomination and Value.			Equivalent in Common Use.
NAME.	Liter.	Cubic Measure.	Dry Measure.
hec′to-stere..	100,000	100 m³	130.8 cu. yds.
kil′o-li″ter (stere)....	1,000	1 m³	1.308 cu. yds.
hec′to-li″ter.	100	1/10 m³	{ 2 bush., 3.35 pecks
dec′a-li″ter..	10	10 dm³	9.08 qts.
li″ter.......	1	1 dm³	0.908 qt.
dec′i-li″ter..	1/10	1/10 dm³	6.1922 cu. in.
cen′ti-li″ter.	1/100	10 cm³	0.6102 cu. in.
mil′li-li″ter..	1/1000	1 cm³	0.061 cu. in.

Metric Denomination and Value.			Equivalent in Common Use.
NAME.	Liter.	Cubic Measure.	Liquid Measure.
hec′to-stere..	100,000	100 m³	26,417 gals.
kil′o-li″ter (stere)....	1,000	1 m³	264.17 gals.‡
hec′to-li″ter.	100	1/10 m⁵	26.42 gals.‡
dec′a-li″ter..	10	10 dm³	2.64 gals.‡
li″ter.......	1	1 dm³	1.0567 qts.
dec′i-li″ter...	1/10	1/10 dm³	0.845 gill
cen′ti-li″ter.	1/100	10 cm³	0.338 fl. oz.
mil′li-li″ter..	1/1000	1 cm³	0.27 fl. dr.

FACTORS FOR CONVERSION: One cubic inch = 0.0164 liter; one bushel = (U. S.) 35.24 or (British) 36.35 liters; one quart (dry measure) = 1.1011 liters; one peck = (U. S.) 8.81 or (British) 9.09 liters; one cubic yard = 765 liters; one fluid dram = 0.00369 liter; one fluid ounce = 0.0296 liter; one gill = 0.1183 liter; one quart (liquid measure) = 0.9463 liter; one gallon standard ‡ (231 cubic inches) = 3.785 liters; one gallon imperial (277 cubic inches) = 4.543 liters.

ABBREVIATIONS*: cl = centiliter, cm³ = cubic centimeter, dal = decaliter, dl = deciliter, dm³ = cubic decimeter, hl = hectoliter, l = liter, m³ = cubic meter, ml = milliliter, mm³ = cubic millimeter.

1: ȧrtistic, ärt; fat, fāre; fạst; get, prēy; hĭt, police; obey, gō; nŏt, ôr; fu̇ll, rūle; but, bûrn.
2: ärt, āpe, făt, fâre, fȧst, whạt, ạll; mē, gĕt, prẹy, fêrn; hĭt, ïce; ĩ=ĕ; ĩ=ē; gō, nŏt, ôr, wŏn,

WEIGHTS.

Metric Denomination and Value.		Water at Maximum Density.	Equivalent in Common Use.
NAME.	Gram.		Avoirdupois Weight.
mil′lier′ (tonneau)	1,000,000	1 m³	2,204.6 lbs.
quin′tal....	100,000	1 hl	220.46 lbs.
myr′i-a-gram	10,000	10 l	22.046 lbs.
kil′o-gram..	1,000	1 l	2.204 lbs.
hec′to-gram.	100	1 dl	3.527 ozs.
dec′a-gram..	10	10 cm³	0.353 oz.
gram......	1	1 cm³	15.432 grs.
deg′i-gram..	1/10	1/10 cm³	1.543 grs.
cen′ti-gram .	1/100	10 mm³	0.154 gr.
mil′li-gram..	1/1000	1 mm³	0.015 gr.

FACTORS FOR CONVERSION: One grain = 0.0648 gram; one avoirdupois ounce = 28.3495 grams; one troy ounce = 31.103 grams; one pound = 453.59 grams.

ABBREVIATIONS*: cg = centigram, dg = decigram, g = gram, kg = kilogram, mg = milligram, q = quintal, t = tonneau (millier).

* Officially adopted abbreviations by International Congress of Metric Weights and Measures.

me-trop′o-lis, 1 me-trŏp′o-lĭs; 2 me-trŏp′o-lĭs, *n.* A chief city.— **met′ro-pol′i-tan,** *a.*

-metry, *suffix.* Denoting the process, science, or art of measuring; as, geo*metry.*

met′tle, } 1 met′l; 2 mĕt′l, *n.* The stuff of
met′l, } which a thing is composed; temperament; disposition.— **met′tle-some,** *a.* Having courage or spirit; ardent; fiery. **met′tled**‡.

mew[1], 1 miū; 2 mū, *vi.* To cry as a cat.

mew[2], *vt.* To shut up or in; confine.

mew[1], *n.* The ordinary cry of a cat.

mew[2], *n.* A European sea-gull.

mewl, 1 miūl; 2 mūl, *vi.* To cry as an infant.

mez′zo, 1 mez′zo; 2 mĕt′zo, *a.* Half; medium; moderate. **mez′za**‡ (*fem.*).— **mezzo soprano,** a voice lower than a soprano and higher than a contralto.

mez′zo-tint, 1 mez′o-tint; 2 mĕz′o-tĭnt, *n.* A method of copperplate engraving, producing a picture like a photograph.

mi, 1 mī; 2 mī, *n.* [It.] The third note of the musical scale.

mi-as′ma, 1 mi-az′mə; 2 mi-ăs′ma, *n.* [-MA-TA, *pl.*] Polluting exhalations; malarial poison. **mi′asm**‡.— **mi-as′mal,** *a.* Abounding in miasma.— **mi-as-mat′ic,** *a.*

mi′ca, 1 mai′kə; 2 mī′ca, *n.* A mineral that cleaves in thin, tough, transparent to translucent scales; isinglass.

mice, 1 mais; 2 mīç, *n.* Plural of MOUSE.

mi′cro-, 1 mai′kro-; 2 mī′cro-. A combining form signifying " small "; as, *micro*scope, *micro*organism.

mi′crobe, 1 mai′krōb; 2 mī′erōb, *n.* A microscopic organism; a bacterium.

mi′cro-cosm, 1 mai′kro-kezm; 2 mī′ero-eŏȝm, *n.* A little world, universe, or community; hence, man.

mi′cro-graph, 1 mai′kro-graf; 2 mī′ero-grȧf, *n.* A microscopic picture; instrument for making the same.

mi-crom′e-ter, 1 mai-krəm′i-tər; 2 mī-erŏm′e-ter, *n.* An instrument for measuring very small dimensions.— **mi′cro-met′ri-cal,** *a.*

mi′cro-mo′to-scope, 1 mai′kro-mō′to-skŏp, 2 mī′ero-mō′to-seŏp, *n.* An instrument for photographing microscopic moving objects.

mi′cro-phone, 1 mai′cro-fōn; 2 mī′ero-fōn, *n.* An apparatus for magnifying faint sounds by means of electrical devices.

mi′cro-scope, 1 mai′kro-skŏp; 2 mī′ero-seŏp, *n.* An instrument for making visible minute objects.— **mi′cro-scop′ic,** *a.* Pertaining to the microscope; visible only through the microscope; exceedingly minute. **-i-cal**‡. **-i-cal-ly,** *adv.*— **mi-cros′co-py,** *n.*

mid, 1 mid; 2 mĭd, *a.* Middle.— **mid′day″,** *a. & n.* Noon.

mid′dle, } 1 mid′l; 2 mĭd′l. **I.** *a.* Equally
mid′l, } distant from the extremes; mean; intermediate. **II.** *n.* The part equally distant from the extremities; something intermediate.— **mid′dle-man,** *n.* One who intervenes, as between producer and consumer.

mid′dling, } 1 mid′lĭŋ; 2 mĭd′lĭng, *a.* Of
mid′ling[2], } middle rank, quality, etc.; medium; tolerable. [fly.

midge, 1 mij; 2 mĭdȝ, *n.* A gnat or small

mldg′et, 1 mij′et; 2 mĭdȝ′ĕt, *n.* **1.** A midge. **2.** A tiny dwarf. **3.** A small, active child.

mid′land, 1 mid′lənd; 2 mĭd′land. **I.** *a.* In the interior country. **II.** *n.* The interior of a country, especially of England.

mid′night″, 1 mĭd′nait″; 2 mĭd′nīt″, *n.* The middle of the night; 12 p.m.

mid′riff, 1 mid′rif; 2 mĭd′rĭf, *n.* The diaphragm.

mid′ship″, 1 mid′ship″; 2 mĭd′shĭp″, *a.* At or pertaining to the middle of a vessel's hull.— **mid′ships,** *adv.*

mid′ship″man, 1 mid′ship″man; 2 mĭd′ship″man, *n.* A naval student, or one holding rank between naval cadet and the lowest commissioned officer.

midst, 1 midst; 2 mĭdst. **I.** *n.* The central part; middle. **II.** *n.* In the middle.

mid′sum″mer, 1 mid′sum″ər; 2 mĭd′sŭm″er, *n.* The middle of summer.

1: ə = final; ı = habĭt; aisle; au = out; oil; iū = feud; chin; go; ŋ = sing; thin, this.

2: wǫlf, dǫ; bŏŏk, bŏŏt; fųll, rųle, cūre, bŭt, bûrn; ŏil, bŏy; ġo, ġem; ịnk; thin, this.

mid'way", 1 mid'wē"; 2 mĭd'wā", *a., n.*, & *adv.* Half=way; middle.

mid'wife", 1 mid'waif"; 2 mĭd'wīf", *n.* [MID'WIVES", 1 -waivz"; 2 -wīvs", *pl.*] A woman who assists at childbirth.—**mid'wife"ry,** *n.*

mid'win"ter, 1 mid'win"tər; 2 mĭd'wĭn"ter, *n.* The middle of winter.

mien, 1 mīn; 2 mēn, *n.* External appearance; manner; bearing.

miff, 1 mif; 2 mĭf. [Colloq.] I[t]. *vt.* To vex. II. *n.* Sudden anger; a huff.

might, 1 mait; 2 mīt, *imp.* of MAY, *v.*

might, *n.* Power; strength; abundant energy.—**might'y,** *a.* [MIGHT'I-ER; MIGHT'-I-EST.] Possessed of might; powerful; strong.—**might'i-ly,** *adv.*—**might'i-ness,** *n.*

mi'gnon-ette', 1 min"yən-et'; 2 mĭn"yon-ĕt', *n.* A North=African annual plant, bearing small fragrant flowers.

mi'grate, 1 mai'grēt; 2 mī'grāt, *vi.* [MI'GRAT-ED[d]; MI'-GRAT-ING.] To remove from one country to another.—**mi-gra'tion,** *n.*—**mi'gra-to-ry,** *a.* Pertaining to migration; roving.

Mi-ka'do, 1 mi-kä'do; 2 mi-kä'do, *n.* The sovereign of Japan.

milch, 1 milch; 2 mĭlch, *a.* Giving milk, as a cow.

Mignonette.

mild, 1 maild; 2 mīld, *a.* Moderate; kind; calm.—**mild'ly,** *adv.*—**mild'ness,** *n.*

mil'dew, 1 mil'diū; 2 mĭl'dū. I. *vt.* & *vi.* To taint, or become tainted, with mildew. II. *n.* A fungus or a mold caused by it, as on walls or clothing.

mile, 1 mail; 2 mīl, *n.* **1.** A measure of distance: 5,280 feet. **2.** A measure of surface: 640 acres.—**mile'age,** *n.* Length measured in miles; compensation per mile for expenses of travel.—**mile'post",** m.=stone, *n.* A post or stone set up to indicate distance.

mil'i-tant, 1 mil'i-tənt; 2 mĭl'i-tant, *a.* Pertaining to conflict; warlike; combative.

mil'i-ta-ry, 1 mil'i-tē-ri; 2 mĭl'i-tā-ry. I. *a.* Pertaining to soldiers or warfare; martial; warlike. II. *n.* A body of soldiers; soldiery.

mil'i-tate, 1 mil'i-tēt; 2 mĭl'i-tāt, *vi.* [-TAT'-ED[d]; -TAT"ING.] To oppose; contend: followed by *against.*

mi-li'tia, 1 mi-lish'ə; 2 mi-lĭsh'a, *n.* Citizens who are enrolled in military organizations other than the regular army.—**mi-li'tia-man,** *n.*

milk, 1 milk; 2 mĭlk. I[t]. *vt.* & *vi.* To draw

milk from; yield milk. II. *n.* The white liquid with which female mammals nourish their young; the white sap of certain plants.—**milk'er,** *n.*—**milk'y,** *a.* [MILK'I-ER; MILK'I-EST.] Containing or like milk; yielding milk.—**milk'i-ness,** *n.*—**Milky Way,** a luminous band encircling the heavens, composed of distant stars and nebulæ.

mill, 1 mil; 2 mĭl, *vt.* **1.** To grind as in a mill. **2.** To indent the edge of (a coin).

mill[1], *n.* A machine or a building for grinding grain, reducing ores, etc.—**mill'=dam",** mill=pond, *n.*—**mill=race,** *n.* The sluiceway of a mill.—**mill'stone",** *n.* One of a pair of stones for grinding.

mill[2], 1 mil; 2 mĭl, *n.* [U. S.] The thousandth part of a dollar.

mil'le-na'ri-an, 1 mil"i-nē'ri-ən; 2 mĭl"e-nā'ri-an. I. *a.* Pertaining to a thousand or to the Millennium. II. *n.* A believer in a millennium.

mil-len'ni-um, 1 mi-len'i- um; 2 mi-lĕn'i-ŭm, *n.* **1.** A period of a thousand years. **2.** [M-] The thousand years of the personal reign of Christ on earth, based on *Rev.* xx, 1-5.—**mil-len'ni-al,** *a.*

mill'er, 1 mil'ər; 2 mĭl'er, *n.* **1.** One who keeps or tends a mill. **2.** A pale moth, with floury wings.

mil'let, 1 mil'et; 2 mĭl'ĕt, *n.* A grass cultivated for forage and as a cereal.

mil'li-gram, 1 mil'li-li"ter, mil'li-me"ter, *n.* See METRIC SYSTEM, under METRIC.

mil'li-ner, 1 mil'i-nər; 2 mĭl'i-ner, *n.* One who makes bonnets, women's hats, etc.—**mil'li-ner-y,** *n.* The goods or business of a milliner.

mil'lion, 1 mil'yən; 2 mĭl'yon, *n.* A thousand thousand; 1,000,000.—**mill'lion-aire',** *n.* A person whose possessions are valued at a million or more.—**mill'lionth,** *a.* & *n.*

milt, 1 milt; 2 mĭlt, *n.* The spleen; sperm of a fish.

mime, 1 maim; 2 mīm, *n.* A mimic play, or actor; a mimic.—**mim'ic.** I. *vt.* [MIM'-ICKED[t], MIM'ICK[s]: MIM'ICK-ING.] To imitate; copy closely. II. *a.* Of the nature of mimicry. III. *n.* An imitator.—**mim'ic,** *n.* [-RIES[z], *pl.*] The act of mimicking; a copy.

mim'e-o-graph, 1 mim'i-o-graf; 2 mĭm'e-o-gräf, *n.* An apparatus for reproducing copies of written or typewritten matter.

min'a-ret, 1 min'ə-ret; 2 mĭn'a-rĕt, *n.* A slender tower near a mosque. See illus. on next page.

mince, 1 mins; 2 mĭns, *vt.* & *vi.* [MINCED[t]; MINC'ING.] To chop fine; lessen; talk or act affectively.—**minc'ing,** 1 mins'ɪŋ; 2

1: **a**rtistic, **ä**rt; fat, fāre; fast; get, prēy; hit, polïce; obey, gō; nøt, ør; full, rūle; but, būrn.

2: **ä**rt, **ā**pe, făt, fâre, fȧst, whạt, ạll; mē, gĕt, prēy, fẽrn; hĭt, īce; ī=ē; ī=ē; gō, nŏt, ôr, wŏn,

mĭnç'ing, *pa*. Showing affected nicety; over-nice; precise.— **mĭnç'ing-ly,** *adv*.

mince, n. Meat chopped fine and mixed with various ingredients. **mince′-meat″‡.** — **mince pie,** a pie made of mince=meat.

mind d, 1 maind; 2 mĭnd. **I.** *vt. & vi* To heed; care for; obey. **II.** *n.* **1.** That w h i c h thinks, feels, and wills; soul; spirit; in-tellect. **2.** Any men-tal state or inclination; determination.— **mind′ed,** *a*. Disposed.— **mind′ful,** *a*. Keep-ing in mind; heedful.— **mind′ful-ly,** *adv*. **mind′ful-ness,** *n*.

Minarets of the Mosque of Suleiman, Istanbul.

mine, 1 main; 2 mĭn, *v*. [MINED; MIN′ING.] **I.** *t*. **1.** To dig out of the earth. **2.** To undermine. **3.** To make by digging. **II.** *i*. To make a mine; engage in mining; burrow.— **min′er,** *n*.

mine, *n*. **1.** An excavation for digging out ore, coal, or the like, or a deposit of such material. **2.** An explosive charge or the cavity containing it. [possessive of *I*.

mine, *pron*. Belonging to me; of me:

min′er-al, 1 mĭn′ẽr-al; 2 mĭn′er-al. **I.** *a*. Pertaining to or resembling minerals; inorganic. **II.** *n.* A substance neither animal nor vegetable, and commonly solid; any inorganic substance.— **min′er-al-i-za′tion,** *n*.— **min″er-al′o-gy,** *n*. **1.** The science of minerals. **2.** A work on minerals. — **min″er-al-og′i-cal,** *a*. Pertaining to mineralogy.— **min″er-al′o-gist,** *n*.

Mi-ner′va, 1 mi-nŭr′va; 2 mĭ-nẽr′va, *n*. *Rom. Myth.* Goddess of wisdom and war; the Greek Pallas and Athena.

min″e′stro′ni, 1 mĭn″ĕ′strō′nĭ; 2 mĭn″e″-strō′nĭ. [It.] A vegetable soup.

min′gle,] 1 mĭn′gl; 2 mĭn′gl, *vt. & vi*. **min′glⁱ,**] [MIN′GL(E)Dᴾ; MIN′GLING.] To unite; mix; blend.— **min′gling-ly,** *adv*.

min′i-a-ture, 1 mĭn′i-a-chur *or* -tiur; 2 mĭn′i-a-chur *or* -tûr. **I.** *a*. Much smaller than reality. **II.** *n*. A small painting; any small copy or model.

min′im, 1 mĭn′im; 2 mĭn′im, *n*. **1.** An apothecaries' fluid measure; roughly, one drop. **2.** *Mus.* A half note.

min′i-mum, 1 mĭn′i-mum; 2 mĭn′i-mum, *n*. [-MA, *pl*.] The least possible quantity,

amount, or degree: used also adjectively. — **min′i-mize,** *vt*. [-MIZED; -MIZ′ING.] To re-duce to the smallest possible amount or degree.

min′ion, 1 mĭn′yan; 2 mĭn′yon, *n*. **1.** A servile favorite. **2.** *Print*. A small size of type: about 7=point. **3.** A minx.

min′is-ter, 1 mĭn′ĭs-tẽr; 2 mĭn′ĭs-ter, *v*. **I.** *t*. To supply. **II.** *i*. **1.** To attend; con-tribute. **2.** To perform a rite of worship.

min′is-ter, *n*. **1.** The head of a govern-mental department; the representative of a foreign government. **2.** A clergyman. **3.** A servant; agent.— **min″is-te′ri-al,** *a*. Pertaining to a minister or to ministry.— **min″is-tra′tion,** The act of ministering; a religious ceremonial.— **min′is-try,** *n*. [-TRIES², *pl*.] **1.** Ministers collectively; the act of ministering. **2.** An executive depart-ment of government.

mink, 1 mĭŋk; 2 mĭŋk, *n*. A small am-phibious carnivore valued for its fur.

min′now, 1 mĭn′o; 2 mĭn′o, *n*. A small fish.

mi′nor, 1 mai′nẽr; 2 mī′nor. **I.** *a*. **1.** Less; secondary. **2.** *Mus.* In the minor key; solemn and plaintive. **II.** *n*. **1.** One under age. **2.** *Mus.* The minor key. — **mi-nor′i-ty,** *n*. [-TIES², *pl*.] **1.** The smaller of two parts or parties. **2.** The state of being under age.

min′ster, 1 mĭn′stẽr; 2 mĭn′ster, *n*. A monastery church; cathedral.

min′strel, 1 mĭn′strel; 2 mĭn′strĕl, *n*. A wandering musician; a lyric poet; mounte-bank.— **min′strel-sy,** *n*. The occupation of a minstrel; ballads or lyrics collectively.

mint d, 1 mint; 2 mĭnt, *vt*. **1.** To coin money by authority. **2.** To fabricate.— **mint′er,** *n*.

mint′, *n*. **1.** A place for the legal coinage of money. **2.** An abun-dance, as of money.

mint², *n*. An aromatic herb, as spearmint or peppermint.

min′u-end, 1 mĭn′yu-end; 2 mĭn′yu-ĕnd, *n*. *Arith.* The number from which another is to be subtracted.

Peppermint.
a, a single flower; *b*, a piece of the square stem.

min″u-et′, 1 mĭn″yu-et′; 2 mĭn″yu-ĕt′,*n*. An old=time stately dance.

mi′nus, 1 mai′nus; 2 mī′nŭs, *a*. **1.** *Math.* (1) Less: indicated by a dash (−). (2) Negative. **2.** [Colloq.] Deprived of; lacking.

min′ute, 1 mĭn′it; 2 mĭn′it, *vt*. [-UT-EDᵈ; -UT-ING.] To make a brief note of.

minute
mitigate

mi-nute′, 1 mɪ-niūt′; 2 mi-nūt′, *a.* Exceedingly small; very exact; punctilious. **-ly,** *adv.* **-ness,** *n.*

min′ute, 1 min′ɪt; 2 min′it, *n.* **1.** The 60th part of an hour, or of a degree. **2.** A memorandum. **3.** *pl.* Official records. — **min′ute·book″,** *n.* A book for recording minutes or memoranda. — **m.·gun,** *n.* A gun fired at intervals of a minute, as on the interment of an officer. — **m.·hand,** *n.* The hand of a watch or clock that marks the minutes.

mi-nu′ti-a, 1 mɪ-niū′shɪ-ə; 2 mi-nū′shi-a, [-Æ, 1 -ɪ; 2 -ē, *pl.*] A small or unimportant detail.

minx, 1 mɪŋks; 2 miŋks, *n.* A saucy girl.

mir′a-cle, } 1 mir′ə-kl; 2 mir′a-cl, *n.* A **mir′a-cl²,** } supernatural event; something wonderful or amazing. — **mi-rac′u-lous,** *a.* Supernatural; strange; wonderful. **-ly,** *adv.* **-ness,** *n.* — **mir′a-cle·play″,** *n.*

mi-rage′, 1 mɪ-räʒ′; 2 mi-räzh′, *n.* An optical illusion, as of a sheet of water in the desert.

mire, 1 mair; 2 mīr. **I.** *vi.* [MIRED; MIR′-ING.] **1.** To fix, stall, or sink in mud. **2.** To defile. **II.** *n.* Wet, yielding earth; deep mud. — **mir′y,** *a.* — **mi′ri-ness,** *n.*

mirk, mirk′i-ly, etc. Same as MURK, etc.

mir′ror, 1 mir′ər; 2 mir′or. **I.** *vt.* To image. **II.** *n.* An object having a reflecting surface.

mirth, 1 mūrth; 2 mirth, *n.* Merriment; jollity; fun. — **mirth′ful,** *a.* Merry. **-ly,** *adv.* **-ness,** *n.*

mis-¹, *prefix.* Less: used with negative or depreciatory force; as, *mis*prize.

mis-², *prefix.* Wrong; wrongly: used with nouns, verbs, and participles; as *mis*conduct.

The following are self-explaining by giving *mis* the sense of wrongly, amiss:

mis″ap-ply′
mis-ap″pre-hend′d
mis-ap″pre-hen′sion
mis″be-have′
mis-cal′cu-lated
mis-charge′, *v.* & *n.*
mis″con-ceive′
mis″con-jec′ture, *v.* & *n.*
mis″con-struc′tion
mis″con-strue′
mis-count′, *v.* & *n.*
mis-date′, *vt.* & *n.*
mis-deem′
mis″de-mean′
mis″di-rec′tion
mis-do′ing
mis″em-ploy′
mis-fit′
mis-got′ten

mis-gov′ern
mis-gov′ern-ment
mis-guide′
mis-judge′
mis-man′age
mis-man′age-ment
mis-match′, *v.* & *n.*
mis-name′, *vt.*
mis-place′
mis″pro-nounce′t
mis-quote′d
mis-send′
mis-shape′
mis-sha′pen
mis-spell′, *v.*
mis-spend′
mis-state′d
mis-time′
mis-treat′d
mis-word′, *vt.*

mis″ad-ven′ture, 1 mis″ad-ven′chur *or* -tiur; 2 mis″ăd-vĕn′chur *or* -tūr, *n.* An unlucky chance; misfortune.

mis″an-thrope, 1 mis′an-thrōp; 2 mis″ăn-thrŏp, *n.* A man-hater. **mis-an′thro-pist**: — **mis″an-throp′ic, mis″an-throp′-i-cal,** *a.* Hating mankind. — **mis-an′thro-py,** *n.* Hatred or distrust of mankind.

mis″ap-pro′pri-ate′d, 1 mis″ə-prō′pri-ēt; 2 mis″ă-prō′pri-āt, *vt.* To appropriate wrongly. — **mis″ap-pro″pri-a′tion,** *n.*

mis-call′, 1 mis-kôl′; 2 mis-eal′, *vt.* To give a wrong or bad name to.

mis-car′ry, 1 mis-kar′ɪ; 2 mis-eăr′y, *vi.* **1.** To fail of an intended effect; go wrong. **2.** To bring forth prematurely. — **mis-car′riage,** *n.* **1.** A premature birth. **2.** Failure to reach an expected conclusion.

mis″cel-la′ne-ous, 1 mis″e-lē′nɪ-us; 2 mis″ĕ-lā′ne-ŭs, *a.* Consisting of several kinds; variously mixed. **-ly,** *adv.* **-ness,** *n.* — **mis′cel-la-ny,** *n.* [-NIES², *pl.*] A miscellaneous collection.

mis-chance′, 1 mis-chans′; 2 mis-chănç′, *n.* An instance of ill luck; a mishap.

mis′chief, 1 mis′chɪf; 2 mis′chif, *n.* Evil; injury; a prank; a prankish person. — **mis′chie-vous,** 1 mis′chɪ-vus; 2 mis′chi-vŭs, *a.* **1.** Inclined to mischief. **2.** Injurious. **-ly,** *adv.* **-ness,** *n.*

mis″con-duct′d, 1 mis″kon-dukt′; 2 mis″-eŏn-dŭet′, *vt.* & *vi.* To behave improperly; mismanage.

mis-con′duct, 1 mis-kon′dukt; 2 mis-eŏn′dŭet, *n.* Improper conduct; bad behavior; mismanagement.

mis′cre-ant, 1 mis′krɪ-ant; 2 mis′ere-ant, *n.* A vile wretch.

mis-deed′, 1 mis-dīd′; 2 mis-dēd′, *n.* A wrong or improper act.

mis″de-mean′or, 1 mis″dɪ-mīn′ər; 2 mis″-de-mēn′or, *n.* Misconduct; an offense less than a felony.

mi′ser, 1 mai′zər; 2 mī′ẓer, *n.* One who saves and hoards avariciously. — **mi′ser-ly,** *a.*

mis′er-a-ble, } 1 miz′ər-ə-bl; 2 mis′er-a-bl, **mis′er-a-bl²,** } *a.* Wretched; unhappy; of mean quality. — **mis′er-a-bly,** *adv.* — **mis′er-a-bl(e-ness)ᵖ,** *n.*

mis′er-y, 1 miz′ər-ɪ; 2 mis′er-y, *n.* [-IES², *pl.*] Extreme distress; wretchedness; also, a cause of wretchedness.

mis-for′tune, 1 mis-iôr′chun *or* -tiun; 2 mis-fôr′chun *or* -tūn, *n.* Ill fortune; calamity.

mis-give′, } 1 mis-giv′; 2 mis-gĭv′, *vt.* & *vi.* **mis-giv′r,** } To cause or feel a lack of confidence; be apprehensive. — **mis-giv′ing,** *n.* A feeling of apprehension.

mis-hap′, 1 mis-hap′; 2 mis-hăp′, *n.* A slight misfortune.

1: ärtistic, ärt; fat, fāre; fɑst, prēy; hit, police; obey, gō; not, ör; full, rūle; but, būrn.
2: ärt, āpe, făt, fâre, fɑst, whɑt, ɑll; mē, gĕt, prey, fērn; hit, īce; i=ē; ī=ē; gō, nŏt, ôr, wŏn,

mis″in-form′, 1 mis″ĭn-fôrm′; 2 mĭs″ĭn-fôrm′, *vt.* To inform falsely.— **mis-in″for-ma′tion,** *n.*

mis″in-ter′pret[d], 1 mis″ĭn-tŭr′pret; 2 mĭs″in-tēr′prĕt, *vt.* To interpret wrongly.— **mis″in-ter″pre-ta′tion,** *n.*— **mis″in-ter′pret-er,** *n.*

mis-lay′, 1 mis-lā′; 2 mĭs-lā′, *vt.* To lay in a wrong or forgotten place; lose.

mis-lead′, 1 mis-līd′; 2 mĭs-lēd′, *vt.* [MIS-LED′; MIS-LEAD′ING.] To lead astray.

mis′le-toe, *n.* Same as MISTLETOE.

mis-no′mer, 1 mis-nō′mər; 2 mĭs-nō′mer, *n.* A name wrongly applied or inapplicable.

mis-og′a-my, 1 mis-ŏg′ə-mi; 2 mĭs-ŏg′a-my, *n.* Hatred of marriage.— **mis-og′a-mist,** *n.*

mis-og′y-ny, 1 mis-ŏj′i-ni; 2 mĭs-ŏg′y-ny, *n.* Hatred of woman.— **mis-og′y-nist,** *n.*

mis-print′, 1 mis-print′; 2 mĭs-prĭnt′. **I**[d]. *vt.* To print erroneously. **II.** *n.* An error in printing.

mis-rep″re-sent′[d], 1 mis-rep″ri-zent′; 2 mĭs-rĕp″re-sĕnt′, *vt. & vi.* To represent wrongly; give a wrong impression.— **mis-rep″re-sen-ta′tion,** *n.*

mis-rule′, 1 mis-rūl′; 2 mĭs-rŭl′, *n.* Bad government; tyranny; disorder.

miss[t], 1 mis; 2 mĭs, *v.* **I.** *t.* **1.** To fail of; come short of. **2.** To feel the loss or absence of. **II.** *i.* To fail of attainment; go wrong.

miss[1], *n.* The act of missing.

miss[2], *n.* A girl or an unmarried woman.

mis′sal, 1 mis′əl; 2 mĭs′al, *n.* *R. C. Ch.* The book containing the service for the mass.

mis′sile, } 1 mis′il; 2 mĭs′il. **I.** *a.* Adapted
mis′sils, } for throwing. **II.** *n.* A weapon intended to be thrown.

mis′sing, 1 mis′iŋ; 2 mĭs′ing, *pa.* Absent from the proper or accustomed place; lost.

mis′sion, 1 mish′ən; 2 mĭsh′on, *n.* **1.** The act of sending, as on special service, or the persons sent. **2.** The work of spreading religious principles.— **mis′sion-a-ry.** **I.** *a.* Pertaining to missions. **II.** *n.* [-RIES[z], *pl.*] A person sent to teach religion and do charitable work.

mis′sive, } 1 mis′iv; 2 mĭs′iv. **I.** *a.* Sent
mis′sivs, } or designed to be sent. **II.** *n.* That which is sent; a letter.

mist, 1 mist; 2 mĭst. **I**[d]. *vt. & vi.* To cloud with mist; be misty. **II.** *n.* Visible moisture in the atmosphere; vapor condensed on a surface; anything that dims or darkens.

mis-take′, 1 mis-tēk′; 2 mĭs-tāk′, *v.* [MIS-

TOOK′; MIS-TAK′EN.] **I.** *t.* To understand wrongly; take or choose wrongly. **II.** *i.* To be in error.— **mis-tak′a-bl(e**[p], *a.* — **mis-tak′en,** *pa.* **1.** Characterized by mistake; incorrect; being in error; erroneous. **2.** Misunderstood.

mis-take′, *n.* An error in action, judgment, perception, or impression; a blunder.

Mis′ter, 1 mis′tər; 2 mĭs′ter, *n.* Master: a title of address for a man: written *Mr.*

mis′tle-toe, } 1 mis′l-tō *or* miz′l-to; 2
mis′tl-toe[F], } mĭs′l-tō *or* mĭs̯′l-to, *n.* A parasitic evergreen shrub.

Mistletoe.

a, male flowers; *b,* female flowers.

mis-took′, 1 mis-tuk′; 2 mis-tōōk′, *imp. & obs. pp.* of MISTAKE, *v.*

mis′tress, 1 mis′tres; 2 mĭs′trĕs, *n.* **1.** A woman in authority. **2.** [M-] A title of a married woman: written *Mrs.* and pronounced *missis.* **3.** A woman who unlawfully fills the place of a wife. **4.** A woman skilled in something.

mis-trust′, 1 mis-trust′; 2 mĭs-trŭst′. **I**[d]. *vt.* To suspect; apprehend. **II.** *n.* Lack of trust; suspicion.— **mis-trust′ful,** *a.* **mis-trust′ful-ly,** *adv.*

mist′y, 1 mist′i; 2 mĭst′y, *a.* [MIST′I-ER; MIST′I-EST.] Dimmed by mist; hazy; obscure.— **mist′i-ly,** *adv.* **mist′i-ness,** *n.*

mis-un″der-stand′, 1 mis-un″der-stand′; 2 mĭs-ŭn″der-stănd′, *vt.* To understand wrongly; fail to understand.— **mis-un″der-stand′ing,** *n.* A misapprehension; disagreement.

mis-use′, } 1 mis-yūz′; 2 mĭs-yŭs̯′, *vt.* To
mis-uze[F], } use wrongly.

mis-use′, 1 mis-yūs′; 2 mĭs-yŭs′, *n.* Improper use; abuse.

mite[1], 1 mait; 2 mīt, *n.* A minute insect.

mite[2,1], *n.* A particle; small coin; trifle.

mi′ter, 1 mai′tər; 2 mī′ter. **I.** *vt. & vi.* **1.** To adorn with a miter. **2.** To join with or form a miter. **II.** *n.* **1.** A divided headdress, as of a bishop. **2.** *Mech.* A slanting joint. **mi′ter-joint″‡;** **mi′tre‡.** — **mi′tral,** *a.* Pertaining to or like a miter.

Miter.

mit′i-gate, 1 mit′i-gēt; 2 mĭt′i-gāt, *vt.* [-GAT′ED[d]; -GAT″ING.] To render milder; alleviate; assuage.— **mit′i-ga-bl(e**[p],

a.— **mit″i-ga′tion,** *n.*— **mit′i-ga″tiv(e⁸,** *a.*
— **mit′i-ga″tor,** *n.*

mi″trai″lleuse′, 1 mī″tra‴yōōz′; 2 mī″trä″-yöös′, *n.* A breech-loading machine gun for firing bullets.

mi′tre, *v. & n.* Same as MITER.

mitt, 1 mīt; 2 mĭt, *n.* **1.** A glove that does not extend over the fingers. **2.** A mitten.

mit′ten, 1 mit′n; 2 mĭt′n, *n.* A covering for the hand, leaving only the thumb separate.

mix, 1 miks; 2 mĭks, *vt. & vi.* [MIXED† or MIXT; MIX′ING.] To mingle; blend; associate.— **mix′er,** *n.*— **mix′ture,** *n.* The act of mixing; something mixed.

miz′zen, 1 miz′n; 2 mĭz′n, *a.* Pertaining to the mizzenmast.— **miz′zen-mast,** *n.* The mast next abaft the mainmast.

mne-mon′ic, 1 ni-mɒn′ik; 2 ne-mŏn′ie, *a.* Aiding the memory.— **mne-mon′ics,** *n.* The science of artificial memory.

moan, 1 mōn; 2 mōn. **I.** *vt. & vi.* To lament; utter a moan. **II.** *n.* A feeble or suppressed groan.

moat, 1 mōt; 2 mōt. **I**ᵈ. *vt.* To surround with a moat. **II.** *n.* A ditch on the outside of a fortress wall.

mob, 1 -mɒb; 2 mŏb. **I.** *vt.* [MOBBED, MOBD⁸; MOB′BING.] To assail, as by a mob. **II.** *n.* A rude, lawless crowd.

mo′bile, 1 mō′bil; 2 mō′bil, *a.* Easily
mo′bil⁸, moving; movable; fickle.—
mo-bil′i-ty, *n.* The state of being mobile.
— **mo′bil-ize,** *vt. & vi.* [-IZED; -IZ′ING.] To make or get ready for active service, as troops. **mo′bil-ise‡.**— **mo″bil-i-za′tion** or **-sa′tion,** *n.*

moc′ca-sin¹, 1 mɒk′ə-sin; 2 mŏe′a-sĭn, *n.* An Indian foot-covering of soft leather.

moc′ca-sin², *n.* A venomous snake of the southern United States.

mock†, 1 mɒk; 2 mŏk. **I.** *vt. & vi.* **1.** To mimic in derision; jeer. **2.** To deceive by false show. **II.** *a.* Merely imitating the reality; sham. **III.** *n.* A jeer; mockery.— **mock′er,** *n.*— **mock′er-y,** *n.* [MOCK′ER-IES², *pl.*] **1.** Mocking-bird. ¹/₂₁ Derisive mimicry. **2.** A false show; sham. **3.** Labor in vain.— **mock′ing-bird″,** *n.* A bird of the southern United States, noted for its power of mimicry.— **mock′ing-ly,** *adv.*

Mocking-bird. ¹/₂₁

mode, 1 mōd; 2 mōd, *n.* **1.** Manner of being or doing; way; prevailing style. **2.** *Gram.* The manner in which the action of a verb is stated.— **mo′dal,** *a.*

mod′el, 1 mɒd′el; 2 mŏd′ĕl. **I.** *vt. & vi.* [-ELED or -ELLED, -ELD⁸; -EL-ING or -EL-LING.] To form or be formed as a model; shape. **II.** *n.* A copy or pattern; example.— **mod′el-er,** *n.*

mod′er-ate, 1 mɒd′ər-ēt; 2 mŏd′er-āt, *vt. & vi.* [-AT″ED⁴; -AT″ING.] To make or become less intense or violent; allay.

mod′er-ate, 1 mɒd′ər-it; 2 mŏd′er-at, *a.* Keeping or kept within reasonable limits; medium; temperate: middling. **-ly,** *adv.* **-ness,** *n.*— **mod″er-a′tion,** *n.*— **mod′er-a″tor,** *n.* The presiding officer of a meeting.— **mod″er-a″tor-ship,** *n.*

mod′ern, 1 mɒd′ərn; 2 mŏd′ern. **I.** *a.* Pertaining to a recent period; not ancient. **II.** *n.* A person of modern times.— **mod′ern-ize** or **-ise,** *vt.* To render modern.— **mod′ern-ly,** *adv.*— **mod′ern-ness,** *n.*

mod′est, 1 mɒd′est; 2 mŏd′ĕst, *a.* Characterized by reserve, propriety, or purity; decorous; chaste; humble.— **mod′est-ly,** *adv.*— **mod′es-ty,** *n.* Decent reserve and propriety; decorum.

mod′i-cum, 1 mɒd′i-kum; 2 mŏd′i-ĕŭm, *n.* [MOD′I-CA, *pl.*] A moderate amount; a little.

mod′i-fy, 1 mɒd′i-fai; 2 mŏd′i-fȳ, *vt.* [-FIED; -FY″ING.] To change somewhat; vary; moderate.— **mod″i-fi-ca′tion,** *n.*— **mod′i-fi″er,** *n.*— **mod′i-fi″a-bl(e²,** *a.*

mod′ish, 1 mɒd′ish; 2 mŏd′ish, *a.* Fashionable. **-ly,** *adv.* **-ness,** *n.*

mod′u-late, 1 mɒd′yu-lēt or med′yu-lēt; 2 mŏj′ụ-lāt or mŏd′yu-lāt, *vt. & vi.* [-LAT″ED⁴; -LAT″ING.] To vary in tone, inflection, pitch, etc.— **mod″u-la′tion.** *n.* **1.** The act of modulating or condition of being modulated. **2.** *Mus.* The change from one key to another during a piece of music.— **mod′u-la″tor,** *n.*

Mo-gul′, 1 mo-gul′; 2 mo-gŭl′, *n.* **1.** A Mongol or Mongolian.— **the Great** or **Grand Mogul. 1.** The former emperor of Delhi. **2.** [g- m-] Any imposing or pretentious personage.

mo′hair, 1 mō′hār; 2 mō′hâr, *n.* The hair of the Angora goat, or a fabric made of it.

Mo-ham′me-dan, 1 mo-ham′i-dən; 2 mo-hăm′e-dan. **I.** *a.* Pertaining to Mohammed, an Arabian reformer and religious teacher (A. D. 570-632), or to his religion. **II.** *n.* A follower of Mohammed.— **Mo-ham′me-dan-ism,** *n.* The Mohammedan religion. [a small part.

moi′e-ty, 1 mɒi′i-ti; 2 mŏi′e-ty, *n.* Half;

moil, 1 mɒil; 2 mŏil, *vt. & vi.* **1.** To soil; be soiled. **2.** To weary; toil.

moist, 1 meist; 2 mŏist, *a.* Slightly wet; damp.— **mois′ten,** *vt. & vi.* To make or become moist.— **moist′ness,** *n.*— **mois′ture,** *n.* Slight sensible wetness.

mo′lar, 1 mō′lər; 2 mō′lar. **I.** *a.* Grinding; fitted for grinding. **II.** *n.* A double tooth.

mo-las′ses, 1 mo-las′ez; 2 mo-lăs′ĕs, *n.* A liquid drained off from crystallizable sugar.

mold¹, ⎰1 mōld; 2 mōld. **I**ᵈ. *vt.* To form
mould, ⎱in a mold. **II.** *n.* A form for shaping anything plastic; a model character.— **mold′er, mould′er,** *n.*

mold², ⎰**I**ᵈ. *vt.* To cover with mold.
mould, ⎱**II.** *n.* Rich earth; constituent material.

mold³, ⎰**I**ᵈ. *vt.* & *vi.* To become, or
mould, ⎱cause to become, moldy. **II.** *n.* Any fungous growth on food, clothing, etc.

mold′er, ⎰1 mōld′ər; 2 mōld′er, *vt.* & *vi.*
mould′er, ⎱To crumble, or cause to crumble.

mold′ing, ⎰1 mōld′ıŋ; 2 mōld′ing, *n.* **1.**
mould′ing, ⎱The act of shaping with a mold. **2.** Anything made in a mold. **3.** An ornamental strip on any structure.

mold′y, ⎰1 mōld′ı; 2 mōld′y, *a.* [MOLD′-
mould′y, ⎱ER; MOLD′I-EST.] Covered with mold; hence, old; musty.— **mold′i-ness,** *n.* The state of being moldy.

mole¹, 1 mōl; 2 mōl, *n.* A small spot on the skin; a stain or spot.

mole², *n.* A small, burrowing mammal.

mole³, *n.* A jetty or breakwater.

mol′e-cule, 1 mel′ı-kiūl; 2 mŏl′e-cūl, *n.* The smallest part of a substance that can exist separately; any small particle.— **mo-lec′u-lar,** 1 mo-lek′yu-lər; 2 mo-lĕc′yu-lar, *a.* Pertaining to or consisting of molecules.

Mole and its Burrow.   1/15

mo-lest′d, 1 mo-lest′; 2 mo-lĕst′, *vt.* To annoy; disturb; injure.— **mo″les-ta′tion,** *n.*

mol′li-fy, 1 mel′ı-fai; 2 mŏl′i-fī, *vt.* & *vi.* [-FIED; -FY′ING.] To make or grow mild, soft, or tender; mitigate.— **mol″li-fi-ca′tion,** *n.*— **mol′li-fi″er,** *n.*

mol′lusk, 1 mel′usk; 2 mŏl′usk, *n.* A bivalve, snail, slug, cuttlefish, or the like.— **mol-lus′can, a.** & *n.*— **mol-lus′cous,** *a.*

mo′loch, 1 mō′lek; 2 mō′lŏc, *n.* **1.** Any destructive influence or system. **2.** An Australian lizard. **3.** *Anc. Myth.* [M-] A god of the Phenicians, worshiped with human offerings, especially of children.

moltᵈ, ⎰1 mōlt; 2 mōlt, *vt.* To cast or
moultᵈ, ⎱slough off, as feathers.

mol′ten, 1 mōl′tn; 2 mōl′tn, *pa.* Melted; molded; cast.   [Much; very.

mol′to, 1 mōl′to; 2 mōl′to. [It.] *Mus.*

mo′ment, 1 mō′ment *or* -mant; 2 mō′ment, *n.* **1.** A very short period of time; an instant. **2.** Consequence or importance.— **mo′men-ta-ry,** *a.* Lasting but a moment.— **mo′men-ta-ri-ly,** *adv.*— **mo′men-ta-ri-ness,** *n.*— **mo-men′tous,** *a.* Of great importance; weighty. -**ly,** *adv.* -**ness,** *n.*

mo-men′tum, 1 mo-men′tum; 2 mo-mĕn′tŭm, *n.* [-TA, *pl.*] The impetus of a moving body.

mon′a-chism, 1 mən′ə-kizm; 2 mŏn′a-ċĭṣm, *n.* The monastic life.

mon′ad, 1 mən′ad; 2 mŏn′ăd, *n.* **1.** An indestructible unit; atom. **2.** *Biol.* A minute simple single-celled organism.

mon′arch, 1 mən′ərk; 2 mŏn′arc, *n.* A sovereign, as a king or emperor.— **mo-nar′chal,** *a.*— **mo-nar′chi-cal,** *a.* Pertaining to a monarch or monarchy. **mo-nar′chic†.**— **mon′arch-ist,** *n.* An advocate of monarchy.— **mon′arch-y,** *n.* [-ARCH-IES²ᶻ, *pl.*] Government by a monarch; a territory ruled by a monarch.

mon′as-ter-y, 1 mən′əs-ter-ı; 2 mŏn′as-ter-y, *n.* [-TER-IES²ᶻ, *pl.*] A dwelling-place occupied by monks.— **mo-nas′tic,** *a.* Pertaining to monks or monasteries. **mo-nas′ti-cal†.**— **mo-nas′ti-cism,** *n.* The monastic life.   [second day of the week.

Mon′day, 1 mʌn′dı; 2 mŏn′dy, *n.* The

mon′ey, ⎰1 mʌn′ı; 2 mŏn′y, *n.* [-EYS²ᶻ or
mun′eyᵖ, ⎱-IES²ᶻ, *pl.*] **1.** A common medium of exchange, as coin or bank-notes. **2.** Wealth; property.— **mon′e-ta-ry,** *a.* Pertaining to money; pecuniary.— **mon′eyed,** *a.* Possessed of money; wealthy. **mon′ied†.**

Mon′gol, 1 mən′gel; 2 mŏn′gŏl. *n.* One of the race inhabiting Mongolia, between China and Siberia; frequently applied to the Chinese generally.— **Mon′gol,** *a.*— **Mon-go′li-an,** *a.* & *n.*

mon′grel, 1 mʌŋ′grel; 2 mŏn′grŏl. **I.** *a.* Of mixed breed. **II.** *n.* An animal of mixed breed.

mo-ni′tion, 1 mo-nish′ən; 2 mo-nĭsh′on, *n.* Friendly counsel; admonition; warning.— **mon′i-tiv(e³,** *a.* Warning. **mon′i-to-ry†.**

mon′i-tor, 1 mən′ı-tər *or* -ter; 2 mŏn′i-tor, *n.* **1.** An adviser; a pupil in temporary charge of a class. **2.** A turreted ironclad with low, flat deck.— **mon″i-to′ri-al,** *a.* **1.** Pertaining to a monitor. **2.** Monitory.

monk, ⎰1 mʌŋk; 2 mŏŋk, *n.* A member
munkᵖ, ⎱of a monastic order; a hermit.

mon′key, ⎰1 mʌŋ′kı; 2 mŏŋ′ky. **I.** *vt.* &
mun′keyᵖ, ⎱*vi.* To ape; play pranks; med-

dle. **II.** *n.* A four=handed mammal; an ape.— **mon'key=wrench"**, *n.* A wrench with a movable jaw.

mon'o-, 1 men'o-; 2 mŏn'o-. One; single: a combining form; as, *monosyllable.*

Monkey=wrench.

mon'o-chro-mat'ic, 1 men'o-krō-mat'ik; 2 mŏn"o-erō-măt'ie, *a.* Of one color.

mon'o-cle, 1 men'o-kl; 2 mŏn'o-el, *n.* An eye=glass for one eye.

mo-noc'u-lar, 1 mo-nek'yu-lər; 2 mo-nŏe'yu-lar, *a.* **1.** One=eyed. **2.** Pertaining to or used for one eye: opposed to *binocular.* **mo-noc'u-lous‡.**

mo-nog'a-my, 1 mo-nŏg'a-mi; 2 mo-nŏg'a-my, *n.* Marriage to but one husband or wife.— **mo-nog'a-mist**, *n.*— **mo-nog'a-mous**, *a.*

mon'o-gram, 1 men'o-gram; 2 mŏn'o-grăm, *n.* A character made up of interwoven letters.

mon'o-graph, } 1 men'o-graf; 2
mon'o-grafᴾ, } mŏn'o-gráf, *n.* A writing on a single subject.— **mon"o-graph'ic**, *a.* **-i-cal'‡.**

Monogram.

mon'o-lith, 1 men'o-lith; 2 mŏn'o-lith, *n.* A single block of stone.— **mon"o-lith'ic**, *a.* **mon"o-lith'al‡.**

mon'o-log, } 1 men'o-leg; 2 mŏn'o-lŏg,
mon'o-logue, } *n.* A soliloquy.

mon'o - ma'ni - a, 1 men'o-mē'ni-ə; 2 mŏn'o-mā'ni-a, *n.* Insanity as regards one subject.— **mon"o-ma'ni-ac**, *n.* A person afflicted with monomania.

mon"o-met'al-lism, 1 men'o-met'əl-izm; 2 mŏn"o-mĕt'al-lism, *n.* The theory or practise of using one metal only, especially gold, as a standard of value.— **mon"o-met'al-ist**, *a.* & *n.* **-al-list‡.**

mon'o-plane, 1 men'o-plēn; 2 mŏn'o-plān, *n.* An aeroplane with but one supporting plane. See plate of AEROPLANES.

mo-nop'o-ly, 1 mo-nep'o-li; 2 mo-nŏp'o-ly, *n.* [-LIES², *pl.*] The exclusive control of a particular traffic, or the persons holding it.— **mo-nop'o-list**, *n.* One who possesses a monopoly.— **mo-nop'o-lize**, *vt.* To secure a monopoly of; control; engross.— **mo-nop'o-liz"er** or **-lis"er**, *n.*

mon'o-syl-la-ble, } 1 men'o-sil-a-bl; 2
mon'o-syl-la-blᴾ, } mŏn'o-sўl-a-bl, *n.* A word of one syllable.— **mon"o-syl-lab'ic**, 1 men"o-sı-lab'ik; 2 mŏn"o-sy-lăb'ie, *a.* Composed of one syllable or of words of one syllable.

mon'o-the"ism, 1 men'o-thī"izm; 2 mŏn'o-thē"ism, *n.* The doctrine that there is but one God.— **mon'o-the"ist**, *n.*— **mon"-o-the-is'tic**, *a.*

mon'o-tone, 1 men'o-tōn; 2 mŏn'o-tōn, *n.* Sameness of utterance or tone.— **mo-not'o-nous**, *a.* Not varied in tone; tiresomely uniform. **-ly**, *adv.*— **mo-not'o-ny**, *n.* Tiresome uniformity.

mon-sieur', 1 ma-syū'; 2 mo-syû', *n.* [MES-SIEURS', *pl.*] **1.** A French title of respect, equivalent to *Mr.* and *Sir:* capitalized when used with a proper name: abbreviated *M.* **2.** [M-] *French Hist.* A title of a French king's eldest brother. **3.** A Frenchman.

mon-soon', 1 men-sūn'; 2 mŏn-sōōn', *n.* **1.** A wind that blows steadily along the Asiatic coast of the Pacific. **2.** A trade-wind.

mon'ster, 1 men'stər; 2 mŏn'ster, *n.* **1.** Anything hideous or abnormal; one atrociously wicked or cruel. **2.** A very large person or thing.— **mon-stros'i-ty**, *n.* [-TIES², *pl.*] Anything monstrous; the character of being monstrous.— **mon'strous**, *a.* Unnatural; huge; hideous; horrible. **-ly**, *adv.* **-ness**, *n.*

month, 1 munth; 2 mônth, *n.* **1.** One of the 12 parts into which the year is divided. **2.** The time of the revolution of the moon.— **month'ly**. **I.** *a.* Continuing a month; done in a month; happening once a month. **II.** *n.* [MONTH"LIES², *pl.*] A monthly publication. **III.** *adv.* Once a month.

mon'u-ment, 1 men'yu-ment *or* -mənt; 2 mŏn'yu-ment, *n.* Something erected as a memorial of a person or of an event; any enduring memorial.— **mon"u-men'tai**, *a.* Pertaining to or like a monument; memorial; grand.

-mony, *suffix.* Used to form nouns from other nouns or from adjectives or verbs; as, testi*mony.*

mood¹, 1 mūd; 2 mōōd, *n.* Same as MODE.

mood², *n.* **1.** Temporary state of the mind; caprice; humor. **2.** The state of being moody.— **mood'y**, *a.* [MOOD'I-ER; MOOD'I-EST.] Given to capricious moods; petulant; melancholy.— **mood'i-ly**, *adv.*— **mood'i-ness**, *n.*

moon, 1 mūn; 2 mōōn, *n.* **1.** A satellite revolving about a planet, as the earth. **2.** A lunar month: 27 days, 8 hours.— **moon'beam"**, *n.* A ray of moonlight.— **moon'light"**, *n.* **I.** *a.* Pertaining to the light of the moon; illuminated by moonlight. **II.** *n.* The light of the moon.— **moon'shine"**, *n.* **1.** Moonlight. **2.** Empty nonsense. **3.** [Local, U. S., & Prov. Eng.] Smuggled or illicitly distilled spirits.— **moon'shin"er**, *n.* An illicit distiller; a smuggler.— **moon'struck"**, *a.* Lunatic.

moor, 1 mūr; 2 mōōr, *vt.* & *vi.* To fasten, as a vessel, to the shore or bottom; tie up;

anchor.— **moor'ing**, *n.* The act of mooring; the place where or fastening by which a vessel or the like is moored.— **mooring=mast**, *n. Aero.* A strong mast=like steel construction, of girderage, steadied by side=stays, to the head of which air=ships may be moored. It consists of several superimposed stages equipped with ladders that lead to a platform at the top.

moor[1], *n.* [Gt. Brit.] A tract of waste land, or a tract kept for hunting.— **moor'ish**[1], *a.* Pertaining to a moor; barren.— **moor'land**, *n.* A moor or marsh.— **moor'y**, *a.*

Moor[2], *n.* One of the mixed race inhabiting Morocco and the adjacent coast.— **Moor'ish**[2], *a.* Pertaining to the Moors.

moose, 1 mūs; 2 mōōs, *n.* [MOOSE, *pl.*] A variety of the elk, of northern North America.

moot, 1 mūt; 2 mōōt. I[d]. *vt.* To debate; argue. II. *a.* Open to discussion.— **a=bl**(e[r], *a.*— **moot'court'**, *n.* A court for the trial of a fictitious case, as a means of practise.

Moose. 1/140

mop, 1 mǝp; 2 mǒp. I. *vt.* [MOPPED[t], MOPT[s]; MOP'PING.] To wipe with a mop. II. *n.* **1.** A piece of cloth, attached to a handle, for washing floors, etc. **2.** A tangled mass of hair.— **mop'board''**, *n.* A board skirting the lower edge of the wall of a room.

mope, 1 mōp; 2 mōp, *v.* [MOPED[t]; MOP'-ING.] I. *t.* To make dull. II. *i.* To be dull and melancholy.— **mop'ing=ly**, *adv.*— **mop'ish**, *a.* Dejected.— **mop'ish=ness**, *n.*

mor'al, 1 mǝr'ǝl; 2 mǒr'al. I. *a.* **1.** Pertaining to right and wrong. **2.** Right; virtuous; chaste. II. *n.* **1.** The lesson of a fable or the like. **2.** *pl.* Conduct or behavior; ethics.— **mor'al=ist**, *n.* **1.** A teacher of morals. **2.** One who practises morality without religion.— **mo=ral'i=ty**, *n.* [-TIES[z], *pl.*] The doctrine of man's moral duties; ethics; moral conduct; virtue.— **mor'al=ize**, *v.* [-IZED; -IZ'ING.] I. *t.* To apply to a moral purpose. II. *i.* To make moral reflections.— **mor'al=ly**, *adv.* [fidence.

mo=rale', 1 mo=rǎl'; 2 mo=rǎl', *n.* Confidence.

mo=rass', 1 mo=ras'; 2 mo=rǎs', *n.* Marsh.

mor''a=to'ri=um, 1 mor''a=tō'rī=um; 2 mǒr''a=tō'rī=ŭm, *n.* An emergency act of legislation authorizing a bank, debtor, etc., to suspend payments for a given period.

mor'bid, 1 mǝr'bɪd; 2 mǒr'bid, *a.* Diseased; abnormal. **-ly**, *adv.* **-ness**, *n.*

mor'dant, 1 mër'dǝnt; 2 môr'dant. I. *a.* Biting; pungent; fixing. II. *n.* A substance for fixing dye.

more, 1 mōr; 2 mōr. I. *a. compar.* [*Positive* wanting; MOST, *superl.*] Greater in amount, degree, number, etc.; additional. II. *n.* A greater quantity, amount, etc.; an added amount. III. *adv.* **1.** To a greater extent or degree. **2.** In addition.

more=o'ver, 1 mōr=ō'vǝr; 2 mōr=ō'ver, *adv.* Besides; further; likewise.

morgue, 1 mȯrg; 2 môrg, *n.* A place where corpses of persons found dead are exposed for identification. [*a.* Dying.

mor'i=bund, 1 mer'i=bund; 2 mǒr'i=bŭnd,

Mor'mon, 1 mer'mǝn; 2 môr'mon, *n.* One of a sect organized in America in 1830, and, until 1890, practising polygamy: named from *Mormon*, a character in the Book of Mormon, the sacred book of the sect.— **Mor'mon=ism**, *n.*

morn, 1 mërn; 2 môrn, *n.* The morning.

morn'ing, 1 mërn'ɪŋ; 2 môrn'ing. I. *a.* Pertaining to the early part of the day. II. *n.* The early part of the day; any early stage.— **morn'ing=glo''ry**, *n.* A twining plant with funnel=shaped flowers.

mo=roc'co, 1 mo=rek'o; 2 mo=rǒe'o, *n.* Leather made from goatskin, and tanned with sumac. [minded person.

mo'ron, 1 mō'rǝn; 2 mō'rǒn, *n.* A feeble=

mo=rose', 1 mo=rōs'; 2 mo=rōs', *a.* Surly; sullen and austere.— **mo=rose'ness**, *n.*

Mor'pheus, 1 mër'fīūs *or* mër'fī=us; 2 môr'fŭs *or* môr'fī=ŭs, *n.* Sleep: named from *Morpheus*, the Roman god of dreams.

mor'phin, } 1 mër'fin, -fin *or* -fīn; 2 môr'-
mor'phine, } fin, -fin *or* -fīn, *n.* A narcotic prepared from opium. **mor'phi=a‡**.

mor'ris, 1 mer'ɪs; 2 môr'is, *n.* An old=fashioned rustic dance in England. **mor'rice‡**.

mor'row, 1 mer'o; 2 môr'o. I. *a.* Next succeeding, as a day. II. *n.* **1.** The first day after the present or after a day specified. **2.** Morning. [food; small piece.

mor'sel, 1 mër'sel; 2 môr'sĕl, *n.* A bit of

mor'tal, 1 mër'tal; 2 môr'tal. I. *a.* **1.** Subject to death; human. **2.** Deadly; fatal. II. *n.* A human being.— **mor=tal'i=ty**, *n.* [-TIES[z], *pl.*] **1.** The quality of being mortal. **2.** Death; the death=rate. **3.** Humanity.— **mor'tal=ly**, *adv.* Fatally; extremely.

mor'tar[1], 1 mër'tǝr; 2 môr'tar, *n.* **1.** A vessel in which substances are pounded. **2.** A short cannon with a large bore.

mor'tar[2], *n.* A mixture of sand and lime for joining bricks, etc.; a cement.

mort'gage, 1 mȯr'gɑj; 2 môr'gag. I. *vt.* [-GAGED; -GAG=ING.] To make over (prop-

erty) by mortgage; pledge. **II.** *n* A pledge of property as security for a loan. — **mort″ga·gee′**, *n.* The one to whom a mortgage is given.— **mort′ga·gor**, *n.* A person who mortgages property. **mort′gag·er‡.**

mor′ti·fy, 1 môr′tɪ·faɪ; 2 môr′tɪ·fī, *v.* [-FIED; -FY″ING.] **I.** *t.* **1.** To humiliate; shame; vex. **2.** To subdue by fasting, etc., as the passions. **3.** To destroy the organic texture of. **II.** *i.* **1.** To lose vitality, as living flesh; gangrene. **2.** To be subdued.— **mor″ti·fi·ca′tion,** *n.* **1.** The state of being mortified; death of one part of a living body. **2.** That which mortifies. **mor′tice‡.**

mor′tise, } 1 môr′tɪs; 2 môr′tɪs. **I.** *vt.*
mor′tisˢ, } [-TISED^d, -TISTˢ;
-TIS·ING.] To make a mortise in; join by a mortise. **II.** *n.* A space hollowed out to receive a tenon. **mor′tice‡.**

mor′tu·a·ry, 1 môr′ċhu-
[or ‑tiu‑]ə‑rɪ; 2 môr′ċhu-
[or ‑tū‑]ā‑rɪ. **I.** *a.* Pertaining to burial. **II.** *n.* A place for the reception of the dead.

Mortise and Tenon.

mo·sa′ic‡, 1 mo·zē′ɪk; 2 mo·sā′ik. **I.** *a.* Pertaining to inlaid work. **II.** *n.* Inlaid work, forming a pattern or picture.

Mo·sa′ic², *a.* Pertaining to Moses, the Hebrew leader (1571–1451 B. C.).

Mos′lem, 1 mɒz′lem; 2 mŏs′lĕm. *a.* & *n.* Mohammedan. [temple.

mosque, 1 mɒsk; 2 mŏsk, *n.* A Moslem

mos·qui′to, 1 mas·kī′to; 2 mos·kī′to, *n.* [TOESᶻ, *pl.*] A two-winged blood-sucking insect.

moss, 1 mɒs; 2 mŏs, *n.* A delicate cryptogamous plant which grows on the ground, on rocks, etc.— **moss″·ag″ate,** *n.* *Mineral.* Quartz containing mineral oxids, arranged in moss-like forms.— **m.·rose,** *n.* A cultivated variety of rose with a mossy calyx and stem. — **m.·trooper,** *n.* A bandit of the borders of England and Scotland (17th cent.); hence, any bandit.— **moss′y,** *a.* Overgrown with, or like, moss.— **mos′si·ness,** *n.*

most, 1 mōst; 2 mōst. **I.** *a.* Consisting of the greatest number, amount, or quantity; greatest. **II.** *adv.* **1.** In the highest degree. **2.** Mostly.— **most′ly,** *adv.* For the most part; principally. [speck.

mote, 1 mōt; 2 mōt, *n.* A minute particle.

moth, 1 mɒθ; 2 mŏth, *n.* **1.** A nocturnal insect resembling a butterfly. **2.** An insect or larva that destroys woolen fabrics or furs.— **moth″·eat″en,** *a.*

moth′er¹, 1 mʊth′ər; 2 mŏth′er, *vt.* To act as a mother toward.

moth′er², *vi.* To form mother, as vinegar.

moth′er, *a.* Native; maternal.

moth′er¹, *n.* A female parent.— **moth′er·hood,** *n.* The state of being a mother.— **moth′er·in·law″,** *n.* The mother of one's spouse.— **moth′er·less,** *a.*— **moth′er·ly,** *a.* Resembling or pertaining to a mother.— **moth′er·li·ness,** *n.*— **moth′er·of·pearl″,** *n.* The hard, iridescent inner layer of a shell, as of the pearl-oyster.

moth′er², *n.* A stringy substance formed in fermenting vinegar; dregs.— **moth′er·y,** *a.*

mo′tion, 1 mō′shan; 2 mō′shon. **I.** *vi.* & *vi.* To make a movement. **II.** *n.* **1.** Change of position; a movement; gesture. **2.** A proposition to be voted on. **-less,** *a.*

mo′tion·pic″ture, *n.* A rapidly changing series of pictures thrown on a screen.

mo′tive, } 1 mō′tɪv; 2 mō′tiv. **I.** *a.* Having
mo′tivˢ, } *ing* power to move; causing motion. **II.** *n.* That which incites to action; incentive; impulse; design; purpose.

mot′ley, 1 mɒt′lɪ; 2 mŏt′lɪ, *a.* Variegated; party-colored; heterogeneous.

mo′tor, 1 mō′tər *or* -ter; 2 mō′tor, *n.* One who or that which produces motion, as a machine.— **mo′tor·boat, ·bus, ·car, ·cycle,** *n.* A boat, an omnibus, a car, or a bicycle propelled by motor-power.— **mo′tor·ist,** *n.* The manager of a motor a chauffeur.— **m.·man,** *n.* One who operates a motor.— **mo′tor·ship,** *n.* A vessel, as a passenger-ship, propelled by motor-power derived from burning oil.

mot′tle, 1 mɒt′l; 2 mŏt′l, *vt.* [MOT′TLED; MOT′TLING.] To spot with different colors.

mot′to, 1 mɒt′o; 2 mŏt′o, *n.* A word or sentence expressing rule of conduct.

mound, 1 maund; 2 mound, *n.* A heap of earth; bank; hillock.

mountᵈ, 1 maunt; 2 mount, *vt.* & *vi.* **1.** To ascend. **2.** To set or get on horseback. **3.** To place on a mounting; equip. **4.** To amount.— **mount′ing,** *n.* **1.** The act of mounting. **2.** That on which something, as a picture, is mounted.

mount¹, *n.* A mountain.

mount², *n.* A saddle-horse; a mounting.

moun′tain, 1 maun′tɪn; 2 moun′tin, *n.* A lofty, rocky elevation.— **moun″tain·eer′,** *n.* One who dwells among or climbs mountains. — **moun′tain·ous,** *a.* **1.** Abounding in mountains. **2.** Like a mountain; huge.

moun′te·bank, 1 maun′tɪ·baŋk; 2 moun′te·băŋk, *n.* A vender of quack medicines; charlatan.

mourn, 1 mōrn; 2 mōrn, *vt.* & *vi.* To sorrow for; grieve; lament.— **mourn′er,** *n.* One who mourns; one who attends a funeral. — **mourn′ful,** *a.* Indicating grief; sad; sorrowful; melancholy; exciting sorrow. **-ly,** *adv.* **-ness,** *n.*— **mourn′ing,** *n.* The manifesting of grief, as in somber dress.

mouse, } 1 mauz; 2 mous, *vt. & vi.* [MOUSED;
mouz⁰, } MOUS'ING.] To hunt for slyly;
prowl; catch mice.— **mous'er,** *n.*

mouse, 1 maus; 2 mous, *n.* [MICE, 1 mais;
2 mi̭ç, *pl.*] A small rodent.

mouth, 1 mauth; 2 mouth, *vt. & vi.* To
speak unnaturally; rant; grimace.

mouth, 1 mauth; 2 mouth, *n.* The orifice
at which food is taken; any opening or
orifice.— **mouth'er,** *n.*— **mouth'ful,** *n.* **1.**
The amount taken into the mouth at one
time. **2.** A small quantity.— **mouth'piece',**
n. **1.** That part of any instrument that is
applied to the mouth. **2.** A spokesman.

move, 1 mūv; 2 mov, *vt. & vi.* [MOVED;
MOV'ING.] **1.** To change or cause to
change place; act; stir; affect; propose;
make a motion; pass; go. **2.** To take
action. **3.** To make progress.— **mov'a-**
ble⁰. **I.** *a.* Capable of being moved. **II.**
n. Anything that can be moved.— **mov'a-**
bil'i-ty, *n.* **mov'a-ble-ness‡.**— **mov'a-**
bly, *adv.*— **mov'er,** *n.*— **mov'ing. I.** *pa.* **1.**
Causing to move; effective; influential. **2.**
Exciting the feelings; touching. **II.** *n.* The act
of moving; change of residence with removal
of household goods, etc.— **mov'ing-ly,** *adv.*—
mov'ing pic'ture, see MOTION-PICTURE.

move, *n.* The act of moving; movement.
— **move'ment,** *n.* **1.** Change of place or
position; rate of moving. **2.** An arrangement of moving parts, as in a watch.

mov'ie, 1 mūv'ı; 2 mov'ı, *n.* [Colloq. U. S.] A
motion-picture show. Used commonly in
the plural, **the movies.**

mow¹, 1 mō; 2 mō, *vt. & vi.* [MOWED,
MOWD⁸; MOWN;
MOW'ING.] To cut
down, as grass; cut
grass from.— **mow'-**
er, *n.* One who or
that which mows; a
machine for mowing
grass.
mow'-
ing-ma-
chine'‡.

mow¹, 1 mō;
2 mau; 2
mow, *n.*
Hay or
grain
stored
in a barn; the place of storage.— **mow²,** *vt.*

Mower.

c, crank-wheel for driving the
knife; *f,* finger-bar; *i,* internal gear;
l, lifting-lever; *lw,* leading-wheel; *t,*
track-clearer.

mow², 1 mō *or* mau; 2 mō *or* mow, *n.*
A grimace.— **mow³,** *vi.*

much, 1 mṷch; 2 mṷch. **I.** *a.* Great in
quantity or amount. **II.** *n.* **1.** A large
quantity. **2.** An important thing. **III.**
adv. **1.** In a great degree. **2.** For the
most part.

mu'ci-lage, 1 miū'sı-lıj; 2 mū'çi-lag̣, *n.* An
adhesive solution of gum in water.— **mu''ci-**
lag'i-nous, *a.* **-ly,** *adv.* **-ness,** *n.*

muck, 1 muk; 2 muk, *n.* Moist manure;
filth.— **muck'y,** *a.*— **muck'i-ness,** *n.*

mu'cous, 1 miū'kus; 2 mū'eus, *a.* Secreting mucus; pertaining to or like mucus.

mu'cus, 1 miū'kus; 2 mū'eus, *n.* A gummy
substance, as in animal⁰ or plant⁰tissues.

mud, 1 mud; 2 mṷd, *n.* Wet and sticky
earth; mire.— **mud'dy. I.** *vt.* [MUD'DIED;
MUD'DY-ING.] To make muddy; muddle.
II. *a.* [MUD'DI-ER; MUD'DI-EST.] Bespat-
tered or beclouded with mud; turbid; confused.— **mud'di-ly,** *adv.*— **mud'di-ness,** *n.*
— **mud'dy-ish,** *a.*

mud'dle, } 1 mud'l; 2 mṷd'l. **I.** *vt. & vi.*
mud'l⁰, } [MUD'DLED; MUD'DLING.] **1.** To
make turbid; confuse, or be confused, as
by drink; mix. **II.** *n.* A muddy or confused condition.

muff¹, 1 muf; 2 mṷf, *vt. & vi.* To do (some-
muf⁰, } act) clumsily; bungle; blunder.

muff¹, *n.* A warm covering, open at both
ends, for the hands.

muff², *n.* A bungling action; failure, as
in catching a ball; a bungler.

muf'fin, 1 muf'ın; 2 mṷf'in, *n.* A light
spongy cake.

muf'fle, } 1 muf'l; 2 mṷf'l, *vt.* [MUF'FLED;
muf'l⁰, } MUF'LD⁰; MUF'FLING.] To wrap up
so as to deaden sound.— **muf'fler,** *n.* **1.** A
wrap for the head or throat. **2.** A mechanism
for deadening sound, as of escaping gases from
a motor⁰engine.

mug, 1 mug; 2 mṷg̣, *n.* A drinking⁰cup
with a handle and no lip.

mug'gy, 1 mug'ı; 2 mṷg̣'y, *a.* [MUG'GI-ER;
MUG'GI-EST.] Warm, moist, and close.

mu-lat'to, 1 miu-lat'o; 2 mū-lă̤t'o, *n.* One
of mingled white and negro parentage.

mul'ber''ry, 1 mul'ber'ı; 2 mul'bĕr''y, *n.*
[-RIES², *pl.*] A tree
bearing a berry⁰like
fruit; the fruit.

mulch, 1 mulch;
2 mulch. **I⁰.** *vt.*
To cover with
mulch. **II.** *n.*
Any loose material,
as straw, spread
about plants, to
protect their
roots.

Black Mulberry.

a, the fruit; *b,* a lobed leaf.

mulct, 1 mulkt;
2 mulkt. **I⁰.** *vt.*
To fine. **II.** *n.* A fine.— **mulct'a-ble,** *a.*

mule, 1 miūl; 2 mūl, *n.* The offspring of
a jackass and a mare; any hybrid; a spin-

ning-machine.— **mu″le-teer′**, *n.* A mule-driver.— **mul′ish**, *a.* Like a mule; stubborn.— **mul′ish-ly**, *adv.*— **mul′ish-ness**, *n.*

mull, 1 mʊl; 2 mŭl, *vt.* To heat and spice, as wine.

mull, *n.* A thin, soft, cotton dress-goods.

mul′len, 1 mʊl′en; 2 mŭl′ĕn, *n.* A tall, stout weed. **mul′lein:**.

mul′let, 1 mʊl′et; 2 mŭl′ĕt, *n.* A food-fish with silvery sides.

mul′lion, 1 mʊl′yən; 2 mŭl′yon, *n.* A division-piece between window-lights or panels.

mul′ti-, 1 mʊl′tɪ-; 2 mŭl′ti-. A combining form signifying many; as, *multitone*.

mul″ti-fa′ri-ous, 1 mʊl″tɪ-fē′rɪ-ʊs; 2 mŭl″ti-fā′ri-ŭs, *a.* Having great variety.

mul′ti-form, 1 mʊl′tɪ-fôrm; 2 mŭl′ti-fôrm, *a.* Having many forms.— **mul″ti-for′mi-ty**, *n.*

mul′ti-ply, 1 mʊl′tɪ-plɑɪ; 2 mŭl′ti-plȳ, *vt. & vi.* [-PLIED; -PLY″ING.] **1.** To make or become more numerous. **2.** To take as many times as there are units in another number.— **mul′ti-ple.** **I.** *a.* Consisting of more than one; manifold. **II.** *n.* *Math.* A quantity exactly divisible by another.— **mul′ti-pli″a-bl**(eᴾ, *a.* That may be multiplied. **mul′ti-pli-ca-bl**(erᶜ.— **mul″ti-pli-cand′**, *n.* *Math.* A number multiplied, or to be multiplied, by another.— **mul″ti-pli-ca′tion**, *n.* The process of multiplying.— **mul″ti-plic′i-ty**, *n.* The condition of being manifold or various.— **mul′ti-pli″er**, *n.* One who or that which multiplies; the number by which another number is multiplied.

mul′ti-tude, 1 mʊl′tɪ-tiūd; 2 mŭl′ti-tūd, *n.* **1.** The state of being many. **2.** A large number of people or things; concourse.— **mul″ti-tu′di-nous**, *a.* Consisting of a vast number.

mum, 1 mʊm; 2 mŭm. **I.** *a.* Saying nothing; silent. **II.** *interj.* Be silent! hush!

mum′ble, } 1 mʊm′bl; 2 mŭm′bl, *vt. & vi.*
mum′biᴾ, } [MUM′BL(E)Dᴾ; MUM′BLING.] To mutter.— **mum′bler**, *n.*

mum′mer, 1 mʊm′ər; 2 mŭm′er, *n.* One who makes sport in a mask.— **mum′mer-y**, *n.* [-IESᶻ, *pl.*] **1.** A masked performance. **2.** Hypocritical parade.

mum′my, 1 mʊm′ɪ; 2 mŭm′y, *n.* [MUM′-MIESᶻ, *pl.*] A body embalmed in the ancient Egyptian manner.

mump′ish, 1 mʊmp′ɪ̌ʃ; 2 mŭmp′ish, *a.* Sullen; sulky; petulant. **-ly**, *adv.* **-ness**, *n.*

mumps, 1 mʊmps; 2 mŭmps, *n. pl.* An epidemic swelling of the parotid glands.

munch¹, 1 mʊnʧ; 2 mŭnch, *vt. & vi.* To chew noisily.

mun′dane, 1 mʊn′dēn; 2 mŭn′dān, *a.* Earthly.— **mun′dane-ly**, *adv.*

mu-nic′i-pal, 1 miu-nɪs′ɪ-pəl; 2 mū′nĭç′i-pal, *a.* Pertaining to a town or city or to local government.— **mu-nic″i-pal′i-ty**, *n.* [-TIESᶻ, *pl.*] An incorporated borough, town, or city.

mu-nif′i-cent, 1 miu-nɪf′ɪ-sent; 2 mū-nĭf′i-çĕnt, *a.* Extraordinarily generous; bountiful. **-ly**, *adv.*— **mu-nif′i-cence**, *n.*

mu′ni-ment, 1 miū′nɪ-ment *or* -mənt; 2 mū′ni-ment, *n.* A defense; stronghold; title-deed.

mu-ni′tion, 1 miu-nɪ̌ʃ′ən; 2 mū-nĭsh′on, *n.* Ammunition; war-material.

mu′ral, 1 miū′ral; 2 mū′ral, *a.* Pertaining to, like, or supported by a wall.

mur′der, 1 mŭr′dər; 2 mûr′der. **I.** *vt. & vi.* To kill with evil intent; commit murder; spoil; mar; destroy. **II.** *n.* The wrongful and intentional killing of one human being by another.— **mur′der-er**, *n.*— **mur′-der-ess**, *n. fem.*— **mur′der-ous**, *a.* Pertaining to murder; destructive; inclined to murder.— **mur′der-ous-ly**, *adv.*

mu″ri-at′ic, 1 miū″rɪ-at′ɪk; 2 mū″ri-ăt′ic, *a.* Pertaining to chlorin.

murk′y, 1 mɜrk′ɪ; 2 mûrk′y, *a.* [MURK′-I-ER; MURK′I-EST.] Darkened; hazy; obscure.— **murk′i-ness**, *n.*

mur′mur, 1 mɜr′mur; 2 mûr′mur. **I.** *vt. & vi.* To utter in a low, suppressed tone; to complain in low tones; mutter; mumble. **II.** *n.* A complaint uttered in a half-articulate voice; a low, repeated sound.— **mur′mur-er**, *n.*

mur′rain, 1 mɜr′ɪn; 2 mŭr′in, *n.* An epidemic disease of cattle; plague.

mus′cle, } 1 mʊs′l; 2 mŭs′l, *n.* Contractile tissue, by which bodily movement is effected.— **mus′cu-lar**, *a.* Pertaining to muscles; strong; powerful.— **mus″cu-lar′i-ty**, *n.*

mus′cle², *n.* Same as MUSSEL.

Mus′co-vite, 1 mʊs′ko-vɑɪt; 2 mŭs′co-vīt, *a. & n.* Of or relating to Muscovy or Moscow, a principality of central Russia; hence, Russian; a Russian.

muse, 1 miūz; 2 mūz, *vt. & vi.* [MUSED; MUS′ING.] To meditate upon; ponder; indulge in reverie.— **muse¹**, *n.* Contemplative thought.— **mus′ing-ly**, *adv.*

Muse², *n.* **1.** [M- *or* m-] The inspiring power of poetry. **2.** One of the nine goddesses of poetry, art, and science.

mu-se′um, 1 miu-zī′um; 2 mū-sē′ŭm, *n.* A place devoted to works of art, curiosities, etc.; also, the collection itself.

mush, 1 mʊʃ; 2 mŭsh, *n.* Thick porridge; anything soft and pulpy.

1: ar̃tistic, ûrt; fat, fãre; fast; get, prēy; hit, police; obey, gō; net, ẽr; full, rūle; but, būrn.

2: ärt, āpe, făt, fâre, fȧst, whạt, ạll; mē, gĕt, prey, fẽrn; hĭt, īce; ĩ=ē; ĩ=ĕ; gō, nŏt, ôr, wọn,

mush′room, 1 mush′rūm; 2 mŭsh′rŏŏm.
I. a. Of or like mushrooms; short=lived.
II. n. Bot. A rapidly growing edible fungus: certain poisonous varieties are called
toadstools.

mu′sic, 1 miū′zık; 2 mū′şie, n. The
rhythmic combination of tones; pleasing
succession of sounds; science of harmony.
— **mu′sl=cal,** a. Pertaining to or producing
music; melodious. **-ly,** adv.— **mu-sl′cian,**
n. One skilled in music.

mu″si-cale′, 1 miū″zı-käl′; 2 mū′şi-eäl′, n.
An informal concert, as at a private house.
mu′sl=cal‡.

musk, 1 musk; 2 mŭsk, n. A substance
of a penetrating
odor, obtained
from the musk=
deer; also, the
odor.— **musk′-
rat″,** n. A North=
American aquatic
rodent, yielding a
valuable fur, and
secreting a sub-
stance with a
musky odor.— **musk′rose″,** n. A cultivated
climbing rose with large white flowers.—
musk′y, a.— **musk′l-ly,** adv.— **musk′l-
ness,** n.

American Muskrat. 1/18

mus′ket, 1 mus′ket; 2 mŭs′kĕt, n. A
former smooth=bore military hand=gun.
— **mus′ket-ry,** n. **1.** Muskets collectively.
2. The science of firing small arms.

musk=mel″on, 1 musk′mel″ən; 2 mŭsk′mĕl″-
on, n. The juicy edible fruit of a trailing
herb, or the plant. Its most common variety is the cantaloup.   [cotton fabric.

mus′lin, 1 muz′lin; 2 mŭş′lin, n. A fine

mus-qui′to, n. Same as MOSQUITO.

mus′sel, 1 mus′l; 2 mŭs′l, n. A small
bivalve mollusk. **mus′cle‡.**

Mus′sul-man, 1 mus′ul-mən; 2 mŭs′ŭl-
man, a. & n. Moslem.

must¹, 1 must; 2 mŭst, vi. [Auxiliary.]
1. To be compelled. **2.** To be necessary.

must²ᵈ, vt. & vi. To make or become
musty.

must¹, n. Mustiness; mold.

must², n. The expressed unfermented
juice of the grape.

mus-tache′, 1 mus-tash′; 2 mŭs-täçh′, n.
The hair on the upper lip of men.

mus′tang, 1 mus′taŋ; 2 mŭs′tăng, n.
The half=wild horse of the American plains.

mus′tard, 1 mus′tərd; 2 mŭs′tard, n.
Either of two annual herbs with yellow
flowers and pods of roundish seeds; also,
the pungent seed, or a condiment, etc.,
prepared from it.

mus′ter, 1 mus′tər; 2 mŭs′ter. **I.** vt. & vi.
To summon and gather together; be assembled. **II.** n. An assemblage, as of
troops.— **mus′ter=roll″,** n.

must′y, 1 must′ı; 2 mŭst′y, a. Having
a moldy odor; stale.— **must′l-ly,** adv.—
mus′ti-ness, n.

mu′ta-ble, } 1 miū′tə-bl; 2 mū′ta-bl, a.
mu′ta-bl¹ᵖ, } Changeable; fickle; unstable.
— **mu′ta-bl(e=ness″,** n. **mu″ta-bil′l-ty‡.**
— **mu-ta′tion,** n. **1.** The act of changing.
2. Modification; change.

mute, 1 miūt; 2 mūt. **I.** a. Speechless;
silent; dumb. **II.** n. **1.** One who is
dumb. **2.** One who does not speak, as a
silent actor. **3.** In Turkey, a dumb
officer of the Seraglio, who acts as executioner. **4.** A letter (as b in dumb) that
is not sounded. **-ly,** adv. **-ness,** n.

mu′ti-late, 1 miū′ti-lēt; 2 mū′ti-lāt, vt.
[-LAT″EDᵈ; -LAT′ING.] To deprive of a
limb or organ; maim; disfigure.— **mu″ti-la′-
tion,** n.— **mu″ti-la″tor,** n.

mu′ti-ny, 1 miū′ti-nı; 2 mū′ti-ny. **I.** vi.
[-NIED; -NY-ING.] To rise against constituted authority. **II.** n. [-NIESᶻ, pl.]
Rebellion, as of soldiers or sailors, against
authority.— **mu″ti-neer′. I.** vi. To mu-
tiny. **II.** n. One who takes part in mu-
tiny.— **mu′ti-nous,** a. Disposed to mu-
tiny; seditious. **-ly,** adv. **-ness,** n.

mut′ter, 1 mut′ər; 2 mŭt′er. **I.** vt. & vi.
To utter in low, sullen tones; murmur.
II. n. An indistinct utterance; murmur.
— **mut′ter-er,** n.— **mut′ter-ing,** pa. & n.

mut′ton, 1 mut′n; 2 mŭt′n, n. The flesh
of sheep as food.— **mut″ton=chop″. I.** a.
Shaped like a mutton=chop. **II.** n. A rib
of mutton, for broiling or frying.

mu′tu-al, 1 miū′chu-əl or -tiu-əl; 2 mū′-
chu-al or -tū-al, a. **1.** Pertaining to
both of two; reciprocally related. **2.**
Joint; common. **-ly,** adv.— **mu″tu-al′l-ty,**
n. The state of being mutual; reciprocity.

mu-zhik′, 1 mu-zik′; 2 mu-zhīk′, n. A
Russian peasant.

muz′zle, } 1 muz′l; 2 mŭz′l. **I.** vt. [MUZ′-
muz′l¹ᵖ, } ZLED, MUZ′LDᵖ; MUZ′ZLING.] To
fasten up the mouth of; silence. **II.** n. **1.**
The snout of an animal. **2.** A guard for
an animal's snout. **3.** The front end of
a firearm.

my, 1 mai; 2 mī, pron. Belonging to me.

my-o′pl-a, 1 mai-ō′pı-ə; 2 mȳ-ō′pī-a, n.
Near=sightedness. **my′o-py‡.**— **my-op′ic,** a.

myr′i-ad, 1 mir′ı-ad; 2 mȳr′i-ad, n. **1.** A
vast indefinite number. **2.** Ten thousand.

myr″i-a-gram, **myr″i-a-li″ter,** **myr″i-a-
me″ter,** etc. In the metric system, 10,-

000 grams, liters, or meters. See METRIC SYSTEM, under METRIC.

myr′i-a-pod, 1 mir′i-ə-pod; 2 mўr′i-a-pŏd, *n.* A worm-like creature with numerous legs; 1 centiped.

Myr′mi-don, 1 mûr′mi-dən; 2 mўr′mi-don, *n.*
1. One of a warlike people of ancient Thessaly, the devoted followers of Achilles in the Trojan war. **2.** [m—] A reckless servitor.

1. Round Myriapod. ¹/₂
2. Flat Myriapod. ¹/₂

myrrh, 1 mûr; 2 mўr, *n.* An Oriental aromatic gum or a shrub or tree yielding it.

myr′tle(eᴾ, 1 mûr′tl; 2 mўr′tl, *n.* A tree or shrub with glossy evergreen leaves, fragrant flowers, and black berries.

my-self′, 1 mai-[or mɪ-]self′; 2 mī-[or my-]-self′, *pron.* I; me: emphatic or reflexive.

mys′ter-yⁱ, 1 mis′tər-ɪ; 2 mўs′ter-y, *n.* [-IESᶻ, *pl.*] Something unknown or incomprehensible.— **mys-te′ri-ous,** *a.* Involved in or implying mystery; incomprehensible. **-ly,** *adv.* **-ness,** *n.*

mys′ter-yᶻ, *n.* [-IESᶻ, *pl.*] A medieval dramatic performance; miracle-play.

mys′tic, } 1 mis′tik, -tɪ-kəl; 2 mўs′tie,
mys′ti-cal, } -tɪ-eal, *a.* Secret; dark; bearing a hidden meaning.— **mys′tic,** *n.* One who trusts to direct divine illumination of the soul, or relies chiefly upon meditation and intuition for the acquirement of truth.—
mys′ti-cal-ly, *adv.*— **mys′ti-cism,** 1 mis′-tɪ-sizm; 2 mўs′ti-çişm, *n.*

mys′ti-fy, 1 mis′tɪ-fai; 2 mўs′ti-fī, *vt.* [-FIED; -FY″ING.] **1.** To confuse, as a person; perplex; bewilder. **2.** To make or treat as obscure.— **mys″ti-fi-ca′tion,** *n.* The act of mystifying.

myth, 1 mith; 2 mўth, *n.* A fictitious narrative for a time received as historical; imaginary person; tradition; popular fable.— **myth′i-cal,** *a.* Pertaining to myth; legendary; fictitious. **myth′ic†.— myth″o-log′i-cal,** *a.* Pertaining to mythology; fabulous. **myth″o-log′ic†.— myth″o-log′i-cal-ly,** *adv.*— **my-thol′o-gist,** *n.*— **my-thol′-o-gy,** *n.* [-GIESᶻ, *pl.*] **1.** The myths and legends of a race. **2.** The scientific collection and study of myths.

N

N, n, 1 en; 2 ĕn, *n.* [ENS, N's, or *N*s, 1 enz; 2 ĕns, *pl.*] The fourteenth letter in the English alphabet.

nab, 1 nab; 2 năb, *vt.* [NABBED, NABDˢ; NAB′BING.] [Colloq.] To catch.

na′bob, 1 nē′bob; 2 nā′bŏb, *n.* A luxurious rich man.

na′dir, 1 nē′dər; 2 nā′dɪr, *n.* The lowest point under foot, measuring downward.

nag, 1 nag; 2 năg, *vt. & vi.* [NAGGED, NAGDˢ; NAG′GING.] To scold or urge continually.

nag, *n.* A small horse; pony.

Na′iad, 1 nē′yad; 2 nā′yăd, *n.* [NA′IA-DES, 1 nē′yə-dīz; 2 nā′ya-dēṣ, *pl.*] *Class. Myth.* A water-nymph.

nail, 1 nēl; 2 nāl. **I.** *vt.* To fasten, as with a nail. **II.** *n.* **1.** A thin horny plate on the end of a finger or toe. **2.** A metal pin with point at one end and head at the other, for driving into wood.

na-ive′, 1 na-īv′; 2 nä-īv′, *a.* Innocently frank and bright.— **na-ive′ly,** *adv.*— **na″ive″-té′,** 1 nä″īv′tē′; 2 nä′īv′tē′, *n.* Innocent frankness.

na′ked, 1 nē′ked; 2 nā′kĕd, *a.* Without
clothing; nude; bare; destitute; plain; evident. **-ly,** *adv.* **-ness,** *n.*

name, 1 nēm; 2 nām. **I.** *vt.* [NAMED; NAM′ING.] To give a name to; call by name nominate. **II.** *n.* The word by which a person or thing is called or known; title; reputation.— **name′less,** *a.* **1.** Having no name or reputation. **2.** Not fit to be named.— **name′ly,** *adv.* That is to say.— **name′sake″,** *n.* One who is named after another. [Chinese cotton fabric.

nan-keen′, 1 nan-kɪn′; 2 năn-kēn′, *n.* A

napⁱ, 1 nap; 2 năp. **I.** *vi.* [NAPPED†, NAPTˢ; NAP′PING.] To take a nap. **II.** *n.* A short sleep; doze.

napᶻ, *n.* The short fibers on the surface of cloth. [neck.

nape, 1 nēp; 2 năp, *n.* The back of the

naph′tha, } 1 naf′thə; 2 năf′tha, *n.* A vola-
naf′tha*, } tile, inflammable oil.

nap′kin, 1 nap′kɪn; 2 năp′kĭn, *n.* A small cloth for use at table, etc.

nar-cot′ic, 1 nar-kŏt′ɪk; 2 năr-eŏt′ie. **I.** *a.* Causing sleep or stupor. **II.** *n.* A narcotic substance, as opium.

nar-rate, 1 na-rēt′; 2 nă-rāt′, *vt. & vi.*

[-RAT′EDᵈ; -RAT′ING.] To tell, as a story — nar·ra′tion, n.— nar·ra′tor, n.

nar′ra·tive, 1 nar′ə-tiv; 2 när′a-tĭv. **I.** nar′ra·tivˢ,) a. Pertaining to narration. **II.** n. An orderly account of some event or events.

nar′row, 1 nar′o; 2 năr′o. **I.** vt. & vi. To make or grow narrow. **II.** a. Having little distance from side to side; limited; illiberal. **III.** n. A narrow passage; strait. **-ly,** adv. **-ness,** n.— nar′row·mind″ed, a.— n.·mindedness, n.

nar′whal, 1 när′whəl; 2 när′whal, n. A large arctic whale·like animal with projecting sword·like tusk. nar′whale‡.

Narwhal. 1/204

na′sal, 1 nē′zəl; 2 nā′sal. **I.** a. Pertaining to the nose; pronounced through or with the aid of the nose. **II.** n. A nasal sound or letter, as m.

nas′cent, 1 nas′ent; 2 năs′ĕnt, a. Beginning to exist or develop.

nas·tur′tium, 1 nas-tûr′shum; 2 năs-tûr′shŭm, n. A flowering plant of the geranium family.

nas′ty, 1 nas′ti; 2 năs′ty, a. [NAS′TI·ER; NAS′TI·EST.] Filthy; indecent.— nas′ti·ly, adv.— nas′ti·ness, n.

na′tal, 1 nē′təl; 2 nā′tal, a. Pertaining to one's birth; dating from birth.

na′tion, 1 nē′shən; 2 nā′shon, n. A people as an organized body; a race; tribe.

ra′tion·al, 1 nash′ən-əl; 2 năsh′on-al, a. Belonging or pertaining to a nation.— na″tion·al′i·ty, n. [-TIESᶻ, pl.] **1.** The quality of being national. **2.** A nation.— na′tion·al·ize, vt.

na′tive,) 1 nē′tiv; 2 nā′tiv. **I.** a. **1.** Of na′tivˢ,) or pertaining to one's birth or birthplace. **2.** Inborn. **3.** Occurring in nature in a pure state. **II.** n. One born in, or any product of, a given place. **-ly,** adv. **-ness,** n.— na·tiv′i·ty, n. [-TIESᶻ, pl.] The coming into life; birth.

nat′ty, 1 nat′i; 2 năt′y, a. [Colloq.] Neatly fine; spruce.

nat′u·ral, 1 nach′u-[or nat′yu-]rəl; 2 năch′u-[or năt′yu-]ral, a. Pertaining to nature or to one's nature; produced by nature; not affected or artificial; normal; common. **-ly,** adv.— nat′u·ral·ism, n.— nat′u·ral·ness, n.— nat′u·ral·ist, n. One versed in natural sciences, as a botanist.— nat″u·ral·i·za′tion, n.— nat′u·ral·ize, vt.

1. To make natural; habituate. **2.** To confer citizenship upon.

nat′u·ral, n. Mus. A note affected by neither a sharp nor a flat; also, the character (♮), which acts upon a sharped note as a flat, and upon a flatted note as a sharp.

na′ture, 1 nē′chur or -tiur; 2 nā′chur or -tūr, n. **1.** The universe. **2.** Inherent or essential qualities; native character.

naught, 1 nêt; 2 nat. **I.** a. **I.** Of no value or account. **II.** n. Nothing; a cipher. **III.** adv. Not in the least.— naugh′ty, 1 nê′ti; 2 na′ty, a. [NAUGH′TI·ER; NAUGH′TI·EST.] Perverse and disobedient.— naugh′ti·ly, adv.— naugh′ti·ness, n.

nau′se·a, 1 nô′shi-ə or -si-ə; 2 na′she-a or -se-a, n. Sickness of the stomach; disgust.— nau′se·ate, vt. [-AT′EDᵈ; -AT′ING.] To sicken; disgust.— nau′seous, a. Nauseating; disgusting. **-ly,** adv.; **-ness,** n.

nau′ti·cal, 1 nô′ti-kəl; 2 na′ti-cal, a. Pertaining to ships, seamen, etc.

nau′ti·lus, 1 nô′ti-lus; 2 na′ti-lŭs, n. [-LI, 1-lai, 2-lī, -LUS·ES, pl.] **1.** A small marine mollusk. **2.** A cuttlefish with a papery shell.

Nautilus. 1/7.

na′val, 1 nē′vəl; 2 nā′val, a. **1.** Pertaining to ships and a navy. **2.** Having a navy.

nave¹, 1 nēv; 2 nāv, n. The main body of a church, between the aisles.

nave², n. The hub of a wheel.

na′vel, 1 nē′vl; 2 nā′vl, n. A small depression in the middle of the abdomen.

nav′i·gate, 1 nav′i-gēt; 2 nä′vi-gāt, vt. & vi. [-GAT′EDᵈ; -GAT′ING.] **1.** To traverse or journey by ship. **2.** To direct a ship; steer.— nav′i·ga·bl(eᵖ, a. Fit to be navigated; capable of navigation.— nav′i·ga′tion, n. **1.** The act of navigating. **2.** The art of ascertaining the position and directing the course of vessels at sea.— nav′i·ga′tor, n.

nav′vy, 1 nav′i; 2 năv′y, n. [Eng.] A laborer on canals, railways, etc.

na′vy, 1 nē′vi; 2 nā′vy, n. [NA′VIESᶻ, pl.] The entire marine military force of a country; also, any fleet or body of ships.

Na′zi, 1 nä′tsi; 2 nä′tsī, n. [G.] The National-Socialist Party of Germany, or a member thereof: a coined word.

neap, 1 nīp; 2 nēp, a. Low; lowest.

near, 1 nîr; 2 nēr. **I.** vt. & vi. To approach. **II.** a. Not far removed; close; familiar; intimate; in riding or driving, placed on the left. **III.** adv. At little distance; nearly; closely. **IV.** prep. Close

by. **-ly,** *adv.* **-ness,** *n.*— **near′-sight″ed,**
a. Short-sighted. **-ness,** *n.*

neat[1], 1 nīt; 2 nēt, *a.* Free from soil or
disorder; tidy; trim; spruce; clever.— **neat′-**
ly, *adv.*— **neat′ness,** *n.*

neat[2], *a.* Pertaining to bovine animals.

neat, *n.* **1.** Bovine cattle collectively. **2.**
A single bovine animal.   [**nib**‡.

neb, 1 neb; 2 nĕb, *n.* A beak; bill; tip.

neb′u-la, 1 neb′yu-la; 2 nĕb′yu-la, *n.*
[**-LÆ,** 1 -lī; 2 -lē, *pl.*] A luminous cloud-
like object in the sky.— **neb″u-lar,** *a.* Pertaining to a nebula.— **neb″u-los′i-ty,** *n.* A
nebulous appearance.— **neb′u-lous,** *a.* Like
a nebula; cloudy; misty.

nec′es-sa-ry, 1 nes′e-sē-rɪ; 2 nĕç′ĕ-sā-ry.
I. *a.* Being such that it must exist,
occur, or be true; essential; unavoidable.
II. *n.* [**-RIES**[z], *pl.*] Something necessary; an essential requisite.— **nec′es-sa″ri-**
ly, *adv.*— **ne-ces′si-tate,** *vt.* [**-TAT″ED**[d];
-TAT″ING.] To make necessary; compel.—
ne-ces′si-tous, *a.* Needy; destitute.— **ne-**
ces′si-ty, *n.* [**-TIES**[z], *pl.*] **1.** The quality of
being necessary; something that is necessary;
fate; fatality. **2.** Poverty.

neck, 1 nek; 2 nĕk, *n.* The part of an
animal connecting the head and trunk;
any similar part, as in a bottle or garment.
— **neck′lace,** *n.* An ornament worn round
the neck.— **neck′tle″,** *n.* A bow or tie worn
under the chin.

ne-crol′o-gy, 1 nɪ-krol′o-jɪ; 2 ne-ĕröl′o-ġy,
n. [**-GIES**[z], *pl.*] A register of deaths.
— **ne-crol′o-gist,** *n.*

nec′ro-man″cy, 1 nek′ro-man″sɪ; 2 nĕe′ro-
măn″çy, *n.* Divination by means of
pretended communication with the dead;
magic.— **nec′ro-man″cer,** *n.*— **nec″ro-**
man′tic, *a.*

ne-crop′o-lis, 1 nɪ-krop′o-lɪs; 2 ne-crŏp′o-
lis, *n.* A city of the dead; an ancient
cemetery.

nec′tar, 1 nek′tɐr; 2 nĕe′tar, *n.* The
fabled drink of the gods; any delicious
drink.— **nec′tar-ine**[s]. **I.** *a.* Sweet and
delicious. **II.** *n.* A variety of the peach.—
nec′ta-ry, *n.* [**-RIES**[z], *pl.*] The organ or
part of a plant that secretes honey.

née, 1 nē; 2 nẹ, *a.* [F.] Born: used to denote
the maiden name of a married woman.

need[d], 1 nīd; 2 nēd, *v.* **I.** *t.* To be in
want of; require. **II.** *i.* To be necessary
or required.

need, *n.* Want or lack; indigence; destitution; necessity; a situation of want or
peril.— **need′ful,** *a.* Needed; requisite; necessary. **-ly,** *adv.* **-ness,** *n.*— **need′less,** *a.*
Useless.

nee′dle, ⎱ 1 nī′dl; 2 nē′dl, *n.* **1.** A small,
nee′dl[F], ⎰ pointed instrument with an eye

to carry thread in sewing. **2.** The rod
used in knitting, etc. **3.** A straight wire,
as in a compass.— **nee′dle-ful,** *n.* The
thread to be used in a needle at one time.—
nee′dle-wo″man, *n.* A seamstress.

needs, 1 nīdz; 2 nēds, *adv.* Necessarily.

need′y, 1 nīd′ɪ; 2 nēd′y, *a.* [**NEED′I-ER;**
NEED′I-EST.] Being in need or poverty; ne-
cessitous.— **need′i-ly,** *adv.*— **need′i-ness,** *n.*

ne′er, 1 nēr; 2 nẹr, *adv.* Never: a contraction.

ne-fa′ri-ous, 1 nɪ-fē′rɪ-us; 2 ne-fā′ri-ŭs, *a.*
Wicked in the extreme; heinous. **-ly,** *adv.*
-ness, *n.*

ne-ga′tion, 1 nɪ-gē′shɐn; 2 ne-gā′shon, *n.*
Negative statement; denial.

neg′a-tive, ⎱ 1 neg′ə-tiv; 2 nĕg′a-tĭv. **I.**
neg′a-tiv[s], ⎰ *vt.* [**-TIV(E)D**[s]; **-TIV-ING.**] To
contradict; veto; deny. **II.** *a.* Express-
ing or implying denial or negation. **III.**
n. **1.** Something expressing negation or
denial. **2.** *Phot.* A picture having the
lights and shades reversed. **-ly,** *adv.* **-ness,** *n.*

neg-lect′, 1 neg-lekt′; 2 nĕg′lĕct′. **I**[d]. *vt.*
To fail to attend to; ignore; overlook; disregard. **II.** *n.* **1.** The state of being
neglected. **2.** Want of attention; disregard; omission; oversight.— **neg-lect′ful,** *a.*
Marked by neglect; heedless; careless. **-ly,** *adv.*

neg″li-gée′, 1 neg′lɪ-zē′; 2 nĕg′li-zhe′. **I.**
a. Informal in dress. **II.** *n.* Unceremonious attire.

neg′li-gent, 1 neg′lɪ-jent; 2 nĕg′li-ġĕnt, *a.*
Neglectful; heedless; unconventional.
-ly, *adv.*— **neg′li-gence,** *n.* The act or
habit of neglecting; heedlessness; careless-
ness.— **neg′li-gi-bl(e**[r], *a.* That may be
disregarded.

ne-go′ti-ate, 1 nɪ-gō′shɪ-ēt; 2 ne-gō′shi-āt,
vt. & vi. [**-AT″ED**[d]; **-AT″ING.**] To bargain
for; arrange; dispose of; sell.— **ne-go′ti-a″-**
tor, *n.*— **ne-go′ti-a-bl(e**[r], *a.* That may be
negotiated.— **ne-go″ti-a-bil′i-ty,** *n.*— **ne-**
go″ti-a′tion, *n.* The act of negotiating.

ne′gro, 1 nī′gro; 2 nē′gro, *n.* [**-GROES,** *pl.*]
[**N-** *or* **n-**] One of the blacks of Africa, or
their descendants.

— **ne′gress,** 1 nī′gres; 2 nē′grĕs, *n. fem.*
[**N-** *or* **n-**]

neigh, 1 nē; 2 nẹ. **I.** *vi.* To cry or call,
as a horse. **II.** *n.* The cry of a horse.

neigh′bor, 1 nē′bɐr; 2 nē′bọr. **I.** *vt.* To
live or be near to. **II**‖. *a.* Neighbor-
ing. **III.** *n.* One who lives near another;
one who is neighborly; a friend. **neigh′-**
bour‡— **neigh′bor-hood,** *n.* The region
near where one is or resides; vicinity; nearness; people in the vicinity.— **neigh′bor-**
ing, *a.* Adjacent; near.— **neigh′bor-ly,** *a.*
Appropriate to a neighbor; sociable.

nei′ther, 1 nī′thər; 2 nē′ther, *a.*, *pron.*, & *adv.* Not either; not at all.

Nem′e-sis, 1 nem′i-sis; 2 něm′e-sĭs, *n.* **1.** *Myth.* The goddess of vengeance. **2.** [n-] Retribution.

ne′o-phyte, 1 nī′o-fait; 2 nē′o-fīt, *n.* A novice.

neph′ew, 1 nef′yu; 2 něf′yu, *n.* The son of a sister or a brother.
nef′ew[r],

nep′o-tism, 1 nep′o-tizm; 2 něp′o-tĭşm, *n.* Favoritism toward nephews or other relatives.

Nep′tune, 1 nep′chūn; 2 něp′chūn, *n.* **1.** *Rom. Myth.* The god of the sea. **2.** The planet farthest from the sun. **3.** The ocean.

Ne′re-id, 1 nī′ri-id; 2 nē′re-ĭd, *n.* *Gr. Myth.* A sea=nymph.

nerve, 1 nūrv; 2 nėrv. **I.** *vt.* [NERV(E)D[s];
nerv[s], NERV′ING.] To imbue with nerve, vigor, or courage. **II.** *n.* **1.** *Anat.* A cord-like structure by which sensations are transmitted through an animal body. **2.** Anything likened to a nerve, as a tendon. **3.** Coolness; courage.— **ner′vin(e[s],** 1 nūr′vin; 2 nėr′vin, **I.** *a.* Pertaining to the nerves. **II.** *n.* A medicine acting on the nerves.— **nerve′less,** *a.* Destitute of nerve or force.
— **nerv′y,** *a.* Full of nerve; brave.

ner′vous, 1 nūr′vus; 2 nėr′vŭs, *a.* **1.** Pertaining to or affected by the nerves. **2.** Unduly excitable; easily agitated. **3.** Full of nerve or vigor. **-ly,** *adv.* **-ness,** *n.*

nes′cience, 1 nesh′ens; 2 něsh′ĕnç, *n.* Ignorance.

-ness. A suffix added to adjectives and participles to form nouns expressing quality.

nest[d], 1 nest; 2 něst, *v.* **I.** *t.* To place in a nest; supply with nests; place, as dishes, one inside another. **II.** *i.* To build a nest; hunt for nests.

nest, *n.* **1.** The place where a bird lays and hatches eggs and rears its young. **2.** Any cozy abode; a home; haunt. **3.** A set of similar things fitting into each other.

nes′tle, 1 nes′l; 2 něs′l, *vt. & vi.* [NES′-
nes′tl[r], TL(E)D[r]; NES′TLING.] To place in a nest; shelter; make a nest; lie close; cuddle; fondle.— **nes′tling. I.** *a.* Recently hatched. **II.** *n.* A young bird in the nest.

net[t], 1 net; 2 nět, *vt. & vi.* [NET′TED[d];
NET′TING.] To make into or catch in a net; make or use nets; ensnare.

net[2d], *vt.* To earn or yield as clear profit.

net, *a.* Free and clear after all deductions.

net, *n.* An open fabric, especially one made for the capture of fishes, birds, etc.
— **net′work″,** *n.* A fabric of openwork; a system of cross-lines. **net′ting[t].**

neth′er, 1 neth′ər; 2 něth′er, *a.* Lower.
— **neth′er-most″,** *a.* *superl.* Lowest.

net′tle, 1 net′l; 2 nět′l. **I.** *vt.* [NET′-
net′tl[r], TL(E)D[r]; NET′TLING.] To sting;

irritate. **II.** *n.* **1.** A common herb, with minute stinging hairs. **2.** A condition of irritation.

neu-ral′gi-a, 1 niu-ral′ji-ə; 2 nū-răl′gi-a, *n.* Acute pain from irritation of a nerve.
— **neu-ral′gic,** *a.*

neu-ri′tis, 1 niu-rai′tis; 2 nū-rī′tĭs, *n.* Inflammation of a nerve.

neu-rot′ic, 1 niu-rot′ik; 2 nū-rŏt′ĭk. **I.** *a.* Relating to or affecting the nervous system. **II.** *n.* **1.** A substance that affects the nerves. **2.** A person afflicted with or predisposed to nervous disease.

neu′ter, 1 niū′tər; 2 nū′ter. **I.** *a.* Of neither gender nor party; sexless; intransitive; neutral. **II.** *n.* **1.** An animal of no apparent sex. **2.** A neuter noun.

neu′tral, 1 niū′trəl; 2 nū′tral. **I.** *a.* Taking neither side; having no decided character or action; neuter. **II.** *n.* One who or that which is neutral. **-ly,** *adv.*— **neu-tral′i-ty,** *n.* [-TIES[z], *pl.*] The state of being neutral.— **neu′tral-ize** or **-ise,** *vt.* To make neutral; counteract.— **neu′tral-i-za′tion** or **-sa′tion,** *n.*

nev′er, 1 nev′ər; 2 něv′er, *adv.* Not ever; at no time; positively not.— **nev″er-the-less′,** *conj. & adv.* None the less; yet.

new, 1 niū; 2 nū, *a.* Lately made, discovered, or brought into use; renewed; different; another. **-ly,** *adv.* **-ness,** *n.*

new′el, 1 niū′el; 2 nū′ĕl, *n.* The central post of a winding stair; end post, as of a stair-rail.

New′found-land″, 1 niū′fənd-land″; 2 nū′-fund-lănd″, *n.* A breed of large, water=loving dogs that originated in Newfoundland.

Newfoundland Dog.

news, 1 niūz; 2 nūş, *n.* Recent intelligence; something new: used always as a singular. **news′mon″ger,** *n.* A vender of news; gossip.— **news′pa″per,** *n.* A daily paper giving news.

newt, 1 niūt; 2 nūt, *n.* A small lizard-like amphibious animal.

next, 1 nekst; 2 někst. **I.** *a.* Being only one step removed; nearest. **II.** *adv.* Immediately succeeding. **III.** *prep.* Nearest to.

nib, 1 nib; 2 nĭb, *n.* A projecting part; beak; point of a pen.— **nibbed′,** *a.*

1: ə = final; ı = habit; aisle; au = out; oil; iū = feud; chin; go; ŋ = sing; thin, this.
2: wolf, do; book, boot; full, rule, cūre, bŭt, bûrn; ŏil, bŏy; ǥo, ǥem; iŋk; thin, this.

nib′ble, } 1 nib′l; 2 nĭb′l. **I.** *vt.* & *vi.*
nib′l[P], } [NIB′BLED, NIB′LD[P]; NIB′BLING.]
To bite off bits of; eat little bits. **II.** *n.*
A nibbling; little bite.— **nib′bler,** *n.*

nice, 1 nais; 2 nĭç, *a.* [NIC′ER; NIC′EST.]
Refined; delicate; exact; accurate. **-ly,** *adv.*
-ness, *n.*— **ni′ce-ty,** *n.* [-TIES[z], *pl.*] The
quality of being nice; something nice; subtlety; delicacy. [as in a wall.

niche, 1 nĭch; 2 nĭch, *n.* A recess or hollow,

nick, 1 nik; 2 nĭk, *vt.* To notch; hit; fit.

nick, *n.* A slight cut or dent; notch; tally;
point of time; critical moment.

nick′el, 1 nik′el; 2 nĭk′ĕl, *n.* **1.** A hard,
silver=like metal. **2.** A United States
five=cent piece.

nick′nack″, *n.* Same as KNICKKNACK.

nick′name″, 1 nik′nēm″; 2 nĭk′nām″. **I.** *vt.*
To give a nickname to. **II.** *n.* A familiar
name given in derision or compliment.

nic′o-tin, } 1 nik′o-tin, -tin *or* -tīn; 2
nic′o-tine, } nĭc′o-tĭn, -tĭn *or* -tīn, *n.* A
poisonous substance contained in tobacco:
from Jean *Nicot,* who introduced tobacco
into France. [brother or a sister.

niece, 1 nīs; 2 nēç, *n.* The daughter of a

nig′gard, 1 nig′ard; 2 nĭg′ard. **I.** *a.*
Stingy; parsimonious. **nig′gard-ly**‡. **II.**
n. A stingy or parsimonious person.— **nig′-
gard-li-ness,** *n.*

nigh, 1 nai; 2 nī, *a., adv.,* & *prep.* Near.

night, 1 nait; 2 nīt, *n.* The time from
sunset to sunrise; darkness.— **night′cap**″, *n.*
A head=covering for sleeping in.— **night′-
fall**″, *n.* The close of day.— **night′gown**″,
n. A loose gown for bed or bedroom wear.
night′dress″‡; **night′shirt**″‡.— **night′ly.**
I. *a.* Pertaining to night; occurring at
night or every night. **II.** *adv.* By night;
every night.— **night′mare**″, *n.* An oppressive condition in sleep, accompanied
usually by bad dreams.— **night′shade**″, *n.*
A poisonous flowering plant.

night′in-gale, 1 nait′in-gēl; 2 nīt′in-gāl, *n.*
A small Eu-
ropean bird,
noted for the
me lo di ous
night = song of
the male.

ni′hil, 1 nai′hil; 2 nī′-
hil, *n.* Nothing.
nil‡.— **ni′hil-ism,** *n.*
A revolutionism, of
Russian origin, bent
on the overthrow of
all government and
existing institutions.— **ni′hil-ist,** *n.*— **ni″-
hil-is′tic,** *a.*— **ni-hil′i-ty,** *n.* Nothingness.

Nightingale. ⅕

nim′ble, } 1 nim′bl; 2 nĭm′bl, *a.* [NIM′-
nim′bl[P], } BLER; NIM′BLEST.] Light and
quick in movement; agile.— **nim′ble-ness,**
n.— **nim′bly,** *adv.*

nim′bus, 1 nim′bus; 2 nĭm′būs, *n.* [NIM′-
BUS-ES or NIM′BI, *pl.*] **1.** *Meteor.* A dark,
heavy, rain=bearing cloud. **2.** *Art.* A halo
of light and glory encircling the head, as of
Christ or a saint.

nine, 1 nain; 2 nīn, *a.* & *n.* Eight plus
one.— **nine′fold,** *a.* Nine times as many.
— **nine′pins**″, *n. pl.* A game similar to ten-
pins, in which nine pins are employed.—
nine-teen″, *a.* & *n.* Ten plus nine.— **nineteenth** . **I.** *a.* Of or pertaining to nine-
teen; being one of nineteen equal parts. **II.**
n. One of nineteen equal parts of anything.
— **nine′ti-eth.** **I.** *a.* Of or pertaining to
ninety; being one of ninety equal parts. **II.**
n. One of ninety equal parts of anything.—
nine′ty, *a.* & *n.* Eighty plus ten.— **ninth.**
I. *a.* Of or pertaining to nine; being one of
nine equal parts. **II.** *n.* One of nine equal
parts.— **ninth′ly,** *adv.*

nin′ny, 1 nin′i; 2 nĭn′y, *n.* [NIN′NIES[z], *pl.*]
A simpleton; dunce.

nip, 1 nip; 2 nĭp. **I.** *vt.* [NIPPED[t], NIPT[s]; NIP′-
PING.] To bite or pinch suddenly; affect
by frost. **II.** *n.* **1.** The act of compressing sharply; a pinch. **2.** A nipping;
pinch; blight.

nip′per, 1 nip′ər; 2 nĭp′ẽr, *n.* **1.** One who
nips; an incisor, as of a horse. **2.** *pl.*
Small pincers.

nip′ple, } 1 nip′l; 2 nĭp′l, *n.* The cone=
nip′l[P], } shaped process of the breast; a
pap; teat; any tubular projection, as to
receive a percussion=cap.

nit, 1 nit; 2 nĭt, *n.* The egg of a small
insect; a speck.

ni′ter, 1 nai′tər; 2 nī′ter, *n.* A crystalline
white salt; saltpeter; potassium nitrate.
ni′tre‡.

ni′trate, 1 nai′trēt; 2 nī′trāt, *n.* A salt of
nitric acid.— **ni′trat-ed,** *a.*

ni′tric, 1 nai′trik; 2 nī′tric, *a.* Pertaining
to or obtained from niter.— **nitric acid,** a
colorless, highly corrosive liquid, used for
dissolving metals, etc. **aqua fortis**‡.

ni′tro-gen, 1 nai′tro-jen; 2 nī′tro-gĕn, *n.*
An odorless, colorless, gaseous element
forming four=fifths of the volume of the
air.— **ni-trog′e-nous,** *a.*

ni″tro-glyc′er-in, 1 nai″tro-glĭs′ər-in; 2
nī″tro-glĭç′er-ĭn, *n.* A light=yellow oily
explosive liquid made by treating glycerin
with nitric acid.

no, 1 nō; 2 nō. **I.** *a.* Not any; none.
II. *n.* [NOES[z], *pl.*] A negative. **III.**
adv. Not so; not; nay; not in any wise°
in no case.

no′ble, 1 nō′bl; 2 nō′bl. **I.** *a.* [NO′BLER;

no′blest.] **1.** Exalted in character or quality; imposing; magnificent. **2.** Belonging to an aristocracy; of exalted rank. **II.** *n.* A nobleman; peer.— **no-bil′i-ty,** *n.* [-TIES²; *pl.*] The state of being noble; the peerage; aristocracy.— **no′ble-man,** *n.* [-MEN, *pl.*] A noble; peer.— **no′ble-ness,** *n.*— **no′bly,** *adv.* In a noble manner. [person.

no′bod-y, 1 nō′bod-ı; 2 nō′bŏd-y, *n.* No noc-tur′nal, 1 nek-tûr′nəl; 2 nŏc-tûr′nal, *a.* Pertaining to night; occurring at night; seeking food by night.

noc′turne, 1 nek′tûrn; 2 nŏc′tûrn, *n.* **1.** *Art.* A painting representing a night=scene. **2.** *Mus.* A dreamy, sentimental composition appropriate to the evening or night.

nod, 1 ned; 2 nŏd. **I.** *vt. & vi.* [NOD′DEDᵈ; NOD′DING.] To bend forward, as the head or top; incline the head, as in assent or drowsiness. **II.** *n.* A forward and downward motion of the head or top.

nod′dle,
nod′l'ᴾ, } 1 nod′l; 2 nŏd′l, *n.* The head.

node, 1 nōd; 2 nōd, *n.* **1.** A knot or knob; swelling. **2.** *Bot.* The joint of a stem. **3.** *Math.* A point at which a curve cuts or crosses itself. **4.** The point where the orbit of a heavenly body intersects the ecliptic.— **no′dal,** *a.* Pertaining to a node.— **nod′u-lar,** *a.*— **nod′ule,** *n.* A little knot, lump, or node.

noise, 1 neiz; 2 nŏiẓ. **I.** *vt.* [NOISED; NOIS′ING.] **1.** To spread by rumor or report. **2.** To disturb with noise. **II.** *n.* **1.** A sound, especially a disturbing sound. **2.** Clamor; discussion.— **noise′less,** *a.* Causing or making no noise; silent. **-ly,** *adv.* **-ness,** *n.*— **nois′y,** *a.* [NOIS′I-ER; NOIS′I-EST.] Making a loud noise; characterized by noise.— **nois′i-ly,** *adv.*— **nois′i-ness,** *n.*

noi′some, 1 nŏi′səm; 2 nŏi′som, *a.* Very offensive; ill=smelling; noxious. **-ly,** *adv.* **-ness,** *n.*

nom′ad, 1 nəm′əd; 2 nŏm′ad. **I.** *a.* Roving; unsettled; nomadic. **II.** *n.* A rover; one of a roving race.— **no-mad′ic,** *a.* Pertaining to nomads; roaming; unsettled.

no′men-cla″ture, 1 nō′men-klē″chur or -tiur; 2 nō′mĕn-elā″chụr or -tūr, *n.* A system of names, as used in any art or science.

nom′i-nal, 1 nəm′i-nəl; 2 nŏm′i-nal, *a.* Pertaining to a name; existing in name only; inconsiderable. **-ly,** *adv.*

nom′i-nate, 1 nom′i-nēt; 2 nŏm′i-nāt, *vt.* [-NAT′EDᵈ; -NAT′ING.] To name; designate as a candidate.— **nom′i-na′tion,** *n.* The act or power of nominating.— **nom′i-na-tiv(es.** **I.** *a.* *Gram.* Naming or being the subject of a sentence. **II.** *n.* The nomina-

tive case.— **nom′i-na″tor,** *n.* One who nominates.— **nom′i-nee′,** *n.* One who is nominated.

non-, *prefix.* Not.

non′age, 1 nən′ij; 2 nŏn′ag, *n.* The period before one is legally of age; minority.— **non′aged,** *a.*

non″a-ge-na′ri-an, 1 nən″ə-jı-nē′rı-ən; 2 nŏn″a-ge-nā′ri-an. **I.** *a.* Pertaining to the nineties. **II.** *n.* A person between the ages of ninety and a hundred.

non″=at-ten′dance, 1 nən″=a-ten′dəns; 2 nŏn″=ă-tĕn′danç, *n.* Failure to attend.

nonce, 1 nəns; 2 nŏnç, *n.* Present time or occasion.

non′cha-lance, 1 nən′sha-lans or (F.) nôn″shə-läns′; 2 nŏn′cha-länç or (F.) nôn″-cha-läng′, *n.* Careless indifference or unconcern.— **non′cha-lant,** *a.*

non″=com-mis′sioned, }
non″=com-mis′siond, } 1 nən″=kə-mish′-ənd; 2 nŏn″=cŏ-mish′ond, *a.* Not having a commission, as a military or naval officer of lower rank.

non″=con-duc′tor, 1 nən″=ken-dŭk′tər or -ter; 2 nŏn″=cŏn-dŭc′tor, *n.* Something that offers resistance to the passage of some form of energy, as of heat or electricity.

non″=con-form′ist, 1 nən″=ken-fêrm′ist; 2 nŏn″=cŏn-fôrm′ist, *n.* One who does not conform to established faith or usage; a dissenter.— **non″=con-form′i-ty,** *n.*

non′de-script, 1 nən′dı-skript; 2 nŏn′de-script. **I.** *a.* Indescribable; odd. **II.** *n.* A person or thing very odd and difficult to describe.

none, 1 nun; 2 nŏn. **I.** *a. & pron.* Not one; no one. **II.** *adv.* In no respect.

non-en′ti-ty, 1 nən-en′tı-tı; 2 nŏn-ĕn′ti-ty, *n.* [-TIES²; *pl.*] Nothingness; nothing; nobody.

non″pa-reil′, 1 nən″pə-rel′; 2 nŏn″pa-rĕl′. **I.** *a.* Of unequaled excellence. **II.** *n.* **1.** Something of unequaled excellence. **2.** The size of type in which this is printed.

non′plus, 1 nən′plus; 2 nŏn′plŭs. **I.** *vt.* [NON′PLUSEDᵗ or -PLUSSEDᵗ, -PLUS′T³.] To bring to a stand mentally; disconcert; perplex. **II.** *n.* A mental standstill; perplexity.

non″=res′i-dent, 1 nən″=rez′i-dent; 2 nŏn″=rĕṣ′i-dĕnt. **I.** *a.* Not resident in a place. **II.** *n.* One not permanently residing in a particular place.— **non″=res′i-dence,** *n.*

non′sense, 1 nən′sens; 2 nŏn′sĕns, *n.* That which is without sense; absurdity.— **non-sen′si-cal,** *a.* [retired place.

nook, 1 nuk; 2 nŏŏk, *n.* A narrow and noon, 1 nūn; 2 nŏŏn, *n.* That time of day when the sun is in the meridian; midday.— **noon′day″,** *a. & n.* Midday.— **nooning,** *n.* A time of rest taken at noon.—

noon'tide". **I.** *a.* Occurring at noon. **II.**
n. The time of midday.

noose, 1 nūs; 2 nŏŏs. **I.** *vt.* [NOOSED^t, NOOST^s;
NOOS'ING.] To catch in or fasten with or
as with a noose. **II.** *n.* A slip-knot.

nor, 1 nôr; 2 nôr, *conj.* And not; likewise not.

nor'mal, 1 nêr'məl; 2 nôr'mal. **I.** *a.*
Conformed to a type or standard; typical;
ordinary; regular. **II.** *n.* **1.** A usual or
accepted rule or process. **2.** Average or
mean value. **-ly,** *adv.*— **normal school,** a
school where pupils are trained to teach.

Nor'man, 1 nêr'mən; 2 nôr'man. **I.** *a.*
Pertaining to Normandy, a former prov-
ince of northwestern France, or its people.
II. *n.* An inhabitant of Normandy.

Norse, 1 nôrs; 2 nôrs. **I.** *a.* Pertaining to
Scandinavian countries, or to their peo-
ples or languages. **II.** *n.* The Scandina-
vian languages, especially the Icelandic.
— **Norse'man,** *n.* An ancient Scandinavian.
North'man‡.

north, 1 nêrth; 2 nôrth. **I.** *a.* **1.** Lying
toward or in the north. **2.** Issuing from
the north. **II.** *n.* **1.** One of the four cardinal points of the compass; at the left
hand of an observer who faces the east;
opposed to *south.* **2.** Any region north
of a given point. **III.** *adv.* Toward the
north; northerly.— **north"east',** *n.* That
point of the horizon lying midway between
north and east; any region lying toward that
point.— **north"east',** *a. & adv.*— **north"-
east'er,** *n.* A gale or storm coming from the
northeast.— **north"east'er-ly,** *a.*— **north"-
east'ern,** *a.*— **north'most,** *a.*— **north star,**
the pole-star. See under POLE².— **north'-
ward,** *a.* Directed or lying toward the
north.— **north'ward, north'wards,** *adv.* In
a northerly direction.— **north'ward-ly,** *a. &
adv.*— **north"west',** *n.* That point of the
compass lying midway between north and
west; any region situated toward that point.
— **north"west',** *a. & adv.*— **north"west'er,**
n. A gale from the northwest.— **north"-
west'er-ly,** *a.*— **north"west'ern,** *a.*

north'er, 1 nêrth'ər; 2 nôrth'er, *n.* A
north wind or gale.— **north'er-ly.** **I.** *a.*
Lying toward or coming from the north;
northern. **II.** *adv.* Toward or from the
north.— **north'ern.** **I.** *a.* **1.** Pertaining to
the north. **2.** Directed toward or coming
from the north. **II.** *n.* A northerner.—
north'ern-er, *n.* One residing in the north.

nose, 1 nōz; 2 nŏz, *vt. & vi.* [NOSED;
NOS'ING.] To smell; scent; track.

nose, *n.* That part of the face containing
the organ of smell; the power of smelling;
a prow; spout, nozle, etc.— **nose'gay",** *n.* A
bouquet.— **nose dive** (*Aero.*), a steep downward plunge by an aviator in an air-plane.

nos'tril, 1 nes'tril; 2 nŏs'tril, *n.* One of
the openings in the nose.

nos'trum, 1 nes'trum; 2 nŏs'trŭm, *n.* A
favorite remedy; quack medicine.

not, 1 net; 2 nŏt, *adv.* In no manner, or to
no extent: used in negation, prohibition,
or refusal.

no'ta-ble¹, } 1 nō'tə-bl; 2 nō'tà-bl, *a.*
no'ta-blᵖ, } Worthy of note; remarkable;
manifest; conspicuous.— **no"ta-bil'i-ty,** *n.*
[-TIES², *pl.*] **1.** The quality of being notable.
2. A person of distinction.— **no'ta-bly¹,** *adv.*

not'a-ble², 1 net'ə-bl; 2 nŏt'à-bl, *a.* Eminently careful or thrifty and skilful, as in
housekeeping.— **not'a-bly²,** *adv.*

no'ta-ry, 1 nō'tə-ri; 2 nō'ta-ry, *n.* [-RIES²,
pl.] An officer who is empowered to administer oaths, take depositions, etc.— **no-
ta'ri-al,** *a.* Pertaining to a notary.

no-ta'tion, 1 no-tē'shən; 2 no-tā'shon, *n.*
1. The process of noting or designating
by figures, etc. **2.** Any system of signs,
figures, etc., as arithmetical characters.

notch, 1 nech; 2 nŏch. **I.** *vt.* To make
nochᵖ, } a notch or notches in; fit in or by a
notch. **II.** *n.* A nick or mark cut in anything.

note, 1 nōt; 2 nōt. **I.** *vt.* [NOT'ED^d;
NOT'ING.] To notice; make a note of.
II. *n.* **1.** A mark; sign; character; anno-
tation; memorandum; brief letter. **2.**
Notice; observation. **3.** High importance;
distinction. **4.** A character indicating a
musical sound; also, the sound. **5.** A
written promise to pay.— **note'-book",** *n.* A
book in which to enter memoranda.— **no'ted,**
a. Well known by reputation or report.—
note'wor"thy, *a.* Worthy of note; remarkable.

noth'ing, 1 nuth'iŋ; 2 nŏth'ing. **I.** *n.*
Not anything; nonentity; a trifle. **II.**
adv. In no degree; not at all.— **noth'ing-
ness,** *n.* **1.** Non-existence. **2.** Worthless-
ness.

no'tice, } 1 nō'tis; 2 nō'tiç. **I.** *vt.* [NO'-
no'tisˢ, } TICED^t, NO'TIST^s; NO'TIC-ING.] To
observe; see; refer to; treat with attention.
II. *n.* **1.** The act of noticing or observing. **2.** Intelligence; news. **3.** Respectful treatment. **4.** An order communicated.— **no'tice-a-bl(eᵖ,** *a.* Worthy of notice.— **no'tice-a-bly,** *adv.*— **no'ti-fy,** *vt.*
[-FIED; -FY'ING.] **1.** To give notice to; inform. **2.** To publish.— **no"ti-fi-ca'tion,** *n.*

no'tion, 1 nō'shən; 2 nō'shon, *n.* A mental
apprehension; an idea; opinion.— **no'tion-al,**
a. Visionary; full of notions or hobbies.

no"to-ri'e-ty, 1 nō"to-rai'i-ti; 2 nō"to-
ri'e-ty, *n.* [-TIES², *pl.*] The fact of being
notorious; common talk; a notorious

1: **ȧ**rtistic, **ä**rt; fat, fāre; fạst; get, prẹy; hit, polīce; obey, gō; nẹt, ôr; fųll, rūle; bụt, bûrn.
2: ärt, āpe, făt, fâre, fȧst, whạt, ạll; mē, gĕt, prẹy, fẽrn; hĭt, īce; ĭ=ē; ĭ=ẽ; gō, nŏt, ôr, wọn.

person or thing.— **no-to'ri-ous,** *a.* Commonly and unfavorably known. **-ly,** *adv.*
-ness, *n.*

not"with-stand'ing, 1 not"with-stand'ıŋ; 2 nŏt"wĭth-stănd'ĭng. **I.** *adv.* & *conj.* In spite of the fact; nevertheless. **II.** *prep.* Without regard to; despite.

nought, 1 nôt; 2 nôt, *a.* & *n.* Same as NAUGHT.

noun, 1 naun; 2 noun, *n.* A word used as the name of a thing; a substantive.

nour'isht, 1 nur'ĭsh; 2 nŭr'ish, *vt.* & *vi.* To feed; support; nurture; educate.— **nour'ish-ment,** *n.* The act of nourishing; food; nutriment.

nov'el, 1 nov'el *or* nov'l; 2 nŏv'ĕl *or* nŏv'l. **I.** *a.* Recent; new; strange; unusual. **II.** *n.* A fictitious tale.— **nov'el-ist,** *n.* A writer of novels.— **nov'el-ty,** *n.* [-TIES², *pl.*] Newness; something novel.

No-vem'ber, 1 no-vem'bər; 2 no-vĕm'ber, *n.* The eleventh month of the year: from the Latin name of the ninth month of the Roman year.

nov'ice, 1 nov'ıs; 2 nŏv'ĭç, *n.* A beginner; one who enters a religious house on probation.— **no-vi'ti-ate,** *n.* The state of being a novice; a period of probation.

no'vo-ca'ine, 1 nō'vo-kā'ın; 2 nō'vo-cā'ĭn, *n.* A substitute for cocain.

now, 1 nau; 2 nou. **I.** *n.* The present time or moment. **II.** *adv.* 1. At once; at the present time. **2.** Things being so. **— now'a-days",** *adv.* In the present time or age.— **now and then,** occasionally; from time to time.

no'where", 1⁸ nō'hwâr"; 2 nō'hwêr", *adv.* In no place or state.

no'wise", 1 nō'waiz"; 2 nō'wĭş", *adv.* In no manner or degree.

nox'ious, 1 nɒk'shus; 2 nŏk'shŭs, *a.* Causing, or tending to cause, injury; pernicious; poisonous.

noz'l(eᵖ, 1 nɒz'l; 2 nŏz'l, *n.* A spout for noz'zle, discharge of liquid, as from a hose.

nu'cle-us, 1 niū'klı-us; 2 nū'cle-ŭs, *n.* [-CLE-I, *pl.*] A center of development; central mass, as of a comet; kernel.

nude, 1 niūd; 2 nūd, *a.* Destitute of clothing; naked; bare. **-ly,** *adv.*— **nu'di-ty,** *n.* [-TIES², *pl.*] Nakedness; anything nude.

nudge, 1 nuj; 2 nŭdg. **I.** *vt.* [NUDGED; NUDG'ING.] To touch gently, as with the elbow. **II.** *n.* The act of nudging.

nu'ga-to-ry, 1 niū'gə-to-rı; 2 nū'ga-to-ry, *a.* Having no power, worth, or meaning; inoperative.

nug'get, 1 nug'et; 2 nŭg'ĕt, *n.* A lump, as of precious metal.

nui'sance, 1 niū'səns; 2 nū'sanç, *n.* That which annoys or harms.

nul(lᵖ, 1 nul; 2 nŭl, *a.* Of no legal force or effect; void; of no avail.

nul'li-fy, 1 nul'ı-fai; 2 nŭl'i-fÿ, *vt.* [-FIED; -FY'ING.] To deprive of force; annul. — **nul"li-fi-ca'tion,** *n.* The act of nullifying.— **nul'li-fi"er,**n.— **nul'li-ty,**n. [-TIES², *pl.*] **1.** The state of being null. **2.** A nonentity.

numb, 1 num; 2 nŭm. **I.** *vt.* To deprive **numb**ˢ, of sensation; benumb. **II.** *a.* Without feeling; torpid; benumbed.— **numb'-ness,** *n.*

num'ber, 1 num'bər; 2 nŭm'ber. **I.** *vt.* To count; reckon; designate by number; amount to. **II.** *n.* **1.** A numeral. **2.** A unit or collection of units. **3.** The science of numerals. **4.** Poetic measure: commonly in the plural. **5.** *Gram.* The form indicating the singular or plural. — **num'ber-less,** *a.* Very numerous; countless; innumerable.— **nu"mer-a-bl(e**ᵖ,*a.* That may be numbered.— **nu'mer-al.** **I.** *a.* Pertaining to number. **II.** *n.* A symbol or word used to express a number.— **nu'mer-ate,** *vt.* & *vi.* [-AT"ED**d**; -AT'ING.] To enumerate; count.— **nu"mer-a'tion,** *n.* The art of reading or naming numbers; enumeration.— **nu'mer-a"tor,** *n.* In a vulgar fraction, the term (written above the line) that denotes how many of the parts of a unit are taken.— **nu-mer'i-cal,** *a.* Pertaining to number; consisting in number. **-ly,** *adv.*— **nu'mer-ous,** *a.* Many. **-ly,** *adv.*

nu"mis-mat'ic, *a.* Pertaining to coins or medals. **nu"mis-mat'i-cal**ᶜ.— **nu"mis-mat'ics,** *n.* The science of coins and medals with reference to their artistic and historical meaning. **nu-mis"ma-tol'o-gy**‡.

num'skull", 1 num'skul"; 2 nŭm'skŭl", **num'skul"**ᵖ, A blockhead.

nun, 1 nun; 2 nŭn, *n.* A woman devoted to a religious life, and living in a convent. — **nun'ner-y,** *n.* [-IES², *pl.*] A convent for nuns.

nun'ci-o, 1 nun'shı-ō; 2 nŭn'shi-ō, *n.* An ambassador of the Pope; a messenger.

nun'cu-pa"tiv(eˢ, 1 nuŋ'kiu-pē"tıv; 2 nŭŋ'cŭ-pā"tĭv, *a. Law.* Oral as distinguished from written.

nup'tial, 1 nup'shəl; 2 nŭp'shal, *a.* Pertaining to marriage or the marriage ceremony.— **nup'tials,** *n. pl.* The marriage ceremony or state.

nurse, 1 nūrs; 2 nûrs. **I.** *vt.* & *vi.* [NURSED**d**; NURST**s**; NURS'ING.] To care for, as a child or a sick person; suckle; nourish; cherish. **II.** *n.* One who nurses a child or a sick person.— **nurs'er-y,** *n.* [-IES², *pl.*] **1.** A playroom for children. **2.** A place where trees, shrubs, etc., are raised for transplanting.—

nurs'er-y-man, *n.* One who has a nursery for trees, etc.—**nurs'ling,** *n.* An infant.

nur'ture, 1 nûr'chur or -tiur; 2 nûr'chur or -tûr. **I.** *vt.* [NUR'-TURED; NUR'TUR-ING.] To give nourishment to; bring up; educate. **II.** *n.* The act of nurturing; that which nourishes or fosters.

nut, 1 nŭt; 2 nŭt. **I.** *vi.* [NUT'TED[d]; NUT'-TING.] To gather nuts. **II.** *n.* **1.** A fruit consisting of a kernel or seed enclosed in a woody shell. **2.** A small block of wood or metal having an internal screw-thread.—**nut'gall",** *n. Bot.*

1. A Hexagonal Lock=, Jam=, or Check=nut above a Square Nut. 2. A Thumb=, Finger=, or Wing=nut.

A gall.—**nut'meg,** *n.* The aromatic kernel of the fruit of various trees; also, the tree itself.—**nut'shell",** *n.* The shell of a nut.—**nut'ty,** *a.*

nu'tri-ent, 1 niū'tri-ent; 2 nū'tri-ĕnt. *a.* Giving nourishment; nourishing.—**nu'tri-ment,** *n.* Food; sustenance. **-al,** *a.*—**nu-tri'tion,** *n.* **1.** The process by which growth is promoted and waste repaired in living organisms. **2.** Nutriment.—**nu-tri'tious,** *a.* Nourishing.—**nu'tri-tiv(e[s],** *a.* **1.** Having nutritious properties. **2.** Pertaining to nutrition.

ny'lon, 1 nai'lon; 2 nȳ'lŏn, *n. Chem.* A man-made chemical product from which fibers, bristles, sheets, etc., may be formed.

nymph, 1 nimf; 2 nȳmf, *n.* **1.** *Myth.* A female divinity inhabiting a grove, spring, etc. **2.** [Poet.] A damsel. **3.** A pupa or chrysalis. **nym'pha[‡].**—**nymph'al,** **nym-phe'an,** *a.*

O

O, o, 1 ō; 2 ō, *n.* [OES, O's, or Os, 1 ōz; 2 ōs, *pl.*] The fifteenth letter in the English alphabet. [in address. **2.** Same as OH.

O, 1 ō; 2 ō, *interj.* **1.** An exclamation used

oaf, 1 ōf; 2 ōf, *n.* A changeling; simpleton.

oak, 1 ōk; 2 ōk, *n.* A hard=wood, acorn-bearing tree; also its wood.—**oak's ap''ple,** *n.* A gall produced on an oak by an insect.—**oak'en,** *a.* Made of oak.

oak'um, 1 ōk'um; 2 ōk'ŭm, *n.* Hemp-fiber obtained by untwisting old rope: used in calking.

oar, 1 ōr; 2 ōr. **I.** *vt.* To propel with an oar; use as an oar. **II.** *n.* A bladed wooden implement for propelling a boat.—**oared,** *a.* Having oars: usually in composition; as, four=oared, etc.—**oars'man,** *n.* One who rows.

Red Oak.

o'a-sis, 1 ō'a-sis or o-ē'sis; 2 ō'a-sĭs or o-ā'-sis, *n.* [O'A-SES, *pl.*] A fertile spot in a desert.

oat, 1 ōt; 2 ōt, *n.* A cereal grass or its edible grain.—**oat'en,** *a.* Made of oats.—**oat'meal",** *n.* The meal of oats; also, porridge made of it.

oath, 1 ōth; 2 ōth, *n.* **1.** A solemn appeal to God or to something holy in support of

a statement. **2.** A blasphemous use of the name of the Deity or of anything sacred.

ob-, *prefix.* Toward; to; against; facing; reversely; over; near; before; up; out; upon; about; as, *object*, *oblique*.

ob'du-rate, 1 eb'diu-rēt; 2 ŏb'dū-rāt, *a.* Hard=hearted; stubborn; impenitent; unyielding. **-ly,** *adv.* **-ness,** *n.*— **ob'du-ra-cy,** *n.* Obstinacy; obdurateness.

o-be'di-ent, 1 o-bī'di-ent; 2 o-bē'di-ĕnt, *a.* Acting according to command; submissive; dutiful.— **o-be'di-ence,** *n.*— **o-be'di-ent-ly,** *adv.*

o-bei'sance, 1 o-bī'[or o-bē']sans; 2 o-bē'[or o-be']sanç, *n.* A courteous bowing or a bending of the knee.

ob'e-lisk, 1 eb'l-lisk; 2 ŏb'e-lĭsk, *n.* **1.** A square monumental shaft with pyramidal top. **2.** The dagger (†) used as a reference-mark.

o-bese', 1 o-bīs'; 2 o-bēs', *a.* Very corpulent; fat.— **o-bes'i-ty,** *n.* **o-bese'ness[‡].**

o-bey', 1 o-bē'; 2 o-bē', *v.* **I.** *t.* To do the bidding of (a pe*r*son); act according to (a command or law); be controlled by. **II.** *i.* To yield obedience.

o-bit'u-a-ry, 1 o-bich'u-[or o-bit/yu-]ē-ri; 2 o-bĭch'u-[or o-bĭt'yu-]ā-ry. **I.** *a.* Pertaining to death. **II.** *n.* A published notice of a death.

ob-ject'[d], 1 eb-jekt'; 2 ŏb-jĕct', *v.* **I.** *t.* To allege as a reason against something. **II.** *i.* To declare oneself opposed to something.

ob'ject, 1 eb'jekt; 2 ŏb'jĕct, *n.* **1.** Any-

thing that may be perceived by the senses. **2.** That which is affected by an action. **3.** A purpose; aim.— **ob-jec′tion,** n. The act of objecting; that which is objected.— **ob-jec′tion-a-bl(e)⁴,** a.— **ob-jec′tion-a-bly,** adv.— **ob-jec′tiv(e)⁵.** **I.** a. **1.** Belonging to an object, purpose, or aim. **2.** External to the mind; outward. **II.** n. **1.** The objective case. **2.** An objective point.— **ob-jec′tiv(e-ly)⁵,** adv.— **ob-jec′tor,** n.

ob′late, 1 ŏb′lēt; 2 ŏb′lāt, a. Flattened at the poles. **-ly,** adv. **-ness,** n.— **ob-la′tion,** n. Anything offered in worship.

ob′li-gate, 1 ŏb′li-gēt; 2 ŏb′li-gāt, vt. [-GAT″ED⁴; -GAT″ING.] To bind by some requirement; compel to as a duty.— **ob″li-ga′tion,** n. **1.** The act of obligating. **2.** Moral or legal constraint; a requirement imposed; debt of gratitude; a bond under penalty.— **ob′li-ga-to-ry,** 1 -ga-to-rɪ; 2 -ga-to-ry, a. Of a nature to impose obligation.

o-blige′, 1 o-blaij′; 2 ŏb′lāt, vt. [O-BLIGED′; O-BLIG′ING.] To constrain; compel; render indebted, as for a favor; gratify.— **o-blig′ing,** pa. Disposed to do favors.

ob-lique′, 1 ɐb-lik′ or ɐb-laik′; 2 ŏb-lĭk′ or ŏb-līk′, a. **1.** Neither perpendicular nor horizontal; slanting; sloping. **2.** Evasive; indirect. **-ly,** adv. **-ness,** n.— **ob-liq′ui-ty,** n. [-TIES², pl.] Oblique quality; inclination; wrong-doing.

ob-lit′er-ate, 1 ɐb-lit′ər-ēt; 2 ŏb-lĭt′er-āt, vt. [-AT″ED⁴; -AT″ING.] To blot or wipe out; efface.— **ob-lit″er-a′tion,** n.

ob-liv′i-on, 1 ɐb-liv′ɪ-ən; 2 ŏ-blĭv′i-on, n. **1.** The state of being utterly forgotten. **2.** The act of forgetting completely; forgetfulness; amnesty.— **ob-liv′i-ous,** a.

ob′long, 1 ŏb′lɔŋ; 2 ŏb′lŏng. **I.** a. Longer than broad. **II.** n. A figure having greater length than breadth.

ob′lo-quy, 1 ɐb′lo-kwɪ; 2 ŏb′lo-kwy, n. **1.** Odium or disgrace. **2.** Vilification.

ob-nox′ious, 1 ɐb-nɒk′shʊs; 2 ŏb-nŏk′shŭs, a. **1.** Calculated to give offense or excite aversion. **2.** Liable, as to penalty.

o′boe, 1 ō′bɵɪ; 2 ō′bŏɪ, n. A wooden flute-like wind-instrument. [It.]

ob-scene′, 1 ɐb-sīn′; 2 ŏb-sēn′, a. Offensive to chastity or decency; foul; vile. **-ly,** adv.— **ob-scen′i-ty,** n. **ob-scene′ness.**

ob-scure′, 1 ɐb-skiūr′; 2 ŏb-scūr′. **I.** rt. [OB-SCURED′; OB-SCUR′ING.] To dim, darken, or hide from view. **II.** a. [OB-SCUR′ER; OB-SCUR′EST.] **1.** Not clear to the eye or to the mind; dim; dark; indistinct. **2.** Little known; lowly. **-ly,** adv. **-ness,** n.— **ob″scu-ra′tion,** n. The act of obscuring; obscurity.— **ob-scu′ri-ty,** n.

ob′se-quies, 1 ɐb′sɪ-kwɪz; 2 ŏb′se-kwĭs, n. pl. Funeral rites.

ob-se′qui-ous, 1 ɐb-sī′kwɪ-ʊs; 2 ŏb-sē′kwi-ŭs, a. Meanly submissive; compliant; cringing.

ob-serve′, } 1 ɐb-zūrv′; 2 ŏb-sĕrv′, vt. [OB-
ob-serv′s, } SERVED′; OB-SERV′ING.] **1.** To take notice of; note; scrutinize. **2.** To celebrate; comply with. **3.** To remark incidentally.— **ob-ser′vance,** n. The act of observing, as a custom.— **ob-ser′vant,** a. Carefully attentive; heedful; watchful; strict; scrupulous.— **ob-ser′vant-ly,** adv.— **ob″ser-va′tion,** n. **1.** The act or habit of observing. **2.** An incidental remark.— **ob-ser′va-to-ry,** n. [-RIES², pl.] **1.** A building or dome for astronomical observations. **2.** A tower built for the view.— **ob-serv′er,** n.— **ob-serv′ing,** pa. Observant. **-ly,** adv.

ob-ses′sion, 1 ɐb-sesh′ən; 2 ŏb-sĕsh′on, n. **1.** A vexing or besieging, as by an evil spirit. **2.** Psychol. An idea that dominates the mind and controls it. **3.** Spiritualism. Possession of one's consciousness by a foreign personality, as in a trance.

ob′so-lete, 1 ɐb′so-līt; 2 ŏb′so-lēt. **I.** a. Gone out of use; discarded; antiquated. **II.** n. An obsolete word or expression. **-ness,** n.— **ob″so-les′cent,** a. Growing obsolete.

ob′sta-cle, 1 ɐb′stə-kl; 2 ŏb′sta-cl, n. That which stands in the way of progress; an obstruction; hindrance.

ob-stet′rics, 1 ɐb-stet′rɪks; 2 ŏb-stĕt′ries, n. The branch of medical science relating to midwifery.— **ob-stet′ri-cal,** a. **-ly,** adv.

ob′sti-nate, 1 ɐb′stɪ-nɪt; 2 ŏb′sti-nat, a. Unreasonably determined; stubborn. **-ly,** adv.— **ob′sti-na-cy,** n. Stubbornness.

ob-strep′er-ous, 1 ɐb-strep′ər-us; 2 ŏb-strĕp′er-ŭs, a. Noisy, as in demand or complaint; clamorous. **-ly,** adv. **-ness,** n.

ob-struct′ᵈ, 1 ɐb-strukt′; 2 ŏb-strŭct′, vt. To block or stop up; hinder; retard. — **ob-struc′tion,** n. **1.** A hindrance; obstacle. **2.** The act of obstructing.— **ob-struc′tiv(e)⁵,** a. Tending to obstruct.

ob-tain′, 1 ɐb-tēn′; 2 ŏb-tān′, v. **I.** t. To bring into one's own possession; get; attain. **II.** i. To have place; be prevalent.— **ob-tain′a-bl(e)⁴,** a.

ob-trude′, 1 ɐb-trūd′; 2 ŏb-trŭd′, vt. & vi. [OB-TRUD′ED⁴; OB-TRUD′ING.] To thrust or be pushed into undue prominence. — **ob-trud′ing,** a.— **ob-tru′sion,** n. The act of obtruding.— **ob-tru′siv(e)⁵,** a. Seeking or tending to undue prominence; thrusting oneself forward. **-ly,** adv.

ob-tuse′, 1 ɐb-tiūs′; 2 ŏb-tūs′, a. Greater than a right angle; rounded; dull; stupid; insensible. **-ly,** adv. **-ness,** n.

ob-verse′, 1 ɐb-vūrs′; 2 ŏb-vĕrs′, a. Noting

1: ə = final; ɪ = habit; ɑisle; ɑu = out; ɵil; iū = feud; ℀hin; go; ŋ = sing; thin, this.
2: wolf, dǫ; bŏŏk, bŏŏt; fŭll, rŭle, cūre, bŭt, bŭrn; ŏil, bŏy; ḡo, ḡem; iŋk; thin, this.

the principal side or face of a medal or coin. **-ly,** *adv.* — **ob′verse,** 1 ŏb′vûrs; 2 ŏb′vẽrs, *n.* The obverse side, as of a coin; an opposite face.

ob′vi-ate, 1 ŏb′vĭ-ēt; 2 ŏb′vĭ-āt, *vt.* [-AT″-ED^d; -AT″ING.] To meet in advance, so as to remove; prevent.

ob′vi-ous, 1 ŏb′vĭ-ŭs; 2 ŏb′vĭ-ŭs, *a.* Immediately evident; manifest.

oc-, *prefix.* Euphonic form of OB- before *c*.

oc-ca′sion, 1 ẽ-kē′ʒɒn; 2 ŏ-cā′zhon. **I.** *vt.* To bring about; cause. **II.** *n.* An occurrence; opportunity for some action; a condition; need; exigency. — **oc-ca′sion-al,** *a.* **1.** Occurring at irregular intervals. **2.** Belonging to some special occasion. **-ly,** *adv.*

Oc′ci-dent, 1 ŏk′sĭ-dent; 2 ŏc′çĭ-dĕnt, *n.* **1.** The countries lying west of Asia and the Turkish empire. **2.** [o-] The west. — **Oc″ci-den′tal,** *a.* Belonging to the West.

oc′ci-put, 1 ŏk′sĭ-pʉt; 2 ŏc′çĭ-pŭt, *n.* The lower back part of the head. — **oc-cip′i-tal,** 1 ŏk-sĭp′ĭ-tɒl; 2 ŏc-cĭp′ĭ-tāl, *a.*

oc-cult′, 1 ẽ-kŭlt′; 2 ŏ-cŭlt′, *a.* Hidden; secret. — **oc-cult′ism,** *n.* — **oc-cult′ist,** *n.* — **oc-cult′ly,** *adv.* — **oc″cul-ta′tion,** *n.* Concealment, as of one heavenly body by another.

oc′cu-py, 1 ŏk′yu-paɪ; 2 ŏc′yu-pȳ, *vt.* [-PIED; -PY″ING.] To use in an exclusive manner; possess; employ. — **oc′cu-pan-cy,** *n.* The act or time of occupying. — **oc′cu-pant,** *n.* One who occupies; a tenant. — **oc″cu-pa′tion,** *n.* One's regular or immediate business; the state of being busy; occupancy.

oc-cur′, 1 ẽ-kûr′; 2 ŏ-eûr′, *vi.* [OC-CURRED′, OC-CURD′S; OC-CUR′RING.] To happen; come into mind. — **oc-cur′rence,** *n.* An event; happening.

o′cean, 1 ō′shɒn; 2 ō′shan, *n.* The great body of salt water on the earth's surface or any one of the great tracts into which it is divided; any unbounded expanse. — **o″ce-an′ic,** *a.*

o′cher, } 1 ō′kɒr; 2 ō′eer, *n.* A native red **o′chre,** } or yellow earth, of iron and clay, used as a pigment and as a paint. — **o′cher-ous,** *a.* **o′chre-ous;** **o′chrous‡.**

-ock, *suffix.* A diminutive; as, hill*ock.*

o′clock, 1 o-klek′; 2 o-elŏk′. Of the clock; a contraction.

oct-, } 1 ŏkt-, ŏk′tɒ-, ŏk′tĭ-, ŏk′to-; 2 ŏet-, **oc′ta-,** } ŏe′ta-, ŏe′tĭ-, ŏe′to-. Combining **oc′ti-,** } forms, signifying "eight"; as, *octagon,* **oc′to-,** } *octangle, octillion, octogenarian, octopus.*

oc′ta-gon, 1 ŏk′tɒ-gɒn; 2 ŏc′ta-gŏn, *n.* *Geom.* A figure with eight sides and eight angles. — **oc-tag′o-nal,** *a.* Eight-sided.

oc″ta-he′dral, 1 ŏk″tɒ-hī′drɒl; 2 ŏc″ta-hē′dral, *a.* Having eight equal plane faces.

oc″ta-he′dron, 1 ŏk″tɒ-hī′drɒn; 2 ŏe″ta-

hē′drŏn, *n.* *Geom.* A solid bounded by eight plane faces.

oc′tave, 1 ŏk′tĭv; 2 ŏe′tav. **I.** *a.* **1.** Composed of eight. **2.** *Mus.* Pertaining to an octave. **II.** *n.* *Mus.* An interval of seven degrees; a note at this interval.

oc-ta′vo, 1 ẽk-tē′vo; 2 ŏe-tā′vo. **I.** *a.* **1.** Folded into eight leaves. **2.** Denoting a certain size of page (commonly 6 x 9½ inches); 8*vo.* **II.** *n.* A book of such leaves or pages.

oc-til′lion, 1 ẽk-til′yɒn; 2 ŏe-tĭl′yon, *n.* A cardinal number: in the French system, represented by a figure 1 with 27 ciphers annexed; in the English system, by a figure 1 with 48 ciphers.

Oc-to′ber, 1 ẽk-tō′bɒr; 2 ŏe-tō′ber, *n.* The tenth month of the year.

oc″to-ge-na′ri-an, 1 ŏk″to-jĭ-nē′rɪ-ɒn; 2 ŏe″to-ge-nā′rĭ-an. **I.** *a.* Being eighty or from eighty to ninety years of age. **II.** *n.* A person of between eighty and ninety years.

oc′to-pus, 1 ŏk′to-pʉs; 2 ŏe′to-pŭs, *n.* [-PUS-ES^z or -PI, 1 -paɪ; 2 -pī, *pl.*] An eight-armed cuttle-fish; a devil-fish.

oc″to-roon′, 1 ŏk″tō-rūn′; 2 ŏe″to-rōōn′, *n.* One who has one-eighth negro blood.

Edible Octopus. ¹⁄₃₀

oc′u-lar, 1 ŏk′yu-lɒr; 2 ŏe′yu-lar. **I.** *a.* Pertaining to or connected with the eye. **II.** *n.* The eyepiece of an optical instrument. **-ly,** *adv.* — **oc′u-list,** *n.* One skilled in treating diseases of the eye.

odd, 1 ŏd; 2 ŏd, *a.* **1.** Not even; not **od^p,** } divisible by two without remainder. **2.** Left over after a division; additional. **3.** Occasional. **4.** Peculiar; queer; eccentric. **-ly,** *adv.* **-ness,** *n.* — **odd′i-ty,** *n.* [-TIES^z, *pl.*] Something odd; singularity; eccentricity.

odds, 1 ŏdz; 2 ŏds, *n. pl. & sing.* Advantage; allowance by way of handicap.

ode, 1 ōd; 2 ōd, *n.* A brief poem; a lyric.

o′di-um, 1 ō′dɪ-ʉm; 2 ō′dĭ-ŭm, *n.* Hatred; repugnance; disgust. — **o′di-ous,** *a.* Detested; detestable.

o′dor, 1 ō′dɒr; 2 ō′dor, *n.* Smell; scent; estimation. **o′dour‡.** — **o″dor-if′er-ous,** *a.* Diffusing an odor. **-ly,** *adv.* — **o′dor-ous,** *a.* Having an odor; fragrant. **-ly,** *adv.*

œc″u-men′ic, etc. Same as ECUMENIC, etc.

o′er, 1 ōr; 2 ōr, *adv. & prep.* Over: contraction.

œ-soph′a-gus, *n.* Same as ESOPHAGUS.

of, 1 ɒv; 2 ŏv, *prep.* **1.** Associated or connected with. **2.** From or out from. **3.** Directed toward or exerted upon. **4.** Concerning; about. **5.** Equivalent to.

---

off, 1 ôf; 2 ôf. **I.** *a.* Farther; aside from. **II.** *adv.* **1.** Away. **2.** Entirely to an end; utterly. **III.** *prep.* **1.** From. **2.** Extending away or out from. **IV.** *interj.* Begone! away! — **off color,** unsatisfactory; inferior. — **off″set′,** *vt.* [OFF′SET′; OFF′SET′TING.] To set off or against; balance.— **off″set″,** *n.* Something set off against something else as an equivalent; a projection; a branch that strikes root. [garbage.

of′fal, 1 ôf′əl; 2 ôf′al, *n.* Refuse of meat;

of-fend′d, 1 e-fend′; 2 ŏ-fĕnd′, *v.* **I.** *t.* **1.** To affront. **2.** To sin against. **II.** *i.* **1.** To transgress laws. **2.** To displease. — **of-fend′er,** *n.*— **of-fense′,** *n.* **1.** Any sin. **2.** That which provokes. **3.** Umbrage. **4.** Assault or attack. — **of-fence′‡.**— **of-fen′siv(e)s.** **I.** *a.* **1.** Serving or intended to give offense. **2.** Disagreeable; injurious. **3.** Serving as a means of attack. **II.** *n.* Aggressive operations or attitude; attack. **-ly,** *adv.* **-ness,** *n.*

of′fer, 1 ôf′ər; 2 ŏf′er, *v.* **I.** *t.* **1.** To present for acceptance. **2.** To propose. **3.** To sacrifice. **II.** *i.* **1.** To present itself. **2.** To make an attempt.— **of′fer,** *n.* The act of offering; a proposal.— **of′fer-ing,** *n.* **1.** The act of making an offer. **2.** That which is offered; sacrifice.

of′fer-to-ry, 1 ôf′ar-to-ri; 2 ŏf′er-to-ry, *n.* **1.** *Rom. Cath. Ch.* A part of the mass. **2.** Words or music during the collection of alms in a church service. **3.** The act of offering, or the thing offered.

off′hand″, 1 ôf′hand″; 2 ôf′hănd″, *a. & adv.* Without preparation; unceremonious or unceremoniously.

of′fice, 1 ôf′is; 2 ŏf′iç, *n.* **1.** A particular duty, charge, or trust. **2.** A service or duty. **3.** A place where business is carried on.— **of′fi-cer. I.** *vt.* **1.** To command as an officer. **2.** To appoint officers for. **II.** *n.* One who holds an office, as in an army.— **of-fi′cial. I.** *a.* **1.** Pertaining to an office. **2.** Authoritative. **II.** *n.* One holding a public office.— **of-fi′ci-ate,** *vi.* [-AT′ED‡; -AT′ING.] To act as an officer, agent, or leader.— **of-fi′cious,** *a.* Intermeddling with what is not one's concern. **-ly,** *adv.* **-ness,** *n.*

off′ing, 1 ôf′iŋ; 2 ŏf′ing, *n. Naut.* That part of the visible sea off shore and beyond anchorage-ground.

off′spring, 1 ôf′spriŋ; 2 ôf′spring, *n.* A child or children; a descendant or descendants; posterity. [ll. *adv.* Often.

oft, 1 ôft; 2 ŏft. [Poet.] **I.** *a.* Frequent.

oft′en, 1 ôf′n; 2 ôf′n, *adv.* On numerous occasions; repeatedly.— **oft′en-times″,** *adv.* At frequent times. **oft′times″‡.**

o′gle, 1 o′gl; 2 ō′gl. **I.** *vt. & vi.* [O′GLED; O′GLING.] To look or glance at fur-

tively, as in coquetry. **II.** *n.* An amorous or coquettish look; a side-glance.

o′gre, 1 o′gər; 2 ō′gĕr, *n.* A demon **o′gers,** fabled to devour human beings. — **o′gre-ish,** *a.*— **o′gress,** *n. fem.*

oh, 1 o; 2 ō, *interj.* An ejaculation.

ohm, 1 ōm; 2 ōm, *n.* The unit of electrical resistance, equivalent to the resistance of 400 feet of common iron telegraph-wire: from Georg Simon *Ohm* (1787?–1854), German physicist.

-old, *suffix.* Like; resembling; having the form of; as, spher*old.*

oil, 1 oil; 2 ŏil. **I.** *vt.* To lubricate or anoint with oil. **II.** *n.* A greasy liquid, of vegetable or animal origin, insoluble in water.— **oil″cake,** *n.* The mass of compressed seeds, etc., from which oil has been expressed, used for cattle-food or as a fertilizer.— **oil′cloth″,** *n.* **1.** Coarse cloth coated with white lead ground in oil, and bearing patterns, for floor-covering, etc. **2.** *Naut.* A tarpaulin.— **oil-painting,** *n.* Painting done in oil-colors: opposed to *water-color* and *fresco-painting.*

oil′y, 1 oil′i; 2 ŏil′y, *a.* [OIL′I-ER; OIL′I-EST.] Pertaining to, containing, or smeared with oil; smooth, as in speech.— **oil′i-ness,** *n.*

oint′ment, 1 eint′ment *or* -mənt; 2 ŏint′-ment, *n.* A fatty medicinal preparation for external use.

o-ka′pi, 1 o-kä′pi; 2 o-kä′pi, *n.* A small African quadruped, giraffe variety: discovered 1900.

o′kra, 1 o′krə; 2 ō′kra, *n.* A herb of African origin or its mucilaginous pods, used in soups. [W. Ind.]

old, 1 ōld; 2 ōld, *a.* **1.** Having a great age; having some specified age; aged. **2.** Antiquated; worthless. **3.** Familiar; customary.— **old′en,** **I.** *vt. & vt.* To render old; grow old. **II.** *a.* Old; ancient.

o″le-ag′i-nous, 1 ō″li-aj′i-nus; 2 ō′le-ăg′i-nŭs, *a.* Oily.

o″le-an′der, 1 ō″li-an′dər; 2 ō′le-ăn′der, *a.* An Old World evergreen shrub with pink or white flowers.

o″le-o-mar′ga-rine, 1 ō″li-o-mär′gə-rin *or* -rīn; 2 ō′le-o-mär′ga-rīn *or* -rīn, *n.* Artificial butter, made from animal fats. **o′le-o‡.**

ol-fac′to-ry, 1 ŏl-fak′to-ri; 2 ŏl-făk′to-ry, *a.* Pertaining to the sense of smell.

Oleander.

ol′i-gar′chy, 1 ŏl′i-gär′ki; 2 ŏl′i-gär′ey, *n.* [-CHIES²; *pl.*] Government by a few.

1: ə = final; ɪ = habit; aisle; au = out; oil; iū = feud; chin; go; ŋ = sing; thin, this.
2: wolf, dog; book, boot; full, rule, cure, but, burn; oil, boy; go, gem; ink; thin, this.

— ol'i-garch, n. A ruler in an oligarchy.— ol'i-gar'chic, a. ol''i-gar'chal‡.

ol'ive, ⎱ 1 ɒl'ɪv; 2 ŏl'ĭv, n. 1. An evergreen
ol'ivᵉ, ⎰ tree, anciently an emblem of peace; also, its oily fruit. 2. A dull yellowish-green color.

-ology, suffix. A suffix used in English words derived from the Greek, denoting (1) a science, as philology; (2) (rarely) a collection, as anthology.

O-lym'pi-an, 1 o-lim'pi-ən; 2 o-lym'pi-an. I. a. 1. Pertaining to the twelve gods of Olympus, especially to Zeus (Jupiter). 2. Pertaining to the Olympic games. II. n. Gr. Myth. Any one of the twelve higher gods who dwelt on Mount Olympus, viz.: Zeus, Hera, Athena, Apollo, Artemis, Hermes, Ares, Aphrodite, Hephæstus, Hestia, Poseidon, and Demeter.

O-lym'pic, 1 o-lim'pik; 2 o-lym'pic, a. 1. Of or pertaining to Mt. Olympus in Thessaly, northern Greece. 2. Of or pertaining to the sacred vale of Olympia in the Peloponnesus, Greece.— Olympic games, athletic games and races held for five days every four years at Olympia, in honor of Olympian Zeus; or the modern revival of these contests.

o-me'ga, 1 o-mī'gə; 2 o-mē'ga, n. The last letter in the Greek alphabet (Ω, ω); figuratively, the end.

om'e-let, 1 em'i-let; 2 ŏm'e-lĕt, n. A dish of eggs and milk, beaten together and fried.

o'men, 1 ō'men; 2 ō'mĕn. I. vt. & vi. To serve as an omen; presage. II. n. Something regarded as a prophetic sign.— om'i-nous, a. Of the nature of an evil omen; ill-omened.— om'i-nous-ly, adv.

o-mit', 1 o-mit'; 2 o-mĭt', vt. [O-MIT'TEDᵈ; O-MIT'TING.] To leave out; leave undone; neglect.— o-mis'sion, n. The act of omitting; anything omitted or neglected.

om'ni-bus, 1 em'ni-bus; 2 ŏm'ni-bŭs. I. a. Covering many and various objects. II. n. A long four-wheeled passenger-vehicle.

om-nip'o-tence, 1 em-nip'o-tens; 2 ŏm-nĭp'o-tĕnç, n. Unlimited and universal power.— om-nip'o-ten-cy, n.— om-nip'o-tent, a. Almighty.

om''ni-pres'ence, 1 em''ni-prez'ens, 2 ŏm''ni-prĕs'ĕnç, n. The quality of being everywhere and always present.— om''ni-pres'ent, a. Everywhere present.

om-nis'cience, 1 em-nish'ens, 2 ŏm-nĭsh'-ĕnç, n. Infinite knowledge.— om-nis'cient, a. Knowing all things; all-knowing; all-wise. — om-nis'cient-ly, adv.

om-niv'o-rous, 1 em-niv'o-rus; 2 ŏm-nĭv'o-rŭs, a. Eating food of all kinds; greedy.

on, 1 en; 2 ŏn. I. adv. 1. So as to cover, overspread, or adhere. 2. Forward,

ahead. II. prep. 1. In or into contact with the top of; by means of. 2. Close behind. 3. Directed toward. 4. In the act of. 5. Comprised in. 6. In reference to. 7. In a state of.

once, ⎱ 1 wuns; 2 wŏnç, adv. One time;
onsᵉ, ⎰ during some past time; at any time. — at once, instantly; simultaneously.

on dit, 1 eñ dī; 2 ŏñ dī. [F.] They say; it is said: used also as a noun.

one, 1 wun; 2 wŏn. I. a. Single; indefinite; this; that; the same. II. n. 1. A unit, or a symbol (1 or I) representing it. 2. A single thing or person; any person indefinitely.— all one, of the same or of no consequence.— at one, in harmony; the same.— one'ness, n. Singleness; unity.

on'er-ous, 1 en'ər-us; 2 ŏn'er-ŭs, a. Burdensome; oppressive.— -ly, adv.

on'ion, 1 un'yən; 2 ŏn'yon, n. An edible underground bulb of the lily family: remarkable for its strong odor.

on'ly, 1 ōn'li; 2 ōn'ly. I. a. Alone in its class. II. adv. 1. Without another; singly. 2. For one purpose alone; simply; merely.

on'set'', 1 en'set''; 2 ŏn'sĕt'', n. An impetuous attack; assault.

on'slaught'', 1 en'slɒt''; 2 ŏn'slat'', n. A violent or overwhelming assault.

on-tol'o-gy, 1 en-tel'o-ji; 2 ŏn-tŏl'o-gy, n. Philos. The science of pure being.— on''to-log'i-cal, a. on''to-log'ic‡.— on''to-log'-i-cal-ly, adv.— on-tol'o-gist, n.

o'nus, 1 ō'nus; 2 ō'nŭs, n. A burden or responsibility.

on'ward, 1 en'wərd; 2 ŏn'ward. I. a. Moving forward or ahead. II. adv. In advance; forward in space or time. on'wards‡.

on'yx, 1 en'iks; 2 ŏn'yks, n. A variegated quartz.

ooze, ⎱ 1 ūz; 2 ōoz. I. vt & vi. [OOZ(E)Dˢ;
oozᵉ, ⎰ OOZ'ING.] To leak out; flow gently; percolate. II. n. 1. Slimy mud, or wet soil. 2. A gentle flow.— oo'zy, a. Miry.

o-pac'i-ty, 1 o-pas'i-ti; 2 o-păç'i-ty, n. [-TIESᶻ, pl.] The state of being opaque; obscurity.

o'pal, 1 ō'pəl; 2 ō'pal, n. A precious stone of changeable colors.— o''pal-es'cent, a. Possessing an iridescent play of pearly colors.

o-paque', 1 o-pēk'; 2 o-pāk', a. That can not be seen through; not transparent or translucent. -ness, n. [To open.

opc, 1 ōp; 2 ōp, vt. & vi. [Archaic or Poet.]

o'pen, 1 ō'pn; 2 ō'pn. I. vt. & vi. To set or become open; unlock; disclose; expand; begin. II. a. 1. Affording approach; unenclosed; expanded; accessible. 2. Ready to receive. 3. Candid. 4. Frank; ingenuous. -ly, adv. -ness

1: **a**rtistic, **ä**rt; fat, f**ā**re; f**a**st; get, pr**ē**y; h**i**t, pol**ī**ce; ob**e**y, g**ō**; n**o**t, **ŏ**r; f**u**ll, r**ū**le; b**u**t, b**ū**rn;

2: ärt, **ā**pe, f**ă**t, f**â**re, f**â**st, wh**a**t, **a**ll; m**ē**, g**ĕ**t, pr**e**y, f**ê**rn; h**ĭ**t, **ī**ce; ĭ=ē; ī=ē; g**ō**, n**ŏ**t, **ô**r, w**ŏ**n,

n.— o′pen-er, *n.*— o′pen-ing, *n.* **1.** A beginning. **2.** An aperture.

op′er-a, 1 ŏp′er-a; 2 ŏp′er-a, *n.* A musical drama.— op″er-a-glass″, *n.* A double telescope of small size.— op″er-at′ic, *a.* Pertaining to or of the nature of the opera.

o″pe′ra′ bouffe′, 1 ŏ″pē″rä′ bũf′; 2 ŏ″pe″rä′ bũf′. Farcical comic operetta.

op′er-ate, 1 ŏp′er-āt; 2 ŏp′er-āt, *v.* [-AT″-ED^d; -AT″ING.] **I.** *t.* To put in action; work; run; conduct; accomplish. **II.** *i.* To effect a result; work.— op″er-a″tion, *n.* **1.** The act of operating; act; mode of action; process. **2.** Surgical treatment, as for removal of a part.— op′er-a″tive^s. **I.** *a.* Exerting power; working efficiently; connected with operations. **II.** *n.* A worker at handicraft; laborer; artizan.— op′er-a″tive(e-ly^s, *adv.*— op′er-a″tor, *n.*

oph-thal′mi-a,) 1 ŏf-thal′mi-a; 2 ŏf-thăl′-
of-thal′mi-a^r,) mi-a, *n.* Inflammation of the eye. oph-thal′my‡.— oph-thal′mic, *a.* Pertaining to the eye or to ophthalmia.

o′pi-ate, 1 ō′pi-ıt; 2 ō′pi-at. **I.** *a.* Consisting of opium; tending to induce sleep. **II.** *n.* A medicine containing opium, or something inducing sleep.

o-pine′‖, 1 o-paın′; 2 o-pın′, *vt. & vi.* [O-PINED′; O-PIN′ING.] To suppose; fancy; conjecture.

o-pin′ion, 1 o-pin′yan; 2 o-pın′yon, *n.* **1.** A confident belief without full certainty. **2.** Reputation.— o-pin′ion-at″ed, *a.* Unwarrantably attached to one's own opinion.

o′pi-um, 1 ō′pi-um; 2 ō′pi-ŭm, *n.* The narcotic juice of the poppy.

o-pos′sum, 1 o-pos′um; 2 o-pŏs′ŭm, *n.* An American arboreal quadruped, the female of which carries its young in a pouch or on the back.

Murine Opossum and Young. 1/4

op-po′nent, 1 e-pō′nent; 2 ŏ-pō′nĕnt. **I.** *a.* Opposing. **II.** *n.* One who opposes; an antagonist.

op″por-tune′, 1 ŏp″ɵr-tiūn′; 2 ŏp″ɵr-tūn′, *a.* Meeting some requirement; seasonable. **-ly,** *adv.* **-ness,** *n.*— op″por-tu′ni-ty, *n.* [-TIES^z, *pl.*] A convenient time; favorable occasion.

op″por-tu′nist, 1 ŏp″ɵr-tiū′nist; 2 ŏp″ɵr-tū′nist, *n.* One who waits for or takes advantage of circumstances or opportunities to gain his ends.

op-pose′, 1 e-pōz′; 2 ŏ-pōs′, *vt. & vi.* [OP-POSED′; OP-POS′ING.] **1.** To act in opposition to; resist. **2.** To object to; to

offer objection. **3.** To stand opposite.— op-pos′a-bl(e^r, *a.*— op-pos′er, *n.*— op′posit(e^s. **I.** *a.* Situated in front of or over against; contrary; radically different. **II.** *n.* One who or that which is in opposition or contrast.— op″po-si′tion, *n.* **1.** The act of opposing. **2.** The state of being opposite or opposed. **3.** An obstacle; obstruction. **4.** *Astron.* The relative position of two bodies that are 180° apart. **5.** The party opposed to an administration.

op-press′^t, 1 e-pres′; 2 ŏ-prĕs′, *vt.* To govern severely and unjustly; weigh down; burden; depress.— op-press′ion, *n.* **1.** Severe and cruel rule; tyranny. **2.** Mental or physical depression; languor.— op-press′-siv(e^s, *a.* Tyrannical; depressive. **-ly,** *adv.* **-ness,** *n.*— op-press′or, *n.*

op-pro′bri-um, 1 e-prō′bri-um; 2 ŏ-prō′-bri-ŭm, *n.* Reproach mingled with disdain; disgrace; shame; a cause of disgrace. — op-pro′bri-ous, *a.* Abusive; contumelious.

op′tic, 1 ŏp′tık; 2 ŏp′tic. **I.** *a.* **1.** Pertaining to the eye or vision. **2.** Optical. **II.** *n.* An eye.— op′ti-cal, *a.* Pertaining to optics or to the eyesight; assisting vision; optic.— op-ti′cian, 1 ŏp-tish′an; 2 ŏp-tish′an, *n.* One who makes or deals in optical goods. — op′tics, *n.* The science that treats of light, vision, and sight.

op′ti-mism, 1 ŏp′tı-mızm; 2 ŏp′tı-mĭsm, *n.* The doctrine that everything is ordered for the best; a hopeful view of things. — op′ti-mist, *n.*

op′tion, 1 ŏp′shan; 2 ŏp′shon, *n.* The right of choosing; choice.— op′tion-al, *a.* Depending on choice; elective. **-ly,** *adv.*

op-tom′e-try, 1 ŏp-tŏm′ı-trı; 2 ŏp-tŏm′e-try, *n.* Measurement of the powers of vision.— op-tom′e-trist, *n.*

op′u-l-ent, 1 ŏp′yu-lent; 2 ŏp′yu-lĕnt, *a.* Wealthy; exuberant; profuse.— op′u-lence, *n.* **1.** Wealth. **2.** Luxuriance. [position.

o′pus, 1 ō′pus; 2 ō′pŭs, *n.* *Mus.* A c.m-or, 1 ŏr; 2 ôr, *conj.* **1.** Either; else: a disjunctive, often preceded by *either.* **2.** Also; alias.

-or, *suffix.* A termination used to form (1) nouns of agent; as, act*or*; (2) comparatives of Latin origin; as, juni*or*; (3) abstract and concrete nouns of Latin origin; as, hon*or*.

or′a-cle,) 1 ŏr′a-kl; 2 ŏr′a-el, *n.* **1.** The or′a-cl^r,) shrine of a divinity, where prophecies were supposed to be given; a prophecy thus given or the deity giving it. **2.** An infallible authority.— o-rac′u-lar, *a.* **1.** Pertaining to an oracle; authoritative. **2.** Enigmatical. **3.** Prophetic.

o′ral, 1 ō′ral; 2 ō′ral, *a.* **1.** Spoken, not written. **2.** Pertaining to the mouth.— o′ral-ly, *adv.* By word of mouth.

or′ange, 1 er′ınj; 2 ŏr′anġ. **I.** *a.* Pertain-

ing to an orange; of the color of an orange.
II. *n.* A large juicy fruit, with a reddish=
yellow rind; also, the tree that bears it or
the color of the fruit.

o-rang'=u-tan", } 1 o-raŋ'=ū-tan", -taŋ";
o-rang'=ou-tang", } 2 o-
răng'=ụ-tăn", -tăng", *n.* A
large red=haired anthro-
poid ape of Borneo and
Sumatra.

or'a-tor, 1 ɔr'ə-tər *or*
-tər; 2 ôr'a-tor, *n.*
One who delivers an
oration; an eloquent
public speaker.— **o-ra'-
tion,** *n.* An elaborate
public speech.— **or"a-
tor'i-cal,** *a.* Pertaining to oratory; dis-
playing oratory.— **or"-
a-to'ri-o,** *n. Mus.* A
sacred composition,
usually semi=dramatic.— **or'a-to-ry,** *n.*
1. The art of public speaking; eloquence. **2.** A private chapel.

Orang=utan.
1/36

orb, 1 ɔrb; 2 ôrb. **I.** *vt.* & *vi.* **1.** To surround; encircle. **2.** To shape into an
orb. **II.** *n.* A rounded mass; a sphere;
globe; circle or orbit; a celestial body, as a
star or planet.— **orbed,** *pa.* **1.** Spherical. **2.**
Encircled; circular. **3.** Having orbs or eyes.
— **or-bic'u-lar,** *a.* Having the form of an
orb or orbit; well rounded.— **or-bic'u-late,**
a. **or-bic'u-lat"ed¹**.— **or-bic"u-la'tion,** *n.*

or'bit, 1 ɔr'bıt; 2 ôr'bit, *n.* **1.** The path in
space along which a heavenly body moves.
2. The cavity of the skull containing the
eye.— **or'bi-tal,** *a.*

or'chard, 1 ɔr'tʃərd; 2 ôr'chard, *n.* A collection of fruit=trees; also, the enclosure
for same.

or'ches-tra, 1 ɔr'kes-trə; 2 ôr'cĕs-tra, *n.*
A band of musicians, their instruments, or
the place occupied by them.— **or"ches-tral,**
a.— **or'ches-trate,** *vt.* & *vt.* [-TRAT"ED⁴;
-TRAT"ING.] To compose or arrange for an
orchestra.— **or"ches-tra'tion,** *n.*

Or'chis, 1 ɔr'kıs; 2 ôr'eis, *n.* A tuber-
bearing plant having dense spikes of
small flowers.— **or'chid,** *n.* Any plant of the
orchis family.

or-dain', 1 ɔr-dēn'; 2 ôr-dān', *vt.* **1.** To
order; decree. **2.** To appoint and consecrate, as a Christian minister.— **or-dain'er,** *n.*

or'de-al, 1 ɔr'dı-al; 2 ôr'de-al, *n.* **1.** A trying experience; severe test. **2.** A medieval
form of trial, as by fire or poison.

or'der, 1 ɔr'dər; 2 ôr'dĕr. **I.** *vt.* To command; put in order; regulate. **II.** *n.*
1. Methodical arrangement; tranquillity;
settled rule; working condition. **2.** A

command; usage. **3.** A class, as of society; a group superior to a genus. **4.**
An honor conferred. **5.** *pl.* The clerical office. **6.** A style of architecture.
— **or'der-li-ness,** *n.*— **or'der-ly. I.** *a.* Systematic; peaceful; well arranged; pertaining to orders. **II.** *n.* A non=commissioned
officer, attendant on a superior.

or'di-nal, 1 ɔr'dı-nal; 2 ôr'di-nal. **I.** *a.*
Denoting position in an order; pertain-
ing to an order. **II.** *n.* That form of
the numeral that shows the order in a
series, as *fifth.*

or'di-nance, 1 ɔr'dı-nəns; 2 ôr'di-nanç, *n.*
1. A municipal law. **2.** *Eccl.* A religious rite.

or'di-na-ry, 1 ɔr'dı-nē-rı; 2 ôr'di-nā-ry.
I. *a.* Common; usual; normal; commonplace. **II.** *n.* [-RIES², *pl.*] That which
is usual or common; a public table; an
ecclesiastical judge.— **or'di-na-ri-ly,** *adv.*

or'di-nate, 1 ɔr'dı-nıt; 2 ôr'di-nat, *a.*
Characterized by regularity or order;
regular.

or"di-na'tion, 1 ɔr"dı-nē"shən; 2 ôr"di-nā'-
shon, *n.* **1.** The act of ordaining; consecration to the ministry; regulation; determination; order. **2.** Ordinance. **3.**
Arrangement in order; disposition; array.
4. Natural or proper order; coordination.

ord'nance, 1 ôrd'nəns; 2 ôrd'nanç, *n.* Implements of war, especially artillery.

or'dure, 1 ɔr'jur *or* ɔr'dıur; 2 ôr'jụr *or*
ôr'dûr, *n.* Excrement; feces.

ore, 1 ɔr; 2 ôr, *n.* A natural substance, as
rock, containing metal.

or'gan, 1 ɔr'gən; 2 ôr'ğan, *n.* An instrument; a musical wind=instrument operated by keys; part of a living structure
performing some special work; newspaper
published in the interest of a party.
— **or-gan'ic,** *a.* **1.** Pertaining to organs or
living organisms, as animals and plants. **2.**
Organized; systematized. **or-gan'i-cal²**.
— **or-gan'i-cal-ly,** *adv.*— **or'gan-ism,** *n.* **1.**
An organized or living being. **2.** The state
of being organized.— **or'gan-ist,** *n.* One
who plays the organ.

or'gan-dy, 1 ɔr'gən-dı; 2 ôr'ğan-dy, *n.* A
very fine translucent muslin dress=goods,
often having figured patterns. **or'gan-die².**

or'gan-ize, 1 ɔr'gən-aız; 2 ôr'ğan-īz, *v.*
[-IZED'; -IZ"ING.] **I.** *t.* To arrange systematically; provide with officers and rules,
as an assembly; form into a living organism. **II.** *t.* To unite in a society. **or'-
gan-ise². — or"gan-i-za'tion, or'gan-i-
sa'tion,** *n.* The act of organizing; a
number of persons or things organized; combination.

or′gies, 1 ŏr′jiz; 2 ôr′ģis, *n. pl.* [OR′GY, *sing.*] Wild or drunken revelry.

o′ri-el, 1 ō′ri-el; 2 ō′ri-ĕl, *n.* A window built out from a wall and resting on a bracket.

Oriel.

o′ri-ent, 1 ō′ri-ent; 2 ō′ri-ĕnt. **I.** *a.* **1.** [O-] Oriental. **2.** Resembling sunrise; bright. **3.** Ascending. **II.** *n.* **1.** [O-] The East, as the countries in Asia east of the Mediterranean. **2.** The eastern sky.— **O′ri-en′tal.** **I.** *a.* Pertaining to the Orient. **II.** *n.* An inhabitant of Asia.

or′i-fice, 1 ŏr′i-fis; 2 or′i-fiçs, } *n.* A small opening into a cavity; an aperture; hole; a perforation.

or′i-gin, 1 ŏr′i-jin; 2 ŏr′i-ġĭn, *n.* Beginning; source; cause; parentage.— **o-rig′i-nal.** **I.** *a.* **1.** Pertaining to the beginning of a thing; new; novel; not copied or imitated. **2.** Having originating power; inventive. **II.** *n.* **1.** The first form of anything. **2.** The language in which a book is first written. **3.** A person of unique character.— **o-rig″i-nal′i-ty,** *n.*— **o-rig′i-nal-ly,** *adv.*— **o-rig′i-nate,** *v.* [-NAT″ED⁴; -NAT″ING.] **I.** *t.* To produce; create. **II.** *i.* To arise from some origin or source.— **o-rig″i-na′tion,** *n.* A beginning; origin.— **o-rig′i-na″tor,** *n.*

o′ri-ole, 1 ō′ri-ōl; 2 ō′ri-ŏl, *n.* One of various black=and= yellow birds of the Old or New World.

or′i-son, 1 ŏr′i-zən; 2 ôr′i-son, *n.* A devotional prayer.

Baltimore Oriole. 1/3

or′na-ment, 1 ŏr′nə-ment *or* -mənt; 2 ôr′na-ment. **I**d. *vt.* To decorate; beautify; adorn. **II.** *n.* Something that adds beauty or elegance; decoration.— **or″na-men′tal,** *a.* Serving to adorn. — **or″na-men′tal-ly,** *adv.* — **or″na-men-ta′tion,** *n.*

or-nate′, 1 ŏr-nēt′; 2 ôr-nāt′, *a.* Made elegant by decoration; ornamented. **-ly,** *adv.* **-ness,** *n.*

or″ni-thol′o-gy, 1 ŏr′ni-thŏl′o-ji; 2 ôr′ni-thŏl′o-ġy, *n.* The scientific study of birds.— **or″ni-thol′o-gist,** *n.* One versed in ornithology.

o′ro-tund, 1 ō′ro-tund; 2 ō′ro-tŭnd. **I.** *a.* Having a full, clear, rounded, resonant quality, as a voice. **II.** *n.* The quality of voice so characterized. **o′ro-tun′di-ty‡.**

or′phan, } 1 ŏr′fən; 2 ôr′fan. **I.** *a.* Deprived of parents by death; pertaining to an orphan or orphans. **II.** *n.* A child deprived of its parents by death. — **or′phan-age,** *n.* **1.** The state of being an orphan. **2.** An orphan asylum.

or′re-ry, 1 ŏr′i-ri; 2 ôr′e-ry, *n.* [-RIES², *pl.*] An apparatus for illustrating the relative size, position, and motions of the sun and planets: named from the Earl of Orrery.

Orrery.

The turning of the crank causes the balls to revolve, in imitation of the natural motions of the planets they represent.

or′tho-dox, 1 ŏr′tho-dŏks; 2 ôr′tho-dŏks, *a.* **1.** Correct in doctrine; approved; accepted. **2.** [O-] Pertaining to the Greek Church.— **or′tho-dox″y,** *n.*

or″tho-ep″y, 1 ŏr′tho-ep″i *or* ⲟr-thō′i-pi; 2 ôr′tho-ep″y *or* ŏr-thō′e-py, *n.* The art of correct pronunciation.— **or″tho-ep′ic,** *a.* Pertaining to orthoepy. **-i-cal‡.**— **or′tho-ep″ist,** *n.* An authority on pronunciation.

or-thog′ra-phy, } 1 ⲟr-thog′ra-fi; 2 ôr-thŏg′ra-fy, } *n.* **1.** A system of spelling; correct spelling. **2.** The science that treats of letters and spelling. — **or-thog′ra-pher,** *n.* One versed in orthography.— **or″tho-graph′ic,** *a.* **-i-cal‡.**— **or″tho-graph′i-cal-ly,** *adv.*

-ory, *suffix.* Used in English to signify place in nouns; as, dormit*ory*; in adjectives, relating to or like, as, amat*ory.*

os′cil-late, 1 ŏs′i-lēt; 2 ŏs′i-lāt, *vt. & vi.* [-LAT″ED⁴; -LAT″ING.] To swing to and fro; vibrate; fluctuate.— **os″cil-la′tion,** *n.* The act or state of oscillating.— **os′cil-la″tor,** *n.* — **os′cil-la-to-ry,** *a.*

os′cu-late, 1 ŏs′kiu-lēt; 2 ŏs′eū-lāt, *vt. & vi.* [-LAT″ED⁴; -LAT″ING.] **1.** To kiss. **2.** *Geom.* To touch, as two curves.— **os″cu-la′tion,** *n.* — **os′cu-la-to-ry,** *a.*

-ose, *suffix.* Same as -OUS; as, verb*ose.*

o′sier, 1 ō′ʒər; 2 ō′zher. **I.** *a.* Consisting of twigs, as of willow. **II.** *n.* Willow for basket=making.

-osity, *suffix.* A suffix, signifying "fulness, abundance of"; as, verb*osity.*

os′prey, 1 ŏs′pri; 2 ŏs′pry, *n.* A dark=brown, hawk=like bird that preys upon fish.

os′si-fy, 1 ŏs′i-fai; 2 ŏs′i-fȳ, *vt. & vi.* [-FIED;

-FY'ING.] To turn into bone.— **os″si-fi-ca′-tion**, *n.*

os-ten′si-bl(e[r], 1 os-ten′si-bl; 2 ŏs-tĕn′si-bl, *a.* Avowed or put forward; seeming; apparent.— **os-ten″si-bil′i-ty**, *n.*— **os-ten′-si-bly**, *adv.*

os″ten-ta′tion, 1 os″ten-tē′shən; 2 ŏs″tĕn-tā′shon, *n.* Boastful display; pretentious parade.— **os″ten-ta′tious**, *a.* Given to ostentation; pretentious; vain. **-ly,** *adv.* **-ness,** *n.*

os″te-ol′o-gy, 1 os″tĭ-ol′o-jĭ; 2 ŏs″te-ŏl′o-gy, *n.* The anatomy of the bones.

os″te-op′a-thy, 1 os″tĭ-op′a-thĭ; 2 ŏs″te-ŏp′a-thy, *n.* **1.** The treatment of bone disease. **2.** A system of the art of healing which emphasizes the power of the body to heal itself and whose therapy majors in manipulation.— **os″te-o-path′ic**, *a.*— **os″te-o-path′i-cal-ly**, *adv.*— **os″te-op′a-thist**, *n.* One who believes in or practises osteopathy. **os″te-o-path‡.**

os′tler, *n.* Same as HOSTLER.

os′tra-cize or **-cise**, 1 os′tra-saiz; 2 ŏs′tra-çĭz, *vt.* [-CIZED′; -CIZ′ING.] To exclude from intercourse or favor.— **os′tra-cism**, *n.* Exclusion from social privilege or favor.

os′trich, 1 os′trich; 2 ŏs′trĭch, *n.* A very large, two-toed bird of Africa and Arabia, noted for its beautiful p l u m e s and its speed in running.

Ostrich. 1/120

oth′er, 1 uth′ər; 2 ŏth′ẽr. **I.** *a.* **1.** Not the same. **2.** Additional. **3.** Second: noting the remaining one of two things; contrary; alternate. **II.** *pron.* A different person or thing. **2.** The opposite one. **III.** *adv.* Otherwise.— **oth′er-wise**. **I.** *a.* Different. **II.** *adv.* **1.** In a different manner. **2.** In other respects. **III.** *conj.* Except for the reason given.

ot′ter, 1 ot′ər; 2 ŏt′ẽr, *n.* A weasel-like, web-footed, aquatic animal, feeding upon fish. [tar‡; ot′ter‡.]

ot′to, 1 ot′o; 2 ŏt′o, *n.* Same as ATTAR. **ot′-**

Ot′to-man, 1 ot′a-mən; 2 ŏt′o-man. **I.** *a.* Pertaining to the Turks. **II.** *n.* **1.** A Turk. **2.** [o-] A low cushioned seat without a back.

ought, 1 ŏt; 2 ôt, *v.* **1.** To be under moral obligation to be or do. **2.** To be fitting or imperative.

ought[1], *n. & adv.* Aught; anything.

ought[2], *n.* A cipher; naught.

ounce[1], 1 auns; 2 ounç, *n.* **1.** A unit of weight; 1/16 of a pound avoirdupois, 1/12 of a pound Troy. **2.** One-sixteenth of a pint.

ounce[2], *n.* A feline carnivorous mammal.

our, 1 aur; 2 our, *poss. pron.* Pertaining to us: *ours* when not followed by a noun.— **our-self′**, *pron.* Myself.— **our-selves′**, *pron. & pl.* We or us.

ours, *poss. pron.* See OUR. [utan.]

ou-rang′, 1 ū-raṇ′; 2 ụ-răṇg′, *n.* The orang.

-ous, *suffix.* **I.** Denoting possession or presence of a quality; as, membran*ous.* **2.** *Chem.* Denoting a compound in which the element to which it is affixed has a less valence than in compounds whose names end in *-ic.*

oust[d], 1 aust; 2 oust, *vt.* To put out; expel.

out, 1 aut; 2 out. **I.** *n.* **1.** An outside place. **2.** A person or thing that is out or omitted. **II.** *adv.* **1.** In a condition of issuance, or as of having issued; on the outside; not in. **2.** Not in harmony or practise. **3.** Completely; thoroughly. **4.** Not at home. **5.** To the uttermost. **III.** *prep.* From the inside of. In numerous self-explaining compound verbs *out* adds the sense of surpassing or exceeding, usually meaning " more than, beyond, in excess "; as, *out*rank, *out*vote, *out*weigh, *out*bid. — **out″and-out′**, *a.* Thoroughgoing; unqualified.— **out″bound′**, *a.* Outward bound; sailing away from a port.— **out-break′**, *vi.* To burst out; break forth.— **out′break″**, *n.* A sudden and violent breaking forth.— **out′burst″**, *n.* A bursting out; a violent manifestation.— **out′cast″**. **I.** *a.* Rejected as unworthy or useless. **II.** *n.* One who is rejected and despised.— **out-class′t**, *vt.* To exceed in skill or powers.— **out-do′**, *vt.* To exceed in performance; surpass.— **out′field″**, *n.* In baseball, etc., the players in the outer part of the field.— **out-grow′**, *vt.* **1.** To surpass in growth. **2.** To grow out of or away from.— **out′growth″**, *n.* An excrescence.— **out′ing**, *n.* The act of going out; a holiday excursion.— **out-last′d**, *vt.* To last longer than: survive.— **out-stretch′t**, *vt.* To stretch or spread out.— **out there** [Recent], on the firing line of an army in action

out′come″, 1 aut′kum″; 2 out′eŏm″, *n.* The consequence or visible result.

out′cry″, 1 aut′krai″; 2 out′erȳ″, *n.* A vehement or loud cry.

out′door″, 1 aut′dōr″; 2 out′dōr″, *a.* **1.** Being or done in the open air. **2.** Outside of certain public institutions. **out′-of-door″t.**— **out′doors″.** **I.** *n.* The world beyond the house. **out″-of-doors‡.** **II.** *adv.* Out of the house.

out′er, 1 aut′ər; 2 out′ẽr. *a.* **1.** External. **2.** Farther from a center.— **out′er-most**, *a.*

out′fit, 1 aut′fĭt; 2 out′fĭt, *n.* A fitting out; equipment.

out-go′, 1 aut-gō′; 2 out-gō′, *vt. & vi.* To go beyond; excel.— **out′go″**, *n.* That which goes out; cost or outlay.— **out′go″ing**, *a. & n.*

out-land′ish, 1 aut-land′ĭsh; 2 out-lănd′-ish, *a.* Strange; barbarous; remote.

out′law″, 1 aut′lô″; 2 out′lạ″. **I.** *vt.* **1.** To put out of the protection of the law. **2.** To deprive of legal force. **II.** *n.* One who is outlawed; a freebooter; bandit.— **out′law″ry**, *n.* The state of being proscribed.

out′lay″, 1 aut′lē″; 2 out′lā″, *n.* A laying out or disbursing; that which is disbursed.

out′let″, 1 aut′let″; 2 out′lĕt″, *n.* A passage or vent for escape or discharge.

out′line″, 1 aut′lain″; 2 out′līn″. **I.** *vt.* To draw the outline of a figure; a sketch giving only the chief lines.

out-live′, 1 aut-liv′; 2 out-lĭv′, *vt.* To
out-liv′⸍ᴾ, *f* live longer than; survive.

out′look″, 1 aut′luk″; 2 out′lŏŏk″, *n.* The expanse in view; place from which a view may be had; prospect; probability; foresight.

out′put″, 1 aut′put″; 2 out′pŭt″, *n.* The quantity put out or produced in a specified time.

out′rage, 1 aut′rēj; 2 out′rāg. **I.** *vt.* [OUT′-RAGED; OUT′RAG·ING.] To commit outrage upon; assault; wrong shamefully. **II.** *n.* An act of shocking violence or cruelty.— **out-ra′geous**, *a.* Of the nature of an outrage; atrocious. **-ly**, *adv.* **-ness**, *n.*

out-ride′, 1 aut-raid′; 2 out-rĭd′, *vt.* To ride faster than; come safely through, as a storm at sea.— **out′rid″er**, *n.* A mounted servant who rides in advance of or beside a carriage.

out′rig″ger, 1 aut′rig″ẽr; 2 out′rĭg″er, *n.* A part built out, as for supporting a r o w l o c k or balancing a canoe.

Polynesian Canoe with Outrigger.

out′right″, 1 aut′rait″; 2 out′rīt″. **I.** *a.* Free from reserve or restraint. **II.** *adv.* Without reservation or delay; at once; utterly.

out′set″, 1 aut′set″; 2 out′sĕt″, *n.* A beginning.

out′side″, 1 aut′said″; 2 out′sīd″. **I.** *a.* External; exterior; extraneous; foreign; utmost. **II.** *n.* **1.** The external part of a thing; superficial appearance. **2.** The

extreme. **III.** *adv.* Without.— **out″sid′er**, *n.* One who is outside; an intruder.

out′skirt″, 1 aut′skŭrt″; 2 out′skĭrt″, *n.* A place on the border; outer verge: commonly in the plural.

out′spo″ken, 1 aut′spō″kn; 2 out′spō″kn, *a.* Bold or free of speech.

out-stand′ing, 1 aut-stand′ıŋ; 2 out-stănd′ing, *a.* Overdue and unpaid, as a debt.

out-strip′ᵗ, 1 aut-strip′; 2 out-strĭp′, *vt.* To outrun; go beyond; escape.

out′ward, 1 aut′wərd; 2 out′wârd, *a.* **1.** Pertaining to the outside; external. **2.** Tending to the outside. **-ly**, *adv.* **-ness**, *n.*

out′ward, *} adv.* **1.** Away from an inner
out′wards, *f* place. **2.** On the surface. **3.** Away from port or home.

out-wit′, 1 aut-wit′; 2 out-wĭt′, *vt.* [OUT-WIT′TEDᵈ; OUT-WIT′TING.] To excel or defeat by cunning.

out′work″, 1 aut′wŭrk″; 2 out′wûrk″, *n.* Any outer defense; bulwark.

o′val, 1 ō′vəl; 2 ō′val. **I.** *a.* Egg-shaped; elliptical. **II.** *n.* An oval figure or object.

o′va-ry, 1 ō′və-rı; 2 ō′va-ry, *n.* [-RIESᶻ, *pl.*] An organ where an egg or seed is developed.— **o-va′ri-an**, *a.*

o′vate, 1 ō′vēt; 2 ō′vāt, *a.* Egg-shaped.

o-va′tion, 1 o-vē′shən; 2 o-vā′shon, *n.* An expression of popular homage, as to a victor.

ov′en, 1 uv′n; 2 ŏv′n, *n.* A cavity for baking, heating, annealing, etc.

o′ver, 1 ō′vər; 2 ō′ver. **I.** *a.* Outer. **II.** *adv.* **1.** From side to side; across. **2.** So as to invert or transpose. **3.** So as to overflow; beyond; completely; excessively. **4.** Once again. **5.** At an end. **III.** *prep.* **1.** Higher than; above; in superiority to; in excess of. **2.** Notwithstanding. **3.** Across.

In a large number of self-explaining compounds, *over* adds the general meaning of "too," "too much," etc.; as, *over*anxiety, *over*act, *over*burden, etc.— **o′ver-alls″**, *n. pl.* Loose, coarse, outer trousers worn by workmen for protection.— **o″ver-awe′**(eᴾ, *vt.* To overpower or restrain by awe.— **o″ver-bal′ance. Iᵗ.** *vt.* **1.** To exceed, as in weight or importance. **2.** To cause to lose balance; tip over. **II.** *n.* Excess of weight or value.— **o″ver-bear′**, *v.* **I.** *t.* To overpower; repress; crush down. **II.** *i.* To bear too much fruit.— **o″ver-bear′ing**, *pa.* Arrogant; dictatorial; crushing.— **o′ver-board′**, *adv.* Over the side of or out of a boat or ship.— **o″ver-cast′**, *vt.* **1.** To cover, as the sky with clouds. **2.** To sew (an edge) with long wrapping stitches.— **o″ver-charge′**, *n.*— **o′-ver-coat″**, *n.* An extra outdoor coat; a great-

---

1: ə = final; ı = habit; aisle; au = out; oil; iū = feud; ᴄhin; go; ŋ = sing; ᴛhin, this.
2: wǫlf, dǫ; bŏŏk, bōōt; fųll, rųle, cūre, bŭt, bûrn; ŏil, bŏy; g̱o, g̱em; iŋk; thin, this.

coat; topcoat.— **o″ver-come′**, *vt. & vi.* To master; control; vanquish; defeat.— **o″ver-do′**, *v.* **I.** *t.* To do excessively; exaggerate; overtax; exhaust. **II.** *t.* To labor too assiduously.— **o″ver-hang′. I.** *vt. & vi.* To project or hang over; menace. **II.** *n.* An overhanging portion; also, the amount of projection.— **o″ver-haul′**, *vt.* To haul over; inspect.— **o″ver-he(a)d′s**, *adv.* **1.** Aloft. **2.** So as to be submerged.— **o″ver-hear′**, *vt.* To hear, as by accident or design.— **o″ver-joy′**, *vt.* To overcome with joy.— **o″ver-land″**, *a. & adv.* Over the land; by land.— **o″ver-lap′t**, *vt. & vi.* **1.** To lie or be folded partly upon. **2.** To lap over.— **o″ver-lay′**, *vt.* To spread something over the surface of; overcast; cloud.— **o″ver-match′. I**t. *vt.* To be more than a match for. **II.** *n.* One who or that which is superior in strength, skill, etc.— **o″ver-night′**, *adv.* During or through the night.— **o′ver-plus**, *n.* A surplus.— **o″ver-shad′ow**, *vt.* **1.** To throw a shadow over. **2.** To cast into the shade.— **o′ver-shoe′**, *n.* A shoe worn over another: usually of india-rubber or felt.— **o″ver-shoot′**, *v.* **I.** *t.* **1.** To shoot over or beyond. **2.** To go beyond; overstep. **II.** *i.* To shoot or fly beyond the mark.— **overshot wheel**, a water-wheel, with buckets that are filled at the top.— **o″ver-state′d**, *vt.* To exaggerate.— **o″ver-state′-ment**, *n.*— **o″ver-top′t**, *vt.* To mount above the top of; tower over; exceed.

o″ver-due′, 1 ō″vər-diū′; 2 ō″ver-diū′, *a.* Remaining unpaid or undone after the appointed time.

Overshot Wheel.

o″ver-flow′, 1 ō″vər-flō′; 2 ō″ver-flō′, *vt. & vi.* To flow over; spread over; flood; overwhelm; abound.— **o′ver-flow′**, *n.* **1.** That which flows over; a flood; profusion. **2.** A passage or outlet for liquid.

o″ver-look′t, 1 ō″vər-lūk′; 2 ō″ver-lŏŏk′, *vt.* **1.** To look down upon; superintend; oversee. **2.** To look over; pardon; fail to see; miss; slight; neglect.

o″ver-pow′er, 1 ō″vər-pau′ər; 2 ō″ver-pow′er, *vt.* To conquer; subdue; overwhelm.

o″ver-reach′t, 1 ō″vər-rīch′; 2 ō″ver-rēch′, *v.* **I.** *t.* To cheat. **2.** To extend over; reach or shoot too far. **II.** *i.* To strike the hind against the fore foot: said of a horse. [To ride down; set aside.

o″ver-ride′, 1 ō″vər-raid′; 2 ō″ver-rīd′, *vt.*

o″ver-rule′, 1 ō″vər-rūl′; 2 ō″ver-rṳl′, *v.* **I.** *t.* To control by superior power; supersede. **II.** *i.* To hold sway.

o″ver-run′, 1 ō″vər-run′; 2 ō″ver-rŭn′, *v.* **I.** *t.* **1.** To run or spread over; infest or ravage. **2.** To run beyond; exceed or go beyond. **3.** *Print.* To carry over (type) to another line. **II.** *i.* To pass just, prescribed, or usual limits.

o″ver-see′, 1 ō″vər-sī′; 2 ō″ver-sē′, *v.* **I.** *t.* **1.** To overlook; superintend. **2.** To fail to see; neglect. **3.** To see too well. **II.** *i.* **1.** To see over things. **2.** To act as overseer.— **o″ver-se′er**, *n.*

o′ver-sight′, 1 ō″vər-sait′; 2 ō″ver-sīt″, *n.* **1.** An error due to inattention. **2.** Watchful supervision; superintendence.

o′vert, 1 ō′vərt; 2 ō′vert, *a.* Open; manifest.— **o′vert-ly**, *adv.*

o″ver-take′, 1 ō″vər-tēk′; 2 ō″ver-tāk′, *vt.* **1.** To come up with by following; catch. **2.** To take by surprise.

o″ver-throw′, 1 ō″vər-thrō′; 2 ō″ver-thrō′. **I.** *vt.* To throw over; throw down; upset; defeat. **II.** *n.* The act of overthrowing; destruction; demolition.

o′ver-ture, 1 ō′vər-chur; 2 ō′ver-chųr, *n.* **1.** A proposal; offer. **2.** A musical composition introductory to an opera, etc.

o″ver-turn′, 1 ō″vər-tûrn′; 2 ō″ver-tûrn′, *vt. & vi.* To cause to fall; upset; overthrow; capsize.

o′ver-turn′, 1 ō′vər-tûrn′; 2 ō′ver-tûrn″, *n.* The act of overturning; overthrow; destruction.

o″ver-ween′ing, 1 ō″vər-wīn′ıŋ; 2 ō″ver-wēn′ing, *pa.* Marked by presumptuous pride or conceit.

o″ver-whelm′, 1 ō″vər-hwelm′; 2 ō″ver-hwĕlm′, *vt.* **1.** To whelm or submerge completely. **2.** To overcome with effusiveness or profusion. [shaped.

o′vi-form, 1 ō′vi-fôrm; 2 ō′vi-fôrm, *a.* Egg-

o-vip′a-rous, 1 o-vip′ə-rus; 2 o-vĭp′a-rŭs, *a.* Producing eggs; propagating by eggs.

o′void, 1 ō′void; 2 ō′vŏid, *a.* Egg-shaped; ovate.

owe, 1 ō; 2 ō, *v.* [OWED (formerly OUGHT or OWN), OWDs; ow′ıNG.] **I.** *t.* **1.** To be under obligation for. **2.** To be indebted for. **II.** *i.* To be indebted; be due.

owl, 1 aul; 2 owl, *n.* A large-eyed nocturnal bird of prey.— **owl′et**, *n.* A small or young owl.— **owl′ish**, *a.* Like an owl; grave; stupid.

Barn-owl.
1/28

1: **a**rtistic, **ä**rt; f**a**t, f**ā**re; f**a**st; get, pr**ē**y; h**i**t, pol**i**ce; **o**bey, g**ō**; n**o**t, **ô**r; f**u**ll, r**ū**le; b**u**t, b**û**rn.

2: **ä**rt, **ā**pe, f**ä**t, f**â**re, f**å**st, wh**ạ**t, **ạ**ll; m**ē**, g**ĕ**t, pr**ey**, f**ê**rn; h**ĭ**t, **ī**ce; **ī**=**ē**; **ĩ**=**ẽ**; g**ō**, n**ŏ**t, **ô**r, w**ŏ**n,

own[1], 1 ōn; 2 ōn, *vt.* To have the rightful title to; possess.   [avow; recognize.

own[2], *vt.* To admit; acknowledge; confess;

own, *a.* Belonging to oneself; individual; real; intimately related.

own'er, 1 ōn'ər; 2 ōn'er, *n.* One who has the right to or possession of a thing.— **own'er-ship,** *n.* The state of being a proprietor or owner.

ox, 1 ŏks; 2 ŏks, *n.* [ox'en, *pl.*] An adult castrated male of domestic cattle.

ox'id, } 1 ŏks'ĭd, -aid; 2 ŏks'ĭd, -ĭd, *n.*
ox'ide, } *Chem.* Any binary compound of

oxygen, as iron-rust.— **ox"i-da'tion,** *n.* The act of uniting with oxygen; also, the state of being so united.— **ox'i-dīze,** *v.* [-dized; -diz'-ing.] **I.** *i.* To cause the oxidation of: rust. **II.** *i.* To unite with oxygen. **ox'i-dise‡.**

ox'y-gen, 1 ŏks'ĭ-jen; 2 ŏks'y-gĕn, *n.* A gaseous element, necessary to combustion and to animal life, existing in both the air and water.— **ox'y-gen-ated,** *vt.* To treat with oxygen.— **ox'y-gen-īze,** *vt.* & *vi.*— **ox"y-gen-a'tion,** *n.*   [salt=water bivalve.

oys'ter, 1 ɔis'tər; 2 ɔys'ter, *n.* An edible

o'zone, 1 ō'zōn; 2 ō'zōn, *n. Chem.* A colorless gas with a pungent odor.

P

P, p, 1 pī; 2 pē, *n.* [pees, P's, Ps, 1 pīz; 2 pēs, *pl.*] The sixteenth letter in the English alphabet.   [*n.* Food.

pab'u-lum, 1 pab'yu-lum; 2 păb'yu-lŭm,

pace, 1 pēs; 2 păç. **I.** *vt.* & *vi.* [paced[b]; pac'ing.] To walk with regular steps; measure by strides; move, as a horse, by lifting both feet on the same side at once. **II.** *n.* **1.** A step in walking. **2.** A measure of length: 3 feet. **3.** Gait; rate of speed. **4.** The movement by a horse of both feet on the same side together.— **pac'er,** *n.* A pacing horse.

pa-cha', *n.* Same as pasha.

pach'y-derm, 1 pak'ĭ-dûrm; 2 păc'y-dĕrm, *n.* A thick-skinned animal, as an elephant.— **pach"y-der'ma-tous,** *a.*

pa-cif'ic, 1 pə-sĭf'ĭk; 2 pa-çĭf'ie, *a.* **1.** Pertaining to peace; peaceable; calm. **2.** [P-] Pertaining to the great western ocean. **-ly,** *adv.*— **Pacific ocean,** vast waters between America and Asia and Australia; 70,000,000 sq. m.; 11,000 m wide at equator.

pac'i-fist, 1 pas'ĭ-fĭst; 2 păç'i-fĭst, *n.* [Recent.] An advocate of peace.— **pac'i-fism,** *n.*

pac'i-fy, 1 pas'ĭ-fai; 2 păç'i-fĭ, *vt.* [-fied; -fy'ing.] To make peaceful; calm.— **pac"i-fi-ca'tion,** *n.* Conciliation.— **pac'i-fi-ca"tor,** *n.* A peacemaker. **pac'i-fi"er‡.**— **pa-cif'i-ca-to"ry,** *a.*

pack, 1 pak; 2 păk. **I**[t]. *vt.* & *vi.* **1.** To fit snugly together; stow; compress; make tight. **2.** To send, load, or carry as or with a pack. **II.** *n.* **1.** A bundle; collection; heap; mass. **2.** A full set, as of cards; a group, gang, or band.— **pack'age,** *n.* The act of packing; a bundle, packet, or parcel.— **pack'er,** *n.*— **pack'et,** *n.* **1.** A small package: parcel. **2.** A fast vessel for mails and passengers.   [compact.

pact, 1 pakt; 2 păet, *n.* An agreement;

pad, 1 pad; 2 păd. **I.** *vt.* & *vi.* [pad'ded[d]; pad'ding.] To stuff with pads or padding; put up in pads; wear or use pads. **II.** *n.* **1.** An elastic cushion. **2.** A flat packet of paper; tablet. **3.** A floating leaf, as of a water-lily.— **pad'ding,** *n.* Stuffing.

pad'dle, } 1 pad'l; 2 păd'l. **I.** *vt.* & *vi.*
pad'l[e], } [pad'dled. pad'ld[p]; pad'dling.] To propel with a paddle; row with or use a paddle; dabble, as in water. **II.** *n.* A short, broad oar, or anything resembling it; blade of an oar; a flipper.

pad'dock, 1 pad'ək; 2 păd'ok, *n.* A small enclosure for horses.   [or growing.

pad'dy, *n.* Rice in the husk, whether gathered

pad'lock", 1 pad'lŏk"; 2 păd'lŏk". **I**[t]. *vt.* To fasten or provide with a padlock. **II.** *n.* A detachable lock, fastened through a staple.   [song of joy.

pæ'an, 1 pī'an; 2 pē'an, *n.* A choral ode;

pa'gan, 1 pē'gan; 2 pā'gan. **I.** *a.* Heathenish; idolatrous. **II.** *n.* A worshiper of false gods; a heathen.— **pa'gan-ism,** *n.*

page, 1 pēj; 2 pāg, *vt.* [paged; pag'ing.] **1.** To number the pages of (a book). **2.** To summon, as by a page.

page[1], *n.* A male attendant, usually a lad.

page[2], *n.* One side of a leaf, as of a book.

pag'eant, 1 paj'ənt; 2 păg'ant, *n.* **1.** An imposing exhibition. **2.** A theatrical spectacle.— **pag'eant-ry,** *n.*

pa-go'da, 1 pə-gō'də; 2 pa-gō'da, *n.* A sacred Oriental tower, profusely adorned.

pail, 1 pēl; 2 păl, *n.* A vessel for carrying liquids, etc., properly having a bail.— **pail'-ful,** *n.* [pail'fuls, *pl.*]

pain, 1 pēn; 2 pān. **I.** *vt.* To hurt: distress. **II.** *n.* **1.** Any distressful feeling; suffering. **2.** *pl.* Care, trouble, or exertion. **3.** Punishment; penalty.— **pain'ful**

1: ə=final; ɪ=habit; aisle; au=out; oil; iū=feud; chin; go; ŋ=sing; thin, this.
2: wolf, do; book, boot; full, rule, cure, but, bûrn; oil, boy; go, gem; ink; thin, this.

a. **1.** Giving pain; distressing. **2.** Requiring care; arduous. **-ly,** *adv.* **-ness,** *n.*
— pain′less, *a.* Free from pain; causing no pain. **-ly,** *adv.* **-ness,** *n.* **— pains′tak″ing.**
I. *a.* Taking pains. **II.** *n.* Diligent and careful endeavor.

paintd, 1 pēnt; 2 pănt. **I.** *vt. & vi.* To apply paint to; color; make (a picture or pictures) in colors. **II.** *n.* A coloring substance to be applied to any surface.
paint′erl, 1 pēnt′ər; 2 pănt′er, *n.* One who paints.
paint′er2, *n.* A rope for mooring a boat.
paint′ing, 1 pēnt′ıŋ; 2 pănt′ing, *n.* The act or art of using paints; a painted picture.
pair, 1 pār; 2 pâr. **I.** *vt. & vi.* To mate; match. **II.** *n.* **1.** Two persons or things of a kind associated; a couple; brace. **2.** A single thing having two like or corresponding parts.
pa-ja′mas, 1 pə-jä′məz; 2 pa-jä′mas, *n. pl.* Loose trousers, especially for night=wear.
pal′ace, 1 pal′ıs; 2 păl′aç, *n.* A royal residence; any stately building.
pal′a-din, 1 pal′ə-din; 2 păl′a-dĭn, *n.* A peer of Charlemagne; a paragon of knighthood.
pa″læ-on-tol′o-gy, *n.* Same as PALEONTOLOGY.
pal″an-quin′, 1 pal′ən-kīn′; 2 păl′an-kĭn′- *n.* An Oriental conveyance borne on the shoulders of men by poles.

pal″an-keen′‡.
pal′ate, 1 pal′ıt; 2 păl′at, *n.* The roof of the mouth; taste; relish.— **pal′at-**
Original Native Palanquin of Hindustan.
a-ble (ə-bl′), *a.* Pleasing to the taste; acceptable.— **pal′at-a-bly,** *aav.*— **pal′a-tal. I.** *a.* Pertaining to or produced by the palate. **II.** *n.* A palatal bone or sound.
pa-la′tial, 1 pə-lē′shal; 2 pa-lā′shal, *a.* Of, like, or befitting a palace; magnificent.
pa-lav′er, 1 pə-lav′ər; 2 pa-lăv′er. **I.** *vt. & vi.* To flatter; cajole; talk idly. **II.** *n.* Empty talk, especially flattery.
palel, 1 pēl; 2 pāl, *vt.* [PALED; PAL′ING.] To enclose with pales.
pale2, *vt. & vi.* To make or turn pale.
pale, *a.* Of a whitish appearance; of a light shade; pallid. **-ly,** *adv.* **-ness,** *n.*
pale, *n.* A pointed stick; a fence=stake; paling; boundary; enclosure.
pa″le-on-tol′o-gy, 1 pē″l-ɒn-tel′o-jı; 2 pā″le-ŏn-tŏl′o-gy, *n.* The branch of biology that treats of fossils. **pa″læ-on-tol′o-**

gy‡.— pa″le-on″to-log′i-cal, *a.*— **pa″le-on-tol′o-gist,** *n.*
pal′et, 1 pal′et; 2 păl′ĕt, *n.* A thin tablet
pal′ette, with a hole for the thumb, for holding an artist's colors in painting.
pal′frey, 1 pɒl′frı; 2 păl′fry, *n.* A gentle, easy saddle=horse, as for a lady.
pal′ing, 1 pēl′ıŋ; 2 păl′ing, *n.* A picket; a picket=fence.
pal″i-sade′. 1 1 pal′ı-sēd′; 2 păl′i-sād′. **I.** *vt.* [-SAD′ED**d; -SAD′-**
ING.] To enclose with a palisade. **II.** *n.* A fence of strong timbers set in the ground.
Artists' Palet as held, showing method of grasping palet=knife and brushes.
pall, 1 pɒl; 2 pal, *vt. & vi.* To make or become insipid; cloy; satiate.
pall, *n.* A cloth thrown over a coffin or a tomb.— **pall′=bear″er,** *n.* One who attends a coffin at a funeral.
pal-la′di-um, 1 pa-lē′dı-ṳm; 2 pă-lā′dĭ-ŭm, *n.* **1.** Any protection or safeguard. **2.** [P] *Class. Antiq. & Myth.* An image of Pallas (Minerva), as that in the citadel of Troy, on which the safety of the city was supposed to depend.
pal′letl, 1 pal′et; 2 păl′ĕt, *n.* A tool, as for mixing clay, or for gilding; a detent of an escapement (see illus. under ESCAPE=MENT); a painters' palet.
pal′let2, *n.* A bed of straw.
pal′li-ate, 1 pal′ı-ēt; 2 păl′i-āt, *vt.* [-AT′-ED**d; -AT′ING.]** To extenuate; mitigate.
— pal′li-a′tion, *n.* Alleviation; mitigation.
— pal′li-a-tive (-tıv). **I.** *a.* Tending to palliate. **II.** *n.* That which serves to palliate.
pal′lid, 1 pal′ıd; 2 păl′id, *a.* Pale; wan; feeble in color.— **pal′lor,** 1 pal′ər; 2 păl′or, *n.* The state of being pale or pallid.
palm, 1 păm; 2 päm, *vt.* **1.** To hide in the hand. **2.** To impose fraudulently; with *off.*
palml, *n.* **1.** The hollow inner surface of

the hand. **2.** The breadth or length of the hand. **3.** That which covers the palm.— **pal′mate, pal′mat-ed,** *a.* **1.** Re-

Palmate Leaves.
1. Palmately parted leaf. 2. Palmately lobed leaf.

sembling an open hand, with the fingers spread. **2.** Web=footed.

palm², *n.* **1.** A tropical tree or shrub having very large leaves. **2.** A branch of the palm, as a symbol of victory or joy; hence, supremacy.— **palm'er**, *n.* A medieval pilgrim who had visited Palestine and brought back a palm=branch.— **palm'y**, *a.* **1.** Marked by prosperity or triumph. **2.** Of, pertaining to, or abounding in palms.

pal-met'to, 1 pal-met'o; 2 pȧl-mĕt'o, *n.* A fan=palm, as of the southern U. S.

palm'is-try, 1 pȧm'ıs-trı *or* pal'mıs-trı; 2 päm'is-try *or* päl'mis-try, *n.* The pretended art of reading one's character or divining one's future by the markings on the palm of the hand.— **palm'ist**. **I.** *a.* Of or pertaining to palmistry. **II.** *n.* One who tells fortunes by palmistry. **palm'is-ter‡.**

palp, 1 palp; 2 pȧlp, *n.* A feeler, esp., one of the jointed sense=organs attached to the mouth=organs of many insects.

pal'pa-ble,) 1 pal'pə-bl; 2 pȧl'pa-bl, *a.*
pal'pa-bl²,) That may be touched or f lt; manifest.— **pal''pa-bil'i-ty**, *n.* **pal'pa-bl(e-ness²‡.— pal'pa-bly**, *adv.*

pal'pi-tate, 1 pal'pı-tēt; 2 pȧl'pi-tāt, *vi.* [-TAT"ED ᵈ; -TAT"ING.] To beat quickly; flutter.— **pal''pi-ta'tion**, *n.*

pal'sy, 1 pôl'zı; 2 pȧl'ṡy. **I.** *vt.* [PAL'SIED; PAL'SY-ING.] To paralyze. **II.** *n.* Paralysis: inefficiency; apathy.— **pal'sied**, *pa.* Paralytic.

pal'ter, 1 pôl'tər; 2 pȧl'ter, *vi.* To trifle; equivocate.— **pal'try**, 1 pôl'trı; 2 pȧl'try, *a.* Trifling; worthless.— **pal'tri-ness**, *n.*

pam'pas, 1 pam'pəz; 2 pȧm'pas, *n. pl.* The great treeless plains south of the Amazon.

pam'per, 1 pam'pər; 2 pȧm'per, *vt.* To feed with rich food; indulge excessively.

pam'phlet,) 1 pam'flet; 2 pȧm'flĕt, *n.* A
pam'flet²,) printed work stitched or pasted, but not bound; a brief treatise or essay.— **pam''phlet-eer'**, *n.* One who writes pamphlets.

pan, 1 pan; 2 pȧn, *n.* A wide shallow vessel.

pan-,) pan-; 2 pȧn-. A combining form signifying all: used before English proper adjectives; as, *Pan=*American.

pan''a-ce'a, 1 pan"ə-sī'ə; 2 pȧn"a-çē'a, *n.* A pretended universal remedy.

pan'cake", 1 pan'kēk"; 2 pȧn'cāk", *n.* A thin batter=cake.

pan''de-mo'ni-um,) 1 pan"dı-mō'nı-um;
pan''dæ-mo'ni-um,) 2 pȧn"dæ-mō'ni-um, *n.* The infernal regions; a noisy and disorderly assemblage.

pan'der, 1 pan'dər; 2 pȧn'der. **I.** *vi.* To minister to the gratification of passions or

prejudices of others. **II.** *n.* One who ministers to the vicious desires of others.

pane, 1 pēn; 2 pȧn, *n.* A piece or plate, as of window=glass.

pan''e-gyr'ic, 1 pan"ı-jir'ık; 2 pȧn"e-ġґr'ie, *n.* A formal public eulogy; encomium; laudation.— **pan''e-gyr'ic, pan''e-gyr'i-cal**, *a.*

pan'el, 1 pan'el; 2 pȧn'ĕl. **I.** *vt.* [PAN'ELED or PAN'ELLED, PAN'ELD ˢ; PAN'EL-ING or PAN'EL-LING.] To form or divide into panels; decorate with panels. **II.** *n.* **1.** A rectangular piece inserted, as in a door. **2.** An official list of persons summoned for jury=duty.— **pan'el-ing**, *n.*

pang, 1 pang; 2 pȧng, *n.* A sudden and poignant pain; a throe of anguish.

pan'ic, 1 pan'ık; 2 pȧn'ie, *n.* A sudden, causeless, overpowering fear, as of a surprised army. [for carrying a load.— **pan'nier**, 1 pan'yər; 2 pȧn'yer, *n.* A basket

pan'o-ply, 1 pan'o-plı; 2 pȧn'o-ply, *n.* [-PLIESᶻ, *pl.*] The full armor of a warrior.— **pan'o-plied**, *a.*

pan''o-ra'ma, 1 pan"o-rū'mə; 2 pȧn"o-rä'ma, *n.* A series of large pictures representing a continuous scene; a complete view in every direction.— **pan''o-ram'ic**, *a.*

pan'sy, 1 pan'zı; 2 pȧn'ṡy, *n.* [PAN'SIESᶻ, *pl.*] A species of violet having many= colored blossoms.

pant, 1 pant; 2 pȧnt. **Iᵈ.** *vi.* To breathe quickly; long eagerly; yearn. **II.** *n.* A short, labored breath; a violent heaving, as of the breast. [loons', *n. pl.* Trousers.— **pan''ta-loons'**, 1 pan"tə-lūnz'; 2 pȧn"ta-

pan'the-ism, 1 pan'thı-ızm; 2 pȧn'the-ı̇sm, *n.* The doctrine that mind and matter, God and the universe, are one.— **pan'the-ist**, *n.*— **pan''the-is'tic**, *a.*

Pan'the-on, 1 pan'thı-ɒn; 2 pȧn'the-ŏn, *n.* **1.** A circular temple at Rome, supposed to have been for all the gods. **2.** [p-] The deities of a people collectively.

pan'ther, 1 pan'thər; 2 pȧn'ther, *n.* A dark=hued leopard.

pan'to-mime, 1 pan'to-maim; 2 pȧn'to-mīm, *n.* Dumb show; a play consisting in action without dialog.— **pan''to-mim'ic**, *a.* **pan''to-mim'i-cal‡.**

pan'try, 1 pan'trı; 2 pȧn'try, *n.* [PAN'-TRIESᶻ, *pl.*] A room or closet for food, etc.

Pan'zer, 1 pȧn'tzer; 2 pȧn'tẑer, *n.* [G.] Armor=plating.— **Panzer Division**. *Mil.* Armored division.— **Pan'zer-schiff"**, armored ship.— **Pan'zer-wa"gen**, military tank.

pap¹, 1 pap; 2 pȧp, *n.* A teat; nipple.

pap², *n* Soft food for babes. [*n.* Father.

pa-pa', 1 pə-pä' *or* pä'pə; 2 pa-pä' *or* pä'pa,

pa'pa-cy, 1 pē'pə-sı; 2 pā'pa-çy, *n.* **1.** The

office of the Pope of Rome. **2.** The Roman Catholic system of church government. — **pa′pal,** 1 pē′pəl; 2 pā′pal, *a.*

pa-paw′, 1 pə-pê′; 2 pa-pâ′, *n.* **1.** A tropical American tree of the passion-flower family. **2.** A small tree of the custard-apple family, bearing edible fruit.

pa′per, 1 pē′pər; 2 pā′per. **I.** *vt.* To put paper upon; cover with paper. **II.** *a.* Of or pertaining to paper. **III.** *n.* **1.** A substance made from fibrous material, as rags in thin sheets or strips; a piece of such material. **2.** A printed or written instrument; newspaper; essay; pledges or promises to pay, collectively. **3.** A package in a paper wrapping.— **pa′per-ing,** *n.* The process of covering walls, etc., with paper, or the paper so applied. **pa′per-hang″ing‡.**

pa′pier′-mä″ché′, 1 pa″pyē′=mȧ″shē′; 2 pä″pyċ′=mä″çhê, *n.* Paper-pulp molded into various forms.

pa′pist, 1 pē′pist; 2 pā′pĭst, *n.* An adherent of the papacy: an opprobrious use.— **pa-pis′ti-cal,** *a.* **pa-pis′tic‡.**

pa-poose′, 1 pə-pūs′; 2 pa-pōōs′, *n.* [Am. Ind.] A North-American Indian infant. **pap-poose′‡.**

pa′pri-ka, 1 pā′pri-kɑ; 2 pä′prĭ-cä, *n.* The [capsicum: Hungarian name.

pa-py′rus, 1 pə-pai′rʊs; 2 pa-pÿ′rŭs, *n.* [-RI, 1 -rai; 2 -rī, *pl.*] The writing-paper of the ancient Egyptians, or plant from which it was made.

par, 1 pūr; 2 pär, *n.* An accepted standard of value; equivalence; parity.— **on a par,** on a level; equal.

par-¹, *prefix.* Per-; as, *par*boil.

par-², 1 1 par-, par′ə-; 2 pär-. **par′a-,** 1 pär′ə-. *prefix.* Besides; near; by: used in certain words of foreign origin and in new scientific terms; as, *para*phrase.

par′a-ble, 1 1 par′ə-bl; 2 pär′-**par′a-bl¹‡,** 1 ə-bl, *n.* A short religious allegory.

pa-rab′o-la, 1 pə-rab′o-lə; 2 pa-răb′o-lä, *n.* A curve formed by the cutting of a cone by a plane parallel to one of its sides: one of the conic sections. — **par′a-bol′ic,** *a.* **1.** Pertaining to a parable. **par″a-bol′i-cal‡.** **2.** Pertaining to or having the form of a parabola.

par′a-chute, 1 par′ə-shūt; 2 pär′a-çhŭt, *n.* A large umbrella-shaped apparatus for retarding the descent of a body through the air, as from a balloon. See illus. in next column.

Papyrus.

pa-rade′, 1 pə-rēd′; 2 pa-rād′. **I.** *vt. & vi.* [PA-RAD′EDᵈ; PA-RAD′ING.] To array or marshal, as in military order; promenade for display. **II.** *n.* A marshaling and review of troops; a ceremonious procession; show; ostentation.

Parachute.

par′a-digm, 1 par′ə-dim; 2 pär′a-dĭm, *n.* A model for the inflection of a class of words, as of a conjugation or declension.

par′a-dise, 1 par′ə-dais; 2 pär′a-dīs, *n.* **1.** [P-] The garden of Eden. **2.** Heaven; supreme felicity; region or state of surpassing delight.— **par″a-di-sĭ′a-cal,** *a.*

par′a-dox, 1 par′ə-dŏks; 2 pär′a-dŏks, *n.* A statement seemingly absurd or self-contradictory in its terms, but really true.— **par″a-dox′i-cal,** *a.* **-i-cal-ly,** *adv.*

par′af-fin, 1 par′ə-fin; 2 pär′a-fĭn, *n.* A translucent, waxy, solid substance prepared from petroleum. **par′af-fine‡.**

par′a-gon, 1 par′ə-gon; 2 pär′a-gŏn, *n.* A model of excellence.

par′a-graph, 1 1 par′ə-graf; 2 pär′a-gråf, *n.* **par′a-grafˢ,** 1 1. A distinct passage in a discourse, treatise, etc.; a short article. **2.** A mark (¶) used to indicate where a paragraph is to be begun.— **par′a-graph″-er,** *n.* A writer of newspaper paragraphs.— **par″a-graph′ic,** *a.* **par″a-graph′i-cal‡.**

par′al-lax, 1 par′ə-laks; 2 pär′a-lăks, *n.* An apparent displacement of an object due to change of an observer's position.

par′al-lel, 1 par′ə-lel; 2 pär′a-lĕl. **I.** *vt.* [-LELED or -LELLED, -LELDˢ; -LEL-ING or -LEL-LING.] To be a parallel for; place parallel to, or in comparison with. **II.** *a.* **1.** Extending or lying in the same direction. **2.** Having a like course; similar. **III.** *n.* **1.** A line extending in the same direction with and equidistant at all points from another line. **2.** Essential likeness; something like or equal to another; a match.— **par′al-lel-ism,** *n.* **1.** Parallel position. **2.** Essential likeness; analogy. **3.** Similarity of construction.— **par″al-lel′o-gram,** *n.* **1.** A four-sided plane figure whose opposite sides are parallel. **2.** Any area or object having such form.

pa-ral′y-sis, 1 pa-ral′i-sis; 2 pa-răl′y-sĭs, *n.* **1.** Loss of the power of voluntary movement; palsy. **2.** Loss of power in general.— **par′a-lyt′ic. I.** *a.* Pertaining to or affected with paralysis. **II.** *n.* A person subject to paralysis.— **par′a-lyze,** *vt.* To make paralytic; deprive of the power to act.

par'a-mount, 1 par'ə-mαunt; 2 păr'ə-mount, a. Superior; supreme; controlling.

par'a-mour, 1 par'ə-mūr; 2 păr'ə-mụr, n. One who unlawfully takes the place of husband or wife.

par'a-pet, 1 par'ə-pet; 2 păr'ə-pĕt, n. A low wall, as about the edge of a roof or bridge; a breastwork.— **par'a-pet-ed,** a.

par'a-pher-na'li-a, 1 par"ə-fər-nē'li-ə; 2 păr"ə-fer-nā'li-a, n. pl. Miscellaneous articles of equipment; trappings.

par'a-phrase, 1 par'ə-frēz; 2 păr'ə-frāṣ.
par'a-frase⁽ᵖ⁾, I. vt. & vi. [-PHRASED; -PHRAS"ING.] To give the sense of in other words. II. n. An explanatory restatement or free translation of a passage or work.— **par"a-phras'tic,** a.— **par"a-phras'ti-cal-ly,** adv.

par'a-site, 1 par'ə-sait; 2 păr'ə-sĭt, n. An organism that lives on or in some other; a hanger-on; sycophant.— **par"a-sit'ic,** a. Living on or in another organism; pertaining to parasites. **par"a-sit'i-cal,** a.— **par"a-sit'i-cal-ly,** adv.— **par'a-sit"ism,** n.

par'a-sol", 1 par'ə-sel"; 2 păr'ə-sŏl", n. A sunshade carried by women.

par'a-troops, par'ə-trūps; 2 păr'ə-trōōps, n. pl. Combat troops equipped with parachutes for descent from aircraft.

par"a-vane", 1 par"ə-vēn'; 2 păr"ə-vān', n. A torpedo-shaped device used by ships to free moored mines.   [boil partially.

par'boil", 1 pär'boil"; 2 pär'bŏil", vt. To

par'cel, 1 pär'sel; 2 pär'çĕl. I. vt. [-CELED οr -CELLED, -CELDˢ; -CEL-ING οr -CEL-LING.] **1.** To divide into parts or shares; distribute. **2.** To combine; make up into a parcel. II. n. **1.** Anything wrapped up; a package. **2.** A part; lot; distinct portion, as of land.   [scorch.

parch⁽ᵗ⁾, 1 pärch; 2 pärch, vt. & vi. To dry;

parch'ment, 1 pärch'ment or -ment; 2 pärch'ment, n. Sheepskin, etc., polished for writing; a writing on parchment.

pard⁽ᴵ⁾, 1 pärd; 2 pärd, n. A leopard; panther.

par'don, 1 pär'dən; 2 pär'don. I. vt. To remit the penalty of; forego; forgive; excuse. II. n. **1.** Remission of penalty incurred. **2.** Courteous forbearance.— **par'don-a-ble⁽ᵉᵖ⁾,** a. That may be pardoned.— **par'don-er,** n.

pare, 1 pär; 2 pâr, vt. [PARED; PAR'ING.] To cut or shave off a covering skin or peel off; diminish by taking away a little at a time.— **par'er,** n.

par"e-gor'ic, 1 par"i-gɔr'ik; 2 păr"e-gŏr'ic, n. A camphorated tincture of opium.

par'ent, 1 pär'ent; 2 pâr'ent, n. A father or a mother; a producer; cause; occasion. — **par'ent-age,** n. The relation of parent to child; descent.— **pa-ren'tal,** a. **-ly,** adv.

pa-ren'the-sis, 1 pə-ren'thi-sis; 2 pa-rĕn'-the-sĭs, n. [-SES, 1 -sĭz; 2 -sĕṣ, pl.] A clause inserted in a sentence that is grammatically complete without it, separated usually by the upright curves ().— **par"en-thet'i-cal,** a. Pertaining to or like a parenthesis. **-i-cal-ly,** adv.   [paralysis.

par'e-sis, 1 par'i-sis; 2 păr'e-sĭs, n. Partial

pa'ri-ah, 1 pē'⁽ᵒʳ⁾ pā'⁽ʳ⁾ri-ə; 2 pā'⁽ᵒʳ⁾ pä'⁾ri-a, n. A Hindu outcast; any social outcast. **pa'ri-aṭ.**

pa-ri'e-tal, 1 pə-rαi'i-təl; 2 pa-rī'e-tal, a. **1.** Pertaining to a wall or walls. **2.** Pertaining to residence within walls, as of a college.

par'ing, 1 pär'ıŋ; 2 pâr'ing, n. **1.** The cutting off of a surface or edge. **2.** The portion pared off; as, apple-parings. **3.** Any worthless scrap.

pa'ri pas'su, 1 pē'rαi pas'ū; 2 pā'rĭ păs'u. With equal pace or movement; in like proportion: a Latin phrase.

par'ish, 1 par'ısh; 2 pär'ish, n. A religious congregation; an ecclesiastical district. — **pa-rish'ion-er,** n. A member of a parish.

par'i-ty, 1 par'i-tı; 2 păr'ĭ-ty, n. Equality.

park, 1 pärk; 2 pärk, n. **1.** A tract of land set apart for ornament or recreation. **2.** An enclosure for artillery, or the artillery there placed.

par'lance, 1 pär'ləns; 2 pär'lançe, n. Mode of speech; language; phrase.

par'ley, 1 pär'lı; 2 pär'ly. I. vi. To hold a conference; argue. II. n. An oral conference, as with an enemy.

par'lia-ment, 1 pär'lı-ment or -mənt; 2
par'la-ment⁽ᵖ⁾, pär'li-ment, n. A legislative body; especially, [P-] the supreme legislature of Great Britain, also of some of her colonies.— **par"lia-men'ta-ry,** a. **1.** Pertaining to a parliament. **2.** According to the rules of Parliament.

Houses of Parliament, London.

par'lor, 1 pär'lər; 2 pär'lor, n. **1.** [U. S.] A guest-room. **2.** [Eng.] A sitting-room.

pa-ro'chi-al, 1 pə-rō'kı-əl; 2 pa-rō'ci-al, a. Pertaining to a parish.

par'o-dy, 1 par'o-dı; 2 păr'o-dy. I. vt.

[-DIED; -DY·ING.] To burlesque; travesty. **II.** *n.* [-D ES², *pl.*] A burlesque composition imitating some serious work; a travesty.— **par'o·dist**, *n.* [pa·role'‡.

pa·rol', 1 pə·rōl'; 2 pa·rōl', *a.* Oral.

pa·role', 1 pə·rōl'; 2 pa·rōl'. **I.** *vt.* [PA·ROLED'; PA·ROL'ING.] To release on parole. **II.** *n.* **1.** *Mil.* A pledge of honor by a prisoner that he will not seek to escape, or will not serve against his captors until exchanged. **2.** *Law.* An oral statement.

pa·rot'id, 1 pə·rŏt'id; 2 pa·rŏt'id. **I.** *a.* Situated near the ear. **II.** *n.* A salivary gland below the ear.

par'ox·ysm, 1 par'ŏks·izm; 2 păr'ŏks·ўsm, *n.* A periodic attack of disease; a fit; convulsion.— **par''ox·ys'mal,** *a.* Convulsive.

par·quet', 1 par·kē'; 2 pär·kẹ', *n.* [U. S.] The main-floor space behind the orchestra of a theater. **par·quette'‡.**

par'ra·keet, 1 par'ə·kīt; 2 păr'ə·kēt, *n.* A small long-tailed parrot. **par'o·quet‡.**

par'ri·cide, 1 par'i·said; 2 păr'i·çĭd, *n.* The murder or the murderer of a parent. — **par''ri·ci'dal,** *a.*

par'rot, 1 par'ət; 2 păr'ot, *n.* A bird having a hooked bill, and able to imitate human speech.

par'ry, 1 par'i; 2 păr'y, *vt. & vi.* [PAR·RIED; PAR'RY·ING.] To ward off, as a blow; avoid, as by repartee.

parse, 1 pärs; 2 pärs, *vt. & vi.* [PARSED†, PARST⁸; PARS'ING.] To describe and analyze according to the rules of grammar.

Par'see, 1 pär'si; 2 pär'sē, *n.* A follower of the Persian religion of Zoroaster. **par'si‡.**

par'si·mo·ny, 1 pär'si·mo·ni; 2 pär'si·mo·ny, *n.* Undue economy; stinginess. — **par''si·mo'ni·ous,** *a.* Meanly economical; stingy. **-ly,** *adv.* **-ness,** *n.*

pars'ley, 1 pärs'li; 2 pärs'ly, *n.* An aromatic herb.

pars'nip, 1 pärs'nip; 2 pärs'nĭp, *n.* A European herb of the parsley family, with edible root.

par'son, 1 pär'sən; 2 pär'son, *n.* The clergyman of a parish or congregation; a minister.— **par'son·age,** *n.* A clergyman's dwelling; a rectory.

part, 1 pärt; 2 pärt. **I**ᵈ. *vt. & vi.* To divide into parts or portions; come apart; sever; separate. **II.** *n.* **1.** A certain portion of anything; a member. **2.** A region; quarter; side; party; cause; duty.

par·take', 1 par·tēk'; 2 pär·tāk', *vt. & vi.* To have a part in; share.— **par·tak'er,** *n.*

par·terre', 1 par·tār'; 2 pär·tār', *n.* **1.** A flower-garden. **2.** The floor of a theater; [U. S.], that part of the floor under the galleries.

par'tial, 1 pär'shəl; 2 pär'shal, *a.* Pertaining to a part only; favoring one side; prejudiced; unfair.— **par''ti·al'i·ty,** 1 par'·shi·al'i·ti; 2 pär'shi·ăl'i·ty, *n.* **1.** The state of being partial. **2.** Unfairness; bias. **3.** A predilection.— **par'tial·ly,** *adv.* **1.** In part only. **2.** With unjust favoritism.

par·tic'i·pate, 1 par·tis'i·pēt; 2 pär·tĭç'i·pāt, *vi.* [-PAT'ED⁴; -PAT'ING.] To share; partake.— **par·tic'i·pant.** *a.* Participating. **II.** *n.* One who participates; a partaker. **par·tic'i·pa'tor‡.— par·tic''i·pa'tion,** *n.* A sharing.

par'ti·ci·ple, 1 pär'ti·si·pl; 2 pär'ti·çi·pl, **par'ti·ci·pl⁵,** *n.* A form of the verb that permits its use as an adjective or as a noun.— **par''ti·cip'i·al,** *a.*

par'ti·cle, 1 pär'ti·kl; 2 pär'ti·cl, *n.* **1.** A minute portion of matter; small amount. **2.** An uninflected part of speech, as a preposition.

par·tic'u·lar, 1 par·tik'yu·lər; 2 pär·tĭc'yu·lar. **I.** *a.* **1.** Pertaining to a part or item; separate; individual; specific. **2.** Specially noteworthy. **3.** Minute; exact; fastidious. **II.** *n.* A separate matter or item; an instance; point; detail.— **par·tic''u·lar'i·ty,** *n.* **1.** The state of being particular. **2.** Something particular.— **par·tic'u·lar·ize,** *v.* [-IZED; -IZ'ING.] **I.** *t.* To mention particularly. **II.** *t.* To give particulars — **par·tic'u·lar·ly,** *adv.*

part'ing, 1 pärt'iŋ; 2 pärt'ing, *n.* Separation; division; a point of separation.

par'ti·san, -ship, *n.* Same as PARTIZAN, etc.

par·ti'tion, 1 par·tish'ən; 2 pär·tĭsh'on. **I.** *vt.* To separate into parts; divide. **II.** *n.* **1.** Division. **2.** A dividing line; separating wall.

par'ti·tive, 1 pär'ti·tiv; 2 pär'ti·tĭv. **I.** **par'ti·tiv⁵,** *a.* Separating; denoting a part. **II.** *n.* A partitive word or case. — **par'ti·tive·ly,** *adv.*

par'ti·zan, 1 pär'ti·zən; 2 pär'ti·zan. **par'ti·san**, *a.* Of or pertaining to a party or partizans; intensely devoted to a party or cause. **II.** *n.* A bigoted adherent of a party or cause.— **par'ti·zan·ship,** *n.*

part'ly, 1 pärt'li; 2 pärt'ly, *adv.* In part; in some degree.

part'ner, 1 pärt'nər; 2 pärt'ner, *n.* One associated with another or others, as in business, a dance, etc.; companion.

Common European Partridge. ¹/₁₆

part'ner·ship, *n.* Association in business.

par'tridge, 1 pär'trij; 2 pär'trĭdg, *n.* **1.** A small game-bird. **2.** [U.S.] A ruffed grouse or a bob-white.

1: artistic, ärt; fat, fare; fast; get, prey; hit, police; obey, gō; net, ôr; full, rūle; but, bûrn.
2: ärt, āpe, făt, fâre, fȧst, whạt, ạll; mē, gĕt, prẹy, fêrn; hĭt, īce; ĭ=ĕ; ĩ=ē; gō, nŏt, ôr, wòn,

par″tu·ri′tion, 1 pär″tiu·rish′ən; 2 pär″-tū·rĭsh′on, *n.* The act of bringing forth young.

par′ty, 1 pär′tĭ; 2 pär′ty, *a.* Divided into parts or of different parties.— **par′ty·col″-ored,** *a.* Variegated.

par′ty, *n.* [PAR′TIES², *pl.*] **1.** A body of persons united for a common purpose, as political ascendency. **2.** A social company. **3.** A small detachment, as of soldiers. **4.** A person interested, as in a contract or a lawsuit; any person.

par′ve·nu″, 1 pär′və·niū″; 2 pär′ve·nū″, *n.* One newly risen to wealth or prominence; an upstart.

pas′chal, 1 pas′kəl; 2 păs′cal, *a.* Pertaining to the Jewish Passover or to Easter.

pa·sha′, 1 pə·shä′; 2 pa·shä′, *n.* A Turkish or Egyptian general, governor, or high functionary. **pa·cha′t.**— **pa·sha′lic,** *n.* The province or jurisdiction of a pasha. **pa·cha′lic‡.**

pass, 1 pas; 2 pás, *v.* [PASSED† or PAST; PASS′ING.] **I.** *t.* **1.** To go by, over, through, or beyond; spend, as time; undergo; endure; surpass. **2.** To move; transfer; convey; put in circulation. **3.** To pronounce, as a judgment; adopt or enact, as a law. **II.** *i.* **1.** To move or glide by; elapse. **2.** To circulate. **3.** To occur. **4.** To go through a course successfully.— **pass′er,** *n.* One who passes. **pass′er·by′‡.**— **pass′ing,** *adv.* In a surpassing degree; exceedingly.

pass, *n.* **1.** A way or opening; defile; waterway. **2.** Permission to pass; a passport. **3.** A state of affairs; crisis. **4.** A lunge.— **pass′a·bl(e″,** *a.* Capable of being passed; fairly good.— **pass′a·bly,** *adv.*

pas′sage, 1 pas′ĭj; 2 păs′ag, *n.* **1.** A passage by, through, or over; the power or right of passing; a way; journey; voyage. **2.** A corridor, hall, etc. **3.** A clause; paragraph. **4.** A personal encounter.

pas″sée′, 1 pä″sē′; 2 pä″ṣe′, *a.* Past the prime; faded: with feminine nouns; in the masculine, *passé.*

pas′sen·ger, 1 pas′en·jər; 2 păs′ĕn·ger, *n.* One who travels in a public conveyance.

pas′si·bl(e″, 1 pas′i·bl; 2 păs′i·bl, *a.* Capable **pas′si·bl‡,** ƒ ble of feeling or of suffering.

pas′sion, 1 pash′ən; 2 păsh′on, *n.* **1.** Intense feeling; strong emotion or impulse. **2.** Suffering; agony. **3.** [P-] The suffering of Christ in Gethsemane and on the cross.— **pas′sion·flow″er,** *n.* A flower, the parts of which are fancied to resemble the instruments of the crucifixion.— **p.·play,** *n.* A medieval mystery or drama representing the Passion of Christ, especially that presented every decade by the peasants of Ober=Ammergau, Germany.— **pas′sion·ate,** *a.* Easily moved to anger; excitable; ardent. **-ly,** *adv.* **-ness,** *n.*— **pas′-sion·less,** *a.* Free from passion; calm.

pas′sive, ⎱1 pas′iv; 2 păs′iv, *a.* **1.** Not **pas′siv‡,** ƒ acting, but acted upon; inactive; unresisting; submissive. **2.** Pertaining to a form of verb that represents the subject of the verb as the object of the action.— **pas′siv(e·ly²,** *adv.*— **pas′siv(e·ness²,** *n.* **pas·siv′i·ty‡.**

Pass′o′ver, 1 pas′ō″vər; 2 pás′ō″ver, *n.* The principal Jewish feast (cp. *Ex.* xii).

pass′port, 1 pas′pōrt; 2 pás′pōrt, *n.* An official protection to a citizen of one country traveling in another.

pass′word″, 1 pas′wŭrd″; 2 pás′wûrd″, *n.* A watchword.

past, 1 past; 2 pást. **I.** *pa.* Belonging to time gone by. **II.** *n.* **1.** Time gone by. **2.** One's antecedents. **III.** *adv.* So as to go by and beyond. **IV.** *prep.* Beyond; after; out of reach of.

paste, 1 pēst; 2 pást. **I.** *vt.* [PAST′ED^d; PAST′ING.] To stick with paste. **II.** *n.* **1.** An adhesive mixture, as of flour and water; moist plastic substance. **2.** A composition for making false gems.— **paste′-board″,** *n.* Stiff, thick sheets of paper pasted together.

pas′tern, 1 pas′tərn; 2 păs′tĕrn, *n.* That part of a horse's foot just below the fetlock joint.

Pas·teur′ize, 1 pas·tūr′aiz; 2 pas·tûr′ĭz, *vt.* [-IZED; -IZ·ING.] To check and prevent fermentation, as of fluids: from the French chemist *Pasteur* (1822–1895).— **Pas·teur″i-za′tion,** *n.*

pas′time″, 1 pas′taim″; 2 pás′tĭm″, *n.* Diversion; amusement; to make time pass agreeably.

pas′tor, 1 pas′tər *or* -ter; 2 pás′tor, *n.* A Christian minister having charge of a congregation.— **pas′tor·al. I.** *a.* **1.** Pertaining to the life of shepherds and rustics. **2.** Pertaining to a pastor and his work. **II.** *n.* **1.** A poem dealing with rural matters; an idyl. **2.** A picture illustrating rural scenes. **3.** A letter from a pastor to his flock.— **pas′-tor·al·ly,** *adv.*— **pas′tor·ate,** *n.*— **pas′tor·ship,** *n.*

past′ry, 1 pēst′rĭ; 2 pást′ry, *n.* Articles of food made with a crust of shortened dough, as pies.

pas′ture, 1 pas′chur *or* -tiur; 2 pás′chur *or* -tûr. **I.** *vt.* & *vi.* [PAS′TURED; PAS′TUR-ING.] To graze. **II.** *n.* Ground for grazing; herbage for cattle.— **pas′tur·age,** *n.* **1.** Pasture. **2.** The business of grazing cattle.

1: ə = final; ɪ = habĭt; aisle; au = out; oil; iū = feud; chin; go; ŋ = sing; thin, this.
2: wǫlf, dǫ; bŏŏk, bōōt; fŭll, rŭle, cūre, bŭt, bûrn; ŏil; bŏy; g̃o, g̃em; iŋk; thin, this.

past'y, 1 pēst'ı; 2 pāst'y. , **I.** *a.* Like paste. **II.** *n.* [PAST'IES², *pl.*] A pie, as of meat.

pat, 1 pat; 2 păt, *vt.* [PAT'TED⁴; PAT'TING.] To strike lightly or caressingly.

pat, *a.* Exactly suitable in time or place; fitting; apt.— **pat'ly,** *adv.*— **pat'ness,** *n.*

pat¹, *n.* **1.** Caressing stroke.— **2.** A pattering.

pat², *n.* A small molded mass.

pat, *adv.* In a fit manner; aptly.

patch, 1 pach; 2 păch. **I**ᵗ. *vt. & vi.* To

pachᴾ, ∫ put a patch on; mend; make hastily or imperfectly. **II.** *n.* A small piece, as of cloth for repairing a garment; a small piece of ground.— **patch'work",** *n.* A fabric made of pieces stitched together, as for quilts, etc.; pieced work.

pate, 1 pāt; 2 păt, *n.* The head.

pa-tel'la, 1 pə-tel'ə; 2 pə-těl'a, *n.* A flattened oval bone in front of the knee-joint; kneepan.

pat'ent, 1 pat'ent; 2 păt'ĕnt. **I**ᵈ. *vt.* To grant or secure by patent. **II.** 1 pat'-ent *or* pē'tent; 2 păt'ĕnt *or* pā'tĕnt, *a.* **1.** Manifest or apparent. **2.** Protected by patent. **III.** *n.* A government protection securing the exclusive right of making and using an invention; also, any government grant or franchise.— **pat'ent-a-ble"(e**ᴾ, *a.*— **pat'en-tee',** *n.* One who holds a patent.

pa-ter'nal, 1 pə-tūr'nəl; 2 pə-tẽr'nal, *a.* **1.** Pertaining to a father; fatherly. **2.** Hereditary. **-ly,** *adv.*— **pa-ter'ni-ty,** *n.* The condition of being a father; ancestry on the male side.

pa"ter-nos'ter, 1 pē"tər-nos'tər; 2 pā"ternŏs'ter, *n.* **1.** The Lord's Prayer: literally, "our father." **2.** A rosary.

path, 1 pɑth; 2 păth, *n.* [PATHS, 1 pɑthz; 2 păths, *pl.*] A walk; way; road; course.— **path'less,** *a.* Having no path; trackless.

pa-thet'ic, 1 pə-thet'ık; 2 pə-thĕt'ıc, *a.* Touching the feelings; arousing compassion. **pa-thet'i-cal‡.**— **pa-thet'i-cal-ly,** *adv.*

pa-thol'o-gy, 1 pə-thol'o-jı; 2 pa-thŏl'o-gy, *n.* [-GIES², *pl.*] The branch of medical science that treats of disease.— **path"o-log'-i-cal,** *a.* Pertaining to pathology. **path"o-log'ic‡.**— **path"o-log'ist,** *n.*— **path"o-log'-i-cal-ly,** *adv.*

pa'thos, 1 pē'thos; 2 pā'thŏs, *n.* That which awakens tender feelings, as of compassion or sympathy. [as PATH.

path'way", 1 pɑth'wē"; 2 păth'wā", *n.* Same

-pathy, *suffix.* Derived from Greek *-patheia:* a combining form, often meaning treatment of disease; as, hydro*pathy.*

pa'tient, 1 pē'shent; 2 pā'shĕnt. **I.** *a.* Possessing quiet endurance under distress

or annoyance; calmly awaiting or enduring; meek; gentle; forbearing. **II.** *n.* A person under treatment for disease or injury.— **pa'tience,** *n.* The quality of being patient; forbearance; gentleness; quiet endurance or expectation.— **pa'tient-ly,** *adv.*

pa"tois, 1 pa"twä'; 2 pä"twä', *n.* An illiterate dialect.

pa'tri-arch, 1 pē'trı-ɑrk; 2 pā'trı-äre, *n.* The head of a family or of a tribe; venerable man.— **pa"tri-ar'chal,** *a.* **pa"tri-ar'chic‡.**

pa-tri'cian, 1 pə-trısh'ən; 2 pa-trĭsh'an. **I.** *a.* Of or pertaining to an aristocracy; noble. **II.** *n.* A nobleman. [Parricide.

pat'ri-cide, 1 pat'rı-said; 2 păt'rı-çĭd, *n.*

pat'ri-mo-ny, 1 pat'rı-mo-nı; 2 păt'rı-mo-ny, *n.* [-NIES², *pl.*] An inherited estate; inheritance.— **pat"ri-mo'ni-al,** *a.*— **pat"ri-mo'ni-al-ly,** *adv.*

pa'tri-ot, 1 pē'trı-ət *or* pat'rı-ət; 2 pā'trı-ot *or* păt'rı-ot, *n.* A lover of his country. — **pa"tri-ot'ic,** *a.* Of or like a patriot.— **pa"tri-ot'i-cal-ly,** *adv.*— **pa'tri-ot-ism,** *n.* Devotion to one's country.

pa-trol', 1 pə-trōl'; 2 pa-trōl'. **I.** *vt. & vi.* [PA-TROLLED', PA-TROLD'³; PA-TROL'LING.] To walk around in order to guard or inspect. **II.** *n.* **1.** A guard or body of guards patrolling a district. **2.** The act of patrolling.— **pa-trol'man,** *n.* [-MEN, *pl.*] One who patrols, as a policeman assigned to a beat, or an inspector who traverses a line of electric wires.

pa'tron, 1 pē'trən *or* pat'rən; 2 pā'tron *or* păt'ron, *n.* A dispenser of patronage; a protector; benefactor.— **pat'ron-age,** *n.* Fostering care and protection; guardianship; control of official appointments.— **pat'ron-ess,** *n.* A female patron.— **pat'ron-ize,** *vt.* [-IZED²; -IZ"ING.] **1.** To act as a patron to; favor. **2.** To treat with offensive condescension. **pat'ron-ise‡.**— **pat'ron-iz"er** *or* **-is"er,** *n.*

pat"ro-nym'ic, 1 pat"ro-nım'ık; 2 păt"ro-nỹm'ic, *n.* A name derived from an ancestor; a family name.

pat'ten, 1 pat'n; 2 păt'n, *n.* A thick-soled wooden shoe.

pat'ter, 1 pat'ər; 2 păt'er, *vi.* To make a succession of light, rattling sounds, as drops of rain.

pat'ter, *vt. & vi.* To mutter; jabber.

pat'ter, *n.* A succession of pats or taps; a pattering sound; glib talk; chatter.

pat'tern, 1 pat'ərn; 2 păt'ern. **I.** *vt. & vi.* To imitate; copy. **II.** *n.* **1.** Something for imitation; a model. **2.** A decorative design; figure; style.

pat'ty, 1 pat'ı; 2 păt'y, *n.* [PAT'TIES², *pl.*] A small pie.

pau'ci-ty, 1 pô'sı-tı; 2 pą'çi-ty, *n.* Fewness. [apostle Paul.
Paul'in(e⁵, *a.* Pertaining to or written by the
paunch, 1 pȧnçh *or* pȯnçh; 2 pänch *or* pạnch, *n.* The abdomen; first stomach of a ruminant.
pau'per, 1 pô'pɚr; 2 pạ'per, *n.* One dependent on charity.— **pau'per-ism,** *n.* 1. Abject poverty; destitution. 2. Paupers collectively.— **pau'per-ize** *or* **-ise,** *vt.* To reduce to pauperism.— **pau″per-i-za**[*or* **-sa'**]**-tion,** *n.*
pause, 1 pôz; 2 pạs. I. *vi.* [PAUSED; PAUS'ING.] To stop; hold back; delay; linger. II. *n.* 1. A cessation or intermission of action. 2. A holding back; hesitation.
pave, 1 pēv; 2 pāv, *vt.* [PAVED; PAV'ING.] To cover with pavement.— **pave'ment,** *n.* 1. A flooring, as of stone, for a road. 2. Material for paving.— **pav'ior,** 1 pēv'yɚr; 2 pāv'yor, *n.* 1. One who paves. 2. Something, as a block or a rammer, used in paving. **pav'er‡; pav'ier‡.**
pa-vil'ion, 1 pɑ-vil'yɒn; 2 pa-vĭl'yon, *n.* A structure for temporary shelter; a canopy.
paw, 1 pô; 2 pạ. I. *vt.* & *vi.* To scrape or strike with the forefoot; touch with the paws. II. *n.* The foot or hand of an animal having nails or claws.
pawl, 1 pôl; 2 pạl, *n. Mech.* A hinged or pivoted piece shaped to engage with ratchet-teeth; a click or detent.
pawn, 1 pôn; 2 pạn, *vt.* To pledge (personal property), as security for a loan.
pawn¹, *n.* Something pledged as security for a loan.— **pawn'brok″er,** *n.* One who makes a business of lending money on personal property.
pawn², *n.* A chessman of lowest rank.

Pawl and Ratchet-wheel. Pawl (p): ratchet-wheel (r); arm (a).

pay, 1 pē; 2 pā, *v.* [PAID; PAY'ING.] I. *t.* 1. To render an equivalent for, as for property or service. 2. To satisfy, as a claim. 3. To expend, as money; deliver; hand over. 4. To profit. II. *i.* To render compensation; yield adequate return.
pay, *n.* Something rendered as an equivalent for property, labor, or loss; requital; reward; compensation.— **pay'a-bl(e⁵,** *a.* Due and unpaid.— **pay-ee',** 1 pē-ī'; 2 pā-ē', *n.* One to whom payment has been or is to be made.— **pay'er,** *n.* One who pays.— **pay'mas″ter,** *n.* One who has charge of the paying of employees.— **pay'ment,** *n.* The act of paying; requital; recompense.
pea, 1 pī; 2 pē, *n.* [PEAS² OR PEASE², *pl.*]

A climbing annual herb, or its edible seed.
— **sweet pea,** an ornamental climber of the bean family, with large, fragrant, variously colored flowers.
peace, 1 pīs; 2 pēc, *n.* Absence or cessation of war; quiet; tranquillity; concord.
— **peace'a-bl(e⁵,** *a.* 1. Inclined to peace. 2. Peaceful; tranquil.— **peace'a-bl(e-ness⁵,** *n.*— **peace'a-bly,** *adv.*— **peace'ful,** *a.* 1. Undisturbed. 2. Inclined to or used in peace.— **peace'ful-ly,** *adv.*
peach, 1 pīch; 2 pēch, *n.* The fleshy, edible fruit of the peach-tree, or the tree itself.— **peach'y,** *a.*
pea'cock″, 1 pī'kȯk″; 2 pī'cŏk″, *n.* A large, crested bird, of which the male is noted for its elongated tail-coverts, marked with beautiful eye-like spots.— **pea'fowl″,** *n.*— **pea'hen″,** *n. fem.*
peak, 1 pīk; 2 pēk, *n.* 1. A point or edge. 2. A mountain summit.— **peak'ed,** *a.* Pointed.
peal, 1 pīl; 2 pēl. I. *vt.* & *vi.* To ring loudly. II. *n.* 1. A prolonged, sonorous, clanging sound. 2. A set of large bells musically attuned; a chime.

Peacock-feathers.

pea'nut, 1 pī'nŭt; 2 pē'nŭt, *n.* A fruit of a trailing plant of the bean family, ripening under ground.
pear, 1 pār; 2 pâr, *n.* The edible, fleshy fruit of a tree of the rose family.
pearl, 1 pɚrl; 2 pĕrl, *n.* A lustrous concretion deposited in the shells of various mollusks: used as a gem.— **pearl'ash″,** *n.* Crude potassium carbonate.— **pearl'y,** *a.* Adorned with or resembling pearls.
peas'ant, 1 pez'ɒnt; 2 pĕṣ'ant, *n.* In Europe, a petty farmer; a farm-laborer.— **peas'ant-ry,** *n.* The peasant class.
pease, 1 pīz; 2 pēṣ, *n. sing.* & *pl.* Peas collectively.
peat, 1 pīt; 2 pēt, *n.* Partially carbonized vegetable matter, found in bogs and used as fuel.— **peat'-bog″,** *n.*— **peat'y,** *a.*
peb'ble, 1 peb'l; 2 pĕb'l, *n.* 1. A small rounded stone. 2. A quartz-crystal lens.— **peb'bly,** *a.* Abounding with pebbles.
pe-can', 1 pı-kan'; 2 pe-eăn', *n.* A large hickory of the United States with olive-shaped nuts, or the nut itself.
pec″ca-dil'lo, 1 pek″ɑ-dil'o; 2 pĕc″a-dĭl'o, *n.* [-LOS² *or* -LOES², *pl.*] A slight or trifling sin.

pec′ca-ry, 1 pek′ə-rı; 2 pĕc′a-ry, *n.* [-RIES², *pl.*] A pugnacious hog = like American mammal.

peckᵗ, 1 pek; 2 pĕk, *vt. & vi.* To strike with or as with the beak.— **peck′er,** *n.*

peck, *n.* A measure; eight quarts or one-fourth of a bushel.

Collared Peccary. ¹/₄₈

pec′to-ral, 1 pek′to-rəl; 2 pĕc′to-ral, *a.* Pertaining to the breast or chest. **-ly,** *adv.*

pec′u-late, 1 pek′yu-lēt; 2 pĕc′yu-lāt, *vi.* [-LAT″ED^d; -LAT″ING.] To embezzle; pilfer; steal.— **pec″u-la′tion,** *n.*— **pec′u-la″tor,** *n.*

pe-cu′liar, 1 pı-kiūl′yạr; 2 pe-cūl′yar, *a.* **1.** Particular; singular; strange; odd. **2.** Belonging particularly to one.— **pe-cu′liar-ly,** *adv.*— **pe-cu″li-ar′i-ty,** *n.* [-TIES², *pl.*] The quality of being peculiar; singularity.

pe-cu′ni-a-ry, 1 pı-kiū′nı-ē-rı; 2 pe-cū′ni-ā-ry, *a.* Consisting of money; monetary.

ped′a-gog,) 1 ped′ə-gog; 2 pĕd′a-gŏg, *n.*
ped′a-gogue,) A schoolmaster.— **ped″a-gog′ic,** 1 ped″ə-gej′ık; 2 pĕd″a-gŏg′ic, *a.* **ped″a-gog′i-cal‡.**— **ped″a-gog′ics,** *n.* The science or art of teaching.— **ped′a-gog-ism,** 1 ped′ə-gog-izm; 2 pĕd′a-gŏg-işm, *n.* The nature, character, or business of a pedagog.— **ped′a-go″gy,** 1 ped′ə-gō″jı *or* -gej′ı; 2 pĕd′a-gō″gy *or* -gŏg′y, *n.* **1.** Pedagogics. **2.** Pedagogism.

ped′al, 1 ped′al *or* pī′dəl; 2 pĕd′al *or* pē′dal, *n.* A lever for the foot, in musical instruments and light machinery.

ped′ant, 1 ped′ant; 2 pĕd′ant, *n.* One who makes needless display of learning.— **pe-dan′tic, -ti-cal,** *a.*— **ped′ant-ry,** *n.* Ostentatious display of knowledge.

ped′dle,) 1 ped′l; 2 pĕd′l, *vt. & vi.* [PED′-
ped′lᴾ,) DLED, PED′Lᴾ; PED′DLING.] To sell from house to house or little by little; do a petty business.

ped′dler, etc. Same as PEDLER, etc.

ped′es-tal, 1 ped′es-tal; 2 pĕd′es-tal, *n.* A base or support, as for a column, statue, or vase.

pe-des′tri-an, 1 pı-des′trı-ən; 2 pe-dĕs′-tri-an. **I.** *a.* Of or pertaining to walking. **II.** *n.* One who journeys on foot; a walker.— **pe-des′tri-an-ism,** *n.*

ped′i-cel, 1 ped′ı-sel; 2 pĕd′ı-çĕl, *n.* A stalk or supporting part, as of a flower.

ped′i-gree, 1 ped′ı-grī; 2 pĕd′ı-grē, *n.* **1.** A line of ancestors. **2.** A genealogical register.

ped′i-ment, 1 ped′ı-ment *or* -mənt; 2 pĕd′i-ment, *n.* A broad, triangular space, as above a portico.— **ped″i-men′tal,** *a.*

ped′ler, 1 ped′lạr; 2 pĕd′ler, *n.* One who sells goods from house to house. **ped′dler‡; ped′lar‡.**

pe″do-bap′tism, 1 pī′do-bap′tizm; 2 pē″-do-băp′tişm, *n.* Infant baptism and the system that teaches it.— **pe″do-bap′tist,** *n.*

pe-dun′cle,) 1 pı-dụŋ′kl; 2 pe-dûŋ′el, *n.*
pe-dun′clᴾ,) The general stalk or support of a flower; any stalk or stem.— **pe-dun′cu-lar,** *a.*— **pe-dun′cu-late, -cu-lat-ed,** *a.*

peel, 1 pīl; 2 pēl. **I.** *vt. & vi.* To strip off the peel of; remove or be detached, as a rind or skin. **II.** *n.* Skin; rind; bark.

peep¹, 1 pīp; 2 pēp. **I**ᵗ. *vi.* **1.** To look slyly; peer. **2.** To be seen partially, as through a crevice. **II.** *n.* A furtive look.

peep². **I**ᵗ. *vi.* To utter a slight, sharp sound. **II.** *n.* The cry of a bird.

peer, 1 pīr; 2 pēr, *vi.* To look at or into something attentively and inquiringly.

peer, *n.* **1.** An equal. **2.** A nobleman.— **peer′age,** *n.* **1.** The rank of a peer. **2.** The nobility.— **peer′ess,** *n.* A woman who holds a title of nobility.— **peer′less,** *a.* Of unequaled excellence. **-ly,** *adv.* **-ness,** *n.*

peeved, 1 pīvd; 2 pēvd, *a.* Annoyed, vexed; disgruntled.

pee′vish, 1 pī′vısh; 2 pē′vish, *a.* Feebly fretful; querulous; petulant.— **pee′vish-ly,** *adv.*— **pee′vish-ness,** *n.*

peg, 1 peg; 2 pĕg. **I.** *vt.* To drive (a peg) into; fasten by pegs. **II.** *n.* A wooden pin.— **pegged,** *a.*

pe-lag′ic, 1 pı-laj′ık; 2 pe-lăg′ic, *a.* Pertaining to or inhabiting the deep sea.

pelf, 1 pelf; 2 pĕlf, *n.* Money; wealth.

pel′i-can, 1 pel′ı-kən; 2 pĕl′i-can, *n.* A large fish=eating bird of warm regions, having a large pouch on the lower jaw, for the temporary storage of fish.

Common Pelican. ¹/₅₄

pe-lisse′, 1 pı-līs′; 2 pe-līs′, *n.* A long outer garment or cloak.

pel′let, 1 pel′et; 2 pĕl′et, *n.* A small round ball, as a small pill.

pel′li-cle,) 1 pel′ı-kl; 2 pĕl′i-el, *n.* A thin
pel′li-clᴾ,) skin, film, or layer.

pell″=mell′,) 1 pel″=mel′; 2 pĕl″=mĕl′, *adv.*
pell″=mel′lᴿ,) In a confused or promiscuous way; with a headlong rush.

pel-lu′cid, 1 pe-liū′sıd; 2 pĕ-lū′çid, *a.* Transparent; clear; translucent.— **pel-lu′cid-ly,** *adv.*— **pel-lu′cid-ness,** *n.*

peltᵈ, 1 pelt; 2 pĕlt, *v.* **I.** *t.* To strike or assail with missiles. **II.** *i.* To throw anything; descend violently.

ɪ: ə = final; ı = habit; aisle; au = out; oil; iū = feud; ɕhin; go; ŋ = sing; ɕhin, this.

2: wolf, do; book, boot; full, rule, cure, but, ûrn; oil, boy; go, gem; iŋk; thin, this.

pelt[1], *n.* The undressed skin of a beast, with the hair or wool on; an undressed fur-skin or sheepskin.

pelt[2], *n.* A blow, as of a missile.

pelt'ry, 1 pelt'rı; 2 pĕlt'ry, *n.* Pelts or undressed skins collectively.

pel'vis, 1 pel'vıs; 2 pĕl'vis, *n.* The bony structure at the base of the abdomen. —**pel'vic,** *a.*

pem'mi-can, 1 pem'ı-kən; 2 pĕm'i-ean, *n.* **1.** Lean, dried venison pounded into a paste with fat and berries. **2.** A similar food now made from beef and dried fruits: used on arctic expeditions, etc.

pen[1], 1 pen; 2 pĕn. **I.** *vt.* [PENNED OR PENT; PEN'NING.] To enclose in a pen. **II.** *n.* A small enclosure, as for pigs.

pen[2]. **I.** *vt.* [PENNED, PEND[S]; PEN'NING.] To write. **II.** *n.* An instrument for writing with a fluid ink.

pen-, *prefix.* Almost; nearly: used in words of Latin origin; as, *pen*ultimate.

pe'nal, 1 pī'nəl; 2 pē'nal, *a.* Pertaining to punishment; liable to punishment.—**pe'nal-ize,** *vt.* To make or declare penal; subject to a penalty.—**pe'nal-ly,** *adv.*—**pen'al-ty,** *n.* [-TIES[Z], *pl.*] Any painful consequence of the transgression of law; punishment.

pen'ance, 1 pen'əns; 2 pĕn'anç, *n.* Suffering voluntarily undertaken as an act of atonement.

pence, } 1 pens; 2 pĕnç, *n.* Plural of penny.
pense[P], } **pen'nies**‡.

pen"chant', 1 pāñ"shāñ' *or* pen'chənt; 2 pän"chän' *or* pĕn'chant, *n.* A strong inclination; bias.

pen'cil, 1 pen'sıl; 2 pĕn'çil. **I.** *vt.* [-CILED OR -CILLED, -CILD[S]; -CIL-ING OR -CIL-LING.] To mark, write, or draw with a pencil. **II.** *n.* **1.** A long, pointed strip of wood enclosing a slip of graphite, slate, etc., used for writing, drawing, etc. **2.** A small, finely pointed paint-brush. **3.** A group of lines or rays diverging from a given point.

pend[d], 1 pend; 2 pĕnd, *vi.* To be awaiting or in process of adjustment: literally, to hang or depend.—**pen'dant,** *n.* Anything that hangs or depends; a short rope, streamer, or pennant. **pen'dent**‡.—**pen'den-cy,** *n.*—**pen'dent,** *a.* **1.** Hanging loosely; pendulous. **2.** Projecting.—**pend'ing. I.** *a.* Awaiting settlement. **II.** *prep.* **1.** During the continuance of. **2.** Awaiting; until.

pen'du-lum, 1 pen'ju-lum; 2 pĕn'ju-lŭm, *n.* A body suspended from a fixed point, and free to swing to and fro.—**pen'du-lous,** *a.* Hanging, especially so as to swing. **-ly,** *adv.* **-ness,** *n.* **pen"du-los'i-ty**‡.

pen'e-trate, 1 pen'ı-trēt; 2 pĕn'e-trāt, *v.* [-TRAT"ED[d]; TRAT"ING.] **I.** *t.* **1.** To enter into the interior of. **2.** To see into; discern; detect. **II.** *i.* To pass into or enter something.—**pen"e-tra-bil'i-ty,** *n.*—**pen'e-tra-bl(e**[P], *a.* That may be penetrated. —**pen"e-tra'tion,** *n.* The act of penetrating; acuteness.—**pen'e-tra-tiv(e**[S], *n.*

pen'guin, 1 pen'gwın; 2 pĕn'gwin, *n.* A sea-bird of the southern hemisphere.

pen"i-cil'lin, 1 pen"ı-sil'ın; 2 pĕn"i-çil'in, *n.* A powerful anti-infective substance found in an earth-mold fungus.

pe-nin'su-la, 1 pı-nin'siu-lə; 2 pe-nin'sū-la, *n.* A piece of land almost surrounded by water.—**pe-nin'su-lar,** *a.*

pen'i-tent, 1 pen'ı-tent; 2 pĕn'i-tĕnt. **I.** *a.* Sorry for sin and desirous of amendment; contrite; repentant. **II.** *n.* One who is penitent. **-ly,** *adv.*—**pen'i-tence,** *n.* The state of being penitent; contrition.—**pen"i-ten'tial,** *a.* Pertaining to penitence, penance, or punishment.—**pen"i-ten'tia-ry, I.** *a.* Penitential. **II.** *n.* A house of correction; state-prison.

pen'knife", 1 pen'naif"; 2 pĕn'nīf", *n.* A small pocket-knife.

pen'man, 1 pen'mən; 2 pĕn'man, *n.* [-MEN, *pl.*] A writer.—**pen'man-ship,** *n.* The art of writing; handwriting.

pen'-name", 1 pen'-nēm"; 2 pĕn'-nām", *n.* An author's assumed name; pseudonym.

pen'nant, 1 pen'ənt; 2 pĕn'ant, *n.* A small flag, especially a very long and narrow one.

pen'nate, 1 pen'ēt; 2 pĕn'āt, *a.* Having wings or feathers.

pen'ni-less, 1 pen'ı-les; 2 pĕn'i-lĕs, *a.* Without a penny; destitute.

pen'non, 1 pen'ən; 2 pĕn'on, *n.* A small flag, borne on his lance by a medieval knight.

pen'ny, 1 pen'ı; 2 pĕn'y, *n.* [PEN'NIES[Z] OR PENCE, *pl.*] **1.** A British coin, one-twelfth of a shilling, or 2 cents United States value. **2.** Any small coin, as a cent (U. S.).—**pen'ny-weight",** *n.* The twentieth of an ounce, troy.

pen"ny-roy'al, 1 pen"ı-rei'əl; 2 pĕn"y-rŏy'al, *n.* A strong-scented herb of the mint family.

pen'sile, 1 pen'sıl; 2 pĕn'sil, *a.* Pendent and swaying; hanging loosely.

pen'sion, 1 pen'shən; 2 pĕn'shon. **I.** *vt.* To grant a pension to; retire on a pension. **II.** *n.* A periodical allowance, as to a disabled soldier or sailor, on account of past services.—**pen'sion-er,** *n.* One who receives a pension. **pen'sion-a-ry**‡.

pen'sive, } 1 pen'sıv; 2 pĕn'siv, *a.* Gravely
pen'siv[S], } or sadly thoughtful. **-ly,** *adv.* **-ness,** *n.*

pent, 1 pent; 2 pĕnt, *pa.* Penned up or in; closely confined.

pen'ta-gon, 1 pen'tə-gən; 2 pĕn'ta-gŏn, *n.*

A figure with five angles and five sides. **— pen-tag′o-nal,** *a.*

Pen′ta-teuch, 1 pen′tə-tiūk; 2 pĕn′ta-tūe, *n.* The first five books of the Bible, collectively.

pen′te-cos″tal, 1 pen′tɪ-kɒs″təl, 2 pĕn′tɪ-cŏs″tal, *a.* Pertaining to or like Pentecost, a Jewish festival, occurring fifty days after the Passover, memorable for the outpouring of the Spirit (*Acts* ii).

pent′house″, 1 pent′haus″; 2 pĕnt′hous″, *n.* A shed having the upper edge of its sloping roof attached to the wall of another building.

pe-nult′, 1 pɪ-nult′ *or* pī′nult; 2 pe-nŭlt′ *or* pē′nŭlt, *n.* The syllable next to the last in a word. **pe-nul′ti-maṭ.— pe-nul′ti-mate,** *a.* Being the last but one.

pe-num′bra, 1 pɪ-num′brə; 2 pe-nŭm′bra, *n.* A margin of a shadow observed in an eclipse, etc.

Planet's Penumbra (exaggerated).

pen′u-ry, 1 pen′yu-rɪ; 2 pĕn′yu-ry, *n.* Extreme poverty or want.**— pe-nu′ri-ous,** *a.* Parsimonious; miserly. **-ly,** *adv.* **-ness,** *n.*

x, the planet; *s,* a satellite; *p, p,* the penumbra; *su.* the sun.

pe′on, 1 pī′ɒn; 2 pē′ŏn, *n.* A common laborer; servant; in Spanish America, a laborer bound to serve until a debt is paid, commonly with little chance of payment; applied in India to certain inferior officers, servants, etc.**— pe′on-age,** *n.* Service in payment of a real or assumed debt: a form of practical slavery.

pe′o-ny, 1 pī′o-nɪ; 2 pē′o-ny, *n.* [-NIES², *pl.*] A plant bearing large showy flowers.

peo′ple, 1 pī′pl; 2 pē′pl. **I.** *vt.* [PEO′-PLED; PEO′PLING.] To stock with inhabitants; populate. **II.** *n.* **1.** The persons, collectively, inhabiting one locality, speaking one language, or living under one government. **2.** Persons collectively. **3.** The populace. **4.** Kinsfolk; attendants, etc.

pep′per, 1 pep′ər; 2 pĕp′er. **I.** *vt.* To season with pepper; pelt; scold. **II.** *n.* A tropical climbing shrub, its pungent aromatic berries, or a condiment prepared from them.**— pep′per-mint,** *n.* A pungent aromatic herb, used in medicine and confectionery.**— pep′per-y,** *a.* Pertaining to or like pepper; pungent; quick-tempered; stinging.

pep′sin, 1 pep′sɪn; 2 pĕp′sin, *n.* The digestive ferment of the gastric juice; also, a medicinal preparation obtained from the stomachs of various animals. **pep′sineṭ.— pep′tic,** *a.***— pep-tic′i-ty,** *n.*

per-, *prefix.* A Romance-Latin prefix meaning (1) through, by, by means of, for; as, *perceive, perjure;* (2) very; extremely; exceedingly; as, *per*acute.

per″ad-ven′ture, 1 per″ad-ven′chur *or* -tiur; 2 pĕr″ăd-vĕn′chur *or* -tūr, *adv.* Perchance; perhaps.

per-am′bu-late, 1 pər-am′biu-let; 2 per-ăm′bū-lāt, *v.* [-LAT″ED^d; -LAT″ING.] **I.** *t.* To walk through or over. **II.** *i.* To walk about.**— per-am″bu-la′tion,** *n.***— per-am′bu-la″tor,** *n.* **1.** One who perambulates. **2.** A baby-carriage.

per-ceive′, } 1 pər-siv′; 2 per-çēv′, *vt.* [PER-**per-ceiv′e,** } CEIV(E)D′S; PER-CEIV′ING.] To know by means of the senses; discern; understand; note.**— per-ceiv′a-bl(e^v,** *a.***— per-ceiv′a-bly,** *adv.***— per-ceiv′er,** *n.*

per cent. By or in the hundred.**— per-cent′age,** *n.* **1.** Rate by the hundred. **2.** The allowance, commission, duty, or interest on a hundred.

per-cep′tion, 1 pər-sep′shən; 2 per-çĕp′-shon, *n.* The act or power of perceiving; that which is perceived: cognition; apprehension.**— per-cep′ti-bil′i-ty,** *n.***— per-cep′-ti-bl(e^v,** *a.* That may be seen or apprehended; perceivable.**— per-cep′ti-bly,** *adv.***— per-cep′tiv(e^s,** *a.* Perceiving, or having the power of perception.**— per″cep-tiv′i-ty,** *n.*

perch¹, 1 pūrch; 2 pĕrch, *vt. & vi.* To place, alight, or sit on a perch; roost.

perch¹, *n.* A small food-fish.

perch², *n.* **1.** A staff, pole, or slat; a roost. **2.** A measure: (1) One rod (16.5 feet). (2) In stonework, about 25 cubic feet.

per-chance′, 1 pər-chɑns′; 2 per-chánç′, *adv.* Perhaps.

per-cip′i-ent, 1 pər-sip′ɪ-ent; 2 per-çĭp′i-ĕnt, *a.* Perceiving.**— per-cip′i-en-cy,** *n.*

per′co-late, 1 pūr′ko-let; 2 pĕr′co-lāt, *vt. & vi.* [-LAT″ED^d; -LAT″ING.] To pass through fine openings; filter; strain.**— per″co-la′tion,** *n.***— per′co-la″tor,** *n.* [On the contrary.

per con′tra, 1 pər kɒn′trə; 2 per cŏn′tra.

per-cus′sion, 1 pər-kush′ən; 2 per-cŭsh′on, *n.* Sudden collision, or the shock or vibration produced by it.**— per-cus′sion-cap″,** *n.* A small cap of thin metal containing a fulminate for firing a charge.**— per-cus′siv(e^s,** *a.*

per-di′tion, 1 pər-dish′ən; 2 per-dĭsh′on, *n.* Destruction; eternal death; hell.

per″e-gri-na′tion, 1 per″ɪ-grɪ-nē′shən; 2 pĕr″e-grĭ-nā′shon, *n.* A traveling about; journey; wandering.

per′emp-to-ry, 1 per′emp-to-rɪ; 2 pĕr′-ĕmp-to-ry, *a.* Decisive; absolute; positive; dictatorial.**— per′emp-to″ri-ly,** *adv.*

---

per-en'ni-al, 1 pər-en'ı-əl; 2 per-ĕn'i-al.
I. *a.* Lasting more than one season. **II.**
n. A plant that lasts year after year.
-ly, *adv.*

per'fect[d], 1 pūr'fekt *or* pər-fekt'; 2 pêr'-
fĕct *or* per-fĕct', *vt.* To make perfect;
finish; complete.— **per-fect"i-bil'i-ty,** *n.*—
per-fect'i-bl(e[p], *a.*— **per-fec'tiv**(es, *a.*

per'fect, 1 pūr'fekt; 2 pêr'fĕct. **I.** *a.* **1.**
Without defect or lack; complete. **2.**
Gram. Noting past or finished action.
II. *n.* *Gram.* The perfect tense.—
per-fec'tion, *n.* **1.** The state of being perfect; supreme excellence. **per'fect-ness**‡.
2. The highest degree of a thing.— **per'fect-
ly,** *adv.*

per'fi-dy, 1 pūr'fi-dı; 2 pêr'fi-dy, *n.*
Treachery; faithlessness.— **per-fid'i-ous,** *a.*
Treacherous. **-ly,** *adv.* **-ness,** *n.*

per'fo-rate, 1 pūr'fo-rēt; 2 pêr'fo-rāt. **I.**
vt. [-RAT"ED[d];-RAT"ING.] To bore through;
pierce. **II.** 1 pūr'fo-rıt; 2 pêr'fo-rat, *a.*
Pierced with a hole or holes.— **per"fo-ra'-
tion,** *n.* **per'fo-rat"ed**‡.— **per'fo-ra"tor,** *n.*

per-force', 1 pər-fōrs'; 2 pêr-fôrç', *adv.*
By force of; necessity.

per-form', 1 pər-fôrm'; 2 per-fôrm', *v.* **I.**
t. **1.** To bring to completion; accomplish;
fulfil. **2.** To act out, as a play; represent; render; play. **II.** *i.* To accomplish an act; do; act on the stage, etc.
— **per-form'ance,** *n.* The act of performing; execution; action; representation.—
per-form'er, *n.*

per-fume', 1 pər-fiūm'; 2 per-fūm'. **I.** *vt.*
[PER-FUMED'; PER-FUM'ING.] To render
odorous; scent. **II.** 1 pūr'fium *or* pər-
fiūm'; 2 pêr'fūm *or* per-fūm', *n.* **1.** A
pleasant odor, as from flowers. **2.** A fragrant substance or mixture.— **per-fum'er,** *n.*
— **per-fum'er-y,** *n.* Perfumes in general.

per-func'to-ry, 1 pər-fuŋk'to-rı; 2 per-
fŭŋc'to-ry, *a.* Done merely for the sake
of getting through; mechanical; formal.
— **per-func'to-ri-ly,** *adv.*— **per-func'to-ri-
ness,** *n.*

per-haps', 1 pər-haps'; 2 per-hăps', *adv.*
It may be; possibly.

pe'ri, 1 pī'rı; 2 pē'ri, *n.* *Per. Myth.* A fairy
or elf.

peri-, *prefix.* Near; around; as, *peri*meter.

Per"i-cle'an, 1 per"ı-klī'ən; 2 pêr"ı-clē'an, *a.*
Pertaining to Pericles, the greatest Athenian
statesman (died 429? B. C.), or to the period
of his supremacy, which was also that of
Greek art, literature, philosophy, and statesmanship.

per"i-gee', 1 per'ı-jī; 2 pêr'ı-gē, *n.* The
point in the orbit of the moon where it is
nearest the earth.

per"i-he'li-on, 1 per"ı-hī'lı-ɒn; 2 pêr"i-
hē'li-ŏn, *n.* The point in the orbit of a
planet or comet
where it is nearest
the sun.

Diagram showing
Perihelion.

per'il, 1 per'ıl; 2 pêr'il.
I. *vt. & vi.* [PER'ILED
or PER'ILLED, PER'-
ILD[s]; PER'IL-ING *or*
PER'IL-LING.] To ex-
pose to danger. **II.**
n. Exposure to
chance of injury, loss,
or destruction.— **per'-
il-ous,** *a.* Full of perils; *s,* sun; *a,* aphelion; *p,*
hazardous. **-ly,** *adv.* perihelion.

pe-rim'e-ter, 1 pı-rim'ı-tər; 2 pe-rim'e-ter,
n. The boundary or rim of a figure or
object.— **per"i-met'ric, -ri-cal,** *a.*

pe'ri-od, 1 pī'rı-əd; 2 pē'ri-od, *n.* **1.** A
definite portion of time; era. **2.** Termination. **3.** The present day. **4.** A dot
(.) marking the end of a sentence; a complete sentence.— **pe"ri-od'ic,** *a.* Pertaining
to a period; returning at regular intervals.—
pe"ri-od'i-cal. I. *a.* Periodic. **II.** *n.* A
publication appearing at regular intervals.—
pe"ri-o-dic'i-ty, *n.*— **pe"ri-od'i-cal-ly,** *adv.*

pe-riph'er-y, 1 pı-rif'ər-ı; 2 pe-rif'er-y,
pe-rif'er-y[p] } *n.* [-IES[z], *pl.*] The outer
surface; circumference.— **pe-riph'er-al,** *a.*

per'ish[t], 1 per'ısh; 2 pêr'ish, *vi.* To be
destroyed; wither; decay.— **per'ish-a-bl**(e[p],
a. Liable to perish; mortal.— **per'ish-a-
bl**(e-ness[p], *n.*— **per'ish-a-bly,** *adv.*

per'i-wig, 1 per'ı-wig; 2 pêr'i-wĭg, *n.* A
head-dress of false hair.

per"i-win'kle, 1 per"ı-wiŋ'kl; 2 pêr'i-
per"i-win'kl[p], } wĭŋ"k l, *n.*
1. A small sea-snail. **2.** [Lo-
cal U. S.] A whelk.

per'jure, 1 pūr'jur; 2 pêr'jur,
vt. & vi. [PER'JURED; PER'-
JUR-ING.] To make or be-
come guilty of perjury;
bear false witness.— **per'jur-
er,** *n.*— **per'ju-ry,** *n.* As- Periwinkle.
sertion of a falsehood under oath.

per'ma-nent, 1 pūr'mə-nent; 2 pêr'ma-
nĕnt, *a.* Continuing without change;
durable.— **per'ma-nence,** *n.* The state of
being permanent; durability; fixity.— **per'-
ma-nen-cy,** *n.*— **per'ma-nent-ly,** *adv.*

per'me-ate, 1 pūr'mı-ēt; 2 pêr'me-āt, *vt.*
[-AT"ED[d]; -AT"ING.] To pass through
the pores or interstices of; be diffused
through.— **per"me-a-bil'i-ty,** *n.*— **per'me-
a-bl**(e[p], *a.* Allowing passage esp'cially of
fluids.— **per"me-a-bly,** *adv.*— **per"me-a'-
tion,** *n.*

per-mis'sion, 1 pər-mish'ən; 2 per-mĭsh'on, *n.* The act of permitting or allowing; license granted.— **per-mis'si-bl**(e^r, **per-mis'siv**(e^s, *a.* **1.** That permits. **2.** That is permitted.— **per-mis'si-bly, per-mis'-siv**(e-ly^s, *adv.*

per-mit', 1 pər-mit'; 2 per-mĭt', *vt. & vi.* [PER-MIT'TED^d; PER-MIT'TING.] To give consent to; allow; give permission.

per'mit, 1 pūr'mit; 2 pēr'mit, *n.* Permission or warrant.

per"mu-ta'tion, 1 pūr"miu-tē'shən; 2 pēr"mū-tā'shon, *n.* Arrangement of a number of things in every possible order; interchange.

per-ni'cious, 1 pər-nish'us; 2 per-nĭsh'ŭs, *a.* Having power to destroy or injure. **-ly,** *adv.* **-ness,** *n.*

per"pen-dic'u-lar, 1 pūr"pen-dik'yu-lər; 2 pēr"pĕn-dĭc'yu-lar. **I.** *a.* Upright; vertical; meeting a given line at right angles. **II.** *n.* A perpendicular line. **-ly,** *adv.*— **per"pen-dic'u-lar'i-ty,** *n.*

per'pe-trate, 1 pūr'pi-trēt; 2 pēr'pe-trāt, *vt.* [-TRAT-ED^d; -TRAT-ING.] To do, or carry through, in a bad sense; be guilty of.— **per"pe-tra'tion,** *n.*— **per'pe-tra"tor,** *n.*

per-pet'u-al, 1 pər-pech'u-əl or -pet'yu-əl; 2 per-pĕch'u-al or -pĕt'yu-al, *a.* Continuing without ceasing; incessant; ceaseless; endless. **-ly,** *adv.*— **per-pet'u-ate,** *vt.* **-AT'ED^d; -AT'ING.**] To make perpetual.— **per-pet"u-a'tion,** *n.*— **per'pe-tu'i-ty,** 1 pūr'pi-tiū'i-ti; 2 pēr'pe-tū'i-ty, *n.* [-TIES^z, *pl.*] Something perpetual; unending time.

per-plex'^t, 1 pər-pleks'; 2 per-plĕks', *vt.* To subject to doubt or difficulty in determining; confuse; puzzle; bewilder.— **per-plex'i-ty,** *n.* [-TIES^z, *pl.*] A perplexed condition; bewilderment.

per'qui-site, 1 pūr'kwi-zit; 2 pēr'kwi-sĭt, **per'qui-sit**^s, *n.* Any profit from service beyond salary or wages.

per'se-cute, 1 pūr'si-kiūt; 2 pēr'se-cūt, *vt.* [-CUT'ED^d; -CUT'ING.] To injure or afflict, as on account of religious belief; harass.— **per"se-cu'trix,** *n. fem.*— **per"se-cu'tion,** *n.* The act of persecuting; oppression.— **per"se-cu'tor,** *n.*

per"se-vere', 1 pūr"si-vīr'; 2 pēr"se-vēr', *vi.* [-VERED'; -VER'ING.] To keep steadily on in doing or striving; persist.— **per"se-ver'ance,** *n.*

Per'sian, 1 pūr'shan; 2 pēr'shan. **I.** *a.* Of or pertaining to Persia, its people, or language. **II.** *n.* A native of Persia.

per-sim'mon, 1 pər-sim-ən; 2 per-sĭm'on, *n.* The plum-like fruit of an American tree, astringent until exposed to frost; also, the tree. See illus. in next column.

per-sist'^d, 1 pər-sist'; 2 per-sĭst', *vi.* To adhere firmly to any course, design, etc.; continue fixed; endure.— **per-sis'tence,** *n.* **per-sis'ten-cy**_t.— **per-sis'tent,** *a.* **1.** Firm and persevering in a course or resolve. **2.** Enduring; permanent. — **per-sis'tent-ly,** *adv.*

per'son, 1 pūr'sən *or* -sn; 2 pēr'son *or* -sn, *n.* **1.** A human being; an individual. **2.** The body of a human being, or its characteristic appearance.— **per'son-age,** *n.* **1.** A man or woman, especially one of rank. **2.** An assumed character.— **per'son-al,** *a.* **1.** Pertaining to or done by a particular person. **2.** Characteristic of human beings.— **per"son-al'i-ty,** *n.* [-TIES^z, *pl.*] **1.** That which constitutes a person. **2.** Anything said of a person, especially if disparaging.— **per'son-al-ly,** *adv.*— **per'son-al-ty,** *n.* Personal property.— **per'son-ate,** *vt.* [-AT'ED^d; -AT'ING.] To assume the character of; impersonate.— **per"son-a'tion,** *n.* The act of personating; impersonation, especially false impersonation.— **per'son-a"tor,** *n.*— **per-son'i-fy,** *vt.* [-FIED; -FY'ING] To attribute human qualities to (something inanimate, an abstraction, etc.); represent or refer to as a person.— **per-son"i-fi-ca'tion,** *n.*— **per"son-nel',** 1 pūr"sə-nel'; 2 pēr"so-nĕl', *n.* The persons collectively employed in any service.

Persimmon-leaves.

a, sterile flowers; *b,* fruit.

per-spec'tive, 1 pər-spek'tiv; 2 per-spĕc'tiv^s, *a.* Pertaining to or drawn in perspective. **II.** *n.* **1.** The art of delineating solid objects on a flat surface, so that they shall appear in relief like the real objects. **2.** A distant view; vista.

per"spi-ca'cious, 1 pūr"spi-kē'shus; 2 pēr"spi-cā'shŭs, *a.* Keenly discerning. **-ly,** *adv.* **-ness,** *n.*— **per"spi-cac'i-ty,** *n.* Mental penetration.

per-spic'u-ous, 1 pər-spik'yu-us; 2 per-spĭc'yu-ŭs, *a.* Clear to the mind; readily understood; clear; lucid. **-ly,** *adv.* **-ness,** *n.* — **per"spi-cu'i-ty,** *n.* Clearness of expression or style; lucidity.

per-spire', 1 pər-spair'; 2 per-spīr', *vt. & vi.* [PER-SPIRED'; PER-SPIR'ING.] To sweat. — **per"spi-ra'tion,** *n.* The act of perspiring; sweat.

per-suade', 1 pər-swēd'; 2 per-swād', *vt. & vi.* [PER-SUAD'ED^d; PER-SUAD'ING.] To influence by entreaty or reasoning; win over; convince; plead successfully.— **per-suad'a-bl**(e^r, *a.*— **per-suad'er,** *n.*— **per-**

sua'sion, 1 pər-swē'zən; 2 per-swā'zhon, *n.* **1.** The act of persuading. **2.** Settled opinion; accepted creed. **3.** Persuasiveness.— **per-sua'sive(e³,** *a.* Having power or tending to persuade. **-ly,** *adv.*— **per-sua'siv(e-ness³,** *n.* Power or tendency to persuade.

pert, 1 pŭrt; 2 pĕrt, *a.* Disrespectfully forward or free; saucy. **-ly,** *adv.* **-ness,** *n.*

per-tain', 1 pər-tēn'; 2 per-tān', *vi.* To belong as an attribute, property, element, etc.; appertain; relate.

per''ti-na'cious, 1 pŭr''tı-nē'shus; 2 pĕr-tı-nā'shŭs, *a.* Stubborn; insistent; incessant. **-ly,** *adv.* **-ness,** *n.*— **per''ti-nac'i-ty,** *n.* Stubborn or undue insistence.

per'ti-nent, 1 pŭr'tı-nent; 2 pĕr'tı-nĕnt, *a.* Related to the matter in hand; relevant.— **per'ti-nence,** *n.* **per'ti-nen-cy‡.– per'ti-nent-ly,** *adv.*

per-turb', 1 pər-tûrb'; 2 per-tûrb', *vt.* To disquiet thoroughly; disturb greatly; agitate.— **per-turb'a-bl(e³,** *a.*— **per''tur-ba'tion,** *n.*

pe-ruke', 1 pe-rūk' *or* per'ūk; 2 pĕ-rŭk' *or* pēr'ŭk, *n.* A wig.

pe-ruse', 1 pe-rūz'; 2 pe-ruş', *vi.* [PE-RUSED'; PE-RUS'ING.] To read attentively. **- pe-ru'sal,** *n.* A careful reading.

Pe-ru'vi-an, 1 pı-rū'vı-an; 2 pe-rū'vi-an, *a.* Of or pertaining to Peru, South America; relating to the ancient realms of the Incas.

per-vade', 1 pər-vēd'; 2 per-vād', *vt.* [PER-VAD'ED⁴; PER-VAD'ING.] To spread through every part of; permeate.— **per-va'sion,** *n.*— **per-va'siv(e³,** *a.* Penetrating; permeating.

per-verse', 1 pər-vûrs'; 2 per-vĕrs', *a.* Wilfully wrong; unreasonable; refractory; petulant.— **per-verse'ly,** *adv.*— **per-ver'sion,** *n.* Perverted use; misapplication.— **per-ver'si-ty,** *n.* [-TIES²; *pl.*] Perverse nature or behavior. **per-verse'ness‡.– per-ver'siv(e³,** *a.* Tending to pervert.

per-vert', 1 pər-vûrt'; 2 per-vĕrt'. **I⁴,** *vt.* To turn from its right purpose, use, or meaning; alter for the worse. **II.** *n.* An apostate.— **per-vert'er,** *n.*— **per-vert'i-bl(e³,** *a.*

per'vi-ous, 1 pŭr'vı-us; 2 pĕr'vi-ŭs, *a.* Penetrable; permeable. **-ness,** *n.*

pes'si-mism, 1 pes'ı-mizm; 2 pĕs'i-mĭşm, *n.* A disposition to take a gloomy view of affairs.— **pes'si-mist,** *n.*— **pes''si-mis'tic,** *a.*

pest, 1 pest; 2 pĕst, *n.* A virulent epidemic; pestilence; a detestable person or thing. **- pest'-house'',** *n.* A hospital for treating infectious diseases. [annoy; irritate.

pes'ter, 1 pes'tər; 2 pĕs'ter, *vt.* To worry; **pes-tif'er-ous,** 1 pes-tif'ar-us; 2 pĕs-tĭf'er-ŭs, *a.* Carrying pestilence; pestilent.

pes'ti-lent, 1 pes'tı-lent; 2 pĕs'ti-lĕnt, *a.* Tending to produce pestilence; hurtful; malignant; vexatious.— **pes'ti-lence,** *n.* Any wide-spread and fatal infectious malady.— **pes''ti-len'tial,** *a.* Having the nature of or breeding pestilence.

pes'tle, ⎱ 1 pes'l; 2 pĕs'l, *n.* An implement **pes'tl(e³,** ⎰ used for pounding or reducing substances in a mortar.

pet, 1 pet; 2 pĕt, *vt.* [PET'TED⁴; PET'TING.] To treat as a pet; fondle.

pet, *a.* Being a pet; indulged; cherished.

pet¹, *n.* A creature fondled or cherished.

Pestle and Mortar.

pet², *n.* A fit of ill temper; peevishness.

pet'al, 1 pet'əl; 2 pĕt'al, *n.* A leaf of a flower.

pe-tard', 1 pı-tärd'; 2 pe-tärd', *n.* An old-time explosive device for making breaches, as in walls.

pet'i-ole, 1 pet'ı-ōl; 2 pĕt'i-ōl, *n. Bot.* The footstalk of a leaf.

pet'it, ⎱ 1 pet'ı; 2 pĕt'i, *a.* Small; less-**pet'ty¹ᵖ,** ⎰ er; minor; petty: used in law phrases.

pe-tite', 1 pa-tīt'; 2 pe-tīt', *a.* [F.] Of small figure; diminutive feminine form.

pe-ti'tion, 1 pı-tish'ən; 2 pe-tĭsh'on. **I.** *vt. & vi.* To present a petition; request. **II.** *n.* A prayer or formal request.— **pe-ti'tion-er,** *n.*

pet'rel, 1 pet'rel; 2 pĕt'rĕl, *n.* A long-winged dusky sea-bird, frequenting the high seas; Mother Carey's chicken.

pet'ri-fy, 1 pet'rı-fai; 2 pĕt'ri-fĭ, *vt. & vi.* [-FIED; -FY'-ING.] To turn to stone; harden.— **pet'ri-fac'tion,** *n.** A turning into stone; something turned to stone.— **pet'ri-fac'tiv(e³,** *a.*

Storm-petrel. 1/12

pe-tro'le-um, 1 pı-trō'lı-um; 2 pe-trō'le-ŭm, *n.* An inflammable oily liquid exuding from the earth; coal-oil.

pet'ti-coat, 1 pet'ı-kōt; 2 pĕt'i-cōt, *n.* A skirt; especially, a woman's underskirt.

pet'ti-fog'ger, 1 pet'ı-fog'ər; 2 pĕt'i-fŏg'er, *n.* An inferior lawyer.

pet'tish, 1 pet'ısh; 2 pĕt'ish, *a.* Capriciously ill-tempered; petulant. **-ly,** *adv.* **-ness,** *n.*

pet'ty², 1 pet'ı; 2 pĕt'y, *a.* [PET'TI-ER; PET'TI-EST.] Having little worth or rank; inferior.— **pet'ti-ly,** *adv.* **pet'ti-ness,** *n.*

1: ə = final; ı = habit; aisle; au = out; oil; iū = feud; chin; go; ŋ = sing; thin, this.
2: wolf, dǫ; book, boot; full, rule, cūre, bŭt, bûrn; ôil, bŏy; go, ĝem; iŋk; thin, this.

pet′u·lant, 1 pet′yu-[or pĕch′u-]lənt; 2 pĕt′yu-[or pĕch′u-]lant, *a.* Capriciously ill-tempered; fretful; pettish. **-ly,** *adv.*—**pet′u·lance, n. pet′u·lan·cy‡.**

pe·tu′ni·a, 1 pɪ-tiū′nɪ-ə; 2 pe-tū′ni-a, *n.* A plant with showy funnel-shaped flowers.

pew, 1 piū; 2 pū, *n.* An enclosed seat in a church.

pew′ter, 1 piū′tər; 2 pū′tẽr, *n.* An alloy of tin and lead.

pha′e·ton, 1 fē′ɪ-tən; 2 fā′e-ton, *n.* A **fa′e·ton**ᴿ, ∫ light four-wheeled carriage, open at the sides.

pha′lanx, ⎰1 fē′laŋks or **fa′lanx**ᴿ, ⎱ fal′aŋks; 2 fā′laŋks or fal′aŋks, *n.* [PHA-LAN′GES or (except in *Anat.* and *Bot.*) PHA′LANX-ES, 1 -gĭz or -ez; 2 -gĕs or -ĕs, *pl.*] **1.** The Macedonian military formation with ranks 8 to 16 deep; any compact body or corps. **2.** One of the bones of the fingers or toes.

American Two-spring Phaeton.

phan′tasm, phan′ta·sy, phan′tom, etc. Same as FANTASM, etc.

Phar′i·see, 1 far′ɪ-sī; 2 făr′i-sē, *n.* One of an ancient Jewish sect excessively devoted to tradition and ceremonies; a self-righteous person.— **phar″i·sa′ic, phar″i·sa′-i·cal,** *a.* **1.** Pertaining to the Pharisees. **2.** Formal; hypocritical; self-righteous.— **phar″i·sa′i·cal·ly,** *adv.*— **Phar′i·sa·ism,** *n.* **phar′i·see·ism‡.**

phar″ma·ceu′tic, 1 fär″mə-siū′tɪk; 2 fär″-ma-çū′tic, *a.* Pertaining to or relating to pharmacy. **phar″ma·ceu′ti·cal‡.**— **phar″-ma·ceu′ti·cal·ly,** *adv.*

phar″ma·co·pœ′ia, 1 fär″mə-ko-pī′yə; 2 fär″ma-co-pē′ya, *n.* A standard book of formulas, drugs, etc. **2.** Drugs collectively.

phar′ma·cy, ⎰1 fär′mə-sɪ; 2 fär′ma-çy, *n.* **far′ma·cy**ᴿ, ∫ [-CIES ᶻ, *pl.*] **1.** The compounding and dispensing of medicines. **2.** A drug-store.

phar′ynx, ⎰1 far′ɪŋks; 2 făr′yŋks, *n.* **far′ynx**ᴿ, ∫ [PHA-RYN′GES, 1 fə-rin′jīz; 2 fa-rŷn′gĕs, *pl.*] The part of the alimentary canal between the palate and the esophagus, serving as an air-passage and also as a food-passage.— **pha·ryn′ge·al,** *a.*

phase, ⎰1 fēz; 2 fāg, *n.* Any one of varying **fase**ᴿ, ∫ manifestations of an object; appearance.— **pha′sis,** *n.* A phase, as of the moon.

pheas′ant, ⎰1 fez′ənt; 2 fĕg′ant, *n.* A **fez′ant**ᴿ, ∫ long-tailed gallinaceous bird; also, a grouse or partridge.

phe′nix, ⎰1 fī′nɪks; 2 fē′niks, *n.* Egypt. **fe′nix**ᴿ, ∫ *Myth.* A sacred bird, fabled to burn itself on the altar once in 500 years, and to rise again from its ashes young and beautiful.

phe·nom′e·non, ⎰1 fɪ-nɒm′ɪ-nɒn; 2 fe-**fe·nom′e·non**ᴿ, ∫ nŏm′e-nŏn, *n.* [-E-NA, *pl.*] An appearance, fact, or incident; marvel; prodigy.— **phe·nom′e·nal,** *a.* Pertaining to phenomena; marvelous.

phi′al, 1 faɪ′əl; 2 fī′al, *n.* Same as VIAL.

phi·lan′thro·py, ⎰1 fɪ-lan′thro-pɪ; 2 fi-**fi·lan′thro·py**ᴿ, ∫ lăn′thro-py, *n.* Love of mankind; effort to mitigate social evils. — **phil″an·throp′ic, -i·cal,** *a.*— **phi·lan′-thro·pist,** *n.* An author or promoter of benevolent projects.

phil″har·mon′ic, ⎰1 fil″här-mən′ɪk; 2 fil″-**fil″har·mon′ic**ᴿ, ∫ här-mŏn′ie, *a.* Fond of harmony or music.

phi·lip′pic, ⎰1 fɪ-lip′ɪk; 2 fi-lĭp′ie, *n.* An **fi·lip′pic**ᴿ, ∫ impassioned and denunciatory speech: named from the orations of Demosthenes (384-322 B. C.) against Philip of Macedon (382-336 B. C.).

Phi·lis′tᴵ·n(ᵉˢ, ⎰1 fɪ-lis′tɪn; 2 fi-lĭs′tin, *n.* **1.** One of a warlike race in southwestern Palestine that opposed the advance of the Israelites. **2.** [P- or P-] A blind adherent to conventional ideas; an uncultured or sordid person.— **Phi·lis′tin**(eˢ, *a.*— **Phi·lis′tin·ism,** *n.*

phi·lol′o·gy, ⎰1 fɪ-lol′o-jɪ; 2 fi-lŏl′o-gy, *n.* **fi·lol′o·gy**ᴿ, ∫ The study of language; linguistic science.— **phil″o·log′ic, -i·cal,** *a.* — **phi·lol′o·gist,** *n.* An expert in philology.

phil′o·mel, ⎰1 fil′o-mel; 2 fil′o-mĕl, *n.* **fil′o·mel**ᴿ, ∫ [Poet.] The nightingale.

phil″o·pe′na, ⎰1 fil″o-pī′nə; 2 fil″o-pē′na, **fil″o·pe′na**ᴿ, ∫ *n.* A pair of twin kernels of a nut, or a social game employing them, and involving a gift made as a forfeit.

phi·los′o·phy, ⎰1 fɪ-los′o-fɪ; 2 fi-lŏs′o-**fi·los′o·phy**ᴿ, ∫ fy, *n.* [-PHIES ᶻ, *pl.*] **1.** Knowledge of forces, causes, and laws. **2.** The rational explanation of anything. **3.** Practical wisdom and rational self-control. **4.** Mental science; metaphysics. — **phi·los′o·pher,** *n.* **1.** A student of philosophy. **2.** A man of practical wisdom. — **phil″o·soph′ic,** *a.* **1.** Pertaining to or founded on the principles of philosophy. **2.** Self-restrained and serene; rational; thoughtful; calm.— **phil″o·soph′i·cal,** *a.* Belonging to or used in the study of natural philosophy or physics. **-ly,** *adv.*— **phi·los′o·phize,** *vt.* To examine or discuss philosophic subjects; theorize.

phlegm, ⎰1 flem; 2 flĕm, *n.* **1.** Mucus, as **flegm**ᴿ, ∫ in the air-passages. **2.** Apathy; indifference.— **phleg·mat′ic,** *a.* Sluggish.

---

indifferent. **phleg-mat′l -cal‡.— phleg-mat′l-cal-ly,** *adv.*

phlox, ⎱ 1 fleks; 2 flŏks, *n.* An American
floxᴾ, ⎰ ʃ herb with clusters
of showy flowers.

phœ′nix, *a.* .See PHENIX.

pho-net′ic, ⎱ 1 fo-net′ik
fo-net′icˢ, ⎰ ʃ fo -nĕt′ic,
a. **1.** Relating to articulate sound. **2.** Directly representing ar-
ticulate sound ; as,
phonetic spelling.—
pho-net′ics, *n.* The
science of articulate
sound. **pho-net′i-cal‡;**
**phon′ics‡;— pho-
net′l-cal-ly,** *adv.* In a phonetic manner.

Phlox.
Flowers of the wild
sweet-william; *a*, its
fruit.

phon′ic, 1 fon′ik *or* fō′nik; 2 fŏn′ie *or*
fon′icˢ, ʃ fō′nie, *a.* Pertaining to or of the
nature of sound.

pho′no-graph, ⎱ 1 fō′no-graf; 2 fō′no-grȧf,
fo′no-grafˢ, ⎰ ʃ *n.* **1.** A mechanism for recording sounds and reproducing them. **2.**
A phonographic character.

pho-nog′ra-phy, ⎱ 1 fo-nŏg′rȧ-fɪ; 2 fo-nŏg′-
fo-nog′ra-fyˢ, ⎰ ʃ rȧ-fy, *n.* The art of
writing by sound; shorthand.— **pho-nog′ra-
pher,** *n.* One skilled in phonography; a
phonetic stenographer.— **pho″no-graph′ic,**
a. Pertaining to a phonograph or to phonography. **pho″no-graph′i-cal‡.**

phos′phate, ⎱ 1 fos′fet; 2 fŏs′fāt, *n.* A
fos′fateᴾ, ⎰ ʃ salt of phosphoric acid, or a
fertilizer containing it.

phos′phor-us, ⎱ 1 fos′fɐr-us; 2 fŏs′for-ŭs,
fos′for-usˢ, ⎰ ʃ *n.* A combustible mineral
element that ignites by moderate heat, as
of friction.— **phos″phor-es′cence,** *n.* The
emission of light without sensible heat, or the
light so emitted.— **phos″phor-es′cent,** *a.*
Glowing faintly without apparent heat.—
phos-phor′ic, *a.* **1.** Pertaining to or derived from phosphorus. **2.** Phosphorescent.

pho′to-graph, ⎱ 1 fō′to-graf; 2 fō′to-grȧf.
fo′to-grafˢ, ⎰ ʃ *t.* *vt.* & *vi.* To take a
photograph of; practise photography. **II.**
n. A picture taken by photography.— **pho-
tog′ra-pher,** *n.* One who practises photography.— **pho″to-graph′ic,** *a.* Pertaining
to or produced by photography **pho″to-
graph′i-cal‡.— pho-tog′ra-phy,** *n.* The
process of forming and fixing an image by the
chemical action of light.

phrase, ⎱ 1 frēz; 2 frās. **I.** *vt.* [PHRASED,
fraseᴾ, ⎰ ʃ PHRAS′ING.] To express in words.
II. *n.* **1.** A few words denoting a single
idea; a brief expression; term; diction. **2.**
M‡s. A fragment of a melody.— **phra″se-
ol′o-gy,** *n.* The choice and arrangement of
words and phrases; diction.— **phras′ing,** *n.*

phre-nol′o-gy, ⎱ 1 frɪ-nel′o-jɪ; 2 fre-nŏl′o-
fre-nol′o-gyᴾ, ⎰ ʃ gy, *n.* A system holding
that the faculties of the mind are located
in separate portions of the brain and may
be estimated by the shape of the head.—
**phren″o-log′ic, phren″o-log′i-cal, a.—
phren″o-log′i-cal-ly,** *adv.—* **phre-nol′o-
gist,** *n.*

phthis′ic, 1 tiz′ik; 2 tĭs′ie, *n.* **1.** Asthma.
2. Disease of the lungs.— **phthis′i-cal,** *a.* **1.**
Consumptive. **2.** Asthmatic. **phthis′ick-y‡.**

phthi′sis, 1 thaɪ′sɪs; 2 thī′sis, *n.* Pulmo-
nary consumption; tuberculosis.

phys′ic, ⎱ 1 fiz′ik; 2 fy̆g′ik **I**ᵗ. *vt.* To
fys′icᴾ, ⎰ ʃ give medicine to; purge. **II.** *n.*
1. Medicine, or the science of medicine.
2. A cathartic.— **phys′i-cal,** *a.* Relating to
the material universe or to the bodily life of
man; corporeal; material.— **phys′i-cal-ly,**
adv.— **phy-si′cian,** 1 fɪ-zish′an; 2 fy-zĭsh′an,
n. One versed in medicine; a doctor.— **phys′-
i-cist,** 1 fiz′ı-sist; 2 fy̆s′ı-çist, *n.* A student of
or specialist in physics.— **phys′ics,** *n.* The
science that treats of the phenomena and
laws of matter.

phys″i-og′no-my, ⎱ 1 fiz″ɪ-ŏg′no-mɪ; 2 fy̆g″-
fys″i-og′no-myᴾ, ⎰ ʃ ɪ-ŏg′no-my, *n.* [-MIES²,
pl.] **1.** The face as revealing character;
the art of reading character by the
face. **2.** The outward look of a thing.—
phys″i-og-nom′ic, phys″i-og-nom′i-cal,
a.— **phys″i-og′no-mist,** *n.* An expert in
physiognomy.

phys″i-ol′o-gy, ⎱ 1 fiz″ı-el′o-jɪ; 2 fy̆g″ı-ŏl′-
fys″i-ol′o-gyᴾ, ⎰ ʃ o-ǵy, *n.* The science of
the organs and functions of living bodies.—
phys″i-o-log′i-cal, *a.* **phys″i-o-log′ic‡.—
phys″i-o-log′i-cal-ly,** *adv.—* **phys″i-ol′o-
gist,** *n.* One versed in physiology.

phy-sique′, 1 fɪ-zīk′; 2 fy-g̈ĭk′, *n.* The
physical structure or organization of a
person.

pi, ⎱ 1 paɪ; 2 pī, *n.* *Print.* Type that has
pie, ⎰ ʃ been thrown into disorder.

pi″a-nis′si-mo, 1 pī″a-nis′ı-mo; 2 pī″a-nis′ı-
mo, *a.* & *adv.* Extremely soft; softly; abbreviated *pp.*

pi-an′ist, 1 pi-an′ıst *or* pī′a-nist; 2 pi-ăn′-
ist *or* pī′a-nist, *n.* A performer on the
pianoforte.

pi-a′no, 1 pī-ā′no; 2 pī-ä′no. **I.** *a.* *Mus.*
Soft. **II.** *adv.* *Mus.* Softly. **III.** 1 pi-an′o;
2 pī-ăn′o, *n.* [Colloq.] A pianoforte.

pi-an″o-for′te, 1 pi-an′o-fōr′tĕ *or* -fōrt; 2
pī-ăn″o-fôr′tĕ *or* -fôrt, *n.* A musical
stringed instrument, played by keys.

pi-az′za, 1 pi-az′a *or* pī-ät′sa; 2 pi-ăz′a *or*
pī-ät′zä, *n.* **1.** In Europe, an open
square or a covered outer walk. **2.** [U.
S.] A veranda.

---

pi′broch, 1 pī′broн; 2 pī′brōн, *n.* **1.** Wild, irregular martial music of the bagpipe. **2.** [Poet.] A bagpipe.

pi′ca, 1 paī′kə; 2 pī′ca, *n. Print.* A size of type six lines to the inch in depth of body; 12-point.

pic″a-yune′, 1 pik″ə-yūn′; 2 pĭe″a-yŭn′, *n.* A small Spanish coin, formerly used in the United States, and worth 6¼ cents.

pick¹, 1 pik; 2 pĭk. **I.** *vt.* & *vi.* **1.** To strike with or as with a pick or point. **2.** To pluck; select; cull. **II.** *n.* **1.** A tool with a pointed head. **2.** Right of selection; choice. **3.** A quantity picked by hand.— **pick′ax″,** *n.* A mattock of which one arm bears a point and the other a chisel-like edge. **pick′axe″‡.**

pick′er-el, 1 pik′ər-el; 2 pĭk′er-ĕl, *n.* A North-American fresh-water fish; a small pike.

pick′et, 1 pik′et; 2 pĭk′ĕt. **I**ᵈ. *vt.* **1.** To fence with pickets. **2.** To place on guard. **3.** To tie to a picket. **II.** *n.* **1.** A pointed stick; fence-paling. **2.** *Mil.* A guard on the outskirts of a camp or the like.

pick′le, ⎱1 pik′l; 2 pĭk′l. **I.** *vt.* [PICK′-
pick′l‡, ⎰ L(E)D²; PICK′LING.] To make pickle of; immerse in pickle. **II.** *n.* **1.** A preserving, flavoring liquid, as brine; diluted acid. **2.** Something in pickle.

pick′pock″et, 1 pik′pok″et; 2 pĭk′pŏk′ĕt, *n.* One who steals from pockets.

pic′nic, 1 pik′nik; 2 pĭe′nĭc. **I.** *vi.* [PIC′-
NICKED; PIC′NICK-ING.] To hold or attend a picnic. **II.** *n.* An outdoor pleasure-party, provided with its own eatables.— **pic′nick-er,** *n.*

pic-to′ri-al, 1 pik-tō′ri-əl; 2 pĭe-tō′ri-al, *a.* Pertaining to or containing pictures; graphic.— **pic-to′ri-al-ly,** *adv.*

pic′ture, 1 pik′chur or -tiur; 2 pĭe′chur or -tūr. **I.** *vt.* [PIC′TURED; PIC′TUR-ING.] To represent, as by a painting or drawing; depict. **II.** *n.* A representation by lines or colors, as a drawing, engraving, painting, or photograph; image; resemblance.— **pic″tur-esque′,** *a.* Suited to make a striking or pleasing picture; figurative; graphic. **-ly,** *adv.* **-ness,** *n.*

pidg′in-En′glish, 1 pij′in-iŋ′glish; 2 pĭdg′-in-ĭŋ′glĭsh, *n.* A jargon of English and Oriental words in Chinese idiom, used in the East. **pidj′in-En′glish‡.**

pie¹, 1 paī; 2 pī, *n.* A magpie or a related bird.

pie², *n.* Prepared food baked either between two crusts of pastry or with only one.

pie′bald″, 1 paī′bōld″; 2 pī′bǎld″, *a.* Having spots, as of white and black.

piece, 1 pīs; 2 pēç. **I.** *vt.* & *vi.* [PIECED‡; PIEC′ING.] To attach a piece or pieces to; fit or join together. **II.** *n.* **1.** A separate part; fragment; section; plot. **2.** A single one of a class or series; a gun; coin; specimen.— **piece′meal″. I.** *a.* Made up of pieces. **II.** *adv.* **1.** Piece by piece; gradually. **2.** In pieces.— **piece′-work″,** *n.* Work done or paid for by the piece or quantity.— **piec′er,** *n.* [ous colors.

pied, 1 paid; 2 pīd, *a.* Mottled with vari-

pier, 1 pīr; 2 pēr, *n.* A mass of masonry serving as a support; projecting portion of a wall; a projecting wharf.

pierce, 1 pīrs; 2 pērç, *vt.* & *vi.* [PIERCED‡; PIERC′ING.] To penetrate or puncture with a pointed instrument; perforate.

Pi′e-tism, 1 paī′ɪ-tizm; 2 pī′e-tĭşm, *n.* **1.** *Ch. Hist.* A religious awakening in the Lutheran Church in the latter part of the 17th century. **2.** [p-] Affected or exaggerated piety.— **Pi′e-tist,** *n.*— **Pi″e-tis′tic,** — **Pi″e-tis′ti-cal,** *a.*

pi′e-ty, 1 paī′ɪ-tɪ; 2 pī′e-ty, *n.* Love and service of God; religious devoutness and faithfulness.

pig, 1 pig; 2 pĭg. **I.** *vt.* & *vi.* [PIGGED, PIGD⁸; PIG′GING.] To litter, as pigs. **II.** *n.* **1.** A hog or hog-like animal, especially when young. **2.** An oblong mass of cast metal. — **pig′gish,** *a.* Acting like a pig; greedy; selfish and rude.— **pig iron,** pigs of iron, collectively, or the iron of which they are composed.

pig′eon, 1 pij′ən; 2 pĭdǵ′on, *n.* A dove or some similar bird.— **pig′eon-hole″. I.** *vt.* To file away. **II.** *n.* **1.** A hole in a pigeon-house. **2.** A small compartment for filing papers.— **pig′eon-En′glish,** *n.* Same as PIDGIN-ENGLISH.

pig′gin, 1 pig′in; 2 pĭg′in, *n.* A small wooden vessel having one stave projecting for a handle.

pig′ment, 1 pig′ment or -mənt; 2 pĭg′ment, *n.* Any coloring-material for paint, etc.

pig′my, 1 pig′mɪ; 2 pĭg′my. **I.** *a.* Diminutive; dwarf-ish. **pig-me′an‡. II.** *n.* [PIG′MIES², *pl.*] A dwarf.

Piggin.

pike¹, 1 paik; 2 pīk, *n.* **1.** A long iron-pointed pole, used in medieval warfare. **2.** A spike or sharp point.

pike², *n.* A slender, long-snouted, voracious fish.

pike³, *n.* A turnpike.

pi-las′ter, 1 pɪ-las′tər; 2 pī-lǎs′ter, *n.* *Arch.* A square column forming part of a wall.— **pi-las′tered,** *a.*

pile, 1 pail; 2 pīl, *vt.* [PILED; PIL'ING.] To gather into a pile; accumulate; amass.

pile¹, *n.* **1.** A quantity heaped together; a heap. **2.** Any great structure.

pile², *n.* A heavy timber driven into the earth to form a foundation.

pile³, *n.* A massive building.

pile⁴, *n.* Hair collectively; fur; raised surface on velvet.

piles, 1 pailz; 2 pīlş, *n. pl. Pathol.* Same as HEMORRHOIDS: the popular term.

pil'fer, 1 pil'fər; 2 pĭl'fer, *vt. & vi.* To take by petty theft; practise petty stealing.

pil'grim, 1 pil'grim; 2 pĭl'grim, *n.* **1.** One who journeys to some sacred place; hence, any wanderer. **2.** [P-] *Am. Hist.* One of the English colonists who in 1620 settled in Plymouth, Mass.— **pil'grim-age,** *n.* A long journey as to a shrine.

pill, 1 pil; 2 pĭl, *n.* A medicinal substance put up in a pellet.— **pill'-box,** *n.* **1.** A small round box for pills. **2.** [Recent.] *Mil.* A round concrete emplacement for a machine gun.

pil'lage, 1 pil'ij; 2 pĭl'aĝ. **I.** *vt. & vi.* [PIL'LAGED; PIL'LAG-ING.] To rob by open force. **II.** *n.* **1.** Open robbery, as in war. **2.** Spoil; booty.— **pil'lag-er,** *n.*

pil'lar, 1 pil'ər; 2 pĭl'ar, *n.* A firm, upright support; column.

pil'lion, 1 pil'yən; 2 pĭl'yon, *n.* A pad on a horse's back, behind the saddle, on which a second person may ride.

pil'lo-ry, 1 pil'o-ri; 2 pĭl'o-ry. **I.** *vt.* [-RIED; -RY-ING.] To set in the pillory; hold up to scorn. **II.** *n.* [-RIES²,*pl.*] A framework in which an offender was fastened and exposed to public scorn.

pil'low, 1 pil'o; 2 pĭl'o. **I.** *vt.* To lay on or support with a pillow. **II.** *n.* A soft cushion for the head; a support.— **pil'low-case",** *n.* A covering drawn over a pillow.

pi'lot, 1 pai'lət; 2 pī'lot. **I**ᵈ. *vt.* To steer; guide. **II.** *n.* One who conducts vessels in and out of port.— **pi'lot-age,** *n.* The act of or the fee for piloting.— **pi'lot-boat",** *n.*— **pi'lot-bread",** *n.* Ship-biscuit.

pim'ple, } 1 pim'pl; 2 pĭm'pl, *n.* A minute
pim'plᴾ, } swelling of the skin.— **pim'ply,** *a.* **pim'pl(e)d**ᴾ‡.

pin, 1 pin; 2 pĭn. **I.** *vt.* [PINNED, PINDˢ; PIN'NING.] To pierce or fasten, as with a pin. **II.** *n.* **1.** A wire, with a point and a head, used in fastening clothing, etc.; a clasp; brooch. **2.** A peg, as for a fastening, support, etc.— **pin'cush'ion,** *n.* A cushion to hold pins.— **pin'-feath"er,** *n.* A rudimentary feather.

pin'a-fore", 1 pin'ə-fōr; 2 pĭn'a-fōr, *n.* A long sleeveless apron.

pin'cers, 1 pin'sərz; 2 pĭn'çerş, *n. sing. & pl.* An instrument with grasping jaws for holding objects; nippets.— **pinch'ers**†.

pinch†, 1 pinch; 2 pĭnch, *vt. & vi.* To squeeze; nip; bind; treat stingily.

pinch, *n.* **1.** The act of pinching; painful pressure; emergency. **2.** So much as can be taken between the finger and thumb.

Pincers.

pinch'beck, 1 pinch'bek; 2 pĭnch'bĕk, *n.* A cheap imitation of gold: from Pinchbeck, the inventor.

pine, 1 pain; 2 pīn, *vt. & vi.* [PINED; PIN'ING.] To languish; waste away with grief.

pine, *n.* A cone-bearing tree, having needle-shaped evergreen leaves; also, its wood.

pine"ap"ple, 1 pain'ap"l; 2 pīn'äp"l, *n.* **1.** The conical edible fruit of a tropical plant. **2.** [U. S. Slang.] A bomb.

pin'ion, 1 pin'yən; 2 pĭn'yon. **I.** *vt.* To confine; bind; shackle. **II.** *n.* **1.** The wing of a bird. **2.** A feather. **3.** A shackle; band. **4.** A cog-wheel.

pink†, 1 pink; 2 pĭnk, *vt.* To decorate with holes; puncture; stab.

pink, *n.* **1.** A garden plant bearing a pink flower; also, the flower. **2.** A pale rose-color. **3.** A type of excellence.

pin'nace, 1 pin'is; 2 pĭn'aç, *n.* **1.** A six-to eight-oared boat. **2.** A small sailing vessel.

pin'na-cle, } 1 pin'ə-kl; 2 pĭn'a-el, *n.* A
pin'na-clᴾ, } small turret; topmost point.

pint, 1 paint; 2 pīnt, *n.* A measure of half a quart.

pin'tle, } 1 pin'tl; 2 pĭn'tl, *n.* A pin upon
pin'tlᴾ, } which something, as a hinge, pivots.

pi'o-neer", 1 pai"o-nīr'; 2 pī"o-nēr'. **I.** *vt. & vi.* To take the lead in; be a pioneer. **II.** *n.* One who prepares the way, as a soldier in advance of an army.

pi'ous, 1 pai'us; 2 pī'ŭs, *a.* Possessed of piety; religious. **-ly,** *adv.*

pip¹, 1 pip; 2 pĭp, *n.* A disease of fowls.

pip², *n.* The seed of an apple, orange, etc.

pipe, 1 paip; 2 pīp. **I.** *vt. & vi.* [PIPED†; PIP'ING.] **1.** To play on or as on a pipe; speak or sing in a high key; whistle. **2.** To convey in pipes. **II.** *n.* **1.** A small bowl with a hollow stem, for smoking. **2.** A tube, as for conveying fluids; a tubular wind-instrument: in the plural,

---

1: ə = *final*; ɪ = *habit*; aisle; au = *out*; oil; iū = *feud*; chin; go; ŋ = *sing*; thin, this.
2: wolf, dọ; bŏŏk, bōōt; fu̇ll, rṳle, cūre, bŭt, bûrn; ȯil, bọ̈y; ĝo, ģem; iŋk; thin, this.

the bagpipe. See illus. **3.** A large cask for wine.— **pi′per,** *n.*— **pip′ing,** *a.* & *n.*

pip′kin, 1 pĭp′kĭn; 2 pĭp′kin, *n.* **1.** A small earthenware jar. **2.** A piggin.

pip′pin, 1 pĭp′ĭn; 2 pĭp′in, *n.* An apple of many varieties.

pi′quant, 1 pī′kənt; 2 pī′kant. *a.* Tart; pungent; smart; racy. **-ly,** *adv.*— **pi′quan-cy,** *n.*

pique, 1 pīk; 2 pīk. **I.** *vt.* [PIQUED⁺; PIQU′ING.] To provoke; make envious; pride (oneself). **II.** *n.* Slight resentment, as from wounded pride.

pi′rate, 1 pai′rīt; 2 pī′rat. **I.** *vt.* & *vi.* [PI′RAT-ED⁴; PI′RAT-ING.] To subject to or practise piracy. **II.** *n.* **1.** A robber on the high seas; a vessel engaged in piracy. **2.** One who appropriates without right the literary work of another.— **pi′ra-cy,** *n.* [-CIES², *pl.*] **1.** Robbery committed on the high seas. **2.** Literary theft.— **pi-rat′i-cal,** *a.*— **pi-rat′i-cal-ly,** *adv.*

Musical Pipes (Scotch Bagpipes)

pir″ou-ette′, 1 pĭr″u-ĕt′; 2 pĭr′u-ĕt′, *n.* **1.** A rapid whirling upon the toes in dancing. **2.** *Manège.* A sudden turn of a horse.— **pir″ou-ette′,** *vt.* [-ET′TED⁴; -ET′TING.]

pis′ca-to-ry, 1 pĭs′kə-to-rĭ; 2 pĭs′ca-to-ry, *a.* Pertaining to fishes or fishing. **pis″ca-to′ri-al‡.**

pis′til, 1 pĭs′tĭl; 2 pĭs′til, *n.* The seed-bearing organ of a flowering plant.

pis′tol, 1 pĭs′tạl; 2 pĭs′tol, *n.* A small fire-arm to be used with one hand. [gold coin.

pis-tole′, 1 pĭs-tōl′; 2 pĭs-tōl′, *n.* An ancient

pis′ton, 1 pĭs′tạn; 2 pĭs′ton, *n.* A disk connected with a rod, and fitted to slide in a cylinder, as in a steam-engine.

pit, 1 pĭt; 2 pĭt, *v.* [PIT′TED⁴; PIT′TING.] **I.** *t.* **1.** To mark with pits or hollows. **2.** To set in antagonism. **3.** To put into a pit. **II.** *i.* To become marked with pits.

pit¹, *n.* **1.** A cavity; depression; abyss. **2.** The main floor of the auditorium of a theater. **3.** An enclosed space, as for the fighting of cocks or dogs. [fruits.

pit², *n.* [U. S.] The kernel of certain

pitch¹, ⎱ 1 pĭch; 2 pĭch, *v.* [PITCHED⁺, PITCHT⁸;
pich⁰, ⎰ PITCH′ING.] **I.** *t.* **1.** To toss; throw. **2.** To fix or arrange, as a tent. **3.** *Mus.* To set the pitch of. **II.** *i.* **1.** To throw; fall or plunge downward. **2.** To settle. **3.** To rise and fall alternately at the bow and stern, as a ship.

pitch²ᵗ, *vt.* To cover or treat with pitch.

pitch¹, *n.* **1.** Point or degree of elevation. **2.** The degree of descent; slope, as of a

roof. **3.** *Mus.* The highness or lowness of a tone. **4.** A toss; throw.

pitch², *n.* A thick, sticky substance obtained from tar or turpentine; the resinous sap of pines.

pitch′blende″, 1 pĭch′blend″; 2 pĭch′blĕnd″, *n.* A brownish-black mineral found in Bohemia, Colorado, Cornwall, and Saxony: important as being the source of radium.

pitch′er¹, ⎱ 1 pĭch′ər; 2 pĭch′er, *n.* One
pich′er⁰, ⎰ who pitches.

pitch′er², *n.* A vessel with a spout and a handle, for holding liquids.

pitch′fork″, 1 pĭch′fŏrk″; 2 pĭch′fôrk″, *n.* A large fork with which to handle hay, straw, etc.

pitch′y, ⎱ 1 pĭch′ĭ; 2 pĭch′y, *a.* Resem-
pich′y⁰, ⎰ bling pitch; intensely dark.

pit′e-ous, 1 pĭt′ĭ-ŭs; 2 pĭt′e-ŭs, *a.* **1.** Exciting pity. **2.** Feeling pity.— **pit′e-ous-ly,** *adv.*— **pit′e-ous-ness,** *n.*

pit′fall″, 1 pĭt′fôl″; 2 pĭt′fạl″, *n.* A pit for entrapping animals; any hidden source of danger.

pith, 1 pĭth; 2 pĭth, *n.* The soft, spongy tissue in the center of the stem of a plant, the shaft of a feather, or the like; essence; gist; force; vigor.— **pith′y,** *a.* [PITH′I-ER; PITH′I-EST.] **1.** Of or like pith. **2.** Forcible; effective.— **pith′i-ly,** *adv.*— **pith′i-ness,** *n.*

pit′tance, 1 pĭt′ạns; 2 pĭt′anç, *n.* A meager allowance.

pit′y, 1 pĭt′ĭ; 2 pĭt′y. **I.** *vt.* & *vi.* [PIT′IED; PIT′Y-ING.] To feel pity for. **II.** *n.* [PIT′IES², *pl.*] **1.** The feeling of grief or pain awakened by the sufferings of others. **2.** Misfortune.— **pit′i-a-bl(e)⁰,** *a.* That may be pitied; pathetic; pitiful.— **pit′i-a-bly,** *adv.*— **pit′i-ful,** *a.* **1.** Calling forth pity. **2.** Contemptible; paltry. **-ly,** *adv.* **-ness,** *n.*— **pit′i-less,** *a.* Destitute of pity; cruel. **-ly,** *adv.* **-ness,** *n.*

piv′ot, 1 pĭv′ạt; 2 pĭv′ot. **I**ᵈ. *vt.* & *vi.* To place or turn on a pivot; hinge. **II.** *n.* A pin on which anything turns.

piz″zi-ca′to, 1 pĭt″sĭ-kä′to; 2 pĭt′sĭ-cä′to. *a.* *Mus.* Notes for a bowed instrument which are to be plucked with the fingers.

pla-card′, 1 plə-kärd′; 2 pla-cärd′. **I**ᵈ. *vt.* To announce by placards; post placards upon. **II.** plak′ard *or* plə-kärd′; 2 plăc′-ard *or* plạ-cärd′, *n.* A paper publicly displayed, as a proclamation or poster.

pla′cate, 1 plē′kēt; 2 plā′cāt, *vt.* [PLA′-CAT-ED⁴; PLA′CAT-ING.] To pacify; appease.— **pla″ca-bil′i-ty,** *n.*— **pla′ca-bl(e)⁰,** *a.* Yielding.

place, 1 plēs; 2 plāç. **I.** *vt.* [PLACED⁺; PLAC′ING.] To put in a place; arrange; appoint; invest. **II.** *n.* **1.** A particular

---

portion of space; position; rank; office; abode. **2.** An open space or square, or a short street in a city. **3.** Vacated room; stead.

plac′er¹, 1 plas′ər; 2 plăç′er, *n.* A place where surface deposits are washed, as for gold. [places.

plac′er², 1 plĕs′ər; 2 plăç′er, *n.* One who

plac′id, 1 plas′ĭd; 2 plăç′ĭd. *a.* Smooth; unruffled; calm. **-ly,** *adv.*— **pla-cid′i-ty,** *n.* Smoothness; tranquillity **plac′id-ness‡.**

pla′gi-a-rize, 1 plē′jĭ-ɑ-rɑiz; 2 plā′gĭ-a-rīz, *vt. & vi.* [-RIZED; -RIZ′ING.] To falsely claim authorship of; commit plagiarism.— **pla′gi-a-rism,** *n.* The unwarranted appropriation of another's literary or artistic work; something plagiarized.— **pla′gi-a-rist,** *n.*

plague, 1 plēg; 2 plāg. **I.** *vt.* [PLAGUED; PLAGU′ING.] To afflict; distress; annoy. **II.** *n.* Anything troublesome; pestilence; calamity.

plaid, 1 plad *or* plēd; 2 plăd *or* plād. **I.** *a.* Having a pattern of stripes crossing in squares. **II.** *n.* A fabric, cross-barred with colors.

plain, 1 plēn; 2 plān. **I.** *a.* **1.** Flat; smooth; easy; readily understood. **2.** Lowly; unlearned; unadorned; unpretending; simple. **3.** Lacking personal beauty. **II.** *n.* An expanse of level land. **-ly,** *adv.* **-ness,** *n.*

plaint, 1 plēnt; 2 plānt, *n.* A mournful complaint; lamentation.— **plain′tiv(e⁵,** *a.* Expressing a subdued sadness; mournful. **-ly,** *adv.* **-ness,** *n.*

plain′tiff, } 1 plēn′tɪf; 2 plān′tĭf, *n.* The
plain′tif⁷, } party that begins an action at law.

plait, 1 plēt; 2 plāt. **Iᵈ.** *vt.* **1.** To double in narrow folds. **2.** To braid. **3.** To mat. **II.** *n.* **1.** A fold fixed in place by sewing or otherwise. **2.** A braid. **pleat‡.**

plan, 1 plan; 2 plăn, *vt. & vi.* [PLANNED, PLANDˢ; PLAN′NING.] To contrive; design; propose.

plan, *n.* **1.** A method; design. **2.** An outline sketch; draft. **3.** A mode of action.

plane, 1 plēn; 2 plān, *vt.* [PLANED; PLAN′-ING.] To make smooth or even; bring to a level; dress with a plane.— **plan′er,** *n.*

plane, *a.* Lying in a plane; level; flat.

plane¹, *n.* **1.** A flat surface. **2.** A grade of development; stage; level. **3.** *Aero.* The principal, or one of the principal supporting elements of an aeroplane.

plane², *n.* A tool for producing a smooth, even surface.

plane³, *n.* The sycamore or buttonwood. **plane′-tree″‡.**

plan′et, 1 plan′et; 2 plăn′ĕt, *n.* One of the bodies of the solar system that revolve around the sun.— **plan′e-ta-ry,** *a.*— **plan′e-toid,** *n.* An asteroid.

plank, 1 plaŋk; 2 plăŋk. **Iᵗ.** *vt.* To cover with planks. **II.** *n.* A broad piece of sawed timber, thicker than a board.

plantᵈ, 1 plant; 2 plănt, *v.* **I.** *t.* **1.** To set in the ground for growth. **2.** To supply (ground) with plants or seeds. **II.** *i.* To sow seeds, or set plants.

plant, *n.* **1.** A vegetable growth. **2.** The appliances required for a factory or other institution.— **plan-ta′tion,** 1 plan-tē′shən; 2 plăn-tā′shon, *n.* **1.** A large farm. **2.** The act of planting; a place planted.— **plant′er,** *n.* One who plants; an owner of a plantation.

plan′tain¹, 1 plan′tɪn; 2 plăn′tin, *n.* A perennial weed with broad, ribbed leaves.

plan′tain², *n.* A tropical perennial herb or its edible, banana-like fruit.

plan′ti-grade, 1 plan′tɪ-grēd; 2 plăn′tĭ-grād. **I.** *a.* Walking on the whole sole of the foot, as man, bears, etc. **II.** *n.* A plantigrade animal.

plaque, 1 plak; 2 plăk, *n.* A plate, disk, or slab, artistically ornamented.

plash, 1 plash; 2 plăsh. **Iᵗ.** *vt. & vi.* To splash. **II.** *n.* A splash; small pool.— **plash′y,** *a.*

plas′ter, 1 plas′tər; 2 plàs′ter. **I.** *vt.* To overlay or treat with plaster; put a plaster on. **II.** *n.* **1.** A composition of lime, sand, and water for coating walls. **2.** Calcined gypsum for making sculptors' casts, etc. **3.** A viscid substance spread upon cloth, for healing purposes.— **plas′ter-er,** *n.*— **plas′ter-ing,** *n.* **1.** The act of applying plaster. **2.** A coating of plaster.

plas′tic, 1 plas′tɪk; 2 plăs′tic, *a.* **1.** Tending to shape or mold. **2.** Capable of being molded. **3.** Pertaining to molding.— **plas-tic′i-ty,** *n.*

platᵈ, 1 plat; 2 plăt. **I.** *vt.* [PLAT′TEDᵈ; PLAT′TING.] To plait. **II.** *n.* A plait.

plat², **Iᵈ.** *vt.* To lay out in plats or plots. **II.** *n.* **1.** A small piece of ground; a plot. **2.** A plotted map.

plate, 1 plēt; 2 plāt. **I.** *vt.* [PLAT′EDᵈ; PLAT′ING.] To coat with metal. **II.** *n.* **1.** A flat, broad, thin body, as of metal; a dish; metallic surface bearing printed matter or the lines of an engraving. **2.** Plated tableware; silverware.

pla-teau′, 1 plə-tō′; 2 pla-tō′, *n.* [-TEAUX′ *or* -TEAUS′, 1 -tōz′; 2 -tōş′, *pl.*] An extensive stretch of elevated level land.

plat'en, 1 plat'en; 2 plăt'ĕn, *n.* The part of a printing-press, or the like, on which the paper is supported in printing.

plat'form, 1 plat'fôrm; 2 plăt'fôrm, *n.* **1.** A raised floor or surface. **2.** A statement of principles, as of a party.

plat'i-num, 1 plat'ı-nŭm; 2 plăt'ı-nŭm, *n.* A whitish metallic element, able to resist heat and acids. **plat'i-na‡.**

plat'i-tude, 1 plat'ı-tiŭd; 2 plăt'ı-tūd, *n.* **1.** A flat commonplace statement. **2.** Dulness.

Pla-ton'ic, 1 plə-tɒn'ık; 2 pla-tŏn'ie, *a.* **1.** Pertaining to the Greek philosopher Plato (427–347 B. C.). **2.** Purely spiritual; as, *Platonic* love.— **Pla-ton'i-cal-ly,** *adv.*— **Pla'to-nism,** *n.*— **Pla'to-nist,** *n.* An adherent of the philosophy of Plato.

pla-toon', 1 plə-tūn'; 2 pla-tōon', *n. Mil.* Half of a company, commanded by a lieutenant. [shallow dish.

plat'ter, 1 plat'ər; 2 plăt'er, *n.* An oblong

plau'dit, 1 plô'dıt; 2 plą'dıt, *n.* An expression of applause.

plau'si-ble, ⎰1 plô'zı-bl; 2 plą'şi-bl, *a.* **plau'si-bil,** ⎰ Seeming likely to be true; specious; calculated to win confidence.— **plau'si-bil'i-ty,** *n.* [-TIES²*, pl.*] **plau'si-bl(e-ness²‡.— plau'si-bly,** *adv.*

play, 1 plē; 2 plā, *v.* **I.** *t.* **1.** To engage in (a game); produce or act in (a drama). **2.** To perform upon, as a musical instrument. **3.** To put into action. **II.** *i.* **1.** To engage in play. **2.** To gamble. **3.** To act with levity; trifle. **4.** To behave; act. **5.** To perform. **6.** To move freely.

play, *n.* **1.** Action for amusement only; exercise; competitive trial; also, gambling. **2.** A dramatic composition. **3.** Freedom of movement.— **play'er,** *n.*— **play'fel'-low,** *n.* An associate in games, etc. **play'-mate"‡.— play'ful,** *a.* Frolicsome. **-ly,** *adv.*— **play'ful-ness,** *n.*— **play'house",** *n.*— **play'thing",** *n.* A toy.

pla'za, 1 plä'zɒ *or* plä'tha; 2 plä'za *or* plä'thä, *n.* An open square in a town.

-ple, *suffix.* A suffix of Latin origin used to form English multiplicatives; as, tri*ple.*

plea, 1 plī; 2 plē, *n.* An act of pleading, or that which is pleaded; entreaty; excuse.

plead, 1 plīd; 2 plĕd, *vt. & vi.* [PLEAD'ED*d or PLEAD, 1 pled, 2 plĕd (irreg. colloq., PLED); PLEAD'ING.] **1.** To advocate; supplicate; argue; urge. **2.** To allege as an excuse or defense. **3.** To make answer, as to a charge.— **plead'er,** *n.*

pleas'ant, ⎰1 plez'ənt; 2 plĕş'ant, *a.* **1. ples'ant,** ⎰ Giving or promoting pleasure. **2.** Merry; gay. **-ly,** *adv.* **-ness,** *n.*— **pleas'-ant-ry,** *n.* [-RIES², *pl.*] Playfulness; jest.

please, 1 plīz; 2 plēş, *vt. & vi.* [PLEASED; PLEAS'ING.] **1.** To give pleasure to. **2.** To be agreeable to. **3.** To have a preference.— **pleas'ing,** *pa.*

plea'sure, ⎰1 plez'ur; 2 plĕzh'ụr, *n.* An **ple'sure²,** ⎰ agreeable sensation or emotion; gratification; amusement in general.— **plea'sur-a-bl(e²,** *a.*— **plea' ur-a-bly,** *adv.*— **plea'sur-a-bl(e-ness²,** *n.*— **plea'-sure·boat",** *n.*— **p.-ground,** *n.*

pleat, 1 plīt; 2 plĕt, *v. & n.* Same as PLAIT.

ple-be'ian, 1 plı-bī'ən; 2 ple-bē'an. **I.** *a.* Pertaining to the common people; common; inferior. **II.** *n.* One of the common people.

pleb'i-scite, 1 pleb'ı-sit; 2 plĕb'ı-sĭt, *n.* An expression of the popular will by vote of the whole people.

pledge, 1 plej; 2 plĕdg. **I.** *vt.* [PLEDGED, PLEDG'D²; PLEDG'ING.] **1.** To deposit as security for a loan. **2.** To promise. **3.** To drink the health of. **II.** *n.* **1.** A guaranty for the performance of an act. **2.** A promise. **3.** The drinking of a health.— **pledg'er,** *n.*

ple'na-ry, 1 plī'nə-rı *or* plen'ə-rı; 2 plē'na-ry *or* plĕn'a-ry, *a.* Full; complete.

plen"i-po-ten'ti-a-ry, 1 plen"ı-po-ten'shı-ē-rı; 2 plen'ı-po-tĕn'shi-ā-ry. **I.** *a.* Possessing or conferring full powers. **II.** *n.* A diplomatic representative invested with full powers by his government.

plen'i-tude, 1 plen'ı-tiŭd; 2 plĕn'ı-tūd, *n.* The state of being full; fulness; abundance.

plen'ty, 1 plen'tı; 2 plĕn'ty. **I.** *a.* Existing in abundance; enough. **II.** *n.* Abundance; a sufficiency; enough.— **plen'te-ous,** *a.* Amply sufficient; abundant; plentiful.— **plen'ti-ful,** *a.* Abundant; yielding in plenty.

ple'o-nasm, 1 plī'o-nazm; 2 plē'o-năşm, *n.* The use of needless words; tautology.— **ple"o-nas'tic,** *a.*

pleth'o-ra, 1 pleth'o-rɒ; 2 plĕth'o-ra, *n.* Excessive fulness; repletion.— **ple-thor'ic,** 1 plı-thor'ık *or* pleth'o-rık; 2 ple-thŏr'ie *or* plĕth'o-rie, *a.*

pleu'ra, 1 plū'rɒ; 2 plų'ra, *n.* [PLEU'RÆ, 1 -rī; 2 -rē, *pl.*] The membrane that infolds the lungs.— **pleu'ri-sy,** *n.* Inflammation of the pleura.

pli'a-bl(e², *n.* Easily bent or persuaded; flexible; yielding.— **pli"a-bil'i-ty,** *n.* Flexibility. **pli'a-bl(e-ness²‡.**

pli'ant, 1 plaı'ənt; 2 plī'ant, *a.* Easily bent; yielding. **-ly,** *adv.* **-ness,** *n.*— **pli'-an-cy,** *n.*

pli'er, 1 plaı'ər; 2 plī'er, *n.* **1.** One who plies. **2.** *pl.* Small pincers. [troth.

plight², 1 plait; 2 plīt, *vt.* To pledge; be-

plight[1], *n.* A pledge; betrothal.

plight[2], *n.* A distressed or complicated situation; predicament.

plod, 1 plŏd; 2 plŏd, *vt. & vi.* [PLOD'DED[d]; PLOD'DING.] To walk over heavily; proceed with toil; drudge. — **plod'der**, *n.*

plot[1], 1 plŏt; 2 plŏt. **I.** *vt. & vi.* [PLOT'-TED[d]; PLOT'TING.] To plan; form a plot; conspire. **II.** *n.* **1.** A secret plan; conspiracy. **2.** The plan of a story, play, or poem.

plot[2]. **I.** *vt.* [PLOT'TED[d]; PLOT'TING.] To make a map of, as lots or plots; divide off in plots. **II.** *n.* **1.** A piece of ground set apart; lot; parcel. **2.** A surveyors' map, as of lots. [tailed wading bird.

plov'er, 1 plŭv'ẽr; 2 plŏv'er, *n.* A short-

plow,) 1 plau; 2 plow. **I.** *vt. & vi.* To
plough,) break up with a plow; work with a plow; cultivate. **II.** *n.* An implement for breaking up or turning over the soil; agriculture.— **plow'boy**, *n.* **plough'-boy**‡.— **plow'man**, *n.* **plough'man**‡.— **plow'share**, *n.* The share or blade of a plow. **plough'share**‡.

pluck[t], 1 pluk; 2 plŭk. **I.** *vt. & vi.* **1.** To jerk up or out; pull; twitch; pick. **2.** To strip completely. **II.** *n.* **1.** Courage; intrepidity. **2.** The heart, liver, and lungs of an animal. **3.** A twitch.— **pluck'y**, *a.* [PLUCK'I-ER; PLUCK'I-EST.] Courageous; intrepid.— **pluck'i-ly**, *adv.*— **pluck'i-ness**, *n.*

plug, 1 plug; 2 plŭg. **I.** *vt.* [PLUGGED; PLUG[s]; PLUG'GING.] To stop with a plug. **II.** *n.* **1.** Anything used to stop a hole. **2.** A cake of tobacco.

plum, 1 plum; 2 plŭm. **1.** The edible fruit of a tree of the rose family; also, the tree. **2.** A raisin. **3.** The best part of anything.

plu'mage, 1 plū'mij; 2 plŭ'maġ, *n.* The feathers that cover a bird; adornment.

plumb,) 1 plum; 2 plŭm. **I.** *vt.* To
plum,) test or adjust by a plumb-line. **II.** *a.* True, accurate, and upright; vertical; perpendicular. **III.** *n.* A plummet. **IV.** *adv.* In a vertical direction.— **plumb'-bob**, *n.* A plummet.— **p.-line**, *n.* A cord by which a weight is suspended to test the perpendicularity of something.

Plumb-bob.

plum-ba'go, 1 plum-bē'go; 2 plŭm-bā'go, *n.* Graphite: used for lead-pencils, etc.

plumb'er,) 1 plum'ẽr; 2 plŭm'er, *n.*
plum'mer[r],) One who makes a business

of plumbing.— **plumb'ing**, *n.* **1.** The art of putting into buildings the tanks, pipes, etc., for conveying water, gas, and sewage. **2.** The pipe-system of a building.

plume, 1 plūm; 2 plụm. **I.** *vt.* [PLUMED; PLUM'ING.] **1.** To dress or arrange the feathers of; adorn. **2.** To felicitate (one-self). **II.** *n.* A feather, or tuft of feathers, worn as an ornament.— **plum'y**, *a.* Covered with feathers.

plum'met, 1 plum'et; 2 plŭm'ĕt, *n.* The weight of a plumb-line.

plump[1], 1 plump; 2 plŭmp, *a.* Full and round; fat. **-ly**, *adv.* **-ness**, *n.*

plump[2], *a.* Blunt; downright; direct.— **plump**, *adv.* Suddenly and forcibly.

plun'der, 1 plun'der; 2 plŭn'der. **I.** *vt.* To despoil or seize by violence; pillage; rob. **II.** *n.* **1.** Property taken by violence; booty; spoil. **2.** The act of plundering.— **plun'der-er**, *n.* One who robs with violence.

plunge, 1 plunj; 2 plŭng, *v.* [PLUNGED; PLUNG'ING.] **I.** *t.* To thrust or throw suddenly into water or the like. **II.** *i.* To jump, dive, or rush, as into water; descend abruptly; leap; fall.

plunge, *n.* The act of plunging; any sudden and violent motion.— **plung'er**, *n.*

plu'per'fect, 1 plū'pūr'fekt; 2 plụ'pẽr"-fĕct. **I.** *a.* Expressing past time prior to some other past time. **II.** *n.* The pluperfect tense.

plu'ral, 1 plū'ral; 2 plụ'ral. **I.** *a.* Containing more than one. **II.** *n.* The plural number. **-ly**, *adv.*— **plu-ral'i-ty**, *n.* [-TIES[z], *pl.*] **1.** The state of being plural. **2.** The larger portion or greater number. **3.** [U. S.] *Polit.* The greatest of more than two numbers when less than a majority; also, the excess of one such number over the next highest number.

plus, 1 plus; 2 plŭs, *a.* **1.** Having an addition (of); increased (by): opposed to *minus.* **2.** More than nothing; above zero; positive.

plush, 1 plush; 2 plŭsh, *n.* A cloth having a soft, velvety surface on one side.— **plush'y**, *a.*

Plu-to'ni-an, 1 plu-tō'nị-ǝn; 2 plu-tō'ni-an, *a.* Pertaining to Pluto or Hades: subterranean; fiery; produced or formed by fire; as, *Plutonian* rocks. From Pluto, god of the underworld or Hades; brother of Jupiter.

plu-toc'ra-cy, 1 plu-tŏk'rǝ-sị; 2 plu-tŏc'-ra-çy, *n.* A wealthy class controlling the administration of the government; the rule of wealth or of the wealthy.

plu'vi-al, 1 plū'vi-ǝl; 2 plụ'vi-al, *a.* Rainy.

ply, 1 plai; 2 plī, *v.* [PLIED; PLY'ING.] **I.** *t.* To work at or use with diligence. **II.** *i.* **1.** To go back and forth. **2.** To be busy. **3.** To proceed in haste.

ply, 1 plai; 2 plī, *n.* [PLIES², *pl.*] A web, layer, or thickness.

pneu-mat'ic, 1 niŭ-mat'ĭk; 2 nū-măt'ĭc. *a.* Pertaining to air or gas. **pneu-mat'I-cal‡.** — **pneu-mat'Ics,** *n.* The branch of physics that treats of the properties of gases.

pneu-mo'ni-a, 1 niu-mō'nĭ-a; 2 nū-mō'ni-a, *n.* Inflammation of lung-tissue.

poach¹ᵇ, 1 pōch; 2 pōch, *vt. & vi.* To cook (eggs) by breaking into boiling water.

poach², 1 pōch, *vt. & vi.* To rob of game; kill game unlawfully. — **poach'er,** *n.*

pock, 1 pɔk; 2 pŏk, *n.* A pustule. — **pock'mark",** *n.* A pit or scar made by smallpox. — **pock'marked",** *a.*

pock'et, 1 pŏk'ĕt; 2 pŏk'ĕt. **Iᵈ.** *vt.* To put into a pocket; appropriate; accept, as an insult without resentment. **II.** *n.* A pouch attached to a garment; a cavity, opening, or receptacle. — **pock'et-book",** *n.* A small book for carrying money.

po'co, 1 pō'ko; 2 pō'co, *adv. Mus.* Slightly; somewhat. [capsule of a plant.

pod, 1 pɔd; 2 pŏd, *n.* A seed-vessel or

po'em, 1 pō'em; 2 pō'ĕm, *n.* A lofty or beautiful composition in verse. — **po'e-sy,** *n.* Poetry. — **po'et,** *n.* One who writes poems. — **po'et-ess,** *n. fem.* — **po'et-as"ter,** *n.* An inferior poet. — **po-et'ic,** **po-et'I-cal,** *a.* — **po-et'I-cal-ly,** *adv.*

po'et-ry, 1 pō'et-rɪ; 2 pō'ĕt-ry, *n.* Beautiful thought in rime or metrical language.

po'go, 1 pō'go; 2 pō'go, *n* A stilt-like stick used for jumping, as across streams.

poign'ant, 1 pein'ent; 2 pŏin'ant, *a.* Severely painful; distressing. — **poign'ant-ly,** *adv.* — **poign'an-cy,** *n.*

poi"lu', 1 pwɑ"lü'; 2 pwä"lü', *a.* [Fr.] Hairy; bearded: used substantively for a French soldier who has served in the trenches.

point⁴, 1 pɔint; 2 pŏint, *v.* **I.** *t.* **1.** To put a point on; sharpen at the tip. **2.** To extend or direct; aim. **3.** To direct attention to. **4.** To punctuate. **II.** *i.* To direct attention, as by the extended finger: with *out*.

point, *n.* **1.** The sharp end of a thing; anything pointed; a promontory. **2.** A place; position; feature; item. **3.** An instant. **4.** A prick; puncture; mark of punctuation, especially a period. — **point'-blank'.** **I.** *a.* Aimed straight at the mark; direct; plain. **II.** *adv.* In a horizontal line; directly. — **point'ed,** *pa.* **1.** Having a point. **2.** Piquant. **3.** Emphasized. — **point'ed-ly,** *adv.* — **point'er,** *n.* One who or that which points; one of a breed of dogs trained to point out game. — **the pointers,** two stars in the constellation Ursa Major (" the Dipper "), whose connecting line points nearly to the north star. See illus. in next column.

poise, 1 peiz; 2 pŏiz. **I.** *vt. & vi.* [POISED;

POIS'ING.] To balance. **II.** *n.* The state of being balanced; a balance-weight; equilibrium; equanimity; repose.

poi'son, 1 pei'zn; 2 pŏi'sn. **I.** *vt.* To put poison into; affect or kill with poison; injure; corrupt. **II.** *n.* A substance that when taken into the system tends to cause death or serious injury. — **poi'son-ous,** *a.*

The Pointers.

poke, 1 pōk; 2 pōk, *v.* Part of the constellation of Ursa Major, showing the stars (Alpha, Beta) called "pointers." [POKED ᵗ; POK'ING.] **I.** *t.* To push against or into; push in or out. **II.** *i.* To go sluggishly or gropingly.

poke¹, 1 pōk; 2 pōk, *n.* A collar with an attachment, to keep animals in restraint.

poke², *n.* The pokeweed.

poke³, *n.* A pocket or bag.

pok'er¹, 1 pōk'ɑr; 2 pōk'er, *n.* A poking instrument, as an iron rod for stirring a fire.

pok'er², *n.* A game of cards in which the players bet on the value of their hands.

po'lar, 1 pō'lɑr; 2 pō'lar, *a.* Pertaining to the poles of a sphere, as of the earth, or the poles of a magnet. — **po-lar'I-ty,** *n.* The quality of having opposite poles. — **po"lar-I-za'tion** or **-sa'tion,** *n.* The act of polarizing, or the state of being polarized. — **po'lar-ize** or **-ise,** *vt.* [-IZED; -IZ'ING.] To develop polarity in.

pole¹, 1 pōl; 2 pōl, *n.* A long slender piece of wood or metal; a rod.

pole², *n.* **1.** An extremity of the axis of a sphere. **2.** One of two points, as of a magnet, at which opposite qualities are concentrated. — **pole'-star",** *n.* The bright star near the north celestial pole. [Poland. north star‡.

Pole³, *n.* One of the Slavic people inhabiting

pole'cat", 1 pōl'kat"; 2 pōl'căt", *n.* A weasel-like carnivore noted for emitting a fetid odor.

European Polecat. 1/20

po-lem'ic, 1 po-lem'ĭk; 2 po-lĕm'ĭc, *a.* Pertaining to controversy; disputatious. — **-I-cal‡.** — **po-lem'Ics,** *n.* The art of controversy or disputation.

po-lice', 1 po-līs'; 2 po-lĭç'. **I.** *vt.* [POLICED ᵗ; PO-LIC'ING.] To place under the control of police. **II.** *n.* A body of civil officers organized under authority to maintain order and enforce law. — **po-lice'-man,** *n.*

pol'I-cy¹, 1 pɔl'ɪ-sɪ; 2 pŏl'ĭ-çy, *n.* [-CIES²,

pl.] **1.** Prudence; sagacity; finesse; artifice. **2.** A course or plan of action, as of a government.

pol'i-cy², *n.* [-CIES², *pl.*] A written contract of insurance.

pol'ish, 1 pŏl'ish; 2 pŏl'ish. **I.** *vt. & vi.* To make or become smooth or lustrous, polite, or refined. **II.** *n.* Smoothness or glossiness of surface; finish; varnish.— **pol'-ish-er,** *n.*

Po'lish, 1 pō'lish; 2 pō'lish. **I.** *a.* Relating to Poland, its inhabitants, or their language. **II.** *n.* The Polish language; a Slavonic speech.

po-lite', 1 po-lait'; 2 po-līt', *a.* Showing consideration for others; elegant in manners; courteous; refined.— **po-lite'ly,** *adv.* — **po-lite'ness,** *n.*

pol'i-tic, 1 pŏl'i-tik; 2 pŏl'i-tĭc, *a.* **1.** Sagacious in planning; judicious; prudent; artful. **2.** Consisting of citizens; pertaining to public polity.

po-lit'i-cal, 1 po-lit'i-kəl; 2 po-lĭt'i-cal, *a.* **1.** Pertaining to public policy. **2.** Belonging to the science of government.— **po-lit'i-cal-ly,** *adv.*— **pol''i-ti'cian,** *n.* **1.** One who is engaged in politics. **2.** One skilled in political science.— **pol'i-tics,** *n.* **1.** The science of civil government. **2.** Party intrigues, etc.

pol'i-ty, 1 pŏl'i-tı; 2 pŏl'i-ty, *n.* [-TIES², *pl.*] The form of government of a nation, church, etc.

pol'ka, 1 pōl'kə; 2 pōl'ka, *n.* A round dance of Bohemian origin, or the music for it.

poll, 1 pōl; 2 pōl. **I.** *vt. & vi.* **1.** To enroll; canvass; vote. **2.** To lop; clip; shear. **II.** *n.* **1.** The head; hence, a person, or a list of persons. **2.** The voting or votes at an election. **3.** A poll-tax. **4.** *pl.* Voting-place.— **poll'-tax",** *n.* A tax on the person.

pol'lard, 1 pŏl'ərd; 2 pŏl'ard, *n.* **1.** A tree that has had its branches cut so that it puts out thick clusters of shoots. **2.** An animal that has lost its horns.

pol'len, 1 pŏl'en; 2 pŏl'ĕn, *n.* The fine powder formed within the anther of a flowering plant.

pol-lute', 1 po-liūt'; 2 pŏ-lūt', *vt.* [POL-LUT'ED⁴; POL-LUT'ING.] To make unclean; defile; stain; soil.— **pol-lu'tion,** *n.* The act of polluting; defilement; ceremonial uncleanness.

po'lo, 1 pō'lo; 2 pō'lo, *n.* A game played on horseback with a light wooden ball and mallets.

po''lo-naise', 1 pō''lo-nēz'; 2 pō'lo-nāṣ', *n.* **1.** A stately Polish dance, or the music for this dance. **2.** A garment for women.

pol-troon', 1 pŏl-trūn'; 2 pŏl-trōōn', *n.* A coward.— **pol-troon'er-y,** *n.* Cowardice.

poly-, 1 pŏl'ı-; 2 pŏl'y-, *prefix.* Many; much; as, *poly*syllable.

po-lyg'a-my, 1 po-lig'ə-mı; 2 po-lȳg'a-my, *n.* The condition of having more than one wife or husband at once.— **po-lyg'a-mist,** *n.*— **po-lyg'a-mous,** *a.*

pol'y-glot, 1 pŏl'ı-glŏt; 2 pŏl'y-glŏt. **I.** *a.* **1.** Expressed in several languages. **2.** Speaking several tongues. **II.** *n.* A book giving versions of the same text, as of scripture, in several languages.

pol'y-gon, 1 pŏl'ı-gən; 2 pŏl'y-gŏn, *n.* A many-sided figure.— **po-lyg'o-nal,** *a.*

pol'yp, 1 pŏl'ıp; 2 pŏl'yp, *n.* A many-armed aquatic animal.— **pol'y-pous,** *a.*— **pol'y-pus,** *n.* [-PI, 1 -paı; 2 -pī, *pl.*] A tumor, as in the nostril.

pol'y-syl'la-ble, } 1 pŏl'ı-sil'ə-bl; 2 pŏl'y-
pol'y-syl''la-bl², } sȳl'a-bl, *n.* A word of several syllables. **II.** *n.* A school of applied science and y-syl-lab'i-caı‡.

pol''y-tech'nic, 1 pŏl'ı-tek'nık; 2 pŏl'y-těc'nie. **I.** *a.* Embracing many arts. **II.** *n.* A school of applied science and the industrial arts.

pol''y-the'ism, 1 pŏl'ı-fhī'izm; 2 pŏl'y-thē'īṣm, *n.* The belief that there are more gods than one.— **pol'y-the'ist,** *n.*— **pol''y-the-is'tic,** and **pol''y-the-is'ti-cal,** *a.*

pom'ace, 1 pum's; 2 pŏm'aç, *n.* The substance of fruit, as apples, crushed by grinding.

po-made', 1 po-mēd'; 2 po-mād', *n.* A perfumed dressing for the hair. **po-ma'tum‡.**

pome'gran-ate, 1 pem'gran-ıt; 2 pŏm'-grăn-at, *n.* The fruit of a tree of the myrtle family, or the tree itself.

pom'mel, } 1 pum'el; 2 pŏm'ĕl. **I.** *vt.*
pum'mel², } [POM'MELED or POM'MELLED, PUM'MELD²; POM'MEL-ING or POM'MEL-LING.] To beat; pound; bruise. **II.** *n.* A knob, as at the front of a saddle or on the hilt of a sword.

po-mol'o-gy, 1 po-mŏl'o-jı; 2 po-mŏl'o-gy, *n.* The science of fruits and the art of fruit-culture.— **po''mo-log'i-cal,** *a.*— **po-mol'o-gist,** *n.*

pomp, 1 pomp; 2 pŏmp, *n.* Magnificent or ostentatious display.— **pom'pous,** *a.* Ostentatious. **-ly,** *adv.* **-ness,** *n.*— **pom-pos'i-ty,** *n.*

pom'pa-dour, 1 pem'pə-dūr; 2 pŏm'pa-dur, *n.* A style of arranging the hair by brushing it straight up from the forehead: named from Marquise de Pompadour (1721–1764), mistress of Louis XV. [still water.

pond, 1 pond; 2 pŏnd, *n.* A small body of

pon'der, 1 pon'dər; 2 pŏn'der, *v.* **I.** *t.* To

weigh in the mind; consider thoughtfully.
II. *i.* To reflect; meditate.— **pon'der-er,** *n.*

pon'der-a-ble, 1 pen'dər-ə-bl; 2 pŏn'der-a-bl, *a.* Capable of being weighed: said of ordinary matter, as opposed to ether, electricity, etc., which are *imponderable.*— **pon'der-a-bil'i-ty,** *n.*

pon'der-ous, 1 pen'dər-us; 2 pŏn'der-ŭs, *a.* **1.** Having weight; unusually weighty or forcible; also, huge; bulky. **2.** Impressive, as by weight of learning. **3.** Heavy to the extent of dulness; lumbering; labored.— **pon'der-os'i-ty,** *n.*—**pon'-der-ous-ly,** *adv.*— **pon'der-ous-ness,** *n.*

pon-gee', 1 pen-jī'; 2 pŏn-gē', *n.* Soft unbleached wash-silk, the product of a wild silkworm. [*n.* A small dagger.

pon'iard, 1 pen'yard; 2 pŏn'yard,
pon'tiff, } 1 pen'tif; 2 pŏn'tif, *n.*
pon'tif ͬ, } **1.** The Pope; a'so, any bishop. **2.** A high priest.— **pon-tif'ic,** *a.*— **pon-tif'i-cal. I.** *a.* Pertaining to or appropriate for a pontiff. **II.** *n.* **1.** A book containing the services conducted by a bishop. **2.** *pl.* The insignia, etc., of a pontiff.— **pon-tif'i-cate,** *n.* The office of a pontiff or pope; also, a pope's term of office.

pon-toon', 1 pen-tūn'; 2 pŏn-tōōn', *n.* A flat-bottomed boat, used as part of a floating bridge; a bridge so supported. **pon-ton'ͭ.** [A very small horse.

po'ny, 1 pō'nı; 2 pō'ny, *n.* [PO'NIES², *pl.*]
poo'dle, } 1 pū'dl; 2 pōō'dl, *n.* One of a
poo'dl ͬ, } breed of curly-haired dogs.

pool, 1 pūl; 2 pōōl, *v.* **I.** *t.* To put into a common fund. **II.** *i.* To form a pool.

pool¹, *n.* A small collection of liquid.

pool², *n.* **1.** A collective stake in a gambling game; a speculative combination; a common fund. **2.** A game played on a six-pocket billiard-table.

poop, 1 pūp; 2 pōōp, *n.* A short deck built over the after part of the deck of a vessel.

poor, 1 pūr; 2 pōōr, *a.* Destitute; indigent; inferior; paltry; pitiable; unhappy. **-ly,** *adv.* **-ness,** *n.*— **poor'house",** *n.* A public establishment for the care of paupers.— **poor'-laws",** *n. pl.* Laws for the care of the poor.

pop, 1 pep; 2 pŏp. **I.** *vt. & vi.* [POPPED ͭ; POP'PING.] **1.** To thrust suddenly. **2.** To issue with a pop. **II.** *n.* A sharp explosive noise. **III.** *adv.* Unexpectedly.

pope, 1 pōp; 2 pŏp, *n.* The supreme pontiff of the Roman Catholic Church.— **pope'dom,** *n.* The office or dominion of a pope.— **po'per-y,** *n.* Opprobriously, the religion of the Roman Catholic Church.— **pop'-ish,** *a.*

pop'-gun", 1 pep'-gun"; 2 pŏp'-gŭn", *n.* A toy gun. [coxcomb.

pop'in-jay, 1 pep'ın-jē; 2 pŏp'in-jā, *n.* A

pop'lar, 1 pep'lər; 2 pŏp'lar, *n.* A tree of rapid growth, and having soft wood.

pop'lin, 1 pep'lın; 2 pŏp'lin, *n.* A lustrous dress-goods of silk and worsted.

pop'py, 1 pep'ı; 2 pŏp'y, *n.* [POP'PIES², *pl.*] A flowering plant having a juice that abounds in opium.

pop'u-lace, 1 pep'yu-lıs; 2 pŏp'yu-laç, *n.* The body of the common people; the masses.

pop'u-lar, 1 pep'yu-lər; 2 pŏp'yu-lar, *a.* **1.** Pertaining to the people at large. **2.** Widely trusted or admired. **3.** Suitable to the common people. **4.** Prevalent among the people. **-ly,** *adv.*— **pop'u-lar'i-ty,** *n.* The condition of being popular: general favor.— **pop'u-lar-ize,** *vt.* To make popular.

pop'u-late, 1 pep'yu-lēt; 2 pŏp'yu-lāt, *v.* [-LAT'ED ͩ; -LAT'ING.] **I.** *t.* To furnish with inhabitants. **II.** *i.* To propagate; breed.— **pop'u-la'tion,** *n.* **1.** The whole number of a people. **2.** The multiplying of inhabitants.— **pop'u-lous,** *a.* Containing many inhabitants.

porce'lain, 1 pôrs'lın; 2 pôrç'lin, *n.* A translucent kind of pottery; chinaware.

porch, 1 pôrch; 2 pôrch, *n.* **1.** A covered entrance to a building. **2.** A veranda.

por'cu-pine, 1 pôr'kiu-pain; 2 pôr'cū-pīn, *n.* A large rodent, having erectile, quill-like spines.

Porcupine. ¹⁄₄₉

pore, 1 pōr; 2 pōr, *vi.* [PORED ͩ; POR'ING.] To ponder or study closely: followed by *over.*

pore, *n.* A minute orifice, as in the skin.

pork, 1 pôrk; 2 pôrk, *n.* **1.** The flesh of swine used as food. **2‖.** A swine, or swine collectively.— **pork'er,** *n.* A pig or hog.

po'rous, 1 pō'rus; 2 pō'rŭs, *a.* Full of pores. **-ly,** *adv.*— **po-ros'i-ty,** *n.* The state of being porous; a pore.

por'phy-ry, } 1 pôr'fı-rı; 2 pôr'fy-ry, *n.*
por'fy-ry ͬ, } [-RIES², *pl.*] An igneous rock enclosing crystals of feldspar.

por'poise, 1 pôr'pus; 2 pôr'pŏs, *n.* A piglike aquatic mammal; a dolphin.

por'ridge, 1 per'ıj; 2 pôr'idg, *n.* A soft food as of meal or flour boiled in water or milk.

por'rin-ger, 1 per'ın-jər; 2 pôr'in-ger, *n.*

1: ạrtistic, ärt; fat, fāre; fạst; get, prēy; hit, police; obey, gō; net, ôr; full, rūle; but, būrn.
2: ärt, āpe, făt, fâre, fâst, whạt, ạll; mē, gĕt, prey, fêrn; hĭt, īce; ĭ=ē; ĭ=ē̆; gō, nŏt, ôr, wŏn,

A small dish, having straight sides, and sometimes ears.

port¹, 1 pērt; 2 pôrt, *n.* A harbor or haven.

port², *n.* **1.** An opening in the side of a ship. **2.** A gate, portal, or door.

port³, *n.* The left side of a vessel as one looks from stern to bow: formerly *larboard.*

port⁴, *n.* The way in which one bears or carries himself; mien.

port⁵, *n.* A class of wines, rich in alcohol: from the Portuguese city, Oporto.

port'a∙ble,⎫ 1 pērt'ə∙bl; 2 *pôrt'a∙bl, a.*
port'a∙bl᷃ᴾ,⎭ That may be readily carried or moved.—**port'a∙bl(e∙ness᷃ᴾ,** *n.* **port'a∙bl'i∙ty‡.**

port'age, 1 pērt'ij; 2 pôrt'aǵ, *n.* **1.** The act of transporting. **2.** The place of such transportation, or that which is transported. [trance; door.

por'tal, 1 pōr'təl; 2 pôr'tal, *n.* An entrance.

por″ta∙men'to, 1 pōr″ta∙men'to; 2 pōr'tä∙men′to, *n.* [It.] *Mus.* To prolong one note into another; slur.

port∙cul'lis, 1 pērt∙kul'is; 2 pôrt∙cŭl'is, *n.* A grating that can be let down suddenly to close the portal of a fortified place.

Porte, 1 pōrt; 2 pôrt, *n.* The Ottoman or Turkish government.

porte″mon'naie, 1 pērt″mo'-nē′; 2 pôrt″mo″nä′, *n.* A pocketbook; small purse.

por∙tend'ᵈ, 1 por-tend′; 2 pŏr-tĕnd′,*vt.* To indicate as about to happen; presage.

Portcullis.

por∙tent', 1 por-tent′ *or* pŏr-tent′; 2 pŏr-tĕnt′ *or* pōr′tĕnt, *n.* Anything that portends what is to happen.— **por∙ten'tous,** *a.* Boding ill; ominous. **-ly,** *adv.*

por'ter¹, 1 pōr′tər; 2 pôr′ter, *n.* One whose business it is to handle travelers' luggage, etc.— **por'ter∙age,** *n.* The business of a porter; cost of carriage.

por'ter², *n.* A keeper of a door or gate.

por'ter³, *n.* A dark brown malt liquor.

port∙fo'li∙o, 1 pōrt-fō'li-ō; 2 pôrt-fō'lĭō, *n.* **1.** A portable case for holding drawings, etc. **2.** The office of a cabinet minister.

port'∙hole″, 1 pōrt'∙hōl″; 2 pôrt'∙hōl″, *n.* A small opening in a ship's side, as for a cannon.

por'ti∙co, 1 pōr'ti-kō; 2 pôr'ti-cō, *n.* [-coesᶻ *or* -cosᶻ, *pl.*] An open space with roof supported by columns; a porch.

por″tière', 1 pōr″tyǟr'; 2 pôr″tyĕr′, *n.* A curtain, or the like, for use in a doorway.

por'tion, 1 pōr′shən; 2 pôr′shon. **I.** *vt.* **1.** To divide into shares; distribute. **2.** To endow with a portion. **II.** *n.* **1.** A part; allotment; share of an estate coming to an heir. **2.** A wife's dowry. **3.** One's fortune or destiny.— **por'tioned,** *a.*— **por'tion∙less,** *a.*

port'ly, 1 pērt'li; 2 pôrt'ly, *a.* Somewhat stout; of imposing appearance and carriage; corpulent.— **port'li∙ness,** *n.*

port∙man'teau, 1 pērt-man'to; 2 pôrt-măn′to, *n.* A case for carrying clothing, etc., behind a saddle; also, a hand∙bag or satchel.

por'trait, 1 pōr′trit; 2 pôr'trit, *n.* A likeness of an individual.— **por'trait∙ure,** 1 pōr′tri∙chur *or* -tiûr 2 pôr'tri∙chur *or* -tūr, *n.* **1.** A representation; portrait. **2.** The act or art of portraying.

por∙tray', 1 por-trā'; 2 pôr-trā', *vt.* To draw or paint; describe vividly.— **por∙tray'al,** *n.* The act of portraying.— **por∙tray'er,** *n.*

por'tress, 1 pōr′tres; 2 pôr′tres, *n.* A female porter.

pose¹, 1 pōz; 2 pōǵ, *vt. & vi.* [POSED; POS′-ING.] **1.** To put into or take an attitude, as for a portrait. **2.** To state as a proposition.

pose², 1 pōz; 2 pōǵ, *vt.* [POSED; POS′ING.] To puzzle.— **pos'er,** *n.* **1.** A puzzling question. **2.** An examiner.

pose, *n.* An attitude or posture to be copied in a portrait or statue.

po∙si'tion, 1 po-zish′ən; 2 po-ǵish′on, *n.* **1.** The manner or place in which a thing is set or stationed. **2.** Disposition of the parts of the body; attitude; posture. **3.** Place in society, government, etc.; office; rank.

pos'i∙tive,⎫ 1 poz'i-tiv; 2 pŏǵ'i-tĭv. **I.** *a.*
pos'i∙tivˢ,⎭ **1.** Real; actual. **2.** Absolute; unquestionable; confident; decided. **II.** *n.* That which is sure; reality; a photograph having the lights and shade of the real object. **-ly,** *adv.* **-ness,** *n.*

pos'se, 1 pos'i; 2 pŏs′e, *n.* **1.** A force aiding a sheriff. **2.** [Colloq.] Any force of men; squad. **3.** Possibility. **posse comitatus‡.**

pos∙sess'ᵗ, 1 pə-zes′; 2 po-ǵĕs′, *vt.* To have; own; control; dominate; impress thoroughly.— **pos∙ses'sion,** *n.* **1.** The act of possessing. **2.** That which one possesses or owns; hence, property; wealth.— **pos∙ses'sive,** *a.* **I.** *a.* Pertaining to or expressive of possession. **II.** *n.* **1.** The possessive case. **2.** A possessive pronoun.— **pos∙ses'sive∙ly,** *adv.*— **pos∙ses'sor,** *n.*

pos'si∙ble,⎫ 1 pos'i-bl; 2 pŏs′i-bl, *a.* That
pos'si∙bl᷃ᴾ,⎭ may be true or may happen; imaginably true.— **pos'si∙bil'i∙ty,** *n.* [-TIESᶻ, *pl.*]— **pos'si∙bly,** *adv.*

post[id], 1 pōst; 2 post, *vt.* To put up in some public place.— **post′er**[1], *n.* A large advertising sheet to be posted in a public place.

post[2d], *v.* **I.** *t.* **1.** To assign to a post position or place. **2.** To mail. **3.** To transfer (items or accounts) to the ledger. **II.** *i.* To travel with speed.— **post′er**[2], *n.*

post[1], *n.* An upright piece of timber or other material used as a support.

post[2], *n.* **1.** A fixed place or station; office; employment. **2.** The mail system; a postman; messenger.

post, *adv.* By post ⸗horses; rapidly; as, to travel *post*. [*ante*⸗; as, *post*script.

post⸗, *prefix.* Behind or after; opposed to *pre*.

post′age, 1 pōst′ij; 2 pŏst′ag, *n.* The charge levied on mail⸗matter.— **post′age⸗stamp″**, *n.* A small printed label in payment of postage.

post′al, 1 pōst′al; 2 pŏst′al. **I.** *a.* Pertaining to the mails or mail⸗service. **II.** *n.* A postal card.— **postal card**, a card bearing a government stamp for sending through the mails.

pos-te′ri-or, 1 pɔs-tī′rɪ-ar; 2 pŏs-tē′ri-or. **I.** *a.* Coming after another. **II.** *n.* The hinder part.

pos-ter′i-ty, 1 pɔs-ter′i-tɪ; 2 pŏs-tĕr′i-ty, *n.* Succeeding generations.

pos′tern, 1 pōs′tarn; 2 pŏs′tern, *n.* A back gate or door; a private entrance.

post″⸗haste′, 1 pōst″⸗hēst′; 2 pōst″⸗hāst′, *adv.* With utmost speed.

pos′thu-mous, 1 pɔs′ḩu-[*or* -tiu-]mʊs; 2 pŏs′ḩu-[*or* -tū-]mŭs, *a.* Born after the father's death; published after the death of the author. **-ly**, *adv.*

pos-til′lon, 1 pɔs-til′yən; 2 pŏs-tīl′yon, *n.* A rider of one of the horses drawing a coach.

post′man, 1 pōst′mən; 2 pōst′man, *n.* A letter⸗carrier; mail⸗carrier.

post′mark″, 1 pōst′mɑrk″; 2 pōst′märk″. **I**[t]. *vt.* To put a postmark on. **II.** *n.* The stamp of a post⸗office on mail⸗matter.

post′mas″ter, 1 pōst′mɑs″ter; 2 pōst′mȧs″ter, *n.* An official having charge of a post⸗office.

post″me-rid′i-an, 1 pōst″mɪ-rid′ɪ-ən; 2 pōst″me-rid′i-an, *a.* Pertaining to the afternoon.

post me-rid′i-em, 1 pōst″me-rid′i-em. [L.] After midday: abbreviated *p. m.* or *P. M.*

post mor′tem, 1 mōr′tem; 2 môr′tĕm. After death.— **post″⸗mor′tem**, *n.* Expert examination of the organs of a body after death.

Postern.

post′⸗of″fice, 1 pōst′⸗ɔf″ɪs; 2 pōst′⸗ŏf″iç, *n.* An office for the receipt, transmission, and delivery of mails; also, the postal service.

post″⸗paid′, 1 pōst″⸗pēd′; 2 pōst″⸗pād′, *a.* Having the postage prepaid.

post-pone′, 1 pōst-pōn′; 2 pŏst-pōn′, *vt.* [POST-PONED′; POST-PON′ING.] To defer to a later time; put off.— **post-pone′ment**, *n.*

post′script, 1 pōst′skript; 2 pŏst′script, *n.* An addition to a written or printed document.

pos′tu-late, 1 pɔs′ḩu-lēt; 2 pŏs′ḩu-lāt. **I.** *vt. & vi.* [-LAT′ED[d]; -LAT′ING.] To assume (something) as self⸗evident or already known. **II.** *n.* Something so assumed.

pos′ture, 1 pɔs′ḩur *or* -tiur; 2 pŏs′ḩur *or* -tūr. **I.** *vt. & vi.* [POS′TURED; POS′TUR-ING.] To place in or assume a posture. **II.** *n.* The position of the parts of the body.

po′sy, 1 pō′zɪ; 2 pō′ġy, *n.* [PO′SIES[2], *pl.*] A bunch of flowers, or a single flower; brief inscription or motto.

pot, 1 pɔt; 2 pŏt, *vt.* [POT′TED[d]; POT′TING.] To put in a pot.

pot, *n.* A round vessel for cooking; a mug for drinking from.— **pot′house″**, *n.* An ale⸗house; tippling⸗house.— **pot′sherd″**, *n.* A broken bit of crockery.

po′ta-ble, 1 pō′ta-bl; 2 pō′ta-bl. **I.** *a.*
po′ta-bl[e], *a.* Suitable for drinking. **II.** *n.* Something drinkable; a drink.— **po-ta′tion**, *n.* The act of drinking; a beverage; a drinking⸗bout.

pot′ash″, 1 pɔt′ash″; 2 pŏt′ăsh″, *n.* **1.** A white, solid, alkaline compound. **2.** The liquid obtained from leached wood⸗ashes; lye.

po-ta′to, 1 pō-tē′to; 2 pɔ-tā′to, *n.* [-TOES[2], *pl.*] One of the edible common tubers of a plant; also, the plant.

po′tent, 1 pō′tent; 2 pō′tĕnt, *a.* Powerful; effective; convincing; controlling. **-ly**, *adv.* **-ness**, *n.*— **po′ten-cy**, *n.* **1.** Inherent ability. **2.** Authority. **3.** Power to influence. — **po′ten-tate**, *n.* One having great power or sway; a sovereign.— **po-ten′tial. I.** *a.* **1.** Possible, but not actual. **2.** Having capacity for existence, but not yet existing. **3.** *Gram.* Indicating possibility or power. **II.** *n.* **1.** Anything that may be possible. **2.** *Elec.* Degree of electrification. **-ly**, *adv.* — **po-ten″ti-al′i-ty**, *n.*

po-ten″ti-om′e-ter, *n. Elec.* An instrument for measuring the potential. [fuss.

poth′er, 1 pɔth′er; 2 pŏth′er, *n.* Bustle or fuss.

po′tion, 1 pō′shan; 2 pō′shon, *n.* A draft, as of liquid medicine.

pot″pour″ri′, 1 pō′pū″rī′; 2 pō′pu″rī, *n.* A heterogeneous mixture. [*or* stew.

pot′tage, 1 pɔt′ij; 2 pŏt′aġ, *n.* A thick broth

pot'ter, 1 pŏt'ər; 2 pŏt'er, *vi.* **1.** To work inefficiently; fuss uselessly. **2.** To walk feebly.

pot'ter, *n.* One who makes earthenware. — **pot'ter-y,** *n.* [-IES²*, pl.*] Earthenware, its manufacture or place of manufacture.

pouch, 1 pauch; 2 pouch, *n.* A small bag or sack; a sac-like organ.

poul'ter-er, 1 pōl'tər-ər; 2 pōl'ter-er, *n.* A dealer in poultry.

poul'tice, 1 pōl'tis; 2 pōl'tiç. **I.** *vt.* [-TICED¹; -TIC-ING.] To cover with a poultice. **II.** *n.* A remedy of a moist, mealy nature, applied to inflamed surfaces.

poul'try, 1 pōl'trɪ; 2 pōl'try, *n.* Domestic fowls, as hens, ducks, etc., whether living or killed and dressed for market.

pounce, 1 pauns; 2 pounç, *vi.* [POUNCED¹; POUNC'ING.] To make a sudden seizure; spring: followed by *on* or *upon.*

pounce¹, *n.* The act of pouncing; a talon.

pounce², *n.* A powder such as was formerly used to absorb excess of ink.

pound¹ᵈ, 1 paund; 2 pound, *vt.* To confine in a pound; restrain.

pound²ᵈ, *v.* **I.** *t.* To beat; break; bruise. **II.** *i.* To hammer; plod.

pound¹, *n.* **1.** A unit of weight: the avoirdupois pound is 16 ounces of 7,000 grains; the troy pound, 12 ounces of 5,760 grains. **2.** An English money of account, worth about $4.86: sign £.

pound², *n.* A place in which stray animals are kept till redeemed.

pour, 1 pōr; 2 pōr, *v.* **I.** *t.* To cause to flow in a continuous stream. **II.** *i.* To flow forth; fall profusely.— **pour,** *n.* A flow or downfall.

pout¹ᵈ, 1 paut; 2 pout, *vt. & vi.* To puff out, as the lips.— **pout'er,** *n.*

pout¹, *n.* A fit of sulkiness or ill humor.

pout², *n.* One of various fishes having a pouting appearance.

pov'er-ty, 1 pŏv'ər-tɪ; 2 pŏv'er-ty, *n.* The state of being poor; destitution.

pow'der, 1 pau'dər; 2 pou'der. **I.** *vt. & vi.* To make or become powder; put powder upon. **II.** *n.* A collection of minute particles; especially, gunpowder. — **pow'der-y,** *a.*

pow'er, 1 pau'ər; 2 pou'er, *n.* **1.** Strength manifested in effective action; energy. **2.** Authority. **3.** Any agent that exercises power.— **pow'er-ful,** *a.* **-ly,** *adv.* **-ness,** *n.*— **pow'er-less,** *a.*

prac'ti-ca-ble, 1 prak'tɪ-kə-bl; 2 prăc'ti-prac'ti-ca-bl², ʃ ca-bl, *a.* That can be put into practise; that may be done.— **prac''ti-ca-bil'i-ty,** *n.*— **prac'ti-ca-bly,** *adv.*

prac'ti-cal, 1 prak'tɪ-kəl; 2 prăc'ti-cal, *a.* **1.** Pertaining to actual experience. **2.** Derived from practise. **3.** Being such in fact or effect.— **prac'ti-cal'i-ty,** *n.* **-ness**: — **prac'ti-cal-ly,** *adv.* In a practical way.

prac'tise, ⎫ 1 prak'tɪs; 2 prăc'tis, *v.* [PRAC-
prac'tice, ⎬ TISED¹, -TICED¹, -TIST⁵; PRAC'TIS-
prac'tis⁸, ⎭ ING, -TIC-ING.] **I.** *t.* **1.** To do or pursue habitually. **2.** To perform by way of training. **II.** *i.* **1.** To do something for amusement or training. **2.** To pursue a profession or calling.— **prac-ti'tion-er,** *n.* One who practises an art or profession.

prac'tise, ⎫ *n.* **1.** Any customary action
prac'tice, ⎬ or proceeding; regular prosecution of a profession; action for exercise or training. **2.** The doing of something thought of or planned.

præ'ter-, *prefix.* Same as PRETER-.

prai'rie, 1 prē'rɪ; 2 prā'ri, *n.* A tract of treeless land covered with coarse grass. — **prai'rie-chick"en,** *n.* The pinnated grouse of North-American prairies.— **p.-dog,** *n.* A marmot of the plains of North America.

praise, 1 prēz; 2 prās. **I.** *vt.* [PRAISED²; PRAIS'ING.] To express approval or adoration of. **II.** *n.* **1.** Commendation; applause. **2.** Thanksgiving for blessings; laudation to the Deity. **3.** The object, reason, or subject of commendation.— **praise'wor"thy,** *a.* Deserving praise.— **praise'wor'thi-ly,** *adv.*— **praise'wor''thi-ness,** *n.*

prance, 1 prans; 2 prånç, *vi.* [PRANCED¹; PRANC'ING.] **1.** To move proudly with high steps. **2.** To ride in a capering manner.

prank, 1 praŋk; 2 prăŋk. **I**¹. *vt. & vi.* To decorate gaudily; make a gaudy show. **II.** *n.* A mischievous or frolicsome act.

prate, 1 prēt; 2 prāt. **I.** *vt. & vi.* [PRAT'ED⁴; PRAT'ING.] To talk about vainly. **II.** *n.* Idle talk.— **prat'er,** *n.*

prat'tle, ⎫ 1 prat'l; 2 prăt'l. **I.** *vt. & vi.*
prat'l¹ᵖ, ⎬ [PRAT'TLED, PRAT'LD¹⁺; PRAT'-
TLING.] To talk artlessly, as a child; prate. **II.** *n.* Childlike talk.— **prat'tler,** *n.*

prawn, 1 prōn; 2 prąn, *n.* A shrimp-like crustacean.

pray, 1 prē; 2 prā, *vt. & vi.* To address [devoutly, as God.

prayer, 1 prâr; 2 prâr, *n.* **1.** The act of offering especially reverent petitions to God; devotion. **2.** A memorial or petition.— **prayer'ful,** *a.*— **prayer'less,** *a.*

pre-, *prefix.* Before, as in time, place, or rank.

In thoroughly naturalized words it takes the form *pre-*; in scientific and recent neo-Latin terms it often takes the form *præ-*.

In the following list *pre-* is a constituent of various nouns, adjectives, and verbs, self-explaining in connection with their second

---

1: ə = *final;* ɪ = *habit;* **aisle;** **au** = *out;* **oil;** **iū** = *feud;* ʧin; go; ŋ = *sing;* ʧhin, **this.**
2: wolf, dǫ; book, boot; fųll, rųle, cūre, bŭt, bûrn; ǫil, bǫy; ḡo, ḡem; iŋk; thin, **this**

elements, in the sense of "before in time; in advance; prior; fore-"; as, *pre*engage, to engage beforehand.

pre"ac·quaint'd
pre"ac·quain'tance
pre·act'd
pre·ac'tion
pre"ad·ap·ta'tion
pre"ad·just'ment
pre"ad·mon'isht
pre"an·nounce't
pre"ap·point'd
pre"ap·point'ment
pre"ar·range'
pre"ar·ran·e'ment
pre·cog'i·tated
pre·cog·ni'tion
pre"cog·niz·a·bl(e⁰
pre·cog'ni·zant
pre·con·sent'd
pre"con·sign'
pre·con·sti·tuted
pre"con·tract'd, v.
pre·con·trive'
pre·date'd
pre"de·lib'er·a'tion
pre'de·sign'
pre·des'ig·nated⁰, v.
pre·des'ig·nate, a.
pre·des'ig·na'tion
pre"de·ter'min·a·bl(e⁰
pre"de·ter'mi·nate, v.

pre"de·ter'mi·na'tion
pre"de·ter'min·(e⁰
pre'di·gest'd
pre"dis·cov'er
pre"dis·cov'er·y
pre·e·lect'd
pre·e·lec'tion
pre·em·ploy'
pre·en·gage'
pre·en·gage'ment
pre·es·tab'lisht
pre·es·tab'lish·ment
pre·ex·am'i·na'tion
pre·ex·am'in(e⁰
pre·ex·ist'd
pre·ex·is'tence
pre·form', v.
pre"for·ma'tion
pre·gla'cial
pre"in·struct'd
pre·in"ti·ma'tion
pre·knowl'edge
pre·na'tal
pre·na'tal·ly
pre"rev'o·lu'tion·a·ry
pre"se·lect'd
pre·sig'ni·fy
pre"sur·mise'
pre·typ'i·fy
pre·view', v.
pre"de·ter'mi·nate, v. pre·warn'

preacht, 1 prĭch; 2 prĕch, v. **I.** *t.* To deliver, as a sermon. **II.** *i.* To discourse publicly on a religious topic.— **preach'er,** *n.*

pre·am·ble,) 1 prī'am·bl; 2 prē'ăm·bl, *n.*
pre'am·blᴾ, ∫ A preliminary statement.

pre·ca'ri·ous, 1 prĭ·kē'rĭ·ŭs; 2 pre·eā'ri·ŭs, *a.* Subject to risk or danger; uncertain. **-ly,** *adv.* **-ness,** *n.*

pre·cau'tion, 1 prĭ·kô'shan; 2 pre·cạ'shon, *n.* Prudent forethought; provision made for a possible emergency.— **pre·cau'tion·a·ry,** *a.*

pre·cede', 1 prĭ·sīd'; 2 pre·çēd', *v.* [PRE·CED'ED⁰; PRE·CED'ING.] **I.** *t.* To go, happen, or exist before. **II.** *i.* **1.** To go before some one else. **2.** To happen first; be prior in existence.

pre·ce'dence, 1 prĭ·sī'dens; 2 pre·çē'den̄çe, *n.* The act or right of preceding.— **pre·ce'den·cy**‡.— **pre·ce'dent,** *a.* **-ly,** *adv.*— **prec'e·dent,** 1 prĕs'ĭ·dent; 2 prĕc'e·dĕnt, *n.* **1.** Previous usage. **2.** An antecedent.

pre'cept, 1 prī'sept; 2 prē'çĕpt, *n.* A prescribed rule of conduct or action.— **pre·cep'tiv(e⁰**, *a.*— **pre·cep'tor,** *n.* A teacher.— **pre·cep·to'ri·al,** *a.*— **pre·cep'tress,** *n. fem.*

pre'cinct, 1 prī'sĭn̄kt; 2 prē'çĭn̄et, *n.* A district.

pre'cious, 1 prĕsh'ŭs; 2 prĕsh'ŭs, *a.* Highly priced or prized. **-ly,** *adv.* **-ness,** *n.*

prec'i·pice,) 1 prĕs'i·pis; 2 prĕç'i·pĭç, *n.* A
preci'pisˢ, ∫ high and steep cliff, or its brink.

pre·cip'i·tate, 1 prĭ·sĭp'ĭ·tĕt; 2 pre·çĭp'i·tāt, *v.* [-TAT'ED⁰; -TAT'ING.] **I.** *t.* **1.** To throw down, as from a height; urge onward rashly; hasten. **2.** To cause to fall, as from a liquid, by condensation. **II.** *i.* To fall headlong; settle down.

pre·cip'i·tate, 1 prĭ·sĭp'i·tĭt; 2 pre·çĭp'i·tat. **I.** *a.* Rushing down headlong; hasty; premature. **II.** *n.* A substance separated from a solution, and deposited. — **pre·cip'i·ta'tion,** *n.*— **pre·cip'i·tous,** *a.* **1.** Similar to a precipice. **2.** Headlong in motion. **-ly,** *adv.* **-ness,** *n.*

pre·cise', 1 prĭ·sais'; 2 pre·çīs', *a.* Strict'y accurate. **-ly,** *adv.* **-ness,** *n.*— **pre·ci'sian,** *n.* A stickler for rules.— **pre·ci'sion,** *n.* Accuracy.

pre·clude', 1 prĭ·klūd'; 2 prē'elụd', *vt.* [PRE·CLUD'ED⁰; PRE·CLUD'ING.] To prevent by previous action.— **pre·clu'sion,** *n.*— **pre·clu'siv(e⁰**, *a.* **-ly,** *adv.* **-ness,** *n.*

pre·co'cious, 1 prĭ·kō'shŭs; 2 pre·cō'shŭs, *a.* Developing unusually early; forward. **-ly,** *adv.* **-ness,** *n.*— **pre·coc'i·ty,** *n.*

pre"con·ceiv'(e⁰, 1 prī'kən·sīv'; 2 prē"ĕon·çēv', *vt.* To conceive or form in the mind beforehand, as an opinion or plan.— **pre"con·cep'tion,** *n.* **1.** The act of preconceiving. **2.** A preconceived notion or opinion. **pre"con·ceit'**‡.

pre"con·cert'd, 1 prī'ken·sūrt'; 2 prē'eŏn·çĕrt', *vt.* To arrange in concert beforehand.

pre·cur'sor, 1 prĭ·kûr'sər *or* -sər; 2 pre·cûr'sor, *n.* A forerunner; harbinger.— **pre·cur'so·ry,** *a.*

pred'a·to·ry, 1 prĕd'a·to·rɪ; 2 prĕd'a·to·ry, *a.* **1.** Characterized by or addicted to plundering. **2.** Living by preying upon others. **pre·da'ceous‡; pre·da'cious‡.**— **pred'a·to"ri·ly,** *adv.*— **pred'a·to"ri·ness,** *n.*

pred"e·ces'sor, 1 prĕd'ĭ·[*or* prī'dĭ·]sĕs'ər; 2 prĕd"e·[*or* prē"de·]çĕs'or, *n.* One who precedes another in time.

pre·des'ti·nate, 1 prĭ·dĕs'ti·nĕt; 2 pre·dĕs'ti·nāt, *vt.* [-NAT'ED⁰; -NAT'ING.] To decree beforehand or from the beginning. **pre·des'tin(e⁰**‡.— **pre·des'ti·na'ri·an. I.** *a.* **1.** Pertaining to predestination. **2.** Holding the doctrine of predestination. **II.** *n.* A believer in predestination.— **pre·des"ti·na'tion,** *n.* **1.** The act of predestinating. **2.** The foreordination of all things by God.

pre·dic'a·ment, 1 prĭ·dĭk'ə·ment *or* -mant; 2 pre·dĭe'a·ment, *n.* A state,

position, or condition; especially, a trying or amusing situation.

pred′i-cate, 1 pred′i-kĕt; 2 prĕd′i-eāt. **I.** *vt.* [-CAT″ED^d; -CAT″ING.] To state as belonging to something. **II.** *n.* The word or words in a sentence that express what is affirmed or denied of a subject. **— pred″i-ca-bl**(e^r, *a.*

pre-dict′^d, 1 pri-dikt′; 2 pre-dĭct, *vt.* To prophesy; foretell.**— pre-dic′tion,** *n.* The act of foretelling, or the thing foretold.

pre″di-lec′tion, 1 prī″di-lek′shən; 2 prē″-di-lĕe′shon, *n.* A favorable prepossession; preference.

pre″dis-pose′, 1 prī″dis-pōz′; 2 prē″dis-pōş′, *vt.* To dispose or incline beforehand; make liable or susceptible.**— pre-dis″-po-si′tion,** *n.* **1.** Propensity; predilection; bias. **2.** Liability to disease.

pre-dom′i-nate, 1 pri-dom′i-nēt; 2 pre-dŏm′i-nāt, *vi.* [-NAT″ED^d; -NAT″ING.] To have superior strength or authority; preponderate.**— pre-dom′i-nance,** *n.* **pre-dom′i-nan-cy**†.**— pre-dom′i-nant,** *a.* Superior in power; prevailing over others.**— pre-dom′i-nant-ly,** *adv.*

pre-em′i-nent, 1 prī-em′i-nent; 2 prē-ĕm′-i-nĕnt, *a.* Supremely eminent; extraordinary. **-ly,** *adv.***— pre-em′i-nence,** *n.*

pre-empt′^d, 1 prī-empt′; 2 prē-ĕmpt′, *v.* [U. S.] **I.** *t.* To secure in advance; gain the right of previous purchase. **II.** *i.* To take up public land by preemption. **— pre-emp′tion,** *n.* The right or act of purchasing public land in advance of others.

pref′ace, 1 pref′is; 2 prĕf′aç, *v.* [PREF′-ACED^t; PREF′AC-ING.] **I.** *t.* To open with a preliminary statement or act. **II.** *i.* To write, speak, or do something as a preface.

pref′ace, *n.* A brief introduction at the beginning of a book; anything introductory.**— pref′a-to-ry,** *a.***— pref′a-to-ri-ly,** *adv.*

pre′fect, 1 prī′fekt; 2 prē′fĕct, *n.* A Roman governor; the head of a French department.**— pre′fect-ship,** *n.***— pre′fec-ture,** *n.* The office, etc., of a prefect.

pre-fer′, 1 pri-fūr′; 2 pre-fĕr′, *vt.* [PRE-FERRED′, PRE-FERD′S; PRE-FER′RING.] **1.** To esteem above others. **2.** To advance; appoint. **3.** To offer.**— pref′er-a-bl**(e^r, *a.* **— pref′er-a-bly,** *adv.***— pref′er-ence,** *n.* The act of preferring, the state of being preferred, or that which is preferred.**— pref″er-en′tial,** *a.***— pref″er-en′tial-ly,** *adv.***— pre-fer′ment,** *n.*

pre-fig′ure, 1 pri-fig′yur; 2 pre-fĭg′yur, *vt.* To represent beforehand by figures or types.**— pre-fig″ur-a′tion,** *n.* **pre-fig′ure-ment**‡.**— pre-fig′ur-a-tiv**(e^s, *a.*

pre-fix′^t, 1 pri-fiks′; 2 pre-fĭks′, *vt.* To put before or at the beginning.

pre′fix, 1 prī′fiks; 2 prē′fĭks, *n.* That which is prefixed.

preg′nan-cy, 1 preg′nən-si; 2 prĕg′nan-çy, *n.* The state of being with young or with child.**— preg′nant,** *a.* Bearing young.

pre-hen′si-ble, 1 pri-hen′si-bl; 2 pre-hĕn′-si-bl, *a.* Capable of being apprehended or grasped.

pre-hen′sile, **pre-hen′sils**^s, } 1 pri-hen′sil; 2 pre-hĕn′sil, *a.* Adapted for grasping or holding.

pre″his-tor′ic, 1 prī″his-tor′ik; 2 prē″his-tŏr′ie, *a.* Belonging to the time before written history.

pre-judge′, 1 pri-juj′; 2 prē-jŭdg′, *vt.* To judge in advance.**— pre-judg′ment,** *n.*

prej′u-dice, 1 prej′u-dis; 2 prĕj′u-diç, **I.** *vt.* [-DICED^t, -DIST^s; -DIC-ING.] **1.** To imbue with prejudice or aversion. **2.** To impair or injure. **II.** *n.* **1.** A premature opinion, favorable or unfavorable. **2.** Detriment.**— prej″u-di′cial,** *a.* Having power or tendency to prejudice. **-ly,** *adv.*

prel′ate, 1 prel′it; 2 prel′at, *n.* One of a higher order of clergy, as a bishop.**— prel′a-cy,** *n.* [-CIES^z, *pl.*] **1.** The system of church government by prelates. **2.** The dignity or function of a prelate.**— prel′ate-ship,** *n.***— pre-lat′ic,** *a.* Of or pertaining to a prelate or to prelacy.

pre-lim′i-na-ry, 1 pri-lim′i-nē-ri; 2 pre-lĭm′i-nā-ry. **I.** *a.* Antecedent or introductory. **II.** *n.* [-RIES^z, *pl.*] An initiatory step.

pre-lude′, 1 pri-liūd′ or prel′yūd′; 2 pre-lūd′ or prĕl′yud, *vt. & vi.* [PRE-LUD′ED^d; PRE-LUD′ING.] To begin with a prelude; precede.**— pre-lud′er,** *n.*

pre′lude, 1 prī′liūd or prel′yūd; 2 prē′lūd or prĕl′yud, *n.* **1.** An opening strain or piece in music. **2.** Anything introductory.

pre″ma-ture′, 1 prī″mə-tiūr′; 2 prē″ma-tūr′, *a.* Happening or done before the proper time. **-ly,** *adv.* **-ness,** *n.***— pre″-ma-tu′ri-ty,** *n.*

pre-med′i-tate, 1 pri-med′i-tēt; 2 pre-mĕd′i-tāt, *vt. & vi.* [-TAT″ED^d, -TAT″ING.] To plan or meditate beforehand.**— pre-med″i-ta′tion,** *n.*

pre′mi-er, 1 prī′mi-ər or prem′yər; 2 prē′mi-er or prĕm′yer. **I.** *a.* First in place or time. **II.** *n.* A prime minister.

pre-mise′, **pre-mize′^p,** } 1 pre-maiz′; 2 pre-mīş′, *vt.* [PRE-MISED′, PRE-MIZED′^p; PRE-MIS′ING.] To state in advance.

prem′ise, **prem′iss**^s, } 1 prem′is; 2 prĕm′is, *n.* **1.** A proposition laid down as a basis

---

1: ə = final; ɪ = habit; ɑisle; ɑu = out; ɒil; iū = feud; ɔhin; go; ŋ = sing; ɔhin, this.
2: wolf, do; book, boot; full, rule, cure, but, bûrn; ŏil, bŏy; g̶o, gem; ink; thin, this.

of reasoning. **2.** *pl.* A distinct portion of land with its appurtenances.

pre'mi-um, 1 prī'mı-ŭm; 2 prē'mi-ŭm, *n.* **1.** A reward for excellence. **2.** A price paid for insurance, etc.; rate, as on stocks, above par.

pre″mo-ni′tion, 1 prī″mo-nish′ən; 2 prē″-mo-nish′on, *n.* A forewarning.— **pre-mon′i-to-ry,** *a.* Giving premonition.— **pre-mon′i-to-ri-ly,** *adv.*

pre-oc′cu-py, 1 prī-ŏk′yu-pai; 2 prē-ŏe′-yu-pŷ, *vt.* To occupy in advance; prepossess; prejudice.— **pre-oc″cu-pa′tion,** *n.*

pre″or-dain′, 1 prī″ŏr-dēn′; 2 prē″ŏr-dān′, *vt.* To foreordain.— **pre-or″di-na′tion,** *n.*

pre-pare′, 1 prı-pār′; 2 pre-pâr′, *vt. & vi.* [PRE-PARED′; PRE-PAR′ING.] To make ready beforehand.— **prep″a-ra′tion,** 1 prep′-ə-rē′shən; 2 prĕp′a-rā′shon, *n.* The act of preparing; the state of being prepared; something that is prepared.— **pre-par′a-to-ry,** *a.* **1.** Serving as a preparation. **2.** Occupied in preparation. **pre-par′a-tiv(e‡.)**

pre-pense′, 1 prı-pens′; 2 pre-pĕns′, *a.* Held beforehand; premeditated.

pre-pon′der-ate, 1 prı-pŏn′dər-ēt; 2 prē-pŏn′dēr-āt, *vi.* [-AT″ED‡; -AT′ING.] To be superior in weight or power: often followed by *over.*— **pre-pon′der-ance,** *n.*— **pre-pon′der-ant,** *a.* **-ly,** *adv.*— **pre-pond′er-a″tion,** *n.*

prep″o-si′tion, 1 prep″o-zish′ən; 2 prĕp′o-sĭsh′on, *n.* The part of speech that denotes the relation of an object to an action or thing.— **prep″o-si′tion-al,** *a.*

pre″pos-sess′‡, 1 prī″po-zes′; 2 prē″pŏ-ses′, *vt.* To make a first impression on, especially a favorable impression.— **pre″pos-sess′ing,** *pa.* Inspiring a favorable opinion from the beginning.— **pre″pos-ses′sion,** *n.*

pre-pos′ter-ous, 1 prı-pos′ter-us; 2 pre-pŏs′ter-ŭs, *a.* Contrary to nature or reason. **-ly,** *adv.*

pre-req′ui-site, 1 prī-rek′wı-zit; 2 prē-rĕk′wi-sĭt, **I.** *a.* Required as an antecedent; necessary to a result. **II.** *n.* A necessary antecedent.

pre-rog′a-tive, 1 prı-rŏg′ə-tiv; 2 pre-rŏg′a-tĭv, *n.* A peculiar right or privilege, as of a king.

pre-sage′, 1 prı-sēj′; 2 pre-sāg′, *vt. & vi.* [PRE-SAGED′; PRE-SAG′ING.] To portend; prophesy.— **pre-sag′er,** *n.*

pres′age, 1 pres′ij; 2 prĕs′ag, *n.* A prognostic; presentiment; an omen.— **pres′age-ful,** *a.*

pres′by-ter, 1 pres′[or prez′]bı-tər; 2 prĕs′[or prĕz′]by-ter, *n.* One of the elders of a church.— **Pres″by-te′ri-an,** *n.* **1.**

One who believes in the government of the church by presbyters. **2.** A member of a protestant body, known as the *Presbyterian Church.*— **Pres″by-te′ri-an,** *a.*— **Pres″by-te′ri-an-ism,** *n.*— **pres′by-ter″y,** *n.* [-IES‡, *pl.*] A body of elders in a church or district.

pre′sci-ence, 1 prī′shı-ens; 2 prē′shi-ĕnç, *n.* Foreknowledge; sagacious foresight. — **pre′sci-ent,** *a.* Foreknowing.

pre-scribe′, 1 prı-skraib′; 2 pre-scrīb′, *vt. & vi.* [PRE-SCRIBED′; PRE-SCRIB′ING.] To direct; order; give directions.— **pre-scrib′er,** *n.*

pre-scrip′tion, 1 prı-skrip′shən; 2 pre-scrip′shon, *n.* **1.** The act of prescribing; that which is prescribed; a physician's formula for compounding and administering a medicine. **2.** Title obtained in law by long possession.— **pre-scrip′tiv(e‡,** *a.* Sanctioned by custom or long use.— **pre-scrip′tiv(e-ly‡,** *adv.*

pres′ence, 1 prez′ens; 2 prĕs′ĕnç, *n.* The state of being present; personal appearance; bearing.

pre-sent′‡, 1 prı-zent′; 2 pre-sĕnt′, *vt.* To introduce; confer a gift upon; give; suggest; offer.— **pre-sent′a-bl(e‡,** *a.*— **pres″en-ta′tion,** *n.* The act or manner of presenting.

pres′ent, 1 prez′ent; 2 prĕs′ĕnt, *a.* **1.** Being in this place or in a place specified as where some event occurs. **2.** Now going on or in mind. **3.** Impending; instant.— **pres′ent-ly,** *adv.*

pres′ent‡, *n.* **1.** Present time. **2.** The present tense. **3.** A matter in hand.

pres′ent‡, *n.* A gift.

pre-sen′ti-ment, 1 prī-sen′tı-ment *or* -ment; 2 prē-sĕn′ti-ment, *n.* A foreboding.

pre-sent′ment, 1 prı-zent′ment *or* -ment; 2 pre-sĕnt′ment, *n.* Presentation; representation; indictment.

pre-serve′, 1 prı-zūrv′; 2 pre-sĕrv′, **I.** *vt.* **pre-serv′‡,** & *vi.* [PRE-SERVED′, PRE-SERVD′‡; PRE-SERV′ING.] To keep; protect; save; put up, as fruit in sugar. **II.** *n.* **1.** Anything preserved, as fruit cooked in sugar. **2.** A place in which game is preserved.— **pres″er-va′tion,** *n.* The act of preserving, or the state of being preserved. — **pre-serv′a-tiv(e‡.** **I.** *a.* Serving or tending to preserve. **II.** *n.* That which serves or tends to preserve.— **pre-serv′a-to-ry,** *a. & n.*

pre-side′, 1 prı-zaid′; 2 pre-sĭd′, *vi.* [PRE-SID′ED‡; PRE-SID′ING.] To sit in authority over others; act as head or ruler.

pres′i-dent, 1 prez′ı-dent; 2 prĕs′i-dĕnt, *n.* One who presides over an organized body; [P-] the chief executive officer of a republic.— **pres′i-den-cy,** *n.* **pres′i-dent-ship‡.**— **pres″i-den′tial,** *a.*

press¹, 1 pres; 2 prĕs, *vt.* & *vi.* [PRESSED^t, PREST^s; PRESS′ING.] **1.** To crush; squeeze; compress; crowd; follow closely. **2.** To embrace. **3.** To insist upon; urge. **4.** To smooth, as with an iron.

press²^t, *vt.* & *vi.* To force into naval or military service.

press, *n.* **1.** A crowd or crowding; throng. **2.** Hurry; urgency. **3.** A movable closet. **4.** A printing-press. **5.** Newspapers or periodicals collectively.— **press′ing**, *pa.* Demanding immediate attention.— **press′ing-ly**, *adv.*— **press′ure**, *n.* The act of pressing, or the state of being pressed; urgency; rush.

pres″ti-dig′i-ta′tion, 1 pres″tɪ-dɪg′ı-tē′-shan; 2 prĕs″tɪ-dĭg′ĭ-tā′shon, *n.* Sleight of hand; legerdemain; jugglery.— **pres″ti-dig′i-ta″tor**, *n.* **pres″ti-dig″i-ta′teur‡.**

pres-tige′, 1 pres-tīg′ *or* pres′tɪj; 2 prĕs-tĭzh′ *or* prĕs′tĭg, *n.* Influence based on past achievements.

pres′to, 1 pres′to; 2 prĕs′to, *adv.* **1.** *Mus.* In quick time. **2.** At once; instantly; suddenly.— **presto! change!** pass quickly; a juggler's formula.

pre-sume′, 1 prɪ-ziūm′; 2 pre-gūm′, *v.* [PRE-SUMED′; PRE-SUM′ING.] **I.** *t.* **1.** To venture on without previous permission; followed by infinitive. **2.** To assume as entitled to belief without proof. **II.** *i.* To behave with arrogance.— **pre-sum′a-bl(e**^P, *a.* Fair to suppose; reasonable.— **pre-sum′a-bly**, *adv.*— **pre-sump′tion**, *n.* **1.** Blind confidence or self-assertion; insolence. **2.** The act of taking for granted; that which may be assumed or taken for granted.— **pre-sump′tiv(e**^s, *a.* Creating or resting upon a presumption; probable.— **pre-sump′tu-ous**, *a.* Unduly confident or bold; audacious; insolent; foolhardy. **-ly**, *adv.* **-ness**, *n.*

pre″sup-pose′, 1 prī″su-pōz′; 2 prē″sŭ-pōg′, *vt.* To suppose in advance; take for granted.— **pre-sup″po-si′tion**, *n.*

pre-tend′^d, 1 prɪ-tend′; 2 pre-tĕnd′, *v.* **I.** *t.* To simulate; feign; claim falsely. **II.** *i.* **1.** To make believe. **2.** To assume a character.— **pre-tend′er**, *n.* **1.** A claimant. **2.** A hypocrite.— **pre-tense′, pre-tence′**, *n.* The act of pretending; a pretext; subterfuge; claim.— **pre-ten′sion**, *n.* **1.** A claim put forward, whether true or false. **2.** Affectation; display.— **pre-ten′tious**, *a.* Making a display; imposing.

pre′ter-, 1 prī′tər-; 2 prē′ter-, *prefix.* Beyond; past; more than.

pret′er-it, } 1 pret′ər-it; 2 prĕt′er-ĭt. **I.**
pret′er-ite, } *a.* Belonging to the past. **II.** *n.* The tense that expresses absolute past time.

pre″ter-mit′, 1 prī″tər-mit′; 2 prē″ter-mĭt′,

vt. [-MIT′TED^d; -MIT′TING.] **1.** To fail to do; neglect. **2.** To give no heed to; pass by. **præ″ter-mit′‡.**

pre″ter-nat′u-ral, 1 prī″tər-nach′u-[*or* -nat′yu-]ral; 2 prē″ter-năch′u-[*or* -năt′yu-]-ral, *a.* Beyond what is natural. **-ly**, *adv.* **-ness**, *n.*

pre′text, 1 prī′tekst *or* prɪ-tekst′; 2 prē′-tĕkst *or* pre-tĕkst′, *n.* A fictitious reason or motive.

pret′ty, 1 prit′ɪ; 2 prĭt′y, *a.* [PRET′TI-ER; PRET′TI-EST.] Characterized by delicate beauty; dainty; pleasing; sweet.— **pret′ti-ly**, *adv.*— **pret′ti-ness**, *n.*— **pret′ty**, *adv.* Moderately; somewhat.

pre-vail′, 1 prɪ-vēl′; 2 pre-vāl′, *vi.* **1.** To triumph; followed by *over.* **2.** To persuade; followed by *on or upon.* **3.** To spread widely.— **pre-vail′ing**, *pa.* **1.** Current; prevalent. **2.** Efficacious.— **prev′a-lence**, *n.* The act, state, or quality of being prevalent. **prev′a-len-cy‡.**— **prev′a-lent**, *a.* **1.** Widely extended; common; general. **2.** Powerful; efficacious.— **prev′a-lent-ly**, *adv.*

pre-var′i-cate, 1 prɪ-var′ı-kēt; 2 pre-văr′ı-eāt, *vi.* [-CAT′ED^d; -CAT′ING.] To pervert or disguise the truth; equivocate.— **pre-var″i-ca′tion**, *n.*— **pre-var′i-ca″tor**, *n.*

pre-vent′^d, 1 prɪ-vent′; 2 pre-vĕnt′, *v.* **I.** *t.* To stop in advance; hinder; check; restrain. **II.** *i.* To take precautionary measures.— **pre-vent′a-bl(e**^P, *a.*— **pre-ven′tion**, *n.* The act of preventing or the state of being prevented.— **pre-ven′tiv(e**^s, *a.* & *n.*

pre′vi-ous, 1 prī′vı-us; 2 prē′vi-ŭs, *a.* Being or occurring before something else. **-ly**, *adv.* **-ness**, *n.* [Foresight.

pre-vi′sion, 1 prɪ-vĭg′ən; 2 pre-vĭzh′on, *n.*

prey, 1 prē; 2 pre. **I.** *vi.* To seize food, as a bird or beast, by violence; plunder; make a victim; wear or waste: followed by *on or upon.* **II.** *n.* Any animal seized by another for food; a victim; booty.

price, 1 prais; 2 prîç. **I.** *vt.* [PRICED^t; PRIC′ING.] **1.** To ask the price of. **2.** To set a price upon. **II.** *n.* An equivalent given or asked in exchange; valuation.— **price′less**, *a.* Beyond price; inestimable.

prick^d, 1 prik; 2 prĭk, *v.* **I.** *t.* **1.** To pierce; sting; goad. **2.** To erect (the ears), as a horse. **II.** *i.* To have or cause a stinging sensation; spur; speed.— **prick′er**, *n.*

prick, *n.* The act of pricking; a point; goad; puncture.— **prick′l(e**^P. **I.** *vt.* & *vi.* [PRICK′L(E)D^P; PRICK′LING.] To prick slightly in many places; have a diffused stinging sensation. **II.** *n.* **1.** A small, sharp point, as on a thistle. **2.** A stinging sensation.— **prick′li-ness**, *n.*— **prick′ly**, *a.*

1: ə = final; ɪ = habit; aɪsle; aʊ = out; oɪl; iū = feud; chin; go; ŋ = sing; thin, this.
2: wǫlf, dǫ; bōōk, bōōt; fųll, rųle, cūre, bŭt, bûrn; ôɪl, bŏy; ḡo, ḡem; iŋk; thin, this.

pride, 1 praid; 2 prīd. **I.** *vt.* & *vi.* [PRID´- EDᵈ; PRID´ING.] To be proud (of); have pride; exult; glory. **II.** *n.* **1.** Undue self=esteem. **2.** A proper sense of personal dignity. **3.** That of which one is proud. **4.** The height of excellence. **5.** Mettle. **6.** Display.

priest, 1 prīst; 2 prēst, *n.* One consecrated to the service of a divinity.— **priest´ess,** *n. fem.*— **priest´hood,** *n.* The priestly office; priests collectively. — **priest´li-ness,** *n.*— **priest´ly,** *a.*

prig, 1 prig; 2 prīg, *n.* A formal, pedantic person.— **prig´gish,** *a.*

prim, 1 prim; 2 prīm. **I.** *vt.* & *vi.* [PRIMMED, PRIMDˢ; PRIM´MING.] To decorate or adjust primly. **II.** *a.* Stiffly proper and neat. **-ly,** *adv.* **-ness,** *n.*

pri´ma, 1 prī´ma; 2 prī´mä. First; principal.— **pri´ma don´na,** a leading female singer, as in an opera company: in English use forming the plural PRIMA DONNAS, as if a compound noun.

pri´ma-cy, 1 prai´ma-sɪ; 2 prī´ma-çy, *n.* [-CIESᶻ, *pl.*] **1.** The state of being first. **2.** The office of a primate. **pri´mate-shipǂ.**

pri´mal, 1 prai´məl; 2 prī´mal, *a.* Primary.

pri´ma-ry, 1 prai´mə-rɪ; 2 prī´ma-ry, *a.* Original; first; fundamental; chief.— **pri´ma-ri-ly,** *adv.*

pri´mate, 1 prai´mēt; 2 prī´māt, *n. Eccl.* The prelate highest in rank in a nation or province.

prime, 1 praim; 2 prīm. **I.** *vt.* [PRIMED, PRIM´ING.] To make ready; supply with priming. **II.** *a.* First; chief; vigorous; excellent. **III.** *n.* **1.** The period between youth and age; fulness of vigor; full perfection. **2.** The beginning of anything.

prim´er¹, 1 prim´ər; 2 prīm´er, *n.* **1.** An elementary reading=book. **2.** Either of two sizes of type, known as **great primer** (18=point) and **long primer** (10=point).

prim´er², 1 praim´ər; 2 prīm´er, *n.* One who or that which primes anything, as a gun.

pri-me´val, 1 prai-mī´vəl; 2 prī-mē´val, *a.* Belonging to the first ages; primitive; primal.

prim´ing, 1 praim´ɪŋ; 2 prīm´ing, *n.* The act of one who primes; powder for igniting the charge in a firearm; a first coat of paint.

prim´i-tive, 1 prim´ɪ-tiv; 2 prīm´i-tīv. **I.** prim´i-tivˢ, *a.* **1.** Pertaining to the beginning; first; earliest. **2.** Old=fashioned. **II.** *n.* A primary or radical word. **-ly,** *adv.* **-ness,** *n.*

pri-mor´di-al, 1 prai-mōr´dɪ-əl; 2 mōr´di-al, *a.* First; original; primitive.

prim´rose´´, 1 prim´rōz´´; 2 prīm´rŏs´´, *n.* **1.** A flowering perennial plant. **2.** A greenish=yellow color.

Common Primrose.

prince, 1 prins; 2 prĭns, *n.* A male monarch; the son of a monarch; a man of exalted rank or power.— **prince´-dom,** *n.* The rank, dignity, or jurisdiction of a prince.— **prince´li-ness,** *n.*— **prince´ly,** *a.*— **prin´cess,** *n. fem.*

prin´ci-pal, 1 prin´sɪ-pəl; 2 prĭn´çi-pal. **I.** *a.* First; chief. **II.** *n.* **1.** A principal person; leader; head. **2.** Property or capital; a sum on which interest accrues. **-ly,** *adv.*

prin´´ci-pal´i-ty, 1 prin´´sɪ-pal´ɪ-tɪ; 2 prĭn´´çi-păl´i-ty, *n.* [-TIESᶻ, *pl.*] The territory of a reigning prince.

prin´ci-ple, 1 prin´sɪ-pl; 2 prĭn´çi-pl, *n.* **1.** A cause; essence. **2.** A general truth; rule of action, especially of right action.

printᵈ, 1 print; 2 prĭnt. **I.** *vt.* & *vi.* To mark, as by pressure; impress; copy by a printing=press; publish. **II.** *n.* An impression; imprint; anything printed, as a newspaper or calico.— **print´er,** *n.*— **print´ing,** *n.* **1.** The act of printing or that which is printed. **2.** The act or process of reproducing an image on sensitized paper, as in photography.— **print´ing-press´´,** *n.* A press by which printing, as of books and papers, is done.

pri´or, 1 prai´ər; 2 prī´or. **I.** *a.* Preceding; previous. **II.** *n.* A monastic officer next below an abbot.— **pri´or-ate,** *n.*— **pri´or-ess,** *n. fem.*— **pri´or-y,** *n.* [PRI´OR-IESᶻ, *pl.*] A convent under charge of a prior or prioress.

pri-or´i-ty, 1 prai-or´ɪ-tɪ; 2 prī-ŏr´i-ty, *n.* Antecedence; superiority.

prism, 1 prizm; 2 prĭşm, *n.* A solid whose bases are similar equal and parallel plane figures, and whose faces are parallelograms; spectrum.— **pris-mat´ic,** *a.* Pertaining to, shaped like, or formed by a prism; exhibiting rainbow tints. **pris-mat´i-calǂ.**— **pris-mat´i-cal-ly,** *adv.*

pris´on, 1 priz´n; 2 prĭş´n. **I.** *vt.* To imprison. **II.** *n.* A place of confinement; jail.— **pris´on-er,** *n.* A captive; one held in custody.

pris´tine, 1 pris´tɪn; 2 prĭs´tin, *a.* First; primeval.

1: artistic, ärt; fat, fāre; fast; get, prēy; hit, police; obey, gō; net, ôr; full, rûle; but, bûrn.

2: ärt, āpe, fặt, fâre, fàst, whạt, ạll; mē, gĕt, prey, fērn; hǐt, īce; ī=ĕ; ĭ=ē; gō, nŏt, ôr, wŏn.

pri′va-cy, 1 praɪ′və-sɪ; 2 prī′va-çy, *n.* [-CIES², *pl.*] Secrecy; seclusion.

pri′vate, 1 praɪ′vɪt; 2 prī′vat. **I.** *a.* Retired; secluded; secret; restricted; personal; without rank. **II.** *n.* A common soldier. **-ly,** *adv.* **-ness,** *n.*— **pri″va-teer′,** *n.* A private vessel commissioned to prey on an enemy's commerce; also, a person conducting or serving on such a ship.

pri-va′tion, 1 praɪ-vē′shən; 2 prī-vā′shon, *n.* Destitution; deprivation.— **priv′a-tive,** **I.** *a.* Depriving; negative. **II.** *n.* A prefix giving a negative meaning.— **priv′a-tive-ly,** *adv.*

priv′et, 1 priv′et; 2 prĭv′ĕt, *n.* An ornamental hedge-plant.

priv′i-lege, 1 priv′i-lɪj; 2 prĭv′i-leg. **I.** *vt.* [-LEGED; -LEG-ING.] To grant a privilege to. **II.** *n.* A right or advantage enjoyed by certain persons only.

priv′y, 1 priv′ɪ; 2 prĭv′y, *a.* Having private knowledge; secret; private.— **priv′i-ly,** *adv.*— **priv′i-ty,** *n.*

prize, 1 praɪz; 2 prīz. **I.** *vt.* To value; esteem. **II.** *n.* Anything won or to be won in a contest; a reward.

Privet.

pro-, *prefix.* Before; fore; forward; for; instead of; as, prolog, pronoun.

prob′a-ble, } 1 preb′ə-bl; 2 prŏb′a-bl, *a.* **prob′a-bl²,** } Likely to be true or to happen; credible.— **prob″a-bil′i-ty,** *n.* [-TIES², *pl.*] The state of being probable; a probable event or statement.— **prob′a-bly,** *adv.*

pro′bate, 1 prō′bēt; 2 prō′bāt, *n.* Formal, official, legal proof, as of a will.

pro-ba′tion, 1 pro-bē′shən; 2 pro-bā′shon, *n.* A period of trial; novitiate.— **pro-ba′tion-a-ry,** *a.*— **pro-ba′tion-er,** *n.* One who is on probation; a novice.

probe, 1 prōb; 2 prōb. **I.** *vt.* [PROBED; PROB′ING.] To explore with a probe; search; scrutinize. **II.** *n.* An instrument for exploring the course of wounds, etc.

prob′i-ty, 1 preb′ɪ-tɪ; 2 prŏb′i-ty, *n.* Tried integrity; strict honesty.

prob′lem, 1 preb′lem; 2 prŏb′lĕm, *n.* A perplexing question.— **prob″lem-at′ic,** *a.* **-i-cal‡.**— **prob″lem-at′i-cal-ly,** *adv.*

pro-bos′cis, 1 pro-bɒs′ɪs; 2 pro-bŏs′is, *n.* [-CI-DES, 1 -sɪ-dīz; 2 -çi-dēs, *pl.*] An animal's trunk.

pro-ce′dure², 1 pro-sī′jur *or* -sīd′yur; 2 pro-çē′jur *or* -çēd′yur, *n.* A method of proceeding; a course of action.

pro-ceed′ᵈ, 1 pro-sīd′; 2 pro-çēd′, *vi.* **1.** To go on or forward; continue. **2.** To issue or come, as from some source

— **pro-ceed′ing,** *n.* **1.** An act or course of action. **2.** *pl.* The records of meetings, as of a society.— **pro′ceeds,** *n. pl.* Product; return; yield.

proc′ess, 1 pres′es; 2 prŏç′ĕs, *n.* **1.** A course or method of operations; progress; course. **2.** An outgrowth; appendage. **3.** A judicial writ.

pro-ces′sion, 1 pro-sesh′ən; 2 pro-çĕsh′on, *n.* **1.** An array, as of persons, moving in order; train; array. **2.** The act of proceeding.

pro-claim′, 1 pro-klēm′; 2 pro-elām′, *vt.* To announce aloud or in a public manner; promulgate.— **pro-claim′er,** *n.*— **proc″la-ma′tion,** *n.* **1.** The act of proclaiming. **2.** That which is proclaimed.

pro-cliv′i-ty, 1 pro-kliv′i-tɪ; 2 pro-clĭz′i-ty, *n.* [-TIES², *pl.*] Natural disposition; propensity; inclination.

pro-cras′ti-nate, 1 pro-kras′tɪ-nēt; 2 pro-erăs′ti-nāt, *vt. & vi.* [-NAT′ED⁰; -NAT′-ING.] To put off; defer; delay.— **pro-cras″ti-na′tion,** *n.*— **pro-cras′ti-na″tor,** *n.*

pro′cre-ate⁰, 1 prō′krɪ-ēt; 2 prō′cre-āt, *vt.* To beget.— **pro″cre-a′tion,** *n.*— **pro′cre-a″tiv⁰²,** *a.*

Pro-crus′te-an, 1 pro-krus′tɪ-ən; 2 pro-erŭs′te-an, *a.* **1.** Pertaining to Procrustes, a legendary Greek robber who was said to stretch or cut off the limbs of his captives as necessary to fit a certain bed. **2.** [-p-] Ruthlessly exacting conformity.

proc′tor, 1 prek′tər *or* -tər; 2 prŏe′tor, *n.* An attorney; proxy; minor officer of a college.— **proc′tor-ship,** *n.*

pro-cure′, 1 pro-kiūr′; 2 pro-eūr′, *vt.* [PRO-CURED′; PRO-CUR′ING.] To come into possession of by effort; bring about; get; obtain.— **pro-cur′a-bl(e²,** *a.* That may be procured.— **pro-cure′ment,** *n.*

prod, 1 pred; 2 prŏd. **I.** *vt.* [PROD′DED⁰; PROD′DING.] To punch; poke. **II.** *n.* **1.** A pointed instrument. **2.** A thrust; punch.

prod′i-gal, 1 pred′ɪ-gel; 2 prŏd′i-gal. **I.** *a.* Wasteful; profuse. **II.** *n.* One who is wasteful or profligate. **-ly,** *adv.*— **prod″i-gal′i-ty,** *n.* [-TIES², *pl.*]

prod′i-gy, 1 pred′ɪ-jɪ; 2 prŏd′i-ğy, *n.* [-GIES², *pl.*] Something extraordinary; a wonder; monstrosity.— **pro-dig′ious,** *a.* Enormous; extraordinary; excessive. **-ly,** *adv.* **-ness,** *n.*

pro-duce′, 1 pro-diūs′; 2 pro-dūç′, *v.* [PRO-DUCED′ᵗ; PRO-DUC′ING.] **I.** *t.* **1.** To bring into existence; cause; make; result in. **2.** To bring forth; yield; bear. **II.** *i.* To be productive.— **pro-duc′er,** *n.*— **pro-duc′i-bl(e²,** *a.*

1: ə = final; ɪ = habit; ɑisle; ɑu = *out*; ɒil; ɪū = feud; chin; go; ŋ = sing; chin, this.
2: wǫlf, dǫ; bŏŏk, bŏŏt; fųll, rųle, cūre, bŭt, bûrn; ŏil, bŏy; ḡo, ǧem; iŋk; thin, this.

prod'uce, 1 prəd'yūs; 2 prŏd'yŭç, n. sing. & pl. A product; farm-products.

prod'uct, 1 prŏd'ukt; 2 prŏd'ŭet, n. Anything produced; result obtained by multiplication.— pro-duc'tion, n. 1. The act or process of producing. 2. That which is produced.— pro-duc'tiv(e³, a. Producing or tending to produce; fertile; remunerative. -ly, adv. -ness, n. [duction.

pro'em, 1 prō'em; 2 prō'ĕm, n. An intro-

pro-fane', 1 pro-fēn'; 2 pro-fān'. I. vt. [PRO-FANED'; PRO-FAN'ING.] To desecrate; pollute; degrade. II. a. 1. Irreverent; blasphemous. 2. Secular; uninspired. -ly, adv. -ness, n.— prof''a-na'tion, n. The act of profaning.— pro-fan'i-ty, n. The state of being profane; profane language; blasphemy.

pro-fess'ᵗ, 1 pro-fes'; 2 pro-fĕs', vt. To make open declaration of; avow; declare. — pro-fess'ed-ly, adv.— pro-fes'sion, n. 1. An occupation that involves a liberal education, and mental rather than manual labor. 2. The act of professing, or that which is professed.— pro-fes'sion-al, a. Pertaining to a profession, or business.— pro-fes'sion-al-ly, adv.— pro-fes'sor, n. 1. A public teacher of the highest grade. 2. One who makes profession, as of religion.— pro''fes-so'ri-al, a. -ly, adv.— pro-fes'sor-ship, n.

prof'fer, 1 prof'er; 2 prŏf'er. I. vt. To offer. II. n. An offer, or the thing offered.

pro-fi'cient, 1 pro-fish'ent; 2 pro-fĭsh'ĕnt. I. a. Thoroughly versed, as in art. II. n. An expert; adept.— pro-fi'cien-cy, n. pro-fi'cience‡.— pro-fi'cient-ly, adv.

pro'file, 1 prō'fīl or -fail; 2 prō'fīl or -fīl, n. An outline, as of a face seen from the side; side-view.

prof'itᵈ, 1 prof'it; 2 prŏf'it, v. I. t. To be of profit to. II. i. 1. To obtain profit. 2. To be of advantage.

prof'it, n. 1. Valuable return from labor; benefit; gain. 2. Excess of returns over outlay.— prof'it-a-bl(eᴾ, a. Remunerative; advantageous.— prof'it-a-bl(e-nessᴾ, n.— prof'it-a-bly, adv.— prof'i-teer, I. vi. To make excessive profits in business. II. n. One given to profiteering.— prof'it-less, a.

prof'li-gate, 1 prof'li-git; 2 prŏf'li-ġat. I. a. Abandoned to vice. II. n. A depraved or abandoned person. -ly, adv.— prof'li-ga-cy, n. prof'li-gate-ness‡.

pro-found', 1 pro-faund'; 2 pro-faund', a. Deep; complete; thorough; abstruse. -ly, adv.— pro-fun'di-ty, n. The state of being profound. pro-found'ness‡.

pro-fuse', 1 pro-fiūs'; 2 pro-fūs', a. Abundant; copious; overflowing. -ly, adv.— -ness, n.— pro-fu'sion, n. Exuberance; prodigality.

pro-gen'i-tor, 1 pro-jen'i-tər or -tẽr; 2 pro-ġĕn'i-tor, n. A forefather or parent.

prog'e-ny, 1 prej'i-ni; 2 prŏġ'e-ny, n. Offspring.

prog-no'sis, 1 prog-nō'sis; 2 prŏg-nō'sis, n. A prediction, as to the result of injury or illness.— prog-nos'tic. I. a. Relating to prognosis; foreshowing. II. n. A sign of some future occurrence; an omen.— prog-nos'ti-cate, vt. & vi. [-CAT'EDᵈ; -CAT'ING.] 1. To foretell. 2. To be an omen of.— prog-nos''ti-ca'tion, n.— prog-nos'ti-ca''tor, n.

pro'gram, } 1 prō'gram; 2 prō'ġram, n. pro'gramme, } A list of exercises, as for an entertainment; any prearranged plan.

pro-gress'ᵗ, 1 pro-gres'; 2 pro-ġrĕs', vt. & vi. To move forward; advance; improve.

prog'ress, 1 prog'res; 2 prŏġ'rĕs, n. A moving forward; advancement.— pro-gres'sion, n. The act of progressing; advancement.— pro-gres'sion-al, a.— pro-gres'-siv(e³, a. -ly, adv. -ness, n.— pro-gres'-sive, n. 1. An advocate of progress. 2. [P-] A member of the political party formed by Theodore Roosevelt in 1912.

pro-hib'itᵈ, 1 pro-hib'it; 2 pro-hĭb'it, vt. To forbid; interdict; hinder.— pro''hi-bi'-tion, n. The act of prohibiting anything, as the sale of intoxicants.— pro''hi-bi'tion-ist, n. One who favors prohibition.— pro-hib'i-tiv(e³, a. Tending to prohibit. pro-hib'-i-to-ry‡.

pro-jectᵈ, 1 pro-jekt'; 2 pro-jĕet', v. I. t. 1. To shoot forth; send out. 2. To contrive or plan. II. i. To stand out; just out.— pro-jec'til(eᴾ. I. a. Impelling forward. II. n. A missile; shot.— pro-jec'tion, n. The act of projecting; a prominence; scheme; project; map or drawing showing something, as in relief.— pro-jec'tor, n. [scheme.

proj'ect, 1 prej'ekt; 2 prŏj'ĕet, n. A plan;

pro''le-ta'ri-at, 1 prō''lĩ-tē'ri-at; 2 prō''le-tä'ri-ăt. 1. Formerly, the lower classes; peasantry. 2. In modern socialistic use, wage-workers collectively; working men and their families.— pro''le-ta'ri-an, a. & n.

pro-lif'ic, 1 pro-lif'ik; 2 pro-lĭf'ic, a. Producing abundantly; fertile.

pro'lix, 1 prō'liks or pro-liks'; 2 prō'liks or pro-lĭks', a. Using or containing too many words; verbose; tedious.— pro-lix'i-ty, n. pro-lix'ness‡.

pro'log, } 1 prō'lŏg; 2 prō'lŏg, n. An pro'logue, } introduction or preface, as to a poem.

pro-long', 1 pro-lŏŋ'; 2 pro-lông', vt. To lengthen; extend.— pro''lon-ga'tion, n.

prom''e-nade', 1 prŏm'i-nād'; 2 prŏm''e-nād'. I. vi. [-NADᵈ; -NAD'ING.] To take a promenade. II. n. 1. A walk for

amusement or exercise. **2.** A place for promenading.

Pro-me'the-an, 1 pro-mī'thi-ən; 2 pro-mḗ'the-an, *a.* Of, pertaining to, or like Prometheus: in Greek mythology, son of the Titan Iapetus, chained to a rock by Zeus because he gave fire to the human race.

prom'i-nent, 1 prom'i-nent; 2 prŏm'i-nĕnt, *a.* Jutting out; projecting; conspicuous; eminent.— **prom'i-nence,** *n.* The state of being prominent; something prominent. **prom'i-nen-cy‡.— prom'i-nent-ly,** *adv.*

pro-mis'cu-ous, 1 pro-mis'kiu-us; 2 pro-mĭs'eū-ŭs, *a.* Mixed; indiscriminate. **-ly,** *adv.* **-ness,** *n.*

prom'ise, 1 prom'is; 2 prŏm'is. **I.** *vt. &*
prom'is, } *vi.* [PROM'ISED‡, PROM'IST‡; PROM'IS-ING.] **1.** To agree to do or not to do. **2.** To afford hope or expectation. **II.** *n.* **1.** A declaration binding to do or not to do a specified act. **2.** Reasonable ground for hope or expectation. **3.** Something promised.— **prom''is-ee',** *n.* The person to whom a promise is made.— **prom'is-or,** *n.* The person who makes a promise. **prom'is-er‡.— prom'is-ing,** *pa.* Giving ground for favorable expectations; affording promise.— **prom'is-so-ry,** *a.* Containing a promise; of the nature of a promise.

prom'on-to''ry, 1 prom'ən-to''ri; 2 prŏm'-on-to''ry, *n.* [-RIES⁷, *pl.*] A high point of land extending into the sea; a headland.

pro-mote', 1 pro-mōt'; 2 pro-mōt', *vt.* [PRO-MOT'ED⁴; PRO-MOT'ING.] **1.** To foster; encourage; advance. **2.** To raise to greater dignity or honor.— **pro-mot'er,** *n.*— **pro-mo'tion,** *n.*— **pro-mo'tiv(e⁵,** *a.*

prompt, 1 prompt; 2 prŏmpt. **I**d. *vt.* To incite; instigate; help by suggestion; suggest. **II.** *a.* Acting, or ready to act, at the moment. **-ly,** *adv.* **-ness,** *n.*— **prompt'er,** *n.*— **prompt'i-tude,** *n.* Promptness; readiness; alertness.

pro-mul'gate, 1 pro-mul'gēt; 2 pro-mŭl'-gāt, *vt.* [-GAT'ED⁴; -GAT'ING.] To announce officially; make known.— **pro''mul-ga'tion,** *n.*

prone, 1 prōn; 2 prŏn, *a.* **1.** Lying flat or with face downward; prostrate. **2.** Inclined; strongly disposed.

prong, 1 prɒŋ; 2 prŏng, *n.* A sharp-pointed instrument, as a tine of a fork.

pro'noun, 1 prō'naun; 2 prō'noun, *n.* A word used instead of a noun.— **perpendicular pronoun,** the pronoun of the first person singular, *I.*— **pro-nom'i-nal,** *a.* Pertaining to, or like, a pronoun.— **ly,** *adv.*

pro-nounce', 1 pro-nauns'; 2 pro-nouncʹ, *vt. & vi.* [PRO-NOUNCED'‡; PRO-NOUNC'-ING.] To articulate; utter formally; declare.— **pro-nounce'a-ble(e²,** *a.*— **pro-**

nounced', *pa.* Of marked character; decided.— **pro-nounc'er,** *n.*— **pro-nun''ci-a'-tion,** 1 pro-nŭn'si-[*or* -shi-]ē'shən; 2 pro-nŭn'çĭ-[*or* -çhi-]ā'shon, *n.* The act or manner of pronouncing words.

proof, 1 prūf; 2 prōof. **I.** *a.* **1.** Employed in or connected with proving or correcting. **2.** Firm; impenetrable. **3.** Of standard alcoholic strength. **II.** *n.* **1.** The act of proving; convincing evidence. **2.** The standard strength of alcoholic liquors. **3.** A printed trial-sheet, as for correction.

prop, 1 prop; 2 prŏp. **I.** *vt.* [PROPPED‡, PROPT⁵; PROP'PING.] To support so as to keep from falling; sustain. **II.** *n.* A support.

prop''a-gan'da, 1 prŏp''ə-gan'da; 2 prŏp'-a-găn'da, *n.* An institution or scheme for propagating a doctrine or system.— **prop''a-gan'dism,** *n.*— **prop''a-gan'dist,** *n.*

prop'a-gate, 1 prop'ə-gēt; 2 prŏp'a-găt, *v.* [-GAT'ED⁴; -GAT'ING.] **I.** *t.* To generate; produce; spread; diffuse; disseminate. **II.** *i.* To be produced or multiplied by generation.— **prop''a-ga'tion,** *n.*— **prop'a-ga''tiv(e⁵,** *a.*— **prop'a-ga''tor,** *n.*

pro-pel', 1 pro-pel'; 2 pro-pĕl', *vt.* [PRO-PELLED', PRO-PELD'⁵; PRO-PEL'LING.] To drive or urge forward; force onward.— **pro-pel'ler,** *n.* One who or that which propels; a screw for propelling, or a vessel driven by it.

pro-pen'si-ty, 1 pro-pen'si-ti; 2 pro-pĕn'-si-ty, *n.* [-TIES⁷, *pl.*] Mental disposition to good or (oftener) to evil; tendency; inclination.

prop'er, 1 prop'ər; 2 prŏp'er, *a.* **1.** Fit; becoming; correct. **2.** Naturally belonging to a person or thing; one's own. **3.** Belonging, as a name, to a single individual. **-ly,** *adv.*

prop'er-ty, 1 prop'ər-ti; 2 prŏp'er-ty, *n.* [-TIES⁷, *pl.*] Anything that may be owned; ownership; a distinguishing quality.

proph'e-cy, } 1 prof'i-si; 2 prŏf'e-çy, *n.*
prof'e-cy⁷, } [-CIES⁷, *pl.*] **1.** An inspired prediction; any prediction. **2.** Discourse under divine inspiration.

proph'e-sy, } 1 prof'i-sai; 2 prŏf'e-sī, *vt. &*
prof'e-sy⁷, } *vi.* [-SIED'; -SY'ING.] **1.** To foretell, as by inspiration. **2.** To speak under divine influence.

proph'et, } 1 prof'it; 2 prŏf'et, *n.* One who
prof'et⁷, } delivers divine messages or foretells the future.— **proph'et-ess,** *n. fem.*— **pro-phet'ic,** *a.* Pertaining to a prophet or prophecy. **pro-phet'i-cal‡.— pro-phet'i-cal-ly,** *adv.*

pro-pin'qui-ty, 1 pro-piŋ'kwi-ti; 2 pro-pĭŋ'kwi-ty, *n.* Nearness; kinship.

---

pro-pi'ti-ate, 1 pro-pĭsh'ĭ-ēt; 2 pro-pĭsh'ĭ-āt, *vt. & vi.* [-AT'ED⁴; -AT'ING.] To appease; conciliate.— **pro-pi''ti-a'tion,** *n.* **1.** The act of propitiating. **2.** That which propitiates.— **pro-pi'ti-a-to-ry,** *a.* Pertaining to or causing propitiation.

pro-pi'tious, 1 pro-pĭsh'ŭs; 2 pro-pĭsh'ŭs, *a.* Kindly disposed; auspicious; favorable. **-ly,** *adv.* **-ness,** *n.*

pro-por'tion, 1 pro-pōr'shən; 2 pro-pôr'shon. **I.** *vt.* **1.** To form; make symmetrical. **2.** To separate into portions. **II.** *n.* **1.** Relative magnitude, number, or degree. **2.** Fitness and harmony; symmetry. **3.** A proportionate share; any share or part. **4.** An equality or identity between ratios.— **pro-por'tion-al,** *a.* Being in due proportion; relating to proportion. **pro-por'tion-ate‡.**— **pro-por'tion-al-ly,** *adv.* **pro-por'tion-ate-ly‡.**

pro-pose', 1 pro-pōz'; 2 pro-pōs', *v.* [-POSED'; -POS'ING.] **I.** *t.* **1.** To offer for acceptance. **2.** To purpose; intend. **II.** *i.* To plan; make an offer, especially of marriage.— **pro-po'sal,** *n.* An offer, or that which is offered.— **pro-pos'er,** *n.*— **prop''o-si'tion,** *n.* **1.** Something proposed; a statement to be proved; the act of proposing. **2.** A statement forming a complete sentence.

pro-pound'd, 1 pro-paund'; 2 pro-pound', *vt.* To state formally for consideration or solution.— **pro-pound'er,** *n.*

pro-pri'e-tor, 1 pro-praī'ĭ-tər or -tər; 2 pro-prī'e-tor, *n.* An owner.— **pro-pri'e-ta-ry,** 1 pro-praī'ĭ-tē-rĭ; 2 pro-prī'e-tā-ry. **I.** *a.* Pertaining to a proprietor. **II.** *n.* [-RIES², *pl.*] A proprietor, or a body of proprietors.— **pro-pri'e-tor-ship,** *n.*— **pro-pri'e-tress,** *n. fem.* **pro-pri'e-trix‡.**

pro-pri'e-ty, 1 pro-praī'ĭ-tĭ; 2 pro-prī'e-ty, *n.* [-TIES², *pl.*] Becomingness; fitness; correctness.

pro-pul'sion, 1 pro-pul'shən; 2 pro-pŭl'shon, *n.* The act or operation of propelling.— **pro-pul'siv(es,** *a.* Tending to propel.

pro ra'ta. In proportion; as, increase or decrease *pro rata.*

pro-rogue', 1 pro-rōg'; 2 pro-rōg', *vt.* [PRO-ROGUED'; PRO-ROGU'ING.] **1.** To terminate by royal command (a session of the British Parliament). **2.** To put off or delay.— **pro''ro-ga'tion,** *n.*

pro-sa'ic, 1 pro-zē'ĭk; 2 pro-sā'ie, *a.* **1.** Unimaginative; commonplace. **2.** Pertaining to or having the form of prose. **-i-cal‡.**— **pro-sa'i-cal-ly,** *adv.*

pro-scribe', 1 pro-skraib'; 2 pro-scrīb', *vt.* [PRO-SCRIBED'; PRO-SCRIB'ING.] To outlaw; ostracize; denounce; condemn.— **pro-scrib'er,** *n.*— **pro-scrip'tion,** *n.* Interdic-

tion; ostracism; outlawry.— **pro-scrip'-tiv(es,** *a.*

prose, 1 prōz; 2 prōs. **I.** *vt. & vi.* [PROSED; PROS'ING.] To write or say in a dull manner. **II.** *a.* Prosaic; prosy. **III.** *n.* Speech or writing without meter.

pros'e-cute, 1 pres'ĭ-kiūt; 2 prŏs'e-cūt, *v.* [-CUT'ED⁴; -CUT'ING.] **I.** *t.* **1.** To pursue or follow up; carry on. **2.** To bring a legal suit or charge against; seek to enforce, as a claim, by legal process. **II.** *i.* To begin and carry on a legal proceeding. — **pros''e-cu'tion,** *n.* The act of prosecuting; the party prosecuting.— **pros'e-cu''tor,** *n.*— **pros'e-cu-trix,** *n. fem.*

pros'e-lyte, 1 pres'ĭ-laĭt; 2 prŏs'e-lȳt. **I.** *vt.* [-LYT'ED⁴; -LYT'ING.] To win over to a different religion, or party. **pros'e-ly-tize** or **-tise‡.** **II.** *n.* A convert.— **pros'e-ly-tism,** *n.* The making of converts.

pros'o-dy, 1 pres'o-dĭ; 2 prŏs'o-dy, *n.* The science of poetical forms.— **pros'o-dist,** *n.*

pros'pect, 1 pres'pekt; 2 prŏs'pĕct. **I**d. *vt. & vi.* To explore; view; survey. **II.** *n.* A view; outlook; reasonable expectation.— **pro-spec'tiv(es,** *a.* **1.** Being still in the future; expected. **2.** Looking to the future. **-ly,** *adv.*— **pros'pec-tor,** *n.* **pros'-pect-er‡.**— **pro-spec'tus,** *n.* A plan; summary; outline.

pros'per, 1 pres'pər; 2 prŏs'per, *vt. & vi.* To make or be successful; thrive; succeed. — **pros-per'i-ty,** *n.* The state of being prosperous.— **pros'per-ous,** *a.* **1.** Successful; flourishing. **2.** Favoring; auspicious.— **pros'per-ous-ly,** *adv.*

pros'ti-tute, 1 pres'tĭ-tiūt; 2 prŏs'tĭ-tūt. **I.** *vt.* [-TUT'ED⁴; -TUT'ING.] To apply to base or vile purposes. **II.** *a.* Surrendered to base or vicious purposes. **III.** *n.* A base hireling; a lewd woman.— **pros''-ti-tu'tion,** *n.* The act of prostituting.

pros'trate, 1 pres'trēt; 2 prŏs'trāt. **I.** *vt.* [PROS'TRAT'ED⁴; PROS'TRAT'ING.] **1.** To lay or throw down flat; overthrow. **2.** To reduce to extreme weakness. **II.** *a.* Lying flat; overthrown or overcome; prostrated.— **pros-tra'tion,** *n.*

pros'y, 1 prōz'ĭ; 2 prōs'y, *a.* [PROS'I-ER; PROS'I-EST.] Tiresome; dull.

pro'te-an, 1 prō'tĭ-ən; 2 prō'te-an, *a.* Assuming various forms; changeable.

pro-tect'd, 1 pro-tekt'; 2 pro-tĕct', *vt.* To preserve in safety; guard; defend.— **pro-tec'tion,** *n.* The act of protecting; a protected condition; that which protects; a system of duties designed to favor home industries.— **pro-tec'tion-ist,** *n.* One who favors protection.— **pro-tec'tiv(es,** *a.* Affording or suitable for protection; sheltering.— **pro-tec'tor,** *n.* One who protects; a defender.

pro-tect'er‡.— pro-tec'tor-ate, *n.* The protection and partial control of a weak nation by a stronger.— **pro-tec'tor-ship,** *n.*— **pro-tec'tress,** *n. fem.*

pro″té′gé′, 1 pro″tē′zē′; 2 prō″tę′zhę′, *n.* [-GÉE′, 1 -zē′; 2 -zhę′, *fem.*] One specially cared for by another.

pro'te-id, 1 prō'tı-ıd; 2 prō'te-id, *n.* A compound essential element of living cells and of the diet of animals.— **pro'te-in,** *n.* A compound obtained from proteids.

pro-test'ᵈ, 1 pro-test′; 2 pro-tĕst′, *v.* **I.** *t.* To assert earnestly; declare solemnly; formally declare the non-payment of. **II.** *i.* To enter a protest; make a solemn asseveration or objection.— **Prot′es-tant. I.** *a.* **1.** Pertaining to Protestants or to Protestantism. **2.** [p-] Making a protest. **II.** *n.* A member of one of those bodies of Christians opposed to Roman Catholicism.— **pro-test′er.— Prot′es-tant-ism,** *n.* The principles and doctrines of Protestant churches.— **prot″es-ta′tion,** *n.* The act of protesting, or that which is protested.

pro'test, 1 prō'test; *n.* The act of protesting; solemn or formal objection; declaration of non-payment.

pro'ton, 1 prō'tŏn; 2 prō'tŏn, *n.* An electrically charged component of an atom.

pro'to-plasm, 1 prō'to-plazm; 2 prō'to-plăsm, *n.* A semiliquid, viscid substance that forms the principal portion of an animal or vegetable cell.

pro'to-type, 1 prō'to-taip; 2 prō'to-tīp, *n.* A primitive form; original.

pro-tract'ᵈ, 1 pro-trakt′; 2 pro-trăct′, *vt.* To extend; lengthen; prolong.— **pro-trac'tion,** *n.*

pro-trude', 1 pro-trūd′; 2 pro-trud′, *vt. & vi.* [PRO-TRUD′EDᵈ; PRO-TRUD′ING.] To push or thrust out; project outward.— **pro-tru'sion,** *n.*— **pro-tru'sive(eˢ,** *a.*

pro-tu'ber-ant, 1 pro-tiū′bǝr-ǝnt; 2 pro-tū′ber-ant, *a.* Swelling out; bulging.— **pro-tu'ber-ance,** *n.*

proud, 1 praud; 2 proud, *a.* **1.** Feeling or manifesting pride; arrogant; haughty. **2.** Being a cause of honorable pride. **-ly,** *adv.*

prove, 1 prūv; 2 prǫv, *v.* [PROVED; PROV′ING.] **I.** *t.* **1.** To establish by evidence. **2.** To test. **3.** To learn by experience. **II.** *i.* To turn out, or be found to be.

prov'en-der, 1 prov'en-dǝr; 2 prŏv'ĕn-der, *n.* Food for cattle; provisions generally.

prov'erb, 1 prov'ǝrb; 2 prŏv'ĕrb, *n.* A brief, pithy saying; a maxim; byword.— **pro-ver'bi-al,** *a.* **1.** Pertaining to or like a proverb. **2.** Well-known; notorious.— **pro-ver'bi-al-ly,** *adv.*

pro-vide', 1 pro-vaid′; 2 pro-vīd′, *vt. & vi.* [PRO-VID′EDᵈ; PRO-VID′ING.] To make, pro-cure, or furnish for future use; supply; stipulate.— **pro-vid'ed,** *conj.* On condition. — **prov'i-dence,** *n.* **1.** The care exercised by the Supreme Being over the universe; also, a providential event or circumstance. **2.** [P-] Hence, the Deity. **3.** The exercise of foresight.— **prov'i-dent,** *a.* Exercising foresight; economical. **-ly,** *adv.*— **prov″i-den′tial,** *a.* Resulting from or exhibiting the action of God's providence. **-ly,** *adv.*— **pro-vid'er,** *n.*

prov'ince, 1 prŏv'ıns; 2 prŏv'inç, *n.* A large division of a country; a department; sphere.— **pro-vin'cial. I.** *a.* Pertaining to a province; local; narrow. **II.** *n.* An inhabitant of a province.— **pro-vin'cial-ism,** *n.* — **pro-vin'cial-ly,** *adv.*

pro-vi'sion, 1 pro-viʒ′ǝn; 2 pro-vĭzh′on. *I.* *vt.* To furnish with food. **II.** *n.* **1.** Measures taken in advance. **2.** A supply of food. **3.** A stipulation.— **pro-vi'sion-al,** *a.* Temporary. **-ly,** *adv.*

pro-vi'so, 1 pro-vai′zō; 2 pro-vī′șō, *n.* A conditional stipulation.— **pro-vi'so-ry,** *a.* Containing or made dependent on a proviso.— **pro-vi'so-ri-ly,** *adv.*

pro-voke', 1 pro-vōk′; 2 pro-vōk′, *v.* [PRO-VOKED′ᵗ; PRO-VOK′ING.] **I.** *t.* **1.** To offend. **2.** To stimulate. **3.** To occasion; to elicit. **II.** *i.* To produce resentment. — **prov″o-ca′tion,** *n.* **1.** The act of provoking. **2.** An incitement to action.— **pro-voc'a-tiv(eˢ,** 1 pro-vok′ǝ-tiv *or* -vō′ka-tiv; 2 pro-vŏc'a-tiv *or* -vō′ca-tiv. **I.** *a.* Serving to provoke. **II.** *n.* That which provokes, or tends to provoke or stimulate.

prov'ost, 1 prev′ost *or* pro′vō′; 2 prŏv'ost *or* pro′vō′, *n.* A magistrate; college officer.— **provost marshal,** a military or naval officer exercising various police functions.

prow, 1 prau; 2 prow, *n.* The fore part of a vessel's hull; the bow; stem.

prow'ess, 1 prau′es; 2 prow'ĕs, *n.* Strength, skill, and intrepidity in battle.

Prow of a Roman Galley.

prowl, 1 praul; 2 prowl, *vt. & vi.* To roam about stealthily, as in search of prey.— **prowl'er,** *n.*

prox'i-mate, 1 prøks′ı-mıt; 2 prŏks'i-mat, *a.* Near; next.— **prox'i-mate-ly,** *adv.*— **prox-im'i-ty,** *n.* The state of being near.

prox'i-mo, 1 prøks′ı-mō; 2 prŏks'i-mō, *adv.*

1: ǝ = final; ı = habit; aisle; au = out; oil; iū = feud; chin; go; ŋ = sing; thin, this.
2: wǫlf, dǫ; bōōk, bōōt; fŭll, rŭle, cūre, bŭt, bŭrn; oil, bŏy; g̅o, g̅em; iŋk; thin, this.

In or of the coming month: abbreviated *prox.*

prox'y, 1 prŏks'ı; 2 prŏks'y, *n.* [PROX'IES², *pl.*] A substitute empowered to act for another, the right so to act, or the instrument conferring it.

prude, 1 prūd; 2 prụd, *n.* One who makes an affected display of modesty.— **prud'er-y,** *n.* Primness; assumed coyness.— **prud'ish,** *a.*— **prud'ish-ly,** *adv.*

pru'dent, 1 prū'dent; 2 prụ'dĕnt, *a.* Cautious; judicious; sagacious; foreseeing; provident; economical. **-ly,** *adv.*— **pru'dence,** *n.* The quality of being prudent; sagacity; economy; discretion.— **pru-den'-tial,** *a.* **-ly,** *adv.*

prune, 1 prūn; 2 prụn, *vt. & vi.* [PRUNED; PRUN'ING.] To cut off superfluous branches; trim; dress, as a bird its feathers.— **prun'er,** *n.* [2. A plum.

prune, *n.* **1.** The dried fruit of the plum.

pru'ri-ent, 1 prū'rı-ent; 2 prụ'ri-ĕnt, *a.* Impure in thought and desire.

Prus'sian, 1 prush'an; 2 prŭsh'an. **I.** *a.* Pertaining to Prussia, in Germany. **II.** *n.* A citizen of Prussia.— **prussian blue,** a coloring substance used in dyeing, etc.— **prus'sic,** 1 prŭs'ık; 2 prŭs'ic, *a.* Pertaining to Prussian blue.— **prussic acid,** an extremely poisonous liquid compound. **hydrocyanic acid‡.**

pry¹, 1 praı; 2 prī. **I.** *vt. & vi.* [PRIED; PRY'ING.] To observe carefully or slyly; scrutinize. **II.** *n.* [PRIES², *pl.*] A sly and searching inspection.

pry², 1 praı; 2 prī. **I.** *vt.* [PRIED; PRY'ING.] To act on or move with a lever. **II.** *n.* A lever.

psalm, 1 säm; 2 säm, *n.* A sacred song or lyric.— **psalm'ist,** *n.* A composer of psalms.— **psal'mo-dy,** *n.* **1.** Psalm-singing. **2.** A collection of psalms.

Psal'ter, 1 sêl'tạr; 2 sạl'ter, *n.* The Book of Psalms.— **psal'ter-y,** *n.* [-IES², *pl.*] **1.** A Hebrew stringed musical instrument. **2.** A Psalter.

pseu'do-nym, 1 siū'do-nim; 2 sū'do-nȳm, *n.* A fictitious name; pen-name, as of a writer.— **pseu-don'y-mous,** *a.*

Psaltery.

psy'chic, 1 saı'kık, -kı-kəl; 2 sī'cie, **psy'chi-cal,** -ci-cal, *a.* Pertaining to the mind or soul.

psy-chol'o-gy, 1 saı-kəl'o-jı; 2 sī-cŏl'o-ğy, *n.* The science of the human soul and its operations.— **psy"cho-log'i-cal,** *a.* **psy"cho-log'ic‡.**— **psy"cho-log'i-cal-ly,** *adv.*— **psy-chol'o-gist,** *n.*

ptar'mi-gan, 1 tär'mı-gən; 2 tär'mi-ğan, *n.* [-GANS² or -GAN, *pl.*] A grouse of elevated

or arctic regions of the northern hemisphere, with winter plumage white.

Ptarmigan. ¹⁄₁₄

pto'ma-in, }
pto'ma-ine, }
1 tō'mə-in; 2 tō'ma-ĭn, *n.* A poisonous alkaloid, derived from decomposing animal matter.

pu'ber-ty, 1 piū'bər-tı; 2 pū'ber-ty, *n.* Opening manhood or womanhood.

pub'lic, 1 pub'lık; 2 pŭb'lic. **I.** *a.* Pertaining to the public at large; open to all; well-known. **II.** *n.* The people collectively.— **public house. 1.** An inn, tavern, or hotel. **2.** [Eng.] A liquor-saloon.— **pub'li-can,** *n.* **1.** [Eng.] The keeper of a public house. **2.** *Rom. Hist.* One who farmed or collected the public revenues; a tax-gatherer.— **pub"li-ca'tion,** *n.* **1.** The act of publishing. **2.** A newspaper, magazine, etc.— **pub-lic'i-ty,** *n.* The state of being public.— **pub'lic-ly,** *adv.*

pub'li-cize, 1 pub'lı-saiz; 2 pŭb'li-çiz, *vt.* [Colloq. 'U. S.] To give publicity to; to make notorious, esp., in newspapers.— **pub'li-cized,** *a. & p. p.* Notorious; publicly known: generally in an invidious sense.

pub'lic-ness, 1 pub'lık-nes; 2 pŭb'lic-nĕs, *n.* The state or quality of being public; publicity.

pub'lish, 1 pub'lısh; 2 pŭb'lish, *vt.* **1.** To make known publicly; circulate. **2.** To issue, as from the press.— **pub'lish-er,** *n.*

puck'er, 1 puk'ər; 2 pŭk'er. **I.** *vt. & vi.* To gather into small wrinkles; corrugate. **II.** *n.* A wrinkle, or group of wrinkles.

pud'ding, 1 pud'ın; 2 pụd'ing, *n.* **1.** A dessert of soft food. **2.** A large sausage.

pud'dle, } 1 pud'l; 2 pŭd'l. **I.** *vt.* [PUD'-
pud'l'ᴾ, } DLED, PUD'LDᴾ; PUD'DLING.] **1.** To convert (melted pig iron) into wrought iron by melting and stirring. **2.** To make muddy. **II.** *n.* A small pool of dirty water.— **pud'dler,** *n.*

pu'er-ile, } 1 piū'ər-il; 2 pū'er-ĭl, *a.* Child-
pu'er-il³, } ish; immature; weak; silly.

puff, } 1 puf; 2 pŭf. **I¹.** *vt. & vi.* To in-
puf³, } flate; swell; praise fulsomely; pant; breathe hard. **II.** *n.* **1.** A sudden, forcible breath; a whiff. **2.** Public and fulsome praise. **3.** A spongy or fluffy article.— **puff'y,** *a.*

pug, 1 pug; 2 pŭg. *n.* **1.** A pug-dog. **2.** A monkey.— **pug'-dog³,** *n.* A small, short-haired dog with upturned nose.— **pug'-nose³,** *n.* A short nose, slightly turned up at the end; a snub-nose.

1: ȧrtistic, ȧrt; fat, fāre; fạst; get, prēy; hit, polīce; obey, gō; nøt, ôr; fùll, rūle; but, būrn.

2: ärt, āpe, făt, fâre, fȧst, whạt, ạll; mē, gĕt, prȩy, fẽrn; hĭt, īce; Ï = ē; Ī = ē; gō, nŏt, ôr, wȯn,

pu′gi-lism, 1 piū′jı-lizm; 2 pū′gi-lĭşm, *n.* The art of boxing or fighting with the fists.—**pu′gi-list,** *n.*—**pu″gi-lis′tic,** *a.*

pug-na′cious, 1 pŭg-nē′shŭs; 2 pŭg-nā′-shŭs, *a.* Disposed to fight; quarrelsome.—**-ly,** *adv.*—**pug-nac′i-ty,** *n.*

pu′is-sance, 1 piū′ı-sans; 2 pū′i-sanç, *n.* Power; ability to fight or conquer.—**pu′is-sant,** *a.* **-ly,** *adv.*

pule, 1 piūl; 2 pūl, *vi.* [PULED; PUL′ING.] To peep; whimper.

pull, 1 pul; 2 pul, *vt.* & *vi.* To draw **pul²,** with force; haul; drag; tug; pluck. **II.** *n.* **1.** The act of pulling; draft. **2.** An advantage, as through political favoritism.

pul′let, 1 pul′et; 2 pul′ĕt, *n.* A young hen.

pul′ley, 1 pul′ı; 2 pul′y, *n.* A wheel for transmitting power by means of a cord or belt.

pul′mo-na-ry, 1 pul′mo-nē-rı; 2 pŭl′mo-nā-ry, *a.* Pertaining to the lungs. **pul-mon′ic‡.**

pulp, 1 pulp; 2 pŭlp, *n.* A moist, soft mass, as the soft, succulent part of fruit.—**pulp′ous,** *a.* **pulp′y‡.**

pul′pit, 1 pul′pit; 2 pul′pit, *n.* **1.** An elevated stand or desk for a preacher in a church. **2.** The preacher's office; the clergy.

pul′sate, 1 pul′sēt; 2 pŭl′sāt, *vi.* [PUL′-SAT″ED; PUL′SAT″ING.] To throb; beat.—**pul-sa′tion,** *n.* A throbbing; a heart-beat.

pulse, 1 puls; 2 pŭls, *vi.* [PULSED; PULSTS; PULS′ING.] To pulsate.

pulse¹, *n.* The rhythmic beating of the arteries; pulsation. [beans, etc.

pulse², *n.* Leguminous plants, as peas,

pul′ver-ize, 1 pul′vər-aiz; 2 pŭl′vẽr-īz, *vt.* & *vi.* [-IZED; -IZ′ING.] To reduce or become reduced to powder; to crush. **pul′ver-ise‡.**—**pul″ver-i-za′tion** or **-sa′tion,** *n.*

pu′ma, 1 piū′mə; 2 pū′ma, *n.* An American carnivore, ranging from Canada to Patagonia.

pum′ice, 1 pum′ıs; 2 pŭm′is, *n.* Volcanic **pum′iss,** lava: used as a polishing-material.—**pu-mi′ceous, pu-mic′i-form, pu′mi-cose,** *a.*

pump, 1 pump; 2 pŭmp, *vt.* & *vi.* To raise with, or as with, a pump; extort information; question closely.

pump¹, *n.* A device for raising, exhausting, or compressing a fluid.

pump², *n.* A light shoe for dancing.

pump′kin, 1 pump′kın; 2 pŭmp′kin (*Colloq.* 1 pung′kın; 2 pŭng′kin), *n.* A trailing vine or its large, yellow fruit.

pun, 1 pun; 2 pŭn, *vt.* & *vi.* [PUNNED; PUNS; PUN′NING.] To make a play on

words. **II.** *n.* The use of a word in two senses. [hole or indentation in.

punch¹t, 1 punch; 2 pŭnch, *vt.* To make a **punch²t,** *vt.* To beat or strike.—**punch′er,** *n.*

punch¹, *n.* A tool or machine for perforating or indenting.

punch², *n.* A drink of wine or spirits, sweetened, flavored, and diluted with water.

punch³, *n.* A blow, thrust, poke, or nudge.

Punch⁴, *n.* The mock-hero in a comic performance of puppets.

pun′cheon¹, 1 pun′chən; 2 pŭn′chon, *n.* **1.** An upright supporting timber. **2.** A punch or perforating tool.

pun′cheon², *n.* A liquor-cask holding from 72 to 120 gallons.

punc-til′i-o, 1 punk-tıl′ı-o; 2 pŭnc-til′i-o, *n.* A nice point of etiquette.—**punc-til′-i-ous,** *a.* Very exact in the forms of etiquette; ceremonious.—**-ly,** *adv.* **-ness,** *n.*

punc′tu-al, 1 punk′chu-[or -tiu-]əl; 2 pŭnc′chu-[or -tū-]al, *a.* Exact as to appointed time. **-ly,** *adv.*—**punc″tu-al′i-ty,** *n.* [-TIES², *pl.*] Promptness. **punc′tu-al-ness‡.**

punc′tu-ate, 1 punk′chu-[or -tiu-]ēt; 2 pŭnc′chu-[or -tū-]āt, *vt.* & *vi.* [-AT″ED; -AT′ING.] To mark, as printed matter, with significant points; use points indicating division or connection.—**punc″tu-a′tion,** *n.* The use of significant points, as comma, period, etc.

punc′ture, 1 punk′chur or -tiūr; 2 pŭnc′-chur or -tūr. **I.** *vt.* [-TURED; -TUR-ING.] To pierce. **II.** *n.* A small hole made by piercing.

pun′dit, 1 pun′dıt; 2 pŭn′dit, *n.* [Anglo-Ind.] A learned Brahmin; any learned man.

pun′gent, 1 pun′jent; 2 pŭn′gĕnt, *a.* Pricking; stinging; caustic; keen. **-ly,** *adv.*—**pun′gen-cy,** *n.*

Pu′nic, 1 piū′nık; 2 pū′nic, *a.* Carthaginian; among the Romans, faithless; untrustworthy.

pun′isht, 1 pun′ısh; 2 pŭn′ish, *vt.* To inflict a penalty upon; requite with penalty; chastise; castigate.—**pun′ish-a-ble‡,** *a.*—**pun′ish-ment,** *n.* Penalty; also, the act of punishing.—**pu′ni-tiv(e‡,** *a.* Pertaining to punishment.

punk, 1 punk; 2 pŭnk, *n.* Decayed wood used as tinder, or an artificial substitute for it. [who puns.

pun′ster, 1 pun′stər; 2 pŭn′ster, *n.* One

punt¹, 1 punt; 2 pŭnt, *v.* **I.** *t.* **1.** To propel, as a boat, by pushing with a pole. **2.** In football, to give a punt to (the ball). **II.** *i.* To go hunting or fishing in a punt.

punt, *n.* **1.** A flat-bottomed boat. **2.** A barge propelled with a pole. **3.** The

---

1: ə = final; ı = habit; aisle; au = out; oil; iū = feud; chin; go; ŋ = sing; thin, this.
2: wolf, dọ; bōōk, bōōt; full, rule, cūre, bŭt, bûrn; öil, böy; go, gem; iŋk; thin, this.

kicking of a dropped football before it strikes the ground.

pu′ny, 1 piū′nı; 2 pu′ny, *a.* [PU′NI-ER; PU′NI-EST.] Weak and insignificant.

pu′pa, 1 piū′pə; 2 pū′pa, *n.* [PU′PÆ, 1 piū′pī; 2 pū′pē, *pl.*] The stage of a transforming insect that precedes the perfect form.

pu′pil[1], 1 piū′pıl; 2 pū′pil, *n.* A person under the care of a teacher; scholar; learner.— **pu′pil-age,** *n.* The state of being a pupil. [eye.

pu′pil[2], *n.* The opening in the iris of the

pup′pet, 1 pup′et; 2 pŭp′ĕt, *n.* A small figure made to move by wires.

pup′py, 1 pup′ı; 2 pŭp′y, *n.* [PUP′PIES[Z], *pl.*] A young dog; whelp; silly fop.— **pup′py-ish,** *a.*— **pup′py-ism,** *n.*

pur′blind″, 1 pûr′blaind″; 2 pûr′blīnd″, *a.* Dim-sighted or near-sighted.— **pur′blind″ness,** *n.*

pur′chase, 1 pûr′ɕhıs; 2 pûr′chas. **I.** *vt.* [PUR′CHASED[t], PUR′CHAST[S]; PUR′CHAS-ING.] To buy. **II.** *a.* **1.** The act of purchasing, or that which is purchased. **2.** An advantage, as of leverage, for moving heavy bodies or the like.— **pur′chas-a-bl**(e[e], **pur′chase-a-bl**(e[r], *a.*— **pur′chas-er,** *n.* A buyer.

pure, 1 piūr; 2 pūr, *a.* Free from mixture or defilement; unmingled; refined. **2.** Absolute; mere; sheer.— **pure′ly,** *adv.* Wholly; very.— **pure′ness,** *n.* Purity.

purge, 1 pûrj; 2 pûrġ. **I.** *vt. & vi.* [PURGED; PURG′ING.] **1.** To cleanse; purify; clear. **2.** To cleanse the bowels by medicinal action. **II.** *n.* A medicine that purges. — **pur-ga′tion,** *n.* A purging, purifying, or clearing.— **pur′ga-tiv**(e[s], **I.** *a.* Efficacious in purging. **II.** *n.* A purging medicine; cathartic.— **pur′ga-to′ri-al,** *a.* Of or pertaining to purgatory.— **pur′ga-to-ry,** *n.* [-RIES[Z], *pl.*] *R. C. Ch.* An intermediate state where souls are made fit for heaven by expiatory suffering.

pu′ri-fy, 1 piū′rı-fai; 2 pū′ri-fy, *v.* [-FIED; -FY″ING.] **I.** *t.* To make clear or pure; cleanse. **II.** *i.* To grow or become pure or clean.— **pu′ri-fi-ca′tion,** *n.*— **pu′ri-fi″-er,** *n.*

Pu′ri-tan, 1 piū′rı-tən; 2 pū′ri-tan. **I.** *a.* Pertaining to the Puritans; scrupulously rigid in morals. **Pu′ri-tan′ic‡**; **Pu′ri-tan′i-cal‡**. **II.** *n.* **1.** One of a sect of English Protestants (1559) who advocated popular rights and opposed ritualism and all laxity of morals. **2.** One of the Pilgrim settlers of New England.— **Pu′ri-tan-ism,** *n.*

pu′ri-ty, 1 piū′rı-tı; 2 pū′ri-ty, *n.* The state of being pure.

purl, 1 pûrl; 2 pûrl, *vi.* To flow with a bubbling sound; ripple.

pur′lieu, 1 pûr′lıū; 2 pûr′lū, *n. pl.* The outskirts of any place.

pur-loin′, 1 pûr-ioin′; 2 pûr-lŏin′, *vt.* To steal.— **pur-loin′er,** *n.*

pur′pl(e, 1 pûr′pl; 2 pûr′pl. **I.** *vt. & vi.* **pur′pl**[P], [PUR′PL(E)D[P]; PUR′PLING.] To make or become purple. **II.** *a.* Of the color of purple. **III.** *n.* **1.** A color of mingled red and blue. **2.** Royal dignity; rank; wealth. **3.** The office of a cardinal.

pur′port, 1 pûr′pōrt; 2 pûr′pōrt. **I**[d]. *vt. & vi.* To signify; mean; imply. **II.** *n.* A meaning intended; import; significance.

pur′pose, 1 pûr′pəs; 2 pûr′pos. **I.** *vt. & vi.* [PUR′POSED[t], PUR′POST[S]; PUR′POS-ING.] To determine; resolve; intend. **II.** *n.* A plan intended to be carried out; design; settled resolution.— **pur′pose-ly,** *adv.*

purr, 1 pûr; 2 pûr. **I.** *vi.* To make a low **purr**[r], murmuring sound, as a cat. **II.** *n.* A prolonged murmur, as of a cat when pleased.— **pur′ring,** *pa. & n.*— **pur′ring-ly,** *adv.*

purse, 1 pûrs; 2 pûrs. **I.** *vt.* [PURSED[t], PURST[S]; PURS′ING.] **1.** To draw into wrinkles. **2.** To place in a purse. **II.** *n.* **1.** A small bag for carrying money. **2.** A treasury. **3.** Money offered as a prize. — **purs′er,** *n.* An officer having charge of the accounts, etc., of a vessel; paymaster.

pur-sue′, 1 pûr-siū′; 2 pûr-sū′, *v.* [PUR-SUED′; PUR-SU′ING.] **I.** *t.* To follow persistently; chase; hunt; seek; continue; keep up. **II.** *i.* To continue; proceed. — **pur-su′ance,** *n.* The act of pursuing; consequence; continuance: usually followed by *of*.— **pur-su′ant. I.** *a.* Conformable. **II.** *adv.* Agreeably; conformably; usually with *to*.— **pur-su′er,** *n.*— **pur-suit′,** *n.* The act of pursuing; a business followed; vocation.

pur′sy, 1 pûr′sı; 2 pûr′sy, *a.* Short-breathed; fat.

pu′ru-lent, 1 piū′ru-lent; 2 pū′ru-lĕnt, *a.* Consisting of or secreting pus.— **pu′ru-lence,** *n.*

pur-vey′, 1 pûr-vē′; 2 pûr-vē′, *vt. & vi.* To provide (supplies).— **pur-vey′ance,** *n.*— **pur-vey′or,** *n.*

pur′view, 1 pûr′viū; 2 pûr′vū, *n.* Extent; sphere; scope.

pus, 1 pus; 2 pŭs, *n.* Secretion from inflamed tissues.

push, 1 pusɦ; 2 push. **I**[t]. *vt. & vi.* To press against; urge forward; thrust. **II.** *n.* **1.** A propelling or thrusting pressure. shove. **2.** An emergency. **3.** Activity; energy.— **push′-ball″,** *n.* A game like foto-

---

1: ȧrtistic, ȧrt; fat, fāre; fȧst; get, prēy; hĭt, police; obey, gō; nŏt, ōr; full, rŭle; bŭt, bûrn.

2: ärt, āpe, făt, fâre, fȧst, whąt, ąll; mē, gĕt, prĕy, fêrn; hĭt, īce; ī = ē; ĭ = ē̆; gō, nŏt, ôr, wŏn,

ball played with a ball six feet in diameter, weighing 48 pounds.

pu″sil-lan′i-mous, 1 piū″si-lan′i-mus; 2 pū″si-lăn′i-mŭs, *a.* Mean-spirited; cowardly. **-ly,** *adv.* **-ness,** *n.* — **pu″sil-la-nim′i-ty,** *n.*

puss, 1 pus; 2 pus, *n.* A cat, hare, or rabbit. — **pus′sy,** *n.* [PUS′SIES², *pl.*] Puss. — **pus′sy-foot″,** *n.* To tread softly and stealthily: used figuratively.

pus′tule, 1 pus′tiūl; 2 pŭs′tūl, *n.* A small pimple. — **pus′tu-lar,** *a.*

put, 1 put; 2 put, *v.* [PUT; PUT′TING.] **I.** *t.* To set; lay; place; express; render; commit; apply; urge. **II.** *i.* To direct one's course; steer; move.

pu′ta-tive, 1 piū′ta-tiv; 2 pū′ta-tĭv, *a.*
pu′ta-tive⁵, Supposed; reputed.

pu′tre-fy, 1 piū′tri-fai; 2 pū′tri-fȳ, *vt. & vi.* [-FIED; -FY′ING.] To rot; decay; decompose. — **pu″tre-fac′tion,** *n.* The act or process of putrefying: decay. — **pu″tre-fac′tiv(e⁵,** *a.* — **pu-tres′cence,** *n.* — **pu-tres′cent,** *a.* Becoming putrid.

pu′trid, 1 piū′trid; 2 pū′trid, *a.* Putrefying; rotten. **-ness,** *n.* — **pu-trid′i-ty,** *n.*

put′ty, 1 put′i; 2 pŭt′y. **I.** *vt.* [PUT′TIED; PUT′TY-ING.] To fill up with putty. **II.** *n.* A mixture of whiting and oil for filling cracks, etc.

puz′zle, 1 puz′l; 2 pŭz′l. **I.** *vt. & vi.*
puz′lᴿ, [PUZ′(Z)L(E)Dᴿ; PUZ′(Z)LINGᴿ.] To confuse or be confused; perplex; mystify. **II.** *n.* A perplexing problem; perplexity; quandary. — **puz′zler,** *n.*

pyg′my, *a. & n.* Same as PIGMY.

py-ja′mas, *n. pl.* [Anglo-Ind.] Pajamas.

pyr′a-mid, 1 pir′a-mid; 2 pȳr′a-mĭd, *n.* A solid having a rectilinear, usually square, base, and with triangular sides meeting in an apex. — **py-ram′i-dal,** *a.* **pyr″a-mid′ic‡; pyr″a-mid′i-cal‡.**

Pyramid.

pyre, 1 pair; 2 pȳr, *n.* A heap of combustibles arranged for burning a dead body.

py-ret′ic, 1 pai-ret′ik; 2 pȳ-rĕt′ic. **I.** *a.* **1.** Affected with or relating to fever; febrile. **2.** Remedial in fevers. **II.** *n.* A remedy in fevers.

py′rite, 1 pai′rait; 2 pȳ′rīt, *n. Mineral.* [PY-RI′TES, 1 pi-rai′tiz; 2 pȳ-ri′tēs, *pl.*] An opaque compound of iron with sulfur, of a pale yellow color, its appearance suggesting gold. Called also *fool's gold*, *pyrites*, or *iron pyrites*.

py″ro-tech′nic, 1 pai″ro-tek′nik; 2 pȳ″ro-tĕc′nic, *a.* Pertaining to fireworks. **py″ro-tech′ni-cal‡.** — **py″ro-tech′nies,** *n.* Fireworks. — **py″ro-tech′nist,** *n.*

Py-thag″o-re′an, 1 pai-thag″o-rē′an; 2 pȳ-thăg″o-rē′an. **I.** *a.* Of or pertaining to Pythagoras, a Greek philosopher of the 6th century B. C. **II.** *n.* A follower of Pythagoras. — **Py-thag″o-re′an-ism,** *n.*

py′thon, 1 pai′thon; 2 pȳ′thŏn, *n.* **1.** A large non-venomous serpent that crushes its prey in its folds. **2.** A soothsayer.

Q

Q, q, 1 kiū; 2 kū, *n.* [QUES, Q's, or Qs, 1 kiūz; 2 kūs, *pl.*] The seventeenth letter in the English alphabet.

quack⁴, 1 kwak; 2 kwăk, *vi.* To utter a quack. [duck.

quack¹, *n.* A croaking sound, as of a

quack², *n.* A pretender, as to medical skill. — **quack,** *a.* **quack′er-y,** *n.* [-IES², *pl.*] Ignorant pretense or practise, as in medicine.

quad′ran″gle, 1 kwed′raŋ″gl; 2 kwad′-răŋ″gl, *n.* A plane figure having four sides and four angles; a court so shaped. — **quad-ran′gu-lar,** *a.* **-ly,** *adv.*

quad′rant, 1 kwed′rant; 2 kwad′rant, *n.* **1.** The quarter of a circle, or of its circumference. **2.** An instrument for measuring angles. — **quad′rant-al,** *a.*

quad′rate, 1 kwed′rēt; 2 kwad′rāt. **I.** *a.* Square. **II.** *n.* Something square. — **quad-rat′ic.** **I.** *a.* Pertaining to a square. **II.** *n. Alg.* An equation of the second degree.

quad-ren′ni-al, 1 kwed-ren′i-al; 2 kwad-rĕn′i-al, *a.* Occurring once in four years; comprising four years. **-ly,** *adv.*

Gunners' Quadrant.

quad′ri-lat′er-al. **I.** *a.* Four-sided. **II.** *n.* A four-sided figure.

qua-drille′, 1 kwə-drïl′; 2 kwa-drïl′, *n.* A square dance for four or more couples, or the music for it.

quad-ril′lion, 1 kwəd-ril′yən; 2 kwạd-rïl′yon, *n.* A cardinal number: (1) In the French (and U. S.) system of numeration, 1 followed by 15 ciphers. (2) In the English system, 1 followed by 24 ciphers.

quad″ri-syl′la-ble, } 1 kwəd″ri-sïl′ə-bl;
quad″ri-syl′la-bl², } kwạd″ri-sỹl′a-bl, *n.* A word of four syllables.

quad-roon′, 1 kwəd-rūn′; 2 kwạd-rōōn′, *n.* A person having one-fourth negro and three-fourths white blood.

quad-ru′ma-na, 1 kwəd-rū′mə-nə; 2 kwạd-ru′ma-na, *n. pl.* An order of four-handed animals, including monkeys. — **quad-ru′ma-nous**, *a.* Four-handed, as monkeys.

quad′ru-ped, 1 kwəd′ru-ped; 2 kwạd′ru-pĕd. **I.** *a.* Having four feet. **II.** *n.* An animal having four feet. — **quad-ru′pe-dal**, *a.*

quad′ru-ple, } 1 kwəd′ru-pl; 2 kwạd′ru-pl.
quad′ru-pl², } **I.** *vt. & vi.* [-PL(E)D³; -PLING.] To make or become quadruple. **II.** *a.* Consisting of or multiplied by four. — **quad′ru-plex**, *a.* Fourfold. — **quad″ru-pli-ca′tion**, *n.*

quaff, } 1 kwaf; 2 kwáf, *vt. & vi.* To
quaf², } drink freely. [boggy.

quag′gy, 1 kwag′i; 2 kwặg′y, *a.* Yielding;

quag′mire″, 1 kwag′mair″; 2 kwặg′mïr″, *n.* Marshy ground that gives way under the foot; bog.

quail, 1 kwēl; 2 kwãl, *vi.* To shrink from facing **t r i a l** or pain; cower; lose heart.

quail, *n.* A small game-bird; a bob-white or the like.

quaint, 1 kwēnt; 2 kwãnt, *a.* Pleasingly odd or old-fashioned. **-ly,** *adv.* **-ness,** *n.*

quake, 1 kwēk; 2 kwãk. **I.** *vi.* [QUAKED²; QUAK′-ING.] To shake; tremble. **II.** *n.* A shaking, tremulous motion. — **quak′er,** *n.* 1. One who quakes. 2. [Q-] A member of the Society of Friends. — **Quak′er-ism,** *n.* — **quak′ing-ly,** *adv.*

European Migratory
Quail. ¹/₇

qual′i-fy, 1 kwol′i-fai; 2 kwạl′i-fỹ, *v.* [-FIED²; -FY′ING.] **I.** *t.* 1. To fit for an office or occupation. 2. To limit or modify; mitigate; restrict. **II.** *i.* To prepare for entering upon a function, employment, etc. — **qual″i-fi″a-bl**(e³, *a.* — **qual″-i-fi-ca′tion,** *n.* 1. The act of qualifying. 2. That which fits a person or thing for something. 3. A restriction; mitigation. — **qual′i-fi″er,** *n.*

qual′i-ty, 1 kwol′i-ti; 2 kwạl′i-ty, *n.* [-TIES², *pl.*] 1. Essential property; characteristic. 2. Degree of goodness. 3. Capacity. — **qual′i-ta″tiv**(e³, *a.* Pertaining to quality; having to do with qualities only: distinguished from *quantitative.*

qualm, 1 kwäm; 2 kwäm, *n.* 1. A feeling of sickness. 2. A twinge of conscience. — **qualm′ish,** *a.* **-ly,** *adv.*

quan′da-ry, 1 kwon′də-ri; 2 kwạn′da-ry, *n.* [-RIES², *pl.*] A state of hesitation or perplexity.

quan′ti-ty, 1 kwon′ti-ti; 2 kwạn′ti-ty, *n.* [-TIES², *pl.*] A certain mass, volume, or number; an object having assignable dimensions or amount. — **quan″ti-ta″tiv**(e³, *a.* Pertaining to quantity or quantities: distinguished from *qualitative.*

quar″an-tine′, 1 kwor″ən-tīn′; 2 kwạr″an-tïn′, *n.* The temporary isolation of persons, ships, or goods liable to bring contagious disease; also, a place for such isolation.

quar′rel, 1 kwor′el; 2 kwạr′ĕl. **I.** *vi.* [-RELED or -RELLED, -RELD³; -REL-ING or -REL-LING.] To dispute; fall out; disagree. **II.** *n.* An angry or violent dispute; also, the cause of dispute. — **quar′rel-some,** *a.* — **quar′rel-some-ness,** *n.*

quar′ry, 1 kwor′i; 2 kwạr′y, *vt.* [QUAR′-RIED; QUAR′RY-ING.] To take, as stone, from a quarry. — **quar′ri-er,** *n.*

quar′ry¹, *n.* [QUAR′RIES², *pl.*] An excavation from which stone is cut.

quar′ry², *n.* A hunted beast or bird; game; prey.

quart, 1 kwôrt; 2 kwạrt, *n.* The fourth part of a gallon, or two pints; a vessel containing this amount.

quar′ter, 1 kwôr′tər; 2 kwạr′ter, *vt.* To divide or separate into four equal parts; to furnish with quarters; lodge. — **quar′tered,** *a.* 1. Divided into quarters. 2. Made of timber cleft or sawed lengthwise into quarters, so as to show the edge-grain; as, *quartered* oak. 3. Provided with quarters; lodged. 4. Having quarters.

quar′ter¹, *n.* 1. One of four equal parts of anything. 2. One of the four principal points of the compass. 3. A place; locality; assigned position; lodging. — **quar′ter-day″**, *n.* A day when quarterly payments become due. — **q.-deck,** *n. Naut.* The elevated rear part of the deck of a war-vessel: for officers only. — **quar′ter-ly.** **I.** *a.* Containing a fourth part. 2. Occurring once every

three months. **II.** *n.* [-LIES^z, *pl.*] A quarterly publication. **III.** *adv.* **1.** Once in a quarter of a year. **2.** In or by quarters.— **quar'ter-mas"ter,** *n.* **1.** A staff-officer, having charge of providing quarters, issuing supplies, etc. **2.** *Naut.* A petty officer who assists the navigator, etc.— **quar'ter-sec'-tion,** *n.* [U.S.] A tract of land half a mile square, containing 160 acres.

quar'ter², *n.* Mercy shown in sparing the life of a defeated enemy.

quar'tern, 1 kwêr'tẽrn; 2 kwạr'tern, *n.* A fourth part, as of certain measures or weights; a four-pound loaf. **quartern loaf‡.**

quar-tet', 1 kwêr-tet'; 2 kwạr-tĕt', *n.* Four things of a kind; a musical composition for four voices or instruments, or the four persons who render it. **quar-tette'‡.**

quar'to, 1 kwêr'to; 2 kwạr'to. **I.** *a.* Having four leaves to the sheet. **II.** *n.* A book or pamphlet whose pages are of the size of the fourth of a sheet.

quartz, 1 kwêrts; 2 kwạrts, *n.* A hard mineral, common in rocks, as in granite.— **quartz'ose,** *a.*

quash, 1 kwosh; 2 kwạsh, *vt.* To set aside, as an indictment; suppress forcibly or summarily.

quas'si-a, 1 kwosh'ı-ə *or* kwash'ı-ə; 2 kwạsh'i-a *or* kwash'i-a, *n.* The wood of the bitter ash: used as a tonic.

qua-ter'na-ry, 1 kwə-tūr'nı-rı; 2 kwa-tĕr'-na-ry, *a.* **1.** Consisting of four things. **2.** Fourth in order.

qua-ter'ni-on, 1 kwə-tūr'nı-ən; 2 kwa-tĕr'-ni-on, *n.* A set, system, or file of four.

qua'ver, 1 kwē'vẽr; 2 kwā'ver. **I.** *vt. & vi.* To sing tremulously; have a tremulous sound or motion; trill. **II.** *n.* A tremulous motion; a shake; trill; an eighth note.

quay, } 1 kī; 2 kē, *n.* A wharf; pier; arti-
key^P, } ficial landing-place.

quean, 1 kwīn; 2 kwēn, *n.* **1.** A low woman. **2.** A young or unmarried woman.

quea'sy, 1 kwī'zı; 2 kwē'sy, *a.* **1.** Sick at the stomach; nauseated. **2.** Nauseating. **3.** Easily nauseated; hence, fastidious. **4.** Difficult: delicate, as a subject or question.— **quea'si-ly,** *adv.*— **quea'si-ness,** *n.*

queen, 1 kwīn; 2 kwēn, *n.* **1.** The wife of a king; a female sovereign of a kingdom; a woman preeminent in a given sphere. **2.** The most powerful piece in chess. **3.** The female of ants, bees, etc.— **queen'ly,** *a.*— **queen bee,** the mother-bee of a hive; a perfectly developed female bee, larger than the undeveloped females called *workers,* and whose sole office is to lay eggs for the maintenance and upbuilding of the colony.— **queen consort,** the wife of a

reigning king, who does not share his sovereignty.— **q. dowager,** the widow of a king who has reigned in his own right.— **q. mother,** the mother of the reigning sovereign when she is entitled to be called queen or is a queen dowager.— **q. regent. 1.** A queen who acts as regent. **2.** A queen regnant.— **q. regnant,** a female sovereign ruling in her own right.— **queen's'ware,** *n.* Fine glazed cream-colored English pottery; hence, any cream-colored pottery.

queer, 1 kwîr; 2 kwēr, *a.* Singular; odd; eccentric; quaint. **-ly,** *adv.* **-ness,** *n.*

quell, } 1 kwel; 2 kwĕl, *vt.* To subdue, **quell^P,** } as by force; put down; calm. **-er,** *n.*

quench^t, 1 kwench; 2 kwĕnch, *vt.* To put out, as fire; subdue, as passion; extinguish. **-a-ble(ᵉʳ,** *a.* [*quirer.*

que'rist, 1 kwī'rist; 2 kwē'rist, *n.* An inquirer.

quer'u-lous, 1 kwer'u-lus; 2 kwĕr'u-lŭs, *a.* Complaining. **-ly,** *adv.* **-ness,** *n.*

que'ry, 1 kwī'rı; 2 kwē'ry. **I.** *vt. & vi.* [QUE'RIED; QUE'RY-ING.] To question; doubt; make inquiry. **II.** *n.* [QUE'RIES², *pl.*] An inquiry to be answered; a doubt; interrogation. [seeking; search.

quest, 1 kwest; 2 kwĕst, *n.* The act of

ques'tion, 1 kwes'chən; 2 kwĕs'chon. **I.** *vt. & vi.* To put a question to; make inquiry; doubt. **II.** *n.* **1.** A sentence calling for an answer; an inquiry. **2.** A controversy; difference; objection. **3.** A proposition under discussion.— **ques'-tion-a-ble(ᵉʳ,** *a.* Liable to be called in question; doubtful. **-ness,** *n.*— **ques'tion-a-bly,** *adv.*— **ques'tion-a-ry,** *a.*— **ques"tion-naire',** 1 kes"chən-nār'; 2 kĕs'chon-när', *n.* A series of questions for formal answer.— **ques'tion-er,** *n.*

queue, 1 kiū; 2 kū, *n.* A pendent braid of hair on the back of the head; a pigtail.

quib'ble, } 1 kwib'l; 2 kwĭb'l. **I.** *vi.* [QUIB'-
quib'l^P, } BLED; QUIB'LD; QUIB'BLING.] To use evasions; play upon words. **II.** *n.* An evasion; equivocation.— **quib'bler,** *n.*

quick, 1 kwik; 2 kwĭk. **I.** *a.* **1.** Done in a short time; rapid; swift; alert; sprightly. **2.** Irritable. **3.** Having life. **II.** *n.* That which has life; any vital or sensitive part. **III.** *adv.* Quickly; rapidly.— **quick'en,** *vt. & vi.* **1.** To make or become alive. **2.** To make quicker; accelerate.— **quick'en-er,** *n.*— **quick'lime,** *n.* Unslaked lime.— **quick'-ly,** *adv.* In a quick manner.— **quick'-ness,** *n.*— **quick'sand,** *n.* A bed of sand so water-soaked as readily to engulf any person or animal that attempts to rest upon it.— **quick'-sight"ed,** *a.*— **quick'sil"ver,** *n.* **1.** Metallic mercury. **2.** An amalgam of tin, used for the backs of looking-glasses.— **quick'step",** *n. Mus.* A march written in the military quick time.

quid, 1 kwĭd; 2 kwĭd, *n.* **1.** A small portion of chewing-tobacco. **2.** A cud, as of a cow.

quid'di·ty, 1 kwĭd'ĭ-tĭ; 2 kwĭd'i-ty, *n.* [-TIES², *pl.*] **1.** The essence of a thing. **2.** A trifling distinction.

quid'nunc, 1 kwĭd'nŭṇk; 2 kwĭd'nūṇe, *n.* An inquisitive busybody.

qui'et, 1 kwai'et; 2 kwī'ĕt. **I**d. *vt. & vi.* To bring to a state of rest; become still. **II.** *a.* Being in a state of repose; silent; tranquil; gentle. **III.** *n.* Freedom from motion, noise, etc.; calm.— **qui·es'cence,** *n.* The state of being quiescent.— **qui·es'cent,** *a.* **1.** Being in a state of repose. **2.** Resting free from anxiety. **-ly,** *adv.*— **qui'et·ism,** *n.* A system of passive religious contemplation as a means of holiness; mystic meditation.— **qui'et·ist,** *n.*— **qui'et·ly,** *adv.*— **qui'et·ness,** *n.* The state or fact of being quiet.— **qui'e·tude,** *n.* Quietness.— **qui·e'tus,** *n.* A silencing; death; repose; quittance.

quill, 1 kwĭl; 2 kwĭl, *vt.* To make or iron (a **quill**ᴾ, fabric) with rounded plaits or ridges.

quill, *n.* **1.** A large, strong feather of a **quill**ᴾ, bird; a hollow, sharp spine of a porcupine. **2.** A pen. **3.** A rounded ridge, or fold, as in a ruffle.

quilt, 1 kwĭlt; 2 kwĭlt. **I**d. *vt. & vi.* To stitch through and through at intervals or in lines or figures. **II.** *n.* A bed-cover made by stitching together two layers of cloth with padding between them.

quince, 1 kwĭns; 2 kwĭnç, *n.* A small tree of the apple family; also, its fruit, used for preserves.

quin'in, 1 kwĭn'ĭn *or* kwai'nain; 2 kwĭn'-
quin'ine, in *or* kwī-nīn,
n. A bitter alkaloid contained in cinchona-bark, or its salts: used for malarial affections.

quin-quen'ni·al, *a.* Occurring every five years; lasting for five years.

quin'sy, 1 kwĭn'zĭ; 2 kwĭn'sy, *n.* Inflammation of the tonsils.

quin'tal, 1 kwĭn'təl; 2 kwĭn'tạl, *n.* **1.** A mass of 100 kilograms. **2.** A hundredweight.

quin-tes'sence, 1 kwĭn-tĕs'ens; 2 kwĭn-tĕs'ĕnç, *n.* A concentrated extract; the most essential part of anything.

quin-tet', 1 kwĭn-tĕt'; 2 kwĭn-tĕt',
quin-tette, *n.* A musical composition ar-

Branch of *Cincho-
na calisaya,* a
source of Quinin.
a, the flower; *b,* a
dehiscent fruit.

ranged for five voices or instruments; also the five persons performing it.

quin-til'lion, 1 kwĭn-tĭl'yən; 2 kwĭn-tĭl'-
yon, *n.* (1) In the French (U. S.) system of numeration, 1 followed by 18 ciphers. (2) In the English system, 1 followed by 30 ciphers.

quin'tu·ple(eᴾ, 1 kwĭn'tiu-pl; 2 kwĭn'tū-pl.
I. *vt. & vi.* [-PL(E)Dᴾ; -PLING.] To multiply by five. **II.** *a.* Multiplied by five.— **quin'tu·plet,** *n.* **1.** Five things of a kind used or occurring together; specif., a bicycle with tandem seats for five riders. **2.** One of five born of the same mother at one birth.

quip, 1 kwĭp; 2 kwĭp, *n.* A sneering or mock- [ing remark.
ery remark.

quire, 1 kwair; 2 kwīr, *n.* Twenty-four (or twenty-five) sheets of paper.

quirk, 1 kwûrk; 2 kwûrk, *n.* A short turn.

quit, 1 kwĭt; 2 kwĭt. **I.** *vt. & vi.* [QUIT or QUIT'TEDᵈ; QUIT'TING.] **1.** To cease or desist; let go; forsake; abandon. **2.** To acquit; free or clear. **II.** *a.* Discharged; released; clear; free.— **quit'claim″.**
I. *vt.* To relinquish or give up all claim or title to. **II.** *n.* A full release and acquit-tance.— **quit'tance,** *n.* **1.** Discharge or release. **2.** Recompense.

quite, 1 kwĭt; 2 kwĭt, *adv.* **1.** To the fullest extent; fully; totally. **2.** To a great extent; considerably. [tremble.

quiv'er, 1 kwĭv'er; 2 kwĭv'ĕr, *vi.* To
quiv'er¹, *n.* A portable case for arrows.
quiv'er², *n.* The act of quivering; a shaking.

qui vive, 1 kĭ vĭv; 2 kī vĭv. Literally, who lives? who goes there? the challenge of a sentinel: the phrase often used as an English noun.— **to be on the qui vive,** to be on the lookout, as a sentinel; to be wide-awake, eager, watchful, expectant.

quix-ot'ic, 1 kwiks-ŏt'ĭk; 2 kwĭks-
ŏt'ie, *a.* Ridiculously chivalrous or romantic.— **quix-ot'i-cal-ly,** *adv.*
Quiver.

quiz, 1 kwĭz; 2 kwĭz. **I.** *vt. & vi.* [QUIZZED⁴; QUIZ'ZING.] **1.** To make game of; chaff. **2.** To peer at. **3.** To examine by questions. **II.** *n.* **1.** An absurd or puzzling question or suggestion. **2.** One given to quizzing.— **quiz'zi-cal,** *a.*

quoit, 1 kwoit; 2 kwŏit, *n.* **1.** A disk of iron, for pitching. **2.** *pl.* A game played by throwing these disks at a short stake.

quon'dam, 1 kwŏn'dəm; 2 kwŏn'dam, *a.* Former.

quo'rum, 1 kwō'rum; 2 kwō'rŭm, *n.* **1.** Number of members necessary for the transaction of business. **2.** [Eng.] Certain designated justices of the peace.

---

quo'ta, 1 kwō'tə; 2 kwō'ta, *n.* A proportional part or share.

quote, 1 kwōt; 2 kwōt, *vt. & vi.* [QUOT'-ED‡; QUOT'ING.] **1.** To repeat, as the words of a book or of a speaker; to cite; make a quotation. **2.** To give the market price of.— **quot'a-bl**(e**r**, *a.*— **quo-ta'-**

tion, *n.* **1.** The act of quoting. **2.** The words or price quoted.

quoth‖, 1 kwōth; 2 kwōth, *vt.* Said or spoke.

quo'tient, 1 kwō'shent; 2 kwō'shĕnt, *n. Math.* A number indicating how often one number is contained in another; the result obtained by division.

R

R, r, 1 är; 2 är, *n.* [ARS, R's, or *R*s, 1 ärz; 2 ärs, *pl.*] The eighteenth letter in the English alphabet.

rab'bet, 1 rab'et; 2 răb'ĕt. **I**d. *vt. Joinery.* To cut a rectangular-groove in. **II.** *n.* A groove cut to receive the edge of an adjoining piece; a joint so made.

Rabbets.

rab'bi, ⎰ 1 rab'ai *or* -ī, -ĭn; 2 răb'ī *or* -i,
rab'bin, ⎱ -ĭn, *n.* Master; teacher: a Jewish title.— **rab-bin'ic, rab-bin'i-cal,** *a.*

rab'bit, 1 rab'ıt; 2 răb'ĭt, *n.* A rodent resembling, but smaller than, the hare.— **Welsh rabbit,** cheese toasted or melted, seasoned, and served on toast. See RAREBIT.

rab'ble, 1 rab'l; 2 răb'l, *n.* A rude crowd; mob; the populace.

rab'id, 1 rab'ıd; 2 răb'id, *a.* **1.** Affected with rabies; mad. **2.** Violent; furious. **-ly,** *adv.* **-ness,** *n.*

ra'bi-es, 1 rē'bi-ĭz; 2 rā'bi-ēş, *n.* An extremely fatal infectious disease, occurring among members of the canine family, communicable to man and other animals by inoculation, as by the bite of a rabid animal: popularly called *hydrophobia.*

rac-coon', 1 ra-kūn'; 2 ră-ēōon', *n.* An American carnivore related to the bear.

ra-coon'‡.

race, 1 rēs; 2 rāç, *vt. & vi.* [RACED‡; RAC'-ING.] To move or cause to move swiftly; match or contend in a contest of speed.

Raccoon. ¹⁄₃₈

race¹, *n.* A series of descendants from a common ancestry; lineage; pedigree.

race², *n.* **1.** A trial of speed. **2.** Movement; career. **3.** A sluice.— **race'±course",** *n.* A track over which a race is run.

ra-ceme', 1 rə-sīm'; 2 ra-çēm', *n.* A cluster of flowers arranged at intervals on a stem.— **rac'e-mose,** 1 ras'ı-mōs'; 2 răç'e-mōs', *a.*

ra'cial, 1 rē'shəl; 2 rā'shal, *a.* Pertaining to or characteristic of race. **-ly,** *adv.*

rack¹ᵗ, 1 rak; 2 răk, *vt.* To torture; pain; stretch; tear; strain. [liquors.

rack²ᵗ, *vt.* To draw off from the lees, as

rack³ᵗ, *vi.* To move, as a horse, with the gait called rack.

rack¹, *n.* **1.** A machine for stretching or straining; an instrument of torture by which the limbs were stretched or strained. **2.** An open grating or frame-work. **3.** A bar having teeth that engage with those of a gear-wheel.

rack², *n.* A quadruped's motion resembling the pace, two feet on a side being moved at once.

rack'er, 1 rak'ər; 2 răk'er, *n.* One who or that which racks, as a racking horse.

rack'et¹, 1 rak'et; 2 răk'ĕt, *n.* An implement for striking a ball, as in tennis.

rack'et², *n.* **1.** A clattering or confused noise; commotion; frolic; spree. **2.** [U.S.] An occupation by which money is made by legitimate means or otherwise.— **rack"et-eer',** *n.* [U.S.] **1.** One who engages in boot-legging, beer-running, or other illegal occupations. **2.** One who terrorizes legitimate business to obtain control, or to collect graft.

rac'y, 1 rēs'ı; 2 rāç'y, *a.* [RAC'I-ER; RAC'I-EST.] **1.** Having a pungent interest; spicy. **2.** Having a special flavor, as wine. **3.** Racial.— **rac'i-ly,** *adv.*— **rac'i-ness,** *n.*

ra'dar, 1 rē'dar; 2 rā'där, *n.* An electro-magnetic device for locating aircraft, ships, and other distant objects.

ra'di-al, 1 rē'di-əl; 2 rā'di-al. **I.** *a.* Pertaining to a ray or to a radius. **II.** *n.* A radiating part. **-ly,** *adv.* [Brightness.

ra'di-ance, 1 rē'di-əns; 2 rā'di-anç, *n.*

ra'di-ant, 1 rē'di-ənt; 2 rā'di-ant, *a.* Emitting or issuing in rays, as of light or heat; beaming, as with joy. **-ly,** *adv.*

ra'di-ate, 1 rē'di-ēt; 2 rā'di-āt. **I.** *vt. & vi.* [-AT"ED⁴; -AT"ING.] To send out in rays; issue in rays. **II.** *a.* Divided or separated into rays; having rays; radiating.— **ra"di-a'tion,** *n.* The act of radiating, or the state of being radiated.— **ra'di-a"tor,** *n.*

rad'i-cal, 1 rad'i-kəl; 2 răd'i-cal. **I.** *a.* **1.** Proceeding from or pertaining to the root; essential; fundamental. **2.** Thoroughgoing; unsparing; extreme. **II.** *n.*

1. An extremist. **2.** The primitive part of a word; a root; radicle. **3.** *Math.* A quantity of which the root is required. — **rad'i-cal-ism,** *n.* The state or character of being radical or a radical.— **rad'i-cal-ly,** *adv.*— **rad'i-cal-ness,** *n.*

rad'i-cle, 1 răd'ĭ-kl; 2 răd'ĭ-el, *n.* **1.** *Bot.* A diminutive root or rootlet. **2.** *Anat. & Zool.* A root or root-like part.

ra'di-o, 1 rē'dĭ-o; 2 rä'dĭ-o. **I.** *a.* Of or pertaining to rays, radiation, or radium. **II.** *n.* **1.** A radio receiving-set and all its accessories, such as wiring, tubes, amplifier, etc. **2.** Wireless telegraphy or telephony. — **ra"di-o-ac-tiv'i-ty,** *n.* The energy, force, or penetrating power of radium.— **ra"di-o-am'pli-fi'er,** *n.* A vacuum-tube used with a radioreceiver to increase the intensity of any communication sent by wireless telegraphy or telephony.— **ra"di-o-broad'cast"-er,** *n.* An apparatus for disseminating concerts, speeches, etc., by radio; also, the person who operates it.— **ra"di-o-broad'cast"ing,** *n.* The act of sending communications by radio.— **ra"di-o-de-tec'tor,** *n.* One of various devices used in discovering the presence of electric waves.— **ra'di-o-gram,** *n.* A radiotelegram.— **ra'di-o-graph,** *n.* An X-ray picture; skiagraph.— **ra"di-o-re-ceiv'er,** *n.* A device for receiving communications by radio.— **ra"di-o-tel'e-gram, ra"di-o-tel'-e-phone,** *n.* A telegram- or telephone-message sent by wireless telegraphy or telephony.

rad'ish, 1 răd'ĭsh; 2 răd'ish, *n.* An annual plant or its pungent, edible root.

ra'di-um, 1 rē'dĭ-um; 2 rä'dĭ-ŭm, *n.* A metallic chemical element of great radioactivity, found in pitchblende.

ra'di-us, 1 rē'dĭ-us; 2 rä'dĭ-ŭs, *n.* [RA'DI-I, 1 -aī; 2 -ī, *pl.*] **1.** A straight line from the center of a circle or sphere to its periphery. **2.** The bone of the forearm on the same side as the thumb.

raf'fle, 1 raf'l; 2 răf'l **I.** *vt. & vi.* [RAF'-FLED, RAF'LD^P; RAF'FLING.] To sell by or take part in a raffle. **II.** *n.* A form of lottery.— **raf'fler,** *n.*

raft, 1 raft; 2 răft. **I.** *vt. & vi.* To transport or travel by raft. **II.** *n.* A float of logs or planks fastened together.— **rafts'-man,** *n.*

raft'er, 1 raft'ẽr; 2 răft'ẽr, *n.* A timber supporting a roof.

rag, 1 rag; 2 răg, *n.* **1.** A torn piece of cloth; fragment. **2.** *pl.* Tattered clothing.— **rag'ged,** *a.* Torn; clothed in rags; shabby; rough. **-ly,** *adv.* **-ness,** *n.*

rag"a-muf'fin, 1 rag'a-muf'in; 2 răg'a-mŭf'in, *n.* A worthless or ragged fellow.

rage, 1 rēj; 2 răg. **I.** *vi.* [RAGED; RAG'ING.] To be furious with anger; rave. **II.** *n.*

1. Violent anger. **2.** Extreme violence, as of a fever. **3.** A fad.— **rag'ing-ly,** *adv.*

ra-gout', 1 ra-gū'; 2 rä-gŭ', *n.* A highly seasoned stew of meat and vegetables; hence, anything spicy or piquant.

raid, 1 rēd; 2 răd. **I.** *vt. & vi.* To invade suddenly; make a raid. **II.** *n.* A hostile incursion; foray. [rails.

rail¹, 1 rēl; 2 răl, *vt.* To enclose or lay with rails.

rail², 1 rēl; 2 răl, *vi.* To use abusive language; scold. — **rail'er,** *n.*— **rail'ing,** *pa.* [on supports.

rail¹, *n.* A bar, as of wood or iron, resting

rail², *n.* A wading bird.

rail'ing, 1 rēl'ĭŋ; 2 răl'ing, *n.* **1.** A series of rails; a balustrade. **2.** Rails, or material for rails.

rail'ler-y, 1 rēl'ẽr-ı or ral'ẽr-ı; 2 răl'er-y or răl'er-y, *n.* Merry jesting; teasing; banter.

rail'road", 1 rēl'rōd"; 2 răl'rōd". **I**d. *vt.* To rush. **II.** *n.* A graded road, having parallel metal rails, for the passage of cars.

rall'way"‡. [Wearing apparel; clothing.

ral'ment‖, 1 rē'ment or -ment; 2 rä'ment, *n.*

rain, 1 rēn; 2 răn. **I.** *vt. & vi.* To pour down; shower. **II.** *n.* Water falling from the clouds in drops.— **rain'bow",** *n.* An arch of refracted and reflected light, seen usually at the close of a shower, exhibiting the spectrum colors.— **Rainbow Division** [U. S.], the first body of American National Guard troops representing the States of the Union, in the World War, 1917–18.

raise, 1 rēz; 2 răs, *vt.* [RAISED, RAIZD^P; RAIZ^P; RAIS'ING.] **1.** To move upward; lift; exalt. **2.** To produce; rear. **3.** To bring to an end, as a siege.

rai'sin, 1 rē'zn; 2 rä'sn, *n.* A dried grape.

ra'ja, 1 rä'jɐ; 2 rä'ja, *n.* A Hindu prince or chief.

ra'jah, } *prince or chief.*

rake¹, 1 rēk; 2 răk. **I.** *vt. & vi.* [RAKED; RAK'ING.] **1.** To scrape together. **2.** To stir with a rake; use a rake; make a search; ransack. **3.** To fire along the length of, as of a vessel or a line of soldiers. **II.** *n.* A toothed implement for drawing together loose material, or smoothing a surface. See page 13, fig. 4.

rake², **I**t. *vi.* To lean, as a mast; incline. **II.** *n.* Inclination from the perpendicular.

rake³, *n.* A dissolute, lewd man.

rak'ish¹, 1 rēk'ĭsh; 2 răk'ish, *a.* Having the masts unusually inclined; as, a *rakish* vessel.— **rak'ish-ness,** *n.*

rak'ish², *a.* Dissolute; profligate; jaunty.

ral'ly¹, 1 ral'ı; 2 răl'y. **I.** *vt. & vi.* [RAL'-LIED; RAL'LY-ING.] To reunite and re-animate; call together; revive; restore. **II.** *n.* [RAL'LIES², *pl.*] **1.** An assembling or reassembling, as of scattered troops. **2.** A recovery, as of health or vigor.

ral'ly², *vt. & vi.* To attack with raillery; joke; tease; banter.

ram, 1 ram; 2 răm. *vt. & vi.* [RAMMED, RAMD⁸; RAM'MING.] **1.** To strike; butt; batter. **2.** To press closely together; stuff.— **ram'mer,** *n.*

ram¹, *n.* A male of the sheep.

ram², *n.* **1.** An instrument for driving, forcing, battering, or crushing, as a projection from the bow of a war-vessel; also, a war-vessel constructed for ramming. **2.** An instrument for raising water by pressure of compressed air: called also *hydraulic ram.*

ram'ble, }1 ram'bl; 2 răm'bl. **I.** *vi.*
ram'bl⁰, }[RAM'BL(E)D⁴; RAM'BLING.] To wander about; roam; talk aimlessly. **II.** *n.* A leisurely stroll; a winding path; maze.— **ram'bler,** *n.*— **ram'bling,** *a.*

ram'ie, 1 ram'i; 2 răm'i, *n.* A shrubby Oriental plant, or a fine fiber yielded by its stem.

ram'i-fy, 1 ram'i-fai; 2 răm'i-fy, *vt & vi.* [-FIED; -FY'ING.] To divide or subdivide into branches.— **ram''i-fi-ca'tion,** *n.*

ra'mose, 1 rē'mōs; 2 rā'mōs, *a.* Branching; full of branches; branch-like. **ra'mous‡.**

ramp, 1 ramp; 2 rămp. **I**ᵗ. *vi.* To rear up; leap; rage; romp. **II.** *n.* A slope or inclination.— **ram'page,** *n.* Boisterous agitation or excitement.— **ram'pan-cy,** *n.*— **ram'pant,** *a.* **1.** Exceeding all bounds. **2.** Rearing; leaping.— **ram'pant-ly,** *adv.*

ram'part, 1 ram'pärt; 2 răm'pärt, *n.* **1.** The embankment around a fort. **2.** A bulwark.

ram'rod'', 1 ram'rod''; 2 răm'rŏd'', *n.* A rod used to drive home the charge of a muzzle-loading firearm.

ram'shack'le, 1 ram'shak'l; 2 răm'shăk'l, *a.* About to go to pieces from age and neglect; shaky hence, disorderly; unsteady.

ranch, 1 ranch, 2 rănch, *n.* A large tract of land with buildings, for keeping stock in large herds.— **ranch'er,** *n.*— **ran-che'ro,** 1 rän-che'ro; 2 rän-che'ro, *n.* A herdsman on a ranch. **ranch'man‡.**

ran'cid, 1 ran'sid; 2 răn'çid, *a.* Having the smell of oily substances that have begun to spoil; rank.— **ran-cid'i-ty,** *n.* **ran'cid-ness‡.**— **ran'cid-ly,** *adv.*

ran'cor, 1 raŋ'kər; 2 răŋ'cor, *n.* Bitter enmity; malice; grudge.— **ran'cor-ous,** *a.* **-ly,** *adv.* **-ness,** *n.* [less; casual.

ran'dom, 1 ran'dəm; 2 răn'dom, *a.* Aimrange, 1 rènj; 2 rāng, *v.* [RANGED; RANG'ING.] **I.** *t.* **1.** To pass through, by, or over; wander along. **2.** To arrange; array. **3.** To classify; rank. **II.** *i.* To lie in the same direction; have equal rank; followed by *with.*

range, *n.* **1.** The area over which anything moves; a tract of grazing land; reach, as of voice or shot. **2.** A line or row; class or series. **3.** A cooking-stove. — **rang'er,** *n.* **1.** A mounted patrolman or guerrilla; a gamekeeper; hunting-dog. **2.** *pl.* An armed band, designed to protect or ravage a country.— **rang'er-ship,** *n.*

rank‡, 1 raŋk; 2 răŋk, *v.* **I.** *t.* **1.** To place in a rank; form in line; range. **2.** To take precedence of. **II.** *i.* To have rank.

rank, *a.* **1.** Vigorous in growth. **2.** Strong and offensive; flagrant. **-ly,** *adv.* **-ness,** *n.*

rank, *n.* **1.** A line or row; a line of soldiers side by side: opposed to *file.* **2.** Relative position; grade; degree. **3.** High degree or position.

ran'kle, }1 raŋ'kl; 2 răŋ'kl, *vi.* [RAN'-
ran'kl⁰, }KL(E)D⁴; RAN'KLING.] To cause lingering distress; inflame; fester.

ran'sack‡, 1 ran'sak; 2 răn'săk, *vt. & vi.* To search through; explore; rummage.

ran'som, 1 ran'səm; 2 răn'som. **I.** *vt.* To secure the release of for a price; redeem. **II.** *n.* **1.** Money paid for the release of a person or property captured. **2.** Release purchased, as from captivity; redemption.— **ran'som-er,** *n.*

rant, 1 rant; 2 rănt. **I**ᵈ. *vi.* To speak loudly and extravagantly; rave. **II.** *n.* Bombastic talk.— **rant'er,** *n.*

rap, 1 rap; 2 răp. **I.** *vt. & vi.* [RAPPED‡, RAPT⁸; RAP'PING.] To strike sharply and quickly. **II.** *n.* A sharp blow or its sound.

ra-pa'cious, 1 rə-pē'shʊs; 2 ra-pā'shŭs, *a.* Given to plunder or rapine; extortionate; grasping. **-ly,** *adv.*— **ra-pac'i-ty,** *n.* **ra-pa'cious-ness‡.**

rape¹, 1 rēp; 2 răp, *n.* Forcible violation; a snatching away by force.

rape², *n.* A weedy Old World annual allied to the turnip, cultivated for feeding cattle.

rap'id, 1 rap'id; 2 răp'id. **I.** *a.* Having great speed; swift; fast; quick. **II.** *n.* A descent in a river less abrupt than a waterfall: usually in the plural.— **ra-pid'i-ty,** *n.* **rap'id-ness‡.**— **rap'id-ly,** *adv.*

ra'pi-er, 1 rē'pi-ər; 2 rā'pi-er, *n.* A light, long, and narrow sword adapted for thrusting.

Spanish
Rapier.

rap'in(e⁸, 1 rap'in; 2 răp'ĭn, *n.* The tak-

ing of property by superior force; spoliation.

rapt, 1 rapt; 2 răpt, *pa.* Enraptured;
transported, as with ecstasy.— **rap'ture,** *n.*
1. The state of being rapt; ecstasy. **2.**
An act expressive of utmost delight.— **rap'-
tur-ous,** *a.* **-ly,** *adv.*

rap-to'ri-al, *a.* **1.** Seizing and devouring
living prey, as hawks, etc. **2.** Adapted
for seizing and holding prey, as talons.

rare[1], 1 rār; 2 râr, *a.* [RAR'ER; RAR'EST.]
1. Infrequent; exceptionally valuable;
choice. **2.** Rarefied; thin.— **rar"e-fac'tion,**
n. The act of rarefying or the state of b ¿ing
rarefied.— **rar'e-fy,** *vt. & vi.* To make rare
or less dense.— **rare'ly,** *adv.*— **rare'ness,** *n.*
— **rar'i-ty,** *n.* The quality of being rare;
something valued for its scarceness.

rare[2], *a.* [U. S.] Not thoroughly cooked:
said especially of beef.

rare'bit, *n.* A Welsh rabbit: the form
rarebit is now generally regarded as erroneous. See RABBIT.

ras'cal, 1 ras'kəl; 2 răs'cal, *n.* An unprincipled fellow; a knave; scoundrel.
— **ras-cal'i-ty,** *n.* [-TIES², *pl.*] **1.** The quality of being rascally. **2.** A rascally act.—
ras'cal-ly, *a.* Unprincipled; knavish; base.

rase, 1 rēz; 2 răs, *vt.* Same as RAZE.

rash, 1 rash; 2 răsh, *a.* Reckless; precipitate. **-ly,** *adv.* **-ness,** *n.*

rash, *n.* A skin¤eruption.

rash'er, 1 rash'ər; 2 răsh'er, *n.* A thin slice
of meat.

rasp, 1 rasp; 2 răsp. I[t]. *vt. & vi.* To
scrape or grate, as with a rasp; treat
roughly; affect harshly. **II.** *n.* A file¤
like tool having coarse pyramidal projections for abrasions.— **rasp'er,** *n.*

rasp'ber"ry, 1 raz'ber'i; 2 răs'bĕr"y, *n.*
[-RIES², *pl.*] A thimble¤shaped berry, or
the shrub producing it.

ra'sure‡, 1 rē'ʒur; 2 ră'zhụr, *n.* Erasure.

rat, 1 rat; 2 răt, *n.* A rodent infesting
houses, barns, ships, etc.

rat'a-bl(e[P], 1 rēt'ə-bl; 2 răt'a-bl, *a.* **1.**
Subject to assessment or tax. **2.** Estimated proportionally. **3.** Capable of
being rated or valued.— **rat"a-bil'i-ty, rat'-
a-bl(e-ness**[P], *n.*— **rat'a-bly,** *adv.*

ratch'et, 1 rach'et; 2 răch'ĕt, *n.* A
notched wheel, the teeth of which engage
with a pawl. See illus. at PAWL. **ratch'-
et=wheel"**‡.

rate[1], 1 rēt; 2 răt, *v.* [RAT'ED[d]; RAT'ING.]
I. *t.* To estimate; assess. **II.** *i.* To be
estimated; have rank or value.

rate²[d], *vt. & vi.* To rail at; scold; reprove
with vehemence.

rate, *n.* Relative measure; degree; value;
price; rank; class; tax.

rath'er, 1 rath'ər; 2 răth'er, *adv.* **1.** With
preference; more willingly. **2.** With more
reason. **3.** Somewhat.

rat'i-fy, 1 rat'i-fai; 2 răt'i-fȳ, *vt.* [-FIED;
-FY"ING.] To sanction; make valid; confirm.— **rat"i-fi-ca'tion,** *n.*

ra'ti-o, 1 rē'shi-o; 2 ră'shi-o, *n.* Relation of
degree, number, etc.; proportion; rate.

ra"ti-oc'i-nate, 1 rash'i-os'i-nēt; 2 răsh"i-
ŏç'i-năt, *vi.* [-NAT"ED[d]: -NAT"ING.] To
draw a conclusion from premises; reason,
— **ra"ti-oc"i-na'tion,** *n.*— **ra"ti-oc'i-na"-
tiv(e**[s], *a.*

ra'tion, 1 rē'shən *or* rash'ən; 2 ră'shon *or*
răsh'on, *n.* A fixed allowance or portion,
as of food, for a day.

ra'tion-al, 1 rash'ən-əl; 2 răsh'on-al, *a.*
Possessing the faculty of reasoning; pertaining to the reason; reasonable; judicious.— **ra"tio-na'le,** 1 rash'o-nē'lī; 2 răsh'-
o-nā'lē, *n.* A rational exposition of principles.— **ra'tion-al-ism,** *n.* The formation
of opinions by relying upon reason alone.—
ra'tion-al-ist, *n.*— **ra"tion-al-is'tic, ra"-
tion-al-is'ti-cal,** *a.*— **ra"tion-al'i-ty,** *n.*
Reasonableness.— **ra'tion-al-ly,** *adv.*

rat'line, 1 rat'lin; 2 răt'lin, *n.* One of the
small ropes fastened across the shrouds of
a ship, used as the rounds of a ladder.
rat'lin‡. [Rat¤poison.

rats'bane", 1 rats'bēn"; 2 răts'băn", *n.*

rat-tan', 1 ra-tan'; 2 ră-tăn', *n.* **1.** The
flexible stem of an Oriental palm. **2.** A
cane or switch of rattan. **ra-tan'**‡.

rat'tle, ⎫ 1 rat'l; 2 răt'l. **I.** *vt. & vi.*
rat'l[P], ⎭ [RAT"TLED, RAT'LD[P]; RAT"TLING.]
1. To make a rattle; clatter. **2.** To utter in a
rapid and noisy manner. **II.** *n.* **1.** A
series of short, sharp sounds in rapid succession. **2.** A plaything or implement,
etc., adapted to produce a rattling noise.
3. Rapid and noisy talk; chatter.—
rat'tle-snake", *n.* A venomous American
snake, having loose bony rings on the tail,
that rattle when shaken.

rav'age, 1 rav'ij; 2 răv'ag. **I.** *vt.* [RAV'-
AGED; RAV'AG-ING.] To lay waste: de-
spoil. **II.** *n.* Violent and destructive
action; ruin; desolation.— **rav'ag-er,** *n.*

rave, 1 rēv; 2 răv, *vt. & vi.* [RAVED; RAV'-
ING.] To say wildly or incoherently;
talk or act wildly or rage as a madman.

rav'el, 1 rav'l; 2 răv'l, *vt. & vi.* [RAV'ELED
or -ELLED, -ELD³; RAV'EL-ING *or* -EL-LING.]
To take apart the threads of; disengage;
disentangle; unravel.— **rav'el-ing,** *n.* **1.** A
thread or threads raveled from a fabric. **2.**
The act of raveling. **rav'el-ling**‡.

rav'en, 1 rav'n; 2 răv'n. **I.** *vt. & vi.* **1.**
To capture by force; ravage. **2.** To eat

voraciously; prey upon; tear. **II.** *n.* The act of plundering; spoliation. **rav'in**‡.

ra'ven², 1 rĕ'vn; 2 rā'vn. **I.** *a.* Black and shining, like the plumage of a raven. **II.** *n.* A large crow=like bird.

rav'en-ous, *a.* Furiously voracious; extremely greedy or eager. **-iy**, *adv.* **-ness**, *n.*

Raven. 1/24

ra-vine', 1 ra-vīn'; 2 ra-vĭn', *n.* A deep gorge.

rav'ish‡, 1 rav'ĭsh; 2 răv'ish, *vt.* **1.** To transport with delight; enrapture. **2.** To violate. **-er**, *n.* **-ment**, *n.*

raw, 1 rē; 2 ra̤, *a.* **1.** Not cooked. **2.** Chafed; abraded. **3.** Bleak; chilling. **4.** Crude; fresh; inexperienced.— **raw'=boned"**, *a.* Bony; gaunt.— **raw'hide"**, *n.* A hide dressed without tanning, or a whip made of it.— **raw'ly**, *adv.*— **raw'ness**, *n.*

ray, 1 rē; 2 rā, *vt.* & *vi.* To provide with rays; send or go out as rays.

ray¹, *n.* A narrow beam of light; anything radiating from an object, as a spine of a fish's fin or a ray=like flower.— **ray'less**, *a.*

ray², *n.* A fish having the body depressed into the form of a flat disk; a torpedo.

ray'on, 1 rē'on; 2 rā'ŏn, *n.* A fabric made of lustrous textile fiber from cellulose.

raze, 1 rēz; 2 rāz, *vt.* [RAZED; RAZ'ING.] To level with the ground; demolish. **rase**‡.

ra'zor, 1 rē'zər; 2 rā'zor, *n.* A cutting-implement for shaving off the beard or hair.— **ra'zor=strop"**, *n.* A strop for sharpening razors. [the musical scale.

re, 1 rē; 2 re̤, *n. Mus.* The second note of

re-, red-, *prefix.* Back; backward; again; again and again; against; anew; over; opposite; as, *re*fit, *re*new.

Numerous compounds, in which *re-* has its unmodified meaning of *back, again, anew,* are practically self-explaining in connection with the definitions of their root-words. Compounds of *re-* which have special meanings will be found in vocabulary place.

re'ab-sorb'
re'ab-sorp'tion
re'ad-just'd, *v.*
re'ad-just'ment
re'ad-mit'd, *v.*
re'ad-mit'tance
re'a-dopt'd, *v.*
re-af-firm'
re-af-for'estd, *v.*
re-am'pu-tated, *v.*
re-an'i-mated, *v.*

re-an'i-ma'tion
re'an-nex't, *v.*
re-an'nex-a'tion
re'ap-pear'
re'ap-pear'ance
re'ap-point'd, *v.*
re'ap-point'ment
re'ap-por'tion
re-ar-range'
re'as-sem'blage
re'as-sem'bl(e)ᵖ
re'at-tach't, *v.*

re'at-tach'ment
re-bap'tism
re'bap-tize'
re-build', *v.*
re-bur'y
re-charge'
re-coin'
re-col"o-ni-za'tion
re-col'o-nize
re'com-bine'
re'com-mence't, *v.*
re'com-mit'd, *v.*
re'com-mit'ment
re'com-mit'tal
re-con'quer
re-con'se-crated, *v.*
re-con'se-cra'tion
re-cop'y
re-curve'
re-ded'i-cated, *v.*
re-ded'i-ca'tion
re'de-pos'itd, *v.*
re'di-gest'd, *v.*
re'dis-cov'er
re'dis-cov'er-er
re'dis-cov'er-y
re'dis-til'
re'dis-trib'uted, *v.*
re-dis'tri-bu'tion
re-ech'o
re'e-lect'd, *v.*
re'e-lec'tion
re'em-bark't, *v.*
re'en-act'd, *v.*
re'en-ac'tion
re'en-act'ment
re'en-dow'
re'en-gage'
re'en-gage'ment
re'en-list'd, *v.*
re'en-list'ment
re-en'ter
re-en'ter-ing
re-en'trant
re'es-tab'lisht, *v.*
re'es-tab'lish-ment
re'ex-am"i-na'tion
re'ex-am'ine
re'ex-port'd, *v.*
re-ex'port, *n.*
re-fash'ion
re-fer'ti-lize
re-fill'
re-flow'
re-hear'
re-hear'ing
re'im-port'd, *v.*
re-im'port, *n.*
re'im-pose'
re'in-aug'u-rated, *v.*
re'in-car'nated, *v.*
re'in-cor'po-rated, *v.*

re'in-fect'd, *v.*
re'in-fec'tion *
re'in-hab'itd, *v.*
re-in'te-grated, *v.*
re-in'te-gra'tion
re'in-ter'
re'in-vest'd, *v.*
re'in-ves'ti-gated, *v.*
re'in-ves'ti-ga'tion
re'in-vest'ment
re'in-vig'or-ated, *v.*
re-is'sue
re-kin'dle
re-land'd, *v.*
re-load'd, *v.*
re-mod"i-fi-ca'tion
re-mod'i-fy
re-mold'd, *v.*
re-name'
re-num'ber
re-nu'mer-ated, *v.*
re-oc'cu-py
re-o'pen
re'or-dain'
re-or'di-na'tion
re-or'gan-i-za'tion
re-or'gan-ize
re-pack't, *v.*
re-paint'd, *v.*
re-pass't, *v.*
re-peo'ple
re'pe-ru'sal
re'pe-ruse'
re-pol'isht, *v.*
re-pop'u-lated, *v.*
re-pop'u-la'tion
re'pos-sess't, *v.*
re'pos-ses'sion
re-pur'chaset, *v.*
re-pur'chase, *n.*
re-read', *v.*
re-sell'
re-set', *v.*
re-set', *n.*
re-set'tle
re-set'tle-ment
re-shape't, *v.*
re-ship't, *v.*
re-ship'ment
re-state'd, *v.*
re-state'ment
re'sup-ply'
re'sur-vey', *v.*
re-sur'vey, *n.*
re-take'
re-tell'
re-tri'al
re-val'u-a'tion
re-val'ue
re-var'nisht, *v.*
re-vis'it'd, *v.*
re-vis"i-ta'tion
re-write'

reach[t], 1 rĭċh; 2 rēch, v. **I.** t. **1.** To stretch out; extend; hand; deliver; pass. **2.** To touch; hit; arrive at; come to; attain; influence; move; affect. **II.** i. **1.** To stretch out the hand, foot, or something held; try to secure something. **2.** To extend to, approach, affect, or equal something.

reach, n. **1.** The act or power of reaching; distance one is able to reach. **2.** Something attained or attainable. **3.** An unbroken extent; expanse.

re-act'[d], 1 rɪ-akt; 2 re-ăct', vi. To act in response, in opposition, or in combination.—**re-ac'tion**, 1 rɪ-ak'shən; 2 re-ăc'shon, n. **1.** Reverse or return action. **2.** The mutual action of chemical agents, or its result.—**re-ac'tion-a-ry,** a. Tending to react or retrograde.

read, 1 rĭd; 2 rēd, v. [READ, 1 red, 2 rĕd; READ'ING, 1 rĭd'ɪŋ; 2 rēd'ing.] **I.** t. To understand, as written or printed characters, or any marks or signs; peruse; interpret; explain; also, to utter audibly what is so learned. **II.** i. To gain information, as from anything written or printed; utter aloud the contents, as of a book or manuscript.—**read,** 1 red; 2 rĕd, pa. Informed as by reading; acquainted with books or literature.—**read'a-bl(e)[r],** 1 rĭd'a-bl; 2 rēd'a-bl, a. Easy and pleasant to read; legible.—**read"a-bil'i-ty,** n.—**read'a-bly,** 1 rĭd'a-blɪ; 2 rēd'a-bly, adv.—**read'er,** 1 rĭd'ər; 2 rēd'er, n. **1.** One who reads. **2.** A text-book for instruction in reading.

read'i-ly, 1 red'ɪ-lɪ; 2 rĕd'i-ly, adv. In a ready manner; promptly; willingly.—**read'i-ness,** n. The quality or state of being ready.

read'ing, 1 rĭd'ɪŋ; 2 rēd'ing, n. **1.** The act of one who reads; study. **2.** That which is read; exact form of a passage or word in a given book; interpretation; rendering.

read'y, 1 red'ɪ; 2 rĕd'y, a. [READ'I-ER; **red'y**[s], READ'I-EST.] **1.** Prepared for use or action; quick; prompt; willing. **2.** Likely or liable; about. **3.** At hand; available; handy.—**read'y-made",** a.

re-a'gent, 1 rɪ-ē'jent; 2 re-ā'gĕnt, n. One who or that which reacts; a chemical agent.

re'al, 1 rĭ'al; 2 rē'al, a. **1.** Actual; genuine; veritable. **2.** Relating to or consisting of lands, or lands and buildings.—**re'al-ism,** n. **1.** In art and literature the depicting of things as they are held really to exist, without reference to any ideal standard. **2.** Philos. (1) The doctrine that the mind perceives real external objects and not merely its own impressions:

opposed to idealism. (2) The doctrine that general conceptions, as mankind, whiteness, virtue, exist as realities, apart from individual objects: opposed to nominalism.—**re-al'i-ty,** 1 rɪ-al'ɪ-tɪ; 2 re-ăl'ɪ-tɪ, n. [-TIES[z], pl.] The state or quality of being real; that which is real; actuality; being; fact.—**re'al-iz"a-bl(e)[r],** a That can or may be realized.—**re"al-i-za'tion** or **-sa'tion,** n.—**re'al-ize,** 1 rĭ'al-aiz; 2 rē'al-ız, v. [-IZED; -IZ'ING.] **I.** t. **1.** To perceive as a reality; feel or appreciate fully. **2.** To make real; accomplish in fact. **3.** To obtain as a profit; convert into cash. **II.** i. To convert property into cash; sell out. **re'al-ise[t].**—**re'al-ly,** 1 rĭ'al-ɪ; 2 rē'al-y, adv. In reality; actually.

realm, 1 relm; 2 rĕlm, n. A kingdom; **relm**[s], empire; domain.

re'al-ty, 1 rĭ'al-tɪ; 2 rē'al-ty, n. [-TIES[z], pl.] Real estate.

ream, 1 rĭm; 2 rēm, vt. To enlarge or taper (a hole) by cutting away material.

Reamers. 1. A reamer for wheel-hubs. 2. A reamer for metal-work.

reem[‡].—**ream'er,** n. One who or that which reams; a reaming-tool. **rim'mer**[‡].

ream, n. Twenty quires of paper.

reap[t], 1 rĭp; 2 rēp, v. **I.** t. To cut, as grain; clear of grain by cutting, as a field; obtain as a result. **II.** i. To cut and gather grain; receive a return or result.—**reap'er,** n. **1.** One who reaps. **2.** A reaping-machine.

rear, 1 rĭr; 2 rēr, v. **I.** t. To raise; elevate; set up; bring up; nurture and train, as children; raise, as animals. **II.** i. To rise upright, as a horse upon its hind legs.

rear, a. Being in the rear; last; hindmost.

rear, n. The hindmost part or position.—**rear'ward,** a. At or toward the rear.

rea'son, 1 rĭ'zn; 2 rē'gn, v. **I.** t. To prove or influence by reasoning; argue; persuade or dissuade. **II.** i. To use the reason; give reasons; argue.—**rea'son-er,** n.

rea'son, n. **1.** A proof; argument; motive; principle. **2.** A cause or condition. **3.** Mind; intellect; rational condition. **4.** Reasonable conduct or speech.—**rea'son-a-bl(e)[r],** 1 rĭ'zn-a-bl; 2 rē'gn-a-bl, a. Sensible; rational; moderate; fair. **-ness,** n.—**rea'son-a-bly,** adv.—**rea'son-ing,** 1 rĭ'zn-ɪŋ; 2 rē'gn-ing, n. The act of giving reasons; reasons given.

re"as-sure', 1 rĭ"a-shūr'; 2 rē"ă-shur', vt. To restore to courage or confidence.—**re"as-sur'ance,** n.

Ré"au"mur', 1 rē"ō"mür'; 2 rē"ō"mür', a. Denoting a thermometric scale, in which

1: ȧrtistic, ärt; fat, fāre, fạst; get, prẹy; hit, police; obey, gō; nɵt, ȯr; full, rūle; but, bûrn.

2: ärt, āpe, făt, fâre, fȧst, whạt, ạll; mē, gĕt, prẹy, fērn; hĭt, īce; ĭ = ē; ī = ē; gō, nŏt, ôr, wȯn.

zero corresponds to the temperature of melting ice, and 80° to that of boiling water: named from the inventor, 1731.

re-bel′, 1 ri-bel′; 2 re-bĕl′, *vi.* [RE-BELLED′, RE-BELD′S; RE-BEL′LING.] To resist forcibly government or authority.— **re-bel′lious,** ˏ ri-bel′yus; 2 re-bĕl′yŭs, *a.* Rebelling or disposed to rebel. **-ly,** *adv.* **-ness,** *n.* [refractory.

reb′el, 1 reb′el; 2 rĕb′ĕl, *a.* Rebellious.

reb′el, *n.* One who rebels.— **re-bel′lion,** 1 ri-bel′yan; 2 re-bĕl′yon, *n.* The act of rebelling; organized resistance to government or authority.

re-bound′d, 1 ri-baund′; 2 re-bound′, *vi.* To bound back; recoil.— **re-bound′,** *n.* A recoil.

re-buff′, 1 ri-buf′; 2 re-bŭf′. **It.** *vt.* To reject abruptly or rudely. **II.** *n.* A sudden repulse; curt denial; check; defeat.

re-buke′, 1 ri-biūk′; 2 re-būk′. **I.** *vt.* [RE-BUKED′t; RE-BUK′ING.] To reprove sharply; reprimand. **II.** *n.* A sharp reproof.

re′bus, 1 rī′bus; 2 rē′bŭs, *n.* [RE′BUS-ESᶻ, *pl.*] A pictorial riddle.

re-but′d, 1 ri-but′; 2 re-bŭt′, *vt. & vi.* [RE-BUT′TEDd; RE-BUT′TING.] To disprove; refute.— **re-but′tal,** *n.*— **re-but′ter,** *n.*

re-cal′ci-trant, 1 ri-kal′si-trant; 2 re-căl′çi-trant, *a.* Rebellious.

re-call′, 1 ri-kôl′; 2 re-eąl′. **I.** *vt.* **1.** To call back; countermand. **2.** To recollect. **II.** *n.* A calling back or countermanding; a signal to call back soldiers, etc.

re-cant′d, 1 ri-kant′; 2 re-cant′, *vt. & vi.* To retract, as a statement or opinion. — **re″can-ta′tion,** *n.*— **re-can′ter** *n.*

re″ca-pit′u-lated, 1 rī″ka-pich′u-lēt; 2 re″ca-pĭch′u-lāt, *vt. & vi.* To repeat concisely; review briefly; sum up.— **re″ca-pit″u-la′tion,** *n.*— **re″ca-pit′u-la-to-ry,** *a.*

re-cap′ture, 1 rī-kap′chur *or* -tiur; 2 rē-eăp′chur *or* -tūr. **I.** *vt.* To capture again. **II.** *n.* The act of retaking; a prize retaken.

re-cast′, 1 ri-sṽ′; 2 rē-eást′, *vt.* To cast again; form or fashion anew.

re-cede′l, 1 ri-sīd′; 2 re-çēd′, *vi.* [RE-CED-EDd; RE-CED′ING.] To move, tend, or incline backward; withdraw. [back.

re-cede′²d, 1 rī-sīd′; 2 rē-çēd′, *vt.* To cede

re-ceipt′, {1 ri-sīt′; 2 re-çēt′, **I**d. *vt. &* **re-ceit′ᴿ,** { *vi.* To give a receipt (for). **II.** *n.* **1.** The act of receiving; that which is received; a written acknowledgment of anything received. **2.** A recipe.

re-ceive′, 1 ri-sīv′; 2 re-çēv′, *vt.* [RE-**re-ceiv′ᴿ,** CEIV(E)D′S; RE-CEIV′ING.] To get; take; accept; admit; hold.— **re-ceiv′a-**

bl(eᴿ, *a.*— **re-ceiv′er,** *n.* One or that which receives: (1) a bell-shaped glass, as for holding gas; (2) one who has official charge of property, etc., under the orders of a court; (3) (*Elec.*) in telephone and telegraph systems, etc., a device for receiving a message: opposed to *transmitter*.

re-cen′sion, 1 ri-sen′shan; 2 re-çĕn′shon, *n.* **1.** A critical revision. **2.** A critique.

re′cent, 1 rī′sent; 2 rē′çĕnt, *a.* Pertaining to time not long past; modern; fresh; new.

re-cep′ta-cle, 1 ri-sep′ta-kl; 2 re-çĕp′ta-el, *n.* Anything that serves to contain or hold other things.

re-cep′tion, 1 ri-sep′shan; 2 re-çĕp′shon, *n.* **1.** The act of receiving, or the state of being received; receipt. **2.** A social entertainment.— **re-cep′tive** (eˢ, *a.* Ready to receive.— **re″cep-tiv′i-ty,** *n.* **re-cep′tiv**(e-ness)‡.

re-cess′, 1 ri-ses′ *or* rī′ses; 2 re-çĕs′ *or* rī′çĕs, *n.* **1.** A depression in a wall; niche. **2.** Cessation from employment; intermission.

re-ces′sion¹, 1 ri-sesh′an; 2 re-çĕsh′on, *n.* The act of receding; withdrawal.— **re-ces′sion-al.** **I.** *a.* Of or pertaining to recession or withdrawal. **II.** *n.* A hymn sung as the choir or the clergyman leaves the chancel after service.

re-ces′sion², *n.* The act of ceding again; a giving back; retrocession.

rec′i-pe, 1 res′i-pī; 2 rĕç′i-pē, *n.* [REC′I-PES, *pl.*] A formula; medical prescription: usually abbreviated to ℞.

re-cip′i-ent, 1 ri-sip′i-ent; 2 re-çĭp′i-ĕnt. **I.** *a.* Receptive. **II.** *n.* One who or that which receives.

re-cip′ro-cal, 1 ri-sip′ro-kal; 2 re-çĭp′ro-eal, *a.* **1.** Mutual; alternating. **2.** Mutually interchangeable, so that each may be the equivalent of the other.— **re-cip′ro-cal,** *n.*— **re-cip′ro-cal-ly,** *adv.*

re-cip′ro-cate, 1 ri-sip′ro-kēt; 2 re-çĭp′ro-eāt, *vt.* [-CAT″ᴇDd; -CAT″ING.] To give and take mutually; interchange.— **re-cip″ro-ca′tion,** *n.*— **rec″i-proc′i-ty,** 1 res′i-pros′i-ti; 2 rĕç″i-prŏç′i-ty, *n.* Reciprocal action or concession.

re-cite′d, 1 ri-sait′; 2 re-çīt′, *vt. & vi.* **1.** To relate; speak from memory; repeat (a lesson). **2.** To quote; cite.— **re-ci′tal,** 1 ri-sai′tal; 2 re-çī′tal, *n.* The act of reciting; a declamation; narration.— **rec″i-ta′tion,** 1 res′i-tē′shan; 2 rĕç″i-tā′shon, *n.* The act of repeating from memory, as a lesson to a teacher; time or occasion of reciting.— **rec″i-ta-tive′,** 1 res′i-ta-tīv′; 2 rĕç″i-ta-tīv′, *n. Mus.* Language uttered as in ordinary speech, but in musical tones.— **re-cit′er,** *n.*

reck[t], 1 rek; 2 rĕk, *vt. & vi.* To care (for); heed; mind.

reck′less, 1 rek′les; 2 rĕk′lĕs, *a.* Heedless of danger; desperate; rash. **-ly,** *adv.* **-ness,** *n.*

reck′on, 1 rek′n; 2 rĕk′n, *v.* **I.** *t.* **1.** To count; compute: often with *up.* **2.** To consider; esteem. **II.** *i.* **1.** To count or depend (*on* or *upon*). **2.** To calculate. **3.** To settle accounts (*with*).— **reck′on-er,** *n.*— **reck′on-ing,** 1 rek′n-ıŋ; 2 rĕk′n-ĭng, *n.* The act of counting; account or indebtedness; a settlement of accounts.

re-claim′, 1 rı-klēm′; 2 re-clām′, *vt.* To get back; regain; recover; reform; cultivate; tame. **-a-ble,** *a.* **-a-bly,** *adv.*— **rec″la-ma′tion,** *n.*

re-cline′, 1 rı-klain′; 2 re-clīn′, *vi.* [RE-CLINED′; RE-CLIN′ING.] To lean; lie down; rest; repose.

re-cluse′, 1 rı-klūs′; 2 re-clus′. **I.** *a.* Secluded; solitary. **II.** *n.* One who lives in seclusion.

rec′og-nize, 1 rek′eg-naiz; 2 rĕc′ŏg-nīz, *vt.* [-NIZED′; -NIZ″ING.] To know again; recollect; acknowledge; confess; admit. **rec′og-nise**[‡].— **rec″og-ni′tion,** 1 rek″eg-nish′en; 2 rĕc″ŏg-nĭsh′on, *n.* The act of recognizing; acknowledgment; salutation.— **rec′og-niz″a-bl(e**[r]**,** *a.*— **re-cog′ni-zance** or **-sance,** 1 rı-keg′ni-zəns; 2 re-cŏg′ni-zanç, *n. Law.* A pledge or obligation to do some particular act, as to appear and answer.

re-coil′, 1 rı-koil′; 2 re-cŏil′. **I.** *vt. & vi.* To start, shrink, or draw back; rebound; retreat. **II.** *n.* A shrinking back; a rebound.

rec″ol-lect′[1d], 1 rek″e-lekt′; 2 rĕc″ŏ-lĕct′, *vt. & vi.* To revive in memory; call to mind; recall.— **rec″ol-lec′tion,** *n.*

re″col-lect′[2d], 1 rī″ke-lekt′; 2 rē″cŏ-lĕct′, *vt.* To collect again.

rec″om-mend′[d], 1 rek″e-mend′; 2 rĕc″ŏ-mĕnd′, *vt.* **1.** To commend to another; make acceptable. **2.** To counsel. **-a-ble,** *a.* **-a-to-ry,** *a.*— **rec″om-men-da′tion,** *n.* The act of recommending; that which recommends or is recommended.

rec″om-pense, 1 rek′em-pens; 2 rĕc′ŏm-pĕns. **I.** *vt.* [-PENSED[t], -PENST[s]; -PENS″ING.] **1.** To repay; require; indemnify. **2.** To pay for. **II.** *n.* An equivalent; payment.

rec″on-cile, 1 rek′en-sail; 2 rĕc′ŏn-çīl, *vt.* [-CILED; -CIL″ING.] To restore to friendship; harmonize; settle.— **rec″on-cil′1a-tion,** *n.* The act of reconciling, or the state of being reconciled; atonement. **rec′on-cile″ment**[‡].— **rec′on-cil″er,** *n.*

rec′on-dite, 1 rek′en-dait; 2 rĕc′ŏn-dīt, *a.* Not easily perceived; abstruse; secret.

re-con′nais-sance, 1 rı-ken′ı-səns; 2 re-cŏn′i-sanç, *n.* The act of reconnoitering; a survey.

rec″on-noi′ter or **-tre,** 1 rek″e-noi′ter; 2 rĕe″ŏ-nŏi′ter, *vt.* To examine; survey or explore, as to learn an enemy's position, etc.

re″con-sid′er, 1 rī″ken-sid′er; 2 rē″cŏn-sĭd′er, *vt.* To consider again, as for reversal of previous action.— **re″con-sid″er-a′tion,** *n.*

re″con-struct′, *vt.* To construct again; rebuild; reorganize.— **re″con-struc′tion,** *n.* — **re″con-struc′tiv(e**[s], *a.*— **re″con-struc′tor,** *n.*

re-cord′[d], 1 rı-kôrd′; 2 re-eôrd′, *vt.* To make a record of; write down; fix in mind; indicate; register.— **re-cord′er,** *n.* **1.** One who records. **2.** A municipal magistrate.— **re-cord′er-ship,** *n.*

rec′ord, 1 rek′erd; 2 rĕe′ord, *n.* **1.** A copy of a document; written memorial; testimony. **2.** One's personal history. **3.** The authorized register of achievements; also, the best recorded achievement.

re-count′[1d], 1 rı-kaunt′; 2 re-count′, *vt.* To relate in detail; recite; tell.

re-count′[2d], 1 rı-kaunt′; 2 rē-count′, *vt.* To count again.

re-count′, *n.* A repetition of a count.

re-coup′, 1 rı-kūp′; 2 re-cup′, *vt.* **1.** To obtain compensation for (a loss); make up; reco er. **2.** To reimburse (a person) for a loss; indemnify. **3.** To keep back (something due) in order to make a counter-claim.— **re-coup′ment,** *n.* **re-coup′**[‡].

re-course′, 1 rı-kôrs′; 2 re-eôrs′, *n.* Resort for help or security in trouble.

re-cov′er[1], 1 rı-kuv′er; 2 re-cŏv′er, *v.* **I.** **re-cuv′er**[2], *t.* To obtain again; regain; retrieve. **II.** *i.* To regain health, prosperity, etc.; succeed in a lawsuit. **-a-ble,** *a.* — **re-cov′er-y,** *n.* [-IES[z], *pl.*] The act of recovering; restoration. [cover again.

re-cov′er[2], 1 rī″-kuv′ər; 2 rē-cŏv′er, *vt.* To **rec′re-ant,** 1 rek′rı-ænt; 2 rĕc′re-ant. **I.** *a.* Apostate; false; craven; cowardly. **II.** *n.* A cowardly or faithless person.— **rec′re-an-cy,** *n.*

rec′re-ate[1], 1 rek′rı-ēt; 2 rĕe′re-āt, *vt.* [-AT″-ED[d]; -AT″ING.] To impart new vigor to; refresh.— **rec′re-a′tion**[1], *n.* Refreshment; diversion.— **rec′re-a-tiv(e**[s], *a.*

re″cre-ate[2d], 1 rī″krı-ēt′; 2 rē″cre-āt′, *vt.* To create anew.— **re″cre-a′tion**[2], *n.*

re-crim′i-nate, 1 rı-krim′ı-nēt; 2 re-crĭm′ĭ-nāt, *vt. & vi.* To accuse in return. — **re-crim′i-na′tion,** *n.*— **re-crim′i-na″-tiv(e**[s], *a.* Of or pertaining to recrimination **re-crim′i-na-to-ry**[‡].

re-cruit′, 1 rı-krūt′; 2 re-crut′. **I**[d]. *vt. &*

vi. To supply, as with soldiers; raise new supplies; build up; refresh. **II.** *n.* A newly enrolled soldier or sailor. — **re-cruit′er,** *n.* — **re-cruit′ment,** *n.*

rec′tan″gle, 1 rek′taŋ″gl; 2 rĕc′tăŋ″gl, *n.*
rec′tan″glᴾ, } *Math.* A right-angled parallelogram. — **rec-tan′gu-lar,** *a.* Having one right angle or more.

rec′ti-fy, 1 rek′ti-fai; 2 rĕc′ti-fỹ, *vt.* [-FIED; -FY″ING.] To correct; amend; purify. — **rec″ti-fi-ca′tion,** *n.* — **rec′ti-fi″er,** *n.*

rec″ti-lin′e-ar, 1 rek″ti-lin′i-ar; 2 rĕc″ti-lĭn′e-ar, *a.* Pertaining to or consisting of a right line or lines; straight. **rec″ti-lin′e-alt.**

rec′ti-tude, 1 rek′ti-tiūd; 2 rĕc′ti-tūd, *n.* Uprightness; integrity; accuracy.

rec′tor, 1 rek′tər *or* -tor; 2 rĕc′tor, *n.* The clergyman of a parish. — **rec-to′ri-al,** *a.* **rec′tor-alt.** — **rec′tor-ship,** *n.* **rec′tor-atet.** — **rec′to-ry,** *n.* [-RIESᶻ, *pl.*] A rector's dwelling.

rec′tum, 1 rek′tum; 2 rĕc′tŭm, *n.* [REC′TA, *pl.*] The terminal portion of the alimentary canal.

re-cum′bent, 1 ri-kum′bent; 2 re-cŭm′bĕnt, *a.* Reclining; leaning. **-ly,** *adv.* — **re-cum′ben-cy,** *n.* The state of being recumbent. **re-cum′bencet.**

re-cu′per-ate, 1 ri-kiū′pər-ēt; 2 re-cū′per-āt, *vt. & vi.* [-AT″EDᵈ; -AT″ING.] To recover. — **re-cu″per-a′tion,** *n.* — **re-cu′per-a-tiv(eˢ,** *a.* Tending or pertaining to recovery. **re-cu′per-a-to-ryt.**

re-cur′, 1 ri-kūr′; 2 re-cûr′, *vi.* [RE-CURRED′, RE-CURD′ˢ; RE-CUR′RING.] To happen again; happen repeatedly; come back, as to the mind. — **re-cur′rence,** *n.* The act or fact of recurring; recourse. **re-cur′ren-cyt.** — **re-cur′rent,** *a.* Recurring; running back.

rec′u-sant, 1 rek′yu-zənt; 2 rĕc′yu-şant. **I.** *a.* Refusing to conform; in English history, refusing to conform to the Anglican church. **II.** *n.* A recusant person; a non-conformist. — **rec′u-san-cy,** *n.*

red, 1 red; 2 rĕd. **I.** *a.* Of the color of blood. **II.** *n.* A color like that of blood, seen at the lower edge of a rainbow; a red pigment. — **red′den,** 1 red′n; 2 rĕd′n, *vt. & vi.* To make red; flush. — **red′dish,** *a.* Somewhat red. — **red′ly,** *adv.* — **red′ness,** *n.* — **red tape,** formal and tedious official procedure: from the tying of documents with red tape. — **red′top″,** *n.* A cultivated grass. **fine′top″t; herd′s'-grass″t.**

re-deem′, 1 ri-dīm′; 2 re-dēm′, *vt.* **1.** To buy back; ransom; recover deliver, as from sin. **2.** To fulfil. **3.** To make amends for. — **re-deem′a-bl(eᴿ,** *a.* **-ness,** *n.* — **re-deem′er,** *n.* **1.** One who redeems. **2.** [R-] Jesus Christ, the Savior. — **re-demp′**-

tion, 1 ri-demp′shən; 2 re-dĕmp′shon, *n.* The act of redeeming, or the state of being redeemed. — **re-demp′tiv(eˢ,** *a.* Serving to redeem, or connected with redemption. **re-demp′to-ryt.**

red′-hot″, 1 red′-het″; 2 rĕd′-hŏt″, *a.* Heated to redness; intense.

re-din′te-grate, 1 re-din′ti-grēt; 2 rĕ-dĭn′te-grāt. **I**ᵈ. *vt.* To restore to a perfect state; renew. **II.** *a.* Restored to a whole or perfect state; renewed. — **re-din″te-gra′tion,** *n.* — **re-din′te-gra″tiv(eˢ,** *a.*

red′o-lent, 1 red′o-lent; 2 rĕd′o-lĕnt, *a.* Full of or diffusing a pleasant odor: followed by *of.* — **red′o-lence,** *n.* **red′o-len-cyt.**

re-doub′le, 1 ri-dub′l; 2 re-dŭb′l, *vt. & vi.* To double again; increase; repeat often.

re-doubt′a-bl(eᴿ, 1 ri-daut′ə-bl; 2 re-dout′-a-bl, *a.* Inspiring fear; formidable; valiant. **re-doubt′edt; re-dout′a-bl(eᴿt.**

re-dound′ᵈ, 1 ri-daund′; 2 re-dound′, *vi.* To contribute; conduce, as to one's credit.

re-dout′, } 1 ri-daut′; 2 re-dout′, *n.* An
re-doubt′, } enclosed fortification; an earthwork.

Redout.

re-dress′, 1 ri-dres′; 2 re-drĕs′. **I**ᵗ. *vt.* To right, as a wrong; make reparation to (a person). **II.** *n.* Satisfaction for wrong done; reparation. — **re-dress′-bl(eᴿ,** *a.* **re-dress′a-bl(eᴿt.**

re-dress′²ᵗ, 1 rī-dres′; 2 rē-drĕs′, *vt. & vi.* To dress again.

re-duce′, 1 ri-diūs′; 2 re-dūc′, *vt.* [RE-DUCED′ᵗ; RE-DUC′ING.] To diminish; lower; degrade; subdue; change the form or denomination of. — **re-duc′i-bl(eᴿ,** *a.* — **re-duc′tion,** *n.* The act of reducing, or its result.

re-dun′dant, 1 ri-dun′dənt; 2 re-dŭn′dant, *a.* Excessive; superfluous; verbose; tautological. — **re-dun′dance, re-dun′dan-cy,** *n.*

re-du′pli-cateᵈ, 1 ri-diū′pli-kēt; 2 re-dū′-pli-cāt, *vt. & vi.* To redouble. — **re-du″pli-ca′tion,** *n.*

red′wood″, 1 red′wud″; 2 rĕd′wʊd″, *n.* An immense California tree of the pine family, or its wood. **Se-quoi′at.**

reed, 1 rīd; 2 rēd, *n.* **1.** *Bot.* The stem of certain tall grasses growing in wet places, or any one of the grasses. **2.** *Mus.* A thin elastic tongue of reed, wood, or metal nearly closing an opening, as of an organ-

Branch of Redwood.

1: ə = final; ɪ = habit; aisle; au = out; oil; iū = feud; chin; go; ŋ = sing; thin, this.
2: wolf, dǫ; book, boot; full, rule, cūre, bŭt, bûrn; oil, boy; ḡo, ḡem; iŋk; thin, this.

14

pipe; also, a rustic musical pipe.— **reed'ed,** *a.*— **reed'y,** *a.*

reef[t], 1 rīf; 2 rēf, *vt.* To take in; fold and fasten down, as a sail or part of a sail.

reef[1], *n.* A ridge of rocks at or near the surface of the water.— **reef'y,** *a.*

reef[2], *n.* The folded part of a sail.— **reef'er,** *n.*

reek[t], 1 rīk; 2 rēk, *vt. & vi.* To smoke; emit vapor.

reel[1], 1 rīl; 2 rēl. **I.** *vt.* To wind on a reel. **II.** *n.* A rotary device for winding rope, etc.

reel[2]. **I.** *vi.* To stagger; dance the reel. **II.** *n.* A lively dance, or its music.

re"en-force'[1t], 1 rī″en-fōrs′; 2 rē″ĕn-fôrç′, *vt.* To give new force or strength to, as with troops. **re"in-force'**[t].— **re"en-force'-ment,** *n.* The act of reenforcing; a fresh body of troops; aid; help. **re"in-force'-ment**[t].

re"en-force'[2t], *vt.* To enforce anew.

re-fec'tion, 1 rī-fek′shan; 2 re-fĕe′shon, *n.* Refreshment; a slight meal.— **re-fec'to-ry,** *n.* [-RIES², *pl.*] A room for eating.

re-fer', 1 rī-fūr′; 2 re-fēr′, *v.* [RE-FERRED′, RE-FER′D'S; RE-FER′RING.] **I.** *t.* To direct, as for information; assign; attribute. **II.** *i.* **1.** To have reference; allude. **2.** To give a reference. **3.** To have recourse; apply; appeal.— **ref'er-a-ble**(e²), *a.* That may be referred. **re-fer'ri-ble**(e²)[t].— **ref'er-ee',** *n.* A person to whom a thing is referred. — **ref'er-ence,** *n.* The act of referring; that which refers; a person or thing referred to; allusion; testimonial.

ref"er-en'dum, 1 ref″ʉr-en′dʉm; 2 rĕf″ʉr-ĕn′dŭm, *n.* **1.** The submission to his own government, by a diplomatic representative, of a proposition he is not authorized to decide. **2.** The submission of a proposed law, after legislative action, to the vote of the whole people.

re-fine', 1 rī-fain′; 2 re-fīn′, *vt. & vi.* [RE-FINED′; RE-FIN′ING.] **1.** To make or become fine or pure; purify; culture. **2.** To make subtle distinctions.— **re-fined',** *pa.* Purified; courteous; cultured; subtle; recondite.— **re-fin'er,** *n.*— **re-fin'er-y,** *n.* A place where some crude material is purified.

re-fine'ment, 1 rī-fain′ment *or* -mənt; 2 re-fīn′ment, *n.* **1.** Delicacy; culture. **2.** The act of refining. **3.** A subtlety.

re-fit'[d], 1 rī-fit′; 2 re-fīt′, *vt. & vi.* To fit or be fitted again; repair.

re-flect'[d], 1 rī-flekt′; 2 re-flĕct, *v.* **I.** *t.* **1.** To throw back, as rays of light. **2.** To return an image of. **II.** *i.* **1.** To send back rays, as of light. **2.** To think upon the past; ponder; meditate. **3.** To cast reproach; blame.— **re-flec'tion,** 1 rī-flek′shan; 2 re-flĕe′shon, *n.* The act of reflecting; an image thrown by reflected light; meditation; blame; censure. **re-flex'ion**[t].— **re-flec'tive**(e⁵), *a.* **1.** Meditative. **2.** Reflecting light, heat, etc. -**ly,** *adv.* -**ness,** *n.*— **re-flec'tor,** *n.* That which reflects; a mirror; a reflecting telescope.

re'flex, 1 rī′fleks; 2 rē′flĕks. **I.** *a.* Turned or thrown backward; reflective. **II.** *n.* Reflection, or an image produced by reflection; a mere copy.— **re-flex'iv**(e⁵), 1 rī-fleks′ıv; 2 re-flĕks′ıv, *a.* Referring to itself or its subject; as, a *reflexive* verb whose object denotes the same person or thing as its subject. -**ly,** *adv.*

ref'lu-ent, 1 ref′lu-ent; 2 rĕf′lu̯-ĕnt, *a.* Flowing or rushing back.— **ref'lu-ence,** *n.*

re'flux, 1 rī′fluks; 2 rē′flŭks, *n.* A flowing back; ebb.

re-form'[1], 1 rī-fērm′; 2 re-fôrm′. **I.** *vt. & vi.* To make better morally; free from evils or abuses. **II.** *n.* An act or result of reformation; change for the better. — **ref"or-ma'tion**[1], *n.* The act of reforming, or the state of being reformed; especially, [R-] the establishment of Protestantism in the sixteenth century.— **re-form'a-tiv**(e⁵, *a.* Reformatory.— **re-form'a-to-ry. I.** *a.* Reforming or tending to reform. **II.** *n.* [-RIES², *pl.*] An institution for the reformation of offenders.— **re-form'er,** *n.*

re-form'[2], 1 rī-fērm′; 2 rē-fôrm′, *vt. & vi.* To form again.— **re"for-ma'tion**[2], *n.*

re-fract'[d], 1 rī-frakt′; 2 re-frăct′, *vt.* To bend from a direct course; turn aside. — **re-frac'tion,** *n.* The change of direction of a ray, as of light or heat. — **re-frac'tiv**(e⁵), *a.* Of or pertaining to refraction.— **re - frac' tiv**(e-ness⁵, *n.*— **re-frac'tor,** *n.* A refracting telescope.

An Experiment showing the Refraction of Light.

re-frac'to-ry, 1 rī-frak′to-rı; 2 re-frăe′to-rry, *a.* Disobedient; unmanageable; obstinate, as a horse.— **re-frac'to-ri-ly,** *adv.*— **re-frac'to-ri-ness,** *n.*

re-frain', 1 rī-frēn′; 2 re-frān′, *vt. & vi.* To hold within bounds; abstain from action; forbear.

re-frain', *n.* A strain repeated at intervals, as in a song; a burden.

re-fran'gi-bl(e²), 1 rī-fran′jı-bl; 2 re-frăn′gi-bl, *a.* Capable of being refracted, as rays of light.— **re-fran"gi-bil'l-ty,** *n.*— **re-fran'gi-bl**(e-ness²)[t].

re-fresh'[t], 1 rī-fresh′; 2 re-frĕsh′, *vt. & vi.*

To make or become fresh again; reinvigorate.— **re-fresh'ment,** *n.* The act of refreshing; the state of being refreshed; that which refreshes, as food or drink.

re-frig'er-ate, 1 rĭ-frĭj'ər-ēt; 2 re-frĭg'er-āt, *vt.* [-AT"ED^d; -AT"ING.] To cause to become cold; cool; chill.— **re-frig'er-ant,** 1 rĭ-frĭj'ər-ənt; 2 re-frĭg'er-ant, *a.* Cooling.— **re-frig'er-a'tion,** *n.* A cooling.— **re-frig'er-a'tor,** *n.* That which makes or keeps cold; a box or room for keeping articles cool by means of ice.— **re-frig'er-a-to-ry,** I. *a.* Reducing heat. II. *n.* That which reduces heat.— **re-frig'er-a'tiv(e^s,** *a.*

reft, *imp. & pp.* of REAVE, *v.*

ref'uge, 1 ref'yuj; 2 ref'yug, *n.* Shelter; protection; that which shelters or protects.

ref'u-gee, 1 ref'yu-jī'; 2 ref'yu-gē', *n.* One who flees to a refuge, as from political or religious persecution, in a foreign land.

re-ful'gence, 1 rĭ-fŭl'jens; 2 re-fŭl'gĕnç, *n.* Splendor; radiance. — **re-ful'gen-cy‡.— re-ful'gent,** *a.* Shining; brilliant; splendid.— **re-ful'gent-ly,** *adv.*

re-fund'^id, 1 rĭ-fŭnd'; 2 re-fŭnd', *vt.* To pay back.

re-fund'^2d, 1 rĭ-fŭnd'; 2 re-fŭnd', *vt.* To fund anew.

re-fuse'^1,) 1 rĭ-fiūz'; 2 re-fūs', *vt. & vi.*
re-fuze'^F,) [RE-FUSED; RE-FUS'ING.] To decline; reject; deny; repel.— **re-fus'al,** *n.* 1. The act of refusing. 2. The privilege of accepting or rejecting; an option.

re-fuse'^2, 1 rĭ-fiūz'; 2 re-fūs', *vt. & vi.* To fuse again.

ref'use, 1 ref'yūs; 2 ref'yūs. I. *a.* Rejected as worthless. II. *n.* Anything worthless; rubbish.

re-fute', 1 rĭ-fiūt'; 2 re-fūt', *vt.* [RE-FUT"ED^d; RE-FUT'ING.] To prove to be false, erroneous, or mistaken; disprove. — **ref"u-ta'tion,** *n.* The act of refuting; disproof. **re-fut'al‡.— re-fut'a-bl(e^p,** *a.*— **re-fut"a-bil'i-ty,** *n.*— **re-fut'a-to-ry,** *a.*

re-gain', 1 rĭ-gēn'; 2 re-gān', *vt.* To recover.

re'gal, 1 rī'gəl; 2 rē'gal, *a.* Belonging to or fit for a king; royal. **-ly,** *adv.*— **re-gal'i-ty,** 1 rĭ-gal'ĭ-tĭ; 2 re-gal'i-ty, *n.* Royalty.

re-gale', 1 rĭ-gēl'; 2 re-gāl', *vt.* [RE-GALED'; RE-GAL'ING.] To feast; delight. **-ment,** *n.*

re-ga'li-a, 1 rĭ-gē'lĭ-ə; 2 re-gā'li-a, *n. pl.* Decorative emblems of royalty, or of some society, order, or rank.

re-gard', 1 rĭ-gärd'; 2 re-gärd'. I^d. *vt.* 1. To observe closely; consider. 2. To esteem. 3. To concern; relate to. II. *n.* 1. Respect; attention; notice. 2. Common repute. 3. Reference. 4. A courteous greeting.— **re-gard'ful,** *a.* Having or showing regard. **-ly,** *adv.*— **re-gard'-**

ing, *prep.* With reference to; with regard to.— **re-gard'less,** *a.* Having no regard or consideration; heedless. **-ly,** *adv.* **-ness,** *n.*

re-gat'ta, 1 rĭ-gat'ə; 2 re-gät'a, *n.* A boatrace.

re'gen-cy, 1 rī'jen-sĭ; 2 rē'gĕn-çy, *n.* [-CIES^z, *pl.*] The government or office of a regent; a body of regents. **re'gent-ship‡.**

re-gen'er-ate, 1 rĭ-jen'ər-ēt; 2 re-gĕn'er-āt. I. *vt.* [-AT"ED^d; -AT"ING.] To produce anew; renew spiritually. II. *a.* Having new life; spiritually renewed; restored; regenerated.— **re-gen'er-a-cy,** *n.* The state of being regenerate.— **re-gen"er-a'tion,** *n.* A renewing; the new birth.— **re-gen'er-a'-tiv(e^s,** *a.* **-ly,** *adv.*

re'gent, 1 rī'jent; 2 rē'gĕnt, *n.* 1. One who rules in the name and place of a sovereign. 2. An officer of a university.

reg'i-cide, 1 rej'ĭ-said; 2 rĕg'i-çīd, *n.* The killing or the killer of a king or sovereign. —**reg'i-ci"dal,** *a.*

ré'gime, 1 rē'zĭm'; 2 re'zhīm', *n.* System of government; social system.

reg'i-men, 1 rej'ĭ-men; 2 rĕg'i-mĕn, *n.* A course of living, as to food, etc.; government.

reg'i-ment, 1 rej'ĭ-ment *or* -mənt; 2 rĕg'i-ment, *n.* A body of soldiers commanded by a colonel.— **reg"i-men'tal.** I. *a.* Of or pertaining to a regiment. II. *n. pl.* Military uniform. **-ly,** *adv.*

re'gion, 1 rī'jen; 2 rē'gon, *n.* A country; district; area.

reg'is-ter, 1 rej'ĭs-tər; 2 rĕg'is-ter. I. *vt. & vi.* 1. To record, as in a register; enroll. 2. To denote according to a scale. II. *n.* 1. An official record; roll; list; schedule. 2. A registrar. 3. Any registering apparatus; a device for regulating the admission of heated air to a room. 4. *Mus.* The compass of a voice or an instrument.— **reg'is-trar,** *n.* The authorized keeper of records.— **reg'is-trar-ship,** *n.*— **reg"is-tra'tion,** *n.* The act of registering; enrolment.— **reg'is-try,** 1 rej'is-trĭ; 2 rĕg'is-try, *n.* [-TRIES^z, *pl.*] 1. Registration. 2. A register, or the place where it is kept.

reg'nant, 1 reg'nənt; 2 rĕg'nant, *a.* Reigning; commanding.

re'gress, 1 rī'gres; 2 rē'grĕs, *n.* Passage back; return. **re-gres'sion‡.— re-gres'siv(e^s,** *a.* **-ly,** *adv.* **-ness,** *n.*

re-gret', 1 rĭ-gret'; 2 re-grĕt'. I. *vt.* [RE-GRET'TED^d; RE-GRET'TING.] To look back to with distress; grieve over; remember with longing. II. *n.* Sorrow for something that can not be recalled or prevented; grief; concern.— **re-gret'ful,** *a.* **-ly,** *adv.*— **re-gret'ta-bl(e^p,** *a.* That is to be regretted.

1: ə = final; ɪ = habit; ɑisle; ɑu = out; oil; iū = feud; ᴄhin; go; ŋ = sing; thin, this.
2: wolf, dǫ; book, boot; full, rule, cūre, bŭt, bûrn; ŏil, bŏy; ḡo, gem; iŋk; thin, this.

reg'u-lar, 1 reg'yu-lər; 2 rĕg'yu-lar. **I.** *a.*
1. Made or done according to rule;
symmetrical; normal. **2.** Uniformly recurring; methodical; usual. **3.** Belonging to a standing army. **II.** *n.* A soldier belonging to a standing army.— **reg"u-
lar'i-ty,** *n.* The state, quality, or character
of being regular.— **reg'u-lar-ly,** *adv.*

reg'u-late, 1 reg'yu-lēt; 2 rĕg'yu-lāt, *vt.*
[-LAT″ED⁴; -LAT″ING.] To order or govern
by rule; put or keep in order; adjust according to a standard.— **reg"u-la'tion,** 1
reg″yu-lē'shən; 2 rĕg″yu-lā'shon, *n.* The act
of regulating, or the state of being regulated; a
prescribed rule.— **reg'u-la″tiv**⁽ᵉ⁾, *a.*— **reg'u-
la″tor,** *n.* One who or that which regulates;
a clock of great accuracy.

re-gur'gi-tate, 1 ri-gūr'ji-tēt; 2 re-gûr'gi-
tāt, *vt.* & *vi.* To throw or pour back; to
surge or be poured back.— **re-gur"gi-ta'-
tion,** *n.*

re"ha-bil'i-tate, 1 rī″hə-bil'i-tēt; 2 rē″ha-
bil'i-tāt, *vt.* To restore to a former status;
reinstate.— **re"ha-bil"i-ta'tion,** *n.*

re-hearse', 1 ri-hūrs'; 2 re-hērs', *vt.* & *vi.*
re-herse'⁽ᴾ⁾, 1 [RE-HEARSED'ᵗ, -HERST'ᵀ; RE-
HEARS'ING, -HERS'INGᴾ.] **1.** To practise in
advance. **2.** To tell over again; relate.
— **re-hears'al,** *n.*

Reich, 1 raiн; 2 rīн, *n.* Germany; literally,
[realm.

reign, 1 rēn; 2 rēn, *n.* *vi.* To have the
authority of a sovereign; rule; control.
II. *n.* Sovereignty; dominion; influence;
the time of a sovereign's rule.

re"im-burse'ᵗ, 1 rī″im-bûrs'; 2 rē″im-bûrs',
vt. To repay.— **re"im-burse'ment,** *n.*

rein, 1 rēn; 2 rēn. **I.** *vt.* & *vi.* To manage
with the rein; check; restrain. **II.** *n.* A
strap attached to the bit for controlling a
horse.

rein'deer', 1 rēn'dīr'; 2 rēn'dēr', *n.* [′REIN-
DEER″, *pl.*] A deer of
northern regions, used as
a draft- and pack-animal.

re"in-for·ce',
-ment, etc.
Same as RE-
ENFORCE, etc.

reins, 1 rēnz;
2 rēns, *n. pl.*
The kidneys;
inward parts;
hence, the af-
fections and
passions.

re"in-state'ᵈ,
1 rī″in-stēt'; 2 rē″in-stāt', *vt.* To restore;
replace. **-ment,** *n.*

re-it'er-ate, 1 ri-it'ər-ēt; 2 re-īt'er-āt, *vt.*
[-AT″ED⁴; -AT″ING.] To say or do again

Reindeer. 1/90

and again; repeat.— **re-it"er-a'tion,** *n.* Repetition.

re-ject'ᵈ, 1 ri-jekt'; 2 re-jĕct', *vt.* To refuse; repel; decline; deny; discard.— **re-jec'-
tion,** *n.*

re-joice', 1 ri-jois'; 2 re-jŏiç', *vt.* & *vi.* [RE-
JOICED'ᵗ; RE-JOIC'ING.] To fill with joy;
gladden; be glad.— **re-joic'ing,** *n.* The
feeling or expression of joy.— **re-joic'ing-
ly,** *adv.*

re-join', 1 ri-join'; 2 re-jŏin', *v.* **I.** *t.* To
join again; return to; reunite. **II.** *i.* To
answer to a reply.— **re-join'der,** *n.* A reply
or retort.

re-ju've-nate, 1 ri-jū'vi-nēt; 2 re-ju've-
nāt, *vt.* [-NAT″ED⁴; -NAT″ING.] To make
young or as if young again.

re-lapse', 1 ri-laps'; 2 re-lăps'. **I**ᵗ. *vi.*
re-laps'ᴾ, } To lapse back, as into disease
or sin; decline; backslide. **II.** *n.* A
lapse into a former evil state.

re-late', 1 ri-lēt'; 2 re-lāt', *v.* [RE-LAT″ED⁴;
RE-LAT′ING.] **I.** *t.* **1.** To narrate; tell.
2. To connect; ally. **II.** *i.* To be in
connection; have reference; refer.— **re-lat'ed,**
a.— **re-lat'ed-ness,** *n.*— **re-lat'er,** *n.* **re-
la'tort.** **re-la'tion,** 1 ri-lē'shən; 2 re-lā'-
shon, *n.* **1.** Connection; reference; regard;
allusion; kinship. **2.** An account or recital.
3. A relative.— **re-la'tion-ship,** *n.*

rel'a-tive, 1 rel'a-tiv; 2 rĕl'a-tīv. **I.** *a.*
rel'a-tivˢ, } Having connection or relationship; referring or relating. **II.** *n.* **1.**
One who is related; a kinsman; relation.
2. A relative word. **-ly,** *adv.*— **rel"a-tiv'-
i-ty,** *n.* The quality of being relative.

re-lax'ᵗ, 1 ri-laks'; 2 re-lăks', *vt.* & *vi.* To
make or become lax, loose, or less rigor-
ous.— **re"lax-a'tion,** *n.* The act of relaxing,
or the state of being relaxed; indulgence;
recreation.

re-lay', 1 ri-lē'; 2 re-lā', *vt.* To lay again.

re-lay', 1 ri-lē'; 2 re-lā', *n.* **1.** A fresh set,
as of horses; a change or shift. **2.** *Elec.*
An electromagnetic device for opening
and closing circuits.

re-lease'¹, 1 ri-līs'; 2 re-lēs'. **I.** *vt.* [RE-
LEASED'ᵗ, RE-LEAST'ˢ; RE-LEAS'ING.] **1.**
To set free; liberate. **2.** To relinquish,
as a right or claim. **II.** *n.* The act of re-
leasing; discharge; relinquishment.

re-lease'²ᵗ, 1 ri-līs'; 2 re-lēs', *vt.* To lease
again.

rel'e-gate, 1 rel'i-gēt; 2 rĕl'e-gāt, *vt.* [-GAT″-
ED⁴; -GAT′ING.] To consign, as to ob-
scurity; banish.— **rel"e-ga'tion,** *n.*

re-lent'ᵈ, 1 ri-lent'; 2 re-lĕnt', *vi.* To
soften in temper; become compassionate;
yield.— **re-lent'less,** *a.* Pitiless. **-ly,** *adv.*
-ness, *n.*

rel'e·vant, 1 rĕl'ĭ-vənt; 2 rĕl'e·vant, *a.* Fitting; pertinent.— **rel'e·van·cy,** *n.* **rel'e·vance‡.**

re·li'a·ble(eᵖ, 1 rĭ-laī'ə-bl; 2 re·lī'a·bl, *a.* That may be relied upon; trustworthy.— **re·li"a·bil'i·ty,** *n.* Trustworthiness. **re·li'a·bl(e·ness‡.— re·li'a·bly,** *adv.*

re·li'ance, 1 rĭ-laī'əns; 2 re·lī'anç, *n.* The act of relying; confidence.— **re·li'ant,** *a.* Confident.

rel'ic, 1 rĕl'ĭk; 2 rĕl'ĭe, *n.* Some fragment of that which has vanished; a memento.

rel'ict, 1 rĕl'ĭkt; 2 rĕl'ĭct, *n.* A widow.

re·lief', 1 rĭ-līf'; 2 re·lēf', *n.* **1.** A relieving; alleviation; aid; release. **2.** The projection of a figure from a surface.

re·lieve', ⎱1 rĭ-līv'; 2 re·lēv', *vt.* [RE-**re·liev'ᵖ,** ⎰LIEV(E)Dᴰ/Bᵇ; RE·LIEV'ING.] **1.** To free from pain or trouble. **2.** To alleviate; lessen; soften; lighten. **3.** To bring out into relief from a surface. **4.** *Mil.* (1) To reenforce. (2) To release, as a sentinel, by substitution.

re·lig'ion, 1 rĭ-lĭj'ən; 2 re·lĭg'ŏn, *n.* A system of faith and worship; devotion; piety.— **re·lig'ious,** 1 rĭ-lĭj'ŭs; 2 re·lĭg'ūs, *a.* Pertaining to or controlled by religion; devout; faithful; conscientious; pious. **-ly,** *adv.* **-ness,** *n.*

re·lin'quish‡, 1 rĭ-lĭŋ'kwĭsh; 2 re·lĭŋ'kwish, *vt.* To let go, especially to let go reluctantly; surrender; abandon; quit. — **re·lin'quish·ment,** *n.*

rel'i·qua·ry, 1 rel'ĭ-kwē-rĭ; 2 rĕl'ĭ-kwā-ry, *n.* [-RIESᶻ, *pl.*] A repository for relics.

rel'ish‡, 1 rel'ĭsh; 2 rĕl'ish, *v.* **I.** *t.* **1.** To like the taste of; enjoy. **2.** To flavor. **II.** *i.* To yield or have a flavor, especially an agreeable flavor.

rel'ish‡, *n.* **1.** Appetite; liking: commonly with *for.* **2.** Flavor; a pleasing taste, in food or drink. **3.** Something that relishes; a slight savory dish.

re·luc'tant, 1 rĭ-lŭk'tənt; 2 re·lŭe'tant, *a.* Disinclined; unwilling.— **re·luc'tance,** *n.* Unwillingness.— **re·luc'tan·cy,** *n.*— **re·luc'tant·ly,** *adv.*

re·ly', 1 rĭ-laī'; 2 re·lȳ', *vi.* [RE·LIED'; RE·LY'ING.] To depend; repose confidence: with *on* or *upon.*

re·main', 1 rĭ-mēn'; 2 re·mān', *vt.* To be left behind; continue; abide; stay.— **re·main'der,** *n.* That which remains, as after subtraction; something left.— **re·mains',** 1 rĭ-mēnz'; 2 re·māns', *n. pl.* That which is left behind; a corpse; skeleton; an author's posthumous works.

re·mand', 1 rĭ-mand'; 2 re·mánd'. **Iᵈ.** *vt.* To order or send back; recommit. **II.** *n.* Recommittal.

re·mark', 1 rĭ-märk'; 2 re·märk'. **Iᵗ.** *vt. & vi.* To express by speech or writing; notice; make remarks. **II.** *n.* A comment or saying; observation; notice.— **re·mark'a·bl(e**ᵖ, *a.* Worthy of special notice; conspicuous; distinguished.— **re·mark'a·bl(e·ness**ᵖ, *n.*— **re·mark'a·bly,** *adv.*

rem'e·dy, 1 rem'ĭ·dĭ; 2 rĕm'e·dy. **I.** *vt.* [-DIED; -DY·ING.] **1.** To cure or heal. **2.** To repair; correct. **II.** *n.* [-DIESᶻ, *pl.*] That which cures or relieves, as a medicine.— **re·me'di·a·bl(e**ᵖ, *a.* That may be remedied.— **re·me'di·a·bl(e·ness**ᵖ, *n.*— **re·me'di·a·bly,** *adv.*— **re·me'di·al,** *a.* Remedying or tending to remedy; curative.— **rem'e·di·less,** *a.* Being beyond remedy.

re·mem'ber, 1 rĭ-mem'bər; 2 re·mĕm'ber, *vt. & vi.* **1.** To retain in memory; recollect. **2.** To have or exercise remembrance.— **re·mem'brance,** *n.* **1.** The act or power of remembering; memory. **2.** That which is remembered; a memento; keepsake.— **re·mem'branc·er,** *n.* A reminder; memento.

re·mind'ᵈ, 1 rĭ-maind'; 2 re·mīnd', *vt.* To bring to mind; recall: with *of.*— **re·mind'er,** *n.*

rem'i·nis'cence, 1 rem'ĭ-nis'ens; 2 rĕm'i·nĭs'ĕnç, *n.* The calling to mind, or that which is recalled.— **rem'i·nis'cent,** *a.*— **rem'i·nis'cent·ly,** *adv.*

re·miss', 1 rĭ-mĭs'; 2 re·mĭs', *a.* Slack or careless; dilatory; negligent.— **re·miss'ly,** *adv.*— **re·miss'ness,** *n.*

re·mit', 1 rĭ-mĭt'; 2 re·mĭt', *v.* [RE·MIT'TEDᵈ; RE·MIT'TING.] **I.** *t.* **1.** To send in return; transmit; refer; submit. **2.** To pardon; forgive. **3.** To release; abate; relax. **II.** *i.* To abate for a time, as a fever.— **re·mis'sion,** 1 rĭ-mĭsh'ən; 2 re·mĭsh'on, *n.* The act of remitting; abatement; pardon.— **re·mit'tance,** *n.* The act of remitting, or that which is remitted, as money.— **re·mit'tent,** *a.* Having remissions, as a fever.

rem'nant, 1 rem'nənt; 2 rĕm'nant, *n.* That which remains; a small remainder.

re·mod'el, 1 rĭ-mod'el; 2 rē·mŏd'ĕl, *vt.* To model again; rearrange.

re·mon'e·tize, 1 rĭ-men't-toiz; 2 rē·mŏn'e·tīz, *vt.* To reinstate as lawful money; opposed to *demonetize.*

re·mon'strate, 1 rĭ-men'strĕt; 2 re·mŏn'străt, *vi.* [-STRAT'EDᵈ; -STRAT'ING.] To protest; expostulate (*with* a person, *against* a thing).— **re·mon'strance,** *n.* The act of remonstrating; expostulation or reproof.— **re·mon'strant. I.** *a.* Of or like a remonstrance. **II.** *n.* One who remonstrates.

re·morse', 1 rĭ-mŏrs'; 2 re·môrs', *n.* The anguish caused by a sense of guilt.— **re-**

morse'ful, a.— re-morse'ful-ly, adv.— re-morse'less, a. Pitiless; cruel; conscience-less.— re-morse'less-ly, adv.— re-morse'-less-ness, n.

re-mote', 1 rı-mōt'; 2 re-mōt', a. **1.** Distant in space, time, or relation. **2.** Not obvious; slight. -ly, adv. -ness, n.

re-move', 1 rı-mūv'; 2 re-mǫv'. **I.** vt. & vi. To move or take away; destroy; change one's residence. **II.** n. **1.** A removal. **2.** An interval. **3.** A course, as at dinner.— re-mov'a-bil'i-ty, n.— re-mov'a-bl(e², a.— re-mov'al, n. The act of removing.

re-mu'ner-ate, 1 rı-miū'nər-ēt; 2 re-mū'ner-āt, vt. [-AT'LDᵈ; -AT'ING.] To compensate; pay; reward.— re-mu'ner-a'tion, n. The act of remunerating; recompense.— re-mu'ner-a'tiv(e², a. Profitable.

Re-nais'sance', 1 rə-nē'sāns'; 2 re-nā'sänç, n. **1.** [r-] A new birth; revival. **2.** The revival of letters and of art marking the transition from medieval to modern history: often used also as an adjective.

re'nal, 1 rī'nəl; 2 rē'nal, a. Of, pertaining to, or near a kidney or the kidneys.

ren'ard, n. Same as REYNARD.

re-nas'cence, 1 rı-nas'ens; 2 re-năs'ĕnç, n. [r- or R-] Renaissance. re-nas'cen-cy‡.— re-nas'cent, a.

ren-coun'ter, 1 ren-kaun'tər; 2 rĕn-coun'ter, n. A sudden hostile collision; unexpected encounter. ren-con'tre‡.

rend, 1 rend; 2 rĕnd, vt. & vi. [RENT or REND'EDᵈ; REND'ING.] To tear forcibly; split; sunder.

ren'der, 1 ren'dər; 2 rĕn'der, vt. **1.** To make of a certain sort; cause to be; furnish; give; interpret; give back. **2.** To melt and clarify, as lard.— ren-di'tion, 1 ren-dish'ən; 2 rĕn-dish'on, n. The act of rendering; a translation; interpretation; surrender.

ren'dez-vous, 1 rän'de-vū or ren'de-vū; 2 rän'de-vǫ or rĕn'de-vǫ. **I.** vt. & vi. [-VOUSED; -VOUS-ING.] To assemble at a given place. **II.** n. [REN'DEZ-VOUS, pl.] An appointed place of meeting; a meeting; appointment.

ren'e-gade, 1 ren'ı-gēd; 2 rĕn'e-ḡād, n. An apostate; deserter. ren''e-ga'do‡.

re-new', 1 rı-niū'; 2 re-nū', vt. & vi. **1.** To make or become new; regenerate. **2.** To begin over again.— re-new'a-bl(e², a.— re-new'al, n.— re-new'ed-ly, adv. Repeatedly; again; afresh.

ren'net, 1 ren'et; 2 rĕn'ĕt, n. The dried stomach of a calf: used for curdling milk.

re-nounce', 1 rı-nauns'; 2 re-nounç', vt.

[RE-NOUNCED'ᵗ; RE-NOUNC'ING.] To refuse to acknowledge longer; forswear; abandon.‡

ren'o-vate, 1 ren'o-vēt; 2 rĕn'o-vāt, vt. [-VAT'EDᵈ; -VAT'ING.] To make as good as new; renew; clean; purify.— ren''o-va'tion, n.

re-nown', 1 rı-naun'; 2 re-nown', n. High distinction; fame.— re-nown(e)d'ˢ, a. Famous.

rentᵗᵈ, 1 rent; 2 rĕnt, v. **I.** t. To obtain or let out for rent; hire. **II.** i. To be rented or leased.

rent², imp. & pp. of REND, v.

rent¹, n. A hole or slit made by rending.

rent², n. The payment periodically made for the use of property. rent'al‡.

re-nun''ci-a'tion, 1 rı-nun'sı-[or -shı-]ē'shən; 2 re-nŭn''çi-[or -shi-]ā'shon, n. The act of renouncing.

re-pair'¹, 1 rı-pâr'; 2 re-pâr', vt. To restore; mend; make amends for.— rep'a-ra-bl(e², a. Capable of repair or reparation.— rep''a-ra'tion, n. The act of making amends; indemnity. [turn.

re-pair'², vi. To betake oneself; resort; re-pair'¹, n. **1.** Restoration; reparation. **2.** Condition after repairing.— rep'a-ra-bly, adv.— re-pair'er, n.

rep''ar-tee', 1 rĕp'ər-tī'; 2 rĕp''ar-tē', n. A witty or apt reply; sharp rejoinder.

re-past', 1 rı-past'; 2 re-pàst', n. The act of taking food, or the food taken; a meal.

re-pay', 1 rı-pē'; 2 re-pā', vt. & vi. To pay back; pay again; requite; retaliate.— re-pay'a-bl(e², a.— re-pay'ment, n.

re-peal', 1 rı-pīl'; 2 re-pēl'. **I.** vt. To rescind; revoke. **II.** n. The act of repealing.— re-peal'a-bl(e², a.— re-peal'er, n.

re-peat'ᵈ, 1 rı-pīt'; 2 re-pēt', vt. To do or say over; reiterate; recite from memory.— re-peat'ed-ly, adv.— re-peat'er, n. One who or that which repeats; a watch that can be made to strike the last hour; a repeating firearm; a voter who repeats his vote.

re-pel', 1 rı-pel'; 2 re-pĕl', vt. & vi. [RE-PELLED', RE-PELD'ˢ; RE-PEL'LING.] To force or keep back; check; repulse; be repulsive.— re-pel'lent, a. Serving or tending to repel.

re-pent'ᵈ, 1 rı-pent'; 2 re-pĕnt', vt. & vi. To sorrow for as sinful; feel sorrow for sin, with desire to amend; regret.— re-pen'tance, n. A turning with sorrow from sin; loosely, regret.— re-pen'tant, a. Showing or characterized by repentance.

rep''er-toire', 1 rĕp''ər-twär'; 2 rĕp'er-twär', n. A list of pieces or the like, ready to be performed; also, such pieces collectively.

rep'er-to''ry, 1 rep'ər-tō'rı; 2 rĕp'er-tō'ry, n. [-RIESᶻ, pl.] A repository; collection.

rep″e-ti′tion, 1 rep″ı-tish′ən; 2 rĕp″e-tĭsh′on, *n.* The act of repeating, or that which is repeated.— **rep″e-ti′tious,** *a.* [U.S.] Characterized by or involving repetition.

re-pine′, 1 rı-pain′; 2 re-pīn′, *vi.* [RE-PINED′; RE-PIN′ING.] To be discontented; complain.— **re-pin′er,** *n.*— **re-pin′ing-ly,** *adv.*

re-place′[t], 1 rı-plēs′; 2 re-plāç′, *vt.* **1.** To put back in place. **2.** To fill the place of. **3.** To refund; repay.— **re-place′ment,** *n.*

re-plen′ish, 1 rı-plen′ısh; 2 re-plĕn′ish, *vt.* To fill again; supply or stock abundantly. — **re-plen′ish-ment,** *n.*

re-plete′, 1 rı-plīt′; 2 re-plēt′, *a.* Filled full; abounding.— **re-ple′tion,** *n.* Fulness; satiety.

rep′li-ca, 1 rep′lı-kə; 2 rĕp′li-ca, *n.* **1.** Art. A duplicate, as of a painting or statue, executed by the artist himself, and regarded as an original. **2.** *Mus.* A passage to be performed a second time.

re-ply′, 1 rı-plai′; 2 re-plȳ′. **I.** *vt. & vi.* [RE-PLIED′; RE-PLY′ING.] To say or do in return; make a reply; answer. **II.** *n.* [RE-PLIES′z, *pl.*] Something uttered, written, or done in return; an answer.

re-port′[d], 1 rı-pōrt′; 2 re-pōrt′, *v.* **I.** *t.* **1.** To bring back, as information; relate; state; circulate publicly. **2.** To prepare a record of; certify. **3.** To inform against. **II.** *i.* To tender a report; announce oneself, as a soldier for duty; act as a reporter.

re-port′, *n.* **1.** That which is reported; an announcement; narration; official statement. **2.** A sudden loud noise.— **re-port′er,** *n.* One employed by a newspaper to gather and report news for publication.

re-pose′, 1 rı-pōz′; 2 re-pōş′. **I.** *vt. & vi.* [RE-POSED′; RE-POS′ING.] **1.** To put to rest; refresh by rest. **2.** To trust; confide. **3.** To lie; recline; rest. **II.** *n.* **1.** The act of reposing; rest; sleep. **re-po′sal**‡. **2.** Calmness; composure.

re-pos′i-to-ry, 1 rı-poz′ı-to-rı; 2 re-pŏş′i-to-ry, *n.* [-RIES‡, *pl.*] A place in which anything is kept.

rep″re-hend′, 1 rep″rı-hend′; 2 rĕp″re-hĕnd′, *vt.* To chide sharply; object to forcibly; blame.— **rep″re-hen′sı-ble**(e[s], *a.* Deserving censure; blameworthy.— **rep″re-hen′sı-bly,** *adv.*— **rep″re-hen′sion,** *n.* Blame; censure; reproof.— **rep″re-hen′sıv**(e[s], *a.* Indicating or conveying reproof. **-ly,** *adv.*

rep″re-sent′[d], 1 rep″rı-zent′; 2 rĕp″re-şĕnt′, *vt.* **1.** To bring before the mind; portray or depict. **2.** To act as agent for; stand in the place of; be an instance of. — **rep″re-sen-ta′tion**[l], 1 rep″rı-zen-tē′shan;

2 rĕp″re-şĕn-tā′shon, *n.* **1.** The act of representing, or the state of being represented. **2.** That which represents; a likeness; model; description; dramatic performance. **3.** Representatives collectively.— **rep″re-sent′a-tiv**(r[s]. **I.** *a.* Representing, or qualified to represent. **II.** *n.* One who or that which represents; a member of a representative body; in the United States, [R-] a member of the popular branch of Congress or of a State legislature.

re″pre-sent′[2d], 1 rī″prı-zent′; 2 rē″pre-şĕnt′, *vt.* To present again.— **re-pres″en-ta′tion**[l], *n.* A second presentation.

re-press′[it], 1 rı-pres′; 2 re-prĕs′, *vt.* To restrain forcibly; crush; quell; overpower. — **re-pres′sion,** *n.* The act of repressing, or the condition of being repressed.— **re-pres′sıv**(e[s], *a.* Tending to repress.— **re-pres′sıv**(e-ly[s], *adv.* [press a second time.

re″press′[2t], 1 rī″-pres′; 2 rē″prĕs′, *vt.* To

re-prieve′, 1 rı-prīv′; 2 re-prēv′. **I.** *vt.* **re-priev′**[r], [RE-PRIEV(E)D′[s]; RE-PRIEV′-ING.] To relieve for a time from punishment, danger, or trouble; respite. **II.** *n.* The temporary suspension of a sentence; respite.

rep″ri-mand′, 1 rep″rı-mand′; 2 rĕp″ri-mănd′. **I.**[d]. *vt.* To reprove sharply or publicly. **II.** *n.* Severe reproof, public or private. [print anew.

re-print′[d], 1 rī-print′; 2 rē-print′, *vt.* To

re′print, 1 rī′print; 2 rē′print, *n.* An exact reproduction of a printed work.

re-pri′sal, 1 rı-prai′zəl; 2 re-prī′şal, *n.* Retaliation.

re-proach′, 1 rı-prōch′; 2 re-prōch′. **I**[t]. *vt.* To censure severely; blame; upbraid. **II.** *n.* The act of reproaching; censure; blame; disgrace.— **re-proach′a-bl**(e[s], *a.*— **re-proach′ful,** *a.* **-ly,** *adv.*

rep′ro-bate, 1 rep′ro-bēt; 2 rĕp′ro-bāt. **I.** *vt.* [-BAT″ED[d]; -BAT″ING.] **1.** To disapprove strongly; reject. **2.** To abandon as hopelessly wicked. **II.** *a.* Abandoned in sin; utterly depraved. **III.** *n.* One abandoned to evil.— **rep″ro-ba′tion,** *n.*

re″pro-duce′[t], 1 rī″pro-diūs′; 2 rē″pro-dūç′, *vt.* **1.** To produce again. **2.** To produce (offspring). **3.** To make a copy of. — **re″pro-duc′tion,** *n.* **1.** The act or power of reproducing. **2.** That which is reproduced; a copy.— **re″pro-duc′tıv**(e[s], *a.*

re-prove′, 1 rı-prūv′; 2 re-prǫv′, *vt.* To censure authoritatively; blame; rebuke. — **re-proof′,** 1 rı-prūf′; 2 re-prōōf′, *n.* The act of reproving; censure.— **re-prov′er,** *n.*

rep′tile, 1 rep′tıl; 2 rĕp′til. **I.** *a.* Crawl-**rep′tıl**[s], ing; groveling; mean. **II.** *n.* **1.** An animal that moves on its belly or by

1: ə = final; ı = habit; aisle; au = out; oil; iū = feud; Chin; go; ŋ = sing; thin, this.

2: wǫlf, dǫ; bōōk, bōōt; fųll, rųle, cūre, bŭt, bûrn; ȯil, bȯy; ḡo, ģem; iṇk; thin, this.

means of short limbs. **2.** A groveling, abject person.— **rep-til′i-an,** *a.*

re-pub′lic, 1 rĭ-pŭb′lĭk; 2 re-pŭb′lie, *n.* A state in which the people rule themselves through officers of their own election: a community; commonwealth.— **re-pub′li-can. I.** *a.* Of or pertaining to a republic. **II.** *n.* One who favors a republican form of government; [r- or R-] a member of a republican party.— **re-pub′li-can-ism,** *n.*

re-pub′lish†, 1 rĭ-pub′lĭsh; 2 re-pŭb′lish, *vt.* To reprint.— **re-pub′li-ca′tion,** *n.* Reprinting; a reprint.

re-pu′di-ate, 1 rĭ-piū′dĭ-ēt; 2 re-pū′di-āt, *vt.* [-AT″ED^d; -AT″ING.] To refuse to acknowledge or pay; disclaim; disavow; discard; put away.— **re-pu′di-a′tion,** *n.*— **re-pu′di-a″tor,** *n.*

re-pug′nant, 1 rĭ-pŭg′nɑnt; 2 re-pŭg′nant, *a.* Offensive; inconsistent; opposed.— **re-pug′nance,** *n.* Aversion; opposition. **re-pug′nan-cy‡.**— **re-pug′nant-ly,** *adv.*

re-pulse′, 1 rĭ-pŭls′; 2 re-pŭls′. **I.** *vt.* [RE-PULSED′, RE-PULST′^s; RE-PULS′ING.] To beat or drive back; repel. **II.** *n.* The act of repulsing; rejection; refusal.— **re-pul′sion,** *n.* Repulse; aversion.— **re-pul′siv(e^s,** *a.* Exciting dislike, disgust, or horror; repellent; offensive. **-ly,** *adv.* **-ness,** *n.*

re-pute′, 1 rĭ-piūt′; 2 re-pūt′. **I.** *vt.* [RE-PUT″ED^d; RE-PUT′ING.] To hold in general opinion; reckon; estimate. **II.** *n.* Reputation; estimation; honor.— **rep′u-ta-bl(e^p,** *a.* Having a good reputation; estimable; honorable.— **rep′u-ta-bl(e-ness^p,** *n.*— **rep′u-ta-bly,** *adv.*— **rep″u-ta′tion,** *n.* The estimation in which a person or thing is held by others; repute.— **re-put′ed-ly,** *adv.*

re-quest′, 1 rĭ-kwest′; 2 re-kwĕst′. **I^d.** *vt.* To ask; solicit. **II.** *n.* **1.** The act of requesting; entreaty; petition. **2.** That which is asked for. **3.** The state of being sought after.

re′qui-em, 1 rī′kwĭ-em; 2 rĕ′kwi-ĕm, *n.* A hymn, dirge, or mass for the dead.

re-quire′, 1 rĭ-kwair′; 2 re-kwīr′, *vt.* [RE-QUIRED′, RE-QUIR′ING.] **1.** To demand, or to request authoritatively; claim. **2.** To need; want.— **re-quire′ment,** *n.*

req′ui-site, } 1 rek′wĭ-zit; 2 rĕk′wi-sĭt. **I.**
req′ui-sit^s, } *a.* Required by circumstances; indispensable. **II.** *n.* A necessity; requirement.— **req″ul-si′tion,** *n.* Any formal request or demand.

re-quite′, 1 rĭ-kwait′; 2 re-kwīt′, *vt.* [RE-QUIT″ED^d; RE-QUIT′ING.] To repay; retaliate upon; punish.— **re-quit′al,** *n.*

re-scind′, 1 rĭ-sind′; 2 re-sĭnd′, *vt.* To make void; abrogate; repeal.

res′cue, 1 res′kiū; 2 rĕs′eū. **I.** *vt.* [RES′-CUED; RES′CU-ING.] To deliver from danger or harm; liberate; save. **II.** *n.* The act of rescuing; deliverance.— **res′cu-er,** *n.*

re-search′, 1 rĭ-sûrch′; 2 re-sẽrch′, *n.* Continued and diligent investigation or study.

re-sem′ble, } 1 rĭ-zem′bl; 2 re-sĕm′bl, *vt.*
re-sem′bl^p, } [-BL(E)D^p; -BLING.] To be like; be of the same or like nature.— **re-sem′blance,** *n.* Likeness.

re-sent′^d, 1 rĭ-zent′; 2 re-sĕnt′, *vt.* To feel or show resentment at; be indignant at. **— re-sent′ful,** *a.* **-ly,** *adv.*— **re-sent′ment,** *n.* Anger at real or fancied injury; persistent displeasure.

re-serve′, } 1 rĭ-zūrv′; 2 re-sẽrv′. **I.** *vt.* [RE-
re-serv′^s, } SERV(E)D′^s; RE-SERV′ING.] To hold or keep back; except. **II.** *n.* **1.** That which is reserved; a body of troops held for emergencies. **2.** Silence or reticence.— **res″er-va′tion,** *n.* **1.** The act of reserving, or that which is reserved. **2.** A tract of land reserved, as for an Indian tribe.— **re-serv(e)d′^s,** *pa.* **1.** Distant in manner; undemonstrative. **2.** Retained; kept back.— **re-serv′ed-ly,** *adv.*— **re-serv′ed-ness,** *n.*

res′er-voir′, 1 rez′ɑr-vwõr′; 2 rĕs′er-vwôr″, *n.* A receptacle, as for keeping water in store.

re-side′, 1 rĭ-zaid′; 2 re-sĭd′, *vi.* [RE-SID′-ED^d; RE-SID′ING.] To make one's abode; live; dwell; inhere.— **res′i-dence,** 1 rez′i-dens; 2 rĕs′i-dĕnc, *n.* **1.** The place where one resides. **2.** The act of residing.— **res′i-dent. I.** *a.* Having a residence. **II.** *n.* One who is resident; a diplomatic representative.— **res″i-den′tial,** *a.*— **res″i-den′ti-a-ry,** *a.* & *n.*

res′i-due, 1 rez′i-diū; 2 rĕs′i-dū, *n.* A remainder; surplus.— **re-sid′u-al, 1 re-zij′yu-al [or -zid′yu-]al; 2 re-sij′u-[or -sĭd′yu-]al,** *a.* **re-sid′u-a-ry‡.— re-sid′u-um,** *n.* [RE-SID′-U-A, *pl.*] A remainder.

re-sign′, 1 rĭ-zain′; 2 re-sĭn′, *vt.* & *vi.* **1.** To give up; surrender; relinquish. **2.** To yield trustfully.— **res″ig-na′tion,** 1 rez″ig-nē′shɑn; 2 rĕs″ĭg-na′shon, *n.* The act of resigning, as an office; submission, as to the divine will.— **re-sign(e)d′^s,** *pa.* Marked by resignation; submissive.

re-sil′i-ence, 1 rĭ-zil′i-ens; 2 re-sĭl′i-ĕnc, *n.* The act, power, or result of springing back to a former position; vigorous elasticity. **— re-sil′i-ent,** *a.*

res′in, 1 rez′in; 2 rĕs′in, *n.* A gummy substance that exudes from plants.— **res′in-ous,** *a.*— **res′in-ous-ly,** *adv.*

re-sist′^d, 1 rĭ-zist′; 2 re-sĭst′, *vt.* & *vi.* To oppose or obstruct; withstand.— **re-sis′-tance,** *n.*— **re-sist″i-bil′i-ty,** *n.* **re-sist-i-bl(e^p,** *a.*— **re-sist′i-bly,** *adv.*— **re-sist′less,** *a.* Irresistible.

res′o-lute, 1 rez′o-liut; 2 rĕs′o-lūt, *a.*

Having a fixed purpose; determined — **res'o-lute-ly,** *adv.* — **res'o-lute-ness,** *n.*

res″o-lu'tion, 1 rez″o-liū'shən; 2 rĕg′o-lū′shon, *n.* **1.** The act of resolving; a re-solve; declaration of an assembly. **2.** The state of being resolute; fortitude; determination. **3.** Separation, as of a substance into its component parts.

re-solve, } 1 rɪ-zɒlv'; 2 re-sŏlv′. **I.** *vt.* & *vi.* **re-solv**s, } [RE-SOLV(E)D′s: RE-SOLV′ING.] **1.** To decide absolutely; form a fixed purpose; determine. **2.** To separate into parts; analyze. **II.** *n.* Fixedness of purpose; a fixed determination; resolution. — **re-solv'a-bl(e**p, *a.*

res'o-nant, 1 rez′o-nənt; 2 rĕs′o-nant, *a.* Sending back or prolonging sound; reverberating; echoing. — **res'o-nance,** *n.*

re-sort', 1 rɪ-zŏrt'; 2 re-sŏrt′. **I.**d *vi.* **1.** To go frequently or habitually; repair. **2.** To have recourse. **II.** *n.* **1.** The act of frequenting a place; a place resorted to or frequented. **2.** A recourse; refuge.

re-sound'd, 1 rɪ-zaund'; 2 re-sound′, *vt.* & *vi.* **1.** To repeat, as a sound; be resonant; reecho. **2.** To celebrate; acclaim.

re-source', 1 rɪ-sōrs'; 2 re-sōrc′, *n.* **1.** That which is resorted to for aid; resort. **2.** *pl.* Available property; natural advantages.

re-spect', 1 rɪ-spekt'; 2 re-spĕct′. **I.**d *vt.* **1.** To have or show respect for; hold sacred. **2.** To relate or refer to. **II.** *n.* **1.** Honor mingled with esteem; deference; regard. **2.** A special aspect or relation. — **re-spect'a-bl(e**p, *a.* **1.** Deserving of respect; honorable. **2.** Fairly good; tolerable. — **re-spect'a-bil'i-ty,** *n.* **re-spect'a-bl(e-ness**p,† **re-spect'a-bly,** *adv.* — **re-spect'-ful,** *a.* Marked by or manifesting respect. **-ly,** *adv.* — **re-spect'ing,** *prep.* In relation to; regarding. — **re-spec'tive**s, *a.* Pertaining severally to each of a group, considered one by one. — **re-spec'tiv(e-ly**s, *adv.*

re-spire', 1 rɪ-spair'; 2 re-spir′, *vt.* & *vi.* [RE-SPIRED′; RE-SPIR′ING.] To breathe. — **re-spir'a-bl(e**p, } rɪ-spair′ə-bl; 2 re-spir′a-bl, *a.* Capable of being respired. — **res″pi-ra'tion,** 1 res″pɪ-rē′shən; 2 rĕs′pi-rā′shon, *n.* Breathing. — **re-spir'a-to-ry,** *a.* Serving for respiration.

res'pite, } 1 res′pɪt; 2 rĕs′pit. **I.** *vt.* **res'pit**s, } [RES′PIT-ED′d; RES′PIT-ING.] To grant a respite to; reprieve; relieve. **II.** *n.* Temporary intermission; postponement, as of the execution of a sentence; reprieve.

re-splen'dent, 1 rɪ-splen′dent; 2 re-splĕn′dĕnt, *a.* Shining; splendid. — **re-splen'-dence, re-splen'den-cy,** *n.* — **re-splen'-dent-ly,** *adv.*

re-spond'd, 1 rɪ-spɒnd'; 2 re-spŏnd′, *vt.* & *vi.* To answer; correspond. — **re-spon'-dent,** *n.* One who responds; a defendant. — **re-sponse',** *n.* An answer; reply.

re-spon'si-ble, } 1 rɪ-spɒn′sɪ-bl; 2 re-spŏn′-**re-spon'si-bl**p, } si-bl, *a.* Accountable; solvent. — **re-spon'si-bil'i-ty,** *n.* [-TIES z *pl.*]. The state of being responsible; a duty or trust. — **re-spon'si-bl(e-ness**p, *n.*

re-spon'sive, } 1 rɪ-spɒn′sɪv; 2 re-spŏn′siv, **re-spon'siv**s, } *a.* Inclined or ready to respond. **-ly,** *adv.* **-ness,** *n.*

restt, 1 rest; 2 rĕst. **I.**d. *vt.* & *vi.* **1.** To cause to cease from labor or exertion; cease; desist. **2.** To support; sustain; trust. **3.** To repose; sleep; be quiet; be still in death. **II.** *n.* **1.** Cessation from exertion or motion; peace; sleep; death. **2.** A support; stopping-place; pause or interval in music. — **rest'ful,** *a.* Full of or giving rest. — **rest'less,** *a.* Uneasy; sleepless. **-ly,** *adv.* **-ness,** *n.*

rest'. 1d. *vi.* To remain; be left. **II.** *n.* A remainder; the residue.

res'tau-rant, 1 res′to-rənt; 2 rĕs′to-rant, *n.* A place where refreshments are provided.

res″ti-tu'tion, 1 res″tɪ-tiū′shən; 2 rĕs′ti-tū′shon, *n.* A restoring; repayment; restoration.

res'tive, } 1 res′tɪv; 2 rĕs′tiv, *a.* **1.** Im-**res'tiv**s, } patient of control; unruly. **2.**‖. Stubborn; balky. **-ly,** *adv.* **-ness,** *n.*

re-store', 1 rɪ-stōr'; 2 re-stōr′, *vt.* [RE-STORED′; RE-STOR′ING.] To bring back; reproduce; return; make restitution or amends for; cure. — **res″to-ra'tion,** 1 res″to-rē′shən; 2 rĕs′to-rā′shon, *n.* The act of restoring, or that which is restored. — **re-stor'-a-tiv(e**s. **I.** *a.* Tending or able to restore. **II.** *n.* A medicine that revives or restores. **-ly,** *adv.* — **re-stor'er,** *n.*

re-strain', 1 rɪ-strēn'; 2 re-strān′, *vt.* To repress; hinder; restrict. — **re-straint',** *n.* A restraining; restriction; imprisonment.

re-strict'd, 1 rɪ-strikt'; 2 re-strĭct′, *vt.* To hold within limits; confine. — **re-stric'tion,** *n.* A restricting; limitation; a restraint. — **re-stric'tiv(e**s, *a.* **-ly,** *adv.*

re-sult', 1 rɪ-zult'; 2 re-sŭlt′. **I.**d. *vi.* To be a result; follow; issue. **II.** *n.* The outcome of an action; consequence; effect. — **re-sul'tant,** *a.* & *n.* Resulting; a result.

re-sume', 1 rɪ-ziūm'; 2 re-zūm′, *vt.* & *vi.* [RE-SUMED′; RE-SUM′ING.] To begin again; reassume; take back. — **re-sum'a-bl(e**p, *a.* **-bly,** *adv.* — **re-sump'tion,** *n.*

ré″su″mé′, 1 rē″zü′mē′; 2 rĕ′sü′mē′. *n.* A recapitulation; summary.

res″ur-rec'tion, 1 rez″u-rek′shən; 2 rĕg′ü-rĕe′shon, *n.* A rising again from the dead; renewal.

re-sus'ci-tate, 1 ri-sus'i-tēt; 2 re-sŭs'i-tāt, *vt. & vi.* [-TAT"ED^d; -TAT"ING.] To bring or come back to life; revive.— **re-sus"ci-ta'tion,** *n.*— **re-sus'ci-ta"tive(e^s,** *a.*

re-tail' 1 ri-tēl'; 2 re-tāl'. **I.** *vt.* To sell in small quantities; tell over, as gossip. **II.** *n.* The selling of goods in small quantities.— **re-tail'er,** *a.*

re-tain', 1 ri-tēn'; 2 re-tān', *vt.* **1.** To hold; keep. **2.** To engage beforehand, as a lawyer, by a fee.— **re-tain'a-bl(e^r,** *a.*— **re-tain'er,** *n.* **1.** A follower. **2.** One who retains. **3.** A retaining fee.

re-tal'i-ate, 1 ri-tal'i-ēt; 2 re-tăl'i-āt, *vt. & vi.* [-AT"ED^d; -AT"ING.] To give like for like; repay evil with evil.— **re-tal'i-a'tion,** *n.*— **re-tal'i-a"tiv(e^s,** **re-tal'i-a-to-ry,** *a.*— **re-tal'i-a"tiv(e-ly^s,** *adv.*

re-tard', 1 ri-tärd'; 2 re-tärd', *vt.* To make slow; hinder; delay; postpone.— **re"tar-da'tion,** *n.* [effort to vomit; heave.

retch^t, 1 rech; 2 rĕch, *vi.* To make an

re-ten'tion, 1 ri-ten'shən; 2 re-tĕn'shon, *n.* The act or power of retaining.

re-ten'tive, 1 ri-ten'tiv; 2 re-tĕn'tiv, *a.* **re-ten'tiv^s,** } Having power or tendency to retain. **-ly,** *adv.* **-ness,** *n.*

ret'i-cence, 1 ret'i-sens; 2 rĕt'i-çĕnç, *n.* The act or habit of being reserved in speech.— **ret'i-cent,** 1 ret'i-sent; 2 rĕt'i-çĕnt, *a.* Reserved in utterance.

re-tic'u-late, 1 ri-tik'yu-lēt; 2 re-tĭc'yu-lāt, *a.* Like network; netted. **re-tic'u-lat"ed‡; re'ti-form‡.**— **re-tic'u-lar,** *a.*— **re-tic"u-la'tion,** *n.*— **ret'i-cule,** *n.* A small bag, used by women to carry needlework, etc.

ret'i-na, 1 ret'i-nə; 2 rĕt'i-na, *n.* The inner coat of the eye, which receives the optical image.— **ret'i-nal,** *a.*

ret'i-nue, 1 ret'i-niū; 2 rĕt'i-nū, *n.* The body of retainers attending a person of rank.

re-tire', 1 ri-toir'; 2 re-tīr', *vt. & vi.* [RE-TIRED'; RE-TIR'ING.] To withdraw; draw back; go away; go to bed.— **re-tire'ment,** *n.* A retiring; seclusion.— **re-tir'ing,** *pa.* Shy; modest; quiet.

re-tort'^d, 1 ri-tôrt'; 2 re-tôrt', *vt. & vi.* **1.** To say in sharp rejoinder; reply sharply. **2.** To bend back.

re-tort'^1, *n.* A vessel with a bent tube, for distillation.

re-tort'^2, *n.* A retaliatory speech.

re-touch't, 1 rī-tuch'; **re-touch'^r,** } 2 rē-tŭch', *vt.* To add new touches to; modify; revise.

Retort.

a, retort; *b,* adapter; *c,* flask; *d,* lamp.

re-trace'^t, 1 ri-trēs'; 2 rē-trāç', *vt.* To trace back; follow backward, as a path.

re-tract'^d, 1 ri-trakt'; 2 re-trăct', *vt. & vi.* To take back; draw back; disavow.— **re-trac'til(e^s,** *a.* That can be drawn back or in, as claws. **re-tract'i-bl(e^r‡.**— **re-trac'tion,** *n.*— **re-trac'tiv(e^s,** *a.* **-ly,** *adv.*

re-treat'^t, 1 ri-trīt'; 2 re-trēt'. **I^d.** *vi.* To withdraw; retire; recede. **II.** *n.* The act of retreating; retirement; seclusion; refuge; a place for retirement.

re-trench'^t, 1 ri-trench'; 2 re-trĕnch', *v.* **I.** *t.* To cut down; reduce. **II.** *i.* To reduce expenses.— **re-trench'ment,** *n.*

ret"ri-bu'tion, 1 ret'ri-biū'shən; 2 rĕt'ri-bū'shon, *n.* Requital; punishment.— **re-trib'u-tiv(e^s,** 1 ri-trib'yu-tiv; 2 re-trib'yu-tiv, *a.* **re-trib'u-to"ry‡.**

re-trieve', } 1 ri-trīv'; 2 re-trēv', *vt.* [RE-**re-triev'^r,** } TRIEV(E)D'S; RE-TRIEV'ING.] To bring back; restore.— **re-triev'a-bl(e^r,** *a.*— **re-triev'a-bly,** — **re-triev'al,** *n.*— **re-triev'er,** *n.* A dog trained to search for and bring back game.

re'tro-, 1 rī'tro- *or* ret'ro-; 2 rē'tro- *or* rĕt'ro-, *prefix.* Back; backward; in return. Many self-explaining words are formed by this prefix, adding the meaning of *back, backward,* *in return* to the meaning of the second element of the compound, as the following:

re'tro-act'd	re'tro-flex
re'tro-ac'tion	re'tro-flex'ion
re'tro-ac'tiv(e^s	re'tro-ject'd
re'tro-cede'd	re'tro-vert'd
re'tro-ces'sion	re'tro-ver'sion

ret'ro-grade, 1 ret'ro-[or rī'tro-]grēd; 2 rĕt'ro-[or rē'tro-]grād. **I.** *vt. & vi.* [-GRAD"ED^d; -GRAD'ING.] To move backward; recede; deteriorate. **II.** *a.* Going backward; declining.— **ret'ro-gra-da'tion,** *n.*— **re"tro-gres'sion,** *n.*— **re"tro-gres'siv(e^s,** *a.* **-ly,** *adv.*

ret'ro-spect, 1 ret'ro-spekt; 2 rĕt'ro-spĕct, *n.* A view or contemplation of something past.— **ret"ro-spec'tion,** *n.* A calling to remembrance.— **ret"ro-spec'tiv(e^s,** *a.*

re-turn', 1 ri-tûrn'; 2 re-tûrn', *v.* **I.** *t.* To put, carry, or send back; repay; answer; yield, as profit. **II.** *i.* To come or go back; revert.— **re-turn'a-bl(e^r,** *a.*

re-turn', *n.* **1.** Returning; response; answer; restoration; requital; profit; repayment. **2.** A report, list, etc.

re-u'nion, 1 ri-yūn'yən; 2 rē-yụn'yon, *n.* **1.** The act of reuniting; harmony. **2.** A social gathering.— **re"u-nite'd,** *vt. & vi.* To unite again. [known.

re-veal'd, 1 ri-vīl'; 2 re-vēl', *vt.* To make **rev"eil-le'e,** 1 rev"e-li' *or* rə-vēl'yə; 2 rĕv'ĕ-lē' *or* re-vĕl'ye, *n.* A morning drum-beat or bugle-call for soldiers.

rev'el, 1 rev'el; 2 rĕv'ĕl. **I.** *vi.* [REV'ELED or REV'ELLED, REV'ELD⁵; REV'EL-ING or REV'EL-LING.] **1.** To feast riotously; carouse. **2.** To delight keenly: followed by *in.* **II.** *n.* A carouse; revelry.— **rev'el-er,** *n.* **rev'el-ler‡.— rev'el-ry,** *n.* Noisy or boisterous festivity.

rev"e-la'tion, 1 rev"ĭ-lē'shan; 2 rĕv"e-lā'shon, *n.* **1.** The act of revealing; that which is revealed. **2.** [R-] The Apocalypse.

re-venge', 1 rɪ-venj'; 2 re-vĕng'. **I.** *vt. & vi.* [RE-VENGED'; RE-VENG'ING.] To take revenge for; retaliate. **II.** *n.* The returning of injury for injury.— **re-venge'-ful,** *a.* **-ly,** *adv.*— **re-veng'er,** *n.*

rev'e-nue, 1 rev'ɪ-niū; 2 rĕv'e-nū, *n.* Income, as of a government; reward.

re-ver'ber-ate, 1 rɪ-vūr'bar-ēt; 2 re-vĕr'-ber-āt, *vt. & vi.* [-AT'ED⁴; -AT'ING.] To return; reecho; reflect.— **re-ver"ber-a'tion,** *n.* **re-ver'ber-a-to-ry‡.**

re-vere', 1 rɪ-vīr'; 2 re-vēr', *vt.* [RE-VERED'; RE-VER'ING.] To adore; venerate.— **rev'er-ence. I.** *vt.* [-ENCED‡; -ENC-ING.] To revere. **II.** *n.* **1.** A feeling of profound respect; veneration. **2.** An act of respect; obeisance. **3.** A reverend person.— **rev'er-end,** *a.* **1.** Worthy of reverence. **2.** Being a clergyman.— **rev'er-ent,** *a.* Feeling or expressing reverence. **-ly,** *adv.*— **rev"er-en'tial,** *a.* Proceeding from or expressing reverence. **-ly,** *adv.*

rev'er-ie, } 1 rev'ar-ɪ; 2 rĕv'er-i, *n.* [-IES²] **rev'er-y,** } *pl.*] Listless musing; a daydream.

re-verse', 1 rɪ-vūrs'; 2 re-vērs'. **I.** *vt. & vi.* [RE-VERSED'⁴, RE-VERST'⁵; RE-VERS'-ING.] To turn back; invert; revoke. **II.** *a.* Reversed. **III.** *n.* **1.** The direct opposite. **2.** The back or secondary side, as of a coin. **3.** A reversing. **4.** A misfortune.— **re-ver'sal,** *n.* The act of reversing.

re-ver'sion, 1 rɪ-vūr'shan; 2 re-vēr'shon, *n.* **1.** A return to some former state. **2.** A reserve.— **re-ver'sion-a-ry,** *a.*

re-vert'd, 1 rɪ-vūrt'; 2 re-vērt', *vi.* To return; recur.— **re-vert'i-bl(e⁰,** *a.*— **re-ver'-tiv(e⁵,** *a.* Tending to revert.

rev'er-y, *n.* Same as REVERIE.

re-view', 1 rɪ-viū'; 2 re-vū', *vt. & vi.* To view or examine carefully; inspect; criticize.— **re-view'er,** *n.* A critic or examiner.

re-view', *n.* **1.** A looking back; retrospection. **2.** Critical examination; survey; an inspection. **3.** A periodical devoted to critical or other essays.

re-vile', 1 rɪ-vail'; 2 re-vīl', *vt. & vi.* [RE-VILED'; RE-VIL'ING.] To attack with or use abusive speech; vilify.

re-vise', } 1 rɪ-vaiz'; 2 re-vīz'. **I.** *vt.* [RE-**re-vize'r,** } VISED'; RE-VIS'ING.] To reexamine; improve; reform. **II.** *n.* A revision.— **Revised Version,** the revised translation of the Bible into English, made in 1870–1884.— **re-vis'al,** *n.* A revision; review for correction.— **re-vi'sion,** *n.* The act of revising; a revised work.

re-vive', 1 rɪ-vaiv'; 2 re-vīv', *vt. & vi.* [RE-VIVED'; RE-VIV'ING.] To restore; refresh; renew; reawaken.— **re-viv'al,** *n.* **1.** The act of reviving, or the state of being revived. **2.** A religious awakening.

re-voke', 1 rɪ-vōk'; 2 re-vōk', *vt. & vi.* [RE-VOKED'⁴; RE-VOK'ING.] To annul; make void; cancel; recall.— **rev'o-ca-bl(e⁰,** *a.* Capable of being revoked.— **rev"o-ca'tion,** *n.* The act of revoking; repeal; reversal.

re-volt'd, 1 rɪ-vōlt'; 2 re-vōlt', *v.* **I.** *t.* To shock or disgust. **II.** *i.* **1.** To rebel. **2.** To be repelled or shocked.

re-volt', *n.* An uprising against established authority.

rev"o-lu'tion, 1 rev"o-liū'shan; 2 rĕv'o-lū'shon, *n.* **1.** The act of revolving; motion around a center. **2.** A radical change as of government.— **rev"o-lu'tion-a-ry,** *a.* Pertaining to revolution.— **rev"o-lu'tion-ist,** *n.*— **rev"o-lu'tion-ize** or **-ise,** *vt.* [-IZED; -IZ'ING.] To change in character, government, or administration.

re-volve', } 1 rɪ-velv'; 2 re-vŏlv', *vt. & vi.* [RE-**re-volv'⁵,** } VOLVED'; -VOLVD'⁵; RE-VOLV'-ING.] **1.** To move in an orbit about a center; move in a circle; rotate; recur. **2.** To turn over mentally.— **re-volv'er,** *n.* **1.** One who or that which revolves. **2.** A repeating firearm.

re-vul'sion, 1 rɪ-vul'shan; 2 re-vŭl'shon, *n.* A strong reaction; recoil.

re-ward', 1 rɪ-wôrd'; 2 re-wa̤rd'. **I**⁴. *vt. & vi.* To give a reward to or for: be a reward for; recompense; requite. **II.** *n.* The act of rewarding; a gift, prize, or recompense.

rey'nard, 1 re̦'nard; 2 re̦'nard, *n.* The fox as the personification of cunning.

rhap'so-dy, 1 rap'so-dɪ; 2 răp'so-dy, *n.* [-DIES²; *pl.*] A disconnected and extravagant composition.— **rhap-sod'ic,** *a.*— **rhap-sod'i-cal-ly,** *adv.*— **rhap'so-dist,** *n.*

rhe'a¹, 1 rī'ə; 2 rē'a, *n.* An ostrich-like bird of the plains of South America, having three toes.

rhe'a², *n.* The ramie-plant.

Rhen'ish, 1 ren'ish; 2 rĕn'ish, *a.* Of or pertaining to the river Rhine or the countries bordering upon it.

rhe'o-stat, 1 rī'o-stat; 2 rē'o-stăt, *n.* A contrivance for measuring current

---

strength of electricity by resistance coils
or the like.

rhet′o·ric, 1 ret′o·rik; 2 rĕt′o·rĭc, *n.* The
art of discourse; pleasing or persuasive
skill in the use of language.— **rhe·tor′i·cal,**
a. Pertaining to rhetoric; oratorical. **-ly,**
adv.— **rhet″o·ri′cian,** *n.* A master or
teacher of rhetoric.

rheum, } 1 rūm, rū′ms; 2 rụm, rụ′ma, *n.*
rheu′ma, } Watery discharge fom the nose
and eyes.— **rheum′y,** *a.*

rheu′ma·tism, *n.* A variable, shifting
inflammation or neuralgia, affecting the
muscles, joints, etc.— **rheu·mat′ic,** *a.* & *n.*
— **rheu·mat′i·cal,** *a.*

rhi·noc′e·ros, 1 raɪ·nes′a·res; 2 rī·nŏç′-
e·rŏs, *n.* [-ES, 1
-ez; 2 -ĕş, *pl.*] A
large mammal,
of Africa and
Asia, with one
or two horns on
the snout, and a
very thick hide. Indian Rhinoceros. ¹/₁₄₀

rho″do·den′dron, 1 rō″do·[*or* rod″o·]den′-
dron; 2 rō″do·[*or* rŏd″o·]dĕn′dron, *n.* A
plant of the heath family, with profuse
clusters of beautiful flowers.

rhomb, 1 remb; 2 rŏmb, *n.* An equilateral
parallelogram having oblique angles, or
a solid bounded by six such parallelograms. **rhom′bus‡.**— **rhom′bic,** *a.*—
rhom′boid, 1 rem′boid; 2 rŏm′boid, *n.* A
parallelogram with oblique angles and un-
equal sides.— **rhom′boid·al,** *a.*

rhu′barb, 1 rū′bärb; 2 rụ′bärb, *n.* **1.** A
hardy perennial herb, the acid stalks of
which are used in cookery. **2.** The medicinal root of certain Oriental plants.

rhyme, rhym′er, etc. See RIME, etc.

rhythm, 1 rithm; 2 rўthm, *n.* Regular
cadence, as in music or poetry.— **rhyth′mic,**
a. Relating to or characterized by rhythm.
rhyth′mi·cal‡.

rib, 1 rib; 2 rĭb. **I.** *vt.* [RIBBED, RIBD⁵; RIB′-
BING.] To mark with or strengthen by
ribs. **II.** *n.* **1.** One of the curved bones
nearly encircling the chest. **2.** A ridge,
strip, or band; a curved timber of a ship.

rib′ald, 1 rib′ald; 2 rĭb′ald, *a.* Pertaining
to or indulging in coarse indecency.—
rib′ald·ry, *n.* Coarse conduct or speech.

rib′bon, 1 rib′ən; 2 rĭb′on, *n.* A narrow
strip of fine stuff, as silk; any long, narrow
strip.

rice, 1 rais; 2 rīç, *n.* An East-Indian annual cereal grass; also, its grain or seeds.
See illus. in next column.

rich, 1 riçh; 2 rĭch, *a.* Wealthy; opulent;

valuable; costly; luxuriant; abundant.
-ly, *adv.* **-ness,** *n.*

rich′es, 1 riçh′ez; 2 rĭch′ĕş, *n. sing. & pl.*
Abundant possessions; wealth;
abundance.

rick, 1 rik; 2 rĭk, *n.* A stack, as
of hay or grain.

rick′ets, 1 rik′ets; 2 rĭk′ĕts, *n.*
A disease of childhood, marked
by softening of the
bones.— **rick′et·y,** *a.*
Ready to fall; affected
with rickets.

ric″o·chet′, 1 rik″o·shā′
or -shet′; 2 rĭc″o·chç′ *or*
-chĕt′. **I.** *vi.* [-CHETED′,
1-shĕd′,2-chĕd′;-CHET′-
TED; -CHET′ING, -CHET′-
TING.] To glance from
a surface, as a cannon-
ball; skip. **II.** *n.* A
bounding, as of a projectile over a surface.

Rice. 1. The
true rice:
a, flower;
b, grain.
2. The Indian rice:
a, a fertile spikelet.

rid, 1 rid; 2 rĭd, *vt.* [RID (sometimes RID′-
DED⁴); RID′DING.] To free, as from a
burden.— **rid,** *pa.* Free; clear.— **rid′dance,**
n. The ridding from something undesirable.

rid′den, *pp.* of RIDE, *q.v.*

rid′dle, } 1 rid′l; 2 rĭd′l. **I.** *vt.* & *vi.* [RID′-
rid′lᶠ, } DLED, RID′LD⁰ᵖ; RID′DLING.] **1.**
To perforate in numerous places. **2.** To
use a sieve; sift down. **II.** *n.* A coarse
sieve.— **rid′dler,** *n.*

rid′dle², **I.** *vt.* & *vi.* To solve, as an
enigma; explain. **II.** *n.* **1.** A puzzling
question. **2.** Anything mysterious.

ride, 1 roid; 2 rīd, *v.* [RODE (formerly also
RID); RID′DEN (formerly also RID), RID′Nᵖ;
RID′ING.] **I.** *t.* **1.** To be supported on
and borne along by. **2.** To traverse, as
on horseback. **II.** *i.* To be carried, as on
a horse or in a conveyance.— **rid′a·ble(eᵖ,** *a.*
ride′a·ble(eᵖ‡.

ride, *n.* **1.** An excursion by any means
of conveyance, especially on horseback.
2. A road intended for riding.— **rid′er,** *n.*
One who rides; a clause added to a bill or
enactment.

ridge, 1 rij; 2 rĭdg. **I.** *vt.* & *vi.* [RIDGED;
RIDG′ING.] To form ridges on. **II.** *n.*
A long elevation; the upper edge of a roof.
— **ridge′pole″,** *n.* A horizontal timber at
the ridge of a roof, against which the rafters
rest.— **ridg′y,** *a.*

rid′i·cule, 1 rid′i·kiūl; 2 rĭd′i·cūl. **I.** *vt.*
[-CULED′; -CUL·ING.] To make fun of;
deride. **II.** *n.* Contemptuous merriment; derision.— **ri·dic′u·lous,** 1 ri·dik′yu·
lus; 2 ri·dĭc′yu·lŭs, *a.* Exciting or calculated
to excite ridicule; absurdly comical. **-ly,**
adv. **-ness,** *n.*

rife, 1 raif; 2 rif, *a.* Abundant; plentiful; abounding; often followed by *with.*

riff′raff″, 1 rif′raf″; 2 rĭf′răf″, *n.* The **rif′raf″**, rabble; rubbish.

ri′fle[1], 1 rai′fl; 2 rī′fl, *vt.* [RI′FLED; RI′FLING.] To despoil; plunder; snatch away.

ri′fle[2], *vt. & vi.* [RI′FLED; RI′FLING.] To groove spirally, as the bore of a gun; rotate when discharged, as a bullet.

ri′fle, *n.* A firearm having spiral grooves within the bore for imparting rotation to the projectile.— **ri′fle-man,** *n.*

rift, 1 rift; 2 rĭft, *n.* A cleft; fissure.

rig, 1 rig; 2 rĭg, *vt.* [RIGGED, RIGD[S]; RIG′GING.] To fit out with what is required; equip.— **rig′ger,** *n.*— **rig′ging,** *n. Naut.* The entire cordage system of a vessel.

rig, *n.* Rigging; equipment.

right[d], 1 rait; 2 rīt, *v.* **I.** *t.* **1.** To make right; set upright; correct; adjust. **2.** To relieve from wrong or injustice. **II.** *i.* To regain an upright position.

right, *a.* **1.** Conformable to the moral law, or to truth, fact, or propriety; righteous; true; accurate; correct; proper. **2.** Pertaining to that side of the body which is toward the south when one faces the sunrise.— **right angle,** an angle of 90°. — **right′=an″gled,** *a.*— **right′ness,** *n.*

right, *n.* **1.** Moral rightness; righteousness: opposed to *wrong.* **2.** A just and proper claim. **3.** The right hand or side. — **right′ful,** *a.* **1.** Characterized by a right or just claim. **2.** Consonant with justice and truth. **-ly,** *adv.* **-ness,** *n.*

right, *adv.* **1.** In a right manner; justly; correctly; suitably; properly. **2.** In a straight line. **3.** In an eminent degree. **4.** Precisely. **right′ly**[‡].

right′eous, 1 rai′chus; 2 rī′chŭs, *a.* Morally right; just; upright; equitable. **-ly,** *adv.* **-ness,** *n.*

rig′id, 1 rij′id; 2 rĭg′ĭd.*a.* Resisting change of form; stiff; inflexible; rigorous; strict. — **ri-gid′i-ty,** *n.* **rig′id-ness**[‡].

rig′ma-role, 1 rig′mə-rōl; 2 rĭg′ma-rōl, *n.* Incoherent nonsense.

rig′or, 1 rig′ər; 2 rĭg′or, *n.* **1.** Stiffness of opinion; strictness; harshness; austerity. **2.** Inclemency, as of weather; asperity.— **rig′or-ous,** *a.* Strict; severe; exact. **-ly,** *adv.* **-ness,** *n.*

ri′gor[2], 1 rai′gor; 2 rī′gŏr, *n.* A violent chill from cold or nervous shock.

rill, 1 ril; 2 rĭl, *n.* A small stream or **rill**[P], rivulet.

rim, 1 rim; 2 rĭm. **I.** *vt.* [RIMMED, RIMD[S]; RIM′MING.] To provide with a rim. **II.** *n.* The edge of an object; a margin; border.

rime[1], 1 raim; 2 rīm. **I.** *vt. & vi.* [RIMED; **rhyme,** RHYMED.] RIM′ING, RHYM′ING.] To put into rime; make rimes; agree in sound. **II.** *n.* **1.** A correspondence of sounds, as at the end of lines in poetry. **2.** Rimed verse.— **rim′er, rhym′er,** *n.* One who makes rimes; a mere versifier.— **rime′-ster, rhyme′ster,** *n.* A maker of inferior verses.

rime[2], 1 raim; 2 rīm. **I.** *vt. & vi.* [RIMED; RIM′ING.] To cover with rime. **II.** *n.* Hoar frost.— **ri′my,** *a.*

rind, 1 raind; 2 rīnd, *n.* The skin or outer coat, as of fruit.

ring[1], 1 riŋ; 2 rĭng, *vt.* To encircle; supply with rings.

ring[2], *vt. & vi.* [RANG (sometimes RUNG); RUNG; RING′ING.] To sound, as a bell; announce or proclaim, as by sounding bells; emit a sonorous sound.

ring[1], *n.* **1.** A circular band, as of gold for the finger. **2.** A circular area or arena. **3.** A group of things or persons in a circle; combination of persons, as in politics.— **ring′=dove″,** *n.* A European pigeon having a cream-colored mark around the neck.— **ring′lead″er,** *n.* A leader in wrong or mischief; head of a party in an unworthy undertaking.— **ring′let,** *n.* A long, spiral lock of hair.— **ring′worm″,** *n.* A skin-disease appearing in circular patches.

ring[2], *n.* The sound of, or as of, a bell.

rink, 1 riŋk; 2 rĭnk, *n.* A floor or surface enclosed, as for skating.

rinse, 1 rins; 2 rĭns. **I.** *vt.* [RINSED[t], RINST[S]; RINS′ING.] To wash anew with clean water. **II.** *n.* The act of rinsing.

ri′ot, 1 rai′ət; 2 rī′ot. **I**[d]. *vi.* To engage in a riot; act riotously. **II.** *n.* **1.** A disturbance on the part of a crowd or mob; turbulent conduct of a large number; tumult. **2.** Revelry; wild, free growth; a medley.— **ri′ot-er,** *n.*— **ri′ot-ous,** *a.* Boisterous; tumultuous; profligate. **-ly,** *adv.* **-ness,** *n.*

rip, 1 rip; 2 rĭp. **I.** *vt. & vi.* [RIPPED[t], RIPT[S]; RIP′PING.] To divide, as along a seam; tear or cut with violence. **II.** *n.* **1.** A rent. **2.** A saw for ripping lumber. **rip′= saw″**[‡].

ripe, 1 raip; 2 rĭp, *a.* Fully matured and fit for food, as fruit; mature.— **ripe′ly,** *adv.* — **ripe′ness,** *n.*— **rip′en,** *vt. & vi.* To make or become ripe.

rip′ple, 1 rip′l; 2 rĭp′l. **I.** *vt. & vi.* [RIP′= **rip′l**[P], PLED, RIP′LD[P]; RIP′PLING.] To make ripples on or in; move with ripples, as running water. **II.** *n.* A wavelet on the surface of water; a sound, as of rippling water.

---

rise, } 1 raiz; 2 rīs. **I.** *vi.* [ROSE, ROZE^P;
rize^P, } RIS'EN, RIZ'N^P; RIS'ING.] To advance from a lower to a higher position;
stand up; to grow or slope upward; to
originate; emerge; prosper; to revolt. **II.**
n. The act of rising; elevation; an elevated place; advance, as in price, rank, etc.

ris'en, 1 riz'n; 2 rĭṣ'n, *pp.* of RISE, *v.*

ris'i-ble, } 1 riz'i-bl; 2 rĭṣ'i-bl, *a.* Pertain-
ris'i-bl^P, } ing to laughter; tending to excite laughter.— **ris"i-bil'i-ty,** *n.* [-TIES^z, *pl.*]
A tendency to laughter.— **ris'i-bly,** *adv.*

risk, 1 risk; 2 rĭsk. **I^t.** *vt.* **1.** To expose
to a risk. **2.** To dare to undertake; ven-
ture. **II.** *n.* A chance of harm or loss;
hazard; danger.— **risk'y,** *a.* **1.** Hazardous.
2. Venturesome.   [ceremony.

rite, 1 rait; 2 rīt, *n.* A solemn or religious

rl"te-nu'to, 1 rī'tē-nū'to; 2 rī'tē-nụ'to, *a.*
Holding back the time at once.

rit'u-al, rich'u-[or rit'yu-]əl; 2 rĭch'ụ-[or
rĭt'yụ-]al. **I.** *a.* Pertaining to rites. **II.**
n. A prescribed form of religious or
solemn ceremony; body of ceremonies.
— **rit'u-al-ism,** *n.* Strenuous insistence upon ritual.— **rit'u-al-ist,** *a. & n.*— **rit'u-al-
is'tic,** *a.*— **rit'u-al-is'ti-cal-ly,** *adv.*

ri'val, 1 rai'vəl; 2 rī'val. **I.** *vt. & vi.* [RI'-
VALED or RI'VALLED, RI'VALD^s; RI'VAL-ING
or RI'VAL-LING.] To strive to equal or excel; emulate. **II.** *a.* Standing in competition or emulation. **III.** *n.* A competi-
tor; an equal.— **ri'val-ry,** *n.* [-RIES^z, *pl.*]

rive, 1 raiv; 2 rīv, *vt. & vi.* [HIVED; RIVED
or RIV'EN; RIV'ING.] To rend or split, as
timber.

riv'er, 1 riv'ər; 2 rĭv'er, *n.* A stream of
water larger than a creek.

riv'et, 1 riv'et; 2 rĭv'ĕt. **I.** *vt.* [RIV'ET-ED^d
or RIV'ET-TED^d;
RIV'ET-ING or
RIV'ET-TING.] To
fasten with or as
with a rivet. **II.**
n. A short soft
metal bolt, hav-
ing a head on
one end, used to join objects, as metal
plates, by passing it through holes and
forming a new head by hammering on its
headless end.

Forms of Rivets.
1. Flat-head. 2. Button-
head. 3. Countersunk but-
ton-head. 4. Boiler-rivet.

riv'u-let, 1 riv'yu-let; 2 rĭv'yụ-lĕt, *n.* A
small brook; streamlet.

roach¹, 1 rōch; 2 rōch, *n.* A European
fish with reddish fins.

roach², *n.* A cockroach.

road, 1 rōd; 2 rōd, *n.* An open way for
public passage; a highway; roadstead.—
road'stead, *n.* A place of anchorage off
shore without harbor protection.— **road'ster,**
n. A horse or bicycle serviceable on ordinary roads.— **road'way",** *n.* A road, over
which vehicles pass.

roam, 1 rōm; 2 rōm, *v.* **I.** *t.* To wander
over; range. **II.** *i.* To wander; rove.
— **roam'er,** *n.*— **roam'ing,** *pa. & n.*

roan, 1 rōn; 2 rōn. **I.** *a.* Of a color consisting of bay, sorrel, or chestnut, sprinkled
with gray or white. **II.** *n.* **1.** A roan
color. **2.** An animal of a roan color.

roar, 1 rōr; 2 rōr. **I.** *vt. & vi* To utter a
roar; vociferate. **II.** *n.* A full, prolonged, resonant cry, as of a beast; any
loud, prolonged sound, as of waves.— **er,** *n.*

roast, 1 rōst; 2 rōst. **I^d.** *vt. & vi.* To cook,
as in an oven; heat intensely or exces-
sively. **II.** *a.* Roasted. **III.** *n.* A
piece of roast meat.

rob, 1 rob; 2 rŏb, *v.* [ROBBED, ROBD^s; ROB'-
BING.] **I.** *t.* To take away from wrong-
fully or injuriously. **II.** *i.* To be guilty
of robbery.— **rob'ber,** *n.*— **rob'ber-y,** *n.*
[-IES^z, *pl.*] The act of robbing; thievery.

robe, 1 rōb; 2 rōb. **I.** *vt. & vi.* [ROBED;
ROB'ING.] To put a robe upon; clothe.
II. *n.* A long, loose, flowing garment; a
lap-covering for use in a carriage.

rob'in, 1 rob'in; 2 rŏb'in, *n.* **1.** A small
European bird; the redbreast. **2.** A
North=American red=breasted thrush.

ro'bot, 1 rō'bot; 2 rō'bŏt, *n.* An automaton
that performs all hard work; hence, one who
works mechanically and heartlessly. Introduced by Karel Capek, Bohemian playwright,
in his "Rossum's Universal Robots" in 1921.

ro-bust', 1 ro-bust'; 2 ro-bŭst', *a.* Characterized by great strength; rugged;
healthy. **-ly,** *adv.* **-ness,** *n.*

rock^t, 1 rok; 2 rŏk, *vt. & vi.* To move
backward and forward, as on a swinging
base; sway; reel.— **rock'a-way,** *n.* [U. S.] A
four=wheeled, two=seated pleasure-carriage.—
rock'er, *n.* One who or that which rocks:
(1) A curved support, as of a rocking-chair.
(2) A rocking-chair.— **rock'ing-chair",** *n.*
A chair supported on curved rockers.

rock, *n.* Any large mass of stone.— **rock'y,** *a.*
Consisting of or abounding in rocks.

rock'et, 1 rok'et; 2 rŏk'ĕt, *n.* A firework
propelled by gases produced as it burns.

rod, 1 rod; 2 rŏd, *n.* **1.** A shoot or twig;
a straight, slim piece of wood or bar of
metal. **2.** A measure of length: 16$^1/_2$ feet.

rode, 1 rōd; 2 rōd, *imp.* of RIDE, *v.*

ro'dent, 1 rō'dent; 2 rō'dĕnt. **I.** *a.* Of
or like a rodent; gnawing. **II.** *n.* A
gnawing mammal, as a rat, squirrel, etc.

ro-de'o, 1 ro-dē'o; 2 ro-de'o, *n.* [Sp.] A
rounding up of cattle for branding.

roe[1], 1 rō; 2 rō, *n.* **1.** The spawn, as of fishes. **2.** A mottled streak in wood.

roe[2], *n.* A small deer of Europe and Asia.

Roent'gen rays, 1 rŭnt'gen rēz; 2 rŭnt'gĕn rāṣ. Rays that can pass through solid substances, and by means of which it is possible to see and photograph the shadows of bones, bullets, etc., through the fleshy parts of the body.

rogue, 1 rōg; 2 rōg, *n.* **1.** A dishonest person; trickster; rascal. **2.** One who is innocently mischievous or playful. — **rogu'er-y**, 1 rōg'ẽr-y, 2 rōg'ẽr-y, *n.* [-IES[z], *pl.*] **1.** Knavery or dishonesty. **2.** Playful mischievousness. — **rogu'ish**, 1 rōg'ish; 2 rōg'ish, *a.* **-ly**, *adv.* **-ness**, *n.*

rôle, 1 rōl; 2 rōl, *n.* A part taken by an actor.

roll, 1 rōl; 2 rōl, *v.* **I.** *t.* **1.** To move onward while rotating; turn about continually; move on rollers. **2.** To wrap round and round upon itself; make into a roll. **3.** To smooth out with a roller. **II.** *i.* **1.** To move onward, like a wheel or as on wheels. **2.** To undulate, fluctuate, or sway, as waves. **3.** To reverberate.

roll, 1 rōl; 2 rōl, *n.* **1.** Anything rolled up in cylindrical form. **2.** A list or register. **3.** Any article of food, as bread, rolled or doubled together in making. **4.** A roller. **5.** A rolling movement or sound. **6.** A trill. — **roll'call**[1], *n.* The calling over of a list of names, as of soldiers or workmen, to ascertain which are present; also, the time of or signal for calling the roll. — **roll'er**, *n.* Anything that rolls or is rolled; a cylinder used in rolling.

Ro'man, 1 rō'man; 2 rō'man. **I.** *a.* **1.** Relating to Rome, the ancient imperial city, the capital of modern Italy, or to the Romans. **2.** Like a Roman; noble; stern. **3.** Roman Catholic. **II.** *n.* **1.** A citizen of Rome or of the ancient Roman empire. **2.** *Print.* A style of perpendicular type, as that in which these words are printed. — **Roman Catholic**, pertaining to the Church of Rome, of which the Pope is the head. — **Ro'man-ism**, *n.* The dogmas, forms, etc., of the Roman Catholic Church. — **Ro'man-ist**, *n.* A member of the Roman Catholic Church. — **Rom'ish**, *a.* Pertaining to the Roman Catholic Church.

ro-mance', 1 ro-mans'; 2 ro-mănç', *vi.* [RO-MANCED'[t]; RO-MANC'ING.] To tell fanciful stories.

Ro-mance', } 1 ro-mans', -man'ik; 2 ro-
Ro-man'ic, } mănç', -măn'ic, *a.* Pertaining to the languages, as Italian, French, Spanish, and Portuguese, descended from the ancient popular Latin.

ro-mance', 1 ro-mans'; 2 ro-mănç', *n.* **1.** A fictitious and wonderful tale, as of chivalry. **2.** Delight in what is chivalrous, adventurous, fanciful, or mysterious. — **ro-manc'er**, 1 ro-mans'ẽr; 2 ro-mănç'er, *n.* A writer of romance; an extravagant story-teller. — **ro-man'tic**, 1 ro-man'tık; 2 ro-măn'tic, *a.* Of or pertaining to romance; fanciful; visionary; improbable. — **ro-man'-ti-cal-ly**, *adv.*

Rom'a-ny, } 1 rem'a-nı; 2 rŏm'a-ny. **I.** *a.*
Rom'ma-ny, } Of or pertaining to the Gipsies or their dialect. **II.** *n.* **1.** A Gipsy. **2.** The Gipsy dialect.

romp, 1 remp; 2 rŏmp. **I**[t]. *vi.* To play boisterously. **II.** *n.* **1.** One who romps **2.** Boisterous play. — **romp'ish**, *a.* **-ly**, *adv.* **-ness**, *n.*

ron'do, ron-deau', 1 ren'do *or* ren-dō'; 2 rŏn'do *or* rŏn-dō', *n.* Composition of several strains; at the end of each strain the first part, or subject, is repeated.

rood, 1 rūd; 2 rōod, *n.* **1.** A cross or crucifix. **2.** A land-measure: one-fourth of an acre.

roof, 1 rūf; 2 rōof. **I**[t]. *vt.* To cover with a roof; shelter; house. **II.** *n.* **1.** The top covering of a building, a car, etc. **2.** A dwelling; home. — **roof'less**, *a.* Shelterless. — **roof'tree**, *n.* The ridge-pole of a roof; hence, the roof.

rook[1], 1 ruk; 2 rŏok, *n.* An Old World crow. — **rook'er-y**, *n.* [-IES[z], *pl.*] **1.** A colony or breeding-place, as of rooks or of sea-birds, seals, etc. **2.** A rambling building.

rook[2], *n.* *Chess.* Same as CASTLE.

room, 1 rūm; 2 rōom. **I.** *vi.* To occupy a room; lodge. **II.** *n.* **1.** Free or open space. **2.** An apartment. **3.** Suitable occasion; ground. **4.** A person's place, function, or office. — **room'ful** *n.* — **room'y**, *a.* Having abundant room; spacious. — **room'i-ly**, *adv.* — **room'i-ness**, *n.*

roost, 1 rūst; 2 rōost. **I**[d]. *vt. & ri.* To perch upon; perch. **II.** *n.* A support upon which birds rest at night; a perch. — **roost'er**, *n.* The male of the domestic fowl.

root[1d], 1 rūt; 2 rōot, *vt. & vi.* To fix or become fixed in the earth by roots.

root[2d], *vt. & vi.* **1.** To turn or dig up with the snout. **2.** To eradicate: followed by *up* or *out.*

root, *n.* **1.** The underground, supporting part of a plant; origin; cause; foundation. **2.** The elementary part of a word. **3.** A factor of a quantity that, multiplied by itself a specified number of times, will

produce the quantity.— **root′let**, *n.* A small root.—**root′y,** *n.* [Eng. Soldiers' Slang.] Bread.

rope, 1 rōp; 2 rōp. **I.** *vt.* [ROPED[t]; ROP′-ING.] To tie up, unite, or enclose with rope. **II.** *n.* **1.** A thick cord of twisted fibers. **2.** A glutinous filament or thread.— **rop′y,** 1 rōp′ɪ; 2 rōp′y, *a.* That may be drawn into threads; stringy.— **rop′i-ly,** *adv.* — **rop′i-ness,** *n.*

ro′sa-ry, 1 rō′zə-rɪ; 2 rō′ṣa-ry, *n.* [-RIES[z], *pl.*] **1.** A string of beads for counting prayers. **2.** A chaplet or garland.

rose, *imp.* of RISE, *v.*

rose, 1 rōz; 2 rōṣ, *n.* **1.** An erect or climbing flowering shrub of numerous varieties, usually spiny-stemmed, and in the wild state bearing white, yellow, pink, or red flowers with five petals each. **2.** A flower of this shrub. **3.** A light pinkish crimson, like the color of many roses.— **brl′er-rose″,** *n.* **1.** The dogrose. **2.** In England any wild rose growing on a spiny stem. **3.** The eglantine.— **ro′se-ate,** *a.* Of a rose-color; rosy.— **rose′bud″,** *n.* **1.** The bud of a rose. **2.** A young girl.— **rose-bush,** *n.* A rose-bearing shrub or vine.— **ro-sette′,** 1 ro-zet′; 2 ro-ṣĕt′, *n.* An ornament resembling a rose.— **rose′-red″,** *a.* Of the color of a red rose; red; ruddy.— **rose′wood″,** *n.* A hard, dark Brazilian wood.— **wild rose,** any rose growing wild.

rose′ma-ry, 1 rōz′mē-rɪ; 2 rōṣ′mā-ry, *n.* A fragrant shrub of the mint family, with usually blue flowers.

ros′in, 1 rez′ɪn; 2 rŏṣ′in, *n.* Resin.— **ros′in-y,** *a.*

ros′ter, 1 rŏs′tèr; 2 rŏs′ter, *n.* A register or list, as of officers and men enrolled for duty.

ros′trum, 1 res′trum; 2 rŏs′trŭm, *n.* [ROS′TRUMS[z] or -TRA, *pl.*] A platform for public speaking.

ros′y, 1 rōz′ɪ; 2 rōṣ′y, *a.* [ROS′-I-ER; ROS′I-EST.] **1.** Like a rose; rose-red; blooming; blushing. **2.** Made of roses.— **ros′i-ness,** *n.*

rot, 1 ret; 2 rŏt. **I.** *vt. & vi.* [ROT′TED[d]; ROT′TING.] To corrupt; decay; putrefy; spoil. **II.** *n.* **1.** That which is rotten, or the process of rotting; decay; putrefaction. **2.** A disease of sheep; also, a disease of plants, as potatoes.— **rot′ten,** 1 rot′n; 2 rŏt′n, *a.* Affected with rot; decayed; putrid. **-ly,** *adv.* **-ness,** *n.*

ro′tate, 1 rō′tēt; 2 rō′tāt, *vt. & vi.* [RO′-TAT-ED[d]; RO′TAT-ING.] **1.** To turn on its axis, as a wheel. **2.** To change about, as crops.— **ro′ta-ry,** 1 rō′tə-rɪ; 2 rō′ta-ry, *a.*

Pertaining to rotation; turning round on its axis, like a wheel.— **ro-ta′tion,** 1 ro-tē′shen; 2 ro-tā′shon, *n.* **1.** The act of rotating; rotary motion. **2.** Change by alternation.

rote, 1 rōt; 2 rŏt, *n.* Repetition of words as a means of learning them, with slight attention to the sense.

ro′tor, 1 rō′tèr or -ter; 2 rō′tor, *n.* **1.** *Elec.* A part of an alternating-current motor which revolves. **2.** A revolving part of a machine, as, in a turbine.— **ro′tor-ship″,** *n.* A vessel propelled by rotors operated by wind-power and auxiliary power when the wind fails: a German invention by Anton Flettner, tested Dec. 3, 1924.

ro-tund′, 1 ro-tund′; 2 ro-tŭnd′, *a.* Round; plump; full-toned.— **ro-tun′da,** *n.* A circular building or hall, surmounted with a dome.— **ro-tun′di-ty,** *n.*

rouge, 1 rūẓ; 2 ruẓh. **I.** *vt. & vi.* [ROUGED; ROUG′ING.] To tint with or apply rouge. **II.** *n.* Any cosmetic for coloring the skin pink or red.

rough[t], 1 ruf; 2 rŭf, *vt. & vi.* **1.** To roughen. **ruf[r]**, ⎫ **2.** To make or shape roughly. **rough,** *a.* Uneven; not smooth; rude; violent; harsh; crude; hasty. **-ly,** *adv.* **-ness,** *n.*— **rough′en,** *vt. & vi.* To make rough; become rough.— **rough′-rid″er,** *n.* A skilled rough and daring horseman.

rough[1], *n.* A crude or rough condition.

rough[2], *n.* A rude, violent fellow.

rou′lade′, 1 rū′läd′; 2 ru′läd′, *n.* **1.** *Mus.* An ornamental run of short notes on one syllable; also, a roll or flourish, as on a drum. **2.** A dish made of slices of beef and bacon, rolled and steamed. [bling game.

rou-lette′, 1 rū-let′; 2 ru-lĕt′, *n.* A gam-

round[d], 1 raund; 2 round, *vt. & vi.* To make or become round; go round; complete.

round, *a.* **1.** Almost or quite circular, spherical, or cylindrical; not angular; curved. **2.** Free from fractions; also, divisible by ten, disregarding the smaller denominations. **-ly,** *adv.* **-ness,** *n.*

round, *n.* **1.** Something that is round, as a globe, ring, or cylinder; an orb; a sphere. **2.** A series of recurrent movements; a circuit; routine; melody in which several voices join at intervals.

round, *adv.* **1.** On all sides; around. **2.** With a rotating motion. **3.** Through a circle or circuit.

round, *prep.* On every side of, or nearly so; in such a manner as to encircle.— **round′-a-bout″,** *a.* Circuitous; indirect.— **round-de-lay,** *n.* **1.** A simple melody. **2.** A musical setting of a poem with a recurrent refrain.— **round′ish,** *a.* Somewhat round.— **round robin,** a paper, bearing signatures written in a circle.

rouse, 1 rauz; 2 rouꜱ, *vt. & vi.* [ROUSED; ROUS′ING.] To waken abruptly; startle; excite; start.

rout, 1 raut; 2 rout. I^d. *vt.* **1.** To defeat disastrously; put to flight. **2.** To drive or drag forth, as from hiding. **II.** *n.* **1.** A disorderly and overwhelming defeat or flight. **2.** A disorderly assemblage; rabble. [road; way.

route, 1 rūt *or* raut; 2 rṳt *or* rout, *n.* A method of procedure, regularly followed.

rove, 1 rōv; 2 rōv, *v.* [ROVED; ROV′ING.] **I.** *t.* To roam over or about. **II.** *i.* To wander.—**rov′er,** *n.* One who roves; a wanderer; pirate.

row, 1 rō; 2 rō, *vt. & vi.* To move or be moved by means of oars.

row[1], *n.* A trip in a rowboat; also, a turn at the oars.—**row′lock,** *n.* Any device in which an oar plays. [line.

row[2], *n.* An arrangement of things in a

row[3], 1 rau; 2 rou, *n.* A noisy disturbance or quarrel.—**row′dy,** *n.* [ROW′DIES[2], *pl.*] A low, quarrelsome fellow; a rough.—**row′dy-ish,** *a.* **row′dy‡.**—**row′dy-ism,** *n.*

row′el, 1 rau′el; 2 row′ĕl, *n.* A toothed wheel, as on a spur; also, the spur so furnished.

row′en, 1 rau′en; 2 row′ĕn, *n.* A second cutting of hay; aftermath.

roy′al, 1 rɷi′əl; 2 rŏy′al. **I.** *a.* Pertaining to a monarch; kingly; regal. **II.** *n.* **1.** A size of paper, 19×24 for writing, 20×25 for printing. **2.** A sail next above the topgallantsail.—**roy′al-ist,** *n.* A supporter of royalty.—**roy′al-ly,** *adv.*—**roy′al-ty,** *n.* [-TIES[2], *pl.*] **1.** Regal authority; royal persons collectively. **2.** A share of proceeds paid, as to an author or inventor, by those using his work or invention.

rub, 1 rub; 2 rŭb. **I.** *vt. & vi.* [RUBBED, RUBD[ꜱ]; RUB′BING.] **1.** To move or pass over with friction and pressure; graze, grate, or scrape. **2.** To polish or erase by friction. **II.** *n.* **1.** A rubbing. **2.** Something that rubs; a hindrance; difficulty.

rub′ber, 1 rub′ər; 2 rŭb′er. **I.** *a.* Made of india-rubber. **II.** *n.* **1.** Caoutchouc or india-rubber. **2.** Anything used for rubbing, erasing, etc. **3.** An article, as an overshoe, made of india-rubber. **4.** One who rubs. **5.** The decisive game in a series. [refuse.

rub′bish, 1 rub′ish; 2 rŭb′ish. *n.* Waste;

rub′ble, 1 rub′l; 2 rŭb′l, *n.* Rough pieces **rub′l**[ᴇ], ‡ of broken stone, or masonry built of them.

Ru′bi-con, 1 rū′bi-kən; 2 rṳ′bi-eon, *n.* A small river of central Italy; boundary of Cæsar's Gallic province, by passing which he committed himself to a war with Pompey; hence, any act done or point passed that decides one's course beyond recall.

ru′bi-cund, 1 rū′bi-kund; 2 rṳ′bi-cŭnd, *a.* Red; rosy.—**ru″bi-cun′di-ty,** *n.*

ru′bric, 1 rū′brik; 2 rṳ′brie, *n.* A liturgical rule, as in a prayer-book; such rules collectively.

ru′by, 1 rū′bi; 2 rṳ′by. **I.** *a.* Pertaining to or like a ruby; crimson. **II.** *n.* **1.** A transparent gem-stone of a deep-red color. **2.** A rich red like that of a ruby.

ruche, 1 rūsh; 2 rṳch, *n.* A quilted or ruffled strip of fine fabric, worn about the neck or wrists of a woman's costume.

rud′der, 1 rud′ər; 2 rŭd′er, *n.* A broad flat device hinged vertically at the stern of a vessel to direct its course.

rud′dy, 1 rud′i; 2 rŭd′y, *a.* [RUD′DI-ER; RUD′DI-EST.] Tinged with red; rosy.—**rud′di-ly,** *adv.*—**rud′di-ness,** *n.*

rude, 1 rūd; 2 rṳd, *a.* [RUD′ER; RUD′EST.] **1.** Rough or abrupt; tempestuous; uncivil; uncouth. **2.** Unskilfully made or done.

ru′di-ment, 1 rū′di-ment *or* -mənt; 2 rṳ′di-ment, *n.* A first principle, step, stage, or condition.—**ru″di-men′ta-ry,** *a.* Pertaining to or of the nature of a rudiment; germinal; undeveloped; abortive. **ru′di-men′tal‡.**

rue, 1 rū; 2 rṳ, *vt. & vi.* [RUED; RU′ING.] To be sorry for; feel remorse; grieve; pity. —**rue′ful,** *a.* Deplorable; pitiful. **-ly,** *adv.* **-ness,** *n.*

rue, *n.* A small bushy herb with bitter leaves; a bitter draft.

ruff, 1 ruf; 2 rŭf, *n.* A ruffle; a collar of **ruf**ᴾ, ‡ projecting feathers around the neck, as of a bird.

ruf′fi-an, 1 ruf′i-ən *or* ruf′yən; 2 rŭf′i-an *or* rŭf′yan, *n.* A lawless, brutal fellow; marauder.—**ruf′fi-an-ism,** *n.*—**ruf′fi-an-ly,** *a.*

ruf′fle, ‡ 1 ruf′l; 2 rŭf′l. **I.** *vt. & vi.* [RUF′-**ruf′l**ᴾ, ‡ FLED, RUF′LD[ᴾ]; RUF′FLING.] **1.** To make into or furnish with ruffles. **2.** To disarrange; rumple; be disordered or rumpled. **3.** To vex; be offended. **II.** *n.* **1.** A plaited strip; frill. **2.** Agitation; discomposure.

rug, 1 rug; 2 rŭg, *n.* A heavy fabric, or dressed skin, to be spread on a floor, or serve as a lap-robe.

rug′ged, 1 rug′ed; 2 rŭg′ĕd, *a.* Rough; rocky; uneven; shaggy; wrinkled; harsh; rude; stern. **-ly,** *adv.* **-ness,** *n.*

ru′in, 1 rū′in; 2 rṳ′in. **I.** *vt. & vi.* To bring to ruin; fall into ruin. **II.** *n.* **1.**

Destruction or a cause of destruction; demolition; decay; desolation. **2.** Remains of something demolished or decayed.—**ru′in·ous**, *a.* **-ly**, *adv.*

rule, 1 rūl; 2 rųl. **I.** *vt. & vi.* [RULED; RUL′ING.] **1.** To control; govern; establish; order. **2.** To mark with lines, as with a ruler. **II.** *n.* **1.** Controlling power; authority. **2.** A direction; command; prescribed form; regular procedure. **3.** A ruler; printers' straight strip of metal. —**rul′er**, *n.* **1.** One who rules. **2.** A straight-edged strip for ruling lines; a rule.

Parallel Ruler.

rum, 1 rum; 2 rům, *n.* An alcoholic liquor distilled from fermented molasses.

rum′ba, 1 rum′ba *or* (*Sp.*) rūm′ba; 2 rŭm′ba *or* (*Sp.*) rųm′bä, *n.* [Sp.] **1.** A dance of violent movements formerly performed by Negroes in Cuba. **2.** [U. S.] A dance in imitation of this. **rhum′ba**.

rum′ble, 1 rum′bl; 2 rŭm′bl. **I.** *vt & vi.* **rum′blF**, [RUM′BL(E)D²; RUM′BLING.] To make a low, rolling sound, as thunder. **II.** *n.* A muffled roar; confused noise.

ru′mi·nant, 1 rū′mi·nənt; 2 rų′mi·nant. **I.** *a.* **1.** Chewing the cud. **2.** Drowsily quiet. **II.** *n.* An animal that chews the cud.

ru′mi·nate, 1 rū′mi·nēt; 2 rų′mi·nāt, *vt. & vi.* [-NAT″ED⁴; -NAT″ING.] **1.** To chew, as a cud; chew the cud. **2.** To meditate (upon); muse.—**ru″mi·na′tion**, *n.*

rum′mage, 1 rum′ij; 2 rŭm′ag. **I.** *vt. & vi.* [RUM″MAGED; RUM″MAG·ING.] To turn over and disarrange things in search. **II.** *n.* A rummaging; disturbance.

ru′mor, 1 rū′mər; 2 rų′mor. **I.** *vt.* To report abroad. **II.** *n.* A report passing from person to person: sometimes personified.

rump, 1 rump; 2 rŭmp, *n.* The buttocks or hinder parts; the fag-end of anything.

rum′ple, 1 rum′pl; 2 rŭm′pl. **I.** *vt.* **rum′plF**, [RUM″PL(E)D²; RUM″PLING.] To wrinkle; tumble. **II.** *n.* An irregular wrinkle; a rumpled fabric or condition.

run, 1 run; 2 rŭn. **I.** *vt. & vi.* [RAN; RUN; RUN′NING.] To go swiftly; move or flow; continue; extend; be reported. **II.** *n.* **1.** The act of running or flowing; swift movement; a brook. **2.** A trip or journey. **3.** A course; succession.—**run′a·way″**. **I.** *a.* Escaped; fugitive. **II.** *n.* **1.** One who or that which runs away; a fugitive. **2.** An act of running away.—**run′ner**, *n.* **1.** One who or that which runs; a mes-

senger. **2.** That part on which an object, as a sled, runs or slides. **3.** A slender, prostrate stem that takes root, forming new plants.

run′die, 1 run′dl; 2 rŭn′dl, *n.* A rung, as of a ladder or chair. [barrel.]

run′dlF, of a ladder or chair.

rund′let, 1 rund′let; 2 rŭnd′lĕt, *n.* A small barrel.

rung, 1 rung; 2 rŭng, *n.* A round, as of a ladder or chair.

rung, *imp. & pp.* of RING², *v.*

run′let¹, 1 run′let; 2 rŭn′lĕt, *n.* A little stream; rivulet.

run′let², *n.* Same as RUNDLET. [dwarf.]

runt, 1 runt; 2 rŭnt, *n.* A stunted animal;

ru·pee′, 1 rū-pī′; 2 rų-pē′, *n.* The standard monetary unit of British India. See COIN.

rup′ture, 1 rup′chur *or* -tiur; 2 rŭp′chųr *or* -tūr. **I.** *vt. & vi.* [RUP′TURED; RUP′TUR·ING.] To burst; break; rend; sever. **II.** *n.* The act of rupturing; ruptured muscle; hernia; breach of friendship.

ru′ral, 1 rū′rəl; 2 rų′ral, *a.* Pertaining to the country; rustic. **-ly**, *adv.*—**ru′ral·ize**, *v.*

ruse, 1 rūz; 2 rųs, *n.* An action intended to mislead or deceive.

rush¹, 1 rush; 2 rŭsh, *vt. & vi.* **1.** To drive or push with violent haste; hurry. **2.** To move or enter precipitately.

rush¹, *n.* **1.** A grass-like herb, having soft, pliant stems. **2.** A worthless thing. —**rush′light″**, *n.* A candle made by dipping a rush in tallow.—**rush′y**, *a.*

rush², *n.* **1.** The act of rushing. **2.** Extraordinary haste or pressure.

rusk, 1 rusk; 2 rŭsk, *n.* A kind of light, sweetened bread or biscuit.

Russ, 1 rus; 2 rŭs, *a.& n.* [Poet.] Russian.

rus′set, 1 rus′et; 2 rŭs′ĕt. **I.** *a.* **1.** Of a reddish or yellowish-brown color. **2.** Made of russet material. **II.** *n.* **1.** A color formed by combining orange and purple. **2.** Russet cloth, leather, etc. **3.** an apple mottled with brown.—**rus′set·y**, *a.*

Rus′sian, 1 rush′an; 2 rŭsh′an. **I.** *a.* Pertaining to Russia, a country or to a republic of eastern Europe and northern Asia, or its people. **II.** *n.* An inhabitant of Russia.

rust, 1 rust; 2 rŭst. **I.** *vt. & vi.* **1.** To affect, or become affected with rust. **2.** To impair by inaction. **II.** *n.* **1.** A reddish coating, as that caused on iron by

Rye.

a, a part of the head in maturity.

oxidation. **2.** *Bot.* Any of the destructive fungi that grow on wheat, oats, barley, etc., or the diseased condition so caused.

rus′tic, 1 rŭs′tĭk; 2 rŭs′tĭc. **I.** *a.* Rural; plain; homely; appropriate to the country. **II.** *n.* A countryman; peasant.— **rus′ti-cal-ly,** *adv.*— **rus′ti-cate,** *vt. & vi.* [-CAT′-ED^d; -CAT′ING.] To send to, dwell in, or go into the country.— **rus″ti-ca′tion,** *n.*— **rus-tic′i-ty,** *n.* [-TIES^z, *pl.*] Rustic simplicity; homeliness.

rus′tle, { 1 rŭs′l; 2 rŭs′l. **I.** *vt. & vi.* [RUS′-
rus′tl^e, } TL(E)D^d; RUS′TLING.] To make or move with a rustling sound. **II.** *n.* A quick succession of small, light, frictional sounds.

rust′y, 1 rŭst′ĭ; 2 rŭst′y, *a.* [RUST′I-ER; RUST′I-EST.] Covered or affected with rust; resembling rust; impaired by inaction.— **rust′i-ness,** *n.*

rut, 1 rŭt; 2 rŭt. **I.** *vt.* [RUT′TED^d; RUT′-TING.] To make ruts in. **II.** *n.* A sunken track made by a wheel; any beaten track.

ruth‖, 1 rūth; 2 ruth, *n.* Sorrow; pity.— **ruth′less,** *a.* Merciless. **-ly,** *adv.* **-ness,** *n.*

rye, 1 raɪ; 2 rȳ, *n.* The grain or seeds produced by a cereal grass nearly allied to wheat; also, the plant. See illus. on preceding page.

ry′ot, 1 raɪ′ət; 2 rȳ′ot, *n.* In India, a tenant; peasant.

S

S, s, 1 es; 2 ĕs, *n.* [s′s, S′s, or *Ss*, 1 es′ez; 2 ĕs′ĕş, *pl.*] The nineteenth letter in the English alphabet.

-s, *suffix.* **1.** The sign of the possessive (with apostrophe); *′s* for singular, *s′* for plural); as, John′s, warriors′. **2.** The common plural sign, becoming *-es*, after sibilants; as, cat*s*, box*es*. **3.** The ending of the third person singular present indicative.

Sab′a-oth, 1 sab′ɪ-ŏth *or* sə-bē′ŏth; 2 săb′a-ŏth *or* sa-bā′ŏth, *n. pl.* Armies; hosts.

Sab′bath, 1 sab′ăth; 2 săb′ath, *n.* **1.** The seventh day of the week, appointed as a day of rest. **2.** Sunday. **3.** A period of rest and peace.— **Sab″ba-ta′ri-an,** 1, *a.* Pertaining to the Sabbath. **II.** *n.* A strict observer of the seventh day as the Sabbath. **-ism,** *n.*— **Sab-bat′i-cal,** *a.* Pertaining to, or like the Sabbath. **Sab-bat′ic†.**

sa′ber, { 1 sā′bər; 2 sā′ber. **I.** *vt.* [SA′-
sa′bre, } BERED, SA′BRED, SA′BERD^s; SA′BER-ING, SA′BRING.] To strike or arm with a saber. **II.** *n.* A heavy cavalry sword.

sa′ble, 1 sē′bl; 2 sā′bl. **I.** *a.* Black or dark-brown. **II.** *n.* **1.** A Siberian carnivore related to the marten; also, its black fur. **2.** The color black; hence, mourning.

sa″bot′, 1 sa″bō′; 2 sä″bō′, *n.* A wooden shoe, as of a French peasant.

sa″bo″tage, 1 sa″bo″täʒ′; 2 sä″bo″täzh′, *n.* [F.] Malicious destruction or damage, as by strikers or malcontents.

Saber.

Sabot.

sac, 1 sak; 2 săc, *n. Biol.* A membranous pouch; a cavity; receptacle.

sac′cha-rin, { 1 sak′ə-rin; 2 săc′a-rĭn. **I.** *a.*
sac′cha-rine, } Pertaining to or like sugar, sweet. **II.** *n.* A chemical substitute for sugar.

sac″er-do′tal, 1 sas″ər-dō′tal; 2 săc″er-dō′tal, *a.* Priestly. **-ism,** *n.* **-ly,** *adv.*

sa″chem, 1 sē′chem; 2 sā′chĕm, *n.* A North-American Indian chief.

sa″chet′, 1 sa″shē′; 2 sä″chē, *n.* A small bag for perfumed powder.

sack¹, 1 sak; 2 săk. **I^t.** *vt.* To put into, cover with, or carry in a sack. **II.** *n.* **1.** A bag for bulky articles. **2.** A loose garment with sleeves.— **sack′cloth,** *n.* A coarse cloth for making sacks, etc.

sack², **I^t.** *vt.* To plunder (a town or city). **II.** *n.* The pillaging of a captured town or city; booty obtained by pillage.

sack′but, 1 sak′but; 2 săk′bŭt, *n.* **1.** A primitive wind‐instrument. **2.** *Bib.* A stringed instrument.

sac′ra-ment, 1 sak′rə-ment *or* -mənt; 2 săc′ra-ment, *n.* A solemn religious rite, as the Lord′s Supper.— **sac″ra-men′tal,** *a.*— **sac″ra-men′tal-ly,** *adv.*

sa′cred, 1 sē′kred; 2 sā′crĕd, *a.* Set apart to religious use; pertaining to deity or religion; consecrated; hallowed; inviolable.— **sa′cred-ly,** *adv.*— **sa′cred-ness,** *n.*

sac′ri-fice, 1 sak′rɪ-faɪz; 2 săc′rĭ-fīz, *v.* [-FICED; -FIC′ING.] **I.** *t.* To offer as a sacrifice; surrender. **II.** *i.* To offer a sacrifice; make an offering.

sac′ri-fice, 1 sak′rɪ-faɪs; 2 săc′rĭ-fīç, *n.* An offering to a deity, or that which is offered; surrender; loss.— **sac″ri-fi′cial,** 1

sak'ri-fish'əl; 2 săc'ri-fish'al, *a.* Pertaining to or of the nature of a sacrifice.

sac'ri-lege, 1 sak'rɪ-lĭj; 2 săc'rĭ-leg, *n.* The profaning of anything sacred; desecration. — **sac'ri-le'gious,** 1 sak'rɪ-lī'jus; 2 săc'rĭ-lē'gŭs, *a.* Impious. — **ly,** *adv.* **-ness,** *n.*

sac'ris-ty, 1 sakʹrɪs-tɪ; 2 săc'ris-ty, *n.* [-TIES², *pl.*] A room, as in a church, where the sacred vessels and vestments are kept. — **sac'ris-tan,** *n.* A church officer having charge of the sacristy, etc.

sad, 1 sad; 2 săd, *a.* [SAD'DER; SAD'DEST.] Sorrowful; mournful; distressing. — **sad'den,** *vt. & vi.* To render or become sad. — **sad'ly,** *adv.* — **sad'ness,** *n.*

sad'dle, ⎱ 1 sad'l; 2 săd'l. **I.** *vt.* [SAD'DLED, **sad'lₚ,** ⎰ SAD'LDₚ; SAD'-DLING.] To put a saddle on; load; burden. **II.** *n.* **1.** A seat or pad to support a rider. **2.** The two hind quarters or the loins, as of mutton or venison. — **sad'dler,** *n.* A maker of saddles, harness, etc. — **sad'dler-y,** *n.* [-IES², *pl.*] **1.** Saddles, harness, and fittings, collectively. **2.** The business of a saddler. — **sad'dle-tree",** *n.* The frame of a saddle.

English Hunting-saddle.

1. Knee-puff, and 2, thigh-puff, of the flap.

Sad"du-ce'an, 1 sad'yu-sī'an; 2 săd'yu-çē'an, *a.* Of or pertaining to the Sadducees, a Jewish party that arose in the 2d century B.C.: opposed to the Maccabees and, later, to the Pharisees (*Acts* xxiii, 6-8). **Sad"du-ce'an‡.** — **Sad"du-cee"ism,** *n.* **Sad'du-cism‡.**

sad'i'ron, 1 sad'ˈaɪ"ərn; 2 săd'ī"ĕrn, *n.* [A flat-iron.

safe, 1 sēf; 2 săf. **I.** *a.* **1.** Free from danger; unharmed. **2.** Not hazardous; prudent, secure. **II.** *n.* A strong iron-and-steel receptacle for protecting valuables; any place of safe storage. **-ly,** *adv.* **-ness,** *n.* — **safe"'con'duct,** *n. Inter. Law.* An official document assuring protection on a journey or voyage. — **safe'g(u)ard"ₛ,** *n.* One who or that which guards or protects. — **safe'ty,** *n.* The state or condition of being safe. — **safe'ty-valve",** *n.* A valve on a steam-boiler, etc., for relieving excessive pressure.

saf'fron, 1 saf'rən; 2 săf'ron. **I.** *a.* Of the color of saffron. **II.** *n.* The dried stigmas of a species of crocus; also, their deep orange color, or the plant producing them.

sag, 1 sag; 2 săg, *vt. & vi.* [SAGGED, SAGDₛ;

SAG'GING.] To bend or cause to bend downward, especially in the middle.

sa'ga, 1 sä'go; 2 sä'ga, *n.* A Scandinavian heroic story; a fragment of ancient history or legend.

sa-ga'cious, 1 sə-gē'shus; 2 sa-gā'shŭs, *a.* Keen; shrewd; wise; quick of scent. **-iy,** *adv.* **-ness,** *n.* — **sa-gac'i-ty,** 1 sə-gas'ɪ-tɪ; 2 sa-găç'i-ty, *n.* The quality of being sagacious; ready and accurate judgment.

sag'a-more, 1 sag'a-mōr; 2 săg'a-mōr, *n.* An Indian tribal chief. [Am. Ind.]

sage, 1 sēj; 2 sāg, *a.* Having calm, far-seeing wisdom; prudent; wise; profound. **-ly,** *adv.* **-ness,** *n.*

sage¹, *n.* A wise and venerable man.

sage², *n.* A plant of the mint family, used for flavoring meats, etc.

sa'go, 1 sē'go; 2 sā'go, *n.* A farinaceous food from inner portions of various palms.

sa'hib, 1 sä'ɪb; 2 sä'ib, *n.* Master; lord; Mr.; sir: a Hindu title of respect.

sail, 1 sēl; 2 sāl, *v.* **I.** *t.* To manage, as a ship, on the water; navigate. **II.** *i.* To move, as in a vessel propelled by sails; travel by water; set sail; float, as a cloud. — **sail'er,** *n.* A vessel that sails. — **sail'or,** *n.* A seaman; mariner.

sail, 1 sēl; 2 sāl, *n.* **1.** A piece of canvas, etc., supported by a mast of a vessel, to secure its propulsion by the wind. **2.** A sailing vessel or craft. **3.** A trip in a vessel.

saint, 1 sēnt; 2 sănt. **I.** *a.* Holy; canonized: as a title, abbreviated to *St.* **II.** *n.* A godly or sanctified person; one of the blessed in heaven. — **saint'ed,** *a.* Numbered among the saints; passed into heaven. — **saint'like,** *a.* — **saint'li-ness,** *n.* — **saint'ly,** *a.* Like a saint; godly; holy.

Saint Ber"nard', 1 sēnt bər'nərd'; 2 sănt ber-nård'. A large, strong, sagacious dog, ordinarily brown and white, trained to rescue travelers lost in the snow on the Alps: named from the hospice of *Saint Bernard* (8,150 ft.), the highest habitation in the Alps.

Rough-coated and Smooth-coated St.Bernard Dogs.

sake, 1 sēk; 2 săk, *n.* Purpose; interest; regard; behalf.

1: ûrtistic, ûrt; fat, fāre; fast; get, prey; hĭt, police; obey, gō; not, ŏr; fŭll, rûle; bᴜt, bûrn.

2: ärt, āpe, făt, fâre, fåst, whạt, ạll; mē, gĕt, prey, fērn; hĭt, īce; ī = ĕ: ĭ = ĕ; gō, nŏt, ôr, wón.

sa-laam′, 1 sə-läm′; 2 sa-läm′, *n.* A respectful Oriental salutation approaching prostration. [Lustful; impure.

sa-la′cious, 1 sə-lē′shŭs; 2 sa-lä′shŭs, *a.*

sal′ad, 1 sal′ad; 2 săl′ad, *n.* A dish of green herbs or vegetables served with a dressing.

sa-lam′, *n.* Same as SALAAM.

sal′a-man″der, 1 sal′ə-man″dər; 2 săl′a-măn″der, *n.* A lizard-like animal fabled to live in fire.—**sal″a-man′-drin(e⁵,** *a.*

sal′a-ry, 1 sal′ə-rɪ; 2 săl′a-ry, *n.* [-RIES², *pl.*] A periodical compensation for services. **-ly,** *adv.*

sale, 1 sēl; 2 säl, *n.* The act of selling; opportunity of selling; market.— **sal′a-bl(e⁵,** *a.* Marketable.— **sal″a-bil′i-ty,** *n.* **sal′a-bl(e-ness‡.**— **sal′a-bly,** *adv.*— **sales′man,** *n.* [-MEN, *pl.*] A man who sells goods.— **sales′-wo″man,** *n. fem.*

Spotted Salamander. 1/8

sal″e-ra′tus, 1 sal″ə-rē′tŭs; 2 săl″e-rä′tŭs, *n.* Cooking-soda.

sa′li-ent, 1 sē′lɪ-ent; 2 sä′li-ĕnt. **I.** *a.* Standing out; projecting. **II.** *n.* A salient angle. **-ly,** *adv.*

sa′line, 1 sē′lain; 2 sä′līn, *a.* Consisting of or containing salt; salty.— **sal″i-nif′er-ous,** *a.* Yielding salt.— **sa-lin′i-form,** *a.* Having the form or nature of a salt.— **sa-lin′i-ty,** *n.* The state or degree of being salt; saltness. **sa′line-ness‡.**

sa-li′va, 1 sə-lai′və; 2 sa-lī′va, *n.* The fluid secreted by the glands of the mouth; spittle.— **sal′i-va-ry,** 1 sal′ɪ-vē-rɪ; 2 săl′i-vā-ry, *a.* [healthy yellowish color.

sal′low, 1 sal′o; 2 săl′o, *a.* Of an unwholesome yellowish color.

sal′ly, 1 sal′ɪ; 2 săl′y. **I.** *vi.* [SAL′LIED, SAL′LY·ING.] To make a sally; set out with spirit. **II.** *n.* [SAL′LIES², *pl.*] **1.** A rushing forth; starting out; sortie. **2.** A sudden overflow of wit or merriment.

salm′on, 1 sam′ən; 2 săm′on, *n.* **1.** A fish of the North Atlantic. **2.** A reddish-orange color.

sa″lon′, 1 sȧ″lôn′; 2 sä″lôn′, *n.* A drawing-room; a fashionable reception.

sa-loon′, 1 sə-lūn′; 2 sa-loon′, *n.* **1.** A drawing-room. **2.** [U. S.] A grog-shop.

salt, 1 sȯlt; 2 sạlt. **I.** *vt.* To apply salt to; cure or season with salt. **II.** *a.* Flavored with salt; briny; containing salt. **salt′ish‡; salt′y‡. III.** *n.* **1.** A compound of chlorin and sodium, abundant in sea-water. **2.** *Chem.* A compound of any base with an acid.— **salt′cel″lar,** *n.* A small receptacle for table-salt.— **salt′ness,** *n.*

sal′ta-rel′lo, 1 sal′tə-rel′o; 2 săl′ta-rĕl′o, *n.* A skipping dance in triple time.

sal′ta-to-ry, 1 sal′tə-to-rɪ; 2 săl′ta-to-ry,

a. Moving by leaps; leaping; bounding.

salt″pe′ter, salt″pe′tre, 1 sȯlt″pī′tər; 2 sạlt″pē′ter, *n.* Niter.

salt′y, *a.* See SALT.

sa-lu′bri-ous, 1 sə-liū′brɪ-ŭs; 2 sa-lū′brɪ-ŭs, *a.* Healthful; wholesome. **-ly,** *adv.*— **sa-lu′bri-ty,** *n.* Healthfulness. **sa-lu′bri-ous-ness‡.**

sal′u-ta-ry, 1 sal′yu-tē-rɪ; 2 săl′yu-tä-ry, *a.* Corrective; beneficial; healthful.— **sa′lu-ta-ri-ness,** *n.*

sal″u-ta′tion, 1 -tē′shən; 2 -tä′shon, *n.* The act of saluting; a greeting.— **sa-lu′ta-to-ry,** *a.* Of or pertaining to salutation.

sa-lute′, 1 sə-liūt′; 2 sa-lūt′. **I.** *vt. & vi.* [SA-LUT′ED⁴; SA-LUT′ING.] To accost; offer a salute (to). **II.** *n.* A greeting with military or naval honors; any salutation.

sal′vage, 1 sal′vɪj; 2 săl′vạj, *n.* The saving of a ship or cargo; the property rescued, or the compensation to the rescuers.

sal-va′tion, 1 sal-vē′shən; 2 săl-vä′shon, *n.* Deliverance from danger or evil, especially from sin and penalty.

salve, 1 säv; 2 säv, *n.* A thick, adhesive ointment for local application.

salv³, ∫

sal′ver, 1 sal′vər; 2 săl′ver, *n.* A tray, as of silver.

sal′vo, 1 sal′vo; 2 săl′vo, *n.* **1.** A simultaneous discharge of artillery. **2.** A successive discharge of guns from right to left, or left to right, at intervals of two seconds.

same, 1 sâm; 2 säm, *a.* Being no different or no other; identical.— **same′ness, same′-li-ness‡,** *n.*

sa′mite, 1 sē′mait; 2 sä′mīt. *n.* A rich silk fabric worn in the middle ages.

sam′pl(e⁵, 1 sam′pl; 2 săm′pl. **I.** *vt.* [SAM′-PL(E)D³; SAM′PLING.] To test by means of a specimen. **II.** *n.* A portion, part, or piece taken as a representative of the whole; a specimen; example.

san′a-tive, 1 san′ə-tɪv; 2 săn′a-tɪv, *a.* Healing. **san′a-to-ry‡.**— **san″a-tiv(e-ly⁵,** *adv.*— **san′a-tiv(e-ness⁵,** *n.*— **san″a-to′ri-um,** *n.* A health retreat.

sanc′ti-fy, 1 saŋk′tɪ-fai; 2 săn̆c′ti-fy, *vt.* [-FIED²; -FY″ING.] To make holy; purify; consecrate.— **sanc″ti-fi-ca′tion,** *n.* Spiritual perfection; holiness.

sanc′ti-mo-ny, 1 saŋk′tɪ-mo-nɪ; 2 săn̆c′ti-mo-ny, *n.* A show of holiness; exaggerated solemnity.— **sanc″ti-mo′ni-ous,** *a.* Making a show of sanctimony. **-ly,** *adv.* **-ness,** *n.*

sanc′tion, 1 saŋk′shən; 2 săn̆c′shon. **I.** *vt.* To approve authoritatively; countenance. **II.** *n.* Authoritative confirmation; justification.

sanc′ti-ty, 1 saŋk′tɪ-tɪ; 2 săn̆c′ti-ty, *n.* [-TIES², *pl.*] The state of being holy; holiness; solemnity. **sanc′ti-tude‡.**

sanc'tu-a-ry, 1 saŋk'chu-[or -tiu-]ē-rı; 2 săp'chu-[or -tū-]ā-ry, *n.* [-IES², *pl.*] **1.** A holy or sacred place. **2.** A place of refuge; asylum; immunity.

sanc'tum, 1 saŋk'tum; 2 săp'tŭm, *n.* A sacred spot; a private room.

sand, 1 sand; 2 sănd, *n.* **1.** A granular rock-material finer than gravel and coarser than dust. **2.** *pl.* Sandy wastes.— **sand'stone",** *n.* A rock consisting chiefly of quartz sand cemented with silica.— **sand'y,** *a.*

san'dal, 1 san'dəl; 2 săn'dal, *n.* A foot-covering, con-sisting of a sole held to the foot by thongs.

san'dal-wood", 1 san'dəl-wud"; 2 săn'dal-wood", *n.* A fragrant wood from India.

sand'wich, 1 sand'wıch; 2 sănd'wich. It. *vt.* To place be-tween other things. **II.** *n.* Two slices of bread, having between them meat, cheese, or the like.

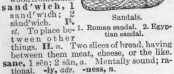

Sandals.
1. Roman sandal. 2. Egyp-tian sandal.

sane, 1 sēn; 2 sāng, *imp.* of SING, *v.*— **-ly,** *adv.* **-ness,** *n.*

sang, 1 saŋ; 2 săng, *imp.* of SING, *v.*

sang'froid', 1 soń'frwä'; 2 săn'frwä', *n.* Calmness amid trying circumstances.

san'guine, 1 saŋ'gwın; 2 săŋ'gwĭn, *a.* **1.** Of buoyant disposition; hope-ful; confident. **2.** Having the color of blood; of, like, or full of blood.— **san'gui-na-ry,** 1 saŋ'gwı-nē-rı; 2 săŋ'gwĭ-nā-ry, *a.* **1.** Attended with bloodshed. **2.** Blood-thirsty. **3.** Consisting of blood.— **san'-guine-ly,** *adv.*— **san'guine-ness,** *n.*

San'he-drin, 1 san'hı-drin, -drim; 2 săn'-he-drĭn, -drĭm, *n.* The supreme council of the Jewish nation.

San'he-drim, 1 he-drĭn, -drĭm, *n.*

san'i-ta-ry, 1 san'ı-tē-rı; 2 săn'ı-tā-ry, *a.* **1.** Relating to the preservation of health. **2.** Curative; sanatory.— **san"i-ta'ri-um,** *n.* [-UMS² or -RI-A, *pl.*] A sanatorium.— **san"i-ta'tion,** *n.* The practical application of san-itary science.

san'i-ty, 1 san'ı-tı; 2 săn'ı-ty, *n.* The state of being sane.

sank, 1 saŋk; 2 săŋk, *imp.* of SINK, *v.*

San'skrit, 1 san's-krit; 2 săn'skrĭt, *n.* The ancient Hindu language.

Sa'or-stat Eire'ann, 1 sē'ar-stath ār'ən; 2 sā'or-stäth ār'an, *n.* Irish Free State.

sap, 1 sap; 2 săp, *vt. & vi.* [SAPPED†, SAPT⁸; SAP'PING.] To weaken; undermine.

sap¹, *n.* **1.** The juice of plants. **2.** Any vital fluid; vitality.

sap², *n.* *Mil.* A deep, narrow ditch in siege-works.

sa'pi-ence, 1 sē'pı-ens; 2 sā'pi-ĕnç, *n.* Wisdom.— **sa'pi-ent,** *a.* Wise.— **sa'pi-ent-ly,** *adv.*

sap'ling, 1 sap'lıŋ; 2 săp'ling, *n.* A young tree.

sa-pon'i-fy, 1 sə-pon'ı-fai; 2 sa-pŏn'i-fȳ, *vt.* [-FIED; -FY"ING.] To convert into soap.— **sap"o-na'ceous,** *a.* Of the nature of soap.

sap'phire, 1 saf'air; 2 săf'īr, *n.* **1.** A hard, transparent gem: usually blue. **2.** Deep pure blue.

saf'fire",

Sar'a-cen, 1 sar'ə-sen; 2 săr'a-çĕn, *n.* Ancient-ly a nomad Arab; hence, one of the Moslem enemies of the medieval Christians.— **Sar"a-cen'ic,** *a.*

sar'casm, 1 sär'kazm; 2 săr'eăṣm, *n.* A keenly ironical or scornful utterance.— **sar-cas'tic,** *a.* **sar-cas'ti-cal‡.**— **sar-cas'-ti-cal-ly,** *adv.*

sar-coph'a-gus, 1 sar-kɵf'ə-gus; 2 săr-eŏf'a-gŭs, *n.* [-GI, 1 -jai; 2 -gī, *pl.*] A stone coffin or chest-like tomb.

sar-dine', 1 sar-dīn'; 2 săr-dīn', *n.* A small herring-like fish.

sar-din'⁸,

sar'di-us, 1 sar'dı-us; 2 săr'di-ŭs, *n.* A red gem stone.

sar-don'ic, 1 sar-dən'ık; 2 săr-dŏn'ie, *a.* Derisive, as a grin; unnatural or forced, as laughter.

sar'do-nyx, 1 sär'do-niks; 2 săr'do-nȳks, *n.* A variety of onyx consisting of alter-nate layers of chalcedony and reddish carnelian.

sar"sa-pa-ril'la, 1 sär"sə-pə-ril'ə; 2 săr"-sa-pa-ril'a, *n.* The dried roots of a tropical American climbing plant, or an infusion made from them.

sash¹, 1 sash; 2 săsh, *n.* A frame in which glass is set.

sash², *n.* An ornamental band for the waist.

sas'sa-fras, 1 sas'a-fras; 2 săs'a-frăs, *n.* A tree of tne laurel fam-ily; also, the bark of the roots, an aromatic stimulant.

sat, 1 sat; 2 săt, *imp.* of SIT, *v.* **sate‡.**

Sa'tan, 1 sē'tən; 2 sā'-tan, *n.* The devil.— **sa-tan'ic,** *a.* Devilish; wicked. **sa-tan'i-cal‡.**— **sa-tan'i-cal-ly,** *adv.*

satch'el, 1 sach'el; 2 săch'ĕl, *n.* A small hand-bag.

sate, 1 sēt; 2 săt, *vt.* [SAT'ED‡; SAT'ING.] To satisfy the appetite of; fill full; satiate.

Leaves and Fruit of the Sassafras.

sat'el-lite, 1 sat'e-lait; 2 săt'ĕ-līt, *n.*

small planet, as the moon, revolving round a larger.

sa'ti-ate, 1 sē'shi-ēt; 2 sā'shi-āt. **I.** *vt.* & *vi.* [SA″TI-AT″ED⁴; SA″TI-AT″ING.] To gratify to the utmost. **II.** *a.* Filled to satiety; satiated.— **sa″ti-a'tion,** *n.* — **sa-ti′e-ty,** 1 sǝ-tai′i-tɪ; 2 sa-tī′e-ty, *n.* [-TIES²*, pl.*] Repletion; surfeit.

sat'in, 1 sat'ɪn; 2 sȧt'ɪn, *n.* A glossy silk fabric of thick texture.— **sa-tin′i-ty,** *n.*— **sat′in-y,** *a.*

sat'ire, 1 sat'air; 2 sȧt'īr, *n.* The employment of sarcasm, irony, or ridicule; any writing in which vice or folly is held up to ridicule.— **sa-tir′ic, sa-tir′i-cal,** 1 sǝ-tir′ɪk, -ɪ-kǝl; 2 sa-tīr′ic, -i-cal, *a.* Of, pertaining to, or employing satire.— **sa-tir′i-cal-ly,** *adv.*— **sat′i-rist,** *n.* A writer of satire.— **sat′i-rize,** *vt.* [-RIZED; - IZ″ING.] To treat with sarcasm; ridicule.

sat′is-fy, 1 sat′ɪs-fai; 2 sȧt′ɪs-fy, *v.* [-FIED; -FY″ING.] **I.** *t.* **1.** To gratify to the full; content. **2.** To free from doubt or anxiety. **3.** To pay off or discharge. **II.** *i.* To give satisfaction.— **sat″is-fac′tion,** *n.* **1.** Complete gratification. **2.** The making of amends or payment. **3.** That which satisfies.— **sat″is-fac′to-ry,** *a.* Giving satisfaction; atoning.— **sat″is-fac′to-ri-ly,** *adv.*— **sat″is-fac′to-ri-ness,** *n.*

sa'trap, 1 sē'trap or sat'rap; 2 sā'trȧp or sȧt'rȧp, *n.* A governor of a province in ancient Persia.— **sa′trap-y,** *n.*

sat′u-rate, 1 sach′u-[or sat′yu-]rēt; 2 sȧch′-u-[or sȧt′yu-]rāt. **I.** *vt.* [-RAT″ED⁴; -RAT″ING.] To soak or imbue thoroughly; fill to the utmost **II.** *a.* Saturated.— **sat″u-ra′tion,** *n.*

Sat′ur-day, 1 sat′ǝr-de; 2 sȧt′ur-da, *n.* The seventh or last day of the week.

Sat′urn, 1 sat′ǝrn; 2 sȧt′urn, *n.* **1.** The planet next beyond Jupiter; marked by concentric rings: in astrology regarded as a melancholy planet. See SATURNINE. **2.** *Myth.* The ancient Italic god o seed-time and harvest: said to have instructed the people of Italy in agriculture; hence, his reign, celebrated as a golden age. **Kron′os‡** [Gr.].— **Sat″ur-na′li-a,** *n. pl.* **1.** The festival of Saturn held in ancient Rome in mid-December. **2.** [s-] Any season of license, revelry, and excess: in this sense treated as a singular.— **Sat″ur-na′li-an,** *a.*— **Sa-tur′ni-an,** *a.* **1.** Pertaining to the god Saturn or to the golden age. **2.** Pertaining to the planet Saturn.— **sat′ur-nin**(e², *a.* **1.** Gloomy; morose; dull. **2.** [S-] Pertaining to Saturn.

sat′yr, 1 sat′ǝr or sē′tǝr; 2 sȧt′yr or sā′tyr, *n. Gr. Myth.* A woodland deity, having goatlike ears and budding horns.— **sa-tyr′ic,** *a.*

sauce, 1 sɔs; 2 sȧc. **I.** *vt.* [SAUCED⁴; SAUC′ING.] To dress with sauce; season.

II. *n.* An appetizing accompaniment of a meal.— **sau′cer,** 1 sɔ′sǝr; 2 sȧ′çer, *n.* A small dish for holding a cup, etc.— **sau′cy,** 1 sɔ′sɪ; 2 sȧ′çy, *a.* [SAU′CI-ER; SAU′CI-EST.] Impudent; piquant.— **sau′ci-ly,** *adv.*— **sau′ci-ness,** *n.*

saun'ter, 1 sȧn′tǝr; 2 sän′ter, *vi.* To walk in a leisurely way; stroll.— **saun′ter-er,** *n.*— **saun′ter-ing,** *pa.* & *n.*

sau′ri-an, 1 sɔ′rɪ-ǝn; 2 sȧ′ri-an, *n.* A lizard or a lizard-like reptile.

sau'sage, 1 sɔ′sɪj; 2 sȧ′saǧ, *n.* **1.** Finely chopped and highly seasoned meat, commonly stuffed into the prepared entrails of some animal. **2.** A type of air-ship.

sav'age, 1 sav′ɪj; 2 sȧv′aǧ. **I.** *a.* Wild and untamed; uncivilized; cruel. **II.** *n.* A wild and uncivilized human being; brutal person; barbarian. **-ly,** *adv.*— **sav′age-ry,** *n.* **1.** The state of being savage. **sav′age-ness**‡. **2.** Savages collectively.

sa-van'na, 1 sǝ-van′ǝ; 2 sa-vän′a, *n.* A **sa-van'nah,** treeless plain; a meadow prairie.

sa′vant‡, 1 sä′vän′; 2 sä′vän′, *n.* [SA′VANTS′, *pl.*] A man of special learning.

save, 1 sēv; 2 sāv, *v.* [SAVED; SAV′ING.] **I.** *t.* To make safe; rescue; protect; preserve. **II.** *i.* To be economical.

save, *prep.* & *conj.* Excepting; unless.

sav'ing, 1 sēv′ɪŋ; 2 sāv′ing. **I.** *pa.* Redeeming; economical; qualifying. **II.** *n.* **1.** Preservation; redemption. 2. Economy. **3.** *pl.* Sums laid away. **III.** *prep.* & *conj.* **1.** With the exception of; save. **2.** Without disrespect to. **-ly,** *adv.* **-ness,** *n.*

Sa′vior, 1 sēv′yǝr; 2 sāv′yor, *n.* **1. Sa′viour,** Jesus Christ, the Redeemer. **2.** [s-] One who saves or rescues.

sa′vor, 1 sē′vǝr; 2 sā′vor. **I.** *vi.* To have a specified flavor or quality: followed by *of.* **II.** *n.* Flavor; relish; specific quality.— **sa′vor-y,** 1 sē′vǝr-ɪ; 2 sā′vor-y, *a.* **1.** Appetizing. **2.** In good repute.— **sa′vor-i-ly,** *adv.*— **sa′vor-i-ness,** *n.*

sa′vor-y, *n.* A hardy annual aromatic herb.

saw[1], 1 sɔ; 2 sȧ, *v.* [SAWED OR SAWN, SAWD⁵; SAW′ING.] **I.** *t.* To cut, shape, or fashion with a saw. **II.** *i.* To be cut with a saw; use a saw; make motions as if using a saw.

saw[2], *imp.* of SEE, *v.*

saw[1], 1 sɔ; 2 sȧ, *n.* A cutting-instrument with pointed teeth.— **saw′dust″,** *n.* Small bits of wood cut or torn out by a saw.— **saw′-mill″,** *n.* **1.** An establishment for sawing logs into lumber. **2.** A large sawing-machine.— **saw′yer,** 1 sɔ′yǝr; 2 sȧ′yer, *n.* One who saws wood.

saw[2], *n.* A proverbial saying.

1: ǝ = fin**a**l; **ɪ** = hab**i**t; **aisle; au** = **ou**t; **oil; iū** = f**eu**d; **chin; go; ŋ** = si**ng; thin, this.**
2: wolf, do; book, boot; full, rule, cure, but, burn; oil, boy; go, gem; ink; thin, this.

sax′i-frage, 1 saks′ı-frıj; 2 săks′i-fraġ, *n.* A perennial herb, growing in rocky places.

Sax′on, 1 saks′ən; 2 săks′on. **I.** *a.* Pertaining to the Saxons. **II.** *n.* **1.** One of a Teutonic tribe that conquered England in the 5th and 6th centuries. **2.** An Anglo-Saxon. **3.** A native of Saxony. **4.** The language of the Saxons.

Purple Saxifrage.

say, 1 sē; 2 sā, *v.* [SAID, 1 sed; 2 sĕd; SAY′ING.] **I.** *t.* **1.** To speak; utter; declare either orally or in writing. **2.** To suppose. **II.** *i.* To make an assertion.

say, *n.* What one has said or has to say.—
say′ing, *n.* An utterance; a maxim.

says, 1 sez; 2 sĕs, *pres. ind. 3d pers. sing.* of SAY, *v.*

scab, 1 skab; 2 scăb, *n.* **1.** A crust formed on the surface of a sore; also, some similar appearance, as on diseased plants; a blister on the surface of a casting, etc. **2.** [Low.] A mean, dirty, paltry fellow: so used by Shakespeare; hence, recently, a workman who refuses to join or acts against a labor-union.— **scabbed, scab′by,** *a.*

scab′bard, 1 skab′ərd; 2 scăb′ard, *n.* A sheath, as of a sword.

scaf′fold, 1 skaf′əld; 2 scăf′old, *n.* A temporary elevated structure for the support of workmen, as in building or for the execution of criminals.— **scaf′fold-ing,** *n.* A scaffold, or system of scaffolds.

scald, 1 skɵld; 2 scɑld. **I**d. *vt.* To burn with a hot fluid; cook or cleanse with very hot water. **II.** *n.* An act of scalding, or the injury inflicted by it.

scale1, 1 skēl; 2 seāl, *v.* [SCALED; SCAL′ING.] **I.** *t.* **1.** To clear of or to cover with scale or scales. **2.** To pare down. **II.** *i.* **1.** To come off, as scales or flakes. **2.** To become crusted.

scale2, *vt.* **1.** To surmount by climbing. **2.** To draw to scale or measure. **3.** To reduce according to a scale.

scale3, *vt.* To weigh.

scale1, *n.* **1.** *Zool.* One of the thin, bone-like, overlapping plates on the skin of fishes or reptiles. **2.** Any incrustation, as of iron-rust; scab.

scale2, *n.* **1.** The ruled lines on a measure, or a measure so ruled; a system of fixed units of measurement; any graded series. **2.** *Mus.* The succession of tones in an octave or more.

scale3, *n.* **1.** The platform or pan of a balance; also, the balance itself. **2.** *pl.* Any form of weighing-machine.

sca-lene′, 1 skē-līn′; 2 seā-lēn′, *a.* Having sides no two of which are equal: said of a triangle.

scal′lop, 1 skɵl′əp; 2 seal′op. **I**t. *vt.* **1.** To cook in a scallop; bake, with crums and seasoning, as oysters. **2.** To shape with scallops. **II.** *n.* A bivalve having a rounded shell with wavy edge; also, its shell; one of a series of curves along an edge.

scalp, 1 skalp; 2 seălp. **I**t. *vt.* To take the scalp from. **II.** *n.* The skin, or skin and hair, of the top of the skull.

scal′pel, 1 skal′pel″; 2 seăl′pĕl, *n.* A small pointed knife used in dissections and in surgery.

sca′ly, 1 skē′lı; 2 seā′ly, *a.* Covered with scales; of the nature of a scale; incrusted; scurfy. [rascal.

scamp, 1 skamp; 2 seămp, *n.* A rogue;

scam′per, 1 skam′pər; 2 seăm′per. **I.** *vi.* To hasten away; flee. **II.** *n.* A hurried flight.

scan, 1 skan; 2 seăn, *vt. & vi.* [SCANNED, SCAND²; SCAN′NING.] **1.** To read metrically; conform to metrical rules. **2.** To scrutinize.

scan′dal, 1 skan′dəl; 2 seăn′dal, *n.* The dissemination of evil reports; slander; reproach.— **scan′dal-ize,** 1 skan′dəl-ɑız; 2 seăn′dal-īz, *vt.* [-IZED; -IZ′ING.] To shock; malign; disgrace.— **scan′dal-ous,** *a.* Causing scandal; disgraceful; injurious to reputation. **-ly,** *adv.* **-ness,** *n.*

Scan″di-na′vi-an, 1 skan″dı-nē′vı-ən; 2 seăn″di-nā′vi-an. **I.** *a.* Of or pertaining to Scandinavia, embracing Norway, Sweden, Denmark, and Iceland. **II.** *n.* A native of Scandinavia.

scant, 1 skant; 2 seănt. **I**d. *vt. & vi.* To limit; stint; become scanty; lessen; fail. **II.** *a.* Scarcely enough; limited; meager; small.

scant′ling, 1 skant′lıŋ; 2 seănt′ling, *n.* Narrow timber, as for studding, etc.

scant′y, 1 skant′ı; 2 seănt′y, *a.* [SCANT′I-ER; SCANT′I-EST.] Limited in extent, quantity, or number; scant; small.— **scant′i-ly,** *adv.*— **scant′i-ness,** *n.*

scape′goat″, 1 skēp′gōt′; 2 seāp′gōt″, *n.* **1.** *Bib.* A goat which symbolically bore the sins of the people into the wilderness. **2.** A person made to bear blame for others.

scape′grace″, 1 skēp′grēs″; 2 seăp′grāç″, *n.* A worthless, dissipated fellow.

scap′u-la, 1 skap′yu-lə; 2 seăp′yu-la, *n.*

[-LÆ, 1 -lī; 2 -lē, *pl.*] The shoulder-blade.— **scap′u-lar,** *a.*

scar, 1 skär; 2 seär. **I.** *vt. & vi.* [SCARRED; SCAR⁸; SCAR′RING.] To mark, or be marked, with a scar. **II.** *n.* The mark left on the skin after the healing of a wound; any mark of past injury.

scarce, 1 skärs; 2 seârç, *a.* **1.** Rare; **scarse′,** } infrequent. **2.** Scant.— **scarce′- ly,** *adv.* Barely; not quite; hardly.— **scar′- ci-ty,** 1 skär′sı-tı; 2 seär′çı-tı, *n.* Scantiness; insufficiency. **scarce′ness‡.**

scare, 1 skār; 2 seär. **I.** *vt. & vi.* [SCARED; SCAR′ING.] To frighten, or take fright. **II.** *n.* Sudden fright; panic.— **scare′crow″, n. 1.** Any image set up to scare crows from growing crops. **2.** A cause of false alarm. **3.** A wretched-looking person.

scarf¹, 1 skärf; 2 seärf, *n. Carp.* A lapped joint for uniting timbers.

scarf², *n.* **1.** A long and wide band, as for the head and neck. **2.** A necktie. **scarf′-skin″,** *n.* The epidermis.

scar′i-fy, 1 skar′ı-fai; 2 seär′ı-fỹ, *vt.* [-FIED; FY′ING.] **1.** To make a number of slight incisions in; scratch. **2.** To criticize severely.— **scar″i-fi-ca′tion,** *n.*

scar″la-ti′na, 1 skär″lə-tī′nə; 2 seär″la-tī′na, *n.* An infectious fever, with a diffused scarlet rash. **scarlet fever‡.**

scar′let, 1 skär′let; 2 seär′lĕt. **I.** *a.* Of a scarlet color. **II.** *n.* **1.** A brilliant red, inclining to orange. **2.** Cloth of a scarlet color.

scarp, 1 skärp; 2 seärp. **I**ᵗ. *vt.* To cut to a steep slope. **II.** *n.* Any steep slope.

scathe, 1 skēth, skaɹh; 2 seăth, seäth. **I.** *vt.* [SCATHED; SCATH′ING.] To injure severely; harm. **II.** *n.* Severe injury.— **sca͡the′less,** *a.* Free from harm.— **scath′ing,** *pa.* Damaging; merciless in severity.

scat′ter, 1 skat′ər; 2 seăt′er, *vt. & vi.* To cast about irregularly; strew; disperse; defeat.

scav′en-ger, 1 skav′en-jər; 2 seäv′ĕn-ger, *n.* A street-cleaner; an animal that feeds on carrion.

scene, 1 sīn; 2 sēn, *n.* A landscape; place and surroundings of an event; place represented on the stage; division of an act of a play; any striking exhibition or display, as of passion.— **scen′er-y,** 1 sīn′ər-ı; 2 sēn′er-y, *n.* [-IES²*, pl.*] The theatrical scenes collectively.— **scen′ic,** 1 sīn′ık *or* sen′ık; 2 sēn′ıc *or* sĕn′ıc, *a.* **1.** Artistic. **2.** Picturesque. **3.** Relating to stage scenery.— **scenic railway,** a miniature pleasure-railway amid artificially built-up scenery.

scentᵈ, } 1 sent; 2 sĕnt, *v.* **I.** *t.* **1.** To **sentᴾ,** } perceive by smell. **2.** To render

odorous; perfume. **II.** *i.* To hunt by scent, as dogs.

scent, *n.* An odor; the sense of smell.

scep′ter, } 1 sep′tər; 2 sĕp′ter. **I.** *vt.* To **scep′tre,** } invest with royal power. **II.** *n.* An ornamental staff as the emblem of sovereignty; kingly office or power.— **scep′tered, scep′tred,** *a.*

scep′tic, -ti-cal, scep′ti-cism, etc. Same as SKEPTIC, etc.

sched′ule, 1 skej′ul *or* sked′- yul; 2 scĕj′ul *or* sĕd′yul. **I.** *vt.* [-ULED; -UL-ING.] To list. **II.** *n.* A written or printed statement; inventory; list.

scheme, 1 skīm; 2 scēm. **I.** *vt. & vi.* [SCHEMED; SCHEM′- ING.] To plan; devise. **II.** *n.* **1.** A plan of something to be done; plot; device. **2.** A list or arrangement; schedule.— **schem′er,** *n.*— **schem′ing,** *a. & n.*

Scepters.
1. King's Scepter. 2. Emperor's Scepter.

scher-zan′do, 1 sker-tsän′do; 2 scĕr-tsän′do, *adv.* In a sportive or lightsome manner. **scher-zo′so‡.**

schism, 1 sızm; 2 sĭşm, *n.* A division of a church into factions; an ecclesiastical faction.— **schis-mat′ic,** 1 sız-măt′ık; 2 sĭş-măt′ıc, *a. & n.*— **schis-mat′i-cal,** *a.*— **schis-mat′i-cal-ly,** *adv.*

schist, 1 shist; 2 shĭst, *n.* Any rock that readily splits or cleaves.— **schist′ic, schis′- tose,** *a.* **schist′ous‡.**

schol′ar, } 1 skol′ər; 2 sĕŏl′ar, *n.* **1.** A **scol′arᴾ,** } pupil; learner. **2.** A person eminent for learning.— **schol′ar-ly,** *a.* Like a scholar; learned; erudite.— **schol′ar-ship,** *n.* **1.** Learning. **2.** Maintenance for a student.— **scho-las′tic,** 1 sko-las′tık; 2 sco-läs′- tıc, *a.* **1.** Pertaining to scholars or schools. **2.** Pedantic.

school¹, } 1 skūl; 2 seŏōl. **I.** *vt.* To teach; **scoolᴾ,** } train; discipline. **II.** *n.* **1.** An educational institution; any place or means of instruction. **2.** A schoolhouse or schoolroom. **3.** A school-session; a body of pupils or of disciples; a sect, etc.— **school′boy″, school′girl″,** *n.* A boy or girl attending school or of school age.— **school′fel″low,** *n.* A schoolmate.— **school′house″, school′room″,** *n.* A building or room in which a school is conducted.— **school′man,** *n.* One of the theologians of the middle ages.— **school′mas″ter,** *n.* A man who teaches school.— **school′- mate″,** *n.* One attending the same school; a fellow pupil.— **school′mis″tress,** *n.* A

woman teacher or principal. **school′ma′am‡** [Colloq., U. S.].— **school′=teach′er,** n. One who teaches in a school of lower grade than a college or university.

school². **I.** v.i. To run together in a school, as fish. **II.** n. A large company, as of fish; shoal.

schoon′er, **scoon′er²,** 1 skūn′ər; 2 seōōn′er, n. A fore= and=aft rigged vessel having two or more masts.

Schooner=yacht.
1. Foretopmast=staysail or jib=topsail. 2. Jib. 3. Fore=staysail. 4. Fore gaff=top=sail. 5. Foresail. 6. Main= topmast=staysail. 7. Main club=topsail. 8. Mainsail.

sci-at′ic, 1 sai-at′ik; 2 sī-ăt′ic, a. Pertaining to the hip or its nerves. — **sci-at′i-ca,** n. Neuralgia of the hip and thigh.— **sci-at′i-cal,** a.

sci′ence, 1 saī′ens; 2 sī′ĕnç, n. **1.** The sum of universal knowledge. **2.** The system of knowledge concerning some subject or group of subjects.— **scī′en-tif′ic,** a. **1.** Pertaining to or used in science. **2.** Systematic; exact. **3.** Versed in science.— **scī′en-tif′i-cal,** a.— **scī′en-tif′i-cal-ly,** adv.— **scī′en-tist,** n. One versed in science; a savant.

scim′i-ter, n. Same as SIMITAR. **scim′i-tar‡.**

scin-til′la, 1 sin-til′ə; 2 sĭn-tĭl′a, n. A spark; hence, a trace; iota.— **scin′til-late,** v.t. & v.i. [-LAT′ED‡; -LAT′ING.] To send forth, as sparks; flash.— **scin′til-la′tio** , n.

sci′o-list, 1 saī′o-list; 2 sī′o-lĭst, n. A pretender to learning.— **sci′o-lism,** n.

sci′on, 1 saī′on; 2 sī′ŏn, n. **1.** A piece cut from a twig, as for grafting. **2.** A shoot. **3.** A child or descendant.

scis′sors, **sis′sors⁸,** 1 siz′ərz; 2 sĭs′orẓ, n. pl. A cutting=implement with a pair of pivoted blades.

Sclav, Sclav′ic, etc. Same as SLAV, etc.

scoff, **scof⁸,** 1 skôf; 2 seôf. **I⁴.** v.t. & v.i. To de= ride; scorn; mock: used with at. **II.** n. An expression of contempt or de= rision.— **scoff′er,** n.

scold, 1 skōld; 2 seōld. **I⁴.** v.t. & v.i. To reprove harshly or noisily; rail at; chide. **II.** n. One who scolds, especially a virago.— **scold′er,** n.

scol′lop, etc. Same as SCALLOP, etc.

sconce, **sconse⁸,** 1 skons; 2 seŏnç, n. **1.** A shelter; fort. **2.** A helmet. **3.** The head. **4.** An ornamental bracket for holding a light.

scoop, 1 skūp; 2 seōōp, v. **I⁴.** v.t. & v.i. To remove with a scoop; use a scoop; hol-

low out; dig. **II.** n. **1.** A shovel=like implement for handling any loose ma= terial. **2.** An act of scooping.

scope, 1 skōp; 2 seōp, n. A range of view or action; outlook; capacity for achieve= ment; aim.

scor-bu′tic, 1 sker-biū′tik; 2 seŏr-bū′tie. **I.** a. Relating to, like, or affected with scurvy. **II.** n. A person afflicted with scurvy. **scor-bu′ti-cal‡.**

scorch¹, 1 skôrch; 2 seôrch, vt. & vi. To burn, or be burnt, superficially; singe; wither by heat.

score, 1 skōr; 2 seōr. **I.** vt. & vi. [SCORED; SCOR′ING.] **1.** To mark with cuts, notches, or the like. **2.** To scourge; cen= sure. **3.** To keep account of; keep tally. **II.** n. **1.** An account; debt. **2.** A grudge. **3.** A tally. **4.** The notes of a musical composition. **5.** The number twenty. **6.** A notch, cut, line, etc.

sco′ri-a, 1 skō′ri-ə; 2 seō′ri-a, n. [-Æ, 1 -Ī; 2 -ē, pl.] Coarsely cellular lava or frag= ments of lava; also, refuse of fused metal; dross; slag: often in the plural.

scorn, 1 skôrn; 2 seôrn. **I.** vt. & vi. To hold in or treat with contempt; despise. **II.** n. Extreme contempt; disdain; de= rision; an object of contempt.— **scorn′ful,** a.— **scorn′ful-ly,** adv.

scor′pi-on, 1 skôr′pi-ən; 2 seôr′pi-on, n. A tropical animal, of lobster=like form, with a poisonous sting in the end of the tail.

Scot, 1 sket; 2 seŏt, n. A native of Scotland.— **Scots.** **I.** a. Scottish. **II.** n. The Scottish dialect.— **Scots′man,** n. A Scotchman.— **Scot′ti-cism,** 1 -siz=m; 2 seŏt′i-çiẓm, n. A form of expression, or an idiom peculiar to the Scotch. **Scot′i-cism‡.**— **Scot′tish,** a. Pertaining to Scotland or its people.

scot‖, n. An assessment; tax.— **scot′=free,** a. Free from scot; untaxed; unharmed.

scotch¹, 1 skoch; 2 seŏch, vt. **1.** To cut or wound slightly. **2.** To dress, as stone, with a pick.

scotch¹, n. A superficial cut; scratch.

Scotch², n. **1.** The people of Scotland: used as a plural. **2.** One of the languages spoken by Scots.— **Scotch,** a. Scottish.— **Scotch′man,** n. A Scot.

scoun′drel, 1 skaun′drel; 2 seoun′drĕl. **I.** a. Rascally. **II.** n. A thoroughgoing rascal.— **scoun′drel-ism,** n.

scour¹, 1 skaur; 2 seour, vt. & vi. **1.** To clean or be cleaned by washing and rub= bing. **2.** To purge.— **scour′er,** n.

scour², vt. & vi. **1.** To traverse thorough= ly; search through. **2.** To skim along.

scourge, 1 skûrj; 2 seûrg. **I.** vt. [SCOURGED, **scourge**ᴾ; SCOURGEDᴾ; SCOUR'ING.] To lash. **II.** n. A whip; hence, severe punishment.

scout¹, 1 skaut; 2 scout. **I**ᵈ. vt. & vi. To follow and spy upon; act as a scout. **II.** n. A person sent out to get information, as of the position or strength of an enemy. —**boy scout,** a member of a world=wide non=military organization of boys for the development of self=reliance.

scout²ᵈ, vt. To reject with disdain; spurn.

scow, 1 skau; 2 scow, n. [U. S.] A large flat=bottomed boat.

scowl, 1 skaul; 2 scowl. **I.** vi. To frown deeply; look threatening; lower. **II.** n. A lowering of the brows; gloomy aspect.

scrab'ble, } 1 skrab'l; 2 serăb'l, vt. & vi. **scrab'l**ᴾ, } [SCRAB'BLED, SCRAB'LDᴾ; SCRAB'BLING.] **1.** To scribble. **2.** To scramble.

scrag'ged, 1 skrag'ed; 2 serăg'ĕd, a. Rough; shaggy; scrawny. **scrag'gly** ‡; **scrag'gy**‡.

scram'bl(eᴾ, 1 skram'bl; 2 serăm'bl, v. [SCRAM'BL(E)Dᴾ; SCRAM'BLING.] **I.** t. To prepare hastily. **II.** i. To clamber with hands and feet; struggle up or along.— **scram'bler,** n. [disorderly performance.

scram'ble, n. The act of scrambling; any

scrap, 1 skrap; 2 serăp, n. A small piece; fragment; clipping.— **scrap'=book",** n. A book in which clippings are pasted.

scrape, 1 skrēp; 2 serāp. **I.** vt. & vi. [SCRAPEDᵗ; SCRAP'ING.] **1.** To scratch with a hard surface or edge, or remove by such process. **2.** To draw together little by little; economize. **II.** n. **1.** The act or effect of scraping. **2.** A predicament.

scratch, } 1 skrach; 2 serăch. **I**ᵗ. vt. & vi. **scrach**ᴾ, } To mark or tear, as with claws or nails; scrape away; write awkwardly. **II.** n. **1.** A shallow mark, groove, etc. **2.** A slight flesh=wound. **3.** Athletics. The line from which contestants start.

scrawl, 1 skrôl; 2 seral. **I.** vt. & vi. To write hastily or illegibly. **II.** n. Irregular or unskilful writing.

scraw'ny, 1 skrô'nı; 2 sera'ny, a. Lean and bony; skinny.

scream, 1 skrīm; 2 serēm. **I.** vt. & vi. To utter in a loud, shrill voice; emit a piercing cry. **II.** n. A shrill, prolonged cry.

screech, 1 skrīch; 2 serēch. **I**ᵗ. vt. & vi. To shriek; scream. **II.** n. A shrill, harsh cry; shriek.

screed, 1 skrīd; 2 serēd, n. **1.** A tirade; harangue. **2.** A strip laid in a wall to gage the thickness of plastering. **3.** A strip or shred.

screen, 1 skrīn; 2 serēn. **I.** vt. **1.** To shield from observation or annoyance. **2.** To sift. **II.** n. **1.** Anything that shields, as a light partition. **2.** A sieve.

screw, 1 skrū; 2 seru, v. **I.** t. **1.** To fasten with a screw or screws. **2.** To oppress; twist; distort. **II.** i. To turn; twist about; practise oppression.

screw, n. **1.** A cylinder grooved in an advancing spiral. **2.** A bladed propeller. **screw pro-peller**‡. **3.** An extortioner.— **screw'=driv"er,** n. A tool for driving screws.

Forms of Screws.
1. Lag=screw. 2. Wood = screw. Thumb=screw.

scrib'ble, } 1 skrib'l; 2 serĭb'l. **I.** vt. & vi. **scrib'l**ᴾ, } [SCRIB'BLED, SCRIB'LDᴾ; SCRIB'BLING.] To write hastily and carelessly; scrawl. **II.** n. Hasty, careless writing; a scrawl.— **scrib'bler,** n.

scribe, 1 skraib; 2 serib, n. **1.** An ancient Jewish instructor in the Mosaic law. **2.** A writer; copyist; penman.

scrim'mage, 1 skrim'ıj; 2 serĭm'ag, n. A rough=and=tumble contest; fracas.

scrimpᵗ, 1 skrimp; 2 serĭmp, vt. & vi. To be niggardly; treat stingily; skimp; stint.

scrip¹, 1 skrip; 2 serĭp, n. A certificate of stock; any written scrap of paper.

scrip‖², n. A wallet or small bag; satchel.

script, 1 skript; 2 serĭpt, n. Writing; printed matter in imitation of handwriting.

This line is in script.

scrip'ture, 1 skrip'chur or -tiur; 2 serĭp'-chur or -tūr, n. Sacred writings; specifically [S-], the Bible: often in the plural. — **Scrip'tur-al,** a.— **Scrip'tur-al-ly,** adv.

scriv'en-er, 1 skriv'n-ər; 2 seriv'n-er, n. One who draws deeds and other writings; a clerk.

scrof'u-la, 1 skref'yu-la; 2 serŏf'yu-la, n. A chronic disease tending to the development of glandular tumors.— **scrof'u-lous,** a.

scroll, 1 skrōl; 2 serŏl, n. A written roll, as of parchment; any similar roll; a spiral line used as an ornament.

Scroll.

scrub, 1 skrub; 2 serŭb. **I.** vt. & vi. [SCRUBBED, SCRUBDᴿ; SCRUB'bING.] To rub vigorously; cleanse by hard rubbing; scour. **II.** a. Stunted; inferior; mean. **III.** n. **1.** A

stunted tree or shrub; brush; jungle. **2.** A small, mean, or worthless thing.— **scrub'by,** a. Stunted; worthless. **scrubbed‡.**

scru'ple(e^F, 1 skrū'pl; 2 scrụ'pl. **I.** vt. & vi. [SCRU'PL(E)D^P; SCRU'PLING.] To entertain scruples; doubt; hesitate. **II.** n. **1.** Doubt regarding a question of moral duty. **2.** An apothecaries' weight of twenty grains. **3.** A minute quantity.— **scru'pu-los'ity,** n.— **scru'pu-lous,** 1 skrū'pṵ-lus; 2 scrụ'pū-lŭs, a. **1.** Nicely conscientious. **2.** Exact; precise. **-ly,** adv. **-ness,** n.

scru'ti-ny, 1 skrū'tɪ-nɪ; 2 scrụ'tĭ-ny, n. [-NIES^z, pl.] The act of scrutinizing; close investigation.— **scru'ti-nize,** 1 skrū'- tɪ-naɪz; 2 scrụ'tĭ-nīz, vt. & vi. [-NIZED; -NIZ'- ING.] To observe carefully in detail. **-nise‡.**

scud, 1 skụd; 2 scŭd. **I.** vi. [SCUD'DED^d; SCUD'DING.] To move, run, or fly swiftly; run before the wind. **II.** n. **1.** The act of scudding. **2.** Light clouds driven rapidly before the wind.

scuf'fle, } 1 skuf'l; 2 scŭf'l. **I.** vi. [SCUF'- **scuf'l‡,** } FLED, SCŬF'LD^P; SCUF'FLING.] To struggle roughly or confusedly. **II.** n. **A** disorderly struggle; fracas.

scull, } 1 skul; 2 scŭl. **I.** vt. & vi. To use **sculp‡,** } a scull or sculls. **II.** n. **1.** An

Scull.

oar worked over the stern. **2.** A light short-handled spoon-oar. **3.** A small boat for sculling.— **scull'er,** n.

scul'ler-y, 1 skul'ər-ɪ; 2 scŭl'er-y, n. [-IES^z, pl.] A room where kitchen utensils are kept and cleaned.— **scul'lion,** 1 skul'yən; 2 scŭl'yon, n. A servant who cleans pots and kettles. [with large, spiny head.

scul'pin, 1 skul'pɪn; 2 scŭl'pin, n. A fish

sculp'ture, 1 skulp'chur or -tiur; 2 scŭlp'- chur or -tūr. **I.** vt. [SCULP'TURED; SCULP'TUR-ING.] To fashion, as statuary. **II.** n. The art of fashioning figures of stone or bronze by modeling, carving, or casting; any sculptured work.— **sculp'tor,** n. One who designs or executes statues.— **sculp'tress,** n.— **sculp'tur-al,** a.

scum, 1 skum; 2 scŭm, n. Impure matter that rises to the surface of boiling or fermenting liquids; froth; refuse.

scup'per, 1 skup'ər; 2 scŭp'er, n. Naut. A hole to let water run off from a deck.

scurf, 1 skūrf; 2 scŭrf, n. Loose scarf-skin thrown off in minute scales.— **scurf'i-ness,** n.— **scurf'y,** a.

scur'ri-lous, 1 skur'ɪ-lus; 2 scŭr'i-lŭs, a. Grossly offensive or vulgar; opprobrious. **scur'ril‡.— scur-ril'i-ty,** n. Coarse, vulgar abuse.

scur'ry, 1 skur'ɪ; 2 scŭr'y, vt. & vi. [SCUR'- RIED; SCUR'RY-ING.] To hurry; scamper. **skur'ry‡.**

scur'vy, 1 skūr'vɪ; 2 scŭr'vy, a. [SCUR'VI-ER; SCUR'VI-EST.] Mean; low; base.

scur'vy, n. A disease characterized by livid spots under the skin, and by great prostration.

scutch'eon, 1 skuch'ən; 2 scŭch'on, n. **1.** An escutcheon. **2.** A shield.

scut'tle, } 1 skut'l; 2 scŭt'l, vt. [SCUT'- **scut'l‡,** } TLED, SCUT'LD^P; SCUT'TLING.] To sink (a ship) by making holes in the bottom.

scut'tle, vi. To scurry.

scut'tle, n. A small opening, as in the roof of a house.

scut'tle, n. A hod for carrying coal.

Scyl'la, 1 sɪl'ə; 2 syl'a, n. Class. Myth. A sea-monster with six heads, represented as dwelling in a cave on the Gulf of Messina, opposite Charybdis.— **to steer between Scylla and Charybdis,** to strike a course between opposing difficulties or dangers.

scythe, } 1 saɪth; 2 sīth, n. A **sithe^s,** } long curved blade fastened to a bent handle, or snath, for mowing.

Scythe and its Snath.

b, blade or scythe proper; n, nibs or handles; s, snath; t, head of blade, showing tang.

sea, 1 sɪ; 2 sē, n. The great body of salt water on the earth's surface; the ocean; also, any large enclosed or inland body of salt water.— **sea'board",** n. **I.** a. Bordering on the sea. **II.** n. The seacoast.— **sea'breeze",** n. A breeze blowing from the sea.— **sea'coast",** n. The seashore.— **sea'far"ing,** a. Following the sea as a calling.— **sea'go"ing,** a. Adapted for use on the ocean; seafaring.— **sea-green. I.** a. Of a bluish-green color. **II.** n. A deep bluish green, as sea-water.— **sea-level,** n. The level continuous with that of the surface of the ocean at meantide.— **sea'man,** n. A mariner; sailor.— **sea'man-ship,** n.— **sea-mew,** n. A gull.— **sea'port",** n. A harbor on or near the sea; especially, a place designated by law where seagoing vessels may enter, anchor, discharge cargoes, and obtain clearance for other voyages.— **sea-room,** n. Sufficient offing for a vessel to be maneuvered.— **sea'shore",** n. Land bordering on the ocean. — **sea'sick",** a. Suffering from seasickness. — **sea'sick"ness,** n. Nausea, dizziness, and prostration caused by the motion of a vessel. — **sea'side". I.** a. Beside the sea. **II.** n. The seashore, especially as a place of resort. — **sea'ward. I.** a. Being toward the sea.

1: ärtistic, ärt; fat, fãre; fast; get, prēy; hit, police; obey, gō; net, ôr; full, rūle; but, būrn.
2: ärt, āpe, făt, fâre, fȧst, whạt, ạll; mē, gĕt, prey, fẽrn; hĭt, īce; ĩ=ē; ĩ=ĕ; gō, nŏt, ôr, wŏn,

II. *adv.* In the direction of the sea.— **sea'-weed"**, *n.* A plant living or growing in the sea.— **sea'wor"thy**, *a.* In fit condition for a voyage: said of a vessel.— **sea'wor"thi-ness**, *n.*

seal¹, 1 sēl; 2 sēl. **I.** *vt.* To fasten with a seal; put a seal upon; close tightly; keep secret; confirm. **II.** *n.* **1.** An instrument used for making an impression upon wax or the like; also, the impression so made, or the substance bearing such impression and affixed to a document. **2.** Anything that fastens securely. **3.** Anything that authenticates; a pledge; guaranty.— **seal'ing-wax"**, *n.* A mixture, as of shellac, turpentine, etc., used for making seals, as on letters.

seal². **I.** *vi.* To hunt seals. **II.** *n.* An

Fur=seal. ¹/₄₀

aquatic carnivorous mammal of high latitudes, yielding valuable fur.

seam, 1 sīm; 2 sēm. **I.** *vt. & vi.* To unite by a seam; make a seam in; become fissured. **II.** *n.* A line where parts or pieces, as of cloth or rock, are joined; a juncture; crack; fissure; scar; wrinkle. — **seam'less**, *a.* Having no seam.— **seam'stress**, *n.* A woman skilled in needlework. — **seam'y**, *a.* Having or showing seams; figuratively, showing the worst aspect; as, the *seamy* side.

sear, 1 sīr; 2 sēr. **I.** *vi.* To wither; cauterize; make callous; harden. **II.** *a.* Dried or blasted; withered.

search, ⎰ 1 sûrch; 2 sêrch. **I**ᵗ. *vt. & vi.* To
serchᴾ, ⎱ explore thoroughly; try; examine; seek or look carefully. **II.** *n.* The act of seeking or looking diligently; investigation; inquiry.— **search'-light"**, *n.* A powerful electric arc-light set in a reflector, so that the rays may be thrown in any direction for search or signaling.— **s.-warrant**, *n.* A warrant directing an officer to search a place, as for stolen goods.

sea'son, 1 sī'zn; 2 sē'ṣn, *v.* **I.** *t.* To give relish or zest to; prepare for use, as lumber by drying; mitigate; moderate. **II.** *i.* To become dry or fit for use; mature. — **sea'son-er**, *n.*

sea'son, *n.* **1.** A division of the year, as spring, summer, autumn, or winter. **2.** A period of time. **3.** A fit time.— **sea'son-a-ble**(eᴾ, *a.* Being in keeping with the season. — **sea'son-a-bl**(e-nessᴾ, *n.*— **sea'son-a-bly**,

adv.— **sea'son-ing**, *n.* **1.** The fitting for use, as lumber by drying. **2.** A relish.

seat, 1 sīt; 2 sēt. **I**ᵈ. *vt.* **1.** To place on a seat; cause to sit down; have seats for; locate. **2.** To fix a seat on or in. **II.** *n.* That on which one sits; location; site; manner of sitting, as on horseback.

se'cant, 1 sī'kant; 2 sē'eant. **I.** *a.* Cutting; intersecting. **II.** *n. Math.* A straight line that intersects a curve or figure.

se-cede', 1 sı-sīd'; 2 se-çēd', *vi.* [SE-CED'-ED**ᵈ**; SE-CED'ING.] To withdraw from association; separate.— **se-ced'er**, *n.*— **se-ces'sion**, 1 sı-sesh'ən; 2 se-çēsh'on, *n.* The act of seceding.

se-clude', 1 sı-klūd'; 2 se-elụd', *vt.* [SE-CLUD'ED**ᵈ**; SE-CLUD'ING.] To withdraw, as from society.— **se-clud'ed**, *pa.*— **se-clu'sion**, 1 sı-klū'ʒən; 2 se-elụ'zhon, *n.* The act of secluding; a secluded place; solitude; retirement.

sec'ondᵈ, 1 sek'ənd; 2 sĕe'ond, *vt.* To support; promote.— **sec'ond-er**, *n.*

sec'ond, *a.* **1.** Next in order after the first. **2.** Inferior; subordinate. **3.** Another; other. **4.** *Mus.* Lower in pitch. — **sec'on-da-ry**, *I. a.* Subordinate; secondrate. **II.** *n.* [-RIES**ᶻ**, *pl.*] **1.** An assistant; deputy. **2.** Anything secondary.— **sec'on-da-ri-ly**, *adv.*— **sec'ond-hand"**, *a.* Received from or through another; previously used; not new; not direct.— **sec'ond-ly**, *adv.* In the second place.— **s. sight**, an assumed power of foretelling the future.

sec'ond¹, 1 sek'ənd; 2 sĕe'ond, *n.* **1.** The one next after the first. **2.** An attendant, as in a duel.

sec'ond², *n.* The ¹/₆₀ of a minute either of time or of angular measure.

sec'ond³, *n. Mus.* **1.** The interval between any note and the next above or below on the diatonic scale. **2.** The second note above the key-note.

se'cre-cy, 1 sī'krı-sı; 2 sē'ere-çy, *n.* [-CIES**ᶻ**, *pl.*] The condition of being secret; secretiveness; privacy; retirement.

se'cret, 1 sī'kret; 2 sē'erĕt. **I.** *a.* Separate; hidden; private; secluded; close-mouthed. **II.** *n.* **1.** Something not to be told or not known. **2.** An underlying reason. **-ly**, *adv.* **-ness**, *n.*

sec're-ta-ry, 1 sek'rı-tē-rı; 2 sĕe're-tā-ry, *n.* [-RIES**ᶻ**, *pl.*] **1.** One who attends to correspondence, records, etc. **2.** A head of a governmental department. **3.** A writing-desk.— **sec"re-ta'ri-al**, *a.*— **sec're-ta-ry-ship**, *n.*

se-crete', 1 sı-krīt'; 2 se-crēt', *vt.* [SE-CRET'ED**ᵈ**; SE-CRET'ING.] **1.** To conceal; hide. **2.** To separate, as a secretion.

— se-cre'tion, 1 sɪ-krī'shən; 2 se-crē'shon, n. **1.** Separation, as of materials from blood or sap; the substance secreted, as saliva or milk. **2.** Concealment.— **se - cre'tiv**(es, 1 sɪ-krī'tiv; 2 se-crē'tiv, a. **1.** Inclined to secrecy. **2.** Producing secretion **-ly,** adv. **-ness,** n. **— se-cre'to-ry,** a. Pertaining to secretion.

sect, 1 sekt; 2 sĕct, n. A religious denomination; an ecclesiastical faction.— **sec-ta'ri-an,** 1 sek-tē'ri-an; 2 sĕc-tā'ri-an, a. Pertaining to a sect; bigoted.— **sec-ta'ri-an-ism,** n.

sec'tion, 1 sek'shən; 2 sĕc'shon, n. **1.** A separate part; division; portion. **2.** A view of something, as if cut through.— **sec'tion-al,** a. **1.** Pertaining to a section; local. **2.** Made up of sections. **-ism,** n. **-ly,** adv.

sec'tor, 1 sek'tər or -tor; 2 sĕc'tor, n. A part of a circle bounded by two radii and the included arc.

sec'u-lar, 1 sek'yu-lər; 2 sĕc'yu-lar, a. **1.** Worldly. **2.** Brought about in the course of ages. **3.** Not bound by monastic vows. **-ly,** adv. **-ness,** n.— **sec'u-lar-ize,** 1 sek'yu-lər-aiz; 2 sĕc'yu-lar-īz, vt. [-IZED; -IZ'ING.] To render secular; make worldly.— **sec''u-lar-i-za'tion,** n.

Sector.

se-cure', 1 sɪ-kiūr'; 2 se-cūr'. **I.** vt. [SE-CURED; SE-CUR'ING.] **1.** To protect; guarantee; fasten; close. **2.** To obtain; acquire. **II.** a. **1.** Guarded against danger. **2.** Overconfident; incautious. **-ly,** adv. **-ness,** n.— **se-cu'ri-ty,** 1 sɪ-kiū'rɪ-tɪ; 2 se-cū'ri-ty, n. [-TIES², pl.] The state of being secure.

se-dan', 1 sɪ-dan'; 2 se-dăn', n. **1.** A closed chair, formerly in use, in which a passenger was carried by two men. **se-dan'chair"‡. 2.** A closed motor-car.

se-date', 1 sɪ-dēt'; 2 se-dāt', a. Habitually calm; sober; staid. **-ly,** adv. **-ness,** n. **— sed'a-tiv**(es, 1 sed'-ə-tiv; 2 sĕd'a-tiv. **I.** a. Soothing. **II.** n. A soothing remedy.

Sedan.

sed'en-ta-ry, 1 sed'en-tē-rɪ; 2 sĕd'ĕn-tā-ry, a. Sitting much of the time.— **sed'en-ta-ri-ly,** adv.— **sed'en-ta-ri-ness,** n.

sedge, 1 sej; 2 sĕdg, n. A coarse rush-like herb growing in a wet place.— **sedg'y,** a.

sed'i-ment, 1 sed'i-ment or -mant; 2 sĕd'i-ment, n. Matter that settles to the bottom of a liquid.— **sed''i-men'ta-ry,** a.

se-di'tion, 1 sɪ-dish'ən; 2 se-dish'on, n. Popular disorder; insurrection; revolt.— **se-di'tious,** a. **-ly,** adv. **-ness,** n.

se-duce', 1 sɪ-diūs'; 2 se-dūç', vt. [SE-DUCED'd; SE-DUC'ING.] To draw into evil; lead astray.— **se-duce'ment,** n.— **se-duc'er,** n.— **se-duc'tion,** 1 sɪ-duk'shən; 2 se-dŭc'shon, n.— **se-duc'tiv**(es, a. Tending to seduce; enticing. **-ly,** adv. **-ness,** n.

see, 1 sī; 2 sē, vt. & vi. [SAW; SEEN; SEE'ING.] **1.** To perceive by the eye; observe; understand; ascertain. **2.** To call on or visit; meet; receive; escort.

see, n. **1.** The jurisdiction of a bishop or pope. **2.** [S-] The Pope; as, a decision by the See of Rome.— **Holy See, See of Rome.** An independent State under the temporal sway of the Roman Pontiffs, originally (1591) 16,000 sq. m., the greater part of which was seized and incorporated with the Kingdom of Italy May 13, 1871. On Feb. 11, 1929, an insignificant part (¹/₅ sq. m.) of this was restored to the Papacy and a new State erected under the jurisdiction of the Pope.

seedd, 1 sīd; 2 sēd. **I.** vt. & vi. **1.** To sow with seed; produce seed; sow seeds; free from seed. **II.** n. **1.** The germ from which a plant may be reproduced; that from which anything springs; a first principle; source. **2.** Offspring; children.— **seed'ling,** n. A plant reared from the seed, instead of from a graft or the like.— **seed'y,** 1 sīd'ɪ; 2 sēd'y, a. [SEED'I-ER; SEED'I-EST.] Abounding with seeds; going to seed; ragged; shabby.— **seed'i-ly,** adv.— **seed'i-ness,** n.

see'ing, conj. Considering; since.

seek, 1 sīk; 2 sĕk, v. [SOUGHT, 1 sōt; 2 sôt; SEEK'ING.] **I.** t. To go in search of; strive for. **II.** i. To search. **-er.** n.

seem, 1 sīm; 2 sēm, vi. To give the impression of being; appear.— **seem'ing. I.** pa. Apparent; not real. **II.** n. Appearance; semblance. **-ly,** adv. **-ness,** n.

seem'ly, 1 -'lɪ; 2 -ly, a. [SEEM'LI-ER; SEEM'LI-EST.] Proper; decorous. **-li-ness,** n.

seer, 1 sīr; 2 sēr, n. One who foretells.

see'saw", 1 sī'sô"; 2 sē'sǎ". **I.** vt. & vi. To move up and down or to and fro; vacillate. **II.** a. Moving like a seesaw; vacillating. **III.** n. A balanced plank on which persons are borne up and down.

seethe, 1 sīth; 2 sēth, vt. & vi. [SEETHED, formerly SOD; SEETHED, formerly SODDEN, or SOD; SEETH'ING.] To boil.

seg'ment, 1 seg'ment or -mant; 2 sĕg'ment, n. A part cut off; a section; the part of a circle included within a chord and its arc.

Segment.

seg're-gate, 1 seg'rɪ-get; 2 sĕg're-gāt. **I.** vt. & vi. [-GAT'ED'd; -GAT'-

1: **artistic.** ärt; fat, fāre; fast; get, prey; hit, police; obey, gō; net, ôr; full, rūle; but, būrn.
2: ärt, āpe, făt, fâre, fȧst, whạt, all; mē, gĕt, prey, fẽrn; hĭt, īce, ī=ĕ; ĩ=ē; gō, nŏt, ôr, wŏn,

ING.] To separate; isolate. **II.** *a.* Separated; select; solitary.— **seg″re·ga′tion,** *n.*

sei′gnior, 1 sēn′yor, *n.* A lord; in southern Europe, used like English *sir.* — **sei′gnior·age,** 1 sēn′yər·ɪj; 2 sēn′yor·ag, *n.* **1.** A governmental charge for coining bullion. **2.** The difference between the cost of bullion and the nominal value of the coin made from it. **3.** A royalty or a commission on sales.

seine, 1 sēn; 2 sēn, *n.* Any large encircling fish=net.

seis′mic, 1 saɪs′mɪk; 2 sīs′mic, *a.* Pertaining to, characteristic of, or produced by earthquakes.— **seis′mo·graph,** *n.* An instrument for recording automatically the phenomena of earthquakes.—**seis″mo·graph′ic,·i·cal,** *a.*— **seis·mol′o·gy,** *n.*

seize, } 1 sīz; 2 sēz, *vt.* [SEIZ(E)D⁸; SEIZ′ING.]
seizᴾ,} **1.** To grasp suddenly or forcibly; take by force; affect suddenly and powerfully. **2.** *Naut.* To bind by turns of cord; lash.— **seiz′a·ble(ᵉ),** *a.*— **seiz′er,** *n.*— **sei′zure,** *n.* The act of seizing; a sudden or violent attack.

sel′dom, 1 sel′dəm; 2 sĕl′dom, *adv.* At widely separated intervals; infrequently.

se·lect′, 1 sɪ·lekt′; 2 se·lĕct′. **I**ᵈ. *vt. & vi.* To take in preference to another or others; choose. **II.** *a.* Chosen; choice. **-ness,** *n.*— **se·lec′tion,** *n.* The act of selecting; choice; anything selected; a collection.

self, 1 self; 2 sĕlf. **I.** *a.* Same; particular; identical. **II.** *n.* [SELVES, *pl.*] **1.** An individual considered as the subject of his own consciousness; a distinct personality. **2.** Personal advantage or gain.— **self″·con·ceit′,** *n.* Vanity; egotism.— **s.·conceited,** *a.*— **s.·conscious,** *a.* Unduly conscious that one is observed by others.— **s.·defense,** *n.* Defense of oneself or one's interests.— **s.·denial,** *n.* Denial of one's own gratification.— **s.·denying,** *a.*— **s.·esteem,** *n.* A good opinion of oneself or of one's abilities.— **s.·evident,** *a.* Carrying its evidence in itself.— **s.·existence,** *n.* Inherent, underived, independent existence: an attribute of God.— **s.·existent,** *a.*— **s.·interest,** *n.* One's own interest or advantage, or the principle of seeking it.— **s.·love,** *n.* The desire to seek one's own well=being.— **s.·possessed,** *a.*— **s.·possession,** *n.* Presence of mind; self=command.— **s.·righteous,** *a.* Righteous in one's own estimation; pharisaic.— **self·same″,** *a.* Identical.— **self·will,** *n.* Adherence to one's own will with disregard of others.— **s.·willed,** *a.*

self′ish, 1 self′ɪsh; 2 sĕlf′ish, *a.* Caring only or chiefly for self. **-ly,** *adv.* **-ness,** *n.*

sell, } 1 sel; 2 sĕl, *vt. & vi.* [SOLD; SELL′ING.]
selᴾ,} To transfer (property) to another for a price; bring a price; be sold.— **sell′er,** *a.*

sel′vage, 1 sel′vɪj; 2 sĕl′vag, *n.* The edge

of a fabric so finished that it will not ravel.

selv(e)s⁸, 1 selvz; 2 sĕlvz, *n.* Plural of SELF, *n.*

sem′a·phore, 1 sem′ə·fōr; 2 sĕm′a·fōr, *n.* An apparatus with movable arms for making signals; a signal=telegraph.— **sem″a·phor′ic,·i·cal,** *a.*

sem′blance, 1 sem′bləns; 2 sĕm′blanç, *n.* Show; likeness; image; appearance.

se·mes′ter, 1 sɪ·mes′tər; 2 se·mĕs′ter, *n.* A college half=year; about five months.— **se·mes′tral,** *a.*   [*semicircle.*

sem′i-, *prefix.* Half; partly; as, *semi*annual.

sem″i-an′nu·al, 1 sem″ɪ·an′yu·al; 2 sĕm″i-ǎn′yu·al, *a.* Half=yearly. **-ly,** *adv.*

sem′i-breve, 1 sem′ɪ·brēv; 2 sĕm′i-brēv, *n. Mus.* A note equal to half a breve; a whole note.

sem″i-cir′cle, 1 sem′ɪ·sûr″kl; 2 sĕm′i-çir″el, *n.* **1.** A half=circle. **2.** Any semicircular structure.— **sem″i-cir′cu·lar,** *a.*

sem′i-co′lon, 1 sem′ɪ·kō″lən; 2 sĕm′i-cō″lon, *n.* A mark (;) of punctuation, indicating a greater degree of separation than the comma.

sem″i-flu′id, 1 sem″ɪ·flū′ɪd; 2 sĕm″i-flu′id. **I.** *a.* Fluid, but thick and viscous. **II.** *n.* A thick, viscous fluid.

sem″i-lu′nar, 1 sem″ɪ·liū′nər; 2 sĕm″i-lū′nar, *a.* Resembling or shaped like a half=moon; crescentic. **sem″i-lu′nate**‡.

sem″i-month′ly, 1 sem″ɪ·munth′lɪ; 2 sĕm″i-mŏnth′ly. **I.** *a.* Taking place twice a month. **II.** *n.* A publication issued twice a month.

sem′i-nal, 1 sem′ɪ·nəl; 2 sĕm′i-nal, *a.* Pertaining to seed; germinal.

sem′i-na·ry, 1 sem′ɪ·nē·rɪ; 2 sĕm′i-nā·ry, *n.* [-RIES², *pl.*] An educational institution; academy.

sem″i-qua′ver, 1 sem′ɪ·kwē″vər; 2 sĕm″i-kwā′ver, *n. Mus.* A sixteenth note.

sem′i-tone, 1 sem′ɪ·tōn; 2 sĕm′i-tōn, *n. Mus.* Half a major tone.

sem″i-vow′el, 1 sem″ɪ·vau′el; 2 sĕm″i-vow′el, *n.* A sound having the character of both a vowel and a consonant, and used as either, as *w* or *y.*

sem″i-week′ly, 1 sem″ɪ·wīk′lɪ; 2 sĕm″i-wēk′ly. **I.** *a.* Issued or recurring twice a week. **II.** *n.* A publication issued twice a week.

sem″pi·ter′nal, 1 sem″pɪ·tûr′nəl; 2 sĕm″pi-tēr′nal, *a.* Everlasting.   [Throughout.

sem′pre, 1 sem′prē; 2 sĕm′pre, *adv. Mus.*

semp′stress, 1 semp′stres; 2 sĕmp′stres, *n.* A seamstress.

sen′ate, 1 sen′ɪt; 2 sĕn′at, *n.* **1.** [S-] The more stable branch of a congress or legislature. **2.** A legislative body; council.— **sen′a·tor,** *n.* A member of a senate.

sen″a-to′ri-al, *a.* **-ly,** *adv.—* **sen′a-tor-ship,** *n.*

send, 1 send; 2 sĕnd, *v.* [SENT; SEND′ING.] **I.** *t.* To cause or command to go; dispatch; forward; throw; inflict; bestow. **II.** *n.* To dispatch an agent, message, or messenger.— **send′er,** *n.*

sen′e-schal, 1 sen′ə-shal; 2 sĕn′e-shal, *n.* A steward.— **sen′e-schal-ship,** *n.*

se′nile, 1 sī′nail *or* -nil; 2 sē′nil *or* -nil, *a.*

se′nil⁵, Of, pertaining to, or affected by old age; infirm; weak.— **se-nil′i-ty,** 1 si-nil′i-ti; 2 se-nil′i-ty, *n.*

se′nior, 1 sīn′yər; 2 sēn′yor. **I.** *a.* **1.** Older; elder. **2.** [U.S.] Pertaining to the closing year of a college course. **II.** *n.* **1.** An elder; elderly person. **2.** A member of a senior class.— **se′ni-or′i-ty,** *n.*

sen′na, 1 sen′ə; 2 sĕn′a, *n.* A leguminous plant, used medicinally as a purgative.

se-ñor′, 1 sē-nyōr′; 2 se-nyŏr′, *n.* A gentleman; Mr.; sir: a Spanish title of respect.— **se-ño′ra,** 1 sē-nyō′rə; 2 se-nyō′ra, *n.* A lady; Mrs.; madam.— **se′ño-ri′ta,** 1 sē″nyo-ri′tɐ; 2 sĕ″nyo-rī′tä, *n.* A young unmarried lady; miss.

sen-sa′tion, 1 sen-sē′shən; 2 sĕn-sā′shon, *n.* **1.** Feeling aroused through the senses; also, stimulation of some organ of sense; sensation. **2.** Interest or excitement, or that which produces it.— **sen-sa′tion-al,** *a.* **1.** Pertaining to sensation. **2.** Causing unnatural emotional excitement; melodramatic; trashy. **-ism,** *n.* **-ist,** *n.*

sense, 1 sens; 2 sĕns, *n.* **1.** The faculty of sensation; feeling; realization. **2.** Any one of the five senses, sight, hearing, taste, smell, or touch. **3.** Good judgment. **4.** Signification; meaning.— **sense′less,** *a.* Without sense; unconscious; also, foolish; meaningless. **-ly,** *adv.—* **sen″si-bil′i-ty,** *n.* [-TIES², *pl.*] Power to feel; sensitiveness.— **sen′si-bl(e⁵,** *a.* **1.** Having good sense; intelligent. **2.** Having sensation; sensitive. **3.** Appreciable. **-ness,** *n.—* **sen′si-bly,** *adv.—* **sen′si-tiv(e⁵,** *a.* **1.** Excitable or impressible. **2.** Pertaining to the senses or sensation. **-ly,** *adv.* **— sen′si-tiv(e-ness⁵,** *n.* **sen′si-tiv′i-ty‡.**

sen′su-al, 1 sen′shu-əl; 2 sĕn′shu-al, *a.* Unduly indulgent to the appetites; lewd; carnal. **-ly,** *adv.* **-ness,** *n.—* **sen′su-al-ist,** *n.* A sensual person.— **sen″su-al′i-ty,** *n.—* **sen′su-al-ize,** *vt.—* **sen′su-ous,** *a.* Pertaining to the senses; luxurious.

sent, 1 sent; 2 sĕnt, *imp. & pp.* of SEND, *v.*

sen′tence, 1 sen′tens; 2 sĕn′tĕnç. **I.** *vt.* [SEN′TENCED†; SEN′TENC-ING.] To pass sentence upon. **II.** *n.* **1.** A group of words expressing a complete thought. **2.** A legal judgment. **3.** A determination; opinion. **4.** A maxim.— **sen-ten′tious,** 1 sen-ten′shus; 2 sĕn-tĕn′shŭs, *a.* Abounding in terse sentences; laconic; axiomatic. **-ly,** *adv.* **-ness,** *n.*

sen′ti-ent, 1 sen′shi-ent; 2 sĕn′shi-ĕnt, *a.* Having sensation and perception; sensitive; feeling.

sen′ti-ment, 1 sen′ti-ment *or* -mənt; 2 sĕn′ti-ment, *n.* **1.** Lofty and refined feeling; sensibility. **2.** An opinion; expressive thought; toast.— **sen″ti-men′tal,** *a.* Characterized by sentiment; emotional. **-ly,** *adv.—* **sen″ti-men′tal-ism,** *n.—* **sen″ti-men′tal-ist,** *n.*

sen′ti-nel, 1 sen′ti-nel; 2 sĕn′ti-nĕl, *n.* A soldier on guard; a watchman. **sen′try‡.**

sep′al, 1 sep′əl *or* sī′pəl; 2 sĕp′al *or* sē′pal, *n.* One of the individual leaves of a calyx.

sep′a-rate, 1 sep′ə-rēt; 2 sĕp′a-rāt, *v.* [-RAT′ED⁴; -RAT′ING.] **I.** *t.* **1.** To disconnect; dissever. **2.** To keep apart. **3.** To consider separately. **II.** *i.* To be disconnected. **-ly,** *adv.* **-ness,** *n.—* **sep′a-ra-bl(e⁵,** 1 sep′ə-rə-bl; 2 sĕp′a-ra-bl, *a.* Capable of being separated.— **sep″a-ra-bil′i-ty,** *n.—* **sep′a-ra-bly,** *adv.—* **sep″a-ra′tion,** *n.* The act of separating; the state of being separated.— **sep″a-ra′tor,** *n.* One who or that which separates; a device or instrument for separating impurities or refuse from a substance, inferior from better grades, etc.— **sep′a-ra-to-ry,** *a.*

sep′a-rate, 1 sep′ə-rit; 2 sĕp′a-rat, *a.* Existing apart from others; considered by itself; unconnected or disconnected.

se′pi-a, 1 sī′pi-ə; 2 sē′pi-a. **I.** *a.* Dark-brown with a tinge of red. **II.** *n.* The cuttlefish, its ink, or a dark-brown pigment prepared from it.

se′poy, 1 sī′pɔi; 2 sē′pŏy, *n.* A native East-Indian soldier equipped and trained in European style.

sep′sis, 1 sep′sis; 2 sĕp′sis, *n.* Poisonous putrefaction, or infection from it.

Sep-tem′ber, 1 sep-tem′bər; 2 sĕp-tĕm′ber, *n.* The ninth month of the year, having 30 days.

sep′te-na-ry, 1 sep′ti-nē-ri; 2 sĕp′te-nā-ry, *a.* **1.** Consisting of, pertaining to, or being seven. **2.** Septennial.

sep-ten′ni-al, 1 sep-ten′i-əl; 2 sĕp-tĕn′i-al, *a.* **1.** Recurring every seven years. **2.** Continuing seven years. **-ly,** *adv.*

sep′tic, 1 sep′tik; 2 sĕp′tic, *a.* Of or pertaining to poisonous putrefaction; putrid. **sep′ti-cal‡.**

1: ɑrtistic, ärt; fat, fāre; fɑst; get, prēy; hit, police; obey, gō; nɔt, ōr; fûll; rūle; bʊt, bûrn.

2: ärt, āpe, făt, fâre, fȧst, whạt, ạll; mē, gĕt, prẹy, fērn; hĭt, īce; ï = ē; ĭ = ĕ; gō, nŏt, ôr, wŏn;

sep-til'lion, 1 sep-til'yən; 2 sĕp-tĭl'yon, *n.* A cardinal number: in the French system (also U. S.) 1 followed by 24 ciphers; in the English system, 1 followed by 42 ciphers.

sep"tu-a-ge-na'ri-an, 1 sep"tiu-a-ji-nē'rɪ-ən; 2 sĕp"tū-ă-ge-nā'ri-an, *n.* A person 70 years old, or between 70 and 80.

Sep'tu-a-gint, 1 sep'tiu-ə-jint; 2 sĕp'tū-a-gĭnt, *n.* An old Greek version of the Old Testament.

sep'tu-pl(e^P, 1 sep'tiu-pl; 2 sĕp'tū-pl, *a.* Consisting of seven; sevenfold; seven times repeated.

sep'ul-cher, ⎰ 1 sep'əl-kər; 2 sĕp'ul-cer.
sep'ul-chre, ⎱ **I.** *vt.* To entomb. **II.** *n.* A burial-place, as in a rock; tomb.— **se-pul'-chral,** 1 sɪ-pul'krəl; 2 se-pŭl'eral, *a.* **1.** Pertaining to a sepulcher. **2.** Dismal; funereal.— **sep'ul-ture,** *n.* The act of entombing; burial.

se'quel, 1 sī'kwel; 2 sē'kwĕl, *n.* A continuing and concluding portion, as of a story; result; upshot.

se'quence, 1 sī'kwens; 2 sē'kwĕnç, *n.* Succession; arrangement; series.

se-ques'ter, 1 sɪ-kwes'tər; 2 se-kwĕs'ter, *vt.* **1.** To separate; seclude. **2.** To sequestrate.— **se-ques'tered,** *pa.* Retired; secluded.

se-ques'trate, 1 sɪ-kwes'trēt; 2 se-kwĕs'trāt, *vt.* [-TRAT-ED^d; -TRAT-ING.] *Law.* (1) To confiscate. (2) To take possession of for a time.— **seq"ues-tra'tion,** *n.* Seizure; confiscation.— **seq"ues-tra'tor,** *n.*

se-quoi'a, 1 sɪ-kwoi'ə; 2 se-kwŏi'a, *n.* Same as REDWOOD.

se-ra'glio, 1 se-rā'lyo *or* sɪ-ral'yo; 2 se-rä'lyo *or* se-räl'yo, *n.* A harem.

ser'aph, ⎰ 1 ser'af; 2 sĕr'af, *n.* [SER'APHS
ser'aph, ⎱ *or* SER'A-PHIM, SER'A-FIM^P, *pl.*] An angel of the highest order.— **se-raph'ic,** 1 sɪ-raf'ik; 2 se-raf'ic, *a.* Angelic.— **se-raph'i-cal,** *a.* **-ly,** *adv.*

sere, *v. & a.* Same as SEAR.

ser"e-nade, 1 ser'ɪ-nēd'; 2 sĕr"e-nād'. **I.** *vt. & vi.* [-NAD'ED^d; -NAD'ING.] To entertain with or engage in a serenade. **II.** *n.* Music rendered as a tribute in the open air at night.

se-rene', 1 sɪ-rīn'; 2 se-rēn', *a.* Clear, or fair and calm; peaceful; tranquil. **-ly,** *adv.* **-ness,** *n.*— **se-ren'i-ty,** n. [-TIES^z, *pl.*]

serf, 1 sürf; 2 sĕrf, *n.* A person whose service is attached to an estate.— **serf'dom,** *n.*

serge, 1 sürj; 2 sĕrg, *n.* A twilled woolen stuff.

ser'geant, 1 sär'jənt; 2 sär'gant, *n.* A non-commissioned military officer next above a corporal.— **ser'gean-cy, ser'geant-cy,** *n.*— **ser'geant-at-arms',** *n.* An officer in legislative bodies who enforces order, etc.

se'ri-al, *a. & n.* See under SERIES.

se"ri-a'tim, 1 sī'rɪ-ē'tɪm; 2 sē"ri-ā'tim, *adv.* One after another; in connected order; serially.

se'ries, 1 sī'rɪz *or* sī'rɪ-īz; 2 sē'rɪs *or* sē'ri-ĕs, *n.* A connected succession.— **se'ri-al,** 1 sī'rɪ-al; 2 sē'ri-al. **I.** *a.* **1.** Of the nature of a series. **2.** Published in a series at regular intervals. **II.** *n.* A literary composition published in parts.— **se'ri-al-ly,** *adv.*

se'ri-ous, 1 sī'rɪ-us; 2 sē'ri-ŭs, *a.* Grave and earnest; thoughtful; sober; of great importance. **-ly,** *adv.* **-ness,** *n.*

ser'mon, 1 sür'mən; 2 sĕr'mon, *n.* A religious discourse, based on a text of the Bible; any serious discourse.— **ser"mon-ette',** *n.*— **ser'mon-ize,** *vt.* [to serum.

se'rous, 1 sī'rus; 2 sē'rŭs, *a.* Pertaining

ser'pent, 1 sür'pent; 2 sĕr'pĕnt, *n.* A scaly, limbless reptile; a snake.— **ser'pen-tine,** 1 sür'pen-tain *or* -tin; 2 sĕr'pĕn-tin *or* -tin. **I.** *a.* Pertaining to or like a serpent; zigzag. **II.** *n.* A variously colored marble-like rock.

ser'rate, ⎰ 1 ser'ēt, ser'ĕt-ed; 2 sĕr'āt,
ser'rat-ed, ⎱ ser'āt-ĕd, *a.* Notched like a saw.— **ser-ra'tion,** *n.*

ser'ried, 1 ser'ɪd; 2 sĕr'ɪd, *pa.* Compacted in rows, as soldiers.

se'rum, 1 sī'rum; 2 sē'rŭm, *n.* A watery animal-fluid, as the watery portion of the blood.

Doubly Serrate Leaves of an Elm.

ser'vant, 1 sür'vənt; 2 sĕr'-vant, *n.* A person who labors for another.

serve, ⎰ 1 sürv; 2 sĕrv, *v.* [SERVED, SERVD^s;
serv^s, ⎱ SERV'ING.] **I.** *t.* **1.** To be in the employment of; work for; be of use to; aid. **2.** To content; satisfy; requite. **3.** To conduct; manipulate; handle; wait on. **II.** *i.* **1.** To act as a servant or under authority. **2.** To be of service; be sufficient.— **serv'er,** *n.*— **ser'vice,** 1 sür'vɪs; 2 sĕr'vic, *n.* **1.** The work or position of one in the army or navy; military or naval duty; also, work performed for another. **2.** One's official work; religious exercise. **3.** A set of vessels, utensils, etc., for use as at table.— **ser'vice-a-bl(e^P,** *a.*— **ser'vice-a-bl(e-ness^P,** *n.*— **ser'vice-a-bly,** *adv.*— **ser'vil(e^s,** 1 sür'vɪl; 2 sĕr'vil, *a.* **1.** Slavish; abject. **2.** Pertaining to slaves or servants. **3.** Being of a subject class. **-ly,** *adv.*— **ser-vil'i-ty,** *n.* Cringing submission; slavishness.— **ser'vi-tor,** *n.* A serving-man; follower.— **ser'vi-tude,** 1 sür'vɪ-tiūd; 2 sĕr'vi-tūd, *n.* The condition of a slave; bondage.

ses'sile, ⎰ 1 ses'ɪl; 2 sĕs'il, *a.* Attached by its
ses'sil(e, ⎱ base, without a stalk, as a leaf.

ses'sion, 1 sesh'ən; 2 sĕsh'on, *n.* A sitting

or meeting of an organized body, or the time during which it remains sitting.

set, 1 set; 2 sĕt, v. [SET; SET'TING.] **I.** t. **1.** To cause to sit; to put in place; place; put; appoint; settle. **2.** To fix (a price). **II.** i. **1.** To pass below the horizon; decline; sink; fade. **2.** To solidify; become fixed. **3.** To tend; incline. **4.** To exert one's powers. **5.** To fit, as a garment.—**set'-off,** n. **1.** An offset or counterpoise. **2.** A decorative contrast or setting.—**set'ter,** n. One who sets; one of a breed of hunting-dogs that crouch to point out game.—**set'ting,** n. **1.** The act of anything that sets. **2.** That in which something is set; a frame.

set, 1 set; 2 sĕt, pa. **1.** Fixed; obstinate. **2.** Established or prescribed. **3.** Rigid; stationary.

set, n. **1.** A collection; class; group. **2.** Position or direction. **3.** The act of sinking below the horizon, as a heavenly body.

set-tee', 1 se-tī'; 2 sĕ-tē', n. A long seat with a high back.

set'tle, 1 set'l; 2 sĕt'l, v. [SET'TLED, SET'-
set'l², ⎱ 1 LD²; SET'TLING.] **I.** t. **1.** To fix; determine; adjust; pay. **2.** To still; calm. **3.** To people; colonize. **II.** i. **1.** To become clarified, as a liquid; sink, as dregs. **2.** To come to rest; adjust differences; subside. **3.** To fix one's abode. **4.** To determine. **5.** To pay one's bill; adjust accounts by payment.—**set'tle,** n. Same as SETTEE.—**set'tle-ment,** n. **1.** The act of settling. **2.** A colonized region.—**set'tler,** n. A colonist.—**set'tling,** n.

sev'en, 1 sev'n; 2 sĕv'n, a. & n. Six and one.—**sev'en-fold,** a.—**sev''en-teen',** 1 sev'n-tīn'; 2 sĕv'n-tēn', a. & n. Seven more than ten.—**sev''en-teenth'. I.** a. **1.** Seventh in order after the tenth. **2.** Being one of seventeen equal parts. **II.** n. One of seventeen equal parts of anything.—**sev'enth,** 1 sev'nth; 2 sĕv'nth, a. & n. Next in order after the sixth; being one of seven equal parts.—**sev'en-ti-eth,** 1 sev'n-ti-eth; 2 sĕv'n-ti-ĕth. **I.** a. **1.** Tenth in order after the sixtieth. **2.** Being one of seventy equal parts. **II.** n. One of seventy equal parts.—**sev'en-ty,** 1 sev'n-ti; 2 sĕv'n-ty, a. & n. Ten more than sixty.

sev'er, 1 sev'ǝr; 2 sĕv'er, vt. & vi. To disjoin; separate; part.—**sev''er-ance,** n.

sev'er-al, 1 sev'ǝr-al; 2 sĕv'er-al, a. **1.** Being of an indefinite but small number; more than two, but not many; divers. **2.** Single; separate.—**sev'er-al-ly,** adv. Individually.

se-vere', 1 si-vīr'; 2 se-vēr', a. **1.** Hard to bear; painful. **2.** Harsh; merciless. **3.** Serious; grave; sedate. -**ly,** adv. -**ness,** n.

— se-ver'i-ty, 1 si-ver'i-ti; 2 se-vĕr'i-ty, n. [-TIES², pl.]

sew, 1 sō; 2 sō, vt. [SEWED, SEWD³; SEWED or SEWN; SEW'ING.] To make, mend, or fasten, as with needle and thread.

sew'age, 1 siū'ij; 2 sū'ag, n. The waste matter carried off in sewers.

sew'er, 1 sō'er; 2 sō'er, n. One who sews or stitches.

sew'er², 1 siū'ǝr; 2 sū'er, n. A conduit to carry off sewage; a large drain.—**sew'er-age,** n. A system of sewers.

sex, 1 seks; 2 sĕks, n. **1.** The difference between male and female. **2.** Males or females of a group, collectively.

sex''a-ge-na'ri-an, 1 seks'ǝ-ji-nē'ri-ǝn; 2 sĕks'a-ge-nā'ri-an, n. A person sixty years old, or between sixty and seventy years of age.

sex'tant, 1 seks'tǝnt; 2 sĕks'tant, n. **1.** An instrument for determining latitude at sea. **2.** The sixth part of a circle; an arc of 60 degrees.

sex-til'lion, 1 seks-til'yǝn; 2 sĕks-til'yon, n. A cardinal number represented in the French system (also U. S.) by 1 followed by 21 ciphers, and in the English system by 1 followed by 36 ciphers.

sex'ton, 1 seks'tǝn; 2 sĕks'ton, n. A janitor of a church; formerly a grave-digger. — **sex'ton-ship,** n. [Sixfold.

sex''tu-pl(e², 1 seks'tiu-pl; 2 sĕks'tū-pl, a.

sex'u-al, 1 sek'shu-al; 2 sĕk'shu-al, a. Of or pertaining to the sexes, or sex. -**ly,** adv. — **sex''u-al'i-ty,** n.

shab'by, 1 shab'i; 2 shăb'y, a. [SHAB'BI-ER, SHAB'BI-EST.] Threadbare; ragged; mean; paltry.—**shab'bi-ly,** adv.—**shab'bi-ness,** n. [of logs.

shack, 1 shak; 2 shăk, n. A rude cabin, as

shack'le, ⎱
shack'l², ⎰ 1 shak'l; 2 shăk'l. vt. [SHACK'-L(E)D²; SHACK'LING.] To fetter. **II.**

Log Shack.

n. **1.** A fetter, especially for the legs; gyve. **2.** A fastening.

shad, 1 shad; 2 shăd, n. A deep-bodied food-fish.

shad'dock, 1 shad'ǝk; 2 shăd'ok, n. A tropical fruit akin to the orange; also, the tree yielding it.

shade, 1 shēd; 2 shād, vt. & vi. [SHAD'ED³; SHAD'ING.] **1.** To screen from light and

1: ȧrtistic, ûrt; fat, fāre; fȧst; get, prēy; hĭt, police; obey, gō; nŏt, ôr; fûll, rūle; bŭt, bûrn.
2: ärt, āpe, făt, fâre, fȧst, whạt, ạll; mē, gĕt, prẹy, fẽrn; hĭt, īce; I = ē; ĭ = ē; gō, nŏt, ôr, wŏn,

heat; shield. **2.** To blend, as colors; modify.— **shad'er,** *n.*

shade, *n.* **1.** Obscurity; gloom; dusk; shadow. **2.** A shady place; retreat. **3.** A blind. **4.** A gradation of color; minute difference. **5.** A ghost. **6.** *pl.* Hades.

shad'ow, 1 shad'o; 2 shăd'o. **I.** *vt. & vi.* **1.** To cast a shadow; shade; darken. **2.** To foreshow dimly: often with *forth* or *out.* **3.** To follow as a spy; dog. **II.** *n.* **1.** Partial darkness caused by the interception of light; shade; gloom; obscurity; sadness. **2.** Something shadowy; a type; faint trace. **3.** Shelter; covert; protection. **-less,** *a.*— **shad'ow-y,** *a.* Full of shadows; dark; vague; unreal; ghostly.

shad'y, 1 shĕd'ĭ; 2 shād'y, *a.* [SHAD'I-ER; SHAD'I-EST.] **1.** Full of shade; casting a shade; shaded. **2.** Dubious; suspicious. — **shad'i-ly,** *adv.*— **shad'i-ness,** *n.*

shaft[1], 1 shaft; 2 shäft, *n.* **1.** A spear; dart; arrow; the stock or stem of such a weapon. **2.** The part of a column between capital and base. **3.** Any long cylindrical bar, as an axle, thill, or the like.

shaft[2], *n.* A well-like opening connected with a mine; the tunnel of a blast=furnace.

shag, 1 shag; 2 shăg, *n.* A rough coat or mass, as of hair.— **shag'bark,** *n.* The white hickory.— **shag'gy,** *a.* [SHAG'GI-ER; SHAG'GI-EST.] With rough hair or wool; ragged; rough.— **shag'gi-ness,** *n.*

sha-green', 1 sha-grēn'; 2 sha-ḡrēn', *n.* The rough skin of various fishes: used for polishing; rough=grained Oriental leather.

shah, 1 shä; 2 shä, *n.* A Persian king or prince.

shake, 1 shĕk; 2 shāk. **I.** *vt. & vi.* [SHOOK; SHAK'EN; SHAK'ING.] **1.** To move rapidly to and fro or up and down; agitate; jolt; wave; tremble; trill. **2.** To weaken; impair; shatter. **II.** *n.* A shaking; agitation; vibration; jolt.— **shak'er,** *n.* **1.** One who or that which shakes. **2.** [S=] A member of a religious sect in the United States.— **shak'y,** *a.*— **shak'i-ness,** *n.*

shale, 1 shĕl; 2 shāl, *n.* A fragile rock resembling slate.

shall, } 1 shal; 2 shăl, *v.* [SHOULD.] [A **shal**[P], } defective auxiliary verb.] **1.** [SHALL, *1st per. sing. & pl.*] Am to, or are to. **2.** [SHALT, *2d per. sing.*; SHALL, *3d per. sing. & pl.*] Art to, is to, or are to.

Shall and *will,* as auxiliaries expressing simple futurity, are used as follows: I *shall*; thou *wilt*; he *will*; we *shall*; you *will*; they *will.* As auxiliaries expressing a promise, determination, command, or permission, their use is precisely the opposite, viz.: I *will*; thou *shalt*; he *shall*; we *will*; you *shall*; they shall.

shal'lop, 1 shal'əp; 2 shăl'op, *n.* A small open boat.

shal'low, 1 shal'o; 2 shăl'o. **I.** *a.* Lacking depth; shoal; superficial. **II.** *n.* A shallow place; shoal. **-ly,** *adv.* **-ness,** *n.*

shalt, 1 shalt; 2 shält, *2d per. sing. pres. ind.* of SHALL, *v.*

sham, 1 sham; 2 shăm. **I.** *vt. & vi.* [SHAMMED, SHAMD⁸; SHAM'MING.] To pretend falsely; feign. **II.** *a.* Pretended; counterfeit. **III.** *n.* **1.** A false pretense; imposture; deception. **2.** A pretender; impostor.

sham'ble, } 1 sham'bl; 2 shăm'bl, *vi.* **sham'bl**[P], } [SHAM'BL(E)D[P]; SHAM'BLING.] To walk with shuffling gait.— **sham'bling,** *pa. & n.*

sham'bles, } 1 sham'blz; 2 shăm'blş, *n. pl.* **sham'bls**[P], } A slaughter=house; formerly, a meat=market.

shame, 1 shĕm; 2 shām. **I.** *vt.* [SHAMED; SHAM'ING.] To make ashamed; disgrace. **II.** *n.* **1.** A painful sense of guilt or degradation; something that makes ashamed; a disgrace. **2.** Modesty.— **shame'ful,** *a.* Disgraceful; scandalous; indecent. **-ly,** *adv.* **-ness,** *n.*— **shame'less,** *a.* Immodest; impudent. **-ly,** *adv.* **-ness,** *n.*

shame'faced″, 1 shĕm'fēst″; 2 shām'fäçt″, *a.* Bashful; abashed. **-ly,** *adv.* **-ness,** *n.*

sham'my, 1 sham'ĭ; 2 shăm'y, *n.* Same as CHAMOIS.

sham-poo', 1 sham-pū'; 2 shăm-pōō'. **I.** *vt.* To wash and rub, as the skin of the head or body. **II.** *n.* The act of shampooing.

sham'rock, 1 sham'rok; 2 shăm'rŏk, *n.* A trifoliolate plant, as the white clover.

shank, 1 shank; 2 shănk, *n.* The leg between the knee and the ankle; the shaft of a tool connecting with the handle.

shan'ty, 1 shan'tĭ; 2 shăn'ty, *n.* [SHAN'TIES[z], *pl.*] A hut; cabin.

shape, 1 shĕp; 2 shāp. **I.** *vt. & vi.* [SHAPED[t] (rarely SHAP'EN); SHAP'ING.] To mold; form; adjust; adapt; imagine. **II.** *n.* Outward form or expression; guise; aspect; statement.— **shape'less,** *a.* Having no definite shape. **-ly,** *adv.* **-ness,** *n.*— **shape'ly,** *a.* Graceful; symmetrical.— **shape'li-ness,** *n.*

Shamrock.

share, 1 shâr; 2 shâr, *v.* [SHARED; SHAR'ING.] **I.** *t.* **1.** To give a part of to another; divide: followed by *with.* **2.** To enjoy or endure in common; participate in. **3.** To distribute: with *between* or *among.* **II.** *i.* To have a part or a share; participate.

share¹, *n.* A portion.— **shar′er, share′hold″-er,** *n.* [cultivator.

share², *n.* A plowshare; a blade, as of a

White Shark. ¹/₂₀₀
a, mouth; *b,* tooth.

shark, 1 shärk; 2 shärk, *n.* A voracious cartilaginous fish.

sharp, 1 shärp; 2 shärp. **I.** *a.* **1.** Having a keen edge or an acute point. **2.** Keen of perception; quick-witted; shrewd. **3.** Ardent; quick; eager. **4.** Painful; harsh; rigorous; sarcastic; bitter; pungent. **5.** Shrill. **6.** Distinct, as in outline. *Mus.* Being above the proper pitch. **II.** *n.* **1.** *Mus.* A note raised a half step in pitch, or a character (♯) indicating this. **2.** A long and slender needle. **3.** A sharper. **III.** *adv.* In a sharp manner; on the very instant. **-ly, -ness,** *n.*— **sharp′en,** 1 shärp′n; 2 shärp′n, *vt. & vi.* To make or become sharp.— **sharp′en-er,** *n.* — **sharp′er,** *n.* A swindler.

shat′ter, 1 shat′ər; 2 shăt′er, *vt. & vi.* To break into many pieces; fall or fly in pieces; smash; shiver; break down body or mind.

shave, 1 shēv; 2 shăv. **I.** *vt. & vi.* [SHAVED; SHAV′EN or SHAVED; SHAV′ING.] **1.** To make smooth by scraping; remove, as beard, with a razor. **2.** To slice very thin; graze past; skim along the surface of. **II.** *n.* **1.** The act of shaving. **2.** A blade, with two handles, for shaving wood, etc. **3.** A shaving.— **shav′er,** *n.* **1.** One who shaves; sharper. **2.** [Colloq.] A lad.— **shav′ing,** *n.* **1.** The act of one who shaves. **2.** A thin paring shaved from anything.

shawl, 1 shôl; 2 shạl, *n.* A wrap, as a square of cloth, worn over the upper part of the body.

she, 1 shī; 2 shē, *pron. fem.* This or that woman or female named or understood.

sheaf, 1 shīf; 2 shēf, *n.* [SHEAVES, 1 shīvz; 2 shēvṣ, *pl.*] The stalks of cut grain, bound together.

shear, 1 shīr; 2 shēr, *vt. & vi.* [SHEARED or SHORE, SHEARD⁸; SHEARED or SHORN; SHEAR′ING.] To clip close with shears or scissors.— **shear′er,** *n.*

shears, 1 shīrz; 2 shērṣ, *n. sing. & pl.* Any large cutting- or clipping-instrument worked by the crossing of cutting edges.

sheath, 1 shīth; 2 shēth, *n.* **1.** A case into which a blade, as of a sword, is thrust when not in use; a scabbard. **2.** Any envelop or case, as the lower part of leaves in grasses.— **sheath gown,** a close-fitting gown sometimes slit at the side.— **sheathe,** 1 shīth; 2 shēth, *t.* [SHEATHED, SHEATHD⁸; SHEATH′ING.] To put into or as into a sheath; cover.— **sheath′ing,** *n.* **1.** A casing, as of a building. **2.** The act of one who sheathes. [wheel.

sheave, 1 shīv; 2 shēv, *n.* A grooved pulley

sheaves, 1 shīvz; 2 shēvṣ, *n.* Plural of **sheavs**², | SHEAF.

shed, 1 shed; 2 shĕd, *vt. & vi.* [SHED; SHED′DING.] **1.** To throw off; turn off, as rain; cast off; molt. **2.** To cause to flow cut, as tears or blood; emit.— **shed′der,** *n.*

shed, *n.* A small low building; cabin; hut.

sheen, 1 shīn; 2 shēn, *n.* A glistening brightness.

sheep, 1 shīp; 2 shēp, *n. sing. & pl.* **1.** A small ruminant quadruped prized for its flesh and wool. **2.** Leather made from its skin. **sheep′skin″‡.— sheep′-cote″,** *n.* A small enclosure for sheep. **sheep′fold″‡.— sheep′ish,** *a.* Awkwardly diffident; abashed. **-ly,** *adv.* **-ness,** *n.*

sheer, 1 shīr; 2 shēr, *vi.* To swerve; turn aside. [right; perpendicular; steep.

sheer, *a.* Unmitigated; absolute; down-

sheer, *n.* A swerving or curving.

sheers, 1 shīrz; 2 shērṣ, *n.* An apparatus of poles and hoisting-tackle, for raising weights.

sheet, 1 shīt; 2 shēt. **I**ᵈ. *vt.* **1.** To furnish with sheets; cover as in a sheet; shroud. **2.** To spread out into a sheet or sheets; expand. **II.** *n.* **1.** A thin and broad piece, as of paper or metal, or of cloth for a bed; any broad, flat surface, as of water. **2.** A rope or chain from a lower corner of the sail to extend or move it; also, a sail.— **sheet′-an″chor,** *n.* An anchor for use only in emergency; a sure dependence.— **sheet′ing,** *n.* Cloth for sheets.

sheik, 1 shīk or shēk; 2 shēk or shĕk, *n.* In Moslem countries, a venerable man; head of a tribe.

shek′el, 1 shek′el; 2 shĕk′ĕl, *n.* **1.** An Assyrian and Babylonian weight. **2.** A Hebrew silver coin worth about 60 cents.

Shekel.

1: ärtistic, ärt; fat, fare; fast; get, prey; hit, police; obey, gō; net, ôr; full, rule; but, bûrn.
2: ärt, āpe, făt, fâre, făst, whạt, ạll; mē, gĕt, prey, fèrn; hĭt, īce; ĭ=ē; ĭ=ĕ; gō, nŏt, ôr, wŏn,

shelf, 1 shelf; 2 shĕlf, *n.* [SHELVES^z, *pl.*] **1.** A board or slab set horizontally into or against a wall. **2.** A flat projecting ledge of rock; a reef; shoal.

shell, 1 shel; 2 shĕl. **I.** *vt. & vi.* **1.** To
shelp, enclose in or separate from a shell, husk, or the like. **2.** To bombard with shells. **II.** *n.* A hard structure, incasing an animal, egg, or fruit; a light racing rowboat; a hollow shot filled with an explosive; a metallic cartridge-case.— **shell'bark",** *n.* Same as SHAGBARK.— **shell'-fish",** *n.* Any aquatic animal having a shell, as an oyster.

shel-lac', 1 she-lak' *or* shĕl'ak; 2 shĕ-lăc' *or* shĕl'ăc, *n.* Crude lac prepared for varnish.

shel'ter, 1 shel'ter; 2 shĕl'ter, *n.* **I.** *vt.* To screen; shield; house. **II.** *n.* A refuge; a cover from the weather; house; home.

shelve¹, 1 shelv; 2 shĕlv, *vt.* [SHELVED,
shelve², SHELVD^s; SHELV'ING.] **1.** To lay on the shelf; postpone; put aside; retire. **2.** To provide with shelves. [beach.

shelve², *vi.* To incline gradually, as a

shep'herd, 1 shep'ərd; 2 shĕp'erd, *n.* A keeper of sheep; a pastor, leader, or guide. — **shep'herd-ess,** *n. fem.*

sher'bet, 1 shūr'bet; 2 shĕr'bĕt, *n.* **1.** A flavored water-ice. **2.** An Oriental drink of fruit-juice. [of pottery.

sherd, 1 shūrd; 2 shĕrd, *n.* A fragment
sher'iff, 1 sher'if; 2 shĕr'if, *n.* The chief
sher'if², administrative officer of a county, who executes the mandates of courts, etc. — **sher'iff-al-ty,** *n.* [-TIES^z, *pl.*]

sher'ry, 1 sher'i; 2 shĕr'y, *n.* [-RIES^z, *pl.*] The wines of Jerez, in Andalusia, Spain.

shew‖, shew'bread", etc. Same as SHOW, etc.

shib'bo-leth, 1 shib'o-leth; 2 shib'o-lĕth, *n.* A party test-word: cp. *Judges* xii, 4–6.

shield, 1 shild; 2 shild. **I^d.** *vt.* To protect; defend. **II.** *n.* A broad piece of defensive armor, commonly carried on the left arm; a defense or defender; shelter.

shift^d, 1 shift; 2 shift, *vt. & vi.* To change; try expedients; manage; evade.

shift, *n.* **1.** The act of shifting. **2.** A substitute; expedient; trick; evasion. **3.** A garment worn by women. **4.** A relay of workmen; also, the working time of each gang.— **shift'er,** *n.*— **shift'i-ly,** *adv.*— **shift'i-ness,** *n.*— **shift'less,** *a.* Inefficient; incapable. **-ly,** *adv.* **-ness,** *n.*— **shift'y,** *a.*

shil'ling, 1 shil'in; 2 shil'ing, *n.* A current silver coin of Great Britain, worth 24 cents.

shil'ly=shal"ly, 1 shil'i=shal'i; 2 shil'y=shăl'y. **I.** *vi.* [SHIL'LY=SHAL"LIED; SHIL'-

LY = SHAL"LY - ING.] To vacillate; trifle. **II.** *n.* Weak vacillation; irresolution.

shim'mer, 1 shim'er; 2 shim'er. **I.** *vi.* To emit a tremulous light; glimmer. **II.** *n.* A tremulous gleam; glimmer.

shin, 1 shin; 2 shin. **I.** *vt. & vi.* [SHINNED, SHIND^s; SHIN'NING.] To climb by the clasp of hands and legs; to trot about. **II.** *n.* The front part of the leg below the knees; the shank.

shine, 1 shain; 2 shin. **I.** *vt. & vi.* [SHONE, SHIN'ING.] To give light; beam; glow; gleam; be illustrious. **II.** *n.* Brightness; fair weather; sunshine.— **shin'ing,** *a. & n.*

shin'gle, 1 shin'gl; 2 shin'gl, *vt.* [SHIN'-
shin'gl², GL(E)D^s; SHIN'GLING.] **1.** To cover with or as with shingles. **2.** To cut (the hair) short.

shin'gle, *n.* One of the thin, tapering pieces of wood, used to cover roofs.

Shin'to, 1 shin'to; 2 shin'to, *n.* The primitive cult of the Japanese; a species of ancestor-worship. [SHIN'I-EST.] Glossy.

shin'y, 1 shain'i; 2 shin'y, *a.* [SHIN'I-ER;

ship, 1 ship; 2 ship, *v.* [SHIPPED^d, SHIPT^s; SHIP'PING.] **I.** *t.* **1.** To transport by ship; also, by rail or other mode of conveyance. **2.** To receive on board ship; hire, as sailors. **II.** *i.* To go on board ship; enlist as a seaman.

ship, *n.* A large seagoing vessel with usually three masts and square sails; loosely, any sailing vessel larger than a boat.— **ship'mate",** *n.* A fellow sailor.— **ship'ment,** *n.* The act of shipping, or that which is shipped.— **ship'per,** *n.*— **ship'ping,** *n.* **1.** Ships collectively. **2.** The act of shipping.— **ship'shape",** *a.* Being in good order as becomes a ship; well-arranged; orderly: also used adverbially.— **ship'wreck".** **I^t.** *vt.* To wreck, as a vessel; ruin; destroy. **II.** *n.* The partial or total destruction of a ship at sea; destruction; ruin.— **ship'wright",** *n.* A ship-carpenter or -builder.

-ship, *suffix.* Condition; office; profession: as, friendship, consulship. [county.

shire, 1 shair *or* shir; 2 shir *or* shir, *n.* A

shirk, 1 shūrk; 2 shirk. **I^t.** *vt. & vi.* To avoid or evade. **II.** *n.* One who shirks.

shirr, 1 shūr; 2 shir. **I.** *vt.* **1.** To gather on parallel gathering = threads. **2.** In cooking, to poach in cream. **II.** *n.* A fulling by means of gathering=threads.

shirt, 1 shūrt; 2 shirt, *n.* A cotton or linen garment worn by men under the outer clothes.

shiv'er¹, 1 shiv'ər; 2 shiv'er. **I.** *vt. & vi.* To break suddenly into fragments; shatter. **II.** *n.* A splinter; sliver.

shiv'er². **I.** *vt. & vi.* To tremble, as with

1: ə = fin<ə>l; ı = habıt; aısle; aυ = out; oıl; ıū = feud; ∤hin; go; ŋ = sing; ∤hin, this.
2: wǫlf, dǫ; bŏŏk, bōōt; fŭll, rūle, cūre, bŭt, bûrn; ŏil, bŏy; go, gem; iṇk; thin, this.

cold or fear; shake; quiver. **II.** _n._ A shivering or quivering from any cause. — **shiv'er-y,** _a._

shoal¹, 1 shōl; 2 shŏl. **I.** _vt._ & _vi._ To make or grow shallow. **II.** _a._ Of little depth; shallow. **III.** _n._ A shallow place in any body of water; a sand-bank or -bar. — **shoal'l-ness,** _n._ — **shoal'y,** _a._

shoal². **I.** _vi._ To throng in shoals. **II.** _n._ A multitude; throng, as of fish.

shoat, 1 shōt; 2 shŏt. **1.** A young hog; a pig. **2.** A worthless fellow. **shot‡; shote‡.**

shock¹ᵗ, 1 shek; 2 shŏk. _vt._ To shake by sudden collision; jar; horrify; disgust. — **shock troops** (_Mil._), seasoned soldiers selected to lead an attack. — **shock'ing,** _pa._ Causing a mental shock; horrible; repugnant; distressing. **-ly,** _adv._ **-ness,** _n._

shock²ᵗ, _vt._ & _vi._ To gather (grain) into a shock or shocks.

shock¹, _n._ **1.** A violent concussion; blow. **2.** A sudden and violent agitation or injury; startling emotion.

shock², _n._ Sheaves of grain, stalks of maize, or the like, set together upright in a field. [gled mass, as of hair.

shock³, 1 shek; 2 shŏk, _n._ A coarse tan-**shock,** _a._ Shaggy; bushy.

shod, 1 shed; 2 shŏd, _imp._ & _pp._ of SHOE, _v._

shod'dy, 1 shed'y; 2 shŏd'y. **I.** _a._ [SHOD'-DI-ER; SHOD'DI-EST.] Made of or containing shoddy; sham. **II.** _n._ Fiber or cloth made of shredded woolen rags; sham.

shoe, 1 shū; 2 shọ. **I.** _vt._ [SHOD; SHOD or SHOD'DEN; SHOE'ING.] To furnish with shoes. **II.** _n._ [SHOES, _pl._] A covering or protection for the foot. — **shoe'mak"er,** _n._

shone, 1 shŏn; 2 shŏn, _imp._ & _pp._ of SHINE, _v._

shook, 1 shuk; 2 shŏok, _imp._ & _pp._ of SHAKE, _v._

shook, _n._ A bundle of barrel staves, or the like, in order for setting up.

shoot, 1 shūt; 2 shŏot, _v._ [SHOT; SHOOT'-ING.] **I.** _t._ **1.** To hit or kill with a missile. **2.** To discharge, as a projectile or a firearm; send forth, as a growth; protrude. **II.** _i._ **1.** To discharge a projectile; dart swiftly; flash along, as a bird or a star. **2.** To grow out rapidly; jut out; protrude.

shoot, _n._ **1.** A young branch; offshoot. **2.** A rapid in a stream. **3.** An inclined passage; a chute.

shop, 1 shep; 2 shŏp. **I.** _vt._ [SHOPPEDᵗ; SHOPTˢ; SHOP'PING.] To visit shops for purchase of goods. **II.** _n._ A place where goods are manufactured, repaired, or sold. — **shop'lift"ing,** _n._ The stealing of goods from a shop or store.— **shop'ping,** _n._

shore, 1 shŏr; 2 shŏr, _vt._ [SHORED; SHOR'-ING.] To support, as a wall, by a prop of timber. See illus. in next column.

shore¹, _n._ A beam set endwise, as a prop.

shore², _n._ The land adjacent to an ocean, sea, lake, or large river.— **shore'less,** _a._ Having no shore, or no visible shore.

Method of Propping a Wall by a Shore (_s_).

shore, 1 shŏr; 2 shŏr, _imp._ of SHEAR, _v._ [of SHEAR, _v._

shorn, 1 shŏrn; 2 shŏrn, _pp._

short, 1 shert; 2 shŏrt. **I.** _a._ Of slight length, height, or duration; not long or tall; brief; scant; curt; crisp. **II.** _n._ **1.** The substance or pith of a matter. **2.** Anything that is short, as a short syllable; a deficiency. **III.** _adv._ In a short manner; petulantly. — **short'age,** 1 shert'ij; 2 shŏrt'ag, _n._ The amount by which anything is short; deficiency.— **short'-com"ing,** _n._ Failure; delinquency— **short'-en,** 1 shert'n; 2 shŏrt'n, _vt._ & _vi._ **1.** To make or become short or shorter; curtail; reduce; lessen. **2.** To make crisp, as pastry.— **short'hand",** _n._ Stenography or phonography.— **short'-lived",** 1 shert'-laivd"; 2 shŏrt'-līvd", _a._ Living but a short time.— **short'ly,** _adv._ **1.** After a short time; quickly; soon. **2.** In few words; briefly. **3.** Abruptly.— **short'ness,** _n._— **short'sight"-ed,** _a._ **1.** Near-sighted. **2.** Lacking foresight. **-ly,** _adv._ **-ness,** _n._

shot¹, 1 shet; 2 shŏt, _vt._ [SHOT'TEDᵈ; SHOT'TING.] To load with shot.

shot², _imp._ & _pp._ of SHOOT, _v._

shot, _n._ [SHOT or SHOTS, _pl._] **1.** A missile, as of iron or lead, to be sent from a firearm; also, such missiles collectively. **2.** The act of shooting; a stroke or hit. **3.** A marksman. **4.** The reach or range of a projectile.

should, 1 shud; 2 shụd, _imp._ & _pp._ of SHALL, _v._

shoul'der, 1 shōl'dɛr; 2 shŏl'der. **I.** _vt._ & _vi._ **1.** To take upon the shoulder; sustain; bear. **2.** To push witn or as with the shoulder. **II.** _n._ **1.** The joint connecting the arm or fore limb with the body. **2.** An enlargement or projection.

shout, 1 shaut; 2 shout. **I**ᵈ. _vt._ & _vi._ To utter with a shout; utter a shout; cry out loudly. **II.** _n._ A sudden and loud resonant outcry.— **shout'er,** _n._— **shout'ing,** _pa._ & _n._

shove, 1 shuv; 2 shŏv. **I.** _vt._ & _vi._ **shuᵛ,** } [SHOVED, SHUVDᵖ; SHOV'ING, SHUV'-INGᵖ.] To push; press against; jostle. **II.** _n._ The act of pushing; a push.

1: ȧrtistic, ärt; fat, fāre; fast; get, prēy; hit, police; obey, gō; net, ȯr; full, rūle; but, būrn.

2: ärt, āpe, fät, fâre, fȧst, whạt, ạll; mē, gĕt, prẹy, fẽrn; hĭt, īce; ĭ=ē; ĩ=ē; gō, nŏt, ȏr, wŏn.

shov′el, } 1 shŭv′l; 2 shŏv′l. **I.** *vt.* &
shuv′el², } *vi.* [SHOV′ELED or SHOV′ELLED,
SHOV′ELD⁸; SHOV′EL-ING or SHOV′EL-LING.]
To take up and move or gather with a
shovel; work with a shovel. **II.** *n.* An
implement with a handle and a broad, flat
blade, for digging.

show, 1 shō; 2 shō, *v.* [SHOWED, SHOWD⁸;
SHOWN or SHOWED; SHOW′ING.] **I.** *t.* To
present to view; exhibit; explain; reveal;
prove; convince; confer; bestow. **II.** *i.*
To become visible; appear; seem.— **show′-
ing,** *n.* Show; display; statement.

show, *n.* A spectacle; exhibition; display;
parade; pretense; semblance; indication;
promise.— **show′bread″,** *n.* In the Jewish
ritual, loaves of unleavened bread set forth in
the sanctuary, and changed every Sabbath.

show′er, 1 shau′ər; 2 shou′er, *vt.* & *vi.* To
sprinkle; pour out; rain; scatter.

show′er¹, *n.* A fall, as of rain, hail, or
sleet, of short duration; abundant supply.
— **show′er-y,** *a.* [shows.

show′er², 1 shō′ər; 2 shō′er, *n.* One who

show′y, 1 shō′ɪ; 2 shō′y, *a.* Making a show;
gaudy; gay; ostentatious.— **show′i-ly,** *adv.*—
show′i-ness, *n.*

shrank, 1 shraŋk, *imp.* of SHRINK, *v.*

shrap′nel, 1 shrap′nel; 2 shrăp′nĕl, *n.* A
shell filled with bullets to be scattered
by its explosion: from the British general,
Shrapnel.

shred, 1 shred; 2 shrĕd. **I.** *vt.* [SHRED or
SHRED′DED⁴; SHRED′DING.] To tear or
cut into shreds. **II.** *n.* A small strip
torn or cut off; a bit; fragment.

shrew¹, 1 shrū; 2 shru, *n.* A scolding
woman.— **shrew′ish,** *a.* Like a shrew; ill-
tempered. **-ly,** *adv.* **-ness,** *n.*

shrew², *n.* A small mouse-like animal.

shrewd, 1 shrūd; 2
shrṳd, *a.* Keen; sharp;
sagacious. **-ly,** *adv.*
-ness, *n.*

shriek, 1 shrik; 2 shrēk.
Iᵗ. *vt.* & *vi.* To utter
with a shriek; utter a shriek. **II.** *n.* A
sharp, shrill outcry; a scream. Shrew. 1/5

shrift, 1 shrift; 2 shrɪft, *n.* The act of
shriving; absolution.

shrill, } 1 shril; 2 shrɪl, *a.* Sharp and
shril², } piercing, as a sound.— **shrill′y,** *a.*
Rather shrill.— **shrill′y,** *adv.* In a shrill manner. **shrill‡.— shrill′ness,** *n.*

shrimp, 1 shrimp; 2 shrɪmp, *n.* A slender,
lobster-like crustacean.

shrine, 1 shrain; 2 shrīn. **I.** *vt.* [SHRINED;
SHRIN′ING.] To enshrine. **II.** *n.* A receptacle for relics; a place of peculiar
sanctity.

shrink, 1 shriŋk; 2 shrĭŋk, *vt.* & *vi.* [SHRANK,
SHRUNK; SHRUNK; SHRUNK′EN; SHRINK′-
ING.] **1.** To draw together; contract; diminish. **2.** To draw back; withdraw; recoil.— **shrink′age,** *n.* Contraction; amount
lost by contraction.

shrive, 1 shraiv; 2 shrīv, *vt.* [SHROVE,
SHRIVED; SHRIV′EN, SHRIVED; SHRIV′ING.]
R. C. Ch. To grant absolution upon con-
fession.

shriv′el, 1 shriv′l; 2 shrĭv′l, *vt.* & *vi.* [-ELED
or -ELLED, -ELD⁸; -EL-ING or -EL-LING.] To
shrink and wrinkle; wither.

shroud⁴, 1 shraud; 2 shroud, *vt.* To clothe
in a shroud; envelop; veil.

shroud¹, *n.* A garment for the dead;
winding-sheet.

shroud², *n.* One of a set of ropes forming
part of the standing
rigging of a vessel. Usu-
ally in the plural.

shrove, 1 shrōv; 2 shrōv,
imp. of SHRIVE, *v.*

Shrove′tide″, 1 shrōv′-
taid″; 2 shrōv′tīd″, *n.*
The three days immedi-
ately preceding Lent.

shrub, 1 shrub; 2 shrŭb,
n. A woody, perennial
plant smaller than a tree;
a bush.— **shrub′ber-y,** *n.*
[-IES², *pl.*] Shrubs collectively.— **shrub′by,** *a.*

shrug, 1 shrug; 2 shrŭg.
I. *vt.* & *vi.* [SHRUGGED, SHRUGD⁸; SHRUG′-
GING.] To draw up (the shoulders), as in
displeasure. **II.** *n.* The act of shrugging
the shoulders.

shrunk, *imp.* & *pp.* of SHRINK, *v.*

shrunk′en, 1 shruŋk′n; 2 shrŭŋk′n, *pa.*;
also *pp.* of SHRINK, *v.* Contracted and
atrophied.

shud′der, 1 shud′ər; 2 shŭd′er. **I.** *vi.* To
tremble, as from fright or cold; shiver.
II. *n.* The act of shuddering; convulsive
shiver, as from horror or fear; aversion.

shuf′fle, } 1 shuf′l; 2 shŭf′l, *v.* [SHUF′-
shuf′l², } FLED, SHUF′LD⁸; SHUF′FLING.] **I.**
t. To shift; mix; confuse. **II.** *i.* **1.** To
change the relative position of cards in a
pack; change position; evade; prevaricate.
2. To scrape the feet along; move awkwardly.— **shuf′fler,** *n.*

shuf′fle, *n.* A shuffling; evasion.

shun, 1 shun; 2 shŭn, *vi.* [SHUNNED,
SHUND⁸; SHUN′NING.] To avoid; refrain
from.

shunt, 1 shunt; 2 shŭnt. **I**ᵈ. *vt.* & *vi.* To
turn aside; switch, as a railway car. **II.**

Shrouds and their
Connections.

c, shrouds; *g,* rat-
lines; *h,* topmast-
backstays.

n. A turning aside; the act of switching; a switch.— **shunt'ing,** *pa. & n.*

shut, 1 shut; 2 shŭt, *v.* [SHUT; SHUT'TING.] **I.** *t.* **1.** To close; stop; obstruct. **2.** To bar out; exclude. **3.** To keep in; confine. **4.** To obscure; hide. **II.** *i.* To be closed.

shut, *pa.* Made fast or closed.

shut'ter, 1 shut'ər; 2 shŭt'er, *n.* One who or that which shuts; a hinged cover for a window.

shut'tle, } 1 shut'l; 2 shŭt'l, *n.* A device
shut'l', } used in weaving to carry the thread to and fro.— **shut'tle-cock",** *n.* A rounded piece of cork, with a crown of feathers, used in the game of battledore and shuttlecock; also, the game itself.

shy, 1 shai; 2 shȳ. **I.** *vi.* [SHIED; SHY'ING.] **1.** To start suddenly aside, as a horse. **2.** To sling; fling. **II.** *a.* [SHY'ER; SHY'EST; or SHI'ER; SHI'EST.] **1.** Easily frightened; timorous; coy. **2.** Circumspect; wary.— **shy'ly, shi'ly,** *adv.*— **shy'ness,** *n.*

shy'ster, 1 shai'stər; 2 shȳ'ster, *n.* [Colloq., U. S.] A lawyer who resorts to low and unprofessional tricks; also, a tricky business man. [the scale.

si, 1 sī; 2 sī, *n.* *Mus.* The seventh note of

sib'i-lant, 1 sib'i-lənt; 2 sĭb'i-lant. **I.** *a.* Having a hissing sound. **II.** *n.* A hissing sound, as of *s*.— **sib'i-lance,** *n.*

sib'yl, 1 sib'il; 2 sĭb'yl, *n.* **1.** *Anc. Myth.* A prophetess. **2.** A sorceress.— **sib'yl-line,** *a.* Of, pertaining to, or like a sibyl.

sick, 1 sik; 2 sĭk, *a.* **1.** Affected with disease; ill. **2.** Nauseated; surfeited. **3.** Longing; languishing.— **sick'en,** *vt. & vi.* To make or grow sick, disgusted, or weary; to deteriorate.— **sick'ish,** *a.*— **sick'ly,** *a.* **1.** Habitually indisposed; ailing. **2.** Faint.— **sick'li-ness,** *n.*— **sick'ness,** *n.*

sick'le, 1 sik'l; 2 sĭk'l, *n.* A reaping-implement with a long, curved blade.

side, 1 said; 2 sīd. **I.** *vi.* [SID'ED; SID'-ING.] To range oneself on the side: followed by *with.* **II.** *a.* Situated at or on one side; lateral; minor; subsidiary. **III.** *n.* **1.** Any one of the bounding lines or surfaces of an object. **2.** A lateral part of a surface or object. **3.** A party; sect. **4.** Either of two opposite opinions.— **si'dle,** *vt. & vi.* [SI'-DLED; SI'DLING.] To move, or cause to move, sidewise.— **side'long".** **I.** *a.* Inclining or tending to one side; lateral. **II.** *adv.* In a lateral or oblique direction.— **side'wise".** **I.** *a.* Directed or moving toward the side; sidelong. **II.** *adv.* Toward or from the side; on one side. **side'ways"**‡.

si-de're-al, 1 sai-dī'ri-əl; 2 sī-dē're-al, *a.* Pertaining to stars; constituted of or containing stars.

siege, 1 sīj; 2 sēg, *n.* The besieging of a town or a fortified place.

si-er'ra, 1 si-er'ə; 2 si-ĕr'a, *n.* A mountain range. [nap.

si-es'ta, 1 si-es'tə; 2 si-ĕs'ta, *n* A mid-day

sieve, } 1 siv; 2 sĭv, *n.* A utensil or ap-
siv's, } paratus for sifting through meshes, as of wire.

sift, 1 sift; 2 sĭft, *v.* **I.** *t.* **1.** To separate with a sieve. **2.** To examine; scrutinize. **II.** *i.* **1.** To fall or pass as through a sieve. **2.** To practise scrutiny.— **sift'er,** *n.*

sigh, 1 sai; 2 sī. **I.** *vi.* **1.** To utter a sigh; lament. **2.** To yearn; long. **II.** *n.* A deep respiration, as in sorrow.

sight, 1 sait; 2 sīt. **I**d. *vt.* **1.** To discover. **2.** To furnish with sights, as a gun; aim. **II.** *n.* **1.** The faculty of seeing; vision. **2.** A view; spectacle. **3.** The range of vision; point of view; estimation. **4.** A device to assist aim, as on a gun, leveling-instrument, etc.— **sight'less,** *a.* Blind. **-ly,** *adv.* **-ness,** *n.*— **sight'ly,** *a.* **1.** Pleasant to the view; comely. **2.** Affording a fine view.— **sight'li-ness,** *n.*

sign, 1 sain; 2 sīn. **I.** *vt. & vi.* To affix one's name to; write one's name; make signs; signal. **II.** *n.* **1.** A pantomimic gesture. **2.** An inscription or the like to indicate a place of business. **3.** A mark; symbol.

sig'nal, 1 sig'nəl; 2 sĭg'nal. **I.** *vt. & vi.* [SIG'NALED or -NALLED, -NALD's or SIG'NAL-ING or -NAL-LING.] To make signals to; communicate by signals. **II.** *a.* Remarkable; conspicuous. **III.** *n.* A sign agreed upon or understood, as conveying information.— **sig'nal-ing,** *n.*— **sig'nal-ize,** } 1 sig'nəl-aiz; 2 sĭg'nal-īz, *vt.* [-IZED; -IZ'ING.] To render noteworthy.— **sig'nal-ly,** *adv.* In a signal manner.

sig'na-ture, 1 sig'nə-chur *or* -tiūr; 2 sĭg'na-chur *or* -tūr, *n.* The signing of one's name or the name signed.

sig'net, 1 sig'net; 2 sĭg'nĕt, *n.* A seal.

sig-nif'i-cant, 1 sig-nif'i-kənt; 2 sĭg-nĭf'i-cant, *a.* Having or expressing a meaning. **-ly,** *adv.*— **sig-nif'i-cance,** *n.* Expressiveness; meaning; consequence.— **sig'ni-fi-ca'tion,** *n.* That which is signified; meaning; the act of signifying.

sig'ni-fy, 1 sig'ni-fai; 2 sĭg'ni-fȳ, *v.* [-FIED; -FY'ING.] **I.** *t.* **1.** To make known by signs or words; betoken in any way. **2.** To amount to; matter. **II.** *i.* To be of importance. [SEIGNIOR *or* SIGNOR.

si'gnior, 1 sī'nyor; 2 sī'nyŏr, *n.* Same as

---

si′gnor, *n.* Anglicized form of the Italian title *signore:* equivalent to *sir* or *Mr.*— **si-gno′ra,** *n.* The equivalent to *madam* or *Mrs.*— **sī′gno-rī′na,** *n.* The equivalent to *Miss.* [LAGE.

sī′lage, 1 sai′lɥ; 2 sī′laɡ, *n.* Same as ENSI-

si′lence, 1 sai′lens; 2 sī′lĕnç. **I.** *vt.* [SI′LENCED⁴; SI′LENC-ING.] To render silent. **II.** *n.* **1.** The state of being silent; a keeping still and silent. **2.** Secrecy.

si′lent, 1 sai′lent; 2 sī′lĕnt, *a.* Noiseless; still; unspoken; not speaking; mute. **-ly,** *adv.* **-ness,** *n.*

sil′hou-ette, 1 sil′u-et′; 2 sĭl′u-ĕt′, *n.* A profile drawing or portrait.

sil′i-ca, 1 sil′i-kə; 2 sĭl′i-ca, *n.* A hard, crystalline substance, the principal constituent of quartz and sand.— **si-li′ceous,** 1 si-lish′us; 2 si-lish′ŭs, *a.* Pertaining to or containing silica.— **si-lic′ic,** 1 si-lis′ik; 2 si-lĭç′ic, *a.* Pertaining to or consisting of silica.

silk, 1 silk; 2 silk. **I.** *a.* Silken; silky. **II.** *n.* **1.** A delicate, glossy, fibrous substance produced by the larvæ of silkworms, to form their cocoons. **2.** Cloth or garments made of silk. **3.** Anything silky.— **silk′en,** *a* **1.** Made of or like silk. **2.** Luxurious.— **silk′i-ness,** *n.*— **silk′-worm,** *n.* The larva of a certain moth that produces a dense silken cocoon.— **silk′y,** *a.* [SILK′I-ER; SILK′I-EST.] Like silk; silken.

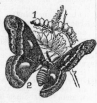

Silkworm (1) and Moth (2). ⅓

sill, ⎱ 1 sil; 2 sĭl, *n.* A horizontal timber at
sil², ⎰ the bottom of a building, door, etc.

sil′ly, 1 sil′i; 2 sĭl′y, *a.* [SIL′LI-ER; SIL′LI-EST.] Destitute of ordinary good sense; foolish; stupid.— **sil′li-ly,** *adv.*— **sil′li-ness,** *n.*

si′lo, 1 sai′lo; 2 sī′lo, *n.* Any close pit in which green fodder is stored.

silt, 1 silt; 2 sĭlt. **I**ᵈ. *vt. & vi.* To obstruct with sediment. **II.** *n.* Fine earthy sediment deposited by a stream.

sil′van, *a.* Same as SYLVAN.

sil′ver, 1 sil′vər; 2 sĭl′ver. **I.** *vt.* To plate with silver; give a silvery hue to. **II.** *a.* Made of silver or resembling silver; having a pure bell-like tone. **III.** *n.* A white, ductile metallic element: one of the precious metals; silver coin or silverware.— **sil′ver-ing,** *n.* A plating or covering of silver.— **sil′ver-smith″,** *n.* A worker in silver; a maker of silverware.— **sil′ver-ware″,** *n.* Articles made of silver.— **sil′ver-y,** *a.* Containing, adorned with, or like silver.

sim′i-an, 1 sim′i-ən; 2 sĭm′i-an. **I.** *a.* Like an ape or monkey. **sim′i-ous‡. II.** *n.* An ape or monkey.

sim′i-lar, 1 sim′i-lər; 2 sĭm′i-lar, *a.* Having resemblance; like.— **sim′i-lar′i-ty,** *n.* [-TIES², *pl.*] Resemblance; likeness.— **sim′i-lar-ly,** *adv.*

sim′i-le, 1 sim′i-lɥ; 2 sĭm′i-le, *n.* A rhetorical figure expressing comparison, by use of such terms as *like*, *as*, *so*, etc.

si-mil′i-tude, 1 si-mil′i-tiūd; 2 si-mĭl′i-tūd, *n.* Similarity; that which is similar; simile.

sim′i-tar, 1 sim′i-tər; 2 sĭm′i-tar, *n.* An Oriental sword or saber of extreme curve.

Turkish Simitar.

sim′mer, 1 sim′ər; 2 sĭm′er, *vt. & vi.* To boil gently or with a singing sound.

si-moom′, 1 si-mūm′; 2 si-mōōm′, *n.* A hot, dry wind of the desert, as in Africa and Arabia. **si-moon′‡.**

sim′per, 1 sim′pər; 2 sĭm′per. **I.** *vi.* To smile in a silly, self-conscious manner. **II.** *n.* A silly, self-conscious smile.

sim′ple, ⎱ 1 sim′pl; 2 sĭm′pl. **I.** *a.* [SIM′-
sim′pl², ⎰ PLER; SIM′PLEST.] **1.** Consisting of one thing; single; plain; unadorned; sincere; artless. **2.** Silly; feeble-minded. **II.** *n.* **1.** That which is simple. **2.** A medicinal plant. **3.** A simpleton.— **sim′ple-ton,** 1 sim′pl-tən; 2 sĭm′pl-ton, *n.* A weak-minded or silly person.— **sim-plic′i-ty,** 1 sim-plis′i-ti; 2 sim-plĭç′i-ty, *n.* [-TIES², *pl.*] The state of being simple. **sim′pl(e-ness‡.** — **sim″pli-fi-ca′tion,** *n.* A simplifying.— **sim′pli-fy,** *vt.* [-FIED; -FY′ING.] To render simple or more intelligible.— **sim′ply,** *adv.*

sim′u-late, 1 sim′yu-lēt; 2 sĭm′yu-lāt, *vt.* [-LAT′ED⁴; -LAT′ING.] To imitate; counterfeit; mimic.— **sim″u-la′tion,** *n.*— **sim′u-la″tor,** *n.*

si″mul-ta′ne-ous, 1 sai″mul-[*or* sim″]tē′ni-us; 2 sī″mŭl-[*or* sĭm″]tā′ne-ŭs, *a.* Occurring, done, or existing at the same time. **-ly,** *adv.* **-ness,** *n.*

sin, 1 sin; 2 sĭn. **I.** *vt. & vi.* [SINNED, SINDˢ; SIN′NING.] To transgress or disregard the moral law. **II.** *n.* Any transgression of a moral law; a fault; offense.— **sin′ful,** *a.* Addicted to sin; wicked. **-ly,** *adv.* **-ness,** *n.*— **sin′less,** *a.* Having no sin; guiltless; innocent. **-ly,** *adv.* **-ness,** *n.*— **sin′ner,** *n.*

since, 1 sins; 2 sĭnç. **I.** *adv.* **1.** From a **sinse²,** ⎰ past time up to the present. **2.** After and in the mean time. **3.** Before now. **II.** *prep.* Ever after, or at a time

after. **III.** *conj.* **1.** From and subsequently to the time when. **2.** Seeing that; because.

sin-cere′, 1 sin-sîr′; 2 sĭn-çẽr′, *a.* Genuine; honest; frank; candid.— **sin-cere′ly,** *adv.*— **sin-cer′i-ty,** 1 sin-ser′i-ti; 2 sĭn-çẽr′ĭ-ty, *n.*— **sin-cere′ness‡.**

sine, 1 sain; 2 sīn, *n.* The perpendicular dropped from one end of a circular arc upon the radius of the other end; the ratio of this perpendicular to the radius.

si′ne-cure, 1 sai′ni-kiūr; 2 sī′ne-eūr, *n.* An office having pay with few or no duties.— **si′ne-cur-ist,** *n.*

sin′ew, 1 sin′yu; 2 sĭn′yu, *n.* **1.** A tendon. **2.** Strength.— **sin′ew-y,** *a.* Of or pertaining to a sinew or sinews; strong.

sing, 1 siŋ; 2 sĭng, *v.* [SANG or SUNG; SUNG; SING′ING.] **I.** *t.* To utter as a song; celebrate in song; charm with singing. **II.** *i.* To utter a song.

singe, 1 sinj; 2 sĭnj. **I.** *vt.* [SINGED; SINGE′ING.] To burn slightly; scorch. **II.** *n.* A singeing. [a poet.

sing′er, 1 siŋ′ər; 2 sĭng′er, *n.* One who sings.

sin′gle, 1 siŋ′gl; 2 sĭn′gl. **I.** *vt. &* **sin′gl‡,** } *vi.* [SIN′GL(E)D‡; SIN′GLING.] To choose out (one); separate. **II.** *a.* **1.** Consisting of one only; individual; alone. **2.** Unmarried.— **sin′gle-ness,** *n.*—**sin′gly,** *adv.*

sing′song′, *n.* Monotonous cadence.

sin′gu-lar, 1 siŋ′giu-lər; 2 sĭng′gū-lar. **I.** *a.* **1.** Standing by itself; peculiar; odd; remarkable. **2.** Denoting a unit; single. **II.** *n.* *Gram.* The singular number, or a word in that number.— **sin′gu-lar′i-ty,** *n.* [-TIES‡, *pl.*] The state of being singular; a peculiarity.— **sin′gu-lar-ly,** *adv.*

sin′is-ter, 1 sin′is-tər; 2 sĭn′is-ter, *a.* Situated on the left; ill-omened; inauspicious; evil.— **sin′is-tral,** *a.* Of, pertaining to, or turned toward the left.— **sin′is-trous,** *a.*

sink, 1 siŋk; 2 sĭŋk, *v.* [SANK or SUNK; SUNK or SUNK′EN; SINK′ING.] **I.** *t.* **1.** To submerge, as in water. **2.** To dig downward, as a well; cause to descend. **3.** To debase or degrade; diminish; depress; suppress. **II.** *i.* To descend by force of gravity, as through a fluid; fall; fail; set; decline; cower; droop; shrink.— **sink′er,** *n.*

sink, *n.* A basin connected with a drain, for waste water, etc.; a cesspool.

Sinn Fein, 1 shin fēn; 2 shĭn fēn. [Ir.] Literally, we ourselves: name of an Irish party originated about 1905 for cultural development and self-government.

sin′u-ous, 1 sin′yu-us; 2 sĭn′yu-ŭs, *a.* Bending; winding. **-ly,** *adv.* **-ness,** *n.*— **sin′u-os′i-ty,** *n.* Sinuous quality; a winding; turn.

-sion, *suffix.* See -TION.

sip, 1 sip; 2 sĭp, *v. vt. & vi.* [SIPPED‡, SIPT‡; SIP′PING.] To take with the lips in very small quantities. **II.** *n.* **1.** A mere taste. **2.** The act of sipping.

si′phon, 1 sai′fən; 2 sī′fon, *n.* A bent **si′fon‡,** } tube for drawing liquids over the intervening side of a vessel.

sir, 1 sūr; 2 sĭr, *n.* **1.** A term of respectful address to men. **2.** [S-] [Eng.] A title of baronets and knights.

sire, 1 sair; 2 sīr. *I.* *vt.* [SIRED; SIR′ING.] To beget, as an animal. **II.** *n.* **1.** An ancestor or progenitor. **2.** A form of address to a king or prince.

Siphon.

si′ren, 1 sai′ren; 2 sī′rĕn, *n.* **1.** A fabulous sea-nymph that lured sailors by song to destruction. **2.** A fascinating, dangerous woman. **3.** A fog-horn.— **si′ren,** *a.*

sir′loin′, 1 sūr′loin′; 2 sĭr′loin′, *n.* A loin of beef. **sur′loin‡‡.**

si-roc′co, 1 si-rɒk′o; 2 si-rŏc′o, *n.* The simoom; so called around the Mediterranean. [in contempt or annoyance.

sir′rah‖, 1 sir′ə; 2 sir′a, *n.* Fellow; sir: used

sir′up, 1 sir′up; 2 sĭr′ŭp, *n.* A thick **syr′up,** } sweet liquid, as the boiled juice of fruits, etc.

sis′ter, 1 sis′tər; 2 sĭs′ter, *n.* **1.** A daughter of the same parents or parent. **2.** A woman or girl allied by some association, as a nun.— **sis′ter-hood,** *n.* **1.** A body of sisters. **2.** The sisterly relationship.— **sis′ter-in-law,** *n.* [SISTERS-IN-LAW, *pl.*] A sister by marriage.— **sis′ter-ly,** *a.*

Sis′y-phus, 1 sis′i-fus; 2 sĭs′i-fŭs, *n.* Gr. Myth. A son of Æolus; condemned to roll up-hill a stone that ever rolls back.

sit, 1 sit; 2 sĭt, *v.* [SAT; SAT; SIT′TING.] **I.** *t.* To have or keep a seat upon. **II.** *i.* **1.** To rest upon, take, or occupy a seat; remain seated. **2.** To hold a session. **3.** To be becoming; fit; suit.— **sit′ter,** *n.*— **sit′ting,** *n.* **1.** The act or position of one who sits; a seat. **2.** A session or term. **3.** An incubation.

site, 1 sait; 2 sīt, *n.* Situation; a plot of ground set apart, as for a building.

sit′u-ate, 1 sich′u-[or sit′yu-]ēt; 2 sĭch′u-[or sĭt′yu-]āt. **I.** *vt.* [-AT′ED‡; -AT′ING.] To fix a site for; locate. **II.** *a.* Situated. — **sit′u-a′tion,** *n.* **1.** Locality; condition; status; complication; plight. **2.** A post of employment.

six, 1 siks; 2 sĭks, *a. & n.* Five and one.— **six′fold,** *adv.*— **six′pence,** *n.* A British silver coin of the value of six English pennies, or about 12 cents.— **six′teen′,** *a. & n.*

Ten and six.— **six″teenth′**, *a.* & *n.*— **sixth**.
I. *a.* **1.** Next after the fifth. **2.** Being one of six equal parts. **II.** *n.* One of six equal parts.— **sixth′ly**, *adv.*— **six′ty**, *a.* & *n.* Ten more than fifty.— **six′ti-eth**, *a.* & *n.*

size[1], 1 saiz; 2 sīz. **I.** *vt.* [SIZED; SIZ′ING.] To gage the size of; distribute according to size. **II.** *n.* Comparative magnitude; bulk; bigness.

size[2]. **I.** *vt.* [SIZED; SIZ′ING.] To treat with size. **II.** *n.* Thin glue for glazing a surface, as of paper. **siz′ing‡**.

skate, 1 skēt; 2 skāt, *vi.* [SKAT′EDᵈ; SKAT′ING.] To move, as over ice, on skates.— **skat′er**, *n.* [pointed snout.

skate[1], *n.* A flat=bodied fish having a

skate[2], *n.* A contrivance for the foot, enabling one to glide rapidly over ice.

skee, *n.* Same as SKI.

skein, 1 skēn; 2 skęn, *n.* A fixed quantity of yarn or thread, doubled and knotted.

skel′e-ton, 1 skel′i-tən; 2 skĕl′e-ton, *n.* **1.** The bony framework of an animal body. **2.** An open framework; sketch; outline. — **skel′e-ton**, *a.*

skep′tic, } 1 skep′tɪk; 2 skĕp′tic, *n.* A
scep′tic, } doubter; one not a believer in the Christian religion.— **skep′ti-cal**, *a.* **scep′ti-cal‡**.— **skep′ti-cal-ly**, *adv.*— **skep′ti-cism**, *n.* **scep′ti-cism‡**.

sketch, } 1 skech; 2 skĕch. **Iᵗ**. *vt.* & *vi.* To
skechᴾ, } make a sketch. **II.** *n.* An incomplete but suggestive picture; a short or incomplete composition; outline.— **sketch′i-ly**, *adv.*— **sketch′i-ness**, *n.*— **sketch′y**, *a.*

skew′er, 1 skiū′ər; 2 skū′er. **I.** *vt.* To pierce with a skewer. **II.** *n.* A long pin, as of wood, for holding meat in shape while roasting.

ski, 1 skī; 2 skī, *n.* A Norwegian snow= or ice=shoe for sliding, consisting of a long and narrow wooden runner, to which the shoe is slightly attached in front, leaving the heel free. **skee‡**; **skī′dor‡**.

ski′a-graph, 1 skaī′ə-graf; 2 skī′a-gräf, *n.* A shadow=picture produced by Roentgen rays passing through the object and falling upon a sensitive photographic plate. See ROENTGEN RAYS. **sko′to-graph‡**.

ski′a-scope, 1 skaī′a-skōp; 2 skī′a-scōp, *n.* Same as FLUOROSCOPE.

skid, 1 skid; 2 skĭd, *n.* **1.** One of a pair of timbers to support an object, as a cask. **2.** *Naut.* A fender over a vessel's side. **3.** A shoe or drag as on an aeroplane tail or a wagon=wheel.

skiff, } 1 skif; 2 skĭf, *n.* A small, light row=
skifᴾ, } boat.

skill, } 1 skil; 2 skĭl, *n.* Knowledge joined
skilᴾ, } with practical efficiency.— **skilled**, *a.*

Expert; proficient.— **skil′ful**, *a.* **1.** Having skill; clever; able. **2.** Showing or requiring skill. **skill′ful‡**.— **skil′ful-ly**, *adv.*— **skil′ful-ness**, *n.*

skil′let, } 1 skil′et; 2 skĭl′ĕt, *n.* A small kettle or frying=pan.

skim, 1 skim; 2 skĭm, *vt.* & *vi.* [SKIMMED, SKIMDˢ; SKIM′MING.] **1.** To remove (floating matter) from the surface of a liquid. **2.** To move lightly over; glance over superficially.— **skim′mer**, *n.* **1.** A ladle for skimming. **2.** One who skims.— **skim′-ming**, *n.*— **skim′-milk″**, *n.*

skin, 1 skin; 2 skĭn. **I.** *vt.* & *vi.* [SKINNED, SKINDˢ; SKIN′NING.] **1.** To strip the skin from. **2.** To cover or be covered with skin. **II.** *n.* **1.** The membranous external covering of an animal; outer covering of fruit; hide; rind; pelt. **2.** A vessel made of skin. **3.** An outside layer; membrane.— **skin′flint″**, *n.* A miser.— **skin′ny**, *a.* [SKIN′NI-ER; SKIN′NI-EST.] **1.** Consisting of or like skin. **2.** Thin; lean; wrinkled.— **skin′ni-ness**, *n.*

skip, 1 skip; 2 skĭp. **I.** *vt.* & *vi.* [SKIPPEDᵗ, SKIPTˢ; SKIP′PING.] To jump lightly over; pass over; omit; caper; spring. **II.** *n.* **1.** A light bound. **2.** A passing over without notice. [or that which skips.

skip′per[1], 1 skip′ər; 2 skĭp′er, *n.* One who

skip′per[2], *n.* The master of a small trading=vessel.

skir′mish, 1 skŭr′mɪsh; 2 skĭr′mish. **Iᵗ**. *vi.* To fight in a preliminary way. **II.** *n.* A light combat, as between small parties.— **skir′mish-er**, *n.*

skirt, 1 skŭrt; 2 skĭrt. **Iᵈ**. *vt.* & *vi.* To lie along the edge of; be on or move along a border. **II.** *n.* **1.** The loose lower part of a garment or of some other object; a petticoat. **2.** Margin; border.

skit′tish, 1 skit′ish; 2 skĭt′ish, *a.* **1.** Easily frightened; timid. **2.** Capricious; tricky. **-ly**, *adv.* **-ness**, *n.*

skulkᵗ, 1 skulk; 2 skŭlk, *vi.* To move about a place furtively or slyly.— **skulk′er**, *n.*

skull, } 1 skul; 2 skŭl, *n.* The framework
skulᴾ, } of the head of a vertebrate animal; cranium.

skull′cap″, 1 skul′kap″; 2 skŭl′căp″, *n.* A plant of wet shady places, with large solitary blue flowers. [skull.

skull′=cap″, *n.* A cap closely fitting the

skunk, 1 skuŋk; 2 skŭŋk, *n.* An American nocturnal burrowing animal having a bushy tail and capable of sending forth a liquid of very offensive odor. See illus. on next page.

sky, 1 skai; 2 skÿ, *n.* [SKIESᶻ, *pl.*] **1.** The blue vault that seems to bend ove

the earth. **2.** The upper air. **3.** Heaven.— **sky′ward,** *adv.* Toward the sky. **sky′-wardst.**

sky′lark″, *n.* A lark of Europe and parts of Africa and Asia that mounts singing toward the sky.

sky′-scrap″er, *n.* A very tall structure.

slab, 1 slab; 2 slăb, *n.* A flat piece, as of timber.

slab′ber, *vt. & vi.* To slaver.

slack¹, }1 slak, slak′n; Skunk. ¹/₆
slack′en, }2 slăk, slăk′n, *vt. & vi.* **1.** To loosen; relax; retard. **2.** To slake, as lime.

slack, *a.* Loose; remiss; careless; listless; feeble.— **slack′ly,** *adv.*— **slack′ness,** *n.*

slack¹, *n.* The part of anything, as a rope, that hangs down loosely between supports; also, a slack condition.

slack², *n.* Small coal; coal-screenings.

slack′er, *n.* One who shirks his duty; specif., one who evades enlistment in the military service.

slag, 1 slag; 2 slăg, *n.* Metallic dross, as from ore; volcanic ashes.

slake, 1 slēk; 2 slāk, *v.* [SLAKED†; SLAK′-ING.] **I.** *t.* **1.** To quench, as thirst; appease; slacken. **2.** To mix with water, as lime. **II.** *i.* To absorb and combine with water: said of lime.

sla′lom, 1 slä′lom; 2 slä′lŏm, *n.* In skiing, a race over a down-hill, zigzag course usually marked by flags. [Norw.]

slam, 1 slăm; 2 slăm. **I.** *vt. & vi.* [SLAMMED, SLAMD⁵; SLAM′MING.] To pull or push to, as a door, with violence and noise; bang. **II.** *n.* A closing or striking with a bang.

slan′der, 1 slan′dər; 2 slăn′dər. **I.** *vt. & vi.* To injure by malicious falsehood; defame; calumniate. **II.** *n.* A false tale or report uttered with malice; defamation.— **slan′der-er,** *n.*— **slan′der-ous,** *a.* **-ly,** *adv.* **-ness,** *n.*

slang, 1 slang; 2 slăng, *n.* Inelegant and unauthorized popular language.— **slang′y,** *a.*

slant, 1 slant; 2 slănt. **I¹.** *vt. & vi.* To give a sloping direction to; incline; lean. **II.** *a.* Lying at an angle; sloping. **III.** *n.* Anything slanting; a slope; incline.

slap, 1 slap; 2 slăp. **I.** *vt.* [SLAPPED†, SLAPT²; SLAP′PING.] To deal a slap to or with. **II.** *n.* A blow delivered with the open hand or with something flat.

slash, 1 slash; 2 slăsh. **I**†. *vt. & vi.* To strike with a slash; slit; gash. **II.** *n.* A sweeping cut or stroke; slit; gash.

slat, 1 slat; 2 slăt, *n.* A thin strip, as of wood.

slate, 1 slēt; 2 slāt. **I.** *vt.* [SLAT′ED†; SLAT′ING.] **1.** To roof with slate. **2.** To put on a political slate. **II.** *n.* **1.** Any kind of rock that splits readily into layers; also, a piece of such rock for roofing, writing upon, etc. **2.** A list of candidates, made up for nomination or appointment.— **slat′er,** *n.*— **slat′y,** *a.*

slat′tern, }1 slat′ərn; 2 slăt′ern, *n.* A negligent or untidy woman.— **slat′tern-ly,** *a. & adv.*

slaugh′ter, }1 slô′tər; 2 sla′ter. **I.** *vt.* To
slau′ter², }kill wantonly or savagely; butcher. **II.** *n.* **1.** Wanton or savage killing; massacre. **2.** Butchering.— **slaugh′-ter-er,** *n.*— **slaugh′ter-house″,** *n.* A place where animals are butchered.

Slav, 1 släv; 2 slăv, *n.* A member of one of various people of northern or eastern Europe, as a Russian, Bulgarian, Pole, or Serbian.— **Slav′ic,** *a.*— **Sla-vo′ni-an. I.** *a.* **1.** Relating to the Slavs or to Slavonia. **2.** Slavonic. **II.** *n.* **1.** A native of Slavonia: Jugo-Slavia. **2.** A Slav.— **Sla-von′ic,** *a.* **1.** Pertaining to Slavs or their languages. **2.** Slavonian.

slave, 1 slēv; 2 slāv. **I.** *vt. & vi.* [SLAVED; SLAV′ING.] To toil; drudge **II.** *n.* A person in slavery; bondman; drudge.— **slave′hold″er,** *n.* An owner of slaves.— **slav′ish,** *a.* Pertaining to or befitting a slave; servile; base. **-ly,** *adv.* **-ness,** *n.*

slav′er, 1 slav′ər; 2 slăv′er, *vt. & vi.* To dribble saliva over; drivel.— **slav′er-er,** *n.*

slav′er¹, 1 slēv′ər; 2 slăv′er, *n.* A person or a vessel engaged in the slave-trade.

slav′er², 1 slav′ər; 2 slăv′er, *n.* Drivel.

slav′er-y, 1 slēv′ər-ɪ; 2 slăv′er-y, *n.* Involuntary servitude; subjection.

slaw, 1 slô; 2 sla, *n.* Cabbage sliced or chopped, served as a salad.

slay, 1 slē; 2 slā, *vt.* [SLEW; SLAIN; SLAY′-ING.] To kill.— **slay′er,** *n.*

sled, 1 sled; 2 slĕd. **I.** *vt. & vi.* [SLED′DED†; SLED′DING.] To convey on a sled; use a sled. **II.** *n.* A vehicle on runners, for use on snow and ice.

sledge¹, 1 slej; 2 slĕdʒ, *n.* A sled or other vehicle, to be drawn over snow and ice by draft-animals.

sledge², *n.* A heavy hammer for blacksmiths′ use, etc. **sledge′-ham″mer†.**

sleek, 1 slēk; 2 slēk, *a.* **1.** Smooth and glossy. **2.** Smooth-spoken; flattering.— **sleek′ly,** *adv.*— **sleek′ness,** *n.*

Siberian Post-sledge.

sleep, 1 slīp; 2 slĕp, **t.** [SLEPT; SLEEP'ING.] **I.** *t.* To rest or repose in (sleep); as, to *sleep* the sleep of death. **II.** *i.* To be asleep, dormant, or dead; slumber.

sleep, *n.* A state or period of unconsciousness; slumber; repose.— **sleep'ing-car",** *n.* A passenger railway-car with accommodations for sleeping.— **sleep'less,** *a.* Wakeful; restless. **-ly,** *adv.* **-ness,** *n.*— **sleep'=walk"-er,** *n.* A somnambulist.— **sleep'=walk"ing,** *n.* Somnambulism.

sleep'er, 1 slīp'ər; 2 slĕp'er, *n.* **1.** One who sleeps. **2.** [U. S.] A sleeping-car.

sleep'er², *n.* A horizontal beam, as a support for rails, etc.

sleep'y, 1 slīp'ī; 2 slĕp'y, *a.* Inclined to sleep; drowsy.— **sleep'i-ly,** *adv.*— **sleep'i-ness,** *n.*

sleet, 1 slīt; 2 slēt. **I**d. *vi.* To let fall sleet. **II.** *n.* A drizzling or driving of partly frozen rain.— **sleet'y,** *a.*

sleeve, 1 slīv; 2 slĕv, *n.* **1.** The part of a **sleeve**r garment that covers the arm. **2.** *Mech.* A tube surrounding something.

sleigh, 1 slē; 2 slĕ, *n.* A light vehicle with runners, for use on snow and ice.— **sleigh'-ing,** *n.* **1.** The act of riding in a sleigh. **2.** The condition of the roads that admits of using a sleigh.

sleight, 1 slait; 2 slīt, *n.* Dexterity in **slight**s, manipulation; a juggler's trick.

slen'der, 1 slen'dər; 2 slĕn'der, *a.* Small in thickness in proportion to height or length; slim; feeble. **-ly,** *adv.* **-ness,** *n.*

slen'der-ize, 1 slen'der-aiz; 2 slĕn'der-īz, *vt. & vi.* [-IZED; -IZ'ING.] To reduce the size of, as ankles; also, to reduce.

sleuth, 1 slūth; 2 slųth, *n.* **1.** The track or trail of man or beast, as followed by the scent. **2.** [Colloq.] A detective.— **sleuth'=hound",** *n.* A bloodhound; figuratively, a detective.

slice, 1 slais; 2 slīṣ. **I.** *vt.* [SLICED; SLIC'ING.] **1.** To cut into thin pieces. **2.** To cut from a larger piece. **II.** *n.* A thin piece cut off from a larger body.

slick, 1 slik; 2 slīk. **I**t. *vt.* To make smooth. **II.** *a.* Smooth; slippery.

slide, 1 slaid; 2 slīd. **I.** *vt. & vi.* [SLID; SLID or SLID'DEN, SLID'NE; SLID'ING.] To pass over a surface with a smooth movement; move easily and smoothly. **II.** *n.* **1.** The act of sliding. **2.** A place for sliding.— **slid'er,** *n.*

slight, 1 slait; 2 slīt. **I**d. *vt.* To neglect; do imperfectly. **II.** *a.* **1.** Of small importance. **2.** Slender; frail. **III.** *n.* A neglectful action; neglect; disregard. **-ly,** *adv.* **-ness,** *n.*

slim, 1 slim; 2 slīm, *a.* [SLIM'MER; SLIM'-MEST.] Slender; thin; flimsy.

slime, 1 slaim; 2 slīm, *n.* Any soft, sticky substance; as mud.— **slim'y,** *a.*— **slim'i-ness,** *n.*

sling, 1 sliŋ; 2 slīng. **I.** *vt.* [SLUNG; SLING'ING.] **1.** To fling from a sling; hurl. **2.** To hang up, as in a sling. **II.** *n.* **1.** A strap with a string at each end, for hurling a stone or other missile; a sudden throw. **2.** A device for suspending or hoisting something.— **sling'er,** *n.*

slink, 1 sliŋk; 2 slīŋk, *vi.* [SLUNK or SLANK; SLINK'ING.] To creep away; move on furtively.

slip, 1 slip; 2 slīp. **I.** *vt. & vi.* [SLIPPEDt or SLIPT; SLIP'PING.] **1.** To slide or cause to glide or slide; lose one's footing. **2.** To let loose; go free. **II.** *n.* **1.** The act of slipping. **2.** A lapse in conduct; a fault. **3.** A narrow piece; strip; long, narrow dock. **4.** A cutting from a plant. — **slip'=knot",** *n.* A bow-knot.— **slip'per,** *n.* A low light shoe, for indoor wear.— **slip'per(e)d**s, *a.*— **slip'per-y,** *a.* **1.** Smooth; so as to slip or cause slipping. **2** Elusive; tricky.— **slip'per-i-ness,** *n.*— **slip'shod",** *a.* Down at the heel; slovenly.

slit, 1 slit; 2 slīt. **I.** *vt.* [SLIT or SLIT'TEDd; SLIT'TING.] To make a long cut in; cut into strips. **II.** *n.* A long cut; a narrow opening.

sliv'er, 1 sliv'ər; 2 slīv'er. **I.** *vt. & vi.* To cut or split into long thin pieces lengthwise; break off, as a splinter. **II.** *n.* A thin strip, as of wood; slip; splinter.

sloe, 1 slō; 2 slō, *n.* A small plum-like fruit; also, the shrub that bears it; the blackthorn. [cry.

slo'gan, 1 slō'gan; 2 slō'gan, *n.* A battle-cry.

sloid, 1 sleid; 2 slŏid, *n* A manual-train-**sloyd,** ing system originating in Sweden.

sloop, 1 slūp; 2 slōop, *n.* A single-masted fore-and-aft rigged vessel, of broad beam.

slop, 1 slŏp; 2 slŏp, *vt. & vi.* [SLOPPEDt or SLOPT; SLOP'PING.] To dash over, as water from a pail; spill.

slop, *n.* **1.** A liquid that has been slopped. **2.** *pl.* Waste and dirty water.— **slop'py,** *a.*

slope, 1 slōp; 2 slōp. **I.** *vt. & vi.* [SLOPEDt; SLOP'ING.] To incline or be inclined; slant. **II.** *n.* Any slanting surface or line; declivity. [opening; slit.

slot¹, 1 slŏt; 2 slŏt, *n.* A narrow groove or **slot**², *n.* The trail of an animal, as a deer.

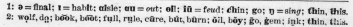

Sloop.

sloth, 1 slŏth *or* slôth; 2 slōth *or* slôth, *n.*
1. Disinclination to exertion; laziness.
2. A slow-moving tree-dwelling mammal of tropical America.— **sloth′ful,** *a.* Sluggish; lazy. **-ly,** *adv.* **-ness,** *n.*

slouch, 1 slauch; 2 slouch. **I**[t]. *vt. & vi.* To hang or droop carelessly; move in negligent and clumsy way. **II.** *n.* **1.** Negligent or clumsy movement. **2.** An awkward, clownish fellow.— **slouch′i-ly,** *adv.* — **slouch′i-ness,** *n.*— **slouch′y,** *a.*

slough[t], **}** 1 sluf; 2 slŭf, *vt. & vi.* To cast
sluf[r], **}** off, or be cast off, as dead tissue.
slough[1], 1 slou; 2 slou, *n.* A place of deep mud or mire.— **slough′y,** *a.* Swampy.

slough[2], 1 sluf; 2 slŭf, *n.* Dead tissue cast off; a skin, as of a serpent, that has been shed.

slov′en, 1 sluv′n; 2 slŏv′n, *n.* One habitually untidy.— **slov′en-li-ness,** *n.*— **slov′en-ly,** *a. & adv.*

slow, 1 slō; 2 slō. **I.** *vt. & vi.* To slacken in speed. **II.** *a.* **1.** Not quick or swift; dull; sluggish. **2.** Behind the standard, as a timepiece. **-ly,** *adv.* **-ness,** *n.*

sludge, 1 sluj; 2 slŭdg, *n.* Slimy mud; slush.

slue, 1 slū; 2 slu. **I.** *vt. & vi.* [SLUED; SLU′ING.] To move sidewise, as if some portion were pivoted; sling around. **II.** *n.* A sluing or turning.

slug, 1 slug; 2 slŭg, *vt. & vi.* To strike heavily.

slug[1], *n.* Any small chunk of metal; especially, one used as a bullet or missile.

Sea-slug.

slug[2], *n.* A snail-like animal of elongated form, having no visible shell.

slug′gard, 1 slug′ard; 2 slŭg′ard, *n.* A person habitually lazy or idle; a drone.— **slug′gish,** *a.* **1.** Slow; inactive; torpid. **2.** Habitually idle and lazy. **-ly,** *adv.* **-ness,** *n.*

sluice, 1 slūs; 2 slus. **I.** *vt.* [SLUICED[t]; SLUIC′ING.] To operate with a sluice; wash in a sluice. **II.** *n.* An artificial channel for conducting water, or the stream so conducted; a flume.

slum, 1 slum; 2 slŭm, *n.* A low, filthy quarter of a city.

slum′ber, 1 slum′bər; 2 slŭm′ber. **I.** *vi.* **1.** To sleep. **2.** To be inactive. **II.** *n.* Sleep; especially light sleep.— **slum′ber-er,** *n.*— **slum′ber-ous,** *a.*

slump, 1 slump; 2 slŭmp, *vi.* To break through a crust and sink into any soft

material, as snow or mud; to fail or collapse.— **slump,** *n.*

slung, 1 slun; 2 slŭng, *tmp. & pp.* of SLING, *v.*

slung′-shot″, 1 slun′-shŏt″; 2 slŭng′-shŏt″, *n.* A weight attached to a thong or cord; used as a weapon by ruffians.

slunk, 1 slunk; 2 slŭnk, *tmp. & pp.* of SLINK, *v.*

slur, 1 slŭr; 2 slŭr. **I.** *vt.* [SLURRED; SLURD[s]; SLUR′RING.] **1.** To slight; disparage; suppress; conceal; run together, as words. **2.** To smear; soil. **II.** *n.* **1.** A disparaging remark; disparagement; stigma. **2.** *Mus.* A curved line (‿ or ⁀) indicating that tones so tied are to be sung to the same syllable.

slush, 1 slush; 2 slŭsh, *n.* Soft, sloppy material, as melting snow; grease for lubrication, etc.— **slush′y,** *a.*

slut, 1 slut; 2 slŭt, *n.* **1.** A female dog. **2.** A slatternly woman.— **slut′tish,** *a.* Slatternly; dirty. **-ly,** *adv.* **-ness,** *n.*

sly, 1 slai; 2 slī, *a.* [SLI′ER *or* SLY′ER; SLI′EST *or* SLY′EST.] Artful in doing things secretly; cunning; crafty.— **sly′ly,** *adv.* **sli′ly**[‡]. **— sly′ness,** *n.*

smack[1], 1 smak; 2 smăk. **I**[t]. *vt. & vi.* To give or make a smack. **II.** *n.* A quick sharp sound; a noisy kiss; a sounding slap.

smack[2]. **I**[t]. *vi.* To have a taste or flavor. **II.** *n.* A taste; flavor.

smack[3], *n.* A small coasting- or fishing-[vessel.]

small, 1 smôl; 2 smạl, *a.* Diminutive; little; unimportant; mean. **-ness,** *n.*— **small′pox″,** *n.* An acute, infectious disease.

smart, 1 smärt; 2 smärt. **I**[d]. *vi.* To experience an acute painful sensation. **II.** *a.* **1.** Quick in thought or action; clever; witty. **2.** Stinging; pungent. **III.** *n.* A stinging sensation. **-ly,** *adv.* **-ness,** *n.*

smash, 1 smash; 2 smăsh. **I**[t]. *vt. & vi.* To break in pieces; shatter. **2.** To put out of shape; crush. **II.** *n.* An act or incident of smashing; destruction.— **smash′er,** *n.*

smat′ter, 1 smat′ər; 2 smăt′er, *vt. & vi.* To have but a smattering of; talk superficially.— **smat′ter-er,** *n.*— **smat′ter-ing,** *n.* A superficial knowledge.

smear, 1 smīr; 2 smēr. **I.** *vt.* To bedaub with a sticky substance. **II.** *n.* A soiled spot made by some gummy substance.

smell, **}** 1 smel; 2 smĕl, *v.* [SMEL(LE)D[s] *or*
smel[r], **}** SMELT, SMELL′ING.] **I.** *t.* To perceive by means of the nose; scent. **II.** *i.* **1.** To emit an odor or perfume. **2.** To use the sense of smell; sniff.

smell, *n.* **1.** That sense by means of which odors are perceived. **2.** An odor.

smelt[d], 1 smelt; 2 smĕlt, *vt. & vi.* To re-

duce (ores) by fusion in a furnace.—
smelt′er, smelt′er-y, *n.*

smelt, *n.* A
small silvery
food=fish.
s m i′l a x, 1
smai′laks; 2
smī′lăks, *n.* A
delicate twin-
ing plant with greenish flowers.

American Smelt. ⅛

smile, 1 smaɪl; 2 smīl. **I.** *vi.* [SMILED;
SMIL′ING.] To give a smile; show approval. **II.** *n.* A pleased or amused expression of the face; favor; blessing.

smirchᵗ, 1 smŭrϛh; 2 smĭrch, *vt.* **1.** To
soil; smear. **2.** To defame.

smirk, 1 smŭrk; 2 smĭrk. **I**ᵗ. *vi.* To
smile in a silly manner. **II.** *n.* An
affected smile.

smite, 1 smaɪt; 2 smīt, *vt.* [SMOTE OR SMIT;
SMIT′TEN OR SMIT; SMIT′ING.] **1.** To
strike with force. **2.** Break by a blow;
afflict. **3.** To affect with sudden feeling.

smith, 1 smiϛh; 2 smĭth, *n.* One who
shapes metals.— **smith′y,** *n.* [-IESᶻ, *pl.*]
A smith's shop; a forge. **smith′er-y**ᵗ.

smit′ten, 1 smit′n; 2 smĭt′n, *pp.* of SMITE, *v.*

smock, 1 smɒk; 2 smŏk, *n.* **1.** A chemise.
2. A smock=frock.— **smock′=frock″,** *n.* An
outside garment resembling a shirt, worn by
some field=laborers.

smoke, 1 smɒk; 2 smŏk, *v.* [SMOKEDᵗ;
SMOK′ING.] **I.** *t.* **1.** To affect, cure, or
flavor by smoke. **2.** To inhale and exhale the smoke of, as tobacco. **II.** *i.* **1.**
To give out smoke. **2.** To use tobacco,
etc., by burning for inhalation.

smoke, *n.* The vapor=like products of
the burning of coal, wood, etc.— **smoke′less,**
a.— **smok′er,** *n.* **1.** One who or that which
smokes. **2.** A smoking=car.— **smoke′=stack″,**
n. A pipe through which the smoke from
a boiler=furnace is discharged.— **smok′y,** *a.*
[SMOK′I=ER; SMOK′I=EST.] Giving forth,
mixed with, or like smoke.— **smok′i-ly,** *adv.*
— **smok′i-ness,** *n.*

smol′der, 1 smōl′dǝr; 2 smōl′der, *vi.* To
burn and smoke in a smothered way.

smooth, 1 smūth; 2 smōōth. **I.** *vt. & vi.*
To make smooth; sotten; extenuate. **II.**
a. Having a surface without irregu-
larities; not rough; calm and unruffled;
bland. **-ly,** *adv.* **-ness,** *n.*

smote, 1 smɒt; 2 smŏt, *imp.* of SMITE, *v.*

smoth′er, 1 smuth′ǝr; 2 smŏth′er. **I.** *vt.
& vi.* To suffocate; stifle. **II.** *n.* That
which smothers; a smothered condition.

smoul′der, *vt.* Same as SMOLDER.

smudge, 1 smuj; 2 smŭdg. **I.** *vt.* [SMUDGED;

SMUDG′ING.] To smear; soil. **II.** *n.* **1.**
A soiling; stain. **2.** A smoky fire.

smug′gle, } 1 smug′l; 2 smŭg′l, *v.* [SMUG′-
smug′lᴾ, } GLED, SMUG′LDᴾ; SMUG′GLING.]
I. *t.* To take (merchandise) into or out of
a country without payment of duties; bring
in underhand. **II.** *i.* To practise smug-
gling.— **smug′gler,** *n.* One who smuggles.—
smug′gling, *n.*

smut, 1 smut; 2 smŭt. **I.** *vt. & vi.* [SMUT′-
TEDᵈ; SMUT′TING.] To affect with smut;
blacken; stain or be stained. **II.** *n.* **1.**
The blackening made by soot or the like.
2. Obscenity. **3.** A parasitic disease
of plants.— **smut′ti-ly,** *adv.*— **smut′ti-ness,**
n.— **smut′ty,** *a.*

snaf′fle, } 1 snaf′l; 2 snăf′l, *n.* A jointed
snaf′lᴾ, } bit, or such bit with its bridle.

snag, 1 snag; 2 snăg. **I.** *vt.* To injure or
impede by a snag. **II.** *n.* **1.** A jagged
or stumpy knot. **2.** The root or remnant
of a tooth. **3.** [U. S.] A tree=trunk
stuck in a river's bed; an impediment.
— **snagged, snag′gy,** *a.* Full of snags.

snail, 1 snēl; 2 snāl, *n.* **1.** A slow=moving
mollusk with a spiral
shell. **2.** A slow
or lazy person.

snake, 1 snēk; 2
snāk, *n.* A ser-
pent.— **sna′ky,** *a.*

Edible Snail. ⅓

snap, 1 snap; 2
snăp, *v.* [SNAPPEDᵗ, SNAPTˢ; SNAP′PING.]
I. *t.* To strike, press, shut, etc., with a
snap; break suddenly with a cracking
noise; seize suddenly. **II.** *i.* **1.** To emit
a sharp, cracking sound. **2.** To part with
a snap.

snap, *n.* **1.** A sharp, quick sound; sudden breaking; sharp, sudden closing, as of
a gun=lock; any fastening, or the like, that
closes with a click. **2.** A sudden snatch,
as with the teeth. **3.** A brief spell, as of
cold weather.— **snap′drag″on,** *n.* A plant
having flowers, likened to dragons' heads.—
snap′per, *n.* **1.** One who or that which
snaps. **2.** A food=fish of the Gulf coast. **3.**
A snapping turtle.— **snap′pish,** *a.* Sharp-
spoken; disposed to snap, as a dog. **-ness,** *n.*
—**snap′shot″,** *n.* **1.** A quick shot taken without deliberate aim. **2.** An instantaneous
photograph.

snare, 1 snâr; 2 snâr. **I.** *vt. & vi.* [SNARED;
SNAR′ING.] To catch with a snare; use
snares. **II.** *n.* A device, as a noose, for
catching animals; allurement; wile.— **snar′-
er,** *n.*— **sna′ky,** *a.*

snarlᵗ, 1 snârl; 2 snärl. **I.** *vt. & vi.* To
growl harshly, as a dog; speak angrily.
II. *n.* A harsh growl.

1: ǝ = final; ɪ = habit; aɪsle; au = out; oɪl; ɪū = feud; ϛhin; go; ŋ = sing; ϛhin, this.
2: wǫlf, dǫ: bŏŏk, bōōt; fṵll, rṵle, cūre, bŭt, bûrn; ōɪl, bŏy; ḡo, ḡem; iŋk; thin, this.

snarl². **I.** *vt. & vi.* To get into a tangle. **II.** *n.* A tangle, as of hair or yarn.

snatch, 1 snăch; 2 snăch. **I**ᵗ. *vt. & vi.*
snachᴾ, } To seize suddenly, hastily, or eagerly; catch something with a sudden motion. **II.** *n.* **1.** An act of snatching; a grab. **2.** A portion snatched.

snathe, 1 snēth; 2 snăth, *n.* The handle of a scythe. Written also **snead, sneed,** etc.

sneak, 1 snīk; 2 snēk. **I**ᵗ. *vi.* To move stealthily; act with covert cowardice. **II.** *n.* One who sneaks; a mean, cowardly fellow.— **sneak'ing,** *pa. & a.* **-ly,** *adv.*

sneer, 1 snīr; 2 snēr. **I.** *vt. & vi.* To utter with a sneer. **II.** *n.* A grimace of contempt; a contemptuous insinuation.— **sneer'er,** *n.*—**sneer'ing,** *pa. & a.*—**sneer'ing-ly,** *adv.*

sneeze, } 1 snīz; 2 snēz. **I.** *vi.* [SNEEZ(E)D⁸;
sneezᴾ, } SNEEZ'ING.] To drive air forcibly through the nose, by a spasmodic action. **II.** *n.* An act of sneezing.

snick'er, 1 snik'ẽr; 2 snĭk'er. **I.** *vt. & vi.* To laugh foolishly; giggle. **II.** *n.* A half-repressed laugh. **snig'ger**‡.

sniff, } 1 snif; 2 snif. **I**ᵗ. *vt. & vi.* To
snifᴾ, } breathe through the nose in short, quick inhalations. **II.** *n.* **1.** An act of sniffing. **2.** Perception as of an odor by sniffing.

snip, 1 snip; 2 snĭp, *v.* [SNIPPED⁸, SNIPT⁸; SNIP'PING.] **I.** *t.* To cut with a short, light stroke of scissors. **II.** *i.* To make snips; clip.— **snip,** *n.* An act of snipping; a clip; bit snipped off.

snipe, 1 snaip; 2 snīp, *vt.* [SNIPED; SNIP'ING.] To shoot snipe; by extension, to shoot an enemy from cover.— **snip'er,** *n.*

snipe, *n.* A small shore-bird having a long beak.

Wilson's
Snipe.
1/₉

sniv'el, 1 sniv'l; 2 snĭv'l. **I.** *vi.* [SNIV'ELED or SNIV'ELLED, SNIV'ELD⁸; SNIV'EL-ING or SNIV'-EL-LING.] To cry in a snuffling manner; run at the nose. **II.** *n.* Discharge from the nose.— **sniv'el-er,** *n.*

snob, 1 snŏb; 2 snŏb, *n.* A vulgar pretender to gentility.— **snob'bish,** *a.* **-ly,** *adv.* **-ness,** *n.*

snooze, } 1 snūz; 2 snōōz. **I.** *vi.* [SNOOZ(E)D⁸;
snoozᴾ, } SNOOZ'ING.] To sleep lightly; doze. **II.** *n.* [Colloq.] A nap.

snore, 1 snōr; 2 snōr. **I.** *vi.* [SNORED; SNOR'ING.] To breathe noisily in sleep. **II.** *n.* An act of snoring.— **snor'er,** *n.*

snort, 1 snôrt; 2 snôrt. **I**ᵈ. *vi.* To force air noisily through the nostrils, as a spirited horse. **II.** *n.* The act or sound of snorting.— **snort'er,** *n.*—**snort'ing,** *pa. & n.*

snout, 1 snout; 2 snout, *n.* The forward projecting part of a beast's head; muzzle.

snow, 1 snō; 2 snō, *v.* **I.** *t.* To cover with snow; let fall like snow. **II.** *i.* To fall as snow.

snow, *n.* Frozen vapor falling through the air; a fall of snow; a snowstorm.— **snow'ball''. I.** *vt. & vi.* To throw snowballs. **II.** *n.* A small round mass of snow, to be thrown.— **snow'bird'',** *n.* A small bird, as the finch, seen in flocks during winter.— **snow'=bound'',** *a.* Hemmed in by snow.— **s.=drift,** *n.* A pile of snow heaped up by the wind.— **snow'drop'',** *n.* A low European early-blooming plant.— **snow'-flake'',** *n.* One of the small feathery masses in which snow falls.— **s.=plow,** *n.* A plowlike structure for clearing roads or railway-tracks of snow.— **s.=shoe,** *n.* A light, spreading support as of network in a frame to be worn on the foot in walking over snow.— **snow'slide'',** *n.* An avalanche.— **s.=storm,** *n.* A storm with falling snow.— **snow'y,** *a.* [SNOW'I-ER; SNOW'I-EST.] **1.** Abounding in or full of snow. **2.** Snow-white; spotless.— **snow'i-ly,** *adv.*—**snow'i-ness,** *n.*

snub, 1 snŭb; 2 snŭb. **I.** *vt.* [SNUBBED, SNUBD⁸; SNUB'BING.] **1.** To check contemptuously; rebuff. **2.** To bring to a sudden stop. **II.** *a.* Short; pug: said of the nose. **III.** *n.* **1.** An act of snubbing. **2.** A snub nose.

snuff, } 1 snŭf; 2 snŭf. **I**ᵗ. *vt. & vi.* To
snufᴾ, } inhale; smell; sniff; take snuff. **II.** *n.* **1.** An act of snuffing; sniff; perception by smelling. **2.** Pulverized tobacco to be inhaled into the nostrils.

snuff². **I**ᵗ. *vt.* To crop the snuff from. **II.** *n.* The charred portion of a wick.

snuf'fle, } 1 snŭf'l; 2 snŭf'l. **I.** *vi.* [SNUF'-
snuf'lᴾ, } FLED, SNUF'LD⁸; SNUF'FLING.] To breathe with difficulty and somewhat noisily through the nose; talk through the nose; snivel. **II.** *n.* An act or sound of snuffling.

snug, 1 snŭg; 2 snŭg, *a.* [SNUG'GER; SNUG'-GEST.] Close or compact; comfortably situated; cozy. **-ly,** *adv.*— **snug'gle,** *vt. & vi.* [SNUG'GLED, SNUG'LD⁸; SNUG'GLING.] To draw close; nestle; cuddle.

so, 1 sō; 2 sō. **I.** *adv.* **1.** To this or that extent. **2.** In such a manner. **3.** Just as said or implied. **4.** Very. **5.** Because; therefore. **6.** Thereabout. **II.** *conj.* Provided that.

soakᵗ, 1 sōk; 2 sōk, *v.* **I.** *t.* To saturate; steep; drench; absorb. **II.** *i.* **1.** To remain in liquid till saturated. **2.** To permeate.

soap, 1 sōp; 2 sōp. **I**ᵗ. *vt.* To rub with

soap; put soap on. **II.** *n.* Any compound formed by the union of a fatty acid with a base: used for cleansing purposes.— **soap′i-ness,** *n.*— **soap′stone″,** *n.* A soft stone, with soapy feeling; talc.— **soap′suds″,** *n. sing. & pl.* Soapy water, as in a foam.— **soap′y,** *a.*

soar, 1 sōr; 2 sôr, *vi.* **1.** To float aloft through the air on wings, as a bird. **2.** To rise in thought; aspire.

sob, 1 sŏb; 2 sŏb. **I.** *vi.* [SOB(BE)D⁸; SOB′-BING.] **1.** To weep with short, catching breaths. **2.** To make a sound like a sob, as wind. **II.** *n.* Act or sound of sobbing.

so′ber, 1 sō′bər; 2 sō′ber. **I.** *vt. & vi.* To make or become sober; render grave or thoughtful. **II.** *a.* **1.** Possessing properly controlled faculties. **2.** Grave; sedate. **3.** Not drunk. **-ly,** *adv.* **-ness,** *n.* — **so-bri′e-ty,** *n.* The state of being sober.

so″bri-quet′, 1 sō′brĭ-kĕ′; 2 sō′bri-ke′, *n.* A nickname.

so′cia-bl(e″, 1 sō′shə-bl; 2 sō′sha-bl, *a.* Inclined to seek company; social; companionable; genial.— **so′cia-bl(e-ness″,** *n.* — **so′cia-bly,** *adv.*

so′cial, 1 sō′shəl; 2 sō′shal, *a.* Pertaining or adapted to society; sociable; companionable. **-ly,** *adv.* **-ness,** *n.*— **so′cial-ism,** *n.* A system that aims at the public collective ownership of land and capital, and public management of all industries.— **so′cial-ist,** *n.* One who advocates socialism.— **so″-cial-is′tic,** *a.*— **so″cl-al′l-ty,** *n.*

so-ci′e-ty, 1 so-sai′ı-tı; 2 so-çī′e-ty, *n.* [-TIES²; *pl.*] **1.** A body of persons composing a community or connected by some tie. **2.** The wealthy and cultured class of a community. **3.** Companionship; fellowship.

so″ci-ol′o-gy, 1 sō″shı-ol′o-jı; 2 sō″shi-ŏl′o-gy, *n.* The science of human society.— **so″cl-o-log′l-cal,** *a.*

sock, 1 sɒk; 2 sŏk, *n.* A short stocking.

sock′et, 1 sɒk′et; 2 sŏk′et, *n.* A cavity or opening adapted to hold some corresponding piece.

So-crat′ic, 1 so-krat′ık; 2 so-crăt′ic, *a.* Pertaining to or characteristic of Socrates, the greatest Athenian philosopher (469–399 B. C.).— **So-crat′l-cal,** *a.*

sod, 1 sɒd; 2 sŏd. **I.** *vt.* [SOD′DED⁴; SOD′-DING.] To cover with sod. **II.** *n.* Grassy soil held together by matted roots; turf.

sod, 1 sɒd; 2 sŏd, *imp.* of SEETHE, *v.*

so′da, 1 sō′də; 2 sō′da, *n.* A white alkaline compound, the basis of salt.— **so′da-wa″-ter,** *p.*

so-dal′i-ty, 1 so-dal′ı-tı; 2 so-dăl′i-ty, *n.*

A brotherhood; especially (*R. C. Ch.*), a lay society of men or women for devotional or charitable purposes.

sod′den, 1 sɒd′n; 2 sŏd′n, *pa.* Soaked with moisture.

sod′den, 1 sɒd′n; 2 sŏd′n, *pp.* of SEETHE, *v.*

so′di-um, 1 sō′dı-um; 2 sō′di-ŭm, *n.* A silver=white alkaline element: the base of soda.

so′fa, 1 sō′fə; 2 sō′fa, *n.* A long seat, upholstered and having a back and raised ends.

soft, 1 sɒft *or* sɒft; 2 sôft *or* sŏft. **I.** *a.* Yielding easily to pressure; pliable; mild; gentle; tender; weak; effeminate. **II.** *adv.* In a soft, easy, or gentle manner. **III.** *interj.* Proceed softly; be quiet or slow.— **soft′en,** *vt. & vi.* To make or become soft or softer.— **soft′ly,** *adv. & interj.*— **soft′ness,** *n.* [liquid; wet; sloppy.

sog′gy, 1 sɒg′ı; 2 sŏg′y, *a.* Soaked with

soil¹, 1 sɒil; 2 sŏil, *vt. & vi.* To make or become dirty; befoul.

soil², *vt.* To feed, as stalled cattle, with freshly cut, green food.

soil¹, *n.* The fertile portion of the surface of the earth; the ground; earth; land.

soil², *n.* That which soils; foul matter.

soi″rée′, 1 swä″rē′; 2 swä″re′, *n.* An evening social party.

so′journ, 1 sō′jûrn *or* so-jûrn′; 2 sō′jûrn **so′journ²,** *or* so-jûrn′. **I.** *vi.* To reside or dwell temporarily. **II.** *n.* Temporary residence; stay.— **so′journ-er,** *n.*

sol, 1 sōl; 2 sōl, *n. Mus.* The fifth note of the scale.

sol′ace, 1 sɒl′ıs; 2 sŏl′aç. **I.** *vt.* [SOL′-ACED⁴; SOL′AC-ING.] **1.** To cheer in trouble. **2.** To alleviate, as grief. **II.** *n.* Comfort in grief, trouble, or calamity.

so′lar, 1 sō′lər; 2 sō′lar, *a.* Pertaining to, connected with, or measured by the sun.

sold, 1 sōld; 2 sōld, *imp. & pp.* of SELL, *v.*

sold′er, 1 sɒd′ər; 2 sŏd′er. **I.** *vt.* To join, as two metallic substances, by solder; unite; repair. **II.** *n.* A fusible alloy used for joining metals.

sol′dier, 1 sōl′jər; 2 sōl′jer. **I.** *vi.* **1.** To be a soldier. **2.** To pretend to work; shirk. **II.** *n.* A man engaged in military service; a warrior; a private as distinguished from an officer.— **sol′dier-ly,** *a.* Brave; martial. **sol′dier-like″** ‡.— **sol′-dier-y,** *n.* **1.** Soldiers collectively. **2.** Military service.

sole, 1 sōl; 2 sōl, *vt.* [SOLED; SOL′ING.] To furnish with a sole; resole, as a shoe.

sole, *a.* Single; only; absolute.— **sole′ly,** *adv.*

sole¹, *n.* The bottom of the foot or of a shoe, boot, etc.

1: ə = final; ı = habit; aisle; au = out; oil; iū = feud; ꞔhin; go; ŋ = sing; ꞔhin, this.
2: wǫlf, dǫ; bōŏk, bōot; fṳll, rṳle, cūre, bṳt, bûrn; ŏil, bŏy; gꞙ, ǧem; iŋk; thin, this.

sole², *n.* A flatfish; flounder: highly esteemed as food.

sol'e-cism, 1 sŏl'ɪ-sizm; 2 sŏl'e-çĭsm, *n.* A violation of grammar or of approved usage; incongruity.

American Sole. ¹/₃₃

1. Upper side.
2. Lower side.

sol'emn, 1 sŏl'em; 2 sŏl'ĕm, *a.* Impressive; awe-inspiring; sacred.— **sol'emn- ness,** *n.* **sol'emn-ness‡.**— **so-lem'ni-ty,** *n.* [-TIES², *pl.*] **1.** The state of being solemn. **2.** Something solemn; a religious rite; legal formality.— **sol'em-nize,** 1 sŏl'em'nɑiz; 2 sŏl'ĕm-nīz, *vt.* [-NIZED -NIZ'ING.] To perform with solemn rites.— **sol'em- ni-za'tion,** *n.*— **sol'em-niz''er,** *n.*— **sol'- emn-ly,** *adv.*

so-lic'it, 1 so-lis'ɪt; 2 so-lĭç'it, *vt. & vi.* To ask earnestly; entreat; beg; allure. — **so-lic'i-ta'tion,** *n.* **1.** The act of soliciting; importunity. **2.** Alluring or enticing influence.— **so-lic'i-tor,** *n.* **1.** An attorney at law; legal adviser. **2.** One who solicits.— **So-lic'i-tor**-Gen''er-al, *n.* [U.S.] An officer who ranks after the Attorney-General in the national Department of Justice.— **so-lic'i-tous,** *a.* Full of anxiety for something; interested; concerned. **-ly,** *adv.* **-ness,** *n.*— **so-lic'i-tude,** *n.* The state of being solicitous; anxiety.

sol'id, 1 sŏl'id; 2 sŏl'id. **I.** *a.* Compact, firm, and unyielding; substantial; not hollow. **II.** *n.* A hard substance; something that has length, breadth, and thickness.— **sol''i-dar'i-ty,** *n.* Coherence and oneness in nature, relations, or interests. — **so-lid'i-fi-ca'tion,** *n.*— **so-lid'i-fy,** *vt. & vi.* [-FIED; -FY'ING.] To make or become solid.— **so-lid'i-ty,** *n.* The state of being solid.— **sol'id-ly,** *adv.*— **sol'id-ness,** *n.*

so-lil'o-quy, 1 so-lil'o-kwɪ; 2 so-lil'o-kwy, *n.* [-QUIES², *pl.*] A talking to oneself. — **so-lil'o-quize,** *vt.* [-QUIZED; -QUIZ'ING.] To discourse to oneself. **so-lil'o-quise‡.**

sol''i-taire', 1 sŏl''i-tār'; 2 sŏl'i-târ', *n.* **1.** A diamond set alone. **2.** A game played by one person.

sol'i-ta-ry, 1 sŏl'i-tē-rɪ; 2 sŏl'i-tā-ry. **I.** *a.* Alone; lonely; secluded; single. **II.** *n.* A hermit.— **sol'i-ta-ri-ly,** *adv.*— **sol'i-tude,** *n.* **1.** Loneliness; seclusion. **sol'i-ta-ri-ness‡. 2.** A deserted place.

so'lo, 1 so'lo; 2 sō'lo, *n.* A musical performance by a single voice or instrument. — **so'lo-ist,** *n.*

sol'stice, 1 sŏl'stɪs; 2 sŏl'stiç, *n.* The **sol'stis⁵,** time of year when the sun is farthest from the equator, usually on June 21 and December 22: called the sum-

mer and winter **solstices;** also, either of the points then attained.— **sol-sti'tial,** *a.*

soi'u-ble, 1 sol'yu-bl; 2 sŏl'yu-bl, *a.* Ca-**sol'u-bl**ᴾ, pable of being dissolved or of being solved.— **sol''u-bil'i-ty,** *n.* **sol'u- bl**(e-ness)ᴾ‡.

so-lu'tion, 1 so-liū'shɐn; 2 so-lū'shon, *n.* **1.** The act or process of dissolving; the preparation made by dissolving a solid in a liquid. **2.** The act or process of solving.

solve, 1 sŏlv; 2 sŏlv, *vt.* [SOLV(E)Dˢ; SOLV'-**solv⁵,** ING.] To obtain an answer to, as a riddle or problem; explain; clear up. — **solv'a-ble,** *a.* — **solv''a-bil'i-ty, solv'a-bl**(e-ness)ᴾ, *n.*

sol'vent, 1 sŏl'vent; 2 sŏl'vĕnt. **I.** *a.* **1.** Having means to pay all debts. **II.** *n.* A fluid capable of dissolving substances.— **sol'ven-cy,** *n.* The state of being solvent.

som'ber, 1 sŏm'bɐr; 2 sŏm'bĕr, *a.* **som'bre,** Dusky; gloomy; melancholy; depressing.

som-bre'ro, 1 sɐm-brē'ro; 2 sŏm-bre'ro, *n.* [Mexican and Southwestern U. S.] A very broad-brimmed hat, usually of felt.

some, 1 sum; 2 sŏm. **I.** *a.* **1.** Of inde-**sum**ᴾ, terminate or moderate quantity or amount. **2.** Not definitely known. **3.** Part, but not all. **II.** *pron.* A portion. **2.** Certain individuals not designated. **III.** *adv.* In an approximate degree; about.— **some'bod''y,** *n.* **1.** A person unknown or unnamed. **2.** A person of consequence or importance.— **some'how',** *adv.* In some way.— **some'thing.** **I.** *n.* A thing indefinitely conceived or stated. **II.** *adv.* Somewhat.— **some'time'',** *adv.* **1.** At some time. **2.** Same as SOMETIMES.— **some'times'',** *adv.* At times; occasionally. — **some'what''.** **I.** *n.* More or less; something. **II.** *adv.* In some degree.— **some'where'',** *adv.* **1.** In or to some place unspecified or unknown. **2.** Approximately. -**some,** suffix. Forming adjectives denoting -**sum**ᴾ, a considerable degree of the quality expressed; as, dark*some*, quarrel*some*.

som'er-sault, 1 sum'ɐr-sŏlt, -set; 2 sŏm'-**sum'er-sault**ᴾ, er-salt, -sĕt, *n.* A leap in **som'er-set,** which a person turns heels **sum'er-set**ᴾ, over head and lights on his feet.

som-nam'bu-lism, 1 sɐm-nam'biu-lizm; 2 sŏm-năm'bū-lĭsm, *n.* The act of walking during sleep.— **som-nam'bu-list,** *n.* One affected with somnambulism.

som-nif'er-ous, 1 sɐm-nif'er-us; 2 sŏm-nĭf'er-ŭs, *a.* Tending to produce sleep; narcotic. **som-nif'ic‡.**

som'no-lent, 1 sɐm'no-lent; 2 sŏm'no-

1: artistic, ärt; fat, fāre; fast; get, prey; hit, police; obey, gō; not, ōr; full, rūle; but, bŭrn.
2: ärt, āpe, făt, fâre, fȧst, whạt, ạll; mē, gĕt, prey, fẽrn; hĭt, īce; ī=ē; ĩ=ē; gō, nŏt, ôr, wŏn,

lĕnt, a. **1.** Inclined to sleep; drowsy. **2.** Tending to induce drowsiness.— **som'no-lence,** n. **som'no-len-cy‡.**

son, 1 sŭn; 2 sŏn, n. A male child or descendant.— **son'-in-law",** n. The husband of one's daughter.— **son'ship,** n.

so'nant, 1 sō'nant; 2 sō'nant. **I.** a. Sounded; sounding; vocal. **II.** n. A sonant letter.

so-na'ta, 1 so-nä'tə; 2 so-nä'ta, n. An instrumental composition, in three or four movements.

song, 1 sĕŋ; 2 sông, n. **1.** The rendering of vocal music; more widely, any melodious utterance. **2.** Poetry; verse. **3.** A mere trifle.— **song'-spar'row,** n. A common North-American sparrow, noted for its song.— **song'ster,** n. A person or bird given to singing.— **song'stress,** n. fem.

son'net, 1 sen'et; 2 sŏn'ĕt, n. A poem of fourteen lines; any short song or poem.— **son'net-eer',** vi. & n.

so-no'rous, 1 so-nō'rus; 2 so-nō'rŭs, a. Sounding; resonant. **-ly,** adv. **-ness,** n.

soon, 1 sūn; 2 sōon, adv. In a short time; speedily.

soot, 1 sut or sūt; 2 sŏot or sōot. **I**d. vt. To soil or over with soot. **II.** n. A black substance, as from the inside of chimneys.— **soot'y,** a. Of or like soot.— **soot'i-ness,** n.

sooth‖, 1 sūth; 2 sōoth, n. Truth; reality.— **sooth'say"er,** n. One who claims to have prophetic insight.— **sooth'say"ing,** n.

soothe, 1 sūth; 2 sōoth, vt. [SOOTHED; SOOTH'ING.] To reduce from excitement to quiet; mitigate; humor.— **sooth'ing-ly,** adv.

sop, 1 sop; 2 sŏp. **I.** vt. & vi. [SOPPED†, SOPT⁸; SOP'PING.] To dip and moisten in a liquid; soak up. **II.** n. **1.** Anything dipped and softened in liquid. **2.** Anything given to pacify.

soph'ism, 1 sef'izm; 2 sŏf'ĭsm, n. A fal-**sof'ism**ᴾ, lacious argument designed to deceive.— **soph'ist,** n. One who argues cleverly but fallaciously.— **so-phis'tic, so-phis'ti-cal,** 1 so-fis'tik, -ti-kəl; 2 so-fis'tic, -ti-cal, a. Of or like sophistry; fallacious; quibbling. **-ly,** adv.— **so-phis'ti-cate,** vt. [-CAT"EDᵈ; -CAT"ING.] **1.** To beguile; mislead. **2.** To adulterate; render artificial.— **so-phis"ti-ca'tion,** n.— **soph'ist-ry,** n. [-RIES⁸, pl.] Subtly fallacious reasoning.

soph'o-more, 1 sef'o-mōr; 2 sŏf'o-mōr, n.— **sof'o-more**ᴾ, In American colleges, a student in the second year of a four-year course.— **soph"o-mor'ic,** a.

so"po-rif'ic, 1 sō"po-[or sop"o-]rif'ik; 2 sō"po-[or sŏp"o-]rĭf'ic. **I.** a. Causing or tending to produce sleep. **sop"o-rif'er-**

ous‡. **II.** n. A medicine that produces deep sleep.

so-pra'no, 1 so-prä'no; 2 so-prä'no, n. [-NOS⁸ or -NI, 1 nōz or -nī; 2 -nōs̬ or -nī, pl.] Mus. **1.** A woman's or boy's voice of high range. **2.** The music intended for such a voice. **3.** A person having such a voice.

sor'cer-y, 1 sôr'sər-ı; 2 sôr'çer-y, n. [-IES⁸, pl.] Magic; witchcraft.— **sor'cer-er,** n. A wizard; conjurer.— **sor'cer-ess,** n. fem.

sor'did, 1 sôr'dıd; 2 sôr'did, a. Meanly avaricious; mercenary; base. **-ly,** adv. **-ness,** n.

sore, 1 sōr; 2 sôr. **I.** a. [SOR'ER; SOR'EST.] **1.** Having a sore; being inflamed or painful; touchy. **2.** Causing extreme distress; also, very great; extreme. **II.** n. A bruised or inflamed spot; boil; ulcer.— **sore'ly,** adv. In a sore manner; greatly; exceedingly. **sore‡.— sore'ness,** n.

sor'ghum, 1 sôr'gum; 2 sôr'g̈ŭm, n. A stout cane-like cultivated grass; also, molasses prepared from its juice.

so-ror'i-ty, 1 so-ror'i-tı; 2 so-rŏr'i-ty, n. [-TIES⁸, pl.] A secret society in a woman's college, corresponding to the fraternity among male students.

sor'rel¹, 1 sor'el; 2 sôr'ĕl. **I.** a. Of a reddish- or yellowish-brown. **II.** n. A sorrel color, or an animal of that color.

Sorghum.

sor'rel², n. A low herb with acid leaves.

sor'row, 1 sor'o; 2 sôr'o. **I.** vi. To be sad. **II.** n. Pain or distress of mind; grief; affliction; trial; lamentation.— **sor'row-ful,** a. **-ly,** adv. **-ness,** n.

sor'ry, 1 sor'ı; 2 sôr'y, a. [SOR'RI-ER; SOR'RI-EST.] **1.** Grieved or pained; regretful. **2.** Poor; paltry.— **sor'ri-ly,** adv.— **sor'ri-ness,** n.

sort, 1 sôrt; 2 sôrt. **I**d. vt. To separate into grades or sizes. **II.** n. **1.** A kind; species; class. **2.** Form; manner.— **sort'er,** n.

sor'tie, 1 sôr'tı; 2 sôr'ti, n. A sally of troops from a besieged place to attack the besiegers.

sos"te-nu'to, 1 sos"tĕ-nū'to; 2 sŏs"te-nu'to, a. Mus. Sustained or continuous in tone.

sot, 1 sot; 2 sŏt, n. A person stupid by habitual drunkenness.— **sot'tish,** a. **-ly,** adv. **-ness,** n. [Softly; in an undertone.

sot'to vo'ce, 1 sot'to vō'chē; 2 sŏt'to vō'che.

sou, 1 sū; 2 su, n. A former French coin: about one cent in United States money.

sou-chong', 1 sū-shoŋ'; 2 su̬-chŏŋ', n. A variety of black tea, or the infusion made from it.

sough, 1 sau *or* suf; 2 sou *or* sŭf. **I.** *vi.* To blow with a sighing sound. **II.** *n.* A deep, murmuring sound, as of wind through tree-tops.

sought, 1 sôt; 2 sŏt, *imp. & pp.* of SEEK, *v.*

soul, 1 sōl; 2 sōl, *n.* **1.** The spiritual nature of man. **2.** The vital principle; essence or life of anything. **3.** Nobleness; generosity.— **soul'ful,** *a.* Emotional; spiritual.— **soul'less,** *a.* Having no soul; heartless; unemotional.

sound¹ᵈ, 1 saund; 2 sound, *vt. & vi.* To make a sound; make known or heard; give a signal by sound.

sound²ᵈ, *v.* **I.** *t.* To try the depth of; examine; test. **II.** *i.* To sink a weight in order to ascertain depth.

sound, *a.* Normal; unimpaired; healthy; true; right; solvent; thorough. **-ly,** *adv.* **-ness,** *n.*

sound¹, *n.* The sensation received through the ear; the waves that affect the ear; noise.

sound², *n.* A long and narrow body of water connecting larger bodies.

sound³, *n.* The air-bladder of a fish.

sound⁴, *n.* Surg. A probe. [sleeping

sound, *adv.* Soundly; profoundly: said of

sound'ing, 1 saund'ıŋ; 2 sound'ĭng. **I.** *pa.* Giving forth a sound. **II.** *n.* **1.** The act of one who or that which sounds. **2.** *pl.* The depth of water as sounded or depth that can be sounded.

soup, 1 sūp; 2 sup, *n.* Liquid food made by boiling meat, vegetables, etc., in water.

sour, 1 saur; 2 sour. **I.** *vt. & vi.* To make or become sour or morose. **II.** *a.* **1.** Sharp to the taste; acid; fermented. **2.** Austere; morose. **III.** *n.* Something sour. **-ly,** *adv.* **-ness,** *n.*

source, ⎱1 sôrs; 2 sōrç, *n.* That from
sourseᵖ, ⎰ which anything proceeds; origin; fountainhead.

souse, 1 saus; 2 sous, *vt. & vi.* [SOUSED⁴, SOUST⁵; SOUS'ING.] To dip into a liquid suddenly; plunge; splash; tipple.

souse, *n.* **1.** Pickled meats, as the head and feet of swine. **2.** A plunge in water.

souse, *adv.* With a plunge; all over.

south, 1 sauth; 2 south. **I.** *a.* Lying or facing toward the south; southern. **II.** *n.* **1.** That point of the compass which is directly opposite to north. **2.** A region lying southward. **III.** *adv.* **1.** Toward or at the south. **2.** From the south.— **south"east',** *n.* That point of the compass midway between south and east.— **south"east'er-ly,** *a. & adv.—* **south"east'ern,** *a.—* **south'er-li-ness,** *n.—* **south'er-ly,** 1 suth'ạr-lı; 2 sŭth'er-ly, *a.* **1.** Situated

in or tending toward the south. **2.** Proceeding from the south.— **south'er-ly,** *adv.—* **south'ern,** 1 suth'ạrn; 2 sŭth'ern, *a.* **1.** Pertaining to the south. **2.** Proceeding from the south, as a wind.— **south'ern-er,** *n.* One born or residing in the south.— **south'ing,** 1 sauth'ıŋ; 2 south'ĭng, *n.* Difference of latitude measured toward the south.— **south'ron,** 1 suth'ron; 2 sŭth'ron, *n.* A person who lives in the south.— **south'ward,** 1 sauth'ward; 2 south'ward. **I.** *a.* Situated in or toward the south. **II.** *adv.* In a southerly direction. **-ly**‡; **south'wards**‡.— **south"west'.** **I.** *a.* **1.** Pertaining to or facing the southwest. **2.** Proceeding from the southwest. **II.** *n.* That part of the horizon which is midway between south and west.— **south"west'er-ly,** *a. & adv.—* **south"west'ern,** *a.*

sou've-nir', 1 sū"vı-nīr'; 2 sụ"ve-nīr', *n.* A memento.

sov'er-eign, ⎱1 sov'[*or* suv']er-ın; 2 sŏv'[*or*
sov'er-enˢ, ⎰ sŏv']er-ĭn. **I.** *a.* Having supreme power; royal; preeminent; paramount; potent. **II.** *n.* **1.** One who possesses supreme authority; a monarch. **2.** An English gold coin of the value of $4.86.— **sov'er-eign-ty,** *n.* The state of being sovereign; supreme authority.

so"viet', 1 sō"vyet'; 2 sō"vy̆et', *n.* [Rus.] A council, as of workingmen or soldiers, or both.

sow, 1 sō; 2 sō, *v.* [SOWED, SOWD⁵; SOWN *or* SOWED; SOW'ING.] **I.** *t.* **1.** To scatter, as seed; disseminate. **2.** To plant with seed. **II.** *i.* To scatter as seed for a harvest.— **sow'er,** *n.—* **sow'ing,** *n.*

sow, 1 sau; 2 sow, *n.* **1.** A female hog. **2.** A small bug. **sow-bug**‡.

soy, 1 soi; 2 sŏy, *n.* A sauce prepared in China and Japan from a bean of the same name. [quented for its mineral springs.

spa, 1 spä; 2 spä, *n.* Any locality fre-

space, 1 spēs; 2 spāç. **I.** *vt. & vi.* [SPACED⁴, SPAC'ING.] To set apart by spaces; also, to arrange into spaces. **II.** *n.* **1.** An interval between points or objects; place; room. **2.** Continuous or unlimited extension. **3.** An interval of time; period. **4.** An occasion or opportunity.— **spa'cious,** 1 spē'shus; 2 spā'shŭs, *a.* Of great extent; roomy; capacious. **-ly,** *adv.* **-ness,** *n.*

spade¹, 1 spēd; 2 spād, *n.* An implement used in digging.— **spade'ful,** *n.*

spade², *n.* A figure like a heart, with a triangular handle, on a playing-card.

spake‖, 1 spēk; 2 spāk, *imp.* of SPEAK, *v.*

span, *imp.* of SPIN, *v.*

span, 1 span; 2 spăn. **I.** *vt.* [SPANNED, SPAND⁵; SPAN'NING.] **1.** To measure with an expanded hand. **2.** To extend over. **II.** *n.* **1.** The space over which the hand can be expanded: about 9 inches; any

small distance. **2.** The space or distance between the supports of an arch. **3.** A pair of matched horses, etc.

span'gle, ⟩ 1 spaŋ'gl; 2 spăŋ'gl. **I.** *vt.*
span'glᴾ, ⟨ [SPAN'GL(E)Dᴾ; SPAN'GLING.] To adorn with spangles. **II.** *n.* **1.** A bit of brilliant metal for decoration. **2.** Any small sparkling object.

Span'iard, 1 span'yᵃrd; 2 spăn'yard. A native or naturalized citizen of Spain.

span'iel, 1 span'yel; 2 spăn'yĕl, *n.* A dog having pendulous ears and silky hair.

Span'ish, 1 span'ish; 2 spăn'ish. **I.** *a.* Pertaining to Spain, the Spaniards, or their language. **II.** *n.* The language of Spain.

spank, 1 spaŋk; 2 spăŋk, *v.* [SPANKEDᵗ, SPANKTˢ; SPANK'ING.] **I.** *t.* To slap smartly. **II.** *i.* To move briskly.— **spank'er,** *n.* **1.** One who or that which spanks. **2.** *Naut.* A fore-and-aft sail on the mizzenmast.— **spank'ing,** *pa.* Moving rapidly; swift; dashing.

spa-ghet'ti, 1 spə-get'ı; 2 spa-gĕt'i, *n.* **1.** [It.] An Italian cord-like flour paste, intermediate in size between macaroni and vermicelli. **2.** *Radio.* An insulated tube through which wiring is passed.

spar¹, 1 spär; 2 spär, *vt.* [SPARRED, SPARDˢ; SPAR'RING.] To furnish with spars.

spar², *vi.* To engage in boxing.

spar¹, *n.* A round timber for extending a sail; a mast, yard, boom, or the like.

spar², *n.* A vitreous, lustrous mineral.

spare, 1 spār; 2 spâr, *v.* [SPARED; SPAR'ING.] **I.** *t.* **1.** To use frugally. **2.** To forbear to injure. **3.** To dispense with; bestow. **II.** *i.* **1.** To be lenient; refrain. **2.** To be frugal. **-ness,** *n.*— **spar'ing.** **I.** *a.* **1.** Scanty; slight. **2.** Bent on saving; frugal; parsimonious. **II.** *n.* Parsimony; frugality. **-ly,** *adv.* **-ness,** *n.*

spare, *a.* **1.** That can be spared. **2.** Held in reserve. **3.** Thin; lean. **4.** Not abundant.— **spare'rib",** *n.* A piece of pork consisting of ribs somewhat closely trimmed.

spark¹, 1 spärk; 2 spärk. **I⁵.** *vt.* & *vi.* To sparkle. **II.** *n.* A luminous particle thrown off from a burning body.— **spark'gap",** *n.* In various forms of electric machines, the space between the electrodes across which the electric discharge leaps.— **s.-plug,** *n.* In motor-engines with electric ignition, a plug screwed into the cylinder-head or body and containing insulated wires connecting the source of current with the spark gap within the cylinder. [A lover; suitor.

spark². **I.** *vt.* & *vi.* To woo; court. **II.** *n.*

spar'kl(eᴾ, 1 spär'kl; 2 spär'kl. **I.** *vt.* & *vi.* [SPAR'KL(E)Dᴾ; SPAR'KLING.] To emit sparks; flash. **II.** *n.* A spark; gleam.

spar'row, 1 spar'o; 2 spăr'o, *n.* One of various small plainly colored birds.— **spar'row-hawk",** *n.* A small hawk that preys on sparrows.

sparse, 1 spärs; 2 spärs, *a.* Thinly scattered. **-sparse'ly,** *adv.*- **sparse'ness,** *n.*

Spar'tan, 1 spär'tan; 2 spär'tᵊn; 2 spär'tan. **I.** *a.* Pertaining to Sparta in ancient Greece, or to the Spartans; heroically brave and enduring. **II.** *n.* A native or citizen of Sparta; a brave and enduring person.

Sparrow-hawk. ¹⁄₁₂

spasm, 1 spazm; 2 spăṣm, *n.* A convulsion.— **spas-mod'ic,** *a.* Of the nature of a spasm; impulsive.— **spas-mod'l-cal-ly,** *adv.*

spat¹, 1 spat; 2 spăt. **I.** *vt.* & *vi.* [SPAT'TEDᵈ; SPAT'TING.] To spawn, as shell-fish. **II.** *n.* Shell-fish spawn; a young oyster.

spat². **I**ᵈ. *vt.* & *vi.* [U.S.] To slap lightly; quarrel. **II.** *n.* **1.** A slight blow; petty quarrel. **2.** A splash.

spat'ter, 1 spat'ᵊr; 2 spăt'er. **I.** *vt.* & *vi.* To sprinkle in drops. **II.** *n.* The act of spattering; a pattering noise.

spav'in, 1 spav'in; 2 spăv'in, *n.* A disease of the hock-joint of horses, stiffening the joint.— **spav'in(e)dˢ,** *a.*

spawn, 1 spôn; 2 spạn. **I.** *vt.* & *vi.* **1.** To deposit eggs or roe. **2.** To produce as offspring. **II.** *n.* **1.** The eggs of fishes, mollusks, etc. **2.** Product; yield.

speak, 1 spīk; 2 spēk, *v.* [SPOKE (SPAKE‖); SPO'KEN; SPEAK'ING.] **I.** *t.* To utter, as a word; articulate; make known; reveal. **II.** *i.* To talk; make a speech.— **speak'er,** *n.* **1.** One who speaks; an orator. **2.** [S-] The presiding officer of a legislative body.— **Speak'er-ship,** *n.*— **speak'ing,** *pa.* Expressive; vivid; telling.

spear, 1 spīr; 2 spēr, *v.* **I.** *t.* To pierce with a spear. **II.** *i.* To send forth spires, as a plant.

spear, *n.* **1.** A weapon for throwing or thrusting, consisting of a pointed head on a long shaft. **2.** A spire, as of grass.— **spear'mint",** *n.* An aromatic herb.

spe'cial, 1 spesh'əl; 2 spĕsh'al,*a.* Singular; unique; particular; specific; differential. **-spe'cial-ist,** *n.* A person devoted to some one line of study or work.— **spe"ci-al'l-ty,** 1 spesh"ı-al'ı-tı; 2 spĕ"sh⁼i-ăl'i-ty, *n.* [-TIESᶻ, *pl.*] Specific or individual character; peculiarity.— **spe'cial-ize** or **-ise,** *v.* [-IZED; -IZ'-ING.]— **spe'cial-ly,** 1 spesh'al-ı; 2 spĕsh'al-y.

adv. **1.** In a special manner; particularly. **2.** For a specific purpose.— **spe'cial-ty,** 1 spesh'al-tı; 2 sĕsh'al-ty, *n.* [-TIES², *pl.*] A special occupation or study; an article chiefly dealt in. [money.

spe'cie, 1 spī'shı; 2 spē'shi, *n.* Coined **ſpe'cies,** 1 spī'shīz *or* spī'shı-īz; 2 spē'shēs *or* spē'shi-ēs, *n. sing. & pl.* **1.** A group of animals or plants subordinate to a genus. **2.** A kind; sort.

spe-cif'ic, 1 spı-sif'ık; 2 spe-çif'ie. **I.** *a.* **1.** Definite; particular; special. **2.** Pertaining to a species. **II.** *n.* A remedy for a particular disease.— **spe-cif'i-cal,** *a.*— **spe-cif'i-cal-ly,** *adv.*

spec'i-fy, 1 spes'ı-faı; 2 spĕç'i-fȳ, *vt.* [-FIED; -FY'ING.] To state in explicit terms; mention particulars.— **spec"i-fi-ca'tion,** 1 spes'ı-fı-kē'shan; 2 spĕç'i-fi-eā'shon, *n.* **1.** The act of specifying. **2.** A statement of particulars; a particular specified.

spec'i-men, 1 spes'ı-men; 2 spĕç'i-mĕn, *n.* One of a class of persons or things regarded as representative of the class; a sample.

spe'cious, 1 spī'shus; 2 spē'shŭs, *a.* Appearing right and true; plausible. **-ly,** *adv.* **-ness,** *n.*

speck, 1 spek; 2 spĕk. **I**ᵗ. *vt.* To spot; speckle. **II.** *n.* A small spot; a little stain; any very small thing.— **speck'l(e**ᵖ. **I.** *vt.* [SPECK'LED, SPECK'LD²; SPECK'LING.] To besprinkle with spots. **II.** *n.* A speck.

spec'ta-cle, } 1 spes'ta-kl; 2 spĕe'ta-cl, *n.*
spec'ta-cl², } **1.** Something exhibited to public view. **2.** *pl.* A pair of glasses, with hinged bows, to secure them before the eyes.— **spec-tac'u-lar,** 1 spek-tak'yu-lər; 2 spĕe-tăc'yu-lar, *a.* Characterized by grand scenic display.— **spec-tac'(e)d**ᵖ, *a.*

spec-ta'tor, 1 spek-tē'tər *or* -ter; 2 spĕe-tā'tor, *n.* One who looks on; an eyewitness.— **spec-ta'tress,** *n. fem.*

spec'ter, } 1 spek'tər; 2 spĕe'ter, *n.* A
spec'tre, } ghost; apparition.— **spec'tral,** *a.* Pertaining to the spectrum or to a specter; ghostly.

spec'tro-scope, 1 spek'tro-skōp; 2 spĕe'tro-seōp, *n.* An optical instrument for forming and analyzing the spectra of the rays emitted by various substances.— **spec"tro-scop'ic,** *a.*

spec'trum, 1 spek'trum; 2 spĕe'trŭm, *n.* [SPEC'TRA, *pl.*] An image formed by rays of light refracted, as through a prism, displaying the colors of the rainbow.

spec'u-lar, 1 spek'yu-lər; 2 spĕe'yu-lar, *a.* Pertaining to a mirror; reflecting.

spec'u-late, 1 spek'yu-lēt; 2 spĕe'yu-lāt, *vi.* [-LAT'ED**ᵈ; -LAT'ING.**] **1.** To theorize;

conjecture. **2.** To make a venturesome investment with hope of gain.— **spec"u-la'tion,** *n.* **1.** The act of theorizing; a theory. **2.** A more or less risky investment.— **spec"u-la-tiv(e³,** *a.* Pertaining to or involving speculation. **-ly,** *adv.*— **spec'u-la"tor,** *n.* One who speculates, in any sense.

spec'u-lum, 1 spek'yu-lum; 2 spĕe'yu-lŭm, *n.* [-LA, *pl.*] A mirror of polished metal, or glass.

sped, 1 sped; 2 spĕd, *imp. & pp.* of SPEED, *v.*

speech, 1 spīch; 2 spēch, *n.* **1.** The power of speaking; a public address; discourse. **2.** A language.— **speech'less,** *a.* Mute; dumb.

speed, 1 spīd; 2 spēd. **I.** *vt. & vi.* [SPED *or* SPEED'ED**ᵈ; SPEED'ING.**] To urge or move on swiftly; expedite; dispatch. **II.** *n.* **1.** Celerity; swiftness. **2.** Rate of motion; degree of prosperity.— **speed-om'e-ter,** 1 spīd-om'ı-tər; 2 spēd-ŏm'e-ter, *n.* An indicator of speed, as for a motor-car.— **speed'y,** *a.* [SPEED'I-ER; SPEED'I-EST.] Swift; immediate.— **speed'i-ly,** *adv.*— **speed'i-ness,** *n.*

spell, 1 spel; 2 spĕl, *v.* [SPELLED *or* SPELT; **spel**ᵖ, } SPELD³; SPELL'ING.] **I.** *t.* **1.** To give the letters of (a word) in their order. **2.** To decipher. **3.** To fascinate; bewitch. **II.** *i.* To frame words out of letters.— **spell'er,** *n.* **1.** One who spells. **2.** A spelling-book.— **spell'ing,** *n.* **1.** The act of one who spells; orthography. **2.** The way in which a word is spelled.— **spell'ing-book**, *n.* A book of exercises in spelling.

spell, *n.* **1.** A turn of duty in relief of another. **2.** Any short period of time.

spell², *n.* An incantation; charm; fascination.— **spell'bound**, *a.* Bound as by a spell.

spelt, 1 spelt; 2 spĕlt, *n.* A cereal intermediate between wheat and barley.

spend, 1 spend; 2 spĕnd, *v.* [SPENT, SPEND'ING.] **I.** *t.* **1.** To pay out, as money, in making purchases. **2.** To squander; waste. **3.** To pass or employ, as time. **4.** To exhaust; use up. **II.** *i.* **1.** To pay out money. **2.** To waste or wear away.— **spend'er,** *n.*— **spend'thrift**, *n.* One who is wastefully lavish of money.

sperm, 1 spūrm; 2 spĕrm, *n.* **1.** A sperm-whale. **2.** Spermaceti.— **sperm'-oil",** *n.* Oil obtained from sperm-whale blubber.— **s.-whale,** *n.* A whale of warm seas.

sper"ma-ce'ti, 1 spūr"mə-sī'tı *or* -set'ı; 2 spĕr"ma-çē'ti *or* -çĕt'i, *n.* A white, brittle, fatty substance contained in the head of the sperm-whale.

spew, 1 spiū; 2 spū, *vt. & vi.* To vomit up; vomit; cast forth. **spue‡.**

sphere, } 1 sfīr; 2 sfer. **I.** *vt.* [SPHERED; **sfere**ᵖ, } SPHER'ING.] To place in a sphere; make spherical; encircle. **II.** *n.* **1.** A

solid every part of whose surface is equidistant from a point within called the center; a globe; planet; star. **2.** Field of action, influence, or existence.— **spher′al,** *a.*— **spher′ic,** 1 sfer′ĭk; 2 sfẽr′ĭc, *a.* **1.** Pertaining to the heavenly bodies; hence, celestial. **2.** Spherical.— **spher′i-cal,** *a.* **1.** Shaped like a sphere; globular. **2.** Pertaining to a sphere.— **spher′i-cal-ly,** *adv.*— **sphe-ric′i-ty,** 1 sfĭ-rĭs′ĭ-tĭ; 2 sfe-rĭç′ĭ-ty, *n.* The state of being a sphere.— **sphe′roid,** 1 sfī′roid; 2 sfe′rŏĭd, *n.* A body having nearly the form of a sphere.— **sphe-roi′dal,** *a.*— **spher′ule,** 1 sfer′ul; 2 sfẽr′ŭl, *n.* A minute sphere; globule.

sphinx, ⎱ 1 sfĭŋks; 2 sfĭŋks, *n.* [SPHINX′ES
sfinxᴾ, ⎰ or SPHIN′GES, 1 -ez or sfĭn′jīz; 2-ĕş or sfĭn′ğĕş, *pl.*] **1.** [s- or S-] *Gr. Myth.* A winged monster that destroyed those unable to guess riddles she propounded. **2.** A moth. **hawk′₌moth″‡.**

spice, 1 spais; 2 spīç. **I.** *vt.* [SPICED‡; SPIC′ING] To season with spice; add zest to. **II.** *n.* **1.** An aromatic vegetable substance, used to flavor food and beverages. **2.** That which gives zest or adds interest. — **spic′y,** *a.* [SPIC′I-ER; SPIC′I-EST.] **1.** Containing, flavored, or fragrant with spices. **2.** Producing spices. **3.** Piquant; vivid.— **spic′i-ly,** *adv.*— **spic′i-ness,** *n.*

spi′der, 1 spai′dər; 2 spī′der, *n.* **1.** An insect₌like creature that makes webs to catch its prey. **2.** One of various implements, as a long₌handled frying₌pan.

spig′ot, 1 spĭg′ət; 2 spĭg′ot, *n.* A plug or faucet for a cask.

spike, 1 spaik; 2 spīk. **I.** *vt.* [SPIKED‡; SPIK′ING] To fasten or provide with spikes; stop with a spike, as the vent of a cannon; disable. **II.** *n.* **1.** A stout, large nail. **2.** An ear, as of grain. **3.** An elongated flower₌cluster.

spike′nard, 1 spaik′nərd; 2 spīk′nard, *n.* An ancient fragrant and costly ointment, or a plant of the same name.

spile, 1 spail; 2 spīl, *n.* **1.** A large timber driven into the ground to serve as a foundation; a pile. **2.** A spigot.

spill, ⎱ 1 spil; 2 spĭl, *v.* [SPILLED OR SPILT,
spillᴾ, ⎰ SPILD⁸; SPILL′ING.] **I.** *t.* To suffer to run out, as a liquid; shed. **II.** *i.* To run out; be wasted.— **spill′er,** *n.*

spin, 1 spin; 2 spĭn. **I.** *vt. & vi.* [SPUN,

Common Spider. ½

formerly SPAN; SPUN; SPIN′NING.] **1.** To draw out and twist into threads. **2.** To form, as thread, by drawing out and twisting. **3.** To compose; tell. **4.** To whirl; twirl. **II.** *n.* An act of spinning; a rapid whirling.— **spin′ner,** *n.*

spin′ach, ⎱ 1 spĭn′ĭj; 2 spĭn′aġ, *n.* A gar-
spin′age, ⎰ den pot₌herb or its fleshy leaves.

spin′dle, ⎱ 1 spin′dl; 2 spĭn′dl. **I.** *vi.*
spin′dlᴾ, ⎰ [SPIN′DL(E)Dᴾ; SPIN′DLING.] To grow long and slender. **II.** *n.* A slender rod or pin, on which thread may be wound, as spun.

spine, 1 spain; 2 spīn, *n.* **1.** The back-bone. **2.** *Bot.* A thorn.— **spi′nal,** 1 spai′-nal; 2 spī′nal, *a.* **1.** Pertaining to the back-bone. **2.** Pertaining to a thorn; thorny.— **spin′y,** *a.* [SPIN′I-ER; SPIN′I-EST.] Having spines; thorny. **spi′nose‡; spi′nous‡.**— **spin′i-ness,** *n.*

spin′ster, 1 spin′stər; 2 spĭn′ster, *n.* An unmarried woman.

spi′ral, 1 spai′ral; 2 spī′ral. **I.** *a.* Winding and receding from a center; winding and advancing. **II.** *n.* Anything of spiral form.— **spi′ral-ly,** *adv.*

spire[1], 1 spair; 2 spīr, *n.* The tapering top of a tower; a steeple; a slender stalk, as of grass.

spire[2], *n.* A spiral; whorl; twist.

spir′it, 1 spir′it; 2 spĭr′it. **I**ᵈ**.** *vt.* To carry off; kidnap; followed by *away.* **II.** *n.* **1.** The part of man that is capable of thought, feeling, and will; the soul. **2.** A rational being not embodied; the Deity or the third person of the Trinity, called the *Holy Spirit.* **3.** A ghost. **4.** Ardor; dash. **5.** Distilled liquor, especially alcohol.— **spir′it-ed,** *a.* Full of spirit; animated. **-ly,** *adv.* **-ness,** *n.*— **spir′it-less,** *a.* Having no spirit; listless; dead. **-ly,** *adv.*

spir′i-tu-al, 1 spir′ĭ-chu-[or -it-yu-]əl; 2 spĭr′i-chu-[or -it-yu-]al, *a.* **1.** Pertaining to spirit. **2.** Affecting the soul. **3.** Coming from the Divine Spirit; holy; pure; sacred; religious. **-ly,** *adv.*— **spir′i-tu-al-ism,** *n.* **1.** The belief that departed spirits communicate with men. **2.** *Philos.* **3.** The doctrine of spiritual existences. **3.** The state of being spiritual.— **spir′i-tu-al-ist,** *n.*— **spir′i-tu-al-is′tic,** *a.*— **spir″i-tu-al′i-ty,** *n.* [-TIES²*, pl.*] The state of being spiritual. — **spir′i-tu-al-ize,** *vt.* [-IZED‡; -IZ′ING.] To render spiritual. **spir′it-u-al-ise‡.**

spir″i-tu-elle′, 1 spir′i-tiu-el′; 2 spĭr′i-tū-ĕl′, *a.* Refined; graceful and delicate: said of women.

spir′i-tu-ous, 1 spir′i-chu-[or -it-yu-]us; 2 spĭr′i-chu-[or -it-yu-]ŭs, *a.* Containing alcohol; distilled, as liquor.

spirt, *v. & n.* Same as SPURT.

1: ə = *final;* **ɪ =** *habit;* **aisle; au =** *out;* **oil; ɪū =** *feud;* **c͡hin; go; ŋ =** *si*n**g;** **t͡hin, this.**
2: wolf, dǫ; bōŏk, bōŏt; fŭll, rŭle, cūre, bŭt, bûrn; ŏil, bŏy; ġo, ğem; iŋk; thin, this.

spit¹, 1 spit; 2 spĭt. **I.** *vt.* & *vi.* [SPIT; SPAT: formerly sometimes SPĬT'TED^d; SPĬT'TING.] **1.** To eject from the mouth; eject saliva. **2.** To come down in drops or flakes. **II.** *n.* **1.** Spittle; saliva. **2.** An act of spitting.— **spit'tle,** *n.* The fluid secreted by the glands of the mouth; saliva; spit.— **spit-toon',** *n.* A receptacle for expectorations.

spit². **I.** *vt.* [SPĬT'TED^d; SPĬT'TING.] To transfix with a spit; string on a stick. **II.** *n.* **1.** A pointed rod on which meat may be turned and roasted. **2.** A point of low land extending into the water.

spite, 1 spaɪt; 2 spīt. **I.** *vt.* [SPĪT'ED^d; SPĪT'ING.] To vex maliciously; thwart. **II.** *n.* Malicious bitterness; grudge; a malicious and vexatious act.— **spite'ful,** *a.* Filled with spite; prompted by spite. **-ly,** *adv.* **-ness,** *n.*

spitz, 1 spits; 2 spĭts, *n.* One of a breed of small Pomeranian dogs with a tapering muzzle. **spitz'-dog'**‡.

splash, 1 splæʃ; 2 splăsh. **I**ᵗ. *vt.* & *vi.* **1.** To make a splash. **2.** To spatter, wet, or soil with a liquid. **II.** *n.* **1.** The act or noise of splashing. **2.** A spot made by a liquid splashed on.— **splash'y,** *a.* Slushy; wet.

splay, 1 sple; 2 splā, *a.* Spread out; displayed; broad and clumsy, as a foot.— **splay'foot',** *a.* Having splay feet. **splay's-foot'ed**‡.

spleen, 1 splin; 2 splēn, *n.* **1.** An organ found in most vertebrates, near the stomach, that modifies the blood. **2.** Ill-temper; spitefulness; melancholy.

splen'did, 1 splen'dɪd; 2 splĕn'dĭd, *a.* Brilliant; magnificent; imposing; illustrious.— **splen'did-ly,** *adv.*— **splen'dor,** *n.* Exceeding brilliancy; magnificence; pomp.

sple-net'ic, 1 splɪ-net'ɪk *or* splen'ɪ-tɪk; 2 sple-nĕt'ĭc *or* splĕn'e-tĭc. **I.** *a.* **1.** Pertaining to the spleen. **2.** Spiteful; peevish. **II.** *n.* A peevish person.— **sple-net'i-cal-ly,** *adv.*

splice, 1 splaɪs; 2 splīç. **I.** *vt.* [SPLICED^t; SPLIC'ING.] To unite so as to form one piece. **II.** *n.* A union of the ends of joined parts; a uniting of ropes by intertwining the strands.

splint, 1 splint; 2 splĭnt. **I**^d. *vt.* To confine with splints, as a fractured limb. **II.** *n.* A thin strip, as of wood, to hold a fractured limb in place; any thin flat piece; splinter.

splin'ter, 1 splin'tər; 2 splĭn'ter. **I.** *vt.* & *vi.* **1.** To separate into splinters; split. **2.** To support by splints. **II.** *n.* A small sharp piece split off from a solid body.

split, 1 split; 2 splĭt. **I.** *vt.* & *vi.* [SPLIT or SPLIT'TED^d; SPLIT'TING.] To divide lengthwise; tear asunder; rend; separate. **II.** *n.* The act or result of splitting; a fissure; rupture; schism.

splut'ter, 1 splʌt'ər; 2 splŭt'er. **I.** *vt.* & *vi.* To speak hastily and confusedly. **II.** *n.* A spluttering sound or utterance.

spoil, 1 spɔɪl; 2 spŏil. **I.** *vt.* & *vi.* [SPOILED or SPOILT, SPOILD^s; SPOIL'ING.] **1.** To make worthless; taint or become tainted. **2.** To rob; despoil. **II.** *n.* Plunder; booty. [SPEAK, *v.*

spoke, 1 spōk; 2 spŏk, spo'ken, *imp.* & *pp.* of

spoke, *n.* **1.** One of the bars joining the hub to the rim of a wheel. **2.** The rung of a ladder.

spokes'man, 1 spōks'mən; 2 spŏks'man. [-MEN, *pl.*] One who speaks for others.

spo"li-a'tion, 1 spo"lɪ-e'shən; 2 spŏ"lĭ-ā'shon, *n.* The act of pillaging; destruction.— **spo"li-a"tor,** *n.*

sponge, 1 spʌndʒ; 2 spŏng, *v.* [SPONGED; spunge^r, SPONG'ING.] **I.** *t.* **1.** To cleanse or absorb with a sponge. **2.** To get at another's expense. **II.** *i.* To depend meanly on another.

sponge. *n.* **1.** A fixed marine animal with porous body or its skeleton of elastic fibers. **2.** Leavened dough. **3.** One who lives at the expense of another.— **spong'y,** *a.* [SPONG'I-ER; SPONG'I-EST.] Like a sponge; elastic; porous.— **spong'i-ness,** *n.*

spon'sor, 1 spɒn'sər; 2 spŏn'sor. **I.** *vt.* To answer or vouch for; to perform the duties of sponsor. **II.** *n.* One who answers for another; a godfather or godmother.— **spon-so'ri-al,** *a.*— **spon'sor-ship,** *n.*

spon-ta'ne-ous, 1 spɒn-te'nɪ-us; 2 spŏn-tā'ne-ŭs, *a.* **1.** Done or acting from one's own impulse; voluntary. **2.** Indigenous. **3.** *Biol.* Arising without external cause; self-produced. **-ly,** *adv.* **-ness,** *n.*— **spon"ta-ne'i-ty,** 1 spɒn'tə-nī'ɪ-tɪ; 2 spŏn"ta-nē'ĭ-ty, *n.* [-TIES^z, *pl.*] Spontaneous quality; freedom.

spool, 1 spul; 2 spŏol, *n.* **1.** A small cylinder upon which thread or the like may be wound. **2.** The quantity of thread held by a spool.

spoon, 1 spun; 2 spŏon. **I.** *vt.* To dip out with a spoon. **II.** *n.* A utensil having a shallow bowl and a handle, used in serving or eating food.— **spoon'ful,** *n.* [SPOON'FULS, *pl.*] The quantity that a spoon will hold.

spoor, 1 spur; 2 spŏor, *n.* [S.-Afr. D.] A track, trail, or other trace of a wild animal.

spo-rad'ic, 1 spo-rad'ɪk; 2 spo-răd'ĭc, *a.* Occurring here and there; isolated.

spore, 1 spɔr; 2 spŏr, *n.* A minute grain

1: **artistic, ärt; fat, fãre; fast; get, prẽy; hĭt, police; obey, gō; net, ôr; full, rūle; but, būrn.**
2: **ärt, āpe, făt, fãre, făst, whạt, ạll; mē, gĕt, prey, fẽrn; hĭt, īce; ĭ=ĕ; ĭ=ẽ; gō, nŏt, ôr, wŏn,**

serving as a seed of a flowerless plant; a germ.

sportd, 1 spŏrt; 2 spôrt, v. **I.** t. To display ostentatiously. **II.** i. To play; frolic; jest.

sport, n. Diversion; pastime; a game or play; pleasantry; raillery.— **spor'tiv**(es), a. Relating to or fond of sport; playful. **-ly,** adv. **-ness,** n.— **sports'man,** n. [-MEN, pl.] A person who is fond of field-sports, as hunting and fishing.— **sports'man-like,** a.— **sports'-man-ship,** n. The art or practise of field-sports.

spot, 1 spot; 2 spŏt. **I.** vt. & vi. [SPOT'-TED d; SPOT'TING.] To mark with spots; stain. **II.** n. **1.** A place or space of small extent; a locality. **2.** A stain; blemish; reproach.— **spot'less,** a. Free from spot or stain; innocent; pure. **-ly,** adv. **-ness,** n.— **spot'ty,** a. [wife.

spouse, 1 spauz; 2 spous, n. A husband or

spout, 1 spaut; 2 spout. **I**d. vt. & vi. To pour out copiously; declaim. **II.** n. A tube, etc., for the discharge of a liquid.

sprain, 1 sprēn; 2 sprān. **I.** vt. To cause a sprain in. **II.** n. A straining or twisting of the ligaments surrounding a joint.

sprang, imp. of SPRING, v. [fish.

sprat, 1 sprat; 2 sprăt, n. A herring-like

sprawl, 1 sprôl; 2 sprạl. **I.** vt. & vi. To lie or move with the limbs stretched out ungracefully. **II.** n. The act or position of sprawling.— **sprawl'ing,** pa.

spray, 1 sprē; 2 sprā, vt. & vi. To disperse (a liquid) in fine particles.

spray[1], n. **1.** Water or other liquid dispersed in fine particles. **2.** An atomizer.

spray[2], n. A small branch; a twig.

spread, } 1 spred; 2 sprĕd. **I.** vt. & vi.
spreds, } [SPREAD; SPREAD'ING.] To extend over; distribute about; publish; expand; unfold; be dispersed or separated. **II.** n. **1.** The act of spreading; an open expanse; extent. **2.** A covering. **3.** [Colloq.] A banquet.

spree, 1 sprī; 2 sprē. **I.** vi. To get drunk. **II.** n. **1.** A drunken carousal. **2.** A gay frolic. [twig.

sprig, 1 sprig; 2 sprĭg, n. A small shoot or

spright'ly } 1 sprait'lı; 2 sprīt'ly, a.
sprite'ly,P } [SPRIGHT'LI-ER; SPRIGHT'LI-EST.] Animated; vivacious; lively.— **spright'li-ness,** n.

spring, 1 spriŋ; 2 sprĭng, v. [SPRANG or SPRUNG; SPRUNG; SPRING'ING.] **I.** t. **1.** To release the spring of, as a trap. **2.** To do or cause to act unexpectedly and suddenly. **3.** To bend forcibly; strain. **II.** i. **1.** To bound; move suddenly. **2.**

To proceed; originate. **3.** To be warped or bent.

spring, n. **1.** An elastic body or contrivance that yields under stress and flies back when the stress is removed. **2.** Elastic quality or energy; recoil. **3.** A jump; bound. **4.** The season in which vegetation starts anew. **5.** A flow or fountain, as of water; a source; origin.— **spring'-tide",** n. **1.** The season of spring; springtime. **2.** A specially high tide that occurs a few days after every new and every full moon, because the attraction of the moon and of the sun are then combined. **3.** Some great flood of feeling, opinion, or influence.— **spring'time",** 1 spriŋ'taim"; 2 spring'tĭm", n. The season of spring.— **spring'y,** a. [SPRING'I-ER; SPRING'I-EST.] **1.** Elastic. **2.** Spongy; wet.— **spring'i-ness,** n.

springe, 1 sprinj; 2 sprĭng, n. A snare.

sprin'kl(eP, 1 spriŋ'kl; 2 sprĭng'kl. **I.** vt. & vi. [SPRIN'KL(E)Df; SPRIN'KLING.] To scatter in drops or small particles; rain in scattering drops. **II.** n. A sprinkling; hence, a small quantity.— **sprin'kler,** n.

sprint, 1 sprint; 2 sprĭnt. **I.** vt. To run, as in a sprint. **II.** n. A short race run at the top of one's speed.— **sprint'er,** n.

sprit, 1 sprit; 2 sprĭt, n. **1.** A small spar for stretching a sail. **2.** The bowsprit.— **sprit'sail,** n. A sail extended by a sprit.

sprite, 1 sprait; 2 sprīt, n. A fairy; elf; goblin.

sprock'et, 1 sprok'et; 2 sprŏk'ĕt, n. **1.** A projection on the rim of a wheel, for engaging with the links of a chain. **2.** A wheel bearing such projections.— **sprock'et=wheel",** n. A wheel with sprockets, as on a bicycle.

sproutd, 1 spraut; 2 sprout, v. **I.** t. To cause to put forth shoots. **II.** i. **1.** To develop shoots. **2.** To grow.

Sprocket (s).

sprout, n. A new shoot or bud on a plant.

spruce, 1 sprūs; 2 sprụç, vt. & vi. [SPRUCED t; SPRUC'ING.] To make oneself spruce. **-ly,** adv. **-ness,** n. [ance.

spruce, a. Having a smart, trim appear-

spruce, n. A cone=bearing evergreen tree; also, its wood.— **spruce'fir",** n.

sprung, 1 spruŋ; 2 sprŭng, imp. & pp. of SPRING, v. [agile.

spry, 1 sprai; 2 sprȳ, a. Quick and active;

spue, vt. & vi. Same as SPEW.

spume, 1 spiūm; 2 spūm. **I.** vi. [SPUMED;

SPUM′ING.] To froth; foam. **II.** *n.*
Froth; scum.— **spu′mous,** *a.* **spum′y†**.

spu-mo′ne, 1 spiu-mō′nē; 2 spū-mō′ne, [-ni, *pl.*] A confection, as of ice-cream or water-ice, containing fruit, nuts, etc.

spun, 1 spun; 2 spŭn, *imp.* & *pp.* of SPIN, *v.*

spunk, 1 spuŋk; 2 spŭnk, *n.* **1.** [Colloq.] Quick, ardent temper; courage. **2.** Punk. — **spunk′y,** *a.* [SPUNK′I-ER; SPUNK′I-EST.] [Colloq.] Spirited; courageous; touchy.

spur, 1 spūr; 2 spûr. **I.** *vt.* [SPURRED, SPURD⁸; SPUR′RING.] **1.** To urge on by the spur. **2.** To furnish with spurs. **II.** *n.* **1.** A pricking or goading instrument worn on a horseman's heel. **2.** Anything that incites or urges. **3.** A stiff sharp spine, as on the leg of a domestic cock. **4.** A projecting crag, ridge, or the like.

spu′ri-ous, 1 spiū′rɪ-us; 2 spū′ri-ŭs, *a.* Not genuine; counterfeit. **-ly,** *adv.* **-ness,** *n.*

spurn, 1 spûrn; 2 spûrn, *vt.* **1.** To reject with disdain. **2.** To kick.

spurt¹, 1 spûrt; 2 spûrt. **I**ᵈ. *vt.* & *vi.* To force out or come forth in a jet; squirt. **II.** *n.* A sudden gush of liquid.

spurt². **I**ᵈ. *vi.* To make a sudden and extreme effort. **II.** *n.* An extraordinary effort of brief duration.

sput′ter, 1 sput′ər; 2 spŭt′er. **I.** *vt.* & *vi.* **1.** To spit out with vehemence and irregular noise. **2.** To speak in a confused, explosive way. **II.** *n.* A sputtering.

spy, 1 spai; 2 spy, *v.* [SPIED; SPY′ING.] **I.** *t.* To see by looking carefully or secretly; discover; discern. **II.** *i.* To act as a spy; investigate; pry.— **spy′-glass″,** *n.* A small terrestrial telescope.

spy, *n.* [SPIES″, *pl.*] **1.** One who enters an enemy's lines covertly to get information. **2.** One who watches others secretly.

squab, 1 skwob; 2 skwąb. **I.** *a.* Fat and short; half-grown. **II.** *n.* A young pigeon; a fat, short person.

squab′ble, 1 skwob′l; 2 skwąb′l. **I.** *vi.* [SQUAB′BLED; SQUAB′BLING.] To quarrel. **II.** *n.* The act of squabbling; a wrangle. — **squab′bler,** *n.*— **squab′bling,** *pa.* & *n.*

squad, 1 skwod; 2 skwąd, *n.* A small detachment of troops or police.

squad′ron, 1 skwod′rən; 2 skwąd′ron, *n.* **1.** An assemblage of war-vessels smaller than a fleet. **2.** A division of a cavalry regiment. **3.** A number of military aeroplanes.

squal′id, 1 skwol′ɪd; 2 skwąl′id, *a.* Dirty, mean, and poverty-stricken.— **squal′id-ly,** *adv.*— **squal′id-ness,** *n.*

squall, 1 skwôl; 2 skwąl. *vt.* & *vi.* To cry loudly, as an angry child.

squall¹, *n.* A loud, screaming outcry.

squall², *n.* A sudden burst of wind.— **squall′y,** *a.* Stormy; blustering.

squal′or, 1 skwel′ər or skwē′ɪər; 2 skwąl′or or skwā′lor, *n.* The state of being squalid.

squan′der, 1 skwon′dər; 2 skwąn′dêr, *vt.* & *vi.* To spend money, etc., lavishly and wastefully.— **squan′der-er,** *n.*

square, 1 skwâr; 2 skwâr, *v.* [SQUARED; SQUAR′ING.] **I.** *t.* **1.** To make square; multiply by itself. **2.** To balance, as accounts; settle; make even. **3.** To cause to conform; adapt. **II.** *i.* **1.** To be at right angles. **2.** To fit; agree.

square, *a.* **1.** Being a square. **2.** Characterized by a right angle. **3.** Just; equitable. **4.** Balanced; even. **5.** Absolute. **6.** Solid; satisfying. **-ly,** *adv.* **-ness,** *n.*

square, *n.* **1.** A figure having four equal sides and four right angles. **2.** Any object that is square. **3.** An instrument by which to measure or lay out right angles. **4.** A block or an open space, as in a city.

squash¹, 1 skwosh; 2 skwąsh, *n.* The fleshy edible fruit of a trailing plant; also, the plant.— **squash′-bee″tle,** *n.* A small American beetle, striped with yellow and black, that feeds upon the squash and similar plants.— **s.-borer,** *n.* The larva of a moth that bores into the stems of squashes.— **s.-bug,** *n.* A large, brownish-black North-American bug, destructive to squash-vines by sucking the sap of the stem.

squash², *n.* **1.** A soft or mashed object. **2.** The sudden fall of a heavy, soft, or bursting body.— **squash′y,** *a.*

squat, 1 skwot; 2 skwąt. **I.** *vt.* & *vi.* [SQUAT′TED⁴ or SQUAT; SQUAT′TING.] **1.** To crouch in a sitting posture. **2.** To settle on a piece of land without right. **II.** *a.* **1.** Short and thick. **2.** Being in a squatting position. **III.** *n.* A squatting attitude.— **squat′ter,** *n.*

squaw, 1 skwô; 2 skwą, *n.* An American Indian woman.

squawk, 1 skwôk; 2 skwąk. **I**ᵗ. *vi.* To utter a squawk. **II.** *n.* A harsh cry, as of certain birds.

squeak, 1 skwīk; 2 skwēk. **I**ᵗ. *vt.* & *vi.* To utter with a squeak; make a squeak. **II.** *n.* A thin, sharp, penetrating sound.

squeal, 1 skwīl; 2 skwēl. **I.** *vi.* To utter a sharp, shrill, somewhat prolonged cry. **II.** *n.* A shrill cry, as of a pig.

squeam′ish, 1 skwīm′ɪsh; 2 skwēm′ish, *a.* Easily disgusted; unduly scrupulous. **-ly,** *adv.* **-ness,** *n.*

squeeze, 1 skwīz; 2 skwēz, *v.* [SQUEEZ(E)D⁸; SQUEEZ′ING.] **I.** *t.* **1.** To press closely; compress. **2.** To draw forth by

pressure. **3.** To crowd. **II. i.** To force one's way by pressing; push.

squeeze, *n.* The act of squeezing.

squelcht, 1 skwelċh; 2 skwĕlĉh, *vt. & vi.* To disconcert; be crushed or subdued.

squib, 1 skwib; 2 skwĭb, *n.* **1.** A mild lampoon; pithy paragraph. **2.** A tube filled with gunpowder. [cuttlefish.

squid, 1 skwid; 2 skwĭd, *n.* A ten=armed

squill¹, 1 skwil; 2 skwĭl, *n.* The sliced bulb of a medicinal plant.

squill², *n.* **1.** A crustacean; shrimp. **2.** A mantis.

squint, 1 skwint; 2 skwĭnt. Id. *vt. & vi.* **1.** To make or be cross=eyed. **2.** To look with half=closed eyes, or with a side glance. **II.** *a.* Having a squint. **III.** *n.* The act of squinting.

squire, 1 skwair; 2 skwīr, *n.* An esquire; justice of the peace; lawyer or prominent citizen; attendant, as of a knight or of a lady.

Squill.

squirm, 1 skwurm; 2 skwẽrm. **I.** *vi.* **1.** To bend and twist the body; wriggle. **2.** To climb by shinning. **II.** *n.* A squirming motion.

squir'rel, 1 skwur'el *or* skwir'el; 2 skwûr'ĕl *or* skwĭr'ĕl, *n.* A slender rodent, with a long bushy tail.

squirt, 1 skwurt; 2 skwĭrt. Id. *vt. & vi.* To force out in a stream. **II.** *n.* **1.** The act of squirting or spurting. **2.** A syringe. **squirt'=gun"**‡.

stab, 1 stab; 2 stăb. **I.** *vt. & vi.* [STABBED, STABDs; STAB'BING.] To pierce with a pointed weapon. **II.** *n.* A thrust made with a pointed weapon; a wound made by stabbing.

sta'ble, 1 stē'bl; 2 stā'bl, *vt. & vi.* [STA'BLED; STA'BLING.] To lodge in a stable.

sta'ble, *a.* Standing firmly in place; fixed; durable.— **sta=bil'i=ty,** *n.*— **sta'ble=ness,** *n.*— **sta'bly,** *adv.*

sta'ble, *n.* A building for horses or cattle.

stac=ca'to, 1 stə-kä'to *or* (*It.*) stäk-kä'to; 2 sta-cä'to *or* (*It.*) stäc-cä'to, *a. Mus.* Rendered in an abrupt, disconnected manner.

stack, 1 stak; 2 stăk. **I**t. *vt.* To gather or place in a pile; pile up in a stack. **II.** *n.* **1.** A large orderly pile of unthreshed grain, hay, or straw. **2.** A smoke=stack.

staff, ⎱1 staf; 2 stäf, *n.* [STAVES, STAFFS, **staff**p,⎰ *pl.*] **1.** A stick, as a shaft or pole; a cane or walking=stick. **2.** *Mil.* A body of officers attached to a commander. **3.** The combined lines and spaces used in written or printed music.

stag, 1 stag; 2 stăg, *n.* **1.** The male of the deer. **2.** [Colloq.] A man, as distinguished from a woman, especially a man not in the company of women; as a *stag=dinner* (one at which only men are present).

Full=grown
Royal
Stag. ¹/₈₃

stage, 1 stēj; 2 stāg. **I.** *vt.* [STAGED; STAG'-ING.] *Theat.* To arrange for the stage; exhibit on the stage. **II.** *n.* **1.** The raised platform on which the performance takes place in a theater; any elevated platform; the profession of an actor; a scene of action. **2.** A step or degree. **3.** One of several regular stopping=places in a route; also, the distance from one to another. **4.** A large four=wheeled conveyance making regular trips. **stage'=coach"**‡.

stag'ger, 1 stag'ẽr; 2 stăg'ẽr. **I.** *vt. & vi.* **1.** To reel or cause to reel; cause to hesitate; waver. **2.** To arrange in groups so as to distribute a mass, as of persons, over a given time. **II.** *n.* A reeling motion.

stag'nant, 1 stag'nant; 2 stăg'nant, *a.* **1.** Standing still; not flowing; foul from long standing. **2.** Sluggish. **-ly,** *adv.*— **stag'nate,** *vi.* [STAG'NAT=ED; STAG'NAT=ING.] To be or become stagnant or inert.—**stag=na'tion,** *n.*

staid, 1 stēd; 2 stād, *imp. & pp.* of STAY, *v.*

staid, *a.* Steady and sober; sedate. **-ly,** *adv.* **-ness,** *n.*

stain, 1 stēn; 2 stān, *v.* **I.** *t.* Toᵉmake a stain upon; impart a stain to; color or discolor. **II.** *i.* To take or impart a stain.

stain, *n.* **1.** A discoloration. **2.** A dye used in staining. **3.** A moral taint; tarnish.— **stain'less,** *a.*

stair, 1 stār; 2 stâr, *n.* **1.** One of a series of steps. **2.** A series of steps: usually plural.— **stair'case",** *n.* A set of stairs. **stair'way"**‡.

stake¹, 1 stēk; 2 stāk. **I.** *vt.* [STAKEDt; STAK'ING.] **1.** To fasten by means of a stake. **2.** To mark off with stakes. **II.** *n.* **1.** A stick or post sharpened for driving into the ground. **2.** A post to which a person was bound to be burned alive; martyrdom.

stake². It. *vt.* To put at hazard; wager; risk. **II.** *n.* **1.** Something wagered; a prize for competition. **2.** An interest.

sta=lac'tite, 1 sta-lak'tait; 2 sta-lăc'tĭt, *n.* An elongated icicle=like form in which cer-

tain minerals are deposited, as from the roof of a cave.— **stal″ac-tit′ic, -i-cal,** *a.*

sta-lag′mite, 1 stə-lag′mait; 2 sta-lăg′mit, *n.* An incrustation on the floor of a cavern; the counterpart of a stalactite, often rising to join it.— **stal″ag-mit′ic, -i-cal,** *a.*

stale, 1 stēl; 2 stăl, *a.* Having lost freshness; decayed; worn out; trite.— **stale′-ness,** *n.*

stalk, 1 stȯk; 2 stạk, *vt.* & *vi.* **1.** To approach stealthily, as in hunting. **2.** To pace in a dignified manner.— **stalk′er,** *n.*— **stalk′-ing≈horse″,** *n.* A horse behind which a hunter hides himself in stalking game: used also figuratively.

stalk, *n.* A stem, as of a plant.

stall, 1 stȯl; 2 stạl. **I.** *vt.* & *vi.* **1.** To place or keep in a stall. **2.** To furnish with stalls. **3.** To stick in mire or snow, as a wagon. **II.** *n.* **1.** A compartment in which a horse or bovine animal is confined and fed. **2.** A small booth, enclosed seat, etc.

stal′lion, 1 stal′yən; 2 stăl′yon, *n.* A male horse kept for breeding.

stal′wart, 1 stȯl′wᵊrt; 2 stạl′wạrt, *a.* Large and strong; of a sturdy build; muscular; brawny.

sta′men, 1 stē′men; 2 stā′mĕn, *n.* [STA′-MENS, rarely STAM′I-NA, *pl.*] The organ that contains the pollen in a flower.

stam′i≈na, 1 stam′i-nə; 2 stăm′i-na, *n.* Strength; vigor. **2.** The supporting part of a body.

stam′mer, 1 stam′ᵊr; 2 stăm′ẽr. **I.** *vt.* & *vi.* To stutter. **II.** *n.* A halting, defective utterance; a stuttering.— **stam′mer-er,** *n.*— **stam′mer-ing,** *pa.* & *n.*— **stam′-mer-ing≈ly,** *adv.*

stampᵗ, 1 stamp; 2 stămp, *v.* **I.** *t.* **1.** To make by impressing. **2.** To impress by a stamp. **3.** To affix a stamp upon. **4.** To bring down quickly and heavily, as the foot. **5.** To crush (ores). **6.** To stigmatize. **II.** *i.* To strike the foot forcibly upon the ground.— **stamp′er,** *n.*, **stamp′ing,** *pa.* & *n.*

stamp, *n.* **1.** A mark made by stamping; device; design. **2.** An implement or machine for stamping. **3.** Kind; sort. **4.** The act of stamping.

stam-pede′, 1 stam-pīd′; 2 stăm-pēd′. **I.** *vt.* & *vi.* [STAM-PED′ED⁰; STAM-PED′ING.] To cause a stampede. **II.** *n.* **1.** A sud-

den starting and rushing off, as of cattle, through panic. **2.** Any sudden tumultuous movement on the part of a crowd.

stanch, 1 stanch; 2 stănch. **I**ᵗ. *vt.* To stop the flow of (blood), as from a wound. **II.** *a.* **1.** Constant: faithful; hearty. **2.** Strong and trustworthy. **-ly,** *adv.* **-ness,** *n.*

stan′chion, 1 stan′shən; 2 stăn′çhon, *n.* An upright bar forming a support; one of two upright timbers for confining cattle in a stall.

stand, 1 stand; 2 stănd, *v.* [STOOD; STAND′-ING.] **I.** *t.* **1.** To place upright. **2.** To put up with; bear. **II.** *i.* **1.** To be or remain upright. **2.** To be in a condition or attitude. **3.** To go; step; pass. **4.** To be situated; lie. **5.** To rest; depend. — **stand′by″,** *n.*— **stand′er,** *n.*— **stand′-ing.** I. *pa.* **1.** Remaining erect. **2.** Maintained for regular use; permanent. **3.** Stagnant. **II.** *n.* **1.** Relative position. **2.** A station. **3.** Duration. **4.** The act of one who stands.— **stand′still,** *n.*

stand, *n.* **1.** A supporting structure; platform; small table, etc. **2.** Position; place. **3.** The act of standing. **4.** A halt; hesitation; resistance.

stand′ard, 1 stand′ᵊrd; 2 stănd′ard, *a.* Accurate and authoritative.

stand′ard¹, *n.* Any established measure; a type, model, or example for comparison.

stand′ard², *n.* An upright timber, post, or the like.

stand′ard³, *n.* A flag, ensign, or banner.

stank, 1 stank; 2 stăŋk, *imp.* of STINK, *v.*

stan′za, 1 stan′zə; 2 stăn′za, *n. Pros.* A group of rimed lines, as a division of a poem.

sta′ple, 1 stē′pl; 2 stā′pl, *a.* Regularly and constantly produced or sold.

sta′ple¹, *n.* **1.** A well≈established article of commerce. **2.** A chief element. **3.** The fiber of cotton or wool. **4.** Raw material.

sta′ple², *n.* A U≈shaped piece of metal with pointed ends.

star, 1 stär; 2 stär, *v.* [STARRED; STARDˢ; STAR′RING.] **I.** *t.* **1.** To set with stars. **2.** To mark with an asterisk. **II.** *i.* To act as a dramatic star.

star, *n.* **1.** A celestial body so distant as to appear like a luminous point. **2.** A figure having radiating points, generally five. **3.** An asterisk (*). **4.** An actor who plays the leading part.— **shoot′ing≈star″,** *n.* See METEOR.— **star′≈cham″ber,** *n.* A tribunal conducted under arbitrary or secret methods.— **star′fish″,** *n.* A marine animal having radiating arms.— **star′≈gaz″er,** *n.*— **star′ry,** 1 stär′ɪ; 2 stär′y,

a. Pertaining to, set with, of, or like a star or stars.— **star′ri-ness,** *n.*

star′board, 1 stär′bōrd; 2 stär′bôrd. I**d.** *vt.* To put or turn (the helm) to the starboard. **II.** *a.* Pertaining to the right of a vessel. **III.** *n.* That side of a vessel on the right hand of one facing the bow.

starch, 1 stärch; 2 stärch. I**t.** *vt.* To apply starch to. **II.** *n.* **1.** A white substance found in the seeds, pith, or tubers of plants. **2.** A solution of the above, for use in stiffening clothes.— **starched,** *a.*— **starch′ed-ly,** *adv.*— **starch′ed-ness,** *n.*— **starch′er,** *n.*— **starch′y,** *a.*

stare, 1 stär; 2 stâr. **I.** *vi.* [STARED; STAR′ING.] To fix the eyes in a steady gaze. **II.** *n.* A steady, fixed gaze with wide⊛open eyes.

stark, 1 stärk; 2 stärk. **I.** *a.* **1.** Stiff or rigid, as in death; stubborn. **2.** Complete; utter. **II.** *adv.* Completely; utterly.— **stark′ly,** *adv.*

star′ling, 1 stär′liŋ; 2 stär′liŋ, *n.* An Old World bird, brown glossed with black.

startd, 1 stärt; 2 stärt, *v.* **I.** *t.* **1.** To set in motion or action; rouse; stir. **2.** To originate; begin. **3.** To call forth; evoke. **II.** *i.* **1.** To make a startled movement. **2.** To set out; begin. **3.** To become loose.

start, *n.* **1.** A quick, startled movement. **2.** A beginning. **3.** Distance in advance.

star′tle,) 1 stär′tl; 2 stär′tl, *vt. & vi.*
star′tlp,) [STAR′TL(E)Dᴾ; STAR′TLING.] To arouse or excite suddenly; be suddenly aroused or excited.

starve,) 1 stärv; 2 stärv, *vt. & vi.* [STARV(E)Dˢ;
starvˢ,) STARV′ING.] **1.** To kill by or die of hunger; famish. **2.** To perish or cause to perish or fail by privation; stunt; dwarf; as, to *starve* the mind. **3.** [Eng.] To kill or perish with cold.— **star-va′tion,** *n.*— **starve′ling,** *n.* A person or animal that is starving.

state, 1 stēt; 2 stät. **I.** *vt.* [STAT′EDᵈ; STAT′ING.] To set forth explicitly, as in speech or writing. **II.** *a.* Pertaining to the state; for use on occasions of ceremony. **III.** *n.* **1.** Mode of existence; condition. **2.** A commonwealth; nation. **3.** A community forming part of a federal monarchy or republic; especially [S-], one of the United States. **4.** Civil government. **5.** Ceremonious style; dignity.— **stat′ed,** *pa.* Established; regular; fixed.— **stat′ed-ly,** *adv.*— **state′ly,** *a.* [STATE′LI-ER; STATE′-LI-EST.] Lofty; dignified.— **state′li-ness,** *n.*— **state′room″,** *n.* A private sleeping-apartment, as in a vessel.— **states′man,** *n.* [-MEN, *pl.*] One who is skilled in the science

and art of government.— **states′man-like″,** *a.*— **states′man-ship,** *n.* The art or skill of a statesman.

state′ment, 1 stēt′ment *or* -mənt; 2 stāt′-ment, *n.* The act of stating; a definite utterance or presentation; narration.

stat′ic,) 1 stat′ik, -ı-kal; 2 stät′ie, -i-cal,
stat′i-cal,) *a.* Pertaining to bodies at rest or forces in equilibrium.— **stat′ics,** *n.* The science of bodies at rest, or of forces in equilibrium.

sta′tion, 1 stē′shən; 2 stä′shon. **I.** *vt.* To assign to a station. **II.** *n.* **1.** An assigned location. **2.** A place or building serving as a starting⊛point or stopping-place, as on a railway. **3.** Social condition; standing.— **sta′tion-a-ry,** *a.* Remaining in one place; fixed.— **sta′tion-er,** *n.* A dealer in stationery.— **sta′tion-er-y,** *n.* Writing-materials.

sta-tis′tics, 1 stə-tis′tiks; 2 sta-tĭs′ties, *n. pl.* Systematized numerical facts collectively.— **sta-tis′ti-cal,** *a.* **sta-tis′tict.**— **sta-tis′ti-cal-ly,** *adv.*— **stat″is-ti′cian,** *n.*

stat′ue, 1 stach′u *or* stat′yu; 2 stäch′u *or* stät′yu, *n.* A sculptured work representing a human or animal figure, as in marble or bronze.— **stat′u-a-ry,** *n.* [-RIESᶻ, *pl.*] **1.** Statues, collectively considered. **2.** A statue-maker. **3.** The art of making statues.— **stat′u-esque′,** *a.* Resembling a statue.— **stat′u-ette′,** *n.* A small statue.

stat′ure, 1 stach′ur *or* stat′yur; 2 stäch′ur *or* stät′yur, *n.* The natural height of the body.

sta′tus, 1 stē′tus; 2 stä′tŭs, *n.* State, condition, or relation.

stat′ute, 1 stach′ut *or* stat′yut; 2 stäch′ut *or* stät′yut, *n.* A legislative enactment; law.— **stat′u-to-ry,** *a.* Pertaining to a statute; created by legislative enactment.

staunch, 1 stanch; 2 stänch, *v., a., & n.* Same as STANCH.

stave, 1 stēv; 2 stäv. **I.** *vt.* [STAVED *or* STOVE; STAV′ING.] **1.** To break in the staves of; smash. **2.** To furnish or fit with staves. **II.** *n.* [STAVES, 1 stēvz; 2 stävz, *pl.*] **1.** A curved strip of wood, forming a part of the sides of a barrel, tub, or the like. **2.** *Mus.* A staff. **3.** A stanza; verse.

stay, 1 stē; 2 stä, *v.* [STAYED *or* STAID; STAY′ING.] **I.** *t.* To stop; prop; postpone. **II.** *i.* To remain; tarry; halt.

stay, *n.* **1.** The act or time of staying. **2.** That which checks or stops. **3.** A prop; support.

stead,) 1 sted; 2 stĕd, *n.* **1.** Place of
steadˢ,) another person or thing; preceded by *in.* **2.** Place of support; service.

stead'y, 1 stĕd'ĭ; 2 stĕd'y. **I.** *vt.* & *vi.*
stead'y⁸, [STEAD'IED; STEAD'Y-ING.] To make, hold, or become steady. **II.** *a.* [STEAD'I-ER; STEAD'I-EST.] **1.** Stable in position. **2.** Constant; uniform. **3.** Free from dissipation. **4.** Stedfast.— **stead'i-ly,** *adv.*— **stead'i-ness,** *n.*

steak, 1 stĕk; 2 stāk, *n.* A slice of meat, as of beef for broiling.

steal, 1 stīl; 2 stēl, *vt.* & *vi.* [STOLE; STO'-LEN; STEAL'ING.] **1.** To take without right; secure dishonestly. **2.** To move stealthily.— **steal'er,** *n.*

stealth, 1 stelth; 2 stĕlth, *n.* The qual-
stealth⁸, ity or habit of acting secretly; secret movement.— **stealth'y,** *a.* Moving or acting secretly or slyly; secret; sly.— **stealth'i-ly,** *adv.*—**stealth'i-ness,** *n.*

steam, 1 stīm; 2 stēm, *v.* **I.** *t.* To cook or otherwise affect by steam. **II.** *i.* **1.** To make, give off, or send out stea . **2.** To move by steam, as a vessel.

steam, 1 stīm; 2 stēm, *n.* **1.** Water in the form of vapor. **2.** Any vaporous exhalation.— **steam'boat″,** *n.* A boat or vessel propelled by steam.— **steam'-en'gine,** *n.* An engine that derives its motive force from the action of steam.— **steam'er,** *n.* **1.** Something moved by steam, as a steamship. **2.** A vessel in which something is steamed.— **steam'ship″,** *n.* A large vessel for ocean traffic, propelled by steam.— **steam'y,** *a.*

ste'a-rin, 1 stī'ə-rĭn; 2 stē'a-rĭn, *n.* A white, pearly compound contained in many fats.

sted'fast, 1 stĕd'fast *or* -fəst; 2 stĕd'-
stead'fast, fåst *or* -fast, *a.* Firm; faithful; constant; steady. **-ly,** *adv.* **-ness,** *n.*

steed, 1 stīd; 2 stēd, *n.* A horse; a war-horse.

steel, 1 stīl; 2 stēl. **I.** *vt.* **1.** To cover with steel; plate with or furnish with steel. **2.** To make hard or unyielding. **II.** *a.* Made or composed of steel; hence, hard; obdurate. **III.** *n.* **1.** A compound of iron (chiefly with carbon) very strong, tough, and elastic. **2.** Something made of steel.— **steel'y,** *a.* Of or like steel.

steel'yard, 1 stīl'yärd *or* (*colloq.*) stĭl'yərd; 2 stēl'yärd *or* (*colloq.*) stĭl'-yärd, *n.* A device for weighing, consisting of a scale=beam, counterpoise, and hooks.

Steelyard.

steep⁸, 1 stīp; 2 stēp, *vt.* & *vi.* To soak, as in a hot liquid; make an infusion of, as tea.

steep. I. *a.* Sharply inclined; precipi-
tous. **II.** *n.* A precipitous place; a hill. **-ly,** *adv.* **-ness,** *n.*

stee'ple, 1 stī'pĭ; 2 stē'pl, *n.* A lofty
stee'pl⁸, structure rising above the roof of a church; a spire.— **stee'ple-chase″,** *n.* A race on horseback across country.

steer, 1 stīr; 2 stēr, *vt.* & *vi.* To guide (a vessel) by means of a rudder; direct one's course.— **steers'man,** *n.* [-MEN, *pl.*] One who steers a boat.

steer, *n.* A young ox.

steer'age, 1 stīr'ĭj; 2 stēr'aġ, *n.* **1.** That part of an ocean passenger=vessel occupied chiefly oy immigrants. **2.** The act of steering.

stel'lar, 1 stel'ər; 2 stĕl'ar, *a.* Pertaining to the stars.— **stel'late,** *a.* Star=shaped or starlike. **stel'lat-ed‡.**

stem¹, 1 stem; 2 stĕm, *vt.* & *vi.* [STEMMED, STEMP⁸; STEM'MING.] To make headway against, as a current.

stem², *vt.* To remove the stems from.

stem¹, *n.* **1.** The stock of a tree, shrub, or plant. **2.** The stalk that supports something, as the fruit, flower, or leaf of a plant. **3.** The stock of a family; lineage.

stem², *n.* A nearly upright timber or metal piece, constituting the forward member of a vessel's hull. [odor.

stench, 1 stench; 2 stĕnch, *n.* An offensive

sten'cil, 1 sten'sĭl; 2 stĕn'çil, **I.** *vt.* [STEN'-CILED *or* -CILLED, -CILD⁸; STEN'CIL-ING *or* -CIL-LING.] To make with a stencil. **II.** *n.* **1.** A thin plate in which letters or figures are cut in such a way that a color applied to the surface marks the characters on a surface beneath. **2.** A marking made by stenciling.

sten'o-graph, 1 sten'o-grȧf; 2 stĕn'o-grȧf,
sten'o-graf⁸, *n.* A character or writing in shorthand.— **ste-nog'ra-pher,** *n.* One who writes stenography.— **sten″o-graph'ic, -I-cal,** *a.*— **ste-nog'ra-phy,** *n.* The art of writing by the use of contractions or symbols; shorthand.

sten-to'ri-an, 1 sten-tō'rĭ-ăn; 2 stĕn-tō'ri-an, *a.* Having a loud voice; very loud and resonant.

step, 1 step; 2 stĕp, *v.* [STEPPED⁺ *or* STEPT; STEP'PING.] **I.** *t.* **1.** To place, set, or move, as the foot. **2.** To set (a mast) in a socket. **II.** *i.* **1.** To take a step or steps; move the feet.— **step'ping-stone″,** *n.* A stone affording a foot=rest, as for crossing a stream.

step, *n.* **1.** A motion by change of position of a foot. **2.** The distance passed over by one movement of the foot. **3.** That upon which the foot is placed in ascending or descending. **4.** An advance or promotion.

---

5. Walk; gait. **6.** A footprint. **7.** *Mus.* An interval between tones.

step-. A prefix denoting relationship through the marriage only of a parent, and not by blood.— **step′broth″er**, *n.*— **step′child″**, *n.* — **step′daugh″ter**, *n.*— **step′fa″ther**, *n.*— **step′moth″er**, *n.*— **step′sis″ter**, *n.*— **step′son″**, *n.*

steppe, 1 step; 2 stĕp, *n.* A vast plain devoid of forest, as in Siberia.

stere, 1 stīr; 2 stêr, *n.* A unit of measure, equal to one cubic meter. See METRIC SYSTEM, under METRIC.

ster″e - op′ti - con, 1 ster′ĭ-op′tĭ-kɒn; 2 stêr′e-ŏp′ti-cŏn, *n.* A double magic lantern: used to bring one image after another on the screen.

ster′e-o-scope, 1 ster′ĭ-o-skōp; 2 stêr′e-o-scōp, *n.* An optical instrument for blending into one image two pictures of an object from slightly different points of view, so as to produce upon the eye the impression of relief.— **ster″e-o-scop′ic, -i-cal**, *a.*— **ster″e-os′co-py**, *n.*

ster′e-o-type, 1 ster′ĭ-o-taip; 2 stêr′e-o-tȳp. **I.** *vt.* [-TYPED‡; -TYP′ING.] **1.** To make a stereotype of. **2.** To furnish stereotype plates for. **II.** *n.* A cast or plate taken in metal from a matrix, as of a page of type, from which the matrix was made. — **ster″e-o-typ″er**, *n.*

ster′ile, 1 ster′ĭl; 2 stêr′il, *a.* Having no reproductive power; barren.— **ste-ril′i-ty**, *n.*— **ster′il-ize**, *vt.* [-IZED; -IZ′-ING.] To free from germs. **ster′il-ise‡.**

ster′ling, 1 stŭr′lɪŋ; 2 stêr′ling, *a.* **1.** Having a standard of value or fineness established by the British government. **2.** Having accepted worth; genuine.

stern, 1 stŭrn; 2 stêrn, *a.* Marked by severity; repelling. **-ly**, *adv.* **-ness**, *n.*

stern, *n.* The aft part of a ship, boat, etc.

ster′num, 1 stŭr′nʊm; 2 stêr′nŭm, *n.* [STER′-NA or -NUMS², *pl.*] The breast-bone.

ster′tor-ous, 1 stŭr′tɒr-us; 2 stêr′tor-ŭs, *a.* Snoring. **-ly**, *adv.*

steth′o-scope, 1 steth′o-skōp; 2 stĕth′o-seōp, *n.* An apparatus for conveying to the ear of an operator the sounds produced within the lungs, heart, etc.

ste′ve - dore, 1 stī′vɪ-dōr; 2 stê′ve-dōr, *n.* A laborer who stows or unloads the hold of vessels.

Binaural Stethoscope, as used.

stew, 1 stiū; 2 stū. **I.** *vt.* & *vi.* To boil slowly and gently. **II.** *n.* **1.** Stewed food. **2.** Mental agitation; worry.

stew′ard, 1 stiū′ərd; 2 stū′ard, *n.* **1.** A person managing the estate or affairs of another. **2.** A man having charge of provisions, etc., on board ship.— **stew′ard-ess**, *n. fem.*— **stew′ard-ship**, *n.*

stick¹, 1 stik; 2 stĭk, *v.* [STUCK; STICK′ING.] **I.** *t.* **1.** To cause to pierce. **2.** To fix in place by inserting. **II.** *i.* **1.** To be held by being thrust in. **2.** To protrude: with *out*, *through*, and *from*.

stick², *v.* [STUCK; STICK′ING.] **I.** *t.* To attach by some adhesive substance. **II.** *i.* **1.** To cleave to a surface; stay attached. **2.** To be stopped, perplexed, or disconcerted.— **stick′y**, *a.* [STICK′I-ER; STICK′I-EST.] Adhering to a surface; adhesive.— **stick′i-ly**, *adv.*— **stick′i-ness**, *n.*

stick¹, *n.* **1.** A piece of wood that is long, compared with its breadth and thickness; a rod, wand, or cane. **2.** *Print.* A metal frame in which type is composed.

stick², *n.* A penetrating thrust; stab.

stick′le, } 1 stik′l; 2 stĭk′l, *vi.* [STICK′L(E)DᵷF; **stick′lᵖ**, } STICK′LING.] To contend about trifles.

stiff, } 1 stif; 2 stĭf, *a.* **1.** Not easily bent or **stifᵖ**, } moved. **2.** Constrained and awkward. **3.** Viscous. **4.** Obstinate; severe. **-ly**, *adv.* **-ness**, *n.*— **stiff′en**, *vt.* & *vi.* To make or become stiff or stiffer.

sti′fle, 1 stai′fl; 2 stī′fl, *v.* [STI′FLED; STI′-FLING.] **I.** *t.* To kill by stopping respiration; extinguish, as a flame; suppress. **II.** *i.* To die from suffocation.

sti′fle, *n.* The joint next the body, in the hind leg of a horse.

stig′ma, 1 stig′mə; 2 stĭg′ma, *n.* [STIG′-MAS² or STIG′MA-TA, *pl.*] **1.** A mark of infamy, or token of disgrace. **2.** That part of a pistil which receives the pollen. **3.** A mark; spot; scar.— **stig-mat′ic**, *a.*— **stig′ma-tize**, *vt.* [-TIZED; TIZ′ING.] To brand as ignominious. **stig′ma-tise‡.**

stile, 1 stail; 2 stīl, *n.* A series of steps for crossing a fence or wall.

sti-let′to, 1 sti-let′o-; 2 sti-lĕt′o, *n.* A small dagger.

still, } 1 stil; 2 stĭl. **I.** *vt.* To cause to be **stilᵖ**, } still; put to rest or silence. **II.** *a.* **1.** Making no sound or movement. **2.** Free from disturbance. **III.** *n.* Stillness; calm. **IV.** *adv.* **1.** Now or then; as previously; yet. **2.** Notwithstanding. **3.** In increasing degree; even yet.— **still′, born″**, *a.* Lifeless at birth.— **still life**, in painting, the representation of fruits, flowers, lifeless animals, and inanimate

objects.— **still′ness,** n.— **still′y. I.** a. [Poet.] Still; silent. **II.** adv. Quietly.

still, n. **1.** An apparatus in which liquors are distilled. **2.** A distillery.

stilt, 1 stilt; 2 stĭlt, n. One of a pair of supports to hold the foot above the ground in walking.— **stilt′ed,** a. Bombastic; inflated.

stim′u-lant, 1 stim′yu-lənt; 2 stĭm′yu-lant. **I.** a. Serving to stimulate. **II.** n. Anything that stimulates, as an intoxicant. — **stim′u-late,** vt. [-LAT′ED; -LAT′ING.] To rouse; excite; animate; intoxicate.— **stim″u-la′-tion,** n.— **stim′u-la″tiv**(es, a. & n.— **stim′u-la″tor,** n.— **stim′u-lus,** n. [-LI, 1 -lai; 2 -lī, pl.] Anything that rouses or excites.

sting, 1 stiŋ; 2 stĭng. **I.** vt. & vi. [STUNG; STING′ING.] **1.** To pierce with a sting; use a sting. **2.** To cause a sensation, as from a sting. **3.** To stimulate. **4.** To be keenly painful. **II.** n. **1.** The act of stinging; the wound made by a sting. **2.** Zoöl. A sharp organ capable of inflicting a painful and poisonous wound. **3.** A spur; goad.

stin′gy, 1 stin′ji; 2 stĭn′ĝy, a. [STIN′GI-ER; STIN′GI-EST.] **1.** Extremely penurious or selfish. **2.** Scanty.— **stin′gi-ness,** n.

stink, 1 stiŋk; 2 stĭnk. **I.** vi. [STANK or STUNK; STINK′ING.] To give forth a foul odor. **II.** n. A stench.

stint, 1 stint; 2 stĭnt. **I**d. vt. **1.** To provide for or serve scantily. **2.** To allot a specific task to. **II.** n. **1.** A fixed amount, as of work; allowance. **2.** Restriction.

sti′pend, 1 stai′pend; 2 stī′pĕnd, n. A salary that affords a bare livelihood.— **sti-pen′di-a-ry,** n. [-RIES², pl.] One who receives a stipend, as a clergyman.

stip′u-late, 1 stip′yu-lēt; 2 stĭp′yu-lāt, v. [-LAT′ED; -LAT′ING.] **I.** t. **1.** To specify as the terms of an agreement. **2.** To particularize. **II.** i. To make stipulations.— **stip″u-la′tion,** n. **1.** The act of stipulating. **2.** Anything stipulated; an agreement or contract.— **stip′u-la″tor,** n.

stir, 1 stŭr; 2 stĭr, v. [STIRRED, STIRD⁸; STIR′RING.] **I.** t. **1.** To mix the components of, by motion. **2.** To move; disturb; rouse. **II.** i. To be active or in motion; move.

stir, n. The act of stirring; activity; excitement; commotion.

stir′rup, 1 stir′up or stŭr′up; 2 stĭr′ŭp or stĭr′ŭp, n. A support for the foot, suspended from a saddle.

stitch,) 1 stiċh: 2 stĭċh. **I**t. vt. & vi. **stich**ᴾ,) To join together with stitches; sew. **II.** n. **1.** A single passage of a threaded needle; also, the thread thus placed. **2.** A sharp sudden pain, as in the side.

stith′y, 1 stiŧh′ĭ; 2 stĭŧh′y. [STITH′IES², pl.] A smithy.

sti′ver, 1 stai′vər; 2 stī′ver, n. A small Dutch coin, worth 2 cents; a mere trifle.

stoat, 1 stōt; 2 stōt, n. The ermine, especially in its summer coat, reddish = brown above, yellow below.

stockᵗ, 1 stek; 2 stŏk, v. **I.** t. **1.** To furnish with stock. **2.** To lay by for the future. **II.** i. To lay in or provide supplies.

Stoat.

stock, a. Continually kept ready; standing.

stock, n. **1.** The trunk or main support of a plant. **2.** Lineage; family. **3.** Domestic animals. **4.** Goods and merchandise employed in trade. **5.** Any reserve supply. **6.** Certificates of shares or indebtedness. **7.** The handle of a gun, etc. **8.** A support, as for a vessel, during construction. **9.** A neckcloth. **10.** A block, stake, or log of wood; anything heavy and senseless.— **stock′bro″ker,** n. Finance. One who buys and sells stocks for others.— **stock company,** n. **1.** An incorporated company that issues stock. **2.** Theat. A permanent dramatic company playing a repertoire.— **stock′dove″,** n. A European wild pigeon.— **stock′ex-change″,** n. **1.** An association of dealers in public stocks. **2.** A place where stocks are publicly bought and sold.— **stock′fish″,** n. A dried fish cured without salt.— **stock′hold″er,** n One who holds certificates of ownership, as in a stock company.— **stock′job″ber,** n. A dealer or speculator in stocks.— **stock′job″ber-y,** n. **stock′job″bing**‡.— **stock′still″,** a. Still as a stock or post; motionless.— **stock′yard″,** n. A large subdivided yard where marketed cattle are kept.

stock-ade′, 1 stok-ēd′; 2 stŏk-ād′. **I.** vt. [STOCK-AD′ED⁴; STOCK-AD′ING.] To fortify with a stockade. **II.** n. A line of stout stakes, set upright to form a barrier.

stock′ing, 1 stok′ıŋ; 2 stŏk′ĭng, n. A woven or knitted covering for the foot.— **stock″I-net,** n. [stout.

stock′y, 1 stok′ĭ; 2 stŏk′y, a. Short and Sto′ic, 1 stō′ĭk; 2 stō′ĭe, n. **1.** A member of a school of Greek philosophy that sternly repressed all emotion. **2.** [-s-] A person indifferent to pleasure or pain:

named from the "Painted Porch" *Stoa Poikilē*, at Athens, frequented by Zeno (344-260 B. C.), founder of the Stoic school.— **Sto'i-cal** [S- or s-], *a.* **-ly,** *adv.* **-ness,** *n.*— **Sto'i-cism,** *n.* **1.** The doctrines of the Stoics. **2.** [s-] Indifference to pleasure or pain.

stoke, 1 stōk; 2 stŏk, *vt.* & *vi.* [STOKED†; STOK'ING.] To supply (a furnace) with fuel; serve as a stoker.— **stok'er,** *n.*

stole, *imp.* of STEAL, *v.*

stole, 1 stōl; 2 stŏl, *n.* *Eccl.* A narrow band worn by an officiating clergyman; any ecclesiastical vestment.

sto'len, *pp.* of STEAL, *v.*

stol'id, 1 stŏl'id; 2 stŏl'id, *a.* Having or expressing no feeling or perception; stupid; dull. **stol'id-ly,** *adv.* **stol'id-ness,** *n.* **sto-lid'i-ty‡.**

stom'ach, } 1 stŭm'ǝk; 2 stŏm'ac. I†. *vt.* **stum'ac‡,** } To accept; put up with; tolerate. **II.** *n.* **1.** A dilatation, of the alimentary canal, serving as an organ of digestion. **2.** The abdomen; belly. **3.** Desire of food; appetite.

stone, 1 stōn; 2 stŏn. **I.** *vt.* [STONED; STON'ING.] **1.** To hurl stones at. **2.** To remove the stones or pits from. **3.** To furnish, as a well, with stone. **II.** *n.* **1.** A small piece of rock, or such pieces collectively. **2.** A gem. **3.** A stony concretion in the bladder. **4.** The hard covering of the kernel in a fruit. **5.** [Brit.] A measure of weight, avoirdupois, usually 14 pounds.— **stone'=fruit",** *n.* A fruit having a stone.— **stone's cast,** the distance a stone may be cast by hand. **stone's throw‡.**— **stone'ware",** *n.* A variety of pottery.— **ston'y,** *a.* [STON'I-ER; STON'I-EST.j **1.** Abounding in stone. **2.** Hard as stone; unfeeling. **ston'i-ness,** *n.*

stood, 1 stud; 2 stōōd, *imp.* & *pp.* of STAND, *v.*

stool, 1 stūl; 2 stōōl, *n.* A backless seat for one person; any low support.— **stool'= pig'eon,** *n.* A decoy pigeon; a person used to decoy others.

stoop†, 1 stūp; 2 stōōp, *vt.* & *vi.* **1.** To bend or lean forward; bow, or be bowed down. **2.** To bring or come down from dignity or rank; condescend. **3.** To swoop.

stoop¹, *n.* **1.** An act of stooping. **2.** Condescension. **3.** A swoop.

stoop², *n.* [U. S.] An uncovered platform at the door of a house; a porch veranda.

stop, 1 stŏp; 2 stŏp, *v.* [STOPPED‡, STOPT⁸; STOP'PING.] **I.** *t.* **1.** To bring from motion to rest; cause to cease; bring to an end. **2.** To check beforehand; prevent. **3.** To close; keep back. **II.** *i.* **1.** To come to rest. **2.** To cease; discontinue.—

stop'=cock", *n.* A faucet having a stop or valve.— **stop'page,** *n.* **1.** The act of stopping. **2.** A deduction from pay.— **stop'per.** **I.** *vt.* To secure with a stopper. **II.** *n.* One who or that which stops up or closes, as a cork.

stop, *n.* **1.** The act of stopping; pause. **2.** An obstruction; hindrance. **3.** A contrivance, in musical instruments, for regulating tones. **4.** A punctuation=mark.

stop'ple, 1 stŏp'l; 2 stŏp'l, *n.* A stopper, plug, or bung.

store, 1 stōr; 2 stŏr. **I.** *vt.* [STORED; STOR'ING.] **1.** To put away for future use. **2.** To provide. **3.** To deposit for safe-keeping. **II.** *n.* **1.** That which is stored or laid up. **2.** *pl.* Supplies. **3.** A place where merchandise is kept for sale.— **stor'age,** *n.* **1.** The depositing of articles for safe = keeping. **2.** Space for storing goods. **3.** A charge for storing.— **store'house",** *n.* A warehouse; depository. — **store'room",** *n.* A room in which things are stored, as household supplies.

sto'ried¹, 1 stō'rid; 2 stŏ'rid, *a.* **1.** Having a notable history. **2.** Related in a story.

sto'ried², *a.* Having or consisting of stories, as a building; as, six=*storied.*

stork, 1 stŏrk; 2 stŏrk, *n.* A long=necked and long=legged wading bird.

storm, 1 stŏrm; 2 stŏrm, *v.* **I.** *t.* *Mil.* To take, or attempt to take, by storm. **II.** *i.* **1.** To take place, as a storm. **2.** To give vent boisterously to passion; move noisily.

storm, *n.* **1.** A disturbance of the atmosphere, commonly accompanied by rain, hail, or snow. **2.** A violent commotion of any sort. **3.** A violent and rapid assault on a fortified place.— **storm'y,** *a.*

sto'ry¹, 1 stō'ri; 2 stŏ'ry, *n.* [STO'RIES², *pl.*] **1.** A narrative or recital; especially, a short tale, novel, etc. **2.** Anything reported or told. **3.** [Colloq.] A lie.

sto'ry², *n.* [STO'RIES², *pl.*] A division in a building comprising the space between two successive floors. **sto'rey‡.**

stout, 1 staut; 2 stout. **I.** *a.* **1.** Strong or firm; tough. **2.** Determined; resolute. **3.** Fat; bulky. **4.** Having muscular strength. **II.** *n.* A strong, very dark porter or beer.— **stout'ly,** *adv.*— **stout'ness,** *n.*

sto'va-ine, 1 stō'vǝ-in; 2 stŏ'va-in, *n.* A local anesthetic used in combination with strychnin.

stove, 1 stōv; 2 stŏv, *imp.* & *pp.* of STAVE, *v.*

stove, *n.* An apparatus, usually of metal, for heating or cooking.

stow, 1 stō; 2 stŏ, *vt.* **1.** To put away compactly; pack. **2.** To hide away; also,

to lodge.— **stow'age**, *n.* **1.** The act or manner of stowing, or the state of being stowed. **2.** Space or charge for stowing goods.— **stow'a-way''**, *n.* One who hides, as on a vessel.

strad'dle, } 1 strad'l; 2 străd'l. **I.** *vt. & vi.*
strad'le, } [STRAD'DLED, STRAD'LDᴾ; STRAD'-DLING.] To stretch the legs widely apart; sit or mount astride. **II.** *n.* A straddling position or movement.

Strad''l-va'ri-us, 1 strad'ı-vē'rı-us; 2 străd'-ı-vä'ri-ŭs, *n.* A stringed instrument made by Antonio Stradivari of Cremona, Italy (1649-1737).

strag'gle, } 1 strag'l; 2 străg'l, *vi.* [STRAG'-
strag'le, } GLED, STRAG'LDᴾ; STRAG'GLING.] **1.** To wander apart from the main body; stray. **2.** To ramble. **3.** To spread out unduly.— **strag'gler**, *n.*

straight, 1 strēt; 2 străt. **I.** *a.* **1.** Extending uniformly in the same direction. **2.** Erect; upright; accurate; true. **II.** *adv.* **1.** In a straight line. **straight'ly‡**. **2.** Correspondingly. **3.** Immediately.— **straight'en**, *vt. & vi.* To make or become straight.— **straight''for'ward**, *a.* Proceeding in a straight course or in a direct manner; frank. **-ly**, *n.*— **straight'ness**, *n.*— **straight'way''‖**, *adv.* Immediately.

strain, 1 strēn; 2 străn, *v.* **I.** *t.* **1.** To exert to the utmost. **2.** To cause a strain in. **3.** To constrain. **4.** To purify by the use of a strainer. **II.** *i.* **1.** To make violent efforts. **2.** To percolate; filter. **3.** To become wrenched or twisted.— **strain'er**, *n.*

strain¹, *n.* **1.** A violent effort or exertion. **2.** The injury due to excessive tension or effort. **3.** A melody; tune. **4.** Prevailing tone. [2. Natural tendency.

strain², *n.* Line of descent; race; stock.

strait, 1 strēt; 2 străt. **I.** *a.* **1.** Of small dimensions; narrow. **2.** Close; tight. **II.** *n.* **1.** A narrow passage of water connecting two larger bodies of water. **2.** Perplexity or distress; necessity. **3.** Any narrow pass or passage. **-ly**, *adv.* **-ness**, *n.*— **strait'en**, *vt.* **1.** To make strait or narrow; contract; restrict. **2.** To distress; hamper.— **strait''jack''et**, *n.* A jacket of strong canvas, for confining the arms of dangerous lunatics or violent prisoners. [aground.

strandᵈ, 1 strand; 2 strănd, *vt. & vi.* To run **strand**¹, *n.* [Poet.] A shore or beach.

strand², *n.* **1.** One of the principal members of a rope. **2.** A fiber, hair, etc.

strange, 1 strēnj; 2 străng, *a.* **1.** Unheard of; unfamiliar. **2.** Unaccountable; remarkable. **3.** Of a different class or kind. **4.** Foreign. **-ly**, *adv.* **-ness**, *n.*— **stran'ger**,

n. **1.** One who is not an acquaintance. **2.** An unfamiliar visitor. **3.** A foreigner.

stran'gle, } 1 strang'gl; 2 străng'gl, *vt. & vi.*
stran'glᴾ, } [STRAN'GL(E)Dᴾ; STRAN'GLING.] **1.** To choke to death; throttle; suffocate; stifle. **2.** To repress; suppress.— **stran''gu-la'tion**, *n.*

strap, 1 strap; 2 străp. **I.** *vt.* [STRAPPEDᵗ, STRAPTˢ; STRAP'PING.] To fasten with a strap. **II.** *n.* A long, narrow, and flexible strip of leather, or the like, for binding about objects; a strop for a razor.

strap'ping, *a.* [Colloq.] Large and muscular.

strat'a-gem, 1 strat'a-jem; 2 străt'a-gĕm, *n.* A maneuver designed to outwit.

strat'e-gy, 1 strat'ı-ji; 2 străt'e-gy. [-GIESᶻ, *pl.*] **1.** The science of military position and movement in war. **2.** The use of stratagem or artifice, as in business.— **stra-teg'ic, stra-teg'i-cal**, *a.* Pertaining to strategy. **strat''e-get'i-cal‡**.— **strat''e-get'i-cal-ly**, *adv.*— **strat'e-gist**, *n.* One versed in strategy.

stra'tum, 1 strē'tum; 2 strā'tŭm, *n.* [STRA'TA, 1 strē'ta, 2 strā'ta, less commonly, STRA'TUMSᶻ, *pl.*] A layer, bed, or thickness, as of rock.— **strat'i-fy**, *vt. & vi.* [-FIED; -FY'ING.] To form or be formed in strata.— **strat''i-fi-ca'tion**, *n.*

straw, 1 stro; 2 strą, *n.* **1.** A dried or ripened stalk; also, stems or stalks of thrashed grain, collectively. **2.** A mere trifle.— **straw'ber''ry**, *n.* [-RIESᶻ, *pl.*] **1.** The scarlet berry-like fruit of a running plant. **2.** The plant that bears this fruit.

stray, 1 strē; 2 strā. **I.** *vi.* To wander; rove; roam. **II.** *a.* **1.** Having strayed; straying. **2.** Irregular. **III.** *n.* A domestic animal that has strayed; an estray.

streak, 1 strīk; 2 strēk. **Iᵗ.** *vt.* To mark with a streak; stripe. **II.** *n.* **1.** A long, narrow mark, line, or stripe. **2.** A vein; trace; dash.— **streaked**, *pa.*— **streak'y**, *a.*

stream, 1 strīm; 2 strēm. **I.** *vt. & vi.* To pour or flow forth in a stream; move in continuous succession; float with a waving movement, as a flag. **II.** *n.* **1.** A current or flow of water or other fluid. **2.** Anything continuously flowing, moving, or passing, as people.— **stream'er**, *n.* An object that streams; a flag that floats extended.— **stream'let**, *n.* A rivulet.— **stream'line**, *a.* Designating an uninterrupted flow or drift; also, designating a form, body, or the like, so constructed as to produce an uninterrupted flow of fluid around it; as, a *stream-line* flow; a *stream-line* shape; a *stream-line* body for a motor-car.

street, 1 strīt; 2 strēt, *n.* A public way, as in a city; also, the roadway between sidewalks.

strength, 1 streᵑſh; 2 strĕngth, *n.* **1.** The quality or property of being strong. **2.** Power; force. **3.** Degree of intensity; concentration.— **strength'en,** *vt.* & *vi.* To make or become strong or stronger.

stren'u-ous, 1 stren'yu-us; 2 strĕn'yu-ŭs. *a.* Pressing; urgent; earnest. **-ly,** *adv.* **-ness,** *n.*— **stren"u-os'i-ty,** *n.*

stress, 1 stres; 2 strĕs, *n.* **1.** Special weight, importance, or significance. **2.** Force exerted; strain; tension; compulsion. **3.** Force of voice; accent.

stretch, } 1 strech; 2 strĕch. Iᵗ. *vt.* & *vi.*
strechᴾ, } **1.** To draw out; draw tight. **2.** To extend or be extended; spread; exaggerate. **II.** *n.* **1.** An act of stretching. **2.** Extent or reach of that which stretches. **3.** A continuous extent of space or of time.— **stretch'er,** *n.* **1.** One who or that which stretches. **2.** A frame for carrying the wounded or dead.

strew, 1 strū; 2 stru, *vt.* [STREWED, STREWDˢ; STREWED or STREWN; ꜱTREW'ING.] To scatter; cover by scattering.

stri'ate, 1 strai'ĕt; 2 strī'āt, *a.* Bearing fine stripes or grooves. **stri'at-ed‡.**

strick'en, 1 strik'n; 2 strĭk'n, *pa.* Wounded; struck down, as by a calamity.

strict, 1 strikt; 2 strĭct, *a.* **1.** Observing or enforcing rules exactly. **2.** Rigidly observed. **3.** Exactly defined or applied. **-ly,** *adv.* **-ness,** *n.*

stric'ture, 1 strik'ĉhur or -tiur; 2 strĭc'chur or -tūr, *n.* **1.** Severe criticism. **2.** *Pathol.* Contraction of some channel.

stride, 1 straid; 2 strĭd, *vi.* [STRODE; STRID'DEN, formerly STRID; STRID'ING.] To walk with strides.

stride, *n.* **1.** A long and sweeping or measured step. **2.** The distance passed over by one complete movement.

stri'dent, 1 strai'dent; 2 strī'dĕnt, *a.* Giving a loud and harsh sound. **-ly,** *adv.*

strife, 1 straif; 2 strīf, *n.* **1.** Angry contention; fighting; rivalry. **2.** Strenuous endeavor.

strike, 1 straik; 2 strĭk, *v.* [STRUCK; STRICK'EN, STRICK'Nᴾ, formerly STROOK; STRIK'ING.] **I.** *t.* **1.** To hit; smite. **2.** To stamp, as coins. **3.** To confirm, as a bargain. **4.** To expunge: followed by *out.* **5.** To haul down, as a flag. **6.** To quit or cease, as work. **II.** *i.* **1.** To come into sudden contact; deliver a blow; beat; sound the hour, as a clock. **2.** To come by accident; happen. **3.** To enter boldly; proceed. **4.** To cease work, as a means of securing some concession. **5.** To surrender.— **strik'er,** *n.* A person who

strikes, especially an employee who leaves his work in consequence of a strike. See STRIKE, *n.*, 2.— **strik'ing,** *pa.* Notable; impressive.

strike, *n.* **1.** An act of striking; a blow. **2.** The quitting of work by a body of laborers to enforce some concession.

string, 1 striᵑ; 2 strĭng, *v.* [STRUNG; STRING'ING.] **I.** *t.* **1.** To suspend on a string. **2.** To fit with a string or strings. **II.** *i.* To stretch out into a long, irregular line.— **stringed,** *a.*

string, *n.* A slender line, thinner than a cord and thicker than a thread; a row or series of things connected.— **string'er,** *n.* **1.** A horizontal supporting timber. **2.** One who strings.— **string'i-ness,** *n.*— **string'y,** *a.*

strin'gent, 1 strin'jent; 2 strĭn'gĕnt, *a.* Rigid; severe; exacting; close.— **strin'gen-cy,** *n.* Strictness; closeness.— **strin'gent-ly,** *adv.*

strip, 1 strip; 2 strĭp, *v.* [STRIPPEDᵗ or STRIPT; STRIP'PING.] **I.** *t.* **1.** To pull off the covering from. **2.** To rob; plunder. **3.** To remove something from. **4.** To tear or cut into strips. **II.** *i.* **1.** To undress. **2.** To come off in strips.

strip, *n.* A narrow piece, comparatively long, as of cloth, wood, etc.

stripe, 1 straip; 2 strīp. **I.** *vt.* & *vi.* [STRIPEDᵗ; STRIP'ING.] To mark with stripes; make stripes. **II.** *n.* **1.** A line, band, or streak. **2.** Kind; sort.

strip'ling, 1 strip'liᵑ; 2 strĭp'ling, *n.* A mere youth.

strive, 1 straiv; 2 strīv, *vi.* [STROVE; STRIV'EN or STRIVED‖, STRIV'Nᴾ; STRIV'ING.] **1.** To make earnest effort. **2.** To contend; fight. **3.** To vie.— **striv'er,** *n.*

strode, 1 strōd; 2 strōd, *imp.* of STRIDE, *v.*

stroke, 1 strōk; 2 strōk, *vt.* [STROKEDᵗ; STROK'ING.] To pass the hand over gently. [a stroking.

stroke¹, *n.* A light caressing movement.

stroke², *n.* **1.** The act or movement of striking; a blow; recurrent movement, as of oars or a piston. **2.** A disaster; attack of disease. **3.** A feat; coup.

stroll, } 1 strōl; 2 strōl. **I.** *vi.* To ramble;
strolᴾ, } wander aimlessly. **II.** *n.* An idle or leisurely walk; a wandering.— **stroll'er,** *n.*

strong, 1 strĕᵑ or stroᵑ; 2 strông or strŏng, *a.* **1.** Having ample strength; muscular; powerful. **2.** Forceful; violent; energetic; effective. **3.** Firm; stable.— **strong'hold,** *n.* A place that nature or art has made strongly defensible.— **strong'ly,** *adv.*

strop, 1 strop; 2 strŏp. **I.** *vt.* [STROPPED, STROPTˢ; STROP'PING.] To sharpen on a

strop, **II.** *n.* An implement, as a strip of leather on which to sharpen a razor.

stro'phe, 1 strō'fĭ or strof'ĭ; 2 strō'fē or strŏf'e, *n.* In poetry, a rhythmical movement; a stanza.— **stroph'ic,** *a.*

strove, 1 strōv; 2 strŏv, *imp.* of STRIVE, *v.*

strowl, 1 strō; 2 strō, *vt.* [STROWED; STROW'-ING; STROWED or STROWN.] Same as STREW.

struck, 1 struk; 2 strŭk, *imp. & pp.* of STRIKE, *v.*

struc'ture, 1 struk'chur or -tiur; 2 strŭk'-chur or -tūr, *n.* **1.** That which is constructed, as a building or machine. **2.** Manner of construction or organization. — **struc'tur-al,** *a.*

strug'gle, ⎱ 1 strug'l; 2 strŭg'l. **I.** *vi.*
strug'l, ⎰ [STRUG'GLED, STRUG'LD²; STRUG'GLING.] To engage in a struggle; strive or labor earnestly. **II.** *n.* A violent effort; contention.

strung, 1 strung; 2 strŭng, *imp. & pp.* of STRING, *v.*

strut, 1 strut; 2 strŭt, *vi.* [STRUT'TED²; STRUT'TING.] To walk with pompous gait.

strut¹, *n.* A proud or pompous step.

strut², *n.* A compression-member in a framework, keeping two others apart.

strych'nin, ⎱ 1 strik'nĭn, -nĭn or -nīn; 2
strych'nine, ⎰ strȳk'nĭn, -nĭn or -nīn, *n.* A white, crystalline, bitter, poisonous compound. **strych'ni-a‡.**

stub, 1 stub; 2 stŭb. **I.** *vt.* [STUBBED, STUBD⁸; STUB'BING.] **1.** [U. S.] To strike, as the toe, against a low obstruction. **2.** To grub up, as roots. **II.** *n.* The stump of a tree, bush, or the like; any short part or piece, as a memorandum left when a check or note is detached; a remnant. — **stub'bed, stub'by,** *a.* Short and thick.

stub'ble, ⎱ 1 stub'l; 2 stŭb'l, *n.* The stubs
stub'l, ⎰ of grain-stalks left after reaping.

stub'born, 1 stub'ɚrn; 2 stŭb'orn, *a.* Unreasonably determined; obstinate; intractable; unyielding. **-ly,** *adv.* **-ness,** *n.*

stuc'co, 1 stuk'o; 2 stŭe'o. **I.** *vt. & vi.* To decorate with stucco. **II.** *n.* A fine plaster for walls or relief ornaments.

stuck, 1 stuk; 2 stŭe, *imp. & pp.* of STICK, *v.*

stud, 1 stud; 2 stŭd, *vt.* [STUD'DED²; STUD'DING.] To set thickly with small points, etc.

stud¹, *n.* **1.** A short intermediate post, as in a building-frame. **2.** A knob, round-headed nail, or the like.— **stud'ding,** *n.* Studs or joists collectively. [ing, etc.

stud², *n.* A collection of horses for breeding.

stu'dent, 1 stiū'dent; 2 stū'dĕnt, *n.* A person engaged in study. [premeditated.

stud'ied, 1 stud'ĭd; 2 stŭd'ĭd, *pa.* Planned;

stu'di-o, 1 stiū'dĭ-ō; 2 stū'di-ō, *n.* The workroom of an artist.

stu'di-ous, 1 stiū'dĭ-us; 2 stū'di-ŭs, *a.* **1.** Given to study. **2.** Assiduous. **3.** Studied. **-ly,** *adv.* **-ness,** *n.*

stud'y, 1 stud'ĭ; 2 stŭd'y. **I.** *vt. & vi.* [STUD'IED; STUD'Y-ING.] To apply oneself to the acquisition of knowledge; examine; meditate upon. **II.** *n.* [STUD'-IES², *pl.*] **1.** The act of studying. **2.** A department of knowledge. **3.** In art, a first sketch. **4.** A room devoted to study. **5.** Earnest endeavor.

stuff, ⎱ 1 stuf; 2 stŭf. **I‡.** *vt.* To fill to
stuff, ⎰ distention; pack full; cram. **II.** *n.* **1.** Raw material; the substance of anything. **2.** Possessions generally. **3.** Rubbish; trashy ideas; nonsense.— **stuff'ing,** *n.* The material with which anything is stuffed; the process of stuffing.

stul'ti-fy, 1 stul'tĭ-fai; 2 stŭl'ti-fȳ, *vt.* [-FIED; -FY"ING.] To cause to appear absurd; make a fool of.— **stul"ti-fi-ca'tion,** *n.*

stum'bl(e)², 1 stum'bl; 2 stŭm'bl. **I.** *vi.* [STUM'BL(E)D²; STUM'BLING.] **1.** To strike the foot against something in walking or running. **2.** To fall (on or upon) by chance. **II.** *n.* A striking or catching of the foot; trip; false step; blunder. — **stum'bling-block",** *n.* An obstacle; a cause of fault or error.

stump‡, 1 stump; 2 stŭmp, *v.* **I.** *t.* **1.** To canvass by making political speeches. **2.** To challenge. **3.** To bring to a halt. **II.** *i.* To walk on or as on stumps; tramp heavily.

stump, *a.* Of or pertaining to a stump.

stump, *n.* **1.** That portion of a tree left standing when the tree is felled. **2.** The end, as of a limb, that remains when the main part has been removed. **3.** *pl.* The legs. **4.** A platform where a stump speech is made.— **stump'y,** *a.*

stun, 1 stun; 2 stŭn. **I.** *vt.* [STUNNED, STUND⁸; STUN'NING.] To stupefy by a blow; shock; astound. **II.** *n.* A stupefying blow or shock.

stung, 1 stung; 2 stŭng, *imp. & pp.* of STING, *v.*

stunk, 1 stunk; 2 stŭnk, *imp. & pp.* of STINK, *v.*

stunt, 1 stunt; 2 stŭnt. **I‡.** *vt.* To check the growth of. **II.** *n.* A check in growth.

stu'pe-fy, 1 stiū'pĭ-fai; 2 stū'pe-fȳ, *vt.* [-FIED; -FY"ING.] To dull the senses of; make stupid; blunt.— **stu"pe-fac'tion,** *n.*

stu-pen'dous, 1 stiu-pen'dus; 2 stū-pĕn'dŭs, *a.* Of prodigious size or degree; astonishing. **-ly,** *adv.* **-ness,** *n.*

stu'pid, 1 stiū'pĭd; 2 stū'pid, *a.* Dull-witted; sluggish; senseless; insensible. **-ly,** *adv.*— **stu-pid'i-ty,** *n.* **stu'pid-ness‡.**

stu'por, 1 stiū'pɚr; 2 stū'por, *n.* A condition of insensibility; dulness; torpor.

---

stur′dy, 1 stŭr′dı; 2 stûr′dy, *a.* [STUR′-DI-ER; STUR′DI-EST.] **1.** Possessing rugged health and strength; hardy. **2.** Firm and unyielding.— **stur′di-ly,** *adv.*— **stur′di-ness,** *n.*

stur′geon, 1 stŭr′jən; 2 stûr′gon, *n.* A

Common Sturgeon. ¹⁄₈₀

large fish of the northern seas and rivers.

stut′ter, 1 stŭt′ər; 2 stŭt′er. **I.** *vt. & vi.* To utter with spasmodic hesitations or repetitions; stammer. **II.** *n.* The act of stuttering.— **stut′ter-er,** *n.* [for swine.

sty¹, 1 staı; 2 stȳ, *n.* [STIES²; *pl.*] A pen

sty², *n.* [STIES²; *pl.*] A small inflamed swelling on the edge of the eyelid.

style, 1 staıl; 2 stȳl, *vt.* [STYLED; STYL′ING.] To give a title to; name.

style¹, *n.* **1.** Manner of conduct or action. **2.** Fashion; mode. **3.** Distinctive use of language or mode of expression. **4.** A sharp point for writing, engraving, etc. **sty′lus‡.** **5.** *Zool.* A pointed process or part.

style², *n.* **1.** A pointer of a sun-dial. **2.** *Bot.* The stem or stalk that bears the stigma. **3.** In joinery, an upright piece in a frame. [**-ly,** *adv.* **-ness,** *n.*

styl′ish, *a.* Having style; fashionable.

sty′lo-graph, 1 staı′lo-grȧf; 2 stȳ′lo-gräf, *n.* A writing-instrument having an ink-reservoir from which ink is fed to a tubular writing-point. **stylographic pen‡.** — **sty″lo-graph′ic,** *a.*

sty′lus, *n.* Same as STYLE¹, 4.

styp′tic, 1 stıp′tık; 2 stŷp′tıc. **I.** *a.* Causing contraction of tissues, as blood-vessels. **II.** *n.* A substance that arrests bleeding. [suasion.

sua′sion, 1 swē′ʒən; 2 swā′zhon, *n.* Per-

suave, 1 swɛv *or* swäv; 2 swäv *or* swäv, *a.* Smooth and pleasant in manner; bland. — **suav′i-ty,** *n.* [-TIES², *pl.*] Geniality; urbanity.

sub-, *prefix.* **1.** Under; from under. **2.** Somewhat; slightly; nearly; as, *sub*vertical. **3.** Subordinate; secondary; inferior; lower; as, *sub*committee.

A large number of words beginning with *sub*- are self-explaining with the sense of (1) somewhat (words marked *); (2) secondary (words marked **).

sub″ab-dom′i-nal*
sub-ac′e-tate*
sub″a-cid′u-lous*
sub-ac′rid*

sub″a-cu′mi-nate*
sub″a-cute′*
sub″a-gen-cy**
sub″a′gent**

sub-an′gu-lar*
sub″as-so″ci-a′tion**
sub″as-trin′gent*
sub″cal-ca′re-ous*
sub-car′bu-ret″ed*
sub″ce-les′tial**
sub″cir′cu-lar*
sub′class″**
sub″co-lum′nar**
sub″com-mis′sion**
sub″com-mit′tee**
sub-con′cave*
sub″con-i-cal*
sub″con′scious*
sub″con-tract″**d, *v.*
sub″con′tract**, *n.*
sub″con-trac′tor**
sub″con-tra-ry*
sub″con′vex″* [& *n.*
sub-del′e-gate**d, *v.*
sub″de-part′ment**
sub-der′mal**

sub-dis′trict**
sub′ed′i-tor**
sub-ed′i-to′ri-al**
sub-en′try**
sub-gla′cial**
sub′head″**
sub′head″ing**
sub-lease′**t, *v.*
sub′lease**, *n.*
sub″les-see′**
sub″les′sor**
sub″lieu-ten′ant**
sub″max′il-la-ry*
sub-o′val*
sub-par′al-lel*
sub′sur″face**
sub′ten″an-cy**
sub′ten′ant**
sub″ter-res′tri-al**
sub′ti′tle**
sub′va-ri′e-ty*

sub-al′tern, 1 sub-ôl′tərn *or* sub′al-tərn; 2 sŭb-ạl′tern *or* sŭb′ạl-tern. **I.** *a.* Subordinate. **II.** *n.* A person of subordinate rank or position; especially, a military officer ranking below a captain.

sub″di-vide′d, 1 sub″dı-vaıd′; 2 sŭb″dı-vīd′, *vt. & vi.* To divide a part of; divide again.— **sub″di-vi′sion,** *n.* Division after division.

sub-dom′i-nant, 1 sub-dom′ı-nạnt, 2 sŭb-dŏm′ı-nant, *n.* *Mus.* The fourth note of the scale in any key.

sub-due′, 1 sub-dıū′; 2 sŭb-dū′, *vt.* [SUB-DUED′; SUB-DU′ING.] **1.** To obtain dominion over, as by war or force; overpower; overcome. **2.** To render mild; soften; tame.

sub-ject′,d, 1 sub-jekt′; 2 sŭb-jĕet′, *vt.* To make subject; submit; subdue; render liable to, as a penalty.— **sub-jec′tion,** *n.*

sub′ject, 1 sub′jekt; 2 sŭb′jĕet, *a.* Being under the power of another; subordinate; liable.

sub′ject, *n.* **1.** One who is under the government of a monarch. **2.** Something subjected to operation, thought, emotion, or discussion; in grammar, the word or phrase denoting the thing spoken of; the nominative case.— **sub-jec′tiv(e³,** *a.* Relating to, proceeding from, or taking place within the thinking subject: opposed to *objective.*

sub-join′, 1 sub-join′; 2 sŭb-jŏin′, *vt.* To add at the end; attach; affix.

sub′ju-gate, 1 sub′ju-gĕt; 2 sŭb′ju-gāt, *vt.* [-GAT″ED]d; -GAT″ING.] To subdue completely.— **sub″ju-ga′tion,** *n.*— **sub″ju-ga″-tor,** *n.*

1: ə = final; ı = habit; aısle; au = out; oıl; ıū = feud; ℭhin; go; ŋ = sing; ℭhin, this.

2: wọlf, dọ; bŏŏk, bōōt; fụll, rụle. cūre, bŭt, bûrn; ōil, bŏy; ğo, ġem; iŋk; thin, this.

sub-junc'tive, ⎱ 1 sub-juŋk'tɪv; 2 sŭb-
sub-junc'tivᵉ, ⎰ jŭŋe'tɪv. **I.** *a. Gram.* Of
or pertaining to that mode of the finite
verb that is used to express doubtful or
conditional assertion. **II.** *n.* The subjunctive mode, or a verb form of this
mode. [to a subordinate; underlet.
sub-let', 1 sub-let'; 2 sŭb-lĕt', *vt.* To let
sub'li-mate, 1 sub'lı-mēt; 2 sŭb'lı-māt.
I. *vt.* [-MAT"ED^d; -MAT"ING.] To convert
from a solid to a vapor by heat and then
solidify again by cooling; refine; purify.
II. *a.* Sublimated; refined. **III.** *n.* A
substance obtained by sublimating.— **sub″-
li-ma'tion,** *n.*
sub-lime', 1 sub-laim'; 2 sŭb-līm'. **I.** *vt.*
& *vi.* [SUB-LIMED'; SUB-LIM'ING.] **1.** To
exalt. **2.** To sublimate. **II.** *a.* Lofty;
grand; solemn; majestic; noble; supreme;
utmost. **III.** *n.* That which is sub-
lime, in any sense: usually with the
definite article. **-ly,** *adv.*— **sub-lim'i-ty,** 1
sub-lim'ı-tı; 2 sŭb-lim'ı-ty, *n.* [-TIES², *pl.*] **1.**
The state or quality of being sublime;
grandeur; loftiness; majesty.   **sub-lime'-
ness‡. 2.** That which is sublime; the acme;
climax; pinnacle.
sub'lu-na-ry, 1 sub'lıu-nē-rı; 2 sŭb'lū-nā-
ry, *a.* **1.** Situated beneath the moon.
sub-lu'nar‡. 2. Terrestrial; earthly.
sub″ma-rine', 1 sub″mə-rīn'; 2 sŭb″ma-
rīn', *a.* Existing, done, or operating beneath the surface of the sea, as a **submarine
boat.**
sub-merge', 1 sub-mŭrj'; 2 sŭb-mĕrg', *vt.*
[SUB-MERGED'; SUB-MERG'ING.] To place
or plunge under water; inundate; drown.
sub-merse'‡.— sub-mer'gence, *n.*   **sub-
mer'sion‡.**
sub-mit', 1 sub-mit'; 2 sŭb-mĭt', *v.* **I.**
t. [SUB-MIT"ED^d; SUB-MIT'TING.] **1.** To
give up to another; yield. **2.** To present
for the judgment of another. **3.** To
offer as one's own opinion. **II.** *i.* To
yield; surrender; be submissive.— **sub-mis'-
sion,** *n.* The act of submitting; obedience;
humility; resignation; meekness.— **sub-
mis'sive(eˢ, *a.* Willing or inclined to submit;
yielding; obedient; docile. **-ly,** *adv.* **-ness,** *n.*
sub-or'di-nate, 1 sub-ōr'dı-nēt; 2 sŭb-ōr'-
di-nāt. **I.** *vt.* [-NAT"ED^d; -NAT"ING.] To
make subordinate. **II.** 1 sub-ōr'd̯.-nıt; 2
sŭb-ōr'di-nat, *a.* Belonging to an inferior
order or rank; secondary; subject; sub-
servient. **III.** *n.* An inferior in rank or
official position. **-ly,** *adv.*— **sub-or″di-na'-
tion,** *n.*
sub-orn', 1 sub-ōrn'; 2 sŭb-ôrn', *vt.* To
induce to commit perjury; incite or instigate to evil; effect by instigation.— **sub″-
or-na'tion,** *n.*— **sub-orned',** *pa.*— **sub-
orn'er,** *n.*
sub-pe'na, 1 sub-pī'nə; 2 sŭb-pē'na. **I.**
vt. Law. To notify by subpena. **II.** *n.*
Law. A judicial writ requiring a person to
appear as a witness. **sub-pœ'na‡.**
sub-scribe', 1 sub-skraib'; 2 sŭb-scrīb', *vt.*
& *vi.* [SUB-SCRIBED'; SUB-SCRIB'ING.] To
write, as a name, underneath a document; sign with one's own name; give
written promise to pay (money); assent or
consent; agree to take a periodical or the
like.— **sub-scrib'er,** *n.*— **sub-scrip'tion,** 1
sub-skrip'shən; 2 sŭb-scrip'shon, *n.* The act
of subscribing, or that which is subscribed.
sub'se-quent, 1 sub'sı-kwent; 2 sŭb'se-
kwĕnt, *a.* Following in time, place, or
order; succeeding; consequent. **-ly,** *adv.*
sub-serve', ⎱ 1 sub-sŭrv'; 2 sŭb-sĕrv', *vt.* &
sub-serv'ˢ, ⎰ *vi.* To serve subordinately;
minister to; help on.
sub-ser'vi-ent, 1 sub-sŭr'vı-ent; 2 sŭb-
sĕr'vi-ĕnt, *a.* Adapted to promote some
end; acting in the interests of another;
obsequious.— **sub-ser'vi-en-cy,** *n.*   **sub-
ser'vi-ence‡.**
sub-side', 1 sub-said'; 2 sŭb-sīd', *vi.* [SUB-
SID'ED^d; SUB-SID'ING.] To quiet down;
abate; cease; sink; settle down.— **sub-si'-
dence,** 1 sub-sai'dens or sub'sı-dens; 2 sŭb-
sī'dĕnç or sŭb'sı-dĕnç, *n.* The act or process
of subsiding; a failing or sinking.
sub-sid'i-a-ry, 1 sub-sid'ı-ē-rı; 2 sŭb-
sĭd'i-ā-ry. **I.** *a.* **1.** Supplementary;
auxiliary. **2.** Of or like a subsidy. **II.**
n. [-RIES², *pl.*] An auxiliary; assistant.
sub'si-dy, 1 sub'sı-dı; 2 sŭb'si-dy, *n.*
[-DIES², *pl.*] Pecuniary aid.— **sub'si-dize,** 1
sub'sı-daiz; 2 sŭb'si-dīz, *vt.* [-DIZED'; -DIZ″-
ING.] To furnish with a subsidy. **sub'si-
dise‡.**
sub-sist', ⎰ 1 sub-sist'; 2 sŭb-sĭst', *v.* **I.** *t.*
To provide with sustenance; support. **II.**
i. **1.** To be furnished with sustenance;
live. **2.** To exist; inhere; continue.— **sub-
sis'tence,** *n.* The act of subsisting; sustenance; support; food. **sub-sis'ten-cy‡.**—
sub-sis'tent, *a.* Existing; inherent.
sub'soil', 1 sub'soil"; 2 sŭb'sŏil", *n.* The
stratum of earth next beneath the surface soil.
sub'stance, 1 sub'stans; 2 sŭb'stançe, *n.* **1.**
The material of which anything is made.
2. The essential part; brief summary;
solid basis. **3.** Wealth; property.— **sub-
stan'tial,** 1 sub-stan'shal; 2 sŭb-stăn'shal, *a.*
1. Solid; strong; important; valuable. **2.**
Possessed of sufficient means; responsible. **3.**
Actual; permanent; lasting. **4.** Conforming
to the essence of a thing; essential; fundamental.— **sub-stan″ti-al'i-ty,** *n.*— **sub-**

1: ȧrtistic, ärt; fat, fāre; fȧst; get, prĕy; hit, police; obey, gō; net, ôr; full, rūle; but, bûrn.
2: ärt, āpe, făt, fāre, fȧst, whạt, ạll; mē, gĕt, prey, fērn; hĭt, īce; ī=ĕ; ĭ=ĕ; gō, nŏt, ôr, wŏn,

stan′tial-ly, *adv.* — **sub-stan′tials,** *n. pl.* Fundamentals; necessities; as, the *substantials* of life.] To establish; verify.

sub-stan′ti-ate, *vt.* [-**AT′ED**ᵈ; -**AT″-ING.**] To establish; verify.

sub′stan-tive, (1 sub′stən-tiv; 2 sŭb′-
sub′stan-tivᵛ,) stan-tĭv. **I.** *a.* Capable of being used as a noun; denoting existence; real. **II.** *n. Gram.* A noun, or something used as a noun. **-ly,** *adv.*

sub′sti-tute, 1 sub′sti-tūt; 2 sŭb′sti-tūt. **I.** *vt.* [-**TUT′ED**ᵈ; -**TUT′ING.**] To put in the place of another; replace. **II.** *n.* One who or that which takes the place of another. — **sub″sti-tu′tion,** *n.*

sub-stra′tum, 1 sub-strē′tum; 2 sŭb-strā′tŭm, *n.* [-**STRA′TA,** 1 -strē′tə; 2 -strā′ta, *pl.*] An underlying stratum; foundation; groundwork.

sub-tend′ᵈ, 1 sub-tend′; 2 sŭb-tĕnd′, *vt.* To extend opposite to.

sub′ter-fuge, 1 sub′tər-fiūj; 2 sŭb′tér-fūg, *n.* A false excuse; pretense; evasion.

sub″ter-ra′ne-an, 1 sub″tə-rē′ni-an; 2 sŭb″tĕ-rä′ne-an, *a.* Underground; hidden. **sub″ter-ra′ne-ous‡.**

sub′tile, (1 sut′til; 2 sŭb′til, *a.* **1.** Deli-
sub′tilˢ,) cate; ethereal; rarefied; refined; hence, penetrating; pervasive. **2.** Subtle. **-ly,** *adv.* — **sub-til′i-ty,** 1 sub-til′i-ti; 2 sŭb-til′i-ty, *n.* The quality or state of being subtile; thinness; fineness. **sub′tile-ness‡.** — **sub′til-ty,** 1 sub′til-ti; 2 sŭb′til-ty, *n.* [-**TIES**ᶻ, *pl.*] Refinement; a nicety.

sub′tle, (1 sut′l; 2 sŭt′l, *a.* **1.** Cunning;
sut′lᴾ,) wily; crafty. **2.** Keen; discriminating; skilful; ingenious; clever. **3.** Subtile. — **sub′tle-ty,** 1 sut′l-ti; 2 sŭt′l-ty, *n.* [-**TIES**ᶻ, *pl.*] Artifice; cunning. **sub′tle-ness‡.** — **sub′tly,** 1 sut′li; 2 sŭt′ly, *adv.* In a subtle manner.

sub-tract′ᵈ, 1 sub-trakt′; 2 sŭb-trăkt′, *vt.* To take away; deduct; withdraw. — **sub-trac′tion,** *n.* The act or process of subtracting; a deducting. — **sub-trac′tivᵛ**(eˢ, *a.*

sub′tra-hend″, 1 sub′trə-hend″; 2 sŭb′tra-hĕnd″, *n.* That which is to be subtracted.

sub′urb, 1 sub′ərb; 2 sŭb′urb, *n.* A place adjacent to a city. — **sub-ur′ban,** *a.*

sub-vert′ᵈ, 1 sub-vŭrt′; 2 sŭb-vĕrt′, *vt.* To overthrow; utterly destroy. — **sub-ver′sion,** *n.* Overthrow; ruin. — **sub-ver′sivᵛ**(eˢ, *a.* Tending to subvert; destructive.

sub′way″, 1 sub′wē″; 2 sŭb′wā″, *n.* **1.** An underground way or passage. **2.** A conduit under a street for electric wires, gasmains, etc. **3.** An underground railroad or the tube in which it is operated.

suc-ceed′ᵈ, 1 suk-sīd′; 2 sŭc-cēd′, *vt. & vi.* **1.** To follow; come next in order. **2.** To meet with success.

suc-cess′, 1 suk-ses′; 2 sŭc-çĕs′, *n.* **1.** A prosperous or advantageous result. **2.** A successful person or affair. — **suc-cess′ful,** *a.* Obtaining success; prosperous. **-ly,** *adv.* — **suc-ces′sion,** 1 suk-sesh′an; 2 sŭc-çĕsh′on, *n.* **1.** A following consecutively. **2.** A sequence. — **suc-ces′sivᵛ**(eˢ, 1 suk-ses′iv; 2 sŭc-çĕs′iv, *a.* Following in succession; consecutive. **-ly,** *adv.* — **suc-ces′sor,** 1 suk-ses′ər; 2 sŭc-çĕs′or, *n.* One who or that which follows in succession.

suc-cinct′, 1 suk-siŋkt′; 2 sŭc-çiŋct′, *a.* Comprised within a narrow compass; concise. **-ly,** *adv.* **-ness,** *n.*

suc′cor, 1 suk′ər; 2 sŭc′or. **I.** *vt.* To go to the aid of; help. **II.** *n.* Help; relief; a helper.

suc′co-tash, 1 suk′o-tash; 2 sŭc′o-tăsh, *n.* [U. S.] A stew of green Indian corn and beans.

suc′cu-lent, 1 suk′yu-lent; 2 sŭc′yu-lĕnt, *a.* Juicy; fleshy, as a plant. — **suc′cu-lence,** *n.*

suc-cumb′ᵖ, (1 su-kum′; 2 sŭ-cŭm′, *vi.*
suc-cum′ᵖ,) To sink down as under a burden; yield; die.

such, 1 such; 2 sŭch. **I.** *a.* Of that kind; being the same. **II.** *pron.* Such a person or thing. **III.** *adv.* So.

suckᵗ, 1 suk; 2 sŭk, *v.* **I.** *t.* **1.** To draw into the mouth by lips and tongue. **2.** To absorb or draw in. **II.** *i.* **1.** To suckle. **2.** To draw in liquid by suction or absorption. — **suck,** *n.* The act of sucking; that which is sucked. — **suck′er,** *n.* **1.** One who or that which sucks; anything used for suction. **2.** One of various fishes. **3.** An adherent disk. **4.** A shoot arising at or near the root. — **suck′l**(eʳ, *vt. & vi.* [**SUCK′-L(E)D**ᴾ; **SUCK′LING.**] To give suck to, as at the breast; suck. — **suck′ling,** *n.* An unweaned babe. — **suc′tion,** 1 suk′shan; 2 sŭc-shon, *n.* The act of sucking. — **suc-to′ri-al,** *a.* Adapted for sucking or for adhesion.

sud′den, 1 sud′n; 2 sŭd′n. **I.** *a.* Happening quickly and without warning; hasty. **II.** *n.* The state of being sudden. **-ly,** *adv.* **-ness,** *n.*

su″dor-if′er-ous, 1 siū″dər-if′ər-us; 2 sū″-dor-ĭf′er-ŭs, *a.* Sweat-producing. — **su″dor-if′ic,** *a. & n.* [foam.

suds, 1 sudz; 2 sŭds, *n. pl.* Soapy water;

sue, 1 siū; 2 sū, *vt. & vi.* [**SUED**; **SU′ING.**] **1.** To bring legal action against. **2.** To entreat; beg.

su′et, 1 siū′et; 2 sū′ĕt, *n.* The fat about the loins of sheep, oxen, etc. — **su′et-y,** *a.*

suf′fer, 1 suf′ər; 2 sŭf′er, *vt. & vi.* **1.** To have a painful experience; feel pain. **2.** To endure. **3.** To undergo; experience. **4.** To sustain loss or injury. **5.** To tolerate; allow. — **suf′fer-a-bl**(eʳ, *a.* Such as can be suffered or endured; endurable. —

suf′fer-ance, 1 sŭf′ər-əns; 2 sŭf′er-anç, n. Negative consent; toleration.— **suf′fer-er,** n.— **suf′fer-ing,** n. Misery; distress.

suf-fice′, 1 su-fais′; 2 sŭ-fīç′, vt. & vi. [SUF-FICED′t; SUF-FIC′ING.] To be sufficient for; be adequate.— **suf-fi′cien-cy,** 1 su-fish′en-sı; 2 sŭ-fish′ĕn-çy, n. **1.** The state of being sufficient. **2.** That which is sufficient.— **suf-fi′cient,** a. Being all that is needful or requisite; enough. **-ly,** adv.

suf-fix′t, 1 su-fiks′; 2 sŭ-fīks′, vt. To add as a suffix.

suf′fix, 1 sŭf′iks; 2 sŭf′iks, n. An addition to the end of a word.

suf′fo-cate, 1 sŭf′o-kēt; 2 sŭf′o-cāt, vt. & vi. [-CAT″ED⁴; -CAT″ING.] To kill by stopping respiration; choke; stifle.— **suf″fo-ca′tion,** n.

suf′frage, 1 sŭf′rıj; 2 sŭf′raġ, n. **1.** A vote; assent. **2.** The right of voting. — **suf′fra-gette′,** n. A woman who advocates the right of women to vote.— **suf′fra-gist,** n. One who exercises the right to vote; a voter.

suf-fuse′, 1 su-fiūz′; 2 sŭ-fūs′, vt. [SUF-FUZE″P, {FUSED′; SUF-FUS″ING.] To overspread, as with a vapor, fluid, or color.— **suf-fu′sion,** n.

sug′ar, 1 shug′er; 2 shŭġ′ar. **I.** vt. To sweeten or cover with sugar. **II.** n. A sweet crystalline compound, chiefly from the juice of the sugar-cane or sugar-beet. — **sug′ar-beet″,** n. A sugar-producing variety of beet.— **s.cane,** n. A tall, stout, perennial grass of tropical regions, rich in sugar.— **s. maple,** n. The hard maple, from the sap of which maple-sugar is made.— **s.plum,** n. A small sweetmeat.— **sug′ar-y,** a.

sug-gest′d, 1 sug-jest′; 2 sŭġ-ġĕst′, vt. To bring up (an idea) by association or indirectly; hint; intimate. — **sug-ges′tion,** n. The act of suggesting; hint; insinuation; intimation.— **sug-ges′tiv**(es, a. Fitted or tending to suggest. **-ly,** adv. **-ness,** n.

su′i-cide, 1 siū′i-said; 2 sū′i-çīd, n. Self-murder or one who commits it.— **su′i-ci′dal,** a.

suit, 1 siūt; 2 sūt. **Id.** vt. & vi. To meet the requirements of; agree; please; prove satisfactory. **II.** n. **1.** The act of suing; solicitation; petition. **2.** A judicial action, as for the recovery of money. **3.** A series of things of like kind.— **suit′a-bl**(er, a. Capable of suiting; appropriate.—

suit″a-bil′i-ty, n. **suit′a-bl**(e-ness**r‡.**— **suit′a-bly,** adv.— **suit′or,** n. **1.** One who institutes a suit in court; a petitioner. **2.** A wooer.

suite, 1 swīt; 2 swīt, n. **1.** A succession of things forming a series; a set. **2.** A retinue.

sul′fur, {1 sŭl′fer; 2 sŭl′fur, n. A pale-**sul′phur,** } yellow, non-metallic, inflammable substance; brimstone.— **sul′fate, sul′phate,** n. A salt of sulfuric acid.— **sul′fid, sul′phid,** n. A compound of sulfur with an element or radical.— **sul′fu-rate, sul′phu-rate.** **I.** vt. [-RAT″ED⁴; -RAT″ING.] To treat with sulfur. **II.** a. Sulfureous. **III.** n. Sulfid.— **sul-fu′re-ous, sul-phu′re-ous,** a. Of or like sulfur.— **sul′fu-ret, sul′phu-ret,** n. A sulfid.— **sul-fu′ric, sul-phu′ric,** a. Pertaining to or derived from sulfur.— **sulfuric acid,** a colorless, corrosive liquid compound of sulfur. **oil of vitriol**t‡.— **sul′fur-ous, sul′phur-ous,** a. Pertaining to or like sulfur.

sulk, 1 sulk; 2 sŭlk. **It.** vi. To be sulky or sullen. **II.** n. A sulky mood or humor: often pl.— **sulk′y,** a. [SULK′I-ER; SULK′I-EST.] Sullenly cross.— **sulk′i-ly,** adv. — **sulk′i-ness,** n.

sulk′y, 1 sulk′ı; 2 sŭlk′ıes², pl.] A light two = wheeled one = horse vehicle for one person.

sul′len, 1 sul′en; 2 sŭl′ĕn, a. Obstinately and gloomily ill-humored. **-ly,** adv. **-ness,** n.

sul′ly, 1 sul′ı; 2 sŭl′ı, vt. & vi. [SUL′-LIED; SUL′LY-ING.] To tarnish; stain. **II.** n. [SUL′LIES², pl.] A stain; spot; blemish.

sul′tan, 1 sul′tan; 2 sŭl′tan, n. The sovereign of Turkey when an empire.— **sul-ta′na,** n. A sultan's wife, daughter, or mother.

sul′try, 1 sul′trı; 2 sŭl′try, a. [SUL′TRI-ER; SUL′TRI-EST.] Hot, moist, and still; close.— **sul′tri-ly,** adv.— **sul′tri-ness,** n.

sum, 1 sum; 2 sŭm. **I.** vt. [SUMMED, SUMD⁸; SUM′MING.] **1.** To recapitulate briefly: with up. **2.** To add into one total. **II.** n. **1.** Math. The result obtained by addition. The whole. **3.** Any indefinite amount. **4.** A problem in arithmetic.

Sugar-cane.

Common Sumacs.
1. A panicle and leaf of the stag-horn sumac. 2. A leaf of the dwarf sumac: a, the flower.

su′mac, 1 sū′mak or shū′mak; 2 sy′mặc or

shụ'măĕ, *n.* A shrub, whose leaves are much used for tanning and dyeing. See illus. on previous page. **su'macht.**

sum'ma-ry, 1 sum'ẽ-rı; 2 sŭm'a-ry. **I.** *a.* **1.** Concise. **2.** Instant; offhand. **II.** *n.* [-RIES², *pl.*] An abridgment or epitome.— **sum'ma-rize,** 1 sum'a-raız; 2 sŭm'a-rīz, *vt.* [-RIZED; -RIZ'ING.] To make a summary of. — **sum'ma-ri-ly,** *adv.*

sum'mer, 1 sum'ẽr; 2 sŭm'er, *n.* The hottest season of the year: including June, July, and August, in the northern hemisphere. [**mer-set‡.**]

sum'mer-sault, *n.* A somersault. **sum'-sum'mit,** 1 sum'ıt; 2 sŭm'ĭt, *n.* The highest point; the top; apex.

sum'mon, 1 sum'ẽn; 2 sŭm'on, *vt.* To command to appear; call; send for; arouse; bid.— **sum'mon-er,** *n.*— **sum'mons,** 1 sum'-ẽnz; 2 sŭm'ons, *n.* A call to attend, act, answer, surrender, etc.

sump'ter, 1 sump'tẽr; 2 sŭmp'tẽr, *n.* A pack-animal; as, a *sumpter*-horse or *sump-ter*-mule.

sump'tu-a-ry, 1 sump'chu-[-or -tıu-]ĕ-rı; 2 sŭmp'chu-[or -tū-]ä-ry, *a.* Pertaining to expense; limiting or regulating personal expenditure.

sump'tu-ous, 1 sump'chu-us *or* -tıu-us; 2 sŭmp'chu-ŭs *or* -tū-ŭs, *a.* Involving lavish expenditure; luxurious. **-ly,** *adv.* **-ness,** *n.*

sun, 1 sun; 2 sŭn. **I.** *vt.* & *vi.* [SUNNED, SUND²; SUN'NING.] To expose to the sun. **II.** *n.* **1.** The heavenly body that is the center of attraction and the main source of light and heat in the solar system. **2.** Any star that is the center of a system. **3.** Sunshine; sunlight. — **sun'beam",** *n.* A ray or beam of the sun; *pl.* sunlight. — **sun'burn",** 1². *vt.* & *vi.* To affect, or be affected, with sunburn. **II.** *n.* Discoloration or inflammation of the skin, produced by exposure to the sun. — **sun'burnt",** *a.* **sun'-burned"‡.**— **sun'-di'al,** *n.* A device that measures time by the movement of a shadow. — **sun'down",** *n.* Sunset. — **sun'flow"er,** *n.* A tall, erect herb of the aster family, with very large, flat, circular heads of flowers.— **sun'less,** *a.* Deprived of the light of the sun; dark; cheerless. — **sun'light",** *n.* The light of the sun. — **sun'ny,** *a.* [SUN'NI-ER; SUN'NI-EST.] **1.** Filled with the light and

Sunflower.

warmth of the sun. **2.** Bright like the sun.— **sun'rise",** *n.* **1.** The daily first appearance of the sun. **2.** The time at which the sun rises. — **sun'set",** *n.* **1.** The daily disappearance of the sun. **2.** The time at which the sun sets; twilight. — **sun'shade",** *n.* Something used as protection from the sun's rays, as a parasol. — **sun'shine",** *n.* The radiance of the sun; brightness. — **sun'shin"y,** *a.*— **sun'stroke",** *n.* Prostration from excessive heat.

Sun'day, 1 sun'dı; 2 sŭn'da, *n.* The first day of the week; the Christian Sabbath.

sun'der, 1 sun'dẽr; 2 sŭn'der, *vt.* & *vi.* To break; part, or be parted; sever.

sun'dry, 1 sun'drı; 2 sŭn'dry, *a.* Various; several.— **sun'dries,** *n. pl.* Items or things not separately specified.

sung, 1 sung; 2 sŭng, *imp.* & *pp.* of SING, *v.*

sunk, 1 sungk; 2 sŭngk, *imp.* & *pp.* of SINK, *v.*

sunk'en, 1 sungk'n; 2 sŭngk'n, *a.* **1.** Deeply depressed. **2.** Beneath the surface.

sup, 1 sup; 2 sŭp, *v.* [SUPPED†, SUPT³; SUP'-PING.] **I.** *t.* To take, as fluid food, in successive mouthfuls. **II.** To partake of (supper). **2.** To sip. **III.** *n.* A mouthful or taste of liquid or semiliquid food.

su'per-, *prefix.* Above; over; beyond. (1) Above in position; as, *super*scription. (2) Above in degree or amount; excessive; as, *super*abundant.

su"per-a-bound'd, 1 süʺpẽr-a-baund'; 2 süʺper-a-bound', *vt.* To abound to excess. — **su"per-a-bun'dance,** *n.*— **su"per-a-bun'-dant,** *a.* Abounding excessively. **-ly,** *adv.*

su"per-add'd, 1 süʺpẽr-ad'; 2 süʺper-ăd', *vt.* To add in addition to what has been added.— **su"per-ad-di'tion,** *n.*

su"per-an'nu-ate, 1 süʺper-an'yu-ēt; 2 süʺper-ăn'yu-āt, *vt.* & *vi.* [-AT"ED⁴; AT'-ING.] To incapacitate by age; retire on account of age.— **su"per-an"nu-a'tion,** *n.*

su-perb', 1 sıu-pûrb'; 2 sü-pêrb', *a.* Having grand, impressive beauty; majestic.

su"per-car'go, 1 süʺper-kär'go; 2 süʺper-eärʹgo, *n. Naut.* An agent sent by owners of goods in charge of a cargo.

su"per-cil'i-ous, 1 süʺper-sil'ı-us; 2 süʺper-çĭl'ı-ŭs, *a.* Haughty; contemptuous; arrogant. **-ly,** *adv.* **-ness,** *n.*

su"per-fi'cial, 1 süʺper-fish'al; 2 süʺper-fĭsh'al, *a.* Pertaining to surface; shallow; hasty; slight. **-ly,** *adv.*— **su"per-fi"ci-al'i-ty,** *n.* **su"per-fi'cial-ness‡.**

su'per-fine', 1 süʺper-faın; 2 süʺper-fīn. *a.* Of surpassing fineness.

su-per'flu-ous, 1 sıu-pûr'flu-us; 2 sü-pêr'flu-ŭs, *a.* More than is needed; needless. **-ly,** *adv.*— **su-per'flu'i-ty,** 1 süʺper-flu'ı-tı; 2 süʺper-fluʹi-ty, *n.* [-TIES², *pl.*] Superabundance; something superfluous. **su-per'flu-ous-ness‡.**

1: ə = final; ı = habit; aısle; au = out; oıl; ıü = feud; chin; go; ŋ = sing; thin, this.
2: wolf, dọ; bŏŏk, bŏŏt; fụll, rụle, cūre, bŭt, bûrn; ŏıl, bŏy; ġo, ġem: ıŋk; thin, this.

su″per-het′er-o-dyne, *a. Radio.* Describing radio-frequency oscillations varying from 50,000 to 100,000.

su″per-hu′man, 1 siū″pər-hiū′mən; 2 sū″per-hū′man, *a.* Exceeding human power or attainment.

su″per-im-pose′, 1 siū″pər-im-pōz′; 2 sū″per-im-pōz̄′, *vt.* To lay or impose on something else.— su″per-im″po-si′tion, *n.*

su″per-in-cum′bent, 1 siū″pər-in-kum′-bent; 2 sū″per-in-cŭm′bĕnt, *a.* Resting upon something else.

su″per-in-duce′t, 1 siū″pər-in-diūs′; 2 sū″per-in-dūc′, *vt.* To induce or give rise to additionally.

su″per-in-tend′d, 1 siū″pər-in-tend′; 2 sū″per-in-tĕnd′, *vt. & vi.* To have the charge and direction of; manage; supervise.— su″per-in-ten′dence, *n.* Direction and management.— su″per-in-ten′dent, *n.* One who superintends; a director.

su-pe′ri-or, 1 siu-pī′ri-ər; 2 sū-pē′ri-or. **I.** *a.* **1.** Surpassing; more excellent; preferable. **2.** Higher; upper. **II.** *n.* One who is superior: a chief.— su-pe″ri-or′i-ty, *n.*

su-per′la-tive, 1 siu-pur′lə-tiv; 2 sū-super′la-tiv̄, *pēr′la-tĭv.* **I.** *a.* Elevated to or expressing the highest degree. **II.** *n.* The highest degree of comparison of the adjective or adverb. -ly, *adv.* -ness, *n.*

su-per′nal, 1 siu-pūr′nəl; 2 sū-pēr′nal, *a.* Heavenly; exalted; lofty.

su″per-nat′u-ral, 1 siū″pər-nach′u-[or -nat′yu-]rəl; 2 sū″per-năch′u-[or -năt′yu-]ral. **I.** *a.* Transcending the forces of nature; miraculous. **II.** *n.* That which transcends nature. -ly, *adv.* -ness, *n.*

su″per-nu′mer-a-ry, 1 siū″pər-niū′mər-ē-rı; 2 sū″per-nū′mer-ā-rı. **I.** *a.* Being beyond a certain number; superfluous. **II.** *n.* [-RIES², *pl.*] A supernumerary person or thing; an actor with no speaking part.

su″per-scribe′, 1 siū″pər-skraib′; 2 sū″per-scrīb′, *vt.* [-SCRIBED′; -SCRIB′ING.] To write on the outside or on the upper part of.— su″per-scrip′tion, *n.* The act of superscribing an address on a letter; the address superscribed.

su″per-sede′, 1 siū″pər-sīd′; 2 sū″per-sēd′, *vt.* [-SED′ED⁴; -SED′ING.] **1.** To take the place of; replace. **2.** To suspend; annul.

su″per-ser′vice-a-ble(e², 1 siū″pər-sūr′vis-ə-bl; 2 sū″pēr-ser′viç-a-bl, *a.* Attempting needlessly or disagreeably to be of service; overofficious.

su″per-sti′tion, 1 siū″pər-stish′ən; 2 sū″per-stĭsh′on, *n.* **1.** A false religion based upon ignorance. **2.** Belief in omens, charms, and signs.— su″per-sti′tious, 1 siū″pər-stish′us; 2 sū″per-stĭsh′ŭs, *a.* Inclined to or influenced by superstition. -ly, *adv.* -ness, *n.*

su″per-struc′ture, 1 siū″pər-struk′chur or -tiur; 2 sū″per-strŭc′chur or -tūr, *n.* A structure built upon something else.

su″per-vene′, 1 siū″pər-vīn′; 2 sū″per-vēn′, *vi.* [-VENED′; -VEN′ING.] To follow closely upon something; to happen.— su″per-ven′tion, *n.*

su″per-vise′, 1 siū″pər-vaiz′; 2 sū″per-vīz̄′, *vt.* [-VISED′; -VIS′ING.] To superintend; inspect.— su″per-vi′sion, *n.*— su″per-vi′sor, *n.* A superintendent; inspector.

su-pine′, 1 siu-pain′; 2 sū-pīn′, *a.* **1.** Lying on the back. **2.** Inactive; indolent. -ly, *adv.* -ness, *n.*

sup′per, 1 sup′ər; 2 sŭp′er, *n.* The last meal of the day; a banquet.— sup′per-less, *a.* Having no supper; hungry.

sup-plant′d, 1 su-plant′; 2 sŭ-plănt′, *vt.* To take the place of, as by treachery; displace.

sup′ple, ⟩ 1 sup′l; 2 sŭp′l, *a.* **1.** Easily
sup′l², ⟩ bent; flexible; pliant. **2.** Compliant; submissive. -ness, *n.*

sup′ple-ment, 1 sup′li-ment or -mənt; 2 sŭp′le-ment. **I**d. *vt.* To make additions to. **II.** *n.* Something added; an addition to a book.— sup″ple-men′tal, *a.* Like a supplement; supplementing. sup″ple-men′ta-ry‡.

sup′pli-ant, 1 sup′li-ənt; 2 sŭp′li-ant. **I.** *a.* Entreating earnestly and humbly. **II.** *n.* One who supplicates.

sup′pli-cate, 1 sup′li-kēt; 2 sŭp′li-cāt, *vt. & vi.* [-CAT′ED⁴; -CAT′ING.] To seek humbly by earnest petition; pray to grant a favor.— sup′pli-cant. **I.** *a.* Asking or entreating humbly. **II.** *n.* One who supplicates.— sup″pli-ca′tion, *n.*— sup″pli-ca″to-ry, *a.*

sup-ply′, 1 su-plai′; 2 sŭ-plȳ′. **I.** *vt.* [SUP-PLIED′; SUP-PLY′ING.] **1.** To furnish with what is needed. **2.** To give; afford. **3.** To occupy temporarily. **II.** *n.* **1.** The available aggregate of things needed or demanded. **2.** An amount sufficient for a given use. **3.** A temporary incumbent.

sup-port′, 1 su-pōrt′; 2 sŭ-pôrt′. **I**d. *vt.* **1.** To bear the weight of; keep up. **2.** To provide for. **3.** To carry on. **4.** To bear or endure; tolerate. **5.** To sustain; defend; aid; nourish. **II.** *n.* **1.** The act of supporting. **2.** One who or that which supports. **3.** Subsistence; living. -er, *n.*— sup-port′a-bl(e², *a.* Endurable.

sup-pose′, 1 su-pōz′; 2 sŭ-pōz̄′, *v.* [SUP-POSED′; SUP-POS′ING.] **I.** *t.* To think or imagine; believe; assume as true.

II. *i.* To frame a supposition; think.—
sup-pos'a-bl(e), *a.* That may be supposed.
sup"po-si'tion, 1 sup"o-zish'an; 2 sŭp'o-
sĭsh'on, *n.* The act of supposing; something supposed: a conjecture.— **sup-pos"i'-**
ti'tious, 1 su-poz'i-tish'ŭs; 2 sŭ-pŏs'i-tish'-
ŭs, *a.* Supposed; fraudulent.

sup-press't, 1 su-pres'; 2 sŭ-prĕs', *vt.* **1.**
To overpower; crush; extinguish. **2.** To
withhold; repress; conceal.— **sup-pres'sion,**
n.— **sup-pres'sor,** *n.*

sup'pu-rate, 1 sup'yu-rēt; 2 sŭp'yu̇-rāt, *vi.*
[-RAT"ED⁴; -RAT"ING.] To form or generate
pus.— **sup"pu-ra'tion,** *n.*   [orbital.

su'pra-, *prefix.* Above; beyond; as, *supra-*
su-preme', 1 siu-prīm'; 2 sū-prēm', *a.* Highest in power, degree, etc. **-ly,** *adv.* **-ness,** *n.*
— **su-prem'a-cy,** 1 siu-prem'a-sı; 2 sū-
prēm'a-cy. *n.* The state of being supreme;
supreme power.

sur-, *prefix.* Same as SUPER-.

sur'cin"gle,) 1 sŭr'siṇ'gl; 2 sûr'çiṇ'gl, *n.*
sur'cin"gle,) **1.** A girth or strap encircling the body of a beast of burden. **2.**
A girdle.

sure, 1 shūr; 2 shur, *a.* **1.** Not liable to
change or failure. **2.** Reliable; trustworthy. **3.** Certain; positive.— **sure's**
foot"ed, *a.* Not liable to fall or stumble.—
sure'ly, *adv.*— **sure'ness,** *n.*— **sure'ty,** *n.*
[-TIES²; *pl.*] **1.** One who becomes responsible
for another; a bondsman; security; pledge.
2. The state of being sure; certainty.—
sure'ty-ship, *n.*

surf, 1 sŭrf; 2 sûrf, *n.* The swell of the sea,
that breaks upon a shore.

sur'face, 1 sŭr'fis; 2 sûr'faç, *n.* **1.** The
outside of anything. **2.** *Geom.* That
which has length and breadth, but not
thickness.— **sur'face=road",** *n.* A railroad
on the surface of the ground; distinguished
from an *elevated railroad* or a *subway.*

sur'feit,) 1 sŭr'fit; 2 sûr'fiit. **I**⁴. *vt. & vi.*
sur'fits,) To overfeed; supply or be supplied to satiety. **II.** *n.* **1.** Excess in eating or drinking. **2.** Satiety. **-ing,** *pa. & n.*

surge, 1 sŭrj; 2 sûrg. **I.** *vt. & vi.* [SURGED;
SURG'ING.] To raise or rise high and roll
onward, as waves. **II.** *n.* **1.** A great
wave; billow. **2.** The act of surging.

sur'geon, 1 sŭr'jan; 2 sŭr'gon, *n.* One who
practises surgery.— **sur'ger-y,** *n.* [-IES²; *pl.*]
The treatment of injuries, deformities, etc.,
by operations or instruments.— **sur'gi-cal,**
a. **-ly,** *adv.*

sur'loin", *n.* Same as SIRLOIN.

sur'ly, 1 sŭr'lı; 2 sûr'ly, *a.* [SUR'LI-ER;
SUR'LI-EST.] Crabbed; cross; rude; gruff.
— **sur'li-ly,** *adv.*— **sur'li-ness,** *n.*

sur-mise', 1 sur-maiz'; 2 sŭr-mīş'. **I.** *vt.*
[SUR-MISED'; SUR-MIS'ING.] To conjecture;

suppose. **II.** *n.* A conjecture; supposition.

sur-mount'd, 1 sur-maunt'; 2 sŭr-mount',
vt. To overcome; conquer.— **sur-mount'a-ble,** *a.*

sur'name, 1 sŭr'nĕm *or* sur-nĕm'; 2
sûr'nām *or* sŭr-nām'. **I.** *vt.* To call by
a surname. **II.** *n.* A name subjoined
to a personal name; family name.

sur-pass't, 1 sur-pas'; 2 sŭr-pàs', *vt.* To
go beyond; excel.— **sur-pass'a-bl(e)**, *a.*—
sur-pass'ing, *pa.* Preeminent; exceeding.
-ly, *adv.*

sur'plice,) 1 sŭr'plıs; 2 sûr'pliç, *n.* A vest-
sur'pliss,) ment worn by the clergy of
certain churches.

sur'plus, 1 sŭr'plus; 2 sûr'plŭs, *n.* That
which remains above what has been used
or is required.

sur-prize',) 1 sur-praiz'; 2 sŭr-prīz'. **I.** *vt.*
sur-prise') [SUR-PRIZED'; SUR-PRIZ'ING.]
To strike with astonishment; take unawares at a disadvantage. **II.** *n.* The act
of surprizing, or the state of being surprized: a sudden and unexpected event.—
sur-priz'ing-ly, *adv.* **sur-pris'ing-ly†.**

sur-priz'al,) 1 sur-praiz'al; 2 sŭr-prīş'al, *n.*
sur-pris'al,) The act of surprizing; surprize.

sur-ren'der, 1 su-ren'dar; 2 sŭ-rĕn'der.
I. *vt. & vi.* **1.** To yield to; give up, as
to an enemy; yield. **2.** To resign; relinquish. **II.** *n.* The act of surrendering.

sur"rep-ti'tious, 1 sur"ep-tish'us; 2 sŭr'-
ĕp-tish'ŭs, *a.* Accomplished by secret or
improper means; stealthy; underhanded.
-ly, *adv.* **-ness,** *n.*

sur'ro-gate, 1 sur'o-gēt; 2 sŭr'o-gāt, *n.* **1.**
A substitute. **2.** [U. S.] A probate judge.

sur-round'd, 1 su-raund'; 2 sŭ-round', *vt.*
To place something around; encompass;
enclose; encircle.— **sur-round'ing,** *n.* That
which environs; the act of one who surrounds.

sur-veil'lance, 1 sur-vē'lans *or* sur-vĕl'-
yans; 2 sŭr-ve'lanç *or* sûr-vel'yanç, *n.*
The act of watching, or the state of being
watched.

sur-vey', 1 sur-vē'; 2 sŭr-ve'. **I.** *vt.* To
view in its entirety; scrutinize; inspect;
measure, as land. **II.** *n.* The operation of surveying; a comprehensive view;
inspection.— **sur-vey'ing,** *n.* The measurement of land.— **sur-vey'or,** *n.*— **sur-vey'or-ship,** *n.*

sur-vive', 1 sur-vaiv'; 2 sûr-vīv', *v.* [SUR-
VIVED'; SUR-VIV'ING.] **I.** *t.* To outlive;
outlast; live through. **II.** *i.* To remain
alive; exist.— **sur-viv'al,** *n.* **1.** The act
of surviving; an outliving. **2.** Something
surviving.— **sur-vi'vor,** *n.*

1: ə = final; ı = habit; aisle; au = out; oil; iū = feud; chin; go; ŋ = sing; chin, this.
2: woḷf, do̜; bōok, bōot; fu̇ll, ru̇le, cūre, bu̇t, bûrn; ŏil, bŏy; g̈o, g̈em; iṇk; thin, this.

sus-cep'ti-bl(e[r], 1 sus-sep'tı-bl; 2 sŭ-çĕp'-ti-bl, *a.* Yielding readily; sensitive; impressionable.— **sus-cep"ti-bil'l-ty,** *n.*— **sus-cep'ti-bly,** *adv.*

sus-pect'[d], 1 sus-pekt'; 2 sŭs-pĕct', *v.* **I.** *t.* **1.** To imagine to exist; mistrust; conjecture. **2.** To infer the guilt of (a person) on slight or no evidence; distrust. **II.** *i.* To be suspicious.

sus-pend'[d], 1 sus-pend'; 2 sŭs-pĕnd', *v.* **I.** *t.* **1.** To cause to hang down from a support. **2.** To interrupt; stay; hold undecided; debar from any privilege. **II.** *i.* To cease from action or operation; stop payment.— **sus-pend'er,** *n.* One who or that which suspends; one of a pair of straps for supporting the trousers.— **sus-pense',** *n.* **1.** The state of being undecided; uncertainty. **2.** The state of being suspended.— **sus-pen'sion,** 1 sus-pen'shan; 2 sŭs-pĕn'shon, *n.* The act of suspending; also, that which is suspended.— **suspension bridge,** any bridge in which the roadway is stretched without support from below over the interval to be crossed.— **sus-pen'so-ry,** *a.* Suspending; sustaining; delaying.

sus-pi'cion, 1 sus-pish'an; 2 sŭs-pĭsh'on, *n.* **1.** The act of suspecting; conjecture; mistrust. **2.** The least particle, as of a flavor.— **sus-pi'cious,** *a.* **1.** Inclined to suspect. **2.** Questionable. **3.** Indicating suspicion. **-ly,** *adv.* **-ness,** *n.*

sus-tain', 1 sus-tēn'; 2 sŭs-tān', *vt.* **1.** To uphold, as a weight; keep up; encourage; support; maintain. **2.** To endure; suffer. **3.** To establish; prove.— **sus'te-nance,** 1 sus'tı-nans; 2 sŭs'te-nanç, *n.* The act or process of sustaining; also, subsistence; food.— **sus"ten-ta'tion,** 1 sus"ten-tē'shan; 2 sŭs"-tĕn-tā'shon, *n.* Support of life; maintenance.

sut'ler, 1 sut'lər; 2 sŭt'ler, *n.* A small trader who follows an army.

sut-tee', 1 su-tī'; 2 sŭ-tē', *n.* A former custom requiring a Hindu widow to immolate herself on the funeral pyre of her husband; also, the widow so immolated.

su'ture, 1 siū'chur *or* -tiur; 2 sū'chur *or* -tūr, *n.* **1.** A seam; junction. **2.** A sewing or joining.

su'ze-rain, 1 siū'ze-rēn; 2 sū'ze-rān, *n.* A person or state invested with paramount authority over another.— **su"ze-rain'ty,** *n.*

swab, 1 sweb; 2 swab. **I.** *vt.* [SWABBED, SWABD[s]; SWAB'BING.] To clean out with a swab. **II.** *n.* A soft substance on the end of a handle, for cleaning.— **swab'ber,** *n.*

swad'dle, 1 swed'l; 2 swạd'l, *vt.* [SWAD'-swad'dl**[r]**, } DLED; SWAD'DLING.] To wrap around with a bandage; swathe.

swag'ger, 1 swag'ər; 2 swăg'er. **I.** *vi.* To walk with a swaying motion; boast; bluster. **II.** *n.* A boastful, blustering manner.— **swag'ger-er,** *n.*

swain, 1 swēn; 2 swān, *n.* A youthful rustic; a lover. [ground.

swale, 1 swēl; 2 swāl, *n.* Low, marshy

swal'low, 1 swel'o; 2 swạl'o, *vt.* **1.** To take into the stomach, as food. **2.** To engulf; take in; accept; believe credulously; endure quietly. **3.** To take back; recant.

swal'low[1], *n.* That which is swallowed at one time; the act of swallowing.

swal'low[2], *n.* A small, swift bird with long, pointed wings, and forked tail.

swam, 1 swam; 2 swăm, *imp.* of SWIM, *v.*

swamp, 1 swomp; 2 swąmp. **I**[t]. *vt. & vi.* To sink, as a boat, by filling with water; ruin; be overwhelmed. **II.** *n.* A tract of low wet land; a bog; morass; marsh.— **swamp'y,** *a.*

swan, 1 swen; 2 swạn, *n.* A large, web-footed, long-necked bird, noted for its grace on the water.— **swans'-down",** *n.* **1.** The down of a swan, often used for dress-trimming. **2.** A soft, thick, woolen cloth.— **swan'skin",** *n.* The unplucked skin of a swan.

Swans. 1/45

Fabrics. 1. The whooping swan. 2. The whistling swan. 3. The trumpeter swan.

swap, 1 swop; 2 swap. **I.** *vt. & vi.* [SWAPPED[t], SWAPT[s]; SWAP'PING.] [Colloq.] To exchange; trade. **II.** *n.* The act of swapping.

sward, 1 swōrd; 2 swạrd, *n.* Grassy land; turf.— **sward'ed, sward'y,** *a.*

sware‖, 1 swār; 2 swâr, *imp.* of SWEAR, *v.*

swarm, 1 swōrm; 2 swạrm. **I.** *vt. & vi.* **1.** To come or bring forth in swarms; throng. **2.** To send out a new colony, as bees. **II.** *n.* A large number, as of bees; a throng.

swarth'y, 1 swōrfh'ı; 2 swạrth'y, *a.* [SWARTH'I-ER; SWARTH'I-EST.] Having a dark hue; tawny. swart‡.— **swarth'l-ly,** *adv.*— **swarth'i-ness,** *n.*

swash, 1 swosh; 2 swąsh. **I**[t]. *vi.* To dash noisily, as water; splash. **II.** *n.* The splash of a liquid.— **swash'buck"ler,** *n.* A swaggering ruffian.

swath, 1 swôth; 2 swạth, *n.* A line of cut grass, as left by a scythe.

swathe, 1 swēth; 2 swăth. **I.** *vt.* [SWATHED; SWATH'ING.] To bind or wrap, as in bandages. **II.** *n.* A bandage for swathing.

sway, 1 swē; 2 swā, *vt. & vi.* **1.** To lean or incline to one side; bend; swing; oscillate. **2.** To direct; influence; rule.

sway, 1 swē; 2 swā, *n.* **1.** Government; dominion. **2.** The act of swaying.

swear, 1 swâr; 2 swâr, *v.* [SWORE or SWARE‖; SWORN; SWEAR'ING.] **I.** *t.* **1.** To affirm solemnly, with an appeal to God or something sacred; make a solemn affirmation. **2.** To utter profanely. **3.** To administer a legal oath to. **II.** *i.* **1.** To give testimony under oath. **2.** To vow. **3.** To blaspheme; curse.— **swear'er,** *n.*— **swear'ing,** *n.*

sweat, 1 swet; 2 swĕt, *v.* [SWEAT or SWEAT'ED^d; SWEAT'ING.] **I.** *t.* **1.** To send forth through the pores. **2.** To cause to perspire. **II.** *i.* To exude moisture through the pores of the skin; perspire; hence, to toil.— **sweat'er,** *n.*— **sweat'shop",** *n.* A place where work, as the manufacture of clothing, is done at unreasonable hours for inadequate pay.— **sweat'i-ness,** *n.*— **sweat'y,** *a.*

sweat, *n.* **1.** Sensible perspiration, or any moisture resembling it. **2.** The act or state of sweating. **3.** Hard labor.

Swede, 1 swīd; 2 swēd, *n.* A native or naturalized inhabitant of Sweden.— **Swed'ish. I.** *a.* Pertaining to Sweden, the Swedes, or their language. **II.** *n.* The language of Sweden.

sweep, 1 swīp; 2 swēp, *v.* [SWEPT; SWEEP'ING.] **I.** *t.* **1.** To collect or clear away with a broom. **2.** To move with a broad, swift action, as of a brush or broom. **II.** *i.* **1.** To brush a floor, etc., with a broom. **2.** To move with a strong, even action.

sweep, *n.* **1.** The act or result of sweeping; a broad, strong, sustained movement, as of a river. **2.** Range, compass, extent of stroke, or of vision, etc.; a curve or bend, or something bent. **3.** A sweeper.— **sweep'er,** *n.*— **sweep'ings,** *n. pl.* Things swept up; refuse.

sweet, 1 swīt; 2 swēt. **I.** *a.* **1.** Agreeable to the taste; tasting like sugar. **2.** Harmonious; lovely; restful. **3.** Agreeable or delightful. **4.** Gentle; kind; amiable. **II.** *n.* Something sweet; a sweetmeat. **-ly,** *adv.* **-ness,** *n.*— **sweet'bread",** *n.* A gland connecting with the alimentary canal, as of a calf.— **sweet'bri"er,** *n.* A stout prickly rose.— **sweet'en,** *vt. & vt.* **1.** To make or become sweet or sweeter. **2.** To make or become more endurable; lighten. **3.** To make or become wholesome.— **sweet'en-**

ing, *n.* **1.** The act of making sweet. **2.** That which sweetens.— **sweet'heart",** *n.* One loved by or as a lover.— **sweet'ish,** *a.* Somewhat sweet. **-ness,** *n.*— **sweet'meat",** *n.* A confection, preserve, or the like.

swell, 1 swel; 2 swĕl, *v.* [SWELLED or swel^P, } SWOL'LEN, SWELD^s; SWELL'ING.] **I.** *t.* To increase the bulk of; enlarge; inflate. **II.** *i.* **1.** To be inflated. **2.** To increase in force, intensity, or volume; rise up; grow.— **swell'ing,** *n.* The act of expanding; enlargement; protuberance.

swell, 1 swel; 2 swĕl, *a.* Pertaining to swells; dandified.

swell, *n.* **1.** A swelling. **2.** A billow. **3.** A person of the ultrafashionable set.

swel'ter, 1 swel'tər; 2 swĕl'ter, *vt. & vi.* To oppress or be oppressed with heat.

swept, 1 swept; 2 swĕpt, *imp. & pp.* of SWEEP, *v.*

swerve, 1 swûrv; 2 swĕrv, *vt. & vi.* swerv^s, } [SWERV(E)D^s; SWERV'ING.] To turn from a course; deflect; deviate.

swift, 1 swift; 2 swĭft. **I.** *a.* **1.** Moving rapidly; fleet; rapid; quick. **2.** Passing rapidly; brief. **3.** Unexpected; sudden. **II.** *n.* A swallow-like bird, as the chimney-swift. **-ly,** *adv.* **-ness,** *n.*

Chimney-swift and its Nest. ⅙

swill, 1 swil; 2 swil. **I.** *vt. & vi.* To drink greedily and to excess; fill; inebriate. **II.** *n.* Liquid food or kitchen refuse given to swine.

swim, 1 swim; 2 swĭm, *vt. & vi.* [SWAM or SWUM; SWUM; SWIM'MING.] To move in or pass through (water) by movements of the limbs, fins, or the like; float.— **swim'mer,** *n.*— **swim'ming,** *ppr. & vn.*— **swim'ming-ly,** *adv.* In a swimming manner; easily, rapidly, and successfully.

swim, *vi.* To be dizzy.

swim, *n.* **1.** The action of swimming. **2.** A gliding, swaying movement.

swin'dler, 1 swin'dlər; 2 swĭn'dler, *n.* A rogue, cheat.— **swin'dle(r,** *vt. & vt.* [SWIN'DL(E)D^d; SWIN'DLING.] To cheat and defraud. **II.** *n.* A cheating; fraud.

swine, 1 swain; 2 swīn, *n. sing. & pl.* A pig or pigs collectively.— **swine'herd",** *n.* A tender of swine.— **swin'ish. -ly,** *adv.* **-ness,** *n.*

swing, 1 swiŋ; 2 swĭng. **I.** *vt. & vi.* [SWUNG or SWANG; SWING'ING; SWUNG.] **1.** To move to and fro while suspended;

move or wave rhythmically. **2.** To turn, as on a pivot; wheel; turn about. **II.** n. **1.** The action of swinging. **2.** A free swaying motion. **3.** A contrivance with a seat, on which a person may swing as a pastime. **4.** Free course; compass; sweep.

swinge, 1 swinj; 2 swĭnj, vt. [SWINGED; SWINGE′ING.] **1.** To weld; forge. **2.** To flog.

swing′ing, ppr. & verbal n. of SWING, v.

swin′gl(e)r, 1 swiŋ′gl; 2 swĭŋ′gl, n. **1.** A wooden implement, for beating flax. **2.** The short wooden bar of a flail.—**swin′-gle-tree″,** n. A horizontal cross-bar, to the ends of which the traces of a harness are attached. **sin′gle-tree″‡.**

Swingletrees.

s, s, swingle-
trees; t, traces;
d, doubletree;
p, plow-beam.

swirl, 1 swûrl; 2 swîrl.
I. vt. & vi. To whirl along, as in eddies. **II.** n. A whirling along, as an eddy; whirl.

swish, 1 swĭsh; 2 swĭsh. **I**t. vt. & vi. To move with a whistling sound, as a whip. **II.** n. A hissing sound.

Swiss, 1 swis; 2 swĭs. **I.** a. Pertaining to Switzerland, an Alpine republic of central Europe. **II.** n. [Swiss or Swiss′es‖, pl.] A native or inhabitant of Switzerland.

switch, 1 swich; 2 swĭch. **I**t. vt. & vi. **1.** To whip or lash with a switch; make a lashing motion. **2.** To shift from one track to another, as a car. **II.** n. **1.** A small flexible rod; light whip. **2.** A tress of hair. **3.** A mechanism for shifting a railway train, an electric current, etc. **4.** The act of switching.—**switch′man,** n. [-MEN, pl.] One who handles railway-switches.

swiv′el, 1 swiv′l; 2 swĭv′l, n. A coupling device, as on a chain, permitting either half of the chain to rotate independently.

swob, swob′ber, n. Same as SWAB, etc.

swol′len, 1 swol′n; 2 swôl′n, pa. Swelled.

swoon, 1 swūn; 2 swōōn. **I.** vi. To faint. **II.** n. A fainting-fit.

swoop, 1 swūp; 2 swōōp. **I**t. vi. To sweep down, as a hawk on its prey. **II.** n. A swooping down, as by a bird of prey.

sword, 1 sōrd; 2 sôrd, n. A long blade fixed in a hilt, as a weapon; military power.—**sword′fish″,** n. A large fish of the open sea, having the bones of the upper jaw consolidated to form an elongated sword-like process.—**swords′man,** n. [-MEN, pl.] One skilful with the sword.

swore, sworn, imp. & pp. of SWEAR, v.

swum, 1 swum; 2 swŭm, imp. & pp of SWIM, v.

swung, 1 swuŋ; 2 swŭng, imp. & pp. of SWING, v.

syc′a-mine‖, 1 sĭk′a-mĭn; 2 sy̆c′a-mĭn, n.

syc′a-more, 1 sĭk′e-mōr; 2 sy̆c′a-môr, n. **1.** A bushy tree of Syria and Egypt, allied to the fig. **2.** [U.S.] The button-wood.

syc′o-phant‖, 1 sĭk′o-fant; 2 sy̆c′-o-fant, n. A servile flatterer.—**syc′o-phan-cy,** n. The practises of a sycophant; base flattery; fawning.—**syc″o-phan′-tic, -ti-cal,** a.

Sycamore.
1/9

a, the fertile
head or "but-
tonball." 1/3

syl′la-ble, 1 sil′a-bl; 2 sy̆l′a-bl. **I.** vt. To utter or express in syllables. **II.** n. A single vocal sound forming a word, or part of a word.—**syl-lab′ic,** a. Pertaining to or consisting of syllables.—**syl-lab′i-cal,** a.—**syl-lab′i-cal-ly,** adv.—**syl-lab′i-cate,** vt. [-CAT′ED‡-CAT′ING.] **syl-lab′i-fy‡.—syl-lab″i-ca′tion,** n. **syl-lab″i-fi-ca′tion‡.**

syl′la-bus, 1 sil′a-bus; 2 sy̆l′a-bŭs, n. [-BI, 1-bai; 2-bī, pl.] A summary or schedule of contents; abstract.

syl′lo-gism, 1 sil′o-jizm; 2 sy̆l′o-gĭṣm, n. The logical form of reasoning, in which two premises lead necessarily to a conclusion.—**syl′lo-gis′tic,** a. **syl′lo-gis′ti-cal‡.**—**syl′lo-gis′ti-cal-ly,** adv.

sylph, 1 silf; 2 sy̆lf, n. **1.** Myth. An ethereal being living in and on the air. **2.** A slender, graceful girl. **3.** A South-American humming-bird.—**sylph′-like″,** a. Like a sylph; slender and graceful. **sylfr.**

syl′van, 1 sil′van; 2 sy̆l′van, a. Forest-like; rustic. **sil′van‡.**

sym′bol, 1 sim′bal; 2 sy̆m′bol, n. **1.** Something that stands for something else; an emblem; a type. **2.** A character, mark, etc., indicating something, as a quantity in mathematics.—**sym-bol′ic,** a. **sym-bol′i-cal‡.—sym-bol′i-cal-ly,** adv.—**sym′bo-lism,** n.—**sym′bo-list,** n.—**sym′bol-ize,** vt.—**sym′bol-iz″er,** n.

sym′me-try, 1 sim′i-tri; 2 sy̆m′e-try, n. [-TRIES², pl.] Due correspondence of parts or elements; harmony.—**sym-met′ri-cal,** a. Harmonious.—**-ly,** adv.—**sym-met′ric,** a.

sym′pa-thy, 1 sim′pa-thi; 2 sy̆m′pa-thy, n. [-THIES², pl.] **1.** Feeling correspondent to that of another; fellow-feeling: followed by with. **2.** Pity; commiseration: followed by for. **3.** Congeniality; accord; affinity.—**sym″pa-thet′ic,** a. **1.** Pertaining

to sympathy. **2.** Having a fellow=feeling for others. **3.** Congenial.— **sym″pa-thet′i-cal,** *a.* **-ly,** *adv.*— **sym′pa-thize,** *vi.* [-THIZED: -THIZ′ING.] **1.** To share the feelings of another. **2.** To be in harmony with another. **sym′pa-thīse‡.— sym″pa-thīz″er,** *n.* **-thīs″er‡.**

sym′pho-ny, 1 sim′fo-ni; 2 sy̆m′fo-ny, *n.* [-NIES², *pl.*] **1.** A harmonious mingling of sounds. **2.** *Mus.* (1) A composition for an orchestra. (2) A subordinate instrumental part, as a prelude, etc.

sym-po′si-um, 1 sim-pō′zi-um; 2 sy̆m-pō′si-ŭm, *n.* [-SI-A, *pl.*] **1.** A drinking together; banquet. **2.** A collection of opinions or essays.

symp′tom, 1 simp′tom; 2 sy̆mp′tom, *n.* A phenomenon of disease; a sign, token, or indication.— **symp″tom-at′ic,** *a.* **symp″tom-at′i-cal‡.— symp″tom-at′i-cal-ly,** *adv.*

syn′a-gog, } 1 sin′a-gog; 2 sy̆n′a-gŏg, *n.*
syn′a-gogue, } A place of meeting for Jewish worship; a Jewish congregation.

syn″co-pa′tion, 1 siŋ″ko-pē′shon; 2 sy̆n″co-pā′shon, *n. Mus.* The continuing of the unaccented last note of a measure through the following accented note of the next measure; characteristic of so=called "ragtime" music.

syn′co-pe, 1 siŋ′ko-pī; 2 sy̆n′co-pē, *n.* **1.** The dropping of a vowel or syllable from the midst of a word. **2.** Sudden faintness.

syn′di-cal-ism, 1 sin′di-kal-izm; 2 sy̆n′di-cal-ism, *n.* A method of enforcing the demands of labor by means of sympathetic strikes.

syn′di-cate, 1 sin′di-kēt; 2 sy̆n′di-cāt, *n.* An association of persons to carry on some enterprise requiring large capital.

syn′od, 1 sin′ad; 2 sy̆n′od, *n.* An ecclesiastical council; hence, any deliberative assembly.— **sy-nod′i-cal,** 1 si-nod′i-kal; 2 sy-nŏd′-i-cal, *a.* **sy-nod′ic‡.— sy-nod′i-cal-ly,** *adv.*

syn′o-nym, 1 sin′o-nim; 2 sy̆n′o-ny̆m, *n.* A word having the same, or nearly the same, meaning as some other; one of two or more words that have one or more meanings in common, but otherwise differ. **syn′o-nyme‡.— sy-non′y-mous,** 1 si-non′i-mus; 2 sy-nŏn′y-mŭs, *a.* Equivalent or similar in meaning.

sy-nop′sis, 1 si-nop′sis; 2 sy-nŏp′sis, *n.* [-SES, *pl.*] A summary.— **sy-nop′tic,** *a.* **sy-nop′ti-cal‡.**

syn′tax, 1 sin′taks; 2 sy̆n′tăks, *n.* **1.** The part of grammar that treats of the sentence and its construction. **2.** The construction of sentences in conformity with rule.— **syn-tac′tic,** *a.* **syn-tac′ti-cal‡.— syn-tac′ti-cal-ly,** *adv.*

syn′the-sis, 1 sin′thi-sis; 2 sy̆n′the-sis, *n.* [-SES, *pl.*] A putting together; construction.— **syn-thet′ic, -i-cal,** *a.* **-i-cal-ly,** *adv.*

sy′phon, sy′ren, *n.* Same as SIPHON, SIREN.

Syr′i-ac, 1 sir′i-ak; 2 sy̆r′i-ăc. **I.** *a.* Pertaining to Syria or its language. **II.** *n.* The language of Syria.

syr′inge, 1 sir′inj; 2 sy̆r′ing. **I.** *vt.* [SYR′-INGED; SYR′ING-ING.] To spray or inject by a syringe. **II.** *n.* An instrument by which to withdraw a fluid from a reservoir and eject it in a stream.

syr′up, syr′up-y. Same as SIRUP, etc.

sys′tem, 1 sis′tem; 2 sy̆s′tĕm, *n.* **1.** Orderly arrangement, as of parts or elements, into a whole; any orderly classification. **2.** A whole as made up of parts, as the human body. **3.** Orderliness; method.— **sys″tem-at′ic,** *a.* **1.** Pertaining to system. **2.** Methodical.— **sys″tem-at′i-cal-ly,** *adv.*— **sys′tem-a-tize,** 1 sis′tem-a-taiz; 2 sy̆s′tĕm-a-tiz, *vt.* [-TIZED; -TIZ″ING.] To reduce to a system; dispose methodically. **sys′tem-a-tise‡.— sys′tem-a-tiz″er,** *n.*

T

T, t, 1 tī; 2 tī, *n.* [TEES, T's, or *T*s, 1 tīz; 2 tēs, *pl.*] The twentieth letter in the English alphabet.

tab, 1 tab; 2 tăb, *n.* A flap, strip, tongue, or appendage of something.

ta-bas′co, 1 ta-bas′ko; 2 ta-băs′co, *n.* [Mex.] A variety of the red pepper plant— *Pimiento de Tabasco:* so called by José Mociño, 1787.

tab′by, 1 tab′i; 2 tăb′y. **I.** *a.* Watered; mottled. **II.** *n.* [TAB′BIES², *pl.*] **1.** Any watered fabric. **2.** A brindled cat; any female cat.

tab′er-na-cle, } 1 tab′ar-na-kl; 2 tăb′er-
tab′er-na-cl‡, } nă-el. **I.** *vi.* To dwell in a tent. **II.** *n.* **1.** A tent, booth, or other slight shelter. **2.** A house of worship; especially, the portable sanctuary used by the Israelites in the wilderness.

ta′ble, 1 tē′bl; 2 tā′bl. **I.** *vt.* [TA′BLED; TA′BLING.] To place or lay on the table. **II.** *n.* **1.** An article of furniture with a flat horizontal top; also, entertainment; fare. **2.** A collection of numbers, signs, or items in condensed form. **3.** A slab; thin plate.— **ta′ble=land″,** *n.* An elevated level region; plateau.— **ta′ble=spoon″,** *n.* A large spoon for table use.— **ta′ble=spoon″ful,** *n.* [TA′BLE-SPOON″FULS, *pl.*]

tab′leau, 1 tab′lo; 2 tăb′lo, *n.* [TAB′LEAUX,

TAB′LEAUS, 1 tab′loz; 2 tăb′lŏṣ, *pl.*] A picture-like scene represented by silent and motionless persons.

tab′let, 1 tab′let; 2 tăb′lĕt, *n.* **1.** A thin solid sheet, as of ivory, for writing on; a pad of writing-paper. **2.** A flat surface, as for an inscription. **3.** A lozenge; troche.

ta′bor, 1 tē′bər; 2 tā′bor, *n.* A small drum or tambourine.

ta-bu′,) 1 ta-bū′; 2 ta-bu′. **I.** *vt.* To
ta-boo′,) forbid; exclude. **II.** *n.* A Polynesian custom, whereby things are set apart as sacred or forbidden to be used.

tab′u-lar, 1 tab′yu-lər; 2 tăb′yu-lar, *a.* Pertaining to a table or list; having a flat surface; tabulated.— **tab′u-late,** 1 tab′yu-lēt; 2 tăb′yu-lāt, *vt.* [-LAT″ED‡; -LAT″-ING.] To arrange in a table; list.— **tab′u-la′tion,** *n.*

tac′it, 1 tas′it; 2 tăç′it, *a.* Inferred or implied, tho unspoken. **-ly,** *adv.*— **tac′i-turn,** 1 tas′i-tūrn; 2 tăç′i-tûrn, *a.* Silent; reserved.— **tac′i-tur′ni-ty,** *n.*

tack‡, 1 tak; 2 tăk, *v.* **I.** *t.* To fasten with tacks; annex; append. **II.** *i.* To change course, as a vessel, so as to bring the wind to the other side; veer.

tack, *n.* **1.** A small sharp nail; a fastening; stitch. **2.** *Naut.* A rope for fastening the corner of a sail; the act of tacking; the course sailed from one such act to the next.

tack′le,) 1 tak′l; 2 tăk′l. **I.** *vt.* [TACK′-
tack′l‡,) L(E)D‡; TACK′LING.] To grapple with; attach by a tackle. **II.** *n.* A hoisting contrivance of ropes, pulleys-blocks, etc.; gear; equipment; the act of tackling.— **tack′ling,** *n.*

tact, 1 takt; 2 tăçt, *n.* An intuitive appreciation of what is fit, proper, or right; discernment; skill; address.

tac′tics, 1 tak′tics; 2 tăç′tics, *n.* **1.** The science and art of military and naval evolutions. **2.** Adroit management.— **tac′ti-cal,** *a.*— **tac-ti′cian,** 1 tak-tish′an; 2 tăç-tish′an, *n.* An expert in tactics.

tac′tile,) 1 tak′til; 2 tăç′til, *a.* **1.** Per-
tac′til‡,) taining to touch; caused by contact. **tac′tu-al‡. 2.** Tangible.

tad′pole, 1 tad′pōl; 2 tăd′pōl, *n.* A young frog or toad, breathing by external gills and having a membranous tail like that of a fish.

taff′rail, 1 taf′rēl; 2 tăf′rāl, *n.* The rail around a vessel's stern.

taf′fy, 1 taf′i; 2 tăf′y, *n.* Molasses candy.

tag‡, 1 tag; 2 tăg. **I.** *vt. & vi.* [TAGGED, TAGD‡; TAG′GING.] **1.** To put a tag on. **2.** To follow persistently. **II.** *n.* Some-

thing attached; a label. **2.** A ragged edge.

tag², 1 tag; 2 tăg. **I.** *vt.* To overtake and touch. **II.** *n.* A juvenile sport in which the object is to keep from being overtaken and touched.

tail, 1 tēl; 2 tāl, *n.* The appendage at the hindmost part of the body of many animals; the hinder part of anything; any flap, stem, appendage, etc.; the reverse of a coin.

tai′lor, 1 tē′lər; 2 tā′lor, *n.* One who makes men's garments.— **tai′lor-ing,** *n.*— **tai′lor-bird″,** *n.* A bird that sews leaves to form a receptacle for its nest.

Tailor-bird and its Nest. 1/6

taint, 1 tēnt; 2 tānt. **I‡.** *vt. & vi.* To take, have, or cause to have a taint; infect; corrupt. **II.** *n.* A trace or germ of decay; corruption.

take, 1 tēk; 2 tāk, *v.* [TOOK; TAK′EN; TAK′-ING.] **I.** *t.* To gain possession of; seize; secure; carry off; convey; abstract; deduct; employ; contract, as a disease. **II.** *i.* To have effect; incline or resort to; please.

take, *n.* The act of taking, or that which is taken.— **tak′ing. I.** *pa.* Fascinating; captivating. **II.** *n.* The act of one who takes. **-ly,** *adv.*

talc, 1 talk; 2 tălk, *n.* A soft, greasy compound of magnesium and silica.

tale, 1 tēl; 2 tāl, *n.* **1.** A story. **2.** A counting.— **tale′bear″er,** One who tells mischievous tales.— **tale′bear″ing,** *a. & n.*

tal′ent, 1 tal′ent; 2 tăl′ĕnt, *n.* **1.** Superior mental ability; a special faculty or gift. **2.** An ancient weight and denomination of money of varying amount. (Roman talent, *talentum*, $500, Attic *talanton*, $1,200, Hebraic, $1,550 to $2,000.)

tales′man, 1 tēlz′man; 2 tălş′man, *n.* [TALES′MEN, *pl.*] A person summoned to make up a jury.

tal′is-man, 1 tal′is-mən; 2 tăl′is-man, *n.* [-MANS², *pl.*] Something supposed to produce magical effects; a charm. **-ic,** *a.*

talk, 1 tôk; 2 tąk. **I‡.** *vt. & vi.* To utter in words; exercise speech; converse. **II.** *n.* The act of talking, or that which is said; familiar speech; conference.— **talk′a-**

tiv(eˢ, *a.* Given to much talking. **-ly,** *adv.* **-ness,** *n.*— **talk′er,** *n.*

talk′ie, 1 tȇk′ı; 2 tak′i, *n.* [Colloq. U. S.] A motion=picture with spoken words or songs. Used commonly in the plural, **the talkies.** Compare MOVIE.

tall, 1 tôl; 2 tạl, *a.* Having more than average height; high.— **tall′ness,** *n.*

tal′low, 1 tal′o; 2 tăl′o. **I.** *vt.* To grease with tallow. **II.** *n.* Solid fat, as of beef or mutton.

tal′ly, 1 tal′ı; 2 tăl′y, *v.* [TAL′LIED; TAL′-LY-ING.] **I.** *t.* To score; register. **II.** *i.* **1.** To agree precisely. **2.** To keep tally.

tal′ly, 1 tal′ı; 2 tăl′y, *n.* [TAL′LIES**ᶻ**, *pl.*] **1.** A piece of wood on which notches are cut; any score; reckoning; account. **2.** A counterpart.

Tal′mud, 1 tal′mud; 2 tăl′mŭd, *n.* The body of Jewish law not in the Pentateuch. — **Tal-mud′ic,** *a.* **Tal-mud′l-cal‡.**

tal′on, 1 tal′ən; 2 tăl′on, *n.* A claw, especially of a bird of prey.

tam′a-bl(eᴾ, 1 tēm′ə-bl; 2 tãm′a-bl, *a.* Capable of being tamed. **-ness,** *n.*

tam′a-rack, 1 tam′ə-rak; 2 tăm′a-răk, *n.* **1.** The American or black larch. **hack′ma-tack‡.** **2.** A North=American pine.

tam′a-rind, 1 tam′ə-rind; 2 tăm′a-rĭnd, *n.* A tropical tree; also, its acid fruit.

tam′bour, 1 tam′būr; 2 tăm′bụr, *n.* **1.** A drum. **2.** A frame for embroidery; embroidery.— **tam″bou-rine′,** 1 tam″bu-rin′; 2 tăm″bu-rĭn′, *n.* *Mus.* An instrument like the head of a drum, with jingles in the rim.

tame, 1 tēm; 2 tãm. **I.** *vt.* [TAMED; TAM′ING.] To make tame; domesticate; subject; conquer; soften. **II.** *a.* [TAM′-ER; TAM′EST.] **1.** Domesticated; docile; subdued. **2.** Dull; inert. **-ly,** *adv.* **-ness,** *n.*

tamp‡, 1 tamp; 2 tămp, *vt.* To ram down.

tam′per, 1 tam′par; 2 tăm′per, *vi.* To experiment officiously or foolishly; meddle; make unjustifiable alterations: followed by *with.*

tan, 1 tan; 2 tăn, *v.* [TANNED, TAND⁸; TAN′-NING.] **I.** *t.* **1.** To convert into leather, by treating with tannin. **2.** To bronze, as the skin. **II.** *i.* To become tanned.— **tan′-ner,** *n.*— **tan′ner-y,** *n.*

tan, *a.* Of a yellowish or reddish brown.

tan, *n.* **1.** Tan=bark. **2.** Yellowish brown tinged with red.— **tan′=bark″,** *n.* A bark, as of oak, containing tannic acid in quantity.

tan′dem, 1 tan′dem; 2 tăn′dĕm. **I.** *a.* Arranged one before the other. **II.** *n.* **1.** Two or more horses harnessed in single file. **2.** A cycle with seat for two persons, one behind the other. **III.** *adv.* One before the other.

tang¹, 1 taŋ; 2 tăŋ, *n.* A slender projecting shank.

tang², *n.* An unusual or disagreeable flavor.

tan′gent, 1 tan′jent; 2 tăn′gĕnt. **I.** *a.* **1.** *Geom.* Touching a line **or** a surface at one point only. **2.** Touching. **II.** *n.* A straight line tangent to a curve.— **tan-gen-cy,** *n.*— **tan-gen′tial,** *a.*

tan″ger-ine′, 1 tan″jər-ın′; 2 tăn″ger-ĭn′, *n.* A small red=skinned orange, a variety of the mandarine.

tan′gi-ble, 1 tan′jı-bl; 2 tăn′gi-bl, *a.* **tan′gi-bl**ᴾ,) Perceptible by touch. **-ness**ᴾ, *n.*— **tan″gi-bil′l-ty,** *n.*— **tan′gi-bly,** *adv.*

tan′gl(eᴾ, 1 taŋ′gl; 2 tăŋ′gl. **I.** *vt. & vi.* [TAN′GL(E)Dᴾ; TAN′GLING.] To intertwine confusedly; snarl. **II.** *n.* A confused intertwining, as of thread; confusion.

tan′go, 1 taŋ′go; 2 tăŋ′gõ, *n.* An Argentinian dance, orig., a diagonal shuffle, elaborated to include a whirl, a dip, and a swing, executed in various ways. [Sp. Am.] **ten′go‡.**

tank, 1 taŋk; 2 tăŋk, *n.* **1.** A large receptacle for containing a fluid. **2.** An armored motor=car. [large mug.

tank′ard, 1 taŋk′ərd; 2 tăŋk′ard, *n.* A

tan′nic, 1 tan′ik; 2 tăn′ic, *a.* Pertaining to or derived from tan.— **tannic acid,** an astringent principle contained in vegetables.

tan′sy, 1 tan′zı; 2 tăn′sy, *n.* A coarse perennial herb, with yellow flowers.

tan′ta-lize, 1 tan′tə-laiz; 2 tăn′ta-lĭz, *vt.* [-LIZED; -LIZ″ING.] To torment by exciting and disappointing hope; harass. **tan′ta-lise‡.** [mount, *a.* Equivalent.

tan″ta-mount, 1 tan″tə-mount; 2 tăn′ta-**tan′trum,** 1 tan′trum; 2 tăn′trŭm, *n.* A petulant fit of passion.

tap¹, 1 tap; 2 tăp. **I.** *vt.* [TAPPED′ᵗ, TAPTˢ; TAP′PING.] To draw liquid from, through an opening. **II.** *n.* A faucet.— **t.=root,** *n.* The principal descending root of a plant.

tap². **I**ᵗ. *vt. & vi.* **1.** To touch or strike gently. **2.** To put leather on a shoe=heel in repair. **II.** *n.* **1.** A gentle or playful blow. **2.** Leather put on a shoe=heel.

tape, 1 tēp; 2 tãp, *n.* A narrow, stout strip of woven fabric; also, a flat strip of paper, etc.— **red tape,** the close observance of forms and routine. **t. line,** a tape for measuring distances. **t. measure‡.**

ta′per, 1 tē′pər; 2 tã′per. **I.** *vt. & vi.* To make or become smaller toward the end; lessen gradually. **II.** *a.* Growing small by degrees toward the end. **III.** *n.* **1.** A small candle. **2.** A gradual lessening.

tap′es-try, 1 tap′es-trı; 2 tăp′ĕs-try. **I.** *vt.* [-TRIED, -TRY-ING.] To hang with tapestry. **II.** *n.* [-TRIES**ᶻ**, *pl.*] A loosely woven, ornamental fabric used for hangings.

---

tap″i-o′ca, 1 tap″ĭ-ō′kə; 2 tăp″ĭ-ō′ca, *n.* A food-product obtained from cassava.

ta′pir, 1 tē′pər; 2 tā′pĭr, *n.* A large mammal, having short, stout limbs and flexible proboscis.

ta′pis, 1 tē′pis *or* tə-pī′; 2 tā′pĭs *or* tä-pī′, *n.* Tapestry: now only in the phrase **on the tapis** (up for consideration).

Malayan Tapir and its Young. ¹⁄₃₃

tap′ster, 1 tap′- stər; 2 tăp′ster, *n.* One who draws and serves liquor.

tar, 1 tär; 2 tär, *vt.* [TARRED, TARD⁸; TAR′- RING.] To cover with tar.

tar¹, *n. Chem.* A dark, viscid, oily liquid obtained from resinous woods, coal, etc.

tar², *n.* [Colloq.] A sailor.

ta-ran′tu-la, 1 tə-ran′tiu-lə; 2 ta-răn′- tū-la, *n.* A large hairy spider of warm regions.

tar′dy, 1 tär′dı; 2 tär′dy, *a.* [TAR′DI-ER; TAR′DI-EST.] **1.** Coming behind time; dilatory: late. **2.** Slow in movement; acting reluctantly.— **tar′di-ly,** *adv.*— **tar′di- ness,** *n.* [weeds, as vetch.

tare¹, 1 tär; 2 târ, *n.* Any one of various

tare², *n.* An allowance for the weight of the receptacle in which goods are packed.

tar′get, 1 tär′get; 2 tär′gĕt, *n.* **1.** A mark to be shot at. **2.** A small shield; buckler. target.

tar′iff, } 1 tar′ıf; 2 tär′if, *n.* A schedule of **tar′iff²,** } charges; system of duties to be paid for import or export of goods.

tar′la-tan, 1 tär′lə-tən; 2 tär′la-tan, *n.* An open, transparent muslin. **tar′le-tan:**

tarn, 1 tärn; 2 tärn, *n.* A small mountain lake.

tar′nish, 1 tär′nısh; 2 tär′nish. **I**ᵗ. *vt. & vi.* To lessen in luster; stain; disgrace. **II.** *n.* Loss of luster; a blemish.

tar-pau′lin, 1 tär-pô′lın; 2 tär-pạ′lin, *n.* **1.** A water-proof canvas for covering merchandise. **2.** A sailors' wide-brimmed storm-hat.

tar′ry, 1 tar′ı; 2 tăr′y, *vi.* [TAR′RIED, TAR′RY-ING.] To put off going or coming; linger; abide; stay. [tar; like tar.

tar′ry, 1 tär′ı; 2 tär′y, *a.* Covered with

tart, 1 tärt; 2 tärt, *a.* **1.** Having a sour taste. **2.** Severe; cutting. **-ly,** *adv.* **-ness,** *n.*

tart, *n.* **1.** [U. S.] A small piece of pastry with fruit filling and without top crust. **2.** [Eng.] A fruit pie.

tar′tan, 1 tär′tən; 2 tär′tan, *n.* A Scotch plaid fabric; also, its design or pattern.

tar′tar¹, *n.* **1.** An acid substance deposited from fermenting grape-juice. **2.** A yellowish incrustation on the teeth.— **tar-tar′ic,** *a.*

Tar′tar², 1 tär′tər; 2 tär′tar, *a. & n.* Same as TATAR.

task, 1 task; 2 tásk. **I**ᵗ. *vt.* To assign a task to; burden with labor. **II.** *n.* A specific amount of labor; burdensome work.— **task′mas″ter,** *n.* One who assigns tasks.

tas′sel, 1 tas′l; 2 tăs′l, *n.* **1.** A pendent ornament, as a tuft of loose thread. **2.** The pendent head of some plants or flowers.— **tas′seled,** *a.*

taste, 1 tēst; 2 tãst, *v.* [TAST′ED⁴; TAST′ING.] **I.** *t.* **1.** To perceive the flavor of. **2.** To test by taking a little of into the mouth. **3.** To have slight experience of. **II.** *i.* **1.** To take a taste. **2.** To have a flavor.

taste, *n.* **1.** The sensation excited when a soluble substance is put into the mouth; flavor. **2.** The sense that gives such sensation. **3.** A small quantity tasted; also, the act of tasting. **4.** Nice perception of artistic excellence. **5.** Inclination.— **tast′er,** *n.*— **taste′ful,** *a.* **1.** Conforming to taste. **2.** Possessing good taste. **-ly,** *adv.* **-ness,** *n.*— **taste′less,** *a.* **1.** Insipid; dull. **2.** Devoid of taste. **-ly,** *adv.* **-ness,** *n.*— **tast′y,** *a.* **1.** Having a fine flavor; savory. **2.** [Colloq.] Tasteful.— **tast′i-ly,** *adv.*

Ta′tar, } 1 tä′tər, tär′tər; 2 tä′tar, tär′tar, **Tar′tar,** } *n.* **1.** One of a people originating in Chinese Tatary (Manchuria and Mongolia); a Turk, Cossack, etc.; also, the dialects spoken by these peoples. **2.** One of the Mongols of the 13th century who ravaged Europe and Asia. **3.** [T- or t-] A person of savage temper: in this sense always *Tartar*.— **to catch a Tartar,** to attack a person who is more than one's match.

tat′ter, 1 tat′ər; 2 tăt′er, *n.* A torn and hanging shred; rag; in the plural, ragged clothing.— **tat′ter(e)d⁸,** *a.*

tat′tle, 1 tat′l; 2 tăt′l. **I.** *vt. & vi.* [TAT′- TLED, TAT′LD²; TAT′TLING.] To tell tales; gossip. **II.** *n.* Idle talk or gossip.— **tat′tler,** *n.*

tat-too″¹, 1 ta-tū′; 2 tă-tōō′. **I.** *vt.* To prick and mark (the skin) in patterns with indelible pigments. **II.** *n.* A pattern so made.

tat-too″², *n.* A continuous drumming.

taught, 1 tēt; 2 tạt, *imp. & pp.* of TEACH, *v.*

taunt, 1 tänt *or* tēnt; 2 tänt *or* tạnt. **I**ᵈ. *vt.* To reproach with insulting words. **II.** *n.* A bitterly sarcastic remark.— **taunt′er,** *n.*— **taunt′ing-ly,** *adv.*

1: ártistic, ärt; fat, fãre; fạst; get, prĕy; hit, police; obey, gō; net, ôr; full, rūle; but, būrn.

2: ärt, āpe, făt, fâre, fạst, whạt, ạll; mē, gĕt, prey, fērn; hit, īce; ĩ=ē; ĭ=ē; gō, nŏt, ôr, wòn,

Tau'rus, 1 tē'rʊs; 2 ta̤'rŭs, *n.* **1.** A constellation, the Bull. **2.** The second sign of the zodiac.— **tau'rine,** *a.* Of or like a bull; oxlike.

taut, 1 tēt; 2 ta̤t, *a.* *Naut.* **1.** Hard-drawn; stretched tight. **2.** Tidy.

tau-tol'o-gy, 1 tə-tel'o-jɪ; 2 ta̤-tŏl'o-ġy, *n.* Unnecessary repetition, whether in word or sense.— **tau"to-log'ic, tau"to-log'i-cal,** *a.*

tav'ern, 1 tav'ərn; 2 tăv'ern, *n.* A public house.

taw, 1 tē; 2 ta̤, *n.* A game of marbles; a [marble.

taw'dry, 1 tē'drɪ; 2 ta̤'dry, *a.* [-DRI-ER; -DRI-EST.] Showy without elegance; gaudy.— **taw'dri-ness,** *n.*

taw'ny, 1 tē'nɪ; 2 ta̤'ny, *a.* Tan-colored; brownish-yellow.— **taw'ni-ness,** *n.*

tax, 1 taks; 2 tăks. **I**t. *vt.* **1.** To impose a tax upon. **2.** To subject to a severe strain. **3.** To ask as a price. **II.** *n.* **1.** A compulsory contribution for the support of government; any assessment. **2.** A heavy demand upon one's resources. — **tax'a-bl(e**p, *a.* Subject to taxation.— **tax-a'tion,** *n.* The act of taxing; also, the amount assessed as a tax.

tax'i-cab, *n.* A motor-cab for hire.

tax'i-der"my, 1 taks'ɪ-dūr"mɪ; 2 tăks'i-dẽr"my, *n.* The art or process of preserving and mounting the skins of dead animals.— **tax"i-der'mal,** *a.* **tax"i-der'mic**‡.— **tax'i-der"mist,** *n.*

tea, 1 tī; 2 tē, *n.* **1.** An evergreen Chinese or Japanese shrub. **tea'-plant"**‡. **2.** The prepared leaves of this plant, or an infusion of them. **3.** A light evening meal.

Flowering Branch of Tea.

teach, 1 tīch; 2 tēch, *v.* [TAUGHT; TEACH'ING.] **I.** *t.* **1.** To impart knowledge to; instruct. **2.** To make known. **II.** *i.* To impart knowledge; give instruction.— **teach'a-bl(e**p, *a.* That may be taught; docile. **-ness,** *n.*— **teach'er,** *n.*

teak, 1 tīk; 2 tēk, *n.* A large East-Indian tree yielding durable timber.

teal, 1 tīl; 2 tēl, *n.* A small river-duck.

team, 1 tīm; 2 tēm, *n.* **1.** Two or more beasts of burden harnessed together. **2.** A set of workers or players.— **team'ster,** *n.*

tear, 1 tār; 2 târ, *v.* [TORE, formerly TARE; TORN; TEAR'ING.] **I.** *t.* **1.** To pull apart, as cloth; rend; sunder; sever; lacerate. **2.** To make, as a hole, by rending. **II.** *i.* **1.** To part or separate on being pulled. **2.** To move or act with precipitate haste.

tear1, *n.* A fissure made by tearing; a rent; an act of tearing.

tear2, 1 tīr; 2 tēr, *n.* A drop of the saline liquid from the eye.— **tear'ful,** *a.* Full of tears; causing tears. **-ly,** *adv.* **-ness,** *n.*— **tear'less,** *n.* Shedding no tears. **-ly,** *adv.* **-ness,** *n.*

tear'-sheet", 1 tār'shīt"; 2 târ'shēt", *n.* A page, as of magazine or newspaper, containing printed matter of particular or personal interest to the person to whom it is sent.

tease, 1 tīz; 2 tēș. **I.** *vt.* [TEASED; TEAS'ING.] **1.** To vex by petty annoyances; annoy; fret; harass; importune persistently. **2.** To comb or card, as wool. **II.** *n.* **1.** A teaser. **2.** The act of teasing. — **teas'er,** *n.* One who or that which teases.

teat, 1 tīt; 2 tēt, *n.* A nipple; pap; dug.

tea'zel, 1 tī'zl; 2 tē'zl, *n.* The rough bur of a plant, or a mechanical substitute: used in dressing cloth. **tea'sel**‡.

tech'ni-cal, 1 tek'nɪ-kəl; 2 tĕc'ni-cal, *a.* Pertaining to some particular art, science, trade, etc.; formal; literal. **-ly,** *adv.*— **tech"ni-cal'i-ty,** *n.* [-TIES^z, *pl.*] **1.** The state of being technical. **2.** A technical point; petty distinction.

tech'ni-col"or, *a.* Describing a type of camera used in producing motion-picture films in colors.

tech-nique', 1 tek-nīk'; 2 tĕc-nīk', *n.* Manner of artistic performance, as in music.

tech-noc'ra-cy, 1 tek-nək'rə-sɪ; 2 tĕc-nŏc'ra-çy, *n.* **1.** A proposed form of government controlled by technical men. **2.** Measurement of industrial output in terms of energy.

tech'y, 1 tech'ɪ; 2 tĕch'y, *a.* Peevish; irritable.— **tech'i-ly,** *adv.*— **tech'i-ness,** *n.*

tedd, 1 ted; 2 tĕd, *vt.* To stir up and spread loosely for drying, as grass.— **ted'der,** *n.*

Te De'um, 1 tī dī'ʊm; 2 tē dē'ŭm. An ancient Christian hymn of thanksgiving.

te'di-ous, 1 tī'dɪ-ʊs; 2 tē'di-ŭs, *a.* Wearisome; slow.— **te'di-ous-ly,** *adv.*— **te'di-ous-ness,** *n.*— **te'di-um,** *n.* Tediousness.

tee, 1 tī; 2 tē, *n.* A mark in some games; in golf, a little heap of earth from which a ball is played.

teem, 1 tīm; 2 tēm, *vi.* To be full; abound; overflow.— **teem'ing,** *pa.* Prolific.

teens, 1 tīnz; 2 tēnș, *n. pl.* The years of one's age ending in *-teen.* [teeth.

teeth, 1 tīth; 2 tēth, *vi.* To cut or develop

tee-to'tal-er, 1 tī-tō'təl-ər; 2 tē-tō'tal-er, *n.* A total abstainer from intoxicating liquors.— **tee-to'tal,** *a.*— **tee-to'tal-ism,** *n.*

tee-to'tum, 1 tī-tō'tʊm; 2 tē-tō'tŭm, *n.* A top with numbers on its side, or a disk pierced by a peg, spun in certain games.

teg'u-ment, 1 teg′yu-ment; 2 tĕg″yu-mĕnt, *n.* An integument; a covering.— **teg″-u-men'ta-ry,** *a.*

tel'e-gram, 1 tel′i-gram; 2 tĕl′e-grăm, *n.* A message sent by telegraph.

tel'e-graph,) 1 tel′i-graf; 2 tĕl′e-grăf. I. **tel'e-graf**ˢ, ſ *vt. & vi.* To send by telegraph; communicate by telegraph. II. *n.* An apparatus for transmitting messages, especially by electricity.— **tel-au'to-graph,** 1 tel-ô′to-graf; 2 tĕl-a′to-grăf, *n.* A telegraph for reproducing writing or drawing at a distance.— **te-leg'ra-pher,** *n.* One who telegraphs. **te-leg'ra-phist:.**— **tel″e-graph'ic,** *a.*— **te-leg'ra-phy,** *n.* The art of conveying intelligence by telegraph.

tel″e-ol'o-gy, *n.* The doctrine that everything in nature is made for a special purpose.

te-lep'a-thy, 1 ti-lep′a-thi; 2 te-lĕp′a-thy, *n.* The sympathetic affection of one mind or person by another at a distance; thought-transference.

tel'e-phone,) 1 tel′i-fōn; 2 tĕl′e-fōn. I. **tel'e-fone**ˢ, ſ *vt. & vi.* [-PHONED; -PHON″-ING.] To send by telephone; talk through the telephone. II. *n.* An instrument for reproducing sound at a distant point, especially by electricity.— **tel″e-phon'ic,** *a.*— **te-leph'o-ny,** *n.* The art of telephoning.

tel'e-scope, 1 tel′i-skōp; 2 tĕl′e-scōp. I. *vt. & vi.* [-SCOPED:; -SCOP″ING.] To drive together, one within another, like the sections of a small telescope. II. *n.* An optical instrument for enlarging the image of a distant object, as a star.— **tel″e-scop'ic,** 1 tel′i-skep′ik; 2 tĕl′e-scōp′ic, *a.* Pertaining to the telescope; visible only through the telescope. **tel″e-scop'i-cal:.**— **tel″e-scop'i-cal-ly,** *adv.*

tel'e-vi″sion, 1 tel′i-viʒ″ən; 2 tĕl′i-vish″on, *n.* The instantaneous transmission to a distance of images, views, etc., by telegraphy or radio.

tell,) 1 tel; 2 tĕl, *v.* [TOLD; TELL′ING.] I. **tel**ˢ, ſ *t.* 1. To relate; make known; inform. 2. To command; to bid. 3. To utter; express. 4. To count; decide; ascertain. II. *i.* 1. To give an account. 2. To produce a marked effect.— **tell'er,** *n.* 1. One who relates. 2. A person who receives or pays out money, as in a bank, or who collects and counts ballots.— **tell'tale″,** 1 tel′tēl″; 2 tĕl′tāl″. I. *a.* Tattling; betraying. II. *n.* 1. A tattler. 2. An indicator.

tel'pher-age, 1 tel′fer-ij; 2 tĕl′fer-ag, *n.* Automatic aerial transportation by electricity, as by independent motors on a conducting cable.— **tel'pher,** *a. & n.*

te-mer'i-ty, 1 ti-mer′i-ti; 2 te-mĕr′i-ty, *n.* Venturesome boldness; rashness.

tem'per, 1 tem′pər; 2 tĕm′per. I. *vt.* 1.

To mix in due proportion; modify; moderate; mitigate; calm; adjust. 2. To soften (a metal) by heating and suddenly cooling. II. *n.* 1. Passion; irritation. 2. Disposition. 3. Self-command; calmness. 4. The condition of a metal as regards hardness and brittleness.

tem'per-a-ment, 1 tem′pər-ə-ment *or* mənt; 2 tĕm′per-a-ment, *n.* Individual constitution; adjustment.

tem'per-ance, 1 tem′pər-əns; 2 tĕm′per-anç, *n.* 1. The state of being temperate: moderation. 2. Total abstinence from intoxicating drinks.

tem'per-ate, 1 tem′pər-it; 2 tĕm′per-at, *a.* 1. Observing moderation; not indulging in intoxicating liquors. 2. Moderate as regards temperature. 3. Not excessive. **-ly,** *adv.* **-ness,** *n.*

tem'per-a-ture, 1 tem′pər-a-chur *or* -tiur; 2 tĕm′per-a-chur *or* -tūr, *n.* Degree of heat or cold; condition as regards heat or cold.

tem'pest, 1 tem′pest; 2 tĕm′pĕst, *n.* A violent wind, with rain, snow, or hail; any violent commotion.— **tem-pes'tu-ous,** *a.* Stormy; turbulent. **-ly,** *adv.* **-ness,** *n.*

tem'ple¹,) 1 tem′pl; 2 tĕm′pl, *n.* A stately **tem'pl**ᵖ, ſ house of worship.

tem'ple², *n.* The region on each side of the head above the cheek-bone.

tem'po, 1 tem′po: 2 tĕm′po, *n.* *Mus.* Time. — **a tempo,** in the proper time.

tem'po-ral¹, 1 tem′po-rəl; 2 tĕm′po-ral, *a.* Secular; earthly; transient. **-ly,** *adv.*

tem'po-ral², *a.* Pertaining to or situated at the temple or temples.

tem'po-ra-ry, 1 tem′po-re-ri; 2 tĕm′po-rā-ry, *a.* Lasting for a short time only; transitory; transient.— **tem″po-ra-ri-ly,** *adv.* — **tem'po-ra-ri-ness,** *n.*

tem'po-rize, 1 tem′po-raiz; 2 tĕm′po-rīz, *vi.* [-RIZED; -RIZ″ING.] To pursue a time-serving policy; delay; procrastinate. **-ri:se:.**

temptᵈ, 1 tempt; 2 tĕmpt, *vt.* 1. To allure, especially for wrong-doing; entice. 2. To provoke; defy.— **temp-ta'tion,** *n.* 1. That which tempts. 2. The state of being tempted.— **tempt'er,** *n.*— **tempt'ing,** *a.*— **tempt'ing-ly,** *adv.*

ten, 1 ten; 2 tĕn, *a. & n.* Nine and one. — **ten'pins″,** *n.* A game in which ten pins are set up to be bowled down by rolling balls.

ten'a-ble,) 1 ten′a-bl; 2 tĕn′a-bl, *a.* Ca-**ten'a-bl**ᵖ, ſ pable of being held or defended. **-ness,** *n.*— **ten'a-bly,** *adv.*

te-na'cious, 1 ti-nē′shus; 2 te-nā′shŭs, *a.* Adhesive; sticky; tough; unyielding. **-ly,** *adv.*— **te-nac'i-ty,** *n.* The quality of being tenacious.— **te-na'cious-ness:.**

ten'ant, 1 ten′ənt; 2 tĕn′ant. Iᵈ. *vt.* To

hold as tenant; occupy. **II.** *n.* One who holds lands or tenements under another; a lessee.— **ten′an-cy,** 1 ten′ən-si; 2 tĕn′an-çy, *n.* [-CIES², *pl.*] The state of being a tenant; occupancy.— **ten′ant-a-bl**(e², *a.* Inhabitable.— **ten′ant-less,** *a.* Without a tenant; unoccupied.— **ten′ant-ry,** *n.* Tenants collectively.

tend¹ᵈ, 1 tend; 2 tĕnd, *vi.* **1.** To have a bent or aptitude; aim; incline. **2.** To move in a certain direction.— **ten′den-cy,** 1 ten′den-si; 2 tĕn′dĕn-çy, *n.* [-CIES², *pl.*] **1.** A tending toward some purpose, end, or result. **2.** That which tends to cause an effect.

tend²ᵈ, *vt. & vi.* To look after; watch over; attend; serve.

ten′der, 1 ten′dər; 2 tĕn′der, *vt. & vi.* To present for acceptance; offer.

ten′der, *a.* Easily crushed, bruised, or injured; sensitive; delicate; considerate. **-ly,** *adv.* **-ness,** *n.* [offer.

ten′der¹, *n.* The act of tendering; an

tend′er², 1 tend′ər; 2 tĕnd′er, *n.* **1.** A vessel attending a larger vessel. **2.** A vehicle for carrying fuel and water for a locomotive. **3.** One who tends.

ten′der-loin″, 1 ten′dər-loin″; 2 tĕn′der-loin″, *n.* The tenderest part of the loin of beef, etc.

ten′don, 1 ten′dən; 2 tĕn′don, *n.* One of the bands forming the terminations of the fleshy portion of a muscle.— **ten′di-nous,** *a.*

ten′dril, 1 ten′dril; 2 tĕn′dril, *n.* A slender organ of a plant; a support in climbing.

ten′e-ment, 1 ten′i-ment *or* -mənt; 2 tĕn′e-ment, *n.* **1.** A room or rooms for a family; usually of an inferior grade. **2.** A dwelling-house.— **ten″e-men′tal,** *a.*

ten′et, 1 ten′et; 2 tĕn′ĕt, *n.* An opinion; doctrine.

ten′fold, 1 ten′fōld; 2 tĕn′fōld. **I.** *a.* Made up of ten; ten times repeated. **II.** *adv.* In a tenfold manner.

ten′nis, 1 ten′is; 2 tĕn′is, *n.* A game played by striking a ball with rackets over a net stretched perpendicularly across a space.

ten′on, 1 ten′ən; 2 tĕn′on, *n.* The end of a timber cut for inserting in a socket.

ten′or, 1 ten′ər; 2 tĕn′or, *n.* **1.** A settled course. **2.** General purport. **3.** *Mus.* The highest adult male voice, or a singer having such a voice.

tense, 1 tens; 2 tĕns, *a.* Stretched tight. **-ly,** *adv.* **-ness,** *n.*

tense, *n.* A form taken by a verb to indicate the time of an action, state, etc.

ten′sile, } 1 ten′sil; 2 ten′sil, *a.* **1.** Per-
ten′silᵉ, } taining to tension. **2.** Capable of extension.

ten′sion, 1 ten′shən; 2 tĕn′shon, *n.* The act of stretching; stress; strain.

tent¹, 1 tent; 2 tĕnt. **I**ᵈ. *vt. & vi.* To cover with or as with a tent: camp out. **II.** *n.* A shelter of canvas or the like, supported by poles, and fastened by cords to pegs in the ground.

tent². *Surg.* **I.** *vt.* To keep open with a tent; also, to probe. **II.** *n.* A small roll, as of lint, to keep a wound, etc., open.

ten′ta-cl(e², 1 ten′ta-kl; 2 tĕn′ta-cl, *n.* A projecting appendage, as on the head of certain insects; a feeler; antenna.— **ten-tac′u-lar,** *a.*

ten′ta-tive, } 1 ten′ta-tiv; 2 tĕn′ta-tĭv. **I.**
ten′ta-tivᵉ, } *a.* Experimental; provisional. **II.** *n.* An experiment; attempt; trial.

ten′ter-hook″, 1 ten′tər-huk″; 2 tĕn′ter-hŏŏk″, *n.* A hook for holding cloth while being stretched.

tenth, 1 tenth; 2 tĕnth. **I.** *a.* **1.** Next in order after the ninth. **2.** Being one of ten equal parts. **II.** *n.* One of ten equal parts.— **tenth′ly,** *adv.*

ten′u-ous, 1 ten′yu-us; 2 tĕn′yu-ŭs, *a.* Thin; delicate; rare; subtile.— **te-nu′i-ty,** *n.*

ten′ure, 1 ten′yur; 2 tĕn′yur, *n.* A holding, as of land.

tep′id, 1 tep′id; 2 tĕp′id, *a.* Moderately warm; lukewarm.— **te-pid′i-ty, tep′id-ness,** *n.*

ter-cen′te-na-ry, 1 tür-sen′ti-nē-ri; 2 ter-çĕn′te-nā-ry. **I.** *a.* Of or belonging to a period of 300 years, or to a 300th anniversary. **II.** *n.* [-RIES², *pl.*] A 300th anniversary.

ter″gi-ver-sa′tion, 1 tür″ji-vər-sē′shən; 2 tĕr″gi-ver-sā′shon, *n.* **1.** Evasion of a point, as by prevarication or subterfuge. **2.** Fickleness or instability of conduct.

term, 1 tûrm; 2 tĕrm. **I.** *vt.* To designate; name. **II.** *n.* **1.** A word or expression to designate some fixed thing. **2.** A fixed period or limit of time. **3.** *pl.* Conditions; basis of agreement.

ter′ma-gant, 1 tür′ma-gənt; 2 tĕr′ma-gant, *n.* A brawling, turbulent woman; shrew.

ter′mi-nal, 1 tür′mi-nəl; 2 tĕr′mi-nal. **I.** *a.* **1.** Pertaining to a boundary or an end. **2.** Pertaining to a term or name. **II.** *n.* A terminating point; station.— **ter′mi-na-ble,** *a.* That may be terminated.— **ter′mi-nate,** *vt. & vi.* [-NAT″ED²; -NAT″ING.] **1.** To put an end to; come to an end; cease. **2.** To be the boundary of; be limited.— **ter″mi-na′tion,** *n.* The act of terminating; the final position; close; end.— **ter′mi-na″tiv**(e³, *a.*— **ter′mi-na″tor,** *n.*

ter″mi-nol′o-gy, 1 tŭr″mĭ-nŏl′o-jĭ; 2 tĕr″-mĭ-nŏl′o-gy, *n.* The correct use of terms; the body of terms used, as in science.

ter′mi-nus, 1 tŭr′mĭ-nus; 2 tĕr′mĭ-nŭs, *n.* [-NI, 1 -naɪ; 2 -nī, *pl.*] The goal; end; terminal; boundary.

ter′mite, 1 tŭr′maɪt; 2 tĕr′mīt, *n.* A white ant. **ter′mes‡.**

tern, 1 tŭrn; 2 tĕrn, *n.* A small gull-like bird with pointed bill.

ter′na-ry, 1 tŭr′na-rɪ; 2 tĕr′-na-ry. **I.** *a.* Formed or consisting of three. **ter′nate‡. II.** *n.* [-RIES², *pl.*] A group of three; a triad.

ter′ra, 1 tĕr′a; 2 tĕr′a, *n.* The earth; earth.— **ter′ra-cot′ta,** *n.* Clay pottery, as for ornamentation.— **terra firma,** dry land.

Common Tern. 1/18

ter′race, 1 tĕr′ɪs; 2 tĕr′aç. **I.** *vt.* [TER′-RACED‡; TER′RAC-ING.] To fashion as a terrace; build in terraces. **II.** *n.* A raised level space, or such levels collectively.

ter′ra-pin, 1 tĕr′a-pɪn; 2 tĕr′-a-pĭn, *n.* One of various tortoises.

ter-ra′que-ous, 1 te-rē′kwɪ-us; 2 tĕ-rā′kwe-ŭs, *a.* Composed of or containing both land and water. [terrestrial; mundane.

Salt-marsh Terrapin. 1/16

ter-rene′, 1 te-rīn′; 2 tĕ-rēn′, *a.* Earthy; **ter-res′tri-al,** 1 te-res′trɪ-al; 2 tĕ-rĕs′tri-al, *a.* **1.** Belonging to the earth. **2.** Pertaining to or living on the land.

ter′ri-ble, 1 tĕr′ɪ-bl; 2 tĕr′i-bl, *a.* Of a **ter′ri-bl‡,** nature to excite terror; appalling. **-ness,** *n.*— **ter′ri-bly,** *adv.*

ter′ri-er, 1 tĕr′ɪ-ər; 2 tĕr′i-er, *n.* A small dog, adapted to pursue burrowing animals.

ter′ri-fy, 1 tĕr′ɪ-faɪ; 2 tĕr′i-fȳ, *vt.* [-FIED; -FY′ING.] To fill with extreme terror; frighten.— **ter-rif′ic,** *a.* Terrifying; alarming.

ter′ri-to-ry, 1 tĕr′ɪ-to-rɪ; 2 tĕr′i-to-ry, *n.* [-RIES², *pl.*] **1.** Any considerable tract of land; domain. **2.** [T-] A division of the national domain of the United States having a separate government in the expectation that it will become a State.— **ter″ri-to′ri-al,** *a.* & *n.* **-ly,** *adv.*

ter′ror, 1 tĕr′ər; 2 tĕr′or, *n.* Extreme fear or that which causes it; fright.— **ter′ror-ism,** *n.* The act of terrorizing; a terrorized condition.— **ter′ror-īze,** 1 tĕr′ər-aɪz; 2 tĕr′or-īz, *vt.* To reduce to a state of terror. **ter′ror-īse‡.**

terse, 1 tŭrs; 2 tĕrs, *a.* Elegantly concise; sententious. **-ly,** *adv.* **-ness,** *n.*

ter′ti-a-ry, 1 tur′shɪ-ē-rɪ; 2 tĕr′shi-ā-ry, *a.* Third in number or degree.

tes′sel-late, 1 tes′e-lēt; 2 tĕs′ĕ-lāt, *vt.* [-LAT′ED‡; -LAT′ING.] To construct in the checkered style of mosaic, as pavement.— **tes″sel-la′tion,** *n.* [ment; prove.

test‡, 1 test; 2 tĕst, *vt.* To try by experiment.

test‡, *vt.* To attest.

test‡, *n.* **1.** An experiment to determine the true character of something. **2.** A trial. **3.** A criterion or standard.

test², *n.* A shell.— **tes-ta′ceous,** *a.* Derived from shells or shell-fish; having a shell.

tes′ta-ment, 1 tes′ta-ment; 2 tĕs′ta-ment, *n.* **1.** A will disposing of property after death. **2.** [T-] One of the two volumes of the Bible, distinguished as the Old and the New Testament.— **tes″ta-men′tal,** *a.* Pertaining to a testament or will.— **tes″ta-men′ta-ry,** *a.* Derived from, bequeathed by, or set forth in a will; appointed by a will.— **tes′tate,** 1 tes′tĕt; 2 tĕs′tāt, *a.* Having made a will before decease.— **tes-ta′tor,** *n.* The maker of a will.— **tes-ta′trix,** *n. fem.*

test′er‡, 1 test′ər; 2 tĕst′er, *n.* One who tests; a device for testing.

tes′ter², 1 tes′tər; 2 tĕs′ter, *n.* A flat canopy, as over a bed.

tes′ti-cle, 1 tes′tɪ-kl; 2 tĕs′ti-cl, *n.* One of the two genital glands of the male.

tes′ti-fy, 1 tes′tɪ-faɪ; 2 tĕs′ti-fȳ, *v.* [-FIED; -FY′ING.] **I.** *t.* To declare on oath or affirmation; make known. **II.** *i.* To give legal testimony; serve as evidence.— **tes′ti-fi″er,** *n.*

tes′ti-mo-ny, 1 tes′tɪ-mo-nɪ; 2 tĕs′ti-mo-ny, *n.* [-NIES², *pl.*] **1.** A statement of fact, as before a court; evidence. **2.** The act of testifying.— **tes″ti-mo′ni-al. I.** *a.* Pertaining to testimony or a testimonial. **II.** *n.* A formal token of regard or approval.

tes′ty, 1 tes′tɪ; 2 tĕs′ty, *a.* [TES′TI-ER; TES′TI-EST.] Irritable; quick-tempered.— **tes′ti-ly,** *adv.*— **tes′ti-ness,** *n.*

tet′a-nus, 1 tet′a-nus; 2 tĕt′a-nŭs, *n.* A nervous affection with spasmodic contraction of muscles; lockjaw.— **te-tan′ic,** *a.*

tête″-à-tête″, 1 tēt″-a-tēt′; 2 tĕt″-ä-tĕt′. [F.] **I.** *a.* Being face to face; confidential. **II.** *n.* A private interview. **III.** *adv.* Privately.

teth′er, 1 teth′ər; 2 tĕth′er. **I.** *vt.* To confine with a tether. **II.** *n.* A rope for fastening an animal so as to limit its range of feeding. [Combining forms.

tet′ra-, combining form. 1 tet′ra-, tetr-; 2 tĕt′ra-, tĕtr-.

tet′ra-gon, 1 tet′ra-gon; 2 tĕt′ra-gŏn, *n.* A figure having four angles.— **te-trag′o-nal,** *a.*

tet′ra-he′dron, 1 tet′ra-hē′dron; 2 tĕt′ra-

he′dron, *n.* [-DRA, *pl.*] A solid bounded by four plane triangular faces.— **tet″ra-he′-dral,** *a.*

tet′rarch, 1 tet′rärk *or* tĭ′trärk; 2 tĕt′rärk *or* tē′träre, *n.* The governor of a fourth part of a Roman province; a tributary prince.— **tet″rarch-y,** *n.* **tet′rarch-ate‡.**

tet′ter, 1 tet′ər; 2 tĕt′er, *n.* An eruptive skin=disease.

Teu′ton, 1 tiū′tən; 2 tū′tŏn, *n.* A German. — **Teu-ton′ic,** *a.* Germanic.

text, 1 tekst; 2 tĕkst, *n.* **1.** The body of matter on a page, as distinguished from notes, illustrations, etc. **2.** A verse of Scripture. **3.** A topic; theme.— **text′=book″,** *n.* A school=book; manual.— **tex′tu-al,** *a.* **-ly,** *adv.*

tex′tile, 1 teks′tĭl; 2 tĕks′tĭl, *a.* Pertaining to weaving or woven fabrics; woven.— **tex′til**ˢ, *ſ*

tex′ture, 1 teks′ĉhur *or* -tiur; 2 tĕks′chur *or* -tūr, *n.* **1.** Manner of weaving or structure of a woven fabric; structural order, as of tissues. **2.** A woven fabric; web.

than, 1 than; 2 thăn, *conj.* When, as, or if compared with: used to express comparison.

thane, 1 ĥēn; 2 thān, *n.* An ancient English nobleman.— **thane′dom,** *n.*

thank, 1 ĥaŋk; 2 thăŋk. **Iᵗ.** *vt.* To express gratitude to. **II.** *n.* The act of thanking; gratitude expressed: generally in the plural.— **thank′ful,** *a.* Grateful. **-ly,** *adv.* **-ness,** *n.*— **thank′less,** *a.* **1.** Not grateful. **2.** Unthanked or unrequited. **-ly,** *adv.* **-ness,** *n.*

thanks″giv′ing, 1 ĥaŋks″giv′iŋ; 2 thăŋks″-ĝĭv′ing, *n.* **1.** The act of giving thanks, as to God. **2.** A public service or celebration in recognition of divine favor.— **Thanksgiving day,** a holiday of the United States in recognition of the year's blessings: usually on the last Thursday in November.

that, 1 that; 2 thăt. **I.** *a.* [THOSE, 1 thōz; 2 thos, *pl.*] **1.** The (one) specially designated. **2.** Such. **3.** The (one) there. **II.** *pron.* **1.** As a demonstrative: the person or thing mentioned or understood. **2.** As a relative: who or which. **III.** *conj.* Noting a fact, reason, or result.

thatch, 1 ĥach; 2 thăch. **Iᵗ.** *vt. & vi.* To cover with a thatch. **II.** *n.* A covering of straw, or the like, for a roof.— **thatch′er,** *n.*— **thatch′ing,** *n.*

thaw, 1 ĥô; 2 tha. **I.** *vt. & vi.* To melt, as ice or snow. **II.** *n.* The act of thawing, as of frozen ground.

theˡ, 1 thī, thi, *or* thə; 2 thē, the, *or* thə, *definite art.* or *a.* Belonging to a distinct and definite class.

the, *adv.* By this; for this; to this extent: a modifier of words in the comparative degree; as, *the* sooner *the* better; *i. e., by as much* as it is sooner, *by so much* it will be better.

the′a-ter, *ſ* 1 ĥī′ə-tər; 2 thē′a-ter, *n.* **1.**
the′a-tre, *ſ* A building for dramatic representations; playhouse. **2.** Any scene of stirring events.— **the-at′ri-cal.** **I.** *a.* **1.** Pertaining to the theater. **2.** Designed for display or effect. **the-at′ric‡.** **II.** *n. pl.* A dramatic performance.

thee, 1 ĥī; 2 thē, *pers. pron.* The objective case of THOU: used in prayer, poetry, etc.

theft, 1 ĥeft; 2 thĕft, *n.* **1.** The act of stealing; larceny. **2.** That which is stolen.

their, *ſ* 1 thâr, thärz; 2 thêr, thêrs, *poss.*
theirs, *ſ pron. pl.* Possessive case of THEY.

the′ism, 1 ĥī′izm; 2 thē′ĩsm, *n.* Belief in one God.— **the′ist,** *n.* A believer in one God. — **the-is′tic, the-is′ti-cal,** *a.*

them, 1 them; 2 thĕm, *pron. pl.* Objective case of THEY.— **them-selves′,** *pron.* Plural of HIMSELF, HERSELF, ITSELF.

theme, 1 ĥīm; 2 thēm, *n.* **1.** A subject, as of discourse; a topic. **2.** An essay.

then, 1 then; 2 thĕn. **I.** *adv.* **1.** At that time. **2.** Next or immediately afterward. **3.** At another time. **II.** *conj.* **1.** For that reason; therefore. **2.** In that case.

thence, *ſ* 1 thens; 2 thĕnç, *adv.* **1.** From
thenseᴾ, *ſ* that place or time. **2.** Therefore.— **thence″forth′,** *adv.* From that time forth. **thence″for′ward‡.**

the-oc′ra-cy, 1 ĥi-ŏk′rə-sı; 2 thē-ŏe′ra-çy, *n.* [-CIES², *pl.*] **1.** A government recognizing the immediate sovereignty of God. **2.** Hence, government by priests or ecclesiastics.— **the″o-crat′ic, -i-cal,** *a.*

the-od′o-lite, 1 ĥi-ŏd′o-lɑit; 2 thē-ŏd′o-lĭt, *n.* A portable instrument for measuring angles, used in land=surveying.

the-ol′o-gy, 1 ĥi-ŏl′o-jı; 2 thē-ŏl′o-ġy, *n.* [-GIES², *pl.*] The branch of religious science that treats of God.— **the″o-lo′gi-an,** 1 ĥī′o-lō′ji-ən; 2 thē″o-lō′ĝi-an, *n.* One versed in theology; a divine.— **the″o-log′i-cal,** 1 ĥī′o-lŏj′i-kəl; 2 thē″o-lŏĝ′i-cal, *a.* Pertaining to theology.— **the″o-log′ic‡.**— **the″-o-log′i-cal-ly,** *adv.*

the′o-rem, 1 ĥī′o-rem; 2 thē′o-rĕm, *n.* A proposition to be proved.

the′o-ry, 1 ĥī′o-rı; 2 thē′o-ry, *n.* [-RIES², *pl.*] A plan or scheme subsisting in the mind only; abstract knowledge of any art; a proposed explanation; speculation. — **the″o-ret′i-cal,** 1 ĥī′o-ret′i-kəl; 2 thē″-o-rĕt′i-cal, *a.* Pertaining to theory; speculative; hypothetical. **the″o-ret′ic‡.**— **the″-o-ret′i-cal-ly,** *adv.*— **the′o-rist,** *n.* One who

theorizes.— **the′o-rize**, *vt. & vi.* [-RIZED;
-RIZ′ING.] To form or express theories;
speculate. **the′o-rise**‡.

the-os′o-phy, 1 thi-os′o-fı; 2 the-ŏs′o-fy,
n. A system of mystical speculation applied to deduce a philosophy of the universe; in modern use, a system that
claims to embrace the essential truth
underlying all systems of religion, philosophy, and science.

ther″a-peu′tic, 1 fher″ə-piū′tık; 2 thĕr″a-
pū′tic, *a.* **1.** Having healing qualities;
curative. **2.** Pertaining to medical science.
ther″a-peu′ti-cal‡.

there, 1 thâr; 2 thêr, *adv.* **1.** In or at that
place. **2.** To that place; thither. **3.** At
that stage.— **there′a-bout″**, *adv.* Near that
number, quantity, etc., approximately.
there′a-bouts″‡.— **there′a-f′ter. I.** *n.* The
time following an event. **II.** *adv.* **1.** Afterward. **2.** Accordingly.— **there-at′**, *adv.*
Upon that.— **there-by′**, *adv.* **1.** Through
the agency of that. **2.** Connected with that.
3. Conformably to that. **4.** Near by.—
there-for′, *adv.* For this or that.— **there′-
fore**, *adv. & conj.* For this or that reason;
consequently.— **there- from′**, *adv.* From
this or that time, place, etc.— **there-in′**, *adv.*
1. In that place. **2.** In that time, matter,
etc.— **there-of′**‖, *adv.* **1.** Of this, that, or it.
2. Therefrom.— **there-on′**, *adv.* On this,
that, or it.— **there-to′**, *adv.* **1.** To this, that,
or it. **2.** In addition.— **there′un-to′**‡.—
there′up-on′, *adv.* Upon that.— **there-
with′**, *adv.* **1.** With this, that, or it. **2.**
Thereupon.— **there′with-al′**, *adv.* Beside.

ther′mal, 1 fhûr′məl; 2 thêr′mal, *a.* Pertaining to, determined by, or measured by
heat.

ther′mo-, therm-. Combining forms.

ther-mom′e-ter, 1 fhər-mŏm′ı-tər; 2 ther-
mŏm′e-ter, *n.* An instrument for measuring degrees of temperature.— **ther″mo-met′-
ric, -ri-cal,** *a.*

ther′mo-stat, 1 fhûr′mo-stat; 2 thêr′mo-
stăt, *n.* A device for the automatic regulation of temperature by the expansion
or differential expansion or contraction
of substances, as for fire-alarms, dampers
of furnaces, etc.

the-sau′rus, 1 thi-sô′rus; 2 the-sa′rŭs, *n.* **1.**
Gr. Antiq. A storehouse. **2.** Hence, a repository of words or knowledge; a lexicon or
cyclopedia.

these, 1 thiz; 2 thês, *a. & pron.* Plural of THIS.

the′sis, 1 thī′sıs; 2 thê′sis, *n.* [THE′SES,
1 -sīz; 2 -sês, *pl.*] **1.** A proposition to be
defended. **2.** An essay; theme.

thew, 1 fhiū; 2 thū, *n.* A sinew or muscle;
in the plural, bodily strength.

they, 1 thē; 2 the, *pron. pl.* [THEIR or

THEIRS, *poss.*; THEM, *obj.*] These or those
understood or mentioned.

thick, 1 fhik; 2 thĭk. **I.** *a.* **1.** Having
relatively great distance from one surface
to its opposite. **2.** Having a specified dimension distinguished from length and
width. **3.** Arranged compactly; close;
dense; abundant. **4.** Foggy; misty; dull.
II. *n.* **1.** The dimension of thickness.
2. The time when or place where anything is thickest or most intense. **III.**
adv. In a thick manner.— **thick′en**, *vt. & vi.*
To make or become thick or thicker.—
thick′et, *n.* A thick growth, as of small
trees.— **thick′ly**, *adv.*— **thick′ness**, *n.*—
thick′set′, *a.* **1.** Having a short, thick
body; stout. **2.** Closely planted.

thief, 1 fhif; 2 thêf, *n.* [THIEVES, 1 fhīvz; 2
thêvs, *pl.*] One who steals.— **thiev(e′**, 1
fhīv; 2 thêv, *vt. & vi.* [THIEV(E)D§; THIEV′ING.]
To steal.— **thiev′er-y**, *n.* The practise of
thieving.— **thiev′ish**, *a.* **-ly**, *adv.* **-ness**, *n.*

thigh, 1 fhai; 2 thī, *n.* The part of the leg
between the hip and the knee.

thill, 1 fhil; 2 thĭl, *n.* One of two light
poles attached to a vehicle between which
a horse is harnessed; a shaft.

thim′ble, 1 fhim′bl; 2 thĭm′bl, *n.* A cap
thim′bl§, of metal, worn on the end of
the finger in sewing.

thin, 1 fhin; 2 thĭn. **I.** *vt. & vi.* [THINNED,
THIND§; THIN′NING.] To make or become
thin or thinner. **II.** *a.* [THIN′NER; THIN′-
NEST.] **1.** Having opposite surfaces very
close to each other; not thick. **2.** Lean.
3. Sparse; rare. **4.** Having little substance or consistency. **-ly**, *adv.* **-ness**, *n.*

thine, 1 thain; 2 thīn, *poss. pron.* Of or
belonging to thee: used now mostly in
poetry, prayer, etc.

thing, 1 fhiŋ; 2 thĭŋ, *n.* **1.** Any distinct
substance; a distinct object of thought.
2. *pl.* Personal belongings, as clothes.

think, 1 fhiŋk; 2 thĭŋk, *v.* [THOUGHT;
THINK′ING.] **I.** *t.* To form or entertain
in mind; to suppose; believe; remember;
purpose. **II.** *i.* To exercise the mind;
consider; meditate; reflect.— **think′er**, *n.*—
think′ing, *n.* Mental action; thought.

third, 1 fhûrd; 2 thîrd, *a. & n.* **1.** Next
in order after the second. **2.** One of
three equal parts.— **third′ly**, *adv.*— **third
rail**, in certain trolley systems, an insulated rail carrying the current, which is
taken from it by various moving contact devices.

thirst, 1 fhûrst; 2 thîrst. **I**. *vt. & vi.* To
have a thirst for; be thirsty; have eager
desire. **II.** *n.* A sensation calling for
relief by drinking; also, any eager desire

or longing.— **thirst'y,** *a.* [THIRST'I-ER; THIRST'I-EST.] **1.** Affected with thirst. **2.** Lacking moisture; parched. **3.** Eagerly desirous.— **thirst'i·ly,** *adv.*— **thirst'i·ness,** *n.*

thir'teen", 1 thûr'tēn"; 2 thir-'tēn", *a. & n.* One more than twelve.— **thir·teenth",** *a. & n.* **1.** Third in order after the tenth. **2.** One of thirteen equal parts.

thir'ty, 1 thûr'tı; 2 thir'ty, *a. & n.* Ten more than twenty.— **thir'ti·eth,** *a. & n.* **1.** Tenth in order after the twentieth. **2.** One of thirty equal parts.

this, 1 this; 2 this. **I.** *a.* [THESE, 1 thīz; 2 thēg, *pl.*] That is here present. **II.** *pron.* The person or thing here present, or as if present. **III.** *adv.* In this way; to this degree.

this'tle, } 1 this'l; 2 this'l, *n.* One of
this'tlᴾ, } various vigorous prickly plants.— **this'tly,** *a.*

thith'er, 1 thith'ər; 2 thith'er, *adv.* **1.** To that place; in that direction. **2.** To that end, point, or result. **thith'er·ward‡.**

Common Thistle.

tho, } 1 thō;
though, } 2 thō, *conj.* **1.** Notwithstanding the fact that. **2.** Even if. **3.** And yet; however. **4.** Nevertheless.

thole, 1 thōl; 2 thōl, *n.* A pin serving as a fulcrum for an oar in rowing. **thole'pin"‡.**

thong, 1 thȯŋ; 2 thȯng, *n.* A long narrow strip of leather, for binding or tying.

tho'rax, 1 thō'raks; 2 thō'räks, *n.* **1.** The part of the body between the neck and the abdomen. **2.** The middle region of the body of an insect.— **tho·rac'ic,** 1 tho-ras'ik; 2 tho-räç'ic, *a.*

thorn, 1 thôrn; 2 thôrn, *n.* **1.** A sharp-pointed outgrowth from a branch. **2.** A spiny shrub or tree. **3.** A discomfort; pain; vexation.— **thorn'y,** *a.* [THORN'I-ER; THORN'I-EST.] Full of thorns; painful; vexatious.

thor'ough, } 1 thur'o; 2 thôr'o, *a.* Going
thor'o⁵, } through and through; complete; perfect. **-ly,** *adv.* **-ness,** *n.*— **thor'ough·bred",** *a.* Bred from the best stock; high-spirited; courageous.— **thor'ough·go"ing,** *a.* Very thorough or efficient.— **thor'ough·paced",** *a.* Perfectly trained; thoroughgoing.

thor'ough·fare", } 1 thur'o-fār"; 2 thôr'o-
thor'o·fare"⁵, } fär", *n.* **1.** A highway. **2.** A passing through.

thor'ough·wort", 1 thur'o-wûrt"; 2 thôr'o-wûrt", *n.* A stout hairy herb, with white flowers.

those, 1 thōz; 2 thōs, *a. & pron.* In present use, plural of THAT.

thou, 1 thau; 2 thou, *pron.* The person spoken to: now superseded in common usage by the plural form *you.*

thought, 1 thȯt; 2 thôt, *imp. & pp.* of THINK, *v.*

thought, *n.* **1.** The act, process, or power of thinking; reason. **2.** A concept, judgment, etc. **3.** Sober reflection; also, a design; purpose; memory.— **thought'ful,** *a.* Full of thought; manifesting thought and care; provident; considerate; attentive. **-ly,** *adv.* **-ness,** *n.*— **thought'less,** *a.* Heedless; giddy; stupid. **-ly,** *adv.* **-ness,** *n.*

thou'sand, 1 thau'zand; 2 thou'sand, *a. & n.* A hundred times ten; ten hundred.— **thou'sandth,** *a. & n.* **1.** Last in a series of a thousand. **2.** One of a thousand equal parts.

thrall, 1 thrȯl; 2 thral, *n.* **1.** A slave; serf. **2.** Slavery; thraldom.— **thral'dom,** *n.* Bondage; servitude. **thrall'dom‡.**

thrash, 1 thrash; 2 thrāsh, *v.* **I.** *t.* To whip. **II.** *i.* To throw oneself about violently; dash. **thresh‡.**— **thrash'er,** *n.*

thread, } 1 thred; 2 thrĕd, *v.* **I.** *t.* To
thread⁵, } pass a thread through. **II.** *i.* To pick one's way, as through a wood.

thread, *n.* **1.** A slender cord, fiber, or line. **2.** The spiral ridge of a screw.— **thread'bare",** *a.* **1.** Worn so that the threads show, as a garment; clad in worn garments. **2.** Commonplace; hackneyed.

threat, } 1 thret; 2 thrĕt, *n.* A declared
thret⁵, } intention to inflict pain, injury, etc.; a menace.— **thre(a)t'en⁵,** *v.* **I.** *t.* To utter menaces or threats against; be ominous or portentous of. **II.** *i.* To employ threats; have a menacing aspect.— **threat'en·ing,** *pa.*

three, 1 thrī; 2 thrē, *a.* Two and one.— **three'fold",** **I.** *a.* Made up of three; triple. **II.** *adv.* In a threefold manner.— **three'score",** *a.* Sixty.

thresh, 1 thresh; 2 thrĕsh, *v.* **I.** *t.* To beat, as stalks of grain, by means of a flail or a machine. **II.** *i.* To beat out grain, etc.— **thresh'er,** *n.*

thresh'old, 1 thresh'ōld; 2 thrĕsh'old, *n.* The plank or stone beneath the door of a building; sill; entrance; starting-point.

threw, 1 thrū; 2 thru, *imp.* of THROW, *v.*

thrice, 1 thrais; 2 thrīç, *adv.* Three times; fully; to the utmost.

thrift, 1 thrift; 2 thrift, *n.* Wise and prudent management; a flourishing condition; vigorous growth.— **thrift'less,** *a.*— **thrift'y,** *a.* [THRIFT'I-ER; THRIFT'I-EST.] Economical; frugal; thriving.— **thrift'i·ly,** *adv.*— **thrift'i·ness,** *n.*

thrill, } 1 thril; 2 thril, *vt. & vi.* To per-
thrilᴾ, } vade, as with a sudden tremor of emotion; be stirred by intense emotion.

thrill[1], *n.* **1.** A tremor of feeling. **2.** A pulsation.

thrill[2], *n.* A trill; warbling.

thrive, 1 thraiv; 2 thrĭv, *vi.* [THROVE, rarely THRIVED; THRIV'EN, rarely THRIVED; THRIV'ING.] To prosper; be successful; be thrifty; grow with vigor.

throat, 1 thrōt; 2 thrŏt, *n.* The part of the neck containing the air-passages; the esophagus or the windpipe; an inlet; orifice.

throb, 1 thrɐb; 2 thrŏb. **I.** *vi.* [THROBBED, THROBD[s]; THROB'BING.] To beat violently, as the heart; palpitate; vibrate; thrill. **II.** *n.* The act or state of throbbing. [pain.

throe, 1 thrō; 2 thrō, *n.* A violent pang or

throne, 1 thrōn; 2 thrōn. **I.** *vt.* [THRONE; THRON'ING.] To enthrone. **II.** *n.* A monarch's chair of state; royal dignity; sovereign power.

throng, 1 thrɐŋ; 2 thrŏng, *v.* **I.** *t.* To crowd into or upon. **II.** *i.* To collect in a throng. [tude.

throng, *n.* A vast, dense crowd; multi-

throttle, 1 throt'l; 2 thrŏt'l. **I.** *vt.* **throt'l**[e], [THROT'TLED,THROT'LD[s]; THROT'TLING.] To choke; shut off, as steam. **II.** *n.* **1.** The throat; windpipe. **2.** A valve closing the steam-supply pipe of an engine.— **throt'tler**, *n.*

through, 1 thrū; 2 thrū. **I.** *a.* Going **thru**[s], from beginning to end; pertaining to an entire distance. **II.** *adv.* **1.** From one end, surface, etc., to or beyond the other. **2.** From beginning to end. **3.** To a termination. **III.** *prep.* **1.** From end to end. **2.** Throughout. **3.** From the first to the last of.— **through-out'. I.** *adv.* Through or in every part. **II.** *prep.* All through.

throve, 1 thrōv; 2 thrōv, *imp.* of THRIVE, *v.*

throw, 1 thrō; 2 thrō, *v.* [THREW; THROWN; THROW'ING.] **I.** *t.* To fling, hurl, or cast forth; overturn; prostrate. **II.** *i.* To send an object through the air by force. — **throw'er**, *n.*

throw, *n.* **1.** An act of throwing; a fling. **2.** The distance a missile is thrown.

thrum, 1 thrum; 2 thrŭm, *vt. & vi.* [THRUMMED, THRUMD[s]; THRUM'MING.] To play on or finger idly, as a stringed instrument.

thrum, *n.* The fringe of warp-threads after the web has been cut off; loose thread.

thrush[1], 1 thruṡh; 2 thrŭsh, *n.* A small migratory song-bird. See illus. in next column.

thrush[2], *n.* **1.** A disease of the mouth and throat. **2.** A disease of a horse's foot.

thrust, 1 thrust; 2 thrŭst. **I.** *vt. & vi.* [THRUST; THRUST'ING.] To push; shove; pierce. **II.** *n.* **1.** A sudden and forcible push; stab; onset. **2.** *Mech.* An outward or sidewise strain.

Thrush. 1/13

thud, 1 thud; 2 thŭd, *n.* A dull, heavy sound, as of a blow on a yielding substance.

thug, 1 thug; 2 thŭg, *n.* **1.** One of a sect of religious assassins in India. **2.** A murderous ruffian; cutthroat.

thumb, 1 thum; 2 thŭm. **I.** *vt.* To **thum**[s], press, soil, or wear with the thumb. **II.** *n.* The short, thick digit of the hand.

thump, 1 thump; 2 thŭmp. **I**[t]. *vt. & vi.* To strike with a heavy dull sound. **II.** *n.* A blow making a dull sound.

thun'der, 1 thun'dɐr; 2 thŭn'der. **I.** *vi.* To give forth a peal or peals of thunder; reverberate. **II.** *n.* **1.** The sound that accompanies lightning. **2.** Any loud, rumbling, or booming noise.— **thun'bolt''**, *n.* A discharge of lightning.— **thun'der-clap''**, *n.* A sharp, violent detonation of thunder.— **thun'der-er**, *n.*— **thun'derous**, *a.* Producing or resembling thunder.— **thun'der-show''er**, *n.* A shower with thunder and lightning. **t.-storm**[?].— **thun'derstruck''**, *a.* Amazed.— **thun'der-y**, *a.*

Thurs'day, 1 thürz'di; 2 thûrg'da, *n.* The fifth day of the week.

thus, 1 thus; 2 thûs, *adv.* **1.** In this or that way. **2.** To such extent. **3.** In this case.

thwack, 1 thwak; 2 thwăk. **I**[t]. *vt.* To slap heavily; whack. **II.** *n.* A blow with a flat instrument.

thwart[d], 1 thwôrt; 2 thwart, *vt.* To prevent by interposition; foil.

thwart, *a.* Lying or extending across.

thwart, *n.* An oarsman's seat.

thy, 1 thai; 2 thī, *pron.* Pertaining to thee: used in poetry, prayer, etc.— **thy'self**, *pron.* [herb.

thyme, 1 taim; 2 tīm, *n.* An aromatic

ti-a'ra, 1 tai-ē'rɐ *or* ti-ā'ra; 2 tĭ-ā'ra *or* ti-ä'rä, *n.* The Pope's triple crown; a coronet.

tib'i-a, 1 tib'i-ɐ; 2 tĭb'i-a, *n.* [-Æ, 1 -Ī, 2 -ē, *or* -As[z], *pl.*] The inner one of the two bones of the leg below the knee.— **tib'i-al**, *a.*

tick[t], 1 tik; 2 tĭk, *vt. & vi.* To sound, as a tick; make a clicking sound or a tapping noise.

---

tick[1], *n.* **1.** A significant mark; check. **2.** One of the recurring sounds made by a watch, clock, or the like.

tick[2], *n.* One of various blood=sucking parasites that infest the skin of animals.

tick[3], *n.* The stout outer covering of a bed or mattress. **tick'ing†.**

tick'et, 1 tik'et; 2 tĭk'ĕt. **I**[d]. *vt.* To fix a ticket to; label. **II.** *n.* **1.** A card showing that the holder is entitled to something, as admission or transportation. **2.** A tag or label. **3.** [U. S.] A ballot; also, the list of nominees of a party.

tick'le, } 1 tik'l; 2 tĭk'l, *v.* [TICK'L(E)D[P]; **tick'l**[P], } TICK'LING.] **I.** *t.* **1.** To excite to spasmodic movement and laughter by light touches. **2.** To please; amuse. **II.** *i.* To cause titillation or tingling.— **tick'-lish,** *a.* Sensitive to tickling; unstable; delicate. **-ness,** *n.*

tĭd'bĭt", *n.* Same as TITBIT.

tide, 1 taid; 2 tīd. **I.** *vt. & vi.* [TID'ED[d]; TID'ING.] To carry, as by a tide; to surmount, as a difficulty; followed by *over.* **II.** *n.* **1.** The periodic rise and fall of the ocean, due to the attraction of the sun and moon. **2.** A current; stream; drift; tendency.— **ti'dal,** 1 tai'dal; 2 tī'dal, *a.*

ti'dings, 1 tai'diŋz; 2 tī'dĭngs, *n. pl.* A report; news.

ti'dy, 1 tai'di; 2 tī'dy. **I.** *vt. & vi.* [TI'DIED; TI'DY-ING.] [Colloq.] To make tidy. **II.** *a.* [TI'DI-ER; TI'DI-EST.] Marked by neatness and order; trim; orderly. **III.** *n.* [TI'DIES[2], *pl.*] A light covering, as for a chair=back.— **ti'di-ly,** *adv.*— **ti'di-ness,** *n.*

tie, 1 tai; 2 tī. **I.** *vt. & vi.* [TIED; TY'ING.] **1.** To fasten, as a cord; bind; lash; fasten; attach. **2.** To form a knot in. **3.** To restrain; confine. **4.** To balance, as opposing votes. **II.** *n.* **1.** A flexible fastening, as of cord. **2.** A bond; obligation. **3.** Exact equality for and against, as in a vote. **4.** *Mus.* A curved line placed over or under two notes of the same pitch, to make them represent one tone length. **5.** *Railroad.* A wooden beam set crosswise to support rails; sleeper.

tier, 1 tīr; 2 tēr, *n.* A rank or row in a series of things placed one above another.

tierce, } 1 tīrs; 2 tērç, *n.* **1.** *Mus.* A **tierse**[P], } third. **2.** A cask. **3.** A sequence of three playing=cards.

tiff, 1 tif; 2 tĭf, *n.* A fit of irritation; pet.

ti'ger, 1 tai'gɐr; 2 tī'gẽr, *n.* A large carnivorous mammal marked with vertical black wavy stripes. See next column.— **ti'ger-ish, ti'grish,** *a.*— **ti'ger-lil"y,** *n.* A tall cultivated lily with purple= or black=spot-

ted flowers.— **ti'gress,** *n.* A female tiger.

tight, 1 tait; 2 tīt, *a.* **1.** Not leaky; impervious. **2.** Closely drawn or fastened; stringent. **3.** Fitting closely.— **tight'en,** *vt. & vi.* To make or become tight or tighter.— **tight'ly,** *adv.*— **tight'ness,** *n.*

Tiger. 1/42

tile, 1 tail; 2 tīl. **I.** *vt.* [TILED; TIL'ING.] **1.** To drain by tiles. **2.** To cover with tiles. **II.** *n.* **1.** A thin piece of baked clay used for covering roofs, floors, etc. **2.** A short earthenware pipe, used in forming sewers.— **til'er,** *n.*— **til'ing,** *n.* **1.** The using of tiles. **2.** Tiles collectively.

till, } 1 til; 2 tĭl, *vt.* To cultivate as soil. **till**[P], } — **till'a-bl(e**[P], *a.*— **till'age,** *n.* Cultiva-

till, *n.* A money=drawer.

till, *prep.* To the time of; up to; until.

till, *conj.* Till such time as; until.

till'er[1], *n.* One who or that which tills.

till'er[2], *n.* A handle for turning a rudder.

tilt[1], 1 tilt; 2 tĭlt. **I**[d]. *vt. & vi.* **1.** To tip; slant; lean. **2.** To aim, as a lance; contend with the lance. **II.** *n.* **1.** An inclination; slant. **2.** A tournament. **3.** A thrust, as with a lance.— **tilt'er,** *n.*— **tilt'=ham"mer,** *n.* A heavy hammer that is raised by machinery and delivers a blow by gravity.

tilt[2]. **I**[d]. *vt.* To furnish with an awning. **II.** *n.* A canvas cover, as for a boat or wagon. [cultivated land.

tilth, 1 tilθ; 2 tĭlth, *n.* Cultivation; tillage;

tim'ber, 1 tim'bɐr; 2 tĭm'bẽr, *n.* Wood suitable for building; standing trees.

tim'brel, 1 tim'brel; 2 tĭm'brĕl, *n.* An ancient Hebrew tambourine=like instrument.

time, 1 taim; 2 tīm. **I.** *vt. & vi.* [TIMED; TIM'ING.] **1.** To adapt to the time or occasion. **2.** To regulate as to time; keep time. **3.** To record the time or rate of. **II.** *n.* **1.** Infinite duration or

its measure. **2.** A definite period of duration; season; era; opportunity. **3.** A point in duration; date; occasion. **4.** *Mus.* (1) Rate of movement. (2) The duration or comparative value of a tone. — **time′keep″er,** *n.* One who or that which keeps time.— **time′ly,** *a.* [TIME′LI-ER; TIME′-LI-EST.] Being or occurring in good or proper time; opportune.— **time′li-ness,** *n.*— **time′piece″,** *n.* A clock or a watch.— **time′serv″er,** *n.* One who yields to the apparent demands of the time, without reference to principle.— **time′serv″ing,** *a.* & *n.*— **time′-ta″ble,** *n.* A tabular statement of appointed times, as of the arrival and departure of railway-trains.

tim′id, 1 tĭm′ĭd; 2 tĭm′id, *a.* Shrinking from danger or from publicity; shy.— **ti-mid′i-ty,** *n.* The state or quality of being timid. **tim′id-ness‡.**— **tim′id-ly,** *adv.*

tim′or-ous, 1 tĭm′ẽr-us; 2 tĭm′or-ŭs, *a.* Fearful of danger; timid. **-ly,** *adv.* **-ness,** *n.*

tim′o-thy, 1 tĭm′o-thĭ; 2 tĭm′o-thy, *n.* A fodder-grass.

tin, 1 tĭn; 2 tĭn. **I**ᵗ. *vt.* [TINNED, TIND˝; TIN′-NING.] To coat or cover with tin; incase in tin. **II.** *n.* **1.** A white malleable metallic element. **2.** Tin-plate or tin-ware.— **tin′-foil″,** *n.* Tin or alloy made into foil.— **tin′man,** *n.* A maker of or dealer in tinware. **tin′ner‡.**— **tin′-plate″,** *n.* Sheet iron plated with tin.— **tin′ware″,** *n.* Household articles, collectively, made of tin-plate.

tinc′ture, 1 tĭŋk′chụr *or* -tiur; 2 tĭŋc′chụr *or* -tūr. **I.** *vt.* [TINC′TURED; TINC′TUR-ING.] To imbue; flavor. **II.** *n.* **1.** A solution of some drug. **2.** A tinge; tint; slight flavor.

tin′der, 1 tĭn′dẽr; 2 tĭn′der, *n.* A highly inflammable substance, as charred linen.

tine, 1 taĭn; 2 tĭn, *n.* A spike or prong, as of a fork.

tinge, 1 tĭnj; 2 tĭng. **I.** *vt.* [TINGED; TINGE′ING.] To color slightly; tint. **II.** *n.* A faint trace of color; a quality or peculiarity.

tin′gle, } 1 tĭŋ′gl; 2 tĭŋ′gĕl, *vi.* [TIN′GL(E)D˝; **tin′gl²,** } TIN′GLING.] To have a stinging sensation.

tink′er, 1 tĭŋk′ẽr; 2 tĭŋk′er. **I.** *vt.* & *vi.* To mend or patch; work in makeshift fashion. **II.** *n.* An itinerant mender of tinware.

tin′kle, } 1 tĭŋ′kl; 2 tĭŋ′kl. **I.** *vt.* & *vi.* [TIN′-**tin′kl²,** } KL(E)D˝; TIN′KLING.] To make a series of quick, slight, metallic sound. **II.** *n.* A sharp, clear, tinkling sound.

tin′sel, 1 tĭn′sel; 2 tĭn′sĕl. **I.** *a.* Superficially brilliant. **II.** *n.* Very thin glittering bits of metal used for ornament.

tint, 1 tĭnt; 2 tĭnt. **I**ᵈ. *vt.* To tinge. **II.** *n.* A slight color; tinge; hue.

tin″tin-nab′u-la′tion, 1 tĭn″tĭ-nab″yu-lā′shạn; 2 tĭn″ti-năb″yu-lā′shon, *n.* The ringing or tinkling of a bell or bells.

ti′ny, 1 taĭ′nĭ; 2 tī′ny, *a.* [TI′NI-ER; TI′NI-EST.] Very small; minute.

-tion, *suffix.* A termination denoting act, state, or agent; as, agita*tion,* tempta*tion.*

-tious, *suffix.* A termination indicating state or manner.

tip¹, 1 tĭp; 2 tĭp, *vt.* & *vi.* [TIPPED˝, TIPT˝; TIP′PING.] **1.** To lean; tilt. **2.** To tap. **3.** To give a small gratuity, or secret information (to).

tip², *vt.* To furnish with or form into a tip; cover the tip of. [tapering; end.

tip¹, *n.* The point or extremity of anything.

tip², *n.* A small gift of money; a hint.

tip′pet, 1 tĭp′et; 2 tĭp′ĕt, *n.* A scarf for the neck, or neck and shoulders.

tip′ple, } 1 tĭp′l; 2 tĭp′l, *v.* [TIP′PLED, TIP′-**tip′l²,** } LD˝; TIP′PLING.] **I.** *t.* To drink, as alcoholic beverages, frequently. **II.** *i.* To sip often, as liquor.— **tip′ple,** *n.*— **tip′pler,** *n.*

tip′sy, 1 tĭp′sĭ; 2 tĭp′sy, *a.* [TIP′SI-ER; TIP′-SI-EST.] Partially intoxicated.

tip′toe″, 1 tĭp′to″; 2 tĭp′to″. **I.** *vi.* To walk on tiptoe. **II.** *n.* The tip of a toe; or of the toes collectively.

tip′-top″, 1 tĭp′-top″; 2 tĭp′-tŏp″, *n.* [Col-loq.] The highest point or degree; the very top: used also as adjective and adverb.

ti-rade′, 1 tĭ-rēd′; 2 ti-rād′, *n.* A prolonged declamatory outpouring, as of censure.

tire¹, 1 taĭr; 2 tīr, *v.* [TIRED; TIR′ING.] **I.** *t.* To weary; fatigue. **II.** *i.* To become weary.— **tired,** *pa.*— **tire′some,** *a.* Wearisome; tedious. **-ly,** *adv.* **-ness,** *n.*

tire², *vt.* To furnish with a tire; put a tire on.

tire¹, *n.* A band on the rim of a wheel.

tire², *n.* A tiara; head-dress.

tis′sue, 1 tĭsh′u; 2 tĭsh′u, *n.* **1.** *Biol.* One of the elementary fabrics of which an organ is composed. **2.** Any light or gauzy woven stuff.— **tis′sue-pa″per,** *n.* Very thin, unsized, almost transparent paper.

tit¹, 1 tĭt; 2 tĭt, *n.* **1.** One of various small birds, as a titmouse, titlark, etc. **2.** A small horse.— **tit′lark″,** *n.* A small bird resembling a lark.— **tit′mouse″,** *n.* [TIT′MICE″, *pl.*] A small bird having a short bill concealed by feathers.

tit², 1 tĭt; 2 tĭt, *n.* A American Titlark. ¹/₁₀ blow; tap: in the phrase **tit for tat,** retort or retaliation in kind.

Ti′tan, 1 taĭ′tạn; 2 tī′tan, *n.* **1.** *Gr. Myth.*

One of a number of divinities of gigantic strength, in conflict with and subdued by the gods of Olympus. **2.** By extension, one having gigantic strength.— **Ti-tan'ic,** *a.*

tit'bit', 1 tit'bit'; 2 tĭt'bĭt'', *n.* A morsel, as of choice food. **tĭd'bĭt''‡.**

tithe, 1 taith; 2 tīth. **I.** *vt.* [TITHED; TITH'ING.] To tax. **II.** *n.* A tax of one=tenth; the tenth part of anything. — **tith'ing,** *n.* **1.** The act of levying tithes. **2.** A tenth part.

tit'il-late, 1 tit'ı-lĕt; 2 tĭt'ĭ-lāt, *vt.* [-LAT''ED‡;-LAT'ING.] To tickle.— **tĭt'ĭl-la'tion,** *n.*

ti'tle, 1 tai'tl; 2 tī'tl. **I.** *vt.* [TI'TLED; TI'TLING.] To confer a title upon; give a name to; entitle. **II.** *n.* **1.** An inscription; name; appellation of rank, etc. **2.** A claim, as to consideration; right, as to property.— **ti'tled,** *a.* Having a title, as of nobility.— **ti'tle=deed'',** *n.* The instrument by which the title to property is evidenced.— **ti'tle=page'',** *n.* A page at the front of a literary production, usually containing the title of the work and the names of the author and the publisher.

tit'ter, 1 tit'ər; 2 tĭt'er. **I.** *vi.* To laugh in a suppressed or silly way; giggle. **II.** *n.* A giggling.

tit'tle, } 1 tit'l; 2 tĭt'l, *n.* The minutest
tit'l², } quantity; iota.

tit'u-lar, 1 tit'yu-lər; 2 tĭt'yu-lar, *a.* Pertaining to a title; being in name or title only; nominal. **tĭt'u-la-ry‡.**

to, 1 tū; 2 to̶. **I.** *adv.* **1.** Toward the end of action. **2.** Into normal condition. **3.** Into place. **4.** In a direction implied. **II.** *prep.* **1.** In a direction=toward. **2.** Noting an indirect object after certain parts of speech. **III.** The sign of the infinitive.

toad, 1 tōd; 2 tŏd, *n.* A tailless, jumping animal, resembling the frog.— **toad'stool'',** *n.* A poisonous mushroom.

toad'y, 1 tōd'ı; 2 tŏd'y. **I.** *vt. & vi.* [TOAD'IED; TOAD'Y-ING.] To fawn upon. **II.** *n.* [TOAD'IES²; *pl.*] An obsequious flatterer.

toast¹, 1 tōst; 2 tŏst. **I^d.** *vt.* To drink to the health of. **II.** *n.* The act of drinking to some one's health or to some sentiment; also, the person or the sentiment involved.

toast², **I^d.** *vt. & vi.* To brown, or become brown, over a fire. **II.** *n.* Toasted bread.

to=bac'co, 1 to-bak'o; 2 to-băe'o, *n.* An annual plant of the nightshade family; also its leaves prepared in various forms. — **to=bac'co=nist,** *n.* A manufacturer or seller of tobacco.

to=bog'gan, 1 to-bŏg'ən; 2 to-bŏg'an. **I.** *vi.* To coast on a toboggan. **II.** *n.* A

sled=like vehicle, consisting of a long thin board or boards curved upward at the forward end. [alarm; alarm=bell.

to=day', 1 tu-dē'; 2 to̶-dā'. **I.** *n.* The present day, time, or age. **II.** *adv.* **1.** On or during this present day. **2.** At the present time.

tod'dle, 1 tod'l; 2 tŏd'l, *vi.* [TOD'DLED; TOD'DLING.] To walk unsteadily, as a little child.— **tod'dler,** *n.*

tod'dy, 1 tod'ı; 2 tŏd'y, *n.* [TOD'DIES²; *pl.*] Sweetened spirits and water; alcoholic liquor.

toe, 1 tō; 2 tō. **I.** *vt.* [TOED; TOE'ING.] **1.** To touch with the toes. **2.** To furnish with a toe. **II.** *n.* One of the digits of a foot; front part of a hoof, shoe, or the like.

to'ga, 1 tō'go; 2 tō'ga, *n.* [TO'GAS² or TO'GÆ, 1 -jī; 2 -gē, *pl.*] The large loose mantle of a Roman citizen.

to-geth'er, 1 tu-geth'ər; 2 to̶-gĕth'er, *adv.* **1.** Into union with each other. **2.** In company. **3.** Simultaneously. **4.** Without cessation.

tog'gle, } 1 teg'l; 2 tŏg'l. **I.** *vt.* [TOG'GLED;
tog'l², } TOG'LD²; TOG'GLING.] To fix or furnish with a toggle. **II.** *n.* A pin for securing a rope. **2.** A toggle=joint.— **tog'gle=joint'',** *n.* A joint having a central hinge like an elbow, and moved by pressure at the junction.

Toggle=joint.

toil, 1 teil; 2 tŏil, *vi.* To labor arduously; work hard.— **toil'er,** *n.*

toil¹, *n.* Fatiguing work; any oppressive task.— **toil'some,** *a.* **-ly,** *adv.* **-ness,** *n.*

toil², *n.* A net, snare, or other trap.

toi'let, 1 tei'let; 2 tŏi'lĕt, *n.* **1.** The process of dressing oneself. **2.** A person's dress. **3.** A dressing=table or dressing=room. **4.** [U. S.] A lavatory.

to'ken, 1 tō'kn; 2 tō'kn, *n.* **1.** Anything indicative of some other thing; a sign; symbol; emblem. **2.** A pledge. **3.** A keepsake.

told, 1 tōld; 2 tŏld, *imp. & pp.* of TELL.

tol'er-ant, 1 tol'ər-ant; 2 tŏl'er-ant, *a.* Indulgent; liberal.— **tol'er-a-bl(e²,** *a.* Passably good; commonplace. **2.** Supportable. **3.** Allowable.— **tol'er-a-bly,** *adv.*— **tol'er-ance,** *n.* The state of being tolerant. — **tol'er-ate,** *vt.* [-AT'ED‡; -AT'ING.] **1.** To allow without opposition; concede, as the right to religious belief and worship. **2.** To bear.— **tol''er-a'tion,** *n.*

toll¹, 1 tōl; 2 tŏl. **I.** *vt. & vi.* To sound, as a bell, with single strokes at uniform

intervals. **II.** *n.* The sound of a bell rung slowly and regularly.

toll². I. *vt. & vi.* To take, as toll; take or pay toll. **II.** *n.* A charge, as for passing on a bridge or turnpike.— **toll'=gate",** *n.* A gate, as across a turnpike, at which toll is paid.

tom'a-hawk, 1 tŏm'ə-hōk; 2 tŏm'a-hạk. **I**t. *vt.* To strike or kill with a tomahawk. **II.** *n.* The North= American Indian war= hatchet.

to-ma'to, 1 to-mē'to *or* to-mä'to; 2 to-mā'to *or* to-mä'to, *n.* [-TOES², *pl.*] The edible fruit of a plant of the night= shade family; also, the plant.

tomb, 1 tūm; 2 tọm, *n.* A place for the deposit of the dead; a vault; grave.— **tomb'stone",** *n.* A stone marking a place of burial.

Pipe=tomahawks.

tom'boy", 1 tŏm'bei"; 2 tŏm'bŏy", *n.* A romping and boisterous girl; hoiden.

tom'=cat", 1 tŏm'=kat"; 2 tŏm'=cắt", *n.* A male cat.

tome, 1 tōm; 2 tōm, *n.* A large volume.

to=mor'row, 1 tu=mŏr'o; 2 to=mŏr'o. **I.** *n.* The morrow. **II.** *adv.* On the next day after to=day. [titmouse.

tom'tit", 1 tŏm'tit"; 2 tŏm'tĭt", *n.* A tit;

ton¹,) 1 tun; 2 tŏn, *n.* **1.** A measure of **tun**P,) weight, either 2,000 pounds (a short ton), or 2,240 pounds (a long ton). **2.** [U. S.] A measure of 40 to 100 cubic feet. See TONNAGE. [fashion.

ton², 1 tŏn; 2 tŏn, *n.* Tone; style; votaries of

tone, 1 tōn; 2 tōn. **I.** *vt.* [TONED; TON'= ING.] To give tone to; modify in tone; tune. **II.** *n.* **1.** A sound having a definite pitch; characteristic sound, as of a voice. **2.** A mood. **3.** Characteristic style. **4.** Vocal inflection; mode of utterance.

tongs, 1 tŏnz; 2 tŏngs, *n. pl.* An imple= ment for grasping, consisting of a pair of pivoted levers.

tongue,) 1 tun; 2 tŏng, *n.* **1.** The organ **tung**s,) of speech and taste. **2.** Some= thing likened to the tongue of an animal, as a promontory, bell=clapper, pin of a buckle, etc. **3.** Speech; utterance; a language.— **tongue'=tied",** *a.* Not able to speak freely.

ton'ic, 1 tŏn'ik; 2 tŏn'ĭe. **I.** *a.* **1.** In= vigorating; bracing. **2.** Pertaining to tone or tones. **3.** Pertaining to tension.

II. *n.* A tonic medicine or anything in= vigorating.

to=night', 1 tu=nait'; 2 to=nīt'. **I.** *n.* The night that follows to=day; also, the present night. **II.** *adv.* In or during the present night or coming night.

ton'nage, 1 tun'ij; 2 tŏa'ag, *n.* The cubic capacity of a vessel in tons of 100 cubic feet each.

ton"neau', 1 to"nō'; 2 to'nō'. **I.** *a.* Barrel= like: said of the body of certain motor=cars. **II.** *n.* A barrel=like body of certain motor= cars.

ton'sil, 1 tŏn'sıl; 2 tŏn'sil, *n.* One of two oval organs situated on either side of the throat.

ton=so'ri-al, 1 tŏn-sō'rı-əl; 2 tŏn-sō'ri-al, *a.* Pertaining to a barber or to his work.

ton'sure, 1 tŏn'shur; 2 tŏn'shụr, *n.* The shaving of the head, or shaven crown, as of a priest; the priestly office.

too, 1 tū; 2 tōo, *adv.* **1.** More than suffi= ciently. **2.** [Colloq.] Exceedingly. **3.** Also; likewise.

took, 1 tuk; 2 tŏok, *imp.* of TAKE, *v.*; also rarely *pp.*

tool, 1 tūl; 2 tōol, *n.* **1.** An implement, as a hammer, file, spade, etc. **2.** A person used to carry out the designs of another.

tooth, 1 tūth; 2 tōoth, *n.* [TEETH, 1 tīth; 2 tēth, *pl.*] **1.** One of the hard, dense structures of the mouth, used for chewing food. **2.** Some'hing resembling the tooth of an animal in form or use, as a project= ing point, pin, or cog.— **tooth'ache",** *n.* Pain in a tooth; also, neuralgia of the teeth. — **toothed,** *a.* Supplied with teeth; indent= ed.— **tooth'less,** *a.* Being without teeth; harmless.— **tooth'pick",** *n.* A small sliver, as of wood, for picking the teeth.— **tooth'= some,** *a.* Having a pleasant taste.

top, 1 tŏp; 2 tŏp, *vt.* [TOPPEDt, TOPTs; TOP'PING.] **1.** To remove the top of. **2.** To provide with a top. **3.** To surmount; surpass; excel.

top¹, *n.* **1.** The upper extremity of any= thing. **2.** That which is first or highest in rank or degree. **3.** *Naut.* A platform at the head of the lower section of a mast.— **top"gal'lant,** *n.* The mast, sail, yard, etc., next above the topmast.— **top'= knot",** *n.* A crest, tuft, or knot on the top of the head.— **top'mast",** *n.* The mast next above the lower mast.— **top'most,** *a.* Be= ing at the very top.— **top'sail",** *n.* A sail on the topmast.

top², *n.* A toy, of wood or metal, with a point on which it is made to rotate.

to'paz, 1 tō'paz; 2 tō'pǎz, *n.* A trans= parent gem of a yellow color.

to-pep'o, 1 to-pep'o; 2 to-pĕp'o, *n.* [-OES, 1 -OZ; 2 -OS, *pl.*] A hybrid plant obtained by crossing the Chinese pepper with a variety of tomato, cultivated for its edible fruit; also the fruit itself.

top'er, 1 tōp'ǝr; 2 tōp'er, *n.* A habitual drunkard; sot.

To'pheth, 1 tō'fĕt; 2 tō'fĕt, *n.* **1.** A place for idolatrous worship and later for burning the city's refuse. *Jer.* xix; 13. **2.** Hence, hell.

top'ic, 1 tŏp'ık; 2 tŏp'ie, *n.* A subject of discourse; a theme.— **top'ı-cal,** *a.*

to-pog'ra-phy, } 1 to-pŏg'ra-fı; 2 to-pŏg'-
to-pog'ra-fy⁷, } ra-fy, *n.* **1.** The description of places, as on a map. **2.** The physical features, collectively, of a region. — **to-pog'ra-pher,** *n.* An expert in topography.— **top'o-graph'ıc, top'o-graph'ı-cal,** *a.*

top'ple, } 1 tŏp'l; 2 tŏp'l, *v.* [TOP'PLED,
top'l⁷, } TOP'LD⁷; TOP'PLING.] To totter and fall.

top"sy-tur'vy, 1 tŏp"sı-tūr'vı; 2 tŏp"sy-tûr'vy, *adv.* Upside down; in confusion.

torch, 1 tōrch; 2 tôrch, *n.* A light made of any combustible substance fastened to a pole, or a lamp so attached.

tore, 1 tōr; 2 tôr, *imp.* of TEAR, *v.* [torture.

tor-ment', 1 tēr-ment'; 2 tôr-mĕnt', *vt.* To inflict extreme pain upon; cause to suffer keenly. **II.** *n.* Intense suffering; agony.

tor'ment, 1 tōr'ment; 2 tôr'mĕnt, *n.* Intense pain or a person or thing that causes it; torture; anguish; distress.— **tor-men'tor,** *n.*

torn, 1 tōrn; 2 tôrn, *pp.* of TEAR, *v.*

tor-na'do, 1 ter-nā'do; 2 tôr-nā'do, *n.* [-DOES⁷; 2 -DOES⁷, *pl.*] A violent local storm.

tor-pe'do, 1 ter-pī'do; 2 tôr-pē'do, *n.* **1.** [-DOES⁷, *pl.*] An apparatus containing an explosive to be fired by concussion or otherwise. **2.** A ray-fish having an electric apparatus with which it stuns or kills its prey.

tor'por, 1 tōr'pǝr; 2 tôr'por, *n.* Complete or partial insensibility; stupor; apathy; torpidity.— **tor'pid,** *a.* Dormant; numb; sluggish.— **tor-pid'ı-ty,** *n.*

tor'rent, 1 tōr'ent; 2 tôr'ĕnt, *n.* A rushing stream. [ing.

tor'rid, 1 tōr'ıd; 2 tôr'ıd, *a.* Sultry; scorch-

tor'sion, 1 tōr'shǝn; 2 tôr'shon, *n.* The act of twisting, the state of being twisted, or the result of twisting.

tor'so, 1 tēr'so; 2 tôr'so, *n.* The trunk of a human body; in sculpture, a statue without head or limbs.

tor'toise, 1 tēr'tıs; 2 tôr'tıs, *n.* A turtle.

tor'tu-ous, 1 tēr'chu-[or -tiu-]us; 2 tôr'-chu-[or -tū-]ŭs, *a.* Winding; twisting; erratic.

tor'ture, 1 tēr'chur *or* -tiur; 2 tôr'chur *or*

To'ry, 1 tō'rı; 2 tō'ry, *n.* [TO'RIES⁷, *pl.*] **1.** A member of an English historic political party, originating with the Cavalier party of Charles I. **2.** One who during the American Revolution adhered to the British cause.— **To'ry-ism,** *n.*

toss, 1 tŏs; 2 tôs, *v.* [TOSSED⁷ or TOST; TOSS'ING.] **I.** *t.* To throw, pitch, or fling up or about. **II.** *i.* To throw oneself from side to side; be moved, rocked, or blown about.

toss, *n.* **1.** The act of tossing. **2.** The state of being tossed about.

tot, 1 tet; 2 tŏt, *n.* A little child; toddler.

to'tal, 1 tō'tal; 2 tō'tal. **I.** *a.* Being a total; complete. **II.** *n.* The whole sum or amount.— **to-tal'ı-ty,** *n.*— **to'tal-ly,** *adv.*

to'tem, 1 tō'tem; 2 tō'tĕm, *n.* *Anthrop.* A natural object, usually an animal, assumed among savages as the emblem of an individual or clan, and regarded as an object of worship.

tot'ter, 1 tet'ǝr; 2 tŏt'er, *vi.* To waver, as if about to fall; walk unsteadily.

tou-can', 1 tu-kän' *or* tū'kǝn; 2 tu-cän' *or* tu'ean, *n.* A tropical American bird with immense beak.

Toucan. 1/18

touch⁷, } 1 tuch; 2
tuch⁷, } tŭch, *v.* **I.** *t.* **1.** To be in or come into contact with, as with the hand; reach; strike; play upon. **2.** To affect with tender feeling. **3.** To relate to; concern. **II.** *i.* To be in contact.— **touch'ing. I.** *pa.* Appealing to the susceptibilities; affecting. **II.** *prep.* With regard to.— **touch'y,** *a.* [Colloq.] Quick-tempered.

touch, *n.* **1.** A touching; contact. **2.** The sense that gives the impression of contact. **3.** Any slight effort or effect, as of brush or pen. **4.** Accord; sympathy. — **touch'-down',** *n.* *Football.* The act or play of touching the ball to the ground behind an opponent's goal.— **touch'stone",** *n.* **1.** A fine-grained dark stone, formerly used to test the fineness of gold. **2.** Any standard or criterion.— **touch'wood",** *n.* Some soft combustible material used as tinder.

tough, } 1 tuf; 2 tŭf, *a.* **1.** Capable of
tuf⁷, } being bent or strained without breaking; tenacious. **2.** Vicious; vulgar.

— **tough′en**, _vt._ & _vi._ To render or become tough or tougher.

tour, 1 tūr; 2 tụr. **I.** _vt._ & _vi._ To make a tour of; travel. **II.** _n._ A round trip or journey; circuit.— **tour′ist**, _n._ One who makes a tour.

tour′na-ment, 1 tūr′nə-ment _or_ -mənt; 2 tụr′na-ment, _n._ In medieval times, a contest of skill between parties of mounted knights; any series of contested games. **tour′ney**‡.

tour′ni-quet, 1 tūr′nĭ-ket; 2 tụr′nĭ-kĕt, _n._ A bandage, etc., for štopping the flow of blood through an artery by compression.

tow, 1 tō; 2 tō, _vt._ To drag, as a boat, through the water by a rope.

tow[1], _n._ A short coarse hemp or flax fiber.

tow[2], _n._ **1.** That which is towed, as a vessel. **2.** The act of towing.— **tow′age**, _n._ The service of or charge for towing.— **tow′boat″**, _n._ A boat for towing.— **tow′path″**, _n._ A path along the river or canal, used in towing boats.— **tow′rope″**, _n._ A rope used for towing. **tow′-line″**‡.

to′ward, 1 tō′ərd; 2 tō′ard, _a._ **1.** Ready to do or learn; apt. **2.** Approaching attainment.

to′ward, } 1 tō′ərd, -ərdz; 2 tō′ard, -ardş
to′wards, } _prep._ **1.** In a course or line leading to; also, facing. **2.** With respect to. **3.** Aiming at or contributing to; for. **4.** Near in time; about.

tow′el, 1 tau′el; 2 tow′ĕl, _n._ A cloth, usually of linen, for wiping or drying.

tow′er, 1 tau′ər; 2 tow′er. **I.** _vi._ To rise like a tower. **II.** _n._ A lofty structure; a citadel; fortress.— **tow′er-ing**, _pa._ **1.** Like a tower; lofty. **2.** Violent; intense; furious.

town, 1 taun; 2 town, _n._ **1.** A collection of houses larger than a village; also, the people of such place, collectively. **2.** [U. S.] A township.— **town′ship**, _n._ **1.** [U. S.] A subdivision of a country. **2.** [Eng.] The district belonging to a town. — **towns′man**, _n._ [**TOWNS′MEN**, _pl._] A resident of a town; also, a fellow citizen.

tox′ic, 1 teks′ik; 2 tŏks′ie, _a._ Poisonous.

tox″i-col′o-gy, 1 teks″i-kel′o-ji; 2 tŏks″i-cŏl′o-gy, _n._ The branch of medical science that treats of poisons.

toy, 1 tei; 2 tŏy. **I.** _vi._ To dally; trifle; play. **II.** _a._ Resembling a toy; of miniature size. **III.** _n._ A plaything; trifle.

trace[1], 1 trēs; 2 trāc. **I.** _vt._ [**TRACED**[t], **TRAC′ING**.] **1.** To follow (a line), as with a pencil; sketch; map out. **2.** To copy, as a drawing or writing, on a superposed transparent sheet. **3.** To track. **II.** _n._ **1.** A vestige or mark; track; trail. **2.** A

barely detectable quantity.— **trace′a-bl(e**[P], _a._ Capable of being traced.— **trac′er-y**, _n._ [-IES[z], _pl._] Any delicate lace-like pattern; scrollwork.— **trac′ing**, _n._ The act of one who traces; that which is traced.

trace[2]. **I.** _vt._ To fasten, as with traces. **II.** _n._ One of two straps or chains of a harness for drawing a load.

tra′che-a, 1 trē′kı-ə _or_ trə-kī′ə; 2 trā′ee-a _or_ tra-eē′a, _n._ [-CHE-Æ, 1 -kı-ī; 2 -ke-ē, _pl._] The windpipe.— **tra″che-ot′o-my**, 1 trē″kı-et′o-mı; 2 trā″ee-ŏt′o-my, _n._ The operation of opening the windpipe, as when choked by a foreign body or by disease.

track[t], 1 trak; 2 trăk, _vt._ **1.** To follow the tracks of; trail. **2.** To make tracks upon; traverse.— **track**[t], _vt._ To tow.

track, _n._ **1.** A mark made by anything that has gone by; trail; series of footprints. **2.** A beaten path; road; racecourse. **3.** A railway.— **track′less**, _a._ Untrodden; pathless. [area.

tract[1], 1 trakt; 2 trăct, _n._ An extended

tract[2], _n._ A short treatise; pamphlet.

tract′a-ble, } 1 trakt′ə-bl; 2 trăct′a-bl, _a._
tract′a-bl[P], } Easily led or controlled; manageable; docile.— **tract″a-bil′l-ty**, _n._

trac′tile[t], 1 trak′tıl; 2 trăe′tıl, _a._ Capable of being drawn out.— **trac-til′i-ty**†, _n._

trac′tion, 1 trak′shən; 2 trăe′shon, _n._ The act of drawing or pulling.

trac′tor, 1 trak′tər; _or_ -ter; 2 trae′tor, _n._ One who or that which draws something, as a motor-vehicle, air-plane, etc.

trade, 1 trēd; 2 trād, _v._ [**TRAD′ED**[d]; **TRAD′-ING.**] **I.** _t._ To dispose of by bargain and sale; barter. **II.** _i._ To engage in trade.

trade[1], _n._ A business; bargain; deal; traffic.— **trad′er**, _n._— **trades′man**, _n._ **1.** A shopkeeper. **2.** A mechanic.

trade[2], _n._ A trade-wind.— **trade′-wind″**, _n._ A wind blowing steadily near the equator, from the northeast on the northern, from the southeast on the southern side of the line.

tra-di′tion, 1 tra-dĭsh′ən; 2 tra-dĭsh′on, _n._ Knowledge transmitted without writing, from generation to generation.— **tra-dĭ′tion-al**, _a._ **tra-dĭ′tion-a-ry**†.

tra-duce′, 1 tra-dūs′; 2 tra-dūç′, _vt._ [**TRA-DUCED**[t]; **TRA-DUC′ING.**] To misrepresent wilfully; defame; slander.— **tra-duc′er**, _n._

traf′fic, 1 traf′ik; 2 trăf′ie. **I.** _vt._ & _vi._ [**TRAF′FICKED**[t]; **TRAF′FICT**[S]; **TRAF′FICK-ING.**] To barter; conduct business; buy and sell. **II.** _n._ The exchange of goods, wares, etc.; transportation, as by rail.

trag′e-dy, 1 traj′ı-di; 2 trăg′e-dy, _n._ [-DIES[z], _pl._] **1.** The form of drama in which the theme is solemn, lofty, or pathetic. **2.** A fatal event; dramatic incident.

— **tra-ge′di-an**, 1 trə-jī′dɪ-ən; 2 tra-gē′di-an, *n.* **1.** An actor in tragedy. **2.** An author of tragedies.— **tra′gē′dienne**, 1 trä″żē′dyen′ *or* trə-jī′dɪ-en′; 2 trä″zhe″dyēn′ *or* tra-gē′di-ēn′, *n. fem.*— **trag′ic**, 1 traj′ɪk; 2 trăg′ic, *a.* Pertaining to tragedy; fatal; calamitous. **trag′i-cal‡.**

trail, 1 trēl; 2 trāl, *vt. & vi.* To draw along lightly; drag or draw after; follow the trail of; trace; creep, as a plant.

trail, *n.* **1.** The track left by anything drawn over a surface; a track; beaten p ṳth. **2.** Anything trailed; a train, as of a gown.

train, 1 trēn; 2 trān, *v.* **I.** *t.* **1.** To develop by instruction and practise; educate; discip.ine. **2.** To direct; point; aim. **3.** To draw along; trail. **II.** *i.* To give or take a course of exercise and instruction.

train, 1 trēn; 2 trān, *n.* **1.** Anything drawn out to a length; a series of things drawn along, as a line of railway carriages; a line, as of combustibles, to conduct fire to a charge; the trailing part of a gown; a comet's tail. **2.** A retinue; suite.

train′-oil′, 1 trēn′-oil′; 2 trān′-öil′, *n.* Oil tried out from the blubber of whales.

trait, 1 trēt; 2 trāt, *n.* A distinguishing feature or quality of mind or character.

trai′tor, 1 trē′tər *or* -ter; 2 trā′tor, *n.* One who betrays a trust; one who commits treason.— **trai′tor-ous,** *a.* Treasonable. **-ly,** *adv.* **-ness,** *n.*— **trai′tress**, *n. fem.*

tram′mel, 1 tram′el; 2 trăm′ěl. **I.** *vt.* [-MELED *or* -MELLED, -MELDˢ; -MEL-ING *or* -MEL-LING.] To hamper; entangle; impede. **II.** *n.* An impediment; fetter.

tramp, 1 tramp; 2 trămp. **I**ᵗ. *vt. & vi.* **1.** To walk with heavy steps. **2.** To travel on foot; walk or wander aimlessly. **II.** *n.* **1.** A heavy, continued tread. **2.** A long stroll on foot. **3.** [U. S] A vagrant.— **tram′ple**(eᵖ, 1 tram′pl; 2 trăm′pl, *v.* [TRAM′-PL(E)Dᵖ; TRAM′PLING.] **I.** *t.* To tread under foot. **II.** *i.* To step heavily.

tran-, trans-, *prefix.* Across; beyond; through; as, *trans*atlantic.

trance, } 1 trans, 2 tráng, *n.* **1.** A state **transe**ᵖ, } in which the soul seems to have passed out of the body; ecstasy; rapture. **2.** A state of insensibility; catalepsy.

tran′quil, 1 traŋ′kwil; 2 trăŋ′kwil, *a.* **1.** Free from agitation or disturbance; calm. **2.** Quiet and motionless **-ly,** *adv.* **-ness,** *n.*— **tran′quil-ize,** *vt.* [-IZED, -IZ′ING.] To make tranquil; soothe. **tran′quil-ise‡.**— **tran-quil′li-ty,** *n.*

trans-act′d, 1 trans-akt′; 2 trăns-ăct′, *vt.* To carry through, as business; accomplish; do.— **trans-ac′tion,** 1 trans-ak′shən;

2 trăns-ăc′shon, *n.* A doing; something done; an affair.

trans-al′pine, 1 trans-al′pɪn *or* -paɪn; 2 trăns-ăl′pɪn *or* -pīn, *a.* **1.** Situated on the other side of the Alps, especially as viewed from Rome. **2.** Crossing or extending across the Alps.

trans″at-lan′tic, 1 trans″at-lan′tɪk; 2 trăns″ăt-lăn′tie, *a.* **1.** Situated on the other side of the Atlantic. **2.** Crossing the Atlantic.

tran-scend′d, 1 tran-send′; 2 trăn-sĕnd′, *vt.* To rise above; surpass.— **tran-scen′dence,** *n.* Surpassing eminence. **tran-scen′den-cy‡.**— **tran-scen′dent,** *a.* Exalted; spiritual. **-ly,** *adv.* **-ness,** *n.*— **tran″scen-den′tal,** *a.* **1.** Of very high degree. **2.** Transcending experience; intuitional.— **tran″scen-den′tal-ism,** *n.*

tran-scribe′, 1 tran-skraɪb′; 2 trăn-scrīb′, *vt.* To write over again; copy or recopy. — **tran-scrib′er,** *n.*— **tran′script,** *n.* A copy.— **tran-scrip′tion,** *n.* A copying; transcript.

tran′sept, 1 tran′sept; 2 trăn sĕpt, *n. Arch.* One of the projections at right angles to the nave of a cruciform church.

trans-fer′, 1 trans-fûr′; 2 trăns-fēr′, *vt.* [TRANS-FERRED′, TRANS-FERD′ˢ; TRANS-FER′RING.] To remove, or cause to pass from one person or place to another; convey.— **trans-fer′a-ble**(eᵖ, *a.* That may be transferred.

trans′fer, 1 trans′fər; 2 trăns′fer, *n.* **1.** The act of transferring. **2.** That which is transferred. **3.** A place, method, or means of transfer.

trans-fig′ure, 1 trans-fig′yur; 2 trăns-fīg′yur, *vt.* [-FIG′URED; -FIG′UR-ING.] To change the outward form or appearance of; make glorious; idealize.— **trans-fig″ur-a′tion,** *n.*

trans-fix′t, 1 trans-fiks′; 2 trăns-fīks′, *vt.* To pierce through.

trans-form′, 1 trans-fôrm′; 2 trăns-fôrm′, *vt.* To give a different form to; to alter; convert; change.— **trans″for-ma′tion,** *n.*— **trans-form′er,** *n. Elec.* An apparatus for changing an electric current from high to low pressure, or the reverse.

trans-fuse′, } 1 trans-fiūz′; 2 trăns-fūṣ′, **trans-fuze′ᵖ,** } *vt.* [TRANS-FUSED′; TRANS-

Ground-plan of Winchester Cathedral.
a, nave; *b, b,* transepts; *c,* choir.

FUS'ING.] To pour out or transfer, as a fluid.— **trans-fu'sion,** *n.*

trans-gress't, 1 trans-gres'; 2 trăns-grĕs', *v.* **I.** *t.* To break over; go beyond; violate. **II.** *i.* To break a law; sin. — **trans-gres'sion,** *n.* The act of transgressing; sin.— **trans-gres'sor,** *n.*

tran'sient, 1 tran'shent; 2 trăn'shĕnt, *a.* Lasting but a short time; evanescent; brief; hasty. **-ly,** *adv.* **-ness,** *n.*

tran'sit, 1 tran'sit; 2 trăn'sit, *n.* The act of passing over or through; passage; especially, the passage of one heavenly body over the disk of another, or over the meridian.— **trans-i'tion,** *n.* Passage from one place, condition, or action to another; change.— **trans-i'tion-al,** *a.*— **tran'si-tiv(e**s. **I.** *a.* *Gram.* Having a direct object, as a verb. **II.** *n.* A transitive verb.— **tran'si-to-ry,** *a.* Existing for a short time only; transient.

trans-late', 1 trans-lēt'; 2 trăns-lāt', *vt. & vi.* [TRANS-LAT'ED^d; TRANS-LAT'ING.] **1.** To give the sense of in another language; interpret. **2.** To change; transform.— **trans-la'tion,** *n.* **1.** A translating. **2.** A reproduction in a different language.— **trans-la'tor,** *n.*

trans-lu'cent, 1 trans-liū'sent; 2 trăns-lū'çĕnt, *a.* Allowing the passage of light, but not of a clear image.— **trans-lu'cence,** *n.*— **trans-lu'cen-cy**†.

trans'ma-rine', 1 trans"mə-rīn'; 2 trăns"-ma-rin', *a.* Being beyond the sea; crossing the sea.

trans'mi-grate, 1 trans"mi-grēt; 2 trăns"-mi-grāt, *vt. & vi.* [-GRAT'ED^d; -GRAT'ING.] To migrate, as from one place or condition to another.— **trans'mi-grant,** *a. & n.*— **trans"mi-gra'tion,** *n.* The act of transmigrating; the passing of the soul from one body, after death, to another.

trans-mit', 1 trans-mit'; 2 trăns-mĭt', *vt.* [TRANS-MIT'TED^d; TRANS-MIT'TING.] To send through or across; transfer; conduct. — **trans-mis'si-bl(e**^p, *a.*— **trans-mis'sion,** *n.*— **trans-mit'ter,** *n.* *Elec.* In telephone and telegraph systems, etc., a device for sending a message: opposed to *receiver.*

trans-mute', 1 trans-miūt'; 2 trăns-mūt', *vt.* [-MUT'ED^d; -MUT'ING.] To change in nature, substance, or form; transform. — **trans-mut'a-bl(e**^p, *a.*— **trans"mu-ta'tion,** *n.* The act of transmuting; a changed state.

tran'som, 1 tran'səm; 2 trăn'som, *n.* A small window above a door.

trans-par'ent, 1 trans-pâr'ent; 2 trăns-pâr'ĕnt, *a.* That can be seen through, as clear glass; easy to understand.— **trans-par'en-cy,** *n.* [-CIES^z, *pl.*] The property of being transparent; a transparent picture or other device.

tran-spire', 1 tran-spair'; 2 trăn-spīr', *vi.* [-SPIRED'; -SPIR'ING.] **1.** To be emitted; exhale. **2.** To become known, as a fact or event.

trans-plant'^d, 1 trans-plant'; 2 trăns-plănt', *vt.* To remove and plant in another place.— **trans"plan-ta'tion,** *n.*

trans-port', 1 trans-pōrt'; 2 trăns-pôrt'. **I**^d. *vt.* **1.** To carry from one place to another; banish. **2.** To fill with enthusiasm, delight, or ecstasy. **II.** *n.* **1.** The act of transporting, or the state of being transported. **2.** A vessel, railway cars, etc., for transporting troops, military supplies, etc. **3.** Emotional excitement; ecstasy; delight.— **trans"por-ta'tion,** *n.*

trans-pose', 1 trans-pōz'; 2 trăns-pōz', *vt.* [TRANS-POSED'; TRANS-POS'ING.] To reverse the order or change the place of; interchange.— **trans"po-si'tion,** *n.*

tran"sub-stan"ti-a'tion, 1 tran"sub-stan"shi-ē'shən; 2 trăn"sŭb-stăn"shi-ā'-shon, *n.* The doctrine that the substance of the bread and wine of the eucharist is changed into the body and blood of Christ; also, such mystical change.

trans-verse', 1 trans-vūrs'; 2 trăns-vẽrs'. **I.** *a.* Lying or being across; athwart. **-ly,** *adv.* **II.** *n.* That which is transverse.

trap^1, 1 trap; 2 trăp, *v.* [TRAPPED^t, TRAPT^s; TRAP'PING.] **I.** *t.* **1.** To catch in a trap; ensnare. **2.** To supply with a trap. **II.** *i.* To set traps for game; operate a trap. — **trap'per,** *n.*

trap^2, *vt.* To adorn with trappings.

trap^1, 1 trap; 2 trăp, *n.* **1.** A snare; stratagem. **2.** A valve-like contrivance in a pipe, etc., for stopping return flow, as of noxious gas. **3.** A trap-door.— **trap'=door,** *n.* A door in a floor or roof.

trap^2, 1 trap; 2 trăp, *n.* A dark rock of columnar structure.

tra-peze', 1 trə-pīz'; 2 tra-pēz', *n.* A short bar, suspended by ropes, for gymnastic exercises.

tra-pe'zi-um, 1 trə-pī'zi-um; 2 tra-pē'-zi-ŭm, *n.* [-ZI-A, *pl.*] A quadrilateral of which two sides are parallel.— **trap'e-zoid,** 1 trap'i-zeid; 2 trăp'e-zŏid, *n.* A four-sided plane figure of which no two sides are parallel.

trap'ping, 1 trap'iŋ; 2 trăp'ing, *n.* An ornamental housing or harness for a horse: in the plural, adornments of any kind.

trash, 1 trash; 2 trăsh, *n.* Worthless matter; rubbish.— **trash'y,** *a.* Worthless.

trav′ail, 1 trav′il; 2 trăv′il, *n.* Labor in childbirth; anguish or distress.

trav′el, 1 trav′el; 2 trăv′ĕl, *v.* [TRAV′ELED or -ELLED, -ELD⁸; TRAV′EL-ING or -EL-LING.] **I.** *t.* To pass or journey over. **II.** *i.* To journey; visit foreign lands; move in space.

trav′el, *n.* **1.** The act of traveling; movement. **2.** *pl.* A narration of traveling experiences.— **trav′el-er,** *n.* **trav′el-ler‡.**

trav′erse, 1 trav′ǝrs; 2 trăv′ers, *vt. & vi.* [TRAV′ERSED‡, TRAV′ERST⁸; TRAV′ERS-ING.] **1.** To move across; pass through or over. **2.** To examine carefully. **3.** To deny; oppose; thwart.— **trav′ers-er,** *n.*

trav′erse, *n.* **1.** Anything that traverses; a crosspiece; screen; barrier. **2.** The act of traversing; a journey; passage; denial.

trav′es-ty, 1 trav′es-tɪ; 2 trăv′ĕs-ty. **I.** *vt.* [-TIED, -TY-ING.] To burlesque. **II.** *n.* [-TIES², *pl.*] A grotesque imitation; burlesque.

trawl, 1 trôl; 2 tral, *v.* **I.** *t.* To drag, as a net; troll. **II.** *i.* To fish by dragging a net or a hooked line behind a boat.

tray, 1 trē; 2 trā, *n.* A flat shallow utensil with raised edges.

treach′er-y, ¦ 1 trech′ǝr-ɪ; 2 trĕch′er-y, *n.*
trech′er-y⁸, ∫ Violation of allegiance or faith; perfidy; treason.— **tre(a)ch′er-ous⁸,** *a.* Traitorous; false.

trea′cle, ¦ 1 trī′kl; 2 trē′el, *n.* The sirup
trea′cl⁸, ∫ obtained in refining sugar; loosely, molasses.

tread, ¦ 1 tred; 2 trĕd. **I.** *vt. & vi.* [TROD;
tred⁸, ∫ TROD′DEN, TROD′N³; TREAD′ING.] To step or walk on; walk. **II.** *n.* **1.** A walking or stepping. **2.** That on which something treads or rests in moving, as the level part of a stair, etc.— **tre(a)d′le⁸,** *n.* A lever operated by the foot.— **tread′mill″,** *n.* A wheel turned by a stepping motion; dreary toil.

trea′son, 1 trī′zn; 2 trē′şn, *n.* Betrayal of, or breach of allegiance toward government; treachery.— **trea′son-a-bl(e⁸,** *a.*

trea′sure, ¦ 1 trezh′ur; 2 trĕzh′ur. **I.** *vt.*
tre′sure⁸, ∫ [TREA′SURED; TREA′SUR-ING.] To lay up in store; accumulate; cherish; prize. **II.** *n.* **1.** The precious metals; money; jewels. **2.** Riches; wealth. **3.** Something very precious.— **tre(a)′sur-er⁸,** *n.* One who has the care of a treasury or funds.— **trea′sure ≈ trove″,** *n.* Money, plate, jewels, or the like, found buried or otherwise hidden, the owner being unknown.— **tre(a)′sur-y⁸,** *n.* [-IES², *pl.*] The place for the keeping of treasure; department having charge of public revenues.

treat⁴, 1 trīt; 2 trēt, *v.* **I.** *t.* To act

toward; deal with; express; present. **2.** To apply a special process to. **3.** [Colloq.] To pay the expense of entertainment, or drink, for. **II.** *i.* **1.** To handle a subject in writing or speaking: followed by *of.* **2.** To negotiate: followed by *with.*

treat, *n.* Some unusual pleasure; entertainment furnished gratuitously.— **treat′ment,** *n.* The act or mode of treating.

trea′tise, ¦ 1 trī′tis; 2 trē′tis, *n.* An elabo-
trea′tis⁸, ∫ rate literary composition on a special subject.

trea′ty, 1 trī′tɪ; 2 trē′ty, *n.* [TREA′TIES²,
pl.] A formal agreement or compact.

treb′le, ¦ 1 treb′l; 2 trĕb′l. **I.** *vt. & vi.*
treb′l⁸, ∫ [TREB′L(E)D³; TREB′LING.] To multiply by three; triple. **II.** *a.* **1.** Threefold; triple. **2.** *Mus.* Soprano. **III.** *n. Mus.* The soprano.— **treb′ly,** *adv.* Three times; triply; exceedingly.

tree, 1 trī; 2 trē. **I.** *vt.* [TREED; TREE′ING.] To force to climb a tree. **II.** *n.* **1.** A perennial woody plant at least 20 feet in height at maturity. **2.** A timber.

tre′foil, 1 trī′foil; 2 trē′fôil, *n.* **1.** A clover. **2.** *Arch.* A three-lobed ornament.

trel′lis, 1 trel′is; 2 trĕl′is, *n.* A grating or lattice as for a climbing plant.

Trefoil.

trem′ble, ¦ 1 trem′bl; 2 trĕm′-
trem′bl⁸, ∫ bl. **I.** *vi.* [TREM′-BL(E)D³; TREM′BLING.] To shake involuntarily; be agitated; quiver; oscillate. **II.** *n.* The act or state of trembling.

tre-men′dous, 1 trɪ-men′dus; 2 tre-mĕn′-dŭs, *a.* Astonishing; terrible; awe-inspiring. **-ly,** *adv.* **-ness,** *n.*

trem′o-lo, 1 trem′o-lō; 2 trĕm′o-lō, *n. Mus.* A vibrating sound produced by the voice or instrumentally.

trem′or, 1 trem′ǝr; 2 trĕm′or, *n.* A quick vibratory movement; a trembling.

trem′u-lous, 1 trem′yu-lus; 2 trĕm′yu-lŭs, *a.* Quivering; trembling; timid.

trench, 1 trench; 2 trĕnch. **I.** *vt. & vi.* To dig a trench in or about; encroach; cut trenches. **II.** *n.* A long narrow excavation in the ground; ditch.

trench′ant, 1 trench′ǝnt; 2 trĕnch′ant, *a.* Sharp; cutting, as sarcasm.

trench′er, 1 trench′ẽr; 2 trĕnch′er, *n.* A wooden plate for use at table.

trend, 1 trend; 2 trĕnd. **I**ᵈ**.** *vi.* To have or take a general direction; incline; lean. **II.** *n.* General course or direction; tendency.

tre-pan′, 1 trɪ-pan′; 2 tre-păn′, *a.* An early form of the trephine.— **tre-pan′,** *vt.*

1: ǝ = *final*; ɪ = *habit*; aisle; au = *out*; oil; iū = *feud*; chin; go; ŋ = *sing*; thin, this.
2: wolf, dǫ; bŏŏk, bōŏt; full, rule, cūre, bŭt, bûrn; ôil, bŏy; ḡo, gem; iŋk; thin, this.

tre-phine′, 1 trĭ-fain′ *or* trĭ-fīn′; 2 tre-fīn′ *or* tre-fĭn′. **I.** *vt.* [TRE-PHINED′; TRE-PHIN′ING.] To operate on with a tre-phine. **II.** *n.* A cylindrical saw for removing a disk of bone from the skull.

trep′′i-da′tion, 1 trep′′ĭ-dē′shən; 2 trĕp′′ĭ-dā′shon, *n.* Agitation from fear; trembling.

tres′pass, 1 tres′pəs; 2 trĕs′pas. **I**[t]. *vi.* To pass the bounds of propriety or rectitude; err; sin. **II.** *n.* **1.** Any transgression of law or rule of duty; offense; sin. **2.** Any invasion of another's rights, as wrongful entry on another's land.— **tres′pass-er,** *n.*

tress, 1 tres; 2 trĕs, *n.* A lock of human hair.

tres′tle(r, } 1 tres′l; 2 trĕs′l, *n.* **1.** A beam
tres′sel′, } supported by four divergent legs. **2.** An open braced framework for supporting a bridge, or the like.

tri-, *prefix.* Three; three times; thrice: as, *tri*lateral. [three persons or things.

tri′ad, 1 trai′ad; 2 trī′ăd, *n.* A group of three.

tri′al, 1 trai′əl; 2 trī′al, *n.* **1.** The act of trying, or the state of being tried; judicial examination. **2.** Affliction; hardship.

tri′an′gle, 1 trai′aŋ′gl; 2 trī′ăŋ′ḡl, *n.* A figure bounded by three sides, and having three angles.— **tri-an′gu-lar,** *a.* Pertaining to, like, or bounded by a triangle.

Triangles.
1. Equilateral. 2. Isosceles.
3. Scalene.

tribe, 1 traib; 2 trīb, *n.* A division or class of people; group of plants or animals. — **tri′bal,** *a.*

trib′′u-la′tion, 1 trib′′yu-lē′shən; 2 trĭb′′-yu-lā′shon, *n.* Affliction; distress; suffering.

tri-bu′nal, 1 trɪ-biū′nəl; 2 tri-bū′nal, *n.* A court of justice; any judicial body.

trib′une[1], 1 trib′yūn; 2 trĭb′yun, *n.* **1.** *Rom. Antiq.* A magistrate chosen by the plebeians to protect them against the patricians. **2.** A public officer of later times.

trib′une[2], *n.* A raised floor for officials or orators; a rostrum; platform.

trib′ute, 1 trib′yut; 2 trĭb′yut, *n.* **1.** Money paid, as to a conqueror; subjection. **2.** A contribution; tax; homage. — **trib′u-ta-ry,** **I.** *a.* **1.** Bringing supply; contributory. **2.** Offered as tribute. **3.** Subordinate; dependent. **II.** *n.* [-RIES[2], *pl.*] **1.** A dependent. **2.** A stream that flows into another.

trice, 1 trais; 2 trĭc, *vt.* [TRICED[t]; TRIC′-ING.] To raise with a rope; tie or lash.

trice, *n.* A very short time; instant: only in the phrase **in a trice.**

tri-chi′na, 1 trɪ-kai′nə; 2 trĭ-cī′na, *n.* [-NÆ, 1 -nī; 2 -nē, *pl.*] A small parasitic worm that sometimes infests the muscles of swine and other mammals, and thence of man.— **trich′′i-no′sis,** *n.* The disease produced by trichinæ.

trick, 1 trik; 2 trĭk. **I**[t]. *vt. & vi.* To play a trick or tricks upon. **II.** *n.* **1.** A petty artifice or stratagem; fraud; cheat. **2.** An annoying act; practical joke. **3.** A characteristic; trait; knack. **4.** In card-playing, the whole number of cards played in one round.— **trick′ster,** 1 trik′-star; 2 trĭk′ster, *n.* One who plays tricks; a cheat.

trick[2t], *vt.* To deck or ornament.

trick′er-y[1], 1 trik′ər-ɪ; 2 trĭk′er-y, *n.* Craft; deception.

trick′er-y[2], *n.* Dressing up; decorations.

trick′l(er, 1 trik′l; 2 trĭk′l, *vt. & vi.* [TRICK′L(E)D[2]; TRICK′LING.] To flow by drops; drip.

trick′y, 1 trik′ɪ; 2 trĭk′y, *a.* **1.** Disposed to tricks; deceitful. **2.** Vicious, as an animal.

tri-col′or, 1 trai′kul′ər; 2 trī′eŏl′or. **I.** *a.* Of three colors. **tri-col′′ored**‡. **II.** *n.* A flag of three colors, as the French.

tri′cy-cle, 1 trai′sɪ-kl; 2 trī′cy-el, *n.* A three-wheeled vehicle of the velocipede class.

tri′dent, 1 trai′dent; 2 trī′dĕnt, *n.* A three-pronged implement; the emblem of Neptune.

tri-en′ni-al, 1 trai-en′ɪ-əl; 2 trī-ĕn′i-al. **I.** *a.* Occurring every third year; also, lasting three years. **II.** *n.* A ceremony observed every three years. **-ly,** *adv.*

tri′fle, 1 trai′fl; 2 trī′fl. **I.** *vi.* [TRI′FLED; TRI′FLING.] To sport; dally. **II.** *n.* Anything of very little value.— **tri′fler,** *n.*— **tri′fling,** *pa.* **1.** Frivolous. **2.** Insignificant.

tri-fo′li-ate, 1 trai-fō′lɪ-ēt; 2 trī-fō′li-āt, *a.* Having three leaves. **tri-fo′li-at′′ed**‡.

trig′ger, 1 trig′ər; 2 trĭg′er, *n.* The fingerpiece of the lock, for discharging a firearm.

trig′′o-nom′e-try, 1 trig′′o-nəm′ɪ-trɪ; 2 trĭg′′o-nŏm′e-try, *n.* The branch of mathematics that treats of the relations of the sides and angles of triangles.— **trig′′o-no-met′ri-cal,** *a.* **ric**‡.

tri-lat′er-al, 1 trai-lat′ər-əl; 2 trī-lăt′er-al, *a.* Having three sides.

tri-lit′er-al, 1 trai-lit′ər-əl; 2 trī-lĭt′er-al, *a.* Consisting of three letters.

trill[1r], 1 tril; 2 trĭl. **I.** *vt. & vi.* To sing

or sound tremulously. **II.** *n.* A tremulous utterance; shake; quaver.

tril′lion, 1 tril′yən; 2 trĭl′yon, *n.* A cardinal number: in the French (also U. S.) system of numeration, a million millions; in the English system, the third power of a million.

trim, 1 trim; 2 trĭm, *v.* [TRIMMED, TRIMD^s; TRIM′MING.] **I.** *t.* To put in shape; prune; clip; decorate; balance, as a vessel. **II.** *i.* **1.** To change sides for gain or safety. **2.** To be or keep in equilibrium: said of a vessel.— **trim′mer,** *n.* One who trims; a time-server.— **trim′ming,** *n.* **1.** Something added for ornament. **2.** The act of a trimmer.

trim, *a.* [TRIM′MER; TRIM′MEST.] Adjusted to a nicety; spruce. **-ly,** *adv.* **-ness,** *n.*

trim, 1 trim; 2 trĭm, *n.* State of adjustment; equipment; condition. **2.** Costume; dress.

trin′i-ty, 1 trin′i-tɪ; 2 trĭn′i-ty, *n.* [-TIES², *pl.*] **1.** [T-] *Theol.* The threefold personality of God: the Father, Son, and Holy Spirit. **2.** Any union of three in one.— **Trin′i-ta′ri-an. I.** *a.* Pertaining to the Trinity. **II.** *n.* A believer in the doctrine of the Trinity.

trin′ket, 1 triŋ′ket; 2 trĭŋ′kĕt, *n.* A small [ornament.

tri-no′mi-al, 1 trai-nō′mi-əl; 2 trī-nō′mi-al. **I.** *a.* Having three terms. **II.** *n.* An algebraic expression consisting of three terms.

tri′o, 1 trī′o *or* traɪ′o; 2 trī′o *or* trī′o, *n.* **1.** Any three things associated together. **2.** *Mus.* A composition for three performers.

trip, 1 trip; 2 trĭp, *v.* [TRIPPED^t, TRIPT^s; TRIP′PING.] **I.** *t.* **1.** To cause (one) to lose balance, stumble, or fall. **2.** To perform (a dance) lightly or nimbly. **3.** *Mech.* To free; release, as a catch. **II.** *i.* **1.** To move with light and nimble steps. **2.** To stumble; err.— **trip′-ham′-mer,** *n.* A tilt-hammer.

trip, *n.* **1.** A short journey; excursion. **2.** A stumble; blunder. **3.** A nimble step.

tri-par′tite, 1 trai-pär′tait *or* trip′ar-tait; 2 trī-pär′tĭt *or* trĭp′ar-tīt, *a.* Divided into three parts or divisions; threefold.

tripe, 1 traip; 2 trĭp, *n.* A portion of the stomach of the ox, as used for food.

triph′thong, 1 trif′thôŋ; 2 trĭf′thông, *n.* Three vowels combined to produce one sound.

tri′plane, 1 traɪ′plēn; 2 trī′plān, *n.* In aviation an aeroplane consisting of three planes.

trip′l(eᵖ, 1 trip′l; 2 trĭp′l. **I.** *vt.* [TRIP′-L(E)D^p; TRIP′LING.] To make threefold; treble. **II.** *a.* Threefold.— **trip′ly,** *adv.*

trip′let, 1 trip′let; 2 trĭp′lĕt, *n.* A group of three of a kind, as of three children at one birth.

trip′li-cate, 1 trip′lɪ-kēt; 2 trĭp′li-eāt. **I.** *vt.* [-CAT″ED^d; -CAT″ING.] To treble. **II.** *a.* Threefold; triple. **III.** *n.* A third of a kind.— **trip″li-ca′tion,** *n.*

tri′pod, 1 traɪ′pɒd; 2 trī′pŏd, *n.* A three-legged stand.

tri-sect′^d, 1 traɪ-sekt′; 2 trī-sĕct′, *vt.* To divide into three parts.— **tri-sec′tion,** *n.*

tri-syl′la-bl(eᵖ, 1 traɪ-sil′ə-bl; 2 trī-sĭl′a-bl, *n.* A word of three syllables.— **tri″syl-lab′-ic,** *a.*

trite, 1 trait; 2 trīt, *a.* Used so often as to be hackneyed; made commonplace by repetition.— **trit′u-rate,** *vt.* [-RAT″ED^d; -RAT′-ING.] To reduce to a fine powder or pulp; pulverize.— **trit″u-ra′tion,** *n.*

tri′umph, } 1 traɪ′umf; 2 trī′ŭmf. **I.**^t *vi.*
tri′umfᵖ, } To obtain or celebrate a victory; exult. **II.** *n.* **1.** Exultation over or celebration of victory. **2.** The condition of being victorious.— **tri-um′phal,** *a.*— **tri-um′phant,** *a.* Exultant; victorious.

tri′une, 1 traɪ′yūn; 2 trī′yun, *a.* Three in one: said of the Godhead.

triv′et, 1 triv′et; 2 trĭv′ĕt, *n.* A three-legged stand, as for kettles or hot irons.

triv′i-al, 1 triv′i-əl; 2 trĭv′i-al, *a.* **1.** Trifling; insignificant. **2.** Commonplace; ordinary; paltry.— **triv″i-al′i-ty,** *n.* **triv′i-al-ness**.

tri-week′ly, 1 trai-wĭk′lɪ; 2 trī-wēk′ly, *a.* **1.** Performed, occurring, or appearing three times a week. **2.** Done or occurring every third week.

tro′che, 1 trō′kɪ; 2 trō′ee, *n.* A medicated lozenge.

tro′chee, 1 trō′kɪ; 2 trō′eē, *n.* *Pros.* A foot comprising a long and a short syllable (— ◡).— **tro-cha′ic,** *a.*

trod, trod′den, *imp. & pp.* of TREAD, *v.*

trog′lo-dyte, 1 treg′lo-dait; 2 trŏg′lo-dȳt, *n.* **1.** A prehistoric cave-dweller or cave-man. **2.** An anthropoid ape, as the gorilla.

troll, 1 trōl; 2 trōl, *vt. & vi.* **1.** To sing or roll out in a free, hearty manner. **2.** To fish by dragging a line near the surface.

troll¹, *n.* **1.** *Mus.* A catch or round. **2.** *Fishing.* A reel; lure used in trolling.

troll², *n.* A giant; a mischievous dwarf.

trol′ley, 1 trol′ɪ; 2 trŏl′y, *n.* **1.** A grooved metal wheel for rolling in contact with an electric conductor (the *trolley-wire*), to convey the current to a motor-car. **2.** A car or system so operated. **3.** A small truck or car.

trom′bone, 1 trem′bōn; 2 trŏm′bōn, *n.* A

powerful brass instrument of the trumpet family, commonly with a U=shaped slide.

troop, 1 trūp; 2 trŏŏp. **I**t. *vi.* To move along together; congregate; depart hastily. **II.** *n.* A body of soldiers; company of cavalry; in the plural, an army. — **troop′er,** *n.* **1.** A cavalryman. **2.** A troop=horse; charger.

trope, 1 trōp; 2 trŏp, *n.* A figure of speech.

tro′phy, 1 trō′fɪ; 2 trō′fy, *n.* [TRO′PHIES², *pl.*] Any memento of victory or success. — **tro′phied,** 1 trō′fɪd; 2 trō′fĭd, *a.* Adorned with trophies.

trop′ic, 1 trŏp′ɪk; 2 trŏp′ĭc. **I.** *a.* Tropical. **II.** *n.* **1.** Either of two parallels of latitude (23° 27′), north and south of the equator, that form the limits of the torrid zone. **2.** *pl.* The regions of the earth between the tropics.

trop′i-cal, 1 trŏp′ɪ-kəl; 2 trŏp′ĭ-cal, *a.* Pertaining to the tropics; torrid; sultry. **2.** Of the nature of a trope or metaphor.

trot, 1 trɒt; 2 trŏt. **I.** *vt. & vi.* [TROT′TED²; TROT′TING.] To ride, drive, or go at a trot; go with a steady, jogging pace. **II.** *n.* A progressive motion of a quadruped, in which each diagonal pair of legs is alternately lifted. — **trot′ter,** *n.* A trotting-horse.

troth, 1 trɒθ or trŏθ; 2 trŏth or trōth, *n.* Good faith; fidelity; betrothal.

trou′ba-dour, 1 trū′ba-dūr; 2 trụ′ba-dụr, *n.* A lyric poet of the middle ages.

trou′ble, | 1 trŭb′l; 2 trŭb′l, *v.* [TROUB′-
trub′le², | LED, TRUB′LD²; TROUB′LING.]
I. *t.* **1.** To give trouble to; vex. **2.** To stir up, as water. **3.** To inconvenience; incommode. **4.** To spoil; mar. **II.** *i.* To take pains; worry. — **trouble-some,** *a.* Causing trouble; vexatious. — **trou′blous,** *a.* Full of commotion, tumult, or trouble.

trou′ble, 1 trŭb′l; 2 trŭb′l, *n.* **1.** The state of being troubled; grief; disturbance. **2.** Something that occasions difficulty, perplexity, or distress. **3.** Exertion; labor; pains.

trough, | 1 trɒf; 2 trŏf, *n.* A long or narrow
trof², | open receptacle, as a log hollowed out on one side, for holding food and water for animals, or for conveying a fluid.

troupe, 1 trūp; 2 trụp, *n.* A troop, as of actors.

trou′sers, 1 trau′zərz; 2 trou′sẹrs, *n. pl.* An outer garment for a man or boy, extending from the waist to the ankles or knees, and divided so as to cover each leg separately; pantaloons.

trous″seau′, 1 trū″sō′; 2 trụ″sō′, *n.* A bride's outfit. [food=fish.

trout, 1 traut; 2 trout, *n.* A fresh=water

American Speckled Trout. ¹/₁₇

trowl, | 1 trō; 2 trō, *vi.*
To suppose; think.

trow′el, 1 trau′el; 2 trow′ĕl, *n.* A flat-bladed implement: used by masons, etc. **2.** A small concave scoop for gardening.

troy, 1 trɔɪ; 2 trŏy, *n.* A system of weights used by goldsmiths and jewelers. See table of weights, under WEIGHT.

tru′ant, 1 trū′ənt; 2 trụ′ant. **I.** *a.* Of or pertaining to a truant; idle; loitering. **II.** *n.* One who absents himself from duty, especially from school without leave. — **tru′an-cy,** *n.*

truce, 1 trūs; 2 trụs, *n.* A temporary suspension of hostilities by agreement; an armistice.

truck¹, 1 trŭk; 2 trŭk. **I**t. *vt. & vi.* To barter; peddle. **II.** *n.* Commodities, as garden produce, for sale.

truck². **I**t. *vt. & vi.* To cart about on a truck; drive a truck. **II.** *n.* **1.** A stout vehicle for moving freight, etc. **2.** A set of wheels or runners bearing a swiveling frame. **3.** A disk; wheel. — **truck′age,** *n.* The conveyance, or the money paid for conveyance, of goods on trucks.

truck′l(e², 1 ¹truk′l; 2 trŭk′l. **I.** *vi.* [TRUCK′L(E)D²; TRUCK′LING.] To curry favor with servility. **II.** *n.* A truck; pulley.

truck′man, *n.* One who drives a truck.

tru′cu-lent, 1 trū′kiu-lent; 2 trụ′eū-lĕnt, *a.* Barbarous; threatening; ferocious. — **tru′cu-lence,** *n.* Ferocity.

trudge, 1 trŭj; 2 trŭdg, *vi.* [TRUDGED²; TRUDG′ING.] To walk laboriously; plod.

true, 1 trū; 2 trụ, *a.* Conformable to fact or reality; genuine; faithful; guileless; right; exact. — **tru′ism,** 1 trū′ɪzm; 2 trụ′ism, *n.* An obvious truth. — **tru′ly,** *adv.*

truf′fle, 1 trŭf′l; 2 trŭf′l, *n.* A fleshy underground fungus resembling the mushroom.

trump¹, 1 trŭmp; 2 trŭmp. **I**t. *vt.* To impose unfairly; obtrude by fraud. **II.** *n.* **1.** [Scot.] A jew's-harp. **2.** [Poetic.] A trumpet. — **trump′er-y.** **I.** *a.* Having a showy appearance, but valueless. **II.** *n.* **1.** Worthless finery. **2.** Rubbish; nonsense.

trump², 1 trŭmp; 2 trŭmp. *Card=playing.* **I**t. *vt. & vi.* To play a trump; take with a trump=card. **II.** *n.* A card of the suit that temporarily ranks above all others.

trum'pet, 1 trum'pet; 2 trŭm'pĕt. **I**[d]. *vt.* & *vi.* To proclaim by trumpet; sound, as a trumpet. **II.** *n.* A wind=instrument with a flaring mouth.— **trum'pet-er,** *n.*

trun'cate, 1 trun'kēt; 2 trŭn'eāt. **I.** *vt.* [-CAT"ED[d]; -CAT"ING.] To cut the top or end from. **II.** *a.* Terminating abruptly; appearing as thus cut squarely off. **trun'cat"ed**‡.— **trun-ca'tion,** *n.*

trun'cheon, 1 trun'chən; 2 trŭn'chon, *n.* A club; staff; baton.

trun'dle, 1 trun'dl; 2 trŭn'dl. **I.** *vt.* & *vi.* [TRUN'DLED; TRUN'DLING.] To roll along, as a hoop; roll on casters. **II.** *n.* **1.** A small broad wheel, as of a caster. **2.** The act of trundling.— **trun'dle-bed",** *n.* A bed with very low frame resting upon casters.

trunk, 1 trunk; 2 trŭnk, *n.* **1.** The main body or stock of a tree; the main body of any structure. **2.** The body, as distinguished from the limbs. **3.** A pack-ing=box with a hinged lid and handles. **4.** A proboscis, as of an elephant.

truss, 1 trus; 2 trŭs. **I**[t]. *vt.* **1.** *Building.* To support by a truss; brace. **2.** To skewer, as a fowl for cook-ing. **II.** *n.* **1.** *Surg.* A support for a rupture. **2.** A frame-work, as for a bridge. A bundle, as of hay.

Bridge=trusses.
1. The Howe truss. 2. The tri-angular truss: *b, b,* braces; *c,* counterbraces; *l,* lower chord; *t,* top chord; *r,* rod.

trust[d], 1 trust; 2 trŭst. *v.* **I.** *t.* **1.** To repose trust in. **2.** To commit to the care of another; entrust; confide. **3.** To sell on credit to. **4.** To believe. **II.** *i.* **1.** To place confidence; rely. **2.** To give credit.

trust, *n.* **1.** Confidence; faith. **2.** A charge or responsibility accepted. **3.** Credit, as for goods. **4.** A combination for the purpose of controlling production, prices, etc.— **trus-tee',** *n.* Any one who holds property in trust.— **trust'ful,** *a.* Disposed to trust.— **trust'wor"thy,** *a.* Worthy of trust; reliable.— **trust'y,** *a.* [TRUST'I-ER; TRUST'I-EST.] Faithful to duty or trust; trustworthy; staunch; firm.

truth, 1 trūth; 2 trŭth, *n.* **1.** The state of being true. **2.** That which is true. **3.** A fact; reality. **4.** Veracity; fidelity; constancy.— **truth'ful,** *a.* Veracious; true.

try, 1 trai; 2 trȳ, *v.* [TRIED; TRY'ING.] **I.** *t.* **1.** To test; experiment with; put on trial. **2.** To undertake; attempt; endeavor. **3.** To strain; distress; afflict. **II.** *i.* To put forth effort; attempt; endeavor. — **try'ing,** *pa.* Testing severely; hard to endure.

tryst, 1 trist *or* traist; 2 trȳst *or* trȳst, *n.* An appointment to meet, or the place for meeting.

tsar, tsar'e-vitch, etc. Same as CZAR, etc.

tub, 1 tub; 2 tŭb, *n.* **1.** A broad open vessel used for washing, etc. **2.** A small cask.

tube, 1 tiūb; 2 tūb. **I.** *vt.* [TUBED; TUB'ING.] To fit or furnish with a tube. **II.** *n.* **1.** A long, hollow cylinder; a pipe. **2.** *Anat.* A tubular organ.— **Crookes tube,** a glass tube for maintaining a high vacuum.— **tub'ing,** *n.* Tubes collectively. — **tu'bu-lar,** *a.* **1.** Tube=shaped. **2.** Made up of or provided with tubes.

tu'ber, 1 tiū'bər; 2 tū'bẽr, *n.* *Bot.* A short, thickened portion of an under-ground stem, as in the potato.— **tu'ber-cle,** *n.* **1.** A small knob, as of bone. **2.** A small tumor, as in the lung.— **tu-ber'cu-lar,** *a.*

tube'rose", 1 tiūb'rōz" *or* tiū'bər-ōs"; 2 tūb'rōs" *or* tū'bẽr-ōs", *n.* A bulbous plant bearing a long raceme of fragrant white flowers.

tuck, 1 tuk; 2 tŭk. **I**[t]. *vt.* **1.** To fold under. **2.** To cover snugly. **3.** To cram; hide. **4.** To make tucks in. **II.** *n.* A fold made in a garment.— **tuck'er,** *n.* **1.** One who or that which tucks. **2.** A covering formerly worn over the neck and shoulders by women.

-tude, *suffix.* State of being; as, grati*tude,* the state of being grateful: a termination of nouns of Latin origin.

Tues'day, 1 tiūz'dɪ; 2 tūȷ'da, *n.* The third day of the week.

tuft, 1 tuft; 2 tŭft. **I**[d]. *vt.* To form into tufts; cover with tufts. **II.** *n.* A bunch of small flexible things, as grass, leaves, or hair, held together at the base.

tug, 1 tug; 2 tŭg. **I.** *vt.* & *vi.* [TUGGED; TUG[d]S; TUG'GING.] To pull with great effort; draw forcibly. **II.** *n.* **1.** The act of tugging. **2.** A struggle; wrestle. **3.** A steam=vessel for towing.

tu-i'tion, 1 tiū-ish'ən; 2 tū-ĭsh'on, *n.* Teaching; instruction or the charge for instruction.

tu'lip, 1 tiū'lɪp; 2 tū'lĭp, *n.* A bulbous plant bearing bell=shaped flowers.— **tu'-lip=tree",** *n.* A large North=American tree allied to the magnolias. See illus. on next page.

tulle, 1 tūl; 2 tul, *n.* A fine silk material, used for veils, etc.

tum'ble(ᵉ², 1 tum'bl; 2 tŭm'bl, *v.* [TUM'-BL(E)Dᵖ; TUM'BLING.] **I.** *t.* To toss carelessly; throw into disorder. **II.** *i.* To roll or toss about; fall in a headlong manner. — **tum'ble**, *n.* **1.** The act of tumbling; a fall. **2.** A state of disorder. — **tum'bler**, *n.* **1.** A drinking-glass without a foot. **2.** One who or that which tumbles; a pigeon that turns somersaults in the air. **3.** In a lock, a latch that engages a bolt.

Flower and Leaf of the Tulip-tree.
a, the fruit: *b*, a carpel of the fruit detached.

tum'brel, 1 tum'brel; 2 tŭm'brĕl, *n.* A rude cart. **tum'bril‡.**

tu'me-fy, 1 tiū'mi-fai; 2 tū'me-fȳ, *vt. & vi.* To swell; puff up; rise as in a tumor. — **tu''me-fac'tion**, *n.*

tu'mid, 1 tiū'mid; 2 tū'mid, *a.* Swollen; protuberant; bombastic. — **tu-mid'i-ty**, *n.*

tu'mor, 1 tiū'mər; 2 tū'mor, *n.* A local swelling on any part of the body. **tu'mour‡.**

tu'mu-lar, 1 tiū'miu-lər; 2 tū'mū-lar, *a.* Having the form of a mound. **tu'mu-lous‡.**

tu'mult, 1 tiū'mʌlt; 2 tū'mŭlt, *n.* Commotion or agitation, as of a multitude; an uproar. — **tu-mul'tu-ous**, *a.* **tu-mul'tu-a-ry‡.**

tun, 1 tun; 2 tŭn. **I.** *vt.* [TUNNED, TUNDˢ; TUN'NING.] To put into a tun. **II.** *n.* **1.** A large cask; fermenting-vat. **2.** A brew. **3.** A varying measure of capacity.

tune, 1 tiūn; 2 tūn. **I.** *vt. & vi.* [TUNED, TUN'ING.] **1.** To put or be in tune; attune. **2.** To celebrate with song. **II.** *n.* **1.** A melody. **2.** Harmony; concord. **3.** Suitable temper or humor. — **tune'ful**, *a.* Musical; melodious. — **tune'less**, *a.* Not being in tune; unmusical; silent. — **tun'er**, *n.* — **tun'ing-fork'**, *n.* A fork-shaped piece of steel having two equal prongs, which vibrate with a definite frequency when struck: used to measure the pitch of musical tones.

tu'nic, 1 tiū'nik; 2 tū'nic, *n.* **1.** An ancient close-fitting garment. **2.** A modern outer garment. [nage.

tun'nage, 1 tun'ij; 2 tŭn'ag, *n.* [Eng.] Ton-

tun'nel, 1 tun'el; 2 tŭn'ĕl. **I.** *vt. & vi.* [TUN'NELED or -NELLED, -NELSˢ; TUN'NEL-ING or -NEL-LING.] To make a tunnel (through). **II.** *n.* **1.** An artificial subterranean passageway. **2.** A funnel; a flue. [Oriental head-covering.

tur'ban, 1 tûr'bən; 2 tûr'ban, *n.* An

tur'bid, 1 tûr'bid; 2 tûr'bid, *a.* Having the sediment stirred up; cloudy; muddy.

tur'bine, 1 tûr'bin *or* -bain; 2 tûr'bin *or* -bīn, *n.* A water-wheel turning on a vertical axis. **turbine wheel‡.** **tur'binˢ,**

tur'bot, 1 tûr'bət; 2 tûr'bot, *n.* A large European flatfish.

tur'bu-lent, 1 tûr'biu-lent; 2 tûr'bū-lĕnt, *a.* **1.** Being in violent commotion. **2.** Insubordinate. **-ly**, *adv.* — **tur'bu-lence**, *n.* **tur'bu-len-cy‡.**

tu-reen', 1 tiu-rīn'; 2 tū-rēn', *n.* A deep, covered dish, as for soup.

turf, 1 tûrf; 2 tûrf. **I.** *vt.* To cover with turf; sod. **II.** *n.* Sod; peat; a grass-plot; race-course. — **turf'y,** *a.* [inflated.

tur'gid, 1 tûr'jid; 2 tûr'gid, *a.* Swollen;

Turk, 1 tûrk; 2 tûrk, *n.* One of the Mohammedan people now dominant in Turkey.

tur'key, 1 tûr'ki; 2 tûr'ky, *n.* A large American bird related to the pheasants. — **tur'key-buz''zard.** An American vulture, of the warmer parts of America, sooty-black, with naked red head and neck: valued and protected as a scavenger. — **t.-cock**, *n.* A male turkey. — **T. red,** a brilliant red pigment, or its color. — **T. stone,** turquoise.

Wild Turkey. 1/45

tur'moil, 1 tûr'meil; 2 tûr'mŏil, *n.* Confused motion; disturbance; agitation.

turn, 1 tûrn; 2 tûrn. **I.** *vt. & vi.* **1.** To move or go round; revolve; rotate. **2.** To change; alter. **3.** To shape in a lathe; round. **4.** To give or take a new direction; reverse; incline; bend. **II.** *n.* **1.** The act of turning; a change; variation; rotation; revolution. **2.** A round; spell. **3.** Shape or form; mold; disposition. **4.** *Mus.* An embellishment formed by playing a note and the accessory notes above and below it. — **by turns. 1.** Alternation; alternately. **2.** At intervals. — **in turn,** in prescribed order; in regular succession. — **turn'coat'**, *n.* One who goes over to the opposite party; a renegade. — **turn'er**, *n.* **1.** One who shapes objects on a lathe. **2.** A gymnast, especially a member of a turnverein. — **turn'ing**, *n.* — **turn'key'**, *n.* A jailer. — **turn'out'**, *n.* **1.** A turning out or coming forth. **2.** An equipage. **3.** A side-track, as along a railway. — **turn'o''ver**, *a.* Folding over; as, a *turn-over* collar. — **turn'o''ver**, *n.* **1.** A small pie having a circular crust turned over on itself. **2.** A utensil for turning over food in a frying-pan. — **turn'pike'**, *n.* **1.** A road

on which are toll=gates; loosely, any high-way. **2.** A toll=bar or toll=gate.— **turn′-sole″**, *n.* Any one of several plants supposed to turn their flowers to the sun; especially, the heliotrope.— **turn′spit″**, *n.* One who turns a spit; a menial.— **turn′-stile″**, *n.* An X=shaped frame, pivoted on an upright post, to turn as people pass through it.— **turn′ta″ble**, *n.* A rotating platform bearing rails which may be connected with any of various tracks as the platform is turned, thus enabling a locomotive or car to be shifted to any set of tracks, and either end foremost.

turn′ing=point″, *n.* The point of a decisive change in direction or action; a crisis.

tur′nip, 1 tŭr′nip; 2 tûr′nip, *n.* The edible root of a biennial plant.

turn′ver=ein″, 1 tŭrn′fer=aīn″; 2 tûrn′fĕr=īn″, *n.* [Ger.] An association of gymnasts.

tur′pen=tine, 1 tŭr′pen=taīn; 2 tûr′pĕn=tīn, *n.* A resinous product of the pine.

tur′pi=tude, 1 tŭr′pĭ=tiūd; 2 tûr′pĭ=tūd, *n.* Inherent baseness; vileness; depravity.

tur-quoise′, 1 tər-keiz′ *or* tŭr′kweiz; 2 tur-kŏis *or* tûr′kwŏis′, *n.* A blue or green gem=stone. **tur-quois′‡.**

tur′ret, 1 tŭr′et; 2 tûr′ĕt, *n.* **1.** A small tower above the main structure, as on a castle. **2.** A low, armored tower, as on a war=ship.— **tur′ret=gun″**, *n.* A large cannon, especially for use in a turret, as on a vessel of war.

tur′tle(e^p), 1 tŭr′tl; 2 tûr′tl, *n.* A reptile, covered with a bony shell; a tortoise.

tur′tle(e^p²), *n.* A dove, noted for its soft cooing. **tur′tle=dove″‡.**

Tus′can, 1 tŭs′kən; 2 tŭs′can. **I.** *a.* Pertaining to Tuscany, a province of west central Italy. **II.** *n.* **1.** One of the people of Tuscany. **2.** The purest type of the Italian language spoken in Tuscany, especially at Florence. **3.** *Arch.* A Roman order of architecture, allied to the Doric.

tusk, 1 tusk; 2 tŭsk, *n.* A long, pointed tooth, especially when protruding, as in the boar or elephant.— **tusked**, *a.*

tus′sle, 1 tus′l; 2 tŭs′l. **I.** *vt. & vi.* [TUS′-SLED; TUS′SLING.] To have a tussle with; contend. **II.** *n.* A disorderly struggle; scuffle.

tus′sock, 1 tus′ək; 2 tŭs′ok, *n.* A tuft or hillock of growing grass or sedge. **tus′suck‡.**

tu′te-lage, 1 tiū′ti=lĭj; 2 tū′te=laǵ, *n.* **1.** State of being under a tutor or guardian. **2.** Act of tutoring.— **tu′te-lar**, *a.* Pertaining to a tutor or guardian. **tu′te-la-ry‡.**

tu′tor, 1 tiū′tər; 2 tū′tor. **I.** *vt.* To act as tutor to. **II.** *n.* An instructor.— **tu′tor-age**, *n.*— **tu′tor-ess**, *n. fem.*— **tu-to′ri-al**, *a.*— **tu′tor-ship**, *n.*

tux-e′do, 1 tuks-ĭ′do; 2 tŭks-ē′do, *n.* A tailless coat for evening wear.

twad′dl(e^p), 1 twed′l; 2 twạd′l. **I.** *vt. & vi.* [TWAD′DL(E)D^p; TWAD′DLING.] To prate. **II.** *n.* Pretentious, silly talk.

twain‖, 1 twēn; 2 twān, *a. & n.* Two; a couple; pair.

twang, 1 twaŋ; 2 twăng. **I.** *vt. & vi.* [TWANGED; TWANGS; TWANG′ING.] To sound with a twang. **II.** *n.* A sharp sound, as of a tense string plucked; a nasal sound of the voice.

tweak, 1 twīk; 2 twēk. **I^t.** *vt.* To pinch and twist sharply. **II.** *n.* A twitch.

tweed, 1 twīd; 2 twēd, *n.* A twilled woolen fabric of unfinished surface.

tweez′ers, 1 twīz′ərz; 2 twēz′ers, *n. pl.* Small pincers for tiny objects.

twelve(e^s, 1 twelv; 2 twĕlv, *a. & n.* Ten and two.— **twelfth**, *a. & n.* **1.** Second in order after the tenth. **2.** One of twelve equal parts.— **twelve′month**, *n.* A year.

twen′ty, 1 twen′ti; 2 twĕn′ty, *a. & n.* Twice ten.— **twen′ti-eth**, *a. & n.* **1.** Tenth in order after the tenth. **2.** One of twenty equal parts.

twice, 1 twais; 2 twīç, *adv.* Two times; doubly. [a tree.

twig, 1 twig; 2 twĭg, *n.* A small shoot of

twi′light″, 1 twai′lait″; 2 twī′līt″. **I.** *a.* Pertaining to twilight; shadowy; dim. **II.** *n.* The faint light diffused over the sky after sunset or before sunrise.

twill, 1 twil; 2 twĭl. **I.** *vt.* To weave with raised lines. **II.** *n.* A twilled fabric.

twin, 1 twin; 2 twĭn. **I.** *a.* **1.** Being a twin or twins. **2.** Double. **II.** *n.* **1.** One of two young produced at a birth. **2.** The counterpart of another.

twine, 1 twain; 2 twīn. **I.** *vt. & vi.* [TWINED; TWIN′ING.] **1.** To twist spirally. **2.** To coil about something; coil around; interlace. **II.** *a.* Of or like twine. **III.** *n.* **1.** A small cord. **2.** The act of twining.

twinge, 1 twinj; 2 twĭnǵ. **I.** *vt. & vi.* [TWINGED; TWING′ING.] To affect with a twinge. **II.** *n.* A darting momentary pain; pang.

twin′kl(e^p), 1 twiŋ′kl; 2 twĭŋ′kl. **I.** *vt. & vi.* [TWIN′KL(E)D^p; TWIN′KLING.] **1.** To shine, as a star, with quivering light. **2.** To wink, or blink, as the eyelids. **II.** *n.* **1.** A sparkle or glimmer. **2.** An instant.— **twin′kling**, *n.* **1.** A scintillating or winking. **2.** An instant.

twirl, 1 twŭrl; 2 twīrl. **I.** *vt. & vi.* To whirl. **II.** *n.* A whirling motion.

twist, 1 twist; 2 twĭst. **I^d.** *vt. & vi.* **1.** To wind (strands, etc.) round each other; intertwine. **2.** To give a spiral form or

---

1: ə = final; ɪ = habit; aɪsle; aʊ = out; ɔɪl; ɪū = feud; ᴄhin; go; ŋ = sing; ᴛhin, this.
2: wọlf, dọ; bŏŏk, bŏŏt; fŭll, rṳle, cūre, bŭt, bûrn; ŏil, bŏy; ǵo, ǵem; iŋk; thin, this.

motion to. **3.** To distort; pervert; writhe. **II.** *n.* **1.** Anything made by twisting. **2.** The act or result of twisting.

twit, 1 twit; 2 twĭt, *vt.* [TWIT′TED⁴; TWIT′TING.] To annoy by reminding of something unpleasant; taunt.

twitch, 1 twĭch; 2 twĭch. **I**ᵗ. *vt. & vi.* To pull sharply. **II.** *n.* A sudden jerk or pull.

twit′ter, 1 twit′ər; 2 twĭt′er. **I.** *vi.* To utter a continuous rapid chirping. **II.** *n.* A succession of light, tremulous sounds.

two, 1 tū; 2 tọ, *a. & n.* One and one.— **two′-fold″.** **I.** *a.* Double. **II.** *adv.* In a twofold manner or degree.— **two′pence,** *n.* [Gt. Brit.] A silver coin of the value of two pennies.— **two′pen″ny,** *a.* Of the price or value of twopence; hence, cheap.

-ty¹, *suffix.* Ten: a termination of numerals; as, thirty.

-ty², *suffix.* A termination of abstract nouns; as, felicity.

type, 1 taip; 2 tȳp, *n.* **1.** Something emblematic, representing, symbolizing, or prefiguring something else; image; emblem; symbol; sign. **2.** A representative of a class or group; an example; pattern. **3.** *Biol.* A fundamental or ideal structure or organism. **4.** A block of metal or of wood, bearing a raised letter or character for use in printing; also, such pieces collectively.— **ty′pal,** *a.*— **type′-bar″,** *n.* **1.** *Print.* A line of type cast in one piece; a linotype; type-slug. **2.** One of a series of bars in a type-setting-machine, bearing a steel type.— **t.-**²**founder,** *n.*— **t.-**²**founding,** *n.* The manufacture of metal type for printing.— **t.-**²**foundry,** *n.* An establishment in which metal type is made.— **t.-**²**metal,** *n.* The alloy of which types are made, usually of lead, tin, and antimony in various proportions.— **type′set″ter,** *n.* A compositor or machine for composing type.— **type′set″ting,** *n.*— **type′writ″er,** *n.* A machine for producing printed characters as a substitute for writing; also, one who operates it.— **type′writ″ing,** *n.*

-type, *suffix.* A termination used to signify "type," "representative form," "stamp."

ty′phoid, 1 tai′foid; 2 tȳ′fŏid. **I.** *a.* **1.** Pertaining to typhoid. **2.** Resembling typhus. **II.** *n.* An infectious, depressing fever. **typhoid fever‡.**

ty-phoon′, 1 tai-fōn′; 2 tȳ-fōōn′, *n.* A wind of cyclonic force, occurring in the China sea.

ty′phus, 1 tai′fus; 2 tȳ′fŭs, *n.* An infectious fever accompanied with extreme prostration.

typ′i-cal, 1 tip′ı-kəl; 2 tȳp′ĭ-cal, *a.* Having the nature or character of a type; symbolical; characteristic. **-ly,** *adv.*— **typ′i-fy,** *vt.* [-FIED‡; -FY′ING.] **1.** To represent by a type; prefigure. **2.** To constitute a type.

ty-pog′ra-pher, } 1 tai-pog′rə-fɪ; 2 tȳ-pŏg′ra-**ty-pog′ra-fy²,** } fy, *n.* **1.** The arrangement of composed type, or the appearance of printed matter. **2.** The act or art of composing and printing from types.— **ty-pog′ra-pher,** 1 tai-pog′rə-fər; 2 tȳ-pŏg′ra-fer, *n.* A printer.— **ty″po-graph′i-cal,** *a.* Pertaining to typography.— **ty″po-graph′ic‡.**

ty′rant, 1 tai′rant; 2 tȳ′rant, *n.* An arbitrary ruler; despot; oppressor.— **ty-ran′ni-cal,** 1 tai-ran′ı-kəl; 2 tȳ-răn′ĭ-cal, *a.* Pertaining to or like a tyrant; arbitrary; despotic; oppressive. **ty-ran′nic‡.**— **ty-ran′ni-cal-ly,** *adv.*— **tyr′an-nize,** *vt. & vi.* [-NIZED; -NIZ′ING.] To domineer over; play the tyrant. **tyr′an-nise‡.**— **tyr′an-nous,** *a.* Despotic; tyrannical.— **tyr′an-nous-ly,** *adv.*— **tyr′an-ny,** *n.* [-NIES², *pl.*] Absolute power unjustly used; despotism.

Tyr′i-an, 1 tir′ı-ən; 2 tȳr′ĭ-an. **I.** *a.* **1.** Pertaining to Tyre, an ancient city of Phenicia. **2.** Having the color of Tyrian dye; purple. **II.** *n.* A native of Tyre.

ty′ro, 1 tai′ro; 2 tȳ′ro, *n.* A beginner; novice. **Tyr″o-lese′,** 1 tir″o-lis′ *or* -liz′; 2 ȳr″o-lēs′ *or* -lēs′. **I.** *a.* Pertaining to Tyrol, an Austrian province. **II.** *n.* A native of Tyrol.— **Ty-ro″li-enne′,** *n. fem.*

tzar, tza-ri′na, etc. Same as CZAR, etc.

U

U, u, 1 yū; 2 yụ, *n.* [UES, U's, *or* Us, 1 yūz; 2 yụs, *pl.*] The twenty-first letter in the English alphabet.

u-blq′ul-ty, 1 yu-bik′wı-tı; 2 yụ-bĭk′wi-ty, *n.* Omnipresence, real or seeming.— **u-blq′-ul-tous,** *a.* Omnipresent.

ud′der, 1 ud′ər; 2 ŭd′er, *n.* The organ that secretes milk; the milk-bag; dug.

ug′ly, 1 ug′lı; 2 ŭg′ly, *a.* [UG′LI-ER; UG′LI-EST.] **1.** Ill-looking; unsightly. **2.** Repulsive; revolting.— **ug′li-ness,** *n.*

uh′lan, 1 ū′lən *or* yū-lən′; 2 ụ′lan *or* yụ-lan′, *n.* A cavalryman and lancer, chiefly employed in reconnoitering, skirmishing, etc.

u-kase′, 1 yu-kēs′; 2 yụ-kās′, *n.* An edict of the Russian government.

u″ku-le′le, 1 ū″kə-lē′le; 2 ụ″ku-lē′le, *n.* [Hawaii.] A guitar-like musical instrument.

ul′cer, 1 ŭl′sạr; 2 ŭl′çẽr, *n.* An open sore. **— ul′cer-ate**[d], *vt.* & *vi.* To become ulcerous. **— ul″cer-a′tion,** *n.* **— ul″cer-ous,** *a.* **1.** Having the character of an ulcer. **2.** Affected with ulcers.

-ule, *suffix.* Of Latin origin indicating a diminutive ; as, glob*ule*. [overcoat.

ul′ster, 1 ŭl′stẽr; 2 ŭl′stẽr, *n.* A long, loose

ul-te′ri-or, 1 ŭl-tī′rĭ-ạr; 2 ŭl-tē′rĭ-or, *a.* More remote; lying beyond; undisclosed.

ul′ti-mate, 1 ŭl′tĭ-mĭt; 2 ŭl′tĭ-mat, *a.* **1.** Final. **2.** Fundamental; primary. **— ul′ti-mate-ly,** *adv.* At last; finally. **— ul″ti-ma′tum,** 1 ŭl″tĭ-mē′tŭm; 2 ŭl″tĭ-mā′tŭm, *n.* [-TA, *pl.*] **1.** A final statement; last proposal or demand. **2.** Anything ultimate.

ul′ti-mo, 1 ŭl′tĭ-mo; 2 ŭl′tĭ-mo, *adv.* In the last month: shortened to *ult.*

ul′tra, 1 ŭl′trạ; 2 ŭl′tra, *a.* Exceeding moderation; extreme; extravagant.

ul′tra-, 1 ŭl′trạ-; 2 ŭl′tra-, *prefix.* A prefix of Latin origin meaning "beyond"; on the other side of; beyond what is usual or natural; as, *ultra*fashionable.

ul″tra-ma-rine′, 1 ŭl″trạ-mạ-rīn′; 2 ŭl″tra-ma-rīn′, *n.* A blue pigment, or its sea-blue color.

ul″tra-mon′tane, 1 ŭl″trạ-mŏn′tēn; 2 ŭl″tra-mŏn′tān, *a.* Situated beyond the mountains, especially south of the Alps, that is Italian or papal. **— ul″tra-mon′ta-nism,** *n.* **— ul″tra-mon′ta-nist,** *n.*

ul″tra-mun′dane, 1 ŭl″trạ-mun′dēn; 2 ŭl″tra-mŭn′dān, *a.* **1.** Pertaining to things exterior to the world. **2.** Pertaining to supernatural things or to another life.

um′bel, 1 um′bel; 2 ŭm′bĕl, *n.* A flower-cluster in which a number of pedicels radiate like the stays of an umbrella. **— um″bel-lif′er-ous,** *a.*

um′ber, 1 um′bạr; 2 ŭm′ber. **I.** *a.* Brownish. **II.** *n.* A brown pigment or color. **— um′bered,** *a.*

um′bra, 1 um′brạ; 2 ŭm′bra, *n.* [-BRÆ, *pl.*] *Astron.* That region of a shadow from which the light is entirely cut off; specif., that part of the shadow of the earth or moon in which the sun is entirely hidden. See PENUMBRA.

um′brage, 1 um′brij; 2 ŭm′brag, *n.* **1.** Resentment; a sense of injury. **2.** Shadow. **— um-bra′geous,** *a.* Shady. **-ly,** *adv.* **-ness,** *n.*

um-brel′la, 1 um-brel′ạ; 2 ŭm-brĕl′a, *n.* A light portable canopy.

um′pire, 1 um′pair; 2 ŭm′pīr. **I.** *vt.* & *vi.* [UM′PIRED; UM′PI-RING.] To decide or act as umpire. **II.** *n.* A person chosen to decide a question or to enforce the rules of a game.

un-[1], *prefix.* Not: used to express negation, incompleteness, or opposition.

un-[2], *prefix.* Back: used to express the reversal of the action of the verb.

The numerous words so formed are mostly self explaining with the sense of denial (UN-[1]), with the force of *not*, or of reversal as denoting the exact opposite (UN-[2]). Compare IN-[2].

un′a-bashed′
un′a-bridged′
un′ac-cept′a-ble(e[p]
un′ac-quaint′ed
un′a-dorned′
un′ad-vis′a-ble(e[p]
un′ad-vised′
un′ad-vis′ed-ly
un′af-fect′ed, -ly, -ness
un-aid′ed
un′al-loyed′
un-al′ter-a-ble(e[p], -bly
un-al′tered
un-an′swer-a-ble(e[p], -ness, -bly
un′ap-pre′ci-a-tiv(e[s]
un′ap-proach′a-ble(e[p], -ness, -bly
un-asked′
un′as-sail′a-ble(e[p], -bly
un′at-tain′a-ble(e[p]
un′at-trac′tiv(e[s]
un-au′thor-ized
un-au′thor-ised‡
un′a-vail′a-ble(e[p], -bly
un′a-vail′ing
un′a-venged′
un′a-vowed′
un′bap-tized′
un′bap-tised′‡
un′bear′a-ble(e[p]
un′blush′ing
un-bound′
un-bound′ed
un-bri′dled
un-bro′ken
un-bus′i-ness-like
un-chain′
un-change′a-ble(e[p]
un-chaste′, -ly, -ness
un-checked′
un-clothe′
un′com-mu′ni-ca-tiv(e[s], -ness
un′com-plain′ing
un′com-pli-men′ta-ry
un′con-demned′
un′con-fined′
un′con-firmed′
un′con-form′a-ble(e[p], -ness
un′con-ge′nial, -ly
un′con-ge′ni-al′i-ty
un′con-nect′ed, -ly
un′con-quer-a-ble(e[p], -ness, -bly
un′con-test′ed

un-con′tra-dict′ed.
un′con-trolled′
un-con′tro-vert′ed.
un′con-vinced′
un′con-vinc′ing
un-curbed′
un-dam′aged
un-dat′ed
un′de-ci′pher-a-ble(e[p], -bly
un-de-filed′
un′de-fin′a-ble(e[p]
un′de-fined′
un′de-mon′stra-tiv(e[s]
un′de-ni′a-ble(e[p]
un-de-served′
un′de-serv′ed-ly
un′de-serv′ed-ness
un′de-serv′ing, -ly
un′de-signed′
un′de-sign′ed-ly
un′de-sir′a-bil′i-ty
un′de-sir′a-ble(e[p], -ness, -bly
un′de-sired′
un′de-vel′oped
un-de′vi-at′ing, -ly
un′di-gest′ed
un′di-min′ished
un′dis-cerned′
un′dis-cern′ing, -ly
un′dis-cov′er-a-ble(e[p], -bly
un′dis-cov′ered
un′dis-guised′
un′dis-guis′ed-ly
un′dis-mayed′
un′dis-put′ed, -ly
un′dis-solved′
un′dis-tin′guish-a-ble(e[p]
un′dis-tin′guished
un′dis-turbed′
un′dis-turb′ed-ly
un′dis-turb′ed-ness
un′di-vid′ed
un-du′ti-ful, -ly, -ness
un-dy′ing
un-earned′
un-ed′u-cat′ed
un′en-cum′bered
un′en-dur′a-ble(e[p]
un-en-light′ened
un′en-ter-pris′ing
un-er′ring, -ly, -ness
un′es-sen′tial
un′ex-pect′ed, -ly, -ness

un˝ex-plored'
un˝ex-tin'guished
un-fad'ing, -ly, -ness
un-fail'ing
un-fall'en
un-fal'ter-ing
un˝fa-mil'iar
un-fash'ion-a-bl(eᴾ
un-fast'en
un-fath'om-a-bl(eᴾ
un-fath'omed
un-feigned'
un-feign'ed-ly, -ness
un-fet'ter
un-fil'ial
un-fin'ished
un-flag'ging
un˝for-bid'den
un˝for-giv'en
un˝for-giv'ing
un-for'ti-fied
un˝fre-quent'ed
un-fur'nished
un-˷en'er-ous, -ly
un-gen'tle-man-ly
un-glazed'
un-˷race'ful, -ly
un˝gram-mat'i-cal,
  -ly, -ness
un-grat'i-fied
un-ground'ed
un-hal'lowed
un-hand'
un-hand'i-ly, -ness
un-hand'y
un-harmed'
un-har'ness
un-health'ful, -ly,
  -ness
un-health'i-ly
un-health'i-ness
un-health'y
un-heed'ing
un-hes'i-tat˝ing, -ly
un-hin'dered
un-hon'ored
un-hurt'
un˝im-ag'i-na-bl(eᴾ
  -ness, -bly
un˝im-ag'i-na-tiv(eˢ
un˝im-ag'ined
un˝im-por'tant
un˝im-proved'
un˝in-formed'
un˝in-hab'it-a-bl(eᴾ
un˝in-hab'it-ed
un˝in-jured
un˝in-spired'
un˝in-spir'ing
un˝in-tel'li-gi-bil'i-ty
un˝in-tel'li-gi-bl(eᴾ,
  -ness, -bly
un˝in-ten'tion-al

un˝in-ter-est-ed, -ing
un˝in-ter-rupt'ed
un-in-vit'ing
un-jus'ti-fi˝a-bl(eᴾ,
  -bly
un-know'ing, -ly
un˝la-ment'ed
un-leav'ened
un-let'tered
un-li'censed
un-lim'it-ed
un-loved'
un-love'ly
un-maid'en-ly
un-man'age-a-bl(eᴾ
un-man'li-ness
un-man'ly
un-man'ner-li-ness
un-man'ner-ly
un-marked'
un-mar'ried
un-matched'
un-mea'sured
un-men'tion-a-bl(eᴾ,
  -ness, -bly
un-men'tioned
un-mer'it-ed
un-mit'i-gat˝ed
un-mo-lest'ed
un-moved'
un-muz'zle
un˝nec'es-sa-ri-ly
un˝nec'es-sa-ry
un-neigh'bor-ly
un-no'ticed
un-num'bered
un-nur'tured
un˝ob-jec'tion·a-bl(2ᴾ
un˝ob-ser'vant
un˝ob-serv'ing
un˝ob-struct'ed
un˝ob-tru'siv(eˢ
un-oc'cu-pied
un-o'pened
un-os˝ten-ta'tious, -ly,
  -ness
un-pack'
un-paid'
un-pal'at-a-bl(eᴾ, -bly
un-par'don-a-bl(eᴾ,
  -ness, -bly
un-peo'pled
un-per-ceived'
un-pit'y-ing
un-pol'ished
un-pol-lut'ed
un˝pre-med'i-tat˝ed
un˝pre-pared'
un˝pre-pos-sess'ing
un˝pre-sent'a-bl(eᴾ
un˝pre-tend'ing, -ly
un˝pre-vent'ed
un-prom'is-ing
un˝pro-nounce'a-bl(eᴾ

un˝pro-pi'tious, -ly
un˝pro-tect'ed
un˝pro-vid'ed
un-pub'lished
un-pun'ished
un-quench'a-bl(eᴾ
un're-al'
un˝rec-og-niz' [or
  -nis']abl(eᴾ
un˝rec'on-ciled
un˝re-gard'ed
un-reg'u-lat˝ed
un˝re-lat'ed
un˝re-lent'ing, -ly
un˝re-li'a-bl(eᴾ, -ness
un-re-lieved'
un˝re-mem'bered
un˝re-mit'ting, -ly
un˝re-mu'ner-a-tiv(eˢ
un-rep're-sent'ed
un˝re-sist'ed
un˝re-sist'ing, -ly
un-rest'ing, -ly
un˝re-strained'
un˝re-strict'ed
un˝re-ward'ed
un-ripe'
un˝ro-man'tic
un-ruf'fled
un-safe', -ly, -ness
un-said'
un-sal'a-bl(eᴾ, -ness
un-san'i-ta-ry
un-sat'is-fac'to-ry
un-sat'is-fied
un-scarred'
un-schol'ar-ly
un-scrip'tur-al
un-scru'pu-lous, -ly,
  -ness
un-seal'
un-sea'wor˝thy
un-seem'ly
un-seen'
un-self'ish, -ly
un-ser'vice-a-bl(eᴾ,
  -bly
un-shack'le
un-shak'en
un-shav'en
un-shel'tered
un-shrink'ing, -ly
un-skil'ful
un-skilled'
un-so'cia-bil'i-ty
un-so'cia-bl(eᴾ, -ness
un-so'cia-bly
un-so'cial, -ly
un-sold'
un-sol'dier-ly
un-so-lic'it-ed
un-sought'

un-sound'
un-spar'ing
un-spec'i-fied
un-spoiled'
un-spoilt'‡
un-spo'ken
un-sports'man-like
un-stained'
un-stead'i-ly, -ness
un-stead'y
un˝sub-stan'tial, -ly,
  -ness
un˝sub-stan'ti-at'ed
un˝suc-cess'ful
un˝sup-port'ed, -ly
un˝sur-passed'
un˝sus-pect'ed
un˝sus-pi'cious
un˝sus-tained'
un-taint'ed
un-tam'a-bl(eᴾ,
  -ness
un-tamed'
un-tan'gled
un-tan'gled
un-tast'ed
un-taught'
un-ten'a-bl(eᴾ
un-ten'ant-ed
un-tend'ed
un-thank'ful
un-tilled'
un-tir'ing
un-touched'
un-trained'
un˝trans-lat'a-bl(eᴾ
un-tried'
un-trod'den
un-troub'led
un-twine'
un-twist'
un-used'
un-u'til-ized
un-u'til-ised‡
un-van'quished
un-va'ried
un-va'ried
un-va'ry-ing, -ly
un-ven'ti-lat'ed
un-war'like'
un-washed'
un-watched'
un-wa'ver-ing, -ly
un-wea'ried, -ly
un-wed'ded
un-wel'come
un-wind'
un-wom'an-ly
un-work'man-like'
un-wrap'
un-writ'ten
un-yield'ing

un-a'bl(eᴾ, a. Not able; incompetent.
un˝ac-count'a-bl(eᴾ, a. Impossible to

be accounted for; extraordinary.— **un″ac-count′a-bly,** adv.

u-nan′i-mous, 1 yu-nan′i-mus; 2 yụ-năn′i-mŭs, a. Agreeing without dissent; harmonious. **-ly,** adv.— **u″na-nim′i-ty,** 1 yū″na-nim′i-ti; 2 yụ″na-nĭm′ĭ-ty, n. Complete agreement; harmony.

un-armed′, } a. Not provided with or
un-armd′s, } bearing arms; defenseless.

un″as-sum′ing, a. Making no pretensions; modest.

un″a-void′a-bl(e⸢r⸣, a. **1.** Inevitable. **2.** That can not be made null and void.

un″a-ware′, a. Giving no heed; not cognizant.— **un″a-wares′,** adv. Unexpectedly; unwittingly.

un-bal′anced, a. Not balanced; lacking mental soundness.

un″be-com′ing, a. Not becoming; unsuitable; improper.

un″be-lief′, n. Lack of belief; incredulity; disbelief.— **un″be-liev′er,** n.

un-bend′, vt. & vi. [UN-BENT′ or UN-BEND′ED⸢d⸣; UN-BEND′ING.] **1.** To straighten after having been bent. **2.** To relax; be affable, condescending, or genial.

un-bi′ased, } 1 un-bai′əst; 2 ŭn-bī′ast, a.
un-bi′assed, } Free from bias; not prejudiced; impartial.
un-bi′asts, }

un-bo′som, 1 un-bu′zəm; 2 ŭn-bọ′som, vt. & vi. [-BO′SOMED; -BO′SOM-ING.] To free one's bosom of; confess.

un-bur′den, vt. To remove as a burden; free from a burden; relieve, as the mind or heart.— **un-bur′den(e)d⸢s⸣,** pa.

un-called′, a. Not asked; not demanded or required.— **uncalled for,** not justified by circumstances; unnecessary.

un-can′ny, a. Not canny. Particularly: (1) Exciting superstitious fear; weird. (2) Unskilful; incautious. (3) Unsafe; dangerous. (4) Severe.

un-cer′tain, 1 un-sūr′tin; 2 ŭn-çẽr′tin, a. Not certain; doubtful; variable; changeful; fitful.— **un-cer′tain-ty,** n. [-TIES⸢z⸣, pl.] **1.** The state of being uncertain. **2.** A doubtful matter; a contingency.

un-char′i-ta-bl(e⸢r⸣, a. Manifesting lack of charity; censorious; severe.

un-civ′il, a. Wanting in civility; discourteous.— **un-civ′i-lized** or **-lised,** a. Destitute of civilization; barbarous.

un′cl(e⸢r⸣, 1 uŋ′kl; 2 ŭŋ′el, n. The brother of one's father or mother; also, the husband of one's aunt.— **Uncle Sam.** A symbolic representative of the United States or its citizens. See JOHN BULL.

un-com′fort-a-bl(e⸢r⸣, a. Causing or feeling discomfort; ill at ease.

un-com′mon, a. Not common; remarkable.

un-com′pro-mis″ing, a. Inflexible; strict.

un″con-cern′, n. Absence of concern; indifference.— **un″con-cerned′,** a.

un″con-di′tion-al, a. Limited by no conditions; absolute. **-ly,** adv.

un-con′scion-a-bl(e⸢r⸣, 1 un-kən′shən-ə-bl; 2 ŭn-cŏn′shon-a-bl, a. Going beyond bounds; unreasonable; intolerable.— **un-con′scion-a-bly,** adv.

un-con′scious, a. **1.** Temporarily deprived of consciousness. **2.** Not cognizant; unaware. **-ly,** adv. **-ness,** n.

un-con″sti-tu′tion-al, a. Contrary to the constitution or fundamental law.

un″con-trol′la-bl(e⸢r⸣, a. Beyond control; ungovernable.

un-couth′, 1 un-kūth′; 2 ŭn-eụth′, a. Outlandish; odd; ungainly. **-ly,** adv. **-ness,** n.

un-cov′er, } v. I. t. To remove the covering
un-cuv′er⸢r⸣, } from; disclose. II. i. To remove the hat, as in respect.

unc′tion, 1 uŋk′shən; 2 une′shon, n. **1.** The act of anointing. **2.** An unguent or a salve. **3.** Religious fervor; divine grace.— **unc′tu-ous,** a. Greasy.— **unc′tu-ous-ness,** n. **unc″tu-os′i-ty‡.**

un-daunt′ed, a. Fearless; intrepid.

un″de-ceive′, } vt. To free from deception.
un″de-ceiv′⸢r⸣, } as by apprizing of the truth.

un′der, 1 un′dər; 2 ŭn′der. **I. a. 1.** Lower or lowermost. **2.** Subordinate. **II.** adv. In a lower position or inferior degree. **III.** prep. **1.** Beneath; covered by. **2.** In a place lower than. **3.** Subject to. **4.** Less than. **5.** By virtue of; in conformity to; in accordance with; authorized, attested, or warranted by.— **un″der-bid′,** vt. To bid lower than, especially in a competitive offer of labor or materials.— **un′der-bred′,** a. **1.** Not thoroughbred. **2.** Lacking in good breeding.— **un″der-brush′,** n. Small trees and shrubs growing beneath the large trees of a forest; brushwood. — **un′der-clothes′,** n. pl. Clothes for wear next the skin. **un′der-clo″thing‡.**— **un′der-cur′rent,** n. A current, as of water, below the surface; a hidden tendency.— **un″der-done′,** a. Partially cooked; rare.— **un″der-go′,** vt. [UN-DER-WENT′; -GONE′; -GO′ING.] **1.** To bear up under. **2.** To pass through, as an experience.— **un″der-grad′u-ate,** n. A student who has not taken the bachelor's degree.— **un″der-ground″. I.** a. **1.** Situated, done, or operating beneath the surface of the ground. **2.** Done in secret. **II.** adv. Beneath the surface of the ground; secretly. — **un′der-growth″,** n. **1.** A thicket in a forest. **2.** The condition of being undergrown.— **un′der-hand″,** a. Done or acting in a treacherously secret manner; unfair;

---

uncomplicated

sly.— **un′der-hand″**, _adv._— **un″der-hand′-ed**, _a._— **un″der-let′**, _vt._ To lease (premises already held on lease); sublet.— **un″der-lie′**, _v._ **I.** _t._ **1.** To be below or under. **2.** To be the ground or support of. **II.** _i._ To occupy a position under; be subject to.— **un′der-line″**, _vt._ To mark with a line underneath.— **un′der-ling**, _n._ A subordinate; an inferior.— **un″der-mine′**, _vt._ **1.** To excavate beneath. **2.** To wear away and weaken.— **un′der-most**, _a._ Having the lowest place.— **un″der-neath′**. **I.** _adv._ In a place directly below. **II.** _prep._ Beneath; under; below.— **un′der-pin″ning**, _n._ A foundation wall or support.— **un″der-prop′**, _vt._— **un″der-rate′**d, _vt._ To rate too low.— **un″der-score′**, _vt._ To underline.— **un″-der-sell′**, _vt._ To sell at a lower price than.— **un″der-shirt′**, _n._ A garment worn next to the skin.— **un″der-sign′**, _vt._ To sign to the foot of; subscribe.— **un″der-signed′**, _pa. & n._— **un″der-state′**, _vt._ To state less than the full fact, truth, or opinion.— **un″der-tone″**, _n._ **1.** A tone of lower pitch or loudness than is usual. **2.** A subdued shade of a color.— **un′der-tow″**, _n._ A flow of water below the surface of the sea in a direction opposite to the surface current.— **un″der-val′ue**, _vt._ To underrate; underestimate.— **un″der-val′u-a″tion**, _n._— **un′der-wear″**, _n._ Underclothing.— **un″der-went′**, _imp._ of UNDERGO, _v._— **un″der-write′**, _vt._ **1.** To write beneath; subscribe. **2.** To insure.— **un′der-writ″er**, _n._ An insurer.

un″der-stand′, _v._ [-STOOD′; -STAND′ING.] **I.** _t._ **1.** To take in or make out the meaning of; perceive; comprehend. **2.** To take or suppose to mean; supply mentally. **3.** To learn; have information of. **II.** _i._ **1.** To comprehend. **2.** To know through information.— **un″der-stand′ing**, _n._ **1.** Intellectual apprehension. **2.** The faculty by which one understands. **3.** The facts of a case as apprehended. **4.** An informal compact.

un″der-take′, _v._ [UN″DER-TOOK′; -TAK′-EN; -TAK′ING.] **I.** _t._ **1.** To take in hand; attempt; try. **2.** To covenant; engage. **II.** _i._ **1.** To make oneself responsible for anything. **2.** To enter into a contract.— **un″der-tak″er**, _n._ One who undertakes; one whose business it is to oversee funerals.— **un″der-tak′ing**, _n._ **1.** An enterprise; task. **2.** The management of funerals.

un-do′, _vt._ [UN-DID′; UN-DO′ING; UN-DONE′.] **1.** To annul or counteract. **2.** To ruin. **3.** To loosen or untie.— **un-do′ing**, _n._— **un-done′**, _pp._

un-doubt′ed,) _a._ Assured beyond ques-
un-dout′eds,) tion. **2.** Not regarded with distrust.

un-dress′t, 1 un-dres′; 2 ŭn-drĕs′, _v._ **I.** _t._

To divest of clothes; strip. **II.** _i._ To remove one's clothing.

un-dress′, 1 un-dres′; 2 ŭn-drĕs′, _a._ Pertaining to every=day attire; hence, informal.

un-dress′, _n._ Ordinary attire; negligee.

un-due′, 1 un-diū′; 2 ŭn-dū′, _a._ **1.** More than sufficient; excessive. **2.** Not justified by law or propriety. **3.** Not due.— **un-du′ly**, _adv._

un′du-late, 1 un′diu-lēt; 2 ŭn′dū-lāt. **I.** _vt. & vi._ [-LAT″ED^d; -LAT′ING.] To move like a wave or in waves; have a wavy appearance. **II.** _a._ Wavy.— **un″du-la′tion**, _n._ A waving motion; a wave.— **un′du-la-to-ry**, _a._

un-earth′t, 1 un-ûrth′; 2 ŭn-ērth′, _vt._ **1.** To dig up from the earth. **2.** To reveal; discover.— **un-earth′ly**, _a._ Supernatural; weird; appalling.

un-eas′y, 1 un-īz′ı; 2 ŭn-ēş′y, _a._ Disturbed; not quiet or comfortable; embarrassed.— **un-eas′i-ly**, _adv._— **un-eas′i-ness**, _n._

un-e′qual, 1 un-ī′kwal; 2 ŭn-ē′kwal, _a._ **1.** Not having equivalent or equal properties. **2.** Inadequate; insufficient. **3.** Not balanced; disproportioned.— **un-e′qualed**, _a._— **un-e′qual-ly**, _adv._

un-e′ven, _a._ **1.** Not even or level. **2.** Not divisible by 2 without remainder; odd. **3.** Not balanced; not fair or just.

un″ex-am′pled, _a._ Without a parallel.

un″ex-cep′tion-a-bl(e^e, _a._ That can not be taken exception to; faultless.

un-fair′, 1 un-fâr′; 2 ŭn-fâr′, _a._ Marked by fraud; not just.— **un-fair′ly**, _adv._— **un-fair′ness**, _n._

un-faith′ful, _a._ **1.** Perfidious; faithless. **2.** Not true to a standard. **-ly**, _adv._

un-fa′vor-a-bl(e^e, _a._ Not favorable. (1) Unpropitious; adverse. (2) Showing no favor.— **un-fa′vor-a-bly**, _adv._ [cruel.

un-feel′ing, _a._ Not sympathetic; hard;

un-fit′. **I**^d. _vt._ To disqualify. **II.** _a._ **1.** Having no fitness; unsuitable. **2.** Not appropriate. **-ly**, _adv._ **-ness**, _n._

un-fledged′, 1 un-flejd′; 2 ŭn-flĕğd′, _a._ Not yet able to fly, as a young bird; callow; immature.

un-fold′d, _vt. & vi._ To open or spread out; reveal itself; develop.

un-for′tu-nate, _a._ Having ill fortune; unsuccessful; disastrous.

un-found′ed, _a._ **1.** Groundless; baseless. **2.** Not founded or established.

un-furl′, _vt._ **1.** To unroll or spread out; expand. **2.** To disclose.

un-gain′ly, 1 un-gēn′lı; 2 ŭn-gān′ly, _a._

Lacking grace or ease; clumsy.— **un-gain'li-ness,** *n.*

un-god'ly, *a.* **1.** Impious; wicked. **2.** Unholy.— **un-god'li-ness,** *n.*

un-gov'ern-a-ble, *a.* That can not be governed.— **un-gov'ern-a-bly,** *adv.*

un-gra'cious, *a.* **1.** Unmannerly. **2.** Not pleasing. **-ly,** *adv.* **-ness,** *n.*

un-grate'ful, *a.* **1.** Making ill return. **2.** Disagreeable. **3.** Thankless. **-ly,** *adv.* — **un-grate'ful-ness,** *n.* Ingratitude.

un'guent, 1 uŋ'gwent; 2 ŭŋ'gwĕnt, *n.* Any ointment for local application.

un-hap'py, *a.* **1.** Sad; depressed. **2.** Causing misery; unfortunate.— **un-hap'pi-ly,** *adv.* — **un-hap'pi-ness,** *n.*

un-heard', *a.* **1.** Not perceived by the ear. **2.** Not granted a hearing. **3.** Not known; not usual: followed by *of.*

un-hinge', *vt.* **1.** To take the hinges from; disconnect the hinges of. **2.** To wrench out of place.

un-ho'ly, *a.* **1.** Not hallowed. **2.** Lacking moral purity.— **un-ho'li-ness,** *n.*

un-horse't, *vt.* To unseat; dismount.

u'ni-corn, 1 yū'nɪ-kôrn; 2 yụ'nɪ-côrn, *n.* **1.** A fabulous horse-like animal with a horn on the forehead. **2.** *Bib.* The wild ox of Palestine.

u'ni-form, 1 yū'nɪ-fêrm; 2 yụ'nɪ-fôrm. **I.** *vt.* **1.** To put into uniform. **2.** To make uniform. **II.** *a.* **1.** Being the same or alike. **2.** Agreeing with each other; harmonious. **III.** *n.* A dress of uniform style and appearance. **-ly,** *adv.* — **u''ni-form'i-ty,** *n.* The state or fact of being uniform.

Unicorn from British Coat of Arms.

u'ni-fy, 1 yū'nɪ-fai; 2 yụ'nɪ-fy̆, *vt.* [-FIED; -FY'ING.] To make uniform; unite.— **u''ni-fi-ca'tion,** *n.*

u'nion, 1 yūn'yən; 2 yụn'yon. **I.** *a.* Pertaining to union. **II.** *n.* **1.** The act of uniting, or the state of being united; a joining; coalescence. **2.** A whole formed by uniting elements previously separate; a combination; consolidation; confederation; league; wedlock. **3.** Agreement.

Union of Soviet Socialist Republics. Official name of Soviet Russia. More popularly known by its abbreviation U.S.S.R.

u-nique', 1 yu-nīk'; 2 yu-nīk', *a.* **1.** Being the only one of its kind; singular; uncommon. **2.** Not complicated. **3.** Sole.

u'ni-son, 1 yū'nɪ-sən; 2 yụ'nɪ-son, *n.* **1.** A condition of perfect accord; harmony. **2.** *Mus.* Coincidence of sounds.

u'nit, 1 yū'nɪt; 2 yụ'nit, *n.* **1.** A single person or thing; an individual. **2.** A least whole number; one; unity.

U''ni-ta'ri-an, 1 yū''nɪ-tē'rɪ-ən; 2 yụ''nɪ-tā'ri-an. **I.** *a.* Pertaining to Unitarians. **II.** *n.* A member of a religious body that rejects the doctrine of the Trinity.— **U''ni-ta'ri-an-ism,** *n.*

u-nite', 1 yu-nait'; 2 yụ-nīt', *vt. & vi.* [U-NIT'ED; U-NIT'ING.] To make or become one; join together; combine; compound; ally; harmonize.— **u-nit'ed,** *pa.* Incorporated in one; harmonious. **-ly,** *adv.* **-ness,** *n.*

u'ni-ty, 1 yū'nɪ-tɪ; 2 yụ'nɪ-ty, *n.* [-TIES^z, *pl.*] **1.** The state of being one; singleness; union; harmony; concord. **2.** The number one.

u'ni-verse, 1 yū'nɪ-vūrs; 2 yụ'nɪ-vêrs, *n.* The aggregate of all existing things; the whole creation; all mankind.— **u''ni-ver'sal,** 1 yū''nɪ-vûr'sal; 2 yụ''nɪ-vêr'sal, *a.* Relating to the universe; unlimited; general; entire; total.— **U''ni-ver'sal-ism,** *n.* The doctrine that all souls will finally be saved.— **U''ni-ver'sal-ist,** *n.* A believer in the doctrines of Universalism.— **u''ni-ver-sal'i-ty,** *n.* The state of being all-embracing.— **u''ni-ver'sal-ly,** *adv.*

u''ni-ver'si-ty, 1 yū''nɪ-vûr'sɪ-tɪ; 2 yụ''nɪ-vêr'si-ty, *n.* [-TIES^z, *pl.*] A school of higher learning.

un-just', *a.* Not just; wrongful; unfair; unrighteous. **-ly,** *adv.* **-ness,** *n.*

un-kempt', *a.* Not combed; untidy.

un-known', 1 un-nōn'; 2 ŭn-nōn'. **I.** *a.* Not known, or not capable of being known. **II.** *n.* An unknown person or quantity.

un-law'ful, *a.* Contrary to law; illegal.

un-learn', ʃ *vt. & vi.* To dismiss from the **un-lern'^{p},** ʃ mind; forget.— **un-learned',** *pp.*

un-learn'ed, ʃ 1 un-lûrn'ed; 2 ŭn-lêrn'ĕd, **un-lern'ed^p,** ʃ *a.* Without learning; illiterate; uncultured.

un-leav'ened, 1 un-lev'nd; 2 ŭn-lĕv'nd, *a.* Not leavened: said specifically of the bread used at the feast of the Passover.

un-less', 1 un-les'; 2 ŭn-lĕs', *conj.* **1.** If it be not a fact that; supposing that ... not. **2.** Save; except.

un-like'. I. *a.* Different. **II.** *adv.* In another manner.— **un-like'ly. I.** *a.* **1.** Improbable. **2.** Not promising success. **II.** *adv.* Improbably.— **un-like'li-ness,** *n.* **un-like'li-hood‡.**

un-lim'ber, *vt.* To detach the limbers from, as a cannon, in readiness for action.

un-load't, *vt.* **1.** To deprive of a load or burden. **2.** To discharge, as a cargo.

---

un-lock′t, *vt.* To unfasten a lock; open.

un-loose′t, 1 un-lūs′; 2 ŭn-lōōs′, *vt. & vi.* To release or be released from fastenings; unfasten.

un-luck′y, *a.* Not favored by luck; unfortunate; disastrous; ill-omened.— **un-luck′-i-ly**, *adv.*— **un-luck′i-ness**, *n.*

un-man′, *vt.* **1.** To deprive of manly power, strength, or courage. **2.** To deprive of men, as a fort.

un-mask′t, *vt.* **1.** To remove a mask from. **2.** To take any disguise from.

un-mean′ing, *a.* Meaningless. **-ly**, *adv.*

un-mer′ci-ful, *a.* **1.** Cruel; pitiless. **2.** Exorbitant. **-ly**, *adv.* **-ness**, *n.*

un″mis-tak′a-ble, *a.* That can not be mistaken. **un″mis-take′a-bl(e)**‡.— **un″mis-tak′**[or **-take′**]**a-bly**, *adv.*

un-nat′u-ral, *a.* **1.** Contrary to nature; monstrous. **2.** Lacking naturalness; artificial. **3.** Destitute of natural affection. **-ly**, *adv.* **-ness**, *n.*   [courage.

un-nerv′(e)′s, *vt.* To deprive of strength or

un-par′al-leled,) *a.* Without parallel; un-
un-par′al-leld′s,) matched; unprecedented.

un-par″lia-men′ta-ry, 1 ŭn-pär″li-men′tạ-ri; 2 ŭn-pär″li-měn′tạ-ry, *a.* Contrary to the rules that govern deliberative bodies.

un-pleas′ant,) *a.* Failing to give plea-
un-ples′ant′s,) sure; disagreeable. **-ly**, *adv.* **-ness**, *n.*

un-pop′u-lar, *a.* Having no popularity; generally disliked. **-ly**, *adv.*— **un″pop-u-lar′i-ty**, *n.*   [*adv.*

un-prec′e-dent-ed, *a.* Unexampled. **-ly**,

un-prej′u-diced, *a.* **1.** Free from prejudice; impartial. **2.** Not injured or impaired.

un-prin′ci-pled, *a.* Unscrupulous; wicked.

un″pro-duc′tiv(e)s, *a.* Barren; yielding no return.

un″pro-voked′, *a.* Having received no provocation; not due to provocation.

un-qual′i-fied, *a.* **1.** Lacking qualification; unfit. **2.** Given or done without limitation; absolute. **-ly**, *adv.*

un-ques′tion-a-bl(e)s, *a.* Being beyond a question or doubt. **-bly**, *adv.*

un-qui′et, *a.* **1.** Not at rest; disturbed. **2.** Causing unrest. **-ly**, *adv.* **-ness**, *n.*

un-rav′el, 1 un-rav′l; 2 ŭn-răv′l, *vt.* To separate the threads of; disentangle; unfold; explain.

un-rea′son-a-bl(e)s, *a.* Acting without or contrary to reason; irrational; immoderate.— **un-rea′son-a-ble-ness**, *n.*— **un-rea′son-a-bly**, *adv.*

un″re-served′,) *a.* **1.** Given without re-
un″re-servd′s,) serve. **2.** Free from reserve; frank; open.— **un″re-serv′ed-ly**, *adv.*

un-rest′, ... Restlessness.

un-right′eous, *a.* Not righteous; wicked.

un-ri′valed, *a.* Having no rival; unequaled; matchless. **un-ri′valled**‡.

un-roll′, *vt.* To spread or open (something rolled up); exhibit to view.

un-ru′ly, 1 un-rū′li; 2 ŭn-rụ′ly, *a.* Disposed to resist control; ungovernable.— **un-ru′li-ness**, *n.*

un-sa′vor-y, *a.* **1.** Having a disagreeable taste or odor. **2.** Suggesting something offensive. **3.** Associated with something morally bad.— **un-sa′vor-i-ly**, *adv.*— **un-sa′vor-i-ness**, *n.*

un-scathed′, 1 un-skē′d′d′; 2 ŭn-seāthd′, *a.* Unharmed; uninjured.

un-scru′pu-lous, *a.* Having no scruples of conscience; unprincipled.

un-sea′son-a-bl(e)s, *a.* Not being in the proper season; inappropriate. **-bly**, *adv.*

un-seat′d, *vt.* To remove from a seat; unhorse; deprive of official position.

un-set′tle, *vt.* **1.** To move from a settled condition. **2.** To confuse; disturb.

un-sex′t, *vt.* To rob of the distinctive qualities of a sex; especially, to make unfeminine, as a woman.

un-ship′t, *vt.* **1.** To unload from a ship. **2.** To move out of place, as a rudder.

un-sight′ly, *a.* Offensive to sight; ugly.

un″so-phis′ti-cat″ed, 1 un″so-fis′ti-kēt″ed; 2 ŭn″so-fĭs′ti-eāt″ĕd, *a.* **1.** Genuine; pure. **2.** Artless; simple; inexperienced.

un-speak′a-bl(e)s, *a.* **1.** Inexpressible; unutterable. **2.** Extremely bad.

un-spot′ted, *a.* Not marked with spots; free from blemishes; immaculate.

un-sta′ble, *a.* Lacking firmness; easily liable to change; wavering; inconstant; fickle.

un-stud′ied, *a.* Unpremeditated; easy; natural.

un-think′ing, *a.* Not having or not exercising the power of thought; thoughtless; heedless.— **un-think′ing-ly**, *adv.*

un-ti′dy, *a.* Showing or characterized by lack of tidiness; not in good order; not neat.— **un-ti′di-ly**, *adv.*— **un-ti′di-ness**, *n.*

un-tie′, *vt.* To loosen, as a knot; hence, to free from any fastening.— **un-tied′**, *a.*

un-til′, 1 un-til′; 2 ŭn-tĭl′. **I.** *prep.* Unto the time of; up to; till. **II.** *conj.* To the time when; to the place or degree that.

un-time′ly, *a.* Coming before time or not in proper time; unseasonable.

un′to, 1 un′tū; 2 ŭn′tụ. *prep.* To: a formal, poetical, or archaic form.

un-told′, *a.* **1.** That can not be described. **2.** That can not be estimated.

un-to′ward, 1 ʊn-tō′ərd; 2 ŭn-tō′ard, *a.* Vexatious; unfavorable; perverse. **-ly,** *adv.*

un-true′, *a.* Lacking truth; not true; false.— **un-truth′,** *n.* **1.** The character of being untrue. **2.** A falsehood; lie.

un-u′su-al, *a.* Not usual; uncommon; rare; infrequent.— **un-u′su-al-ly,** *adv.*

un-ut′ter-a-bl(e^r, *a.* That can not be uttered; inexpressible; unspeakable.

un-veil′, *vt.* To remove the veil from; uncover; disclose; unfold.

un-war′rant-a-bl(e^r, *a.* That can not be warranted; unjustifiable; indefensible.

un-war′rant-ed, *a.* **1.** Unwarrantable. **2.** Being without warranty.

un-wa′ry, 1 ʊn-wē′ri; 2 ŭn-wā′ry, *a.* Not being on one's guard; incautious.

un-well′, *a.* Somewhat ill; indisposed.

un-whole′some, *a.* **1.** Injurious to health; deleterious; also, mentally or morally injurious; pernicious. **2.** Impaired in health; sickly.

un-wield′y, 1 ʊn-wild′ı; 2 ŭn-wēld′y, *a.* Moved with difficulty; bulky; clumsy.

un-will′ing, *a.* Not willing; reluctant. **-ly,** *adv.* **-ness,** *n.*

un-wise′, *a.* Lacking wisdom; injudicious; foolish. **-ly,** *adv.*

un-wit′ting, *a.* Having no knowledge of the thing in question. **-ly,** *adv.*

un-wont′ed, *a.* Not according to wont or custom; unusual. **-ly,** *adv.*

un-wor′thy, } *a.* Not worthy; not becoming; wrong.— **un-wor′thi-ly,** **un-wur′thy^r,** } *adv.*— **un-wor′thi-ness,** *n.*

up, 1 ʊp; 2 ŭp. **I.** *a.* Moving or sloping upward. **II.** *n.* That which is up: chiefly in the phrase **ups and downs. III.** *adv.* **1.** Toward a higher place or level. **2.** In or on a higher place. **3.** In or to an upright position; risen from bed. **4.** So as to be level (to) or even (with) in space, degree, etc. **5.** Aroused; astir. **6.** In or into prominence. **7.** At an end or close. **IV.** *prep.* **1.** From a lower to a higher point or place. **2.** At, on, or near a higher place or part of.— **up-heave′,** *v.* **I.** *t.* To heave up; raise or lift with effort. **II.** *i.* To be raised or lifted.— **up-heav′al,** *n.*— **up-held′,** *imp. & pp.* of UPHOLD, *v.*— **up′-hill′,** *a.* Going up a hill; extending upward; difficult; laborious. — **up-hold′,** *vt.* To hold up; support; encourage.— **up-lift′d,** *vt.* To lift up or raise aloft; elevate.— **up′lift,** *n.* A movement upward; upheaval; exaltation.

u′pas, 1 yū′pɑs; 2 yu̧′pas, *n.* A tall tree, of the island of Java, with an acrid, milky poisonous juice. See illustration in next column.

up-braid′d, 1 ʊp-brēd′; 2 ŭp-brād′, *vt. & vi.* To reproach; accuse.

up-hol′ster, 1 ʊp-hōl′stər; 2 ŭp-hōl′-ster, *vt.* **1.** To fit, as furniture, with coverings, cushioning, etc. **2.** To provide or adorn with hangings, curtains, etc., as an apartment.— **up-hol′ster-er,** *n.*— **up-hol′ster-y,** *n.* **1.** Goods used in upholstering. **2.** The act or business of upholstering.

up′land, 1 ʊp′lənd; 2 ŭp′land. **I.** *a.* Pertaining to an upland; elevated. **II.** *n.* The higher portions of a region, district, etc.

Upas-tree.
a, a spray of leaves.

up-on′, 1 ʊp-ɒn′; 2 ŭp-ŏn′, *adv. & prep.* On.

up′per, 1 ʊp′ər; 2 ŭp′er. **I.** *a.* Higher than something else. **II.** *n.* **1.** That part of a boot or shoe above the sole and welt. **2.** *pl.* Gaiter=tops for wearing above the shoe.— **up′per-most,** *a.* Highest in place, rank, etc.; first thought of.

up′pish, 1 ʊp′ish; 2 ŭp′ish, *a.* [Colloq.] Snobbish; pretentious.

up′right, 1 ʊp′rait; 2 ŭp′rīt. **I.** *a.* **1.** Vertical; erect. **2.** Just and honest. **II.** *n.* Something having a vertical position. **-ly,** *adv.* **-ness,** *n.*

up-ris′ing, 1 ʊp-raiz′iŋ; 2 ŭp-rīz′ing, *n.* The act of rising; revolt; insurrection.

up′roar, 1 ʊp′rōr; 2 ŭp′rōr, *n.* Violent disturbance and noise; tumult.— **up-roar′l-ous,** *a.* **-ly,** *adv.*

up-root′d, 1 ʊp-rūt′; 2 ŭp-rōōt′, *vt.* To tear up by the roots; eradicate; destroy utterly.

up-set′, 1 ʊp-set′; 2 ŭp-sĕt′, *vt.* **1.** To overturn. **2.** To discompose; confuse.

up′set, *a.* Set up; required; as, the *upset* price.

up′set, *n.* The act of upsetting, or state of being upset.

up′shot, 1 ʊp′shɒt; 2 ŭp′shŏt, *n.* The final outcome or result.

up′side, 1 ʊp′said; 2 ŭp′sīd, *n.* The upper side.

up′stairs″, 1 ʊp′stārz″; 2 ŭp′stârz̧. **I.** *a.* Pertaining to an upper story. **II.** *n.* The upper story or stories. **III.** *adv.* In or to an upper story; up the stairs.

up′start″, 1 up′stärt″; 2 ŭp′stärt″. **I.** *a.* Suddenly raised to wealth or prominence; pretentious. **II.** *n.* One who has risen suddenly to consequence.

up′ward, 1 up′wẽrd; 2 ŭp′ward, *a.* Turned or directed toward a higher place.

up′ward, } *adv.* **1.** Toward a higher
up′wards, } place or price. **2.** In excess; more. **3.** Toward that which is better or nobler.

u-ra′ni-um, 1 yu-rē′nı̆-um; 2 yu̇-rā′nı̆-ŭm, *n.* A heavy, hard, white, metallic element found in pitchblende. Compare RADIUM.

U′ra-nus, 1 yū′ra-nus; 2 yu̇′ra-nŭs, *n.* **1.** *Gr. Myth.* The son and husband of Ge (Earth) and father of the Titans and the Cyclops. **Ou′ra-nos̗. 2.** *Astron.* Except Neptune, the outermost planet of the solar system.

ur′ban, 1 ûr′ban; 2 ûr′ban, *a.* Pertaining to or like a city; situated or dwelling in a city.

ur-bane′, 1 ûr-bēn′; 2 ûr-bān′, *a.* Civil; refined; polite; suave.— **ur-ban′i-ty,** *n.*

ur′chin, 1 ûr′chin; 2 ûr′chin, *n.* **1.** A mischievous boy. **2.** A hedgehog. **3.** A sea-urchin.

urge, 1 ûrj; 2 ûrg, *vt.* [URGED; URG′ING.] To press earnestly; drive; impel; hasten; hurry.— **ur′gen-cy,** *n.*— **ur′gent,** *a.* Pressing; imperative; importunate. **-ly,** *adv.*

u′rine, 1 yū′rın; 2 yu̇′rin, *n.* The fluid secreted from the blood by the kidneys. — **u′ri-na-ry,** *a.* [foot.

urn, 1 ûrn; 2 ûrn, *n.* A vase having a

ur′sa, 1 ur′sa; 2 ûr′sa, *n.* [L.] A she bear. — **Ursa Major,** the Great Bear: a large, northern constellation containing seven conspicuous stars, popularly called the Dipper, the line joining two of these stars indicating the position of the pole-star or north star. See POINTERS.— **U. Minor,** the Little Bear: a northern constellation including the pole-star.

ur′sine, 1 ûr′sın *or* -saın; 2 ûr′sin *or* -sīn, *a.* **1.** Pertaining to or like a bear. **2.** Densely bristled, as certain caterpillars.

us, 1 us; 2 ŭs, *pron.* The objective case plural of the personal pronoun of the first person.

use, } 1 yūz; 2 yu̇s, *v.* [USED; US′ING.] **I.**
uze᙭, } *t.* To make use of; put into practise; treat; accustom. **II.** *i.* To be accustomed.— **us′a-ble,** 1 yūz′a-bl; 2 yu̇s′a-bl, *a.* Such as can be used.— **us′age,** 1 yūz′ıj; 2 yu̇s′ag, *n.* **1.** The manner of using or treating a person or thing. **2.** A custom.

use, 1 yūs; 2 yu̇s, *n.* **1.** The act of using; application to an end. **2.** Serviceableness. **3.** Necessity. **4.** Custom.— **use′ful,** *a.* Serving a use or purpose; beneficial. **-ly,**

adv. **-ness,** *n.*— **use′less,** *a.* Being of no use. **-ly,** *adv.* **-ness,** *n.*

ush′er, 1 ush′ẽr; 2 ŭsh′er. **I.** *vt.* To attend as an usher; introduce. **II.** *n.* **1.** One who acts as doorkeeper, conducts persons to seats, etc. **2.** An under teacher.

u′su-al, } 1 yū′ʒu-al; 2 yu̇′zhu̇-al, *a.* Or-
u′zu-al᙭, } dinary; frequent; common.— **u′su-al-ly,** *adv.*

u′su-fruct, 1 yū′ʒu-frukt; 2 yu̇′zhu̇-frŭet, *n.* The right of enjoying things belonging to another and of drawing from them all profit they produce without wasting their substance.

u-surp′᙭, 1 yu-zûrp′; 2 yu̇-sûrp′, *vt.* To seize and hold without right; assume arrogantly.— **u″sur-pa′tion,** *n.*— **u-surp′er,** *n.*

u′su-ry, 1 yū′ʒu-rı; 2 yu̇′zhu̇-ry, *n.* [-RIES᙮, *pl.*] Illegal interest; originally, interest in general.— **u′su-rer,** *n.*— **u-su′ri-ous,** 1 yu-ʒū′rı-us; 2 yu̇-zhu̇′ri-ŭs, *a.* Of the nature of usury.

u-ten′sil, 1 yu-ten′sıl; 2 yu̇-tĕn′sil, *n.* An implement or vessel, as for domestic or farming use.

u′ter-us, 1 yū′tẽr-us; 2 yu̇′ter-ŭs, *n.* [-RI, 1 -raı; 2 -rī, *pl.*] The organ of a female mammal in which the young are developed before birth; the womb.— **u′ter-in(e᙮, *a.* **1.** Pertaining to the uterus. **2.** Born of the same mother, but having a different father; as, a *uterine* brother.

u-til′i-ty, 1 yu-til′ı-tı; 2 yu̇-tīl′i-ty, *n.* [-TIES᙮, *pl.*] Fitness for some practical use; serviceableness; usefulness.— **u-til′i-ta′ri-an,** *a.* Relating to mere utility. **-ism,** *n.*— **u′til-ize,** *vt.* [-IZED; -IZ′ING.] To make useful.— **u″til-i-za′[or -sa′]tion,** *n.*

ut′most, 1 ut′mōst; 2 ŭt′mōst. **I.** *a.* **1.** Of the highest degree or the largest amount. **2.** Most remote; last. **II.** *n.* The greatest possible extent; farthest boundary.

U-to′pi-a, 1 yu-tō′pı-a; 2 yu̇-tō′pi-a. *n.* An imaginary island, the seat of an ideally perfect life; any state of ideal perfection. — **U-to′pi-an,** *a.* Pertaining to or like Utopia; ideal.

ut′ter, 1 ut′ẽr; 2 ŭt′er, *vt.* To speak; say publicly; put in circulation; publish.

ut′ter, *a.* Absolute; total; unqualified. — **ut′ter-a-ble(᙮, *a.*— **ut′ter-er,** *n.*— **ut′ter-ly,** *adv.*— **ut′ter-most,** *a. & n.* Same as UTMOST.

ut′ter-ance, 1 ut′ẽr-ans; 2 ŭt′er-anç, *n.* **1.** The act of uttering. **2.** A thing uttered; a word; expression; statement.

ux-o′ri-ous, 1 uks-ō′rı-us; 2 uks-ō′ri-ŭs, *a.* Extravagantly devoted to one's wife. **-ly,** *adv.* **-ness,** *n.*

1: **a**rtistic, **ä**rt; f**a**t, f**ā**re; f**a**st; get, pr**ē**y; h**i**t, pol**ī**ce; obey, g**ō**; n**o**t, **ô**r; f**u**ll, r**ū**le; b**u**t, b**û**rn.
2: **ä**rt, **ā**pe, f**ă**t, f**â**re, f**å**st, wh**a**t, **a**ll; m**ē**, g**ĕ**t, pr**ey**, f**ẽ**rn; h**ĭ**t, **ī**ce; **ī**=**ē**; **ĭ**=**ē**; g**ō**, n**ŏ**t, **ô**r, w**o**n,

V

V, v, 1 vī; 2 vē, *n.* [VEES, V's, or *V*s, 1 vīz; 2 vēs, *pl.*] The twenty-second letter in the English alphabet.

va'cant, 1 vē'kənt; 2 vā'eant, *a.* **1.** Containing nothing; empty. **2.** Not occupied; void of thought or expression.— **va'cancy,** *n.* [-CIES², *pl.*] Emptiness; empty space; a gap.— **va'cant-ly,** *adv.*

va'cate, 1 vē'kēt; 2 vā'eāt, *vt. & vi.* [VA-CAT-EDᵈ; VA'CAT-ING.] To make vacant; set aside; annul; quit; leave.— **va-ca'tion,** *n.* An intermission; period of recreation.

vac'cin(e⁵, 1 vak'sɪn; 2 văe'çin. **I.** *a.* Pertaining to cows or to cowpox. **II.** *n.* The virus of cowpox, for vaccination.— **vac'ci-nate,** *vt.* [-NAT'EDᵈ; -NAT'ING.] To subject to vaccination.— **vac'e'i-na'tion,** *n.* Inoculation with cowpox as a preventive of smallpox.

vac'il-late, 1 vas'ɪ-lēt; 2 văç'ĭ-lăt, *vi.* [-LAT-EDᵈ; -LAT'ING.] To fluctuate in mind; be irresolute; waver.— **vac'il-la'tion,** *n.*

va-cu'i-ty, 1 va-kiū'ɪ-tɪ; 2 va-eu'i-ty, *n.* [-TIES², *pl.*] Emptiness; a void; vacuum.

vac'u-ous, 1 vak'yu-us; 2 văe'yu-ŭs, *a.* Vacant.

vac'u-um, 1 vak'yu-um; 2 văe'yu-ŭᵐ, *n.* [-UMS² or -U-A, *pl.*] Vacant or empty space; a space or vessel from which the air has been exhausted.

va'de-me'cum, 1 vē'dɪ-mī'kum; 2 vā'dē-mē'eum, *n.* Anything that is carried on the person for constant use, as a manual: a Latin phrase, meaning "go with me."

vag'a-bond, 1 vag'a-bɔnd; 2 văg'a-bŏnd. **I.** *a.* Wandering; homeless; vagrant. **II.** *n.* A tramp; vagrant.— **vag'a-bond-age,** *n.*

va-ga'ry, 1 va-gē'rɪ; 2 va-gā'ry, *n.* [-RIES², *pl.*] A wild fancy; whim.

va'grant, 1 vē'grant; 2 vā'grant. **I.** *a.* Wandering about as a vagrant. **II.** *n.* An idle wanderer; vagabond.— **va'gran-cy,** *n.*

vague, 1 vēg; 2 văg, *a.* Indefinite; indistinct; ambiguous. **-ly,** *adv.* **-ness,** *n.*

vain, 1 vēn; 2 văn, *a.* **1.** Conceited; ostentatious; showy. **2.** Empty; unreal; ineffectual; fruitless. **-ly,** *adv.* **-ness,** *n.*— **vain-glo'ry,** *n.* Unfounded pride; vain pomp.— **vain-glo'ri-ous,** *a.* **-ly,** *adv.*

vale, 1 vēl; 2 văl, *n.* A valley.

val'e-dic'tion, 1 val'ɪ-dik'shən; 2 văl'ē-dĭe'shon, *n.* A bidding farewell.

val'e-dic'to-ry, 1 val'ɪ-dik'to-rɪ; 2 văl'ē-dĭe'to-ry. **I.** *a.* Farewell. **II.** *n.* [-RIES², *pl.*] A parting address; address first in honor at graduation.— **val'e-dic-to'ri-an,** *n.* One who delivers a valedictory.

va'lence, 1 vē'lens; 2 vā'lĕnç, *n.* *Chem.* The combining power of elements or radicals. **va'len-cy‡.**

val'en-tine, 1 val'ən-tain; 2 văl'en-tīn, *n.* **1.** A letter or token sent on St. Valentine's day (Feb. 14). **2.** A sweetheart.

val'et, 1 val'et; 2 văl'ĕt, *n.* A gentleman's body-servant.

val"e-tu'di-na'ri-an, 1 val'ɪ-tiū'dɪ-nē'rɪ-ən; 2 văl'ē-tū'dĭ-nā'ri-an. **I.** *a.* Seeking to recover health; infirm. **II.** *n.* A chronic invalid. **val"e-tu'di-na-ry‡.— val"e-tu'di-na'ri-an-ism,** *n.*

Val-hal'la, 1 val-hal'a; 2 văl-hăl'a, *n.* **1.** *Norse Myth.* The hall of the slain; the palace of immortality. **2.** A building for preserving the remains or memorials of deceased national heroes. **Wal-hal'la‡.**

val'iant, 1 val'yənt; 2 văl'yant, *a.* **1.** Strong and brave. **2.** Heroic. **-ly,** *adv.* **-ness,** *n.*

val'id, 1 val'ɪd; 2 văl'id, *a.* Based on sound evidence; sound; just.— **va-lid'i-ty,** *n.*— **val'id-ly,** *adv.*

va-lise', 1 va-līs'; 2 va-līs', *n.* A traveling-bag.

val'kyr, 1 val'kir; 2 văl'kÿr, *n.* *Norse Myth.* One of the maidens that serve in the banquets of Valhalla. **val-kyr'i-a‡; val-kyr'ie‡; wal'kyr‡.** [between hills.

val'ley, 1 val'ɪ; 2 văl'y, *n.* A depression between hills.

val'or, 1 val'ər; 2 văl'or, *n.* Intrepid courage; personal bravery. **val'our‡.— val'or-ous,** *a.* Courageous; valiant. **-ly,** *adv.*

val'ue, 1 val'yū; 2 văl'yu. **I.** *vt.* [VAL'UED; VAL'U-ING.] To estimate; appraise; esteem; prize. **II.** *n.* **1.** Intrinsic worth; utility. **2.** The market price. **3.** Esteem; regard.— **val'u-a-bl(e⁵,** 1 val'yu-a-bl; 2 văl'yu-a-bl. **I.** *a.* Costly; worthy. **II.** *n.* A thing of value.— **val'u-a'tion,** 1 val'yu-ē'shən; 2 văl'yu-ā'shon, *n.* The act of valuing or the value estimated.— **val'u-a'tor,** 1 val'yu-ē'tər or -ter; 2 văl'yu-ā'tor, *n.* An appraiser.— **val'ue-less,** *a.* Worthless.

valv(e⁵, 1 valv; 2 vălv, *n.* **1.** An arrangement that permits the flow of a fluid in one direction, and closes against its return. **2.** One of a pair of folding doors. — **valved,** *a.*— **val'vu-lar,** *a.*

vamp, 1 vamp; 2 vămp. **Iᵗ.** *vt.* To provide with a vamp; hence, to furbish up; modernize; repair. **II.** *n.* The upper front part of a boot or shoe.— **to vamp up,** to make up, as from odds and ends, or from nothing; concoct; improvise.

vam'pire, 1 vam'paɪr; 2 văm'pīr, *n.* **1.** A ghostly being fabled to suck the blood of

---

1: ə = final; I = habit; aisle; au = out; oil; iū = feud; chin; go; ŋ = sing; thin, **this.**
2: wolf, do; book, boot; full, rule, cure, but, burn; oil, boy; go, gem; ink; thin, **this.**

the living during sleep. **2.** A blood=suck= ing bat. **3.** A coquet; flirt.

van¹, 1 van; 2 văn, *n.* A large covered wagon, as for removing furniture.

van², *n.* A vanguard; the front; advance.

Van'dal, 1 van'dal; 2 văn'dal, *n.* **1.** One of a race that in the fifth century ravaged Gaul and pillaged Rome. **2.** [v=] Any ruthless plunderer or destroyer.— **van'dal, van=dal'= ic,** *a.*— **van'dal=ism,** 1 van'del=izm; 2 văn'= dal=iṣm, *n.* Wanton and wilful destruction.

vane, 1 vēn; 2 văn. *n.* **1.** A thin plate, pivoted out of center, on a vertical rod, so as to turn its shorter end toward the point from which the wind blows. **2.** An arm or blade, as of a windmill, propeller, etc. **3.** The shaft and barbs of a feather.

van'guard", 1 van'gärd"; 2 văn'ġärd", *n.* The advance= guard of an army; the van.

Vane.

va=nil'la, 1 va=nil'a; 2 va=nĭl'la, *n.* A tall=climbing orchid or its fruit, known as the **vanilla=bean;** also, a fla= voring extract prepared from it.

van'ish⁺, 1 van'ish; 2 văn'ish, *vt.* To disappear; fade away; depart.

a

van'i=ty, 1 van'i=ti; 2 văn'i=ty, *n.* [-TIES²*, pl.*] The condition of being vain; some= thing vain; conceit; ostentation; show.

van'quish⁺, 1 vaŋ'= kwish; 2 văŋ'kwish, *vt.* To subdue, as in battle; conquer; confute. **-er,** *n.*

van'tage, 1 van'tij; 2 văn'taġ, *n.* Superiority over a com= petitor; advantage.

vap'id, 1 vap'id; 2 văp'id, *a.* Having lost sparkling quality and flavor; flat; dull; insipid. **-ly,** *adv.*— **va=pid'i=ty,** *n.*

A Flowering Branch of Vanilla. *a,* a pod.

va'por, 1 vē'pər; 2 vā'pŏr, *n.* **1.** Floating moisture in the air; the gaseous form of any substance. **2.** Something fleeting and unsubstantial.— **va'pour⁺;— va'por=ize,** *vt. & vi.* [-IZED, -IZ'= ING.] To convert or be converted into vapor. — **va'por=i=za'tion,** *n.*— **va'por=ous,** *a.*— **va'po=ry,** *a.*

va=que'ro, 1 va=kē'ro; 2 vä=ḳe'ro, *n.* In Spanish=speaking countries, a herdsman or cowboy.

va'ri=a=bl(e⁺, 1 vē'ri=a=bl; 2 vā'ri=a=bl. **I.** *a.* Varying; changeable. **II.** *n.* That which varies or is liable to change.— **va'ri=a= bil'i=ty,** *n.*— **va'ri=a=bl(e=ness⁺,** *n.*— **va'ri= a=bly,** *adv.*

va'ri=ant, 1 vē'ri=ənt; 2 vā'ri=ant. **I.** *a.* Varying; variable; fickle. **II.** *n.* A vari= ant form of the same thing; in this Dic= tionary, a word or phrase of the same meaning but of different form: denoted by ‡.— **va'ri=ance,** *n.* The act of varying; dissension; discord.— **va'ri=a'tion,** 1 vē'rī= ē'shən; 2 vā'ri=ā'shon, *n.* The act or state of varying; modification; diversity.

va'ried, 1 vē'rid; 2 vā'rid, *pa.* **1.** Partially or repeatedly altered. **2.** Consisting of diverse sorts. **3.** Differing from one another. **-ly,** *adv.*

va'ri=e=gate, 1 vē'ri=1=gēt; 2 vā'ri=e=ġāt, *vt.* [-GAT'ED⁴; -GAT'ING.] To diversify with different colors; spot; streak.— **va'ri=e=ga'= tion,** *n.*

va=ri'e=ty, 1 va=rai'i=ti; 2 va=rī'e=ty, *n.* [-TIES², *pl.*] **1.** The state of being varied; diversity. **2.** A collection of diverse things; a subdivision of a species.

va'ri=o=coup"ler, *n. Radio.* A tuning coil in which the secondary winding rotates within the primary winding.

va'ri=o=loid, 1 vē'ri=[or var'i=]o=loid; 2 vā'ri= [or vär'i=]o=löid. **I.** *a.* Resembling small= pox. **II.** *n.* A mild form of smallpox, espe= cially as modified by previous vaccination.

va'ri=ous, 1 vē'ri=us; 2 vā'ri=ŭs, *a.* **1.** Different from one another; diverse. **2.** Several. **-ly,** *adv.*

var'let, 1 vär'let; 2 vär'lĕt, *n.* A low menial; formerly, a page.

var'nish, 1 vär'nish; 2 vär'nish. **I⁺.** *vt.* To cover, as with varnish; polish; gloss over. **II.** *n.* A solution of certain gums or resins: used to produce a shining coat on a surface; superficial polish.

va'ry, 1 vē'ri; 2 vā'ry, *vt. & vi.* [VA'RIED; VA'RY=ING.] **1.** To make different; diver= sify; differ. **2.** To deviate to one side; depart.

vas'cu=lar, 1 vas'ḳiu=lər; 2 văs'cū=lar, *a.* Per= taining to, consisting of, or containing vessels or ducts.— **vas'cu=lar'i=ty,** *n.*

vase, 1 vēs *or* vāz; 2 vāṣ *or* väṣ, *n.* An urn= like vessel.

vas'sal, 1 vas'əl; 2 văs'al, *n.* A feudal re= tainer; bondman; servant.— **vas'sal=age,** *n.*

vast, 1 vast; 2 vást, *a.* Of great extent or degree; immense; numerous. **-ly,** *adv.*— **-ness,** *n.* [liquids.

vat, 1 vat; 2 văt, *n.* A large vessel for liquids.

Vat'i=can, 1 vat'i=kən; 2 văt'i=can, *n.* **1.** The palace of the popes in Rome: a vast as= semblage of buildings rich in art=treasures. **2.** The papal government.

vaude′ville, 1 vōd′vil; 2 vōd′vĭl, *n.* A miscellaneous theatrical entertainment.

vault[1], 1 vŏlt; 2 vạlt. **I**[d]. *vt.* To form with an arched roof. **II.** *n.* An arched apartment or chamber; subterranean compartment; arched ceiling or roof.

vault[2]. **I**[d]. *vt. & vi.* To leap, as with the aid of the hands. **II.** *n.* A springing leap, as one made with the aid of the hands.

vaunt, 1 vänt *or* vŏnt; 2 vänt *or* vạnt. **I**[d]. *vt. & vi.* To boast; exult; glory. **II.** *n.* Boastful assertion or ostentation.

veal, 1 vēl; 2 vēl, *n.* The flesh of a calf as food.

Ve′das, 1 vē′dạz *or* vī′dạz; 2 vē′dạs *or* vĕ̄′dạs, *n. pl.* The four Hindu holy books.

ve-dette′, 1 vɪ-det′; 2 ve-dĕt′, *n.* A mounted sentinel. **vi-dette′‡.** [wind] vary.

veer, 1 vīr; 2 vēr, *vt. & vi.* To shift, as the

veg′e-ta-bl(e[r], 1 vej′ɪ-ta-bl; 2 vĕg′e-ta-bl. **I.** *a.* **1.** Pertaining to, of the nature of, or resembling plants. **2.** Pertaining to garden vegetables. **II.** *n.* **1.** The edible part of a garden plant. **2.** Any plant.

veg′e-tal, 1 vej′ɪ-tạl; 2 vĕg′e-tạl, *a.* **1.** Pertaining to plants. **2.** Common to plants and animals, as growth, nutrition, etc.

veg″e-ta′ri-an-ism, 1 vej″ɪ-tē′rɪ-an-izm; 2 vĕg″e-tä′ri-an-iṣm, *n.* The theory that man's food should be exclusively vegetable. **— veg″e-ta′ri-an,** *a. & n.*

veg′e-tate, 1 vej′ɪ-tēt; 2 vĕg′e-tāt, *vi.* [-TAT**′**ED[d] ; -TAT**′**ING.] To grow, as a plant; live in a monotonous, passive way.**— veg″e-ta′tion,** *n.* **1.** The process of vegetating. **2.** Plants collectively.**— veg′e-ta′tiv(e[s], *a.* Pertaining to or producing plant-life.

ve′he-ment, 1 vī′he-ment; 2 vē′he-mĕnt, *a.* Impetuous; ardent; energetic; violent; furious. **-ly,** *adv.***— ve′he-mence, n.**

ve′hi-cl(e[r], 1 vī′ɪ-kl; 2 vē′ɪ-cl, *n.* A conveyance, as a carriage, wagon, car, or sled. **— ve-hic′u-lar,** *a.*

veil, 1 vēl; 2 vēl. **I.** *vt.* To cover with a veil; hide; disguise. **II.** *n.* A piece of thin fabric, worn over the face; a screen; also, a disguise. **vail‡.**

vein, 1 vēn; 2 vēn. **I.** *vt.* To furnish, traverse, or fill with veins. **II.** *n.* **1.** One of the vessels that convey blood to the heart; loosely, any blood-vessel. **2.** A rib, as of an insect's wing, or of a leaf. **3.** A seam of ore. **4.** A colored streak, as in wood. **5.** A trait; humor; mood.

veld, 1 velt; 2 vĕlt, *n.* [S Afr.] The open country or any land that can be used as pasturage. Low-lying wooded land is known as **bush-veld,** and the high treeless plains as **high veld. veldt‡.**

vel′ium, 1 vel′um; 2 vĕl′ŭm, *n.* Fine

parchment, or a manuscript written on it.

ve-loc′i-pede, 1 vɪ-los′ɪ-pīd; 2 ve-lŏc′ɪ-pēd, *n.* An early form of bicycle; a child's tricycle.

ve-loc′i-ty, 1 ve-los′-ɪ-tɪ; 2 ve-lŏc′ɪ-ty, *n.* [-TIES[z], *pl.*] **1.** Swiftness; speed. **2.** Rate of motion.

ve′lo-drome, 1 vī′lo-drōm; 2 vē′lo-drōm. *n.* A place where motor-car or bicycle races are held.

Velocipede of 1817.

vel′vet, 1 vel′vet; 2 vĕl′vĕt. **I.** *a.* Made of velvet; smooth; velvety. **II.** *n.* A fabric of silk closely woven with thick, short, smooth nap on one side.**— vel′vet-een′,** *n.* A fabric imitating silk velvet.**— vel′vet-y,** *a.*

ve′nal, 1 vī′nạl; 2 ve′nạl, *a.* Ready to sell honor or principle; mercenary. **-ly,** *adv.***— ve-nal′i-ty,** *n.*

ve-na′tion, *n.* Arrangement of veins.

vend[d], 1 vend; 2 vĕnd, *vt.* To dispose of; sell; carry about for sale.**— vend′er,** *n.* One who vends; a pedler. **ven′do̤r‡.— vend′i-bl**(e[r]. **I.** *a.* Marketable. **II.** *n.* A thing exposed for sale.**— vend′i-bl(e-ness[r],** *n.***— vend′i-bly,** *adv.***— ven-due′,** *n.* A public sale at auction. [Private warfare or feud.

ven-det′ta, 1 ven-det′ə; 2 vĕn-dĕt′a, *n.*

ve-neer′, 1 vɪ-nīr′; 2 ve-nēr′. **I.** *vt.* To cover, as with veneer. **II.** *n.* A thin layer as of choice wood, upon a commoner surface; mere outside show.**— ve-neer′ing,** *n.*

ven′er-a-bl(e[r], 1 ven′ər-a-bl; 2 vĕn′er-a-bl, *a.* Meriting or commanding veneration. **— ven′er-a-bl(e-ness[r],** *n.***— ven′er-a-bly,** *adv.***— ven′er-ate,** *vt.* [-AT**′**ED[d]; -AT**′**ING.] To look upon or regard with honor and reverence; revere.**— ven″er-a′tion,** *n.* Profound reverence.

Ve-ne′tian, 1 vɪ-nī′shan; 2 ve-nē′shan. **I.** *a.* Pertaining to Venice, or to its typical style of architecture. **II.** *n.* A native of Venice or Venetia.

ven′geance, 1 ven′jans; 2 vĕn′ganç, *n.* The infliction of punishment; retribution; revenge.**— venge′ful,** *a.* Vindictive. **-ly,** *adv.* **-ness,** *n.*

ve′ni-al, 1 vī′nɪ-əl; 2 ve′ni-al, *a.* That may be pardoned; excusable.**— ve″ni-al′i-ty,** *n.* **ve′ni-al-ness‡.— ve′ni-al-ly,** *adv.*

ven′i-son, 1 ven′ɪ-zən; 2 vĕn′ɪ-ṣon, *n.* The flesh of deer.

ven′om, 1 ven′əm; 2 vĕn′om, *n.* **1.** The poison of serpents, scorpions, or the like. **2.** Malignity; spite.**— ven′om-ous,** *a.***— ven′om-ous-ly,** *adv.*

ve′nous, 1 vī′nʊs; 2 vē′nŏs, *a.* **1.** Pertaining to the veins. **2.** Marked with or having veins.

vent, 1 vent; 2 vĕnt. **I**ᵈ. *vt.* To let out; emit; pour forth; utter. **II.** *n.* **1.** An opening, as for gas or steam; outlet. **2.** Utterance.

ven'ti-late, 1 ven'tı-lēt; 2 vĕn'tı-lāt, *vt.* [-LAT″EDᵈ; -LAT″ING.] To admit fresh air into; purify; make public.— **ven″ti-la'-tion,** *n.*— **ven'ti-la″tor,** *n.* An opening for supplying fresh air.

ven'tral, 1 ven'trəl; 2 vĕn'tral, *a.* Pertaining to or situated on the abdomen.

ven'tri-cl(eʳ**,** 1 ven'trı-kl; 2 vĕn'tri-el, *n.* A cavity, as of the brain or heart.— **ven-tric'u-lar,** *a.*

ven-tril'o-quism, 1 ven-tril'o-kwizm; 2 vĕn-tril'o-kwĭṣm, *n.* The act of speaking so that the sounds seem to come from some source other than the speaker. **ven-tril'o-quy‡.**— **ven-tril'o-quist,** *n.*— **ven-tril'o-quize,** *vt.*

ven'ture, 1 ven'chur *or* -tiur; 2 vĕn'chur *or* -tūr. **I.** *vt. & vi.* [VEN'TURED; VEN'-TUR-ING.] To hazard; risk; dare. **II.** *n.* **1.** A hazard; risk; speculation. **2.** Property risked.— **ven'ture-some,** *a.* **1.** Bold; daring. **2.** Risky.— **ven'tur-ous,** *a.* Adventurous. **-ly,** *adv.* **-ness,** *n.*

ven'ue, 1 ven'yū; 2 vĕn'yu, *n.* The place where a crime is committed or a trial held.

Ve'nus, 1 vī'nus; 2 vē'nŭs, *n.* **1.** *Myth.* The Roman goddess of love, identified with the Greek Aphrodite. **2.** The second planet from the sun.

ve-ra'cious, 1 vı-rē'shus; 2 ve-rā'shŭs, *a.* Truthful; true. **-ly,** *adv.*— **ve-rac'i-ty,** *n.* Habitual regard for truth; truthfulness; truth.

ve-ran'da, 1 vı-ran'də; 2 ve-rǎn'da, *n.* An open portico. **ve-ran'dah‡.**

verb, 1 vûrb; 2 vĕrb, *n.* That part of speech which asserts, declares, or predicates something.— **ver'bal,** *a.* **1.** Pertaining to words rather than ideas; literal. **2.** Spoken; not written; oral. **3.** Pertaining to or derived from a verb.— **ver'bal-ism,** *n.* An expression in words; also, a meaningless form of words.— **ver'bal-ist,** *n.* A critic of words.— **ver'bal-ly,** *adv.*— **ver-ba'tim,** *adv.* In the exact words; word for word.— **ver'bi-age,** *n.* Use of unnecessary words. **ver-bos'i-ty‡.**— **ver-bose',** *a.* Wordy; prolix. **-ness,** *n.*

ver-be'na, 1 vər-bī'nə; 2 ver-bē'na, *n.* An American plant having dense terminal spikes of showy flowers.

ver'dant, 1 vûr'dənt; 2 vĕr'dant, *a.* Green with vegetation; fresh; unsophisticated. **-ly,** *adv.*— **ver'dan-cy,** *n.*

ver'dict, 1 vûr'dikt; 2 vĕr'dĭct, *n.* The decision of a jury; any decision or conclusion.

ver'di-gris, 1 vûr'dı-grīs; 2 vĕr'di-grĭs, *n.* The green rust of copper.

ver'dure, 1 vûr'jur *or* -diur; 2 vĕr'jur *or* -dūr, *n.* Fresh green vegetation, or its bright hue.

verge, 1 vûrj; 2 vĕrg, *vi.* To approach; border; followed by *on* or *upon.*

verge, *n.* **1.** The extreme edge; margin. **2.** A rod or staff.— **ver'ger,** *n.* An usher in charge of a church.

Ver-gil'i-an, 1 vûr-jil'ı-ən; 2 vĕr-gĭl'i-an, *a.* Of or pertaining to the Roman poet Vergil (70–19 B. C.), author of the Æneid. **Vir-gil'i-an‡.**

ver'i-fy, 1 ver'ı-fai; 2 vĕr'i-fy, *vt.* [-FIED; -FY′ING.] To prove to be true; confirm; authenticate.— **ver'i-fi″a-bl(e**ʳ**,** *a.*— **ver″i-fi-ca'tion,** *n.*— **ver'i-fi″er,** *n.*

ver'i-ly, 1 ver'ı-lı; 2 vĕr'i-ly, *adv.* In truth; beyond all doubt; assuredly; really.

ver″i-si-mil'i-tude, 1 ver″ı-sı-mil'ı-tiūd; 2 vĕr″i-si-mĭl'i-tūd, *n.* Appearance of truth or reality.— **ver″i-sim'i-lar,** *a.* Seeming to be true; likely.

ver'i-ty, 1 ver'ı-tı; 2 vĕr'i-ty, *n.* [-TIES², *pl.*] The quality of being correct or true; a truth.— **ver'i-ta-bl(e**ʳ**,** *a.* Genuine; true; real.— **ver'i-ta-bly,** *adv.*

ver'juice, 1 vûr'jūs; 2 vĕr'jŭç, *n.* The sour juice of green fruit; sourness; acidity.

ver'mi-, 1 vûr'mı-; 2 vĕr'mi-. A combining form.— **ver-mic'u-lar,** *a.* **1.** Pertaining to a worm; having the form or motion of a worm. **2.** Resembling the tracks of worms, as a style of tracery in stone.— **ver-mic'u-late,** *vt. & a.*— **ver-mic″u-la'tion,** *n.*— **ver'mi-form,** *a.* Having the form of a worm; long, thin, and flexible; as, the *vermiform* appendix. See APPENDIX.— **ver'mi-fuge,** 1 vûr'mı-fiūj; 2 vĕr'mi-fūg, *n.* Any remedy that destroys intestinal worms.— **ver-miv'o-rous,** *a.* Eating worms or grubs, as some birds, etc.

ver″mi-cel'li, 1 vûr″mı-sel'ı *or* ver″mı-chel'lī; 2 vĕr″mi-cĕl'i *or* vĕr″mī-chĕl'lī, *n.* A paste made into slender pipes.

ver-mil'ion, 1 vər-mil'yən; 2 ver-mĭl'yon, *n.* A brilliant durable red.

ver'min, 1 vûr'mın; 2 vĕr'min, *n. sing. & pl.* A troublesome small animal, as a rat, mouse, roach, etc., or such animals collectively.

ver-nac'u-lar, 1 vər-nak'yu-lər; 2 ver-nǎc'yu-lar. **I.** *a.* Pertaining to one's native land; indigenous. **II.** *n.* One's mother-tongue. **-ly,** *adv.*

ver'nal, 1 vûr'nəl; 2 vĕr'nal, *a.* Belonging to spring; also, pertaining to youth.

ver'sa-til(eˢ**,** 1 vûr'sə-til; 2 vĕr'sa-tĭl, *a.* **1.** Having an aptitude for new occupations. **2.** Inconstant.— **ver″sa-til'i-ty,** *n.*

verse, 1 vûrs; 2 vĕrs, *n.* **1.** A line of poetry; loosely, a stanza. **2.** Poetry.

1: **a**rtistic, **a**rt; f**a**t, f**a**re; f**a**st; get, pr**e**y; h**i**t, pol**i**ce; **o**bey, g**o**; n**o**t,**o**r; f**u**ll, r**u**le; b**u**t, b**u**rn.
2: **a**rt, **a**pe, **a**t, f**a**re, f**a**st, wh**a**t, **a**ll; m**e**, g**e**t, pr**e**y, f**e**rn; h**i**t, **i**ce; **i**=**e**; **i**=**e**; g**o**, n**o**t, **o**r, w**o**n,

3. A short division of a chapter in the Bible.— **ver'si-fy,** *vt. & vi.* [-FIED; -FY-ING.] To put into or tell in verse; write verses.— **ver"si-fi-ca'tion,** *n.*— **ver'si-fi"er,** *n.*

versed, ⟨1 vŭrst; 2 vĕrst, *a.* Thoroughly **verst**ˢ, ⟩ acquainted with a subject or art; proficient.

ver'sion, 1 vūr'shan; 2 vĕr'shon, *n.* A translation; description; statement.

ver'sus, 1 vūr'sus; 2 vĕr'sŭs, *prep.* Against.

ver'te-bra, 1 vūr'tɪ-bra; 2 vĕr'te-bra, *n.* [-BRÆ, 1 -brī; 2 -brē, *pl.*] One of the small bones that form the spinal column or back-bone.— **ver'te-bral,** *a.* **1.** Pertaining to a vertebra. **2.** Vertebrate.— **ver'te-brate. I.** *a.* Having a back-bone. **II.** *n.* An animal with a back-bone.

ver'tex, 1 vūr'teks; 2 vĕr'tĕks, *n.* [VER'-TEX-ES, 1 -ɪz, 2 -ez; VER'TI-CES, 1 -tɪ-sīz; 2 -tɪ-çĕs, *pl.*] The highest point of anything; apex; top.— **ver'ti-cal,** *a.* **1.** Being at the highest point, or directly overhead. **2.** Perpendicular; upright. **-ly,** *adv.* **-ness,** *n.*

ver'ti-go, 1 vūr'tɪ-go; 2 vĕr'tɪ-go, *n.* Dizziness.

verve, 1 vūrv; 2 vĕrv, *n.* Artistic spirit and enthusiasm; poetic rapture.

ver'y, 1 ver'ɪ; 2 vĕr'y. **I.** *a.* [VER'I-ER; VER'I-EST.] Real; actual; true; same. **II.** *adv.* In a high degree; extremely.

ves'i-cl(e)ᵃ, 1 ves'ɪ-kl; 2 vĕs'ɪ-cl, *n.* Any small bladder-like cavity, cell, etc.— **ve-sic'u-lar,** *a.*— **ve-sic'u-lose,** *a.*

ves'per, 1 ves'par; 2 vĕs'per. **I.** *a.* Pertaining to the evening or to the service of vespers. **II.** *n.* **1.** *pl.* Evening worship. **2.** [V-] Venus when an evening star.

ves'sel, 1 ves'el; 2 vĕs'el, *n.* **1.** A hollow receptacle. **2.** A ship or other craft for navigation. **3.** *Anat. & Zool.* A duct for fluid.

vestᵈ, 1 vest; 2 vĕst, *v.* **I.** *t.* **1.** To endow as with authority; invest. **2.** To confer ownership of. **II.** *i.* **1.** To put on vestments. **2.** To take effect, as a title.— **vest'ed,** *pa.* **1.** Having vestments; robed. **2.** *Law.* Held by a tenure subject to no contingency. [coat; vesture.

vest, *n.* A short sleeveless jacket; waist-

Ves'ta, 1 ves'ta; 2 vĕs'ta, *n.* The goddess of the hearth and the hearth-fire, and protectress of the state; in her temple in Rome the sacred fire, brought by Æneas from Troy, was kept up and guarded day and night by the vestal virgins. **Hes'ti-a‡** [Gr.].— **ves'tal. I.** *a.* **1.** Pertaining to Vesta. **2.** Suitable for a vestal or a nun; chaste; pure. **II.** *n.* **1.** *Rom. Antiq.* One of the virgin priestesses of Vesta. **2.** A virgin; nun.

ves'ti-bule, 1 ves'tɪ-biūl; 2 vĕs'tɪ-būl, *n.* An antechamber; porch; enclosed entrance.

ves'tige, 1 ves'tɪj; 2 vĕs'tig, *n.* A visible trace or impression; originally, a footprint; track.

vest'ment, 1 vest'ment *or* -mant; 2 vĕst'-ment, *n.* An article of dress; robe of state.

ves'try, 1 ves'trɪ; 2 vĕs'try, *n.* [VES'TRIESᶻ, *pl.*] **1.** A room where vestments are kept. **2.** A chapel. **3.** A body administering the affairs of the parish.— **ves'try-man,** *n.* A member of a vestry.

ves'ture, 1 ves'chur *or* -tiur; 2 vĕs'chur *or* -tūr, *n.* Something that invests or covers; garments collectively; a robe.

vetch, 1 vech; 2 vĕch, *n.* A plant of the bean family.

vet'er-an, 1 vet'ar-an; 2 vĕt'er-an. **I.** *a.* **1.** Old in service. **2.** Belonging to a veteran. **II.** *n.* One long in service, as an old soldier; an ex-soldier.

vet'er-i-na-ry, 1 vet'ar-ɪ-nē-rɪ; 2 vĕt'er-i-nā'ry, *n.* Pertaining to diseases or injuries of domestic animals, and their treatment.— **vet"er-i-na'ri-an,** *n.* One who treats diseases of domestic animals; a horse-doctor. **vet'er-i-na-ryt.**

ve'to, 1 vī'to; 2 vē'to. **I.** *vt.* To check by a veto. **II.** *n.* [VE'TOESᶻ, *pl.*] **1.** The refusal of an executive officer to approve a legislative enactment. **2.** Any authoritative prohibition.

vexᵗ, 1 veks; 2 vĕks, *vt.* **1.** To provoke or irritate by small annoyances; annoy. **2.** To cause grief to; afflict; distress. **3.** To agitate; disturb.— **vex-a'tion,** *n.* **1.** The act of vexing, or the state of being vexed. **2.** That which vexes.— **vex-a'tious,** *a.* Vexing; troublesome; annoying. **-ly,** *adv.* **-ness,** *n.*

vi'a, 1 vai'a; 2 vī'a, *prep.* By way of, as a route or place.

vi'a-duct, 1 vai'a-dukt; 2 vī'a-dŭct, *n.* A bridge-like structure, to carry a road-way or the like over a valley or ravine.

vi'al, 1 vai'al; 2 vī'al, *n.* A small bottle, commonly of glass and cylindrical. **phi'al‡.**

Viaduct.

vi'and, 1 vai'and; 2 vī'and, *n.* An article of food.

vi'brate, 1 vai'brēt; 2 vī'brāt, *vt. & vi.* [VI'-BRAT-ED⁴; VI'BRAT-ING.] To move or swing back and forth, as a pendulum; oscillate; fluctuate; vacillate.— **vi-bra'tion,**

n. **1.** The act of vibrating; oscillation. **2.** A complete motion back and forth.— **vi′bra-to-ry,** *a.* Pertaining to or causing vibration.

vic′ar, 1 vik′ər; 2 vĭc′ar, *n.* One who is authorized to perform functions in the stead of another; a parish priest.— **vic′ar-age,** *n.* The benefice, office, or residence of a vicar.— **vic′ar-ship,** *n.*

vi-ca′ri-ous, 1 vai-kē′rĭ-us; 2 vĭ-cā′rĭ-ŭs, *a.* **1.** Made or performed by substitution. **2.** Acting for another. **-ly,** *adv.*

vice[1], 1 vais; 2 vĭç, *n.* **1.** Depravity; gross immorality. **2.** A bad trick, as of a horse.

vice[2], *n.* Same as **VISE.** [the place of.

vi′ce, 1 vai′sī; 2 vī′çē, *prep.* Instead of; in

vice-, 1 vais-; 2 vĭç-, *prefix.* Substitute; subordinate; sub-; second.— **vice-ge′rent. I.** *a.* Acting in the place of another. **II.** *n.* One authorized to exercise the powers of another; a deputy.— **vice-ge′ren-cy,** *n.*— **vice-pres′i-den-cy,** *n.* The office or term of vice-president.— **v.-president,** *n.* One who is to act, on occasion, in place of a president.— **vice-re′gal,** *a.* Of or relating to a viceroy.— **vice′roy,** *n.* A ruler acting with royal authority in the place of a sovereign. **-al-ty, -ship,** *n.*— **vice′₋reine′,** *n. fem.*

vi′ce ver′sa, 1 vai′sī vūr′sə; 2 vī′çē vēr′sa. [L.] The order or relation of terms being reversed.

vic′i-nage, 1 vis′i-nij; 2 vĭç′i-naġ, *n.* The vicinity; neighborhood.— **vi-cin′i-ty,** *n.* Nearness; proximity; neighborhood.

vi′cious, 1 vĭsh′us; 2 vĭsh′ŭs, *a.* **1.** Addicted to vice; depraved; wicked. **2.** Unruly; faulty; malignant. **-ly,** *adv.* **-ness,** *n.*

vi-cis′si-tude, 1 vɪ-sis′i-tiūd; 2 vi-çĭs′i-tūd, *n.* A change, as of fortune; mutation.

vic′tim, 1 vik′tim; 2 vĭc′tĭm, *n.* A living creature sacrificed or made to suffer; a sufferer; a dupe. **-ize,** *vt.*

vic′tor, 1 vik′tər *or* -tər; 2 vĭc′tor, *n.* One who wins a victory; a conqueror.

vic′to-ry, 1 vik′to-rɪ; 2 vĭc′to-ry, *n.* [-RIES[Z], *pl.*] The overcoming of an enemy or of opposition or difficulty.— **vic-to′ri-ous,** *a.* Conquering; triumphant. **-ly,** *adv.* **-ness,** *n.*

vict′ual, 1 vit′l; 2 vĭt′l. **I.** *vt. & vi.* [VICT′-UALED *or* VICT′UALLED; VICT′UAL-ING *or* VICT′UAL-LING.] To furnish or store with victuals. **II.** *n. pl.* [VICT′UALS, 1 vit′lz; 2 vĭt′lz.] Food for human beings. **-er,** *n.*

vi-del′i-cet, 1 vɪ-del′i-set; 2 vi-dĕl′i-çĕt, *adv.* [L.] To wit; namely: abbreviated *viz.*

vi-dette′, *n.* Same as **VEDETTE.**

vie, 1 vai; 2 vī, *vi.* [VIED; VY′ING.] To strive for superiority: followed by *with.*

view, 1 viū; 2 vū. **I.** *vt.* To look at scrutinizingly; inspect; see. **II.** *n.* **1.** The act of viewing; survey; examination.

2. Range of vision. **3.** A spectacle; landscape. **4.** Intention; opinion; motion. **-er,** *n.*— **view′less,** *a.* Invisible; unseen.

vig′il, 1 vij′il; 2 vĭg′il, *n.* **1.** The act of keeping awake; watchfulness. **2.** Religious devotions: usually plural.— **vig′i-lance,** *n.* Alertness; watchfulness.— **vig′i-lant,** *a.* Being awake and on the alert; watchful; heedful. **-ly,** *adv.*

vi-gnette′, 1 vin-yet′; 2 vĭn-yĕt′, *n.* **1.** A running ornament of leaves and tendrils. **2.** An engraving, or the like, having a background that is shaded off gradually.

vig′or, 1 vig′ər; 2 vĭg′or, *n.* Active strength; force; energy.— **vig′or-ous,** *a.* **1.** Full of vigor; robust. **2.** Pertaining to vigor. **-ly,** *adv.* **-ness,** *n.*

vi′king, 1 vai′[*or* vī′]kiŋ; 2 vī′[*or* vī′]king, *n.* A freebooter; pirate: one of the Scandinavian warriors of the 8th to the 11th century, who harried the coasts of Europe.

vi′la-yet′, 1 vī′lɑ-yet′; 2 vī′lä-yĕt′, *n.* One of the chief political divisions of the Republic of Turkey.

vile, 1 vail; 2 vīl, *a.* [VIL′ER; VIL′EST.] **1.** Shamefully wicked; sinful. **2.** Mean; objectionable; disgusting. **-ly,** *adv.* **-ness,** *n.*— **vil′i-fy,** *vt.* [-FIED; -FY′ING.] To defame; slander.— **vil″i-fi-ca′tion,** *n.*— **vil′i-fi-er,** *n.*

vil′la, 1 vil′ə; 2 vĭl′a, *n.* An elegant country house.

vil′lage, 1 vil′ij; 2 vĭl′aġ, *n.* A collection of houses smaller than a town; also, its inhabitants collectively.— **vil′lag-er,** *n.*

vil′lain, 1 vil′in; 2 vĭl′in, *n.* **1.** A basely wicked person; scoundrel. **2.** Formerly a serf; farm-servant.— **vil′lain-ous,** *a.* Wicked; vile; atrocious. **-ly,** *adv.*— **vil′lain-y,** *n.* Moral depravity; extreme wickedness.

vim, 1 vim; 2 vĭm, *n.* [Colloq.] Strength; vigor; force; spirit.

vin′di-cate, 1 vin′dɪ-kēt; 2 vĭn′di-eāt, *vt.* [-CAT″ED[d]; -CAT′ING.] To assert or defend against attack; maintain successfully; justify.— **vin″di-ca′tion,** *n.* Justification; defense.— **vin′di-ca″tive(e[s],** *a.* Tending to vindicate.— **vin′di-ca-to″ry,** *a.*

vin-dic′tive(e[s], 1 vin-dik′tɪv; 2 vĭn-dĭe′tiv, *a.* Revengeful. **-ly,** *adv.* **-ness,** *n.*

vine, 1 vain; 2 vĭn, *n.* Any climbing or twining plant, especially a grape-vine.

vin′e-gar, 1 vin′ɪ-gər; 2 vĭn′e-ġar, *n.* An acid liquid obtained from the fermentation of an alcoholic liquid, as cider; figuratively, anything sour.

vin′er-y, 1 vain′ər-ɪ; 2 vĭn′er-y, *n.* **1.** A greenhouse for grapes. **2.** Vines in general.

vine′yard, 1 vin′yərd; 2 vĭn′yard, *n.* A **vin′yard[p],** place where grape-vines are cultivated in numbers.

---

vi′nous, 1 vai′nʊs; 2 vī′nŭs, *a.* Pertaining to wine; wine=producing.

vin′tage, 1 vin′tɪj; 2 vĭn′tᴀg, *n.* The yield of a vineyard or wine=growing district; also, the act or time of gathering it.—**vint′ner,** *n.* A wine=merchant.

vi′ol, 1 vai′əl; 2 vī′ol, *n.* A stringed instrument of the violin class played with a bow; a violoncello.— **vi′o-la,** 1 vai′o′la *or* vi-ō′la; 2 vī′o-la *or* vĭ-ō′la, *n.* A stringed instrument somewhat larger than the violin.

vi′o-late, 1 vai′o-lēt; 2 vī′o-lāt, *vt.* [-LAT-ED^d; -LAT′ING.] **1.** To break, as a law or an oath; transgress. **2.** To treat irreverently; do violence to; abuse.—**vi″o-la′tion,** *n.*—**vi′o-la″tiv**(e^s, *a.*—**vi′o-la″tor,** *n.*

vi′o-lent, 1 vai′o-lent; 2 vī′o-lĕnt, *a.* Forcible; furious; intense. **-ly,** *adv.*—**vi′o-lence,** *n.* Violent exercise of force; injury; outrage.

vi′o-let, 1 vai′o-let; 2 vī′o-lĕt. **I.** *a.* Of the color of violet. **II.** *n.* **1.** A low=growing plant, with flowers typically of a purplish blue color. **2.** A color seen at the end of the spectrum opposite the red.

vi″o-lin′, 1 vai′o-lin′; 2 vī′o-lĭn′, *n.* **1.** A musical instrument having four strings, and played with a bow. **2.** A violinist.— **vi″o-lin′ist,** *n.* One who plays on the violin.

vi″o-lon-cel′lo, 1 vī″o-lon-ᴄhel′lo *or* vai″o-lon-sel′o; 2 vī″o-lŏn-ᴄhĕl′lo *or* vī″o-lŏn-çĕl′o, *n.* A bass violin having four strings. **cel′lo‡.**—**vi″o-lon-cel′list,** *n.*

vi′per, 1 vai′pər; 2 vī′pẽr, *n.* A venomous Old World snake; adder.— **vi′per-ous,** *a.* Having the qualities of a viper; venomous.

vi-ra′go, 1 vi-rē′go; 2 vi-rā′go, *n.* [-GOES^z, *pl.*] A turbulent woman; vixen.

Vir-gil′i-an, *a.* Same as VERGILIAN.

vir′gin, 1 vūr′jin; 2 vîr′gĭn. **I.** *a.* **1.** Pertaining or suited to a virgin; maidenly; chaste. **2.** Uncorrupted; pure. **3.** Untried; new; maiden. **II.** *n.* A chaste unmarried woman; a maiden.— **vir′gi-nal,** *a.* — **vir-gin′i-ty,** *n.* Maidenhood.

vir′il(e^s, 1 vir′il; 2 vîr′il, *a.* Having the characteristics of mature manhood; masculine.— **vi-ril′i-ty,** *n.*

vir-tu′, 1 vir-tū′*or* vūr′tū; 2 vĭr-tṳ′*or* vîr′tṳ, *n.* Rare, curious, or beautiful quality: as in the phrase *objects* or *articles of virtu.*

vir′tue, 1 vūr′ᴄhu *or* -tiu; 2 vîr′chṳ *or* -tū, *n.* **1.** Moral excellence; virtuousness; morality; chastity. **2.** Any admirable quality.— **vir′tu-al,** *a.* Being in effect, but not in form or appearance. **-ly,** *adv.*— **vir′tu-ous,** *a.* Characterized by or having the nature of virtue; moral; upright. **-ly,** *adv.* **-ness,** *n.*

vir″tu-o′so, 1 vir″[or vūr″]tu-ō′so; 2 vîr″[or vîr″]tṳ-ō′so, *n.* One having skill in, or a

critical knowledge of, the fine arts; especially, a highly skilled musician.

vi′rus, 1 vai′rus; 2 vī′rŭs, *n.* A morbid poison that is the means of communicating infectious disease.— **vir′u-lence,** *n.*— **vir′u-lent,** 1 vir′u-lent; 2 vīr′u-lĕnt, *a.* Having the nature of virus; poisonous; malignant. **-ly,** *adv.*

vis′age, 1 viz′ij; 2 vĭs′ag, *n.* The face or look of a person; distinctive aspect.— **vis′aged,** *a.*

vis″-à-vis′, 1 vīz″=ɑ=vī′; 2 vĭs″=ä=vī′. [F.] **I.** *n.* One of two persons or things that face each other. **II.** *adv.* Face to face.

vis′cer-a, 1 vis′ɛr-ə; 2 vĭs′er-a, *n. pl.* The internal organs of the body.— **vis′cer-al,** *a.* **1.** Pertaining to or enclosing the viscera. **2.** Abdominal.

vis′cid, 1 vis′id; 2 vĭs′id, *a.* Sticky or adhesive; viscous.— **vis-cid′i-ty,** *n.*

vis′count, 1 vai′kaunt; 2 vī′count, *n.* **1.** In England, a nobleman next below an earl. **2.** In continental Europe, the son or younger brother of a count.— **vis′count.ess,** *n.* The wife of a viscount; a peeress.

vis′cous, 1 vis′kus; 2 vĭs′eŭs, *a.* **1.** Glutinous; sticky. **2.** Imperfectly fluid, as tar or wax.— **vis-cos′i-ty,** *n.*

vise, 1 vais; 2 vīs, *n.* An instrument of two jaws closed together by a screw or the like. **vice‡.**

vi-sé′, 1 vi-zē′; 2 vi-sē′, *n.* An official indorsement, as on a passport, certifying that it has been inspected and found correct.— **vi-sé′,** *vt.* [VI-SÉED; VI-SÉ′ING.]

Vise.

vis′i-bl(e^p, 1 viz′i-bl; 2 vĭs′i-bl, *a.* Such as may be seen; perceptible; evident. — **vis″i-bil′i-ty,** *n.* **vis′i-bl**(e=ness^p‡.— **vis′i-bly,** *adv.*

vi′sion, 1 viz′ən; 2 vĭzh′on, *n.* **1.** The sense of sight; act of seeing. **2.** Something seen; an apparition; dream; fantasy; specifically, an inspired revelation.— **vi′sion-a-ry. I.** *a.* Impracticable; dreamy; unreal. **II.** *n.* [-RIES^z, *pl.*] A theorist; dreamer.

vis′it^d, 1 viz′it; 2 vĭs′it, *v.* **I.** *t.* **1.** To make a visit to. **2.** To send or come upon, as good or evil. **II.** *i.* To call; make calls.

vis′it, *n.* The going to see a person, place, or thing; a sojourn; call.— **vis′i-tant,** *n.* A visitor; that which comes and goes or makes a transient appearance.— **vis″i-ta′tion,** *n.* **1.** The act or fact of visiting; a visit. **2.** An official inspection. **3.** A divine dispensation. — **vis′i-tor,** *n.*— **vis″i-to′ri-al,** *a.*

vis′or, *n.* Same as VIZOR.

vis′ta, 1 vis′tə; 2 vĭs′ta, *n.* An outlook shut

in at the sides and reaching into the distance, as along an avenue; view; prospect: often used figuratively.

vis′u-al, 1 vĭg′u-əl; 2 vĭzh′u̯-al, *a*. **1.** Pertaining to or serving sight. **2.** Visible.

vi′tal, 1 vai′tal; 2 vī′tal, *a*. Pertaining to life: essential to or affecting life; of utmost importance.— **vi-tal′i-ty,** *n*. Vital principle or force; power of continuing in force or effect.— **vi′tal-ly,** *adv*.— **vi′tals,** *n. pl*. The vital parts, as the heart and brain.

vi′ta-min, ⎱ 1 vai′ta-mɪn; 2 vī′ta-mĭn, *n*. A
vi′ta-mine, ⎰ substance found in fresh fruits, vegetables, etc., essential to the diet of man and other animals as a nutritive force.

vi′ta-scope, 1 vai′tə-skōp; 2 vī′ta-seōp, *n*. A device by which the pictures on kinetoscope-films are enlarged and exhibited upon a screen.

vi′ti-ate, 1 vĭsh′ı-ēt; 2 vĭsh′ĭ-āt, *vt*. [-AT′ED^d; -AT′ING.] To impair or spoil by corruption; contaminate; destroy the validity of, as a contract.— **vi′ti-a′tion,** *n*.

vit′re-ous, 1 vĭt′rı-us; 2 vĭt′re-ŭs, *a*. **1.** Pertaining to glass: glassy. **2.** Obtained from glass.— **vit′ri-fy,** *v*. [-FIED; -FY′ING.] **I.** *t*. To make vitreous: glaze. **II.** *i*. To become glass or glassy.— **vit′ri-fac′tion,** *n*.

vit′ri-ol, 1 vĭt′rı-ol; 2 vĭt′rĭ-ol, *n*. Sulfuric acid, or any of its salts.— **blue vitriol,** a copper v.; copper sulfate.— **green v.,** copperas.— **vit′ri-ol′ic,** 1 vĭt′rı-ol′ık; 2 vĭt′rĭ-ŏl′ĭe, *a*. Of or like vitriol; caustic.

vi-tu′per-ate, 1 vai-tiū′pər-ēt; 2 vī-tū′per-āt, *vt*. [-AT′ED^d; -AT′ING.] To find fault with abusively; censure; assail; upbraid; rail at.— **vi-tu″per-a′tion,** *n*.— **vi-tu′per-a″tiv**(e^s, *a*. Defamatory.

vi-va′ce, 1 vi-vä′chē; 2 vī-vä′che̱, *adv. Mus*. Lively; quickly.

vi-va′cious, 1 vai-vē′shus; 2 vī-vā′shŭs, *a*. Full of life; lively; active. **-ly,** *adv*. **-ness,** *n*.— **vi-vac′i-ty,** *n*. [-TIES^z, *pl*.] The state of being vivacious; liveliness.

vi′va vo′ce, 1 vai′və vō′sĭ; 2 vī′va vō′çē. [L.] By spoken word; orally: used both as an adjective and an adverb.

viv′id, 1 viv′ıd; 2 vĭv′ĭd, *a*. Lifelike; intense; spirited. **-ly,** *adv*. **-ness,** *n*.

viv′i-fy, 1 viv′ı-fai; 2 vĭv′ĭ-fỹ, *vt*. [-FIED; -FY′ING.] To endue with life; animate.

vi-vip′a-rous, 1 vai-vip′ə-rus; 2 vī-vĭp′a-rŭs, *a*. Bringing forth living young, as most mammals.

viv″i-sec′tion, 1 viv″ı-sek′shən; 2 vĭv″ĭ-sĕc′shon, *n*. The dissection of a living animal.

vix′en, 1 viks′n; 2 vĭks′n, *n*. **1.** A turbulent, quarrelsome woman. **2.** A female fox.

viz., *abbr*. Abbreviation for VIDELICET, "*that is to say*": generally read *namely* or *to wit*.

vi-zier′, ⎱ 1 vı-zīr′; 2 vi-zēr′, *n*. A high of-
vi-zir′, ⎰ ficial in a Mohammedan country.

viz′or, 1 viz̞′ər; 2 vĭz′or, *n*. A projecting piece on the front of a cap or helmet. **vis′or‡**.

vo′ca-bl(e^r, 1 vō′kə-bl; 2 vō′ca-bl, *n*. A word or a vocal sound.

vo-cab′u-la-ry, 1 vo-kab′yu-lē-rı; 2 vo-cǎb′yu̯-lā-ry, *n*. [-RIES^z, *pl*.] **1.** A list of words in alphabetical order. **2.** An aggregate of words.

vo′cal, 1 vō′kəl; 2 vō′cal, *a*. **1.** Having voice; oral. **2.** Pertaining to the voice; uttered or modulated by the voice; sonant. — **vo′cal-ist,** *n*. A singer.— **vo′cal-ize,** *vt. & vi*. [-IZED; -IZ′ING.] To make vocal; utter sound with the voice.— **vo″cal-i-za′tion,** *n*. — **vo′cal-ly,** *adv*.

vo-ca′tion, 1 vo-kē′shən; 2 vo-cā′shon, *n*. A regular occupation.

vo-cif′er-ate, 1 vo-sif′ər-ēt; 2 vo-çĭf′er-āt, *vt. & vi*. [-AT′ED^d; -AT′ING.] To utter loudly and vehemently; roar out.— **vo-cif″er-a′tion,** *n*.— **vo-cif′er-ous,** *a*. Making a loud outcry; clamorous. **-ly,** *adv*.

vogue, 1 vōg; 2 vōg, *n*. The prevalent way or fashion; popular temporary usage.

voice, 1 vois; 2 vŏiç, *n*. **I.** *vt*. [VOICED^t; VOIC′ING.] **1.** To put into speech; give voice to. **2.** To tune. **II.** *n*. **1.** The sound produced by the vocal organs of a person or animal. **2.** The power of vocal utterance. **3.** Opinion or choice expressed. **4.** The form of a verb, as active or passive.— **voice′less,** *a*. Having no voice; silent.

void, 1 void; 2 vŏid. **I**^d. *vt*. **1.** To render null; annul. **2.** To send out; emit; evacuate. **II.** *a*. **1.** Vacant; empty; unoccupied; destitute; clear. **2.** Having no legal force; ineffective; null: often in the phrase *null and void*. **III.** *n*. A vacuum; emptiness.— **void′a-ble,** *a*. That may be declared void, or set aside.

vol′a-til(e^s, 1 vol′ə-til; 2 vŏl′a-tĭl, *a*. **1.** Evaporating readily. **2.** Easily influenced; fickle; changeable; transient.— **vol′a-til**(e-ness^s, *n*. **vol″a-til′i-ty‡**.— **vol′a-til-ize** or **-ise,** 1 vol′ə-til-aiz; 2 vŏl′a-til-īz, *vt. & vi*. To cause to pass off in vapor; become volatile.— **vol″a-til-i-za′tion,** *n*.

vol-ca′no, 1 vol-kē′no; 2 vŏl-eā′no, *n*. [-NOES^z, *pl*.] A mountain, having a crater from which lava is or has been ejected. — **vol-can′ic,** *a*.

vo-li′tion, 1 vo-lish′ən; 2 vo-lĭsh′on, *n*. The power of willing; resolve; decision; will.

vol′ley, 1 vol′ı; 2 vŏl′y. **I.** *vt. & vi*. To discharge with a volley; be let fly together. **II.** *n*. A simultaneous discharge of many missiles.

1: ɑrtistic, ärt; fat, fāre; fast; get, prēy; hit, police; obey, gō; net, ȯr; fụll, rūle; but, bũrn.
2: ärt, āpe, fảt, fâre, fȧst, whạt, ạll; mē, gĕt, prey, fẽrn; hĭt, īce; ı̇̄=ĕ; ĩ=ĕ; gō, nŏt, ȯr, wȯn,

vo'lo-drome, 1 vō'lo-drōm; 2 vō'lo-drŏm, n. A place where flying machines are tested.

vol'plane", 1 vel'plān"; 2 vŏl'plān", n. A flight downward from a height at an angle considerably greater than the gliding angle.— **vol'plane,** vi.

volt, 1 vōlt; 2 vōlt, n. The practical unit of electromotive force: from Volta, Italian physicist (1745–1827).— **volt'age,** 1 vōlt'ij; 2 vōlt'ag, n. Electromotive force as measured or expressed in volts.— **vol-ta'ic,** 1 vel-tē'ik; 2 vŏl-tā'ic, a. Pertaining to electricity developed through chemical action or contact; galvanic.

vol'u-bl(e², 1 vel'yu-bl; 2 vŏl'yu-bl, a. **1.** Having a ready flow of words; fluent. **2.** Turning readily.— **vol''u-bil'i-ty,** n.— **vol'u-bly,** adv.

vol'ume, 1 vel'yum; 2 vŏl'yum, n. **1.** A book; anciently, a written roll. **2.** Bulk; quantity; fulness of sound or tone.— **vo-lu'mi-nous,** a. **1.** Consisting of many volumes; of great bulk. **2.** Having written much; productive.

vol'un-ta-ry, 1 vel'un-tē-ri; 2 vŏl'ŭn-tā-ry. **I.** a. **1.** Unconstrained; intentional; volitional; free. **2.** Possessing or exercising will. **3.** Subject to will, as a muscle or movement. **II.** n. [-RIES², pl.] **1.** Any work or performance not compelled. **2.** Mus. An organ solo before, during, or after a religious service.— **vol'un-ta-ri-ly,** adv.— **vol'un-ta-ri-ness,** n.

vol''un-teer', 1 vel''un-tīr'; 2 vŏl''ŭn-tēr'. **I.** vt. & vi. To offer one's service voluntarily. **II.** a. Voluntary. **III.** n. One who volunteers, as for service in the army.

vo-lup'tu-a-ry, 1 vo-lup'chu-[or -tiu-]ē-ri; 2 vo-lŭp'chu-[or -tū-]ā-ry. **I.** a. Pertaining to sensual desire or indulgence. **II.** n. [-RIES², pl.] One addicted to sensual pleasures.

vo-lup'tu-ous, 1 vo-lup'chu-[or -tiu-]us; 2 vo-lŭp'chu-[or -tū-]ŭs, a. Belonging to sensuous gratification; luxurious; sensual. -ly, adv. -ness, n.

vom'it, 1 vem'it; 2 vŏm'it. **I^d.** vt. & vi. To throw up (matter) from the stomach. **II.** n. **1.** Matter thrown up from the stomach. **2.** An emetic. **3.** The act of emitting.

voo'doo, 1 vū'dū; 2 vōō'dōō, n. **1.** The superstitions (collectively) prevalent among West-Indian and southern United States negroes, and dealing with charms, conjuring, witchcraft, etc. Compare HOODOO. **2.** A conjurer. **vou'dou.**— **voo'doo-ism,** n.

vo-ra'cious, 1 vo-rē'shus; 2 vo-rā'shŭs, a. Eating greedily; ravenous. -ly, adv.— **vo-ra'cious-ness,** n. **vo-rac'i-ty‡.**

vor'tex, 1 vŏr'teks; 2 vôr'tĕks, n. [VOR'TI-CES, 1 vŏr'ti-sīz, 2 vôr'ti-çēṣ, or VOR'-TEX-ES, pl.] A mass of rotating fluid; a whirl in a fluid; whirlpool; whirlwind. — **vor'ti-cal,** a.

vo'ta-ry, 1 vō'ta-ri; 2 vō'ta-ry, n. [-RIES², pl.] One who is devoted to a particular worship, pursuit, etc.— **vo'ta-ress,** n. fem.

vote, 1 vōt; 2 vōt. **I.** vt. & vi. [VOT'ED^d; VOT'ING.] To determine by vote; cast a vote. **II.** n. **1.** A formal expression of choice, as by a show of hands, or ballot. **2.** The aggregate of votes.— **vot'er,** n. One who votes, or is qualified to vote.

vo'tiv(e², 1 vō'tiv; 2 vō'tiv, a. Dedicated by a vow. -ly, adv.

vouch^t, 1 vauch; 2 vouch, v. **I.** t. To support; confirm; warrant. **II.** i. To become surety for another.— **vouch'er,** n. **1.** Anything (as a receipt) that serves to attest an alleged act. **2.** One who vouches for another.— **vouch-safe',** vt. [-SAFED'^t; -SAF'-ING.] To grant; permit; deign.

vow, 1 vau; 2 vow. **I.** vt. & vi. To promise solemnly, as to God; make a vow. **II.** n. A solemn promise, as to God; solemn pledge.

vow'el, 1 vau'el; 2 vow'ĕl. **I.** a. Pertaining to a vowel. **II.** n. An open vocal sound or a character representing it, as a, e, i, o, u.

voy'age, 1 voi'ij; 2 vŏy'ag. **I.** vt. & vi. [VOY'AGED; VOY'AG-ING.] To travel over; make a voyage. **II.** n. A journey by water.— **voy'ag-er,** n.

Vul'can, 1 vul'kan; 2 vŭl'can, n. Rom. Myth. The god of fire and of the arts of forging and smelting; deformed husband of Venus.

vul'can-ite, 1 vul'kan-ait; 2 vŭl'can-īt, n. A dark-colored hard variety of vulcanized india-rubber.

vul''can-i-za'tion, 1 vul''kan-i-zē'shan; 2 vŭl''can-i-zā'shon, n. The process of treating crude india-rubber with sulfur at a high temperature.— **vul'can-ize,** vt.

vul'gar, 1 vul'gar; 2 vŭl'gar. **I.** a. Pertaining to the common people; coarse or common; low; inelegant; unrefined; vernacular. **II.** n. The common people.— **vul'gar-ism,** n. **1.** Vulgarity. **2.** A word or phrase of bad taste.— **vul-gar'i-ty,** 1 vul-gar'i-ti; 2 vŭl-găr'i-ty, n. The quality of being vulgar; coarseness.— **vul'gar-ize,** vt.

Vul'gate, 1 vul'gĕt; 2 vŭl'găt, n. The ancient Latin version of the Bible made by St. Jerome (340–420), and now used (with some modifications) as the authorized version by the Roman Catholic Church.

1: ə = final; ɪ = habit; aisle; au = out; oil; iū = feud; chin; go; ŋ = sing; thin, this.
2: wolf, do; book, boot; full, rule, cūre, bŭt, bûrn; ŏil, bŏy; go, ġem; iŋk; thin, this.

vul'ner-a-bl(er, 1 vul'nər-a-bl; 2 vŭl'ner-a-bl, *a*. **1.** Capable of being wounded. **2.** Liable to attack; assailable.— **vul'ner-a-bil'i-ty, vul'ner-a-bl**(e-ness)ᵣ, *n*.

vul'ner-a-ry, 1 vul'nər-ē-rɪ; 2 vŭl'ner-ā-ry. **I.** *a*. Tending to cure wounds. **II.** *n*. A healing application for an external wound.

vul'pine, 1 vul'pɪn *or* -pain; 2 vŭl'pin *or* -pīn, *a*. Foxlike; crafty.

vul'ture, 1 vul'chur *or* -tiur; 2 vŭl'chur *or* -tūr, *n*. One of certain birds that feed on carrion.— **vul'tur-ine,** *a*. **vul'tur-ish**‡; **vul'tur-ous**‡.

vy'ing, 1 vaɪ'ɪŋ; 2 vȳ'ing, *ppr*. of VIE, *v*.

W

W, w, 1 dub'l-yū; 2 dŭb'l-yu, *n*. [w's, W's, or W's, 1 dub'l-yūz; 2 dŭb'l-yuẓ, *pl*.] The twenty-third letter in the English alphabet.

wab'ble, 1 wob'l; 2 wạb'l. **I.** *vt*. & *vi*. [WAB'BLED; WAB'BLING.] To sway or move unsteadily, as a top turning at a low speed; vacillate. **II.** *n*. A wabbling motion. — **wab'bly,** *a*.

wad, 1 wod; 2 wạd. **I.** *vt*. [WAD'DEDᵈ; WAD'DING.] To press into a mass; pack; put a wad in. **II.** *n*. A small compact mass of soft substance, as used for packing, etc.— **wad'ding,** *n*. Wads collectively; carded cotton in sheets used for padding.

wad'dle, 1 wod'l; 2 wạd'l. **I.** *vi*. [WAD'-DLED; WAD'DLING.] To sway from side to side in walking. **II.** *n*. A clumsy rocking walk.— **wad'dler,** *n*.

wade, 1 wēd; 2 wād, *vt*. & *vi*. [WAD'EDᵈ; WAD'ING.] To walk through water or other yielding substance; plod.— **wad'er,** *n*.

wa'fer, 1 wē'fər; 2 wā'fer, *n*. **1.** A thin hardened disk of paste for sealing letters, etc. **2.** A small, flat disk as of unleavened bread.

waf'fle, 1 wof'l; 2 wạf'l, *n*. A batter cake baked between hinged iron plates called **waffle-irons.**

waft, 1 waft; 2 wȧft, *vt*. To carry lightly with waving motion, as in air or water.

wag, 1 wag; 2 wăg, *vt*. & *vi*. [WAGGED; WAGDˢ; WAG'GING.] To move quickly in alternate opposite directions.

wag¹, *n*. The act or motion of wagging.

wag², *n*. A droll fellow; wit; a joker.— **wag'ger-y,** *n*. Fun; drollery.— **wag'gish,** *a*. Jocose. **-ly,** *adv*. **-ness,** *n*.

wage, 1 wēj; 2 wāg. **I.** *vt*. [WAGED; WAG'ING.] To engage in vigorously, as a conflict. **II.** *n*. [WA'GES, *pl*.] Payment for service rendered: usually in the plural.

wa'ger, 1 wē'jər; 2 wā'ger. **I.** *vt*. & *vi*. To stake; bet. **II.** *n*. **1.** The staking of something, as money, upon the happening or not happening of an uncertain event; a bet. **2.** The thing pledged.

wag'on, 1 wag'ən; 2 wăg'on, *n*. A four-wheeled vehicle. **wag'gon**‡ [Eng.].— **wag'-on-er,** *n*. A wagon-driver.

waif, 1 wēf; 2 wāf, *n*. **1.** A homeless wanderer. **2.** Anything found and unclaimed.

wail, 1 wēl; 2 wāl. **I.** *vt*. & *vi*. To moan. **II.** *n*. A prolonged moan; plaintive cry.

wain‖, 1 wēn; 2 wān, *n*. A wagon.

wain'scot, 1 wēn'skot; 2 wān'scŏt, *n*. A lining for the lower portion of inner walls, usually of paneled wood.

waist, 1 wēst; 2 wāst, *n*. **1.** That part of the body between the chest and the hips, or a garment covering it. **2.** The middle part of a ship or other object.— **waist'band,** *n*. A band for the waist, constituting the upper part of trousers, skirts, etc.— **waist'coat,** 1 wēst'kōt *or* wes'kət; 2 wāst'cōt *or* wĕs'cot, *n*. A man's vest.

waitᵈ, 1 wēt; 2 wāt, *v*. **I.** *t*. To delay action for (something); await. **II.** *i*. **1.** To rest in expectation. **2.** To stand in readiness. To be or act as a waiter. — **wait'er,** *n*. **1.** One who waits; an attendant, as at table. **2.** A tray for dishes, etc.— **wait'ress,** *n*.

waiv(er, 1 wēv; 2 wāv, *vt*. [WAIV(E)Dˢ; WAIV'ING.] To relinquish, especially temporarily, as a claim; put aside; yield. — **waiv'er,** *n*. The voluntary relinquishment of a right, privilege, or advantage.

wake, 1 wēk; 2 wāk, *v*. [WAKEDᵈ *or* WOKE; WAK'ING.] **I.** *t*. To rouse from slumber; awake; arouse; resuscitate. **II.** *i*. **1.** To be aroused from sleep, etc. **2.** To be set in action. **3.** To keep watch at night. — **wake'ful,** *a*. **1.** Remaining awake, especially at night. **2.** Attended by want of sleep. **-ly,** *adv*. **-ness,** *n*.— **wak'en,** *vt*. **1.** To arouse from sleep; awaken. **2.** To incite to activity.

wake¹, *n*. A watching all night over the body of a dead person. [water.

wake², *n*. The track left by a vessel in the

wale, 1 wēl; 2 wāl. **I.** *vt*. [WALED; WAL'-ING.] **1.** To lash; flog. **whale**†. **2.** To mark with wales or strakes. **II.** *n*. **1.**

A ridge made by flogging. **2.** A ridge or strake, as in the planking of a vessel.

walkt, 1 wŏk; 2 wạk, v. **I.** t. **1.** To pass through or over at a walk. **2.** To lead, ride, or drive at a walk, as a horse. **II.** i. **1.** To advance by steps, without running; take a walk. **2.** To behave; live.

walk, n. **1.** The act of walking; a movement in which a quadruped has always two or more feet on the ground, and a biped always one foot on the ground. **2.** The manner of walking; a promenade or stroll. **3.** A place for walking; path; sidewalk; range. **4.** A course of life; conduct.— **walk′ie=talk′ie,** n. A portable radio for transmission and reception.

wall, 1 wŏl; 2 wạl. **I.** vt. To provide with a wall; enclose; fortify; defend. **II.** n. A continuous structure, as for the side of a house; also, a fence of stone or masonry.

wall′=eye″, n. **1.** An eye in which the iris is light=colored or white. **2.** A large, staring eye, as of a fish; also a fish so marked.— **wall′= eyed″,** a.— **wall′flow″er,** n. **1.** A garden flower of the mustard family. **2.** A woman who at a ball or party is in want of a partner.

wal′la-by, 1 wŏl′ɑ-bɪ; 2 wạl′a-by, n. One of the smaller kangaroos. [Austral.]

wal′let, 1 wŏl′et; 2 wạl′ĕt, n. **1.** A pocket-book. **2.** A bag; knapsack.

wal′low, 1 wŏl′o; 2 wạl′o. **I.** vi. To roll about, as swine, etc., in mud or mire. **II.** n. The act of wallowing; place where animals wallow.

wal′nut, 1 wŏl′nut; 2 wạl′nŭt, n. A valuable timber=tree, its edible nut, or its wood.

wal′rus, 1 wŏl′rus or wŏl′rus; 2 wạl′rŭs or wạl′rŭs, n. A large marine seal=like mammal having tusk=like canines in the upper jaw.

waltz, 1 wŏlts; 2 wạlts. **I.** t. vi. To dance a waltz. **II.** n. A round dance in triple time, or the music for it.

wam′pum, 1 wom′pum; 2 wạm′pŭm, n. Beads formed of shells strung on threads, formerly used by the American Indians as currency, and worn also as ornaments.

Leaf and Fruit of the Black Walnut.

a, nut, as it grows: *b,* nut, with shuck removed.

wan, 1 wen; 2 wạn, a. **1.** Pale, as from sickness; pallid. **2.** Dismal. **-ly,** adv. **-ness,** n.

wand, 1 wend; 2 wạnd, n. **1.** A long slender rod. **2.** A musician's baton.

wan′der, 1 won′dɚ; 2 wạn′der, vi. **1.** To roam hither and thither; ramble; stray. **2.** To ramble mentally; stray from a subject; also, to be delirious.— **wan′der-er,** n.

wane, 1 wŏn; 2 wān. **I.** vi. [WANED; WAN′ING.] To diminish; decline. **II.** n. Decrease, as of the moon's visible surface; decline.

wantd, 1 wŏnt; 2 wạnt, v. **I.** t. **1.** To feel the need of; desire. **2.** To be without; be in need of; lack; require. **II.** i. To be needy; be deficient; be lacking or absent.— **want′ing,** pa. **1.** Not at hand; missing. **2.** Lacking something; deficient.

want, n. **1.** Lack or absence of something; scarcity. **2.** Privation; poverty. **3.** Something lacking or desired.

wan′ton, 1 won′tɚn; 2 wạn′ton. **I.** vt. & vi. To squander; waste; revel. **II.** a. **1.** Unrestrained; frolicsome; licentious. **2.** Inexcusable. **III.** n. A licentious person. **-ly,** adv. **-ness,** n.

wap′i-ti, 1 wŏp′ɪ-tɪ; 2 wạp′i-ti, n. A large North=American deer: often erroneously called *elk.*

war, 1 wŏr; 2 wạr. **I.** vi. [WARRED; WARDS; WAR′RING.] To be at war; make war; contend. **II.** n. An armed contest between nations or states.— **war′fare″,** n. The waging of war; armed conflict; contest.— **war′like,** a. Of, like, or disposed for war; martial; military.— **war=plane,** n. An armed military aeroplane.

war′bl(ep, 1 wŏr′bl; 2 wạr′bl. **I.** vt. & vi. [WAR′BL(E)Dp; WAR′BLING.] **1.** To sing, as a bird; trill. **2.** To make a liquid, murmuring sound. **II.** n. The act of warbling; a song.— **war′bler,** n. A singing bird.

ward, 1 wŏrd; 2 wạrd. **I**d. vt. To repel or turn aside, as a blow; defend. **II.** n. **1.** A person who is under the guardianship of another. **2.** A section of a city; division in a hospital, prison, etc.; division in a lock or key.— **ward′ship,** n. The state of a ward; pupilage.

-ward, -wards, suffix. Denoting motion to or from a point; as, up*ward,* out*ward.*

war′den, 1 wŏr′dn; 2 wạr′dn, n. A keeper; guardian; chief officer of a prison.— **war′-den-ry,** n. **war′den-ship**‡.

ward′er1, 1 wŏr′dɚ; 2 wạr′der, n. A keeper; guard; sentinel.

ward′er2, 1 wŏr′dɚ; 2 wạr′der, n. An official staff or baton.

ward′robe″, 1 wŏrd′rōb″; 2 wạrd′rōb″, n. A closet for clothes; one's wearing=apparel.

ware, 1 wâr; 2 wār. **I.** vt. To guard against; beware of. **II.** a. Conscious; aware; wary.

ware, n. **1.** Manufactured articles collectively; as, table*ware,* glass*ware.* **2.** pl. Articles of commerce; goods.— **ware′-house″,** n. A storehouse.

wa′ri-ly, wa′ri-ness. See WARY.

warm, 1 wŏrm; 2 warm. **I.** *vt.* & *vi.* To make or become warm; heat slightly. **II.** *a.* **1.** Having moderate heat. **2.** Ardent; zealous; passionate.— **warm′ly,** *adv.*— **warmth,** 1 wŏrmth; 2 w·rmth, *n.* The state or sensation of being warm.

warn, 1 wŏrn; 2 warn, *vt* & *vi.* To give notice of danger (to); notify authoritatively.— **warn′ing. I.** *pa.* Serving as a warning. **II.** *n.* **1.** Notice of danger. **2.** An admonition. **3.** Something that warns.

warp[t], 1 wŏrp; 2 warp, *vt.* & *vi.* **1.** To twist out of shape, as by shrinkage; distort; bias. **2.** To move (a vessel) by hauling on a rope attached to some fixed object.

warp, *n.* **1.** The state of being warped; a twist. **2.** The threads that run the long way of a fabric. **3.** A light cable.

war′rant, 1 wŏr′ant; 2 war′ant. **I**[d]. *vt.* To guarantee the quality or character of; assure; justify. **II.** *n.* **1.** A judicial writ authorizing arrest, search, seizure, etc. **2.** A voucher; guaranty; sanction. — **war′rant-a-ble**(e[r], *a.*— **war′rant-a-bly,** *adv.*— **war′ran-ty,** *n.* [-TIES[z], *pl.*] A written warrant by a seller.

war′ren, 1 wŏr′en; 2 war′ĕn, *n.* A place where rabbits or small game live and breed.

war′rior, 1 wŏr′yər *or* wor′i-ər; 2 war′yer *or* war′i-or, *n.* A man engaged in or experienced in warfare; a soldier.

wart, 1 wŏrt; 2 wart, *n.* A small excrescence rooted in the skin; a protuberance on a plant.— **wart′y,** *a.*

wa′ry, 1 wē′ri; 2 wā′ry, *a.* [WA′RI-ER; WA′RI-EST.] **1.** Carefully watching and guarding. **2.** Shrewd; wily.— **wa′ri-ly,** *adv.* — **wa′ri-ness,** *n.*

was, 1 wez; 2 waz, *v.* A form of a defective verb, used as the imperfect tense of the verb *be.*

wash[t], 1 wesh; 2 wash, *v.* **I.** *t.* **1.** To cleanse, as with water; purify. **2.** To sweep over or dash against, as waves. **3.** To supply with a thin coat, as of metal, or color. **II.** *i.* To perform one's ablutions.— **wash′er,** *n.* **1.** One who or that which washes. **2.** *Mech.* A small flat perforated disk, as for placing beneath a nut.— **wash′er-wo″man,** *n.* A laundress.

wash, *n.* **1.** The act or process of washing. **2.** The articles washed at one time. **3.** A preparation used in washing; a thin coating. **4.** The breaking of waves on a shore.

wasp, 1 wesp; 2 wasp, *n.* A stinging insect, having membranous wings. See illus. in next column.— **wasp′ish,** *a.* Irritable; irascible. **-ly,** *adv.* **-ness,** *n.*

was′sail, 1 wes′il *or* was′il; 2 wǎs′il, *n.* A drinking revel; carousal.

wast, 1 west; 2 wast, *2d per. sing. imp. ind.* of BE, *v.*

waste, 1 wēst; 2 wāst, *vt.* & *vi.* [WAST′ED[d]; WAST′ING.] **1.** To expend thoughtlessly or idly; squander. **2.** To lose or cause to lose strength or substance gradually, as by disease or training.

Social Wasp and Section of its Nest. ¹⁄₄

waste, *a.* **1.** Worthless; useless; refuse. **2.** Unproductive; desert; made desolate.

waste, *n.* **1.** The act of wasting or squandering. **2.** A continuous diminishing or failing; wasting; decline. **3.** Refuse. **4.** A wilderness; desert.— **waste′ful,** *a.* **-ly,** *adv.* **-ness.** *n.* [waster.]

wast′rel, 1 wēst′rel; 2 wāst′rĕl, *n.* A waif; a

watch[t], 1 wech; 2 wach, *v.* **I.** *t.* To observe closely; keep in view; guard. **II.** *i.* **1.** To be on the alert; be wakeful; serve as a watchman. **2.** To wait expectantly: followed by *for.*

watch, *n.* **1.** Vigilant observation; wakefulness. **2.** A watcher; watchman; guard; also, watchmen collectively. **3.** *Naut.* The period of time that one set of men is on duty; a division of the night; also, the men on duty. **4.** A pocket mechanism for keeping time.— **watch′er,** *n.* One who watches, as a nurse.— **watch′ful,** *a.* Vigilant. **-ly,** *adv.* **-ness,** *n.*— **watch′man,** *n.* [-MEN, *pl.*] One whose business is to keep watch or guard, as at night.— **watch′word″,** *n.* A secret password; a rallying-cry.

wa′ter, 1 wŏ′tər; 2 wa′ter, *v.* **I.** *t.* To pour water upon; treat with water; dilute. **II.** *i.* **1.** To be watery, as the eyes; have a longing. **2.** To take in water.

wa′ter, *n.* **1.** A limpid liquid compound of hydrogen and oxygen, constituting the bulk of the ocean, rivers, lakes, etc. **2.** Any particular body of water. **3.** Any one of the watery secretions of animals. **4.** A watery appearance, as in precious stones; luster; sheen in certain textiles; hence, purity.— **wa′ter-col″or,** *n.* A color for painting, rendered semifluid with water for use; a painting in such colors or the art of painting in them.— **wa′ter-course″,** *n.* A stream of water; river; brook.— **wa′ter-cress″,** *n.* A creeping perennial herb of the mustard family. See illus. on following page.— **wa′ter-fall″,** *n.* A cataract; cas-

1: **ȧ**rtistic, **ă**rt; fat, fāre; fast; get, prēy; hit, police; obey, gō; not, ôr; full, rūle; but, bûrn.

2: ärt, āpe, făt, fâre, fȧst, what, ȧll; mē, gĕt, prey, fẽrn; hĭt, īce; ĭ=ē; ĭ=ĕ; gō, nŏt, ôr, wọo

cade.— **w.-fowl**, *n.* A bird that lives on or about the water.— **w.-lily**, *n.* An aquatic plant that bears a flower, rising just above or floating on the water.— **w.-logged**, *a.* Heavy and unmanageable on account of the leakage of water into the hold, as a ship; also, water-soaked.— **wa'ter-man**, *n.* A boatman.— **wa'ter-mel''on**, *n.* The large edible fruit of a trailing plant of the gourd family.— **w.-power**, *n.* **1.** The power of moving water as applied to the driving of machinery. **2.** A fall in a stream from which motive power may be obtained.— **wa'ter-proof''**, *n.* Material rendered impervious to water; a garment made from such material.— **w.-proof**, *a.* Allowing no water to enter or pass through, as a fabric. — **wa'ter-shed''**, *n.* A ridge from which streams flow in opposite directions.— **w.-tight**, *a.* So closely made that water can not pass through.— **w.-wheel**, *n.* A wheel so arranged with floats, buckets, etc., that it may be turned by flowing water.— **w.-works**, *n. pl.* A system of machines, buildings, and appliances for furnishing a water-supply.— **wa'ter-ing-place''**, *n.* A place affording a supply of water, or one having mineral springs, or near a lake or ocean.— **wa'ter-y**, *a.* Containing much water; thin or liquid; consisting of or pertaining to water. — **wa'ter-i-ness**, *n.*

Common Watercress.

wa'ter-spout'', 1 wô'tẽr-spout''; 2 wạ'ter-spout'', *n.* A moving column of spray with water in the lower parts, due to a whirlwind at sea.

watt, 1 wŏt; 2 wạt, *n.* The practical unit of electrical activity, corresponding to the horse-power in mechanics; 746 watts are equal to one horse-power: from the Scottish inventor, James Watt (1736–1819).

wat'tle, 1 wŏt'l; 2 wạt'l. **I.** *vt.* [WAT'-TLED; WAT'TLING.] To weave, as twigs, into a network; form, as baskets, of flexible twigs. **II.** *n.* **1.** A frame of rods or twigs platted together, or a twig so used. **2.** A fleshy growth depending from the head or neck of a bird, as a cock.

wave, 1 wĕv; 2 wāv, *vt. & vi.* [WAVED; WAV'ING.] **1.** To move to and fro in the air. **2.** To move with undulations, as water.

wave, *n.* A moving ridge on the surface of a liquid; an undulation of air or light; an undulating or wavy line.— **w.-length**, *n. Radio.* The distance between corresponding points on any two consecutive electric waves;

as, a *wave-length* of 200 meters.— **wave'let**, *n.* A little wave.— **wa'ver**, *vt. & vi.* To move one way and the other; sway; falter.— **wav'y**, *a.*

wax, 1 waks; 2 wăks. **I.** *vt.* To coat or treat with wax. **II.** *n.* A fatty solid substance of animal, vegetable, or mineral origin.— **wax'en**, *a.* Consisting of wax; wax-like; waxy.— **wax'y**, *a.* **1.** Resembling wax; hence, plastic. **2.** Made of or coated with wax.— **wax'i-ness**, *n.* [grow.

waxt, *vi.* To become larger gradually;

way, 1 wē; 2 wā, *n.* **1.** A path; course; track; road; channel. **2.** Distance; direction. **3.** A method of procedure; manner; style; plan; particular.— **way'-bill''**, *n.* An accompanying list of goods or passengers carried by any common carrier, as by a train on a railway.— **way'far''er**, *n.* One who journeys along a way on foot.— **way'far''ing**, *pa.* — **way'lay'**, *vt.* [WAY'LAID'; WAY'LAY'ING.] **1.** To watch for by the way, as with a view to rob. **2.** To accost on the way.— **way'side''**, *n.* The side or edge of the road or highway.— **way'ward**, *a.* Wandering away; wilful; unsteady; vacillating. **-ly,** *adv.* **-ness,** *n.*— **way'worn''**, *a.* Worn or wearied by travel.

we, 1 wī; 2 wē; *pron. 1st per. pl.* Plural of I.

weak, 1 wīk; 2 wēk, *a.* Lacking in strength or force; feeble; yielding; deficient.— **weak'en**, *vt.* **1.** To render weak or weaker; enfeeble. **2.** To dilute.— **weak'fish''**, *n.* An American food-fish.— **weak'ling**, *n.* A feeble person or animal.— **weak'ly.** **I.** *a.* Sickly. **II.** *adv.* In a weak manner.— **weak'ness**, *n.*

weal, 1 wīl; 2 wēl, *n.* Welfare; health; prosperity.

wealth,) 1 welth; 2 wĕlth, *n.* A great
wealths,) amount of property; riches; exuberance; profusion.— **wealth'y**, *a.* [WEALTH'-I-ER; WEALTH'I-EST.] Possessing wealth; affluent.

wean, 1 wīn; 2 wēn, *vt.* **1.** To accustom (the young of any animal) to relinquish its mother's milk for other nourishment. **2.** To alienate the affections of; reconcile to some privation.

weap'on,) 1 wep'an; 2 wĕp'on, *n.* Any
wep'ons,) implement of war or combat. — **weap'on-less**, *n.*

wear, 1 wār; 2 wâr, *v.* [WORE; WORN.] **I.** *t.* **1.** To carry on the person; have on; maintain; exhibit. **2.** To impair by use; efface or rub off. **II.** *i.* **1.** To be impaired gradually by use. **2.** To bear using; endure.— **wear'er**, *n.* [wind astern.

wear, *vt. & vi. Naut.* To go about with the wind astern.

wear, *n.* **1.** The act of wearing, or the state of being worn. **2.** Impairment from use or time.

wea'ry, 1 wī'rı; 2 wē'ry. **I.** *vt. & vi.*

[WEA'RIED; WEA'RY-ING.] To make or grow weary; fatigue; tire. **II.** *a.* [WEA'-RI-ER; WEA'RI-EST.] **1.** Worn with exertion, vexation, or endurance; tired. **2.** Discontented· vexed.— **wea'ri-ly,** *adv.*— **wea'ri-ness,** *n.*— **wea'ri-some,** *a.* Tiresome. **-ly,** *adv.* **-ness,** *n.*

wea'sel, 1 wī'zl; 2 wē'zl, *n.* A small elongated reddish-brown quadruped, that preys on smaller mammals and birds.

Weasel. 1/10

weath'er, ⎰ 1 weth'ạr; 2
weth'erˢ, ⎱ wĕth'er. **I.** *vt.* **1.** To pass successfully; survive. **2.** To expose to the weather. **3.** *Naut.* To go to the windward of. **II.** *n.* Atmospheric conditions, as regards heat, cold, dampness, rain, winds, storms, etc.— **weath'er=beat″en,** *a.* Bearing the effects of exposure to weather. — **w.=board,** *n.* A board prepared for the outside covering of wooden buildings.— **w.= bound,** *a.* Detained by unfavorable weather. — **weath'er-cock″,** *n.* A vane. **weath'er= vane″:**— **w.=gage,** *n. Naut.* A position to windward; an advantage gained.— **w.=glass,** *n.* A barometer.— **w.=wise,** *a.* Experienced in observing the weather.

weav(eˢ, 1 wīv; 2 wēv, *vt.* [WOVE or WEAV(E)Dˢ; WO'V(E)Nᴾ or WOVE or WEAV(E)Dˢ; WEAV'ING.] To entwine, as threads, in a loom; make, as a fabric, by this process.— **weav'er,** *n.*

wea'zen, 1 wī'zn; 2 wē'zn, *a.* Same as WIZEN. **wea'zened‡.**

web, 1 web; 2 wĕb, *n.* **1.** A woven fabric. **2.** A cob veb; a scheme or snare. **3.** A membrane connecting the toes of an animal.— **web(he)dˢ,** *a.*— **web'bing,** *n.* A woven strip.— **web'=foot″,** *n.* **1.** A foot with webbed toes. **2.** A bird with webbed feet.— **web'=foot″ed,** *a.*

wed, 1 wed; 2 wĕd, *vt.* [WED'DEDᵈ or WED; WED'DING.] **1.** To marry. **2.** To devote (oneself) permanently to something.— **wed'ding,** *n.* **1.** A marriage ceremony. **2.** The anniversary of a marriage.— **wed'lock,** *n.* Matrimony.

wedge, 1 wej; 2 wĕdg. **I.** *vt. & vi.* [WEDGED; WEDG'ING.] To act upon by a wedge; split; fasten. **II.** *n.* A V=shaped piece, as for splitting or for fastening.

Wednes'day, 1 wenz'dī; 2 wĕnş'da, *n.* The fourth day of the week.

wee, 1 wī; 2 wē, *a.* [Colloq. & Scot.] Very small; little; tiny.

weed¹, 1 wīd; 2 wēd. **I.** *vt.* To remove the weeds from; root out, as weeds. **II.** *n.* Any troublesome useless plant.—

weed'er, *n.*— **weed'y,** *a.* **1.** Having weeds. **2.** Resembling a weed.

weed², *n.* A token of mourning worn as part of the dress.

week, 1 wīk; 2 wēk, *n.* A period of seven days.— **week'=day″,** *n.* Any day of the week except Sunday.— **week'ly. I.** *a.* **1.** Reckoned by the week. **2.** Occurring once a week. **II.** *n.* [WEEK-LIES²*, pl.*] A publication issued once a week. **III.** *adv.* Once a week.

ween, 1 wīn; 2 wēn, *vt.* [WEENED or WENT‡; WEENDˢ.] To think; guess; fancy.

weep, 1 wīp; 2 wēp, *vt. & vi.* [WEPT; WEEP'ING.] **1.** To let fall, as tears; shed tears. **2.** To lament; grieve. **3.** To be pendulous and drooping.— **weep'er,** *n.*

wee'vil, 1 wī'vil; 2 wē'vil, *n.* An insect destructive to plants.

weft, 1 weft; 2 wĕft, *n.* The cross=threads in a web of cloth; woof.

weigh, 1 wē; 2 wȩ, *v.* **I.** *t.* **1.** To find the weight of. **2.** To estimate the worth or importance of. **3.** To press upon heavily; burden. **4.** To lift up, as an anchor. **II.** *i.* **1.** To have a specified weight. **2.** To be of value; avail. **3.** *Naut.* To raise anchor.— **weigh'er,** *n.*— **weight. I**ᵈ. *vt.* To add weight to; burden. **II.** *n.* **1.** The measure of the force with which bodies tend toward the earth's center. **2.** A definite mass used, as of metal in weighing. **3.** Any heavy mass; efficacy; preponderance; oppressiveness.— **weight'less,** *a.* Having no weight; imponderable.— **weight'y,** *a.* [WEIGHT'I-ER; WEIGHT'I-EST.] Having great weight; important; influential.— **weight'i-ly,** *adv.*— **weight'i-ness,** *n.*

Apothecaries' Weight

(used in compounding medicines).

20 grains (gr.)	= 1 scruple (℈).
3 scruples	= 1 dram (ʒ).
8 drams	= 1 ounce (℥).
12 ounces	= 1 pound (℔).

NOTE.— The pound, ounce, and grain have the same weight as those of Troy weight.

Avoirdupois Weight

(used in weighing all articles except drugs, gold, silver, and precious stones).

27 u/₃₂ grains	= 1 dram (dr.).
16 drams	= 1 ounce (oz.).
16 ounces	= 1 pound (lb.).
25 pounds	= 1 quarter (qr.).
4 quarters ⎰ 100 pounds ⎱	= 1 hundredweight (cwt.).
20 hundredweight or ⎰ 2,000 pounds ⎱	= 1 ton (T.).

NOTE.— 1 lb. Avoirdupois = 7,000 grs.

The ton and hundredweight above given (often called the *short ton* and the *short hun-*

1: ạrtistic, **ạ̈**rt; fạt, fāre; fạst; get, prēy; hit, police; obey, gō; net, ôr; fụll, rūle; but, būrn.
2: ärt, **ä**pe, fặt, fâre, fȧst, whạt, ạll; mē, gĕt, prey, fẽrn; hĭt, īce; ī=ē; ĭ=ĕ; gō, nŏt, ôr won.

dredweight) are those in common use in the United States.

The ton of 2,240 lbs., and the hundred-weight of 112 lbs. (often called the *long ton* and the *long hundredweight*), are used at United States custom=houses and in whole-sale transactions in coal and iron, and are in general use in Great Britain. When the long ton is the standard, 1 qr. = 28 lbs.

Troy Weight

(used in weighing gold, silver, and precious stones).

24 grains (*gr.*)   = 1 pennyweight (*dwt.*).
20 pennyweights   = 1 ounce (*oz.*).
12 ounces   = 1 pound (*lb.*).

NOTE.— 1 lb. troy = 5,760 grains. In weigh-ing diamonds 1 carat = 3.168 troy grains, and is divided into quarters, which are called car-at=grains.   See also CARAT in vocabulary.

weir, 1 wīr; 2 wēr, *n.* A dam; a wattled enclosure in a stream to catch fish. **wear‡.**

weird, 1 wīrd; 2 wērd, *a.* Pertaining to witchcraft; unnatural; awakening super-stitious feeling; uncanny.

wel'come, 1 wel'kəm; 2 wĕl'eom. **I.** *vt.* [WEL'COMED, WEL'COMDˢ; WEL'COM=ING.] To give a welcome to. **II.** *a.* **1.** Ad-mitted gladly. **2.** Pleasing. **3.** Made free to use. **III.** *n.* A hearty greeting; hospitable reception.

weld, 1 weld; 2 wĕld. **I**ᵈ. *vt.* To unite, as heated metal, in one piece by hammering or pressure. **II.** *n.* The act of welding; also, the closed joint so formed.

wel'fare", 1 wel'fâr"; 2 wĕl'fâr", *n.* The state of faring well; prosperity.

wel'kin, 1 wel'kin; 2 wĕl'kin, *n.* [Poet.] The vault of the sky; the region of the clouds.

well, 1 wel; 2 wĕl, *vt. & vi.* To flow up, as water in a spring.

well, *a.* [BET'TER; BEST.] **1.** Suitable; fit; right. **2.** Having good health; free from trouble.

well, *n.* **1.** A hole sunk into the earth for water, oil, or natural gas. **2.** A spring. **3.** A depression, cavity, etc.— **well'=spring",** *n.* An inexhaustible fountain.

well, *adv.* [BET'TER; BEST.] **1.** Excel-lently; suitably; prosperously. **2.** To a great extent.— **well'=be"ing,** *n.* Happiness or prosperity; welfare.— **w.=born,** *a.* Of good lineage.— **w.=bred,** *a.* **1.** Having good ancestry. **2.** Well brought up; polite.— **w.=favored,** *a.* Of attractive personal appear-ance; handsome; comely.— **w.=nigh,** *adv.* Very nearly; almost.— **w.=read,** *a.* Having a wide knowledge of books by perusal.— **w.=to=do,** *a.* In prosperous circumstances. **w.=off‡.**   [Alas! **well'a=way‡.**

well'a=day, 1 wel'ə-dē; 2 wĕl'ȧ-dā, *interj.*

Welsh, 1 welsh; 2 wĕlsh. **I.** *a.* Pertain-

ing to Wales, its people, or their language. **II.** *n.* The people or language of Wales.

welt, 1 welt; 2 wĕlt. **I**ᵈ. *vt.* **1.** To sew a welt on or in. **2.** To flog severely. **II.** *n.* **1.** A strip of material, to cover a seam. **2.** A swollen stripe on the skin, made by a lash.

wel'ter, 1 wel'tər; 2 wĕl'tẽr, *vi.* To roll or tumble about, as in mud; wallow.

wen, 1 wen; 2 wĕn, *n.* An encysted tumor; a protuberance or prominence.

wench, 1 wench; 2 wĕnch, *n.* A girl of humble condition; serving=maid.

wendᵈ, 1 wend; 2 wĕnd, *vt. & vi.* To direct one's course; go.

went, 1 went; 2 wĕnt, *vt.* An obsolete im-perfect of *wend,* now used as imperfect of *go.*

wept, 1 wept; 2 wĕpt, *imp. & pp.* of WEEP, *v.*

wer(eᵖ, 1 wûr; 2 wēr. Indicative plural and subjunctive singular and plural of WAS, imperfect of BE, *v.*

wert, *2d per. sing. ind. & subj.* of WAS, *v.*

west, 1 west; 2 wĕst. **I.** *a.* **1.** Located at the west; facing the west. **2.** Coming from the west. **II.** *n.* **1.** That point of the compass or quarter of the heavens where the sun sets. **2.** Any western region. **III.** *adv.* In a westerly direc-tion.— **west'er=ly,** *a.* **2.** Approximately western. **II.** *adv.* Westward.— **west'ern,** *a.* **1.** Being in the west; pertaining to the west. **2.** Proceeding from the west.— **west'-ward,** *a.*— Tending or lying toward the west. — **west'ward,** **west'wards,** *adv.* Toward the west. **west'ward=ly‡.**

wet, 1 wet; 2 wĕt. **I.** *vt.* [WET'TED⁴ or WET; WET'TING.] To moisten or soak with liquid. **II.** *a.* Moistened or satu-rated with water or other liquid; watery; moist; rainy. **III.** *n.* A considerable degree of moisture; rain.— **wet'ness,** *n.*— **wet'=nurse",** *n.* A woman who is hired to suckle the babe of another woman.

weth'er, 1 weth'ạr; 2 wĕth'ẽr, *n.* A castrated ram.— **bell'=weth"er,** *n.* A wether bearing a bell, as leader of the flock.

whale, 1 hwēl; 2 hwāl, *n.* A marine mammal of fish=like form.— **whale'back",** *n.* A form of vessel built for rough seas, having the main decks covered in and rounded over.— **whale'bone",** *n.* The horny substance from the palate of certain whales.— **whal'er,** *n.* A person or a vessel engaged in whaling.— **whal'ing,** *n.* The industry of capturing whales.

wharf, 1 hwôrf; 2 hwarf, *n.* [WHARVES or WHARFS, *pl.*] A landing=place for vessels and their cargoes.— **wharf'age,** *n. Com.* **1.** Charge for the use of a wharf. **2.** Wharf accommodations.— **wharf'in=ger,** *n.* One who keeps a wharf for landing goods.

1: ə = final; ɪ = habɪt; aɪsle; aᴜ = out; ŏɪl; ɪū = feud; chin; go; ŋ = sing; thin, this.
2: wọlf, dọ; bŏŏk, bōōt; fụll, rụle, cūre, bŭt, bûrn; ŏɪl, bŏy; ğo, ġem; iŋk: thin, this.

what, 1 hwet; 2 hwąt. **I.** *a.* **1.** In interrogative construction, asking for information as to a person or thing. **2.** How surprizing, ridiculous, great, or the like. **II.** *interrog. pron.* Which circumstance, event, relation, or the like. **III.** *rel. pron.* That which: a double relative. **IV.** *adv.* **1.** In what respect; to what extent. **2.** In some measure; partly. **V.** *conj.* **1.** So far as; as well as. **2.** That: especially in the phrase *but what.*— **what-ev'er,** *pron.* The whole that; all that; anything that.— **what″so-ev'er,** *a. & pron.* Whatever. [skin.

wheal, 1 hwēl; 2 hwēl, *n.* A welt on the

wheat, 1 hwēt; 2 hwēt, *n.* A grain, from which flour is made; also, the plant producing this grain.— **wheat′en,** *a.* Made of wheat.

whee′dle, 1 hwī′dl; 2 hwē′dl, *vt. & vi.* [WHEE′DLED; WHEE′DLING.] To persuade by flattery; coax; deceive.— **whee′dler,** *n.*— **whee′dling,** *n.*

wheel, 1 hwīl; 2 hwēl. **I.** *vt. & vi.* To carry or move on wheels; roll; turn; rotate; revolve. **II.** *n.* **1.** A circular framework or a disk, made to rotate on its axis. **2.** A wheeling; turning.— **wheel′bar″row,** *n.* A box-like vehicle with ordinarily one wheel and two handles.— **wheel′wright″,** *n.* A man whose business is to make or repair wheels and wheeled vehicles.

wheeze(er, 1 hwīz; 2 hwēz, *vi.* [WHEEZ(E)D⁸; WHEEZ′ING.] To breathe with a husky, whistling sound.— **wheeze(**er, *n.* A wheezing sound.— **wheez′y,** *a.* Subject to wheezing.

whelk, 1 hwelk; 2 hwĕlk, *n.* A marine mollusk having a spiral shell.

whelm, 1 hwelm; 2 hwĕlm, *vt.* To submerge; overpower; destroy; overwhelm.

whelp, 1 hwelp; 2 hwĕlp. **I.** *vt. & vi.* To bear whelps. **II.** *n.* A cub; puppy; worthless young fellow.

when, 1 hwen; 2 hwĕn, *adv.* **1.** At what or which time. **2.** At the time that; while; altho; after that.— **when-ev'er,** *adv. & conj.* At whatever time. **when″so-ev'er‡.**

whence, } 1 hwens; 2 hwĕnç, *adv.* **1.** From
whenseer, } what place or source. **2.** For which reason; wherefore.

where, 1 hwār; 2 hwêr, *adv.* At or in what place, relation, or situation; to what place; whither; whence.— **where′a-bouts″. I.** *n.* The place in or near which a person or thing is. **where′a-bout″‡. II.** *adv.* Near or at what place; about where.— **where-as′,** *conj.* **1.** Seeing that. **2.** The fact of the matter being that.— **where-at′,** *adv.* **1.** At what. **2.** At which.— **where-**

by′, *adv.* **1.** By what; how. **2.** By, near, through, or by means of which.— **where′-fore,** *adv.* **1.** For what reason; why. **2.** Therefore.— **where-in′,** *adv.* **1.** In what particular or regard. **2.** In which thing, place, etc.; in whatever.— **where-of′,** *adv.* **1.** Of or from what. **2.** Of which or whom. — **where-on′,** *adv.* **1.** On what or whom. **2.** On which.— **where″so-ev′er,** *adv.* **1.** Wherever. **2.** To what place soever.— **where-to′,** *adv.* **1.** To what place or end. **2.** To which; whither.— **where″up-on′,** *adv.* **1.** Whereon. **2.** Conjunctively, upon which or whom; after which.— **wher-ev′er,** *adv. & conj.* In or at whatever place.— **where-with′,** *adv.* **1.** With what. **2.** With which. — **where″with-al′,** *n.* The necessary means or resources.

wher′ry, 1 hwer′ı; 2 hwĕr′y, *n.* [WHER′-RIES², *pl.*]
A light, sharp rowboat; also, a decked fishing-vessel with two sails.

Thames Wherry.

whet, 1 hwet; 2 hwĕt. **I.** *vt.* [WHET′TED⁴; WHET′TING.] To sharpen; excite. **II.** *n.* The act of whetting; something that whets or excites.— **whet′stone″,** *n.* A fine-grained stone for whetting edged tools. — **whet′ter,** *n.*

wheth′er, 1 hweth′ar; 2 hwĕth′er. **I.** *a. & pron.* [Archaic.] Which: properly of two. **II.** *conj.* In case; if: introducing an alternative clause, followed by a correlative *or,* or *or whether.*

whey, 1 hwē; 2 hwę, *n.* A clear liquid that separates from the curd when milk is curdled.— **whey′ey, whey′ish,** *a.*

which, 1 hwich; 2 hwĭch, *interrog. or rel. pron.* What particular one of a certain number or class referred to.— **which-ev′er,** *pron.* Whether one or another (of two or of several). **which″so-ev′er‡.**

whiff, 1 hwif; 2 hwĭf. **I.** *vt. & vi.* To send forth whiffs, as of smoke; throw out, as whiffs. **II.** *n.* A slight gust, as one bearing an odor; puff, as of smoke.

whif′fle, 1 hwif′l; 2 hwĭf′l, *vt. & vi.* [WHIF′-FLED; WHIF′FLING.] To waver; sway; shift; vacillate.— **whif′fle-tree″,** *n.* Same as SWINGLETREE.

Whig, 1 hwig; 2 hwĭg, *n.* **1.** A member of the Liberal party in England in the 18th and 19th centuries; also, a Covenanter or a Roundhead. **2.** An American colonist who supported the Revolutionary war; later, a

member of a party opposed to the Democratic.— **Whig'ger-y,** *n.* The doctrines of Whigs.

while, 1 hwail; 2 hwîl. **I.** *vt.* [WHILED; WHIL'ING.] To spend pleasantly, as time: commonly followed by *away*. **II.** *n.* A short time; also, a period of time. **III.** *conj.* **1.** During the time that. **2.** At the same time that; sometimes; tho.— **whilst,** *conj.* While: old form.

whi'lom, 1 hwai'lom; 2 hwi'lom, *a.* & *adv.* Former; formerly; at times. [freak.

whim, 1 hwim; 2 hwĭm, *n.* A caprice;

whim'per, 1 hwim'pər; 2 hwĭm'per. **I.** *vt.* & *vi.* To whine; complain. **II.** *n.* A low, broken, whining cry; whine.

whim'sy, 1 hwim'zı; 2 hwĭm'sy, *n.* [-SIES^z, *pl.*] A whim. **whim'sey‡.— whim'si-cal,** *a.* Having eccentric ideas; capricious; odd. **-ly,** *adv.* **-ness,** *n.—* **whim"si-cal'i-ty,** *n.*

whine, 1 hwain; 2 hwîn. **I.** *vt.* & *vi.* [WHINED; WHIN'ING.] To utter with a whine; give forth a whine; find fault in a weak or childish way. **II.** *n.* A plaintive, complaining cry; a suppressed nasal drawl.

whin'ny, 1 hwin'ı; 2 hwĭn'y. **I.** *vi.* [-NIED; -NY-ING.] To neigh. **II.** *n.* [-NIES^z, *pl.*] The cry of a horse; a neigh.

whip, 1 hwip; 2 hwĭp, *v.* [WHIPPED^t or WHIPT; WHIP'PING.] **I.** *t.* **1.** To strike with a whip; flog. **2.** To effect by or as by blows of a whip. **3.** To move or sweep with a lashing motion. **II.** *i.* To move nimbly.

whip, *n.* **1.** An instrument consisting of a handle and lash, or the like, used for driving draft-animals or for administering punishment. **2.** A driver. **3.** A rope and pulley used for hoisting, etc. — **whip'per,** *n.—* **whip'ping,** *n.* The act of one who whips or the condition of being whipped; castigation.

whip'ple-tree", 1 hwip'l-trī"; 2 hwĭp'l-trē", *n.* A swingletree; whiffletree.

whip'poor-will", 1 hwip'pur-wil"; 2 hwĭp'poor-wil", *n.* A goat-sucker of the eastern United States, named from its cry.

Whippoorwill. ¹/₁₀

whir, 1 hwûr; 2 hwîr. **I.** *vt.* & *vi.* [WHIRRED, WHIRD^s; WHIR'RING.] To whirl; move or fly with a whir. **II.** *n.* A trilling, swishing sound, produced by the sudden rising of birds. **whirr‡.**

whirl, 1 hwûrl; 2 hwîrl. **I.** *vt.* & *vi.* To turn, or cause to turn; twirl; spin; rotate.

II. *n.* **1.** A swift rotating or revolving motion. **2.** Something whirling.— **whirl'-i-gig,** *n.* **1.** A toy that revolves rapidly upon an axis. **2.** A merry-go-round.— **whirl'pool",** *n.* An eddy or vortex where water moves with a gyrating sweep.— **whirl'-wind",** *n.* A moving funnel-shaped column of air, causing waterspouts, dust-whirls, etc.

whisk, 1 hwisk; 2 hwĭsk. **I.** *vt.* & *vi.* To move or be moved along with a light, sweeping movement. **II.** *n.* **1.** A light, sweeping movement. **2.** A little broom; wisp.

whisk'er, 1 hwisk'ər; 2 hwĭsk'er, *n.* **1.** *pl.* The hair that grows on the sides of a man's face; loosely, the beard. **2.** One of the long bristles about the mouth of some animals, as the cat.— **whisk'ered,** *a.*

whis'ky, } 1 hwis'kı; 2 hwĭs'ky, *n.* **whis'key,** } [-KIES^z, *pl.*] An alcoholic liquor obtained by the distillation of grain.

whis'per, 1 hwis'pər; 2 hwĭs'per, *v.* **I.** *t.* To utter in a whisper. **II.** *i.* To speak in a whisper; speak with caution; devise mischief; rustle.— **whis'per-er,** *n.*

whis'per, *n.* An articulated but not sonant breath; also, a low, rustling sound; a secret communication. [quiet; calmed.

whist, 1 hwist; 2 hwĭst, *a.* Made silent or

whist, *n.* A game of cards played by four persons.

whist, *interj.* Hush! be still!

whis'tle(r), 1 hwis'l; 2 hwĭs'l. **I.** *vt.* & *vi.* [WHIS'TL(E)D^d; WHIS'TLING.] To sound as a whistle; call or guide by a whistle. **II.** *n.* The sound of air, steam, etc., forced through a narrow aperture or against a thin edge; also, an instrument for producing such a sound.— **whis'tler,** *n.*

whit, 1 hwit; 2 hwĭt, *n.* The smallest particle; speck.

white, 1 hwait; 2 hwît. **I.** *vt.* & *vi.* To whiten. **II.** *a.* **1.** Having the color of pure snow. **2.** Having a light complexion; blond. **III.** *n.* **1.** A color devoid of any tint, the opposite of *black*. **2.** Anything white, as the *white* portion of the eyeball, a *white* person, etc.— **whit'en,** *v.* **I.** *t.* To make white or whiter; bleach. **II.** *i.* To become white.— **white'-ness,** *n.—* **white'wash".** **I^t.** *vt.* **1.** To coat with whitewash. **2.** To attempt to excuse or defend a corrupt person, act, or thing. **II.** *n.* A mixture of slaked lime and water, used for whitening walls, etc.— **white'wash"er,** *n.—* **whit'ing,** *n.* A white powdered chalk used as a pigment and for polishing.— **whit'ish,** *a.* Somewhat white. — **whit'ish-ness,** *n.*

whith'er, 1 hwith'ər; 2 hwĭth'er, *adv.* **1.**

As an interrogative, to which or what place. **2.** As a relative, to which or what. **3.** Wheresoever.— **whith′er-so-ev′er,** *adv.*

whit′low, 1 hwit′lo; 2 hwĭt′lo, *n.* An inflammatory tumor, as on a finger.

whit′tle, 1 hwit′l; 2 hwĭt′l, *vt. & vi.* [WHIT′-TLED; WHIT′TLING.] To cut, carve, or shape by hand with a knife.

whiz, 1 hwiz; 2 hwĭz. **I.** *vi.* [WHIZZED, WHIZD⁸; WHIZ′ZING.] To move swiftly with a hissing or humming sound. **II.** *n.* A sound such as is produced by a flying missile.

who, 1 hū; 2 họ, *pron.* **I.** *interrog.* Which or what person. **II.** *rel.* **1.** That. **2.** He, she, or they that.— **who-ev′er,** *pron.* Any one without exception who. **who″so-ev′er‡.** [still!]

whoa, 1 hwō; 2 hwọ, *interj.* Stop! stand

whole, 1 hōl; 2 hōl. **I.** *a.* **1.** Containing hole⁸, ∫all; entire; total; complete. **2.** Sound; healthy. **II.** *n.* The sum total of all the parts or elements of anything; totality.— **whole′ness,** *n.* Entireness; completeness.— **whole′sale′,** *a.* **1.** Selling in quantity. **2.** Pertaining to wholesale trade; made or done on a large scale.— **whole′some,** *a.* **1.** Tending to promote health. **2.** Salutary. **-ly,** *adv.* **-ness,** *n.*— **whol′ly,** *adv.* Totally; exclusively.

whom, 1 hūm; 2 họm, *pron.* The objective (formerly dative) case of *who.*— **whom″-so-ev′er,** *pron.*

whoop, 1 hūp; 2 hōōp. **I**ᵗ. *vi.* To utter whoops; hoot. **II.** *n.* **1.** A shout of excitement, derision, etc.; a hoot. **2.** A loud convulsive inspiration after a paroxysm of coughing.— **whoop′ing-cough″,** *n.* A contagious disease, marked by violent coughing, ending with a whoop.

whorl, 1 hwŭrl; 2 hwûrl, *n.* **1.** *Bot.* A set of leaves, etc., distributed in a circle in a single plane. **2.** A turn, as of a spiral shell.

whor′tle-ber″ry, 1 hwŭr′tl-ber′ĭ; 2 hwûr′tl-bĕr′y, *n.* **1.** [U. S.] Same as HUCKLEBERRY. **2.** [Eng.] A dwarf hardy shrub and its blue=black fruit.

Whorl of Leaves of the Starry Campion.

whose, 1 hūz; 2 họz, *pron.* The possessive case of *who* and often of *which.*

who′so‖, 1 hū′so; 2 họ′so, *pron.* Whoever.— **whose″so-ev′er,** *pron.* Possessive case of *whosoever.*

why, 1 hwai; 2 hwĭ. **I.** *adv.* For what cause, purpose, or reason. **II.** *conj.* **1.**

Because of which; for which. **2.** As a relative, the reason or cause for which. **III.** *interj.* An introductory expletive.

wich′=ha″zel, 1 wĭch′=hē″zl; 2 wĭch′=hā″zl, *n.* An American shrub, used in pharmacy. **witch′=ha″zel‡.**

wick, 1 wik; 2 wĭk, *n.* A band, as of woven fibers, to draw up oil to a flame.

wick′ed, 1 wik′ed; 2 wĭk′ĕd, *a.* Evil; depraved; vicious; sinful. **-ly,** *adv.* **-ness,** *n.*

wick′er, 1 wik′er; 2 wĭk′er. **I.** *a.* Made of twigs, osiers, etc. **II.** *n.* **1.** A pliant young shoot or rod. **2.** Ware made of such shoots.

wick′et, 1 wik′et; 2 wĭk′ĕt, *n.* **1.** A small door or gate beside or in a larger entrance. **2.** *Cricket.* An arrangement of three upright rods, with two crosspieces on top.

wide, 1 waid; 2 wĭd. **I.** *a.* [WID′ER; WID′EST.] **1.** Having relatively great extent between sides; broad. **2.** Extended; ample. **II.** *adv.* **1.** To a great distance.— **wide′=a-wake″,** *a.* Marked by vigilance and alertness.— **wide′ly,** *adv.*— **wid′en,** *vt. & vi.* To make or grow wide.— **wide′ness,** *n.*— **width,** *n.* Space between sides.

widg′eon, 1 wij′an; 2 wĭj′ạn, *n.* A short=billed river=duck. **wig′eon‡.**

wid′ow, 1 wid′o; 2 wĭd′o. **I.** *vt.* To make a widow. **II‖.** *a.* Widowed. **III.** *n.* A woman who has lost her husband by death and is still unmarried.— **wid′ow-er,** *n.* A man whose wife is dead and who has not married again.— **wid′ow-hood,** *n.*

wield, 1 wild; 2 wēld, *vt.* **1.** To use, control, or manage, as a weapon. **2.** To command.

wife, 1 waif; 2 wĭf, *n.* [WIVES, 1 waivz; 2 wĭvz, *pl.*] **1.** A woman joined to a man in wedlock. **2.** A housewife.— **wife′hood,** *n.*— **wife′ly,** *a.*

wig, 1 wig; 2 wĭg, *n.* A covering of false hair closely fitting the head.— **wigged,** *a.*

wight, 1 wait; 2 wĭt, *n.* A person: used generally in good=humored contempt.

wig′wam, 1 wig′wem; 2 wĭg′wạm, *n.* **1.** A lodge or tent of the North= American Indians. **2.** [U. S.] A large public building.

Indian Wigwam of Bark.

wild, 1 waild; 2 wild. **I.** *a.* **1.** Not

tamed; uncivilized; uncultivated; uninhabited. **2.** Dissolute; prodigal. **3.** Stormy; turbulent; keen; eager. **II.** *n.* An uninhabited or uncultivated place; a wilderness.— **wild′ly,** *adv.*— **wild′ness,** *n.*— **wild rose,** see under ROSE, *n.*

wil′der-ness, 1 wil′dər-nes; 2 wĭl′der-nĕs, *n.* An uncultivated or uninhabited region; a waste.

wild′ing, 1 waild′ıŋ; 2 wīld′ing. **I.** *a.* [Poet.] Growing wild; uncultivated; undomesticated. **II.** *n.* An uncultivated plant; a fruit-tree growing from its own roots among grafted trees.

wile, 1 wail; 2 wīl. **I.** *vt.* [WILED; WIL′-ING.] **1.** To mislead; delude; dupe. **2.** To pass divertingly, as time. **II.** *n.* A trick; artifice; stratagem.

wil′ful, 1 wil′ful; 2 wĭl′ful, *a.* **1.** Headstrong; self-willed. **2.** Voluntary. **-ly,** *adv.* **-ness,** *n.*

will[1],) 1 wil; 2 wĭl, *vi.* [*pres. sing.*, WILL,
wil[2],) WILT, WILL (cp. WILLS, under WILL[2]); *pl.*, WILL; *imp. sing.*, WOULD, WOULDEST or WOULDST, WOULD; *pl.*, WOULD.] **1.** To be desirous; have a wish: mostly in the form *would*. **2.** As an auxiliary verb, in the first person a sign of purpose, and in the second and third persons, of futurity. See SHALL.

will[2], *vt. & vi.* [WILLED, WILD[s]; WILL′ING; *3d per. sing. pres.*, WILLS (confused with WILL[1]).] **1.** To produce by the exercise of will; exercise volition; resolve. **2.** To bequeath by a will.

will, *n.* **1.** The power of willing; also, a choice; volition; purpose. **2.** Energy of character; resolution; determination. **3.** A document by which one provides for the disposition of his property after his death.

will′ful, -ly, -ness. Same as WILFUL, etc.

will′ing, 1 wil′ıŋ; 2 wĭl′ing, *a.* **1.** Having the mind favorably inclined or disposed. **2.** Compliant. **3.** Gladly proffered or done. **-ly,** *adv.* **-ness,** *n.*

will′-o′-the-wisp, 1 wil′-ə-thə-wisp′: 2 wĭl′-o-the-wĭsp′, *n.* The ignis fatuus.

wil′low, 1 wil′o; 2 wĭl′o, *n.* A tree or shrub having slender, pliant, and sometimes pendent branchlets.— **weeping willow,** an Old World willow remarkable for its long, slender, pendulous branches.— **wil′low-y,** *a.* **1.** Abounding in willows. **2.** Having supple grace.

wilt[1], 1 wilt; 2 wĭlt, *vt. & vi.* To cause to droop; droop; wither.

wilt[2], *2d per. sing. pres. ind. act.* of WILL, *v.*

wi′ly, 1 wai′li; 2 wī′ly, *a.* [WI′LI-ER; WI′LI-

EST.] Full of wiles; sly; cunning; deceptive.— **wi′li-ly,** *adv.*— **wi′li-ness,** *n.*

win, 1 win; 2 wĭn, *vt. & vi.* [WON, WUN[s]; WIN′NING.] **1.** To gain in contest or competition; achieve; attain; be victorious. **2.** To charm; allure; persuade.— **win′ner,** *n.*— **win′ning.** **I.** *pa.* **1.** Successful in competition. **2.** Capable of winning affection; attractive; charming; winsome. **II.** *n.* **1.** The act of one who wins. **2.** That which is won: usually in the plural.

wince, 1 wins; 2 wĭnç, *vi.* [WINCED[t]; WINC′ING.] To shrink back; flinch.

winch, 1 winch; 2 wĭnch, *n.* A windlass; a crank.

wind[1], 1 waind; 2 wīnd, *vt. & vi.* [WOUND; WIND′ING.] To pass around; twine; twist; turn; wreathe; encircle.— **wind′ing,** *pa.* **1.** Turning spirally about an axis. **2.** Having bends; twisting.— **wind′ing-sheet**″, *n.* The sheet that wraps a corpse.

wind[2], 1 wind *or* waind; 2 wīnd *or* wĭnd, *vt. & vi.* [WIND′ED[d] (not WOUND); WIND′ING.] To blow, as a horn; sound by blowing.

wind[3d], 1 wind; 2 wĭnd, *vt.* **1.** To detect or follow by scent. **2.** To exhaust the breath of, as by running; put out of breath.

wind[1], *n.* **1.** A current of air. **2.** Lung-power; breath. **3.** Idle talk.— **wind′fall**″, *n.* **1.** Something, as ripening fruit, brought down by the wind. **2.** A piece of unexpected good fortune.— **wind′gall**″, *n.* A soft swelling near the fetlock-joint of a horse.— **wind′mill**″, *n.* A machine turned by the wind and designed to furnish motive power.— **wind′pipe**″, *n.* The duct by which the breath is carried to and from the lungs.

wind[2], 1 waind; 2 wīnd, *n.* A winding; a bend, turn, or twist.

wind′lass, 1 wind′las; 2 wĭnd′las, *n. Mech.* A drum turned by a handle so as to wind up a rope and raise a weight.

win′dow, 1 win′do; 2 wĭn′do, *n.* An opening in a building for the admission of light or air.

wind′row, 1 wind′rō; 2 wĭnd′rō, *n.* A long ridge, as of hay raked into rows.

wind′ward, 1 wind′wərd; 2 wĭnd′ward. **I.** *a.* Being on the side exposed to the wind. **II.** *n.* The direction from which the wind blows. **III.** *adv.* In the direction from which the wind blows.

wind′y, 1 wind′i; 2 wĭnd′y, *a.* [WIND′I-ER; WIND′I-EST.] **1.** Abounding in wind; stormy. **2.** Exposed to the wind. **3.** Bombastic; pompous.— **wind′i-ness,** *n.*

wine, 1 wain; 2 wīn. **I.** *vt. & vi.* [WINED; WIN′ING.] To entertain or treat with wine. **II.** *n.* The fermented juice of the

grape or other fruit; also, the unfermented juice of the grape.— **wine′=bib″ber,** n. A tippler.— **w.glass,** n. A small goblet from which to drink wine.

wing, 1 wiŋ; 2 wĭng, v. **I.** t. **1.** To accomplish by the aid of wings. **2.** To impart rapid motion to. **3.** To furnish with wings. **4.** To shoot in the wing; disable. **II.** i. To fly with or as with wings.— **wing(e)d⁸,** a. **1.** Having wings; passing swiftly. **2.** Soaring; lofty; rapt.

wing, n. **1.** The fore limb of a bird, adapted for flight, or something resembling or acting like it. **2.** Flight. **3.** An extension of a building at the side; the right or left division of an army. **4.** A sustaining surface of an air=plane.

wink, 1 wiŋk; 2 wĭnk. **I**ᵗ. vt. & vi. **1.** To close and open (the eyelids) quickly. **2.** To pretend not to see; as, to wink at wrong=doing. **3.** To twinkle. **II.** n. **1.** The act of winking. **2.** The time necessary for a wink. **3.** A twinkle. **4.** A nap.

win′ner, win′ning. See WIN, v.

win′now, 1 win′o; 2 wĭn′o, vt. & vi. To separate grain from chaff by a current of air.— **win′now=er,** n.

win′some, 1 win′sᵃm; 2 wĭn′som, a. Having a winning appearance or manner.

win′ter, 1 win′tᵃr; 2 wĭn′ter. **I.** vt. & vi. To care for during the winter; pass the winter; be affected by winter weather. **II.** n. The coldest season of the year.— **win′ter=green″,** n. A small creeping evergreen plant with red berries.— **win′try,** a. Belonging to winter; cold.— **win′ter=y‡.**

win′y, 1 wain′ı; 2 wīn′y, a. Having the taste, smell, or other qualities of wine.

wipe, 1 waip; 2 wīp. **I.** vt. [WIPED⁴; WIP′ING.] **1.** To rub or dry, as with a towel. **2.** To remove by rubbing; brush. **II.** n. The act or process of wiping.

wire, 1 wair; 2 wīr, vt. & vi. [WIRED; WIR′-ING.] **1.** To furnish with wire; fasten with wire. **2.** To telegraph.

wire, 1 wair; 2 wīr, n. **1.** A slender strand or thread of metal, formed by drawing through dies or holes. **2.** A telegraphic system using wires; a telegram. **3.** The string′of a musical instrument. **4.** [Colloq.] A secret means of influence; as, to pull the wires.— **wire′draw″,** 1 wair′drō″; 2 wīr′drᴀ″, vt. [WIRE′DREW″; WIRE′DRAWN″; WIRE′DRAW′ING.] **1.** To draw, as a metallic rod, into wire. **2.** To draw out, as a subject or thought, by fine distinctions; strain; spin out.— **wire′less,** a. Without wires; not using wires; as, **wireless telegraphy,** telegraphy without the use of connecting wires.— **wireless message,** a message sent by

wireless telegraphy.— **wir′y,** a. **1.** Thin, but tough and sinewy. **2.** Like wire; stiff.— **wir′i-ness,** n.

wis‖ᵗ, 1 wis; 2 wĭs, vt. To suppose; think.

wis′dom, 1 wiz′dᵃm; 2 wĭz′dom, n. **1.** The power of true and just discernment; the right use of knowledge; sound, practical judgment. **2.** A high degree of knowledge; erudition.

wise, 1 waiz; 2 wīz, a. [WIS′ER; WIS′EST.] Possessed of wisdom; sagacious; prudent; sensible; shrewd; erudite; sage. **-ly,** adv.

-wise, suffix. Way or manner: used as a termination; as, nowise, likewise: often confused with -way, -ways.

wise′a″cre, 1 waiz′ā″kᴇr; 2 wīz′ā″eer, n. One who affects great wisdom; hence, a dunce.

wish, 1 wiꞩ; 2 wĭsh. **I**ᵗ. vt. & vi. To desire; have a wish or longing. **II.** n. **1.** A desire or longing. **2.** A request or petition. **3.** Something wished for.— **wish′ful,** a. Full of longing (for).

wisp, 1 wisp; 2 wĭsp, n. A small bunch, as of hay.

wist‖, 1 wist; 2 wĭst, imp. of WIT, v.: sometimes used incorrectly for the present tense. Compare WIS.

Wis-ta′ri-a, 1 wis-tā′rı-ᵃ; 2 wĭs-tä′ri-a, n. Bot. **1.** A genus of climbing shrubs of the bean family, with clusters of purplish flowers. **2.** [w-] A plant of this genus. **Wis-te′ri-a‡** [Erroneous]

wist′ful, 1 wist′ful; 2 wĭst′ful, a. **1.** Wishful; longing. **2.** Musing; pensive. **-ly,** adv. **-ness,** n.

wit‖, 1 wit; 2 wĭt, vt. & vi. [WIST, imp.] To be or become aware of; learn.— **to wit,** that is to say.

wit, n. **1.** Sudden and ingenious association of ideas or words, causing surprize and merriment. **2.** A witty person; formerly, a person of learning or genius. **3.** The reasoning power or faculty; sense.

witch, 1 wiꞩ; 2 wĭch. **I**ᵗ. vt. To bewitch.

wichᴾ, ‖ **II.** n. One supposed to have dealings with evil spirits; playfully, a bewitching girl or woman.— **witch′craft″,** n. **1.** Sorcery. **2.** Extraordinary fascination.— **witch′er-y,** n. [-IES²; pl.] Power to charm.

with, 1 with; 2 wĭth, prep. **1.** In the company of; in the case of; in the same direction or sense as. **2.** By the use of; by; because of. **3.** Attended, accompanied, or followed by; having. **4.** From; as, to part with. **5.** In opposition to; against; as, to fight with.— **with-al′.** **I.** adv. With the rest; in addition. **II**‡. prep. With.— **with-draw′,** v. **I.** t. **1.** To draw or take away; remove; recall. **2.** To keep or abstract from use. **II.** i. To draw back; retire.— **with-draw′al,** n.

with-, prefix. Against; as, withstand.

withe, 1 with; 2 with, n. **1.** A willow;

supple twig. **2.** A band made of twisted
flexible shoots or the like.

with'er, 1 with'ər; 2 wĭth'er, *vt. & vi.* **1.**
To cause to become limp or dry, as a plant.
2. To waste, as flesh. **3.** To droop or perish.

with'ers, 1 with'ərz; 2 wĭth'ers, *n. pl.* The
ridge between the shoulder=blades, as of a
horse.

with=hold', 1 with-hōld'; 2 wĭth-hōld', *vt.
& vi.* To hold back; restrain.

with=in', 1 with-in'; 2 wĭth-ĭn'. **I.** *adv.*
1. In the inner part; interiorly. **2.** At
home; indoors. **II.** *prep.* **1.** Inside. **2.**
In the limits, range, or compass of. **3.**
Not going beyond.

with=out', 1 with-aut'; 2 wĭth-out'. **I.**
adv. **1.** In or on the outer part. **2.** Out
of doors. **3.** External. **II.** *prep.* **1.** Destitute of; lacking. **2.** On the outside of; external to. **3.** Beyond the limits of.

with=stand', 1 with-stand'; 2 wĭth-stănd',
vt. & vi. To oppose with any force;
endure. [wit; foolish.

wit'less, 1 wit'les; 2 wĭt'lĕs, *a.* Lacking

wit'ness, 1 wit'nes; 2 wĭt'nĕs. **I.** *vt. &
vi.* To see or know by personal experience;
testify; attest; give evidence. **II.** *n.*
1. A person who has seen or known
something; a spectator. **2.** One who
or that which furnishes evidence or proof;
attestation.

wit'ti=cism, 1 wit'i-sizm; 2 wĭt'i-çĭşm, *n.*
A witty or clever saying.

wit'ting=ly, 1 wit'iŋ-li; 2 wĭt'ing-ly, *adv.*
Knowingly and designedly.

wit'ty, 1 wit'i; 2 wĭt'y, *a.* [WIT'TI-ER;
WIT'TI=EST.] Having or displaying wit.
— **wit'ti=ly,** *adv.* — **wit'ti=ness,** *n.*

wive, 1 waiv; 2 wīv, *vt. & vi.* [WIVED;
WIV'ING.] To furnish with a wife; mate;
marry.

wives, 1 waivz; 2 wīvz, *n.* Plural of WIFE.

wiz'ard, 1 wiz'ərd; 2 wĭz'ard, *n.* A male
witch; sorcerer; juggler. [withered.

wiz'en, 1 wiz'n; 2 wĭz'n, *a.* Shrunken

wo, 1 wō; 2 wō, *n.* Overwhelming sor-
woe, row; heavy affliction or calamity.
— **wo'be=gone',** *a.* Overcome with wo;
mournful; sorrowful. **woe'be=gone'‡.**— **wo'-
ful,** *a.* Accompanied by or causing wo;
melancholy; sorrowful; doleful. **woe'ful‡.**
-ly, *adv.* **-ness,** *n.*

woke, 1 wōk; 2 wŏk, *imp. & pp.* of WAKE, *v.*

wolf, 1 wulf; 2 wolf, *n.* [WOLVES, 1 wulvz;
2 wolvş, *pl.*] A wild and savage dog=like
animal.— **wolf'ish,** *a.* Having the qualities
of a wolf; rapacious; cruel.— **wolf's'=bane'‡,**
n. A species of aconite of the Alps; also, a
species of arnica.

wol"ver=ene', 1 wol"vər-īn'; 2 wọl'ver-ēn',
n. A rapacious and cunning carnivore
of northern for-
ests; the glut-
ton. **wol"ver-
ine'‡.**

Wolverene. ¹/₆₇

wo'man, 1 wu'-
mən; 2 wọ'-
man, *n.* [wo'-
MEN, 1 wim'en; 2 wĭm'ĕn, *pl.*] **1.** An
adult human female. **2.** Women collectively. **3.** Womanly character; feminin-
ity.— **wo'man=hood,** *n.* **1.** The state of a
woman or of womankind. **2.** Women collectively.— **wo'man=ish,** *a.* Characteristic of
a woman; effeminate.— **wo'man=kind,** *n.*
Women collectively.— **wo'man=ly.** **I.** *a.*
Having the qualities becoming to a woman.
II. *adv.* In the manner of a woman.— **woman suffrage,** suffrage as belonging to or
exercised by women.— **w. suffragist,** see SUF-
FRAGIST.— **women's rights,** rights, as of
suffrage, property, education, etc., claimed
for women equally with men.

womb, 1 wūm; 2 wọm, *n.* **1.** The organ
in which young are developed; the place
where anything is brought into life. **2.**
A cavern.

wo'men, 1 wim'en; 2 wĭm'ĕn, *n.* Plural
wim'en‡, of woman.

won, 1 wun; 2 wŏn, *imp. & pp.* of WIN, *v.*

won'der, 1 wun'dər; 2 wŏn'der. **I.** *vt.*
wun'der‡, & *vi.* To be affected or filled
with wonder; marvel. **II.** *n.* **1.** Surprise mingled with curiosity; astonishment.
2. Something extraordinary; a prodigy.
— **won'der=ful,** *a.* Of a nature to excite
wonder or admiration; marvelous. **-ly,** *adv.*
-ness, *n.*— **won'der=ment,** *n.*— **won'drous,**
a. Wonderful. **-ly,** *adv.* **-ness,** *n.*

wont, 1 wunt; 2 wŏnt. **I.** *vt. & vi.* To
wunt‡, habituate: used reflexively. **II.** *a.*
Using or doing habitually; accustomed;
used. **III.** *n.* Ordinary manner of
doing or acting; habit.— **wont'ed,** *pa.* Commonly used or done; habitual; accustomed.

won't, 1 wōnt; 2 wŏnt. [Colloq.] Will not.

woo, 1 wū; 2 wōō, *vt. & vi.* To make love
to; court; entreat.— **woo'er,** *n.*

wood, 1 wud; 2 wŏŏd, *v.* **I.** *t.* **1.** To
furnish with wood for fuel. **2.** To convert
into a forest. **II.** *i.* To supply wood.

wood, *n.* **1.** A large and thick collection
of trees; forest; grove: often in the plural.
2. The substance of which a tree is composed, or something made of this substance, as lumber, etc.— **wood'bine',** *n.*
1. The common European honeysuckle. **2.**
The Virginia creeper.— **wood'cock",** *n.* A
small game=bird.— **wood'craft",** *n.* Skill in

such things as belong to woodland life.— **wood'cut"**, *n.* An engraving on wood; also, a print from such a block.— **wood'-cut"ter**, *n.* One who chops wood.— **wood'ed**, *a.* Having a supply of wood; abounding with trees.— **wood'en**, *a.* **1.** Made of wood. **2.** Like a block of wood; stupid; mechanical.— **w.-engraving**, *n.* The art of making wood-cuts.— **wood'land**, *n.* Land occupied by woods or forests.— **wood'man**, *n.* [-MEN, *pl.*] **1.** A wood-cutter; lumberman. **2.** A forester.— **wood'peck"er**, *n.* A bird having a chisel-like bill, that pecks holes in bark in search for insects.— **wood-thrush**, *n.* A North-American thrush of a prevailing cinnamon-brown color, noted for the sweetness of its song.— **wood'work"**, *n.* The wooden part of any structure, especially interior wooden parts.— **wood'y**, *a.* **1.** Of the nature of wood. **2.** Pertaining to or resembling wood. **3.** Wooded.

wood'chuck", 1 wud'chŭk"; 2 wŏŏd'chŭk", *n.* A marmot of eastern North America.

woo'er, 1 wū'ẽr; 2 wōō'er, *n.* See WOO.

woof, 1 wūf; 2 wōōf, *n.* The cross-threads of a woven fabric; weft.

wool, 1 wul; 2 wŏŏl, *n.* The soft, long, curly, or crisped hair obtained from sheep and some allied animals; also, something resembling this.— **wool'en.** **I.** *a.* Consisting of wool. **II.** *n.* Cloth or clothing made of wool. **wool'len‡.**— **wool'-gath"er-ing**, *n.* Any trivial or purposeless employment; idle, wandering reverie: also used as adjective or adverb.— **wool'ly**, *a.* Consisting of, covered with, or resembling wool.— **wool'sack"**, *n.* A sack of wool, especially as the seat of the Lord Chancellor in England; hence, the office of Lord Chancellor.

word, 1 wũrd; 2 wûrd. **I**d, *vt.* To express in words. **II.** *n.* **1.** A vocal sound or combination of sounds, used as a symbol to signify a thought. **2.** A brief remark; conversation; talk. **3.** A message; command; promise. **4.** [W-] (1) The Scriptures; (2) Christ.— **word'ing**, *n.* The act or style of expressing in words; phraseology.— **word'y**, *a.* **1.** Of the nature of words; verbal. **2.** Using many words; verbose.— **word'i-ly**, *adv.*— **word'i-ness**, *n.*

work, 1 wũrk; 2 wûrk, *v.* [WORKED‡, WORK‡S, or WROUGHT; WORK'ING.] **I.** *t.* **1.** To expend labor on. **2.** To cause to act, labor, or produce; influence. **3.** To investigate or solve, as a problem. **II.** *i.* **1.** To labor; toil. **2.** To make progress; be effective; move. **3.** To ferment.— **work'er**, *n.* One who or that which works, as a working ant or bee.

work, *n.* **1.** Manual labor; occupation. **2.** An undertaking; task. **3.** That which

is produced by labor. **4.** *pl.* A manufacturing or other industrial establishment. **5.** *pl.* Running-gear.— **work'-bag"**, **w.-box**, *n.* A small bag or box for needle-work, etc.— **w.-day**, *n.* Any day not a Sunday or holiday. **work'ing-day"‡.**— **work'-house"**, *n.* An almshouse; also, an industrial prison.— **work'ing-man"**, *n.* One who earns his bread by manual labor; an artisan; mechanic.— **work'man**, *n.* A man who works; a worker.— **work'man-like"**, *a.* Like a skilled workman.— **work'man-ship**, *n.* The quality, manner, or style of work; the work produced.

world, 1 wũrld; 2 wûrld. *n.* **1.** The earth; any planet. **2.** A division of things; department; sphere. **3.** Mankind. **4.** The practises and ways of men. **5.** Secular affairs; worldly pleasures.— **World Court** [Colloq.], the Permanent Court of International Justice established at the Hague, Dec. 16, 1920, for the purpose of arbitrating international disputes.— **world'ling**, *n.* One who lives merely for this world.— **world'ly.** **I.** *a.* Pertaining to the world; earthly; temporal. **II.** *adv.* In a worldly manner.— **world'li-ness**, *n.*

worm, 1 wũrm; 2 wûrm, *v.* **I.** *t.* **1.** **wurm**ᴾ, insinuate (oneself or itself) into, as a worm; effect as by crawling: with *in* or *into.* **2.** To draw forth by artful means, as a secret: followed by *out.* **II.** *i.* To work or proceed stealthily.

worm, *n.* **1.** A small, legless, invertebrate crawling animal. **2.** A despicable person. **3.** A short screw formed to mesh with a gear-wheel; the thread of a screw; the spiral condensing pipe of a still. **4.** *Anat.* An organ or part that resembles a worm in shape.— **worm'-eat"en**, *pa.* Eaten or bored through by worms.— **worm'y**, *a.* Infested with worms; earthy; groveling.

1. The Common Earth-worm.
2. The Young, escaping from its case.

worm'wood", 1 wũrm'wud"; 2 wûrm'wŏŏd", *n.* **1.** A bitter herb formerly used as a vermifuge. **2.** That which embitters.

wor'ry, 1 wur'ı; 2 wŏr'y, *v.* [WOR'RIED; **wur'ry**ᴾ, WOR'RY-ING.] **I.** *t.* **1.** To harass or vex; make anxious; annoy. **2.** To shake and tear; as, a dog *worries* a rat. **II.** *i.* To become uneasy in mind; fret.

wor'ry, *n.* [WOR'RIESᶻ.] A state of perplexing anxiety; vexation.— **wor'ri-some**, *a.*

worse, 1 wũrs; 2 wûrs, *a.* & *adv.* [Used **wurse**ᴾ, as compar. of *bad, ill, evil,* and the

1: ärtistic, ärt; fat, fāre; fast; get, prēy; hit, polïce; obey, gō; net, ôr; full, rūle; but, bũrn.

2: ärt, āpe, făt, fâre, fȧst, whạt, ạll; mē, gĕt, prev, fẽrn; hït, ïce; ï=ē; ĭ=ē; gō, nŏt, ôr, wŏn,

like.] More evil, unworthy, objectionable, unfortunate, etc.; in a more evil manner.

wor'ship, 1 wŭr'ship; 2 wûr'ship. **I.** *vt.*
wur'shipᴾ, } & *vi.* [WOR'SHIPEDᵗ or WOR'-SHIPPEDᵗ, WOR'SHIPTˢ; WOR'SHIP-ING or WOR'SHIP-PING.] **1.** To pay worship to; perform acts or have feelings of worship. **2**‖. To honor. **II.** *n.* **1.** Religious homage; prayer. **2.** Deference, respect, etc. **3.** Excessive or ardent admiration. **— wor'ship-er,** *n.* **wor'ship-per‡.— wor'-ship-ful,** *a.* Worthy of honor.

worst, 1 wŭrst; 2 wûrst. **I**ᵈ. *vt.* To get
wurstᴾ, } the advantage over in a contest.
II. *a.* Bad, ill, or evil in the highest degree. [Used as the superlative of *bad, ill,* or *evil.* Compare WORSE.] **III.** *n.* The most evil or calamitous state or result. **IV.** *adv.* In the worst manner or degree.

wors'ted, 1 wus'ted or wurs'ted; 2 wọs'tĕd or wors'tĕd. **I.** *a.* Made of worsted. **II.** *n.* Woolen yarn, with fibers combed parallel and twisted hard; also, a lightly twisted woolen yarn. [plant.

wortᵗ, 1 wŭrt; 2 wûrt, *n.* A cabbage-like
wort², *n.* The unfermented infusion of malt that by fermentation becomes beer.

worth, 1 wŭrᵺ; 2 wûrth. **I.** *a.* **1.**
wurthᴾ, } Having value; equal in value (to); exchangeable (for). **2.** Deserving (of). **II.** *n.* **1.** That quality which renders a thing useful or desirable; value; excellence. **2.** High personal character; merit; virtue.— **worth'less,** *a.* Having no worth; valueless. **-ly,** *adv.* **-ness,** *n.*

wor'thy, 1 wŭr'ᵺi; 2 wûr'thy. **I.** *a.*
wur'thyᴾ, } [WOR'THI-ER; WOR'THI-EST.] **1.** Possessing worth; having valuable qualities. **2.** Fit; suitable: followed by *of.* **II.** *n.* [WOR'THIESᶻ, *pl.*] A person of eminent worth.— **wor'thi-ly,** *adv.* In a worthy manner.— **wor'thi-ness,** *n.*

wot‖, 1 wet; 2 wŏt, *vt.* & *vi.* *1st* & *3d pers. sing. pres. ind.* of WIT, *v.*

would, 1 wud; 2 wụd, *v., imp.* of WILL, *auxiliary.* Expressing desire, assertion, or action.

woundᶦᵈ, 1 wŭnd or waund; 2 wụnd or wound, *vt.* & *vi.* To inflict a wound upon; hurt; pain.

wound², 1 waund; 2 wound, *imp.* & *pp.* of WIND, *v.*

wound, 1 wŭnd or waund; 2 wụnd or wound, *n.* A hurt or injury caused by violence; as a stab, etc.

wove, *imp.* & *pp.* of WEAVE, *v.*

wov'en, 1 wōv'n; 2 wŏv'n, *pp.* of WEAVE, *v.*

wrack, 1 rak; 2 răk, *n.* **1.** Floating material, as seaweed, cast ashore. **2.** Wreck; ruin; wreckage. **3.** A rack, as of clouds. See RACK³, *n.*

wraith, 1 rēᵺ; 2 rāth, *n.* **1.** A fantom of a living person, supposed to be ominous of that person's death. **2.** Any ghost or specter.

wran'gl(eᴾ, 1 raŋ'gl; 2 răŋ'gl. **I.** *vt.* & *vi.* [WRAN'GL(E)Dᴾ; WRAN'GLING.] To dispute noisily; brawl. **II.** *n.* An angry or noisy dispute.— **wran'gler,** *n.*

wrap, 1 rap; 2 răp, *vt.* & *vi.* [WRAPPEDᵗ or WRAPTᵗ; WRAP'PING.] To fold or draw together; cover by infolding; infold.

wrap, *n.* An article of dress intended to be drawn or folded about a person; a wrapper.— **wrap'per,** *n.* **1.** An outer covering. **2.** A loose, flowing garment.

wrath, 1 raᵺ; 2 răth, *n.* Determined and lasting anger; rage.— **wrath'ful,** *a.* **-ly,** *adv.* **-ness,** *n.*

wreakᵗ, 1 rīk; 2 rēk, *vt.* To inflict; satiate.

wreath, 1 rīᵺ; 2 rēth, *n.* A garland of leaves or flowers.— **wreathe,** 1 rīᵺ; 2 rēth, *vt.* [WREATHED; WREATH'ING.] To form into a wreath; infold; encircle; embrace.

wreck, 1 rek; 2 rĕk. **I**ᵗ. *vt.* To shipwreck; destroy; ruin; bring destruction upon. **II.** *n.* **1.** The act of wrecking; total ruin; shipwreck. **2.** That which has been wrecked or ruined, as a stranded ship, etc. **— wreck'age,** *n.* **1.** The act of wrecking. **2.** Material from a wreck.— **wreck'er,** *n.*

wren, 1 ren; 2 rĕn, *n.* A small bird, having short wings and tail.

wrench, 1 rench; 2 rĕnch. **I**ᵗ. *vt.* To twist violently; wrest; sprain; distort. **II.** *n.* **1.** The act of wrenching. **2.** A tool for twisting bolts, etc.

wrest, 1 rest; 2 rĕst. **I**ᵈ. *vt.* To twist; wrench; turn from the true meaning, etc. **II.** *n.* **1.** An act of wresting. **2.** A key for tuning a stringed instrument.— **wrest'er,** *n.*

wres'tl(eᴾ, 1 res'l; 2 rĕs'l, *vi.* [WRES'-TL(E)Dᴾ; WRES'TLING.] To contend or grapple, as opponents striving each to bring the other to the ground.— **wres'tl(e**ᴾ, *n.* An act of wrestling.— **wres'tler,** *n.*

wretch, 1 rech; 2 rĕch, *n.* **1.** A base
wrechᴾ, } person; despicable character. **2.** A miserable or unhappy person.— **wretch'-ed,** *a.* Miserable; unhappy; mean; despicable. **-ness,** *n.*

wrig'gle, 1 rig'l; 2 rĭg'l, *vt.* & *vi.* [WRIG'-
wrig'lᴾ, } GLED, WRIG'LDᴾ; WRIG'GLING.] To squirm; twist; writhe.— **wrig'gler,** *n.*

wright, 1 rait; 2 rīt, *n.* A mechanic: used chiefly in compounds; as, ship*wright.*

wring, 1 riŋ; 2 rĭŋ, *vt.* [WRUNG, WRINGED, or WRANG (Prov.); WRING'ING.] To com-

press or squeeze out by twisting; to extort; torture.— **wring'er,** *n.*

wrin'kl(e^P, 1 riŋ'kl; 2 rĭŋ'kl. [WRIN'KL(E)D^P; WRIN'KLING.] To contract into furrows and ridges. **II.** *n.* A small ridge or crease.— **wrin'kly,** *a.*

wrist, 1 rist; 2 rĭst, *n.* The part of the arm immediately adjoining the hand.— **w.-watch,** *n.* A watch worn on the wrist.— **wrist'band,** *n.* The band or part of the sleeve that covers the wrist.

writ, 1 rit; 2 rĭt, *n.* An order of a court to a person addressed.— **Holy Writ,** the Bible.

write, 1 rait; 2 rīt, *v.* [WROTE; WRIT'TEN; WRIT'ING.] **I.** *t.* **1.** To mark or trace on a surface, in letters. **2.** To describe, compose, or produce in writing. **II.** *i.* To mark letters on a surface; compose in writing.— **writ'er,** *n.* One who writes; espe-

cially, an author.— **writ'ing,** *n.* **1.** The act of one who writes. **2.** Written characters; handwriting. **3.** Anything written, as a legal document, literary composition, book, etc.

writhe, 1 raith; 2 rīth, *vt. & vi.* [WRITHED; WRITH'ING.] To twist with violence; wrench; distort, as the body in pain.

wrong, 1 rŏŋ; 2 rông. **I.** *vt.* To injure; oppress; misrepresent; defraud. **II.** *a.* **1.** Violating right or justice. **2.** Erroneous; improper. **III.** *n.* An injury; mischief; crime; error.— **wrong'ful,** *a.* Characterized by wrong or injustice. **-ly,** *adv.* **-ness,** *n.*— **wrong'ly,** *adv.*

wrote, 1 rōt; 2 rŏt, *imp.* of WRITE, *v.*

wroth‖, 1 rŏth; 2 rŏth, *a.* Full of wrath; angry.

wrought, 1 rŏt; 2 rŏt, *imp. & pp.* of WORK, *v.*

wrung, 1 ruŋ; 2 rŭng, *imp. & pp.* of WRING, *v.*

wry, 1 rai; 2 rȳ, *a.* Bent out of position; contorted; perverted. **-ly,** *adv.* **-ness,** *n.*

X

X, x, 1 eks; 2 ĕks, *n.* [EXES, X's, or Xs, 1 eks'es; 2 ĕks'ĕş, *pl.*] The twenty-fourth letter in the English alphabet.

xan'thic, 1 zan'thik; 2 zăn'thĭc, *a.* Having a yellow or yellowish color.

xiph'oid, 1 zif'eid; 2 zĭf'ŏid, *a.* Shaped like a sword.

X'-rays". *n. pl.* Same as ROENTGEN RAYS.

xy'lo-graph,) 1 zai'lo-graf; 2 zȳ'lo-gråf, *n.*
xy'lo-graf^P,) An engraving on wood, or a

print from such engraving.— **xy-log'ra-pher,** 1 zai-leg'ra-fər; 2 zȳ-lŏg'ra-fer, *n.*— **xy"lo-graph'ic, xy"lo-graph'i-cal,** *a.* Pertaining to wood-engraving.— **xy-log'ra-phy,** *n.* **1.** Wood-engraving. **2.** The making of prints showing the grain of wood.

xy'lo-phone, 1 zai'lo-fōn; 2 zȳ'lo-fōn, *n.* A musical instrument with graduated metallic or wooden bars sounded by small mallets.

Y

Y, y, 1 wai; 2 wȳ, *n.* [WYES, Y's, or Ys, 1 waiz; 2 wīş, *pl.*] The twenty-fifth letter in the English alphabet.

y-, *prefix.* Used in Middle English as the sign of the past participle; as, *yclept.*

yacht, 1 yet; 2 yat, *n.* A vessel built for pleasure; a light, sailing or steam vessel.— **yachts'man,** *n.*— **yacht'ing,** *n.*

yak'a-lo, 1 yak'a-lō; 2 yăk'a-lō, *n.* A hybrid between an Asiatic yak and an American buffalo; still in the experimental stages; a portmanteau-word.

yam, 1 yam; 2 yăm, *n.* A tropical plant having a fleshy edible tuberous root.

Yan'kee, 1 yaŋ'ki; 2 yăŋ'ke. **I.** *a.* Pertaining to Yankees. **II.** *n.* A New Englander; any citizen of the United States.

yard¹, 1 yård; 2 yärd, *n.* **1.** The standard English measure of length: 36 inches. **2.** *Naut.* A spar suspended crosswise on a

mast.— **yard'-arm",** *n. Naut.* Either end of a yard.— **yard'stick",** *n.* A graduated measuring-stick a yard in length.

yard², *n.* A tract of ground enclosed near a residence or other building.

yarn, 1 yärn; 2 yärn, *n.* **1.** Spun fiber, as for knitting, etc.; loosely, thread. **2.** [Colloq.] A long extravagant story.

yar'row, 1 yar'o; 2 yăr'o, *n.* A perennial herb, having small white flowers, with a pungent odor and taste.

yawl, 1 yŏl; 2 yal, *n.* **1.** A small sailing vessel rigged like a sloop, with a small additional mast in the stern. **2.** A ship's boat.

yawn, 1 yŏn; 2 yan. **I.** *vi.* **1.** To open the mouth wide and draw in the breath, as when drowsy. **2.** To stand wide open; gape. **II.** *n.* A wide opening of the mouth, as from weariness.

1: artistic, ärt; fat, fāre; fast; get, prēy; hit, police; obey, gō; net, ōr; full, rūle; but, būrn.

2: ärt, āpe, făt, fâre, fâst, whąt, ąll; mē, gĕt, prȩy, fērn; hĭt, īce; ĭ = ē; ī = ē; gō, nŏt, ôr, wŏn,

y-clept′, } 1 ɪ-klept′; 2 y-elĕpt′, *pp.* [Ar-
y-cleped′, } chaic or Humorous.] Called;
named.

ye, 1 yī; 2 yē, *pron.* The nominative plural of
the personal pronoun of the second person.

ye, ye, 1 thī; 2 thē. The: a contraction in
which *y* represents the Anglo-Saxon
character for *th:* sometimes incorrectly
pronounced like the pronoun *ye.*

yea, 1 yē; 2 yā. **I.** *adv.* Yes; verily. **II.**
n. An affirmative vote.

year, 1 yīr; 2 yēr, *n.* **1.** The period of
time in which the earth completes a revolution around the sun: about 365 days,
used as a unit of time, and divided into 12
months. **2.** Any period of 12 months.
— **year′ling. I.** *a.* Being a year old. **II.** *n.*
An animal between one and two years old.—
year′ly. I. *a.* **1.** Occurring once a year;
annual. **2.** Continuing a year. **II.** *adv.*
Annually.

yearn, } 1 yûrn; 2 yĕrn, *vi.* To desire
yernᵖ, } something anxiously; long.—
yearn′ing, *a. & n.*— **yearn′ing-ly,** *adv.*

yeast, 1 yīst; 2 yēst, *n.* **1.** A fungous
growth rapidly propagated in saccharine
liquids, producing alcoholic fermentation.
2. Such a substance as prepared for raising dough; a ferment. **3.** Froth or
spume.— **yeast′y,** *a.*

yelk, 1 yelk; 2 yĕlk, *n.* [Dial.] Same as **YOLK.**

yell, 1 yel; 2 yĕl. **I.** *vt. & vi.* To express
yelᵖ, } with a yell; utter a yell. **II.** *n.* A
sharp, loud, and often inarticulate cry.

yel′low, 1 yel′o; 2 yĕl′o. **I.** *a.* Having
the color of brass, gold, etc. **II.** *n.* The
color of the spectrum between green and
orange.— **yellow fever,** an acute infectious
fever, endemic in various tropical countries.—
yel′low-ish, *a.* Somewhat yellow. **-ness,** *n.*
— **yel′low-jack″et,** *n.* A social wasp marked
with yellow.— **yel′low-ness,** *n.*

yelp, 1 yelp; 2 yĕlp. **Iᵗ.** *vi.* To give a
yelp. **II.** *n.* A sharp, shrill cry or bark.

yeo′man, } 1 yō′mən; 2 yō′man, *n.* [YEO′-
yo′manˢ, } MEN, *pl.*] [Eng.] A freeholder,
next under the rank of gentleman; in
modern usage, a farmer. [U. S. N.] A petty
officer.— **yeo′man-ry,** *n.* The collective body
of yeomen; freemen; farmers. [just so.

yes, 1 yes; 2 yĕs, *adv.* As you say; truly;

yes′ter-day, 1 yes′tər-dē; 2 yĕs′ter-dā.
I. *n.* **1.** The day preceding to-day. **2.**
Loosely, the near past. **II.** *adv.* On the
day last past.

yes′ter-night″, 1 yes′tər-naɪt″; 2 yĕs′ter-
nīt″. **I.** *n.* The night last past. **II.** *adv.*
In or during the night last past.

yet, 1 yet; 2 yĕt. **I.** *adv.* **1.** In addition;

besides. **2.** Before or at some future
time: eventually. **3.** Still. **4.** At the
present time; now. **5.** After all the
time that has or had elapsed. **6.** Hereto-
fore. **II.** *conj.* **1.** Nevertheless; notwithstanding. **2.** But. **3.** Altho.

yew, 1 yū; 2 yu, *n.* An Old World evergreen tree of slow growth
and long life.

yield, 1 yīld; 2 yēld. **Iᵈ.** *vt.*
& vi. **1.** To furnish in return for labor. **2.** To give
way; surrender; relinquish.
3. To admit; assent; grant.
II. *n.* The amount yielded;
product; result.— **yield′ing,**
pa. Disposed to yield.

yoke, 1 yōk; 2 yōk. **I.** *vt.*
[YOKEDᵗ; YOK′ING.] To at-
tach by means of a yoke; put
a yoke upon; enslave. **II.** *f.* a single
n. **1.** A curved timber having sterile catkin.
a bow at each end to receive the neck of
a draft-animal. **2.** Something that supports, binds, or connects. **3.** Servitude;
bondage. **4.** *sing. & pl.* A couple or pair,
as of oxen.

Spray of Eu-
ropean Yew.

yolk, 1 yōk *or* yōlk; 2 yōk *or* yōlk, *n.* The
yellow portion of an egg.

yon, 1 yen; 2 yŏn, *a. & adv.* Yonder:
chiefly poetic.— **yon′der,** 1 yen′dər; 2 yŏn′-
dēr. **I.** *a.* Being at a distance indicated.
II. *adv.* In that place; over there; there.

yore, 1 yōr; 2 yōr, *n. sing. & pl.* [Archaic &
Poet.] Old time: originally, years.

you, 1 yū; 2 yu, *pron.* The personal pronoun of the second person plural: used
in modern English to denote a single person, but retaining its plural construction,
you are, were, etc.

young, } 1 yuᵑ; 2 yŭng. **I.** *a.* Being in
yungᵖ, } the early period of life; youthful;
vigorous; immature. **II.** *n.* Offspring,
especially of the lower animals.—
young′ster, *n.* A young person.

your, 1 yūr; 2 yur, *pron.* Belonging to
you: the possessive case singular and
plural of YOU: in use preceding the noun.
— **yours,** *pron.* Possessive case of YOU: used
when the noun is omitted.— **your-self′,** *pron.*
[YOUR-SELVES′, *pl.*] A reflexive and often emphatic form of the second-personal pronoun.

youth, 1 yūth; 2 yuth, *n.* [YOUTHS, 1 yūths;
2 yuths, *pl.*] **1.** The state of being young.
2. The period when one is young.
3. A young man.— **youth′ful,** *a.* Pertaining
to youth; being still young. **-ly,** *adv.* **-ness,** *n.*

Yule, 1 yūl; 2 yul, *n.* Christmas time, or
the feast celebrating it. **Yule′tideᵗ.**

1: ə = final; ɪ = habit; aɪsle; au = out; oɪl; iū = feud; ċhin; go; ŋ = sing; ṫhin, this.
2: wǫlf, dǫ; bōŏk, bōōt; ᶠu̇ll, ru̇le, cūre, bŭt, bûrn; ŏɪl, bŏy; ġo, ġem; iŋk; thin, this.

Z

Z, z, 1 zī; 2 zē, *n.* [ZEES, Z's, or Zs, 1 zīz; 2 zēg, *pl.*] The twenty=sixth letter in the English alphabet.

zeal, 1 zil; 2 zēl, *n.* Ardor for a cause; enthusiastic devotion; fervor.— **ze(a)l'ot⁸,** 1 zel'ət; 2 zēl'ot, *n.* One unduly zealous; a fanatic.— **ze(a)l'ous⁸,** *a.* Filled with or incited by zeal.— **zeal'ous-ly,** *adv.*

ze'bra, 1 zī'brə; 2 zē'bra, *n.* An African ass=like mammal marked with stripes.

Zebra.
1/60

ze-na'na, } 1 zə-nä'nə;
za-na'na, } 2 ze-nä'na, *n.* In India, the women's apartments; the East=Indian harem.

Zend'-A-ves'ta, 1 zend'ə-ves'tə; 2 zĕnd'=ə-vĕs'ta, *n.* The sacred writings of the religion of Zoroaster.

ze'nith, 1 zī'nⁱᵗʰ or zen'ⁱᵗʰ; 2 zē'nith or zĕn'ith, *n.* **1.** The point in the celestial sphere that is exactly overhead. **2.** The culminating=point, as of prosperity.

zeph'yr, 1 zef'ər; 2 zĕf'yr, *n.* **1.** The west wind; poetically, any soft, gentle wind. **2.** Anything light and airy.

ze'ro, 1 zī'ro; 2 zē'ro, *n.* **1.** The numeral 0; a cipher. **2.** The absence of quantity; nothing. **3.** The lowest point, as on the scale of a thermometer.

zest, 1 zest; 2 zĕst, *n.* Agreeable excitement of mind or something that imparts it; an agreeable and piquant flavor.

Zeus, 1 zūs; 2 zūs, *n.* The supreme deity of the Greeks, corresponding to the Roman Jupiter.

zig'zag", 1 zig'zag"; 2 zĭg'zăg". [ZIG'-ZAGGED", ZIG'ZAGD"⁸; ZIG'ZAG"GING.] **I.** *vt. & vi.* To form a zigzag; move in zigzag. **II.** *a.* Having a series of zigzags. **III.** *n.* A series of short, sharp angles from one side to the other; something, as a path, having such angles. **IV.** *adv.* In a zigzag manner. [metal.

zinc, 1 ziŋk; 2 zĭŋc, *n.* A bluish=white

Zi'on, 1 zai'ən; 2 zi'on, *n.* **1.** A hill in Jerusalem, site of the royal residence of David and his successors. **2.** Metaphorically: (1) The Hebrew theocracy; (2) The church of Christ; (3) The heavenly Jerusalem; heaven.— **Zi'on-ism,** *n.* The movement among the Jews to give separate political form to Judaism, as by organizing a Jewish commonwealth in Palestine.— **-ist,** *n.*

zith'er, } 1 zith'ər, zith'ərn; 2 zĭth'er,
zith'ern, } zĭth'ern, *n.* A stringed instrument, having a flat sounding=board, and played with the fingers.

zo'di-ac, 1 zō'di-ak; 2 zō'di-ăe, *n.* **1.** *Astron.* An imaginary belt encircling the heavens and extending about 8° on each side of the ecliptic, within which are the larger planets. It is divided into twelve parts, called **signs of the zodiac,** which formerly corresponded to twelve constellations bearing the same names. **2.** Figuratively, a complete circuit; round. — **zo-dī'a-cal,** *a.* Pertaining to the zodiac.

zone, 1 zōn; 2 zōn, *n.* **1.** One of five divisions of the earth's surface, bounded by lines parallel to the equator, and taking their names from the prevailing climate. **2.** A belt, band, stripe, etc., distinguished by any characteristic. **3.** [Archaic or Poetic.] A belt or girdle.— **zoned,** *a.* **1.** Wearing a girdle. **2.** Marked with zones.

zo-ol'o-gy, 1 zo-ol'o-ji; 2 zo-ŏl'o-gy, *n.* **1.** The science that treats of animals with reference to their structure, functions, etc. **2.** The animal kingdom. **3.** A treatise on animals.— **zo⁸o-log'i-cal,** *a.*— **zo-ol'o-gist,** *n.*— **zo⁸o-log'i-cal-ly,** *adv.*

zo'o-phyte, 1 zō'o-fait; 2 zō'o-fȳt, *n.* An invertebrate animal resembling a plant, as a coral or sponge.

Zo"ro-as'tri-an, 1 zō"ro-as'trⁱ-ən; 2 zō"or-ăs'tri-an. **I.** *a.* Of or pertaining to Zoroaster or Zoroastrianism. **II.** *n.* One of the followers of Zoroaster, anciently known as *Magi.*— **Zo"ro-as'tri-an-ism,** *n.*

Zou-ave', 1 zu-äv'; 2 zu-äv', *n.* **1.** A light=armed French infantryman, wearing an Oriental uniform. **2.** [z-] [U. S.] In the Civil War a member of a volunteer regiment that assumed the name and characteristic uniform.

Zu'lu, } 1 zū'lū; 2 zu'lu, *n.* A
Zoo'loo, } member of one of certain tribes in southeastern Africa, or the language of these people: often used adjectively.

Zouave.

zy-mot'ic, 1 zai-met'ik; 2 zȳ-mŏt'ie, *n.* Relating to or produced by or from fermentation, as a disease.

1: urtistic, **ä**rt; f**a**t, f**ā**re; f**a**st; g**e**t, pr**ē**y; h**ĭ**t, pol**ī**ce; **o**bey, g**ō**; n**o**t, **ŏ**r; f**ṳ**ll, r**ū**le; b**u**t, b**ū**rn.
2: ärt, **ā**pe, f**ă**t, f**â**re, f**à**st, wh**ạ**t, **ạ**ll; m**ē**, g**ĕ**t, pr**ȩ**y, f**ē**rn; h**ĭ**t, **ī**ce; ĭ=ē; ĭ̃=ẽ; g**ō**, n**ŏ**t, **ô**r, w**ŏ**n,

APPENDIX

FAULTY DICTION.

a

a, **an.** A immediately before a consonant *sound*, whatever the spelling (as, *a* peach, *a* song); *an* immediately before a vowel sound, whatever the spelling, or before beginning with silent *h* (as, *an* apple, *an* honor, *an* honest man). A word beginning with the long sound of *u*, where *u* has the sound of *you*, takes *a* (as, *a* unit, *a* university); the short sound of *u* takes *an* (as, *an* unknown quantity).

"No man can be at the same time *a* patriot and traitor." Since "patriot" and "traitor" denote different persons, this sentence should read, either "No man can be at the same time *a* patriot and *a* traitor," or "No man can be at the same time patriot and traitor."

ac-cept', **ex-cept'.** To *accept* is "to take, receive"; to *except* is to "take out, reject"; as, "All the specimens were *accepted, except* one." Avoid confusion of these two words.

ad-mis'si-ble. Never spell this word *admissable*.

adverbs should be kept as close as possible to the word or words they are to modify. Instead of, "I meant to write to Tom *all day*," say, "I meant *all day* to write to Tom."

af-fect', **ef-fect'.** Do not confuse these words, as is frequently done. To *affect* is "to influence"; to *effect,* "to accomplish, achieve."

a half an hour. "I will do it in *a half an hour*." If *a* is used, the expression should be, *"in a half-hour"*; but it is better to say, "I will do it in *half an hour*." So, *half a minute*, etc.

ain't. A modification of *am not* or *are not,* always inelegant, becomes atrocious when used for *is not, has not,* or *have not;* as, "He *ain't* here," *"Ain't* you seen him?" "They *ain't* had it." Better say: "He is not," "Aren't you?" "They're not." See ARE N'T.

all of. "He drank *all of* it." "I saw *all of* them." "Take *all of* it." *All of* is allowable, to emphasize totality when contrasted with *a part of, some of,* etc. The best literary usage, however, omits the *of* in most cases as needless, preferring "He drank it *all,*" "I saw them *all,*" "Take it *all,*" etc.

and. "A language like the French *and* German" implies that the same language is both French and German. Repeat the article, and say: "A language like the French *or* the German"; or you may use the plural, and say: "Languages like the French *and* the German."

an'y. Instead of "The mother is better than *any* of the family," say: "— better than *any other one* of the family" or "— better than *all the others* (or *all the rest*) of the family."

carry

"The blacksmith is stronger than *any* man," or "stronger than all men," would imply that the blacksmith is not a man. Say, "The blacksmith is stronger than any *other* man," or "than *all other* men."

aren't. A correct form, but harsh; to be avoided when possible. "We're *not,*" "They're *not,*" etc., have a much pleasanter effect than "We *aren't,*" "They *aren't.*"

an'y-way, **an'y-where.** Frequently misspelled with a superfluous *s: anyways, anywheres,* probably in imitation of such adverbial forms as *forwards, backwards.*

at, **in.** Always *in* a *c*ountry; either *at* or *in* a city, town, or village; *at,* if the place is regarded as a point; *in,* if it is inclusive. "We arrived *at* Paris"; "He lives *in* London"; "There are three churches *in* this village." The sense of *at* is virtually included in *there* and *where,* so that in the phrase "Where is it *at?*" — common in some parts of the United States — the *at* is redundant, and the expression somewhat grotesque.

aw'ful, **aw'ful-ly.** In colloquial or slang use, for *very, exceedingly,* to be avoided; as, "an *awful* good time"; "an *awfully* jolly crowd"; "thanks *awfully.*"

back. Do not say, "He returned *back.*" *Back* is included in *return.* Say simply: "He *returned,*" or "He came *back.*"

bad or **badly.** Instead of "He felt *badly,*" better say: "He felt *bad.*" Instead of "It needs to be mended *badly,*" say: "It *badly* needs to be mended," or, better still: "It *greatly* needs to be mended."

be back. Instead of "I'll *be back* in a moment," say: "I'll *come back,*" or "I'll *be here* (or *there*) again, in a moment."

be-side', **be-sides'.** These words should be discriminated carefully. "There were two *beside* him" (*i.e.,* by the side of him); "There were two *besides* him" (*i.e.,* in addition to him).

between you and I. Say: "Between you and *me.*" *Between,* as a preposition, is followed by the objective case. Similarly, say: "That will be good for you and *me*"; not "—— for you and *I.*"

bit. A *bit* is primarily a *bite,* and applies to solids. Say, "a *bit* of bread," "a *bit* of money," but not "a little *bit* of water"; "a *bit* of soap," but not "a *bit* of soup."

blame on. Instead of "Don't *blame* that *on* me," say: "Don't *blame* me for that."

bring, **car'ry.** Will I *bring* this plant into the house, sir?" Here "*Will*" should be "*Shall*" and "*bring*" should be "*carry*"; "*Shall* I *carry* it into the house?" If an object is to be moved *from* the place we occupy,

551

we say *carry;* if *to* the place we occupy, we say *bring.*

can, may. Instead of "*Can* I come in?" say: "*May* I come in?" *Can* refers to possibility, *may* to permission.

can but, } Both are correct, but with a dif-
cannot but. } ference of meaning. *Can but* is the feebler form. "I *can but* protest" means "I can *only* protest" (that is all I am able to do). "I *cannot but* protest" means, "I *cannot help* protesting" (I must enter my protest.).

considerable. An adjective often misused as an adverb; as, "*considerable* hot"; "*considerable* tired." The adverb *considerably* should be used in such connections.

don't, a contraction of *do not,* should be used only in the first person singular or in the plural; as, "I *don't* (do not) know," "They *don't* (do not) care." Never say: "He *don't*," "It *don't*," but, "He *doesn't*," "It *doesn't*." In the interrogative form, do not say: "*Don't* he" or "*Don't* it," but "*Doesn't* he," "*Doesn't* it."

each. Instead of "*Each* of the men *were* paid a dollar," say: "*Each* of the men *was* paid a dollar"; instead of, "*Each* of the students have *their* own room," say: "*Each* student has *his* (or *her*) own room." Remember that *each* denotes an individual, and is always singular.

else but. Instead of "It is nothing *else but* pride," say: "It is nothing *else than* pride."

em'i-grant, } Not infrequently confounded
im'mi-grant. } by some educated persons of careless speech. If a person is considered as migrating from a country, he is an *emigrant;* if to a country, he is an *immigrant.*

eq'ua-ble, } Study these words in the dic-
eq'ui-ta-ble. } tionary and avoid confusing them. An *equable* mind is one that is calm and self-poised; an *equitable* decision is one that is fair or just.

every one. "So *every one* had something to please *them.*" This is incorrect. How can "every one" be "them"? Better change the construction, and say: "So there was something to please *every one,*" or the like.

ex-pect'. *Expect* refers to the future. One should not say: "I *expect* it is," still less "I *expect* it *was.*" We can not *expect* the present or the past. Better say: "I *think* (*believe* or *suppose*) it is," or "—— was."

first'ly. *First,* being itself an adverb, does not need the *-ly* that is frequently added. In an enumeration say *first, secondly, thirdly,* etc., rather than *firstly,* etc.

for, at, to dinner. "We will have a friend *for dinner*" would imply that the "friend" is to be eaten. Say: "We will have a friend *at dinner,*" or "We have invited a friend *to dinner.*"

had have. Improperly used in such expressions as "*Had* I *have* known it," "*Had* he *have* done that," "If I *had have* known." Say: "*Had* I *known* this," "*Had* he *done* that," "If I *had known.*"

had (or hadn't) ought. Incorrect. See OUGHT.

help. Instead of "I will use *no more than I can help,*" better say: "—— *no more than is necessary,*" "—— *no more than I must,*" or the like.

hope. "I *hope* he arrived in time." Better say: "I *trust* he arrived in time." *Hope* refers to the future.

how-ev'er. Instead of "*However* did you come here?" say: "*How* did you *ever* come here?" *However* is properly used as an adverb; as, "*However* wise one may be, there are limits to his knowledge"; but its use for *how* and *ever* should be avoided as a vulgarism. *However* is also in approved use as a conjunction; as, "I believed the statement accurate. I find, *however,* that it contained some errors."

I am, } yours truly. Say, "*I am,*" if this
I remain } is your first letter to that correspondent; "*I remain*" if you have previously written.

If I were you. "Were" in this expression is not the indicative plural agreeing with "you," but the subjunctive singular agreeing with "I." It is employed also for the third person singular, "If I *were,* if he, she, or it *were.*" *Were,* so used, always implies that the fact is otherwise, "If I *were* a dog, I might bay the moon"; "If he *were* here, I would tell him to his face."

in, in'to. Instead of "He fell *in* the pond," say: "He fell *into* the pond." *In* denotes position, state, etc.; *into,* tendency, direction, destination, etc.; as, "I throw the stone *into* the water, and it lies *in* the water."

kind of. Does not require the indefinite article before the following noun. Not "What *kind of a* man is he?" but "What *kind of* man." Not "It is a *kind of an* animal," but "A *kind of* animal."

know, } Either is correct, but they mean
know of. } different things. I *know* my friend; I may *know of* a stranger.

lay, *v.t.* } "I will *lay* down and rest." No: "I will
lie. *v.i.* } *lie* down and rest." But one may say: "I will *lay* my head down on the pillow, and rest." The identity in form of the present tense of *lay,* a transitive verb, with the imperfect tense of *lie,* an intransitive one, has led to the frequent confounding of the two. The principal parts of the two verbs are:

Present.	*Imperfect.*	*Past Participle.*
lay, *vt.*	laid	laid
lie, *vt.*	lay	lain

Lay, in "I *lay* upon thee no other burden," is the present tense of *lay, vt.,* having as its object *burden;* in "I *lay* under the sycamore-tree," *lay* is the imperfect tense of *lie, vi.,* having no object. *Lay* (imperfect of *lie*) never takes an object; *laid* (imperfect of *lay*) always takes an object. "The soldier *laid* aside his knapsack and *lay* down." *Laid* and *lain* are similarly distinguished. "The hen has *laid* an egg"; "The egg has *lain* too long in the nest." *Lie,* to falsify, is regular: *lied, lied.*

learn, ⎱ "If I set out to *learn* a man the
teach. ⎰ river, I'll *learn* him," said Mark
Twain's Mississippi pilot. He should have
said *teach.* The instructor *teaches;* the pupils
learn.

lit'tler, ⎱ These are colloquialisms, and should
lit'tlest. ⎰ be avoided. *Less* and *least* are the
approved comparative and superlative of
little.

lives. Instead of "I'd just as *lives* as not,"
say: "I'd just as *lief* as not."

love, ⎱ Although their distinction in meaning is
like. ⎰ one of the peculiar felicities of the
English language, these words are often confounded in use. We *love* that which ministers
to our affections; we *like* what ministers to
appetite, taste, fancy, etc. A man *loves* his
wife and children; he *likes* roast beef; he
likes some good-natured acquaintance whom
he could not be said to *love*, except as he
should *love* all men; he *likes* a fleet horse, a
fine house, a pleasing picture, a brisk walk;
the Christian *loves* God.

mile, ⎱ In some parts of New England these
mild. ⎰ two words are confused, and persons
say, "He ran a *mild,*" or the like. *Mile* is
a noun denoting distance, *mild* an adjective
signifying "moderate, gentle," etc.

most. Never use *most* for *almost.* Instead of
"*most* everybody," "*most* always," say:
"*almost* everybody," "*almost* always." The
former use is a colloquialism.

nei'ther. Do not say "*Neither* he nor his wife
were there." *Neither,* like *either,* when it
introduces two nominatives in the singular
number, takes a verb in the singular; as,
"*Either* James *or* Henry *was* there"; "*Neither*
Germany *nor* Italy *is* a republic."

new beginner. In the sentence "I'm a *new*
beginner," *new* is included in *beginner,* and
the addition of the adjective is tautological.
Say simply: "I'm a *beginner.*"

no use. Instead of "It was *no use* to argue
with him," say "*of* no use."

of, ⎱ Two prepositions often oddly confounded
off. ⎰ *Of* properly denotes source: as, "I bought
the horse *of* the farmer." *Off* denotes removal; as, "To take the crop *off* the land";
"To cut the hair *off* the head." "Shall I
cut a slice *off* the ham?" is correct; "Shall
I get a steak *off* the butcher?" is ludicrous.

off of. In "Cut a yard *off of* the cloth," the
of is redundant, and should not be used.
Say: "Cut a yard *off* the cloth."

one. Instead of "Not *one* of our friends *were*
present," say: "—— *was* present." We may
say: "*None* of our friends were present,"
since *none* can be used in the plural sense.

or. When *or* connects subjects that require
different persons or numbers of the verb, as,
"Either you *or* I am (are) wrong"; "Either
they *or* he was (were) here"; "This man *or*
those men are (is) guilty," the rule is that the
verb shall agree with the nearest subject;
but then we seem to be saying "you am,"
"they was," "this man are." It is better

to change the construction, saying: "Either
you are wrong *or* I am," etc. Then the verbs
will take care of themselves. *Or* does not
pluralize connected subjects, as *and* does:
"A woman *and* a child (two persons) *are*
lost, but "A woman *or* a child (one of the
two) *is* lost."

ought, the verb for duty, can never take *have,*
be, do, or any other auxiliary; expressions like
"I *had* ought," "I *hadn't* ought," "You *don't*
ought," etc., are, therefore, erroneous. To
express past obligation use the simple *ought*
followed by the *perfect infinitive* of the verb
required; as, "I ought *to have gone.*"

per'fect. *More perfect* and *most perfect* are
condemned by some grammarians, since
what is perfect can not be *more so.* But
every adjective of this kind that strictly
means an absolute and unsurpassable degree, becomes gradually weakened in force in
colloquial use so that a secondary meaning is
developed, and in that sense such adjectives
may properly be compared like other adjectives. Phrases of this kind are common in
popular use to signify "having *more* or *most*
of the qualities that constitute perfection."

place. This noun is improperly used as adverb in some parts of the United States.
Instead of "Are you going any *place?*" say,
"anywhere." "Where have you been?"
"No *place.*" Say, "*Nowhere.*" Some even
say: "Go different *places*" instead of "Go *to*
different *places,*" which latter is the correct
form.

plurals — nouns. When two nouns are united
to form a compound, the first, as a general
rule, is not pluralized. We say *toothache,*
not *teethache; woman=hater,* not *women=*
hater. When a noun follows a numeral in a
compound word, the noun is not pluralized;
as, a ten=*foot* (not ten=*feet*) pole; a two=*mile*
(not two=*miles*) race. A compound word
generally forms its plural by adding *s* at the
end of the whole word, as *handfuls, spoonfuls.*
Nouns ending in *y* preceded by a vowel form
the plural by adding *s*; as *donkey, donkeys:*
chimney, chimneys; monkey, monkeys, etc.
Where the *y* is preceded by a consonant, the
y is changed into *ie,* and *s* added to this; as,
mercy, mercies; pony, ponies; supply, sup-
plies.

A collective noun, as *audience, congrega-*
tion, family, flock, multitude, people, public,
etc., tho singular in form, may take a verb
either in the singular or the plural number,
according as it refers to the objects included
as one aggregate or as separate individuals;
as, "The audience *was* large"; "The audience *were* divided in opinion."

Possessives. A noun ending in *s* properly
takes another *s* with the apostrophe to form
the possessive; thus, *Dickens's* novels,
"*Pepys's* Diary," "*James's* heir," etc. Some
exceptions are commonly made; as, "for
conscience' sake," "for *Jesus'* sake," where
the apostrophe alone is added. Also in words

of many syllables, where the added syllable with 's would have a disagreeable effect; as, "*Empedocles*' sandals," "*Themistocles*' services," instead of "*Empedocles's* sandals," "*Themistocles's* services." In the sentence "The *horses* feet were sore," if you refer to one *horse*, write "the *horse's* feet"; if to more than one, "the *horses'* feet." The apostrophe precedes the *s* for the singular, but follows the *s* for the plural.

quan'ti-ty. Instead of "A great *quantity* of fossil remains *were* found," say: "—— *was* found." Omit the qualifying phrase "of fossil remains," and it is evident that we must say "A great *quantity* —— *was* found."

raise, ⎫ Instead of "He was so weak that he
rise. ⎭ could not *raise*," say: "—— so weak that he could not *rise*." *Raise*, meaning "to cause to rise," is never to be used intransitively. Say: "He could not *rise* in the saddle," but "He could not *raise* himself, his hand, or his head."

raise chil'dren. *Raise*, "to rear (an animal)," is never to be applied to human beings; a misuse common in the southern and western United States. Cattle are *raised; human beings are *brought up*, or, in older phrase, *reared*.

right, *n.* "If you do that, you've a *right* to be arrested." This use of *right* in the sense of "liability" is a barbarism. The true phrase would be: "You are *liable* to be arrested," or, "You *deserve* to be arrested."

sales'la'dy. An inadmissible term. Why not also "*salesgentleman*"? If salesman is a worthy term to apply to a man, its appropriate counterpart is *saleswoman*, which is the only correct term.

set, ⎫ In strict grammatical usage *sit* is always
sit. ⎭ intransitive when referring to posture; *set*, transitive. The uses meaning "to *sit* on eggs" ("the hen *sets*") and "to fit" ("the coat *sets* well or badly") are colloquialisms.

shall, ⎫ The misuse of these little words is very
will. ⎭ prevalent. The simplest brief explanation is the inflection of the two verbs, viz.:

SIMPLE FUTURE.	PURPOSE, COMMAND, OR OBLIGATION.
I *shall*	I *will*
Thou *wilt*	Thou *shalt*
He *will*	He *shall*
We *shall*	We *will*
You *will*	You *shall*
They *will*	They *shall*

Will should never be used interrogatively in the first person. Instead of "*Will* I come in?" say: "*Shall* I come in?" *Shall*, in an interrogative sentence, asks for the consent or approval of the person addressed. Do not say, "*Will* we go in to dinner?" but, "*Shall* we go to dinner?"

sort of. Instead of "I felt *sort of* weak," say: "I felt *rather* weak," or "*somewhat* weak." *Sort of* in such use is a colloquialism, and, as corrupted to *sorter*, a vulgarism.

splen'did. Instead of "He is a *splendid* player," say: "—— a *fine, accomplished*, or *skilful* player." *Splendid* is applied properly to something characterized by splendor; hence, its indiscriminate application to anything admired or agreeable; as, "a *splendid* hat," "a *splendid* beefsteak," is a gross misuse.

stop, ⎫ Instead of "He is *stopping* in Washing-
stay. ⎭ ton this winter," say: "He is *staying* in Washington." To *stop* is to cease moving or acting: the reverse of *start*. "I shall *stop* at Baltimore on my way to Washington" is correct; but "How long will you *stop*?" is as unreasonable a question as "How long will you *start*?" The proper question is: "How long will you *stay* (or *remain*)?"

sure. "I *sure* did"; "It *sure* was." *Sure* is not an adverb. Say "*surely*" or "*certainly*."

than, *conj.* Has the office of connecting a subordinate proposition, as an adverbial modifier, with an adjective or adverb of comparison in a principal proposition; hence its use is improper where there is no comparison.

their, ⎫ Instead of "If any one has been over-
they. ⎭ looked, *they* may raise *their* hand," better say: "Any one who has been overlooked may raise *the* hand," or "*his* hand" ("*his*" including "*her*"); or, "If any of you has been overlooked, you may raise *your* hand."

went for gone. Instead of "If I had *went*," say: "If I had *gone*." The imperfect *went* is often vulgarly used for the past participle *gone* in conjunction with the verb *have; as, "I *have went* there many times," instead of "I *have gone*," etc.

where. *Where* is not to be followed by *at* or *to*. Not, "*Where* is it *at?*" but, "*Where* is it?" not "*Where* are you going *to?*" but simply, "*Where* are you going?"

who. Instead of "*Who* do you refer to?" say: "*Whom* do you refer to?" *Whom* is the object: "You refer to *whom?*" The more formal question is: "*To whom* do you refer?"

with. "The man with his two sons *were* present." The addition of a noun or a pronoun following *with* does not pluralize the subject; consequently, the correct phrase here is "*was* present." The subject might be made plural by using the conjunction *and* instead of the preposition *with; as, "The man *and* his two sons *were* present."

with-out'. Instead of "I'll come *without* it rains," say: "I'll come *unless* it rains."

wit'ness. A verb sometimes misused as a synonym of *see*. We can *witness* an assault, a murder, a theft, a sunrise, anything that is of the nature of an event or is subject to change — but not a thing — not a river, a house, a fire, or a star.

RULES FOR SPELLING

1. Final Consonants Doubled.— Monosyllables ending in *f, l,* or *s,* immediately preceded by a single vowel, double the final consonant; as, *cliff, bell, brass.*

Exceptions: *clef, if, of, sol, as, gas, has, his, is, thus, us, was, yes.*

2. Final Consonants Not Doubled.— Monosyllables ending in any other consonant than *f, l,* or *s,* immediately preceded by a single vowel, do not double the final consonant; as, *cab, bin, dip, hit,* etc.

Exceptions: *abb, ebb, add, odd, egg, inn, err, shirr, burr, purr, mitt, butt, fizz, buzz, fuzz.*

3. Consonants Doubled Before Suffix.— Monosyllables ending in a single consonant, preceded by a single vowel, double the consonant before a suffix beginning with a vowel; accented final syllables follow the same rule; as, *dip, dip'per;* a-*bet'*, a-*bet'tor*.

Exceptions: (1) Syllables ending in *x* do not double the final letter; as, *box, boxes, boxing;* (2) when the accent in the derivative is carried further back, the consonant is likely to remain single; as, *pre-fer', pref'erence;* but *pre-fer'ring, re-fer', ref'er-a-ble;* but also, *re-fer'ri-ble;* (3) the derivatives of the word *gas* (except *gassed, gassing,* and *gassy*) are written with but one *s;* as, *gaseous.*

4. Silent e Omitted Before Vowel-Suffix.— Silent *e* final is ordinarily omitted before a suffix beginning with a vowel; as, *love, loving, lovable.*

Exceptions: (1) Words ending in *ce* or *ge* retain the *e* before -*able* or -*ous,* in order to avoid hardening of the *c* or *g;* as, *effaceable, changeable, advantageous;* (2) the *e* is retained in *hoeing, shoeing,* and *toeing;* (3) also in the derivatives of *dye, singe; springe, swinge,* and *tinge,* thus distinguishing *dyeing* from *dying,* etc., and keeping the *g* soft in *tingeing.*

5. Silent e Retained Before Consonant-Suffix.— Silent *e* final is ordinarily retained before a suffix beginning with a consonant; as, *dire, direful; fine, finely; amaze, amazement.*

Exceptions: The *e* is always dropped in *duly, truly, wholly, argument,* and commonly in *abridgment, acknowledgment, awful, judgment,* and *lodgment.*

6. Final y Unchanged in Plurals.— Nouns ending in *y,* when the *y* is preceded by a vowel, form the plural regularly by simply adding *s;* as, *donkey, donkeys; monkey, monkeys.*

7. Final y Changed in Plurals.— Nouns ending in *y,* when the *y* is preceded by a consonant, form the plural by changing *y* into *i* and adding *es;* as, *mercy, mercies; sky, skies; pity, pities.*

8. Change of y to i Before Suffix.— Words ending in *y,* when the *y* is preceded by a consonant, change the *y* into *i* before any suffix except one beginning with *i;* as, *icy, icily; mercy, merciful; pity, pitiable, pitiful;* but *marry, marrying.*

Exceptions: Adjectives of one syllable ending in *y* preceded by a consonant ordinarily retain the *y;* as, *shy, shyly.*

9. Full as Suffix Changed to -ful.— The word *full,* used as a suffix, drops one *l;* as, *cupful, mouthful, spoonful,* etc. (plurals *cupfuls, mouthfuls, spoonfuls,* etc.).

10. How to Choose Between ei and ie.— When *ei* or *ie* has the sound of ī (= *ee* in *feel*), the usage may be discriminated as follows: After *c* the combination is *ei;* as, *ceiling, perceive, receive;* after any other letter than *c* the combination is *ie;* as, *believe, grieve, reprieve.*

Exceptions: The combination *ie* is used in *ancient, deficient, efficiency,* etc. In *leisure, neither, seize, weir,* and *weird, ei* is used, tho not following *c.*

NOTE.— *ei* sounded as ê (= ā in *fäte*) may follow any consonant; as, *neighbor, sleigh, weigh.*

PROPER NAMES OF ALL KINDS

WITH THEIR RESPELLING AND ACCENTS, OR WITH ACCENTS ALONE WHEN THE SYLLABICATION AND ACCENTUATION SEEM SUFFICIENT TO INDICATE PRONUNCIATION.

Rare names, and also many familiar names that are readily pronounced, are here omitted.

Geographical names are spelled according to the forms adopted by the "United States Board on Geographic Names."

A

Aa'chen, 1 ä'нen; 2 ä'hĕn.
Aal'borg, 1 ôl'bôrg; 2 ạl'bôrg.
Aar, 1 är; 2 är.
Aar'gau, 1 är'gou; 2 är'gou.
Aar'on, 1 âr'un; 2 âr'ŭn.
A'ba-co, 1 ä'bȧ-kō; 2 ä'bȧ-cō.
Ab'a-na, 1 ab'ȧ-nȧ; 2 ăb'ȧ-na.
Ab'a-rim, 1 ab'ȧ-rim; 2 äb'a-rim.
Ab'bas', 1 ä'bäs"; 2 ä'bäs'.
Ab-bas'sides, 1 a-bas'ȧidz; 2 ȧ-bäs'īdş.   Ab-bas'sids†.
Ab-de'rus, 1 ab-dī'rus; 2 ăb-dē'rŭs.
Ab'di-el, 1 ab'di-el; 2 ăb'dĭ-ĕl.
A-bed'ne-go, 1 ȧ-bed'nĭ-gō; 2 a-bĕd-ne-gō.
Ab'é-lard, 1 ab'ı-lärd; 2 äb'e-lärd.   [äb'er-dēn'.
Ab'er-deen', 1 ab'ȧr-dīn'; 2 ab'er-neth-y, 1 ab'ȧr-neth-ı; 2 äb'er-nĕth-y.
A-bi'a-thar, 1 ȧ-baï'ȧ-thär; 2 a-bī'a-thär.   [ä'bī-ē'zer.
A'bi-e'zer, 1 ē'bı-ī'zer; 2
Ab'i-gail, 1 ab'ı-gēl; 2 äb'ī-gāl.
Ab'i-ha'il, 1 ab'ı-hē'il; 2 äb'ī-hā'īl.   [lēn.
Ab'i-lene, 1 ab'ı-līn; 2 äb'i-A-bim'e-lech, 1 ȧ-bim'ı-lek; 2 a-bĭm'e-lĕc.
Ab'i-shag, 1 ab'ı-shag; 2 äb'ī-shăg.   [a-bĭsh'a-ī.
A-bish'a-i, 1 ȧ-bish'ȧ-ï; 2
A'bo, 1 ē'bo; 2 ạ'bo.   Aa'bo†.
A'bra-ham, 1 ē'bra-ham; 2 ä'bra-hăm.
A'bu-kir', 1 ä'bū-kīr', 2 ä'bu-kĭr'.   A'bou-kir'†.
A-by'dos, 1 ȧ-baï'dos; 2 a-bȳ'dŏs.   A-by'dus†.
Ab'ys-sin'i-a, 1 ab'ı-sın'ı-ȧ; 2 äb'y-sĭn'i-a.

A-chæ'a, 1 ȧ-kī'ȧ; 2 a-cē'a.
A-cha'ia‡ [Gr.], 1 ȧ-kä'yȧ; 2 a-cä'ya.
Ach''æ-men'i-dæ, 1 ak'ı-men'ı-dī; 2 ăc'e-mĕn'ĭ-dē.
A-chæ'us, 1 ȧ-kī'us; 2 a-cē'ŭs.
A-cha'tes, 1 ȧ-kē'tīz; 2 a-cā'tēş.   [äc'e-rōn.
Ach'e-ron, 1 ak'ı-ron; 2
A-chil'les, 1 ȧ-kil'īz; 2 a-cĭl'ēş.
A-chit'o-phel, 1 ȧ-kit'o-fel; 2 a-cĭt'o-fĕl.
A'con-ca'gua, 1 ä'kon-kä'gwȧ; 2 ä'cŏn-cä'gwä.
A'cre, 1 ē'ker or ä'ker; 2 ä'cer or ä'cer.
Ac-tæ'on, 1 ak-tī'ȧn; 2 ăc-tē'ŏn.   [äc'shi-ŭm.
Ac'ti-um, 1 ak'shi-um; 2
A-da'iah, 1 ȧ-dē'yȧ or a-daï'ȧ; 2 a-dä'ya or a-dī'a.
A'den, 1 ä'den or ē'den; 2 ä'dĕn or ā'dĕn.
A'di-ge, 1 ä'di-jē; 2 ä'dī-ġe.
Ad''i-ron'dacks, 1 ad'ı-ron'daks; 2 ăd'ī-rŏn'dăks.
Ad''o-ni'jah, 1 ad'o-naï'jȧ; 2 ăd'o-nī'ja.
Ad''o-ni'ram, 1 ad'o-naï'rȧm; 2 ăd'o-nī'ram.   [nĭs.
A-do'nis, 1 ȧ-dō'nis; 2 a-dō'A-dras'tus, 1 ȧ-dras'tus; 2 a-drăs'tŭs.   A'dra-stos† [Gr.].
A'dra-stos, 1 ä'dra-stŏs.
Ad''ri-a-no'ple, 1 ad'ri-a-nō'pl; 2 ăd'rĭ-a-nō'pl.
A'dri-at'ic, 1 ē'dri-at'ik; 2 ä'dri-ăt'ic.
Æ'a-cus, 1 ī'ȧ-kus; 2 ē'a-cŭs.
Ai'a-kos‡ [Gr.], 1 aï'ȧ-kos; 2 ī'a-kos.
Æ-e'tes, 1 ī-ī'tīz; 2 ē-ē'tēş.
Æ-ge'an, 1 ī-jī'ȧn; 2 ē-ğē'an.
Æ-gi'na, 1 ī-joï'nȧ; 2 ē-ğī'na.
Æ'gle, 1 ī'glī; 2 ē'glē.

Æ-ne'as, 1 ī-nī'ȧs; 2 ē-nē'as
Æ-ne'id, 1 ī-nī'id; 2 ē-nē'id.
Æ'o-lus, 1 ī'o-lus; 2 ē'o-lŭs.
Æs'chy-lus, 1 es'kı-lus; 2 ĕs'cy-lŭs.
Æs''cu-la'pi-us, 1 es'kiu-lē'pı-us; 2 ĕs'cū-lā'pĭ-ŭs.
Æ'sop, 1 ī'sȧp; 2 ē'sop.
Af-ghan'i-stan', 1 af-gan'ı-stan'; 2 ăf-găn'i-stän'.
Ag''a-mem'non, 1 ag'ȧ-mem'nen; 2 ăg'a-mĕm'nŏn.
Ag''a-nip'pe, 1 ag'ȧ-nip'ı; 2 ăg'a-nĭp'e.
Ag'as-siz, 1 ag'ȧ-sī; 2 ăg'a-sĭ.
A-ges'i-la'us, 1 ȧ-jes'ı-lē'us; 2 a-ğĕs'ĭ-lä'ŭs.
A''gin'court', 1 a'zän'kūr'; 2 ä'zhän'cur'.   [ğiä'ya.
A-gia'la, 1 ȧ-glē'yȧ; 2 a-A'gra, 1 ä'grȧ; 2 ä'gra.
A''gui-lar', 1 ä'gī-lär'; 2 ä'gī-lär'.   [ä-ğul'yäs.
A-gul'has, 1 a-gŭl'yaş; 2
Ah''med Fu'ad, 1 ä'med fū'ad; 2 ä'mĕd fu'äd.
A-has'u-e'rus, 1 a-haz'yu-ī'rus; 2 a-hăş'yu-ē'rŭs.
A'i, 1 ē'aï or aï; 2 ä'ī or ī.
Ai'ja-lon, 1 ē'[or aï']jȧ-lon; 2 ä'[or ī']ja-lon.
A'in, 1 ē'in; 2 ä'in.
Ain, 1 an; 2 än.
Ain-tab', 1 aïn-täb'; 2 īn-täb'.
Aisne, 1 ēn; 2 än.
Aix, 1 ēks; 2 äks.
Aix''-la-Cha''pelle', 1 ēks'-lȧ-shȧ'pel'; 2 äks'-lä-chä-pĕl'.   [yä'cho.
A-jac'cio, 1 a-yä'cho; 2 ä-Al''a-ba'ma, 1 al'ȧ-bä'mȧ; 2 äl'a-bä'ma.   [a-läch'u-a.
A-lach'u-a, 1 ȧ-lach'u-ȧ; 2
A-la-me'da, 1 ä'la-mē'dȧ; 2 ä'la-me'da.

A'la-mo, 1 ä'lä-mō; 2 ä'lä-mŏ.
Al'a-ric, 1 al'ə-rik; 2 ăl'a-rĭc.
Al-ba'ni-a, 1 al-bē'ni-ə; 2 ăl-bā'nĭ-a.　　　　[bä'no.
Al-ba'no, 1 al-bä'no; 2 äl-
Al'ba-ny, 1 ôl'bə-nı; 2 ạl'-
ba-ny.
Al'bi-on, 1 al'bı-ən; 2 ăl'bı-on.
Al'bu-e'ra, 1 äl'bu-ē'ra; 2 äl'bu-ē'rä.
Al'bu-quer'que, 1 al'bū-ker'kē; 2 äl'bu-kër'ke or
(city) 1 al'bū-kūr'kı; 2 äl'-bu-kër'ke.　　　[çē'ūs.
Al-cæ'us, 1 al-sī'us; 2 äl-
Al-can'ta-ra, 1 al-ses'tıs; 2 äl-
Al'ci-bi'a-des, 1 al'sı-baī'ə-dīz; 2 äl'çi-bī'a-dēs.
Al-ci'des, 1 al-saī'dīz; 2 äl-çī'dēs.　　[äl'çi-frŏn.
Al'ci-phron, 1 al'sı-frən; 2
Alc-me'na, 1 alk-mī'nə; 2 äle-mē'na.
Al'cott, 1 ôl'kət; 2 al'cŏt.
Al-cy'o-ne, 1 al-sı̄'o-nı; 2 äl-çī'o-nē.
Al'der-ney, 1 ôl'dər-nı; 2 al'der-ny.
Al'drich, 1 ôl'drĭch or ôl'drij; 2 al'drĭch or al'drij. [lĕe'to.
A-lec'to, 1 ə-lek'to; 2 a-
A-len'çon, 1 ə-len'sən or (F.) a'lań'sôń'; 2 a-lĕn'son or
(F.) ä'läń'sôń'.
Al've-u'ti-an, 1 al'ı-ū'shı-ən; 2 ăl'e-ū'shın.　　　[e'rĭ.
Al'fi-e'ri, 1 al'fī-ē'rī; 2 äl'fī-
Al'ford, 1 ôl'ford; 2 al'ford.
Al-ge'ri-a, 1 al-jī'rı-ə; 2 äl-gē'rĭ-a.　　　　[äl'ger-nŏn.
Al'ger-non, 1 al'jər-non; 2
Al'giers, 1 al-jīrz'; 2 äl-gērs'.
Al'li-can'te, 1 a'lı-kän'tē; 2 ä'lĭ-cän'te.　[ä'lĭ pa-shä'.
Al'li Pa-sha', 1 ä'lī pə-shä';
Al'la-ha-bad', 1 äl'ə-hə-bäd'; 2 äl'a-ha-bäd'.
Al'le-gha'ny, 1 al'ı-gē'nı; 2 äl'e-gä'ny.　　[äl'e-gĕn'y.
Al'le-ghe'ny, 1 al'ı-gen'ı; 2
Al'len-by, 1 al'ən-bı; 2 äl'en-by.　　　[2 äl'en-shtīn.
Al'len-stein, 1 äl'len-shtaın;
All'ston, 1 ôl'stən; 2 al'ston.
Al'mon, 1 al'mən; 2 äl'mon.
Aln'wick, 1 an'ık; 2 än'ıe.
Al-phe'us, 1 al-fī'us; 2 äl-fē'ūs.　Al-phæ'us.
Al-sace', 1 al-sās' or al'sās'; 2 äl-säç' or äl'säç'.
Al'tai, 1 äl'taı; 2 äl'tī.

Alt'kirch, 1 ält'kırн; 2 ält'-kırн.　　　[va-rĕs.
Al'va-rez, 1 äl'və-res; 2 äl'-
Am'al-thæ'a, 1 am'al-thī'ə; 2 äm'al-thē'a.　　　[a-sa.
Am'a-sa, 1 am'ə-sə; 2 äm'-
Am'a-zi'ah, 1 am'ə-zaī'ə; 2 äm'a-zī'a.　　　　[erst.
Am'herst, 1 am'ərst; 2 äm'-
Am'i-ens, 1 am'ı-enz or (F.) a'mī'äń'; 2 äm'ı-ĕnѕ or (F.) ä'mī'äń'.　　[äm-fī'on.
Am-phi'on, 1 am-faī'ən; 2
Am'ster-dam, 1 am'stər-dam; 2 äm'stər-däm.
A-nac're-on, 1 ə-nak'rı-on; 2 a-näe're-ŏn.　　　[kım.
An'a-kim, 1 an'ə-kım; 2 än'a-kım.
An'ax-ag'o-ras, 1 an-äks-ag'o-rəs; 2 än'äks-ăg'o-ras.
An-cæ'us, 1 an-sī'us; 2 än-çē'ūs.　　　[äŋ-cī'sēs.
An-chi'ses, 1 äŋ-kaı'sīz; 2
Ancre, 1 ăŋkr; 2 äner.
An'do-ver, 1 an'do-vər; 2 än'do-ver.　　　[än'dro-cīes.
An'dro-cles, 1 an'dro-klīz; 2
An-drom'a-che, 1 an-drom'ə-kī; 2 än-dröm'a-cē.
An-drom'e-da, 1 an-drom'ı-də; 2 än-dröm'e-da.
An'dros-cog'gin, 1 an'dros-kog'ın; 2 än'drŏs-cŏg'ĭn.
An'gers, 1 äń'ĕ'; 2 äń zhę'.
An'gle-sey, 1 aŋ'gl-sı; 2 äŋ'gl-sy.　　　　[gŏ'la.
An-go'la, 1 aŋ-gō'lə; 2 äŋ-gō'ra.　　　[2 äń'ĝu'lēm'.
An'gou-lême', 1 añ'gū'lēm';
An'jou, 1 an'jū or (F.) äń'ЗŪ'; 2 än'jŭ or (F.) äń'zhŭ'. [tıl'ĕs.
An-tæ'us, 1 an-tī'us; 2 än-tē'-
An-tie'tam, 1 an-tī'təm; 2 än-tī'tam.　　　[tıl'ĕs.
An-til'les, 1 an-til'īz; 2 än-
Ant'werp, 1 ant'wərp; 2 änt'-werp.
A-pel'les, 1 ə-peı'īz; 2 a-pĕl'ēs.
Ap'en-nines, 1 ap'e-naınz; 2 äp'ĕ-nīnѕ.　[2 ăf'ro-dī'tē.
Aph'ro-di'te, 1 af'ro-daī'tī;
A'pis, 1 ē'pıs; 2 ä'pıs.
Ap'pa-lach'i-an, 1 ap'ə-lach'ı-ən; 2 äp'a-lǎch'ı-an.
Ap'po-mat'tox, 1 ap'o-mat'əks; 2 äp'o-măt'oks.
Ap'u-lei'us, 1 ap'yu-lı'us; 2 äp'yu-lē'ūs.
A-rach'ne, 1 ə-rak'nı; 2 a-räe'ne.　　　[rä-gwī'.
A'ra-guay', 1 ä'ra-gwaī'; 2
Ar'al sea, 1 ar'əl or a-räl'; 2 är'al or ä-räl'.

Ar'a-rat, 1 ar'ə-rat; 2 är'a-rät
Ar'buth-not, 1 är'buтн-not; 2 är'bŭтн-nŏt.　[är'ee-lä'ūѕ
Ar'che-la'us, 1 är'kı-lē'us; 2
Ar'chi-me'des, 1 är'kı-mī'dīz; 2 är'ei-mē'dēѕ.　[är dĕn'.
Ar'dennes', 1 or'den'; 2
A"re-op'a-gus, 1 ē'rı[or är'ı]-op'ə-gus; 2 ä're[or är'e]-ŏp'a-gŭs.
A-rez'zo, 1 a-red'zo; 2 ä-rĕd'zo.　　　　[lĭs.
Ar'go-lis, 1 är'go-lis; 2 är'go-
Ar"gonne', 1 är'gŏn'; 2 är'-gŏn'.
Ar-gyll', 1 ar-gaıl'; 2 är-gīl.
A"ri-ad'ne, 1 ä'rı-ad'nı; 2 ä'ri-äd'ne.
A'ri-el, 1 ē'rı-el; 2 ä'rı-l.
Ar"i-ma-thæ'a, 1 ar'ı-mə-thī'ə; 2 är'ı-ma-thē'a.
A-ri'on, 1 ə-raī'ən; 2 a-rī'on.
Ar'is-tar'chus, 1 ar'ıs-tär'kus; 2 är'ıs-tär'eūѕ.
Ar"is-ti'des, 1 ar'ıs-taī'dız; 2 är'ıs-tī'dēѕ.
Ar'is-tot-le, 1 ar'ıs-tɒt-l; 2 är'ıs-tŏt-l.　　[är'kan-sạ.
Ar'kan-sas, 1 är'kən-sô; 2
Ar"ma-ged'don, 1 är"mə-ged'ən; 2 är"ma-gĕd'on.
Ar"men"tières, 1 aı'măń'tyär'; 2 är"măń'tyēr'.
A-roos'took, 1 ə-rūs'tuk; 2 a-rōōѕ'tōōk.
Ar"ras', 1 ä'räs'; 2 ä'räs'.
Ar"tax-erx'es, 1 är"tag-zŭrk'sız; 2 är"tag-zērk'sēѕ. [nĕth.
As'e-nath, 1 as'ı-nath; 2 äs'e-
A-shan'ti, 1 ə-shan'tı or a-shän'tı; 2 a-shän'tĭ or a-shän'tī.　[2 äsh'tə-bü'lạ.
Ash'ta-bu'la, 1 ash'tə-bü'lə;
Ash'ta-roth, 1 ash tə-roth; 2 äsh'ta-rŏth.　[äsh'to-rēth.
Ash'to-reth, 1 ash'to-reth; 2
A'sia, 1 ē'sha; 2 ä'sha.
As"saye', 1 a'saī'; 2 ä'sī'.
As-tar'te, 1 as-tär'tī; 2 äs-tär'tē.　　[2 äs'trä-kän'.
As"tra-khan', 1 as'trä-kŭn';
A-sun"ci-on', 1 a-sŭn'sı-ŏn'; 2 ä-ѕŭn"çi-ŏn'.　[ä'tä-cä'mä.
A"ta-ca'ma, 1 ä'ta-kä'ma; 2
A"ta-hual'pa, 1 ä'ta-hwäl'pa; 2 ä"tä-hwäl'pa.
A"ta"türk', 1 ä"tä"türk'; 2 ä"tä"türk'.
A'te, 1 ē'tı or ä'tē; 2 ä'tĕ or ä'te.　　　　[äтн'a-lı'a.
Ath-a-li'ah, 1 aтн'ə-laı'ə; 2
Ath"a-na'sius, 1 aтн"ə-nē'shus; 2 äтн'a-nä'shūѕ.　[na
A-the'na, 1 ə-thī'nə; 2 a-thē'-

Ath″e-næ′us, 1 ăth′ĭ-nī′ŭs; 2
  ăth″e-nē′ŭs.
Ath′ens, 1 ăth′enz; 2 ăth′ĕnş.
Ath′os, 1 ăth′ŏs; 2 ăth′ŏs.
At-lan′ta, 1 ăt-lăn′tȧ; 2 ăt-
  lăn′tȧ.
A′tre-us, 1 ē′trŭs or ē′trĭ-ŭs;
  2 ā′trŭş or ā′tre-ŭs.   [lŭs.
At′ta-lus, 1 ăt′ȧ-lŭs; 2 ăt′ȧ-
Au″ber′, 1 ō′bĕr′; 2 ō′bĕr′.
Au″bi′gné′, d′, 1 dō′bĭ′nyē′;
  2 dō′bĭ′nyĕ′.   [a′dụ-bŏn.
Au′du-bon, 1 ō′dụ-bon; 2
Au′er-städt, 1 ou′ẽr-shtĕt; 2
  ou′ẽr-shtĕt.
Augs′burg, 1 augz′bụrH; 2
Au-gus′ta, 1 ȯ-gŭs′tȧ; 2 a-
  gŭs′tȧ.
Au′gus-tine, 1 ō′gŭs-tǐn or ȯ-
  gŭs′tǐn; 2 a′gŭs-tǐn or a-gŭs′-
  tǐn.
Aus′ter-litz, 1 ŏs′[or ous′]tẽr-
  lǐts; 2 aş′[or ous′]tẽr-lǐts.
Aus′tin, 1 ŏs′tǐn; 2 aş′tǐn.
Aus″tral-a′sia, 1 ŏs″trȧl-ē′-
  shȧ; 2 aş″tral-ā′shȧ.
Au″vergne′, 1 ō′vãr′nye; 2
  ō′vĕr′nye.   [ä′ve′rŏn′.
A″vey′ron′, 1 ȧ′vē′rŏn′; 2
A″vi′gnon′, 1 ȧ′vĭ′nyŏn′; 2
  ä′vĭ′nyŏn′.   [or ăv′on.
A′von, 1 ē′von or av′on; 2 ā′von
Ayr, 1 âr; 2 âr.
Ayr′shire, 1 âr′shǐr; 2 âr′shǐr.
A-zof′, 1 a-zŏf′ or ē′zŏv; 2
  ä-zŏf′ or ā′zŏv.
A-zores′, 1 ȧ-zōrz′; 2 a-zōrş′.

B

Ba′al, 1 bā′ăl; 2 bā′al.
Baal″bek′, 1 bāl″bek′; 2 bäl″-
  bĕk′.   [2 bä′al-zē′bŭb.
Ba′al-ze′bub, 1 bē′al-zī′bŭb;
Ba′den, 1 bä′dĕn; 2 bä′dĕn.
Bage′hot, 1 baj′ŏt; 2 băg′ot.
Ba-ha′ma, 1 ba-hē′[or hä′]mȧ;
  2 ba-hä′[or hä′]ma.
Bah-i′a, 1 bä-i′ȧ; 2 bä-ī′ä.
Bai′kal, 1 bai′kal; 2 bī′käl.
Bail′leul, 1 bai′yöl′; 2 bī′yŭl′.
Bal-reuth′, 1 bäl-reit′; 2 bī-
  rŏit′.   [2 bäl″lä-klä′vä.
Ba″la-kla′va, 1 ba″la-klä′vȧ;
Bâle, 1 bäl; 2 bäl.
Bal″e-ar′ic, 1 băl′ĭ-ar′ĭk; 2
  băl′e-ăr′ĭc.
Ba-lize′, 1 ba-līz′; 2 bä-lĭz′.
Bal-kan′, 1 bal-kăn′ or băl′-
  kȧn; 2 bäl-kän′ or bȧl′kȧn.
Bal-mor′al, 1 bal-mŏr′ȧl; 2
  băl-mō′ral.   [bäl-thä′zar.
Bal-tha′zar, 1 băl-thē′zẽr; 2
Ba-lu″chi-stan′, 1 ba-lū′chĭ-
  stän′; 2 ba-lụ′chi-stän′.

Bal″zac′, 1 bȧl′zăk; 2 bäl′-
  zăc′.   [băng′kŏk′.
Bang″kok′, 1 băŋ′kŏk′; 2
Ban′gor, 1 băn′gẽr; 2 băn′gŏr.
Ba″paume′, 1 ba″pōm′; 2 bä″-
  pōm′.
Bar-ba′dos, 1 bar-bē′doz; 2
  bär-bä′dŏş. Bar-ba′does‡.
Bar″ce-lo′na, 1 bär′sĭ-lō′nȧ
  or (Sp.) bär″thĕ-lō′na; 2
  bär″çe-lō′na or (Sp.) bär″-
  thₑ-lō′nä.   [rĕzh′.
Ba″règes′, 1 ba″râ′; 2 bä″-
Bar″le-Duc′, 1 bär″le-dŭk′;
  2 bär″le-dük′.
Bar′ne-veldt, 1 bär′na-velt;
  2 bär′ne-velt.
Bar″the′lé″mont′, 1 bär″te″
  lē″mon′; 2 bär″tē″le″mŏn′.
Bar″ti-mæ′us, 1 bär′tĭ-mī′-
  ŭs; 2 bär″tĭ-mē′ŭs.
Ba′ruch, 1 bē′rụk; 2 bä′rŭk.
Bar-zil′la-i, 1 bar-zĭl′ȧ-ī or
  -zĭl′ē; 2 bär-zĭl′a-ī or -zĭl′ä.
Ba′sel, 1 bä′zel; 2 bä′şĕl.
Ba′shan, 1 bē′shȧn; 2 bä′-
  shan.
Bas′il, 1 băz′ĭl or bē′zĭl; 2
  bäş′ĭl or bā′şil. [băs-sä′nĭ-o.
Bas-sa′ni-o, 1 bas-sä′nĭ-o; 2
Bas′sein′, 1 ba″sēn′; 2 bä″şen′.
Bas′so-ra, 1 băs′o-ra; 2 băs′-
  o-ra.   [bä-tä′vĭ-ä.
Ba-ta′vi-a, 1 ba-tä′vĭ-ȧ; 2
Bath-she′ba, 1 bath-shī′ba
  or bath′shĭ-ba; 2 băth-
  shē′ba or băth′she-ba.
Bat′on Rouge, 1 băt′on rūż;
  2 băt′on rụżh.
Bat′ter-sea, 1 băt′ẽr-sī; 2
  băt′ẽr-sē.   [ba-vä′rĭ-a.
Ba-va′ri-a, 1 ba-vē′rĭ-a; 2
Bay′ard, 1 bai′ẽrd; 2 bī′ard.
Ba″yeux′, 1 ba″yẽ′; 2 bä″yụ′.
Ba″yonne′, 1 ba″yon′; 2 bä″-
  yŏn′.   [ba-a-trīç.
Be′a-trice, 1 bĭ′a-trĭs; 2
Beau″champ′, 1 bō″shŏn′; 2
  bō″shän′ (in England, 1 bĭ′-
  chum; 2 bē′chŭm).
Beau′fort, 1 biū′fẽrt or bō′-
  fẽrt, 2 bū′fort or bō′fort.
Beau′re-gard, 1 bō′rĭ-gärd; 2
  bō′re-gärd.
Beau″vais′, 1 bō″vē′; 2 bō″vā′.
Be-er′she-ba, 1 bĭ-ẽr′shĭ-ba
  or bē′ẽr-shĭ′ba; 2 be-ẽr′she-
  ba or bē′ẽr-shē′ba.
Bee′tho-ven, 1 bē′tō-ven; 2
  bē′tō-vĕn.
Beh′ring. See BERING.
Be′i-ra, 1 bē′ĭ-ra; 2 bē′ĭ-rä.
Bei-rut′, 1 bē-rūt′; 2 be-rụt′.
Be-lem′, 1 bē-leñ′; 2 bē-lĕñ′.

Bel-grade′, 1 bel-grēd′; 2
  bĕl-gräd′.   [2 bĕl′ĭ-sä′rĭ-ŭs.
Bel″i-sa′ri-us, 1 bel′ĭ-sē′rĭ-ŭs;
Be-lize′, 1 bē-līz′; 2 be-lĭz′.
Bel″leau′, 1 bĕl″lō′; 2 bĕl″lō′.
Bel″ler′o-phon, 1 be-ler′o-
  fon; 2 bĕ-lĕr′o-fŏn.   [lō′na.
Bel-lo′na, 1 be-lō′na; 2 bĕ-
Be-na′iah, 1 bĭ-nē′ya or bĭ-
  naī′a; 2 be-nā′ya or be-nī′a.
Be-na′res, 1 bĭ-nä′rĭz; 2 be-
  nä′rĕş.   [găl′.
Ben-gal′, 1 ben-gôl′; 2 bĕn-
Ben-gue′la, 1 ben-gē′la; 2
  ben-gē′lä.   [2 bĕn″hä′däd.
Ben″-ha′dad, 1 ben″he′däd;
Ben-in′, 1 ben-ĭn′; 2 bĕn-ĭn′.
Ben Ne′vis, 1 nĭv′is or nev′ĭs;
  2 nĕ′vĭs or nĕv′ĭs.
Ber″e-ni′ce, 1 ber′ĭ-naī′sī; 2
  bĕr″e-nī′çē.
Be′ring Sea, 1 bē′rĭng or bẽr′ĭŋ;
  2 bē′rĭng or bē′rĭng.
Ber′lin, 1 bẽr′lĭn or (G.) ber-
  lĭn′; 2 bĕr′lĭn or (G.) bĕr-lĭn′.
Ber-mu′das, 1 bẽr-miū′dȧz;
  2 ber-mū′däş.
Ber-ni′ce, 1 bẽr-naī′sī; 2 ber-
  nī′çē.   [2 be-şän″çŏn′.
Be-san″çon′, 1 .ba-zäñ″sŏn′;
Beth-ab′a-ra, 1 beth-ab′a-ra
  or beth′a-bē′ra; 2 bĕth-äb′a-
  ra or bĕth′a-bā′ra.
Beth′pha-ge, 1 beth′fȧ-jī or
  beth′fĭj; 2 bĕth′fȧ-gē or
  bĕth′fag.   [2 bĕth-sā′ĭ-da.
Beth-sa′i-da, 1 beth-sē′ĭ-da;
Bey′rout. Same as BEIRUT.
Be-zal′e-el, 1 bĭ-zal′ĭ-el; 2 be-
  zäl′e-ĕl.   [äŋ′ca.
Bi-an′ca, 1 bĭ-aŋ′ka; 2 bĭ-
Bi″ar′ritz′, 1 bĭ″a′rĭtz′; 2
  bĭ″ä′rĭtz′.
Bie′la, 1 bĭ′la; 2 bē′la.
Bil-ba′o, 1 bĭl-bā′o; 2 bĭl-bä′o.
Bing′en, 1 bĭng′en; 2 bĭng′ĕn.
Bi-ron′, 1 bĭ-rēn′; 2 bĭ-rŏn′.
Bis′marck, 1 bĭs′märk; 2
  bĭs′märk.
Bis′sing, 1 bĭs′sĭŋ; 2 bĭs′sĭŋg.
Bi-thyn′i-a, 1 bĭ-thĭn′ĭ-a; 2
  bĭ-thŷn′ĭ-a.
Blanc, Mont, 1 mĕñ blŏñ; 2
  mŏñ blän.   [blĕn′hĭm.
Blen′heim, 1 blen′hoim; 2
Bloem″fon-tein″, 1 blüm-
  fon-tēn″; 2 blōōm″fŏn-tₑn″.
Blois, 1 blwä; 2 blwä.
Blount, 1 blunt; 2 blŭnt.
Blü″cher, 1 blü″hẽr, blū′chẽr
  or blü′kẽr; 2 blü′Her, blụ′-
  cher or blụ′cer.
Bo″a-di-ce′a, 1 bō′a-dĭ-sī′a;
  2 bō′a-di-çē′a.

Bo″ba-dil′la, 1 bō″ba-dîl′ya; 2 bŏ″bä-dĭl′yä.

Boc-cac′cio, 1 bok-kä′cho; 2 bŏc-eä′cho. [bō″go-tä′.

Bo″go-ta′, 1 bō″go-tä′; 2

Bol′se, 1 bŏl′zī; 2 bŏl′sĕ.

Bo-kha′ra, 1 bo-kä′ra; 2 bo-kä′ra. [2 än bŏl′yn.

Bol′eyn, Anne, 1 an bul′in;

Bol′ing-broke, 1 bŏl′ĭn-bruk; 2 bŏl′ing-brŏk.

Bol′i-var, 1 bol′i-vər or (Sp.) bo-lī′vär; 2 bŏl′i-var or (Sp.) bo-lī′vär. [bo-lō′nyä.

Bo-lo′gna, 1 bo-lō′nya; 2

Bon′heur′, 1 bȯn′ȯr′; 2 bȯn″ȗr′. [bȯr′dȯ′.

Bor′deaux′, 1 bȯr′dō′; 2

Bor-ghe′se, 1 bȯr-gē′zē; 2 bȯr-gē′se. [bȯr′o-dī′no.

Bor″o-di′no, 1 bȯr′o-dī′no; 2

Bos′po-rus, 1 bŏs′po-rus; 2 bŏs′po-rŭs. [bŏs′pho-rŭs‡.

Bos′phor-us‡, 1 bo′swē′; 2 bŏ″-swę′.

Bos′sut′, 1 bo″sü′; 2 bŏ′sü′.

Bo′tha, 1 bō′ta; 2 bō′tä.

Both′ni-a, 1 bŏth′ni-ə; 2 bŏth′ni-a. [bu′dī-net.

Bou′di-not, 1 bū′dĭ-net; 2

Bou-logne′, 1 bu-lōn′ or (F.) bū′lō′nya; 2 bu-lōn′ or (F.) bu̇′lō′nya.

Bourges, 1 bûr3; 2 bu̇rzh.

Bou-vier′, 1 bū-vir′ or (F.) bū″vyē′; 2 bu̇-vir′ or (F.) bu̇″vyę′. [bow′dich.

Bow′ditch, 1 bau′dich; 2

Bow′doin, 1 bō′din; 2 bō′dn.

Boz′za-ris, 1 bŏt′sa-rĭs or bo-zar′ĭs; 2 bŏt′sä-rĭs or bo-zär′ĭs.

Bra′bant, 1 brä′bant or (F.) bra″bäñ′; 2 brä′bänt or (F.) brä′bäñ′.

Bra′he, Ty′cho, 1 taī′ko brä′he or 1 brä′ma-pū′tra; 2 brä′ma-pu̇′tra.

Brah″ma-pu′tra, 1 brä″ma-pū′tra; 2 brä″ma-pu̇′tra.

Brase′nose, 1 brēz′nōz; 2 bräʒ′nōʒ.

Bra′zos, 1 brä′zos; 2 brä′zŏs.

Bre-genz′, 1 brĭ-gens′; 2 bre-gĕns′.

Brem′en, 1 brem′en or (G.) brē′men; 2 brĕm′ĕn or (G.) brē′mĕn.

Bre′mer, 1 brī′mər; 2 brē′mer.

Bres′cia, 1 bresh′a; 2 brĕsh′ä.

Bres′lau, 1 brez′lau; 2 brĕʒ′lou. [bre-tä′nye.

Bre-tagne, 1 bra-tä′nye; 2

Bret′on, 1 bret′an or bri′ten; 2 brĕt′on or brē′tŏn.

Bret′on, Cape, 1 bret′ən or brit′an; 2 brĕt′on or brit′on.

Bri″an′çon′, 1 brī″añ″sōñ′; 2 brī″äñ″çōñ′. [brī-ä′re-ùs.

Bri-a′re-us, 1 braī-ē′rĭ-us; 2

Bri′enz′, 1 brī′äñ; 2 brī′änʒ′.

Brin′di-si, 1 brĭn′dĭ-zī; 2 brĭn′dĭ-sĭ. [sē′is.

Bri-se′is, 1 braī-sī′is, 2 brī-brĭn′dĭ-sĭ.

Bron′te, 1 brȯn′tē; 2 brŏn′tę.

Brook′line, 1 bruk′laīn; 2 brŏŏk′laīn. [brō′am.

Brough′am, 1 brō′əm; 2

Bru′ges, 1 brü′jiz or (F.) brüʒ; 2 bru̇′ges or (F.) brüzh.

Bu-ceph′a-lus, 1 biu-sef′a-lus; 2 bū-çĕf′a-lùs.

Bu″cha-rest′, 1 biū′ka-rest′; 2 bū′ca-rĕst′. [bu̇′dä-pĕst.

Bu′da-pest′, 1 bū′da-pest′; 2

Bue′na Vis′ta, 1 bū′na vis′ta or (Sp.) bwē′na vis′ta; 2 bu̇′na vis′ta or (Sp.) bwę′nä vis′tä.

Bue′nos Ai′res, 1 bō′nas ē′rĭz or (Sp.) bwē′nōs aī′res; 2 bō′nos ā′rēʒ or (Sp.) bwę′nŏs ī′rēs.

Bu″la-wa′yo, 1 bū″lə-wä′yo; 2 bu̇″lə-wä′yo.

Bul-ga′ri-a, 1 bul-gē′rĭ-ə; 2 bu̇l-gä′ri-a.

Bul′len. See BOLEYN.

Bü′low, von, 1 fon bü′lo; 2 fon bü′lo.

Butte, 1 büt; 2 bu̇t.

By-zan′ti-um, 1 bĭ-zan′shĭ-um; 2 by-zän′shĭ-ùm.

C

Cab′ot, 1 kab′ət; 2 eäb′ot.

Ca-bul′. See KABUL.

Ca′diz, 1 kē′dĭz or (Sp.) kä′thĭth; 2 eä′dĭz or (Sp.) eä′thĭth.

Caen, 1 käñ; 2 eäñ.

Ca″gay-an′, 1 kä″gaī-än′; 2 eä″gī-än′. [lyä-rī.

Ca′glia-ri, 1 kä′lya-rī; 2 eä-

Ca-glios′tro, 1 ka-lyōs′tro; 2 eä-lyōs′tro.

Cai′a-phas, 1 kē″[or kaī′]ə-fəs; 2 eä′[or eī′]a-fas.

Cai′ro, [Egypt] 1 kaī′ro, 2 eī′ro; [U. S.] 1 kē′ro, 2 eä′ro.

Cal′us, 1 kē′us or kē′yus; 2 eä′ús or eä′yùs.

Ca″lais′, 1 ka′lē′; 2 eä′lä′.

Ca-lig′u-la, 1 ka-lig′yu-la; 2 ea-lig′yu-la.

Cal-la′o, 1 ka-lä′o or kal-yä′o; 2 eä-lä′o or eäl-yä′o.

Ca-lyp′so, 1 kə-lĭp′so; 2 ea-lypso.

Cambrai, 1 kañ″brē′; 2 eäñ′brä′. [eäm-bī′sēʒ.

Cam-by′ses, 1 kam-baī′sīz; 2

Cam′e-lot, 1 kam′i-lot; 2 eäm′e-lŏt. [mīl′.

Ca″mille′, 1 ka″mīl′; 2 eä-

Cam′o-ens, 1 kam′o-ens; 2 eäm′o-ens. [2 eäm-pā′nyä.

Cam-pa′nia, 1 kam-pā′nya;

Cam-pe′che, 1 kam-pī′chi or (Sp.) kam-pē′chē; 2 eäm-pē′che or (Sp.) eäm-pę′chę.

Ca′na, 1 kē′na; 2 eä′na.

Can″an-dai′gua, 1 kan″an-dē′gwa; 2 eän′an-dä′gwa.

Can-ber′ra, 1 kan-ber′a; 2 eän-bĕr′a. [ean′da-çē.

Can′da-ce, 1 kan′da-sī; 2

Cannes, 1 kän; 2 eän. [nō′va.

Ca-no′va, 1 ka-nō′va; 2 eä-

Ca-nute′, 1 kə-nūt′; 2 eä-nu̇t′.

Cap″pa-do′ci-a, 1 kap′ə-dō′shĭ-a; 2 eäp′a-dō′shi-a.

Cap′u-a, 1 kap′yu-ə or (It.) kä′pu̇-a; 2 eäp′yu-a or (It.) eä′pu̇-ä. [eär′a-eäl′a.

Car″a-cal′la, 1 kar″a-kal′a; 2

Ca-rac′as, 1 kə-rak′əs or (Sp.) ka-rä′kas; 2 ea-räe′as or (Sp.) eä-rä′eäs.

Car″chem-ish, 1 kär′ki-mish; 2 eär′ee-mish. [eär′de-näs.

Car′de-nas, 1 kär′dē-nas; 2

Car″ib-be′an, 1 kar′i-bī′an. 2 eär′i-bē′an. [RUHE

Carls′ru″he. See KARLS-

Car′mi, 1 kär′maī; 2 eär′mī.

Car-nar′von, 1 kar-när′von; 2 eär-när′von.

Car′ne-a-des, 1 kar-nī′ə-dīz; 2 eär-nē′a-dēʒ.

Car′not′, 1 kar′nō′; 2 eär′nō′

Car-ra′ra, 1 kar-rä′ra; 2 eäl-rä′rä. [rụ′so.

Car″ta-ge′na, 1 kär″tə-jī′nə or (Sp.) kär′tu-hē′na; 2 eär′ta-gē′na or (Sp.) eär′tü-hē′nä.

Ca-ru′so, 1 ka-rü′so. 2 eä-rü′so.

Cash-mere′. See KASHMIR.

Cas″si-o-pe′ia, 1 kas′i-o-pī′yə; 2 eäs′i-o-pē′ya.

Cas-ta′li-a, 1 kas-tē′li-ə; 2 eäs-tä′li-a.

Cas″ti-glio′ne, 1 käs″tĭ-lyō′nī; 2 eäs″tī-lyō′nē.

Cas′tile′, 1 kas-tēl′; 2 eäs-tīl′.

Cas′tle-reagh, 1 kas′l-rē; 2 eäs′l-rē.

Ca-ta′ni-a, 1 ka-tē′ni-ə or (It.) ka-tä′ni-a; 2 ea-tä′ni-a or (It.) eä-tä′ni-ä.

1: ə = final; ɪ = habit; aɪsle; aυ = out; oɪl; ɪu̇ = feud; ᴄhin; go; ŋ = sing; ᴛhin, this.

2: wǫlf, dǫ; bŏŏk, bo͞ot; fu̇ll, rụle, cūre, bŭt, bûrn; ŏɪl, bŏy; ᵹo, ᵹem; iŋk; thin, this.

Ca-taw'ba, 1 kə-tô'bə; 2 ca-tạ'ba.

Ca-thay', 1 kə-thē'; 2 ea-thā'.

Cau'ca-sus, 1 kô'kə-sus; 2 eạ'ca-sŭs.

Ca'val'gnac', 1 kạ'vē'nyŭk'; 2 eā'vā'nyäe'.

Cav'ell, 1 kay'l; 2 eäv'l.

Ca-vour', 1 kạ-vūr'; 2 eä-vur'.

Cawn-pur', 1 kôn-pūr'; 2 eạn-pur'.

Cay-enne', 1 kē-en' or kai-en'; 2 eä-ĕn' or eï-ĕn'.

Cec'il, 1 ses'il or sī'sil; 2 çĕç'il or çē'çil.

Ced'ric, 1 sed'rik or ked'rik; 2 çĕd'ric or eĕd'ric.

Cel'e-bes, 1 sel'ı-bīz; 2 çĕl'e-bēs. [lïï'nï.

Cel-li'ni, 1 chel-lï'nï; 2 chĕl-lïï'nï.

Cen'ci, 1 chen'chï; 2 chĕn'chï.

Ce-nis', Mont, 1 môn sə-nï'; 2 môn çe-nï'.

Ce'res, 1 sï'rïz; 2 çē'rēs.

Cer-van'tes, 1 sər-van'tïz or (Sp.) ther-vän'tēs; 2 çer-vän'tĕs or (Sp.) thĕr-vän'tẹs.

Cet"e-wa'yo, 1 set'ı-wā'yo or kech-wā'yo; 2 çĕt"e-wä'yo or eĕch-wä'yo.

Ceu'ta, 1 sïü'tə or (Sp.) thē'ü-tä; 2 çü'ta or (Sp.) thẹ'ü-tä.

Ce'vennes', 1 sē'ven'; 2 çẹ'vĕn'.

Cey-lon', 1 sı-lən'; 2 çe-lŏn'.

Chad, 1 chăd; 2 chăd.

Chær'o-ne'a, 1 ker'o-nï'ə; 2 eĕr'o-nē'a.

Chai'ce-don, 1 kal'sı-dən; 2 eăl'çe-dŏn. [dē'a.

Chal-de'a, 1 kal-dï'ə; 2 eăl-(Sc.) chē'mərz; 2 chăl'mẹrz or (Sc.) chạ'mẹrz.

Cham-be'si, 1 cham-bē'zï; 2 chäm-bē'sï.

Cha"mo'nix', 1 sha"mō'nï'; 2 chä"mō'nï'. **Cha"mou'ni'**‡.

Cham"plain', 1 sham"plēn' or (F.) shaṇ"plaṇ'; 2 chäm"plän' or (F.) chäṇ"plän'.

Cham"pol"lion', 1 shäṇ"pōl'yŏṇ'; 2 chäṇ"pōl'yŏṇ'.

Cha-pul'te-pec', 1 chä-pul'tē-pek'; 2 chä-pul'te-pĕc'.

Cha'rente', 1 sha'räṇt'; 2 shä'räṇt'.

Char"le-magne', 1 shär'le-mēn' or (F.) sharl'mä'nyẹ; 2 shär'le-män' or (F.) shärl'mä'nye.

Char"le-roi', 1 shär'le-rwä'; 2 chär'le-rwä'. [2 chär"le-vïl'.

Char"le-ville', 1 shar'le-vïl';

Cha'ron, 1 kē'rən; 2 eā'ron.

Chartres, 1 shärtr; 2 chärtr.

Cha-ryb'dis, 1 kə-rib'dis; 2 ea-ryb'dis.

Cha"teau"bri'and', 1 sha"tō"brï'äṇ'; 2 chä"tō"brï'äṇ'.

Chat'ham, 1 chat'əm; 2 chăt'am.

Chat"ta-noo'ga, 1 chat"ə-nū'gə; 2 chăt"a-nōō'ga.

Chau"mont', 1 sho"môṇ'; 2 cho"môṇ'.

Chaun'cey, 1 chôn'sı or chôn'cı; 2 chän'çy or chạn'çy.

Chau-tau'qua, 1 shə-tô'kwa; 2 chạ-tạ'kwa. [2 che-bŏy'gan.

Che-boy'gan, 1 shı-boi'gan;

Chel'sea, 1 chel'sı; 2 chĕl'se.

Chem'nitz, 1 kem'nits; 2 cĕm'nits. [chе-mŭng'.

Che-mung, 1 shı-muṇ'; 2

Che-nan'go, 1 shı-naṇ'go; 2 che-nän'go.

Che'ops, 1 kï'ops; 2 cē'ŏps.

Cher"bourg', 1 sher"būr'; 2 chĕr"būr'.

Cher"so-ne'sus, 1 kŭr"so-nï'sus; 2 eĕr"so-nē'sŭs.

Che-ru-bi'ni, 1 kē'ru-bï'nï; 2 çĕ"rụ-bï'nï. [2 chĕs'a-pēk.

Ches'a-peake, 1 ches'ə-pïk;

Chev'i-ot, 1 chev'ı-ot; 2 chĕv'ï-ot. [chï-ēn'.

Chey-enne', 1 shai-en'; 2

Chich"es-ter, 1 chich'es-tər; 2 chïch'es-ter. [chï-wä'wä.

Chi-hua'hua, 1 chï-wä'wa; 2

Chi'le, 1 chï'lē; 2 chï'le.

Chil'lon', 1 shï'yŏṇ'; 2 chï'yŏṇ'.

Chil"pe-ric, 1 chil'pə-rik or (F.) shïl'pē'rïk'; 2 chïl'pe-ric or (F.) chïl'pe'rïe'.

Chim"bo-ra'zo, 1 chim"bo-rä'zo; 2 chïm"bo-rä'zo.

Chi'os, 1 kai'os or kï'os; 2 eï'ŏs or eï'ŏs.

Chi'ron, 1 kai'rən; 2 eï'ron.

Chis'holm, 1 chiz'əm; 2 chïz'om.

Chis'wick, 1 chiz'ık; 2 chïg'le.

Chlo'e, 1 klō'ı; 2 elō'e.

Chol"seul', 1 shwa'zŭl'; 2 chwä'sŭl'. [cho"pän'.

Cho"pin', 1 sho"paṇ'; 2

Chris"ti-a'ni-a, 1 kris"tı-ä'-nı-ə; 2 eris"tı-ä'ni-a.

Ci"en-fue'gos, 1 sï"en-fwē'gos or (Sp.) thï"en-fwē'gos; 2 çï"en-fwẹ'gos or (Sp.) thï"en-fwẹ'gos.

Cir'ce, 1 sŭr'sı; 2 çïr'çe.

Ci'ren-ces'ter, 1 sai'rən-ses'ter or (local) sis'e-ter; 2 çï'ren-çĕs'ter or (local) çis'e-ter.

Ci'vi-ta-vec'chi-a, 1 chï'vï-tä-vek'kı-a; 2 chï'vï-tä-vĕe'eï-ä. [nus; 2 eạ'dï-a'nŭs.

Clau'di-a'nus, 1 klô'dı-a'-

Cle-an'thes, 1 klı-an'thïz; 2 ele-än'thēs.

Clé"men'ceau, 1 klē'maṇ'-sō; 2 elẹ"män"çō'.

Cle"o-bu'lus, 1 klï"o-biü'lus; 2 elē"o-bü'lŭs.

Cle-om'e-nes, 1 klı-om'ı-nïz; 2 elē-ŏm'e-nēs. [päs.

Cle'o-pas, 1 klï'o-pas; 2 elē'o-

Cle"o-pa'tra, 1 klï"o-pē'trə; 2 elē"o-pä'tra.

Cli'o, 1 klai'o; 2 elï'o.

Clis'the-nes, 1 klis'thı-nïz; 2 elis'the-nēs.

Cli'tus, 1 klai'tus; 2 elï'tŭs.

Cly"tem-nes'tra, 1 klai'tem-nes'tra; 2 elï"tem-nĕs'tra.

Clyt'i-e, 1 klit'ı-ı; 2 elỹt'ï-ē.

Cni'dus, 1 naï'dus; 2 nï'dŭs.

Co'blenz, 1 kō'blents; 2 eō'blents.

Co-cy'tus, 1 ko-sai'tus; 2 eo-çï'tŭs.

Cod'rus, 1 kod'rus; 2 eŏd'rŭs.

Cœur de Li'on, 1 kûr də lï'oṇ'; 2 eûr de lï'ŏn'.

Col'ches-ter, 1 kōl'ches-tər; 2 eŏl'chĕs-ter. [rïdg.

Cole'ridge, 1 kōl'rij; 2 eōl'-

Co"li'gny, 1 ko'lï'nyï'; 2 eo"lï'nyï'.

Co-logne', 1 ko-lōn'; 2 eo-lōn'.

Co-lon', 1 ko-lōn'; 2 eo-lōn'.

Col"o-ra'do, 1 kel"o-rä'do; 2 eŏl"o-rä'do.

Col"u-mel'la, 1 kel"yu-mel'ə; 2 eŏl"yu-mĕl'a.

Combe, 1 kūm or kōm; 2 eụm or eōm. [eo"mïn'.

Co"mines', 1 kō"mïn'; 2

Com"mer"cy', 1 ko"mär'sï', 2 eo"mĕr'çỹ'. [eŏm'o-dŭs.

Com'mo-dus, 1 kəm'o-dus;

Com"pi-ègne', 1 kōṇ"pï-ĕ'-nyẹ; 2 eŏṇ"pï-ç'nye.

Con'go, 1 keṇ'go; 2 eŏṇ'go.

Con-nect'i-cut, 1 kə-net'ı-kut; 2 eŏ-nĕt'ı-eŭt.

Con'stan-tine, 1 kən'stan-tïn; 2 eŏn'stan-tïn.

Co"pen-ha'gen, 1 kō"pn-hē'-gn; 2 eō"pn-hä'gn.

Co-phet'u-a, 1 ko-fet'yu-ə; 2 eo-fĕt'yu-a. [eo-kïm'bo.

Co-quim'bo, 1 ko-kïm'bo; 2

Cor'do-ba, 1 kôr'do-ba; 2 eôr'do-bä. **Cor'do-va**‡.

Cor"i-o-la'nus, 1 kôr"ı-o-lē'-nus; 2 eôr"i-o-lä'nŭs.

Cor-neille', 1 kər'nē'yẹ; 2 eôr'ng'ye.

1: artistic, ärt; fat, fâre; fast; get, prēy; hit, police; obey, gō; net, ôr; full, rūle; but, bûrn.
2: ärt, āpe, fät, fâre, fȧst, whạt, ạll; mē, gĕt, prẹy, fērn; hit, ïce; ï = ē; ï = ē; gō, nŏt, ôr, wòn,

Cor-reg'glo, 1 kər-rej'o; 2 côr-rĕg'o.

Cor'tez, 1 kôr'tez or (*Sp.*) kor-tĕs'; 2 côr'tĕz or (*Sp.*) côr-tĕs'.

Co-ru'ña, 1 ko-rū'nya; 2 eo-rṳ'nyä. **Co-run'na‡.**

Cos'ta Ri'ca, 1 kos'ta rī'ka; 2 côs'ta rī'ca. [2 cŏ″to-pāks'ī.

Co″to-pax'i, 1 kō″to-paks'ī;

Cou'sin', 1 kū'zañ'; 2 eṳ-säñ'.

Cow'per, 1 kau'pər or kū'pər; 2 eou'pĕr or cū'pĕr.

Cra'cow. See KRAKOW.

Cré″bil'lon', 1 krē'bī'yôn'; 2 erẹ'bī'yôn'.

Cré″cy', 1 krē'sī'; 2 erẹ'çȳ'.

Cre-u'sa, 1 krı-ū'sǝ; 2 ere-ṳ'sa.

Crich'ton, 1 krai'tǝn; 2 eri'ton. [mē'a.

Cri-me'a, 1 krı-mī'ǝ; 2 eri-

Crœ'sus, 1 krī'sus; 2 erē'sus.

Cron'stadt, 1 krŏn'stat; 2 erŏn'stät.

Cuen'ca, 1 kwen'ka; 2 ewĕn'eä. [eū-lō'dĕn

Cul-lo'den, 1 ku-lō'den; 2

Cu-nha, 1 kū'nya; 2 eṳ'nyä.

Cu″ra-ça'o, 1 kū″ra-sā'o or kū″ra-sō'; 2 eṳ″rä-sä'o or eṳ″rä-sō'. [2 eū″ri-ä'shi-a.

Ɔu″ri-a'ti-l, 1 kiū'ri-ä'shi-ai;

Cu″vier', 1 kū'vyē'; 2 eū'vyē'.

Cuy″a-ho'ga, 1 koi'ǝ-hō'gǝ; 2 eī'a-hō'ga.

Cuz'co, 1 kūs'ko; 2 eṳs'eo.

Cyb'e-le, 1 sib'ı-lī; 2 çȳb'e-lē.

Cyc'la-des, 1 sik'la-dīz; 2 çȳc'la-dēs.

Cy-re'ne, 1 sai-rī'nī; 2 çī-rē'nē.

Cyr'il, 1 sir'ıl; 2 çȳr'ıl.

Cyth″e-re'a, 1 sith'ı-rī'ǝ; 2 çȳth″e-rē'a.

Czer'no-witz, 1 ĉher'no-vits; 2 ĉhĕr'no-vits.

Czech″o-slo'vak, 1 ĉhek'o-slō'vak; 2 ĉhĕk″o-slō'väk.

D

Dæd'a-lus, 1 ded'ǝ-lus; 2 dĕd'a-lûs. [dä'gĕr'.

Da″guerre', 1 da'ger'; 2

Dahl, 1 däl; 2 däl.

Dahl'gren, 1 dal'gren; 2 däl'grĕn. [da-hō'my.

Da-ho'mey, 1 dǝ-hō'mı; 2

Da″la″dier', 1 dä″lä'dyē'; 2

Dal-hou'sie, 1 dal-hū'sı; 2 däl-hṳ'sī. [däl-mā'sha.

Dal-ma'tia, 1 dal-mē'sha; 2

Dal'ton, 1 dŏl'tǝn; 2 dạl'ton.

Da'mi'ens', 1 dɑ'mī'añ'; 2 dä'mī'äñ'. [dăm'o-clēs.

Dam'o-cles, 1 dam'o-klīz; 2

Dan'te, 1 dän'tē or dan'tı; 2 dän'tẹ or dän'te. [tslH.

Dan'zig, 1 dän'tsıH; 2 dän'-

Dar″da-nelles', 1 där'dǝ-nelz'; 2 där'da-nĕlç'.

Da″ri-en', 1 dē'rı-en'; 2 dä'-rī-ĕn'. [därm'shtät.

Darm'stadt, 1 därm'shtat; 2

Deb'o-rah, 1 deb'o-rǝ; 2 dĕb'o-ra. [dĕb'rĕt-sın.

Deb'rec-zin, 1 deb'ret-sin; 2

Del'a-ware, 1 del'ǝ-wār; 2 dĕl'a-wār.

Del'hi, 1 del'ī; 2 dĕl'ī.

Del'phi, 1 del'fai; 2 dĕl'fī.

Dem″a-ra'tus, 1 dem'ǝ-rē'-tus; 2 dĕm'a-rā'tûs.

De'mas, 1 dī'mǝs; 2 dē'mas.

De-me'ter, 1 dı-mī'tǝr; 2 de-mē'ter. [ford.

Dept'ford, 1 det'fǝrd; 2 dĕt'-

Des″cartes', 1 dē'kärt'; 2 dẹ'eärt'. [mŏln.

Des Moines, 1 dē mǫın; 2 dē

Des″mou″lins', 1 dē″mū″lañ'; 2 dẹ″mṳ'läñ'.

Des″saix', 1 de'sē'; 2 dẹ'sä'.

Deu-ca'li-on, 1 diū-kē'lı-ǝn; 2 dū-eä'lı-on. [vĕt-e.

De Wet'te, 1 dǝ vet'ǝ; 2 dǝ

Di'az, 1 dī'as; 2 dī'äs.

Di-eppe', 1 dı-ep'; 2 dī-ĕp'.

Di″jon', 1 dī'jŏn'; 2 dī'zhŏn'.

Di″nant', 1 dī'nän'; 2 dī'näñ'.

Di-o'ne, 1 dai-ō'nī; 2 dī-ō'nē.

Di″o-nys'i-us, 1 dai'o-nish'ı-us; 2 dī-o-nish'ı-ûs.

Di'rœ, 1 dai'rī; 2 dī'rē. [shou.

Dir'schau, 1 dīr'shau; 2 dīr'-

Dix″mude', 1 dīs″[or dī″]mūd'; 2 dīs'[or dī']mūd'.

Dnie'per, 1 nī'pər; 2 nē'per.

Dnies'ter, 1 nıs'tǝr; 2 nē'ster.

Do'lo″mieu', 1 do'lo″myū'; 2 do'lo″myū'.

Don Juan, 1 dǝn jū'ǝn or dŏn hwän; 2 dŏn jṳ'an or dŏn hwän.

Don Quix'ote, 1 dǝn kwiks'ǝt or (*Sp.*) dŏn kı-hō'tē; 2 dŏn kwiks'ot or (*Sp.*) dŏn kı-hō'tẹ. [dôr'dō'nye.

Dor′do'gne, 1 dôr'dō'nyǝ; 2

Dou′ai', 1 dū'ē'; 2 dṳ'ä'.

Dou″au″mont', 1 dū'ō″moñ'; 2 dṳ'ō″moñ'.

Dra′ve, 1 drä'vǝ; 2 drä've.

Du-buque', 1 du-biūk'; 2 dṳ-būk'. [dū'ĉhen'.

Du'chesne', 1 dū'shen'; 2

Du″clos', 1 dū'klō'; 2 dū'elō'.

Dul-cin'e-a, 1 dʌl-sin'ı-ǝ or (*Sp.*) dul'ĉhi-nē'a; 2 dʌl-çin'e-a or (*Sp.*) dul'ĉhi-ne'ä.

Dul'wich, 1 dʌl'ıj or -ıĉh; 2 dūl'ıj or -ıĉh.

Du″mas', 1 dū'mä'; 2 dū'mä'.

Dum-fries', 1 dʌm-frīs'; 2 dûm-frīs'. [dū'môñ'.

Du″mont', 1 dū'môñ'; 2

Dun-dalk', 1 dʌn-dôk'; 2 dûn-dạk'. [däs'.

Du″quesne', 1 dū'kēn'; 2 dṳ'ken'.

Dü'rer, 1 dṳ'rǝr; 2 dū'rer.

Düs′sel-dorf, 1 düs'el-dôrf'; 2 düs'ĕl-dôrf. [dīk'ıŋk.

Duyck'ink, 1 daik'ıŋk; 2

Dwi'na, 1 dwī'nǝ; 2 dwī'na.

E

Eau Claire, 1 ō klār; 2 ō elâr.

E'bro, 1 ī'bro or (*Sp.*) ē'bro; 2 ē'bro or (*Sp.*) ẹ'bro.

Ec'ua-dor, 1 ek'wǝ-dor; 2 ĉc'wa-dōr. [2 ĕd'ın-bûr'o.

Ed'in-burgh, 1 ed'ın-bur-o;

E'ger, 1 ē'gǝr; 2 ē'ger.

E-ge'us, 1 ı-jī'us; 2 e-gē'ûs.

Eh″ren-breit'stein, 1 ē'ren-brait'shtain; 2 ẹ'rĕn-brīt'shtīn. [fon ı'nĕm.

El'nem, von, 1 fon aı'nem; 2

Ek'ron, 1 ek'rǝn; 2 ĕk'ron.

E'lah, 1 ī'lǝ; 2 ē'la. [eä-nē'.

El Ca-ney', 1 el kɑ-nē'; 2 ĕl

El'e-a-nor, 1 el'ı-ǝ-nor or el'ǝ-nǝr; 2 ĕl'e-a-nor or ĕl'a-nor.

El'gin, [Sc.] 1 el'gın, 2 ĕl'gın; [U. S.] 1 el'jın, 2 ĕl'jın.

E'li-a, 1 ī'lı-ǝ; 2 ē'lı-a.

E-lim'e-lech, 1 ı-lim'ı-lek; 2 e-lim'e-lĕe. [e-lif'a-lät.

E-liph'a-lat, 1 ı-lif'a-lat; 2

El Pa'so del Nor'te, 1 el pä'so del nôr'tē; 2 ĕl pä'so dĕl nôr'te. [mäs.

El'y-mas, 1 el'ı-mas; 2 ĕl'y-

El'ze-vir, 1 el'zı-vǝr or -vīr; 2 ĕl'ze-vir or -vīr.

Em'ma-us, 1 em'ı-us or e-mā'us; 2 ĕm'a-ûs or ẹ-mā'ûs.

Em-ped'o-cles, 1 em-ped'o-klīz; 2 ĕm-pĕd'o-clēs.

En-cel'a-dus, 1 en-sel'ǝ-dus; 2 ĕn-çĕl'a-dûs.

En-dym'i-on, 1 en-dim'ı-ǝn; 2 ĕn-dȳm'ı-on. [gland.

En'gland, 1 iŋ'glǝnd; 2 iŋ'-

E-paph″ro-di'tus, 1 ı-pof″ro-dai'tus; 2 e-pạf″ro-dī'tûs.

E'phra-lm, 1 ī'frı-ım; 2 ē'-fra-ta.

Eph'ra-ta, 1 ef'rǝ-tǝ;

1: ǝ = final; ı = habit; aisle; ɑu = out; oil; iū = feud; ĉhin; go; ŋ = sing; thin, this.

2: wolf, dǫ; bōok, bōot; full, rṳle, cūre, bṳt, bûrn; ôil, bǫy; ḡo, ḡem; iŋk; thin, this.

Ep'i-cu'rus, 1 ep'ı-kiū'rus; 2 ĕp'ĭ-cū'rŭs.

Ep"i-me'theus, 1 ep'ı-mī'-thǐŭs or -thi-ŭs; 2 ĕp'ĭ-mē'thŭs or -the-ŭs. [nȧl'.

E"pi'nal', 1 ē'pï'nȧl'; 2 ę'pī'-

Er'furt, 1 er'furt; 2 ĕr'fŭrt.

Es-co'ri-al, 1 es-kō'rı-əl or (Sp.) es-kō'rī-äl'; 2 ĕs-cō'rĭ-al or (Sp.) ĕs-cō'rī-äl'.

Es"dra-e'lon, 1 es'dra-ē'lon; 2 ĕs"dra-ē'lon. [ō'pi-a.

E"t i-o'pi-a, 1 ī"thi-ō'pı-a; 2 ē"tĭ-

Eu'ler, 1 yū'lər or (G.) oi'lər; 2 yụ'lẹr or (G.) oi'lẹr.

Eu'nice, 1 yū'nıs; 2 yụ'nĭs.

Eu-phra'tes, 1 yu-frē'tīz; 2 yu-frā'tēs.

Eu-ter'pe, 1 yu-tūr'pı; 2 yu-tûr'pē.

Eux'ine, 1 yūks'ın; 2 yŭks'ĭn.

F

Fah'ren-helt, 1 fä'ren-hait; 2 fä'rĕn-hĭt. [fäl'muth.

Fal'mouth, 1 fal'məth; 2

Fal'staff, 1 fôl'staf; 2 fạl'stȧf.

Fan'euil, 1 fan'l or fun'l; 2 fân'l or fŭn'l. [ne'se.

Far-ne'se, 1 far-nē'sē; 2 fär-

Far'quhar, 1 fär'kwər or -kar; 2 fär'kwar or -kar. [chis'tī.

Fas"cis'ti, 1 fa"shis'u; 2 fa"-

Faust, 1 foust; 2 foust.

Fay-al', 1 foi-äl'; 2 fī-äl'.

Fé"ne-lon', 1 fē'nə-lôṅ'; 2 fę'ne-lôn. [rä'ra.

Fer-ra'ra, 1 fer-rä'ra; 2 fẹr-

Fes"tu"bert', 1 fes'tü'bär'; 2 fĕs"tü'bẽr'.

Fez-zan', 1 fe-zän'; 2 fĕ-zän'.

Fich'te, 1 fīн'tə; 2 fīн'te.

Fi-de'le, 1 fı-dī'lı; 2 fī-dē'le.

Fi'ga'ro', 1 fī'ga'rō'; 2 fĭ'-gä'rō'.

Fi'ji, 1 fī'jī; 2 fī'jī. [fin'ıs-tẽr'.

Fin"is-tère', 1 fin'ıs-tär'; 2

Fin'land, 1 fin'lənd; 2 fĭn'-land.

Fismes, 1 fīm; 2 fēm.

Fi-u'me, 1 fı-ū'mē; 2 fi-ụ'mę.

Fleu'ry', 1 flö'rī'; 2 flö'rў'.

Flü'gel, 1 flü'gel; 2 flü'gĕl.

Foch, 1 fosh; 2 fŏsh.

Foix, 1 fwä; 2 fwä. [fôṅ'tän'.

Fon'taine', 1 fôṅ'tän'; 2

Fon"taine'bleau', 1 fôṅ'-tĕn'blō'; 2 fôṅ'tän'blō'.

Fon'te-noy, 1 fon'tı-noi or (F.) fôṅt'nwä'; 2 fŏn'te-nöy or (F.) fôṅt'nwä'.

Foo'chow', 1 fū'chou'; 2 tōō'chow'. Fu'chau'‡.

For'tin-bras, 1 fôr'tin-bras; 2 fôr'tĭn-bräs.

G

Fou"cault', 1 fū'kō'; 2 fụ'cō'.

Fou"ri-er', 1 fū'rı-ê'; 2 fụ'rı-ȇ'.

Fran-ces'ca, 1 fran-ches'ka; 2 fran-chĕs'cä.

Fraun'ho-fer, 1 fraun'hō-fər; 2 froun'hō-fer.

Frei'berg, 1 froi'berн; 2 frī'bẽrн. [frī'bụrн.

Frei'burg, 1 froi'burн; 2

Fre'ling-huy"sen, 1 frī'lıṅ-hai'zen; 2 frē'lĭng-hī'sĕn.

Fre-mont', 1 frī-mont'; 2 frē-mōnt'. [nĕl'.

Fres"nel', 1 frē'nĕl'; 2 frē-

Froe'bel, 1 frö'bel; 2 frû'bĕl.

Frois"sart', 1 frwa'sär'; 2 frwä'sär'.

Froude, 1 frūd; 2 frụd.

Fun-chal', 1 fun-shäl'; 2 fun-chäl'.

G

Gab'a-tha, 1 gab'ə-тhə; 2 găb'a-тha.

Ga-la'pa-gos, 1 ga-lä'pa-gōs; 2 gä-lä'pä-gōs.

Gal"a-te'a, 1 gal'a-tī'ə; 2 găl'a-tē'ȧ.

Ga'latz, 1 gä'lats; 2 gä'läts.

Ga'li-le'i, 1 gä'lı-lē''ı; 2 gä'lĭ-lē'ī. [yē'nī'.

Gal"lie'nī', 1 gal'yē'nī'; 2 găl-

Gal-va'ni, 1 gal-vä'nı; 2 găl-vä'nī. [găl'vĕs-ton.

Gal'ves-ton, 1 gal'ves-tən; 2

Gal'way, 1 gôl'wē; 2 gạl'wā.

Ga-ma'li-el, 1 ga-mē'lı-el; 2 ga-mā'lĭ-el.

Gan'ges, 1 gan'jīz; 2 găn'gēs.

Gan'y-mede, 1 gan'ı-mīd; 2 găn'y-mēd.

Gar-ci'a, (Cuban) 1 gar-sī'a; 2 gär-çī'ä; (Sp.) 1 gar-тhī'a; 2 gär-тhī'ä.

Ga'ri-bal'di, 1 ga'rı-bäl'dı; 2 gä'rı-bäl'dī. [rôn'.

Ga'ronne', 1 ga'ron'; 2 gä'-

Ga-tun', 1 ga-tūn'; 2 gä-tụn'.

Ga'za, 1 gē'za; 2 gä'za.

Ge-ha'zi, 1 gı-hē'zai; 2 ge-hä'zī. [e-sē'.

Gen"e-see', 1 jen'ı-sī'; 2 ĕ-sē'

Gen-nes'a-ret, 1 ge-nes'ə-ret; 2 gĕ-nĕs'a-rĕt.

Gen'o-a, 1 jen'o-ə; 2 ğĕn'o-ȧ.

Ge-rard', 1 jı-rärd'; 2 ge-rärd'.

Ger"i-zim, 1 ger'ı-zim; 2 ğĕr'-i-zim. [ğĕr'shom.

Ger'shom, 1 gūr'shəm; 2

Ge'ry-on, 1 jī'rı-on; 2 ğē'ry-ŏn.

Geth-sem'a-ne, 1 geth-sem'ə-nī; 2 gĕth-sĕm'a-nē.

Ghent, 1 gent; 2 gĕnt.

Gib'e-ah, 1 gib'ı-ə; 2 ğĭb'e-a.

Gi-bral'tar, 1 jı-brôl'tər; 2 gi-brạl'tar.

Gi'la, 1 hī'lə; 2 hī'la.

Gil-bo'a, 1 gil-bō'ə; 2 ğĭl-bō'a.

Gil'gal, 1 gil'gal; 2 ğĭl'gal.

Gi-rard', 1 jı-rärd'; 2 gi-rärd'.

Gil"ven'chy', 1 gī'van'shī'; 2 ğī'vän'chў'.

Glouces'ter, 1 glos'tər; 2 glŏs'tẽr.

Go'bi, 1 gō'bī; 2 gō'bī.

Goe'thals, 1 gō'thalz; 2 gō'-thäls.

Goe'the, 1 gū'tə; 2 gū'te.

Gol'go-tha, 1 gol'go-тhə; 2 gŏl'go-тha.

Goltz, von der, 1 fon der gölts; 2 fon dẽr gölts. [go-môr'a.

Go-mor'rah, 1 go-mor'ə; 2

Go'na"ives', Les, 1 lē gō'-na'īv'; 2 le gō'nä'īv'.

Gor'gas, 1 gôr'gas; 2 gôr'gas.

Go'shen, 1 gō'shen; 2 gō'shĕn.

Go'tha, 1 gō'ta; 2 gō'tä.

Göt'ting-en, 1 gūt'ıṅ-en; 2 gūt'ing-ĕn.

Gough, 1 gof; 2 gŏf.

Gra-na'da, 1 gra-nä'da; 2 grä-nä'dä.

Grätz, 1 grēts; 2 gräts.

Green'wich [Eng.], 1 grin'ıj; 2 grĭn'ĭj; [U. S.], 1 grīn'-wich; 2 grēn'wich.

Gries'bach, 1 grīs'baн; 2 grēs'bäн. [sôн'.

Gri'sons', 1 grī'zôṅ'; 2 grī'-

Gua"da-la-ja'ra, 1 gwä'тhä-la-hä'ra; 2 gwä'thä-lä-hä'rä.

Gua"dal-quiv'ir, 1 gä"dal-kwiv'er or (Sp.) gwa"тhäl'-kī-vīr'; 2 ğä"dal-kwiv'er or (Sp.) gwä"тhäl'kī-vīr'.

Gua"da-lupe', 1 gā'də-lūp' or (Sp.) gwä"тha-lū'pē; 2 ğä"da-lụp' or (Sp.) gwä'-тha-lụ'pē. [gwä'тhī-ä'nä.

Gua"di-a'na, 1 gwä' ĭ-ä'na; 2

Gua"te-ma'la, 1 gō"tu-mä'la or (Sp.) gwä"tē-mä'la; 2 gä"te-mä'la or (Sp.) gwä'te-mä'lä. [ğwī'ä-kīl'.

Guay"a-quil', 1 gwai'a-kīl';

Guern'sey, 1 gûrn'zı; 2 gûrn'sy.

Gui-a'na, 1 gı-ä'nə; 2 ğī-ä'na.

Guin'ea, 1 gin'ı; 2 ğĭn'e.

Guise', 1 gīz; 2 ğīs.

Gu'ten-berg, 1 gū'ten-berg; 2 ğụ'ten-bẽrн.

Guth'rie, 1 guтh'rı; 2 gŭтh'rı.

H

Ha-bak'kuk, 1 hə-bak'ụk or hab'ə-kuk; 2 ha-băk'ŭk or hăb'a-kŭk. [vä'nä.

Ha-ba'na, 1 ha-vä'na; 2 hä-

1: artistic, ärt; fat, fāre; fast; get, prëy; hit, police; obey, gō; not, ör; full, rūle; but, būrn.

2: ärt, āpe, făt, fâre, fȧst, what, gɪl: mē, gĕt, prēy, fẽrn; hĭt, īce; ī=ĕ; ĭ=ē; gō, nŏt, ôr, wǒn,

Hag'ga-l, 1 hag'ı-al: 2 häg'a-ĭ.
Hague, 1 hēg; 2 hāg.
Hah'ne-mann, 1 hä'nə-mɔn; 2 hä'ne-män.
Haig, 1 hēg; 2 häg.
Hai"naut', 1 ē'nō'; 2 ā'nō'.
Hai'ti, 1 hē'tı; 2 hā'ti.
Ha-mil'car, 1 ha-mil'kar; 2 hä-mil'cär.
Ha'nau, 1 hä'nau; 2 hä'nou.
Ha-ro'sheth, 1 hə-rō'sheth; 2 ha-rō'shĕth.
Har'pa-gus, 1 har'pə-gus; 2 här'pa-gŭs. [häs'dru-bal.
Has'dru-bal, 1 haz'dru-bəl; 2
Ha-van'a, 1 hə-van'ə; 2 ha-vän'a.
Have'lock, 1 hav'lɔk; 2 häv'-lŏk. [hä'vər-il.
Ha'ver-hill, 1 hä'vər-il; 2
Ha'vre, 1 hä'vər; 2 hä'vre.
Le Ha'vre [F.], 1 lə ä'vr; 2 le ä'vr.
Hav're de Grace, 1 hav'ər də grās; 2 häv'er de gräc.
Ha-wai'i, 1 ha-wai'ī; 2 hä-wī'ī. [äz'bruk.
Haze"brouck', 1 az'brūk'; 2
He'be, 1 hī'bı; 2 hē'be.
Heb'ri-des, 1 heb'rı-dīz; 2 hĕb'ri-dēş.
Hec'a-te, 1 hek'ə-tī or hek'ıt; 2 hĕe'a-tē or hĕe'at.
Hec'u-ba, 1 hek'yu-bə; 2 hĕe'yu-ba.
He'gel, 1 hē'gel; 2 hẹ'gĕl.
Hel'dei-berg, 1 hai'dl-bürg or (G.) hal'del-berH; 2 hī'dl-bẽrg or (G.) hī'dĕl-bĕrH.
Hei'ne, 1 hai'nə; 2 hī'ne.
Hel'e-na, 1 hel'ı-nə; 2 hĕl'e-na.
He'li-os, 1 hī'lı-os; 2 hī'li-ŏs.
Hé"lo"ise', 1 ē'lō'īz'; 2 ę'-lō'īş'. [hĕn-lō'pen.
Hen-lo'pen, 1 hen-lō'pen; 2
Hen"ri'ot', 1 ãn'rī'ō'; 2 än'-rī'ō'.
He-phæs'tus, 1 hı-fes'tus; 2 he-fĕs'tŭs. [hĕf'zi-ba.
Heph'zi-bah, 1 hef'zı-bə; 2
He-rat', 1 hı-rāt'; 2 he-rät'.
Her-ml'o-ne, 1 hər-mai'o-nī; 2 her-mī'o-nē.
Her-mog'e-nes, 1 hər-məj'ı-nīz; 2 her-mŏg'e-nēş.
Her'schel, 1 hür'shel; 2 hĕr'shĕl.
Hes'per-us, 1 hes'pər-us; 2 hĕs'per-ŭs.
Hes'se, 1 hes'ə; 2 hĕs'se.
Hes'sen‡ [G.], 1 hes'en; 2 hĕs'en.
Hi'a-wa'tha, 1 hai"[or hī"]ə-wä'thə; 2 hī'[or hī"]a-wä'tha.

Hi"er-on'y-mus, 1 hai"ər-ɔn'ı-mus; 2 hī'er-ŏn'y-mŭs
Hi-ma'la-ya Mts., 1 hı-mä'-lə-yə; 2 hı-mä'la-ya.
Hin'du-stan', 1 hin'du-stän'; 2 hin'dụ-stän'. [hı-pŏl'y-ta.
Hip-pol'y-ta, 1 hı-pɔl'ı-tə; 2
His-pa'ni-a, 1 his-pē'nı-ə; 2 hīs-pā'ni-a.
Hit'ler, 1 hit'lär; 2 hit'lĕr.
Hoang"ho'. Same as HWANG.
Ho'garth, 1 hō'garth; 2 hō'gärth. [stín.
Hol'stein, 1 hōl'stain; 2 hōl'-
Hol'yoke, 1 hōl'yōk; 2 hōl'-yōk. [hŏn-dy'ras.
Hon-du'ras, 1 hen-dū'ras; 2
Hong'kong', 1 heŋ'keŋ'; 2 hóŋ'kóŋ. [hŏn'o-lụ'lụ.
Hon"o-lu'lu, 1 hen'o-lū'lū; 2
Hoo'ver, 1 hū'vər; 2 hōō'ver.
Hoph'ni, 1 hof'nai; 2 hŏf'nī.
Ho'reb, 1 hō'reb; 2 hō'rĕb.
Ho'tzen-dorf, von, 1 hō'tsen-dorf; 2 hō'tsĕn-dôrf.
Hough'ton, 1 hō'tən or hau'-tən; 2 hō'ton or hou'tŏn.
Hous'ton, 1 hūs'tən or haus-tən; 2 hūs'ton or hous'ton.
Hu'di-bras, 1 hiū'dı-bras; 2 hū'di-brăs.
Hu"é', 1 ū'ē'; 2 ü'ę'.
Hu'shai, 1 hiū'shai; 2 hū'shī.
Huy, 1 hoi; 2 hōy.
Hwang, 1 bwäŋ; 2 hwäŋg.
Hy'a-des, 1 hai'ə-dīz; 2 hī'a-dēş.
Hy"me-næ'us, 1 hai'mı-nī'-us; 2 hī'me-nē'ŭs.
Hy-pa'ti-a, 1 hai-pē'shı-ə; 2 hī-pā'shi-a.
Hy-pe'ri-on, 1 hai-pī'rı-on or hai'pər-ai'ən; 2 hī-pē'ri-ŏn or hī'per-ī'ŏn.
Hy"perm-nes'tra, 1 hai"-pərm-nes'trə; 2 hī'perm-nĕs'tra.

I

I-ac'chus, 1 ai-ak'us; 2 ī-āe'ŭs.
I-a'go, 1 ı-ā'go; 2 ī-ā'go.
Ic'a-rus, 1 ik'ə-rus; 2 īe'a-rŭs.
Ich'a-bod, 1 ik'ə-bɔd; 2 īe'a-bŏd. [dä'lı-a.
I-da'li-a, 1 ai-dē'lı-ə; 2 ī-
I-dom'e-neus, 1 ai-dom'ı-niūs; 2 ī-dŏm'e-nūs.
I"du-mæ'a, 1 ai'dıu-mı'ə; 2 ī'dū-mē'a.
Il"li-nois', 1 il'ı-nɔi' or -nɔiz'; 2 il'i-nôi' or -nôiş'. [eŭs.
In'a-chus, 1 in'ə-kus; 2 in'a-
In'ge-low, 1 in'jı-lo; 2 in'ge-lō.

I'o, 1 ai'o; 2 ī'o.
Iph"i-ge-ni'a, 1 if'ı-jı-nai'ə; 2 if'i-ge-nī'a.
I-ran', 1 ı-rän'; 2 ī-rän'.
I'raq, 1 ī'rak or ı-räk'; 2 ī'räk or ı-räk'. I'rakț.
Ire'land, 1 air'lənd; 2 īr'land.
Ir-kutsk', 1 ir-kutsk'; 2 ir-kutsk'. [ır"o-kwôi'.
Ir"o-quois', 1 ir"o-kwoi'; 2
I-sa'iah, 1 ai-zē'yə or ai-zai'ə; 2 ī-şā'ya or ī-şī'a.
Ish'ma-el, 1 ish'mı-el; 2 īsh'ma-ĕl.
I'sis, 1 ai'sıs; 2 ī'sis.
Is"pa-han', 1 īs'pa-hän'; 2 īs'pä-hän'.
I"stan-bul', 1 ı'stan-būl'; 2 ı'stän-bül'; 2 ı"stan-rē'a.
It"u-ræ'a, 1 it'yu-rī'ə; 2 it'yu-rē'a.
I-u'lus, 1 ai-yū'lus; 2 ī-yụ'lŭs.
Ix-i'on, 1 iks-ai'en; 2 īks-ī'ŏn.

J

Ja'bez, 1 jē'bez; 2 jā'bĕz.
Ja'el, 1 jē'el; 2 jā'ĕl.
Jane Eyre, 1 ūr; 2 êr.
Ja'nus, 1 jē'nus; 2 jā'nŭs.
Ja"pu-ra', 1 ʒä"pū-rā'; 2 zhä"pụ-rä'. [yä"ro-släf'.
Ja"ro-slav', 1 yä"ro-släf'; 2
Jas'sy, 1 yäs'ī; 2 yäs'y.
Ja'va, 1 jä'va; 2 jä'va.
Jech"o-ni'as, 1 jek"o-nai'əs; 2 jĕe"o-nīs. [je-dū'thŭn
Je-du'thun, 1 jı-diū'thun; 2
Je'na, 1 yē'nə; 2 yę'na.
Jeph'thah, 1 jef'tha; 2 jĕf'-tha. [jĕr"ŭ-bä'al.
Jer"ub-ba'al, 1 jer"u-bē'al; 2
Jesh'u-run, 1 jesh'yu-run or jı-shū'run; 2 jĕsh'yụ-rŭn or je-shụ'rŭn.
Jeth'ro, 1 jeth'ro or jı'thro; 2 jĕth'ro or ję'thro.
Jez're-el, 1 jez'rı-el; 2 jĕz're-ĕl. [a-cîm.
Jo'a-chim, 1 jō'ə-kim; 2 jō'-căs'ta.
Jo-cas'ta, 1 jo-kas'tə; 2 jo-căs'ta.
Joffre, 1 ʒɔfr; 2 zhôfr.
Jo-rui'lo, 1 ho-rū'lyo; 2 ho-rụ'lyo. [zhụr"dän'.
Jour"dan', 1 ʒūr"däñ'; 2
Ju'an Fer-nan'dez, 1 jū'an fər-nan'dīz or (Sp.) hū-än' fer-nän'dĕth; 2 jụ'än fer-nän'dĕz or (Sp.) hụ-än' fer-nän'dĕth.
Ju-a'rez, 1 ju-ä'rez or (Sp.) hū-ä'rĕth; 2 jụ-ä'rĕz or (Sp.) hụ-ä'rĕth.
Ju"go-Slav'i-a, 1 yū"go-slav'-ı-ə; 2 yū"go-släv'i-a.

1: ə = final; ı = habit; aisle; au = out; oil; iū = feud; ɔhin; go; ŋ = sing; thin, **this.**
2: wọlf, dọ; bōōk, bōōt; fụll, rụle, cūre, bụt, bûrn; ôil, bọy; go, ġem; iŋk; thin, **this.**

Jung, 1 yuŋ; 2 yung.
Jung'frau, 1 yuŋ'frau; 2 yung'frou.
Ju"not', 1 zü'nŏ'; 2 zhü'nŏ'.
Ju'ra, 1 jū'rə; 2 jy'ra.

K

Ka-bul', 1 ka-būl'; 2 ka-bul'.
Ka'desh, 1 kē'dĕsh; 2 kä'dĕsh.
Kam-chat'ka, 1 kam-chat'kə; 2 käm-chät'ka.
Kam"e-run', 1 kam'ı-rūn'; 2 käm'e-run'.
Ka"mi"mu"ra, 1 ka'mi"mū'ra'; 2 kä'mi'mu'rä'.
Ka-na'wha, 1 kə-nô'wə; 2 ka-nä'wa. [2 kän'ka-kē'.
Kan'ka-kee', 1 kan'ka-ki';
Ka-no', 1 ka-nŏ'; 2 kä-nŏ'.
Karls'ru-he, 1 kärls'rū-ə; 2 kärls'ru-e. [käsh-gär'.
Kash-gar', 1 kash-gär'; 2
Kash-mir', 1 kash-mir'; 2 käsh-mir'. [ka-tä'din.
Ka-tah'din, 1 ka-tä'din; 2
Kat'rine, 1 kat'rın; 2 kät'rin.
Ke'ble, 1 kī'bl; 2 kē'bl.
Ke'dron, 1 kī'drən or kĕd'rən; 2 kē'dron or kĕd'rŏn.
Ke'nya, 1 kī'nya; 2 kĕ'nyä.
Ke-ren'sky, 1 ke-ren'skı; 2 kĕ-rĕn'sky.
Ker'gue-len Land, 1 kür'gı-len; 2 kĕr'ge-lĕn. [ty'ra.
Ke-tu'rah, 1 ke-tū'rə; 2 kē-
Ke'we-naw, 1 kī'wı-nô; 2 kĕ'we-nä. [kär-tụm'.
Khar-tum', 1 kar-tūm'; 2
Khi'va, 1 kī'va; 2 kī'vä.
Kho"ra-san', 1 kŏ'ra-sän'; 2 kŏ'rä-sän'. [äk'tä.
Ki-akh'ta, 1 kı-äk'ta; 2 kı-
Ki-ao"chow', 1 kı-au'chau'; 2 kī-ou'chow'.
Ki-ef', 1 kı-ef'; 2 kī-ĕf'.
Kiel, 1 kīl; 2 kēl.
Kil-mar'nock, 1 kil-mär'nək; 2 kil-mär'nok. [2 kir-gīz'.
Kir-ghiz' Steppe, 1 kir-gīz';
Ki-ung"chow', 1 kı-uŋ'chau'; 2 kī-ung'chou'.
Kjö'len, 1 kyü'len or chü'len; 2 kyü'lĕn or chü'lĕn.
Kluck, von, 1 kluk; 2 klụk.
Ko'be, 1 kŏ'bĕ; 2 kŏ'bẹ.
Koch, 1 koH; 2 kŏH.
Kon'go, 1 keŋ'go; 2 kŏŋ'go.
Kö'nigs-berg, 1 kü'niHs-berH; 2 kü'niHs-bĕrH.
Ko'rah, 1 kŏ'rə; 2 kŏ'ra.
Kos"ci-us'ko, 1 kəs'ı-us'ko; 2 kŏs'ı-us'ko.

Kos'suth, 1 kəs'uth; 2 kŏs'-uth.
Kra"ka-tau', 1 krä'ka-tau'; 2 krä'kä-tou'.
Kra'kow, 1 krä'kau; 2 krä'-kow.
Kur'di-stan', 1 kür'dı-stän'; 2 kụr'dı-stän'.
Ku'ril Islands, 1 kū'rıl; 2 kụ'rıl.
Kwa'sind, 1 kwä'sınd; 2 kwä'sind.
Kyo'to, 1 kyŏ'to; 2 kyŏ'to.
Kyu-shu', 1 kiū-shū'; 2 kū-shụ'.

L

La Bru"yère', 1 la brü'yär'; 2 la brü'yār'.
Lac"e-dæ'mon, 1 las'ı-dī'mən; 2 läc'e-dē'mon.
Lach'e-sis, 1 lak'ı-sıs; 2 läc'e-sis.
La'chish, 1 lē'kish; 2 lä'eish.
La-co'ni-a, 1 lə-kŏ'nı-ə; 2 lä-cō'ni-a.
La Crosse, 1 lə krŏs; 2 la erōs.
Lad'is-laus, 1 lad'ıs-lôs; 2 läd'is-läs. [do-gä.
La'do-ga, 1 lō'do-go; 2 lä-
La-drone' Islands, 1 lə-drŏn' or (Sp.) lä-drō'nĕ; 2 lä-drōn' or (Sp.) lä-drō'ne.
La-er'tes, 1 lē-ür'tīz; 2 lä-ēr'tēs.
La'fay-ette', 1 la'fē-et'; 2 lä'fä-ĕt'. [fŏl'ĕt.
La Fol'lette, 1 lə fŏl'et; 2 lä
La Fon"taine', 1 la fŏn'tēn'; 2 lä fŏn'tän'.
La Hague, 1 lə hĕg or (F.) lä äg; 2 lä häg or (F.) lä äg.
La-hore', 1 lə-hŏr'; 2 la-hōr'.
Lal'la Rookh, 1 lä'lä rūk; 2 lä'lä rōōk.
La"mar'tine', 1 la'mar'tīn'; 2 lä'mär'tēn'.
La'mech, 1 lē'mek; 2 lä'mĕe.
La'mi-a, 1 lē'mı-ə; 2 lä'mi-a.
Lam-prid'i-us, 1 lam-prid'ı-us; 2 läm-prid'ı-ūs.
Lan'cas-ter, 1 laŋ'kəs-tər; 2 läŋ'cas-ter.
Lan'ce-lot, 1 lan'sı-lət; 2 län'çe-lŏt.
Lan'gue-doc', 1 laŋ'gə-dŏk'; 2 läŋ'ge-dōc'.
La-nier', 1 lə-nīr'; 2 la-nēr'.
La-oc'o-on, 1 lē-ŏk'o-ŏn; 2 lä-ōc'o-ŏn.
La-od"a-mi'a, 1 lē-ŏd'ə-mal'ə; 2 lä-ōd'a-mī'a.

La-od'i-ce, 1 lē-ŏd'ı-sī; 2 lä-ŏd'i-çē.
La-od'i-ce'a, 1 lē-ŏd'ı-sī'ə; 2 lä-ŏd'i-çē'a.
Lap'i-thæ, 1 lap'ı-thī; 2 läp'i-thē. [shūs.
Lar'tius, 1 lär'shus; 2 lär'-
Las Cases, 1 las käz; 2 läs cäg.
Las"si"gny', 1 las'sī'nyī'; 2 läs'sī'nyī'. [shi-ŭm.
La'ti-um, 1 lē'shı-um; 2 lät'ı-um.
Lat'vi-a, 1 lat'vı-ə; 2 lät'vi-a.
Laun'fal, 1 lên'fəl; 2 lan'fal.
Lau'sanne, 1 lo'zan'; 2 lo'-sän'.
Lau"ter-brun"nen, 1 lau'tər-brun'en; 2 lou'ter-brun'-ĕn. [vä'ter.
La-va'ter, 1 la-vä'tər; 2 lä-
La"voi"sier', 1 la'vwa'zyē'; 2 lä'vwä'sye'. [zhändr'.
Le-gendre', 1 lə-zändr'; 2 le-
Leg'horn, 1 lĕg'hôrn or lĕg'-ərn; 2 lĕg'hôrn or lĕg'orn.
Le-gna'go, 1 lē-nyä'go; 2 le-nyä'go. [nits.
Leib'nitz, 1 laip'nits; 2 līp'-
Leices'ter, 1 lĕs'tər; 2 lĕs'ter.
Leigh, 1 lī; 2 lē.
Leigh'ton, 1 lē'tən; 2 lē'ton.
Lein'ster, 1 len'stər; 2 lĕn'-ster.
Leip'zig, 1 laip'sık; 2 līp'sie.
Le'nine, 1 lyē'nin; 2 lyē'-nīn.
Le'nin-grad', 1 -grad; 2 -gräd.
Len'tu-lus, 1 lĕn'tiu-lus; 2 lĕm'in-ster.
Leom'in-ster, 1 lem'ın-stər; 2 lĕm'in-ster.
Le'on, 1 li'en or (Sp.) lē-ŏn'; 2 lē'on or (Sp.) lẹ-ōn'.
Le'o-pold, 1 lī'o-pŏld; 2 lē'o-pōld. [pän'o.
Le-pan'to, 1 lı-pan'to; 2 le-
Lep'ti-nes, 1 lep-tı-nīz; 2 lĕp'ti-nēs.
Le-sage', 1 lə-säz'; 2 le-säzh'.
Les'bos, 1 lez'bos; 2 lĕs'bos.
Les Cayes, 1 lē kē; 2 lẹ cä.
Les Mi"sé"ra'bles, 1 lē mī'-zē'rä'bl; 2 lẹ mī'sẹ'rä'bl.
Le'the, 1 lī'thī; 2 lē'thē.
Lett'o-ni-a, 1 let'o-nı-ə; 2 lĕt'-o-ni-a.
Leu-co'the-a, 1 liu-kō'thı-ə; 2 lū-cō'the-a.
Lew'es, 1 liū'es; 2 lū'ĕs.
Ley'den, 1 lai'den; 2 lī'dĕn.
Li-be'ri-a, 1 lai-bī'rı-ə; 2 lī-bē'ri-a.
Li'chas, 1 lai'kas; 2 lī'cas.
Li-cin'i-us, 1 lı-sın'ı-us; 2 nüs.
Lic'i-nus, 1 lis'ı-nus; 2 liç'i- li-çin'i-ūs.

1: artistic, ärt; fat, fâre; fast; get, prey; hit, police; obey, gō; net, ōr; full, rūle; but, būrn.
2: ärt, āpe, fät, fâre, fåst, whąt, ąll; mē, gĕt, prey, fĕrn; hĭt, īce; ī=ē; ĭ=ĕ; gō, nŏt, ôr, wŏn,

Lie'big, 1 lī'bĭh; 2 lē'bĭh.
Ll''ège', 1 ll''ēȝ'; 2 lī''ȇȝh'.
Li-ge'a, 1 laı-jī'ə; 2 lī-gē'a.
Lille, 1 lĭl; 2 lĭl.
Li'ma, 1 lī'ma; 2 lī'mä.
Li''moges', 1 lī''mōȝ'; 2 lī''mōzh'. [nä'rĕs.
Li-na'res, 1 lī-nä'rĕs; 2 lī-
Lin-næ'us, 1 lĭ-nī'us; 2 lĭ-nē'ŭs.
Li'nus, 1 laı'nus; 2 lī'nŭs.
Lip'a-ri, 1 lĭp'a-rı or lī'pa-rī; 2 lĭp'a-ri or lī'pä-rī.
Lith''u-a'ni-a, 1 lĭth''yu-ē'nı-ə; 2 lĭth''yu-ä'nı-a.
Lla'no, 1 lä'no or (Sp.) lyä'no; 2 lä'no or (Sp.) lyä'no.
Llew-el'lyn, 1 lu-el'ın; 2 lu-ĕl'yn. [erīn'.
Lo-crine', 1 lo-krain'; 2 lo-
Lo'di, 1 lō'dı; 2 lō'dı.
Lo-dore', 1 lo-dōr'; 2 lo-dōr'.
Lo-fo'den, 1 lo-fō'den; 2 lo-fō'dĕn. [lō'ĕn-grin.
Lo'hen-grin, 1 lō'en-grin; 2
Loire, 1 lwär; 2 lwär.
Lo'ĭs, 1 lō'ıs; 2 lō'ıs [Gr., desirable].
Lo'mond, 1 lō'mənd; 2 lō'mond. [lŏn-gī'nŭs.
Lon-gi'nus, 1 lon-jaı'nus; 2
Long''wy', 1 lŏn'vī'; 2 lŏn'vȳ'.
Lo're-lei, 1 lō'ra-laı; 2 lō're-lī.
Los An'ge-les, 1 los an'jı-līz or (Sp.) lōs än'hē-les; 2 los än'ge-lēs or (Sp.) lōs än'he-lĕs. [thär'.
Lo-thair', 1 lo-thār'; 2 lo-
Lo-tha'ri-o, 1 lo-thē'rı-ō; 2 lo-thä'ri-ō.
Lou''is' Phi'lippe', 1 lū'ī' fī'lĭp'; 2 lu'ī' fī'lĭp'.
Lou'is-ville, 1 lū'ıs-vıl or lū'ı-vıl; 2 lu'ıs-vıl or lu'ı-vil.
Lou''vain', 1 lū'vaṅ'; 2 lu'-väṅ'.
Lo-yo'la, 1 lo-yō'la; 2 lo-yō'lä.
Lu-ca'ni-a, 1 liu-kē'nı-ə; 2 lū-cä'ni-a.
Luc'ca, 1 lūk'ka; 2 lu̇e'eä.
Lu-cerne', 1 lu-sern'; 2 lu-çĕrn'. [çı'na.
Lu-ci'na, 1 liu-saı'na; 2 liu-
Luck'now, 1 lŭk'nau; 2 lŭk'now. [lū-cŭl'us.
Lu-cul'lus, 1 liu-kul'us; 2
Lu''né''ville', 1 lū'nē'vīl'; 2 lü''ne'vīl'. [lū'per-cal.
Lu'per-cal, 1 liū'pər-kal; 2
Lu''si-ta'ni-a, 1 lū''sı-tē'nı-ə; 2 lū'sı-tä'ni-a.
Lu-zon', 1 lū-zən' or (Sp.) lū-thon'; 2 lu-zŏn' or (Sp.) lu-thŏn'.

Ly-ca'on, 1 laı-kē'ən; 2 lī-eä'ŏn.
Lyc''o-me'des, 1 lĭk'o-mī'dīz; 2 lȳe'o-mē'dĕs.
Ly-cur'gus, 1 laı-kūr'gus; 2 lī-cür'gus.
Ly'ell, 1 laı'el; 2 lī'ĕl.
Ly'ons, 1 loı'ənz or (F.) lī'ŏṅ'; 2 lī'ong or (F.) lȳ'ŏṅ'.
Ly-san'der, 1 laı-san'der; 2 lī-sän'der.
Lys'i-as, 1 lĭs'ı-əs; 2 lȳs'i-as.

M

Ma-ca'o, 1 mə-kā'o; 2 ma-eä'o. [mäe-pē'la.
Mach-pe'lah, 1 mak-pī'la; 2
Mac-leod', 1 mək-laud'; 2 mae-loud'.
Ma'con, 1 mē'kən or (F.) ma'kōṅ'; 2 mä'eon or (F.) mä'eŏṅ'.
Ma-dei'ra, 1 ma-dī'ra or (Pg.) ma-dē'ra; 2 ma-dē'ra or (Pg.) mä-de'rä. [dräs'.
Ma-dras', 1 ma-drăs'; 2 ma-
Ma-drid', 1 ma-drid' or (Sp.) ma-drīth'; 2 ma-drid' or (Sp.) mä-drīth'.
Mæ-ce'nas, 1 mī-sī'nas; 2 mē-çē'nas.
Mag'da-lene, 1 mag'də-līn or mag'də-lī'nī; 2 mäg'da-lēn or mäg'da-lē'nĕ.
Ma-gel'lan, 1 ma-jel'ən; 2 ma-gĕl'an. [mäd-gō'rĕ.
Mag-gio're, 1 mad-jō'rē; 2
Ma'gog, 1 mē'gog; 2 mä'gŏg.
Ma-hom'et, 1 ma-hom'et; 2 ma-hŏm'ĕt. Same as Mo-HAMMED.
Mainz, 1 maints; 2 mīnts.
Ma-kas'sar, 1 ma-kas'ər; 2 ma-käs'ar. Ma-cas'sar‡.
Mal'a-ga, 1 mal'ə-gə or (Sp.) mä'la-gə or (Sp.) mäl'ä-ga or (Sp.) mäl'lä-gä.
Ma-lak'ka, 1 ma-lak'ə; 2 ma-läk'a. Ma-lac'cat. [dĕn.
Mal'den, 1 mēl'den; 2 mal'-
Mal'mö, 1 mal'mö; 2 mäl'mü.
Mal'ta, 1 mēl'tə; 2 mạl'ta.
Mal''te-Brun', 1 mal''te-brụn' or (F.) malt''-brụn'; 2 mäl'-te-brụn' or (F.) mält''-brụn'.
Mam're, 1 mam'rı; 2 mäm're.
Ma-nas'seh, 1 ma-nas'ə; 2 ma-näs'e.
Man''chu-kuo', 1 män''jo-gwō'; 2 män''go-gwō'.
Man-chu'ri-a, 1 man-chū'rı-ə; 2 män-chu'ri-a.

Ma-nil'a, 1 mə-nil'ə or (Sp.) ma-nī'la; 2 ma-nil'a or (Sp.) mä-nī'lä.
Man'tu-a, 1 man'chu-ə or -tiu-ə; 2 män'chu-a or -tū-a.
Ma''ra-cal'bo, 1 mä'ra-kaı'bo; 2 mära-eī'bo.
Ma''ran-hão', 1 mä'ran-youn'; 2 mä'rän-youn'.
Ma''ra-nham'‡.
Mar'i-on, 1 mar'ı-ən; 2 mär'i-on.
Marl'bor-ough, 1 märl'bur-o or märl'bra; 2 märl'bŭr-o or märl'bru.
Mar'mo-ra, 1 mär'mo-ra; 2 mär'mo-rä.
Mar-que'sas Islands, 1 mar-kē'sas; 2 mär-kę'säs.
Mar'quette', 1 mar'ket'; 2 mär'kĕt'. [mär-selz'.
Mar-seilles', 1 mar-sēlz'; 2
Mar'shal-sea, 1 mär'shəl-sī; 2 mär'shal-sē.
Mar'sy-as, 1 mär'sı-əs; 2 mär'sy-as.
Mar''ti-nique', 1 mär'tı-nīk'; 2 mär'ti-nīk'.
Mas'ke-lyne, 1 mas'ka-laın; 2 mas'ke-lin.
Mat''a-be'le-land, 1 mat'ə-bī'lı-land; 2 mät'a-bē'le-länd.
Ma-tan'zas, 1 ma-tan'zas or ma-tän'sas; 2 mä-tän'säs.
Mau''beuge', 1 mo'bȳ̆ȝ'; 2 mo'bŭzh'.
Mauch Chunk, 1 mȯk chunk; 2 mäe chŭnk.
Mau'i, 1 mau'ı; 2 mou'ī.
Mau'na Lo'a, 1 mau'na lō'a; 2 mou'nä lō'ä.
Mau''re-pas', 1 mo'rə-pä; 2 mo're-pä'.
Mau-ri'tius, 1 ma-rish'us; 2 mạ-rish'ŭs.
Maz''a-rin', 1 maz'ə-rīn' or (F.) maz'ra'ran'; 2 mäz'a-rīn' or (F.) mäz'zä'rän'.
Maz'za-roth, 1 maz'ə-roth; 2 mäz'a-rŏth. [sī'nī.
Maz-zi'ni, 1 mat-sī'nī; 2 mäz-
Med'i-ci, 1 med'ı-chı or (It.) mē'dī-chī; 2 mĕd'i-chi or (It.) mę'dī-chī.
Me-du'sa, 1 mı-diū'sə; 2 me-dū'sa.
Mee'rut, 1 mī'rut; 2 mē'rŭt.
Me-gid'do, 1 mı-gid'o; 2 me-gĭd'o. [mę'kong.
Me''kong', 1 mē''koṅ'; 2
Me-lanch'thon, 1 mı-laŋk'thən; 2 me-läŋe'thon.

Mel'bourne, 1 mel'bərn; 2 mĕl'burn.
Mel-chis'e-dec, 1 mel-kiz'i-dek; 2 mĕl-cĭş'e-dĕc.
Mel'e-a'ger, 1 mel'i-ē'jər; 2 mĕl'e-ā'ger.
Men'ai Strait, 1 men'ai; 2 mēn'ī. [nām'.
Me-nam', 1 mɪ-nām'; 2 me-
Men'dels-sohn, 1 men'del-sōn; 2 mĕn'dĕl-sōn.
Men'do-ci'no, 1 men'do-sī'no; 2 mĕn'do-çī'no.
Men"e-la'us, 1 men'i-lē'us; 2 mĕn'e-lā'ŭs.
Mer'i-bah, 1 mer'i-bə or me-rī'ba; 2 mĕr'ĭ-ba or mē-rī'ba.
Me'ri-da, 1 mā'rī-tha; 2 mẹ'rī-thä. [o-pē.
Mer'o-pe, 1 mer'o-pī; 2 mĕr'-
Mes-si'na, 1 me-sī'nə; 2 mĕ-sī'na.
Meuse, 1 miūz or [F.] mūz; 2 mūş or [F.] mûş. [mī'er-bēr.
Mey'er-beer, 1 mai'ər-bēr; 2
Mé"zières', 1 mē'zyâr'; 2 mĕ'-zyêr'.
Mi-ca'iah, 1 mai-kē'ya or -kai'a; 2 mi-cā'ya or -cī'a.
Mi'chael, 1 mai'kel or mai'ki-el; 2 mī'cĕl or mī'ca-ĕl.
Mi"chel-an'ge-lo, 1 mai'kel-an'ji-lo or (It.) mi'kel-än'jē-lō; 2 mī'cĕl-ăn'ge-lo or (It.) mī'cĕl-än'ge-lō. [mĭch'lẹ'.
Miche'let, 1 mĭsh'lē'; 2
Mig'ron, 1 mig'rən; 2 mĭg'rŏn.
Mi'lan, 1 mī'lan; 2 mī'lăn.
Mi-le'tus, 1 mɪ-lī'tus; 2 mi-lē'tŭs.
Mil-lais', 1 mi-lē'; 2 mi-lā.
Mille"rand', 1 mīl'rän'; 2 mīl'-rän'.
Mil'let', 1 mī'yē'; 2 mī'yẹ'.
Mi'lo, 1 mai'lo; 2 mī'lo.
Mil-ti'a-des, 1 mil-tai'a-dīz; 2 mil-tī'a-dēş. [mi-nĕr'va.
Mi-ner'va, 1 mi-nūr'va; 2
Mi'nos, 1 mai'nos; 2 mī'nŏs.
Min'o-taur, 1 min'o-tôr; 2 min'o-ta̤r. [mī'rä'bō'
Mi'ra'beau, 1 mī'ra'bō'; 2
Mis"so-lon'ghi, 1 mis'o-lon'-gī; 2 mis'o-lŏṇ'gī.
Mis-sou'ri, 1 mi-sūri or mi-zū'ri; 2 mi-su̱'ri or mi-şu'ri.
Mith'ri-da'tes, 1 mĭth'ri-dē'tiz; 2 mĭth'rĭ-dä'tēş.
Mit"y-le'ne, 1 mĭt'i-lī'nī; 2 mit'y-lē'nē. [miz'ra-im.
Miz'ra-im, 1 miz'ri-im; 2
Mna'son, 1 mai'nəs; 2 nā'nŏs.
Mne-mos'y-ne, 1 nɪ-mos'i-nī; 2 ne-mŏs'y-nē.

Mo'de-na, 1 mō'dē-na; 2 mō'de-nä. [mō'lyêr'.
Mo"llère', 1 mō'lyâr'; 2
Mo"lo-ka'i, 1 mō'lo-kā'ī; 2 mō'lo-kā'ĭ.
Molt'ke, 1 mōlt'kə; 2 mōlt'ke.
Mon-taigne', 1 mən-tēn' or (F.) mŏn'tē'nyə; 2 mŏn-tān' or (F.) mŏn'tā'nye.
Mont-calm', 1 mənt-kām'; 2 mŏnt-cäm'. [mŏn'te-rẹ'.
Mon"te-rey', 1 mon'ti-rē'; 2
Mon"tes-quieu', 1 mon'tes-kiū' or (F.) mŏn'tĕs'kī'ū'; 2 mŏn'tĕs-kū' or (F.) mŏn'-tĕs'kī'ū'.
Mon"tes-so'ri, 1 mən'tes-sō'-rī; 2 mŏn'tĕs-sō'rī'.
Mon"te-vid'e-o, 1 mon'ti-vid'i-o or (Sp.) mon'tē-vī-thē'o; 2 mŏn'te-vid'e-o or (Sp.) mŏn'tĕ-vī-thē'o.
Mon"te-zu'ma, 1 mon'ti-zū'ma; 2 mŏn'te-zu̱'ma.
Mont-pel'li-er, 1 mənt-pī'li-ər or -pēl'yər; 2 mŏnt-pĕl'li-er or -pĕl'yer.
Mon"tre-al', 1 mən'tri-ôl' or (F.) mŏn'trē'äl'; 2 mŏn'tre-al' or (F.) mŏn'trẹ'äl'.
Mor'de-cai, 1 môr'di-kai or mər'di-kā'ai; 2 mŏr'de-cī or mŏr'de-cā'ī.
Mos'cow, 1 məs'ko; 2 mŏs'co.
Mo-selle', 1 mo-zel'; 2 mo-gĕl'.
Mo-sul', 1 mo-sūl'; 2 mo-sul'.
Moul'trie, 1 mōl'[mūl' or mū']tri; 2 mōl'[mu̱l' or mu']tri.
Mo"zam-bique', 1 mō'zam-bīk'; 2 mō'zam-bīk'.
Mo'zart, 1 mō'zärt or (G.) mō'tsärt; 2 mō'zärt or (G.) mō'tsärt. [2 mül'hou-gen.
Mül'hau-sen, 1 mül'hau-zen;
Mun-chau'sen, 1 mun-chô'-zen; 2 mŭn-cha̤'şen.
Mu'nich, 1 miū'nɪk; 2 mū'nĭc.
Mu'rat', 1 mü'rä' or (Eng.) miu-rat'; 2 mü'rä' or (Eng.) mū-rät'.
Mur'ci-a, 1 mūr'shi-ə or (Sp.) mür'thī-a; 2 mŭr'shi-a or (Sp.) mu̱r'thī-ä.
Mu-ril'lo, 1 miu-ril'o or (Sp.) mū-ril'yo; 2 mū-ril'o or (Sp.) mu̱-ril'yo.
Mu-sæ'us, 1 miu-sī'us; 2 mu̱-sē'ŭs.
Mus"so-li'ni, 1 mus'o-lī'ni; 2 mus'o-lī'nī. [çē'nä.
My-ce'næ, 1 mai-sī'nī; 2
My'si-a, 1 mish'i-ə; 2 mỹsh'i-ä.
My'sore', 1 mai-sōr'; 2 mỹ-sōr'.

N

Na'a-man, 1 nē'ə-mən; 2 nä'a-man.
Na'in, 1 nē'in; 2 nä'in.
Na-ma'qua-land, 1 na-mä'kwə-land; 2 nä-mä'kwa-länd.
Na"mur', 1 na'mür'; 2 nä'-mür'. [nän'king'.
Nan'king, 1 nan'kin; 2
Nantes, 1 nants or (F.) nänt; 2 nänts or (F.) nänt.
Naph'ta-li, 1 naf'ta-lai; 2 năf'ta-lī. [när'bŏn'.
Nar'bonne', 1 nar'bon'; 2
Na-tal', 1 nə-tal'; 2 na-täl'.
Nau'cra-tis, 1 nē'krə-tis; 2 na̤'cra-tis. [vär'.
Na-varre', 1 na-vär'; 2 nä-
Ne"ze'ra, 1 nɪ-ī'ra; 2 ne-ē'ra.
Ne-ap'o-lis, 1 nɪ-ap'o-lis; 2 nē-ăp'o-lis.
Ne-ba'joth, 1 nɪ-bē'jəth or -baɪ'ōth; 2 ne-bä'jōth or -bī'ōth.
Neb"u-chad-rez'zar, 1 neb'-yu-kad-rez'ar; 2 nĕb'yu-cad-rĕz'ar. **Neb"u-chad-nez'-zar‡.**
Nel'son, 1 nel'sən; 2 nĕl'son.
Nem'u-el, 1 nem'yu-el 2 nĕm'yu-ĕl.
Ne"op-tol'e-mus, 1 nɪ'op-tol'i-mus; 2 nē'ŏp-tŏl'e-mŭs.
Ne-pal', 1 nɪ-pôl'; 2 ne-pal'.
Ne'pos, 1 nī'pos; 2 nē'pŏs.
Neu"cha'tel', 1 nū'sha'tel'; 2 nū'chä'tĕl'.
Neuve Chapelle, 1 nūv'sha'-pel'; 2 nūv'chä-pĕl'. [vä'da.
Ne-va'da, 1 nɪ-vä'də; 2 ne-
New"found-land', 1 niū'-fənd-land'; 2 nū'fund-länd'.
Ney, 1 nē; 2 ne. [çã'nōr.
Ni-ca'nor, 1 nai-kē'nər; 2 ni-
Nic"a-ra'gua, 1 nik'ə-rä'gwə; 2 nic'a-rä'gwa.
Nice, 1 nīs; 2 nĭç.
Ni"cho-lo'vitch, 1 nĭkko-lō'-vich; 2 nī'co-lō'vi̱ h.
Nic"o-me'di-a, 1 nik'o-mī'-di-ə; 2 nic'o-mē'di-a.
Nie'buhr, 1 nī'būr; 2 nē'bur.
Nie'der-wald, 1 nī'dər-valt; 2 nē'der-vält.
Nie'men, 1 nī'men; 2 nē'měn.
Nietzsch'e, 1 nĭch'ə; 2 nēch'e.
Ni'gel, 1 nai'jel; 2 nī'gĕl.
Ni'ger, 1 nai'jər; 2 nī'ger.
Nimes, 1 nīm; 2 nĭm.
Nim'shi, 1 nim'shai; 2 nim'-[pō'.
Ning'po', 1 nin'pō'; 2 ning'-

1: ȧrtistic, ärt; fat, fāre; fast; get, prēy; hit, police; obey, gō; nŏt, ör; full, rūle; but, bûrn;
2: ärt, āpe, făt, fâre, fâst, what, all; mē, gĕt, prẹy, fèrn; hit, īce; ī=ē; ĩ=ē̃; gō, nŏt, ôr, wòn,

Ni'nus, 1 naı'nus; 2 nī'nŭs.	**Or'lé-ans,** 1 ŏr'lı-ənz *or* (*F.*) or'lē'äṅ'; 2 ŏr'le-ans *or* (*F.*) ŏr'le'äṅ'.	**Par'a-guay,** 1 par'ə-gwē *or* pä'rag-waı'; 2 pär'a-ḡwä *or* pär'ä-ḡwī'. [pä'rä-nä'.
Ni'o-be, 1 naı'o-bɪ; 2 nī'o-bē.	**Or'pheus,** 1 ŏr'fīus *or* ŏr'fı-us; 2 ŏr'fūs *or* ŏr'fe-ŭs.	**Pa''ra-ná',** 1 pä'ra-nä'; 2
Niph'a-tes, 1 nıf'ə-tīz; 2 nıf'a-tēs.	**Or''te-gal', Cape,** 1 ŏr''tē-gäl'; 2 ŏr'te-gäl'.	**Par'me-nas,** 1 par'mı-nas; 2 bär'me-näs.
Nord'kyn, Cape, 1 nŏrt'kın; 2 nŏrt'kŷn.	**O-sage',** 1 o-sēj' *or* ō'sıj; 2 o-sāg' *or* ō'sag.	**Par-nas'sus,** 1 par-nas'us; 2 pär-năs'ŭs.
Nor'folk, 1 nŏr'fək; 2 nŏr'fok.	**Os''ce-o'la,** 1 ɒs'ı-ō'lə; 2 ŏs'e-ō'la. [ŏsh'kŏsh.	**Par-rha'si-us,** 1 pa-rē'shı-us; 2 pä-rä'shi-ŭs.
Nor'ge, 1 nŏr'gə; 2 nŏr'ye.	**Osh'kosh,** 1 ɒsh'kɒsh; 2	**Par-then'o-pe,** 1 par-then'o-pı; 2 pär-thĕn'o-pē.
Nor'walk, 1 nŏr'wŏk; 2 nŏr'wǫk.	**O-si'ris,** 1 o-saı'rıs; 2 o-sī'ris.	**Par-va'im,** 1 par-vē'ım; 2 pär-vä'im.
Nor'wich, [Eng.] 1 nɒr'ıch; 2 nŏr'ıch; [U. S.] 1 nŏr'wıch; 2 nŏr'wich.	**Os'lo,** 1 ɒs'lō; 2 ŏs'lō.	**Pa-siph'a-e,** 1 pə-sıf'ə-ı; 2 pa-sıf'a-ē. [mŏs.
Nour'ma-hal, 1 nūr'mə-hal; 2 nur'ma-hăl. [yŏn.	**Os-we'go,** 1 ɒs-wī'go; 2 ŏs-wē'go.	**Pat'mos,** 1 pat'mos; 2 păt'-
Noy''on', 1 nwa'yŏn'; 2 nwä'-	**O'tho,** 1 ō'tho; 2 ō'tho.	**Pa-tro'cius,** 1 pə-trō'klus; 2 pa-trō'clŭs.
Nu'bi-a, 1 niū'bı-ə; 2 nū'bi-a.	**Ot-se'go,** 1 ɒt-sī'go; 2 ŏt-sē'go.	**Pat'ti,** 1 pat'ı; 2 păt'i.
Nue'ces, 1 nwē'ses; 2 nwe'çĕs.	**Ouach'i-ta,** 1 wɒsh'ı-tô; 2 wäch'i-tä.	**Pau,** 1 pō; 2 pō.
Nu-man'ti-a, 1 niu-man'shı-ə; 2 nū-măn'shi-a.	**Gudh,** 1 aud; 2 oud.	**Pau-sa'ni-as,** 1 pô-sē'nı-as; 2 pa-sä'ni-as.
Nu'rem-berg, 1 niū'rem-bûrg; 2 nū'rĕm-bērg.	**Ourcq,** 1 ûrk; 2 ųrk.	**Pa-vi'a,** 1 pa-vī'a; 2 pä-vī'ä.
	O-we'go, 1 o-wī'go; 2 o-wē'go.	**Pe-chi-li',** 1 pē-chı-lī'; 2 pe-chī-lī'. [pǣ'a-sŭs.
O	**O'zark,** 1 ō'zärk; 2 ō'zärk.	**Peg'a-sus,** 1 peg'ə-sus; 2
O-a'hu, 1 o-ä'hū; 2 o-ä'hu.		**Pe''i-ping',** 1 pē'ı-pıŋ'; 2 pe'ē-pıŋ'.
Oa-xa'ca, 1 wa-hä'ka; 2 wä-hä'çä.	**P**	**Pe'kin,** 1 pē'kın; 2 pē'kin.
O''ce-an'I-a, 1 ō'shı-an'ı-ə; 2 ō'she-än'i-ä.	**Pac-to'lus,** 1 pak-tō'lus; 2 păc-tō'lŭs.	**Pe-king',** 1 pī-kın; 2 pē-king'.
Oc-ta'vi-us, 1 ɒk-tē'vı-us; 2 ŏc-tā'vi-ŭs.	**Pa''dan-a'ram,** 1 pē'dən-ē'rəm *or* ä'rəm; 2 pä'dan-ä'ram *or* ä'ram.	**Pe''lée',** 1 pē'lē'; 2 pe'le'.
O-dys'seus, 1 o-dis'yus *or* o-dis'ı-us; 2 o-dŷs'yus *or* o-dŷs'e-ŭs.	**Pa''de-rew'ski,** 1 pa''de-rev'ski *or* -res'kı; 2 pä''dĕ-rĕv'ski *or* -rĕs'ki. [yu-a.	**Pe'leus,** 1 pī'lius *or* pī'h-us; 2 pē'lē-us *or* pē'le-ŭs. [pe-lū'.
Od'ys-sey, 1 ɒd'ı-sı; 2 ŏd'y-sy.	**Pad'u-a,** 1 pad'yu-ə; 2 păd'-	**Pe-lew' Islands,** 1 pı-lū'; 2
Œd'i-pus, 1 ed'ı-pus *or* ī'dı-pus; 2 ĕd'i-pus *or* ē'di-pŭs.	**Pæs'tum,** 1 pes'tum; 2 pĕs'tŭm.	**Pe'li-as,** 1 pī'lı-əs *or* pel'ı-as; 2 pē'li-as *or* pĕl'i-as. [dĕs.
Œ-no'ne, 1 ī-nō'nı; 2 ē-nō'ne.	**Pa''ga-ni'ni,** 1 pä'ga-nī'nī; 2 pä'gä-nī'ni.	**Pel'i-des,** 1 pel'ı-dīz; 2 pĕl'-
Of'fen-bach, 1 ɒf'en-bäɦ; 2 ŏf'ĕn-bäн.	**Pa-læ'mon,** 1 pə-lī'mən; 2 pa-lē'mon.	**Pe'li-on,** 1 pē'lı-ən; 2 pē'li-ŏn
Oise, 1 wäz; 2 wäs.	**Pal'a-me'des,** 1 pal'ə-mī'dīz; 2 păl'a-mē'dĕs.	**Pei''o-pon-ne'sus,** 1 pel'o-pə-nī'sus; 2 pĕl'o-po-nē'sŭs.
O-khotsk', 1 o-kɒtsk'; 2 o-kŏtsk'.	**Pa-len'que,** 1 pä-leŋ'kē; 2 pä-lĕŋ'ke.	**Pe'lops,** 1 pē'lɒps; 2 pē'lŏps.
O-man', 1 o-män'; 2 o-män'.	**Pa-ler'mo,** 1 pə-lûr'mo *or* (*It.*) pa-ler'mo; 2 pa-lĕr'mo *or* (*It.*) pä-lĕr'mo.	**Pe-nel'o-pe,** 1 pı-nel'o-pı; 2 pe-nĕl'o-pe.
Om'pha-le, 1 ɒm'fə-lı; 2 ŏm'fa-le.	**Pal'es-tine,** 1 pal'es-taın; 2 păl'ĕs-tīn.	**Pe-ni'el,** 1 pı-naı'el *or* pen'ı-el; 2 pe-nī'el *or* pĕn'i-ĕl.
O-nei'da, 1 o-naı'də; 2 o-nī'da.	**Pal'i-nu'rus,** 1 pal'ı-niū'rus; 2 păl'i-nū'rŭs.	**Pen''thes-i-le'a,** 1 pen'thes-ı-lī'ə; 2 pĕn'thĕs-ı-lē'a.
O-nes'i-mus, 1 o-nes'ı-mus; 2 o-nĕs'i-mŭs.	**Pall Mall,** 1 pal mal; 2 päl mäl. [păm'fı-lŭs.	**Per'a-zim,** 1 per'ə-[*or* pı-rē']zim; 2 pär'a-[*or* pe-rä']zim.
On''e-siph'o-rus, 1 ɒn'ı-sif'o-rus; 2 ŏn'e-sif'o-rŭs.	**Pam'phi-lus,** 1 pam'fı-lus; 2	**Per'ga-mos,** 1 pûr'gə-mos; 2 pĕr'ga-mŏs.
On''on-da'ga, 1 ɒn'on-dô'ga; 2 ŏn'ŏn-dä'ga. [tä'rı-ō.	**Pan'a-ma',** 1 pan'ə-mä'; 2 pän'a-mä'.	**Per'nam-bu'co,** 1 per'nam-bū'ko; 2 pĕr'näm-bų'co.
On-ta'ri-o, 1 ɒn-tē'rı-ō; 2 ŏn-	**Pan'da-rus,** 1 pan'də-rus; 2 pän'da-rŭs. [păr-dō'ra.	**Per-seph'o-ne,** 1 per-sef'o-nı; 2 per-sef'o-nē.
O'phir, 1 ō'fer; 2 ō'fır.	**Pan-do'ra,** 1 pan-dō'rə; 2	**Per'seus,** 1 pûr'sius *or* -sı-us; 2 pĕr'sŭs *or* -se-ŭs.
Oph'rah, 1 ɒf'rə; 2 ŏf'ra.	**Pan'o-pe,** 1 pan'o-pı; 2 păn'-o-pe.	**Per'shing,** 1 pûr'shıŋ; 2 pĕr'shing.
O-por'to, 1 o-pôr'to; 2 o-pōr'to. [tĕg.	**Pa'phos,** 1 pē'fos; 2 pä'fŏs.	**Pe-ru',** 1 pı-rū'; 2 pe-ru'.
O-res'tes, 1 o-res'tīz; 2 o-res'-	**Pa-ra',** 1 pa-rä'; 2 pä-rä'.	**Pe''tain',** 1 pē'taṅ'; 2 pe'täṅ'
Or-get'o-rix, 1 ɒr-jet'o-riks; 2 ŏr-gĕt'o-rĭks. [ō'rī-nō'co.		**Pe'trarch,** 1 pı'trärk; 2 pĕ'trärk.
O''ri-no'co, 1 ō'rı-nō'ko; 2		
O''ri-za'ba, 1 ō'rı-zä'ba; 2 ō'rī-zä'bä.		

1: ə = final; ı = habıt; aisle; au = out; oil; iu = feud; chin; go; ŋ = sing; thin, this.

2: wolf, dǫ; book, boot; full, rule, cure, bŭt, bûrn; oil, bǫy; ḡo, ḡem; ınk; thin, this.

Pe'tro-grad, 1 pē'tro-grad; 2 pĕ'tro-gräd.
Phæ'dra, 1 fī'drə; 2 fē'dra.
Pha'e-thon, 1 fē'ı-thon; 2 fā'e-thŏn. [ris.
Phal'a-ris, 1 fal'ə-ris; 2 făl'a-
Pha'raoh, 1 fē'ro or fē'rı-ō; 2 fā'ro or fā'ra-ō. [nish'ı-a.
Phe-ni'ci-a, 1 fı-nish'ı-ə; 2 fe-
Phid'i-as, 1 fid'ı-əs; 2 fid'i-as.
Phi-le'mon, 1 fı-lī'mən; 2 fi-lē'mon. [lip'ī.
Phi-lip'pi, 1 fı-lip'ai; 2 fi-
Phil'ip-pine Islands, 1 fil'ı-pin or -pīn; 2 fil'i-pin or -pīn.
Phil'oc-te'tes, 1 fıl'ək-tī'tīz; 2 fĭl'ŏc-tē'tĕs.
Phleg'e-thon, 1 fleg'[or flej']-ı-thon; 2 flĕg'[or flĕj']-e-thŏn.
Pho'ci-on, 1 fō'shı-ən; 2 fō'-shi-on.
Pi-a've, 1 pı-ä'vē, 2 pī-ä've.
Pied'mont, 1 pīd'mənt; 2 pēd'mont. [2 pī-rith'o-ūs.
Pi-rith'o-us, 1 paı-rith'o-us;
Pi'sa, 1 pī'za; 2 pī'sä.
Pis'gah, 1 piz'gə; 2 pĭs'ga.
Pi-sis'tra-tus, 1 pı-sis'tra-tus; 2 pi-sis'tra-tŭs.
Pi'son, 1 paı'sən; 2 pī'son.
Pi'thom, 1 paı'thəm; 2 pī'thŏm.
Plan-tag'e-net, 1 plan-taj'ı-net; 2 plăn-tăg'e-nĕt.
Plei'a-des, 1 plaı'[or plī']ə-dīz; 2 plī'[or plē']a-dēs.
Plo-ti'nus, 1 plo-taı'nus; 2 plo-tī'nŭs. [pwän'cä'rē'.
Poin'ca'ré, 1 pwaṅ'ka'rē'; 2
Poi'ti'ers, 1 pwa'tī'ē'; 2 pwä'tī'ẽ'. Polc'tiers'‡.
Po-lyb'i-us, 1 po-lıb'ı-us; 2 po-lŷb'i-ŭs.
Pol'y-ni'ces, 1 pol'ı-naı'sīz; 2 pŏl'y-nī'cēs.
Pol'y-phe'mus, 1 pol'ı-fī'-mus; 2 pŏl'y-fē'mŭs.
Po-lyx'e-na, 1 po-liks'ı-na; 2 po-lŷks'e-na. [mō'na.
Po-mo'na, 1 po-mō'nə; 2 po-
Pom-pe'ii, 1 pem-pē'yī; 2 pōm-pē'yī.
Pon'ce de Le'on, 1 pŏn'thē dē lē'ŏn or pons də lī'an; 2 pŏn'the dĕ le'ŏn or pŏṅc de lē'on.
Pon'di-cher'ry, 1 pen'dı-sher'ı or -cher'ı; 2 pŏn'di-chĕr'y or -chĕr'y.
Pont'char'train, 1 pŏn'-shar'trän'; 2 pŏn'chär'trăn'.
Po-po'ca-te'pet-l, 1 po-pō'-ka-tē'pet-l or -tē'pet'l; 2 po-pō'cä-tĕ'pĕt-l or -tĕ-pĕt'l.

Por'se-na, 1 pôr'sı-nə or per-sen'ə; 2 pôr'sē-na or pŏr-sēn'a. [2 pôr'to rī'co.
Por'to Ri'co, 1 pōr'to rī'ko;
Po-sei'don, 1 po-saı'dən; 2 po-sī'don. [pòt'ı-dē'a.
Pot'i-dæ'a, 1 pet'ı-dī'ə; 2
Pot'i-phe'rah, 1 pet'ı-fī'ra; 2 pŏt'ı-fē'rä.
Po'to-si', 1 pō'to-sī'; 2 pō'to-sī'.
Pough-keep'sie, 1 po-kip'sı; 2 po-kip'sī.
Prax-ag'o-ras, 1 praks-ag'o-rəs; 2 prăks-ăg'o-ras.
Prax-it'e-les, 1 praks-it'ı-līz; 2 prăks-ĭt'e-lēs.
Pri'am, 1 praı'am; 2 prī'am.
Proch'o-rus, 1 prek'o-rus; 2 prŏc'o-rŭs.
Pro-crus'tes, 1 pro-krus'tīz; 2 pro-crŭs'tēs.
Pro-me'theus, 1 pro-mī'thiūs or -thı-us; 2 pro-mē'thŭs or -the-ūs.
Pros'er-pine, 1 pros'er-pin or -pīn; 2 prŏs'er-pin or -pīn.
Pro-tes'i-la'us, 1 pro-tes'ı-lē'us; 2 pro-tĕs'i-lā'ŭs.
Pro'teus, 1 prō'tiūs or -tı-us; 2 prō'tŭs or -te-ūs.
Pro'vence, 1 pro'väṅs'; 2 pro'väṅç'.
Prze'mysl, 1 pshe'mishl; 2 pshĕ'mŷshl.
Psy'che, 1 saı'kı; 2 sī'ee.
Ptol'e-ma'is, 1 tel'ı-mē'is; 2 tŏl'e-mā'is. [my.
Ptol'e-my, 1 tol'ı-mı; 2 tŏl'e-
Pue'bla, 1 pwē'bla; 2 pwg'blä.
Puer'to Prin'ci-pe, 1 pwer'-to prin'sī-pē; 2 pwēr'to prin'çi-pe.
Puer'to Ri'co, 1 pwer'to; 2 pwēr'to. Same as Porto Rico.
Pu'get Sound, 1 piū'jet; 2 pū'gĕt. [läs'ki.
Pu-las'ki, 1 piu-las'kı; 2 pū-
Put'nik, 1 pūt'nık; 2 put'nĭk.
Pyl'a-des, 1 pil'ə-dīz; 2 pŷl'a-dēs.
Py'los, 1 paı'ləs; 2 pŷ'lŏs.

Q

Que-bec', 1 kwı-bek'; 2 kwē-bēc'. [ke-rĕ'ta-ro.
Que-ré'ta-ro, 1 kē-rĕ'ta-ro; 2
Quin'cy, 1 kwin'sı; 2 kwin'çy.
Qui-ri'nus, 1 kwı-raı'nus; 2 kwı-rī'nŭs. [kwis'ling.
Quis'ling, 1 kwis'lin; 2
Qui'to, 1 kī'to; 2 kī'to.

R

Rab'sha-keh, 1 rab'sha-ke or rab-shē'ke; 2 răb'sha-kĕ or răb-shā'kĕ.
Ra'cine', 1 ro'sīn'; 2 rä'çīn'.
Raf'fa-el, 1 raf'ı-el; 2 răf'a-ĕl Ra'pha-el‡.
Ra-gu'el, 1 rə-giū'el or rag' yu-el; 2 ra-gū'ĕl or răg'yu-ĕl
Ra'hab, 1 rē'hab; 2 rä'häb.
Raj'pu-ta'na, 1 räj'pū-tä'nə; 2 räj'pu-tä'na.
Ra'leigh, 1 rô'lı; 2 rạ'le.
Ra'ma, 1 rē'mə; 2 rä'ma.
Ra'mah‡.
Ram'e-ses, 1 ram'ı-sīz; 2 răm'e-sĕs. [gōōn'.
Ran-goon', 1 raṅ-gūn'; 2 răṅ-
Ra-ven'na, 1 ra-ven'ə or (It.) ra-ven'na; 2 ra-vĕn'a or (It.) rä-vĕn'nä.
Read'ing, 1 red'ın; 2 rĕd'ing.
Ré'au'mur', 1 rē'ō'mür'; 2 rē'ō'mür'.
Re'gem-me'lech, 1 rı'gem-mi'lek or -mel'ek; 2 rē'gĕm-mē'lĕc or -mĕl'ĕc.
Re-gil'lus, 1 rı-jil'us; 2 re-gil'ŭs. [rĕg'ı-nald.
Reg'i-nald, 1 rej'ı-nald; 2
Re'ho-bo'am, 1 rı'ho-bō'am; 2 rē'ho-bō'am.
Reims, 1 rimz or (F.) raṅs; 2 rēms or (F.) räns.
Rem'brandt, 1 rem'brant; 2 rĕm'bränt.
Rennes, 1 ren; 2 rĕn.
Reph'a-im, 1 ref'ı-im or ri-fē'im; 2 rĕf'a-im or re-fā'im.
Re-thondes, 1 rə-tŏnd'; 2 re-tŏnd'.
Rhad'a-man'thus, 1 rad'ə-man'thus; 2 răd'a-män'thŭs.
Ri'che-lieu', 1 rı'sha-lyū' or (Eng.) rish'a-lū; 2 rī'çhe-lyū' or (Eng.) rĭch'e-lụ.
Ri'ga, 1 rī'gə; 2 rī'ga.
Ri'o de Ja-nei'ro, 1 rı'o dē ʒə-nē'ro; 2 rī'o dĕ ʒha-nẹ'ro
Ri'o Gran'de, 1 grän'dē; 2 grän'dĕ. [nẹ'gro.
Ri'o Ne'gro, 1 nē'gro; 2
Ro'a-noke, 1 rō'a-nōk; 2 rō'a-nŏk.
Ro'bes-pierre, 1 rō'bəs-pır or (F.) rō'bes'pyär'; 2 rō'bes or (F.) rō'bĕs'pyĕr'.
Roche'fort', 1 rōsh'fôr'; 2 rōçh'fôr'.
Roche'fou'cauld', La, 1 la rōsh'fu'kō'; 2 lä rōçh'fu'cō'.
Ro-chelle', 1 ro-shel'; 2 ro-çhĕl'.

Roo'se-velt, 1 rō'zə-velt; 2 rē′ze-vĕlt.

Ros'ei-us, 1 rŏsh′ı-us; 2 rŏsh′i-ŭs. [sĕt′tl.

Ros-set'tl, 1 ro-set′tı; 2 ro-

Ros-si'ni, 1 ros-sī′nĭ; 2 rŏs-sī′nĭ.

Roths'child, 1 rŏṭhs′child or (G.) rŏt′shilt; 2 rŏṭhs′child or (G.) rŏt′shilt.

Rou″en', 1 rū'äṅ'; 2 ru̇′äṅ'.

Rou″lers', 1 rū'lē'; 2 ru̇''lē'.

Rou-ma'ni-a, 1 ru-mē′nı-ə; 2 ru̇-mā′ni-a. Ru-ma'ni-a‡. Ru-ma'mah, 1 ru-hē′[or -hä′]-mə; 2 ru̇-hā′[or -hä′]ma.

S

Saar'brück, 1 zär′brük; 2 sär′brük. [bī′na.

Sa-bi'na, 1 sə-baı′nə; 2 sa-

Sa'bines, 1 sē′baınz; 2 sā′bīns.

Sa-bi'nus, 1 sə-baı′nus; 2 sa-bī′nŭs.

Sa'co, 1 sē′ko; 2 sạ′eo. [ı-nạ.

Sag'i-naw, 1 sag′ı-nē; 2 săg′-

Sa-gun'tum, 1 sə-gun′tum; 2 sa-ğŭn′tŭm. [hä′rä.

Sa-ha'ra, 1 sɑ-hä′rɑ; 2 sä-

Sal-gon', 1 sal-gen' or (F.) sa'ī'gōñ'; 2 sĭ-ğōn' or (F.) sä′ī'ğōñ′.

Saint Au'gus-tine' (city), 1 sēnt ẽ'gus-tīn'; 2 sänt ạ′ğŭs-tīn'. [he-lē′nạ.

Saint He-le'na, 1 hı-lī′nə; 2

Saint'-Mi'hiel', 1 saṅ′-mī′′-yel'; 2 saṅ′mī′yĕl'.

Saint'-Pierre', 1 saṅ′-pyär′; 2 saṅ′-pyêr'.

Saint'-Quen'tin', 1saṅ′kaṅ′-taṅ'; 2 săṅ′käṅ′tặñ'.

Sais, 1 sēs; 2 sās.

Sal'a-din, 1 sal′ə-dın; 2 săl′a-dĭn. [săl′a-mĭs.

Sal'a-mis, 1 sal′ə-mis; 2

Sa-la'thi-el, 1 sə-lē′ṭhı-el; 2 sa-lā′ṭhĭ-ĕl.

Sa-line', 1 sə-līn′; 2 sa-līn'.

Salis'bur-y, 1 sōlz-bər-ı; 2 sạls′ber-y. [lō′me.

Sa-lo'me, 1 sə-lō′mı; 2 sa-

Sa'lo-ni'kl, 1 sä′lo-nī′kī; 2 sä′lo-nī′kī. [mō′ä.

Sa-mo'a, 1 sɑ-mō′ɑ; 2 sä-

Sa'mos, 1 sē′mos; 2 sā′mŏs.

San-bal'lat, 1 san-bal′at; 2 săn-băl′ăt.

San Di-e'go, 1 san dī-ē′go; 2 sän dī-ē′go. [sän ho-sē'.

San Jo-sé', 1 săn ho-sē′; 2

San Ju-an', 1 săn hu-än′; 2 sän hu-än'.

San Ma-ri'no, 1 sän mɑ-rī′no; 2 sän mä-rī′no.

San Sal'va-dor, 1 san sal′və-dōr or (Sp.) sän säl′va-thōr'; 2 sän säl′va-dōr or (Sp.) sän säl′vä-thōr'.

San'ta Cruz, 1 sän′ta krūs; 2 sän′tä erụs.

San'ta Fé, 1 san′tə or (Sp.) sän′tə fē; 2 sän′ta or (Sp.) sän′tä fẹ. [sän′tĭ-ä′ğo.

San'ti-a'go, 1 sän′tı-ä′go; 2

Sar'da-na-pa'lus, 1 sär′də-nə-pē′lus; 2 sär′da-na-pä′-lŭs. [sär-pē′dŏn.

Sar-pe'don, 1 sar-pī′dєn; 2

Sas - katch ' e - wan, 1 sas-kach′ı-wєn; 2 săs-kăch′e-wan.

Sault Sainte Ma'rie, 1 sū sēnt mē′rī; 2 sụ sänt mä′rī.

Save, 1 sāv; 2 sāv.

Sa-voy', 1 sə-voı′; 2 sa-vŏy'.

Scæv'o-la, 1 sev′o-lə; 2 sĕv′o-la.

Sche-nec'ta-dy, 1 skı-nek′tə-dı; 2 sce-nĕe′ta-dy.

Schuyl'kill, 1 skūl′kil; 2 scụl′kĭl.

Scip'i-o, 1 sip′ı-ō; 2 sĭp′i-ō.

Scyl'la, 1 sil′ə; 2 sȳl′a. [i-a.

Scyth'i-a, 1 siṭh′ı-ə; 2 sȳth′-

Se-at'tle, 1 sı-at′l; 2 se-ăt′l.

Se-bas'to-pol, 1 sı-bas′to-pōl or sĕb′as-tō′pєl; 2 se-băs′to-pōl or sĕb′as-tō′pŏl.

Seine, 1 sēn; 2 sēn.

Se'ir, 1 sī′ir; 2 sē′ir.

Se-leu'cus, 1 sı-liū′kus; 2 se-lū′eŭs. [e-lē.

Sem'e-le, 1 sem′ı-lı; 2 sĕm′-

Se-mir'a-mis, 1 sı-mir′ə-mis; 2 se-mir′a-mis.

Sen'e-ca, 1 sen′ı-kə; 2 sĕn′-e-ca. [sĕn′e-ğal'.

Sen'e-gal', 1 sen′ı-gôl′; 2

Sen'lis', 1 saṅ′līs' or lī'; 2 säṅ′līs' or lī'.

Sen-nach'e-rib, 1 se-nak′ı-rib; 2 sĕ-năe′e-rib.

Se-oul', 1 sē-ūl'; 2 se-ụl'.

Seph'ar-va'im, 1 sef′ər-vē′im; 2 sĕf′ar-vā′ĭm.

Se'ra-je'vo, 1 sē′ra-ye′vo; 2 sä′rä-ye′vo. [vē′rụs.

Se-ve'rus, 1 sı-vī′rus; 2 se-

Sev'ille, 1 sev′ıl or sı-vil′ or (Sp.) sĕ-vil′yĕ; 2 sĕv′ĭl or se-vil′ or (Sp.) se-vil′ye.

Sè'vres, 1 sä′vr; 2 sĕ′vr.

Sha'drach, 1 shē′drak; 2 shā′dräc.

Shang'hai, 1 shaṅ′haı or shäṅ-hä′ī; 2 shäng′hī or shäng-hä′ī.

Shar'on, 1 shar′єn; 2 shăr′on.

Shawan'gunk Moun'tains, 1 shєṅ′gum; 2 shŏṅ′ğŭm.

Shen″an-do'ah, 1 shen′ən-dō′ə; 2 shĕn′an-dō′a.

Shi-ko'ku, 1 shī-kō′kū; 2 shī-kō′kụ.

Sieg'fried, 1 sīg′frid or (G.) zīh′frīt; 2 sēğ′frēd or (G.) sēh′frēt.

Si-er'ra Ma'dre, 1 mä′drē; 2 mä′dre. [lē′nŭs.

Si-le'nus, 1 saı-lī′nus; 2 sī-

Si-lo'am, 1 sı-lo′[or saı-]lō′əm; 2 sĭ-[or sī-]lō′am.

Sil-va'nus, 1 sıl-vē′nus; 2 sĭl-vä′nŭs. Syl'vi-a‡ (fem.), 1 sil′vı-ə; 2 sȳl′vi-a.

Si-mon'i-des, 1 saı-mon′ı-dīz; 2 sī-mŏn′i-dēş.

Si'nai, 1 saı′naı or saı′nı-aı; 2 sī′ni or sī′na-ī.

Sin'ga-pore', 1 sıṅ′gə-pōr′; 2 sĭṅ′ğa-pōr'.

Si'non, 1 saı′non; 2 sī′nŏn.

Sioux Cit'y, 1 sū; 2 sụ.

Sis'er-a, 1 sis′ər-ə; 2 sĭs′er-a.

Sis'y-phus, 1 sis′ı-fus; 2 sĭs′y-fŭs.

Si-ut', 1 sı-ūt′; 2 sī-ụt'.

Skan″e-ate'les, 1 skan′ı-at′les; 2 skăn′e-ăt′lĕs.

Smyr'na, 1 smur′nə; 2 smẏr′na.

So-fi'a, 1 so-fī′ɑ; 2 so-fī′ä.

Sois'sons', 1 swɑ′sєn'; 2 swä′sŏñ'.

So'pa-ter, 1 sō′pə-[or sєp′ə-]tєr; 2 sō′pa-[or sŏp′a-]ter.

Sos'tra-tus, 1 sos′trə-tus; 2 sŏs′tra-tŭs.

Sou'fri'ère', 1 sū′frī′är'; 2 sụ′frī′êr'.

South'ey, 1 sauth′ı or suth′ı; 2 south′y or sŭth′y.

Spo-kane', 1 spo-kan′; 2 spo-kän'.

Stet'tin, 1 stet′ın or (G.) shte-tin′; 2 stĕt′ĭn or (G.) shte-tin'.

Stil'i-cho, 1 stil′ı-kō; 2 stil′-i-cō.

Stock'holm, 1 stok′hōlm or (Sw.) stok′helm; 2 stŏk′-hōlm or (Sw.) stŏk′hŏlm.

St. Pe'ters-burg, 1 pī′tarz-bürg; 2 pē′ters-bürğ.

Stra'bo, 1 strē′bo; 2 strā′bo.

Strass'burg, 1 shträs′burh; 2 shträs′bụrh.

Strauss, 1 straus; 2 strous.

Stutt'gart, 1 stut′gärt or (G.) shtut′gärt; 2 stŭt′gärt or (G.) shtụt′gärt.

Stuy've-sant, 1 staī'və-sənt; 2 stī've-sant.
Su'cre, 1 sū'krē; 2 sụ'erẹ.
Su-dan', 1 sū-dän'; 2 sụ-dän'.
Su-de'ten, 1 sū-dē'tən; 2 sụ-de'ten.
Sue-to'ni-us, 1 swī-tō'nɪ-us; 2 swē-tō'nĭ-ŭs.
Su-ez', 1 sū-ez'; 2 sụ-ĕz'.
Su-ma'tra, 1 su-mä'trə; 2 sụ-mä'tra.
Swa'bi-a, 1 swē'bɪ-ə; 2 swä'bi-a.
Swan'sea, 1 swon'sī; 2 swän'sē.
Syr'i-a, 1 sīr'ɪ-ə; 2 sĭr'i-a.
Sze'ge-din, 1 se'ge-dīn; 2 sĕ'gĕ-dīn.

T

Ta'gus, 1 tē'gus; 2 tä'gŭs.
Ta'hi-ti, 1 tä'hɪ-tī; 2 tä'hī-tī.
Tai'wan', 1 taī'wän'; 2 tī'wän'.
Tan'gan-yi'ka, 1 tän'gan-yī'kä; 2 tän'gän-yī'kä.
Tan-gier', 1 tan-jīr'; 2 tän-gēr'. [tän'ta-lŭs.
Tan'ta-lus, 1 tan'ta-lus; 2 tän'ta-lŭs.
Tauch'nitz, 1 tauн'nits; 2 touн'nĭts.
Te-cum'seh, 1 tɪ-kum'sə; 2 te-eŭm'se. [tç'hä-rän'.
Te'he-ran', 1 tē'he-rän'; 2 tç-wän'te-pēk'.
Te-huan'te-pec', 1 tē-wän'te-pek';
Te-ko'a, 1 tɪ-kō'ə; 2 te-kō'a.
Te-lem'a-chus, 1 tɪ-lem'ə-kus; 2 te-lĕm'a-eŭs.
Tel'e-phus, 1 tel'ɪ-fus; 2 tĕl'e-fŭs. [tĕm'esh-vär.
Tem'es-var, 1 tem'esh-vär;
Ten'e-riffe', 1 ten'ər-if'; 2 tĕn'er-if'. [tĕn'ĕ-sē'.
Ten'nes-see', 1 ten'e-sī';
Terp'sich'o-re, 1 tẽrp-sĭk'o-rĭ; 2 tẽrp-sĭe'o-rē.
Ter're Haute, 1 ter'ɪ hōt; 2 tẽr'e hōt.
Te'thys, 1 tī'fhɪs; 2 tē'thys.
Teu'cer, 1 tiū'sər; 2 tū'çer.
Tha'les, 1 thē'līz; 2 thä'lēg.
Tha-li'a, 1 tha-laī'ə; 2 tha-lī'a.
Thames, 1 temz; 2 tĕmg.
The-re'sa, 1 ta-rī'sə; 2 te-rē'sa.
Ther-mop'y-læ, 1 fhẽr-mop'ɪ-lī; 2 thẽr-mop'y-lē.
The'seus, 1 fhī'sius or -sɪ-us; 2 thē'sūs or -se-ŭs.
Thl'er''ry, 1 tī'ar'rī'; 2 tĭ'ẽr'rỵ'.
Thiers, 1 tyer; 2 tyẽr.
Thion'ville, 1 tyeň'vīl'; 2 tyôn'vīl'.

Thor, 1 fhōr; 2 thôr.
Tho'reau, 1 fhō'ro or fho-rō'; 2 thō'ro or tho-rō'.
Thorn, 1 tôrn; 2 tôrn.
Thor'wald-sen, 1 tôr'wald-sen; 2 tôr'wald-sēn.
Thras'y-bu'lus, 1 fhras'ɪ-biū'lus; 2 thräs'y-bū'lŭs.
Thu-cyd'i-des, 1 fhiu-sid'ɪ-dīz; 2 thū-çŷd'ĭ-dēg.
Ti-bet', 1 tɪ-bet'; 2 tĭ-bĕt'.
Ti-flis', 1 tɪ-flīs'; 2 tĭ-flīs'.
Ti-gra'nes, 1 tai-grē'nīz; 2 tī-grä'nēg. [mē'ŭs.
Ti-mæ'us, 1 tai-mī'us; 2 tī-mē'ŭs.
Tim-buk'tu, 1 tim-buk'tū; 2 tim-bŭe'tụ. [ti-mō'le-ŏn.
Ti-mo'le-on, 1 tɪ-mō'lɪ-on; 2 tī-mō'li-ŏn.
Ti-re'si-as, 1 tai-rī'shɪ-əs; 2 tī-rē'shi-as.
Tis'a-pher'nes, 1 tis'ə-fẽr'nɪz; 2 tis'a-fẽr'nēg.
Ti'tian, 1 tish'ən; 2 tish'an.
Tmo'lus, 1 tmō'lus; 2 tmō'lŭs. [bōlsk'.
To-bolsk', 1 to-bolsk'; 2 to-bōlsk'.
To'ky-o, 1 tō'kɪ-ō; 2 tō'kỵ-ō.
To'ma-szow", 1 tō'ma-shof'; 2 tō'mä-shôf'.
Tor-quay', 1 ter-kī'; 2 tôr-kỵ'.
Tor-tu'ga, 1 ter-tū'gə; 2 tôr-tū'gä.
Toul, 1 tūl; 2 tụl.
Tou'lon', 1 tū'lôň'; 2 tụ'lôň'.
Tou'louse', 1 tū'lūz'; 2 tụ'lụs'.
Tra-fal'gar, 1 trə-fal'gər or traf'al-gär'; 2 tra-fäl'gar or träf'al-gär'.
Treb'i-zond, 1 treb'ɪ-zond; 2 treb'ĭ-zond. [trich'ke.
Treit'sch'ke, 1 traich'ke; 2 trīch'ke.
Treves, 1 trīvz; 2 trēvg.
Trip'o-li, 1 trip'o-lɪ; 2 trip'o-li.
Tro'as, 1 trō'as; 2 trō'as.
Trond'hjem, 1 tron'yem; 2 trôn'yĕm. [2 tro-fō'nɪ-ŭs.
Tro-pho'ni-us, 1 tro-fō'nɪ-us;
Trotz'ky, 1 trots'kɪ; 2 trôts'kỵ.
Tro'va-to're, 1 trō'va-tō'rē; 2 trō'vä-tō'rẹ.
Troyes, 1 trwä; 2 trwä.
Tsl-nan', 1 tsɪ-nän'; 2 tsĭ-nän'.
Tsing'tau', 1 tsiŋ'tau'; 2 tsiŋ'tou'.
Tü'bing-en, 1 tü'biŋ-en; 2 tü'bing-ĕn.
Tu'nis, 1 tiū'nɪs; 2 tū'nĭs.
Tu'rin, 1 tiū'rɪn; 2 tū'rĭn.
Tur'ke-stan', 1 tur'ke-stän'; 2 tụr'kĕ-stän'.
Tus'cu-lum, 1 tus'klu-lum; 2 tŭs'eū-lŭm.

Tyb'alt, 1 tib'əlt; 2 tўb'alt.
Ty'burn, 1 taī'bɚn, 2 tī'burn.
Ty'deus, 1 taī'diūs or tid'ɪ-us; 2 tī'dūs or tўd'e-ŭs.
Tyr-tæ'us, 1 tər-tī'us; 2 tyr-tē'ŭs.

U

U-cal'e-gon, 1 yu-kal'ɪ-gon; 2 yu-eăl'e-gŏn.
U'ca-ya'll, 1 ū'ka-yä'll; 2 ụ'eä-yä'll.
Ulm, 1 ulm; 2 ụlm.
U-lys'ses, 1 yu-lis'īz; 2 yu-lys'ēg. [bri-a.
Um'bri-a, 1 um'brɪ-ə; 2 ŭm'-
Un-dine', 1 un-dīn' or un'dīn; 2 ŭn-dīn' or ŭn'dīn.
U'ral, 1 yū'ral; 2 yụ'ral.
U-ra'ni-a, 1 yu-rē'nɪ-ə; 2 yụ-rä'ni-a. [ra-nŭs.
U'ra-nus, 1 yū'rə-nus; 2 yụ'-
U'ri, 1 yū'rai; 2 yụ'rī.
U'ri-el, 1 yū'rɪ-el; 2 yụ'rĭ-ĕl.
Ur'su-la, 1 ūr'sɪu-lə; 2 ụr'sū-la.
U'ru-guay, 1 ū'ru-gwē or ū'ru-gwaī'; 2 ụ'ru-gwä or ụ'ru-gwī'.
U'trecht, 1 yū'trekt or (D.) ü'trent; 2 yụ'trĕct or (D.) ü'trĕnt.
Uz'bek, 1 uz'bek; 2 ŭz'bĕk.

V

Va'len'ciennes', 1 va'loň'-syen'; 2 vä'läň'çyĕň'.
Val'en-ti'nus, 1 val'en-tai'nus; 2 väl'ĕn-tī'nŭs.
Val'jean', 1 val'zhäň'; 2 väl'-zhäň'.
Val'pa-rai'so, 1 val'pə-raī'so or -raī'zo; 2 väl'pa-rī'so or -rī'so.
Van Dyck, 1 van daīk; 2 vän dīk.
Vaud, 1 vō; 2 vō.
Vau'dois', 1 vo'dwä'; 2 vo'-dwä'.
Ve'glia, 1 vě'lya; 2 vẹ'lyä.
Ve'il, 1 vī'yai; 2 vē'yī.
Ve-las'quez, 1 vē-läs'kēth; 2 vẹ-läs'kĕth.
Ven'e-zue'la, 1 ven'ɪ-zwī'lə; 2 vĕn'e-zwē'la.
Ve'ra Cruz, 1 vē'ra krūz; 2 vẹ'rä erụz.
Ver'dun', 1 ver'dűň'; 2 vẽr'-dűň'.
Ver'net', 1 ver'nĕ'; 2 vẽr'nę'.
Ve-ron'l-ca, 1 vɪ-rən'ɪ-kə; 2 ve-rŏn'i-ca.

1: artistic, ûrt; fat, fâre; fast; get, prêy; hĭt, police; obey, gō; nȯt, ôr; full, rūle; but, bûrn.
2: ärt, āpe, făt, fâre, fȧst, whạt, ạll; mē, gĕt, prẹy, fērn; hĭt, īce; ĭ = ē; ĩ = ē; gō, nŏt, ôr, wȯn.

Ver-sailles′, 1 vər-sēlz′; 2 ver-säls′.

Ver″vlers′, 1 ver′vyē′; 2 vėr′vyē′.

Vesle, 1 vēl; 2 veḷ.

Vi-en′na, 1 vi-en′ə; 2 vi-ën′a.

Vin′ci, 1 vin′chī; 2 vin′chī.

Vis′tu-la, 1 vis′chu-[or -tiu-]-lə; 2 vis′chu-[or -tū-]la. [tär′.

Vol″taire′, 1 vōl′tār′; 2 vōl′-

Vosges, 1 vōz; 2 vōzh.

W

Wa′bash, 1 wō′baʃh; 2 wą′-bäsh.

Wag′ner, 1 vɑg′nər or (Eng.) wag′nər; 2 väg′nėr or (Eng.) wäg′ner. [wɑ-lä′ei-a.

Wai-la′chi-a, 1 we-lē′kı-ə; 2

War′wick, 1 wor′ık; 2 wąr′ık.

Wei′mar, 1 vai′mar; 2 vī′mär.

Wet′ter-horn, 1 vet′ər-hōrn; 2 vėt′er-hōrn.

Wemyss, 1 wīmz; 2 wēmṣ.

Wey′mouth, 1 wē′məth; 2 wä′muth.

White′field, 1 hwit′fīld; 2 hwit′fēld. [vēs-bä′dën.

Wies-ba′den, 1 vīs-bä′den; 2

Wilkes′-bar″re, 1 wilks′-bar″ı; 2 wilks′-bär′e.

Will′kie, 1 wil′ke; 2 wil′kí.

Win″ne-pe-sau′kee, 1 win′ı-pı-sô′kī; 2 win′e-pe-są′kē.

Wo″evre′, 1 wo′ē′vr; 2 wo′-e′vr.

Worces′ter, 1 wus′tər; 2 wǫs′ter.

Wurt′tem-berg, 1 vür′tem-berʜ; 2 vür′tĕm-bėrʜ.

Wurz′burg, 1 vürts′burʜ; 2 vürts′bųrʜ.

Wy-o′ming, 1 wɑi-ō′mıŋ or wɑi′o-miŋ; 2 wī-ō′ming or wī′o-ming.

X

Xan′thus, 1 zan′ɟʰus; 2 zăn′thüs. [zăn-tip′e.

Xan-tip′pe, 1 zan-tip′ı; 2

Xav′i-er, 1 zav′ı-ər or (Sp.) ha-vyer′; 2 zăv′i-er or (Sp.) hä-vyēr′.

Xe-noph′a-nes, 1 zı-nof′ə-nīz; 2 ze-nŏf′a-nēş.

Xen′o-phon, 1 zen′o-fən; 2 zĕn′o-fŏn.

Xi-me′na, 1 hī-mē′na; 2 hī-me′nä. [ĝu′.

Xin-gu′, 1 ʃhın-gū′; 2 shǐn-

Y

Ya″chow-fu′, 1 yä′chɑu-fū′; 2 yä′chow-fų′. [tsę.

Yang′tze, 1 yāŋ′tsē; 2 yäng′-

Yap, 1 yap; 2 yăp.

Yen″i-se′i, 1 yen′ı-sē′ı; 2 yĕn′i-sē′ī.

Yo″ko-ha′ma, 1 yō′ko-hä′-mɑ; 2 yō′ko-hä′mä.

Yo-sem′i-te, 1 yo-sem′ı-tı; 2 yo-sĕm′i-tē.

Y′pres, 1 ī′pr; 2 ÿ′pr.

Yu-an′ Shi Kai, 1 yu-än′ ʃhī kɑi; 2 yu-än′ shī kī.

Yu″ca-tan′, 1 yū′kə-tan′; 2 yų′ca-tän′.

Yu′go-Sla′vi-a, 1 yū′go-slä′-vı-ə; 2 yų′ĝo-slä′vi-a.

Yu′kon, 1 yū′kɒn; 2 yy′kŏn.

Z

Za″ca-te′cas, 1 sɑ″kɑ-tē′kas; 2 sä″eä-te′eäs.

Zac-chæ′us, 1 za-kī′us or zak′ı-us; 2 ză-cē′ŭs or zăc′e-ŭs.

Zam-be′zi, 1 zam-bē′zi or zam-bī′zı; 2 zäm-be′zī or zäm-bē′zi.

Zan′zi-bar, 1 zan′zı-bār; 2 zän′zi-bär.

Ze′no, 1 zī′no; 2 zē′no.

Zeus, 1 ziūs; 2 zūs.

Zeux′is, 1 ziūks′ıs; 2 zūks′ıs.

Zip′por, 1 zip′er; 2 zip′ŏr. [zip-po′rah‡.

Zos′i-mus, 1 zɒs′ı-mus; 2 zŏs′i-mŭs.

Zul′der Zee, 1 zɑi′dər zı or (D.) zœi′dər zē; 2 zī′der zē or (D.) zōi′der zę.

Zu′rich, 1 zū′rik; 2 zy′rīe.

Zwing′li, 1 tsving′lī; 2 tsving′lī.

1: ə = final; ı = habit; ɑisle; ɑu = out; ǫil; iū = feud; ɟhin; go; ŋ = sing: ɟhin, this.
2: wǫlf, dǫ; bŏŏk, bōōt; fųll, rųle, cūre, bŭt, bûrn; ŏil, bŏy; ĝo, ĝem; iŋk; thin, this.

FOREIGN WORDS, PHRASES, ETC., CURRENT IN ENGLISH LITERATURE

ab

ab. [L.] From; by.

à bas. [F.] Down with: opposed to *vive.*

ab extra. [L.] From without.— **ab initio.** From the beginning.— **ab intra.** From within.   [cheap.

à bon marché. [F.] At a good bargain;

ab origine. [L.] From the origin.— **ab ovo.** From the egg; from the origin.— **ab ovo usque ad mala.** From egg to apples (as in Roman banquets); from beginning to end of a feast.

absit invidia. [L.] No offense intended.

absque. [L.] Without.— **absque hoc.** Without this.   [all.

ab uno disce omnes. [L.] From one learn

ab urbe condita. [L.] From the building of the city (Rome).

à cheval. [F.] On horseback.

à compte. [F.] On account.

ad. [L.] To; toward; with regard to.— **ad arbitrium.** At will.— **ad astra.** To the stars (to exalted place or state).— **ad astra per aspera.** To the stars through bolts and bars. (Motto of Kansas.) — **ad captandum vulgus.** To catch the crowd.

à demi. [F.] Half (*i. e.,* to the extent of one-half); by halves (*i. e.,* imperfectly).

à dessein. [F.] On purpose.

ad finem. [L.] To the end.— **ad hoc.** With respect to this.— **ad hominem.** To the (individual) man.— **ad infinitum.** To an infinite degree or extent; endlessly.— **ad interim.** In the mean time; during the interval.

à discrétion. [F.] At discretion; without limit.

ad libitum. [L.] At will; as much as one pleases. — **ad nauseam.** To the point of disgust or revulsion.— **ad patres.** [Gathered] to his fathers (*i. e.,* dead).— **ad rem.** To the thing; to the point; direct.

à droite. [F.] To the right; to the right hand.

ad unguem. [L.] To the finger-nail; to a nicety. — **ad valorem.** According to the value, as certain customs duties.

æquo animo. [L.] With equal [tranquil] mind.   [bronze.

ære perennius. [L.] More enduring than

affaire d'honneur. [F.] Affair of honor.

affaire du cœur. [F.] Affair of the heart.

à fin. [F.] Incorrectly written for A LA FIN.

a fortiori. [L.] By a stronger reason; all the more.

Agnus Dei. [L.] The Lamb of God.

à la. [F.] To the; at the; in the, etc.: used in phrases.— **à la bonne heure.** Good; excellent.— **à la fin.** To or at the end; finally. — **à la française.** In the French style.— **à la**

aut Cæsar aut nihil

mode. According to the mode; in the fashion.

allez-vous-en! [F.] Go! off with your begone!

allons! [F.] Let us go! come!

à l'outrance. [F.] To the uttermost; erroneous for À OUTRANCE.

alter ego. [L.] My other self; bosom friend.

alter idem. [L.] Another self.

amende honorable. [F.] Public reparation or apology.

amor patriæ. [L.] Love of country.

amour propre. [F.] Self-love; self-esteem

ancien régime. [F.] Ancient order of things.

anno ætatis suæ. [L.] In the year of his or her] age.— **anno Domini (A. D.).** In the year of our Lord; in the Christian era. — **anno mundi.** In the year of the world. — **anno urbis conditæ (A. U. C.).** In [such or such a] year [reckoned] from the founding of the city (*i. e.,* Rome).

à outrance. [F.] To the bitter end.

à peu près. [F.] Nearly.

a posteriori. [L.] From that which follows; from effect to cause.

appartement. [F.] Two or more rooms *en suite;* a "flat."

a priori. [L.] From what is before; from cause to effect.

à propos. [F.] Suited to time, place, or occasion; pertinent; appropriate.— **à propos de rien.** Apropos of nothing; without pertinency.

arc en ciel. [F.] Rainbow.

argumentum ad hominem. [L.] An argument to the man [addressed] (*i. e.,* founded on the principles or practises of an opponent himself).   [revoir.

a rivederci. [It.] Until we meet again; au

arrectis auribus. [L.] With erect ears; attentively.

ars est celare artem. [L.] Art consists in hiding art.— **ars longa, vita brevis.** Art is long, life is short.

à tout prix. [F.] At any price; whatever the cost.

au contraire. [F.] On the contrary.

audi alteram partem. [L.] Hear the other side.

au fait. [F.] To the act or fact; skilled; expert.— **au fond.** At bottom; fundamentally.— **au revoir.** Till we meet again; good-by.   [good-by.

auf Wiedersehen. [G.] Till we meet again;

auri sacra fames. [L.] Accursed greed of gold.   [or nothing.

aut Cæsar aut nihil. [L.] Either Cæsar

au troisième. [F.] On the third floor; in the third story. [quer or to die.

aut vincere aut mori. [L.] Either to conquer or to die.

aux armes! [F.] To arms!

avant-coureur. [F.] Forerunner.

avant propos. [F.] Preliminary matter; preface.

avec plaisir. [F.] With pleasure.

a vinculo matrimonii. [L.] From the marriage bond.

à votre santé [F.]; **a vuestra salud** [Sp.]. To your health.

B

bas-bleu. [F.] A literary woman; bluestocking.

beau monde. [F.] The fashionable world.

beneplacito. [L.] By [your] leave.

ben trovato. [It.] Well invented.

bête noire. [F.] Black beast; object of abhorrence.

bienvenu. [F.] Welcome.

bis dat qui cito dat. [L.] He gives twice who gives promptly.

bon ami. [F.] Good friend.— **bon gré, mal gré.** With good grace or with ill grace; willynilly.— **bon jour.** Good day; good morning.

bonne foi. [F.] Good faith.

bon soir. [F.] Good evening.— **bon voyage.** Prosperous voyage to you! [bolt.

brutum fulmen. [L.] Ineffectual thunder-**buona mano.** [It.] Small gratuity.

C

caput mortuum. [L.] A worthless residue, as of distillation.

carpe diem. [L.] Enjoy the present moment. [condition.

causa sine quâ non. [L.] Indispensable

cause célèbre. [F.] Celebrated case.

caveat emptor. [L.] Let the buyer beware.

cave canem. [L.] Beware of the dog.

cela va sans dire. [F.] That is a matter of course.

ce n'est que le premier pas qui coûte. [F.] It is only the first step that costs.

c'est à dire. [F.] That is to say.— **c'est magnifique.** That is magnificent.— **c'est une autre chose.** That is a different affair.

ceteris paribus. [L.] Other things being equal. [his taste.

chacun à son goût. [F.] Every man to

chapeaux bas! [F.] Hats off!

château en Espagne. [F.] A castle in Spain; a castle in the air.

chef de cuisine (or simply **chef**). [F.] Male head cook.

chemin de fer. [F.] Railway.

cher ami (*masc.*), **chère amie** (*fem.*). [F.] Dear friend.

chevalier d'industrie. [F.] Literally, knight of industry; a swindler; sharper.

cogito, ergo sum. [L.] I think, therefore I am: a famous first principle of Descartes.

coiffeur. [F.] Hair-dresser.

comme il faut. [F.] As it should be.

compagnon de voyage. [F.] Traveling companion. [clergy.

concio ad clerum. [L.] Discourse to the

confer (cf.). [L.] Compare.

contra bonos mores. [L.] Against good morals. [guard-room.

corps de garde. [F.] A body of guards; a

corpus. [L.] Body.— **C. Christi.** Body of Christ.— **c. delicti.** The essential fact of the commission of a crime.

coup. [F.] Stroke.— **c. de maitre.** Masterstroke.— **c. de pied.** A kick.— **c. de soleil.** Sunstroke.

crème de la crème. [F.] The very best.

cui bono? [L.] For whose advantage? to what end? of what use?

cum grano salis. [L.] With a grain of salt: with some allowance.

currente calamo. [L.] With running pen; offhand.

D

d'accord. [F.] Agreed; in tune.

das heisst (d. h.). [G.] That is.

de bonne grâce. [F.] With good grace; cheerfully.

de gustibus non est disputandum. [L.] There is no disputing about tastes.

déjeuner à la fourchette. [F.] Breakfast with the fork (*i. e.*, meat breakfast).

delenda est Carthago. [L.] Carthage must be destroyed.

de mortuis nil nisi bonum. [L.] Of the dead [say] nothing but good.

Deo favente. [L.] God favoring.— **Deo juvante.** [L.] God helping.— **Deo volente.** God willing.

de profundis. [L.] Out of the depths.

de retour. [F.] Back again; returned.— **de rigueur.** Imperative; not to be dispensed with.

dernier ressort. [F.] A last resource.

desunt cetera. [L.] The remainder is wanting.

de trop. [F.] Too much; too many; out of place; not wanted.

deus ex machinâ. [L.] A god [let down] from a machine: as in ancient theaters.

Deus vobiscum! [L.] God be with you!

dies iræ, dies illa. [L.] Day of wrath, that [dreadful] day: first words of ancient Latin hymn on the Day of Judgment.

Dieu et mon droit. [F.] God and my right.

dignus vindice nodus. [L.] A knot worthy of being loosed by such hands.

disjecta membra. [L.] Scattered parts.

distingué. [F.] Distinguished.

distrait. [F.] Absent-minded.

dit. [F.] Called (*e. g.*, "Ant. Allegri dit Il Correggio").

divide et impera. [L.] Divide and govern.

dolce far niente. [It.] Sweet doing nothing; delightful idleness.

Dominus vobiscum. [L.] The Lord be with you.

double entente. [F.] Double meaning; equivocal sense.

drap d'or. [F.] Cloth of gold.

ducit amor patriæ. [L.] Love of country leads [me].

dulce est desipere in loco. [L.] It is delightful to unbend upon occasion.— **dulce et decorum est pro patriâ mori.** Sweet and seemly is it to die for one's fatherland.

dum vivimus, vivamus. [L.] While we live, let us live.

E

eau-de-vie. [F.] Water of life; brandy.

ecce. [L.] Behold.— **ecce homo!** Behold the man!— **ecce signum!** Behold the sign! here is the proof.

ecco. [It.] Here is [or are]; there is [or are]; look here; look there; see.

edition de luxe. [F.] An elaborate and costly edition.

editio princeps. [L.] First edition.

égalité. [F.] Equality.

en. [F.] In; into; within; like; as; by means of.— **en arrière.** In the rear; behind.— **en avant.** Forward; onward.— **en déshabillé.** In undress.— **en effet.** In effect; virtually; substantially.— **en famille.** In the family; at home.

enfant terrible. Terrible child.

en grande tenue. [F.] In full dress.— **en masse.** In a body.— **en passant.** In passing; by the way.— **en rapport.** In sympathetic relation.— **en règle.** According to rule; in due order.— **en route.** On the road; on the way.— **en suite.** In a series or set.

entre nous. [F.] Between ourselves; confidentially.

e pluribus unum. [L.] Out of many, one. (Motto of the United States.)

errare humanum est. [L.] To err is human.

est modus in rebus. [L.] There is a limit in things.

esto perpetua. [L.] May it [or mayst thou] last forever.

et sequentia (et seq.). [L.] And what follows.— **et tu, Brute!** And *thou*, Brutus! (Cæsar's exclamation on seeing his friend Brutus among his assassins.)

eureka! [Gr.] I have found it! (Exclamation attributed to Archimedes.)

ex cathedrâ. [L.] Officially, or with authority.

excelsior. [L.] Higher.

exceptio probat regulam. [L.] The exception proves the rule.

exceptis excipiendis. [L.] The proper exceptions having been made.

ex dono. [L.] By the gift.

exegi monumentum ære perennius. [L.] I have reared a monument more enduring than bronze.

ex necessitate rei. [L.] From the necessity of the case.— **ex nihilo nihil fit.** Out of nothing nothing is made.

experto credite. [L.] Believe one who speaks from experience.

ex uno disce omnes. [L.] See AB UNO, etc.

F

facilis descensus Averni. [L.] Easy is the descent to Avernus (*i. e.*, to the lower world).

facta, non verba. [L.] Deeds, not words.

factum est. [L.] It is done.

fait accompli. [F.] An accomplished fact; a thing already done.

falsus in uno, falsus in omnibus. [L.] False in one point, false in all.

Fata obstant. [L.] The Fates oppose.

femme. [F.] Woman; wife.— **f. de chambre.** A chambermaid; lady's-maid.— **f. de charge.** Housekeeper.

fervet opus. [L.] The work glows (*i. e.*, goes on actively).

festina lente. [L.] Make haste slowly.

fête champêtre. [F.] An open-air or rural festival. [to express public joy.

feu de joie. [F.] A bonfire or firing of guns

fiat justitia, ruat cœlum. [L.] Let justice be done, tho the heavens fall.

fidus Achates. [L.] Faithful Achates; trusty friend. [of the crime.

flagrante delicto. [L.] In the commission

functus officio. [L.] Having fulfilled his office; out of office.

G

garde du corps. [F.] Body-guard.

gens. [F.] People; race.— **g. d'affaires.** Business men.

gloria. [L.] Glory: a title of certain doxologies beginning with this word, as the **Gloria in Excelsis** [Deo], "Glory to God in the highest," and the **Gloria Patri**, "Glory be to the Father."

gnothi seauton. [Gr.] Know thyself.

grande parure or **toilette.** [F.] Full dress.

H

hac lege. [L.] With this law; under this condition.

hic et ubique. [L.] Here and everywhere.

hinc illæ lacrumæ or **lacrimæ.** [L.] Hence those tears.

hoc signo vinces. See IN HOC, etc.

hoc tempore. [L.] At this time.

hoi polloi. [Gr.] The masses; the herd.

homme d'affaires. [F.] Business man.

homme de lettres. [F.] Man of letters; literary man.

homme d'esprit. [F.] Man of intellect; wit.

honi soit qui mal y pense. [F.] Evil be to him who evil thinks. (Motto of Order of the Garter.)

honores mutant mores. [L.] Honors change (men's) manners.

horribile dictu. [L.] Horrible to be told.

hors de combat. [F.] Out of the struggle; disabled. [petition.

hors de concours. [F.] Out of the com-

hortus siccus. [L.] Literally, a dry garden; a herbarium.

hôtel de ville. See HOTEL, in vocabulary.

humanum est errare. [L.] To err is human.

I

ich dien. [G.] I serve. (Motto of the Prince of Wales.) [here.

ici on parle français. [F.] French is spoken

id est. [L.] That is: abbreviated *i. e.*— **id genus omne.** All that class; all of that sort.

imperium in imperio. [L.] Empire within empire; realm within realm.

in. [L.] In.— **in æternum.** Forever.— **in armis.** In arms.— **in articulo mortis.** At the point of death.— **in camerâ.** In secret.— **in flagrante delicto.** In the very act of committing the crime.— **in foro conscientiæ.** In the forum of conscience.

infra dignitatem. [L.] Beneath one's dignity.

in hoc signo vinces. [L.] By this sign thou wilt conquer. (Motto of Constantine.)— **in limine.** On the threshold.— **in memoriam.** In memory [of]; as a memorial [to]. — **in nomine Domini.** In the name of the Lord.— **in nubibus.** In the clouds; not clear.— **in nuce.** In a nutshell.— **in omnia paratus.** Prepared for all things.— **in pace.** In peace.— **in perpetuum.** Forever.— **in præsenti.** At the present time.— **in propriâ personâ.** In one's own person; in person.— **in secula seculorum.** To ages of ages.

inter alia. [L.] Among other things.

in terrorem. [L.] By way of intimidation or warning.

inter se. [L.] Between [or among] themselves.

in totidem verbis. [L.] In so many words. — **in transitu.** In transit; during transmission.— **in vino veritas.** In wine [there is] truth (*i. e.,* intoxication makes one communicative).

invita Minerva. [L.] Minerva being unwilling (*i. e.,* without genius or inspiration).

iterum. [L.] Again.

J

je ne sais quoi. [F.] I know not what.

je suis prêt. [F.] I am ready.

jet d'eau. [F.] Jet of water; fountain.

jeu. [F.] Play; diversion.— **jeu de mots.** Play on words.

jeunesse dorée. [F.] Gilded youth; rich young men.

jour de fête. [F.] A fête=day; a festival.

jubilate Deo. [L.] Rejoice in God.

Juppiter (Jupiter) tonans. [L.] Jupiter Thunderer.

juste milieu. [F.] Golden mean.

K

Kulturkampf der Menschheit. [G.] Culture=conflict of humanity.

L

labor omnia vincit. [L.] Labor conquers all things.

læsa majestas. [L.] Lese=majesty; treason.

laisser= (or laissez=) faire. [F.] Let alone.

laissez=nous faire. Let us alone; let us be.

lapsus linguæ. [L.] A slip of the tongue.

lares et penates. [L.] Household gods.

laus Deo. [L.] Praise be to God.

le pas. [F.] The step; precedence.

le roi le veut. [F.] The king wills it.— **le roi s'avisera.** The king will deliberate.

les absents ont toujours tort. [F.] The absent are always in the wrong.

le tout ensemble. [F.] The whole taken together.

lex non scripta. [L.] Unwritten law; the common law.

lex scripta. [L.] Written or statute law.

lex talionis. [L.] Law of retaliation.

l'homme propose, et Dieu dispose. [F.] Man proposes, and God disposes.

lite pendente. [L.] During the trial.

longe absit. [L.] Far be it.

longo intervallo. [L.] With a long interval.

lucus a non lucendo. [L.] Something whose properties do not correspond to its name: alluding to an absurd derivation of *lucus* (a grove) from *luceo* (be bright).

M

ma chère. [F.] My dear (feminine).

macte novâ virtute. [L.] Go on in fresh deeds of valor: often *macte virtute,* meaning "Go on in virtue."

ma foi. [F.] My faith; upon my faith.

magna est veritas, et prævalet. [L.] Great is truth, and it prevails. (*Prævalebit* "will prevail," a form frequently used, is inaccurate.)

magnum opus. [L.] The chief work of an author.

maître d'hôtel. [F.] A house=steward.

mal. [F.] Evil; disease; ailment.— **mal de dents.** Toothache.— **mal de mer.** Seasickness.— **mal de tête.** Headache.

malgré nous. [F.] In spite of us.

malum in se. [L.] A thing evil in itself.

mania a potu. [L.] Delirium tremens.

mare clausum. [L.] A closed sea.

me judice. [L.] In my judgment.

memento mori. [L.] Remember that you must die.

mens sana in corpore sano. [L.] A sound mind in a sound body.

meum et tuum. [L.] Mine and thine.

mirabile dictu. [L.] Wonderful to be told.

mirabile visu. [L.] Wonderful to be seen.

misericordia Domini inter pontem et fontem. [L.] 'Twixt bridge and wave the Lord may save.

modus. [L.] Mode; manner.— **modus operandi.** A mode of operating.— **modus vivendi.** A mode of living; temporary arrangement.

mon ami. [F.] My friend.

mon cher. [F.] My dear (masculine).

mutatis mutandis. [L.] The necessary changes having been made.

mutato nomine. [L.] The name being changed.

N

necessitas non habet legem. [L.] Necessity has no law.

nemine contradicente (nem. con.). [L.] No one speaking in opposition.

nemo me impune lacessit. [L.] No one attacks me with impunity.

nil admirari. [L.] To wonder at nothing.

nil desperandum. [L.] Nothing to be despaired of; never despair.

n'importe. [F.] It does not signify; no matter.

nitor in adversum. [L.] I struggle against adverse circumstances.

noli me tangere. [L.] Touch me not.

nom de guerre. [F.] Literally, a war-name; a pseudonym.— **nom de plume.** Literally, a pen-name; a pseudonym.

non est. [L.] It is not; it is wanting.— **non est inventus.** He has not been found.— **non libet.** It does not please me.— **non passibus æquis.** Not with equal (*i. e.*, with shorter) steps.   [notice.

nota bene (N. B.). [L.] Note well; take notice.

nous verrons. [F.] We shall see.

novus homo. [L.] A new man; upstart; parvenu.

nunc aut nunquam. [L.] Now or never.

O

obiit (ob.). [L.] He [she] died.

obiter dictum. [L.] A remark in passing.

obsta principiis. [L.] See PRINCIPIIS OBSTA (which gives the true order).

omnia vincit amor. [L.] Love conquers all things.

onus probandi. [L.] The burden of proof.

ora pro nobis. [L.] Pray for us.

ore rotundo. [L.] With full utterance.

O tempora! O mores! [L.] O the times! O the manners!

otium cum dignitate. [L.] Leisure with dignity.

P

pallida mors. [L.] Pale death.

par. [F.] By; out of; in.— **par accès.** By fits and starts.— **par accident.** By accident.— **par accord.** By agreement.— **par exemple.** For example.

pâté de foies gras. [F.] A pie of fat goose-livers.

pater patriæ. [L.] Father of his country.

pax vobiscum! [L.] Peace be with you!

peccavi. [L.] I have sinned.

pendente lite. [L.] Pending or during suit.   [sanctuary.

penetralia. [L.] The inmost parts; secrecy;

per diem. [L.] By the day; daily.

per fas et nefas. [L.] Through right and wrong.

petitio principii. [L.] A begging of the question.

peu à peu. [F.] Little by little.

peu de chose. [F.] A small matter.

pinxit. [L.] He [or she] painted [it].

pis aller. [F.] Last shift; end of resources.

poëta nascitur, non fit. [L.] The poet is born, not made.

poste restante. [F.] To remain [at the post-office] until called for; the general delivery.   [take leave.

pour prendre congé (P. P. C.). [F.] To

prima facie. [L.] At first view; as far as first appears.   [nings.

principiis obsta. [L.] Withstand begin-

pro aris et focis. [L.] For altars and for firesides.— **pro et con.** For and against.

profanum vulgus. [L.] The profane herd.

pro patriâ. [L.] For native land.— **pro tanto.** For so much; to that extent.— **pro tempore (pro tem.).** For the time being; temporary.

Q

quantum sufficit. [L.] As much as suffices; enough.

quid pro quo. [L.] Something for something; an equivalent.

quid rides? [L.] Why do you laugh?

quien sabe? [Sp.] Who knows? (*i. e.*, I do not know, or do not care to say.)

qui facit per alium facit per se. [L.] He who acts through another acts through himself.

qui va là? [F.] Who goes there?

quoad hoc. [L.] To this extent; so far.

quod erat demonstrandum (Q. E. D.). [L.] Which was to be proved.

quot homines, tot sententiæ. [L.] Minds as many as the men.

R

rara avis. [L.] Rare bird; prodigy.

reductio ad absurdum. [L.] Reduction to an absurdity; proof of a proposition by showing the absurdity of its contradictory.

rentes. [F.] Stocks: funds bearing interest.

répondez s'il vous plait (R. S. V. P.). [F.] Reply, if you please.

requiescat in pace. [L.] May he [she] rest in peace!

res angusta domi. [L.] Straitened circumstances.— **res gesta.** A thing done; transaction.— **res gestæ** (*pl.*). All the essential circumstances.

respublica. [L.] The commonwealth.

resurgam. [L.] I shall rise again.

revenons à nos moutons. [F.] Let us return to our sheep (*i. e.*, to our subject).

ruse de guerre. [F.] A stratagem of war.

rus in urbe. [L.] Country in city.

S

sans. [F.] Without.— **s. cérémonie.** Without ceremony.— **s. doute.** Without doubt.— **s. façon.** Informally.— **s. pareil.** Without equal.— **s. peur et s. reproche.** Without fear and without reproach.— **s. souci.** Without care.

sauve qui peut. [F.] Let him save himself who can (indicating an utter disorganized rout).

savoir faire. [F.] The knowing how to do; address; tact.— **savoir vivre.** The knowing how to live; good breeding.

scripsit. [L.] He [or she] wrote [it].

sculpsit. [L.] He [or she] sculptured [it].

secundum naturam. [L.] According to nature.— **secundum ordinem.** In order.

semper. [L.] Always.— **s. eadem.** [*fem.*] Always the same.— **s. felix.** Always fortunate.— **s. idem.** [*masc.*] Always the same. — **s. paratus.** Always prepared.

sic itur ad astra. [L.] Thus one may rise to the stars (*i. e.,* to immortal fame).— **sic passim.** Thus everywhere.— **sic semper tyrannis.** Thus ever to tyrants.— **sic transit gloria mundi.** Thus passes away the glory of the world.

similia similibus curantur. [L.] Like [ailments] are cured by like [remedies]. (Motto of homeopathy in medicine.)

simplex munditiis. [L.] Plain in neatness; of simple elegance.

sine. [L.] Without.— **s. curâ.** Without charge; without care.— **s. die.** Without a day being appointed; indefinitely.— **s. morâ.** Without delay.— **s. odio.** Without hatred.

siste, viator! [L.] Stop, traveler!

si vis pacem, para bellum. [L.] If you wish peace, prepare for war.

sponte suâ. [L.] Of one's own accord.

statu quo ante bellum. [L.] As it was before the war.

sauviter in modo, fortiter in re. [L.] Gently in the manner, firmly in the act.

sui generis. [L.] Forming a kind by itself; unique. [chief good.

summum bonum. [L.] The supreme good;

sursum corda! [L.] Lift up your hearts!

sutor ne supra crepidam (judicaret). [L.] "The cobbler should stick to his last." *Ultra* is sometimes less correctly written for *supra.*

suum cuique. [L.] To each one his own.

T

tabula rasa. [L.] A blank tablet.

tædium vitæ. [L.] Weariness of life.

tant mieux. [F.] So much the better.— **tant pis.** So much the worse.

tempora mutantur, et nos mutamur in illis. [L.] Times are changed, and we are changed in them.

tempus, edax rerum. [L.] Time, consumer of things.

tempus fugit. [L.] Time flies.

tertium quid. [L.] A third something; a conjectural medium between two opposites; hence, a nondescript.

tiers état. [F.] The third estate; the common people.

timeo Danaos et dona ferentes. [L.] I fear the Greeks, even when they bring gifts.

totidem verbis. [L.] In so many words.

toto cælo. [L.] By the whole heaven; very far apart.

tout-à-fait. [F.] Entirely.

tu quoque. [L.] You too; you're another.

U

ubique. [L.] Everywhere.

ubi supra. [L.] Where above mentioned.

Ultima Thule. [L.] Farthest Thule, utmost bound.

unâ voce. [L.] With one voice.

und so welter (u. s. w.). [G.] And so forth.

usque ad nauseam. [L.] To the point of nausea.

usus loquendi. [L.] Usage in speaking.

ut infra. [L.] As below.

ut supra. [L.] As above.

V

vade in pace. [L.] Go in peace.— **vade mecum.** Go with me; constant companion.

væ victis. [L.] Wo to the vanquished.

vale. [L.] Farewell.

valet de chambre. [F.] A man servant; body-servant.

variæ lectiones. [L.] Various readings.

variorum notæ. [L.] Notes from various authors. [quered.

veni, vidi, vici. [L.] I came, I saw, I con-

verbatim et literatim. [L.] Word for word and letter for letter.

verbum sat sapienti. [L.] "A word to the wise is sufficient."

vestigia. [L.] Vestiges; footsteps; traces.

vestigia nulla retrorsum. [L.] No backward steps.

vi et armis. [L.] By force and arms.

vinculum matrimonii. [L.] The bond of matrimony.

vis a tergo. [L.] Force (or compulsion) from behind. [public!

vivat respublica! [L.] Long live the re-

vivat rex! [L.] Long live the king!

vive! [F.] Long live!— **v. la république!** Long live the republic!— **v. l'empereur!** Long live the emperor!— **v. le roi!** Long live the king!

voilà! [F.] There! there it is! see there!

voilà tout. [F.] There, that is all; that is the whole of it.

volente Deo. [L.] God willing.

vox, et præterea nihil. [L.] A voice, and nothing more.— **vox populi, vox Dei.** The voice of the people is the voice of God.

vulgo. [L.] Commonly.

W

Weltliteratur. [G.] World-literature.

wie gewonnen, so zerronnen. [G.] As won, so flown; "light come, light go."

Y

y á Roma por todo. [Sp.] And to Rome for everything.

yeux doux. [F.] Sweet eyes; soft glances.

Z

Zeitgeist. [G.] The spirit of the times.

zum Beispiel (z. B.). [G.] For example.

SYMBOLIC FLOWERS AND GEMS

Flowers and gems have from earliest times been invested with symbolic expression, and the interpretations of their supposed characteristics constitute a sentimental philology amusing if not instructive, as shown in the partial list here given. In some cases the different sentiments given to the same flower are not at all compatible.

FLOWERS

Abutilon. Meditation.
Acacia. Friendship; Platonic love.
Aconite, Crowfoot. False security.
Adder's-tongue. Jealousy.
Allspice. Compassion.
Almond, Common. Indiscretion.
Almond, Flowering. Hope.
Aloe. Grief; misplaced devotion.
Alyssum, Sweet. Exemplary modesty.
Amaranth. Immortality.
Amaryllis. Beautiful, but timid; pride.
Ambrosia. Love returned.
Anemone. Fading hope.
Apple-blossom. Preference.
Arbor-vitæ. I never change; live for me.
Arbor-vitæ, American. Immortality.
Arbutus. You only do I love.
Ash. Prudence; with me you are safe.
Aspen. Excess of sensibility; fear.
Aster, China. Afterthoughts.
Azalea. Temperance; moderation.
Bachelor's-button. Celibacy; hope in love.
Balm. Sympathy; social intercourse.
Barberry. Sharpness of temper.
Basil, Sweet. Good wishes.
Bayberry. Instruction; discipline.
Bay-leaf. I change but in death.
Bee-orchis. Industry; error.
Bellflower. Constancy; gratitude.
Bellwort. Hopelessness.
Bittersweet. Truth.
Bluebell. Sorrowful regret; constancy.
Bramble. Lowliness; remorse.
Burdock. Importunity.
Buttercup. Riches.
Butterfly-orchis. Gaiety.
Cactus. Grandeur; warmth.
Calla-lily. Beauty; maiden modesty.
Came lia, Red. Innate worth.
Camellia, White. Perfected loveliness.
Camomile. Energy in adversity.
Candytuft. Indifference.
Canterbury-bells. Acknowledgment.
Cape jasmine. I am too happy.
Catalpa. Beware of the coquette.
Catchfly. Pretended love; snare.
Cedar. Think of me; I live but for thee.
Celandine. Joys to come.
Cherry-blossom. Spiritual beauty.
Chestnut-blossom. Do me justice.

Chrysanthemum, Chinese. Loveliness and cheerfulness.
Chrysanthemum, Red. I love.
Chrysanthemum, White. Truth.
Chrysanthemum, Yellow. Dejection.
Cinquefoil. Maternal affection.
Citron. Ill-natured beauty.
Clematis. Mental beauty.
Clematis, Evergreen. Poverty.
Clover, Four-leafed. Be mine.
Clover, Red. Industry.
Clover, White. Think of me.
Columbine. Desertion; folly; inconstancy.
Convolvulus, Great. Despondency.
Convolvulus, Pink. Worth sustained by affection.
Coreopsis. Always cheerful.
Cowslip. Winning grace; comeliness.
Crab-apple blossom. Irritability.
Cranberry. Cure for heartache.
Crocus. Gladness; abuse not.
Currant. Your frown will kill me.
Cyclamen. Diffidence.
Cypress. Despair; mourning.
Daffodil. Deceitful hope; unrequited love.
Dahlia. Elegance and dignity; forever thine.
Daisy. Innocence.
Dandelion. Love's oracle; coquetry.
Dogwood. Love undiminished by adversity; faithfulness.
Eglantine. Poetry; talent; I wound to heal.
Elder. Compassion; zealousness.
Everlasting. Always remembered.
Eyebright. Cheer up.
Fern. Fascination; magic; sincerity.
Fig. Argument; I keep my secret.
Fir. Time.
Flax. Domestic industry; fate.
Forget-me-not. True love; constancy.
Four-o'clock. Timidity.
Foxglove. Youth; insincerity.
Fuchsia. Confiding love; taste.
Gentian, Closed. Sweet be thy dreams.
Gentian, Fringed. I look to heaven.
Geranium. Gentility.
Geranium, Fish. Failure.
Geranium, Ivy. Bridal favor.
Geranium, Lemon. Unexpected meeting.
Geranium, Rose. Preference.
Geranium, Scarlet. Comforting.

Gillyflower. Bonds of affection; she is fair.
Gladiolus. Ready-armed.
Goldenrod. Encouragement; precaution.
Grape, Wild. Charity; mirth.
Grass. Submission.
Hazel. Reconciliation.
Heliotrope. Devotion; eagerness.
Hellebore. Calumny; scandal.
Hemlock. You will cause my death.
Holly. Domestic happiness; am I forgotten?
Hollyhock. Ambition; fruitfulness.
Honey-flower. Love sweet and secret.
Honeysuckle. Bonds of love.
Horse-chestnut. Luxury.
Hyacinth, Blue. Constancy.
Hyacinth, White. Modest loveliness.
Hydrangea. A boaster; heartlessness.
Iris. Message; my compliments.
Iris, German. Aflame; I burn.
Ivy. Fidelity; friendship; wedded love.
Jacob's-ladder. Come down.
Jasmine, Night-blooming. Love's vigil.
Jasmine, White. Amiability. [wear me.
Lady's-slipper. Capricious beauty; win and
Lantana. I am inflexible.
Larch. Audacity; boldness.
Larkspur, Pink. Fickleness.
Laurel. Treachery.
Laurel, Mountain-. Ambition.
Lemon. Discretion.
Lettuce. Cold-hearted.
Lichen. Dejection; refusal; solitude.
Lilac, Purple. First love; fastidiousness.
Lilac, White. Youthful innocence.
Lily-of-the-valley. Perfect purity.
Lily, White. Purity and sweetness.
Lobelia. Arrogance; malevolence.
Locust. Affection beyond the grave.
Lotus. Estranged love.
Magnolia. High-souled.
Magnolia, Swamp-. Perseverance.
Maple. Reserve; retirement.
Marigold. Cruelty in love; inquietude.
Marjoram. Blushes.
Marshmallow. Beneficence; consent.
Mignonette. Your qualities surpass your
  charms.
Mint. Let us be friends again; virtue.
Mistletoe. You are a parasite.
Mock-orange. Counterfeit.
Monk's-hood. Chivalry.
Moonflower. I but dream of love.
Morning-glory. Affectation.
Moss. Ennui.
Motherwort. Concealed love.
Mountain-ash. Prudence.
Mulberry, Black. I shall not survive you.
Mulberry, White. Wisdom.
Mullen. Take courage.
Musk-plant. Be bolder.
Mustard. I smart.
Myrtle. Love in absence. [well.
Narcissus. Egotism; you love yourself too
Nasturtium. Patriotism.
Night-blooming Cereus. Transient beauty.
Nightshade. Your thoughts are dark.
Oak. Hospitality.

Oleander. Beware.
Olive. Peace. [worthy.
Orange-blossom. You are pure and
Orchid. You are a belle; you flatter me.
Palm. Victory.
Pansy. Pleasant thoughts; think of me.
Parsley. Festivity; useful knowledge.
Passion-flower. Holy love; religious fervor.
Pea, Everlasting. Appoint a meeting.
Pea, Sweet. Departure; remember me.
Peach-blossom. I am your captive.
Pear-blossom. Not altogether lovely.
Pennyroyal. You had better go.
Peony. Anger; indignation. [by and by.
Persimmon-blossom. I shall surprize you
Petunia. You soothe me.
Phlox. Unanimity.
Pine. Pity.
Pink, Carnation. Woman's love.
Pink, Double red. Ardent love.
Pink, Mountain. Aspiration.
Pink, White. Fascination; talent.
Plum-blossom. Keep your promises.
Plum-blossom, Wild. Independence.
Poppy, Red. Consolation.
Poppy, Variegated. Flirtation.
Poppy, White. Forgetfulness.
Primrose. Believe me; youth and sadness.
Primrose, Evening. Inconstancy.
Privet. Prohibition.
Quince-blossom. Temptation.
Rhododendron. I am dangerous; beware.
Rose, Austrian. You are all that is lovely.
Rose, Bridal. Happy love.
Rose, China. Beauty always new.
Rose, Damask. Young and brilliant.
Rose, Full-blown. Engagement.
Rose, Jacqueminot. I am true. [soul.
Rose, Maréchal Niel. Yours, heart and
Rose, Moss-. Superior merit.
Rose, Wild. Charming simplicity.
Rosebud, Moss-. Confession of love.
Sage. Domestic virtues.
Salvia, Red. Untiring energy.
Scabious, Sweet. Widowhood.
Sensitive-plant. Fine sensibility.
Shamrock. Loyalty.
Shepherd's-purse. I offer you my all.
Snapdragon. Presumption; no.
Snowball. Bound; thoughts of heaven.
Snowdrop. Friendship in trouble; hope.
Sorrel, Wood-. Secret sweetness.
Star-of-Bethlehem. Atonement.
Sumac. I shall survive the change.
Sunflower, Dwarf. Adoration.
Sunflower, Large. You are splendid.
Sweet-william. Grant me one smile.
Syringa. You shall be happy yet.
Thistle. Austerity.
Thistle, Scotch. Retaliation.
Thyme. Courage.
Tiger-lily. I dare you to love me.
Trumpetflower. Fame.
Tuberose. You are perfectly lovely.
Tulip, Red. Declaration of love.
Tulip-tree blossom. Rural happiness.
Venus's fly-trap. Duplicity.

Verbena. Tender and quick emotion.
Violet, Blue. Love; faithfulness.
Violet, White. Modesty; candor.
Virginia creeper. I cling to you.
Virgin's-bower. Filial love.
Wake-robin. Ardor; zeal.

Water-lily. Purity of heart.
Wheat. Prosperity.
Wich-hazel. Mysticism; inspiration.
Wistaria. Cordial welcome.
Woodbine. Fraternal love.
Zinnia. Thoughts of absent friends.

GEMS

Agate. Health; longevity; wealth.
Amethyst. Deep and pure love; prevents intoxication.
Beryl. Happiness; everlasting youth.
Bloodstone. Courage; wisdom.
Carnelian. Prevents misfortune.
Cat's-eye. Warns of danger and trouble.
Chalcedony. Disperses melancholy.
Chrysolite. Gladdens the heart.
Diamond. Purity; preserves peace; prevents storms.
Emerald. Immortality; incorruptible; conquers sin and trial.

Garnet. Insures power, grace, and victory.
Hyacinth. Gives second sight.
Jacinth. Modesty.
Jasper. Courage; wisdom
Moonstone. Good luck.
Onyx. Conjugal felicity.
Opal. Hope; innocence; purity; ill omen.
Pearl. Purity; innocence.
Ruby. Charity; dignity; divine power.
Sapphire. Constancy; truth; virtue.
Sardonyx. Conjugal happiness.
Topaz. Friendship; happiness.
Turquoise. Prosperity; soul-cheerer.

ABBREVIATIONS AND CONTRACTIONS

AS COMMONLY USED AMONG THE ENGLISH-SPEAKING PEOPLES, WITH
THEIR MEANING AND WITH INDICATION OF THE PRE-
FERRED USAGE AS TO CAPITALIZATION

A. Academy, America, Augustus.— **a.** Adjective, acre, are, arc.— **A. B.** Same as B. A. — **ab init.** From the beginning.— **A. C.** *Ante Christum* (before Christ), Arch-chancellor, Army-Corps.— **acc.**, **acct.** Account, accountant.— **A. D.** *Anno Domini* (in the year of our Lord).— **ad fin.** *Ad finem* (at the end, to the end).— **ad inf.** *Ad infinitum* (to infinity).— **ad init.** *Ad initium* (at the beginning.)— **ad int.** *Ad interim* (in the mean time).— **ad lib.** *Ad libitum* (at pleasure).— **ad loc.** *Ad locum* (at the place).— **aero.** Aeronautics.— **æ.**, **æt.**, **ætat.**, *Ætatis* (of age, aged).— **agr.** Agriculture.— **Ala.** Alabama (official).— **Alas.** Alaska.— **A. M.** *Anno Mundi* (in the year of the world), *ante meridiem* (before noon).— **A.M.** Same as M.A. — **Am.**, **Amer.** America, American.— **Anon.** Anonymous.— **A.N.Z.A.C.** Australian and New Zealand Army Corps.— **app.** Appendix — **A.R.A.** Associate of the Royal Academy. — **Ariz.** (official), **Arl.** Arizona.— **Ark.** Arkansas (official).— **A. S.** Academy of Science, Anglo-Saxon.— **A. U. C.** *Anno Urbis Conditæ*, or *Ab Urbe Condita* (in the year of, *i. e.*, counted from, the building of the city [Rome]) — **Auth. Ver.**, **A. V.** Authorized Version.

B. A. Bachelor of Arts, British America.— **Bart.**, **Bt.** Baronet.— **B. C.** Before Christ, Board of Control, British Columbia.— **B. C. L.** Bachelor of Civil Law.— **B. D.** Bachelor of Divinity.— **B. I.** British India.— **Bib.** Bible, Biblical.— **bot.** Botanical, botanist, botany, bought.— **B. Ph.** Bachelor of Philosophy.— **B. Sc.** Bachelor of Science.

C. Cæsar, Catholic, Centigrade, Congress.— **Cal.** (official), **Calif.** California.— **Can.** Canada.— **can.** Canon, canto. **C. B.** Cape Breton, Companion of the Bath.— **C. E.** Civil engineer.— **Cent.** Central, centum (hundred), century.— **cf.** *Confer* (compare). — **cg.** Centigram (see METRIC SYSTEM).— **ch.** Chaldron, chapter, child, children.— **Chap.** Chapter.— **chem.** Chemical, chemist, chemistry.— **Chin.** China, Chinese.— **cl.** Centiliter (see METRIC SYSTEM).— **cm.** Centimeter (see METRIC SYSTEM).— **Co.** Cobalt, company, county.— **C.O.D.** Cash (or collect) on delivery.— **Colo.** (official), **Col.** Colorado.— **Con.** Consul.— **con.** Conclusion,*contra* (in opposition to),conversation.— **Conn.** Connecticut (official).— **cos.** *Consiliarius* (counselor), cosine.— **cp.** Compare—**cres.** Crescendo.— **Ct.** Connecticut (see CONN.), Count, Court.— **ct.** [CTS., *pl.*] Cent, centum. — **cwt.** Hundredweight or hundredweights.

Dak. Dakota (official).— **dal.** Decaliter (see METRIC SYSTEM).— **D. C.** *Da capo* (from the beginning), Deputy Consul, District Court, District of Columbia.— **Del.** Delaware (official).— **D. G.** *Dei gratia* (by the grace of God).— **dg.** Decigram (see METRIC SYSTEM).— **dial.** Dialect, dialectal, dialectic, dialectical.— **Dict.** Dictator, dictionary.— **dl.** Deciliter (see METRIC SYSTEM).— **dm.** Decimeter (see METRIC SYSTEM).— **do.** Ditto. —**doz.** Dozen, dozens.—**Dr.** Debtor, doctor. — **D. S.**, **D. Sc.** Doctor of Science.— **D.V.** *Deo volente* (God being willing).— **dwt.** A pennyweight.

E. Earl, east, eastern, English.— **ea.** Each.— **E. C.** Eastern Central (London postal district).— **e.g., ex. gr.** *Exempli gratia* (for the sake of example; for instance).— **E. I.**, **E. Ind.** East India, East Indies.— **E. N. E.** East-northeast.— **Eng.** England, English. — **E. S. E.** East-southeast.— **esp.**, **espec.** Especially.— **Esq.**, **Esqr.** (ESQRS., ESQS., *pl.*] Esquire.— **et al.** *Et alibi* (and elsewhere), *et alii*, *aliæ*, or *alia* (and others).— **etc.**, **&c.** *Et cetera*; and so forth.— **et seq., sq.**, or **sqq.** *Et sequentes*, *et sequentia* (and the following).— **etym.**, **etymol.** Etymological, etymologically, etymology.— **Eur.** Europe, European.

F. France, French.— **F.**, **Fah.**, **Fahr.** Fahrenheit.— **fl.** Florin, flourished.— **Fla.** Florida (official).— **Flem.** Flemish.— **fm.** Fathom.—**fo.**, **fol.** Folio.—**f. o. b.** Free on board —**F.R.S.** Fellow of the Royal Society.

G., **Ger.**, **Germ.** German, Germany.—**g.** Gram (see METRIC SYSTEM).— **Ga.** Gaelic, Gallium.— **Ga.** (official), **Geo.** Georgia.— **Gael.** Gaelic.— **G. A. R.** Grand Army of the Republic.— **GI, G.I.** Government issue (used to denote any equipment used by the U.S. Army); hence, any enlisted man.— **Gr.** Greek.

ha. Hectare (see METRIC SYSTEM).— **hhd.** Hogshead.— **H. I.** Hawaiian Islands.— **hl.** Hectoliter (see METRIC SYSTEM).— **H. M. S.** His (or Her) Majesty's Ship or Service.— **Hon.** Honorable, honorary.— **H. R. H.** His (or Her) Royal Highness.

I. Idaho (see Ida.), Island.— **i.** *Immortalis* (undying), intransitive.— **Ia.** Iowa (official). — **ib.**, **ibid.** *Ibidem* (in the same place).— **Id.** *Idem* (the same).— **Ida.** Idaho.— **i. e.** *Id est* (that is).— **I. H. S.** *Jesus Hominum Salvador* (Jesus Savior of Men).— **Ill.**, **Ills.** (official). Illinois.— **incog.** Incognito.— **Ind.** India, Indian, Indiana (official), index.

(581)

— **Ind. T.** Indian Territory (official).— **in loc.** In its place.— **inst.** Instant, institute, institution, present (month).— **I. O. U.** I owe you.— **Ir.** Ireland, iridium, Irish.— **Ire.** Ireland.— **Is., Isl.** [ISLS., *pl.*] Island, islands, isles.— **It., Ital.** Italian, Italic, Italy.

J. P. Justice of the Peace. — **jr., jun., junr.** Junior.

Kan., Kans. (official), **Kas.** Kansas.— **K. C. B.** Knight Commander of the Bath.— **K. G.** Knight of the Garter.— **kg., kilo., kilog.** Kilogram (see METRIC SYSTEM).— **kl.** Kiloliter (see METRIC SYSTEM).— **km., kilo., kilom.** Kilometer (see METRIC SYSTEM).— **Knt., Kt.** Knight.— **Ky.** (official), **Ken.** Kentucky.

l. Liter (see METRIC SYSTEM).— **L., Lat.** Latin.— **La.** Lanthanum, Louisiana (official).— **lat.** Latitude.— **lb.** [LBS., *pl.*] *Libra* (pound). — **L. C.** Lower Canada.— **l. c.** Left center, letter of credit, lower case.— **L. H. D.** Doctor of the more Humane Letters or university studies.— **lib.** *Liber* (book).— **LL.B.** Bachelor of Laws.— **LL.D.** Doctor of Laws. — **Lon., Lond.** London.— **lon., long.** Longitude.— **L. S.** Linnean Society, *locus sigilli* (the place of the seal).— **l. s.** Left side. — **L.** (or **£.**) **s. d.** *Libræ, solidi, denarii* (pounds, shillings, pence).— **LXX.** Seventy, Septuagint.

M. Marcus, Marius, Marquis, member, middle, *Mille* (one thousand), Monsieur.— **m.** Masculine, *meridian, meridies* (noon), meter (m.², square meter; m.³, cubic meter) (see METRIC SYSTEM), mile.— **M. A.** Master of Arts.— **Mass.** Massachusetts (official).— **M. C.** Master Commandant, Member of Congress, Member of Council.— **M. D.** Doctor of Medicine, Middle Dutch.— **Md.** Maryland (official).— **mdse.** Merchandise.— **M. E.** Methodist Episcopal, Middle English.— **Me.** Maine (official).— **mech.** Mechanic, mechanical, mechanics.— **Messrs., MM.** *Messieurs* (gentlemen).— **Mex.** Mexican, Mexico.— **mg.** Milligram (see METRIC SYSTEM).— **Mich.** Michaelmas, Michigan (official).— **mil.** Military.— **Minn.** Minnesota (official).— **misc.** Miscellaneous, miscellany. — **Miss.** Mission, missionary, Mississippi.— **ml.** Milliliter (see METRIC SYSTEM).— **Mlle.** Mademoiselle.— **mm.** Millimeter (see METRIC SYSTEM).— **Mme.** [MMES., *pl.*] Madame.— **Mo.** Missouri (official), Molybdenum.— **Mont.** Montana (official).— **M. P.** Member of Parliament, Methodist Protestant, Metropolitan Police.— **Mr.** Mister (Master).— **Mrs.** Missis (Mistress).— **MS.** [MSS. *pl.*] Manuscript.— **Mt.** [MTS., *pl.*] Mount, mountain.— **myth.** Mythology.

n. Name, noun, noon.— **N. A., N. Am.** North America, North-American.— **N. B.** New Brunswick, North Britain, North British, *nota bene* (note well).— **N. C.** New Church, North Carolina (official).— **N. Dak.** North Dakota (official).— **N. E.** Northeast, northeastern.— **N. E., N. Eng.** New England.— **Nebr.** (official), **Neb.** Nebraska.—

nem con. *Nemine contradicente* (no one contradicting, *i. e.,* unanimously).— **Nev.** Nevada (official).— **N. H.** New Hampshire (official).— **N. I. R. A.** National Industrial Recovery Act.— **N. J.** New Jersey (official). —**N. Mex.** (official), **N. M.** New Mexico.— **N. N. E.** North-northeast.— **N. N. W.** North-northwest.— **nol. pros.** *Nolle prosequi* (to be unwilling to prosecute).— **non. seq.** *Non sequitur* (it does not follow).— **norm.** Normal.— **N. R. A.** National Recovery Administration.— **N. S.** New School, New Series, New Side, New Style, Nova Scotia.— **N. S. W.** New South Wales.— **N. T.** New Testament, new translation.— **N. V.** New Version.— **N. W.** Northwest, northwestern. —**N. W. T.** Northwest Territory.— **N. Y.** New York (official).— **N. Z., N. Zeal.** New Zealand.

O. Ohio, oxygen.— **ob.** *Obiit* (died), *obiter* (by the way).— **O. K.** All correct. (Oll korrect.)— **Okla.** Oklahoma (official).— **Ont.** Ontario.— **Ore.** (official), **Oreg.** Oregon.— **O. S.** Old Saxon, Old Style.— **oz.** [oz. or ozs., *pl.*] Ounce.

p. Page, part, participle, past, *piano* (soft), pint, pipe, pole, population.— **p. a.** Participial adjective.— **Pa.** (official), **Penn.** Pennsylvania.— **per an.** *Per annum* (by the year).— **per ct.** Per cent.— **Pg.** Portugal, Portuguese.— **Ph. D.** Doctor of Philosophy. — **Phil. Soc., Ph. S.** American Philological Society.— **P. I.** Philippine Islands.— **pinx., pnxt., pxt.** *Pinxit* (painted [it]).— **P. J.** Justice of the Peace, Police Justice, Presiding Judge, Probate Judge.— **pkg.** [PKGS., *pl.*] Package.— **pl.** Plural, place.— **P. M.** Past Master, paymaster, peculiar meter, postmaster, *post meridiem* (afternoon).— **pm.** Premium.— **P. O.** Post-office, Province of Ontario.— **P. O. D.** Pay on delivery, Postoffice Department.— **p. p.** Past participle. — **pp.** pages, *pianissimo* (soft).— **P. P. C.** *Pour prendre congé* (to take leave).— **p. pr.** Present participle.— **P. R.** Porto Rico, Paradise Regained.— **pro tem.** *Pro tempore* (for the time being).— **prox.** *Proximo* (next [month]).— **P. S.** *Post scriptum* [PSS., *pl.*] (postscript), Privy Seal.— **psych.** Psychology.— **pwt.** Pennyweight.

q. Quasi, query, quintal (see METRIC SYSTEM). —**q. e. d.** *Quod erat demonstrandum* (which was to be demonstrated).— **Q. M.** Quartermaster.— **qr.** [QRS., *pl.*] *Quadrans* (farthing), quarter (weight or measure), quire.— **Q. S.** Quarter-sessions.— **qt.** Quantity, quart.— **qts.** Quarts.— **qu., qy.** Query. —**q. v.** *Quantum vis* (as much as you will), *quod vide* (which see).

R. Rex (king).— **R. A.** Rear-admiral, right ascension, Royal Academy, Royal Arch, Russian America.— **R. C.** Red Cross, Roman Catholic.— **R. E.** Reformed Episcopal, Right Excellent, Royal Engineers, Royal Exchange.— **Réaum.** Réaumur.— **Rec.** Recipe, record, recorded, recorder.— **rec'd, recd.** Received.— **Rec. Sec.** Recording Secretary.

— **Rect.** Rector.— **Ref.** Reformation.— **ref.** Reference, referred, reformed, reformer.— **Ref. Ch.** Reformed Church.— **refl.** Reflection, reflective, reflex, reflexive.— **Reg.** Register, Registrar.— **reg.** Registry, regular.— **Reg., Regt.** Regent, regiment.— **rel.** Relative, relatively, religion, religious, *reliquæ* (remains, relics).— **rel. pron.** Relative pronoun.— **rem.** Remark.— **Rev.** Revelation, Reverend [REVS., *pl.*].— **Rev. Ver.** Revised Version (of the Bible).— **R. H.** Royal Highness.— **R. I.** Rhode Island (official).— **R. I. P.** *Requiescat in pace* (may he [or she] rest in peace).— **Rom.** Roman.— **R. R.** Railroad.— **R. S.** Recording Secretary, Revised Statutes.— **r. s.** Right side.— **rs.** Rupees.— **R. S. S.** *Regiæ Societatis Socius* (Fellow of the Royal Society).— **R. S. V. P.** *Répondez, s'il vous plaît* (answer, if you please).— **Rt. Hon.** Right Honorable.— **Rt. Rev.** Right Reverend.— **R. V.** Revised Version (of the Bible).

S. Saxon, scribe, segno, Servius, Sextus, sign, Signor, society, south, sulfur, Sunday.— **S., Sa., Sat.** Saturday.— **S., Sab.** Sabbath.— **s.** Second, section [ss., *pl.*], series, set, shilling, singular, sinister, substantive.— **S. A.** South Africa, South America, South Australia.— **S. Am.** South America, South-American.— **Sam., Saml.** Samuel.— **Sam., Samar.** Samaritan.— **San., Sans., Sansc., Sansk., Skr., Skt.** Sanskrit.— **Sar.** Sardinia, Sardinian.— **Sax.** Saxon, Saxony.— **S. B.** South Britain, steamboat.— **Sb.** Stibium.— **S. C.** South Carolina, Supreme Court.— **s. c., s. caps., sm. caps.** Small capitals.— **Sc.** Scandium, Scotch.— **sc.** Scene, *scilicet* (namely, to wit).— **Scan., Scand.** Scandinavian.— **sch., schol.** School, *Scholium* (a note).— **sch., schr.** Schooner.— **sci.** Science, scientific.— **Sclav.** Sclavonic.— **Scot.** Scotch, Scotland, Scottish.— **scr.** Scruple.— **Script.** Scriptural, Scripture. **sculp., sculpt.** *Sculpsit* (engraved [it]), sculptor, sculptural, sculpture.— **s. d.** *Sine die* (without day).— **S. Dak.** South Dakota (official).— **S. E.** Southeast, southeastern.— **Se.** Selenium.— **Sec.** Secretary.— **sec.** Secant, second.— **sec., sect.** Section.— **sel.** Selected, selection.— **Sem.** Seminary, Semitic.— **sem.** *Semble* (it seems).— **Sen.** Senate, Senator.— **Sen., senr.** Senior.— **Sen. Doc.** Senate Document.— **sep.** Separate.— **seq.** *Sequentes, sequentia* (the following).— **S. I.** Sandwich Islands, Staten Island.— **Si.** Silicium, silicon.— **Sib.** Siberia, Siberian.— **Sic.** Sicilian, Sicily.— **S. J.** Society of Jesus.— **sq.** *Sequens, sequentes* (the following), square.— **sq.** Same as ET SEQ.— **sq. ft., sq. in.,** etc. Square foot (or feet), square inch, etc.— **S. R. S.** *Societatis Regiæ Socius* (Fellow of the Royal Society).— **S. S.** Sabbath-school, Sunday-school.— **s. s.** Screw steamer, steamship.— **SS.** Saints.— **ss.** *Semis* (half).— **S. S. E.** South-southeast.— **S. S. W.** South-southwest.— **St.** Saint, strait, street.— **Ste.** *Sainte* (fem.).— **S. W.** Southwest, southwestern.— **Sw.** Sweden, Swedish.— **Swit., Switz.** Switzerland.

t. Transitive, Tonneau (see METRIC SYSTEM).— **Tenn.** Tennessee (official).— **Ter., Terr.** Territory.— **Tex.** Texan, Texas (official).

U. C. Upper Canada.— **U. K.** United Kingdom.— **ult., ulto.** *Ultimo* (last [month]).— **Univ.** University.— **U. S.** Uncle Sam, United States.— **U. S. A.** United States Army, United States of America.— **U. S. M.** United States Mail, United States Marines.— **U. S. N.** United States Navy.— **ut. sup.** *Ut supra* (as above).

v. Verb, verse, volume.— **Va.** Virginia (official).— **va.** Viola.— **vi.** Verb intransitive.— **viz.** *Videlicet* (to wit, namely).— **vol.** [VOLS., *pl.*] Volume, volunteer.— **Vt.** (official). Vermont.— **vt.** Verb transitive.— **Vul., Vulg.** Vulgate.

Wash. Washington (State: official).— **W. I.** West India, West Indies.— **Wis.** (official), **Wisc.** Wisconsin.— **W. N. W.** West-northwest.— **W. S. W.** West-southwest.— **wt.** Weight.— **W. Va.** West Virginia (official).— **Wyo.** Wyoming (official).

Xm., Xmas. Christmas.

yd. [YDS., *pl.*] Yard.

x 4 - 5 - 10
1,50

alternative